THE
DONNING
INTERNATIONAL

ENCYCLOPEDIC
PSYCHIC
DICTIONARY

THE
DONNING
INTERNATIONAL

ENCYCLOPEDIC
PSYCHIC
DICTIONARY

A division of Schiffer Publishing, Ltd.
1469 Morstein Road
West Chester, Pennsylvania 19380 USA

To the urgency
of human progress

Copyright © 1986 by June G. Bletzer

Edited by Richard A. Horwege

Library of Congress Cataloging-in-Publication Data

Main entry under title:
    The Donning international encyclopedic psychic dictionary.

    Bibliography: p.
    1. Psychical research—Dictionaries. I. Bletzer,
June G., 1921- .II. Howege, Richard A.
BF1025.D66   1986   133.8'03'21   84-13808
ISBN: 0-89865-372-X
ISBN: 0-89865-371-1 (pbk.)

Printed in the United States of America

The Donning International
Encyclopedic
PSYCHIC DICTIONARY

TABLE OF CONTENTS

PREFACE

When I have been all alone, I would go into this waking trance, by repeating my own name to myself silently till all at once, as it were, out of the intensity of the consciousness of the individuality, individuality itself seemed to dissolve and fade away into nothingness. And this is not a confused state, but the opposite, the very clearest and surest state, utterly beyond words, where death was an almost laughable impossibility...and this loss of personality seemed never to be extinct, and the only true likeness. I am ashamed of my feeble description. Have I not said the state is utterly beyond words?

ALFRED, LORD TENNYSON

Alfred Lord Tennyson is not the only person through the ages to find himself unable to describe a psychic state. Standard dictionaries and grammar books do not offer adequate language when it comes to describing invisible mind impressions, internal body sensations, and altered states of consciousness.

Newly awakened interest in psychics, mystics, shamans, mediums, their philosophy of life and their experiences within invisible dimensions has extended everywhere. Organizations, seminars, weekend workshops, classes, and therapies in parapsychology and humanistic psychology spring up over night. Medical doctors and researchers in holistic health are assembling a startling body of evidence that intimately connects parapsychological theories with both physical and mental well-being. One may now "openly" speak about one's new attitudes, changes in beliefs, successful alternative healings, meditative and psychic experiences, and one's personal quest of a more qualitative lifestyle, without "under the breath" ridicule and harrassment.

This is a global shift in consciousness occurring in all levels of awareness. Legions of individuals and other living organisms are beginning to sense the surge of a consciousness shift within themselves, from the ant and the tree, to the layman and government official. Some name this shift in consciousness the "age of transformation." Whatever one names it, it is here! Changes....change....changed.........and *semantic confusion!* People are groping for words to express new dimensional concepts, sensations, and experiences with third-dimensional language. Instructors, authors, psychics, and laymen in this field are coining new words and giving standard words new meanings in trying to explain the variety of experiences of other levels of consciousness and new inner levels of awareness. Mankind has not yet evolved a language or a communication system that can adequately explain these new experiences, sensations, and concepts. This is quite normal in a pioneer field—*but these descriptive terms are multiplying faster than research and study can evolve.* The written media system is flooded with newly coined words.

The aim of this volume is to make the groping for words easier when describing noncustomary experiences and theories with the customary language. Any situational shift requires a shift in language variety. This book contains a concise grouping of the present day shift in language variety and a comparison of this new language variety to words and phrases used in the past in similar philosophies, activities, and inner-dimensional experiences. To accomplish this I have recorded words and phrases from 2000 B.C., the *I Ching,* to the present interviews of new-age workers such as seen on the "Phil Donahue Show." Terms used in the mystical and parapsychological field over the years are defined, described, annotated, or theorized.

This literary reference volume is a twofold book in which a textbook interweaves with a dictionary. The "same wordage" synchronizes a dictionary, a textbook, and a psychic skill development course. This means no unnecessary reading of valueless words. The material is concise and to the point. *Every word is important!* You could say, this volume is a shift in a literary style of writing to accommodate the new global shift in consciousness. It is a tool for an accelerated style of learning!

As a teacher in this field for some three decades, I have found that students drawn to the study of parapsychology are people of all ages and all walks of life. I have observed this human potential movement and consciousness shift becoming "alive" among my students with an accelerated speed in the last few years. From the sixteen hundred students I taught to develop psychically over the past, the amount of time to acquire good psychic skills has lessened by half over the past two years.

I am finding that the public demand for information relating to parapsychology is coming faster than anyone can teach it. Advertisements regarding new-age organizations, small groups, workshops, lectures, and parapsychological cassette tape mail order houses flood the mail. I find a strong desire to understand the multitude of new terms and new meanings for standard words used to describe new and rediscovered states of awareness and experiences. I also find a concrete need for a comprehensive study of the parapsychological field. Human beings all over the world will continue to seek means to transform themselves under the new vibrations of the Aquarian Age and common-ground communication will make this easier.

With no standard textbooks in this field, during my many years of teaching metaphysics and psychic development, I researched and prepared all my class lectures, experiments, and course material. With knowledge gleaned from this research, I taught psychic development, and received feedback from the students being instructed. I also read and scanned hundreds of additional books written in the past and present. Words and phrases have been taken, not only from these books, but also from magazines, pamphlets, newspaper articles, lectures, seminars, television and radio programs, record jackets, and even from herb tea boxes. Therefore one will find colloquialisms, as well as technical and philosophical terms. The bibliography at the end of the volume describes many of these sources. Because astrology, demonology, psychology, mythology, and many religions have their own glossary, these words are not reprinted in this volume, unless the term frequently interfaces parapsychology.

This book is intended to serve as a reference tool for the beginning student, the researcher, and the professional.

First, consider this volume as an easy-to-use, comprehensive, annotated, technical dictionary, complete with cross references to ninety percent of the entries. The cross references add to the meaning, description, annotation, or sometimes simply presents another person's viewpoint to the reader. Although the definitions emphasize simplicity and clarity, I tried to retain and reflect the beauty and profoundness given by the mystic, philosopher, and parapsychologist. The annotations are concise and to the point in order to get all the categories in one volume. This gives a holistic view of the parapsychology field. One may feel there are too many relating subjects, but once one is open to this field, he or she will be exposed to many of these fields.

There are guidelines as to the format used in the dictionary wordage. I also suggest that one turn to the categories of his or her interest to see what terms exist. In spite of acceleration of popular growth in this field, one can quickly acquaint her or himself with the many words which have recently come into usage.

Secondly, consider this volume as a condensed, comprehensive, technical, parapsychology textbook, complete with "do-it-by-yourself" instructions. Because the entries are "categorized" under their particular field and in alphabetical order, one can very quickly find much information about the subject of their choice. And for a full basic, but in capsule form, education in this field, there are instructions outlining graduated steps for not only the individual just becoming interested but also the long-time instructor.

Language varies in different cultures, time periods, and even in small groups of one cause. It varies because the users of language change it to adapt to their needs. Words are alive, powerful, and constantly growing. As a dictionary researcher it is my duty to record the words as they are used, not to pass judgment and offer corrections. I tried to keep the definition, description, or annotation as unvarnished and natural as possible so one can more easily understand the philosophy, or a new dimension, that may be completely foreign to him.

My overall aim is to make some kind of common-ground, melding, psychic-knowledge-pot, which will bring together time periods and cultures showing similarities and differences in psychic skills and philosophies.

Language today is being individually designed, different meanings and different parts of speech are being given to standard words, and old words are being revitalized. The reason for this is because there is no common-ground, melding, psychic-knowledge-pot. Humankind needs a synthesization of communication in this discipline today more than ever before. Hosts of individuals are finding an inner desire to increase their psychic skills in order to better understand themselves, and to understand how and why the planet is bringing a consciousness shift. Psychic skills and parapsychological information are "tools" to help understand this consciousness shift and these accelerated times. They are also good tools for those who wish to add to the shift in the earth's consciousness.

I hope in some small way this volume will aid compatibility, co-operation, and conformity in parapsychological affairs among psychics, humanistic psychologists, holistic health practitioners, scientists, researchers, ministers, meditators, etc.—*and lessen the semantic confusion!*

I have contributed this well-researched dictionary and comprehensive textbook knowing full well that there are additional words being coined before I get this off the press.

Please write to me if you have easily and joyously been able to use this as a twofold reference book. I also urge that you consider this simply a beginning and if you know of words or phrases that you would like to go in the next edition, please write the word or phrase along with its explanation and mail it to: June G. Bletzer, P.O. Box 7036, St. Petersburg, FL 33734.

As you study from these references, I hope you find it as comforting and educational as I have in learning that man, as a universal creature, has been using psychic skills, holistic health therapies, etheric world intelligences, etc., in other time periods and in every culture of the world.

Confucius said: "Without knowing the force of words, it is impossible to know men."

Etheric oneness,

June G. Bletzer

ACKNOWLEDGMENTS

As this volume has evolved and taken shape, I have received the help and support of my friends, family, and students. Thanks to them, I have been able to accomplish my vision of creating a parapsychology reference work that is both comprehensive and lasting.

Typing of the manuscript was done by Margaret Anderson, Jane Annis, Marion Bennett, Vivienne Fellows, Peggy Frank, Maxiene Meilleur, Roberta Rabon, Janet Rogers, Brenda Scott, Margaret Sturgess, and Shirley Walter. Thank you!

Clarence Casto, Sylvia Heller, Loretta Kunke, Heidi Jones, and Alice Wink helped with proofreading, copy-editing, and alphabetizing of the entries. Thank you all!

My thanks to Sylvia Heller, Diana Peridotti, Shirley Walter, Loretta Kunke, and the computer staff (Randy, Nancy, Paul) at the Science Center of Pinellas County, Inc., for computerizing the entries in alphabetical and categorical order.

I received special encouragement to carry out my vision from my writing teacher, Martha Monigle, and a friend forever, Andrew Galet. Floyd Fellows gave me a lot of support as to my knowledge and understanding of this work and handled many responsibilities associated with the Psychic Research Institute of Florida while I researched much of this material for this volume. A thank you to these three and also to Helen Morris for her astrological counseling regarding the book's production.

My daughter Siri stood firmly behind me with the assurance that she would come in from Texas to see the book through to completion if I were physically unable to continue. My son Keith's words, "Mother, write something that will be lasting," remained with me during the late hours.

My grateful thanks to the consistent and endless hours of "love energy" that was supplied to me by three friends: Alice Wink, who organized the entire bibliography and wrote its introduction; Clarence Casto and Loretta Kunke, who came regularly to the writing workspace to check and recheck for accuracy in alphabetizing and categorizing until the manuscript was finalized; Loretta Kunke encouraged me when there were disruptions, delays, and disappointments—she spent many hours helping me straighten out potential catastrophes and worked continually until the manuscript was packaged for mailing.

From my first vision concerning this book, I had thought that with hard work and determination we could some day hold this book in our hands. Visions shape thought-forms, thought-forms shape events. This vision supplied me with determination and with support from my family, friends, and students. To all of you, I give an appreciative thank you!

GUIDE TO USING THE PSYCHIC DICTIONARY

In the field of parapsychology, new words continue to be coined, and it is impossible to record them all. Also, when using the names that psychics and researchers have given to the hundreds of types of psychic skills, one finds that they do not always adhere to standard grammar. These names were coined because they bring forth the essence of a particular psychic talent. There are also standard words and rules, however, that describe the psychic and his or her talent without violating the coined phrases that are presently being used.

If one does not find the word in this psychic dictionary as written in a particular book or article, look in Appendix 2 under the type of skill one is reading about, or look in Appendix 5 if one is reading about related subjects. The types of psychic skills or related subjects are listed alphabetically. Under each particular category is a list of various phrases or words used in connection with that category. By scanning word entries one may run across a word similar to what one is referring to. If not, read the starred words.

Arrangement of Entries

1. Words and terms are alphabetized using the word-by-word format. For example, *human potential movement* is entered before *humanist*. The entries are also alphabetized according to computer ASCII code. The computer considers punctuation to be a part of the alphabet and punctuation characters precede letters in this code: ! " # % & ' ( ) * + , — . / 0 1 2 3 4 5 6 7 8 9 : ; = ? a b c d e f g, etc.; for example, *a priori* is entered before *a. muscaria* and *!kia* is entered before *ka*. A hyphenated word is recognized as one word by the computer, and *e-matrix* is entered before *earth magnetism*.

2. *(esoteric)* frequently precedes the definition. This designates that the world relates to the psychic element and is not able to be scientifically examined, or is not accepted by the masses.

3. Parentheses which directly follow the entered word are used to: **(a)** enclose a time period or an area where the word originated; **(b)** give the derivation and meaning of the derivation of the word; **(c)** state the field of parapsychology the word pertains to in order to eliminate lengthy information under the explanation, e.g., *(seance)* would eliminate repeating that the skill is performed in the dark and with etheric world intelligences.

4. *(Inconcl.)* is the abbreviation for *inconclusive*. This is found at the end of the definition, description, or annotation, to indicate that the subject is "known" to be under investigation at the present time and the definition will be more extensive in the future.

5. *(do not confuse with . . .)* is given because there is another skill so similar that the general public frequently mistakes the two to be identical. Only the pronounced difference is stated. If more clarification is necessary, one is referred to Appendix 4 in the back of the dictionary.

6. *Syn.* is the abbreviation for *synonym*. Synonyms are given following the word, if a term is known to be identical. In the case of multiple synonyms, a few are chosen to

represent various cultures and time periods as much as possible. If the term is synonymous with a popular word which has a lengthy annotated definition, the entry will say "see. . . ." For example: ETHEREAL SMOKE—see ECTOPLASM. If the word has numerous synonyms, it will read "see Appendix 3."

7. *Sim.* is the abbreviation for *similar*. It is written in place of *synonym* if the word is assumed to be identical, but due to differences in culture, language translation, and subjective definitions, one is not sure.

8. *[cf.]* directs the reader to compare the defined term with other phrases and words which will aid in one's comprehension of the entry. Sometimes the term is to suggest another author's point of view. Once in a while it is suggested that one look up a whole category, for example: [*cf.* BOTANE Appendix 2].

A CALL—a request, silently or verbally, to the subconscious mind or the etheric world intelligence for psychic information; anyone, anywhere, and at any time can get psychic help but only if one makes "a call" for it; the law of free will in action; the subconscious mind will not surface information nor will the etheric world intelligence thrust impression in the mind unless it is consciously willed, secretly desired, or karmically willed. [cf. KARMICALLY WILLED, LAW OF FREE WILL Appendix 7, PSYCHIC INFORMATION]

A COURTESY—(dowsing) to verbally or silently say "thank you" when resetting the dowsing rod or pendulum back to normal; helps to clear or neutralize the mind, making it ready for the next question and clear channel tuning. [cf. DOWSING, PENDULUM, NONSWING RESPONSE]

A PRESENCE—1. any invisible energy field that is psychically sensed and felt to be a life-form (as man knows life) as opposed to an inert energy field (such as an aura, a thought-form, or colored energies); e.g., a dead bird in one hand and a live bird in the other hand give two distinct feelings; 2. used as an umbrella word if one is unable to discern whether the soul-mind from the etheric world is a ghost, a poltergeist, a UFO intelligence, a personal guide, or a deceased friend; etheric world soul-mind can be perceived by clairvoyance, a cold chill in the atmosphere, a fragrance not relative to anything in the vicinity, a touch on the shoulder, a surge of warmth flooding the body, etc. Usage: "I feel 'a presence' around me making me feel safe." [cf. SPIRIT, ETHERIC WORLD INTELLIGENCE]

A PRIORI ACTION—an awareness of ideas and events existing in the mind, which manifest in the outer environment just as they existed in the mind, without any physical action in that direction from the perceiver of the events. Syn. PROPHECY, PREDICTION. [cf. SUBJECTIVE CLAIRVOYANCE, INNER-MIND ACTIVITY]

A-PK—see ARTICLE PSYCHOKINESIS.

A. MUSCARIA—(esoteric) a type of mushroom plant (red with white spots) used as a drink offering for the Greek gods to induce visions and other psychic phenomena. Syn. FLY AGARIC, SOMA. [cf. FORCED PSI, PLANES]

AANROO—(esoteric) an invisible iron wall that separates the higher planes from the lower planes in the etheric world; can be perceived clairvoyantly. Syn. VEIL. [cf. ASTRAL PLANE, DENSITY]

AARON'S ROD—1. (esoteric) a wand entwined with serpents in a cadeuceus fashion; has the vibrational frequency to be a psychic tool for healing, dowsing, and promoting an alchemical change of atomic structure in transmutation; e.g., "(the rod) cast before the Egyptian Pharaoh, turned into a serpent." 2. (ancient belief) an actual rod created on the sixth day for Adam, handed down to Aaron, and later used as the beam on Jesus' crucifixion cross. [cf. RADIESTHESIA, DOWSING ROD, ALCHEMY]

AB—(ancient Egypt) the heart; the seat of good or evil thoughts. Syn. CONSCIOUS MIND. [cf. BRAIN, WILL, HEART]

AB-I-HAYAT—(esoteric) special water believed to have the atomic structure that will bring eternal youth to the bather. [cf. WATER, VIBRATIONS, MAGNETIZED WATER]

AB-SOO—see VITAL LIFE FORCE.

ABADDON—(Hebrew) evil, satan.

ABAKA—(ancient Egypt) a special geometric relation to the earth; used in placing the pyramids. (Inconcl.) [cf. PYRAMIDOLOGY; GOLDEN SECTION]

ABATUR—(esoteric) an etheric world entity who works subordinately with the creator to make the visible universe; recognized as the father of evil, meaning matter. [cf. MATTER, DEMIURGE]

ABBOT—(Tibet) highest office in the lamasery; usually senior administrator.

ABDOMINAL BRAIN—mass of substance similar to the head brain located behind the stomach; (esoteric) the seat of feeling and sensation; broadcasts this to all parts of the body; used by some psychics as the mechanism to obtain psychic information instead of the third-eye area, an important connection between the sympathetic nervous system and the astral body. Syn. BACK BRAIN. [cf. EMOTIONAL-ASTRAL-SEED-ATOM, SILVER CORD, ASTRAL BODY, NADIS]

ABHAMSI—(angel kingdom) (esoteric) intelligent energy form, aware of its intelligence; capable of manipulating cosmic forces; has eternal existence; four types: gods, pitris, demons, and men. **Syn.** BEINGS. [**cf.** ANGEL KINGDOM, PITRIS]

ABHYANTARA VRITTI—(Yoga) a method of holding one's breath; used in breathing exercises given for higher attainment of the soul-mind. [**cf.** VAGUS NERVE, RESONANT BREATHING)

ABIGOR—(esoteric) 1. psychic, prophet; 2. Duke of Hell commanding sixty legions; depicted by a handsome rider bearing a scepter.

ABLANATHTANALBA—(Egypt)a word with the proper vibrational frequency to persuade one in a certain direction, and to protect one when written or verbalized; same when written backward. **Sim.** ABRACADABRA. [**cf.** WORDS-WITH-POWER, CEREMONIAL MAGIC]

ABNORMAL BEHAVIOR—1. to act in a manner contrary to the mores, laws, social judgment, and standards of the majority of one's culture; 2. depends upon the judgment of the doctor or psychiatrist one chooses; 3. courts say abnormal behavior is the inability to know right from wrong; right or wrong principles vary in countries, cities, organizations, religions, etc. [**cf.** NEW-AGE PSYCHOLOGY, NEGATIVE THOUGHT]

ABOMINABLE SNOWMAN—(Himalayas) a huge, half-human creature, rarely seen, but gives evidence of its existence by its large footprints in the snow and destructive actions; seen with red hair; capable of shifting dimensions. (Inconcl.) **Sim.** YETI, SASQUATCH, LOCH NESS MONSTER. (**cf.** DIMENSION-SHIFTING, NATURE SPIRITS, MONSTER ACTIVITY, UNDERWORLD]

ABORIGINE—(Australia) highly developed psychic who communicates with the etheric world entities for guidance and information; works with dreams. **Syn.** See Appendix 3 PSYCHICS. [**cf.** MEDIUMSHIP, SHAMAN, DREAM THERAPY]

ABRACADABRA—1. (Hebrew *ab*, "father"; *ben*, "son"; *ruach Acadsch*, "the Holy Spirit") written in the form of a triangle referring to the trinity; 2. (Arabic, "speak the blessing"); used as an amulet when written in the form of a triangle, and worn around the neck; protects the wearer and brings him or her good experiences; 3. (Aramaic) used for the disappearance of sickness from the world: because of its magical vibrational frequency, it is used to ward off afflictions; powerful when written or verbalized; 4. later used as a tool for many kinds of psychic feats; has the same power written backward. **Sim.** ABLANATHTANALBA. [**cf.** WORDS-WITH-POWER Appendix 2]

ABRAMS BOX—see BLACK BOX.

ABRAXAS—(Gnostic) the supreme God; depicted with the head of a rooster and snakes for feet; the name has the vibrational frequency that enhances psychic skills. [**cf.** SYMBOLS, WORDS-WITH-POWER]

ABREACTION—to release psychic tension, through verbalizing or acting out an adequate resolution of a repressed traumatic experience with an appropriate emotion or effect; the moment of a breakdown; sometimes it is possible to relive the original experience in hypnotherapy and dissipate the repression. [**cf.** BLOCKS, HYPNOTHERAPY, PAST LIVES THEORY, REVIVIFICATION]

ABRED—(Celtic) three circles of the same size, overlapping in such a manner as to make a center; the center represents Totality of being; this shape has the vibrational frequency to be used in psychic skills and in spiritual attainment. [**cf.** FORMS-WITH-POWER Appendix 5, AMULETS]

ABSENT DREAMS—picture language in the mind which occurs during sleep, but one does not choose to remember it upon awakening. (Inconcl.) [**cf.** THINKING DURING SLEEP, FALSE AWAKENING]

ABSENT HEALING—(mental healing) to use one's brain energy that emanates from the head constantly to heal an individual in another locality; healer should receive permission to send this energy, as everyone has a right to their state of well-being; accomplished by healer when in a physically relaxed state and the conscious mind is passive; research found that this energy is capable of changing body chemistry in the patient; distance is no barrier; see specific methods for details: MENTAL TELEPATHIC HEALING, VISUALIZATION, PRAYER TEAM, PRAYER GROUP, PETITION. (Inconcl.) [**cf.** PARAELECTRICITY, MENTAL HEALING Appendix 2]

ABSENT SITTING—to receive a psychic reading from a psychic for someone else who is not in the vicinity. **Syn.** PROXY SITTING. [**cf.** PSYCHIC INFORMATION, READING]

ABSOLUTE—1. (Latin *absolutum*, "freed, loosened"); **2.** (Sanskrit **mukti**, "obtaining of freedom") free from bondage of the material world; **3.** the perfected Total completed. **Syn.** GODHEAD, ALL-THERE-IS; TOTALITY Appendix 3 [**cf.** REINCARNATION, PLANES, MICROCOSM]

ABSOLUTE BEING—that which always was, and always will be in charge of bringing perfect order to the entire universe; see TOTALITY. [**cf.** MACROCOSM, MONAD]

ABSOLUTE ENERGY—(esoteric) an invisible, primal life force found in the atmosphere; necessary for the existence of all life in the universe; see VITAL LIFE FORCE. (Inconcl.) **Syn.** SPIRIT, PRANA, TUMO, BIOCOSMIC ENERGY. [**cf.** VIBRATIONS, PRANA]

ABSTRACT DANCING—classical dance steps designed for particular melodies that put the dancer in various levels of consciousness. [**cf.** MOVEMENT-FOR-ALTERED-CONSCIOUSNESS Appendix 2]

ABULIA—the level of consciousness in hypnosis in which the conscious mind becomes passive and one then relinquishes their will. [**cf.** HYPNOTHER-APY Appendix 5, INDUCTION, POST-HYPNOTIC SUGGESTION]

ABYSSUM—(esoteric) an herb that has the vibrational frequency to ward off evil; used in exorcising a haunted house and when making the sign of the cross. [**cf.** HOUSE SWEEP, BOTANE]

ACAUSAL COINCIDENCE—see SYNCHRONICITY.

ACAUSAL RELATIONSHIPS—(*acausal*, "without cause"); (clinical) events in the world which cannot be attributed to a cause and effect theory nor to "chance," and yet seem to blend together simultaneously in a meaningful way. (Inconcl.) **Syn.** SYNCHRONICITY. [**cf.** RADIESTHESIA, CYCLIC LAWS, CASTING OF LOTS]

ACCIDENTAL PSYCHIC ATTACK—1. strong emotional thoughts of fear for another's safety or health, forms a thought-form that travels to the person thought about; even though the sender is sincerely concerned about their friend, the thought-form of fear and anxiety is picked up by the friend, who thinks they are his or her own emotions; **2.** victims of a psychic attack can unconsciously pass this force to another person in their area. [**cf.** PSYCHIC TRANSFER Appendix 2]

ACCLIMATIZING—(astral projection) to take time with one's self to eliminate any fear or anxiety about taking an astral projection; a necessary step before one begins a "willed projection." [**cf.** SKY-WALKER, SEPARATION, SECOND STATE]

ACCOMMODATION—(trance manifestations) an advanced step in trance development when the guides are so accomplished that they can perform to the preplanning of the medium even though the medium changes the routine. Usage: "Are your guides at the stage of accommodation? Will they be able to perform with you on the platform instead of the seance room?" [**cf.** DESIRED-CONTROL, GUIDE, DEEP TRANCE]

ACCUMULATED KARMA—(Sanskrit) an individual's pattern of life formed from past experiences in the current life and the past incarnations, which is lying dormant; pattern is made from thoughts, attitudes, and actions; the pattern will unfold and manifest when that individual is ready to handle it. **Syn.** DELAYED KARMA. [**cf.** RIPE KARMA, MASS KARMA, REINCARNATION Appendix 5]

ACETYLCHOLINE—(esoteric) a fluid produced by a nerve segment allowing psychic information to transfer itself from one nerve segment to another; sometimes called **acetyl cholinesterase**. (Inconcl.) [**cf.** SYNAPSES, SYMPATHETIC NERVOUS SYSTEM]

ACHETA—(Japan) a consciousness discipline in the martial arts, blending forces of the mind, body, and spirit; see KARATE. **Sim.** AKETA, BLACK BELT, JUDO. [**cf.** MARTIAL ARTS]

ACOMA-PUEBLO—(Native American, Pueblo) an area in the etheric world which is inhabited by the gods (etheric world intelligences) who communicate with earthlings through eagles. **Syn.** SKY CITY. [**cf.** ETHERIC WORLD, BODIES AND PLANES Appendix 5.]

ACONCINNITOUS PSYCHISM—1. fuzzy, muddled psychic information; to perceive combinations of mental and physical psychic information at one time and to be unable to make it fit the target or make a whole theme; e.g., the vision does not correspond to the movement of the stone in the hand; **2.** (astral projection) projector is able to clairvoyantly perceive the environment and is also capable of moving a light article in the environment upon his or her destination.

ACORN—(esoteric) (world-wide) a seed that has the vibratory rate to be used as a talisman to induce psychic experiences; (ancient) eaten before prophesying; worn or carried to help preserve youthfulness, bring marriage harmony, and cure rheumatism. [**cf.** AMULET, HOLED STONE]

ACOMISM—(esoteric) theory: at one time the universes were nonexistent except in essence; intelligent, energized atoms vibrated around without any order, just "being." **Syn.** CHAOS, PERFECTNESS. [**cf.** MACROCOSM, MICROCOSM, ABSOLUTE, POLARITY, VIBRATIONS]

ACROSS THE THRESHOLD—(esoteric) 1. an expression to relay that one has died; used by those who believe the soul-mind leaves the physical body and enters into the etheric world very much alive. Usage: "Jan has passed over the threshold." **Syn.** MADE THE TRANSITION. [**cf.** DISCARNATE BEINGS, ASTRAL WORLD, DEATH ANGEL] 2. the passing of psychic information from the etheric world to the perception of the psychic, e.g., "A stream of thought came pell-mell across the threshold." [**cf.** INSPIRATIONAL THOUGHT, GOING-TO-LEVEL]

ACROSS TIME—the occurrence of subjective and objective events simultaneously. [**cf.** SYNCHRONICITY, RADIESTHESIA, TIME Appendix 5]

ACTINIC RAYS—(ufology, Kirlian effect) ultraviolet and infrared radiation. [**cf.** COLOR, KIRLIAN PHOTOGRAPHY]

ACTINISM—(ufology) noticeable changes and burns on parts of one's skin after an exposure to a UFO close-encounter-of-the-second-kind; area of skin appears as if it is sunburned which is not discovered until the next day; a similar result of the majority of contactees; e.g., one half of the face is redder than normal. [**cf.** UFOLOGY, CONTACTEE SYNDROME, CONTACTEE]

ACTION—(multidimensional) theory: a constant, vital, invisible, moving force of the inner universe that materializes matter and destroys it; this force serves as identification for man to exist and learn in the earth world; involves the law of change and activity. [**cf.** MULTIDIMENSIONAL, EARTH PLANE, MATTER]

ACTION TELEPATHY—to control or influence bodily movements of living organisms (including mankind) by densifying one's thought and sending it to the organism; e.g., to will the cat to come over to one's lap; to will one's daughter to come home immediately. **Syn.** MOTION TELEPATHY, KINETIC TELEPATHY. [**cf.** TELEPATHY Appendix 2]

ACTIVE AND PASSIVE PHASES—(biorhythm charts) the four divisions of each cycle. [**cf.** BIORHYTHM, MOOD-PATTERN]

ACTIVE RITUAL—(psi tasks) involvement of direct discharge of energy from agent to target; to psychically discharge concentrated energy to the target. [**cf.** PSI-CONDUCIVE STATE, OBJECTIVE PROGRAMMING]

ACTIVE IMAGINATION—(Carl Jung) symbols that seem to arise in dreams and fantasies from the depth of the unconscious. [**cf.** COLLECTIVE UNCONSCIOUS]

ACTIVE MENTAL INACTIVITY—(mental psychism) a state of consciousness necessary for psychic information to flow, wherein one stills the conscious mind to outer stimuli and allows the subconscious mind to be alert to inner information. **Sim.** NON-THOUGHTS. [**cf.** THOUGHTS, VISUALIZATION, OUTER MENTAL ACTIVITY]

ACTIVE TRANCE—(hypnosis) to compose music, to write, or to paint with special characteristics of a deceased famous artist while in a deep state of hypnosis; subject's work far exceeds his own ability; e.g., the subject is directed to paint pictures as if he were the famous painter himself. **Syn.** SUPERCREATION. [**cf.** INSPIRATIONAL THOUGHT, POST-HYPNOTIC SUGGESTION, SPELLED]

ACTIVE VOLITION—coined by Elmer Green; to will one's self to activity and motion during the daytime without thinking about it; the normal awake state of consciousness. [**cf.** BIOFEEDBACK TRAINING, PASSIVE VOLITION, SLEEP ALERT]

ACTIVE WILLING—to deliberately still the conscious mind to outer stimuli with a strong desire to use the subconscious mind only; 1. (biofeedback training) to will one's self to reach an alpha state (or lower) while hooked up to the instruments; an approach of "making it happen." [**cf.** PASSIVE WILLING] 2. (meditation) to repeat a mantra during the meditation period to purposely still the conscious mind; 3. (psychic process) to formulate a method for one's self in which the conscious mind goes through a ritual until it is inactive or neutralized and then wills a stream of non-thoughts to enter the subconscious mind for psychic perception; (do not confuse with mediumship in which passive willing is necessary to call in one's guide). **Syn.** SENSE-WITHDRAWAL. [**cf.** THOUGHTS, PASSIVE WILLING, NON-THOUGHTS, BRAIN WAVE RHYTHM]

ACTIVE-AGENT TELEPATHY—(laboratory) intentional or unintentional mental or behavioral influence regarding the target given by the agent in an ESP experiment. **Syn.** MOBIA. [**cf.** MENTAL TELEPATHY, TELEPATHY Appendix 2]

ACTIVE-AGENT-ACTIVE-SUBJECT—(psi tasks) a controlled experiment in which the subject is capable of psychically perceiving the information as intended, which is sent by the agent. [**cf.** TARGET, CHANCE]

ACTIVISM—(esoteric) theory: the continuous unconscious thoughts in the mind have a relation to outer reality in some way. **Sim.** SYNCHRONICITY. [**cf.** CASTING OF LOTS, DOWSING, INNER-DIALOGUE, COLLECTIVE UNCONSCIOUS]

ACTIVITY—(esoteric) theory: conscious and unconscious thoughts have an effect on outer manifestations and this effect corresponds to the type and kind of thought. [**cf.** THOUGHT, THINKING, VISUALIZATION, LAW OF ACTIVITY Appendix 7]

ACTIVITY AND REST CYCLES—the rhythmic functions of man's body systems repeating themselves every twenty-four hours regardless of his location; see CIRCADIAN RHYTHM. [cf. BIOLOGICAL CYCLES, BIORHYTHM, CYCLES Appendix 5]

ACTUALISM—(esoteric) theory: everything in all the universe is in a flux of constant movement and change making all things alive. [**cf.** CYCLES, LAW OF VIBRATION Appendix 7, SPIRIT, EMOTION]

ACTUALIZATION—(humanistic) theory: all people are related through a universal essence consciousness; there is a need to let go of the stereotypical image of what relationships should be in order to fully experience and express one's self in reality, which is the here and now; (Gestalt)freedom to be in the here and now [**cf.** HOLOGRAM GESTALT, HOLISTIC, LAW OF MICRO/MACROCOSM Appendix 7]

ACUPOINTS—abbr. ACUPUNCTURE PRESSURE POINTS; see same.

ACUPRESSURE—(China) a method of contact healing that creates a smooth flow of vibratory energy throughout the body; to use compression with the hands and fingers on the acupuncture points of the meridians in the body which releases the flow of nerve fluid where there is disease; stimulates the body cells to normalize and heal themselves; the diagnosis is the treatment. [cf. MERIDIAN LINES, ACUPUNCTURE, TRANSRECEIVER POINTS, NODES]

ACUPUNCTURE—(ancient China) to influence the body to heal itself by inserting tiny electric needles into the body in specific invisible energy fields; theory: the body fluid flows in invisible meridian lines extending from the brain to the toes and fingers; these meridians have many concentrated energy fields called acupuncture points that act as transreceivers to distribute the body fluids; electric needles stimulate and unlock any blocked acupuncture point that is congested and causing a disease in the body; once the flow is restored the body can heal itself more easily; variations of other methods used in place of needles: ointments, chemicals, sound, laser beam, and massage. [cf. ACUPRESSURE, NEUROMUSCULAR MASSAGE, TWELVE PULSES, ACUPUNCTURE Appendix 5]

ACUPUNCTURE CHANNEL DETECTOR—invented by Adamenko; instrument that graphs variations of the bioplasmic energy in the body and the intensity of reaction; used after applying needles to acupuncture points; instrument is attached to points in the body to detect bodily energy as emotions and consciousness change. [**cf.** ACUPUNCTURE Appendix 5, MERIDIAN LINES]

ACUPUNCTURE POINTS—tiny, invisible, concentrated centers of energy and intellect, located in the nervous system (electrical system) of the body which distribute its emotional load; 741 points in the body act as transformers and transmitters; points accept the rate of vibrational frequency that comes into them and change the frequency to form various parts of the body; each organ and tissue in the body is made by a different rate of vibration; emotion runs along these invisible lines (meridian lines) in a universal pattern throughout the nervous system in all humans; congestions in these points, caused by imbalanced emotions, clog up the flow and manifest as a disease; treatment on the points to repair the electrical system frees the flow, cells normalize, and heal themselves: acupoints correspond to nodes in the air and act as a continuation of the electrical system in the air; makes man a part of the universal system. [cf. MERIDIAN LINES, TWELVE PULSES, NODES, ACUPRESSURE, BLOCKS]

ADAM—(esoteric) represents the period of evolution when the living organism "involved" down the scale to earth, a soul-mind entered it, clothed itself with a third-dimensional form and a mechanism to make decisions; Adam is the turning point when man began its "evolvement" up the scale on its return trip. [cf. EVOLUTION, SOUL-MIND, MONAD]

ADAM KADMON—1. (Hebrew) the prototype of the original man; primal humanity; 2. (Kabbalah) a body formed by the Sefiroth of the Tree of Life, represents God, the creator, of which man is a miniature image. [cf. ATMAN, MACROCOSM, MICROCOSM]

ADAPT—one who is skilled in the field of mastership, either residing in the earth plane or in the angelic kingdom; one who has a devotion for world progress or universal evolution. [cf. ANGEL KINGDOM, MASTER, GODHEAD]

ADAPTIVE REACTION—(psychology) the same response of the nervous system to environmental change repeated until it becomes a basic pattern to that same environmental change, regardless of whether it is the proper or improper response. [cf. LAW OF SUGGESTION Appendix 7, DESTRUCTIVE BRAINWASHING CULT]

ADARO—(Buddhism) the head on the astral body; 2. (Tibet) the astral body of man. [cf. BODIES AND PLANES Appendix 5]

ADARSAJNANA—(Buddhism) to see a form within the mind like a reflection, isolated from materiality. **Syn.** SUBJECTIVE CLAIRVOYANCE, MIRROR-LIKE WISDOM, WISDOM OF THE GREAT MIRROR. [cf. MEDITATION, CLAIRVOYANCE Appendix 2]

ADDITOR—a device which uses a pencil and the fingertips to bring psychic information from an etheric world intelligence in the form of automatism; similar to the Ouija board. [cf. PLANCHETTE, OUIJA BOARD, AUTOMATIST]

ADEPT—1. one who has prepared himself to assist in ruling the world in an earthly body; accomplished by self-denial and consistent self-development; one who has been illuminated by applying his knowledge of cosmic laws to the affairs of earth living; now has control over his own being and the cosmic forces; 2. a soul-mind in the etheric world who has

earned the rank of adeptship and works from that vibration to help earth civilization advance. [cf. ADEPT MATERIALIZATION, GREAT WHITE BROTHERHOOD]

ADEPT MATERIALIZATION—1. projection of the adept's astral or mental body to a location other than his earthly body and functions in both bodies simultaneously; adept uses matter from the surrounding ethers in the location of the ethereal body to help make the astral or mental body dense enough to see physically; sometimes astral body splits and more than one is seen in different locations; **Syn.** MULTIFORM, BILOCATION. 2. A full-blown vision perceived clairvoyantly by those ready for a message from the higher realms; shows himself during sleep, or when psychic is needing his presence; (do not confuse with ECTOPLASM MATERIALIZATION in the seance room). (Inconcl.) [cf. ASTRAL PROJECTION Appendix 2, APPARITION]

ADI—(Sanskrit) the beginning; the first. Symbol is a circle with a dot for a center point. **Syn.** ADI-BUDDHI. [cf. LAW OF CENTER Appendix 7, TOTALITY]

ADI PLANE—the seventh level of consciousness; the highest plane; the world as it was first formed by Totality; an impulse of perfectness in the creative process. **Syn.** DIVINE, TOTALITY. [cf. PLANES, CHAOS, MONAD]

ADI-BUDDHI—(Sanskrit) pertaining to the beginning of creation; primeval Buddhi; see TOTALITY.

ADI-BUDHA—(Buddhism) the highest consciousness man can understand in his present state of evolution; a feeling of emerging into the Monad. **Syn.** WISDOM MIND. [cf. CONSCIOUSNESS Appendix 5]

ADIDACTOS—(Greece) psychic talent that one was born with which reacts normally when applied properly. **Syn.** ATECHNOS. [cf. PSYCHIC INFORMATION, PSYCHIC]

ADITYAS—(angel kingdom) a high order of etheric world intelligences with the purpose of carrying out the divine plan among the universes. [cf. ANGEL HIERARCHY, LARGE-GOOD ANGEL]

ADONAI—(Hebrew, "the Lord," God of Israel) because the Jewish people had deep awe for this name and understood the power of spoken words, they avoided pronouncing this name which led to the name of Jehovah to replace it; both names have extreme power when written or spoken. [cf. WORDS-WITH-POWER Appendix 2]

ADORATION—(esoteric) an inner process that draws one constantly to work for perfectness. Syn. GRACE. [cf. MONAD, MANKIND SEED, FIFTH PLANE]

ADORE—to use a personal belonging or its replica to communicate to a deity; belonging or replica serves as a psychic channel to receive deity's revelation or phenomena; theory: God is the worker, the relic is the occasion; the personal belonging contains special attributes of the deity himself. [cf. ADORATION, MANTRAM]

ADORNATION OF ASHES—(Yoga) to wear only ashes as a body covering with the belief that "one who owns everything, therefore, possesses nothing." [cf. ASSOCIATION MAGIC Appendix 2]

ADRENERGIA—inner excited state of mind, when sending mental messages, which helps make the process successful. [cf. SHEEP AND GOAT EFFECT, EMOTIONS, BEAMED ENERGY]

ADROGYNOUS—(Yoga) the channel of the holy breath located in the solar plexus; active vagus nerve when trying for higher attainment of soul-mind growth. [cf. BIORHYTHMS, TWENTY-EIGHT DAY CYCLE, HOLY BREATH]

ADVANCED SPIRIT—an etheric world helper from the higher planes in charge of deceased persons· helps them adjust in their new vibration. [cf. DEATH ANGEL, BIRTH OF THE BARDO-BODY, DEATH-BED EXPERIENCES]

ADVERSARIES—(density) earthbound entities from the lower etheric world planes who try to influence earthlings in the wrong direction. [cf. BODIES AND PLANES Appendix 5, DENSITY, HAUNTING]

ADYTUM—a sacred place where only special people may enter.

ADZE—(Africa) an evil psychic who projects his soul-mind to suck blood from an innocent sleeping victim; usually detected by a swarm of red lights where the work is being done. Syn. VAMPIRE.

AERIAL BODY—(B.C.) (esoteric) a form of evil energy showing itself in a fiery, human-like shape, brought to psychics who entertain low-quality etheric world entities. Syn. DEMON, EARTHBOUND ENTITIES. [cf. DENSITY, DEATH MIST, APPARITION]

AERIAL PLANE—(B.C.) the lower division of the etheric world believed to house demons. Syn. DENSITY. [cf. ETHEREAL PLANE, SOUL-MIND, ASTRAL SHELL]

AERIAL TRANSLATION—to move an inert body through space in its original form without the help of physical matter. Syn. TELEPORTATION. [cf. AERIAL TRANSLATION MEDIUM, GUIDES]

AERIAL TRANSLATION MEDIUM—one who can move an inert body through space without the help of physical matter when in a state of trance; medium has the proper body chemistry and is capable of allowing an etheric world intelligence to intervene and use his or her ectoplasm to move an article from one area to another; (do not confuse with PSYCHOKINESIS in which the subconscious mind does the moving). Syn. TELEPORTIST. [cf. TELEPORTATION TELEKINESIS, GRAVITY CONTROL Appendix 2]

AEROFORMS—(ufology) living organisms in the sea of space; seem to be made of etheric substance having pecular sizes and shapes; visible to people in aircraft. (Inconcl.) Syn. BIOLOGICAL UFOS, BIO-FORMS. [cf. UFO PHENOMENA, ETHER SHIPS]

AEROLITE—a messenger from the etheric world who is desirous to communicate with an earthling. [cf. ETHERIC WORLD INTELLIGENCE Appendix 3, GUIDE, CONTROL]

AESTHETIC PERCEPTION—a forty-three-day cycle of emotion and sensation in which man and woman have a pattern of twenty-one and one-half days of low emotional or stagnant emotional days and twenty-one and one-half days of becoming emotional very easily. [cf. CYCLES, BIORHYTHM Appendix 5]

AETHER—1. (esoteric) a vibrational frequency of space where it is postulated that ether does not exist; the vibrational frequency which is responsible for the flow of electro-magnetic waves; space on into infinity; 2. (Greece) personification given to what was believed to be pure clear air in the sky; 3. (physics) used until approximately 1932 representing the space or substance in which bodies exist or move, postulating the existence of some manner for the transmission of heat, light, magnetic, and radio signals (all of which may be accomplished in a perfect vacuum); 4. an existence where the power of space (as man knows space) is not. [cf. ETHERIC WORLD]

AETHEREAL—see AETHER; also spelled **aetherial**.

AETHERIAL—see AETHER; also spelled **aethereal**.

AETHROBACY—to raise objects or persons in the air by the removal of normal influence of the law of gravity while in a state of trance; psychic allows an etheric world intelligence to intervene, use his or her ectoplasm to levitate the object or person; phenomena can be seen with physical eyes; the first step in teleportation. [**cf.** MOTOR LEVITATION, TELEKINESIS LEVITATION, TELEPORTATION]

AETHYR—see VITAL LIFE FORCE.

AFFERENT SCHIZONEUROSIS—(clinical) a break in the response of a patient reacting from the stimulus object and the central process which includes a clairvoyance experience, passive telepathy, veridical hallucination, or communication from the etheric world. [**cf.** SNAPPING, CLICK, MENTAL PSYCHIC PROCESSES Appendix 2]

AFFINITIES—(Rudolf Steiner) two entities who have been together through many earth and etheric lives; leads to a special fondness for one another, either in marriage, job relations, friendship, or an exchange of abilities. **Sim.** SOUL-MATES. [**cf.** REINCARNATION, EMOTIONAL KARMA, ROUND, PERIOD PIECES]

AFFIRMATIONS—planned grouping of words of Truth repeated daily, silently or verbally, to stir up the divine spark of perfectness within the human seed and change outward manifestions; instigated by the conscious mind but aimed at the subconscious mind to change one's belief system; brings words of Truth into being that are not manifesting in reality; can be designed for any aspect of one's life, harmony, abundance, health, or education; verbiage should not be lengthy; more effective if used for one's self and decreed with emotion or repeated after meditation; (can be said with rote but takes longer to be effective); Truth words change one's auric pattern by gradually taking its place in the subconscious mind. [**cf.** PLOY, WORDS-WITH-POWER, TRUTH, REALITY]

AFFIRMATIVE HEALING—(mental healing) to repeat daily, silently or verbally, a grouping of words decreeing the good health potential within one's self when one is manifesting illness; said by rote frequently during the day; preferably said with emotion or while in an alpha state of consciousness; words gradually change one's pattern and the body reacts in a healing process; e.g., "I am a perfect child of God and therefore inherit perfect lungs."; "My body is whole, perfect, energetic, vibrantly alive, and manifesting good health now." [**cf.** MENTAL HEALING Appendix 2]

AFFLATUS—to receive knowledgeable information that one could not have been known from past education or experiences; comes through the superconscious mind direct to the conscious mind, psychically, when in a relaxed state of consciousness. **Syn.** INSPIRATIONAL THOUGHT. [**cf.** SUPERCONSCIOUS MIND, KUNDALINI, INSPIRATIONAL MUSIC]

AFTER IMAGE—the natural form seen with eyes closed after staring at a visual picture in a type of meditation; non-psychic; (do not confuse with CLAIRVOYANCE).

AFTER-DEATH WORLD—(Tibet) umbrella word; any level of the etheric world that is alive, vibrating, and full of soul-minds without physical bodies. **Syn.** ETHERIC WORLD, OVERWORLD, THE BARDO, HEAVEN, BEYOND. [**cf.** ASTRAL PLANE, REINCARNATION]

AFTER-DEATH-DREAM-STATE—(Tibet) a sleep-like trance condition that the soul-mind is put into after death if the soul-mind does not realize he or she is dead; frequently the soul-mind feels he or she is still alive because they can see the physical world as they left it and wonder why earth persons do not speak to them; happens when one dies suddenly or is indoctrinated into a different kind of etheric world than he or she perceives when there. [**cf.** DEATH ANGEL, ETHEREAL HYPNOSIS]

AFTER-HUMAN-DEATH-STATES—theory: various levels or vibrational frequencies of body substance and its inhabitant in the etheric world that shows differences and similarities; as opposed to one great big world encompassing all soul-minds. [**cf.** REINCARNATION, DENSITY, ASTRAL PLANE]

AGALA—(Germany) to verbalize this word brings protection to the person repeating it; sound of word has psychic properties. **Sim.** ABRACADABRA. [**cf.** VIBRATIONS, WORDS-WITH-POWER, PSYCHIC ENERGY]

AGAMI KARMA—(Vedic) the mental and physical acts performed in this life will reap results in the future of this life and in future incarnations. **Syn.** KARMA. [**cf.** REINCARNATION Appendix 5]

AGAMENT—(Ethiopia) a nature spirit in charge of water and its various phases; ability to reflect on a water surface; shows itself clairvoyantly in human form with black skin.

AGAPE—(Greece) a gathering for the purpose of performing an ethereal type of love-making; highest form of sex; (not physical sex); later degenerated into an orgy of physical sex and feasting. **Syn.** LOVE FEAST. [**cf.** SEXUAL MYSTICISM]

AGARTHA—an underground sanctuary camp hidden under the Himalayas where the Masters of the world assemble; a place of prayer and goodness; considered the great initiatory university of Asia; its ruler, the Hahatma, is known as the Sovereign Universal Pontiff; Agartha has knowledge of a physical science that would enable it to destroy the world and its psychic science is equally advanced: Asian history says it was established in 1800 B.C. but was kept concealed until the nineteenth century because their science would expose mankind to evil and the eternal reign of anarchy; no one ever takes the textbooks from the Agartha—their contents must be kept in memory only. [**cf.** AQUARIAN AGE, TRANSFORMATION]

AGATE—(esoteric) a mineral that acts as a transmitter of Mercury's radiations for the earth; offers protection from any air disturbance for those who understand this; known for healing qualities. [**cf.** MINERAL KINGDOM, AMULETS]

AGATHION—a nature spirit that only appears at mid-day; makes itself known clairvoyantly as a man, beast, bottle, or magic ring.

AGATHODEMON—(Greece) an etheric world intelligence serving in a protective manner to one particular person during his or her incarnation. **Syn.** DOCTOR TEACHER, CELESTIAL GUARDIAN. [**cf.** GUIDES, INNER BAND, SOUL JURY, ETHERIC WORLD INTELLIGENCES Appendix 3]

AGE—1. (esoteric) denotes a cycle of civilization; a period of approximately 26,000 years wherein the soul-mind of man grows and progresses. **Syn.** CIVILIZATION CYCLE; 2. (astrology) one-twelfth of the platonic year or 2,190 years; a period of approximately 2,000 years during which the point of the spring equinox proceeds through one sign of the zodiac of constellations; a time area while our sun is passing through each sign of the zodiac of the "Greater Solar System" of a parent sun in a reverse cycle of our zodiac signs (approximately 2,500 years between each sign). [**cf.** PLATONIC YEAR, AQUARIAN AGE, CYCLES, CHAIN OF GLOBES, CELESTIAL]

AGE OF AQUARIUS—see AQUARIAN AGE.

AGE OF BRAHMA—(Hinduism) one hundred cycles of 311,040,000,000,000 years each.

AGE OF COSMIC CONSCIOUSNESS—a period of time in which the planet will go through a struggle to purify itself on its own evolutionary path; some people say it began in the 1920s, and others say it began in 1952; this transformation of the planet brings with it a change in man's evolution also; opens man to an awareness of higher states of consciousness, and more use of the mind mechanism, in every aspect of his lifestyle. **Syn.** AGE OF AQUARIUS. [**cf.** EVOLUTION, EVOLUTION OF THE SOUL-MIND, CYCLES, CONSCIOUSNESS]

AGE OF LOVE, LIGHT, AND LIFE—name given to the tremendous transformation on planet earth and all the inhabitants on it; all living things feel the thrust of the mother planet trying to purify herself and sense a change; the earth is not only swinging from the Piscean Age to the Aquarian Age but the Milky Way system is also swinging into a new global cycle. **Syn.** AGE OF COSMIC CONSCIOUSNESS, AGE OF AQUARIUS. [**cf.** GREAT YEAR, CIVILIZATION CYCLES, AGE]

AGE OF REASON—(1642-1727) brought about by Sir Isaac Newton, who carefully published nothing which was not firmly supported by experimental proofs.

AGE REGRESSION—1. (hypnotherapy) to recall a past experience from one's present life while under a deep hypnotic state; (a) to relive it in the same emotional attitude and the same age of the experience with all future knowledge blocked from memory; (b) to verbalize the experience to the hypnotherapist as a bystander watching the past scene; 2. (meditation) the surfacing of incidents of one's past life after a deep meditation period; 3. to surface past incidents that have meaning to one's present lfie by a physical manipulation of rubbing the legs to stimulate the awakening of the subconscious mind; (do not confuse with COMPLETE REGRESSION, which involves past incarnations. [**cf.** REVIVIFICATION, FULL RECALL, AWARENESS TECHNIQUES]

AGELESS WISDOM—Truth that will always be saved, even though civilizations fall, only to rise again to great heights in another civilization; divine truths of man's being; knowledge which builds in the minds of great men through inspiration, dwindles through civilization, and is then picked up again by other great soul-minds.

AGENERES—(Greece, alchemy, *geinomai*, "to bring into existence") a complete life-like vision of an etheric world intelligence which the intelligence assumes momentarily for the earthling to perceive. **Syn.** TANGIBLE APPARITION. [**cf.** ALCHEMY Appendix 2, SHAPE-SHIFTING, GLORIFIED BODY]

AGENT—1. (psi tasks) the sender in a mental telepathic experiment; person who looks at the target object and initiates telepathic communication; [**cf.** ESP, MENTAL TELEPATHY] 2. any individual who receives spontaneous psychic information through telepathic communications or through clairsentience. **Syn.** PSYCHIC. [**cf.** SPONTANEOUS PSI] 3. (mediumship) (a) one who contacts the etheric world intelligences for psychic information and physical phenomena, acting as a "go-between" or an agent for the two worlds. **Syn.** MEDIUM. (b) the etheric world intelligence who communicates with the medium, the agent or "go-between" for the medium and the etheric world." **Syn.** GUIDE, INNER BAND; 4. (poltergeist) the individual that is generating the energy for the poltergeist to exist and do his pranks. **Syn.** FOCUS. [**cf.** POLTERGEISTERY, GHOSTS]

AGENT-PERCIPIENT PAIR—(psi tasks) two individuals who are emotionally linked by friendship, love, or relations and work successfully together in mindreading experiments. [**cf.** ESP, TELEPATHIC TWIN, SOUL-RAPPORT TELEPATHY]

AGENTINUM ASTRUM—written A∴ A∴ ; refers to the inner circle of the Order of the Golden Dawn. [**cf.** WORDS-WITH-POWER, LAW OF ASSOCIATION Appendix 7]

AGENTS OF THE LORDS OF KARMA—(esoteric) believed to be helpers in the etheric world who design or mold the blueprints of ethereal substance, planning a kind of life for the soul-mind getting ready to incarnate to earth. [**cf.** REINCARNATION, ACCUMULATED KARMA]

AGHARTA—(Buddhism) the subterranean world in the hollouw of the earth connected by two places on earth proper; believed to be first colonized many thousands of years ago by those who fled there to be saved from the sinking of Atlantis; colonists are far advanced of our civilization today; hypothesis of some scientists: the home base of some types of flying saucers; capital is Shamballah. (Inconcl.) [**cf.** SUBTERRANEAN WORLD, HOLLOW EARTH]

AGLA—(Hebrew, "thou are powerful and eternal, O Lord"); used as an invocation before opening psychic doors or as an inscription written on an amulet; has the vibrational frequency that protects the one who wears the inscription or utters the words. [**cf.** WORDS-WITH-POWER, TALISMAN, AMEN, ABRACADABRA]

AGLOW—1. (Bible) a radiance of incandescent light around a physical body that has purified their soul-mind; this makes the physical body so refined that the radiance can be seen with physical eyes at times; 2. golden radiant energies seen by physical eyes when there is a spontaneous fulfillment of the Holy Spirit to an earthling; fulfillment is so meaningful and powerful that it spills over in the physical realm. (Inconcl.) [**cf.** GLORIFIED BODY, ALCHEMY]

AGNI—1. (Latin *ignis*) an etheric world intelligence who works between gods and men giving guidance, protection, and psychic information; 2. (Hinduism) god of fire, one of the chief divinities of the Vedas; 3. (Bhagavad Gita) using a god as a principle of behavior. **Syn.** GUIDE, DEVA, ANGEL. [**cf.** BRAHMANA, SPIRIT, INNER BAND]

AHAM BRAHMASMI—(Yoga) an affirmation or mantra which one repeats in meditation to help raise his state of consciousness; i.e., "I am Brahma." [**cf.** SOUNDS-WITH-POWER Appendix 2, CHANTING]

AHOLA—(Native American, Hopi) 1. etheric world intelligence known as the Germ God; in charge of all types of reproduction; communicates to the Indian as an invisible human being; 2. an etheric world ancestor in control of agriculture. **Syn.** LOKI, MAGNIFICENT DEVA. [**cf.** GUIDE, DEVA, MEDIUMSHIP]

AHRIMAN—(Zoroastrianism) an etheric world intelligence; the supreme god in the underworld level of the etheric world; an evil god; opposite of AHURA MAZDAH. **Syn.** DEVIL. [**cf.** OVERWORLD, UNDERWORLD, DENSITY]

AHURA MAZDAH—(Zoroastrianism) an etheric world intelligence; the supreme god in the overworld; good god, opposite of AHRIMAN. **Syn.**

MAGNIFICENT DEVA. [**cf.** OVERWORLD, DIMENSIONS, ANGEL HIERARCHY]

AHYRAS—(India) lower-quality entities from the density of the etheric world who desire to bring harm to man; earthbound entities or young soul-minds on the planes close to earth. **Syn.** ASURAS. [**cf.** DENSITY, EARTHBOUND ENTITIES]

AIA—an individual who has successively progressed through the necessary laws of earth life during their many incarnations; has earned a habitation in the higher realms and no longer has to reincarnate in earth. **Syn.** MASTER. [**cf.** PLANES, FIFTH PLANE]

AIKDO DOJO—(martial art) name of the halls where one practices the art of aikido. [**cf.** EMPTY HANDS, BLACK BELT]

AIKIDO—1. (Oriental, *aie*, "oneness"; *ki*, "environment"; *do*, "path"): a martial art that teaches a unique method of self-defense stressing wholistic self-discipline through mind-body awareness; 2. (Japan) a martial art that trains one to become sensitive to another person's energy field and to detect an energy field when it is not normal, thereby enabling the student to sense danger before it happens; objective: to help form universal harmony. **Syn.** ART OF THE VELVET FIST. [**cf.** KAMI, CHUAN]

AIN SOPH—(Kabbalah) that which is limitless; a nameless god; see TOTALITY.

AIO—(Native American, Hopi) an etheric world guide who helps the Indian psychic contact other entities in the etheric world when he seeks guidance, protection, and information. **Syn.** DOOR KEEPER. [**cf.** INNER BAND, DOCTOR TEACHER, MEDIUM]

AIR—(esoteric) 1. the second primary element of creation; a condition of gases; a construct manifesting energy, intelligence, order, and thousands of frequency levels; 2. essence of all manifestations, including life, sustained by the atoms making the air; an area without boundaries where all life begins and ends; 3. a faster, finer vibrational frequency than earth, surrounding earth, within earth, and everywhere else; 4. an element of energy, breath, soul-minds, and liberation from earth; an aggregate of decisions. (Inconcl.) **Sim.** HEAVEN, SPACE, ATMOSPHERE. [**cf.** ATOMS, VIBRATIONS, CHAOS]

AIR FAIRIES—nature spirits who work and reside in air; have charge of wind and storms; can be perceived clairvoyantly as centers of energy above the clouds resembling great dragons.

AIR-ELEMENT PSYCHIC SOUND—the noise of a thousand thunders reverberating all at once; caused by unity of a certain kind of negative globular thinking which stirs the vital life force into aggrevation; can be perceived clairaudiently. (Inconcl.) [**cf.** CLAIRAUDIENCE, MUSIC OF THE SPHERES]

AIR-SPIRIT—see AIR FAIRIES or SYLPHS.

AIRPORT DEVA—a highly intelligent dynamic life force in charge of designing etheric blueprints for earth's airports; a magnificent life form; see ANGELS. (Inconcl.) [**cf.** DEVAS, NATURE KINGDOM, ANGEL HIERARCHY]

AIR WRAITHS—(Scotland) nature spirits who are seen lurking around ruined or deserted castles or haunting the cobblestone streets of towns. **Syn.** WHORLEY.

AIWASS—name of the etheric world intelligence who worked through Aleister Crowley when he went into trance; Aiwass claimed he was the life force ruling the earth at that time; a Holy guardian angel of the world; also spelled **Aiwaz.**

AJIVA—(Jainism) an etheric world intelligence, who has had many earthly incarnations and now communicates to the psychic earthling bringing valuable information from the etheric world; any nonliving entity that is anywhere that jiva (earth entity) is not; without jiva. **Syn.** ETHERIC WORLD INTELLIGENCE. [**cf.** GUIDES, INNER BAND, ANCESTRAL SPIRITS, MENTAL PSYCHISM, PLANES]

AJNA CHAKRA—(Hinduism) an invisible force center important for psychic work, located in the center of the forehead, almost between the eyes. **Syn.** EYE OF BRAHMAN, THIRD-EYE, BROW CHAKRA. [**cf.** THIRD-EYE AREA Appendix 5]

AKA—(Huna) the three invisible bodies that interpenetrate the human physical body and extend outward; the etheric double, astral and mental bodies. **Sim.** LOWER BODIES. [**cf.** SILVER CORD, ETHERIC THREAD, AKA FINGER]

AKA FINGER—(Huna) a projection of ethereal substance that follows the cord which connects the astral body with the physical body; function is to send duplications of the sense organs; a tiny part of the astral body. [**cf.** AKA, NADIS, SILVER CORD, SINGLE-EYE]

AKAM'S SLIMY EARTH—(alchemy) the primary substance from which all things in existence are made; atoms. **Sim.** PRIMA MATERIAL. [**cf.** ATOM, ALCHEMY Appendix 2]

AKASA—1. (Pythagoras) a primordial spatial substance that penetrates all the atmosphere and beyond; vital to all living and nonliving things; primeval element created in the atoms in the beginning; see VITAL LIFE FORCE; 2. (Brahma) a pure energy that flows up the sushumna and passes into the Ida and Pingala. [**cf.** KUNDALINI, BRAHMANICAL THREAD] 3. (parapsychology) fifth cosmic element. [**cf.** ZOETHER, VITAL LIFE FORCE]

AKASHA—see OVAL.

AKASHIC CHRONICLE—tiny, ethereal records of the soul-mind's past incarnations that provide the earthling with the type of life he or she is now experiencing; records of one's attitudes, thoughts, concepts, and actions of the mental mind as one goes through events during earth incarnations; stored similar to a computer's compartments; see AKASHIC RECORD. [**cf.** MENTAL MIND, ACCUMULATED KARMA, RIPE KARMA, REINCARNATION]

AKASHIC CURRENTS—emanations of electromagnetic energy forming planes and their subplanes interpenetrating and surrounding the physical world; superior in nature to the earth. [**cf.** ASTRAL LIGHT, EARTH'S ETHERIC DOUBLE, AKASA]

AKASHIC RECORD OF THE EARTH—(esoteric) an ethereal energy force field surrounding the earth containing minute, detailed pictures of every person and happening of earth and orderly arranged according to the earth's history; on rare occasions it can be perceived by psychics, but it is shown at such a rapid speed that it is barely recognizable. (Inconcl.) **Sim.** ASTRAL ART GALLERY. [**cf.** AGE, X-NESS IN SPACE, MENTAL-REFLECTING-ETHER, REINCARNATION]

AKASHIC RECORDS—(Sanskrit *akasha*, "primary substance") that out of which all things are formed; 1. tiny, ethereal records that store attitudes, emotions, and concepts from the mental mind as the physical body experiences tastes, smells, sights, sounds, emotions, and thoughts during each earthly incarnation; (a) files are kept until they become ripe and are then used to make the experiences in other incarnations, regardless of the levels of existence, in earth or in the etheric world; utilizes the law "for every action there is a reaction" and one finds he or she makes their new experiences out of their past experiences from these orderly, accurate ethereal records; (b) the total of these records compose the stage of evolution one is in as one progresses toward perfectness; holds the picture images of all events, occurrences, and knowledge one has accepted and encountered throughout all lives; (c) recognized as a part of the soul-mind construct, comparable to a large computer; takes in exactly what is fed by the conscious mind and feeds back these records into the bloodstream without being noticed until one reaps negation in his life. 2. "akasha" is the first state of the crystallization of the spirit (all primordial substance is spirit); akasha is of exquisite fitness and so sensitive that the slightest vibrations of an ether, any place in the universe, registers an indelible impression upon it; 3. akashic impressions are wholly in the domain of Supreme Intelligence; one can enter into a conscious recognition of these akashic impressions if one is in close touch with the Holy Spirit; when every thought vibration is instantly felt in every fiber of their being, then these impressions can be translated into any language the reader is familiar with. (Inconcl.) [**cf.** REINCARNATION Appendix 5, KARMA, MENTAL-REFLECTING-ETHER]

AKETA—see ACHETA and KARATE.

AKH—(ancient Egypt) a glorified soul-mind that has been purified through its many incarnations on earth and is now ready for the monad; individual has correctly balanced with experiences and learned all there is to know, which in turn perfects the soul-mind and refines its encasement. **Sim.** OVERSOUL. [**cf.** MONAD, SOUL-MIND, AKASHIC RECORD, GLORIFY, ALL-AGLOW, WISDOM]

AKSHARA—(Rig-Veda) a level of consciousness where the least balancing of outer stimuli is necessary, making it possible to tune into unmanifested, perfectly correlated intelligence. **Sim.** SATORI, SIDHIS, SUTRAS OF PANANJALI, THE SILENCE, DETACHMENT. [**cf.** QUANTUM VACUUM, SELF-GENERATED, MEDITATION]

AKSHI—(Hinduism) the human eye, a neutral organ which serves the human as a psychic tool; under the direction of the mind, thus, it is used for both good and evil intentions; eyes work unconsciously and selectively; 1. eye psychically beams energy from the person to an object or another person in healing, hexing, energizing amulets, and hypnosis; **2.** psychically receives energy from an object in point of focus, radiesthesia, colorology, scrying, etc. **Syn.** THIRD-EYE, EYE OF HORUS. [**cf.** EVIL-EYE, BEAMED ENERGY, AMULET]

AKUA—(Huna) an etheric world intelligence who communicates with humans; superior to the middle self (conscious mind); a very highly evolved soul-mind. **Sim.** MASTER, DEVA, ANGEL. [**cf.** DEVA NATURE KINGDOM, MASTER, GUIDE, ASTRAL PLANE, AVATAR]

AKUALELES—a nature spirit who lives easily in fire and has charge of fires on earth; endowed with qualities of a deva elemental; its energy is like a ball of fire; as it strikes an object it acts like a cut in a broken electric wire, sizzling and sparking. **Syn.** SALAMANDER]

AKUHAIAMIO—(Huna, "the god who speaks silently") knowledge brought psychically to guide, warn, or give approval of one's actions; inner knowing of what to do and which decision to make; see CLAIRSENTIENCE and INTUITION. [**cf.** SUPERCONSCIOUS MIND, MASTER]

AKWA—(Huna) the force that manifests itself as light; symbolized by the sun; see TOTALITY. [**cf.** SUN, INTELLIGENCE]

AKWALU—(Huna) an invisible energy found in all space, vital to all organisms, inanimate or animate; see VITAL LIFE FORCE. (Inconcl.) **Syn.** KI, L-FIELD, SPIRIT, BIOCOSMIC ENERGY.

AKWALUPO—(Huna, "without life and light") a mass of intelligent energy hovering close to earth looking for an opportunity to psychically communicate with an earthling; see ASTRAL SHELL. **Sim.** SHADOW, SHADE. [**cf.** ETHERIC WORLD INTELLIGENCE, ASTRAL CEMETERY, ELEMENTAL]

ALABASTER—(esoteric) a stone with the appearance of marble; has the vibrational frequency that allows it to isolate, select, and draw to it that which is desired by the owner; used to enhance the psychic ability and other talents of the owner. [**cf.** MINPSI, AMULET, BEAMED ENERGY]

ALAISIAGAE—(Germany) a female etheric world intelligence whose function is to help earthlings who are slain in a battle during war; helps them adjust to their foreign inhabitation and understand that they are dead. [**cf.** ANGEL BEING KINGDOM, DEATH ANGEL]

ALAYA—**1.** (Sanskrit) the indissoluble, universal Soul; Total Intelligence; see TOTALITY. **Syn.** MACROCOSM, GOD, DIVINE MIND; **2.** (Theosophy) the divine intelligence in every atom. **Syn.** MICROCOSM, MONAD.

ALAYA-VIJNANA—(Buddhism) to experience the universal light during meditation; begins with forms rising in the mind, passing over a great mass, and continuing until one experiences pure emptiness of space and then universal light. **Sim.** SATORI, SIDHIS, DETACHMENT, SENSE WITHDRAWAL, IS-NESS. [**cf.** ZEN MEDITATION, SEED MEDITATION, TRANSCENDING]

ALCHEMICAL FORMULA—similarities of all formulas: directions, using the four basic ingredients fire, earth, air, and water, plus other ingredients; each written formula is missing one ingredient deliberately, so that the next chemist will desire to use the formula for good ends by the time he or she pursues and finds the missing link. [**cf.** ALCHEMY Appendix 2]

ALCHEMICAL LIQUOR—(alchemy) a chemical liquid in the body produced by mind concentration until it rises to the brain to be distilled as the "alchemical liquor of transcendence"; this liquid is produced in one's body by a special method of heating body ingredients that are internally manufactured through physical processes by intensified mind concentration; liquid then rises upward through various stages until it is distilled in the brain. **Syn.** CELESTIAL DEW. [**cf.** ALCHEMY, PURIFIED BODY, TRANSCENDANCE]

ALCHEMICAL MATERIALIZATION—see TRANSMUTATION.

ALCHEMICAL PRINCIPLES—**1.** there is a relationship between total creation and the position of the parts which compose it; all substance is produced from one by the one, so all can be reproduced by one through similarity; **2.** process of life or growth goes on in all substance, organic and inorganic, as the universe is constantly expressing its potential, subjected to the law of thought; the nature of the activity of growth follows the nature of thought; to make gold one must start with the thought of gold; **3.** there is a force that the mind can control that can act on solid matter; more powerful than an outside force; sometimes acts instantaneously. [**cf.** ALCHEMY, MATERIALIZATION, TRANSMUTATION Appendix 4]

13

ALCHEMICAL SYMBOLISM—theory: the nature of activity (experiences) of a person comes from the nature of his or her thoughts; number formulas cannot be used to denote changes in attitudes and emotions of one's thoughts, so pictures are used to show one's evolutionary progression; pictures of objects and things that can represent a state of emotions of one's soul-mind are used as opposed to numbers; pictures are used to show the necessary steps the soul-mind must go through to be refined. [**cf.** ALCHEMY, PARABLES]

ALCHEMICAL THEORY—when a substance is heated, a spirit comes out of the substance because of the heat; then the substance will condense itself to a stage in which it can be manipulated. (Inconcl.) [**cf.** ALCHEMY Appendix 2]

ALCHEMIST—1. a scientist who studies how to transmute anything from a lower form to a higher form using both a chemical process and a spiritual process; he or she begins with the transmutation of metals with the desire to eventually transmute the self from one vibrational frequency to another, thereby having life immortal; they can then help soul-minds on various frequencies and quicken their own fusing with the perfect, beautiful primordial state. [**cf.** ALCHEMICAL PRINCIPLES, ALCHEMY Appendix 2, TRANSMUTATION, BODIES AND PLANES Appendix 5] **2.** (mediumship) an etheric world intelligence serving as a guide in each person's inner band, whose main function is to keep a chemical balance in the physical body; capable of attaching to the pineal gland to help with one's psychic development and to add elements to the physical body for better health. [**cf.** INNER BAND, KARMA, PSYCHIC DEVELOPMENT, DOCTOR TEACHER]

ALCHEMIST OF SACRED FIRE—a burning fire that doesn't consume but vivifies; an accomplishment of an inner degree illumination before becoming a candidate for the outer court of the Great Brotherhood; theory: one cannot succeed in attaining the secret of transmutation unless one has an upright and honest soul. **Syn.** AGLOW, FIRE OF THE SAGUS. [**cf.** TRANSMUTATION, ALCHEMY, SIXTH BODY]

ALCHEMIST'S EGG—see RAVEN'S WING.

ALCHEMY—(ancient Egypt *al Khem,* "a mixture to create a mixture"; *qem,* "black mud of the Nile" or "to form from primary substance"); (Latin, "all composition"); **1.** a science regarding the altering of the structure of an object to another vibrational frequency by mind power and mind control; an art dealing with the control of mutations and trans-mutations within matter, substance, energy, and life itself, by the mental mind; to change baser metals to gold; (Hermes) a mental art to change universal phenomena; **2.** a spiritual process blended with a chemical process to transform one's own state of consciousness to a higher vibrational frequency by purification of the atoms in one's body; this is accomplished by first knowing how to transmute lesser metals to higher metals with intense mind control; mind control is then focused on raising one's state of consciousness permanently by assimilating the same processes in one's body which was used for transmutation of metals; alchemist can then dematerialize this purified body at will into an invisible vibrational frequency and go from plane to plane in the etheric world; a purified body can also rematerialize into a physical form at will; sometimes at a different time period; gives the alchemist life immortal. [**cf.** GLORIFIED BODY, LEVITATION MATERIALIZATION, ALCHEMICAL PRINCIPLES, TRANSMUTATION, ELIXIR OF LIFE, LAW OF THOUGHT Appendix 7] **3.** (physical psychism) the process of dematerializing and rematerializing an object using mind control; to use intense concentration upon an object until its atomic structure is changed to a vaporized ethereal vibrational frequency with the mind; the object reappears but changed in form; (do not confuse with APPORTATION in which it is returned exactly as it was dematerialized; see Appendix 4). [**cf.** ECTOMAPLASM MATERIALIZATION]

ALERT ALPHA WAVES—(biofeedback training) fast, small jerky lines showing on the EEG graph readouts when the subject is in an alpha state but also in a state of arousal; normal alpha lines are rhythmic and smooth. (Inconcl.) **Sim.** DESYNCH-RONIZATION. (**cf.** EEG, BIOFEEDBACK TRAINING, ALPHA STATE OF CONSCIOUSNESS]

ALERT-ASLEEP—(meditation) a state of complete relaxation of the physical body, but the mind is more awake than usual; descriptive of meditation; accomplished by pinpointing one's concentration to one small thing which makes the mind super-sensitive to outside disturbances and inside subjective thoughts. [**cf.** MEDITATION Appendix 5]

ALERT-PASSIVITY—a state of consciousness wherein the physical body systems have slowed down, the emotions have quieted, and the conscious mind is passive; conscious mind is aware of outer stimuli but will not make a decision regarding it; occurs in meditation and hypnotherapy. [**cf.** ALPHA STATE, ZEN MEDITATION, ALERT SLEEP]

ALERT-WAKEFULNESS—a state of consciousness wherein the conscious mind is perceiving with the five senses and making decisions accordingly; the normal beta state. [**cf.** MEDITATION, ALPHA STATE OF CONSCIOUSNESS, DELTA STATE OF CONSCIOUSNESS, THETA STATE OF CONSCIOUSNESS]

ALEURANTHROPY—(alchemy) to transform one's self into a life form of the animal kingdom; accomplished by a disciplined mind that changes the molecular structure of the body rapidly, performs an activity, and transforms back into the self; most frequent changes result in cats (domestic and wild), wolves, and dogs; (do not confuse with MULTIFORM). **Syn.** SHAPE-SHIFTING. [**cf.** ALCHEMIST, WEREWOLF]

ALEXANDRITE—(esoteric) a stone that draws radiations from Mercury to itself; capable of polarizing light rays. [**cf.** VIBRATIONS, MINPSI]

ALFHEIM—(Europe) 1. a nature spirit that takes the form of a tiny person with light skin; desires to work for humanity; can be mischievous; frequently allows her or himself to be perceived clairvoyantly. **Sim.** WEE PEOPLE. 2. the level of consciousness in the overworld that houses the elves who work with this world. [**cf.** NATURE SPIRIT, DIMENSION-SHIFTING]

ALIEN TONGUES—to utter sounds that are foreign to the native tongue when in a state of ecstasy; sounds are believed to be sent by the Holy Spirit; occurs frequently at Evangelistic or Charismatic services wherein the person is self-hypnotized into a highly joyful state of religious "high." **Sim.** GLOSSOLALIA, TALKING-IN-TONGUES. [**cf.** INTERPRETATION OF TALKING IN TONGUES, UTTERANCES]

ALIEN VOICE—(trance) an etheric world intelligence speaking through a medium, using the tone and quality of his or her own voice from memory of a past incarnation, as opposed to using the medium's voice. [**cf.** TRANCE VOICE MEDIUM, TRUMPET CONTROL]

ALIVE BUT ASLEEP AND DEAD—refers to those entities in the astral world who have recently passed from this world and have been put to sleep until the soul-mind can establish a period of calmness. [**cf.** MADE HIS TRANSITION, DEATH SCIENCE]

ALKAHEST—(Arabic) (alchemy) universal solvent, the higher spiritual self. [**cf.** ALCHEMIST, GLORIFIED BODY, ASCENSION]

ALL—(capitalized) the only source of intelligence and energy in one total construct; expresses itself in different vibrational frequencies throughout all the universes, and each expression, whether huge or minute, contains all the attributes of the "All." **Syn.** TOTALITY Appendix 3. [**cf.** MICROCOSM, TOTAL CONSCIOUSNESS, VIBRATIONS]

ALL AGLOW—a large, solid, colored light (white, yellow, or orange) without pattern, surrounding a person or psychic event; brought on by: 1. a positive emotional event or a deep meditational session which puts the psychic in an altered state of consciousness of high ecstasy; 2. a purified body or a purified event that emanates radiance bright enough to be seen by physical or clairvoyant eyes. [**cf.** GLORIFIED BODY, ASCENSION, CROWN OF GLORY]

ALL SOUL'S DAY—(Tibet) the anniversary of Siddhartha's death, celebrated in respect of all people who have made their transition; (Catholic) day of prayer for souls in purgatory.

ALL-ACCOMPLISHING WISDOM—(Buddhism) a movement in meditation that is known as "karma-free"; a selfless action dedicated to the realization of universal enlightenment that benefits all living things or a willingness to take the consequences. [**cf.** REINCARNATION, MEDITATION]

ALL-AT-ONCE—(esoteric) a phrase used by psychics who perceive the past, present, and future simultaneously, believing there is no time-space but "all is now." Usage: "I saw the baby new and aged all-at-once." **Syn.** MULTIDIMENSIONAL. [**cf.** CLAIRVOYANT, TIME-SPACE]

ALL-IS-WITHIN DOCTRINE—all phases of manifestation of matter on the earth plane including the earth is held together by a massive collection of man's past and present thoughts; corresponds with the expression *man has dominion over the world* ("man's mind is the controller"). [**cf.** LAW OF THOUGHT Appendix 7, MATTER]

ALL-SEEING EYE—a region located in the center of the forehead etherically connected to the pituitary

15

gland and pineal gland; a sense faculty of humans allowing them to perceive information from the etheric world and Totality in many psychic ways; the subjective part of humans that knows how to tune into Universal Mind for unknown information to be revealed. **Syn.** EYE OF HORUS, SIXTH SENSE. [**cf.** THIRD-EYE AREA, THALAMUS]

ALL-SELF—1. a totally selfless person; 2. (esoteric) that invisible part of one that is perfect; see MONAD. [**cf.** TOTALITY Appendix 3; MONADOLOGY, MACROCOSM]

ALL-THAT-IS—see TOTALITY.

ALL-THERE-IS—see TOTALITY.

ALLADIN—(esoteric) symbol to represent a psychic using a ritual to conjure up one' guide to reveal higher wisdom; the lamp is the light of pure knowledge; to rub the lamp and ask one's genie to bring this knowledge to oneself. **Sim.** GOING-TO-LEVEL. [**cf.** MENTAL PSYCHIC PROCESSES Appendix 2]

ALLAH—(Islam) (Sufi) the one God of all; that which is not separated from Truth and Reality; the Supreme Being. [**cf.** SUFISM, TOTALITY]

ALLEGED PHENOMENA—a psychic feat which is scientifically tested and found to be a fact, according to those who believe it is not a psychic feat unless it can be scientifically tested; it is then described to be real psychism. [**cf.** PSYCHIC READING, PHYSICAL PSYCHISM]

ALLEGORY—materialistic or concrete form to represent a spiritual or abstract meaning; form can be an animal, object, plant, scene, etc.; (parapsychology) an objective vision to portray subjective and meaningful knowledge; dreamstuff and psychic information is more readily given in picture form of worldly things because pictures can represent emotions, character, and attitudes; picture forms expend less energy of the etheric world and the psychic; can be shown faster than words heard clairaudiently in the head or reading words like a book, e.g., a vision of a table lavishly set with plenty of food and no one at the table suggests a different story about that individual than a table with very little on it and many people gathered there to enjoy themselves. [**cf.** DREAMS, PSYCHIC INFORMATION, VISIONARIES, METAPHYSICAL, SYMBOLS]

ALLOBIOFEEDBACK—(laboratory) the transference of thoughts between two persons, each hooked up to a GSR; at the exact time one sent a thought to the other person, both instruments registered reactions. [**cf.** GALVANIC SKIN RESPONSE, BIO-STAT MONITOR, EEG]

ALLOPATHY—a method of treating disease by the use of agents producing effects different from those in the disease being treated, as opposed to homeopathy; treatment is by the law of contraries. [**cf.** CURATIVE EDUCATION]

ALMIGHTY CREATIVE POWER—(esoteric) the one source of all intelligence, power, and love which is broken down into atoms (and smaller particles); each atom has all the attributes of the one source and co-creates as its parent the Almighty Creative Power; see TOTALITY. **Syn.** GOD, UNIVERSAL MIND. [**cf.** VIBRATIONS, MICROCOSM, POLARITY, ATOMS, MATTER]

ALOGICAL—without logic, beyond logic.

ALPHA BLOCKING—an outer stimulus that normally helps one reach an alpha state of consciousness, does not react on the subconscious mind, but instead it reacts on the conscious mind; a new brain wave grouping identified by the mindmirror EEG instrument. (Inconcl.) [**cf.** SPLIT BRAIN Appendix 5]

ALPHA BRAIN—(esoteric) a section of the brain where man thinks psychic information is received; see THIRD-EYE AREA. (Inconcl.) [**cf.** ALPHA SENSES, ALPHA WAVES]

ALPHA CREATURES—(ufology) life-form constructs that float and live in the atmosphere; appear in various sizes and shapes, looking like animals; invisible to the physical eye but capable of being photographed by infrared camera exposures. (Inconcl.) **Sim.** SPACE ANIMALS, EXTRATERRESTRIAL ANIMALS. [**cf.** ETHER SHIPS, SPHEROIDS]

ALPHA INDEX—(biofeedback training) large wave patterns shown on the readout graphs of the EEG instrument, as compared to the frequent and fast waves at other times; makes it possible to determine special groupings and therefore make a scale. (Inconcl.) [**cf.** SCALE OF BRAIN RHYTHM, BIO FEEDBACK TRAINING]

ALPHA MODE—a state of consciousness in which the body is relaxed, the emotions are quiet, and the mind is controlled; reached by meditating; can be detected on a biofeedback instrument. [**cf.** DELTA STATE OF CONSCIOUSNESS, THETA STATE OF CON-

SCIOUSNESS, SCALE OF BRAIN WAVE CYCLES, PASS-ING-THE-MANTRA, COLLECTING THE MIND]

ALPHA SENSES—(esoteric) an invisible intelligent mechanism that can detect and impress information psychically on the brain; a subjective awareness. (Inconcl.) **Sim.** PSYCHIC SENSE. [**cf.** ALPHA BRAIN, SUPERCONSCIOUS MIND, SUBCONSCIOUS MIND]

ALPHA STATE OF CONSCIOUSNESS—(biofeedback training) a brain wave frequency of approximately eight to fourteen cycles per second as registered on the brain rhythm scale used with the electroencephalograph instrument; 1. universal characteristics of humans that register this state: awake but not actively moving about; resting, relaxed, composed, meditative, approaching the hypnotic state, or becoming less alert to outer stimuli than normal; 2. an awareness of invisible, emotional reactions, psychic information, and inspirational thought; 3. to use the conscious, subconscious, and superconscious minds alternately, unintentionally shifting back and forth. (Inconcl.) [**cf.** BIOFEEDBACK TRAINING Appendix 5, BETA WAVES]

ALPHA WAVES—(biofeedback training) a universally suggested grouping of the patterns of brain wave activity when hooked up to the electroencephalograph instrument; recognized by a consistent outburst of lines similar enough from thousands of persons while in a parallel state of awareness to form a grouping; people's patterns vary in length and duration of ups and downs but are still universally similar enough to name it a state of consciousness, recognized on the biofeedback earphones by a slowing of the electrical hum or electrical discord; registers on the readout graphs between eight and fourteen cycles per second. (Inconcl.) [**cf.** BRAIN ELECTRICAL EVENTS, AUTOCONTROL OF CONSCIOUSNESS, EEG]

ALPHA-ESP—to paint or draw better than one's normal capabilities because one was programmed while in an alpha state of consciousness; suggestions given to the subconscious mind when in a passive-alert state carry over into waking consciousness and allow the individual to bring out hidden potential in the area that is programmed. [**cf.** ALERT PASSIVITY, HYPNOTHERAPY, ALPHA BRAIN]

ALPHABETIC TYPTOLOGY—to receive information from etheric world intelligences by means of rappings on a table or object; knocks occur within walls, on walls, tables, chairs, and other furniture, preferably wooden furniture; a code is worked out by medium and sitters relating to yes and no answers or numbered raps for letters of the alphabet. **Syn.** TAPS. [**cf.** TABLE-TIPPING, PERCUSSION Appendix 2]

ALPHOID PATTERN—(biofeedback training) a new grouping of readout patterns on the EEG biofeedback instrument occurring when a person is having an astral projection. [**cf.** SCALE OF BRAIN RHYTHM, ASTRAL PROJECTION]

ALPIEL—(Talmud) a nature spirit who shows itself as a tiny life form decorated in bright colors; has charge of the fruit trees in the earth plane.

ALRUNE—(Germany) (esoteric) a mannequin made from the roots of the mandrake plant into various female statues about a foot high; has the vibrational frequency making it possible to give out psychic information; if not held sacred this mannequin could make an audible noise and cause misfortune to the household where stationed. **Syn.** MANDRAKE AMULET. [**cf.** AMULETS, WORDS-WITH-POWER, VIBRATIONS, BOTANE.]

ALTA MAJOR CENTER—(esoteric) a nerve center at the top of the spine that makes approximate contact with the cranium; forms a center of communication between the sushumna working its way up the kundalini and the two head chakras. [**cf.** NERVE FLUID, KUNDALINI, MEDULLA OBLONGATA, BROW CHAKRA, CROWN CHAKRA]

ALTAR—(esoteric) a physical place or object used as a point of focus where one can raise or alter one's state of consciousness, gaining higher ground within oneself; 1. a special design made of wood, believed to be magical and used for psychic information; 2. a place made of stone that has never been worked or hewn or touched by the hammer so its vibrations are virgin and neutral and can be used for upliftment into a higher consciousness. [**cf.** LAW OF RITUAL Appendix 7, TRADITION, PSYCHOMETRY]

ALTER EGO—(esoteric) theory: man has more than one personality or construct of intelligence which is capable of surfacing into his present life; can be detected. (Inconcl.) [**cf.** PAST LIVES THEORY, AKASHIC RECORD]

ALTERATION OF VIBRATION PHENOMENA—to dematerialize an object or one's own body and rematerialize it in another location; to change the vibrational frequency of matter into an ethereal state, move it to the desired area, and change it back to its original state of atomic structure and drop it into the third dimension. **Syn.** APPORTATION. [**cf.** SYMPATHETIC VIBRATION, MEDIUMSHIP]

ALTERED STATE OF AWARENESS—any state of consciousness in which the conscious mind or the five senses are inactive, i.e., dreaming, sleeping, meditation, hypnosis, trance, or under the influence of drugs. **Syn.** ALTERED STATES OF CONSCIOUSNESS. [**cf.** HYPNOTHERAPY, MEDITATION, MOVEMENT-FOR-ALTERED-CONSCIOUSNESS, BETA]

ALTERED STATE OF CONSCIOUSNESS—(esoteric) any state of mind activity differing from that which is considered the normal awake state in which decisions are made from the input of outer stimuli on the five senses; acquired by: 1. deliberately willing the different state through meditation, hypnosis, going-to-level, calling in guides, sleeping, dreaming, going into trance, taking LSD or other narcotic drugs; 2. a spontaneous experience happening to one who has an "inner peace" or one who is able to allow the superconscious mind to flow with inspirational thought regarding lifestyle demands. **Syn.** STATE OF NON-ORDINARY REALITY, ALTERED STATES OF AWARENESS. [**cf.** TRANCE, MEDITATION, SUPERCONSCIOUS MIND, ALTERNATE REALITIES, ECSTASY, MOVEMENT-FOR-ALTERED CONSCIOUSNESS Appendix 2]

ALTERNATE EARTHS—(ufology) prescience assumption: there are planets very similar to earth because some UFO intelligences appear to resemble earth man. [**cf.** UFOLOGY Appendix 5]

ALTERNATE REALITIES—levels of energy known as planes in the etheric world where the soul-mind can reach by mind expansion when the individual is in an altered state of consciousness; soul-mind feels compatible and at home under the laws of the new vibrational frequency. **Syn.** SOUL TRAVEL, MENTAL PROJECTION. [**cf.** SEED MEDITATION, ECKANKAR, ASTRAL PLANE, MENTAL PLANE]

ALTERNATIVE—(holistic health; healing) any unorthodox or unconventional remedy, treatment, medicine, practice, or change in life habits, environment, personal relationships, and attitude, that aim toward a more "preferred" qualitative lifestyle and "correct" health for a specific individual; some of the current choices are: acupuncture, acupressure, psychic healers, spiritual healers, hypnotherapists, aerobic dancing, biofeedback training, running,

jogging, color therapy, natural foods, homeopathy, yoga, naturopathy, meditation, body-self-awareness, radionics, dream analysis therapny, music therapy, rolfing, neuromuscular massage, reflexology, primal scream therapy, rebirthing, isolation tanks, past lives therapy, regression rational living, psychic reading, polarity balancing, aura balancing, psychoanalysis, inner-dialogue therapy, and an abundance of laughter. [**cf.** HOLISTIC HEALTH, CURATIVE EDUCATION]

AMAIMON—an exalted, magnanimous deva who presides over one of the four parts of the universe: air, earth, water, fire. [**cf.** ANGEL KINGDOM, DEVA]

AMANITA MUSCARIA—(esoteric) 1. (Vedic) a type of mushroom (red with white spots) that has the vibratory rate which makes it a hallucinogenic drug; used to reach a state of bliss or to see visions of heaven; held sacred and only given under supervision to those who desire to learn the art of seeing into the etheric world at will. 2. (Siberia) a white-stalked, red-capped fungus planted in circle by peasants; those who sat inside the cirlce experienced long-lasting psychic visions; 3. (Greece) used to make a drink offering for the Greek gods to induce visions and other psychic phenomena. **Syn.** FAIRY RINGS, FLY AGARIC, SOMA PLANT. [**cf.** ACTIVE RITUAL, FORCED PSI, FORMS-WITH-POWER, PLANES]

AMATL PAPER—(Otomi Indian, Mexico) an ancient paper used as a basic ingredient in psychic rituals because the paper has the properties to invoke etheric world entities for healing, clairvoyance, and other psychic phenomena. [**cf.** TALISMANS, MEDIUMSHIP, VIBRATIONS, PSYCHIC HEALING]

AMBER—(esoteric) a yellow to brown fossilized resin from prehistoric evergreens that is linked with the moon's vibrations giving it "positive" electrical charges, making it helpful in hypnotherapy and other psychic phenomena; can be highly polished, and becomes charged with static electricity when rubbed with a cloth. [**cf.** MINPSI, MINERAL KINGDOM]

AMBIENT GRAVITATIONAL RADIATION—(esoteric) an energy field that completely encompasses the earth and surrounds objects on the earth, holding the earth and everything on it in orbit; (do not confuse with the AURA or ETHERIC DOUBLE). (Inconcl.) [**cf.** GRAVITY CONTROL Appendix 2]

AMBIENT VISION—a psychic perception attributed to blind persons; to intuitively know where one is in relation to one's surrounding, e.g., to avoid a wall or chair without the use of a cane or outstretched arm. [**cf.** EYELESS SIGHT Appendix 2]

AMBROSIA—(esoteric) (Greece) a red mushroom plant with white spots, used in a special drink to favor the Gods; has the properties to induce visions and other psychic phenomena. **Syn.** FLY AGARIC, MUSCARIA. [**cf.** TRANCE, PSYCHOTROPIC PLANTS, BOTANE]

AME NO MA-HITOTSU NO KAMI—1. (Japan) one God of All, located in the sky; 2. the village blacksmith who performs psychic healings and other psychic skills. [**cf.** BLACKSMITH, TOTALITY]

AMEN—1. (ancient Egypt) representative of the Main Soul; expression of the hidden invisible God; Lord of Space and Breath; used sacredly; depicted by a disc or by fire as "the giver of light"; 2. (Sanskrit) all the world, taken from the chant *aum* or *amin;* 3. (Christianity) used after a prayer, creed, or formal statement as a commitment of consent; synonymous with "so be it"; that which was said beforehand was the Truth; 4. (Hebrew) this I have faith in; 5. (metaphysics of Egypt, Greece, Rome, Jews, Christians) synonymous with the Word or God; and enforces the power of the Word when spoken after statements, e.g., God was the Word, and the Word was God. [**cf.** WORDS-WITH-POWER, AUM, TOTALITY]

AMETHYST—(esoteric) (ancient) a jewel that has the vibrational frequency to protect the wearer from external negative activity, and bring him power over the masses; recognized as a sacred jewel and worn only by the high priest; influenced by the radiations from Jupiter. [**cf.** MINERAL KINGDOM, MINPSI, AMULET]

AMIDA—(Japan, Buddhism) name of the avatar who reached perfection before the time of Siddhartha. [**cf.** AVATAR, MASTER]

AMITABHA—(Japan) the supreme deity; the one main source. [**cf.** TOTALITY, MICROCOSM]

AMNESIA'S GRIP—(ufology) a period of time in which the contactee has no memory of what happened regarding his or her visit with the outer space living intelligences. (Inconcl.) [**cf.** UFOLOGY Appendix 5, HYPNOTHERAPY, STROBE LIGHT, CONTACTEE]

AMON-RA—(Egypt) the primal invisible energies: fire, earth, air, and water.

AMORC—the Rosicrucian order, or the Ancient Mystic Order Rosae Crucis.

AMPING—to tune into one's subconscious mind to receive psychic information; skills using the subconscious mind work with the electrical system in the body (the nervous system), therefore the name *amping*; skills requiring amping are: PENDULUM POWER, DOWSING, RADIONICS, CASTING OF LOTS, MANTIC ARTS, PSYCHOMETRY, HUMAN OMENS, and MAGNETIC HEALING. **Syn.** GOING-TO-LEVEL.

AMPLITUDE DIAL—(biofeedback training) a switch on the biofeedback instrument regulating the intensity of the ergs of energy put into the instruments by the body or brain; that part of the instrument that expands the electrical energy from the brain to its fullest, making the electricity readable in either sound, color, or graph readouts (depending upon the type of instrument); the maximum dial readout. [**cf.** GSR, EEG, EMG, ALPHA STATE OF CONSCIOUSNESS]

AMPLITUDE INTEGRATION—(biofeedback training) a special switch on some instruments that combines the two frequences of brain rhythm cycles usually separated, enabling a more accurate readout. [**cf.** BIOFEEDBACK TRAINING Appendix 5]

AMRIT—(kundalini) the divine nectar of immortality that is produced where the Ganges, Jumna, and Saraswati rivers meet; represents the Ida, Pingala, and Sushumna meeting invisibly in man's neck as one can feel the spiritual current flowing into the center of the spine in this location. [**cf.** KUNDALINI, SUSHUMNA, MEDULLA OBLONGATA]

AMSU—1. (Egypt) god of the productive force of nature, identified with Horus; 2. (Greece) identified with Pan; depicted in human form with a plume on the head and holding a flail above the shoulder. [**cf.** ANGEL KINGDOM]

AMULET—an object left in its virgin state, psychically energized and used as a protection against negative vibrations or to enhance one's psychic skills; natural object may be a stone, gem, shell, or a piece of wood; energized by owner's thoughts, emotions, psychic energy, and nature's radiations, for a specific purpose; can be worn as a charm, carried on the body, or kept covered or protected until owner wishes it to release its psychic energy; serves as protection against disease, mischief, and evil spirits, etc.; aids opening of psychic doors for. knowledge and visions; aids in healings, etc.; (do not confuse with a TALISMAN). [cf. AMULET Appendix 4, BEAMED ENERGY, WORDS-WITH-POWER, MINERAL CONSCIOUSNESS]

AMULET ENERGIZING—1. to psychically store energy in an inert object to be used later for specific purposes; energy used for storing can come from: (a) human thoughts, emotions, eyes, verbal words, and breaths; (b) etheric world intelligences' energies and thoughts; (c) natural life forces; sun, water, rain, lightning, wind; (d) music and dancing vibrations; (e) form energy, pyramid, square, sphere, etc.; energy is induced by dancing, singing, meditation, special breathing, rituals and ceremonies; before storing psychic energy it is consecrated to be used for a specific purpose for its owner; object is wrapped in a protective covering until ready for its release of energy; amulets worn on a body are constantly being energized by emotion from one's body; 2. (future science, Czechoslovakia) tools, natural objects, and instruments are being used to draw psychic energy from man, and then stored for use elsewhere. (Inconcl.) [cf. AMULET, SYMPATHETIC MAGIC, LAW OF BEAMED ENERGY Appendix 7, RITUAL]

AMULETING—to use an energized amulet or talisman for psychic purposes; process can enhance psychic skills, increase healing ability, enhance one's potential, be the healing agent itself, serve as a protecting agent, or be an aid in any way it has been decreed to be useful; amuleting is accomplished by wearing the object, keeping it wrapped until ready to use, or carrying it on one's self; amulets must be used by their owner; amuleting can be performed by a group; e.g., the totem pole for psychic purposes and use of communion articles repeatedly. [cf. TALISMAN, TOTEM, BEAMED ENERGY, MEDICINE BUNDLE]

AMULETIZING—see AMULET ENERGIZING.

AN INTELLIGENCE—(esoteric) an energy field that makes itself known to an individual through psychic skills when called upon; brings information or aid in physical phenomena; does not name itself but shows intelligence by its ability to communicate and assist the psychic; if clairvoyantly perceived energy field may take a human form or an object form; but always gives the sensation that it is alive, as opposed to an inert object. [cf. APPARITION, DISCARNATE, GUIDE, UFO CONSTRUCTS, ENTITY, PERSONALITY]

AN-KHEFT-KA—(Egypt, 3,700 B.C.) a symbol of polarity necessary for all things; depicted by a royal person with rods in each hand. [cf. YIN AND YANG, POLARITY]

ANACHITIS—(esoteric) a stone with the vibrational frequency that enables it to contact nature spirits living in water, who in turn help mankind; enhances psychic skills and healing energies for its owner. [cf. MINPSI, AMULET]

ANAGAMAI—one who has purified oneself to a state where one does not have to return to the earth but now abides in the higher planes. **Sim.** ANGEL, MASTER. [cf. ANGEL HIERARCHY, GLORIFIED BODY]

ANAGOGER—1. one who can interpret psychic symbols to help in everyday life situations; 2. one who can find hidden meaning in scripture symbols. [cf. SYMBOLOGY, ASSOCIATION MAGIC]

ANAGOGICAL—pertains to: 1. actions reflecting idealistic thoughts surfacing from the subconscious mind; 2. mysterious and hidden meaning coming through the subconscious mind; 3. spiritual interpretations of words.

ANAHAT CHAKRA—1. (Hinduism) located in the heart area; perceived clairvoyantly as deep red, with twelve petals; represents "air"; 2. (Vedanta) the flower of the human body representing the consciousness in man; symbolized by the lotus flower. **Syn.** heart Chakra. [cf. KUNDALINI, ETHERIC DOUBLE]

ANAHATA SHABDA—(Vedic) sound vibrations above the threshold of normal hearing for the physical ear but very beautiful music when heard by the clairaudient ear. **Syn.** COSMIC MUSIC, MUSIC OF THE SPHERES. [cf. VIBRATION, CLAIRAUDIENCE]

ANALYST—one who separates the elements of an entity or object to study the nature of the elements, as opposed to synthesis. **Syn.** PSYCHOANALYST. [cf. GESTALT, METAPHYSICS]

ANALYTICAL MIND—(parapsychology) the part of the mind that conceives data and studies data conceived; forms a judgment or concept and drops this concept into the subconscious mind, and becomes emotional to the degree the reasoning provides; happens simultaneously; has a physical counterpart, the brain. **Syn.** CONSCIOUS MIND, MENTAL MIND.

ANAMORPHOSIS—coined by Ludwig von Bertalanffy (1967); see VITAL LIFE FORCE.

ANANCITHIDUS—(esoteric) a mineral believed to have the vibrational frequency that helps it protect the owner against the lower entities in the density. [**cf.** MINERAL KINGDOM, MINPSI]

ANANDA—(Sanskrit, Brahmanism) a highly transcended state of consciousness; experienced when the kundalini rises to the top of the brain during meditation; accomplished through righteous living and repeated meditation; a permeation within the body of extreme rapture, called "pure bliss." **Syn.** SAMADHI. [**cf.** MEDITATION, KUNDALINI]

ANANISAPTA—(Kabbalah) special words written on parchment with the vibrational frequency that will ward off negative vibrations in the area where placed. [**cf.** WORDS-WITH-POWER]

ANCESTOR WORSHIP—1. (Native American) to communicate psychically with the intelligences in the higher realms of the etheric world, and to respect and follow the instructions and guidance given; psychic information offers aid in all phases of the tribe's life-style, and at the same time benefits mother earth; invisible intelligences understand the overall needs of the earth and universe, and give counsel accordingly; 2. (Asia, Eastern) a circle of people meeting in a home, repeatedly, for the purpose of invoking etheric world intelligences who have lived many lives on earth and have more knowledge than themselves; these intelligences communicate psychically in the circle with new knowledge and guidance and a blessing on the members. **Syn.** PSYCHIC DEVELOPMENT CIRCLES, SEANCE. [**cf.** MEDIUMSHIP, SHAMANSHIP, CLAIRVOYANCE]

ANCESTRAL BODY—(esoteric) theory: the life-cord-seed-atom of the baby-to-be enters the new forming fetus and attracts into its etheric double, atoms that were in the etheric double in his past incarnation; this is known as the "ancestral body"; this body reflects the record from the past atoms into the genes of the baby-to-be; the new baby now has "inherited" traits and will react in many instances similar to actions in his past life. [**cf.** BIRTH SCIENCE]

ANCESTRAL GHOST—a discarnate being that communicates or makes his presence known to an earthling who is capable of psychism. [**cf.** REINCARNATION, GUIDE, MEDIUMSHIP]

ANCESTRAL MEMORY—(Native American) there is an energy field that everyone on earth can tune into for information regarding the earth and growth of the soul. **Sim.** COLLECTIVE UNCONSCIOUS. [**cf.** ARCHETYPAL IMAGE, SUBCONSCIOUS MIND, EARTH, AKASHIC RECORD]

ANCESTRAL SPIRITS—1. (Slavic) deceased ancestors who bring guidance, protection, and new information to tribe members through psychic skills; perceived psychically in the form of a bird or animal; recognized by a similar behavioral pattern of the deceased or a familiarity connected to the deceased, e.g., send an odor that could be connected with that particular person; animal would limp if the deceased person had limped. [**cf.** SOUL-SHIFTING] 2. (South Africa) etheric world intelligences who have lived many earth lives and now have earned the privilege to communicate with witch doctors and tribe members; does not necessarily pertain to their particular deceased tribesman; bring guidance, counsel, protection, and instructions for the benefit of the whole tribe. [**cf.** WITCH DOCTOR, TRIBAL DANCING]

ANCESTRALS—(inspirational thought) (Native American, Cherokee) living souls "out there" (etheric world) who communicate with the Indian bringing guidance, counsel, protection, abundance, and prophecy; souls have been incarnated many times and earned the right to inspire earthlings; intelligences from the higher realms, not necessarily souls that had incarnated as an Indian. [**cf.** RELATIONS, INITIATORY SICKNESS, INSPIRATIONAL THOUGHT]

ANCIENT DISCIPLINES—theory and rules of conduct and thinking that helped the individual to become enlightened.

ANCIENT MAGIC—wisdom concerning the laws of the universe and how to incorporate these laws into psychic skills and psychic healings; given only to those who were in higher states of consciousness and would use the wisdom for the benefit of civilization.

ANCIENT WISDOM—superior knowledge of the universe and the growth of the soul-mind that is preserved and held sacred; taught only to those who are ready to use it for mankind; taught to the individual on the level of his soul-mind evolvement by advanced soul-minds who enjoy full contact with their akashic record and have an understanding of universal needs. **Syn.** WISDOM OF THE MYSTERIES, MYSTICISM. [**cf.** PARAPSYCHOLOGY, METAPHYSICS]

ANDRIAMANITRA—(Philippines, Malagasy) see VITAL LIFE FORCE.

ANDROID—(esoteric) an artificial visible manlike mannequin made with the belief that the owner can imbue it psychically with enough energy to respond to their subconscious mind and do menial tasks for them; (do not confuse with an ELEMENTAL.) [**cf.** BEAMED ENERGY, AMULET, THOUGHTS, SOULLESS PSYCHISM Appendix 2]

ANESTHETIC HOLD—(Tibet, judo) a special kind of body grasp that makes one unconscious and anesthetizes the body, enabling a medical operation to take place. [**cf.** MARTIAL ARTS]

ANGAKOOS—(Eskimo) a shaman who specializes in bringing-in-the-animals, controlling the weather, finding lost objects, and healing psychically. **Syn.** PSYCHIC Appendix 3. [**cf.** BRINGER-OF-THE-ANIMALS, PSYCHIC ENERGY, ATMOSPHERE CONTROL]

ANGAS—(India) external aids to better meditation; e.g., mandala, image of a deity.

ANGEL—(Latin *angelus*); (Greek *angelos*, "supernatural being"); (Hebrew *malak*, literally signifies "a person sent, a messenger") an instrument of divine justice, a guide for men of goodwill; 1. the name of an office or an earned rank, not a name of the nature of the form; an etheric world intelligence who has lived many earthly lives and purified his or her soul-mind in these incarnations until the soul-mind has earned the privilege of administering rewards and arousing the higher faculties in man; can be given only when the conditions are adaptable to the giving and receiving of man; (a) manifests no personality separate from the message it bears; serves selflessly; (b) stays within its own property; functions with its own principles as symbols of good influence; administers to the aspirations of the soul-mind; (c) manipulates earth matter when necessary. Usage: "protecting angel" is behind an accident which almost occurred but didn't; "comforting angel" is behind a peaceful state of mind; 2. an intelligence who has never lived an earthly life; evolved from a nature spirit or from pure air; 3. living intelligences found everywhere in the etheric world; sometimes perceived psychically in human form; neuter in gender but can take a gender for the human form. **Syn.** DEVA, GUIDE, MASTER, ETHERIC WORLD

INTELLIGENCES Appendix 3. [**cf.** ANGEL HIERARCHY, ANGEL CONSCIOUSNESS]

ANGEL AXIR—a highly evolved etheric world intelligence that psychically worked through the Magus of long ago; brought knowledge of psychic skills and wisdom of the earth for the earth. [**cf.** MAGI, ANGEL]

ANGEL BEING KINGDOM—(esoteric) 1. a dimension of dynamic, intelligent, loving energies in the etheric world who have charge of the human being's evolution on earth and their own evolution in the invisible world; interested in earth people, earth living organisms, and earth nonliving organisms; 2. consists of angels, deceased human beings, and nature spirits; 3. a highly intelligent life force necessary and capable of designing the etheric blueprints for every form of nature and its sustenance, which interpenetrates and surrounds the earth; 4. a division of degrees of intelligences, each having his own purpose, life form, and life-style; 5. the invisible planes of the home of the nature spirits and angels working harmoniously with the nature elements of fire, earth, air, and water, collectively and separately; angels divide the earth into thousands of units for easier manipulation of aid and guidance, e.g., an angel overseeing trees and forests, an angel in charge of pollution, an angel in charge of education; 6. capable of appearing in human form for communication with earthlings; exalted angels appear as light beings without human form if perceived clairvoyantly. **Syn.** DEVIC KINGDOM, KINGDOM OF ELEMENTS, KINGDOM OF NATURE. [**cf.** ANGEL, ANGEL KING; MINOR DEVAS, NATURE SPIRITS]

ANGEL CONSCIOUSNESS—an etheric world intelligence who has purified his or her body through thousands of earthly incarnations, and his or her level of awareness is now living in the faster vibrational frequencies in the etheric world without human form; exists as light and color with a few characteristics of the human; does not have to reincarnate to earth but may choose to; sees and perceives by thought vertically, with their whole being; as opposed to seeing horizontally as humans see; varies in size and shape, depending upon their function. [**cf.** ANGEL, SINGLE EYE, CONSCIOUSNESS Appendix 5]

ANGEL DOCTOR—an etheric world intelligence who administers guidance and protection to one specific earthling throughout the earthling's incarnation. **Syn.** DOCTOR TEACHER, CELESTIAL GUARDIAN [**cf.** GUIDE, INNER BAND]

ANGEL EVOLUTION—(esoteric) **1.** theory: human beings incarnate in the earth plane to go through special processes of purifying and perfecting their soul-minds, which will eventually be so purified that their casings will adapt more readily to the subtle vibrations of the etheric world, and there they will continue their progression; human beings and angel beings belong to the same soul-mind family; **(a)** one goes through seven stages of righteous living, toil, strife, overcoming adversaries until one's desires are to work selflessly for the universe; some lessons are conquered in earth and some conquered in the etheric world; substance of a purified body is a very fine ethereal vibration; **(b)** growth steps allow angels to design blueprints for that which is on the earth, and to oversee and sustain them, e.g., a minor angel oversees parking lots; a magnificent angel oversees the Grand Canyon; (600 B.C.) Michael oversaw Israel; **2.** theory: angels evolve from the nature spirits, unfolding from the lower nature spirits to the magnificent angels of Godhood; acquired through joyousness and service to humanity; angels grow until they are free from destructive emotions and can be responsible over large, important areas, e.g., mountains, controlling pollution, etc. [**cf.** DEVA, ANGEL BEING KINGDOM, MINOR DEVAS]

ANGEL HIERARCHY—a ranking of highly evolved etheric world soul-minds; **1.** grouped into nine orders or choirs; starting at the bottom, moving upward: seraphim, cherubim, thrones, dominations-dominions, virtues, powers, principalities, archangels, angel princes; **2.** the first five initiations of purification are taken in a physical life; the fifth (Mastership) is worked through in either the etheric world or on earth; the sixth (Lordship) and the seventh (Godship) are earned in the etheric world; **3.** celestial orders: (first) angels of nature, (second) builders of form, (third) angels of inspiration, (fourth) angels of love, guardian angels, healing angels, religious angels, and song angels; (fifth) angels of birth and death. **Syn.** DEVA EVOLUTION. [**cf.** ANGEL, NATURE SPIRIT, HUMAN KINGDOM]

ANGEL KING—(esoteric) a soul-mind who has gone through eons of degrees of purification until the highest rank, called angel king, is earned; an angel king is in charge of maintaining the largest areas in the universe because he is more illumined,

has understanding of the principles of the solar system, and has showed selfless toil and love in incarnations and ethereal duties; last three ranks in the angel hierarchy are archangel, angel prince, and angel king. **Sim.** SOLAR LOGAS. [**cf.** ARCHANGEL, DEVAS, EXALTED ONES, EYE LANGUAGE]

ANGEL KINGDOM—see ANGEL BEING KINGDOM.

ANGEL OF BIRTH—an etheric world intelligence who inhales vivifying properties and uses the electrical force to unite the new soul-mind with his or her new physical body at birth. [**cf.** BIRTH SCIENCE Appendix 2]

ANGEL OF DEATH—an etheric world intelligence who inhales vivifying properties and uses this electrical force to free the soul-mind from the worn-out physical body during an earth death. **Syn.** ANGEL OF TRANSITION. [**cf.** DEATH SCIENCE Appendix 2]

ANGEL OF RIGHTEOUSNESS—(Hermes) an etheric world intelligence attached to each man who helps inspire good actions in the earthling's present incarnation; stays throughout one incarnation. **Syn.** DOCTOR TEACHER, CELESTIAL GUARDIAN. [**cf.** GUIDE, ANGEL]

ANGEL OF THE SUN—(esoteric) a king angel, evolved to the highest order in angel evolution, earning the function of wielding and energizing the power of the sun on the higher etheric body of human beings. **Syn.** SOLAR LOGAS. [**cf.** ANGEL EVOLUTION, MAGNIFICENT DEVA]

ANGEL OF TRANSITION—see ANGEL OF DEATH.

ANGELHOOD—(capitalized) one who has earned a supreme rank in the hierarchy of the etheric world evolutionary scale; the last three orders under God. **Syn.** GODHOOD, LARGE SCALE DEVA, MAGNIFICENT DEVA, MASTERSHIP. [**cf.** ANGEL CONSCIOUSNESS, CELESTIAL PHENOMENA, COURIERS OF HEAVEN]

ANGELIC CONVERSATION—(mediumship) to communicate with understanding with an etheric world intelligence; to perceive visions and impressions from one's invisible helper. **Syn.** MEDIUMSHIP. [**cf.** MENTAL PSYCHISM, GUIDES, ANCESTRAL COMMUNICATION]

ANGELIC FORCES—see ANGELS.

ANGELIC HOST—a group of synchronized etheric world intelligences desiring to offer assistance to civilization and who thrust their energy upon an individual or a gathering; the tremendous power of their number usually enables everyone in the gathering to witness or feel their presence; brought about by a need of many to change in attitude, or a need to execute a warning or a comfort. [cf. OMEN, ANGEL]

ANGELIC SENTRIES—(Mohammedan) three personal world intelligences who are in charge of each man during an incarnation; two guard the individual during the daytime and one during the nighttime. **Syn.** DOCTOR TEACHER, GUIDE, CELESTIAL GUARDIAN. [cf. INNER BAND, SOUL JURY]

ANGELICA—(esoteric) a plant with the properties to bring protection to the children who play in its presence. [cf. BOTANE Appendix 2, SENSATION CONSCIOUSNESS, WATCH-PLANTS]

ANGELICA ARCHANGELICA—(Latin) (esoteric) an herb felt to have properties to be able to protect one against evil psychic attacks; sometimes linked with Saint Michael, the archangel, and called "the root of the Holy Ghost." [cf. BOTANE, ARCHANGEL]

ANGELICAL STONE—(esoteric) a small crystal globe, sometimes egg-shaped, used for obtaining psychic information in the same fashion as crystal ball gazing. [cf. CRYSTAL GAZING, HYDROMANCY]

ANGELOLOGY—1. study of the higher intelligent life beings in the etheric world and their relationship to earth beings and nature spirits; includes: their life-styles, laws, functions, levels of existence, and vibrational frequencies; 2. study of intelligent invisible energies around animate and inanimate things; theory: when properly understood, these intelligent energies can be contacted to protect, to guide, and to help in earth matters. [cf. ANGELOLOGY Appendix 5; HUMAN BEING KINGDOM]

ANGELS OF THE FOUR CARDINAL POINTS—four exalted intelligences who have earned the highest rank in the ANGEL HIERARCHY in earth's solar system; have charge of the four elements: FIRE, EARTH, AIR, and WATER, on the overall scale; this includes the function of manipulating mankind's accumulated KARMA and directing the essence of nature spirits. **Syn.** CHATUR MAHARAJAS, REGENTS OF EARTH. [cf. ANGEL EVOLUTION]

ANGES—(Voodoo, Haiti) the saints they worship, including Saint Anthony, Saint Michael, and Saint Patrick. [cf. VOODOOISM, ANGELS]

ANGLE-ROD—(radiesthesia) a dowsing rod made of heavy wire and shaped in a ninety-degree angle; has a shorter end to be gripped by the hands and a longer part running parallel to the earth; commonly made of wire coat hangers; more elaborately made with a wooden handle for easier gripping and freer flow of the wire. **Syn.** L-RODS. [cf. RADIESTHETIC GRIP, DOWSING, PENDULUM]

ANGOKOK—(Eskimo) one who performs mediumship healings and mediumship counseling; see MEDIUM and PSYCHIC.

ANGUTTARA NIKAYA—(Tibet) to project the astral body to a distant place on earth and carry on activity at that place while the physical body is also carrying on activity; the soul-mind splits and allows itself to function in two places simultaneously; usually brought on by an emotional desire to be in another place and worldly obligations preventing this, so the astral body fills in; both bodies are identifiable by others. **Syn.** MULTIFORM, BRAHMANA VAGGA, BILOCATION. [cf. ASTRAL PROJECTION Appendix 2]

ANI—(Pacific, Ponape) see VITAL LIFE FORCE.

ANIMA—(Latin) (esoteric) 1. a life-force found in all atoms, giving movement to the atom; 2. soul; an inner personality that unconsciously turns toward Totality. [cf. VITAL LIFE FORCE]

ANIMA HUMANA—an umbrella word; psyche, soul, spirit, heart, mind; see SOUL-MIND.

ANIMA MUNDI—(Latin) (esoteric) 1. theory: a main Soul of the universe which split into many soul-minds, detaching from the main source and still containing all the attributes of the main Soul; so all soul-minds are etherically connected. **Syn.** UNIVERSAL MIND, DIVINE MIND. 2. a hidden, all-pervading, all-uniting influence which connects heaven and earth. **Syn.** JACOB'S LADDER, GOLDEN CHAIN, MAGICIAN'S FIRE.

ANIMAL BIRTH—(reincarnation) the incarnation of a soul-mind on earth in a human body, with unadmirable inclinations stimulated by the animal traits from which it evolved; a new soul-mind who is born behind its time with personality traits unsuitable for the civilization he or she incarnated into and with seemingly animalistic actions. Usage: "He belongs to 'the beasts of the field.'" [cf. KARMA, REINCARNATION]

ANIMAL BRAIN—(esoteric) the cerebellum, the functioning organ of the conscious mind; also known as the lower mind. **Syn.** MAN-BRAIN. [**cf.** INSTINCTUAL THOUGHTS, ARCHETYPAL THOUGHTS]

ANIMAL CONTROL—to have a psychic rapport with all animals; the ability to have dominion over the animal kingdom through psychic means; usually an inborn trait to have harmony with animals, e.g., to go into a lion's cage with no weapon and not be harmed; to ask the cockroaches to move out of the house and they obey without having to use poison. [**cf.** ANPSI, ATMOSPHERE CONTROL, BODY CONTROL]

ANIMAL ESP—the innate ability of all species of animals to know the intentions of other animals, plants, and the thoughts and emotions of man's mental mind; an instinctual ability given to the animal kingdom to take care of themselves so they can sense danger or frustration before it happens. (Inconcl.) **Sim.** ANPSI. [**cf.** PRIMARY PERCEPTION, INSTINCT CONSCIOUSNESS, SIMPLE CONSCIOUSNESS]

ANIMAL FAMILIAR—an elemental shaped like an animal, usually a cat, made by a witch, from condensed, repititious thoughts; elemental thought form is invisibly attached to the witch to be used as an agent for her psychic work that is to be carried on at a distance; animal familiar is mentally sent to a home or an area, psychic energy is transferred along the invisible cord to the familiar and dissipated into the area; witch uses familiar to place a healing or a hex in another locale. **Syn.** FAMILIAR SPIRIT.

ANIMAL GROUP-SOUL—an energy field that contains an overall collected consciousness of each particular classification of animals; consciousness works through each individual animal, maintaining, sustaining, and helping it advance through each incarnation; energy field absorbs accumulated experiences from each individual animal to add to the overall collected consciousness; when energy field has perfected itself, each animal monad evolves to a higher animal species' energy field, and the overall collected consciousness in the new field repeats its cycle; accounts for animal evolvement in general. [**cf.** ANIMAL OVERSOUL, ANPSI]

ANIMAL KARMA—1. animals function under the consciousness of mankind and are subject to humanity's karma; this makes the animals responsible for their rapport with people individually, and with human evolution collectively; animals act from instinct and are incapable of making decisions, so they do not have to work out past life experiences; 2. animals function from a group soul to which they are responsible to help the group soul evolve; any reaction from instinct, good or bad, is absorbed into the group soul and can be used by all other animals in that group for their present incarnation; in this way, learned instincts become strengthened and more keen to all members of the group; badly chosen instinct activity is also usable by all members. [**cf.** ANIMAL KINGDOM, ANTELOPE CHARMING, SIMPLE CONSCIOUSNESS, ANPSI]

ANIMAL KINGDOM—a vibrational frequency designed and held together by the human mind as a necessary tool for lessons one can learn in no other way; 1. animals feed human emotions through mankind's guardianship (dominion) over them; animals have a primal instinct to look up to humans as their deities and adore them; 2. (Native American; Tibet) animals strain and strive to attain equality to man in speech and work, without malice or jealousy, only to be his joyous companion; they offer up sacrifice of themselves as food or as workers in their desire to be of service to man; this is an instinctual striving to raise themselves to a higher state of consciousness, in which the law of subservience is active; "man is subservient to the animals"; 3. in ancient times, man abused animals and they became wild and ferocious, and now man must learn to respect them and their right to live; 4. the animal kingdom includes creatures that fly, swim, crawl, and walk (any organism that is not a plant). [**cf.** LAW OF SUBSERVIENCE Appendix 7, ANPSI Appendix 2, SIMPLE CONSCIOUSNESS, ANIMAL ESP]

ANIMAL LIBERATION—a striving for more respect to be given the undomesticated and the farm animals in regard to the methods of killing, fishing, and using their parts. [**cf.** NONHUMAN, ANIMAL KINGDOM]

ANIMAL MAGNETISM—term coined by Franz Anton Mesmer (1774); see VITAL LIFE FORCE.

ANIMAL OVERSOUL—that part of the group soul for that particular species that has absorbed the actions from each animal's incarnation and added it to the overall collected consciousness for that species. [**cf.** ANIMAL GROUP SOUL, ANPSI]

ANIMAL PSYCHISM—see ANPSI.

ANIMAL SOUL—an invisible energy field evolving parallel to the human form; will not be absorbed into the "human being line" until it has evolved enough times to raise in consciousness to learn through emotions; 1. animal soul is fully aware of cosmic consciousness but will not become one with it (as will the human soul); animals' awareness of cosmic consciousness is through instinct from which it is continually sustained; 2. functions under many laws similar to human beings, especially the law of opposites; 3. animal soul has no memory bank because it has no mental mind to make a decision, so it is not responsible for its karma; animal souls work under man's conscious mind and his karma; 4. animal souls reincarnate from the same group soul or transmute from one species to another; always contributing to and receiving from the group soul; animal's soul is always trying to raise itself in consciousness, but humans do not know the animal hierarchy scale. [cf. GROUP SOUL, SIMPLE CONSCIOUSNESS, INSTINCT CONSCIOUSNESS, ANPSI]

ANIMAL SPIRITS—1. an invisible energy field that is composed of the intelligence of the psychic and acts as an agent to bring new data to the psyshic; energy field takes the form of an animal with the characteristics of the psychic; works as an intermediary between the etheric world and the psychic; animals function similarly to an inner band guide (do not confuse with an animal familiar which is a thought-form and must be constantly fed with thought-energy). (Inconcl.); 2. see ECTOPLASM; 3. a deceased animal perceived clairvoyantly by his past owner, bringing a message; capable of being perceived by a psychic reader. [cf. ANIMAL ESP, ANPSI, ANIMAL KINGDOM]

ANIMAL TRANSMIGRATION—(Hinduism) belief: animal's soul can be born from one species of animal to another, e.g., the soul of the horse is reborn into a dog. [cf. REINCARNATION]

ANIMAL-HEADED DEITIES—(Tibet, Egypt) sub-human thought-forms surfacing from one's own inner mental thoughts when in the Bardo state during the death process; an initiation to clairvoyantly perceive these thought-forms and to dissipate them and pass the initiation. Sim. SEA-OF-FACES. [cf. BARDO STATE, TRANSITION, HYPNOGOGIC STATE]

ANIMALIZED FLUID—the substance in a human being used in physical phenomena; that which serves as the instrument for physical manifesta-

tions to flow. Syn. ECTOPLASM. [cf. TRANCE, SEANCE]

ANIMATE—(esoteric) matter that is endowed with vitality and intelligence; refers to man, a thinking entity, and nondecision-making entities, plants and animals; living organisms. [cf. INANIMATE THINGS]

ANIMATE BEINGS—(esoteric) includes humans, animals, plants, birds, fish, minerals, which are higher intelligences of life whose change in evolutionary growth is noticeable. [cf. CYCLES, LAW OF PROGRESSION Appendix 7]

ANIMISM—(esoteric) (Latin *animus, anima,* "soul, spirit, life-breath"); theory: all natural objects and natural occurrences have a soul (monad) that stands apart from the object or occurrence, but very necessary for the function of that object or occurrence, e.g., found in the wind, fish, plants, and the universe, etc. [cf. LAW OF PERSONIFICATION Appendix 7, SOUL, NATURE SPIRITS]

ANJA CHAKRA—a vortex of ethereal energy pulsating between the eyebrows in the region of the pineal gland; if perceived clairvoyantly it has two petals that bend down and out as the Kundalini rises; symbolized by the winged globe or global crowned serpent; see BROW CHAKRA. [cf. CHAKRAS, KUNDALINI, MENTAL PSYCHIC PROCESSES]

ANKH—(ancient Egypt) a short-armed cross shaped like a **T** with a drop-shaped loop on top; represents "life" and immortality; the circle stands for the Godhead, or the three upper chakras; the vertical line represents the other four chakras; the crossbar represents the horizontal division of male and female or the balancing of polarity; this special shape gives it properties to help heal, induce psychic energy, and protect the owner from negative vibrations; considered a very powerful tool; and even more so when a charged gem is placed in the loop; worn by all Egyptian deities. Syn. CRUX ANSATA. [cf. FORMS-WITH-POWER, TALISMAN, MINPSI, IMITATIVE MAGIC]

ANNAMAYA-KOSHA—(Vedic) the physical body.

ANNIVERSARY SYMPTOMS—(psychology) a feeling from within saying to repeat a response when certain outer stimuli occurs, which form a pattern which is usually not desirable. Syn. CONDITIONAL LEARNING. [cf. BLOCKS, GORDIAN KNOTS]

ANOINTED ONES—ones who have accomplished self-control and mastery over their thinking, actions, talents, and psychic energies; qualifies them to work for the better evolution of civilization; the rank is earned through toil and strife through many incarnations; works toward the progress of the planet in a physical incarnation or from the etheric world; the fifth initiation toward Godhood. **Syn.** MASTER. [**cf.** HUMAN BEING KINGDOM, ANGEL BEING KINGDOM]

ANNOUNCING DREAMS—(Haida) (reincarnation) a dream that indicates who a new baby was in its last incarnation; usually dreamt by the pregnant mother.

ANNU—(ancient Egypt) (esoteric) a beautiful, peaceful place in the etheric world where righteous soul-minds may live; the capital and source of Divine instruction. [**cf.** PLANES, MENTAL BODY]

ANNU COLLEGE—(ancient Egypt, Unas) a school of the most influential of beliefs for all ancient Egypt where the dogma was established.

ANNUIT COEPTIS—the Great Seal of the United States printed on the one-dollar bill; picture of a pyramid with a detached capstone and an eye in the capstone; radiations are around the capstone; (esoteric) the unfinished pyramid of the Great Seal is surmounted by the white triangular capstone in which is placed the "all-seeing eye"; the four-square pyramid is representative of matter; the triangular stone is an emblem of spirit; man's task is to complete the structure by uniting the two. [**cf.** SYMBOLOGY]

ANNWN—(Celtic) the veil or door to the underworld of fairy folk of lower quality; sometimes known as the door to hell. [**cf.** DENSITY, ANNWYL]

ANNWYL—(Celtic) the negative underworld where nature spirits dwell which are made from negative elemental essence. **Sim.** HELL, DENSITY. [**cf.** DENSITY, NATURE SPIRITS, ELEMENTAL ESSENCE]

ANOINTING—to have an unguent or oily liquid applied to one's body by an authoritative figure in a ceremonial manner; 1. a mundane symbolic expression in which oils or other ingredients are used to consecrate one for a specific purpose (usually to raise one's state of consciousness); the oil represents the fluid in the kundalini that rises as one purifies one's body through righteous service to mankind; utilizes the law of similarity; 2. to spread fragrances or oils on one's body before psychic work as the etheric world intelligences can readily use fragrances in their spiritual psychic skills; fragrances have an ethereal counterpart easily

detectable in the etheric world. [**cf.** CEREMONIAL MAGIC, CLAIRSCENT]

ANOLIST—a medium who synchronizes with etheric world intelligences for performing physical phenomena, with either good or evil intentions. [**cf.** CONJURING UP, PHYSICAL PSYCHISM]

ANOMALOUS SHADOWS—(ufology) a black haze on aeroform photographs that seems to take meaningful shapes or forms, yet is not identifiable to humans at this time. (Inconcl.) [**cf.** EXTRATERRESTRIAL ANIMALS, SPACE ANIMALS]

ANORM—coined by June Bletzer; a life-style and accomplishments of what "should be" for each individual according to his or her own uniqueness, potentials, and karma, as opposed to a stereotyped pattern made from the average behavior of thousands; one should establish a personal norm so one can evaluate one's activities in this perspective; each person's norm changes as he or she grows and should be reestablished periodically; every year divisible by seven is a sensible period. [**cf.** NEW-AGE PSYCHOLOGY]

ANPSI—abbr. ANIMAL PSYCHISM; the innate ability that animals have to communicate psychically with other animals, humans, plants, minerals, and other aspects of nature; animals perceive auras of all things and have an alpha sensitivity; animals have a mental telepathic ability to transfer thought back and forth with humans without bodily motions or speech form the human; (Inconcl.); the anpsi category in this dictionary includes the transfer of psychic energy between humans and all species of animals, birds, and fish, and the transference of psychic energy between animals, plants, and minerals. [**cf.** ANIMAL CONSCIOUSNESS, AURAS, MINPSI, BOTANE, ANIMAL SOUL, ANPSI Appendix 2]

ANPSI PREMONITIONS—animals have a sensitivity to predict environmental changes, e.g., before hurricanes or earthquakes, birds stop singing, cattle become uneasy, unmanageable, and head for shelter, and dogs show fear; rats will leave a ship before it sails if the rat predicts a future storm. [**cf.** ANIMAL KINGDOM, ANIMAL GROUP-SOUL]

ANPU—(ancient Egypt) an etheric world angel believed to be in charge of dawn and twilight; depicted as a man with a jackal's head, standing guard. [**cf.** ANGEL OF THE SUN, MAGNIFICENT DEVA]

ANRAKUSHI—(Japan) to make one's transition with ease and comfort when it is time to die;

theory: this is possible if one has the proper instructions long before the time comes. [cf. DEATH ANGEL, ANUHIS, ANSHI-JUTSU]

ANSHI-JUTSU—(Japan) instructions on how to go through the death process easily and comfortably. [cf. DEATH ANGEL, BARDO STATE]

ANSWER CASES—(electronic voices) 1. to carry on a telephone conversation with a dead person which seems like a normal conversation; after the telephone conversation the caller discovers the person had died before the call was made; voice and information transacted pertained to the person who called; 2. to call one's friend, carry on a telephone conversation, and later find that the person was not at home at the time; conversation and voice pertained to the one who was called. (Inconcl.) [cf. BILOCATION, INTENTION CASES, ELECTRONIC VOICES]

ANTAHKARANA—see ANTASKARANA.

ANTASKARANA—(Sanskrit, "within") 1. an invisible region that acts like a bridge between the superconscious and conscious minds; utilized in the skills such as inspirational thought, clairsentience, and intuition; 2. an ethereal bridge between the higher manas and lower manas, linking the soul-mind with the material man. **Syn.** ANTAHKARANA, VEIL, ETHERIC WEB. [cf. SUPERCONSCIOUS MIND, INSPIRATIONAL THOUGHT]

ANTELOPE CHARMING—(Native American) a special dance that is performed as an offering for mother earth; prayers are said asking for food to eat, thanking mother earth for past food, and offering oneself back to earth one day; intent of the dance is to psychically tune into the antelope and an antelope will walk into the corral to offer its body to be eaten; to understand the balance of nature is an instinct among creatures. [cf. MOVEMENT-FOR-ALTERED-STATES-OF-CONSCIOUSNESS, ANIMAL KINGDOM]

ANTHROPOFLUX—coined by Farny; emanation from the human body can decrease the resistance in an electrical circuit; the maximum emission is from the inner surfaces of the left hand fingers, and in the breath. [cf. BREATHING, GALVANIC SKIN RESPONSE INSTRUMENT, RADIONICS]

ANTHROPOMORPHIC CREATIONS—an etheric world intelligence showing itself in a human form, in order for man to feel compatible and comfortable in relating to it, as opposed to a pulsating white

light energy which may be its present vibrational frequency. [cf. GEOMETRIC FORMS, LIGHT BODY, ANGELS, SIXTH PLANE]

ANTHROPOMORPHISM—to ascribe a human form or human attribute to a nonhuman thing, e.g., object, mineral, animal, plant, or to a deceased deity; to make a carving or statue to resemble a human form. [cf. TOTEM, ETHERIC WORLD INTELLIGENCE, SYMBOL, MANDRAKE]

ANTHROPOMORPHON—(Greece) (esoteric) a plant with roots that resemble a human form; capable of making a noise heard by the physical ear; has the vibrational frequency enabling it to bring psychic information to humans. **Syn.** MANDRAKE, SEMIHOMO PLANT. [cf. AMULET, BOTANE]

ANTHROPOSCOPY—(esoteric) (ancient) the art of determining personal characteristics of a person from the shape of his or her head, facial features, and profile. **Syn.** PHYSIOGNOMY. [cf. POINT-OF-FOCUS, HANDREADING Appendix 2, LAW OF REPETITION Appendix 7]

ANTHROPOSOPHY—(Greece *anthropos*, "man"; *sophis*, "wisdom") 1. theory: the root of all things comes from the etheric world and branches out in the physical world of life and actions; a study of the relationship of the source of all in man to the source of all in the universes; utilizes the law of mobility of thought. **Syn.** SPIRITUAL SCIENCE. [cf. BODIES OF MAN, MICROCOSM, MACROCOSM] 2. refers to the discipline as taught by the Anthroposophical Society founded by Rudolf Steiner; aims to liberate man from selfishness by the development of his responses to the subtle influences of the spiritual world; emphasis is put on the significance of color and rhythm. [cf. COLOR, DANCING, BOTANE]

ANTIDOTAL MEDICINE—testimony of people who have found answers to their life problems or physical ills and who give evidence in public as to how this came about; this proves helpful to others, as opposed to a great person solving their problems for them, which still makes the problem insurmountable. [cf. CURATIVE EDUCATION, HOLISTIC HEALTH, UNORTHODOX HEALING]

ANTIFRAUD PRECAUTION—an infrared network installed to surround the mediumistic physical phenomena in a seance dark room to detect mundane interference. [cf. DARKNESS, ECTOPLASM]

ANTIGOD—(Greece, Rome) an inferior etheric world entity of little intelligence and low standards who intrudes occasionally on the medium or psychic, and simulates a higher entity; happens to the inexperienced or ritually impure. **Syn.** ASTRAL SHELL, CONFUSED SOUL-MIND, NONHUMAN SPIRIT. [**cf.** ETHERIC WORLD INTELLIGENCE Appendix 3, ASTRAL CEMETERY, SOULLESS]

ANTIGRAVITY PHENOMENA—to reverse the laws of gravity to perform physical phenomena; executed by intense densification of the mind activity or by one's guides; theory: atoms are capable of moving backward in time; concentration is on the auric construct of the material object until it is no longer under gravitational laws, then manipulated as desired and allowed to fall back in its original form; used in LEVITATION, TELEPORTATION, and APPORTATION. (Inconcl.) [**cf.** TIME, ANTIMATTER, GRAVITY CONTROL Appendix 2]

ANTILIFE—1. without life as scientists know life to be; inert matter, e.g., a chair, a building; 2. (parapsychology) life in a lesser degree than the plant, mineral, animal, or human. [**cf.** LAW OF PERSONIFICATION Appendix 7]

ANTIMATTER—(esoteric) 1. ethereal substance functioning free from gravity in space; gaseous in nature; believed to be the fourth dimension; "matter in a reversed time flow" (Bob Toben). (Inconcl.) [**cf.** ANTIGRAVITY, SPACE FORMS] 2. theory: atoms can move backward in time and make a physical object ethereal substance; intense mental energy is concentrated on the object until it goes back into its pattern form, its invisible pattern form is moved through space and then reconstructed in its original form of a material object; used in the skills of APPORTATION, TRANSMUTATION, and MATERIALIZATION. (Inconcl.) [**cf.** GRAVITY CONTROL Appendix 2]

ANTINODES—the periodic disturbance of two superimposed vibrations traveling in opposite directions in the atmosphere, also known as loops. [**cf.** STANDING WAVE, NODES]

ANTIPAN—(nature spirits) 1. the intelligence in charge of negative energies that give form around the earth; 2. pseudoelementals which have an earthly function and can be evoked by negative thoughts; depicted with horns, goat's legs, coarse hair, offensive odor, and vicious looks. [**cf.** DENSITY, EARTH FAIRY, ELEMENTAL]

ANTIPSI—to obstruct or confuse the normal flow of psychic information and prevent it from getting through to other psychics; a powerful psychic can release thoughts, emotional energy, or psychic energy (unconsciously or deliberately) which is so strong that it spills over into others in the room; not always negative but just an overabundance of energy, e.g., The party had an anxious atmosphere for about ten minutes that was felt by all, when a powerful psychic had a very jealous reaction. **Sim.** SPLODGING, BROADCASTING. [**cf.** PSI BLOCK, CLOAK OF INSULATION, APOPSI]

ANTISURVIVALISTS—psychic researchers who do not believe that life continues after death; they believe that the phenomena that appears to have a living entity behind it are the workings of the psychic's mind and its ability to trick the psychic into believing he or she has contacted a living soul-mind from the etheric world. [**cf.** SURVIVALISTS, REINCARNATION]

ANTITHEOI—(Greece) an evil etheric world entity able to intrude at times to the psychic or medium and bring poor-quality information. [**cf.** ASTRAL SHELL, DENSITY]

ANTITHESIS OF SLEEP—(hypnotherapy) to act sanely but have all the personality traits of another person, while under the influence of hypnosis; subject is given instructions that for a short time he or she will perform like a special celebrity or great artist; subject is capable of imitating this person, feeling that this is reality while performing; unaware of not being the self; has partial recall upon awakening. **Syn.** ARTIFICIAL REINCARNATION. [**cf.** HYPNOTHERAPY]

ANU—1. (Sanskrit) a generic term for the basic pattern of all monads, including atoms (H. P. Blavatsky); 2. (Chaldea) highest of Babylonian deities. [**cf.** TOTALITY, GOD, MICROCOSM, MONAD]

ANUBIS—(Egypt) an etheric world angel whose function is to guide the dying person during his or her death process, making it easier for the soul-mind to slip from the physical body into the etheric world in a peaceful state. **Syn.** DEATH ANGEL, ANRAKUSHI. [**cf.** REINCARNATION, DEATH]

ANUT—(Pacific, Kusaie) see VITAL LIFE FORCE.

ANXIETY ATTACK—(possession) a tremendous feeling of apprehension and psychic tension that occurs in one who has possessional attacks; can only be relieved by allowing the etheric world entity of low quality to enter the body, possess it, and have the hysterical fit. **Syn.** POSSESSION,

29

AVESHA, PHOWA. [cf. HYPERVENTILATION SYNDROME, FREE-FLOATING DREAD, EXORCISM]

ANXIETY STATION—(future science) coined by Marvin Karlins and Lewis M. Andrews; a special area needed for persons to learn what is causing their anxiety and how to balance with situations so as not to build anxiety in the future; currently biofeedback training is providing stress knowledge. [cf. BIOFEEDBACK TRAINING, MEDITATION, EMOTIONAL STRESS]

AP THMOP—(Cambodia) a psychic who specializes in auric clairvoyance and predicts the future of nations and countries by tuning into the aura of sections of civilization. **Syn.** FORECASTER, PROPHET. [cf. VIBRATIONS, CLAIRVOYANT, PROPHECY Appendix 2[

APAS—a silver-colored crescent, drawn with the points of the crescent facing up, aimed to reach the basic part of the subconscious mind; the second tattwa symbol which represents the primordial element, water. **Syn.** CRESCENT. [cf. TATTWAS, TATTWA CHART, CLAIRVOYANCE, FORMS-WITH-POWER]

APERTURE OF BRAHMA—top of the head where the life force leaves the body in the death process via the silver cord. **Syn.** CROWN CHAKRA. [cf. DEATH, KUNDALINI, SUSHUMNA]

APHRODITE—(Greece) the angel in charge of fertility, working with beauty, love, and the moon phases. [cf. MAGNIFICENT DEVA, ANGEL]

APOCALYPSE—alternate name for the book of Revelation, final book of the Bible.

APOCALYPTIC ZODIAN—teaching regarding the etheric world and the Solar God; knowledge that the inner nature of man reflects the science of the heavens; used as necessary instructions for the initiate of the mysteries. [cf. MICROCOSM, MACROCOSM, MONADOLOGY]

APOCRYPHA—(Greek, "hidden") ancient writings given through psychic inspirational thought regarding the etheric world, psychic attunement, and psychology of the soul-mind growth; found only in the Septuagint version of the Old Testament; kept secretive except for the initiates of a distinctive sect; currently in print; singular **Apocryphon.**

APOPSI—to make one's self completely immune from perceiving psychic energy of any kind (positive or negative vibrations); to consciously or unconsciously surround one's self with an impenetrable shield that eliminates all psychic information; skepticism and fear of psychism, and lack of desire to learn about one's self are emotions that build a shield; e.g. "while talking to Jane, her secretiveness made a wall around her and prevented me from tuning into her feelings, so I could not help her with her problem." (do not confuse with ANTIPSI). [cf. CLOAK OF INSULATION, TALISMANS]

APOTHECARER—an etheric world intelligence that takes care of the blending of chemicals in the human body; recognized to be a part of the inner band who is with the individual through one incarnation. **Syn.** ALCHEMIST. [cf. INNER BAND, OUTER BAND, GUIDE]

APOTROPAIC ACTION—to employ a physical symbol to eliminate negative vibrations in an area or in future activity; to take physical action or make bodily motions with the intent of keeping out, or dissipating negative vibrations; e.g., 1. to knock on wood to keep the good flowing inward; 2. to make the Christian "sign of the cross" to seal that which took place with good; 3. to put a four-leaf clover over one's door to keep out evil; 4. to perform a ritual ceremony designed to allow only the good etheric world intelligences to enter one's psychic arena; 5. to execute a tribal dance to cleanse tribe members mentally and physically, so the visions that enter as a result will be of the highest quality. [cf. IMITATIVE MAGIC, LAW OF MIMICRY and LAW OF SYMPATHETIC MAGIC Appendix 7]

APOTROPAIC HEALING PRAYER—(holistic health) to incorporate in one's method of healing a decree that this healing only take place if the patient has already learned the necessary lessons from this manifestation, if the patient may learn the lessons presented from the sickness in another manner, or if the karmic debt may be worked off in a different manifestation; otherwise the patient will have to repeat suffering to this point in the future; to be used in mental and magnetic healing; a usable simple affirmation: "If it is for his highest good and the highest good of all concerned." [cf. MAKE A PRAYER, MAGNETIC HEALING, MENTAL HEALING]

APPARENT PSYCHIC PHONE CALLS—(electronic voices) the most common type of telephone calls from the dead, in which the dead person initiates the phone call; telephone rings, is answered, and two persons talk in a normal way; a parallel factor of all these reported calls: the receiver knows the caller is dead, but for the time period of the conversation this is blocked from his or her memory. (Inconcl.) [**cf.** INTENTION CASES, ANSWER CASES, WITNESS]

APPARITION—(Latin, "to appear") 1. a phantom, misty-like vision perceived clairvoyantly in outer space; psychic manifestation of a scene, an object, or a human resemblance; occurs suddenly, or startling and uninvited, when in a relaxed state, i.e., after meditation, during sleep, or during concentration; appears full-blown but unclear; if a human resemblance, it acts as if it wants to communicate; 2. a collective word covering all visions perceived outside the mind, clairvoyantly and hallucinating: 3. (laboratory) random electrical flickers in the brain. **Sim.** ASTRAL SHELL, SHADES, CONFUSED SOUL-MIND, VISIONARY APPEARANCE, SPECTER. [**cf.** ASTRAL BODY, SPIRIT, ETHERIC WORLD INTELLIGENCE, APPARITION Appendix 4]

APPARITION MEDIUM—see ECTOPLASM MATERIALIZATION MEDIUM.

APPARITION OF THE LIVING—a clairvoyant appearance of a friend or relative, so vivid that it suggests the real presence of the individual; a short-lived duplication of an individual in another location caused by a highly emotional state of the person duplicating himself; occurs unknowingly to the duplicator; duplicator could be undergoing a traumatic situation and desires to announce it to someone or duplicator could strongly desire to see the friend but circumstances make it impossible; duplicator will be fully clothed in the same clothes he is wearing where he is; receiver must be in a relaxed state to perceive the vision. [**cf.** ASTRAL PROJECTION, BILOCATION, EMOTIONAL PSI, NEED-DETERMINED RESPONSE]

APPARITIONAL LIGHT—(materialization) the visibility of a vaporous semimaterial that exudes from the medium before the personality is formed; within the semimaterial a full vision, in an outline form, appears before the personality develops; this indicates enough substance has exuded and the form commences. **Syn.** PERISPRIT. [**cf.** ECTOPLASM, MATERIALIZATION]

APPERCEPTION—1. to comprehend a new idea with the assimilation of knowledge and experience one has had in one's life to formulate a concept; the opposite of PSYCHIC INFORMATION; 2. (esoteric) to interpret psychic information in symbolic form by combining aspects of impressions with conscious knowledge, e.g., "I can see the music in that visionary picture"; "The vision of the lion tells me you are angry"; "The butterfly around your head tells me you have a question." [**cf.** LAW OF SIGNATURES and LAW OF ACTIVITY Appendix 7] 3. (Baron Gottfried Wilhelm von Leibnitz) to convey the meaning that "nerve-sensation expresses the state of monadic conscoiusness through all the kingdoms up to man." [**cf.** MONADOLOGY, TOTALITY]

APPLE—(esoteric) a fruit which has the vibrational frequency that promotes discernment of love matching, e.g., used in games at Halloween parties. [**cf.** BOTANE, CEREMONIAL MAGIC]

APPLIED KINESIOLOGY—a form of chiropractic examination wherein the doctor locates a malfunctioning nerve by testing and using the patient's own hand to add or subtract energy to nerve centers; a method of correlating the total nervous system, including the autonomic nervous system; this sometimes includes evaluation of nerve, vascular, and lymphatic systems, nutrition, acupuncture, cerebral spinal fluid function. [**cf.** THERAPY LOCALIZATION, PERIPHERAL NERVE SYSTEM, CURATIVE EDUCATION]

APPORT MEDIUM—one who has proper body chemistry and an alchemist guide in his or her inner-band who can perform apportations; ectoplasm apportation can be developed by sitting in seances for same; conscious apportation is usually an inborn ability. [**cf.** APPORTATION-TELEKINESIS, APPORT OBJECT]

APPORT OBJECT—any living or inert thing that appears from the air without or with the will of the psychic or medium; object can be jewelry, stone, gem, arrowhead, flower, fruit, bird, mouse, etc.; 1. appears spontaneously in the close vicinity of the psychic while the psychic is conscious but unaware of the happening, e.g., a few pennies falling in front of one without physical means; 2. appears in one's path, noticed as it is out of its element; has significance to the finder, e.g., an arrowhead appearing in the hotel lobby for one who is collecting Indian things; 3. appears in the room where medium is sleeping and the treasure is found upon awakening; (theory: aported object was a personal belonging of the medium in another life); 4. appears in the seance room; willed by the medium in a trance state. [**cf.** APPORTATION-PSYCHOKINESIS, MOTOR APPORTATION]

APPORTATION PSYCHOKINESIS—abbr. APPOR-TATION-PK; **1.** to deliberately dematerialize an object and rematerialize it in a different location under mind power; an alchemical process in which one focalizes undivided attention upon an object until the atomic structure is at a frequency that is ethereal and vaporous in nature, capable of passing through solid substance (walls or buildings); mind power transports it to another location and puts it back in its original atomic structure in the new location; (do not confuse with APPORTATION-TK, wherein the etheric world intelligences do the work). [cf. Appendix 4] **2.** (alchemy) to intensely concentrate on one's vibrational frequency until the body is in its ethereal pattern form; concentration is held to transport oneself in ethereal form to another location; vibrational frequency is slowed down by mind power until body is in its original human form; a necessary step to learn before true "transmutation." [cf. APPORTATION-TK, LEVITA-TION-TK, ALCHEMY, TRANSMUTATION]

APPORTATION TELEKINESIS—abbr. APPORTA-TION-TK; to make things appear from the atmos-phere through the intervention of a personal etheric world intelligence without physical means; personal intelligence is an ethereal alchemist who can use the psychic energy of the medium to dematerialize and rematerialize solid matter; **1.** (seance apportation) to bring matter (sometimes foreign to earth matter) into the seance room and have an apported object for each sitter; one theory: etheric alchemist produces hot, high tension cur-rents that disintegrate the object from a distant place (not disclosed to the sitters); transport it in an ethereal vibration, and reconvert it into solid matter again; it is dropped in a huge sheet in the center of the seance (still hot to the touch); apport objects are gems, shells, stones, jewelry, flowers, etc.; sometimes an object vibrates in an ectoplasm ball in front of the sitter until it cools and the ectoplasm disappears; this skill is developed by the desire of the medium. **Syn.** SEANCE APPORTATION; **2.** to frequently find an apport object in one's path without looking for it; recognized because object is out of its element; occurs randomly but is useful to the medium, e.g., to find extra money in a book when it is especially needed; waking up to find a strange ring on one's finger; **3.** to allow the etheric world alchemist to change one's vibrational fre-quency until it is intact but ethereal in nature, transport the invisible body to another location and change the vibrational frequency to its original human form, capable of performing one's earthly activity; always preplanned and willed by the medium; (do not confuse with TELEPORTATION in which the body moves through air in its natural state). **Syn.** MOTOR APPORTATION. [cf. APPORT MEDIUM, ALCHEMY, ALCHEMIST, SEANCE, PSYCHO-KINESIS, APPORTATION-PK]

APSARAS—**1.** a nature spirit who finds a home and purpose for life in the water; has charge of bodies of water in earth. **Syn.** WATER NYMPH; **2.** (esoteric) a plant used to induce sleep. [cf. BOTANE, FAIRY]

AQUA FLEUR—a solution discovered by Louis VanDecar that keeps him living a much longer life than the normal earthling, looking young and very active. [cf. PHILOSOPHER'S STONE, ELIXIR OF LIFE; ALCHEMY]

AQUAMARINE—(esoteric) a mineral that has the properties which allow the vibrations of Venus to enter the earth; works with human beings to affect water to be used for healing and psychic skills. [cf. MINPSI, MINERAL KINGDOM]

AQUARIAN AGE—a new magnetic field that human evolution is entering; a spiritual age and an air sign; depicted by a man in the sky emptying a pitcher of higher cosmic influence upon all mankind; **1.** as the sign enters, a cleansing of the earth will take place; civilization will go through a tremendous change in morals, values, essential living materials, economic changes, social structures, etc.; this has already begun with terrorism, hijackings, restless violence of youth, and a breakdown of homes; in the 1980s civilization turned about and began providing an opportunity for free-spirited soul-minds to grow into an expanded state of consciousness; there are fewer restrictions in the once rigid social structure and broader communications in which individuals admit their frailties and personal feelings; **2.** the mind will be considered and take preference in many aspects of life, i.e., mind-body health link, biofeedback training, meditation, computer recre-ation, psychic experiments, and a Western interest in the martial arts, etc.; **3.** (astrology) Aquarius is the eleventh sign of the Zodiac; some astrologers say mankind entered this age approximately A.D. 1900 and it will continue approximately 2,600 years to A.D. 4500; some feel the earth began its preparation when Benjamin Franklin worked the kite and key and it built momentum when Thomas Edison invented the electric light bulb; when people no longer had to regulate their activities to the sun, they became free for self-expression; *4.* in the early 1970s the consciousness awareness movements swept across the country, and today the mind is being fed so rapidly, it is difficult to keep up with the changes; expectations of esotericists are that new laws and values will build the action rather than harness it; the youth of today have come to furnish mankind with talents so that a better world can evolve and bridge the gap between the ages of Pisces and Aquarius; (Edgar Cayce) souls born during 1943 to 1956 were from Atlantis and have come into earth again to pay their karma. **Syn.** NEW-AGE. [**cf.** COSMIC CYCLE, AGE, PERIOD]

ARAHANT—(Buddhism) a monk; an enlightened soul-mind.

ARC EMANATIONS—the electromagnetic field surrounding humans; concept that the mental aura is like a rainbow; see AURA. [**cf.** KIRLIAN EFFECT, MENTAL AURA, SOUL-MIND AURA]

ARCANE RECORDS—(*arcanus,* "that which is hidden") (ancient) secret knowledge regarding the etheric world, universal laws, and mankind's relationship to them; mystery of alchemy and psychism; kept sacred and given only to those who are ready to understand and receive it.

ARCHANGELS—1. ETHERIC WORLD INTELLIGENCES who have purified their soul-minds from all imperfection before earth came into being; 2. etheric world intelligences of a very high order who have always existed; 3. (Kabbalah) term used to personify the ten divine emanations that were steps in creation in the SEPHIROTH; recognized as the OVERSOUL; 4. eighth rank in an ANGEL HIERARCHY of nine. [**cf.** ARCHDEMONS, ANGEL KINGDOM, ANGEL KING]

ARCHDEMONS—(Kabbalah) the ten infernal emanations that were created in the beginning; an energy field that serves as the opposite of the archangels, in a universe that is bipolar. [**cf.** POLARITY, ARCHANGELS]

ARCHEO-CORTEX—(esoteric) (*archeo,* "primitive") a storage place in man's brain where his past animal, survival instincts spring from. [**cf.** SYMPATHETIC NERVOUS SYSTEM, INSTINCT CONSCIOUSNESS, HERD INSTINCT]

ARCHETYPAL DREAMS—(Carl Jung) scenes of places, dress, customs, myths, that one cannot identify with; comes from the infinite memory

bank or collection of past lives of mankind, but still relay a message. [**cf.** UNIVERSAL SYMBOLS, ARCHETYPAL IMAGES]

ARCHETYPAL EXPERIENCE—outer actions and manifestations that happen automatically with a natural ability to accomplish correctly; individual has no previous training in that type of activity; does not function under the law of cause and effect; springs from deep within buried layers of the subconscious mind. [**cf.** COLLECTIVE UNCONSCIOUS, SOUL-MIND, REINCARNATION]

ARCHETYPAL FANTASY-FORMS—a spontaneous, clairvoyant vision, that appears to be ancient and senseless; comes from the pre-rational or primitive soul-mind of the psychic's personal memory bank or the collective unconscious. [**cf.** COLLECTIVE UNCONSCIOUS, SUBCONSCIOUS, MENTAL PSYCHISM, SYMBOLISM]

ARCHETYPAL MIRACLE—(Carl Jung) a special quality intuitive feeling that something wonderful is expected to happen; the soul-mind process begins to change its pathway and from then on the soul-mind will be working from a higher plateau. [**cf.** REINCARNATION, PLANES, CONSCIOUSNESS, SOUL-MIND EVOLUTION]

ARCHETYPAL PATTERN—the blueprint for all forms around mankind in the earth plane, held together and sustained by the devic kingdom; designed by man's thoughts. [**cf.** NATURE SPIRITS, ELEMENTALS, AURA, COLLECTIVE UNCONSCIOUS]

ARCHETYPAL PERFECTION—theory: basically man came from one source of perfectness in the beginning; see TOTALITY.

ARCHETYPAL REGION—an area in the subconscious mind where primitive experiences were recorded; can evolve and chose to become a part of the heritage of this incarnation. [**cf.** COLLECTIVE UNCONSCIOUS, SOUL-MIND, REINCARNATION]

ARCHETYPAL SYMBOLS—1. images and scenes dating back to the beginning of primitive mankind, which are perceived clairvoyantly in flashes during sleep, psychic readings or biofeedback training; theory: these flashes stem from a grouping of historical experiences and thoughts in a collective consciousness that each man or woman can dip into; 2. psychic clairvoyant messages clothed in symbols of religion and mythology to bring meaning to the interpretation. [**cf.** THOUGHT, TOTALITY]

33

ARCHETYPAL UNCONSCIOUS—(Carl Jung) a universal memory bank built by the mental activity of mankind since earth began, which man responds to instinctively, but unknowingly; memory bank has an input of all the ideas, thoughts, images, pat-terns, community forms, etc., that are now an in-heritance in everyone's subconscious mind. [cf. SUBCONSCIOUS MIND, MEMORY BANK, REINCARNATION]

ARCHETYPAL WOMB—theory: there is a basis, or root, from which all things come; there is an original first form of all objects and things happen-ing at creation. [cf. ATOMS, VIBRATIONS]

ARCHETYPES—(Greek *arche*, "basic"; *typos,* "type of form") 1. (Plato) a basic form or pattern on which all objects of a certain category are built; 2. (Carl Jung) everything is preexistent in identical form everywhere, making up the collective uncon-scious and manifests through the ability to organize images and ideas operating from the soul-mind; 3. symbols emerging independent of individual memory of the stages of psychological develop-ment; not an individual but universal unconscious, identical in all mankind; 4. the group soul. [cf. COLLECTIVE UNCONSCIOUS, GROUP SOUL, IN-STINCT CONSCIOUSNESS, TOTALITY, SUBLIMINAL LEVEL]

ARCHIVISTS—persons entrusted with the very sacred material wisdom in the ancient great mys-tery schools.

ARCHON—a highly evolved soul-mind in the etheric world who has a purified body through righteousness and goodness. [cf. PLEROMA, ANGEL EVOLUTION]

ARCTURUS—(esoteric) a star belonging to the "great bear" constellation where members of the Great White Brotherhood gather to learn and discuss how to take care of planet earth. (Inconcl.) [cf. GREAT WHITE BROTHERHOOD, MASTERS, ANGEL HIERARCHY]

ARDAT-LILE—(Semitic) a female etheric world entity who is capable of having a form of psychic sex relations with a human male during the nighttime. **Syn.** SUCCUBUS. [cf. ASTRAL PROJEC-TION, DIMENSION-SHIFTING, MENTAL MANIFESTA-TION Appendix 2]

ARETALOGY—(ufology) the study of encounters with nonterrestrial beings and their influence, taken from biographies of ancient writings.

ARHAT—(Buddhism) one who is worthy of being paid homage of an exalted being; one who feels he is enlightened. **Syn.** SAINT. [cf. SAINT, MASTER, REINCARNATION]

ARIEL—an etheric world intelligence that desires to communicate with an earthling to help in his psychic work. [cf. ETHERIC WORLD INTELLIGENCES Appendix 3]

ARIOSOPHIE—(Germany) an esoteric teaching pertaining to ASTROLOGY, PHRENOLOGY, FRINGE MEDICINE, diet reform, PSYCHIC SCIENCE, and the KABBALAH, established by Lanz about 1900.

ARJUNA—(Hinduism) the disciple and prince to whom Sri Krishna delivers his religious wisdom and basic theories of how to live; written in the famous literature called *Bhagavad Gita.*

ARK OF THE COVENANT—(Old Testament) (eso-teric) rectangular box made of acacia wood and covered inside and out with a layer of pure gold: on top were placed two Cherubs in such a way as to create an electrical spark gap; theories: 1. a highly charged box filled with crystals, which gave off electricity used in connection with the great pyra-mid; so highly charged with electricity that only initiates could touch it; all others would be electro-cuted; also charged with antigravity power; 2. a device that magnified voices from the etheric world to give knowledge, confidence, and prophecy through special qualified leaders; 3. a prescience tool manipulated from outer space. (Inconcl.)

ARKALEEN—(Sufi) a psychic who teaches the wisdom that is hidden from the masses; works psychically with the etheric and natural forces to promote a more full and meaningful life.

ARMAGEDDON—the place where the final battle of the earth will be fought; theory: some day the Satanic and angelic forces will have to battle out the destiny of the earth. [cf. COSMIC TIME-TABLE]

ARMORED ORGANISM—(ufology) (Trevor James Constable) pertains to the rigid structure that humans have built around themselves from thousands of years of socio-religious taboos in-tended to protect themselves from painful stimuli and from one's natural organism sensations; hu-mans should be compatible to UFO phenomena because it has the same bioenegetic movement but instead this armor makes humans intolerant to UFOs regardless of evidence. [cf. CONSTRUCT, UFOLOGY Appendix 5]

ARNQUAGSSAQ—(Eskimo) an etheric world intelligence who earned the rank of angel; has charge of all the sea animals. [cf. ANGEL EVOLUTION, MAGNIFICENT DEVA]

AROUSAL—(biofeedback training) the degree of emotional activity within the body, capable of being measured on instruments; intensity dimension of behavior revealed by one's moods, anxiety, excitement, effects of drugs or smoking, feeling of fatigue and the time of the day; a drowsy, inactive subject is low in arousal, and the alert, active subject is high in arousal; measured by the sweat glands on a GSR and by passing a minute amount of electricity through the body on the metabolic monitor. [cf. GSR, EEG, BIOFEEDBACK TRAINING, BIO-STAT MONITOR]

ARRHYTHMIA—lack of rhythm; (esoteric) a condition of the body when the etheric world control of the medium is switching the normal flow of the physical body to his workable flow; the heart beats rapidly and spasmodically. [cf. MENTAL MANIFESTATIONS/MISCELLANEOUS, PHYSICAL MANIFESTATIONS/MISCELLANEOUS, MEDIUMSHIP]

ARRIVAL CASE—to be psychically impressed that one would soon meet a specific person and shortly after the spontaneous impression, the person arrives in one's presence. **Sim.** PREMONITION. [cf. CLAIRSENTIENCE, MENTAL PSYCHISM]

ARS MORIENDI—the craft of dying properly; to learn the process of death before one makes his or her transition, so one can go through it without pain and suffering. [cf. DEATH, REINCARNATION, DEATH ANGEL]

ARS NOTORLA—the science of the Tarot signs and their application to nature and philosophy, in regard to predicting the future. [cf. POINT OF FOCUS, LAW OF SIGNATURES and LAW OF REPETITION Appendix 7]

ART OF DYING—(ancient, esoteric) theory: dying is a form of initiation, and one should take instructions in the dying process before approaching death to be able to sensibly and intelligently pass the initiation that death offers. [cf. DEATH ANGEL, FIRST DEATH, LAW OF DYING Appendix 7]

ART OF LIVING—(esoteric) to balance with the experiences encountered in planet earth by resolving each encounter as it presents itself; in this way one's experiences become more qualitative and enriching; theory: earth experiences are totally the result of one's own decision, thoughts, and actions throughout all incarnations; to realize that one is in command of his or her entire life and to correctly handle each situation as it comes, brings happiness. [cf. KEY TO LIFE, FREE WILL, BRAIN]

ART OF PRECIPITATION—see VISUALIZATION.

ART OF TEA—(Zen) to use a tea made of a special herb to keep one's self awake during long meditation periods. [cf. MEDITATION, SEED MEDITATION]

ART OF THE VELVET FIST—see AIKIDO.

ARTEMIS—(Greece) one who has earned the rank of angel in the etheric world, and is in charge of the nature spirits who oversee water, mountains, meadows, and forests; recognized as a great goddess; depicted as a bear. [cf. DEVA-LOKA, EXALTED ONES]

ARTEPHIUS—(Hermetic) a human being who is said to have lived more than a thousand years by means of alchemical secrets; died in the twelfth century.

ARTHAME—(esoteric) the knife used in Solomon's temple to draw circles for invocation and evocation of etheric world intelligences; it was properly imbedded with psychic vibrations for such ceremonies. [cf. CEREMONIAL MAGIC, SYMBOLISM, EVOCATION]

ARTICLE PSYCHOKINESIS—abbr. A-PK; 1. to deliberately concentrate on a specific energy field to change or alter its position or form; used in experiments to determine power of the mind and to practice mind control, e.g., Uri Geller bends spoons and fixes clocks with mind intensification; laboratories work with moving matchsticks and altering thrown dice; 2. (Russia) the ability to change the energy of the bioplasma around matter to undo the flow, and this allows the article to bend; mind and emotions have an effect on the bioplasmic force in the experiment; in this kind of PK the law of gravity is intact. Usage: "Can you PK a grain of dust?" (Inconcl.) **Syn.** NONHUMAN-PK. [cf. NATURE-PK, LEVITATION-PK, LEVITATION-TK; MENTAL HEALING]

ARTIFACT—1. (biofeedback training) an electrical charge from a source other than that which is being tested, giving a different level of signals on the printouts; caused by bodily muscular movements, such as unnoticed twitches or sweating in the electrode area; also caused by interference from

35

electronic equipment or fluorescent lighting; any signal that does not come from brain thoughts. [cf. BIOFEEDBACK TRAINING, ELECTRODES] 2. (laboratory) a skeptical attitude in a controlled psychic experiment which produces an effect not totally accurate. [cf. SHEEP AND GOATS EFFECT]

ARTIFACTUAL ESP—(laboratory) that which can push the subject away from his conscious task and interfere with a good ESP target. [cf. TARGET, ESP, CHANCE EXPECTATION]

ARTIFICIAL ANXIETY WAVES—(Thomson and Ward) a transmitter instrument that makes fear and aggression vibrations similar to a human's negative thoughts; to be used to aid in curing patients who have a great deal of anxiety tension. (Inconcl.) [cf. CASECRACKING, HABITUAL KARMA, MENTAL BLOCK]

ARTIFICIAL ASTRAL PLANE—a large mass of various types of semiintelligent entities in the etheric world lacking in order and completeness; made by man's negative thoughts interrelated with bad karmic experiences; half-human entities taking their abode in the lower astral planes. **Syn.** DENSITY. [cf. PLANES, DENSITY, THOUGHTS]

ARTIFICIAL BRAIN WAVE PATTERN—a telepathic thought originated by one person and picked up by another, quite unaware of where the thought came from and why; occurs especially in the case of twins, or two people in very good rapport psychically. [cf. TELEPATHY, ASTRAL LINK, AGENT-PERCIPIENT PAIR]

ARTIFICIAL ELEMENTAL—(esoteric) 1. an invisible intelligent mass of energy created by an individual to be used psychically; hovers close to its owner taking the shape of a personality or animal that the owner desires; made by constant consistent thoughts of one theme and must be recharged daily to exist; once formulated, it possesses a distinct and independent life of its own, but soulless; functions under the direction of the owner but can react on past suggestions with no warning: this thought mass can be helpful in traveling to bring healing energies to an individual in another location or perform menial tasks for its owner; thought mass can be destructive and travel to put a hex on another individual if directed to do so. **Syn.** RUPA. 2. an invisible entity from the etheric world encased with elemental essence into a thought-form caused by strong invocations of the psychic; assists the psychic in physical phenomena. [cf. THOUGHT-FORMS, ELEMENTAL ESSENCE]

ARTIFICIAL FIELDS—(Russia) the use of complex equipment designed to put magnetic energy around the psychic to improve the psychic's ability. (Inconcl.) [cf. PSYCHIC TRANSFER, SHIELDING, UP-FOR-GRABS, PSYCHIC DOORS, SANCTUARY]

ARTIFICIAL GROUP ELEMENTAL—a large energy field hovering over the heads of individuals in a gathering which has a strong influence on each individual; 1. energy field is composed of thought energy coming from the individuals; field is formed and sustained because of the unity of thoughts and emotions; all minds are focused on one subject, one goal, one concept, or one attitude brought about telepathically by the tone and pitch of the words of the leader or music; elemental becomes recharged as the meeting progresses if the group keeps this unity of emotion and thought; 2. elemental has an independent existence outside the consciousness of the thinkers and is capable of influencing each person individually to react emotionally in a manner one could not or would not be capable of individually away from the group; 3. elemental disperses as rapidly as it is formed when the group is dismissed as the crowd no longer has continuity of existence; 4. e.g., individuals at a concert frequently weep because the oneness, joy, and awe become overwhelming; young adults at a rock festival scream and tear off clothing because the music is choreographed to tune into these levels of the brain and the massness of feelings thrust them into this; soldiers attend military drills frequently in the sameness of uniform; this, along with the saluting and music reinforces their patriotism; destructive-brainwashing cult members meet daily or bi-daily to engage in repetitious verbiage and phrase shouting to keep the "cult programming" at an emotional peak. [cf. ELEMENTAL, MASS HYPNOSIS, DESTRUCTIVE-BRAINWASHING CULTS]

ARTIFICIAL MAGNET—any object that is purposely charged by a human's psychic energy and used as an amulet, or in a ritual; object can be a stone, part of a tree, or a treasure, etc.; psychic beams energy to object in a variety of methods until object has more magnetism than it originally had; intent of its usage is necessary to establish when energizing it; **Syn.** TALISMAN. [cf. BEAMED ENERGY, MAGNETISM, AMULET ENERGIZING]

ARTIFICIAL PARADISE—visionary scene accompanied by a wonderful feeling of being in a heavenly location brought on by the use of a hallucenogenic drug; considered a "good trip";

useful if experienced under the guidance of a teacher who then explains the various levels of the etheric world. [**cf.** PEYOTE CACTUS, IPOMEA, PSILO-CYBIN MUSHROOM, THORNAPPLE]

ARTIFICIAL REINCARNATION—(hypnosis) to act like a deceased person in mannerisms, intelligence, speech, and talent, while under the influence of a hypnotic state; e.g., to assume the characteristics of one's mother in expression and speech; subject does not necessarily have to be acquainted with the person he imitates; subject can paint like a great painter himself. (Inconcl.) [**cf.** REINCARNATION, SUBCONSCIOUS MIND, HYPNOTHERAPY]

ARTIFICIAL SYMBOLS—psychic information showing through in visionary symbols using mundane objects that have a communality or universal meaning; e.g., a national flag shown to portray a victory over something one has already begun; an old black upright telephone may indicate one will be communicating with an old friend; a roof without anything underneath could be emblematic of one being protected in his problem. [**cf.** CLAIR-VOYANCE, MENTAL PSYCHISM, IMAGE]

ARTIKA CEREMONY—a ritual performed in one of the destructive-brainwashing cults to induce a "snapping" state of mind; consists of offering a candle to the deity, jumping up and down, singing, dancing, chanting, repetitiously for a prolonged time, and then concentrating immediately on six statues of deities; overindulgence in the above activities forces one's psychic doors to open in an unnatural way; one may see visions, pleasant or fierce, but believed (or told) to be spiritual because the individual has never experienced an altered state of consciousness like it before; the mind has snapped and from that time on the individual floats in and out of the altered state which makes him easier to be controlled by the organization. [**cf.** DESTRUCTIVE-BRAINWASHING CULT, SNAPPING, FORCED PSYCHISM]

ARTIST OF THE HEART—(Egypt) priest who does psychiatric work.

ARTISTIC TELEPATHY—an experiment wherein the teacher draws on paper or traces a picture and the students draw in line form on their paper what they are feeling; the teacher is hidden from sight of the students. [**cf.** TELEPATHY Appendix 2]

ARUNQUILTHA—(Australian aborigines) see VITAL LIFE FORCE.

ARUPA—(Sanskrit, "formless") that which is bodiless, formless, dimensionless in space and time; name given to the etheric world intelligences who communicate with mankind from the higher levels of consciousness where they no longer take on a human-like body; exist in a shape far beyond the narrow limits of language. [**cf.** ARUPA-LOKAS, EYE LANGUAGE, SIXTH PLANE]

ARUPA-LOKAS—(Sanskrit) spheres in the higher realms of the etheric world, which is a finer and more subtle vibration than its lower spheres; a habitation where more highly evolved soul-minds abide. [**cf.** PLANES, BODIES OF MAN, MANSIONS]

ARUSPEX—to predict the future for a nation or an individual by the formation, number, and direction of birds in flight. **Syn.** ORNITHOMANCY. [**cf.** MANTIC ARTS Appendix 6, DIVINATION, PROPHECY]

ARY—suffix meaning "belonging to."

ARYAN RACE—(Hinduism) earliest ancestors of India responsible for writing the Veda, the sacred book of the Hindus; believed to be the first sub-race inhabiting India and Egypt in prehistoric times.

AS ABOVE, SO BELOW, AS BELOW SO ABOVE—coined by Hermes; shortened from "what is below is like that which is above, and what is above is like that which is below." [**cf.** LAW OF PARALLELISM Appendix 7]

AS IF TECHNIQUE—(ancient) to psychically influence an individual to act according to one's wishes without the individual being aware of an outside influence; psychic charges himself with psychic energy and visualizes being inside the victim's body acting out a desired plan; must be repeated frequently with strong emotions and a disciplined mind; (do not confuse with POSSESSION). [**cf.** PSYCHIC TRANSFER]

ASANA—1. (Yoga) body positions patterned after an animal, or plant, used for exercise and meditation; named after the animal or plant which describes the quality and appearance of the position; techniques are used for becoming limber, toning muscles, giving relief from tension, and normalizing other bodily functions by stretching and relaxing; 2. (Sanskrit, "to sit"); referring to an effortless and comfortable position to meditate; 3. (Vedic) the posture of the body during meditation and the place used for this posture. [**cf.** MEDITATION Appendix 5]

ASAT—(Sanskrit) that which is unreal, false, illusory. [**cf.** HALLUCINATION, MAYA]

ASC—abbr. ALTERED STATES OF CONSCIOUSNESS; an awareness or unawareness whereby its quality differs from a normal mental or sleep state; a subconscious, superconscious, or subliminal level of mind activity brought on by meditation, psychic development, or drugs (medical or drugs for the purpose of a change in consciousness). [**cf.** HALLUCINATION, MEDITATION, PSYCHIC DEVELOPMENT, CONSCIOUSNESS]

ASCEND—1. (esoteric) to float or suspend one's body in the air by temporarily releasing all negation from the body cells which in turn releases the pull of gravity and the body rises easily. [**cf.** LEVITATION, FLY, ASCENSION-THROUGH-MEDITATION] 2. to mount; to climb upward and onward; to rise to a higher level of consciousness through righteous living and actions which change the body chemistry making it possible to free itself from the law of gravity and float upward. [**cf.** TRANSCEND, TRANSCENDENT, GLORIFIED BODY, ASCENSION, GRAVITY CONTROL]

ASCENDED BEING—1. a collective word meaning any etheric world intelligence who communicates with earthlings; 2. one who has earned the privilege of inhabiting the higher realms in the etheric world by purifying his or her body while on the earth plane. [**cf.** ASCENSION, DEATH SCIENCE, ETHERIC WORLD INTELLIGENCES]

ASCENDED MASTER—(esoteric) a human being who has earned the rank of Masterhood and abides on the fifth plane in the etheric world but chooses to reincarnate in a physical body as a great leader to promote spiritual understanding and growth for civilization, e.g., Buddha, Krishna, Jesus. [**cf.** ANGEL HIERARCHY, REINCARNATION, CHRISTED]

ASCENDING ARC—(Theosophy) the life-waves of all the celestial globes in the whole galaxy evolving upward making a chain effect.

ASCENSION—(esoteric) 1. to physically purify one's body from all negativity until the body chemistry becomes refined and is eliminated from the law of gravity and rises in the air; body is purified from all the gross vibrations by righteous thoughts, actions, and high qualitative living over many incarnations; when all the worthless actions and memories and thoughts are resolved and dissipated, the soul-mind in the body, desiring to return to its source, will lift in the air as if floating and head upward; 2. other psychic and alchemical skills are necessary to achieve before one can ascend; to free the mind from materialistic thoughts is to free the body from the law of gravity; the internal physical process carried on by the mind causes certain parts of the body to become heated up within the body; this heat goes up to the brain producing celestial dew and the person appears to be all "aglow" as he ascends; (do not confuse with levitation or teleportation); see Appendix 4 for clarification. [**cf.** ALCHEMIST, PURIFIED BODY, AGLOW, HUMAN BEING, EVOLUTION]

ASCENSION-THROUGH-MEDITATION—(Transcendental Meditation) to rid one's self of much of the worthless vibrations in the atoms of the body by prolonged meditation until the body rises a few inches or feet off the floor and hops around like a frog; occurs at meditation retreats because of long daily periods of meditation; body is cleansed and/or released from the material world for that time and rises easily; (do not confuse with prolonged meditational periods in the destructive-brainwashing cults where they have no feedback, evaluation, or proper supervision, as one has at a TM retreat). (Inconcl.) **Sim.** LEVITATION, FLY. [**cf.** APPORTATION Appendix 4, SELF-NONSELF, SATORI]

ASCENT—(Buriat) a very important ritual in which a shaman climbs a birch tree, after he has earned his shamanship; it means that from that time on, he is protected whenever he communicates to the etheric world intelligences; symbol that the shaman goes to heaven to receive his psychic information. **Sim.** LADDER TO HEAVEN. [**cf.** SHAMANSHIP, SYMBOLISM, CLOAK OF INSULATION]

ASCETIC—(esoteric) one who renounces the worldly way of life and disciplines himself or herself in a rigid, religious way of life, believing this is the way to purify oneself more quickly. [**cf.** EVOLUTION, SOUL-MIND, THE PATH]

ASCETICISM—theory: to live a simple life and abstain from normal pleasures will increase one's psychic skills and healing abilities.

ASEXUAL—an entity that is neither gender; without sex organs; angels are neuter and all deceased human beings are without either gender while living in the etheric world. [**cf.** ANGEL KINGDOM, ETHERIC WORLD, IMPERISHABLE ONES]

ASHES—a residue of deliberate fire used in ceremonies as a symbol of the fire in the beginning of creation from which everything came; seeds of fire will purify and regenerate, so the ashes are capable of bringing new life and strength to the wearer; used over the entire body or on the forehead. [**cf.** CEREMONIAL MAGIC, SYMBOLISM]

ASHRAM—(Sanskrit, Vedic, Hinduism) a monastery, a spiritual colony, a place where a special teaching experience is held; a religious retreat headed by a guru or a teacher. [**cf.** SOUL-MIND EVOLUTION]

ASHTAR—(ufology) personal name of an etherian being from Venus who communicated through a tranced psychic; brought thousands of volumes of knowledge on etherian psychism and all phases of space. (Inconcl.)

ASIYYAH—the sublunar universe; the vibrational frequencies directly under the sun.

ASOMATIC EXPERIENCE—to mentally project one's consciousness to another location and feel a part of one's self in the location but cannot associate with a body there; feeling a sense of "point consciousness"; clairvoyant perception is vivid; stimulated by deep meditation beforehand. (Inconcl.) [**cf.** PARASOMATIC EXPERIENCE, MENTAL PROJECTION Appendix 2]

ASPECT OF SELF-SOURCE—theory: personalities that come to man in an altered state of consciousness are given to man from the Universal Mind or the total picture; stem from a grouping of thoughts in the ethereal world formed by everyone. (Inconcl.) [**cf.** COLLECTIVE UNCONSCIOUS, SUBCONSCIOUS MIND, GUIDES]

ASPECTS OF WISDOM—(Tibet) (esoteric) theory: contents of the soul-mind mechanism: 1. mirrorlike wisdom symbolized by white; 2. wisdom of equality symbolized by yellow; 3. light path of discriminating wisdom, red; 4. all performing wisdom, green.

ASPIRANT—one who desires to seek higher knowledge and follow the path he or she feels is the righteous one to take that will lead to perfectness. Sim. DISCIPLE. [**cf.** RIGHT PATH]

ASPORT—the disappearance of a physical object from a location that the psychic frequents or from the seance room if an apport medium is present; the object is dematerialized into its original ethereal form by an ethereal world guide; object can be transported through space and rematerialized in another location (process that must take place before apportation); (do not confuse with POLTERGEIST activity wherein there is no cause for disappearing objects and it happens frequently). (Inconcl.) [**cf.** MEDIUMSHIP, SEANCE, APPORTATION Appendix 4]

ASPORT TO APPORT—passing of solids through solids; to dematerialize an article by resolving it into its component atoms, transport it through space regardless of walls or furniture, and reassemble it into mundane substance in its original form; performed by the medium's guide while medium is in deep trance; (do not confuse with ALCHEMY transmutation in which the mind is the tool). (Inconcl.) **Sim.** APPORTATION. [**cf.** DEMATERIALIZATION, APPORTATION Appendix 4]

ASPORTATION—to allow an etheric world intelligence to intervene and dematerialize an object into its original atomic components; this can be held in abeyance until a future date or future incarnation when it is rematerialized or it can be immediately rematerialized in a different location; occurs in a seance room or when medium is in an altered state. [**cf.** GRAVITY CONTROL Appendix 2]

ASSESSING—(magnetic healing) 1. to become aware of energy flow differences in the patient's physical body as a preparation before LAYING-ON-OF-HANDS; palms of the hands are run over the patient's body a few inches above body to detect different sensations; at the same time healer tunes in psychically to the patient to allow associated ideas to surface to help the cure; when a different sensation of energy flow is felt in the healer's hands it is recognized as a congested area that needs attention; 2. (Delores Krieger) theory: hands pick up positive ions which are formed when an atom loses an electron making a disease; one may sense a fullness in the tissues making the skin drawn and tight that cannot be detected by the naked eye or may sense a tingling, hot, cold, or puzzling feeling. (Inconcl.) [**cf.** RUFFLED, THERAPEUTIC TOUCH, LAYING-ON-OF-HANDS]

ASSIAH—(Kabbalah) an ethereal substance that lies immediately behind matter and gives rise to matter; planes close to earth are of a lower evolutionary state; emblematic of the root chakra as mankind operates from the materialistic level. [**cf.** DENSITY, ATZILUTH, BRIAH, YETZI-RAH, SEPHIROTH]

ASSIMILATION—the transference of a sick person's disease to a psychic; sick person will feel well if the psychic accepts it; willed or unconsciously given and willed or unconsciously received; psychic may send it back to where it came from if he realizes it is not his own illness; otherwise it will disappear in a few days. (Inconcl.) [cf. SCAPEGOAT, ANTIPSI, PSYCHIC ATTACK]

ASSISTANT DOWSING—to extend one's radiesthetic sense (if an accomplished dowser), to a student; dowser stands behind the student and puts his hands on the dowsing rods over the student's hands; both concentrate on the target; the rods will dip as if the accomplished dowser were working alone. (Inconcl.) [cf. RADIESTHETIC SENSE, DOWSING, L-RODS, PENDULUM]

ASSOCIATION FLUIDITY—a quick verbal response by the patient when the therapist names an object in the subject's dream, in a psychoanalyzing session; the spontaneous answer is believed to be useful to get at hidden feelings in the subconscious mind of the subject. **Syn.** FREE ASSOCIATION. [cf. DREAM SYMBOLS, BLOCKS, DREAMSTUFF]

ASSOCIATION MAGIC—theory: "the symbol of the thing is the thing; the real can be influenced through the simulated"; 1. to use a thing and go through activity with the thing similar to what one wants to happen to the real; similar actions produce similar results, regardless of distance; thing must be an object, person, or event that bears resemblance in color, shape, smell, action, or sequence of events; 2. to use an article that belongs to the person or animal that one is psychically working with which creates a psychic link between the article and the person or animal; association magic utilizes the laws of imitation, contagion, parallelism, signatures, and symbolism, see Appendix 7. [cf. ASSOCIATION MAGIC and SYMBOLS Appendix 2]

ASSOCIATION TELEPATHY—(laboratory) to pick up both ideas in the mind of the agent even though only one idea was voiced verbally in the experiment; subject picks up untold associated idea telepathically. [cf. ESP, AGENT, TARGET, MENTAL TELEPATHY]

ASSOCIATION THEORY—each subconscious mind has its own characteristic features and is linked to a huge mind in which all other subconscious minds are linked; each subconscious mind draws from this huge mind also revealing characteristics of others;

reason for many similarities in the world. (Inconcl.) **Sim.** COLLECTIVE UNCONSCIOUS. [cf. UNIVERSAL MIND, MONAD, SUBCONSCIOUS MIND]

ASSUMED—indicates that an intelligence from the invisible world is using a physical body to work through psychically in the earth plane. Usage: the medium's body is "assumed" by the unseen operator for physical phenomena. (Inconcl.) [cf. MEDIUMSHIP, TRANCE, GUIDE IMPERSONATION]

ASSUMPTION OF GOD FORMS—(ancient Egypt) to psychically merge one's consciousness with an etheric world intelligence (called gods at that time) in an animal form that could be detected by physical eyes; to function for a time in the new form and then return to one's normal consciousness for normal living. **Sim.** SHAPE-CHANGING. [cf. DIMENSION-SHIFTING, LAW OF ATTENTION Appendix 7]

ASTARTE—(Semitic, Phoenicia) an etheric world intelligence who earned the rank of goddess; in charge of beauty, love, and fertility on earth; works in rapport with the vibrations from the moon; a symbol of sex; goddess is sometimes used for evoking passion for oneself and one's lover. [cf. ANGEL, EVOCATION, ETHERIC WORLD INTELLIGENCES]

ASTRAL—(Latin *astar,* "star") refers to the level of awareness in the etheric world that is close to the mundane world; a vibration faster than the earth vibration but looks similar to earth when one perceives it clairvoyantly; easiest frequency for psychics to tune into. [cf. ASTRAL PLANE, ASTRAL INHABITANTS]

ASTRAL ART—to put on paper with charcoal or paint that which one's higher self sees around him or her while one is painting; psychic artist tunes into the higher realms and senses energies that come to him or her in supersensual forms, shapes, and colors of eloquence beyond words; (do not confuse with AUTOMATISM in which the hand is moved by an etheric world intelligence). [cf. PORTRAIT ARTIST, PSYCHIC ART]

ASTRAL ATTENDANT—a constant, persistent thought of one emotional aspect of his or her life which builds a mass elemental for the thinker; influences the thinker constantly until the persistent thought is dropped from his or her mind; elemental can become so forceful that it prevents the thinker from deviating in thought; built deliberately for beneficial purposes, e.g., to give one courage, healing, etc.; built unconsciously from discouragement and keeps one at a low level or depressed. See ELEMENTAL. [**cf.** SOULLESS, DENSITY, ELEMENTAL ESSENCE]

ASTRAL BELL—a clairaudient sound which comes to a medium to announce that an etheric world intelligence is ready to bring assistance or communicate; astral bell is any noise from a tiny click to a large bell, or a knock on glass or something in the area. [**cf.** CLAIRAUDIENCE, ANGELIC CONVERSATION, DIVINE WHISPER]

ASTRAL BODY—1. while a human is alive: the astral body is an invisible, ethereal substance interpenetrating the physical body and extending outward about five to eight inches; lives under the principles of this frequency (not earth principles), learning and growing and being influenced by the physical existence; in turn contributes to the physical existence in an unrecognizable manner; capable of separating from the physical body in an astral projection during sleep, during the daytime at will, or unconsciously in bilocation; if psychically perceived when projected it looks identical to the physical body; 2. when human is dead: astral body envelopes the soul-mind in the etheric world; composed of semifluidic astral material, less dense, porous, and weightless; sensitive to thought; astral body has the emotions of the physical body but in the form of memory, only; looks human-like and clothed if perceived clairvoyantly; because of its fast vibration the five senses are not stabilized through an organ and one sees with their entire body; astral brain recognizes both the physical and the astral experiences; has no conscious mind or nervous system per se but is subject to memories of earth's strong desires and habits so it can hover close to earth and influence earthlings for its own pleasures if it chooses. (Inconcl.) **Syn.** see Appendix 3. [**cf.** HAUNTING, ASTRAL PLANE, GHOSTS, ASTRAL PROJECTION]

ASTRAL BODY WANDERINGS—to slip out of one's physical body and perform activity in another location appearing as if it were the real person; astral body leaves the physical body without having knowledge of how to do this or how to sense that it is happening; physical body keeps on performing its normal activity; later many persons verify seeing the astral-projected body; e.g., the split-form singing a hymn in a church with the same clothes on as the normal body which is not in the church. (Inconcl.) **Syn.** bilocation [**cf.** ASTRAL PROJECTION, MULTIFORM, EMOTIONAL PSI]

ASTRAL BRAIN—a counterpart of the physical brain located in the astral body head but not used to make astral decisions; connected to the physical body by an invisible, ethereal cord but not used as a brain to help physical decisions nor is it connected to a cerebrospinal nervous system in the astral body. [**cf.** ASTRAL VISION, ASTRAL LIGHT, NADIS]

ASTRAL BRUISES—(astral projection) physical swellings, teeth marks, and bruises found on one's body in the morning after an astral projection in which one encountered difficulty on the astral plane or was struck by an earthling who saw the subtle body and was afraid; [**cf.** ASTRAL PROJECTION, PSYCHIC ATTACK]

ASTRAL CABLE—an invisible, tenuous, cobweb-like elastic cord made of ethereal substance; runs from the base of the spine through to the crown chakra and extends to the monad; contains vibrant life energy; difficult to see when not in use; attached to the astral body when it is on an astral projection and will stretch as far as the astral body goes. (Inconcl.) **Syn.** SILVER CORD, ASTRAL CORD. [**cf.** BIRTH SCIENCE, DEATH SCIENCE, ASTRAL PROJECTION]

ASTRAL CATALEPSY—(astral projection) a period of time in which both the physical and astral bodies are "set and stiff"; occurs when the astral body first lifts out of the physical body to a horizontal position above the physical body to begin its journey. [**cf.** ASTRAL PROJECTION Appendix 2]

ASTRAL CEMETERY—a low subplane in the etheric world in which the astral shell will stay until it dissipates, after the soul-mind has left for a higher plane; similar to an earth cemetery. [**cf.** ASTRAL SHELL, REINCARNATION, MENTAL PLANE, ASTRAL PLANE]

ASTRAL COADJUTOR—(mediumship) an etheric world intelligence whose function is to regulate the time and quality of intelligences who enter the mind of the medium; responsible for the health of the medium in regard to this regulation; a member of the inner band and subject to guidance of the main guide. **Syn.** DOORKEEPER. [**cf.** INNER BAND, DOCTOR TEACHER, MEDIUMSHIP]

ASTRAL CONSCIOUSNESS—a feeling of lightness and seeing with one's whole body; information is difficult to sort out if one is not aware of this reality but while in this consciousness one feels like it is reality; obtained in an astral projection, a mental projection, or dream state; infrequently one is born with the ability to see on the mundane and astral planes simultaneously; a freedom from balancing with mundane vibrations. [cf. CONSCIOUSNESS, ASTRAL PLANE]

ASTRAL CORD—an invisible, elastic, tenuous cobweb-like cable attached to the kanda at the base of the spine and the monad in the etheric world; runs along the spinal cord and extends through the crown chakra; during an astral projection, this cord stays attached to the astral body and stretches as far as the astral body travels (its ability for infinite stretching is perplexing to man); pulsation is seen along the cord when one is projecting as if heartbeat and breath are transferred from the physical body to the astral body or vice versa. (Inconcl.) **Syn.** SILVER CORD, ASTRAL CABLE. [cf. ASTRAL PROJECTION, IN-THE-RANGE-OF-CORD-ACTIVITY, SOUL-MIND]

ASTRAL CORPSE—see ASTRAL SHELL.

ASTRAL COUNTERPART—an exact duplication in the etheric world of everything in this world but functioning under different laws "as above, so below." (Inconcl.) [cf. ASTRAL PLANE, REINCARNATION, DENSITY, GRAVITY]

ASTRAL CURRENTS—an ethereal substance able to act upon the physical and astral plane atoms to bring about a coherent agreeable vibrational frequency that the psychic can perceive; a number of parallel lines of astral substance extending from the psychic to the scene of viewing; a tube is formed according to the will of the psychic whether he or she intends to see into the past, present, or future; tubes cause a physiological process to take place in the psychic's body to bring him or her the clairvoyant pictures and impressions. (Inconcl.) **Syn.** ASTRAL TELESCOPE. [cf. EMOTIONAL PLANE, CLAIRVOYANCE, EARTH MEMORY]

ASTRAL DIVING POOL—an electric insulated chamber built to test the electrical fields of a person taking an astral projection flight. (Inconcl.) [cf. ASTRAL PROJECTION, DENSITY, PLANES]

ASTRAL FAIRIES—beautiful, radiant nature spirits that stand eight feet high; if perceived clairvoyantly, rays of light are seen streaming from them.

ASTRAL FANTASIES—see CLAIRVOYANCE.

ASTRAL FIRE—see MAGNETISM.

ASTRAL HALLUCINATIONS—(Tibet) to perceive unsightly visions, in the death process, that are one's own negative thoughts being worked out for one to overcome; visions are grotesque, distorted, and unrecognizeable, e.g., a green light around an image defying one's own jealous thoughts. [cf. DEATH SCIENCE, BARDO]

ASTRAL HEALING—an earned privilege in which one travels to the astral world during sleep to take part in an ethereal healing or surgery; psychic works on an astral body of one unknown to him or her in earth life; unwilled by the psychic and usually not recalled except for parts of the scene in dreamstuff or meditation; the similarity in most cases is that the psychic feels tired in the morning and knows something unusual took place. (Inconcl.) [cf. PSYCHIC HEALING, DREAMS, ASTRAL PROJECTION]

ASTRAL INITIATION—to forceably go through an artificial death process in order to obtain a better understanding of life's function, purpose, and responsibility; a prepared method for students studying to become an abbot. **Sim.** CEREMONY OF LITTLE DEATH. [cf. DEATH ANGEL, INITIATION, HYPNOGOGIC STATE]

ASTRAL LAND OF LIGHT—see ASTRAL PLANE.

ASTRAL LIGHT—1. a continuous twilight-like glow psychically perceived over the astral plane; has no variation of day or night; diffused throughout the astral ether; 2. (parapsychology) the second kind of psychic energy of a higher vibrational frequency than the physical or etheric-double plane; capable of being transmitted over great distances instantaneously; travels outside physical space/time; exists within man's physical body as well as outside. (Inconcl.) [cf. ETHERIC ENERGY, MIND ENERGY] 3. a part of the spectrum of cosmic energies within the range of frequencies grouped as the astral plane. **Sim.** LINGA-SARIRA, ASTRAL PLANE. [cf. RESURRECTION BODY, SEMIMATERIAL, ANTIGRAVITY PHENOMENA, DENSITY]

ASTRAL LIGHT RECORDS—tiny pictures of everything that ever happened throughout the history of the planet; a scenic representation of every thought, feelings, and activity with the smallest detail recorded in linear form, since the beginning of the world; a duplicate of the akashic records reflected from the original akashic records in the higher realms. (Inconcl.) [cf. AKASHIC RECORDS,

REINCARNATION, KARMA, BODIES AND PLANES, MASS KARMA]

ASTRAL LINE OF FORCE—see ASTRAL CORD.

ASTRAL LINK—the unconscious transference of thoughts and feelings between two people, frequently regardless of distance; to tune into the other person's upset and ills without willing it; theory: they have spent time together in another incarnation; happens frequently between mother and offspring. (Inconcl.) **Syn.** TELEPATHIC TRANSMISSION. [**cf.** SOUL-MATES, MIND-LINKING, ETHERIC LINK, ASSOCIATION TELEPATHY]

ASTRAL LOTUSES—(Hinduism) see CHAKRAS.

ASTRAL MATTER—a level of energy more refined than physical matter, influenced by and subject to the thoughts and emotions of mankind; makes a counterpart of everything in the physical world before it manifests in the physical world. (Inconcl.) [**cf.** EMOTIONAL PLANE, ENERGY, THOUGHTS]

ASTRAL MEDICINE—(parapsychology) to be taken to the astral planes by one's guide during sleep and shown demonstrations or taught lessons to aid in changing one's attitude that will heal the sickness; only occurs to those who truly desire to follow a righteous path and progress; impressions received in the astral world aid in changing one's belief system which in turn mends the physical body; the emotion of desire to do what is right furnishes the energy for the guides to use in this manner. (Inconcl.) [**cf.** PSYCHIC HEALING, MENTAL HEALING, KARMA]

ASTRAL PERCEPTION—in the etheric world; 1. one sees with the whole body in all directions at once, seeing inside and outside buildings; similar to the way animals and trees see; 2. one does not hear sound with the astral ear but the thought is changed into wordy impressions, similar to dream-stuff; i.e., no sound is uttered, but one knows what the other means. (Inconcl.)

ASTRAL PICTURE GALLERY—see ASTRAL LIGHT RECORDS.

ASTRAL PLANE—a level of awareness in the etheric world having its own principles, inhabitants, and purpose for existing; 1. the second body of earth vibrating faster than earth or earth's etheric double; this plane interpenetrates earth to its core and extends out from the earth surrounding it; 2. looks similar to earth's plane, when clairvoyantly perceived; contains people clothed,

modes of travel, schools, buildings, etc., as if man is duplicating himself; but one does not consume food or have eliminations; all entities are neuter gender; love prevails but no physical sex; 3. a continuous twilight glow that does not vary for day or night; one does not experience distance or time and travels by the speed of thought; a constant temperature without seasons; 4. no procreation but a transition of soul-minds from this plane to the higher planes or to earth, constantly; 5. easy for soul-minds to change forms, and go from level to level of the astral plane which is divided into hundreds of levels of awareness (each having its own principles with a little variation); 6. free from the law of gravity; 7. recognized as the fourth dimension; 8. considered a halfway house, neither entirely mundane or entirely ethereal but a mixture of the two; 9. in the disciplines postulating seven principles of man, the astral plane is divided into two levels of consciousness quite distinct when perceived clairvoyantly; felt to be separated by an etheric veil; lower level (kama rupa) would be the counterpart of earth's lower class of society who have animalistic actions and thoughts; upper astral level would be the counterpart of earth's society which has good character traits (nothing to do with prestige or wealth). (Inconcl.) **Syn.** ASTRAL WORLD. [**cf.** ASTRAL BODY, ASTRAL LIGHT, MENTAL PLANE]

ASTRAL PLANE INHABITANTS—intelligent energy fields that abide in or temporarily visit the astral level of awareness; the astral plane is divided into many levels of awareness within itself and each energy field will reside in, or visit, that level which is compatible with his or her or its vibrational frequency; 1. deceased human beings whose soul-minds are presently encased in astral matter: (a) masses of confused soul-minds floating in an ocean, going where their mundane thoughts take them; (b) soul-minds learning and performing constructive activity while waiting for their next incarnation; (c) bewildered soul-minds staying close to earth to attach onto earthlings to recapture memories of their earth life; (d) soul-minds hovering close to earth to be helpful as a means of working out negative karmic acts, such as suicide; (e) highly evolved soul-minds who visit from higher planes to teach those who desire it; 2. human beings living in the earth plane: (a) individuals who have astrally projected in their sleep in a normal manner, flying aimlessly about; (b) pupils of an etheral adept who astrally project in their sleep to receive his or her teachings; (c) the mind of a psychic who has tuned in to receive psychic information; (d) the mind of a student who has deliberately tuned in to the astral world for information of the astral world; (e) the astral body of a psychic who deliberately preplanned his or her flight; (f) the mind of an individual who has consumed enough drugs, medicinal or recreational, to hallucinate; 3. nonhuman beings: (a) astral bodies of animals; (b) protean forms with an intelligent purpose belonging to an evolution of their own; (c) vitalized astral shells; (d) many kinds of nature spirits; 4. artificial energy fields: (a) elementals formed unconsciously; (b) elementals formed consciously; (c) human artificials; (d) thought-forms of all shapes, sizes, and colors; (e) color energies floating in an order unknown to man; 5. UFO travelers. (Inconcl.): (a) intelligent constructs; (b) drivers of constructs; (c) beings from other planets whose planet is similar to earth; (d) protean forms not belongng to mankind's evolution; (e) intelligences who seem to abide in air.

ASTRAL PROJECTION—1. to will one's soul-mind to leave the physical body enclothed in an astral body and travel to distant localities; (a) journey is preplanned and preprogrammed; requires a relaxed state of consciousness to begin; technique varies with each person; transpires in a conscious or unconscious state; (b) astral senses are fully alert while the physical body resembles a corpse; silver cord keeps the two bodies attached and breathing and heart pulsation synchronized; (c) astral body moves about in the astral plane, a foreign planet, or another location on this planet; detached body is physically visible, clairvoyantly visible, or invisible; (d) length of travel is preplanned; individual feels refreshed and more knowledgeable upon return; 2. see INVOLUNTARY ASTRAL PROJECTION and AUTOMATIC ASTRAL PROJECTION. **Syn.** OUT-OF-BODY-EXPERIENCE, OBE, SOUL FLIGHT, EXTERIORIZATION. [**cf.** ASTRAL PROJECTION Appendix 2]

ASTRAL PROJECTION HEALING—to unconsciously heal an ill person in one's sleep; the astral body slips out of the physical body during sleep, unaware to the sleeper unless the dreamstuff shows this visit; patient sees, feels, or dreams of the psychic healing and awakens the next day feeling healed. (Inconcl.) [**cf.** ASTRAL HEALING, MULTILOCATION]

ASTRAL PROJECTION MODE OF TRAVEL—normal walking, fast walking without effort, taking giant steps, sliding down a hill or slide, running up steps, swimming, sailing without arms moving in a prone position, sailing with arms flapping, or standing still but the objects appear to move backward; whatever mode, similarity is to travel in supernormal speed over great distances. (Inconcl.) [**cf.** ROLLED OUT, SEES-IN-SLEEP]

ASTRAL PROJECTIONIST—the psychic who takes astral projections. **Syn.** ASTRAL PROJECTOR, TRAVELER, PROJECTIONIST, EXTERIORIST. [**cf.** AUTOMATIC ASTRAL PROJECTION, PROJECTION ART]

ASTRAL PROJECTOR—see ASTRAL PROJECTIONIST.

ASTRAL ROUTE—1. the programmed-path suggestion given to the subconscious mind if the projectionist has a special place he or she wants to visit; 2. an energy filmy substance following the projectionist as if he or she stirred up the ethers and left a trail behind, recognizable by the clairvoyant or another projectionist in flight. [**cf.** UPRIGHT FORCE, ZIGZAGGING]

ASTRAL SEED ATOM—(esoteric) an invisible, tiny, concentrated center of energy located in the solar plexus; believed to contain the "quality" of emotions encountered in every life the soul-mind has ever lived; often referred to as one of the three books of life. **Syn.** EMOTIONAL-ASTRAL-SEED-ATOM. [**cf.** SILVER CORD, LIFE-CORD-HEART-SEED-ATOM, AKASHIC RECORDS]

ASTRAL SENSES—a corresponding counterpart of the five physical senses in the astral body, but have no nerve matter to respond like the physical senses; vibrate so rapidly they cannot be utilized as organs; whole astral body is the faculty for perceiving information corresponding to the physical five senses. (Inconcl.) **Sim.** SINGLE-EYE VISION. [**cf.** ZONE OF QUIETUDE, REASSOCIATED, NADIS]

ASTRAL SHELL—an astral corpse in the etheric world after a soul-mind low on the evolutionary scale who has left for reincarnation in earth; 1. the entire human-like shape holds together if the soul-mind had strong negative materialistic thoughts; to retain one's materialistic desires and habits gives the astral shell cohesive glue that binds it together until these low-grade negative thoughts that make the shell dissipate and dissolve; 2. in the meantime, the semblance will float away from the astral cemetery and manifest dimly in earth with a repetitive, mechanical intelligence; this shell is responsible for many hauntings, apparitions, Ouija board and automatic writing material; can be easily stimulated by psychics or mediums who do not protect themselves or open their psychic doors in a negative area; astral shells cannot always be detected at first, but eventually the information becomes abusive and vulgar and it can be discovered. **Syn.** VITALIZED SHELL. [**cf.** OUIJA BOARD, DENSITY, LOWER MAN, ASTRAL CEMETERY]

ASTRAL SPECTRUM—corresponds to the colors of earth's rainbow, but colors are brighter and indescribable; a blending of the seven radiant columns of color. (Inconcl.) [**cf.** MANSIONS OF LIGHT, COLOR, SEMITRANSPARENT]

ASTRAL SPHERE—see ASTRAL PLANE.

ASTRAL SUBSTANCE—the vibrational frequencies that can be classified as the material or elements that constitute the astral plane; etheric, superetheric. [**cf.** SEMIMATERIAL, ASTRAL BODY]

ASTRAL TELESCOPE—see ASTRAL CURRENT.

ASTRAL THREAD—see ASTRAL CABLE.

ASTRAL TRAVEL see ASTRAL PROJECTION.

ASTRAL VAMPIRISM—(Slavic *vampire,* "he flies away"); the deliberate act of an etheric world entity to prey upon a sleeping victim in invisible form, and drain blood from the sleeper; not detectable by the sleeping victim, except to feel exhaustion upon awakening in the morning. (Inconcl.) [**cf.** VAMPIRE, DIMENSION-SHIFTING, EARTHBOUND ENTITIES, DENSITY]

ASTRAL VISION—1. to see right through everything and in all directions simultaneously; objects are seen from the inside and outside at the same time; a view which absolutely lays open to the gaze of the seer, every point in the interior of a solid unit; comparable to the gaze of one looking down upon the interior of a circle and every point of the interior lies open to view. (Inconcl.) **Syn.** SINGLE-EYE VISION. 2. the privilege to clairvoyantly use the astral light which magnifies one's vision one can then see the minute pictures of the duplicate akashic records of the earth, (not a talent but a privilege one must earn). [**cf.** ASTRAL PROJECTION, SINGLE EYE, ASTRAL LIGHT]

ASTRAL WORLD ARTIST—a psychic artist who draws, paints, etc., what he or she perceives about the etheric world regarding a subject, while in a slightly altered state of consciousness; needs a human to sit for the point of focus and to get inspirations about the person; finished product could be the person's guides, or forms and shapes that developed from his or her presence; perceived through clairvoyance and clairsentience; (do not confuse with INSPIRATIONAL ART in which the artist produces mundane objects on canvas; do not confuse with an AUTOMATIC PAINT MEDIUM whose hand is used by the guides to paint). **Sim.** PSYCHIC ART. [**cf.** PORTRAIT CLAIRVOYANCE, ASTRAL PLANE, CLAIRVOYANCE, GUIDES]

ASTRO—a prefix meaning "star."

ASTRO-SOUL—a study of the soul-mind as to its function on the fifth plane in the etheric world; a spiritual science of the fifth dimension. (Inconcl.) [**cf.** FIFTH PLANE, OVERSOUL, SUBCONSCIOUS MIND, SOUL-MIND Appendix 3]

ASTROBIOLOGY—the study of the movements of heavenly bodies and how these patterns affect living systems in earth; the study of the relationship of all living things to the universe. **Sim.** COSMOBIOLOGY. [**cf.** METAPHYSICS, LAW OF CORRESPONDENCE Appendix 7]

ASTROLOGER—one who studies, teaches, or makes astrological charts for human beings and group activities on the planet, in relationship to the influence of the stars and planets; studies this influence for the individual and group activity in regard to their characteristics, involvements, and progress. [**cf.** PLANETARY SOUL, ASTROLOGICAL CHARTS]

ASTROLOGICAL BIRTH CONTROL—(Czechoslovakia) theory: woman's fertile days can be determined with her relationship to the sun and moon according to her birth date. (Inconcl.) [**cf.** CURATIVE EDUCATION, NEW-AGE PSYCHOLOGY, BIRTH CONSCIOUSNESS, BIRTH SCIENCE]

ASTROLOGICAL CHART—see HOROSCOPE.

ASTROLOGICAL HERB HEALING—to prepare a mixture suitable for healing the disease by blending herbs, according to their own astrological sign; the mixture is then astrologically "favorable"; principles of KABBALAH, TAROT, YOGA, and HERBOLOGY. (Inconcl.) [**cf.** HOLISM, CURATIVE EDUCATION, PSYCHIC HEALING]

ASTROLOGICAL INFLUENCES—(Tibet) cosmic rays which can alter the nature of one's body

45

chemistry and electrical polarity according to the rapport of the body with the twelve sun signs. (Inconcl.)

ASTROLOGICAL TYPE—to ascertain one's strengths, weaknesses, and body chemistry according to one's astrological chart; types have been scientifically researched.

ASTROLOGIST—one who studies and shows an interest in astrology; the student of astrology. [cf. LIFE WAVE, LUNAR CYCLE, SEVEN PLANETARY CHAIN LOGOI]

ASTROLOGY—(ancient) a science and art that brings guidance and counsel to mankind based on one's birth date; helps one understand personal relationships and how to work in harmony with the sun, moon, planets, and stars; a study of the heavens at the birth of an idea, place, or person will tell the nature or character of the adversaries, and the possibilities of the idea, place, or person; necessary to know date, hour, and location of birth; divides the heavens into twelve sections called the Zodiac signs; most organized system known dealing with the movements of stars and planets. [cf. ZODIAC, ASTROLOGICAL CHART]

ASTROMENTAL—pertains to the sidereal influences on man's thoughts and feelings.

ASTROMETEOROLOGY—study of the behavior of planets in the solar system and this relationship to the weather.

ASTRONAVIGATION—the study of UFOLOGY and the possibility of living beings traveling between planets and stars.

ASTRONICS PITCHES—1,080 cosmic sounds related to the psychic energy of the earth that a trained clairaudient can hear. (Inconcl.) [cf. NUMEROLOGY, COSMIC SOUNDS, ASTROLOGY]

ASTROPHYS—(ufology) the physical body of a celestial being from outer space. [cf. UFOLOGY Appendix 5]

ASTROPHYSICS—the branch of astronomy that deals with the physical properties of celestial bodies and with the interaction between matter and radiation, in the interior of celestial bodies.

ASTROPHYSICS STATION—(Russia) a laboratory designed to study time.

ASTROSONICS—coined by Michael C. Heleus (Greek *astro*, "star") (Latin *sonus*, "sound; making

star sound"); an inaudible noise that comes from the planets and stars and effects a psychological and physical response in human beings; studies show it can be predictable; represents the "aspects" in astrology; capable of being heard by clairaudients. (Inconcl.) Syn. STAR-SOUND, COSMIC MUSIC. [cf. CLAIRAUDIENCE, MUSIC OF THE SPHERES, RESONANCE PRINCIPLE]

ASTROTHEOLOGY—a study of the celestial bodies, their functions and laws. [cf. ASTROPHYSICS, ASTROMETEOROLOGY, ASTROSONICS]

ASURA-LOKA—(Hinduism) 1. planes of the etheric world where the asuras dwell; 2. plane of hell, wherein one endures suffering, incapable of passing on until purgation is completed. [cf. SPIRIT, DENSITY, PLANES]

ASURAS—1. (Sanskrit) etheric world intelligences recognized as gods, both the good and evil gods; 2. (Iran, Zoroastrian) very highly evolved deities that have earned the rank of angels; 3. (India) etheric world entities that have accomplished black magic when incarnated in earth and now choose to harm men from the etheric world. Syn. AHYRAS; 4. (Tibet) individuals who have fallen from the estate of the heavenly gods, and are now seeking enlightenment in earth under the teachings of Buddhism. [cf. ASURA-LOKA, DENSITY, ANGEL]

ASWATTHA—(Sanskrit) (esoteric) picture of a tree growing in reverse position with the roots extending upward; signifies a tree of cosmic knowledge and a man growing in relationship to the overall cosmic plan; the unfolding from within going back to one's primal roots. Syn. TREE OF KNOWLEDGE, TREE OF COSMIC LIFE. [cf. MONADOLOGY, CHAOS, ABSOLUTE]

AT—(current slang) used by those who are seeking a path of enrichment; "at" is how one feels at this very moment; to be aware of this very moment in one's life and aware that one is aware of it. Usage: "I don't know where I am *at* today, but I will go to the lecture with you anyway." [cf. AQUARIAN AGE, CONSCIOUSNESS AWARENESS MOVEMENT]

AT-ONE-MENT—(esoteric) to undergo a union with the Divine or Cosmic Consciousness, during meditation. Syn. SATORI. [cf. SOUND KASINA, PRAYER BEADS]

ATAVISM PSYCHISM—theory: memories of prehuman ancestry are stored in the subconscious mind and can resurface to the conscious mind motivating animalistic activity; 1. a spontaneous or willed change in appearance to a half-animal, half-man manifestation; see WERE-WOLF and SHAPE-CHANGING; 2. regression while under hypnosis to a primitive life and speaking in grunts, with loss of ability to understand the hypnotist; 3. barbarianistic traits of character brought on psychically without logical reason or conscious intention. [cf. COLLECTIVE UNCONSCIOUS, UNIVERSAL SYMBOLS, PRIMAL PERCEPTION]

ATAVISTIC RESURGENCE—psychic information for one's self that resurfaces from the prehuman consciousness as symbols to fit the needs of the psychic; e.g., visions of lions when physical strength is needed. [cf. ATAVISTIC PSYCHISM, SYMBOLISM]

ATECHNOS—(Cicero) inborn psychic ability as opposed to psychic ability that one develops. Syn. ADIDACTOS. [cf. MENTAL PSYCHISM, MENTAL TELEPATHY, TELEPATHY, GUT FEELING, INTUITION, SOLAR PLEXUS]

ATLANTIS—(esoteric description) 1. a continent that occupied most of what is now the north Atlantic Ocean and was completely sunk in the waters in three major catastrophes; approximately 1,000,000 years ago this civilization was at its peak with technologies now unknown to humanity; politics, science, customs, and religion were conducted in a harmonious manner; people were twelve feet tall and beautiful; degeneration began to set in and the civilization deteriorated in size and morals; approximately 800,000 B.C. a large part of the land sank into the sea; minor upheavals hit frequently; in 200,000 B.C. the continent split in two; the major catastrophe occurred in 80,000 B.C. and left only a small remnant of what had been Atlantis; before each catastrophe priests led large groups into Europe, Asia, and north Africa; 9564 B.C. (determined through psychic means) Atlantis sank with its last 60 million people; this was the Poseidonis of Plato's *Critias; 2.* (Master Onargo, a highly evolved etheric world intelligence, who worked through voice trance in seances, in 1969) about 10,000 years ago outside planetary beings came to inhabit the earth; earth culture was illiterate; the outside beings had knowledge far beyond mankind's present civilization; they came to save the earth from turning too far on its axis and crashing into another planet; (at that time, living people-like organisms traveled from planet to planet easily and were interested in the evolvement of the entire universe); the two cultures

intermarried; the supertechnology (computerized world) was eventually used for materialistic desires; because their high technologies were misused for power, self-satisfaction, with a total disregard for human life, the thought-forms of the continent caused it to sink into the ocean; archaeology findings indicate that these two cultures could have existed at that time; 3. (Edgar Cayce) before 50,000 B.C. many lands had appeared and disappeared on earth; five races were on earth representing the five senses that human beings may become conscious from their spiritual form to the physical form; humanity had attained great technological progress surpassing that which exists today; mankind's misuse of scientific and material achievements brought physical destruction in the earth as they triggered off volcanic eruptions and earthquakes resulting in the changing of the earth; 4. (Native American, Hopi) destruction of this first world came about because the people used the "vibratory centers of their bodies solely for earth purposes, forgetting their creator"; destruction of the second world occurred when again the people did not show reverence to the creator; the earth teetered off balance and spun crazily around, rolled over twice, and mountains plunged into the sea and the seas sloshed over the land; the world spun through lifeless space and froze into solid ice; 5. name used to refer to a long stage in human development and civilization when the primary focus of human growth was nurturing an expression of the astral body and emotions; 6. (Ignatius Donnelly, 1822) approached the subject with scientific accuracy and detailed inquiry; his writing on Atlantis ranks next to Plato in importance and influence.

ATMA—1. (capitalized) (Sanskrit, Hinduism, Vedic) the universal Soul encompassing all knowledge, all-power, all love, and the patterns of everything that will ever be thought of, acted upon, or discovered, etc.; divine wisdom; all-there-is. Syn. MACROCOSM, GODHEAD, PURE CONSCIOUSNESS. [cf. TOTALITY, MONAD, LAW OF REPETITION Appendix 7]; 2. (uncapitalized) (Sanskrit, Hinduism) the divine spark of Totality within the physical body; the inner part of the soul-mind expressing itself toward perfecting the soul-mind to its original state of perfectness. Syn. PSYCHE, RUH, "I AM," MICROCOSM. [cf. MONADOLOGY, MACROCOSM]

ATMA-VIDYA—(Hinduism) the highest form of spiritual knowledge; cosmic laws.

ATMAN BODY—(Eastern) the fifth invisible body of a human being in the "principles of seven bodies"; interpenetrates and extends out quite a distance from the physical body; when this body has earned the right to abide in the fifth plane, and other bodies have been discarded, this energy field has an unknown form; body acts as a strainer, as it separates the waste of unnecessary reactions from karma that is now overcome, and this dross is dissolved so the soul-mind is purified; the purified body works from a group soul known to us as the brotherhoods of earth; engages in activities that encompass all of humanity from a universal point of view; they may choose to incarnate as a great world master to do selfless service but it is not necessary; their objective is to help earthlings understand the purpose of universal love and to flow with universal will; one may rest and recuperate here if desired; incarnation is rare. [**cf.** BODIES and PLANES Appendix 5]

ATMIC MATTER—the third grouping of seven planes of energy existing for the expression of the monad on its journey upward; a vibrational frequency where the force of will finds expression; see MENTAL PLANE. [**cf.** BODIES AND PLANES Appendix 5, SPHERES]

ATMOSPHERE—(science) a section of the etheric world with various levels of energy within it which penetrate space.

ATMOSPHERE CLEARING—to remove all past imbedded emotional vibrations (loving and hostile) from a home, business building, or area; executed before new tenants start a business or change residency to allow new tenants to build their own personality into the environment; walls, furniture, and surrounding environment are exorcised by powerful evocation rituals, mantras, prayers, and ceremonial magic; this activity removes imbedded vibrations on objects and building to bring it back to virgin state; when necessary ghosts are dissipated; performed by one person or a group working as a unit; dangerous procedure for one not well-grounded in psychism or magic. **Syn.** HOUSE SWEEP, EXORCISM. [**cf.** GHOSTERY, VIBRATIONS, SECONDARY WAVES]

ATMOSPHERE CONTROL—to use powerful intensified concentration, CEREMONIAL MAGIC procedures, or the aid of etheric world nature spirits, to control one's environment and the laws of nature; performed for humanity's overall benefit; see Appendix 2 for types of these skills.

ATMOSPHERE OF AFFECTION—(destructive-brainwashing cults) a thought enclosure built around the newly approached victim-to-be by bombarding him with love, compliments, and an answer to his highest goals, by a recruiter; conversation is kept on an emotional level aimed at the above, until the victim experiences with "his heart totally"; this encounter psychically connects the recruiter to the new victim and later that night the recruiter sends thoughts of him joining the group or attending the mass meeting while he sleeps, which influence his decision to join the group because of this emotional bond during the encounter. [**cf.** LOVE-LINE, MENTAL TELEPATHY, THOUGHT ATMOSPHERE, MASS ELEMENTAL]

ATMOSPHERE PHENOMENA—(ufology) pertains to thin white objects that look like snowflakes (only larger) and fall to the ground, even in warm weather; presumed to be connected to spacecraft. [**cf.** UFOLOGY, MUTATION OF ENERGY, DAWN ANGELS, DOR CLOUDS]

ATMOSPHERE SHIELDING—to put a wall of mental energy around one's self to protect one's self in a crowd of people or an area containing objects; wall is built by silently or verbally saying positive affirmations, beautiful poetry, or other pleasant thoughts; this aids in freeing one from a psychic impact or collision or having to balance with that which is against one's tastes or moods. [**cf.** CLOAK OF INSULATION, MENTAL ACTIVITY, PSYCHIC TRANSFER]

ATMOSPHERIC AMOEBA—a spheroidal, plasmatic living organism, amoeba-like in appearance, inhabiting the sea of ethers; a life form on a different level of awareness from a human being; visible only on an infrared camera; returns a radar echo. (Inconcl.) **Syn.** BIOLOGICAL UFOS. [**cf.** ETHERIAN PHYSICS, UFOLOGY Appendix 5]

ATMOSPHERIC PHYSICS—(ufology) the study of outer space; includes the sea of etheria, its life forms (both creatures and higher intelligences), the mode of travel, functions, and the vibrational frequency. **Syn.** ETHERIAN PHYSICS. [**cf.** COSMIC PULSE, ELECTROGRAVITIC WAVES]

ATOM—1. (esoteric parapsychology); (**a**) a minute, indestructible, unduplicatable, concentrated, center of energy and intelligence which makes up the essence of all levels of space and degrees of density of matter; functions and generates under the law of thought; (**b**) comprises electricity, magnetism, and chemicals which make it adaptable to psychic work and thought; (c) vibrates at thousands of different vibrational frequencies caused by the differing numbers of protons and electrons which are generated to change in number according to the nature and emotional value of man's thought; atoms aggregate to form degrees of density of matter under the LAW OF LIKE ATTRACKS LIKE. [cf. LAW OF THOUGHT Appendix 7, MATTER]; 2. (metaphysics) (a) a minute, concentrated, consciousness center of Total Intelligence plus a memory bank of all the rates of vibration it has been involved in since creation; (b) a minute speck of energy composed of light particles held within its orbital path under the dominion of mankind's thoughts; emotions that accompany humanity's thinking form its units of electrons, protons, and neutrons; influenced by the human heart and mind, linking it to UNIVERSAL MIND; (c) each atom is an individual living entity having a soul (intelligence), a spirit (energy or movement), and a pattern (aura); a miniature duplicate of man; atoms vibrate under the law of constant movement but make sense in the universes because their intelligence keeps them vibrating at various rates making order and purposefulness to the "all"; 3. atoms perform as tiny radio transceivers working on ultrashort waves; atoms give and receive radiations from all other atoms influencing the ALL. (Inconcl.) [cf. POLARITY, LAW OF VIBRATION Appendix 7, CONDENSED CONSCIOUSNESS, ATOM-MEMORY BANK]

ATOM-MEMORY BANK—theory: the ability of each atom to store within itself all the experiences and information it has gained from the hundreds of vibrational frequencies it has participated in since the beginning of creation; acts as God's little bookkeepers. [cf. MACROCOSM, SOUL-MIND MEMORY BANK, CONDENSED CONSCIOUSNESS]

ATOMIC AND MOLECULAR ATTRACTION—scientific name given to the aura around objects; see AURA.

ATOMIC ETHER—(esoteric) an invisible substance with extremely rapid vibrations; interpenetrates earth, human bodies, and air; records in picture form all the events of everything that happens on earth and everything that each goes through in each incarnation; stores these minute pictures in the akashic records. **Syn.** MENTAL-REFLECTING-ETHER. [cf. KARMA, BLOODSTREAM, REINCARNATION]

ATOMIC ETHEREAL MATTER—see ATOMIC SUBSTANCE.

ATOMIC PICTURE IMAGES—(esoteric) minute, flat, ethereal, still pictures of each person's life experiences in each earthly incarnation since the beginning of earth; complete in historical detail and attitudinal emotions; taken by the MENTAL-REFLECTING-ETHER and stored in one's personal AKASHIC RECORD file; karmically timed when to be released; atomic images then flow through one's bloodstream in such a manner as to make up one's current world of manifestations and one's body; adheres to the LAW OF KARMA. (Inconcl.) [cf. EVOLUTIONARY MAN, MENTAL-REFLECTING-ETHER, BEHAVIORAL MEMORIES]

ATOMIC SUBSTANCE—1. (esoteric) the fastest, most subtle, peaceful, intellectual vibrational rate known to man; one of the seven compositions of the physical body; invisible; essence of the monadic plane; capable of transferring thought from mind to mind; 2. (physics) known as electronic. **Syn.** ATOMIC ETHEREAL MATTER. [cf. BODIES AND PLANES Appendix 5, MENTAL TELEPATHY]

ATOMIC-MOLECULAR MATTER—(esoteric) vibrational frequencies that compose the physical body and the etheric world; comprised of solids, liquids, gases, and invisible ether, super-ether, sub-atomic, and atomic frequencies.

ATOMIC-PSYCHOKINESIS—(alchemy) to dematerialize third-dimensional matter into an invisible state, transport it through space, and rematerialize it in the same form or a different form; see APPORTATION PSYCHOKINESIS [cf. ALCHEMY Appendix 2, ASCENSION, PURIFIED BODY, MATERIALIZATION]

ATOMISTS—(ancient Greece) men who believed that atoms composed everything contained in the universes and declared them to be the "foundation-bricks" of the universes.

ATOPICAL LOCALIZATION—(poltergeistry) supernormal activity in a home generated by a poltergeist focus that begins in one area and keeps extending itself to larger areas with an increase in matter manipulation; e.g., movement of the bed; later, manipulation and flying objects in the bedroom; later, disturbances by weird noises and matter being readjusted and manipulated irregularly in the whole house; as opposed to supernormal activity localized; e.g., bath powder on the floor each morning with no apparent physical cause. [cf. PROXIMAL, FOCI, POLTERGEIST]

ATOUTS—(Persia) picture cards used as a guide to tell one's future and bring other psychic information in an "atout card reading"; first used by the gypsies in A.D. 1300. **Sim.** TAROT CARDS. [cf. MONADOLOGY, CASTING OF LOTS, POINT OF FOCUS]

ATROPA BELLADONNA—(gravity control) one of the ingredients used by witches to rub on themselves as preparation to fly in the air; has the vibrational frequency that releases matter from its gravitational hold. **Sim.** FLYING OINTMENT. [cf. GRAVITY CONTROL Appendix 2, TELEPORTATION]

ATROPINE—(esoteric) a psychedelic drug with the properties to make one feel as if he or she were gloriously soaring through the air in the midst of a religious experience of ecstasy; used by European witches and North American healing practitioners. [cf. ASTRAL PROJECTION, ECSTASY, EMOTIONAL PSI, FORCED PSI]

ATTENTIVE-EYE—theory: one eye is more observant and useful according to the direction one is facing in alignment with the earth's magnetism; both eyes do not see equally the same even with perfect vision; one eye picks up the rays of what is in view when one faces a certain direction according to the point on the magnetic compass; the other eye picks up what is in view when the person is facing in the opposite direction. **Syn.** MASTER EYE. [cf. RADIESTHESIA, PENDULUM, COLOR]

ATTITUDINAL HEALING—to help one understand the reason for life and to change in attitude toward the emotional aspects of life to alter one's body chemistry; this gives the body cells an opportunity to normalize and heal themselves; theory: one's attitude toward one's self, lifestyle, and sickness has a great influence on one's state of health; the more informed one is regarding attitude and how to balance with them, the more normal state of health one manifests. [cf. LAW OF HEALING Appendix 7, BLOCKS]

ATTRACTION CONSCIOUSNESS—(mineral kingdom) (esoteric) the instinct or primal perception of the mineral constantly attracts radiations from its environment to eternally seek self-expression; stones, as living entities, draw to themselves vibrations from miles around their area and from the planets; this includes other minerals, plants, animals, humans, and atmospheric conditions; in return the mineral gives out psychic signals to its environment regarding the dangers and pleasures of future involvements; uses the radiations it draws in to evolve to a higher state of consciousness; because of its give and take properties, the stone makes an excellent psychic and healing tool. **Sim.** OVER-ALL CONSCIOUSNESS, MINERAL KINGDOM, MINPSI.

ATTRACTION-ACTION-REACTION—(astral projection) (Robert Monroe) principle: the atoms are attracted to opposite poles, they intermingle until they equalize and then tranquilize all in a split second; occurs in the beginning of an astral projection. [cf. ASTRAL PROJECTION, POLARITY, SOUL-MIND]

ATTUNEMENT—1. (psychic reading) (a) to synchronize one's self with the person one is reading for in order to perceive facts regarding that person; psychic blends his or her brain rhythm, aura, and body chemistry with the subject's brain rhythm, auric pattern, and body chemistry; this blending enables the psychic to relate back to the subject facts, future and present conditions, and characteristics that the subject is not aware of; the above properties differ with each "attunement" making some readings better than others; the more compatible these properties are the better the reading; (b) to deliberately sense the conscious and subconscious mind of another person to give out psychic information regarding the other person; 2. to still the conscious mind and allow the subconscious and superconscious mind to connect to higher planes; 3. (psychic healing) to know inwardly that a healing energy from a healing practitioner has touched one's self; outer signs are warmth, coldness, prickly sensations, or moisture on the body; 4. to blend one's mind activity and ectoplasm with an etheric world intelligence in a trance state of consciousness. [cf. CONSCIOUS COOPERATION, PSYCHIC READING, GOING-TO-LEVEL, FLOW FREE, ETHERIC LINK]

ATUA—(New Zealand Maoris) see VITAL LIFE FORCE.

ATZILUTH—(Kabbalah) one of ten Holy names of God assigned to each Sephira; considered to be the highest plane in the etheric world; an archetypal plane of pure divine vibrations, which was assigned the alchemical element "fire." [cf. TREE OF LIFE IN KABBALAH, BRIAH, YETZIRAH, ASSIAH]

AUAPICIA—see AUGURY.

AUDIO—(biofeedback training) the opening in the instrument where the earphones are plugged. [**cf.** BIOFEEDBACK TRAINING Appendix 5]

AUDITIVE MEDIUM—one who hears sounds, music, and voices within his or her mind or in the atmosphere which come from an etheric world intelligence; capable of interpreting the message. **Syn.** HEARING MEDIUM, CLAIRAUDIENT. [**cf.** MEDIUMSHIP, ANGELIC CONVERSATION, CLAIRAUDIENCE]

AUDITORY HALLUCINATION—1. to hear sounds or voices within the interior of the mind or within the atmosphere nearby bringing psychic information; more apt to occur to the blind person as opposed to seeing visions; 2. to hear noises that are a reactivated memory of noises heard previously in one's life. **Syn.** CLAIRAUDIENCE, SENSORY AUTOMATISM. [**cf.** SEEDS OF SOUND, ULTRASOUND]

AUGOEIDES—(Greek *auge*, "radiant sunlight"; *eides*, "form or shape"); a luminous clear vision appearing to a teen-ager that portrays an ideal image of his or her desires or portrays the goal-to-be of his or her designated path. [**cf.** APPARITION, CLAIRVOYANT, PATH, SOUL JURY]

AUGUR—1. (Rome) a psychic who predicts the future and perceives helpful counsel for an individual or for their country through the use of things of nature; one of a body of Roman officials whose function it was to observe and interpret "omens" for guidance in public affairs. [**cf.** MANTIC ARTS Appendix 6] 2. (Latin) a psychic who used tablets with special instructions and advice inscribed upon them to predict one's future and offer counsel; used with lots. [**cf.** SORTES, CASTING OF LOTS] 3. one who divines and tells the future by "omens" that occur in his or her proximity. **Syn.** PORTENDER, LITUS, TEMPLUM, SOOTHSAYER, DIVINER, ORACLE, PSYCHIC Appendix 3. [**cf.** HUMAN OMENS, AUGURY]

AUGURY—(Rome) 1. (a) to psychically obtain information from Totality using signs of nature and weather to give counsel and predict the future for one's country; e.g., government officials were responsible for observing unusual, unpredictable occurrences in nature in their proximity and use them for prognostication for the country's future welfare; (b) to use the pattern of growing things of nature to forecast future events; e.g., to kill an animal and examine its entrails for abnormality; theory: vibrations of the cosmos repeat in all life, and this is a matter of identifying the things of the earth in relation to the things of the heavens; augury was taught professionally by Julius Caesar in the college of his day; 2. to use tablets with special inscriptions designed to predict the future; lots were cast and the pattern of their "fall" was the indication of which tablet would answer the problem; 3. used loosely to mean "divination" by means of whatever is handy; to take anything and everything as a "sign" to be used for whatever one likes. Usage: "I saw a white cat and this was an omen that my sister would come to see me this summer." **Syn.** SOOTHSAYING, DIVINATION. [**cf.** LITUS, SORTES, DOMESTIC AUGURY, PUBLIC AUGURY, OMENS, MANTIC ARTS, RADIESTHESIA, I CHING]

AUM—1. (Eastern) a powerful, yet delicate sound designed to be chanted to help one experience many levels of consciousness simultaneously; most well-known chant of the eastern philosophies but now used universally in conjunction with any spiritual endeavor; represents all the world because it uses every part of the voice organs of every language; i.e., *A* is guttural, *U* comes from the palate, and *M* is labial; when chanted correctly it vibrates through the universe; 2. chanted singularly or in groups to be used for healing or psychic attunement; sound psychically charges the air with prana which is under the direction of thought and can be directed specifically; 3. to repeat this sound in meditation fills the mind and at the same time sets it free to explore inner thoughts; 4. (Native American) recognized as the primal sound and chanted to control natural manifestations; represents the three manifestations of all life; creation, preservation, and destruction; 5. emblematic of the universe functioning as a whole unit; *A* is father beckoning creation, *U* is son, the evolution of individual souls, and *M* is absorbing of all that is created; also spelled **OM, OHM**; 6. (Hinduism) the Word, God. **Syn.** HUM, AMIN, AMEN. [**cf.** SOUNDS-WITH-POWER, CHANTING]

AUMAKAU—(Huna *au*, "cord"; *makau*, "older"; "god who is father"; "an utterly trustworthy parental spirit") psychic information which is brought from the High Self (superconscious mind) to the middle self (conscious mind) via the silver cord; information brought this way comes direct from Totality without interference from the low self (subconscious mind) and its karma; "pure" information. **Sim.** INSPIRATIONAL THOUGHT, CLAIR-SENTIENCE. [**cf.** SUPERCONSCIOUS MIND, HIGH SELF]

AURA—(esoteric) 1. an invisible, electromagnetic, intelligent energy field completely surrounding an entity, living and nonliving, functioning as a blueprint and battery for that entity; field gives direction to the entity to grow, mature, maintain its cell structure and die; 2. different frequencies emanate from every entity (or system) that blend with the magnetism in its proximity making its electromagnetic field; entity radiates out according to its rate of vibration and level of intelligence and awareness which constantly arranges and rearranges the blueprint and increases or decreases the battery energy; 3. the field returns the radiations making the entity's body form; 4. human aura is bi-polar: receives negative polarity from the physical body (conscious consciousness), and its positive polarity from the soul-mind (subconscious consciousness); 5. the electromagnetic field cannot exist without the entity and vice versa; auric field gives entity the rate and mode of vibrational frequency to behave in third-dimensional matter; 6. major functions of aura: pattern and battery, protection from other invisible radiations (acts as a shield in the etheric world), communication with plants, animals, and etheric world intelligences (mode of communication before sound utterance and language), and connection (nodes in aura connect to nodes in atmosphere); 7. attitudes, thought, and state of health; 8. field around non-living entities and in immediate proximity of living entities looks like luminous fur without much motion or differences; known as the etheric double; another field extends farther outward that contains patterns and colors: both levels are perceivable clairvoyantly; Kirlian high-voltage camera picks up the colorful aura level; 9. believed to interpenetrate the body but not capable of being perceived inside the entities; 10. types of auras: (a) human being aura which divides into two, the soul-mind aura and the mental aura; (b) narrow aura surrounding objects; (c) colorful aura around living entities. (Inconcl.) **Syn.** Appendix 3. [**cf.** ETHERIC DOUBLE, CORONA, OBJECT AURA]

AURA BALANCING—to perceive the aura around the client, detect energy blocks that could be preventing normal flow of energy; use special magnetic passes over the congested area a few inches from patient's body; when aura looks changed from healing energy emanated from hands, patient's cells will begin to normalize so the body can heal itself more quickly. [**cf.** GORDIAN KNOTS, AURIC CLAIRVOYANCE, PASSES]

AURA COLORS—(human being) many colors and patterns perceived clairvoyantly around an individual reveal the state of evolution of the soul-mind, health of the person, and the quality of the person's concepts. [**cf.** AURA, SOUL-MIND AURA, MENTAL AURA, KIRLIAN EFFECT]

AURA ENERGY—a dense ethereal substance which forms a figure eight over the solar plexus; varies in tone, rhythm, color, and vibrational frequencies; changes with the emotional mood of the person; detectable with instruments. [**cf.** ETHERIC DOUBLE, SCHLIEREN SYSTEM, SOLAR PLEXUS CHAKRA]

AURA MEMORY—to psychically release information one heard years previously (even as a baby) through talking-in-tongues, trance, hypnotherapy, automatic writing, or xenography. [**cf.** LINGUISTIC RESTITUTION, ETHERIC SCRIPT]

AURA OF RESPECTABILITY—(medieval) the transference of the evil vibrations of one's sickness to an inanimate object; object is then buried in a special ritual; performed because of belief that God is on the side of the suffering. **Syn.** AURA RESPONSIBILITY. [**cf.** PSYCHIC TRANSFER, SCAPEGOAT, BOOMERANG, PSI]

AURA PHOTOGRAPHY—the study and photographing of radiations surrounding objects and living organisms, including human beings, using a high-voltage camera; camera invented by Semyon D. Kirlian of Soviet Russia; research recognizes it to be the aura or corona or both. (Inconcl.) [**cf.** CONTACT PHOTOGRAPHY, AUTOEMISSIVE IMAGE]

AURA READING—to psychically perceive emanations surrounding an object, living organism, or human being and understand its meaning in rapport with the thing it surrounds; human aura reading shows character, health, and future events of individual; object reading is under study; emanations vary in color, pattern, size, and density of light; colors perceived by clairvoyance differ from colors attained by Kirlian photographs, but show similarities in pattern. [**cf.** ETHERIC DOUBLE, ENERGY FIELD PHOTOGRAPHY, ELECTRODYNAMIC THEORY]

AURA-MIST—the first layer of vibrations of the human aura or object aura that is more easily seen with physical eyes; as opposed to the other layers of the soul-mind aura. [**cf.** MENTAL AURA, SOUL-MIND AURA]

AURA-VISION—to perceive clairvoyantly, at will, a luminous ridge or a many-colored-flare around a person, living organism, or object; luminous ridge projects a few inches from the construct and is viewed by tuning into the etheric realm; colored-flare projects from two inches to a few feet and is viewed by tuning into the astral realm; flare will vary in patterns, color, and density according to the construct; both radiations give meaning to the construct and take emanations from the construct. [**cf.** AURA, ETHERIC DOUBLE, BIOPLASMA BODY, BIOENERGENICS THERAPY, KIRLIAN EFFECT Appendix 5]

AURA-VISION TRAINER—a device that prepares the eyes for better aura-viewing by stimulating the rods and cones. **Syn.** INTEGRAL STIMULATING INTENSITY STROBOSCOPE (ISIS). [**cf.** KILNER GOGGLES, ULTRAOUTER AURA, LOST LEAF]

AURA MEMORY—to psychically release information one heard years previously (even as a baby) through talking-in-tongues, trance, hypnotherapy, automatic writing, or xenography. [**cf.** LINGUISTIC RESTITUTION, ETHERIC SCRIPT]

AURASCOPE PAINTINGS—to paint a picture revealing the subject's or individual's aura; artist deliberately attunes to subject's or individual's aura for a better understanding of how to paint the object or person; artist puts on canvas or paper psychic auric emanations that enhance the picture and have meaning to artist or subject. [**cf.** INSPIRATIONAL ART, PSYCHIC READING]

AURATIST—a clairvoyant who perceives the auric colors around living and nonliving things and understands its meaning; gives pertinent information about thing based on the colors, size, density, and vibrational speed of aura. (Inconcl.) [**cf.** CLAIRVOYANT, ASTRAL ART, CONTROLLED RELAXATION]

AUREOLA—emanations of a golden radiance projecting out from an individual's body or head; perceived, physically or clairvoyantly, around a highly evolved soul-mind. **Syn.** GLORIA, HUMAN AURA. [**cf.** PURIFIED BODY, HALO, CROWN OF GLORY, GLORIFICATION]

AURIC AUREOLA—a luminous "surround" in the immediate space around the entire human body; changes continually with the moods and attitudes

of the human: see ETHERIC DOUBLE. [*cf.* AURA Appendix 3, HEALTH AURA, AURIC EGG]

AURIC CHARGE—(radiesthesia) to perceive body feelings going from the hand to one's head or from the head to one's hand or both when using a pendulum or dowsing rod; body feelings can be tingly, hot, cold, or twitching sensations; comes from the radiation of object or person under the radiesthetic tool as it travels to the subconscious mind and back to the tool; this charge makes the tool act in a tangible meaningful way to the dowser or pendulumist; happens in body whether felt or not. [*cf.* RADIESTHESIA, DOWSING, PALLOMANCY]

AURIC CLAIRVOYANCE—to perceive with psychic eyes, the electromagnetic energy field surrounding objects, living organisms, including humans; variations of color, patterns, density, and speed of vibrations distinguishable through clairvoyance; more easily seen while in an alpha state or after meditation; an inborn talent, but can be learned; occurs spontaneously or willed. [*cf.* AURIC READING, FINGER PAD ELECTROGRAPHS, KIRLIAN EFFECT, AURA COLORS]

AURIC CLAIRVOYANT—see AURATIST.

AURIC DIAGNOSIS—(magnetic healing) to detect a congested area in a physical body by following the outline of the body with the palms of the hands; palms facing inward are passed over the entire body until a different sensation is felt, which is the area needing attention; sensation can be cold, hot, tingling, or sticky. [*cf.* PSYCHIC HEALING, AURIC HEALING]

AURIC EGG—see SOUL-MIND AURA.

AURIC HEALING—(magnetic healing) to unruffle or smooth over with magnetic passes the congested area in the patient, until the psychic practitioner senses a difference in the area of congestion; area of congestion is first diagnosed by one's palms or clairvoyant perception; palms face the body proximate to the congestion and make the proper maneuvering into the etheric double; psychic energy from practitioner's palms is transferred to etheric double under the law of thought; consequently the etheric double is repaired, which leads to normalizing of body cells, and in turn the body heals itself more quickly. [**cf.** AURIC DIAGNOSIS, MAGNETIC PASSES, MAGNETIC HEALING Appendix 2]

AURIC LIGHT—see AURA.

AURIC RAYS—emanations extending at right angles to the body, going straight out from pores of the body; drooping rays designate illness in the body. [**cf.** FLARE PATTERNS, HEALTH AURA, FIELD SHIFTS]

AURIC RETREAT—the withdrawing or curling up of the electromagnetic emanations around an individual when he is frightened or under stress; if situation worsens the aura temporarily isolates itself. [**cf.** HAIRCUT EFFECT, AURA, COLD ELEC-TRON EMISSION]

AURIC SENSE—to perceive clairvoyantly the electromagnetic force field surrounding all things; see AURA READING]

AURORA AUSTRALIS—(esoteric) an expression of energy lighting up the sky in the Southern Hemisphere; gives the appearance of fire; caused by the bombardment of electrically charged particles with the upper atmosphere; occurs nightly in the Antarctic. **Syn.** SOUTHERN LIGHTS. [**cf.** AU-RORA BOREALIS, AURA]

AURORA BOREALIS—(esoteric) an expression of force lighting up the sky in the Northern Hemisphere sometimes forms an arc in the earth's atmosphere sending out rays of bright green, pink, and yellow; and other times it looks like a curtain of colored lights; caused by electrically charged particles emitted by the sun clashing with the upper atmosphere. **Syn.** NORTHERN LIGHTS. [**cf.** AURORA AUSTRALIS, AURA]

AUSTERITY—(Tibet) a self-discipline in which one refrains from materialistic experiences believing this is a method of maintaining one's self on his path toward perfectness; practiced by monks in the monastery.

AUTO—prefix meaning "self."

AUTOCONTROL OF CONSCIOUSNESS—(biofeedback training) to obtain mastery of one's emotional states by learning to understand one's attitudes while in a biofeedback training session; subject is hooked up to one of the biofeedback instruments and meditates or ponders over the problems of his world; instruments feedback tangible evidence of his levels of anxiety which aid subject in changing his attitude and bringing control of emotions; see following kinds of instruments individually: EEG, GSR, METABOLIC MONITOR and TEMPERATURE CONTROL. [**cf.** BIOFEEDBACK TRAINING, FEEDBACK, AUTOGENIC TRAINING]

AUTOEMISSIVE IMAGE—(Kirlian effect) a similar discharge of electromagnetic energy surrounds all the members of one species; capable of being photographed on Kirlian cameras. [**cf.** KIRLIAN EFFECT Appendix 5]

AUTOGENIC RELAXATION SEQUENCE—(Europe; Johannes Hans Schultz; early 1920s) a technique of suggestions to help the subject to relax body and quiet the mind and emotions; practitioner verbalizes special phrases designed to alter the consciousness to an alpha state; subject concentrates on the practitioner's voice and follows instructions with his or her mind; key phrases were to feel one's hands become heavy and warm and to decree one's self to become quite quiet; entire process is currently being used extensively with biofeedback training sessions. [**cf.** AUTOGENIC TRAINING, BIO-STAT MONITOR]

AUTOGENIC STATE—scientific name for THE SILENCE; see same. **Syn.** QUIETUDE. [**cf.** MEDITATION, IS-NESS, SENSE-WITHDRAWAL, ZEN]

AUTOGENIC TRAINING—abbr. A.T.; 1. (biofeedback training) a method to help master stress by putting the mind in charge of one's bodily functions while being monitored by an EEG or GSR instrument, under the direction of a therapist or biofeedback attendant; therapist verbalizes key phrases for the subject to adhere to and obey which relaxes the physical body and quiets the mind and emotions; after many training sessions, subject is capable of having control over specific bodily functions and anxiety thoughts. [**cf.** EMG INSTRUMENT, BIOFEEDBACK TRAINING Appendix 5, FORMULA-RECEIVE MODE] 2. (hypnotherapy) a formula phrased to promote self-generated control over one's muscles and body tensions when anxious, upset, or excited; given to one's self in self-hypnotic procedure. [**cf.** SELF-HYPNOSIS, AUTOSUGGESTION] 3. to speak affirmations designed to modify one's behavior, especially to handle stress situations calmly; spoken verbally or silently frequently throughout the day and evening. [**cf.** AFFIRMATIONS, INNER-DIALOGUE] 4. visualization or imagery exercises emphasizing behavior modification executed after meditation while in an alpha state of consciousness. [**cf.** IMAGERY, VISUALIZATION]

AUTOGENICS—a study of mechanisms and the substances in the human body which contribute to self-generation of the human body. **Syn.** AUTOGENIC SCIENCE. [**cf.** BIOFEEDBACK TRAINING]

AUTOGRAPHY—1. to receive psychic messages written on an old-fashioned child's slate by etheric world intelligences; ectoplasm is used by intelligence to move the slate pencil while the slate is being held by the medium or is placed in the center of a seance circle; messages are short but meaningful. 2. see DIRECT WRITING. **Sim.** SLATE WRITING, DIRECT SPIRIT WRITING. [**cf.** PRECIPITATION, ETHERIC SCRIPT, SEANCE]

AUTOHYPNOSIS—to put one's self in a relaxed, suggestible, hypnotic state by silently verbalizing the necessary induction steps, offering suggestions for desired behavior or body modifications and ending by the induction release; subject will not go as deep as if he were hypnotized by a guide, but suggestions will influence his subconscious mind; (do not confuse with MEDITATION). **Syn.** AUTOSUGGESTION, SELFSUGGESTION. [**cf.** HYPNOTHERAPY]

AUTOMAGRAPH—a type of planchette designed with a special arm to hold the pencil that gives the pencil freer movement and does not require it to be placed in the planchette. [**cf.** AUTOMATISM, PLANCHETTE]

AUTOMAT—one who allows an etheric world intelligence to intervene and use his arm and hand or feet to write, paint, or draw on paper, canvas, slates, etc.; medium has the proper body chemistry for synchronization of intelligence and her or himself; material is beyond the comprehension of medium and usable for mankind; skill performed while in a deep trance, ten percent trance, or a light state of consciousness that is unnoticeable to outsiders; true automat preplans sessions, otherwise his or her psychic doors are inviting inferior entities to interfere, which can easily happen in this particular skill. [**cf.** MEDIUMSHIP, AUTOMATIC WRITING, AUTOMATIC SCRIPTS]

AUTOMATIC ART—see AUTOMATIC WRITING.

AUTOMATIC ASTRAL PROJECTION—1. to involuntarily and unconsciously move out of one's physical body and float over it; life-force that left the physical body is usually quite aware of the presence of the body below; occurs in anesthesia, fainting, accident, severe pain, or a deep trance state; see SPONTANEOUS ASTRAL PROJECTION and INVOLUNTARY ASTRAL PROJECTION. 2. to involuntarily and unconsciously step to one side of the physical body during prolonged or deep meditation; person sees himself meditating. **Syn.** SLIGHTLY OUT-OF-BODY-EXPERIENCE. 3. to slide out of one's physical body during sleep and move to the astral planes to take care of universal functions or to educate one's self; occurs with and without recall upon awakening. [**cf.** ASTRAL PROJECTION, ASTRAL PLANE, DREAMS]

AUTOMATIC AUTOSUGGESTION—see INNER-DIALOGUE.

AUTOMATIC MUSICAL MEDIUM—one who has the proper body chemistry and agrees to be taken over partially or in whole by a deceased great musician; deceased musician uses the hands and arms of medium to play the piano or another instrument; medium may or may not understand music but feels compatible with synchronization of etheric world intelligence and is willing to share this music with mankind; more frequently an inborn ability but can be learned; executed in deep trance or ten percent trance. [**cf.** AUTOMATISM Appendix 2, MEDIUMSHIP, TEN PERCENT TRANCE]

AUTOMATIC PAINT MEDIUM—a person who agrees to a complete or partial takeover of his physical body by a great deceased painting artist; deceased artist uses medium's hands or feet to paint exceptional pictures in one-third the time an artist can paint; talent of medium lies in the proper body chemistry, ability of synchronization of etheric world intelligence, and willingness to share pictures with mankind; (do not confuse with INSPIRATIONAL PAINTING in which medium must be an artist and receives impressions). [**cf.** AUTOMAT, FACSIMILE WRITING]

AUTOMATIC SCRIPT—description of styles of writing used by etheric world intelligences in automatism: 1. written in reverse; words are spelled backward; 2. decipherable only by holding it up to a mirror. **Syn.** MIRROR WRITING. 3. written in etheric world intelligence's own handwriting, styled from one of his past incarnations in earth; 4. hieroglyphics; picture symbols; 5. presented in unknown language. **Syn.** XENOGLOSSIA, ETHERIC SCRIPT. [**cf.** AUTOMATISM Appendix 2]

AUTOMATIC SPEECH—to bring psychic information through one's voice box from an etheric world intelligence; information could not have been known from earthly experiences or education of the medium; information is meant to be utilized by mankind; intelligence helps medium go into a trance, anesthetizes his voice organs to use as an amplification system; more easily obtainable in an

organized seance circle; see DEPENDENT VOICE.
[**cf.** DISSOCIATED STATE, SEANCE, INDEPENDENT
VOICE]

AUTOMATIC TRANCE WRITING—to allow an
etheric world intelligence to intervene and use
one's hand to write psychic messages on paper for
an individual or for mankind; information totally
unknown previously to medium; medium understands trancing, DESIRED-CONTROL, and is willing
to use information for constructive purposes; see
AUTOMATIC WRITING. [**cf.** DESIRED-CONTROL,
PARTIAL ANESTHESIA, AUTOMAT]

AUTOMATIC TYPEWRITING—to sit at a type-
writer and allow an etheric world intelligence to
intervene and use one's hands to type information
that one did not know beforehand; knowledge is
usually meant to be published for the masses;
medium must be an expert typist, have the proper
body chemistry, know how to relax and keep a
neutral mind for the etheric world intervention;
e.g., Ruth Montgomery uses this method for her
recent writings; "The writing flows through the
subconscious mind and into the fingertips as if it
were all one process"; the control does not press
the keys but triggers the subconscious, and this
automatically works through the fingers to press
the correct keys. [**cf.** AUTOMATISM, MEDIUMSHIP,
GUIDE, LIGHT TRANCE]

AUTOMATIC WRITING—to allow an etheric world
intelligence to intervene in one's hand and arm and
write on paper information that one had no way of
knowing from formal education or life experiences;
medium must have the proper body chemistry,
know how to relax and keep the conscious mind
neutral; medium holds pen in hand over the paper
until the intelligence enters and moves the hand
and pen/pencil; writing is swift, and frequently
runs together as if the entity would lose control if
he or she picked the pen up from word to word;
writing could be large and slanting (see ETHERIC
SCRIPT); accomplished in trance state or an awareness state appearing that the medium was entirely
conscious. **Syn.** DIRECT PSYCHOGRAPHY, INVOL-
UNTARY WRITING. [**cf.** CEREBRAL MATERIAL,
SCRIPT INTELLIGENCE, ASTRAL SHELL, COMPLI-
MENTARY CROSS-CORRESPONDENCE]

AUTOMATIC-EYE CONTROL—(radiesthesia) theory of Howard St. L. Cookes: a system within the
eyes that gives each eye an individual opportunity
to be in charge of the present job based on the
direction the individual is facing; instead of each

eye seeing equally, one eye aligns itself to the
earth's magnetism and is master of the seeing
process according to the points of the compass one
is facing; each eye knows when it should take
precedence, and if the body changes, the master eye
reacts accordingly. (Inconcl.) [**cf.** ATTENTIVE EYE,
RADIESTHETIC SENSE, MAGNETISM]

AUTOMATISM—1. to will an etheric world intelligence to intervene and use a part or all of one's
body to write, paint, play a musical instrument,
dance, walk, run, or perform an experiment;
intelligence brings forth information, knowledge,
beauty, or an expression of Totality that one could
not have accomplished by one's self, known from
formal education, or life experiences in this incarnation; a dissociation from the life force of the
medium with the part or whole of the body being
used; can be used for private psychic counseling or
producing paintings and other great arts; (a)
performed while medium is in a deep state of
trance, whereby the mind is unaware of what the
body is doing and does not recall what transpired
upon awakening; medium preplans the length of
time the intelligence will use the body; (b) performed while medium is in light trance and knows
through his or her brain, but may not have full
recall later; arm that is used is anesthetized and
medium has no control over it; able to induce and
terminate at will. [**cf.** AUTOMATIC WRITING, DE-
SIRED-CONTROL, AUTOMATIC TYPEWRITING, TEN-
PERCENT TRANCE] 2. to will an etheric world
intelligence to make use of a nonhuman agent
(Ouija board or planchette) to bring psychic information to the medium or group; a code is established or letters on board are used; all members are
in a conscious awareness, but the mind is passive;
one in group must be a physical medium; usually
used for answering personal questions. [**cf.**
PLANCHETTE, OUIJA BOARD, ASTRAL SHELLS,
GUIDE, DISCARNATE ENTITIES]

AUTOMATIST—a medium who has the proper
body chemistry and desire to allow the etheric
world intelligence to enter his or her body, in whole
or in part, and use it for a preplanned time period;
intelligence uses medium's psychic energy (ectoplasm) to bring psychic information or psychic art
that could not have been known in any other way;
executed while the medium is in an altered state or
an aware state of consciousness. (Inconcl.) **Syn.**
AUTOMAT. [**cf.** OUIJA BOARD, AUTOMATIC PAINT-
ING, ASTRAL SHELL]

AUTOMATON—(destructive-brainwashing cults) an individual who reacts easily to simple, long-term, child-like tasks without questioning because he or she no longer has the ability to make decisions; performs contrary and erroneous activity to his or her previous life-style and belief system without the ability to realize it is not his or her idea to behave this way; victim has been coerced and influenced by cult leaders with clever destructive mind activity methods until his or her belief system is altered to suit the desires of the cult leaders; former compartments in the subconscious mind are repressed through constant repetitious ploys to keep the focus on the cult duties twenty-four hours a day, and other brainwashing methods that dull the mind, making it easy to manipulate. **Syn.** MENTAL PSYCHOLOGICAL PRISON. [**cf.** ON-THE-SPOT-HYPNOSIS, MASS ELEMENTAL, LOVE-BOMBING, MENTICIDE]

AUTONOMIC NERVOUS SYSTEM—a construct in the human body serving organs that function involuntarily; i.e., digestion, circulation, respiration, urination, and endocrine glands; connects all to the spinal cord and brain; has two divisions, sympathetic and parasympathetic; see SYMPATHETIC NERVOUS SYSTEM for esoteric meaning. [**cf.** SUBCONSCIOUS MIND, SYMPATHETIC NERVOUS SYSTEM]

AUTONOMOUS SECONDARY PERSONALITY—an intelligence that communicates with a psychic through inspirational thought by writing or speaking while the psychic is in a relaxed state or an altered state of consciousness; theory: this higher intelligence is a hidden personality trait or past incarnation personality of the psychic as opposed to the theory that another individual (guide or discarnate being) is impressing the psychic to write or speak. (Inconcl.) [**cf.** MEMORY-BANK, REINCARNATION]

AUTOPHONIC ORACLE—(Greece, Rome) an etheric world entity who has learned to construct his own invisible voice box mechanism in the air near the medium whose ectoplasm he is using; voice comes through this mechanism and not the medium's voice box; accomplished in the seance room; see DIRECT VOICE or INDEPENDENT VOICE. [**cf.** TRANCE, ECTOPLASM, TRANCE VOICE Appendix 2]

AUTOPHOTOGRAPHY—(botane) the innate ability of plants to transfer energy from themselves to film taking a picture of themselves without the aid of a camera; plants are placed directly on the film in a dark room. [**cf.** PLANT KINGDOM, BOTANE]

AUTOPROCEDURE—(hypnosis) to tell one's self what one would like to accomplish after one has hypnotized her or himself; the suggestions to change one's thinking or modify one's behavior are planned beforehand so the conscious mind does not fully enter into the process after the self-induction period. [**cf.** HYPNOTHERAPY, AUTOSUGGESTION]

AUTOSCOPE—(Rudolf Steiner) any mechanical means whereby communication from an unknown source psychically reaches one; i.e., Ouija board, table tippings, etc. [**cf.** above individually, PHYSICAL PSYCHISM, MEDIUM]

AUTOSCOPIC HALLUCINATION—1. (medical) to view one's body from outside the body during an accident, operation, or severe pain; occurs spontaneously and unwilled; recognized as a hallucination. 2. (esoteric) the soul-mind in its astral body slips out of the physical body to free itself from shock or severe pain; a built-in mechanism. [**cf.** AUTOSCOPY, ASTRAL PROJECTION]

AUTOSCOPIC VISION—see AUTOSCOPY.

AUTOSCOPY—to view one's physical body from a position outside the physical body; 1. the soul-mind encased in its astral body slips out of the physical body to free itself from the pain of the physical body caused from an accident, operation, other severe pain causes, or from too many drugs; soul-mind hovers over the physical body much aware of the physical body, activity of people and voices beneath it; occurs spontaneously and unwilled; 2. the soul-mind slips out of the physical body induced deliberately in a hypnotherapy session or in a programmed slightly-out-of-body projection; 3. to mentally view one's self; the mind only steps outside the body and, as if turning around, sees one's self sitting or lying down; occurs willed and unwilled; accomplished under hypnosis, in an imagery exercise, during meditation and biofeedback training. **Syn.** AUTOMATIC ASTRAL PROJECTION, AUTOSCOPIC VISION. [**cf.** CLAIRVOYANCE, ASTRAL PROJECTION, MENTAL PROJECTION]

AUTOSUGGESTION—to deliberately give one's own subconscious mind orders, information, or instructions with purposeful intentions; 1. e.g., to suggest to one's self to go to the store when the chore is finished; a normal mental activity one carries on constantly; 2. a planned ploy to change the subconscious mind's belief system and then feed the subconscious mind in self-hypnotherapy, visualization, or affirmations; (do not confuse with AUTOMATIC AUTOSUGGESTION). [cf. INNER-DIALOGUE, THOUGHTS, MATTER, SELF-HYPNOTHERAPY, VISUALIZATION, PROGRAMMING]

AUTOSUGGESTION HEALING—(metaphysics) to change one's body chemistry by speaking, audibly or silently, to the body suggestions to function correctly which aid normalization of body cells allowing the body to heal itself more quickly; 1. to repeat affirmations frequently of universal Truths that portray the potential within the human specie seed and universal seed, even though the body is not manifesting perfection at the time; this quickens the potential of good health within the human seed and gradually changes one's belief system resulting in good physical health; 2. to speak healing and complimentary words to the congested area of the body when in an alpha state of consciousness after meditation or during biofeedback training; when the conscious mind is passive, the subconscious mind is very receptive. [cf. MENTAL HEALING, AFFIRMATIONS, HOLISTIC HEALTH, SOUL-MIND, LISTENING MODE]

AUXILIARIES TO THE SPIRITS—(Allan Kardec) sitters in a seance circle whose bodies contain animal fluid that is easily accessible for the etheric world intelligences to use in their physical phenomena; animal fluid is emanated from sitters according to their desire, body chemistry, and length of time attending the circle; animal fluid was later called ectoplasm. **Syn.** BATTERIES. [cf. SEANCE, MATERIALIZATION, TRANCE, TRUMPET]

AVATAR—a human being who has perfected and purified his soul-mind through thousands of earthly incarnations to an exalted order in the angel kingdom and then functions to help evolution through mass progression of civilization; by: 1. a normal incarnation into an earth family; becomes a great leader over a large area; accomplishes a gigantic step for the benefit of civilization; recognized for his magnetic personality and capabilities; remembered and revered for hundreds of years later; the highest form man can attain and still reincarnate in an earthly body (and only if he chooses); the magnetism that surrounds his physical body when on earth can be felt and seen for miles; 2. materializing himself in an earthly body for a time long enough to help promote an issue important for the progress of civilization; e.g.,

appears to aid in getting a document signed at a diplomatic conference or to accomplish the air pollution solution, etc.; 3. acting as a great magnetic force from the etheric world who is connected to disciples in earth; the disciples psychically receive impressions through inspirational thought and inner-world telepathy to carry on the avatar's work. [cf. GODHEAD, MASTERSHIP, ANGEL HIERARCHY]

AVATAR MEDITATION—to repeat the name of one's chosen personal deity over many times while meditating; e.g., Jesus, Krishna, Buddha; helps the meditator fix his mind on the divine because of the natural urge to love his chosen deity. [cf. JAPA, MEDITATION Appendix 5]

AVATARA—a very highly evolved soul-mind incarnated from a female womb by an invisible process from the etheric world instead of earthly intercourse. [cf. AVATAR, MIRACULOUS CONCEPTION]

AVERAGE EVOKED RESPONSE—(biofeedback training) a universal pattern of waves registering on the EEG instrument due to the brain activity that occurs when the subject hears the rhythmic sound of the instrument. [cf. SUBJECT, BIOFEEDBACK TRAINING, EMG]

AVERAGE SCORE—(laboratory) expressed as a percentage; the total amount of hits divided by the number of runs of an experiment conducted in the laboratory. [cf. RUN, SCORE, TOTAL SCORE]

AVERROES—wisdom in its entirety, held in the subconscious mind of man, of which man is not aware; the world soul. **Syn.** GROUP SOUL, COLLECTIVE UNCONSCIOUS, COSMIC MIND, MACROCOSM]

AVESHA—(obsession) the process of an etheric world entity entering a physical body and working within it; this new consciousness is so powerful to the earthling that it eventually kills the old consciousness; the soul-mind of the earthling gradually slips out of the physical body leaving the etheric entity full control of the physical body. [cf. REINCARNATION, POSSESSION, INCARNATION EXCHANGE, WALK-IN, OBSESSION]

AVIATION-TYPE DREAM—an airplane shown in one's dream fabric that is the result of an astral projection; the movement of the projector stimulates the dream symbol. [cf. DREAMS, ASTRAL PROJECTION]

AVITICHI—(Sanskrit) 1. a state of hell in the etheric world where one remains in his physical body after death with the same desires of the flesh;

2. a division of the density where energy stagnates, no movement or waves; 3. a level of consciousness lacking in any form of happiness which continues until the entity reaches for help or begins to mend his attitude; also spelled **avichi**. [**cf.** HELL, DENSITY, REINCARNATION, KARMA]

AWAKE CONTROL—(Silva method) 1. a special mind-technique used to awaken oneself without an alarm clock; 2. a special mind-technique to rid oneself of a drowsy feeling. [**cf.** PROGRAMMING]

AWAKE-DREAMING—a dream surfacing during the daytime whenever the person sits and relaxes or is quiet; occurs from a shortage of necessary REM dream time due to lack of sleep; the body is trying to balance itself, as a certain amount of dream-time is necessary each night. [**cf.** DREAMS, REM STATE, NREM]

AWAKENED—see RESURRECTION.

AWARE ENERGY—(esoteric) atoms full of intelligence and energy with a consciousness of their intelligence and their function; atmosphere of consciousness that has the realization of its own identity. [**cf.** CONDENSED CONSCIOUSNESS, ATOMS MEMORY BANK]

AWARENESS—to recognize and be mindful of that which comes before one and to have a consciousness of its existence; to be altered by the stimuli of the five senses and record same in the conscious mind; until it is dropped into the subconscious mind it remains awareness only; has no independent existence, but neither is it separate from what it is aware. [**cf.** CONSCIOUSNESS]

AWARENESS NOTEBOOK—(biofeedback training) a record kept by the subject of his experiences and progress during the biofeedback training on the instruments both in the office and at home. **Syn.** PERIOD LOG. [**cf.** BIOFEEDBACK TRAINING, ELECTROENCEPHALOGRAPH]

AWARENESS-RAISING—to bring out a desire for more aspirational theories and activities. **Syn.** NEW CONSCIOUSNESS MOVEMENT. [**cf.** AQUARIAN AGE, CONSCIOUSNESS, PLANETARY HELPERS]

AWD GOGGIE—(Britain) a nature spirit that is a tiny, man-like creature who has charge of the berry bushes; swift to change dimensions when perceived by man.

AYIK—(Africa, Elgonyi) see VITAL LIFE FORCE.

AZILUT—(Kabbalah) a primal source; one of the divine emanations from the ensoph making one of the four worlds. [**cf.** BERIAH, YETZIRAH, MERKABAH]

AZOIC ROCK—(esoteric) a rock that has the vibrational frequency that can awaken animal forms. [**cf.** ANPSI, MINPSI]

AZOTH—(alchemy) name of the missing link in formula for alchemical transmutation; the x quantity. [**cf.** KABBALAH, ALCHEMY]

B

BA—(Egypt) the principle of life, found dwelling in physical form on earth, and dwelling in the Ka in the etheric world; an immortal, indestructible, refined mass of intelligence, containing all the attributes of the gods; pure spirit; the soul; symbolized in the form of a human-headed hawk carrying the ankh. **Sim.** SOUL, ATMAN, HEART, JIVA. **Syn.** SOUL-MIND. [**cf.** PRIMITIVE BRAIN, ROOT ASSUMPTIONS]

BAALZEPHON—(esoteric) etheric world entities who stand guard in the density, and are willing to communicate with earthlings. [**cf.** PRETA-LOKA WORLD, PRINCE OF DARKNESS, DENSITY]

BAARAS—(alchemy) a plant which has properties that help in the transmutation of metals; used by alchemists in their experiments; referred to as the golden plant. [**cf.** ALCHEMICAL PRINCIPLES, IMMORTAL DRAUGHT]

BABBLER—coined by Dick Sutphen; the voice within that keeps talking whether one pays attention or not; gets one in trouble or gives one sane guidance; under the influence of hypnotherapy regression, the babbler is usually very accurate. **Syn.** INNER-DIALOGUE. [**cf.** THOUGHT, SELF-OBSERVATION THERAPY, REGRESSION]

BACK BRAIN—see ABDOMINAL BRAIN.

BACK-IN-MEMORY—to relive or review as a bystander, past experiences of this life or other lives, while in a hypnotic state or in a relaxed state brought on by various methods of regression; see REGRESSION. [**cf.** REVIVIFICATION, PARTIAL REGRESSION]

BACK-IN-TIME—to relive or review, past experiences of this life, or other lives, only as a bystander or third person, instead of an emotional regression method; objective is to understand one's traits of character, or the experiences of this life; brought on by various methods of regression, through hypnotherapy, mental procedure, mechanical motions, or induction by one's self after meditation. **Syn.** BACK-IN-MEMORY, REGRESSION. [**cf.** REINCARNATION, CELESTIAL SEEING, GERM PICTURES, FLASHBACK]

BACK-TOGETHER—a term meaning the astral body is back in the physical body, and the projectionist no longer feels immobile, after taking an astral projection. [**cf.** ASTRAL TRAVEL, LOOPING THE LOOP, ROLL-IN]

BACKGROUND FILL—(esoteric) 1. sound used to remove the quietness in an area; 2. special sound or music used to promote special moods; i.e., to assist concentration while studying or meditating, etc.; 3. all noise and sound influences the etheric bodies, unknown to the conscious mind, and in turn have an emotional affect on the physical body; music that is pleasurable to the mental mind is not always harmonious to the etheric bodies, and makes one change his mood for no logical reason. [**cf.** WHITE NOISE, PRINCIPLES OF MAN, PSYCHOACOUSTICS]

BACKLASH—negative psychic energies sent out by an individual and returned to the sender with the same force with which they were sent; occurs when the receiver recognizes these negative psychic energies as not being his own and silently commands them to return to the sender. [**cf.** PSYCHIC TRANSFER, MIRROR CURSE, SICKNESS TRANSFER]

BACKSLIDING—(destructive-brainwashing cults) to rejoin the cult organization after having been deprogrammed; can be triggered by something said, by seeing an old member, or by an emotional event that resurfaces memories of past cult experiences; the ex-cultist then runs away to rejoin the organization. [**cf.** FLOATING, SUDDEN PERSONALITY CHANGE, SNAPPING, DEPROGRAMMING]

BACKSTER PHENOMENA—refers to the reactions of plants to man's thoughts; Cleve Backster found scientific evidence by using the polygraph instrument. [**cf.** PLANT PERCEPTION, SENSATION CONSCIOUSNESS]

BACKWARD CAUSATION—(laboratory) to produce the same physical effect that is the target of the experiment which is kept a secret until the experiment is over. **Syn.** BACKWARD PSI. [**cf.** ESP, PREDICTION]

BACKWARD DISPLACEMENT—(psi tasks) to pick up psychic information regarding the target before the target is given. [**cf.** PRESAGED, WAITING TECHNIQUE, TARGET PREFERENCE]

BACKWARD PSI—(laboratory) to telepathically perceive physical movement that is the target of the experiment; percipient tunes into physical body motion or physical matter that has been moved or rearranged and performs the same act; the target is then made known. **Syn.** BACKWARD CAUSATION, RETROACTIVE PK. [**cf.** MOMENTARY ABILITY, MOTOR TELEPATHY]

BACKWARDS TIME—theory suggesting that a signal traveling forward (seemingly faster than light) could (when viewed from another point of reference) travel backward in time. (Inconcl.) [**cf.** TIME Appendix 5]

BACOTI—(North Vietnam) see PSYCHIC and MEDIUM.

BAD TRIP—1. to experience distorted visions and emotions, as a result of taking a hallucinogenic drug; a feeling of dismemberment, dissociation from reality, a feeling of being lost, etc. (lasting hours to months). [**cf.** HALLUCINATION, HYPNO-GOGIC] 2. (meditation) overwhelming body-feelings, clairvoyance, and clairaudience from the superconscious or subconscious minds which the conscious mind cannot accept in its present level of understanding. [**cf.** CAVE MEDITATION]

BADI—(Malaya) see VITAL LIFE FORCE.

BAGUETTE DIVINATOIRE—(France) see DOWSER.

BAHYA VRITTI—(Yoga) a special method of expelling one's breath to bring about an increase in strength and mind activity. [**cf.** BREATHING, LOW BREATHING]

BAKA—(Haiti) a huge mass of thoughts formed together as a result of the unity of the motive of the thoughts; held together as long as this motive is concentrated on daily; thought-form will have enough intelligence to be useful for the one making it; purposely built for good or evil intent. **Syn.** SHUG. [**cf.** GOLEM, SOULLESS, ELEMENTAL]

BALANCE CONTROL—the dial on a biofeedback instrument that can be regulated to the subject's own electrical impulse cycles, establishing a baseline for that training system. **Syn.** FREQUENCY CONTROL. [**cf.** BIOFEEDBACK TRAINING, BASELINE DRIFT, MONITOR SWITCH]

BALANCING OF ENERGY FIELDS—(acupuncture) a special technique of working with the meridian lines of the physical body; puts the body in a state of harmony, using needles or hand pressure to equalize the polarity in the body. **Syn.** POLARITY THERAPY. [**cf.** COMPRESSION MASSAGE, MERIDIAN LINES]

BALCONY—(esoteric) an energy level in the etheric world that appears to take on the characteristics of both the astral plane and the earth plane and vibrates at a rate between these two planes. **Syn.** MEZZANINE, EARTH'S ETHERIC DOUBLE. [**cf.** BODIES AND PLANES Appendix 5, ASTRAL PLANE]

BAND OF COLLABORATORS—(mediumship) a personal group of etheric world entities, who constantly administer guidance, protection, and psychic development to the earthling, if asked to do so. **Syn.** INNER BAND. [**cf.** GUIDE, MEDIUMSHIP, OUTER BAND]

BANISHING—(esoteric) 1. an important ritual performed by the psychic when the work is finished, which closes the psychic doors, so the etheric world entities will not spill over into normal living. [**cf.** GUIDES, MEDIUMSHIP, CLOAK OF INSULATION] 2. (exorcism) a necessary ritual, with a special formula, performed by the psychic who is in charge of the exorcism; sends the evil entities back to their level of consciousness, so they will not turn and attack the psychic. [**cf.** EXORCISM, EVOCATION]

BANISHING RITUALS—see BANISHING.

BANSHEE—(Ireland) a female etheric world intelligence who desires to warn families of an approaching death and to be of assistance; sometimes recognized by her terrifying wail. [**cf.** DEATH ANGEL, ETHERIC WORLD INTELLIGENCES]

BANTERING SPIRIT—(possession) the etheric world entity capable of taking control, or influencing an earthling for evil intent, by seizures of distorted and abnormal behavior. [**cf.** POSSESSION, COMPULSION, DUAL PERSONALITY]

BAPTISM BY FIRE—(esoteric) the moment of arousal and rising of the kundalini power, felt by the person as a surge of energy enters the chakras. [**cf.** SACRED RIVER IN MAN, MUSICAL LIGHTS]

BAPTISM IN THE SPIRIT—see SLAYING-IN-THE-SPIRIT.

BAQUET—a wooden tub filled with magnetized water, iron filings, and iron rods (that extend to the diseased areas of the patient's body), to help cure disease. [**cf.** MAGNETISM, POLARITY, MAGNETS Appendix 5]

BARADUC'S BIOMETER—(inventor, Hyppolite Baraduc) an instrument that measures nervous force and unknown vibrations which are connected to the human body during psychic experiments in a seance (early 1900s) [cf. SEANCE, MENTAL PSYCHIC PROCESSES]

BARAKA—1. (Sufi, A.D. 600) see VITAL LIFE FORCE; 2. a form of grace or blessing, said for one who needs healing. **Sim.** BARUCH. [cf. MENTAL HEALING, BLESSING]

BARDO BODY—(Tibet) astral substance clothing itself around the soul-mind, while in the astral plane; see ASTRAL BODY. [cf. DESIRE BODY, REALM OF ILLUSION]

BARDO CONSCIOUSNESS—(Buddhism) the various mental states experienced in the earth plane and the etheric world plane, which are aspects of the flux of that part of man that dies, and is reborn every minute; divided into degrees: chik-hai, sidpa, chonyd, bsamgtan, skye-gnas. [cf. MOLECULAR MEMORY, CONSCIOUSNESS, SYSTEM OF MENTAL WAVES]

BARDO THODOL—(Tibet) a book of instruction, showing man the correct way to go through the initiation of dying, enter the new life, and live in the etheric world. **Syn.** THE EGYPTIAN BOOK OF THE DEAD.

BARDOS—(Tibet *bar,* "between," *do,* "two") between two states; the experiences which occur in the period of time when one is dying (in the physical world), and being reborn (in the etheric world); a twilight state of very real events to the dying person. **Syn.** INTERMEDIATE STATE, TRANSITIONAL STATE. [cf. DEATH, HYPNAGOGIC STATE]

BAREHANDED DOWSING—a method of extending the arms in search for underground substance, instead of using a dowsing rod; arms are extended at right angles and there is a "pull" felt within the arms or hands to know when one has located the water or oil. [cf. RADIESTHETIC SENSE, DOWSING]

BARHISHAD—(Sanskrit) intelligent forms of energy in the etheric world, belonging to the moon chain, called lunar pitris, concerned with physical evolution on earth. [cf. PITRIS, GREAT WHITE BROTHERHOOD]

BARON SAMEDI—(Haiti) etheric world entities, believed to guard tombs and burial places; in control of zombies. [cf. ZOMBIES]

BARRIER—(esoteric) energy that acts as a curtain, keeping information of the astral world from man's mental consciousness, during dreams, as-

tral flights, clairvoyancy, etc. **Syn.** VEIL, BLACK CLOUD, ETHERIC WEB. [cf. SOLID ASTRAL MATTER, DENSITY]

BARUCH—(Hebrew) a form of blessing or grace, administered to one who is in need of a healing. **Syn.** BARAKA. [cf. MENTAL HEALING, WORDS-WITH-POWER]

BASELINE DRIFT—(biofeedback training) the readout is no longer registering on the instrument because the subject is producing in another range level. Usage: "He has drifted from the alpha level to the theta level, and we must change his baseline range." [cf. RANGE SWITCH, LOWER FREQUENCY]

BASELINE READING—(biofeedback training) a gauge on the readout of the biofeedback instrument which indicates the normality level of the subject at the beginning of the session. [cf. LEVEL-OFF, METABOLIC MONITOR]

BASIC BUZZ OF THE UNIVERSE—that which manifests is everything, in the universe; see VITAL LIFE FORCE.

BASIC CONSCIOUSNESS—that innate desire within man to move forward and improve himself in the world. **Syn.** GRACE. [cf. LAW OF MACRO/MICROCOSM Appendix 7]

BASIC ELEMENTS—(esoteric) atoms and their breakdown particles, believed to be in various vibratory rates, composing everything in all the universes. [cf. ATOMS, VIBRATIONS]

BASIC LIMITING PRINCIPLES—(laboratory) those concepts that are taken for granted, buried in the subconscious mind, which prevent the proper examination of ESP, i.e., an event will not have an effect before it happens; one can only perceive with the visible senses. [cf. SHEEP AND GOATS EFFECT]

BASIC TECHNIQUE—abbr. BT; (laboratory) a system of psi testing, using cards; each card is laid aside by the experimenter, as it is called by the subject (receiver), until the run is ended and then a checkup is made for psi ability. [cf. ESP, ZENER CARDS, TRAIL, STACKING EFFECT]

BASKET—(automatism) a homemade tool holding a pencil; used by the etheric world entity to write messages to the medium. **Syn.** CORBEILLE-TOUPIE. [cf. PLANCHETTE, INDIRECT PSYCHOGRAPHY]

BASKET DRAWINGS—messages and pictures drawn on small cards by the etheric world intelligences in the presence of a precipitation medium; cards and colored pencils are placed in a basket near the medium, and during a seance or lecture, there is movement in the basket; when the session is finished, many participants receive a personal written message on a card. [**cf.** PRECIPITATION, ETHERIC SCRIPT, SLATE WRITING]

BAT—(Eastern) a winged mouse-like creature that has the vibratory rate which makes it helpful for psychic phenomena; (Austria) to wear the bat's left eye enhances the skill of becoming invisible; to wear the bat's heart, bound to the arm with red thread, guides one on the right path. [**cf.** ANPSI, BAT'S BLOOD]

BAT KOL—(Hebrew, "daughter of voice") a medium who has the proper body chemistry and the ability for concentration, which allows an etheric world intelligence to speak through the medium's voice box to bring counsel, knowledge, and protection. [**cf.** DIRECT VOICE, MEDIUMSHIP]

BAT'S BLOOD—used in witches' brew to make an ointment to help them fly; law of similarity: any object bearing a similarity to the psychic event will aid in the psychic event (bats fly, witches fly). [**cf.** ASSOCIATION MAGIC, LAW OF MIMICRY Appendix 7]

BATES METHOD—system of eye exercises and eye philosophy that enables one to see without glasses. [**cf.** CURATIVE EDUCATION, NATUROPATHY]

BATH OF REBIRTH—(esoteric) water found in certain places that is believed to have special magnetic qualities; when bathed in the water, one is stripped of the old self and new life is stirred up on the bloodstream; considered a baptismal to some. [**cf.** WATER, HOLY WATER, LOURDES OF FRANCE]

BATTERIES—see SITTERS.

BATTERY—a psychic acting as a human generator (in a seance or psychic development circle) for another psychic in the circle, to help the information come through. [**cf.** SITTER, GUIDE, DARK-ROOM SESSIONS]

BATTLE GROUND—(kundalini) the heart chakra, located between the three lower and three higher chakras; one stays here the longest in his or her development, as one struggles to cleave to the lower chakras; the lower chakras eventually become purified and transmute into the energies of the higher chakras and one moves along their path. [**cf.** KUNDALINI, OCCULT FIRE, ROOT CHAKRA]

BATTLE GROUND PLANE—the middle section of the mental plane, that separates the causal section from the mental section; where the mind struggles because it is not always in agreement, to give up the material world and the astral plane below. [**cf.** ASTRAL PLANE, MENTAL PLANE]

BATYSPHERE—(Thailand) name of a plane in the etheric world. **Syn.** SPHERE. [**cf.** STRATA OF CREATION]

BC/AB—known as the symbol of Sacred Proportion because it appears throughout all nature, and is the basis of measurement of the human body; the governing ratio of the pyramid. [**cf.** LAW OF REPETITION Appendix 7, PYRAMIDOLOGY]

BE'AL—(Druid) the one God, life of everything. [**cf.** MACROCOSM, TOTALITY]

BEAM OF HEAT—(ufology) streaks of redness on the face and upper parts of the body, similar to suntan streaks, noticeable on many UFO contactees the day after the encounter; one is unaware of this heat during the encounter. **Syn.** RADIATION BURN. [**cf.** CONTACTEE, MAGNETIC ANOMALY]

BEAMED IN—to tune into the aura of a person or thing, where information about that person or thing can be perceived; (do not confuse with beaming energy *to* the object or person). [**cf.** PSYCHIC READING, PSYCHOMETRY]

BEANS—(Egypt) 1. have a vibrational frequency to make them a useful tool for psychic skills because they are a seed of potential life; 2. used as markers in the casting of lots; 3. worn around the neck as a protecting agent. 4. Pythagoras believed beans to contain souls and blood and would not consume or crush them. [**cf.** CASTING OF LOTS, SORTES]

BEAR CLAW—(Native American) has the vibratory rate enabling it to psychically draw power to one's self; represents power for the one who wears a claw as an amulet. [**cf.** AMULET, PSYCHIC SHOCK ARTICLES]

BEAR PAW—(Native American) used as an amulet; the paw is considered to be a complete replica of the bear; therefore, if one endows the paw with love, the paw will become protection against bear attacks for the wearer. [**cf.** LAW OF CORRESPONDENCE Appendix 7]

BEASTIES—1. (Scotland) see NATURE SPIRIT; 2. (Peggy Frank) negative thoughts that cause unpleasant and unwanted activity in a person's life; shortened from the phrase BEASTS OF THE FIELD [**cf.** LAW OF THOUGHT Appendix 7]

BEASTS OF THE FIELD—1. (biblical) human beings who have not been incarnated as many times as the rest of the culture in which they live; they engage in unethical behavior, such as lust, envy, greed, and crudity; appear to the etheric world intelligences with an aura similar to that of an animal, from which the name comes. **Syn.** BRUTE WORLD. [**cf.** REINCARNATION, SOUL-MIND EVOLUTION] 2. (metaphysical interpretation of Bible) negative thoughts mingled among other thoughts, silently or audibly spoken. [**cf.** INNER-DIALOGUE, NEGATIVE THOUGHTS]

BEATING DOWN THOUGHT—to use a word or short phrase to put worldly thoughts and worldly activity out of the mind; used in meditation or as inner-dialogue when disturbed; e.g., "love, love, etc." or "Jesus" or "happy and lovable am I." [**cf.** MANTRA, INNER-DIALOGUE]

BEAUTIFICATION—to earn a very high rank, such as "sainthood," through the purification of the body, by righteous living and thinking. **Syn.** CANONIZATION. [**cf.** GLORIFIED BODY, AGLOW, REINCARNATION]

BECHARM—to cast a spell; to beam concentrated thoughts to an object or person, and gain a certain amount of control over that object or person; see SPELL. **Syn.** BEWITCH, CHARM. [**cf.** BEAMED ENERGY, LAW OF ASSOCIATION and LAW OF QUANTUM CONNECTION Appendix 7]

BEELZEBUB—(density) an etheric world entity who is considered evil, and communicates with earthlings; ranked sometimes with Satan. **Syn.** LORD OF THE FLIES. [**cf.** DENSITY, PLANE]

BEGGAR MONK—(Tibet) one whose job in the monastery is to meditate all day long. [**cf.** THOUGHTS ARE THINGS, QUIETUDE]

BEHAVIOR-CONTROL—(humanistic psychology) to focus one's awareness on the subjective self; to expand inner awareness and potentials, as opposed to focusing attention on one's environment. [**cf.** HUMANISTIC PSYCHOLOGY]

BEHAVIORAL MEMORIES—(reincarnation) 1. actions and speech of a child that pertain to one's past life identity, surfacing as a part of one's daily function; 2. past life experiences in the subconscious mind that spill into the conscious mind and unknowingly influence one's actions and thoughts. [**cf.** REINCARNATION, KARMA, AKASHIC RECORDS]

BEING—1. (capitalized); God; see TOTALITY; 2. (uncapitalized); finite existence.

BEING OF LIGHT—an etheric world intelligence who no longer uses a form of a physical body and shows itself to the earthling as a lighted atmosphere when perceived clairvoyantly; abides in the highest realms. [**cf.** INNER-BAND, PSYCHIC LIGHTS, CLAIRVOYANCE]

BEINGS—(esoteric) 1. an eternal intelligent mass of energy, conscious of its intelligence, and living within its own principles on its own plane of vibration; capable of manipulating cosmic forces; has an irreducible existence, endowed with an inner law of upward evolution; placed in a sphere of multitudinous energies coming from every direction, influencing its vibrational rate, and being influenced by these same energies; has a soul or a soul-mind and a state of consciousness of living reality in relation to itself; 2. man, or having a similarity to man; classes: human beings, discarnate human beings, angel beings, etheric space beings, craft occupant beings, nature spirit beings, deva beings, demon beings, sentient beings (subhuman), and pritris; (do not use interchangeably with ENTITY). **Syn.** ABHAMSI. [**cf.** KINGDOMS]

BELIEF SYSTEM—1. one's inner or basic ideas, concepts, values, and theories about the "here and now," in regard to one's self, the world, and one's relation to the world; this is formulated from the total of one's past thinking, emotions, and experiences (from the present incarnation and from past incarnations), that are imbedded in the subconscious mind and resurface to make one's world and body what it is, in the present; 2. can be categorized into two groupings for each individual: (**a**) a core belief: a strong ideas about one's own existence; (**b**) a blanket belief: subconscious ideas that combine with other belief systems all over the world, to make thought-forms that hold the earth and material matter together; 3. (Seth) "thoughts reinforced by imagination and emotion, concerning the nature of one's reality"; 4. a mental structure of thoughts from unconditioned responses from past living

63

experiences, as a basis from which emotions develop; 5. every new experience blends with one's belief system, changes it a little, or strengthens what is already there; if it is completely foreign, it is rejected or begins a new compartment. [cf. THOUGHTS, EMOTIONS, HOLISM, SUBCONSCIOUS MIND]

BELL—(esoteric) tiny, soft-toned bells are used as a tool for psychic work, especially when one is in an altered state of consciousness; can be heard by etheric world intelligences and by the subconscious mind without jarring one's nervous system; used by: 1. Catholic priests, during mass; 2. monks in the monastery; 3. Spiritualist churches, during the message service; 4. meditators; 5. magicians, to summon an etheric world intelligence for psychic help. [cf. MAGIC WAND, NECROMANTIC BELL]

BELL, BOOK, AND CANDLE—(Roman Catholic, fourteenth century) a ceremony of excommunication from the church: the book of curses was closed, the bell was tolled for the dead man, and the candles were lighted, then extinguished, to represent the removal of the offender's soul from the sight of God. [cf. CEREMONIAL MAGIC, SYMBOLISM]

BELLY DANCING—(Egypt) 1. special body movements, performed to a chosen rhythm, in costumes which expose the navel area; the navel is used as a point of focus for hypnotizing the spectators; 2. muscular movements designed to make childbirth easier; 3. a special art for inducing an altered state of consciousness in the dancer or in the spectator. [cf. MOVEMENT-FOR-ALTERED-CONSCIOUSNESS]

BELOW LEVELS OF AWARENESS—the sights and sounds one is tuned into, and which affect one subconsciously, even though they are not in one's conscious path of awareness. **Syn.** SUBLIMINAL LEVEL. [cf. VIBRATIONS]

BENEFICENT DAEMON—(Neoplatonism) an etheric world intelligence who communicates with earthlings, and is willing to help, guide, and protect them. **Syn.** ETHERIC WORLD INTELLIGENCES Appendix 3. [cf. GUIDE, MEDIUMSHIP]

BENEVOLENT SPIRIT—(angel) an etheric world intelligence who has progressed in morality (rather than intelligence), and offers assistance in character building to the earthling. **Syn.** ANGEL, GUIDE. [cf. INNER BAND, OUTER BAND]

BEOWULF—(esoteric) an etheric world entity of low quality, who takes an animal form to communi-

cate with an earthling; of evil intent, and shows himself mostly at night. [cf. SHAPE-CHANGING]

BERBERLANGS—a human who needs to feed on human flesh periodically in order to survive; takes astral flights (in the form of a bird) to a sleeping person and feeds on the victim's entrails; can be seen physically. **Syn.** VAMPIRE. [cf. NIGHT FLYING, BLOODSUCKERS]

BERGER RHYTHM—(biofeedback training) name given to the alpha rhythm of the brain, for Hans Berger who discovered it; inventor of the EEG instrument which detects the various brain rhythms. [cf. BRAIN WAVE SCALE, EEG, EMG, THETA STATE OF CONSCIOUSNESS, BETA STATE OF CONSCIOUSNESS]

BERIAH—a high vibrational plane in the etheric world; one of the four worlds of thrones and palaces; a subdivine sphere of angel beings. [cf. AZILUT, YETZIRAH, MERKABAH]

BERMUDA TRIANGLE—(esoteric) an area in the Atlantic Ocean with enough underwater suction power to periodically pull down objects from the surface of the sea and to periodically pull down airplanes from the air; believed to be a type of huge tunnel or vast cave under the surface of the sea; ships and airplanes disappear mysteriously, never to return; however, many ships sail and craft fly over this area safely; how and why these disappearances occur has not yet been discovered; an area in the Atlantic Ocean whose boundaries exist somewhere between Bermuda, Miami, San Juan, and a small part of the Gulf of Mexico (along the coast of West Central Florida). (Inconcl.) [cf. UFOLOGY, ATLANTIS]

BERYL—(esoteric) a mineral associated with water and Venus; has a vibrational frequency to help a psychic summon his or her guide, and to bring psychic visions in the mineral. [cf. MINPSI, INVOCATION]

BESOM—a broom made from birch or heather twigs tied to a stick; used by fairies and witches to ride on. [cf. LAW OF SIMILARITY Appendix 7, GRAVITY CONTROL, DIMENSION SHIFTING]

BETA BODY—see ETHERIC DOUBLE.

BETA SENSES—(esoteric) the intelligence mechanism that detects and impresses information of the beta part of the brain; called the objective senses. (Inconcl.) [cf. LITTLE LOCAL SELF, MIND EXPERIENCE]

BETA STATE OF CONSCIOUSNESS—(biofeedback training) the brain rhythm between fourteen and thirty cycles per second; shows a rough, jerky print-out on the biofeedback electroencephalograph; the conscious mind in a normal waking state: sorting and compiling from sight, sound, smell, touch, taste, time, and space. [**cf.** SCALE OF BRAIN RHYTHM, EEG]

BETHOR—(esoteric) an angel of the major hierarchies in the etheric world; in charge of Jupiter. [**cf.** ANGEL, AVATAR]

BEWITCHER—a psychic specializing in spelling; see SPELLER.

BEWITCHERY—see SPELL. **Syn.** SPELLCRAFT, ENCHANTMENT, WITCHWORK. [**cf.** ON-THE-SPOT-HYPNOSIS, DESTRUCTIVE-BRAINWASHING CULT, BEAMED ENERGY]

BEWITCHING—to use one's psychic influence over another person for the purpose of manipulating his thoughts and actions; bewitcher uses beamed energy from an eye-stare, incantations, or rituals of magic to put his victim in a transfixed state; this beamed energy is either an icy, destructive, fearful stare or a pleasurable, enticing, lovable stare; verbiage and chants are accompanied appropriately; results in the victim experiencing events that cannot be attributed to his own personal efforts; sometimes the victim is unaware that his actions are not his own; lasts from a few hours to many years. **Syn.** CASTING A SPELL. **Sim.** CHARMING, ENCHANTING, FASCINATING. [**cf.** LAW OF MIMICRY Appendix 7, CANTATIONS, CHARMS]

BEYOND—refers to all invisible space, including all levels of energy interpenetrating each other; see ETHERIC WORLD.

BEYOND PERSONAL CONSCIOUSNESS—pertains to any type of perception that does not come through normal thought processes; an altered state of consciousness; see INSPIRATION, PSYCHIC INFORMATION, APPARITIONS, PROPHECY, HYPNOTHERAPY.

BFT—abbr. BIOFEEDBACK TRAINING; see same.

BHAGAVAD-GITA—the gospel of Hinduism; dated between the fifth and second centuries B.C.; dialogue between Sri Krishna (the divine incarnation) and his disciple Arjuna; scriptures dealing with the aspects of human life, leading to the whole man, with a spiritual teacher to guide.

BHAIRAVA RAGA—(Hinduism) a fixed melodic scale; played in the mornings during the months of August, September, and October, to achieve tranquility. [**cf.** MUSICAL SCIENCE, LISTENING FATIGUE]

BHAKTI-MARGA—(India) a method of expressing true love by following the path to the devotion of the divine. **Sim.** PEYOTE ROAD, THE PATH, TREE OF LIFE. [**cf.** LAW OF PERFECTIBILITY Appendix 7, GRACE]

BHAVANA—(Sanskrit) constant brooding over a problem which the conscious mind has dropped, but which the subconscious mind is anxious to solve; thus the problem keeps surfacing. [**cf.** OUTLAW MEMORY, INNER-DIALOGUE, SELECTIVE AMNESIA]

BHIKKHU—(Buddhism) a psychic and holy man of India, capable of healing, counseling, and prophesying; a spiritual teacher and guide.

BHUT—(Hinduism) an etheric world entity believed capable of having sexual intercourse with an earthling; see INCUBUS. **Syn.** SUCCUBUS. [**cf.** DIMENSION-SHIFTING]

BHUTAS—(Sanskrit) see ASTRAL SHELL.

BI—prefix meaning "twice" or "two."

BIBLE—(King James, Revised Standard, George Lamsa, tr.) (June Bletzer's interpretation) a textbook for the development and growth of one's soul-mind; its literary style and choice of words make it a practical textbook; one can read it at any level of their development and find rules and principles that will bring him or her encouragement and direction to raise the self to a higher level of existence; most of the passages have various meanings, parallel to the stages a man or woman goes through to perfection, bringing information regarding these stages; its instructions, knowledge, and wisdom permeate such subjects as: metaphysics, science, psychology, psychism, history, literature, mathematics, astrology, numerology, music, curative medicine, healing methods, sex evolution, angelic kingdoms, and cosmology.

BIBLICAL NUMEROLOGY—a belief which attributes special significance to each number, and the way it is used in the Bible. [**cf.** numbers ONE to NINE]

BIOCORPOREITY—(astral projection) name given to the astral body when it is projected; is visible and appears a duplicate of the physical body; see

65

ASTRAL PROJECTION and BILOCATION. **Syn.** DOUBLE-MEN. [**cf.** INTERGLOBE TROTTING, SPECTRAL EVIDENCE]

BIDIRECTIONALITY OF PSI—see DIFFERENTIAL EFFECT.

BIENERGY—another name for AURA; felt to be caused by self, and the cause of self; (do not confuse

BIFROST—(Scandinavian) a rainbow linking heaven and earth; made of fire, air, and water; a sacred bridge for the guides to cross over when counselling with earthlings. **Syn.** REQUITER. [**cf.** FIRMAMENT, SYNAPSE]

BIFURCATION THEORY—see LAW OF CATAS-TROPHE Appendix 7.

BIG BANG THEORY—(cosmology) all matter in the universe came from a tiny, superdense object, which hurled its fragments in all directions at enormous speeds, following a cataclysmic explosion, ten to twenty billion years ago. [**cf.** PRIMEVAL ATOM]

BIG BIRD—(Texas, 1975) a creature seemingly half-human/half-bird; reported to look like a flying ostrich; leaves footprints visible from the air and flies without using its wings; appears to shift dimensions. (Inconcl.) **Sim.** SASQUATCH, ABOM-INABLE SNOWMAN, LOCH NESS MONSTER. [**cf.** MONSTER ACTIVITY, DIMENSION-SHIFTING]

BIG BREAKTHROUGH—see SUDDEN PERSON-ALITY CHANGE.

BIG FOOT—(ufology) (Western United States) a creature reported to resemble a large, hairy giant, sometimes ten feet tall; gives evidence of his presence by destruction of surroundings, large foot-prints in the dirt, and a foul smell; sometimes seen crashing around trees and in logging camps, terrorizing people; when it appears it is after a UFO-sighting and in the same area; capable of shifting dimensions; some believe it belongs to the nature kingdom, and some believe it is a throwback from another civilization. **Sim.** BIG BIRD, YETI, LOCH NESS MONSTER [**cf.** NATURE SPIRITS, DIMENSION-SHIFTING, MONSTER ACTIVITY]

BIG MAMA—(ufology) an assemblage of nocturnal lights which break up into separate small lights, speed off for a time, and then return to the parent; believed to be a type of space craft; often seen before cattle mutilations on farms in one area. [**cf.** SCOUT SHIP, UFOLOGY]

BIG OWL—(Native American) a creature who is half owl/half man; giant in size; similar to BIGFOOT. [**cf.** DIMENSION-SHIFTER, MONSTER ACTIVITY]

BIJA MANTRA—a special word or syllable or a group of words, used in meditation; believed to be an aspect of God within these words; the sound that governs the syllable manifests itself. **Syn.** SEED-MANTRA. [**cf.** MANTRA, POWER OF THE WORD, PSYCHOSPIRITUAL POWERS]

BIJAKSHARA MANTRA—a special monosyllabic sound with the vibratory rate that, when spoken repetitively, silently or aloud, will bring on psychic power which may be used for psychic work or healing. [**cf.** TRANCE, PASSING-THE-MANTRA]

BILATERAL ALPHA RHYTHMS—one of the five brain-wave signatures resulting from the read-out of the "mind-mirror EEG instrument", showing calm, detached alertness, no thoughts, and no visions. (Inconcl.) [**cf.** ALPHA BLOCKING, MIND-MIRROR, EEG]

BILLET READING—to psychometrize, while blind-folded, a question written on a slip of paper and to give the answer to the question; individual writes a question on a slip of paper and folds it over; blind-folded psychic holds it between the palms of his or her hands and psychically tunes into an answer for the recipient; usually performed in group meet-ings. [**cf.** PRACTICAL PSYCHOMETRY, PURE PSY-CHOMETRY]

BILOCATION— to appear in more than one body, at the same time; the soul-mind appears to split in half for a period of time; appears in two physical bodies simultaneously but in different locations; both bodies function totally, are able to speak, and behave normally during this period; can be willed; usually happens spontaneously, triggered by an emotional desire; the soul-mind wants to fulfill its needs, or it performs to protect its continuity; usu-ally the psychic is not aware of the other body until someone from the other location describes having witnessed his presence, clothing, etc.; the ability to transcend every obstacle of gross matter at will, for a soul-mind purpose; (do not confuse with a nor-mal astral projection or mental projection). (Inconcl.) [**cf.** SOUL-MIND, SPLIT-OFF, REDOUBLED]

BILOCATION OF CONSCIOUSNESS—see TRAVEL-ING CLAIRVOYANCE and CLAIRVOYANCE-IN-SPACE.

BINAH—(Kabbalah) in the supreme triangle; the three sides are symbolic of reason, necessity, and liberty. [**cf.** FORMS-WITH-POWER, LAW OF THREES Appendix 7]

BINDING DEITIES—inferior or low-grade etheric world entities who help a psychic cast a spell and hold a person in one place for years; see SPELL. **Sim.** FASCINATION, BEWITCHED, ENCHANT. [**cf.** SPELL, DESTRUCTIVE-BRAINWASHING CULT]

BIO—a prefix meaning "life."

BIO-STAT MONITOR—innovated by J. Bletzer and invented by Maury Bonnain; a sophisticated, tiny biofeedback instrument that measures both physiological and neurological responses in the body fed back in two thousand increments of visual, calibrated, digital number readouts; eliminates the use of sound and baseline adjustments; because of the instantaneous feedback with every change in emotion from second to second, it not only determines the kind of stimuli associated with stress, but the degree of that stress; two electrodes are attached to the finger of each hand; uses both pulsating and direct current for more accuracy; see METABOLIC MONITOR. [**cf.** GSR, EEG]

BIOACCUMULATOR—invented by Robert and Jana Paviltova; a device constructed to extract psychic energy from the hands of people, store it, and then transmit it through matter and space; controls the quality and quantity of this energy; operates by the law of mutual effect. [**cf.** BEAMED ENERGY, LAW OF MUTUAL EFFECT Appendix 7]

BIOCHEMICAL—(esoteric) the relationship of the body chemistry to psychic work, and the changes in body chemistry during hypnotherapy, meditation, biofeedback training, psychic readings, and psychic and mental healings. [**cf.** PSYCHIC DEVELOPMENT, MENTAL HEALING, BIOFEEDBACK TRAINING]

BIOCHEMIC SYSTEM OF MEDICINE—a method of treating and preventing disease with cell salts; theory: disease is a deficiency in one or more of the inorganic chemical compounds in the body cells. **Syn.** CELLULAR THERAPY. [**cf.** CELL SALTS, CURATIVE EDUCATION]

BIOCHEMISTRY THERAPY—the use of inorganic mineral substances which are essential to good health; used for their curative properties in treating disease; the chemistry of living tissue. **Syn.** CELLULAR THERAPY. [**cf.** TISSUE SALTS]

BIOCLIMATOLOGY—(Europe) the study of the influence of atmospheric changes and earthly environment on the human body, and how to use this information for the betterment of individual health as used in preventative medicine. **Syn.** MEDICAL CLIMATOLOGY. [**cf.** CIRCADIAN RHYTHM, ASTROLOGY]

BIOCLOCKS—pertains to the study of biorhythms, and the part they play in the living systems of humans, animals, and plants. **Sim.** PERIODICITY. [**cf.** BIORHYTHM, EARTH RADIATIONS, CYCLES]

BIOCOMMUNICATION—1. (laboratory) the rapport of two living organisms in a laboratory experiment who have organic changes relating one to another; e.g., one heart gaining beats and the other losing beats; 2. (esoteric) an individual drawing energy psychically from another individual when in the other's presence, consciously or unconsciously. [**cf.** PSYCHIC TRANSFER] 3. (Russia) name for various types of telepathy, requiring studies of cybernetics, information processing theory, neurophysiologic science, and quantum physics. (Inconcl.)

BIOCOMPUTER—human life computer: 1. (current science) the conscious mind; the brain; 2. (esoteric) the invisible subconscious mind; (a) functions like the hardware of a man-made computer, programmed by the conscious mind; the brain sifts, sorts, labels, categorizes, and forms opinions regarding the information from the outside stimuli obtained through the five senses; this information is then sent to the subconscious mind for storage; instantaneously the subconscious mind prints out material from the past that is similar to the present activity, and surfaces it for use by the conscious mind in making judgments in the present situation; if the material coming in is completely foreign, there will be no compartment for it to be stored, and the computer will not accept it, until the material has some similarities to an already-established compartment; branches off into new compartments "gradually" with new information; (b) cannot make decisions; accepts ideas and opinions exactly as stated by the brain in normal states of consciousness; (c) in an altered state of consciousness: accepts and stores emotions and words from other people and conditions from the environment as presented without any judgment or opinion. (Inconcl.) **Syn.** SOUL-MIND. [**cf.** LAW OF SUGGESTION Appendix 7, BRAIN, SUBCONSCIOUS MIND]

BIOCOSMIC ENERGY—see VITAL LIFE FORCE.

BIOCURRENTS—(esoteric) an energy emanating from (and generated by) living cells; appears to be electrochemical in nature.

BIOCYBERNETICS—research in the combined fields of bionics, physiology, and biology, and their relationship to one another.

BIOCYCLE—abbr. for BIOLOGICAL CYCLES; a rhythmic pattern "within" the physical body, synchronizing with the heartbeat and the earth's revolution around the sun, influencing both the mind and the body. **Syn.** BIOLOGICAL RHYTHM, INTERNAL TIME, CIRCADIAN RHYTHM; (do not confuse with BIORHYTHM). [**cf.** CYCLES, CIRCADIAN RHYTHM]

BIODETECTORS—the use of plants and animals for detecting lies and behavioral changes in humans by studying the reactions of plants and animals as they tune into the energy radiations around individuals. (Inconcl.) [**cf.** BOTANE, ANPSI]

BIODYNAMIC FARMING—founded by Rudolf Steiner; to allow the plant, animal, and soil to live in a natural relationship makes them happier, healthier, and better for human consumption. [**cf.** CURATIVE EDUCATION]

BIODYNAMICS—branch of physiology that deals with the life processes of plants, animals, and humans; a study of energies and forces, and their capacities within the human body. [**cf.** RADIONICS, HOLISTIC HEALTH]

BIODYNAMO-CHROMATIC—a method of understanding the aura by means of colors and their relationship to the magnetic meridian lines. [**cf.** MERIDIAN LINES, AURA, COLOR]

BIOELECTRIC—theory that all living organisms (including the human body) are full of electricity. [**cf.** NERVOUS SYSTEM, THOUGHT, ATOM]

BIOELECTRIC PHENOMENA—(esoteric) to release from one's body an abnormal quantity of electricity causing unpleasant psychic events at random; performed unconsciously and unavoidably; psychic reacts like a high voltage wire to any person or object that touches him or her; this body chemistry is inborn and sometimes cannot be altered to alleviate this effect; a rarity. [**cf.** ELECTRIC GIRLS, PHYSICAL MANIFESTATIONS/MISCELLANEOUS Appendix 2]

BIOELECTRIC SIGNS—(biofeedback training) the actions of the brain and muscles as they are amplified and reported by the biofeedback instrument. [**cf.** EEG, EMG, UPPER FREQUENCY]

BIOELECTRICAL PHENOMENA STUDY—pertains to the electrical fields around the psychic or medium during psychic experiences. [**cf.** SEANCES, PSYCHIC READINGS, EEG INSTRUMENT]

BIOELECTRICAL SYSTEM—(esoteric) the nervous system in the human body. [**cf.** SYMPATHETIC NERVOUS SYSTEM, CEREBROSPINAL NERVOUS SYSTEM, VAGUS NERVE]

BIOELECTRODE—(Kirlian effect) the discharge from living organisms which appears to be like a complex electrode, having channels that carry a spectrum of life electricity and its components; differs for each organism. [**cf.** KIRLIAN PHOTOGRAPHY, COLD ELECTRIC EMISSION, ELECTROGRAPHY]

BIOELECTROMAGNETIC INTERACTIONS—the relationship between the cycles of light and darkness, the central nervous system, and the influence of the environment on the human body. [**cf.** CIRCADIAN RHYTHM, BIORHYTHM, GEOMAGNETIC FIELD]

BIOELECTRONICS—(Poland) the study of electricity in living organisms and earth radiations, and how this influences a subject of hypnosis and one receiving psychic information. [**cf.** SYMPATHETIC NERVOUS SYSTEM, MENTAL PSYCHIC PROCESSES]

BIOENERGETIC AND REICHIAN THERAPY—(Wilhelm Reich) a method of establishing the proper relationship between love, depression, anxiety, transcendental experiences, and the body's energy flow.

BIOENERGETIC BEACON—(ufology) an individual who uses her or himself psychically as a radar signal for contacting life and objects in outer space. [**cf.** UFOLOGY, SPACE CRAFT, SPACE-BEING]

BIOENERGETIC BENDS—the unusual preplanned contortions a therapist helps a patient perform; a method of freeing the emotional blocks stored in the body muscles. [**cf.** BIOENERGETIC THERAPY, LOCKED-IN, FROZEN]

BIOENERGETIC PROPULSION—(ufology) theory that creatures in outer space (and their vehicles) are traveling under thought vibrations; the same as man lives under his thought vibrations. [**cf.** LAW OF THOUGHT Appendix 7, UFOLOGY]

BIOENERGETICS—1. theory: man's emotional reactions register within the body cell; this reaction changes the growth of one's posture, facial expression, muscles, etc.; 2. (Russia) replaces the term *psychokinesis* in the Russian psychic dictionary. [**cf.** BIOENERGETICS THERAPY, CURATIVE EDUCATION]

BIOENERGETICS THERAPY—1. a method of releasing the physical constrictions in the cells and muscles of the body, which was stored there by unresolved emotional reactions to experiences in life, thus allowing the energy to flow and normalize the body. [**cf.** BIOENERGETICS CLUSTER, ENERGY BLOCK] 2. (Russia) study of the electromagnetic field around objects and living organisms. [**cf.** AURA]

BIOENERGY—1. (esoteric) a force within man's body (more subtle than electromagnetic waves) which man can control and direct outward for the performance of physical psychism (using concentration of the mind); presently associated with psychic impulses and the psychic components of a living organism; an energy in man, connecting him with the same energy in the universe, with man acting as the generator; 2. (science) whether the force is already within man or whether he draws it from outer space is not yet scientifically determined. (Inconcl.) **Syn.** PSYCHIC ENERGY. [**cf.** BIOACCUMULATOR, OCCULT PHILOSOPHY, MYSTICISM]

BIOFEEDBACK DESENSITIZATION—to learn to relax through biofeedback training, when one is reminded of a past situation that was a painful, traumatic experience and has been repressed; when hooked up to a metabolic monitor or a GSR, one can tell one's state of relaxation or arousal when stressful experiences are thought about; through meditative practice in biofeedback training sessions, one can learn to break up the repressed patterns and free oneself of the stress block. [**cf.** PROGRESSIVE RELAXATION, AUTOGENIC TRAINING, NEUTRAL INNER FEELINGS]

BIOFEEDBACK INSTRUMENTS—sensitive electronic devices that are attached to the human body by tiny electrodes; electrodes are attuned to one's brain or nervous system, depending upon the type of instrument; subject who is "hooked-up" meditates or ponders over certain aspects of his or her life; the electrical system of the instrument and electrical system of the body become one, and therefore the instrument shows what is happening within the body with regard to thoughts and emotional states; the signals are amplified in color, sound, lights, digitals, and in graphical recordings; used for the purpose of stress management and behavioral modification; subject learns to understand their emotional state and attitudes by logging his or her accomplishments in each session. [**cf.** MIND-BODY-DISCIPLINE, RANGE CONTROL, PATTERNS]

BIOFEEDBACK TRAINING—abbr. BFT; coined by Barbara Brown; daily or weekly sessions in which one is "hooked-up" to one of the various types of biofeedback instruments in order to learn how the physical body reacts to mind activity and emotions; the instruments give tangible evidence showing that thoughts, attitudes, and emotions influence changes in the physical body; tangibility of instrumentation results in: graphic lines, blinking colored lights, digital readouts, audible tones (varying in density of pitch and sound), and (currently) the moving of small electrical toys by the mind's electrical activity; tangibility varies with different types of instrumentation; 1. major part of the training session consists of: (a) quieting the emotions, controlling the mind, and relaxing the body; therapist gives special instructions in autogenic relaxation or meditation techniques; (b) subject thinks of situations and traumatic experiences in his life at the present or in the past, to determine changes in his physical body from the feedback; serves as a diagnostic tool; 2. training centers have found that: (a) biofeedback instruments serve as a "tool" for learning control of one's attitudes, thoughts, and emotions; (b) man is capable of learning control of his body functions, even those assumed to be automatic; (c) man must consider a new philosophy that there is a definite mind/body relationship; mind and mood fluctuations indicate subtle changes in the body chemistry (instruments show this interior reaction within the skin); (d) man does not react universally to the same traumatic situations; (e) one can "see" the relationship of thoughts and body functions as a synthesis and can then figure out an efficient and effective way to change one's internal and external processes; (f) subjects find a new way to learn about the self, by turning into the body during training sessions; they relearn what the body already knows (the relationship between the perceived world and self); (g) training sessions easily open one up psychically;

(h) one can reach a deeper state of meditation more rapidly than in normal training (wherein one would not be aware of which level one had attained); 3. dangers of biofeedback training sessions occur if the doctor or therapist who is monitoring the readouts and session is not familiar with parapsychological principles; he or she could: (a) allow the subject to meditate too long, causing the subject to reach an altered state of consciousness which he is not ready to handle (to reach an altered state of consciousness with no formal education in other levels of awareness can be overwhelming and frightening); (b) ignore or not understand the subject's psychic experiences and leave the subject more mixed up than when he started, or leave the subject thinking he is ill, etc. [cf. EEG, EMG, GSR, METABOLIC MONITOR, BIOFEEDBACK TRAINING Appendix 5]

BIOFORMS—(ufology) live, pulsating, unicellular organisms of various sizes and shapes, living in the etheria substance in outer space; capable of shifting dimensions and changing shapes; visible at times to earth aircraft. (Inconcl.) **Syn.** AEROFORM, BIO-LOGICAL UFOS. [cf. CRITTERS, ETHEREAN BEINGS]

BIOGENERATOR—(laboratory) the use of animals (especially frogs) as living organisms for electrical generators. (Inconcl.) [cf. ANPSI, SPINAL CON-SCIOUSNESS, NATURE TELEPATHY]

BIOGENETIC LAW—theory: the development of the individual is replicated in the development of the race. [cf. REINCARNATION, MASS KARMA, LAW OF REPETITION Appendix 7]

BIOGRAM—(biofeedback training) a diagram showing the possible experiences that can occur during the biofeedback training session. [cf. TIME LAG, ZEROING, SWISHING, PSYCHIC SOS SYSTEM]

BIOGRAVITATIONAL FIELD—a fluctuating force generated by humans and things (animate and inanimate) that interpenetrates their systems, enabling them to function on the earth; (D. W. Scaima) "acts in two distinct ways: can be 'seen' inside the light cone, and 'felt' outside the light cone". (Inconcl.) [cf. PSYCHOKINESIS, LEVITATION, GRAVITY CONTROL, LIFE]

BIOINFORMATION—1. study of the brain and its many components, and capabilities; 2. data, visions, prophecy, and other psychic information coming through the psychic senses; 3. (Russia) extrasensory perception; 4. (Bulgaria) research in the combined field of bionics, physiology, and biology. **Syn.** PSYCHIC INFORMATION, BIOLOGICAL INFORMATION.

BIOINTROSCOPY—1. the ability to see with the fingertips; see EYELESS SIGHT; 2. (Russia) X-ray clairvoyance. [cf. EYELESS SIGHT Appendix 2]

BIOLOGIC FILTER—(biofeedback training) a special device that screens out extraneous brain waves that prevent pure expression from coming through in a genuine transduction of energy from the subject. [cf. ARTIFACT, BIOLOGIC FILTER]

BIOLOGICAL CLOCK—1. an internal, automatic timer "within" people which causes a pattern that repeats itself approximately every twenty-four hours and synchronizes with the heartbeat and the earth's revolution around the sun; appears to influence both the mind and the body, regardless of outer environment and stimuli. (Inconcl.) **Syn.** INTERNAL TIME, BIOLOGICAL RHYTHM, CIRCADIAN RHYTHM, BIOLOGICAL CYCLE; (do not confuse with BIORHYTHM). [cf. CYCLES] 2. a catch-all word meaning any rhythmical, organized change in animals, plants, and humans, including biorhythm.

BIOLOGICAL COMPATIBILITY—1. the clashing or harmonizing or body chemistry between two people who are lovers, friends, relatives, acquaintances, or co-workers; results in personality bonds or differences without one being aware that this relationship is influenced by each person's body chemistry. [cf. PARASITISM, PSYCHIC TRANSFER] 2. (Russia) spontaneous telepathy: the brain of one person imposing its rhythm on the brain of another, causing an immediate like or dislike for each other. [cf. TELEPATHY, SYMBIOTIC RELATIONSHIP]

BIOLOGICAL CONTACT—(science) tuning into another person's aura to psychically pick up information regarding that person. **Syn.** TUNED-IN, STEP-INTO-YOUR-VIBRATION. [cf. READING, PERCEPTUAL DEFENSE, NONINTENTIONAL ESP]

BIOLOGICAL CYCLE—see BIOLOGICAL CLOCK.

BIOLOGICAL FIELD—see AURA. [cf. KIRLIAN EFFECT]

BIOLOGICAL GENERATOR—(Czechoslovakia) an instrument devised to draw psychic energy out of man, store it, and then send it out in condensed form, in emergencies, for reuse. (Inconcl.) [cf.

BEAMED ENERGY, PALMED POWER, AMULET ENER-
GIZING, PRAYER POWER]

BIOLOGICAL INFORMATION—see BIOINFORMA-
TION and ESP.

BIOLOGICAL MARKER—the "eye-roll" test given
by some psychiatrists who use hypnotherapy in
their practice; this test indicates how the patient
rates on the hypnotizability scale. [**cf.** EYE-ROLL
TEST, HAND LEVITATION]

BIOLOGICAL PHENOMENA—to control the
growth of living tissue and organisms, including
one's physical body; 1. to use intense mind focalization on a seed to accelerate its sprouting; to hold a
sprout in the hand and through concentration it
reverses back into a seed; 2. to arrest the decomposition of one's organic body after death; (the bodies
of great saints have been exhumed years after death
and found in good condition); 3. to halt the
destruction of bacteria on plants; 4. to heal a severe
wound or a severed finger by placing the severed
parts together, and the healing is instantaneous.
[**cf.** INCORRUPTABILITY, NATURE-PK, PSYCHIC
HEALING]

BIOLOGICAL PLASMA—(Kirlian effect) name
given to the electrical discharge appearing around
objects and small parts of the human body showing
on the prints taken with a high-voltage camera;
1. believed to be a field of excited negatively
charged electrons and other subatomic particles
which react to magnetic fields. (Inconcl.); 2. (Russia) the emanations around an organism showing
corona discharges, believed to change according to
the individual's emotional state. (Inconcl.) **Syn.**
AURA. 3. theory: elementary charged particles living within man and living within things; have
elementary charged particles in a living system
within themselves; these particles seem to be dominant in all biodynamic relationships of living
organisms; strongly influenced by changes in temperature and environmental factors; (do not confuse with nonorganic plasma). [**cf.** KIRLIAN EFFECT,
CORONA]

BIOLOGICAL PLASMA BODY—see AURA.

BIOLOGICAL RADIATION—see AURA.

BIOLOGICAL RADIO COMMUNICATION—see
AURA.

BIOLOGICAL RHYTHM—see BIOLOGICAL CYCLE.

BIOLOGICAL SIGNAL TRANSDUCER—(ufology) a
device (weighing three tons) built by scientists,
using a signal to scan and detect any form of life in
the galaxy. [**cf.** UFOLOGY, SPACECRAFT, CRITTERS]

BIOLOGICAL TIME OF DAY—an innate, invisible
mechanism within the physical body that tells the
body its pattern of behavior, every hour of the
twenty-four-hour cycle, regardless of mundane
time; e.g., one may feel sleepy at three o'clock every
afternoon even though the workday is not finished;
one may feel hungry every morning at eleven
o'clock even though he eats at twelve noon; (do not
confuse with biorhythm). [**cf.** CIRCADIAN RHYTHM,
DIURNAL CYCLE]

BIOLOGICAL TRANSMUTATION—theory: the
atoms and molecules change in the organic systems
of one's body, giving it a different chemical
composition, without any outward changes such as
eating, exercising, or sleeping habits; one's thoughts
with their accompanying emotions change body
chemistry every moment. [**cf.** CONSCIOUS CON-
SCIOUSNESS, THOUGHTS, EMOTIONS, PURIFIED
BODY]

BIOLOGICAL UFO'S—(ufology) invisible living
organisms, detected by infrared photography, appearing to be plasmatic, spheroidal, varying in
shapes and sizes; a composition capable of returning a radar echo on the detector. (Inconcl.) **Syn.**
BIOFORMS, AEROFORMS. [**cf.** FUSIFORM, RADAR
ANGELS]

BIOLOGOGRAM—refers to the idea that the physiology and mental state of the body are recorded in
a code, somewhere within, and it is up to the
individual to decipher it and use it, e.g., IRIDOLOGY,
HAIR ANALYSIS, REFLEXOLOGY, AURA. [**cf.** BODY
READING Appendix 5]

BIOLUMINESCENCE—colored rays that surround
the person or object; invisible to the physical eye
but picked up on the Kirlian photograph; named by
the Drs. Semyon and Valentina Kirlian. [**cf.**
KIRLIAN THEORY, ULTRAFAINT LUMINESCENCE,
PYROTECHNICS]

BIOLUMINESCENT—the light energy released
from certain animal species, such as glowworms,
fireflies, corals, etc. (Inconcl.) [**caf.** PSI TRAILING,
ANPSI]

BIOLUMINESCENT ELECTRICAL FIELD—see
AURA.

BIOMAGNETICS—the science that deals with all magnetic fields: permanent, electromagnetic, constant, pulsed, terrestrial, or extraterrestrial, and their influence or effect on the systems of living organisms; based on the nature of the living thing itself. **Sim.** MAGNETOTHERAPY, MAGNETOBIOLOGY. [**cf.** MAGNETIZING, TELLURIC ENERGY]

BIOMECHANISMS—the division of living organisms into many systems according to their variance in function.

BIOMETER—an instrument that measures the radiations of an unknown form of energy in all substances; used in radiesthesia; invented by Andre Bovis. [**cf.** SPIRITOSCOPE, RADIONICS, RADIESTHESIA, PENDULUM]

BIOMETER OF BARADUC—an instrument that detects the polarity and exteriorization of the psychic energy emanating from the body and hands of a medium who is in a state of trance. [**cf.** EXTERIORIZATION OF SENSITIVITY, SPIRITOSCOPE, HUMAN POLARITY, PALMED POWER, STHENOMETER]

BIOMUSIC—theory: one can translate one's own biofeedback brain wave patterns into music to use for soothing and healing purposes at a later date. [**cf.** BIOFEEDBACK TRAINING, MENTAL HEALING]

BIONICS OF MAN—theory: the human mind represents a computer and the body an electronic device which one can control to receive psychic information; phrase used in place of parapsychology at times.

BIONOMY—the ability to predict a person's reactions to a situation, using the knowledge of cyclic changes. [**cf.** BIORHYTHM, SENSITIVITY, CYCLES]

BIONS—(Wilhelm Reich) the basic units of orgon energy; approximately one-millionth of a meter. [**cf.** ORGONE ENERGY]

BIOPHYSICAL EFFECT METHOD—abbr. BPE; (Russia) the use of the dowsing rod for discovering untapped national resources; name for dowsing in USSR. [**cf.** RADIESTHESIA, SURFACE DOWSING, MENTAL PROBE]

BIOPHYSICS—the study of the relationship of matter and energy, and its reaction to and influence on the human physical body.

BIOPLASMA—1. (Russia) psychic energy; presumed to be a fourth state of matter that constantly interacts with other states of matter, and transforms itself into them from time to time; an invisible energy that seems to have molding characteristics (future science). 2. see VITAL LIFE FORCE.

BIOPLASMA BODY—coined by Dr. Semyon Kirlian; see KIRLIAN EFFECT. **Syn.** ETHERIC DOUBLE.

BIOPLASMA FORCE FIELD—the invisible etheric rays which have shape, color, pattern, and polarization, that surround all living organisms and objects; acts as a whole system with its own rules, yet these rays are definitely related to the organism and object they surround (as if the organism or object is causing the field and the field is causing the object or organism); experiments show that human activity, emotions, and health change the system for humans; can be photographed by high-voltage cameras. (Inconcl.) **Syn.** AURA. [**cf.** X-BIOENERGIES, COSMIC OCTAVES, ULTRAOUTER AURA]

BIOPSYCHIATRIC—the relationship between all life in the universe and its influence on man's mind, behavior, and emotions. [**cf.** EMOTIONS, STRESS]

BIOPSYCHIC—1. pertains to the combination of biological and psychological happenings. **Syn.** MIND/BODY. 2. pertains to the relationship of all life to the psychic energy in man. [**cf.** PSYCHIC ENERGY]

BIOPSYCHIC ENERGY FIELD—(esoteric) theory: the human species has seven bodies interpenetrating each other in different vibrational frequencies simultaneously; six are invisible to the physical eye; each body has its own purpose and laws for functioning, and each contributes to an overall purpose and utilizing an overall law. [**cf.** PRINCIPLES OF MAN, ASTRAL BODY, BUDDHIC BODY, MENTAL BODY]

BIORAPPORT—(esoteric) the psychic influence of one individual on others when in a group; not recognizable utilizing the laws of psychology, but detectable using the laws of psychism; i.e., 1. to put one's self in a wall of psychic protection, making one's self a misfit in the group because the wall is felt by members of the group; the individual is labeled an introvert or a poor sport; 2. to psychically spread one's personal attitude over the crowd, with each member tuning into this attitude but feeling it is his or her own; 3. to psychically draw energy from the aura of the group as a whole for one's own physical gain, leaving many members drained.

(Inconcl.) [cf. PSYCHIC TRANSFER, NEGAPSI, SPLODGER, CLOAK OF INSULATION]

BIORESONANCE—theory: the body of each living organism is structured like a musical chord, vibrating at its own unique frequency and co-creating the natural harmony most easily sustained by it; each person's and each living organism's bioresonance is as individual as a person's fingerprints. [cf. ATOMS, SOUND, NATURAL INFRASOUND]

BIORHYTHM—(esoteric) theory: a man or woman is subject to the influence of vibrations from the planets, the sun, and the moon, based on his or her date of birth; this influence makes a well-defined pattern of physical, emotional, and intellectual capabilities that are subject to dramatic fluctuations over a period; this pattern triggers at birth and repeats itself immutably throughout a person's life; one is usually aware that the highs and lows of one's life follow specific patterns, regardless of outside stimuli; e.g., one may cut a finger when one's emotional pattern is below the line and one reacts in a childish manner; the same person, receiving a whiplash injury from an automobile accident when his emotional pattern is above the line, takes it in stride. (Inconcl.) [cf. PERSONALITY CYCLE, SENSITIVITY CYCLE, INTELLECTUAL CYCLE]

BIORHYTHM CHART—a calculated graph of one's emotional, intellectual, and physical cycles based on one's birthdate; shows when to expect the high and low performance days in that particular cycle. [cf. KEY BIRTHDATE FIGURES, REVERSAL SLEEP, THIRTY-THREE DAY CYCLE]

BIORHYTHM CURVES—the lines on a biorhythm chart which fall above and below the critical line, signifying for each cycle when one will have peak performance or regenerative performance. [cf. ZERO-LINE, SYNC]

BIORHYTHM CYCLEGRAPH—chart cards used for figuring individual biorhythm cycles. [cf. BIORHYTHM DIALGRAPH, PSYCHOCYCLES]

BIORHYTHM DIALGRAPH—a pocket-sized metal computer used to chart biorhythm patterns for a month at a time by switching dials.

BIORHYTHMIC SPAN—the only point in one's life when all three rhythms in a biorhythm chart will begin on the same day, as it did on the day of one's birth; found by multiplying 23 x 28 x 33, which equals 21,252 days from one's date of birth. [cf. BIORHYTHM CHART, EMOTIONAL CYCLE, CRITICAL DAYS]

BIORHYTHMIC YEAR—(biorhythm) a period of 644 days when both the 23- and 28-day cycles begin on the same day. [cf. POSITIVE DAY, ETERNAL RHYTHM]

BIOSONE—an intrument that can detect and inform the subject when he is producing alpha or theta brain waves. [cf. PRINT-OUTS, BRAIN WAVE PATTERNS]

BIOSPHERE—(esoteric) a vibrational frequency which forms an invisible plane in the etheric world where all mundane expressions of life emerge. (Inconcl.) [cf. MENTAL PLANE, FIFTH PLANE]

BIOTELECOMMUNICATION—life systems, animate and inanimate things, influencing one another regardless of distance; research into the combined fields of bionics, physiology, biology, and parapsychology; to tune into the electromagnetic field of all things, at will, and be aware of its subtle and known effects on one's self and other things. [cf. ETHERIC DOUBLE, GRAVITY FIELDS, PSYCHIC SENSITIVITY]

BIOTELEPATHY—the action of one living organism upon another in a relationship of empathy and help; e.g., one plant existing in the shade sharing its water with another plant close by, which is exposed to the sun; the rapid heartbeat of one twin will synchronize with the other twin, regardless of distance, until both hearts are beating at the same rate. [cf. INSTINCTUAL TELEPATHY, ANPSI, HERD IMPULSES, SENSUOUS ELEMENT, SELECTIVE TELEPATHY]

BIOTENSOR FIELD—coined by Patrick Flanagan; see AURA.

BIOTRANSDUCER—(electronic voices) a tape cassette recorder which acts as a device for recording inaudible voices from invisible soul-minds; so called because it receives energy from one system, such as an etheric world intelligence or an intelligence from outer space, into a different form, an audible sound; tape recorder is left by the psychic while sleeping or put in the center of a circle of persons dedicated for this purpose; while voice or sound is being recorded, it cannot be heard with physical ears; whether energy is coming from the invisible intelligence or the psychic has not been established. (Inconcl.) [cf. ELECTRONIC VOICES, TAPED VOICE PHENOMENA, ETHERIC WORLD INTELLIGENCE]

BIOTRONICS—the study and use of the human body to its full capacity.

BIPOLAR—(esoteric) having two definite aspects which function as opposites, both vital to the function of the whole; negative and positive polarity. [**cf.** YIN AND YANG, POLARITY, PHYSICAL BODY POLARITY]

BIPOLAR AURA—the auric field around each human being; shows manifestations of two opposite or contrasting principles making the physical body bipolar; the conscious consciousness gives the physical body a negative, feminine polarity aspect, and the soul-mind consciousness and its memory-bank give the physical body a masculine, positive polarity aspect. [**cf.** AURA, POLARITY, LINGAM AND YONI, MAGNETISM]

BIRCH—(esoteric) a tree believed to have a vibratory rate that can protect a home against weather hazards; (Native American, Sioux) used ashes for protection against thunder. [**cf.** TREE, SWEET GRASS]

BIRDS OF PREY—(esoteric) low-quality etheric world entities who need to feed on flesh periodically, so they incarnate as birds and carry off pieces of flesh from dead bodies. **Sim.** VAMPIRE. [**cf.** SHAPE-SHIFTING, DENSITY, EARTHBOUND ENTITIES]

BIRTH—(esoteric) (human) the transition from an ethereal functional system with its purpose and form, to a mundane functional system with a different purpose and form; when the life force of the human specie seed is ready to move into a higher form of existence, the thrust from within will push the life force on its journey, in a natural way and at the natural time in evolution; a change in vibrational frequency that begins a new pattern of lessons to benefit the growth of the soul-mind. [**cf.** BIRTH SCIENCE, EVOLUTION]

BIRTH BY HEAT AND MOISTURE—(Tibet) the germination of spores and seeds in the manner of the vegetable kingdom. [**cf.** BOTANE, IMMACULATE CONCEPTION]

BIRTH BY SUPERPSYCHIC WOMB—(Tibet) the process of transferring the consciousness-principle from its invisible plane of existence to the womb desire; the ability of the etheric world entity, who is ready to reenter into the earth plane, to build a physical body in a womb of an earthling, from memory of past incarnations; etheric entity uses persistent concentration and then transfers its life force into the body it built; no physical sex is required for conception. **Sim.** MIRACULOUS BIRTH. [**cf.** CONSCIOUSNESS-PRINCIPLE, ALCHEMY]

BIRTH CONSCIOUSNESS—(Tibet) a subconscious level of awareness and thinking; the new baby is in the astral plane state of mind activity when born; the mental mind consciousness gradually takes over during the first seven years of the child's life, until it is completely in charge; during these seven years, the child must rely on the decisions of the adults around it because its logical reasoning facility is still growing. [**cf.** CONSCIOUSNESS, SPINAL CONSCIOUSNESS, BIRTH TRAUMA, EMOTIONAL CONSCIOUSNESS]

BIRTH KARMA—(esoteric) tendencies peculiar to one's culture and immediate environment; a goal-direction that for no apparent reason influences one's life; believed to stem from past incarnations, and a predecision of what is to be accomplished in the present incarnation. [**cf.** RIPE KARMA, KARMA]

BIRTH OF THE BARDO BODY—(Tibet) a realization of shedding the physical world and graciously accepting the astral body in the death process. [**cf.** ASTRAL BODY, ASTRAL CEMETERY, DEATH, DENSITY]

BIRTH PRIMAL—a release through the verbalization or acting out of the tension or pain that was stored in the subconscious mind at birth, especially if the birth process was in any way traumatic or unnatural. [**cf.** BLOCKS, BIRTH TRAUMA, PRENATAL EXPERIENCE, CAUL]

BIRTH SCIENCE—(esoteric) the scientific study of how, why, and when a soul-mind changes vibrational frequencies from the ethereal world to the earth world; investigation into the soul-mind's preparation for the transition, the process of transition, and the aftermath; kinds of birth: 1. by egg; 2. by womb; 3. by superpsychic womb; 4. by heat and moisture. [**cf.** BIRTH SCIENCE Appendix 2]

BIRTH SYMBOL—the birth of a baby, flower, or animal, as seen in dreams or perceived in psychic visions, means that something new is going to occur; a universal symbol that infers a beginning; i.e., the birth of a job, marriage, car, etc. [**cf.** DREAMSTUFF, SYMBOLS, ARCHETYPAL IMAGES, PSYCHIC INFORMATION, VISIONS]

74

BIRTH TRAUMA—the shock of being expelled from the comfortable state in the mother's womb, to a totally unfamiliar environment, without a gradual period of adjustment; to lock-in negative, unnatural emotions that occur in a hospital birth; i.e., from a dark womb to immediate exposure of bright lights. [**cf.** BIRTH SCIENCE Appendix 2]

BIRTH WITHOUT VIOLENCE—coined by Frederick LeBoyer; the removal of traumatic influences in the birth process, such as: improper conversation, loud noise, bright light, unnatural cutting of the cord and other unnatural practices; prevents negative vibrations from entering the subconscious mind and influencing behavior during the life to come. [**cf.** PERINATAL EXPERIENCE, REBIRTHING, BIRTH CONSCIOUSNESS, AGE REGRESSION]

BIRTHING RELEASE—to rid one's self of negatives stored in the subconscious mind from birth trauma, by simulating conditions similar to being in the womb; i.e., to submerge in warm water, assume the fetal position, and breathe through a snorkel; this helps to surface any trauma that one experienced prenatally or during the birthing process. [**cf.** HARMONIOUS INFANT, PRENATAL RECALL]

BISEXUALITY—(biorhythm) the inherited characteristics of both sexes which are found in both sexes; used as a basis to establish the twenty-eight- and twenty-three-day cycles. [**cf.** BIORHYTHM CHARTS, BIORHYTHMS]

BISHOP'S RING—(esoteric) a ring with an amethyst and a special design in gold; has the vibratory rate that, when worn, it will aid in psychic understanding, in protection, and in bringing power. [**cf.** MINPSI, FORMS-WITH-POWER, SYMBOLS]

BITUMEN—(esoteric) (Asia) an asphalt containing hydrocarbons, which has the vibrational frequency that makes it conducive to psychic work; 1. used in making statues and talismans for sympathetic magic; 2. sprinkled on floors as an aid in a house sweep; in its natural form it absorbs negative vibrations. [**cf.** HOUSE SWEEP, CEREMONIAL MAGIC, ATMOSPHERE CLEARING, INCENSE, TALISMAN]

BLACK—(esoteric) the absence of light, the absence of intelligence (light being intelligence); dull black represents the negative aspects of the color: death, depression, evil intentions; shiny black represents the positive aspects: strength, good power, and spirituality. [**cf.** COLOROLOGY Appendix 5, WHITE LIGHT, GOLD, SEVEN MAJOR RAYS]

BLACK ANNIS—a cannibalistic creature that belongs to the nature kingdom. **Sim.** HAG. [**cf.** NATURE SPIRITS]

BLACK ART—to deliberately use psychic energy for evil intent; to unjustly acquire something for oneself, or to bring harm to another person or situation by special rituals and mind concentration; see BLACK MAGIC. [**cf.** SYMBOLISM, CEREMONIAL MAGIC]

BLACK BEANS—(esoteric) (Italy) a seed believed to have the properties to assist the soul-mind of the deceased to make a peaceful entry into the etheric world planes; given away at funerals. [**cf.** BOTANE, DEATH, DEATH ANGEL]

BLACK BELT—(Japan) a special belt worn during practice or teaching of karate; can be used synonymously with karate to mean one who has attained the eight levels of proficiency in the art of karate discipline and has earned the right to wear this black belt; other colored belts are worn progressively until one reaches this level. **Sim.** ACHETA, KARATE. [**cf.** KARATE, MARTIAL ARTS]

BLACK BOX—invented by Dr. Albert Abrams (1900); a simple box-shaped apparatus designed to diagnose and prescribe for a patient, whether present or absent; a sample of blood or urine is placed in the proper container on top (according to sex); the dials are moved until a "stick" is felt; this means the proper attunement with the patient has been made, and it is time to read the dials; the dials read out the type of disease and prescription for the treatment. **Syn.** ABRAM'S BOX. [**cf.** MIND MACHINES, STICK]

BLACK BOX CONCEPT—(radionics) 1. the operator uses radiesthetic sense as in radionics; the operator's human nervous system tunes into the radiations given off from the blood and urine samples of the patient placed on top of the box; the dials amplify these radiation signals and act differently, as a code to tell the operator to stop turning; one then reads the dials to diagnose and prescribe for the patient; 2. a unique electronic system that emits a signal when a signal is received into it; a transmitter/receiver for the mind which is plugged into "the Source" at one end, and the other end into the samples on top of the box; 3. some black boxes can diagnose an illness by taking photographs by psychic means. **Sim.** DELAWARR CAMERA. [**cf.** FORMS-WITH-POWER, RADIONICS, STICK, MEDICAL RADIESTHESIA]

75

BLACK CROWN—(Tibet) a sacred crown worn only by special holy men, and believed to bring them psychic ability; designed after a crown seen clairvoyantly many years earlier; made of hair from 100,000 celestial beings. [**cf.** SYMBOLISM, LAW OF SIMILARITY Appendix 7, SACRAMENTAL HEALER]

BLACK CROWN CEREMONY—(Tibet) a special ceremony for thousands of people where the black crown is worn by a holy man, giving him the ability to release tremendous power through himself, and to put thousands in a state of ecstasy, making it possible for many healings of the mind and body to occur. [**cf.** TRADITION, BEAMED ENERGY, MENTAL HEALING]

BLACK CURTAIN—see VEIL or ETHERIC WEB.

BLACK DIAMOND—(esoteric) a mineral believed to be influenced by the vibrations of Saturn; 1. used symbolically to represent the chaos or void from which "all" emerged; 2. placed in the pupil of an eye of a talisman, making it more endowed with psychic energies; used to ward off evil and to accelerate psychic ability in the owner. [**cf.** SIGHT IN DARKNESS, UNSEEN SEER, EVIL EYE]

BLACK GLANCE—see EVIL EYE.

BLACK HOLE—a huge, super-dense, massive force in the sky that sucks objects into its center; a hole with gravity so intense that it warps time, curves space, and imprisons light; concentrated within a small area provided by giant stars. (Inconcl.) **Syn.** CELESTIAL GHOSTS. [**cf.** STATIC UNIVERSE, TIME, GRAVITY CONTROL]

BLACK LODGES—1. groups of individuals who take the left-hand path and work for evil intent; 2. etheric world entities who intrude in the earth vibrations with a selfish desire to accomplish massive evil. [**cf.** DENSITY, EARTHBOUND ENTITIES, DEVILS OF ALL AGES, INFERNAL BEINGS]

BLACK MAGIC—(*black,* "lack of intelligence"); to deliberately use psychic energy for evil intent; to unjustly and wickedly acquire something for one's self, or bring harm to another person or situation by special rituals and mind concentration; everything has an opposite and every psychic principle can be used in reverse; i.e., one can psychically send energy decreed to be healing in quality or decreed to be destructive in quality; (do not confuse with LOW MAGIC). **Syn.** BLACK ART. [**cf.** SYMBOLISM, CLOAK OF INSULATION, CEREMONIAL MAGIC]

BLACK MASS—a ritual of magical powers; powerful ceremonies used for unusual evil by black magicians, but not related to Satanism; opposite to the orthodox celebration of the Eucharist.

BLACK MUD OF OCCULTISM—refers to the use of the words *magical, mysterious, supernormal,* and *occultism* and their effect on people, giving the impression that psychic energy is evil.

BLACK NIMBUS—drawn around a person's head to symbolize that he is evil. [**cf.** BLACK, COLOR, MENTAL AURA, AUREOLA]

BLACK ONYX—(esoteric) a mineral believed to be influenced by the vibrations of Saturn, due to the gloomy nature of both; used by psychics who specialize in forecasting death and detecting the person responsible for casting a spell. [**cf.** HEX, EXORCISM, ATMOSPHERE CLEARING, SPELLED]

BLACK SACK—(Huna) a storage place in the subconscious mind for the ideas and memories of experiences that were never reasoned with logically when the event or experience happened; these memories cause problems in one's life as they come to the surface. [**cf.** BLOCKS, SUBCONSCIOUS MIND, OUTLAW MEMORIES, GRAPES, PRIMAL SCREAM]

BLACK SERPENT—opposite of SERPENT POWER; symbolic of the descending path of involution. [**cf.** EVOLUTION, SERPENT FIRE, KUNDALINI]

BLACK SHAMAN—(Biriat, Yakut, Siberia) psychics and healers who are willing to astrally project into the density to encourage soul-minds to desire a higher state of consciousness; etheric world intelligences help protect the psychic from harm and help find the lost and new soul-minds; purpose of trip is to give understanding, stimulate desire for growth, and give instructions how to rise above their present level of awareness; a difficult and honored art; (do not confuse with shaman working in BLACK MAGIC or confuse this with skin color). (Inconcl.) [**cf.** ERLIK, SPIRITUALIZING THE ETHERIC WORLD, DENSITY, EVOLUTION]

BLACK SHELL CREATURES—(Buddhism) (esoteric) sea shells that are black; represent the yoni: negative polarity. [**cf.** ANPSI, FISH PSI, ANIMAL GROUP SOUL, ROBIN]

BLACK-BEADED ELECTRODE—(biofeedback training) the electrical ground that must be placed in the center of the forehead or over one ear, for proper monitoring of the EEG instrument. [cf. SENSORS, ELECTODES, EEG, EMG, TIME INTERVAL CONTROL]

BLACK-SAILED SHIP OF DEATH—a sailors' belief that the soul-minds of deceased sailors who are buried on land, and should be rotting in hell, would be sucked up from the inland by this invisible boat and brought back out to sea. [cf. THETA PHENOMENA, DEATH ANGEL, PHANTOM CARS]

BLACKBIRD—(Britain) (esoteric) birds used by etheric world entities to carry psychic messages to earth entities. [cf. EAGLE POWER, PEACOCK, ANIMAL SOUL]

BLACKED-OUT ROOM—name given to a room used for seances; black-out material or heavy, dark-colored material is used to cover doors, windows, and every crack of light; no light is allowed to enter because light is believed to destroy the ectoplasm that emanates from the medium and sitters; this also eliminates the doubt that what is seen with physical eyes is a dimension of the etheric world, and not a shadow or light ray of the physical world. [cf. MATERIALIZATION, SEANCE, ECTOPLASM]

BLANK AWARENESS—to feel that nothing is going on and yet one is awake; a state of consciousness in which one is not aware of anything in particular, and yet one is not asleep. [cf. NONBEING, PURE AWARENESS]

BLANK MIND—a state of consciousness wherein one can actually stop all thoughts; usually after long concentration during meditation. **Syn.** SEED MEDITATION. [cf. THE SILENCE, QUIETUDE, SITTING ZEN]

BLANK MOOD—a state in which the mind is active, yet neutral or devoid of opinion; necessary for psychic and radiesthetic work. [cf. MANTRA, MEDITATION, BIOFEEDBACK TRAINING, GOING-TO-LEVEL, MONKEY CHATTER]

BLANK PERIODS—a break in one's stream of consciousness with no present apparent reason; to be in a state of daydreaming, mulling over, or reasoning out a situation and the mind activity stops for a brief moment; the conscious mind finds no logical reason for this, but the theory is that the subconscious mind has had orders previously (probably repeatedly in many incarnations) to suppress this aspect of one's life. [cf. DAYDREAMING, INNER-DIALOGUE, THOUGHT-FORMS, MENTAL ACTIVITY]

BLANK STARE—the eyes are "fixed" and the person seems lost in thought; ocular fixation on nothing and nowhere; 1. occurs in a state of daydreaming or conscious fantasy, lasting a short period; 2. occurs when under the influence of a destructive-brainwashing cult organization and lasts for days or years. [cf. FANTASY, DAYDREAMING, TRANSFIXED, DESTRUCTIVE-BRAINWASHING CULT]

BLESS—(metaphysics) to burst into bloom; to call forth the potential within the seed of a person or object blessed; to sincerely desire that perfection come into fruition for a person. [cf. WORDS-WITH-POWER, MENTAL HEALING, SACRED LANGUAGE]

BLESS YOU—to verbally speak these words: 1. seals an experience or omen with a decree of good, e.g., said after a sneeze; a sneeze is believed to be an expulsion of breath (the life of man), and the expression seals this good omen; 2. seals a favor received from another; the receiver seals the gesture with a desire for it to be returned to the giver. [cf. OMEN, PRAYER POWER, HOLISTIC HEALTH]

BLESSED BE—a phrase used by witches as a greeting and a farewell. [cf. AFFIRMATIONS, MAGIC VERSE, SIGIL]

BLESSING—(esoteric) 1. a mass of energy psychically produced that is healing, soothing, and pleasant to receive; (a) densified and consecrated through a ritual or an individual personally and sent to benefit another; (b) received by being in the presence of a Master or Saint (given unconsciously); 2. to decree that the electrical impulses coming from one's head be changed from neutral or negative to a vibrational frequency of benevolence; to direct these electrical impulses to a certain designation to improve health or to bring about good experiences. [cf. SPELL, MENTAL HEALING, POWER OF THE WORD]

BLESSING WAY—(Native American, Navaho) a special ceremony in which the whole tribe participates; raises positive vibrations which can be used to heal, to exorcise, and to bring an abundance to the tribe. **Sim.** PSYCHIC ART. [cf. RITUAL VIBRATIONS, CEREMONIAL MAGIC, ECSTASY]

BLIND AWARENESS—a state experienced by a blind person who is helped to see psychically by blending the teachings of dermoptics, aura-viewing, and clairvoyance. [cf. EYELESS SIGHT Appendix 2, CLAIRVOYANCE]

BLIND EXPERIMENTS—laboratory experiments in which precautions are taken so no one knows what the target is; several targets are put into sealed envelopes, and the percipient (psychic) selects one at random at the given time; this prevents the workers from telepathically passing on information to the percipient. [**cf.** ESP, SUBLIMINAL PROCESS, SCREENED TOUCH MATCHING, MUDDY CONDITIONS]

BLIND FAITH—belief founded without knowledgeable facts or tangible proof, and without having complete acceptance in the belief system; the mental mind desires to believe, and/or logically reasons, something to be true; then it forms a concept and tries to register it in the subconscious mind; from lack of proof, this concept just mingles in the subconscious mind with past learnings, and does not become solidified; this incomplete acceptance of a concept rises to the surface at times and interferes with the happening of the desired event; (do not confuse with FAITH). [**cf.** FAITH, CONSCIOUS MIND, SUBCONSCIOUS MIND]

BLIND MENTAL PSYCHISM—(laboratory) to know the answer to the test or to perform the target with success, in a controlled psychic experiment; the percipient (psychic) just thinks the word *success,* and succeeds. [**cf.** PROPHECY, COGNITION, PUTTING OUT FEELERS, OPEN DOOR]

BLIND SPOT—(psychic reading) the lack of a perfect answer or misinformation given by a psychic to his or her client; caused by an inner urge within the psychic, which refuses to see or feel certain things; occurs because of the psychic's own shortcomings and blocks becoming linked with the information received for the client. [**cf.** PSYCHIC INFORMATION, PSYCHIC READING, CLAIRSENTIENCE]

BLIP—(ufology) the infinitesimal portion of energy reflected back from the electromagnetic microwave energy sent by radar. **Syn.** ECHO. [**cf.** FIREFLIES, PROJECT MAGNET, PROPULSION, RADAR ANGELS]

BLISS—1. a peak, spiritual experience; a moment of euphoria, usually encountered in the meditative state; 2. a personal, mundane, unbelievable, and unexpected instant; 3. a revelation of universal Truths; 4. (Maharishi Mahesh Yogi) "a state when one is not feeling anything; not a state of profound pleasure but a level of awareness devoid of all thought and feeling"; 5. a critical situational response that raises one's consciousness sky-high.

[**cf.** FIFTH STATE OF CONSCIOUSNESS, BLISSED OUT, MEDITATION]

BLISS BODY—see BUDDHIC BODY.

BLISS CONSCIOUSNESS—(esoteric) to be at one with Totality, to be aware of it, and to be aware of its wonderfulness; to pass the state of pure consciousness where one feels that pure consciousness is one's own; to no longer be a part of Totality, but to *be* Totality; a level that is difficult to obtain, and then only from prolonged meditation; to reach the extreme state of quietude. [**cf.** SYMBIOTIC PROTOPLASMIC CONSCIOUSNESS, PURE ALERTNESS]

BLISSING-OUT—1. a state of stupor-high ecstasy, that is deliberately planned by a destructive-brainwashing cult, to be achieved by their members; explained to the member to be "from the divine" which helps keep his or her thoughts centered on the organization; 1. can be recognized by: (a) eyes that appear to be on fire; (b) a personality that is "out of this world"; (c) breaking out in laughter or tears; (d) talking-in-tongues; (e) loss of consciousness for a short period; 2. brought on by prolonged meditation, overindulgence in chanting, rhythmic movements, and other preplanned methods that are performed to extremes; 3. member feels: (a) a short period of inexplicable happiness, joy, peace, or wonderment; (b) a short period of bewilderment and total confusion; 4. achieved by a "good trip" with hallucinogenic drugs. [**cf.** BIG BREAKTHROUGH, ARTIKA CEREMONY, AUTOMATON]

BLOCK—a pseudo-process in which man feels he is not accepting a painful emotion that reminds him of a past unpleasant experience (which was not resolved when it happened); theory: every activity that one becomes involved in, voluntarily or involuntarily, must be put into the proper perspective according to one's belief system as all involvement is automatically written in one's nervous system; "to block out," or ignore, a replica of an unpleasant emotion is impossible; painful emotions are not put "aside" by ignoring them, but are put "inside," and repressed, until the encounter is handled harmoniously according to one's value system, regardless of the time elapsed; these blocked-out emotions show up eventually in unwanted physical and mental behavioral patterns. [**cf.** BLOCKS, GRAPES, GORDIAN KNOTS]

BLOCKED PATH—(Huna) repressed ideas; experiences or thought-forms that are entirely or partially repressed; these restraints prevent the conscious mind from going into a higher level of understanding. **Syn.** SIN MEMORIES, OUTLAW MEMORIES, FIXATIONS. [**cf.** PSYCHOLOGICAL-DETERMINED AMNESIA]

BLOCKING—1. (blocks) to suppress and implode ideas, concepts, and memories of past unpleasant, negative experiences that repeat themselves throughout life; this causes a hold-pattern or "locked-in" area of cells that stagnate and cause abnormal behavior of mind and body systems; triggers off from environmental stimuli; reactions are sometimes unconscious. [**cf.** ROLFING, CONDITIONED AVOIDANCE RESPONSE, BLOCKS] 2. (mental psychism) to surround one's self with an energy field of scepticism, doubt, and a desire for privacy, when receiving a psychic reading; this prevents a good reading unless the psychic can break through the wall. [**cf.** PSYCHIC READING, VIBRATIONS, PSYCHIC DOORS] 3. (reincarnation) to allow guilt and other negative complexes from past lives to prevent one from rising up from the lower self, along the path of evolution. Usage: "Something is blocking your abundance. You could be regressed to understand what happened in your past to cause constant poverty." [**cf.** PATH, REINCARNATION, KARMA] 4. (dowsing) to use protection when dowsing if one is sensitive to earth's vibrations; a manmade shield has been designed to protect the dowser who is supersensitive to earth radiations and unable to control these vibrations, which lead to illness. [**cf.** EARTH MAGNETISM, DOWSING]

BLOCKS—unwanted emotions, "locked-in" the body cells and subconscious mind, which prevent one from optimum performance; these locked-in emotions grow in mass as years pass, hindering one's preferred mental and physical behavioral pattern and hindering one's growth in consciousness; begins with a distasteful, painful, emotional incident that is not resolved at the time it happens (interpreted with a correct attitude) or brought into balance with the individual's belief system; as life repeats itself, similar experiences occur that resurface that memory, and the individual represses these emotions as the body and mind refuse to accept the same pain; this negative emotional repressed stress gathers inside the body until it explodes in nervous, unwanted behavioral patterns, or in muscle tension; the pain and neurosis is capable of being triggered off from environmental stimuli; personal experience is constantly being recorded into man's nervous system and reflects in

the muscles, movements of the body, facial expressions, sensory acuteness, breathing habits, and various types of illnesses; these traits go unnoticed as the years go by, even if the original encounter is consciously forgotten; the cells gather together as grapes in a bunch; implosive gathering acts as explosive activity; compression becomes expression; 1. (psychiatry) chronic muscle tension is a learned response because of a past occurrence, and stops normal muscle reaction; 2. (Huna) ideas stored in the subconscious mind in a negative concept which the conscious mind was in no condition to rationalize when formed; e.g., incidents occuring when one is a child; 3. (Sigmund Freud) an emotional colored idea or idea pattern that has been repressed; 4. (metaphysics) memories of a negative experience from a past life that was never resolved correctly, surfacing in one's current life to be rehandled until it can be harmoniously resolved; brings with it into a current life physical and mental manifestations that are now wanted. **Syn.** FIXATION, OUTLAW MEMORIES, GRAPES, CLUSTERS, GORDIAN KNOTS. [**cf.** BLOCKS Appendix 5]

BLOOD—(esoteric) (Eastern) a mechanism in the physical body that releases the electronic, microscopic, karmic pictures from the mental-reflecting-ether; these pictures come from the heart which is a temporary akashic record file and flow throughout the blood stream with their information on the pattern of the body's condition and individual's life-style; a tool in administering good and bad karma. [**cf.** MENTAL-REFLECTING-ETHER, KARMA]

BLOOD-COVENANT—an exchange of blood in a sacred ritual between the chief of the tribe and one who desires to become a new member; the new member now attains a psychic rapport with all other members. [**cf.** BLOOD-SOUL, CEREMONIAL MAGIC, LAW OF QUANTUM CONNECTION Appendix 7]

BLOOD-FLOW SURGE—(astral projection) a quick sensation that occurs in the mind just before taking an astral projection; a way of informing the person that something is going to happen; it is as if the soul-mind is notifying the conscious mind of its intention. [**cf.** ASTRAL PROJECTION, ROLLED-OUT, SKYING, SHOOT, SEPARATION]

BLOOD-SOUL—one who has exchanged blood with another person, in a sacred, wrist-slashing ritual; this outward physical procedure binds them together and brings on a telepathic relationship by which each one can perceive the other's thoughts and emotions, regardless of distance; objective is for each one to be concerned about the other. [cf. BLOOD-COVENANT, CEREMONIAL MAGIC, LAW OF QUANTUM CONNECTION Appendix 7, TELEPATHY]

BLOWING UPON THE SICK—(Native American) to cure the sick by blowing one's breath upon them; "with breath and hands they cast out infirmity." [cf. SPIRIT HEALING, BREATH RETENTION, RHYTHMIC BREATHING, BREATHING]

BLUE—(esoteric) a primal, basic color; means Father, the highest of the Lords of the mind, ruler of the universe; symbol chosen from the concept that God comes on a blue ray from the blue sky; peace, tranquility, Truth. [cf. COLOROLOGY, SEVEN MAJOR RAYS]

BLUE AIR—(Tibet) a vibrational frequency that makes blue ethers at the base of each universe. Syn. WARP AND WOOF. [cf. VIBRATIONS, WARMTH ETHER]

BLUE BLOOD—(Sanskrit) (esoteric) pertains to an individual born into a family where a master has incarnated in the physical body. [cf. SOUL JURY, BIRTH SCIENCE Appendix 2]

BLUE BOOK—(ufology) a record of data concerning UFO intelligences or sightings; recorded and kept by the Air Force. [cf. NEW KNOWLEDGE, SIGHTINGS, SOLID STATE LIFE FORMS, MIB]

BLUE HOLES—(esoteric) (Bahamas) a tunnel-like effect or vast cave that exists underneath the surface of the sea; believed to have existed above sea level at one time; capable of enough suction power to pull objects down from the surface of the sea. (Inconcl.) Syn. BERMUDA TRIANGLE.

BLUE-BLACK-EGG—a formulation of energy enveloping a person who is going through the death process; makes him invisible as he travels through the density. Sim. BLUE-BLACK OF HIPPOCRATES. [cf. DEATH ANGEL, SHADES, VOID]

BLUEPRINT—see AURA.

BLUR—see HOLY.

BO AND PEEP—two individuals capable of getting many people to follow them and live in a commune together with the belief that UFO intelligences would come and gather all earth people who were ready to be saved; they would go in the UFO vehicle to another planet; group was called UFO Cult; the group disbanded. Syn. THE TWO. [cf. UFOLOGY, MIB, DAWN ANGELS, LANDING]

BO-TREE—(Buddhism) (esoteric) a fig tree that bears a fruit which is very potent in serotonin and seems to influence consciousness; chosen by Siddhartha Gautama to sit under, in a still position, meditating until he became enlightened. [cf. ENLIGHTENMENT, MEDITATION, SILENCE]

BOANTHROPY—to change from a human into an animal; in this case, a cow. [cf. DIMENSION-SHIFTING, WEREWOLF]

BOAT OF THE SEEKER—(Egypt) an egg-shaped ganglion of the inner brain; the optic thalamus; Egyptians recognized this as a symbol of immortality because it resembles a beetle if crosscut, similar to their beetle of immortality. Syn. SINGLE EYE, EGG OF IMMORTALITY, HEART OF THE LOTUS, OPEN EYE. [cf. THIRD-EYE AREA Appendix 5]

BOB—(pendulum) weight on the end of the suspension of a pendulum; made of various materials but should be lightweight, flexible, and equally balanced; kinds of bobs: spool, spoon, ring, stone, button, crystal, monocle, brazil nut, glass bead, or a small container in which a sample of the element to be hunted is put; suspension is thread, chain, white hemp, fishing line, black silk, cord, twine, or string. [cf. PENDULUM POWER, RADIESTHETIC SENSE]

BOBBER—see BOB.

BOCOR—(Voodoo) a psychic who is proficient in psychic counseling and healing; see PRACTITIONER and PSYCHIC. [cf. PSYCHIC HEALING]

BODHI TREE—the famous fig tree where Siddhartha Gautama sat for many days, until he attained Nirvana and became enlightened. Syn. BO TREE. [cf. MEDITATION, ZERO VIBRATION, PROFOUND WAKEFULNESS]

BODHISATTVA—1. (Tibet) a lama who attains Nirvana in the etheric world and no longer has to be reincarnated but instead, he chooses to be reborn in the earth plane as a spiritual leader; 2. (China) one who is intent on enlightenment; works to overcome imperfections on the level of earth; one who works with civilization as a whole, destroys that which needs to be destroyed, and increases that which needs to be strengthened. [cf. ANGEL HIERARCHY, MASTER]

BODIES OF AIR—(Plato) see ASTRAL PROJECTION.

BODIES OF FIRE—(Plato) see ASTRAL PROJECTION.

BODIES OF LIGHT—the envelope around the soul-minds in the causal plane, where the soul-mind is in its own soul form. [**cf.** THIRD PLANE, CAUSAL BODY, MENTAL BODY]

BODIES OF MAN—(esoteric) 1. the seven states of consciousness that man functions in, simultaneously; while in the physical body, man has six ethereal bodies that interpenetrate and protrude from him with their own set of principles, shapes, density, and vibrational frequency; each frequency knows its function and contributes to the overall goal of completing the monad (the finest body); each mundane activity performed influences the progression of the other bodies; no body is aware of what the other bodies are doing; 2. refers to the seven energy levels of matter that envelop the soul-mind during its life in the etheric world; as one learns, and progresses, the bodies are peeled off on a graduated scale until the monadic body is earned; one inhabits a body in the etheric world after transiting according to one's state of consciousness; one earns each body by many earthly incarnations and many ethereal lessons; 3. common names given to the bodies from the disciplines using seven principles of man: **(a)** physical body (lower—physical, higher—etheric double); **(b)** astral body (lower—kama rupa, higher—astral); **(c)** mental body (lower—mental, higher—causal); **(d)** Buddhic body; **(e)** atman body; **(f)** monad; **(g)** Divine (etheric oneness); 4. some disciplines use a scale of firve principles and some use twelve principles of man, enveloping the soul-mind. [**cf.** BODIES AND PLANES Appendix 5]

BODILESS DEVAS—angel beings who belong to the higher mental planes and no longer have a form, shaped similar to an earth body; their bodies blend into the mental atmosphere and yet each one maintains his purpose and individuality; composed of mental elemental essence belonging to the first elemental kingdom. [**cf.** ANGEL HIERARCHY, ELEMENTAL ESSENCE, PLANES, FORM DEVAS]

BODILY FIRES—(alchemy) to internally make one's body chemistry rise to a higher qualitative body substance through alchemical processes, using the power of the mind; (bodily fire is the normal heat in the body); to cause an internal physiological process by which the internal ingredients manufactured within the body are heated to an "even heat" by the bodily fires; causes them to rise upward through various stages; accomplished by synchronization of the conscious and subconscious minds from consistent concentration. [**cf.** ALCHEMIST, PURIFIED BODY, GLORIFICATION]

BODILY INCORRUPTION—to prepare one's body and soul-mind before death, so that after death, the physical body is preserved and when exhumed many years later, it is found in perfect condition; body is neither mummified, embalmed, nor preserved by other methods; more common among saints. [**cf.** GLORIFIED BODY, ALCHEMY, DEATH SCIENCE]

BODY—see PHYSICAL BODY.

BODY ARMOR—(Wilhelm Reich) theory: life's experiences which write themselves into the muscles, organs, and tissues of the body; this influences bodily reactions as to one's characteristics and health; these reactions are solidified, when things of like nature occur. **Syn.** CHARACTER ARMOR. [**cf.** BLOCKS, EMOTIONS, STRESS, SYMPATHETIC NERVOUS SYSTEM]

BODY BREAKERS—(Tibet) men, highly skilled in the anatomy of the body, whose job it is to cut up the deceased body and find the cause of death; the body is then prepared for the vultures for quick disposal into another vibrational frequency. **Syn.** DISPOSERS OF THE DEAD COLONY. [**cf.** DEATH SCIENCE, CREMATION, THREE EGG CEREMONY, TOMB]

BODY CATALEPSY—(physical psychism) to reach a state of deep trance so one's body can be used by an etheric world intelligence to perform physical psychism; medium relaxes, allows the etheric world intelligence to intervene, induce the trance state, and then utilize his body; medium feels loss of contact with his physical body and becomes unaware of his physical body; many mediums take an astral flight while in this altered state of consciousness; this state is used for etheric surgery, impersonation, and performing automatism of some types. [**cf.** HYPNOSIS, IMPERSONATION, TRANCE MANIFESTATION/MISCELLANEOUS Appendix 2]

BODY CHANGE—(Lobsang Rampa) the departing of one ego (soul-mind) from his physical body and permitting another ego from the etheric world to take over and reanimate the body; occurs when earthling has grown past childhood, as if the etheric intelligence desired to eliminate youth experiences; etheric intelligence is an advanced soul who is needed by mankind; earthling has lost his desire to live; planned by both parties; etheric intelligence usually finishes working out karma started by the earthling and then gets on with his needed task. **Syn.** INCARNATIONAL EXCHANGE, WALK-IN. [**cf.** SUPREME GUIDES OF HUMANITY, SCIENCE OF SERVICE, PRE-BIRTH]

BODY CHEMISTRY—(esoteric) 1. atoms vibrating in a frequency which makes and sustains a third-dimensional envelope around a life-force consciousness; this frequency is a result of evolution from the thinking and acting of the masses who existed in earth in past incarnations; although each individual's body chemistry is generally similar for purposes of compatibility of life-style, each individual's vibrational frequency varies in degrees; this variance is in accordance with the state of evolution of the soul-mind; the growth of the soul-mind speeds the frequency of the body chemistry which determines its vibrational rate for the next incarnation; during each incarnation, chemistry changes minutely with each thought and emotion; this is recognized in holistic health research and verified in biofeedback training (each individual shows a different electrical conductivity rate); 2. special body chemistry is necessary for psychic work; natural-born psychics are born with the essential body chemistry; others can sit for development because "desire" is the emotion necessary to change body chemistry for psychic skills. [**cf.** METABOLIC MONITOR, BIOFEEDBACK INSTRUMENTS, AKASHIC RECORD, SOUL-MIND]

BODY CONTROL—to alter the functioning of specific parts of the body and involuntary body systems in order to perform physical phenomena or in order to learn mind control; performed at will, for short or long periods; accomplished by intensified focalization of the mind on the activity; some psychics also use breathing techniques; skill extends into the afterlife; this is an alchemical skill and does not require the help of guides. [**cf.** see individual types under this category in Appendix 2]

BODY DNAs—(esoteric) cells containing the body pattern, which is made from a person's thoughts and words from every incarnation; capable of penetrating the entire universe when one tunes in psychically; "God's little bookkeepers" for the body. [**cf.** MICROCOSM, MACROCOSM, TOTALITY, WORDS-WITH-POWER]

BODY FEATS—(Yoga) "complete" control of body functions through mind discipline; to endure extreme conditions or postures of the body for long periods of time; i.e., to stand on one foot for months; to remain submerged in a stream up to one's waist for long periods with no ill effect. [**cf.** FAKIR, MAGIC SLEEP, HUNGER CONTROL, ELONGATION, BREATH CONTROL]

BODY IS TURNED ON—(Kinesiology) an expression used after chiropractor manipulation denoting that the muscle is strong again. [**cf.** FRINGE MEDICINE, LAW OF HEALING Appendix 7, HOLISM]

BODY OF GLORY—the fastest, the most pure, and the most subtle vibrational frequency to envelop the soul-mind before liberation; this body substance encompassing the soul-mind is earned through righteous living and pure thinking during earthly incarnations; this vibrational frequency gives the soul-mind the ability to materialize and dematerialize at will, on all seven planes; objective is to materialize in earth when needed to serve mankind; body will appear and disappear without a childhood or without a death; a purified body chemistry is the goal of the alchemist. **Sim.** GLORIFIED BODY OF CHRIST, RAINBOW BODY. [**cf.** ASCENSION, PURIFIED BODY, GLORIFICATION]

BODY OF LIFE AND VITALITY—the etheric double; earned this name because it acts similar to a battery, drawing energy from the cosmos and feeding it to the physical body; draws energy from the mind activity of the individual, stores it, and feeds it back to the body. [**cf.** AURA]

BODY OF LIGHT—1. (astral projection) a phantom body made of light substance, in which the projectionist places his astral body for protection; deliberately made with the mind before the trip commences; 2. the monadic body where one's consciousness blends into divine intelligence or the "light" of creation; light signifying intelligence as it was in the beginning (all intelligence). [**cf.** LIGHT, LIBERATION, ASTRAL PROJECTION]

BODY POLARITY—(esoteric) the manifestation of two contrasting, but balancing, principles within the body; mental consciousness gives the negative, feminine principle, and the subconscious gives the positive, masculine principle of polarity. [**cf.** LAW OF POLARITY Appendix 7, BIPOLAR, MAGNETIC POLES, BYELBOG AND CHERNOBOG]

BODY READING—to isolate parts of the human body for the purpose of studying one's physical health, life-style situations, or characteristics, in reference to the past, present, and future; these findings can be changed if desired; uses a combination of formal education and psychic skills; body reading utilizes four principles together or singularly; 1. the law of repetition that claims, "everything is a replica of the whole"; 2. the body is a product of the mind; 3. the sympathetic nervous system records and retains the history of the individual; 4. point of focus that encourages psychic information to surface. [cf. Appendix 5 for individual skills]

BODY RHYTHM DIARY—daily records of answers to specific questions regarding daily activities over a period of thirty days or more; used to pinpoint one's body cycles and learn about one's behavioral patterns. [cf. CYCLES, BIOFEEDBACK TRAINING]

BODY SCANNING—1. (magnetic healing) to detect the congested area in the body of one's self or another by using the palms of the hands; practitioner slowly runs his or her hands (palms facing body) a few inches above the surface of the body, going over the whole etheric double; a different sensation felt in the palms indicates the congested area or the base of the illness; sensations can be heat, cold, tingling, a pull, a stickiness, etc. [cf. MAGNET HEALING, CURATIVE EDUCATION, PALMED POWER, ETHERIC DOUBLE] 2. (pendulum power) to detect the congested area of a patient by using a pendulum; pendulumist slowly dangles the pendulum over the entire surface of the etheric double; if the pendulum swings in the opposite direction of the polarity of a specific area of the body, this indicates that area is not functioning normally. [cf. POLARITY, PALLOMANCY] 3. (psychic counseling) to mentally go over the body using x-ray clairvoyance to detect any areas that need attention; psychic can either perceive it as it is, or has worked out a code with his or her guide or subconscious mind to locate the trouble. [cf. X-RAY CLAIRVOYANCE, PSYCHIC COUNSELING]

BODY SENSATIONS—see BODY-FEELING.

BODY TRANSCEIVERS—energy points running along the meridian lines in the nervous system, that are necessary to distribute the system's emotional load; these compare to the nodes in the air and are a continuation of the nodes which make man and the universe one system; when the electrical energy in the body blows a fuse from an overload of negative emotions, it causes congestion or a disease; this blocks the electrical flow and the emotion that blew the fuse must be "balanced" to repair the fuse. **Syn.** ACUPUNCTURE POINTS. [cf. LAW OF HEALING Appendix 7, ACUPUNCTURE, EMOTIONS, NEGATIVE THOUGHT]

BODY ZONES—twelve invisible electrical energy lines in the body connecting the major organs and glands and major acupuncture points; divide the body in twelve divisions that run from the feet to the head, from the hands to the head, and are in line with the fingers and toes; see MERIDIAN LINES. [cf. REFLEXOLOGY, ACUPRESSURE POINTS]

BODY-FEELINGS—1. to sense what is going on inside the skin by attuning to the physical sensations of the body systems, as opposed to picturing what the body systems look like; to centralize concentration on one area of the body and to become one with this area; used in mental mediumship readings when the etheric world intelligences talk to the medium by giving him or her a little physical body stimulus to impart the following information: (a) to relate that the etheric world intelligence has entered into the reading, and the medium can feel the information coming through will be accurate; (b) that the sensations in the medium's body are part of the message being given: e.g., sensing a heavy weight on his right foot may indicate not to advance in the aspect in question; (c) to let a physical condition be known about the client, while the medium is scanning the client's body for illnesses. **Syn.** BODY SENSATIONS. 2. see HUMAN OMENS. [cf. GOING-TO-LEVEL, BRAIN WAVE TRAINING, SUBLIMINAL PERCEPTION]

BODY-FLAPPING—(dreams) sensations of the arms moving and the body twisting; brought about by the push and pull of the silver cord when one is taking an astral projection in one's sleep; this triggers a dream in which the upper part of the body is having similar movements. [cf. ASTRAL PROJECTION, REASSOCIATED, ROLLED-OUT]

BODY-TIME—a rhythmic pattern of internal body functions that repeats itself approximately every twenty-four hours; it comes from "within" the physical body, synchronizing with the heartbeat and the earth's revolution around the sun; this pattern has an influence on the mind and the body processes; (do not confuse with BIORHYTHM). (Inconcl.) **Syn.** BIOLOGICAL CYCLE, INTERNAL-

TIME. [**cf.** CYCLES, CIRCADIAN RHYTHM, JET LAG, CIRCADIAN HALF-WAVES]

BOGEY BEAST—a nature spirit who plays jokes on earthlings; takes the form of an animal when seen clairvoyantly; see NATURE SPIRITS.

BOGEY MAN—(Slavic) nature spirit in charge of the areas of decayed vegetable matter; seen hovering over these areas in apparition or goblin form; see NATURE SPIRIT. [**cf.** ELEMENTAL KINGDOM]

BOGGART—(Scotland, Highland) a nature spirit that acts both good and maliciously toward humans. **Sim.** PUCK.

BOGGLE—see POLTERGEIST.

BOGIE—a nature spirit that is shaped like a goblin; usually acts dangerously, mischievously, and maliciously.

BONDAGE OF THE FLESH—1. (metaphysical) refers to humanity's belief that one is dependent upon mundane materials and actions for health, abundance, and happiness and acts accordingly; 2. (alchemy) theory: one cannot be free from this world and one's material desires until one "frees himself" by accomplishing purification of the mind. [**cf.** ALCHEMY, MUNDANE, GLORIA, ELIXIR OF LIFE, MERCURY]

BONE-SYMMETRY HEALING—to heal by the movement and realignment of bones in the physical body by merely touching the area; performed by a practitioner who understands the law of gravitation and is influenced by his or her guide; theory: when bones are out of alignment, they cause pressure on nerve endings, which leads to internal organs reacting and forming a disease. [**cf.** CURATIVE EDUCATION, PSYCHOLOGICAL FIELD]

BONE-THROWING—(South Africa) to toss bones into the air and use their pattern of fall to obtain psychic information; theory: the bones themselves know how to make patterns that will reveal the future, characteristics of the person tossing the bones, and answers to his questions. [**cf.** SYNCHRONICITY, CASTING OF LOTS]

BONPA—(Australian aborigine) see PSYCHIC.

BOOK OF CHANGES, THE—see I CHING.

BOOK OF ENOCH—(Kabbalah) pertains to seventy-two angels, their sins, and the consequences, after they took human wives and taught them psychic arts.

BOOK OF FORMATION—(Kabbalah) recognizes the doctrine that man is exiled from God; man descends through the ten spheres that comprise the universe; man ascends through the ten spheres to return to God; contains knowledge regarding creation based on numbers, certain letters, and knowledge on how to create animals. **Syn.** SEPHER YETZIRAH. [**cf.** PATH, INVOLUTION, EVOLUTION]

BOOK OF GOD'S REMEMBRANCE—the records, in tiny picture form, of all that has happened on the planet earth since it was formed; see AKASHIC RECORDS and MENTAL-REFLECTING-ETHER. **Syn.** COSMIC MEMORY, AKASHIC RECORD. [**cf.** REINCARNATION]

BOOK OF RATES—information concerning every known part and disease of the human body; used in conjunction with the DE LA WARR BOX to diagnose the patient's illness. [**cf.** RADIONICS, BLACK BOX, DE LA WARR BOX]

BOOK OF THE DEAD—(ancient Egypt) composed of four versions of the four periods of the history of the Egyptian religions; refers to the process of death, the burial ritual of the physical body, and the entry of the soul-mind into the etheric world. [**cf.** DEATH SCIENCE, SIDPA BARDO, READER]

BOOK OF THE GOLDEN PRECEPTS—written material regarding universal laws, psychism, purpose of life, and life in the etheric world; given to those in the East studying to be mystics.

BOOK OF THE LAW—founded by Aleister Crowley (1905); dictated by an etheric world entity, Hoor-Paar-Kraat, in charge of the adversities of the earth at that time; main theme: "Do what thou wilt shall be the whole of the Law. Love is the Law, love under will."

BOOK OF THE SECRET—(Persia) contains material regarding the cosmos and methods of becoming psychic.

BOOK OF THE YELLOW EMPEROR—(China, about 200 B.C.) contains information of the ACUPUNCTURE theory.

BOOK OF THOTH—(ancient Egypt) believed to be the basic book for telling fortunes with cards; book of Tarot. [**cf.** POINT OF FOCUS]

BOOK READING—(mediumship) the skill of an etheric world intelligence to quote information from a book that is helpful to the medium in answering a question or problem; to name a book and page number where the medium can look for an answer to the question or problem. [**cf.** CROSS-CORRESPONDENCE, MEDIUMSHIP]

BOOK TESTS—(mediumship, early 1900s) psychic proof that the psychic information received by a medium was not telepathically perceived but actually given by an etheric world inteligence: 1. in a seance, the guide came through to sitters giving one a part of a sentence, another sitter fragments of the meaning of a quotation, and another the name and page number of a book; when this was put together, the quotation was found on that page of the book. [**cf.** CROSS-CORRESPONDENCE] 2. in a seance, the etheric world intelligence read material from a book that the medium never had access to; then gave the name and page number of the book; when verified, the words were verbatim. [**cf.** GUIDE, MEDIUMSHIP]

BOOKS OF LIFE—(Eastern) tiny invisible concentrated centers of energy at the end of three strands of the silver cord, which are nestled in man's physical body; located in the solar plexus, pineal gland, and heart; this energy contains records of man's past experiences which will be worked out in this incarnation; see HEART-SEED ATOM, ASTRAL-SEED ATOM, MENTAL-SEED ATOM. [**cf.** REINCARNATION, DEATH, BIRTH]

BOOMERANG CURSE—to return a psychic transfer of an illness, or an emotion of jealousy, anger, or hate to the sender; negative vibrations are transferred unknowingly between the two subconscious minds or sent consciously with evil intent; when the receiver realizes it is not his own illness or emotion, he has the ability to send it back to the sender; this will return with a strong jolt; to return a psychic transfer, these words are repeated silently or verbally: "Send it back to where it came from." [**cf.** ASSIMILATION, PSYCHIC ATTACK, PSYCHIC TRANSFER, CLOAK OF INSULATION]

BOOMERANG PSI—see BOOMERANG CURSE.

BORDER—an ethereal line between the physical world and the etheric world that is closed off by a curtain or purple veil; awareness of this line and the drawing of the curtain can happen in the transition of the soul-mind and in the receiving of psychic information; a necessary mass of energy that prevents the earthling from being constantly tuned into the other world, which would make earth life even more chaotic; this ethereal line will be lifted as man evolves and can handle both worlds simultaneously. [**cf.** BORDERLAND]

BORDER PHENOMENA—phases of physical psychism that show tangibly in the mundane world but are produced by invisible means, e.g., POLTERGEISTRY, GHOSTERY. [**cf.** POLTERGEIST, FOCUS, GHOSTS, CONFUSED-SOUL-MINDS, ASTRAL SHELLS]

BORDER REDCAP—a nature spirit that seems to be in charge of the tower houses along the border of land and water; capable of being harmful or helpful to travelers; see NATURE SPIRIT.

BORDERLAND—an imaginary space between the physical world and the etheric world measured by time; a subjective line of awareness when ethereal visibility ends and physical visibility begins. [**cf.** WALL, NONDURATION, SIMULTANEOUS, VEIL]

BORDERLAND SLEEP STATE—see HYPNAGOGIC STATE.

BORDERLINE SCIENCE—the study of anything that has been detected in outer space that shows evidence of life or/and intelligence; study of inhabitants of the ethereal world (exclusive of human beings as we know human being life in the etheric world), vehicles in space, occupants of the vehicles, nonliving and living aeroforms of all sizes; this life makes its abode in the atmosphere, aerosphere, or comes from other planets. **Syn.** UFOLOGY. [**cf.** UFOLOGY Appendix 5]

BORDERLINE STATE—see HYPNAGOGIC STATE.

BOREAS—the angel intelligence who rules the north wind; capable of making the north wind destructive or helpful, according to man's thoughts on planet earth. [**cf.** MAGNIFICENT ANGEL, ANGEL HIERARCHY, MINOR DEVA]

BORN IN DISGUISE—(Tibet) to wake up in the etheric world after physical death, endowed with supernormal psychic powers. **Sim.** SPRINGING FORTH. [**cf.** LORDS OF DEATH, PRESERVING OF SACREDNESS]

BORN WITH A VEIL—a baby born with a thin membrane that envelopes the fetus; it is believed that this child is psychic; technical term is *caul*. [**cf.** BIRTH SCIENCE]

BORROWED—(mediumship) the act of an etheric world intelligence stepping into a medium's body for a designated time to perform physical phenomena; the medium is in a deep trance state and has no control over his or her autonomic nervous system; medium controls the length of time, the type of activity, and then puts complete trust in the etheric world's righteous intent to use his or her body; this mutual agreement results in no harm done to the medium; to allow one's body to be borrowed is usually for the purpose of healing. [cf. IMPERSONATION, VOICE TRANCE, AUTOMATIC WRITING]

BOSSES—(hand reading) a puffiness or raised section of the hand or fingers, having a correlation to astrology and a significant meaning to the palmist. **Syn.** MOUNTS. [cf. CHIROGNOMY, PALMISTRY]

BOSWELLIA—(esoteric) a plant that grows mainly in East Africa; produces frankincense. [cf. PLANT KINGDOM, BOTANE]

BOTANE—(Hellene religion, B.C.) the ability of the plant kingdom to react psychically to humans, animals, atmosphere, environment, etc.; a subtle shifting network of energies psychically attuned to all other systems in nature; ability of plants to react to the attitudes, emotions, and health changes in humans which is demonstrated by a change in growth activity and unnatural performances of itself; different psychic skills of different plants: cause genuine or distorted hallucinations, heal the body, bring clairaudience to the surface, calm the nerves (herb teas), promote skin healing, strengthen eyes, accelerate one's psychic ability, forecast the weather (by changing with atmospheric conditions). (Inconcl.) [cf. SENSATION CONSCIOUSNESS, PRIMARY PERCEPTION, BOTANE Appendix 2]

BOTANE ENERGY—an exuberent, vibrating force found in gardens or woods that are left virgin or where a great deal of love and respect for life is given to the flowers or vegetables, e.g., Findhorn: "There is a pronounced feeling of power vibrating among the gardens like no other place on planet earth." [cf. PLANT MAGIC, LAW OF SUBSERVIENCE Appendix 7, CELLULAR CONSCIOUSNESS]

BOTTLE IMPS—(Germany) see FAMILIAR SPIRIT.

BOUNDLESS—(theosophy) abstract time; to have an essence of continuation; found during meditation. [cf. FIFTH DIMENSION, FOURTH DIMENSION, TIME-DISPLACEMENT, PRESENT MANIFESTED]

BOUNDLESS VISION—(Buddhism) mental activity in the mind showing a picture of the distant future; ability to see the future in akashic records. See CELESTIAL EYES. [cf. CLAIRVOYANCE, REINCARNATION, VISIONARY, SPIRITUAL SIGHT]

BOW PALLOMANCY—(Ceylon, Vedas) to use a bow belonging to a bow and arrow set as a pendulum tool for yes and no answers; the string part is lightly suspended over the forefingers with perfect balance, while in the squatting position; the question is asked and the bow will tip or swing on one side for yes and the opposite side for no. [cf. PALLOMANCY, RADIESTHESIA, BOB, WARM UP THE MOTOR]

BOWLS—an accessory used in many different kinds of ceremonies; began when bowls were first made of metal with wide openings; this shape is symbolic of the heavens. [cf. IMITATIVE MAGIC, CEREMONIAL MAGIC]

BOYS DOWNSTAIRS—(ufology) intelligent entities from outer space whose intent is believed to be to pull humans down and control them; this is reflected by their type of UFO encounters; (do not confuse with discarnate human beings who can only be contacted psychically). [cf. OTHER WORLD INTELLIGENCES, MIB, ETHERICALLY PROPELLED SHIPS, HOMO MECHANICUS]

BOYS FROM TOPSIDE—(ufology) intelligent entities from outer space whose whole intent (it is believed) is to help raise mankind on planet earth to higher states of consciousness; this is reflected by their type of UFO encounters; (do not confuse with discarnate human beings who can only be contacted psychically). [cf. COSMOLOGICAL COMMUNITY, GODS FROM THE SKY]

BPE—abbr. for BIOPHYSICAL EFFECT METHOD; (Russia) name for dowsing; used mainly for discovering their national natural resources in the ground. [cf. RADIESTHESIA, DOWSING]

BRAHAMARANDA CHAKRA—(Sanskrit) the crown or seventh chakra at the top of the head, connected to the pineal gland, considered the "king in man." [cf. CHAKRAS, KUNDALINI, SERPENT POWER]

BRAHMA—(Hinduism, Sanskrit) God, in His aspect as Creator; God, as one of the Hindu trinity; depicted by a statue having four faces and four arms, each holding special symbols representing his deity; masculine form. **Syn.** sometimes **Brahman.** [cf. TOTALITY Appendix 3]

BRAHMA CONSCIOUSNESS—to become one with the "All"; a state beyond unity consciousness; a blending with perfectness; experienced during meditation. **Sim.** DIVINE CONSCIOUSNESS, SATORI, NIRVANA. [**cf.** CONSCIOUSNESS, MEDITATION]

BRAHMADANDA—(India) name of the spine, as it functions for the kundalini; the stick of Brahma. [**cf.** CADUCEUS OF MERCURY, KUNDALINI, SUSHUMNA, MEDULLA OBLONGATA]

BRAHMAN'S EYE—(Sanskrit) an energy force-center of etheric substance, located in the low central forehead of everyone; invisible to the physical eye; serves as a tool to see into the etheric world; the pineal gland (an organ in the third-eye area). **Syn.** THIRD-EYE. [**cf.** THIRD-EYE AREA, PINEAL GLAND, PSYCHIC ENERGY]

BRAHMANA—(Sanskrit) 1. a priest and philosopher belonging to the top four classifications in the Vedic, Hindu religion; they have mediumistic abilities and are capable of communicating with the fire god, Agni; 2. signifies proper usage of the mantras and their purposes. [**cf.** SAGE, MENTOR, SHAMAN, FILLED WITH THE SPIRIT]

BRAHMANA VAGGA—(Buddhism) the psychic process of making oneself seen in more than one place at the same time; see MULTIFORM. **Syn.** BILOCATION, ANGUTTARA NIKAYA.

BRAHMANICAL THREAD—(Sanskrit) a fluid, made of semi-material, that flows up the center of the spine; can be seen with physical eyes; carries an invisible force from the base of the spine to the crown chakra; necessary to man; shows the state of one's soul-mind evolution by its location. **Syn.** SUSHUMNA. [**cf.** KUNDALINI, CADUCEUS WINDING]

BRAIN—(esoteric) 1. a physical muscle in the head, that serves as a liaison organ for intelligence to surface to a "now" awareness; sustains this "now" awareness that the rest of the body inhabits for compatibility; 2. generates a reality produced by thought; gives off a radiation of energy responding to the nature of thoughts, which make this (world) reality, everything in it, and hold it in place for manipulation; 3. functions of this liaison organ: (a) to sift, sort, label, categorize, reason, intellectualize, and form concepts and opinions from the information that comes in through the five physical senses (stimulated by the environment); files these opinions and concepts in the invisible, subconscious mind, for the future; (b) to surface back learned material from the subconscious mind; to remember learned information when needed for the "now" awareness and to interpret it in a meaningful way;

(c) to recognize "pure information" as it comes from Totality, through the superconscious mind, and use it properly; (d) to interpret in a meaningful way, psychic information brought through the subconscious mind and to keep the psychic information disciplined; (e) to electrically translate and rearrange cosmic energy into formulas and vibrational frequencies (within its boundaries) and radiate these formulas out (past its boundaries), to change the atoms around the body into frequencies that manifest a third-dimensional reality; 4. acts with instant rapidity, automatically, and with conscious deliberate mental activity; 5. needs information for fuel, and deprivation of information can cause insanity; can co-create information of its own; 6. a mechanism that makes a decision, which is unique only to the human race; 7. governing body for the nervous systems; uses the CEREBROSPINAL NERVOUS SYSTEM for receiving action and information; uses the sympathetic nervous system for sending out mundane action and information; 8. generates a consciousness; 9. not "intelligence" itself, but a "temporary intelligence" that transfers to the permanent intelligence upon death; 10. is space-bound, unable to imagine anything outside its third-dimension. (Inconcl.) **Syn.** MENTAL MIND, CONSCIOUS MIND. [**cf.** BRAIN HEMISPHERES, SUBCONSCIOUS MIND, SUPERCONSCIOUS MIND]

BRAIN DEWS—a vital, invisible, gaseous fluid from cosmic consciousness, which enters into and flows through the head region, down the spinal cord, and throughout all the nerves in the body; absorption of this fluid in the body depends upon the level of evolution of the soul-mind; it can be directed by conscious thought to heal and soothe one's self and others. [**cf.** SOUL-MIND EVOLUTION, CHRISM OIL, MAGNETIC HEALING]

BRAIN ELECTRICAL EVENTS—(biofeedback training) brain wave patterns that differ each time a man or a woman learns something new; a new pattern of electrical brain frequencies that become set when new information is accumulated by a man or a woman, giving evidence that a human being could be an evolving creature. (Inconcl). [**cf.** BIOFEEDBACK TRAINING, ALPHA WAVES]

BRAIN ELECTRICITY—ergs of energy constantly being sent out from the brain; thought impulses, that can be detected on the EEG instrument, give evidence that the body has an electrical system geared by the brain. (Inconcl.) [**cf.** EEG, MIND INSTRUMENT]

BRAIN FREQUENCY ALTERATION—(biofeedback training) the interplay of all three levels of consciousness: alpha, theta, delta, during sleep; can be measured by hooking-up sleeping subjects to the electroencephalograph, overall results are universally the same. (Inconcl.) [**cf.** EEG, REM DREAMS]

BRAIN HEMISPHERES—the division of the brain into two main sections, each having its own function and operating semi-independently, even though physically connected; each section has its own private sensations, perceptions, impulses, etc.; details: see RIGHT HEMISPHERE and LEFT HEMISPHERE. (Inconcl.) **Syn.** SPLIT BRAIN. [**cf.** SPLIT BRAIN HEMISPHERES Appendix 5]

BRAIN MAGNETISM—(esoteric) the magnetic currents that pass around and through the brain, connecting both hemispheres; this magnetism rises and falls "within" each hemisphere. (Inconcl.) [**cf.** BRAIN, SPLIT BRAIN, MAGNETOMETER]

BRAIN PRINT-OUTS—(biofeedback training) pen or pencil lines made on a graph, generated by the electrical ergs of energy emanating from the brain of a person hooked-up to an electroencephalograph; these lines form patterns with enough universal similarity to make groupings; the groupings make the experience more meaningful, as significance can be given to each group. (Inconcl.) [**cf.** BRAIN WAVE PATTERNS, CLEAN RECORDS, NEURAL COMMUNICATION]

BRAIN SAND—(esoteric) substance found in the pineal gland, similar to apparatus in a wireless telegraph; felt to be necessary to transmit and receive waves of mental thought impulses. (Inconcl.) [**cf.** PINEAL GLAND, THIRD-EYE AREA, BRAIN DEWS, KINGLY CENTER]

BRAIN SCALE OF REVOLUTIONS—see SCALE OF BRAIN RHYTHM.

BRAIN SOOTING—a slang expression, used to refer to meditation by those who do not approve of meditation. [**cf.** MEDITATION Appendix 5]

BRAIN SUBSTRATE—an acknowledgment that the brain is not the only intelligence accessible to man; there is at least one other place which man can "dip into" for intelligence: the soul-mind is the substrate for the physical brain. (Inconcl.) [**cf.** SUBCONSCIOUS MIND, UNIVERSAL MIND]

BRAIN WAVE HIGH—special patterns made on the biofeedback print-outs, when the subject who is hooked-up is experiencing a reaction to hallucinogenic drugs. [**cf.** BIOFEEDBACK TRAINING, FIXED-BRAIN-WAVE-STATE, LEVEL DRIFT]

BRAIN WAVE PATTERNS—lines drawn on graph paper, made by brain wave activity that is amplified by an EEG instrument; these lines vary in length and depth, and behave similarly for long enough intervals that they form a phase, or groupings of mental brain activity; these lines are made by the amplification, through the electroencephalograph, of ergs of energy that constantly emanate from one's brain; electrodes are placed on various areas of the head, and then attached to a wire and jack, so the person can be hooked-up to the EEG instrument; these amplified lines are found to be affected by outside stimuli, reactions of the five senses, and changes in emotions and thoughts; after hooking-up thousands of persons, it has been found that a man or a woman makes four definite "universal" patterns from his or her brain emanations. (Inconcl.) [**cf.** EEG, METABOLIC MONITOR, SCALE OF BRAIN RHYTHMS]

BRAIN WAVE RHYTHM—electrical impulses emanating from one's brain, in definite patterns, as opposed to having no order or similarity; these impulses are amplified on the EEG instrumentation by graphs or colored lights; these graphs or lights show little variation from person to person, which makes it possible to form a scale; by isolating the phases on a scale made from the read-outs of the instrumentation they can be studied. (Inconcl.) [**cf.** SCALE OF BRAIN RHYTHM]

BRAIN WAVE SYNCHRONIZER—a flashing strobe light that can be adjusted to a person's brain wave electrical frequencies; used to induce instant or quick hypnosis, by making them both synchronize; believed to be the purpose of the UFO craft's flashing light that comes with each encounter. (Inconcl.) [**cf.** HYPNOTHERAPY, CLOSE-ENCOUNTERS-OF-THE-THIRD-KIND]

BRAIN WAVE TRAINING—(biofeedback training) daily or weekly sessions, in which one is hooked-up to an electroencephalograph instrument, to learn what happens to the physiology of the body in relationship to one's thinking; one learns how to control body changes according to the thoughts and emotions; these sessions are a tool for learning how to take charge of one's self; special exercises are given by a therapist to assist the person in learning mind and emotional control; the EEG gives tangible evidence of a mind/body relationship. **Sim.** BIO-FEEDBACK TRAINING. [**cf.** SELF-CONTROL OF INNER STATES, EMOTIONS, THOUGHT]

BRAIN WAVES—ergs of electrical energy, emanating from the mental mind (brain), caused by constant, unnoticed thinking, and deliberate thinking; capable of being detected by the EEG biofeedback instrument; this electrochemical activity in the brain has been found to generate many different electrical frequencies; these frequencies interact with each other and transmit information throughout the body in the form of emotion, psychic information, and motor activity; see BRAIN WAVE RHYTHM SCALE. [**cf.** EEG; ALPHA, BETA, THETA, AND DELTA STATES OF CONSCIOUSNESS]

BRAIN-BOUND CONSCIOUSNESS—concepts and opinions that one implants in the subconscious mind, from authoritative sources, but are not necessarily Truths; these may constantly rise to the conscious mind for alteration, but one does not recognize them as untruths; when one does recognize them, they are difficult to change because the authoritative source implanted at the same time gives them (pseudo) validity. [**cf.** PSYCHOSIS, INNER-STREAM OF CONSCIOUSNESS, NOETIC SCIENCE]

BRAIN/MIND—also written **brain-mind**; 1. (current) to indicate that the brain is not the only source of man's intelligence; however, without the physical organ, the brain, the other source of intelligence would not be possible, thus it is all one system; 2. (parapsychology) mind is an invisible energy field, that intermingles and meshes, within the brain area; *mind* means "subconscious mind." [**cf.** SUBCONSCIOUS MIND, SOUL-MIND, CONSCIOUS MIND, BRAIN]

BRAINWASHING—1. (Webster's Dictionary) "a method of indoctrination so intensive and thorough as to effect a radical transformation of beliefs, morals, and mental attitudes"; 2. (Random House Dictionary) "any accelerated method of controlled systematic indoctrination based on 'repetition' and 'confusion'"; 3. a special systematic technique used to accelerate a change in one's attitude, morals, and beliefs, happening unknown to the subject and without the subject's permission; the objective in brainwashing is to bypass the logical, reasoning, decision-making mind, and go directly to the subconscious mind, where the suggestions are accepted and stored exactly as given; (**a**) "confusion" method is produced with drugs, torture, and forced

lack of sleep; these weaken the conscious mind, making it step aside; (**b**) the "repetition" method is accepted in today's culture, with an increase in usage; the repetition method of making the conscious mind step aside: (1) to gain one's undivided attention by repeating planned phrases; (2) holding one transfixed in an eye-stare; (3) overuse of the pronoun *you;* (4) pointing the finger at the listener, and; (5) a repeated appeal to one's primal emotional nature; these tactics cause the decision-making mind to become passive and allows the subconscious mind to accept and file the suggestions, opinions, and information "as given"; the subject acts in favor of the lecturer, minister, salesperson, destructive-brainwashing cult recruiter, or the authoritative figure administering the planned verbiage; (this is brainwashing but not destructive at this point). See Appendix 4 for clarification. [**cf.** SNAPPING, SUGGESTION, POWER-OF-THE-WORD, DESTRUCTIVE-BRAIN-WASHING CULT, ATMOSPHERE OF AFFECTION]

BRAIN WAVE SIGNATURES—(Maxwell Cade and Nona Coxhead) five groupings of various types of patterns found by using the Mind-Mirror instrument and the EEG instrument; named: UNILATERAL PATTERN, ALPHA STATE OF CONSCIOUSNESS, ALPHA BLOCKING, MEDITATION, LUCID AWARENESS. (Inconcl.) [**cf.** SPLIT BRAIN, BRAIN, CONSCIOUSNESS]

BREAKERS OF THE DEAD—(Tibet) highly skilled lamas, whose job is to find the cause of a death by cutting open the physical body of a deceased person; later, they prepare the body for the vultures. [**cf.** SHRADDA CEREMONIES, SHIP-BURIAL, THREE EGG CEREMONY]

BREAKFALLS—(Judo) the skill of landing gently from a high fall, without bringing harm to one's body. [**cf.** MARTIAL ART]

BREAKTHROUGH—(taped voices) coined by Dr. Konstantin Raudive; refers to the voices of intelligences capable of putting sound and words on tape, either from those who have made their transition from this plane, or Intelligences from other planets. [**cf.** TRACKING VOICES, VOICE-PHENOMENA, TELE-PHONE CALLS FROM THE DEAD]

BREASTPLATE OF JUDGMENT—(ancient Hebrew) a tool, imitative of the high priest's breastplates, consisting of two parts: a lower stationary part, cast as a plate engraved with the letters of the alphabet; the upper part functions as a pointer; used to seek psychic information (as one uses the

Ouija board or planchette). [**cf.** AUTOMATISM, IMITATIVE MAGIC, TALKING BOARD]

BREATH CONTROL—to use the vagus nerve for a special technique of "inner breathing"; supports life without taking air into the lungs; easterners use the vagus nervous system to stay alive without suffocating, when buried under the ground for many days; the finer vibrations of the mind control the lower vibrations of chemical matter. [**cf.** LAW OF SUBSERVIENCE Appendix 7, BODY CONTROL]

BREATH FORM—pertains to the physical body, one phase of the soul-mind's awareness. **Syn.** HUMAN BEING.[**cf.** SOUL-MIND, BREATHING, INNER-SOUND CURRENT]

BREATH HEALING—see SPIRIT HEALING.

BREATH LEVITATION—(Hereward Carrington) to lift a person by the fingertips, with one coordinated breath; (during an experiment, the individual being raised lost sixty pounds). [**cf.** LEVITATION-TK, GRAVITY CONTROL]

BREATH OF GOD—pertains to the substance found in the air, that man cannot destroy or duplicate; necessary for all life, organic and inorganic; see VITAL LIFE FORCE. [**Syn.** VITAL LIFE FORCE Appendix 3]

BREATH OF LIFE—(Christianity) see VITAL LIFE FORCE.

BREATHATERIAN—one who lives without food or water; to employ special breathing techniques that enable an individual to be sustained by the "spirit" in the air, for a physical life in earth. [**cf.** VEGETARIAN, HOLISTIC HEALTH, DIAPHRAGMIC BREATHING]

BREATHED INTO—(ancient Greece) to be impressed with psychic knowledge from an etheric world deity while in a trance state of consciousness; medium speaks out the impressions in his or her own voice, as they proceed within the mind; knowledge is beyond formal education of the present era and is usually meant for the masses; sometimes it is prophecy for the country. **Sim.** GOD-FILLED, ENTHUSED. 2. to receive impressions in the mind more rapidly than one can think; impressions can be in the form of poetry or information that the psychic could not have known by any other means; knowledge is not personal but meant to be shared. **Sim.** INSPIRATIONAL WRITING. [**cf.** POET, RETROCOGNITION, MANTIC TRANCE]

BREATHING—(esoteric) 1. one of the processes of putting "spirit" into the body, which is absolutely necessary for the life of that body; the master function of the body, all other functions are secondary; the nervous system extracts the "spirit" from the breath, and uses it with an importance similar to the oxygen in the blood; oxygen and carbon dioxide are a secondary necessity; the more deeply one breathes the better one's physical health and longevity will be; 2. deep breathing helps to amplify the psychic signals in the mind. [**cf.** SPIRIT, LOW BREATHING]

BREATHING RELEASE—(rebirthing) a technique performed by a teacher and student, for the student to reexperience the learning process of breathing similar to what he or she experienced during birth; personal instructions are given by the teacher, to surface this experience; the student then tries to pattern his or her breathing accordingly; theory: one will indraw more "spirit" from the air from this time on, leading to more vigorous health. [**cf.** REBIRTHING, DRY REBIRTHING, BREATH]

BRIAH—(Kabbalah) considered to be a product of creation; the second highest plane in the etheric world, where "air" is assigned; a primal alchemical element; the home of the archangels. [**cf.** TREE OF LIFE, ATZILUTH, YETZIRAH, ASSIAH]

BRIDGE OF CONSCIOUSNESS—(mediumship) an exchange of awareness, from the alert-awake state to a deep level of unconsciousness; occurs when a medium goes into a deep trance; phrase used among mediums because they all seem to go through a sensation of mixed emotions and visions while the two minds exchange roles and synchronize with the etheric world guide; the conscious mind steps out of control, so the subconscious mind or guide can take over for the physical phenomenon at hand. **Sim.** BORDERLINE STATE. [**cf.** HYPNAGOGIC, OUTER CONSCIOUS LEVEL]

BRIGHT ANGEL—1. a superior etheric world intelligence, who appears to stand behind the right shoulder of each earthling, ready to help the earthling at any time, if the earthling asks it to do so; 2. the superconscious mind in everyone; the source of universal intelligence; available at all times, when one learns how to tap into it. **Syn.** HIGHER SELF, HOLY GUARDIAN ANGEL. [**cf.** ANGEL KINGDOM, GUIDE]

BRIGHT SPOT OF THE DAY—(Yoga) to focus one's consciousness always on the good in life; accomplished by recording the most pleasurable events or peak experiences of each day in a diary; this improves one's memory of happy times, and decreases the chance of becoming depressed. [cf. CURATIVE EDUCATION, HASSLE-LOG]

BRIMSTONE—(esoteric) (ancient) an element that has the properties to burn away negative vibrations and evil spirits; was used in a home to make it "holy," and a safe place in which to live. [cf. MINERAL KINGDOM, SULPHUR]

BRINGER-OF-THE-ANIMALS—(Eskimo, early hunting cultures) a shaman who is sensitive to nature and understands the power of the mind; he psychically maneuvers the movements of the game animals into a position for easy hunting; works for the good of the whole tribe. [cf. SHAMAN, NATURE TELEPATHY]

BROADCASTING—to psychically release (deliberately or unknowingly) personal feelings and attitudes in a group; this causes an uncomfortable feeling within all members of the group, unless they are aware of what is happening. Usage: "Mary is broadcasting again, and we are not reaching any decisions at our meeting." Sim. SPLODGING. [cf. PSYCHIC TRANSFER, PSYCHIC INVASION]

BROOMSTICK—1. (ancient) symbolic of the "rod" used in magic; the shape gives the stick psychical energy, so it can be used as a tool in magic; helps the witches in their conquest of teleportation, from place to place; 2. (cavemen) symbolic of power and strength, as the "club" is used; 3. a step in the graduation of the shape of a long stick: from the club, to the rod, to the broomstick, to the sword. [cf. TELEPORTATION, FORMS-WITH-POWER]

BROTHERHOODS—a group soul that consists of lofty intelligences who are incarnates, discarnates, and walk-ins; their function is to work together to aid the growth of the planet; each brotherhood has from fifty to several hundred in its number, specializing in every field; e.g., mathematical calculations, harmonic vibrations, managerial counseling, etc.; these exalted soul-minds are so attuned to the universe and each other that they can communicate with each other through mental telepathy when necessary; each soul-mind member of the group soul contributes to the group soul and may draw knowledge from it; occurs among all three types of intelligences; some who are incarnates

have made their status known to earthlings; they tell of a Federation serving world-wide in its outreach, composed of sixty brotherhoods; branches of the Federation that have made themselves known: White Feather, Gold Circle, the Overall Mind, the Spiral, and the Great White Brotherhood. [cf. GROUP SOUL, GREAT WHITE BROTHERHOOD, MASTER, GODHEAD]

BROTHERS OF THE LIGHT—(Sanskrit) those on the right-hand path; magicians who use white magic for counseling, healing, foretelling the future, and other psychic phenomena to help civilization. Syn. DAKSHIACHARINS. [cf. HIGH MAGIC, PSYCHIC]

BROTHERS OF THE SHADOW—(Sanskrit) those who learned magic to use it for evil intent, called black magic; those treading on the left-hand path. Syn. WEARERS OF THE RED CAP, DUGPAS. [cf. MAGIC Appendix 4]

BROUGHT DOWN—(etheric surgery) an expression meaning that the operation, given to the etheric double, is now happening in the physical body; the physical body is reacting as if it had been cut into, and is now mending (as was performed on the etheric double). [cf. ETHERIC SURGERY, PSYCHIC SURGERY]

BROW CHAKRA—(Sanskrit) a concentrated cosmic energy force, located in the forehead; when perceived clairvoyantly, it emanates ninety-six streams of radiation; it is divided into two sections, by an outer cosmic force: the left side houses the pituitary gland, is feminine, negative in polarity, and shows itself in an indescribable violet color; the right side houses the pineal gland, is masculine, positive, and shows itself in a glorious golden hue; all of this blends into the crown chakra attached to the silver cord. Syn. AJNA, AGYAN. [cf. SILVER CORD, CHAKRAS, PRANA]

BROWN MAN OF THE MUIRS—(England) a nature spirit whose function is to protect the wild beasts; see FAIRIES.

BROWN STUDY—slang expression used for daydreaming.

BROWNIE—(Scotland *daoine sithe,* "men of peace") a nature spirit known for its hard work within a home or on a farm, for one particular family; endowed with a helpful energy that is easily given in a steady flow, bringing a feeling of security; shows itself clairvoyantly with dark skin; can be felt clairsentiently by heat on one's skin;

generally helpful and not mischievous; (Wales; Scotland, Highlands, Lowlands) shows itself as very small in size (sometimes only twenty-five inches tall), is shabbily dressed, wrinkled and brown in appearance, and is either naked or clothed; Highland brownies have no fingers or toes; Lowland brownies have no noses; all brownies have a tremendous sense of responsibility, once they adopt a household to look after; they do their chores at night, and expect food in return; see NATURE SPIRIT.

BRUJO—(Native American, Southwest) the medicine man who heals the soul, foretells the future, and gives psychic counsel. **Syn.** YAQUI, SORCERER, MEDICINE MAN. [**cf.** SHAMANSHIP, PSYCHIC HEALING, MEDIUMSHIP HEALING, PSYCHIC, HAND-TREMBLER]

BRUTE WORLD—(Tibet) (esoteric) relates to the human beings whose soul-minds have not evolved to the degree of the masses; to the masses they are acting in an unethical manner, with materialistic and animalistic behavior. **Syn.** BEASTS OF THE FIELD. [**cf.** REINCARNATION, BODIES AND PLANES]

BRUXA—(Portugal) see VAMPIRE.

BSAM-GTAN BAR-DO—(Tibet) a deep state of meditation; to feel detached from the physical body, and to feel like a unit of eternity. [**cf.** MIND EXPANSION, PURE AWARENESS, SILENT INTONING]

BSM—abbr. for BIOPHYSICAL METHODS; see same.

BT—(psi tasks) abbr. for BASIC TECHNIQUE; the experimenter lays aside the cards as they are called by the subject (the one being tested for ESP ability); at the end of the experiment, the answers are verified and compared to change. [**cf.** ESP, COGNITION]

BUBBLE—an energy field surrounding each person; it forms a circle, fluctuates, pulsates, reaches out and draws vibrations of like nature to itself; when seen clairvoyantly, it differs with sexes; is fully developed around middle age; (do not confuse with AURA). [**cf.** BODIES OF MAN]

BUBBLE MACHINE—(laboratory) a device designed to test PK hits; uses an electric-eye, and a continuous stream of water. [**cf.** ESP, PK, COGNITION]

BUCANS—(Scotland, Highlands) see NATURE SPIRIT.

BUCCA DHU—(Cornwall, England) a nature spirit which instructs schools of fish to swim into the nets when the fisherman are deserving; in charge of the fishing industry; can be a good helper if one stays on the good side of it.

BUCCA GWIDDEN—(Cornwall, England) see BUCCA DHU.

BUCKIE—(Scotland) see NATURE SPIRIT.

BUDA—(Ethiopia) one who practices psychic skills with evil intent; capable of changing into an animal; see LYCANTHROPY. [**cf.** WEREWOLF, DEMONOLOGY, DIMENSION-SHIFTING]

BUDDHA—(Sanskrit, "to awaken"; to become enlightened) 1. refers to Prince Siddhartha Gautama who founded Buddhism, and became enlightened; 2. is a title, not a person; one who reaches Nirvana: one who is spiritually awakened, who has the highest of principles, and who has nothing more to learn; 3. compared to being "Christed" in Christianity; (do not confuse with BUDDHI). [**cf.** CHRISTED, PURIFIED BODY]

BUDDHA AMIDA BUTSU—(Zen, Japan, "boundless, light, and love") to repeat these words continually during meditation is to show adoration to the Buddha principle; this brings one's self to a higher understanding of life, and a desire to work with civilization as a whole. [**cf.** WORDS-WITH-POWER, MANTRA, CHANTING]

BUDDHA'S BRAIN—(Buddhism) the southern teaching of Prince Gautama, the Buddha; a philosophy for the general world; outer symbols of forms and ceremonies, sometimes called "Eye-doctrine," or "Doctrine of Forms and Ceremonies."

BUDDHI—(Sanskrit) "to perceive" on the level of the oversoul; the mechanism in human beings that opens them to wisdom from the universal mind; this wisdom comes directly to their consciousness, without picking up any material in the subconscious mind; it is "pure" information; works with the very highest principles. **Sim.** INSPIRATIONAL THOUGHT. [**cf.** SUPERCONSCIOUS MIND]

BUDDHI AMITABHA—to see psychic visions, or to be psychically impressed during meditation; this knowledge comes directly from Totality, as in clairsentience or inspirational thought. [**cf.** MEDITATION, CLAIRVOYANCE, INSPIRATIONAL SPEAKING]

BUDDHI OF INFINITE LIGHT—see INSPIRATIONAL THOUGHT.

BUDDHIC BODY—(Eastern) fourth invisible body of a human being in the "principles of seven bodies;" a very subtle energy field interpenetrating and extending quite a distance from the human body; when this body has earned the right to abide in the etheric world, and other bodies have been discarded, the soul-mind works with constructive imagination for the causal plane, seen clairvoyantly as a beautiful colored energy vibrating swiftly; when incarnating from this plane the soul-mind is interested in evolving humanitarian desires among earthlings; corresponding chakra is the brow chakra. [**cf.** MENTAL BODY, CAUSAL BODY, MONAD]

BUDDHIC PLANE—(Sanskrit, "wisdom") the fourth plane on the scale of varying vibrational frequencies of worlds, which the varying bodies inhabit; consciousness on this plane begins to promote universal love and humanitarian deeds for soul-mind growth; and works down the superconscious mind to the pineal gland and reaches the human psychically through intuition and inspirational thought; geniuses function from this plane more frequently than others; many schools of wisdom give instructions in constructive imagination to feed into the abstract ideas of the causal plane to help promote proper living conditions and peace in earth; soul-minds exude energy for this plane making its existence possible but they are also a motivator of the third plane. **Syn.** FOURTH PLANE. [**cf.** MENTAL PLANE, SEVENTH PLANE]

BUDDHISM—one of the great religions of the world; most predominant philosophy in the east; founded by Prince Siddhartha Gautama; divided into two branches 1. Buddha's brain; 2. Heart-doctrine; a metaphysical teaching that believes in life in the etheric world, the development of mankind's soul-mind, and that suffering is inseparable from existence.

BUDO—see MARTIAL ART; similar to jujitsuism; founded by Hikitsuchi.

BUFFALO POWER—(esoteric) (Native American) the buffalo is worshipped for its psychic energy; the buffalo acts as an etheric world guide, to bring psychic information to man, and to give him protection; psychic energy flows through the buffalo, similarly to man. [**cf.** ANPSI, PEACOCK]

BUG-A-BOOS—(Scotland, Highlands) see NATURE SPIRIT.

BUGABOO—(England) see NATURE SPIRIT.

BUGS—see NATURE SPIRIT.

BUILDING BLOCKS—(esoteric) atoms were given this name in very ancient times, with the belief that everything in the universe was comprised of atoms. [**cf.** MONAD, MICROCOSM, MACROCOSM]

BUILT-IN ALARM SYSTEM—(anpsi) an animal's sensitivity to changes in the earth's electromagnetic field, which tells it to prepare for the danger before it occurs; e.g., the ability to detect an impending earthquake, and to move to another area before it happens. [**cf.** SIMPLE CONSCIOUSNESS, ANIMAL PSYCHISM]

BUILT-IN DIRECTIONAL SENSE—an invisible mechanism in humans, that keeps them in tune with the radiations given off from the earth's electromagnetic field, and tells them which direction is north and south, without landmarks, and without looking in the sky for sun or moon placement; attributed to radiesthetic sense. (Inconcl.) [**cf.** RADIESTHESIA, RADIONICS]

BUKOR—(Voodoo) (West Africa, Haiti) see PSYCHIC. **Syn.** NECROMANCER.

BULL ROARER—(Africa, South Pacific, New Guinea) a whistle (carved from wood or rock) that is thrown into the air, where it lingers; etheric world intelligences use it to amplify their voices to communicate with earthlings, bringing psychic information. [**cf.** TRANCE VOICE, TRUMPET, INDEPENDENT VOICE]

BUMPING—(biofeedback training) a spasmodic or jerky sound, given off by the brain of the person hooked-up to the EEG instrument; a signal for the subject to change his or her thoughts and attitude; gives an indication that certain phases of one's life are causing one tension. [**cf.** RAMP FUNCTION, BIOLOGICAL FILTER, EXPECTANCY WAVE, SWISHING]

BUMPS—(phrenology) raised areas on the skull that have a definite meaning in interpreting one's character. [**cf.** BODY READING]

BUN FESTIVAL—(China) a celebration held in honor of the etheric world intelligences; they are presented with a sixty-foot mountain made of buns, many prayers, and lit joss sticks.

BUR—(Wynn Kent, England) an energy field of low intelligence that attaches itself to one's aura and influences one in a negative way; utilizes the law of "like attracts like"; also called **creature**; (do not confuse with a soul-mind haunting). [cf. ELE-MENTAL, THOUGHT-FORM]

BURIAL WITH FEET TO THE EAST—an ancient Christian custom to bury a dead person with his feet toward the east and his head toward the west; imitates the posture of prayer; corpse was placed thus in preparation for the resurrection when the dead will rise with their faces toward the east. [cf. DEATH SCIENCE]

BURIED LIFE—past experiences, in this life and in past incarnations, that are repressed in the subconscious mind; believed to be the cause of fears, anxieties, and neuroses, that have no other basis for their existence. [cf. BLOCKS, PSYCHIC PAIN, CASE-CRACKING, ENERGY BLOCK, MUSCLE TENSION PATTERNS]

BURMESE MEDITATION—a discipline without ritual, whereby one works by oneself until one works through one's own individuality to the universal whole, in similation during meditation; brings about a change in one's attitude. [cf. JUST SITTING, MUDRA, CAVE MEDITATION]

BURNING HANDPRINTS—an imprint of a hand of a dead person on a handkerchief, communion cloth, or in a book, etc., that was not put there by a human hand; it appears as if a red-hot hand burned the imprint; early studies show a theory: the person is in purgatory, and concerned about himself; and later theory: the person is emotionally tied to the earth, and desires to contact a loved one; this burning desire could be strong enough to transfer onto tangible material. (Inconcl.) [cf. PSYCHIC PHOTOGRAPHY, FIRES WITH BOUNDARIES, ELECTRIC GIRLS]

BURNING KARMA—to bring to fruition the results of past experiences, and be free from anxiety, anger, shame, and censuring. [cf. REINCARNATION, BLOCKS, RIPE KARMA]

BURSTS—(biofeedback training) waves, with similar lengths and forms, shown on the EEG readouts over a given time; this makes it possible to group the waves for further study. [cf. EEG, READOUTS, EMG]

BUTTERFLY—(esoteric) used frequently to represent man's soul-mind; the caterpillar must be "reborn," and become a butterfly, before it is finished; the human soul-mind must be reborn many times before it too becomes a finished human being. [cf. IMITATIVE MAGIC, ANPSI, SYMBOLISM]

BYELBOG AND CHERNOBOG—(Slavic) deities in the etheric world, who personify light and darkness, or good and evil; used together, as if both were part of the one. **Sim.** GOD and SATAN. [cf. POLARITY, LAW OF OPPOSITE Appendix 7]

BYO-KI—(Japan, means "sick ki") a congested acupressure point indicating the area of the illness. [cf. ACUPRESSURE, MERIDIAN LINES, REFLEXOLOGY]

CAAPI—(esoteric) (Native South American) a hallucinogenic agent (in liquid form) drunk by a medicine man before counseling his people, thus putting him in an altered state of consciousness making it easier to see visions and receive psychic impressions. [**cf.** BOTANE, MEDICINE MAN, FORCED PSI]

CABALA—(Hebrew) a Jewish doctrine telling the importance of humanity's role in God's universe; how each individual will unfold from within to the fullness of God; originated in the twelfth century in Spain and France, but now used universally to inform humanity about the angels and demons in the etheric world, and of their communications with mankind; see KABBALAH and QABALAH; also spelled **Cabbala, Kabala, Kabalah, Kabbala, Qabala, Quabalah, Quaballah,** and **Quabbalah.** [**cf.** DEUS ABSCONDITIUS, EN SOPH, TREE OF LIFE, SEFIROTH]

CABINET—(materialization seance) an area in a corner of the seance room which is enclosed with wood or heavy black drapes and blacked-out for the materialization session; medium needs the blacked-out corner so the ectoplasm will not be destroyed and needs the privacy because the ectoplasm emanates from the orifices of his or her body (eyes, ears, nose, mouth, genitals, and navel); medium wears loose-fitting clothing and stays quite immobile in a slouched position for the full session; cabinet also serves as a protection to the medium from outside disturbances, which could shock the medium and cause physical harm to the medium. [**cf.** ETHEREALIZATION, ECTOPLASM, PARTIAL MATERIALIZATION]

CADUCEUS OF MERCURY—(India) see CADUCEUS WINDING SYMBOL.

CADUCEUS WINDING SYMBOL—(Latin) a staff, or wand, with two snakes entwined around the staff (crossing it six times), then a pair of wings, and topped with a globe; the special winding represents the kundalini power, the Ida and Pengala winding up the spine, crossing at the six chakra points on the body; the globe represents the brain, and kundalini power takes the shape of the wings; used by those who had earned royal office; associated with the Greek god Hermes; used as a symbol for the Medical Corps of the United States Army; chiropractors use the symbol showing only one snake. **Syn.** CADUCEUS OF MERCURY. [**cf.** KUNDALINI POWER, IDA, PENGALA, WINGS, CHAKRAS]

CAIRN DRUIDS—(England) a culture of highly intelligent people, many of whom were genius-level; excellent psychics and with an understanding of universal laws that far surpassed that of individuals of today. [**cf.** HUMAN OMENS, PSYCHIC, SHAPE-CHANGING, DIMENSION-SHIFTING, CYCLES, NUMEROLOGY, ASTRAL PROJECTION]

CAKRAS—see CHAKRAS.

CALL—1. (laboratory) a specific guess given by the subject trying to psychically identify a target in an ESP test; a person's cognitive answer when being tested to identify turned-over cards. [**cf.** ESP, COGNITION] 2. (ancient) (mediumship) an expression to denote that an etheric world intelligence had spoken to one with psychic knowledge. Usage: "I had a call to go to Palestine; a man will meet me there, with further instructions." [**cf.** GUIDES CLAIRAUDIENCE] 3. (scrying) a message; perceived clairsentiently in the mental mind from the entity which is seen in a crystal ball. [**cf.** CRYSTAL BALL, MENTAL PSYCHISM, SCRYING] 4. (capitalized) (Native American) to receive shaman instructions in an unwilled initiation of good and bad experiences by the etheric world intelligences; begins with an unexpected ecstatic experience of continual visions and vivid dreams; this graduates into a loss of mundane consciousness which could last for days; during this loss of consciousness, the individual goes through physical and mental suffering and must heal his or her own body and mind; instructions for shamanship are also given in the loss of mundane consciousness state; occurs at a young adult age; when boy or girl awakens they can perform psychic healing and psychic skills for the tribe. [**cf.** HEREDITARY TRANSMISSION, INITIATORY SICKNESS, SHAMANSHIP]

CALL DOWN—(ceremonial magic) to petition or to invoke an etheric world intelligence to possess one's body, in part or in whole, in order to perform psychic acts to help persons who are in trouble or are ill. **Syn.** INVOCATION. [**cf.** EVOCATION, CEREMONIAL MAGIC]

CALL PHASE—(ufology) a special tone or sound with power to extend above the psychic background noise which reaches to intelligences in outer space and opens the door for communication. [cf. UFOLOGY Appendix 5, CLOSE ENCOUNTERS OF THE THIRD KIND, CONTACTEES]

CALL UP—(ceremonial magic) to draw forth inferior etheric world entities who are bothering an individual for the purpose of exorcism; magician teases the entities and entices them to enter his or her body; when in his or her body the magician can more easily dissipate their energy so they cannot bother anyone else. **Syn.** EVOCATION. [cf. CALL DOWN, INVOCATION, EXORCISM]

CALL UP SPIRITS—see CALL UP.

CALLED PERSON—an individual given psychic abilities (from the etheric world) to prophesy, heal, counsel, and guide. [cf. CALL, HIGH DREAM, PEAK EXPERIENCE]

CALM MEDIUM—one who serves as a vehicle for an etheric world intelligence without displaying the usual indications of an intelligence taking over; medium writes with a certain slowness and without body agitation; executed in a deep trance state. [cf. MEDIUMSHIP, GUIDE, TRANCE, SEMITRANCE]

CALM WAVES—(Ward and Thompson) artificial vibrations similar to a human being's positive thoughts; they are soothing, and cheerful but are made by a transmitter. (Inconcl.) [cf. BIOFEEDBACK TRAINING, EEG,. BRAIN WAVE TRAINING]

CALUNDRONIUS—(esoteric) a stone believed to have the vibratory rate that enhances psychic powers and meditative states for the owner. [cf. MINPSI, OVERALL CONSCIOUSNESS]

CAMBODIAN SPIRIT—see ASTRAL BODY.

CAMERON CONE—conoid shapes, regardless of size and material, generate a condensed field of energy in their center; this field is built from the vital life force in the air and vibrates faster than normal within the cone shape; being studied for its practicality to humans; used by witches for a hat and Indians for a teepee to enhance psychic energy, and by dunces to stimulate brain activity. (Inconcl.) [cf. FORMS-WITH-POWER, PYRAMIDOLOGY, CUBE]

CAMOUFLAGE—the physical body and the physical world that encompasses the soul-mind and give a vibrational frequency for the soul-mind to work with on its evolutionary path. **Sim.** ILLUSION. [cf. BODIES AND PLANES Appendix 5, SOUL-MIND EVOLUTION]

CANCER ELEMENTAL—(future science) belief that cancer is brought on by a lower elemental infesting

the etheric double and manifesting itself in the physical body. [cf. CURATIVE EDUCATION, THOUGHTS, ELEMENTAL]

CANDLE FLAME—(esoteric) 1. popular ancient and modern symbol used for purification; the flame burns up negative vibrations in the area; 2. flame is neutral and responds quickly to mind thoughts, taking and releasing energy; makes a good tool for psychic development, as a point of focus for mind energy to work and manipulate. [cf. MENTAL PSYCHISM, MEDITATION]

CANDLE LIGHT—(esoteric) see FOOLISH FIRE.

CANDOMBLE—(West Africa) an independent shrine where priests and priestesses go to communicate with etheric world entities; a sacred area where vibrations have been built up to make voice trance and other physical psychism easier, bringing faith and inspiration to the people. [cf. MEDIUMSHIP, VOICE TRANCE, ORACLE, DEPENDENT VOICE]

CANTERBURY TALES—famous literary work by medieval English poet, Geoffrey Chaucer; appears to have metaphysical and parapsychological levels of interpretation.

CANTRIP—(Scotland) see PSYCHIC ART.

CAPITAL P—abbr. for PSYCHIC PAIN; stored stress from painful experiences in childhood reasserts itself in adulthood in painful ways such as mental disorders and neuroses. [cf. PSYCHIC PAIN, PRIMAL THERAPY, BLOCKS]

CAPSTONE—(pyramidology) the apex of the Great Pyramid of Giza, occupying one-fifth of its whole, and made in as precise proportions as the bottom; acts as the chief corner stone (all other corners converge into it); some theorize it was made of a metallic alloy of gold combined with a number of other elements; other theories say it was crystalline in nature; its function was to act as an antenna, to absorb cosmic energy, and store it for vehicles in outer space; it acts as a tuning device for communication in a huge system, bringing outer space into a unified whole. (Inconcl.) [cf. PYRAMIDOLOGY, FORMS-WITH-POWER]

CAPTIVATION—see SPELL.

CAPTURING THE VISION—(Findhorn, Scotland) an inner desire to participate collectively in making the world a better place to live, so strong that one starts in the process immediately with one's whole being. [cf. PATH, RIGHT-HAND-PATH, NEW-AGE PSYCHOLOGY, PLANETARY WORKERS]

CAPUT AUREOLA—the radiance of magnetic rays around the heads of human beings who are in a higher evolutionary stage than the masses. **Syn.** NIMBUS. [cf. AURA]

CARD-BASKET—1. (precipitation) to allow an etheric world intelligence to intervene and write messages to members of a gathering without the use of the medium's body; file cards and colored pencils are placed in a basket before the seance or church service; at the end of the meeting, each card bears a personal message for those present; intelligence levitates the pencils swiftly and writes in words or pictures on the cards; intelligence uses the medium's ectoplasm while medium is in a semi-trance state. Usage: "I have card-basket." 2. a normal basket that is filled with file cards and colored pencils to be used for the process of precipitation during a church service or seance. [cf. PRECIPITATION, GUIDE, SLATE WRITING]

CARNAL MAN—a person whose mind is filled with mundane thoughts, e.g., greed, resentment, anxiety, jealousy, etc.; person is said to be operating from the lower three chakras. **Syn.** MATERIALISTIC MAN. [cf. SPIRITUAL, HUMAN BEING]

CARNATE ENTITY—a person in the physical body living in earth as opposed to an entity living in the etheric world (referred to as a discarnate entity). [cf. ETHERIC WORLD INTELLIGENCES, ETHERIC WORLD, MAKING-THE-TRANSITION]

CAROLE—a circle of dancers holding hands purposely to form a link with an intent to bring a oneness to humanity, and to raise each individual to a higher state of consciousness. [cf. CIRCLE, FORMS-WITH-POWER, MOVEMENT-FOR-ALTERED-CONSCIOUSNESS]

CARRY-ON-TALKING—(electronic voices) to receive a human-like voice on a tape cassette recorder with no physical sounds in the area; voice records itself electronically with no help from the owner of the recorder; voices come from outer space itself, other planets, and places foreign to our understanding. [cf. TAPED VOICE PHENOMENA, ELECTRONIC VOICES, TELEPHONE CALLS FROM THE DEAD]

CARRYING AN EVIL—(South Africa) a psychic who specializes in exorcism for the tribe; psychic calls down a guardian angel and allows the angel to work through his body in order to chase away or dissipate the evil demon who is working among the tribe. [cf. PSYCHIC, MAZENGE, GUARDIAN SPIRIT, MERCY BAND, EARTHBOUND ENTITIES]

CASECRACKING—discovering the subconscious thoughts that make negative conditions in one's life. [cf. BLOCKS, GRAPES, INNER-DIALOGUE, THOUGHT-FORMS, ELEMENTAL]

CASSETTE VOICE RECORDING—to receive a human-like voice electronically recorded on a tape cassette recorder with no physical sounds in the vicinity; psychic displays desire, genuine interest, and patience; tape recorder is placed by one's bed at night or in the center of a circle of persons meeting for this purpose; each time the tape is played back the voice or sounds are louder and clearer; voices can be from deceased friends or relatives of the psychic, from one's etheric world guides, or from an intelligent source somewhere in the universe or from another planet; see TAPED VOICE PHENOMENA.

CASTING A SPELL—to hold a person captive to the point that the victim experiences events and thoughts which they cannot account for; and yet feels that they are from his or her own personal effort; done by one of the following processes: 1. beaming energy out of the eyes: staring at the victim with intentional threat; the victim becomes fearful and transfixed, losing his or her resistance in anticipation that the speller will do something destructive; 2. beaming energy out of the eyes by using the eye-stare in the exact opposite manner: keeping the victim enthralled by the power of pleasing them, coming from deep within the eye-starer; delighting the victim to a high degree with tender loving ploy, making the victim easily held captive; 3. using special magic chants and songs that were written to weaken a person's will, and to allure the victim into an easily manipulated state of consciousness; this psychic skill can be used in reverse: to hold an individual captive for their protection, so they cannot be manipulated. **Syn.** FASCINATION, BEWITCHED, SPELLED. [cf. SPELLER, CEREMONIAL MAGIC, SPELL, CASTING A SPELL Appendix 2]

CASTING OF LOTS—(ancient) to divine by throwing multiple objects and interpreting the pattern of their fall to answer the question; used by government officials and by lay persons to make important decisions and to foretell the future; multiple objects used were stones, coins, beads, shells, bones, etc.; before the throw, psychic would pose a clear, concise question in his mind (verbally or silently); mind was kept unopinionated; the pattern formed by the landing of the multiple objects was studied for a correct answer to the question; theory: principle of acausal relationships; there is a synchronization of the nervous system and the earth's magnetism which unfolds in a meaningful answer; two events take place having no effect on one another and yet combine to give a meaningful answer. **Syn.** LOTS, DRAWING LOTS, LITHOMANCY. [**cf.** SORTES SANCTORUM, ASTRAGALOMANCY Appendix 6, RADIESTHESIA, SYNCHRONICITY]

CASTING OUT AN EVIL SPIRIT—to remove an etheric world entity who enters an earthling's body intermittently with evil intent, causing spasmodic seizures; magic rituals force the inferior entity out of the body and dissipate them; see EXORCISM. [**cf.** POSSESSION, OBSESSION]

CASTING RUNES—see CASTING OF LOTS.

CASTLES-IN-SPAIN—a slang expression for day-dreaming; see DAYDREAMING.

CASTOR—see ST. ELMO'S FIRE]

CAT—(biofeedback training) abbr. COMPUTER OF AVERAGE TRANSIENTS; an instrument that automatically averages all electrical emanations from the brain, under the electrodes of the EEG instrument, and gives a baseline which is then used for comparison for that biofeedback training session, and for others to come. [**cf.** BIO-STAT MONITOR, BIOFEEDBACK TRAINING, HASSLE-LOG]

CAT'S EYE—(esoteric) a mineral believed to be influenced by vibrations from the sun; has the vibrational frequency capable of bringing the wearer courage, loyalty, and leadership, implying the lower man is under control; used to symbolize the astrological sign of Leo. [**cf.** MINPSI, OVER-ALL CONSCIOUSNESS]

CATALEPSY—a state of suspension of vital functions in which it is impossible to move; sometimes spontaneous, sometimes brought on artificially by hypnosis, and dissipated by same; do not confuse with the normal hypnotic state; feeling of loss of contact with environment; a temporary loss of consciousness; vitality is suppressed and body is in a fixed position. [**cf.** TRANCE MANIFESTATION, PHYSICAL PSYCHISM]

CATALEPSY PHENOMENA—physical phenomena in which the psychic feat is conducted by the etheric world intelligence while he or she is using the medium's body; see CATALEPTIC TRANCE.

CATALEPTIC STAGE OF HYPNOSIS—see MEDIUM STATE OF HYPNOSIS.

CATALEPTIC TRANCE—(mediumship, seance) a state of body consciousness in which the medium's body is used by an etheric world intelligence to perform physical phenomena; etheric world intelligence synchronizes and assists the medium into a deep hypnotic state; medium's condition involves a suspension of normal sensation and partial suspension of vital functions; sometimes the medium's soul-mind slips out in an astral projection; body becomes very limp before the etheric world intelligence enters it; body could become rigid, or behave differently; intelligence uses the medium's eyes as a point of focus, their voice box to speak, and their arms and legs to execute the necessary phenomenon; when the allotted time is up, the intelligence slips out of the body and the medium slips back in; the body is completely limp during the switch; medium returns to normalcy but remembers nothing; session is always preplanned, willed, and desired-controlled; can be performed in semilight or a seance; this state is necessary for impersonation, etheric surgery, and some types of psychic surgery. [**cf.** TRANCE MANIFESTATIONS/MISCELLANEOUS, DESIRED-CONTROLLED]

CATALYSTIC HEALING—the fusing of two forces; the strong desire within the healer to be useful and the desire of the patient to be healed; when this energy is fused, it changes the chemistry of the patient so the body can more easily heal itself, and healer remains unaffected from the action. [**cf.** MENTAL HEALING, MAGNETIC HEALING, CLOAK OF INSULATION, CELL ACTIVITY]

CATAPSI—the generating of a "static" psychic energy in such a large quantity that it cancels out all psychism in the vicinity and blocks the psychic senses of others too; e.g., a skeptic sends out enough static to block the psychic senses of others. SPLODGING. [**cf.** ANTIPSI, ATMOSPHERE SHIELDING, BACKLASH]

CATHARSIS—1. (Greece) name of a sacred ritual used for purification of the mind and body; 2. (clinical) help experienced from talking out a problem with a therapist or psychiatrist. [**cf.**

CURATIVE EDUCATION, HOLISTIC HEALTH, CONDITIONED AVOIDANCE RESPONSE]

CAUCASIAN YOGA—the basic technique of breathing into the body the ga-llama, or prana, that is believed to be so necessary to the human nervous system and to one's very existence. [**cf.** PRANA, BREATH HEALING, BREATHING]

CAUL—(esoteric) a thin membrane that sometimes envelopes the head of a newborn infant, which indicates in some cultures that this child has psychic ability. **Syn.** VEIL. [**cf.** BIRTH SCIENCE Appendix 2]

CAUSAL ANALYSIS—(dreams) to integrate the unknown parts of one's personality with a dream so one can find the purpose of the dream. [**cf.** DREAMS Appendix 2, LATENT CONTENT, DREAM DIARY]

CAUSAL BODY—the higher mental body encompassing a human while one is in a physical body; from the "principles of seven bodies"; a vehicle of abstract thought in a vibration one cannot comprehend while alive; function of this body on its level of reality is to analyze the lives of the soul-mind as presented by the mental body, find the cause of the various happenings, and separate the karmic conditions; those which have been learned and experienced correctly become WISDOM and head upward, those which must be corrected are karmic liabilities which head downward for more earthly incarnations to be corrected; this abstract force field actually makes the physical form come alive. **Syn.** INTELLIGENT BODY. [**cf.** BODIES AND PLANES Appendix 5, KARMA]

CAUSAL PLANE—the upper area of the mental plane; a region of concrete thought where the soul-mind designs the patterns or blueprints of ideas, and plans for new incarnations; then sends it to the lower half to give it substance; depicted by fire; felt to have crystal mountains from which fiery flashes issue and there is a tremendous exchange of power, containing treasuries of sound, creative inspiration, and energy; believed that the archetypal patterns originate here. [**cf.** MENTAL PLANE, CAUSAL BODY]

CAUSATION—that which happens as a result of another action as opposed to synchronicity; for every action there is a reaction. [**cf.** SYNCHRONICITY, KARMA, RIPE KARMA, DELAYED KARMA]

CAVE MEDITATION—overindulgence in meditation; practicing meditation for its own sake, to escape one's worldly problems; to get into a level where one has no problems; a mental cop-out. Usage: "Charlie has gone into cave meditation again, and I won't see him for half the day"; (do not confuse with SEED MEDITATION). [**cf.** MEDITATION Appendix 5]

CAVE OF ENERGY—(China) a state of quiet when all shadows and echoes have disappeared, and one can feel returned to one's roots. **Syn.** SEED MEDITATION. [**cf.** MEDITATION Appendix 5, SILENCE, SELF-NONSELF, SOUND CURRENT]

CAVE PHENOMENON—(T. Kostrubala) a state of aesthetic arrest that happens to a runner after an hour of running; runner feels a mystical unity with his or her surroundings, an organic loosening of the unconscious, a feeling of pure sensation, emotion, and beauty, as opposed to intellectual thought; during or after running, the runner finds it easier to solve problems. [**cf.** MOVEMENT-FOR-ALTERED-CONSCIOUSNESS, TM, TAMING THE MIND, WHIRLING DERVISH, ZEN OF RUNNING]

CAZZAMALLI WAVES—sounds coming from the minds of people who were not talking; e.g., people were visualizing themselves in a violent scene; named after the Italian neurologist who could clairaudiently hear the sounds. [**cf.** VISUALIZATION, THOUGHT-FORMS, CLAIRAUDIENT]

CCAP—abbr. for CONDUCTIVITY OF THE CHANNELS OF ACUPUNCTURE POINTS; an instrument invented by Adamenko which graphs variations of the bioplasmic energy in the body, its intensity, and reaction to changing moods, with proximity to the acupuncture points. [**cf.** ACUPUNCTURE POINTS, MERIDIAN LINES]

CELESTIAL—1. pertaining to the sky; as sky, or as visible heaven; 2. (esoteric) pertaining to an invisible world of a very subtle force of energies and life intelligences that must be perceived clairvoyantly; an invisible heaven of many levels of energies. [**cf.** ETHERIC WORLD, UFOLOGY]

CELESTIAL BEINGS—intelligent entities in the etheric world that one can perceive psychically, where they communicate with him or her; does not mean our known ancestors who have made their transition. [**cf.** ETHERIC WORLD INTELLIGENCES, ANGELS, PROTECTOR, DOOR-KEEPER]

CELESTIAL CHORUSES—(esoteric) groups of angels working together in great numbers for mankind, healing the sick, bringing protection, or counsel; detected by sounds similar to a chant or hum; express their energies in tones without words. **Sim.** MUSIC OF THE SPHERES. [**cf.** CLAIRAUDIENCE, COSMIC MUSIC, AIR ELEMENT PSYCHIC SOUND]

CELESTIAL CITY—a state of consciousness one has grown and progressed into while in the physical body; one can project one's soul-mind mentally to this place in the etheric world at night, or during meditation; objective is to meet other advanced soul-minds to discuss progression of civilization. [**cf.** PATH SYMBOLISM, MENTAL PROJECTION, MASS KARMA]

CELESTIAL DESCENT—to astrally project to the density in the etheric world with the intent of helping the soul-minds inhabiting there to desire to ascend to the higher realms; a dangerous and rare feat; always preplanned. [**cf.** ASTRAL PROJECTION, ERLIK, SPIRITUALIZING THE ETHERIC WORLD]

CELESTIAL DEW—see ALCHEMICAL LIQUOR.

CELESTIAL EYES—to clairvoyantly perceive the akashic records because one has earned the privilege; psychic then predicts one's future life experiences or reveals information regarding one's past lives. **Syn.** EYES-OF-THE-TRUTH, DIVINE EYES. [**cf.** THIRD-EYE AREA, EVIL EYE, X-RAY CLAIRVOYANCE]

CELESTIAL GUARDIAN—see DOCTOR TEACHER.

CELESTIAL HEADACHE—(astral projection) a warning experienced when in a complete somatic dissociation state of consciousness, given as a signal by the astral body indicating it is time to snap back into the physical body. [**cf.** PERCUSSION, IN-THE-RANGE-OF-CORD ACTIVITY]

CELESTIAL HIERARCHY—see ANGEL HIERARCHY.

CELESTIAL LIGHT—a brilliance seen in the air over an area out in space, or encompassing a person or group of people; a beautiful elemental produced by the thoughts of a group of soul-minds living in earth, or in the etheric world; seen by those in a relaxed and high state of consciousness. **Sim.** MENTAL PSYCHIC LIGHTS. [**cf.** CLAIRVOYANT LIGHTS, GROUP ELEMENTAL]

CELESTIAL MAGIC—theory: planets are controlled by magnanimous, exalted etheric world intelligences, as are all other units in the solar system, and these planets and units have influence over persons and things in earth. [**cf.** STONE KINGDOM, NATURE KINGDOM, ASTROLOGY]

CELESTIAL PHENOMENA—ancient name given to any type of psychic events believed to have come from the atmosphere and without invitation; it comes as a guide, protection, or informative assistance for the earth being. [**cf.** PSYCHIC ART, CLAIRAUDIENCE, CLAIRVOYANCE, OMEN]

CELESTIAL RECORDERS—(Sanskrit) angel beings in the etheric world who are in charge of mechanically recording and analyzing events of earth, making the tablets of the astral light. [**cf.** MENTAL-REFLECTING-ETHER, KARMA]

CELESTIAL SEEING—to psychically tune into an earthling's akashic record by one who has earned the right to do this, for the purpose of helping the earthling find information about the past or future. [**cf.** PROPHECY, PATH, REINCARNATION, CELESTIAL EYES, CLAIRVOYANCE, MENTAL-REFLECTING-ETHER]

CELESTIAL SMITH—(Ireland) an etheric world entity whose function is to be in charge of craftsmanship. [**cf.** ANGEL HIERARCHY, MINOR DEVAS]

CELESTIAL SPIRITS—intelligences in the celestial terrain; each in a different level of consciousness and whose function is to oversee the ethereal bodies in that particular consciousness. [**cf.** ANGEL HIERARCHY, ANGEL EVOLUTION]

CELL—(esoteric) a group of atoms which aggregated together to form a unit within a living tissue; without relinquishing their own individuality consciousness, the atoms take on the unit consciousness; their free will is now to act as a unit, subject to the physical, psychical, and intellectual impulses of the parent organ and their own innate desire to evolve. [**cf.** ATOM, NOETIC, PSYCHIC HEALING]

CELL ACTIVITY—(esoteric) behavior of the molecular structure in a human tissue influenced by the intelligence of the conscious, subconscious, and superconscious minds; directs human structure psychically from one cell to another; cells have a structure, are alive, and react to stimuli, and organize their own classification; every body cell is duplicated and replaced every six months; behavior of the cell is governed by psychic force from "without, within" and soul-mind force "within, without"; cells thrive on association. (Inconcl.) [**cf.**

MENTAL HEALING, BODY CHEMISTRY, ATOMS, CURATIVE EDUCATION, THOUGHTS ARE THINGS]

CELL RHYTHM—the vibrational frequency of a group of atoms aggregated to perform a function in a living tissue; can be perceived clairaudiently, a part of the music of the spheres. [**cf.** COSMIC MUSIC, INTONING]

CELL SALTS—(healing) inorganic substance found in minute quantities in the body, which are essential in rebuilding cells, fighting disease, and keeping the body chemistry balanced; principal ingredients of activity in the body and necessary in certain quantities according to the signs of the Zodiac; used in preventive and alternative healing medicine. (Inconcl.) **Syn.** TISSUE SALTS, MINERAL SALTS. [**cf.** CELLULAR THERAPY, CURATIVE MEDICINE]

CELLAR GHOST—a nature spirit that helps with chores in the home; adopts one home in particular and becomes a part of the family. [**cf.** ELEMENTAL ESSENCE]

CELLULAR CONSCIOUSNESS—a group of atoms that make up a plant and have a memory-bank of all that has transpired through the life of that plant; this memory-bank will intermesh with the present outer stimuli and influence the plant's growth and movements. [**cf.** BOTANE, ATOM MEMORY BANK, SENSATION CONSCIOUSNESS]

CELLULAR MEMORY—(Seth) "tiny, complex unit of protoplasm, made up of a nucleus, a semifluid living matter, and a membrane"; comparable to man's brain, having memories of every type of vibrational frequency they have ever been active in; these units of protoplasm can die and be reborn from memory just as man builds his body in the womb. [**cf.** LAW OF CORRESPONDENCE Appendix 7, ATOMS, PERCEPTUAL DATA, ENERGY FIELDS]

CELLULAR PSYCHOKINESIS—(laboratory) to change the organs or tissue of man, animal, or plant, by willing the change through intense concentration; accomplished by talking aloud or visualizing the "end-result" desired; used for healing and promoting growth. **Syn.** VISUALIZATION. [**cf.** MENTAL HEALING, NATURE-PK, PSYCHOKINESIS]

CELLULAR THERAPY—to supply the blood with tissue cell salts in the treatment and prevention of disease; the body is a huge chemical plant and needs certain inorganic chemical constituents found in

tissue salts. [**cf.** CELL SALTS, BIOCHEMIC SYSTEM OF MEDICINE]

CENTAUR—a nature spirit that oversees the hunters of the forest to protect the forest wild life against unnecessary killing; depicted by the trunk and head of a man and the four legs of a horse.

CENTER—1. the level or state of consciousness in which the psychic feels comfortable that the psychic information coming in will be accurate. **Syn.** GOING-TO-LEVEL. 2. to pinpoint or intensify the focalization point to help one reach a deeper state of meditation. [**cf.** SEED MEDITATION]

CENTERING—1. coined by Delores Krieger; (magnetic healing) to be aware and in control of one's dynamics; to go to a level within one's self where one can feel that they can call upon their physical and psychodynamic energies on command; one calms their own nervous system, relaxes all tension, and goes deep within their consciousness until they attain a sense of inner equilibrium; these energies are then directed for healing another person. [**cf.** THERAPEUTIC TOUCH, UNRUFFLING] 2. (destructive-brainwashing cult) to focus all one's thoughts on the specific teachings of the organization, excluding all other thoughts and feelings, using the leader's definition of God as a focal point; this takes precedence over all activities, and all situations are acted upon in favor of the organization. [**cf.** DESTRUCTIVE-BRAINWASHING CULT, BRAINWASHING, AUTOMATON, BACKSLIDING]

CENTERS OF CONSCIOUSNESS—refers to the seven bodies of a human being that the soul-mind is in simultaneously; bodies are formed from substance made from the conscious and subconscious mind; a person is aware of only the body which their consciousness level supports at any given time. [**cf.** BODIES AND PLANES, AWARENESS, CONSCIOUSNESS, LAW OF CENTERING Appendix 7]

CENTRAL AXIS OF CREATION—(Yoga) the invisible kundalini connecting human beings to the universe and the visible spine holding them in place in earth. [**cf.** KUNDALINI Appendix 5, MEDULLA OBLONGATA, PINEAL GLAND, CHAKRAS]

CENTRAL NERVOUS SYSTEM—voluntary nervous system; includes the brain and the nerves that direct skeletal muscle activity; concerned with thought, voluntary action, and manipulation of the external environment through the limbs. **Syn.**

CEREBROSPINAL NERVOUS SYSTEM. [cf. SYMPA-THETIC NERVOUS SYSTEM]

CENTRAL PREMONITIONS REGISTRY—an organization interested in collecting and filing prophetic premonitions and prophetic dreams for examination by the general public, giving evidence of the information coming psychically before the fact; located in New York City. [cf. PROPHECY Appendix 2]

CENTRAL SUN—(capitalized) a universal storehouse of all potencies and energies necessary for the various solar systems; corresponds to the sun in our solar system necessary for our planets; all solar systems revolve around a Great Universal Sun. Syn. SPIRITUAL SUN. [cf. ROUND, LAW OF REPETITION Appendix 7]

CERBERUS—(Greece, Parthian religion) a nature spirit whose function is to guard the underworld; depicted by a three-headed dog. [cf. FETISH, EUMENIDES, IMP]

CERE—prefix; derived from the word *seed*.

CEREBRAL CLICK—(astral projection) noise heard in the brain, occuring simultaneously with the astral body entering into the physical body. Syn. CLICK-CLACK. [cf. ASTRAL PROJECTION Appendix 2, MYCLONIC JERK]

CEREBRAL CORTEX—(esoteric) the layer of gray matter that forms the outermost part of the brain; has its own size and rhythm on the printouts when individual is hooked-up to the EEG biofeedback instrument. [cf. EEG, ELECTRO-DERMAL RESPONSE, ELECTRIC FABRIC, BIOLOGIC FILTER]

CEREBRAL HEMISPHERES—the two separate functions of the brain; the left major hemisphere and the right minor hemisphere. (Inconcl.) Syn. SPLIT BRAIN. [cf. SPLIT BRAIN, CONSCIOUS MIND]

CEREBRAL LATERALIZATION—separation of the brain into two hemispheres, each having its own function, seeming to be separate from the other, yet connected and functioning as a whole. [cf. CEREBRAL HEMISPHERES, SPLIT BRAIN Appendix 5, BILATERAL ALPHA RHYTHMS, MIND-MIRROR]

CEREBRAL LOCALIZATION—separation of the human being senses and the attributing of a specific area in the brain to the function of each sense. [cf. HUMAN BEING, BRAIN, CEREBROSPINAL NERVOUS SYSTEM, UNILATERAL PATTERN, LUCID AWARENESS]

CEREBRAL MATERIAL—an ethereal substance emanating from the medium and sitters to be used for physical phenomena, similar to ectoplasm but the medium is in a conscious state instead of a trance state; e.g., used for automatic writing, percussion. [cf. TABLE-TIPPING, BASKET DRAWINGS]

CEREBRAL RECORDING—(esoteric) a temporary memory-bank within the brain, acting as a way-station for the akashic record; brain sorts information for filing in the akashic records and pinpoints needed information to surface from the akashic records. (Inconcl.) [cf. MENTAL-REFLECTING ETHER, CONSCIOUS MIND]

CEREBRAL VISION—see EYELESS SIGHT.

CEREBROSPINAL NERVOUS SYSTEM—(esoteric) a network of electrical wires in the human body covering all body areas; governed by the brain but under the direct control of the mental body (one of the seven bodies of a human being); brings information from outer stimuli via the five senses and decides the degree of stress that should be carried throughout the body; makes the human organism differ in personalities; evolved later than the sympathetic nervous system but much faster; positive-masculine in polarity for the body. [cf. POLARITY, MENTAL MIND, STRESS, SYMPATHETIC NERVOUS SYSTEM, MENTAL-CONSCIOUSNESS-SEED-ATOM]

CEREMONIAL MAGIC—(ancient, Middle Ages) psychic skills brought about by rituals, traditions, and formal methods; utilizes laws of mother nature instead of the soul-mind of the psychic; rituals consist of consecrations, symbolic motions, use of tangible objects, and cantations of words aimed at specific goals; ceremonies are directed to conjure up etheric world intelligences and demand their services according to the prescribed law of tradition; (Dion Fortune) "forms and symbols are psychological devices to enable the mind to get a grip on the intangible; it is exceedingly difficult to take off from sense consciousness without the use of a psychological device to act as a springboard; most people cannot rise to higher planes unaided"; used to prophesy, heal the sick, bring forth psychic information, bring prosperity, control the elements, dissipate a hex, perform exorcisms, and sometimes used for evil to create a hex. [cf. LAW OF SYMPATHETIC MAGIC and LAW OF MIMICRY Appendix 7, IMITATIVE MAGIC, WORDS-WITH-POWER, RITUALS]

CEREMONIAL MAGICIANS—those who understand the laws of the universe and use these laws in designed rituals to perform psychic art as a service or disservice to man. [cf. CEREMONIAL MAGIC, WITCH, WHITE MAGIC]

CEREMONIAL MAGNETISING—every instrument or object used in a ceremony (whether the clergy or performers know it or not) is being energized with the vibrations of the ceremony, the overall emotions, and concept of the ceremony held by each person, as they put and take from these instruments and objects; every thing associated with any form of ceremony or repetitious motion is invariably highly charged with magnetism and intimately linked with the force they have served. [cf. RITUAL MAGIC, PSYCHOMETRIZING, VIBRATIONS, BEAMED ENERGY, AMULETING]

CEREMONY—1. patterned activity repetitiously performed in an objective way having a subjective purpose; a ritual having a symbolic or metaphysical meaning; use of the same tools makes the intent stronger each time the ritual is performed because vibrations are imbedded within the tools; (a) group ceremonies: designed formality so those who participate will centralize their thoughts on purpose of ceremony, making the activity more effective; (b) individual ceremony: a ritual designed to manipulate and control the emotions of the psychic by changing the neural system and altering his state of consciousness; this promotes the accomplishment of the psychism; 2. (Native American, Chippewa) the highest way of giving back to earth mother so earth mother can replenish her supply for mankind; a necessary act for people to put balance back into the earth (earth gives people power); a time set aside preferably during the equinox, solaris, and under a full moon; each member of the tribe is required to participate, including children; rituals offer prayers of thanks to earth mother; 3. (Seth) habits, or actions which the establishment expects one to do. [cf. RITUALS, POWER-OF-THE-WORD, MAGIC CIRCLE, WINGED DISC, SWORD, CHANTING]

CEREMONY OF LITTLE DEATH—(Tibet) a forced method through the death process without physically dying; performed by the Abbots as an initiation to help them understand the reality of life. Sim. ASTRAL INITIATION. [cf. DEATH SCIENCE, HALL OF TRUTH, NEAR-DEATH EXPERIENCE, CHIKHAI BARDO, BARDOS, DEATH MIST]

CERENUNNOS—(Celtic) a nature spirit usually depicted with horns.

CEREOSCOPY—(ancient) divination process wherein wax is melted to a fine liquid, then poured on cold water; the wax congeals into tiny discs on the surface of the water; these tiny formations are used by the psychic to interpret psychic information for the querant. Syn. CEREOMANCY. [cf. MANCY suffix Appendix 6, DIVINATION]

CH'I—(China) an immutable principle in the air needed for life, taken in by breathing; circulates throughout the entire body making up the twelve meridian lines in the body; this vital force is found in the ethers divided into opposite but complimentary halves and appears in the body as positive and negative areas; see VITAL LIFE FORCE. Syn. TCH'I, QI, PRANA, L-FIELDS, BIOCOSMIC ENERGY. [cf. YIN AND YANG, BREATHING]

CHA-NO-YU—(Zen) special tea used in solemn rituals to help keep the meditator awake. Syn. ART OF TEA. [cf. MEDITATION, ZA-ZEN]

CHAC—(Mexico, Native American, Otomi) an etheric world intelligence in charge of rain. [cf. MAGNIFICENT DEVAS, DEVA, ANGEL HIERARCHY]

CHAIN OF BEING—(Plato, Aristotle) all things in the physical and etheric worlds are maintained by the one principle, God, projecting from the one main principle through the ranks of etheric world beings to physical beings. [cf. ANGEL HIERARCHY, HUMAN BEING KINGDOM, REINCARNATION]

CHAIN OF GLOBES—(esoteric) a planetary link of spherical bodies, consisting of the first seven planets; three are physical planets and four are ethereal, invisible planets; earth is the most dense of the lower manifestations in this chain. (Inconcl.) [cf. CYCLES, EARTH EVOLUTION]

CHAIN PERIOD—1. (C. W. Leadbeater) length of time required for the life wave to pass seven times around the seven globes in the Chain of Globes; 2. philosophy: all manifestations are cyclic in nature, having a rhythmic pattern of manifestation. [cf. CYCLES, GLOBES, LIFE WAVE]

CHAIR TEST—to prophesy, in a psychic development circle, regarding the person who will choose to sit in the chosen chair at the next meeting. [cf. CLAIRVOYANCE, CLAIRSENTIENCE, PROPHECY]

CHAKRA—(Sanskrit) a whirling vortex of concentrated etheric energy; perceived clairvoyantly as a colorful wheel or flower, with a hub in the center; invisibly attached along the spine, from the base to the top of the head, held in place by the crossing of the invisible Ida and Pengala; these crossings act as electric sockets into which a physical gland is plugged; chakras have counterparts in the astral body but are fed astrally and physically by the etheric double; chakras indraw the "spirit" from the air, distribute it to the physical gland in the body, where it transmutes into physical substance and flows throughout the bloodstream and nervous system; the older the soul-mind, the more "spirit" the chakra will assimilate; each chakra has its own rate of vibration, making a distinct difference in pattern and color; a human being functions from the lowest chakra for many incarnations until their behavior warrants the absorption of this energy into the next chakra; this continues until all the energy is absorbed into the crown chakra, after many incarnations and proper evolutionary growth; see each of the seven chakras below for details: 1. ROOT, MULDHARA; 2. SPLEEN (No Sanskrit term); 3. SOLAR PLEXUS, MANIPUR, SVADHIS-THANA; 4. HEART, ANAHAT; 5. THROAT, VISUDDA; 6. BROW, AJNA; 7. CROWN, SAHASRARA; sometimes known as psychic centers channeling a person's psychic energies. **Syn.** (Bible, Revelation) SEVEN STARS AND SEVEN CHURCHES. [**cf.** KUNDALINI, SUSHUMNA, IDA, PENGALA, SERPENT FIRE, SUPERCONSCIOUS MIND]

CHAKRA ANALYSIS—a human measurement of one's level of reality, psychological state, karmic debts and karmic assets. [**cf.** CHAKRA, GATEWAY TO THE HEART, CROWN CHAKRA]

CHAKRA STEM—invisible force running from the mouth or opening of the flower-like chakra to the spinal cord. [**cf.** VAGUS NERVE, THROAT CHAKRA]

CHAKRA SYSTEM—an invisible, interdimensional transducing system, running up and down the spine, being directed by man's thoughts; has seven concentrated centers of energy from the base of the spine to the crown of the head which convert cosmic energy into body energy, and vice versa; transcends the constraints of time and space; connects man to the universe making man and the universe all one system. [**cf.** SPLEEN CHAKRA, THROAT CHAKRA, INNER BOWL]

CHAKRAM—see CHAKRA.

CHALCEDONY—(esoteric) stone in the onyx family; put on earth with the forming of earth; influenced by Saturn; has properties to dissolve sadness by quickening the energy in the body;

prevents attack by evil spirits, helps induce abundance; black variety clears the voice. [**cf.** MINPSI, PRIMARY PERCEPTION, OVER-ALL CONSCIOUSNESS]

CHALCHIHUITLICUE—(Mexico) an angel in charge of spring rains, whirlwinds, and whirlpools in the water, for the Aztec Indians. [**cf.** AHURA MAZDAH, MAGNIFICENT DEVAS, NATURE SPIRITS]

CHALDEAN—(Mesopotamia, 600 B.C.) group with an understanding of cosmic knowledge beyond their time; so noted for psychic talent, mediumship ability, and astrological knowledge that the word came to mean a "psychic." Usage: "You are a Chaldean." **Syn.** PSYCHIC. [**cf.** PSYCHIC ART, MENTAL PSYCHISM, ASTROLOGY]

CHALDEAN ORACLES—sacred books of classical antiquity containing wisdom of the cosmos, mysteries, and astrology; basis for theurgy (magic) religion. [**cf.** CHALDEAN, ORACLE, PATH]

CHALICE—an elaborate cup or vase used only for rituals or ceremonies; made of a material suitable for the purpose of the ritual; frequently engraved with special words contributing to the aim of the ritual. [**cf.** WORDS-WITH-POWER, FORMS-WITH-POWER, RITUAL MAGIC]

CHAMBER OF THE HEART—(India) refers to a human being functioning from the heart chakra. [**cf.** KUNDALINI, CHAKRAS]

CHANCE—(psi tasks) the most likely score if only chance is involved; to be correct approximately one-fifth of the time in any game or experiment that involves five variables is the normal percentage, having nothing to do with ESP; a significant number of answers over one-fifth is considered psi energy; one-fifth and under correct answers is considered chance. [**cf.** ZENER CARDS, ESP, PSI-HIT]

CHANCE AVERAGE—(laboratory) one-fifth or fewer correct answers in a five-variable experiment when one speculates or guesses the answers; used as a basis to judge when ESP is coming through in ESP experiments. [**cf.** ESP, PSI-TASKS, ERROR PHENOMENON]

CHANCE EXPECTATION—(Rhine laboratory) the most likely score figured in a guessing experiment, not concerned with ESP; determined from the mathematics of probability. [**cf.** DOWN THROUGH, VARIANCE, BACKWARD CAUSATION]

CHANCE LEVEL—(clinical) the average for the goal to be reached in the law of averages or the law of chance; the amount of guesses out of the number of tries that could be expected without using ESP; needed as a guide to know whether one was tuned into the psychic realm during the experiment. [cf. ESP, DECLINE EFFECT]

CHANG TANG HIGHLANDS—(Tibet) a secluded, difficult-to-reach area having drastic changes in climate and life growth inhabited by subhuman creatures that are felt to be throwbacks of the human race who refuse to try to attain a higher status. [cf. PATH SYMBOLISM, YETIES, DIMENSION-SHIFTING]

CHANGE EFFECT—a temporary drop in scoring level, associated with a change of environmental conditions during an experiment, or from experiment to experiment. [cf. ESP, PSI-TASK, MENTAL PSYCHIC PROCESS]

CHANGELING—a nature spirit found in the baby bed instead of the baby; exchanged by a fairie; child appears stupid, ugly, and strange-looking. [cf. ELEMENTAL ESSENCE, NATURE SPIRIT KINGDOM]

CHANGING LINES—(I Ching) a throw of three tails or three heads which makes a line that is used in the first hexagram passage and then is reversed in the second hexagram passage; the line changes and brings about a new hexagram. **Syn.** MOVING LINES. [cf. CASTING OF LOTS, SYNCHRONICITY, LOTS]

CHANGING THE SKIN—(West Indies) see ASTRAL PROJECTION.

CHANGING WOMAN—(Native American, Navaho) respected as a holy person; has psychic ability to summon etheric world angels in charge of nature to help the people when in need of rain, wind, and other natural events necessary for their existence. **Syn.** PSYCHIC Appendix 3. [cf. ATMOSPHERE CONTROL Appendix 2]

CHANNEL—a person who allows his body and mind to be used as a mechanism for the etheric world intelligences to bring psychic information or healing energy to others; comes through in physical and mental psychic skills, while the person is in a deep or semi-trance state; used in inspirational speaking, writing, psychic surgery, etc. **Syn.** PSYCHIC. [cf. CHANNELING]

CHANNELING—to allow an etheric world intelligence to enter one's mind and impress thoughts upon the consciousness to be spoken aloud, using

one's own voice; medium's body is relaxed and mind is uncluttered and free of former concepts and opinions; awareness is heightened and medium senses another presence operating through him or her but does not sense the significance of the material until afterward; the knowledge brought through is beyond normal comprehension of the medium and must be studied to be understood; currently becoming very popular. [cf. GUIDE, MEDIUMSHIP, INSPIRATIONAL THOUGHT]

CHANOYU—see CHA-NO-YU.

CHANTING—an intoning of a chosen sound to accomplish a definite purpose; 1. sound is repetitive in rhythm, uttered in monotone, and varying in intensity and length of time; performed alone or in a group; 2. a spiritual practice of the highest order leading to an inner sound current resulting in a higher state of consciousness; enhances the process of meditation, healing disease, harmony among persons, or conjuring up etheric world intelligences for psychic information and psychic phenomena; 3. sensations of heat are felt within the body; activates the kundalini to rise in the spine; 4. chanting increases the coherence and harmony in brainwave patterns; nerve cells are recruited into rhythm until all regions of the brain seem to be throbbing as if choreographed and orchestrated; the two brain hemispheres become synchronized through entrainment; brainwave activity in older, deeper brain structures may also show an expected synchronicity with the new cortex; 5. prolonged chanting: the mind dissolves into the liquid current of energy and becomes purified for the altered state; 6. (Native American, Chippewa) chanting brings life energy down from the sky and up from the earth into one's being; runs through the chakras; gives energy back to the earth mother from the dancers and chanters. [cf. SOUNDS-WITH-POWER, PSYCHIC HEALING, OHM]

CHAOS—(Greece) creation of perfectness consisting of indestructible, intelligent, energetic atoms (and smaller particles) not having order, as mankind knows order; essence of all things made in the universes; mish-mash of the original principles of humanity; the formless void of primordial matter; the essence of all things made; some call it chaos, others call it perfectness as mankind knows no other. [cf. TOTALITY, DIVINE]

CHARACTER—(esoteric) mannerisms, habits, lifestyle, action, and reactions to stimuli of environmental stresses; these traits of action are always based on one's ethical standard; one's ethical standard is based on one's belief system; one's belief system is based on all the experiences one encountered and his attitude toward the experiences in the sum total of incarnations; objective is to purify one's character each incarnation; some theorize that this character will not be lost when one blends into Totality. **Syn.** INDIVIDUALITY. [**cf.** HUMAN BEING, SOUL-MIND EVOLUTION]

CHARACTER ARMOR—(Wilhelm Reich) life's experiences which write themselves into the muscles, organs, and tissues of the body; these experiences influence man's or woman's bodily reactions, as characteristics and health, solidifying these reactions when things of like nature occur. **Syn.** BODY ARMOR. [**cf.** BLOCKS, EMOTIONS, STRESS]

CHARGE—1. abbr. for electrical charge; quantity of electricity upon an object noting an excess or deficiency of electrons; (human) pertains to the emotional electricity in the acupuncture points that are working in excess, or working deficiently, causing unwanted physical or mental behavior. [**cf.** BLOCKS Appendix 5] 2. (esoteric) (magnetic healing) an electric tingle or shock as it emanates from the hand of the healer in magnetic healing; hand comes in direct contact with or is a little above the body to receive this feeling; brought about by intensified thought and the desire to help another, which builds in the healer's mind and is directed out through the palms of the hands; sometimes felt by both healer and healee; if not felt by healee, heelee is not psychic or is not ready to be healed, but this does not mean the healing energy was not emanated. [**cf.** PSYCHIC HEALING, MAGNETIC HEALING, BEAMED ENERGY, THERAPEUTIC TOUCH]

CHARGED GLOBULE—a very tiny sphere containing vitality from the brilliance of the sunshine, making a subatomic element, capable of being absorbed by a living creature. [**cf.** LAW OF THOUGHT Appendix 7, ENERGY, VIBRATIONS]

CHARGING—(botane) to talk to a new plant when first put in a room, welcoming it, and treating it as a new pet until it begins to respond; plants work with human emotions and feel emotions themselves. [**cf.** BOTANE, PRIMARY PERCEPTION]

CHARIOT—(Jewish) a soul flight through the celestial spheres until the soul has an ecstatic vision of divine splendor of a tremendous, numinous light; technique learned by an "adept" in mystic school as their initiation; sometimes called RIDING THE CHARIOT TO THE EXALTED THRONE. [**cf.** EXALTED THRONE, MYSTICISM, MENTAL PROJECTION]

CHARIOT OF THE SOUL—(Cornelius Agrippa) one of the highest bodies of the seven bodies found in humans; represents perfectness in its proper portions. **Syn.** MONAD. [**cf.** TOTALITY, MACROCOSM, MICROCOSM]

CHARISMA—(Greek, "gift," giving) an inborn quality of spiritual power and leadership magnetism that draws masses to one; includes subtle, pleasant, and influential characteristics; persons who have charisma usually preach the gospel to large gatherings and sometimes heal at these gatherings; this type of personality easily hypnotizes his congregation without them knowing it for the length of time of the gathering; leader emanates psychic energy and magnetism and refers to it as the Holy Spirit; many persons who have charisma use this quality to serve mankind and others use it to serve their personal needs. [**cf.** CHARISMS, CHARISMATIC MOVEMENT]

CHARISMATIC—Greek *charismata,* "gifts of grace") pertains to the instantaneous transference of beneficial condensed energy to a desirous lay person by a religious leader; (energy is from Totality and not from the leader); referred to as gifts of the Holy Spirit; executed in LAYING-ON-OF-HANDS, PROPHECY, TALKING-IN-TONGUES, and SLAYING-IN-THE-SPIRIT. [**cf.** HOLY SPIRIT, MAGNETIC HEALING]

CHARISMATIC HEALER—one whose ultimate essence is a magnetic, pleasant personality; healer is capable of influencing many types of individuals through their religious preaching, their ploy, and the angelic forces which work through them; healer leads a special style of charismatic meeting in which the congregation's expectations are focused on the healings to take place; this plus the emotional state the members of the congregation are in, from the preplanned meeting, makes them open and receptive to the tremendous flow of healing energy emanated from the leader; at the end of the meeting, healer gently touches the forehead of the individual and many are instantaneously healed; healing energy is named the Holy Spirit. [**cf.** SLAYING-IN-THE-SPIRIT]

CHARISMATIC HYMN—a chant or song composed in a special vibrational frequency so that its tone and rhythm stir the emotions of each member of the gathering; music is played extremely loud and the words are repetitious; puts congregation in an altered-state-of-consciousness and encourages one to talk-in-tongues and to rise up and give prophecy. [cf. RAISE THE VIBRATIONS, MASS MUSIC]

CHARISMATIC MOVEMENT—(current) laymen gathering together on a weeknight in the church to help develop the Holy Spirit among themselves; use special songs and instruments that make a peppy atmosphere conducive to outbursts of talking-in-tongues, prophecy, and beaming healing energy (similar to LAYING-ON-OF-HANDS); a revival of the Holy Spirit groups. [cf. PSYCHIC ENERGY, GLOSSOLALIA, RAISE THE VIBRATIONS]

CHARISMATIC RENEWAL—an emotional inner feeling that, in a profound way, God touched one, releasing the power of the Holy Spirit in one's life; an emotion that fills one's spiritual hunger; a personal encounter with God; similar to "being born again." **Syn.** EMOTIONAL HIGH, HYPNOTIC ECSTASY. [cf. MASS ELEMENTAL, EMOTIONAL PSI]

CHARISMS—(Catholicism, "gifts of the Spirit") TALKING-IN-TONGUES, PROPHECY, and the LAYING-ON-OF-HANDS; some add SLAYING-IN-THE-SPIRIT; others add any kind of psychic skill. (Inconcl.) [cf. MENTAL PSYCHISM, PHYSICAL PSYCHISM]

CHARM—1. to psychically act upon a living entity, human, animal, or plant, using a compelling magical force with an intent to change its course of action; (a) (plants, animals) to use rhythmic chants, songs, or music (that are in a key for absorption by the plant or animal) and a loving eye-stare, until the entity is under the psychic influence of the magician; entity is kept for a set time to be manipulated by the magician or to stay lifeless. **Syn.** ENCHANT. (b) (human) to attract one's self to or to allure one's own desires upon an individual by a talisman, pleasing, and rhythmic chant or song, magically composed verse, or by casting a spell using the eye stare; these put the individual in a transfixed state of awareness; then the charmer promises something emotionally pleasurable and delightful from the depths of his or her being; eventually the victim is enticed and in a state for easy manipulation and influential control for a set time; victim is not aware that his or her actions are not performed under their own volition. **Syn.** SPELL. 2. (Latin *carmen*, "song") a song, verse

(magical formula), or chant, composed for magical purposes; it stirs or disrupts the consciousness for its intended purposes; 3. to use a song, chant, or verse because of its ethereal qualities to raise the vibrations in order to contact etheric world intelligences for psychic information or physical phenomena. **Sim.** INVOCATION. 4. something worn for its psychical value; a trinket that has been infused with psychical energy with specific intent on how and when this energy will be used. **Sim.** TALISMAN. [cf. ON-THE-SPOT-HYPNOSIS, CASTING A SPELL]

CHARM-BOUND—see SPELLED.

CHARM-STRUCK—to be under the influence of another's wishes; victim has a new pattern of actions and personality behaviorisms, but he or she is unaware that these new actions are not of their own volition; one does not stay under the influence of another for a great length of time because it is very tiring and time-consuming for the charmer. **Syn.** SPELL-BOUND. [cf. SPELL Appendix 4]

CHARMER—a magician or psychic who has the ability and understanding of how to cast a spell or to charm another person, animal, or plant; spells are used for good or evil. **Syn.** SPELLER. [cf. TRANSFIX]

CHARMING—1. energizing a talisman; to impregnate an article or object with psychic energy with the intent that it will bring good fortune to the owner; frequently performed by a priest in a special ritual. [cf. TALISMAN, AMULET ENERGIZING, RITUAL, ENERGY] 2. exercising psychic energy to change the movement or action of a living organism, including humans, for a set length of time; an object that has been energized with cantations, chanting, rituals, etc., can be used. **Syn.** CASTING A SPELL. [cf. IMITATIVE MAGIC, ACTIVE RITUAL, SPELL]

CHATERSON COILS—man-made device that generates energy as a result of the special coiling of the wires which is patterned after the caduceus. [cf. FORMS-WITH-POWER]

CHATTERBOX ORGAN—(biofeedback training) see SKIN TALK.

CHATUR MAHARAJAS—(Hinduism) the four highly advanced intelligences who rule over earth's solar system, in charge of the four elements, fire, earth, air, and water, with their indwelling nature spirits to help them. (Hindu names: Dhritarashtra, Virudhaka, Virupaksha, Vaishravana.) **Syn.** RE-

107

GENTS OF THE EARTH, ANGELS OF THE FOUR CARDINAL POINTS. [cf. ANGEL EVOLUTION, MAGNIFICENT DEVA]

CHAYOTH—(Hebrew) an animal considered holy, sacred, and in psychic rapport with man, and treated as such. [cf. ANPSI]

CHECK—procedure used in TM that tells the meditator if he is meditating correctly. [cf. MEDITATION, ZAZEN]

CHECKER—1. (meditation) a person who is trained to help the meditator determine if he is meditating correctly; 2. (laboratory) a person who matches targets and responses in a psi experiment to determine the score. [cf. MEDITATION, CHANCE RESPONSE, CHECKING, DETACHMENT]

CHECKING—a set, systematic procedure of asking questions to be answered by the meditator to indicate where re-instruction is needed. [cf. QUIET ATTENTIVENESS, PROCESS MEDITATION]

CHEIROGNOMY—see CHIROGNOMY.

CHELA—(India, Tibet) 1. a disciple or person serving a teacher or a philosophy, and desirous of instructions from a teacher; 2. boy pupil studying to become a priest; plural **chelas**. [cf. LAW OF THE PATH Appendix 7]

CHEMICAL AURA—one of the seven electromagnetic energy fields surrounding a human, making up the entire human aura. [cf. SOUL-MIND, AURA, KIRLIAN EFFECT]

CHEMICAL ETHER—the third level of vibrational frequencies in the atmosphere evolved from light ether; indraws liquid, interlocks with cold, and contracts giving form to objects in the world; produces sound to the physical ear and takes an active part in chemical processes of all kinds. **Syn.** SOUND ETHER, NUMBER ETHER. [cf. VIBRATIONS, ETHERIC WORLD]

CHEMICAL MARRIAGE—(alchemy) to develop dualities of the mind; to use the right and left hemispheres simultaneously to achieve harmony, balance, and peace of mind. [cf. SPLIT BRAIN, ALCHEMY]

CHEMICAL PHENOMENA—peculiar activity in a seance that defies normal laws of physics; attributed to chemical reactions of the medium, sitters, and etheric world intelligences; e.g., lights moving around, cold spots appearing for no logical reason, ozone smells occuring, and phosphorus fires seen in the dark. [cf. SEANCE, BLACKED-OUT, PHYSICAL MANIFESTATIONS/MISCELLANEOUS]

CHEMICOGRAPH—a picture taken without a camera; the use of film to photograph a picture as if a camera were used; etheric world intelligences direct the process for the medium. [cf. PSYCHIC PHOTOGRAPHY, DELAYED PHOTO IMPRESSION PHENOMENA, SKOTOGRAPH]

CHEMILUMINESCENT AND ELECTRO-PHOTO-GRAPHIC TECHNIQUES—term used by United States government regarding the study of auras using high-voltage cameras similar to Kirlian cameras. [cf. KIRLIAN EFFECT Appendix 5, ETHERIC DOUBLE]

CHEMIPHYSICAL—refers to the physical chemistry of the body.

CHERNOBOG AND BYELBOG—(Slavic) deities in the etheric world personifying darkness and light, symbolizing evil and good; used together as if both were a part of the one; compares to God and Satan. [cf. POLARITY Appendix 5, YIN AND YANG]

CHERUB—(Greece, Hebrew) a member of the second order of etheric world angels, known for their knowledge and help in carrying out the Divine plan; represented by a beautiful, innocent-looking chubby face or chubby whole body, with wings at the shoulders; sometimes depicted with two or more faces; frequently mentioned in the Bible; delighted to intercede between man and God. [cf. ANGELHOOD, Angels of The Four Cardinal Points]

CHERUBIM AND SERAPHIM MOVEMENT—(West Africa) a ceremony of hymns, drums, and dancing to raise the vibrations in a church service until psychics in the congregation go into an altered state of consciousness and bring forth information from etheric world intelligences to inspire, teach, and protect their people. [cf. TEMPLE DANCERS, MERCY GROUND, WATCH SERVICES]

CHHAYA—(Sanskrit) 1. an etheric world image resembling a human when perceived clairvoyantly. **Syn.** ASTRAL BODY. 2. an intelligent pattern coming to planet earth in the time of the moon chain; mankind was formed from this pattern, beginning the ancestral race. **Syn.** SHADE, SHADOW, LUNAR PITRIS. [cf. BODIES AND PLANES Appendix 5]

CHHOS-NYID BAR-DO—(Tibet) to reach a state in which one experiences Reality and realizes it; occurs during meditation. [**cf.** ESSENCE OF REST, EQUALIZING WISDOM]

CHI—see CH'I.

CHIEF DEITIES—thought-forms in the etheric world that one gives a personal name or character when perceived clairvoyantly; attributed to coming collectively from the mass-mind of mankind;, i.e., the collective unconscious; personified thought-forms of Jesus, Buddha, or monks made by the masses in similar shapes with similar features, are held together and float around due to the emotion of the masses from which they are built. [**cf.** COLLECTIVE UNCONSCIOUS, ELEMENTALS, THOUGHT-FORMS]

CHIKAHAI BARDO—(Tibet) the first period of the death process, an unrecognizable transcendental state in which one perceives tiny karmic pictures of a past incarnation; if aware of the purpose of this, the one making the transition attempts to dissolve these pictures into the clear light for purification. [**cf.** FIRST STAGE OF CHIKHAI BARDO, SECOND STAGE OF CHIKHAI BARDO]

CHILD FROM THE EGG—(Gnostic) the creator of the universe.

CHILDREN OF THE EAST—(ancient Egypt) two root races, Caudoic and Avidic Children, who live to feed lust and the ego. [**cf.** ROOT RACE, CHILDREN OF THE WEST]

CHILDREN OF THE FIRE MIST—(Theosophy) entities coming from Venus to guide the process of evolution for planet earth. [**cf.** WHITE BROTHERHOOD, BODILESS DEVAS]

CHILDREN OF THE WEST—(ancient Egypt) two root races, Godoic and Zodoic Children; the race of Egyptians; emphasized love and the will. [**cf.** CHILDREN OF THE EAST, ROOT RACE]

CHINESE MASSAGE—(China) a method of releasing muscle tension, thus breaking up the blocks in the body; to use the fingers and fists, in a special technique, along the meridian lines and acupuncture points. **Syn.** TUI-NA. [**cf.** ACUPUNCTURE POINTS, BLOCKS, MERIDIAN LINES]

CHIROGNOMY—science of the shape and formation of the hand, fingers, thumb, nails, and texture of the skin; correlated to astrological signs; determines character, intelligence, emotional tendencies,

and general disposition as well as kinds of situations one will draw into one's life on earth; also spelled **cheirognomy**. [**cf.** BODY READING Appendix 5, MOUNTS, SET HIS SEAL]

CHIROGNOMY GRAPH—a chart or rough graph of one's character, intelligence, general disposition, and expectations for one's future; determined by the lines, formation, and mounts on the hand, thumb, fingers, and nails; correlates with the astrological signs. [**cf.** CHIROGNOMIST, PALMISTRY, MIRRORS OF DESTINY, SET HIS SEAL]

CHIROGNOSY—(*chiro,* "hand"; *gnosy,* "knowledge") study of formation, structure, texture, and lines of the hand in relation to one's experiences and personality in this incarnation; sometimes means both chirognomy and chiromancy, bringing forth both scientific and psychic information. **Syn.** HAND-ANALYSIS. [**cf.** BODY READING Appendix 5]

CHIROGNOMIST—one qualified to make a chirognomy chart, which deals with the study of the hand; correlated with astrology; see CHIROGNOMY; (do not confuse with CHIROMANT). [**cf.** CHIROSOPHY, BODY READING Appendix 5]

CHIROPRACTIC—(The Council on Chiropractic Education) the science which concerns itself with the relationship between structure, primarily the spine, and function, primarily the NERVOUS SYSTEM, of the human body as that relationship may affect the restoration and preservation of health.

CHIROPRACTIC ADJUSTMENT—(esoteric) the alignment of the physical body's spinal cord and mental body's kundalini, with concentration on the neck area; the medulla oblongata and main (invisible) ethereal organs, and (visible) physical organs meet or cross in the neck area; this alignment allows the body to normalize so any malfunctions can heal themselves. [**cf.** MENTAL BODY, KUNDALINI, CADUCEUS WINDING SYMBOL]

CHIROSOPHIST—a psychic who studies the science of the hand; uses both this scientific information and psychic information to determine the future and characteristics of the person whose hand is being analyzed; a hand analysis counselor. [**cf.** CHIROGNOSY]

CHIROSOPHY—(Greek *chiro,* "hand") to receive information regarding a person by analyzing their hand; includes both types of palmists: chiromancy, information by psychic means, and chirognomy, information by formal scientific means. **Syn.** PALM-ISTRY, HAND-ANALYSIS. [**cf.** IRIS PHOTOGRAPHY, HAIR ANALYSIS]

CHIT—1. (Brahmanism) pure thought of the Absolute; 2. (Sanskrit) an ultimate, pure, abstract consciousness. [**cf.** LAW OF MICRO/MACROCOSM Appendix 7]

CHITRINI—(Yoga) one of the fine invisible channels made of ethereal substance and which runs up the kundalini; vital to man's physical functioning. [**cf.** KUNDALINI, VAJRINI, SUSHUMNA, CADUCEUS WINDING SYMBOL]

CHITTA—(Sanskrit) conscious mind; brain; carnal mind of man which one struggles to control. **Syn.** MENTAL MIND, BRAIN. [**cf.** SUBCONSCIOUS MIND, UNIVERSAL MIND]

CHOLINERGIA—see MENTAL TELEPATHY.

CHONS—(ancient Egypt) a celestial deity known as "The Lord of Time"; the moon god who has counted the years of kings and men. [**cf.** ANGEL-OLOGY Appendix 5, TIME]

CHONYID BARDO—(Tibet) the third state of the death process; to psychically perceive "real reality" wherein one views the karmic illusions of one's previous thoughts and events of one's past incarnations and then views the karmic leftovers of previous lives; one making the transition should attempt to dissipate these karmic illusions as much as possible, before going further into the etheric world. [**cf.** DEATH SCIENCE, THOUGHT-FORMS, DENSITY]

CHRISM OIL—(Eastern) an invisible, mysterious, gaseous fluid filtering with the physical magnetic fluid that travels throughout each nerve-ending in the body, carrying the vital life force from the air; starts at the kanda, traveling up the kundalini to the medulla oblongata, branching off in the nerves; regulated by the subconscious and conscious minds, having nothing to do with food and drink; called the brain dews when it enters the body and travels downward; (do not confuse with the SUSHUMNA which stays in the kundalini). [**cf.** BRAIN DEWS, MAGNETIC FLUID, SYMPATHETIC NERVOUS SYSTEM]

CHRIST—(Greek *Kristos,* "anointed") (Hebrew *Messiah*) the word *Christ* per se does not refer to any particular person; every person earning the right to become anointed is christed; after being anointed, *Christ* is used as his or her title; the Logos of Infinities. [**cf.** CHRISTED]

CHRIST CONSCIOUSNESS—see COSMIC CONSCIOUSNESS.

CHRIST WITHIN—an invisible seed within a human containing the perfectness of Totality; involuted down from Totality or God, to grow and develop mankind back to a perfect state through evolution upward; a Divine spark of perfectness that motivates one to do better each day. **Syn.** MONAD. [**cf.** EVOLUTION, INVOLUTION, MONAD]

CHRISTAMORPHIC—the combination of Christian beliefs, inner consciousness, and psychic art.

CHRISTED—an earned rank by one who has learned all the lessons there are to learn; the rank of one whose higher principles have reached nirvana and abides as close to Totality as possible without becoming Totality; to earn the highest rank of human and angel beings by righteous thinking and acting; to acquire pure knowledge by many incarnations in earth and other planets until the soul-mind has become purified. [**cf.** ANGEL HIERARCHY, PERFECTNESS, BUDDHA, CROWN OF GLORY]

CHRISTIAN MYSTIC—one who follows the teaching of Jesus Christ, who studies the Bible for its psychical scripts, soul-mind growth information, and metaphysical interpretations, rather than the literal meaning; one who follows the Christ teachings and is still in rapport with Eastern sects; one whose inner life is much more important than their outer life; one who practices psychic skills and psychic healing to grow spiritually. [**cf.** PSYCHIC, HEALING PRACTITIONER]

CHRISTIAN PRAYER—generalized classification not attributed to any one sect: 1. vocal prayer, adorations of God, thanksgiving, penitence, petition; 2. mental prayer, intellectual pondering, affective prayer; 3. contemplative prayer, prayer of loving regard, prayer of faith.

CHRISTIAN SPIRITISTS—mediums whose main goal is to help the progression of the planet and society, and then to help themselves grow in understanding and in deeds and acts using one's mediumship as a tool to help this progression. [**cf.** CHRISTIAN MYSTIC]

CHRISTIANITY—a religion of beliefs and practices that claims to come from the teaching of Jesus; hundreds of variations of professed ways to worship Jesus, all important to the person who feels their Bible interpretation is correct.

CHRISTOS—(Greek *Christed,* "anointed") an initiation through the secret doctrines to help one operate from their Higher Self; the highest rank the human being can earn through earthly incarnations of righteous living and thinking; those who have gone through this mystery rite are high on the hierarchy of evolution; few choose to incarnate, but those who do will be serving as messiahs and teachers. [**cf.** CHRIST WITHIN, FIFTH PLANE]

CHROMA—a measure of the "purity" and "saturation" or intensity of a color; the scale runs from 000 for the achromatics to 100 for the spectrum colors. Usage: "White has more value than black; neither has any purity." [**cf.** CHROMOTHERAPY, COLOR]

CHROMATOGRAM—a picture showing a colored pattern of a certain object, e.g., a vitamin telling the story of itself. [**cf.** PAPER CHROMATOGRAPHY]

CHROME PRACTITIONER—one who understands color rays and the anatomy of the body; administers color therapy for a patient. [**cf.** CHROMOTHERAPY]

CHROMO—prefix meaning "color" or "pigment."

CHROMOPATH—see CHROMOTHERAPY PRACTITIONER.

CHROMOPATHY—theory: color has an influence on all aspects of a human being, physical, emotional, mental, and spiritual; therefore, color can be helpful in healing through body harmony; disease involves body inharmony just as much as it involves microbes. [*cf.* CHROMOTHERAPY, COLOR BREATHING, COLOR HEALING, GOLD, RAY THERAPY]

CHROMOTHERAPY—(esoteric) the use of colors to heal disease; color is pure cosmic rays full of energy; the flow of colors can be regulated and absorbed into the etheric double; if the correct colors are chosen the etheric double will normalize the body cells, encouraging the physical body to rebuild and heal itself; other tools used with color: solarized water, nutritional food, color lamps, transparencies, color meditation, color breathing, and gems. **Syn.** COLOR HEALING. [**cf.** COLOR, COLOROLOGY Appendix 5]

CHROMOTHERAPY PRACTITIONER—one who understands the power of color rays and is capable of using these rays to heal disease. [**cf.** COLOR ACTIVITY, CHROMOPATHY, COLOR SCIENCE, WHITE LIGHT]

CHRONIC PAIN—(new-age psychology) a continuous physical hurt brought about by a psychological hurt that is hidden and suppressed; as long as the feelings are not dealt with and resolved, the pain remains and becomes so great that one's whole existence is on the pain; one's entire life activities are focused around the pain, making a change in the personality; the focus on the pain takes the focus away from the real cause which is what the patient subconsciously wants and makes the pain more acute; incidents that could cause chronic pain: performing tasks with hidden resentment, feeling one was unjustly treated and can do nothing about it, wanting to change an experience that happened but cannot be changed. [**cf.** PAIN, PSYCHOSOMATIC SELF-REGULATION, ILLNESS, LAW OF HEALING Appendix 7]

CHRYSOLITE—(esoteric) a mineral with the vibrational frequency to be a good transmitter of solar energy for man and helps the wearer acquire wealth. [**cf.** MINPSI, CALUNDRONIUS, CAT'S EYE]

CHTHONIAN—an invisible intelligence living buried beneath the earth and whose function is to help maintain earth. [**cf.** BODIES AND PLANES Appendix 5, HOLLOW EARTH]

CHUA K'A—(Mongolia) a special kind of facial massage to rid one of fear. [**cf.** CURATIVE EDUCATION]

CHUAN—(Chinese, "fist") a slow gymnastic medicine to maintain good health; to use the entire physical self in slow, nonstrenuous exercises in a pattern designed to condition mind and body; shortened name for TAI-CHI CHUAN. [**cf.** BREAK-FALLS, MARTIAL ART]

CHUCHUNAA—(Siberia, "fugitive" or "outcast") a grotesque human-like monstrous creature which is seldom seen but makes itself known by the destruction it leaves from its visits; cannot be captured. **Sim.** TAKUHE, ABOMINABLE SNOWMAN. [**cf.** MONSTER ACTIVITY]

CHUKU—(Nigeria, "sky being") see ETHERIC WORLD ENTITY.

CHUNTZU—(China) all there is: Totality, Superior Man; God. [**cf.** LAW OF MICROCOSM/MACROCOSM Appendix 7, TOTALITY]

CHURINGA—(Australian aborigines) a slab of stone or wood carved with patterns representing the emergence of the totem ancestor; used as a marker where the soul-mind rests until a likely mother passes by; these stones and slabs have magical properties chosen to represent the owner's soul-mind and then hidden in a secret place to bring good fortune to the owner. [cf. MINPSI, AMULET, TALISMAN, TOTEM]

CINQUEFOILS—(Egypt) a plant with five-fingered leaves noted for its properties to keep evil vibrations away from the owner and his household. [cf. BOTANE, HOUSE LEEK, MIDSUMMER MAN, MANDRAKE FRUITS]

CIRCADIAN HALF-WAVES—a cycle of thirty-seven hours after a negative act has been done, trouble activity begins undoing it; sometimes curtailing others to help work out the karma. **Syn.** HOMEO-STASIS. [cf. CYCLES, KARMIC DEBTS, RIPE KARMA, DELAYED KARMA]

CIRCADIAN RHYTHM—(Latin *circa*, "around"; *dies*, "day") around a day; the period of approximately twenty-four hours, in harmony with the turning of the earth; has an effect on animals, man, and plants resulting in biological rhythmic patterns of action; (do not confuse with BIORHYTHM.) **Syn.** BIOLOGICAL CYCLE, BIOLOGICAL RHYTHM, INTERNAL TIME. [cf. DAILY CYCLE, CYCLES, BIORHYTHM]

CIRCLE—(esoteric) 1. a primary symbol representing the first level of the atmosphere, warm ether, red color; a heat state giving man heat; 2. (Tattwa symbol) third symbol of the Tattwa, representing air, primordial element, blue in color; used in clairvoyance to help reach the depths of the subconscious mind. **Syn.** VAYU. 3. a symbol representing infinity and eternity; has no beginning and no ending; 4. used in psychic ritual ceremonies of all kinds as a cut-off place between good and evil vibrations; the evil is on the outside and all inside are safe; 5. term meaning "psychic development circle" for both physical psychism and mental psychism; each person sits facing the center of the circle to lock out negative energies. [cf. TATTWA VISION, PSYCHIC DEVELOPMENT CIRCLE, SEANCE, FORMS-WITH-POWER]

CIRCULAR STONE DANCE—(Africa) a dance performed by many people who circle around a group of trees or stones to impregnate them with psychic energy; dance continues with a pronounced rhythmic beat until the people become excited into a wild frenzy state; this state generates power which is absorbed and stored by the trees or stones; energy used later to attract etheric world intelli-

gences for psychic information or for healing the sick. [cf. MOVEMENT-FOR-ALTERED-CON-SCIOUSNESS, FORMS-WITH-POWER, AMULET]

CIRCULATION OF THE KOSMOS—(ancient mysticism) signifies paths of soul-minds as they travel from planet to planet, from plane to plane, and from sun to planet; occurs after one has reached a finer vibrational frequency of a glorified body impacted with universal love, to help the growth of the planets. [cf. ALCHEMY Appendix 2, GLORIFIED BODY, RESURRECTION]

CITTAVISUDDHIPRAKARANA—(Tantric) principles and knowledge of Tantraism Sect.

CITY OF MAN—the physical body vibrational frequency wherein mankind was given a mechanism to have sensations and feelings as compared to other bodies of the soul-mind, wherein one does not feel sensations. [cf. BODIES OF MAN, MENTAL BODY, BUDDHIC BODY]

CIVILIZATION CYCLE—(esoteric) a pattern of the lives of a population, the culture, knowledge, emotional state, values, etc.; a period between 2,160 and 2,190 years, consisting of one-twelfth of the platonic year, constituting a larger cycle of changes in humanity's growth. [cf. PLATONIC YEAR, ROUND]

CLAIR—(French) prefix meaning "clear."

CLAIR SENSES—(French *clair* "clear") a collective word meaning any one or all types of psychic sensitivity that correspond to the normal five senses; CLAIRVOYANCE, CLAIRAUDIENCE, CLAIRSENTIENCE, CLAIRSCENT, CLAIRSAVORANCE.

CLAIRAUDIENCE—(French, "clear audio") to perceive sounds or words when no person present is speaking or no article is causing the disturbance; sounds that are inaudible to the normal hearing range appear to come from "within the head" or from "out in the atmosphere," perceived singly; 1. types: (a) delicate sounds and music of nature and the cosmos; subtle organ chords, or sounds emitted from the growth of nature; (b) profound words, whole sentences, knocks, music, bells, or other noises that portray a message: etheric world intelligences transmit impressions in the head that can be "heard"; 2. these cosmic sounds and impressions register on the spirillae of the pineal gland and go through the same process that normal hearing goes through in the third-eye area of the head; 3. easier to perceive when in an alpha state or after meditation; 4. should be controlled at all times; to hear sounds at random could interfere with one's task or cause an accident from the startling effect; (do not confuse with PERCUSSION or noises in the seance room that are heard by all present). See OBJECTIVE CLAIRAUDIENCE and SUBJECTIVE CLAIRAUDIENCE. [**cf.** COSMIC MUSIC, VIBRATIONS]

CLAIRAUDIENT—a psychic having the sensitivity to hear the cosmic vibrations of nature, or to hear sounds within or away from the mind that others do not hear. [**cf.** SUBJECTIVE CLAIRAUDIENCE, OBJECTIVE CLAIRAUDIENCE]

CLAIREMPATHIC—1. a psychic who, knowingly or unknowingly, senses within their body, the attitudes, feelings, or emotions of another person and can recognize it as not their own; uses this psychic information to help and guide the other person, or uses it discreetly for reasons of friendship with the person; 2. a psychic who senses the feelings and emotions clinging to an area or an object (from past visitations); ability to recognize these vibrations for what they are and act accordingly; (do not confuse with PURE PSYCHOMETRY wherein touching the object is necessary). [**cf.** CLOAK OF INSULATION, CLAIREMPATHY, CLAIRSENTIENCE]

CLAIREMPATHY—(French, "clear emotion") a type of telepathy: 1. to sense or feel within one's self, the attitude or emotion of another person and recognize it as not belonging to one's self; 2. to tune into the vibrations of an object, or area of one's surroundings, picking up the attitude or feelings of those who have previously visited that area, and act accordingly; spontaneous or willed; used in police work; (do not confuse with PSYCHOMETRY wherein handling is necessary). [**cf.** PSYCHIC TRANSFER, CLAIREMPATHIC]

CLAIRGUSTANCE—(French, "clear tasting") to taste a substance or food without putting anything in the mouth; occurs more easily when psychic is in an alpha state of consciousness and desirous of psychic information; can indicate a human omen (warning or pleasurable event), symbolic information for oneself or another, the presence of a guide, or can relate a message of a soul-mind going through trauma; happens spontaneously or is willed; frequently a psychic smell is perceived with the taste; occurs only to the one who is psychic; (do not confuse with "tastes in the seance room" when

all partake of the phenomena). [**cf.** PSYCHIC INFORMATION, FOOD OF ETHEREAL ESSENCE]

CLAIRGUSTANT—a psychic who can taste a substance or food without putting anything in the mouth; frequently the food or substance is smelled simultaneously; happens spontaneously or can be developed and willed. [**cf.** EMOTIONAL PSI, PROPHESY, HUMAN OMEN, CLAIRGUSTANCE]

CLAIROLFACTION—see CLAIRSCENT.

CLAIRSAVORANCE—(French, "clear tasting") see CLAIRGUSTANCE.

CLAIRSAVORANT—a psychic who experiences tastes in the mouth without putting anything in the mouth and has the ability to interpret the psychic information this intends to relay. **Syn.** CLAIRGUSTANT. [**cf.** CLAIRSAVORANCE, MENTAL PSYCHIC PROCESSES Appendix 2]

CLAIRSCENT—(French, "clear smelling") to smell a fragrance or odor of a substance or food which is not in one's surroundings; occurs more easily when psychic is in an alpha state of consciousness and desirous of psychic information; can indicate a human omen (warning or pleasurable event), symbolic information for oneself or another, the presence of a guide, or can relate a message of a soul-mind going through trauma; happens spontaneously or can be willed; frequently a psychic taste is perceived with the smell; occurs only to the one who is psychic; (do not confuse with "smells in the seance room" when all partake of the phenomena); e.g., to smell an onion at the same time a friend is choking on one; to smell incense when a guide enters the psychic's presence; to smell a death odor before a friend dies. [**cf.** EMOTIONAL PSI, GUIDES, PSYCHIC READING, INCENSE, ODOR OF SANCTITY]

CLAIRSCENT DIAGNOSIS—to detect a disease of the patient by the etheric odor it gives off; each physical disease has an etheric odor of its own and can be smelled by a sensitive clairscentrist. [**cf.** CLAIRSCENT, MENTAL PSYCHIC HEALING]

CLAIRSCENTRIST—a psychic who can smell fragrances or odors when the substance or food is not in his surroundings and has the ability to interpret these smells. [**cf.** ODOR, GUIDE, CLAIRSCENT]

CLAIRSENTIENCE—(French, "clear sensation or feeling") to perceive information by a "feeling within the whole body" without any outer stimuli

113

related to this feeling or information; 1. a nonthought bypasses the process of thinking by bringing through information one did not know before, logically think out, or reason with; an "inner" knowing that the psychic information is true or should be followed; happens spontaneously, is willed, or unwilled; 2. information comes from the superconscious mind, with or without the help of the etheric world intelligences; 3. this is the only kind of psychism that is harmless in coming at any time to the psychic because it comes within the body, down the kundalini to the stomach area, and does not disturb the psychic nor take his attention away from what he is doing, as other types of psychism do; the easiest type of psychism to develop but the one that is doubted the most; 4. specialization: functional clairsentience, precognitive clairsentience, cognitive clairsentience. **Syn.** HUNCHABILITY, INTUITION, GUT FEELING. [**cf.** CLAIRVOYANCE, KUNDALINI, SUBCONSCIOUS MIND]

CLAIRSENTIENT—one who perceives, intentionally or unintentionally, information through a feeling in the stomach or throughout the entire body, with an urge to obey or interpret its meaning; information or feeling was not stimulated by outer environment that one was aware of; information comes "out of the blue" and proves to be correct; psychic perceives best in an alpha state unless born with the ability, and then he or she perceives even during anxiety. **Syn.** IMPRESSIBLE MEDIUM, INTUIT. [**cf.** CLAIRSENTIENCE, SUPERCONSCIOUS MIND, INTUITION, INSPIRATIONAL THOUGHT]

CLAIRSENTIMENT PEOPLE—psychics who can fall in with the character and sentiments of another person and become involved with and use those features as their own personality for a while; a method of helping out another person. [**cf.** CLAIRSCENT, CLAIREMPATHY]

CLAIRTANGENCY—(French, "clear touching") more commonly known as PSYCHOMETRY, see same.

CLAIRVOYANCE—(French, "clear vision") to see into an ethereal dimension without using physical eyes; to reach into another vibrational frequency and visually perceive "within the head" or "in outer space" something significant to this incarnation; eyes opened or closed; 1. to see psychically a full-blown picture, part of a person or scene, an object, lights, words, colors, auras, geometrical figures,

thought-forms, deceased friends, living friends, animals, or etheric world intelligences, all with a message or purpose; visions are shown regarding the past, present, future, etheric realms, and in symbolic form to be interpreted by the psychic; 2. clairvoyance should be kept under control, perceiving only when desired; seeing a full-blown vision can take one's attention away from the job at hand or startle one and disaster might follow; 3. more easily perceived when in an alpha state, in one's sanctuary, after a meditation period, or during sleep; occurs from the subconscious mind or with the help of guides; 4. two main classifications: objective clairvoyance and subjective clairvoyance. **Syn.** DIVINE EYES, EYES OF WISDOM. [**cf.** VISIONARY, MENTAL PSYCHISM, CLAIRVOYANCE Appendix 2]

CLAIRVOYANCE-IN-SPACE—to psychically see a vision of what is happening at present beyond one's line of physical sight; distance is no barrier; vision will not be symbolic but actually happening; willed or unwilled; eyes open or closed; within the head or out in space; easier to tune into if the desired space has an emotional tie; vision can be full-blown or in part. **Syn.** EXTENDED CLAIRVOYANCE, TRAVELING CLAIRVOYANCE, BI-LOCATION OF CONSCIOUSNESS. [**cf.** SPONTANEOUS PSI, FOURTH DIMENSION]

CLAIRVOYANCE-IN-TIME—to psychically see a vision of an event that has already happened or has not occured yet; eyes may be open or closed; seen within the head or out in space; will not be in symbolic form but an actual activity; (do not confuse with TRAVELING CLAIRVOYANCE or CLAIRVOYANCE-IN-SPACE), spontaneous or willed. [**cf.** PROPHET CLAIRVOYANT, REGRESSION, MULTIDIMENSIONAL]

CLAIRVOYANT—a psychic who can tune into the etheric world and perceive an ethereal vision of that which is desired, at will; one who knows how to tune into the proper vibrational frequency for their answer, and interpret the vision; visions are most frequently symbolic and a clairvoyant can understand their own symbols; used in psychic readings and counseling. [**cf.** APPARITION, REMOTE VIEWING]

CLAIRVOYANT DREAM—a psychic vision appearing between dreams during sleep, while in the lower alpha and theta states; psychic visions during sleep are vivid, clear, full-blown, detailed, authentic to the time phase, and easily recalled and remembered. [cf. SLEEP EXPERIENCE, REM, NREM]

CLAIRVOYANT LIGHT—an etheric vibrational frequency of filmy white light, seen psychically over a person, a group of people, a section of a city, or a very large area, by a clairvoyant psychic; (not an aura); a type of mental psychism as it is perceived only by one person; unknown as to its classification; speculation: emotional thought-forms. [cf. PSYCHEDELIC CLAIRVOYANCE]

CLAIRVOYANT MODE—(psi tasks) performing an experiment without the AGENT concentrating on the target symbol. [cf. CONSTRUCTIVE IMAGINATION, TARGET]

CLAIRVOYANT PROJECTION—see CLAIRVOYANCE-IN-SPACE.

CLAIRVOYANT RECONNAISSANCE—to use a psychic with extended clairvoyance ability to tune into a military enemy and look into the plans of the enemy. [cf. CLAIRVOYANCE Appendix 2]

CLAIRVOYANT SWEEP—(laboratory) to perceive a vision of a chosen area and determine what is in that area. Syn. CLAIRVOYANCE-IN-SPACE, CLAIRVOYANT PROJECTION, EXTENDED CLAIRVOYANCE, TRAVELING CLAIRVOYANCE. [cf. X-RAY CLAIRVOYANCE, CLAIRVOYANCE-IN-TIME]

CLASS MANTRA—to call into manifestation a certain action in a large gathering by chanting a mantra; the sound of the mantra is controlled by the unison of the utterance or chant; this unity of sound utilizes the principle of sympathetic vibration which, in turn, results in achieving the goal of those gathered. [cf. MANTRA, SOUNDS-WITH-POWER, SYMPATHETIC VIBRATION]

CLASSIC CLAIRVOYANT—an expert clairvoyant who uses his or her talents professionally. [cf. PSYCHIC Appendix 3]

CLASSICAL SORCERERS—(Rome) educated psychics who were knowledgeable in astrology, astronomy, medicine, alchemy, and divination. [cf. PSYCHIC ART Appendix 3]

CLASSICAL WITCHES—(early witchcraft) highly respectable psychic women who were educated in healing with roots and herbs, midwifery, abortions, love potions, blessings, weather predictions, prophecy, and psychic counseling; descendants of the medicine men of European tribes or pagan priestesses. [cf. SHAMANSHIP, MEDICINE MEN, WITCHCRAFT]

CLAW OF THE DRAGON—(China) noxious and harmful rays coming from underground, which are detectable through the dowsing rod. [cf. DOWSING, RADIESTHESIA, IRRITATION ZONES]

CLEAN RECORDS—(biofeedback training) tabulations made under the proper biofeedback settings, with no artifacts, as opposed to wiring up a jogger. [cf. BIOFEEDBACK TRAINING, ARTIFACTS]

CLEAN SLATE PSYCHOLOGY—to take the analysis of past experiences out of the subconscious mind, bury the old consciousness, and never speak of it again; one is then ready to go in a new direction. [cf. BLOCKS, NEW-AGE PSYCHOLOGY]

CLEAR—1. (rebirthing) to rid one's self of undesirables in the subconscious mind through a rebirthing process; i.e., old theories, repressed emotions, and guilt feelings; one is then free to function in a smooth consciousness. [cf. BIRTH SCIENCE, PRIMAL SCREAM] 2. a forced method of interrogation on a one-to-one basis whereby the ultimate goal is to get the blocks out of the victim's head so he can have a clear state of awareness. [cf. DESTRUCTIVE-BRAIN-WASHING CULT, ENGRAM]

CLEAR CONSCIOUS STATE—(astral projection) to will one's self to project and to program one's self beforehand to make a decision if necessary while traveling in the astral body, and to have recall upon return. (Inconcl.) [cf. ASTRAL PROJECTION Appendix 2]

CLEAR LIGHT—(capitalized) a very vivid, dazzling, brilliant white light that human eyes cannot tolerate up close, and yet it gives off no heat; light of pure intelligence; pure Reality, Nirvana, all-there-is. (Inconcl.) [cf. TOTALITY, MONAD]

CLEAR LIGHT OF REALITY—(Tibet) see ASTRAL PLANE.

CLEARING—to release, flush out, or break up complexes in the subconscious mind so they do not cause problems in one's personality, life-style, or physical body; complexes are feelings of guilt, hate, anxiety, resentment, jealousy, or the clinging to old theories, standards, and life-styles; because of emotional pain when an event happened, or because of today's cultural restraint, unpleasant, unwanted emotions are repressed repeatedly; these repressed emotions grow until they are forced to surface and be put in their proper perspective; clearing is to examine unbalanced, unpleasant events, and take the (electric) charge out of them so they will dissipate and not return; one is then "clear" and the conscious mind feels free and begins a new image; methods of surfacing complexes: (hypnotherapy) REGRESSION, PAST LIVES THERAPY, PRIMAL SCREAM, ISOLATION TANKS, NEUROMUSCULAR MASSAGE, CHIROPRACTIC ADJUSTMENTS, ROLFING, COLOR THERAPY, SOUND HEALING, MASSAGE THERAPY, ACUPUNCTURE, ACUPRESSURE, DREAM ANALYSIS, and BIOFEEDBACK TRAINING. [**cf.** BURIED LIFE, DESENSITIZED, MONKEY CHATTER, PSYCHIC PAIN, BLOCKS]

CLEARING PASS—(magnetic healing) to use the magnetism from one's hands to cleanse the aura of the patient, relaxing the patient and making him or her ready for the next healing pass. [**cf.** MENTAL HEALING, MAGNETISM]

CLEVER MAN—(Australia) psychic who heals and gives counsel to those in need; see PSYCHIC. **Syn.** SHAMAN, MEDICINE MAN. [**cf.**MEDIUMSHIP, CURATIVE EDUCATION, PSYCHIC HEALING]

CLICK—1. a pronounced turning point in one's life in which one spontaneously goes in the exact opposite direction; occurs with a complete change in one's beliefs; results from the written or spoken word or from an experience. Usage: "Something clicked, and I could see my error." (Inconcl.) **Syn.** RANG A BELL. [**cf.** SNAPPING, PEAK EXPERIENCE] 2. (holistic health) a spontaneous turning point in a patient's attitude detected by doctors and nurses; something "clicks," and from this time on, the patient begins to get well regardless of the type of therapy; recognized by the patient's facial expression, the lighting up of the eyes, and the skin becoming "alive." [**cf.** ATTITUDINAL HEALING, LAW OF HEALING Appendix 7, CURATIVE EDUCATION]

CLICK-CLAK—(astral projection) a noise heard in the head simultaneously with the astral body's re-entering the physical body upon its return. **Syn.** CEREBRAL CLICK, HEAD-SNAPPING. [**cf.** ASTRAL PROJECTION Appendix 2]

CLICK-OUT—(trance) a pronounced quickening sensation within the mind and body as one reaches the level wherein the etheric world intelligence moves into the body and the medium loses all mundane awareness; guides move into the body quickly, which causes a "click" sensation. [**cf.** TRANCE, PSYCHIC HEALING, GOING-TO-LEVEL]

CLICKATION—(astral projection) vivid sensation that seems to "click" in the mind when the soul-mind slips out of the physical body into the astral body ready for projection; a feeling of being "locked out" of the physical and being "locked in" the astral body. **Syn.** CLICK-CLAK, CEREBRAL CLICK. [**cf.** CELESTIAL HEADACHE, PARTIAL SOMATIC DISSOCIATION]

CLIENT—one who receives a psychic counseling reading from a professional psychic; individual brings their questions to the psychic and the guidance given is received from the etheric world intelligence who works with the psychic in such matters. **Sim.** COUNSELEE. [**cf.** PSYCHIC INFORMATION, PSYCHIC COUNSELING, SITTING]

CLOAK OF INSULATION—genuine, expedient, pleasant, positive, affirmative thoughts said verbally or silently before calling forth psychic energy, psychic information, or etheric world intelligences; these good ergs of energy sent out from the brain will surround the psychic or medium and prevent negative, harmful, or erroneous psychic energy from entering the psychic's mind; theory: like attracts like; (Bible) St. Paul called it the "whole armor of God"; if said each morning, it helps prevent accidents during the day and deters negative thoughts from cluttering one's mind; below is sample of cloaking oneself used universally: "I am surrounded by the great all good of Totality; only good do I send out and only good do I receive." **Syn.** COAT OF PROTECTION. [**cf.** THOUGHT-FORMS, ELEMENTALS, WORDS-WITH-POWER, BRAIN, THOUGHTS]

CLOCK—(biorhythm) a mechanism in all human beings that makes a rhythmical repetition of physical, mental, and emotional states. [**cf.** BIORHYTHM CHART, CYCLES, BIOLOGIAL RHYTHM, CIRCADIAN RHYTHM]

CLOSE BRUSHES—(death science) situations in which people whose death has been verified by clinical testing, have come back to life, telling others about their experience. [**cf.** SURVIVALISTS, DEATHBED EXPERIENCE, DEATHBED VISIONS]

CLOSE-ENCOUNTER-OF-THE-FIRST-KIND—(ufology) a close-range sighting of a UFO which leaves no noticeable effect on the viewers except excitement and shock; a luminous object without wings hovers close by the persons for a short period, usually within less than 500 feet, and then takes off at a high speed. (Inconcl.) [**cf.** UFOLOGY Appendix 5]

CLOSE-ENCOUNTER-OF-THE-FOURTH-KIND—(ufology) a continuation of the close-encounter of the third kind with the addition of impregnating a woman or having the man impregnate one of their species. (Inconcl.) [cf. CLOSE-ENCOUNTER-OF-THE-SECOND-KIND, FLASHING STROBE LIGHT, INDIVIDUAL METAMORPHOSIS, PULSED-WAVE ACTIVITY]

CLOSE-ENCOUNTER-OF-THE-SECOND-KIND—(ufology) a close-range sighting of a UFO which results in effects on animate and inanimate things; object seen is luminous, without wings, usually oval in shape, hovers in one area for a short period in which earth things are agitated; vegetation is pressed down or scorched, animals become frightened, excited, and out of control, automobile radios, engines, and headlights are momentarily disabled, people are terrorized and go into shock; days later, contactees find physical effects on the body (usually burned skin). (Inconcl.) [cf. BIG-FOOT SIGHTINGS, BEAM OF HEAT]

CLOSE-ENCOUNTER-OF-THE-THIRD-KIND—(ufology) the landing of a UFO and its occupants in which they contact the earthling and leave him with ill physical effects and a program in his mind; occupants differ in colors, shapes, and sizes but all show intelligence and give a feeling of a living presence (as opposed to a robot or machine); earthling is transfixed by the flashing strobe light, approached, and taken aboard the construct; the physical body is tampered with and examined, to the best conclusion of the abductee (abductee's mind draws a blank for this period of encounter); when the abductee relates his experience, it is as if a recording had been placed in his mind, as each story is told in exactly the same words and fluctuations of tone; earthling is in a state of shock for days and later finds biological changes on or in his body; many abductees live only three or four years longer. (Inconcl.) [cf. CLOSE-ENCOUNTERS-OF-THE-FIRST-KIND]

CLOSED PACK—(laboratory) a deck of twenty-five cards, designed by E. Karl Zener, consisting of five symbols, with five cards of each symbol; used in Rhine laboratories. [cf. ESP, PSI TASKS]

CLOSET—(capitalized) (Christianity) 1. see MEDITATION; 2. see MONAD.

CLOTH PHOTOGRAPHY—see CLOTHOGRAPHY.

CLOTHOGRAPHY—spiritual images psychically impressed on handkerchiefs or similar fabric occurring from no known physical means; picture is outlined in black similar to a negative; occurs randomly but necessitates a psychic in the vicinity; e.g., the Shroud of Turin; the face on the altar cloth occurring on Holy Thursday in a church in Wyalusing, Penn. (Inconcl.) [cf. EASTER PHENOMENA, SHROUD, PSYCHIC PHOTOGRAPHY]

CLOUD BEINGS—(Native American, Pueblo) groups of etheric world intelligences who have ties among the various sects, thus criss-crossing and overlapping their appearances, information, and bringing peace among all. [cf. RAIN-MAKERS, CORN MAIDENS, STAR SPIRITS]

CLOUD CHAMBER—an instrument invented by Charles T. R. Wilson; designed to trace or detect invisible high-energy subatomic particles; instrument uses condensation of water vapor to trace the paths of electrically charged particles from radioactive elements and cosmic rays; also used to register the wavelengths which emanate from a psychic healer's hands. (Inconcl.) [cf. MAGNETIC HEALING, PHYSICAL ETHERS]

CLOUD OF UNKNOWING—the etheric world that is invisible for most persons. [cf. BODIES AND PLANES Appendix 5]

CLOUD SHIFTING—to move a cloud by the power of concentration; usually a small piece of the larger cloud breaks off and slides away; easier to do on a sunny day, with a cumulus cloud. [cf. ATMOSPHERE CONTROL Appendix 2]

CLOUD SPIRIT—nature spirit that lives among the clouds and whose function is to be a sculptor of the fairy kingdom.

CLOVER—(esoteric) a wild, green plant having a varying number of petals on its stem; has the property to aid one in their karmic path; 1. three-leaf clover is symbolic of the Trinity; helps raise the owner's state of consciousness; brings protection against negative vibrations in regard to vegetation; 2. four-leaf clover begins to open up good karmic experiences for the owner; accelerates psychic energy for owner; helps one judge between good and evil; 3. five-leaf clover leads one to overcome their bad karma more quickly when they are seriously on this "path." [cf. BOTANE, NUMEROLOGY]

CLURICAUN—a nature spirit of the leprechaun species known to work at night raiding wine cellars.

CLUSTERS—(Huna) a gathering of thoughts, emotions, and opinions in the subconscious mind that are negative and painful; these began with an unpleasant emotional event that was not handled at the time it happened and because of its emotional hurt was suppressed; each event that carried emotional similarities from that time on was also suppressed; these emotional thoughts gather together and form a cluster in the body or mind and surface as unwanted reactions, a complex, or a neurosis. **Syn.** BLOCKS, GRAPES, GORDIAN KNOTS. [**cf.** BLOCKS Appendix 5]

CMS—abbr. CORTICALLY MEDITATED STABILIZATION; meditation used as a means to reduce anxiety. [**cf.** MEDITATION Appendix 5, STRESS, AUTOGENIC TRAINING, MANTRA]

CO—prefix meaning "complement of."

CO-CREATIVE QUIETNESS—level of the subconscious mind wherein the psychic information seems to flow with accuracy and purpose. **Syn.** GOING-TO-LEVEL. [**cf.** PSYCHIC INFORMATION, SUBCONSCIOUS MIND, PSYCHIC DOORS]

CO-CREATOR—a person's thoughts, comprised of conscious and subconscious activity; 1. deliberate, instigated thoughts, unconscious inner-dialogue, sleep thinking, and one's belief system constructed from past incarnations; all of the above from mankind as a whole, builds or co-creates the universe and its various vibrational frequencies; a person's mind activity constantly sends out ergs of energy and intelligence that connect to Total Intelligence and change the vibrational rate of the atoms; see MATTER, ATOMS, THOUGHTS; 2. a person's mind, through the process of thinking, uses the Creation (the atoms) to design, construct, build, destroy, transform, rebuild, and rearrange substance mankind calls *reality;* an individual does not create but uses the Creation in various ways (Creation happens only once); one cannot create but only unfolds and surfaces that which was created in the beginning; (do not confuse with NON-THOUGHTS, i.e., PSYCHIC EXPERIENCE, DREAMS, HYPNOTIC SUGGESTION, HALLUCINATION, and IMAGERY that come from outside into the mind; these do not contribute to one's co-creation of vibrational frequencies of the three-dimensional world). [**cf.** LAW OF THOUGHT Appendix 7, POLARITY, VIBRATIONS]

COAT OF PROTECTION—see CLOAK OF INSULATION.

COBLYNAU—(Wales) a nature spirit belonging to the goblin species living in the mines; cousins to the Cornish Knockers.

COCKROACH—(esoteric) an insect having a perfect system for its purpose; has never evolved but is the same as when created; will never become extinct as it can change dimensions, thus saving its life from destruction in the third plane dimension. (Inconcl.) [**cf.** DIMENSION-SHIFTING]

COEXISTENCE—"all" is happening at one time, the past, the present, and the future. **Syn.** MULTIDIMENSIONAL. [**cf.** TIME Appendix 5]

COFFEEOGRAPHY—to predict the weather for the day by using the pattern of the bubbles in one's first cup of coffee; if the bubbles form a circle around the edge of the cup, it will be rainy; if the bubbles form no pattern, the weather will be changeable during the day. [**cf.** CASTING OF LOTS, FALL, MANTIC ARTS]

COFFER—a lidless, empty box found in the Great Pyramid and made of red granite, with geometrical proportions; now under investigation. [**cf.** PYRAMIDOLOGY]

COFFIN RITUALS—(Egypt, Freemasonry) an organized method in which the initiate who desires to understand life more fully is put through a simulation of the death process. [**cf.** DEATH SCIENCE, DWELLERS IN THE BARDO]

COGNIT—see COGNITANT.

COGNITANT—one who psychically perceives information pertaining to the present through any one of the psychic skills. [**cf.** COGNITION, PRECOGNITION, RETROCOGNITION]

COGNITION—see PSYCHIC COGNITION.

COGNITIVE CLAIRSENTIENCE—to perceive an "exact" short fact that the conscious mind is having trouble bringing to the surface; happens instantaneously when the conscious mind has given up or is in a neutral state; comes directly from Totality through the superconscious mind, by-passing the subconscious mind: occurs to those who know they are psychic and those who are not aware of being psychic; e.g. a missing link in a scientific formula, words for a blank line in a poem, title for a new concerto, a new way to cut hair; (do not confuse with INSPIRATIONAL THOUGHT). [**cf.** COGNITANT, CLAIRSENTIENCE, PSYCHIC INFORMATION]

COGNITIVE PSYCHOPHARMACOLOGY—(future science) discovery of the peptides to modify behavior in the field of cognition. (Inconcl.) [**cf.** PSYCHIC COGNITION, TELEPATH, NEW-AGE PSYCHOLOGY]

COGNITIVE REVOLUTION—the shift of scientific interest in the field of psychology from that of one's behavior to that of one's thoughts and subjective experiences. (Inconcl.) [**cf.** SUBJECTIVE BEHAVIORISM]

COGNIZE—to perceive. [**cf.** PSYCHIC COGNITION Appendix 2]

COILED SERPENT—(kundalini) an invisible/visible concentrated energy field that lies dormant in the invisible kanda at the base of the human spine; this energy is subject to thought and rises up the spine during one's evolutionary path as they perfect themselves in earth incarnations; see SUSHUMNA. [**cf.** KUNDALINI, CHAKRAS, PATH]

COINCIDENCE—1. (esoteric) (Carl Jung) two events occurring simultaneously having no known cause-and-effect connection and unrelated in nature but showing a meaningful response, indicating some kind of intelligence link. **Syn.** SYNCHRONICITY. [**cf.** CASTING OF LOTS, I CHING, RADIESTHESIA] 2. (clinical, laboratory) a simultaneous occurrence or repeated occurrence of two or more events at the same time, or close to the same time, which are meaningfully related; accredited to the law of chance. [**cf.** CHANCE, ESP, PSI TASKS] 3. (astral projection) the realignment of the astral body (subconscious mind) with the physical body after the projection is over. Usage: "The astral body snapped back into coincidence with the physical body." [**cf.** REPERCUSSION]

COINCIDENTAL MATCHING—the environment and the genes of a human being working together in a meaningful way for evolutionary survival. [**cf.** SYNCHRONICITY, RADIESTHESIA]

COLD—to give psychic information or psychic messages to the public without any previous notice; results in a lesser performance than usual and is an insult to one's guides; stems from misconceptions and ignorance of the public as to how and why psychism functions; superior etheric world intelligences have such fine vibrations that preparation is preferable for the medium's health and accuracy of message; "cold" messages performed frequently call into performance inferior guides who have a vibrational frequency more closely related to earth vibrations; (do not confuse with INTUITION). [**cf.** MENTAL PSYCHISM PROCESS]

COLD ELECTRON EMISSION—(Kirlian effect) theory: the emanations being picked up on the high frequency camera are caused by the high frequency of the light current, making it look as if the body is radiating electrified particles; as opposed to the theory that these electrified particles are responsible for radiating the body. (Inconcl.) **Syn.** CORONA DISCHARGE. [**cf.** ETHERIC DOUBLE, VITALITY GLOBULES, MITOGENETIC RADIATION, RADIATION-FIELD PHOTOGRAPHY]

COLD LIGHT—(Kirlian effect) light that is 100 percent efficient. [**cf.** KIRLIAN EFFECT Appendix 5]

COLD READER—mental psychic who gives psychic messages in public and is accused of watching eye and body movements of the subject to reveal information anyone knowledgeable in body language could reveal; psychic reads with eyes open and gives generalized statements. [**cf.** HOT READING]

COLLABORATOR—in invisible etheric world intelligence that works through a medium to bring psychic information, guidance, and healing. **Syn.** GUIDE. [**cf.** MEDIUMSHIP, GUIDE, INNER BAND]

COLLECTING THE MIND—(Zen) to sit still, watch, and observe the stillness of the mind for long periods of time. **Sim.** SESSHIN. [**cf.** ZAZEN, KOAN]

COLLECTIVE APPARITION—a nonphysical form or scene perceived psychically in outer space by many people, simultaneously and spontaneously; usually occurs when the psychics are in a relaxed and receptive state of consciousness with unity of thought; e.g., an apparition appearing in the night sky seen by four children, but the adults present saw nothing (Fatima prophecy); life-forms hovering over the platform in church services perceived clairvoyantly by only a few of the congregation. [**cf.** CLAIRVOYANCE, APPARITION, ANGEL HIERARCHY]

COLLECTIVE AURA—an energy field hovering over areas such as cities, factories, forests, etc., as the result of the mind activity of those who frequent that area; the unison of the most common basic attitude, purpose, cognitive knowledge, and emotion makes the auric pattern of the area; this energy field contributes to the welfare of the area, regardless of the size of the mundane project below. [**cf.** MASS KARMA, COLLECTIVE UNCONSCIOUS, ETHERIC FILM]

COLLECTIVE CLAIRAUDIENCE—the spontaneous perception of sound by many people simultaneously, with no physical evidence present; sounds can be music, voices, or noise appearing to come from outer space; occurs to psychics and untrained psychics depending upon one's emotional state; usually an omen meant for that locale; (do not confuse with "physical phenomena" in which the noise is heard with physical ears). [**cf.** COLLECTIVE APPARITION, OBJECTIVE CLAIRAUDIENCE]

COLLECTIVE CLAIRVOYANCE—see COLLECTIVE APPARITION.

COLLECTIVE HALLUCINATIONS—sharing similar psychic visions or clairauditory noises among a number of persons simultaneously; a telepathic transfer due to a unison of emotions and thoughts among those psychically perceiving. [**cf.** TELEPATHY Appendix 2, CLAIRVOYANCE]

COLLECTIVE PRAYER—(1. (West Africa) special verbiage designed by the Seraphim and Cherubum movement to be said in unison with the group to open the majority of the group to clairvoyance. [**cf.** CLAIRVOYANCE, MASS ELEMENTAL, CELESTIAL LIGHT] 2. words said in unison when everyone in the group has been emotionally attuned to unity of thought; will induce healing, physical phenomena, and stir up whatever the words speak. [**cf.** POWER-OF-THE-WORD, CHANTING]

COLLECTIVE PSYCHE—(Carl Jung) see COLLECTIVE UNCONSCIOUS.

COLLECTIVE TRANCE—an entire group or tribe inducing a state of ecstasy together at the same time; members of the tribe dance to a unison of rhythm for a prolonged period until each one drifts into a state of frenzy; this unison of trance gives the psychic performance more power. [**cf.** MOVEMENT-FOR-ALTERED-CONSCIOUSNESS, ECSTASY]

COLLECTIVE UNCONSCIOUS—(Carl Jung) 1. the sum-total consciousness of all mankind's knowledge and experience throughout the history of the earth, collected unconsciously; includes the primitive experiences and early phases of humanity's evolution up to current thoughts coming from the works of art, legends, fairy tales, myths, and instincts, forming universal symbols buried deep in the subconscious mind; 2. inherited by all mankind; this consciousness has a tendency to emerge in dreams, psychic sessions, meditation, daydreaming, and in actual experiences; relates to the past,

expressing humanity's deepest awareness of life energy; 3. a cross-culture of Western and Eastern philosophies hard-wired in the neuronal architecture of our brain; a giant pot of knowledge collected from beliefs, objects, symbols, famines, abundance, jealousies, love, friendships, peacetime, wars, emotions to which every person is connected; 4. not caused by the guiding principle but rather by what the individual self has dumped there. [**cf.** CONSCIOUSNESS Appendix 5, ARCHETYPAL PATTERN]

COLLECTIVE UNCONSCIOUS CONSCIOUSNESS—a law of cosmic consciousness that holds all that human beings have ever done and thought in an energy field of cosmic awareness; similar thoughts are repeatedly saved, increasing in strength as to their meaning; this awareness is buried deep in man's subconscious mind and is used to intermesh with conscious mind thoughts to make the world of form; e.g., when one speaks *chair*, immediately in his or her mind and the listener's mind the form of a chair takes place and because of the past concerted thoughts, a chair appears; (conscious mind thoughts make the style of chair); when man does not need a chair, the idea of a chair will dissipate and fall away because of its uselessness, and then something else will be strong in the mind of the individual and will manifest. [**cf.** COLLECTIVE UNCONSCIOUS, MATTER, MASS KARMA, RACE CONSCIOUSNESS, SYMPATHETIC NERVOUS SYSTEM]

COLLOIDAL SYSTEM—(Greek, "glue") specks of energy working as a unit to hold atoms together in the body; capable of being transposed into physical substance. [**cf.** THOUGHTS, CONSCIOUS MIND, ATOMS]

COLOR—(esoteric) 1. powerful cosmic energy named "white"; when white is broken down by a prism to various intensities, each new frequency has its own different appearance to a human and is then named red, orange, yellow, green, blue, indigo, and violet; each subcolor has its tones, shades, tints, and mixtures; 2. an interpretation of the way in which photons hit the retina; 3. the boundary or edge between light and darkness; the edge where light is admitted will make the color; 4. the rays radiating down to earth at their particular rate of vibration make the color by reflecting back all the colors except the one seen; color is visible light vibrating at a frequency, as one octave in the center of seventy in the electromagnetic spectrum; 5. each layer of air has its own color, depending upon density and temperature; 6. a powerful primal cosmic force dependent upon the central sun and found in all matter; one characteristic of each atom is color; 7. each color, shade, tone, and tint has a separate frequency; 8. there is only one color, white, and everything else is an extension of white; white represents pure love and pure intelligence; 9. each sound shows a different color or tone of color. [cf. COLOROLOGY Appendix 5, COLOR BREATHING, COLOROLOGY]

COLOR ACTIVITY—color is sensation, an emotional and mental interpretation of what the eye records in the nature of feeling; each color represents a constructive and destructive emotional effect. [cf. COLOR BREATHING, COLOR THERAPY]

COLOR BARRIER—(eyeless sight) present research has found that certain degrees of light and other objects can hinder the eyeless sighted person from seeing; the lighting of a room must be bright to get the best results from eyeless sight. [cf. EYELESS SIGHT Appendix 2]

COLOR BREATHING—to heal one's body using breathing and various colors; to draw into the body a certain permanence of color balance by using the right color and consciously making it impossible for the body to respond to future circumstances with the wrong color. (Inconcl.) [cf. THOUGHT, PRANA]

COLOR ELEMENTALS—etheric world intelligences in charge of the seven major rays. [cf. ANGEL HIERARCHY, RAYS]

COLOR HEALING—(Greece, Egypt) to heal the body by applying the correct color vibrations to the chakras and the etheric double; color is pure cosmic rays full of power, and by applying the color through special colored lights, the etheric double rebuilds, restores, and revitalizes the body, giving the cells an opportunity to heal themselves. Syn. CHROME THERAPY, COLOR THERAPY. [cf. COLOR SPECTRUM, COLOR MEDITATION]

COLOR ORGAN—an instrument that flashes color on a screen when musical notes are being played upon it. (Inconcl.) [cf. COSMIC OCTAVES, VIBRATIONS]

COLOR PSYCHOLOGY—the study of the conscious and unconscious effect that the color of one's clothing and environment has on one's moods and emotions. [cf. COLOR THERAPY, EMOTIONS]

COLOR SCIENCE—1. (ancient Egypt, China, India, Greece, Healing Temples of Light and Color at Heliopolis) the study of the seven rainbow colors, their sub-colors, and their functions in correlation to the sevenfold nature of man; the seven planes in the etheric world, and the seven chakras; 2. (science) the study based on the principle that matter and light are inseparable, and when matter returns to its essence, it goes back into a radiation identical to light. [cf. COLOROLOGY Appendix 5]

COLOR SPECTRUM—(esoteric) light and color transmit and register in the brain by means of the optic nerve; color oscillates so minutely that it passes through the eye lens; red is the slowest vibration and violet is the fastest vibration of color that humans can perceive; each color has three aspects: hue, value, and chroma. (Inconcl.) [cf. COLOR, COLOR ACTIVITY, CHROMOTHERAPY]

COLOR STARVATION—(esoteric) personality traits can impair proper circulation of cosmic life forces which emanate the various colors, resulting in a disease; a bad habit, trait, vice, and continued bias cause a blind spot in the consciousness; this in turn screens off some of the cosmic light and prevents circulation through the brain, relating to the negative personality traits, and the corresponding areas of the body, opening it to disease. [cf. MENTAL HEALING, COLOR HEALING, DARKNESS]

COLOR TELEPATHY—to send the sensation of the color from one mind to another; thus the receiver knows the color being sent without perceiving it clairvoyantly. [cf. CLAIRSENTIENCE, TELEPATHY, COLOR]

COLOR THERAPY—(Egypt, Greece) using color to promote a natural body healing; wavelengths known by their color, tones, and hues, have an effect on body tissue, and this color can be regulated into the chakras or the etheric double, the pattern; this changes the pattern which, in turn, stimulates the physical body by normalizing the cells and the body can more easily heal itself. Syn. COLOR HEALING, CHROMOTHERAPY. [cf. PSYCHIC HEALING, HUE, GREEN RAYS]

COLOR VISUALIZATION—to use the proper color as a point of focus in a visualization exercise; the color serves as a yantra (visible symbol) for focusing attention during the meditation part; later the color is sent to the end-result of the desired action; e.g., to send color to the afflicted part of the body for a healing; to send the color to the pocketbook when asking for abundance. [cf. GOLD, SIMONTON METHOD, VISUALIZATION]

121

COLOROLOGY—the study of color in its invisible and visible state in its relation to man and the universe; theory: color is a strong subtle force shaping human behavior; color has three functions: 1. sensation; a mental and emotional interpretation of what the eye records; each color represents destructive and constructive emotions; 2. chemical; color one wears is infused with the electrical and magnetic qualities of the wearer and attracts to one according to the strength of the color; 3. light. [cf. COLOR ACTIVITY, COLOR THERAPY]

COMBUSTIBILITY—to eat fire, or walk on burning coals, without burning the body; see FIRE IMMUNITY. [cf. FIRE WALKING, INSENSIBILITY TO FIRE, TEMPERATURE CONTROL, BODY CONTROL]

COME CLOSE TO YOU—a common expression used by public psychics giving standing reading messages; e.g., as psychic tunes into the subject's aura, he or she says, "As I come close to you, I sense money coming to you." [cf. STANDING READER, PSYCHIC INFORMATION]

COME INTO YOUR VIBRATION—common phrase used by public psychics giving verbal messages from the platform as they tune into the rhythm of the subject's auric pattern to bring psychic information. [cf. STANDING READER, COME CLOSE TO YOU, MESSAGE]

COMFORTING ANGEL—to feel a psychic source of energy nearby and have an inner knowing that it is an etheric world intelligence; it is there to guide, protect, or help in the problem at hand, as opposed to a negative force; intelligence can be perceived as light, two eyes, an apparition in a flowing gown, or swirling, moving energies. [cf. OUTER BAND, CELESTIAL GUARDIAN, INDIAN GUIDE]

COMING FORTH FROM THE DAY—(Egypt) a revivification of a corpse equipped with psychic energy and immune from decay; acts as if it is under a "spell"; comes forth each day from the tomb to see the sun and feed on the offerings put by his tomb by his friends. [cf. DEATH SCIENCE, MUMMIFICATION, HOUSE OF ETERNITY]

COMA STATE—(hypnotherapy) the deepest level of an altered consciousness one can attain and be alive; accomplished under hypnosis wherein the pulse slows to almost nothing: the subject will: take commands from the guide to be effective when in a normal awake state, not be able to move or talk, not recall what transpired when back in a normal state,

drift in and out of this state; an effective state for operations, and physical and mental therapy; not everyone can accomplish this state. Syn. SOMNAMBULISM HYPNOTHERAPY. [cf. HYPNOTHERAPY, MEDIUM STATE]

COMMENTARY—(I Ching) that part of the hexagram passage which more thoroughly interprets the judgment section of the hexagram. Syn. TUAN CHUAN. [cf. JUDGMENT, GREAT SYMBOLISM, MOVING LINES, THE RULERS]

COMMON AURIC FIELD—an electromagnetic field found around a group of persons, compounded from the greatest common measure of the thinking and feeling qualities of the people; usually brought on intentionally by the main leader; a necessary factor in mass healing or in organizations to bind the members to the purpose of the organization; this energy field feeds back to the individuals who will respond in mannerisms capable only under group influence. [cf. MASS ELEMENTAL, THOUGHTFORMS, GROUP KARMA]

COMMUNAL SEANCE—a development circle of mediums in which each one desires to increase his own abilities; kept under control by a developed medium, but concentration is on individual talent; unity of theme is important. (Inconcl.) [cf. SEANCE, GUIDE, TRUMPET, KNOCKS]

COMMUNAL WORSHIP—a gathering of persons having common religious beliefs and each one desirous of participating in the service; i.e., 1. charismatic movements wherein each member puts forth effort to talk-in-tongues, to prophesy, and to heal; 2. snake-handling cults wherein each member handles the snakes; 3. church services in which laymen take turns in giving the sermon.

COMMUNICANT—see ETHERIC WORLD ENTITY.

COMMUNICATOR—an etheric world intelligence desirous of helping man while in an earthly incarnation and capable of using the medium as a channel for inspirational thought, trance voice, mental psychism, etc. Syn. GUIDE, IMPERATOR, MENTOR, DYNATYPE. [cf. ANGEL HIERARCHY, DOCTOR TEACHER, VOICE TRANCE, SEANCE]

COMMUNITY OF SENSATION—(hypnotherapy) the sensation of the subject in a hypnotic state that he or she is participating in the same experience the hypnotist is going through even though they are not programmed to do so; e.g., the hypnotist answers the telephone and subject feels they are talking to the other party on the phone, or the hypnotist smokes a cigarette and subject feels they are smoking. [cf. HYPNOTHERAPY Appendix 5]

COMPANIES OF GODS—(Tibet) the organizing of circles into mandalas containing the four colors which correlate with the four aspects of wisdom. [cf. ASPECTS OF WISDOM, MIRROR-LIKE WISDOM, MANDALAS]

COMPANION GLOBES—each sidereal body and planet has six visible and invisible globes that are necessary to the life of that planet. [cf. EVOLUTION, GROUP SOULS, CYCLES]

COMPASSION CYCLE—every thirty-eight days a human has something happen that he thinks of as a misfortune or a suffering; every nineteen days a human has something happen that he thinks is very wonderful, making this a cycle of ups and downs of compassion. [cf. BIORHYTHM CHARTS, CYCLES, YEARLY CYCLE, WHEEL OF TIME]

COMPATIBILITY—(radiesthesia) the harmonious interaction of two or more given force fields working together: 1. the auric field of the object one is measuring; 2. the subconscious ability of the eyes to pick up this invisible energy field with regard to the magnetic relationship to the object and send it instantaneously throughout the sympathetic nervous system; 3. the reaction of the pendulum or dowsing rod to this sympathetic nervous system vibration in an outward movement. [cf. MASTER EYE, SYNCHRONICITY]

COMPATIBILITY PERCENTAGE—(biorhythm chart) to determine if two people are compatible by using biorhythm cycles; the distance between the three sets of curves on each biorhythm chart is computed to find the average percent of distance. [cf. BIORHYTHM CHART]

COMPENSATORY DREAMS—picture language during REM sleep that makes up for some of the action one has done during the previous day; 1. dream themes that will lift the conscious mind out of a state of "down" feeling or lower the level of the conscious mind when in a state of "high" egotism; 2. dreamstuff that releases stress so it does not have to be dealt with the next day; 3. dream themes that point out character traits that are out of balance. [cf. DREAM DISSOLUTION, DREAM-MOTIFS, DREAMS FOR BALANCE]

COMPENSATORY HALLUCINATIONS—psychic experiences that make up or fill in for body parts no longer there; e.g., one without normal vision on the left side will perceive clairvoyantly on his left side; a man blind from birth will not perceive clairaudiently but develop clairvoyance; one with an amputated leg will see himself in his dreams with two legs. [cf. AUDITORY HALLUCINATION, CLAIRVOYANCE]

COMPITA—(Rome) small towers built within a home or building as a shrine for the etheric world intelligences to inhabit to protect that household or public building. [cf. ANGELS, ETHERIC WORLD INTELLIGENCES]

COMPLEMENTARY CROSS-CORRESPON-DENCE—(early 1900s) preplanned etheric world dependent communications by etheric world intelligences who were desirous to prove their existence and authenticity; intelligences worked through two or more mediums with and without time intervals and always with great distance between mediums; used mediumistic skills such as VOICE TRANCE, INSPIRATIONAL THOUGHT, AUTOMATISM; each medium perceived fragments or sections of information which, when put together, made a clear and worthwhile message. [cf. PHYSICAL PSYCHISM, AUTOMATISM, GUIDE, SIMPLE CROSS-CORRESPONDENCE]

COMPLETE AGE REGRESSION—(hypnotherapy) to relive a traumatic event from a past experience of one's present life under deep hypnosis; one goes through the same emotional and attitudinal feelings that he went through at that time with all later knowledge blocked from his subconscious mind; e.g., to relive a birthday party at the age of four and speak in the same language and voice quality as the four-year-old; subconscious mind takes subject back to a situation that pertains to his present physical or mental problem; hypnotherapist guides the subject to reconcile the event and balance with it at the age level it happened; this takes the charge out of the event, surfaces any repression, and erases it from the akashic record; subject is then free from that particular problem; (do not confuse with PARTIAL AGE REGRESSION or COMPLETE REGRESSION). [cf. HYPNOTHERAPY, DEEP HYPNOSIS, REVIVIFICATION]

COMPLETE BREATH—(Yoga) to breathe from the lower part of the diaphragm; a special method of drawing in air using the nostrils to fill the pit of the stomach and the lungs; air is held a few seconds, and then let out through the nostrils by emptying the lungs first until the air in stomach is also released; this deep breath aids one if performed before meditation, opening psychic doors, biofeed-back training hook-up, performing on the stage, and before a sports race. [cf. BREATH CONTROL, CURATIVE EDUCATIN, HYPERVENTILATION]

COMPLETE IMPERSONATION—to allow an etheric world intelligence to use one's body and mind for a time to perform physical phenomena; the soul-mind of the medium slips out of the physical body while in deep trance with the help of the etheric world intelligence; session is preplanned and programmed by medium beforehand as to objective and length of session; intelligence uses the eyes, hands, voice, and body of medium to walk, talk, for necessary activity, as if it were its own; the soul-mind returns seconds after purpose is accomplished to the satisfaction of etheric world intelligence; medium remembers nothing and need not be educated in the activity the body performs; used in painting beautiful pictures with feet, some psychic surgery, voice trance, etheric dancing, some teleportation; (do not confuse with POSSESSION that is accomplished for evil intent at the discretion of the inferior etheric world entity and against the conscious will of the earthling). [cf. CATALEPIC TRANCE, POSSESSION, PSYCHIC SURGERY]

COMPLETE MEDIUM—a person who has developed the mediumistic faculties of transmitting to and communicating with the etheric world entities and has accomplished the goal desired; e.g., TRANCE VOICE, TRUMPET, AUTOMATIC WRITING, etc.; now shares respect for the etheric world entities and vice versa; capable of working together when the medium desires. **Syn.** FORMED MEDIUM. [cf. TRANCE MANIFESTATIONS]

COMPLETE REGRESSION—(hypnotherapy) to relive a traumatic event from a past incarnation under deep hypnosis; one goes through the same emotional and attitudinal feelings that they went through at that time with all subsequent knowledge blocked from their subconscious mind; education, beliefs, and life experiences from future incarnations are not contributing to the regression; subject can speak in a language they no longer remember, become the opposite sex, be a different skin color, be any age, etc.; subject goes through the same emotions, e.g., hysteria, anger, hostility, joy, sadness, etc.; under the guidance of the therapist, the subject reconciles or puts the attitude and feelings in their proper perspective; this takes the charge out of the event and it is erased from the akashic record; subject does not usually regress to a

pleasurable event as the soul-mind is usually interested in correcting itself and in a hypnotic state the soul-mind is not bothered by the decision-making mind and can do this; event relates to the present life-style behaviors; the subject is now free from incarnational carry-overs and unwanted physical and mental behavior. **Syn.** REVIVIFICATION. [ct. PARTIAL REGRESSION, KARMA, FINGER RESPONSE, AGE REGRESSION]

COMPLEX—a congregation of emotional feelings and memories in the subconscious mind, all relating to a central theme of an unpleasant experience which is repressed; individual did not want to or was not capable of correcting or resolving the situation when it happened and suppressed it so as not to handle it; hidden emotional pain is now causing unwanted nervous behavior or unwanted habits; memory clusters are frequently carried over into the next incarnation until resolved correctly and in harmony with both minds. **Syn.** BLOCKS, FIXATION, CLUSTERS. [cf. BLOCKS Appendix 5]

COMPOUND OF CONSCIOUSNESS—(Tibet) the present character of the person, compiled from all the past lives and thoughts stored in their akashic record. **Syn.** SOUL-MIND. [cf. PATTERN, MEMORY BANK, REINCARNATION]

COMPRESSION MASSAGE—to use the first finger and thumb of the hand to work on the foot to break up the crystal deposits, which in turn breaks up congestion in the body, normalizing the body cells and allowing the body to heal itself. **Syn.** REFLEXOLOGY. [cf. ACUPUNCTURE, MERIDIAN LINES]

COMPRESSION SYMBOL—(psychic reading) information given to the psychic that is condensed into one vision, making the vision at first seem to be incorrect; e.g., "I see a necessity to take money out of both your bank accounts, as I see two passbooks"; the querent has only one account but does end up taking goodly sums of money out of the savings at two different times, making the vision correct but easily misinterpreted; two separate acts at different times put together in one vision. **Syn.** CONDENSATION. [cf. PSYCHIC INFORMATION, READING]

COMPULSION—(possession) a strong body and mind sensation that precedes a possession attack; victim acts from an irresistible impulse to perform an act contrary to their will, as if being pushed into their convulsion; this psychic experience comes upon the earthling victim to the degree of voluntary resistance of the victim. [**cf.** POSSESSION, OBSESSION]

COMPUTERISTS—(esoteric) soul-minds who choose to live in the etheric world vibration in an energy field similar to a manmade computer after making their earthly transition; advanced soul-minds who are in an awareness of numbers and can comprehend the thousands of vibrational frequencies of the atmosphere; desire universal love evolvement. [**cf.** EXTRATERRESTRIAL BEINGS, SOLID STATE LIFE FORMS]

CONCAVATION—(astral projection) to experience a tunnel effect as one leaves the physical body in an astral projection; one feels as if they are going through a dark tunnel with a light at the end; the tunnel effect sometimes appears again when the projector reenters his physical body. (Inconcl.) [**cf.** PINEAL DOOR, CEREBRAL CLICK, SUSPENDED ANIMATION]

CONCENTRATED THOUGHT—(laboratory) to give one's undivided mental activity to a unified theme (the target) for a few minutes before shooting this mental activity to the target; a psychic expression to mean one is deliberately paying attention to the target (objective of the experiment) only; needed in all psychic skills and some mediumistic skills; emphasized in PK, MENTAL and MAGNETIC HEALING, ENERGIZING AMULETS, BODY CONTROL, MEDITATION, VISUALIZATION, HYPNOSIS, and ALCHEMY.

CONCENTRATION—to gather all of one's attention by focusing the conscious mind on one point, one object, one condition, one principle and all other faculties and interests are subordinate; with eyes closed or open; to direct the mental mind toward a common center, one-pointedness; used in meditation, psychic and mediumistic skills, healings and hypnotherapy. (Inconcl.) [**cf.** LAW OF CENTER Appendix 7, POINT-OF-FOCUS, MIND-DRIFT]

CONCENTRATION/CONTEMPLATION/SAM-YAMA-TYPE—intense focusing of the mind on one single object during meditation long enough to blend oneself with the object itself. [**cf.** ATORI, BLANK MIND, NONATTACHMENT]

CONCENTRIC SPHERES—(astronomy) the spheres of the sun, moon, planets, and fixed stars rotating around the earth. **Syn.** HEAVEN. [**cf.** PLANETARY CYCLES, ASTROLOGY]

CONCEPT—(esoteric) a construct, notion, or idea that grew like a tree, slowly and strongly, from knowledge obtained through education and life experiences.

CONCEPT RECALL—(clinical) to return experiences of the past to the conscious mind memory. [**cf.** AGE REGRESSION, AKASHIC RECORD, PREBIRTH]

CONCEPTUAL BLOCKBUSTING—to think through "body blocks" within one's mind or body by using logic, reasoning, and modern psychological techniques; to rid one's self of unwanted behavior, habits, complexes, and neuroses by finding the cause of the block and breaking it up by conscious mind reasoning, thereby freeing one's self of unwanted actions. (Inconcl.) [**cf.** CLUSTERS, BLOCKS, DRAINING OFF, MISSION CONTROL]

CONCEPTUAL SENSE—to perceive the "feeling of the concept" of a psychic experience, regardless of logical reasoning of the intellect, and apply it to life. [**cf.** CLAIRSENTIENCE, SUBJECTIVE SENSATION, SOUL ACTION]

CONCEPTUALIZATION—(laboratory) to find a theory that will not raise other problems but appears to fit the psychic experiment's findings; to form subjective ideas or principles. [**cf.** TAPPING INTO, LIMITATION, PSI-MEDITATED EXPERIMENTAL EFFECTS]

CONCEPTUALIZE THE EXPERIENCE—(biofeedback training) to interpret a psychic event that happened while hooked-up to a biofeedback instrument; to put intellectual thought into a subjective experience. [**cf.** BIOFEEDBACK TRAINING, CORTICAL INTEGRATIONS, BIOLOGICAL FILTER]

CONCLAVE—a secret place in the etheric world where the exalted angels meet to discuss their functions. [**cf.** ANGELS, OVERLORDS, SPIRITS OF THE SEVEN RAYS]

CONCLUSION-LEAPING—(laboratory) a tendency to look at the results of laboratory testing and form conclusions based on only a few experiences instead of a balanced answer based on many experiments, under all kinds of conditions. [**cf.** ESP, PSYCHO-PHYSIOLOGICAL PRINCIPLE]

CONCORDANT AUTOMATISM—1. a message coming through a medium from an etheric world intelligence in automatic writing, with words of similar sound repeated one after another until the intelligence comes into agreement with his message; as if the intelligence was learning the English language; e.g., Maureice, Morris, Mors. (Inconcl.)

2. two or more mediums getting pieces that must be put together to make knowledgeable information. [**cf.** CROSS-CORRESPONDENCE, ETHERIC SCRIPT, AUTOMATISM]

CONCRETE MIND—see CONSCIOUS MIND.

CONCUSSION—see RAPS.

CONDENSATION—to perceive psychic information in a psychic reading condensed into one vision, making the answer seem to be incorrect when given; e.g., "I see three people belonging to the family sitting around your table, indicating that three family members will be coming to visit you;" the querent already had had an aunt visit, later a nephew came to visit, and still later a girlfriend of the daughter came, thus combining three different time periods into one vision. **Syn.** COMPRESSION SYMBOL. **2.** (automatism) a number shorthand used in automatic writing; e.g., b4, they 2, 4told. [**cf.** ETHERIC SCRIPT, AUTOMATIC WRITING]

CONDENSATION DREAM—a manifestation of two or more dream messages that have been dormant, now condensed into a single disguised theme. (Inconcl.) [**cf.** DREAMS Appendix 2, HEART THOUGHTS, CRITICAL FACILITATE]

CONDENSED CONSCIOUSNESS—(esoteric) total intelligence, or all there is to know, aggregated in completeness and stored within an atom or the smallest particle; a realization within each particle that it knows all there is to know but this awareness is not full-blown at all times; the smallest particle also stores with this intelligence a record of all its experiences at the many rates of vibration it has moved since the beginning of time. Usage: "Atoms have a condensed consciousness and seem to oscillate where they have existed before as if they desire to learn all that is necessary in that vibrational frequency before moving on." (Inconcl.) [**cf.** DIVINE ENERGY, LIFE WAVE, ATOM, MATTER]

CONDITIONED AVOIDANCE RESPONSE—(psychology) to repress emotions repeatedly to please another, or to meet the requirements of the culture, until the repressed emotions are locked in an area of the muscles or in the subconscious mind; this reacts in an illness or unwanted behavioral pattern. (Inconcl.) [**cf.** CONDITIONED LEARNING, BLOCKS]

CONDITIONED CONSCIOUSNESS—to transfer one person's desires to the mind of another, through repeatedly programming, with or without permission, until the subject responds to the psychic's desires; used for good in healing illness and for evil in personal manipulation; programming can be accomplished by hypnosis, mental telepathic suggestions, mass lecturing, or sleep training; a good tool if subject has consented to the conditioning process. (Inconcl.) [**cf.** NONCONSCIOUS LEVEL, ON-THE-SPOT-HYPNOSIS, MENTAL HEALING, BIOCOMPUTER]

CONDITIONED LEARNING—to attain patterned responses of the mind and body by frequent repetition of an experience; accomplished by repetitious stimuli aimed at one's primal emotional and preservation needs; occurs through autosuggestion (affirmations), self-hypnosis, hetero-hypnosis, mental telepathic suggestion, or repetition of an activity which touches the Achilles heel of the subject. [**cf.** PSYCHOLOGICAL BIND, AFFIRMATIONS]

CONDITIONED REFLEXES—an automatic response of mind and body to specific stimuli because of an already learned condition response which relates to the present stimuli. [**cf.** CONDITIONED LEARNING]

CONDITIONED RESPONSE—(laboratory) repeated stimuli produces action by the subject when there are minimal hints of the stimuli; the subject reacts as if the stimuli were complete. (Inconcl.) [**cf.** SELECTIVE AMNESIA]

CONDITIONING—(Silva Mind Control) to learn to function at lower brain wave frequencies in order to use more of the brain. [**cf.** ALPHA WAVES, PSYCHIC DEVELOPMENT, SELF-HYPNOSIS, THREE FINGER TECHNIQUE]

CONDITIONING BIOFEEDBACK—to learn to reach an alpha level of awareness by hearing verbal appraisal when alpha level is reached; a special tone sounds when subject hooked up to a biofeedback instrument reaches an alpha level, and if human appraisal is given, subject reaches this level more quickly. (Inconcl.) [**cf.** CONDITIONED LEARNING, PASSIVE CONCENTRATION]

CONE OF POWER—1. concentration of energy co-created by a circle of people or objects; an unbroken circle forces energy to gather in the center; energy can be released and used for psychic needs by directing it with the mind; (a) psychics sitting in a development circle form an energy that can be perceived clairvoyantly as a silvery, blue light in spiral shape coming from the center of the circle, having the most energy at the tip; (b) (medieval) a circle was drawn on the floor for its energy to be utilized by the etheric world intelligences in their work; conjured up entities use the circle to raise a cone-shaped psychic energy field in the center; (c) a circle of persons around a patient, all concentrating on the patient's good health, results in more healing energies than standing in a line or sitting in an assembly; 2. diagnosing of disease: magnetic rays shaped like a megaphone over the diseased part of the body can be seen by clairvoyants; the colors of the cone reflect how the area is accepting the treatment. [cf. PYRAMID, STONEHENGE, CONICAL SHAPE, FORMS-WITH-POWER, MENTAL HEALING, PSYCHIC DEVELOPMENT CIRCLE]

CONFERRING OF POWER—(Tibet) psychic energy and knowledge given to the aspirant as he earns it but without awareness of it not being his own; teachers on this plane and in the etheric world stimulate and influence spiritual development when one is desirous and shows honest effort to advance. Syn. GIFT-WAVES. [cf. VIBRATIONS, THOUGHT-FORMS, BEAMED ENERGY]

CONFIDENCE CALL—(laboratory) 1. to feel, without doubt, that what one has perceived is correct before the score is taken. [cf. ZENER CARDS, MENTAL TELEPATHY] 2. a forceful vision or impression in a psychic development circle bringing an exact interpretation; what all psychics strive for. [cf. PSYCHIC INFORMATION]

CONFIGURATIONISM PARAPSYCHOLOGY—a doctrine that psychological phenomena do not occur through the summation of individual elements as reflexes or sensations, but through energy intelligences functioning separately or interrelatedly. [cf. STATES OF NONORDINARY REALITY, ETHERIC WORLD INTELLIGENCES]

CONFORMANCE BEHAVIOR—(laboratory) subject's desire or wish can alter the result of the psychic energy on the target. (Inconcl.) [cf. PSI-CONDUCTIVE STATE, MUDDY CONDITIONS, SHEEP AND GOATS EFFECT]

CONFRONT AND CONQUER—(dreams) (Malaysia, Senoi) to change the negative energies in an unpleasant or frightening dream and use them for one's benefit; ability to have a partial conscious awareness in a dream and to go toward the dream danger until it is conquered, and to manipulate the dream to end in something favorable for the

dreamer. [cf. LUCID DREAMING, OBJECTIVE DREAM, RELEASE-TYPE DREAMS]

CONFUCIANISM—a philosophy founded by Confucius (K'ung Fu'tzu) about 550 B.C.; teaches that man should adjust the heaven with the earth and preserve a balance; did not believe in reincarnation but that worldly harmony would help harmony in the etheric planes; "when spontaneous tradition breaks down it must be replaced with deliberate tradition"; gave rules for this in conduct, etiquette, ceremony, character, and a guide for social action in earth; also spelled **Confuciusism.**

CONFUSED SOUL-MINDS—1. a deceased human being who is earthbound, floating aimlessly among earthlings, and needing understanding and help; responsible for some hauntings; can be perceived clairvoyantly or clairaudiently as an apparition and a nuisance; confused because: (a) their earth beliefs emphasized one life only; (b) their earthly teachings presented a different-appearing etheric world; (c) they do not realize they are dead; (d) they are so imbedded by materialistic desires that they cannot let them go, and hover close to earthlings to recapture the memory of these desires; (e) they can see earth activities and do not realize earthlings cannot see them; (f) they are absorbed with a traumatic experience of death that causes them to search for answers to its cause, or the desires to let earthlings know more about this event; (g) mourners in earth keep them bound by constant thoughts about them and will not release their image or emotional memories; 2. earthbound entities can be released by psychics so that they can begin the learning process in the etheric world and be happy; 3. one form of ghost. [cf. EARTHBOUND ENTITY, ASTRAL SHELL, HAUNTING]

CONGESTED AREA—(magnetic healing) a static condition in the body where energy is not flowing through the meridian lines properly; manifests as a disease; area can be detected by: 1. a different color and pattern in the aura; 2. pendulum will change its swing pattern over static condition; 3. palm of hand will feel a "sticky" sensation in scanning person. (Inconcl.) [cf. ASSESSMENT, THERAPEUTIC TOUCH, ACUPUNCTURE, RADIONICS]

CONGREGATIONAL HEALING—(mental healing) a method of changing body chemistry of many persons through mass meditation and formulaic healing; the psychic minister, or healing practitioner, leads a guided meditation in front of the gathering, and when the majority is in alpha state,

127

utters words to change everyone's mental energy to healing energy; unity of thought creates a healing elemental, which hovers over the group, that reacts on the body chemistry of the persons individually; healings are usually gradual and persons feel better the next day. (Inconcl.) [cf. MENTAL HEALING, AFFIRMATION, MENTAL TELEPATHIC HEALING, MASS ELEMENTAL]

CONGRESS OF SPIRITS—(Nettie Colburn, 1862) name given by a group of deceased earth leaders who worked through Nettie, the medium of White House seances with Abraham Lincoln; group helped to counsel and guide the country during that administration. [cf. ANGEL HIERARCHY, MASTERS]

CONICAL SHAPE—a cone or megaphone form (of any substance) contains strong power in the middle of the shape which can be used by man for special work; understood and used in other cultures; e.g., DUNCE HAT, WITCHES-HAT, INDIAN TEEPEE. (Inconcl.) **Syn.** CAMERONA CONE. [cf. SHAKING TENT, ORACLE OF DELPHI, PYRAMID POWER, OVAL, FORMS-WITH-POWER]

CONJUNCTION—(astral projection) a feeling that one is again in a worldly vibration when the soul-mind returns to the physical body after an astral projection. [cf. CLICK, UPRIGHTING FORCE, SLOW-VIBRATORY DROP]

CONJURATION—1. to arouse an intelligence from the etheric world to come to an earth vibration for a special task or to assist an earth person; 2. to remove an etheric world entity with evil intent from the body of a person who has seizures of possession; accomplished by ritual and incantations; 3. to remove an etheric world entity (ghost) from a haunted area, and help them to overcome their emotional disturbance and go into higher learnings in the etheric world; 4. to prevent a poltergeist from using the energies of an earthling for their mischievous purposes. **Syn.** EXORCISM. [cf. POSSESSION, GHOST HAUNTING, POLTERGEIST, GUIDES, INVOCATION, EVOCATION]

CONJURE—(occult) to bring into existence by magic; to command, call upon, or raise up etheric world intelligences with an earnest desire for assistance, through incantations and rituals; to either invoke or evoke etheric world entities from one's subconscious thought-forms for definite purposes. [cf. CEREMONIAL MAGIC, CONJURING UP PHILLIP, EXORCISM]

CONJURE MAN—(United States black culture) a psychic who has recipes and capabilities to call upon etheric world entities; hires him or herself out for psychic purposes of good or evil intent. **Syn.** HOODOO DOCTOR, PRACTITIONER, VOODOO MAN. [cf. WHITE MAGICIAN, EVOCATION, LOW MAGIC]

CONJURE UP—(magic ceremony) a special learned ritual and densified thought used to bring etheric world intelligences into action for a desired task; theory: to become involved with real entities who are brought to life by personification of patterns of the psychic's collective subconscious which comes from inside and outside of the mind; it is sometimes more convenient to acknowledge the existence of an angel that performs this function than to recognize possession of a supernormal power within one's self that could be awakened by an invocation; "beings within and beings without." (Inconcl.) [cf. LICENSE TO DEPART, MUMBO-JUMBO, MUSING]

CONJUROR'S WAND—see DOWSING ROD.

CONJURING LODGES—(Native American) a hut or tent used by the early Indians for mediumistic purposes, to call down the etheric world intelligences for their guidance and psychic help. [cf. CONJURATION, TOTEM POLE, RITUAL, SWEAT LODGE]

CONJURING UP PHILLIP—name of an experiment by eight people in Toronto, Canada, who gathered weekly around a table for table-tipping phenomena; (1972) they used a pretend person in the etheric world to talk through the table; group decided to investigate the parapsychological happenings in their endeavor; success came about a year later when an alleged entity moved the table and continued to do so; (also name of their book). **Syn.** PK BY COMMITTEE. [cf. PHILLIP, TABLE TIPPINGS, RAPPING SPIRITS]

CONJUROR—a psychic, medium, or priest specializing in exorcism; see EXORCIST. [cf. EXORCISM, POLTERGEISTS, GHOSTS, INVOCATION]

CONSCIOUS ASTRAL PROJECTION—a willed projection wherein one is aware that their astral body is out of the physical body, and of what the astral body is experiencing; able to remember what transpired when back in the physical body; this is unusual. (Inconcl.) **Syn.** WILLED ASTRAL PROJECTION. [cf. VOLUNTARY ASTRAL PROJECTION]

CONSCIOUS AWARENESS—the normal process of learning for the physical body existence by using the five senses; to be alerted to environmental stimuli through the five senses and carried by the cerebrospinal nervous system to the brain; the stimuli are then sorted and judged; some information is stored and some reacted to immediately; beta level functioning; mental activity when awake and thinking. (Inconcl.) [cf. SYMPATHETIC NERVOUS SYSTEM, BRAIN]

CONSCIOUS COOPERATION—to accept help for one's self from etheric world intelligences by recognizing the psychic energy or psychic information as it is administered, similar to accepting help from people on the physical plane, without being in an altered state of consciousness. [cf. CLAIRSENTIENCE, INSPIRATIONAL THOUGHT]

CONSCIOUS COOPERATION CONSCIOUSNESS—principle: when atoms and smaller particles are colonized into molecules, cells, organs, or any compounds, they retain their individual function even though this congregation of atoms works together for the reason they have gathered as a unit. (Inconcl.) [cf. LAW OF FUNCTION Appendix 7, HOLISTIC BIOLOGY, GESTALT]

CONSCIOUS DEZGOSIS—(astral projection) a partial separation of the soul-mind from the physical body, usually for a short time, with the individual aware of this; a cerebral or neurological process taking place in the brain and adjacent area. (Inconcl.) **Sim.** SLIGHTLY OUT-OF-BODY. [cf. OUT-OF-RANGE OF CORD-ACTIVITY, SPONTANEOUS ASTRAL PROJECTION]

CONSCIOUS EXPLOSION—a spontaneous full-blown vision or a highly impressionable awareness happening unexpectedly, bringing out the cause of the restraining problem that has been repressed repeatedly; this in turn heals the mental or physical sickness; brought about by many new types of therapy; PSYCHODRAMA, GESTALT, PRIMAL THERAPY, GUIDED FANTASY, ROLFING, PAST LIVES THEORY, HYPNOTHERAPY. (Inconcl.) [cf. CURATIVE EDUCATION]

CONSCIOUS FANTASY—inner-mind pictures of scenes, images, or people pertaining to the subject's life; controlled deliberate activity brought about when alone; accomplishes psychological needs of the subject, such as gratification of wishes, exploration of concerns for the future, and consumption of time; these pictures build into future behavior as any thoughts do even though subject realizes it is not reality at the time they are entertained; classifications: 1. ongoing stream of associations; 2. recurring scenes; (do not confuse with VISUALIZATION, MEDITATION, or PSYCHIC DEVELOPMENT, **Syn.** DAYDREAMING. [cf. See Appendix 4 for clarification; BLANK STARE]

CONSCIOUS MIND—(esoteric) 1. a place in the physical body to manipulate information, located in the brain; a central station where environmental stimuli of hearing, seeing, tasting, smelling, feeling, and experiencing is brought to be sorted, sifted, reasoned with, logically thought about, classified, and categorized; these concepts and ideas are either acted upon immediately or stored in the akashic record; accumulated stress is stored in the sympathetic nervous system; 2. allows a person to become aware of their thoughts and mental operations in earth; a mechanism of the physical body in charge of the cerebrospinal nervous system to help the evolutionary path of soul-mind growth; 3. acts as the programmer, the software for the computer, the subconscious mind; responsible for the compartments in the subconscious mind; 4. a necessary physical organ for the invisible subconscious and superconscious mind to function through; 5. a liaison, using its own pineal gland as the center of receiving and distributing knowledge, emotions, mental-reflecting-ether, akashic records, from the five senses; 6. positive-masculine in polarity; 7. temporary intellect that transfers its knowledge to the invisible life force (subconscious mind) upon death; see BRAIN and CEREBROSPINAL NERVOUS SYSTEM; 8. (Descartes) the rational soul. (Inconcl.) **Syn.** MENTAL MIND, BRAIN. [cf. SYMPATHETIC NERVOUS SYSTEM, SOUL-MIND]

CONSCIOUS MOTOR PSYCHISM—(telekinesis) to allow the etheric world intelligences to intervene in one's body lightly and manipulate action within it, making the movement visible; the medium is in a light state of trance, not noticeable to the sitters or audience; preplanned and willed; used in some AUTOMATISM, MEDIUMSHIP HEALING, EXORCISM, STANDING READING. [cf. PARTIAL ANESTHESIA, MOTOR TELEPORTATION, PSYCHIC SURGERY, HUMAN-TK]

CONSCIOUS OF BEING—the state of atoms in the "beginning," in the perfect stage, which consisted of total consciousness; this total consciousness was aware of its total intelligence and of its function; intelligence knew it was intelligent. Usage: "There is 'conscious of being' in the tree, telling it to grow

129

to be a tree; there is 'conscious of being' in my liver, telling it to function as my liver should." (Inconcl.) [cf. OVERALL CONSCIOUSNESS, TOTALITY]

CONSCIOUSNESS—(esoteric) 1. a primal, nebulous, invisible energy comprising all of Totality, endowed with intelligence, energized with emotion; a forever-changing energy with interaction between the brain (physical senses), the soul-mind (instinctual senses), and cosmic mind (perfectness sense); changes according to the awareness of knowing as each entity evolves, making matter for one's present life; 2. invisible matter made of free atoms, alive, endowed with energy and intelligence, subject to the thought and emotions of one's mind, utilizing the law of polarity and vibration; various levels of matter correspond to levels of thought; 3. consciousness extends beyond time and space and is used in all kinds of "form" making reality of current thoughts; functions to constantly seek self-expression; 4. a total composite of what a person thinks, feels, and senses, accumulated from all that one has ever tasted, smelled, heard, felt, and seen, and one's responses to these, labeled "life"; 5. emotion is the activating force behind consciousness, and consciousness is the force behind all matter, in the physical, astral, etheric, etc., planes; what consciousness forms is always dependent upon the emotion behind the consciousness; feeling is the energy of consciousness; consciousness does not take up space; 6. (Annie Besant) "consciousness is an attribute or characteristic; knowing that we know"; 7. (Carl Jung) "consciousness arises from the psychoid of personality, depending upon the patterns of behavior and psychic contents that are primarily unconscious"; 8. (Seth) "a dimension of action, made possible by a series of creative dilemmas"; 9. the sum total of all ideas accumulated and affecting one's being; constantly renewing pattern of all one has thought and experienced; 10. consciousness and life are identical; 11. definition is constantly changing. (Inconcl.) Syn. LIFE. [cf. SOUL-MIND EVOLUTION, CONSCIOUSNESS Appendix 5]

CONSCIOUSNESS AWARENESS MOVEMENT—1. a large percentage of people in the United States and the world making sharp changes in their lifestyles and standards; people searching for "something else"; a life with more meaning to it; a desire to express one's self and to work with one's mind; 2. blending of the old with the new, East and West, science and psychology, philosophy and physics, logic and intuition, science and mysticism; 3.

science to investigate man's unused portion of the brain; people desiring to use more of their potential; 4. young people leading the adults in a change in life-style. [cf. AQUARIAN AGE, TRANSFORMATION, PLANETARY WORKER, NEW-AGE PSYCHOLOGY Appendix 5]

CONSCIOUSNESS CORD—(esoteric) one of the strands of the silver cord, running from the soul-mind to the pineal gland; carries the attributes and weaknesses from one's akashic records into one's present incarnation; returns the quality of knowledge learned from this incarnation to the soul-mind. (Inconcl.) Sim. MENTAL-CONSCIOUSNESS-CORD. [cf. MENTAL-CONSCIOUSNESS-SEED-ATOM, SILVER CORD, SOUL-MIND EVOLUTION]

CONSCIOUSNESS EVOLUTION—an explosion of interest in the activity of the brain and mind in the decade of the 1970s; scientists studying altered states of consciousness, not through intellect but through experience, found that the brain can be coaxed into various levels of awareness; the brain can turn in on itself, can realize other realities, and can be trained to control involuntary functions of the body; the brain has two hemispheres that show one's intellectual and sensational nature, and how one learns from each. (Inconcl.) [cf. AQUARIAN AGE, SPLIT-BRAIN HEMISPHERES, CONSCIOUSNESS, REALITY, BIOFEEDBACK TRAINING, TRANSFORMATION]

CONSCIOUSNESS JUNKIE—a person "hooked" on finding the new mind/body awareness and how to attain altered states of consciousness; attends workshops, seminars, intensives, group therapies, new exercise-concentration movements, and psychic development groups; seeks a life with more depth to it; e.g., GESTALT THERAPY, SUFI, ROLFING, TM, PAST LIVES THERAPY, KARATE, PYRAMID SEMINARS, HOLISTIC HEALTH, etc. [cf. AQUARIAN AGE, SOUL-MIND, EVOLUTION]

CONSCIOUSNESS OF INFINITE SPACE—a degree of meditation in which the meditator feels nothing but calmness and composure, and relates to the oneness of Totality. [cf. SAMADHI, WITHDRAWAL, SEED MEDITATION, MANTRA]

CONSCIOUSNESS OF SELF—to realize that one's life experiences are coming from within, not from without; to know one's world is a by-product of one's own imbalances; to realize that one is totally guided if one so desires and acts accordingly; to recognize that one must drop the mental mind struggle, a goal of earth incarnations. [cf. AWARENESS, TOTALITY, EVOLUTION]

CONSCIOUSNESS PROJECTION—see MENTAL PROJECTION.

CONSCIOUSNESS SHIFT—a gradual or sudden change in one's life-style and attitude that indicates one is functioning from another level of awareness; occurs in all living organisms and inanimate things (but much less noticeable); one can change by themselves as they sense a thrust of restlessness within or one can allow it to come about involuntarily with an emotional traumatic event; when it is time for one to raise their level of awareness, the consciousness festers like a boil or a flower trying to bloom, and bursts forth regardless of any restraint; recognizable by a change in one's choices of friends, colors, food, vocation, behavioral patterns, and attitude. **Sim.** TRANSFORMATION. [cf. NEW-AGE PSYCHOLOGY, PERSONALITY TRANSFORMATION, MIND-AWARENESS MOVEMENT]

CONSCIOUSNESS TRAVEL—see MENTAL PROJECTION.

CONSCIOUSNESS-CONTROL PROGRAMS—workshops and seminars now popular all over the United States that cater to levels of mind awareness and altered states of consciousness. [cf. CONSCIOUSNESS AWARENESS MOVEMENT, TRANSFORMATION, BLOCKS, HOLISTIC HEALTH, BIOFEEDBACK TRAINING, MEDITATION]

CONSCIOUSNESS-PRINCIPLE—(Tibet) that which makes one individual different from another individual; characteristics expressing in this incarnation formed from thinking and acting in other incarnations; expresses through the cerebrospinal nervous system mingled with the akashic record. [cf. SOUL-MIND, MEMORY BANK, TOTALITY, MONAD]

CONSCIOUNESS-SEED-ATOM—(esoteric) an invisible, tiny, concentrated center of energy located in the pineal gland; contains all the attributes and weaknesses from one's akashic record to use in this incarnation; (accomplished from one's many lives); attached by the consciousness cord to the soul-mind, accumulates new qualities of knowledge learned from this incarnation; (Bible) one of the books of life. (Inconcl.) **Sim.** MENTAL-SEED-ATOM. [cf. SILVER CORD, MENTAL-CONSCIOUSNESS-SEED-CORD, OVERSOUL]

CONSECRATED MAN—see MEDIUM.

CONSECRATED STATUS—(Egypt, Greece) a statue of an enchanted deity used as a protective talisman; had power to avert natural disaster or military defeat; derived from the statue used for oracle purposes. [cf. ORACLE, TALISMAN, AMULETING Appendix 2]

CONSTANT SENSORY INPUT—an environmental low-key hum or noise that reacts on etheric bodies, favorably or unfavorably; not always detectable to the physical ear; in constant duration and capable of being physically suppressed; e.g., air conditioner hum; sixty-cycle hum. (Inconcl.) **Syn.** WHITE NOISE STIMULI. [cf. MEDITATION, COSMIC MUSIC, CLAIRAUDIENCE]

CONSTITUTING RULERS—(I Ching) a part of the hexagram passage giving a characteristic meaning to the reading. [cf. GOVERNING RULER, CASTING OF LOTS]

CONSTRUCTIVE IMAGINATION—to mentally process a controlled stream of thought for special purposes; to deliberately call forth and use inner-mind pictures to solve one's problems, working out the many "ifs"; to use the imagination faculty in imagery or fantasy which will manifest in one's world if repeated often enough and if emotion is behind it. [cf. INNER-MIND PICTURES, NON-THOUGHT, IMAGERY]

CONSTRUCTS—(ufology) (T. J. Constable) vehicles of a highly intelligent technical design, made of substance unknown to science, seen in outer space; viewer feels that intelligent life of some kind is driving them; either they travel through space or have their abode in space; capable of shifting dimensions; vary in size, shape, and color; (do not confuse with CRITTERS that resemble animals). (Inconcl.) [cf. UFOLOGY, SPACE-BEING, PLAS-MATIC FAUNA, FLYING FLAPJACK, PROPULSION]

CONSULTANT—(casting of lots) psychic who uses dice or lots in a form of divination to answer problems of the querent. [cf. NONCHANGE, LOTS, PATTERNING ACROSS TIME, SYNCHRONICITY]

CONTACT HEALER—psychic or healing practitioner who administers magnetic healing; practitioner understands how to release magnetism from within their body by concentration and decreeing its healing ability to come forth; magnetic energy is released from the palms of the healer's hands into the patient's nervous system when they are passed over the patient's body; promotes the normalization of the cells, and the body can more easily heal itself. (Inconcl.) [cf. MAGNETIC HEALING, SCANNING, THERAPEUTIC TOUCH]

CONTACT HEALING—(magnetic healing) to touch the patient or the patient's auric field to promote a change in body chemistry so that the body can more easily heal itself; the practitioner touches the diseased area of the patient, the patient's temples, forehead, hands, or simulates touching same, a few inches above the patient; touching the patient's body per se has a psychological effect if the local law allows this; magnetic energy passes through the practitioner, directed by thought, into the nervous system of the patient, gradually normalizing body cells; sometimes instantaneous and sometimes takes a few days to be noticed; patient can feel hot, cold, tingles and physical sensations within the body, differing with each application and each practitioner; (term is sometimes misused to mean psychic, spiritual, or mediumistic healing, because of the lack of scientific investigation of unorthodox healings.) (Inconcl.) **Syn.** LAYING-ON-OF-HANDS. [cf. MAGNETIC HEALING and MENTAL HEALING Appendix 4, EARTH MAGNETISM]

CONTACT PHOTOGRAPHY—see KIRLIAN PHOTOGRAPHY.

CONTACT TELEPATHY—to physically touch the recipient's hand or wrist to make synchronization with the recipient, while or before giving a psychic reading. **Syn.** PSYCHOMETRIC READING. [cf. PURE PSYCHOMETRY, PRACTICAL PSYCHOMETRY, TELEPATHY]

CONTACTEE—(ufology) persons who have been contacted by a UFO vehicle or the life forms from the vehicle; anyone who is a part of a close-encounter-of-the-second- or third-kind. [cf. DISK SKY CRAFT, AMNESIA'S GRIP]

CONTACTEE SYNDROME—(ufology) a constant, peculiar feeling within the body, after having a close encounter with a UFO; one feels as if their body is possessed by an entity from outer space; contactee feels they are functioning at another's will. (Inconcl.) [cf. SPOTTER, CLOSE-ENCOUNTER-OF-THE-SECOND-KIND, RADIATION BURN]

CONTAGIOUS ENTHUSIASM—(laboratory) an attitude of anxious desire to hit the target produces better results in experiments. [cf. ESP, CHANCE EXPECTATION, DOWN THROUGH, RECEIVER OPTIMIZATION]

CONTAGIOUS MAGIC—(West Africa) **1.** to employ something that belongs to or has contact with the person one wants to send psychic energy to; when an object or person comes in contact with another object or person, the two will continue to act upon each other and be held together by an etheric thread (regardless of distance); this object or person and invisible thread can be used to contact the person or object after separation for psychic means; i.e., nail clippings, cloth containing the sweat from one's body, a footprint left in the sand, or hair from animal or person make good tools to transfer psychic energy for purposeful or evil intent; e.g., nail clippings are talked to, held, blessed, and comforted, which is picked up by the patient whose nail clippings they were; to distract a bothersome dog through the boy it bothers by distracting the boy and never seeing the dog; **2.** to use an object which was involved in an emotional act between living persons or animals to influence another person or object; objects retain emotional vibrations; e.g., a piece of garment taken from one who just argued to promote unrest in another; to use one's meditation chair for a distraught neighbor to sit in to become calmed. [cf. LAW OF CONTAGION and LAW OF RITUAL Appendix 7]

CONTAINERS OF MAGICAL POWER—(Native American, Pueblo) stones, mountains, rivers, flowers, and all of nature contains psychic energy that is attuned to mankind and can be tapped, used, or redirected by the Native American for the benefit of mankind. [cf. BOTANE, MINPSI, TALISMANS, TOTEMS, MANTIC ART, SYNCHRONICITY]

CONTEMPLATION—to reach an alpha state of consciousness, during a period of quietude with one's self, by giving undivided attention to one idea; methods: **1.** (Rosicrucian) to use judgment and reason which comes from the center of one's being after becoming quiet; to discriminate and evaluate imaginative constructions; **2.** to dwell upon one philosophical concept for many minutes allowing many meanings and variations to spring forth; **3.** to let the mind wander from one idea to the next with no particular direction, while the body is very relaxed and quiet; **4.** to direct one's attention to a project, study it, and ponder upon it with the attitude that one cannot fail. [cf. MEDITATION, CONCENTRATION]

CONTINUITY—(cycles) theory: every thing constantly moves in cyclic order; the time span differs with each thing and person; the repetition of movement exists. [cf. CYCLES Appendix 5, BIO-RHYTHM, SYSTEM OF WAVES, TIME SERIES ANALYSIS]

CONTINUITY OF LIFE—survivalist theory: some kind of life form or life awareness of each person exists in the etheric world after the person is dead; the soul-mind contains the individual's personality, achievements, and liabilities, which make a life form existence after the physical body is shed on earth; this life form keeps living on in the etheric world; (do not confuse with the theory of REINCAR-NATION). (Inconcl.) [cf. REINCARNATION, SOUL-MIND EVOLUTION, SURVIVALIST]

CONTOUR THEORY—(esoteric) people live in a world with cosmic vibrations constantly affecting them, but have freedom of choice; by learning about the nature of these vibrations, they can change their own destinies within the bounds of the cosmic universes. (Inconcl.)

CONTRA-GRAVITATIONAL—that which is no longer under the law of gravitation, such as levitation of a chair. Usage: "The stones of the pyramid were contra-gravitational due to their precise alignment." (Inconcl.) [cf. GRAVITY CON-TROL, GRAVITATIONAL WAVES, BENDING LIGHT, ANTI-MATTER]

CONTRADISTINCTION TO SEE—the urge of the psychic to see a certain thing when giving a psychic reading; his or her own inner conflict and desire to prove their own reactions to an event influences the reading; the information comes through showing a contrast to the event. [cf. SETTING THE MOOD, PSI-CONDUCIVE STATES, SURFACING]

CONTROL—1. (mediumship) an etheric world intelligence that has learned to synchronize with a medium to perform physical phenomena; intelligence can be trusted to carry out the desires of the medium without harm to the medium during and after the trance state; intelligence takes full charge during the trance when the medium puts aside free will; medium preplans as to length of the session and type of phenomena to take place. [cf. DESIRED-CONTROL] 2. (laboratory) a dissociation effect comes through the psychic as a secondary person-ality talking and acting as if it were an etheric world intelligence; theory: repressed characteristics of psychic are capable of taking over in an altered state of consciousness. [cf. GUIDE, TESTING MEDIUM-SHIP, MEMORY STORAGE SYSTEM]

CONTROL PERSONALITY—(taped voice phenom-enon) a life intelligence that repeatedly takes charge of the subject matter and is a help to other intelligences who want to project sound on tape; (do not confuse with a GUIDE or DISCARNATE ENTITY as the tape personality is still under study, and its abode has not been determined). (Inconcl.) [cf. TAPED VOICE PHENOMENON, VOICE BROAD-CAST CONTROLLER]

CONTROLLED CLAIRVOYANT—a psychic who has trained to see psychic visions at will and is in charge if these visions occur, as opposed to visions flashing whenever the etheric world desires. [cf. GOING-TO-LEVEL, CLOAK OF INSULATION, MISCARRIAGES]

CONTROLLED COINCIDENCES—advantageous and pleasant events happening, one right after another, to a person who believes very devotedly and intensely in a power higher and more intelli-gent than the self, who will guide one through this incarnation, and it happens; as long as one keeps this faith and belief steady and frees the self from worry, these beneficial experiences will continue. (Inconcl.) [cf. LAW OF LIKE ATTRACTS LIKE Ap-pendix 7, NEGATIVE THOUGHT, POSITIVE THOUGHT]

CONTROLLED EMPATH—one who is capable of clairempathy and can drain other people of their psychic power; psychic thus gains psychic power or physical energy for the self. (Inconcl.) [cf. SPLODG-ER, PARASYTE, PSYCHIC TRANSFER, PSYCHICAL INVASION]

CONTROLLED MULTIPLE HAUNTINGS—execu-tion of distress to householders by a clever powerful psychic who beams psychic energy for evil intent; subordinate psychic chooses varied antics to cause disturbances within the furnishings of the house-hold continually; householders feel they are being attacked by ghosts, poltergeists, and nightmares; (do not confuse with a HAUNTING from an ethereal entity). (Inconcl.) **Syn.** HEX. [cf. SPELLED, GHOSTS, CURSE]

CONTROLLED PSYCHISM—to perceive psychic information or psychic activity at one's own discre-tion only; psychic has earned the right to communi-cate with a superior intelligence and has domination over his conscious and subconscious minds; natural-born psychic is more apt to have psychic events occur at random; uncontrolled psychism leads to an unhealthy body and spills over into and interferes with one's daily lifestyle; daily sittings for a short time to open one's psychic doors, and only after meditation, is the best method of taking charge of one's psychic skills; one exception to this statement is the skill of CLAIRSENTIENCE (intuition, hunchability) which is not harmful to one when it happens unexpectedly. **Syn.** WILLED PSYCHISM. [**cf.** CONTROL, GUIDE, COORDINATED PSYCHICAL FUNCTIONS]

CONTROLLED RELAXATION—to will an altered state of consciousness when desired; to dominate one's conscious mind activity so it will become passive and step aside, allowing the subconscious or superconscious mind to take over upon command only; to go into meditation, hypnosis, or opening of psychic doors quickly. [**cf.** MEDITATION, INSPIRATIONAL THOUGHT, AWAKE CONTROL, ATTUNEMENT, IDEOMOTOR ACTION]

CONTROLLER—(medieval) see PSYCHIC.

CONVENTIONAL DOWSING—to use the rules and method with the pendulum or dowsing rod which works best for one's self, regardless of what others do or recommend. [**cf.** RADIESTHESIA, PENDULUM, DOWSING]

CONVERGENT—left hemisphere thinkers. (Inconcl.) [**cf.** SPLIT BRAIN Appendix 5]

CONVERGENT OPERATIONS—(dreams) to awaken the sleeping person in the sleep research laboratory to record their dream. [**cf.** MIRRORED, DREAMS, NREM, DREAM RESEARCH LABORATORIES]

CONVERSION HYSTERIA—the psychic transfer of the psychiatrist's unconscious desires and expectations to the patient, surfacing as subpersonalities in the patient; traits of character thrust into the patient's life-style intermittently which they did not know they had; not recognizable by the psychiatrist to be his or her own traits; patient psychically tunes into the psychiatrist while in a subdued state at therapy sessions. [**cf.** PSYCHIC TRANSFER, SPONTANEOUS SYMPTOM SHIFTING]

CONVULSIONARY—(possession) one who is possessed by a low-grade entity which frequently shows itself in seizures; individual goes into an involuntary cataleptic trance without the power to stop it; body does contortions, and voice says words the individual would not normally say. (Inconcl.) [**cf.** DUAL PERSONALITY, RESCUE CIRCLES, STATIC ELECTRICITY]

CONVULSIVE MEDIUM—one who trembles and becomes feverish and overexcited when the etheric world entities are intervening for communication. [**cf.** TRANCE, MEDIUMSHIP, INITIATORY SICKNESS, FORCED PSI]

COOCCURRENCE—two separate events happening with one central theme that are meaningfully related and yet not having a cause and effect connection, nor either one affecting the other. (Inconcl.) **Syn.** SYNCHRONICITY. [**cf.** I CHING, SORTES, CASTING OF LOTS]

COOL DOWN STAGE—(laboratory) (astral projection) a short period of relaxation before one attempts to astrally project proves to be inducive to projection. [**cf.** STRETCH, EXTERIORIZATION, AUTOSCOPIC HALLUCINATION, ASTRAL PROJECTION]

COOPERANTS—members of a seance circle, sitting for a special purpose; see SITTERS. [**cf.** SEANCE, PHYSICAL PHENOMENA]

COOPERATIVE KINGDOMS—term used by Findhorn for the *kingdom* classifications: 1. human being kingdom; 2. nature kingdom, devic and elemental; 3. inanimate kingdom, devic and elemental. [**cf.** PLANES, ANGEL HIERARCHY, NATURE SPIRITS]

COOPERATIVE SUGGESTION—(hypnosis) to be under the influence of a hypnotist's suggestions, knowing or not knowing one is being hypnotized; to give undivided attention to the hypnotist's stare and verbiage, which plays on one's emotional and basic needs, puts the conscious mind in a passive state, and allows the subconscious mind to accept data as is; one is easily swayed to the beliefs and suggestions of the hypnotist and gradually absorbs them and believes they are one's own. [**cf.** POWER OF THE GAZE, SUGGESTION, EGO STRENGTHENING, ON-THE-SPOT-HYPNOSIS]

COORDINATE POINTS—(Seth) pure, minute, ethereal energy centers (created at creation), acting as transformers and supports in the atmosphere; connecting one level of existence to another making creation continuous. (Inconcl.) **Syn.** SUBORDINATE POINTS, NODES. [**cf.** ELECTRONS, PLANES, NODES]

COORDINATED PSYCHICAL FUNCTIONS—to use more than one psychic talent as a unit to bring forth psychic information; e.g., automatic writing, plus seeing the entity who is taking over the hand to perform the task; seeing a vision and hearing inner voices at the same time. [**cf.** MENTAL PSYCHIC PROCESS, SUBJECTIVE DIMENSION, PSI-INTERACTIVE BIO-MOLECULES]

COPAL—(Maya) used as an incense; invokes etheric world intelligences and encourages blessings for the burner. [**cf.** BOTANE, ROSEMARY, FRANKINCENSE, EMOTIONAL CONSCIOUSNESS]

COPARTICIPANTS—members of a seance circle, frequently called this in place of "sitters," because they are being used in conjunction with the phenomena, and it cannot take place if one were absent; members' bodies are used as a battery or used for the ectoplasm they exude. [cf.SEANCE, SITTERS, ETHERIC WORLD INTELLIGENCES, ETHEREAL SMOKE, HUMAN BATTERIES]

CORAL CASTLE—a structure built by one man without machinery from stones heavier and larger than those used in the pyramids; used native coral of Florida taken out of the ground located near Miami; builder is Edward Leedskalnin; believed that he knew the secret of levitation of huge rocks (similar to the methods used to build the pyramids). (Inconcl.) [**cf.** MINPSI, PYRAMIDOLOGY]

CORBEILLE-A-BEC—(French, "basket with a beak") a tool used by etheric world intelligences to write words on paper with the help of the medium's finger tips; a homemade instrument made from an ordinary basket or from wood, with a pencil attached, so that it writes similar to a PLANCHETTE; see CORBEILLE-TOUPIE. [**cf.** AUTOMATISM]

CORBEILLE-TOUPIE—an ordinary basket with attached pencil used by etheric world intelligences to write a message; medium lightly places fingertips on basket and it moves to form letters, bringing psychic information in the skill of automatism. [**cf.** OUIJA BOARD, INDIRECT PSYCHOGRAPHY, PLANCHETTE, AUTOMATISM]

CORD-ACTIVITY RANGE—(astral projection) an ethereal string attached to the astral body in an astral projection, stretching as far as the projector desires to go; ethereal energy, breath, and "spirit" runs back and forth through this thread while bodies are detached; can be perceived clairvoyantly when extended but it is not known where it is stored when not in use. (Inconcl.) [**cf.** SILVER CORD, IN-THE-RANGE-OF-CORD-ACTIVITY]

COREAD—to perceive psychic information about the subject who is being counseled without any questions being asked by the subject. [**cf.** PSYCHIC INFORMATION, READING, CLIENT]

CORN MAIDENS—(Native American, Pueblo) nature spirits who live in the atmosphere and clouds that are in charge of the corn harvest; also called CLOUD BEINGS. [**cf.** STAR SPIRITS]

CORONA—1. (scientific) a white or colored circle or several circles ranging in color from red outside to blue inside; seen around a luminous body, i.e., the sun or moon; attributed to the diffraction caused by thin clouds, dust, or mist. **Syn.** AUREOLA, AUREOLE. 2. the upper half seen over heads of very religious people by clairvoyants; depicted by artists as a white half circle (over masters' or saints' heads); 3. (esoteric) emanations around an object perceived clairvoyantly as white glowing lines; believed to be the emanations picked up on the Kirlian camera. (Inconcl., opinions differ in all countries) [**cf.** KIRLIAN EFFECT, NIMBUS, ETHERIC DOUBLE, ULTRAFAINT LUMINISCENCE, ULTRA OUTER-AURA]

CORONA OF THE SUN—the protrusion of flames extending millions of miles from the sun. (Inconcl.)

CORONA PATTERNS—a variation of colors around objects and organisms seen from the photographs taken by the Kirlian camera; form similarities according to the similar nature of the objects and organisms photographed. (Inconcl.) [**cf.** RADIATION-FIELD PHOTOGRAPHY, EARTH'S ELECTRICAL FIELD, LUMINESCENCE]

CORONA PHOTOGRAPHY—1. to use a special high-voltage camera to photograph electromagnetic emanations (invisible to the physical eye) coming from organisms or objects; 2. radiations photographed by the high-voltage camera are discharges caused by the high-frequency currents of the camera, as opposed to belief that the radiations are coming from a person, varying with each person. (Inconcl.) **Syn.** KIRLIAN PHOTOGRAPHY, RADIATION FIELD PHOTOGRAPHY. [**cf.** COLD LIGHT, TELSA COIL

CORPOREAL—belonging to the material world; pertaining to the third dimension, physical matter, mundane. [**cf.** BUDDHIC PLANE, ATOMIC MATTER, HAPPY HUNTING GROUND]

CORPOREAL ENVELOPE—the physical body encompassing the soul-mind while living in the earth plane. [**cf.** ASTRAL BODY, BODIES AND PLANES

135

Appendix 5, MENTAL PLANE, GREY LAND, DARKNESS OF IGNORANCE]

CORPOREAL SUBJUGATION POSSESSION—(mediumship) the provoking of involuntary body movements of a medium by an inferior etheric world entity; entity acts on the physical organs of medium, consistently, to bring forth psychic information or physical phenomena; information or actions are not necessarily incorrect or in poor taste, but it becomes a nuisance and rules one's life; e.g., writing medium made to write on the wall or paper at any time whether convenient or proper. **Syn.** POSSESSION OF A MEDIUM. [**cf.** SIMPLE OBSESSION, MORAL SUBJUGATION]

CORPOREAL VISION—(Roman Catholic) to perceive a person, looking real and fleshlike, capable of speech and movement, who has passed from this earth plane; perceived by more than one psychic: usually a great leader in his or her past life; i.e., a crisis operation or need-determined phenomena, e.g., vision of Jesus walking and talking to the disciples when he appeared in the flesh after the resurrection; theories: disciples were seeing the etheric resurrection body of the Christ, or were seeing a kind of wraith fashioned by the angels; (do not confuse with BILOCATION which happens to a living person). (Inconcl.) [**cf.** PHYSICAL TRANSFIGURATION, SPONTANEOUS PHYSICAL MANIFESTATION, INCORRUPTIBILITY]

CORPSE ASPECT—(astral projection) describes the physical body when the astral flight lasts a long time; the physical body does not get much cosmic energy and will look very much as if the person is dead, but actually the physical body is hibernating. [**cf.** SUSPENDED ANIMATION, OUT-OF-RANGE-OF-CORD-ACTIVITY, SOLID DOUBLES]

CORPSE CADAVER—(Haiti, Voodoo) see ZOMBIE.

CORPSE CANDLE—a nature spirit taking the form of a tiny flame to prophesy a coming death; hovering at dawn over the place where the death will take place. [**cf.** FETCH LIGHT]

CORPSE LIGHT—1. pale, cloudy, phosphorous lights flitting or hovering over a graveyard at night; can be seen with physical eyes; (a) (folklore) an etheric world entity misleading a night traveler; (b) (Germany) a deceased person who is confused about their death and doesn't understand their new home; (c) an ASTRAL SHELL of one of the persons buried in the graveyard, still clinging to material

life; 2. misty lights in cloudy formation that appear when a tomb, catacomb, or grave which has been long closed is first opened. **Syn.** FOOLISH FIRE, IGNIS FATUUS, JACK-O'-LANTERN, FAIRY FIRE. [**cf.** DEATH SCIENCE, PLANES, CONFUSED SOUL-MIND]

CORPSE POSE—see PALMING THE EYES.

CORPUS CALLOSUM—the connection between the two hemispheres of the brain. (Inconcl.) [**cf.** SPLIT BRAIN Appendix 5]

CORRECT HEALTH—(holistic health) theory: the condition of one's physical body when both the soul-mind and conscious mind agree to that condition; does not necessarily mean good health; the body encompasses the soul-mind, as a tool for each incarnation, but does not need perfect health to serve as this tool; there are earthly experiences that can only be found in physical conditions; correct health means: 1. the conscious mind has accepted the body condition with an attitude that this is an opportunity to grow and learn; 2. or the subconscious mind accepts the conscious mind's desire to abuse the body and/or think negatively, to indraw negative conditions, as an opportunity to manifest as ill health in order to perfect itself; correct health is recognizable if an individual lives a productive life and maintains a cheerful outlook toward life regardless of physical afflictions. [**cf.** CURATIVE EDUCATION Appendix 5, HOLISTIC HEALTH, LAW OF HEALING Appendix 7]

CORRELATION—(dreams, Carl Jung) a method of balancing the images in a dream as symbology with the inner and outer movements of the individual to make the dream meaningful. [**cf.** PARADOXAL SLEEP, DREAM GLOSSARY, COMPENSATORY DREAMS, PICTURE METAPHORS]

CORRESPONDENCE—see LAW OF CORRESPONDENCE Appendix 7.

CORRESPONDENCE-IN-TIME—two events happening simultaneously bringing about a significant end result, able to be tuned into with psychic skills; events are not related under the law of cause and effect according to today's technology; occurs in casting of lots and the pendulum's swing. **Syn.** MAGIC CAUSALITY. [**cf.** CASTING OF LOTS, SORTES, I CHING, RADIESTHESIA, PENDULUM POWER]

CORROBORATOR—(laboratory) a witness to a case of spontaneous psi; one who observed the subject during the psychic experience, observed events connected with it, or received a report about it soon after the occurrence; witness is in a position to confirm in whole or in part the subject's account of the psi experience. [cf. EMOTIONAL PSI, SPONTANEOUS OCCURRENCE, SHOCK WAVES, RANDOM PSYCHISM]

CORTICAL INTEGRATION—(biofeedback training) to control a single cell in one's body while hooked-up to a biofeedback instrument; to give recognition to the mingling in the brain of the sensory system, motor system, and memory bank and to control these systems until a single cell is under the conscious will of the subject; the instrument tells the subject what is happening in the body, making it easier to do. [cf. BIOFEEDBACK TRAINING, BRAIN, FOCUSED ATTENTION, CYBERNETIC LOOP, PROGRAMMER]

CORTICALLY MEDIATED STABILIZATOIN—abbr. CMS; to use meditation to reduce anxiety. [cf. QUIET REFLECTION, REVERIE, SELF-GENERATED STIMULUS]

COSMIC—pertains to the vastness of ALL-THERE-IS and the laws that maintain all-there-is; includes infinite wisdom that all in the vastness has access to; total; macrocosm. [cf. MONAD, DIVINE, TOTALITY, COSMOS]

COSMIC ATOM—the seed of the universe that has the potential of perfecting the universes and is constantly manifesting in this direction; divine spark of Totality; motivation of evolution. **Syn.** COSMIC MONAD. [cf. TOTALITY, ONE, NOUS]

COSMIC AXIS—(Native American) a vertical line which connects the levels of heaven with the levels of earth and the levels below the earth; a physical place in earth from which extraordinary emanations rise; (emanations were seen by a Native American priest coming from that spot). [cf. SHAKING TENT, NANABUSH, HOLLOW EARTH, PLANE OF DESIRES]

COSMIC BAND—an exalted, lofty rank in angel hierarchy in charge of keeping harmony in the universe; sends messengers of lower rank to communicate with mankind through various psychic skills to offer assistance and guidance to build and maintain this harmony. [cf. ETHERIC WORLD INTELLIGENCES, ANGELS]

COSMIC BEING—(esoteric) 1. an intelligent, eternal mass of energy living within its own plane of vibration; a life form evolved enough to have a soul or evolved past a soul; comes from outer space where it appears to live; unfamiliar to human beings in looks and actions; see BEING; 2. a human being who has earned the rank of angel and inhabits the air; communicates with earthlings. [cf. MAG.:IFICENT DEVAS, PLANETARY ANGEL, SEVEN SPIRITS OF GOD]

COSMIC BIOLOGY—a study of the effects of the solar cycles and how the periodic radiations of energy from the sun have an influence on the behavior of earth people. [cf. BIOLOGICAL CYCLES, CIRCADIAN RHYTHM]

COSMIC CHORD—music and sounds in the atmosphere of moving energies of nature; detectable by clairaudient perception and modern instruments; theory: everything emits a sound and when peace prevails, the sounds are like a harmonious chord; the sound is indescribable in present language. **Syn.** MUSIC OF THE SPHERES. [cf. CLAIRAUDIENT, VIBRATION]

COSMIC CHRIST—1. a primal invisible energy field that mankind cannot duplicate, rearrange, or destroy; necessary for all existences; the motivating force behind evolution, broken up into individual motivation within each seed species; dominating factor for all things to grow into perfectness; 2. (Bible) the center of divinity within all things that makes all things possible; cosmic seed; (humans) the "I AM" and the CHRIST WITHIN. **Syn.** MONAD. [cf. MONADOLOGY, VITAL LIFE FORCE]

COSMIC CLOCK—see CIRCADIAN RHYTHM; (do not confuse with BIORHYTHM).

COSMIC COMMUNION—to become integrated into the whole; not feeling at one with Totality, but being Totality itself; highest state one can experience in the physical body; takes much meditation practice to achieve. **Syn.** BLISS, MEDITATIVE ECSTASY. [cf. SILENCE, SATORI, NIRVANA]

COSMIC COMPUTER—(esoteric) a gigantic guiding intelligence that has order and plans for itself and its inhabitants; within the etheric invisible vibrations is a huge memory bank that records all ideas, experiences, and events that occur in all the worlds; available for one to use when one learns how to tap into it; intelligence is sorted and filed orderly for convenience; an invisible grandiose mechanism of all the knowledge to make people function, giving them a place to function and containing all the information they will ever need and desire; mankind is the software and needs to learn how to tune into the correct program compartment and how to read the printouts. **Syn.** TOTALITY. [**cf** CONSCIOUS MIND, SUBCONSCIOUS MIND]

COSMIC CONSCIOUSNESS—(esoteric) 1. an invisible, intelligent, living energy without direction, limits, or boundaries in its primeval form; a state of perfection making Totality; 2. intelligence and energy vibrating at such a speed that it penetrates within and around all things, animate and inanimate, capable of being directed by man's mind to slow down to thousands of different vibrational frequencies to form varying levels of matter; 3. that which constructs time, space, and beyond; contains atoms, smaller particles, and vital life force; aware of its function, that it can be broken up and manipulated into different aspects for humanity's schooling and progression; for this reason, all matter is minutely connected and never detached from the whole; immeasurable, perfect, intelligent, whole, constantly moving and changing; 4. (Bob Toben) pure consciousness; what is beyond space-time is within everything and can connect with man and influence man within space-time; 5. (meditation) (Maharishi Mahesh Yogi) a state of being aware well above normal wakefulness but below the highest state of consciousness; 6. total energy that transcends time-space and constructs time-space. (Inconcl.) [**cf.** TOTALITY, METAPHYSICS, MONAD, VIBRATION]

COSMIC CREATIVITY—see TOTALITY.

COSMIC CYCLE—(esoteric) every 26,000 years earth's solar system working as a unit completes one revolution around a Great Central Sun; earth's solar system is parallel to the Great Central Sun as a planet is to earth's sun. **Syn.** ONE AGE. [**cf.** PISCEAN AGE, AQUARIAN AGE, PLANETARY INITIATION]

COSMIC DESTINY—to become a perfect cosmos of universes motivated by the potential within the cosmic seed; the unfolding of the cosmic seed by an evolutionary process of each atom; length of time required is not predestined but depends upon the choice of men and women and their free will; each has one predestination which is to become a perfect specimen of humanity according to the potential within their seed which is to add to the evolvement of the perfect cosmos.

COSMIC DYNAMICS—the study of invisible and visible universal motion.

COSMIC EDUCATION—the study of the universal laws and their relation to the whole as a unit; study of humanity's place, responsibility and benefits to and from the whole. **Sim.** COSMOLOGY.

COSMIC EGG—1. the substance permeating throughout all infinity, which is used to form all things in infinity. **Syn.** TOTALITY. 2. (Native American, California) an egg-shaped symbol containing two supernatural beings representing heaven and earth uniting to produce images and thoughts, making our earth world a reality. [**cf.** HUMAN AURA, POLARITY, TOTALITY]

COSMIC ELECTRICITY—see PSYCHIC ENERGY. (Inconcl.)

COSMIC ELECTRONICS—esoteric theory: essence of mankind's spiritual evolution is governed by the laws of electronics; the atmosphere and humanity are full of electrical particles which aid each one in their spiritual path. (Inconcl.) [**cf.** ENERGY CURRENTS, NODES, ATOM, PRIMAL ENERGY]

COSMIC ENERGY—1. the law of movement that keeps all atoms vibrating; 2. an energy permeating all space necessary to all forms of life, known and unknown; see VITAL LIFE FORCE. [**cf.** TOTALITY, MICROCOSM, PRIMAL ENERGY]

COSMIC ENTITY—an intelligent life form coming from the etheric world making itself known to an earthling; possibilities: 1. a space being; 2. an extraterrestrial being; 3. a high-ranking angel. [**cf.** UFOLOGY, ANGEL HIERARCHY, STAR TRAVELERS, MENTAL INTERCHANGE]

COSMIC FIRE—1. the primal source in its unorganized form emanating as the divine being before it became the universe. **Syn.** GREAT WHITE LIGHT, IMPERISHABLE ONE, GOD. 2. the potential energy lying dormant in the base of the kundalini that has the potential to become ignited and help the human race evolve on its path to Totality. **Syn.** KUNDALINI FIRE. [**cf.** SERPENT FIRE, FIRE, KANDA]

COSMIC GENERATOR—(Czechoslovakia) an instrument that will be able to collect psychic energy out of the air, store it until it is needed, and send it out for reuse; now being invented. (Inconcl.) [**cf.** COSMIC ELECTRICITY, ATOMS, BEAMED ENERGY]

COSMIC GOD—(esoteric) the intelligence behind the pattern or aura of the celestial planes that governs all things in the universe; that which puts the potential within the seed of all things and then sustains and motivates that potential development. **Syn.** TOTALITY.

COSMIC GUSHERS—see WHITE HOLES.

COSMIC HOSTS OF LIGHT—intelligences of the higher etheric realms in charge of physical worldly trials that earthlings can do little about, such as mass karma; will guide the earthling if called upon. [cf. ANGEL HIERARCHY, BODIES AND PLANES Appendix 5, CONGRESS OF SPIRITS, ANOINTED ONES, ASCENDED BEING]

COSMIC INTERVAL—the time one spends in the etheric world from one death in the earth world until rebirth into the earth world. [cf. REINCARNATION, PRINCIPLES OF MAN]

COSMIC LIGHT—see VITAL LIFE FORCE.

COSMIC LOVE—to be in love where one is essentially beyond the vicissitude of love responses of a beloved person; an unconditional love that says, "If it is your pleasure, it is my pleasure to see you be pleasurable"; a heart love that grows into a spirit love. [cf. UNIVERSAL KISS]

COSMIC MAGNETIC FORCES—energy radiations that come from earth's sun in earth's solar system; masculine-positive force dealing with the law of polarity to the magnetic forces of the earth (feminine-negative). [cf. VIBRATIONS, POLARITY]

COSMIC MAINSTREAM—all knowledge known about the universe to this point in time and the inner urge that thrusts everything to keep moving upward and onward.

COSMIC MASS—(Sufi) see TOTALITY.

COSMIC MASTER—(AMORC) a soul-mind who no longer has to reincarnate on earth due to its attainment and the wisdom acquired through its many incarnations on earth. [cf. MASTERSHIP, WISDOM, KARMA, OVERSOUL]

COSMIC MEMORY—(esoteric) a huge ethereal system working like a computer that carefully organizes and stores records of all intelligence stemming from the solar system; used when needed by the solar systems; the means of expression by the solar systems at this time; held together by the law "for every action there is a reaction." **Sim.** MEMORY BANK, AKASHIC RECORD. [cf. REINCARNATION, CYCLES, KARMA, CONDENSED CONSCIOUSNESS]

COSMIC MESSIAH—theory: there is one soul-mind in the etheric world who has earned the rank to be overseer of the one family, the world. [cf. ANGEL HIERARCHY, AVATAR]

COSMIC MIND—the sum total of all intelligence that ever was and ever will be; all ideas, formulas, pictures, sounds, colors, shapes, living organisms, non-living things, numbers, human-being life forms, other intelligent life forms, emotions, planets, stars; in fact, manifestations of any nature and the laws that govern them. **Syn.** TOTALITY, DIVINE MIND, UNIVERSAL MIND, GOD. [cf. TOTALITY, MONAD]

COSMIC MUSIC—sound in space that does not register upon the normal hearing of a human being; 1. everything throughout nature, from the atom to the largest planet, emits sounds at frequencies that cannot be heard physically, but can be perceived clairaudiently and by modern instruments; 2. cosmic sound registers on the spirillae of the pineal gland via the superconscious mind, and influences the ethereal bodies of human beings, playing a part in their physical life. (Inconcl.) 3. cosmic sound has power to create, destroy, and recreate manifold universes, reaching throughout eternity, carrying information as it goes; this sound brings news of the vast stellar nebulae and interstellar spaces of all the existing spatial firmaments; 4. a harmonic wave of sound of the entire cosmos; a sytem of unheard music; a rhythm in structure and movements from the molecule to the solar system; possessing a keynote of its own; whatever is manifesting harmoniously in earth will produce a harmonious chord in the etheric world. **Syn.** NONMANIFEST SOUND, SEEDS OF SOUND. [cf. SOUL-MIND KEY NOTE, PSYCHOACOUSTICS, SPHERES OF RESONANCE]

COSMIC OCTAVES—(estoeric) groupings of vibrational frequencies in the electromagnetic spectrum; man has discovered how to harness and use ultra-violet rays, x-rays, gamma rays, and cosmic rays at the higher frequency end of the scale, and the infra-red, radio waves and broadcasting band of the lower frequencies, with the visible light forming colors in the center. [cf. COLOR, ULTRA-VIOLET, KIRLIAN EFFECT]

COSMIC PICTURE GALLERY—ethereal records in still picture form in the higher planes of the etheric world that record every thought, action and event of earth since earth was first formed; comparable to tiny microfilm; reflects itself in exact duplicate on the astral planes where the clairvoyant can perceive it at times. (Inconcl.) [cf. AKASHIC RECORD OF THE EARTH, REINCARNATION, MENTAL-REFLECTING-ETHER]

139

COSMIC PROCESS—(Egypt) (esoteric) belief that the evolutionary progress of each human being is important to the total substance; symbolized by a circle divided in half; one half represents the period of the development of the inner-man or psychic level, and the other half represents the development of the outer-man, the conscious level. [cf. RIGHT-HAND PATH, LOWER SELF, STAGE OF EVOLUTION]

COSMIC PULSE—theory: the cosmos is a living entity as a whole and its beat or vibrations are the biological energy behind UFOs as well as all other existence. (Inconcl.) [cf. UNSHIELDED PLANETARY BODIES, TIME TRAVELERS, SAUCERNAUTS]

COSMIC RAY—an extreme penetration of radiation energy being picked up on ufology radar that seems to originate somewhere in outer space. (Inconcl.) [cf. UFOLOGY, ELECTROGRAVITATION, ETHER SHIPS, FREQUENCY BARRIER'S CREATION]

COSMIC RECEIVER—name given to plants and animals because they automatically respond to the variance in radiations from the sun and moon and from terrestial magnetism [cf. BOTANE, ANPSI]

COSMIC RHYTHM—(esoteric) the periodicity cyclic beat of vibrations that seem to be a part of the governing of the universe. [cf. CYCLES, NUMEROLOGY, VIBRATIONS]

COSMIC SNAKE—(antiquity) a semi-divine nature spirit showing itself with a serpent body, usually wanting to help mankind; (not having demonic intentions as many believe). **Syn.** MIDGARD, SESHA. [cf. SYMBOLISM, JACOB'S LADDER, SEVEN-KNOTTED WAND, MAGIC WHEELS]

COSMIC STREAM—1. a gathering of energy in the etheric world, held in abeyance, to be used for each new culture in earth to take shape and form; waits to be called upon by earthlings interested in change for earth. **Syn.** ETHERIC POWER POINTS. [cf. VIBRATIONS, NODES, ENERGY CURRENTS] 2. the potential within the seed of the cosmos that urges every solar system to grow to perfection and to blend into perfectness for all. [cf. MONAD]

COSMIC SWEEP—(new term) represents the new interest in humanity's relation to the cosmos and what is happening as earth cleanses itself; interest in galaxies, stars, black holes, etc. Usage: "The cosmos is making one big sweep in evolution." [cf. PLANETARY INITIATION, ASTROLOGY]

COSMIC TIME-TABLE—1. the cyclic laws have brought about a New Age as a stepping stone toward a more enriched life; 2. (Bible, in Book of Revelation) an impending judgment day is coming soon where God's wrath will take over earth; 3. see TRANFORMATION.[cf. PLANETARY SCHEME, ONE AGE]

COSMIC TREE—(Persia) the haoma tree; (Native American) the soma tree; (India) the fig tree; 1. (ancient) a tree that bore fruit which the gods ate to ensure themselves of immortality; 2. twelve psychic trees laden with diverse fruits; 3. (Siberia, India) wood used to construct a drum which when beaten would bring ecstatic psychic experiences; 4. (Bible, Genesis) the tree of knowledge.

COSMIC WHEEL—1. (Persia, Manichaean) a wheel with twelve spokes is used to link time with the twelve signs of the zodiac; the creator built a cyclic world; 2. the wheel contains twelve buckets for the raising of the soul-minds. [cf. ZODIAC, SOUL-MIND, EVOLUTION, TWELVE]

COSMIC WILL—the thrust behind the transformation that takes place as each solar system and planet makes a shift in their cycle of growth; this thrust is felt within all living things in the planet; the innate drive in all things, animate and inanimate, to progress up the spiral of development as the law of change and regeneration evolves. [cf. LAW OF DESTINY Appendix 7, UNIVERSAL LIFE CYCLE]

COSMIC ZONES—most common large groupings: EARTH PLANE, HEAVEN, and HELL; all having many subdivisions.

COSMO—(Greece) prefix, pertains to world or universe. **Syn.** KOSMO.

COSMO RAYS—invisible, electrical particles in the air, few and far apart; contain tremendous energy and penetrating power, constantly changing in intensity and direction. [cf. LIFE UNITS, PRIMAL ENERGY]

COSMO-BIOLOGICAL BIRTH CONTROL—the study of astrology, the movement of the planets and stars and their relationship to birth control. (Inconcl.) [cf. ASTROLOGY, NATURAL BIRTH CONTROL]

COSMOBIOLOGY—new study of the relationship between body chemistry, human thinking processes and the science of astrology. **Syn.** SCIENTIFIC ASTROLOGY. [cf. ASTROLOGICAL INFLUENCES]

COSMOGENESIS—study of evolutionary process

140

of the development of the universe according to the book of Genesis in the Bible; the universe created as a harmonious whole, and the part earth plays in this universe. [cf. TRANSFORMATION, PREESTABLISHED HARMONY, GESTALT]

COSMOGONIC CYCLES—patterns of creation as told in mythology repeating themselves in a pattern of cycles. [cf. CYCLIC PRINCIPLE, PERIODICITY]

COSMOGONIC MYTHS—stories handed down and believed, that give evidence of and the steps in, the creation of the universe. [cf. COSMOGONY, PREARRANGED HARMONY]

COSMOGONIC SYMBOLS—objective drawings, carvings, or paintings that man can relate to regarding a theory of how the universe was created, as in mythology. [cf. ARCHETYPAL UNCONSCIOUS, UNIVERSAL SYMBOLS]

COSMOGONY—(Greek *cosmo* "the universe as an orderly whole") the study of how the universe was created according to Genesis; the story of steps of development. [cf. PRIMORDIAL SUBSTANCE, VIBRATIONS, EVOLUTION, CHAOS, TOTALITY, NODE]

COSMOGRAPHY—(esoteric) a study of the universe, its functions and relationship to mankind; the relationship of the stars to earth using geology, geography, and astronomy. Syn. COSMOLOGY.

COSMOLOGICAL COMMUNITY—entities comparable to human beings; find their abode in space, the atmosphere. [cf. THIRD FORM OF LIFE, UNKNOWN FORCES, TIME TRAVELERS]

COSMOLOGY—(esoteric) the study of the primordial elements; FIRE, AIR, WATER, EARTH, SPACE, TIME, and GRAVITY; the laws governing their functions in relation to mankind. [cf. see above individually, METAPHYSICS]

COSMOS—1. the universe seen as a complete orderly, harmonious whole functioning with purpose and meaning; 2. (Plato) a central point of condition, surrounded by concentric spheres of mingled light and darkness, bounded by a sphere of fire; 3. (Plotinus) the central point of emanation; 4. a complete orderly system that knows its functions; all that man knows to exist; see TOTALITY.

COUNCIL OF MASTERS—etheric world intelligences who have earned an exalted, lofty, magnanimous rank whereby they are assigned to watch over each new age as it unfolds in the earth plane. [cf. WHITE BROTHERHOOD, MASTER, PISCEAN AGE, SPACE BROTHERS]

COUNSELEE—one who receives a psychic counseling or psychic reading from a professional psychic; individual inquires about his or her problems and the psychic tunes into his or her own etheric world intelligence(s) for guidance, encouragement, and alternatives to help solve the problems. Sim. CLIENT. [cf. SUBJECT, SITTING]

COUNSELING MEDIUM—one who is capable of summoning and working with etheric world guides in order to receive psychic information regarding problems and questions of the seeker. [cf. MEDIUMSHIP, READING, PSYCHIC INFORMATION]

COUNTERFEIT—see ASTRAL SHELL.

COUNTERPART BODY—an ethereal body having a vibrational frequency that cannot be seen with physical eyes, and is absolutely necessary for the existence of the physical body; interpenetrates and protrudes outward from the physical body; cannot be felt physically or psychically; does interfere at the subliminal level with brain decisions; see ETHERIC DOUBLE. Syn. AURA. [cf. SUBLIMINAL LEVEL, MENTAL BODY, CAUSAL BODY]

COUNTERSPACE—see ETHERIC WORLD.

COUNTERSPELL—to intercede and break a spell or glamour that is imposed upon a victim; to free the victim by using reverse and contrary magic rituals with intense mind concentration on loosening the bondage. [cf. CHARM-STRUCK, LOOSENING DEITIES, GLAMOUR, EXORCISM]

COUNTS OF HELL—etheric world entities of the density who rank in a superior order of the density hierarchy and are in charge of numerous legions; they are more easily evoked in a wild, unfrequented spot. [cf. DENSITY, PURGATORY, HADES, EARTHBOUND SOUL-MINDS]

COURIERS OF HEAVEN—see ANGELS.

COURT CARDS—(Tarot) the king, queen, page and knight standing for the sacred name in Hebrew YHVH. [cf. YHVH, TAROT CARDS]

COURTESY—(radiesthesia) to stop and hold the pendulum and say, "thank you" before going on with the next question; this is called "the courtesy"; every time one resets the pendulum one should say a word of kindness, or express one's appreciation; this lets the subconscious mind know it seeks a new answer and prevents the previous answer from spilling over into the next question. Syn. RESET. [cf. PENDULUM POWER, NONSWING QUESTIONS, MENTAL PROBE]

141

COVALENT BONDING—(esoteric) the sharing of the outer electrons of one atom with another until the atoms of the same vibration frequency congregate together, making an ethereal plane of a different dimension. (Inconcl.) [cf. ATOM, ASTRAL PLANE, SUBSTATES OF MATTER, WAVE-VIBRATION CONCEPT]

COVARIANCE EFFECT—(lboratory) when psychism is noticed in two laboratory experiments associated with one another, the score will be similar in both experiments, high in both or low in both. (Inconcl.) [cf. DIFFERENTIAL EFFECT, DUAL TASK]

COVEN—(esoteric) a group of thirteen people working for a secret society or special theory or purpose; a workable number considered magical or lucky, as this number cannot be divided against itself; (Wicca) a group of thirteen members with a priest in charge. [cf. NUMBER POWER]

COYOTE—(Native American, Plains) an etheric world intelligence taking the form of a bird or animal when perceived clairvoyantly by a Native American; desirous of helping an communicating with the Indian. Usage: "My coyote advised me to plant in this plot of ground." [cf. ETHERIC WORLD INTELLIGENCE, MENTAL MANIFESTATION, OMEN]

CPS—abbr. CYCLES PER SECOND; a means of groupings on a scale for study purposes of the electrical activity in the brain; measured in patterns per second when hooked-up to the EEG instrument; e.g., alpha consciousness is between 9-13 cycles per second. (Inconcl.) [cf. ALPHA STATE OF CONSCIOUSNESS, BRAIN WAVE SCALE]

CRAB DIVINATION—(ancient) to determine future events for the querist by studying the movement of crabs placed in a bowl. [cf. MANTIC ART, POINT-OF-FOCUS]

CRAFT OF THE SMITH—(past cultures) psychic skills performed by the village blacksmith, who served as a priest and was called upon to perform religious duties concerning psychic work; his knowledge of the blacksmith craft, and how to control fire, worked well with controlling his psychic talent (fire purified the area and induced etheric world intelligences to the scene). [cf. MASTER OF FIRE, FIRE IMMUNITY]

CRAFTERS—see NEOPAGAN WITCHES.

CRAMBION—a child born as a result of an etheric world entity having intercourse with an earthling. [cf. VAMPIRES, DENSITY, SUCCUBUS]

CREATION—1. (esoteric) theory: implies the universe had a beginning; the universe was brought into existence containing all the knowledge that ever was and ever will be as a unified whole; creation consisted of highly intelligent vibrating atoms in a chaotic order which can be used in an orderly way to make-over, form, discover, invent, develop, design, compose, arrange, establish, construct, organize, incorporate, press out, or deconstruct; "creation" happened only once; 2. (Pythagorean) a diversity with deities representing the various universal principles of birth, love, strife, fertility, growth, maturity, death, and renewal, etc.; 3. (Egypt) the division of primordial unity into multiplicity, and the function and principle of polarity; 4. creation was a need for an engender relationship; 5. a continuous, cyclically recurring process throughout the universe.

CREATIVE—1. (esoteric) pertains to a NON-THOUGHT evolving through one's conscious mind bringing a new idea from a higher source than that person's normal intellect could bring into being; psychic information that comes through the superconscious mind directly from Totality to the conscious mind; psychism by-passes the subconscious mind as it flows, as opposed to other psychic information that passes the subconscious mind and is subject to some of its stored information; creative non-thoughts are pure, untampered information, known to psychics as inspirational thought, writing, art, music, speaking, etc. Usage: "creative flow, creative insight"; (a better choice of adjective is "inspirational" inflow); 2.(I Ching) the half of mankind that is masculine, active, represented by the seed of Christ consciousness showing itself through man at special times. [cf. INSPIRATIONAL WRITING, INSPIRATIONAL ART, CLARISENTIENCE, POLARITY]

CREATIVE INSIGHT—see INSPIRATIONAL THOUGHT.

CREATIVE INTELLIGENCE—a conglomoration of all there ever was and all there ever will be; the single flow of energies stemming from one energy with directness. **Syn.** TOTALITY, ALL-THERE-IS, INFINITE MEMORY BANK, UNIVERSAL MIND. [cf. COLLECTIVE UNCONSCIOUS, MONAD]

CREATIVE MEDITATION—co-creative ideas that are sparked during meditation; the stillness of meditation allows non-thoughts to be recognized; when meditation turns into co-creative ideas, it becomes psychic activity and no longer meditation; see Appendix 4. [cf. CO-CREATE, MEDITATION, PSYCHIC ENERGY]

CREATIVE MENTAL PROCESS—theory: man's subconscious and conscious minds give the earth and everything on it form, shape and density; continued thought holds all this together. (Inconcl.) [cf. LAW OF THOUGHT Appendix 7, SOUL-MIND, BRAIN, ATOMS]

CREATIVE POTENTIAL—see TOTALITY.

CREATIVE QUIET—a level of consciousness in which psychic information can be perceived with accuracy; level is reached after one has been meditating long enough and the psychic recognizes the sensation of this level; the more one reaches his or her creative level of consciousness the less meditation time it takes beforehand; the listening mode. (Inconcl.) **Syn.** GOING-TO-LEVEL. [cf. MENTAL PSYCHIC PROCESSES]

CREATIVE SYNTHESIS—see TOTALITY.

CREATIVE UPWELLINGS—see INSPIRATIONAL THOUGHT; (do not confuse with CLAIRSENTIENCE)

CREATOR—(capitalized) the supreme one intelligence that made Totality, is the essence of Totality, and is the laws that sustain Totality; one main principle behind all-there-is and everything being a part of that one main principle. **Syn.** GOD, TOTALITY. [cf. MONAD, TOTALITY, VIBRATIONS, CHAOS]

CREATURES OF STRATOSPHERE—(ufology) various pulsating living shapes and forms using space as their home, some attractive, some grotesque, some visible to the eye and some visible only on special camera pictures. (Inconcl.) **Syn.** CRITTER FAMILY. [cf. MAGNETIC ANOMALY, ATMOSPHERIC AMOEBA, BIOFORMS, ETHERIC FAUNA]

CREDOLOGY—one's belief system, belief patterns, or formula of beliefs; e.g., "I believe . . . ." [cf. BELIEF SYSTEM, AKASHIC RECORD]

CREMATION—process of using fire to burn the corpse shortly after death to purify the atoms of the physical body from their dross negative thoughts impinged within; 1. frees the soul-mind more quickly from the magnetic pull of the bone and cell structure to allow the soul-mind to go about its new tasks in the etheric world; 2. hastens the reduction of material elements of the physical body to the primal elements again. (Inconcl.) [cf. SURVIVAL ELEMENTS, MUMMIFICATION, DEATH ANGEL]

CRESCENT—the second tattwa symbol representing water; a primordial element drawn with the points of the crescent facing up; this is aimed to reach the very basic part of the subconscious mind; silver in color. **Syn.** APAPS. [cf. TANS, TATTWA VISION, SQUARE, FORMS-WITH-POWER]

CRESCOGRAPH—(Latin, "to increase") an instrument that measures, amplifies, and records the nervous impulses in animals and plants; invented by Sir Jagandis Chandra Bose in early 1900s; demonstrates the indivisible unit of all kinds of life; a wireless coherer and an instrument used for indicating the refraction of electric waves, magnifying them ten million times; e.g., one can see a snail move like an express train, or the minute life movements of a plant. (Inconcl.) [cf. STRIP-CHART RECORDER, OSCILLATING RECORDER]

CRICK STONE—(Cornwall, England) a large stone with a hole in the center; has the vibratory frequency that can attune to the bones of the physical body and help cure back diseases and bone defects. **Syn.** MEN-AN-TOL. [cf. NATURAL MAGNETS, STONE CIRCLE, LEVITATION, GEMS]

CRIONICS—(1963) program of extended life; corpse theory: death is a disease; the body is taken right after it is pronounced clinically dead; the body temperature is reduced to below zero by special methods and put into the second state of crionics suspension; objective: to preserve life. (Inconcl.) [cf. SOUL-MIND]

CRISIS APPARITION—a vivid, clear vision of an accident, death, unexpected trauma, or the victim himself, perceived clairvoyantly by a friend or loved one of the victim; vision says what is happening, or about to happen; perceiver is in a relaxed state when the vision is received; emotional soul-mind realizes the unexpected experience will happen and is desirous to let someone know about it; soul-mind splits and is in two or three places simultaneously; victim is unaware of the soul-mind split; distance is no barrier. (Inconcl.) **Sim.** EMOTIONAL PSI, DEATH APPARITION. [cf. APPARITION, SOUL-MIND, BI-LOCATION]

CRISIS CALLS—(electronic voices) to receive a phone call from one who is about to die without the individual going to a phone to make the call; usually comes at the moment of the death or within

143

twenty-four hours of the death; caller does not mention their death but carries on what appears to be a normal conversation; the emotional state of a soul-mind, ready to make its transition, is great enough to split and contact a close associate; dying person is not consciously aware of the conversation; receiver learns at a later date that the individual died at the precise hour of the call, or a little later; research is being done to see how a split soul-mind can operate a telephone. [cf. TELEPHONE CALLS FROM THE DEAD]

CRISIS ESP—see CRISIS TELEPATHY.

CRISIS PHENOMENA—to encounter supernormal strength and intelligence at a time of a traumatic shock, allowing one to perform tasks impossible in a normal state; during a siege of panic, all concentration is accelerated and all forces of energy are mobilized at once; (relaxation is not involved); when the meaning of the physical world is so important to existence, information comes across psychically and one reacts extraordinarily and sometimes in a state of amnesia; e.g., in an automobile accident, a mother frees herself, picks up the side of the automobile with a crowbar, and frees her child. (Inconcl.) [cf. EMERGENCY PSI, NEED-DETERMINED RESPONSE]

CRISIS SITUATION—(Pir Vilayat Inayat Khan) "a time when the greatest changes take place in one's life; caused by one making compromises repeatedly in an unpleasant situation and it boils up until it results in a climax or an emergency; one feels moved and makes a decision; unless one promotes a life crisis situation one does not progress; one is being tested in one thing, 'making a decision.'"[cf. NEW-AGE, PSYCHOLOGY, TENSION, SUFFERING]

CRISIS TELEPHATHY—freakish happenings to material objects or persons that cannot be explained by normal causation; theory: the soul-mind can split when in an emotional state and connect with objects and persons with which there has been meaningful previous connections; e.g., 1. the stopping of a clock at the exact time of one's death in the home of a friend or relative; the falling of one's picture at the same time one went through a traumatic experience; 2. the smelling of the death odor when a loved one is about to die (distance is no barrier); the tasting of metal before a steel bridge collapses and many persons are killed. (Inconcl.) **Syn.** HUMAN OMENS, OBJECT OMENS. [cf. PHANTASMS OF THE LIVING, LAW OF CONTAGION Appendix 7, SPONTANEOUS PSI]

CRITICAL DAYS—(biorhythm chart) the day when the body system switches from a discharging phase into a recuperative phase, or vice versa; this day is exactly one half of the twenty-three, twenty-eight, and thirty-three day cycle; the body makes a complete switch in a twenty-four hour period from one phase to the other, instead of a gradual change; this makes the individual's activity least reliable to that particular cycle; e.g., if the physical cycle is crossing, one may have an accident; if the emotional cycle is crossing, one is more apt to cry or shout for an occurrence that would not bother one at any other time; designated on the biorhythm chart by the cycle line crossing on the O-line. (Inconcl.) **Syn.** FLUX. [cf. EMOTIONAL DAYS, BIORHYTHM CHART, OUT OF SYNC]

CRITICAL FACILITATE—(mental psychism) 1. to mentally hold a vision and silently converse with it for understanding, during a psychic development sitting; 2. to allow the vision to flow, hang onto the flow psychically, and at the same time ask silently for clarification. [cf. PSYCHIC DEVELOPMENT CIRCLE, IMAGE, LISTENING MODE]

CRITICAL MIND—(destructive brainwashing cult) the conscious mind; the decision-making mind; means to infer that decisions are not always good for the individual. [cf. MENTAL-PSYCHOLOGICAL PRISON, MENTICIDE]

CRITICAL SITUATIONAL RESPONSE—(destructive brainwashing cult) strange disorders of personality which cannot be diagnosed as medically based mental illness or traditional psychological uneasiness; new type of mental and emotional disturbance which renders traditional methods of psychiatry ineffective; brought about by new and intense experiences that quickly dull one's emotions, make glassy eyes, accelerate changes in one's belief system and drastically alter one's personality; e.g. psychedelic drug trips; overindulgence in mystical practices; or repetitious coercion of ploy given to one unknowingly after inducing a disguised hypnotic state. (Inconcl.) [cf. SNAPPING, LOVE-BOMBING, ARTIKA CEREMONY, BREAKTHROUGH]

CRITTER FAMILY—see CRITTERS.

CRITTERS—(ufology) living organisms inhabiting the sea of outer space, at a vibrational frequency that the physical eyes can see only at times; vary in shape, size, color and density; range from tiny to huge, from attractive to grotesque; (compare with earth's fish, birds and animals); propel themselves in and out of dimensions, visible and invisible; can be photographed when visible with a special camera; research indicates they have a special function to etheria space. (Inconcl.) **Syn.** CRITTER FAMILY, SPACE CREATURES, BIOFORMS, AEROFORMS. [**cf.** MUTANTS, BIOLOGICAL UFO'S, SPHEROIDS]

CROSS—(esoteric) a structure of an upright and transverse piece, varying in size, texture and style; used as an emblem or symbol of a religious order; has a vibrational frequency so powerful that each cross, no matter the style, from a newspaper drawing to the most elaborate large, gold structure, is minutely connected; every cross sends its emanations which have an effect on its surroundings. [**cf.** CEREMONIAL MAGIC, FORMS-WITH-POWER, TRIANGLE]

CROSS OF LIFE—see ANKH.

CROSS REFERENCE—(early 1900s) simultaneous, similar delivery of psychic information to mediums located distantly around the country; came in the form of automatism and dependent voice; given from the same etheric world intelligence; etheric world willingly performed this phenomena to prove the psychic information was coming from a soul-mind who lived in many earth incarnations and did not come from the subconscious mind; see CROSS-CORRESPONDENCE]

CROSS-CAUSALITY OF INTERACTION—(Carl Jung) the synchronicity of the many events of causal history happening simultaneously across time that influences humanity subconsciously and individuals can attune into consciously. (Inconcl.) [**cf.** MULTIDIMENSIONAL, MOMENT POINT, TIME]

CROSS-CORRESPONDENCE—psychic information coming through more than one medium, with each working independently in distant areas; information received must be compared or put together to become clear and meaningful; perceived through voice trance, automatism, and inspirational thought; sometimes happening spontaneously without much time interval, but usually requested of the etheric world intelligences; began in early 1900s when psychic research was being tested for evidence of discarnate entity's psychic skills and validity of subconscious mind psychic skills; see SIMPLE CROSS-CORRESPONDENCE and COMPLIMENTARY CROSS-CORRESPONDENCE. [**cf.** INSPIRATIONAL THOUGHT, VOICE TRANCE, AUTOMATIC WRITING]

CROSS-EXCITATION—(biofeedback training) (Russian research) negative emotional impulses transferred to the subject using the EEG instrument showed definite changes of the wave formations in all four ranges. (Inconcl.) [**cf.** OCCIPITAL HEMISPHERE BRAINWAVE MONITORING]

CROSS-TALK—(biofeedback training) one cell activity reacting to another cell activity, seeming to influence an effect on the two body halves proportionately, governed by the brain cortex; monitored on the EEG instrument. (Inconcl.) [**cf.** SUBCONSCIOUS LEVEL, CORTICAL INTEGRATION]

CROSSROADS—the area of two roads crossing on earth is conducive to psychic and ghostly activity; the number of accidents that happen at crossroads renders the section in the middle vulnerable for unhappy deceased victims to cling to and periodically haunt. [**cf.** ENVIRONMENTAL HAUNTING, IRRITATION ZONES]

CROWN CHAKRA—(Yoga) an invisible, whirling vortex of energy located on the top of the head in the cerebrum; emanates 960 petals on the outside of a circular shape, with a subsidiary central whirlpool of twelve gleaming white petals, fused with gold in its heart; becomes stirred into activity as the soul-mind gradually becomes purified, making ready to be glorified for the higher realms; each of the lower chakras unfolds energy into this chakra by graduated steps, giving this chakra the brilliance, power and intelligence it needs for man's ascension; when fully developed it radiates a most splendent of chromatic effects forming what Yogis call the Lotus flower; (Jesus called it the "crown of glory"); a continuity of consciousness showing itself as a man or woman unfolds; can be perceived clairvoyantly in all its stages. (Inconcl.) **Syn.** SAHASRARA. [**cf.** KUNDALINI, HEART CHAKRA, KANDA, ASCENSION]

CROWN—(capitalized) (the top and "Christos") the whirling vortex of energy that emanates a huge glow surrounding the head; seen visibly when one has purified the soul-mind to earn the rank of being Christed; i.e., the light around Jesus, especially at the time of the ascension. (Inconcl.) **Syn.** CROWN OF GLORY, CROWN CHAKRA, SAHASRARA. [**cf.** ALCHEMY, GLORIFIED BODY, PURIFIED BODY, NIMBUS]

CRUCIFICATION—(alchemy) to make changes through elimination. [**cf.** ALCHEMIST, ASCENSION, TRANSMUTATION, ALCHEMICAL PRINCIPLES]

145

CRUTCH—common symbol shown in a psychic reading; there is something one is leaning on for security, ego-building, a karmic tie, or pseudo-needs. [cf. PSYCHIC INFORMATION, SYMBOLS]

CRUX ANSATA—(Egypt) a cross with a large loop on the top; symbolizes life eternal and the key to heaven; energized as a talisman and used in healing, protection, and psychic attunement; worn by all pharoahs; sometimes found with a special jewel in the circle. **Syn.** ANKH. [cf. TALISMAN, CROSS, FORMS-WITH-POWER]

CRYPTESTHESIA—(Greek *crypto*, "hidden") coined by Charles Richet; all mental psychic skills that use the subconscious mind only; a hidden sensitivity; a perception of events, persons, and objects by a mechanism of which mankind is not aware; mysterious external vibrations which are vibrations of reality; i.e., premonitions, monitions, clairvoyance, clairaudience, psychometry, mental telepathy and dowsing; (do not confuse with MENTAL MEDIUMSHIP subject to etheric world intelligences). [cf. Appendix 2 MENTAL PSYCHIC PROCESSES]

CRYPTIC—hidden, secret, occult, puzzling.

CRYPTO—(Greek) prefix meaning "hidden" or "secret."

CRYPTOGRAPHERS—(biofeedback training) persons studying brain currents that register on the electroencephalograph to see if they have a specific meaning. (Inconcl.) [cf. BIOFEEDBACK TRAINING, SCALE OF BRAIN RHYTHMS, READOUTS, FREQUENCY CONTROL, BRAIN WAVE TRAINING]

CRYPTOMENESIA—(Greek *crypto*, "hidden") to summon back into the conscious level of awareness information that has been forgotten or suppressed; e.g., data which one has read, seen or heard in formal education or experiences, data that entered the subliminal level of awareness, suggestions given a UFO contactee, suggestions given one in hypnosis, or knowledge received in trance; surfaced into consciousness through the following means: 1. hypnotherapy regression; 2. electrical stimulation; 3. trance regression; 4. after a deep, prolonged meditation. (Inconcl.) [cf. SUBCONSCIOUS MEMORY, AGE REGRESSION, CONSCIOUS MIND, SUBLIMINAL LEVEL]

CRYPTOPHYSICAL—that which is unexplainable to the science and technology of today.

CRYPTOPSYCHISM—to use psychic talent without knowing about psychic work, such as, sending messages to a child to call you on the phone and child responds; or to rub a wound with the palm of the hand and it hastens its healing. [cf. PARENT-CHILD TELEPATHY, MENTAL TELEPATHY]

CRYPTOSCOPY—(laboratory) to perceive clairvoyantly what is in the sealed envelope that is the target of the experiment (a drawing or inscription), or what is in the contents in a closed drawer. **Syn.** X-RAY CLAIRVOYANCE. [cf. MENTAL PSYCHISM, SEE, SEEING-EYE VISION]

CRYSTAL BALL GAZING—(1,000 B.C.) to stare into a perfectly round shaped ball of natural crystal with intensified concentration until a vision is seen within the ball; meditation beforehand enhances the vision; lighting should strike the ball from a certain angle; a white cloudy formation begins at first and when this moves the visions appear; picture within the ball is the answer to questions. **Sim.** HYDROMANCY, CYLICOMANCY Appendix 6. [cf. SCRYING, LECONOMANCY Appendix 6, SOLOMON'S MIRROR]

CRYSTAL DEPOSITS—(reflexology) a formation of nerve fluid at the nerve endings on the bottom of the foot, forming a tiny hardness, indicating malfunction of some other place in the body which is known by the reflexologist. [cf. ACUPUNCTURE Appendix 5, MERIDIAN LINES, REFLEXOLOGY]

CRYSTAL LAMP—(Egypt) the optic thalamus; an egg-shaped ganglion of the inner brain; when cross-sectioned it looks like a beetle; symbolizes immortality. **Syn.** SINGLE EYE, HEART OF THE LOTUS, BOAT OF THE SEEKER, SACRED BEETLE. [cf. THIRD-EYE AREA, PINEAL GLAND]

CRYSTAL PENDULUM—a tiny crystal ball, artificial or natural, used as the bob from the cord on a pendulum; used for answering questions and measuring energies over objects. [cf. BOB, MUTUAL LANGUAGE, PENDULUM SEARCHING]

CRYSTALLINE LEVEL—a superior degree in the angel hierarchy encasing the soul-mind in a purified consciousness; earned by a long evolvement of sincerity, righteousness, and singleness of purpose, in the soul-mind's thoughts, deeds and acts during both earth incarnations and etheric world incarnations. [cf. STEPS TO GODLINESS]

CRYSTALLO—a natural crystal mineral in the shape of a ball used for crystal-ball gazing. [cf. SCRYING, QUARTZ]

CRYSTALLOGRAPHY—see CRYSTAL BALL GAZING.

CRYSTALS—(esoteric) a natural mineral formed by a balance of forces around a central axis of symmetry giving the mineral a particular shape; that shape then has a vibrational frequency that endows it with extra power depending upon the shape of each individual mineral; the octahedron has the most added energy; crystals have a natural, universal, interconnecting property from within boundaries of the earth's energy field to the higher realms of awareness; crystals hold a human's energy and thought when actively used within the range of one's electromagnetic field, then organizes and aligns this thought energy as it processes through the crystal structure, then amplifies and emits this thought energy in a focused form where designated, making it a useful tool for psychic healing, or mental work; (Aline Vergano) "crystals are a life being, continuing to grow, reproduce, and regenerate by itself." (Inconcl.) [**cf.** FORMS-WITH-POWER, CAPSTONE, ROCK CRYSTAL, MINPSI]

CS.—abbrev. CONDITIONING STIMULUS; a color, object, taste, smell, sound, or an event that makes the body react in the same way every time; brought on by the imbedding of similarity in the subconscious mind to the original emotion from the above outer stimulus; occurs unconsciously or consciously.

CUANNADERO—(Mexico) a person with psychic talents; a human channel for psychic healing. **Syn.** PSYCHIC. [**cf.** MENTAL HEALING]

CUBE—represents the life ether in the etheric world; vibrates in a violet color; symbol of the new age. [**cf.** SQUARE, CONICAL SHAPE, FORMS-WITH-POWER]

CULT—a system of persons who work together and are bound together by the same ideal, principle, and leader, usually of a religious nature; system or sect becomes object of devotion; (do not confuse with OCCULT or DESTRUCTIVE-BRAINWASHING CULT). [**cf.** see Appendix 4 for clarification]

CULT OF THE DEAD—(Slavic) those etheric world intelligences who surround the people of the earth and desire to be a part of furthering earth's evolvement; intelligences who communicate with earthlings through psychic skills, bringing information to help the earth survive. [**cf.** ETHERIC WORLD INTELLIGENCES, REGENT OF THE EARTH]

CULT SYNDROME—refers to destructive-brainwashing cults and their ability to drastically change the beliefs, morals, and personalities of young adults with abnormal swiftness; victim's new personality is unrecognizable to friends and family; cult recruiters snare and coerce millions of young adults into joining their organizations through false statements given through on-the-spot-hypnosis, mental telepathy at a distance, mass hypnosis, and constant repetition of planned ploy aimed at one's basic emotional needs; because of the cult's disguised methods all persons are vulnerable who are not educated in parapsychological principles. (Inconcl.) [**cf.** DESTRUCTIVE-BRAINWASHING CULT MASS ELEMENTAL, ON-THE-SPOT-HYPNOSIS, AUTOMATION, PLOY]

CULTURAL NOISE—sounds of the times and place that interfere with a good meditation and an accurate biofeedback reading; e.g., airplanes, motorcycles, newspaper thump, birds, automobiles, children talking, etc. [**cf.** EEG, GSR, ARTIFACT, METABOLIC MONITOR, SIXTY-CYCLE HUM]

CULTURAL TRANCE—to consciously or subconsciously hold on to outmoded beliefs and values from a past society; acts as a mental block and prevents the individual from expressing themselves in modern beliefs and personal desires, hindering his or her evolvement. [**cf.** PERSONALITY TRANSFORMATION, BELIEF SYSTEM]

CULTURAL TRANSFORMATION—a collective evolutionary change brought on by birth pains of a new time period; individuals subconsciously feel the birth pains and look for new potentials within their lifestyle, standards, habits, etc.; as people evolve individually and interact with others, one follows the other and whole cultures change; those who live in the past hold back these birth pains and prevent a smooth growth of the planet. [**cf.** LAW OF TRANSFORMATION and LAW OF LETTING GO Appendix 7, SOUL-MIND EVOLUTION, EVOLUTION]

CUNNING FOLK—see PSYCHIC and PSYCHIC HEALER. **Syn.** WHITE WITCHES.

CUP—1. symbol of "life"; used in ceremonies to help control the forces of nature in bringing the Higher Self through into manifestation in the conscious consciousness, making a more purified life; 2. symbol of water, therefore, brings one with the cup in rapport with Venus and its emotional receptive nature. [**cf.** SYMBOLS, LAW OF RITUAL Appendix 7]

147

CUP OF DIVINATION—a special cup owned by Dr. George M. Lamsa; when he put water in it, and the vibrations were right between him and the cup, the cup would utter sounds of a human voice, bringing psychic information and answering questions for Dr. Lamsa. [**cf.** POINT-OF-FOCUS, BEAMED ENERGY]

CUP OF DJEMSCHEED—(Persia) a special cup found while digging the foundations of Persia that contributed to the prosperity of Persia; believed to be filled with the elixir of immortality, and mirrored within was revelation of all the good and evil in the world. [**cf.** AMULETS, ALCHEMY, PHILOSOPHER'S EGG]

CUPID—(esoteric) a special nature spirit deva in the etheric world that earned the rank of having charge of love affairs in the earth plane; identified by a beautiful winged boy with a bow and arrow hovering over those to be blessed with love. [**cf.** NATURE SPIRITS, DEVAS, ANGELS]

CURANDERA—(Mexico, Native American, Otomi) 1. the name of the homes denoting that a psychic lives there. [**cf.** ORACLE] 2. the psychic of the village, specializing in applied psychology, prayer meetings and mental psychism; sometimes administered physical psychism and healings. **Syn.** WISE WOMAN. [**cf.** PSYCHIC READING, PHYSICAL PSYCHISM]

CURANDERISM—the use of psychic and faith healing techniques as practiced in Spain, Latin America, and North America. [**cf.** MENTAL HEALING, PSYCHIC HEALING, SPIRITUAL THERAPY, CATALYSTIC HEALING]

CURANDEROS—(Native American) see PARANORMAL HEALER]

CURATIVE EDUCATION—the study of the cause of disease, and the value and effectiveness of unorthodox healing alternatives and wellness programs; 1. to find the "cause" of energy flow blockage that presents a physical or mental disease for that individual; modern theory: both mental and physical disease is a deficiency in one or more of the inorganic chemical constituents of the physical body which is caused by a person's mind and their attitude toward their daily experiences; one should balance with each experience daily and resolve the unpleasurable ones; when one doesn't, there is a stoppage in the energy flow, which builds over the years and causes illness; objective is to find

the original attitudinal cause and eliminate it, even if it goes back to other incarnations; 2. scientific study of natural means to treat the body to help the cells normalize and heal themselves more quickly; 3. to encourage individuals to take charge of one's own well being and practice wellness habits to suit one's desires and needs. (Inconcl.) [**cf.** FRINGE MEDICINE, HOLISTIC, BLOCKS, NATURALIST, SYNERGETIC, LAW OF HEALING Appendix 7, CURATIVE EDUCATION Appendix 5]

CURATIVE MEDICINE— any treatment, therapy, activity change, or education that can help one bring about an attitudinal change toward an emotional experience that was never correctly resolved and is constrained over the years and now causes the mental or physical disease; e.g., neuromuscular massage, holistic health course, past lives therapy, hypnotherapy regression, isolation box, dream therapy, Gestalt therapy; see Appendix 5 for further listings. (Inconcl.) [**cf.** HOLISTIC HEALTH THEORY, ALTERNATIVES, POSITIVE EXPECTATION, BIOFEEDBACK TRAINING, BLOCKS Appendix 5]

CURATIVE MESMERISM—to use magnetic passes over a patient with the palm of the hand to relieve pain, remove disease, or give vitality; takes effect more quickly when patient is in a state of hypnosis. [**cf.** HYPNOTHERAPY, LONG PASSES, MAGNETIC HEALING, PALMED POWER]

CURRENT KARMA—see RIPE KARMA.

CURSE—to use an elemental for the transference of evil psychic energy; psychic intensifies mind activity by focusing on a thought-form until it is dense enough to mold into an elemental, into which he or she pours a part of themselves; this gives the elemental intelligence and connects it to her or him; psychic aims at a chosen object, person, or area they want to bring harm; the elemental thought-form is then invoked in the names of an activity and an entity; e.g., "I curse you, Bob, to break a bone," which endows the elemental with an independent life of its own; as long as the psychic keeps their mind activity on this elemental and keeps it solidified with anger and evil intentions, the elemental will hover over the head of the victim and bring its intent to pass; a curse employs no physical article, but is a product of inner tension of the psychic which is released in negativity; some psychics use a plant or animal in the victim's house from which substance is drawn to influence the victim; (do not confuse with HEX or SPELLED; see

Appendix 4 for clarification). [**cf.** ARTIFICIAL ELEMENTAL, THOUGHT-FORMS, FAMILIAR]

CURSUS—a long building used in ancient times for great leaders to assemble and exchange their learned wisdom with each other.

CUTANEOUS VISION—to see without the use of physical eyes; see EYELESS SIGHT.(Inconcl.) **Sim.** BIOINTROSCOPY, DERMO-OPTICAL PERCEPTION. [**cf.** FINGER READING, BLIND AWARENESS, SENSATION]

CYBERNETIC LOOP—(biofeedback training) a pattern of physical sensory awareness that causes a mental, emotional, limbic, hypothalamic and pituitary reaction in humans; subject begins a physiological change, then an inside-the-skin response, allowing voluntary control to body parts that were involuntary. [**cf.** FEEDBACK, PASSIVE CONCENTRATION, ELECTRODES]

CYBERNETIC MACHINE—a complex, electronic calculating machine that compares with the human brain and human nervous system; the brain is like a calculator machine and the subconscious mind is like a computer. [**cf.** SUBCONSCIOUS MIND, AKASHIC RECORD, MEMORY BANK, MENTAL MIND]

CYBERNETICS—the study of communication and control of animals and machines; science of automatic control systems, mechanical, electronic and biological structures that regulate their own internal processes and correct their own errors in operation; the study of human control functions and man-made designs of mechanical and electrical systems designed to replace them. [**cf.** THOUGHT-FORMS, SYMPATHETIC NERVOUS SYSTEM]

CYCLE—a series of occurrences which repeats itself in a specific pattern with precision timing and no regard to outer changing conditions; an action of anything in the universe that repeats itself with a similarity at constant intervals; all life is held together in concentric patterns. (Inconcl.) [**cf.** Appendix 5 CYCLES, LAW OF CYCLES Appendix 7]

CYCLE OF MOVEMENTS—(radiesthesia) (Howard St. L. Cookes) the swing of the pendulum in either oscillations or gyrations made by the natural rhythmical vibrations of the human nervous system as it reacts to the radiations of the object being measured or questioned; pendulum amplifies in a tangible way for the brain to decipher; pendulum differs in direction of oscillations and gyrations for

each color and mineral when measuring energy. (Inconcl.) [**cf.** PENDULUM POWER, GYRATE, NON-SWING, UP-AND-DOWN MOTION]

CYCLE OF PERSONAL LIFE SITUATIONS—a period from birthday to birthday; divides 365 days by seven, making periods 52 1/7 days, out of which one period is expecially good for expressing the inner nature of the person, like traveling, strengthening of the psychic powers, etc. (Inconcl.) [**cf.** BIORHYTHM CHARTS]

CYCLE OF SOUL-MIND PROGRESSION—(esoteric) theory: every eighteen years, seven months and a few days there occurs a particular relationship between a person's soul-mind and the etheric world; beginning at the age of 18/19 and then following at the ages of 37/38, 55/56, 74/75. [**cf.** PSYCHIC ENERGY, POSITIVE DAYS, RACES, SOUL-MIND CYCLE, CYCLE RULER]

CYCLE OF THE AGES—(esoteric) theory that every 26,000 years our solar system makes one revolution around a Great Central Sun, and the completion of one such cycle constitutes one age. [**cf.** PISCEAN AGE, AQUARIAN AGE]

CYCLES OF PROGRESSION—the periodicity of material or worldly affairs which will have its lows and highs, regardless of the people on the planet; people will influence the degree of lows and highs, but will not influence a smooth running world; e.g., history repeats itself every 100 years. [**cf.** CYCLE OF THE AGES, LIFE GROWTH CYCLE, RELIGIOUS CYCLES]

CYCLIC PRINCIPLE-(esoteric) everything vibrates at, responds to, or is moved in, a certain definite rhythm; a repetitive motion transferring energy in patterns; e.g., planetary motions are measured in cycles per year, audible sound is measured in cycles per second. [**cf.** PERIODICITY, ENERGY PATTERNS, CYCLES Appendix 5]

CYCLIC REVERSAL—(esoteric) 1. refers to half of the cycle in any given rhythmic pattern that is on the negative side of that activity; 2. a period of time in the history of the world that will be difficult to live through, as prophesied by Edgar Cayce, Native Americans, the Biblical Revelations, and other prophets. [**cf.** CHAIN PERIOD, SUN-SPOTS, PLANETARY SCHEME, OUT OF SYNC]

CYCLIC RULER—a special ruler used in making biorhythm charts; designed with a sine curve representing one of the three cycles necessary for

149

charting one's biorhythms. [**cf.** BIORHYTHM CHARTS, EMOTIONAL CYCLE]

CYCLICITY-SERIALITY-SYNCHRONICITY—(laboratory) theory: the statistically out-of-portion hits of mental psychism infers there is an involvement of the rhythmic cycles of the physiological metabolic state. [**cf.** MENTAL PSYCHISM, PHASE SHIFT]

CYNANTHROPY—to change one's vibrational frequency and appear as a wolf, emotionally charged in anger. [**cf.** WERE-WOLF, SHAPE-CHANGING]

CYPHER CHARACTERS—(esoteric) pictures of an object, plant or animal representing a direct plan or subjective idea; shown clairvoyantly when giving a reading or bringing in psychic information from the etheric world; similar to the ancient way of writing sacredotal language. [**cf.** PSYCHIC MESSAGES, SYMBOLS]

d-ASC—(laboratory) abbr. for DISCRETE ALTERED STATES OF CONSCIOUSNESS; if a specific degree of detachment would be agreed upon by scientists, ASC would become a special science.

D-State—abbr. for DREAM STATE; the third state of existence; occurs during sleep, when picture language is entertaining the subconscious mind. **Syn.** REM DREAMS. [**cf.** ALPHA STATE OF CONSCIOUSNESS, NREM SLEEP]

DABTARAS—(Arabic) church deacons who have psychic ability, specializing in prophecy, exorcism and healing. [**cf.** FILLED WITH THE SPIRIT, SPASMODIC CONTROL, COUNSELING MEDIUM]

DACTYL—psychic who studied under Pythagorus; excellent craftsman and wizard; also clalled **Iaean actyl.**

DACTYLOMANCER—psychic or medium who is successful using the Ouija Board. [**cf.** MEDIUMSHIP, AUTOMATISM, PLANCHETTE, AUTOMATIC WRITING]

DAEMON—1. (2000 B.C., I Ching) the relationship between the consciousness of the soul-mind and the consciousness of outside time (etheric world); able to talk to a person within their mind giving him or her information that their conscious minds do not have access to; 2. (Greece) an etheric world entity capable of communication with an earthling, for good or evil; (Hermetic) identical with the angels; (Socrates) name of Socrates personal guide; a demigod, part human and part divine, but not of evil intent; also spelled **daimon.** [**cf.** ETHERIC WORLD INTELLIGENCES Appendix 3, MENTAL BODY, ASTRAL BODY]

DAEMON IN THE DIE—name given to an etheric world intelligence working with physicist J.C. Maxwell, giving him secrets of entropy and thermodynamics. [**cf.** MEDIUMSHIP, INSPIRATIONAL THOUGHT, DEPENDENT VOICE]

DAEMONOLOGIE—treatise written by King James I of England, giving theories on etheric world entities.

DAGGER—symbol of fire because the shape resembles a flame; made of iron, steel, or made in the mind (visualized); used in magical ceremonies: 1. to control the forces of nature; to bring the higher self into manifestation within the conscious mind; 2. to help in resurrecting the dead; associated with sacrifice and death. [**cf.** LICENSE TO DEPART, BANISHING RITUAL, GUARDIAN OF THE DOOR]

DAILY BREAD—(Bible) the "spirit" in the air, the vital life force needed for all things, animate and inaminate, to exist; see VITAL LIFE FORCE. **Syn.** PRIMARY ENERGY, ELOPTIC ENERGY, KA-LA, RAUCH. [**cf.** SOUL, ATOM, VIBRATION]

DAILY CYCLE—a period of twenty-four hours (midnight to midnight) which affects animals, plants and humans, regardless of environment, habits, hunger, fatigue, and physical ability; in man, the intellectural capacity, meditative state, psychic ability, and emotional stability can be charted by the individual to establish the natural time for life activities. **Syn.** CIRCADIAN RHYTHM. [**cf.** CYCLES, INTUITIVE INFLUENCE, CIRCADIAN HALF-WAVES]

DAIMOKU—(Zen) act of practicing how to chant. [**cf.** MEDITATION, OHM]

DAIMON—1. etheric world genius who communicates with man for the good of all mankind; 2. an evil spirit (spelled **demon**). **Syn.** DAEMON, ETHERIC WORLD ENTITY. [**cf.** GUIDE, ANGEL, MEDIUMSHIP, CLAIRAUDIENCE]

DAIRY MAGIC—ability to psychically milk a cow from a distance, and obtain the milk; performed either by putting a pail under the cow, with the psychic at a distance, or with both the pail and the psychic at a distance from the cow; accomplished by power of the mind; used in ancient times to steal milk. [**cf.** ANPSI, NATURE CONTROL, PHYSICAL PSYCHISM, PK]

DAIVAS—(Zoroastrianism) inferior etheric world entity who lives in the atmosphere surrounding and interpenetrating the earth; because of his or her low level of consciousness their communication with mankind is considered to be maleficent. [**cf.** DENSITY, ANGEL HIERARCHY, DISCARNATE ENTITY, GUIDE]

DAIVIPRAKRITI—(Sanskrit) divine, God, the total of all-there-is; (Tibet) the primordial light in the beginning which is "all intelligence"; see TOTALITY. [**cf.** MONAD, UNIVERSAL MIND]

DAKINIS—(Tibet) 1. fairy-like intelligences that can be seen in various places by humans as they desire to show themselves; see NATURE SPIRIT. 2. psychic forces in the centers of the body (throat, brain, and heart chakras). [cf. CHAKRAS]

DALKARL—(Sweden) psychic who has dowsing ability. [cf. FORKED BRANCH, WIZARD ROD]

DAMBALLAHWEDO—(Voodoo) nature spirit in the form of a snake; has charge of the water on earth, regulating it to the needs of man; can be seen by man when the snake so desires; see fairie.

DANA O'SHEE—fairies which personify the lost gods of the land when perceived clairvoyantly; see NATURE SPIRIT. [cf. ANGEL HIERARCHY]

DANCE OF LIFE—(primitive) a special dance with concentration on rhythm, beat, and duration, rather than the steps; practiced throughout all civilizations; used to: tune into higher realms of life; to connect with spirits, God, and demons; to prepare one's self to be a channel for healing; to bring prophetic visions; to help exorcise evil entities; and to communicate with the dead. [cf. MOVEMENT-FOR-ALTERED-CONSCIOUSNESS Appendix 2, WHIRLING DERVISH, HYSTERIA]

DANCE THERAPY—rhythmic movement in a non-competitive atmosphere, encouraging grace with exercise in many different styles; believed to help participants work out their problems through the activity of dance. [cf. BELLY-DANCING, ESOTERIC MOVEMENT, DERVISH]

DANCED HIM—(!Kung tribe, Kalahari Desert) to psychically support a healer who has lost self-control during a healing dance around the camp-fire, while preparing himself to become a channel for healing energies; his colleagues dance around him in a circle, which extends energies to hold him up until the fear has left him, and he is again self-supporting. [cf. HEALING DANCE, HYSTERIA]

DANCING MANIA—(middle ages, Europe) a group of people whirling and dancing in wild delirium to the beat of a drum, until close to exhaustion, which puts them in a hypnotic trance; this opens each one to be a channel for healing, for prophetic visions, or for communicating with the dead. [cf. TRANCE, HYPNOSIS, MOVEMENT-FOR-ALTERED-CONSCIOUSNESS]

DANCING SORCERER—earliest known image of psychic; depicted as a half-animal/half-man per-forming a magical dance; had an understanding of and could use the forces of nature. [cf. MOVEMENT-FOR-ALTERED-CONSCIOUSNESS, CEREMONIAL MAGIC, ELICITING PSI]

DANGER-CHARGED WORDS—words that are spoken over and over, or are repeated in the mind silently, build up power; according to the nature of the thought, they bring a situation into being, whether one wants it to happen or not. [cf. EVIL MOUTH, HOLD THE THOUGHT, BABBLER]

DARK ANGEL—(metaphysics) the lower self of each individual, standing behind the left shoulder; catches one off-guard with temptations of the flesh or with negative thoughts. [cf. MENTAL CON-SCIOUSNESS, SUBCONSCIOUS MIND]

DARK NIGHT OF THE SOUL—term used to mean that one has experienced a spiritual crisis during the initiation; the darkness before the dawn may be the next step in the transformation of the individual. [cf. TRANSFORMATION, TRANSMUTATION, RIGHT-HAND PATH]

DARK OUTSIDE-PERSONALITIES—etheric world entities who have grey or darkness around them when perceived clairvoyantly; bring havoc or nega-tive vibrations to the earthling whom they use for communication. [cf. POSSESSION, OBSESSION, PLANES OF DARKNESS]

DARK ROOM—a room prepared by extinguishing as much light source as possible; darkness is required for most physical psychism to occur, and to permit the sitters to be more comfortable; (do not confuse with BLACKED-OUT ROOM needed for materialization). [cf. PHYSICAL PSYCHIC PROCESSES Appendix 2, APPARITIONAL LIGHT]

DARKNESS—(esoteric) 1. (Johann Wolfgang von Goethe) an agent in the production of color that is active (as opposed to passive); 2. lack of light, or lack of intelligence; 3. (psychic circles) physical psychism is believed to develop more easily in a darkened room, as the ectoplasm for physical phenomena requires less psychic energy to mani-fest in the dark. [cf. COLOR, ECTOPLASM, INTELLI-GENCE, LIGHT]

DARKNESS OF IGNORANCE—(Buddhism) a plane that surrounds and interpenetrates the earth plane; invisible to the naked eye, inhabited by new soul-minds, who out of ignorance, do not care to move to a higher plane, but who live in uncouth, barbarian conditions, **Sim.** DENSITY. [cf. BODIES AND

PLANES Appendix 5, ASTRAL PLANE, REALMS OF FORM, SANGSARIC REGIONS, PHANTASM]

DARKROOM SESSIONS—ongoing, weekly meetings of a closed group, interested in developing physical, mediumistic phenomena within themselves, under the guidance of a developed medium; sitting in a circular formation, in a blacked-out or dimly lit room, for one or two hours; compatibility and harmony among the sitters is the most important factor for success; second factor is the "desire" to learn about the etheric world, its functions and relationship to humanity and to surface untapped potential of humans for individual well-being and the well-being of the planet. [**cf.** MEDIUMSHIP, GUIDES, SEANCES, BLACKED-OUT ROOM]

DARSHAN—(Hinduism) the blessing vibrations which flow from the mere sight of a Saint; pleasant emanations around the picture of a highly evolved person which flow to receptive individuals; (India) pleasant energy which flows from a Saint or Master, which can be felt by those in his or her physical presence.

DART—(mental healing) a very strong thought given by the healer that is felt as a sharp pain (for a split second) as it penetrates the diseased area of the patient; helps to change the body chemistry of the patient so his or her body can heal itself. (Inconcl.) [**cf.** MENTAL HEALING, BEAMED ENERGY, CURATIVE EDUCATION]

DATURA INOXIA—see JIMSON WEED.

DATURA STRAMONIUM—abbr. DATURA, (Mexico, Native American, Navaho) a plant with a vibrational frequency that puts it in the category of hallucinogenic drugs; held sacred by the natives; can induce trance or visions; has illuminating qualities; contains scopolamine and atropine. **Syn.** JIMSON WEED, THORNAPPLE. [**cf.** HALLUCINATORY EXPERIENCES, FORCED PSI]

DAUGHTER OF VOICE—(Hebrew) a medium who is capable of synchronizing with the etheric world intelligence so that the intelligence can anesthetize the medium's voice box, and speak through it with information that could not have been know through earth's schooling. **Syn.** DIRECT VOICE MEDIUM [**cf.** MEDIUMSHIP, GUIDE, TRANCE VOICES]

DAVY JONES—(West Indies) *davy* taken from the spirit "duppy" and *Jones,* taken from "Jonah and the Whale"; an etheric world intelligence who comes from the sea to guide the sailors. [**cf.** ETHERIC WORLD INTELLIGENCES Appendix 3]

DAWN ANGELS—(ufology) moving energy in the atmosphere that shows on radar screens, usually at dawn; when seen it manifests shapes that are unrecognizable to human beings. (Inconcl.) [**cf.** ECHO, RADAR ANGELS, BEAM OF HEAT]

DAWN OF CONSCIENCE—(ancient Egypt) the emergence of judgement, flowing into the conscious mind upon death, weighing out one's qualities. [**cf.** HOUSE OF ENTERNITY, DEATH WISH, DEATH PROCESS]

DAWN SPIRITS—(Native American, Pueblo) etheric world intelligences who communicate with Native Americans to help them; related to the CLOUD BEINGS. [**cf.** CORN MAIDENS]

DAWNING CONSCIOUSNESS—the emergence of an inspirational thought, coming from Totality directly to the conscious mind; see INSPIRATIONAL PSYCHISM. [**cf.** INSPIRATIONAL ART, INSPIRATIONAL SPEAKING, COGNITIVE CLAIRSENTIENCE.]

DAY DREAM OF HOMAGE—the daydreamer pictures her or himself doing a service to win approval from society, or from a specific individual. [**cf.** DAYDREAMING, FANTASY]

DAY OF JUDGEMENT—(theory) the last day of 12,000 years of manmade time, when the cosmic clock has completed a full cycle. [**cf.** CYCLES, TIME]

DAYDREAMING—controlled thought, usually emerging when alone to fill in time, characterized by a blank stare; the daydreamer realizes that it is not reality; the conscious mind, influencing innermind pictures pertaining to the subject's life; brought on deliberately for psychological needs; an experience with thoughts that will manifest in the physical world of the daydreamer, as other thoughts do; (do not confuse with VISUALIZATION, PSYCHIC INFORMATION, IMAGERY, FANTASY, or HALLUCINATION; see Appendix 4 for clarification). **Syn.** CONSCIOUS FANTASY, MEMORY-VISUAL DISPLAYS, OBJECTIVE CONTROLLED IMAGERY.

DAYDREAMS—consciously controlled thoughts of two types: 1. repetition of the same scene many times over; 2. an ongoing stream of scenes, images or people with a fluidity of association; brought on for gratification of wishes and exploration of practical concerns for the future. [**cf.** DAYDREAMING, FANTASY]

153

DAYLIGHT DISCS—(ufology) objects (sometimes in pairs) seen in the atmosphere, appearing to be oval or elipsoid, shiny or glowing, but showing no discernable light source; yellowish white or metallic in color; possess the ability to accelerate rapidly and soundlessly (except for a faint swish); appear to have a purpose behind their movement. (Inconcl.) [cf. FIREFLIES, DOR CLOUDS, PROJECT MAGNET]

DAZHBOG—(Slavic) principal deity personifying fire (Svarozhich), and sun (Tsar) from which all earth people have their beginning. [cf. TSAR, SVAROZHICH, FIRE]

DAZZLEMENT—(Tibet) the clear colorless light of the oneness. [cf. TOTALITY, CHIT, LOGOS, VOID, WEB]

DE DEVELESKI—(gypsies) name for the divine mother of all earth; a celestial being. **Sim.** GOD. [cf. TOTALITY, UNIVERSAL MIND, AVATAR]

DE LA WARR BOX—(England) instrument designed to diagnose disease, using the principle of radiesthesia; a sample of the patient's blood is used, or the patient is wired directly to the instrument; the dials are turned until the operator feels a "stick" from the turning, which indicates the dials should be read for the diagnosis. **Sim.** BLACK BOX. [cf. RADIESTHETIC SENSE, ENERGY FIELDS, STICK]

DE-TUNED—(Steven Halpern) to be out of psychological and physical harmony and balance resulting from noises, sound, and music that one rarely gives a second thought to; environmental sound pollution of today's culture can induce stress and deafness. [cf. CLAIRAUDIENCE, SOUNDS-WITH-POWER]

DEAD FOOD—foods that are referred to by nutritionists as "dead to nutrition"; foods that lose a large percentage of nutrients through processing and preparation for marketing. [cf. CURATIVE MEDICINE, HERBOLOGY]

DEAD MATTER—(science) inanimate objects; (parapsychology) inanimate objects are alive but to a lesser degree than what scientists call living organisms; alive because it has motion and intelligence; has a slower vibrational frequency than living organisms. [cf. ATOMS, MATTER, SOUL]

DEAD PEOPLE—(esoteric) soul-minds who have shed their physical bodies and are now in the etheric world, functioning under a different set of laws, with a new awareness, and very much alive. [cf. REINCARNATION, BODIES AND PLANES

Appendix 5, ASTRAL VISION, EDGE OF THE UNKNOWN, HAPPY HUNTING GROUND]

DEAD SEA SCROLLS—a number of leather, papyrus and copper scrolls collaborating on the books in the Old Testament of the Bible; found in 1948 in caves on the northwest coast of the Dead Sea; believed to have been written between 168 B.C. and A.D. 233; they predate all existing records by hundreds of years; include psalms, hymns, commentaries and apocryphal writings of the hidden mysteries, angel kingdom and keys to psychism.

DEATH—(esoteric) a painless, enriching experience which has been earned by the soul-mind; a change from one state of consciousness to another; an initiation into another form of existence, body and environment; letting the old life end and moving into a new home; no one dies too early, everything is in divine order; (don Juan) "death is an eternal companion at our left, watching us at arms length, always with us, considered to be able to give us advice." [cf. DEATH SCIENCE, DEATHBED VISIONS, DEATH ANGEL, SURVIVALISTS]

DEATH ANGEL—(esoteric) a soul-mind who has earned the rank of angel; assigned to help with the death process of a given area; administers and assists with death according to karmic debts and soul-mind evolution. [cf. MAGNIFICANT DEVA, ANGEL HIERARCHY, DEATH PROCESS]

DEATH COINCIDENCES—psychic experiences that appear to be caused by the soul-mind who realizes it will make its transition and wishes to reassure a loved one that everything will be all right; comes through various types of psychic skills: 1. nonhuman omens: a clock stopping at the exact time an individual dies; a relative or close friend of a dying person, awakens in the night and perceives a full blown vision of the dying person; 2. human omens: an odor of death is smelled shortly before death occurs by a close associate in another city; an unexplainable desire to telephone a person not heard from in a long time, and later learn that he died the next day; 3. mass omens: many individuals perceiving a prophetic vision of a coming disaster, during sleep; (a) a soul-mind with a magnetic personality psychically sends a notice of his forthcoming death, to thousands of people, e.g., the deaths of President John Kennedy and Elvis Presley were psychically perceived the nights before they happened; (b) soul-minds involved in an up-coming airplane crash, collapse of a bridge, or an earthquake send out disturbed, uneasy, or depressed vibrations which can be picked up by those who are very psychic; after the catastrophe the psychics feel in good spirits again; distance is no barrier. [cf. OMENS, EMOTIONAL PSI]

DEATH COMA—(esoteric) a state of consciousness during the death process in which the body is still breathing, but the mental capacity has left; the MENTAL-CONSCIOUSNESS-SEED-ATOM has departed along the silver cord, but the LIFE-CORD-HEART-SEED-ATOM has not yet left the body. [cf. DEATH SCIENCE, DEATH ANGEL, ETCHING OF THE SEED ATOM]

DEATH COMPACT—an agreement between two or more people before they pass on, to endeavor to give evidence of their continued existence, after they make their transition. [cf. DEATH HORMONE, GO-BEYOND DEATH EXPERIENCES, HALL OF INCARNATIONS]

DEATH CONSCIOUSNESS—(esoteric)1. the period of time that it takes a man or woman to go through the process of dying, approximated at two hours to one day. (Inconcl.) 2. the awareness of the dying person that he or she is passing over the threshold. **Syn.** CHONYID. [cf. DEATH SCIENCE, DEATH PROCESS]

DEATH DEMONS—(Celtic) belief that an etheric world entity can cause a death on the earth plane, if there is a karmic tie. [cf. DAWN OF CONSCIENCE, BIRTH OF BARDO BODY, KARMIC REFLEXES]

DEATH FEASTS—(Tibet) a large meal given in honor of the deceased, one year after his or her death, to help the deceased attain a higher rebirth in the etheric world. [cf. DEATH SCIENCE Appendix 2]

DEATH FETCH—an apparation of a dying person, seen by another at the exact time of, or shortly before the death occurs; believed to be caused by an overly emotional soul-mind who wants a loved one to know; the soul-mind splits and is in two places at once. [cf. BILOCATION, ASTRAL PROJECTION, DEATH PROCESS PHENOMENA]

DEATH GLOW—emanations of light that seem to flow from the top of the head of the individual who is going through the process of death; can be perceived clairvoyantly by those close by. **Syn.** GOLDEN BOWL. [cf. BIRTH OF THE BARDO BODY, CORPSE LIGHTS, DEATH HORMONE, ETCHING OF THE SEED ATOMS]

DEATH HORMONE—(esoteric) an invisible substance emitted by the endocrine glands during the process of death, which helps to loosen the three seed-atoms belonging to the silver cord. [cf. LIFE-CORD-HEART-SEED-ATOM, EMOTIONAL-ASTRAL-SEED-ATOM, MENTAL-CONSCIOUSNESS-SEED-ATOM]

DEATH MIST—(Anglo-Saxton) a film of darkness surrounding the person who will descend to the lower planes during his or her death process. [cf. DEATH SCIENCE, DENSITY, DEATH ANGEL]

DEATH PROCESS—(esoteric) to end one expression of life ready to give rise to another expression of life; an evolutionary step in soul-mind growth, from one completed area into another; (not a set method) similarities: the soul-mind painlessly slips out of the physical body, assisted, if desired, by loved ones from the etheric world who have gathered; viewing a kind of micro-film which shows experiences from the life just passed; seeing a great light, or a tunnel with a tremendous light at the far end (which draws one to it); the soul-mind reaches an ethereal plane level according to it's development; a pleasurable, beautiful experience, or an unpleasant one, depending on the accumulated karma, but always physically painless. (Inconcl.) **Syn.** MADE THE TRANSITION. [cf. DEATH SCIENCE Appendix 2, LAW OF DYING Appendix 7]

DEATH PROCESS PHENOMENA—a paranormal act happening at the instant of death, such as, a plant which is owned by the dying person, bowing its flowers and dying, a full blown vision of the dying person showing himself in another locale; believed that the soul-mind is in such an emotional state that it can split and release a nonphysical force affecting physical objects, in an area it wants to notify of its oncoming transition; not consciously willed. (Inconcl.) **Sim.** EMOTIONAL PSI, DEATH-PK. [cf. DEATH PROCESS, DEATH SCIENCE, DEATH ANGEL]

DEATH SCIENCE—an esoteric study of the death process from the standpoint of the universe; a change in the speed of the soul-mind vibrational frequency to one of a faster speed, changing the location of the soul-mind in the cosmos (from a physical body in a physical plane, to an ethereal body in an ethereal plane); an initiatory step on the path of the monad; a forward status of the soul-mind on the evolutionary scale; the release of a

155

nonphysical energy, the three permanent seeds, in three periods closely related, (except in accidents when the energies are released simultaneously); loosening from the physical body the three books of life; the "quality" of knowledge and emotion is taken from these three books to be added to the akashic records and oversoul, according to a law, thus forming the new total personality, now alive in the soul-mind in the etheric world. (Inconcl.) [cf. DEATH PROCESS, MENTAL-REFLECTING-ETHER, DEATH, EMOTIONAL-ASTRAL-SEED-ATOM, LAW OF DYING Appendix 7]

DEATH TRANCE—(esoteric) a time of sleep for the person who has died, believed to be the three-day period after the loosening of the silver cord; there is a period of adjustment and judgement lasting three days, while the new arrival is in a sleep state or in a hypnotic state. [cf. DEATH ANGEL, DIE WITH DIGNITY, OPENING OF THE MOUTH CEREMONY, HOUSE OF ENTERNITY]

DEATH WISH—(Sigmund Freud) theory: within man is the instinct of death which provides energy for the soul-mind aura, leading one to eventually die. [cf. SOUL-MIND AURA, REINCARNATION]

DEATH-LIKE TRANCE—(esoteric) a physical body lying as still as a corpse, not needing food, water, or breath, but capable of rising if necessary; a technique of resting in a hypnotic state for many years, without need of nourishment, without movement, but able to wake up and become normal again; accomplished by a psychic spell or perfect body control. [cf. MAGIC SLEEP INDUCEMENT]

DEATH-PK—(esoteric) the movement of physical objects which have a relationship to a dying person: clock stopping at time of death, picture of the dying person falling, etc.; some theories: 1. (laboratory) if the dying person is awake as death approaches, the heart could act as a storage for the blood being pumped into its chambers, causing abnormal quantities of energy and this energy could act on adjacent or surrounding physical objects; 2. the death process could release an ethereal force which is capable of affecting physical objects; 3. the soul-mind, in an emotional state, could split, and be in two places at one time, and perform paranormal acts. (Inconcl.) **Sim.** DEATH PROCESS PHENOMENA. [cf. EMOTIONAL PSI, DEATH SCIENCE Appendix 2]

DEATHBED EXPERIENCE—the soul-mind slips from the body in an astral projection and exper-iences the death process in the etheric world; the patient is pronounced clinically dead; the soul-mind then returns to the body; the patient lives, and has vivid memory of both their invisible death activity and what happened in the room where the doctors were caring for them; an expression of rapture on the features of the patient is frequently noticeable. [cf. DEATH PROCESS, DEATH ANGEL, MENTAL-REFLECTING-ETHER, INVOLUNTARY ASTRAL PROJECTION]

DEATHBED VISIONS—scenes and images of loved ones who have passed on, or kind angels (sometimes recognized as a personal deity, such as Jesus or Krishna, etc.); visions are often accompanied with murmerings to the dead; appear at the bedside as one prepares to make one's transition. **Syn.** SURVIVAL RELATED APPARITIONS. [cf. DEATH ANGEL, FREEING OF THE SOUL]

DEATHLIKE—term used to describe the appearance of the physical body when the astral body has slipped out, on a long astral projection. [cf. ASTRAL PROJECTION, OUT-OF-RANGE-OF-CORD-ACTIVITY]

DECLINE EFFECT—(laboratory) 1. the lowering of scores on a series of runs in an experiment, when the recipient is not fed back his hits and misses of the target, until the end of the experiment; 2. the tapering off of ability to hit the target, after much repetition of experiments. [cf. SHEEP AND GOAT EFFECT, TARGET, CHANCE]

DECOMPOSE—to allow every muscle in the body to relax, and the mind to become free from any thought of the outside world; concentrating on the smallest possible target until the body does not seem to be there; a state necessary for trancing for physical psychism. [cf. MEDITATION, TRANCE MANIFESTATION]

DECONDITIONING PROCESS—(psychology) consciously trying to do away with previous concepts, believed to be good at a previous time, but which no longer apply; going through a transformation process with the pull inside to adopt new beliefs and a slight pull from the subconscious mind to hang on to the old ones. [cf. LAW OF LETTING GO Appendix 7, TRANSFORMATION, CULTURAL EVOLUTION]

DEEP LEVEL OF CONSCIOUSNESS—when the subconscious mind can function normally without the conscious mind in control; see SUBCONSCIOUS MIND. [cf. DEEP HYPNOTHERAPY, MEDITATION]

DEEP PSYCHOPHYSIOLOGICAL RELAXATION—
abbr. DPR: a restful hypnometablic state reached by decreased activity of the sympathetic nervous system; mental and bodily stillness; relieves stress symptons and provides physical benefits; reached in meditation and when working with biofeedback training sessions. [cf. RELAXATION RESPONSE, RISING TO THE SURFACE, SLEEPLESS SLEEP]

DEEP SLEEP—refers to a very deep trance state; see TRANCE.

DEEP STATE OF HYPNOSIS—to function within the "depth" of the subconscious mind without the conscious mind interfering, and with the physical body completely relaxed, limp and pliable; awareness is that of euphoria and joy; accomplished by lying flat on one's back or sitting ina chair; more easily attained with a hypnotherapist guide than by one's self; body's automatic functions slow down to almost nil; ability to open eyes without awakening; 1. deep state is determined by the following signs: subject feels detached from his physical body and suspension of his mind; superconscious mind can surface knowledge that is advanced to current science; capable of revivification regression; complete amnesia upon awakening; control of bodily movements by the hypnotherapist; time distortion as to length of time in the hypnotic state; whole body is anesthesized; capable of perceiving psychic visions; hearing background noise is acute or nil; subject will carry out posthypnotic suggestion upon awakening; subject must be programmed to verbalize; subject cannot make a decision but can state facts at this new level of awareness; 2. at this level the subconscious mind accepts suggestions verbatim, so it is used for therapeutic purposes; habits, attitudes, and body cells can be altered by proper wording of the prescription. **Syn.** SOMNAMBULISTIC HYPNOTHERAPY. [cf. HYPNOTHERAPY Appendix 5]

DEEP TRANCE—to prepare one's physical body with the assistance of the etheric world intelligence, so he or she is free to enter and use it for performing physical phenomenon; medium's body no longer functions on its own; medium becomes very relaxed through self-hypnosis, shutting out all objective life, allowing the conscious mind to become passive; the subconscious mind either steps out close by, or takes an astral projection; intelligence slides into the medium's body and uses it to speak through, as a channel for healing, or other preplanned psychic phenomenon. **Syn.** HEAVY

TRANCE. [cf. SELF-HYPNOSIS, DESIRED-CONTROL, PHYSICAL PSYCHISM PROCESS, GUIDES, SEANCE]

DEEP-DREAM MEDITATION—sitting for psychic development; name used by those who prefer not to use the word *psychic* to refer to visions they did not instigate. [cf. PSYCHIC INFORMATION, VISIONARY, MEDITATION]

DEEPAKA RAGA—(Hinduism) music of a fixed melodic scale, played during summer evenings to arouse compassion among the people. [cf. SOUNDS-WITH-POWER, QUIETISM, MOLECULAR CHORUS]

DEEPER DREAMLAND—a deep state of sleep when one sees only with the subconscious mind; subjective thinking, with no decision making; the mind uses only memories and imagination, with the same quality of intelligence used while awake, except that the five senses do not react to outer stimuli. **Syn.** DELTA STAGE. [cf. SLEEP BRAIN WAVE PATTERNS, DREAMS]

DEER—(Scotland) (esoteric) an animal having the vibrational frequency to communicate between the etheric world and mankind; every part of the deer's body has a medicinal purpose, and the antlers are able to ward off negative vibrations; seeing pictures of half-man/half-deer suggests that a person could transform themselves into a deer at will. [cf. DEER ANTLERS, SHAPE-CHANGING, VIBRATIONS]

DEER ANTLERS—(Scotland, England) belief that deer antlers can store psychic energy; when hung over a doorway or in a building, will prevent negative entities from influencing the room. [cf. ANPSI, ENERGY, FAIRY STONE]

DEHUMANIZE—1. (new-age therapy) to deprive an individual of their basic normal needs with the intention of releasing fears, anxieties, or psychosomatic problems; patient is put into a room without sound, light, or furniture; therapist is close by to decipher his reaction, such as screaming, crying, perceiving visions, etc.; this takes the charge out of the emotional blocks that have been surpressed over the years and the patient works through his or her problem. [cf. PRIMAL SCREAM, BLOCKS, ISOLATION TANK] 2. (destructive-brainwashing cult) to use hypnosis and psychic techniques to forceably alter the individual's belief system so they know themselves as a member of the organization only; this process of evil intent is performed upon the victim without their knowledge or permission; makes the victim act without emotions or without the ability to make decisions; deprives victim of normal human experiences; members of destructive-brainwashing cults are dehumanized or automatons. [cf. MASS HYPNOSIS, SUGGESTION, AUTOMATON]

DEHYPNOTIZING—1. the process of eliminating a conditioned reflex through hypnotherapy; the use of regression sessions to discover the stimuli and the original cause of the conditioned reflex; 2. the act of bringing back into the subject's mental consciousness that which the hypnotist had removed during the session; e.g., "You will now react normally to all sounds." [cf. HYPNOTHERAPY Appendix 5]

DEIFICATION—godlike; deify: to personify as a god; to exalt to the rank of a deity. [cf. CHRISTED, GLORIFIED BODY, PURIFIED BODY]

DEILS—(Scotland) see NATURE SPIRIT.

DEINDIVIDUALIZED—(esoteric) the ability to leave the "self" out of life and merge into the great cosmic conscious, with dependence on the cosmos. [cf. THE PATH, MEDITATION]

DEISM—1. theory: God created the world, but from then on, intends to interfere as little as possible; 2. theory: the world consists of three distinct things, the human mind, God, and matter, each independent of God and each separate from the other.

DEITIES—(Tibet) an etheric world god in one of three aspects: lotus, peaceful, and wrathful; held together by thought; visible to one according to one's own thoughts; perceived clairvoyantly as coming from within to the without. [cf. LAW OF CENTER Appendix 7, SOLAR LOGOS, GREAT ONES, LADY OF HEAVEN]

DEITY—1. that which serves as God to a particular man; 2. one who has reached the rank of god or goddess in the angel kingdom in the etheric world. [cf. DEVA, ETHERIC WORLD INTELLIGENCES, PITRIS, MASTERS]

DÉJÀ—the feeling of familiarity, divorced from any evidential reason; an experience when one feels that the present moment, in all its exact detail, has been lived before. [cf. DÉJÀ ENTENDU, DÉJÀ VU, PAST LIVES THEORY, REINCARNATION]

DÉJÀ ENTENDU—(France) the feeling that what is now being heard for the first time, has been heard before. [cf. DÉJÀ VU, REINCARNATION]

DÉJÀ VU—(French, "already seen"); to sense an innate feeling that where one is for the first time, one has been before, or to meet an individual for the first time and sense that one knows that individual already; theories: 1. (science) a momentary alteration of consciousness, caused by a minor seizure of the temporal lobe in the brain; 2. (psychology) the subconscious mind is working faster than the conscious mind; perceives what is happening, and quickly relates it to the conscious mind; 3. (parapsychology) (a) to meet an individual or to visit a location that one had visited or met in a past incarnation; (b) to experience the same "emotional sensations" from a situation or person that one experienced in another lifetime or the past of this lifetime, (having nothing to do with the actual location or person); the subconscious mind is activated by the memory of this duplication of emotions; body cells have a condensed memory bank of every life the soul-mind lived which could make this possible. (Inconcl.) [cf. REINCARNATION, CLAIRSENTIENCE, KARMA, DÉJÀ ENTENDU]

DELAYED KARMA—see ACCUMULATED KARMA.

DELAYED PHOTO IMPRESSION PHENOMENA—the appearance of etheric world entities on film not seen by the photographer at the time the picture was taken; can only take place if the photographer has a mediumistic body chemistry; (do not confuse with SKOTOGRAPHY, when a camera is not used). (Inconcl.) [cf. EXTRAS, MIND PHOTOGRAPHY]

DELILAH—describing the negative, feminine principle of an object of living organism. [cf. POLARITY]

DELPHI—(B.C.) a famous temple in Greece where a trance medium, Pythia, sat on a tripod over a vapor that came from the earth; she was able to bring guidance, prophecy, and protection for her people from the voice of the god, Apollo, speaking through her. [cf. DEPENDENT VOICE, PROPHECY]

DELTA STATE OF CONSCIOUSNESS—a level of awareness in which the conscious mind is passive, the subconscious mind, or the superconscious mind is acute, alert, and active and the body is completely relaxed, limp, and pliable, large body movements are impossible; the brain rhythm produces waves every three cycles per second on the EEG instrument; psychic mechanism is easily utilized; the mind is more readily programmed from outside stimuli; 1. occurs in the first two hours of a normal night's sleep and does not occur again during the night; children can be carried around in this state without awakening; sleep learning from cassette tapes is at its highest peak; **2.** occurs in a deep hypnotherapy session in which revivification can occur, and in which the subject can be programmed with post hypnotic suggestions, and can be operated on without pain; (do not confuse with a DEEP TRANCE state in which the soul-mind leaves the body for the skill of IMPERSONATION. [**cf.** BRAIN SCALE OF REVOLUTIONS, BIOFEEDBACK TRAINING, DREAMS]

DELTA WAVES—(biofeedback training) a long symmetrical wave, occuring about three to four times per second when recorded by the EEG instrument; a continuous movement of electrical changes in the brain activity forms groups or "bursts" of wavey lines on the printout, with enough uniformity to know they represent different states of consciousness. [**cf.** DREAMS, DELTA STATE OF CONSCIOUSNESS, THETA WAVES, BIOFEEDBACK TRAINING]

DELUSION—controlled inner-mind pictures; a false interference in daydreams; conscious fantasy usually based on reasonable accurate perception. [**cf.** FANTASY, DAYDREAMING, VISIONS, NON-THOUGHT]

DEMAND CHARACTERISTICS—(laboratory) outward environmental influences that affect the results of an ESP experiment; usually picked up unintentionally, e.g., the attitude, tone of voice, or mannerisms of the experimenter, or certain behaviors expected of the percipient; (do not confuse with PSI-LEAKAGE). [**cf.** TIP-OFFS, SHEEP AND GOAT EFFECT]

DEMANDED PSI-TRY—to compel one's psychic ability to surface immediately because someone needs proof of this ability; this is an abnormal characteristic of mental or physical psychism and mediumship that could cause physical disorders or mental imbalance within the psychic; psychic and mediumship information or beaming energy from one's hands or eyes should be preplanned, and the environment scanned preceeding the turning on of any psychic skill (except intuition); preplanning can be subconsciously willed if all things are favorable; an unknowledgeable and criticizing public sometimes demands or challenges the psychic to give a psychic answer or to perform a psychic feat which can lead a good psychic to fake an answer because of his or her desire to verify that psychism is factual; hastiness prevents the psychic from

reaching his or her normal low state of consciousness needed to manipulate matter. [**cf.** CLAIRSENTIENCE, MENTAL PSYCHIC PROCESS, GOING-TO-LEVEL]

DEMATERIALIZATION—**1.** (ectoplasmic) the process of a materialized form being returned into the medium's body through the ectoplasmic cord, during a materialization seance; begins when the medium's trance time is complete (prearranged with etheric world intelligence); the cord which extends from the medium's navel to the materialized form, makes a few movements, and looks like it "sinks into the floor" or is sucked back into the orifices of the medium's body. [**cf.** SEANCE, SYMPATHETIC NERVOUS SYSTEM, MATERIALIZATION] **2.** (alchemy) to intensely focalize attention on an aura of an object, which in turn changes the objects rate of vibration, causing it to appear in ethereal form; gradually or rapidly; the first step in apportation and transmutation. (Inconcl.) [**cf.** ALCHEMIST, APPORTATION] **3.** (ufology) a process used by spacecraft intelligences to cause their vehicle to disappear from one place and reappear in another; (similar to DIMENSION-SHIFTING). (Inconcl.) [**cf.** FLASHING STROBE LIGHT, ETHEREANS, PROPAGATION ANOMALIES]

DEMIGOD—(French *demi*, "half") **1.** an ANGEL of lesser rank, an inferior DEITY, or minor ETHERIC WORLD INTELLIGENCE; **2.** an offspring of a deity and a mortal. [**cf.** ASTRAL PLANE, GOD (uncapitalized), DEVA]

DEMIURGE—**1.** (Gnostic) believed to be an etheric world intelligence in charge of organizing matter; creator of the visible universe; builder of the material world; a necessary subordinate of the invisible world, therefore, considered by some to be evil; a life form inferior to a god. [**cf.** SOPHIA, ABATUR]

DEMON—**1.** (ancient Greece) "genius," intelligence; a name used indiscriminately for all entities in the etheric world, whether their behavior was good or bad. **Syn.** DAEMON. **2.** (current) an intelligence in the etheric world, low (or new) on the evolutionary scale, therefore its life style appears to be evil or ignorant; capable of communicating with mankind, or being manipulated by them or manipulating them, which ends in harm to people or their worldly situations; a soul-mind who pursued inferior activities in physical life, now abides in the lower planes and haunts men; **3.** (Zoroastrianism)

159

("Dev," designation of invisible entities under the orders of Ahriman); the genius of evil in the invisible world. [cf. PRINCE OF DARKNESS, DENSITY, HAUNTING]

DEMONESS—female demon; see DEMON.

DEMONIAC—1. pertains to evil; possessed by an inferior spirit; raging; frantic. [cf. POSSESSION, DENSITY, ANGEL HIERARCHY]

DEMONIC—pertains to being inspired by an etheric world intelligence of either kind: one who works with evil intent or one who is a genius of good intent. [cf. ETHERIC WORLD INTELLIGENCE, DENSITY, GENIUS]

DEMONICAL SOMNAMBULISM—(possession) the seizure of a physical body by an inferior etheric world entity with evil intent; occurs with such rapidity and force that the victim loses consciousness and the body takes on the personality of the entity; facial features become twisted, language is obscene and vulgar, even though the person is well-bred; body performs physical contortions normally impossible to human beings; sometimes behaves like an animal; body becomes so strong that it takes many to subdue it; not willed consciously. **Syn.** DIABOLIC POSSESSION [cf. POSSESSION, LUCID POSSESSION, HOLY SPIRIT POSSESSION]

DEMONIFUGE—see SPELL; in this case the spell is used for ill intent.

DEMONOLOGIST—1. (current) one who investigates and researches haunted houses; records and examines cases for study with the objective being to find some answers to the reason for poltergeist and ghost activity. [cf. POLTERGEISTRY, LOW-ORDER-PSI-FORCE, GHOSTOLOGY] 2. (ancient) one who calls upon inferior etheric world entities to perform psychic feats for evil intent. [cf. DENSITY, LAND OF THE SHADOWS, BLACK MAGIC]

DEMONOLOGY—study of low intelligent life beings in the etheric world: their function, life style, levels of existence, laws, relationship to earth beings and nature spirits, and their vibrational frequency; study of invisible energies of an unpleasant nature, around animate or inanimate things; this knowledge is used to prevent inferior intelligences from wrongly influencing earth persons and earth matters; (do not confuse with PARAPSYCHOLOGY, ANGELOLOGY, PSYCHISM,

SATANISM). **Sim.** DEMONRY, DEMONOMANCY, DEVILRY, DEMONISM. [cf. OUIJA BOARD, EARTH-BOUND ENTITIES]

DEMONOMANIA—an individual behaving as if in a convulsive seizure; believed to have an inferior or evil etheric world entity in his or her body, which uses it for its benefit; see POSSESSION. [cf. DUAL PERSONALITY, DIABOLIC POSSESSION]

DEMONOPATHY—see DEMONOMANIA.

DEMONSTRATION—the outward manifestation of an object, event or change in one's life, brought about by using a special method and a deliberate attempt for this manifestation to happen. [cf. VISUALIZATION, THOUGHT-FORMS, DAYDREAMING]

DEMOS—a psychic demonstration; mental psychic information. [cf. MENTAL PSYCHIC PROCESS, PSYCHIC DEVELOPMENT]

DENDRITES—many short fibers radiating from the body of a nerve cell through which impulses enter from other nerve cells; transmitters of electrical currents in the brain. [cf. BIOFEEDBACK TRAINING, BRAIN]

DENIAL—1. an unconscious defense mechanism used frequently to make life manageable on the surface; diminishing or hiding a past unpleasant experience as an alternative to facing its hurts and complexes; denying that an activity ever happened; evading a task by substituting other things to occupy time; not performing in accordance to one's ability; not handling an underlying current of resentment and jealousy; finding alternatives to settle the spur of the moment feelings in place of looking at the overall picture (always looking for short answers). [cf. BLOCKS, CLUSTERS, HOLISTIC HEALTH, LAW OF AVOIDANCE Appendix 7] 2. (Unity) the act of erasing, cleansing or releasing from the soul any concepts, beliefs, or thoughts that are contrary to the perfectness of Totality; accomplished by consciously willing the belief away, usually through affirmations or hypnotherapy. [cf. AFFIRMATION, PATTERN, BELIEF SYSTEM]

DENIZENS IN SPACE—refers to any inhabitant of space made known either by the physical senses or by the psychic senses, i.e., star, planet, discarnate entity, angel, space intelligent being, or space critter. [cf. UFOLOGY, ETHERIC WORLD ENTITIES, BEINGS]

DENSE—(esoteric) atoms vibrating at a slower vibrational frequency, producing third dimensional matter; each piece has it's own vibrational rate necessary to express itself. [**cf.** Appendix 5 VIBRATIONS, ATOMS]

DENSE BLACK-CLOUD—a mass of energy functioning as a curtain, separating the astral world from the physical world; one does not have to be concerned with one's astral existence while in the physical body. **Syn.** VEIL, BARRIER, ETHERIC WEB. [**cf.** PLANES, LOWER ASTRAL WORLD, ASTRAL BODY]

DENSE BODY—(esoteric) another name for physical body, because it is vibrating slower than the ethereal body and inhabits the plane of dense matter called earth. [**cf.** PLANES, ASTRAL BODY, MENTAL BODY]

DENSELY PACKED REALM—(Tibet) an etheric world plane where seeds of all universal forces and objects are closely knit together. **Syn.** NO-DOWN, OG-MIN, THICKLY-FORMED. [**cf.** SEEDS, BODIES AND PLANES Appendix 5, MENTAL PLANE]

DENSITY—(esoteric) 1. slowest rate of vibration of the atoms, forming the lower planes in the ETHERIC WORLD; inhabited by soul-minds who are too new on the evolutionary scale to understand physical life while in the physical body, and who desire to take the unrighteous path; create their own hell plane that they go to after death; divided into levels: HADES, HELL, PURGATORY, INFERNO, LIMBO, etc; these planes are dark, evil, and uncouth; lowest experiences are nonhuman and animalistic forms inhabiting the slime; 2. light-waves, lacking intelligence, form the lower planes for new soul-minds who have not yet acquired intelligence; 3. a vibrational frequency of dark earth disfiguration reflecting the waste products of the human body, its viruses and other impurities; makes the demonic entities in the etheric world; 4. the end of INVOLUTION and the beginning of EVOLUTION. [**cf.** DENSITY Appendix 5, PRETA-WORLD, SURVIVAL ELEMENTS, INFERNAL ANIMALS]

DENSITY ELEMENTALS—(esoteric) living entities in the density who take shapes relating to the earth, e.g., animals, nonhumans, half-humans, with grotesque and artificial forms; their law and intelligence comes from the slums, ghettoes, cannibalistic tribes, etc., which literally feeds this plane of existence; see DENSITY. [**cf.** SOULLESS, ARTIFICIAL ELEMENTAL, LEFT-HAND PATH]

DENTAL PSYCHISM—an instantaneous healing in the mouth area by a psychic; intense concentration

on the molecular structure of the gums or teeth causes changes to take place, e.g., a filling appears where needed, a silver filling changes to gold, diseased gums are healed, and a tooth falls out that needed to be pulled. (Inconcl.) [**cf.** MENTAL HEALING, PSYCHIC HEALING, CURATIVE EDUCATION]

DEO—prefix taken from the Latin meaning "with God."

DEOSIL MOVEMENT—that which goes in the same direction as the sun; clockwise; belief that one brings God into the sphere of the operator in psychic work, if one makes movements in the same direction as the natural forces; opposite of WIDDERSHIN MOVEMENT. [**cf.** WIDDERSHINS, CEREMONIAL MAGIC, FORMS-WITH-POWER]

DEPARTED SPIRITS—see ETHERIC WORLD INTELLIGENCES.

DEPENDENT CLAIRVOYANCE—to produce psychic visions at will, when giving a psychic reading or asking a personal question in a hypnotherapy session. [**cf.** WELL-GROUNDED MEDIUM, X-RAY CLAIRVOYANCE, EMOTIONAL PSI]

DEPENDENT VOICE—to allow an etheric world intelligence to intervene and use one's vocal cords as an amplification system to bring forth information and knowledge so others can hear it; occurs in or out of a seance if conditions are correct; medium, with the aid of the intelligence allows himself or herself to go into a deep trance so the intelligence can anesthetize his vocal cords before using them; occurs by desired-control of the medium only; see VOICE TRANCE. [**cf.** INDEPENDENT VOICE, DESIRED-CONTROL, MEDIUMSHIP, TEN PERCENT TRANCE]

DEPERSONALIZATION—to feel a loss of one's personal identity with the material world and to feel opened to an awareness of one's place in the universe; acquired by: 1. an astral projection; 2. deep meditation. [**cf.** ASTRAL PROJECTION, DOUBLE APPEARANCE]

DEPERSONALIZED EXPERIENCE—see ASTRAL PROJECTION.

DEPOSITED MATTER—(ectoplasm telekinesis) the production of useful and worthwhile artwork or messages, on paper or canvas, by an etheric world intelligence without the use of the medium's body; tools are set close by the medium beforehand; while medium sleeps at night or is in a deep trance state in a seance, the intelligence uses the ecto-plasm that has emanated from the medium; the tools are levitated and descend upon the paper or canvas and hastily write the message; later the medium awakens to a finished product. Usage: "He is a deposited matter medium." **Syn.** PRECIPITA-TION. [**cf.** ETHERIC SCRIPT, INDEPENDENT PAINT-ING, SLATE WRITING, PHYSICAL PHENOMENA]

DEPROGRAMMING—(destructive-brainwashing cult) a method of interrogation to help a destruc-tive cult victim "regain" his or her inborn freedom of decision or thought; (Ted Patrick) on a one-to-one basis, the deprogrammer (a former destructive cult victim himself) forces the victim to think and reason by shooting questions at him that he has not been preprogrammed to answer by the destructive cult organization; "it is like a stab in the heart with a dagger"; deprogrammer keeps the victim off balance by the questions he cannot respond to in his automaton personality; this challenges the victim's mind, frustrates him and his mind begins to make decisions of its own; basically, the depro-grammer gets the suppressed thoughts and ques-tions regarding the cult life-style to surface and the victim begins to see through all the lies he or she has been programmed to believe. [**cf.** SURRENDER OF WILL, EGO DESTRUCTION, FLOATING]

DEPTH PSYCHOLOGISTS—name given psychol-ogists who are interested in investigating the psychic realm.

DEPTH PSYCHOLOGY—(Carl Jung) the study of one's actions in relation to their philosophy of life, centered around the deep center, the ego, or the soul-mind. [**cf.** METAPHYSICS, SOUL-MIND]

DERMAL OPTICAL SENSITIVITY—(eyeless sight) (Greek *dermo*, "skin"); (Russia) the ability to distinguish colors and words through the skin, usually the fingers and hands; the hands are placed on or above the object to detect the vibrational frequency of the polarity movement of the elec-tromagnetic field of that color; object is not handled for its shape or surface texture. (Inconcl.) **Syn.** DERMO-OPTICAL PERCEPTION, DERMAL VISION. [**cf.** EYELESS SIGHT Appendix 2, ELEC-TROSTATIC SENSITIVITY, AURAS]

DERMAL VISION—see DERMAL OPTICAL SENSITIVITY.

DERMATOGLYPHIC—a description of of one's latent feelings, psi talents, suitable vocations,

mental and psychological balance, etc.; determined by analyzing the fingerprint and skin patterns from an ink print. [**cf.** BODY READING Appendix 5]

DERMO-OPTICAL PERCEPTION—see DERMAL OPTICAL SENSITIVITY.

DERMOGRAPHY—a message written on the flesh of an arm or hand, by an etheric world intelligence; a form of physical motor psychism, performed with the medium in trance; the flesh is raised with writing which describes an appropriate psychic message; in a short time the medium's skin is back to normal and the writing disappears; the medium awakens with no harm to the skin; (do not confuse with STIGMATA). **Syn.** SKIN WRITING. [**cf.** AUTO-MATISM, SPIRITISTIC, GOLDEN PLATES]

DERMOGRAPHY ARM—see DERMOGRAPHY.

DERMOPTIC—see DERMAL OPTICAL SENSITIVITY.

DERVISH—a Mohammedan holy man (and psy-chic) following an order of the Sufi philosophy and culture; noted for raising his state of consciousness by special group dancing in which one whirls and twirls while chanting until he experiences a state of bliss, ecstasy, or psychic help and guidance for his daily life; dance, chants, and circle formation work in harmony with a polarity energy that keeps the dancer from becoming tired or dizzy. **Syn.** WHIRLING DERVISH. [**cf.** SUFISM, MOVEMENT-FOR-ALTERED-CONSCIOUSNESS]

DESENSITIZATION—a method of bringing re-pressed emotions and feelings to the surface so they can be acknowledged and dealt with; treating blocks in the body which resist conventional treatment with various therapies; psychotherapy, hypnotherapy, meditational techniques, encounter groups, biofeedback training, etc. [**cf.** BLOCKS Ap-pendix 5, HYPNOTHERAPY DESENSITIZATION]

DESENSITIZING PAIN—a therapy whereby one airs their pent up feelings regarding a traumatic experience that has not been dealt with properly; patient verbalizes the event repeatedly; this helps to rationalize intelligently so the patient can accept what happened with the correct attitude, dissolving any physical or mental pain it causes. [**cf.** NEW-AGE PSYCHOLOGY, BLOCKS, ENCOUNTER GROUPS]

DESERT FATHERS—(A.D. 400) Christian monks who lived in remote parts of the Egyptian desert and are thought to be the originators of meditation in the Christian religion; used the mantra meditation method. [cf. MANTRA MEDITATION, JESUS PRAYER]

DESIGN BODY—see ASTRAL BODY.

DESIRE—(esoteric) the strongest and most influential emotion; believed to have been born with creation; responsible for the monad *involuting* into a soul-mind forming the world of matter caused by the basic need of the monad, as if it requested to express its full potential; desire is an expression of a wish for the soul-mind to *evolute* back to Totality experiencing its full potential; 1. the emotion that is the basis for the mankind seed en masse; 2. desire makes it possible to feel pleasurable and unpleasurable communication at both the subliminal and tangible level; 3. a silent request (a desire) to become psychic changes the body chemistry to be adaptable to psychic skills; 4. affects body chemistry with silent feelings, suppressed feelings, karmic feelings, and outward feelings; wishes and requests inwardly and unconsciously stimulate the hormones in the body constantly to run on the ongoing-life-process or the ongoing-death-process; 5. (Hinduism) desire is depicted by a youth riding an elephant or a bird; known as Kama, the god of love. [cf. ASTRAL BODY, EMOTION, HOLISTIC HEALTH, SOLAR PLEXUS, BRAIN, LAW OF HEALING Appendix 7]

DESIRE BODY—see ASTRAL BODY.

DESIRE ELEMENTAL—thought-forms built up around the earth formed by the desires and passions of the material world; people feel they should identify with these, which causes the world to be held back by adding more negative vibrations to it. [cf. ELEMENTAL, VIBRATIONS]

DESIRE WORLD—matter in the astral planes formed by the semiconscious thoughts of earth people, making a place for discarnate entities who want to hold on to the habits and desires of the earth plane, even after they have died; lower astral planes inhabited by the discarnate entities who cannot let go of earthly habits and material pleasures. [cf. DESIRE BODY, ASTRAL PLANE]

DESIRED-CONTROL—to make arrangement with one's etheric world intelligence (guide) as to what is expected of one, before one goes into a trance state for physical phenomena; medium silently tells his or her guide the length of time he wants to be in a trance, and what type of physical psychic feats the intelligence should do; the medium then

relaxes, hypnotizes himself, and allows the etheric world guide to enter his body, with faith and trust that the guide will work according to the program set up, in the highest interest of all concerned. **Syn.** ACCOMMODATION [cf. MEDIUMSHIP, CONTROL, TELEKINESIS, UNCONSCIOUS MOTOR PSYCHISM, ECTOPLASM]

DESSOUNIN RITE—(Haiti, Voodoo) a ritual designed to disassociate a soul-mind from a physical body which has been enchanted with the evil intent of zombification; then the physical body is brought back to half-life. [cf. ZOMBIES, SOULLESS PSYCHISM Appendix 2]

DESTRUCTIVE MANIPULATION—(destructive-brainwashing) to deliberately implant suggestions and ideas into the mind of another without his consent or knowledge that it is happening; ideas, suggestions, or statements are given directly to the subconscious mind, while the conscious decision-making mind is passive; victim receives a mental telepathic suggestion when asleep during the night, or during a hypnotic state (that he or she is unaware of being in); destructive because the victim reacts with an inner consent and willingness to obey the suggestion or to believe the statement without feeling the necessity to logically reason with it; members of destructive cults are kept moving swiftly to a preplanned life-style which prevents them from normal thinking and reacting, and keeps them highly suggestible to the subconscious implanted ideas. [cf. DESTRUCTIVE-BRAIN-WASHING CULT, BRAINWASHING, HYPNOTHER-APY, ON-THE-SPOT HYPNOSIS, LAW OF SUGGES-TION, Appendix 7]

DESTRUCTIVE-BRAINWASHING CULT—any organization or group, massive or small, which works on the minds of their members twenty-four hours a day (for months and even years) to prevent members from making their own decisions; 1. techniques used: group hypnosis, mental telepathic suggestion, coercive repetitious suggestion, sleep learning, low protein diet, and forced wakefulness; keeps member metally worn and physically fatigued until member has a drastic shift in consciousness and the victimized member then works solely for the benefit of the organization, with his or her "total being"; this is accomplished by keeping the member in an alpha state of consciousness most of the time, which makes it possible to force a complete change in his or her belief system; member is not aware that he or she is being hypnotized daily, nor have they ever given their consent to these techniques; 2. with this sensory overload in the subconscious mind, the victim's "complete" focus is now on the objective of the organization with his or her mind, emotion, and energy; member is to the point of automation, unable to make a decision of his or her own or to think like a thinking being; 3. characteristics of the goal, or material put into the head of the victim, does not make a group or organization destructive; only if the methods and techniques are used consistently with the intent to deprive him or her of their conscious, decision-making mind makes it a destructive cult; member functions with his or her instinctual level of awareness (like an animal); 4. (dangers) the fuel of the subconscious mind is new information, and with the same repetitious rudimentary information, year after year, the mind can become *burned-out* or dulled to the point of no return. (Inconcl.) [cf. SNAPPING, ON-THE-SPOT HYPNOSIS, LAW OF SUGGESTION Appendix 7, TELEPATHIC SUGGESTION, MASS HYPNOSIS, BRAINWASHING]

DESYNCHRONIZATION—to become out of harmony with the rhythm of the twenty-four-hour cycle that attunes one's mind and body to the turning of the earth; this affects the action patterns of the physical body, e.g., flying through time zones does not change the five senses and they will desire their normal attention regardless of the time of day where one is; a night worker requires more sleep than when he or she works days. **Syn.** JET LAG. [cf. CYCLES Appendix 5, CIRCADIAN RHYTHM]

DESYNCHRONIZED WAVES—(biofeedback training) small, fast, active waves on printouts of the electroencephalograph indicating arousal of the subject hooked up to the instrument; large, slow rhythmic waves indicate passive activity. [cf. BIO-FEEDBACK TRAINING, EEG]

DETACHMENT—1. (healing) the ability of the healer to be understanding but not sympathetic; personal involvement opens the etheric web, making the disease easily transferable to the practitioner when he is in a healing state of consciousness; 2. (Zen) a meditative state where one notices one's thoughts without pursuing them, wherein one can resist attraction but still remain attentive to it, giving up desires; 3. (Buddhism) a meditational state wherein one is both intellectually and emotionally aware of real Reality but no longer aware of one's body or environment; 4. (hypno-

therapy) the pleasurable sensation of being without a body, having only a mind, and having no fear. **Syn.** DISASSOCIATION. [cf. PSYCHIC PRACTITIONER, HYPNOTHERAPY, SEED MEDITATION]

DETECTOR—1. (radiesthesia) scientific name for pendulum and dowsing rod). [cf. Appendix 2. DOWSING]. 2. (biofeedback training) a small device that is attached to the external physical body to detect the amount of electrical activity in that area; feeds it to the instrument for amplification to be interpreted for practical application. **Syn.** ELECTRODE, SENSOR. [cf. BIOFEEDBACK TRAINING, ARTIFACT, GSR]

DETERIORATING SELF-CONCEPT SYNDROME—a feeling of worthlessness experienced by an individual because of scientific advances which provide improved methods of accomplishing his or her job, e.g., new machinery that does the work faster and better than he or she can. [cf. VALUES, CULTURAL TRANSFORMATION, ABNORMAL BEHAVIOR]

DETERMINISM—a belief contrary to that of metaphysics; 1. a theory that the events in one's life are ruled by cosmic forces; 2. a doctrine that all events in the world are not due to one's free will but have other underlying natural causes; 3. an assumption that everyone is conditoned and entirely dependent upon preceding circumstances; 4. theory that individuals are cosmic puppets, intelligent beings moving along in an unconscious cooperation with universal forces that constantly impinge upon them causing them to take paths they think they are choosing. [cf. REINCARNATION, KARMA, FREE WILL]

DETERMINISTIC PSYCHOLOGY—the theory that individuals will react in a predetermined, automatic fashion when given specific stimuli that relate to their primary emotions. **Syn.** RAT PSYCHOLOGY. [cf. DESTRUCTIVE-BRAINWASHING CULTS, MENTAL PSYCHOLOGICAL PRISON]

DETUNED—see DE-TUNED.

DETUNING—a point where psychic energy reaches wavelengths in the ethers that obliterate or weaken them. [cf. APO PSI, ANTI-PSI, TUNING OF THE MIND]

DEUS ABSCONDITIUS—(Kabbalah) "the hidden God"; a self-revealing dynamic intelligence and energy; an inaccessible and unknowable God. [cf. TOTALITY, MONAD]

DEUTEROSCOPY—(Greek *deutero*, "second") second sight; to see visions without the use of the physical eyes; see CLAIRVOYANCE. [cf. PERIPHERAL VISION, PSYCHIC LIGHTS, SEEING MEDIUM]

DEVA—1. (Sanskrit, "shining one") (English, "angel") (a) part of the whole hierarchy of beings, visible and invisible; dynamic centers of energy and intelligence moving along with other life forces in the etheric world, givng and receiving; this kingdom is open to one when he or she has purified their soul-mind enough through the process of evolution; (b) the deva's main purpose is to design the blueprints of all things in the earth plane, animate and inanimate, in regard to mankind's karma, sending out highly focused beams of energy of appropriate intensity and quality to make life forms, whether it be a grove of trees, an airline pilot, a praying congregaton, a city, a valley, or a continent; responsible for bringing forth from thought energy physical bodies of minerals, vegetables, animals, and humans; (c) has no particular form of its own, but is capable of establishing form for people to see (form reflects their etheric function); limitless, free, and insubstantial but delighted to communicate with mankind if deserving; (d) responsible for the four elements: fire, earth, air, and water, and their indwelling nature spirits and essences. 2. (Hinduism, Buddhism) a divine being; 3. (Zoroastrianism) a magnificent supernatural being; a semi-divine being in the etheric world who has earned a very high rank in the angel hierarchy and has important functions for the earth; a selfless, unselfconscious spark of Totality that can penetrate matter and contact earthlings; does so for the good of the universe. Syn. ANGEL, ETHERIC WORLD INTELLIGENCE, MASTER. [cf. NATURE DEVAS, MAGNIFICENT DEVAS, MINOR DEVAS, FORMLESS DEVAS, BODILESS DEVAS, PASSION DEVAS]

DEVA EVOLUTION—see ANGEL EVOLUTION.

DEVA OF COMMUNICATION—distributes one's inner energy into responsibilities for his or her soul-mind growth, knowingly and unknowingly to the individual; can be contacted for higher learning experiences and knowledge through desire, anticipation, and preparation for contact. [cf. ETHERIC WORLD ENTITIES, ANGEL KINGDOM, PSYCHIC DEVELOPMENT]

DEVA WORLD—the higher state of consciousness of the nature kingdom where the gods and angels abide.

DEVA-LOKA—(Hinduism, Tibet) a vibrational frequency in the etheric world where one abides in a god body and is believed to experience paradise. [cf. BODIES AND PLANES Appendix 2, DEVA, GREAT LOGI, RACIAL ANGELS]

DEVA-YANA—(India) the god-path that the soul-mind may take after transition if one's incarnations on earth warrant it because one has led a life without sin. Sim. PEYOTE ROAD, BHAKTI-MARGA, HINAYANA. [cf. PATH SYMBOLISM]

DEVACHAN—1. a happy state of consciousness wherein one feels one is dwelling in heaven; 2. an inner feeling of peace and security when one knows one's function in the great Totality; 3. a faster rate of vibration, invisible to mankind; known to those in the etheric world as the devachanic plane, where the devas abide and work. Syn. HEAVEN WORLD. [cf. ANGEL HIERARCHY, MAGNIFICENT DEVAS]

DEVANCHAN—see DEVACHAN.

DEVANCHANIC BREAK—the time one spends in the etheric world between earth incarnations; theory: an individual rests in a state of bliss, free from negative action. [cf. REINCARNATION, KARMA, PLANES]

DEVANIC—having characteristics of a deva or angel.

DEVELOPMENT PATTERNS—(human) at certain ages in a child, psychic experiences are more prominent than in others, e.g., when the child is from one to two years of age, the mother can easily tune into the child knowing where and what he or she is doing; at puberty, poltergeists are more capable of using the child for their foci, as if to relate to the psychological and emotional stresses of this age. [cf. MENTAL PSYCHIC PROCESSES]

DEVI—1. the female negative creative principle of the universe, as opposed to the positive masculine principle in the law of polarity, necessary in all manifestations; 2. refers to a female god, a goddess; 3. (Vedic) written at the end of a name with a capital *D*, to command respect. [cf. POLARITY, DEVIL]

DEVIL—1. (Greek *diabolos*, "slanderer"); supreme spirit of evil; an enemy of both God and mankind; 2. a god displaying his bad attributes; 3. an etheric world entity in an early state of evolution; working in an earthbound state of consciousness, haunting and tempting earthlings to act against their conscious thinking, not realizing it is wrong; 4. a force of energy that seems to well up inside an individual, leading him or her to perform work contrary to that which is for one's highest good; sometimes out of control of the conscious mind; 5. an etheric world entity rebelling against discipline and knowledgeable progression due to their ignorance, not having incarnated as many times as others in their present time period; 6. personification of evil in the mind of man; 7. opposite of God, but still a part of God; necessary for the opposite polarity of the earthly vibrations and manifestations. **Syn.** OLD ONE, LUCIFER, PRINCE OF DARKNESS, OLD NICK. [**cf.** EVIL, THE LEFT-HAND PATH, DEVI]

DEVIL'S GIRDLE—(medieval) a magnetic belt worn by witches that assists them in their psychic work. [**cf.** MAGNETS, ENEMY WAY, RITUAL WORK]

DEVIL'S HEAD—(ufology) a plant growing in the ground where a UFO has recently been sighted; looks like a human face with eyes and ears and has blood within it. [**cf.** DISC OCCUPANTS, SPACE ANIMALS]

DEVIL-LIKE GOBLIN—(ufology) creature of intelligence from outer space who looks like a goblin and a devil, pictured from compilations of descriptions made by those who have encountered UFOs. [**cf.** UFOLOGY, LIVING CREATURES OF OUR ATMOSPHERE, SIGHTINGS]

DEVILS OF ALL AGES—humans who have made their transition and are now living in the lower density because of their ignorance and past lives of ill intent; have a tremendous pull to earthly sensations and haunt earthlings when possible to revive the memory of uncouth deeds; will not shed their astral bodies but will incarnate back to earth from this plane. [**cf.** DENSITY, HELL, LAW OF SOUL-MIND EVOLUTION Appendix 7]

DEVOTEE—one who commends all of his or her time and energy to a spiritual leader, sacrificing one's tastes, habits, and pleasures to further the disciplines one believes in; usually lives in a monastery or ashram.

DEZYGOTIC PHENOMENA—(astral projection) the moving of material objects in a room by an astral projectionist who is slightly out of the body, hovering close to it; projectionist can be conscious or unconscious; one theory is that a cerebral or neurological process is taking place in the brain or area adjacent to it whereby the astral body is capable of affecting objects telekinetically for a short period (Inconcl.) [**cf.** IN-THE-RANGE-OF-CORD-ACTIVITY]

DGONGS-PA—(Tibet) thoughts, conscious mind; see BRAIN.

DHAMMACHAKKAPPAVATTANA SUTTA—(Buddhism) the equivalent of the word *chakra*; see CHAKRA.

DHAMMAPADA—(Zen, Buddhism) a teaching of the Sutta-Pitaka, the second movement in meditation, when one no longer feels like the observer but has good rapport and compassion for all other living things, recognizing we are all one.

DHARANSIS—(Sanskrit) 1. one-phrase-creeds or short profound statements of belief; frequently used as mantras; 2. a state of concentration when the conscious mind is held firmly on the object of attainment, taught in psychotechnology disciplines. [**cf.** MEDITATION, VISUALIZATION]

DHARMA—(Yoga *dhri*, "to hold, that which upholds") an unknown quantity or principle by which the universe is upheld; that which pervades the whole universe and regulates its harmonious action; that which is the cause of the universe, its preservation, and its final dissolution or absorption into the Supreme. **Sim.** SCHEME OF THINGS. [**cf.** MONAD, SPIRIT]

DHARMA-KAYA—(Buddhism) 1. feminine-negative aspect of the ultimate reality from which all things are born; 2. highest of the three bodies; to reach a state of consciousness of immutable light within, sometimes called **perfect enlightenment**. **Syn.** SEELE. [**cf.** COLLECTIVE UNCONSCIOUS, POLARITY, BODIES AND PLANES Appendix 5]

DHARMAS—(Buddhism) the ultimate elements of existence having no space extension or time duration; source of the order of all things; impersonal simple entities. **Syn.** POINT-INSTANTS. [**cf.** ELECTRONS, ATOMS, NODES]

DHARMIC—(Vedic) not what one says about one's self, but what one actually does and thinks; that which is true about one's self, one's morality, one's merit, and one's righteousness. [**cf.** BELIEF SYSTEMS, INNER-DIALOGUE]

DHIKR—(Sufi) a dance or method of worship to produce a state of ritual ecstasy to accelerate the contact of one's mind with the world mind, or to

166

put oneself in a state ready for trancing; a series of exercises repeated in unison; bodily movements linked to a thought and a sound, or a series of sounds, in relation to musical rhythm. [cf. MANTRA, PHYSICAL PSYCHIC PROCESS, WHIRLING DERVISHES]

DHYAN CHOHANS—an order of angels in the etheric world whose function is to carry out one aspect of the plan of Totality. [cf. ANGEL KINGDOM, REINCARNATION]

DHYANA—(Tibet, Sanskrit, Zen) the ability to meditate and "hold" the conscious mind on a single thought; the feeling of detachment from material objects; being in a subjective state. [cf. MEDITATION, BLISS, MANTRA]

DHYANI BUDDHAS—(Buddhism) angels who helped to create the phenomenal universe or our material world, who keep looking after their creation. [cf. ANGEL KINGDOM, ETHERIC WORLD ENTITIES]

DI—(Greek) prefix meaning "two, twice, double."

DI-ELECTRIC BIO—see VITAL LIFE FORCE.

DIA—prefix meaning "passing through," thoroughly or completely.

DIABOLIC—pertains to the characteristic traits of what mankind calls the "devil." [cf. DEVIL, EVIL, DENSITY, EARTHBOUND ENTITIES]

DIABOLIC POSSESSION—see DEMONICAL SOMNABULISM.

DIABOLIST—a psychic who uses his or her psychic talents for evil intent. [cf. EVIL, WITCHCRAFT, CEREMONY MAGIC, NECROMANCER]

DIAGNOSTIC PALMISTY—(hand analysis) to use lines in the hands to identify problems of health within the person [cf. BODY READING Appendix 5]

DIAKKA—mischievous, ignorant, and undeveloped etheric world entities that come uninvited, squeezing through in a seance or in a medium's message work, gaining attention by being undignified, e.g., kicking a sitter; (do not confuse with POLTERGEIST). [cf. ASTRAL SHELLS, EARTHBOUND ENTITY]

DIALOGUE—to mentally and silently question the psychic information that is coming through; to ask for more information, for its symbolic meaning, or for its validity; a sort of talking to oneself with an expectation of perceiving psychic answers. [cf. MENTAL PSYCHIC PROCESSES Appendix 2]

DIALOGUE TECHNIQUE—(dreams) 1. the ability to be aware enough while dreaming to talk to the symbols in the dream for help in interpretation; dreamer asks the symbols, whether objects or living characters, to clarify their purpose as the dream proceeds, e.g., "Ladder, what do you represent?" 2. to converse to the symbols during the daytime, orally or silently, and listen for their answers to help in dream analysis; e.g., "Sneaker, why did you appear in my dream last night?" [cf. DREAMS Appendix 2]

DIAMAGNETIC—completely magnetic, as opposed to electromagnetic.

DIAMOND BODY—a higher plane etheric world intelligence who comes to a psychic after a deep meditation and an attunement to his or her psychic level, showing itself by a tremendous, beautiful, luminous display; instead of a physical form. [cf. PSYCHIC LIGHT, Appendix 2 MENTAL MANIFESTATIONS MISCELLANEOUS]

DIANETICS—(Greek dianoua, "thought") pertains to thought and aimless, rambling reasoning; a sum of one person's behavior today is a result of what is in the soul-mind's memory prior to birth; also called time-track memory. (Inconcl.) [cf. REINCARNATION, KARMA]

DIBBUK—(Kabbalah) an etheric world intelligence who is capable of entering an earthling's physical body to work from the earth plane. [cf. IMPERSONATION, HAUNTING, EARTHBOUND ENTITY, GUIDE]

DICE DIVINATION—(ancient) to forecast the future and receive answers to life-style psychological problems by throwing dice; numbers of landed dice are referred to on a chart of number combinations and answers. [cf. CASTING OF LOTS, RADIESTHESIA, DIVINATION]

DICE-PK—(laboratory) to "will" certain numbers to appear on dice whether thrown by oneself or the experimenter; (do not confuse with DICE DIVINATION). [cf. DIVINATION, CASTING OF LOTS]

DICHOTOMOUS—(Greek dicho "in two parts") name given to the brain after the discovery of the two hemispheres; the discovery of dichotomy in human consciousness was subsequently made. [cf. SPLIT BRAIN Appendix 5]

DICYANAIN SCREENS—special chromatic plates

167

of glass used to help see auras by making the eye more sensitive to other wavelengths; invented by Walter J. Kilner; works to induce eye fatigue in the short visible purple range, making the eye temporarily more sensitive to waves beyond the normal visibility. [cf. KILNER GOGGLES, KIRLIAN EFFECT]

DIDJAN—(Cornwall, England) a small piece of food left at night for the "wee people." [cf. FAIRIES, NATURE SPIRITS]

DIE—(Native American) a special initiation ritual to become a channel for healing energy and psychic ability by lying in solitude for a few days; to allow weather elements and animals to dismember the body; then heal the body, and return to life and work for the tribe. [cf. SHAMANSHIP, FORCED PSI, INITIATORY DEATH]

DIELECTRIC BIOCOSMIC ENERGY—coined by Oscar Brunler (1950) see VITAL LIFE FORCE.

DIES, MIES, JESCHET, BENEDOEFET, DOWIMA, ENITEMÁUS—(Jewish) an utterance used in coscinomancy divination which seems to have power to compel an etheric world entity to turn the sieve in the direction of the guilty one. [cf. MANCY, WORDS-WITH-POWER]

DIETS FOR PSYCHICS—see FOOD SCALE.

DIFFERENTIAL EFFECT—(laboratory) to score above chance in one type of psychism, and below chance in another, when working with two contrasting targets or modes of response; the results are related to emotional preferences, attitudes, or inborn tendencies toward one particular skill. (Inconcl.) Syn. BIDIRECTIONALITY OF PSI. [cf. ESP, MENTAL PSYCHISM]

DIFFUSION—the psychic ability of a high plane etheric world intelligence to destruct his or her atoms as they exist for that plane, and rebuild him or herself to relate to the medium on the level that the medium can perceive their intelligence. [cf. MEDIUMSHIP, BODIES AND PLANES Appendix 5, DEMATERIALIZATION]

DIKER—see DHIKR.

DILATION—a type of physical psychism whereby one makes one's body larger by using mind power. [cf. BODY CONTROL Appendix 2, ELONGATION, SHAPE-CHANGING]

DIMENSION-SHIFTING—1. to disappear at will from the physical world without moving from one's space and without disrupting one's structure of existence; to change the vibrational frequency of one's physical body or visible structure into a faster vibrational frequency, and to slide one's whole structure instantaneously into another dimension of life invisible to the physical world; structure or physical body stays in the invisible dimension or reappears again in the physical world with no damage to its living structure, regardless of existing in the invisible or visible world; time in invisible dimension varies from minutes to years; change of dimension occurs in a matter of minutes, according to man's sense of time; 2. requires the ability to hold one's focus on one's bodily vibrations and to maintain this focus in the invisible frequency so the body or structure will stay intact and can reappear in the same form; always willed by the shifter; an innate characteristic of nature spirits and of UFO with TRANSMUTATION of the alchemists). (Inconcl.) 3. (Native American) to change dimensions, one changes levels of attention and goes through a "crack" in the atmosphere, a subtle division between the two worlds; the secret is in the "art of attention" and awareness. [cf. Appendix 2 DIMENSION-SHIFTING AND SHAPE-CHANGING]

DIMENSIONS—1. (Latin dimensio, "measuring") a term used by authoritative metaphysicians and psychics who have grouped the varying vibrational frequencies into seven different states of matter; each contains living forms, special functions and laws; interpenetrates the earth and its surroundings; necesssary for and related to all of earth life and its third-dimensional matter. Syn. PLANES, SPHERES, LEVEL, PLATEAUS, MANSIONS. [cf. BODIES AND PLANES Appendix 5] 2. another variation of the planes; first dimension is linear, moving in one direction, flat; second dimension is moving back and forth, flat; third dimension is moving with height, width, and depth, up and down and back and forth; fourth dimension is time and space. (Inconcl.) [cf. FIRST, SECOND, THIRD DIMENSION]

DIMONION—name of Plato's etheric world intelligence who constantly guided and inspired him throughout his life. [cf. ETHERIC WORLD INTELLIGENCE]

DINHINH DYONRD—(China) (esoteric) flat plates of jade which give off musical tones, believed to have the vibrational frequency capable of healing certain diseases. Syn. SINGING STONES. [cf. MINPSI]

DIRECT ARTISTRY—paintings and drawings put on canvas or paper by etheric world intelligences while medium is nearby, sleeping or relaxed, without using medium's body; performed rapidly; intelligence remains invisible but the results of the motions are seen; see PRECIPITATION PAINTINGS; (do not confuse with automatic painting.) [**cf.** PSYCHIC ARTIST]

DIRECT KNOWLEDGE—"pure" information given to the psychic to benefit mankind and further their evolution, through the skill of INSPIRATIONAL THOUGHT.

DIRECT MEDIUM—a medium who allows his or her ectoplasm (but not their body) to be used by etheric world guide to paint, draw, or write on paper or canvas using tools laid out for this purpose; work is accomplished faster than an earth artist, while the medium is either asleep or in a trance state; sometimes the etheric world guides materialize their own tools; (do not confuse with AUTOMATISM or INSPIRATIONAL ART). [**cf.** MEDIUMSHIP, PRECIPITATION Appendix 2]

DIRECT PARAGNOSTIC OBSERVATION—see MENTAL TELEPATHY.

DIRECT VISION—to perceive clairvoyantly every point in the interior of a solid physical body, or any object of third dimensional construction; similar to looking down upon a circle and seeing every point of the interior of the circle. **Sim.** ASTRAL VISION. [**cf.** CLAIRVOYANCE Appendix 2]

DIRECT VOICE—(seance) to allow an etheric world intelligence to intervene and build an invisible amplifier in the seance room with one's ectoplasm; voice amplifier is used to convey information and knowledge beyond formal education; each session, the invisible amplification box is built in one corner of the blacked-out room; ectoplasm from the medium and sitters is used; box is dissolved after each session and sucked back into the medium's body; this invisible box neither reflects nor obstructs light, but is capable of setting up vibrations in the atmosphere that affect the sitters as sound; takes years of sitting in a blacked-out room to perfect; medium uses desired-control; (do not confuse with DEPENDENT VOICE in which the intelligence depends upon the physical voicebox of the medium). **Syn.** INDEPENDENT VOICE. [**cf.** ECTOPLASM, TRUMPET, VOICE TRANCE Appendix 2]

DIRECT WRITING—to produce psychic information written by an etheric world intelligence on paper or an object without the aid of the medium's arm or hand, bringing important material that the psychic or medium could not have known beforehand; 1. controlled, willed situation in a seance, church service, or at a bedside with supplied materials by the medium; sometimes the levitation of a pencil can be seen and the scratchings on paper heard; sometimes accomplished without the help of the supplied tools; ectoplasm from the medium and sitters levitates the tool and descends it upon the paper, guided by the intelligence; performed with abnormal speed. [**cf.** BASKET DRAWINGS, SLATE WRITING, PRECIPITATIONS Appendix 2] 2. spontaneous writing occurring without the support of the materials or a medium close by, e.g., writings on tombstones, vegetables, unfinished letters; (Bible) e.g., "a hand came out and wrote upon the wall." (Inconcl.) **Syn.** PNEUMATOGRAPHY, INDEPENDENT ETHERIC WRITING. [**cf.** PRECIPITATION, ETHERIC SCRIPT]

DIRECTED-THOUGHT—to deliberately project densified ergs of mental energy onto an individual or object by one who has developed good mind concentration, e.g., 1. to transfer mental or emotional energy between two persons; 2. to beam energy directly upon an object to be used for an amulet; 3. to channel healing energy from the mind to the patient's body cells. [**cf.** DIRECTED-THOUGHT TRAINERS, AMULETS, MENTAL PSYCHIC HEALING]

DIRECTED-THOUGHT TRAINER—a small box with a blinking light used as a tool to increase one's concentration ability; blinking light sits in the box behind a groove that holds pictures; sender concentrates on the action, emotion, sound, smell, color, taste, or object in the picture; receiver is in another area; blinking light accelerates one's ability to attain telepathic accuracy. (Inconcl.) [**cf.** MENTAL TELEPATHY, BEAMED ENERGY]

DIRECTIONAL INSTINCT—a cosmic law built within all animals giving guidance to survive, flourish, and perform their functions in the universe, e.g., sends homing pigeons back to their starting point; guides a dog back miles to its original master; tells rats to scuttle the ship which will be in danger on a trip. **Sim.** PRIMARY PERCEPTION. [**cf.** COSMIC CONSCIOUSNESS, PRIMARY PERCEPTION, ANPSI]

DIRECTIVE INTELLIGENCE—see TOTALITY.

DIRECTOR—(angel kingdom) an adept from a high plane in the etheric world who is devoted to

169

world progress and returns to earth in a physical body consciousness (as opposed to helping in an angelic consciousness); classified in two groupings: 1. designers; 2. initiators; believed to come from the fifth dimension. **Syn.** MASTER. [**cf.** ANGEL HIERARCHY, ADEPT]

DISASSOCIATE—(astral projection) to separate the consciousness from the physical body; the main part of the consciousness stays with the astral body when projecting, in sleep, or in a controlled situation. [**cf.** EXTERIORIZE, DUAL CONSCIOUSNESS, AUTOSCOPE VISION]

DISASSOCIATION—(hypnosis, meditation) when the consciousness is no longer aware of the physical environment; a feeling that the entire being is "thought." **Syn.** DETACHMENT. [**cf.** MEDITATION, HYPNOTHERAPY, SEED MEDITATION]

DISASSOCIATION TRANCE—(Socrates 470-399 B.C.) to travel to the higher etheric world planes in a subconscious level of consciousness; accomplished after long periods of meditation which causes the mental mind to withdraw its activity. [**cf.** MENTAL PROJECTION, SELF-DISIDENTIFICATION]

DISC OCCUPANT—(ufology) an intelligent application of an energy form; to recognize an intelligent living presence managing the air construct. (Inconcl.) [**cf.** UFOLOGY, CONSTRUCT, TIME TRAVELERS]

DISC SKY CRAFT—UFO air construct shaped like a saucer or disc; believed by some to belong to the etheric region of Venus. (Inconcl.) [**cf.** Appendix 5 UFOLOGY, SCOUT SHIP, SPACE ANIMALS, BLIP, BIOLOGICAL UFOs]

DISCARNATE ENTITY—(esoteric) the soul-mind of a person who has lived one or more lives on planet earth, or other planets now living in the etheric world; sometimes means the soul-mind of a dead relative or friend. **Syn.** DISCARNATE INTELLIGENCE, APPARITION. [**cf.** Appendix 4 to differentiate between a GUIDE, GHOST, SPIRIT and DISCARNATE]

DISCARNATE ENTITY SLEEP EXPERIENCE—to see, feel, or talk to a deceased loved one during sleep; a psychic experience in which the dreamer is actually close to and communicating with the deceased person; occurs in the theta level of consciousness between REM dreams; experience appears vivid, clear, lifelike, is easily recalled, and has an obvious meaning; can be instigated by the desire of the dreamer or the deceased loved one, who comes to alleviate a problem or let the dreamer know he or she is alive; (do not confuse with a normal dream of a deceased person which is fuzzy, difficult to remember, and has a symbolic meaning). (Inconcl.) [**cf.** SLEEP EXPERIENCE, REM, NREM, THETA STATE OF CONSCIOUSNESS]

DISCARNATE INTELLIGENCE—see DISCARNATE ENTITY.

DISCIPLE—(root word *discipline*) a pupil; a follower of the teachings of a great leader; one who follows an incarnated master and is motivated to improve himself or herself by the magnetism one absorbs from one's individual, spiritual closeness with the master (not from verbal ploy). **Syn.** CHELA. [**cf.** EARTH MAGNETISM, EGYPTIAN MYSTERY SCHOOLS]

DISCIPLINE—a set of rules and values to which a group of people train, practice, and live accordingly, regardless of its inconventional life-style or hardships, e.g., yogis, Indians, Buddhists, parapsychologists, magicians, etc.

DISCOINCIDENCE—(astral projection) the separation of the astral body and consciousness from the physical body during sleep, or in a controlled projection, even if the astral body only extends an inch. **Syn.** DISASSOCIATE, EXTERIORIZATION. [**cf.** ASTRAL PROJECTION Appendix 2, NATURAL COINCIDENCE, PARTIAL SOMATIC DISSOCIATION]

DISEASE—(esoteric, holistic health) the word tells its story, *dis-ease:* 1. an energy field meant to bring: **(a)** pain, abnormal behavior or appearance, or incapacitation of normal functions, to remind one to change one's thinking (attitude), life-style, or both, to further soul-mind growth; **(b)** particular lessons that only a malformed or diseased body would negotiate, so the disease or malformation is nourished until the lessons are learned. 2. (E. Arthur Winkler) "health and disease are an expression of personality; any disturbance to the body involves all levels of organization, biochemical, psychological, and social." 3. basic cause is one's belief system (built from this incarnation and from past incarnations); belief systems cause the emotional attitude one takes toward life activity and experiences, these emotions change body chemistry, body chemistry causes imbalance in the physical body or mental behavioral patterns; belief systems can cause a war between the soul-mind and conscious mind and this disagreement causes one to engage in health-destroying habits, to become judgments regarding diseases, which in turn weakens resistance in the body cells; 4. there is only *one* disease, but it manifests in different symptoms; (Hippocrates) "the same evil with different manifestations." (Inconcl.) [cf. BELIEF SYSTEM, ILLNESS, HOLISTIC HEALTH, LAW OF HEALING Appendix 7]

DISEMBODIED SOUL—1. a soul-mind without a physical body; refers to one in the etheric world; 2. a human being who has passed into the low subplanes; appears inhuman when perceived clairvoyantly. **Syn.** DISCARNATE ENTITY. 3. (Eastern disciplines) earthlings are disembodied from Reality, using the physical body as a vehicle for a short time. [cf. ASTRAL BODY, MAYA-RUPA, ENTITY]

DISEMBODIED SPIRIT—an apparition perceived clairvoyantly or clairsentiently which could be *any* living being in the etheric world: 1. a deceased loved one; 2. an unknown astral body; 3. an astral shell; 4. an earthbound, confused soul-mind; 5. an astral body on an astral flight. [cf. ETHERIC WORLD ENTITY, ASTRAL SHELL, APPARITION]

DISENTANGLEMENT—to change the vibrational frequency of one's body and transform the energy to another aspect of existence; to perform physical psychism, e.g., levitation. [cf. GRAVITY CONTROL, LEVITATION]

DISGUISED HYPNOSIS—to become hypnotized during normal activity and to be unaware that one is in an hypnotic state of consciousness; steady, consistent concentration on a minimal amount of outer stimuli makes the conscious mind passive, and one operates by the subconscious mind, e.g., watching the white line and listening to the hum of the motor while night driving, one does not remember which towns one passed; being so intensely engrossed in a TV program that one is unaware of a family member passing by. [cf. SLEEP-WAKE HYPNOSIS, EMOTIONAL HYPNOSIS]

DISINTEGRATION—(alchemy) to prepare an object for transformation or movement by dematerializing it; alchemist gives undivided attention to the auric field of the object until it vibrates more rapidly and can no longer be seen; it is now ready for apportation or transformation of a baser metal to a finer one. [cf. ALCHEMIST, SYMPATHETIC VIBRATIONS, DEMATERIALIZATION]

DISPENSATION—2,600 years; an age is 2,000 years, and there is a carry-over of 600 years from the magnetic field, making a total of 2,600 years. **Syn.** COSMIC CYCLE. [cf. CYCLES, FIRST ROUND OF PLANET EARTH, CIVILIZATIONS CYCLES]

DISPLACEMENT—1. (laboratory) predicting what *follows* in a series, or calling the *past* of the series, when using cards, drawings, or other objects, instead of identifying the target; 2. (laboratory) perceiving something psychically other than the target, e.g., in a mental telepathy experiment, instead of picking up what the sender is sending, the receiver picks up the name of one of the experimenters who is on the phone making an appointment at that time; 3. (psychic reading) information unknowingly suppressed by the psychic because of its unpleasant nature; the psychic message is revealed vicariously, e.g., "I see an advertisement in the newspaper for cleaning carpets"; the querient has no carpets to be cleaned, but a few days later, an obituary notice of a good friend is next to the carpet cleaning advertisement in the newspaper; 4. (dreams) interpreting a dream by shifting the importance of one symbol or image to another symbol which is more neutral, thus avoiding the message of the dream because of an unconscious desire not to face the message. **Syn.** MISPLACED PSI. [cf. DREAM SYMBOLS, ZENER CARDS, PSYCHIC READINGS, ESP]

DISPLAY DAYDREAMING—to picture oneself performing a feat which wins applause; if pictured with strong emotion it will eventually come about. [cf. BRAIN, THOUGHTS, VISUALIZATION]

DISPOSERS OF THE DEAD COLONY—(Tibet) monks who were assigned to a special area for the purpose of dismembering and preparing dead bodies for the vultures. **Syn.** BODY BREAKERS. [cf. SCIENCE OF DEATH, SOUL-MIND]

DISSOCIATED STATE—1. (laboratory) the working of an etheric world guide through a medium in such a way that it seems the mind is split, and one or more parts behave independently, each functioning as a separate unit; 2. an awareness coming from the subconscious mind without the aid of the conscious mind, bringing in psychic information. (Inconcl.) [cf. TRANCE MEDIUM, PLANES, PSYCHIC INFORMATION, EXTERIORIZATION OF A SENSATION]

DISTAL LOCALIZATION—(poltergeistry) activity of the poltergeist implies the presence of an

171

extended field, apparently supplied by the poltergeist generator who can extend his or her energies over the whole house. (Inconcl.) [cf. PROXIMAL, FOCUS, POLTERGEIST]

DISTANT HEALING—(mental healing) to use mental telepathic procedures to heal another; practitioner meditates, builds energy in the mind by concentration, decrees it to be of a healing nature, and beams it to the patient; the following make the treatment more effective: 1. prearranged time between both parties; 2. performed after 11:00 p.m.; 3. practitioner sends a love-line just before beaming energy; 4. practitioner says first name of patient repeatedly; distance is no barrier; should never be performed without consent of patient; researchers found telepathic healing changes body chemistry. (Inconcl.) [cf. MENTAL HEALING, MAGNETIC HEALING]

DISTANT HYPNOSIS—see ETHEREAL HYPNOSIS.

DISTANT-POINT ASTRAL PROJECTION—to astrally project to another planet at will; see ASTRAL PROJECTION. [cf. OUT-OF-RANGE-OF-CORD-ACTIVITY, FRINGE OF SPACE-TIME, BODIES OF AIR, BLOOD-FLOW SURGE]

DISTANT-POINT VISION—to perceive clairvoyantly at will what is happening in areas not visible to the physical eyes. **Syn.** EXTENDED CLAIRVOYANCE, TRAVELING CLAIRVOYANCE. [cf. X-RAY CLAIRVOYANCE, BILOCATION OF CONSCIOUSNESS]

DISTINGUISHING WISDOM—(Buddhism) considered to be the third movement in meditation; when one is no longer concerned with the mundane, but intuitively begins to perceive visions from Totality, and recognizes them as such. [cf. INSPIRATIONAL THOUGHT, FREE-RESPONSE SETTING]

DISTORTED MUSIC—sounds and music which affect one's etheric bodies, sounding normal to the physical ears; songs recorded on a system that is not equipped with the range of the song being played; this music gradually affects the etheric bodies which in turn changes one's mood and attitude without one's knowledge of its influence. (Inconcl.) **Syn.** LISTENING FATIGUE. [cf. SOUNDS-WITH-POWER, MENTAL BODY, CAUSAL BODY]

DISTRESS—(Hans Seleye) unpleasant or disease-producing stress; details see STRESS.

DIURNAL CYCLE—a twenty-four-hour pattern that is built within all living things, repeating itself daily

regardless of where the organism is located. **Syn.** CIRCADIAN CYCLE. [cf. Appendix 5 CYCLES, EMOTIONAL CYCLE]

DIVER—(Bible) see PSYCHIC.

DIVINATI—(Latin *divus,* "divine or of the gods").

DIVINATION—1. (ancient) (root, "gift from the divine") information received from God; the ability to receive this information (this gift) is acquired by one's own initiative; a process or ritual performed with natural things, living organisms, human parts, or man-made objects to receive information regarding the future of a person or country; see MANTIC ART; 2. (Dr. B. J. Fitzgerald) "the faculty of moving into states of awareness of time-bending; foretelling future conditions and events"; 3. (current) an umbrella word referring to a science and an art; to use psychic skills or practices to gain knowledge presently unknown; to receive information of the past, present, and future, and to be given healing instructions, psychic reading information, and a radiesthetic sense ability. **Syn.** PSYCHISM. [cf. CASTING OF LOTS, SORTES, DOWSING, and MANTIC ARTS Appendix 6]

DIVINATION DREAMING—a special incubation ritual performed by ancient Greeks in consecrated rooms of the temple; ritual stimulates a psychic clairvoyant vision in the sleep state to answer a specific question or diagnose an illness. [cf. SLEEP EXPERIENCES, INCUBATION, CEREMONIAL MAGIC]

DIVINATION WITH THE SPIRIT—(South Africa) to call upon etheric world intelligences for counsel and aid in dealing with the problems of the tribe by the sangoma (psychic). [cf. MEDIUMSHIP, GUIDES, PSYCHISM]

DIVINE—(Greece) 1. (capitalized); God, Totality, Creator; neutral in nature; the Divine is both good and evil because it is all-there-is; mankind names activity good or evil in order to have a scale of standards in which they can improve; 2. (uncapitalized); "to find the godlike or the sacred"; to use the skill of divination to find hidden factors which are only known by God. Usage: "I will divine into the future and see if we will have rain on our vacation." [cf. DIVINATION, LOTS, TOTALITY]

DIVINE AURA—(esoteric) primal vibrations of color filling all space, contributing to make the Great White Light, and dispersion of the Great White Light. [cf. COLOROLOGY Appendix 5]

DIVINE BODY—the universe; a living entity; corresponds to one's physical body. [**cf.** MACROCOSM, MICROCOSM, LAW OF CORRESPONDENCE Appendix 7]

DIVINE BODY OF TRUTH—(Buddhism) to reach the ultimate end in a state of meditation and come into a oneness of bliss. **Syn.** DHARMA-KAYA.]

DIVINE BREATH—see VITAL LIFE FORCE.

DIVINE CONSCIOUSNESS—(esoteric) "conscious of being"; the *one* consciousness that divided and permeates all things, animate and inanimate; controlled by the thoughts of all soul-minds in the universe. **Syn.** COSMIC CONSCIOUSNESS, UNIVERSAL MIND. [**cf.** Appendix 5 CONSCIOUSNESS]

DIVINE DOG—theory: a nature spirit in the form of a dog capable and willing to guide an earthling through the darkness of the underworld when the earthling enters there to help its inhabitants. [**cf.** SHAPE-CHANGING, NATURE SPIRITS]

DIVINE ENERGY—ceaseless movement of the atoms created with creation; the *only* energy in the universe; therefore, it is neutral in nature; all energy is a manifestation of this *one* energy, subject to a person's thoughts which makes good or bad activity. **Syn.** TOTALITY. [**cf.** ENERGY, THOUGHTS, MATTER, KARMA, ATOMS]

DIVINE EYES—to psychically perceive throughout and within millions of world-periods, gathering information regarding the past and future events of the universes. [**cf.** PROPHECY, AKASHIC RECORDS, CLAIRVOYANT, MULTIDIMENSIONAL]

DIVINE FIRE IN MAN—see KUNDALINI.

DIVINE IDEA—information, knowledge, suggestions, and concepts that come psychically to an individual using the skill of inspirational thought. [**cf.** INSPIRATIONAL SPEAKING, INSPIRATIONAL WRITING]

DIVINE INITIATIVE—a person who has earned the right to receive perpetual instructions and guidance from a saint or a Master in the etheric world as to the path he or she is to take in the present incarnation, e.g., Uri Geller, the Caddy's of Findhorn. [**cf.** DISCIPLE, MASTERSHIP]

DIVINE INTELLIGENCE—the overall pattern containing all mankind will ever invent, discover, become, do, make, learn, smell, taste, hear, say, see, and feel; ALL-THERE-IS; the total of all intelligence located in the atoms of the visible and invisible, minutely connected to each other, making them responsible to the overall pattern; total intelligence spread out in every atom. **Syn.** GOD, TOTALITY, UNIVERSAL MIND.

DIVINE INTERVENTION—see INSPIRATIONAL PSYCHISM, CLAIRSENTIENCE, CLAIRVOYANCE.

DIVINE INTOXICATION—(ancient) to receive a mass of enfolding psychic experiences within a short time, resulting in a spiritual upliftment; brought on deliberately or occurs without a consciously known reason, e.g., to be flooded with vivid dreams each night; to become entranced with the awe of the beauty and accuracy of the psychic experiences. [**cf.** FORCED PSI, INITIATORY SICKNESS, MOVEMENT-FOR-ALTERED CONSCIOUSNESS]

DIVINE LIGHT—(ancient) a psychic vision which comes with a special purpose for civilization; a divine intervention. [**cf.** PROPHECY, CLAIRVOYANCE]

DIVINE LOVE—(Hinduism) love without condition, without boundary, and without change.

DIVINE MARRIAGE—(esoteric) (Yoga) a special technique of drawing the kundalini power up the sushumna in the spine, which then escapes through the top of the head becoming the silver cord and bringing one into a period of enlightenment. [**cf.** KUNDALINI, CHAKRAS, SILVER CORD]

DIVINE MIND—see DIVINE INTELLIGENCE.

DIVINE MOTHER—(Vedic) that part of the Godhead that is spectacular; sometimes appearing as Shiva or Vishnu.

DIVINE NOSTALGIA—coined by Pir Vilayat Inayat Khan; the heavenly condition that was in the beginning, now showing through all organisms with the desire to be divine again; the potential within each seed to keep growing and evolving until it goes back to its perfect state; i.e., comes through the mature plant, showing all that is in it. [**cf.** TOTALITY, MACROCOSM, EVOLUTION, GUIDING PRINCIPLE]

DIVINE ORDER—1. the overall plan of everything in the universe (from the minutest particle to the Great Solar System); everything has a special function in this overall plan, and "everything knows this function," as though a guiding principle has been built within everything, directing it to perfectness in its due time and with purposeful action; 2. individual activity that comes to one, unconsciously or consciously, desired and planned for; all experiences are brought about by one's attitude and thinking according to divine law, therefore, all is in *divine order* because all adheres to the divine law.]

DIVINE PLANE—the fastest vibrational frequency interpenetrating all-there-is, but so fast as to be inconceivable to a human being's finite mind; theorized to contain total perfectness; the Great Light of Intelligence, the Great Spirit of Energies, and the All Powerful essence of Love in every aspect; in this plane one will be in a vibrational frequency free from the wheels of rebirth, all negation strained away and an ultimate blending of soul-minds in a large creative center. **Syn.** SEVENTH PLANE, PLANE OF LIBERATION. [**cf.** BODIES AND PLANES Appendix 5]

DIVINE PROGENITORS—(Hinduism) the first human beings on earth believed to be incarnated from the higher planes of the etheric world having the rank of Gods; serve as models for one to copy and give one direction in living.

DIVINE PSYCHOLOGY—a study of: how the state of evolution of the soul-mind has an influence on man's environment, his physical body, earthly experiences and his attitude toward life; how his reaction and attitude toward the past, plus his reaction and attitude toward his new experiences, influence the growth of the soul-mind in its evolutionary state, making it ready for a better incarnation the next time.

DIVINE RULERS OF THE GOLDEN GATE—a lodge of highly evolved soul-minds who teach occult studies prior to the initiation into higher levels of wisdom; started by what is believed to be reincarnated adepts interested in world progression; began in America, transferring the headquarters from country to country; uses the hidden material of the Atlanteans; exists today.

DIVINE SPARK—1. the overall plan-pattern of Total Intelligence in a very concentrated energy from (imbedded within every atom) with a functional direction to evolve to its fullest potential; the outer aspect of what the Great Cosmos will eventually become is stamped as a *thought* within each atom; 2. minute specks of perfect light buried everywhere, in animate and inanimate objects, that yearn to return to the original Light Source. **Syn.** COSMIC ATOM, MONAD. [**cf.** MONADOLOGY, MACROCOSM, MICROCOSM]

DIVINE THRONE—(Kabbalah) name given to the higher realms where the angels abide; see SEVENTH PLANE.

DIVINE WHISPERS—(ancient) the rustling of leaves, gushing of fountains, whipping of the wind and other nature sounds that are answers to questions from the etheric world; ability of angels to manipulate nature, contrary to natural law, to be used to answer questions posed to them by earthlings; a code can be established between the angels and earthlings. [**cf.** CLAIRAUDIENCE, NATURE OMENS, BOTANE Appendix 2]

DIVINER—see PSYCHIC.

DIVING POOL—(laboratory) (astral projection) an enclosed device which is electronically isolated for testing out-of-body experiences; contains an object suspended in it that will register the slightest movement of the psychic being tested. (Inconcl.) [**cf.** Appendix 2, ASTRAL PROJECTION, ASTRAL PLANES]

DIVINING—1. to use radiesthetic sense in a ritual-like process with natural or manmade objects to acquire psychic information of a personal or historic nature; 2. to move one's self into an awareness of Totality and believe the information received; 3. (current) process of psychically tuning into the future. [**cf.** CASTING OF LOTS, SORTES, DOWSING, MANTIC ART]

DIVINING ROD—(radiesthesia) a long narrow tool used in the hands of a dowser that gives him or her tangible signals in answer to their questions; the rod picks up the undetectable, minute signal running down the nerve canal from the brain to the arm and hand, amplifies it, and makes the stick point to the covered treasure in the ground, or move according to a code to answer the question in the mind; (ancient) the straight stick, or the forked stick, cut from a live tree, (hazel or bamboo); (modern) two wire coat hangers bent in an *L* shape, one used in each hand. **Syn.** DOWSING ROD, WAND, WITCHSTICK. [**cf.** DOWSING, PENDULUM, RADIESTHETIC SENSE]

DIVYA DRISTI—(Yoga) term used to designate the third-eye area in the head of a human being; see THIRD-EYE. [**cf.** PINEAL GLAND, PITUITARY GLAND]

DJINNI—(Islam) a nature spirit believed to have been existing 2,000 years before Adam; made of smoke; inhabits the seashore and wild places, capable of flying rapidly, assuming shapes and imitating sounds of animals or humans; has a desire to work for earthlings, e.g., attaching to a lamp as in Aladdin's lamp; plural **Djinn**; also spelled **Jinni**. [**cf.** JANN, MARID, NATURE SPIRITS, FIRE ELEMENTAL]

DMT—psychedelic drug that induces micropsia and macropsia, the sense of the world shrinking or expanding; similar to what happened to Alice after she obeyed the instructions on the small container that read "eat me" in *Alice in Wonderland* by Lewis Carroll. [**cf.** SHAPE-CHANGING, DIMENSION-SHIFTING, WHALE]

DNA BODY CELLS—(esoteric) minute pictures, or the mental-reflecting-ether in the body cells; memory of the body activity stored in each cell. (Inconcl.) [**cf.** MOVIE-MICROFILM FORM, NERVE ETHER, THOUGHT BODY]

DNA MOLECULES—(esoteric) new theory: belief that the DNA in atoms is a code that operates through words; the word becomes the code, so one can change the coding or application by changing the word; (Bible, New Testament John 1:1). "In the beginning was the Word". [**cf.** ATOMS, INTELLIGENCE, ELECTRICAL ACTIVITY]

DO-IN—(Japan) form of massage therapy designed to promote strength and quality of the *Ki* flow throughout the body, establishing more harmony within the systems of the body. [**cf.** CURATIVE EDUCATION, JOGGING, TAI CHI CHUAN, ACUPUNTURE Appendix 5]

DOCTOR OF THE SPIRIT—a master whose function is to heal the entire universe of its worries; works at this through an incarnation on earth, teaching universal love; incarnated for this purpose only. [**cf.** ANGEL HIERARACHY, HOLY ONES, LADY OF HEAVEN]

DOCTOR TEACHER—"guardian angel"; an etheric world intelligence assigned to each earthling during the entire incarnation; in charge of four other guides, who constitute the *inner band*; principle functions are to assist the earthling to accomplish the purpose of the incarnation and bring inspirational information and guidance; has access to the akashic records and may dole out karmic experiences **as** the earthling needs and can understand them, but never makes a decision for the earthling; a link in a chain of intelligences; one in a system of

energies given to help soul-minds evolve. **Syn.** CELESTIAL GUARDIAN. [**cf.** INNER BAND, OUTER BAND, ANGEL HIERARCHY]

DOCTORING SESSION—(Native American, Cherokee) the time period in which the patient is being treated by the medicine man, whether it be the tribal session or a personal visit. [**cf.** MAGNETIC HEALING, PSYCHIC HEALING]

DOCTRINAL COMPLIANCE—see TELEPATHIC LEAKAGE.

DOCTRINE—the collective teachings or principle of any science or subject.

DOCTRINE OF FORMS AND CEREMONIES—name given to the outer philosophy of Buddhism, which is taught to the general public; southern teachings of Gautama Buddha.

DOCTRINE OF LOCALIZATION OF SOUL—belief of survival after death and the study of what happens to one's individuality.

DOCTRINE OF SUBLIMINAL—(F.W.H. Myers) each human being has one psyche controlling his body, and each has one or more streams of consciousness flowing into this psyche. (Inconcl.) [**cf.** SUBLIMINAL PERCEPTION, BRAIN]

DOER—human being seed that gives a person motivation to live, and to improve the quality of each life. **Syn.** MONAD, ATMAN. [**cf.** MONADOLOGY, DIVINE SPARK]

DOG-GHOST—(esoteric) etheric energy in the form of a dog assigned to each earthling as a means of protection during each incarnation. [**cf.** GUIDE, ASTRAL WORLD, DOMESTIC SPIRITS, WIND PEOPLE]

DOG-GODS—(esoteric) etheric world intelligences from the faster vibrational frequencies taking the form of a dog when appearing to a human; believed to be deities in charge of the sun, moon, stars and water for the earth; protects one from evil influences if called upon. [**cf.** BODIES AND PLANES Appendix 5, GUIDE, ANGEL HIERARCHY]

"doing JAPA"—(Hinduism) repeating a short phrase or a mantra constantly during meditation to help quiet the mind and to reach a high state of consciousness; sometimes beads are used to count the repetition. [**cf.** JAPA, MANTRA, MEDITATION]

DOMESTIC SPIRITS—etheric world intelligences, who in some cultures are believed to be ancestors who will protect the earthling's home and family, when called upon to do so. **Sim.** ANCESTRAL SPIRITS. [**cf.** SHAPE-SHIFTING, ETHERIC WORLD INTELLIGENCES]

DOMICILIUM POLTERGEIST—an etheric world entity making themselves known as an earthbound, noisy spirit who performs within the walls of the home only instead of the usual procedure of following the poltergeist generator around; the conclusion of researchers is that some poltergeists use a combination of individual's energy for their pranks. [**cf.** EXTRADOMICILIATION, POLTERGEIST GENERATOR, GHOSTS, FOCUS]

DOMINANT PERSONA CONSCIOUSNESS FACTOR—principles or ideas that are acquired without the ability to logically think them out or without making a rational decision about the experience before filing the idea in the subconscious mind, e.g., in early years, when the conscious mind is not fully developed, the birth trauma could cause erroneous thoughts; at the age of four years, to see a jungle on television and not have anyone there to tell you that jungles are not around the corner. [**cf.** BLOCKS, SUBCONSCIOUS MIND, CONSCIOUS MIND]

DOMINANTS OF THE UNCONSCIOUS—(Carl Jung) a collection of universal indentical forms, archetypal in nature, which make up a layer of the subconscious mind; capable of springing forth spontaneously in psychic experiences, in non-thought visions, and in dreams. (Inconcl.) [**cf.** COLLECTIVE UNCONSCIOUS, SUBLIMINAL LEVEL, SUBCONSCIOUS MIND]

DOMINATIONS—a graded order of etheric world intelligences who help carry out the divine evolutionary plan; (Theosophy) one of the nine orders of celestial attendants of God. [**cf.** ANGEL HIER-ARCHY, EVOLUTION]

DOMINO DIVINATION—(radiesthesia) a method of getting solutions to one's problems, predicting the future, and receiving psychic information by the use of a standard set of dominoes; a book is used in which answers to many questions are listed under possible number combinations; dominoes are drawn by the querist from dominoes lying face down, and this number combination will be the solution to his or her problem, as it is written in the book. [**cf.** CASTING OF LOTS, SORTES]

DOODLEBUG—(radiesthesia) another name for the dowsing rod or pendulum; see PENDULUM.

DOORKEEPER—(mediumship) an etheric world

intelligence, belonging to the inner band, whose responsibility is to allow only certain entities to enter the mind of the medium working when the medium is working with mental and physical psychism; regulates the entities' time with the medium; oversees so that only high qualitative psychic information is presented; acts under the guidance of the main guide; contributes to keeping the medium cheerful. **Syn.** JOY GUIDE, ASTRAL COADJUTOR. [**cf.** INNER BAND, DOCTOR TEACHER, MEDIUM]

DOORKEEPERS—(Tibet) 1. etheric world faith-guarding, peaceful, tranquil deities ready to serve mankind; depicted seated on the great mandala as representing north, south, east and west. [**cf.** ANGELS, RAPHAEL]

DOPPELGANGER—(Germany) see ASTRAL BODY.

DOR—(Wilhelm Reich) abbr. for *orgone energy* in a deadly form: "Deadly ORgone"; the product of exhausted orgone energy when used as fuel in the UFO vehicles; it is black, in cloud formation, radioactive and in need of water, and oxygen; will attack plants, animals, rocks, soil, and humans. (Inconcl.) [**cf.** ORGONE ENERGY, DOR CLOUDS]

DOR CLOUDS—(Wilhelm Reich) (ufology) visible dark clouds over any area of the planet after the passage of UFOs; believed to be a product of exhausted orgone energy which is used as fuel in UFO spacecraft; geometrically shaped, flat with sharp edges, looks like steel wool; capable of preventing normal buildup of rain clouds. (Inconcl.) [**cf.** DOR, ORGONE ENERGY, UFOLOGY]

DORJE—1.(Sanskrit) a three-pronged instrument (a trident), symbolizing power; used to repel evil influences, in the same manner as ozone purifies the air by a storm; 2. (Tibet) an electric device, made of metal, shaped like the three-pronged sceptor of medievil kings, globed at each end; symbolizes lotus buds of purity; believed to be capable or recharging like a psychotronic generator; used for psychic phenomena. (Inconcl.) 3. gesture and posture used in meditation; 4. a symbol of power used for both good and evil. [**cf.** ELECTRICITY, ARK OF THE CONVENANT, FORMS-WITH-POWER]

DORMANT ESP—(laboratory) psychic information coming through spontaneously, e.g., correct answers to questions on tests taken in school; see CLAIRSENTIENCE.

DOUBLE APPEARANCE—see BILOCATION.

DOUBLE EGOS—(astral projection) the unconscious splitting of a soul-mind in order to give a message to a loved one, and resulting in the individual being in two locations at the same time; stimulated by a highly emotional state of the soul-mind; astral body appears with the message in clairvoyant form, clairaudient words, or clairscent fragrance; see BILOCATION. (Inconcl.) [**cf.** SPLIT PERSONALITY, NEED-DETERMINED PHENOMENON]

DOUBLE HEAVY—(Tai Chi) theory: when weight is evenly distributed on both feet, the mind and body are stagnant. [**cf.** MOVEMENT-FOR-ALTERED-CONSCIOUSNESS, HEALING DANCE, GYMNASTIC MEDICINE]

DOUBLE MEN—(astral projection) the astral and physical body are exact duplications in the astral projection; even as to clothing. **Syn.** BICORPOREITY. [**cf.** BILOCATION, ASTRAL PROJECTION]

DOUBLE PLANCHETTE WRITING—(automatic writing) to use a planchette on each hand simultaneously; one hand will write normally and the other hand will produce mirror-writing. [**cf.** AUTOMATISM, PLANCHETTE]

DOUBLE SIGHT—a state of ecstasy wherein one can see into the astral world at the same time one sees the physical environment; the astral world looks like a part of the scenery, only in the air. [**cf.** CLAIRVOYANCE Appendix 2, EIDETIC IMAGES, EXTERNAL AUTOSCOPY, FOURTH DIMENSIONAL CLAIRVOYANCE]

DOUBLE TRIANGLE—one triangle is pointing toward the top and another triangle is superposed on it with the point facing the bottom; it makes a six pointed star; this is the Seal of Solomon. [**cf.** FORMS-WITH-POWER, SQUARE, CAMERON CONES, MAGIC CIRCLE]

DOUBLE WAVE—(Johann Wolfgang von Goethe) the pulsating or breathing of the earth; occurs in the morning and evening; gives the concept that the earth is a living organism; a cyclic reaction. (Inconcl.) [**cf.** CYCLES, LAW OF PERSONIFICATION AND LAW OF CORRESPONDENCE Appendix 7]

DOUBLEGANGER—ASTRAL BODY.

DOUBLE-BLIND EXPERIMENTS—1. (laboratory) a testing technique in which both experimenter and subject are kept ignorant of particular conditions of a control group in the test, e.g., in testing for drug use, the alternate administration of the drug and a placebo; 2. (laboratory) an experiment in which neither the psychic nor the assistant knows what the target is. (Inconcl.) [**cf.** ESP, RANDOM NUMBER GENERATOR]

DOUBLING—(astral projection) when the astral body leaves the physical body and hovers over it; occurs during surgical operations, sudden accidents and sometimes when the subject is in deep meditation. [**cf.** EMOTIONAL PSI, DOUBLE EGOS, IN-THE-RANGE-OF-CORD-ACTIVITY]

DOUBT VIBRATIONS—an energy field made by viewers, experimenters, or others in the area, who have doubts about the psychic's ability and/or scepticism about the reality of psychism; this field hinders the psychics performance (from the dowser to the trance medium). [**cf.** PSYCHIC DEVELOPMENT CIRCLE, SHEEP AND GOAT EFFECT]

DOVES—(ancient) noted for their ability to send psychic messages to earthlings. [**cf.** ANPSI, HORSE WHISPERS, BLACKBIRD]

DOWN THROUGH—(laboratory) an experiment for testing psychic cognition; the subject names the cards in a deck, starting from the top and going to the bottom, before any cards are removed or matched with the calls. (Inconcl.) [**cf.** UP THROUGH, ZENER CARDS]

DOWNWARD CURVE OF THE ARC—process of the monad pressing downward until it develops a soul-mind; then encased in a soul-mind presses downward again until it becomes entangled into matter of the earth plane. **Syn.** INVOLUTION, ELEMENTAL EVOLUTION. [**cf.** MONADOLOGY]

DOWSER—a psychic with radiesthetic sense; 1. detects oil, water, or anything underground by means of the reaction of his or her dowsing rods; 2. receives answers to questions from their rods; theory: man is the instrument or the machine, the dowsing rods are the amplifier, and the tuning dial is the mind, i.e., a question is proposed in the mind of the dowser, then a minute, undetectable answer flows from the mind to the dowsing rod and it amplifies the answer by a reaction in the rod that is detectable. (Inconcl.) [**cf.** DIVINING ROD, RADIESTHETIC SENSE, DOWSING, PENDULUM POWER]

DOWSING—branch of radiesthesia; 1. study and practical use of nonliving energy fields and their effect on the human sympathetic nervous system; 2. to psychically perceive answers to questions in one's mind from a rod held in the hand(s); dowsing operator holds the dowsing tool in his or her

177

hand(s) while concentrating on a question, (usually concerning the location of oil, water, or other minerals underground) until they sense the answer by a downward pull of the rod in their arms; this visible motor reaction is understood by the dowser; dowser uses radiesthetic sense; theory: nervous system (including motor system), earth's magnetic field, and the dowsing rod work harmoniously to bring a meaningful answer to a proposed question by the dowser. (Inconcl.) [**cf.** PALLOMANCY Appendix 6, DIVINING ROD, DOWSER, RADIESTHETIC SENSE]

DOWSING QUESTION—an inquiry or request relating to a human need, made orally or silently by the operator before using the dowsing rod or pendulum; inquiry or request must require a yes or no answer only, must be concise, clear, specific, simply worded, ungeneralized, and must be free of ambiguous words that could have many meanings in one's belief system; operator poses the question, takes the necessary position with the instrument in hand(s), and keeps his or her mind neutral and uncluttered until the instrument gives the answer. [**cf.** WITNESS, BLOCKING, DOWSING RESPONSE]

DOWSING RESPONSE—a visible and invisible reaction of the divining rod or pendulum after a question has been posed by the dowser or pendulum operator; reaction varies: e.g., an inward pulling sensation of the rod, as the rod tips downward over an area, indicates underground minerals, sometimes so forceful the hands let go of the rod; L-rods bend downward or crisscross excitedly; pendulum reverses the direction of its swing or increases the speed or size of its swing; instrument obeys a code that is prearranged between the subconscious mind and the conscious mind of the operator; with the visible outward reaction to the question by the divining rod or pendulum, there is also a sensation of the frequency registration in the hands, arms, or body of the operator; amount of body sensations depends upon the ability of the operator. [**cf.** A COURTESY, DOWSING QUESTION, ASSISTANT DOWSING]

DOWSING ROD—an implement designed to use in the hands to detect minerals underground, find lost objects, and to answer questions which require a yes or no reply; instrument can be made from natural wood in a stick or forked branch shape, copper wire, or bent wire coathangers; see DIVINING ROD. [**cf.** TAMING WAND, STRIPPED ROD, L-RODS]

DOWSING ZONE—an energy field under the earth's surface (i.e. water, oil, etc.) which can be detected by radiesthetic sense; causes a tangible reaction in the dowsing rod or pendulum activity. [**cf.** TELLURIC FORCE]

DRAG AND DRAG—(Anglo-Saxon) radiesthetic term explaining the strong pull of the divining rod felt by the dowser, which continues to pull as long as the dowser moves in the correct direction. **Syn.** DOWSER RESPONSE. [**cf.** RADIESTHESIA, FORKED BRANCH]

DRAGON—(ancient) one of the four spiritual creatures. [**cf.** FENG-HWANG, TORTOISE, UNICORN]

DRAINING OFF—(Huna) to bring that which is blocking one's path to the surface where it can be rationalized with to untangle memories of unpleasant experiences. [**cf.** OUTLAW MEMORY, GRAPES, PAST LIVES THEORY, ROLFING]

DRAPERIES—simple, loose, one piece garments, from neck to floor, belted with a sash; most common clothing worn by etheric world intelligences when presenting themselves to psychics or mediums; used because it is easier to manifest something simple, rather than conventional styled clothing, enabling them to conserve energy for more useful purposes. [**cf.** INNER BAND, OUTER BAND, CREATIVE UPWELLINGS, APPARITION]

DRAWING MEDIUM—an automatist who draws meaningful and useful pictures, instead of receiving word messages, sometimes revealing the higher planes. [**cf.** AUTOMATISM, ETHERIC SCRIPT, FACSIMILE WRITING MEDIUM]

DRAWING OF LOTS—(Ancient Israel) to make a decision or a choice by using multiple objects, e.g., stones or straws; objects are shaken in the hand and thrown on the ground to determine the decision which is indicated by their *fall*, according to a prearranged fall code. **Syn.** LOTS, URIM, CASTING OF LOTS. [**cf.** RADIESTHESIA]

DREAM ANALYSIS—methods of interpreting a written recalled dream into a meaningful experience for the dreamer; 1.professional opinions of dream analysis: (Sigmund Freud) all dreams are related to sex and its conflicts; (Carl Jung) dreams contain archetypal symbols that relate to the world's great myths; (Frederick S. Perls) dreams are related to man's personality of top/dog-under/dog connotations and to what man avoids in his life; (Edgar Cayce) dreams are meant to improve man's life; (Ann Faraday) dreams relate to man's present life and day to day concernments; with honest effort, dreamer can interpret his or her own dreams; 2. categories of dreams: dreams for balance, for immediacy, for physical problems, for psychic development, for sustenance of life, for character improvement. (Inconcl.) [cf. DREAMS Appendix 2]

DREAM AVOIDANCES—theory: the symbols and scenes shown in dreams, referring to portions of waking life that the dreamer would like to forget or evade, will be forgotten or evaded in dream interpretation also: 1. dreamer will awaken before the dream is finished to block out the unwanted section; 2. dreamer will forget that part of the dream upon awakening; 3. dreamer will omit that section of dream when telling the dream more than once; these are the dream symbols and activities that need working on for a more meaningful life. (Inconcl.) [cf. DREAM ANALYSIS, DREAM CONTROL]

DREAM BODY—name sometimes given to the astral body because more astral flights are taken at night during sleep, than are consciously willed.

DREAM CLAIRVOYANCE—(dreams) a psychic experience of EMOTIONAL CLAIRVOYANCE happening during sleep; experienced at the theta level with no rapid eye movement; a very clear, vivid, detailed vision which is easy to recall. [cf. SLEEP EXPERIENCES, EOG, DELTA STATE OF CONSCIOUSNESS, NIGHT LANGUAGE]

DREAM CONSCIOUSNESS—1. (dream laboratory) a level of awareness in which the conscious mind is passive, the body is relaxed, and the subconscious mind is functioning; printout on the electroencephalograph indicates brain wave rhythm to be in a low beta level and a high alpha level. [cf. EEG, BRAIN RHYTHM, NREM CONSCIOUSNESS] 2. (parapsychology) an alert and active awareness of the subconscious mind without interference from the conscious mind; in this state the individual is in a PSYCHE CONSCIOUSNESS wherein the soul-mind has free rein to improve and perfect itself without interference; dreams are for this purpose and give scenes and symbols to present one's life up to that night; it is as if the psyche is providing aid for the next day's decisions. [cf. OBJECTIVE INTERPRETATION, SUBJECTIVE INTERPRETATION, COMPENSATORY DREAMS]

DREAM CONTROL—the ability to manipulate dream energies; to talk to the subconscious mind just prior to the oneset of sleep and give instructions that any negative dream scenes or symbols be reversed to positive symbols and scenes, e.g., if the sleeper dreamt that a lion was attacking him or her, they would go after the lion until they ended up riding the lion to a safe place. (Inconcl.) [cf. DREAM PROGRAMMING, DREAMING TRUE, HYPNAGOGIC DREAMS]

DREAM CYCLE—a biological rhythm of dream visions occuring in approximately ninety-minute intervals regardless of the length of one's sleep; mind is between the alpha and beta levels of consciousness. **Syn.** SLEEP CYCLE. [cf. BRAIN WAVE RHYTHM, EEG INSTRUMENT, SLEEP EXPERIENCES]

DREAM DIARY—a journal, notebook, or filebox used for recording dreams and their interpretation; properly kept diary contains: the date, a one-sentence summary of emotions and experiences of the day before the dream, the dream and dream fragments (as accurately as can be recalled), the mood the dream left one in, and the interpretation (entered at a later time). **Syn.** DREAM LOG, DREAM JOURNAL. [cf. Appendix 2 DREAMS]

DREAM DICTIONARY—see DREAM GLOSSARY.

DREAM FORMS—see DREAM SYMBOLS.

DREAM FABRIC—the framework or structure of one's dream; that which produces and connects one's sleeping scenarios together. **Syn.** DREAMSTUFF. [cf. LUCID DREAMING, NINETY-MINUTE CYCLE, NONRECALLERS]

DREAM FRAGMENTS—parts of a dream appearing by themselves or appearing unfinished, e.g., scenes that stop and start in different settings, symbols that are scattered in pieces, or out of their normal setting; these are normal dream characteristics of the dream and can be used for interpretation when the dream is not in story form or cannot be fully recalled. [cf. SYMBOL AMPLIFICATION, FREE ASSOCIATION]

DREAM GLOSSARY—a *personal* list of objects and characters that appear frequently in one's dreams; when symbols are out of context, one uses *free association* with each symbol; this aids the subject to determine more accurately what the symbol means to him or her; then the meaning is related to rest of the dreamstuff; glossaries printed in books have no value for the dreamer; each sleeper chooses their own symbols from his or her subconscious mind. [cf. FREE ASSOCIATION, SYMBOL AMPLIFICATION]

DREAM GUIDE—(American Native, Iroquois) an etheric world intelligence who is skilled in working with dreams, bringing guidance and help to the dreamer. [cf. INCUBATION, FEAST OF THE FOOLS]

DREAM INTERPRETATION—to analyze and study a dream for its value and worth to the dreamer: 1. find theme of dream by action in the dream (is sleeper searching, running, laughing, playing, etc.?); 2. find why sleeper chose the symbols and what they mean to him or her; 3. determine how dreamstuff can be used for advancement of dreamer; interpretation should be done within a day or two of dream; suggestions from therapist, colleagues, or friends open new avenues for each of the above steps, but final decision is made by dreamer. [cf. DREAMMAKERS Appendix 2]

DREAM JOURNAL—see DREAM DIARY.

DREAM LOG—see DREAM DIARY.

DREAM REALITY—a level of consciousness that is real to the dreamer at the time of the dream; when dream is finished for dreamer, its energies go into other levels of dimensions, just as all thoughts do, working with one's other six bodies. [cf. DREAM-MAKERS, LUCID DREAMING]

DREAM RECALL—the skill of recording a dream story or its fragments before it fades from memory; to write the dream on paper, to verbalize it to a laboratory monitor when awakened, or to voice it into a tape recorder; skill lies in the ability to stay still physically, and to be able to record it before it eludes; skill increases if one retires with the necessary tools prepared for recording, if one programs one's mind during the daytime to remember the dream fabric, and if one takes time to interpret the dream during the day; (do not confuse with a PSYCHIC EXPERIENCE DURING SLEEP which is easy to recall, not having the peculiarity of elusion as dreams). (Inconcl.) [cf. Appendix 2 DREAMS, DREAM FRAGMENT]

DREAM RESEARCH LABORATORIES—a building designed with small sleeping rooms and necessary electronic equipment to study dreamstuff and the dream period; usually established at universities or hospitals, under the supervision of psychologists and psychiatrists; physical facilities provide cubicles large enough to accomodate the subject and required equipment; technician observes and controls the equipment from outside a large window to the cubicle so he can awaken the subject when the eyeballs are moving and listen to the dream he or she has just experienced; laboratory is run with precision; subject returns at the same hour each night, is free from psychotic problems, and takes no caffine or drugs during the day; pajamas are worn and the EEG and EOG instruments are appropriately attached to subject; print-outs from instruments are visible for logging and recording at the various levels of consciousness; subjects are used from every walk of life and various ages to make the statistics more accurate; research began in the early 1960s. [cf. DREAM THINKING, NONRECALLERS, NOCTURNAL PARALYSIS]

DREAM STAGE—a level of consciousness during sleep, in which one's mind activity is busy producing visions of people, colors, objects and scenery, along with impressions of speaking and emotions; occurs at ninety-minute intervals throughout a normal night of sleep; visions of stories or fragments last between five to forty-five minutes, increasing in length toward morning; this awareness level displays low beta waves and high alpha waves in the EEG readouts; sleeper's eyeballs move rapidly under closed lids, which is detectable; large muscles are in a state of temporary paralysis, but fingers, toes, eyes, and genitals can move; blood temperature and blood pressure rises, pulse increases, breath is faster and adrenaline flows quickly, all equivalent to the waking state; biological functions are universal, as if it is a part of the overall pattern of human functions; see DREAMS for their worth. Syn. PARADOXAL SLEEP, REM SLEEP. [cf. DREAMS Appendix 2]

DREAM SYMBOLISM—the use of visual pictures, scenes, objects, things, people, colors, and feelings to arouse thought in the dreamer by the power of suggestion, causing the hidden truth in the subconscious mind to reveal itself; symbols may be studied from many points of view; sleeper interested in improvement will discover his or her meaning in the symbol according to the logic of their own conception; symbols are unconsciously chosen by the dreamer, and can have more than one meaning; pertains to all phases of the dreamer's life. [cf. UNIVERSAL SYMBOLS, THOUGHTS OF THE HEART,

LOSING MONEY DREAMS]

DREAM THERAPY—1. to use one's dream diary as an aid to psychotherapy by analyzing one's dreams for hidden talents and repressed experiences; theory: one continues one's same feelings and attitudes in one's dreams and when the conscious mind is passive (as in sleep) the subconscious mind surfaces that which needs attention; 2. (advanced therapy) to program one's self through incubation dreaming, to experience a needed attitudinal change which eliminates the necessity of experiencing this attitudinal change in the waking state. [cf. DREAMS, LUCIDITY, INCUBATION]

DREAM-WHISKEY—to remember the physical sensation of drinking alcohol while in the physical body, by a discarnate entity who was a heavy drinker in earth life, and who is now dissatisfied in the astral world, looking for earthlings to haunt to revive his memory. [cf. HAUNTING, ASTRAL PLANE]

DREAMED AWAKE—a psychic experience occurring during the sleep period: the vision is so intense, clear and vivid that one feels as though one is awake while it is happening. [cf. SLEEP EXPER-IENCES, THINKING, EXPOSURE DREAM, DELTA STATE OF CONSCIOUSNESS, THETA STATE OF CONSCIOUSNESS]

DREAMING—an uninitiated process occuring during a person's sleep in which their mind shows them black and white or colored, moving or still pictures, that relate to their lifestyle and personality; pictures bring impressions of the speech and intent of activity without bringing actual conversation; an absolute vital function of the human and animal species to maintain balance in their lives; denial of dreams by frequently forcing the sleeper to awaken during a dream period causes neural disorder, and the continuation of this disruption causes insanity. [cf. NIGHTLY RHYTHM, DREAMLETS, DREAMSTUFF, DREAMS, SENSE IMAGERY]

DREAMING MIND—(parapsychology) the subconscious mind.]

DREAMING TRUE—to purposely picture a scene before falling asleep, stepping into the scene without a break in consciousness and remembering what transpired in the dream upon awakening; (do not confuse with LUCIDITY or CONFRONT AND CONQUER dreaming). [cf. DREAM AVOIDANCES, INCUBATION DREAMING]

DREAMLETS—coined by Ann Faraday; see HYPNAGOGIC]

DREAMMAKERS—(esoteric) the guiding principle buried deep within every human being seed; a motivating force that says one will grow until one reaches perfection in the human being species; works within the subconscious mind when the conscious mind is passive (during sleep) via the superconscious mind, to promote the growth of the organism (without interference from the conscious mind); presents this information in symbolization (universal to all humans) to be interpreted for the benefit of the sleeper, if she or he so chooses. [cf. DREAMS Appendix 2]

DREAMS—mind activity during sleep (between the lower beta and upper alpha levels), resulting in fuzzy, fragmented, nonsensical visions accompanied by emotions; 1. present themselves in: (a) still scenes or story form; (b) using the dreamer as subject or spectator; (c) black and white or color; (d) conversations understood by dreamer without subjects in dream uttering words; (e) an awareness of the five senses being used; (f) symbols and images; (g) elusive and paradoxal form; 2. theories for purpose of dreams: (a) to compensate for the activity of the day just passed, bringing balance to mind and body; (b) to provide a workshop for repair of self-esteem and competency; (c) to provide information of where and how the dreamer stands in his or her life, according to past decisions; to provide help for new decisions and activities; (d) to emphasize unbalanced character traits, unrealized potentials, and give encouragement when these are acted upon; 3. dreams work with the present; are a form of psychic energy originating from the guiding principle, entering through the subconscious mind, relating material to help the soul-mind advance for the highest good of the individual. (Inconcl.) Syn. PARADOXAL SLEEP, REM SLEEP. [cf. DREAMS Appendix 2, DREAM RESEARCH LABORATORIES]

DREAMS FOR HEALTH—directions and instructions to improve one's good health given in dream fabric during sleep; 1. symbols representing a negative physical condition in the body shown to the dreamer before the physical condition is actually manifested in the body; 2. symbol and theme describes how to heal one's self; 3. symbol or image gives a diagnostic clue to the prevailing disease; 4. dream fabric occuring simultaneously with an actual healing of the body; e.g., one dreams one is

181

standing in wavy water up to the knees, and the next day their sprained ankle is better). [cf. DISPLACEMENT, RECURRING DREAMS, REDUCTIVE ANALYSIS, PREMONITORY DREAMS]

DREAMSTUFF—material of which the dream is made; the essence of contents of the visions and feelings occurring during the rapid-eye-movement stage of consciousness. [cf. DREAM REALITY, NIGHT LANGUAGE, SECOND VISION]

DREAMTIME—(Australian Aborigines) a belief that dreams are stimulated by a past period of time when the world was unorganized; men and animals were indistinguishable, land and water was not properly separated; this stimulation through dreaming is to be interpreted as a reminder for the dreamer to continue to advance themselves and his or her surroundings.

DRIFTERS—human beings who have made their transition into the etheric world but will not accept that fact, and who are infatuated with material sensations; float in the astral world, ready to reexperience former sensations by latching on to an earthling. (Inconcl.) **Syn.** HAUNTERS, EARTH-BOUND ENTITIES. [cf. ASTRAL BODY, DENSITY, ASTRAL SHELLS, CONFUSED SOUL-MINDS]

DRIZA—(Tibet) a nature spirit that abides in a shaped cloud, vanishing in the rain; coming from the planes of odour-eaters. [cf. NATURE SPIRITS Appendix 3]

DROLL—a nature spirit, sometimes visible to mankind as a giant or a saint; usually amusing; capable of working for a person or against him or her. [cf. NATURE SPIRITS]

DROP-IN COMMUNICATORS—etheric world entities who come into the vibration of a seance, a psychic development circle, or a medium, unexpected and uninvited; sometimes giving good psychic information and sometimes giving trouble. [cf. SEANCE, MEDIUMSHIP, DESIRED CONTROL]

DROPS IN—(pendulum map dowsing) the movement of the pendulum over the area where the mineral can be found underground that one desires to locate; sometimes it follows the underground trail of this mineral. [cf. PENDULUMIST, MAP DOWSING]

DROWSINESS ALARM CONTROL—(biofeedback training) an attachment to a biofeedback instrument that makes a sound when the subject has fallen asleep. [cf. BIOFEEDBACK TRAINING, SLEEPITATE]

DRUGGER—(medieval) healer, psychic; see PSYCHIC.

DRUID—(*daur*, "oak tree") (ancient Britain) originally Buddhists who invaded Britain during the iron age (third century); learned class of Celtic people of Gaul; advanced mystic teachings classify them as: philosophers, magistrates, priests, psychics, astrologers, and mediums. [cf. MEDIUMSHIP, STONEHENGE]

DRUIDISM—ancient religion practiced by Celtic speaking people of Ireland, England, Scotland; mystics seeking to manifest the higher self while in the physical body; specialized in the more difficult psychic skills, like dimension-shifting and shape-changing; work harmoniously with nature spirits. [cf. DRUID, SHAPE-CHANGING, MYSTICISM]

DRUM—a percussion instrument used by magicians, priests, and shamans as an aid to invoke communication with etheric world intelligences, to induce trance states, and to frighten evil entities; because of its pulsating rhythm, it has an effect on the nervous system. [cf. SOUNDS-WITH-POWER, GREGORIAN CHANTS, SYMPATHETIC VIBRATION]

DRUZES—(Moslem) a sect noted for mediumship; believe in etheric world hierarchies, transmigration of souls and auric energy fields. [cf. MEDIUMSHIP, REINCARNATION, KARMA]

DRY REBIRTHING—a special breathing technique in the rhythm of the pulsating umbilical cord, which takes one back to the prenatal awareness and birth process; if there is any trauma associated with the birth experience which has been repressed, it will surface and can be dealt with. [cf. REBIRTHING, BIRTHING RELEASE]

DRYAD—(Greece) a nature spirit that presides over trees, woods, and forests; believed to die when the tree dies. **Syn.** WOOD NYMPH, HAMODRYADS. [cf. DRYAD FIELDS]

DRYAD FIELDS—coined by T.C. Lethbridge, who discovered that the wood nymphs create an energy field around the tree while they work with the tree. [cf. NATURE SPIRITS Appendix 3]

DUAL ASTRAL VISION—to see with astral and physical vision at the same time, when on an astral projection; this makes the two worlds look criss-crossed. [cf. ASTRAL VISION]

DUAL CONSCIOUSNESS—to be aware of being in two places at the same time; to be aware of one's surroundings and still be fully aware of the message coming through; see LIGHT TRANCE, STANDING READER, INSPIRATIONAL THOUGHT, and HYP-NOTHERAPY.

DUAL GERMS—see SOUL-MATES.

DUAL PERSONALITY—see POSSESSION.

DUAL TASK—(laboratory) an ESP experiment in which the results obtained under two conditions, are contrasted. [**cf.** RUN SCORE, ESP SHUFFLE, SERIES]

DUAL UNCONSCIOUSNESS—theory: a human mental mind can tap into two separate functions of the unconscious mind: 1. personal unconsciousness, built from one's attitudes regarding past experiences; 2. collective unconsciousness, built from the attitudes of present and past civilizations (autonomous). [**cf.** CONSCIOUSNESS Appendix 5]

DUGPA SECT—(Tibet) those who are studying the left hand path; a force that pulls one matterward; (Dugpaship). [**cf.** LEFT-HAND PATH]

DUGPAS—(Tibet) those who attend a semi-reformed school and study tantric magic; sometimes misused to mean those who study black magic. **Syn.** RED CAPS, BHONS. [**cf.** TANTRIC MAGIC]

DUNKUN—(Indonesia) see PSYCHIC and HEALER.

DUNCE HAT—(esoteric) a conical structured hat (type of material is insignificant) which has the properties similar to the pyramid; worn by slow learning pupils while sitting on a wooden stool; condensed energy from the center stimulates mind activity, quickening one's learning ability. [**cf.** WITCHES HAT, PYRAMID POWER, FORMS-WITH-POWER]

DUNNY—wee one; see NATURE SPIRIT.

DUSIL—(Celtic) etheric world entity capable of having sexual intercourse with earthlings. **Syn.** INCUBUS, SUCCUBUS. [**cf.** SEXUAL MYSTICISM, DIMENSION-SHIFTING]

DUST DEVILS—particles of dust in cyclic motion, appearing in connection with severe windstorms (hurricane, tornado, etc.): have electromagnetic frequencies which can project on television sets, thirty miles away. [**cf.** GRAVITY CONTROL]

DWARF—(Greece, Scandinavia, Germany) a nature spirit that is short, dark, ranging in height from two inches to two feet tall, very strong and powerful; depicted with a pickaxe and beard; mature at age three; works with the mineral kingdom in mines; cannot survive above ground because sunlight will turn him into stone; some spend the day as toads; shape-changers and dimension-shifters.

DWARF TROLLS—hideous featured, humped back, red-haired nature spirits; good mechanics, clever dancers, sharp-witted and possess beautiful wives. [**cf.** DIMENSION-SHIFTING, NATURE SPIRITS]

DWELLER IN THE ABYSS—(Choronzon), a very vicious demon.

DWELLER IN THE BODY—the divine spark of Totality within every human being; the potential within the human being seed; also spoken of as the MONAD, the "I AM" and the CHRIST WITHIN.

DWELLER ON THE THRESHOLD—1. (Occultism) an individual making his or her transition as an initiate; the soul-mind slips out of the body and is confronted with the accumulated karma of its entire past; this manifests as shadows and debt thought-forms, varying as to the nature of the debt; the past becomes the present; these debt thought-forms are absorbed as a part of the personality of the initiate; if it is unpleasant to see, the initiate must face it knowing it must be overcome before she or he can progress. **Syn.** DWELLERS IN THE BARDO. 2. a discarnate in the etheric world, not realizing they are dead, floats close to earth, trying to be a part of it; 3. an astral shell. [**cf.** HAUNTING, EARTHBOUND ENTITIES, ASTRAL SHELL, BARDO, REINCARNATION, KARMA, EATER OF HEARTS]

DWELLERS IN THE BARDO—see DWELLERS OF THE THRESHOLD def. 1.

DYBUK—(Jewish) (esoteric) a confused deceased person wandering around in the etheric world not realizing he or she is dead. **Syn.** EARTHBOUND ENTITY. [**cf.** BODIES AND PLANES Appendix 5, GHOST APPARITION]

DYING—1. (esoteric) the transition from one vibrational frequency to another vibrational frequency (nothing every dies, it just changes form); 2. (human) the change from one level of existence to another level of existence; 3. (holistic health) the dying process of each individual is regulated by one's self as to the time and the method; theory: emotion changes body chemistry and emotion follows thought; each thought a person thinks contributes to the on-going-life-process or the on-going-death-process by releasing the hormones to correspond to these thoughts; there is no neutrality; body chemistry changes constantly; individual chooses the method of his or her passing by their subconscious inner desires, e.g., a long drawn out sickness gives the loved ones an opportunity to gradually get used to living without the individual; 4. steps in dying result in a growth experience; **(a)** shock (individual knows he or she is dying); **(b)** denial (individual puts it aside); **(c)** anger; **(d)** bargaining to stay alive to take care of unfinished business; **(e)** depression (reactive depression and preparatory grief); **(f)** acceptance (positive submission); 5. everyone subconsciously knows they are going to die. [**cf.** DEATH SCIENCE Appendix 2]

DYNAMIC TRANSITIONS—(ufology) the changing from one state of force to another state of force; the ability to change vibrational frequencies, going from dimension to dimension, with rapid speed, e.g., the UFO aircraft are visible and then seem to disappear into thin air. [**cf.** DIMENSION-SHIFTING]

DYNAMICS—1. branch of mechanics that deals with the motion and equillibration of systems, under the action of forces, usually from outside the system; 2. (Michael H. Braddford) potential energy in a state of conversion to kinetic energy; opposite of static; "bio-state conditions of life; potential of the human."

DYNAMISTOGRAPH—invented by J.L.W.A. Matlo and G.J. Zaalberg Van Zelst; an instrument very delicately balanced constructed under etheric world guidance (similar to the tickertape) made for etheric world intelligences to punch out messages for the medium during his or her sleep or during a seance. [**cf.** GUIDE, MEDIUMSHIP, PRECIPITATION]

DYNAMIZE THE WILL—(astral projection) to make a firm, positive decision to induce an astral projection when one is sure he wants to work with the

moving force; the firmness assists in freeing the astral body; law: "It is the suggestion that bursts forth, not the subconscious will." [**cf.** ASTRAL PROJECTION Appendix 2]

DYNAMOMETER—(hypnosis) an instrument that records the degree of muscular reaction when a hypnotized person is perceiving colors, clairvoyantly. (Inconcl.) [**cf.** HYPNOTHERAPY Appendix 5]

DYNAMOSCOPE—instrument invented by Dr. Collongues; capable of detecting the human polarity of a medium in a state of deep trance; used to test and explain the force emanated to make objects move or store energy; proven to have similar findings as other instruments when tested. [**cf.** STHENOMETER, FLUID MOTORS, MAGNETOMETER, HUMAN POLARITY, PALMED POWER]

DYNATYPE—(Greek *dyna,* "power"); (Ira Progoff) an etheric world intelligence bringing in principles of life unknown to earthlings at this time, keeping a balance in the mediumship of the medium working with physical phenomena. [**cf.** MEDIUMSHIP, INNER BAND]

DYS—prefix, meaning "bad, ill" or "incorrect."

DYSPONESIS—(Whatmore) to unknowingly misdirect one's energy through wrong decisions, ending in illness. [**cf.** HOLISTIC HEALTH, LAW OF HEALING Appendix 7, CURATIVE EDUCATION]

DYSRHYTHMIA—to be out of balance with the twenty-four hour cycle because of working nights or flying into other time zones. (Inconcl.) **Syn.** DESYNCHRONIZED, JET FATIGUE. [**cf.** CIRCADIAN CYCLE, JET LAG]

DYSRHYTHMIC PREVENTION—the study and practical application of one working with their own relationship to circadian rhythm when their job puts them in a state of desynchronization. (Inconcl.) [**cf.** JET LAG, CIRCADIAN RHYTHM]

E-MATRIX—(radionics) bioplasmic energy that both interpenetrates and encompasses the entire human body, making radionics possible; the human body reacts like an electronic device; the radiesthesist can feel outer stimuli within the circuits of his or her body as it comes into contact with the outside matrix; this in turn reacts upon the divining rod or pendulum, giving tangible evidence of what the radiesthesist feels within his or her body; can be consciously willed or happen spontaneously. (Inconcl.) [**cf.** RADIESTHESIA, RADIONICS]

E.R.A.—abbr. the ELECTRONIC RADIATION OF ABRAMS (1900-1923); a black box with dials that was capable of diagnosing and prescribing for one's illness, from a blood sample; invented by Dr. Albert Abrams, see BLACK BOX CONCEPT. [**cf.** PSYCHIC HEALING, RADIONICS]

EA—1. (Mesopotamia) a god in charge of the cedar tree and the *oracle* of the tree which revealed psychic information to the public; his name is believed to be nature-carved into the core of the tree. [**cf.** BOTANE, TREE] 2. (Babylonia) one of three deities credited with the invention of magic; god of wisdom; depicted as the man from clay. **Syn.** ENKI, ORACLE, WISDOM.

EAGLE—1. (Egypt) highly honored bird in many cultures connected with psychism, as far back as records were kept; considered to be a deity; linked psychically with the invisible powers of the sky, sun, and the etheric world in general; 2. (Native American) belief that energy flows from Totality through the eagle; eagle frequently acts as an etheric world guide, giving a person psychic information and guidance; power that emanates from its body, feathers, and claws is held sacred and used for special purposes. [**cf.** ANPSI, COYOTE, DEER, DOVES]

EAR-RING—a pendant or amulet worn in the ears, by both sexes; amulet has the vibrational frequency which prevents evil entities from entering the ear bringing disease; belief: diseases enter the ear by evil etheric world entities. [**cf.** AMULET ENERGIZING, KACHINA DOLL, GARNETS, SCARAB]

EARTH—(esoteric) 1. a vibrational frequency forming a solid *quality*, which mankind calls earth; held together by mankind's thought energy; made of the primary elements needed for human existence, and their manipulation, for learning certain evolutionary lessons; 2. has its special function in the solar system, being the lowest manifestation; 3. the fourth globe in the planetary chain; 4. passive, negative-feminine .polarity, with the sun as its opposite pole; 5. has a musical keynote of *F* in relationship to music of the cosmos; it's harmonical chord becomes visible as green; 6. a living entity comparable to humans; has an etheric double and an astral body that interpenetrates from the core outward; has ethereal akashic records that have been recording and working themselves out since earth began; 7. currently; earth is cleansing itself as it manifests through a great evolutionary transformational process. [**cf.** EVOLUTION, GROUP SOULS, LAW OF FORM Appendix 7]

EARTH CHAKRAS—huge, concentrated fields of energy and intelligence hovering close to the earth, absorbing the spirit in the air and transmuting it into material energy, to be utilized by the earth; functions in a fashion similar to the function of the chakras for the human body, e.g., area around Glastonbury in southeastern England. [**cf.** ETHERIC DOUBLE EARTH, ELECTROMAGNETIC ENERGY]

EARTH COSMIC SOUND—the noise made by the world as it rotates in the solar system; heard by the clairaudient ear, as a noise like the crumbling of a mountain. [**cf.** CLAIRAUDIENCE, MUSIC OF THE SPHERES]

EARTH EVOLUTION—the cyclic pattern of the continual change, and growth of our world globe, working to purify and perfect itself; includes all animate and inanimate things that are a part of the earth; motivated by the earth seed that is unfolding from within, out. [**cf.** LAW OF EVOLUTION Appendix 7, MONAD]

EARTH FAIRIES—a general term used to include all nature spirits on the surface of the earth, and underground, which developed through etheric emanations of the earth; main classifications: 1. tree; 2. garden; 3. wood; 4. rock. (Inconcl.) [**cf.** NATURE SPIRITS Appendix 3]

EARTH MAGNETIC HEALING—to use the magnetism that involuntarily enters the palm of the left hand and will it to be directed out of the right palm,

185

right eye, or right hip toward the patients congested area; this in turn helps to balance the patient's body chemistry so the body can heal itself; see MAGNETIC HEALING. (Inconcl.) [cf. CURATIVE EDUCATION, HEALING, GAUSS MAGNETICS]

EARTH MAGNETISM—an invisible ethereal fluid, interpenetrating the nervous system of the physical body, carrying magnetism; a universal substance vital to life; involuntarily enters the left palm, runs through the body, and exits from the right foot; subject to the law of thought and can be voluntarily directed to exit the right palm and used in healing and psychic skills. [cf. HEALING, EARTH MAGNETIC HEALING, PSYCHIC HEALING]

EARTH MEMORY—theory: located within one of the earth's auras are the records of all the happenings, discoveries, wars, births, thoughts, and attitudes, etc., of the people from all its civilizations, etc., recorded from the beginning of earth's formation; these past experiences contribute to the earth's experiences now. **Syn.** EARTH'S AKASHIC RECORDS. [cf. REINCARNATION, KARMA, MENTAL-REFLECTING-ETHER]

EARTH MOTHER—1. an etheric world angel, manifesting as a female, who personifies the fertility of the earth, and can be called upon for matters of this nature. [cf. ANGEL HIERARCHY, GUIDES] 2. (Native American) see PLANET EARTH; 3. see THIRD DIMENSION.

EARTH PLANE—the first and the most dense of all seven planes of matter; reveals itself in three dimensions; slowest of all vibrational frequencies; contains all the components of the other six planes as they interpenetrate earth plane, which are solids, liquids, gases, ether, super-ether, sub-atomic, and atomic. [cf. BODIES AND PLANES Appendix 5]

EARTH SPIRIT—1. belief that the earth has the properties that can help psychism and healing, when the body comes in contact with it; e.g., placing a newborn baby on the ground, to absorb the earth energies; walking barefoot in the morning dew, for balanced energies. (Inconcl.) [cf. EARTH-BREATHING, MOON PHASES] 2. a highly intelligent, invisible, formless, powerful energy force working with the etheric blueprints of all nature on earth; capable of forming into a tiny person with differing characteristics, to communicate with mankind. **Syn.** NATURE SPIRIT, FAIRIE.

EARTH TELEPATHY—see MENTAL TELEPATHY.

EARTH'S ELECTRICAL FIELD—an energy surrounding the planet, which shifts gears twice a day, as it changes its cyclic pattern of rest and activity; felt within one's physical body by some people; e.g., becoming sleepy at 3:00 P.M. and waking up at 3:00 A.M. (Inconcl.) [cf. CYCLES, COSMIC CLOCK, CIRCADIAN HALF-WAVES, HIGHS AND LOWS]

EARTH'S ELECTROSTATIC FIELD—a high voltage electrical field surrounding the earth, extending from the ionsphere to the surface; (esoteric) believed to contain the reflected-picture-gallery of world happenings, from the beginning of time; miniscule pictures of every event of earth, recorded and played back as earth karma; can be perceived clairvoyantly at times. (Inconcl.) **Syn.** MENTAL-REFLECTING-ETHER. [cf. EARTH MEMORY, REINCARNATION, ASTRAL PICTURE GALLERY]

EARTH'S ETHERIC DOUBLE—see ETHERIC DOUBLE/EARTH.

EARTH-BIOLOGY PLANE—the virbrational frequency making third-dimensional matter, and all other parts that pertain to its growth, and structure. [cf. BODIES AND PLANES Appendix 5, SECOND DIMENSION, FOURTH DIMENSION]

EARTH-BREATHING—the pulsation and rhythmic pattern of the earth that changes in the morning, and again in the evening; performs like a living organism having definite similar vibrational frequencies that correspond to human alpha, beta, theta, and delta brain waves. (Inconcl.) **Syn.** DOUBLE WAVE. [cf. LAW OF PERSONIFICATION Appendix 7, RADIESTHETIC SENSE]

EARTHBOUND ENTITIES—deceased human beings that inhabit the etheric world in a lower astral body; hover close to the earth plane, instead of going on into their new expression of life; make their presence known in various ways (sometimes unpleasantly); reasons why soul-minds choose to stay close to earth: 1. the deceased person does not realize they are dead, and tries to live with their family, unaware that he or she cannot be seen; 2. earthly habits and desires are so solidified in their subconscious mind that he or she tries to relive the same pleasures of earth and haunts earth people who have the pleasures they are trying to relive; 3. earth person or persons continue to mourn and these emotional mourning thought patterns hold the deceased person to earth. (Inconcl.) [cf. PSYCHIC DRIFTERS, DENSITY, SPECTER, GHOST, HAUNTING]

EARTHBOUND PHANTOM CARS—automobiles and trucks that are seen on the highway and appear as real as other cars, but have no drivers; sometimes appearing and disappearing very easily. [cf. EARTH-BOUND ENTITIES, GHOSTS]

EARTHIAN—see EARTHLING.

EARTHLING—a soul-mind enveloped in a physical body, living in the earth plane; belongs to the human being kingdom. **Syn.** EARTHIAN. [cf. HUMAN BEING, KINGDOM]

EARTHQUAKE FORECASTERS—animals that predict earthquakes; research shows that cockroaches, dogs, goldfish, and cats change their behavior radically just before an earthquake; this behavior is exhibited only at the time of earthquakes, making it a true forecaster. [cf. ANPSI Appendix 2]

EAST—(esoteric) the east point of the compass is symbolic of *unity*; by facing east: 1. one turns toward the light, which brings psychic illumination more easily; 2. one can invoke the Oriens, the ruling etheric world helpers of the east; 3. (under a pyramid) one can help the body to heal or one can bring on a meditative state. [cf. MAGIC CIRCLE, WITHERSHINS]

EASTER EXTRAS—pictures taken during the Easter season, are known to show *extras* on the developed print (in the form of religious symbols), which were not in the area where the picture was taken; e.g., a crucifix, a biblical face, a cross. (Inconcl.) [cf. PSYCHIC PHOTOGRAPHY, EXTRAS]

EASTERN PHILOSOPHY—the term has come to mean any of the disciplines in the Eastern world, such as Hinduism, Buddhism, Yoga, Confucianism, Vedanta, and Taoism, all seem to have similar threads, as opposed to Western philosophy.

EASTERN ROSARY—a string of 108 beads, used in meditations, for counting the number of times the mantra is said. **Syn.** PRAYER BEADS. [cf. DOING JAPA, MANTRA]

EATER OF HEARTS—(Egypt, Tibet) see DWELLER ON THE THRESHOLD.

EATING COMPANIONS—(Huna) an etheric world entity that invisibly attaches itself to an earthling; capable of drawing the vital life force from the earthling, without the victim's knowledge of what is making his or her weak and ill. [cf. OBSESSION,

SECONDARY PERSONALITY, VAMPIRE, PSYCHIC TRANSFER]

EATING MINDFULLY—(Zen, Hinduism) eating a meal in silence with reverence, and concentrating on the chewing and eating itself. [cf. MEDITATION, QUIET ATTENTIVENESS, TEA]

EC—prefix meaning "out of."

ECHO—1. (acupuncture) vibration or impulse stimulated by the inserted needle and transmitted along the meridian line to the other end of the line; detectable to both the acupuncturist and patient. [cf. ACUPUNCTURE, ACUPRESSURE, MERIDIAN LINES] 2. (ufology) infinitesimal portion of energy, reflected back from the electromagnetic microwave energy sent by the radar, announcing an energy mass in the atmosphere. **Syn.** BLIP. [cf. RADAR ANGELS, UFO RADIATION]

ECK—the audible life current; the Holy Spirt, the essence of God; see TOTALITY, PSYCHIC ENERGY.

ECK MASTER—one who believes themselves to be born to teach Eckankar; executes soul travel to the higher planes, and administers help to eckankar members who call upon him or her. [cf. MENTAL PROJECTION]

ECKANKAR—a discipline that teaches the ancient science of mental projection, termed soul travel; student is taken by steps through the lower etheric states of consciousness into the ecstatic states to experience an awareness of the religious experience of being; (do not confuse with ASTRAL PROJECTION). [cf. MENTAL PROJECTION Appendix 2]

ECSTASY—(*ec,* "out of, from") 1. (mediumship) pleasurable, religious, meaningful trance state brought on by scientific prayer; the conscious mind exits so the etheric world entity can enter the body of the medium, and carry on the beautiful work they came for; capable of using this in preaching, or other occupational services. **Syn.** PERSONIFICATION. 2. a spontaneous cosmic attunement occuring in deep prayer, in church, or some other fulfilling situation, whereby the ecstatic person consciously experiences a variety of thoughts, feelings, visions, and a sense of union with the benign cosmic power; usually accompanied by a feeling of loss of contact with surroundings; 3. (meditation) a feeling of union with the deity through a transcending of the mind and body during meditation; (do not confuse with HYSTERIA TRANCE). **Syn.** RAPTURE, BLISS.

[**cf.** EMOTIONAL PSI, SUPERCONSCIOUS MIND, ECSTATIC MEDIUM, TRANSCENDING]

ECSTAT—see PSYCHIC.

ECSTATIC—a psychic with universal attunement abilities who takes astral flights to other planets or to the subterranean world in the density; has tremendous physical psychic skills; also spelled exstatic. **Sim.** SHAMAN, PSYCHOPOMP. [**cf.** MOMENTARY ABILITY]

ECSTATIC MEDIUM—one who has earned the privilege to blend with an etheric world intelligence of an extremely high level of consciousness; intelligence brings knowledge, healings, and physical phenomena beyond normal comprehension. [**cf.** ECSTASY, TRANCE MEDIUMSHIP, PERSONIFICATION]

ECSTATIC VISION—(Jewish) to perceive a tremendous *light* while in a meditative state; the feeling of being one with the light and the divine glory of God. [**cf.** PERFECTNESS, LIGHT]

ECTENIC FORCE—coined by Thury: (Greek *ekteneie*, "extended"); the emission of psychic power from the psychic's body, directed by his or her will, to perform feats that defy natural laws; phenomena of parapsychology. [**cf.** PSYCHIC ENERGY]

ECTOPLASM—coined by Charles Richet, a Frenchman, (Greek *ectos* and *plasmos*, "exteriorized substance"); a living material, full of intelligence and energy, capable of generating and directing its own power, which can be willed to exude from the orifices and cells of the medium and sitters; 1. attached to the medium by etheric tenuous threads but still being a part of him or her; used by the etheric world intelligences to perform physical phenomena; interiorized into the medium's body when the seance is over; 2. characteristics of ectoplasm vary with the different mediums; i.e., can be visible or invisible, intangible or tangible, and combinations of same; takes the form of gas, liquid, solid, or more commonly, an ethereal smoke that is stringy, like muslin or paste jelly; sensitive to light (except infrared); appears grey, white, or black; 3. studied by French scientists when used to materialize etheric world intelligences in human form; found to contain albumoid matter and fatty matter (same as human cells, except for sugar and starch); smells similiar to ozone; capable being weighed and measured; coming from advanced mediums, it contains white blood cells, calcium phosphate,

membraneous cell detritus, and nitrogen; 4. analyzed by Massachusett's Institute of Technology and found to contain properties of: sodium, potassium, water, chlorine, albumen, epithelial cells, and alive red blood corpuscles; 5. sometimes takes the form of long rods; extends from the medium or hovers close by; is manipulated to form a replica of a human, in full or in part, or (in lesser degrees), to raise a trumpet, or knock on walls, etc,; 6. takes from one sitting to twenty years for a medium to develop the ability to exude ectoplasm necessary for the desired weekly seance phenomenon; sessions with the basic same sitters are necessary. (Inconcl.) **Syn.** QUASI-PHYSICAL, TELEPLASM. [**cf.** MEDIUMSHIP, MATERIALIZATION Appendix 2, PLASMOLOGY]

ECTOPLASM ENERGY—a lower form of prana; see VITAL LIFE FORCE. (Inconcl.)

ECTOPLASM MATERIALIZATION—to bring about, at will, a manifestation of a deceased person, in whole or in part, in a seance setting, using ectoplasm; visible to the physical eye under infrared lighting; ectoplasm that exudes from the medium's body and sitters (in lesser degrees) is utilized by the etheric world intelligence and the person manifesting; medium is in deep trance; accomplished in progressive steps over a period of years; begins with partial materialization, then etherealization, and finally full materialization. [**cf.** CABINET, ECTOPLASM, ETHEREALIZATION, ECTOPLASMIC MATERIALISTIC FORMS, DESIRED-CONTROL, FULL MATERIALIZATION]

ECTOPLASM PHANTOM—the etheric world intelligence who blends with the medium and uses his or her ectoplasm to make a life form to represent themselves; occurs in a seance. **Syn.** SPIRIT PERSONALITY. [**cf.** ECTOPLASM MATERIALIZATION Appendix 2]

ECTOPLASM PSYCHIC SURGERY—a type of operation, performed by former doctors now in the etheric world, which is totally invisible to the patient; they work through an earthling, using her or his arms and hands to go through maneuvers above the patient's body with unbelievable swiftness; patient lies on a bed or board, as a psychological necessity to let him or her know they are having an operation; many operations are performed in one evening as they are completed in minutes; body is not opened but healed through a change made in the etheric double. [**cf.** PSYCHIC SURGERY, MEDIUMSHIP HEALING Appendix 2]

ECTOPLASM TELEKINESIS—(seance) to manipulate physical matter without using normal physical means but by using one's ectoplasm and the blending of an etheric world intelligence; living organisms and inanimate articles are altered in size, shape, moved in space, or changed in vibrational frequency; ectoplasm emanating from the medium and sitters is used by the intelligence; medium is in a semi or deep trance state; occurs in a seance after repeated sessions of the same sitters with this intent; always desired-control and prearranged between the medium and intelligence; e.g., a candy dish could levitate and move across the room; (do not confuse with PSYCHOKINESIS, in which mind power is used instead of etheric world aid); see TELEKINESIS PSYCHISM. [**cf.** DESIRED-CONTROL, GUIDE, SEANCE, LEVITATION, TELEPORTATION]

ECTOPLASMIC CORD—an ethereal solidified rod or cord of ectoplasm in physical phenomena sessions that seems to be the main connection of the manifestation to the medium; brings injury to the medium if handled and death if severed; cord is needed by the medium to suck the ectoplasm back into her or his body when seance is over. (Inconcl.) **Syn.** FLUIDIC LINK. [**cf.** SINKS INTO THE FLOOR, VAPOR ECTOPLASM, ECTOPLASMIC WISPS]

ECTOPLASMIC DEMATERIALIZATION—when the programmed-time for the plasmic form is over, the ectoplasm must be taken back into the medium's body; occurs in different ways: 1. the cord makes a few movements, and the form (whether in part or whole) SINKS INTO THE FLOOR and disappears; 2. begins with a rumbling sound and the form melts gradually within the piercing light which brought it; first the legs and feet vanish, then the torso and head (like a scroll being rolled up) until nothing remains but the light, and that soon fades; 3. the ectoplasm is sucked back into the orfices of the medium, with a loud swish; the medium gradually comes out of the deep trance state, feeling fine and very hungry. [**cf.** TANGIBLE APPARITION, FULL MATERIALIZATION, CABINET, VAPOR ECTOPLASM, PRESEANCE PHENOMENON]

ECTOPLASMIC FLOW—used to describe ectoplasm because it appears to always be active and alive coming from the medium; when withdrawn into the medium's body, it is still very active, sometimes snapping with vigor, as the seance is over. [**cf.** MATERIALIZATION Appendix 2]

ECTOPLASMIC HAND—a human hand produced out of the medium's ectoplasm, during a material-ization seance; when fingerprints were tested, they were found to be those of the deceased person whose hand was materialized. [**cf.** ECTOPLASMIC WISPS, PUTTY IMPRESSIONS, PSYCHIC IMPRINTS]

ECTOPLASMIC MATERIALIZATION FORMS—manifestations within the ectoplasm, in a materialization seance; varies in density, shape, size, color, and texture according to the stage of development of the medium, and the ability of the etheric world personality coming through; 1. visible in infrared lighting or clairvoyant vision; appears gossamer in quality or close to a third-dimensional vibration; 2. utilizes the ectoplasm exuding in large quantities from the medium and lesser quantities from the sitters; attached to the medium at all times by the ectoplasmic cord; medium is sensitive to the handling of the forms by the sitters and becomes ill or traumatically shocked if handled; 3. when forms are dense enough for the sitters to touch, they feel like a spider web, or stiff and elastic; forms last from a few minutes to two hours; 4. shows itself as: (a) partial sections of an etheric world entity's body; i.e., wisps of hair, eyes, arms, or hands, (capable of intelligent movements); or a whole face without a body; all varying in size (from tiny to giant), density and shape (from flat, raised on one side, to normal); gives a feeling of a *living presence.* (b) a whole personality from the etheric world (miniature to giant in size); a deceased person known to sitters or medium, an entity completely foreign to all, or the guide of the medium; capable or incapable of speech; varying in characteristics as to: weight, heartbeat, and breathing; features and mannerisms can reflect the medium; gives a feeling of a *living presence.* (c) a replica of the medium himself, in part or in whole; can be fully dressed as the one in the CABINET; shows mannerisms of medium; medium is visibly still in the cabinet. (Inconcl.) [**cf.** SPIRIT PERSONALITY, PSEUDORODS, SINKS INTO THE FLOOR]

ECTOPLASMIC STRUCTURES—(seance) ectoplasm in the form of bars, ribbons, or other shapes necessary to perform the physical phenomena intended; extended from the medium to the object that is to be manipulated and become densified as they are used to raise the trumpet, the table, etc.; forms can be seen in the blacked-out room in infrared lighting. [**cf.** TRUMPET, TABLE-TIPPING, LEVITATION]

ECTOPLASMIC WISPS—(materialization) densified ectoplasm making parts of a human body in a

189

materialization seance; ectoplasm colonizes into clouds that gradually form hair, eyes, head, or hands of the etheric world personality that will materialize full blown eventually; hover close to medium or extend out into circle; parts of body may materialize many sessions before the etheric entity and medium accomplish the full body form. [cf. PSYCHIC NAVAL CORD, PARTIAL MATERIALIZATION, PARAFFIN MOLDS]

ECTOPLASY—see ECTOPLASM.

EDB—abbr. for EXTRADIMENSIONAL BEING; see ETHERIC WORLD INTELLIGENCE.

EDDA—(Germany, Scandinavia) sacred, profound literature written by a famous mystic, Meister Eckhart (c. 1260-c. 1328); gives full instructions on how to become skilled in psychism.

EDDY CURRENT—a whirling electric force, created around the magnetic current that enters the body in magnetic healing; believed to ionize the protoplasm in the body. (Inconcl.) [cf. MENTAL PSYCHIC HEALING, MAGNETIC HEALING Appendix 2]

EDGE OF THE UNKNOWN—an imaginary line between the physical world and etheric world, measured by feelings and two different states of consciousness. **Syn.** BORDERLAND, ACROSS THE THRESHOLD. [cf. ASTRAL WORLD, VEIL]

EDUCATED CONSCIOUSNESS—see MENTAL MIND.

EDUCATED GUESS—see CLAIRSENTIENCE, and HUNCH.

EDUCATION—(esoteric) a process of bringing to the surface that which potentially exists; a manner of enhancing intelligence through actual experience, through schooling, or through books and lectures, etc.; provides the mind with an abundance of material to work with; education cannot give the mind the aptitude necessary for using the material it has acquired, intelligence alone does that. [cf. ACTUALIZATION, ART OF LIVING, WISDOM]

EEG—abbr. for ELECTROENCEPHALOGRAPH; a biofeedback instrument made to detect and amplify the electrical impulses which the human brain is constantly emitting; these impulses vary with one's thoughts and feelings; some measure up to 1/200,000 of a volt; records brain activity from precise sections of the brain by attaching three electrodes to the head; the instrument amplifies brain impulses onto a graph, into audible sound, or into colored lights; information is recorded (as to states of consciousness, emotional states, and brain wave cycles) in a tangible form, making the study of brain activity possible. [cf. BIOFEEDBACK TRAINING, ARTIFACTS, ELECTRODES, BRAIN WAVE RHYTHM, TOPSY]

EEG MIND-MIRROR—invented by C. Maxwell Cade and Nona Coxhead; a sophisticated electroencephalograph designed to give an almost immediate display of the brain wave activity coming from both hemispheres of the brain, simultaneously; capable of reading brain wave patterns from a psychic during paranormal communication and from a healer who is emitting a healing energy; these new states of consciousness are temporarily named by Cade and Coxhead, the *fifth* and *seventh* states. [cf. SPLIT BRAIN Appendix 5]

EFFERENT SCHIZONEUROSIS—(clinical) "breaks" in the response between the central process and the motor response of body and mind, resulting in action upon the environment; known as *telepathy* from the agent, or *poltergeistry*; e.g., a book falling off the shelf when the agent is in the room, without any conscious concentration on this activity from him or her. [cf. POLTERGEISTERY, TELEPATHY, PSYCHOKINESIS]

EFFUVIUM—see ECTOPLASM.

EGG OF IMMORTALITY—(Egypt) the optic thalamus located in the third-eye area in the human head which is necessary for physical and psychic vision; this was known by Egyptians, who gave it symbolic credance; symbol is shaped like an egg, making it emblematic of immortality; when cross-sectioned, it is shaped like a beetle and used to represent the sacred beetle. **Syn.** CRYSTAL LAMP, LIGHT OF THE WORLD, OPEN-EYE. [cf. THIRD-EYE AREA Appendix 5]

EGGS—(ancient) have the vibrational frequency to be used for divination purposes and fertility potency; psychic information is received from the formation of the raw egg white, as it is poured out of the shell. [cf. PHILOSOPHER'S EGG, POINT OF FOCUS, Appendix 6, MANTIC ART]

EGO—(esoteric) 1. representative of the combination of the conscious and subconscious mind; an intangible mechanism, within a human, that stimulates his or her mannerisms and characteristics, into outer actions and reactions under life conditions; established from all one's past incarnation experiences, this incarnation's past experiences, and one's attitude toward these experiences; an individual takes this ego with him or her in other planes of expression, building and changing it as they go; (Vedic) two kinds of ego working together: **(a)** the *I* consciousness, the waking consciousness that says *me* this and *me* that; **(b)** *I*, the subconscious mind that carries the seed of perfection, the hidden awareness striving to better one's self. **Syn.** BELIEF SYSTEM. **2.** (conscious mind) **(a)** (Latin) the *I* awareness of self; a person recognizing themselves as separate from the total, *I am I*; **(b)** (Seth) that portion of waking consciousness that feels an inner identity with all-there-is; deals with physical manipulation, sometimes refusing to focus directly on the inner identity; **(c)** (Cosmic Fire) the thinking entity, the self-conscious identity is in essence a *Truth Love-Wisdom*, but manifests primarily as intelligent consciousness. **Syn.** INDIVIDUALITY. **(d)** (Carl Jung) the surface level of the psyche where analysis take place; **(e)** (Sigmund Freud) one of the three aspects of the total personality which administers daily interactions of the personality with the environment. [**cf.** ID, SUPEREGO] **3.** (subconscious mind) **(a)** (AMORC) the *Subconscious Self*, as separate from the *Objective Self*, **(b)** (Buddhism) the mind of a human felt to already contain the knowledge of the great universal mind. **Syn.** MONAD. [**cf.** CONSCIOUSNESS, SUBCONSCIOUS MIND, MONADOLOGY]

EGO METAPROGRAMMING—(brainwashing) a belief in an untruth, or an action to an untrue belief (according to one's belief system), forced into the subconscious mind, without the victim's consent or knowledge of this happening. [**cf.** BRAINWASHING, BRAIN, SUBCONSCIOIUS MIND, DESTRUCTIVE-BRAINWASHING CULT]

EGO PSYCHOLOGY—philosophies and disciplines that pertain to the growth of the whole person: soul-mind, body, and mental mind. [**cf.** CONSCIOUSNESS AWARENESS MOVEMENT, CURATIVE EDUCATION, HOLISTIC HEALTH]

EGO-DESTRUCTION—to destroy one's inner desire to grow and advance; to dull one's motivation mechanism; the loss of one's identity and personality; one no longer thinks in terms of personal health and growth but can only think of one's self as part of an organization, blending in with the movements of the organization; one loses all sense of self and experiences identity only through that of the group; occurs in the destructive-brainwashing cults.

[**cf.** DESTRUCTIVE-BRAINWASHING CULT Appendix 5]

EGO-ID—(Sigmund Freud) the simultaneous reaction of the ego and id in a necessary relationship; the conscious mind thinks and reasons out the process of the new experience with mental activity; the subconscious mind's memory and instinct surfaces to help the decision. [**cf.** SUBCONSCIOUS MIND, SOUL-MIND, MENTAL MIND]

EGO-KILLING PRACTICE—(Zen) (doing Zen meditation); to change one's attitude toward civilization, ending a materialistically oriented personality by using daily discipline regarding meditation. [**cf.** JUST SITTING, THE ART OF TEA, CHECKER]

EGO-SPLITTING—see ASTRAL PROJECTION.

EGO-STRENGTHENING—(hypnosis) to reinforce the hypnotherapeutic suggestion in the subject's subconscious mind by repeating words or praise and encouragement after the suggestion is given; a beneficial part of the therapy because the subconscious mind responds favorably to compliments; i.e., "you, and your friends, will notice the change in you and be pleased." [**cf.** HYPNOTHERAPY, BELIEF SYSTEM, AURA]

EGOIC—1. common usage: SOUL-MIND; 2. see EGO.

EGYPTIAN BOOK OF THE DEAD—translated by E. A. Wallis Budge; the principle reference to the sacred Egyptian art of passing an initiation, for the individual making his or her transition into the etheric world; originally written over 5,000 years ago in hieroglyphic text on papyrus with interline transliteration and word-for-word translation of the religious views of the people; proclaims the resurrection of a spiritual body and immortality of a soul; gives instructions for preserving the dead body, teaching what to expect beyond the grave, and describes how one's soul-mind goes unhindered through the passage to the Godhead. [**cf.** DEATH SCIENCE Appendix 2]

EGYPTIAN GODS AND GODDESSES—those who have earned the rank from their many earth and ethereal incarnations, that allows them to express specific cosmic functions in the etheric world; e.g., in charge of birth maturation, assimilation, death, evacuation, etc. [**cf.** ANGEL KINGDOM, FIFTH DIMENSION]

EGYPTIAN MYSTERY SCHOOLS—a place where only royalty and priests could attend, to learn advanced knowledge, and its practice; studies were related to the etheric world, growth of the soul-mind, and the use of psychic art as a tool for this progression.

EGYPTIAN TEMPLE DANCERS—a group of dance artists who perform so both the dancers and the audience attain a higher level of consciousness; accomplished by repeated rhythmic movements to special music choreographed to alter one's state of consciousness. [cf. LIGHT TRANCE, MOVEMENT-FOR-ALTERED-CONSCIOUSNESS, ABSTRACT DANCING, ALPHA STATE OF CONSCIOUSNESS]

EGYPTIAN YOGA—the basic teaching, in various techniques, for breathing in the ga-llama (vital life force) so necessary for a healthy existence. [cf. VITAL LIFE FORCE, BREATHING]

EIDETIC—(Greek *eidos,* "form") pertains to visual inner-mind pictures which are retained in the memory bank and readily recalled clairvoyantly with vivid detail and accuracy. [cf. THOUGHTS, NON-THOUGHT, PSYCHISM]

EIDETIC BIOFEEDBACK—1. to psychically see visions from one's past activity, from a previous life or in this life during biofeedback training; believed to spring from the collective unconscious; easily recalled later; 2. to psychically tune into one's visceral nervous system and observe how it reacts to worldly activity and outside stimuli; helps the subject regain better control over his or her life. [cf. BIOFEEDBACK TRAINING Appendix 5]

EIDETIC IMAGE—an intense memory image of an object or scene once perceived, or lived, so vivid as to be almost photographic in nature; seen *within* the mind as though still before the eyes. [cf. CLAIRVOYANCE, IMAGERY, DAYDREAMING Appendix 4]

EIDETIC LANGUAGE—1. psychic information in the form of inner-mind pictures (scenes, colors, or people), as opposed to receiving impressions or hearing utterances. [cf. VISIONARY, SUBJECTIVE IMAGES] 2. (biofeedback training) clairvoyant pictures seen within the mind or in front of one, that are not intentionally brought to one's awareness, while HOOKED-UP to a biofeedback instrument. [cf. BIOFEEDBACK TRAINING, COLLECTIVE UNCONSCIOUS, REINCARNATION]

EIDETIKERS—highly suggestible people, whose imaginative, inner visual activity is more fluid, and more vivid and clear in form than others, detected in imagery exercises. (Inconcl.) [cf. IMAGERY, FANTASY, DAYDREAMING, NATURAL SYMBOLS]

EIDOLA—1. the astral shell of a deceased person, so solidified from the materialistic thoughts of earth experiences, that it keeps the human form, and hovers over the earth plane, wanting to relive physical experiences; see ASTRAL SHELL. [cf. HAUNTING, APPARITION] 2. (Plato) forms in the mind.

EIDOLON—1. (B.C., early A.D.) an image of a person in a psychic vision or dream portraying no one in particular; 2. (Greece) a pale copy of a human when on earth, perceived clairvoyantly as: an apparition, a shadow, a shade or an astral shell. (Inconcl.) [cf. APPARITION, DREAM IMAGES, SHADE]

EIDOLONGIC KINESIS—1. the outward movement of the phantom body, in an astral projection; 2. the movement of the invisible poltergeist. [cf. GHOST, ASTRAL PROJECTION, POLTERGEIST]

EIDOLONICS—the study of the behavior of visual images in mental activity: concerning physiological, psychological, and parapsychological aspects. [cf. BRAIN Appendix 5, FANTASY Appendix 4, HALLUCINATION, LUMINOUS PHENOMENA]

EIDOPHONE—an instrument built with a taut drumlike surface; when sand is placed upon the surface and sounds are tapped on it, the sand will produce geometrical designs according to the tone and volume of the sound vibrations. [cf. CLAIRAUDIENCE Appendix 2, INVISIBLE DRUM, OBJECTIVE CLAIRAUDIENCE, UNHEARD MELODIES]

EIGHT—(esoteric) 1. vibration of this number relates to involvment in material matters for power and money; emblematic of mankind, upon finding his or her soul-mind, must turn back to earth life, and learn to combine power, organization and constructive leadership backed by spiritual inspiration; 2. (numerology life cycle) the most powerful of all the numbers; symbolized by both strength and success, war and destruction; the planetary link is Mars. [cf. NUMBER POWER, SEVEN, TWELVE]

EIGHTH SPHERE—(esoteric) a plane between the earth and the moon. [cf. BODIES AND PLANES Appendix 5, SEVENTH PLANE, MENTAL PLANE]

EKA-KSANA—(Buddhism) an instantaneous surge of illumination; a state of feeling one with the eternal presence, happening as quickly as a flash of lightning. [cf. KSANA, MOTIONLESSNESS]

EL—1. (Canaanite) a supreme deity; depicted as a young and vigorous male, armed with an axe and spear, symbolizing lightning; 2. (Herbrew) God; 3. soul-mind of a deceased person.

ELAN VITAL—coined by Henri Bergson (1920) see VITAL LIFE FORCE.

ELDER BROTHERS—men, of earth race, who are from a very high plane in the etheric world and who have chosen to incarnate for no other purpose but to serve mankind; will have no personal life of their own; excellent psychics. [**cf.** WHITE BROTHERHOOD]

ELDER TREE—(esoteric) has the vibrational frequency to protect humans against evil; wherever an elder tree grows, witches are powerless; these trees are planted in the entrances, and around the home for protection. [**cf.** BOTANE Appendix 2, PLANT ENERGIES, SENSATION CONSCIOUSNESS]

ELECTION—(shamanism) the process of receiving instructions in psychism and healing techniques by first experiencing torture, from an extreme accident or illness, and then proving one's ability to use these new skills in healing oneself. [**cf.** INITIATORY SICKNESS, RESURRECTION, SHAMANSHIP INSTRUCTIONS]

ELECTRIC ACTUALITY—(esoteric) the recording of one's thoughts, attitudes and experiences within the atoms of the body, taken from the dream and awake state; this recording surfaces and reacts in one's life style; makes each man or woman unique, according to their own chosing, as opposed to being a victim of circumstances. [**cf.** AKASHIC RECORD, ATOMS, LAW OF THOUGHT Appendix 7]

ELECTRIC AURA—see AURA.

ELECTRIC BODY—see ETHERIC DOUBLE.

ELECTRIC CHAIR EFFECT—a physical handicap that affects the subject sitting in the biofeedback chair because of the many electrodes attached to her or him; this hinders their learning self-regulation during the session. [**cf.** ELECTROSTATIC SENSITIVITY, FOCUSED ATTENTION]

ELECTRIC CLAIRAUDIENCE—to bring voices through a tape recorder, either from outer space, or from the etheric world. **Syn.** TAPED VOICE PHENOMENON. [**cf.** ELECTRIC VOICES Appendix 2]

ELECTRIC ETHER—an invisible, subtle agent which flows through the bloodstream. (Inconcl.) **Syn.** PHYSICAL ETHER. [**cf.** KARMA, ETHER, MENTAL-REFLECTING-ETHER, HEART]

ELECTRIC FABRIC—(biofeedback training) psychic visions that appear to the subject hooked-up to a biofeedback instrument, when in a very relaxed state of consciousness. **Syn.** VISION. [**cf.** EEG, EMG, ALPHA STATE OF CONSCIOUSNESS]

ELECTRIC FIELDS—see AURA.

ELECTRIC FLUID—an element within universal substance that is absorbed by all humans and nonhumans, to sustain life. (Inconcl.) **Syn.** VITAL PRINCIPLE, MAGNETIC FLUID, NERVE FLUID.

ELECTRIC GIRLS—(documented case) two human beings who were born with an over abundance of electricity within their bodies. They could sit at opposite poles and do things known to the laws of electricity; e.g., make sparks crackle from their fingertips, give electrical energy as if they were a battery, and if anyone touched them they would receive an electric shock. [**cf.** EATING COMPANIONS, GHOST SHIP, FIRES WITH BOUNDARIES]

ELECTRIC MAGNETIC ENERGY—concentrated power in each atom, lying between the central nucleus and its surrounding electrons; see ETHERIC DOUBLE. [**cf.** VIBRATIONS Appendix 5, ATOMS, MATTER]

ELECTRIC MAGNETIC MATRIX—see AURA.

ELECTRIC PERSON—an individual who is endowed with an abundance of natural electricity and walks around like an open circuit; one cannot touch him or her without getting an electrical shock; (do not confuse with MAGNETIC FLUID needed to make etheric world contacts). [**cf.** ELECTRIFIED, FLAMES OF DIVINE LOVE, SPIRIT LIGHTS]

ELECTRIC PICTURE RECORDS—(esoteric) miniscule pictures, of all the experiences that a person has ever gone through in their present life and past lives, recorded in the etheric world; have been clairvoyantly perceived by some on their death bed and by some in trance states. (Inconcl.) **Syn.** MENTAL-REFLECTING-ETHER. [**cf.** REINCARNATION, DEATH SCIENCE]

ELECTRIC RHYTHM—(biofeedback training) the patterns of brain impulses that show enough similarity in all people, at various levels of consciousness, to say there is a definite rhythm in consciousness levels; this information provided a scale, that was made for further study, called **scale**

of brain rhythm. [cf. CONSCIOUSNESS ELECTRO-PHYSIOLOGY, SCALE OF BRAIN RHYTHM]

ELECTRIC SKIN RESISTANCE—abbr. ESR: a biofeedback instrument that will measure arousal of emotions from the sweat glands of fingers caused by the polarization of blood flow, as in the fight or flight responses; sweat gland activity is the secondary effect; subject is HOOKED-UP to the instrument by applying two electrodes to fingertips; see GSR. [cf. METABOLIC MONITOR, BIO-STAT]

ELECTRIC STATE—(Kirlian effect) the discharge of radiations from the whole living organism that can be photographed by high frequency cameras. [cf. KIRLIAN EFFECT Appendix 5, AURA]

ELECTRIC VAMPIRISM—to absorb into one's physical body enough voltage from a man-made electrical system to put the apparatus out of commission; rare but possible. [cf. PSYCHIC TRANSFER]

ELECTRICITY—(esoteric) an aspect of energy; natural electricity is the result of radiations from the sun, which runs through the atoms in all the universe's manifestations; artificial electricity can be produced through chemical, and mechanical action. (Inconcl.)

ELECTRIFIED—(esoteric) 1. to become suddenly charged with an exuberant amount of psychic energy while going through an exhilarating psychic experience; shows evidence in the physical condition, such as: the heart racing, mind activity accelerating, physical body feelings of light, heat, cold, tingling sensations along the spine, and other unusual physical sensations; comes from the sixth dimension where the atmosphere is very energizing, and lasts only a short time; 2. a state of super-consciousness, wherein all internal organs remain in a state of suspended animation, charged with cosmic energy; an individual can dispense with sleep while in this state; 3. an intense vibration; the difference between the power which exists as reality in the sixth plane and the use to which it has been put in life in the physical plane; life energy that permeates every form on earth extending from the sixth plane to physical things, animate or inanimate; makes it possible for discarnates to project thoughts of the higher etheric world intelligences into the minds of incarnates, and vice versa. [cf. ENERGY POTENTIAL, HYPERSYN-CHRONIZED WAVES]

ELECTRO—a combining form of electricity.

ELECTRO-OCULAGRAM—abbr. EOG; an instrument that records the movements of the eyeballs while an individual is sleeping; used in dream research laboratories; tiny electrodes are placed around the eyes which record the rapid movement of the eyeballs that occur in the dream state. 9 [cf. NREM, TIME LAPSE PHOTOGRAPHY, REM]

ELECTROAURAGRAM—(Russia) an instrument capable of measuring a neuron, in animals and humans. (Inconcl.)

ELECTROBIOLOGY—the science of the electrical properties of living organisms; the electrical system within, and the electricity emanating out. [cf. KIRLIAN EFFECT, BIO-PLASMA, CORONA, PSYCHISM, BOTANE, ANPSI]

ELECTROBIOLUMINESCENCE—see AURA.

ELECTROCHEMICAL—pertains to chemical changes produced by electricity, and electrical changes produced by chemistry.

ELECTROCULTURE—the use of electrodes and biofeedback instruments for studying the growth and behavior of the plant kingdom. (Inconcl.) [cf. BOTANE, SENSATION CONSCIOUSNESS]

ELECTRODE CREAM—(biofeedback training) a salve applied to the area of the body that is to make contact with the electrodes; makes a more even contact with the biofeedback instrument throughout the training session. [cf. ARTIFACTS, BIOFEEDBACK TRAINING, GSR]

ELECTRODE RETENTION BAND—(biofeedback training) an elastic band that is worn around the head to hold the electrodes to the scalp, when hooked-up to the EEG instrument. [cf. SENSOR, MIND-BODY ART]

ELECTRODE WINDOWS—(biofeedback training) the areas on the scalp that seem most adaptable for electrode placement, to detect the brain activity for biofeedback instruments. [cf. BRAIN PRINTS, BIO-ELECTRIC SIGNS, PERCEPTAL DATA, RED-BEADED ELECTRODES]

ELECTRO-DERMAL RESPONSE—abbr. EDR; a biofeedback instrument that detects mood changes, attitudes, and truths, by measuring the activity of the sympathetic nervous system through the sweat glands in the hands; obtained by attaching the EDR instrument to the skin by tiny electrodes; see GSR. [cf. SUBCONSCIOUS MIND, ELECTRONIC ANALYZ-ER, METABOLIC MONITOR]

ELECTRODES—(biofeedback training) tiny conductors of electricity which are attached to the body in specific places depending upon the biofeedback instrument in use; transmit an electrical flow from the body into a series of amplifiers; amplifiers magnify this electrical flow into signals detectable to the five senses. **Syn.** SENSORS. [**cf.** PRINTOUTS, POLYGRAPH, RECEIVING MODE]

ELECTRODYNAMIC FIELD—coined by H.S. Burr (Yale University) an energy around humans and other objects which creates a force field (like an electrical mold); as the body renews itself, this mold insures that the new tissue takes the proper shape, no matter how often the material is changed. **Syn.** L-FIELD, ETHERIC DOUBLE, HEALTH AURA. [**cf.** AURA Appendix 3]

ELECTRODYNAMIC THEORY—(science) the electromagnetic field, around living tissue, seems to guide and repair the living protoplasm of the organism. [**cf.** KIRLIAN EFFECT, PHANTOM PAINS, ETHERIC DOUBLE]

ELECTROENCEPHALOGRAM—see ELECTROENCEPHALOGRAPH.

ELECTROENCEPHALOGRAPH—abbr. EEG; a biofeedback instrument made to detect and amplify the electrical impulses which the human brain is constantly emitting, varying with thoughts and feelings; some EEGs measure up to 1/200,000 of a volt, and can be recorded from precise sections of the brain; three electrodes are attached to the scalp and these electrodes pick up the impulses of the mind activity, which is then fed into an instrument, where it is amplified onto graph paper, into audible sound, or into colored lights, providing tangible material with which to work and study. [**cf.** BIOFEEDBACK TRAINING Appendix 5, ELECTRODES, EMG, MIND-MIRROR]

ELECTROENCEPHALOGRAPHY SCIENCE—a study of the electrical activity of the brain in all three states of consciousness: awake, sleep, and dream state. [**cf.** SENSITIVITY CONTROL, PRECONSCIOUS LEVEL, EXPECTANCY WAVE, BRAIN ELECTRICAL EVENTS]

ELECTROGRAPHY—(Kirlian effect) (Czechoslovakia) a highly sensitive camera, using high frequency currents, that can photograph (in color to some degree) the electromagnetic emanations coming from any living organism (including humans), or inanimate object that the physical eye cannot see; (do not confuse with psychic photography EXTRAS). (Inconcl.) **Syn.** KIRLIAN PHOTOGRAPHY, CORONA DISCHARGE PHOTOGRAPHY. [**cf.** PRANA, CORONA, ETHERIC DOUBLE]

ELECTROGRAVITATION—(T. Townsend Brown) a new field which studies the behavioral relationship of the combined forces of electricity, magnetism, and gravitation; sometimes relating this to ufology. (Inconcl.) [**cf.** UFOLOGY, QUASARS, PLASMAS]

ELECTROGRAVITIC WAVES—(T. Townsend Brown) a study of gravity, and its control; an energy field in the ethers capable of being transmitted, through concentric layers of electromagnetic and electrostatic shielding, without apparent loss of power; believed to have a relationship to make matter weightless by being linked to a condensor, etc., and be used for planetary travel. (Inconcl.) [**cf.** GRAVITY CONTROL, POSITIVE PRIMARY ENERGY, PHONY STARS]

ELECTROKINETIC—the conversion of electrical energy into mechanical energy, and then converting this to the required task.

ELECTROMAGNET HEALING—a method of connecting a magnet to electricity, and applying it to the diseased area. [**cf.** MAGNET HEALING, POLARITY]

ELECTROMAGNETIC BODY WAVES—the nature of the emanations coming from a person's head, heart and every organ of their body. [**cf.** AURA, BRAIN, RADIATIONS]

ELECTROMAGNETIC CIRCUIT—(esoteric) electricity and magnetism of the planets are connected to the electricity and magnetism in the human body, and this electromagnetic circuit flows through all things, connecting every thing to every other thing; this circuit makes psychism possible. (Inconcl.) [**cf.** BRAIN, PSYCHISM, TOTALITY]

ELECTROMAGNETIC IMAGE—a vision perceived clairvoyantly; theory: one communicates with the etheric world through electrical currents because everything is plugged into a central electronic system. (Inconcl.) **Syn.** VISION. [**cf.** CLAIRVOYANCE, ELECTROMAGNETIC UNIVERSE]

ELECTROMAGNETIC RADITATION—(ufology) the waves produced by radar equipment, which shoot out from earth, and are capable of being seen by other planets. (Inconcl.) [**cf.** ENERGY TRAILS, RADAR ANGELS]

ELECTROMAGNETIC REALITY—thought energy transformed from one level of existence to another, but never dissipated. (Inconcl.) [cf. THOUGHT ENERGY, BRAIN, THIRD DIMENSION]

ELECTROMAGNETIC SPECTRUM—a band or range of frequencies running from below six cycles per second to well over fifty billion cycles per second; everything mankind is familiar with is registered in this range; above and below this range are vibrational frequencies of life in the atmosphere occupying the same space at the same time with orderly interpentration; mankind can tune into frequencies above and below this range with psychic skills and instruments; (alpha and theta waves of the human brain are below this range). (Inconcl.) [cf. COLOR, SOUND, VIBRATIONS]

ELECTROMAGNETIC THEORY—(electronic voices) one theory as to how one can receive a telephone call from a dead person: the witness (receiver) hears only a pattern of electrical oscillations that imitate human speech; this is generated by a PK force from their own mind as they have tuned into a telepathic message unconsciously; this in turn liberates the PK force; this force is strong enough and intelligent enough to manipulate the telephone apparatus. (Inconcl.) [cf. PARAPHYSICAL THEORY, WITNESS, ELECTRONIC VOICES Appendix 2]

ELECTROMAGNETIC UNITS—thought patterns formed by emotions making a new vibrational level, or frequency, according to the clarity, quality and nature of the thought. [cf. THOUGHT-FORMS, BRAIN, ENERGY]

ELECTROMAGNETIC UNIVERSE—(esoteric) the total of All is made up of atoms, and each atom has an electromagnetic field around its nucleus, making the universe and everything in it electromagnetic in nature; even though each atom vibrates at different vibrational frequencies, manifesting shapes, forms, colors, sounds and varying degrees of matter, the electromagnetic field never leaves the atom; each atom is electrically coded to all other atoms by this field and all are attached to the "great electronic switchboard," so to speak; a man or woman has their electromagnetic field being made of the same atoms and, therefore, can tune into anything in the universe if they learn how; this is known as psychic skills; research found that each thing, animate or inanimate, has this electronmagnetic field around it, similar to the atom, making it easy for each thing to tune into the other, and explains the theory that all is a sea of electricity and magnetic vibrations. (Inconcl.) [cf. VIBRATIONS, AURA]

ELECTROMAGNETIC WAVES—(esoteric) thousands of frequencies which form thousands of levels of realities; some are in the range of physical perception through sound, color or form; e.g., violet is 4/10,000 of a millimeter; red is 7/10,000 of a millimeter which a human can see, but outside this range, it becomes invisible to the eye. [cf. COLOR, AURA, SOUND]

ELECTROMAGNETISM—pertains to the relationship between electric current and magnetism; magnetic fields are always accompanied by electric fields and described as electromagnetic.

ELECTROMEDIANIMIC—(Allan Kardec) a combination of animal magnetism and electricity which runs through the medium, when entranced, that is used by the etheric world intelligences in the performance of physical phenomena [cf. MEDIUMSHIP, PERISPRIT, TABLE-TIPPING]

ELECTROMETRIC—"electrically measured."

ELECTROMOTIVE FORCE—(esoteric) energy available for conversion from nonelectric to electric, or vice versa; when the potential difference becomes zero, the electrons stop flowing because they are equalized; this force exists only during the time that electrons are unevenly distributed between the two bodies; a man or woman has an invisible body of a finer electromotive vibration which occupies the same space as the physical body and has its seat in the lymphatics; it is this nonelectric energy that is contacted in magnetic healing and converted to electric energy to change the body's chemistry so the body can heal itself. [cf. MAGNETIC HEALING, GAUSS MAGNETICS]

ELECTROMYOGRAPHY—abbr. EMG; a biofeedback instrument used to detect restricted muscle tension caused from stress conditions; uses sensors attached to the skin over the congested muscle area; these sensors detect tiny electrical signals from nerves that activate the muscles sending these signals to the instrument which then amplifies the signals in sounds, colors, or graphs, making it tangibly possible to detect when tension is released. [cf. BIOFEEDBACK TRAINING, MEDITATION, ARTIFACTS]

ELECTRON—(esoteric) minute concentrated centers of energy which fill space, under the direction of mental thought activity; manifestations of the original substance of Totality, which has not yet been formed into matter; has two aspects, positive and negative, correlating with emotional and mental mind activity. (Inconcl.) [cf. POLARITY, ATOMS, VIBRATIONS, THOUGHT]

ELECTRON MICROSCOPE—(esoteric) an instrument designed to allow the physical eyes to see the aura around people and objects. (Inconcl.) [cf. AURA, CORONA DISCHARGE, FLARE PATTERNS]

ELECTRON MICROSCOPY—(Russia) a sophisticated apparatus, using high frequency currents, that results in Kirlian motion pictures; Kirlian closed-circuit TV. (Inconcl.) [cf. CORONA PATTERNS, KIRLIAN CAMERA]

ELECTRONIC ANALYZER—(Russia) an instrument that decodes brain wave patterns. [cf. BRAIN WAVE RHYTHM, ALPHA WAVES, THOUGHT, EMOTIONS]

ELECTRONIC FINGER—(ufology) a sensitive beam, from radar equipment shot in a straight line that detects aircraft of any nature within that beam. [cf. FLAPS, RADIATION, FIREFLIES, RADAR ANGELS]

ELECTRONIC GHOSTS—voices of deceased persons capable of electronically recording voice-like utterances on a tape recorder; recorders are placed in a psychic development circle, by a bedside, in a graveyard, etc. (Inconcl.) **Syn.** TAPED VOICES. [cf. ELECTRONIC VOICES Appendix 2]

ELECTRONIC MEDITATION—(biofeedback training) to learn to quiet the emotions, relax the body, and control the mind while hooked-up to a biofeedback instrument; instrument gives feedback instantaneously to the meditator so he or she knows how well they are doing each session; this feedback enhances one's capability to reach lower states of consciousness more quickly than if one is not being monitored with an instrument. [cf. BIOFEEDBACK TRAINING Appendix 5, FULL BLOWN SOLUTION, EXTERNALIZED THOUGHT, RANGE CONTROL]

ELECTRONIC PLASMA—the electrical system in the brain; any mind activity. [cf. BRAIN, THOUGHT, BIOFEEDBACK TRAINING]

ELECTRONIC RADIATION OF ABRAMS—abbr. E.R.A.; pertains to the black box that utilizes the principles of radionic vibrations; capable of diagnosing and prescribing for the disease of a patient by using a blood sample from the patient; this blood sample knows the story of the patient and its radiations will tell the operator when to stop so as to read the dials for the diagnosis; invented by Dr. Albert Abrams; see BLACK BOX. [cf. RADIONIC HEALING, STICK, BLACK BOX CONCEPT]

ELECTRONIC SENSING DEVICES—see BIOFEEDBACK INSTRUMENTS.

ELECTRONIC VOICES—human speech, raps, clicks, whistles, musical sounds, and foreign languages which come through electronic instruments and cannot be heard with physical ears at the time of recording; instruments include telephones, tape recorders, record player amplifiers, between radio stations, magnetic tape, flashes on TV screens and over telegraph keys; theories: 1. a PK force comes from an emotional wish of a deceased person trying to contact a loved one; this initiates a series of electrical impules on the electronic system that imitates a human voice; 2. a thought-form, created by the witnesses; is endowed with an energy all its own and the intelligence in this thought-form is sensitive enough to motivate itself to manipulate the electronic system to bring an informative message to the witnesses; 3. the voice is impressed directly onto the tape via some sort of psychokinetic, mediated, electromagnetic manipulation; 4. the voice is being parapsychically created (though inaudible to the human ear), directly in front of the electronic amplifier or microphone; 5. in the cases of radio and TV flashes; speculation suggests that extraterrestrial soul-minds or the constructs themselves are trying to communicate with us, or they are so close to earth that our electronic systems pick up their noise. (Inconcl.) [cf. TAPED-VOICE PHENOMENA, PSYCHIC PHONE CALLS, Appendix 2 ELECTRONIC VOICES]

ELECTRONIC YOGA—the practice of mental mind activity of the Yoga disciplines while hooked-up to a biofeedback instrument. [cf. BIOFEEDBACK TRAINING, BUMPING, ELECTRIC FABRIC, EIDETIC LANGUAGE]

ELECTRONOGRAPHY—(Kirlian effect) the study of high voltage cameras and their possibility of photographing other invisible parts of the body; found that acupuncture points, and organs in the thoracic and abdominal cavity can appear visible on the photograph; (do not confuse with an x-ray machine). (Inconcl.) [cf. CONTACT PHOTOGRAPHY, HIGH-VOLTAGE PHOTOGRAPHY]

ELECTROPHOTOGRAPHY—see ELECTROGRAPHY.

ELECTROPHYSIOLOGIST—one who studies the electrical system in the human body in relation to emotions, attitudes, and tangible evidence given by biofeedback instruments and Kirlian photograph cameras. [**cf.** BIOFEEDBACK TRAINING, KIRLIAN EFFECT]

ELECTROPHYSIOLOGY—the study of the flow of the electrical system in the physical body, by the use of the biofeedback instruments and the Kirlian camera, in relationship to its behavior influenced by mind activity. [**cf.** BRAIN, HUMAN BODY, KIRLIAN EFFECT]

ELECTROSLEEP—the application of a weak pulsating electrical current passing over the eyes and mastoid processes causing a pleasant experience; this induces relaxation and later sleep; used with people who have anxiety and insomnia. [**cf.** DREAMS]

ELECTROSTATIC—electricity that is not in motion.

ELECTROSTATIC ARTIFACT—(biofeedback training) noise or sound coming into the electrode and registering on the instrument but not emanating from the person or plant hooked-up to the biofeedback device; e.g., fluorescent lights whose sixty-cycle hum can cause erroneous readings. [**cf.** BASELINE DRIFT, EVOKED POTENTIALS, GSR, EEG]

ELECTROSTATIC FIELD—a quiet electrical energy around people; appears to be enmeshed in the aura; fluctuates with changes in emotions and attitudes and can be activated for more subtle tasks, such as physical phenomena. (Inconcl.) [**cf.** PK, PHYSICAL PSYCHIC PROCESSES]

ELECTROSTATIC FIELD METER—an instrument used to measure the part of the aura that is quiet electrical energy, waiting to be called upon. (Inconcl.) [**cf.** AURA, PK, PHYSICAL MANIFESTATION, MISCELLANEOUS, LEVITATION]

ELECTROSTATIC SENSITIVITY—to determine what kind of vibrations are hitting the skin and to recognize environment much as a sighted person; to tell colors, textures, people and objects close by, etc.; see EYELESS SIGHT; (do not confuse with PSYCHOMETRY). **Syn.** HYPERESTHESIA, CUTANEOUS VISION, BIOINTROSCOPY. [**cf.** EYELESS SIGHT Appendix 2]

ELECTROSTATIC-PK—(laboratory) to move an object by using power of mind concentration and hand movements; theory: it is the electrical energy field around the object and hand that causes the object to move, as opposed to the theory that the bioelectrical force used is coming from within the psychic. (Inconcl.) [**cf.** PSYCHOKINESIS, NATURE-PK, NONHUMAN-PK]

ELECTROSUROGRAM—invented by Pavel Gulyaiev (Russia) an instrument with high-resistance detection electrodes that can measure force fields as small as the force field around a nerve. [**cf.** SYMPATHETIC NERVOUS SYSTEM, BRAIN]

ELEMENTAL—(esoteric) 1. a constant, persistent thought on one subject, idea, person, or situation; can be good or bad; thinker gives the thought their undivided attention throughout the entire day; this consistency builds a thought-form, a mass of intelligence so forceful that it can work for or against the thinker, until the theme is dropped; deliberately formed and controlled or can be unknowingly formed and rampant; utilized by: (a) the thinker, to form the shape of a person (invisible and soulless) which is capable of performing menial tasks for its owner; lasts many years if the thought remains strong enough; diminishes when the theme of the thought diminishes; capable of turning on its owner when the thought activity is weakened; (do not confuse with a FAMILIAR). **Syn. TULPA.** (b) the thinker's guides, as an extra amount of energy to manipulate mundane activity in case of an oncoming accident or stressful time; (c) the thinker, to send a sick person healing energies; (d) the psychic, to put a hex on another person for evil intent; capable of having enough intelligence to be destructive and frightening to the receiver; finds a weak point through which it can operate in the victim; dissipates only when the hexer neglects its repetition; (e) a negative thinker, unwanted and unknowingly, bringing negative and chaotic activity repeatedly in her or his life; happens to a depressed person or one who is resentful, angry, envious, or hateful; unpleasant happenings will continue until he or she drops the consistency in their attitude; 2. synonymous with NATURE SPIRITS; see same; 3. an umbrella word meaning any or all nonhuman intelligences in the etheric world, from god-like devas, down through the ranks to the density; 4. thought-forms which will continue to work where directed as long as it is persistently nourished; when weakened by thinker, they stay in the etheric world with less force but are still able to latch onto thoughts of like nature. [**cf.** MASS ELEMENTAL, THOUGHT-FORM, SOULLESS]

ELEMENTAL ASTRAL SHAPES—grotesque, distorted, fleeting forms found interacting on the horizontal planes of the etheric world; sensitive to the temperament of a person's thoughts; show themselves (in dreams and visions) to those who are depressed or engulfed in negative thinking. **Syn.** MULTIFORM WAVES. [**cf.** SOULLESS Appendix 2, DWELLERS IN THE BARDO]

ELEMENTAL BEINGS—life forms, from very high intelligences to low forms of intelligence, made of etheric world elemental essence; live in either the etheric world, the overworld, or the underworld: 1. nature devas (angels); 2. nature spirits (fairies); 3. animal; 4. subhuman beings (underworld); 5. half-animal, half-human; 6. artificial (man-made). [**cf.** SOULLESS, NATURE SPIRITS, ANGEL KINGDOM]

ELEMENTAL ESSENCE—1. aggregations of molecular matter which make up the six non-atomic subplanes of the mental and astral planes; a substance, gathered from the life around the physical body and earth plane, holding together the astral shells and the underworld in general; molecules working down into the arc of matter, warring against the law of the mind of man, resisting regeneration; lower molecular division of each of the basic types of matter, a step finer than physical matter; 2. name given to living matter amenable to being shaped into living forms and performing special duties by the power of the mind; see TULPA. [**cf.** BODIES AND PLANES Appendix 5, SOULLESS, DENSITY, ASTRAL PLANE]

ELEMENTAL EVOLUTION—the process of the monad (human being seed) pressing downward, taking on a soul-mind, and still pressing downward until it becomes entangled into matter of the earth plane. **Syn.** INVOLUTION. [**cf.** MONADOLOGY]

ELEMENTAL WEAPONS—the four basic instruments represented by the primordial elements used in ceremonial magic: WAND (fire); DAGGER (air); CUP (water); PENTACLE (earth).

ELEMENTALS—(angel kingdom) 1. nature spirits composed of the *elements* in which they live and of which they are in charge; e.g., a tree elemental is made to interpenetrate the tree and its physical substance; as they evolve, they become ethereal, but still remain the tree substance; 2. meant to be only the low or evil nature spirits.

ELEMENTARIES—(Theosophy) soul-minds who go off their path in this incarnation and must take a lower form in the etheric world; inhabitants of the density. [**cf.** ASTRAL WORLD, DENSITY]

ELEMENTARY—a collective word referring to any and all of mankind's possible etheric world states of consciousness. [**cf.** BODIES AND PLANES Appendix 2]

ELEMENTS—(esoteric) the four basic primary substances belonging to the human being kingdom: FIRE, EARTH, AIR, and WATER; found in every substance known to mankind; each element contains nature spirits and angels who help in the function of the elements, and in their relationship to mankind. [**cf.** NATURE SPIRITS]

ELEMENTS OF OCCULTISM—conditions in which psychic energy can exist: 1. gas (air); 2. electricity (fire); 3. solid matter (earth); 4. liquid (water). [**cf.** AIR, FIRE, EARTH, WATER]

ELEVATED SPIRITS—(Allan Kardec) etheric world entities having purified terrestrial fluid, perfected senses, and are capable of high quality psychism. **Syn.** SUPERIOR SPIRITS. [**cf.** ANGEL HIERARCHY, MEDIUMSHIP]

ELEVEN—(numerology) symbolizes faithfulness, courage, clairvoyance, and a desire to inspire others. [**cf.** NUMEROLOGY]

ELF—see ELVES.

ELF ARROW—a tool used by the elf to harm a human when the elf is angry with him or her. [**cf.** NATURE SPIRITS, SHAPE-CHANGING]

ELF BULL—a tiny animal nature spirit; makes itself known where fairies abide; kind, gentle, and playful; desires to be perceived clairvoyantly.

ELF FIRE—(Druids) see VITAL LIFE FORCE.

ELF WAVES—(Russia) extremely low-frequency electromagnetic radiations that broadcast extrasensory perception and communication of human mental energy from one to another. [**cf.** WIDE-BAND TUNING, VERIDICAL HALLUCINATION]

ELF-MARKED—(Europe) a deformity in a young child; happening during birth or at a very young age; blamed on a nature spirit. [**cf.** ELF, GNOME, NATURE SPIRITS]

ELICITING PSI—(laboratory) a controlled experiment wherein the experimenter is psychic, making it more conducive for the subject to hit the target. [**cf.** ESP, MENTAL TELEPATHY]

ELIMA—(Congo) see VITAL LIFE FORCE.

ELIXIR—(esoteric) 1. an amulet, perfume, food, or anything enabling one to live forever; 2. an agent sought by medieval alchemists for transmuting base metal into gold; 3. a drug that can restore youth; 4. the intelligence found in all substance; the quintessence of Totality; the soul. **Syn.** PHILOSOPHER'S STONE. [**cf.** ALCHEMY, AMULETS]

ELIXIR OF LIFE—a transmuting agent; a special formula for the soluable form of the Philosopher's Stone which is to be discovered by each alchemist for her or himself; the process of making a mixture of many ingredients which is tested, heated, and changed many times until a liquid is discovered to have life-giving properties to cure all disease and restore youth; this same process is then simulated by the alchemist to transmute his or her body to an ethereal state. [**cf.** GLORIFIED BODY, ALCHEMIST, PHILOSOPHER'S STONE]

ELOHIM—(Hebrew) 1. God, Jehovah, Lord; 2. the sound of this word has the vibrational frequency to invoke only divine etheric world entities when in a psychic circle; sometimes spelled **Eloah**. [**cf.** WORDS-WITH-POWER]

ELONGATION—to alter one's body in size and shape when in an altered state of consciousness without harming the the body; body of medium can be stretched out (sometimes as much as a foot longer), looking as if pulled up by the neck and as if the muscles were in a state of tension; body can expand, contract, and swell; legs lengthen, body separates at the ribs and then shrinks to smaller than normal size; occurs when in a trance state in a seance, with the aid of an etheric world intelligence, when asleep, awake, or in ecstatic state; can be willed or occur spontaneously. [**cf.** BODY CONTROL Appendix 2]

ELOPTIC ENERGY—coined by Thomas Galen Hieronymus; (*el* taken from *electricity; optic* meaning energy); has some, but not all, of the characteristics of electricity; combines light and electricity; energy used by witches, mediums and psychics; see VITAL LIFE FORCE. (Inconcl.)

ELOPTIC RADIATION—see AURA.

ELUSIVE PSI—(laboratory) refers to the fact that psi is not necessarily reliable when experiments are repeated, even though conditions are the same in each experiment. [**cf.** PSYCHIC, ZERO VIBRATION, PSYCHIC ATTUNEMENT]

ELVES—(Europe) joyous nature spirits, appearing in a transparent texture when seen by mankind; height ranges from four inches to four feet; help the growth of nuts and flowers; come from the pure elemental group of nature spirits; two types: 1. light elves (live in air) are benign, happy creatures; their energy feels cooling, gentle, and pleasant; energies blend easily to enhance romances, gentle love, and platonic friendships; 2. dark elves (live underground) are swarthy, evil and blighting. (Inconcl.) [**cf.** NATURE SPIRITS, ELF-ARROWS, ELF-MARKED, ALFHEIM, SWARTHEIM]

ELYSIUM—(Orpheus) 1. Elysian Fields: an underworld of strange brightness; a happy resting place for pure spirits; 2. (current) means a place in the sky. [**cf.** HAPPY HUNTING GROUND, CONCENTRIC SPHERES]

EMANATION—(esoteric) 1. an extension of what is within the form, animate or inanimate, given off in vibrations that can be detected as rays; used in radiesthesia and other types of physical psychism. (Inconcl.) [**cf.** RADIESTHESIA, RADIONICS, PK] 2. defined in various ways: subtle, fluidic, astral influence, psychic force, physical effluence, magnetism, radiations and vibrations which proceed from and surround all bodies and objects; when brought into contact with a medium or psychic, both radiation and psychic influence and react upon each other; the result being either interpenetration or repulsion, and the psychic skill is brought into play; 3. (Kabbalah) the creation; that which has flowed out; 4. (Theosophy) the seed of every organic entity is perfectness, expressing its abilities through the ages in various vibrational frequencies; these abilities improve with the ages, through a process of evolution.

EMANATIONS—(psychometry) inert objects that easily reveal psychic information to a psychometrist about an animal or human because they have been repeatedly used or have been close to the human or animal in the course of its life; inert objects can be a lock of hair, a tooth, jewelry, watch, glasses, a horse's saddle, bird cage, walls of a dog house, etc.; these inert objects have been impregnated with radiations from their owner and the emotion and intelligence from these radiations are picked up by the hands of the psychometrist; the psychometrist touches the object with the palms of his hands when in an alpha state of consciousness; present and past conditions are revealed but the future is not as these radiations are not yet present. (Inconcl.) **Syn.** TOKEN OBJECT, PSYCHOMETRIC SPECIMEN. [**cf.** PURE PSYCHOMETRY, PRACTICAL PSYCHOMETRY, SECONDARY WAVES]

EMBER WALK—(fire) the beginning session for the initiate into fire walking; done on a bed of hot coals, with unprepared bare feet; one theory: a learned technique to take four steps at a steady pace, bring each foot down in exactly the same length, and with the same amount of pressure, establishing a rhythm which keeps the feet cool and unharmed. [**cf.** BODY CONTROL Appendix 2, MASTERS-OF-FIRE]

EMBLEMATIC—pertains to psychic information or dreamstuff that does not mean itself per se but represents a situation, activity, characteristic, quality, or state that has the same main nature; to perceive something psychically to identify intangible information; may occur clairvoyantly, clairaudiently, or clairsentiently; e.g., vision of a flag is the emblem for success; feeling a heaviness on one foot is the emblem to stop whatever one is planning to do. **Syn.** SYMBOLIC. [**cf.** MENTAL PSYCHIC PROCESS]

EMBODIED ANEW—pertains to the birth of a baby, and knowing that the soul-mind of that child has had other physical and ethereal lives. [**cf.** REINCARNATION, GERM PICTURES, KARMA OF FUNCTION] FUNCTION]

EMBRYONIC AURIC CLOUD—to clairvoyantly perceive something new being formed in the astral world, with its casing of thought energy still around it; seems to grow from within the thought energy, similar to a physical embryo growing within the mother. (Inconcl.) [**cf.** THOUGHT-FORM CLUSTER, THOUGHTSMANSHIP]

EMERALD—(esoteric) a mineral influenced by the vibrations of Venus; has the vibrational frequency to give it talisman properties to assure a good reincarnation to earth and to be helpful in transferring the vital force from one organism to another; used with the symbol of the Eye of Horus. [**cf.** TALISMAN, AMULET, MINPSI]

EMERALD TABLET—a construction of substance that possesses the properties of the emerald, transmuted by Hermes from a type of glass, upon which was carved an alchemical formula; formula was believed to be the Philosopher's Stone; was found in the hand of the corpse of Hermes Trismegistus but is now lost; believed to contain the formula for life eternal. [**cf.** PHILOSOPHER'S STONE, ALCHEMY, ELIXIR]

EMERGENCY PSI—an instinctual function in humans that gives one exaggerated strength and illogical but correct decisions when the situation calls for immediate action; the conscious mind is shoc'ed to a standstill and the superconscious mind can flow through clairsentiently with psychic information and strength. (Inconcl.) **Syn.** SURVIVAL PROGRAM, SYMPATHETIC NERVOUS SYSTEM.]

EMETIC RITUAL—(Native American) to swallow an herbal medicine to clear the stomach before one seeks clairvoyant visions and enlightenment. [**cf.** CEREMONIAL MAGIC, PHYSICAL PSYCHIC PROCESS]

EMG—abbr. for ELECTROMYOGRAPHY; see same.

EMIGRATIONS—(esoteric) the incarnated soul-minds who have returned to earth from the etheric world. [**cf.** REINCARNATION, DELAYED KARMA]

EMISSARY—(esoteric) a highly intelligent, strong formless energy capable of communicating with a human being; represents the interests and the consciousness of the nature spirit kingdom, making possible the growth of the natural forms from the powers of Totality; provies a special earthly environment for higher forms of life to enter and be comfortable within this physical dimension; believed by some to be cosmic in origin. [**cf.** ANGEL KINGDOM, ETHERIC WORLD ENTITY]

EMOTION—(esoteric) 1. a highly concentrated form of energy consciousness which stimulates a pattern of organic responses in the body; can be felt physically and experienced mentally; 2. emotion is the fundamental manifestation of the vital life force: it cannot be seen or touched but can be felt in a powerful form; every form of life possesses it in varying degrees; cannot be concretely identified; 3. reacts in the body from outside stimuli, according to one's entire belief system; 4. instantaneous feelings, moods, and attitudes (good, bad and in-between) stemming from within, without volition; responds and relates to all phases of life experiences; emotions change from moment to moment, having roots and instinct from cosmic consciousness; 5. emotions of the body come from the endocrine and gland activity and manifest as electrical transmitter points along the path of the nervous system, connected to the electrical system in the etheric world; 6. emotional energy is transmuted to the mental plane in the etheric world to help make the blueprints of a human's physical body and physical outer environment; uses astral matter for its transmission, linking and influencing astral growth;

7. emotions are a feeling sensation, a mental awareness, and a physical change taking place simultaneously in the body. (Inconcl.) [cf. LAW OF EMOTION Appendix 7, DESIRE, PSYCHOPHYSIO-LOGICAL PRINCIPLE, SYMPATHETIC NERVOUS SYSTEM, KEY TO LIFE]

EMOTIONAL ASTRAL CORD—(esoteric) a strand of the invisible silver cord running through the body from the soul-mind; enters the top of the head and ends in te emotional-astral-seed-atom located in the solar plexus of the body; takes care of the emotions and their relation to the soul-mind while in this incarnation. (Inconcl.) [cf. EMOTIONAL-ASTRAL-SEED-ATOM, EMOTIONAL STRESS, SILVER CORD]

EMOTIONAL BODY—see ASTRAL BODY.

EMOTIONAL CLAIRAUDIENCE—a spontaneous, emphatic utterance associated with an urgent message, heard by the psychic *within* his or her head and seems to come from nowhere; relates information of a warning, much-needed comfort, or a prediction regarding a traumatic situation of a loved one; believed to be stimulated by 1. the emotion of the soul-mind of an individual in a traumatic experience and her or his close bond with the psychic; e.g., the voice of a boy screaming for help, heard by the mother, at the exact time he is being struck by a war bullet; 2. a need of the psychic and therefore his or her guides utter words to them. (Inconcl.) [cf. EMOTIONAL PSI, CLAIRAUDIENCE, CRISIS ESP, EMOTIONAL-PK]

EMOTIONAL CLAIRVOYANCE—a spontaneous, clear vision in detail, bringing an urgent message to a psychic; indicates a traumatic experience about to happen either to her or himself or a loved one, or vision occurs at the exact time the experience is happening; believed to be stimulated by the emotions of the soul-mind about to venture into the traumatic experience, and the close bond between the two, or by the psychic's own disturbed soul-mind, as in the case of his or her own prediction; e.g., Abraham Lincoln seeing his own casket laid out three days before he was assassinated. (Inconcl.) [cf. CLAIRVOYANCE, DREAM CLAIRVOYANCE, EMOTIONAL PSYCHISM Appendix 2]

EMOTIONAL CONSCIOUSNESS—an instinctual awareness existing in all plants; see SENSATION CONSCIOUSNESS.

EMOTIONAL CYCLE—(biorhythm) a rhythmic pattern of moods, emotions, attitudes, sensibility, and creativeness within the mechanism of the body; works in a twenty-eight day period, having fourteen days in the pleasurable high moods and fourteen days in the lower state of emotions. **Sim.** SENSITIVITY CYCLE. [cf. BIORHYTHM CHARTS, TWENTY-THREE-DAY CYCLE]

EMOTIONAL FORCE FIELD—(esoteric) a concentrated invisible energy located in the solar plexus and under the influence of emotions; begins the flow of psychic energy which is brought about by a highly emotional state of consciousness and directed out from the solar plexus. (Inconcl.) [cf. SYMPATHETIC NERVOUS SYSTEM, SOUL-MIND, SOLAR PLEXUS CHAKRA]

EMOTIONAL HEALING—See SLAYING-IN-THE-SPIRIT.

EMOTIONAL HIGH—(esoteric) a beautiful, ecstatic self-hypnotic state of joyful joy; a concentrated exhilaration of happiness; a feeling of detachment from the body and a oneness with Totality; usually accompanied by an outpouring of psychic energy, resulting in a very pleasurable experience; brought on by effort, or occurs spontaneously from a good meditation session, a long fervent prayer, a period of chanting, or specially designed music such as concerts, loud, continuous charismatic hymns, or from gatherings for religious, metaphysical, philosophical, or consciousness awareness purposes. (Inconcl.) [cf. EMOTIONAL PSYCHISM Appendix 2]

EMOTIONAL HYPNOSIS—(disguised hypnosis) a short time-period wherein a single powerful motive or preoccupying thought towers over all sensations and the individual acts irrationally; there is a loss of wakeful rational consciousness because the conscious mind is blocked out and the subconscious mind takes over; brought about by an intense situation: great fear, anger, sensations of ecstatic rapture, or a reaction to a repetitive repressed feeling from outer stimuli; in this situation, the conscious mind is literally forced to step aside for a few minutes and let the subconscious mind release concentrated stored emotions because the present experience will not fit in the storage compartment in the subconscious mind; outside stimuli triggered the already full compartment in that area, the lid comes off, and the person reacts according to the stored emotions; reactions can be pleasant or harmful; e.g., for months the child lets a door bang each time he enters; one day the mother rises in anger and fiercely shakes the child (which is not her normal nature); a spiritual feeling repressed until a special song releases it and one bursts into happy tears. [cf. SPONTANEOUS HYPNOSIS, HYPNOTHERAPY Appendix 5, EMOTIONAL HIGH]

EMOTIONAL KARMA—a strong feeling or attitude about a special person or experience from another incarnation which is stored in the adrenal glands and shows itself when one comes close to a similar situation; the person's reactions may not seem explainable to those who do not know it is a karmic emotion. [cf. REINCARNATION, ACCUMULATED KARMA, RIPE KARMA, SOUL-MIND]

EMOTIONAL NOISE—disturbing unwanted thoughts that wander through and pester the mind, especially when time is pressing, when in meditation, doing psychic work, or when concentration is of importance; wastes time that is meant for something else. **Syn.** INNER-DIALOGUE. [cf. THOUGHTS, NON-THOUGHTS, DAY-DREAMING, MONKEY CHATTER]

EMOTIONAL PLANE—see ASTRAL PLANE.

EMOTIONAL PSI—(current usage) a clear, psychically perceived indication that a traumatic or unexpected crisis is about to happen to a loved one; brought to a psychic by means of a vision, voice, smell, taste, or feeling; instigated by the person who is about to experience the traumatic crisis because this disturbed soul-mind desires to let someone know about the happening; the soul-mind is able to telepathically project this emotion because of the bond between the two or else the soul-mind splits due to the highly emotional state; usually occurs spontaneously; (do not confuse with BILOCATION or an ASTRAL PROJECTION). (Inconcl.) [cf. EMOTIONAL CLAIRAUDIENCE, EMOTIONAL CLAIRVOYANCE, CRISIS APPARITION, SPONTANEOUS SYMPTOM SHIFTING]

EMOTIONAL PSYCHISM—mental and physical psychism brought on by a highly emotional state of the sympathetic nervous system (transmitter for the soul-mind); results in various outbreaks of concentrated energy in many forms; manifests within one's self, within a loved one, or within mundane matter; brought on spontaneously or by effort; comes through any of the five psychic senses, or through exaggerated physical strength; see Appendix 2 EMOTIONAL PSYCHISM for listings of same.

EMOTIONAL PSYCHOKINESIS—physical phenomena occurring as a result of someone going through a very highly emotional state: 1. matter being manipulated at the same time, or shortly before, a very traumatic experience or crisis occurs (by the person who is experiencing it); e.g., a person dies and simultaneously (miles away) his picture falls off the wall; 2. matter being manipulated while the person is experiencing a personal high; e.g., a communion wafer flying into the recipient's mouth. (Inconcl.) [cf. EMOTIONAL PSYCHISM Appendix 2, SHROUD]

EMOTIONAL STRESS—positive and negative feelings, moods, and attitudes; (esoteric) emotional stress runs through the body's nervous system like electrical wiring connected to the central cosmos system for electrical power; negative attitudes draw the lower frequencies causing chemical corrosion which short-circuits the inflow in the body's wiring system resulting in unwanted mental or physical behavior; positive attitudes reach into the higher frequencies and these frequencies run through the system as they should, and the body runs smoothly. (Inconcl.) [cf. DESIRE, EMOTION, CEREBROSPINAL NERVOUS SYSTEM, BLOCKS, EUSTRESS]

EMOTIONAL TELEPATHY—the transference between two persons of one's feeling nature (mood or emotion), one's sickness, one's conscious attitude, or one's karmic accident-to-be, regardless of distance; occurs between two persons who have a close bond of friendship, hate, love, or business relationships; performed intentionally or unintentionally; sometimes an inborn trait; e.g., husband going through pseudo-labor pains the same time as the wife; sensing the fear of others in a gathering; feeling symptoms of a disease but upon examination, the physical body is well. (Inconcl.) **Syn.** SPONTANEOUS SYMPTOM-SHIFTING. [cf. NONINTENTIONAL PSI, NEED-DETERMINED PHENOMENA, MOMENTARY ABILITY, CLOAK OF INSULATION, SYMPATHETIC INDUCTION]

EMOTIONAL-ASTRAL-SEED-ATOM—(esoteric) an invisible concentrated center of energy located in the solar plexus, attached to the silver cord; contains the quality of the emotions of the present and future for the present incarnation; acts as an agent for the development of the soul-mind. (Inconcl.) **Syn.** BOOK OF LIFE. [cf. EMOTIONAL-ASTRAL-CORD, ASTRAL BODY, MENTAL-CONSCIOUSNESS-SEED-ATOM]

EMOTIONAL-SEED-ATOM—see EMOTIONAL-ASTRAL-SEED-ATOM.

EMPATH—one who psychically tunes into the emotional state of a person, group, animal, nature, or a nation; unconsciously or deliberately; e.g., 1. to wake up in the middle of the night sensing disaster, feeling fear, anxiety, and cold; the next morning reading about a hurricane in a cold climate and many were hurt; 2. feeling ill at ease for three days before the president was shot and when it actually happened, the feeling left; 3. one who is skilled at clairempathy; (do not confuse with EMOTIONAL PSI). [cf. CLAIRSENTIENCE, INNER-DIRECTED]

EMPATHY CLAIRSENTIENCE—to psychically perceive the emotional feelings of another person or animal, at the same time they are feeling that particular emotion; willed or spontaneous; e.g., one may not know the wife, but, while talking to the husband one feels a hate for the wife, because one is sensing what the husband feels for his wife. [cf. CLAIRSENTIENCE, INTUITION, EMPATH]

EMPATHY-PK—(laboratory experiments) the rapport of two living organisms who experience organic changes relating one to another; e.g., two frogs, one heart gaining beats and the other losing beats, simultaneously, until the hearts beat at the same speed; baby rabbits were taken miles away from the mother rabbit and ruffled up and at the same moment, the mother rabbit became very uneasy. [cf. PSYCHIC TRANSFER, PARASITISM]

EMPIRICAL ENERGY—psychic skills which occur willed and spontaneously, not determined through scientifically proven facts, but just because practice makes it work; psychic phenomena that defies all laws known to man; (PARAPHYSICAL law: if it works for you, it's a law for you). [cf. Appendix 7 LAWS]

EMPIRICAL KNOWLEDGE—psychism experienced and perceived by oneself that becomes knowledge to oneself, regardless of science or theory.

EMPTINESS—to realize one is treading the middle path between *being* and *non-being*; 1. a sensation of *something lacking* when a portion of one's lifestyle does not include giving to the universe; 2. lack of an overall, long-range, constructive goal.

EMPTY HANDS—(Japan) a technique of defending oneself without the use of weapons. **Syn.** KARATE, JUDO, JUJITSU. [cf. MARTIAL ARTS]

EMPTY SPACE—see ETHERIC WORLD.

EMPYREAN ZONE—the upper half of the etheric world making an abode for intelligences without form as they rise into pure consciousness. **Syn.** MYSTIC ZONE. [cf. COSMIC CONSCIOUSNESS, ANGEL HIERARCHY]

EN SOPH—(Kabbalah) represents the God of traditional religion; "infinite one." [cf. UNIVERSAL MIND, TOTALITY]

EN SOPH, AIN SOPH, EIN SOPH—everywhere and beyond, the unknowable.

ENCHANT—1. (Latin *cantare,* "to sing") to reach and invoke the etheric world intelligences by singing and chanting; songs and chants are composed with the proper rhythm, pitch, and tone to stir up vibrations in the atmosphere and prepare the conscious mind of the magician (to be passive and neutral) making etheric world communication easier. [cf. GOING-TO-LEVEL, PHYSICAL PSYCHIC PROCESS Appendix 2, SOUNDS-WITH-POWER] 2. to subject one to psychic energy; to impart a magic quality or effect in the atmosphere around a person, by intensified concentration of one's mind; e.g., (a) to psychically concentrate on a patient, consistently, imparting healing energy into their aura until the patient shows much relief; (b) to psychically concentrate on a victim and send energy with evil intent until the victim is in an accident. (Inconcl.) **Syn.** CHARM, SPELL. [cf. THOUGHT ATMOSPHERE, SPELLCRAFT, IMITATIVE MAGIC]

ENCHANTER—a male psychic who specializes in the skill of influencing or manipulating people for good or evil by creating a thought atmosphere around his subject by a technique using songs, chants or rhythmic sounds. [cf. ENCHANT, THOUGHT ATMOSPHERE]

ENCHANTRESS—a female psychic, see ENCHANTER.

ENCOUNTER GROUP—a small gathering of people under leadership who ventilate and express their emotions in front of others in order to rid themselves of blocks in their personalities. [cf. BLOCKS, GRAPES]

END-RESULT—(visualization) to formulate in the mind, a visual picture of the *finished* product or the *finished* accomplishment one desires to manifest in his or her life or another person's life; this visionary picture is held in the mind for a period of time during a visualization exercise, after meditation; expectation of this manifestation is necessary, with no consideration of how it is to happen; e.g., to mentally picture a new red automobile, running smoothly, with yourself as the driver, as opposed to picturing one's self earning the money for the automobile. **Syn.** HO-ANO, SOLEMNIZING THE MIND. [**cf.** BRAIN, THOUGHTS, MENTAL HEALING, PSYCHIC ATTACK, VISUALIZATION]

END-STATE—(meditation) a method for attaining quietude; achieved by sitting with eyes closed and just watching one's thoughts go by, not correcting, not suppressing but simply watching, attentive and attentionless at the same time. [**cf.** MEDITATION Appendix 2]

ENDOGENTIC PSYCHISM—includes all types of psychic skills in which the psychic manufactures the energy needed from within the body; e.g., to beam energy to energize an amulet; to create a mental thought atmosphere around a sick person for healing; to send a telepathic message to a daughter to write a letter; to use mind power to move a matchstick. [**cf.** EXOGENIC PSYCHISM]

ENDOCRINE SYSTEM—(esoteric) an automatic defense mechanism under the leadership of the pituitary and pineal glands, connected to the great central communication system (Totality) which is found in every living organism, giving a motive for self-preservation; in a human sometimes known as the *fight or flight* mechanism; also known to bring exaggerated physical strength in crisis telepathy. (Inconcl.) [**cf.** EMOTIONAL PSI, CRISIS TELEPATHY]

ENDURANCE TESTS—(Australian aborigine, Ananda tribe) extreme body postures and undue exposure to weather or environment to learn mind discipline and the realization that mind controls all; to enter a state of profound sophistication in human awareness that tests one's physical endurance, spiritual satisfaction, and psychic mind control, as marks of advanced evolution in a tribe; e.g., to stand on one leg for hours, completely motionless, in a waking, detached state so deep that flies may crawl across the eyeballs without causing them to blink. [**cf.** FORCED PSI, ISOLATION TANK, PERSONAL QUEST, THIRD-EYE ATTAINMENT]

ENEMY WAY—(Native American, Navaho) an important ceremony held before a war, designed to stir up vibrations and to put positive vibrations around each warrior (like a cloak of insulation) to protect him in battle and against vengeful ghosts of slain enemies. [**cf.** CEREMONIAL MAGIC, ELEMENTAL, CLOAK OF PROTECTION]

ENERGEOLOGY—the study of all phases of energy.

ENERGETIC MEDICINE—(magnetic healing) to direct the magnetism, that daily passes from the cosmos through one's body, to the patient, to accelerate her or his healing; this magnetism utilizes the law of thought and may be directed out through one's palms to touch the aura or body of the patient; helps in the healing process or gives the patient extra vitality; can be redirected back into one's own body in the same way. (Inconcl.) [**cf.** CURATIVE MEDICINE, ENERGY EXCHANGE]

ENERGY—(esoteric) (*energeia*, "active") vital activity; that which moves or quickens inert matter; literally means "of itself, motivationalness"; **1.** (ancient Egypt) primeval spirit of the universe; fundamental life force; an innate law from the beginning of creation that makes all particles comprehend, vibrate, oscillate, or shake at different speeds (subject to mind thought); **2.** (Eastern science) the *physical ultimate*, underlying all forms of matter; **3.** (East Indian science) a limited manifestation of the Almighty as the changeless aspect of the one; **4.** energy is magnetism; found everywhere moving throughout all the universe in every direction; located in earth and in air; **5.** a force or action communicated by vibrations or waves, having its source in the mind; all force, power, or action is derived from the thinking mechanism and generated by its constant companion *emotion* (synonomous with energy); this energy / emotional force follows the thought through vibratory radiations, speed, and duration, regulated by the degrees of emotion; it flows through space, subject to the law of like attracts like, etc.; see THOUGHT; **6.** an expression of Totality in dense matter; thought / intellect / electricity (synonomous) plus emotion / energy / magnetism (synonomous) holds the world together and everything thereon. (Inconcl.) [**cf.** CONSCIOUSNESS, VIBRATIONS Appendix 5, BRAIN, LAW OF LIKE ATTRACTS LIKE Appendix 7]

ENERGY ACCUMULATOR—see ASTRAL BODY.

ENERGY BLOCK—see BLOCKS.

ENERGY BODY—see ETHERIC DOUBLE.

ENERGY CURRENTS—an invisible force that aggregates and flows in waves and shapes under and over the surface of the earth only in certain places which is connected with the UFO sightings. (Inconcl.) [**cf.** VIBRATIONS Appendix 5, UFOLOGY]

ENERGY FIELD PHOTOGRAPHY—see KIRLIAN PHOTOGRAPHY.

ENERGY FIELDS—(radiesthesia) radiations given off by all things, animate and inanimate, that are picked up by the dowsing rod and pendulum; radiations know their function and move in cycles; radiesthetic tools tune into these radiations and move meaningfully, in a code decided upon beforehand by the pendulumist or dowser. [**cf.** DOWSING ROD, PENDULUM POWER]

ENERGY GESTALTS—(esoteric) patterns of force in the great Totality which know their function individually and collectively, under the supervision of a guiding principle. (Inconcl.) [**cf.** HOLISM, GESTALT, LAW OF FUNCTION Appendix 7]

ENERGY GRID—(esoteric) an invisible network in the atmosphere of perpendicular and horizontal electrical lines, uniformly spaced and of equal length; connect at minute energy field points which act as transmitting and receiving stations; when perceived clairvoyantly they appear to be suspended in space with no break in the network and no collisions. [**cf.** NODES, VIBRATIONS, ACUPUNCTURE POINTS]

ENERGY MATRIX—1. see ETHERIC DOUBLE; 2. abbr. E-MATRIX; bioplasmic force that exists independently outside the mind and bioenergy field; has form and origin and appears to serve the thing it encloses. (Inconcl.) [**cf.** RADIONICS, ENERGY CURRENTS]

ENERGY MATRIX MACHINES—(radionics) instruments currently being constructed without the use of electronics, components, symbols, or moving physical attachments, as opposed to former radionic machines that had attachments; some function without an operator. (Inconcl.) [**cf.** RADIONICS, RADIESTHESIA]

ENERGY PATTERNS—1. (science) motions in the universe; 2. (esoteric) patterns of molecular structure held together by thought. (Inconcl.) [**cf.** SOUL-MIND, THOUGHT-FORMS]

ENERGY POTENTIAL—(esoteric) a storehouse of latent power in matter, from the subtle to the gross; capable of being transformed into useable energy. (Inconcl.) [**cf.** VIBRTIONS, EARTH BREATHING, MITOGENTIC RADIATION, RADIATION PATTERN]

ENERGY SHIELD—see ETHERIC DOUBLE.

ENERGY SINK—a cavity that assists energy to flow from a higher potential to a lower one. (Inconcl.)

ENERGY SURROUND—see ETHERIC DOUBLE.

ENERGY SYSTEMS—(esoteric) a congregated activity of motion that can be put into categories with special functions, properties and aspects; scientific name given to the various laws governing specific fields, such as, gravitation, time, space, crystalization, light, etc. (Inconcl.)

ENERGY TRAIL—1. a mist or cloud-like formation that follows a discarnate entity in the etheric world, if perceived clairvoyantly; 2. (ufology) a mist extending out from the vehicles or critters in photographs of UFO sightings. (Inconcl.) [**cf.** FLYING FLAPJACK, FLYING SHIELDS, CLAIRVOYANCE]

ENERGY-ELECTRICAL FIELD—see ETHERIC DOUBLE.

ENERVATED—(esoteric) deprivation of cosmic energy in the body, caused by one's negative thinking, which weakens the nerve force in the body. [**cf.** SPIRIT, COSMIC ENERGY, CLOAK OF INSULATION, NEGATIVE THOUGHT]

ENGRAMS—(esoteric) 1. a flimsy substance (sometimes causing waves) created by the mind; visible to a psychic; 2. records of stored stress in the subconscious mind, made from unpleasant experiences and attitudes toward the experiences that were not logically reasoned with before being recorded, this causes a neurosis or complex for the person. (Inconcl.) [**cf.** THOUGHT FORMS, BLOCKS Appendix 5]

ENIGMATIC PHENOMENA—happenings that are puzzling and inexplainable in scientific terms; see PSYCHIC ART.

ENKI—Ea, the god of magick; an etheric world intelligence skilled in working with earthlings to increase their psychic talent; called upon especially for exorcism and protection. [**cf.** MEDIUMSHIP, GUIDE, EXORCISM, PROTECTOR, DOORKEEPER]

ENLIGHTENMENT—(esoteric) 1. a realization of a higher attainment than one is in, leaving one with an attitudinal change; happens for a brief moment or happens by working toward it, never quite knowing what one is working for; 2. knowledge of certain universal Truths and the ability to live them; 3. realization that one is on the path one came for; 4. a state of finding peace for one's self; daily serenity; a specific permanent enjoyment; 5. realization of the "I AM" within, resulting in a change in one's life; perfect harmonious functioning in all aspects of one's life based on the full growth of consciousness; **6.** flowing with natural laws and being supported by them; **7.** (during meditation) aware of a wonderful nothingness; an emptiness of consciousness without loss of consciousness; **8.** meaning differs with different philosophies, and means different things to different people within those philosophies.

ENOCH—(ancient) seers for the books of Enoch; the title went to anyone who had authentic seership ability; see PSYCHIC. [**cf.** PSYCHIC Appendix 3, MEDIUMSHIP]

ENOCHIAN—a language having its own alphabet and grammar, coming through the psychic skill of crystal gazing. [**cf.** CALL, ETHERIC SCRIPT]

ENRICHING EXPERIENCE—coined by Siri Bletzer; a choice phrase to use in a negative situation, as opposed to using words of anger or disgust; prevents a wrong attitude that could easily take over and bring negative karmic reactions; to be used in an unpleasant emotional experience, when a chore is thrust upon one at an inconvenient time, or when one must handle a problem that is a nuisance. Usage: "I had a very enriching experience this summer," instead of "It was a pain in the neck when my purse was snatched from me; it cost $175.00 and a week of extra time to take care of credit cards and to replace my personal belongings." [**cf.** NEGATIVE THOUGHT, KARMA]

ENTECHNOS—**1.** (Cicero) psychic intuition that can be taught to those who are not born with psychic abilities. **Syn.** INDUCTIVE DIVINATION. [**cf.** MENTAL PSYCHIC PROCESSES Appendix 2]

ENTELECHY—**1.** (Hans Driesch) see VITAL LIFE FORCE; **2.** (Aristotle) a pattern or mold of innate design within the life of a human being influencing them and their mechanism of free will; **3.** a guiding principle within a human being seeming to come from the subconscious mind that directs the functioning of the body.

ENTENCEPHALIC VISIONS—clairvoyant perception of colors or geometric forms, and the ability to make sensible psychic information from them. [**cf.** GOLDEN BEAMS, MULTIVALUED PERCEPTION, SPIRITUAL SIGHT]

ENTHUSED—(ancient Greece) to bring forth psychic information, especially in the form of poetry, by allowing an etheric world intelligence to inspire one with information and knowledge that one could not have known from conventional learning; comes through in a relaxed state or light trance state. **Syn.** INSPIRED, BREATHED INTO. [**cf.** POET, PROPHET, MANTIC TRANCES]

ENTITIES OF SEANCES—guides, controls, and other etheric world intelligences who bring psychic knowledge and psychic phenomena into the seance circle; can be perceived; **1.** tangibly but not visibly; **2.** visibly but not tangibly; **3.** both visibly and tangibly. [**cf.** KNOCKS, MATERILIZATION, SEANCES, CLAIRVOYANCE]

ENTITY—**1.** the whole of something existing, animate or inanimate, e.g., a system of roads, a tree, or a person; **2.** (human entity) the sum total that a soul-mind has acquired in individuality, making its own existence, its own rules and its own rate of vibration; draws from the cosmos its own wave length and sends out its own individual wavelengths and emanations; correctly used to mean a deceased person or a live person; **3.** (Seth) the total of many personal fragments, directing and giving them purpose. [**cf.** EGO, INDIVIDUALITY, FRAGMENTS]

ENTRANCEMENT—**1.** a hypnotic trance state of consciousness to be used for performing physical phenomena; **2.** a transfixed, hypnotic stupor that one psychically acquires unknowingly from a person, without his or her consent or knowledge of it happening; in this state of consciousness one can be manipulated for the benefit of the psychic; see SPELLED. **Syn.** BEDEVILMENT, FASCINATION, BEWITCHMENT. [**cf.** SPELLBOUND, EYE-STARE]

ENTRANCER—a psychic who specializes in techniques for manipulating other persons; builds a thought atmosphere around the victim, creating a dazed state of consciousness; skill used for evil intent or revenge. [**cf.** FASCINATING, PSYCHIC ATTACK, BEWITCHER]

ENVELOPE—**1.** the physical body encasing the soul-mind; **2.** any one of the seven bodies encasing the soul-mind. **Syn.** VEHICLE, MATERIAL BODY. [**cf.** ASTRAL BODY, MANSIONS, PSYCHIC CABLE, SUBLIMINAL WORLD, MENTAL BODY]

ENVIRONMENTAL HAUNTING—**1.** the ghostly activity of an earthbound entity, making its presence known repeatedly, in the same area or around the same object; an area or material object can become imbedded with unpleasant strong emotional vibrations created from a mental atmosphere by the person who is experiencing a powerful and emotional event; this mental atmosphere holds that person to the environment after he or she has made their transition; it can be used for energy for the earthbound entity to use to return periodically seeking understanding; entity makes noises, human grunts, a cold atmosphere, and makes the earthling feel that a living presence is invisibly in the room; 2. a very pleasant feeling of serenity experienced by earthlings, in old churches which are visited periodically by very religious persons who have made their transition; they desire to re-experience the feelings of comfort and ecstasy they went through in the church; this pleasant mental atmosphere is strongly imbedded and draws them back to it. **Syn.** GHOST HAUNTING. [**cf.** APPARITION, EARTHBOUND ENTITIES, GHOST]

ENVIRONMENTAL NOISE—a sixty cycle hum in the air at all times, coming from the electronic and electrical systems civilizations use; capable of being picked up on tape recorders and biofeedback instruments. [**cf.** BIOFEEDBACK TRAINING, METABOLIC MONITOR, ELECTRONIC VOICES, ARTIFACT]

EOG—abbr. ELECTRO-OCULOGRAM; (dreams) an instrument used in the dream research laboratories which is hooked-up to the eyeballs by tiny electrodes around the eyes; detects fast movement of the eyeballs, indicating that the subject is dreaming and subject can be awakened to report the dream. [**cf.** DREAMS Appendix 2, NREM, DREAMED AWAKE, EXPOSURE DREAM]

EON DEGREES—the highest rank in the order of the angel kingdom. **Syn.** ANGEL KING. [**cf.** ANGELOLOGY, HUMAN BEING KINGDOM, HIERARCHY]

EPATOSCOPY—divination by means of the innards of animals. **Syn.** EPATOSCOMANCY. [**cf.** MANTIC ARTS Appendix 6]

EPHEMERAL PROJECTION—(astral projection) an unconscious, spontaneous, astral projection occurring when one is in a state of shock, in tremendous pain, or in a coma; astral body slips out of the physical body for a short period, taking the life force with it, to relieve the person of his or her pain; astral body hovers close to the physical body and snaps back into it before the person dies. [**cf.** DEATHBED VISIONS, NEAR DEATH EXPERIENCES, IN-THE-RANGE-OF CORD-ACTIVITY]

EPHEMERIDES—(astrology) the position of the planets, based on the day, month and the year at Greenwich, England, at high noon.

EPHIDROSIS—(ufology) excessive perspiration, frequently experienced by UFO contactees and low-level witnesses. [**cf.** CLOSE-ENCOUNTERS-OF-THE-THIRD-KIND, DAYLIGHT DISCS, POWER SYSTEM, FLASHING STROBE LIGHT]

EPI—(Greek) prefix meaning "outside, over, after," or "anterior."

EPIGENESIS—(cycles) theory: young organisms develop from a formless mass of living material. [**cf.** CYCLES Appendix 5, MONAD]

EPIPHENOMENALISM—(*epi,* "outside of the event") 1. materialistic theory: (Rudolf Steiner) consciousness is a by-product of the basic process; consciousness is in relation to the neutral process which underlies it; 2. theory: the soul-mind survives after death. [**cf.** DEATH ANGEL, DEATH SCIENCE]

EPIPNEUMA—the astral body after it separates from the physical body in the process of death, after the silver cord is loosed. [**cf.** DEATH SCIENCE Appendix 5, FUNIS, PNEUMA]

EPIPNEUMA SPHERE—see ETHERIC WORLD.

EQUALIZING WISDOM—(meditation) the second movement in meditation; an awareness that one is no longer an observer but one becomes compassionate with all that lives. [**cf.** MEDITATION Appendix 5, BUDDHIC PLANE, UNIVERSAL LOVE]

EQUI-LIMBED CROSS—(occult) a construction with four equal crossbars to represent nature; i.e., the four quarters of the globe, and the four elements (air, earth, water, and fire); when used in magic ritual it affirms that God is believed to be the sole creator and supreme law of the universe and invokes him into the psychic skill; used with thought-forms, artificial elementals, and nature spirits; can be used for exorcism of the above when evil is intended or for enhancement; bodily gestures in a simulated cross is as effective as a tangible cross; the first two fingers of the right hand are used to touch the forehead, the solar plexus, the right and left shoulders respectively while repeating the incantation and facing east. [**cf.** ASSOCIATION MAGIC, CEREMONIAL MAGIC, SIGN OF THE CROSS]

EQUINOXES—the time when the sun crosses the plane of the earth's equator, making night and day of equal length all over the earth, occurring about March 21 and September 22.

ERA—see E.R.A.

ERGOSPHERE—coined by Bob Toben, (*ergu,* "radiates and absorbs") source of rotational energy. [**cf.** LAW OF GIVE AND TAKE Appendix 7]

ERHARD SEMINARS TRAINING—abbr. **est;** a mass group therapy that is supposed to transform one's life in sixty hours; strict discipline during training; a conglomeration of techniques and principles from encounter groups, psychodrama, Gestalt, Scientology, Zen, Buddhism, Dale Carnegie, and marine boot camp; lectures are aimed at erasing the trainee's "tapes" or past belief systems, into a more modern way of thinking; theories seem to fit the new culture that is trying to emerge.

ERINNYES—three goddesses living in the etheric world, depicted with their heads wreathed with serpents; in charge of punishing criminals.

ERLIK—(esoteric) the state of consciousness of the lower planes; the density and all its divisions. **Sim.** DENSITY, UNDERWORLD. [**cf.** BODIES AND PLANES Appendix 5, ANGEL KINGDOM, UNDERWORLD]

EROS—1. Greek god of love living in the etheric world; usually depicted by a chubby cherub; 2. forceful energy capable of both love and fear; 3. see ETHERIC WORLD INTELLIGENCES.

ERRANT SPIRIT—an etheric world entity who wanders about aimlessly bothering earthlings with no desire to go onward, until its next incarnation. **Syn.** EARTHBOUND ENTITY. [**cf.** HAUNTING, GHOST]

ERROR PHENOMENON—(psi tasks) a procedural error made by the experimenter or by the subject during a psi experiment; the error has been felt to occur as a result of psi or as activating psi results. [**cf.** ESP Appendix 2, SYNCHRONICITY, ACAUSAL COINCIDENCE, GOING-TO-LEVEL]

ESCHATOLOGY—(ancient) a system of doctrines concerning death, judgement, heaven, and hell.

ESOTERIC—(Greek *esoterikos,* "within, withheld, fuzzy, not clear") 1. pertains to inner or subjective information, as opposed to objective information; 2. pertains to information and knowledge that can be intellectualized but will not be accepted by the individual unless they feel comfortable and compatible with it when the belief system is ready for its incorporation; 3. pertains to information and knowledge that is better understood by the feeling nature rather than the intellect; 4. cannot necessarily be proven by present scientific means, but its value is not discredited for this reason; 5. refers to Ancient Wisdom: knowledge of the etheric world, and one's inner life, intended for or understood by only a chosen few; knowledge of the soul-mind, its purpose and growth; 6. not publically disclosed.

ESOTERIC DEVELOPMENT—see PSYCHIC ART.

ESOTERIC HEALERS—those who use unorthodox methods to heal people by following various occult or "hidden" teachings, such as alchemy, astrology, the Kabbalah, the Tao, and Tantra. [**cf.** PSYCHIC HEALING, MAGNETIC HEALING, HOLISM]

ESOTERIC HEALING—ancient method of manipulating the subtle energy forces to transform the whole person, bringing the body and mind together in one relationship; a humanistic approach to health and wellness. [**cf.** HOLISTIC HEALTH, ALTERNATIVES]

ESOTERIC HYPNOTISM—(antiquity) an advanced technique by the hierophants of the mystery schools, to send their subjects to the higher planes to receive lessons and initiations for the advancement of mankind; hierophants knew how to transfer their magnetic fluid to the subject, to influence the superconscious mind and cerebrospinal column of the subject; in this deep state of hypnosis, the subject could contact their mental body and oversoul and receive knowledge beyond earth education, regarding relationship of the earth to the universe, etc.; subject has full retention of their new knowledge when in the alert state, as this knowledge works down the spinal column; (do not confuse with normal HYPNOSIS that contacts the subconscious mind). **Syn.** OCCULT HYPNOTISM. [**cf.** HYPNOTHERAPY, HYPERACUTE, DETACHEMENT]

ESOTERIC MOVEMENT—activity of old soul-minds, working with earthlings, collectively in groups, and/or singularly to change or to alter the consciousness of the peoples of the world and to prepare them for the transformation of the planet at this time; objective and desire is for the transformation to run smoothly, joyfully, and with understanding, while mother earth purifies herself. **Syn.** CONSCIOUSNESS AWARENESS MOVEMENT. [**cf.** PARAPSYCHOLOGY, METAPHYSICS, MYSTICISM, CYCLES, EVOLUTION]

ESOTERIC PHILOSOPHIES—(ancient) sacred, mystical teachings regarding a human being's soul-mind and his or her relationship to the universe; Truths reserved for desirous and sincere students of worthy character; theories, not necessarily based on scientific facts, but subjective theories with depth, understanding, communication, and brotherly love between those living in mankind's world, those living in the etheric world, and between those from both worlds; uses the principles of metaphysics, mysticism, and physical science. [cf. PARA-PSYCHOLOGY, SPIRITUALISM, CULTURAL TRANS-FORMATION]

ESOTERIC PSYCHOLOGIES—research of consciousness, psychic phenomena, meditation, altered states of consciousness, humanistic psychology, ancient concepts and traditions, and how these influence and modify one's behavior. [cf. CURATIVE EDUCATION, NEW-AGE PSYCHOLOGY]

ESOTERIC SCIENCE—considers consciousness a function of mental energy, and recognizes that everything in the universe has its own consciousness, making everything related; the study and teaching of mechanistic aspects of control, limitation, projection and focusing of this mental energy to make progression in the world. [cf. MATTER, LAW OF THOUGHT Appendix 7, COSMIC MAINSTREAM]

ESOTERICISM—theory: all religions are necessary; each religion recognizes a different state of evolution, and therefore, each man or woman can find a religion to help them handle their present awareness and to advance to another state of awareness; does not take issues in what another man chooses; suffers not from superstitions or fear; works for balance in one's lifestyle; emphasizes freedom of choice for one's lifestyle, beliefs and religions. [cf. SOUL-MIND, GESTALT PSYCHOLOGY]

ESOTERISTS—those who study the inner meaning of mankind, his or her purpose, function, and relationship to the universe; interests lie in the subjective meaning of an object or place; have a sincerity regarding the in-depth meaning of things and happenings regardless of the mass thinking. Syn. PLANETARY HELPERS. [cf. NEW-AGE PSYCHOLOGY, CURATIVE EDUCATION, FUTURISTS, EVOLUTIONARY NECESSITY]

ESP—abbr. EXTRA SENSORY PERCEPTION; 1. coined by J. B. Rhine of Duke University; to experience a response to, or be influenced by a target, object, state, or event without using the five senses; the transmission of thought and feeling from one mind to another mind over a distance, without physical means; 2. after years of experiments, the meaning changed to encompass mental telepathy, clairsentience, precognition, psychic cognition, or any combination of same. [cf. see each above individually] 3. (current) (a) an umbrella word meaning *parapsychology;* (b) perceptual data; (c) in laboratories: clairvoyance, precognition, and retrocognition; 4. (Russia) biological information or bioinformation. Syn. PARAGNOSIS.

ESP ATTUNEMENT—to bring psychic information to another by psychically reaching into his or her thought atmosphere and auric field; psychic uses clairvoyance and clairsentience skills. [cf. CLAIRSCENT, SUBJECTIVE CLAIRVOYANCE]

ESP CARDS—a deck of cards, containing twenty-five cards, with five symbols: a star, circle, square, cross, and wavy lines; used for over thirty years in the Rhine laboratory as the main means of testing psi ability. Syn. ZENER CARDS. [cf. DOWN THROUGH, CHANCE LEVEL, RANDOM TESTING]

ESP PHENOMENA UNDER LSD—to experience a pronounced noticeable change in awareness, loss of time reality, and an extension of mind consciousness to realms that are not always like earth; in a good trip one perceives the astral plane as it is, similar to earth, only more beautiful; in a bad trip one perceives the astral planes and density mixed and distorted as if one is tuned into many stations at one time. [cf. FORCED PSI Appendix 2, DENSITY]

ESP PROJECTION—see ASTRAL PROJECTION.

ESP SHUFFLE—(psi tasks) the subject shuffles the deck of cards for their own experiment, instead of the experimenter. [cf. DECLINE EFFECT, BACKWARD CAUSATION]

ESPA TESTER—an automatic testing device designed for laboratory use of parapsychological research, especially ESP. [cf. ESP, PSYCHIC COGNITION]

ESPIRITISMO—(Africa, southwestern United States, Chicanos) a religion dealing in psychism.

ESPIRITISTA—(Philippines) a religion noted for performing psychic surgery; works with other types of hidden psychic phenomena. [cf. PSYCHIC SURGERY, TEN PERCENT IMPERSONATION]

ESPIRITISTA GROUP—religious organization that most psychic surgeons belong to, which has headquarters in Manilla. [cf. PSYCHIC SURGERY]

ESPRIT—see ASTRAL BODY.

ESS—suffix meaning "feminine," as in *goddess* or *prophetess.*

ESSAY DREAM—dreamstuff is shown in picture language and an interpreter appears and explains the dream in verbal commentary. [cf. DREAMS Appendix 2]

ESSAYING TO LIVE—the consciousness of a new soul-mind on its first incarnation on the planet. [cf. REINCARNATION, GROUP KARMA]

ESSENCE OF MIND—(esoteric) the atoms in the universe subject to the mental activity of mankind for manipulation. [cf. ENERGY, ATOMS, BRAIN, LAW OF LIKE ATTRACTS LIKE Appendix 7]

ESSENCE OF REST—(Yoga) a meditation done in a prone position with emphasis on expanding the consciousness; accomplished by complete relaxation, breathing rhythmically, concentrating on the body going into the air, and the inner sound current; one feels a buoyancy or lightness of body or feels a cave of energy surrounding them. [cf. MEDITATION Appendix 5]

ESSENES—a pre-Christian sect capable of communicating with the etheric world, working toward initiation of the highest mysteries; appeared first in 150 B.C.; organization noted for their strict rules, initiations, separate grades of divinity, deviation of the beliefs of that time, and exercise of great benevolence; knowledge recorded in the Dead Sea Scrolls; a discipline, believed by many, that Jesus studied.

ESSENTIAL BODY—see ASTRAL BODY.

est—abbr. ERHARD SEMINARS TRAINING; see same.

ESTHETIC STATE—a feeling of being highly elated; an extreme feeling of beauty and joy; pure sensation as opposed to intellect; happening during meditation or at a religious gathering. **Syn.** SATORI, BLISS. [cf. MEDITATION, ONE-POINTEDNESS, ZEN MEDITATION]

ESTRIE—see STRIGA.

ETCHING OF THE SEED ATOMS—process during death wherein the three seed-atoms gradually withdraw from the physical body and move along the silver cord, each in their own turn. [cf. DEATH SCIENCE Appendix 2]

ETERNAL BRAHMAN—God, the Absolute, all-there-is; bliss and perfect harmony. see TOTALITY.

ETERNAL FORMS—a "being" in its entirety; a feeling that a human usually perceives only partially. [cf. MONAD, CONSCIOUS OF BEING, TOTALITY, MULTIDIMENSIONAL]

ETERNAL NOW—1. theory: everything happens simultaneously; past, present, and future is happening at the same time; see MULTIDIMENSIONAL; 2. (Australia) a dream time experience when one joins his or her ancestors and becomes at one with the all. [cf. TIME Appendix 5]

ETERNAL PRESENT—(esoteric) concept where "time" is nonexistent. **Syn.** STASIS, NONDURATION, MULTIDIMENSIONAL.

ETERNAL RHYTHM—1. (esoteric) the internal pulsating rhythm of the earth as a continuation of the rhythm of the universe; everything in the earth, in lesser and stronger degrees, beats in time with the earth; the particular tempo of a human's heartbeats beat to the same rhythm, making everything all one system. (Inconcl.) 2. (Native American) beat of the earth is played on the drum to put one in a state of tranquility; capable of chasing evil spirits out of one's body. [cf. SOUNDS-WITH-POWER Appendix 2]

ETERNAL WORLD—see ETHERIC WORLD.

ETERNITIES—(esoteric) soul-minds who are now living in the density part of the etheric world, because they do not want to progress, or are ignorant of the ability to progress; they ask for help from no one, and therefore, will live in their own hell for a very long time. [cf. DENSITY, ASTRAL PLANE, DEMONOLOGY, SOUL-MIND]

ETERNITY—without end, limitless; (Oriental) a period of 100 years; (Hinduism) the AGE OF BRAHMA, a period of 311,040,000,000,000 years.

ETH—abbr. EXTRATERRESTRIAL HYPNOSIS of mass thinking, that all unidentified flying objects come from other planets; much evidence gives theory that some live in space. (Inconcl.) [cf. UFO SIGHTINGS, DISC OCCUPANTS, RADAR ANGELS]

ETHER—1. (esoteric) a very fine (indefinable) matter or substance believed to support the earth and atoms of the air; (Greece) an energy necessary for all life and things found in the atmosphere since creation; see VITAL LIFE FORCE; 2. (capitalized) invisible atoms evenly distributed through all space; any region beyond the earth; (Bible) the invisible world; a state of physical matter; a sort of elastic solid, more rarefied than gases, in which light waves vibrate transversely to their direction. **Syn.** ETHERIC WORLD, HEAVENS, ATMOSPHERE; **3.** (Isaac Newton and Rene Descartes) "a hypothetical substance which permeates the entire universe, responsible for gravitation and electromagnetism as well as sensations and nervous stimuli; a living spirit"; **4.** an all-pervading fluidic substance, which fills the universe and is responsible for the transmission of light and heat. (Inconcl.)

ETHER GOER—one who takes astral projections. [**cf.** ASTRAL PROJECTIONIST, SPIRAL DROP, CONJUNCTION, ROLLED-OUT]

ETHER IN NATURE—orgone energy; see VITAL LIFE FORCE.

ETHER OCEAN—see ETHERIC WORLD.

ETHER PRESSURE—(esoteric) invisible vibrational frequencies of ether substance interpenetrates matter, and creates its own special pressures in earth matter; can be detected and observed by isolating the ether from matter; speculation: these pressures are the astral world. (Inconcl.) [**cf.** LAW OF VIBRATION and LAW OF POLARITY Appendix 7, ETHER, SUPER-ETHER]

ETHER SHIP—(ufology) forms in outer space that mankind recognizes as a vehicle living in space (as opposed to being from another planet); visible to the physical eye; construct with an intelligent design, varying in color, shape, and size; travels at all speeds; changes shape in air, dwindles in size, and dematerializes its whole construct; has some type of life intelligence for a driver; lives in sea of etheria. (Inconcl.) [**cf.** PHONY STARS, VENTLA-TYPE VEHICLE, CONSTRUCTS, ANOMALOUS SHADOWS]

ETHER-SHIP BEING—(ufology) an intelligent energy form which manages the construct of an intelligent functional design, known to mankind as an unidentified flying object. [**cf.** INTERPLANETARY COLONIZATION, FLYING FLAPJACK]

ETHEREAL—pertains to heavenly or celestial; that which is refined; the upper regions of space; also spelled **etherial**. [**cf.** ETHERIC WORLD, ANGEL KINGDOM]

ETHEREAL BODY—a collective term used to refer to any living entity perceived in the etheric world; pertains to the astral body, mental body, or etheric double; used by psychics and writers. [**cf.** BODIES OF MAN, PLANES]

ETHEREAL HYPNOSIS—to be hypnotized by a hypnotist that is not in one's point of vision; disguised hypnosis wherein the hypnotist sends telepathic suggestions to the subject; planned beforehand or unknowingly to the subject; suggestions are for the subject to relax the conscious mind and be submissive to the hypnotist's suggestions and directions; involvement in a close relationship beforehand is helpful for the hypnotist to get into the thought atmosphere of the subject; used in psychic experiments and used for evil intent. **Syn.** TELEPATHIC HYPNOSIS. [**cf.** RESPONSE ATTENTIVENESS, HYPNOTIC SUGGESTION, ARTIFICIAL REINCARNATION]

ETHEREAL MUSIC—(esoteric) beautiful, indescribable sounds constantly going on in the etheric world that cannot be heard by physical ears; can be heard with psychic ears. **Syn.** MUSIC OF THE SPHERES, COSMIC MUSIC. [**cf.** CLAIRAUDIENCE, DIVINE WHISPERS, CELESTIAL CHORUS, HARMONY OF THE UNIVERSE]

ETHEREAL PLANE—(B.C.) the highest division of the etheric world; houses the gods. [**cf.** AERIAL PLANE, ANGELS]

ETHEREAL PSYCHISM—(north Tibet) **1.** supernormal vision; **2.** supernormal hearing; **3.** thought-reading; **4.** knowledge of miraculous power; **5.** recollection of former existences; **6.** knowledge of the destruction of the passions. [**cf.** PATH]

ETHEREAL SMOKE—see ECTOPLASM.

ETHEREALIZATION—(materialization, seance) a step before full ectoplasmic materialization, in which the etheric world intelligence is not sufficiently condensed to produce a more solidified form; it takes many weeks for the medium and sitters to produce enough ectoplasm for the etheric world intelligence to use; in etherealization, the form is phantomish, unspeakable, untouchable, immovable, transparent, and capable of being seen under infrared light; intelligence however, shows the same characteristics each week. [**cf.** FULL MATERIALIZATION, CABINET, SEANCE]

ETHEREAN BEINGS—(ufology) intelligences made of ETHERIA substance, making their abode in the ethers; although features, size, shape, and density are different from earthlings, they appear to be a living soul-mind; invisible to mankind, but capable of materializing for one to perceive; theory: in existence forever in the ether as opposed to a discarnate human being who returns to the earth. (Inconcl.) [**cf.** ETHERS, HUMAN BEING KINGDOM]

ETHERIA—(esoteric) the essence of all substances vibrating at different rates, forming levels of worlds, and manifestations within the worlds; works under the law of intelligence. [**cf.** ETHERIC WORLD, BODIES OF MAN, PLANES]

ETHERIAL—see ETHEREAL, both spellings are correct.

ETHERIAN COMMUNICATION—(ufology) the study or communication of etherians among themselves and among earthlings which is biological and bioelectrical. (Inconcl.) [**cf.** UFOLOGY Appendix 5]

ETHERIAN PHYSICS—(ufology) the study of etheria substance, the life it contains and its functions, etc., which includes the vehicles, creature forms, and all aspects of the etheria. (Inconcl.) [**cf.** ETHER SHIPS, AEROFORMS, UFOLOGY Appendix 5]

ETHERIC—1. (esoteric) pertains to the invisible world, the etheric world; 2. a vibrational frequency wherein sound and ordinary currents of electricity are transmitted; composed of tenuous matter by the vibrations of which the sensation of light is conveyed to the eye; 3. the most dense of the four substances necessary to compose etheric matter: solids, liquids, gases, etheric, super-etheric, sub-atomic, atomic; 4. (physics) atomic substance. [**cf.** THOUGHT SPHERE, SUPERPHYSICAL ORDER OF MATTER]

ETHERIC ACTIVITY—to engage in rhythmic body movement continuously until one alters his or her state of consciousness, which enduces psychic experiences; basis for a consciousness change is rhythm and repitition; disciplines use dancing, twirling, running, chanting, clapping of hands, and jumping; without need of conscious mind decisions, the conscious mind becomes passive and the subconscious mind takes charge. [**cf.** MOVEMENT-FOR-ALTERED-CONSCIOUSNESS]

ETHERIC AURA—see ETHERIC DOUBLE.

ETHERIC BOWL—see KANDA.

ETHERIC BRIDGE—(esoteric) etherial matter that separates the astral world from mankind's vision, believed to be created by the mind. **Syn.** VEIL. [**cf.** PLANES, UNDERWORLD, SEVENTH HEAVEN]

ETHERIC CENTERS—(Native American, Hopi) the solar plexus, heart, throat, the brow, and the crown of the head. [**cf.** KUNDALINI, CHAKRAS]

ETHERIC CLAIRVOYANCE—to tune into the auric field of a material object and understand its counterpart in the etheric world; accomplished by staring at an object until the object disappears and one perceives the astral counterpart only; (do not confuse with X-RAY CLAIRVOYANCE). [**cf.** VISIONARY, MENTAL PSYCHISM]

ETHERIC CONTROL—(trance) an etheric world intelligence who works with a medium each session for physical phenomenon; intelligence synchronizes with medium's body helping the medium reach a deep trance state; intelligences screen out etheric world entities who would not benefit the physical psychic feat; protects the medium from the sitters who do not abide by the rules of trance; some controls also perform the desired phenomenon; brings the medium out of the trance state at the time alloted by the medium. [**cf.** DESIRED-CONTROL, TRANCE MANIFESTATIONS MISCELLANEOUS]

ETHERIC COUNTERPART—an invisible, refined order of matter that surrounds every material object and living organism (including humans) in earth, which is an exact replica of that object or organism; this refined order of matter consists of various kinds of astral matter and is formed following the pattern of the mental plane; astral objects and organisms are formed before they manifest in earth; the psychic can, therefore, tune into the future of earthlings and earth objects by reaching an (astral) alpha level of awareness; this can also be seen in gay colors as the outer part of the aura; (do not confuse with the luminous mist or ETHERIC DOUBLE section of the aura that clings close to the object or organism). [**cf.** ASTRAL VISION, CLAIRVOYANCE, ASTRAL PLANE]

ETHERIC CURRENTS—(esoteric) waves of semi-physical substance sweeping over the surface of the earth in a powerful movement, subject to utilization by human beings. (Inconcl.) [**cf.** VIBRATIONS Appendix 2, FLOW PATTERN, WAVELENGTH, SUBTLE]

ETHERIC DIAGNOSING—see AURIC DIAGNOSIS.

ETHERIC DOUBLE—(Eastern) 1. an invisible electromagnetic field surrounding and interpenetrating each thing in the universe, animate and inanimate, from the atom to the Great Central Sun; electromagnetic field gives energy to each thing's electrical system serving as a battery; field absorbs

213

emanations from each thing forming a pattern for its future existence; perceived clairvoyantly as very colorful, in neutral colors, or looking like luminous fur. **Syn.** AURA. **2.** (human being) an invisible electromagnetic field that surrounds each human and interpentrates his or her body at a faster vibrational frequency than the body; (**a**) serves as a pattern for one's future lifestyle in the present life and in future incarnations; pattern is built from one's emotions, (moods and attitudes), traits of character and activity; can be changed as easily as it is built; breaks up harmonious thoughts and inharmonious thoughts into elements for the body and lifestyle of the individual; (**b**) serves as a battery for the body's health and vitality; houses the chakras, that take the "spirit" from the air, assimilates it, and sends it throughout one's nervous system; (**c**) known before the days of Kirlian photography as an individual's second body; but it is now known that it does not encase the soul-mind in death but stays with the physical body until it fully decays; (**d**) affected by outside radiation, forces of light and darkness, cycles of the moon, magnetic storms, sunspots, and cosmic radiation; these radiations can be controlled and used for humanity's benefit; (**e**) perceived clairvoyantly as a luminuous fur or like an array of colors (Native American headdress), or an array of neutral tones; it is this field that the Kirlian camera photographs. (Inconcl.) **Syn.** AURA Appendix 5. [**cf.** BIOPLASMIC ENERGY FIELD, ASTRAL BODY, ETHERIC COUNTERPART]

ETHERIC DOUBLE/EARTH—the aura, or electromagnetic field encompassing and interpenetrating the earth, moving at a faster vibrational frequency; contains the blueprint of what is to happen on the planet earth in the future, including the earth's rotation and climatic conditions, and civilization in general; made from the energy emananting from the minds of mankind, throughout all the ages since the beginning of the earth. [**cf.** MENTAL-REFLECTING-ETHER, AKASHIC ART GALLERY]

ETHERIC ENERGY—(esoteric) one of the three types of psychic energy, usually called ectoplasm, vibrating at a slower frequency; found present in bioplasmic energy of the etheric double; in sufficient quantities, can act directly on the physical matter, as in physical psychism; see ECTOPLASM. **Syn.** PSYCHOTRONIC ENERGY. [**cf.** ASTRAL LIGHT, MIND ENERGY, PRANA]

ETHERIC ENERGY FIELD—see ETHERIC DOUBLE.

ETHERIC ENVELOPE—see ETHERIC DOUBLE.

ETHERIC EXTRAS—see EXTRAS.

ETHERIC FAUNA—(ufology) animal forms that live in the ethers, made of etherial substance, invisible to the physical eye. [**cf.** UFOLOGY Appendix 5, CRITTERS, TRANSITION OF SUBSTANCE]

ETHERIC FILM—(esoteric) **1.** an invisible record in picture form of events and inert objects found hovering over areas, situations and objects; perceived clairvoyantly as being clear-cut or cloud-like depending upon the emotions attached to the event or object; pictures are made from a person's thoughts which draw ethereal energy to them, form a blueprint conforming to the nature of the thought; blueprint activates more ethereal energy and makes the object or event manifest; **2.** an ethereal energy field capable of photographing all events that occur in the earth plane; see MENTAL-REFLECTING-ETHER. (Inconcl.) [**cf.** IRRADIANCE PHENOMENA]

ETHERIC FLUID—see VITAL LIFE FORCE.

ETHERIC FORCE—coined by John Worrell Keely; see VITAL LIFE FORCE.

ETHERIC FORMATIVE FORCES—(Rudolf Steiner, 1900) see VITAL LIFE FORCE.

ETHERIC GUARDIAN—see DOCTOR TEACHER.

ETHERIC LIFE FORMS—(ufology) various shapes, sizes and formations that swim or float in the ethers, constructed from glowing gaseous, liquid, and solid state substance; life that lives in the ethers, unable to be seen with physical eyes, but can be detected on film. [**cf.** AEROSPACE FORMS, PLASMATIC FAUNA, FIREFLIES]

ETHERIC LIGHTS—the human aura, as seen by etheric world entities; each person is known to the etheric world by the light he bears. **Syn.** HUMAN AURA. [**cf.** GUIDE, AURAS]

ETHERIC LINK—invisible ergs of energy that form an arc from one mind to another mind, from thought; arc extends from one's mind to the person one is thinking about, speaking to, or sending a mental telepathic message to; happens when two people are in same vicinity or at a distance. (Inconcl.) **Sim.** ASTRAL LINK. [**cf.** ABSENT HEALING, THOUGHTS]

ETHERIC MAGNETIC CURRENT—nerve fluid flowing from one person to the nerve fluid of another person, in hypnotherapy or in magnetic healing; could feel like an electric current, cold, hot, prickly, or even like a shock on the skin. [cf. HYPNOTHERAPY, MAGNETIC HEALING, GAUSS MAGNETICS]

ETHERIC MATERIALIZATION—a full blown psychic vision; 1. to perceive clairvoyantly one's doctor teacher, or a personal friend or relative who is deceased and desires to say he or she is still alive (crisis apparition); occurs after deep meditation or during sleep; 2. to perceive clairvoyantly an etheric world entity who can for a split second materialize and show her or himself; occurs spontaneously; entity appears in a normal setting; they disappear as quickly as they came; (why and how is under study). [cf. EMOTIONAL PSI, NEED-DETERMINED PSI]

ETHERIC MATRIX—see ETHERIC DOUBLE.

ETHERIC MATTER—(esoteric science) elements of four grades of different vibrational frequencies which interpenetrate each other throughout the atmosphere; invisible to the physical eye; 1. ether; 2. super-ether; 3. sub-atomic; 4. atomic. [cf. PLANES]

ETHERIC MENTOR—a soul-mind in the higher planes who chooses to work with an earthling to bring her or him knowledge. **Syn.** TRANCE CONTROLS, DOCTOR TEACHER. [cf. GUIDE, INNER BAND, OUTER BAND]

ETHERIC MOULD—(England) see ETHERIC DOUBLE.]

ETHERIC PHYSICAL AURA—see ETHERIC DOUBLE or AURA.

ETHERIC PLANE—see ETHERIC WORLD.

ETHERIC POWER POINTS—(esoteric) concentrated centers of energy and intelligence which act as transmitters and receivers of electricity in the atmosphere; believed to be created with creation of the electron; run along invisible lines (meridian lines) which connect one with another in a four-dimensional formation; subject to the law of thought; necessary to make this culture take form and shape; (acupuncture points in the human body are an extension of these). (Inconcl.) **Syn.** NODES. [cf. COSMIC STREAM, MERIDIAN LINES]

ETHERIC PROJECTION—1. (astral projection) to will etheric matter to form around the astral body after it lands at its destination, giving the astral body more opportunity to experience the physical surroundings; makes the astral body more easily seen by the clairvoyant eye, (a difficult skill for the projectionist); 2. a clairvoyant form of a living person standing close by; happens in a dream state or in a very relaxed state; occurs when one has strong emotional thoughts about that person; can be willed or spontaneous, unknown to the visionary personality. (Inconcl.) [cf. EMOTIONAL PSI, ETHERIC MATERIALIZATION] 3. to project ectoplasm from one's body at will, to a person in another area; when done with evil intent, makes an evil form at the end of the projection; when done with good intent, extends vitality to the distant person; strong, intense emotion is needed by the sender. **Syn.** PSYCHIC ATTACK. [cf. PSYCHIC TRANSFER]

ETHERIC RUNNING—to run at high speed, for hours without tiring; accomplished by centralizing one's attention on the upper part of the body, or on one subject (that has nothing to do with the run) and the lower part of the body carries on automatically, with the feet hardly touching the ground, and without fatigue. [cf. MOVEMENT-FOR-ALTERED-CONSCIOUSNESS, PROLONGED JOGGING, DETACHMENT]

ETHERIC SCRIPT—various styles of writing that have come through physical psychism from different etheric world entities, using different kinds of psychic writings; 1. scripts written in reverse, words spelled backwards; 2. scripts produced in mirror writing, which can be read only by holding it in front of a mirror and reading from the mirror; 3. scripts written in the handwriting style of the etheric world entity's previous life on earth; 4. scripts presented in an unknown language, called XENOGLOSSIA. [cf. AUTOMATISM, AUTOMATIC WRITING]

ETHERIC SPACES—(esoteric) the space between the atoms in the air and in matter; the path which energy travels that man has pronounced to be good energy. **Syn.** ETHERIC WARP. [cf. SYNAPSE, THOUGHT, POLARLITY]

ETHERIC STEEL—(ufology) name given to an unidentified flying object that appears to have just one body, because of its hard outer shell in one piece. [cf. UFOLOGY Appendix 5, HOMO MECHANICUS, SCOUT SHIP, ETHER SHIP]

ETHERIC SURGERY—(William Brown, an etheric surgeon) the act of etheric world doctors working through a physical body to perform invisible surgery on a patient; the psychic healing practitioner goes into a cataleptic trance, vacates the physical body, and allows the etheric world doctors to enter his or her body and use it; they perform surgery on the etheric double of the patient; the hands are held a few inches above the patient and look like they are performing a physical operation, only through simulation; the hands never touch the patient; the patient has a short recovery time. [**cf.** MIRACLE HEALING, ECTOPLASMIC PSYCHIC SURGERY, TEN PERCENT IMPERSONATION]

ETHERIC THREAD—(ancient Egypt) an invisible cord made by a psychic when she or he beams energized thought out of their hands; can be perceived clairvoyantly extending from the palms of the psychic to the object or person that they desire to reach. **Syn.** TELEPATHIC WIRE. [**cf.** BEAMED ENERGY, CONTACT HEALING, THAUMATURGISTS]

ETHERIC VISION—1. to perceive clairvoyantly creatures of a nonhuman nature, living just outside the normal range of vision in the etheric world; 2. to perceive clairvoyantly the chakras of the human. [**cf.** X-RAY CLAIRVOYANCE, OBJECTIVE CLAIRVOYANCE]

ETHERIC WARP—(esoteric) the spaces between the atoms in the air and in all matter; 1. the path of travel of energy that mankind has pronounced good; 2. the path of travel of psychic energy. (Inconcl.) **Syn.** ETHERIC SPACE. [**cf.** THOUGHTS, VIBRATIONS]

ETHERIC WEB—(esoteric) a dense, ethereal network of fine, fiery threads spreading itself over the counterpart of the physical body chakras, acting as a curtain or sheath to separate the astral body and astral experiences; prevents exposure to constant astral vision; can be removed, at times through desire and practice, by a person who choses to develop psychism. **Syn.** VEIL, BLACK CLOUD, BARRIER. [**cf.** CLAIRVOYANCE, ASTRAL WORLD]

ETHERIC WIRES—interlacing of ethereal strands that compose the etheric double. [**cf.** ETHERIC DOUBLE, KIRLIAN PHOTOGRAPHY]

ETHERIC WORLD—(esoteric) 1.overall picture of invisible space, containing its many kinds of life forms, and its many levels of intelligences, who communicate with mankind psychically; 2. the place where humans live after they make their transition from planet earth; 3. atoms or lesser particles in outer space vibrating all around man, faster than his physical eyes can see, forming layers of energy that have different characteristics and

functions, interpenetrating each other; 4. the atmosphere that contains seven levels of energies, with their functions and life forms, called **planes**; 5. contains four essential kinds of vibrational frequencies: (a)warmth ether; (b) light ether; (c) chemical ether; (d) life ether, which is used to form the many layers. **Syn.** HIGHER SIDE, INVISIBLE WORLD, ATMOSPHERE, HEAVEN, OTHER DIMENSIONS, UNKNOWN, SPIRIT WORLD. [**cf.** BODIES AND PLANES Appendix 5]

ETHERIC WORLD COMMUNICATIONS—assistance given by etheric world intelligences who have chosen for their own personal progression to work with individual earthlings; the assistance consists of: personal protection, guidance, psychic lessons for the masses; knowledge of disease and healing methods, advanced scientific knowledge, and collaboration with the medium who desires physical phenomena; the medium must show inner desire for this assistance and take time to sit for development. [**cf.** PSYCHIC DEVELOPMENT CIRCLE, SEANCE]

ETHERIC WORLD ENTITY—any soul-mind living in the etheric world at present who belongs to the human/angel kingdom; includes those who will incarnate again and those who have no need to: 1. advanced soul-minds who communicate with earthlings through psychic or mediumship skills; 2. advanced soul-minds who bring guidance and protection to earthlings without formal communication; 3. earthbound soul-minds who haunt and disturb earthlings; 4. inferior soul-minds from the density who deliberately haunt and disturb earthlings with evil intent; 5. deceased friends, relatives, and spouses; 6. poltergeists; 7. ghosts; (although this term is broad, it does not include nature spirits because they are soulless, nor does it include extraterrestrial beings who are still foreing to man's study). [**cf.** ETHERIC WORLD INTELLIGENCES, DISCARNATE BEING, ETHERIC WORLD]

ETHERIC WORLD INTELLIGENCES—soul-minds living in the etheric world who are higher on the human/angel evolutionary scale than the mass of earthlings; 1. have lived innumerable lives in earth and have chosen and earned the privilege to serve earthlings; some incarnate in earth again and some are past this necessity; 2. personal communication between etheric world intelligences and earthlings is in the form of: psychic information skills, physical psychic skills, healing skills, and bodily and and environmental protection; some serve one earthling for his or her entire incarnation and some serve for the time they are needed according to mutual talents and interests; intelligences evolve themselves by working with earthlings; intelligences do not intercede unless called upon and do not make choices for earthlings but do offer guidance; 3. general communication brought through seances, darkroom sessions, and psychic development circles; laws of the universe, guidance for the masses, metaphysical philosophies, ethereal physics, self-awareness instructions, and knowledge of soul-mind growth; 4. intelligences utilize the law of like attracts like and superior qualitative intelligences are not drawn to earthlings who are low on civilization's moral scale; (do not confuse with EXTRATERRESTIAL BEINGS who have not been studied enough to know if they belong to the same soul-mind species that humans belong to); see Appendix 3 for listing of names of intelligences in various cultures and time periods. [cf. INNER BAND, OUTER BAND, GUIDE, CONTROL]

ETHERIC WRITING—see PRECIPITATION.

ETHERICALLY PROPELLED SHIPS—(ufology) an invisible UFO that appears to live in the ethereal space instead of on a planet, shown by special photography. Syn. CONSTRUCTS. [cf. MUTANTS, INTRUDERS, SCOUT SHIPS]

ETHERICO-PHYSICAL BODY—see ETHERIC DOUBLE; name designates that a human's physical body and etheric body do not separate at death. [cf. ETHERIC DOUBLE, KIRLIAN EFFECT]

ETHERTRICITY—(esoteric) a basic form of energy, like electricity, but derived directly from the "ether"; travels inside a tube as a concentrated, high potential, high frequency electricity, as opposed to outside of its conductor; seems to favor doing or being active; capable of generating certain types of engines, producing kinetics, "heat," and conditions akin to "light." Syn. ETHER ENERGY. [cf. VIBRA-TIONS Appendix 5]

ETHNOMYCOLOGY—the science of attitudes of different reactions toward mushrooms; the plant that induces altered states of consciousness. [cf. MYCOPHAGES, MYCOPHOBES]

ETIMMU—(Mesopotamia) the personality who has died, and then returns by communicating through a psychic. Syn. DISCARNATE ENTITY. [cf. DEATH SCIENCE, PHANTOM COACH]

ETP—abbr. for EXTRATEMPORAL PERCEPTION; receiving information regarding the future of the world, through many types of mental psychism. Syn. PROPHESYING. [cf. CLAIRVOYANCE, CLAIR-AUDIENCE, PREDICTIONS, PROPHECY]

EU—(Greek) prefix meaning "good" and "well."

EUCALYPTUS TREE—(esoteric) a plant that stimulates the nerve fluid in the body by its aura, e.g., a person with nervous imbalance could feel better by sitting near the tree to absorb its emanations, which seem to regenerate the nerve fluid of the human. [cf. BOTANE, HOLISTIC HEALTH]

EUDEMON—see ETHERIC WORLD ENTITY.

EUMENIDES—a goddess in the etheric world who administers to humans when they need help. Syn. FURIES. [cf. ANGEL KINGDOM, FAIRIES, ETHERIC WORLD ENTITIES]

EURYTHMY—(Rudolf Steiner) a therapeutic art of movement of the human body based upon speech, making speech visible, and intoning untapped sound. (Inconcl.) Syn. VISIBLE SPEECH.

EUSTRESS—coined by Hans Selye; stress that works for one's benefit and health; stress that makes one come alive; e.g., excitement before a play helps one give a good performance; anxiety of eagerness makes a better outcome of a situation. (Inconcl.) [cf. STRESS, EMOTIONS, HOLISTIC HEALTH]

EUTHANASIA—(Greek *eu*, "good; *thantos*, "death") 1. the right to end suffering when a disease is considered clinically incurable, either by the permission of the patient or the family members; 2. the right to die the way one wants to and the right to spend one's last days on earth as one choses when the disease is diagnosed as being clinically incurable. Syn. MERCY KILLING, DIE WITH DIGNITY. [cf. DEATH SCIENCE, INITIATORY DEATH]

EVERGREEN TREE—(botane) a plant used as a symbol of continuity of life; has foliage which remains green all year round. [cf. BOTANE Appendix 2, SENSATION CONSCIOUSNESS]

EVERYDAY TRANCE—to hypnotize oneself by being deeply absorbed in, or preoccupied with, what one is doing at the present; for this time period, which can last from ten minutes to hours, one is one-pointed focused and in a hypnotic state, oblivious to what is happening in one's surroundings. Syn. SPONTANEOUS HYPNOSIS. [cf. ON-THE-SPOT-HYPNOSIS TRANCE]

EVIL—(esoteric) 1. a neutral energy in the form of an activity or object that the beholder interprets to be bad or sinful; 2. purposeful inaccuracies of life activity; man-made decisions about another individual's evolutionary growth experience; one unfolding in his or her own path according to their own speed, but not in accord to another person's lifestyle or opinion; 3. God fulfillment in a dormant state; 4. a name used to designate a step in evolution for growth that one does not approve of, nor feel compatible with at that time; 5. imperfect intelligence; ignorant actions; 6. manifestations of mixed consciousness; evil is not, it is in the mind; 7. graduations of good; scale of evil depends upon contemporary mass belief system; 8. duality of balance, method of checking balances of polarity; bad opinionated experiences are necessary to understand and appreciate good opinionated experiences; 9. evil is not real, as it is destructible and can be converted into good energies (good is indestructible); 10. opposite aspects of the one energy, necessary to produce power and manifestations. [**cf.** LAW OF POLARITY Appendix 7, GOOD, NEGATIVE THOUGHT]

EVIL EYE—to capture one's full attention with an eye-stare; to fix one's eyes upon another as if one's eyes are piercing through like a pointed weapon, and to fasten one's attention to another by a stare; a magnetic fluid emanates from everyone's eyes as they talk, and this fluid is subject to the law of thought; it is more emphatic and influential in some persons; 1. if used simultaneously with thoughts of evil intent, the victim will experience unpleasant and wicked activity occurring in his or her life; victim is hypnotized for the length of the stare and their subconscious mind is open to mental telepathic suggestions. [**cf.** SPELLED, TRANSFIXED] 2. used by hypnotists to help induce the hypnotic state in normal HYPNOSIS, in ON-THE-SPOT-HYPNOSIS (for evil intent), and in MASS HYPNOSIS. [**cf.** see above individually, MAGNETISM, MASTER EYE] 3. pertains to psychic information (the third-eye); (ancient) most psychic information was about the future and because the unknown was feared, the name evil eye was given psychism. [**cf.** GAUSS MAGNETICS, THIRD-EYE AREA]

EVIL GENIUS—an elevated soul-mind who chose a path in his or her earthly incarnation to help correct and overcome undesirable and neglected deeds performed; to lift up those who are in a low-scale level of society. [**cf.** GOOD GENIUS]

EVIL MOUTH—gossip about one's neighbor is an involuntary agent of evil and an unconscious working of black magic; adverse news is an assault on one's peace of mind; negative talking can give an unconscious psychic attack to the listener of the talk. [**cf.** POWER-OF-THE-WORD, PSYCHIC TRANSFER]

EVOCATION—(magic) to summon an inferior entity from the etheric world by performing a ceremonial ritual using incantations, verse, and magical tools, such as a wand or sword; two main objectives; 1. magician is hired to perform evil activity; an entity who is unbalanced and incomplete is summoned to execute the task; magician keeps her or himself in complete control and separated from the evoked entity; because of their knowledge and control, he or she is able to do the job and not become possessed by the entity; 2. magician is hired to exorcise an individual who is possessed by an inferior etheric world entity; magician summons the entity into his or her own body; from here they can either help the entity to go on into higher realms or dissipate her or him so they will not possess another individual; (do not confuse with INVOCATION). [**cf.** CEREMONIAL MAGIC Appendix 2]

EVOKE RESPONSES—(botane) the response of plants to peoples thoughts, emotions and actions. [**cf.** BOTANE Appendix 2, PRIMARY PERCEPTION]

EVOKED POTENTIALS—(laboratory, biofeedback training) temporary brain responses, minutely detected all over the head when hooked up to an EEG instrument; present themselves when stimulated by sensory input. [**cf.** BIOFEEDBACK TRAINING Appendix 5, ELECTRODES, EEG INSTRUMENT]

EVOLUTION—(esoteric) 1. the unfolding of the potential of the seed of Totality, until it remanifests as a perfect Totality; the attributes of perfect Totality within each atom will motivate each atom to unfold, grow, and progress, until they have experienced the wholeness of Totality and end in their original state of perfectness; 2. (B. J. Fitzgerald) an upward movement of consciousness to eventual oneness with the Source, God. 3. common theory: the higher forms of life are derived from the earlier and simpler forms; growth of progression from slower vibrational frequencies to faster vibrational frequencies; progression from one state of consciousness to a higher state of consciousness, converting a lesser form of life to a more sophisticated form of life; 4. the progressive growth and perfecting of all that is manifest in the universes, with no regard to time; the making of quality but not quantity. [**cf.** SIMPLE CONSCIOUSNESS, OVER-ALL CONSCIOUSNESS, SENSATION CONSCIOUSNESS, SOUL-MIND]

EVOLUTIONARY MAN—(esoteric) 1. theory; there is a human being seed within every man and woman that motivates them to become a perfect specimen of a human being, (as every living organism is unfolding the potential within the seed); 2. (Theosophy) a man or woman is responsible for perfecting the personality to fold into the soul-mind (the ego) in these many incarnations; the soul-mind is responsible to the Planetary Angel; the Planetary Angel is responsible to the Solar Deity Himself (perfection); 3. speculation: the cycle then reverses and we have involution. [**cf.** REINCARNATION, SOUL-MIND, KARMA]

EVOLUTIONARY NECESSITY—an activity or event that occurs at an inappropriate time, happens unexpectedly, and consumes money, energy, and thoughts that were intended for another project; passage of time will help one to understand why this distraction had to be dealt with in one's life; these events have an overall objective, instead of personal reasons. [**cf.** TRANSFORMATION, NEW-AGE PSYCHOLOGY]

EVOLVING PRINCIPLE—the potential within the seed of Totality extending itself into every thing in the universes, keeping the universes alive and growing to fulfill this potential; this potential of Totality is the motivating force within all things, keeping them forever moving; each thing strives to absorb knowledge and understanding of its own nature, directing to perfect that state of evolution so it can progress to a higher state. [**cf.** TOTALITY, MONADOLOGY]

EX—prefix meaning "out of, from, off, former, thoroughly," or "imparting."

EXACTITUDE CRITERIA—to perceive an "inner knowing" of the validity of facts, ideas, or names that are forced upon one with persistency and exclusiveness. **Syn.** INTUITIVENESS, CLAIRSENTIENCE. [**cf.** INSPIRATIONAL THOUGHT, HUNCHABILITY]

EXALTED ONES—(angel kingdom) those in the etheric world who have earned the rank of the Lordhood group. [**cf.** ANGEL HIERARCHY, PLANES]

EXALTED THRONE—(Jewish) a tremendous, awesome, numinous display of supreme and blinding light, seen by achieving the technique of a visionary experience through the celestial spheres; an ascension to the highest; used as an initiate rite for adepts; this skill is known as RIDING THE CHARIOT TO THE EXALTED THRONE. [**cf.** CHARIOT, SOUL FLIGHT]

EXCARNATE—a human being that has made his or her transition to the etheric world. **Syn.** DISCARNATE. [**cf.** DEATH ANGEL, DEATH SCIENCE, REINCARNATION

EXCITABILITY CYCLE—cyclic periods when the mass of people can more easily be induced to act in a more intense state of emotion than usual, *e.g.*, during stock market buying, war, and mob demonstrations.

EXCITABLE MEDIUM—one who allows the etheric world entity to intervene at any time the entity desires, frequently interfering with other plans; only inferior entities will do this and soon the information brought through is worthless and the medium becomes mentally or physically ill, (superior entities only intervene if the medium desires and preferably are told ahead of time). [**cf.** TRANCE Appendix 2]

EXCLUSIVE MEDIUM—a psychic or medium who has only one etheric world intelligence who works through them on all occasions, and in all types of psychic skills, (as opposed to having different guides for different types of skills). [**cf.** DOCTOR TEACHER, CONTROL, SPIRIT GUIDANCE]

EXECUTIVE ORDER—a subordinate or inferior group of earthbound entities who are communicating with politicians and business people, bringing them incorrect and incomplete information; happens to those who do not have the proper knowledge of psychism, regardless of their social status; earthbound entities are felt to be those who had practiced black magic in earth or were business failures in their last incarnations. [**cf.** EARTH-BOUND ENTITIES, HAUNTING]

EXO—(Greek) prefix meaning "outside, outer, external," when used in compound words.

EXOBIOLOGY—a study of action and life beyond the limits of the earth; study of extraterrestrial life; a discipline which believes that life exists throughout the universe and will develop where conditions are suitable or hostile. [**cf.** UFOLOGY Appendix 5]

EXOGENIC PSYCHISM—types of psychic skills stimulated by forces outside the body, such as receiving energy from a tree leaf, receiving a message given telepathically from another, or allowing an etheric world entity to use one's hands in psychic healing. [**cf.** MEDIUMSHIP HEALING, BOTANE, MENTAL TELEPATHY]

EXORCISM—to remove evil forces or negative influences from a person or an area, using a special technique or a ritual, e.g., 1. to remove a low-grade inferior entity from the body of someone who has seizures of possession, and to dissipate the entity so it will not reenter the victim's body; 2. to remove a confused soul-mind (a ghost) from an environment that he or she is frequently haunting; 3. to discourage a poltergeist from returning to play their pranks; 4. to repair the aura of one who is a victim of a psychic attack; 5. to clear the negative vibrations from a building's walls, ceiling, floors, etc., where emotional trauma has taken place; 6. to dissipate and destroy the evil energy field that is following one who is being hexed. [**cf.** EXORCISM Appendix 2]

EXORCIST—a person, usually a psychic, medium, or priest capable of performing the act of exorcism. **Syn.** EXORCISER. [**cf.** CONJUROR, HEX, GHOST, POSSESSION]

EXOTERIC—(Greek, *exo*, "without, external") information that is visible and suitable for the general public; worldly knowledge; information that is popularly understood by all and has been accepted as true.

EXOTERICISM—belief in the external world as it is perceived by the physical senses.

EXPANSION OF CONSCIOUSNESS—umbrella term to express what happens in meditation or psychic development; an awareness of life beyond the earthly world, awareness of one's place in Totality, awareness of one's soul-mind as eternal, awareness of feeling very light and disassociated. [**cf.** NEW-AGE PSYCHOLOGY, AWARENESS MOVEMENT, AWARENESS]

EXPECTANCY WAVE—(biofeedback training) an electrical wave showing in the cerebral cortical area that seems to precede a willed muscle movement. (Inconcl.) [**cf.** BIOFEEDBACK TRAINING, EEG, EMG]

EXPECTATION—(psi tasks) the score that is figured by averages of chance in a controlled ESP experiment. [**cf.** COGNITION, ESP, CONFIDENCE CALLS]

EXPERIENCER—(Maharishi Mahesh Yogi) the subconscious mind viewing action from its pure state, unaware of it being presently clothed in a physical body; happens during a good meditation session. [**cf.** MEDITATION, TRANSCENDENT, ECSTASY, SITTING ZEN, TAMING OF THE MIND]

EXPERIENT—(psi tasks) the one who receives the psychic energy that is given off from a psychic. [**cf.** UNCARING ALERTNESS, PUTTING OUT FEELERS, NONINTENTIONAL ESP]

EXPERIENTIAL—(biofeedback training) (derived from experience) to experience the emotion that goes with the vision. [**cf.** PROBLEM SOLVING STATE OF CONSCIOUSNESS]

EXPERIENTIAL HISTORIES—events that have happened in one's life, and one's reactions to those events, which seem to influence the present situation. [**cf.** REINCARNATION, HOLISTIC HEALTH, PAST-LIVES THEORY]

EXPERIENTIAL PHILOSOPHY—theory: one can learn by experiencing an event or action rather than understanding it by the intellect.

EXPERIMENT EXPECTANCY—(psi tasks) the outcome of tests can be easily swayed by the experimenter's attitude toward the outcome; found to influence the scoring of the ESP tests. [**cf.** RANDOM PROCESSES, STACKING EFFECT, PARAGNOSIS]

EXPERIMENT-EXPERIMENTER INTERACTIONS—(psi tasks) concept that the thoughts and attitudes of one's mind are a part of the experiment and must be considered in each experiment; also it must be considered that thoughts and attitudes change daily. [**cf.** SHEEP AND GOATS EFFECT]

EXPERIMENTAL SENSOR—(Patrick Flanagan) a flattened, circular metal that can regulate and radiate energy like the pyramid shape, called a pyramid energy generator; can be worn as an adornment and at the same times gives one the energy as if one is sitting under a pyramid. [**cf.** FORMS-WITH-POWER, PYRAMID ENERGY]

EXPERIMENTAL SPIRITISTS—psychics and mediums who believe in the physical manifestations of the etheric world and discarnate soul-minds, but who cannot go along with the philosophy.

EXPERIMENTER—(psi tasks) one who conducts, assists, or judges the psi experiment. [**cf.** COGNITION, CLAIRVOYANCE, ESP]

EXPERIMENTER BIAS—(laboratory) theory: personal prejudices of the experimenter can influence the manner in which data is reported by the subject or can cause motivational experimenter errors. [cf. CLOAK OF INSULATION, MISS, SHEEP AND GOATS EFFECT]

EXPERIMENTER EFFECT—(laboratory) even though subjects are chosen from the same group of people and work under the same objective conditions, they get conflicting and different target results because their target results show a conformity to individual expectations, even though the experiment is controlled. [cf. NONRANDOM BEHAVIOR, SUBJECT VARIANCE, TECHNICAL MUSE]

EXPERIMENTER PATTERN—(psi tasks) characteristics or mannerisms of the experimenter leave temporary vibrations on the experiment material which can have an influence on the psi perception in the experiment. [cf. BLIND PK, MISS, RECEIVER OPTIMIZATION]

EXPERIMENTER-SUBJECT PARANORMAL COMMUNICATION—(psi tasks) the subject picks up the attitude or thoughts of the experimenter. [cf. MENTAL TELEPATHY, CLAIRSENTIENCE, PERSONAL MIND PRINTS]

EXPLICIT MEDIUM—one who has the body chemistry for and allows an etheric world intelligence to intervene for psychic communication and who finds this communicated knowledge has the fullness and extent of a perfect author. [cf. INSPIRATIONAL WRITING, GUIDES, MEDIUMSHIP]

EXPLOITATION OF INSTINCT—to utilize one's inner feelings, hunches, and intuitive knowledge without questioning, due to belief that psychic information is from Totality and that Totality is above human reasoning and logic; to be divinely guided, to realize it, and to use the guidance. [cf. CLAIRSENTIENCE, INTUITION, PSYCHIC ART]

EXPOSURE DREAM—to see one's self nude and engage in activity, in a dream; is a common dream which can be interpreted to refer to honesty or refer to being unprepared. [cf. DREAM SYMBOLS]

EXPRESSIONS—see BODIES OF MAN.

EXPRESSIVE STEREOTYPE—(possession) a possessed person maintains the same activity and expression throughout each attack, as opposed to the more common type of possession in which each attack is unpredictable. [cf. POSSESSION, OBSESSION, EXORCISM]

EXSUFFLATION—see EVOCATION.

EXTENDED CLAIRVOYANCE—to see psychically beyond the normal range of vision and know what is happening in another place at the same time, e.g., to see in the mind's eye an accident two miles up the road; to see a tornado in another country at the same time it is happening; (do not confuse with CLAIRVOYANCE-IN-TIME). **Syn.** CLAIRVOYANCE-IN-SPACE. [cf. REMOTE VIEWING, X-RAY CLAIRVOYANCE]

EXTERIOR PNEUMATOPHONY—to hear spontaneous sounds in the air expressing intelligence; imitates a person or a nature creature; come from an etheric world intelligence in the presence of a medium. [cf. INTERIOR PNEUMATOPHONY, MEDIUMSHIP, OBJECTIVE CLAIRAUDIENCE]

EXTERIORIZATION—see ASTRAL PROJECTION.

EXTERIORIZATION OF MOTORICITY—(1860-1920) to project, energize, and store nervous emotional energy onto material, e.g., wood, water, linen, and cardboard; medium holds item in their palms and wills the emotion to enter the material. **Syn.** PALMED POWER [cf. BIOMETER OF BARADUC, MAGNETOMETER, SPIRITOSCOPE, HUMAN POLARITY]

EXTERIORIZATION OF SENSATION—(seance) to sense what is transpiring in a blacked-out seance room; ability of the sitters or medium to recognize a living presence, movement of ethereal substance or material objects, and the general atmosphere of the quality of the etheric activity. [cf. SEANCE, GUIDE, PSYCHIC LIGHTS]

EXTERIORIZATION OF SENSITIVITY—(hypnosis experiment) to experience (while in a hypnotic state) sensations similar to the activity of the hypnotist at the same time the hypnotist performs the activity; e.g., feeling pain and armstroking simultaneously when the hypnotist sticks a pin in a doll and strokes the doll's arm. [cf. HYPNOTHERAPY, HYPNOTIC SUGGESTION, RESPONSE ATTENTIVENESS, PSYCHOMETRIC TELEPATHY]

EXTERIORIZED PROTOPLASM—see ECTOPLASM.

EXTERNAL ALCHEMY—(Taoist) manufacture of elixirs of immortality. [cf. ALCHEMY, ELIXIR]

EXTERNAL AUTOSCOPY—to see past the skin as if there were no skin there; distance no barrier; to see into the body of a patient while in a trance state and be able to describe the organs in regard to their state of health. **Sim.** X-RAY CLAIRVOYANCE. [cf. INTERNAL AUTOSCOPY, TRANCE MEDIUM]

221

EXTERNAL WORLD—coined by Charles Richet; "nothing but the total of actual or past vibrations." [**cf.** VIBRATIONS Appendix 5]

EXTERNALIZED THOUGHTS—to receive answers to everyday problems shortly after a meditative state, through biofeedback training, meditation, prolonged jogging, etc. [**cf.** ALTERED STATES OF CONSCIOUSNESS]

EXTINCTION OF A CONDITIONED RESPONSE—(psi tasks) to weaken the stimuli gradually until there is no more action on the part of the person. [**cf.** PSI TASKS]

EXTINCTION PROCEDURE—(laboratory) theory: sets of internal conditions within a person's mechanism that makes them hit the target by "chance" alone, which have no connection to psi; these chance-correct successes constitute a kind of hindrance in psi procedure and constitute an inherent "extinction procedure" built into any repeated experiment. [**cf.** PSI TASKS, ESP, CHANCE, INTUITION]

EXTISPICIUM—divination using the intestines and bowels or internal parts of an animal as the point of focus for psychic examination. [**cf.** DIVINATION, POINT-OF-FOCUS, SYNCHRONICITY]

EXTRA—prefix meaning "beyond."

EXTRABRAIN-MIND COMPUTER—an entity from the higher planes of the etheric world that the medium can count on for added knowledge, above and beyond the ability of the medium's education; uses the skill of dependent voice or inspirational thought. **Syn.** CONTROL, GUIDE. [**cf.** GUIDES, DEPENDENT VOICE, INDEPENDENT VOICE]

EXTRACHANCE—(laboratory) psychic answers to experiments in a controlled situation that are not due to chance alone. [**cf.** MEANS, CHANCE, COGNITION]

EXTRACORPOREAL INTELLIGENCES—those in the etheric world who have made their transition from the earth. **Syn.** DISCARNATE ENTITIES. [**cf.** REINCARNATION, PLANES, ASTRAL BODY]

EXTRADOMICILIATION—a poltergeist who prefers to perform outside the house. [**cf.** POLTERGEIST, FOCUS, GHOSTS, APPARITIONS]

EXTRAORGAN—a tool for psychism endowed in some mediums, located in the solar plexus; one person known to be so well organized that the voice could speak through the solar plexus as if the medium had two mouths. [**cf.** MEDIUMSHIP, DEPENDENT VOICE]

EXTRARETINAL VISION—see EYELESS SIGHT.

EXTRAS—that which appears on the finished photograph or negative that was not visible by the naked eye when the picture was taken, e.g., one's guides, words, lights, streaks, hidden faces; believed to be accomplished because of synchronization of the psychic picture taker and the psychic's guides; now happens on colored film; (do not mistake this for the electromagnetic field taken with a high voltage camera). [**cf.** PSYCHIC PHOTOGRAPHY, SPIRIT PHOTOGRAPHY]

EXTRASENSITIVE PERCEPTION—later suggested to replace extrasensory perception by Dr. J.B. Rhine.

EXTRASENSORIMOTOR—the ability of behavioral and personal exchanges with the environment, coming through any one of the five psychic senses; the earth telepathically sending its vibrations to human telepaths who sense what is going on within nature in the world, e.g., knowing a tornado is coming, sensing death and anxiety during a hurricane in another part of the country. **Syn.** INTUIT TELEPATHY. [**cf.** TELEPATH, EMPATHY, CLAIRSENTIENCE]

EXTRA SENSORIMOTOR INTERACTION—see PARAPSYCHOLOGY.

EXTRASENSORY EPISODES—see MENTAL PSYCHISM.

EXTRASENSORY PERCEPTION—abbr. ESP; 1. term coined by J. B. Rhine; the concept that one mind can transfer thought and emotions to another mind over any distance without physical means. **Syn.** MENTAL TELEPATHY, EMPATHY CLAIRSENTIENCE. 2. (J. B. Rhine) the ingoing effect; information goes this information is then related back by the organism, e.g., ability to name the order of a deck of cards handled by another person; information traveling from cards to psychic. **Syn.** PSYCHIC COGNITION. 3. (Edgar Mitchell) the experience of, or response to, an external event, object, state, or influence without contact through the known senses; sometimes unconsciously occuring without awareness of it by person involved. **Syn.** TELEPATHY. 4. (Seth) are initially nonverbal and nonvisual, more like pure feeling that is only later interpreted in sense terms. **Syn.** CLAIRSENTIENCE. [**cf.** TELEPATHS, EMOTIONAL TELEPATHY, PSI TASKS]

EXTRASENSORY SIGNALS—(laboratory) information coming to a psychic that was not known before. [cf. PSYCHIC COGNITION, TELEPATHY, CLAIRSENTIENCE]

EXTRATEMPORAL PERCEPTION—abbr. ETP; to perceive information psychically through time and space, e.g., to intuitively receive information that will happen in the future or that has happened in the past. Syn. PROPHECY. [cf. CLAIRVOYANCE-IN-TIME, EXTENDED CLAIRVOYANCE, PREDICTIONS]

EXTRATERRESTRIAL—action that happens outside the earth; the earth being one boundary.

EXTRATERRESTRIAL ANIMALS—(ufology) biological UFOs that take the form of animals; varying from tiny to very large in size; some pleasant to see and some grotesque; realization by their movements that they are a pulsating life. Syn. SPACE ANIMALS. [cf. ATMOSPHERE AMOEBAE, DAWN ANGELS, BIOFORMS, DAYLIGHT DISCS]

EXTRATERRESTRIAL BEINGS—(ufology) intelligent life forms that seem similar to human beings, coming from outer space; differ in appearance from earth people but seem to be a body encompassing a soul-mind; come from other planets or live in the etheria. (Inconcl.) [cf. UFOLOGY Appendix 5]

EXTRATERRESTRIAL CRAFT—(ufology) foreign objects other than space ships seen in the atmosphere. [cf. FLYING SHIELDS, POWER SOURCE, GOOSEGG INSTRUMENTS]

EXTRATERRESTRIAL LIFE—(Trevor James Constable) organisms living in the earth's upper atmosphere; elemental creatures who live in an ocean atmosphere, existing in the infrared portion of the spectrum beyond the range of visible light. Syn. CRITTERS. [cf. PLASMATIC FAUNA, SOLID STATE LIFE FORMS, ECHO]

EXTRATERRESTRIAL VISITATION—broad term used for any type of UFO craft sighted, or any type of UFO craft landing with or without their craft beings; see CLOSE-ENCOUNTERS-OF-THE-FIRST-KIND, SECOND-KIND, THIRD-KIND, FOURTH-KIND. [cf. UFOLOGY, Appendix 5]

EXTREME EXALTATION—to journey to the higher spheres and be fully alert as to what one is experiencing; a state of altered consciousness wherein the soul-mind takes a soul flight; happens during deep meditation or in an emotional religious setting; (do not confuse with ASTRAL PROJECTION). Syn. SOUL FLIGHT. [cf. MENTAL PROJECTION Appendix 2]

EYE—(esoteric) represents intelligence, spirituality, terror, sun, moon; if shown in the middle of the forehead, eye represents the third-eye or psychic sense; sends out electromagnetic energies in streams, forming like a beam where directed, meeting the "antennas" of the object one wants to see, which is the electromagnetic field around the object, and brings this field back to the head for interpretation; this makes it possible for a psychic to beam energy to an object and implant it there, as in amulet rituals; this is the magnetism that enters the nerve fluid in the hypnotherapist's subject. [cf. THIRD-EYE AREA, EYELESS SIGHT, THALAMUS, BEAMED ENERGY, AMULET]

EYE DOCTRINE—(Buddhism) the southern teachings of Guatama Buddha, the exoteric or outer philosophy for the general world.

EYE OF BALOR—(Ireland) the power that comes from the eyes when staring. [cf. EYE-FIXATION, EVIL EYE, BEAMED ENERGY]

EYE OF HORUS—(Egypt) a symbol believed to possess the strength to ward off evil; represents Osiris, the Supreme Deity; male, positive polarity. Syn. EYE OF ISIS, THIRD-EYE, UDJAT EYE. [cf. POLARITY, THIRD-EYE AREA]

EYE OF ISIS—(ancient Egypt) female, negative; see EYE OF HORUS.

EYE OF LIGHT—to reveal personal psychic information, especially regarding one's past incarnations, by staring steadfastly into the eyes of the recipient; the principle that the eyes are the window of the soul-mind. [cf. REINCARNATION, POINT OF FOCUS]

EYE OF SIVA—(Hinduism) represents the place where both destructive and constructive cosmic forces become energized; a famous and popular symbol of God. [cf. POLARITY, VIBRATIONS, COSMIC FORCES]

EYE OF THE SOUL—a fully developed third-eye area; when cosmic energy enters the head of a fully developed third-eye area, the pituitary gland and pineal gland will fuse together this cosmic energy, giving humanity a new mechanism to use; humanity will be able to transmit vibrations of a more refined, subtle, and discriminative nature; these he or she will interpret and rearrange giving them access

223

to higher knowledge and they will use clairvoyance, clairaudience, clairscent, and clairsentience as easily as they use their five physical senses; humanity will develop this in the coming age. [cf. THIRD-EYE AREA Appendix 5, SPIRILLA, PITUITARY GLAND]

EYE OF WISDOM—collective name for psychic ability; pertains to the third-eye.

EYE SINGLE—to see with the whole body; having no point of focus; fairies, insects, and animals are believed to see this way. **Syn.** ASTRAL VISION. [cf. EYES OF INSTINCT]

EYE-FIXATION—(hypnosis) to stare at an object with eyes open to induce a hypnotic state; 1. to roll one's eyes back in the head and stare at an object on the ceiling until the eyes tear and close; 2. to stare straight forward at a revolving hypnodisc composed of two-toned spiraling lines; 3. to stare at a swinging pendulum until the eyes close. [cf. SELF-HYPNOTHERAPY, MASS HYPNOSIS, SPONTANEOUS HYPNOSIS]

EYE-LANGUAGE—to speak with emotions of love and understanding through one's eyes, without verbalizing; to be so full of love that the eyes express this emotion; a way of communicating between angels; to just see two eyes when sitting for psychic information, can be interpretated that a high etheric world intelligence wants to bring love to one. [cf. PSYCHIC DEVELOPMENT, MEDITATION, GUIDE]

EYE-ROLL TEST—(hypnosis) a method of determining the hypnotizeability of a subject before the hypnosis session; the subject is to roll his eyes backward while gradually closing the eyelids; the more white of the eye that shows, the more hypnotizeable the subject is; used by psychiatrists as a biological marker. [cf. HYPNOTHERAPY, INDUCTION, SELF-HYPNOTHERAPY]

EYE-TYPE ANGELS—the highest rank of soul-mind intelligence belonging to the sun and star kingdom; believed to exist on light; known to earthlings, when perceived clairvoyantly, by a pair of eyes (rare occasion). [cf. ANGEL KINGDOM, DEVA, PLANETS, EYE-LANGUAGE]

EYELESS SIGHT—(Canada, United States) ability of a blind person or blindfolded person to distinguish color, mass, size, and distance without using the organ of sight; a psychic ability varying with individuals and requiring concentration; reports of this study: finger tips and cheeks detect the thermal and density feelings of color; negatives are imprinted on the inside of the forehead; an awareness is felt with the whole consciousness; (do not confuse with PSYCHOMETRY or X-RAY CLAIRVOYANCE) (Inconcl.) The following are other names given to this study and practice: DERMOPTIC, DERMO-OPTICAL PERCEPTION, PARAOPTIC SIGHT, BIOINTROSCOPY, HYPERESTHESIA, CUTANEOUS VISION, EXTRA-RETINAL VISION, X-RAY VIDEO CLAIRVOYANCE, FINGERTIP VISION, SKIN SIGHT, DERMAL OPTICAL SENSITIVITY.

EYELESS VISION—see EYELESS SIGHT.

EYELID FATIGUE—inability to open the eyes when meditating, engaged in psychic sensitivity, or in a hypnotic state; means the body is very relaxed and tuned into the alpha state of consciousness; occurs when concentration is single-pointed. [cf. HYPNOTHERAPY, PSYCHIC DEVELOPMENT]

EYES OF INSTINCT—to see with a large scope of vision, as if one is seeing with one's whole body, not needing a point of focus; ability to see as birds and beasts do. **Sim.** EYES OF THE FLESH. [cf. ASTRAL VISION, ANPSI]

EYES OF THE FLESH—see EYES OF INSTINCT.

EYES OF TRUTH—to preceive the past and future of hundreds of world-periods through the psychic skill of inspirational thought, automatic writing, voice trance or clairvoyance-in-time. **Sim.** FORE-SEER, PROGNOSTICATOR, RETROGRESSOR, PROPHET. [cf. CELESTIAL SEEING, PROPHECY]

EYES OF WISDOM—to be so attuned to Totality that one is fed psychically to know what is going on throughout all eternity; avatars are believed to have this perception. [cf. MULTIDIMENSIONAL, EYES OF TRUTH]

"F"—the musical note which is a combination of sounds of everything on earth, making the harmoic chord which is the keynote of planet earth; perceived as the key of "F"; when played musically, produces the vibrations that make green color; considered by modern physicists to be the actual tone of nature; (Chinese) known as the "Kung," the great tone. [**cf.** CLAIRAUDIENCE, COLOR]

FACHAN—(west Highlands of Scotland) see NATURE SPIRIT.

FACING THE SHADOW—(occult) implies a realization of the reality of the subconscious mind; an acceptance of the material world, often at variance with that of the conscious mind and the necessity of integrating the two minds. [**cf.** SHADOW, SUBCONSCIOUS MIND, BRAIN]

FACSIMILE WRITING—a reproduction of a famous deceased person's work by an etheric world intelligence or the author her or himself or working through an automatist; two cases that have been tested and proven: Oscar Wilde, Blance Abercrombi. [**cf.** PAINTING MEDIUM, AUTOMATIC WRITING]

FACULTAS FORMATRIX—(Galen, A.D. 170; Johannes Kepler, circa 1600) see VITAL LIFE FORCE.

FAINT—(botane) an action by a plant that compares to a human faint; occurs when the owner is going through a catastrophe. [**cf.** WATCH PLANTS, SENSATION CONSCIOUSNESS, SYMBIOTIC RELATIONSHIP]

FAIR WITNESS—(John C. Lilly) functioning of the minds wherein the conscious mind remains uninvolved and objective, letting what happens go into the subconscious mind without making decisions upon it; when necessary to call it from the subconscious mind, it is unhampered by the original experience; as in hypnotherapy, guided meditation, under anesthesia, and in unknown hypnotic influence. [**cf.** ON-THE-SPOT-HYPNOSIS, HYPNOTHERAPY, MASS HYPNOSIS]

FAIRIE—(Latin *fata*; Archaic *fay*, "enchanted or bewitched") a small, ethereal replica of a human in appearance and mannerisms; desires a rapport with humans but lives in its own invisible culture; a collective word to mean the whole lower-half of the angel being kingdom of over 1,000 varieties;

1. work with and have charge of the four elements of air, fire, water, and earth under the supervision of the angels; pure elemental vortexes of energy; 2. light energy field capable of forming an etheric body of substance drawn from the etheric double of the earth to carry out its function; 3. live in the rhythm of nature; synchronizes its heartbeat to that of the work at hand; concerned with the process of nature's evolution and its service to humanity; 4. at times it gives off a luminous reflection and at times it takes on the shape of a human form, altered in size; human form changes with locale; appears in either gender but prefers male gender; body appears loosely knit and felt to have a dense body inside the light body; 5. can be perceived clairvoyantly and seen with physical eyes; cannot be touched; materializes and dematerializes itself going from dimension to dimension very quickly; 6. an energetic vapor-like ethereal substance using the same material that feelings are made of; responds quickly to human emotions; has a sensation consciousness similar to the plant kingdom; posesses the ability of sending an electric charge to stimulate the human intellect and emotions in order to communicate with them; actions and thoughts influence mankind's ethereal bodies; 7. loveable, joyous entity but unpredictable; 8. neither an angel nor a devil but mediate space between mankind and angels; also spelled **faerie, elf fayerye, fairye, fayre, faerie, faery, fairy, fay, fey**; see NATURE SPIRITS. [**cf.** NATURE SPIRITS Appendix 3 for individual types]

FAIRIE LAND—a vibrational frequency very close to the physical world, considered to be the etheric double of the earth. [**cf.** NATURE SPIRITS]

FAIRY CHANGELING—an ugly, strange looking baby found in place of the mother's own beautiful child; a fairy baby exchanged by the fairies. [**cf.** NATURE SPIRITS, BROWNIES, RED CAPS]

FAIRY FIRE—a misty, phosphorescent light flitting at night: 1. when seen in the graveyard, believed to be an astral shell or confused soul-mind; 2. when seen on the road, believed to be an etheric world entity misleading night travelers; 3. (Russia) the soul-mind of an unbaptized child. **Syn.** FRIAR'S LANTERN, FOOLISH FIRE, IGNIS FATUUS. [**cf.** CORPSE LIGHT, WILL-O-THE-WISP]

FAIRY MIDWIFE—a nature spirit that materializes in time to help an earthling have a baby; produces itself because of the strong intense thought of the couple; is capable of stealing the baby or mother. [**cf.** FAIRIES, BROWNIES, MIDDAY WOMAN, HWANG]

FAIRY MOUNDS—(Scotland) actual physical earth hills, but hidden; believed to be the homes of the wee people. [**cf.** FAIRY RING, FAIRIES, NATURE SPIRITS Appendix 3]

FAIRY RINGS—1. bare spots in lawns and fields in the form of a ring; an area where the fairies dance in the physical world when humans are not around; this dance strengthens their power and brings good luck to the owner of the land; 2. (Siberia) circles of white-stalked, red-capped fungus; used by peasants to provoke intense, long-lasting, hallucinations. **Syn.** AMANITA MUSCARARIA. [**cf.** HALLUCINATIONS, FORMS-WITH-POWER]

FAIRY STONE—(minpsi) a stone containing a nature-formed hole; has the vibrational frequency making it suitable to be used as a healing agent and protective amulet for its owner. [**cf.** AMULET ENERGIZING, MINPSI]

FAIRY WEED—(botane) plants that have the proper vibrational frequency to help the fairies have psychic manifestations. [**cf.** NATURE SPIRITS Appendix 3, SENSATION CONSCIOUSNESS]

FAITH—(esoteric) 1. to have an automatic understanding of knowledge of a system; a law of function of an entity; perfect knowing; 2. the conscious mind is aware of scientific proof, tangible proof, or its acceptance by the masses, of a certain principle or happening in the outer world; this concept is dropped into the subconscious mind and solidified with repetition; the conscious mind reacts accordingly to this belief and it is so; e.g., expectance that the sun will rise every morning simply because it hasn't yet failed to do so, keeps the sun rising; 3. "positive" expectation that "it" will happen and it does; (do not confuse with BLIND FAITH). [**cf.** NEW-AGE PSYCHOLOGY]

FAITH HEALING—to "expect" that one will get better is one of the necessary factors in every type of cure; this confidence that one will be cured comes from a "desire to live"; this desire of the patient allows the treatment she or he chooses to change their body chemistry so the body can heal itself, at the time one is seeking healing; method chosen can be a medical doctor, aspirin, herbs, diet, a religious practioner, reflexologists, manipulation of the body, prayers, biofeedback training, hypnotherapy, and others; if the patient has a desire to live, one automatically expects the chosen method of cure to heal them, and any type of chosen cure, will; this desire is "faith" or automatic knowing that one will get better; (if one does not have a strong desire to get well, no method chosen will cure them); (do not confuse with INSTANTANEOUS HEALING). [**cf.** LAYING-ON-OF-HANDS, MENTAL HEALING AFFIRMATIONS]

FAKIR—1. (Sufi) both the follower and the traveller; one who has spent hours in meditation learning to quiet the brain and body activity so as to fuse the pineal and pituitary glands to bring psychic information for use in healing and guiding his or her people; 2. (Islam) an order for those who aspire to acquire psychism to use for the benefit of their people; 3. (Arabic *faqir*, "poor") poor in the sight of God; originally applied to dervishes under a vow of poverty; 4. (Moslem) a yogi; 5. (India) former pupils of Agartha who stopped their studies before reaching the "upper" levels of the organization. [**cf.** PSYCHIC SKILL, DERVISHES]

FALL—(casting of lots) the pattern of the landing of the thrown lots; this pattern has a bearing on the answer to the question; coins, stones or ming sticks are used as lots to throw and the psychic uses the position of their "fall" in regard to the question asked. [**cf.** I CHING, SYNCHRONICITY]

"FALL IN WITH"—to tune into the vibrations around the recipient in a psychic reading; each psychic has a silent routine that brings him or her into the thought atmosphere and electromagetic pattern around the person who is seeking answers. Usage: "As I fall in with your vibrations I find you have a question about a friend named Helen." **Syn.** COME INTO YOUR VIBRATION. [**cf.** RECIPIENT, QUERANT, PSYCHIC INFORMATION]

FALLEN ANGELS—discarnate entities who live close to earth and are desirous and capable of haunting earthlings; ancient history tells that they have fallen out of favor with God and want to get back at the gods for not giving them mankind privileges. **Syn.** EARTHBOUND ENTITIES, UNGODLY SPIRITS, GHOSTS. [**cf.** HAUNTING, DISCARNATE ENTITY, REINCARNATION]

FALLING DREAMS—to perceive during sleep that one is falling: 1. to become aware that one is taking an astral flight in the night and when interiorizing

226

the astral body the sensation is that of falling; 2. to have a normal dream and the dreamstuff scene pertains to the dreamer falling; to be interpreted to mean that the dreamer has fallen down in one aspect of his life. [cf. DREAMS, PERSONAL PSYCHIATRIST, DREAMSTUFF]

FALLING SPIRITS—(Native American, Senoi) entities in the etheric world who have been given the responsibility of having charge of man in his falling dreams. [cf. DREAM RESEARCH LABORATORIES, DREAM INCUBATION, ONDINNONK]

FALSE AWAKENING—(dreams) 1. to think one has awakened from the dream and keeps on dreaming as if it were daytime living; later finds he or she was still sleeping; 2. (astral projection) the astral body gets up and goes through the motions of dressing and later the dreamer finds instead that she or he is still in bed. [cf. LUCID DREAMS, SLEEP CONTROL, ESSAY DREAMS]

FALSE-FACE SOCIETY—(Native American, Iroquois) tribal members with the psychic ability to conjure away the evil etheric world entities whom they feel are causing some of their brother tribesmen to do cruel acts. [cf. ORENDA, EXORCISM, CONJURE]

FALSE-SERIOUS COMMUNICATIONS—psychic information brought through a medium that is difficult to distinguish from serious true information, except for its lack of continuity; the beginning messages are spoken in intelligent language and appear to be authentic material, but later the information contradicts itself. [cf. AUTOMATIC WRITING, INSPIRATIONAL WRITING, DEPENDENT VOICE, TRANCE]

FAMA FRATERNITATIS—a book, printed in 1614, telling about the Rosicrucian Order of the Brotherhood, and the founder of the Rosicrucian discipline, Christian Rosenkreuz. [cf. ROSY CROSS, SEVEN-SIDED VAULT]

FAMILIA—an etheric world intelligence that does all the chores in every aspect of the medium's life. **Syn.** DOCTOR TEACHER, CELESTIAL GUARDIAN. [cf. INNER BAND, CONTROL, MASTER]

FAMILIAR—a live cat or other animal owned by a witch upon which she transfers psychic energy in cases of evil-oriented activities; the witch summons etheric world forces to possess the animal, which then has the intelligence needed to help carry out the witch's evil action; animal is sent to the area

where the evil is intended and performs in mannerisms directed by the witch to release the evil vibrations; if the animal will stay in the area, the witch keeps sending evil vibrations by way of the animal; plants, garments, and inert objects can also be used as a familiar; (do not confuse with a FAMILIAR SPIRIT). [cf. ANPSI, POSSESSION, WITCHCRAFT, HEX]

FAMILIAR SPIRIT—1. a thought-form used psychically by a witch to carry evil vibrations to an area; an artifical elemental purposely made by the witch through repetitious densification of thought until it becomes strong enough to form the shape of an animal or a grotesque formation; witch sends this thought-form to the desired area where she intends evil to prevail; though-form is attached to the witch by an ethereal cord making it possible to be willed anywhere; witch psychically transfers evil vibrations through the cord to the thought-form which expels it according to her will; one concept: it is an extension of the witch itself under full control; if witch breaks her train of thought before she recalls the animal thought-form, it snaps back and expels the evil vibrations on her. **Syn.** ANIMAL FAMILIAR. [cf. ELEMENTAL, MASS ELEMENTAL] 2. a deceased person who is summoned by a witch to serve as an evil spirit to bring harm to an individual; witch summons one who was her friend while living and because of this earthly bond between them, she is able to transfer her evil vibrations to the deceased person who transfers it to the enemy; (do not confuse with a FAMILIAR that is visible). [cf. WITCH]

FAMILY GHOST—1. an aggregate of atoms that mimics, entirely or in part, a highly traumatic event which previously happened in the home; household members are unable to handle this trauma, keep talking about it and its disturbance to them; their constant rememberance and repetitious retelling of the story collectively holds these atoms together, forming an elemental (or thought-form) with enough intelligence and power to reenact the event; thought-form is perceived by visible activity or by observing the results of unseen activity. **Syn.** ELEMENTAL. 2. an earth-bound entity, former resident of the home, who reenacts parts of a traumatic scene he or she encountered while alive; the grossly emotional vibrations of the experience impregnated the area of the occurrence; this impregnation, plus their desire to return, gives them ample energy to periodically show their

227

presence; identified by gruntings, walking sounds, and movement of physical objects. [cf. GHOSTS, HAUNTED LOCALITIES]

FAMILY KARMA—(Sanskrit) a series of happenings centering around the family household that cannot be accounted for by member's activities or which occur for no logical reason; a collective result of the family's past actions; made from members individually and also from a similarity of attitudes of all members, which gives the actions energy to react as a whole; e.g., each member has a flat tire on his car the same week. [cf. KARMA, ACCUMULATED KARMA, GROUP KARMA]

FAMULATION—poltergeist activity; causing an entire family harassment because the family as a unit is the focus or generator for the poltergeist. [cf. GHOSTS, POLTERGEIST, FOCUS EXORCISM]

FANA—(Sufi) to lose one's own identity and become one with the divine essence; occurs during meditation or in Sufi twirling; to reach the supreme goal; to accomplish paradise. [cf. SEED MEDITATION, MOVEMENT-FOR-ALTERED-CONSCIOUSNESS]

FANTASY—uncontrolled inner-mind pictures of scenes, objects and people; the thinker starts the picture deliberately and then lets it flow to grow and become pleasurable; can be performed with others around; individual "can" distinguish it from reality; fills a psychological need for wish fulfillment, frustration, deferred gratification, or is used as a defense mechanism; does not contribute to the manifestation of future events as other thoughts do; (do not confuse with CONSCIOUS FANTASY or VISUALIZATION; see Appendix 4 for clarification with PSYCHIC INFORMATION, IMAGERY, HALLUCINATION and DAYDREAMING). [cf. THOUGHT-FORMS Appendix 2]

FAR-MEMORY—a technique of recalling or seeing visions of one's past (either this life or past incarnations) without being under hypnosis; one can find out their sex, historical dates, vocations, and country of their past incarnations; one is not apt to choose a traumatic scene and will not revivify as in hypnosis; see BACK-IN-TIME. [cf. LEVEL-SHIFT, MULTI-DIMENSIONAL]

FARADAY CAGE—the use of Michael Faraday's theory for psychic experiments; a cubicle, large enough for one or two persons, built out of concrete, steel, or other metals; designed so that whatever is placed in it would resist penetration of radio and electromagnetic waves; e.g., a psychic was placed in this cubicle and performed PK experiments; objective was to determine whether the increase in psychic energy comes from within the body or from the outside environment. [cf. RADIONICS, PK, NONHUMAN-PK]

FASCIA—(Rolfing) connective tissue which has set into place over the years, retaining and holding unresolved emotional patterns that could not be dealt with at the time of occurrence, and cause the body to be out of alignment. [cf. ALTERNATIVE, BLOCKS]

FASCINATE—(Latin *fascinare*, "to enchant, to charm") to allure and hold an individual captive until they are deprived of their resistance and slide under the control of the fascinator for manipulation, until released; accomplished by: 1. capturing one's eyes with a forceful stare and at the same time promising the victim something unusual and extremely pleasurable; the stare is constant and the fascinator's personal charm emanates while the attention is held with the constant stare until the victim is enthralled by the power and promises of pleasure; 2. arousing one's interest and then holding them captive by a fixed eye-stare with a desire to put fear into the victim; fear energy is beamed out of the eyes and the ploy of the fascinator, until the victim relinquishes their power of resistance for fear that the fascinator will do something destructive. **Syn.** SPELL. [cf. BEWITCHMENT, OVERLOOKING, CAPTIVATION, CHARM]

FASCINATED MEDIUM—one who brings forth a low quality entity when summoning from the etheric world; is easily deceived by the communications of such entities because of their tremendous desire to communicate. [cf. MEDIUMSHIP, GUIDE, DISCARNATE ENTITY, ASTRAL SHELL]

FASCINATION OBSESSION—the action directly on a medium's thoughts by an inferior, malicious etheric world entity, constantly urging communications; brings through low quality information but it is clever enough to deceive the medium. [cf. SIMPLE OBSESSION, GUIDE]

FASCINATOR—one who is capable of holding another person captive by their piercing eye-stare and clever allurability. **Syn.** CHARMER, SPELLER, ENCHANTER. [cf. FASCINATE, ENCHANT]

FASTING—to eat less or no food in order to break down and remove the toxins in the tissues before they are recycled back into the bloodstream; nature's way to cleanse and purify the inside of the body; an aid to accelerate one's psychic skills and healing abilities; (do not confuse with DIETING; see Appendix 4). [cf. ALTERNATIVE, HOLISTIC HEALTH]

FATAL PSYCHIC ABILITY—to constantly use one's psychic powers for evil intent; to overuse this power and allow one's mediumship to get out of control; could unintentionally wind up in self-destruction or harming other people. [cf. PHYSICAL MANIFESTATIONS/MISCELLANEOUS and PHYSICAL PSYCHIC PROCESSES Appendix 2]

FATE—(Latin *fatum*, "a spoken decree presumed to come from the gods") a destiny created by oneself but denied as being one's own creation; that which is inevitable and unavoidable in one's life, due to one's own past thinking and acting. [cf. KARMA, DELAYED KARMA]

FATEFUL COMMUNICATION—information that tells of a death happening at the precise moment of the death or an announcement of a death coming soon, perceived through a psychic skill. **Syn.** HUMAN OMEN. [cf. PROPHECY, EMOTIONAL PSI, PORTENDER]

FATES—1. (Nordic) male nature spirits believed to be older and more potent than the gods; 2. three goddesses in the etheric world who have power over one's future; they can spin the destiny for one and cut it off when they desire.

FATHER-MOTHER GOD—a salutation used in prayer with the inner belief that Totality or God is complete and has perfect male and female balance in polarity.

FATICARIA—see WITCH or PSYCHIC.

FATIMA—a Roman Catholic Shrine located in Fatima, Portugal in honor of the many psychic events that happened there; e.g., a light shone and dried up all the rain instantly; discs seen in the sky emitted a power so strong it deprived the people in the area of their bodily senses; a superior being appeared in the sky; the Fatima prophecy. [cf. FATIMA PROPHECY]

FATIMA PROPHECY—(1917) at the exact moment that the Bolshevik Revolutionary Army entered a church in Moscow, and killed those in prayer, Mother Mary appeared to three young children in Portugal and gave a special prophecy; prophecy regarded wars and the infiltration of Communism in the Catholic Church; some of the prophecies have already materialized.

FAUDEUR—a mischievous elf; see NATURE SPIRITS.

FAUNS—1. (Greek mythology) a class of rural deities in the nature kingdom represented as men with ears, horns, tails, and hind legs, similar to a goat; 2. (pre-Christian) etheric world male entity who sought out women with whom to fulfill his sexual desires. **Sim.** SATYRS, LORDS OF EVIL]

FAUNUS—(Latin, "divinities") deities in the etheric world who are similar to Pan, that are in charge of the nature kingdom. **Syn.** SYLVANUS.

FAUST—1. a German magician, alchemist, and astrologer; 2. a character of medieval legend used in many plays; represented as selling his soul to the devil in exchange for knowledge and psychic powers.

FAWN—(Spain) a young deer is regarded as a sign of divine protection for the area where seen; depicted with horns; belief that people can be charmed and then transformed into deer. [cf. CHARM, ANPSI, NATURE SPIRITS]

FAY—see FAIRIE.

FC—see FIELD CONSCIOUSNESS.

FEAST OF FOOLS—(Native American, Iroquois) (dreams) a community-wide event wherein everyone acts out their dreams in charades, while others try to guess the content; a method of getting rid of personal conflicts and improving one's personality. **Syn.** ONONHAROIA. [cf. ONEIROS, RECALLER]

FEATHER CROWN—a ball of feathers in a unique pattern, found in beds or pillows after a person has died; feather ball is about six inches in diameter and two inches thick; feathers are closely overlapped, turning in a clockwise direction with no apparent visible adhesive. [cf. DEATH SCIENCE Appendix 2]

FEE—(Normandy) a mischievous nature spirit in charge of bridges.

FEEDBACK—any method that tells one what one is doing; e.g., a mirror tells one how one looks in one's outfit; the coach tells one how one is shooting the baskets, etc. [cf. BIOFEEDBACK INSTRUMENT]

FEEDBACK CONTROL SYSTEM—a built-in body mechanism that gives an order for the body to perform an action; body picks up sensations from the five senses, and this is relayed to the brain, which is a control center; here it intermeshes with other information; the brain then gives an order for the body to act. [**cf.** BRAIN, SUBCONSCIOUS MIND, CONSCIOUS MIND]

FEEL-AND-SEE-COMBINATION—to telepathically communicate the feeling of touch to another; the sender touches an object with an unusual surface such as a furry toy, ice cube, sand paper, etc.; the receiver located in a remote area tunes into the sensation of the touch. **Sim.** PSYCHOMETRIC TELEPATHY. [**cf.** TELEPATHY, MENTAL TELEPATHY, INTUIT, TELEPATHY]

FEELING THERAPY—concept: a change in consciousness and attitude can come from getting in touch with one's feelings and to become aware of these feelings. [**cf.** HOLISTIC HEALTH]

FEELINGS—(esoteric) 1. fundamental, conscious, emotional states; an emotional awareness of every experience one has, and the "degree" of this emotion is influenced by one's evaluation of the experience; evaluation of the situation is influenced by one's point of view; one's point of view is influenced by one's conscious and subconscious belief system; conclusion: feelings and their degree of emotion are caused by one's belief system; 2. the expression of Totality in astral matter. [**cf.** BELIEF SYSTEM, CURATIVE EDUCATION, FEELING THERAPY]

FEMALE HAMADRYADS—1. nature spirits that live in trees and have charge of greenery; 2. (Greece) "wives of the silent" during the time of Aphrodite. [**cf.** TROLLS, LEPRECHAUN]

FENG—a nature spirit in the form of a bird that expresses the element of fire; works, lives and has its being in fire; see FENG-HWANG. [**cf.** FOOLISH FIRE]

FENG-HWANG—1. a nature spirit in the form of a bird that expresses the element of fire for humans to use; works, lives and has its being in fire; can be perceived clairvoyantly when music is played; most exalted of the three spiritual creatures; 2. used as an emblem in primitive cultures; bears on its body the characteristics for virtue, righteousness, humanity, sincerity, and integrity; male bird resembles the western phoenix; **feng** is male, **hwang** is female bird. [**cf.** NATURE SPIRITS, FOX FIRE, FIRE ELEMENTAL]

FERMENTAL AETHER—atmosphere as it was created in the beginning with its governing laws and functions. [**cf.** TOTALITY, VIBRATIONS, ATOMS]

FERMIE'S FIRE—see ST. ELMO'S FIRE.

FETCH—1. (England, Ireland) an apparition of a living person perceived clairvoyantly in an area other than where the physical body is at the exact time of that person's death; the emotional soul-mind splits in two or more parts because of the strong desire that its transition be known to someone. [**cf.** HUMAN OMEN, EMOTIONAL PSYCHISM] 2. (astral projection) the person's astral body clairvoyantly showing as a shadowy counterpart when astral projecting; 3. an apparition that resembles a human form and gives the feeling of a living presence, not always clear as to who it is. [**cf.** ASTRAL PROJECTION, EMOTIONAL TELEKINESES]

FETCH LIGHT—see CORPSE CANDLE and NATURE SPIRITS.

FETISH—an object that has been energized with psychic energy and used to induce psychism for the wearer; accomplished by intensified focusing of energy from the eyes and hands; e.g., witches energized their rings, lockets or other trinkets to accelerate their skills. **Syn.** TALISMAN. [**cf.** AMULET, WAND]

FETISHISM—see PSYCHISM.

FEY—common name for NATURE SPIRIT; function is to absorb prana or vitality from the sun and distribute it to a human's physical body; fey's body comprises the finest state of physical matter; form is so sensitive and fluidic that it can be molded by such tenuous things as thought and feelings; fey's normal state is a pulsating sphere of light with a bright nucleus which can be used as a collective consciousness; capable of traveling through air and matter at will and changing levels of planes. **Syn.** FAERIE, ELF FAYERYE, FAIRYE, FAYRE, FAERIE, FAERY, FAIRY.

FIDDLER'S GREEN—the sailors believe there is a level of consciousness in the etheric world where, after death, they can have constant music, dancing, and women. [**cf.** HAPPY HUNTING GROUND, SEVENTH PLANE]

FIELD—(Kirlian effect) that which surrounds a person, living organism, or object; having special functions within a boundary, either visibly or invisibly; relates to that object, person or organism, and the universe; (Kurt Lewin) "a field is the totality of co-existing facts which are conceived of as mutually interdependent." [**cf.** ELECTROMAGNETIC FIELD, BIOLOGICAL PLASMA, AURA]

FIELD BIOLOGY—the study of life or activity in the area that surrounds human and other forms of life. [**cf.** PLASMATIC FAUNA, CRITTERS]

FIELD CONSCIOUSNESS—abbr. FC; (laboratory) (Edgar Mitchell) "an altered state of consciousness in which an individual seems to experience an enlargement of the ordinary boundaries of self, so that part of all of the individual's environment becomes merged with his awareness of self." [**cf.** ALTERED STATES OF CONSCIOUSNESS, CONSCIOUSNESS, AWARENESS]

FIELD DOWSING—(radiesthesia) to locate underground substance by being in the area where one feels there is an underground substance, as opposed to MAP DOWSING; psychic grasps the device in the prescribed manner, poses the question to the subconscious mind as to what he or she is looking for, clears their mind of previous conceptions, and allows the dowsing rod to react as he or she walks slowly over the field; the rod will notify the psychic of the underground substance by a tangible response of movement. [**cf.** REMOTE DOWSING, INFORMATION DOWSING METHOD, RADIESTHESIA]

FIELD EFFECT MONITORS—(W. A. Schafer) a sensitive device that picks up electromagnetic waves produced by heartbeats, at a distance of over four feet away from the body. [**cf.** KIRLIAN EFFECT, PHYSICAL BODY]

FIELD INDEPENDENCE—the ability to concentrate attention on the specific activity or problem without letting the environment of the activity get in the way; to concentrate on one's own psychic perceptions and recognize what is irrelevant to the problem without the conscious mind cutting in. **Syn.** COGNITION. [**cf.** CLAIRSENTIENCE]

FIELD OF BEING—a state of consciousness when one is full of the reality of one's own self. [**cf.** REALITY, AWARENESS]

FIELD OF MIND—(R. Alexander) an electromagnetic field around the earth, made from a collection of humanity's thoughts as a whole; responsible for the activity on the earth; a give-and-take energy field; "the energy that is round the earth and makes

the planet, is a field of mind." **Syn.** CREATIVE REALISM. [**cf.** ETHERIC DOUBLE/EARTH]

FIELD OF PEACE—(ancient Egypt) the eternal land in the etheric world where one stays with great gods and lives a life of bliss. [**cf.** MANSIONS OF LIGHT, THOUGHT BODY, X-NESS IN SPACE]

FIELD SHIFTS—variance of electrical charges emanating from things, inanimate or animate; detectable by the following parapsychological methods; RADIESTHESIA, KIRLIAN PHOTOGRAPHY, CLAIRVOYANCE, and PALMING. [**cf.** ELECTROMETRIC, AURA]

FIELD SPIRITS—(Slavic) nature spirits that are dwarf in size and which live in the forest and oversee the trees.

FIELDS OF LIFE—see AURA.

FIERCE ONE—the village blacksmith who was also the village psychic; his psychic skills and psychic information were known as the "fire of the iron doctor." [**cf.** VILLAGE BLACKSMITH, MASTER OF FIRE]

FIERY FURNACE—see KUNDALINI POWER.

FIERY INTELLIGENCE—see VITAL LIFE FORCE.

FIERY LIVES—1. specks of light charged with prana that can be seen with physical eyes in the seance room or in subdued lighting; perceived clairvoyantly in normal light during psychic sensitivity periods. **Syn.** SEANCE LIGHTS. [**cf.** SEANCE] 2. seventh and highest subdivision of the plane of matter; corresponds in the plane of matter to the monad in the individual. [**cf.** ETHER, SUPER-ETHER, SEMIMATERIAL]

FIERY POWER—see KUNDALINI.

FIERY RIVER—(angel kingdom) the higher light substance of a very fine vibration, used by the higher order of angels. [**cf.** ANGEL BEINGS, HIERARCHY]

FIFTH DIMENSION—(esoteric) 1. a faster rate of vibration than earth that makes a transparent plane running through the earth plane and throughout the atmosphere; 2. principles the fact of designs, patterns, and plans for all which takes shape and place on the physical plane; a level of consciousness where plans, original design, and individuality set up radiations that send forth rays with a tremendous force behind them, holding the plans, design, and individuality in manifestation;

where plans come into being; 3. known as the mental or mind plane; mind of the universe containing myriads of designs, prototypes, life forms, activity and plans before physical earth; 4. interpenetrates the other planes' vibrational frequencies but exists independently; 5. artists and composers receive inspirational thought and work from this plane. (Inconcl.) **Syn.** KINGDOM OF THE MIND. [**cf.** PLANES, SPIRITUAL PLANE, REALMS OF FORM, NONFORM-PRODUCING MATTER]

FIFTH ELEMENT—(esoteric) (Hinduism) ether in its primal form; vibrational frequency that transmits psychism; depicted by the green lighted path. (Inconcl.) [**cf.** ETHER, SUPER-ETHER, SPEED OF THOUGHT, SIXTH DIMENSION]

FIFTH FORCE—see PSYCHIC ENERGY.

FIFTH FORM OF PSI—(laboratory) to dream of an experience that another person is going through; occurs where there is a strong emotional tie. [**cf.** DREAMS Appendix 2]

FIFTH PLANE—(Eastern) a level of consciousness in the etheric world of self-realization, through universal "will," wherein the monad reaches close to perfection; monad loses all thought of self and finds the purpose of becoming one with Totality; Total love is for the sole purpose of progression of the universal seed; group souls function from this plane working as a unit to maintain balance in the solar systems; this group counsciousness is involved in motivating earthlings to desire and do that which is for their highest good in the overall plan. **Syn.** SPIRITUAL PLANE, PLANE OF SELF, ATMAN PLANE. [**cf.** BODIES AND PLANES Appendix 5, MASTERS]

FIFTH STATE OF CONSCIOUSNESS—(C. Maxwell Cade and Nona Coxhead) brainwave level of awareness when healing energy is being transferred between the healer and the patient; nondetectable on the EEG instrument but detectable on the mind-mirror EEG instrument, showing both patient's and healer's brainwaves change to a similar pattern; the alpha and theta reactions, generally associated with meditation, are present, and the beta reactions of ordinary wakefulness. [**cf.** SCALE OF BRAIN RHYTHMS, READOUTS, EEG]

FIFTH TYPE OF MATTER—see PRANA and SPIRIT.

FILI—a psychic who specializes in prophesying, reading the past, and writing poetry. **Syn.** FATES,

PSYCHIC. [**cf.** PRECOGNITION, CLAIRVOYANCE-IN-TIME]

FILLED WITH THE SPIRIT—to be under the influence of a powerful religious emotion and feel surges of love, impressions of messages, and feel a desire to express joy; brought about by a large religious gathering, with music of a proper tempo, and a charismatic evangelistic leader; members who become filled with powerful religious emotion, talk-in-tongues, move the body, and experience psychic impressions; leader is able to extend his or healing abilities to the individuals and the gathering as a whole. [**cf.** TALKING-IN-TONGUES, CLAIRVOYANCE, SLAYING-IN-THE-SPIRIT, HOLY SPIRIT]

FILLY FOAL—see FAIRY.

FINDER—a psychic who specializes in finding lost persons, animals or articles, using a psychic skill. [**cf.** PSYCHIC Appendix 3]

FINDHORN FOUNDATION—a spiritual community in the northeast area of Scotland; based on the belief in the oneness of all life; teachings: the task of the human race is to deepen the understanding of human integrity and relationship with nature and other dimensions of consciousness; community members work with the etheric world gods and nature spirits to bring unity between the cosmic forces and this planet; this is being done through the growing of extraordinary food and flowers, and changing attitudes and body chemistry of members; their work is a three-part co-operation. [**cf.** FAIRIES, PLANETARY DEME, INSPIRATIONAL THOUGHT]

FINDHORN HONEYMOON—the beginning of one's stay at Findhorn where the experience is one of complete faith, ecstasy, and understanding among one another before one realizes the necessity of its application. [**cf.** FAITH, ONEARTH, NEW BIRTH, AWARENESS, CONSCIOUSNESS]

FINE MEDIA—a primordial force capable of setting into motion the particles or units of the atom by the mental-emotional activity of humanity; see VITAL LIFE FORCE. [**cf.** VITAL LIFE FORCE Appendix 3]

FINGER—(Huna) an ethereal substance projected by the subconscious mind that follows along the invisible thread connecting the astral body of the psychic with the object or person being contacted for psychic information. [**cf.** PSYCHIC READING, PSYCHOMETRY, MENTAL HEALING, WAVE LENGTH]

FINGER PAD ELECTROGRAPHS—(Kirlian effect) photographs taken of the finger patterns and their emanations by electrophotography (high voltage camera) that shows the intensity and luminosity of the person's health; theory: photographs show time-related cyclic changes in relationship to illness and surgery. [cf. KIRLIAN EFFECT, MENTAL AURA]

FINGER READING—the ability to read and detect color with the fingertips; see EYELESS SIGHT and FINGER-TIP VISION.

FINGER RESPONSE—(hypnosis) a truthful reaction to questions given a hypnotic subject through the movement of two fingers, one indicating *yes* and one indicating *no*; a code is made with the subconscious mind designating which two fingers are to move; the subconscious mind flows through the sympathetic nervous system with a truthful response if the question is properly worded. **Syn.** IDEOMOTOR RESPONSE. [cf. HYPNOTHERAPY, RADIESTHESIA, FINGERS]

FINGER TIP VISION—a type of eyeless sight in which blind people can distinguish colors of objects; believed possible because colors induce thermal and density feelings which could give various dynamometrid reactions. **Syn.** DERMAL OPTICAL SENSITIVITY. [cf. EYELESS SIGHT Appendix 2, FINGERS, HANDS]

FINGERPRINTS OF PSI—(laboratory) to isolate the following aspects of the controlled psi experiment: 1. study the effects of the position; 2. identify the source of the psychic energy, whether from the subject or th experimenter; 3. discover differences from, and similarities to, other cognitive processes; 4. examine the sporadic nature of psi performance itself. [cf. PSI TASKS, MENTAL PSYCHIC PROCESSES, PSYCHIC COGNITION]

FINGERS—human transmitters and receivers of psychic and healing energies; when tips of fingers of both hands are touching, the psychic impressions in the brain are amplified; the forefinger of the right hand picks up condensed psychic energy from the brain, amplifies it and shoots it out in the direction toward which it is pointed; forefinger and thumb of both hands are more receptive to receive and transmit psychic and healing energy than the others; middle finger under investigation; fingertips are used for eyeless sight, table-tipping, psychometrizing, etc. (Inconcl.) [cf. PALMING, LAYING-ON-OF-HANDS, PENDULUM POWER, REFLEXOLOGY]

FINKELRUT—(Denmark) see DOWSING ROD.

FIR DARRIG—a nature spirit that enjoys playing practical jokes on humans. **Syn.** LEPRECHAUN.

FIRE—(esoteric) 1. a primordial substance existing as the void in the beginning; also known as the Clear Light of the beginning; a condition necessary for the primary element electricity to exist; 2. first of the primary elements fire, earth, air, and water that make up the universe; evolved in the first round of the planet; assumed a rotary motion becoming a blazing globular body of undifferentiated primeval forces; 3. emblematic of a deity, in many cultures; symbolic of purification, transformation, passion, and aspiration; 4. an element of emotional energy, a nature spirit, is the only organism that can live in fire. [cf. AIR, EARTH, WATER, SALAMANDER, FIRE WORSHIP]

FIRE HANDLING—to hold one's hands in a burning flame without causing harm to them; fire psychics have handled ignited kerosene torches and miner's acetylene lamps and received only smoke blackened hands; used as a method of learning body control; performed in religious rituals as an act of faith in God; believed to prove that the fire psychic has power over the devil. [cf. FIRE, FIRE ORDEAL, BODY CONTROL Appendix 2]

FIRE IMMUNITY—to eat fire, handle hot coals, walk through a log fire, run or walk over live, hot coals or red-hot stones without bodily harm or destroyed clothing; the skill to become engulfed with fire which would burn or scorch the average person's skin or clothing but results in no singed hair or clothing and no odor of fire on self or clothing; investigations assume the following methods: 1. fire immunitor is a medium who works in a deep or semi-trance state allowing the guides to anesthetize the mouth, throat, hands, or feet according to the job at hand; 2. fire immunitor is a medium whose guides produce a thin layer of etheric elemental essence around the area handling the fire, hot coals or heated stones; 3. fire immunitor is a psychic who emanates a magnetic nerve fluid to surround the area of the body that needs protection or around the object itself; documented cases in history: St. Francis of Paula, St. Catherine of Siena, and Clovis, in the rise against Louis XIV, in which he stood in burning pyre until it burnt out and he was found unscathed; six hundred men watched the procedure. (Inconcl.) **Syn.** COMBUSTIBILITY. [cf. FIRE-WALKING, BODY CONTROL, MASTER OF FIRE]

FIRE OF CREATION—see KUNDALINI.

FIRE OF THE SAGES—(alchemy) the last step in the process of refining of metals and in processing soul-minds; a fire that does not burn but "vivifies"; procedure kept secret by the alchemist. **Syn.** PHILOSOPHER'S FIRE. [**cf.** ALCHEMY Appendix 2, AWAKENED, ILLUMINATION, SULPHUR]

FIRE OF WISDOM—see KUNDALINI.

FIRE ORDEAL—(ancient) firewalking or fire eating; used as a ritual or initiation ceremony from the earliest of times; may have arisen from the conception of the influence of purification from fire; used by suspects to prove their innocence. [**cf.** FIRE IMMUNITY, STONE WALK]

FIRE WALKING—(Spain, Greece, Tibet, Taiwan, Asia, Polynesia, Japan, Huna, New Zealand, India, Malay, Fiji, South Pacific Islands, Tahiti) to walk or run over live, hot coals or a bed of red-hot stones without the feet or legs becoming burned, scorched or singed; used as a ritual, or initiaion for various disciplines and religious ceremonies; investigators differ as to method used; 1. walker is in a deep trance state, and while a guide is using his or her body, it is not subject to mundane laws; 2. walker releases a vital magnetic force through their nervous system that surrounds the body and soles of the feet to insulate against the heat; 3. hot coals or fire are coated with cooling atoms, bathed in a flame of cooling breezes, with or without the aid of the etheric helpers; 4. walker increases their body temperature to the temperature of the coals; 5. walker coats him or herself with a thin layer of etheric elemental essence so the heat cannot penetrate; 6. (Huna) the high voltage of the High Self controls the heat of the flames to prevent burning; 7. the soles of the walker's feet cut off the oxygen when they touch the coals because when the coals reach the point of pure carbon, they are flattened. (Inconcl.) [**cf.** COMBUSTIBILITY]

FIRE WORSHIP—(ancient) based on the belief that fire occupied all space before anything else; the first of the primeval elements which make up the universe; i.e., fire, earth, air and water; unanimous feeling in cultures that fire has properties to cleanse, purify and heal; types of sacred rituals differ with cultures. [**cf.** FIRE IMMUNITY, HOLY FIRE, ICE-SITTERS]

FIRE-ELEMENT PSYCHIC SOUND—a noise perceived clairaudiently which sounds like burning foliage and trees, as if an entire jungle was burning. [**cf.** OBJECTIVE CLAIRAUDIENCE]

FIRE ELEMENTAL—see SALAMANDER.

FIREFLIES—(ufology) plasmatic creatures or shapes that resemble fireflies; capable of being seen at dawn in outer space. [**cf.** UFOLOGY Appendix 5, SPACE ANIMALS]

FIRES WITH BOUNDARIES—fires that start for no apparent reason and burn only a particular area with no damage to surrounding environment; occur in the area of a psychic; (do not confuse with fire that does not consume). (Inconcl.) [**cf.** PSYCHIC PYROTECHNICS, HUMAN ELECTRIC WIRE]

FIRES WITHOUT CAUSE—1. a fire that is triggered from some unknown cause and burns an area near the psychic's body; believed that the psychic's body is overly filled with electricity. (Inconcl.) **Sim.** FIRES WITH BOUNDARIES. 2. a fire that is from a psychic attack or hex, using a nonhuman elemental to carry the evil energy to the situation, environment, or person under attack. [**cf.** HEX, FAMILIAR, ELECTRIC GIRLS]

FIRMAMENT—(esoteric) made from the fire, in the beginning, by rhythmic reversion; sextillion worlds passed into translucent and transparent luster and fire became firmament. [**cf.** EVOLUTION, CYCLES]

FIRST AURA—a narrow dark band about one-quarter inch wide surrounding the body and next to the skin. [**cf.** KIRLIAN EFFECT, ETHERIC DOUBLE]

FIRST DEATH—symbolizes the letting-go of the physical body during the earth dying process. [**cf.** DEATH SCIENCE, DEATH ANGEL, ENVELOPE, REINCARNATION]

FIRST DIMENSION—a line moving straight unto itself has one dimension, length; if the straight line or simple basic vibration moves in its own direction, it remains only a basic vibration; motion only is all that exists and motion only in the same dimension on which the basic vibration exists; e.g., a leaf growing, sense of sight; elementary movement through space was in one direction only, linear measurement. [**cf.** SECOND DIMENSION, THIRD DIMENSION]

FIRST FOOTING—(Scotland) to use a principle that whatever happens in the first few moments of the New Year will influence the rest of the year. [**cf.** SYNCHRONICITY, FATE, CYCLES]

FIRST MATTER—(Wilhelm Reich) vibrational frequencies caused by two spinning waves, positive and negative, approaching one another until they superimpose, forming a very elemental substance; these two opposing, yet complimentary, forces are responsible for the creation of all physical manifestation. [**cf.** YIN AND YANG, POLARITY]

FIRST PERSONALITY—(F.W.H. Myers) the conscious mind.

FIRST PLANE—see PHYSICAL PLANE.

FIRST RING OF POWER—(Carlos Castenada) "one's awesome ability to impart order to one's perception of one's daily world"; to place one's awareness on the tonal of the world; the act of perceiving and "being" is the act of awareness. [**cf.** SECOND-RING-OF-POWER]

FIRST ROUND OF PLANET EARTH—the evolvement of fire element. [**cf.** FIRMAMENT, CYCLE]

FIRST STAGE OF THE CHIKHAI BARDO—(Tibet) the procedure of the consciousness-principle passing out of the physical body during the death process; a reader is present to direct and guide the consciousness-principle. [**cf.** DEATH SCIENCE, BARDOS]

FIRST TEMPLE OF THE MYSTERIES—The Great Pyramid; a keeping place for secret truths. [**cf.** PYRAMIDOLOGY]

FISH—1. (astrology) represents the Piscean Age in the ZODIAC; 2. (Christianity) symbol of Jesus Christ signifying conversion to the Christian religion; made into jewelry to be worn by those converted as a means of mutual identification; sculpted upon a number of Christian monuments and on the ancient sarcophagi; used on amulets, jewelry, and other ornaments.

FISH GATE—chakra with four petals located at the base of the spine; symbolized by earth; see ROOT CHAKRA. [**cf.** KUNDALINI, CHAKRAS, IDA, PINGALA]

FISH PSI—the study of fish response to human thought. [**cf.** FISH TELEPATHY]

FISH TELEPATHY—1. to train fish by means of communicating psychically with them; 2. to psychically predict what fish will do. [**cf.** ANPSI, NATURE TELEPATHY, SHELLS]

FIVE—numerology meaning: experience, travel, variety and drama needed for life and progress; life cycle is associated with quickness of thought, impulsive action, body, and daring adventure; represents the five senses; planetary link is with Mercury. [**cf.** NUMBER POWER Appendix 5]

FIVE POINTED STAR—1. see PENTAGRAM; 2. symbolizes love; known as Krishna's star of love; symbol has a four-petaled lotus in the center. [**cf.** FORMS-WITH-POWER, CEREMONIAL MAGIC]

FIXATIONS—see BLOCKS.

FIXED THOUGHT—a deliberate belief, desire, or idea so intense and persistent that its manifestation is stagnated and solidified to the extent that it will not dissipate by itself; e.g., 1. thoughts of material objects and things on earth are held together by collective fixed thoughts; while the majority of men continue to need a chair, every time one says *chair,* it is visualized as a chair, and so earth has chairs; when man no longer needs a chair and another object is visualized as a substitute, man no longer will sit on "chairs"; 2. to desire something to happen with such strong emotion that it possesses one's thinking and causes the atoms to solidify and stop flowing and one's desire never occurs; 3. a collective belief that manifests as long as it is held collectively by humanity; e.g., the mass of people believe the human body is susceptible to disease and therefore mankind maintains sickness on earth. [**cf.** THOUGHTS, THINGS, BRAIN, COLLECTIVE UNCONSCIOUS]

FIXED-BRAIN-WAVE-STATE—(biofeedback training) a brain wave pattern that does not do its normal fluctuating because the subject hooked-up to the instrument is capable of "holding" one particular thought. [**cf.** NEUTRAL INNER FEELINGS, INTEGRATION, FIXED THOUGHT, SEED MEDITATION]

FIXITY—(radiesthesia) the reaction of the dowsing rod and pendulum at a point where the past and future are gathered to a meaningful coincidence. [**cf.** SYNCHRONICITY, PENDULUM, MEANINGFUL COINCIDENCE THEORY]

FLAME AND THE FIRE—sacred symbol representing the most important aspect of the creative energy (God); theory: everything came into being through fire, warmth and purification; depicted by the sun. [**cf.** SYMBOLS, FIRE]

FLAME BILLETS—to use the flame blaze, the smoke, and the ashes to serve as a means to perceive psychic information; accomplished by the querant writing a question on a paper and this paper is burned over a candle flame; the shape and density of the blaze, smoke, and ashes are used as a point of focus for the psychic, giving the answer to the question. **Syn.** SPODOMANCY, TEPHRAMANCY, CAPNOMANCY. [**cf.** POINT-OF-FOCUS, MANTIC ART, SYMBOLS]

FLAMES OF DIVINE LOVE—heated blood oozing out of an extremely warm body or a high fever, brought about by an intense subconscious love for a deity; usually happens at a religious function or in a religious setting by one's self, which brings on a hysteria-trance. **Syn.** INCENDIUM AMORIS. [**cf.** PARTIAL INCENDIUM AMORIS, HYSTERIA, STIGMATA, LAW OF ACTIVITY Appendix 7]

FLAMING SWORD—(ancient, esoteric) symbol of the top of the medulla oblongata where the nerve fluid (sushumna) flows into the brain; looks like a flaming Greek torch; many physical systems cross at the medulla oblongata area. [**cf.** SUSHUMNA, BRAIN, CHRISM OIL]

FLARE PATTERNS—(Kirlian effect) the radiations shown on the photographs from a high-voltage camera, which shows that different species have their own aura; the bright part of the aura that stands out from the rest of it shows parallelism with each species; does not completely prove the basis of the behavior of either the separate parts of the systems or the entire species; on humans, this shows where the acupuncture points are located. [**cf.** KIRLIAN EFFECT, NIMBUS, HAIRCUT EFFECT]

FLASHBACK—the spontaneous remembrance of a past experience in a previous life, occurring without programming one's self as in mental or hypnotherapeutic regression. **Syn.** SPONTANEOUS RECALL. [**cf.** REINCARNATION, RIPE KARMA, ACCUMULATED KARMA]

FLASHES—see HUNCHES.

FLASHING FIRE—see FORMLESS FIRE.

FLASHING LIGHT—a light that flashes on and off at regular, rhythmic intervals and can be regulated as to speed of flashes; serves as a tool for meditating and for sending telepathic messages; light is also timed to one's heart beat, making it very hypnotic; dangerous if used too long at one sitting; used by UFO craft to hypnotize the subject in a close encounter so he will not run away. [**cf.** EYE-FIXATION, DIRECTED-THOUGHT TRAINER, STROBE LIGHT, CLOSE-ENCOUNTERS-OF-THE-THIRD-KIND]

FLAW-DETERMINED PHENOMENA—(laboratory) an experimental, forced-choice psi effect or incident; e.g., card-guessing type, which has a trivial, indifferent nature, possessing no survival advantage. [**cf.** NEED-DETERMINED, PROCEDURAL IRREGULARITIES]

FLESH FOOD—pertains to meat of animals; beef, fowl, lamb, pork, veal.

FLEXIBLE MEDIUM—one who has developed the ability to do many kinds of physical phenomena; allows the etheric world guides to intervene spontaneously, or by invocation, for the various types of communication. [**cf.** CONTROL, TRUMPET TRANCE, LEVITATION]

FLICK—(psychic healing) to jerk or snap the fingers or hands to shake off the diseased vibrations when performing AURIC HEALING, LAYING-ON-OF-HANDS, or MAGNETIC HEALING. [**cf.** HOLISTIC HEALTH, PSYCHIC HEALING, MAGNETISM]

FLINT ARROW HEADS—(Ireland, Scotland) fairy weapons; used to cure mankind's ills by dipping them in a special water. [**cf.** FAIRIES]

FLOAT OFF—1. to reach a state of consciousness where the mind expands and travels to unusual realms of the etheric world; 2. to experience supernormal and subnormal visions and emotions. [**cf.** PSYCHOTROPIC PLANTS, MEDITATION, EMOTION, STRESS, ELONGATION]

FLOATING—(destructive-brainwashing cult) to fluctuate back and forth between the cult personality and one's own personality after one has been deprogrammed and has left the commune; after the breakthrough in the deprogramming and the victim regains his or her ability to use their free will again, they are not completely free; former cult member goes through periods of uncertainty and periods of being vulnerable to suggestions along the cult line of thinking; cult personality occurs as a spontaneous flashback, or memory is triggered by a similarity of the past and cult personality lasts from one day up to a few weeks; former cult member is confused as to his or her religious beliefs and can be easily swayed to rejoin; fluctuation will continue until the compartments in the subconscious mind have been completely reasoned with, changed, and a corrected attitude toward the cult solidified; the mind of the previous cult victim must be kept active and free from guilt feelings in order to quickly erase the compartments in the subconscious mind, which were "forced" into their belief system. [**cf.** SUBCONSCIOUS MIND, BACK SLIDING]

FLOOD OF NEW WORDS—see TALKING-IN-TONGUES.

FLOW—1. the thread, or continuous stream, in nature that connects every living and nonliving thing in all the universes to each other and to the whole circulation of force; 2. the energy moving within a person throughout the course of the day; variations of energy flow through the body meridians in association with the season of the year; 3. the movement of psychic energy in a seance or in a psychic's body which gives out psychic information; when the "flow" stops, the information stops; 4. to become lost in one's activity, experiencing an altered sense of time; person is aware of their actions but not aware of their awareness; 5. to be versatile, to go along with whatever comes across one's path; by not boxing-in one's desires or plans, one is not disappointed if they do not occur; 6. (Russia) flow has a pattern and a rate (of flow). [**cf.** CYCLES, ELECTRICITY, MERIDIAN LINES, PSYCHIC ENERGY]

FLOW FREE—pertains to how the mind should function to receive psychic information; psychic begins with a neutral or empty mind, without any preconceptions of what should or will transpire, or what the message will be; this makes the mind flow without garbling. [**cf.** PSYCHIC DEVELOPMENT CIRCLE, PSYCHIC INFORMATION, PENDULUM POWER]

FLOW OF SOUL—the alignment and vivification of one's three lower bodies, the mental, astral, and physical, in tune with the center of Self; in this state, controlling one's outer states of consciousness becomes easy. [**cf.** CONSCIOUSNESS, BODIES OF MAN]

FLOW PATTERN—(time) an orderly pattern of cycles creating a constant movement in time; caused by the repititious contracting and repulsing of the positive and negative energy in the universe. [**cf.** TIME Appendix 5]

FLOWER CLAIRSENTIENCE—to use a bouquet of flowers to reach a level of consciousness wherein one can perceive psychic information for the recipient; bouquet is brought to the psychic by the recipient and then used as a point of focus by the psychic; (do not confuse with FLOWER PSYCHOMETRY. [**cf.** BOTANE, POINT-OF-FOCUS, CLAIRSENTIENCE]

FLOWER PSYCHOMETRY—to hold a flower in one's hands that came from the home of the recipient for psychometrizing psychic information for the recipient; flower should be one the recipient attends to as it will be attuned to the emotions of the owner and will carry the vibrations of the owner; a form of practical psychometry. [**cf.** PRIMARY WAVES, BOTANE, SENSATION CONSCIOUSNESS]

FLOWER THERAPY—(esoteric) to use specific plants to heal specific diseases; (does not mean eating them). (Inconcl.) [**cf.** CURATIVE EDUCATION, ALTERNATIVES, SWEET GRASS]

FLOWERS—(esoteric) flowers have the vibrational frequency to be a good tool to accelerate psychic skills and healing ability; etheric world intelligences can use flowers placed in the area to invervene more easily with the psychic; flowers may be fresh-cut, artificial or simply a plant but fresh-cut flowers are preferable. (Inconcl.) [**cf.** MANDRAKE, SENSATION CONSCIOUSNESS, POINT-OF-FOCUS, PLANT MAGIC]

FLUCTUATION—(hypnotherapy) pertains to normal variations of level of consciousness which occur in a hypnotherapy session. [**cf.** HYPNOTHERAPY, REGRESSION, MASS HYPNOSIS]

FLUID MOTOR INSTRUMENT—(Tromelin) a device capable of testing the force emanating from the medium and the medium's hand while in a trance state when he or she is working with psychokinesis and exteriorization of motoricity. [**cf.** MAGNETOSCOPE, BIOMETER OF BARADUC, STHENOMETER, PALMING, PSYCHOKINESIS]

FLUIDIC APPARITION—a hazy, vague vision that resembles a person; perceived clairvoyantly in a psychic skill period or during a dream. [**cf.** PSYCHIC DEVELOPMENT, CLAIRVOYANCE, GHOSTS]

FLUIDIC ASSOCIATION—a therapeutic method for revealing one's inner blocks during a psychoanalysis session: the analyst verbalizes words meaningful to the patient; the patient responds spontaneously and his or her response is used as a clue for the analyst's next word; to elicit spontaneous response from patient's subconscious rather than a considered response from his or her conscious thinking; such response reveals hidden emotions of the patient. **Syn.** FREE ASSOCIATION. [**cf.** DREAM THERAPY, BLOCKS]

FLUIDIC BODY—see ETHERIC DOUBLE.

237

FLUIDIC ENERGY—see AURA.

FLUIDIC LINK—1. see SILVER CORD; 2. an invisible vaporous substance that unites the medium to the etheric world guide when working in physical psychism. [**cf.** PERISPRIT, MANIFESTATIONS]

FLUX DAYS—(biorhythm charts) trying, disturbing, and uneasy days that occur for unknown reasons; when the body system changes from the discharging phase into the recuperative phase of the biorhythm cycles; this change takes one day; occurs exactly at the halfway point of the twenty-three-, twenty-eight-, and thirty-three-day cycles; indicated on the biorhythm chart when the curve crosses the 0-line; on these days, one should be cautious of their activities. **Syn.** CRITICAL DAY. [**cf.** BIORHYTHM CHART, EMOTIONAL CYCLE]

FLY—(Trancendental Meditation) to rise in a vertical direction while meditating; occurs after prolonged days of deep and serious meditation in which some of the dross substance, subject to the laws of gravity, is removed, making the body buoyant; occurs while in the lotus position; the body rises and sometimes jumps around like a frog. (Inconcl.) [**cf.** PATANJALI'S SUTRAS, LEVITATION, MOTOR LEVITATION]

FLY AGARIC—(Siberia, ancient East) a psychotropic drug recognized by its circles of white-stalked, red-capped fungus; used to help reach a state of bliss or to see intense, long-lasting visions of heaven. **Syn.** SOMA PLANT, AMANITA MUSCARIA, FAIRY RINGS. [**cf.** FORCED PSI, WRAITHFUL ORDER OF THE DEITIES, JIMSON WEED]

FLYER—(Native American, Algonquin) represents the medicine man who is the go-between of the etheric world and his tribesmen; depicted by a medicine man with a bird on his head and wearing a belt containing magic charms. [**cf.** SAND READER, NOCTURNAL BIRD, ORACLE, OWLS IN MADAGASCAR]

FLYING DREAMS—to dream one is floating, swimming, flying, sailing; occurs when one is taking an astral projection; the sensation of the astral body moving from side-to-side, or through the air could trigger a dream of the same nature; (symbolic interpretation) the dreamer is rising above a situation or is on top of a situation. [**cf.** DREAMS, LUCID DREAM, INCUBATION]

FLYING FLAPJACK—name used to identify a certain type of UFO which is seem repeatedly. [**cf.** UFOLOGY Appendix 5]

FLYING FROM CLOUD TO CLOUD—(Book of Job in the Bible) descriptive of unidentified flying objects. [**cf.** SAUCER FLAP, TRANSITION OF SUBSTANCE]

FLYING IN THE SKY—(ancient India) one of the eight Siddhis (psychic skills). **Syn.** ASTRAL PROJECTION. [**cf.** INTERIORIZATION, REPERCUSSION, SPONTANEOUS ASTRAL PROJECTION]

FLYING OINTMENT—(magic) special ingredients used to make a mixture that induces a dissociation of consciousness and aids one to fly through the air; witches rubbed this mixture on the mucous membranes of the nasal and sexual orifices before they flew. [**cf.** GRAVITY CONTROL, PHYSICAL MANIFESTATIONS/MISCELLANEOUS Appendix 2, ASTRAL PROJECTION]

FLYING SAUCER—coined in 1947 by an American, Kenneth Arnold; an object that was seen repeatedly in the sky and could not be identified; object looked like two huge saucers connected face-to-face; currently a collective word to identify any object seen in the sky by people all over the world; varies in shape, color, size and capabilities. **Syn.** UNIDENTIFIED FLYING OBJECTS. [**cf.** UFOLOGY Appendix 5]

FLYING SAUCER DISEASE—similar symptoms of failing health which come to people who have had an encounter with a UFO. [**cf.** CONTACTEE, CLOSE-ENCOUNTER-OF-THE-THIRD-KIND]

FLYING SCROLL—name given by Zachariah to the unidentified flying objects in the Bible. [**cf.** STAR TRAVELERS, WINDOW AREA, RADAR ANGELS]

FLYING SHIELDS—name given to flying saucers by the early Romans. [**cf.** GUARDIANS, DISC SKY-CRAFT, ETHER-SHIP BEINGS]

FLYING SPIRITS OF RED MEN—(Native American) psychics who are adept in astral projection. [**cf.** SUPERCLAIRVOYANCE, EXPERIENCER, SPIRAL DROP]

FO-TI-TIENG—an herb with psychic properties used in the alchemists' formula of elixir of life; found only in certain districts in Eastern tropics. **Syn.** HYDACATYLE ASIATICA. [**cf.** BOTANE, ALCHEMY]

FOCAL POINT—that which is used to keep one's attention narrowed to the least possible oneness in order to induce an altered state of consciousness; a spot, a tiny object, music, body movements, or words spoken (silently or verbally) can be used; 1. (psychic sensitivity) a flower, picture, candle, crystal ball, or the third-eye area in the head are good focusing points to keep one's mind neutral and allow the psychic information to flow; 2. (meditation) music, mantra, picture, object, beads, or body movements are good to focus on for a deep altered state of consciousness; 3. (hypnotherapy) centering one's attention on the guide's voice or a hypnotic disc makes it easier for reaching a deep state of hypnosis. [**cf.** SELF-GENERATED REPEATED STIMULUS, SILENT INTONING, TAMING OF THE MIND]

FOCALIZER—see PSYCHIC.

FOCUS—an individual whose energy is being used by a poltergeist; an individual who has emotions that cannot be coped with on a conscious level or who has emotions which society keeps him or her from expressing, this emotional energy is suppressed within the body on a subconscious level where it can easily be generated by the invisible, mischievous poltergeist; possible candidates: 1. teenager who has an abnormal abundance of emotional energy; 2. one who is frustrated by jealousy, hostility, and hate; 3. one involved in sibling rivalry; 4. one who stays on a religious emotional high; 5. one going through a mental breakdown; plural **foci. Syn.** POLTERGEIST GENERATOR, AGENT. [**cf.** GHOSTS, POLTERGEIST MISSLES, POLTERGEIST]

FOCUS ATTENTION—a psychic term: to tune out all worldly vibrations that could cloud accurate psychic information; to free one's self of the environment and personal thoughts, making the flow of psychism more fluent. [**cf.** MENTAL PSYCHIC PROCESSES, STATES OF CONSCIOUSNESS]

FOCUS FIFTEEN—(astral projection) a state of consciousness, reached in a professionally induced astral flight, where you are there, taking the flight; time-space does not exist or is not important. [**cf.** ROLLED OUT, CLICK-CLACK, IMMOTIVE CONSCIOUSNESS, ASTRAL PROJECTION]

FOCUS ONE—(astral projection) C-one; the first state of consciousness in a professionally induced astral flight. [**cf.** CONSCIOUS DEZGOSIS, DISTANT-POINT ASTRAL PROJECTION, ASTRAL PROJECTION]

FOCUS TEN—a state of consciousness reached in a professionally induced astral flight when the body seems asleep and the mind fully awake. [**cf.** REDOUBLED, PROPULSION]

FOCUS TWELVE—a state of consciousness reached in a professionally induced astral flight wherein one no longer feels he or she has a body; a nonphysical awareness. [**cf.** DEPERSONALIZATION, MIND-DRIFT, ORAL BREATHING]

FOCUSING EFFECT—theory: the more one centers one's attention on a form of energy, concept, or an object, the easier it is to tune in pyschically; occurs consciously or unconsciously; e.g., unconsciously, to bring blood through the pores of the skin in psychic surgery; consciously, to bend a key in the palm of the hand. (Inconcl.) [**cf.** POINT-OF-FOCUS, MANDALA, COLLECTING THE MIND, PK]

FOG—coined by don Juan; an aura of psychic energy put around one's self to close off or lose one's past identity, leaving one a free agent; induced by erasing all personal history and not revealing what one is doing; this new attitude breaks the tie of thoughts of the past and of the people of the past; e.g., Jesus said "be *in* this world but be not *of* this world." [**cf.** FLOW, HOLD THE THOUGHT, MATTER]

FOHATIC POWER—see VITAL LIFE FORCE.

FOLK CONSCIOUSNESS—generalization of collective conscious thinking of each special area making that area what it is; pertains to concepts of economics, government, and all things in general, which make the karma for that area. **Syn.** GROUP KARMA. [**cf.** ACCUMULATED KARMA, MASS KARMA]

FOLK MEDICINE—remedies and customs that have been handed down through the ages for a particular culture; may seem ridiculous for the outsider, but they work for the people of that area; usually uses part of the environment and the herbs of the field; e.g., a dirty sock around the neck during sleep for relief of a sore throat. [**cf.** LICORICE, ALTERNATIVES, MINERAL SALTS]

FOLK MONSTER—(Arkansas) see BIG FOOT.

FOLLOWER—(Norway) see ASTRAL BODY.

FOO FIGHTERS—(ufology) luminous small objects, seemingly intelligent, that hovered over the airplanes during World War II. (Inconcl.) [**cf.** FLYING SAUCERS, UFOLOGY, RADAR ANGELS]

239

FOOD OF ETHEREAL ESSENCE—an invisible substance in the form of an odor or fragrance which can be picked up psychically; extracted from material objects and used to identify its own object in a psychic message or to identify with a particular discarnate being or guide. **Syn.** CLAIRSCENT. [**cf.** CLAIRSCENTRIST, CLAIRSAVORANCE]

FOOD SCALE—(esoteric) foods have been tested for their vibrational rate and then grouped on a scale; scale of decreasing vibrational frequencies shows the following order: fruit, vegetables, seeds and nuts, dairy products, whole grain cereals, fish with fins, flesh food (meat), shell fish, honey and molasses. (Inconcl.) [**cf.** VEGETARIAN, ONIONS, SAGE]

FOOLISH FIRE—a flitting, flickering light, sometimes phosphorescent, sometimes pale and misty, taking on the shape of a person; at times looks like small balls of light or candle flames; seen mostly hovering around graveyards and marshy grounds; named foolish because only fools follow it; 1. (folk-belief) a discarnate entity misleading night travellers; 2. (Germany) a wandering soul-mind not finding refuge in either heaven or hell; 3. (Russia) the soul-mind of an unbaptized child; 4. (Europe) the soul-minds of dead warriors guarding the treasure which was buried with them; 5. a helpful light that leads one out of danger; 6. an earthbound entity wandering around in an erratic manner; 7. an astral shell that cannot disintergrate because of the past owner's love for earthly desires; 8. a nature spirit wanting to be heard; 9. (science) spontaneous gas caused from decomposed matter. **Syn.** CORPSE LIGHT, FRIAR'S LANTERN, FOXFIRE, WILL-O-THE-WISP, JACK-O-LANTERN, IGNIS FATUUS. [**cf.** GHOSTS, NATURE SPIRITS, ASTRAL SHELLS]

FOOLS IN CHRIST—(Slavic) Christian psychics.

FORCE—(capitalized) pertains to the highest power there is; encompasses "all" as a whole; an energy field generated within all living things; infinite intelligence that penetrates all life and holds the galaxies together; neutral in character but can be switched to have good or bad characteristics when utilized by the human mind. **Syn.** GOD. [**cf.** DIVINE ENERGY, COSMIC GOD, GUIDING PRINCIPLE]

FORCE CENTERS—see CHAKRAS.

FORCE ZONE—(pyramidology) the area in the pyramid where the energy is most dense and will influence whatever is put into the area; pyramid energy is located at a point about one-third up from the bottom. [**cf.** PYRAMIDOLOGY, FORMS-WITH-POWER]

FORCE-FEED—(Tibet) a special physical operation on the third-eye area in the middle of the forehead performed to open one's psychic door to enable one to see into the invisible world immediately, at will; strict training is administered before this operation in order to give instructions on how to use this ability properly and to protect one's self from it spilling over when not willed. [**cf.** PROVED INCARNATION, THIRD-EYE AREA, ADEPT, INITIATE]

FORCED IMPRESSIONS—non-thoughts, feelings, and visions coming through to the psychic at random; happens more frequently in the natural-born psychic; uncontrolled psychism which can, however, be controlled. [**cf.** CONTAGIOUS ENTHUSIASM, GROKKING IN FULLNESS, CLOAK OF INSULATION]

FORCED PSI—abbr. for FORCED PSYCHISM.

FORCED PSYCHISM—to induce or compel oneself to open-up psychically or mediumistically; to strengthen, intensify, and accelerate one's psychic and mediumship sensitivity by special methods or techniques accepted by one's culture; many cultures have figured out methods of attaining psychic skills faster than allowing them to develop normally; these cultures understand, teach, and use para-psychological or metaphysical philosophy regularly, therefore, it is already in an individual's belief system and such an individual can handle any psychic activity he or she experiences; (in the West, forced psychism is looked upon as "taboo" since the average Westerner does not live in a culture that understands, teaches, and uses psychism philosophy; therefore, a Westerner should "sit" for development and allow her or himself to "unfold" until their mental and subconscious minds can harmoniously accept this philosophy; otherwise, forced methods could be physically or mentally harmful); forced psychism examples: operation on the third-eye, over-stimulating dancing, psychotropic plants, isolation areas, and extreme initiations; see FORCED PSYCHISM Appendix 2.

FORCED-CHOICE—1. (psi tasks) to will the target to occur spontaneously at the present time, because time-dependence is a factor; 2. (personally) to will psychic information to come through immediately when the conscious mind desires it. [**cf.** MENTAL PSYCHIC PROCESSES, DESIRED-CONTROL, FORCED PSYCHISM]

FORCED-CHOICE TEST—(laboratory) an experiment of cognition whereby the participant is required to tune into one of a fixed number of items which have been previously chosen as the targets. [**cf.** ESP, PSYCHIC COGNITION Appendix 2]

FORCES—invisible intelligences that make themselves psychically available to reveal guidance and information for a psychic or medium. **Syn.** ETHERIC WORLD INTELLIGENCES. [**cf.** MEDIUMSHIP, SECRET CHIEFS, GUIDE, LEGION]

FORCES OF THE UNSEEN—see FORCES.

FORE-AND-AFT-SWING—(penduluming) a sideways movement of the pendulum as opposed to a circular movement; each has a different meaning. [**cf.** PREFLIGHTING, PALLOMANCY, OSCILLATION]

FORECASTING—see PREDICTIONS.

FOREKNOWLEDGE OF THE FUTURE—psychic skill allowing one to predict future events in various psychic methods; see PROPHECY. **Syn.** PRECOGNITION, PREDICTIONS.

FORERUNNER—(Scotland, astral projection) a manifestation of a psychic's presence occuring at the destination of the astral projectionist before the projectionist arrives. [**cf.** FALSE AWAKENING, ETHER-GOER]

FORETELLING—see PREDICTION.

FORGOTTEN LANGUAGE—pictured symbols, emblems, and metaphors used as the dreamstuff of dreams; picture metaphors, symbols, and emblems can be understood by children, the literate and illiterate of any country, making it a universal language. [**cf.** DREAMS Appendix 2, TRUE ACTION DREAMS, PERSONAL PSYCHIATRIST]

FORK—a three-pronged branch, newly-cut from a tree, used as a tool by the magician and witch in performing psychic work; fork preferably cut from a hazel or almond tree with a single blow from an unused knife. **Syn.** TRIDENT. [**cf.** NECROMANCY, RITUAL]

FORKED BRANCH—(dowsing) see DOWSING ROD.

FORKED DIVINING ROD—a Y-shaped dowsing rod as opposed to an L rod; the oldest type was made from a newly-cut tree branch; later made from metal wire, whale baleen, oxhorn, or ivory, irrespec-

tive of whether the material is conductive or not. [**cf.** WIZARD'S ROD, DOWSING, WATERLOPER]

FORKED DOWSING WAND—see FORKED DIVINING ROD.

FORM—(esoteric) matter built out of consciousness that is shaped to the direction of human thought; an illusory manifestation of underlying causes. (Inconcl.) [**cf.** CONSCIOUSNESS, MATTER, SHAPES]

FORM DEVAS—angel beings that belong to the lower mental planes, with a rate of vibration that makes their bodies composed of mental elemental essence; belong to the second elemental kingdom. [**cf.** BODILESS DEVAS, NATURE SPIRITS, ELEMENTAL ESSENCE, ANGEL HIERARCHY]

FORM LEVELS—grades of matter making various levels of form, influenced by trend of a human's thoughts and the disposition and character of his or her personality. (Inconcl.) [**cf.** CONSCIOUSNESS, MATTER, BRAIN]

FORMATIVE CAUSE—(Aristotle, 350 B.C.) see VITAL LIFE FORCE.

FORMATIVE ENERGY—coined by Paul Kammerer (1920); see VITAL LIFE FORCE.

FORMATIVE-FORCE BODY—see AURA.

FORMED MEDIUM—one in whom the medianimic faculties have been completely developed with entities of the higher planes, and with whom the transmitting of the communications is done with respect and with proper sharing. **Syn.** COMPLETE MEDIUM.

FORMLESS FIRE—a high order of nature spirits that dart and flash through the very depths of the universe giving one a feeling that one is being spoken to; known as HOLY FIRE when seen in a darkened psychic development circle; can be heard clairaudiently and seen physically when in an alpha or theta state. **Syn.** FLASHING FIRE. [**cf.** OBJECTIVE CLAIRAUDIENCE, FAIRIES]

FORMLESS LEVELS—the plane that makes a home for the casual body. [**cf.** PLANES, BODIES OF MAN]

FORMLESS VISIONS—clairvoyant perception that shows itself as just color, dancing lights, vibrations, symmetrical shapes, energy in action, or other hazy formations. [**cf.** CLAIRVOYANT LIGHTS, X-RAY CLAIRVOYANCE]

FORMS—1. (esoteric) shapes that have a hollow within their boundaries and therein produce a captured, concentrated special energy within that hollow that can be utilized for meaningful purposes; i.e., the pyramid, circle, cone, sphere, square and other geometric forms; theories: **(a)** these shapes act as an antenna which tunes into the master patterns of the universe that match that structure's shape and brings condensed energy into the hollow of the structure; **(b)** the energy within a form generates some unknown energy and/or creates a force-field which can focus on already existing energy fields and amplify them; e.g., energy could work on the aura and bring the object back to its proper condition as much as is possible; if a bruised apple whose original condition was good is placed in a form, the bruise would not grow but neither would it disappear. (Inconcl.) **Syn.** FORMS-WITH-POWER. [**cf.** SQUARE, MAGIC CIRCLE, CAMERON CONES] 2. (Tai Chi) specific patterns of movements in the dance have meaning which bring a feeling of oneness. [**cf.** MOVEMENT-FOR-ALTERED-CONSCIOUSNESS]

FORMS-WITH-POWER—shapes that are used as psychic tools because of the potential within their areas or because of their character or their metaphoric value, due to their peculiar structure; "form" is the external appearance of a clearly defined area as distinguished from color or material; a particular way of being that gives something its nature or character; since antiquity, there have been forms, shapes, and formations that people have found to be useful for their information, guidance, or protection when working psychically; shapes that exude energy include the cross, swastika, sword, circle, cone and pyramid; shapes known for protection are the circle and the hexagram; see Appendix 5 FORMS-WITH-POWER for more listings. (Inconcl.)

FORMULA—(biofeedback training) a short phrase used to aid in curing a health problem when hooked-up to a biofeedback instrument; special phrase for each problem helps to pinpoint where one should center his or her thoughts; (Elmer Green) "to use a specific phrase for a specific problem, rather than a divinity affirmation, obtains the most satisfactory results"; e.g, "My heart pumps normally," rather than "I am filled with the great white light." [**cf.** WORDS-WITH-POWER, CEREMONIAL MAGIC, AFFIRMATION]

FORTEAN EVENTS—(twentieth century) (Charles Fort) "any event that does not have a scientific or rational explanation"; Fort researched the unusual and absurd phenomena which includes psychic phenomena and called it "fortean." [**cf.** METAPHYSICAL, PARAPSYCHOLOGICAL]

FORTEAN PHENOMENA—see PSYCHIC ART.

FORTEAN PHILOSOPHY—"Nothing is impossible—we should examine this." Charles Fort was a collector of odd facts; he believed that everything is possible and "nothing is ever wholly true or false."

FORTUNE TELLER—one whose psychic messages are all about the future of the recipient; type of psychic skill varies with fortune teller. [**cf.** CLAIRVOYANCE, PROPHECY, TAROT CARDS]

FORTY—1. (ancient, "many") because the masses of people could not count, forty came to mean "many"; 2. (numerology, "completion") well-understood; e.g., "forty days in the wilderness"; 3. forty means well-balanced because four means balance; e.g., when one arrives at a four-sided or balanced state of mind. [**cf.** NUMBER POWER Appendix 5]

FORTY-NINE—(numerology) the square of the sacred number seven; symbolic of the seven worlds of Maya within the seven globes of the planetary chain. [**cf.** CYCLES, SEVEN]

FORWARD DISPLACEMENT—(psi tasks) to pick up psychic information regarding the target, after the target is decided upon but before the experiment begins. [**cf.** ESP, RHINE CARDS]

FORWARD-PK—(psi tasks) see PRECOGNITION.

FOUL-SCENTED ROHUTU—(Leeward Islands) a place in the etheric world where the lower class of society will go in a soul-mind form, according to their rank. [**cf.** SWEET-SCENTED ROHUTU, DENSITY, ASTRAL PLANE]

FOUR—(esoteric) 1. ("balance") a solid number; a basic number; e.g., four directions of the compass, four gospels, four elements, four legs on an animal, four wheels to a vehicle and four corners to a building; balance and earth; 2. numerology meaning: solid framework of life; those with a numerological number four are the foundations or backbone of the country; they are patient, reliable, and plodders; 3. life cycle four means the person is affectionate, talented, popular; 4. planetary link is with Jupiter; 5. (ancient Egypt) found to be the number most used with nine; 6. symbolic of creation as every creature has the mark of four within them. [cf. NUMBER POWER Appendix 5]

FOUR CORNERS—(Native American, Hopi) a sanctuary in the etheric world for the day of Purification when all the good and righteous people will go there. [cf. REINCARNATION, RIGHTHAND PATH]

FOUR CORNERS AREA—the Colorado Plateau; known as Telos; believed to be the location of underground vaults with valuable records and secrets of the scientific knowledge of Lemuria; center of power in America because of the natural energies of the earth. (Inconcl.)

FOUR-POINTED STAR—see TETRAGRAM.

FOURTH CHAKRA—see HEART CHAKRA.

FOURTH DIMENSION—(esoteric) 1. that part of the etheric world that is filled with thought formations from the earth entities; a plane in which the actual life forces play and reach their concrete forms, both influential and causative; 2. the cause of growth; the link between mind (ultimate mind) and matter (fifth and third planes); radiates motion and life energy through mankind; 3. a single motion in all directions, simultaneously, formlessness with continuous radiatory movement; 4. a plane of successive existence, being three dimensional in space as is also each successive instant of time; 5. (AMORC) "nothing more or less than the rate of electronic vibrations"; electricity, telephone communication, radio voices, x-ray, and ultraviolet ray; 6. mundane substances which cannot be measured or weighed; has the power of movement; 7. relates to the astral plane and its functions and peculiarities. (Inconcl.) [cf. PLANES, BODIES OF MAN, FIRST DIMENSION, SECOND DIMENSION]

FOURTH DIMENSIONAL CLAIRVOYANCE—to perceive everything at once in a visionary mode; the inside and outside is seen simultaneously; it is as if the psychic was in the object perceived, or in all places at once; (Charles W. Leadbeater) "astral vision lays every point in the interior of every solid body absolutely open to the gaze of the seer, just as every point in the interior of a circle lies open to the gaze of a man looking down"; (do not confuse with X-RAY CLAIRVOYANCE). **Syn.** SINGLE-EYE VISION, ASTRAL VISION. [cf. SUBJECTIVE CLAIRVOYANCE, VISIONARY]

FOURTH PLANE—1. a level of consciousness recognized for its wisdom, with emphasis on constructive thought and the full development of the use of the imagination faculty; here constructive imagination is taught because the etheric atoms of the third plane use the thought of the fourth plane; 2. one's consciousness develops universal love and humanitarianism which motivates the plane below, where the earth blueprints are drawn; 3. the monad (human seed) forms soul-mind energy here to begin the involutionary journey of the soul-mind to earth; this soul-mind fourth plane energy motivates the third plane energy; 4. the center of intuition, spiritual awareness, discrimination, and Reality perception; 5. geniuses on earth function from this plane to receive their illumination of earth knowledge unknown to mankind in any other way; 6. intuition (clairsentience) tunes into information from this plane and this information in turn runs along the superconscious mind to the pineal gland to be perceived by mankind. **Syn.** BUDDHIC PLANE, INTUITIONAL WISDOM PLANE. [cf. BODIES AND PLANES Appendix 5]

FOURTH ROUND OF PLANET EARTH—the evolution of earth mixed with fire, air and water. [cf. ROUND, CYCLES, EARTH]

FOURTH STATE OF CONSCIOUSNESS—1. (Transcendental Meditation) a deep meditative state; 2. delta; the very deep state of sleep wherein the muscles are very relaxed, and the sleeper rarely moves; brainwaves show about three cycles per second; see DELTA STATE OF CONSCIOUSNESS. [cf. TRANSCENDENTAL MEDITATION, SEED MEDITATION]

FOURTH STATE OF MATTER—see AURA.

FOURTH WAY—(George Ivanovich Gurdjieff) the desire to work on one's consciousness using relations with people, animals, and ideas; begins with self-observation learning to divide one's attention so as to direct a portion of it back on one's self, until one learns there is no "I" within but an internal cast of characters; these characters, in turn, dominate the stage and add to one's personality. **Syn.** SLYMAN MEDITATION. [cf. PATH]

FOX SISTERS—two American girls who publicly commenced the practice of spirit-rapping and life-beyond-death belief in America; 1847, Arcadia, New York. [cf. KNOCKINGS, SPIRITUALISM]

FOX SPIRITS—(Japan) etheric world intelligences capable of contacting earth people and bringing

243

them psychic information. **Syn.** GUIDES, CONTROL, SPIRIT. [**cf.** DISCARNATE BEING, PHYSICAL PSYCHISM, MEDIANIMIC]

FOX-FIRE—see FOOLISH FIRE.

FOXGLOVE—(botane) a psychotropic weed used for psychic manifestations, connected to the fairies and elves. [**cf.** BOTANE, EARTH FAIRIES, HALLUCINATIONS]

FRAGMENT—(esoteric) all things being segments of a One. [**cf.** HOLOGRAM, METAPHYSICS, GESTALT]

FRANKINCENSE—(ancient Egypt) (botane) a gum resin of trees of the Boswellia family used to invoke the etheric world helpers for guidance and protection; when burned slowly, the patterns of smoke have a soothing effect and burn negative vibrations in the area; valued highly by Egyptians. **Syn.** INCENSE. [**cf.** SENSATION CONSCIOUSNESS, BOTANE, INVOCATION]

FRATERNITY OF THE ROSE CROSS—the original name of the Rosicrucian Society; courses in knowledge of the Wisdom of the Mysteries. [**cf.** SEVEN-SIDED VAULT, ROSE CROSS]

FRAU HOLLE—(Grimm's Fairy Tales) identified as queen of the elves. **Syn.** HOLDA. [**cf.** NATURE SPIRITS]

FREE ASSOCIATION—a method developed by Sigmund Freud for use in psychoanalysis: the analyst verbalizes, in a constant flow to the patient, specific words; the patient is required to respond spontaneously with the first word which comes to him or her; such response prompts the next word from the analyst; objective: to reveal to the analyst the patient's subconscious reaction to the first-stated words which, in turn, discloses to the analyst hidden (buried) emotions of the patient. **Syn.** FLUIDIC ASSOCIATION. [**cf.** DREAM THERAPY, BLOCKS]

FREE CHOICE—to make a voluntary decision, consciously or unconsciously, to perform an action, or to think a thought of one's preference; (metaphysics) a human is the only organism that does everything of his or her own accord and has complete charge of their body and affairs; voluntary decisions made over many incarnations make his or her world today and voluntary decisions made today can change it; one's free choice is utilizing the law of karma and so one must live by their decisions; (Ross) "free choice is a sacred universal law

and no one should be deprived of it." [**cf.** ON-THE-SPOT-HYPNOSIS, HOLISTIC HEALTH]

FREE ENERGY—**1.** motion that gives power and is unlimited insofar as the supply will not become extinct; little or no cost is associated with its production; i.e., solar energy, windpower, geothermal energy, tidal energy, etc. (Inconcl.) **2.** (esoteric) the electron floating in space subject to the law of thought. (Inconcl.) **3.** made from positive ions and can be used for everything and anything. (Inconcl.) **4.** men from outer space. (Inconcl.) **5.** (America) see VITAL LIFE FORCE. [**cf.** FREE ENERGY, ENERGY]

FREE FLOWING—see FLOW FREE.

FREE RUN—the automatic function of human and animal organisms on a twenty-four-hour cycle, even though they are free of environmental influences which make a sun and moon day; e.g., a man living in a cave or a bear hibernating have a twenty-four-hour cycle of body systems regardless of whether or not they see the sun shine. **Syn.** CIRCADIAN RHYTHM. [**cf.** PHASE SHIFT, BIOLOGICAL CYCLES]

FREE STATE OF CONSCIOUSNESS—when the two minds have changed prominency in their roles and the conscious mind is allowing the subconscious mind to be fed from an outside source. [**cf.** HYPNOTHERAPY, ON-THE-SPOT-HYPNOSIS, MENTAL PSYCHISM, PSYCHOMETRY, PENDULUM POWER]

FREE WILL—see LAW OF FREE WILL Appendix 7.

FREE-ASSOCIATION UNCONSCIOUS—(hypnotherapy) to elicit repressed feelings in the subconscious mind while in a hypnotic state; hypnotherapist questions the subject allowing one thought to bring up another thought, with all material being related; subject reveals things that the conscious mind would not reveal in the awake state, which helps resolve the present problem. [**cf.** HYPNOTHERAPY, PAST-LIFE RECALL]

FREE-FLOATING ANXIETY—an uneasy feeling that cannot be related to any one event or any one person. [**cf.** HOLISTIC HEALTH]

FREE-FLOATING DREAD—(possession) a violent and unconquerable feeling of anxiety that sometimes precedes an attack of possession that results in a faint; feeling is relieved when the etheric world entity enters the body. [**cf.** POSSESSION, HYPERVENTILATION SYNDROME, ANXIETY ATTACKS]

FREE-RESPONSE TEST—(laboratory) an experiment of cognition wherein the participant is to tune into the correct target even though he or she is not informed of the target range. [**cf.** PSYCHIC COGNITION Appendix 2]

FREE-SOUL—(Eskimo) an immortal substance that lives on in the etheric world; see soul-mind. [**cf.** ASTRAL PLANE, ASTRAL BODY]

FREEING THE SOUL—(Tibet) to help a dying person go through the initiation ritual as they make their transition, to assure them of an easy birth in the etheric world; performed in countries where it is the custom, by one who is knowledgeable in the science of death. [**cf.** DEATH SCIENCE, DEATH ANGEL, REFLECTING]

FREEMASONRY—a metaphysical secret society that documents a system of morality through symbols embracing a supreme being; a combination of psychism, religion, metaphysics, and Kabbalah. **Syn.** MASONRY.

FRENZIED HYSTERICAL POSSESSION TRANCE—(ancient Greece) the possession of one's body by an etheric world intelligence for use in physical phenomena or to bring forth psychic knowledge; accomplished by emotional arousal such as prolonged dancing, twirling, chanting, snake handling, etc., which puts the subject in a state of hypnotic trance. **Syn.** ECSTASY TRANCE. [**cf.** IMPERSONATION, TRANCE, MILD DISSOCIATION, TRANCE OF INDIFFERENCE]

FREQUENCY—1. (biofeedback training) sufficient similar EEG brainwaves occurring per second to establish identification; 2. (Patrick Flanagan) "the number of repetitions of a periodic process per unit of time, usually denoted in cycles per second"; 3. (biological cycle) the expression of mutual relationships within the period. [**cf.** BRAIN WAVES, BIOLOGICAL CYCLES]

FREQUENCY ANALYSIS—(biofeedback training) the study of various levels of consciousness of the subject who is hooked-up to a biofeedback instrument; levels of consciousness from the brain or from the finger tips are amplified and recorded on a graph device or auditory system. [**cf.** BIOFEEDBACK TRAINING, EEG, GSR, LISTENING MODE, ALPHA STATE OF CONSCIOUSNESS]

FREQUENCY CONTROL—(biofeedback training) the dial on an EEG instrument that can be regulated to the subject's own electric impulse cycles, establishing a baseline for that training session. [**cf.** THRESHOLD CONTROL, RESTING ELECTRICAL LEVEL, BASELINE READING]

FREQUENCY REGISTRATIONS—(dowsing) to measure the interaction of a given force field with one's owns nervous system to determine information regarding that particular force field; pendulum or dowsing instrument is held over the force field to be tuned into, radiations register through the instrument traveling up the nervous system to the brain and down the nervous system to the instrument which amplifies the answer by its movement; radiesthesist may feel body sensations in the hand, arm, or entire body but interpretation is from the movement of the instrument. **Syn.** RADIESTHETIC SENSE. [**cf.** DOWSING, PENDULUM POWER, GYRATION]

FREYJA—a nature spirit in charge of fertility and the health of a household; desirous of communicating to all ranks of the human species; has a twin called FREYR. [**cf.** FAIRIES]

FREYR—see FREYJA.

FRIAR'S LANTERN—see FOOLISH FIRE.

FRINGE MEDICINE—(Canada) any unorthodox remedy, treatment, medicine, practice, or change in life habits that aims toward a more qualitative life. **Syn.** NEW-AGE MEDICINE, UNORTHODOX MEDICINE. [**cf.** HOLISTIC HEALTH, CURATIVE MEDICINE]

FRINGE OF CONSCIOUSNESS—a state of awareness in which the individual is tuned into the etheric world and the physical world simultaneously; the subconscious mind is predominant and perceives the astral planes, but the conscious mind never fully left, so the individual is still aware of his or her environment; obtained by MEDITATION or HYPNOSIS. [**cf.** ALPHA STATE OF CONSCIOUSNESS, SELF-HYPNOTHERAPY]

FRINGE OF SPACE-TIME—a state of consciousness wherein one's conscious mind is quiet and the subconscious mind has expanded into another level, and the time concept is distorted; e.g., an astral flight or a deep hypnotherapy session. [**cf.** ASTRAL PROJECTION, THETA STATE OF CONSCIOUSNESS, HYPNOTHERAPY, MENTAL PROJECTION]

245

FRINGE SCIENCES—study of the occult, metaphysics, parapsychology, mysticism, radiesthesia, pyramidology, ufology and any other subjects that have philosophical concepts interrelated with science.

FRIVOLOUS COMMUNICATIONS—witty, sarcastic, mischievous, nonimportant psychic information coming from inferior etheric world entities that have not evolved enough for more worthwhile information. [cf. CLOAK OF INSULATION, MEDITATION, INNER BAND]

FRIVOLOUS SPIRITS—nature spirits in the etheric world that annoy earthlings because they are ignorant, mischievous and unaware of their purpose in life. Syn. HOBGOBLINS, GNOMES, WILL-O-THE-WISPS. [cf. POLARITY, FAIRIES]

FROM THE WORLD OF SPIRIT—common phrase used by the mental psychic to express that the information is coming from the etheric world intelligence and not her or himself. [cf. STAND-UP READER, CLOAK OF INSULATION]

FRONTAL GAZE—to look with eyes half-closed and the eye-balls turned up focusing on an imaginary point just inside and above the center of the eyebrows; puts one in an alpha state more quickly. [cf. ALERT-PASSIVITY, CONCENTRATION, INTERIOR SILENCE]

FRONTALIS MUSCLES—(biofeedback training) a place where an electrode is positioned when using the EEG biofeedback instrument, located one inch above the eyes, in the middle of the forehead. [cf. BIOFEEDBACK TRAINING, ELECTRODES, EEG, EMG]

FRONTIERLESS—(Theosophy) pertains to abstract space or time. [cf. MULTIDIMENSIONAL, TOTALITY]

FROZEN—pertains to places in the body where the flow of energy current is blocked by repressed memories of a traumatic experience that went unresolved when it occurred. Syn. LOCKED-IN. [cf. HOLISTIC HEALTH, REGRESSION, PRIMAL SCREAM, ROLFING]

FRUITITARIAN—one whose entire diet is varieties of fruit. [cf. FOOD SCALE]

FU HSI PATTERN—a symbol of a circle representing the Absolute; divided into overlapping positive and negative sections, each containing the seed of its own opposite. Sim. YIN AND YANG. [cf. SYMBOLS, FORMS-WITH-POWER, FOHAT]

FUGA DAEMONUM—(botane) a yellow plant similar to a miniature sun believed to have the vibrational frequencies that will repel evil vibrations; called "flight of demons." Syn. ST. JOHN'S WORT. [cf. BOTANE, INSTINCT PERCEPTION, VEGETATION MAGIC]

FULFILL THE SCRIPTURES—(Bible, metaphysics) (to complete the monad") to fulfill the potential within the seed: the potential of perfectness is within every species of seed, and the life of every seed "evolves" from within, out; the human seed or the monad "involuted" to earth, gathered up material matter to evolve itself back to a perfect human; the scriptures are the "potential of perfectness" or the path back to perfectness. [cf. MONADOLOGY, METAPHYSYICAL, HUMAN BEING KINGDOM]

FULFILLMENT—an emotion of satisfaction and joy when one realizes their inherent capacities and uses these potentials to build a personality and lifestyle that contributes to humanity. [cf. WELLNESS, GESTALT]

FULL-BLOWN SOLUTION—to psychically perceive a vision showing the person, object, or scene in detail as an answer to a problem or in a setting of activity revealing its purpose of showing itself, as opposed to seeing things in snatches and then having to decipher the reason for their appearance; willed or unwilled; e.g., seeing an out-of-town friend ill in bed as opposed to seeing just the friend's face and not knowing why they appeared. [cf. MENTAL PSYCHISM, CLAIRVOYANCE, BIOFEEDBACK TRAINING]

FULL CLAIRVOYANCE—to physically see what is around one and, simultaneously, clairvoyantly perceive levels in the astral world and be aware of both so as to relate astral activity for recording (rare skill). [cf. FULL ETHERIC VISION, AURIC CLAIRVOYANCE]

FULL ETHERIC VISION—to be sensitive to matter other than physical matter; to psychically see objects and people transparently as if one were looking through them, or one was looking from the front and back simultaneously; things appear as if they were flattened out and nothing is hidden from view; in full etheric vision, one can see through the ground and detect the nature spirits that inhabit the earth (rare skill); (do not confuse with X-RAY CLAIRVOYANCE). **Syn.** ASTRAL VISION. [**cf.** PSYCHIC TELESCOPE, SPIRITUAL SIGHT]

FULL MATERIALIZATION—(ectoplasm materialization) the process of an etheric world personality made physically visible in whole, from the ectoplasm exuding from the medium and sitters in a seance; some personalities have been dense enough to walk, talk, have weight, lungs to breath and other normal parts of a body; size varies from tiny to a giant personality; body exists from two minutes to two hours; body is sensitive and when touched, the medium feels pain; personalities can be a known deceased person, the medium's guide, or a stranger; final accomplishment comes after years of sitting for materialization by the sitters and medium; see ECTOPLASM MATERIALIZATION. [**cf.** ETHERIALIZATION, ECTOPLASM, SEANCE]

FULL RECALL—(hypnotherapy) to remember what transpired while in the hypnotic state of consciousness after the session is over; one should be programmed while in the hypnotic state to have "full recall" so the subconscious mind will surface the experiences later; sometimes the subject remembers suggestions that go against their belief system or experiences of a traumatic past life, because these disturb their consciousness; a tape recording of the session played back later will freshen the memory in the conscious mind. [**cf.** SELF-HYPNOTHERAPY, AGE REGRESSION, INDUCTION]

FULL TRANCE—a somnambulistic state of hypnosis wherein the soul-mind of the medium leaves their body and allows the etheric world intelligence to use it for the physical phenomena at hand; soul-mind takes an astral projection to the ceiling or a far-off place; etheric world intelligence uses the medium's eyes, arms, legs, hands and voice box; medium has no memory of what transpired when phenomena is over; always planned, willed, and desire-controlled by the medium. **Syn.** DEEP TRANCE. [**cf.** IMPERSONATION, SEANCE, DESIRED-CONTROL]

FUNCTIONAL BODY—see AURA.

FUNCTIONAL CLAIRSENTIENCE—a strong impulse or urge to change one's plans or to spontaneously do something without any apparent cause; e.g., a hunch to go home a different way and find you have avoided an accident. **Syn.** HUNCHABILITY. [**cf.** INTUITION, PROPHECY]

FUNCTIONAL INTEGRATION—(Moshi Feldenkrais) the altering of habitual movement response through education of the central nervous system. [**cf.** ALTERNATIVES, FRINGE MEDICINE, BIOFEEDBACK TRAINING]

FUNERARY GEOGRAPHY—see ETHERIC WORLD.

FUNIS—see SILVER CORD.

FURIES—1. (Greece) three goddesses in the etheric world who are in charge of punishing criminals; known as the kindly ones; depicted with their heads wreathed with serpents; 2. (Rome) nature spirits capable of being stirred into existence as a product of the imagination; frequently used for evil; female gender; 3. (Tibet) impulses of emotions of inferior quality, emotions that are tormentors and eventually take one's life. [**cf.** FAIRIES, EMOTIONS, THOUGHTS]

FUROR—(Latin) a state of consiousness necessary to attain for psychic information to flow; see ECSTASY. [**cf.** DEEP TRANCE, PROPHECY, ALPHA STATE OF CONSCIOUSNESS]

FUSIFORM—(ufology) a living organism found in outer space which is capable of being melted. (Inconcl.) [**cf.** UFOLOGY Appendix 5]

FUTURISTS—those who have the ability to predict the future and are willing to spend much of their time to help purify the planet in the years of the transformation; one who thinks globally and sees things in a huge scope, by-passing personal interest; capable of many psychic skills. [**cf.** PLANETARY HELPERS, AQUARIAN AGE]

FUZZY FEELING—to realize that one is being fed psychic information but it is not coming in clear enough to decipher. [**cf.** CLAIRSENTIENCE, MENTAL PSYCHISM]

FYE—(British Isles) identifies a living presence from the etheric world when one is not sure what one is psychically perceiving, as opposed to perceiving an energy field that is not alive; an umbrella word encompassing a deceased known person, a guide, an earthbound entity, an UFO personality, or a poltergeist. **Syn.** SPIRIT, APPARITION. [**cf.** INNER BAND, GUIDE, GHOSTS]

FYLGJA—(Norway) see ASTRAL BODY.

GA-LLAMA—see VITAL LIFE FORCE.

GABRIEL—the planetary archangel in charge of the moon's oversoul; a genius of mysteries, who has worked psychically through the great masters during their earthly incarnations, such as: Mohammed dictating the KORAN; Heron, a Greek scientist, giving inspirational thought to write "The Recitation"; and with Daniel (Bible) coming as the Holy Spirit with wisdom and understanding. [cf. ANGEL HIERARCHY, GODHOOD, ANGEL KINGDOM]

GAIN SETTING—(biofeedback training) adjustment knob on a biofeedback instrument giving desired sensitivity of response. [cf. ELECTRODE CREAM, CLEAN RECORDS, CONDITIONING BIOFEEDBACK]

GALACTIC CONFEDERATION—(esoteric) believed to be a brotherhood of intelligences that restored order to earth's solar system between the Lemurian and Atlantean periods, leaving large antenna systems to monitor the planet; these could be seen from all other planets, and earth could then be monitored from the air; these antenna systems are the pyramids. [cf. GIZEH, PYRAMID TEXTS, KING'S CHAMBER, HOUSE OF GOD]

GALACTIC WAVE FIELD—bombardment of vibrations from the stars or any space substance. [cf. ENERGY CURRENTS, HYPERSYNCHRONIZED WAVES]

GALAXIAL DEITY—a magnanimous, exalted intelligent energy whose rank has been earned in the purification process, and is now in charge of one of the galaxies; an energy field whose function is the highest principal of order in the universe; acts as a huge angel ruling over the supergalaxies; having many solar deities under that law. [cf. MAGNIFICENT DEVAS, CENTRAL SUN, STEPS TO GODLINESS, LADY OF HEAVEN, GABRIEL]

GALAXY—(esoteric) an outward, successive, repetitive process containing billions of smaller processes, each with essentially the same structure and purpose of individuality and hologramic goals; a constant transformation of energy divided into four parts: active, receptive, function, and result; a large system of stars held together by mutual gravitation revolving around a Central Sun, which is part of a Supergalaxy. [cf. ISLAND UNIVERSE, SYSTEM OF REALITIES, COSMIC RAY]

GALLEN MACHINE—an instrument invented by Thomas Gallen Hieronymous, an American, that detects invisible emanations from inert matter; projects and transmits many energies which are unknown to mankind at this time, but which have an influence on matter. (Inconcl.) [cf. PSYCHOTRONIC GENERATORS, RADIESTHESIA, TELLURIC ENERGY]

GALVANIC SKIN RESISTANCE—abbr. GSR; the measurement of fluctuation of the conductivity of the skin; the body constantly gives off minute quantities of water through the sweat glands, usually unnoticeable; this water is generated by the nervous system in the body and regulated by emotions, feelings, and attitudes; electrodes placed on the fingertips monitor the amount of sweat one is producing; through instruments that amplilfy these signals, one can get information as to what makes one aroused, excited, calm, happy or peaceful. [cf. METABOLIC MONITOR, BIOFEEDBACK TRAINING, LOG BOOK, CROSS-EXCITATION]

GALVANIC SKIN RESPONSE INSTRUMENT—abbr. GSR; invented by Luigi Galvani; the first type of biofeedback instrument to measure emotional activity in the body, in its minute quantities, and amplify it tangibly, to be isolated and studied; an instrument that is attached to the fingers or toes by tiny electrodes; monitors skin conductivity through sweat glands, produced by the sympathetic nervous system which is affected by thoughts, emotional responses, attitudes, truths, indirect physical tensions, and arousal; sends these signals to the box for amplification to be heard as sounds or seen on a meter. [cf. METABOLIC MONITOR, BASELINE DRIFT, SKIN RESISTANCE]

GALVANOMETER—invented by Puyfontain; an instrument to test the psychic power and body changes in the medium while in the seance room; capable of detecting a change of polarity in the human body. [cf. STHENOMETER, SPIRITOSCOPE, HUMAN POLARITY, EXTERIORIZATION OF SENSITIVITY]

GANDHARVAS—1. (Tibet) celestial nature spirits that live in the world of sound, song, and music, functioning as great musicians who can be perceived clairaudiently, singing the glories of the

Great Deities; 2. (Buddhism) nature spirits that have their abode in cities and in clouds; in charge of shaping the clouds; perceived clairvoyantly but vanish with rain. [cf. DEVA WORLD, COSMIC MUSIC, SAINT]

GANZFELD EXPERIMENTAL TECHNIQUES— (Germany) a method of forming sensory deprivation of the brain to create a clearer channel for psi information to flow, especially in clairvoyance; the psi-receiving subject is usually lying down wearing halved Ping-Pong balls over the eyes and receiving white noise over headphones; objective is to eliminate patterned visual and auditory stimulation and thereby achieve a quiet and introspective mental state; experiments are intended to research to find out if ESP is flowing through a human being at all times but being blocked by the five senses; in this condition the psi signal could be sensed more strongly and manifest in the form of a vision. [cf. MENTAL PSYCHISM PROCESSES Appendix 2]

GARLIC—(esoteric) plant used extensively for curing many diseases because of its healing qualities; known as a cure-all; used to ward off evil humans from entering a home by placing buds over the threshold. [cf. BOTANE, CEREMONIAL MAGIC]

GARNETS—(esoteric) minerals used as amulets to bring the wearer happiness and loyalty from subjects and friends; known as the "happy stones." [cf. AMULET, BEAMED ENERGY]

GARUDA—(Hinduism) a symbol shown in paintings as part man and part bird; in charge of wind and birds. [cf. ANGEL KINGDOM, KINGDOMS OF LIVING CREATURES, NATURE SPIRITS]

GASSHO—(Japan) a gesture of placing palms of the hands together with the fingers outstretched, as Christians do when in prayer. [cf. PALM UPWARD DURING MEDITATION, BLESSING, HANDS]

GATE CONTROL MECHANISM—(acupuncture) an area in the spinal cord and in the thalmus in which the nerves carrying sensations and pain signals must pass to reach the brain; by use of an acupuncture needle this area (gate) can be opened and shut to allow the pain signals to preceed or halt, so no pain is experienced; works similarly to hypnotic anesthetization. [cf. HYPNOSIS, GATEWAY TO MEDITATION]

GATES—(Yoga) inner principle that keeps the three lower chakras separated from the higher chakras; will open when the person has given up

materialistic thoughts and acts, and is concerned with earning higher enlightment. [cf. KUNDALINI, CHAKRA, LOWER MAN]

GATEWAY TO THE HEART—(heart chakra, Yoga) theory: when one overcomes the consciousness of the three lower chakras, one enters the heart chakra where one can stay awhile before proceeding to the consciousness of the three higher chakras. [cf. BATTLE GROUND, CARNAL MAN, SUSHUMNA]

GATEWAYS TO THE MIND—five physical senses that bring vibrations from outer stimuli to the conscious mind where they are interpreted as sensation. Syn. SENSE DATA, SENSA. [cf. BRAIN]

GATHERING DIFFUSENESS OF THOUGHT— (Buddhism) ability to pinpoint or direct the usual mundane thoughts that come and go, to a place beyond intellect. [cf. INNER-DIALOGUE, SUBTALK]

GAUSS MAGNETICS—an invisible electromotive energy interpenetrating the nervous system of all living organisms; carries the vital life force necessary for all life; is positive and negative; enters the left palm and exits the right foot involuntarily and constantly; can be directed by thought out of the right palm, eye and hip as a healing agent; known as Gauss magnetism after its inventor Karl Friedrich Gauss, who invented a meter that could measure the density of magnetism. Syn. EARTH MAGNETISM, MAGNETIC FLUID. [cf. MAGNETIC HEALING, NADIS, POLARITY]

GAYATRI MANTRA—a special sound or chant considered to be the most powerful of all mantras; usually given to the aspirant to help him or her develop realization of the yoga theory; was given psychically to Sri Rama, a Vedic Sage. Syn. VEDAMATA. [cf. CHANTING, MUSIC OF THE SPHERES, SOUNDS-WITH-POWER]

GAZE—the normal function of the eyes, which is to send out rays that penetrate the aura of objects and people; these rays can be intensified by concentration and emotion, making a greater effect on the person than a normal conversation. [cf. ON-THE-SPOT-HYPNOSIS, SPELL, RADIESTHETIC SENSE, MAGNETISM]

GAZING CRYSTAL—a perfect crystal in the shape of a ball; ideal tool for scrying. [cf. CRYSTAL BALL GAZING, SCRYING]

GEIST—(Germany) spirit, soul, heart, mind, and psyche. [cf. POLTERGEIST, RATTLING GHOST]

GELLER-TYPE PHENOMENA—pertains to psychokinesis in relation to Uri Geller who is capable of exuding more than the normal amounts of energy to move material objects, and is noted for NON-HUMAN-PK, bending of spoons, and fixing watches and clocks. [**cf.** NATURE-PK, HUMAN-PK, LEVITATION, TELEPORTATION]

GELOSCOPY—to perceive psychic information regarding a person by the way he or she laughs. **Syn.** GELOSCOMANCY. [**cf.** MANTIC ARTS Appendix 6]

GELUGPA—(Tibet) see PSYCHIC.

GEMATRIA—(Kabbalah) a system of interpreting divine literature by substituting numbers for the letters or words, e.g., Torah, biblical verses. [**cf.** NUMEROLOGY]

GENERAL EXTRASENSORY PERCEPTION—abbr. GESP; to perceive psychic information through two or more kinds of psychism operating at the same time, e.g., CLAIRSENTIENCE and CLAIRVOYANCE. [**cf.** ESP, MUDDY CONDITIONS, PSYCHIC POTENTIAL]

GENIUS—plural **geni, genii;** 1. a person born with an exceptional intellectual capacity, shown by creative ability in art, music or scientific discoveries, bringing knowledge or art beyond his or time period; one who works from the superconscious mind most of the time, operating from the fifth plane; earned and obtained this ability through many incarnations; (Henry Ford) "It is the fruit of long experiences in many lives"; 2. (Latin, England) "each man's guardian spirit; a protective force in man"; a superior class of etheric world intelligences who help humans by giving guidance; a demi-god who presides over birth and is a constant companion until death; 3. sometimes God of nature and sometimes Nature itself; has the ability to protect everything, animate or inanimate; the three orders of genii in the etheric world: nature spirits, guardians, and regular gods; female is called **juno.** **Syn.** LARS OF ANCIENTS, DOCTOR TEACHER, DAEMON. [**cf.** REINCARNATION, WHEEL OF LIFE]

GENIUS LOCI—(Rome, Greece) 1. nature spirits that guard families; 2. etheric world entities that guard specific localities. [**cf.** ETHERIC WORLD INTELLIGENCES, WIND PEOPLE, WRAITH, SILENT WATCHER]

GEOBIOLOGY—science of Pathology (sickness); includes: geobiological origins and radiations, anomalies in the soil such as clay, subterranean water-veins (springs), radioactive rocks, lines of the global grid, ley lines, uranium deposits, fissures in the rocks, earth anomalies due to earthquakes and imbalances in the earth's magnetic field; these can have a detrimental effect on the biological system of mankind, animals and plants. [**cf.** LEY LINES, HOLISTIC HEALTH]

GEOMAGNETIC FIELD—the magnetic field around the earth, emanating from and giving to the earth; the earth's etheric double containing the blueprint of the earth. **Syn.** ETHERIC DOUBLE/EARTH, ELECTROMAGNETIC FIELD]

GEOMANCER—a psychic who communicates with nature spirits, especially the GNOMES; also skilled in PALMISTRY and CLAIRVOYANCE.

GEOMANTIC ART—to communicate with the nature spirits, especially the GNOMES. [**cf.** FAIRY RINGS, DIMENSION-SHIFTING]

GEOMETRODYNAMICS—(John A. Wheeler) "the fabric through which our universe tunnels in a multiconnected way, is described by a structured curved empty space, in which *before* and *after* have no meaning." [**cf.** HYPERSPACE, WHITE HOLES]

GERM GOD—(Native American, Hopi) an etheric world intelligence who controls the growth and reproduction of all growing things. [**cf.** THUNDER PEOPLE, WISE SPIRITS]

GERM PICTURES—the negatives of the pictures of the AKASHIC RECORDS. [**cf.** MENTAL-REFLECTING-ETHER, THALAMUS]

GERMAN HASIDISM—(twelfth century) mysticism of MERKABAH, dealing in sacred secrets of psychism, disciplines and meditation in the Hebrew letters.

GESP—abbr. GENERAL EXTRASENSORY PERCEPTION; psychic information obtained through two or more psychic skills at the same time, usually mental telepathy and clairvoyance. [**cf.** ESP, DOUBLE-BLIND EXPERIMENTS, ELICITING PSI]

GESTALT—a pattern or organized field having specific properties that cannot be derived from the summation of its component parts, a unified whole; the whole has a different function than the simple sum of its parts. [**cf.** GESTALT THERAPY, GESTALT PSYCHOLOGY, HOLISTIC HEALTH]

GESTALT PSYCHOLOGY—a theory of perception that includes the interrelationships between the form of the object and the processes of the perceiver; concerns itself with humanistic as opposed to behavioristic terms; views problems in living as difficulties in relating and communicating; understanding and learning to be more fully present, whole, or centered, making one more alive. [cf. GESTALT, GESTALT THERAPY, CURATIVE EDUCATION]

GESTALT THERAPY—an aim for positive directions and goals of living and using techniques directly and immediately designed to produce them; includes processes that help to unite observable events and the personal, important part of personality; brings certain behaviors into awareness by changing internal processes and fantasies into overt behavior; blocks in awareness and behavior will emerge in this process; uses the patient's experiential knowledge for its value and enhancement.

GESTALTUNG—coined by Johann Woolfgang von Goethe (1800); see VITAL LIFE FORCE.

GESTATION IN HUMANS—the human being seed begins in the mother's womb as mineral, progresses to vegetable, fish, and animal to human being, when examined in stages. [cf. LAW OF REPETITION Appendix 7]

GESTIC MAGIC—see BLACK MAGIC.

GHANTA NADAM—the ringing of a tiny bell when meditation is over so as not to startle the meditator. [cf. CAVE OF ENERGY, INWARD ART, INNER-ATTENTION]

GHOST—an energy field that makes its presence known periodically in the same area, giving the awareness of a "living presence"; brings a drop in temperature with its presence; perceived clairaudiently or audiently by its activity and movements; perceived clairvoyantly as a fluffy, transparent human-like mass, moving very slowly; kinds: 1. a confused soul-mind; a discarnate entity floating in the etheric world; dazed and puzzled; held earthbound by: (a) an emotional tie from the past incarnation he or she does not understand; (b) belief he or she is not dead because of former education that misinformed them about the etheric world; (c) mourners who do not stop thinking and talking about them; ghost receives energy from an environment (a room or furniture) that holds emotional ties regarding their past life; ghost performs in an area that relates to their earth life; 2. astral shell: a human-like semblance held together by the memory of earthly desires of the soul-mind that just left it; earthly habits and desires are so strongly

imbedded within the shell that it holds its human-like form for a long time; floats close to earth and uses energy from psychics to make its presence known; see ASTRAL SHELL. [cf. EARTHBOUND ENTITY, POLTERGEIST Appendix 4, EXORCISM] EXORCISM]

GHOST DANCE—(Native American, late 1800s) the central ritual of a messianic religion began by WOVOKA, a Paiute, circa 1870 which quickly spread to most western tribes; performed by all members of the tribe to induce the opening of psychic skills; dancing is done in a circle to the rhythmic beat of a drum until tribal members achieve an ALTERED STATE OF CONSCIOUSNESS and can communicate with etheric world intelligences (called ancestors); some are: 1. shown clairvoyant visions; 2. hypnotized for preparation for the medicine man's healing energy; 3. put into a trance state to receive direct guidance, and counsel, through direct voice. **Syn.** TRIBAL DANCING, SUN-DANCE. [cf. WHIRLING DERVISHES, TRIBAL DANCING]

GHOST HAUNTING—an etheric world incarnate that makes its presence known by noise activity or is perceived clairvoyantly, in the same area periodically; receives its energy from great earth emotions connected to that area, and needs to have that earth problem resolved before it can rest and go on in its new vibration in the etheric world; some of the noises are rustling, foot steps, knocks, all moving slowly; accompanied by a drop in temperature and the feeling of a cold chill; there is always a feeling of life as opposed to dead presence. **Syn.** ENVIRONMENTAL HAUNTING. [cf. GHOSTS, EARTHBOUND ENTITIES, PHOTOGRAPHIC PLATE OF NATURE, HAUNTING]

GHOST IN THE MACHINE—(Rene Descartes) a highly intellectual energy force that is "in contact with the brain" or "in the brain" but is not the brain; receives information from the sense organs and controls the workings of the brain; in turn, the brain controls the working of the glands, the vocal apparatus, the skeletal musculature, and all the other parts, causing one to act as a human being. (Inconcl.) **Syn.** SOUL-MIND. [cf. MIND, SUBCONSCIOUS MIND, SYMPATHETIC SYSTEM]

GHOST SEERS—belief: those born at twilight will have the psychic ability to perceive clairvoyantly and to prophesy deaths. [cf. VILLAGE WISE-WOMAN, THAUMATURGIST, NATURAL MEDIUM]

GHOST SHIPS—(Nova Scotia) a phantom ship that appears to live on the water; can be seen by sailors, either up close or at great distances; theories: the boat and its crew are capable of DIMENSION-SHIFTING or the observer is temporarily out of step with the stream of time, or the ship is. (Inconcl.) [cf. PHANTOM ARMIES, SPOOK, SPIRIT INFLUENCE]

GHOST VEIN—(dowsing) a dried up water vein that causes the rod to react and bring a false signal to the dowser; water vein retains some of its magnetism in its surrounding environment which a dowsing rod can detect. [cf. INTERNAL DIRECTION, BLOCKING, SOIL RADIATIONS]

GHOSTERY—see GHOSTOLOGY.

GHOSTLY ODORS—a fragrance or odor, pleasant or unpleasant, perceived psychically in an area where its source is not physically present; made psychically perceivable by: 1. an etheric world guide to introduce his or her presence; 2. a discarnate being to introduce his or her presence; 3. an omen, to announce a coming emotional event, e.g., smell of death a few days before a friend dies; a smell of fire a few hours before the fire breaks out. [cf. GUIDE, OMEN, CRISIS PHENOMENA, CLAIRSCENT]

GHOSTOLOGY—the study of phantom bodies; human-like apparitions, shadowy substances, or feelings of a live presence in the area, that are perceived psychically. [cf. SURVIVALISTS, POLTERGEIST, GHOST HAUNTING]

GHOSTS OF THE GIBBET—etheric world entities capable of shifting dimensions who take the form of swine-like creatures; in this form they rush into earthly vibrations at night where there is foul crime, and do their share of fighting and rooting. [cf. DIMENSION-SHIFTING AND SHAPE-CHANGING Appendix 2, EARTHBOUND ENTITIES, DENSITY]

GHOSTS' PRINTS—(Vatican theory, 1979) "spirit hands"; the genuine mark of the dead; handprints left by dead people as a warning or as a comforting omen; e.g., once prints were left on a desk (1731) and once on a nun's sleeve. [cf. CLOTH PHOTOGRAPHY, SKIN WRITING, STIGMATA, ELECTRIC GIRLS]

GHUL—(Koran) a nature spirit created out of tremendous heat and abiding in the heat; assumes human form and hids in places ready to harm humans; belongs to the jinn family.

GI—(karate) a two-piece cotton uniform that hangs nearly to the feet; worn while taking karate lessons. [cf. MARTIAL ARTS Appendix 5]

GIANT AMOEBA—(ufology) a very large, glowing, super-performing critter, pulsating in space; when seen could be mistaken for a space ship. [cf. CRITTERS, ECHO, CREATURES OF STRATOSPHERE]

GIANT TROLL—(Norway, Sweden) nature spirit living in mountains, in charge of building mighty structures such as castles, bridges and churches; desire human souls for their wages.

GIANT-STRIDE DREAM—astral projection taken during sleep wherein the traveler moves in the air, under the direction of the subconscious will; goes great distances with each astral stride, corresponding to strides in the dream. [cf. BODIES OF AIR, ROLL-IN, HEAD-THUMPING DREAM]

GIANTS—a huge nature spirit; represents mankind's core, collective thoughts and deeds, making overwhelming and uncontrollable forces in the world; usually personifies dissatisfaction, but can also make manifestations for good in the world. [cf. BIG FOOT, MONSTER ACTIVITY, MATTER, LAW OF THOUGHT Appendix 7]

GIB GHOSTS—see GHOSTS OF THE GIBBET.

GIDDINESS—(Old English *gidig*, "possessed by a god") a state of ecstasy; an emotional high; a feeling of being in paradise; usually influenced by a very advanced soul-mind or a religious experience. [cf. PEAK EXPERIENCE]

GIFT OF HEAVEN—(Aztec) see IRON and TAMING OF FIRE.

GIFT OF TONGUES—see TALKING-IN-TONGUES.

GIFTED EXPERIMENTERS—see PSYCHIC and MEDIUM.

GIFTS OF THE SPIRIT—see PSYCHIC SKILL.

GILA MONSTER—(Native American) etheric world god responsible for helping with development of "motion-in-the-hand" psychic skill. [cf. CONTROL, DOORKEEPER, CONTAGIOUS ENTHUSIASM, CELESTIAL DESCENT]

GINSENG—(China) (botane) an herb having the vibrational frequency to help one live a long life and maintain wellness. [cf. ELIXIR, OAK TREE, LAW OF DOCTRINE OF SIGNATURES Appendix 7, HEALING]

GISMO—(Ted Serios) a funnel, or means of channeling one's thoughts into the camera lens, in thought photography. [cf. PSYCHIC PHOTOGRAPHY Appendix 2]

GIZA PYRAMID—also spelled **Gizeh**; most studied pyramid on earth; largest of all pyramids, covering thirteen acres; linked to King Cheops; located near Cairo, Egypt; 1. noted for its exactness of measurement which is responsible for its pyramid energy; (Coptic language *pyr,* "division"; *met,* "ten, the division of ten"); a system of fives that runs through the Giza pyramid and its measure also runs throughout all nature; 2. believed to be constructed by psychic skills, such as LEVITATION, DEMATERIALIZATION, and rematerialization, because the stones are so perfectly aligned that slave power could not have built it; 3. (esoteric) reasons why the pyramid was built: (a) to serve as an antenna to accumulate and refocus cosmic light into two directions, so the earth could be identified from other planets; (b) to serve as a communication center for interterrestrial flights; to act as a transmitter and receiving station; (c) to store energy to be used for machinery on this planet; (d) to induce healing; pyramid energy restores and normalizes cells in the physical body; (e) to increase psychic sensitivity; (f) to store food; pyramid energy inhibits bacterial growth; (g) to serve as a meeting place for great leaders on our planet; in this atmosphere of pyramid energy, leaders in ancient times were allowed to open the akashic records of the earth and plan how to promote a higher state of consciousness within all civilizations.

GIZEH COMPLEX—also spelled **Giza**; an area in Egypt that contains the GREAT PYRAMID, two smaller pyramids next to the large one, and six smaller pyramids close by. [**cf.** PYRAMIDOLOGY Appendix 5, GOLDEN SECTION]

GLAMOUR—(Scotland) to put an individual under a spell; see CASTING A SPELL.

GLAMOURIE—an abnormal feeling of "being fixed and unable to move," even when the conscious mind is saying to be active; a state of consciousness in which the subject is being manipulated by a GLAMOURIZER; begins when the eyes of the psychic penetrate a person's mind intensely with a state of fear or of extreme pleasure; victim stays in this state of glamourie consciousness until the psychic lets up on his or her constant concentration to manipulate the subject; distance no barrier; see SPELLED. **Syn.** GLAMOURED. [**cf.** SPELLED, TRANSFIXED, ON-THE-SPOT-HYPNOSIS]

GLAMOURIZER—a psychic who specializes in casting of spells; see SPELL CASTER. [**cf.** SPELL, PSYCHIC, HYPNOSIS]

GLANDS—(esoteric) physical transmitters and transformers between the spiritual, divine, cosmic-self, and the gross earth and physical self; guardians and controllers of the human body; build vitamins for the body. [**cf.** CHAKRAS, THIRD-EYE AREA, SYMPATHETIC NERVOUS SYSTEM]

GLASTONBURY TOR—(Britain, Celtic) a hill on an island that emanates a sacred aura over an area where prominent dead people were buried. [**cf.** ANNWN, GWYN-AP-NUDD]

GLOBE—(esoteric) a rational, living being taking the form of a sphere; a system of life and intelligence to serve God; known to us as a planet, e.g., Jupiter, Mars, Earth; one seventh part of a planatary chain in a solar system. **Syn.** PLANET. [**cf.** GLOBE-ROUND, SOLAR CYCLE]

GLOBE-ROUND—(Theosophy) one evolutionary cycle that the globe earth will pass through with the seven root-races. [**cf.** ROOT-RACES, CYCLES, AGE, ROUND]

GLOBULAR SPIRITS—an appearance of tiny opaque bodies in the form of points or discs, floating in the air, coming from the eye or center of the globe; perceived clairvoyantly day or night; (do not confuse with SPIRIT LIGHTS seen near mediums at night). **Syn.** OPAQUE POINTS. [**cf.** UFOLOGY, CLAIRVOYANCE, NODES]

GLOBULES—(Yoga) evidence of prana and atmospheric orgone; dancing dots of light; pinpricks which assume an arc-like configuration against a blue sky during the day. [**cf.** VIBRATIONS, MITOGENIC RADIATION]

GLORIA—1. (Christian) a luminosity drawn in pictures around the head of highly evolved humans, usually religious figures; symbolizes this person's brilliance, understanding and extraordinary service to humankind; perceived clairvoyantly on these persons when alive; 2. (esoteric) the concentrated energy in the CROWN CHAKRA flowing from the top of the head of the enlightened soul-mind; occurs when one is on the final steps of ascension and working from the crown chakra level of consciousness. **Syn.** HALO, GLORY, PRANA HALO. [**cf.** AGLOW, GLORIFIED SOUL-MIND, GLORIFICATION]

GLORIFIED BEINGS—advanced adepts from other solar systems who mingle and blend with our etheric world higher planes. [**cf.** GREAT ONES, SOLAR LOGOS, SEVEN SPIRITS OF GOD]

GLORIFIED BODY—(Bible) an intelligence that through many incarnations on earth has so purified his or her soul-mind that they can now transmute to all planes of the etheric world, and function properly under the laws of each plane; when appearing in the earth plane, he or she takes a physical grouping of atoms, but the texture of the body is not as a normal physical body is known to be; appears to clairvoyants as a beautiful radiance encompassing a perfect physical form, with an intensified brilliance around the head; i.e., Jesus called it a "crown of glory"; a purified soul-mind in a glorified body does not die, but when ready to return to the etheric world rises and ascends. **Syn.** BLISS BODY. [**cf.** AGLOW, GLORIFIED SOUL-MIND, GLORIA]

GLORIFIED SOUL-MIND—the OVERSOUL; contains learned and experienced knowledge that is ready to return to the monad; called WISDOM. [**cf.** GLORI-FIED BODY]

GLORY—(uncapitalized) means HALO; see GLORIA.

GLOSOPERTA—(minpsi) a stone which comes from a meteor; has properties which help the owner to accelerate his or her psychic skills and healing abilities. [**cf.** MINPSI Appendix 2, QUARTZ, RUNE STONES]

GLOSSOLALIA—(Christianity) see TALKING-IN-TONGUES.

GLOSSOLALIC UTTERANCE—see TALKING-IN-TONGUES.

GLOSSOLALIST—a psychic who specializes in TALKING-IN-TONGUES.

GLOTTOLOGUE—medium who speaks a language foreign to her or himself, but which is a valid language; works with etheric world intelligences in the level of consciousness of trance. **Syn.** XENO-GLOSSIST. [**cf.** TRANCE VOICE Appendix 2, TALK-ING-IN-TONGUES]

GLOW—an internal, alchemical body process; out of one's own gross substance, its quintessence is brought about by an airtight distillation from the bodily fluids, with the body acting as the instru-ments and utensils; this subtle quintessence sub-stance can reinvigorate the physical frame and make the body show a whitish light surrounding it; see AGLOW. (Inconcl.) [**cf.** ALCHEMY, ALCHEMIST, ASCENSION, GLORIFIED BODY]

GNOMES—nature spirits made of pure elemental substance, living underground, in mines, and in rocks, absorb the sun through earth and rocks; gnomes have their own homes and government in another vibrational frequency which allows them to pass through stone and rocks easily; usually show themselves about twelve to eighteen inches tall but are capable of elongating and shifting dimensions quickly; gnomes have an energy compatible with humans and unselfishly help humans, urging them to be in control of body health and psychic skills; the gnome brings strength with a flash, and is persistent in his or her good intent to change the human; addicted to mockery and sometimes can be annoying and frivolous in their communication with humans; see FAIRIES. [**cf.** EARTH SPIRITS, ELVES]

GNOSIS—(Greece) suffix meaning "mystical and spiritual knowledge"; seeking to know; that which one cannot perceive with one's five senses; this knowledge formed at the same time Christianity assumed an esoteric character; primarily teaches a metaphysical meaning of God and creation, not attained intellectually but through feeling and prophecies from God. [**cf.** METAPHYSICAL, PARA-PSYCHOLOGICAL]

GNOSTIC—(Greece, Rome) one who knows; see PSYCHIC.

GNOSTIC GEMS—talismans or medallions that are made of stone; found by the thousands in Egypt, but their use is unknown. [**cf.** MINPSI, AMULETS, CALUNDRONIUS]

GNOSTICISM—a religion of beliefs coming from ZOROASTRIANISM, formed about the same time as Christianity; theory: mankind originated in the celestial realms where only pure spirits dwell; has taken on a material body, binding her or himself to the material world, its values and motives; mankind can evolve back to the celestial realms through the superknowledge he or she receives from the etheric world intelligences who communicate with them regarding the etheric world, psychism, metaphysics and control of the mind; includes ALCHEMY, ASTROLOGY, and MYSTICISM.

GO WITH THE FLOW—instructions to stay at one-pointedness and once the psychic information starts coming, to show no emotion and let it keep coming. [**cf.** MENTAL PSYCHIC PROCESSES Ap-pendix 2]

GO-BETWEENS—see MEDIUM.

255

GO-BEYOND-DEATH EXPERIENCE—the preparation for the death process; teaches what happens in the etheric world when one slips out of the physical body; then, when physical death time comes, one slips easily into the other vibrational frequency and past the density. [**cf.** DENSITY, BARDO THODOL, BODY BREAKERS, DEATH-BED VISIONS]

GOAT—used to personify the devil; presides over the witches' Sabbath; the emblem of sinful humanity at the day of judgment. [**cf.** SYMBOLISM, SCAPEGOAT, ASSOCIATION MAGIC]

GOATS—(psi tasks) people who do not believe in ESP; see SHEEP AND GOAT EFFECT. [**cf.** TIME BARRIER, PSI-COGNITION, DISPLACEMENT]

GOBLIN—a nature spirit showing itself as small, swarthy, and malicious; capable of shape-shifting to become an animal, thief, or villain; name given to the more mischievous and grotesque-looking fairies. **Syn.** HOBGOBLIN.

GOD—(capitalized) activity (energy) and intelligence; 1. infinite soul and infinite spirit; both a monad and a whole; 2. God is neutral, both good and evil, because God is all there is or ever will be; God has an opposite in order to balance in polarity; (Anglo-Saxon) God means "good," so both God and Satan are good; Satan is good in a lesser manifestation; 3. God is all the power, all the love, and all the wisdom in the universe; perfectness because that is all mankind knows; 4. that which is behind all things; the essence of all matter; in all things but only in some, more or less excellent; 5. universal principle; "the scheme of things"; a guiding intelligence; the evolutionary drive of consciousness in the universe; 6. the nature of God is electrical impulses, as thought is electrical; (Bible) "in the beginning was the word [thought] and the word was God"; 7. (Hinduism) the Father is the Absolute Unmanifested, existing "beyond" vibratory creation. **Syn.** TOTALITY. [**cf.** TRINITY, EVIL]

GOD—(uncapitalized) 1. (ancient Greece) all etheric world intelligences who communicated with humans; named god because they could accomplish more than ordinary human feats, gave protection and guidance and their intelligence was beyond human intelligence; 2. (mythology) angels who were given charge over various areas and activities of earth and the universe to distinguish from angels in charge over lesser capacities; duties involved good and adverse situations. [**cf.** DEVA, ANGEL, ANGEL HIERARCHY, SAINT]

GOD CONSCIOUSNESS SUPREME—(Transcendental Meditation) the seventh state of consciousness found in MEDITATION; attitude of detachment and sensing an indescribable feeling of "one." **Syn.** BLISS, SATORI, NIRVANA. [**cf.** TRANSCENDENT, INTUITIVE LEVEL OF THE PSYCHE]

GOD SPOKE—(Hebrew) psychic communication of a very high quality, bringing Truth and Wisdom. [**cf.** SUBLIMINAL PERCEPTION, SUPERSENSUAL, THRONE MYSTICISM]

GOD WITHIN—(Christianity) the real self; the spark of divinity within all things; the core of the one source; see HUMAN BEING SPECIES SEED. [**cf.** I AM, KNOWER, LIFE-ATOM, NOUS]

GOD'S FLESH—(botane) (Mexico) an hallucinogenic drug held sacred; has properties to induce clairvoyance and altered states of consciousness; contains psilocybin. **Syn.** PSILOCYBE MUSHROOM, TEONANACTL. [**cf.** BOTANE, SENSATION CONSCIOUSNESS, MOUNTAIN ASH, WATCH-PLANTS]

GOD-AS-THE-STONE—(esoteric) 1. (Ireland) nature spirits that live in stones; imps living in a stone make the stone speak and move, especially on calendar occasions; 2. (Central America) stones on a mountain were shaped like a jaguar; capable of transforming themselves into a live jaguar at will; 3. rocks have been known to grow at will; dead persons have been known to inhabit their own tombstones. [**cf.** RED CORALS, RUNE STONES, STAR-RUBY]

GOD-BRAIN—see SUPERCONSCIOUS MIND.

GOD-FILLED—(ancient Greece) the flow of poetry; see INSPIRATIONAL MEDIUMSHIP, INSPIRATIONAL THOUGHT. **Syn.** BREATHED INTO, INSPIRED. [**cf.** POET]

GOD-IN-THE-STONE—(Native American, Celtic, Asia, Australia) belief that stones have psychic power and properties to influence the human to accelerate his or her psychic powers. [**cf.** GOD-AS-THE-STONE, MINPSI, MOONSTONE]

GODDESSES—(uncapitalized) 1. (Tibet) thought-forms made from high human sentiments; energy fields of beautiful impulses in the collective unconscious; 2. female gods, see GODS (uncapitalized). [**cf.** CELESTIAL GUARDIAN, CHIEF DEITIES, EIDOLON]

GODFORM POSITION—a posture good for meditation, psychic information, astral projection, or hypnotherapy; to sit in a chair, relaxed, back straight, knees a little bit apart, hands relaxed in the lap, eyes closed. [**cf.** OBJECTIVE PROGRAMMING, SITTING, SOUL FLIGHT]

GODHEAD—(Sanskrit) 1. emblematic of the upper three chakras (CROWN, BROW and THROAT), depicted by drawing a circle with a line vertically through the chakras; represents both Father/Mother God, positive/negative; 2. see GOD (capitalized).

GODHOOD—(capitalized) the highest rank an angel can earn by working through the seven steps of unfoldment, after many initiations; presumably thousands of incarnations when one's monad is wholly united with the top source, God, but is not God; Godhood angels blend with the Spirit of God and are used as channels of His thought, His benevolence and His laws, which direct the universes. **Syn.** GREAT LOGI. [**cf.** LORDSHIP, MASTERSHIP]

GODS FROM THE SKY—(ufology) intelligences who drive the constructs that come to earth from outer space; these intelligences have properties similar to a human. [**cf.** ETHER SHIP BEINGS, MUTATION OF ENERGY, DISC OCCUPANTS, CONSTRUCT]

GOETIA—a GRIMOIRE which catalogues seventy-two etheric world entities who were put away and sealed up by Solomon and which gives the techniques for invoking them to bring guidance, counsel, protection, and one's desires. [**cf.** GOETRIC ART]

GOETRIC ART—1. to exorcise, evoke and dislodge evil haunters from earthlings; 2. to invoke the gods for assistance and guidance by the use of symbols and rituals; noted for the foundation of high magic. [**cf.** OVERLAP, HIGH MAGIC, EVOCATION, INVOCATION, RITUALS]

GOHONZON—1. the box that sets upon the altar which contains a small sacred scroll; 2. (Soka Gakkai) a ritual drawing used to place on the altars in temples and homes as a symbol to encourage only good vibrations to enter that vicinity; drawing consisted of the name of the Lotus Sutra in the center and names of the divinities mentioned in the sutra arranged around it. [**cf.** WORDS-WITH-POWER, RING OF WOODEN POSTS, TOTEMISM, SYMBOL, SIMILE]

GOING INTO THE SILENCE—see MEDITATION.

GOING WITHIN—the ability to turn off all outside stimuli and be completely absorbed with the body, inner-mind, and the etheric world; time is irrelevant; peace encompasses the new awareness. [**cf.** INNER SOUND CURRENT, INTERIOR SILENCE, INTERNALIZATION]

GOING-TO-LEVEL—a personal process for each psychic which brings him or her to a state of consciousness felt within the self to be the level from which their messages will be correct; accomplished through practice. [**cf.** ALTERED STATES OF CONSCIOUSNESS, THREE-FINGER TECHNIQUE]

GOINMUI—(Celtic) 1. divine warrior in the etheric world who is in charge of wars; 2. a divine blacksmith in the etheric world who is in charge of the village blacksmiths. [**cf.** FIRE DOCTOR, CELESTIAL SMITH, EXECUTIVE ORDER]

GOLD—(esoteric) a mineral that has strengthening properties; brings the wearer self-confidence; a good conductor of resonance; as a color, it stands for WISDOM. [**cf.** COLOROLOGY, MINPSI]

GOLDEN BEAMS—yellow or orange rays of light extending from the candle used in a psychic development exercise which will follow the command of the voice and hands; has nothing to do with normal vision. [**cf.** PEAK EXPERIENCES, GOLD, COLOR]

GOLDEN BOWL—(Bible) the emanations flowing out of the top of the head during the death process. **Syn.** DEATH GLOW. [**cf.** INITIATORY DEATH RITE, BORN IN DISGUISE, RIGHT TO DIE]

GOLDEN CHAIN—1. the invisible, all-pervading, all-uniting Totality influence, which connects all things of heaven and earth. **Syn.** JACOB'S LADDER, MERCURIUS PHILOSOPHORUM. 2. (Greece) living beings, from the Godhood Divinities to those in the density below mankind; each intelligence, ethereal and earthly, teaches, instructs, and inspires the living chain below itself. **Syn.** HERMETIC CHAIN. [**cf.** EVOLUTION]

GOLDEN DAWN—(England) founded in 1887; an esoteric by-product of the Rosicrucian Society; felt to be the outer order of the GREAT WHITE BROTHERHOOD receiving guidance, Truths, and instructions from the SECRET CHIEFS of a very high angel rank; pertains to psychic development circles, astral projection, energizing talismans, mediumship, and other psychic feats.

257

GOLDEN LANE—(Czechoslovckia) a section of homes where ancient ALCHEMISTS lived; located near the Gothic Cathedral of St. Vitus. [**cf.** ELIXIR]

GOLDEN LOTUS—(Bible) see CUP.

GOLDEN MONEY SPIDER—(esoteric) a special spider which symbolizes the golden coin; honors with riches anyone on whose body it runs. [**cf.** AMULET, LAW OF MIMICRY Appendix 7, ANPSI, ROBIN]

GOLDEN MOUNTAIN—(Hinduism) see GIZA PYRAMID.

GOLDEN OIL—(esoteric) an invisible, ethereal, mysterious, gaseous fluid, traveling upward along with the magnetic fluid in the SUSHUMNA in the spine; filters outward throughout the nervous system; is not influenced by food, but by one's thinking; on the trip downward, it is the brain dews. **Syn.** GOLDEN OIL. [**cf.** BRAIN DEWS, COSMIC ENERGY, MEDULLA OBLONGATA]

GOLDEN PLATES—plates that bear hieroglyphics describing how the Book of Mormon material was given from the etheric world. [**cf.** ETHERIC SCRIPT, MONOSYLLABIC ANSWERS, POLYGLOT WRITINGS]

GOLDEN ROD—(Germany) (folklore) see DOWSING ROD.

GOLDEN RODS—yellow-orange or golden cylinders, similar to organ pipes which extend downward from nowhere to an individual; denotes the degree of spirituality for that individual according to the circumferences of the cylinders, their number, and density of color; capable of being perceived clairvoyantly in development circles and seances. [**cf.** GIFT WAVES, DIVINE EFFECT, CLOAK OF INSULATION]

GOLDEN SECTION—see MAGICAL PROPORTIONS OF MAN.

GOLDEN TREATISE—one of the writings of the ancient Egyptian king and noted alchemist, Hermes Trismegistus.

GOLDEN URN—(Yoga) represents the human head.

GOLEM—(Hebrew, "a robot brought to life through magic") discovered by Rabbi Yehuda Low; an artificial humanlike being created by carving wood, wax, clay, metal, or by sewing together pieces from dead bodies; given a personality by carving a sacred name into the forehead, and then infusing it psych-ically with concentrated thought energy and direction to do menial tasks for its master. [**cf.** ANDROID, ELEMENTAL, ZOMBIE]

GONG—(Zen) a sounding instrument used to trigger the mind to stay with the mantra of the meditation. [**cf.** JUST SITTING, SLEEPITATE, TOTAL ABSORPTION, TEA]

GONGYO—the practice of CHANTING. [**cf.** PINK SOUND, SHOOTING CHANT, DRUM]

GOOD—an individual opinion of the thinker; a neutral energy but interpreted by the beholder to be upright and proper by his or her morals and standards; 1. any change in vibrational frequencies of anything in the universe is a step to the one source and considered *good* (beneficial) by God; graduations of progression; 2. a scale of correctness depends upon the mass belief system for that time period; good is *not*, it is in the mind; 3. duality of balance, a method of checking balance of the polarities; 4. name one uses to designate a step in evolution for growth, that he or she approves of and feels comfortable with, for that time period; presumably intelligent actions; manifestations of a clear conscience; 5. *good* (desirable) opinionated experiences are necessary to understand and to enable one to move up from *bad* opinionated experiences; 6. *good* is the "perfection of the beginning," indestructible but yet to be understood by mankind; an aspect of energy necessary to produce power. [**cf.** GOOD GENIUS, EVIL]

GOOD GENIUS—(Buddhism) a deity or an advanced soul-mind born in this incarnation with a task of determining which deeds would be mankind-evaluated as good for this time period. [**cf.** SIN, EVIL, EVIL GENIUS]

GOOSEGG INSTRUMENTS—(ufology) equipment developed during the Apollo Flights in the 1970s to monitor the effects of mysterious "lights" which periodically afflicted the astronauts; to record any suspected damage from cosmic radiation to the brain tissue. [**cf.** UFOLOGY]

GORDIAN KNOTS—see BLOCKS.

GOSSAMER VEIL—a cloud-like substance appearing in the mind when sitting for psychic development; further concentration will give it energy to develop into an image, or some kind of psychic information. [**cf.** PLANE OF ILLUSION, VEIL, PINEAL, PUTTING OUT FEELERS]

GOTHIC WITCHES—(1450-1750) (Roman Catholics) psychics who were burned at the stake because they could not correctly repeat the printed material in the specially written manuals as the Catholics desired them to be repeated; only ten percent of these psychics were followers of Satan, and ninety percent were psychics, healers, and psychiatrists. [**cf.** WITCHCRAFT, SATANISM]

GOVERNING RULERS—(I Ching) a part of the hexagram passage that indicates good character, becoming the ruler, and emphasizing the time element of the QUERANT. [**cf.** CONSTITUTING RULERS, I CHING]

GRACE—a level of consciousness in which all growth is effortless; an open, frank, joyful, agreement between the soul-mind and conscious mind desiring growth which makes existence easy. [**cf.** LAW OF GRACE Appendix 7, GRACE OF GOD]

GRACE OF GOD—a directive intelligence motivating everything to move onward and upward; the potential within every seed that motivates that unit or entity to become a perfect unit or entity of its kind; mankind is inwardly perfect so one now has to make oneself outwardly perfect; grace of God is "motivation" that all humans are born with.

GRAND MAN OF THE UNIVERSE—see TOTALITY.

GRAPES—(Huna) unresolved ideas and concepts which the conscious mind was not in condition to rationalize when formed and are suppressed and stored in the subconscious mind; ideas and concepts unresolved because the emotional content was too much to handle at the time of the experience; as time goes on, emotions of like nature join these, making a larger group which will keep growing until the conscious mind resolves the original experience; cause mental and physical illnesses, and are capable of being passed on from one incarnation to another, accumulating like a bunch of grapes. **Syn.** BLOCKS, HOLD PATTERNS, MEMORY CLUSTERS, TIME TRAINS. [**cf.** MUSCLE TENSION PATTERNS, PRIMAL PAINS, REBIRTHING, ROLFING]

GRAPHOLOGY—(ancient Egypt) the study of one's handwriting; by analyzing the various characteristics of one's style of writing one's character, one's past, and future is revealed. **Syn.** HANDWRITING ANALYSIS. [**cf.** BODY READING Appendix 5]

GRAPHOLOGY THERAPY—a technique of studying one's handwriting that reveals subconscious abilities, goals, talents, ambitions and thinking patterns which do not surface normally; because each person's handwriting is unique, this therapy aids in one's state of maturity. [**cf.** HANDWRITING ANALYSIS, CHEIROGNOMY]

GRAVEYARD GHOSTS—human-looking apparitions seen around graveyards; caused by: 1. the astral shell of the newly buried person; 2. an astral projection of a friend of the newly buried person; 3. a materialized thought-form created by grievers paying respects to the deceased; grief thoughts hovering close to earth. [**cf.** HAUNTED LOCALITIES, PHOTOGRAPHIC PLATE OF NATURE]

GRAVITATIONAL SPINNING WAVE—a principle pervading matter on the earth, or wherever there is third-dimensional vibrational frequency, holding it in the third-dimension. [**cf.** GRAVITY CONTROL Appendix 2, STRUCTURAL INTEGRATION, TELEKINESIS LEVITATION]

GRAVITATIONAL WAVES—1. (Albert Einstein) "radiation generated by stellar explosions; rotation of binary stars and the gravitational collapse of stellar masses into black holes"; 2. the various kinds of rays pouring down from ethereal space which appear to cause a measurable reaction of weight when striking earth, and are then absorbed by the materials of the earth's surface; 3. (René Descartes) loose bodies driven into the earth by impact, or aerial corpuscles in the center of the earth's energy field, formed by trillions of energy ray atoms from space, the combination of which produces the force called gravity. (Inconcl.) [**cf.** GRAVITONS, LAW OF GRAVITY Appendix 7, GRAVITATIONAL-FIELD SENSE]

GRAVITATIONAL-FIELD SENSE—the innate ability to sense the location of the sun and moon, even when out of their vicinity, (such as being buried); present in land creatures and fish. (Inconcl.) **Syn.** PRIMARY PERCEPTION. [**cf.** GRAVITATIONAL WAVES, LAW OF GRAVITY Appendix 7]

GRAVITONS—gravitational waves (currently under study) which show a relationship between the rotary motion of atomic structures and the rotation of the planets in our solar system; may be gravitational force, or a separate gravitational force which could be the second force of gravity. (Inconcl.) [**cf.** LEVITATED RUNNING, GRAVITY CONTROL]

GRAVITY—(under study) 1. present science assumes the existence of a constant hydrostatic pressure transmitted through the ethers; 2. believed

259

one function is to reorganize light to interpenetrate other universes; 3. (Patrick Flanagan) gravity is a tensor field; 4. (Nikolai Kozyrev) gravity is a time-field. (Inconcl.) [cf. GRAVITY CONTROL Appendix 2]

GRAVITY CONTROL—to psychically release the force of gravity in an object or human, move the person or object in a particular direction; performed by intense concentration of the will, intervention of the guides, or magical skills; occurs in an aware or trance state of consciousness; suggested theories: 1. to neutralize or reverse the action of gravity in a person or object; 2. to change the rate of vibration of the object by concentrating on the auric field of the object until the atoms are weightless, changing the object to antimatter; if the normal influence of gravity is removed, the object will move easily; 3. to change the "rate of time flow" throughout the substance which makes a weight loss; 4. to change the molecular structure of the object or body until object or body is invisible in its ethereal form, gravity is dissipated and object or body rises; 5. to move the matter faster than the speed of light; this takes the matter out of the third-dimension where gravity prevails; executed by subconscious mind or guides; 6. to allow the guide to intervene, when in a tranced state, and use body ectoplasm to lift the object or medium in the air; 7. to allow one's guide to nullify the normal gravitational effect and raise the object or medium; 8. (law of mimicry) to simulate the object moving off the ground. [cf. GRAVITY CONTROL Appendix 2]

GRAVITY FREE FLIGHT—an unlimited quantity of energy in the universe waiting to be tapped. (Inconcl.) [cf. GRAVITY CONTROL, ENERGY]

GREAT AWAKENING—(alchemy) the time when the alchemist accomplishes the transmutation of his or her internal organs. **Syn.** IMMORTAL DRAUGHT, THE SUPREME BLISS. [cf. ASCENSION, QUINTESSENCE, BODILY FIRES]

GREAT BEAST—(Bible) represents the 666 of Revelation; also the personal name given to a great psychic and medium of his day, Aleister Crowley, by his mother. [cf. NUMBER POWER, DENSITY]

GREAT BODY OF RADIANCE—see GLORIFIED BODY.

GREAT BROTHERHOOD OF SAGES AND SEERS—Association of the Masters of Wisdom and Compassion: the purest example of teachers uninterruptedly instructing a disciple. [cf. FAMA FRATERNITATIS, DOCTRINE OF FORMS AND CEREMONIES, DISCIPLINES]

GREAT CAMP—(Neur tribe, Upper Nile) a wonderful place in the sky where everyone lives after they die. [cf. THOUGHT SPHERE, MANSIONS OF LIGHT, PROGRESSIVE LYCEUMS]

GREAT COUNTENANCE—(Kabbalah) represents the Universe; see TOTALITY.

GREAT DOCTRINE OF LIBERATION—(Tibet) to clairaudiently or clairvoyantly view one's own thought-forms in the Bardo, during the death process; begins to change the attitude of the viewer which is what it is supposed to do. [cf. BOOK OF THE DEAD, GO-BEYOND DEATH EXPERIENCE, CHIKHAI BARDO]

GREAT EYE—see THIRD-EYE and PSYCHISM.

GREAT JOURNEY—(Buddhism) the whole and complete cycle of existence; one ROUND. [cf. AGE, WHEEL OF TIME]

GREAT KARMIC BOARD—etheric world intelligences who have taken on the responsibility of helping civilizations work out their MASS KARMA, RACE KARMA and GROUP KARMA. [cf. REINCARNATION, ACCUMULATED KARMA, RIPE KARMA]

GREAT LAW OF COSMIC JUSTICE—a motivational excitement within the "stream of things" that keeps the universe working out its KARMIC DEBTS and enjoying its karmic assets. [cf. RIPE KARMA, REINCARNATION, CYCLES, LORDS OF JUSTICE]

GREAT LOGI—see TOTALITY or GOD.

GREAT MANITOU—(Native American, Algonquin) (capitalized) the God over all things; the directing force found within all living and nonliving things. [cf. MANITOU] see TOTALITY.

GREAT MASTER—common phrase used by chelas (students); because they feel their leader is a Master incarnated in the flesh to be their teacher; teacher operates from the HIGHER SELF. **Sim.** CHRISTOS, ATMAN, HIGHER SELF. [cf. GURU DEV, LOGOIDAL WILL]

GREAT MOTHER—a name for the sea based on the belief that the first forms of life came from water; represents the positive force in the world. [cf. POLARITY, EVOLUTION]

GREAT ONES—angels who have risen to be working on the fifth initiation toward MASTERSHIP;

accomplished from an earthly incarnation or from an ethereal vibration. **Syn.** MASTERS. [**cf.** ANGEL HIERARCHY, LORDSHIP]

GREAT PICTURE GALLERY—an energy field in the etheric world which contains a complete record of every thought, act, and emotion of all living things; this includes all living things to date and will include all living things that ever will be. [**cf.** MENTAL-REFLECTING-ETHER, ETHERIC DOUBLE/ EARTH]

GREAT PYRAMID—see GIZA PYRAMID.

GREAT SCIENCE—(ancient) study and practice of psychic and healing powers using laws of META-PHYSICS, ELECTRICITY, MAGNETISM, GRAVITY, and ALCHEMY. **Syn.** MAGIC, HIDDEN SCIENCE. [**cf.** PARAPSYCHOLOGY, MYSTICISM]

GREAT SOUL—involving and evolving "total" motivated by the potential within itself to perfect and purify itself through its many universes; see TOTALITY.

GREAT SPIRIT—(Native American) see GOD and TOTALITY.

GREAT TONE OF NATURE—the combined sounds of everything on earth composing a harmonic chord, considered the keynote of planet earth; perceived clairaudiently as the key of *F*; perceived clairvoyantly in sound-form as the color green (making earth's basic color green). **Syn.** KUNG. [**cf.** COSMIC SOUND, MUSIC OF THE SPHERES, F, SOUND, LAW OF VIBRATION Appendix 7, CLAIRAUDIENT]

GREAT UNMANIFEST—the LOGOS; see TOTALITY.

GREAT WHEEL—(William Butler Yeats) a diagrammatic system which relates historical cycles and human character to the twenty-eight phases of the moon; resembles the system by Eliphas Levi, which is related. [**cf.** MOON, SHIFT THE PHASE, CYCLE RULER, CYCLES Appendix 5]

GREAT WHITE BROTHERHOOD—(capitalized) a group of soul-minds in the etheric world who lived long and arduous incarnations in planet earth and other planets many times; 1. became advanced soul-minds after much stern self-discipline, self-denial and consistent self-development, until they transcend humans in all avenues of life; have fitted themselves to assist in ruling the world from the etheric world; their activities are multifarious, being concerned with teaching, and guiding civilization on earth; known as adepts; 2. extraordinary

capabilities: **(a)** able to control natural forces in both the etheric and mundane realms; **(b)** understand alchemy and can transmute their bodies; **(c)** able to prolong their lives for centuries; **(d)** make themselves known in mediumship development circles; **(e)** earnest truth seekers by the chain system; Jesus was both an adept and a master in charge of the Great White Brotherhood. **Syn.** RISHIS, RAHATS, MAHATMAS. [**cf.** ADEPTS, MASTERSHIP]

GREAT WHITE LIGHT—(esoteric) the primal source in its unorganized indestructible state; "in the beginning there was light," CHAOS, perfection, TOTAL INTELLIGENCE; eventually it diffused into many various vibrational frequencies; all manifestations are a diffusion of this light. **Syn.** SHINING ONE, COSMIC FIRE, IMPERISHABLE LIGHT.

GREAT WHITE LODGE—a collection of adepts and masters in the etheric world, whose function is to work with the main religions of the world and keep guard over the HIDDEN WISDOM; members incarnate in earth as great religious leaders if necessary; provide substitute teachings for these who need higher knowledge than the masses; incarnate members work psychically with the ethereal members constantly; reveal knowledge to the masses through mediumship by the chain system, sending lesser intelligences as their messengers. [**cf.** GREAT WHITE BROTHERHOOD]

GREAT WHITE SPIRIT—(Native American) see TOTALITY.

GREAT YEAR—a period of approximately 26,000 years; equal to the time required for our solar system to revolve once around a Great Central Sun; equal to the time required for a complete revolution of the equinoxes. **Syn.** AGE, PLATONIC YEAR. [**cf.** EQUINOXES, CYCLES Appendix 5, AQUARIAN AGE]

GREAT-GIFT WAVES—(Tibet) psychic energy sent telepathically from gurus, in the etheric and physical worlds, which stimulates the spiritual development of the aspirant who acknowledges and desires to follow the esoteric doctrines. [**cf.** HIDDEN DOOR, HOMING IN, GUIDE, ETHERIC LINK]

GREATER MIND—the subconscious mind or soul-mind, as opposed to the conscious mind; see SUBCONSCIOUS MIND.

GREATER MYSTERIES—(Rome, Greece) compositions of doctrines, based on study and personal experience during the initiations; make up the secrets of mythologies and some ancient religions; based on the concept that one must live righteously in order to have a noble life after death and in their next reincarnation. [cf. LAW OF COMPENSATION Appendix 7, KARMA, REINCARNATION]

GREEK LOVE FEAST—a religious gathering as a form of ritual to enhance working with the gods; participants indulge in eating, drinking, having a good time, and spiritual love making of a higher form of sex love than mankind knows. [cf. SEX TRANSMUTATION, CEREMONIAL MAGIC]

GREEN—the vibrational frequency that promotes growth, harmony, sympathy, balance, and new beginnings. [cf. COLOR, GREAT TONE]

GREEN MAN—a nature spirit in charge of vegetation and forests; shows itself as a face among the green foliage; see FAIRY.

GREEN RAY PERIOD—(esoteric) the fourth period wherein mankind is now, midway in the scheme of things; red, orange, and yellow periods have passed. [cf. COLOROLOGY, AQUARIAN AGE, SPIRILI]

GREEN RAYS—(chromotherapy) color energies that excite and encourage the activity of the pituitary gland. [cf. COLOR HEALING, PITUITARY GLAND, VISUALIZATION]

GREENISH TURQUOISE—(minpsi) a mineral influenced by the vibrations of Venus; has the properties that deteriorate into green gas, which the alchemist can use to putrefy his or her substances and the psychic can use to foretell disaster. [cf. MINPSI, PROPHECY]

GREGORIAN CHANTS—instituted by Pope Gregory in the Middle Ages for use in the Catholic Mass; each of the many chants have been very carefully composed to set the mood for that particular religious service, putting the congregation into the alpha state (a very pleasurable and receptive state); some chants produce an absolutely calm, tranquil, almost emotionless tone with no single personal note, a series of events without commentary; some of which are very grave and solemn, and some show grace and freshness. [cf. HYPNOTHERAPY, CHANTING, SOUNDS-WITH-POWER]

GREY TWILIGHT LANDS—the second highest division of the four spheres in the etheric world. [cf. BODIES AND PLANES Appendix 5]

GREYLAND—a dim, grey, fog-like cloud causing temporary restlessness and discomfort as it surrounds the deceased entity, while he or she is between the physical and astral worlds, during the death process. [cf. DEATH SCIENCE Appendix 5, VEIL, DISEMBODIED]

GRIFFIN—nature spirit that guards against theft and fierce attacks; depicted with head, wings and feet of an eagle and the hind-part of a lion; the female is winged with a bird-like beak. [cf. GRYPHON, HIPPOGRIFF]

GRIMMS FAIRY TALES—the overtone of the stories portrays the life force at many levels of an entity's existence; the hero or heroine is capable of going back and forth between these levels, shifting dimensions, until perfection is achieved; shows belief in PSYCHISM, life after death, and DREAMS.

GRIMOIRE—(European) (*gramarye*, "magic and enchantment") a magician's handbook containing collections of magic lore, traditions, spells, rituals, secret symbols of Kabbalah, alchemy, astrology, secret knowledge for making powerful talismans, and instructions for summoning etheric world entities and performing many psychic skills. **Syn.** BLACK BOOK.

GRIS-GRIS—(jungle) a wooden talisman with the image of a tribal protector carved in it; worn around the neck; has the properties that ward off negative vibrations and protect the wearer. [cf. TALISMAN, AMULET, TOTEM, FETISHES]

GROK—to take time; to experience with one's whole self. [cf. GROKKING IN FULLNESS, DENIAL, FULFILLMENT]

GROKKING IN FULLNESS—and LSD expression meaning to take time to make the experience a part of one's self. [cf. GROK, MEDITATION, CLOAK OF INSULATION]

GROS BON ANGE—(Haiti, Voodoo) the soul-mind or LARGE GOOD ANGEL, which manifests in the breath and shadow of a sick or bewitched individual; coexists with the CONSCIOUS MIND, or conscience, or spirit referred to as the little good angel; believed that the gros bon ange can become affected by emotions of greed, anger, hate, lust, or jealousy which makes one ill, or a BEWITCHER; object of MAGIC HEALING is for the MEDICINE MAN to change the soul-mind of the victim or prosecutor, whoever needs it the most; magic changes the attitude of the one causing the trouble. **Syn.** LARGE GOOD ANGEL. [cf. 'TI BON ANGE, SPELL]

GROSS BODY—physical body filled with carnal thoughts; materialistic thoughts slow down the vibrations of atoms into third dimension manifestation. [**cf.** BUDDHIC PLANE, SEVENTH PLANE, GLORIFIED BODY, HUMAN BEING KINGDOM]

GROSS COMMUNICATIONS—obscene, trivial and malevolent information coming from etheric world entities on a lower plane who still contain impurities of matter; one tunes into these entities when not following the rules of psychism or if still in a very materialistic level when opening one's psychic doors. [**cf.** CLOAK OF INSULATION, THOUGHTS]

GROSS LEVEL—state of consciousness of the material plane in the mass grouping; the overall consciousness of planet earth. [**cf.** CONSCIOUSNESS, ETHERIC DOUBLE/EARTH]

GROSS SOUL—(Allan Kardec) the soul-mind while it is in the physical envelope.

GROTESQUES—the stream of faces, some ugly, some beautiful, seen clairvoyantly at the onset of sleep or deep relaxation; lasts for a few minutes, while the conscious mind and subconscious mind are exchanging prominence in their respective roles. **Syn.** HYPNAGOGIC STATE, SEA OF FACES, SURREALISTIC PHANTOMS. [**cf.** HYPNAGOGIC, HYPNAPOMPIC]

GROUP BRAINWASHING—see GROUP-ELEMENTAL.

GROUP DENTISTRY PSYCHISM—an instant change in the molecular structure in one's mouth occurring to many of the participants in a planned gathering; psychic talks a little and plays music, to build a mass healing thought-form; this healing thought-form is shot to the congregation in an instantaneous mental gesture; healings vary: a tooth filled, silver filling changed to gold, gums healed, tooth extracted, etc., when accomplished, each participant's mouth is examined with normal dentistry tools to see what has taken place; participants do not make their needs known; the healing thought-form appears to know where it is needed. (Inconcl.) [**cf.** MAGNETIC HEALING, MENTAL HEALING]

GROUP ELEMENTAL—a thought-form hovering over the heads of a gathering or an assembly; 1. thought-form is charged with a stimulus that causes mutual emotion between members and leader pulling them into unity of purpose; thought-form intensifies in strength as the meeting lengthens if the "theme" is constantly being dwelled upon and directed toward one's emotional needs; everyone becomes emotionally pulled into the vortex of the thought-form; 2. this elemental or thought-form is capable of an independent existence outside the consciousness of the members and causes them to perform acts they would not perform individually under normal circumstances; (many leaders understand this and intentionally build this elemental for derogative intent); acts and suggestions put in the minds of the members during the gathering will usually be carried out; 3. an "artificial" elemental because it disperses as rapidly as the crowd breaks up (unity of thought disperses also); 4. formed by: (a) loud, rhythmical music; (b) monotone, tranquil, or concert music; (c) hand clapping, singing, chanting, shouting, body twisting, and; (d) cleverly planned ploy using repetitive statements to reinforce the theme; used advantageously or with evil intent; 5. e.g., mass healing gatherings, mass screaming at rock festivals, mass hypnotism in the destructive-brainwashing cult meetings, unity of patriotism by army drills, the following of The Pied Piper of Hamlin. (Inconcl.) **Syn.** ARTIFICIAL ELEMENTAL. [**cf.** ELEMENTAL, THOUGHT-FORMS, GROUP HYPNOSIS]

GROUP ENERGY—an energy field of strong psychic energy which flows fluently among a group whether willed or unwilled; 1. concentration of a group on one particular activity accomplishes this activity more quickly than single concentration; 2. developing of psychic skills is easier in a group than by oneself; the question under investigation is whether this abundant psychic energy is dependent upon PSYCHIC ABILITY of the members or whether the strength depends upon the HARMONY of the members. [**cf.** GROUP ELEMENTAL, LAW OF THOUGHT Appendix 7]

GROUP HYPNOSIS—to induce a light, hypnotic state of consciousness in the majority of participants of a gathering wherein participants are not aware that they are being hypnotized; 1. when a number of persons are gathered in a unity of purpose, they can easily become hypnotized by an intense consistent concentration on the leader and what he or she is saying; the intense concentration quiets the conscious mind and allows the subconscious mind to absorb the material as it is presented without first sifting it out in the conscious mind; 2. induced by a leader with CHARISMA; the verbiage is carefully planned, and structured to touch one's emotional needs, and the pronoun *you* is emphasized and used repeatedly with a pointed finger at the group; music and chanting frequently aid in the inducement of the hypnotic stage; 3. almost all lectures and sermons, whether for good or evil intent, have a hypnotic effect; the larger the group and the longer the lecture with no break, the more easily the hypnotic state is accomplished without one realizing he or she is being hypnotized; if one can trust their leader and there is no need for decision-making regarding its contents, it is a good method to more easily remember what one heard. [cf. HYPNOSIS, ELEMENTAL, DESTRUCTIVE-BRAIN-WASHING CULT]

GROUP KARMA—purpose of every group gathering is to work off and build new karma for each person that participates in the gathering; each member is held responsible for the "main goal" of the organization, regardless of one's personal opinion; karma is relative to the job performed and attitude toward the job and organization; all groups influence karma; e.g., family, church, job, clubs, school, bowling leagues, baseball teams, etc.; karma between members could mean they were together in a situation in another incarnation; if one does not try to correct or promote the intent of the gathering, one partakes of this karma anyway by simply being sociable. [cf. ACCUMULATED KARMA, REINCARNATION, RIPE KARMA]

GROUP MIND—an aggregation of highly evolved soul-minds who are on the same wavelength in values, intellect, and dedicated purpose because of their advanced accomplishments earned through past earth incarnations; includes individuals in the etheric world and earth world; connected by a psychic thread; this energy field is a consensus of all the experiences of these soul-minds AKASHA; each advanced soul-mind contributes to it and may draw upon it; others who are able to fine tune their vibrations can tap into this energy field with answers to one's problems being fed back almost as rapidly as the question telepathically is fed in (works with the speed of thought); each one within the group may draw upon the intellect of another within the group, if the intent is to serve mankind; an inner branch of the Brotherhood. [cf. GROUP SOUL, GROUP KARMA]

GROUP SOUL—a number of monads or soul-minds in the same consciousness bound together by this consciousness with the same specialization flowing through each MONAD; this creates an envelope of monadic essence which serves as the mother parent, nourishing the souls until each is ready for independence; each monad must learn all the experiences of every category within the envelope through sharing the KARMA of each member of the group before it can evolve to a higher level; individual monads may call upon the knowledge of others; when all lessons have been learned the essence will dissolve and each monad will seek another group where higher lessons for evolvement may be learned. [cf. ANIMAL GROUP SOUL, MONADIC ESSENCE]

GROUP SOUND—music and sounds composed for group gatherings that influence members in the manner the leader intends; music with a particular pitch, tone, speed, or rhythmic beat affects certain areas of the brain, and etheric bodies of the listeners which intensifies until the group is telepathically connected; 1. psychologically the members get into the FLOW by clapping or stamping their feet or by concentrated listening; the sound and unison of emotions puts individuals in a light hypnotic state; 2. the members of the group are capable of doing individually that which they would not do without getting in this mass mood; 3. group music can be used for beneficial or undesireable intent; e.g., misconduct stimulated by rock concerts; altered states of consciousness for psychism stimulated by tribal drumming; patriotism enhanced by a military band; healings encouraged by charismatic loud music and clapping; healings brought about by chanting. [cf. GROUP ELEMENTAL, GROUP HYPNOSIS]

GROUP TELEPATHY—the transference of thought, words, pictures, color or movement among members of a gathering; when many persons concentrate on the same thing at the same time, the idea or thought-form becomes larger and more powerful in order that the receiver or receivers will be more apt to perceive it; can be executed with MENTAL TELEPATHY, MOTOR TELEPATHY, PSYCHOMETRIC TELEPATHY. [cf. TELEPATHY Appendix 2]

GROUP TONE—a common denominator that each participant of a group will carry away in his or her belief system from that encounter with others; sometimes it seems insignificant and is unrecognizeable at the time, but the ideas, suggestions, and emotional sensations that were experienced will be added to one's storage system and used in future decisions; (do not confuse with GROUP ELEMENTALS which disperse with the group). [cf. GROUP KARMA, HYPNOSIS]

GROUP TOTEM—a long, large piece of wood upon which has been carved forms of animals and birds; once it is finished and consecrated it can be used as an AMULET of hidden power for the group as a whole; it magnetizes its surrounding area so it can be used for sacred rituals or serve as an outdoor church; e.g., the eagle or lion which is noted for strength and leadership is always carved at the top of the totem. [cf. CHURINGA, ORENDA MEDICINE BAG, TALISMAN, TOTEM]

GROWTH GAMES—experiential exercises and group discussions designed to offer opportunities for the participants to explore their own thoughts and feelings about life; helps devise strategies for creative living regardless of environmental conditions; gives hints for solving problems, and helps the individuals have control of their own lives. [cf. NEW-AGE PSYCHOLOGY, CURATIVE EDUCATION]

GRYPHON—a nature spirit that guards against theft and fierce attacks; depicted with a head, wings, and feet of an eagle and the hind-part of a lion. **Syn.** GRIFFIN.

GSR—abbr. for GALVANIC SKIN RESPONSE; see same.

GUARDIAN ANGELS—see ETHERIC WORLD INTELLIGENCES.

GUARDIAN OF THE DOOR—(Siberia) a piece of birch which extends from the hearth, inside the tent, to the hole in the ceiling of the tent; represents the door to the etheric world; indicates that a SHAMAN lives there. [cf. SHAMANSHIP INSTRUCTIONS]

GUARDIAN SPIRIT—see ETHERIC WORLD INTELLIGENCES.

GUARDIAN WALL—(Yoga) an ethereal wall of protection around civilization created by the adepts and saints to shield mankind from worse evils than those found on earth. **Syn.** WALL OF PROTECTION. [cf. VEIL, TUNING IN]

GUARDIANS—1. highly evolved soul-minds who are now incarnated in the earth vibration and who are entrusted with knowledge of secret vaults scattered around the earth; these vaults hold sacred knowledge of the universes which will be released when the time is right; 2. (ufology) ethereans living in the ETHERIA matter in space who will

guide, help, and enlighten earthlings. [cf. EXTRA-TERRESTRIAL BEINGS, DISC OCCUPANTS, SPACE BROTHERS]

GUERWITSCH RAYS—see THIRD-EYE.

GUETTISTE—(France) see DIVINER and DOWSER.

GUFFAW—(Zen) a ten-minute meditation period before breakfast, to aid in balancing one's self with the negativity of life's destructive ways. [cf. ART OF TEA, DHYANA]

GUIDE—1. a highly evolved etheric world intelligence who administers guidance, protection, assistance, psychic information, and hidden knowledge to an EARTHLING; this intelligence has lived many incarnations on planet earth and is more evolved than the earthling he or she serves; the guide will never intercede unless called upon by the earthling; the guide's presence can be perceived by: (a) a full-blown CLAIRVOYANT vision of the guide in attire he or she has chosen to portray; (b) clairvoyant vision of parts of the guide's clothed body, e.g., head, hands performing an activity, or just the clothing pieces; (c) clairvoyant vision of a characteristic geometric symbol; (d) sensations within the psychic's body; (e) the guide touching the psychic's skin; (f) noise in the area of the psychic; (g) a CLAIRSCENT fragrance; (h) CLAIRAUDIENT noise, or words, in the psychic's head or out in the room; (i) evidence of his or her work without giving an outward sign; frequently the guide will give the psychic a name that can be used to summon him or her, the guide may use either gender when manifesting; the guide will be (1) from the INNER BAND, spending an entire incarnation with one earthling; guides could have specific names, e.g., DOCTOR TEACHER, ALCHEMIST, HEALER, PROTECTOR, JOY GUIDE, or DOORKEEPER; (2) from the OUTER BAND, spending only that time in which he or she can be of assistance; guides from the outer band are drawn to one's vibration when their talent and knowledge will be of an aid to the earthling to enhance earthling's new interest and needs. **Sim.** DOCTOR TEACHER, ANGEL, GENIUS (male), JUNO (female), CELESTIAL GUARDIAN, ALCHEMIST. [cf. INNER BAND, OUTER BAND] 2. (hypnosis) one who leads the subject into a hypnotic state; THERAPEUTIST, OPERATOR, HYPNOTIST. [cf. HYPNOTHERAPY, INDUCTION]

GUIDE SERIES—(Tibet) the book of directions that is read to the deceased person's body after the soul-mind has left it; executed to help the soul-mind through the bardo. [**cf.** DEATH SCIENCE, HPHO-BO SERVICE, COFFIN RITUALS]

GUIDED FANTASY—see GUIDED IMAGERY.

GUIDED HYPNOSIS—to alter one's state of consciousness to a deep, relaxed level by influence or verbal suggestions from a hypnotist operator; hypnotist uses verbal suggestions in the form of imagery, simile, or commands, influences by moving an object back and forth in front of the subject's eyes or has the subject stare at a spot that puts a strain on the eyes; these techniques induce the subject to relax, to release the conscious mind to passivity, and to allow the subconscious mind to surface and rule; subject goes deeper when he or she gives their undivided attention to the hypnotist's voice than when hypnotizing themselves; types: 1. STAGE or SENSATIONAL HYPNOSIS; 2. MEDICAL HYPNOSIS; 3. HETEROHYPNOTHERAPY; 4. MASS HYPNOSIS; 5. ETHEREAL or DISTANT HYPNOSIS; 6. ON-THE-SPOT-HYPNOSIS. [**cf.** HYPNOTHERAPY, Appendix 5, SUBJECT]

GUIDED IMAGERY—an exercise to help students develop their imagination faculty; a group leader suggests the kind of pictures the students are to visualize as he or she leads them on a fantasy trip; broad suggestions are given and the students use these cues, and let their minds wander in that direction; this exercise helps them become acquainted with symbology interpretation which is needed for psychic work. [**cf.** COLLECTING THE MIND, ESSENCE OF REST, AUTOGENIC TRAINING]

GUIDED MEDITATION—a process used by a leader to induce a state of quietude in the minds and bodies of a group of people; the leader of a group quietly speaks words that maintain the members' attention; conscious concentration is narrowed down to the leader's directions only; leader uses imagery in story form, muscle tension relaxation exercises, chants, or words of inspiration; gradually the group is in a state of consciousness in which their minds are passive, their bodies relaxed, and their emotions quieted; the leader's words and tone of speech are the point of focus for concentration. [**cf.** GUIDED HYPNOSIS, GUIDED FANTASY]

GUIDING PRINCIPLE—see TOTALITY.

GUIDING THE GHOST SERVICE—(Tibet) a large gathering of lamas performing a ritual to exorcise a ghost from an area; objective is to understand the ghost's emotional problem, and motivate him or her to move to a higher expression in the etheric world, otherwise the ghost could reappear in another area; accomplished by telepathic communication. [**cf.** GHOSTS, EXORCISM, ENVIRONMENTAL HAUNTING]

GUNA—(Hinduism) see VITAL LIFE FORCE.

GUANS—(Sanskrit) manifestations in the MATERIAL WORLD.

GURDJIEFFIAN MAN—(George Ivanovich Gurdjieff) "the awake man, a higher level of man is to stay awake in order to store positively and negatively reinforced experiences"; to integrate the highest states of consciousness into the ordinary life is the goal. [**cf.** CARNAL MAN, MENTAL PLANE, BATTLEGROUND]

GURU—(Sanskrit *gu*, "dark"; *ru*, "light") a spiritual teacher working on a one-to-one basis; inspires his or her disciple to follow along the disciple's intended path by pointing out the correct way to live; sometimes gives assignments in life experiences for teaching lessons; establishes a very sacred personal relationship wherein one learns much about life and one's inner self; the guru is capable of destroying the undesirable habit-mechanisms in the brain of the disciple; the grooves in the disciple's brain formed by worldly tendencies are beneficially disturbed and new attitudes are put into the brain; a spiritual teacher who dispels darkness (ignorance). [**cf.** DARKNESS, TEACHER]

GURU DEV—"Divine Teacher," Master Divine, a guru who guides a disciple on his or her path; a very close relationship of mind-to-mind and heart-to-heart. [**cf.** GURU]

GURUDEVA—(Hinduism) sometimes used in combination with GURU or "illumined teacher" to denote profound reverence and respect. **Syn.** MASTER. [**cf.** ANGEL KINGDOM, GODHEAD, MASTER]

GURUESQUE—a guru appearing in the traditional fashion of gurus.

GURUMUKHI—("tongue of the Guru") sacred literature in a book of hymns, composed in metric form.

GUT FEELING—a very definite impression regarding future plans or an answer to a problem that comes from the stomach, or is felt "within one's bones," which says this message is important; information that one did not logically think out, or have any way of knowing beforehand; see CLAIRSENTIENCE.

GUT LEVEL VALUES—judgments and decisions based on one's total belief system; past historical events, past inhabitations, blend in with one's ASKASHIC RECORDS from other lives making one's total BELIEF SYSTEM; each comment, judgment, decision, and acceptance of a new belief is based on one's total information and knowledge within their belief system; this makes each person's basic set of values differ even though one is now inhabiting the same area.

GWRAGEDD ANNWN—(Wales) a nature spirit that lives in the water; perceived psychically as a beautiful lake maiden; capable of taking earthlings to be her husband. **Syn.** GWRAGETH ANOON.

GWYN-AP-NUDD—(Celtic) a nature spirit that has charge of wild hunts; also recognized as lord of the fairies of the underworld.

GYMNASTIC MEDICINE—(China) slow, nonstrenuous exercises used for conditioning the entire organism via specific patterns. **Syn.** TAI CHI. [**cf.** MOVEMENT-FOR-ALTERED-CONSCIOUSNESS]

GYPSY—abbr. for EGYPTIAN, but means "Little Egypt" or "lesser Egypt"; noted for excellent fortune telling, love potions, charms, herbal medicine, and psychic skills; a cast of turbulent wanderers who travelled through Europe during the Middle Ages migrating from India; they have brown skin, black hair, and their language and appearance suggest affinities with Hindustan. **Syn.** KALDERASH, GITANOS, MANUSH, SINTI, ZIEGUNAR, CIGAN, SARACEN.

GYRATE—(penduluming) a circular movement of the pendulum; varies in size and direction of rotation (clockwise or counter-clockwise) depending upon data sought; all movements have meaning to pendulumist regarding the information desired and this meaning differs with each PENDULUMIST. [**cf.** OSCILLATION, RADIESTHETIC SENSE, CYCLE OF MOVEMENT]

HABIT—a well established compartment in the subconscious mind which reacts automatically at times, causing physical movement, unless censored by the conscious mind; wanted or unwanted activity; compartment is established by conscious repetitious activity and emotional reactions to similar situations and is easily triggered when outside activity is similar. [**cf.** BIOCOMPUTER, CURATIVE EDUCATION]

HABIT FOCUS—the way one perceives one's reality, not as REALITY really is; the subconscious mind packages impressions received in symbols (words and images); these symbols are the "average representations" of millions of similar symbols of millions of other individuals; from this, one experiences life, not as a reality but as a *synthetic* reality that the subconscious mind has been conditioned to create by habit focusing through the years; thinking of one's self as one is not. [**cf.** LAW OF ATTENTION Appendix 7]

HABITS OF THOUGHT—accepted concepts having roots in historical culture or social usage, with no decisions of one's own; has an influence on one's personality, choice of current decisions and health. [**cf.** COLLECTIVE UNCONSCIOUS, SUBTALK]

HABITUAL KARMA—(Buddhism) repeated actions, thoughts, and emotions that react automatically, proper or unpleasant, always bringing expected consequences. [**cf.** KARMA, SUBCONSCIOUS MIND, REINCARNATION, HABIT]

HABITUATED STIMULUS—a repeated, constant noise in the background, that one has classified as unimportant and dismissed from the mind; then it is like having no stimulus and has no influence upon one's mind; e.g., the hum of the refrigerator or air conditioner. [**cf.** MEDITATION, WHITE NOISE]

HABITUATES—(biofeedback training) to stop reacting to the same outer situation each time it occurs because one has become used to it and no longer needs the original emotional response. [**cf.** BIOFEEDBACK TRAINING, EMOTION]

HABITUATION—1. (psychology) that small portion of any total experience that reaches one's awareness; an aspect of human consciousness; 2. (W. Brugh Joy) the filtering of sensory awareness in a sequence of events that usually reach the brain; the filtering takes place between the receptive centers of the brain and the awareness of the individual; 3. caused by one's ordinary consciousness being asleep, as it is so highly filtered by past conditioning.

HADES—one of the seven planes that make up the density in the etheric world; a counterpart of crime and other inferior characteristics of earth life; has an opposite higher plane; interpenetrates earth at its core with living intelligent forms considered to be new soul-minds; (Greece) the first plane one enters during the death transition; no punishment except by the soul-mind's own spiritual discomfort. **Syn.** UNDERWORLD, INFERNAL REGIONS, PURGATORY. [**cf.** DENSITY Appendix 5]

HAG—(Britain) a nature spirit that takes astral projections in the form of a hideous woman, bringing harm to humans; can turn into a beautiful maiden instantaneously; larger than a man when perceived clairvoyantly; capable of SHAPE-CHANGING and DIMENSION-SHIFTING.

HAGG—(Islam, Sufi) reality or Truth; "there is no reality but Reality."

HAGGING—(West Indies) to sing special charm songs to induce an astral projection at will. [**cf.** ASTRAL PROJECTION, FORCED PSI]

HAGIOGRAPHERS—one who writes about the lives of saints.

HAGRIDDEN—one who is held under a spell by another person; see SPELLBOUND.

HAGRIDE—a spell cast by a HAG; see SPELL.

HAIR—1. (ancient, esoteric) has psychical powers that act as a protection from evil entities of the etheric world; cutting of the hair was done in a ritual to discontinue this protection; 2. symbolic of strength; can physically sap one's body energy when it is too thick and too long; 3. contributes to one's personality, and is a mark of identification; to shave one's head is to remove one's self-image so one can begin a new self-image, as in the convent or monastery; 4. a duplication of the entire body's health. [**cf.** HAIR ANALYSIS, CURATIVE EDUCATION, PERSONAL HISTORY]

HAIR ANALYSIS—to examine a small section of healthy hair, cut from the head, to determine how that person's body is assimilating its food and drink; using the analysis, the practitioner prescribes the necessary minerals needed by that person at that particular time. [**cf.** LAW OF REPETITION Appendix 7, IRIDOLOGY, SYMPATHETIC NERVOUS SYSTEM]

HAIRCUT EFFECT—(Kirlian effect) a sharp gap in the auras of fingers of two people hostile toward each other, showing in a high voltage photograph. [**cf.** KIRLIAN PHOTOGRAPHY, HEAT CONVECTION CURRENTS, PHANTOM LEAF]

HALF-CYCLES—see CIRCADIAN HALF-WAVES.

HALF-MOON SHAPE—a primary symbol representing the third level of the atmospheric substance (liquid in nature); a primeval substance, sometimes called CHEMICAL ETHER, SOUND ETHER, or NUMBER ETHER; perceived clairvoyantly as blue; produces audible sound. [**cf.** SHAPES, CROSS, CRESCENT]

HALF-SLEEP—see HYPNAGOGIC STATE.

HALL OF INCARNATIONS—(Tibet) a large sacred building where deceased Lamas of the highest order were preserved in gold, in a sacred ritual. [**cf.** DEATH SCIENCE, MUMIFICATION, DAWN OF CONSCIENCE]

HALL OF LEARNING—schools in the astral planes where one can go during sleep or when deceased; similar to earth schools, but teaches higher wisdoms. [**cf.** WISDOM, TRANSCENDENTAL WORLD OF IDEAS]

HALL OF SORROW—name given to planet earth, from the astral point of view. [**cf.** PHYSICAL PLANE, MENTAL PLANE, DESIRE PLANE]

HALL OF TRUTH—(Egypt) a state of consciousness in the etheric world in which the soul-mind, on its last journey from earth during the transition process, meets OSIRIS to be judged. [**cf.** DEATH SCIENCE, ETCHING OF THE SEED ATOMS, REBIRTH, SECOND STAGE OF THE CHIKHAI BARDO]

HALLOWEEN—1. stems from the worlds *all hallows*; the night before the Christian festival of All Saints Day; began as a day when the powers of darkness were prevelant; a festival of fire and the dead; 2. (Britain) derived from the great Fire Festivals "All Hollow's Eve"; begins the witches new year; the etheric world has tremendous power on that night.

HALLUCINATION—(esoteric) 1. to perceive an uninstigated NON-THOUGHT triggered by delerium, extreme pain, or drugs; to see INNER-MIND PICTURES or perceive CLAIRAUDIENT noises that are false, distorted, uncontrollable, temporary and do not correspond to one's normal range of perception or surrounding environment; (a) to tune into the ETHERIC WORLD, but to have too many stations on at one time, causing confusion within the mind; (b) (Dion Fortune) to perceive repressed instincts in visionary and clairauditory form, giving rise to dissociated complexes of ideas in the patient's own subconscious mind; (c) insane hallucination: patient does not understand that the visions are not real; (d) sane hallucination: subject realizes the nature of the impressions. (Inconcl.) [**cf.** ASTRAL PLANES, IMAGERY] 2. (Tibet) to clairvoyantly view the contents of one's consciousness as psychic reflexes of THOUGHT-FORMS; outer mental activity coming into the mind from the etheric world as one's seeds of karma from physical world experiences; (do not confuse with VISUAL DISPLAYS or CLAIRVOYANCE; see Appendix 4 for clarification with PSYCHIC INFORMATION, IMAGERY, FANTASY and DAYDREAMING). (Inconcl.) [**cf.** MIND WANDERING, KARMA, NON-THOUGHT, PSYCHOTROPIC PLANTS, FORCED PSI]

HALLUCINOGEN—a substance that activates a mechanism in the body which opens psychic centers and releases the chemical in the brain that is used in dreammaking; brings mental activity from the ETHERIC WORLD beyond the normal range of vision and comprehension; mental activity can be distorted and ungovernable, or be seeing the etheric world as it really is. (Inconcl.) [**cf.** PSYCHOTROPIC PLANTS, HALLUCINATION]

HALLUCINOGENIC INDEX—(psi tasks) a file on persons who are reported cases in survival-after-death-experiences, and who have no medical reason in their situations to hallucinate, i.e., a high fever, on many drugs, or having a disease that is characteristically hallucinogenic. [**cf.** DEATH SCIENCE, DEATHBED VISIONS]

HALO—a radiant, luminous, glowing circle of light surrounding the head of a deity, or highly evolved soul-mind; denotes a brilliant, inspired, enlightened, understanding, extraordinary human serving his or her fellow human; perceived clairvoyantly as an arc shape; 1. (Eastern) belief that an enlightened soul-mind is operating from the CROWN CHAKRA preparing for his or her ascension and this potency spills out of the head as that soul-mind evolves; 2. (Moslem) a symbol of flames around a person's head denoting spiritual power; 3. (Turkey) denotes an angel or a holy man; 4. (Christianity) denotes a SAINT. **Syn.** NIMBUS GLORIA; (do not confuse with the AURA). (Inconcl.)

HALO EFFECT—1. (clinical) a feathery plume, about five inches above the head, caused by the convection currents that move up from the soles of the feet to the shoulders; the current traps bacteria or microscopic bits of skin, and when it reaches the shoulders, it spurts out. (Inconcl.) 2. (Kirlian effect) a diffused ring shown in a Kirlian photograph, larger in circumference than the object photographed, with the proximal area unexposed and the ring displaying a stress pattern. (Inconcl.) 3. a clairvoyant psychic experience to please the teacher, by a student who has found it difficult in the past to tune into the psychic realm. [**cf.** KIRLIAN PHOTOGRAPHY, SCHLIEREN SYSTEM]

HAM-SA—(Vedic) life energy; vital force embodied in the breath; its guided circulation through the body stimulates the arousal of spiritual energy; see VITAL LIFE FORCE.

HAMADRYADS—1. a nature spirit that presides over the trees; lives in a tree and is said to die when the tree dies; 2. (Greece) nymphs involved with trees and tree cults. **Syn.** DRYADS.

HAMATMAS—highly evolved intelligence from the etheric world whose function is to communicate with humans to teach, guide, and protect them. [**cf.** GUIDE, ANGELS, GOLDEN DAWN]

HAMMER—the shape of the hammer gives it a vibrational frequency capable of being used as a psychic talisman; protects the area against lightning, fire, theft, floods, and other calamities; to make the sign of the hammer, is to convey a blessing to another. [**cf.** THOR, AMULET, TALISMAN]

HAN—(Pacific, Ponape) see VITAL LIFE FORCE.

HAND ANALYSIS—to examine one's hands, fingers, and nails to relate back to the individual information about his or her past, present, and future; their character, and potential; theory: each appendage of the body is a complete story of the body and mind; hand analysis means chiromancy or chirosophy or both methods are being used; 1. CHIROMANCY: the use of a person's hand to psychically attune into that person; 2. CHIROSOPHY: to study one's hand, as to the lines on the palm, shapes of fingers, and condition of nails, to relate back scientific informa-

tion as to that one's character, emotional attitude, past and future experiences; see each individually for details. **Syn.** PALMISTRY. [**cf.** BODY READING Appendix 5]

HAND ANALYST—one who uses CHIROMANCY and/or CHIROGNOMY to bring information to a person for guidance in self-improvement by studying their hand. [**cf.** GRAPHOLOGY THERAPY, PALMISTRY]

HAND LEVITATION—(hypnosis) the raising of the subjects hand or leg automatically during the deep stages of hypnosis, which remain elevated all through the session with no discomfort to the subject. [**cf.** NERVE FLUID, HYPNOTIC ANETHESIA]

HAND OF GLORY—(ancient Europe) a candle holder made from a pickled or dried hand taken from a man who was hanged; used to charm a person to sleep for a long time; the victim would only awake when milk was used to extinguish the candle in the hand of glory; sleep was linked with death; see LAW OF SIMILARITY Appendix 7.

HAND REFLEXOLOGY—see REFLEXOLOGY.

HAND-TREMBLER—(Native American, Navajo) a SHAMAN of the tribe who specializes in using his bare hand skillfully as a psychic tool; uses the hand and arm in the same manner one uses a pendulum; the shaky hand has many uses for the Indian, such as locating lost articles and diagnosing illnesses; hand-trembler also has ability to crystal gaze, to prophesy, to perceive clairvoyantly and to perceive clairaudiently. **Syn.** MOTION-IN-THE-HAND. [**cf.** SHAMANSHIP, HAND-TREMBLER DIAGNOSTICIAN]

HAND-TREMBLER DIAGNOSTICIAN—(Native American, Navajo) a SHAMAN whose main function is to find the cause of the illness, and then refer the patient to the proper healer: the SINGER, HERBALIST or himself; accomplished by rubbing corn pollen on the body of the patient, then the hand-trembler runs his hand along the outline of the body, a few inches above the body, until the hand trembles; this indicates the diseased area; hand-trembler can also use SAND WRITING for psychiatric diagnosing. [**cf.** MAGNETIC HEALING, APPLIED KINESIOLOGY]

HAND-TREMBLING SICKNESS—(Native American, Navajo) the process of developing psychic and shamanship skills by undergoing an unpleasant illness, appears to be thrust upon one in the teenage years; symptoms; the body swells, feels like it is rising in the air, and becomes feverish; person goes through some difficult psychic experiences; illness lasts for one day to three weeks until the body returns to normal; the Indian then knows the skill is within him and is to be used for the benefit of his tribe. [cf. SOLITARY TRANCE, INITIATORY SICKNESS]

HANDKERCHIEF HEALING—to use a piece of cloth on which healing magnetism has been emanated for healing purposes; to energize the cloth with healing ability, the practitioner holds the cloth between his or her hands, with eyes open, and verbalizes healing words; this releases magnetism from the palms; the cloth is to be placed over the diseased area or carried on the patient; if the cloth is protected by a covering, it may be sent through the mail without losing its potency. (Inconcl.) [cf. MAGNETIC HEALING, MENTAL HEALING]

HANDLING OF FIRE—to handle red-hot, burning coals with bare hands, and/or to put hot coals in the mouth without damage to the body; to place red-hot coals on another person or object without scorching the person or object; see FIRE IMMUNITY. (Inconcl.) [cf. FIRE WALKING]

HANDS—(esoteric) an inborn psychic tool; one's hands and fingers are an intermediary for receiving psychic radiations from outer stimuli and for relaying inner PSYCHIC ENERGY to the outer environment; psychic runs from the hands through the SYMPATHETIC NERVOUS SYSTEM to the BRAIN, and vice versa; 1. palms, forefingers, and thumbs are the most adaptable parts of the hand to send and receive psychic energy; used in PSYCHOMETRY, CASTING OF LOTS, RADIESTHESIA (dowsing and pallomancy), RADIONICS, energizing an AMULET, ACUPRESSURE, MAGNETIC HEALING, and REFLEXOLOGY; 2. a pointed finger of the right hand emanates and directs condensed psychic energy when thrust forward with much emotion; 3. palms of hands are pressed together in a wringing fashion to amplify information coming into the brain for psychic information and normal thinking; 4. by interlacing one's fingers beind the palms of the hands and placing the palms against the occipital lobe, located in the back of the head, with a gentle push, one may amplify the psychic information or normal thinking message in the brain; used when sitting for psychic answers or to solve a serious problem when the answer doesn't seem to come; 5. the right hand automatically and unconsciously goes in the direction of one's consciousness if

allowed to do so; 6. (biofeedback) electrodes are attached to the fingertips as the best indicators for stress throughout the body (GSR, metabolic monitors); 7. (meditation) position of fingers and hands is important in the results of meditation. [cf. PSYCHOMETRY, HAND-TREMBLER, PALMED POWER, MATERIALIZED HANDS, HEALING HANDS, FINGERS]

HANDS AT THE HEART LEVEL—(meditation) (Buddhism) left palm turned inward, and right palm turned outward, representing the uniting of the outer and INNER-WORLD; responsible for setting the UNIVERSAL LAW in motion. **Syn.** RADIATING ONE. [cf. PALM UPWARD DURING MEDITATION]

HANDS OF SPIRIT—to manifest human-like hands to perform acts of normal human hands; can be seen with the physical eyes, and seem to appear out of the etheric world without a body; occurs in the presence of a medium; authenticated cases: a hand has been seen writing on a wall, a building, and a fence; a hand manifested in the seance room and shook hands with the sitters; (Bible) a hand appeared around a candle, and a hand wrote on the wall. [cf. HANDS, TRANCE MANIFESTATION, PHANTOM DOG, PSYCHIC THEFT, MATERIALIZED HANDS]

HANDWRITING ANALYSIS—theory: one's personal style of handwriting portrays information about oneself; handwriting is studied for its size, slant, and letter formation; reveals one's personality, character, health, and life situations. **Syn.** GRAPHOLOGY. [cf. BODY READING Appendix 5]

HAPPINESS—1. to feel comfortable with one's self and feel it unnecessary to make excuses for one's actions; a contented state of mind; 2. (Murray Banks) happiness is a by-product of living a life fully and effectively; 3. ability to accept (with both the conscious and subconscious mind) decisions one has made and to balance with the outcome; 4. one is not born happy or unhappy, one learns happiness; to accept the fact one has chosen this time to be reincarnated and to work contentedly with the earth situations; 5. ability to live up to one's personal standards of ethics and not comprise these standards for the sake of adapting or earning a living; 6. a rare moment of superior emotions. [cf. JOY, STRESS, MATURITY]

HAPPY HUNTING GROUND—(Native American) 1. a level of consciousness in the higher astral planes of the etheric world where Native Americans gather together after they make their transition; **2.** (Native American, Sioux) a place where warriors come through the sky to communicate with the tribe. [**cf.** SKY PEOPLE]

HARA—(Japan) the one point, the vital center, around which the whole body is centered; visualized as a single point about two inches below the navel in the middle of the pelvis. [**cf.** LAW OF CENTER Appendix 7, ABDOMINAL BRAIN, SOLAR PLEXUS CHAKRA]

HARD SCIENCE—what is measurable and repeatable is true.

HARE—symbol of the moon; performs as deity and devil; helps give shape to witches. [**cf.** ANPSI Appendix 2]

HARMONIC INTERVALS OF MAN—(Robert Fludd) a diagram showing all aspects of the universe, having their counterpart in man; the upper part of man is day, the lower part of man is night, the sun is the heart, etc. [**cf.** LAW OF REPETITION Appendix 7]

HARMONIOUS INFANT—(Taoism) a child produced by a method of intense concentration which creates an embryonic seed within one's body; this seed forms the nucleus of a physical body making ready for a soul-mind from the etheric world to enter; one becomes pregnant without sexual intercourse. [**cf.** BIRTH SCIENCE Appendix 2, IMMACULATE CONCEPTION]

HARMONY—(esoteric) a comfortable, pleasurable sensation "within" one's being when both the conscious mind and subconscious mind agree upon one's decision and its outer manifestation; congruent vibrations make Truth, and harmony is synonymous with Truth (real Reality); synchronization between lifestyle, belief system, and personal desire is the end-product of one's individual life; (a by-product is correct health). [**cf.** HOLISTIC HEALTH, HOLISM, KEY TO LIFE]

HARMONY OF THE UNIVERSE—inaudible sounds, noises, and music which occupy all space; can only be perceived clairaudiently or with instrumentation; comes from inert objects, living organisms, and atmospheric conditions; theory: everything emits a sound according to its unit frequency; each unit begins by drawing to it atoms with the music that will play harmonious chords when the unit is complete; that which is unfinished, nonbeneficial, low in quality, or when persons quarrel and think negatively toward one another, makes the music

play dischords. [**cf.** CLAIRAUDIENCE, LISTENING FATIGUE, INVISIBLE DRUM]

HARP—a musical instrument whose tones are of such a high vibrational frequency level that negativity cannot tolerate it, and the negativity dissolves; a neutral sound used in healing the body; used in ancient times to ward off evil forces. [**cf.** TONING, QUIETNESS, WATER-ELEMENT]

HARPAKRAD—The Greco-Egyptian god whose function is to work with the harmony of the earth vibration while he is in the etheric world. [**cf.** HOOR-PAA-KRAAT]

HARPIES—(Greece, Tibet) **1.** a nature spirit in charge of wind, who lives in the air; **2.** when showing itself to humans, looks like a bird from the waist down, or like woman with eagle claws and a beak; known to swoop down viciously, seize a man, depart, and use him for food; leaves a stench wherever it has been.

HARUSPEX—(first millenium B.C.) (Etruscan) to receive psychic information by inspecting the liver or other internal organs of an animal. **Syn.** HARUSPIMANCY, HARUSPICATION. [**cf.** DIVINATION, CASTING OF LOTS, RADIESTHESIA]

HARUSPICATION—see HARUSPEX.

HARUSPICES—(ancient) psychics specializing in obtaining prophetic information by the inspection of livers and other organs of an animal; called HARUSPEX. [**cf.** MANTIC ARTS]

HASSLE-LOG—(psychology, biofeedback training) a personal record of daily incidents: pleasant, argumentive, financial, work problems, etc.; used to determine which incidents are stress related. [**cf.** BRIGHT SPOT OF THE DAY]

HATAHLI—(Native American, Navajo) medicine man for his tribe; noted for his timelessness with one patient, prescribing food, prescribing sex habits, and prescribing a total transformation of life patterns. [**cf.** HAND-TREMBLER, SHAMAN, INITIATORY SICKNESS]

HATHA YOGA—(*hatha*, "force"; *yoga*, "union"); also means "sun/moon"; teaches a special way to do physical exercise with a complete integration of mind and body; usually results in a subtle change in personality. [**cf.** KRIYAS, ASANAS, PRANAYAMA TECHNIQUES]

HAUGHTY MEDIUM—one who pays no attention

to the psychic knowledge that is imparted to him or her from the etheric world, but who is always striving for more and more psychic phenomena. [**cf.** UP-FOR-GRABS, PSYCHIC TRANSFER]

HAUNTED HOUSE—a building, empty or occupied, in which an earthbound entity makes her or himself known periodically by noises, apparitions, or an eerie feeling of a life presence in the area; entity is invisibly attached to a piece of furniture or a room in which a traumatic event happened when he or she was alive; lack of understanding of this event or the desire to make others understand it, keeps him or her returning; haunter seeks to be heard by an earthling to work out a problem; haunter uses the emotional impregnation of energy on the walls or furniture, to be recognized; therefore the entity will stay even if residents move; the best way to exorcise a haunted house is to get the earthbound entity to reveal his or her problem in some psychic manner or to burn the house down. [**cf.** EARTHBOUND PHANTOM CARS, CONFUSED SOUL-MIND, FAMILY GHOST]

HAUNTED LOCALITIES—an area where a great deal of emotion is connected to an earth experience or many earth experiences, impregnating the area so strongly that the energies of the environment can be used by dead people to activate or reenact these mundane emotional events, repeatedly; emotion can be desirable or undesirable; brings the deceased person the memory of this event, some for further understanding and some for further pleasure; e.g., chorus girls dancing in their etheric bodies on the stage long after they were dead and the theater was closed, (Baltimore, Maryland). [**cf.** GHOST, EARTHBOUND ENTITIES, HAUNTING]

HAUNTING—abnormal, periodic mundane interruptions that cannot be explained by physical means; two categories: 1. ENVIRONMENTAL HAUNTING: a particular place or object, so impregnated with ecstatic emotions or disturbed, unpleasant emotions from a former incarnation of one person or several persons, that this area brings disturbances and interferences to living people; theory: the incident was photographed by the MENTAL-REFLECTING-ETHER when it occurred in the mundane world, and because of its highly emotional content, lingers on, and is played repeatedly, coming through audibly or visibly to sensitive persons; (a) this allows the deceased entity to reenact fragments of the scene to get a better under-

standing of the incident or to become thrilled again from the memory; entity holds her or himself earthbound; (b) living relatives and friends that grieve so emotionally and frequently, hold the deceased entity earthbound to an area, because love bonds always exist (dead or alive); 2. PERSONAL HAUNTING: a living being with negative thinking or materialistic desires can draw to her or himself an etheric world entity of like desires who wants to recapture the memory of past wordly habits; negative thinking makes it possible for the deceased entity to attach her or himself to the earthling for short periods, encouraging this habit, e.g., an inward impression to have another cigarette comes through to the living person from the inferior earthbound entity who had enjoyed cigarettes when alive. [**cf.** GHOSTOLOGY, GRAVEYARD GHOSTS, HAUNTED LOCALITIES, ASTRAL SHELLS, FOOLISH FIRE]

HAVE YOU BEEN READ—a common phrase used to question an individual in a public gathering where psychic stand-up messages are being given; the psychics concentrate to achieve an alpha state when their turn comes and do not know who in the gathering has had a message; the above question is used so as to give as many as possible a reading. [**cf.** STANDING READER, MESSAGE]

HAWK—a large white bird seen around Uri Geller, believed to be connected with a space craft or working in rapport with Uri.

HAWKWEEK—(botane) an herb believed to have the vibrational frequency to ward off evil events and evil people. [**cf.** BOTANE Appendix 2]

HAZEL WOOD—(botane) a plant which has tremendous psychic energy and relates well to humans; used for making dowsing forks, wands, scepters, witches' broomsticks, and other ritual tools. [**cf.** DAGGER, DOWSING FORK, AARON'S ROD]

HCHHI-KHA BAR-DO—(Tibet) going through the death process. [**cf.** DEATH SCIENCE Appendix 5]

HEAD-SNAPPING—a click frequently felt in the head, as the conscious mind reenters to assume charge of the body, after a quiet period when the subconscious mind was in charge (as in sleeping, deep trance, or in astral projection); appears similar to the shifting of gears. [**cf.** CLICK-CLACK, CEREBRAL CLICK, HYPNAGOGIC]

HEAD STONE—see CAPSTONE.

HEAD-THUMPING DREAM—a dream about bang-ing one's head that is induced by the defined pulsations of the heart as it travels along the silver cord, during a sleep astral projection. [cf. TRIP PROJECTION, ZIGZAGGING, GIANT STRIDE DREAM]

HEAD-TRIPPING—(Findhorn, Scotland) one spouting off to other community members about the ecstasy one has found at Findhorn, and accusing them of not being appreciative of it, as if he is the only person experiencing it. [cf. PEAK EXPERIENCE, ECSTASY, HIGH DREAM]

HEADACHE CONTROL—technique taught by Silva Mind Control to stop migraine or tension headaches. [cf. THREE-FINGER TECHNIQUE, AFFIRMATIONS]

HEALEE—the patient who is being healed in a psychic or other unorthodox healing method. [cf. HEALING PRACTITIONER, MAGNETIC HEALING, CONTACT HEALING]

HEALER—1. a psychic person with an inner desire to help sick people get well and is willing to take time to prepare his or her body and mind beforehand; must have an understanding of the method he or she uses; must be dedicated to perform a service without the ego interfering, to have the healing take. [cf. MAGNETIC HEALER, MENTAL HEALER, PSYCHIC SURGEON, ALTERNATIVE] 2. one of the guides in the inner band of an earthling; function is not to heal the earthling but to heal mankind in general; interested in human kindnesses and humanitarianism; e.g., guide is working through the earthling when earthling is contributing to a cancer drive, Red Cross work, etc. [cf. GUIDE, ANGEL, INNER BAND]

HEALING—all physical body healings are done by the body itself; no person, method, or medicine, (whether it be surgery, antibiotics, chiropody, psychiatry, psychic, mental, faith, acupuncture, hypnotherapy, etc.) can heal the body; the intelligence in the cells easily responds to the human being seed, which is motivated to be a perfect specimen, and directs the cells to heal themselves; theory: all methods of orthodox and unorthodox medicine and therapies are designed to help change the body chemistry in their particular way, making the cells normalize to make it easier for the body to heal itself. [cf. CURATIVE EDUCATION Appendix 5, LAW OF HEALING Appendix 7]

HEALING BASKET—see HEALING PETITIONS.

HEALING BY EVOCATION—(ancient Egypt) to exorcise an evil entity out of the victim: 1. to pretend or to HOLD THE THOUGHT that the evil force is immunized and healthy, by the use of affirmations (similar to the use of affirmations today); 2. to draw out the evil force by suggesting it come out by means of vomit, sneezes, or urination. [cf. SLAYING-IN-THE-SPIRIT, PSYCHIC HEALING Appendix 2]

HEALING BY IMPERSONATION—to allow one's body to be used as an instrument for an etheric world intelligence to perform healing, diagnosing, and prescribing for the patient; medium has no control over the healing per se, but does have control over their deep trance state, the length of time he or she is entranced and how often they perform. (Inconcl.) **Syn.** MEDIUMSHIP HEALING. [cf. PSYCHIC SURGERY, GUIDE, PARTIAL ANESTHESIA

HEALING BY PROXY—(ancient) disease is psychically transferred to an animal and this animal is destroyed or psychically worked upon until revived. [cf. PSYCHIC TRANSFER, SCAPEGOAT]

HEALING BY THE SUN—(esoteric) to use the sun as a battery to recharge the body cells; the sun carries a complete band of psychic energy which makes a rich treatment source for many human ills, cancer included; sun has healing qualities unknown in other sources. [cf. ALTERNATIVES, SUN WORSHIP, SUN RAYS]

HEALING CRISIS—to become ill the first few days of a fast; the process of the debris removing itself from the tissues as the body detoxifies itself; a necessary aspect of the fast, when FASTING is used for healing and rejuvenating. [cf. GINSENG, FOLK MEDICINE, FOOD SCALE]

HEALING CURRENT—the normal, neutral, cosmic energy that enters the head daily; can be "decreed" to have a healing quality and directed by mind concentration to the congested area of the patient in various mental healing techniques; can be performed for one's self and for others; (do not confuse with HEALING FLUID that is used in MAGNETIC HEALING). [cf. VISUALIZATION, AFFIRMATIONS, DISTANT HEALING]

HEALING DANCE—(Kalahari Desert) a ritual dance around the campfire in the night, in which "everyone" in the community shares in the spiritual power of oneness called N/UM; this energy is activated by the dance, until it boils up in the healer's spine, preparing him for his cures; a method for healing virtually every kind of illness, mental, physical, and lifestyle disharmony. [**cf.** !KUNG, !KIA, N/UM]

HEALING FLUID—(esoteric) an invisible ethereal fluid which runs through the nervous system, endowed with healing properties and subservient to thought; when used in healing, it is transferred from the nervous system of the healing practitioner to the patient's nervous system, emanating from the eyes and hands of the healer; for details see MAGNETIC HEALING [**cf.** SPIRIT, NADIS]

HEALING FORCES—ETHERIC WORLD INTELLIGENCES that work through earthlings in various types of healing methods, using the earthling as a channel to help others; intelligences have been doctors in past incarnations; some specialize in certain diseases or a particular part of the body. [**cf.** PSYCHIC HEALING Appendix 2, PSYCHIC SURGERY, !KIA HEALING, ETHERIC SURGERY, CHARISMATIC HEALING]

HEALING HANDS—hands of a healing practitioner who specializes in channeling healing energies through his or her hands in various techniques. [**cf.** LAYING-ON-OF-HANDS, PSYCHIC SURGERY, MAGNETIC HEALING, APPLIED KINESIOLOGY]

HEALING MEDIUM—one who has the proper body chemistry and willingness to allow ETHERIC WORLD INTELLIGENCES to use his or her body as a healing agent; medium goes into a deep or semi-trance, permits the intelligence to step into his or her body in part or in whole and use it as an instrument to perform the healing; method used for some PSYCHIC SURGERY, ETHERIC SURGERY, LAYING-ON-OF-HANDS (sometimes), tribal healing, etc. **Syn.** HEALING BY IMPERSONATION. [**cf.** IMPERSONATION, HOLISTIC HEALTH, ALTERNATIVE]

HEALING MOON-DEITY STONE STATUE—(Egypt) noted for its vibratory rate which is a help in performing exorcism. [**cf.** POSSESSION, EARTHBOUND ENTITIES]

HEALING OF MEMORIES—1. (Ruth Carter Stapleton) to release emotional "hell" of painful and disturbing memories that one has repressed, making room "without conflict," for Jesus to heal the emotions of these memories; theory: repressed memories are the inner child of the past, who lives in the unconsious of everyone. [**cf.** BLOCKS, CHARISMATIC HEALING] 2. to erase the memory of traumatic experiences from one's past life or lives

in order to heal one's body or mind; to uncover the root of a negative attitude which was repressed over the years through a method of regression: **(a)** one can rationalize the cause of the negative attitude by viewing the trauma as a bystander; then putting the incident in its proper perspective and the body will mend; **(b)** one can re-experience the event in the same time frame as it happened and while in that time frame of consciousness change one's attitude toward the event; this takes the charge out of the event and the body mends. [**cf.** HYPNOTHERAPY, REVIVIFICATION, AGE REGRESSION]

HEALING PETITIONS—small slips of paper on which are written the nature of the healing desired and the signature of the person in need, or the first name written by a friend; a method of healing at a distance in which healer's mental energy changes patient's body chemistry gradually and promotes a change in the patient's attitude; the need could be for healing of an illness, for harmony among two persons, or for abundance; papers are placed in a container and: 1. taken home for the healing practitioner to pray over daily; 2. container used in a congregational healing service as a POINT-OF-FOCUS for everyone's mental healing energy; key lies in the desire of the healing practitioner to be of service and in the desire of the patient to be healed. [**cf.** CONGREGATIONAL HEALING, MENTAL HEALING, PRAYER SLIPS, PARAELECTRIC]

HEALING REFLEXES—involuntary reflexes of the body working to put themselves back in order after accepting healing energy from a healing session, in which people are the healing instrument; body can shake, move, twitch muscles, skin can change in color, and breathing can accelerate or lessen. [**cf.** SLAYING-IN-THE-SPIRIT, !KIA HEALING, PULLING OUT THE SICKNESS]

HEALING-AT-A-DISTANCE—to heal persons that are not in one's presence by sending mental healing energies, regardless of distance; the natural electrical energy that emanates from one's head constantly is intensified, consolidated, decreed to be a healing agent and sent to the patient; (this is known as paraelectric energy and has been tested and found to change the body chemistry of the patient); methods used include: MENTAL TELEPATHY, VISUALIZATION, CONGREGATIONAL HEALING, PRAYER LISTS. [**cf.** PARAELECTRICITY]

HEALTH—(esoteric) 1. the condition of one's

physical body or mental mind as the end result of one's thinking and acting over the years and over past incarnations; a necessary phase of earthly incarnations for special lessons that only good or poor health can teach; 2. a by-product of one's personal destiny; 3. one's health should be the "correct" physical and mental condition for harmony between the soul-mind and conscious mind; what constitutes "good" health for one's self differs with each person's opinion; 4. health is not a gauge of one's spirituality, but one's "attitude" toward one's health is. [cf. HOLISTIC HEALTH, HOLISM, ATTITUDINAL HEALING]

HEALTH AURA—both human auras denote the condition of the physical body and mental mind; mental aura around one's head and shoulders indicates the current condition of the body by its colors and patterns; the human aura surrounding the entire body gives a read-out of any chronic, karmic, or leading-to-death illnesses; this is detected by the auric emanations pointing downward. [cf. AURIC CLAIRVOYANCE, SCANNING, KIRLIAN EFFECT]

HEARING MEDIUMS—persons who are aware of voices or sounds not heard by others which come from the etheric world intelligences; occur within the mind or out in the atmosphere. **Syn.** CLAIRAUDIENT, AUDITIVE MEDIUM. [cf. LISTENING WITH WITH THIRD EAR, OBJECTIVE CLAIRAUDIENCE]

HEART—1. (ancient Eastern) the seat of the SOUL; the secret hidden center; a storage place for the temporary duplicate AKASHIC RECORDS to distribute the KARMA throughout the bloodstream as it becomes ripe, forming one's body and lifestyle; 2. (Bible) heart symbolizes the SOUL-MIND, the subconscious mind. Usage: "Out of the abundance of the heart, the mouth speaketh." "As a man thinketh is his heart, so is he." 3. (contemporary) heart symbolizes the conscious mind; dominates love and hate. Usage: "I haven't got the heart to do that." "She wears her heart on her sleeve." 4. (Aristotle) the center of intelligence. [cf. MENTAL MIND, SUBCONSCIOUS MIND]

HEART CHAKRA—a vibrant, fast-moving energy field which superimposes the thymus gland between the shoulder blades and pulse point of the heart; if perceived clairvoyantly it has twelve petals; begins with pink color, and becomes golden as one progresses; the center of compassion; one dwells in this chakra the longest, as it separates the higher and lower states of consciousness; see CHAKRAS. **Syn.** ANAHAT, ANAHATA.

HEART DOCTRINE—the northern teachings of Gautama the Buddha; pertains to that which is hidden, the inner life; the heart-blood of the religion.

HEART FIRE—the appearance of a flame emanating from the heart of a man or woman when perceived clairvoyantly; reflects a replica of one perfected; the hidden potential of the MONAD. [cf. LAW OF REPETITION Appendix 7, BODY READING]

HEART OF THE LOTUS—(Sanskrit) the optic thalamus, a necessary section of the third-eye, working with perception from the psychic senses; an egg-shaped ganglion of the inner brain, when cross-sectioned, looks like a beetle; symbolizes IMMORTALITY. **Syn.** OPEN-EYE, SACRED BEETLE, EGG OF IMMORTALITY, BOAT OF THE SEEKER, SINGLE EYE. [cf. THIRD-EYE AREA, THALAMUS, PITUITARY GLAND]

HEART THOUGHTS—(dreams) repressed emotions of the past day brought out in the dream to be recognized and dealt with by the dreamer; heart thoughts symbolize conscious mind thinking. [cf. PERSONAL PSYCHIATRIST, WAKING THINKING, LUCID DREAMS]

HEART-SEED-ATOM—(Eastern) a tiny, invisible, concentrated center of energy in the heart that contains the same pictures as the AKASHIC RECORDS; these pictures are the RIPE KARMA that is distributed throughout the bloodstream to make up one's physical body and one's daily events; symbolized in the Bible as one of the books of life. **Syn.** LIFE-CORD-HEART-SEED-ATOM, PHYSICAL-SEED-ATOM. [cf. BOOKS OF LIFE, SILVER CORD, EMOTIONAL-ASTRAL-SEED-ATOM]

HEARTH DIVINATION—to use the burning fire in the hearth as a tool to foretell the future and the present condition of the household; the fire is a duplicate of the entire household's vibrations and burns accordingly, using the LAW OF REPETITION; substitutes for the parent sun, symbolizing the group soul of the family. [cf. GROUP SOUL]

HEAT AURA—see HUMAN AURA.

HEAT CONVECTION CURRENTS—air waves produced by normal body heat, forming a density of one to three inches surrounding the human body; invisible to the physical eyes but shows on the

277

Schlieren plates; looks like a shimmering rainbow-covered aura or halo; (do not confuse with the KIRLIAN EFFECT) (Inconcl.) **Syn.** INNER AURA, SECOND AURA. [**cf.** SCHLIEREN SYSTEM]

HEAT ENVELOPE—see AURA.

HEAT GENERATION—(Tibet) to show control over body temperature as a candidate for the title of RESPAS; psychic concentrates on the TUMO force in the body until it generates a tremendous amount of heat and forces through minute channels in the body, called TSAS; candidate is then wrapped in wet cotton sheets and is tested for his ability to dry them rapidly.

HEAT-UP—(Kalahari Desert) describes the necessary reaction of the N/UM energy in the spine before it can be used for healing the sick; n/um energy begins at the base of the spine, reaches a boiling point through ritual dancing, vaporizes and rises up the spine to the head, tingling as it goes, and is then ready to be transferred to the sick. [**cf.** !KIA HEALING]

HEAVEN—1. a word used loosely to mean "entire etheric world"; 2. state of consciousness while in the physical body, wherein one feels in harmony with God and realizes his or her personal function and importance in the universe; 3. an attainment which is completely satisfying; a level of consciousness one gravitates to; created by one's self for one's self from one's beliefs, actions, and attitudes of many incarnations; 4. a selective place; a place of goodness; this place is not a reward, but a place attained by one's self; (do not confuse with PARADISE); 5. the top four planes in the etheric world where the orders of the genii and junos dwell; (mystics) a doctrine of the upper regions in general; 6. a place where God is; the source of all good, final happiness, and the final beatific visions of God; 7. (Old Testament) a lost garden on earth; 8. (Christianity) an eternal, blissful abode of all those among the dead whose lives have earned such reward; 9. a place in the sky where God sits enthroned among his angels; 10. (Rabbinic) Garden of Eden; 11. (Astronomy) the spheres of the sun, moon, planets and fixed stars rotating around the earth Sun; concentric spheres; 12. (Greece) a doctrine of disembodied existence for souls between now and the resurrection; 13. (Osiris) (gnostic) a place to rise for purification after this earth life; 14. (Enoch) a resting place of the righteous in a realm of angels above the sky; 15. (Judaism) a future paradise on earth; 16. a celestial dwelling of God; 17. a visible system outside of earth's system, to live blissfully with gods and fellow initiates forever.

HEAVEN COUNTRY—an orthodox setting, in alignment with one's belief system, formed while on earth, to which one will go after the death process. [**cf.** KARMIC RECALL, ASTRAL PLANE, MENTAL PLANE]

HEAVEN OF FIRE—the atmosphere; the many invisible planes in the air.

HEAVEN OF STARS—the many layers of spheres.

HEAVENLY COMPUTERS—a mechanism or system in the etheric world that matches earthly opportunities to suit the candidate who is ready for reentry as a baby. **Syn.** SOUL JURY. [**cf.** ETHERIC WORLD, REINCARNATION]

HEAVENLY DECEIT—(destructive-brainwashing cult) to use Bible verses in persuasive and coercive methods to change the member's belief system; well-known Bible verses are taken out of context and interpreted to fit the needs of the organization; verses chosen touch one's basic emotional needs, and with the cult explanation, the verses stimulate one in the direction of focusing wholly on the cult and its needs; used in personal recruiting, weekend seminars, mass meetings, and repeated continually throughout all aspects of the cult movement to reinforce the change in the member's belief system. [**cf.** DEHUMANIZED, EGO-DESTRUCTION, BLISSING OUT]

HEAVENLY FIELDS—(Tibet) the etheric world.

HEAVENLY MAN—the universe considered to be a replica of man; the sun of the solar system represents the heart in man; man the microcosm, universe the macrocosm; see TOTALITY.

HEAVENLY STUFF—see PSYCHIC INFORMATION.

HEAVY TRANCE—see DEEP TRANCE.

HECATE—(Greece) goddess of ghosts and spectres; in charge of physical psychism performed in the dark; meets with etheric world entities in lonely places to transact earthly business. **Syn.** ANATAIA, EINODIA, TRIODOS. [**cf.** ETHERIC WORLD INTELLIGENCES]

HEDGE-WIZARD—classical witch who uses herbs, roots, stage magic, and psychic skills to perform her tasks; capable of mid-wifery, healing, inducing abortions, predicting the weather, providing love or poisonous potions, and giving blessings or curses. [cf. BOTANE, PSYCHOTROPIC DRUGS, HERBALISTS, CEREMONIAL MAGIC]

HEDLEY KOW—see NATURE SPIRIT.

HEI-TIKI—(New Zealand) a talisman, resembling a little man, to symbolize the human embryo (life force in man). [cf. AMULET, HOLED STONE, UNICORN, BEAR PAW]

HEIMDALL—an etheric world deity considered to be watchman of the gods; the "father of all mankind." [cf. LOGOI OF A PLANETARY CHAIN, SAINT, CHRISTOS]

HEKHALOTH TEXTS—(Kabbalah) the main part pertains to the ascent of the soul to heaven and the perils the soul encountered during these ascents.

HELICOPTER MOTIONS—(dowsing) the L-rods rotating in even, circular movements designating information regarding that which is underground; occurs over ley lines; refers to the direction of flow of water, strength of line, the down shoots, or answer to any questions regarding the grounds. [cf. RADIESTHESIA, DOWSING, LEY LINES]

HELIOTHERAPY—1. use of infrared and ultraviolet light in therapy for natural healing. (Inconcl.) [cf. CURATIVE EDUCATION, WELLNESS, COLOR HEALING] 2. (Tantrism) invigorating the body by adoration of the sun, by means of exposure of the body to the sun. [cf. ICE SITTERS, TEMPERATURE CONTROL]

HELL—1. one of the seven planes in the density in the etheric world; 2. a level of consciousness while in the physical world created by one's own thinking and acting; a chaotic period of time when everything goes wrong; a "burning sensation within" created for one's self from guilt, hate, resentment, jealousy, and fear; 3. not a place of eternal torment from punishment of a law, but the out-working of the law; for every action there is a reaction (LAW OF COMPENSATION); 4. a level in the density for the weak and limited in intelligence; one will stay here until he or she reaches out for advancement and then moves into another incarnation on a higher plane; 5. (Tibet) a crescendo of confusing emotions that generate a paranoid terror; 6. (Annie Bessant) a darkness radiating from within oneself causing one's existence to be passed in a perpetual night of evil and horror; 7. (B. J. Fitzgerald) a state of mind comparable to the low etheric world after passing from this world, in which untruth and disharmony

are known; results in feelings of extreme deprivation and separateness. [cf. DENSITY Appendix 5]

HELOIDIC RAYS—see AURA.

HELPERS—1. earthlings who are incarnated at the present time but have previously been incarnated in other planets; have chosen to help planet earth in her transitional times; the amount of their awakening and use of their built-in program will depend on the cultural need, their own self-development, and their immediate environment; they have excellent psychic abilities. [cf. STAR PEOPLE] 2. (Mexico) etheric world intelligences who have chosen to help earth at this time and communicate technical and advanced knowledge to earthlings in seances; 3. (Native American) (Rolling Thunder) name for the herbs and plants which are used for curing illnesses. [cf. BOTANE, HERBOLOGY]

HEMLOCK—(ancient) a plant that is a powerful sedative; can be made into a poisonous drink; characterized by its pyramidal manner of growth. [cf. BOTANE Appendix 2]

HEN-EGGS—used as a tool to induce psychic clairvoyance by a method of breaking the eggs. [cf. ANPSI, DOVES, OWL, TROUT-OF-THE-WELL]

HENBANE—(botane) a plant known to have the vibrational frequency that can be used as a psychic tool; wards off evil spirits in the area where placed; used as a love potion and as an aid to perceive clairvoyantly; used by herbalists and physicians. [cf. HOLISTIC HEALTH, INSANE ROOT, LOVE-APPLES]

HEPATOSCOPY—to perceive psychic information by examining the livers of animals. Syn. HEPATOMANCY. [cf. MANTIC ARTS]

HERBALIST—a practitioner who understands plants for their medicinal use; knows where they grow, how to prepare them for healing various kinds of diseases, and how to use them in everyday life for wellness programs [cf. CELL SALTS, FOOD SCALE, BOTANE, ALTERNATIVES]

HERBOLOGY—the science of healing, using herbal formulas; theory: there is no illness, mental or physical, that nature's herbs cannot aid in healing. [cf. HOLISTIC HEALTH, CURATIVE EDUCATION]

HERD IMPULSES—unconscious telepathy transferred between the minds of men and women telling them similar thoughts; e.g., females of all ages wear slacks; crazes and fads that impact on all levels

279

of society. [cf. COLLECTIVE UNCONSCIOUS, GROUP SOUL]

HERD INTOXICATION—to join a mob or group because one feels uncomfortable as a single unit; this helps one to transcend his or her consciousness to feel like one with the multitude; individuals work out mass karma as a group project. [cf. MASS KARMA, GROUP KARMA, TIME PLAN, KARMA OF FULFILLMENT]

HEREDITARY TRANSMISSION—(Native American) process of becoming the SHAMAN for the tribe because one is chosen by the deceased ancestors of that clan; chosen candidate is taught how to take an astral flight into the higher realms, where he is given instructions in how to heal, how to perform psychic skills, and how to use the secret language of the tribe; at this time the etheric world intelligences who are to work for him make themselves known. [cf. SHAMANSHIP INSTRUCTION, SPONTANEOUS VOCATION, INITIATORY SICKNESS]

HEREDITY—one's own AKASHIC RECORDS built by one's own self through past incarnations, mingled with everyday experiences in the present. [cf. REINCARNATION, ACCUMULATED KARMA]

HERESY—(Greek *hairesis,* "selection of choice") **1.** (Essenes, ancient) adhering to the established philosophy or religion of that time; **2.** (New Testament) not adhering to the established religion of that time.

HERETIC—one who does not conform with the established religion of the time; (at one time, these people were called witches).

HERMES TRISMEGISTUS— (Greece, Egypt) an Egyptian King noted as the father of alchemy; author of the GOLDEN TREATISE, the EMERALD TABLET, and the SMARAGDINE TABLETS, the source of all ALCHEMY; an astrologer and psychic; HERMES means "thrice greatest"; later the Egyptian god, THOTH was given this name, as he was god over wisdom, learning, and literature; this god is depicted as the Greek winged messenger of magic.

HERMETIC—(Greece) literature consisting of later versions of the BOOK OF THE DEAD worshipping the god THOTH. [cf. DEATH SCIENCE Appendix 2]

HERMETIC BOOKS—sacred literature and wisdom of the mysteries, psychic skills, psychology, and healing arts, specializing in ALCHEMY.

HERMETIC CHAIN—(Greece) living beings serving as teachers, making a chain in the overall Totality; each teacher instructs and inspires the living chain below itself; begins with the Archangels, then angels, then lesser intelligences in the etheric world, then mankind and below mankind. **Syn.** GOLDEN CHAIN. [cf. ANGEL HIERARCHY, LAW OF SUBSERVIENCE Appendix 7, UNDERWORLD]

HERMETIC PHILOSOPHY—the writings of HERMES TRISMEGISTUS, noted for his esoteric thinking; believed in psychic energy, astrology, and in God as one huge unit; taught the evolution of man through working upward in degree initiations; studied by the Egyptians; used today for occult teachings. [cf. PARASYCHOLOGY, MYSTICISM, METAPHYSICS, NATURAL LAWS]

HERMETIST—see PSYCHIC.

HERMIT—(Tibet) one who enters into darkness and solitude for a period, without communicating with other men; objective is to lose mundane identification, increase one's psychic skills, gain healing abilities, and learn strict mind discipline. [cf. HERMIT'S CELL, PRIMAL SCREAM, THINK TANKS]

HERMIT'S CELL—(Tibet) a small room, without sound and light and with only a small opening for food, located in an isolated area; a place where one spends time to rid one's self of blocks in the body and personality, accelerate psychic skills, and find a oneness with the universe; an initiation process. [cf. HERMIT, ISOLATION TANK]

HERTZ—abbr. HZ; the symbol for the number of electrical charges per second, used to measure brain rhythms. [cf. EEG, EMG]

HESYCHASM—(fifth century Christianity), a sect founded by Hesychius of Jerusalem, noted for prayer and mediation; word was then used in orthodox monasteries as a MANTRA; to repeat *hesychasm* over and over silently in every waking moment, brings one closer to Jesus by silencing the mind. **Syn.** JESUS PRAYER. [cf. MEDITATION, KYRIE ELEISON, THOUGHTS, DESERT FATHERS]

HET KA—(ancient Egypt) meaning the house of the "ka"; the tomb where the physical body is buried. [cf. CREMATION, MUMMIFICATION]

HETEROHYPNOTHERAPY—to enter into a hypnotic state under the guidance of another person for a physical or mental therapy session; an induction process is given by a hypnotherapist to put the subject in a deep or medium hypnotic state of consciousness whereby the subconscious mind is given therapeutic instructions and suggestions; can be used to improve physical health, to eliminate undesirable mental or physical habits, to increase the potentiality of the subject, or to regress the subject to experiences from his or her past life or lives (to uncover the cause of unwanted repetitious life patterns); the hypnotist transfers the magnetism from his or her nervous system to the nervous system of the subject making the treatment more successful. [cf. MAGNETISM, SELF-HYPNOTHERAPY]

HETEROSUGGESTION—(Greek *hetero*, "different or other") instructions or information given by "someone else" to the conscious mind, in a waking state, for decision making or reasoning; given through the spoken or written word; this is the normal way to receive and learn information. [cf. HYPNOTHERAPY, DESTRUCTIVE BRAINWASHING CULT, SUBCONSCIOUS MIND, CONSCIOUS MIND, WORDS-WITH-POWER]

HEX—(United States) to use BLACK MAGIC to harm another person's body, family, or property by means of deep concentration, rituals, and utilizing the LAW OF MIMICRY and the LAW OF CONTAGION; bodily harm can show as marks on the neck, bruises on the body, odors coming from the victim, sexual impotence, breaking out in a sweat for no apparent reason, vomiting, pricking pains, kidney or stomach pains; property damage can result in fire, the smell of rotting flesh around the house, and animals getting sick or dying for no reason; (do not confuse with SPELLED). [cf. PSYCHIC ATTACK, BEWITCHING, ASSOCIATION MAGIC Appendix 2]

HEX DOCTOR—a psychic who understands how a hexist performs his or her evil work and knows how to counteract these negative, harmful vibrations; prescribes antidotes to help the victim overcome the hex, and establish harmony in his or her life once again; psychically puts a stop to the hexist. [cf. HEX, SPELL, PSYCHIC ATTACK, EXORCISM]

HEX-SIGNS—symbols, symbol drawings, and amulets used to counteract or prevent evil vibrations from entering a room; used over the threshold, on the door proper, and around the entire home; common hex-signs are SALT, GARLIC, the HEXAGRAM and SIGN OF THE CROSS. [cf. HEX, SPELL, PSYCHIC TRANSFER]

HEXAGONAL FORM—a polygon having six sides and six angles; the natural shape of quartz crystals, but with no two being alike in length of sides and in size; this shape gives the crystal the vibrational frequency that enhances its healing qualities, and enhances pyramid energy when placed in the pyramid apex. (Inconcl.) [cf. FORMS-WITH-POWER Appendix 2]

HEXAGRAM—two interlaced equilateral triangles, one apex pointing up and one apex pointing down, making a sixpointed star: 1. the STAR OF DAVID, or David's shield; 2. represents the LAW OF POLARITY, male and female, fire and water, God and man, spirit and matter; 3. represents the soul of man, the upper point is the OVERSOUL, full of wisdom and ready for the monad, and the lower point is the AKASHIC RECORDS wanting to be rectified; 4. used as an amulet symbol in ritual ceremonies, to induce help from the etheric world intelligences and to banish evil vibrations (as if the helpers put a blockage wherever the hexagram is drawn); 5. (I Ching) unbroken and broken lines forming sixty-four different patterns that represent the throw of objects by the querant; the querant's throw gives his or her human condition and its guidance as presented in the book of I Ching from the particular hexagram pattern made by the throw. [cf. POLARITY, AMULET, CASTING OF LOTS, SYNCHRONICITY, SYMBOLISM, FORMS-WITH-POWER, [cf. TRIGRAMS, JUDGMENT, MOVING LINES]

HEXIST—one who uses psychic energy for evil intent; sends evil forces to upset a family or person, their life style or physical body; performs for hire or for her or himself. [cf. HEX, SPELL, PSYCHIC TRANSFER, ASSOCIATION MAGIC, LAW OF CONTAGION and LAW OF MIMICRY Appendix 7]

HIDDEN DIMENSION—see ETHERIC WORLD.

HIDDEN DOOR—(esoteric) the optic thalamus in the head that serves as the dark room for developing impressions into pictures; impressions are perceived by the eyes and by cosmic energy entering the head; constitutes a part of the THIRD-EYE AREA and works the same for physical vision as for psychic vision; see THALAMUS. **Syn.** SACRED TEMPLE.

HIDDEN MASTERS—highly evolved ETHERIC WORLD INTELLIGENCES who come to mediums in physical psychism to provide great wisdom for those who need more education than the masses can understand, and/or provide a substitute for religion in areas where religion has not reached. [**cf.** ANGEL, COSMIC ENTITY, WHITE BROTHERHOOD]

HIDDEN SCIENCE—see MYSTICISM.

HIDDEN WISDOM—(ancient) philosophies and religions that taught advanced laws of the universe that were not necessarily proven by scientists but found to be Truths by actuality; named "hidden" because these teachings were only given to those who would use the knowledge discreetly and wisely; the teachers were aware of the danger of giving this knowledge to the masses; lessons included: the evolution of man, transcendental awareness, functions of the higher realms, how to contact Self, psychic skills for spiritual growth and protection, and how to perform healings. [**cf.** HOLISTIC HEALTH, PARAPSYCHOLOGY]

HIERARCHY—1. a system of delegated power in a self-contained body, directed and guided by One Supreme authority, called the Hierarch; 2. the innumerable degrees or steps of evolving soul-minds in the cosmos, under a directive intelligence; all steps are vital and will happen but the rate of progression is in accord with the choices of the soul-mind; steps are all subject to a fairness code that recognizes the accomplishments of the individual soul-mind; see ANGEL HIERARCHY; 3. Greek divisions of hierarchy descending: (**a**) DIVINE; (**b**) Gods; (**c**) Demigods; (**d**) Heroes proper; (**e**) Men; (**f**) Beasts or Animals; (**g**) Vegetable world; (**h**) Mineral world (**i**) DENSITY (Hades). [**cf.**HUMAN BEING KINGDOM, KINGDOMS]

HIEROGLYPHS—1. (Greece) "sacred carvings" on religious and important buildings which contributed to psychic vibrations emanated by etheric world gods; 2. (ancient Egypt) pictographic script; symbols meant to convey words; 3. (psychism) spiritual symbols used in DIRECT WRITING (writing without any physical agent); commonly found on walls, ceilings, vegetables, etc., portraying messages of guidance and other important information. [**cf.** DIRECT WRITING, ETHERIC SCRIPT]

HIEROMANTIS—seer of sacred things; see PSYCHIC.

HIERONYMUS DETECTOR—invented by Thomas Galen Hieronymus; an instrument used to show a correlation of wavelengths of the instrument and the mind of the operator. (Inconcl.) [**cf.** BIOFEEDBACK TRAINING Appendix 5, BRAIN ELECTRICAL EVENTS]

HIEROPHANT—(Egypt) the high priest of the Temple, serving as the instructor of psychic skills and officiator over initiation ceremonies. [**cf.** CEREMONIAL MAGIC Appendix 2, INITIATION RITES, EVOLUTION]

HIGH DREAM—a psychic experience occuring during the NREM state of sleep, leaving the dreamer with a change of attitude or with a change in personality; a distinct feeling of transcending to a high level of consciousness; recognized by one's perception of a deity taking him or her to the higher realms, or by a state of EMOTIONAL HIGH ecstasy; in the higher realms the belief system is changed or enlarged upon; differs from a dream as it leaves a clear, vivid impression. [**cf.** DREAMS, PSYCHIC EXPERIENCES DURING SLEEP, THETA STATE OF CONSCIOUSNESS]

HIGH FREQUENCY FIELDS—(Kirlian effect) lights in the camera pulsating at 200,000 times per second; makes it possible to pick up radiations coming from the bodies of plants, animals, and humans; used in the original Kirlian camera. (Inconcl.) [**cf.** COLD EMISSION, STREAMER REPULSION, ETHERIC DOUBLE, PATTERN]

HIGH MAGIC—the accomplished art of white magic whereby one knows what to do, what to expect, and no longer has to depend on ceremonies and tools of the trade but relies on his or her own psychic powers. [**cf.** LOW MAGIC, MAGIC]

HIGH PLATEAU—(Findhorn) to see oneself as a tiny part of the planetary system, but tremendously important; being able to distinguish between the worldly and the sacred. [**cf.** NEW-AGE PSYCHOLOGY, HOLISM]

HIGH SELF—(Huna) see SUPERCONSCIOUS MIND.

HIGH SPIRIT—an entity in the invisible world who has a high degree in scientific knowledge, wisdom, and goodness: works through an earthling with noble words and wisdom. **Syn.** MASTER, ANGEL. [**cf.** ETHERIC WORLD INTELLIGENCES]

HIGH VOLTAGE PHOTOGRAPHY—the use of high voltage spark discharges from a camera to capture on film the auras of objects and living things; a method of conversion of nonelectrical properties of an object into electrical properties; see KIRLIAN PHOTOGRAPHY. [**cf.** KIRLIAN EFFECT, ETHERIC DOUBLE]

HIGHER INTELLIGENCES—those in the etheric

world who have evolved to a higher plane and do not have to incarnate in the earth plane again, but choose to help earthlings from their realm; work through PHYSICAL PSYCHISM. [**cf.** ETHERIC WORLD INTELLIGENCES, HELPERS, SAINTS]

HIGHER MIND—see SUPERCONSCIOUS MIND.

HIGHER PLANE—levels of consciousness that vibrate faster than the physical vibration and cannot be detected by mankind's five senses but can be perceived by one's psychic senses.

HIGHER REALITIES—1. (Marilyn Ferguson) identifies with a wider dimension than one's usual fragmented consciousness; encompasses all the lower dimensions in its circumference; a circle of circles to see with different vision; 2. a more inclusive dimension than earth. [**cf.** FOURTH DIMENSION, MENTAL PLANE, BUDDHIC PLANE, FIFTH DIMENSION]

HIGHER SELF—see MONAD.

HIGHER SIDE—see ETHERIC WORLD.

HIGHER SIDE OF LIFE—(Spiritualism) see ETHERIC WORLD.

HIGHER SOUL-MIND—see OVERSOUL.

HIGHER STATE OF CONSCIOUSNESS—to be aware of universal consciousness and to unify it with personal consciousness; comes through intuition and clairsentience skills. [**cf.** KUNDALINI, SUPERCONCIOUS MIND, CONSCIOUSNESS Appendix 5]

HIGHER VISION—to magnify, clairvoyantly, at will, the minutest physical particle to any size, similar to a microscope. [**cf.** CLAIRVOYANCE Appendix 2]

HIGHLAND BANSHEE—a nature spirit meaning "fairy woman"; a tutelary fairy who guards one family or clan; gives a wailing cry to the family when one of them is about to die.

HIGHLAND GLAISTIGS—a nature spirit appearing like a fairy but acting like a vampire; see FAIRY. [**cf.** VAMPIRE]

HIGHS AND LOWS—all life forms seem to have a divided period, of "better than" and "lesser than" cycles in all phases of their lives. [**cf.** CYCLES, FLUX DAYS, CRITICAL LINE]

HINAYANA—(India) the lesser course or the wrong path. [**cf.** PATH SYMBOLISM, DEVA-YANA, PEYOTE ROAD, TREE OF LIFE]

HINDOLE RAGA—(Hinduism) one of the six fixed melodic scales heard only at dawn in the spring; played to evoke the mood of universal love. [**cf.** MEGHA RAGA, SRI RAGA, RAGAS]

HINDU YOGA—teachings of techniques for breathing in PRANA for many health measures. [**cf.** HOLISTIC HEALTH, ALTERNATIVES]

HINDUISM—(Persia) (India) ageless, founderless religion of India; philosophy based on the Vedas: teaches REINCARNATION as it relates to the ultimate union of the soul of man with God; the soul moves through several material worlds, higher and lower than this present world until it reaches the final liberation from all material worlds; length of time it takes depends upon the soul's behavior in each incarnation.

HINE—(Hawaii) etheric world deity who is assigned to help people through the death process. [**cf.** DEATH SCIENCE Appendix 2, DEATH ANGEL, DEATHBED VISIONS]

HIPPOGRIFF—a nature spirit who is seen with the hindquarters of a horse and the head and wings of a griffin; also spelled **hippogryph**.

HIS HOLINESS—title given only to the Pope of the Roman Catholic Church. [**cf.** MASTER, LORDHOOD]

HISTORICAL MEDIUM—one whose intervention with the etheric world results in information regarding historical developments, past, present, and future. [**cf.** AUTOMATIC WRITING, INSPIRATIONAL WRITING]

HIT—(laboratory) to psychically perceive the target of the psychic experiment. [**cf.** ESP, LOW VARIANCE, ESPATESTER, RUN]

HLAMBULULU EMADLOTI—(Africa) to hiss, spit and growl like an animal while in an altered state of consciousness; this releases inner turmoils of the tribe as interpreted by the ancestral spirits; performed to the wishes of the ancestral spirits and accomplished by prolonged tribal dancing. [**cf.** MOVEMENT-FOR-ALTERED-CONSCIOUSNESS, FORCED PSI, MEDIUMSHIP]

HO-ANO—(Huna, "making the seed") to deliberately begin an outer manifestation by planting the seed of the desire in the mind; putting attention on one main desire through visualization or affirmations; see VISUALIZATION. **Syn.** SOLEMNIZING THE MIND. [**cf.** THOUGHT-FORMS Appendix 2]

HOBGOBLIN—a nature spirit, very frivolous, ignorant, mischievous, and unreasonable; delights in making its presence known in a mischievous way; perceived clairvoyantly hopping on one leg. **Syn.** GOBLIN.

HOBS—a nature spirit usually attached to one home or farm. **Syn.** ROBIN GOODFELLOW.

HOCUS POCUS—1. (Latin *hoc est corpus*); words having a vibrational frequency that impart psychic energy; an imitation of the act of transubstantiation practiced by the priests of the Catholic Church; 2. derived from Ochus Bochus, a magician and demon, from the north. [**cf.** TRANSUBSTANTIATION, WORDS-WITH-POWER, RITUAL, TRADITION]

HOLD PATTERNS—see BLOCKS.

HOLD THE THOUGHT—to put one's attention on a desired manifestation or a Truth, in the silence of the mind, without deviating from its significance; can be done by repeating a statement, verbally or silently, to reinforce the attention; to know something so well that one's thoughts do not deviate from that fact, desire or need, until it becomes manifested in the mundane world; to remind one's self to think the best for a person or a situation, regardless of reality, in order to prevent negative vibrations from entering that person or situation. Usage: "Hold the thought that I will be home in time for the wedding." [**cf.** THOUGHT-FORMS Appendix 2, THOUGHTS ARE THINGS, INNER-DIALOGUE]

HOLD-OFF POINT—(astral projection) (Robert Monroe) the borderline of sleep where one wants to remain relaxed, but not fall asleep, in order to be aware of astral travel. [**cf.** CLICKATION, LIFT-OUT, MIND-DRIFT]

HOLDA—a nature spirit known as queen of the elves; leader of the wild ring. [**cf.** FRAU HOLLE]

HOLE—the interface between the etheric world and the physical world. **Syn.** VEIL, WALL.

HOLED STONE—a hole put in a stone by nature; has the vibrational frequency to make a good psychic tool and amulet; can be used as a healing agent for physical illness and as a protecting agent to ward off evil vibrations for the wearer. [**cf.** AMULET, TALISMAN, BEAMED ENERGY]

HOLISM—1. (Greek *holos*, "all-encompassing, total, complete") wholeness within and without; 2. whole entities have a responsibility to the sum total of their individual existence, to the sum total of all existences, and to their individual components; theory: the universe (especially living humans, animals, plants, and minerals) is correctly understood as more than the sum of its parts; the universe has a total over-all purpose; the universe is also a living, growing, evolving unit that must burst into full bloom some day, to be beneficial to Totality; each living thing must burst into full bloom, or perfection, to be of benefit to the universe in its progress; 3. all universes are one huge system and one change in any thing, animate or inanimate, miniscule or huge, will make a change in the whole system of universes; 4. nothing in the universe is ever lost or gained, it only changes form but is still a part of the universe. **Syn.** GESTALT. [**cf.** HOLISTIC HEALTH, HOLISTIC BIOLOGY]

HOLISTIC—pertains to emphasis of the importance and significance of each unit to a greater unit with each unit having individual importance and significance; this chain of importance holds true from the miniscule particle to the vastness of Totality. [**cf.** HOLISTIC MEDICINE, HOLISM, GESTALT, METAPHYSICS]

HOLISTIC BIOLOGY—theory: each atom colonizing together to make a life or an inert thing, has more responsibility than to just make up that life or thing. [**cf.** HOLISM, GESTALT, LAW OF PERFECTABILITY Appendix 7]

HOLISTIC EDUCATION—see CURATIVE EDUCATION.

HOLISTIC HEALTH—1. the degree of physical and mental well-being that is "correct" for an individual and is judged to be correct by them; 2. encompasses the whole person, physically, mentally, and emotionally, in relation to their "preferred" lifestyle, their cosmic environment, and their soul-mind growth; each is totally responsible for her or himself and has a say in the degree of health they wish to maintain and in the methods of healing they choose; 3. correct health is produced when the two minds are in harmony and the individual functions as a whole, leading a life that is constructive, valuable, joyful, working out karma, and ever-evolving "to him"; e.g., (a) the conscious mind must feel comfortable and satisfied with the body and its condition (constructed from the memory bank of the subconscious mind from past incarnations) and is able to use this body to learn the proper lessons, whether it is by being blind, crippled, or vigorously well; (b) the subconscious mind must feel comfortable and satisfied that the decisions the conscious mind is making toward sleep, diet, vitamins, drugs, attitudes, lifestyle activity, and positive and negative thinking are producing conditions in the physical body which contribute toward the lessons needed and the universe. [cf. HOLISTIC MEDICINE, CURATIVE EDUCATION, PRIMAL SCREAM, HOLISM]

HOLISTIC HEALTH HEALER—any doctor, practitioner, spiritual healer, or psychic who is interested in a person's "correct" health, or "their desire" for good health; he or she then suggests healing remedies and practices which will lead to the lifestyle preferences of the patient, whether they are orthodox or unorthodox therapies and medicines. [cf. HOLISM, ALTERNATIVES, HOLISTIC, NEW-AGE PSYCHOLOGY]

HOLISTIC HEALTH THEORY—good health, disease, life, and its meaning are to be treated as one purposeful unit; 1. one's physical and mental health is related to one's lifestyle, one's attitude toward that lifestyle, one's desire to grow, one's desire to live, and to one's value of life per se; 2. a disease cannot be isolated from one's emotions, state of evolution, karma, ability to balance with life stresses, and one's inner desires; 3. human life is more than the sum of mental, emotional and physical states; one cannot isolate the man or woman from friends, family, job, environment, inner desires, or their attitude toward these contacts and their lifestyle; one must look at all parts together. (Inconcl.) [cf. ALTERNATIVE, HOLISM, GESTALT THERAPY, FRINGE MEDICINE, MENTAL HEALING, VISUALIZATION]

HOLISTIC MEDICINE—1. any external change in one's life-style or environment, or any method that works for attitudinal change which aims to alter the patient's body chemistry and belief system; should keep the body chemistry altered to the degree of well-being to satisfy the patient's preference; lifestyle changes include alterations in one's residence, job, friends, living companions, medicine, exercise, diet, pleasures, education, and the release of hidden potentials; 2. anything that is added or subtracted from the patient's physical body, or mundane-activities that helps him or her have a more qualitative life for their desires and needs; 3. (Old English *halig,* "Holy") the reunion between medi-

cine and religion; 4. to unlock a HOLD PATTERN through various techniques of revealing the past emotional event that was not resolved at the time it happened, and now causes the illness; to reeducate the belief system behind this event so the disease will not repeat itself, or travel somewhere else in the body; 5. to encourage body systems by stimulating the body's own healing energies by "balancing" with emotional stress as it comes along; to encourage efficient interaction with the environment. (Inconcl.) [cf. BLOCKS, HOLISM, SYMPTOM SUBSTITUTION, WELLNESS, LAW OF HEALING Appendix 7]

HOLLOW BOB—the object at the end of the cord of a pendulum (the bob) is constructed so it can be uncapped and a sample of the substance to be dowsed for is put inside; this sample of substance utilizes the LAW OF LIKE ATTRACTS LIKE and makes it easier to locate the substance; e.g., when dowsing for oil, oil is put into the hollow bob. [cf. BOB, NONSWING, OSCILLATION, WARM UP THE MOTOR]

HOLLOW EARTH—coined by Admiral Richard E. Byrd; by theory: the middle of the earth is hollow and inhabitable; perhaps even suitable for mankind; Byrd discovered earth to have two openings, one at the north pole and one at the south pole that mankind could enter. (Inconcl.) **Syn.** SUBTERRANEAN WORLD. [cf. AGHARTA]

HOLOGRAM ENERGY—(Bob Toben) "the description of any part of a unit is inseparable from the description of the whole." Questionable theory: the universe is focused on the self and the self is focused on the universe. (Inconcl.) **Syn.** GESTALT. [cf. VIBRATIONS, CELLS, LAW OF MICRO/MACROCOSM Appendix 7, PROTOPLASMIC, SYMPATHETIC MAGIC]

HOLOGRAM BRAIN THEORY—(Karl Pribram) each part of a living entity, essentially represents the whole entity, continuing throughout nature; each part is completely intertwined with the entire thing, to which it belongs, having characteristics of the whole thing; a leaf represents the whole tree, the foot represents the whole body, therefore, the brain represents the whole universe; the brain is a hologram interpreting a holographic universe; the brain mathematically constructs what one knows as reality by interpreting frequencies of the cosmos, and gives it to one in a third-dimensional manifestation to perceive and manipulate; (a meaningfully patterned primary reality transcending time and space). (Inconcl.) [cf. HOLOGRAPH, HOLOGRAM OF ENERGY, HOLISTIC, BODY READING Appendix 2]

HOLOGRAPH—oneness of all things; a unified, interrelated living whole unit having no beginning or ending, constantly printing its likeness in all sizes, shapes and forms of living material; everything is a small piece of the whole, containing the same information and life as the whole, only reduced in size, shape, texture, speed, etc. [cf. LAW OF PERSONIFICATION and LAW OF REPETITION Appendix 7, GESTALT, HAIR ANALYSIS, IRIDOLOGY]

HOLOGRAPHIC MODEL—(Karl Pribram) accounts for normal perception, by simultaneously taking paranormal and transcendental experiences out of the SUPERNATURAL, and explains them as a part of nature, for mankind's practical use. (Inconcl.) [cf. FOURTH DIMENSION, FIFTH DIMENSION, HOLISM]

HOLON—1. (Arthur Koestler) a unit of whole, versus a part being relative; e.g., molecules are parts of cells, but wholes of atoms; 2. (metaphysics) a group of thoughts belonging to the intellect of mankind. [cf. HOLOGRAPH, HOLISM, LAW OF MICRO/MACROCOSM Appendix 7]

HOLY—(same meaning written **Holy** or **holy**) 1. pertains to that which is correct, righteous, sacred, good, helpful, and religious; determined by its use or by its authority; 2. dedication to the service of God; 3. that which works toward righteousness. [cf. HOLY SPIRIT]

HOLY BODY—see ST. ELMO'S FIRE.

HOLY BREATH—1. (ancient Hebrew) see VITAL LIFE FORCE; 2. (Yoga) a way of breathing internally using the vagus nerve, appearing to one's self to not be breathing; happens after prolonged and deep meditation or when working for higher spiritual attainment; 3. the meeting of the Ida and Pingala at the solar plexus chakra which makes an alchemical formula that is circulated throughout the body in a 29 1/3 day cycle, and in accord with one's birth date; 4. a mechanism within a human being that makes the conception and the birth of a child possible; 5. ancient masters called it the Supreme Intelligence or UNIVERSAL MIND, the HOLY BREATH or HOLY SPIRIT.[cf. VAGUS BREATHING, BIORHYTHM CYCLES, HOLY SEED, RAUCH, IDA AND PENGALA, SPIRIT]

HOLY EGGS—(esoteric) optic thalamus: an impor-

tant area of the third-eye section of the brain, necessary for perception; believed to be symbolic of the dark room for developing pictures for both physical and psychic vision. [cf. THIRD-EYE AREA Appendix 2]

HOLY FIRE—1. (Greece) inspiration from God; to "breath out" psychic information when in an altered state of consciousness; theory: God is a globe of fire, and to approach fire is to receive light from God; the baptism of fire; 2. the fire that burns but doesn't consume, necessary to the alchemical formula. **Syn.** HOLY BREATH. [cf. ALCHEMY, INSPIRATIONAL SPEAKING]

HOLY FOOLS—(Native American, Pueblo) those who dance in mud, screech obscenities, mock chants, etc., representative of one's evil thoughts; a purging for those who yearn to break free of the demands of society. **Syn.** KOYEMSHI, TRICKSTER-TRANSFORMER. [cf. HABIT, HETEROSUGGESTION, EVIL, SHADOW]

HOLY GHOST—see HOLY SPIRIT and SPIRIT (capitalized).

HOLY GRAIL—1. (Bible) the holy cup used in Jesus Christ's last supper; 2. quest for one's deeper slef; 3. deals with the search for a vessel of great sanctity; 4. a cup or chalice used symbolically to represent purity or a reward for purity; 5. symbolic of man himself. **Syn.** GRAIL, HOLY GRAIL. [cf. TRUTH, HOLY BREATH, PATH]

HOLY GUARDIAN ANGEL—1. (metaphysics) the superconscious mind; the HIGHER SELF; 2. (magic) the elevated mind of one's self communicating psychically with the lower self (conscious mind) to liberate the lower mind; 3. an etheric world intelligence from the higher realms communicating through psychism to the earthling, with knowledge not intended for the masses. [cf. CELESTIAL GUARDIAN, GUIDE, SUPERCONSCIOUS MIND.]

HOLY KISS—(Snake-Handling Cult) to identify with the spirit within another by a friendly kiss and hug; men kiss men, women kiss women, and men kiss women; see UNIVERSAL KISS. [cf. GESTURES, SYMBOLS]

HOLY MEN OF GOD—(Bible) see PSYCHICS.

HOLY MOTHER EARTH—(Slavic) represents the worshiping of earth; to recognize earth as a pure element; pregnant in the spring with new life;

willing to receive the bodies of sinners, black magicians, or suicide victims, back into her womb.

HOLY MOUNTAIN—one mountain in a link of mountains in England, that has been psychically charged with spiritual man power; visited by space people in ancient times who left it psychically charged; in 1972 George King took people there to charge themselves with psychic energy, and stored this psychic energy in his camera-like battery designed to store human psychic energy. [**cf.** OPERATION PRAYER POWER, PSYCHIC TRANSFER]

HOLY OILS—(Catholic) to charge the oils with odic force making them potent for healing and soothing; performed in a ritual by the Bishop and his attendant priests by breathing over the oils and making the sign of the cross; the breath, impregnated with odic force, has an effect on the oils. [**cf.** MAGNETISM, SPIRIT, MAGNETIZED WATER]

HOLY ONES—the highest rank of angel princes in the etheric world; see ANGEL KINGDOM for division of ranks. **Syn.** WATCHERS.

HOLY QUABALLAH—see KABBALAH.

HOLY SEED—(ancient Egypt) (esoteric) an energy potential found in the gossamer sac in the posterior lobe of the PITUITARY GLAND, part of the THIRD-EYE AREA. [**cf.** HOLY EGGS, PINEAL GLAND]

HOLY SPIRIT—1. neutralizing force between a positive and negative polarity energy field; connecting link in the LAW OF THREES, making two separate units capable of functioning as one unit; this connecting link is called Holy Spirit when working with mankind (Father, Son, Holy Spirit); 2. to decree a psychic experience to be of ultimate good, in a universal sense, working toward the evolution of mankind (versus INVOLUTION), e.g.: (a) Father (God, Totality); (b) Son (man, Monad); (c) Holy Spirit (connection between God and mankind is psychic communication). [**cf.** LAW OF THREES Appendix 7] 3. Usage: (John 20:22) "receive ye the Holy Spirit" and Jesus transferred to them the ability to be psychic and receive the higher communications from God. [**cf.** PSYCHIC TRANSFER, BLESSING] (St. Luke 12:11) "and when they bring you into the synagogues and into magistrates and powers, . . . ye take not thought of how or what thing you shall answer, or what you shall say for the Holy Spirit will teach you the same hour what ye ought to say"; i.e., INSPIRATIONAL SPEAKING; (II Peter 1:21) "for the prophecy came

not in old time by the will of man, but holy men of God spake as they were moved by the Holy Spirit"; they were able to predict the future, not by calculations or by logical thinking (by the will of man) but psychic skills (moved by the Holy Spirit); 4. ancient Masters used this term meaning UNIVERSAL MIND or God. **Syn.** HOLY BREATH.

HOLY TRINITY—represents the LAW OF THREES; very powerful symbol; (Hinduism) 1. Father, Sat (God the Father is the absolute, unmanifested, existing "beyond" vibratory creation); 2. Son, Tat (God the Son is the Christ Consciousness, existing "within" vibratory creation, and this Christ Consciousness is the "only begotten," or sole reflection of the uncreated infinite; outward manifestation of the Christ Consciousness is "witness"); 3. Holy Ghost, AUM (AUM or the word of Holy Ghost is the "outward" manifestation of invisible divine power, the only doer, the sole causative and activating force that upholds all creation through vibration). [**cf.** LAW OF THREES Appendix 7]

HOLY WATER—water that has been blessed by a priest to change its properties, making it a suitable tool for healing and psychic skills; the priest's right hand is held over the water, and magnetism is released from his palm by the spoken word of will. [**cf.** MAGNETISM, MAGNETIZED WATER]

HOLY WATERS—(esoteric) to accelerate the vitality in the energy pouring into the body by inducing methods of a Yoga exercise, using the uvula in the back of the mouth.

HOME CIRCLE—(America, Europe) a gathering of sincere persons who meet weekly in a home for an indeterminate period to help one member develop full mediumship or to develop themselves individually; to sit in a circle formation is necessary to keep the psychic energy concentrated in the center and to lock out negative vibrations; through one fully developed medium whether it is TRUMPET or VOICE TRANCE, etc., the group will be given knowledge of the etheric realm, information on developing psychism, and personal counsel; when developing each member individually whether mental or physical mediumship, it is necessary to be guided by a developed medium in the circle; group work with etheric world intelligences; a home setting is conducive to this type of development whereby a room can be set aside just for that meeting; approximately fifty percent of all the knowledge the Westerners now know was acquired from home circles. [cf. SEANCE, MEDIUMSHIP, GUIDE]

HOME GALAXY—(esoteric) the milky way, a storehouse of soul-minds waiting to be incarnated [cf. WAVES OF REINCARNATION, PATTERNS, THIRD ROUND OF PLANET EARTH]

HOMELAND—see ETHERIC WORLD.

HOMEOPATHY—founded by German physician Samuel Hahnemann (1775); to cure diseases by using medicines made from natural sources, and given in minute doses to the sick patient; if given to a healthy person it would produce symptoms similar to those of the disease; curing disease under the law of "like cures like," and each person is treated as an individual (as opposed to mass medication).

HOMEOTHERMIC ANIMALS—animals that keep the same body temperature within a narrow range regardless of the external temperature; known as warm blooded animals; the most readily acceptable to anpsi, communicating with humans. [cf. ANPSI, SIMPLE CONSCIOUSNESS, INSTINCT CONSCIOUSNESS, EAGLE]

HOMING IN—to tune into another person's vibrations to pick up psychic information about that person. [cf. COME INTO YOUR VIBRATION, COME CLOSE TO YOU, COLD READER, DETUNING]

HOMO MECHANICUS—(ufology) (NASA) lifelike robots created to go into outer space and to other planets where humans cannot go; made to have tremendous power, human movements, electrical responses like the human nervous system and with a muscle-like mechanism; some have small, advanced computers. [cf. UFOLOGY Appendix 5]

HOMUNCULUS—(Medieval) (Theophrastus Paracelsus) a small child-like life form created by the alchemists, using artificial means; child grew to about two feet high and it was necessary to keep it in a glass jar in a rarified atmosphere; sperm was placed in sealed vessels with certain ingredients and incubated in horse manure for forty days to develop the child.

HOODOO DOCTOR—(a sect of black people in the United States) one who is very psychic and will hire out for healings, blessings, or hexing; rituals are copied from the Voodoo religion. **Syn.** CONJURE MAN, VOODOO PRACTITIONER. [cf. HOODOOISM, ASSOCIATION MAGIC, CALLED PERSON, CARRYING AN EVIL]

HOODOOISM—sect of black people in the United States who established a religion similar to Voodooism; teach psychic skills, mediumship; worship saints; use talents for good experiences and if necessary use them against an enemy; (has nothing to do with Satanism). [cf. HOODOO DOCTOR, UDJAT EYE, WITCH BOTTLE, TRIBAL DANCING]

HOOKED-UP—the attachment of a person to a biofeedback instrument; the person wears the electrode on the fingers, the head or other places on the body where it can connect to the electrical system of the body; on the other end of the electrical wire is a plug which is put in the jack in the instrument. Usage: when one is hooked-up to a GSR, the effect of one's thought on the physical body can be monitored. [cf. BIOFEEDBACK Appendix 5]

HORIZONTAL GLIDING—(astral projection) to will one's self to stay in the horizontal position and to stay in that position throughout the travel. [cf. ASTRAL PROJECTION, CONSCIOUS DEZGOSIS, SECOND BODY, REDOUBLED, SHOOT]

HORMIC ENERGY—coined by William McDougall (1920) see VITAL LIFE FORCE.

HORMONES—(esoteric) chemical messengers within the body, whose function is to keep the body's chemistry in balance, acting automatically with the thoughts of the brain; pleasant, benevolent, sincere thoughts secrete a different substance than thoughts of anxiety, anger, resentment, and worry; hormones keep the body working with the "on-going-life-process" or with the "ongoing-death-process" with each thought. (Inconcl.) [cf. HOLISTIC HEALTH, BODY TRANSRECEIVERS, NEGATIVE THOUGHT.]

HORNED SORCERER—(Stone Age) a nature spirit that is half-man and half-deer; brings protection and fertility to humans; some cultures connected horned animals with the sun and some with the underworld.

HORNS—(Greece, Egypt) worn on one's head to signify that the wearer is sacred; has psychic powers, and is capable of communicating with etheric world intelligences for counsel, information, and protection. [cf. INCONONGRAPHY, CONTAGIOUS MAGIC, SKULLS, CONICAL SHAPE]

HOROSCOPE—(Latin, Greek *horo*, "hour"; *scope*, "watcher") a chart of the heavens frozen at a particular time of a birth (birth of an idea, place, or person); (person) based on a mathematical statement or equation showing the relationships of various factors in a person's character or soul-mind as revealed by the relationships of the symbols; reveals the structure of the state of the soul-mind evolution in clear, concise, symbolic form; a systematized body of knowledge of the movements of planets and their relationship to humanity on earth by a diagram showing the geocentric positions of the sun, moon, and planets at an exact certain time. **Sim.** ASTROLOGICAL CHART. [**cf.** ZODIAN, ASTROLOGY]

HOROSCOPIC THEORY—at the moment of birth, a pattern of tendencies is given to that baby, in accordance with the planetary arrangements he or she chose to come to earth with. [**cf.** HOROSCOPE]

HORSE SHOE—(Middle Ages) has the properties to ward off evil because of its shape; placed over the threshold of a home or barn to prevent negative entities from entering and to attract good experiences for that household. [**cf.** FORMS-WITH-POWER Appendix 2, MAGIC SYMBOLS, HALF-MOON SHAPE]

HORSE WHISPERER —(Britain) (anpsi) a horseman who has psychic telepathic ability with the wildest beast by just using a whispered word; known to tame an unbroken steed, to stop runaways in their tracks, and to lure horses toward himself to his choosing. [**cf.** ANPSI Appendix 2, ANIMAL KINGDOM]

HORUS —1. (antiquity) the sun-god representing day and night, sun and moon; Horus the great, Horus of the two eyes; **2.** (Egypt) ruler of Egypt, son of Isis and Osiris, Horus the child; used the name Harpocrates also. [**cf.** EYE-OF-HORUS]

HOST WOMAN—(Kalanga, Botswana, South Africa) a female SHAMAN who exorcises an etheric world demon who has been disturbing the tribe; allows the demon to enter her body and work out demonic activity in order to find the causes; from the causes, she can eliminate the situation for tribe. [**cf.** MERCY-BAND, PULLING OUT SICKNESS, OBSESSION, EXORCISM]

HOT READER—a pseudo-medium who keeps files on people who seek readings, to be used for information for future readings; this information is sometimes exchanged among other pseudo-mediums in town. [**cf.** COLD READER]

HOT SEAT—(Frederick S. Perls) the chair next to the leader in Gestalt group psychotherapy, which means the person sitting in it will be the next person to be questioned during the session. [**cf.** ENCOUNTER GROUP, DISTRESS, GROWTH GAMES, NEW-AGE PSYCHOLOGY]

HOTBRUSH—see NATURE SPIRIT.

HOUNGEMAN—(Haiti) a medicine man who psychically detects the one responsible for transferring bad luck vibrations to others and then psychically takes care of the situation. **Syn.** HEX-DOCTOR [**cf.** PSYCHIC TRANSFER, BLESSING, HEXIST, LAW OF MIMICRY Appendix 7]

HOUSE BLESSING—exorcism of a home by a priest before one moves into the house; priest visits the house, performs a ritual emphasizing certain words that will rid the house of negative vibrations on the walls, floors, etc., that could have been impregnated there from previous owners; insulates the home with good vibrations by praying and chanting. [**cf.** HOUSE SWEEP, ATMOSPHERE CLEARING]

HOUSE OF ETERNITY—(Egypt) a tomb where the body is buried after mummification, which can be used only by those whose corpse has gone through a special "opening of the mouth" ritual; in this tomb the etheric double will live on and be revisited by the soul-mind that left it at death; revisitation is done when the soul-mind desires to help earthlings and the etheric double energy is there to use. [**cf.** COMING FORTH, OPENING OF THE MOUTH]

HOUSE OF GOD—(ancient) name given to the GIZA PYRAMID.

HOUSE SWEEP—to sever all unwanted, invisible circuit-potentials in a home or building before the new owners or tenants move in; executed by one or more psychics who go through special rituals and dialogue that eliminates the negative vibrations from the walls, ceilings, floors, and furniture that could have been impregnated by a catastrophic event or a highly emotional person; if desired by the new residents, the positive vibrations can be removed also and the interior neutralized to almost the virgin state, ready for their personal individualized impregnations of vibrations; (do not confuse with a HOUSE BLESSING). [**cf.** GHOST, LAW OF CONTAGION Appendix 7, SECONDARY WAVES]

HOUSEHOLD LAR—see LAR.

HOUSELEEK—(botane) a plant recognized as sacred; has the properties that will ward off fire, lightning and evil persons. [cf. INSANE ROOT, PLANT SENSING SYSTEMS]

HOWLING DERVISHES—(Sufi) those who use chanting with their dancing when seeking an altered state of consciousness; the rites of the Rufai order. [cf. WHIRLING DERVISH, SUFI, GHOST DANCE, HYSTERIA]

HPHO—(Tibet) ("transference") dissolving of total karmic debts into the clear light during the process of death. [cf. BARDO THODOL, BIRTH OF THE BARDO BODY]

HPHO-BO SERVICE—(Tibet) ritual performed by the priest to extract the soul-mind of the dying person during the process of death, and direct it to the proper place in the etheric world. [cf. DEATH SCIENCE Appendix 2]

HPHO-WA—(Tibet) see ASTRAL PROJECTION.

HSIANG CHUAN—(I Ching) part of the HEXA-GRAM that interprets the images associated with the TRIGRAMS. **Syn.** TREATISE ON SYMBOLISM, IMAGE. [cf. JUDGMENT, COMMENTARY]

HU—1. (Sufi) the creative sound found in all nature; can be heard by a keen clairaudient ear; 2. (Eckankar) secret and unknown name of the life force within all living organisms; all sounds of nature are a form of the Hu. [cf. COSMIC SOUND, GREAT TONE, SYMPATHETIC VIBRATION, MOLEC-ULAR CHORUS]

HUACA—(Peru) an oracle; see PSYCHIC.

HUE—(color) the position in the spectrum of visible light, running from 7,000 angstrom units for red to 4,000 angstrom units for indigo purple. [cf. COLOR, ODIC COLOR, COLOR STARVATION]

HUGAN—(Haiti) also spelled **hungan**; see PSY-CHIC and HEALER.

HULA—(Hawaii) rhythmic movement dance, performed with or without chanting, that puts one in an altered state of consciousness. [cf. DERVISH, RHYTHMIC EMOTION, MEDITATION IN MOTION]

HUM—(Tibet) see AUM.

HUMADRYAD—a nature spirit that takes his abode within a tree; is born and dies with the life of the tree.

HUMAN AIR SURROUND—invisible patterns of shimmering silver and colots, that can be seen around humans by the SCHLIEREN SYSTEM; shows various layers of air, recognized by their density, temperature and color. (Inconcl.) [cf. AURA, ETH-ERIC DOUBLE]

HUMAN ATMOSPHERE—see AURA.

HUMAN AURA—(esoteric) an invisible energy field that interpenetrates the physical body and extends a few feet from it like a shell, comprising the pattern of the physical body and the pattern of an overall lifestyle of that physical body during the earth life (the AKASHIC RECORD); 1. can be perceived clairvoyantly and the first layer can be photographed on the Kirlian camera showing colors, pattern, and density; 2. this invisible energy field belongs to one individual only and is the responsibility of that individual to feed it with thoughts, attitudes, emotions, and actions; in re-turn this field forms the condition of the body and lifestyle; the human aura forms the embryo in the womb and does not leave until the individual dies; 3. the object of life is to alter the human aura to a higher vibrational frequency during the incarna-tion; it changes slowly as one changes in character, attitudes, and intelligence; 4. aura regulates body energy flow and energy flow returns emanations into it; emanations protrude from the pores of the body in a perpendicular stream of light or color; whether the emanations are pointing outward, upward, or downward reveals the condition of the individual; 5. the extension outward consists of the invisible bodies of man; first layer is the etheric double, second layer is the PSYCHOLOGICAL AURA, third layer is the SPIRITUAL AURA; 6. total aura consists of seven energy fields: (a) electric field; (b) magnetic field; (c) infrared radiation; (d) sound and infrasound; (e) ultraviolet radiation; (f) chemi-cal aura; (g) psychic aura; 7. (do not confuse with the MENTAL AURA which changes rapidly in alignment with emotional changes and the mental mind) human aura changes with the subconscious mind and belief system. **Syn.** SOUL-MIND AURA. [cf. AURA, MENTAL AURA, KIRLIAN EFFECT]

HUMAN BATTERIES—1. sitters in a seance who give their electrical energy to the medium to be used in the physical phenomena; occurs naturally with no special effort on their part; 2. persons who are born with so much electricity that no one can touch them; cause much damage as they go through life, through no willing of their own; 3. persons whose electrical energy is accelerated while in a

trance state and is used for extraordinary phenomena experiments; e.g., extending an arm toward
another to give him an electric jolt. [**cf.** ELECTRIC
GIRLS, FLAMES OF DIVINE LOVE, SITTERS, IN-
VISIBILITY]

HUMAN BEING—(esoteric) 1. an intelligent energy
mass, forming a reality of a third-dimensional
vibrational frequency, endowed with a decision-
making mechanism and an innate desire to evolve;
functions under principles of a third-dimensional
world, constructed by soul-minds throughout the
universe; has the capacity to feel emotions and to
understand these feelings; the only organism that
changes its pattern-of-being because of its decision-
making mechanism and its emotional system; 2. a
miniature of Totality, having all the attributes of
Totality, linked to Totality and all its lesser rates of
vibration; 3. an intelligent organism placed in the
center of multitudinous energies, coming from
every direction; given the honor to constantly
change its own dimensional frequency by its existence, which requires thinking and acting; 4. has a
mechanism to tune into knowledge in the invisible
atmosphere, thoughts of others, consciousnesses,
and energy fields of all natures; acts like the condensor in a radio set picking up transmission signals in the cosmos, according to the voltage of the
soul-mind; see SOUL-MIND; 5. (Beal) an insynergis-
tic higher order of mental and psychic patterns; 6.
(Allan Kardec) **(a)** spirit and soul; **(b)** physical; **(c)**
perisprit; 7. human gyroscope who maintains both
an internal and external balance with a series of
forces and energies; 8. what one calls human is
nothing but biology, chemistry and machinery;
humanity lies in the space between. [**cf.** Appendix
5 HUMAN BEING, PHYSICAL BODY, HUMAN BEING
KINGDOM, MAN]

HUMAN BEING CONSCIOUSNESS—1. humans
view life horizontally as opposed to angels, who
view life vertically; 2. consists of sensory information, feelings and emotions, inductive and deduc-
tive reasoning, memory, psychic sensitivity, and
imagination, through the process of thinking. [**cf.**
CONSCIOUSNESS, LAW OF THINKING Appendix 7,
MATTER, BRAIN, SUBCONSCIOUS]

HUMAN BEING KINGDOM—(esoteric) 1. a vibrational frequency producing matter in a third-
dimensional form, functioning as a unit with its
own laws and principles; a unit of energy; a life
force moving along with other life forces; 2. influ-

enced by all other rates of vibration and influencing
all rates of vibration in the universe; a unique
kingdom with a personal mechanism to function
intelligently in this vibration, with the intention
this kingdom will contribute to the universal evolution; 3. an inferior aspect of the angel kingdom,
working toward the higher aspect of the angel
kingdom. [**cf.** BEINGS, ANGEL KINGDOM, HUMAN
BEING, PHYSICAL BODY]

HUMAN BEING SPECIES SEED—coined by June
Bletzer; 1. a minute invisible concentrated mass of
energy and intelligence within each human, containing the "pattern" of a perfect human being
specimen; included in the intelligence are the
attributes of Totality in its perfect state, endowed
with a governing principle that keeps it in perpetual movement toward the expression of that
perfect state in a perfect human being specimen
form; 2. Divine Spark of God within humanity,
giving them all the attributes of God, and urging
them to evolve and unfold these attributes "from
within, out"; 3. cannot be tampered with, nor can
its perpetual evolvement be stopped; has all the
time of eternity to develop quality of a perfect
specimen; 4. the motivation that keeps one growing, and gives one the desire to improve one's self
and environment. **Syn.** HUMAN MONAD, MAN-
KIND SEED, STAINLESS INDIVIDUALITY, MICRO-
COSM. [**cf.** IN THE BODY PENT, LAW OF GRACE
Appendix 7, SEED OF IMMORTALITY]

HUMAN BODY—(esoteric) 1. a workable, transmutation laboratory with chemical apparatus and insulated wiring system, complete with frequency
changers and transreceiver stations; this laboratory
takes food, drink, breath, cosmic energies, and
thoughts, to separate their constituents and chemicals to make and sustain a formula that completes a
body unit; this main formula is separated into
smaller formulas that form the thousands of parts
of the body distributed throughout the body unit by
the insulated wiring system (nervous systems); 2.
its amazing adaptability and non-predictable flexi-
bility indicates that the laboratory does not run
automatically; its boss is one's reasoning mechanism, making each one a unique pattern unto her or
himself; research found that every emotion and
thought changes body chemistry (minute changes),
making one an independent unit in full control of
his or her body unit. (Inconcl.) [**cf.** HOLISTIC
HEALTH, BEINGS, HUMAN BEING KINGDOM, HOL-
ISM, ETHERIC DOUBLE]

291

HUMAN ELECTRIC WIRE—formed by individuals linking their right hand over the left hand of the other person making an unbroken circle; unites a single current of psychic energy that flows through each body, transferred from hand to hand, whereby healing energy or psychic information can be passed. [**cf.** BEAMED ENERGY, PSYCHIC DEVELOPMENT CIRCLE, SPIRIT HEALING, FORMS-WITH-POWER]

HUMAN ENERGY TRANSFER—(magnetic healing) the movement of invisible magnetic fluid from the practitioner's body to the patient's body; healing practitioner must modulate the energy flow in relation to the healee's (patient) condition; one can receive too much at one time which is not harmful, but could be overwhelming to the patient. (Inconcl.) [**cf.** MAGNETIC HEALING, MENTAL HEALING, THERAPEUTIC TOUCH]

HUMAN GENERATOR MACHINES—instruments designed to transfer psychic energy from psychics, store it, and then use it to perform psychic feats; human psychic energy from these instruments is capable of moving objects, turning on electric motors, performing telepathically and attracting objects like a magnet; depends upon the shape of the instrument. (Inconcl.) [**cf.** OPERATION PRAYER POWER, BIOACCUMULATOR]

HUMAN HAND—(called the second brain, the visible mind) 1. channel for psychic energy to enter and exit the body, traveling to the brain for interpretation; psychic parts of hand are the palm, forefinger and thumb; 2. (Yoga) hand gesture articulates and concentrates the internal forces, directing them outwards; receives cosmic energies from the etheric world; 3. extremely sensitive for the blind person to perceive colors; 4. excellent informers of lingering vibrations on articles; see PSYCHOMETRY; 5. how hands are placed is important in healing, psychic work, and meditation. (Inconcl.) [**cf.** HANDS, PALMS, HUMAN BATTERY]

HUMAN INFORMATION PROCESSING SYSTEM—(American Society for Psychical Research) a mechanism of human beings, the mind, and its five senses; mind accepts inputs, extracts information from the inputs in a sequence of specific stages, and stores this information for future use; when necessary, this information is activated to generate output. **Syn.** INFORMATION PROCESSING THEORY. [**cf.** SUBCONSCIOUS MIND, REACTIVE MIND, EGO METAPROGRAMMING, INNER-MIND PICTURES]

HUMAN MAGNETISM—invisible fluid running through the nervous system; capable of emanating through hands and other extremities, directed by thought; see MAGNETIC FLUID. **Syn.** NERVE FLUID, HEALING FLUID. [**cf.** GAUSEE MAGNETICS, EARTH MAGNETISM, SPIRIT, CHAKRAS]

HUMAN MONAD—see HUMAN BEING SPECIES SEED.

HUMAN OMENS—to feel bodily sensations and reactions to environmental situations, other persons, and universal changes; a normal function of the body is to sense and know what is going on in the universe because body and universe are all one system; a change in one thing in the universe affects all other things; the body constantly tells the individual what is happening around it, but humanity has blocked this out over many incarnations, as each became concerned with personal affairs; this was mankind's protective mechanism; as a protective mechanism, the body now only emphasizes some things to call one's attention to it; e.g., 1. hair standing on end, goose pimples or duck bumps occurring when the individual is listening to statements that are truthful as opposed to a lie, and statements that bear a universal Truth, whether being surfaced by one's self or another; this is the most common of all human omens; 2. chills running up and down the spine indicating a warning of oncoming activity; 3. tingling in the spine or neck area indicating that the kundalini is acting and soon a hunch or intuitive thought will surface; 4. the meaning of itches and sneezes are individual to their owner and outside their usual category; each individual has these signals and his own personal signals, which should be recognized and learned. [**cf.** NATURE OMENS, PORTENT]

HUMAN ORIENTATION—to inwardly sense the clock time of day or night, and to sense the direction in which one is facing. [**cf.** BODY CONTROL, ATMOSPHERE CONTROL, IMMUNITY TO FIRE, INTERNAL INTONATION]

HUMAN POTENTIAL MOVEMENT—a search by masses of people all over the continent for a more satisfying life, deeper personal happiness, and greater opportunities to use one's potentials; this search began to spread rapidly in all walks of life since approximately 1972; large and small organizations are still springing up all over the country offering new alternatives to one's lifestyle, regarding exercise, recreation, eating habits, the healing of disease, and a sincere interest in psychic phenomena; all this relates to parts of the mind which mankind has not been using. [**cf.** NEW-AGE PSYCHOLOGY, HOLISTIC HEALTH, MEDITATION, VISUALIZATION]

HUMAN PSYCHOKINESIS—abbr. HUMAN-PK; to change, move, or alter the cells, or chemistry of a human body (one's self or another person) while at the conscious level of awareness without using mundane methods; performed by disciplined concentration of the conscious and subconscious minds; includes types of physical phenomena such as, ALCHEMY, ASCENSION, RADIONICS, MOTOR APPORTATION, MENTAL HEALING, MAGNETIC HEALING, and PSYCHIC DENTISTRY; (do not confuse with some of the same types of physical phenomena in which guides are used in place of the subconscious mind). [**cf.** HUMAN TELEKINESIS]

HUMAN SOUL—see SOUL-MIND.

HUMAN TELEKINESIS—abbr. HUMAN-TK; to allow one's body to be used, in part or in whole, by an etheric world intelligence, to perform physical psychism; the intelligence intervenes and moves, changes, or alters the medium's body for the planned activity; divided into two groupings: 1. light trance (seeming to onlookers to be an awareness state); necessary for STAND-UP READING, AUTOMATISM, TALKING-IN-TONGUES, TRANSFIGURATION; 2. deep trance state; necessary for DEPENDENT VOICE, LEVITATION, TELEPORTATION, AUTOMATISM, TRANSFIGURATION, IMPERSONATION, PSYCHIC SURGERY, ETHERIC SURGERY.

HUMAN TEMPERATURE CONTROL—(Tibetan Yoga) to keep one's body warm while sitting in freezing weather with little or no clothes on; the mind must be disciplined and single-pointed to concentrate on body temperature for the entire period; a form of initiation. [**cf.** BODY CONTROL Appendix 2]

HUMAN TRANSMITTER—one who unconsciously allows others to draw magnetic energy from his or her body while in their presence; 1. some individuals are endowed with an abundance of magnetism and need to share it or it would prove too overwhelming for lifestyles of the present age; these individuals do not realize they feed others and maintain their vivaciousness regardless; 2. some individuals transmit magnetism and feel devitalized and tired after a meeting with an absorber; not

realizing why, he or she usually blames the conversation or has a dislike for the other party; this magnetic transfer is caused by body chemistry interplay and has nothing to do with the topic of conversation or personalities per se; 3. one who has the body chemistry to draw energy feels elated and revitalized after a meeting with a transmitter; when in need for this magnetic energy they are drawn to persons who have the proper body chemistry for transmitting; 4. these body chemistries attract and hold together, stimulating a marriage or close friendship and yet the relationship in other ways is not necessarily compatible. [**cf.** PARASYTE, PSYCHIC TRANSFER Appendix 2, EMPATHY-PK, INTUIT TELEPATHY]

HUMAN X-FACTOR-(laboratory) see ESP.

HUMANIST—one who aims to serve as a bridge between theoretical philosophical discussions and the practical application of humanism to ethical and social problems. [**cf.** HUMANISTIC PSYCHOLOGY, HUMAN BEING KINGDOM]

HUMANISTIC PSYCHOLOGY—theory: one's human behaviorisms should not be isolated, but acted upon as a whole, as opposed to treating one as a mechanism; recently psychologists with this theory broke away from scientific psychology; use phenomenogical methods which better answer human concerns than the scientific method; gives human behavior a holistic approach; recognizes that humanity does not know enough, and the salvation of mankind requires the advancement of knowledge of humans; tends to improve human and social values and the quality of knowledge which results in more holistic interconnections; rejects the robot model of man and explores the "why" of mankind's unique human capabilities; offers new techniques to human awareness; an offshoot of the HUMAN POTENTIAL MOVEMENT.

HUMANIST THERAPY GROUPS—1. a small gathering of individuals who hold regular sessions for the purpose of helping one another to stand on their own, and not to rely on outside help or the ENCOUNTER GROUP; theory: all people are here to express themselves fully and not to subserve others; the process of an individual's experience is more important than any end-product of behavior; 2. (Carl Rogers) the group leader places the power and control of the group experience in the hands of each participant as opposed to mass induction, such as evangelists and charismatic movements do. [**cf.**

293

HUMANISTS, ABNORMAL BEHAVIOR, ART OF
LIVING]

HUMANIZED TECHNOLOGY—theory: everything
is alive, even inanimate things such as machinery;
because everything is in motion and has a consciousness, everything is a living entity; the atoms
store in their memory bank all the vibrational
frequencies they experience ready to experience
higher states of frequencies; which inert objects are
higher than others hasn't been established. [**cf.**
LAW OF PERSONFICATION Appendix 7, CONSCIOUS
OF BEING, CONSCIOUSNESS]

HUMANOIDS—(ufology) metallic looking entities
that have been seen getting out of UFOs that have
landed on earth. [**cf.** MAGNET ANOMALY, SCOUT
SHIP, DOR CLOUDS, SPACE BROTHERS, PROJECT
MAGNET, POWER SYSTEM]

HUNCH—a thrust of information or a premonition
coming from "within" one's own body and mind,
without willing it; information one did not logically
think out, reason with or know from formal education or life experiences, but a certain feeling that
the information is correct. **Syn.** INTUITION. [**cf.**
HUNCHABILITY, CLAIRSENTIENCE, INSPIRATIONAL
THOUGHT, PRESENCE, SUGGESTION, GUT FEELING]

HUNCHABILITY—to receive and understand psychic information when it is given spontaneously
throughout the whole body; one senses an "inner
knowing" that the information is correct; to perceive feelings or body sensations that something is
about to happen, that one should change plans, that
this is the right thing to do despite outside opposition, or that this is the right place or right person;
none of these suggestions were reasoned with, logically thought out, or could have come from past
education or life experiences; a safe psychism to
occur at any time, in contrast to those types that
should be under control at all times. **Syn.** CLAIR-
SENTIENCE, INTUITION. [**cf.** COSMIC CONSCIOUS-
NESS, SUPERCONSCIOUS MIND, INSPIRATIONAL
THOUGHT]

HUSKS—(Kabbalah) counterparts of the human
body that make up the density and demonic intelligences; e.g., viruses, impurities and waste products.
[**cf.** HADES, PURGATORY, HELL, DENSITY]

HWANG—a female nature spirit; see FAIRIES. **Sim.**
FENGHWANG.

HYDRONICS—an energy that is versatile and can

be conducted through most everything; the same
energy that radiates from the ends of an antenna;
found to be useful in fish psychism; used under
water to record fish talking, (a feat that is immeasurable by conventional means). (Inconcl.) [**cf.**
ANPSI Appendix 2]

HYDROTHERAPY—scientific application of water
to the body in all of its three physical states, for
purposes of therapy and rehabilitation; e.g.. saunas,
steam baths, hot packs, ice packs, friction sprays,
contract baths. [**cf.** CURATIVE EDUCTION]

HYLOZOISM—doctrine that all matter has life and
that life is a property of matter. [**cf.** LAW OF PER-
SONIFICATION Appendix 7, ENERGY, SPIRIT]

HYPER—prefix meaning "overabundance, in excess, above."

HYPER-META-PROTO-ELEMENTAL MATTER—
(Theosophy) groupings of esoteric atoms on the
very highest plane. [**cf.** THOUGHT SPHERE, UN-
KNOWN PLANE, SPIRITUAL LIGHT, SEVENTH
PLANE]

HYPERACUITY—to psychically recognize mental
and physical impressions that are not one's own; a
heightened sensitivity to the cosmos; see PSYCHIC
SKILLS. [**cf.** PSYCHOPHYSICAL PHENOMENA, PSY-
CHOSENSORY, OBEAH, MAGIC ART]

HYPERACUTE—pertains to the heightened awareness of hearing, tasting, and smelling while in a
deep state of hypnosis; e.g., someone breathing
from across the room is easily heard by the hypnotic subject. [**cf.** HYPNOTHERAPY, DISPLACE-
MENT PHOBIA, FLUCTUATION]

HYPERAESTHESIA—1. to perceive an external
feeling in the senses when no visible stimuli is
there; e.g., to feel a heavy shoe on one's foot and no
one is nearby; 2. the acceleration of the normal
senses in a state of hypnosis or meditation; e.g., to
hear a lawn mower outside the window sounding
like it is in the room; paper falls and it sounds like a
thud. [**cf.** SEVENTH SENSE, EXTERNALIZATION OF
SENSITIVITY]

HYPERAMNESIA—1. to have an extension of
memory power when in a hypnotic state; ability to
be regressed back to infancy and recall the tiniest
details; 2. to bring forth knowledge psychically that
could not have been known by any earthly education, when in a theta state of consciousness; the
quickening of the mind's sensitivity by hypnosis or

meditation. [cf. HYPNO-REPRODUCTION, PARTIAL AGE REGRESSION, COSMIC MEMORY]

HYPERCATHOLIC—a catholic who is psychic.

HYPERCOGNITION—to think, reason, and speak at a superfast speed and not be aware of this speed; to speak as if a lot of study went into one's words but actually without planning the conversation before speaking; occurs at a subconscious alpha level, unintentionally, when one is talking at a beta level; subject floats in and out of the alpha state unknowingly. [cf. INSPIRATIONAL SPEAKING, LIGHT TRANCE]

HYPERESTHESIA—increased sensitivity to the sense of touch; to sense colors, and fabrics with one's own skin; to see with the skin without the use of eyes; a form of eyeless sight. [cf. CUTANEOUS VISION, PARAOPTIC SIGHT, EYELESS SIGHT]

HYPERGEOMETRICAL—a shape that can be conducive to PK, or other psi energies. [cf. UNINTENTIONAL-PK, PSYCHOKINETIC, MIND-OVER-MATTER]

HYPERMETABOLIC—pertains to an aroused physiological state brought about by increased sympathetic nervous system activity, invoked by the fight-or-flight response. [cf. BIOFEEDBACK TRAINING, RESTFUL ALERTNESS, SOUND CURRENT]

HYPERPHYSICS—see METAPHYSICS.

HYPERSENSITIVE—a psychic with an excess of psychic ability which is difficult to turn off; happens to a natural-born psychic or one who had an accident that opened their psychic ability to an acute state; these persons spontaneously tune into the earth and its changes, such as tornadoes, hurricanes, political situations, and prominent people's deaths; can size up their environment psychically; occurs unwilled, and can be a nuisance and cause poor health.

HYPERSPACE—a level of consciousness where no time elapses; an atmosphere where everything is multiconnected, interwoven with every other thing. **Syn.** FOURTH DIMENSION. [cf. TIME FLOW, TIME STRUCTURE, WOMB OF TIME]

HYPERSPACE THEORY—special forms and shapes in this world that are capable of harnessing energy in the center of their form and keeping it concentrated in one spot, e.g., the pyramid shape, the circle. [cf. MAGIC CIRCLE, SHAPED POWER, TANS]

HYPERSYNCHRONIZED WAVES—the over-blending of two or more vibrational frequencies, causing a good situation to be overwhelming and appear to be destructive, e.g., sitting under a pyramid for so long, that the change in body harmony that is received is too drastic to handle. [cf. SYNCHRONICITY, VITALISM, VIBRANALYSIS, OCTAVES]

HYPERTRANCE STATE—a level of consciousness in which the subject has quieted their emotions, stilled their mind and relaxed their physical body, but the psychic senses are very alert; happens in MEDITATION, HYPNOSIS, and BIOFEEDBACK TRAINING. [cf. THETA STATE OF CONSCIOUSNESS, MANTRA, SELF-NONSELF, RESTFUL ALERTNESS]

HYPERVENTILATION—excessive, rapid deep breaths, making one feel dizzy or lightheaded; occurs because of decreased carbon dioxide in the bloodstream which the diaphragm is unaccustomed to. **Syn.** OXYGEN JAG, OXYGEN INTOXICATION. [cf. HYPERVENTILATION SYNDROME]

HYPERVENTILATION SYNDROME—a preparation that sometimes precedes impersonation, trance, or other physical phenomena causing this over-breathing; an entity from the etheric world, coming to a medium to bring in a psychic message, can cause this overbreathing until they both become synchronized. [cf. HYPERVENTILATION, POSSESSION, CONTROL, TRANCE MANIFESTATIONS/MISCELLANEOUS]

HYPNAGOGIC STATE—a short time span just before sleep takes over, when the conscious and subconscious mind are changing dominancy in their roles; the conscious mind becomes passive and the subconscious mind takes control of the thinking; this process sets up an equilibrium of mind activity and when the two minds are on the same level of activity, there seems to be an unplugging and plugging of circuits in the head; lasts from a few seconds to a few minutes; it goes unnoticed to many; to some, it is a fusing of electrical sparks in the head; to some, a host of energies is perceived clairaudiently as voices and sounds unfamiliar to the sleeper; to others a host of scenes, images, or faces are perceived clairvoyantly and appear grotesque, friendly, unfriendly, pleasant, hazy, vivid, unknown, and seemingly make no sense; as sleep takes over, this disappears from view and memory; also spelled **hypnogogic** (Inconcl.) [cf. HYPNAGOGIC Appendix 2, TOPOSCOPE, HYPNAPOMPIC STATE]

HYPNAPOMPIC STATE—a short period which precedes a full awakening state, at the end of the sleep cycle, when the conscious mind and subconscious mind are changing dominancy in their roles; the subconscious mind is giving up control and the conscious mind is starting to take control of the thinking mechanism; this process sets up an equilibrium of mind activity, and when the two minds are on the same level of activity, there seems to be an unplugging and plugging of circuits in the head, lasting from a few seconds to a few minutes; it goes unnoticed by many; to some it is a fusing of electrical sparks in the head; to others, it is a host of energies perceived clairaudiently as voices and sounds unfamiliar to the sleeper; and to some it is a host of scenes, images, or faces perceived clairvoyantly which appear grotesque, friendly, unfriendly, pleasant, hazy, vivid, unknown, and seemingly to make no sense; as one becomes fully awake, this disappears from view and memory, also spelled **hypnopompic**. [cf. HYPNAGOGIC Appendix 2, REM REBOUND PHENOMENA]

HYPNOANALYST—a hypnotherapist who uses regression as a possible means of finding the cause of today's illnesses or unwanted lifestyles, by traveling back into the subject's past life or lives, while in a state of deep hypnosis. **Syn.** HYPNOTHERAPIST. [cf. REVIVIFICATION, AGE REGRESSION, HYPNOTHERAPY]

HYPNOCAMPAL—a region of the brain that stores basic animal survival programs. [cf. COLLECTIVE UNCONSCIOUSNESS, SYMPATHETIC NERVOUS SYSTEM, FLIGHT OR FIGHT SYSTEM]

HYPNOGOGIC STATE—see HYPNAGOGIC STATE.

HYPNOGOGOSTAT—(biofeedback training) a biofeedback instrument designed to monitor the state between waking and sleeping, the HYPNAGOGIC STATE: the sleeper is made aware of their hypnagogic state by a buzzer from the instrument when he or she is being monitored at this level of consciousness. [cf. REM REBOUND, TOPSY, HYPNAGOGIC]

HYPNOGRAPHY—to write or paint spontaneously while in a deep hypnotic state; a form of psychoanalysis wherein the hypnotherapist is given valuable clues as to the patient's disturbances and emotional conflicts by the manner in which he or she proceeds and what is on the paper; theory: when one is in a PSYCHIC CONSCIOUSNESS level,

the subconscious mind is always trying to better itself and this will surface. [cf. IMPERSONATION, FINGER RESPONSE, GUIDED FANTASY]

HYPNOIDAL—1. a mild state of hypnosis acquired unknowingly by one's self (not by induction); one reaches a low ALPHA STATE OF CONSCIOUSNESS and is unaware of what is happening around him or her, by single-pointed concentration on a book, thrilling TV program, or putting together a mechanical device, etc; 2. see HYPNAGOGIC STATE. [cf. FLUCTUATION, AUTOHYPNOTIC, PULSING]

HYPNOLOGY—the study of psychic skills while parties involved are under the state of hypnosis; e.g., to send a mental telepathic message to one in a hypnotic state. [cf. GROUP HYPNOSIS, POSTHYPNOTIC SUGGESTION]

HYPNOMOTIVATION—the use of formative suggestions during hypnotherapy to motivate the student. [cf. PRESCRIPTION, INDUCTION, EGO-STRENGTHENING]

HYPNOPEDIA—see SUGGESTOPEDIA.

HYPNOPERSONATION—to assume the personality and characteristics of a deceased foreign entity, for a temporary time, while under the hypnotic effect of suggestion; subject chooses who he or she is to imitate; suggestions stimulate the subject to perform and produce work like the great person agreed upon, capable of doing great things in this state of consciousness; e.g., playing the piano like the great pianist, herself; painting like the famous artist, himself; (do not confuse with TRANCE IMPERSONATION) **Syn.** ARTIFICIAL REINCARNATION. [cf. PRESCRIPTION, SLEEP-AWAKE HYPNOSIS, MAGNETIC SLEEP]

HYPNOPHOBIA—anziety resulting in an inability to sleep because one does not like the dreams that occur; these dreams are believed to be suppressed desires one does not want to face. [cf. DREAMS, NIGHTMARES, LOSING MONEY DREAMS, FALLING DREAMS]

HYPNOPLASTY—to mold spontaneously from a piece of modeling clay while in a hypnotic state; the mold serves as a valuable clue for the therapist to diagnose the mental conflicts, and to reach the cause of the disturbance of the patient. [cf. PSYCHIC CONSCIOUSNESS, BLOCKS, FLUIDIC ASSOCIATION]

HYPNOPOMPIC STATE—see HYPNAPOMPIC STATE.

HYPNOPSYCHEDELIC—pertains to experiential investigation of factors which affect the production of parapsychological phenomena in altered states of consciousness.

HYPNOREPRODUCTION—(Russia) see HYPNO-PERSONATION.

HYPNOS—(Greece) the god of sleep, felt to be responsible for the dreams in which etheric world entities come to the sleeper with guidance. [**cf.** DREAMS, SLEEP EXPERIENCES, HIGH DREAM, THETA STATE]

HYPNOSCOPE—a design of black and white winding circles, spiraling to a small center, which is used for the induction period of a hypnotic state of consciousness; the subject stares at the design that appears to be moving, until the eyes become tired and close; sometimes design used in a twirling movement. [**cf.** MAGNETIZER, MESMERIC FLUID, SUGGESTION]

HYPNOSENTIENCE—to recall memories of places, names or experiences of former lives without a hypnotherapy session or without other deliberate methods. [**cf.** REINCARNATION, KARMA, REGRESSION]

HYPNOSIS—(antiquity) (Greek *hypnos*, "sleep") represents the alpha and theta levels of consciousness that one also reaches during sleep; a deliberate technique or a nondeliberate process of narrowing the CONSCIOUS MIND to such a degree that it relinquishes its role of decision making and becomes passive; this puts the SUBCONSCIOUS MIND in control of the person, with a heightened sense of response to suggestions and an acute awareness of PSYCHIC SENSES; usually the physical body is relaxed; 1. **Degrees of hypnosis: (a)** LIGHT STATE OF HYPNOSIS (lethargic); **(b)** MEDIUM STATE OF HYPNOSIS (cataleptic); **(c)** DEEP STATE OF HYPNOSIS (somnambulistic); 2. **Types of hypnosis: (a)** SELF-HYPNOSIS: (1) SELF-HYPNO-THERAPY; (2) EMOTIONAL HYPNOSIS; (3) SPONTANEOUS SELF-HYPNOSIS: **(b)** GUIDED HYPNOSIS: (1) STAGE HYPNOSIS; (2) MEDICAL HYPNOSIS; (3) HETEROHYPNOTHERAPY; (4) MASS HYPNOSIS; (5) ETHEREAL HYPNOSIS (distant); (6) ON-THE-SPOT HYPNOSIS.

HYPNOSPELL—to deliberately put an individual in a state of narrowed awareness so they can be manipulated; the hypnotist uses a planned ploy attacking the victim's vulnerable emotional desire and an eye-stare to stimulate attentive concentration of the victim on him or her until the hypnotist has the victim in a hypnotic state; the hypno-speller stimulates the victim's brain by thought transference so the resistance of the nerve gap is reduced and the acetylcholine is undissolved, making the resistance to the other person's message more acute; as long as the hypnospeller can keep their concentration on the necessary ploy and the eye-stare, they can control the victim; to lengthen the hypnospell, posthypnotic suggestions are given; see SPELLED. [**cf.** TRANSFIXED, GLAMORIE, BECHARM]

HYPNOTELEPATHY—to influence another person's mind activity, silently by unobserved means, causing the person to think they are their own thoughts; distance is no barrier. **Syn.** MENTAL TELEPATHY. [**cf.** HYPNOSPELL, TELEPATHY]

HYPNOTHERAPIST—one who induces a hypnotic state in another person for mental and physical therapy; must be skilled in various induction methods, know how to correctly word the hypnotic prescription, and know the induction release; has knowledge of the five minds: CONSCIOUS MIND, SUBCONSCIOUS MIND, SUPERCONSCIOUS MIND, UNIVERSAL MIND, and the SUBLIMINAL LEVEL of the mind; has knowledge of KARMA and knows how to handle regression of past lives in case the subject slips into a past life without suggestion. **Syn.** OPERATOR, GUIDE. [**cf.** REVIVIFICATION, AGE REGRESSION, SYMPTOM SUBSTITUTION, EYE-LID TEST]

HYPNOTHERAPY—to use a hypnotic state of consciousness for physical and mental therapy; an induction process into a deep or medium hypnotic state, whereby the subconscious mind of the subject is given therapeutic instructions or suggestions: 1. to improve the subject's physical health; 2. to rid the subject of undesirable mental or physical habits; 3. to increase the subject's potential; 4. to regress the subject into the past of the present life or other incarnations for the purpose of uncovering the cause of repetitious, unwanted life patterns; see SELF-HYPNOTHERAPY and HETEROHYPNO-THERAPY. [**cf.** SYMPTOM SUBSTITUTION, GUIDED HYPNOSIS, MEDIUM STATE, DEEP STATE, AGE REGRESSION, REVIVIFICATION]

HYPNOTHERAPY DESENSITIZATION—to use a hypnotic state of consciousness to urge repressed problems and feelings to surface repeatedly from the subconscious mind; when the repressed feelings are no longer accompanied with negative emotions, the subject is free from their hold pattern in the body, and from future repressions from the original experience. [cf. HYPNOTHERAPY, BLOCKS]

HYPNOTIC ANESTHESIA—see MEDICAL HYPNOSIS.

HYPNOTIC CLAIRVOYANCE—to put one's self in a hypnotic state to perceive visions easily; the psychic senses are more acute in this state. [cf. HYPERAESTHESIA, HYPNOVISION, EYE-FIXATION]

HYPNOTIC DISC—a twelve-inch cardboard circle with heavy black swirling lines that spiral toward a small center, used for the induction period to put the subject in a hypnotic state; can be spun on a phonograph for emphasized inducement. [cf. GUIDED FANTASY, NERVE FLUID, EYE-FIXATION]

HYPNOTIC ECSTASY—to use rhythmic dancing, chanting, loud music, or singing to induce an ALTERED STATE OF CONSCIOUSNESS, leaving the individual feeling elated and on an emotional high; the rhythmic beat and prolonged span of movement subdues the conscious mind and brings the subject to an alpha state in which he or she may perceive visions or have other psychic experiences; done in religious ceremonies or traditional gatherings. [cf. WHIRLING DERVISHES, TRIBAL DANCING, CHARISMATIC]

HYPNOTIC PALLOMANCY—to put a subject through the induction process of hypnosis by the use of the pendulum; pendulum bob is usually a crystal, and is swung in front of the subject's eyes; the subject stares at the swinging bob until his or her concentration is narrowed down and his or her eyes close, making the subconscious mind ready for the suggestions. [cf. PENDULUM BOB, HYPNODISC, INDUCTION]

HYPNOTIC PHENOMENA—to have a psychic experience while under the influence of hypnosis. [cf. HYPERAESTHESIA, HYPERAMNESIA, HYPNOVISION]

HYPNOTIC PRESCRIPTION—suggestions that have been carefully planned and worded for a particular person, to be given when in a hypnotic state to help heal their symptoms; prescription tells the body or mind how it wants it to behave when in the awake state; designed to help change what the subject wants to overcome in their life; given after the induction and before the induction

release. [cf. SUGGESTION, REEDUCATION, SELF SUGGESTION]

HYPNOTIC SPEECH PATTERN—method of induction for a hypnotic state whereby a breath is taken and the speech is given on the exhalations of the breath; makes it easy for the subject to become relaxed, and the conscious mind to become passive; used personally or in a group; leaders who talk this way normally put their audience in a state of hypnosis while lecturing. [cf. INDUCTION, HYPNOTIC PALLOMANCY]

HYPNOTIC SUGGESTION—1. orders, instructions, or information given to the subject during the hypnosis period, during the induction, prescription, or induction release; 2. any message, instructions or ideas given to the subconscious mind when the conscious mind is passive; the subconscious mind accepts the material without criticism or judgment; hypnosis is based on the law of suggestion. [cf. PRESCRIPTION, LAW OF SUGGESTION Appendix 7]

HYPNOTIC TOUCH—to reach a relaxed state of consciousness with only a touch of the hypnotist's hand, after being conditioned in many hypnotic sessions to respond to this. [cf. COOPERATIVE SUGGESTION, PULSING, REEDUCATION]

HYPNOTISM—to prepare the conscious mind of another person to relinquish its role of control and decision-making and allow the subconscious mind to be in charge; the magnetism from the hypnotist's eyes is transferred to the subject's nervous system, making him or her very relaxed and receptive to the suggestions of the hypnotist; the subconscious mind of the subject will take the data and suggestions, just as it is given, and store it; can be used for therapeutic or destructive means; see HYPNOTHERAPY and HYPNOSIS. [cf. LIGHT STATE OF HYPNOSIS, MEDIUM STATE OF HYPNOSIS, CATALEPTIC STATE OF HYPNOSIS]

HYPNOTIST—one who knows various techniques that will put another individual in a very relaxed state of consciousness, in which the mental mind is passive and the subconscious mind is all-absorbing; the subject is then ready to accept the suggestions and beliefs of the hypnotist given verbally or silently; ability to hypnotize another can be learned or can be inborn (in which case hypnotist is not always aware of his or her ability); knowledge of hypnosis techniques does not necessarily mean the hypnotist understands the functions of the two minds, nor does it involve one's value system; how the hypnotist handles the subject after he or she is in a hypnotic state, does reveal his or her knowledge of the two minds, and his or her intent reveals his or her value system; a good or poor hypnotist should be judged by how the subject is handled in the hypnotic state. **Syn.** HYPNOTHERAPIST, OPERATOR, GUIDE. [**cf.** ON-THE-SPOT-HYPNOSIS, GUIDED HYPNOSIS, MASS HYPNOSIS, SYMPTOM SUBSTITUTION]

HYPNOTIZABILITY—the response to an induction test (of which there are many), given to the subject before the hypnotic session to determine whether the person responds quickly to suggestion and whether they can be easily put into a hypnotic state; e.g., those who cannot unclasp their hands in the hand-clasp test are highly hypnotizable. [**cf.** EYE-ROLL TEST, MAGNETIZER, INDUCTION]

HYPNOTIZABLE—pertains to a person who is capable of being hypnotized without a great deal of effort or without needing many sessions. [**cf.** HYPNODISC, MAGNETIZER, MAGNETIC FLUID, HYPNOTIC TOUCH]

HYPNOTIZED TEAMS—(psi tasks) see AGENT PERCIPIENT TEAM.

HYPO—prefix meaning "under, less, shortening"; opposite of *hyper*; written *hyp* is preceding a vowel.

HYPOCHONDRIAC—one who has imaginary illnesses; the body does not show what the mind is feeling; (not the same as PSYCHOSOMATIC). [**cf.** PSYCHOMATIC ILLNESS, DISEASE, CURATIVE EDUCATION]

HYPOMETABOLIC STATE—a decrease in activity in the sympathetic nervous system and other systems in the body, making the person feel very relaxed, rejuvenated and pleasurable; brought on by meditation, biofeedback training session, or a hypnotic state. [**cf.** METABOLIC MONITOR, GSR, MEDITATION]

HYPONEDIA—to learn new material, or change one's belief system while sleeping; correct wordage for one's desire to accomplish is taped on the cassette; the cassette is listened to at the onset of sleep for an hour or two or played on an endless tape all night; the amount of nights necessary to learn the material or to see a difference in one's behavior varies; researchers found this beneficial in activating cells to heal one's body and to change

one's karmic pattern to show a difference in behavioral patterns; the conscious mind is passive during the night and during the first few hours the subconscious mind is at its lowest level, and therefore, accepts information or suggestions without question; tapes should not be played too frequently so that the normal, necessary, dream-stuff becomes inhibited; (do not confuse with SUGGESTOPEDIA). [**cf.** SUBCONSCIOUS MIND, SOUL-COMPLEX, WISDOM MIND, DREAMSTUFF]

HYPOPHENOMENALISM—theory: the soul-mind survives after the physical body is dead. [**cf.** DEATH SCIENCE, ETHERIC WORLD, INTELLIGENCES, DEATHBED VISIONS]

HYPOTHALAMUS—(clinical) a cluster of cells tucked away in the dark, intricate recesses of the middle of the head, located over the pituitary gland; oozes pinpricks of peptides that release the peptides from the pituitary gland; serves as an executive over the pituitary gland (the master gland of the physical body); peptides in the hypothalamus also influence human behavior. (Inconcl.) [**cf.** HIDDEN DOOR, THIRD-EYE AREA Appendix 2]

HYPOTHERMIA—artificial reduction of body temperature to slow metabolic processes; usually done for heart surgery; similar to the slow metabolic processes found during hypnosis and meditation. [**cf.** HYPNOTHERAPY, MEDITATION]

HYSTERIA—a violent, emotional, trance state of consciousness, which brings one an excess of psychic skills and healing abilities; 1. brought on willingly by persistent rhythmic twirling, dancing, singing or other emotional-physical actions; 2. brought on gradually by a subconscious, obsessive, attitude concerning one's religion; possible results in either method before skills are mastered: temporary blindness, deafness, or paralysis, loss of or excessive sensitivity of the skin, short-period coma, fainting, fits, spasms, and/or miscellaneous aches and pains. [**cf.** AUTOSUGGESTION, OBSESSION, INITIATORY SICKNESS, SUFI TWIRLING]

HYSTERICAL ABSENCES—a sudden loss of full consciousness, resulting in hysterical movements of the body and voice, air being sucked involuntarily into the stomach, abdominal swelling, convulsive fits, insensitivity in regions of the skin, muscular spasms, and a sudden recovery that is unexplainable. **Sim.** POSSESSION. [**cf.** SECONDARY PERSONALITY, EXORCISM]

HZ—abbr. HERTZ; a unit of measure, equal to one cycle per second; used on the biofeedback instruments.

"I"—(Transcendental Meditation) the SELF; a part of CREATIVE INTELLIGENCE, the EGO, the INDIVIDUALITY; the INNER-SELF. **Syn.** SOUL-MIND.

I AM—the divine spark of Totality in all individuals; the intelligent potential in the HUMAN BEING SPECIES SEED giving the human being motivation to unfold to a perfect human being; a sacred connection with the ultimate; one's true self. **Syn.** SELF, MONAD, CHRIST WITHIN. [**cf.** MONADOLOGY, CHRIST]

I CHING—(China, 2498-1150 B.C.); a divination process wherein one uses the patterns of three tossed objects to receive an answer to one's psychological, business, or social problem from the BOOK OF CHANGES; objects can be coins, dice, stones, etc.; see LOTS; the three objects are tossed into the air by the querant and the pattern they make on the ground is recorded; this is repeated six times and is matched with the hexagram in the book for the answer to the problem; book consists of lines, TRIGRAMS, and HEXAGRAMS with their statements and commentaries regarding answers to people's life problems; the querant must have a clear, simple question in his mind, although it need not be written, voiced, or answerable by yes or no; this process utilizes the principle that two separate events will occur at the same moment, neither being causally connected or having an effect one on the other, yet meaningfully related, when consciously or subconsciously willed. [**cf.** SYNCHRONICITY]

I-NESS—("man's individuality") one's concern about oneself and one's self-preservation; that which separates one from his identity with the ALL. **Syn.** EGO, CONSCIOUS-MIND. [**cf.** SOUL-MIND, CONSCIOUS MIND]

I-PROCESS—(Buddhism) the continuance of the personality unfolding from one incarnation to another. [**cf.** MONADOLOGY, REINCARNATION, TRANSMIGRATION]

IAO—(esoteric) symbols used for the male and female generative principles. **Syn.** POLARITY. [**cf.** YIN AND YANG]

IATROMANTIS—(ancient) a seer, who is also skilled in diagnosing and curing illness. **Syn.** PSYCHIC. [**cf.** MENTAL HEALING, PSYCHIC HEALING]

IB—(ancient Egypt, "heart"; "the god in man") the spark of divine Totality in all human beings; that which lives on after death. **Syn.** MONAD. [**cf.** SOUL-MIND, TOTALITY]

IBLEES—(Greek, "devil") a nature spirit created of and living in fire; capable of assuming human form; works for and against humans; belongs to the jinn family [**cf.** JINNI]

ICE-SITTER—(Tibet) psychic who sits on ice in the nude and keeps his body warm and sometimes makes it hot enough to melt the ice. [**cf.** BODY CONTROL Appendix 2]

ICEBOX EFFECT—(destructive-brainwashing cults) (Father Kent Burtner) repression of normal developmental conflicts and resolutions, that young adults have about their parents and themselves that are typical for their age group, while in the cult organizations; these conflicts need to be resolved and they are not; when one goes into a cult, it is like taking a block of ice and putting it in the icebox, the conflicts are frozen; the mind is now indoctrinated twenty-four hours a day to center on the needs of the cult; when the victim is deprogrammed or comes out on his or her own, it is like taking the block of ice out to thaw; the unresolved conflicts begin to thaw out or come to the surface; these conflicts must now be dealt with along with their new feelings regarding their cult experience. [**cf.** DESTRUCTIVE-BRAIN WASHING CULT Appendix 2]

ICELAND SPAR—(esoteric) a mineral that transmits vibrations from Mercury to the earth; capable of polarizing light rays. [**cf.** MINPSI, POLARITY]

ICONOCLAST—one who destroys another person's ideas or beliefs without the victim knowing it is being done; uses hypnosis and mental telepathy to attack the subconscious mind directly; objective is usually to destroy the victim's religious beliefs so they can replace them with their own religious beliefs. [**cf.** SPELLER, INFORMATION DISEASE, WITNESSING, DESTRUCTIVE-BRAINWASHING CULT]

ICS—suffix pertaining to the matter, facts, principles, and knowledge of a subject.

ID—suffix meaning "belonging to" or "connected with."

301

ID—(Sigmund Freud) one of three aspects of the total personality; a channel of energies and tensions; (psychoanalysis) the part of the psyche residing in the unconscious that is the source of instinctive energy; its impulses, which seek satisfaction in accordance with the pleasure principle are modified by the EGO and SUPEREGO before they are given overt expresssion; a primal urge. **Syn.** SUBJECTIVE MIND, UNCONSCIOUS MIND, SUBCONSCIOUS MIND. [**cf.** PRIMARY PERCEPTION, INSTINCT]

IDA—1. (Eastern) one of two ethereal nerve canals; runs along the left side of the spinal column, crossing at each chakra; feminine-negative in nature; contributes energy to the nervous systems and the plexus that are at the base of the invisible chakras; its right side companion is the PENGALA. [**cf.** CHAKRAS, KUNDALINI, SUSHUMNA] 2. (Trans-Himalayan) the sharps and flats of *F* in the scale of human nature. [**cf.** SOUNDS-WITH-POWER]

IDDHI or IDDHIS—(Buddhism) see PSYCHIC ENERGY.

IDEA CONSTRUCTION—(Seth) "man projects ideas into an object so he can deal with it and know just where he has progressed in this world by these objects and experiences."

IDEA PATTERNS—a collection of thought patterns in the subconscious mind of the masses with one central ideal; this gives massive energy to a pattern field which can be perceived by psychics as an apparition, etc., e.g., fairies seen dancing in the forest. [**cf.** GHOST, ARCHETYPES]

IDEALISM—that which is comfortable to one is the real material world; the real depends upon one's belief system. [**cf.** REALITY]

IDEAS—all plans, conceptions, forms, shapes, sizes, notions, suggestions, etc., were created with creation; start in Totality and flow thoughout creation; flow through mankind as human intent, generating emotion and imagination which activates interior patterns; these interior patterns motivate force of action exteriorizing the interior events; (Seth) "an event whether physically materialized or not"; (Plato) idea is reality; the invisible pattern behind all tangible events in the physical world. [**cf.** LAW OF THOUGHT and LAW OF SUGGESTION Appendix 7]

IDEATION—an association of the various impressions had by the mind both internally and externally and then arranged in a new order. [**cf.** THOUGHTS, THINGS]

IDENTIFICATION—the attempt to be like a parent produces similar traits bringing massive similarities and slows down the process of evolution. **Syn.** DRAMATIZATION. [**cf.** FUTURISTS, FLOW, HUMAN POTENTIAL MOVEMENT]

IDENTITY—(Seth) personality accumulated from action within action, and unfolding action upon itself, conscious of itself, using earth plane experiences, from the many incarnations. **Syn.** PERSONALITY. [**cf.** CEREBROSPINAL NERVOUS SYSTEM, FREE WILL]

IDENTITY THEORY—theory: mental and physical brain processes are one and the same thing, that is, they are identical to each other; empirical possibility and a scientific proposition which cannot be ruled out on logical grounds alone.

IDEO—prefix meaning "idea."

IDEOELASTICITY—takes its shape from the mind; used to express transfiguration and materialization; see ECTOPLASM. [**cf.** MATERIALIZATION]

IDEOGRAM—an ancient way of sacred writing using symbol or hieroglyph to represent a direct idea or object. **Syn.** CYPHER CHARACTERS. [**cf.** SYMBOLISM]

IDEOGRAPH—a written symbol that represents a direct object or idea, as opposed to a particular word or speech sound. **Syn.** LOGO.

IDEOMORPH—(seance materialization) melted parafin or another substance which is used for the imprint of materialized hands in the seance room; this was done to prove the materialized person's identity; see PSYCHIC MOLD, PSYCHIC IMPRINT. [**cf.** SEANCE, MATERIALIZATION, BLACKED-OUT ROOM, ECTOPLASM]

IDEOMOTOR ACTION—(hypnosis) to condition the conscious and subconscious minds that one will go into a hypnotic state every time there is a special body movement; meant to shorten the induction period; accomplished through practice of the stimulus; e.g., every time I count on my fingers silently I will reach a deep state of hypnosis. [**cf.** SELF-HYPNOTHERAPY, MEDIUM STATE OF HYPNOSIS]

IDEOMOTOR RESPONSE—(hypnosis) to establish a body reaction while in a hypnotic state, that will answer a yes and no question; belief: the subconscious mind knows the answer and will give a truthful replay (and not repress experiences that the conscious mind may repress); used with UFO contactees to find the blank spots in their memory, regression of one's past lives, and to find the cause of an illness; e.g., designate one finger to move for *yes* and one finger for *no*. **Syn.** FINGER METHOD RESPONSE. [**cf.** HYPNOTHERAPY, PAST LIVES THEORY, REGRESSION]

IDEOMOTOR THEORY—(Russia) to make an individual have slight unconscious muscle movements in facial expressions, changes in breathing and other bodily movements, by intensification and consolidation of that particular thought. [**cf.** CONCENTRATION, FOCAL POINT.]

IDOIHO—(Tahiti) see TOTALITY.

IEMANJA—(Brazil) a nature spirit considered goddess of the sea and mother of all the Yoruba spirits. [**cf.** NYMPHS, FAIRIES]

IFREET—(Koran) a nature spirit living in fire and using fire to function; capable of assuming a human form to bring good or evil to humans; belonging to the jinn family.

IGNIS FATUUS—see FOOLISH FIRE.

IKRA—The International Kirlian Research Association; purpose: for the advancement of multidisiplinary research in ELECTROPHOTOGRAPHY, ELECTROPHYSIOLOGY, BIOLOGICAL FIELDS, photobiology and photochemistry as applied in the biomedical, engineering and physical sciences.

ILL-WISHING—to use mind concentration and magic rituals and principles to bring misfortune to another; results in such evil as: bruises on the victim's body, anxiety and distress within the victim's mind for no cause, an odor of rotting flesh or another foul smell exuding from the victim's body, and outbreaks of fire in the victim's home. **Syn.** HEX. [**cf.** CURSE, PSYCHIC ATTACK, BEWITCHING, IMITATIVE MAGIC, PSYCHIC TRANSFER]

ILLITERATE MEDIUM—one who cannot read or write, but allows an etheric world intelligence to intervene and speak or write through her or him; knowledge that is psychically perceived surpasses the intellect of the masses as if this is what the illiterate was incarnated for. [**cf.** PLANETARY HELPERS, TRANSFORMATION]

ILLNESS—(esoteric, holistic health) a neutral energy field in motion, occuring in various vibrational frequencies which brings physical or mental pain, abnormal behavior, abnormal appearance, or incapacitation of normal body functions; manifested by one's self for one's personal growth needs (karmic or present); 1. an energy field in varying degrees that appears to cause annoyance or displeasure to the patient; affects organs and parts of the body in conjunction with one's present lifestyle, environment, associates, and one's attitude toward this lifestyle; a body activity one needs or desires, consciously, subconsciously, or karmically; e.g., an illness to some may make it easier to interact with others; 2. opposite of WELLNESS; caused by disagreement between the conscious mind and soul-mind over a period of time; this makes an imbalance in the physical chemistry; caused by one's own belief system and activity in relation to that belief system; making it a reality; 3. a short circuit in the body's energy terminals caused by an emotional psychological event that went unresolved or incorrectly interpreted at the time it happened; the mind suppressed it (into the body) and added to it when similar experiences occurred that the mind did not want to feel; happens consciously or unconsciously; this eventually blows a fuse in the nerve circuit and body chemistry falters; (see BLOCKS); 4. illness is a constructed challenge leading one towards greater fulfillment; a method of fulfilling a function as a purposeful activity in one's evolvement; 5. a sanctuary for fear or anxiety and a refuge for hurts. (Inconcl.) **Syn.** SICKNESS, DISEASE. [**cf.** CURATIVE EDUCATION, HOLISTIC HEALTH, ALTERNATIVES, EMOTIONS, THOUGHTS, ACUPRESSURE]

ILLUMINATI—1. see PSYCHIC: 2. one who has been enlightened.

ILLUMINATION—(esoteric) 1. as close to perfection, as the alignment of the three minds, conscious, subconscious, and superconscious can come to absorb and enjoy the ultimate wholeness; 2. when the conscious and subconscious minds think equally or are synchronized there is illumination; the CONSCIOUS MIND is the pupil of the SUBCONSCIOUS MIND, the tutor.

ILLUMINATORS—see GUIDE and ETHERIC WORLD INTELLIGENCES.

ILLUMINED.—(esoteric) the realization that within one is a spark of divinity or perfectness that can be fed and made to unfold for one's own good; when one begins to see the light (light pertains to SPIR-

303

ITUALITY); the enlightenment of the mind which includes knowledge, experience, and understanding.

ILLUMINED MIND—see SOUL-MIND.

ILLUMINOUSITY—(Sufi) when there is no end to being illuminous; the individual keeps becoming more and more ILLUMINED until one reaches TOTALITY.

ILLUSION—1. (laboratory) an erroneous interpretation of the normal five senses data, or perception of the psychic sense data, usually brought on by emotion. (Inconcl.) 2. (Seth) solidified vitality capable of changing its shape; 3. some disciplines believe mankind's reality of earth and the third dimension is an illusion, the real being the astral world. [**cf.** MAYA, DESIRE]

IMAGE—1. (psychic information) person, object or scene that is perceived clairvoyantly "within" the mind or "outside" the mind (in the air); person, object or scene remains static or has movement of patterns; represents itself as the real physical person, object or event, or represents a kind of parallelism; psychic may silently ask, "Is this symbol or image?," e.g., the vision is a tall straight woman: (image interpretation) a tall straight woman, (symbol interpretation) a female who is stern, strong, dominant and who towers over others; 2. (Democritus) particles in the etheric world representing the mental activities and emotions of an entity; capable of being perceived clairvoyantly by another human being. [**cf.** SUBJECTIVE CLAIRVOYANCE, PSYCHIC INFORMATION, SYMBOLISM]

IMAGE MAGIC—see IMITATIVE MAGIC.

IMAGED MEMORIES—(reincarnation) to perceive clairvoyantly a scene that is accompanied by feelings of familiarity, that are later learned to be scenes from one's own past; individual describes the area with accuracy, and sometimes gives the names of people and buildings inhabiting it; visions flash back unexpectedly, unintentionally, or are brought about by regression techniques. [**cf.** DÉJÀ VU, BEHAVIORAL MEMORIES, REINCARNATION]

IMAGERY—1. a mind exercise to strengthen the imagination faculty; uncontrolled INNER-MIND PICTURES of images, figures, or scenes, deliberately started by the student, induced by music or staring at an abstract picture; the mind then wanders along with the music or picture, flowing freely with any inner-mind pictures, impressions, or sounds that come into it; this exercise helps one to relate to PSYCHIC INFORMATION perceived in symbol form; does not manifest in future behavior as other thoughts do. **Syn.** MIND-WANDERING. 2. to ask one's higher mind a question while in a relaxed state of consciousness; picture that enters the mind is believed to be inner guidance for that person by analyzing its meaning; used sometimes as a diagnostic tool and as an aid to one's problems; 3. (biofeedback training) term used to mean psychic information. [**cf.** Appendix 4 differentiates from FANTASY, DAYDREAMING and IMAGERY]

IMAGES MUNDO—image of the universe: a microcosm. [**cf.** MACROCOSM, MICROCOSM]

IMAGINARY GHOST—an energy field that is brought into being by the sitters of a psychic circle who meet regularly; sitters decide upon a name, make up personal history for it, concentrate on it and encourage the name to perform physical phenomena; eventually, the energy field created by the unity, desire, and persistence of the group will perform for them; e.g., tip a table or rap on the wall, and bring psychic information; it may be that an etheric world intelligence steps in to fill the desires of the sitters. [**cf.** PHILLIP GROUP, SITTERS, RAPS]

IMAGINARY SPIRIT—sufficient concentrated thought in a seance or PSYCHIC DEVELOPMENT CIRCLE to conjure up an entity from the etheric world which would be the control of the circle, substituting for the absent main medium. [**cf.** PHYSICAL MANIFESTATIONS/MISCELLANEOUS]

IMAGINATION—1. a concentrated form of mental energy; ability of the brain to produce new mental concepts, ideas, forms, shapes, and symbols from what appears to be nowhere; ideas are felt by the individual but are not actually present to the senses; begins with an innate desire of the individual and the brain then takes out of storage from that individual's belief system, memories of past sights, sounds, and feelings, to formulate new sights, sounds, beliefs and ideas; from this imagination faculty springs forth new manifestations, and goals become reality. (Inconcl.) [**cf.** LAW OF IMAGINATION Appendix 7] 2. (magic), to manifest new activity by the use of one's imagination faculty, one's will, and a magic ritual; used to reproduce images and activity through suggestion and images that associate with objects and activities which are stored in the memory of the magician; this mind concentration and simulation then directs the will; imagination must be coequal with the will in order to reproduce the rituals properly; without the will, the force created by the mind will hang in the ethers until it is directed by the will; imagination creates the image or force and the will directs it. [cf. ASSOCIATED MAGIC, THOUGHTS ARE THINGS] 3. (Carl Jung) visual forms having the character of archetypal images. [cf. CREATION, CO-CREATOR, SYMBOLS]

IMAGINATIVE FREEDOM—to not use that part of nature which is perceived by the physical senses but to rely on one's psychic senses when the conscious mind is temporarily suspended and INTUITION flows freely; using art to express true feeling. **Syn.** INSPIRATIONAL THOUGHT, PURE PSYCHIC AUTO-MATISM, SURREALISM. [cf. INSPIRATIONAL PAINT-ING, PSYCHIC ARTIST, CLAIRSENTIENCE]

IMAGINATIVE VISION—(Roman Catholic) a pure-ly mental image coming into the mind, very vivid in detail, believed to be induced by the action of God. **Syn.** DIVINE INTERVENTION. [cf. ALPHA STATE OF CONSCIOUSNESS. MENTAL PSYCHIC PROCESSES Appendix 2]

IMAGINE—see VISUALIZATION.

IMAGING FACULTY—located in the nerve center between the eyes or in the PINEAL GLAND where ideas come directly from Totality; the input is to be distributed in the consciousness perception, and is referred to as non-thoughts or PSYCHIC INFORMA-TION. **Syn.** THIRD-EYE. [cf. Appendix 2 MENTAL PSYCHIC PROCESSES]

IMITATIVE MAGIC—theory: by using psychic skills the real can be influenced through the simulated, "the symbol of a thing is the thing"; through traditional occult rituals, mind control, and using a thing of a similar sensation, color, odor, shape, or function to represent that which the psychic desires to happen; e.g., hanging a fish on a tree to bring a good catch of fish; using a doll stuck with pins to make a person receive pain (in hexing); healing a person by sending healing energy to a photograph of that sick person, the photo having been taken when the person was very healthy. **Syn.** MIMICRY, IMAGE MAGIC. [cf. PSYCHIC ATTACK, SYMBOLISM, LAW OF CONTAGION and LAW OF SIMILARITY Appendix 7]

IMMATERIAL DIMENSIONS—see ETHERIC WORLD.

IMMATERIAL FORCE—see VITAL LIFE FORCE.

IMMOBILITY—motion too fast to be measured; past, present, future simultaneously; heaven-earth-hell at one time. [cf. MULTIDIMENSIONAL]

IMMORTAL DRAUGHT—to transmute oneself through internal alchemy to a higher level than the physical body. (Inconcl.) **Syn.** GREAT AWAKEN-ING, SUPREME BLISS. [cf. TRANSMUTATION, PURI-FIED BODY, ALCHEMIST]

IMMORTAL SOUL—see SOUL-MIND.

IMMORTALITY—a continuous existence of being; (Vedic) beyond time, space and causation. [cf. REINCARNATION, ETHERIC WORLD, SURVIVALISTS]

IMMOTIVE CONSCIOUSNESS—(astral projec-tion) an astral projection stopped due to fear; the astral body projects to the horizontal position, lowers itself to the standing position, becomes rigid, unable to release itself from the cataleptic state and withdraws into the physical body without taking the trip. [cf. REPERCUSSION, IN-THE-RANGE-OF-CORD-ACTIVITY]

IMMUNITY TO FIRE—see FIRE IMMUNITY.

IMMUNOBIOLOGY—the science of aging, with emphasis on the possibility of the body's immunity to it. [cf. WELLNESS, HOLISTIC HEALTH]

IMMUTABILITY—to psychically prepare one's body so that after death the body will preserve itself; when the body is exhumed years later it shows no sign of decay, odor, discoloration, etc. **Syn.** INCOR-RUPTIBLE BODY. [cf. SEVEN-SIDED VAULT, SAINT, MASTER]

IMMUTABLE LIGHT—(Eastern) the oneness of all-there-is; total ultimate consciousness blending into the whole. **Syn.** CLEAR LIGHT OF PURE REALITY, VOID, CHRIST CONSCIOUSNESS. [cf. TOTALITY]

IMMUTABLE ONE—(Buddhism) a figurine of a divine individual with the right hand pointing down toward the earth; emblematic of inward direction or INTUITION. [cf. PALM DOWN, IMITA-TIVE MAGIC]

IMP—1. a nature spirit who does more harm than good to the earthling; 2. an etheric world intelli-gence working psychically with a medium, usually connected with witches; sometimes takes the form of an animal. [cf. DENSITY, EARTHBOUND ENTITY]

IMPERATOR—see DOCTOR TEACHER, CONTROL, GUIDE.

IMPERATOR BAND—a group of intelligences from the invisible world or a higher plane than most etheric help, who communicate with individuals in development circles, bringing knowledge for mankind. **Syn.** MASTERS. [**cf.** WHITE BROTHERHOOD]

IMPERFECT SPIRITISTS—mediums who take advantage of physical manifestations of psychism from the etheric world for personal enjoyment, but who never absorb etheric world teachings. [**cf.** MEDIUMSHIP]

IMPERISHABLE LIGHT—a primal energy vibrating throughout all the universes, showing illumination and radiance beyond description, when perceived clairvoyantly. **Syn.** DIVINE BEING, GREAT WHITE LIGHT. [**cf.** TOTALITY]

IMPERISHABLE ONES—angels represented as the circumpolar stars in the west, that never set. [**cf.** ANGEL HIERARCHY]

IMPERSONATION—to allow an etheric world intelligence to use one's body in part or in full to perform physical phenomena; medium preprograms the length of time and what is to transpire while her or his body is being occupied; medium trusts the intelligence (guide) to use good judgment in: 1. case of danger from outside stimuli; 2. programming other intelligences who are needed for the feats; 3.preventing inferior entities from slipping in any psychic openings; 4. only doing that which balances with the medium's chemistry to maintain his or her health; whether body entry is in part or in full, the medium takes on the characteristics and mannersims of the guide, during the allotted time; feats are performed that would be impossible for an individual to do by her or himself; some types require a seance setting and some are performed individually; phenomenon is meant to benefit the masses; two kinds: PARTIAL ANESTHESIA and COMPLETE IMPERSONATION; (do not confuse with POSSESSION or TRANSFIGURATION). [**cf.** LEVITATION, ETHERIC SURGERY, DESIRED-CONTROL]

IMPRESSIBLE MEDIUM—one who receives psychic information throughout his or her body; occurs in different areas bringing varying sensations; information is given by one's guide and can be interpreted into useful information; e.g., the body feeling heavy may mean to stop what one is doing; a twitching of eyes may mean to examine the situation very carefully. [**cf.** INSPIRED MEDIUM, CALLED PERSON, CHANNEL, BODY-FEELINGS]

IMPRESSION—(esoteric) a fourth dimensional technology that is innate in all human beings, functioning as a brain awareness; brain activity that was not brought about by a thinking process, but yet it directs an individual to speak, act, or rethink purposely; parallel to dreamstuff, inasmuch as one knows what the person in the dream is saying, but the words per se are not spoken; 1. happens if one reaches an ALPHA STATE OF CONSCIOUSNESS during one's daily affairs; upon analysis one finds the mindstuff illogical or beyond one's normal ability to know; if directions are followed or ideas rationalized, the mindstuff is for the highest good of all concerned; theories: (a) enters from the subconscious mind through the instinct channel; (b) enters from the superconscious mind as need-determined; (c) carefully placed in the mind by an etheric world intelligence; 2. normal brain activity when one opens one's psychic doors for answers after meditating; comes from the subconscious mind or from one's guide; 3. (psi tasks) message sent to another in an ESP experiment. [**cf.** CLAIRSENTIENCE, INSPIRATIONAL THOUGHT, PSI TASKS]

IMPRINT—coined by E. Arthur Winkler; the interpretation of an event or verbal remark received at the subconscious level of the mind; has a direct influence on an individual's health; an emotionally disturbing event occurs or an unkind remark is heard and if improperly interpreted, it will be processed to the centers of one's being incorrectly; similar experiences are then repressed to escape the original emotional pain; eventually these interpretations are (imprints) expressed through the body as a disease; imprints of properly interpreted events and remarks preserve the harmony of the body and result in good health. [**cf.** LAW OF ILLNESS Appendix 7, BLOCKS Appendix 5, REGRESSION]

IMPURE SPIRITS—earthbound etheric world entities who hover very close to the earth plane because of their materialistic desires; this makes it easy for them to influence an EARTHLING by clinging to the earthling's body to experience earthly sensations again; usually done with evil or ignorant intentions. [**cf.** HAUNTING, GHOSTS]

IN PROTECTION—to instigate mental thoughts, visualize a picture, or speak words that are positive, protective, and that give one a feeling of security; it can be used as a shield that negation will bounce off, can be used as energy for one's guides to manipulate for the thinker's highest good; e. g., to say the cloak of insulation or to picture one's self in a sphere of gold light; to be used in crowds, in the automobile, before opening one's psychic doors, or before any event if one feels the need. [**cf.** CLOAK OF INSULATION, THOUGHT ENERGY]

IN QUIETUDE—see MEDITATION.

IN STREAM—a shift to a more expanded awareness where one can channel information or receive answers psychically; the focus of the psychic must be kept on the theme of the speaking or writing; the material will flow as long as the psychic is *in stream*; ; questions, whispering, etc., break this stream. [**cf.** INSPIRATIONAL THOUGHT]

IN THE BODY PENT—an entity in an earthly existence; a human being.

IN THE MOOD—(radiesthesia) the actual time during which the pendulum or dowsing rod is responding correctly; one's radiesthetic sense is activated by: an ALPHA STATE OF CONSCIOUSNESS, an uncluttered and neutral mind, and faith in one's ability. [**cf.** RADIONICS, RADIESTHESIA, GYRATE]

IN THIS WORK—an expression used frequently by the psychic when referring to PSYCHISM.

IN TRANSITION —(Rosicrucian) pertains to an individual living in the etheric world; life in between earth lives. [**cf.** SOUL JURY, DISCARNATE, MADE THE TRANSITION]

IN VISION—1. (Emanuel Swedenborg) to see a scene, a place, or people in another vibrational frequency while walking down the street; happens spontaneously or can be willed; theory: another world penetrates ours at a frequency which mankind cannot normally perceive. [**cf.** OBJECTIVE CLAIRVOYANCE] 2. to see into the astral plane while in a BETA STATE OF CONSCIOUSNESS (normal awareness); rare but possible. [**cf.** CLAIRVOYANCE, EYES OF INSTINCT]

IN-DEPTH SPIRIT READING—personal psychic information brought through a medium in VOICE TRANCE. [**cf.** PHYSICAL PSYCHISM, DEPENDENT VOICE]

IN-THE-RANGE-OF-CORD-ACTIVITY—(astral projection) refers to a projection when the SILVER CORD is extended to approximately fifteen feet or less; cord seems to take dissimilar characteristics; i.e., more thickness in size and more elasticity in its pull; at this short distance, projectionist finds it more difficult to keep his or her astral body stable, enjoys it less and the possibility of snapping his or her repercussion upon return is stronger. (Inconcl.) [**cf.** OUT-OF-RANGE-OF-CORD-ACTIVITY]

INANIMATE COGNITION—1. to use an object as the querant as in psychometry and penduluming which brings forth psychic information regarding the object only; 2. psychically perceived information of the moment regarding an inanimate, nonemotional object, without touching, seeing, or hearing the object; e.g., in the laboratory, knowing which zener card is next in the deck. [**cf.** COGNITION, PSYCHOMETRY, ESP]

INANIMATE ENTITIES—see ELEMENTAL.

INANIMATE POLES—(radiesthesia) theory: each inanimate object, form, and color has its own magnetic poles in accordance with the earth's magnetism; this causes the pendulum to react differently when held over different objects; operator attunes to the color, size, shape, and density of the object and this is related back to them by the swing of the pendulum in size, speed, and direction. [**cf.** RADIESTHESIA, PENDULUM POWER, OSCILLATION]

INANIMATE THINGS—(esoteric) a manifestation of matter imbued with an intelligence and life of a lesser nature than mankind, animals, plants, and minerals; their growth and change in evolution is not very noticeable, such as in tables, cars, houses, etc. [**cf.** LAW OF PERSONIFICATION Appendix 7]

INCAL—the supreme God in Atlantean days.

INCANTATION—(Latin *canatare*, "to sing") 1. to sing and chant formulaic words, phrases or sounds to special rhythm and tonation, which are composed to stir and build psychic energy for manipulation; energy obeys the thought and intent for which it was built; chanting has to be repeated daily to keep energy strong; (a) (medieval) used to keep another person under one's spell (usually for selfish reasons); (b) (current) used for healing another person, distance no barrier; 2. formulaic phrases that have the vibrational frequency to summon etheric world intelligences for guidance and counsel; 3. to chant or sing certain secret sacred words and tones that were composed to join the two brain hemispheres; helps psychic information to flow more easily, and helps send healing energies to others. (Inconcl.) [**cf.** SOUNDS-WITH-POWER Appendix 2]

307

INCARNAL—1. pertains to an innate part of a human being that thinks and feels spiritual and religious; 2. description of the soul-mind that lives a continuous life.

INCARNATION—(Latin *in carne*, "in flesh; to make flesh") pertains to a life spent in physical flesh living on the earth; theory: humans go through a repetitious pattern of living in the etheric world and living on the earth many times. Usage: "In my last incarnation I was a woodcutter with nine children." [**cf.** REINCARNATION, TRANSMIGRATION OF SOULS]

INCARNATIONAL EXCHANGE—(Tibet) a soul-mind from the etheric world enters the body of a grown earthling, to use it until it wears out; the earthling's soul-mind slips into the etheric world; exchange is agreeable to both parties; the new soul-mind will finish the highlights of the karma of its new body, and then give the new body an entirely new personality. (Inconcl.) **Syn.** WALK-IN. [**cf.** REINCARNATION, RIPE KARMA, ACCUMULATED KARMA]

INCENDIUM AMORIS—a high fever, or heated oozing blood, caused by a hysterical trance; brought about by an extreme subconscious love for a deity. **Syn.** FLAMES OF DIVINE LOVE. [**cf.** HYSTERIA, STIGMATA, LAW OF ACTIVITY Appendix 7]

INCENSE—an odoriferous wood or herb reduced to a fine powder, pressed into shapes to be burned; 1. disintegrates negative vibrations in the area where burned; 2. heightens the consciousness of the psychic; 3. used as a symbol of purification or its opposite, sacrifice; 4. used in conjunction with the dead; it is felt the soul-mind will ascend to heaven upon a cloud of incense-smoke; 5. has an aroma that will bring etheric world helpers; 6. chases away the earthbound soul-minds; 7. the patterns of the smoke have a soothing effect for some. [**cf.** FRANKINCENSE, ALL SOUL'S DAY]

INCLINE EFFECT—(laboratory) ability to perceive better psychic information or hit the target more frequently as the tests progress, or through a progression of tests made at the same time. [**cf.** PSI TASKS, ESP]

INCOMBUSTIBILITY PHENOMENA—see FIRE IMMUNITY.

INCOMPLETE PROJECTION—(astral projection) a state in which the astral body never becomes free from ASTRAL CATALEPSY, remaining in the horizontal position over the physical body; is interiorized before it is liberated. [**cf.** ASTRAL PROJECTION, IN-THE-RANGE-OF-CORD-ACTIVITY]

INCORPORATION—see POSSESSION.

INCORRECT MEDIUMS—those who allow the etheric world to intervene, but the psychic information brought forth has a diffused style and is incorrect and repetitious. [**cf.** CLOAK OF INSULATION, GUIDE, CONTROL]

INCORRUPTIBILITY—(Yoga) to preserve one's own body after death; when the body is exhumed, it is in perfect condition due to the excellent mind control of the person who left the body which enabled them to preserve it; there is no odor, discoloration, or decay; accomplished by great saints, masters, etc. **Syn.** IMMUTABILITY. [**cf.** ALCHEMIST, BODY CONTROL]

INCUBATION DREAMING—1. (Egypt, Greece, Rome; 3000 B.C.) a traditional method used to deliberately induce the nature of a dream where one spent the night in a sacred temple designed for dream incubation; people came to the temple for answers to problems, and to be healed physically; the problem was posed, or the healing need requested, before retiring; priest interpreted the meaning of the dream in the morning; methods of stimulating the dream: (a) to rub the body with special oils; (b) to sleep in the skin of a freshly killed animal; (c) to burn incense; 2. indeliberate dreaming in which an inventor or artist receives his or her answer to their daytime work in symbol form, or clearly and vividly in an image form, to be used as presented in the dream; the sleep state of mind allows answers to come to problems that do not flow during conscious thinking, but which surface when the conscious mind is passive; 3. to elicit specific dreams at will; one makes a request for an answer to a problem, or for personal guidance, before falling off to sleep; the dream will bring an answer, usually in symbolic form. [**cf.** INCUBATION PHRASE, LANDMARK IMAGERY, LUCID DREAMING, RELEASE-TYPE DREAMS]

INCUBATION PHRASE—(dreams) a one-line sentence that sums up and expresses one's clearest presentation of the question one wants answered in the dream. [**cf.** INCUBATION DREAMING, VISITATION DREAM]

INCUBUS—an etheric world male entity capable of

having sexual intercourse with a person in one of three ways: by remaining invisible, by entering in a dream, or by assuming a human form for that time. **Syn.** SPIRIT LOVER. [**cf.** SUCCUBUS]

INDEPENDENT BELLS—bells that ring without mechanical means, human intervention, or without a medium or psychic in the vicinity to cause the action; e.g., the pealing bells that rang for fifty-three days without mundane means. [**cf.** PERCUSSION]

INDEPENDENT ETHERIC WRITING—to supply psychic energy (ECTOPLASM) to an etheric world intelligence so they can use it to write messages on paper without using any parts of the medium's physical body; 1. (seance) medium places writing tools close to their body and then puts her or himself in a trance state of consciousness; ectoplasm is used to raise the pencil and the pencil swiftly writes a useful message on the paper; messages are for the sitters personally or for publication; 2. (personal) medium places the tools close to their bed; during the night, the intelligence lifts the pencil and writes a message without awakening the sleeping medium. [**cf.** BASKET DRAWINGS, SLATE WRITING, PRECIPITATION]

INDEPENDENT SPIRIT—see GUIDE and CONTROL.

INDEPENDENT VOICE—(seance) to allow an etheric world intelligence to use one's ectoplasm to build a temporary, invisible VOICE BOX in the seance room to amplify utterances and chants from the etheric world intelligences; voice box is built from the ECTOPLASM that emanates from the medium in charge and the sitters; voice box hovers over the heads of the group, and is clairvoyantly visible at times; box must be rebuilt each session, which requires the same sitters to attend repeatedly; etheric world intelligences audibly bring forth information and knowledge of advanced science which must be studied by the group for their understanding and is then intended to be published for the masses; it is "independent" of the medium's vocal cords; (do not confuse with TRUMPET skill in which the trumpet is a tangible amplifier). **Syn.** DIRECT VOICE. [**cf.** SEANCE, TRUMPET, DEPENDENT VOICE]

INDEX—(radiesthesia) the signal or specific movement of the pendulum or dowsing rods that indicates an answer to the operator's question; operator understands how to interpret the direc-tion, speed, size, number of swings or pulling sensations of this tool beforehand; operator asks the question and when he or she has the answer in their body, this tool which is in tune with the body amplifies the answer by a favorable or unfavorable INDEX or movement. [**cf.** WITNESS, COURTESY, PENDULUMIST, DOWSING]

INDIAN GUIDE—one of the five etheric world intelligences in the inner band of the individual; known in either gender; believed to come into the individual's band at birth, and if events go as anticipated, he or she stays until death; guide encourages respect and love for nature; their other function is to protect one from accidents if the individual's karma permits, if called upon for help, and if the individual has enough positive thought substance to use for the prevention. **Syn.** PROTECTOR. [**cf.** INNER BAND, OUTER BAND, GUIDE]

INDIAN MEDICINE WHEEL—(Native American) any idea, person or object which comes into one's path becomes a medicine wheel for that person; this object or person acts as a mirror which reflects one's objectives in life and can be psychoanalyzed for that individual; the universe is a mirror of people, and each person is a mirror to every other person. [**cf.** MANTIC ART, BODY READING]

INDIAN PIPE—(Native American, Chippewa) a pipe that is smoked to accomplish specific ends more frequently than it is smoked for pleasure; recognized as an altar and the herbs placed in it are offered as a blessing, e.g., one prayer Rolling Thunder makes when he smokes his pipe, "these herbs are offered for all the earth and mental beings." [**cf.** AFFIRMATION, WORDS-WITH-POWER]

INDIAN WHEEL OF THE LAW—see PROPHECY.

INDIFFERENT MEDIUM—a person with the ability to communicate with the etheric world intelligences, but this fact has no influence on his or her everyday life; individual takes the mediumistic sessions in stride acting as if it were normal activity. [**cf.** MEDIUMSHIP, VOICE TRANCE]

INDIGO—color of intuition; borderland where wisdom and saintliness are attained through meditation; a meeting ground for all colors; also indicates dignity and spiritual aspirations. [**cf.** COLOR, VIOLET]

INDIRECT PSYCHOGRAPHY—to receive psychic information from an etheric world intelligence by using a tool similar to a planchette; the medium has only to lightly touch the movable tripod and the intelligence spells out the message; see PLANCH-ETTE. [cf. BASKETS, CORBEILLE-TOUPIE, CORBEILLE-A-BEC, OUIJA BOARD]

INDIVIDUAL CELLULAR CONSCIOUSNESS—(eso-teric) three levels of awareness within the mech-anism of each cell: 1. an innate intelligence present in all living organisms, that "knows its function"; each cell is aware of its job as an individual cell; 2. a record of what the cell experienced when it functioned as one of a group, making an organ, and all the parts of living organisms it ever contributed to; 3. an inner thread of total intelligence coming from each atom within the cell that keeps moti-vating it to better itself. (Inconcl.) [cf. INDIVIDUAL CONSCIOUSNESS, INSTINCT CONSCIOUSNESS, PRIMAL PERCEPTION]

INDIVIDUAL CONSCIOUSNESS—a deceptive in-dividuality tied to a body of life and death; an ILLUSION; 2. a fragment of a HOLOGRAM contained in the whole; a miniature version of the whole; indestructible and timeless; 3. that which builds personality out of experiences on the various planes of existence; each person is a part of the one consciousness, functions as a separate distinct important entity, but also functions as if it were the whole consciousness. (Inconcl.) [cf. BRAIN THEORY, TOTALITY, TIME, INSTINCT CONSCIOUSNESS]

INDIVIDUAL METAMORPHOSIS—(ufology) theory of the UFO cults: by freeing oneself of all human emotions and earthly attachments, the body would be converted into a new vehicle that would resist disease and decay, giving the life force within the body eternal life. [cf. GLORIFIED, LIGHT BODY, SOUL-MIND]

INDIVIDUAL ORACLE—(Greece, Spain) see MEDIUM.

INDIVIDUALITY—(esoteric) the immortal soul-mind that contains the higher or DIVINE SPARK of Totality, the real person, the perfect seed within. **Syn.** MONAD, IMMORTAL EGO, SOUL-MIND, DIVINE EGO. [cf. EGO, MONAD, TOTALITY]

INDIVIDUALIZED CONDITIONED RESPONSE—a personalized ritual or distinct format which each psychic feels is helpful in reaching his or her level of consciousness wherein truthful and accurate psychic information is obtained; psychic repeats same method each time the etheric world is tuned

into, and eventually the body and mind go to that level with no hesitancy; e.g., to perform special breathing exercises before opening psychic doors; or to touch one's necklace while cloaking one's self; to turn clockwise three times close to a glass of water and a cut flower. [cf. MEDITATION, INCANTA-TION, WITHERSHINS]

INDIVIDUATION—(Carl Jung) "integrating the per-sonality so that the person becomes in the true sense an 'individual'; reconciliation of the opposites of human nature in a complete self, the archetype of unity." [cf. POLARITY, MONADOLOGY]

INDIVIDUATION PROCESS—a dream interpreta-tion method that requires the use of many dreams in a series, for proper interpretation. [cf. DREAMS Appendix 2]

INDUCED PHYSICAL MANIFESTATIONS—to move mundane matter by deep concentration and a strong will while in the conscious state of con-sciousness. **Syn.** PSYCHOKINESIS. [cf. TELEPOR-TATION-PK, MIND-OVER-MATTER]

INDUCTION—(hypnosis) a highly suggestible tech-nique used in the beginning of a hypnotherapy session which puts the subject into a hypnotic state of consciousness, in preparation for the prescrip-tion; takes from five minutes to a half hour, depending upon the hypnotizability of the subject; performed by voice guidance, a hypnodisc, or other methods. [cf. PRESCRIPTION, INDUCTION RELEASE]

INDUCTION PROFILE—(hypnosis) different methods that hypnotists try with their subjects before beginning the hypnotism session, to deter-mine the hypnotizability of the subject. [cf. EYE-ROLL TEST, EYE-LID FATIGUE]

INDUCTION RELEASE—to bring the hypnotized subject back to the waking state of consciousness by suggestions which are the opposite of the induc-tion; this encourages the conscious mind to get back in control of the mind and body. [cf. INDUCTION, HETEROHYPNOTHERAPY]

INDUCTIVE DIVINATION—teaching psychism to someone who is not a natural-born psychic. **Syn.** ENTECHINOS. [cf. MENTAL PSYCHIC PROCESSES]

INDUCTOPYREXIA—(ufology) a fever or sensation of heat felt by a UFO contactee; produced by exposure to the electromagnetic induction given off by the UFO vehicle in a close encounter. [cf. CLOSE-ENCOUNTERS-OF-THE-SECOND-KIND]

INDUCTOR—1. (psychometry) the article that is used for the psychometric reading because of its many imbedded vibrations; 2. (Russia) the sender in a mental telepathic experience. [**cf.** TELEPATHY, PSYCHOMETRY]

INDWELLING LIFE—see SOUL-MIND.

INEDIA—to survive without food. **Syn.** BREATHATERIAN. [**cf.** HOLISTIC HEALTH, CURATIVE EDUCATION, BREATHING]

INEFFABLE—an aspect of mental psychism which describes a direct feeling that cannot be imparted to others. [**cf.** MENTAL PSYCHIC PROCESSES Appendix 2]

INEFFECTIVE KARMA—(Buddhism) those experiences and thoughts from present and past incarnations that are accumulated, but fail to produce ripe karma because the necessary auxiliary causes fail to appear; (do not confuse with DELAYED KARMA or RESERVED KARMA). [**cf.** KARMA OF FULFILLMENT, RIPE KARMA]

INERGY—(1973) see VITAL LIFE FORCE.

INFERIOR SPIRITS—etheric world entities who still contain their terrestrial fluids, making it very easy for a psychic communication; entity does not have more intelligence than the psychic; this makes a purposeless experience and sometimes a dangerous one. [**cf.** ANTIGOD, ASTRAL SHELL, NARROW BAND TUNING, COAT OF PROTECTION]

INFERNAL ANIMALS—living organisms that take forms similar to creatures or animals; sometimes appearing grotesque; live in the section of the density called the INFERNO. [**cf.** DENSITY Appendix 2]

INFERNAL BEINGS—soul-minds living in the INFERNO section of the density, whose evolvement is very young. [**cf.** HELL, EARTHBOUND ENTITIES]

INFERNO—(Latin, "lying beneath") one of the levels of the density, or lower plane regions; serves as an opposite for one of the higher planes in the above regions. [**cf.** HELL, DENSITY, PURGATORY, DISEMBODIED SOUL]

INFINITE—that which cannot be measured or is never limited; the unmanifest; space in which the LAW OF OPPOSITES exists, dissolving into reality which in turn gives rise to these opposites. [**cf.** TOTALITY, POLARITY]

INFINITE CREATOR-CREATRIX—see TOP FORCE.

INFINITE MEMORY BANK—(esoteric) an invisible collection in an overall ethereal essence of all of mankind's knowledge and experiences from the past; records the present which makes the future; uses the past to make the present; utilizes the law: for every action, there is a reaction; memory bank is an active intelligent energy throughout all the universes. **Syn.** CREATIVE INTELLIGENCE, UNIVERSAL MIND, TOTALITY. [**cf.** COLLECTIVE UNCONSCIOUS, ASTRAL PICTURE GALLERY]

INFINITE VISION—(Japan) see THIRD-EYE.

INFINITESIMAL LIGHT DOTS—minute centers of energy floating in space (not the electron); act as transreceivers for the overall electrical system in the atmosphere; believed to have been there in the beginning; considered to be the "suns" for the molecular solar system. **Syn.** NODES. [**cf.** ELECTRODE, MATTER]

INFINITY—all of space, all the universes, and then more so; the INVISIBLE WORLD; the essence of God, TOTALITY.

INFLUENCED WRITING—see INSPIRATIONAL WRITING.

INFORMATION CAPACITY AT THE FIRST LEVEL—(clinical) a series of symbols stored from the past which are used to transmit the meaning of psychic information; not the knowledge itself. [**cf.** MENTAL PSYCHIC PROCESSES Appendix 2]

INFORMATION DISEASE—coined by Flo Conway and Jim Siegelman; (destructive-brainwashing cult) an alteration of a person's fundamental information processing capacities; a lasting alteration of human awareness at the most basic level of an individual's personality; a severe quick change in one's belief system and a severe decline in one's decision-making mechanism; disease does not destroy the sturdy biological machinery of the brain but it does greatly alter the complex organization of the brain; brought on by an unethical indoctrination using hypnosis and parapsychological skills for evil intent; personalities are transformed abnormally fast. (Inconcl.) [**cf.** ON-THE-SPOT-HYPNOSIS, BRAINWASHING, SNAPPING]

INFORMATION DOWSING METHOD—a technique used to carry on the searches after the oil or water has been located; used to get yes and no answers as to the rate of flow in gallons per minute, the distance down, or the depth of the vein, and other answers pertinent to the location. [cf. MAP DOWSING, FIELD DOWSING]

INFORMATION PROCESSING THEORY—(Laboratory) the subconscious mind is a system which processes information; it accepts input from the conscious mind, extracts information from this input in a sequence of specifiable states, and stores this information for future reference according to category; if necessary, it acts upon the stored information to assist the conscious mind to generate output. [cf. CONSCIOUSNESS, MENTAL MIND, SUBCONSCIOUS MIND]

INFRADIAN RHYTHMS—a pattern that repeats itself over a period longer than the twenty-four hour cycle, pertaining to one's biological functions. (Inconcl.) [cf. BIORHYTHM Appendix 5]

INFRARED—the electromagnetic radiation that is outside the color spectrum range of visibility on the lower end, next to the visible red. [cf. COLOR]

INFRARED FILM—film that has been sensitized to the electromagnetic radiation that occupies the spectrum before the color red; found to be workable for PSYCHIC PHOTOGRAPHY, showing ectoplasmic words, substance, or etheric world intelligences that were not in the normal vision at the time of the picture taking. (Inconcl.) [cf. SPIRIT PHOTOGRAPHY, KIRLIAN PHOTOGRAPHY, EXTRAS]

INFRARED NETWORK—the use of infrared lighting in the seance room to detect mundane interference or fraud; also makes it possible for the sitters to see what physical phenomena is taking place without interfering with the ectoplasm, which is destroyed by normal light. [cf. DARKNESS, ECTOPLASM, SEANCE]

INFRARED RADIATION MAN—one of the seven energy fields in the human aura. [cf. AURA, KIRLIAN EFFECT, INFRARED]

INGHAM REFLEX METHOD OF COMPRESSION MASSAGE—to use finger manipulation on one's feet to heal, diagnose, and keep one well; certain spots on the feet represent and are attached to various areas of the body; by a special creeping movement of the fingers and compression on the tender spots, the practitioner releases the flow of electrical energy in the nerve endings of the congested area; this hastens the cells to normalize and heal themselves. **Syn.** ZONE THERAPY, REFLEXOLOGY. [cf. MERIDIAN LINES]

INHERITED COMPLEXES—(Carl Jung) "primordial images or archetypes tending to mold all attempts to interpret the universe as a whole, incorporating mythology, religion, philosophy and science."

INITIANT—a beginner in the mystery schools or a similar discipline; one who desires the path of righteousness; name given to the student until he or she passes the first test. [cf. ADEPT, MASTER, RIGHT-HAND PATH]

INITIATE—one who desires to grow in consciousness and joins a chosen discipline, e.g., the mystery schools; one who desires to intensify the direction of their present growth, or to further their growth in a different direction; one who has passed their first test of initiation (from INITIANT to initiate). [cf. GURU DEV, GROUP SOUL]

INITIATION RITES—1. (Vedic) a sacred ceremony that symbolizes the beginnning of a spiritual life; 2. (Egypt, Assyrian) the process of experiencing one of the seven steps necessary for accomplishment in the mystery schools; these schools were open only to the special few whose character was worthy of this knowledge, determined by his or her akashic record; steps were designed to test one's mentality, and one's physical endurance; i.e., one must use their knowledge to keep themselves alive in very painful and frightening situations; 3. (Native American) a process of going through very difficult and painful mental and physical endurance tests before one is fully accepted into the community; these tests are oriented to eliminate one's present beliefs from past karma and past lifestyles spent in other lives; the initiate can then be reoriented to the beliefs of the community; e.g., techniques of gestures, chants, dances, isolation, and other procedures designed to react similarly to a hospital shock treatment; these startle the initiate out of habitual behavioral patterns; initiate then focuses on the present moment and the shaman of the tribe immediately inserts the beliefs he determined the initiate needs. [cf. TRADITIONAL INSTRUCTIONS, WILL OF THE CLAN, MYSTICISM]

INITIATOR—a person trained by Maharishi Mahesh Yogi to teach TRANSCENDENTAL MEDITATION. [cf. MEDITATION, ZEN MEDITATION, BRAIN SOOTING]

INITIATORY CEREMONIES—rituals patterned to work on the soul-mind of the candidate to further their knowledge, to change their thought patterns, to elevate them to a higher state of consciousness, or to a higher lifestyle. [cf. CERMONIAL MAGIC, INITIATORY RITES]

INITIATORY DEATH—(primitive Native American) a mystical ordeal whereby one goes through the death process by torture, such as having the flesh scraped off the bone; then by the power of thought and with the efforts of one's etheric world helpers, one has a change of beliefs, is healed, resurrected, and consecrated with new knowledge; one then earns the right to heal the sick, perform psychic skills, and assist others through the death process. **Sim.** INITIATORY SICKNESS. [cf. RESURRECTION, SHAMANSHIP]

INITIATORY DEATH-RITE—to control one's own process of dying by staying in the awareness of the CONSCIOUS MIND and using previously learned instructions. [cf. DEATH SCIENCE, DEATH ANGEL, SILVER CORD]

INITIATORY SICKNESS—(primitive Native American) a patterned procedure for an attitudinal change using severe illness, or a psychopathological state, brought on purposely by the ancestors of the clan; initiate is tortured by demons and experiences hell; this brings on a changed and understanding mind, whereby the initiate earns the ability to cure disease and perform psychic phenomena. [cf. RESURRECTION, SHAMANSHIP INSTRUCTIONS, CALL]

INMOST ONE—(capitalized) (Tibet) the highest rank in the lamasary of the priesthood order; the MASTER. [cf. INITIATE, THE RIGHT-HAND PATH]

INNATE RESPONSE—occurs in a very relaxed state of consciousness, preceded by meditation or a biofeedback training period; when the SUPERCONSCIOUS MIND is reached and psychic information and visions flow to the surface. **Syn.** INSPIRATIONAL THOUGHT. [cf. MENTAL PSYCHIC PROCESSES Appendix 2, CONCENTRATION, MEDITATION, PSYCHIC INFORMATION]

INNER-ADVISOR—the GUIDING PRINCIPLE, PSYCHE, or SOUL-MIND that dwells within each individual to guide that individual to PERFECTNESS; brings information when in an ALTERED STATE OF CONSCIOUSNESS if asked and sometimes unexpectedly if subconsciously asked; responsible for one's inner-dialogue. [cf. HUMAN BEING SPECIES SEED, BABBLER]

INNER-ATTENTION—the skill of knowing the nature of one's thoughts that ramble through the mind without conscious instigation; one must be alert to the stream of pell-mell thoughts that occupy one's thinking without one realizing it; takes much discipline to have one's inner thoughts under control; these thoughts have an effect on one's body and lifestyle just as purposely instigated thoughts do. [cf. INNER-DIALOGUE, COLLECTIVE UNCONSCIOUS, THOUGHTS ARE THINGS]

INNER-AURA—see ETHERIC DOUBLE.

INNER-AWARENESS—psychic information flowing through an ALPHA STATE OF CONSCIOUSNESS, with the conscious mind having sufficient awareness of it to relate the psychic information to the recipient. [cf. MIND-AWARENESS MOVEMENT, STREAM OF HALF-CONSCIOUSNESS]

INNER-BAND—a system of easy access to energy, protection, guidance, and knowledge for each EARTHLING during an entire incarnation; a chain of individual intelligences or graduated energies given to mankind to assist in the evolutionary process; 1. usually a group of five to seven soul-minds who have lived many lives on planet earth previously and have earned enough rank to permit them to help earthlings; each member is drawn to the earthling by a parallelism of abilities or interests and their function is to assist in these capacities; inner-band attunes themselves to the individual at birth and remains subservient until the death process is over; give aid only when called upon but one does not necessarily have to call them by name; to verbalize mentally or aloud that one desires help is enough invitation for them to enter and bring invisible help; 2. member uses the ergs of energy from the earthling's head to manipulate and alter physical activity and can only do this if earthling has positive energy around them; 3. allowed to read the AKASHIC RECORDS in order to know what is for the highest good of the earthling; 4. members work cooperatively as a team; help is given in every phase of one's life, such as, education, sports, recreation, eating, employment, sleeping, and personal relationships; 5. make themselves known in mediumship circles; come through all the various types of mental and physical mediumship; sometimes reveal their name; 6. mediumship circles in United States have established the names of the following invisible helpers in the inner-band: DOCTOR TEACHER or CELESTIAL GUARDIAN, ALCHEMIST or METAPHYSICAL PHYSICIAN,

HUMANITARIAN HEALER, PROTECTOR, and DOOR-KEEPER or JOY GUIDE. **Syn.** GUIDE, ANGEL, SPIRIT GUARDIAN.

INNER-BEING—see SOUL-MIND.

INNER-BOWL—an invisible area, shaped like a triangle, at the base of the spine where the KUNDALINI POWER begins; energy coiled like a serpent; see KANDA. [**cf.** SUSHUMNA, IDA, PENGALA]

INNER-BROTHERHOOD—(Ruth Montgomery) a closed or smaller group within each Brotherhood; these smaller groups have their own individual group-mind and a specific goal; they have been growing and evolving for untold thousands of years. (Inconcl.) [**cf.** GROUP SOUL, GROUP MIND, WHITE BROTHERHOOD, ANGELS]

INNER-CONSCIOUSNESS—see SUBCONSCIOUS MIND.

INNER-DIALOGUE—thoughts which flow fluidly through one's MENTAL ACTIVITY mechanism when one is not speaking of or actuating a deliberate plan; these thoughts go unnoticed more frequently than they are noticed; occupies time in between constructed thought, as if the minds (conscious and subconscious) must never stop producing; some-times, they appear to have no logical purpose; researchers found they affect one's behavior, lifestyle and body chemistry in the same manner as one's deliberate thoughts, due to their repetitious nature, and the emotion they carry; believed to surface from one's present and past incarnations, past and present cultural beliefs, feelings of self-worth and one's values; (do not confuse with NON-THOUGHTS or PSYCHIC IMPRESSIONS). (Inconcl.) **Syn.** SUBTALK, INNER-TALKING, BABBLER. [**cf.** CURATIVE EDUCATION, BRAIN, THOUGHTS, SELF-SUGGESTION, SUGGESTION, SELF-OBSERVATION THERAPY]

INNER-DIRECTED—to act upon one's hunches and intuition instead of being influenced by other people and outer visible circumstances; one must be attuned to one's body feelings and understand the difference between them and personal desires. [**cf.** HUNCHABILITY, GUT FEELING, BODY-FEELINGS, INTUITING]

INNER-EARTH CIVILIZATION—theory: intelligent beings live within the bowels of the earth; they carry on at their level of consciousness, whether it be above or below mankind's level; archeologists found underground cities connected by cave tunnels which could substantiate evidence of this theory. (Inconcl.) **Sim.** INTERIOR LANDS, HOLLOW EARTH. [**cf.** CONSCIOUSNESS, PLANES]

INNER-EGO—(Seth) "the unconscious mind; correlates the information that is perceived through invisible senses; carries the memory of each of one's past existences; looks into subjective dimensions that are literally infinite, and from these subjective dimensions all objective realities flow; all necessary information is given to one through these inner channels."

INNER-KINGDOMS—the many levels of energy or the many vibrational frequencies in the etheric world; each frequency or level has its own living inhabitants, functions, and principles. **Syn.** PLANES. [**cf.** ASTRAL PLANE, MENTAL PLANE, CAUSAL BODY]

INNER-LIGHT—pertains to the essence of the HUMAN BEING SPECIES SEED; theory: all things began of one perfect light; light is synonomous with intelligence; each seed contains this perfect light (INTELLIGENCE) and all things are a manifestation of light; each thing uses a percentage of the total light. [**cf.** MONADOLOGY, TOTALITY, WHITE LIGHT]

INNER-MIND ACTIVITY—includes both THOUGHTS and NON-THOUGHTS; any kind of sensation, constructed intelligence, unconscious intelligence, emotion, imagery, dreamstuff, or psychic information that originates in or passes through the brain organ. [**cf.** BRAIN, DREAMS, SUBCONSCIOUS MIND]

INNER-MIND PICTURES—to provoke thoughts about things that have not happened, using symbols such as images, scenes, events, colors and fragments; to use the imagination faculty without sufficient emotion to create thought-forms; controlled and uncontrolled; includes HALLUCINATIONS, IMAGERY, FANTASY, DAY-DREAMING, VISUAL DISPLAYS; (do not use interchangably; do not confuse with PSYCHIC INFORMATION or VISIONS, which are non-thoughts). [**cf.** NON-THOUGHTS, THOUGHTS]

INNER-PLANES—see ETHERIC WORLD.

INNER-PSYCHIC CLIMATE—(Seth) that part of each individual which forms the seasons.

INNER-SELF—refers to the perfectness imbedded in the human seed within each human being that is the motivating factor for constant desire to improve. **Syn.** SUBCONSCIOUS MIND. [**cf.** SOUL-MIND, BRAIN]

INNER-SENSES—the intangible counterparts of the five physical senses: CLAIRAUDIENCE (invisible ears), CLAIRVOYANCE (invisible eyes), CLAIRSENTIENCE (intuitive feeling), CLAIRSCENT (a nonevident odor), CLAIRSAVORANCE (a nonevident taste); pertains to psychic information through the above. **Syn.** PSYCHIC SENSES, SUPERSENSES, PARASENSES. [**cf.** THIRD-EYE AREA]

INNER-SIGHT—see PSYCHIC INFORMATION.

INNER-SILENCE—an advanced state of MEDITATION whereby the meditator has become so disenchanted with their own mind that they wish for a total quieting of all mind activity; ripe for NIRVANA. [**cf.** PURE ALERTNESS, SATORI, TAMING OF THE MIND]

INNER-SOUND CURRENT—a constant steady stream of the same sound used for MEDITATION, e.g., rain falling, air conditioner noise, hum of a fan. **Syn.** WHITE NOISE, NADAM. [**cf.** REVERIE, INNER-ATTENTION, SELF-GENERATED REPEATED STIMULUS]

INNER-SPACE OF MAN—1. see PSYCHIC INFORMATION; 2. see MONAD.

INNER-STREAM OF CONSCIOUSNESS—constant mind activity provoked by the thinker consciously or unconsciously; to think thoughts encompassed with enough emotion to make a thought-form and to think thoughts with emotion too weak to make a thought-form; normal function of the mind; thought-forms eventually manifest in one's lifestyle and body, but this inner-stream of consciousness evades giving one a clue as to what degree of emotion is needed to make a thought-form; (do not confuse with non-thoughts that belong to the psychic realm). **Syn.** THOUGHTS. [**cf.** INNER-MIND PICTURES, NON-THOUGHT]

INNER-TALKING—see INNER-DIALOGUE.

INNER-VIBRATIONAL TOUCH—to perceive directly; being able to feel or see the experience one chooses to see; more of a psychic counseling nature than foretelling the future. [**cf.** INSTANT COGNITION, PSYCHIC COUNSELING]

INNER-WISDOM—see PSYCHIC INFORMATION.

INNER-WORLD—1. the level of consciousness where one finds psychic information; 2. level in meditation where one finds peace and purpose. [**cf.** SEED MEDITATION, MENTAL PSYCHIC PROCESSES Appendix 2]

INNER-WORLD TELEPATHY—to receive information from the mind of an ETHERIC WORLD INTELLIGENCE or DISCARNATE ENTITY; earthling can be attuned to the etheric world when in deep thought and receive ideas that no outside stimuli could have triggered; when one talks with her or himself and receives answers in another level of thought, one is holding a conversation with an etheric world intelligence; (do not confuse with a PSYCHIC MESSAGE). [**cf.** EARTH TELEPATHY, INNER-DIALOGUE]

INNERGY—coined by Patrick Flanagan (1975); the energy found within the smallest particle of matter; also found within mankind's LAW OF THOUGHT; innergy is short for "inner energy." [**cf.** THOUGHT, MATTER, ELECTRODES]

INSANE ROOT—(William Shakespeare) (botane) the mandrake plant, known for its scream when pulled from the earth; believed to have the power to drive men mad; has other psychic power. **Syn.** MANDRAKE PLANT. [**cf.** BOTANE, SENSATION CONSCIOUSNESS]

INSENSIBILITY TO FIRE—see FIRE IMMUNITY.

INSIDERS—(Tibet) those who believe in the Tibetan religion which consists of metaphysics, occultism, mysticism, parapsychology and astrology. [**cf.** OUTSIDERS, THIRD-EYE]

INSIGHT—see PSYCHIC ART.

INSINCERE MEDIUM—one who works with an etheric world entity but who also fakes some phenomena abilities which are not yet developed. [**cf.** MEDIUMSHIP, REDCAPS, NATURAL MEDIUM, OBEAH DOCTOR]

INSPIRATIONAL ART—to psychically paint or draw a picture that is more exquisite or unusual than one's own talent; performed with more speed than one normally paints or draws; artist is required to be passive, emotionally engrossed in his or her work, and desiring a specific end-result; the passivity of the CONSCIOUS MIND and strong desire activates the SUPERCONSCIOUS MIND; impressions flow from the superconscious mind throughout the KUNDALINI telling the hand what to paint or draw; work moves along easily and rapidly until the art is finished or interrupted; the art is the same style each time but far superior than the natural ability of the artist; artist must trust and follow his or her inner directions quickly; performed in an ALPHA STATE OF CONSCIOUSNESS and if artist is disturbed by noise the rest of the inner feeling could be lost. [cf. INSPIRATIONAL THOUGHT]

INSPIRATIONAL COMPOSITION—see INSPIRATIONAL WRITING.

INSPIRATIONAL MEDIUMSHIP—to bring forth a level of knowledge that is greater than one's education or experience in this lifetime from a superior ETHERIC WORLD INTELLIGENCE; knowledge comes in the form of writing, speaking, painting, drawing, poetry, music, and counseling in order to enhance the medium's own talents in these fields; knowledge is usually meant for the enjoyment or education of the masses; usually accomplished through impressions and visions made by the etheric world intelligence attaching his or herself to the PINEAL GLAND of the MEDIUM; many genii, mathematicians, scientists, philosophers, musicians, and counselors use this skill, at least part of the time; occurs in a LIGHT TRANCE, SEMI-TRANCE, or DEEP TRANCE, or sleep state of consciousness; knowledge may be willed or occur when the individual has exhausted his or her own personal talent and unexpectedly falls into a very relaxed state; seances are not necessary but can be used; intelligence only intervenes when called upon. [cf. INSPIRATIONAL THOUGHT, GUIDE, GENIUS, EGO]

INSPIRATIONAL MEDIUMSHIP ART—to draw or paint a picture more elegant or rare than one's own ability; medium/artist allows an ETHERIC WORLD INTELLIGENCE to intervene with impressions; takes practice to synchronize with the intelligence who attaches to the PINEAL GLAND of the artist, art work flows rapidly, finishing in one tenth of the normal time; MEDIUM is in a light or SEMI-TRANCE state; medium may plan the theme of the picture but the end result of the picture is decided upon by the intelligence; style of picture could vary making a few definite styles as if different ethereal artists take turns using the same medium; many of the world's great artists have had the privilege of having a highly evolved etheric world artist work through them; (do not confuse with AUTOMATISM in which the intelligence uses the hand of the medium). [cf. INSPIRATIONAL THOUGHT]

INSPIRATIONAL MEDIUMSHIP SPEAKING—1. (light trance) to speak a stream of words that was not in one's prepared speech, nor thought about beforehand, and sometimes not the beliefs of the speaker; ETHERIC WORLD INTELLIGENCE flows in and out of the speaker's mind with impressions to enhance the prepared material; MEDIUM appears to be fully conscious to the listeners; sometimes the new thoughts blend so well with the medium's style that only the medium knows the information was not in his or her intended speech; 2. (semi-trance) to allow an etheric world intelligence to intervene and give the whole lecture through one's self; information is brought through at the level of the medium's philosophy and intelligence, but flows more swiftly than he or she could present the material; theme of material is decided upon by either the medium or the intelligence; but the style of presentation is that of the intelligence; 3. (deep trance) to bring through information and knowledge that is above the level of one's own education or lessons from life's experiences while in a heavy state of trance; an etheric world intelligence attaches to the PINEAL GLAND or SOLAR PLEXUS of the medium and speaks by giving impressions to the medium; knowledge is intended for the masses and only given to mediums who will share it with others; medium is not aware of what is said until in the awake state and listens to themselves recorded on cassette tape; 4. in all of the above states of consciousness: (a) the voice is that of the medium, sometimes in a lower pitch; (b) hand, foot, or torso could be rhythmically moving and indicates when the guide becomes involved; (c) words sound jumbled when the guide's impressions come too fast; (d) sometimes called CHANNELING; (do not confuse with VOICE TRANCE in which intelligence's voice is used). **Syn.** INSPIRED BY GOD. [cf. CLAIRSENTIENCE, DUAL CONSCIOUSNESS]

INSPIRATIONAL MEDIUMSHIP WRITING—to write knowledge beyond one's formal education or results of life experiences by inviting an ETHERIC WORLD INTELLIGENCE to intervene; one sits with paper and pencil and intelligence impresses knowledge upon the mind more swiftly than one can think and must be written rapidly or the material is lost; information is meant for the benefit of mankind; performed by one's self after MEDITATION or in a SEANCE; if MEDIUM is disturbed the flow is broken and usually will not return (even to the extent of a few words that have passed the brain but are not yet written); information is usually not remembered and must be deciphered when in a BETA STATE OF CONSCIOUSNESS because it is not always written legibly or words spelled correctly; medium is in light or SEMI-TRANCE state of consciousness; style of writing sometimes changes from sitting to sitting as if a different intelligence enters for special purposes; many great authors have had the privilege of having a highly evolved etheric world intelligence work through them; not necessary to be a writer; intelligence does not let themselves be known in this type of PSYCHISM and one cannot be sure if he or she is using the SUPERCONSCIOUS MIND or an intelligence; believed that the intelligence attaches to the brain or in close proximity to the brain; (do not confuse with AUTOMATIC WRITING in which the intelligence uses the hand of the medium). (Inconcl.) [cf. INSPIRATIONAL WRITING]

INSPIRATIONAL SLEEP—to take a short nap or sleep a full night with the intention of waking up with information that had been elusive during the logical thinking state; information comes immediately upon awakening as impressions in the mind but not with clairvoyant or clairaudible perceptions nor through the dreams of the sleep; impressions can be the climax of a story or poem, an ingredient in an experiment, a key word in an advertisement, a lecture theme for an oncoming class, or even an answer to a political problem; impressions must be recorded quickly or they could fade. [cf. SLEEP EXPERIENCES, DREAMS, INSPIRATIONAL SPEAKING]

INSPIRATIONAL SPEAKING—to be interrupted while speaking with unplanned words that flow spontaneously and swiftly as if one is being pushed to say this information; occurs when one is emotionally caught up in the subject; could be a few important sentences in a personal conversation or in between notes in a lecture or lesson; could be the whole lecture without using notes; information is new to psychic and cannot be remembered once it is said; sometimes it comes too swiftly to enunciate correctly and sounds jumbled; information comes through the SUPERCONSCIOUS MIND and bypasses the SUBCONSCIOUS MIND making it pure or truthful; (do not confuse with VOICE TRANCE or INSPIRATIONAL MEDIUMSHIP SPEAKING). [cf. INSPIRATIONAL THOUGHT, IMPRESSION, JABBERWOCKY TRANCE]

INSPIRATIONAL THOUGHT—to be psychically stimulated with impressions that move the intellect and/or the emotions to bring new art, knowledge, or scientific information; mind impressions extend beyond one's normal ability, are nonpersonal, and are intended to benefit or bring joy to the public;

knowledge or wisdom flows like a stream from the potential within the HUMAN BEING SPECIES SEED via the SUPERCONSCIOUS MIND, to the RIGHT BRAIN HEMISPHERE and travels down the KUNDALINI; information is "pure" or the Truth because it bypasses the subconscious mind and therefore, is not infiltered with one's BELIEF SYSTEM; information could not have been known by psychic's formal education or results of his or her past experiences; talent may be learned; occurs from a strong desire, deliberately willed, and preparation by relaxing the body and quieting the CONSCIOUS MIND; impressions well-up and drive swiftly to their intended base, sometimes in an unpredictable manner; impressions come more clearly and quickly than the brain can think; information can be perceived for stories, poetry, music, drawings, painting, lecturers, lessons, symbols, or mathematics; not easy to distinguish from INSPIRATIONAL MEDIUMSHIP unless the intelligence makes her or himself known; **Syn.** DIVINE IDEA. [cf. INSPIRATIONAL THOUGHT Appendix 2, BREATHED INTO, INSPIRATIONAL SPEAKING]

INSPIRATIONAL WRITING—to write or type information that flows into the MIND in a steady stream that has nothing or little to do with one's own thoughts or ability; the conscious mind must be centered on the writing as it comes rapidly and must be written as rapidly because it is elusive and if not captured immediately it cannot be retracted; outside stimuli breaks the flow; body feelings are usually nil; knowledge is from the SUPERCONSCIOUS MIND working in the RIGHT BRAIN HEMISPHERE and flowing down the KUNDALINI; some of the writing is not legible, nor the spelling correct, so it must be deciphered when in the alert or BETA STATE OF CONSCIOUSNESS; performed after MEDITATION when the mind is passive and lasts from a few minutes to hours; 1. information is foreign to the psychic, not learned from formal education or past life experiences, or logically reasoned; 2. information could be known by the psychic and is now being organized and points being emphasized; (do not confuse with INSPIRATIONAL MEDIUMSHIP WRITING). [cf. ACTIVE MENTAL INACTIVITY, IN STREAM]

INSPIRED—(ancient Greece) to reveal information from an etheric world intelligence, while in a semitrance state, which the etheric world wants earthlings to know; see INSPIRATIONAL MEDIUMSHIP. **Syn.** ENTHUSED, BREATHED INTO. [cf.

317

RETROCOGNITION, POET, PROPHET, MANTIC TRANCE]

INSPIRED BY GOD—ancient phraseology meaning that there was communication between the etheric world and an earthling. [**cf.** PSYCHIC INFORMATION, ETHERIC WORLD INTELLIGENCES, DIVINE IDEA, PROPHECY]

INSTANT COGNITION—to psychically perceive what is going on in one's immediate surroundings, in the "here and now," without deliberately thinking about it; (do not confuse with CLAIRSENTIENCE). **Syn.** INNER VIBRATIONAL TOUCH. [**cf.** PSYCHIC, PRECOGNITION]

INSTANTANEOUS HEALING—to experience an extreme change in one's physical health and/or mental attitude within a very short time; triggered by an outside stimulus or force; occurs when the patient is in an emotional state and the "foremost" desire to both the subconscious and conscious mind is to become well; the patient's body chemistry and attitude would change no matter what the cure or who the doctor or practitioner is, at that time; "mind(s) (and emotions) over matter." (Inconcl.) [**cf.** CHARISMATIC HEALER, MIRACLE HEALING, INTERCHANGE OF MAGNETISM, LAW OF HEALING Appendix 7]

INSTINCT—(esoteric) 1. a flow of intelligent motivations, sometimes unrecognizable, built within the living organism, which promotes growth, life sustenance, death, and change in the evolutionary path; a higher degree of intelligence coming into the prehuman kingdoms and the mankind kingdom which works toward the overall plan through an independent existence of each; 2. "something" causing an unconscious movement that is responsible to cosmic consciousness; a rudimentary intelligence in that its manifestations are almost always spontaneous, built-in, and meaningful; a minimum ability of an organism pattern construction for physical survival. [**cf.** INSTINCT CONSCIOUSNESS, SENSATION CONSCIOUSNESS, SYMPATHETIC NERVOUS SYSTEM]

INSTINCT CONSCIOUSNESS—(anpsi) the awareness level of animals, directing them to existence on the planet with a built-in desire to preserve and protect themselves; 1. given to animals to take the place of knowledge and decision making; animals react spontaneously from a built-in awareness of intelligence from cosmic consciousness with regard to environmental functions. **Syn.** SPINAL CON-

SCIOUSNESS. [**cf.** ANPSI, INSTINCT PERCEPTION, OVERALL CONSCIOUSNESS] 2. an innate intelligence that directs the animal's physical structure, its digestion, elimination, breathing, ability to obtain food and shelter, under the influence of man's consciousness. (Inconcl.) **Syn.** INSTINCT, ANIMAL SEED. [**cf.** COSMIC CONSCIOUSNESS, SIMPLE CONSCIOUSNESS, MONAD]

INSTINCT PERCEPTION—(animal and plant kingdoms) to sense and distinguish between beneficial and destructive energy; innate intelligence of what is good or bad for its particular structure, which makes it react accordingly. (Inconcl.) **Syn.** PRIMARY PERCEPTION. [**cf.** BOTANE, MINSPI, ANPSI]

INSTINCTUAL TELEPATHY—the ability of the animal to psychically sense feelings and intentions between other animals and itself, and between itself and humans. **Syn.** ANPSI, ANIMAL ESP. [**cf.** ESP, INSTINCT CONSCIOUSNESS]

INSTITUTIONALIZED MEDIUMSHIP—(B.C. and early A.D., Rome) the use of public oracles confined to the holy places and working professionally for certain officials of the government. [**cf.** ORACLE, PROPHET]

INSTRUCTIVE COMMUNICATIONS—informative material regarding morals, philosophy, and science, with a continual high standard; comes from the ETHERIC WORLD INTELLIGENCES by many varieties of mediumship; intended to be published and used by the masses.

INSTRUMENT—1. a psychic in good rapport with the etheric world GUIDE or guides, and able to perceive psychic information and guidance from them at will; i.e., acting as an INSTRUMENT to portray the message. **Syn.** AGENCY, FORETELLER, GO-BETWEEN PROGNOSTICATOR. 2. a medium who allows an etheric world intelligence to use their vocal organs as a voice box for etheric world knowledge; i.e., an instrument or amplifier for the message they want known. **Sim.** MEDIUM, LAMA, SIBYL. [**cf.** PSYCHIC]

INSUFFLATION—(ancient occult) to breathe on the diseased area for healing; a warm breath corresponds to positive electricity, and a cold breath corresponds to negative electricity; the cold breath is directed downward from above, swiftly; the warm breath is dispersed from below, upward; the two are performed alternately over the diseased area which neutralizes the congestion. [**cf.** CURATIVE EDUCATION, ALTERNATIVES]

INTEGRAL STIMULATING INTENSITY STROBO-SCOPE—(Isis) a device used for AURA-VISION training which prepares the hues for better vision by stimulating the rods and cones of the eyes. [cf. COLOROLOGY Appendix 5, AURA]

INTEGRATED PHYSIOLOGICAL RESPONSE—(biofeedback training) a change in both the body and mind which results from intense pinpointed concentration; body becomes very relaxed and the logical, reasoning, mind becomes passive and the subconscious mind is more acute to outside stimuli. [cf. BIOFEEDBACK TRAINING Appendix 5, BRAIN]

INTEGRATION—the harmonious blending of two normally opposed forces, to form an integral whole; 1. (biofeedback training) the logical and emotional functions of the mind working together to bring better understanding of self to the subject; 2. (holistic health) the subconscious and conscious minds agreeing on attitudes, concepts and beliefs to bring a healing into the body; 3. the monad and the personality realizing that they belong to the universe and must begin to give some energy to the universe for perfecting it. [cf. CURATIVE EDUCATION, KARMA, TOTALITY]

INTEGRATION CONTROL—a switch on some biofeedback instruments used to blend rough-textured sounds into smoother sound as it comes through the machine. [cf. BIOFEEDBACK TRAINING, ELECTRODES]

INTEGRATIVE TENDENCY—(Arthur Koestler) "the ghost in the machine"; the SOUL-MIND.

INTELLECTUAL CYCLE—(biorhythm) a rhythmic pattern "within" the human body that reacts to mental productivity (memory alertness, reasoning, reaction, and ambition); the organism gives out peak performance for 16½ days and relaxed performance for 16½ days, making 33 days; begins at birth and ends at death, repeats itself constantly; used in charting one's biorhythms. [cf. BIORHYTHM, CRITICAL LINE]

INTELLECTUAL SOUL—(Allan Kardec) principle of intelligence peculiar to animals and human beings [cf. SOUL, SOUL-MIND]

INTELLIGENCE—(esoteric) 1. a coordination and blending of the forces of life, being chemical in action, used in degrees by each individual and inanimate things; an orderly formation and action of energy in the infinitesimal particle knows its own function; that which is in all matter to sustain it;

CONSCIOUS OF BEING throughout all infinity (intelligence knows it is intelligent); life; matter; 2. (Maury Bonnain) act of doing, kinetic energy; purposeful application of energy; "the use of energy by living organisms to change or alter the form of substance; a purposeful orderly organized sphere of activity being the result of the use of one of the major forms to alter the other form"; 3. the innate ability of the mind to respond to new conditions and keenly realize what it perceives; to make new things, views, and courses of action, out of its accumulated impressions. [cf. SUBCONSCIOUS MIND, NEW-AGE PSYCHOLOGY, BRAIN, ENERGY]

INTELLIGENCE IN THE SKY—(Ufology) a space craft or UFO needing an intelligent entity, similar to a human, to propel it, as opposed to the amoebas or critters in the atmosphere. [cf. EXTRATERRESTRIAL BEINGS, CREATURES OF STRATOSPHERE]

INTELLIGENCE, AN—see AN INTELLIGENCE.

INTELLIGENT AGENT—an etheric world entity that acts as an agent for an earthling, bringing in physical or mental psychism, guidance, and protection; see GUIDE. [cf. DOCTOR TEACHER, SPIRIT]

INTELLIGENT BODY—see CAUSAL BODY.

INTELLIGENT SLEEP—(astral projection) astral flights taken to the astral plane for visits before the period of one's transition, to make ready for the soul-mind's new home. [cf. DEATH, DEATH ANGEL, DEATHBED VISIONS]

INTENTION CASES—(psychic phone calls) to receive a telephone call and carry on a conversation, only to learn later that the person never made the call but had been planning to do so. (Inconcl.) [cf. BILOCATION, ANSWER CASES, APPARENT PSYCHIC PHONE CALLS]

INTENTIONAL SUFFERING—self-imposed limitations to which one becomes indoctrinated by one's own volition, because of cultural beliefs, past teachings, and personal uncomplimentary comments; one then sits back complacently and lives beneath one's potential in an unhappy lifestyle and in ill health. [cf. WELLNESS, HOLISTIC HEALTH]

INTER-ETHERIC FORCE—(Helena Petrovna Blavatsky) an energy controlled by the use of sound vibrations, capable of ultimately providing mankind with a free source of energy; could enable humans complete control over their physical environment. (Inconcl.) [cf. SOUNDS-WITH-POWER, VIBRATIONS]

INTER-GALACTIC UFO'S—theory: an intelligence from another planet, or from SPACE, can adjust his or her vibrational frequency to visit our system of stars; at a distance, this would be recognized as a "star." [cf. MUTATION OF ENERGY, ETHER SHIP, GODS FROM THE SKY]

INTER-GLOBE-TROTTING—(slang) see ASTRAL PROJECTION.

INTERCEPTOR—a third person who intrudes during a psychic act; this intrusion is felt by the psychic and makes a difference in the information delivered; see GUIDE.

INTERCEREBRAL COMPETITION—(split-brain) pertains to a discipline problem people have using both hemispheres of the brain equally in mankind's present evolutionary stage; belief that using one hemisphere much more than the other brings an imbalance in one's life. (Inconcl.) **Syn.** INTERCEREBRAL DOMINANCE, INTERCEREBRAL INHIBITION.

INTERCEREBRAL DOMINANCE—see INTERCEREBRAL COMPETITION.

INTERCEREBRAL INHIBITION—see INTERCEREBRAL COMPETITION.

INTERCHANGE OF MAGNETISM—(healing) the transfer of the disease from the patient to the practitioner in a healing session; happens because the practitioner does not take on the proper PSYCHIC PROTECTION for her or himself. [cf. MAGNETISM IMMUNITY, SPIRIT HEALING, MAGNETIC HEALING]

INTERDISCIPLINARY APPROACH—the use of data and techniques from many different arts and sciences in analyzing psychic phenomena.

INTERFACE—(ufology) 1. an overlapping of high frequency radio waves on radar when studying human beings, animal organisms, and microwaves in outer space preventing accuracy. [cf. ECHO, CREATURES, PROTEAN FORMS] 2. facts, problems, theories that are shared by two or more disciplines of study. [cf. SPIRITUALISM]

INTERGALACTIC CONSCIOUSNESS—occurrences in outer space relating to a oneness of harmony among the galaxies. [cf. UNIVERSAL LIFE CYCLE, DIVINE CONSCIOUSNESS, TOTAL EXACTITUDE CONSCIOUSNESS]

INTERIOR COHESION—a principle that holds a pattern of any thing or event together that operates "within" and maintains the pattern as it should be; expressed in the psychic skill CASTING OF LOTS. (Inconcl.) [cf. I CHING, DICE-PK, Appendix 6 MANTIC ARTS]

INTERIOR LANDS—areas "within" the center of the earth that are inhabited with living intelligent beings, carrying on a civilization; tunnels leading to these cities were found by archaeologists. (Inconcl.) [cf. UNDERWORLD, HOLLOW EARTH, GUARDIANS]

INTERIOR MONOLOGUE—to talk to or to question one's self silently, between conversations; a constant flow of ideas and comments in the mind's activity; if such conversation is in two different levels, it is believed one is conversing with their inner or outer band of intelligences; this is one method used by them to help mankind. [cf. SUBCONSCIOUS MIND, INNER-DIALOGUE, INNER-MIND PICTURES]

INTERIOR ORDEREDNESS—the SCHEME OF THINGS; the pattern of the universes; intellectual in nature, seeming that everything has a purposeful function and evolutionary time period. [cf. TOTALITY, POLARITY]

INTERIOR PNEUMATOPHONY—to perceive words from within one's head without anyone in the area speaking; while in an ALPHA STATE OF CONSCIOUSNESS one perceives words from an etheric world GUIDE or a nature spirit with one's psychic ears; occurs spontaneously or when willed; see SUBJECTIVE CLAIRAUDIENCE. [cf. OBJECTIVE CLAIRAUDIENCE]

INTERIOR SILENCE—(meditation) to control the mind, to relax the body, and to quiet the emotions to the point where one can see emptiness. [cf. MEDITATION Appendix 5]

INTERIOR TYPTOLOGY—(development circle) to receive psychic information from the etheric world intelligences through sounds coming from within wood itself, without visible movement; a code is worked out from the sounds by the sitters and medium to obtain purposeful information. [cf. ALPHABETIC TYPTOLOGY, LANGUAGE OF SIGNS, RAPPINGS]

INTERIOR VISION—see SUBJECTIVE CLAIRVOYANCE.

INTERIORIZING—(astral projection) the return of the astral body to the physical body after the astral projection is finished; the projectionist feels a pulling backward sensation at this time, whether he or she is dreaming, aware or unaware of the flight. [**cf.** IN-THE-RANGE-OF-CORD-ACTIVITY, REPERCUSSION]

INTERLINKED SCRIPTS—(early 1900s) an experiment suggested by the etheric world intelligences in which they would work through automatists in different cities to prove their validity; automatists received information through automatic writing simultaneously; information was related and each automatist's information needed to be used as a whole to be efficient. **Syn.** CROSS-CORRESPONDENCE. [**cf.** AUTOMATISM, AUTOMATIC WRITING, BOOK TESTS]

INTERMEDIARIES—1. see GUIDES; 2. see MEDIUMS.

INTERMEDIARY AGENCY—see PERISPRIT.

INTERMEDIARY BODY—see ASTRAL BODY.

INTERMEDIATE DUAD—(Theosophy) the mortal aspects of man; see SOUL-MIND.

INTERMEDIATE NATURE—see SOUL-MIND.

INTERMEDIATE STATE—(Christianity) the lower planes one enters immediately after death. **Syn.** PURGATORY. [**cf.** ADVERSARIES, HELL, HADES, DIABOLIC]

INTERMEDIATE WORLD—see DENSITY.

INTERNAL AUTOSCOPY—to see through one's own skin and give a description of what one sees; performed in a state of trance. **Syn.** X-RAY CLAIRVOYANCE. [**cf.** ETERNAL AUTOSCOPY]

INTERNAL AWARENESS—to be conscious of one's silent mind activity, and to have the ability to control it to some degree. [**cf.** BLANK PERIODS, CONSCIOUS MIND, INNER-DIALOGUE]

INTERNAL DIALOGUE—(psychic information) to consciously talk, silently or verbally, to one's CONSCIOUS MIND, SUBCONSCIOUS MIND, and SYMPATHETIC NERVOUS SYSTEM before opening one's psychic doors; enhances control and discipline of one's mind; (do not confuse with INNER-DIALOGUE which is nondeliberate). [**cf.** DESIRED-CONTROL, MENTAL PSYCHIC PROCESSES Appendix 2]

INTERNAL DIRECTION—(dowsing) the RADIESTHETIC SENSE of the person responding tangibly by the swing of the pendulum or the tipping of a dowsing rod as an amplification of the answer to the question. **Syn.** DOWSING RESPONSE. [**cf.** EMA-

NATIONS, PENDULUM POWER, ACASUAL RELATIONSHIPS]

INTERNAL EXERCISES—(Tantrism) a subtle process of motionless stances, with the limbs fixed in prescribed symbolic attitudes, while the internal exercises are carried out. [**cf.** BODY CONTROL Appendix 2]

INTERNAL INTONATION—(Tantrism) a technique whereby the psychic uses an abbreviated kind of spelling or holy MANTRA, minimizes the voicing of the mantra like a chant, and then carries it on internally in harmony with their body. [**cf.** CHANTING, BODY CONTROL, BREATHING RELEASE]

INTERNAL SEX—(Tantrism) a sexual experience using breathing techniques during sexual intercourse which cause the subtle fluids manufactured and potentialized in the body to travel up to the head area, and to be reabsorbed into the system, where the climax is experienced. [**cf.** KUNDALINI]

INTERNAL STATES—(biofeedback training) (Elmer Green) body functions going on inside the skin; used in reference to special areas on which one is concentrating for behavioral change. [**cf.** ELECTRONIC ANALYZER, THRESHOLD CONTROL, BIOFEEDBACK DESENSITIZATION]

INTERNAL TIME—a rhythmic pattern "within" the human body which synchronizes the heartbeat and the earth's revolution around the sun which affects the mind and body; approximately every twenty-four hours these biological and mental functions seem to move in their own time frame; (do not confuse with BIORHYTHM) **Syn.** BIOLOGICAL CYCLE, CIRCADIAN RHYTHM. [**cf.** CYCLES]

INTERNALIZATION—(meditation) to draw external situations to activity, within the mind, using a special meditation technique which prevents these external situations from working against one's self; turns the uncomfortable situations into more comfortable situations. **Syn.** MIND EXPERIENCE. [**cf.** ART OF TEA, DHARANA, MENTAL SYMBIOSIS]

INTERNALIZATION AWARENESS—(biofeedback training) to study and analyze one's external conditions, values, and the like, in regard to how they affect one's biological condition internally while HOOKED-UP to a biofeedback instrument; all styles of biofeedback instruments report on one's stress levels as an indication of what is going on inside the skin or how one "internalizes" outer stimuli. [**cf.** FOCUS ATTENTION, EIDETIC BIOFEED-BACK, EVOKED POTENTIALS]

INTERPLANETARY—going from one planet to another.

INTERPRETATION-OF-TALKING-IN-TONGUES—to instantaneously perceive the inner meaning of the foreign jibberish while in the area of one TALKING-IN-TONGUES; the interpreter must also be in a highly emotional state or a state of ecstasy; the skill lies in perceiving the feeling nature of the utterances rather than the words per se. [**cf.** FORCED PSI, ZENOGLOSSLIA, EMOTIONAL PSYCHISM]

INTERRUPTED UNCONSCIOUS ASTRAL PROJECTION—while in a somnambulistic traveling state, the traveler may consciously have flashes of where he or she is and what is going on and be able to recall these snatches later on in a waking state. [**cf.** ASTRAL PROJECTION Appendix 2]

INTERSTELLAR SPACE—space between stars. (Inconcl.)

INTERVENTION—to perceive a psychic feeling within the whole body or within the stomach area which is strong enough for one to heed its warning; occurs before an event is to take place, telling one to change plans; requires the ability to distinguish from one's own preferences and the real warning; later one finds that the activity or event did not run smoothly and the warning was for their highest good. **Syn.** CLAIRSENTIENCE. [**cf.** PRECOGNITION, GUT FEELING, HUMAN OMEN]

INTERVIEWER—(dreams) an individual one knows or a foreign character that appears in one's dreams to verbally explain the meaning of the dream to the dreamer as he or she is dreaming; used as a method of DREAM CONTROL; dreamer asks the subconscious mind to put someone in their dream to accompany them and interpret the dream as it flows. [**cf.** INCUBATION, LUCID DREAMING, THETA STATE OF CONSCIOUSNESS]

INTIMATE ZONE—a space bubble around a human being, discovered by scientists in 1974; research says it is the first layer of energy around an individual; includes one's daily life, which one cannot evade. (Inconcl.)

INTIMATION DREAMS—scenes of what the dreamer could achieve if the effort was made during waking hours. [**cf.** HEART THOUGHTS, HIGH DREAM, DREAMS Appendix 2]

INTONING—to sing in a monotone or chant in harmony with the body.

INTRA—prefix meaning "within, inside, interior."

INTRADIMENSIONALITY—(ufology) levels of energy penetrating one another with life organisms of many kinds, on all levels. [**cf.** UFOLOGY, CRITTERS, CREATURES OF THE STRATOSPHERE]

INTRAPSYCHIC CONFLICT—a deep-seated subconscious belief; see BLOCKS.

INTRAPSYCHIC MACHINERY—(psychology) a subjective part of the working mechanism of the mind.

INTRAUTERINE ORIGIN MEMORIES—experiences of other lives stored within a person's AKASHIC RECORDS. [**cf.** KARMA, SUBCONSCIOUS MIND, REINCARNATION]

INTRO AND INTER—prefix meaning "within, between."

INTROJECTION—(Karl Pribram) private sensations of thought and feeling intermingled with the projections that make up one's experience of oneself as a human being. [**cf.** HOLOGRAM, TIME]

INTRUDERS—(ufology) UFO intelligent beings who manipulate the aircraft. [**cf.** UFONAUT, UNKNOWN FORCES, FUSIFORM]

INTUIT—1. a psychic sensitive to emotional feelings, who specializes in receiving psychic information through hunches and intuition. **Syn.** HUNCHER, CLAIRSENTIENT. [**cf.** CLAIRSENTIENCE] 2. (anpsi) a psychical reaction of a mother animal when her babies are hurt, sick, or killed; distance no barrier; e.g., in an experiment: baby rabbits were "roughed up" miles away from their mother and the mother rabbit paced nervously up and down in her cage. Usage: "Watch the mother rabbit closely and she will intuit at the exact time the babies are mishandled." *Intuit* covers all types of animal reactions, as all animals will react differently. [**cf.** ANPSI Appendix 2]

INTUIT TELEPATHY—to transfer emotions and feelings from one person to another; the receiver goes through the same sensations as the sender; consciously willed or unconsciously spontaneous; e.g.: 1. (laboratory) senders in the experiment send the feelings and attitudes of the target (a person or picture); the receivers try to receive feelings of the same sensations; 2. a receiver spontaneously feels the same anguish as a close friend involved in an accident; the husband feels labor pains with the wife; 3. the receiver feels depressed, sad or as if death is close by, simultaneously with the eruption of a volcano which kills many people and has taken place in another part of the world. [**cf.** TELEPATHY, PSYCHOMETRIC TELEPATHY, EMPATHY CLAIRSENTIENCE]

INTUITING—1. to perceive emotional feelings about one's self and one's actions; to sense right from wrong; to receive sensations about universal activity and other happenings, to which the average person is not attuned; 2. to psychically feel the sensations, moods, and attitudes that belong to another person; see INTUIT TELEPATHY. [**cf.** CLAIRSENTIENCE, CLAIREMPATHY]

INTUITION—a non-thought which by-passes the process of thinking and brings through a whole body sensation of "this information is important"; information that one did not know before through education or past experiences, did not logically think out or reason with; an "inner" knowing; happens spontaneously, willed or unwilled; comes from the SUPERCONSCIOUS MIND making it "pure" information, unclouded by the subconscious belief system; comes with or without the help of the etheric world intelligences; soul-mind guidance; instinct guidance that appears naturally in all human beings, if one could only recognize it; the most common type of MENTAL PSYCHISM and the most easily developed. **Syn.** CLAIRSENTIENCE, HUNCHABILITY. [**cf.** CLAIRSENTIENCE Appendix 2]

INTUITIONAL WISDOM PLANE—see FOURTH PLANE.

INTUITIONAL WORLD—see FOURTH PLANE.

INTUITIONIST—a psychic who specializes in receiving psychic information through their intuition or feeling nature; see CLAIRSENTIENCE. **Syn.** INTUIT, CLAIRSENTIENT, HUNCHER. [**cf.** HUNCHABILITY, NON-VERBAL COMMUNICATION, SPONTANEOUS OCCURRENCES]

INTUITIVE ARCHAEOLOGY—the supersensitivity of the archaeologist to unexplicably analyze the artifact of his or her findings or to know which area to dig; skills that could be used: PSYCHOMETRY, RADIESTHETIC SENSE, and INTUITION.

INTUITIVE AWARENESS—see INTUITION.

INTUITIVE EXPERIENCES—see CLAIRSENTIENCE.

INTUITIVE HEALERS—those born with the ability to be used as a channel for healing; respond to a feeling within to "lay-on-hands" or to pray for the sick with no special training or initiation ceremonies. [**cf.** MENTAL HEALING, MAGNETIC HEALING, ALTERNATIVES, LAYING-ON-OF-HANDS]

INTUITIVE INFLUENCE—the cycle of highs and lows that one has in the perception of intuitive flashes; cycle repeats itself in a fifty-two day period. (Inconcl.) [**cf.** CYCLES, BIORHYTHM, MINOR CYCLES]

INTUITIVE KNOWING—see INTUITION.

INTUITIVE LEAP—(Barbara Weber) any information perceived through INSTINCT or through psychic inspiration that pertains to a future or past time period; e.g., Albert Einstein foresaw theories far out of his time and was capable of putting them into formulas. [**cf.** CLAIRSENTIENCE, INNER-DIRECTED]

INTUITIVE LEVEL OF THE PSYCHE—(Carl Jung) that part of the soul-mind which reflects a part of the human being and the universe. **Syn.** NONCONSCIOUS LEVEL. [**cf.** MEMORY CONSCIOUSNESS, PURE CONSCIOUSNESS]

INTUITIVE MEDIUM—one who receives intuitive flashes from one's etheric world helper instead of from one's subconscious mind; unlike most clairsentience, the medium wills this to happen and understands when the etheric world helpers are responsible. [**cf.** INTUIT TELEPATHY, INTUITION, PSI-MEDIATED INSTRUMENTAL RESPONSE]

INTUITIVE MIND—see SUPERCONSCIOUS MIND.

INUA—(Eskimo) see AURA.

INVASION—an attack of POSSESSION: a possession seizure. [**cf.** POSSESSION Appendix 2]

INVERSION OF TIME—(emotional psychism) an apparition of the astral body of a deceased person directly after his or her death; occurs between those who are closely related; soul-mind is still in an emotional state and desires someone to know he or she is all right; (do not confuse with EMOTIONAL PSI in which the apparition comes as a warning previous to the death). [**cf.** NEED-DETERMINED PHENOMENA, BILOCATION]

INVISIBILITY—(Tibet) to make one's self invisible to the physical eye by the suspension of one's brain waves; see DIMENSION-SHIFTING. [**cf.** ATMOS-

PHERE CONTROL, FLASHING STROBE LIGHT, EARTHBOUND PHANTOM CARS, PHYSICAL TRANSFORMATION]

INVISIBLE—see ETHERIC WORLD.

INVISIBLE COLLEGE—a symbol to represent the basic teachings of the Rosicrucian discipline.

INVISIBLE CONSCIOUSNESS—an "inner knowingness" of the various invisible bodies interpenetrating one's self and the bodies' inhabitancy on other levels of vibrational frequencies. [cf. CONSCIOUSNESS, BODIES AND PLANES, Appendix 5]

INVISIBLE DRUM—(Native American) the beating of a drum that is heard with physical ears coming from a tent when there is no physical drum inside; Indian priest is in a deep trance state inside the tent and when the drum beats come through him, while in trance, the tent shakes; sound comes from the ETHERIC WORLD INTELLIGENCES using the priest as a channel. [cf. PSYCHIC VOICES, REGULATED SITUATION, TRANCE]

INVISIBLE INTELLIGENCE—an ambiguous term designating someone who is now in the etheric world: 1. a discarnate human being who has transited; 2. a soul-mind acting as a guide; 3. a being from outer space who seems comparable to earth's human being species; 4. a nature spirit. **Syn.** SPIRIT. [cf. ETHERIC WORLD ENTITY, PILOTING INTELLIGENCES, GHOST]

INVISIBLE MASTER—a human being who has earned an exalted rank of mastership in the angel kingdom and is now helping earthlings from an etheric plane, rather than from an earth incarnation. [cf. MASTER, FIFTH PLANE, ANGEL HIERARCHY, INNER BAND]

INVISIBLE TRANSMUTATION—(alchemy) to internally manufacture body processes that will make one's body glow, similar to a glorified body; the skilled alchemist is capable of mixing and heating up his or her body processes with extreme mind discipline; the dream of every alchemist. [cf. GLORIFIED BODY, ASCENSION, ALCHEMIST, RESURRECTION]

INVISIBLE WORLD—see ETHERIC WORLD.

INVISIBLE-PHYSICAL EXISTENCE—(ufology) a belief that some UFOs are composed of a substance capable of inhabiting the atmosphere as their home; a human being cannot detect this with his or her eyes but the UFOs can make themselves visible so they can be detected. [cf. PLASMATIC FAUN, CRITTERS, ETHERICALLY PROPELLED SHIPS]

INVISIBLES—(Haiti, Voodoo) dead ancestors who cause plagues, sickness, and other negation in one's life until there is an attitude change in the personality of the earthling; the energy from the ancestors is then transformed into power to be used for good accounts; referred to as "gods" which make up one's personality. [cf. VOODOOISM, THOUGHTS ARE THINGS, LAW OF CONSCIOUSNESS Appendix 7]

INVOCATION—(Latin *invocatia,* "to call upon") 1. (magic) a preplanned ritual performed by a trained magician to invite forces from the cosmos to help perform beneficial physical psychic feats that the magician could not perform alone; using incantations, formulas, and amulets that have proven workable. The magician CALLS DOWN into her or himself a particular force who personifies himself as a god; the "god" possesses the magician's body to execute the task; (do not confuse with POSSESSION in which the entity works for evil). [cf. IMPERSONATION] 2. (West Africa) a ceremony with drums, dancing and sacrifices performed by the tribe, or individually, in order to invite the LOA (god) to intercede within their bodies; this god then brings guidance and counsel for the tribe. [cf. MOVEMENT-FOR-ALTERED-CONSCIOUSNESS] 3. (France) to call upon superior gods with earnest desire by prayer, incantation or repetitious formulaic phrases when in need of a higher order of assistance than one can give oneself; 4. a prayer given verbally at the onset of a church service or lecture; 5. formulaic thoughts, incantations, or affirmations used to stir a shift in consciousness; 6. (scrying) mental conversation which can be heard from the intelligence that is seen in the CRYSTAL BALL. [cf. SCRYING]

INVOCATION OF THE HOLY GUARDIAN ANGEL—(magic) see SUPREME AND COMPLETE RITUAL.

INVOCATOR—a psychic who specializes in calling etheric world helpers through the process of incantations, magic rituals or chanting. [cf. INVOCATION, GUARDIAN OF THE DOOR, CEREMONIAL MAGIC]

INVOLUNTARY ASTRAL PROJECTION—an unwilled separation of the SOUL-MIND from the physical body, encased in the ASTRAL BODY: 1. caused by an accident, severe pain, fainting, or while under anaesthesia; astral body leaves as if to relieve the physical body from pain and anxiety; astral body usually hovers above the physical body quite alert as to what is taking place with the physical body below; ASTRAL VISION is so vivid individual can relate this experience when out of danger; see NEAR-DEATH EXPERIENCE; **2.** slight movement of the astral body to one side of the physical body, during MEDITATION or BIOFEEDBACK TRAINING allowing the person to view him or herself; astral body is about two inches from physical body, similar to when one sleeps; normal reaction to a deep meditation; **3.** a separation of the astral body from the physical body during sleep, traveling to: (a) the higher etheric world planes to perform a task that was not consciously preplanned; PROJECTIONIST can become bewildered because the task is not understandable to third dimensional thinking; (b) places in the earth world either close by his other home or to far away countries; sleep projectionist may have no recall, partial, or full recall, upon awakening. [**cf.** SPONTANEOUS ASTRAL PROJECTION, SLEEP ASTRAL PROJECTION, SLIGHTLY-OUTOF-BODY]

INVOLUNTARY FUNCTIONS—(esoteric) body systems that take care of themselves without conscious help from the human, i.e., circulation, elimination, digestion, breathing; controlled by the SOUL-MIND via the SYMPATHETIC NERVOUS SYSTEM; developed through evolution of thousands of incarnations until they became automatic to mankind's conscious awareness; recently found to be controllable by deep meditation and intense concentration. [**cf.** STRESS, ARCHETYPAL EXPERIENCE]

INVOLUNTARY INTERVENTION—psychic physical phenomena occuring to a medium who does not consciously prepare for it or will it to happen; could prove disastrous as this is usually attributed to lower quality entities. [**cf.** UP-FOR-GRABS, SPONTANEOUS PHYSICAL MANIFESTATIONS]

INVOLUNTARY MEDIUM—a natural-born medium who has the ability to produce physical psychism without willing it; caused by an inferior etheric world entity as no superior intelligence will go against the medium's free will; can result in physical complications in the medium; inborn talents can be brought under control through self-discipline. [**cf.** OPTIONAL MEDIUM, SUSCEPTIBLE MEDIUM, INVOLUNTARY INTERVENTION]

INVOLUNTARY WRITING—see AUTOMATIC WRITING.

INVOLUTION—(esoteric) to work downward from the top source; the descent of the monads (created with creation) from Totality when Totality was in its chaotic/perfect form; the descent to a lesser existence with an intent and desire to work upward and return to the chaotic/perfect form; involution begins at the top source and ends at earth; earth is the critical-line-expression or the "snapping" of the monad when it reverses its path completely and begins evolution; descent of the monad utilizes its own law, and on the ascent upward it utilizes the LAW OF THE SOUL-MIND (which envelopes it while in the earth vibrational frequency). [**cf.** LAW OF INVOLUTION Appendix 7, EVOLUTION]

INWARD ART—see MEDITATION.

INWARD ATTENTION—to still one's mind activity to outer stimuli and size up one's body-feelings at that precise moment in order to be open and receptive to incoming psychic information energies; this mind process is easier after meditation but as the transformation period of the earth grows, mankind will be able to discipline the mind to this process quickly without much preparation. [**cf.** BODY-FEELINGS, MENTAL PSYCHIC PROCESSES Appendix 2]

IO—(New Zealand, Maoris) see TOTALITY.

IOA—(Greece) "the lady of the sirens": a nature spirit living in an ocean-consciousness; deity in charge of the oceans. [**cf.** NATURE SPIRIT, WATER BABIES, NYMPHS]

ION—(Latin) suffix denoting "action" or "condition" of the noun used. **Syn.** SION.

IPOMEA—(botane) (Mexico) a psychotropic plant held sacred for its quality to induce CLAIRVOYANCE; contains a relative to LYSERGIC ACID (LSD). [**cf.** BOTANE, FORCED PSI, PLANT MAGIC]

IPSISSIMUS—(Golden Dawn) the highest level for the psychic to reach where she or he becomes master of their own power. [**cf.** FROM THE WORLD OF SPIRIT, DISCIPLINE, FAVORABLE STATES]

IRIDOLOGY—the study of the eyes and their corresponding body parts; the iris areas of the eyes correspond to and reveal structural defects, latent toxic inherent weaknesses, and the activity of body organs of the past and present; helps to determine the locations of the congestion, the stage of congestion, and the causes and steps to overcome it. [**cf.** ALTERNATIVE, CURATIVE EDUCATION, IRIS PHOTOGRAPHY]

IRIS—(Greece) goddess of the rainbow; a golden-winged intelligence working as a messenger of the gods and communicating these messages to earthlings. [**cf.** LADY OF HEAVEN, PLANETARY ANGEL]

IRIS PHOTOGRAPHY—a specially designed camera used as an analytic tool; takes colored, detailed pictures of the eyes; can be enlarged for study; used in IRIDOLOGY analysis to detect the health level of various organs and tissues. [**cf.** LAW OF CORRESPONDENCE Appendix 7, HOLISTIC HEALTH, ALTERNATIVE]

IRISH BANSHEE—*Banshee* means "fairy women"; a TUTELARY FAIRY, guardian of one particular family or clan. [**cf.** NATURE SPIRITS, JINN, GNOME]

IRON—(minpsi) 1. (Germany) a mineral which has a vibrational frequency to help benefit the new child; see IRON RING; 2. (Vietnam) used to contact deceased loved ones; 3. objects made of iron have a vibrational frequency that will protect one against witchcraft, evil spirits, and malevolent influences; used in evocation rituals to call out evil entities; 4. (alchemy) an agent used in the transmutation process. [**cf.** MINPSI Appendix 2]

IRON DOCTOR—(Vietnam) considered to be a very important person in his town as iron doctors were psychic and could be called upon for various psychic skills. [**cf.** MASTER-OF-FIRE, CAT'S EYE, BLACK DIAMOND, IRON]

IRON RING—(Vietnam) an iron chain attached to a sleeping newborn child; iron has the properties to protect one against evil spirits. [**cf.** MASTER OF THE FIRE, MINERAL KINGDOM, ATTRACTION CONSCIOUSNESS]

IRON-WALL SHELL—(esoteric) a cloak around each universe, invisible to the physical eyes; closes off the light of the sun, stars, and moon to separate one universe from another. **Syn.** PERPETUAL DARKNESS. [**cf.** PLANES, VEIL, KINGDOM OF THE MIND]

IRRADIANCE PHENOMENA—the formation of a yellow, white or orange light around a psychic event, or an individual in an ALTERED STATE OF CONSCIOUSNESS, or in a high state of ECSTASY; (do not mistake for the AURA). **Syn.** ALL AGLOW. [**cf.** GLORIFIED BODY, GREAT BODY OF RADIANCE, LIGHT BODY]

IRRATIONAL SHELL—an invisible floating body-like form that has recently enveloped a soul-mind in the ETHERIC WORLD; held together with materialistic thoughts which belong to neither the earth world nor the astral world; see ASTRAL SHELL. [**cf.** SOULLESS PSYCHISM Appendix 2]

IRRITATION ZONE—(dowsing) a spot where two or more underground streams intersect; this area has a direct influence on individuals who spend many hours directly over the spot; it has been found to be the cause of different types of illnesses, e.g., bed wetting, cancer, arthritis; suspected areas are checked by the DOWSING ROD, and if such intersections of water are detected, and the patient no longer sits, stands or sleeps there, or if he or she moves to another building, the illness clears up with no medication. [**cf.** DOWSING, LEY LINES, MERIDIAN LINES]

IS—abbr. INTELLIGENCE IN THE SKY; (ufology) term used for both the space-craft and the driver. [**cf.** CONSTRUCTS, BIOFORMS, GODS FROM THE SKY, PHONY STARS]

IS-NESS—1. (Zen) the universe seen as an indissoluble unit; a single TOTALITY of which mankind is but a part; 2. (Buddhism) to experience "pure being"; going into the void in a state of meditation; no feeling of time, space or movement. **Syn.** SUNYATA. [**cf.** VOID, METAPHYSICAL EMPTINESS, GOING INTO THE SILENCE]

ISANGOMA—(South Africa) see WITCH DOCTOR and PSYCHIC.

ISHTAR—1. (Summeria) goddess representing womanhood and maidenhood, possessing psychic skills (2350 B.C.); symbolized by an eight-pointed star; 2. (Babylonia) goddess of the moon, fertility, beauty, and love. [**cf.** ANGELOLOGY Appendix 2]

ISIS—(ancient Egypt) the DIVINE MOTHER; a mistress of enchantment depicted in the form of a woman wearing a headdress composed of a solar disc and four cow's horns; the mother of HORUS; wife of OSIRIS, who put the pieces of Osiris together and brought him to life again with her psychic powers. [**cf.** PSYCHIC CASUALTIES]

ISIS' VEIL—the part of the invisible world that seems to pertain to the wisdom of the Egyptians.

ISLAM—an Arabic religion of the desert people, founded by Mohammed; basis of five great religions; belief: there is one supreme being who made the world and presides over the destiny of mankind; that the world is full of ETHERIC WORLD INTELLIGENCES engaged in natural phenomena to help earthlings believe in REINCARNATION.

ISLES OF THE BLEST—Pythagorean theory: a place in the etheric world where a SOUL-MIND, who has been purged after death, can go to rest and be warmed by the sun before going to a higher level or back to earth for REINCARNATION; located away from the dangerous disembarkation on the moon where customs officers might rob the soul-mind of its assets. [**cf.** INEFFECTIVE KARMA, ACCUMULATED KARMA]

ISOLATION BOOTH—see ISOLATION BOX.

ISOLATION BOX—a small enclosed area containing only a mattress, where one goes for SENSORY DEPRIVATION; all sight, light, food, odor, and touch is cut off; operation of the brain can become totally disrupted and disoriented; used under supervision as an aid to bring on psychic experiences, uproot BLOCKS, gain insight for a new lifestyle, reach a high state of BLISS, unravel oneself and find one's position with the universe. [**cf.** SENSORY DEPRIVATION, INITIATORY SICKNESS]

ISOLATION INITIATION—(Tibet) a method of mental torture whereby one is placed in an underground tomb, totally cut off from sight, sound, touch, and light; person stays there for days; the objective is to commune with the INNER-SELF, seeing all aspects of oneself that were never before noticed; escape is impossible; those who survive are made priests, capable of psychic healings and skills; through this experience, they are purified and stripped of entangling KARMA. [**cf.** PRIMAL SCREAM, ISOLATION TANK]

ISOLATION TANK—a small construction that contains a floor of shallow, salted water and is free from sound, light, odor, and human touch; designed for one person to float on their back in order to induce an ALTERED STATE OF CONSCIOUSNESS; a method of deprivation; the body-temperature water nullifies all impressions of hot and cold; adequate oxygen is assured; an effect of weightlessness is produced by the highly salt-saturated water; individual relaxes for approximately one hour; tank is conducive to deep meditation, a psychic experience, surfacing repressed thoughts, and producing solutions to problems. [**cf.** SOLITARY TRANCE, HERMIT'S CELL]

IST—suffix meaning "doer."

IT—(George Groddeck, 1890) see VITAL LIFE FORCE.

IUPPITER FULGAR—(Rome) an etheric world angel in charge of lightning. [**cf.** ANGELOLOGY, MAGNIFICENT DEVAS]

IUPPITER PLUVIALIS—(Rome) an etheric world angel who has charge of rain for the planet. [**cf.** MAGNIFICENT DEVAS, COSMIC MASTER, HOLY ONES]

IUPPITER TONANS—(Rome) etheric world angel in charge of the thunder for our planet. [**cf.** IUPPITER FULGAR, LORDS OF HUMANITY, PLANETARY ANGEL]

IVORY—(esoteric) a mineral held sacred by many; contains the vibrational frequency that induces INSPIRATIONAL WRITING, especially POETRY. [**cf.** MINPSI, BOTANE, INSPIRATIONAL THOUGHT]

IVORY ROD—an ornament and tool used for psychic skills; used to express the supernatural authority vested in a king. [**cf.** DOWSING ROD, AARON'S ROD, WIZARD ROD, DIVINING ROD]

IZANA-GI—(Shinto, Japan) the male angel in the etheric world in charge of propagating Japan's race, working with the IZANA-MI. [**cf.** POLARITY]

IZANA-MI—(Shinto, Japan) the female angel in charge of propagating Japan's race, working with the IZANA-GI. [**cf.** ANGEL OF BIRTH, COMFORTING ANGEL, EARTH MOTHER]

J-COINCIDENCE—(psi tasks) abbr. "JUST" A COIN-CIDENCE; an event occuring in which identical elements fall together, and applies the theory that it is merely a chance event and should be forgotten. [cf. SYNCHRONICITY, MEANINGFUL COINCIDENCE, CHANCE]

JABBERWOCKY TRANCE—coined by Lewis Carroll; to bring forth profound Truths and wisdomic thoughts by verbalizing simple, spontaneous, unconstructed words repeatedly for a length of time; accomplished by conscious repetitious rambling of simple words that normally would be considered useless and do not need actuating, to put the psychic in an alpha state of consciousness; session must be taped on a cassette recorder; upon investigating the tape, one finds within this supposed nonsense, material that is worth studying, as if the superconscious mind has deliberatly seeped through; (do not confuse with a TRANCE that requires the assistance of the guides). [cf. LIGHT TRANCE, INSPIRATIONAL THOUGHT]

JACK—a name frequently given to a etheric world intelligence or a human because he has psychic skills; a good connection to COSMIC CONSCIOUS-NESS with the vibration *J*, e.g., Jack and the beanstalk, Jack the Giant Killer, JACK-O'-LANTERN: James in the Bible, King James, Jeremiah, JESUS. [cf. WORDS-WITH-POWER]

JACK OF THE BRIGHT LIGHT—see FOOLISH FIRE.

JACK-IN-IRONS—the village blacksmith who is also the town psychic; see BLACKSMITH.

JACK-O'-LANTERN—see FOOLISH FIRE.

JACOB'S LADDER—1.(esoteric) the underlying motivating force that drives mankind to a higher state of consciousness; to work toward ASCENSION to the higher spheres, representing mankind's purpose on earth; 2. (alchemy) a metaphorical representation of the powers of ALCHEMY; power of ascension through the visible nature; a rainbow or prismatic staircase set up between the etheric world and the earth; 3. (Yoga) the spinal column in a human being; advancement through the chakras; 4. (Unity) step-by-step realization by means of which one assimilates the divine ideas of Truth that come to one from God. Syn. GOLDEN CHAIN, VITAL MAGNETIC SERIES, ANIMA MUNDI. [cf. IMI-TATIVE MAGIC, SYMBOLISM]

JACOB'S ROD—see DOWSING ROD.

JADE—1. (esoteric) toughest stone on earth; helpful in curing diseases, especially of kidneys, gall-stones, and spleen; used as a talisman of prevailing good; 2. (China) the counterpart of a human; see ETHERIC DOUBLE. Syn. PEARLY EMPEROR. [cf. ALTERNATIVES, HOLISTIC HEALTH]

JAGRAT—(Hinduism) waking state of consciousness; BETA STATE OF CONSCIOUSNESS. [cf. CON-SCIOUSNESS, THETA WAVES, STREAM OF HALF-CONSCIOUSNESS]

JANN—(Islam) a nature spirit considered to be the weakest of the five types of Jinn.

JAPA—(Yoga, Vedic, Hinduism, "mantra recita-tion") signifying one's private mantram, a set of words or a certain sound, to be repeated aloud in a chanting nature each day; given to the ASPIRANT by a MASTER who chooses a special sound that will help the aspirant grow spiritually. [cf. MANTRA, JAPA-MALA]

JAPA YOGA—a prayer, a statue, or picture of a holy person; a MANTRA or a holy symbol that can be used in MEDITATION to inspire the meditator to the goal of TOTAL ABSORPTION. [cf. ZIKR]

JAPA-MALA—(Sanskrit, "muttering chaplet") a string of 108 beads used in meditation to keep track of how many times one has said one's MANTRA through a special process of fingering and handling. Syn. PRAYER BEADS, SANDALWOOD BEADS. [cf. ROSARY, JAPA, SELF-GENERATED STIMULUS]

JAPAM—(Vedic) to "make Japam" is to repeat in MEDITATION the name of one's own personal deity, over and over, for a prescribed time. Sim. DEVOTIONAL MEDITATION. [cf. QUIET ATTENTIVE-NESS, SATORI]

JEHOVAH—(Hebrew) name for God.

JERK—(dreams, meditation) see MYCLONIC JERK.

JESSE TREE—symbolic of the spiritual heritage of JESUS the Christ. [cf. SYMBOLISM]

JESUS—(esoteric) the main DEITY of Christian religions; felt to be the greatest MEDIUM, PSYCHIC, ALCHEMIST, and CHANNEL for healing that the earth planet has ever experienced; could use the Holy Spirit fluently; knew all the laws of this world and the etheric world and how to harmonize them for practical purposes; a LIFE WAVE from the rank of LORDSHIP in the angel hierarchy, manifesting in a physical body, to teach mankind the power of the mind and the importance of human evolution. [cf. WORDS-WITH-POWER]

JESUS PRAYER—"Lord Jesus Christ, Son of God, have mercy on me, a sinner." Advocated by some religions that if said repeatedly in meditation and during the day, it will be protective and help that person grow spiritually; in its Latin form: KYRIE ELEISON. **Syn.** HESYCHASM. [cf. DESERT FATHERS]

JET FATIGUE—see JET LAG.

JET LAG—a desynchronization of the CIRCADIAN RHYTHM in one's body causing one to feel peculiar, fatigued and less mentally alert when there is a change in one's nightly sleeping habit to sleeping during another part of the twenty-four hour cycle; happens when flying across time zones and with shift-workers; an interruption in the pattern of the internal body functions which seem to flow more smoothly when in tune with the earth's rotation. **Syn.** JET FATIGUE. [cf. CYCLES]

JET SYNDROME—the adjustment period of the internal body causing a change in attitude and bodily functions when one has flown over time zones and there is quite a difference in time and activity. [cf. JET LAG, BIOLOGICAL CYCLES]

JETTATORE—(Italy) also spelled **jettatura;** see PSYCHIC.

JEWEL OF THE LOTUS—(Tibet) the diamond; used to symbolize what the LOTUS stands for. [cf. CEREMONIAL MAGIC, SYMBOLISM]

JI—(Yoga) a suffix meaning "customary and respectful"; added to the end of a word of direct address, e.g., swamiji, guruji, Sri Yukteswarji.

JIJI-MU-GE—(Japanese, "each thing no hindrance") the interaction of FORM and SPACE, form and EMPTINESS, as seen in MEDITATION. [cf. CAVE OF ENERGY, DISSOCIATION]

JIMSONWEED—a PSYCHOTROPIC PLANT used to induce a TRANCE state; used by Native Americans in the midst of a religious ceremony to bring an elated state of ECSTASY; used by European witches to take astral flights. **Syn.** DATURA. [cf. EMOTIONAL PSI, FORCED PSI]

JIN SHIN JYUTSU—(Japan) a type of finer-pressure massage to the ACUPUNCTURE POINTS in the body; used for energy, breaking up blocks, sexual vitality and relief from tension and pain. [cf. SHIATZU, NEUROMUSCULAR MASSAGE]

JINNI—(North Africa, Arabia, Egypt, Korea) NATURE SPIRIT which lives underground all over the world; believed to be here before Adam; created out of tremendous heat, sometimes having a body of smoke, monstrous in size; assumes different forms to communicate with humans by attaching to a light; capable of flying rapidly and imitating sounds of humans or animals; found inhabiting dust storms, deserts, hot burning sand, trees, woods and thickets, and seashores; willing to work for the benefit of mankind or to harm them, depending upon the situation; five types in the Jinn kingdom; also spelled **Djinni, djini, jini, djinni;** plural is **jinn.** [cf. JANN, MARIDS, SATYRS, CENTAUR, DRYADS, WOOD NATURE SPIRITS, ALADDIN'S LAMP]

JIUJITSU—see JUJITSU.

JIUJUTSU—see JUJITSU.

JIVA—(Yoga, Vedic, Sanskrit, Jainism) the human being living in a physical body, having as its life force a monad of infinite energy; uncreated and indestructible. **Syn.** LIFE-MONAD, HUMAN BEING. [cf. MICROCOSM/MACROCOSM, BODIES AND PLANES Appendix 5, MONADOLOGY]

JIVANMUKTA—1. (Sanskrit) the highest form of feeling free an INITIATE can attain in a physical body or without a physical body; 2. one who has reached NIRVANA while still in the physical body, usually during meditation. [cf. ESTHETIC STATE, BLANK PERIODS, COSMIC LIGHT]

JIVATMAN—(Sanskrit) see MONAD.

JIZO—(Japan) (Buddhism) an etheric world god whose function is to protect and guide children who have made their transition. [cf. EARTH MOTHER, ANGEL, ANGELIC SENTRIES]

JNANA—1. (Yoga) the incessant focusing of one's mental activity on the desired end-result to a problem, without instigating a mental solution, whereby one can arrive at the right solution to anything life tosses one's way; 2. (Vedic) true knowledge of REALITY. **Syn.** VISUALIZATION. [cf. MENTAL MIND, THOUGHT-FORMS]

JND—written **jnd,** just-noticeable difference," (Gustav Theodor Fechner) the smallest observable difference between two different outward stimuli of different intensities which has been found to have an effect on the SOUL-MIND and PHYSICAL BODY. [cf. CURATIVE EDUCATION, HOLISTIC HEALTH]

JOGGING MEDITATION—prolonged running, from forty to sixty minutes, causing one to lose ability to organize thoughts; ideas flash in from the periphery of the runner's consciousness, visual perception changes, colors blend together and thought patterns shift into a free-form creative shorthand; problems are solved and answers tumble into the mind.

JOGI-FEATS—(Yoga) to have extreme and complete self-control of one's bodily functions; accomplished through mind control and self-discipline; e.g., standing on one foot for months, remaining immersed for days waist-deep in a stream of water. **Syn.** FAKIR. [cf. BODY CONTROL]

JOINT HYPNOSIS TELEPATHY—the ability of two subjects in different areas being hypnotized at the same time, to send mental telepathic messages to one another. [cf. HYPNOTHERAPY, PARENT-CHILD TELEPATHY]

JOLLY BACCUS—(Rome) the god in the etheric world who is in control of wine; uses NYMPHS and SATYRS to carry out his functions.

JOSS-STICK—(China) (botane) a slender stick of dried fragrant paste burned as incense in front of a statue of a Chinese deity; burns out one's negative vibrations and brings harmony into the body through a connection with that deity. [cf. HOLISTIC HEALTH]

JOULE'S HEAT—see MAGNETIC NERVE FLUID.

JOURNEY—(Yoga) the sushumna (kundalini power) flowing up the spine of the human, purifying the human as it goes; see SUSHUMNA. [cf. KUNDALINI, SERPENT POWER, COSMIC FIRE]

JOURNEY OF THE MOON—the awakening of consciousness to a higher state, causing the KUNDALINI energy to begin its flow upward past the lower chakras. [cf. ROOT CHAKRA, SPLEEN CHAKRA, SOLAR PLEXUS CHAKRA]

JOY—(esoteric) the sensation of PLEASURE regarding one's growth; to accept each experience, whether good or bad, as a step in the process of one's unfoldment and to be content with the outcome as a learning experience; (unknown) "the unfolding of perfectness is the joy of the world."

[cf. CURATIVE EDUCATION, ENRICHING EXPERIENCE]

JOY GUIDE—a highly intelligent ETHERIC WORLD INTELLIGENCE belonging to the INNER BAND and assigned to a human for one incarnation; function is to bring gaiety to the human, guide his or her lifestyle to balance with recreation and work; manifests as a very young person of either gender; eager to serve when summoned. **Syn.** DOORKEEPER. [cf. OUTER BAND, GUIDE]

JTB—(laboratory) "justified true belief" in physical research. [cf. LAW OF EXCLUSIVENESS Appendix 7]

JUDAISM—a religion which holds the belief that every human being has a right to justice, purity, and truth which even the power of kings cannot erase.

JUDEL—(Germany) see ASTRAL BODY.

JUDGMENT—(I Ching) that part of the tossed HEXAGRAM that discusses the attributes of the symbol, its impact on the questioner, and related advice. **Syn.** TUAN, TEXT. [cf. COMMENTARY, GREAT SYMBOLISM]

JUDO—(Japanese *ju*, "soft"; *do*, "art") a form of JUJITSU developed by Jigoro Kano (1882), a Japanese jujitsu expert, as a sport and as a means of self-defense by modifying or eliminating many holds too dangerous for use in sport; uses an opponent's weight and strength against him which allows a light or weak person to overpower a physically stronger opponent; see JUJITSU, KARATE, and EMPTY HANDS. [cf. MARTIAL ARTS]

JUDO TOUCH—a special technique, used in the MARTIAL ARTS, which can make one unconscious; used for medical purposes or to free the SOUL-MIND from the body for an ASTRAL PROJECTION. [cf. KARATE]

JUGAMENTUM—(astral projection) because of differences of opinions as to where the SILVER CORD is attached to the physical body during an ASTRAL PROJECTION, the area is arbitrarily known as the jugamentum. [cf. OUT-OF-RANGE-OF-CORD-ACTIVITY]

JUGGERNAUT—1. see NATURE SPIRIT; 2. (ufology) the large, overpowering objects or craft that overwhelm an earthling by sending out a beam that vibrates in an hypnotizing motion, causing loss of memory. [cf. FOO-FIGHTING, BEAM OF HEAT, BRAIN WAVE SYNCHRONIZER, FIREFLIES]

JUJITSU—(Japanese *ju*, "soft, pliant"; *jutsu*, "art") a system of wrestling which applies the knowledge of anatomy and the principle of leverage to use an opponent's strength and weight against him; developed over a 2,000 year period by Buddhist monks in China, Tibet, and Japan to be used as defense against armed marauders without violating their own religion; also spelled **jiujitsu, jiujutsu,** and **jujutsu;** see JUDO and KARATE. [**cf.** MARTIAL ARTS]

JUJU—(West Africa) see SPELL, e.g., "I put a juju on him."

JUMBIE—(Trinidad) see LOOGAROO or VAMPIRE.

JUMPING MAGICIANS—a special kind of jumping for a long period of time which induces an emotional state of ECSTASY, TRANCE, or other psychic experiences. [**cf.** MOVEMENT-FOR-AL-TERED-CONSCIOUSNESS, PROLONGED JOGGING]

JUNCTIONS—thirty-eight areas in the human body where PSYCHIC ENERGY enters. [**cf.** MERIDIAN LINES]

JUNG ACTIVE IMAGINATION—to induce a psychic experience; "letting the symbol extend itself from within." [**cf.** VERIDICAL HALLUCINATION, PSYCHIC MESSAGE SYMBOLS]

JUNGIAN—pertaining to theories brought to the world by Carl Jung.

JUNO—1. (Latin) a blanket name given to each female's main guardian angel; opposite of GENIUS for the male. **Syn.** DOCTOR TEACHER, CELESTIAL GUARDIAN. [**cf.** GUIDES, INNER BAND] 2. (mythology) a female, the first God; 3. (Roman) queen of heaven and protectress of females; associated with childbirth and the month of June, making the month of June a good time in which to marry.

JURGENSON VOICES—see TAPED VOICES PHENOMENON.

JUST NOTICEABLE DIFFERENCE—abbr. jnd; (Gustav Theodor Fechner) the smallest observable differences between two objects of different intensities and how they affect the PHYSICAL BODY and SOUL-MIND of an individual. [**cf.** EXPERIENTIAL PHILOSOPHY]

JUST SITTING—1. to quiet the mind, quiet the body, and quiet the emotions in a MEDITATION period, with no special direction; helps one deal with controversy in life by not trying to resolve it but rather to explore it in a quiet way; 2. (Zen) another name for the use of KOAN riddles where the student is forced to a greater awareness of reality through contemplation. [**cf.** END-STATE, GOING WITHIN, LOW BREATHING]

JUSTIFIED TRUE BELIEF—(laboratory) abbr. JTB; that which cannot be proven by normal scientific means but shows enough evidence of its possibility by it actually happening; see LAW OF EXCLUSIVENESS Appendix 7. [**cf.** METHOD+PATTERN, SPIRITUAL CIRCLE]

!KIA—(!Kung tribesman) a trancelike state of emotional ECSTASY wherein the SHAMAN has enhanced awareness; psychically sees over great distances, and inside other people's bodies; shaman can connect to the gods and be used for a healing channel; brought about by tribal singing, chanting, and dancing around a fire until the !kia fire boils up the spine. [**cf.** X-RAY CLAIRVOYANCE, !KIA HEALING, N/UM, SHAMANSHIP, FORCED PSI]

!KIA FIRE—(!Kung, Kalahari Desert) an energy in the body that can be activated and used for healing illnesses, performing psychic feats, and for SEEING PROPERLY, brought on by tribal dancing and singing; begins at the pit of the stomach and base of the spine, heats up to a boiling point by repetitious dancing, and then rises up the spine until thoughts are "nothing in the head." **Syn.** N/UM. [**cf.** SEPARATE REALITIES, MOVEMENT-FOR-ALTERED-CONSCIOUSNESS]

!KIA HEALING (!Kung, Kalahari Desert) tribal primitive healing performed in steps: 1. SEEING PROPERLY which allows the healer to locate and diagnose the sickness; 2. pulling out the sickness by LAYING-ON-OF-HANDS; 3. arguing with the ghosts to free the patient. [**cf.** N/UM, !KIA]

!KUNG HEALER—(Kalahari Desert) an accomplished PSYCHIC who cures disease by treating the patient's lifestyle, attitudes and their resulting physical effects, through the knowledge of N/UM energy; the HEALER forces the n/um energy at the base of his spine to boil up and travel up the spine to the head, by constant excited tribal dancing; when he reaches a state of transcendence or painful ecstasy, his psychic powers are accelerated, so he can diagnose the conditions causing the disease, and then channel healing energies to the patient. [**cf.** !KIA, SEEING PROPERLY, PULLING OUT THE SICKNESS, !KIA HEALING]

K-COMPLEX—(dreams) a safety mechanism in human beings that allows them to sleep through trivial noises, no matter how loud, but alerts them to awaken for a noise of an emergency nature; research shows that one chooses the noises he or she wishes to be aware of during sleep; e.g., loud train rumbles will not phase a person who lives near a railroad. [**cf.** DREAMS Appendix 2]

K-OBJECT—(laboratory)(psychometry) the object which is held in the palm of the hands by the participant to help them psychically perceive the target in the experiment; the target is related to the object, and this association makes it easier. [**cf.** LAW OF ASSOCIATION Appendix 7, PRACTICAL PSYCHOMETRY]

KA—(Egypt) the exact double of the physical body, surrounding and interpenetrating it; found around animals and inanimate objects; every mortal received Ka at birth; depicted by a holder of the body and two upstretched arms; name given to OSIRIS; see ETHERIC DOUBLE.

KA-HE-A—(Huna, "to call") to ask for information that cannot be attained by earthly means, by psychically tuning into the etheric world. **Syn.** KE-HE-A. [**cf.** TAPPING INTO, OPEN-EYE, HEAVENLY STUFF]

KA-LA—(Burma) spirit; the life energy of a person; see SOUL-MIND.

KABBALAH—(Hebrew, "doctrines received from tradition") Jewish doctrine or system of theosophy; tells the importance of humanity's role in God's universe, and how an individual is the unfolding of God unto fullness; depicted by an inverted tree, designed to relate to concepts of how the world came into being; theory: the soul existed in a state of complete knowledge before reluctantly accepting a body; symbolism is used throughout the teachings; see CABALA and QABALAH; also spelled **Cabbala, Kabala, Kabalah, Kabbala, Qabala, Quabalah, Quaballah,** and **Quabbalah.** [**cf.** DEUS ABSCONDITIUS, EN SOPH, TREE OF LIFE, SEFIROTH]

KACHINA—(Native American, Hopi) an ETHERIC WORLD INTELLIGENCE of an ancestral heritage that communicates with the tribe in various kinds of psychism; brings counsel for the tribe's prosperity and problems, and gives protection over the tribe's land. [**cf.** KACHINA DOLL, MANITOU, CELESTIAL GUARDIAN]

KACHINA DOLL—(Native American: Hopi, Pueblo) a carved image of an etheric world intelligence, similar to a doll, given to each child in the tribe; this is carved to look like the child's own personal etheric world guide or like the tribal

Kachina god; as the child plays with the doll, she or he is reminded of the tribal etheric world guide or their own personal guide, and should show honor and respect for the help and protection that the guides give them and their tribe. [**cf.** TALISMAN, TOTEM]

KAHUNA—(Hawaiian *ka* and *huna*, "the secret"; *kahu* and *na*, "guard"; "guardian of the secret") an ancient religious faith that brings illuminating knowledge and information regarding psychic skills, (that which is unknown becomes known); a strict discipline for only those who are willing to learn and accept discipline; children are carefully selected before being taught this discipline; specializes in INSPIRATIONAL THOUGHT and attunement to the SUPERCONSCIOUS MIND.

KAHUNA NUI—(Hawaii) the high priest and psychic; see PSYCHIC.

KAIDAN—(Soka Gakkai) a temple used for teaching the art of CHANTING. [**cf.** SEED-MANTRA, SHOOTING CHANT]

KAIROS—(Greece) the divine moment; characterized by awesome sensations and celestial visions; this word is used by all major religions, including ISLAM, HUNDUISM, BUDDHISM, and ZOROASTRIANISM. **Syn.** THE HIGH PEAK, BREAKTHROUGH. [**cf.** SATORI, PURE LAND, HIGH PLATEAU]

KAIROS DIMENSION—to deliberately enlarge one's normal state of consciousness through MEDITATION. [**cf.** MENTAL PROJECTION Appendix 2]

KALA—(Hinduism) the smallest unit of TIME; the period taken by an atom to traverse its own unit of SPACE. [**cf.** PRESENT, TIME, TIME-SPACE]

KALEVALA—(Finland) a book containing 4,200 verses of poetry that are used for "spelling" another person; beneficial for every aspect of one's life. [**cf.** SPELLBOUND, CHARM, ENCHANT]

KALI—a female etheric world intelligence in charge of destruction; see ETHERIC WORLD INTELLIGENCE.

KALIT—(Pacific, Palau) see VITAL LIFE FORCE.

KALPA—1. (Buddhism, Hinduism) 120,000 years representing one day of BRAHMA; 1,000 hahayuga or 12,000 years make a kalpa; that one day spanned the whole period of creation of a world; 2. (Tibet) world periods; 3. (Sanskrit) a cycle of time, but not a definite number. [**cf.** CYCLES, ROUND, AGE]

KAMA—(Sanskrit) the seat of electric impulses caused by desire; the principle of desire used advantageously or subordinately. [**cf.** EMOTION, LAW OF THOUGHT Appendix 7, ETHERIC MAGNETIC CURRENT]

KAMA RUPA—(Sanskrit) known as the lower astral body; see ASTRAL BODY.

KAMA-KALI—a special method of sexual intercourse whereby the seminal fluid and sexual release is brought back into the body through mind concentration, and runs up the KUNDALINI until it reaches a climax in the CROWN CHAKRA. [**cf.** SEXUAL MAGIC, INTERNAL EXERCISES]

KAMA-LOKA—(Sanskrit) the density plane where mankind will make their abode after death, while one is in a mortal man or woman consciousness and has material desires; one will incarnate from this plane directly to the physical body. **Syn.** HADES. [**cf.** BODIES AND PLANES Appendix 5, DENSITY]

KAMA-MANAS—the animal center in mankind (or the lower mind) that one is trying to overcome in this plane. [**cf.** CARNAL MAN, ROOT CHAKRA]

KAMI—(Shinto, Japan) 1. see VITAL LIFE FORCE; 2. any kind of psychic phenomena that is the unusual. [**cf.** PSYCHIC CASUALTIES, PSYCHIC VOICES]

KAMIC BODY—see ASTRAL BODY.

KAMMA—(Buddhism) see KARMA.

KANALOA, KU, KANE—(Huna) exalted, lofty etheric world angels who have a part in fulfilling the trinity; highly evolved soul-minds who have earned the rank to serve over worlds and the peoples of these worlds. [**cf.** ANGEL HIERARCHY, MAGNIFICENT DEVAS]

KANDA—(Sanskrit) an ethereal triangle at the base of the spine, located in the sacrum, housing the concentrated stored energy of the SUSHUMNA; sushumna will work itself up the KUNDALINI as one evolves; the three points of the triangle represent that which is required of a man or woman to accomplish this: will, power and action. **Syn.** MULDHARA, ROOT CHAKRA, COILED SERPENT]

KARANA-SARIRA—(Sanskrit) see CAUSAL BODY.

KARATE—(Japanese *kara*, "empty"; *te*, "hand") a martial art, known in JUDO as *atemi*, that has been separately developed; 1. a physical method of attaining power over another person without wasting any physical movements; over fifty basic techniques are taught in karate discipline; techniques thwart any known attack from an assailant, and provide a stunning counterattack; performed for recreation, exercise, and self-defense; 2. method used of applying pressure to a sensitive area on an attacker's body, usually by means of blows with the side of the hands and feet, to put them out of control without the use of weapons; see JUDO, JUJITSU, and EMPTY HANDS. [cf. MIND-CLEANSING MEDITATION, OPEN-HANDED CHOP, GI]

KARATE PRACTITIONER—one who has learned the techniques and discipline of the karate lessons. Syn. KARATEKA. [cf. MARTIAL ARTS Appendix 5]

KARDEC SYSTEM—material brought through Allan Kardec from the ETHERIC WORLD INTELLI-GENCES over one hundred years ago; this knowledge included: laws to govern human behavior, information of life after death, instructions of MEDIUMSHIP, and information regarding the dangers and practicality of mediumship; from this Kardec wrote many books which are still in print. [cf. KARDEKIAN CENTERS, SPIRITUALISM]

KARDEKIAN CENTERS—(Paris, Brazil, Portugal) groups of people interested in following Allan Kardec's famous teachings of MEDIUMSHIP. [cf. KARDEC SYSTEM, HIGH MAGIC]

KARDICISM—a metaphysical religion based on the accomplished medium, Allan Kardec, who received the many laws governing mediumship from the ETHERIC WORLD INTELLIGENCES: especially popular in Brazil. Sim. SPIRITUALISM. [cf. MEDIUMSHIP, MYSTICISM]

KARETEKA—one who is skilled in the movements, techniques and discipline of KARATE. Syn. KARATE PRACTITIONER. [cf. EMPTY HANDS, ART OF THE VELVET FIST]

KARMA—(Sanskrit, Buddhism, Hinduism, Theosophy) the principle that makes every man or woman the cause of their present global location, lifestyle, intelligence, relatives and physical body condition; this principle is governed by one's entire activities, thoughts, and emotions throughout all incarnations; 1. a law of action: (a) for every action there is a reaction; (b) action and its fruits; (c) deeds, acts, and attitudes of one resulting in future deeds, acts, and attitudes, making one completely responsible for oneself; 2. karma represents the sum total of the causes one has set into motion in past lives, making the pattern for this life and for future lives; this pattern can be changed, and rearranged purposely through preplanned deeds, acts, and attitudinal changes; 3. karma works in one's favor or against one, doling out good or poor physical bodies and experiences; while living the results of the past, one is processing the condition of the future; 4. Buddhist aspects: (a) KARMA OF FULFILLMENT; (b) KARMA OF FUNCTION; (c) KARMA OF PRIORITY; (d) KARMA OF ITS REALM. Syn. LORDS OF JUSTICE, LAW OF COMPENSATION Appendix 7. [cf. REINCARNATION Appendix 5, LAW OF KARMA Appendix 7, KARMIC BOARD, ACCUMULATED KARMA, GROUP KARMA, RIPE KARMA]

KARMA OF FULFILLMENT—(Buddhism) experiences and thoughts that produce consequences which fail to produce "cancellation" of past experiences and thoughts, due to auxiliary causes that are not outwardly known; these can occur in the same lifetime as accumulated karma or in future lifetimes. Syn. RIPE KARMA. [cf. ACCUMULATED KARMA, INEFFECTIVE KARMA]

KARMA OF FUNCTION—(Buddhism) experiences of past incarnations that will determine current events, new birth situations, modification of ripe karma, and cancellation of some experiences, replacing it with new karma. Syn. RIPE KARMA. [cf. DELAYED KARMA, MASS KARMA]

KARMA OF ITS REALM—(Buddhism) those particular experiences that must be worked out on the plane where they were sown. Sim. LAW OF KARMIC BALANCE Appendix 7.

KARMA OF LIVING ORGANISMS—(Hinduism) non-human organisms living in the present time period are the outworking of past deeds and acts through the congregations of atoms in the same evolutionary system. [cf. EVOLUTION, KARMIC BOARD]

KARMA OF PRIORITY—(Buddhism) the degrees and quality of one's actions and thoughts when happening, determine the immediacy and impact of their reaction. [cf. LORDS OF JUSTICE, LAW OF COMPENSATION Appendix 7]

KARMA YOGA—(Vedic) daily activity that is for the DIVINE and not for the person performing it; a path of joining oneself with the Divine, one of selflessness. [cf. THIRD ROUND OF THE PLANET, WEARY WHEEL OF EXISTENCE]

KARMA-KANDA—that part of the VEDAS, the Hindu basic manual, called "Section of Works."

KARMA-MARGA—(India) a path for doing good

335

works that one chooses to take. [cf. PATH SYM-BOLISM]

KARMAN—see KARMA.

KARMIC BOARD—a group of ETHERIC WORLD INTELLIGENCES who have earned the right to look into the AKASHIC RECORDS of earthlings when called upon; serves as a liaison between the evolution of an EARTHLING and the evolution of the planet. [cf. LAW OF KARMA Appendix 7, SOUL JURY]

KARMIC DEBT—(Sanskrit) an unpleasant and uncomfortable experience one must go through to learn a lesson one did not learn, to compensate for something one should not have done, or to compensate for something one left undone, in one of their past incarnations or in the past of their present life. [cf. TRANSFERENCE, NEGATIVE THOUGHT, SPINNING THE WEB]

KARMIC PROPENSITIES—lower desires and thoughts which come from the SUBCONSCIOUS MIND, instigated from past lives; the logical mind will not consciously allow the person to carry them out, thus causing an uneasiness not thoroughly understood. [cf. SURVIVAL OF PERSONALITY, SCIENCE OF SERVICE]

KARMIC RECALL—a short time period when tiny, ethereal microfilm pictures are being clairvoyantly flashed before a dying person's mind; these show the lessons, achievements and failures of the life just led. [cf. REINCARNATION, KARMA, DEATH SCIENCE]

KARMIC REFLEXES—(Tibet) psychic visions which one sees while going through the death process, and that portray the results of the activities of the life just led from the results of past karma. [cf. DEATH ANGEL, DEATHBED VISIONS]

KARMICALLY DESIRED—(psychism) pertains to the occurrence of PSYCHIC INFORMATION and physical psychic phenomena that happens frequently, spontaneously, and randomly, to one who does not make a request for these psychic experiences; examples of uninvited PSYCHISM: knocks and noises with no physically relevant means, apparitions, flashes of other people's problems, etc.; psychic is not aware, consciously or unconsciously, of asking for these events to happen; ETHERIC WORLD INTELLIGENCES of a superior quality do not make decisions for an individual nor perform psychic acts at random, and the SUBCONSCIOUS MIND cannot make a decision of its own accord; therefore, the following concepts: 1. there is an innate wish from a past incarnation to become a great psychic and this would warrant SPONTANEOUS PSYCHISM; 2. there is an inner need from past experiences to feed one's EGO and this is one way of accomplishing it; 3. psychic could have been a WITCH, Celt, CHALDEAN, MYSTIC or SHAMAN in another life, in a time period, when spontaneous psychic events were a natural occurence; occurs more frequently in a NATURAL-BORN PSYCHIC; one can discipline her or himself and learn to control one's psychic experiences, even if they are karmically instigated. [cf. ACCUMULATED KARMA, SOUL JURY, KARMA]

KARMICALLY SELF-GENERATED—pertains to frequent spontaneous psychic events, happening to a psychic or medium, that cannot be attributed to AWARENESS, CONSCIOUS MIND decisions, and cannot be traced back to subconscious desires; felt to be instigated from past lives, as opposed to being instigated from the etheric world intelligences. Syn. KARMICALLY DESIRED. [cf. RIPE KARMA, GROUP KARMA, MASS KARMA]

KARMICALLY WILLED—see KARMICALLY DESIRED.

KASINA MEDITATION—a method of quieting the mind, body and emotions by which one tries for a fixation of consciousness; to use an image in the mind and have that image remain permanently in one's consciousness for the meditation time; helps the individual to direct the forces of their being toward a single goal; image could be a mood, hallucination, unappeasable hatred, amorous attachment or whatever one cherishes; types: water kasina, SOUND KASINA, nature kasina, color kasina, space kasina. [cf. LAW OF CENTER Appendix 7]

KASINGE—(Pacific, Palau) see VITAL LIFE FORCE.

KAT (Egypt) the symbol for the physical body, depicted by a curled up dead fish. [cf. SYMBOLISM]

KATHARSIS—(Greece) the first three steps in a cleansing initiation; discipline in the spiritual, mental, psychic, and physical realm. [cf. GURU, PATH]

KAUSTUBHA—(Hinduism) a gem worn by KRISHNA and VISHNU; believed to have the vibrational frequency that would grant the wearer their wishes. [cf. MINPSI Appendix 2]

KEISAKU—(Zen) the stick carried by the master of the monastery, used to beat the shoulder of one who dozes off during MEDITATION. **Syn.** WARNING STICK. [**cf.** ZAZEN, OUT-BREATH, SESSHIN, ZEN MEDITATION, SLEEPITATE]

KELPIE—(Scotland) a nature spirit that is given charge over WATER; seen by psychics as a horse; communicates with earthlings; performs both good and bad activities.

KEN—see MENTAL PSYCHISM.

KENDO—a type of sword fighting without attacking; swords are used for control only, not for striking; a defensive moving MEDITATION. [**cf.** MARTIAL ARTS]

KENSHO—(Zen, Buddhism, "seeing into one's own nature") a time during meditation when the nature of all things and one's self is revealed, yet one remains personally detached from it. **Syn.** ENLIGHTENMENT. [**cf.** TOTAL ABSORPTION, CHECKING, GOING WITHIN]

KERAUNIOS—(Greece) an etheric world deva who was given charge over the lightning for the earth. [**cf.** DEVA, MAGNIFICENT DEVAS]

KERES—(Greece) an etheric world angel and guardian in charge of old age and death. [**cf.** DEATH ANGEL]

KETAB—(Ethiopia, Arabic) long strips of leather which are inscribed with words; worn as a TALISMAN to ward off illnesses; must be frequently energized by intensified concentration. [**cf.** AMULET, WORDS-WITH-POWER]

KETAMINES—psychedelic drug that can induce an OUT-OF-BODY-EXPERIENCE by dissociative anaesthetics; in times of mortal danger, it is released in the body naturally, and people returning from such an experience induced either way always provide the same account of heaven and God. (Inconcl.) [**cf.** DEATHBED VISIONS, INVOLUNTARY ASTRAL PROJECTION]

KETHER—(Kabbalah) 1. a mineral; represents the number ONE; the crown, the top-most SEPHIROTH of the TREE OF LIFE; has properties that can be used for protection and psychism, so it adorned the crowns of earthly priests and kings; 2. represents the LIGHT that moved upon the face of the waters; the first manifestation, the flowing force that poured down throughout the systems of the world. [**cf.** ATZILUTH]

KEY—symbol used in many religions and philosophies; has properties that will unlock WISDOM and PSYCHIC ABILITY. [**cf.** MENTAL PSYCHIC PROCESSES, SYMBOLISM, IMITATIVE MAGIC]

KEY BIRTHDATE FIGURES—(biorhythm) numbers that have been mathematically computed so one will not have to refigure one's BIO-RHYTHM CHART by the long method each month; these numbers remain constant throughout life. [**cf.** BIORHYTHM, BIOLOGICAL CYCLES]

KEY OF SOLOMON—a text book of magic rituals written by the king of Israel; contains the proper time, place, weapons, dress, cabalistic pentacles, incantations and the MAGIC CIRCLE which the psychic needs for releasing PSYCHIC ENERGY. [**cf.** CERMONIAL MAGIC, RITUAL]

KEY TO HEXAGRAM—a chart used to locate the number of one's passage in the I CHING book for an answer to one's problems; uses the upper and lower TRIGRAMS of the throw. [**cf.** CASTING OF LOTS.]

KEY TO LIFE—(June Bletzer) to "balance" with emotional stress every day, whether the stress is good or bad: 1. to have the correct attitude toward each experience that life presents, resolving any unpleasant experience at the time it happens; to handle all personal emotions (pleasant or unpleasant) comfortably, intelligently, and satisfactorily in accord with one's belief system; to put each undesirable subordinate or traumatic experience in its proper perspective, integrating it into the whole, as opposed to putting it aside without attitudinally resolving it; unresolved emotions are not put "aside" as supposed, but rather they go "inside" the body, to turn up later in the form of a disease or a chaotic life situation; 2. it is just as important not to repress experiences that are painful, as it is to not dwell upon the activity with resentment, jealousy, condemnation or pity; 3. principle: nothing in the world can hurt a person, no death of a loved one, no accident, no environmental catastrophe, no chronic illness, no loss of job or marriage; it is only the attitude one takes toward these experiences that hurts the person. [**cf.** ENRICHING EXPERIENCE, KARMA, BLOCKS]

KEY-NOTE—every object, organism and person has a special musical chord that is the sum total of that entity's vibrational frequency expressing itself; can be heard by other units in the cosmos, and by the psychic's clairaudient ear; it is as unique as an individual's fingerprint. [**cf.** CLAIRAUDIENCE, MUSIC OF THE SPHERES]

337

KEYS TO THE KINGDOM—spiritual studies or scriptures that tend to help one uplift one's concepts, and lead one to higher aspirations, e.g., the BIBLE, the UPANISHADS, the KORAN.

KHAIBIT—(Egypt); see ASTRAL BODY.

KHALB—(Egypt) the shadow, which at death leaves the body to continue a separate existence of its own; see SOUL-MIND.

KHAT—(Egypt) the physical body.

KHEPERA—(Egypt) (death science) the state between inertness and life; the time period in the death process when the soul-mind has left the physical body but has not yet been glorified in its new form; depicted by a man with a beetle's head. [cf. BIRTH OF THE BARDO BODY, DEATH TRANCE, COMING FORTH FROM THE DAY]

KHEPRI—(Egypt) the sun god, felt to be self-existent; generator of all forms of life in earth. Syn. RA. [cf. SPIRIT, PRANA]

KHIKR—("remembering" of God) the attainment of ecstasy through a hypnotic repetitive activity, such as twirling to music, or chanting; also spelled **kikr**. [cf. WHIRLING DERVISHES, MOVEMENT-FOR-ALTERED-CONSCIOUSNESS Appendix 2]

KHU—(ancient Egypt) the AURA which the Egyptians perceived clairvoyantly like a shining translucent body; named this aura "the glorious intelligent shining one"; they understood that this was the ETHERIC DOUBLE and preserved it for the future use of the deceased when they returned to earth, by mummifying the physical body. [cf. DEATH SCIENCE Appendix 2, MUMMIFICATION, INCORRUPTIBLE BODY]

KI—pronounced "chi," (Japan, China) 1. see VITAL LIFE FORCE; 2. (Mesopotamia) god of the earth.

KI-LIN—one of the four spiritual nature spirits, the UNICORN; see FAIRIE. [cf. DRAGON, FENG-HWANG, TORTOISE]

KIA—see !KIA.

KIA FIRE—see !KIA FIRE.

KIA HEALING—see !KIA HEALING.

KICHI-MANITOU—(Native American) the GREAT SPIRIT in heaven who is willing to communicate with earthlings, bringing guidance, counsel and protection. [cf. MEDIUMSHIP, DESIRED-CONTROL, DIVINE INTOXICATION]

KILCROP—a child born from the result of the sexual relations between an INCUBUS and woman. [cf. HAG]

KILNER GOGGLES—special colored glasses used to see auras; filters out the regular spectrum of colors, so colors on both ends of the spectrum come into view. [cf. AURA, COLOR.]

KILNER SCREEN—a device invented by Walter Kilner in the early 1900s to allow nonpsychic people to see further along the color scale; used in COLOR THERAPY to help diagnose diseases; the screen filters out the normal colors, leaving the emotional aura and physical aura visible. [cf. PSYCHIC HEALING, AURA, CURATIVE EDUCATION]

KINDLY ONES—(Greece) FURIES; see NATURE SPIRITS.

KINEMATICS—to move an object through space by nonphysical means; similar to poltergeistery activity, except that kinematics has special characteristic patterns. [cf. POLTERGEIST, FOCUS]

KINESIOLOGY—the science dealing with the interrelationship of physiological processes and anatomy of the human body, with respect to movement; theory: humans are equilateral triangles; good health is achieved when the structural, chemical and emotional sides of that triangle are harmoniously balanced; accomplished by aligning the MERIDIAN LINES, loosening muscle spasms, and treating muscle imbalances; study of muscles, joints, and tendons. [cf. HOLISTIC HEALTH, APPLIED KINESIOLOGY]

KINESIS—a suffix meaning "physical movement"; includes quantitative, qualitative, and positional change; sometimes movement caused by stimulation, but not directionally aimed; e.g., TELEKINESIS, PSYCHOKINESIS.

KINESTHETIC EXPERIENCE—an awareness of sensations of the muscles, joints and tendons. [cf. BODY-FEELINGS]

KINESTHETIC FEEDBACK—a normal function in which conscious information is given to the senses via the nervous system and the brain, telling the muscles how to act; research shows that muscle strength changes after color, sound and food is applied to the individual. [cf. SENSATION, BRAIN, COLOR]

KINETIC ENERGY PHENOMENA—the movement of objects spontaneously, unwilled, and without mundane means; occurs simultaneously with the performance of other types of psychism or with the presence of one who is endowed with an overabundance of PSYCHIC ENERGY; the conditions which produce these phenomena are currently under investigation; see KARMICALLY SELF-GENERATED; e.g., documented case: when Uri Geller was on TV in Florida, two stations went off the air at the time of his interview; this occurred unintentionally and unknowingly to Geller. (Inconcl.) [cf. PSYCHO-KINESIS, TELEKINESIS, ARTICLE-PK]

KINETIC TELEPATHY—1. (receiver) to foretell another person's physical movements before they move; e.g., an arm, leg or body location; 2. (sender) to make another person move in the direction or manner which the psychic desires, by giving a thought command for this movement; e.g., wiggle his nose; see MOTOR TELEPATHY, MUSCULAR ESP. [cf. PSYCHOKINESIS, MENTAL TELEPATHY, INTUIT TELEPATHY, HUMAN PSYCHOKINESIS]

KING IN HEAVEN—the OVERSOUL of each individual; WISDOM that has been accomplished from all incarnations of the soul-mind, and is perfected and ready to return to the MONAD.

KING OF THE PENDULUMISTS—Mermet, a French Abbot, considered "king," because of his persistance in congressional conferences to increase the scientific knowledge of many uses for pendulums, particularly in diagnosing diseases. [cf. PALLOMANCY, RADIESTHESIA.]

KING PEPI—(ancient Egypt) the king who reigned during the composition of the BOOK OF THE DEAD. [cf. DEATH SCIENCE]

KING SCALE—a diagram containing circles and paths which are painted special colors; used in a ritual by the devotee to assist him or her in becoming attuned to the universal power. [cf. FORMS-WITH-POWER Appendix 2, CEREMONIAL MAGIC]

KING SOLOMON—(Bible) considered to be the greatest MAGICIAN or PSYCHIC in the BIBLE, second to JESUS.

KING'S CHAMBER—(pyramid) the largest known room in the GIZA PYRAMID, where the energy is condensed, solidified and more potent; located in the middle of the pyramid; presently under investigation for its formation of a granite air condensor, for energy storage, and for the reason the atoms in this area absorb an increase of energy. (Inconcl.) [cf. PYRAMIDOLOGY Appendix 5]

KINGDOM—(esoteric) consists of a realm of living organisms which inhabit a particular plane, all having a core state of consciousness that includes the function, purpose, basic laws, symbols, and density of matter; operates under a sphere of power or influence from the same jurisdiction of a higher realm of other living units; major kingdoms of the following worlds are: 1. PHYSICAL WORLD: (a) HUMAN BEING KINGDOM, (b) ANIMAL KINGDOM, (c) PLANT KINGDOM, (d) MINERAL KINGDOM, (e) bird kingdom, (f) fish kingdom, and (g) insect kingdom; 2. ETHERIC WORLD: (a) ANGEL BEING KINGDOM, (b) NATURE SPIRITS kingdom, (c) discarnate human being kingdom, (d) NATURE DEVA kingdom, (e) ANIMAL KINGDOM, (f) SUBHUMAN BEINGS kingdom, (g) ARTIFICIAL ELEMENTAL kingdom; 3. aerial SPACE world: (a) CREATURES OF STRATOSPHERE kingdom, (b) CONSTRUCTS kingdom, (c) ETHERSHIP being kingdom, ETHEREAN BEINGS kingdom. (Inconcl.) [cf. PLANES, SPHERES, LAW OF KINGDOMS Appendix 7]

KINGDOM OF ELEMENTS—the ANGEL KINGDOM; so named because the angels must consider the AIR, WATER, FIRE and EARTH in cooperation with their responsibilities. [cf. ANGELOLOGY Appendix 5]

KINGDOM OF THE MIND—the FIFTH PLANE in the etheric world where plans are conceived and prepared for execution; great artists and composers receive their inspiration from this plane, through the skill of INSPIRATIONAL THOUGHT. [cf. INSPIRATIONAL ART, INSPIRATIONAL WRITING]

KINGDOMS OF LIVING CREATURES—1. the life in the element FIRE; 2. the life in the element AIR; 3. the life in the element WATER; 4. the life in the element EARTH. [cf. KINGDOM OF ELEMENTS, NATURE SPIRITS]

KINGLY CENTER—(ancient Eastern) the PINEAL GLAND; so named because it is the master gland of the etheric bodies, and the generator of the PITUITARY GLAND that has charge of the physical body; pineal gland is the main center for perceiving psychic information. [cf. THIRD-EYE AREA]

KINHIN—(Japan) ZEN type of walking meditation. [cf. MEDITATION, MOVEMENT-FOR-ALTERED-CONSCIOUSNESS]

KIRLIAN EFFECT—an energy that forms a field of brilliant colors surrounding all things (inanimate and animate), invisible to the naked eye, but can be photographed by high voltage cameras; this energy field changes patterns, shapes, density and size, and is predominantly indigo, blue, aqua, pink, and pale yellow; this field interpenetrates the object or organism, and extends out according to the shape of the organism or object, acting as a system of its own, with its own principles; has been investigated and studied since the invention of high voltage cameras; can be perceived clairvoyantly. (Inconcl.) [cf. KIRLIAN EFFECT Appendix 5, HIGH VOLTAGE PHOTOGRAPHY]

KIRLIAN PHOTOGRAPHY—the process for taking pictures of the emanations and radiations surrounding objects and persons, which the human eye does not see; made possible by a high voltage camera invented by Semyon and Valentina Kirlian, in Russia; the camera provides a method for the conversion of nonelectrical properties of an object into electrical properties, which are captured on film, by means of high-voltage spark discharges. (Inconcl.) **Syn.** HIGH VOLTAGE PHOTOGRAPHY; ELECTRO-PHOTOGRAPHY; (do not confuse with PSYCHIC PHOTOGRAPHY). [cf. STREAMER REPULSION, SUPERSENSITIVE PHOTO MULTIPLIERS, ELECTRON MICROSCOPY, KIRLIAN EFFECT Appendix 5]

KIRLIAN THEORY—(Russia) all organisms and objects are charged with electricity of a high voltage frequency, which interpenetrates and emanates out from the whole system; these emanations follow the natural lines of force as they leave the object and organism; the lines of force are sub-atomic particles, a "cold" PLASMA that makes an electromagnetic field "surrounding" the entire unit. (Inconcl.) [cf. MITOGENTIC RADIATION, ETHERIC DOUBLE, PRANA]

KIRTAN—(India) a special rhythmic dance choreographed for the purpose of putting the dancer in an ALTERED-STATE-OF-CONSCIOUSNESS; the objective is to bring spiritual enlightenment, psychic experiences and an increased dream power and recall. [cf. FORCED PSYCHISM, DIVINE INTOXICATION, MOVEMENT-FOR-ALTERED-CONSCIOUSNESS]

KISMET—to have one's fortune told in prophetic form, and then submit to it objectively; to be caught in a fatalistic syndrome. [cf. PREDICTIONS, PROPHECY]

KITE-FLYING—(Europe, Orient) the popular pastime of flying kites to stir up the atoms in the sky, with the belief that this keeps the negative vibrations away from that area. [cf. PSYCHIC THEFT, TELEPATHY]

KIVA—(Native American: Hopi, Pueblo, "sacred circle") a highly symbolic, ritualistic ceremony that sets the gods to work, tapping into psychic information, guidance, counsel and protection for the tribe. [cf. KIVAS, CEREMONIAL MAGIC, MEDIUMSHIP, HYPERTRANCE STATE]

KIVAS—(Native American, Pueblo) an underground sacred chamber where the tribal members go to communicate with their spiritual protectors or etheric world guides. [cf. TRANCE, GUIDE, DELTA STATE OF CONSCIOUSNESS]

KLIEG CONJUNCTIVITIS—(ufology) an "eyeburn"; inflammation, itching and soreness of the eyes as a reaction to ULTRA VIOLET RAYS, after contact with certain UFOs. [cf. CLOSE-ENCOUNTERS-OF-THE-THIRD KIND, SPOTTER, DOR CLOUDS]

KLU—(Egypt) the radiance of the human being in eternal life; see THE BUDDHIC BODY.

KNACKER—(Cornwall, England) see KNOCKER and NATURE SPIRITS.

KNIFE SIDE—(karate) a term to designate the use of the hand in a certain position to strike and stop blood. [cf. EMPTY HANDS]

KNOCKER—(Cornwall, England) a nature spirit in charge of the mines; seen singing and knocking in rich mines; capable of being both mischievous and helpful. **Syn.** KNACKERS.

KNOCKS—(percussion) 1. noise that sounds like a human knocking on a wall, chair, or within the walls heard while sitting in a SEANCE; sometimes a code of *yes* and *no* is established, so questions can be asked by the SITTERS; comes from the etheric world intelligence who uses the ECTOPLASM from the MEDIUM and sitters to perform; 2. to be psychically responsible for sounds, similar to a knock on a door, or furniture; occurs spontaneously in a medium's home who has the skill of PERCUSSION; heard by many household members; usually meant to convey a message to the medium; e.g., the medium is being reminded that they forgot to do something, being notified of a traumatic event to come, or complimented on a recent deed or decision to reassure the medium it was correct; (do not confuse with CLAIRAUDIENCE which is heard by the psychic only). **Syn.** RAPS. [cf. LANGUAGE OF RAPPINGS, INDEPENDENT BELLS, PERCUSSION Appendix 2]

KNOT OF BRAHMA—(Hinduism) an invisible, inverted triangle energy field housing the KUNDA-

LINI power at the base of the spine; compared to a knot because of its cluster of energy, and because this energy must be loosened before its journey up the kundalini. **Syn.** KANDA.[**cf.** IDA, PINGALA]

KNOT OF SHIVA—(Hinduism) an invisible, inverted triangle found in the SOLAR PLEXUS CHAKRA, similar in nature to a tied knot. [**cf.** LOWER MAN, COILED SERPENT]

KNOT OF VISHNU—(Hinduism) an invisible triangle found in the SPLEEN CHAKRA, similar to a tied knot. [**cf.** ROOT CHAKRA, KNOT OF BRAHMA, KANDA, COSMIC FIRE]

KNOTS—used symbolically in magical work in conjunction with the LAW OF MIMICRY and the LAW OF SIMILARITY; **1.** a continuous knotting in the form of horizontal figure eight, represents infinity; can be drawn on paper, visualized in the mind, or tied with a cord; **2.** anything, in the form of a simile, that can be used to bind the body of the doll or picture of the subject being treated, has the power to bind the etheric world entities either in or out; e.g., "Gordian knots which were wrought so intricately around his image, and could not be undone, helped protect him from evil entities"; **3.** to conjure up good etheric intelligences in a ritual, and their knot a cord around the image of the subject being treated, to keep the etheric world helpers always around the subject for protection and guidance; **4.** knots are usd for keeping one SPELLBOUND for a long time; when the doll is untied, the negative vibrations of the subject are released. [**cf.** SPELL, THREAD, CONJURE UP, SYMPATHETIC MAGIC]

KNOWER—the Godhead; see TOTALITY.

KNOWER OF THE FIELD—that spark within all people which gives energy to the body and mind substance; that which motivates people in a direction of improvement; see MONAD. [**cf.** HUMAN BEING SPECIES SEED, INTUITION]

KNOWLEDGE—**1.** a scope of AWARENESS of varying degrees of information, which one feels good about, and then learns accordingly from memory; **2.** is not what one teaches another, but what one causes another to remember; "all KNOWLEDGE is remembering." **3.** (Maharishi Mahesh Yogi) a structured consciousness brought to light; **4.** material that is proven either by the power of the intellect or by evidence of the SENSES; **5.** (esoteric) not facts that can be or have been proven necessarily, but repeated results that are obvious; **6.** infor-

mation which cannot be separated from action; the step before WISDOM; "knowledge is the beginning of practice, and doing is the completion of knowledge or wisdom." [**cf.** LAW OF KNOWLEDGE and LAW OF SELF-KNOWLEDGE Appendix 7]

KNOWLEDGE BEYOND THAT TIME PERIOD—INSPIRATIONAL THOUGHT given to the geniuses or scientists as answers to their questions regarding discoveries that are correct, but will not be accepted until future years; pertains to being born in a time period with access to information and understanding of future science. [**cf.** FIFTH PLANE, COGNITIVE CLAIRSENTIENCE]

KOAN—(Zen, "authoritative") (pronounced "Ko-an") an unanswerable question or riddle used as a tool for stopping the useless inner MENTAL CHATTER that goes on in the minds of humans throughout the day; forces the student to a greater awareness of REALITY through contemplation; the nonverbal and illogical answer cannot be found, so eventually this point-of-focus, over a period of time, breaks the normal inner mental chatter, making room for a more qualitative inner chatter when it resumes; e.g., a koan: "What is the sound of one hand clapping?"; also called JUST SITTING. [**cf.** POINT-OF-FOCUS, INNER-DIALOGUE, CLEAR]

KOAN THEORY—nothing exists but the here and now. [**cf.** NEW-AGE PSYCHOLOGY Appendix 5]

KOBOLD—(Germany) a nature spirit who lives below the earth's surface, and who despises the light; generally troublesome, mischievous and frustrating when dealing with humans. **Sim:** KNOCKER.

KOILON—(Annie Bessant, Charles W. Leadbeater) the ultimate physical ATOM that fills all space; the spiralling vortex of about 14,000 million bubbles in koilon; the atoms alter themselves in their capacity to resound to vibrations as the cycles proceed. [**cf.** VIBRATIONS, ATOMS]

KOKYSYU—(China, "preventative medicine") given by the superior physician who has been trained to intercede before the early building of a disease, (the inferior physician begins to help when the disease has already developed). [**cf.** HOLISTIC HEALTH, ALTERNATIVES, WELLNESS]

KOLAM—(India, Hinduism) an intricate geometrical pattern used to invoke good vibrations into one's home; special symbols used that attract a desired result, e.g., an ALTAR drawn on the door of the threshhold is used to safeguard that home; a drawn angel placed in front of the guest's chair is used to prevent evil spirits from jumping down his or her mouth. [cf. CEREMONIAL MAGIC, SYMBOLISM, HEXAGRAM]

KOMMASSO—a NATURE SPIRIT that lives within trees; can be mischievous or helpful to humans; see FAIRIES.

KOOT HOOMI—the great master of the etheric world who brought great inspiration to Madame Blavatsky for the THEOSOPHICAL SOCIETY.

KORAN—the sacred books of ISLAM; divided into 114 suras; believed to have been dictated to Muhammad by St. Gabriel; regarded by the Muslims as their law and religion. **Syn.** QURAN.

KOSMIC LIFE—existences that are limitless, boundless, infinite, and perhaps without beginning. [cf. TOTALITY, LAW OF MICRO/MACROCOSM Appendix 7]

KOSMIC NOUS—the source of divinity; the higher MANAS or spiritual monad; see MONAD. [cf. TOTALITY, DIVINE]

KOSMON REVELATION—a sacred history of the kingdoms in the higher and lower PLANES in the etheric world; begins with the submersion of the continent PAN, in the Pacific Ocean.

KOSMOS—(Greece) 1. (capitalized) refers to the entire infinite galaxies; the universe as an orderly, organized, whole unit; see TOTALITY; 2. (uncapitalized) refers to the galaxy of the earth. [cf. UNIVERSE]

KOYEMSHI—("holy fools") see PSYCHIC.

KRISHNA, BHAGAVAD LORD—(India) a beloved AVATAR who came in a physical body in 3,000 B.C.; teacher of the BHAGAVAD-GITA; also known as **Hari Krishna, Lord,** and **Vishnu-Krishna;** supreme God of the HINDUISM philosophy; considered to be the incarnation of God, or the perfect man specimen; known as "one who plays the flute."

KRIYA SAKTI—(Sanskrit) a method of MEDITATION used to awaken the NADIS, the etheric nerve fluid within the astral nervous system, to be used for healing. [cf. ASTRAL BODY, QUIET ATTENTIVENESS]

KRIYA YOGA—(Yoga, Sanskrit *kri,* "to do, to act and react") a technique taught by Lahiri Mahasaya, whereby the sensory tumult is stilled, permitting one to achieve an ever-increasing identity with COSMIC CONSCIOUSNESS; the Yogi who faithfully practices the technique is gradually freed from KARMA, the natural principle of cause and effect; a simple psychophysical method by which human blood is decarbonated and recharged with oxygen; the atoms of this extra oxygen are transmuted into life currents to rejuvenate the brain and spinal centers; by stopping the accumulation of venous blood, the yogi is able to lessen or prevent the decay of tissues; this transmutes his or her cells into energy, e.g., Elijah, JESUS, Kabir, and other prophets were past masters of the use of Kriya, by which they caused their bodies to materialize and dematerialize at will. [cf. ALCHEMIST, ASCEND, APPORTATION, HUMAN PSYCHOKINESIS]

KRIYA-MARGA—(India) a path of ritual that the worshipers must follow. [cf. PATH SYMBOLISM, HINAYANA, TREE OF LIFE, PEYOTE ROAD]

KRIYAS—a HATHA YOGA technique of postures and MEDITATION for cleansing vital organs, such as the lungs, sinuses, kidneys, colon, and stomach; helps them function properly and have greater resistance to disease.

KRU—(Cambodia) psychics, medicine men and exorcists; see PSYCHIC.

KSANA—(Buddhism, "the highest pleasure") a state of consciousness wherein one is in the favorable moment; eternal present, when every instant of time is past, present, future; one is stabilized, and all time and all space surrounds one; a state of non-motion, stability, or motion too fast to be measured. [cf. TIME, EKA-KSANA, ETERNAL PRESENT, POINT-OF-FOCUS]

KU—(Hawaii) an ETHERIC WORLD INTELLIGENCE who earned the rank of DEITY, and is given charge over wars. [cf. SUPREME GUIDES OF HUMANITY]

KU, KANE, KANALOA—(Huna) highly evolved etheric world angels who serve over worlds and people, and who work to fulfill the TRINITY of EVOLUTION. [cf. PLANETARY ANGEL, MICHAEL]

KU-HE-A—(Huna, "to call") to ask for higher information and spiritual assistance by tuning into the etheric world helpers. **Syn.** KA-HE-A. [cf. INVOCATION, EVOCATION, CEREMONIAL MAGIC]

KUAN TI—(nineteenth century China) an ETHERIC WORLD INTELLIGENCE in charge of preventing wars.

KUANTHROPY—to transform one's self into a dog

and take on the characteristics of the dog; see SHAPE-CHANGING. **Syn.** LYCANTHROPY. [**cf.** DIMENSION-SHIFTING]

KUKLOS GENESEON—see REINCARNATION.

KUKULCAN—(Mayan, Yucatan Indian) a very highly evolved etheric world intelligence who takes on the symbolic form of a huge serpent, and acts as a protecting agent for earthlings who call upon him. [**cf.** PROTECTOR, DOORKEEPER]

KUMBHAKAM—also spelled **kumbhaka;** (Yoga) a method of breathing whereby the breath is held to allow the toxic gases to be replaced by fresh energy. [**cf.** COMPLETE BREATH, HYPERVENTILATING]

KUNDALINI—(Sanskrit *kund,* "to burn"; *kunda,* "to coil or to spiral") a concentrated field of intelligent, cosmic, invisible energy absolutely vital to life; beginning in the base of the spine as a man or woman begins to evolve in their first incarnation; fed by the chakras along the spine and by the cosmic energy entering through the feet from the earth; as WISDOM is earned in each incarnation, this electromagnetic, ultrapotent energy moves slowly upward through the spine; it is directed by the speed of the SOUL-MIND as the soul-mind meets the requirements of each CHAKRA, according to the needs and thinking of the individual; eventually this energy is unspiralled through the MEDULLA OBLONGATA, PITUITARY GLAND, PINEAL GLAND and through the CROWN CHAKRA to unite with the SILVER CORD; one will ascend to the higher realms to finish their evolutionary cycle; kundalini is feminine polarity in nature. **Sim.** COILED SERPENT, COSMIC FIRE, CHI, BIOPLASMA, HOLY SPIRIT. [**cf.** Appendix 5 KUNDALINI]

KUNDALINI PRANA—an energy emanating from the sun and moon, to the earth, where it is transformed into negative kundalini prana; it then travels up the feet of mankind to the base of the spine, feeding power to the kundalini. [**cf.** KANDA, COSMIC FIRE, KUNDALINI Appendix 5]

KUNDALINI SHAKTI—(Yoga, Sanskrit) the cosmic, ethereal, electromagnetic, ultrapotent, intelligent energy in condensed form sleeping at the base of the spine; located in the (lower) MULDHARA CHAKRA before it is aroused, and travels up the spine. **Syn.** COILED SERPENT. [**cf.** COSMIC WATERS, FIRE OF WISDOM]

KUNDALINI YOGA—(Tibet) a special technique used to bring harmony between the kundalini power and psychic energy, to increase psychic energies. [**cf.** MENTAL PSYCHIC PROCESSES Appendix 2]

KUNG—(ancient China) represents the musical tone of *F,* and is considered the great tone of nature. [**cf.** F, CLAIRAUDIENCE, MUSIC OF THE SPHERES]

KUNG HEALER—see !KUNG HEALER.

KUNG-FU—(Zen Buddhism) a combination of recreation, exercise and self-defense; a learned power, with no wasted movement; comes from a repertoire of more than fifty basic techniques, which can thwart any known attack from an assailant, and which provides a stunning counter-attack. **Syn.** BLACK BELT, KARATE. [**cf.** KNIFE SIDE, MIND-CLEANSING MEDITATION, GI]

KUPHI—a mixture of incense consisting of sixteen ingredients, one of which is FRANKINCENSE. [**cf.** LAND OF PUNT]

KURMOS—(Greece) a NATURE SPIRIT making itself known as half-human/half-animal; shows itself with pointed chin and ears, two small horns, and shaggy legs with hooves; comes from a higher plane of existence, with a purpose to help trees grow; capable of communicating with humans. [**cf.** PAN]

KWOTH—(Egypt) an ETHERIC WORLD ENTITY from either the higher or lower PLANES; plural **kuth.** [**cf.** Appendix 3 ETHERIC WORLD IN-TELLIGENCES]

KYPHI—(botane) an aromatic plant that has prop-erties of tranquility and healing; prepared from sixteen materials, according to the prescription of the sacred books.

KYRIE ELEISON—words used for silent repetition in MEDITATION; used as a MANTRA in Christian monasteries; means "Lord Jesus Christ, Son of God, have mercy on me a sinner." **Syn.** JESUS PRAYER. [**cf.** MANTRA, JAPAM]

KYUNGRAK SYSTEM OF DUCTS—the network of MERIDIAN LINES which compose the electrical system in the human body; used by the ACU-PUNCTURE practitioner. **Syn.** MERIDIANS. [**cf.** ACUPRESSURE, BODY TRANSRECEIVERS, BLOCKS, REFLEXOLOGY]

"L" PARTICLE—see VITAL LIFE FORCE.

L & T FIELDS—abbr. for LIFE-AND-THOUGHT FIELDS, coined by C. Baxter, Harold Saxton Burr, L. Raviz; see HUMAN AURA.

L-FIELD—abbr. for LIFE-FIELDS; coined by Harold Saxton Burr; "an energy field inside, outside, above, below, and completely surrounding every chromosome, molecule and atom in the body, as well as every other organism, in, on, or under the earth"; (Joseph Goodavage) "a reflection or component of supersentient force that measures emotion." **Syn.** ELECTRODYNAMIC FIELD [**cf.** AURA Appendix 3]

L-ROD—(dowsing) a stiff wire, bent at a right angle about one-third the way down, that is used for DOWSING; also written **"L" rod. Syn.** ANGLE-ROD. [**cf.** REMOTE DOWSING]

L-ROD RESPONSE POSITION—abbr. RP; (dowsing) the correct way to hold the L-ROD, whether in the open field or asking a question; upper arms close to the body, and forearms at right angles with a rod in each hand pointing straight ahead; the body is relaxed and the mind is in a neutral state ready for the response; rods can point downward, cross each other, or one hold its place and the other cross over it. [**cf.** DOWSING]

L-TRYPTOPHON—(dreams) a new chemical found in milk, certain meats, and other protein rich foods which facilitates sleep and allows normal dreaming. (Inconcl.) [**cf.** DREAMS, NEW-AGE PSYCHOLOGY, CURATIVE EDUCATION]

LA PRISE DES YEUX—(Haiti, Voodoo) to remain conscious and allow the LOA (Godguide) to possess one's body and give one enormous power; at this time one can see visions clearly and hear whispers in one's CLAIRAUDIENT ear; attributed to be a skill of the high priest in which he is given instructions and guidance for his people; (do not confuse with Western IMPERSONATION, whereby the medium is unconscious). [**cf.** COMPLETE INPERSONATION, FULL TRANCE, PHYSICAL OBSESSION IN A MEDIUM, INSPIRATIONAL THOUGHT]

LA REPRODUCTION INTERDITE—("forbidden double") A SPONTANEOUS ASTRAL PROJECTION when one's astral body slides out of the physical body, hovers close by, and is aware of the physical body below. (Inconcl.) **Sim.** SPONTANEOUS ASTRAL PROJECTION. [**cf.** IN-THE-RANGE-OF-CORD-ACTIVITY]

LA VECCHIA—(Italian) witchcraft includes both black and white witchcraft, used for both good and evil. [**cf.** PARAPSYCHOLOGY, PSYCHIC ARTS Synonyms Appendix 3]

LABUNI—(New Guinea) coined by Gelaria; see VITAL LIFE FORCE.

LABYRINTH SUBCONSCIOUS—confusing and mixed up events that randomly surface from the MEMORY BANK, that the individual cannot find a way out of or understand, therefore the confusion cannot be resolved and keeps on surfacing. (Inconcl.) [**cf.** FREE ASSOCIATION, UNCONSCIOUSNESS]

LACONIC MEDIUM—individual who lacks patience when SITTING for development and therefore allows any ETHERIC WORLD ENTITY to intervene for communication; the messages are brief and meaningless; if not stopped, inferior entities will oblige and enter medium's mind frequently, as they do not care if they cause harm to the medium's body or mind. [**cf.** COAT OF PROTECTION, SERIOUS MEDIUM, SUBCONSCIOUS FORCE, UP-FOR-GRABS]

LADDER—a symbol used in psychic messages and in dreams to represent: 1. mankind rising above the human conditions of earth; 2. mankind's need to ascend to a higher state of consciousness; 3. mankind connecting to superior spiritual power; depicted as being located in the sky. [**cf.** SYMBOLISM, TOTEM, RIGHT-HAND PATH]

LADDER OF LIFE—(Theosophy) pertains to the expressions of the upward stages of manifestations of existences in the universe. **Syn.** HERMETIC CHAIN. [**cf.** TOTEMISM, EVOLUTIONARY SCALE]

LADDER TO HEAVEN—(Native American) a special, earned ritual in which the shaman-to-be climbs a birch tree, typifying ascending to heaven; from this day on they will only communicate with the superior ETHERIC WORLD INTELLIGENCES, will be protected by them, and will be given guidance for their tribe. **Sim.** ASCENT. [**cf.** SHAMANSHIP INSTRUCTIONS, GUARDIAN OF THE DOOR, ASCEND]

LADY OF DARKNESS—(death science) a special angel, capable of making a dying person invisible as she travels through the density, which eases that step of the death process. [**cf.** DEATH SCIENCE, DEATH ANGEL, SURVIVALISTS, NEAR-DEATH EXPERIENCES]

LADY OF HEAVEN—1. (Sumeria) the goddess Venus Inanna; 2. (Babylon) Ishtar, the morning star who presided over war and carnage. [**cf.** GREAT ONES, MAGNIFICENT DEVAS]

LAIBON—(East Africa, Masai) the religious leader who is a PSYCHIC, a HEALER, an herbal practitioner and PROPHET. **Syn.** MEDICINE MAN. [**cf.** SHAMAN-SHIP, FILLED WITH THE SPIRIT]

LAM—a SEED-MANTRA inscribed at the chakra's center; mantra is pronounced "ong." [**cf.** CHAKRAS, KUNDALINI, REVERIE, MEDITATION]

LAMA—("religious superior") those monks in the lamasery who have reached priesthood and developed psychic skills. **Sim.** MASTER, GURU. [**cf.** ANGEL HIERARCHY, MASTERSHIP, SHAMANSHIP]

LAMAISM—religion of the Tibetans; a form of BUDDHISM. [**cf.** OUTSIDERS, INSIDERS]

LAMASERY—(Tibet) the school where one enters to become a priest, to advance spiritually, and to increase one's psychic skills.

LAMEN—a small round table kept sacred for the use of SCRYING, magnetizing water, or for other paraphernalia used in healing and for gaining PSY-CHIC INFORMATION; also called **the holy table.** [cf. MAGNETIZED WATER, SYMBOLS]

LAMIA—(Tibet) see PSYCHIC.

LAND OF DARKNESS—(Egypt) 1. an area where evil is practiced; 2. a land of rich black soil from which all life and good stems. [**cf.** BRIMSTONE, PRIMARY PERCEPTION, ATTRACTION CON-SCIOUSNESS]

LAND OF PUNT—an area in ancient Egypt where FRANKINCENSE was grown. [**cf.** INCENSE, SYM-BOLS, FORCED PSI, BOT'ANE]

LAND OF THE GOLDEN LIGHT—see ASTRAL PLANE.

LAND OF THE SHADOWS—a state of consciousness in the etheric world that is dark, dense, and active with crime, inhabited by ignorant new SOUL-MINDS; made from mankind's foul, evil and other' negative vibrations, and mankind's viruses and

waste products while living in earth. (Inconcl.) **Syn.** DENSITY. [**cf.** HELL, ASTRAL SHELL, SHADE, SUBHUMAN BEING]

LAND SPIRITS—(ancient) nature spirits found inhabiting mountains, rocks, forests, marshes, and rivers; belonging to a minor ELEMENTAL group; will communicate with mankind to help or harm them.

LANDING—(ufology) an area where a UFO craft has landed at least one time; designates a special place on earth, because UFO craft seem to use the same area for landing more than once. [**cf.** LEY-LINES, ETHERIAN PHYSICS, PLANETIZATION, SPOT-TER, CLOSE-ENCOUNTER-OF-THE-FIRST-KIND]

LANDMARK IMAGERY—(dreams, incubation) a special symbol requested to be shown in the specific dream that answers the incubated question; e.g., to put a pink ribbon somewhere in the DREAMSTUFF that answers the question. [**cf.** INCUBATION DREAMING, MOTIVE UNCONSCIOUSNESS, DREAM-ING TRUE]

LANDSCAPE PAINTINGS—drawings, or paintings appearing on a public wall or building with information on how the land should be cared for; believed to be drawn by the DEVA in charge of that area. [**cf.** WANDJINA, PRECIPITATION]

LANGUAGE OF DREAMS—clairvoyant, fuzzy, mixed-up snatches of pictures that show mundane scenes, mundane objects, plots not carried out, friends, relatives, and strangers; used as symbols and metaphors to represent the personality of the dreamer, his or her lifestyle, and to give guidance and indicate dangers for that lifestyle and per-sonality. (Inconcl.) [**cf.** PSYCHIC CONSCIOUSNESS, REM]

LANGUAGE OF RAPPINGS—(seance) monosyl-labic answers to questions given through knocks on walls, tables, chairs, and "within" the walls by the ETHERIC WORLD INTELLIGENCES in the SEANCE room; a code is established between the SITTERS, MEDIUM, and ETHERIC WORLD to receive informa-tion not available through MUNDANE education. (Inconcl.) **Syn.** TYPTOLOGY. [**cf.** PHILLIP GROUP, PERCUSSION, RAPS, KNOCKS]

LANGUAGE OF SIGNS—movement of objects in a pantomine manner in the SEANCE room by the etheric world intelligences to show their feelings; e.g., a gentle floating hanky means they are in agreement; rocking of one's chair means to pay attention; loud, fast knocks mean anger. **Syn.** SEMATOLOGY. [**cf.** PRECIPITATION, LEVITATION-TK, TELEKINESIS, KNOCKS]

LANOO—(Asiatic) see DISCIPLE.

LANSUIR—(Malay) a female psychic who is capable of changing the form of her body to that of a night owl and suck blood from children while they sleep; known by her long nails and ankle-length hair. [**cf.** PENANG-GALAN, SELF-TRANSFORMATION, WERE-LEOPARD, VAMPIRE]

LAO TAN—see LAO TSE.

LAO TSE—(China, 604 B.C.) supreme ruler and author of the Tao te ching, a great religious classic containing guidance for the improvement of man's soul-mind; also spelled **Lao Tzu.** [**cf.** LAOTSE]

LAOTSE—a Chinese classic composed of mystical and metaphysical scripture written in eighty-one stanzas of poetry, also called the TAO TE CHING. **Syn.** LAO TAN. [**cf.** LAO TSE, I CHING]

LAPIS—(esoteric) a mineral composed of the same elements of the HUMAN BODY, SOUL-MIND and SPIRIT; considered to be the earthly aspect of the PHILOSOPHER'S STONE; depicts a reentry into the womb of the earth. [**cf.** MINPSI, ALCHEMY Appendix 2, ELIXIR OF LIFE]

LAPIS LAZULI—(esoteric) a mineral that can increase one's psychic abilities, and give one self-assurance and strength; influenced by the highest vibrations from Jupiter; emblematic of the feminine aspect and sex. [**cf.** MINPSI, LAPIS, ATTRACTION CONSCIOUSNESS]

LAPIS NOSTER—(alchemy) a primary substance used by the ALCHEMIST because it has the property to germinate and develop the final substance in his formula for producing the PHILOSOPHER'S STONE. (Inconcl.) [**cf.** OUR STONE, TRANSMUTATION, PRIMA MATERIAL]

LAPIS PHILOSOPHICUM—(alchemy) the final objective of the ALCHEMIST in all operations, both mentally and spiritually; to perfect the PHILOSOPHER'S STONE. [**cf.** TRANSMUTATION, ELIXER OF LIFE, RESURRECTED]

LAR—(Rome) an ANGEL from the etheric world who is in charge of a household's activity and guardian of its inhabitants, to help maintain health and happiness. [**cf.** EXECUTIVE ORDER, ELEVATED SPIRITS, FRIVOLOUS SPIRITS]

LAR FAMILIARIS—an ETHERIC WORLD ENTITY attached to a special household, giving it protection and guidance. **Syn.** HOUSEHOLD LAR. [**cf.** ANGEL HIERARCHY, DOMESTIC SPIRITS, EARTH MOTHER]

LAR SEMITALES—(Rome) etheric world angels in charge of paths and highways, and who help maintain them and keep them safe. [**cf.** PLANETARY SPIRITS, REGENTS OF THE EARTH, MINOR DEVAS]

LARES—etheric world angels who come in pairs to guard the household, and to bring psychic information. **Syn.** LAR FAMILIARIS, LARES COMPITALES. [**cf.** DOMESTIC SPIRITS, COMFORTING ANGEL, ETHERIC WORLD INTELLIGENCES Appendix 2]

LARES COMPITALES—angels from the etheric world in charge of rural cross roads and busy urban intersections. **Syn.** CROSSROAD DEVAS. [**cf.** MAGNIFICENT DEVAS, ANCESTRAL SPIRITS, BENEFICENT DAEMON, CROSS ROADS]

LARES OF ANCIENTS—(Rome) see DOCTOR TEACHER and GENIUS. [**cf.** GUIDES, CONTROL, INNERBAND]

LARES PRAESTITES—(Rome) angels who have earned the rank by their many incarnations, to be guardians of the entire Roman people. [**cf.** HOLY ONES, ASCENDED BEING, LEGION]

LARGE GOOD ANGEL—(Haiti, Voodoo) see GROS BON ANGE.

LARVA—see GHOST.

LASER MICROPHONE MATRIX—invented by Patrick Flanagan; a special device that allows a tape recorder to "hear" inaudible sound in its vicinity, and to locate it and record it. [**cf.** COSMIC MUSIC, CLAIRAUDIENCE, TAPED VOICE PHENOMENA]

LATENT CONTENT—(dreams) the parts of a dream that are elusive but very significant to the dreamer; must be brought to the surface through HYPNOTHERAPY or through PSYCHOANALYSIS because the CONSCIOUS MIND evades their recall. (Inconcl.) [**cf.** DREAMS, DREAMS FOR HEALTH]

LAUDANUM—(botane) a narcotic plant used to reduce pain, to make one passive and to induce INSPIRATIONAL THOUGHT. (Inconcl.) [**cf.** PLANT CONVERSATIONS, MANDRAKE FRUITS, PSYCHOTROPIC PLANTS]

LAUREL—(botane) (Greece) a flower which induces an excitable and emotional trance state of consciousness, by chewing it or inhaling its smoke. [**cf.** FORCED PSI, JIMSON WEED, PSYCHOPATHOLOGY]

LAURIN—(Scandinavia) a nature spirit that is king of the dwarfs. [**cf.** WEE PEOPLE, FAIRIES]

LAW OF THE WHEEL—(Kabbalah) the never ending evolutionary path of universal life. [**cf.** JACOB'S LADDER, RIGHT-HANDED PATH, EVOLUTION]

LAY—(esoteric) to exorcise; see EXORCISM.

LAY GHOSTS—to exorcise EARTHBOUND ENTITIES that are haunting an EARTHLING; see EXORCISM.

LAY THE SPIRITS—(Voodoo) name of the ceremony used to put the zombies back in their graves when the master is through with them. [**cf.** ZOMBIE, VOODOOISM, SOULLESS PSYCHISM Appendix 2]

LAYA YOGA—1. (Yoga, "latency") one method of practicing RAJA YOGA meditation by use of a MANTRA; 2. (Tibet) to teach one to become master of their mind; e.g., to remember permanently something read only once. [**cf.** MENTAL BRAIN PROGRAMMING, MENTAL PSYCHIC PROCESSES]

LAYING-ON-OF-HANDS—(magnetic healing) to use one's hands to accelerate the normalizing of the patient's cells, so the patient's body can heal itself more quickly; the most common cross-cultural technique of healing and as old as civilization; the healing practitioner or psychic uses the magnetism within his or her own nervous system; this magnetism is concentrated upon to intensify its healing qualities, and is then transferred through their palms or fingertips to the patient; the healer's hands are placed over the congested area making physical contact or contacting a few inches above the body, or touching the head of the patient sending the magnetism to the diseased area; healing occurs gradually or instantaneously; patient feels heat, cold, prickles, and energy surge or nothing; a biochemical reaction takes place in the body chemistry of the patient; overstimulation can occur (but does not cause damage) if both healer and patient are psychic; (do not confuse with MENTAL HEALING, SPIRIT HEALING, or MEDIUMSHIP HEALING; see Appendix 4 for clarification). (Inconcl.) **Syn.** THERAPEUTIC TOUCH, CONTACT HEALING. [**cf.** MAGNETIC HEALING Appendix 2]

LAYOUT—the format for placing cards when giving a psychic reading in CARTOMANCY; the style of each deck of cards has its own pattern of placement on the table, and its own special handling by the reader or recipient. [**cf.** POINT-OF-FOCUS, SHUSUTAH, LOTS, TAROT CARDS]

LEA—see VITAL LIFE FORCE.

LEADER—(laboratory) (healing) an individual who questions the psychic in a PSI SCAN; chosen because he or she knows nothing about the patient's background, and therefore, cannot influence the psychic's information through unconscious telepathy. [**cf.** HEALING CURRENT, SENSITIVITY TRANSFER, SHEEP AND GOATS EFFECT]

LEAGUE—(esoteric) a group of ETHERIC WORLD INTELLIGENCES who help those who have just made their transition to adjust to their new home and conditions. [**cf.** WHITE BROTHERHOOD, DEATH ANGEL, DEVAS, PEACEFUL ORDER OF DEITIES, DEATH PROCESS]

LEARNED SPIRITS—ETHERIC WORLD INTELLIGENCES who bring higher degrees of philosophy and scientific knowledge to earthlings through psychic communication. [**cf.** GOD SPOKE, SUPERHUMAN BEING, SUPERIOR SPIRITS]

LEARNING TO LEARN—(esoteric) process of cells that seem to be able to learn more readily than other cells; particularly those cells that are useful for survival, and therefore have a survival memory, because they have been used more often. (Inconcl.) [**cf.** LAW OF INFORMATION and LAW OF INTELLIGENCE Appendix 7, PRIMARY PERCEPTION, SYMPATHETIC NERVOUS SYSTEM]

LEAST ACTION PRINCIPLE—to follow one's divine guidance to reach one's path in each incarnation in the shortest possible time; the objective is to be aware of one's informative intuitive mechanism, be able to separate it from instigated thoughts, and to desire to follow it. [**cf.** RIGHT-HAND PATH, EVOLUTION OF THE SOUL-MIND]

LECHIE—a nature spirit in charge of rural areas. **Syn.** FAUNS, SATYRS.

LED MEDITATION—see GUIDED MEDITATION.

LEDI SAYADAW—(Buddhism) a method of MEDITATION using the word PHYIT-PYET for a MANTRA, wherein one notices the endlessly changing particles and waves in the body. [**cf.** POLYSENSORY INCANTATION, BLESSED BE]

LEFAFA SEDO—(Ethiopia) an AMULET that is buried with a dead person to help him or her ascend to a paradise level of consciousness in the etheric world. [**cf.** DEATH SCIENCE, DISCARNATE ENTITY]

LEFT BRAIN HEMISPHERE—research shows that each half of the brain has its role as to the various phases of one's emotions, activities, abilities, and information processing; such as: 1. predominates during daytime, waking hours; 2. is attached to the five senses; 3. analyzes outer stimuli; 4. uses logical reasoning; 5. rationalizes stimuli input; 6. categorizes sensory input for the correct compartments of the SUBCONSCIOUS MIND; 7. uses rational language, both spoken and written; 8. processes linear information; 9. takes charge of orderliness in MUNDANE WORLD activity; 10. reacts objectively to science, mathematics, and time-sequential analysis; 11. controls the relationship in contemporary orientation; 12. focuses eye movement; 13. arouses physical motor ability; 14. dominates over the fight or flight mechanism of the SYMPATHETIC NERVOUS SYSTEM; 15. controls right side of the body; 16. dominates over the SUPRALIMINAL level of the mind; 17. is susceptible to cognitive diseases; 18. dominates over PSYCHOSOMATIC illnesses (mental disorders that affect the rational intellectual perception of the mundane); 19. causes a surge of blood in psychic tasks; 20. takes charge of the speech of a TRANCE PERSONALITY; 21. during this predominancy the RIGHT BRAIN HEMISPHERE is enlarged, showing inactivity. (Inconcl.)

LEFT PSYCHIC NERVE—see IDA.

LEFT-HAND PATH—(Sanskrit) a road of darkness that is taken by those who follow a direction of evil (called BROTHERS OF THE SHADOW); the direction one follows when having intentions of evil doings, and when following BLACK MAGIC religions and rituals; the road that leads to HELL on earth, and after death. [**cf.** PATH CULT, SEPHIROTH, DENSITY, LAW OF SOUL-MIND EVOLUTION Appendix 7]

LEGAROU—(Haiti) a WITCH who is capable of changing shape into an animal form; attacks sleeping persons to suck their blood. [**cf.** HAG, SHE-WOLF, GHOSTS OF THE GIBLET, DIMENSION-SHIFTING]

LEGBA—(Haiti, Voodoo) an angel who is guardian over the passage between the ETHERIC WORLD and the EARTH PLANE, and who has charge of whether the SOUL-MIND entering the earth for a new

INCARNATION has earned the good or bad LOA. [**cf.** DEATH ANGEL, SOUL JURY]

LEGION—(Bible) the hundreds of inferior, undesirable etheric world entities who abide in the DENSITY, and who are capable of possessing earthlings. [**cf.** POSSESSION, EARTHBOUND ENTITIES, DEVILS OF ALL AGES]

LEMON—(esoteric) a sour, acid fruit that vibrates at the fastest frequency of any of mankind's foods; used over the centuries in physical healing remedies. [**cf.** FOOD SCALE]

LEMUR—see GHOST.

LEMURIA—also called MU; a gigantic continent that was believed to have once been located on planet earth and was lost; covered an area from the foot of the Himalayas, Tibet, Mongolia, and the Gobi Desert; extended south across India, Ceylon, Sumatra, to Madagascar on its right, and to Australia and Tasmania on its left; located beyond Easter Island; believed by some to be the evolution of the first physical man, about 18,000,000 years ago, (before the time of ATLANTIS); relics have been found on Easter Island of the most astounding and eloquent memorials of primeval giants; some of the heads of the colossal statues have remained unbroken and the features are recognized to be the type and character attributed to the Fourth Race giants; cities seem to have been built out of rare metals and the lava that the fires vomited; (Helena Petrovna Blavatsky) archaeology findings show that they worshipped images of themselves in size and likeness, cut out of white stone of the mountains and black stone of the subterranean fires. [**cf.** EVOLUTION, ROOT RACE]

LEPANTHROPY—to temporarily change one's shape and form into that of a hare, conduct business, and then change back into the human form. [**cf.** DIMENSION-SHIFTING, SHAPE-CHANGING]

LEPRECHAUN—(Ireland) a NATURE SPIRIT that shows himself in human form, wears green clothing, and appears from two inches to two feet in height; lives in solitude but enjoys darting in and out of the THIRD DIMENSION for humans; known to spin like a top using his headgear as an axis; has characteristics of being sly, tricky, and helpful to humans; (past) repaired shoes for earthlings; belief: leprechauns know where gold is hidden. **Syn.** ELF, FAY, PIXIE, BROWNIE.

LESHY—(Slavic) a NATURE SPIRIT that appears to

humans as a DWARF; has green eyes burning like coals, a long white beard and white hair, and wears a green robe and crown; his function is to guard the woods and take care of the animals.

LESSER KEY OF SOLOMON—a GRIMOIRE based on ancient writings dealing with the demons and their powers, attributed to KING SOLOMON. [cf. INFERNAL ANIMALS, NON HUMAN REALMS, EARTH-BOUND ENTITIES]

LESSER MYSTERIES—a book composed of dramatical ceremonies, rituals, teachings, and information preparing one for DEATH. [cf. CEREMONIAL MAGIC Appendix 2]

LETHARGIC STAGE OF HYPNOSIS—see LIGHT STATE OF HYPNOSIS.

LETTERS TO THE DEAD—(Egypt) messages written to the dead on pottery vessels that were used to hold food for the person after they had transited (died). [cf. DEATH SCIENCE, OPENING OF THE MOUTH CEREMONY, SECONDARY CLEAR LIGHT, LORDS OF DEATH]

LEVEL AND BEINGNESS—an ETHERIC WORLD INTELLIGENCE of strong formless energy existing on the higher planes of consciousness, and who communicates with earthlings. **Syn.** ANGEL. [cf. ANGEL HIERARCHY, JUNO, THOR, BOUNDLESS IMMORTALS]

LEVEL OF BEING—1. the awareness of REALITY for the moment; a state of consciousness one can relate to, at the time one is in it; e.g., when one is dreaming, the activity feels very real; 2. to be aware of existing in the universe; 3. mankind can change his or her level of being, from mundane existence to ethereal existences, by altering their attention and by focusing on higher realms, because mankind is composed of all the elements of all the ethereal realms: e.g., to achieve a DISSOCIATED STATE during meditation; to take a soul-projection to higher planes. **Syn.** REALITY. [cf. MENTAL PROJECTION, CONSCIOUSNESS]

LEVEL SHIFT—(hypnotherapy) a change in one's attention from the present life to a previous life or to a future life, where one retains sufficient normal waking consciousness to dictate a running commentary of these emotions, thoughts, and sensations that are being experienced in these lives. (Inconcl.) [cf. PARTIAL REGRESSION, COMPLETE REGRESSION, REINCARNATION, KARMA]

LEVEL-OFF—(biofeedback training) to reach a state of consciousness, when one is hooked-up to a biofeedback instrument, wherein one feels he or she has reached normalcy, as much as possible; this state of consciousness has a relationship to the electrical current level in the instrument and to the electrical current in the subject, and is necessary for an accurate reading on any one of the instruments; to obtain this relationship, the subject must do nothing but just "be" for a few minutes, until the instrument comes to a stable reading point, and the subject agrees that this feels like his or her norm. **Syn.** RESTING ELECTRICAL LEVEL. [cf. BASELINE READING, ARTIFACT, AROUSAL]

LEVELS—(esoteric) see PLANES.

LEVELS OF REALITY—pertains to the ability of the SOUL-MIND to realize where he or she is on each plane of existence, simultaneously; does not infer that the human brain is aware of these existences, but does infer that the soul-mind has many AWARENESS levels at once. (Inconcl.) [cf. TIME, MULTIDIMENSIONAL, REALITY, RELATIVE IMMORTALITY]

LEVITATED DANCING—to dance for hours, about an inch above the floor or ground, without becoming tired; accomplished by undivided attention on the music, or on the upper part of the body, this puts one in control of the speed of descent. (Inconcl.) [cf. LEVITATED RUNNING, PROLONGED JOGGING, ASTRAL PROJECTION]

LEVITATED RUNNING—(Tibet) to run great distances without touching one's feet to the ground and without tiring; accomplished by focalizing one's entire attention on the upper part of the body and allowing the feet to take care of themselves; the focalizing of attention puts one in a semitrance making the skill easier; can also be accomplished by allowing an etheric world intelligence to interpenetrate one's body, and use it to run because of the intelligence's ability to contol gravity. **Sim.** LEVITATED DANCING. [cf. PROLONGED JOGGING, FORCED PSI, SEMITRANCE, MOVEMENT-FOR-ALTERED-CONSCIOUSNESS, WALKING-ON-WATER]

LEVITATION—to elevate one's self or an object in the air; the object or one's self is kept suspended for a time without the use of physical means; performed by PSYCHIC or MEDIUM while in a SEMITRANCE or FULL TRANCE state of consciousness; levitation is always willed and "desired-controlled";

accomplished by the undivided concentration of the SUBCONSCIOUS MIND or by the guides; the first step to teleportation. (Inconcl.) Various hypothesis of investigators: 1. the psychic's subconscious mind or the medium's guides neutralize or reverse the attraction of GRAVITY in the medium, the psychic, or the object; 2. medium synchronizes with the guides, so the guides can nullify the normal gravitational effect, and raise the object; 3. psychic concentrates on the auric field of the object until the rate of vibrational frequency changes and the atoms seem weightless, as in ANTIMATTER; 4. psychic or GUIDE changes the rate of "time flow" throughout the substance, making a weight loss; 5. many guides of the medium invisibly lift the medium or object in the air; see LEVITATION PSYCHOKINESIS and LEVITATION TELEKINESIS. [cf. ANTIMATTER, VIBRATIONAL FREQUENCY, GRAVITY CONTROL, SYMPATHETIC VIBRATION, TELEPORTATION Appendix 4]

LEVITATION GEMS—(Buddhism) stones and gems that are endowed with the special property that, when placed in one's mouth, will cause one to become weightless and rise in the air. [cf. MINPSI, GRAVITY CONTROL Appendix 2, LEVITATION-TK]

LEVITATION PSYCHOKINESIS—abbr. LEVITATION-PK; 1. to elevate an object or one's self vertically in the air; one's self or the object is kept suspended in one spot for a short time without physical means; accomplished by the undivided concentration of the SUBCONSCIOUS MIND, while in an ALPHA or THETA STATE OF CONSCIOUSNESS; planned, willed, and controlled; the first step in teleportation-PK; (object or one's self) (a) to neutralize or reverse the attraction of gravity in the entity allowing a natural elevation; (b) to change the rate of vibrational frequency, making the atoms weightless, by focalizing attention on the auric field of the object or one's self; entity becomes antimatter; (c) to change the rate of time flow through the substance, co-creating a weight loss. [cf. GRAVITY CONTROL, ALCHEMY, ANTIMATTER, TELEPORTATION-PK] 2. (one's self) to rise in the air while in a state of "spiritual ecstasy"; theory: the rate of vibration changes during the spiritual devotional period; happens spontaneously and uncontrolled; documentation exists in which it has occurred to priests and nuns; 3. (one's self) to overcome and release the grossness in the body by prolonged MEDITATION; as one frees one's self of materialistic thoughts, the atoms are simultaneously freed of the

LAW OF GRAVITY, and the body rises and hops about like a frog. [cf. MOTOR SUSPENSION, TM, ASCENSION, ALCHEMY]

LEVITATION TELEKINESIS—abbr. LEVITATION-TK; (mediumship) to synchronize one's body chemistry with the ETHERIC WORLD INTELLIGENCES, who vertically lift an object or the medium's body into the air, and keep it suspended in the air without physical means for a short time; always programmed and willed; first step to accomplish for TELEPORTATION TELEKINESIS; hypothesis: 1. while medium is in a SEMITRANCE or DEEP TRANCE state of consciousness, a group of guides invisibly lift the object or medium's body into the air; 2. (seance) ECTOPLASM is used from the MEDIUM and SITTERS to lift the entity into the air; 3. the etheric world intelligences affect the attraction of GRAVITY by neutralizing or reversing it, which allows the entity to rise; 4. the guides nullify the normal gravitational effect, and raise the object or body; 5. guides concentrate on the auric field of the entity until changes in the vibrational rate make it ANTIMATTER, and capable of rising; 6. guides concentrate on the time flow through the substance, co-creating a weightless entity. [cf. TELEPORTATION-TELEKINESIS, GRAVITY CONTROL Appendix 2]

LEVITATION-PK—see LEVITATION PSYCHOKINESIS.

LEVITATION-TK—see LEVITATION TELEKINESIS.

LEVITY—negative GRAVITY or the absence of gravity; a primary force that is characteristic of the ETHERIC WORLD, which streams inward to the earth from the COSMOS; e.g., the principle that put Newton's apple up in the tree in the beginning. [cf. GRAVITY CONTROL Appendix 2]

LEY LINES—abbr. LL; a path of power extending around the world and marked on the earth's surface by the great megalithic sites, which were built thousands of years ago, e.g., STONEHENGE and the pyramids; megalithic sites have mysterious properties ascribed to the locations where they intersect, implying that these LL have special powers; were used for their power in ancient rituals. [cf. CEREMONIAL MAGIC Appendix 2, FORMS-WITH-POWER, MINPSI Appendix 2]

LIA-FAIL—(Tara, Ireland; "stone of fail") a stone used in the inauguration ceremonies which accompanied the enthronement of the High Kings, because it was known to scream when a rightful king was being crowned. **Syn.** SCREAMING STONE. [**cf.** BISHOPS RING, TOPAZ, STONE OF LAZ]

LIBER JUGORUM—(Aleister Crowley) a strict discipline whereby one punishes her or himself by razor slicing one's wrist each time one violates a principle; object is to "train the will" in steps to unite the MICROCOSM(mankind) to the MACROCOSM (Totality). [**cf.** FORCED PSI, CEREMONIAL MAGIC, DISCIPLINE]

LIBERATION—1. (esoteric) to release one's self and feel the freedom of not being, but "just allowing"; to follow a surge from within that wants to become detached, and to disengage one's self from the present REALITY; 2. (alchemy) the act of fusing one's SOUL-MIND with COSMIC ENERGY. [**cf.** ALCHEMIST, MEDITATION, UNITY CONSCIOUSNESS]

LIBIDO—1. (esoteric) the force of TOTALITY which pulses through all the forms and activities of the psychic system and establishes communication between them; distinguishes between PSYCHIC ENERGY and physical energy; 2. an energy derived from general emotions, such as: sex, fear, anger, desire, and the like, as merely some of its specialized forms; 3. name given to KUNDALINI power; 4. a property of Totality, providing energy, life and growth for all; 5. see VITAL LIFE FORCE. [**cf.** INSTINCT, CLAIRSENTIENCE]

LICENSE TO DEPART—(magic) a ritual performed to close one's psychic doors, when through with one's psychic activity, thus preventing any overlap of spirits coming into ordinary life affairs. [**cf.** CLOAK OF INSULATION, BANISHING RITUALS, EVOCATION, POWER-OF-THE-WORD]

LICORICE—(esoteric) 1. (China, 3000 B.C.) used in religious ceremonies, as it has the properties to induce psychic energy; 2. (Egypt) packed in tombs with the deceased because it has the psychic power to ward off evil spirits; root was found by archaeologists in Tutankhamen's tomb; 3. makes a healthful sweet tea. [**cf.** HERBS, BOTANE, CURATIVE EDUCATION]

LIE—(Zoroastrianism) a principle of disruption and then DEATH; opposite of TRUTH.

LIEKKIO—(Finland, "flaming one") the soul of a child who has been buried in the forest. [**cf.** SOUL-MIND]

LIFE—(esoteric) changes occuring in an organism that are noticeable, and which show a maturation and growth process, as opposed to inert or dead matter; 1. (earth man) a time span of experiences of a SOUL-MIND, clothed in a PHYSICAL BODY made by itself, and abiding in a world consciousness made by itself for the special lessons this earth body and world consciousness can give back to the soul-mind for absorption toward its total growth; total growth is accomplished by the attitude of likes and dislikes in varying degrees regarding the food, families, peoples, health, money, education, and all other major and minor details that go with one's lifestyle in the earth consciousness; 2. (earth things) a state of CONSCIOUSNESS in a continuing, evolving, growing process working from within, outward, until perfection is reached at each level in the process; 3. (Alfred Korzybski) "the amount of energy any nervous system contains." (Inconcl.) [**cf.** LAW OF LIFE Appendix 7, TIME, MULTIDIMENSIONAL, VIBRATIONS, ENERGY]

LIFE CHANGE INDEX—a scale designed to measure the factors causing anxiety or STRESS that have been found to be a contributing factor to illnesses, e.g., death of a spouse = 65 points, traffic ticket = 11 points, foreclosure of mortgage = 30 points, the more points accumulated at a given time the greater one's risk of becoming ill. **Syn.** RAHE SCALE. [**cf.** WELLNESS, ALTERNATIVES, HOLISTIC HEALTH, NEW-AGE PSYCHOLOGY]

LIFE CYCLES—various phases of one's life and lifestyle flow in equally divided periods, repeating themselves constantly, e.g., primary cycle, personal cycle, worldly affairs cycle. (Inconcl.) [**cf.** CYCLES Appendix 5, BIORHYTHM]

LIFE ENERGY—see VITAL LIFE FORCE.

LIFE ETHER—(esoteric) the fourth level of CONSCIOUSNESS in the atmosphere which evolved out of the CHEMICAL ETHER; a more subtle, more complex, solid, contractive and suctional vibrational frequency than the lower levels; radiates to the earth by the sun; purple/violet in color; manifests in the shape of a SQUARE. (Inconcl.) [**cf.** FORMS-WITH-POWER, PHYSICAL ETHERS, PARADISE REALMS]

LIFE FIELD—see AURA.

LIFE FLUID—an invisible cosmic energy emanating from the sun, necessary for the human nervous system, and which enters the body through the SPLEEN CHAKRA. [**cf.** SUSHUMNA, NADIS]

LIFE FORCE—coined by Luigi Galvani (eighteenth century); see VITAL LIFE FORCE.

LIFE FORCE SYMBOL—(ancient Egypt) a PYRA-MID built to scale, having a CIRCLE sitting on top, with the pyramid apex intersecting the circle; the circle represents eternal life; designed to give the wearer PSYCHIC ABILITY and pyramid energy. [cf. SYMBOLISM, CEREMONIAL MAGIC, FORMS-WITH-POWER]

LIFE FORMS—(ufology) an energy field in the atmosphere that has a reasonable amount of intelligence, comparable to fish, animals, birds, plants or humans in earth; new discoveries to science that have not yet been named, but are called life forms in order to distinguish them from a dead image, such as a geometric figure or color mass. [cf. BIOFORMS, DAWN ANGELS, FLYING SHIELDS]

LIFE GROWTH CYCLE—as one matures, one's mind takes on a different set of attitudes every seven years. [cf. CYCLES Appendix 5]

LIFE READING—1. information about one's past incarnations, that could be affecting the present life, given by a MEDIUM while in a DEEP TRANCE state; one to six past life incarnations are dealt with to reveal personality traits, vocations, successes, failures, or traumatic experiences that could relate to the present life; one inquires of the past lives, if one had drifted or reached their goal, if one is to overcome karmic debts, or if one is to pursue talents from these past lives. [cf. PSYCHIC INFOR-MATION, READING] 2. (parapsychology) to use scribblings from a child to foretell the child's characteristics and give insight into his or her future; scribblings come from the SUBCONSCIOUS MIND, revealing the child's past lives and revealing their auric blueprint. [cf. AURA, SUBCONSCIOUS MIND, POINT-OF-FOCUS, IMITATION MAGIC]

LIFE SOUL—(Eskimo) see AURA.

LIFE UNITS—(Thomas Edison) theory: myriads of tiny LIFE UNITS make up the physical body; the body itself is not the unit of life, but these tiny entities, which may be cells, are the units of life. [cf. HOLOGRAM, EVOLUTION, LAW OF LIFE Appendix 7]

LIFE WAVE—(Theosophy) denotes the manifesta-tion of active life, with a multitude of monads, in one complete chain or circle in EVOLUTION; consists of seven journeys around the chain of seven globes of a SOLAR SYSTEM. **Syn.** ROUND.

LIFE WISH—an ongoing life process from within, that one never gets too much of; comes with BIRTH.

LIFE-AND-THOUGHT FIELDS—abbr. L & T FIELDS, coined by C. Baxter, L. Ravitz, and Harold Saxton Burr; see AURA.

LIFE-ATOM—(esoteric) the primeval potential of PERFECTNESS in every seed (in every group of atoms) regardless of its stage of EVOLUTION; motivates the seed to reach total growth. (Inconcl.) **Syn.** MONAD. [cf. MONADOLOGY, LAW OF MICRO-COSM/MACROCOSM Appendix 7, TOTALITY]

LIFE-CORD—(esoteric) an invisible etheric strand, running from the invisible MONAD to the perman-ent seed in the HEART; its function is to carry the invisible, minute, electronic karmic pictures from the individual's AKASHIC RECORDS to the heart, for distribution; one of the five strands making the SILVER CORD. (Inconcl.) [cf. LIFE-CORD-HEART-SEED-ATOM, MENTAL-REFLECTING-ETHER]

LIFE-CORD-HEART-SEED-ATOM—(esoteric) a min-ute, invisible, heavily concentrated field of energy, located in the HEART, containing minute, invisible, electronic, karmic pictures; a temporary replica of the AKASHIC RECORDS which are distributed through the bloodstream in their due season; kar-mic pictures promote karmic experiences; attached to the MONAD by the life-cord. (Inconcl.) **Syn.** (Bible) BOOK OF LIFE. [cf. SILVER CORD, EMO-TIONAL-ASTRAL-SEED-ATOM, TEMPORARY AKASH-IC RECORDS, MENTAL-REFLECTING-ETHER]

LIFE-FLUX—the motivating energy/intelligence within all living organisms, directing them to evolve back into the Total; (Hinduism, Buddhism) an invisible intelligent force that directs the lowest form of organism to keep evolving in conscious-ness until it reaches man, and then PERFECTNESS. **Syn.** GRACE OF GOD. [cf. MONADOLOGY]

LIFEIT—coined by Richard Simmons; the correct foods to eat for keeping well and for improving good health; has a positive connotation meaning alive; pronounced life-it, as opposed to die-it; foods should and can be chosen to enhance the on-going life process. [cf. CURATIVE EDUCATION]

LIFETRONS—subtle life forces, or finer-than-atomic energies, intelligently charged with the five distinc-tive sensory idea substances; see PRANA, SPIRIT. [cf. VIBRATIONS Appendix 5]

LIFT—(dreams) suggestions from outsiders that help the dreamer interpret the meaning of his or her dream; although the final interpretation is up to the dreamer, one needs suggestions from interested individuals that differ from one's own reaction to one's dream; if the dreamer knew immediately what the symbols represented, they would know their daytime frailties and would not be dreaming about them. [**cf.** SURREALISTIC PHANTOMS, MOTIVE UNCONSCIOUSNESS]

LIFT-OUT—(astral projection) pertains to the ASTRAL BODY sliding out of the physical body. [**cf.** ASTRAL PROJECTION Appendix 2]

LIFTER OF SPELLS—one who can free the victim from a CURSE, SPELL, or PSYCHIC ATTACK; one who exorcises. [**cf.** HEX, SPELLED, PSYCHIC TRANSFER, EXORCISM]

LIGHT—(esoteric) (capitalized) 1. an unorganized, luminous, radiant, electromagnetic energy presenting itself in the beginning (recognized as a state of CHAOS or a state of PERFECTNESS); a primeval source of TOTAL INTELLIGENCE; indestructable in its original state, but capable of breaking up into manifestations of other shapes, textures, and sizes with varying degrees of this intelligence; 2. essence of all MATTER; a wave motion of particles within the ETHER which is within matter; now manifests in all the universes in an orderly intelligent manner; 3. (Bob Toben) "light vibrates in a ring; chases itself in gravitational collapse"; 4. light signifies INTELLIGENCE, therefore, DARKNESS is the absence of intelligence, e.g., the DENSITY in its darkness is inhabited by new soul-minds who are still ignorant; 5. synonymous with FIRE and THE WORD in the Christian Bible. (Inconcl.) **Syn.** GODHEAD, TOTALITY, TOTAL INTELLIGENCE, IMPERISHABLE LIGHT, COSMIC FIRE, SHINING ONE, GREAT WHITE LIGHT. [**cf.** LAW OF MICROCOSM/MACROCOSM Appendix 7, COLOR, VIBRATIONS Appendix 5]

LIGHT APPARITION—a psychic vision which begins as a huge light, and then develops into a particular person, usually full blown; occurs when the PSYCHIC is in a relaxed state, such as, the middle of the night or after meditation; gives the psychic messages through impressions; an OMEN of good or a prophetic message; occurs instantaneously, willed or unknowingly willed; (do not confuse with EMOTIONAL PSI regarding DEATH). [**cf.** HUMAN OMENS, APPARITION, PRECOGNITIVE DREAM]

LIGHT BEARER OF THE PISCEAN AGE—a master who incarnated on earth to reawaken the multitudes to the necessary spiritual consciousness, for their highest growth in this age, and to carry on for future generations, e.g., JESUS, Moses, Siddhartha, KRISHNA. [**cf.** MASTER, WALK-IN, GODHEAD]

LIGHT BEINGS—angels of a very high order; soul-minds who have evolved to such a superior state of consciousness that their coating no longer is in the form of a human body, but now expresses as different densities of light. [**cf.** ANGEL HIERARCHY, KINGDOMS]

LIGHT BODY—1. (human) a human body living in earth that is a purified atomic structure, making it extremely sensitive to the higher etheric realms; accomplished by a transference of the dense physical substance into light and lightness by: eating foods and liquids of a higher vibrational rate, eliminating junk and dead foods, exercising and resting properly, taking the proper attitude toward its self, the mind and universe; the refined and purified body requires less solid food and becomes more receptive to absorbing energies from the sun, sea, air, and NATURE KINGDOMS; soul-minds with a light body receive psychic communications from the superior ANGEL HIERARCHY to be used for mankind, e.g., Eileen and Peter Caddy from FINDHORN. [**cf.** GLORIFIED BODY, ASCENSION] 2. (nature spirit) a misty, glowing, luminous, radiant energy field whirling in constant motion; most frequently seen as golden, but can change colors easily; the primary state of life of a NATURE SPIRIT; capable of changing to a human-like form when communicating with humans. **Syn.** FAIRIE.

LIGHT DOT—a minute energy field of highly concentrated intelligence throughout the atmosphere, which acts as a sending and receiving station for the electrical system in atoms, giving them direction; believed to have been created with CREATION; functions as the sun for the molecular system, parallel to the sun's function for earth's solar system. **Syn.** NODE. [**cf.** VIBRATIONS, ACUPUNCTURE POINTS, MERIDIAN LINES]

LIGHT ETHER—(esoteric) a gaseous, aeriform substance used in the physical body as an invisible subtle agent of the bloodstream; extracted from breath and the COSMIC ENERGY entering the body; a PHYSICAL ETHER evolved from WARMTH ETHER; a second level of vibrational frequency in the atmosphere; can be seen with physical eyes as expansive light, and produces a triangle shape and yellow color. [**cf.** SECOND PLANE, ETHERIC DOUBLE, SPIRIT]

LIGHT HIEROGLYPHS—(Kirlian effect) special patterns that appear on the Kirlian photographs, showing the human being's AURA, but which do not appear on the photographs of auras of inanimate objects, thus suggesting "inner life" activities of some kind. [cf. HIGH-VOLTAGE PHOTOGRAPHY, COLOR]

LIGHT INTELLIGENCE—(Uri Geller) a highly evolved, exalted soul-mind that once had a physical body millions of light years ago, and is now Pure Light, intensified with pure intelligence; travels using their own cosmic galactical energy in the form of a light without a human shape. [cf. ANGEL KINGDOM, GODHEAD, TOTALITY, LIGHT]

LIGHT OF THE WORLD—(Egypt) the optic THALAMUS; an egg-shaped ganglion of the inner brain; when cross-sectioned it looks like a beetle, which symbolizes IMMORTALITY; part of the THIRD-EYE AREA. **Syn.** SINGLE EYE, SACRED BEETLE, HEART OF THE LOTUS. [cf. QUEEN PITUITARY]

LIGHT PENCIL—a compact device that is used for finding the acupressure points in the body. **Syn.** TOBISCOPE. [cf. YIN/YANG, POLARITY, ACUPRESSURE POINTS, MERIDIAN LINES]

LIGHT STATE OF HYPNOSIS—a state of CONSCIOUSNESS in which the CONSCIOUS MIND has stepped aside, allowing the SUBCONSCIOUS MIND to accept outer stimuli input as received, without any decisions being made regarding the material; easily brought on whenever an individual narrows their focus and prolongs this narrowed attention without making a conscious mind decision for an hour or more; occurs from concentraing on: a hypnotist's suggestions, a book, an invention, creative writing, a TV program, outer stimuli such as a constant monotonous sound, a voice, or a steady gaze from one who demands full attention while they speak; characteristics that differentiate a light state from a DEEP STATE and MEDIUM STATE OF HYPNOSIS: not easily recognizable, can happen when subject is standing, sitting or lying down, vitality of body is suppressed, attitude toward outside influences is passive, subject is fully aware of conversation but has incomplete recall afterwards, ability to verbally respond if not required to make a decision, only a slight change in appearance, no realization that one is in a hypnotic state; subject is highly suggestible as the conscious mind has relinquished its role of decision making; (do not confuse with LIGHT TRANCE, in which the ETHERIC WORLD INTELLIGENCES play a role). **Syn.** LETHARGIC

STATE OF HYPNOSIS. [cf. ON-THE-SPOT-HYPNOSIS, TRANCE, MEDITATION, INDUCTION, SELF-HYPNO-THERAPY]

LIGHT TRANCE—a state of consciousness in which an ETHERIC WORLD INTELLIGENCE is allowed to interpenetrate one's body and use it for physical phenomena; MEDIUM speaks and acts in an altered state of consciousness in which the CONSCIOUS MIND is inactive, the PHYSICAL BODY is active, and the intelligence uses the SUBCONSCIOUS MIND; intelligence moves and speaks through the medium in a manner that is only recognizable to those who know the situation; medium is fed through CLAIRVOYANCE, CLAIRAUDIENCE, CLAIRSCENT, body feeling, body movements, and impressions in speech; willed purposely under DESIRED-CONTROL or willed karmically and occurs spontaneously; intelligence is responsible for the activity and speech for the allotted time; impressions are given more rapidly than a person normally thinks; full recall is elusive unless it is related back later; conscious mind is close by to intercede immediately in an emergency, such as an abrupt disturbance or loud noise; this causes the intelligence to snap out of the medium's body; light trance is used in prolonged running, dancing, stand-up reading and performing in front of an audience. [cf. MEDIUM TRANCE, DESIRED-CONTROL, GUIDES, STAND-UP READER]

LIGHT WAVES—(esoteric) a harmonious vibration of etheric matter that projects through space in perfect rhythmic waves, strikes a surface, and the homogeneous particles are thrown into sympathetic vibrations with the incoming current; a form of manifestation of cosmic law, visible and invisible, dependent upon the Great Central Sun. [cf. RAYS, COLOR, MAGNETIC LIFE FORCE, WAVELENGTH, DARKNESS]

LIGHT WITHIN—see MONAD.

LIGHT-BULB GEMS—(Greece) (minpsi) ancient jewels found in the foreheads of statues, so brilliant they could light up the whole temple at night, and easily light up the underground palaces. [cf. AMULET, MINPSI Appendix 2, QUARTZ CRYSTALS]

LIGHTNING PHOTOGRAPHY—a picture of a deceased person which is etched on a glass window during an electrical storm, without human methods. [cf. PSYCHIC PHOTOGRAPHY Appendix 2]

LILI—(Assyria) a female ETHERIC WORLD ENTITY

355

who is capable of having sexual relations with earth men during the night. **Syn.** SUCCUBUS, NIGHT HAG, WOOD NYMPH, MONSTER LILITH. [**cf.** SHE-WOLF, DIMENSION-SHIFTING Appendix 2]

LILITH—(Jewish) chief of the demonesses in the etheric world. [**cf.** LILI, DENSITY, HADES, SHEOL, WATCHFUL SPIRITS]

LIMB CATALEPSY—(hypnosis) the ability of the subject's body muscles, during a DEEP or MEDIUM STATE OF HYPNOSIS, to be extremely rigid or extremely loose, with a tendency to stay in any position in which they are placed by the hypnotist. [**cf.** HYPNOTHERAPY, HAND LEVITATION, HYPER-ACUTE, FINGER RESPONSE, SOMNAMBULISTIC STAGE]

LIMBIC SYSTEM—(esoteric) a series of structures ranging down from the cortex of the brain through the midbrain; key to emotional response, memory and attention. [**cf.** BRAIN, EMOTION, KEY TO LIFE]

LIMBO—a level of CONSCIOUSNESS which comprises one of the seven planes in the DENSITY in the ETHERIC WORLD; an area of awareness for those who have died, placed in the middle of two extremes; 1. an area on the edge of HELL, which is not a place of physical torment but of banishment from GOD; 2. a vibrational frequency in the etheric world reserved for the righteous who lived before CHRIST; 3. the border of hell and HEAVEN serving those who do not know which way to go. [**cf.** SOUL-MIND, EVOLUTION, EARTHBOUND ENTITIES]

LINEAR DIMENSIONS—thoughts perceived in a line, and in length; also called **one-dimensional**. [**cf.** TIME, SECOND DIMENSION, FOURTH DIMENSION]

LINEAR THINKING—to use in one's thoughts, only that which one can see with the physical eyes. [**cf.** THOUGHTS, MATTER, BRAIN]

LINGA—(India) a symbol of primal force, divided so half extends down in earth and half extends above the earth; seen in front of the temple of SHIVA in India. [**cf.** YIN AND YANG, POLARITY, LINGAM]

LINGA SHARIRA—see ETHERIC DOUBLE.

LINGA-SAIRIRA—ASTRAL LIGHT which is a soft glow, similar to earth's twilight; never varies for night or day; can sometimes be seen during MEDITATION. [**cf.** ASTRAL VISION, ASTRAL PLANE, VEIL]

LINGAM—(Hinduism) the male symbol for positive POLARITY. [**cf.** YONI, YIN AND YANG]

LINGAM AND YONI—(Hinduism) the male and female symbols for positive and negative POLARITY. [**cf.** YIN AND YANG, LAW OF POLARITY Appendix 7, SHIVA]

LINGER EFFECT—(laboratory) the temporary retainment of VIBRATIONS from the PSYCHIC, EXPERIMENTER, and helpers in an area where a psychic experiment was performed, which may have an influence on the next psychic. [**cf.** PSYCHOMETRY, RITUALS, MENTAL PSYCHIC PROCESSES]

LINGUISTIC NEOFORMATION—a form of NEOPHASIA (TALKING-IN-TONGUES) using a new language; usually done to satisfy the requirements of this language and to help accelerate its growth. [**cf.** XENOGLOSSIA]

LINGUISTIC RESTITUTION—a form of TALKING-IN-TONGUES which is revealed in a language of the world, but which is foreign to the talker; theory: the talker learned this language in a past INCARNATION, heard it in childhood, or when a baby; sometimes hypnotic REGRESSION, AUTOMATIC WRITING, or DREAMS will reveal when the talker was exposed to the language. [**cf.** CRYPTOMNESIA, AURAL MEMORY, XENOGLOSSIA, MEMORY ABILITY]

LIPIKAS—(Sanskrit) etheric world intelligences whose function is to record KARMA, known as "the scribes." [**cf.** RIPE KARMA, ACCUMULATED KARMA]

LISTENING—1. (Native American, Navajo) see CLAIRAUDIENCE; 2. (Tibet) to view the THOUGHT-FORMS of one's own making, as they take shape in the ETHERIC WORLD (similar to a human, sub-human, and superhuman activity); first stage of discipleship; a technique of hearing the teachings of the GURU with the HEART. [**cf.** REFLECTING, MEDITATING, THOUGHT-FORMS Appendix 2, LAW OF THOUGHT Appendix 7]

LISTENING FATIGUE—tiredness caused by background music to which one is not paying much attention; caused by music which was recorded on a recording system that was not equipped with a range wide enough for that piece of music; this brings a disturbance in the etheric bodies, which can be felt by the physical body. [**cf.** MUSIC OF THE SPHERES, CLAIRAUDIENCE, SOUNDS-WITH-POWER]

LISTENING MODE—an ALTERED STATE OF CONSCIOUSNESS in which one feels comfortable that this is the proper level of awareness wherein the SUBCONSCIOUS MIND listens to incoming information; when the body is relaxed, the CONSCIOUS MIND passive, and the emotions quieted, the subconscious mind records incoming information as it is, and uses it from that time on; the altered state is to be used for VISUALIZATION, and for talking to the body cells for a HEALING; a personal technique to reach this level is accomplished by repetition and deliberation. [cf. RECEIVING MODE, MEDITATION, BIOFEEDBACK TRAINING]

LISTENING TO THE SKIN—the perception of things and people through the sensitivity of the skin; a way to see without eyes. (Inconcl.) [cf. EYELESS SIGHT Appendix 2]

LISTENING WITH THE THIRD EAR—see CLAIRAUDIENCE.

LITANY—a long PRAYER or INCANTATION which contains a refrain that is repeated constantly, and which has the power to induce psychic phenomena or a hypnotic state. [cf. SOUNDS-WITH-POWER, CHANTING]

LITE PROGRAM—abbr. LIFE-THREATENING ILLNESS THERAPY AND EDUCATION; theory: constructive attitudes and habits can strengthen the natural immunity of the body against disease. [cf. NEW-AGE PSYCHOLOGY Appendix 5]

LITERARY MEDIUM—one who is capable of allowing an ETHERIC WORLD INTELLIGENCE to intervene in some form of psychic skill, and the resulting communications are teachings of WISDOM; information is correct, and has an elegant style, displaying a very high intelligence. [cf. MEDIUMSHIP, INNER BAND, CONTROL, PSYCHIC DEVELOPMENT CIRCLE]

LITHOSPHERE—(Pierre Teilhard de Chardin) one level of CONSCIOUSNESS in the ETHERIC WORLD; has its own function and inhabitants. [cf. BODIES AND PLANES Appendix 5]

LITTLE BLACK DEMON—(Tibet) an evil ETHERIC WORLD ENTITY who hinders an individual from the time he or she is born; theory: this is the person's lower nature in action. [cf. LITTLE WHITE GOD, SUBCONSCIOUS MIND, AKASHIC RECORDS, EARTHBOUND ENTITY, HAUNTING]

LITTLE EGYPT—the imaginary homeland of the first gypsies who told fortunes and gave psychic readings with cards. [cf. POINT-OF-FOCUS, CARTOMANCY]

LITTLE GOOD ANGEL—(Haiti, Voodoo) see 'TI BON ANGI.

LITTLE LOCAL SELF—the surface mind; see CONSCIOUS MIND.

LITTLE MAN—materialistic, linear thoughts that limit one to a very small potential. [cf. MENTAL MIND, BRAIN, MATERIALISTIC MAN, LINEAR THINKING]

LITTLE PEOPLE—(Cornwall, Stonehenge, England) name used when referring to the FAIRIES, when not wanting to invoke them; see NATURE SPIRITS. **Syn.** PEOPLE OF PEACE.

LITTLE SNAKE—pertains to the uvula in the mouth; used to induce psychic skills by special exercises and chants concerning the uvula, and which send the vibrations from the uvula to the brain and throughout the body. [cf. THIRD-EYE AREA Appendix 5, CHANTING, SOUNDS-WITH-POWER]

LITTLE WHITE GOD—(Tibet) the ANGEL that helps an individual from the time he or she is born; theory: this is the person's higher nature in action. **Sim.** GOOD GENIUS, CELESTIAL GUARDIAN, DOCTOR TEACHER. [cf. LITTLE BLACK DEMON, GUIDE, SUPERCONSCIOUS MIND]

LITURGY—prescribed forms of ritual for public worship. [cf. RITUALS, CEREMONIAL MAGIC, TRADITION]

LITUUS ROD—(Rome) a special arched shaped rod used by the AUGUR for DOWSING; the curved rod was used to mark a place in the sky, for a POINT-OF-FOCUS to be used by him when doing psychic work. [cf. ANGEL RODS, AUGURY TEMPLUM]

LIVE SILVER—see QUICKSILVER.

LIVER GAZING—the art of giving a psychic reading using the liver of an animal. [cf. DIVINATION, MANTIC ARTS, CASTING OF LOTS]

LIVING CLOCKS—an innate, internal timer within a human being that makes him or her repeat patterns of energy and regeneration; reacts the same in all people; affects their physical, emotional, mental and spiritual capabilities with no intentional outside influence. **Sim.** BIORHYTHMS. [cf. BIORHYTHM CHARTS, CIRCADIAN RHYTHM]

LIVING CREATURES OF OUR ATMOSPHERE—see CRITTERS.

LIVING DEAD—1. (Buddhism) earthlings who are

very materialistic and not highly enough evolved to understand the ESOTERIC truths and WISDOM; they have no idea they should improve themselves over a lifetime; 2. soul-minds in the etheric world. [cf. EVOLUTION, MATERIALISTIC MAN, ETHERIC WORLD ENTITIES]

LIVING INCARNATION—(Tibet) an advanced SOUL-MIND whose body, birth, and childhood gave certain signs that prompted tracing their previous incarnations; past incarnations are used to guide this life to one of importance for mankind. [cf. KARMA, REINCARNATION, RIPE KARMA]

LIVING ORGANISM—(esoteric) a system operating in TOTALITY; consists of: blood that feeds it, chemical energy that gives it mobility, an innate potential that directs its independent growth, and an innate mechanism that handles external forces that impinge upon it, making it responsible to its environment. [cf. GESTALT, SYNERGISM, SOUL-MIND, SPIRIT, MONADOLOGY, HOLOGRAM]

LIVING PHENOMENA—(ufology) anything seen in a UFO sighting, or in the atmosphere by airplane pilots, that appears to be alive, and is not normal to earth life. Sim. UNIDENTIFIED FLYING OBJECTS. [cf. CRITTERS, FLAPS, FOO FIGHTERS]

LIVING SOLID FACE—(Native American, Delaware) an ETHERIC WORLD INTELLIGENCE that communicates with the tribe and is known to wear a mask instead of a face, when perceived clairvoyantly; assists the tribe in their hunts and in their healings. Syn. MISINGHALIKUN. [cf. INNER BAND, OUTER BAND, CLAIRVOYANCE]

LIVING TISSUE—(esoteric) a manifestation of the complex patterns of atoms which comes from the inherent nature of the living tissue under the laws of the higher planes. (Inconcl.) [cf. MENTAL BODY, MENTAL PLANE, CAUSAL PLANE, THOUGHTS]

LL—see LEY LINES.

LLEU—(Wales) an ETHERIC WORLD god who can be summoned psychically to help the warriors in time of war, and other times, for guidance and protection. [cf. GUIDE, ETHERIC WORLD INTELLIGENCES]

LOA—(Haiti, Voodoo) an etheric world intelligence who communicates with earthlings; is recognized as a "god" and the god is recognized as a part of one's personality; the gods bring guidance, knowledge, protection, healings, or evil activities according to one's attitude; each god also has a particular dance pattern and drum rhythm necessary for entering the earthling in order to perform physical psychism. Syn. INVISIBLES. [cf. RIDES, RITUALS, ETHERIC WORLD INTELLIGENCES, GUIDE]

LOB—a nature spirit who helps with domestic work in the home; see FAIRIES. Sim. ROBIN GOODFELLOW. [cf. NATURE SPIRITS]

LOCALE I—(astral projection) (Robert Monroe) the astral world where one can visit and perceive the current physical world, while in the astral body; one of the environments of the SECOND STATE; the "here-now." [cf. LOCALE II, ASTRAL PROJECTION]

LOCALE II—(astral projection) (Robert Monroe) part of the astral world that consists of non-material, vastness, different laws of motion and depth, and is inhabited by those etheric world entities who communicate with earthlings; one of the environments of the SECOND STATE. [cf. LOCALE I, ASTRAL PLANE]

LOCALIZED FIELD—(magnetic healing) magnetic energy that is deliberately built up in the hands of the practitioner by a special technique, to be transferred to the patient for healing. [cf. MAGNETIC HEALING, HEALEE, LAYING-ON-OF-HANDS]

LOCH NESS MONSTER—(Scotland) nicknamed Nessie; see MONSTER ACTIVITY.

LOCKED IN—1. pertains to muscle tension that has settled in the body and increases as time goes on; caused by a traumatic experience that was not resolved when it happened; each time a similar emotional experience occurs and the emotion is again repressed, it tends to shape the body and make a hold-pattern in the body. [cf. BLOCKS, ROLFING, HOLD-PATTERN] 2. pertains to the closing of the magnetic circuit within one's self when administering MAGNETIC HEALING to one's self to prevent the MAGNETISM from escaping; the feet are crossed and flat on the floor; hands are clasped in the lap.

LOCKING-OUT—a protective measure to prevent the mind from absorbing what is being said when one cannot physically walk away from the speaker; the arms and/or hands are crossed and placed on the solar plexus, thereby short-circuiting the body; the verbiage bounces back to the speaker; used in lecture halls or with individuals. [cf. DESTRUCTIVE-BRAINWASHING CULTS, MASS ELEMENTAL]

LOCOMOTION—traveling in the ASTRAL BODY;

see ASTRAL PROJECTION. **Sim.** HORIZONTAL GLIDING.

LODESTONE—also spelled **loadstone;** (minpsi) a variety of magnitite possessing a magnetic polarity; (esoteric) nature's own magnet, emanating a magnetic quality similar to body magnetism; draws its qualities from the sun, moon, and stars; capable of influencing the human body by withdrawing disease from the patient, and then drawing in elements from the ethers that the body needs for that healing; some magnetic healers know how to use this stone to store magnetism in the nerve fluid in their body, to be used later for healing others. [**cf.** MAGNETISM, MAGNET HEALING, GAUS MAGNETICS]

LODGES—(esoteric) groups in the ETHERIC WORLD whose members are highly developed soul-minds, and who work together for benefit of a particular area in the earth. [**cf.** WHITE BROTHERHOOD, SAINT, GABRIEL]

LOGOI OF A PLANETARY CHAIN—an exalted, magnanimous, mighty, etheric world intelligence who has earned the privilege of ruling the chain of worlds. [**cf.** PLANETARY CHAIN, EVOLUTION, CYCLES]

LOGOIDAL ENERGY—an all-pervading dynamic force that generates the consciousness or LOGOIDAL PLASM since the beginning of CREATION; the generating power behind logoidal plasm, so it can express the LOGOS; see VITAL LIFE FORCE. **Syn.** SPIRIT, PRANA. [**cf.** ORGONE ENERGY]

LOGOIDAL PLASM—pure CONSCIOUSNESS; the raw material that was there in the beginning now expressing itself, making up all things in the UNIVERSE; see TOTALITY. **Syn.** GOD, INFINITE INTELLIGENCE. [**cf.** LOGOIDAL ENERGY, LOGOS, TOTALITY Appendix 3]

LOGOIDAL WILL—mankind's FREE WILL; the mechanism in one that gives one the power of decision. [**cf.** CEREBROSPINAL NERVOUS SYSTEM, WILL, BRAIN]

LOGORHYTHMIC—the repetitious beat, or the emphasis of a word or group of words, spoken in the mind or out loud to induce MEDITATION, or to induce a psychic skill. [**cf.** FORCED PSI, MENTAL PSYCHIC PROCESSES, MANTRA, SOUNDS-WITH-POWER]

LOGOS—(Greek *logo* "word, speech") therefore meaning the CREATOR, GOD; (in the beginning was the WORD, and the word was God); one force of the COSMOS; creator responsible for all other forces in the cosmos; see TOTALITY. **Syn.** DEITY, ALL-THERE-IS, DIVINE INTELLIGENCE. [**cf.** TOTALITY Appendix 3, LOGOIDAL PLASM, LOGOIDAL ENERGY]

LOGOS OF THE SYSTEM—see TOTALITY.

LOGURIST—a MENTAL HEALER specializing in VISUALIZATION and control of his or her mind; see PSYCHIC. [**cf.** LOGURY, MENTAL HEALING, AFFIRMATIONS]

LOGURY—(ancient) (*lo* "look, see, behold") to visualize the patient in a perfectly healthy and active state, and holding that thought in the mind at length; also, beholding the thought of perfect health for that patient, to prevent sick thoughts, which give a sickness power. **Syn.** VISUALIZATION, HOLD THE THOUGHT. [**cf.** MENTAL HEALING, NON-THOUGHT]

LOKA—1. (Buddhism) the ETHERIC WORLD; 2. (Sanskrit) the world; a sphere divided in two: RUPA-LOKAS and ARUPA-LOKAS. [**cf.** POLARITY, PLANES]

LOKI—(Germany, Scandinavia, ancient) a NATURE SPIRIT belonging to the giant race in the ETHERIC WORLD; DEITY of mischief, fraud, and jester; capable of shifting dimensions to be seen by humans; see FAIRIES.

LOMI-LOMI—(Huna) body manipulation for loosening the BLOCKS in the body to promote a HEALING, such as, NEUROMUSCULAR MASSAGE. [**cf.** ACUPUNCTURE, ACUPRESSURE, MERIDIAN LINES]

LONELINESS—1. mental suffering caused from: (a) attachment to a specific person, location, group, job, or thing, for happiness and a particular lifestyle; nothing goes on forever and when something happens to the attachment, one feels lost; (b) inability to realize that the world is full of wonderful, loving, kind, persons and one will never lose his or her ability to appreciate and love other things and persons; 2. a state of being uncomfortable about oneself and not being able to relate to oneself; the individual continually seeks company to win approval from another, to make up for disapproval of oneself. [**cf.** WELLNESS, HOLISTIC HEALTH, NEW-AGE PSYCHOLOGY]

LONG PASS—(magnetic healing) a movement by the PRACTITIONER to release the NERVE FLUID

359

from his or her hands to the patient, to promote a HEALING; practitioner begins at the head of the patient and ends at the feet, by stroking the body or stroking the ETHERIC DOUBLE; causes the cells to normalize and heal more quickly. [cf. MAGNETIC HEALING, MENTAL HEALING, CURATIVE EDUCATION]

LONG-STEMMED UNFOLDED LOTUS—(Buddhism) a symbol referring to the spinal column in a human being. [cf. KUNDALINI, CADUCEUS WINDING, IDA, PINGALA]

LOOGAROO—(Grenada) a witch who feeds on the blood of humans during the night; changes her shape by shedding her skin and then travels as balls of light; characterized by red lights swarming around the area of the person where she is working. [cf. ASTRAL VAMPIRISM, SHAPE-CHANGING]

LOOK FIXEDLY—(Carlos Casteneda) to focus with the entire body and mind. [cf. SINGLE-POINTED, LAW OF ATTENTION Appendix 7, ASTRAL VISION]

LOOPING THE LOOP—(astral projection) the process of the ASTRAL BODY completely turning around and going back over covered territory, during an ASTRAL PROJECTION (an unusual process). [cf. ASTRAL PROJECTION Appendix 2]

LOOSENED—(magnetic healing) to use special magnetic passes with the palms of the hands to break up the blockage in the congested area; allows the NERVE FLUID to begin its regular flow. Usage: "Did you get the disease loosened?" [cf. SIDEWAY PASSES, LAYING-ON-OF-HANDS, EARTH MAGNETISM]

LOOSING DEITIES—the higher ETHERIC WORLD INTELLIGENCES who are assigned the task of helping to unbind those earthlings who are victims of a major psychic attack, a hex or a spell. [cf. KNOTS, HEX, SPELLED]

LOPHOPHORA WILLIANSII—see PEYOTE.

LORD OF EVIL—(early Christian) a low quality ETHERIC WORLD male entity capable of having sexual intercourse with a human female during the night; occurs by coming in a dream, or by changing dimensions and assuming a human body for that time. **Syn.** INCUBUS, SATYRS. [cf. DIMENSION-SHIFTING AND SHAPE-CHANGING Appendix 2]

LORDHOOD—(angel) a rank in the ETHERIC WORLD that is the last step before GODHOOD; taken after the sixth INITIATION has been passed;

soul-minds who have elevated to this rank are of an ethereal substance not understood by mankind; Lordhood angels are overshadowed by the Godhood angels, but supervise the Masters; their function is to radiate power, love and pure thought into space, giving attention to guiding the world to help the overall COSMOS evolutionary plan; cannot enter earth dimension, but can send a MASTER to intercede when called upon; constantly send out energy of inspiration and encouragement to encompass the world; those who have reached this step in the etheric world, and have incarnated to help from this plane: Lord JESUS, Lord Siddartha (BUDDHA), Lord Maitreya, Logos OSIRIS. **Syn.** EXALTED ONES. [cf. INITIATE, INITIATION RITES, MASTERSHIP, ANGELOLOGY]

LORDS OF DEATH—the mental activity of one's own CONSCIOUSNESS while incarnated in earth, that brings one to the DENSITY of evil inhabitants when going through the DEATH PROCESS; one must face all levels of consciousness of their own making after leaving the physical body. **Syn.** MINOR DEITY. [cf. BARDO THODOL, CEREMONY OF LITTLE DEATH]

LORDS OF HUMANITY—soul-minds in the etheric world who have evolved to the rank of MASTERS and have passed the steps known as humanity; do not have to be incarnated in earth again. [cf. ANGEL HIERARCHY, GODHEAD, MASTER]

LORDS OF JUSTICE—(*Lords* synonymous with *laws*) see LAW OF KARMA and LAW OF COMPENSATION Appendix 7.

LORDS OF KARMA—(*Lords* synonymous with *laws*) see LAW OF COMPENSATION Appendix 7.

LORDS OF LIGHT—soul-minds in the ETHERIC WORLD who have earned a lofty, grandoise rank in the angel hierarchy, and whose function is to guide the evolutionary cycles of mankind; one ANGEL is in charge of each of the seven major rays, e.g., (Bible) "Seven angels which stood before God." **Syn.** SPIRITS OF THE SEVEN RAYS, SEVEN SPIRITS OF GOD. [cf. ANGEL HIERARCHY]

LORDS OF MIND—exalted, lofty, magnanimous angels in the ETHERIC WORLD who earned an extremely high rank, and whose function is to rule over the UNIVERSE from beginning to the end. [cf. HOLY ONES, IMPERISHABLE ONES, LOGOI OF THE PLANETARY CHAIN]

LORDS OF THE DARK FACE—a highly specialized

ARTIFICIAL ELEMENTAL with a peculiarly venomous ability, and one that mediums were able to communicate with at the time of ATLANTIS. [cf. SOULLESS PSYCHISM Appendix 2, ELEMENTAL]

LORDS OF THE ENVIRONMENT—ETHERIC WORLD INTELLIGENCES who have been assigned to guide earth through its environmental change, e.g., replacing trees that were cut down to make a shopping center; making laws so hunting and fishing will be seasonal. [cf. ANGEL HIERARCHY, GREAT ONES]

LORDS OF THE NATURE KINGDOM—ANGELS who are more advanced in EVOLUTION than humans, and whose function is to oversee the activities of NATURE SPIRITS; nature spirits in turn are in charge of nature activities in earth. [cf. GNOMES, UNDINES, SALAMANDERS, FAIRIES]

LORDSHIP—(angel) the sixth step in rank toward GODHOOD in the ETHERIC WORLD; Lordship angels are composed of ethereal substance, have an extremely high intelligence and whose function is to be in charge over nature in manmade civilizations, e.g., to preserve the grand canyon, or to clear the air pollution for the earth; Lordship angels have huge bodies, and are known to be as large as the area which they serve; they blend into their area and emanate harmony and guidance. **Syn.** NATURE LORDS. [cf. MASTERSHIP, ANGEL HIERARCHY]

LORELEI—1. a NATURE SPIRIT that lives in WATER and has charge over water. **Syn.** NYMPH. 2. (minpsi) a tall rock on the Rhine river that has properties that cause an echo. [cf. MINPSI Appendix 2, FAIRIES]

LOSING MONEY DREAMS—interpreted by some to mean the dreamer has a fear of, or is losing something of value, either a trait of character or material property. [cf. DREAMS Appendix 2]

LOST LEAF—see PHANTOM LEAF.

LOST WORD—theory: special words or sounds have a vibrational frequency capable of unblocking a "hold pattern" in a sick person's body, bringing a balance to that sick body so it can heal itself. [cf. TONING, BLOCKS, SOUNDS-WITH-POWER, HOLD PATTERNS]

LOTS—(Anglo-Saxon) 1. markers used to identify persons taking part in the skill of CASTING OF LOTS; markers could be stones, pebbles, sticks, die, dominoes, cards, straws, or coins; each person had their own personal marker so the FALL could be easily explained; used in I CHING and SORTES SANCTORUM; cliche: "my lot in life" originated from throwing lots to divide cattle or land during biblical times, meaning "my portion as my marker indicated"; 2. "lots" is a short form of saying "casting of lots." [cf. SYNCHRONICITY, ASTRAGALOMANCY, SORTES]

LOTUS—a white water lily, with many petals, blooming up to ten inches in diameter during the night; native of Africa, but held sacred as a cosmic symbol by many disciplines; used as a metaphor to represent: 1. centers of CONSCIOUSNESS; 2. beauty and holiness; 3. the causal body; 4. (India) a holy plane associated with the life-giving Ganges; 5. (Egypt) the female life principle, shown with OSIRIS and HORUS; 6. (Hinduism) the invisible CROWN CHAKRA located on the human head, symbolic of the time when the crown chakra will emanate in a beautiful white radiance that comes from one's evolvement; as each CHAKRA is absorbed into the one above it, this KUNDALINI energy will be in such abundance, and of such fast vibrations, that when it reaches the crown chakra it will radiate like a lotus, and one will be capable of ascending into the ethers without going through physical death, e.g., JESUS called it the "crown of glory." **Syn.** THOUSAND PETAL LOTUS. [cf. BOTANE, SYMBOLS]

LOTUS OF THE HEART—(Vedic) a metaphor representing one of the CENTERS OF CONSCIOUSNESS in the body; its unfolding petals suggest the expansion of the soul; the growth of the flower's pure beauty from the root chakra, or the mud of its source, makes it a spiritual promise. [cf. SYMBOL, TRADITION, CONSCIOUSNESS Appendix 5]

LOTUS ORDER OF DEITIES—(Tibet) ETHERIC WORLD gods typifying the glorified principles of the vocal functions within mankind; held together by THOUGHT. [cf. ETHERIC WORLD INTELLIGENCES, LAW OF LIKE ATTRACTS LIKE Appendix 7]

LOTUS POSTURE—(Yoga) position of the body used for MEDITATION; one sits on the floor or bench with legs crossed and locked, back straight, and hands on knees; lotus posture holds the spine upright and locks the body securely against the dangers of falling backwards or forward during long periods of meditation; YOGI can view the varicolored lotuses of the cerebrospinal centers in this position. **Syn.** PADMASANA. [cf. ESSENCE OF REST, HESYCHASM, ILLUMINATION]

LOURDES—a Roman Catholic shrine in the region of Hautes-Pyrenees, France; built because of a VISION which showed that the spring water had the vibrational frequency to heal sick people; thousands go there each year to be healed, and thousands are healed, but not all. [**cf.** MENTAL HEALING, HOLISTIC HEALTH, FAITH HEALING, LAW OF VIBRATIONAL FREQUENCIES Appendix 7]

LOVE—a neutral energy that can be used by mankind beneficially or nonbeneficially; the "intent" behind the energy of love determines whether it is used for GOOD or for bad; an energy created in the beginning, under a principle that is available when there is a bond between two atoms or two units; 1. mankind's love has many degrees which have been isolated and named; the positive degrees of love are: (a)respect, (b)admiration, (c)like, (d)concern for, (e)affection, (f)passion, (g)enamored of, (h)enjoy, (i)adore, (j)regard for, (k)fondness, (l)reverence for, (m)friendliness, (n)worship, (o)crazy about, (p)adulation, (q)kindnesses, (r)thoughtfulness, and (s)empathy with; 2. negative love occurs when there is a lack of harmony between the two people engaged in these degrees of love; (a)the receiver of energy may not desire the attention, as the attention may be stunting the receiver's growth (smother love); (b)the giver may give, believing it should be returned; (c)the giver may give because the society says they should; or (d)the giver may give, trying to win a place in the other's heart; 3. love that is not returned, strengthens or weakens one's character depending upon the intent in which it is administered; 4. the highest form of love is to give love unconditionally, without depending upon or expecting any return; universal love that is given to any living organism or inert object, because one is giving to the UNIVERSE, not to the person or object, per se; 5. that which one loves will come and go, but the capacity to love will never go. [**cf.** NEW-AGE PSYCHOLOGY Appendix 5]

LOVE FEAST—(ancient Greece) a gathering for the purpose of performing an ETHEREAL type of love making, that does not include physical relations; the highest degree of making love; in later history, the love feast degenerated into an orgy of sex and feasting on foods. **Syn.** AGAPE. [**cf.** BODY CONTROL, SEX TRANSMUTATION]

LOVE-APPLES—(Egypt) a fruit that has properties which raise one's sexual desires, when eaten. **Syn.** MANDRAKE FRUIT. [**cf.** BOTANE Appendix 2]

LOVE-BEAM—see LOVE-LINE.

LOVE-BOMBING—(destructive-brainwashing cult) the overly abundant showing of concern for the new recruit's happiness, well-being, interests and goals, which is incorporated in the ploy of the cult member when he or she is recruiting a new member; objective is to show personal affection and attentiveness from their whole being, thereby making it impossible for the new victim to say no to someone who apparently cares that much about them. [**cf.** SPELLED, ON-THE-SPOT-HYPNOSIS, WORDS-WITH-POWER]

LOVE-LINE—complimentary and loving thoughts sent along a pink imaginary beam to the individual one wants to receive a telepathic message; objective is to create a thought atmosphere around the person who is to receive a telepathic message before sending the message; this opens the receiver's AURA so he or she is receptive to the real message; compliments and loving thoughts alert the CONSCIOUS MIND and SUBCONSCIOUS MIND to pay attention to the wave-lengths; however, compliments must be in compliance with the receiver's personality, or the receiver's subconscious mind will reject it, similar to a computer which will reject material if it has no compartment for it. [**cf.** MENTAL TELEPATHY, THOUGHT ATMOSPHERE, SOUL-RAPPORT TELEPATHY]

LOW BREATHING—to use the abdominal muscles for breathing, causing air to enter deeper into the lungs, as opposed to shallow breathing. **Syn.** DIAPHRAGMATIC BREATHING. [**cf.** PSYCHIC DEVELOPMENT, MEDITATION]

LOW MAGIC—to use amulets, talismans, handed-down rituals, chants, and incantations as an aid to help the MAGICIAN perform his or her psychic feats; these tools help stimulate the magician's PSYCHIC ENERGY until it bubbles up and becomes known from a feeling "within" their body; eventually the magician receives the same surge of psychic energy without using the tools; this is known as HIGH MAGIC, e.g., a magician uses a chalked circle or salted circle and eventually they can get the same effects from an imaginary circle drawn with their pointed finger, or magician uses fortune-telling cards and their interpretation only, and eventually cards stimulate psychic information and are no longer used for the rules of the cards; (do not confuse with BLACK MAGIC). [**cf.** MAGIC, TRADITION, CEREMONIAL MAGIC]

LOW SELF—(Huna) the SUBCONSCIOUS MIND; does not mean it is lower than the CONSCIOUS MIND (middle self), but rather, that much of the mind is involuntary; that part of the human being that incarnates over and over. [**cf.** SYMPATHETIC NERVOUS SYSTEM, OVERSOUL]

LOW VARIANCE—(psi tasks) the fluctuation of scores below mean chance variance in a controlled experiment. [**cf.** MEAN CHANCE EXPECTATION, ESP]

LOW-ORDER-PSI-FORCE—(laboratory) soul-minds who are ignorant, criminals and earth-bound, residing in the DENSITY of ETHERIC WORLD. [**cf.** DENSITY Appendix 5, HAUNTINGS]

LOWER FREQUENCY—(biofeedback training) the lowest level one's mind reaches in the BIOFEEDBACK TRAINING session; measured in cycles per second on the brain wave scale. [**cf.** BRAIN WAVE RHYTHM]

LOWER SELF—that part of a man or woman that has thoughts of selfishness, jealousy, greed, hate, dissatisfaction, resentment, etc.; functions from the lower three chakras; a materialistic person. **Syn.** CARNAL MAN. [**cf.** ROOT CHAKRA, PHYSICAL PLANE]

LOWERED STATE OF CONSCIOUSNESS—an awareness when one's mind is under control, the body is relaxed and the emotions are quiet; a state of MEDITATION and a state for perceiving psychic information more fluently. **Syn.** LISTENING MODE. [**cf.** MENTAL PSYCHIC PROCESSES Appendix 2, BIOFEEDBACK TRAINING, METABOLIC MONITOR]

LUCID AWARENESS—(biofeedback training) the fifth brain wave signature discovered on the Mind-Mirror EEG instrument (invented by C. Maxwell Cade); a sophisticated EEG that involves high amplitude alpha accompanied by bands of beta and theta; fifth brain wave level observed in metaphysical healers while they are sending the healing energy; in this lucid awareness, one can walk around with eyes open, converse, solve mathematical problems, induce emotional states, read and understand what was read. (Inconcl.) [**cf.** SPLIT BRAIN, CONSCIOUSNESS, MIND-MIRROR]

LUCID DREAMING—dreams occurring in the normal DREAM CYCLE, but the dreamer is confidently aware that she or he is dreaming; one feels in full possession of waking consciousness, and yet is aware that one is asleep in bed; dreamer knows when a lucid dream is happening, and with practice can be in control of the dream if they desire. [**cf.** LUCIDITY, INCUBATION]

LUCID POSSESSION—a possession seizure, wherein the victim is aware of an evil ETHERIC WORLD ENTITY within her or himself, but cannot do anything about it; sometimes the two personalities make conversation with each other; two distinct levels of thought in the seizure; one theory: this evil entity is a second self within the victim. [**cf.** POSSESSION, OBSESSION]

LUCIDITY—to manipulate dream energies during the dream state in the direction one desires, similar to making up one's own mind in the daytime; to steer the dream makers with a conscious reaction during the dream, and retain awareness throughout the dream without awakening, or falling into a natural dream state. [**cf.** LUCID DREAM, INCUBATION, DREAM CONTROL]

LUCIFER—(esoteric) ("light-bearer" or "bringer of the light") to be identified with Satan or Lucifer is to begin at the bottom of the evolutionary scale and deal with the lowest quality of the earth consciousness; objective is to bring mankind out of a rigid order, up into a state of BLISS or ENLIGHTENMENT. [**cf.** DENSITY, NEGATIVE THOUGHTS, HAUNTING]

LUGH—(Ireland) an ETHERIC WORLD INTELLIGENCE whose main function is to be guardian over wars and to communicate with humans when they desire guidance and protection. [**cf.** CELESTIAL GUARDIAN, OUTER BAND]

LUMINESCENCE—see ETHERIC DOUBLE.

LUMINOSITY—(esoteric) the quality of being intellectually brilliant; enlightened.

LUMINOUS ARC—(Theosophy) refers to the life-waves of all the celestial globes, which evolve upward in a chain effect, in the whole galaxies. [**cf.** CYCLES, ROUND, EVOLUTION, LIFE WAVE]

LUMINOUS BODY—see AURA.

LUMINOUS DISCS—(Greece) name given to the UNIDENTIFIED FLYING OBJECTS seen in the sky. [**cf.** UFOLOGY, CONSTRUCTS, CRITTERS]

LUMINOUS EGGS—see ETHERIC DOUBLE.

LUMINOUS PHENOMENA—see PSYCHIC LIGHTS.

LUMINOUS SPIRITS—(Voodoo, Haiti) ETHERIC

363

WORLD guides who are communicated with psychically to bring guidance, protection, and information. [cf. INNER BAND, GUIDE, OUTER BAND]

LUMINOUS TRAIN—magnetic energy that is emanated from the bodies of avatars or great masters, and can be felt and perceived clairvoyantly by those in their presence. [cf. GODHEAD, MASTER, AVATAR, ANGEL HIERARCHY]

LUM-GOM-PA RUNNERS—(Tibet) couriers who cover enormous distances, moving with vast strides, and who seem to hardly touch the ground; accomplished by BREATH CONTROL and undivided attention to the top half of the body, thus allowing the feet to take care of themselves. [cf. PROLONGED JOGGING, MOVEMENT-FOR-ALTERED-CONSCIOUSNESS, DERVISH]

LUNAR CYCLE—a period measured by the moon's revolutions around the sun; a pattern of approximately nineteen years, when the new moon appears at the same time of the year as at the beginning of the cycle; symbolic of the awakening of the PSYCHIC CENTERS in human beings. **Syn.** METONIC CYCLE. [cf. CYCLES, AQUARIAN AGE, TRANSFORMATION]

LUNAR MONADS—(Helena Petrovna Blavatsky) theory: the present inhabitants of the earth were inhabitants of the moon, many millions of years ago, before it became barren; LUNAR MONADS are intelligences who have ended their life-cycle on the lunar chain and have now incarnated on the earth plane. [cf. SEVEN PLANETARY CHAIN LOGOI, PLANETARY CHAIN]

LUNG-TA—(Tibet) (myth) a winged horse that was a messenger traveling thoughout the universe, bringing helpful things from the gods to humans; believed to be a spaceship. (Inconcl.) [cf. UFOLOGY Appendix 5]

LYCANTHROPY—(Greek *wol* and *man*) to psychically transform oneself into an animal, e.g., a wolf, leopard, bear, tiger, jaguar; one develops a taste for raw or putrid meat, a desire to howl, and takes on other characteristics of the animal; in this animal form, the psychic kills, rapes, and eats young girls; different theories: 1. the psychotic feeling that one is an animal, without actually being one; 2. the skill of changing one's own vibrational frequency, for a set time, into another vibrational frequency of one's own making; dematerializing and rematerializing (through deep concentration) and then taking on the new characteristics that have overcome one's mind thoughts; utilizes the law of identity. (Inconcl.) 3. the skill of moving into an animal's body, and using its eyes and ears to see and hear; similar to POSSESSION, except that the psychic takes on the characteristics of the new body which is that of the animal. **Syn.** SHAPE-SHIFTING, METAMORPHOSIS. [cf. WEREBOARS, WERELIONS, WEREBEARS]

LYING POSTURE OF THE LION—(Tibet) a process whereby the Lama turns the dying person on their right side for better manipulation during the ritual for a successful, peaceful transition in the DEATH PROCESS. [cf. INITIATORY DEATH RITE]

LYING SPIRIT—an inferior ETHERIC WORLD ENTITY who manages to usurp the place of a normal high entity's intervention; uses vulgar language, and gives misinformation during a SEANCE or PSYCHIC DEVELOPMENT CIRCLE; may be due to an ill MEDIUM or disharmony among the SITTERS, which causes a broken circuit in the circle. [cf. ETHERIC WEB, PSYCHIC ATTACK, LAW OF LIKE ATTRACTS LIKE Appendix 7]

LYSERGIC ACID—(botane) a psychotropic drug capable of bringing about a psychedelic clairvoyant experience, in which the mind activity resembles a state of madness or functions at its edge; sometimes called PSYCHOSOMATIC. [cf. FORCED PSI, PSYCHOTROPIC PLANTS]

M-RAYS—see MITOGENIC RAYS.

MA—(Egypt) nature, recognized as the eternal mother. [**cf.** TOTALITY, MONADOLOGY]

MA-AT—(Egypt) a temple used to train disciples how to properly use their psychic senses; depicted by a vulture-headed human because the vulture has a very keen psychic sense. [**cf.** INITIATION RITES, MYSTICISM, ORACLE AT DELPHI]

MAAT—(Egypt) goddess personifying law and righteousness; begot by air, appearing as an egg in the beginning; later adopted a more conventional shape; fool of the Tarot cards; controls breathing the air that is connected with life; goddess of Truth. [**cf.** DIVINE THRONE, GREAT LOGI, LORDHOOD]

MACRO—(Greece) prefix meaning "excessive, great" or "long."

MACROBACTERIA—(ufology) immense foreign material living in the atmosphere which is new to earth's scientists. (Inconcl.) [**cf.** UFOLOGY, SPHEROIDS, CRITTERS, MUTANTS]

MACROCOSM—(esoteric) (Greek *Kismos*, "the world") the UNIVERSE; is a gigantic living being and everything in this orderly system is alive; 1. eternal reality; indestructable; invisible in its primordial form; the absolute whole; all energy under total law; 2. unmanifested, interdependent intelligence; consists of all the VIBRATIONAL FREQUENCIES that ever will exist that mankind will ever comprehend and find necessary to use; composed of every thought conceived by the individual minds of humanity and all the inhabitants of the universe; all manifestations within its boundaries are made from the emotions and knowledge of mankind; macrocosm is crystallized thought; 3. a replica of a physical human being or vice versa; likewise divided into minute microcosmic duplications of various vibrational frequencies of shapes, sounds, and thicknesses (as the body is); 4. depicted by the six pointed star formed by two triangles, the emblem of the world; see TOTALITY. (Inconcl.) [**cf.** SOLOMON'S SEAL, PROTOPLASMIC, SYMPATHETIC MAGIC, LAW OF MICRO/MACROCOSM Appendix 7, GOD, DIVINE INTELLIGENCE]

MACROMOLECULAR BASIS OF MEMORY—memory in the COSMOS plan; ability of the atom to

remember; see TOTALITY. [**cf.** AKASHIC RECORD, DNA MOLECULES]

MACROPROSOPUS—(Kabbalah) the GREAT COUNTENANCE; a symbol of the UNIVERSE. [**cf.** SYMBOLS, ASSOCIATION MAGIC]

MACROPSIA—to sense the world expanding; occurs during an ALTERED STATE OF CONSCIOUSNESS. [**cf.** MENTAL PROJECTION Appendix 2]

MACROTELLURICALLY—pertaining to the EARTH.

MADAME ZENOIBIA—a general name given to those who profess to have great psychic talent but whose lust for psychic experience and attention far exceeds their competence or honesty; they usually appear with an excess of makeup, jewelry and odd clothing. [**cf.** UP-FOR-GRABS, PSYCHIC ATTACKS]

MADAN—(Hinduism) a nature spirit believed to assist psychics. [**cf.** FEY]

MADE HIS TRANSITION—(metaphysics) the DEATH of an individual; phrase used as opposed to *died* by those who believe the LIFE FORCE leaves the physical body to live on in the ETHERIC WORLD; theory: an earthly death is just the natural and automatic shifting of the elements of survival (the SOUL-MIND) to a different plane of CONSCIOUSNESS; elements of survival continue life from a different level of AWARENESS. (Inconcl.) **Syn.** ACROSS THE THRESHOLD. [**cf.** DEATH SCIENCE Appendix 2, SURVIVALISTS]

MAGE—see MAGICIAN, MAGUS, MAGIAN.

MAGGANA—(Ethiopia) the ETHERIC WORLD INTELLIGENCE that was assigned to oversee buildings and houses, whether occupied or vacant. [**cf.** HOUSE SWEEP, HAUNTED LOCALITIES]

MAGGID—(Judaism, Kabbalah) a teacher or spiritual leader who gives special instructions in MEDITATION and psychic work; instructions are an offshoot of the normal prayers of the devout Jew. [**cf.** SELF-NONSELF, PRAYER, NON-THOUGHT, CONTEMPLATION]

MAGI—(Persia) class of Zoroastrian priests noted for their supernatural powers; worked with ALCHEMY and ASTROLOGY; psychics who could control the forces of nature, heal the sick, predict the future, and perform many other psychic skills; singular **magus**. [**cf.** CEREMONIAL MAGIC, ALCHEMIST, ROD, SACRAMENT, LADDER TO HEAVEN, MASTERSHIP]

MAGIANISM—philosophy of psychic art; see MAGIC.

MAGIC—(Greek, Zoroaster *magein*, "great, the great science and religion") now, also considered an art; **1.** comprises a system of concepts and methods of using the more subtle forces of nature to help individuals balance with their emotions; teaches how to alter the ELECTROCHEMICAL aspect of the body metabolism, using association techniques and objects to concentrate and focus the emotional energy; attempts to help one achieve a higher state of consciousness and improvements in environmental atmosphere; **2.** develops control of the human WILL; uses some alchemical procedures; **3.** utilizes the psychic skills that use the energy emanating from one's body, adjusting it to interact with other energy patterns, animate or inanimate, according to one's will; **4.** belief: the SOUL-MIND lives on after physical death and can be called upon for help in the MUNDANE WORLD; uses techniques to CONJURE UP their assistance; **5.** uses incantations, ceremonies, symbols, nature objects, manmade objects, to simulate and therefore stimulate the more subtle forces to obey; relies on these two laws: (HERMETIC) "as above so below"; "respect nature and have control over it"; **6.** two kinds: BLACK MAGIC used for evil intent; WHITE MAGIC used for righteous purposes; (do not confuse with HIGH MAGIC and LOW MAGIC which are steps in white magic). **Syn.** HIDDEN SCIENCE, GREAT SCIENCE, MYSTICISM, PARAPSYCHOLOGY. [**cf.** CEREMONIAL MAGIC Appendix 2; LAW OF ASSOCIATION, LAW OF SIGNATURES and LAW OF CONTAGION Appendix 7]

MAGIC ART—see MAGIC, PARAPSYCHOLOGY.

MAGIC CAUSALITY—**1.** the end result of two events happening together with a very significant meaning to the person and yet neither event is the cause of, or related to, the happening; **2.** the end result of the pattern or patterns in the CASTING OF LOTS, I CHING, ASTRAGALOMANCY and other similar MANTIC ARTS; finds a parallelism with the MACROCOSM and MICROCOSM which reshuffles the entire environment in question. (Inconcl.) [**cf.** SYNCHRONICITY, CORRESPONDENCES-IN-TIME, LOTS, SORTES]

MAGIC CIRCLE—**1.** an imaginary circle drawn with a pointed finger or a real circle made with substance (e.g., string, rock-salt, chalk) around the person, persons, or objects that desire protection; performed with or without ritual or ceremony; belief: no EVIL forces can penetrate the circle line; **2.** mandala-mudra combination used around an area where something spiritual is to take place; builds energy and isolates the activity in the center of the circle so the individual or group can more easily control the energy generated, e.g., Sufi twirling; **3.** (Buddhism) represents four steps of unfoldment in various states of consciousness that one goes through in MEDITATION; **(a)** MIRROR-LIKE WISDOM; **(b)** EQUALIZING WISDOM; **(c)** DISTINGUISHING WISDOM; **(d)** ALL-ACCOMPLISHING WISDOM. [**cf.** FORMS-WITH-POWER, TRIANGLE, WITHERSHINS, MANDALA]

MAGIC EFFECT—(Carl Jung) an intuitive feeling of a special "quality of expectation" of the MONAD process being urged into its more perfect state; from this time on, the individual changes their pathway and is a happier person. **Syn.** ARCHETYPE OF THE MIRACLE. [**cf.** TRANSFORMATION, SPONTANEITY DISCIPLINE, SELF-ACTUALIZATION]

MAGIC HEALING—**1.** to find the sick person's SOUL-MIND and return it to that body or replace it with another person's soul-mind; **2.** see PSYCHIC HEALING. [**cf.** SHAMANISM, WALK-IN, INCARNATIONAL EXCHANGE, POSSESSION]

MAGIC MIRROR—a mirror painted black on the back; used for the purpose of seeing visions in the front. [**cf.** SCRYING, CRYSTAL GAZING]

MAGIC OF LIGHT—(esoteric) to mentally surround one's self and one's area with a WHITE LIGHT before performing any psychic skills; to mentally surround a sick person with a white light to induce a healing; theory: the vibratory rate of white light is capable of destroying all negative forces that interfere with superior quality mental and physical psychism. [**cf.** LIGHT, LISTENING MODE, MEDITATION, COLOR]

MAGIC PASSES—**1.** to move the hands back and forth over the CRYSTAL BALL with the palms facing the ball; the psychic energy emanating out of the palms helps stir the energy and bring forth visions on the crystal. [**cf.** SCRYING Appendix 2] **2.** see MAGNETIC PASSES. [**cf.** MAGNETIC HEALING]

MAGIC SLEEP—to psychically rest in a hypnotic

state of consciousness for many years; individual remains alive but appears like a corpse; no need for food, body elimination, or emotional stimulation; individual wakes up and lives in a new time period without body deterioration. **Syn.** DEATH-LIKE TRANCE, SLEEPERS. [**cf.** MAGIC SLEEP INDUCEMENT, TEMPERATURE CONTROL, IMMUTABILITY]

MAGIC SLEEP INDUCEMENT—(Slavic) to put one-self or another in a DEATH-LIKE TRANCE which lasts for many years without body deterioration; no need for food, elimination, personal touch, noise, educational stimulation; body looks lifeless, as if hybernating; executed by: 1. elementary principles of HYPNOSIS; 2. combing one's hair, chanting and singing lullabies endlessly until the body behaves in this manner; (charm songs have been versed for this purpose). (Inconcl.) [**cf.** INCANTATIONS, POETRY, JOGI-FEATS]

MAGIC SYMBOLS—objects, real or imaginery, used because of their peculiar properties to induce and produce psychic phenomena; objects used in psychic skills, meditation, rituals, and spiritual growth exercises are carefully chosen for their color, form, and parallel meaning, to produce the vibrational frequency necessary for that which one wishes to achieve. [**cf.** Appendix 2 ASSOCIATION MAGIC, FORMS-WITH-POWER, SYMBOLS]

MAGIC VERSE—rhythmic or musical poetry using symbols, similes, and analogies, very skillfully designed to: 1. cure; 2. rid one of a HEX or other negative vibrations; 3. entice one to do what the MAGICIAN or PSYCHIC bids; e.g. (a) the pied piper of Hamlin; (b) the Psalms in the BIBLE originally had a musical background and are known, even today, to heal various diseases. [**cf.** WORDS-WITH-POWER, HEXED, SPELLED, INCANTATIONS, AFFIRMATIONS]

MAGIC WAND—(antiquity) a long, slender instrument used by magicians and psychics to transfer power in a specific direction; symbol of authority and master of psychic energies; used as an outward agency of intense psychic power which holds psychic vibrations from the magician and his or her rituals until it is aimed and released; good substances to use for rods are HAZEL WOOD, YEW, and hawthorn; known uses: 1. priests used a staff for healing the ill; 2. knights used a sceptre as a symbol of knighthood; 3. Hermes carried a caduceus wand; 4. shepherd's crook was the emblem of royal authority; 5. medieval magician's rod was tipped with a magnetized cap which projected an extremely powerful magnetic force for psychic purposes. [**cf.** AARON'S ROD, MAGIC SYMBOLS, ANKH]

MAGIC WHEEL—a motif of a wheel in various forms and designs used in many cultures for varying symbology; e.g., 1. (Greece) a wheel with four spokes and jagged edges to represent the rays of the sun and the four points of the compass; 2. (alchemy) four wheels within one design to represent the basic four elements of the ALCHEMIST. [**cf.** PRAYER WHEEL, WHEEL OF FORTUNE]

MAGIC WITH MAGIC CURE—(theory) in order to send psychic activity to another individual, one must send the psychic activity at the level of CONSCIOUSNESS of the receiver; unless there is some compatibility between the psychic activity and the receiver's AURA and mental atmosphere, the receiver will subconsciously refuse to accept it; 1. (exorcism) to exorcise a victim of a CURSE, SPELL, or HEX, put on them by the use of BLACK MAGIC, one must use black magic rituals to free the victim; the victim accepted the negative activity in the beginning because they thought along these lines; 2. (healing) to heal one's health, wealth or relationships, the magician must know the state of consciousness of the receiver in order to organize psychic activity that is compatible in some degree to the receiver. [**cf.** LAW OF AN EYE FOR AN EYE Appendix 7, SUGGESTION]

MAGICAL—pertains to the performance of a psychic function.

MAGICAL CORRESPONDENCE—to use a parallel symbol in a simulated activity with the same gestures of an activity that one wants to happen in reality. **Syn.** IMITATIVE MAGIC. [**cf.** LAW OF ASSOCIATION Appendix 7, CEREMONIAL MAGIC, PSYCHODRAMA WHITE MAGIC, MIMICRY]

MAGICAL CREATURES—(nature kingdom) ELEMENTAL forces composed of chaotic thought energies which have no definite structure or real moral determination; capable of existing in both the THIRD DIMENSION and FOURTH DIMENSION so they are vulnerable to psychic thought and can blend their emotional strength and nervous excitement in either direction; used for EVIL or GOOD. **Syn.** FAIRIES. [**cf.** Appendix 3 NATURE SPIRITS]

MAGICAL DIAGRAMS—geometrical designs that represent the mysteries of the DEITY and CREA-

367

TION which give the designs the proper vibrational frequency to be helpful in the rites of evocation and conjuration; the main magician's diagrams are: 1. TRIANGLE; 2. DOUBLE TRIANGLE which forms a six-pointed star and is known as the Seal of Solomon; 3. HEXAGRAM, a four-pointed star formed by the interlacement of two pillars; 4. PENTAGRAM, a five pointed star. [cf. FORMS-WITH-POWER, CONJURATION]

MAGICAL GIFT—see PSYCHIC SKILL.

MAGICAL PROPORTIONS OF MAN—the human structure is the sacred ratio that appears throughout nature, BC/AB = 1; the governing ratio of the Great Pyramid, depicted by a man with outstretched arms and legs in a SQUARE, a CIRCLE, and an inverted TRIANGLE; also symbolic of man bridging the gap between the solid PHYSICAL WORLD (the square), and the eternal ETHERIC WORLD (the circle with no beginning and no ending), and the triangle outlining it all. Syn. GOLDEN SECTION. [cf. NUMBER POWER, FORMS-WITH-POWER]

MAGICIAN—(Zoroastrianism, 600 B.C.) one who studies supernormal scientific knowledge and masters psychic skills in the quest to understand mankind's purpose in earth; not highly religious but interested in raising their consciousness, exploring the universe, and helping their brother and sister humans; an educated scientist and ALCHEMIST; receives their power from NATURE and its laws; uses special doctrines and ritualistic techniques to CONJURE UP angels, nature elementals, nonhuman entities, and uses their influence for his or her purposes; practices GEOMANCY; manufactures and consecrates talismans; utilizes the power of thought and sound; performs psychic healings. Syn. PSYCHIC. [cf. RITUAL, SYMBOLIC MAGIC, OIL FOR ANNOINTING, SEVEN-KNOTTED WAND, SACRED MAGIC]

MAGICIANS' FIRE—the hidden all-pervading all-uniting influence which connects HEAVEN and EARTH and everything on the earth. Syn. GOLDEN CHAIN, JACOB'S LADDER, ANIMA MUNDI. [cf. ALCHEMY, PRAYER WHEEL, SCARAB BEETLE, SCHEME OF THINGS]

MAGISM—one who is skilled in magic arts; see PSYCHIC.

MAGISTER—see MASTER, TEACHER, or MAGICIAN.

MAGISTRATE OF GOD—(ancient) name of SATAN;

(more recent) Keeper of Karma and Numbers; from these records, he deals out lawful effects of one's imbalances. [cf. KARMA, LORDS OF JUSTICE, AKASHIC RECORDS]

MAGLOIRE—(France) a manikin made from the roots of the MANDRAKE plant to be used as a psychic tool; this manikin was used as a home for a psychic elf who would bring protection and psychic information to the household. Syn. MAIN-DE-GLOIRE, ALRUNE, MANDRAKE AMULET. [cf. BOTANE, MAGNETIZED OBJECTS, PINE TREE]

MAGNALE MAGNUM—coined by Jan Baptista van Helmont (1620); see VITAL LIFE FORCE.

MAGNET DISPENSARY—(eighteenth century) an institution in which huge magnets were used for the sick person to pull on, sending the MAGNETISM through the body to hasten the healing; theory: magnets have healing effects on the physical body. [cf. Appendix 5 MAGNETOLOGY]

MAGNET HEALING—to use magnets that have been designed and tested, to repair living tissue; magnets have a positive energy on one side and a negative energy on the other; in healing living tissue in humans or animals, the positive or south pole energy activates, increases, rejuvenates, accelerates, and expands; the north pole or negative energy checks, arrests, retards, and reduces swelling and pain. (Inconcl.) [cf. MAGNETOMETER, MAGNETOLOGY, CURATIVE EDUCATION]

MAGNET PRACTITIONER—one who uses magnets or lodestones to heal another's body by placing them on the patient (or on the self) which transfers the energy to the patient. [cf. NATURAL MAGNETS]

MAGNET SLEEP—(method introduced by Franz Anton Mesmer) a state of HYPNOSIS reached by using MAGNETIZED OBJECTS in the induction process. [cf. INDUCTION, DEEP HYPNOTIC STATE, SUBJECT, HYPNOTHERAPY]

MAGNET SOMNAMBULISM—(late 1700s) to use a material object to put one's self in a deep hypnotic state of consciousness in preparation for trancing; object may be a HYPNOTIC DISC, metronome, PENDULUM, etc.; material objects are especially helpful for SELF-INDUCTION; a deep hypnotic state is necessary for ETHERIC WORLD INTELLIGENCES to intervene for physical phenomena. [cf. DEEP TRANCE, MEDIUMSHIP]

MAGNETIC ANOMALY—1. an odd or strange phenomena according to the laws of magnetics, as physicists now know them; an inconsistency or deviation from the known magnetic laws; 2. (ufology) an area on the earth that is different in nature in a physical sense and is conducive of UFO materializations. [**cf.** UFO SIGHTINGS, SPACE CONTINUUM, PLASMAS]

MAGNETIC ATMOSPHERE—vital force or auric emanations surrounding the entire UNIVERSE; the result of the internal energy of things and the activity of the universe, binding all things together in the universe. (Inconcl.) **Sim.** AURA. [**cf.** ETHERIC DOUBLE/EARTH, RADIATION FIELD PHOTOGRAPHY, NODE]

MAGNETIC BODY—1. (Tibet) part of the human ETHERIC DOUBLE that is influenced by one's emotions whether they are hateful and greedy, or passions of love and kindness; 2. consists of chemical-electro-magnetic forces around each person, object, or celestial entity; see AURA. (Inconcl.) [**cf.** STRIATIONS, KIRLIAN PHOTOGRAPHY, ULTRAVIOLET AURIC LIGHT]

MAGNETIC DISTANT HEALING—to transfer the MAGNETISM from one's self to a patient who is in another locale, with the intent of healing the patient's body; healing practitioner holds their right hand over the patient's photograph or a PETITION (a slip of paper in which the patient has written their name); the left palm is open to the magnetism flowing in through the atmosphere; the magnetism travels through the body and out the right hand to the petition or photograph and keeps traveling to the patient's nervous system by thought-direction of the PRACTITIONER; practitioner decrees the magnetism to possess healing qualities; patient does not need to know when the process is taking place; (do not confuse with MENTAL DISTANT HEALING; see Appendix 4 for differences). (Inconcl.) [**cf.** REMOTE TREATMENT, NERVE FLUID, PALMS]

MAGNETIC EMANATIONS—lines of energy reflected from objects that differ in color, patterns and density according to the object form; electro-magnetic light waves that can be photographed with a high frequency camera. [**cf.** KIRLIAN EFFECT, ULTRAFAINT LUMINESCENCE, X-BIOENERGIES, NIMBUS]

MAGNETIC FIELDS—1. one of the seven ENERGY FIELDS surrounding the human body that are affected by the SOLAR PLEXUS, emotions, and physical and mental states of the individual; can be measured by a sensitive MAGNETOMETER; 2. an energy field surrounding the earth and pulsating at frequencies similar to the ALPHA BRAIN waves of the human. (Inconcl.) [**cf.** ETHERIC DOUBLE, MAGNETIC BODY, ULTRAOUTER AURA]

MAGNETIC FLUID—coined by Franz Anton Mesmer (1775); see VITAL LIFE FORCE.

MAGNETIC FLUX—see MAGNETIC NERVE FLUID.

MAGNETIC FORM RESONANCE—coined by Patrick Flanagan; the energy that is found within a PYRAMID; this energy creates effects similar to MAGNETISM, heat and luminous radiations, but of itself it is none of these. [**cf.** Appendix 5 PYRAMIDOLOGY, FORMS-WITH-POWER]

MAGNETIC HEALING—(esoteric) to transfer the MAGNETIC NERVE FLUID from one's hands to the patient, under the direction of thought; this helps the cells to normalize so that the intelligence in the cells will direct a healing to itself more quickly; types: 1. the magnetic nerve fluid from the healer's nervous system is transferred from the palms of the hands to the nervous system of the patient; 2. nerve fluid is directed out of the hands to the congested area of the patient, and with special motions the nerve fluid loosens the block in the MERIDIAN LINES and the patient starts to heal; 3. hands are laid on the patient's forehead or shoulders to bring a soothing effect which puts harmony into the patient's body; the magnetic nerve fluid, the healing agent, can be intensified, stored, or liberated by deep breaths; magnetic fluid contacts the physical, astral and etheric double bodies, therefore, hands may touch the body or preferably be held a little above the body per se; methods utilizing magnetic healing: REFLEXOLOGY, ACUPRESSURE, NEUROMUSCULAR MASSAGE, AURA BALANCING, DISTANT HEALING. See Appendix 4 to differentiate from other healing methods. (Inconcl.) **Syn.** THERAPEUTIC TOUCH, LAYING-ON-OF-HANDS. [**cf.** GAUSS MAGNETICS, MAGNETISM, PASSES, POWWOW HEALING]

MAGNETIC LIFE FORCE—see VITAL LIFE FORCE.

MAGNETIC NERVE FLUID—1. (esoteric) an invisible, electro-motive energy field which runs throughout all three nervous systems (CEREBROSPINAL, SYMPATHETIC, and vagus); carries a universal substance vital to sustain life; flows involun-

369

tarily, or flows voluntarily when directed by thought; capable of being measured by the Gauss meter; used more abundantly in sports and for healing purposes. (Inconcl.) **Syn.** ANIMAL MAGNETISM, HEALING FLUID, NERVE FLUID, EARTH MAGNETISM, GAUSS MAGNETICS; **2.** (ancient Egypt) **(a)** an ethereal energy field that acts as tubes throughout the whole nervous system to carry and blend: (1)cosmic energies that enter the head; (2) SPIRIT taken through breathing and through the chakras; (3) the MENTAL-REFLECTING-ETHER; (4) the bone marrow; (5) the chemicals of the glands; (6) the emotions and their degree of electricity; **(b)** MAGNETIC NERVE FLUID enters the body involuntarily in a constant stream, through the left hand, and goes to "ground" through the right foot unless it is redirected by thought; when directed to be utilized for healing, it exudes out the right hand, right eye and right hip; **(c)** perceived clairvoyantly as BLUE in color; **(d)** an internal working of the externalization of the astral nervous system; connects and interpenetrates the physical and astral nervous system. (Inconcl.) **Syn.** NADIS, ETHERIC MAGNETIC CURRENT. [**cf.** MAGNETIC HEALING Appendix 2, THERAPEUTIC TOUCH, GOLDEN OIL, BRAIN DEWS]

MAGNETIC PASSES—(magnetic healing) to move one's hands back and forth in a parallel manner over the congested area of the patient with the intent of loosening the blockage in the energy flow; palms of practitioner's hands face the patient and work with the patient's ETHERIC DOUBLE, about one or two inches above the body: PRACTITIONER has previously scanned and evaluated the patient's etheric double for a sticky feeling indicating the blockage; patient may or may not feel any sensations during process; once the congestion is loosened, practitioner uses another technique to put MAGNETISM from her or his body into this area so the cells can normalize and heal more quickly. [**cf.** ALTERNATIVES, ASSESSING, HOLY FIRE, UNRUFFLING THE FIELD]

MAGNETIC PRACTITIONER—one who has a genuine desire to heal another person as opposed to a special way of moving the hands; subconscious and conscious desire will automatically exude MAGNETIC FLUID from the palms regardless of the technique of movements. [**cf.** HEALEE, PUMPING, REFLECTED HEALING]

MAGNETIC RADIATION—see MAGNETIC EMANATIONS.

MAGNETIC SELF-HEALING—to intensify the MAGNETIC NERVE FLUID within one's self and use it to energize or heal one's body; the MAGNETISM that normally flows in the left hand is concentrated upon and directed out the right palm, right palm is held a few inches above the congested area to loosen and break up the congestion, or is held a few inches over the head to energize the whole body; deep breaths will increase the magnetism as it flows; (do not confuse with MENTAL HEALING, see Appendix 4). [**cf.** LOOSENED, EARTH MAGNETISM, CONGESTED AURA]

MAGNETIC SENSE—to psychially see the AURIC RAYS that surround people and objects. **Syn.** AURIC CLAIRVOYANCE. [**cf.** AURA, ETHERIC DOUBLE, AURA GOGGLES]

MAGNETIC WAVES—see AURA.

MAGNETISM—(esoteric) **1.** an ethereal primordial ELECTROMOTIVE FORCE that finds a way to penetrate every system on earth, living and nonliving; functions throughout the UNIVERSE under the laws of polarity and thought; a necessary conjunction to electricity; the MITOGENTIC RAYS or power are released from the human body, or objects, according to the change of polarities of the physical vitality. (Inconcl.) [**cf.** POLARITY, ELECTRICITY, AURA] **2.** (prescience) *magnetism* is synonomous with *emotions*; i.e., stir the emotions and the magnetic flow increases; induce magnetic flow and emotions rise; a fluid within the nervous system; can be liberated from the body by physical rhythmic movement and certain forms of music, or by PSYCHIC TRANSFER; see MAGNETIC HEALING. (Inconcl.) **3.** (prescience) the ENERGY in the atom that keeps it vibrating; works in harmony with the electricity in the atom that is telling the atom the rate to vibrate. (Inconcl.) [**cf.** ATOM, MAGNETS, POLARITY, MAGNETIC HEALING, MAGNETIC NERVE FLUID]

MAGNETISM IMMUNITY—(psychic healing) individuals living with a healing practitioner are less susceptible to her or his healing magnetism as they are sustained by the magnetism all the time; an individual who is foreign to the healer is affected more readily. [**cf.** BODY SCANNING, HEALING BY IMPERSONATING, BODY IS TURNED ON]

MAGNETIZATION—**1.** to methodically use an iron magnet to heal sicknesses; PRACTITIONER puts magnets on patient's body in places where the magnets will bring a balance of polarity to the body;

treatments must be continuous; healings are gradual; **2.** to use a MAGNETIZING OBJECT to hypnotize one's self or another person, as opposed to the method of using words of commands and imagery. [**cf.** MAGNETOLOGY Appendix 5]

MAGNETIZED OBJECTS—things of nature or manmade articles that have been energized by a psychic to be used for psychic purposes; psychic releases the MAGNETISM from palms of hands to the article by thought and rhythmic breathing; one way to energize an amulet or talisman. (Inconcl.) [**cf.** AMULET Appendix 2]

MAGNETIZED WATER—water activated and energized by a psychic or religious figure to be used in healings, rituals, or blessings; psychic places the right hand over the water, or sprinkles the fingers over the water while breathing rhythmically and directing the spirit from the body into the water by thought. [**cf.** BLESSING, HOLY WATER, ALTERNATIVES, PUMPING]

MAGNETIZER—**1.** a HYPNOTIST or HYPNOTHERAPIST; **2.** an ETHERIC WORLD ENTITY who works in physical MEDIUMSHIP; **3.** a PSYCHIC or MAGNET HEALER; **4.** (Russia, Japan) a device that concentrates energy and allows it to flow through to the patient with a healing effect. [**cf.** ELECTROMAGNETISM]

MAGNETIZING OBJECT—(hypnosis) a tangible form that is capable of putting an individual into a hypnotic state of consciousness because of its design, color, or activity potential; object is used in front of the subject's eyes, until the subject's eyes water, and a tired and relaxed state occurs; most common articles used: the PENDULUM, HYPNOTIC DISC, and STROBE LIGHT. [**cf.** INDUCTION, SUBJECT, MESMERIC FLUID]

MAGNETOBIOLOGY—a science which deals with the effects of MAGNETIC FIELDS on the biological systems; includes permanent, electromagnetic, constant, pulsed, terrestrial or EXTRATERRESTRIAL fields. **Syn.** BIOMAGNETICS, MAGNETOTHERAPY.

MAGNETOCARDIOGRAPH—(future science) abbr. MCG; an instrument that records rhythmical changes of the heart's magnetic field; this instrument found that the magnetic field varies in parallel with its electrical field; both fields arise from the same source, originating from the rhythmical flow of positive and negative charges in the nerve and muscle fibers of the heart. (Inconcl.) [**cf.** Appendix 5 POLARITY]

MAGNETOELECTRICITY—coined by William T. Tiller (1973); see VITAL LIFE FORCE.

MAGNETOENCEPHALOGRAPH—abbr. MEG; an instrument similar to the ELECTROENCEPHALOGRAPH except it does not distort the brain's magnetic field when it measures it; (brain's magnetic field is one ten-billionth the intensity of the Earth's own field. [**cf.** BIOFEEDBACK TRAINING Appendix 5]

MAGNETOISM—coined by A. Wendler (1920); see VITAL LIFE FORCE.

MAGNETOLOGY—the study of the effect of MAGNETS, their energies of POLARITY and how these two energies affect living organisms; theory: magnets have two types of energy, north and south poles; when applied to living systems, such as human beings, animals, or plants, these energies will influence the biological system according to the pole that touches the living tissue. (Inconcl.) **Syn.** BIOMAGNETISM. [**cf.** MAGNETS, MAGNET HEALING, IRON, Appendix 5 MAGNETOLOGY]

MAGNETOMETER—an instrument used in seances to test the energy emanating from the MEDIUM; invented by A. Fortin; capable of finding a change in the POLARITY of the medium while the medium is in a TRANCE state of unconsciousness; instrument is able to detect MAGNETIC FIELDS one ten-billionth of the intensity of the earth's own magnetic field. [**cf.** BRAIN MAGNETISM, DYNAMOSCOPE, TELEKINESIS, BIOMETER OF BARADUC, ECTOPLASM, PALMED POWER, EXTERIORIZATION OF SENSITIVITY]

MAGNETOTHERAPY—a science which deals with the effects of MAGNETIC FIELDS on the biological systems, including constant, pulsed, electromagnetic, terrestrial or EXTRATERRESTRIAL fields. **Syn.** BIOMAGNETICS, MAGNETOBIOLOGY. [**cf.** MAGNETS, POLARITY]

MAGNETOSCOPE OF RUTER—an instrument used in the SEANCE room to understand PK, PALMING energy, and EXTERIORIZATION OF SENSITIVITY; capable of investigating the energy emanating from the MEDIUM. [**cf.** FLUID MOTOR INSTRUMENT, STHENOMETER, GALVANOMETER, TRANCE, POLARITY]

MAGNETOTHERAPEUTIC DEVICE—(Japan) an instrument designed by Maeshima for transmitting MAGNETISM into the human body in order to help the body normalize so it can heal itself more quickly. [cf. MAGNETIC HEALING, MAGNETS]

MAGNETS—(esoteric) magnetized pieces of metal or other products of various sizes; each side has different qualities of polarized magnetism; the south pole presents positive energy, and the north pole presents a negative electronic energy, each having a different function on living organisms; used in MAGNET HEALING. (Inconcl.) [cf. POLARITY, MAGNETOLOGY Appendix 5]

MAGNIFICENT DEVA—an exalted SOUL-MIND who has earned a high rank on the HIERARCHY of the ANGEL KINGDOM by achieving WISDOM; wisdom is acquired through lessons experienced in hundreds of incarnations in earth and other levels of awareness; a "magnitude being" relating to a measurement of spiritual stature and capacity; 1. this state of EVOLUTION results in an enormous, ethereal, formless life-force, who is dynamically powerful and who has an extremely high qualitative intelligence; deva form can also be organized to resemble, in some aspects, a human form; e.g., only eyes, a head, or outstretched arms; 2. psychically perceived if one is in a THETA STATE OF CONSCIOUSNESS and if the DEVA desires to be visioned, impressionable, or clairaudible; when clairvoyantly perceived, the colors surrounding them are out of the earth realm of colors; 3. function: deva oversees entire regions, e.g., a country, all the forests of the world, all the mountains in the earth, etc.; this magnanimous center of energy receives and transmits energy to their specific unit; capable of sending out a highly focused beam of energy appropriate in intensity and quality needed by the life forms in their care; e.g., sent to an individual airline pilot by a deva in charge of airplanes; sent to an individual city by a deva in charge of its country; sent to congregations of all the churches in an area by a deva in charge of harmony among the churches. [cf. WISDOM, GREAT ONES, MINOR DEVAS, ANGEL HIERARCHY]

MAGNUM OPUS—(Latin, "the great work") 1. the task of working for SELF-REALIZATION and LIBERATION; 2. (alchemy) to study and experiment with one's mind, chemicals, and formulas until one can transmute her or himself to a higher state of consciousness. [cf. PHILOSOPHER'S STONE, TRANSMUTATION, ALCHEMIST]

MAGOS—(Greek) synonomous with MAGI; see PSYCHIC.

MAGUS—singular form of MAGI; see PSYCHIC.

MAHA—prefix meaning "great."

MAHA KUMBHA MELA—(India) a giant fair held every twelve years, put together by thousands of organizations; each one participating demonstrates the best of their spiritual knowledge and their own particular type of psychic skill for contacting God; sometimes thirty million people meet at one time. [cf. TRADITION, RITUALS]

MAHA MAYA—a great ILLUSION; the objective UNIVERSE as mankind inhabits it; see TOTALITY.

MAHAPARANIRVANIC—see SEVENTH PLANE.

MAHARISHI—(Yoga) a great SAGE and SEER; see PSYCHIC.

MAHAT—(Vedanta) see TOTALITY.

MAHATMAS—1. (Sanskrit, "great soul") used as a title of reverence to one who has risen above the masses and emanates universal love; men who have perfected themselves and now serve as teachers, masters, sages, seers, and ELDER BROTHERS; 2. (Theosophy) one who has passed all seven aspects of the initiation. **Syn.** PSYCHIC. [cf. LORDSHIP, SOUL-MIND, MASTER]

MAHAYUGA—(Hinduism, Buddhism, India) a period of 12,000 years, pertaining to the years of the gods; each year of one god is 360 earth years. [cf. KALPA, CYCLES, EVOLUTION]

MAIN-DE-GLOIRE—(France) a manikin made from the roots of the MANDRAKE plant; an elf then moves into the human-like form to live and brings psychic information and protection to the owner. **Syn.** MAGLOIRE, SEPARATE REALITIES, ALRUNE. [cf. SOULLESS, PLANT CONVERSATIONS]

MAITHUNA—(Tantrism) to arouse the KUNDALINI through controlled, ritual sexual intercourse; a psychic sexual union in which the semen is not released but instead the energy is sent up the kundalini to the CROWN CHAKRA by mind concentration and a special breathing technique; a powerful way to arouse the kundalini so that the self-disciplined YOGI can raise the energy to his higher CHAKRAS converging the energy to a higher form; performed in an alpha state. [cf. BODY CONTROL Appendix 2]

MAITREYA ASANA—(Buddhism) the correct MEDITATION posture when using a chair; keep back straight, feet flat on floor, and hands comfortable in the lap, preferably palms turned upward on knees. [cf. ZEN SITTING, PALM DOWNWARD, QUIETUDE]

MAJESTIC MUSIC—see MUSIC OF THE SPHERES.

MAJOR ARCANA—twenty-two cards of the TAROT, each with an allegorical figure of complicated symbolic meaning; connect to the twenty-two paths that a human being travels to the GODHEAD in his or her ASTRAL BODY. **Syn.** MAJOR TRUMP CARDS. [cf. POINT-OF-FOCUS, SYCHRONICITY]

MAJOR TRUMP CARDS—see MAJOR ARCANA.

MAKE A PRAYER—(Sun Bear, Native American) four important parts of a "request" to the GREAT SPIRIT for a healing, a good lecture, rain, harmony, etc.; 1. ask that the request be granted if it is the will of the UNIVERSE at this time; 2. make one's needs be known by verbalizing them silently or aloud; ask that these needs balance with the life forces; 3. thank the Great Spirit; 4. tell how one will return the energy to the universe that is given to them through this request. [cf. APOTROPAIC HEALING PRAYER, KARMA, PRAYER]

MAKING MEDICINE—(Native American) to deliberately and mindfully try to improve or alter a situation whether it be tribal, atmospheric, between individuals, or the health and potential of an organism; prayer, psychic skills, herbs, amulets, visualization, shamanship, physical labor, etc. may be used; e.g., when one is doing his job, training a horse, delivering a baby, taking care of crops, leading a ceremony, healing the sick, teaching the young, etc., one is making medicine.

MAKING STRONG THE KHU—(ancient Egypt) a book telling about the process of dying; one in the set of the BOOK OF THE DEAD. [cf. DEATH SCIENCE Appendix 2]

MALADAPTIVE BEHAVIOR—(clinical) a nonsensical or undesirable PSYCHIC EXPERIENCE; brought on by forced choice or by a PSYCHIC ATTACK through lack of knowledge of how to protect one's self. [cf. SHIELDING, CLOAK OR INSULATION, PSYCHIC TRANSFER Appendix 2]

MALKOUNSA RAGA—(Hinduism) a fixed melodic scale played during the middle of the night in winter time to help induce valor among the people. [cf. SOUNDS-WITH-POWER Appendix 2]

MAMBO—(Voodoo) the female PSYCHIC and HEALER.

MAN—(esoteric) pertains to the physical being one can see and feel: 1. (Levi) "Lord of all the planes, manifests of protoplast, of mineral, of plant, of beast"; (Dion Fortune) "a perfect microcosm of the macrocosm with all its aspects and the only animal as such"; (Seth) "an individualized portion of energy materialized within physical existence to learn to form ideas from energy and make them physical"; (Greg Nielsen and Joseph Polansky) "a mental, emotional, and physical being functioning as a unit with all the parts interconnected and interacting, each affecting and affected by the other"; (ancient Egypt) man was believed to be a divine creation into whom were inscribed laws of the universe and of evolution; 2. man, the HUMAN BEING, is one stage of unfoldment of his seed species; this seed species belongs to his parent, the universal system species, so man has all the attributes of the universal system within him; man must unfold into a perfect specimen as a contribution to the universal system which is also an entity growing to perfectness; 3. man is a co-creator of his world as an inheritance from his parent, the universal system, which was created by THOUGHT, (the WORD); man, as a co-creator who has access to thought, made his third-dimensional body and a place to inhabit (the EARTH and everything on it); man needs EMOTION, which accompanies every thought to keep the atoms moving in the direction of his thought; (emotion is the ENERGY of the universe). [cf. TOTALITY, ANGEL KINGDOM, SOULMIND, PHYSICAL BODY, MONAD]

MAN FORCE—see GUIDE.

MAN SHOCK TREATMENT—(Huna) a form of EXORCISM whereby a tremendous amount of SPIRIT from one's invisible nervous system, and from breathing techniques, is used to dislodge the evil ETHERIC WORLD ENTITY that is possessing or obsessing an EARTHLING; influences the brain similar to an electric shock treatment used for the mentally ill. [cf. EXORCISM Appendix 2]

MANA—1. (Polynesia) an invisible, all pervasive ENERGY found in the air, imponderable, but extremely powerful and necessary for all beings and objects; (Melanesia) a power felt to be derived from SPIRIT, capable of being controlled, transferred and directed to human ends; innate in both animate and inanimate objects; 2. (Huna) one of the three parts of the energy vital for life, moving like waves, flowing from person to person, or person to substance, under the influence of the mind, a vital force of life which depends upon the activities of the mind; 3. (Buddhism) the THINKING mechanism in mankind; the thinking principle. [cf. VITAL LIFE FORCE, DAILY BREAD]

MANA LOA—(Huna, Hawaii) a highly evolved PSYCHIC ENERGY which has an influence on all things; used knowingly and unknowingly by the SUBCONSCIOUS MIND; symbolized by the sun to show the parallelism that the sun influences all things. [cf. PSYCHOKINESIS, THIRD-EYE]

MANA SURCHARGE—(Huna) an abundance of vital energy (SPIRIT) taken into the body and stored; capable of being used as a whole unit at one time, to unlock a block in the body. [cf. BLOCKS Appendix 5]

MANA, MANA-MANA, MANA LOA—(Huna, Hawaii) a vital energy found in the atmosphere that is necessary for all things, inanimate and animate; taken into one's body by breathing; distributed through one's body waves as MANA, through thinking waves as MANA-MANA, and through his psychic waves as MANA LOA. [cf. VITAL LIFE FORCE, BREATHING]

MANA-MANA—(Huna, Hawaii) one part of the VITAL LIFE FORCE which is drawn into the body, shared by the BRAIN WAVES, and absolutely necessary for thinking and willing activities. [cf. BRAIN Appendix 5]

MANAS—1. (Buddhism) the psychic sense; 2. (Theosophy) a level of the SOUL-MIND which reflects the UNIVERSAL MIND where thinking is abstract, inspirational, and profound; 3. CONSCIOUSNESS and its various levels; 4. the MIND.

MANAS-KAMA—1. (Sanskrit) mankind in the lowest state of EVOLUTION; 2. (Buddhism) the human EGO. [cf. NEW-AGE PSYCHOLOGY, MATERIALISTIC MAN]

MANASAPUTRAS—(Sanskrit, "sons of mind") a highly evolved ETHERIC WORLD INTELLIGENCE who communicates with earthlings bringing knowledge to aid in mankind's ENLIGHTENMENT. [cf. INNER BAND, OUTER BAND, DOCTOR TEACHER]

MANCY—(Greek *mania*, "hidden things, sacred") a suffix pertaining to one form of the mantic arts. [cf. MANTIC ARTS Appendix 6 for definitions of entire grouping of mantic skills]

MANDALA—1. (Sanskrit, "circle, the mystic circle"); a picture that contains archetypal images from the depths of the mind expressing the SOUL-MIND itself; represents a time when sound, light, color and form, appeared in the mind in a rhythmic harmonious nature; 2. (Oriental Art) a schematized representation of the COSMOS, chiefly characterized by geometric shapes that can be recognized as a DEITY or an attribute of a deity; 3. a picture constructed to be used as a point of focus for MEDITATION; always characterized by a center or has symmetry and cardinal points; takes many forms: **(a)** a circle of animals or deities; **(b)** geometrical or nongeometrical pictures of animals or deities; **(c)** a MYSTICAL (abstract) diagram; can be black and white or colorfully painted; when stared at in meditation, the meditator's awareness is restricted to the center from which the form-creating energy flows and is one of constant self-renewal because of its design. [cf. LAW OF CENTER Appendix 7, MANTRA, FORMS-WITH-POWER, SYMBOLS]

MANDRAKE—(botane) 1. (Rome) a plant with roots that resemble a human form; capable of making a noise to the threshold of hearing if uprooted; endowed with the property that mankind can use when seeking psychic advice; 2. a plant that has the vibrational frequency to help induce DEPENDENT VOICE for its owner; 3. (Europe, North America) used as a psychedelic drug in religious ceremonies to aid in the experience of a glorious ASTRAL PROJECTION; psychics and healers can reach the higher realms of awareness when in the state of religious ecstasy during the ceremony. [cf. PLANT MAGIC, PSYCHOTROPIC PLANTS]

MANDRAKE AMULET—a MANNIKIN made from the roots of the MANDRAKE plant for the purpose of an elf using the mannikin as his or her home; the elf then gives the householders psychic advice. [cf. AMULET, BOTANE]

MANDRAKE FRUITS—(botane) (Egypt) believed to have the VIBRATIONAL FREQUENCIES that would make one more desirous of sex. **Syn.** LOVE-APPLES. [cf. ROSEMARY, SAGE, THORNAPPLE]

MANDUNUGU—(East Africa) see PSYCHIC.

MANES—1. (Rome) a community of departed soul-minds in the astral world functioning as a unit; see GROUP-SOUL; 2. a discarnate intelligence who communicates with an earthling; see ETHERIC WORLD INTELLIGENCE. **Syn.** SPIRIT, LORELEI, ODIN, WODAN.

MANI PADME—jewel in the lotus flower; see LOTUS.

MANIA—(Greece) see TRANCE.

MANIFEST—to bring into form; to make evident to the senses; to give evidence of.

MANIFESTED IN THE LIGHT—(ancient Egypt) name used in the BOOK OF THE DEAD for the process of dying. **Syn.** MAKING THE TRANSITION. [**cf.** ASTRAL INITIATION, DWELLERS IN THE BARDO, FREEING THE SOUL]

MANIMALA—("chain of the gems") the study of the vibratory rate of gems and their relationship to the human mind and physical body. [**cf.** MINPSI Appendix 2]

MANIPUR—(Yoga) see SOLAR PLEXUS CHAKRA and SVADHISTHANA.

MANITOU—(Native American, Algonquin) a highly evolved SOUL-MIND who communicates through a SHAMAN and a MEDICINE MAN to bring healing methods, knowledge, and prophecy for the tribe. **Syn.** GUIDE. [**cf.** GREAT MANITOU]

MANITU—(Native American, Algonquin) see VITAL LIFE FORCE.

MANJURSI—(Zen Buddhism) the god of WISDOM; this personification of wisdom is made into a sword-from similar to a small oar; used by the presiding priest to strike the meditators in the hall when they seem to be falling asleep during the long MEDITATION periods. [**cf.** ZEN MEDITATION, WISDOM, ART OF TEA, SLEEPITATE]

MANKIND—1. (esoteric) massive field of energetic intelligent matter, co-created by itself, to benefit itself, and to benefit the growth of the planet; chief function of mankind is to purify itself and become a higher STATE OF CONSCIOUSNESS as an entire unitary system; this requires the purification of each individual who chooses to work within this structure; each one is individually responsible to the mankind structure and must perfect her or himself to the state of consciousness that cleanses the vibrational frequency of the planet; the planet can then evolve in consciousness that influences the unitary universal structure, in its unfoldment into purification; 2. (Sufi) one family, one body, the whole of life being one in its source and its goal. [**cf.** HUMAN BEING Appendix 5, GROUP SOUL]

MANKIND SEED—a "subjective motivation" that surfaces and thrusts itself throughout each individual life, continually encouraging each to perfect her or himself and to contribute to their environment; this invisible flow brings an interrelationship which bears the one unitary goal of the purpose of the masses in earth and in the lower three PLANES in the ETHERIC WORLD; motivation is frequently unrecognizable individually; this massive energy field functions as a GROUP SOUL, encasing thousands of soul-minds; each individual's responsibility is as important as any other's but many refuse to take this responsibility; motivation never stops its innate push to alert the individual to better itself in a way that will benefit the entire population of earth; (do not confuse with the HUMAN BEING SPECIES SEED that functions mainly for the individual). [**cf.** MONADOLOGY, MICROCOSM]

MANNA—1. (esoteric) that which is miraculously and unexpectedly supplied when one's need is great and the logical means of obtaining it is obstructed; 2. (Bible) Exodus 16: 14-36; theories: **(a)** COSMIC ENERGY of superior quality, necessary for life sustenance, continually pours down through the head or CROWN CHAKRA; each individual utilizes this cosmic energy in degrees according to their state of EVOLUTION; this energy normally would sustain mankind but because of their materialistic thinking in biblical times, it had to take the form of a more solid substance, capable of being eaten through the mouth; "gathered every man according to his eating"; each individual could only absorb what he or she was ready to absorb; the process is a type of physical phenomena that took place because Moses was obedient to the law (the Lord); **(b)** Moses psychically produced a subtle substance that was strong enough to be seen, handled, and eaten; through his ability to work with the law (the Lord) he materialized small bits of substance from the atoms by changing their vibrational frequency; an alchemical process of APPORTATION PSYCHOKINESIS or MATERIALIZATION; **(c)** a manna machine could have produced a manna-like food by intensive cultivation of small water plants similar to projects now under development by the United States and USSR Space Agencies. [**cf.** HUMAN BEING, UFOLOGY]

MANNIKIN—a TALISMAN made like a monster of half chicken and half man; originally made in the image of a NATURE SPIRIT; the talisman serves as an aid in inducing psychic information when it is treated with respect. [**cf.** AMULET]

MANPSI—the exercise of one's psychic ability upon animals; the use of telepathy to talk to animals instead of speech; any type of psychic transfer to an animal initiated by man. [cf. ANPSI Appendix 2]

MANSIONS—(Bible) see PLANES.

MANSIONS OF LIGHT—the higher astral planes; see ASTRAL LIGHT.

MANTIC ART—(Rome, China, B.C.) (Greece *mania*, "sacred, Godlike, hidden") to ask a question, silently or verbally, and immediately use a mundane system (nonhuman or human organism, or an inert object) in a manner that will reveal the hidden answer; an aspect of the religion; 1. theory originated from I CHING in 2000 B.C.: "there is no chance; all things in the universe follow a definite order; symbols (human, nonhuman organisms and objects) serve as models or patterns from which physical objects evolve; Heavens are symbols there complete, Earth are the shapes and features there formed; Heaven and Earth interweave and are constantly overcoming one another by exact rule; all movements of the world are constantly subject to the same rule; symbols come into existence in precedence of substance"; 2. MANTIC ART skills in ancient times were used to predict and guide the conduct of persons and nations, settle disputes and uncover personal problems; symbols are formed in the atmosphere that precede earth doings and are sent to man to announce or warn of these earth doings; in ancient times, everyone believed that the orderly universe writes its patterns in all things and the lay person became proficient in the skill of DIVINATION by the use of whatever was at hand; one tacked the suffix *mancy* on the word representing what one used; see Appendix 6 for hundreds of types of MANTIC ARTS. [cf. CASTING OF LOTS, RADIONICS, SYNCHRONICITY, MANTIS, POINT-OF-FOCUS]

MANTIC ARTIST—a psychic who can use nonhuman objects as a POINT-OF-FOCUS or a radionic detector to bring forth psychic information. [cf. MANTIC ARTS Appendix 6]

MANTIC TRANCES—(Greece, 350 B.C.) to allow an ETHERIC WORLD INTELLIGENCE to intervene and reveal knowledge or psychic information that the MEDIUM or SHAMAN could not have known through normal means; kinds: 1. ORACULAR POSSESSION TRANCE: 2. FRENZIED HYSTERICAL POSSESSION TRANCE; 3. shamanistic trance (DISASSOCIATION). [cf. MEDIUMSHIP, SHAMANISM, IMPERSONATION]

MANTIKE—(Greece) psychic information derived from a mania or frenzied STATE OF CONSCIOUSNESS whereby one purposely induces a DEEP TRANCE to bring forth extraordinary information. [cf. MYSTICAL ECSTASY, TRIBAL DANCING, TRANCE, POSSESSION]

MANTIS—(Greece) a psychic who is skilled in one of the many types of mantic arts; a seer of hidden things. **Syn.** DIVINER, SEER, PLURAL MANTES. [cf. MANTIC ARTS Appendix 6]

MANTRA—(Sanskrit, India) a significant sound which is psychically and scientifically known to affect human beings; used as a POINT-OF-FOCUS while meditating; sound can be a syllable, word, or a series of words or syllables; objective is to repeat it continuously for the entire MEDITATION period, either verbally or silently; 1. the sound is designed to assist one to attain higher states of consciousness, evoke COSMIC ENERGY to manifest within the meditator, dispel disease or create a blessing; 2. a sound uttered by a never silent SOUL-MIND expressing devotion to DIVINE CONSCIOUSNESS; 3. (Steven Halpern) "the mantric formula resonates and thereby, repatterns states in the nervous system and glands, or by other names, in the subtle electronic or 'etheric' forces in and around the physical body"; 4. language properly chosen and tested could have the vibrational frequency to co-create, sustain, or destroy; words and sounds utilize the law of SYMPATHETIC VIBRATION; mantra should be a tongue twister so one has to concentrate on its pronounciation; one does not have to understand what the mantra means for its effectiveness. [cf. SOUNDS-WITH-POWER Appendix 2]

MANTRAM—a symbol of supreme reality; a holy name, a name of God, or a spiritual formula in one's religion used as a device to alter one's mental activity; assists one to direct one's attention at will, to shift one's attention from negative to positive channels, or to steady a tense or troubled mind; used as a MANTRA in meditation; symbol must have meaningful roots for the meditator. [cf. QUIET ATTENTIVENESS, MIND EXPANSION, ONENESS]

MANTRAM YOGA—see TRANSCENDENTAL MEDITATION.

MANTRIC SCIENCE—a study of the principle that "thinking is making." [cf. LAW OF THOUGHT and LAW OF LIKE ATTRACTS LIKE Appendix 7, LOTS, SYNCHRONICITY]

376

MANUAL PSYCHOGRAPHY—to allow an ETHERIC WORLD INTELLIGENCE to use one's hand to write psychic information or knowledge on paper that one could not know in any other way. **Syn.** AUTOMATIC WRITING. [**cf.** ETHERIC SCRIPT, PLANCHETTE AUTOMATISM]

MANUS—great ethereal beings; the prototype of the ideal man of his ROOT RACE; supreme cultural leaders of the great root races on the INNER-PLANES in the ETHERIC WORLD; these ethereal beings hold within themselves the principle and function of their root race, overseeing mankind's root race to aid in bringing it to this ideal prototype. **Syn.** ARCHANGEL. [**cf.** ANGEL KINGDOM, ANGELOLOGY]

MAP DOWSING—(radiesthesia) 1. to locate water, oil, etc., underground by using a map of the area instead of physically being in the area; a map, sketch or copy of a surveyor's drawing can be used; the SUBCONSCIOUS MIND is silently told what the search is for; the PENDULUM or L-ROD is held over the map and moved slowly around in the area which is suspected; theories: **(a)** the SUPERCONSCIOUS MIND "visits" the area and relates the finding back through the pendulum swing or the dip of the L-rods; **(b)** the map utilizes the LAW OF ASSOCIATION in which it states that the real can be simulated by a thing if the thing has something in common with the real; map simulates for the area; 2. to find a missing person or animal by using a map of the suspected area, a pendulum and a WITNESS (an article that frequently came in contact with the missing person or animal). [**cf.** PENDULUM POWER]

MARGINAL STATES OF AWARENESS—see UNCONTROLLED INNER-MIND PICTURES and HYPNAGOGIC STATE.

MARID—(Islam) a NATURE SPIRIT that belongs to the Jinn grouping; the most powerful of the five types.

MARTIAL ARTS—(Orient) a special training in body and mind control between two persons for self-defense; results in accomplishing mind discipline in daily activities; methods teach how to deprive one of mental consciousness for medical purposes; philosophies emphasize that this strong physical and mental training be used for self-defense only. [**cf.** MARTIAL ARTS Appendix 5]

MARTINET—1. an ETHERIC WORLD ENTITY who specializes in helping lost travelers find their way; 2. (Switzerland) an invisible ambassador from HELL who tries to influence earthlings to do wrong things. [**cf.** HAUNTING, ETHERIC WORLD INTELLIGENCE]

MASS CONSCIOUSNESS—1. (temporary) a new state of AWARENESS of each individual in a gathering, brought on by the "collective" thoughts, emotions, and attitudes of the majority of the members; the larger the group, the more influential the new awareness; this collection of thoughts and attitudes influences each individual into activity and forms each individual's new beliefs for the length of the gathering; during this gathering each individual's sense of reasoning is not entirely their own; there is a psychic tie or mental telepathic thread that connects each one in the gathering; happens at a large store sale, parade, lecture, church picnic, etc.; 2. (permanent) a SUBLIMINAL LEVEL of awareness that influences one's activity and decisions as a result of the present collective thoughts and attitudes of everyone who inhabits the planet; what is held in consciousness by the majority of earth inhabitants will be recognized in the activity of the majority of earth inhabitants; a type of herd consciousness; e.g., women and men adhering to a fashion, persons traveling by automobile and airplane, persons eating processed foods, each large community having a form of government to keep the people organized, etc.; a psychic telepathical beam minutely connects all persons who live in earth at the same time. [**cf.** CONSCIOUSNESS Appendix 5]

MASS DREAMS—a PSYCHIC EXPERIENCE pertaining to an event of national or worldly interest occuring the same night to hundreds of people while they sleep; psychic experience could refer to the economic or political situation of the country, a catastrophe encompassing hundreds of persons, or a tragedy occurring to a prominent person of the world; psychic experience comes through any of the five PSYCHIC SENSES and is usually disturbing enough to make the sleeper have good recall; happens immediately preceding the event, or at the time of the event, as if to prepare the masses for the traumatic news; e.g., to smell the odor of burning flesh before a huge fire, to feel very sad and depressed before an earthquake that leaves thousands homeless, to perceive clairvoyantly an attempt to assassinate a high ranking governmental official, to clairaudiently perceive the shouting or upheaval

377

in a stock market crash. [**cf.** PSYCHIC EXPERIENCE DURING SLEEP, PRECOGNITION, SLEEP EXPERIENCES, EYES OF INSTINCT, WARNING DREAMS]

MASS ELEMENTAL—a large unbroken thought form hovering over the heads of a gathering of people that displays unity of interest and emotion; each member contributes to the thought form, making it grow as the meeting progresses; as long as the attention of the majority is centered on this sity, size and intelligence; it psychically influences the feelings and reasoning of each individual participating; members are capable of individual behavior that would be impossible on their own; this thought form is only kept alive by the unity of purpose and will dissipate when the crowd disbands; as members leave the gathering the elemental no longer has this influence over them; e.g., 1. an individual born crippled could receive the faith and change of attitude in a religious meeting and become instantaneously healed; 2. young people disregard their privacy and make love openly at rock festivals. **Syn.** ARTIFICIAL ELEMENTAL. [**cf.** MASS HYPNOSIS, ELEMENTAL, THOUGHT-FORMS]

MASS HYPNOSIS—1. to hypnotize the majority of people at a lecture without them realizing that their level of awareness is altered; occurs, unconsciously or deliberately, if a leader is very impressive and charismatic; (a) deliberate techniques: (1) leader commands undivided attention to his or her speech; (2) rhythmic pacing and hand flinging movements are used; (3) ploy is preplanned to reach one's basic emotional needs (personal acceptance, self-preservation, patriotism, service to others, and cultural acceptance) through fear, guilt, or excessive love; (4) to overly repeat the pronoun *you* and continually point a finger at the audience; (b) all this narrows one's concentration to the theme of the lecture which automatically relinquishes the conscious mind from its role and allows the uncritical subconscious mind to surface and accept the material as presented, and the leader makes her or his point; the more clever the leader is with the above tactics, the more hypnotized each member becomes, and the more unlikely to question the material of the lecture; (c) most ministers and lecturers capture their audience's attention by using some of the above methods of delivery; this is a good way for the audience to grasp the meaning of the speech; it is absolutely necessary in a healing program as one is more receptive to healing energies when in an alpha (hypnotic) state of consciousness; e.g., slaying-in-the-spirit meetings; 2. to hypnotize the majority of people at a gathering by playing loud, rhythmic music; music has been composed in a special key that will have a hypnotic effect on the audience; chanting special chants also put members in an alpha state of consciousness; (a) music is deliberately played if the meeting is meant for healings to take place; (b) music is deliberately played at meetings designed for brainwashing the audience; 3. dangers: one should know how to shield one's self from this during the first encounter with the speaker so one can keep from being put in the hypnotic state and be able to make a clear-cut decision regarding the speaker's intelligence, integrity and intent; (this all is a form of brainwashing but do not confuse it with destructive-brainwashing). (Inconcl.) [**cf.** MASS ELEMENTAL, MASS-KARMA, BRAINWASHING, SUGGESTION, DESTRUCTIVE-BRAINWASHING CULT]

MASS KARMA—(Sanskrit) the series of consequences pertaining to a country as a whole; the present thoughts, activities, moral standards, government, and cultural systems of a neighborhood, city, country, and the world; these are manifestations of the mental and emotional equivalent held by the citizens of that society and culture based on a collection of each individual's AKASHIC RECORDS and present state of emotion; 1. each citizen builds into his or her future lifestyle and incarnations by their attitude of these events and moral standards; 2. members are held responsible individually for the basic goals of their neighborhood, city, country and world whether they approve of them or not, "unless" they are doing something about correcting the actions; 3. one is incarnated in the country, culture, and time period that is best suited for one's karmic challenges, individually and as a whole; all EVOLUTION must go through cycles and individuals contribute to various group cycles by their thoughts and actions and must return to that situation to complete the CYCLE in another INCARNATION if necessary. [**cf.** GROUP KARMA, ACCUMULATED KARMA, REINCARNATION, KARMA]

MASS MUSIC—sound, rhythm, and music that portray the overall feelings and emotions of the various sections of the world; as history changes and cultures advance, the rhythm and music change to disclose the feeling of the majority; e.g., in 1920, jazz bands became popular as the war was over and

378

everyone was living to the heights without caring, and the music showed abandonment and joy; folk or country music gives a feeling of "poor me," and emphasizes the struggles of life; in this way the music holds the majority of people in this state of consciousness, but it also brings a unity of thought from the telepathic message; like a circle, the attitude feeds the song and the music feeds the attitude.

MASS STRENGTH—SUPERNORMAL power that is accomplished when groups of people work as one unit, each individually sharing the same emotion, goal, and discomfort; brought about through mind concentration and unison of rhythmic motion, which builds up to a crescendo and makes the "impossible" happen; e.g., soldiers have been known to show superhuman strength, enduring blows that would kill the strongest oxen or overpower an army twice their size. (Inconcl.) [cf. MASS CONSCIOUSNESS, MASS ELEMENTAL, VISIBLE CONSCIOUSNESS, EXPANSION OF CONSCIOUSNESS]

MASS SUFFERING—1. (Native American, Chippewa, Sun Bear) caused by the narrow and selfish viewpoint of one's activities in which one considers their immediate benefit from the activity; individuals on up to larger groups should consider and evaluate how the activity performed will affect others in their family, neighborhood, city, nation, and "future" generations, otherwise EARTH MOTHER gets sick from lack of respect and lack of replacement of human PSYCHIC ENERGY; earth mother cannot replenish herself without reenergizing, and an attitude of respect, and thanks from her children; mankind is a transmitter as well as a receiver of energy and when earth has been abused and misused, it gets sick, such as, floods, draughts, volcanoes, mixed up seasons, etc., earth mother needs human respect to replenish herself; the world is going through a (fourth) cleansing at this time because of this; 2. sometimes caused when many individuals in the same area have an inner desire to share with, care for, and love others more, but do not know of an outlet for these emotions; a catastrophic event will occur in that area so these individuals' inner desire will be carried out; e.g., an airplane crashes in the water and hundreds run to help the survivors, by bringing hot soup, blankets, and offering temporary homes, etc. (this does not discard the theory that these victims could also be working out KARMA or a MIND-CAUSED ACCIDENT at this time); individuals should recognize this inner desire to help others and form an organiza-tion to do so to prevent a catastrophic event. . [cf. CONSCIOUSNESS SHIFT, PERSONAL TRANSFORMATION, SUCCESS]

MASSAGE THERAPY—(ancient, Greece, Rome, China, Egypt, Hippocrates) an art that employs body manipulation by a therapist to another person to restore and maintain balanced circulation; therapist is trained in hand movement on the skin and muscularity of the body; these manipulations tone and relax muscles, aid in elimination of toxins, stimulate nerve activity, and soothe small nerve endings contained in the skin; this reacts in reflexes to all internal organs; there is an energy circuit whereby the electromagnetic energy passes between the patient and therapist. [cf. POLARITY BALANCING, KI, NEUROMUSCULAR MASSAGE, ACUPUNCTURE POINTS]

MASTER—1. a SOUL-MIND who has earned the right to inhabit the FIFTH PLANE and chooses to incarnate (although one does not have to do so from this plane) in an earthly body to help mankind; soul-mind returns to earth by an immaculate birth, a WALK-IN, or an INCARNATIONAL EXCHANGE; performs selfless service to humanity and lifts the states of consciousness of the masses for evolutionary evolvement of civilization; these soul-minds with their supreme wisdom and psychic abilities form organizations among themselves around the earth; known to mankind as the GREAT ONES, the Secret Brotherhood, the Inner Government of the World, the HIERARCHY, MAHATMAS, the GREAT WHITE LODGE of Masters and Wisdom; 2. a soul-mind inhabiting the fifth plane in the etheric world who chooses to earn his or her LORDSHIP from the etheric world; these intelligences communicate with earthlings through PHYSICAL PSYCHISM, i.e., TRUMPET, VOICE TANCE, INDEPENDENT VOICE, IMPERSONATION, MEDIUMSHIP HEALING, etc.); usually bring knowledge to raise the consciousness of the masses and make spiritual leaders within cultures that are ready for advancement; 3. a human being who retreats to solitude to become established in the SELF and earn their mastership; he or she then returns to the world to serve civilization in a leadership capacity. **Sim.** SAINTS. 4. INITIATE in an earthly body who leads disciples through a path of wisdom and advice that is otherwise unattainable; helps by communion and inspiration; known as the **father guru;** 5. ETHERIC WORLD INTELLIGENCE who is in charge of governments in earth, guardian of a nation, originator of a system, and a distributor of power. [cf. ANGEL HIERARCHY, AVATAR, LORDS OF HUMANITY]

MASTER EYE—(radiesthesia) coined by and currently discovered by Howard St. L. Cookes; the physical eye that influences the direction of the PENDULUM swing; with both eyes open and artificial lighting being equal in both eyes, one eye takes charge of the beams of energy that are emitted from the eyes, according to the direction of the compass one is facing; this causes a clockwise or counterclockwise gyration. (Inconcl.) [cf. PENDULUM POWER, EYE, PENDULUM GYRATION, OSCILLATION]

MASTER OF FIRE—1. (Africa, Germany) one who uses one's knowledge of fire to heal, rejuvenate, change another's attitude, and to perform psychic skills; knowledgeable about circumcision and sexual behavior necessary for procreation; protects persons by fire energy; changes into an animal if necessary to perform psychic duties; known as the VILLAGE BLACKSMITH, a PSYCHIC, craftsman, and/or a priest; depicted with devils or saints; e.g., (Bible) St. Peter and Christ "appear in the forge of the blacksmith possessed of miraculous powers"; 2. (India) creator of the world; 3. (Japan) smith is god. **Syn.** IRON DOCTOR, SMITH, KING OF TRADES. 4. those shaman, priests, fakirs, and medicine men who are capable of walking on fire, handling or eating it without having bodily harm. [cf. SHAMANSHIP, FIREWALKING, BODY CONTROL]

MASTER SENSE—(Silva Mind Control) to psychically tune into brain cells and perceive information that was stored there by the other five physical senses. **Syn.** PSYCHIC ART.

MASTER SOUL—see TOTALITY.

MASTERSHIP—the fifth rank of the ANGEL HIERARCHY (before Godship); one shows proof of mastery over SELF, one's talents, right use of psychic skills, and ability to work harmoniously with universal will; selfish self is completely destroyed; earthly karmic debts have been worked off (which means one does not need to incarnate in earth again); accomplished by endless experiences of toil and strife for wisdom and self-control during earthly incarnations; these experiences are used to guide leaders of earth civilization: 1. an INITIATE may serve from an earth incarnation as a great leader, guiding and informing the masses; 2. an initiate may serve from the ETHERIC WORLD

through psychic communication, in which he or she attaches to the earth leader's PINEAL GLAND to guide and protect them so that they can complete their earth mission, but without making decisions for the earth leader; 3. initiate's objective is to acquire greater qualifications to work with the external power for civilization evolvement; Pythagoras and LAO-TSE were masters working to achieve Lordship. **Syn.** ANNOINTED ONES. [cf. DIRECTORS, GODHEAD, ANGEL HIERARCHY]

MATE TEA—(Native American) an herb with the properties that when taken in tea form will induce an ALTERED STATE OF CONSCIOUSNESS which brings forth psychic information. [cf. BOTANE, PSYCHOTROPIC PLANTS, PLANT CONVERSATIONS]

MATERIAL FLUIDIC ENVELOPE—(late 1800s) the SEMIMATERIAL that encompasses the SOUL-MIND while in the ETHERIC WORLD; a blanket name given to any entity who has made their transition and shows her or himself in apparitional form to an earthling. **Syn.** APPARITION. [cf. PERISPRIT, ASTRAL BODY, FLUIDIC LINK]

MATERIAL WORLD—the planet earth and all in it that one can see, hear, taste, smell and feel with the five physical senses. [cf. ETHERIC WORLD, MUNDANE WORLD, BODIES AND PLANES, THIRD DIMENSION]

MATERIALISTIC MAN—an individual who is engrossed in objects, things, activities, and money as necessary gains for their happiness. **Syn.** CARNAL MAN. [cf. PHYSICAL REALITY, SUBTLE BODY, MUNDANE WORLD]

MATERIALIZATION—1. see ECTOPLASM MATERIALIZATION (physical phenomena which is performed in the SEANCE room); 2. see ALCHEMICAL MATERIALIZATION (the use of ALCHEMY for DEMATERIALIZATION and rematerialization of an object or the alchemist); 3. see MENTAL PSYCHISM (to perceive clairvoyantly a full blown DISCARNATE ENTITY) usually non-requested; occurs in a meditative state, during sleep, or when the need is great; discarnate entity could be a loved one or one's guide. **Syn.** APPARITION. [cf. HIGH DREAM, LAW OF ATTENTION Appendix 7, CLAIRVOYANCE]

MATERIALIZATION FORMS—see ECTOPLASMIC MATERIALIZATION FORMS.

MATERIALIZATION MEDIUM—one whose AURA, BODY CHEMISTRY and power of CONCENTRATION can synchronize with an ETHERIC WORLD INTEL-

LIGENCE so the intelligence can use the ECTOPLASM for building her or himself a body in the SEANCE room; intelligence uses the ectoplasm that exudes from the orifices of the MEDIUM with the medium's permission and desire; through many sessions with a dedicated group of SITTERS, the medium produces the etheric world intelligence in full body form. [**cf.** PRESEANCE PHENOMENON, PSYCHIC HANDS, BLACKED-OUT]

MATERIALIZED PERSONALITY—(ectoplasmic materialization) ETHERIC WORLD INTELLIGENCE who is capable of building him or herself from the ECTOPLASM exuded from the orifices of the MEDIUM and SITTERS; intelligence begins by building only parts of their body; intelligence builds from a tiny head to a full blown person; takes years before the personality is full blown; varies in size from a foot tall to a giant; same intelligence manifests in each SEANCE; some personalities can walk, talk, and breathe; intelligence's parts (or full body) are dissolved into the medium's body when the session is over; 1. can only be seen in the seance room when INFRARED light is used, as light destroys the ectoplasm; 2. medium is in deep trance and knows nothing of what transpires, so the etheric world personality does all the work; 3. objective is to reveal the power of the mind over matter, the nature of atoms and their control by mankind, knowledge of the etheric world and life continuity, and the desire of the etheric world intelligences to help humanity. [**cf.** ECTOPLASMIC MATERIALIZATION, ETHEREALIZATION, PSYCHIC NAVAL CORD]

MATRIX—1. (Sanskrit) the mother goddesses of early HINDUISM; 2. means that which gives form to a thing, so it is used as a term to name the AURA. [**cf.** KIRLIAN EFFECT]

MATTER—(esoteric and future science) 1. the colonization of atoms in a vibrational frequency that a human being's five SENSES can perceive; brought about by mankind's thoughts to serve all of humanity; (**a**) the peculiarity of human THOUGHT, the intent and EMOTION behind the thought, excites the atomic particles to arrange patterns of various forms, shapes, and colors; when each individual's thought meshes with enough thoughts having similar properties from humanity as a whole, matter comes into existence; this matter will stay in existence until mankind no longer needs this matter, e.g., houses, clothes, chairs, trees; (**b**) matter is used for growth and expansion of the entire human race; matter is a tool to express ENERGY with humanity in control of the energy; matter is made from mankind's CONSCIOUSNESS and for that consciousness; (**c**) all matter is under the influence of an ETHEREAL blueprint or PATTERN which works to fulfill itself; this pattern is made by human thoughts and emotions and is constantly changing as easily as human emotions change; difference in patterns comes from the peculiarity of the thought, and the energy or movement is caused by human emotions; (Seth) "a substance that can be transformed and rearranged by thought"; 2. matter is destructible, temporary, and changeable, but the essence from which it is made is indestructible, unchangeable, and permanent; (Allan Kardec) "matter is the element which enchains SPIRIT, the instrument which serves it, and upon which, at the same time, it exerts its action"; 3. (Elmer Green) "matter is crystalized thought"; (R. Gammon) "mind and matter are one, poles of one continuum; matter is the human mind in action"; 4. matter is condensed radiant energy, atomic in nature, composed of particles of LIGHT as extensions of the Great Light; (Bob Toben) "gravitational trapped light"; bound energy; 5. matter is thousands of vibrational waves in the ATMOSPHERE colonizing invisible levels of energy; made by thoughts, emotions, and a pattern; 6. (B.C.) matter has three divisions: (**a**) etherial, Gods; (**b**) aerial, devils; (**c**) terrestrial, people. (Inconcl.) [**cf.** LAW OF VIBRATIONS and LAW OF THOUGHT Appendix 7, ATOM, THOUGHT-FORMS]

MATTER DUPLICATION—(alchemy) to concentrate on a material object already in existence until copies of the same article materialize in three-dimensional form; material object is used as a POINT-OF-FOCUS to intensify the MIND-ENERGY and to create the PATTERN of duplication in the mind, e.g., JESUS multiplied the loaves and fish. [**cf.** APPORTATION, PSYCHOKINESIS, NONHUMAN-PK]

MATTER THROUGH MATTER—(mediumship, early 1900s) to perform supernatural feats with mundane materials that a human could not do with his or her physical five SENSES or body movement; executed in the SEANCE room by the ETHERIC WORLD INTELLIGENCES to prove their true existence; uses the ECTOPLASM of the MEDIUM and SITTERS as in other phenomena, e.g., tied knots in a rope that was circular in shape without an end; linked two large wooden rings together with no signs of breaks in either ring; took clothes off sitters without unbuttoning them and without hurting the sitters. [**cf.** MEDIUMSHIP, GUIDES, NONHUMAN TELEKINESIS, HUMAN TELEKINESIS]

MATURITY—(holistic health) the ability to live with the decisions one has made without frustration, resentment, condemnation or guilt; and to balance daily with the outcome of one's decisions. [**cf.** STRESS, HAPPINESS, KEY TO LIFE]

MAULAVI—see WHIRLING DERVISHES.

MAXIN STONE—used in the days of ATLANTIS to cremate bodies after death. [**cf.** DEATH SCIENCE, CREMATION]

MAYA—1. (Sanskrit, Vedic, Hinduism) ("to affect; to limit; to form") an illusionary vibration, the earth, where nothing is permanent, just ILLUSION; mankind feels quite real while existing in illusion; a necessary step for EVOLUTION; a universal principle of MIND and MATTER; imperfect knowledge of REALITY; 2. the magical power in CREATION by which limitations and divisions are apparently present in the Immeasurable and Inseparable; the false impressions of the universe because the universe is composed of interference patterns of energy and events, and mankind only sees the interference; humanity cannot perceive the invisible field creating these patterns; 3. COSMIC apprehension; a deception of the ONE consciousness with its different aspects of this consciousness shown to man's perception in various rates of vibration. (Inconcl.) 4. (Native American, Yucatan, Guatemala, British Honduras, El Salvador) maya is a rhythm in the universe that makes recurrences. [**cf.** TIME, MULTIDIMENSIONAL, NODES, SHAPED ENERGY]

MAYA-RUPA—(Sanskrit) see ASTRAL BODY.

MAYAVI-RUPA—(Sanskrit) see ASTRAL PROJECTION.

MAZE—(Egypt) a labyrinth used as a ritual center and symbol of magical powers. [**cf.** SYMBOLIC MAGIC, RITUAL MAGIC, PILLARS]

MAZENGE—(South Africa) an ETHERIC WORLD INTELLIGENCE who protects the tribe during one of their rituals; intelligence works through a female PSYCHIC who allows help to come to the tribe by not permitting evil entities to enter the ritual. [**cf.** CARRYING AN EVIL, DOORKEEPER]

MDA—a special psychedelic drug that tends to induce age regression; shows a succession of events that happened when the individual was a youth or baby and that have long been forgotten. [**cf.** REINCARNATION, AGE REGRESSION, KARMA]

MEAN CHANCE EXPECTATION—abbr. MCE; (psi tasks) the average number of hits expected if only chance factors are involved; used as a scale in ESP experiments. [**cf.** HIT, ESP Appendix 2]

MEAN VARIANCE—(psi tasks) the expected variance of the theoretical mean score. [**cf.** TIME DISPLACEMENT, CHANCE, TARGET, RANDOM-EXPERIMENT]

MEANINGFUL COINCIDENCE THEORY—(Carl Jung) the occurrence of two separate events having neither a causal connection nor having an effect on each other, yet having a significant relationship; the occurrence of two separate events that do not have a cause and effect relationship but rather a blending together simultaneously in a meaningful, but unexplainable way. **Syn.** SYNCHRONICITY. [**cf.** CASTING OF LOTS, SORTES, RADIESTHESIA]

MEANINGLESS NOISE—(dreams) theory: DREAMS have no significance as a psychological effect on the dreamer, but come as a necessary function of the electrical mechanism of the brain; (as noise is necessary to a person's electrical mechanism). [**cf.** NIGHT LANGUAGE, NIGHTMARE, SENOI DREAM THERAPY]

MECHANICAL PSYCHOGRAPHIC MEDIUM—one who allows his or her hand to be used by an ETHERIC WORLD INTELLIGENCE to bring forth psychic information on paper; MEDIUM can be in a LIGHT TRANCE, SEMITRANCE, or DEEP TRANCE state. **Syn.** PASSIVE PSYCHOGRAPHIC MEDIUM, AUTOMATIST. [**cf.** AUTOMATIC WRITING, ETHERIC SCRIPT]

MECHANICAL WRITING MEDIUM—see INSPIRATIONALIST.

MECHANICO-MYSTICAL COGNITION—a normal psychic vision; see CLAIRVOYANCE.

MECHANIZED-PK—(psi tasks) machine monitored PSI TASKS. [**cf.** NONHUMAN-PK, NATURE-PK, GRAVITY CONTROL]

MEDIAMIZED—(Allan Kardec) an ALTERED STATE OF CONSCIOUSNESS whereby the MEDIUM allows the ETHERIC WORLD INTELLIGENCE to use her or his body for physical phenomena; e.g., VOICE TRANCE, TRUMPET, INDEPENDENT VOICE, PRECIPITATION, IMPERSONATION, TELEKINESIS, etc.;

altered state of consciousness can be a LIGHT TRANCE, SEMITRANCE, or DEEP TRANCE state; body metabolism changes while mediamized, e.g., heart could slow down or speed up, stomach muscles tighten or loosen, etc., body changes according to how the etheric world intelligence synchronizes with the medium. [**cf.** PHYSICAL PHENOMENA MISCELLANEOUS Appendix 2]

MEDIAN-NERVE—(Tibet) see SUSHUMNA.

MEDIANIMIC—the animalized fluid in a medium which gives her or him the properties for easy performance of physical psychism. [**cf.** PSYCHIC DEVELOPMENT CIRCLE, SEANCE, ECTOPLASM]

MEDIANIMIC PHENOMENA—see PHYSICAL PSYCHISM and MEDIUMSHIP.

MEDIANIMIZATION—(Allan Kardec) the harmonious interaction between the MEDIUM and the ETHERIC WORLD INTELLIGENCE so he or she can perform the physical phenomena desired; medium must know how to deeply relax or how to hypnotize the self to allow the intelligence to either enter their body or to use the ECTOPLASM emanating from their body; medianization takes repeated sessions in a BLACKED-OUT ROOM with the same SITTERS each week; medium gives permission for the intelligence to enter and programs the length of the session; the intelligence does most of the work, as he or she changes the chemistry of the medium to suit their entry, and performs the phenomena. [**cf.** PHYSICAL PSYCHIC PROCESS, MEDIUMSHIP]

MEDIATE—to perform in the capacity of a MEDIUM.

MEDIATOR—see MEDIUM.

MEDICAL CLIMATOLOGY—(England) the study of the influence of atmospheric changes and earthly environment on human health as a form of preventive medicine. [**cf.** HOLISTIC HEALTH, ALTERNATIVES, WELLNESS]

MEDICAL HYPNOSIS—to use hypnotic techniques for putting a patient in a state of anesthesia or partial anesthesia for a surgical operation such as setting a bone or pulling a tooth; the patient feels no pain, bleeding can be controlled, etc. [**cf.** INDUCTION, HYPNOTHERAPY]

MEDICAL INCUBATION—(ancient Egypt) to deliberately ask for a dream that would give instructions for curing one's illness while one was sleeping in the healing temple; healing god visited the sleeper's dreams while in the temple; sacrifices and rituals were often performed, before the sleeper retired, to invoke the god, pay tribute to him and return the energy to the ETHERIC WORLD; sleeper could awaken already healed or with a vivid dream that told him or her how to be healed. [**cf.** INCUBATION DREAMING, LANDMARK, REDUCTIVE ANALYSIS]

MEDICAL MEDIUM—one who diagnoses or prescribes for an illness through a psychic reading; executed through any one of the MENTAL MEDIUMSHIP skills; medium lacks knowledge in medicine and relies entirely on the information from the ETHERIC WORLD INTELLIGENCE; (do not confuse with PHYSICAL MEDIUMSHIP in which the intelligence heals the patient). [**cf.** MENTAL PSYCHIC HEALING, CLAIRVOYANT]

MEDICAL RADIESTHESIA—to use a PENDULUM to locate the area of the disease in the body; PRACTITIONER understands the POLARITY divisions in the body and the normal direction of the gyrational swing of the pendulum over each polarity division; pendulum is held a few inches above the body over each polarity division while patient lies on their back and on their abdomen, respectively; if the pendulum swings in reverse of the normal polarity, this indicates congestion in that area. [**cf.** RADIESTHESIA, PENDULUM POWER, POLARITY, RADIONICS]

MEDICAL REINCARNATION—(Russia, psychotherapy) the patient is given posthypnotic suggestions while in a hypnotic state of consciousness, stating that he or she is one of their past personalities; the intent is that they will reveal information from past lives that is helpful to this life's problems; patient believes he or she is this former personality and acts like them in a seemingly normal wakeful state of consciousness. [**cf.** REINCARNATION, PRESCRIPTION, POSTHYPNOTIC SUGGESTIONS, KARMA]

MEDICINE—(Native American) one's own unique talent or skill that is used to heal brother tribesman and animals; Indians with "medicine" have the ability to blend with the natural forces of nature, and have a good bond with the Creator and the spirit realm; talent received through formal tribal education and/or through a natural born trait; special talents using the natural remedies for healing; one conducts the sweat lodge, another heals with herbs, another leads the prayer pipe ritual, etc.

Usage: 1. "That is not my medicine to heal the horse" (skills have a relationship to one's karma); 2. "It is not my medicine to die at this time." [**cf.** MEDICINE PATH, SINGER, NATURAL HEALING, PIPE]

MEDICINE BAG—(Native American) a pouch or drawstring bag made of the skin of that Indian's personal TOTEM (the animal that represents him or her); inside the bag are pieces of that animal's dead body; the bag is worn on one's belt; this bag is used as a protection for the Indian, to induce their guide to enter their vibration, and to help them perform psychic feats. [**cf.** AMULET, LAW OF CONTAGION Appendix 7, MAGNETIZED OBJECTS]

MEDICINE BUNDLE—(Native American) a personal collection of odd objects and relics which pertain to the Indian's personal etheric world guide; some articles have been chosen because they were perceived clairvoyantly to represent the guide's personality or talent and others have been apported in the Sun Dance ceremony; carried in the medicine pouch on the Indian's belt; brings protection for the Indian; used for psychic guidance, health cures, and as an aid to perform physical psychic skills. [**cf.** PRIMARY WAVES, TALISMAN, LAW OF ASSOCIATION Appendix 7, KACHINA DOLL]

MEDICINE MAN—1. (Native American) one who studies formally for many years (sometimes twenty years) to learn the ceremonial rituals of his particular tribe and how to handle mental and physical illnesses; formal education includes knowledge of healing with herbs, preventing disease, exorcising hexes, communicating with ETHERIC WORLD INTELLIGENCES, supervising religious affairs, guiding one in psychological problems, prophesying, performing crop ceremonies, controlling atmospheric conditions, going into trance, preparing a sweat lodge, and other forms of psychic skills; acquires WISDOM and universal understanding; medicine man must have so much compassion and empathy that he makes hate go away; (similar to a Christian priest or minister, except for the healing and psychic powers); in large tribes, the SHAMAN (psychic) and HERBALIST help with his duties; uses unorthodox methods of healing with plants, bones, stones, feathers, words, chants, and dancing; 2. (Central Africa) a shaman who can raise and alter his STATE OF CONSCIOUSNESS with tribal ceremonies; goes into VOICE TRANCE state to bring needed cures, PSYCHIC INFORMATION and PROPHECY for his tribe; 3. sometimes used as a blanket name for a

priest, shaman, PSYCHIC, PRACTITIONER, exorcist or herbalist. [**cf.** PRIESTS, WITCH DOCTOR]

MEDICINE PATH—(Native American) to center one's LIFE FORCE in ONE direction; Indians know the "power of the medicine path." [**cf.** NEW-AGE PSYCHOLOGY, LAW OF CENTER Appendix 7, KARMA]

MEDICINE WHEEL—(Native American, Plains) a picture of a wheel that depicts the total UNIVERSE and the sacred way that all CREATION balances; a tool used to gain wisdom, guidance and growth from external clues; the wheel teaches gentle dealing and respect for nature, its creatures and people, and teaches one to sing the song of the world to become whole people and one with the universe; wheel tells of the responsibilities of all to "return" good to EARTH MOTHER in order to keep her balanced and prevent her from becoming sick. [**cf.** SOUL CYCLES, PLANETARY CYCLES, HOLISM]

MEDITATION—a disciplined mind technique for a set time to achieve a high STATE OF CONSCIOUSNESS; accomplished by a prolonged CONCENTRATION of an unbroken flow of thought toward the object of concentration, allowing confused and disjointed thoughts to melt away and be replaced by the chosen FOCAL POINT; focal point may be a MANTRA, a MANDALA, a YANTRA, PRAYER BEADS, music, a visual object, a divine person, personal chosen words, or words from a leader; 1. objective is to quiet the emotions, control the mind, and relax the physical body; the CONSCIOUS MIND awareness is narrowed down to the focal point, the SUBCONSCIOUS MIND is bypassed and the SUPERCONSCIOUS MIND becomes activated; each experience varies; normal awarenesses are: (a) a sense of DISASSOCIATION, (b) a oneness with the COSMOS, or (c) a unifying healthful and loving experience of the INNER-SELF: 2. benefits of daily MEDITATION: (a) improved general health, (b) mental alertness, a positive attitude toward life and a feeling of general well-being; 3. (C. Maxwell Cade and Nona Coxhead) medical testing found there is a definite change in BODY CHEMISTRY and metabolism during meditation; scientists are calling this the FOURTH STATE OF CONSCIOUSNESS; a sophisticated EEG, the MIND-MIRROR, found a fifth brain wave signature on the readouts which results from a calm, detached, inward and outward awareness; lines were symmetrical ALPHA WAVES and some THETA WAVES. (Inconcl.) 4. beneficial postures for meditation: (a) the LOTUS POSTURE in YOGA, (b) sitting on a chair with back straight, legs and arms uncrossed, hands on knees, palm up or down, and eyes closed or open; (do not confuse with PRAYER or PSYCHIC DEVELOPMENT, see Appendix 4). [cf. BRAIN WAVES, GUIDED MEDITATION, LAW OF MEDITATION Appendix 7, PASSIVE VOLITION, Appendix 5 MEDITATION]

MEDITATION-IN-MOTION—(Sufi) a dance performed by many persons moving in a circular direction while chanting and rhythmically keeping in step; choreographed so one does not become dizzy but one experiences a spiritual elevation; the repetition tends to raise one's ego-self to a higher dimension with a feeling of floating and identifying with the UNIVERSE; each one in the circle has a different experience. **Syn.** SUFI TWIRLING. [cf. WHIRLING DERVISH, TEMPLE DANCERS, DANCE THERAPY]

MEDITATIVE PALMING—(Buddhism) the placing of both palms upward on the lap, one resting on the other, during MEDITATION; represents wisdom of inner vision; palms are recognized as the doors of psychic inspiration. [cf. CORPSE POSE, HANDS, SEED MEDITATION]

MEDIUM—("mediator," go between) one who serves as an instrument through which the personality of an intelligence in the ETHERIC WORLD can help earthlings; individual must have the proper MAGNETIC FLUID within the nervous system, proper chemicals in the body, and be desirous and capable of synchronizing with the intelligence; 1. if the BODY CHEMISTRY is not suitable for the intelligence's entry, the intelligence changes it during repeated sittings of the individual; sittings may be done privately in one's home or in a PSYCHIC DEVELOPMENT CIRCLE; 2. one becomes a medium by choice, (superior ETHERIC WORLD INTELLIGENCES never force or even make the decision for their communication); 3. once developed, medium is in control of the etheric intelligence(s), or GUIDE(S); guide(s) relays messages back and forth and blend the two energy fields together, bringing new KNOWLEDGE, PSYCHIC INFORMATION, and guidance for the medium's and for others' healing abilities, protection, and the manipulation of matter; 4. kinds: (a) mediums for physical effects; (b) mediums for intellectual effects; (do not confuse with a PSYCHIC, see Appendix 4). **Syn.** SHAMAN. [cf. PHYSICAL PSYCHISM, MENTAL MEDIUMSHIP, DOCTOR TEACHER, SEANCE, TRANCE, ETHERIC WORLD INTELLIGENCE]

MEDIUM FOR INTELLECTUAL EFFECTS—one whose guide (etheric world intelligence) works through mental mediumship skills, i.e., INSPIRATIONAL THOUGHT, INSPIRATIONAL SPEAKING, CLAIRVOYANCE, CLAIRSENTIENCE, CLAIRAUDIENCE, CLAIRSAVORANCE and CLAIRSCENT; guide uses his or her own energy and only the medium perceives the information given; MENTAL MEDIUMSHIP is used for counseling, bringing new knowledge to the masses, diagnosing mental or physical illnesses, guidance, and PROPHECY. [cf. GUIDE, INNER BAND, OUTER BAND]

MEDIUM FOR PHYSICAL EFFECTS—one whose guide (etheric world intelligence) intervenes within the physical body of the medium and brings forth physical phenomena; i.e., AUTOMATIC WRITING, VOICE TRANCE, TRUMPET, RAPPINGS, PSYCHIC HEALING, APPORTATION TELEKINESIS, LEVITATION; guide uses energy of the medium, called ECTOPLASM, and the medium must be in a deep state of trance; everyone in the area perceives the psychism; physical mediumship is used for counseling, bringing new information for the masses, healing mental and physical illnesses, guidance, PROPHECY, and for manipulating matter. [cf. BLACKEDOUT ROOM, SEMITRANCE, VOICE TRANCE, UNDER]

MEDIUM FOR SPONTANEOUS DICTATIONS—see INSPIRATIONAL MEDIUMISTIC WRITING.

MEDIUM FOR TRIVIAL COMMUNICATIONS—one who can only attract etheric world entities from the lower astral planes to communicate with; mediumship utilizes the LAW OF LIKE ATTRACTS LIKE and the medium cannot attract a high, superior intelligence if their own lifestyle and morals are low on the scale of society. [cf. THOUGHTS, SPIRIT COMMUNICATION, OUTER BAND, EARTHBOUND ENTITIES]

MEDIUM STATE OF HYPNOSIS—a level of CONSCIOUSNESS in which the CONSCIOUS MIND has relinquished its role of decision making and the SUBCONSCIOUS MIND is accepting any verbalization given it; brought on by a HYPNOTIST or by one's self (as in SELF-HYPNOTHERAPY); characteristics of the subject's body and mind that distinguish this state from the LIGHT or the DEEP STATE OF HYPNOSIS: 1. body is very relaxed and limp like a rag doll; body will assume different positions without tiring if commanded to do so by the hypnotist; body will become anesthetized in part or in whole upon suggestion; if pain was in the body beforehand, it will either be more pronounced or completely gone; subject's lips and mouth become dry during session; subject has difficulty swallowing; **2.** subject has feelings of indifference and DISASSOCIATION with their environment; **3.** subject is aware of what the hypnotherapist is saying but will not remember all of it upon awakening; subject will answer hypnotist without waking, if questions do not require a decision; voice is soft; **4.** subject responds to PARTIAL REGRESSION or AGE REGRESSION; **5.** upon awakening, subject has distortion of time he or she was in this state. **Syn.** SEMI-STAGE HYPNOSIS, CATALEPTIC STAGE OF HYPNOSIS. [**cf.** MASS HYPNOSIS, INDUCTION, PRESCRIPTION]

MEDIUM TRANCE—see SEMITRANCE.

MEDIUMISTIC COMMUNICATION—to have a good rapport with one's guides, angels, doctor teacher, inner band or outer band for bringing psychic information, guidance, good health, and personal desires into being. [**cf.** SPIRITUALISM, PARAPSYCHOLOGY]

MEDIUMISTIC SERVITOR—see MEDIUM.

MEDIUMISTIC SLEEP—a deep state of trance brought about by the cooperation of both the MEDIUM and the ETHERIC WORLD INTELLIGENCE; the medium's LIFE FORCE takes an astral flight and the etheric world intelligence moves into the medium's body to use it for the tasks; tasks can be HEALING, giving a lecture, PSYCHIC SURGERY, DEPENDENT VOICE, etc. [**cf.** DESIRED-CONTROL, ASTRAL PROJECTION, IMPERSONATION]

MEDIUMISTIC TRANCE—**1.** see MEDIUMISTIC SLEEP; **2.** (clinical) a deep ALTERED STATE OF CONSCIOUSNESS in which one performs physical phenomena; clinical theory: in this state the medium's unconscious complexes, repressed desires, anxieties, past lives, loved ones, and internal drives are given free externalization power: these are expressed, giving the appearance that it is another entity working through the medium. (Inconcl.) [**cf.** NEED-DETERMINED RESPONSE]

MEDIUMIZED—pertains to one who has mediumistic, PERISPRIT fluid within their nervous sytem which allows the etheric world GUIDE to use them as an instrument for physical phenomena; one is born mediumized or acquires it through SITTING for development over a period of time; etheric world ALCHEMIST changes the medium's BODY CHEMISTRY so it contains this perisprit fluid; medium must have the DESIRE to sit patiently and repetitiously, and allow it to unfold. [**cf.** DARKROOM SESSIONS, BLACKED-OUT ROOM]

MEDIUMSHIP—a compatible sharing of time, energy, talent, and intellect between an EARTHLING and an ETHERIC WORLD INTELLIGENCE; objective is to bring knowledge to the earth world that cannot be obtained through normal educational sources; a human body is used as a psychic instrument for etheric communication and matter manipulation to enrich mankind's education regarding the growth of the SOUL-MIND, the progression of civilization and individual well-being; the desire and willingness of the etheric world intelligence and the earthling to work together is shared, regardless of difficulties and time, until there is the proper synchronization both physically and mentally for the relaying of the PSYCHIC INFORMATION and the manipulation of matter that can be beneficial in some manner; (Allan Kardec) "mediumship is a human potential, not proof of superiority or moral advancement"; etheric world intelligences help in both mental and physical psychism; see Appendix 4 to differentiate from psychic skills that require the SUBCONSCIOUS MIND. **Syn.** SHAMANSHIP. [**cf.** GUIDE, INNER BAND, ORACLE, AUGUR, ETHERIC WORLD INTELLIGENCE Appendix 3]

MEDIUMSHIP DEVELOPMENT—**1.** (physical phenomena) a group of people who meet regularly with a desire that one or more of them will be mediumized and physical phenomena will occur; **(a)** room is darkened or blacked-out; group sits in a circle formation to keep the psychic energy that builds within the circle, and negative energy (if any) outside; repetition of meetings weekly, with no absences and no new attenders, moves the development along more swiftly; **(b)** everyone concentrates on those who desire to be developed and the desired type of physical phenomena; SITTERS are relaxed, passive, and patient; **(c)** ETHERIC WORLD INTELLIGENCES have charge of synchronizing the body chemistries of the sitters; harmony among the members of the group during the meeting and outside the meeting is absolutely necessary for physical phenomena; this harmony contributes to SYNCHRONIZATION of body chemistries; **(d)** facets that induce development: using the room for mediumship circles only, metaphysical lesson preceding blacked-out circle, singing peppy songs, classics, and hymns, and meditating during the session. [cf. SEANCE, BLACKED-OUT ROOM, CONTROL] 2. (mental mediumship) (a) a group of people and one well-grounded MEDIUM who meet weekly to individually learn how to give psychic messages; (1) group members sit in a circle to keep themselves protected from negative ethereal INTRUDERS; room has subdued lighting or normal lighting; (2) basic nucleus of group remains the same but a gradual flow of newcomers can be handled; (3) lesson precedes the circle meeting; (4) sitters take turns giving messages for one another and giving PROPHECY for the group, or regarding the world; (5) etheric world intelligences work individually with each sitter to harmonize with their BODY CHEMISTRY; (6) meditating or singing loud, peppy songs helps to raise the vibrations for MENTAL MEDIUMSHIP; guides feed sitters PSYCHIC INFORMATION through CLAIRVOYANCE, CLAIRSENTIENCE, CLAIRSCENT, CLAIRSAVORANCE, and CLAIRAUDIENCE; (b) one sits daily by one's self in a consecrated area in one's home to develop a rapport with one's guide(s); one makes their desire to contact his or her GUIDE known, verbally or silently, and then sits patiently to perceive; meditation always precedes opening of PSYCHIC DOORS: sitter sits passively and keeps a NEUTRAL MIND; guide makes his or her presence known and answers questions through clairvoyance, clairaudience, clairscent, clairsavorance or clairsentience; (1) short daily sittings are more advantageous than one long weekly SITTING; (2) intelligences should be questioned if one feels he or she is not of superior quality; (3) both types of mental mediumship can be developed by anyone, but the quality of psychic information one receives depends upon the medium's morals and lifestyle; invisible entities are drawn to one utilizing the LAW OF LIKE ATTRACTS LIKE; a sitter who is low on the scale of human society or does not meditate beforehand will draw inferior etheric world helpers or intruders and the information will prove to be inaccurate. [cf. DOCTOR TEACHER, INNER BAND, OUTER BAND, MEDITATION]

MEDIUMSHIP HEALING—to serve as an instrument for an ETHERIC WORLD INTELLIGENCE to use his or her healing skills on earthly patients; healing techniques are beyond the reach of conventional medicine; medium PRACTITIONER has the proper BODY CHEMISTRY, mental makeup, and has earned this privilege in a past life or in this life; the etheric world intelligence usually has been a great physician in a past incarnation; sometimes more than one etheric world intelligence works through for one healing. [cf. MEDIUMSHIP HEALING Appendix 2, Appendix 4 for differentiating common healing methods]

MEDULLA OBLONGATA—(esoteric) an area in the neck where the invisible NERVE FLUID, IDA and PINGALA, cross, affecting all the nervous systems in the body, including the vagus nerve. [cf. IDA, PINGALA, SYMPATHETIC NERVOUS SYSTEM, VAGUS NERVE]

MEGBE—(Ituri Pygmies) see VITAL LIFE FORCE.

MEGHA RAGA—(Hinduism) music of a fixed melodic scale, composed to summon courage when played; Hindus understand the power of music, so it is played as a melody for midday in the rainy season. [cf. BHAIRAVA RAGA, MALKOUNSA RAGA, SOUNDS-WITH-POWER]

MELCHIZEDEK—an archangel who presided over and was in charge of the Chaldean race, an early Semitic race, which had a connection to the Atlantean race. [cf. GABRIEL, ANGEL HIERARCHY]

MEMORY AND ESP—(clinical) to bring into one's CONSCIOUSNESS through the ability of the PSI field, an event which one experienced a long time ago. **Syn.** REGRESSION. [cf. AGE REGRESSION, REINCARNATION, BACK-IN-TIME]

MEMORY BANK—see AKASHIC RECORD.

MEMORY CLUSTERS—(Huna) an idea or attitude regarding an unpleasant emotional event that is continually repressed and stored in the body; this REPRESSION surfaces in unwanted mental and physical behavior; see BLOCKS. [cf. REINCARNATION, PROGRAMMED BIOCOMPUTERS, INNER-MIND ACTIVITY]

MEMORY CONSCIOUSNESS—theory: each ATOM has stored within it all the experiences that it has ever gone through; the atom knows all the rates of vibration it has performed. **Syn.** CONDENSED CONSCIOUSNESS. [cf. PRIMARY PERCEPTION, SYMPATHETIC NERVOUS SYSTEM]

MEMORY OF THE LOGOS—see AKASHIC RECORD.

MEMORY RECORD—(biofeedback training) a log

of the subject's experiences, outward and inward, each time he or she is HOOKED-UP to an instrument in their training; this log provides a method of helping the subject analyze their body feelings, subjective thought, and the outward results of the instrument, so that they can understand what causes arousal of internal behavior; thus the subject can learn how to correct unnecessary arousal of internal states. [cf. BIOFEEDBACK TRAINING, HASSLE LOG, NEUTRAL MIND, RECALL]

MEMORY STORAGE SYSTEM—the SUBCONSCIOUS MIND, which functions like a computer; when the subconscious mind is given instructions from the CONSCIOUS MIND as each new event happens, the subconscious mind stores the instructions in categories into a "hold" file; when future orders are given from the conscious mind for that program to be activated, the computer surfaces that category material to be used in the new decision; the button to surface this material seems to be labeled "related activity" and the conscious awake mind is not aware of this function; (John Lilly) "a dimension always infiltrating with the moment's experience so that the experience of the present moment is altered according to the individual's memory storage system." [cf. SUBCONSCIOUS MIND Appendix 5, BIOCOMPUTER, INFORMATION PROCESSING THEORY]

MEMORY TIME—(biofeedback training) an estimate of how long in clock time, one was experiencing visions while HOOKED-UP to the BIOFEEDBACK INSTRUMENT; at the end of the session the subject is asked to give their estimate because it is relative to how deep he or she was in an ALTERED STATE OF CONSCIOUSNESS; distorted clock time says the subject was in a deep altered state. [cf. PERCEPTUAL DATA, RECEIVING MODE, RELIABLE FLOW]

MEMORY-VISUAL DISPLAY—to play-back pictures in INNER-MIND ACTIVITY fashioned of past experiences; deliberately or unintentionally reminiscing to occupy time, feel rewarded, or please one's self; flashbacks usually relate to emotionally pleasurable scenes; occurs as time stallers because the work at hand is difficult or undesirable and one plays back a happy moment to assure one's self that one deserves pleasure. **Syn.** DAYDREAMING. [cf. NON-THOUGHTS, FANTASY, IMAGERY Appendix 4]

MEN IN BLACK—(ufology, 1975-76) abbr. MIB; a group of poker-faced men dressed in black who drove black sedans and traveled in groups of three;

appeared repeatedly after a UFO sighting or encounter and used hostile tactics to warn and dissuade the contactee and UFO investigators to silence their information. [cf. UFOLOGY, UNKNOWN FORCES, TIME TRAVELERS]

MEN OF GOD—(Slavic) see PSYCHIC.

MEN OF THE OAK TREE—another name given to the Druids of the ancient Celtic country because of their understanding of the trees, the inner lives of the trees and the use of trees in psychic work. [cf. WEATHER MAGIC, NATURE-PK, ATMOSPHERE CONTROL, TREE, DRUID]

MEN-AN-TOL—(Cornwall, England) a large stone with a hole in the center; because of its structure it has a vibratory rate that is suitable to cure back diseases and bone defects. **Syn.** CRICK STONE. [cf. MINPSI, FORMS-WITH-POWER]

MENT—suffix meaning a "result," a "means," the "act," or the "condition of."

MENTAL ACTIVITY—encompasses any movement of electrical energy in the brain; electrical energy is stimulated deliberately and unconsciously by the conscious, subconscious and superconscious minds; since the SUBCONSCIOUS MIND and SUPERCONSCIOUS MIND are invisible they must enmesh within the brain energy to be recognizable by the CONSCIOUS MIND; mental activity is divided into two groupings: 1. thoughts or inner-mental activity: THINKING and thoughts that belong to the owner of the brain in which they occur; instigated thoughts that the individual is aware of stimulating and thoughts he or she is not aware of stimulating, coming from the individual's memory storage compartments, or from his or her connection with TOTALITY; 2. non-thoughts or outer mental activity: psychic information that does not belong to the owner of the brain in which it occurs; psychic information is free data which one did not have to learn or make a decision about from the past or make a decision about in the present; non-thoughts "come into" the brain by way of the superconscious or subconscious minds because these minds are ethereal and provide a means of entry for information that is ethereally structured. [cf. NON-THOUGHT, THOUGHT]

MENTAL ARENA—see THIRD-EYE AREA.

MENTAL AURA—light-like beams of colored energy surrounding the head, portraying one's current health, emotional state, and momentary thinking; beams extend outward from the shoulders like an Indian headress (as opposed to ARC EMANATIONS); beams of colors change their tone, intensity, length and color constantly, denoting one's moods; mental aura can be activated to change during periods of meditation; easily seen by auric clairvoyants; (do not confuse with the SOUL-MIND AURA that extends around the whole body). [cf. HUMAN AURA, EMOTIONS]

MENTAL AVENUE—an attunement between the universal mind and the subjective mind that brings forth psychic information in the form of INSPIRATIONAL THOUGHT and CLAIRSENTIENCE. [cf. SUPERCONSCIOUS MIND, KUNDALINI]

MENTAL BODY—1. in earthly existence: a subtle, ethereal energy field that interpenetrates the human physical body at the hip line and extends upward and outward into the ETHER; mental body controls the CEREBROSPINAL NERVOUS SYSTEM; mental body brings PSYCHIC INFORMATION from Totality in the form of INTUITION, GUT FEELINGS, and INSPIRATIONAL THOUGHT; chiropractors and osteopaths are trained to take care of this body, whether they realize it or not; some religions know this body as the SPIRITUAL BODY as it carries cosmic energies more freely than the other bodies; recognized by parapsychologists as the third body in the principles of bodies; 2. in etheric existence: when one abides in the ETHERIC WORLD and has shed the other two bodies, this body is exposed to the life that just transpired in earth and must evaluate it to plan future lives; function is to solidify one's emotional and mental nature; retains its human form while abiding in the etheric world. [cf. THIRD PLANE, MENTAL PLANE, CAUSAL BODY]

MENTAL BRAIN PROGRAMMING—to logically reason with oncoming stimuli and information, make a decision, react emotionally with the decision and drop it into the SUBCONSCIOUS MIND (the computer, the hardware); a normal function of the mental brain is to act like the software of the computer and program the computer; occurs continually; see BRAIN; the functions can be separated for study but the two minds are never completely separated; (Silva Mind Control) "the conscious mind is telling the subconscious mind what to do even though one is functioning at the subconscious level." [cf. INNER-DIALOGUE, VERBAL MISER, SUBJECTIVE PROGRAMMING, PSYCHIC ATTUNEMENT, BABBLER]

MENTAL CHATTER—thoughts within; see INNER-DIALOGUE.

MENTAL CULTURE—a study of METAPHYSICS and BORDERLINE SCIENCE; see PARAPSYCHOLOGY.

MENTAL CYCLE—(biorhythm) see INTELLECTUAL CYCLE.

MENTAL DISSOCIATION—clinical theory: a STATE OF CONSCIOUSNESS caused by a reduction of one's conscious control of their unconsciousness, repressed thoughts, motivations, and impulses, which could lead to involuntary behavior patterns; e.g., TALKING-IN-TONGUES, AUTOMATIC WRITING and OUIJA BOARD. [cf. AUTOMATISM]

MENTAL ELEMENTAL—a solidified thought-form that hovers close to the thinker who builds it and has a great influence on the thinker; solidified thought-form is formed by "constantly dwelling" on one subject with no deviation while one sleeps, eats, works, exercises, etc.; elemental grows in intelligence and energy until the thinker breaks his or her train of thought; angelic elementals built from happy, positive thoughts aid in furthering joy and happiness in one's life; beastly elementals formed by jealousy, resentment, etc., result in hazardous and unpleasant events; THOUGHT-FORMS are capable of growing so large that they perform acts of their own; majority of people think both positive and negative thoughts during the day and therefore never build a large elemental. [cf. ELEMENTALS, COUNTERFEIT, SHADOW, LAW OF LIKE ATTRACTS LIKE Appendix 7]

MENTAL ENERGY—(metaphysics and future science) electrical impulses that constantly emanate from the human head resulting from conscious thoughts, subconscious thoughts (purposely or unknowingly), inner-dialogue, and dreamstuff; these electrical impulses are full of INTELLIGENCE and ENERGY, compatible with atoms in the atmosphere; atoms from the head aggregate with atoms of the same number of protons making molecules; molecules aggregate to make elements, elements to compounds, and compounds to three-dimensional matter; thus, one's mental energy directs the course of the atoms and forms one's environment, body, and activities; number of protons from the atoms of the MIND are determined by the emotion and characteristic of the thought output. (Inconcl.) [cf. MENTAL-EMOTIONAL ACTIVITY, ATOM, EEG, MATTER, LAW OF THOUGHT AND LAW OF DOMINION Appendix 7.]

389

MENTAL ENZYMES—physical body chemicals that act as generators for thought. (Inconcl.) [**cf.** THIRD-EYE AREA, PITUITARY GLAND, PINEAL GLAND, CEREBROSPINAL NERVOUS SYSTEM]

MENTAL EPIDEMIC—a group of people who perform body movements as a unit to induce an ALTERED STATE OF CONSCIOUSNESS; the group dances, whirls, chants, claps hands, stamps feet, or shouts until many are exhausted from working themselves into a frenzy; this results in a TRANCE STATE, HYPNOTIC STATE, or DISASSOCIATION that brings on PSYCHIC INFORMATION through some skill; e.g., throbbing of the tom-toms while tribe dances around a fire, WHIRLING DERVISHES, CHARISMATIC meetings designed for TALKING-IN-TONGUES or instant healings. [**cf.** EMOTIONAL PSI, ECSTASY]

MENTAL ETIQUETTE—(Seth) on the invisible planes where all thoughts are known to one another, one chooses their thoughts with "discrimination and finesse." [**cf.** LAW OF THOUGHT Appendix 7, THINKING]

MENTAL FIELD—1. see MENTAL BODY; 2. the ergs of energy that a human being gives out of their brain by thinking. (Inconcl.) [**cf.** INNER-DIALOGUE, EEG, MENTAL-SEED-ATOM, MENTAL PLANE]

MENTAL HEALER—(esoteric) a PSYCHIC, PRACTITIONER, or religious figure who uses their mind to aid BODY CHEMISTRY or attitude change in a patient, thus hastening the healing process; HEALER gathers together an abundance of energy, declares it to be of a healing quality, and sends it to the patient by proper wordage; healer contacts patient's wavelength by complying with the patient's belief system and directs his or her MENTAL ENERGY to the AURA, MIND, or diseased area of patient, depending upon the disease; distance is no barrier; attitude of healer must be one of service to their fellow human beings or one of empathy, but not a desire to feed their own ego (which destroys the energy). [**cf.** LOVE-LINE, MENTAL TELEPATHY, VISUALIZATION, MENTAL-EMOTIONAL ACTIVITY]

MENTAL HEALING—(esoteric) a form of PSYCHOKINESIS wherein the natural electrical energy that emanates steadily from the brain is used for healing purposes; this electrical energy is intensified in the healer's brain by different methods, depending upon the healer or type of mental healing, and is then transmuted in the healer's brain to contain healing characteristics before it is sent to the patient; healing energy is directed either to the MIND, diseased area, or AURA of the patient where it reacts on body or mind cells; 1. healing can be instantaneous or gradual; healing is more effective if both parties are in an ALPHA STATE STATE OF CONSCIOUSNESS: 2. distance is no barrier as to strength of healing energy; 3. diseased tissue has been medically examined and found that this energy does make changes in cell activity, aiding the body cells to normalize, so the intelligence in the cells makes the cells heal themselves; 4. can be used to heal one's self or others; permission should be received before sending healing to another because it could be overwhelming, frightening, or unwanted and will have little effect; 5. utilizes the theories that "energy follows thought" and "the higher always acts on the lower," (the subtle vibrations of the healer's mind acts on the diseased tissue); 6. types of mental healing: (a) VISUALIZATION; (b) MEDITATION; (c) HYPNOTHERAPY; (d) MENTAL TELEPATHY; (e) AFFIRMATIONS; see Appendix 4 to differentiate types of psychic healing. [**cf.** PARAELECTRIC, LAW OF SUBSERVIENCE Appendix 7, HOLISTIC HEALTH, ALTERNATIVES, MENTAL HEALING Appendix 2]

MENTAL INTERCHANGE—(ufology) an inner feeling and intuitive knowing that the object close by is a living entity of some kind and not a robot; e.g., a dead bird in the hand is not the same feeling as a live one; to recognize that the image that gets out of a UFO construct is a living entity and not a machine. [**cf.** CONSTRUCTS, ETHER SHIP BEING, FUSIFORM, GODS FROM THE SKY]

MENTAL MANIFESTATION—to clairvoyantly perceive a picture that is so life-like and clearly defined that one thinks it is real; can be a person, animal, object, scene or partial scene; occurs spontaneously when in a state of spiritual ECSTASY, MEDITATION, DREAMING, or when SITTING for psychic answers; can only be perceived by the PSYCHIC; frequently startles the consciousness back to the beta state; whether symbol or image, the message is always important; (do not confuse with PHYSICAL MANIFESTATION in which one sees with the physical eyes). **Syn.** MENTAL MATERIALIZATION. [**cf.** CLAIRVOYANCE, VISIONARY, APPARITION, PSYCHIC EXPERIENCES DURING SLEEP]

MENTAL MANIFESTATIONS/MISCELLANEOUS—a category in this dictionary that lists psychic skills that do not have enough research, or happen frequently enough, to warrant an individual category; see Appendix 2.

MENTAL MEDIUM—one who relies on their ETHERIC WORLD INTELLIGENCES to work cooperatively with them in performing many psychic skills pertaining to MENTAL PSYCHISM; most mental mediums are also psychics. [**cf.** PHYSICAL PSYCHISM, MEDIUM, PSYCHIC]

MENTAL MEDIUMSHIP—to use ETHERIC WORLD INTELLIGENCES when performing mental psychic skills; intelligences use their energy and only the medium perceives (as opposed to PHYSICAL MEDIUMSHIP in which the intelligences use the medium's energy); the following mental psychic skills can be performed by either the SUBCONSCIOUS MIND or the etheric world intelligences: CLAIRVOYANCE, CLAIRAUDIENCE, CLAIRSCENTIENCE, INSPIRATIONAL THOUGHT, CLAIRSCENT. [**cf.** PHYSICAL MEDIUMSHIP, GUIDE, MENTAL PSYCHISM]

MENTAL MEDIUMSHIP HEALING—to call upon one's ETHERIC WORLD INTELLIGENCES when sending healing to many at one time and over great distances; intelligences intercede if called upon when meditating over PETITION slips or a prayer list and use the healer's mental energy to extend the healing beam (without interference) and direct it to the correct area of the patient; intelligences also use their mental energy if necessary. **Syn.** PETITION SLIP HEALING. [**cf.** MENTAL HEALING, MEDIUMSHIP, GUIDE, INTER-WORLD TELEPATHY]

MENTAL MIND—see CONSCIOUS MIND and BRAIN.

MENTAL NOISE—(clinical) the normal, waking conscious mind at work, in an inner-dialogue, reading, or speaking. [**cf.** INNER-DIALOGUE, WORDS-WITH-POWER, THOUGHT-FORMS, INNER-MIND ACTIVITY]

MENTAL OR BEHAVIORAL INFLUENCE OF AN AGENT—abbr. MOBIA; coined by Stanford University researchers; theory: the AGENT plays an active role in telepathy and telepathy is actually a form of PSYCHOKINESIS; sometimes phrased ACTIVE-AGENT TELEPATHY. [**cf.** TELEKINESIS ARTICLE-PK, MENTAL TELEPATHY, LOVE-LINE]

MENTAL OSMOSIS—to psychically absorb material written in a book by glancing at it; psychic understands what is written and can comment on it as if he or she had read it. (Inconcl.) [**cf.** SLEEP OSMOSIS, MENTAL MANIFESTATIONS/MISCELLANEOUS Appendix 2]

MENTAL PLANE—see THIRD PLANE.

MENTAL POWER—(esoteric) to have control over one's brain activity and make it do what one wills it to do; process: 1. gather together (electrical) mind energy in one area of the head before it emanates from the head in the normal process; 2. keep concentrating until the energy is intensified; 3. focus the mind on the target whether an invisible or visible target; 4. decree the built up energy to perform in a particular manner, invisibly, or to show evidence visibly; 5. shoot it with enough emotion to hit the target or perform its psychic feat; 6. executed in seconds or minutes. (Inconcl.) [**cf.** WORDS-WITH-POWER, CONSCIOUS MIND, ATOMS, MENTAL PSYCHISM, DIRECTED-THOUGHT TRAINER]

MENTAL PROBE—(dowsing and penduluming) the desired target held in the SUBCONSCIOUS MIND of the DOWSER and PENDULUMIST; operator tells her or himself what they are looking for or the questions they want answered, and this, then projects into the ethers; e.g., looking for oil, water, or a missing person; when the instrument comes close to this target, the radiations bounce off the instrument as if it were a radar screen; the SYMPATHETIC NERVOUS SYSTEM carries the radiations to the subconscious mind and the instrument reacts in a movement that tells the operator the mental probe is found; the subconscious mind does not seem to get mixed up and locate the wrong material. (Inconcl.) [**cf.** RADIESTHETIC SENSE, TELLURIC ENERGY]

MENTAL PROCESSES—(Carl Jung) all brain action results from four primary activities: SENSING, feeling, INTUITING and THINKING. [**cf.** STREAM OF HALF-CONSCIOUSNESS, TEMPORARY MEMORY BANK, MENTAL ENCLOSURE, CHRYSALIS]

MENTAL PROJECTION—to will one's SUBCONSCIOUS MIND to travel to higher realms in the etheric world; PSYCHIC focuses on raising their CONSCIOUSNESS to the fastest vibrational frequency possible; intense concentration gradually expands mind activity and it soon reaches the higher levels of existence; one has an awareness of normal reality at the same time, so one can remember what is attained or learned during this trip; objective: to learn from the highly evolved intelligences for exploratory education and understanding of earth life; one sees scenes of color, floating energies and angel beings that are indescribable in current language; (do not confuse with ASTRAL PROJECTION, see Appendix 4 for differences). **Syn.** SOUL PROJECTION. [**cf.** MENTAL PROJECTION Appendix 2, TRANSCENDENCE, PERILS OF THE SOUL, FLOAT-OFF]

MENTAL PSYCHIC PROCESSES—a category in the appendices which lists the various methods and techniques one can use to become adept in various psychic skills; how-to directions and cautions that are necessary for everyone, and some suitable only for advanced students, instructions to obtain one's level for perceiving psychic information, for improving one's skills, and for helping natural-born psychics keep their talent under control. [**cf.** Appendix 2 MENTAL PSYCHIC PROCESSES, CLOAK OF INSULATION, LAW OF EXCLUSIVENESS and LAW OF TRUE FALSEHOODS Appendix 7]

MENTAL PSYCHISM—one of the two major categories of psychic skills (mental psychism and physical psychism); can be identified from physical psychic skills by the following characteristics; these features are listed below under two sub-groupings, **mental personal psychism** and **mental mediumship: 1.** (both) (a) require the activity of any of the five minds of the psychic singularly or in combinations; (CONSCIOUS, SUBCONSCIOUS, SUPERCONSCIOUS, and UNIVERSAL MINDS, and the SUBLIMINAL LEVEL of the mind); (b) tunes into the three minds of other persons and the universal mind (personally or with the help of ETHERIC WORLD INTELLIGENCES); (c) only the PSYCHIC perceives; no one knows exactly what the psychic is sensing; (d) psychic is aware of what is transpiring while the PSYCHIC INFORMATION is coming through; (e) psychic information can come through in symbols as well as in true image form; **2.** (**mental personal psychism**) (a) skills improve with practice and also with an interest shown in the philosophy behind the skill by attending classes and reading books; (b) executed by will or spontaneously; (c) requires a relaxed BETA or ALPHA STATE OF CONSCIOUSNESS; (d) ability can be increased or decreased by an accident of the spine or head; **3.** (**mental mediumship**) (a) requires regular sittings; psychic sits quietly and patiently, allowing the etheric world intelligences to do the unfolding; (b) completely controlled by psychic (superior etheric world intelligences only come when asked); (c) etheric world intelligences and discarnate entities use their own energy for the feats; (d) requires an alpha state of consciousness and preparation between both the etheric world intelligences and psychic. **Syn.** CRYPTETHESIA. [**cf.** see Appendix 2 for listing of the skills which belong under this classification]

MENTAL PSYCHOLOGICAL PRISON—(destructive-brainwashing cult) an extremely low state of consciousness wherein the subject has no profile of her or himself outside of being functional to the cult organization and its leader; sometimes the subject reaches the level of instinctual awareness (similar to an animal) and can no longer make decisions about eating, vocation, religious beliefs, friends, and lifestyle; this is brought about by the clever technique of the mechanics of the DESTRUCTIVE-BRAIN-WASHING CULT systems; the planned ploy and key phrases are repeated continuously night and day to keep the victim from thinking of her or himself; all verbiage is planned to reach an emotional level of the victim and results in their desire to work for the leader of the cult; victim is unable to realize he or she is entrapped and will therefore have no desire to leave the cult organization or change their lifestyle. [**cf.** Appendix 5 DESTRUCTIVE-BRAINWASHING CULT]

MENTAL RADIO—the human being can be compared to a radio because one sends and receives electronic messages on various frequencies all the time. (Inconcl.) [**cf.** TELEPATHY, MENTAL TELEPATHY, PSYCHIC ATTACK, FEEL-AND-SEE-COMBINATION, TELEPHONE TELEPATHY, HERD IMPULSES]

MENTAL RAYS—six nonphysical energy fields in the higher realms of the ETHERIC WORLD that are closely connected to the body; feed into the CHAKRAS lending a variety and complexity to the body. [**cf.** TRIPLE-WARMER, KUNDALINI, BODY CONTROL]

MENTAL REGRESSION—to take a subject back in time by an OPERATOR rubbing the subjects legs and arms or by giving the subject a GUIDED IMAGERY exercise (but without hypnosis); subject can reveal information regarding their past lives or past events of this incarnation without bringing in the traumatic events or becoming emotional; operator asks questions and takes the subject from one life to another; subject views their lives as a bystander and reaches some of the better highlights of past lives as opposed to the traumatic scenes that surface in

HYPNOTHERAPY. (Inconcl.) [cf. REVIVIFICATION, AGE REGRESSION, PAST LIVES THEORY]

MENTAL SCREEN—a deliberate, imaginary, large, blank screen that one projects in their MIND'S EYE when they want to focus their attention on one spot with expectation to perceive psychic visions. [cf. LAW OF ATTENTION Appendix 7, UPPER FREQUENCY, PSYCHING-UP]

MENTAL SELF-HEALING—(esoteric) to heal one's self through the power of the mind; 1. to change one's BELIEF SYSTEM through new attitudes and thoughts so the CONSCIOUS MIND and SUBCONSCIOUS MIND are in agreement regarding one's well-being; this is accomplished by repeating AFFIRMATIONS frequently, while in the BETA STATE OF CONSCIOUSNESS, that declare the Truth of one's body and emphasizing the area that needs attention; 2. to change the chemistry of one's body through AUTOSUGGESTION which allows it to heal itself more quickly; performed while in the ALPHA STATE OF CONSCIOUSNESS, after meditation or after the induction in SELF-HYPNOTHERAPY: (a) see VISUALIZATION; (b) to talk to one's body cells directing their behavior toward the healing process; consider the cells an entity and tell them what is expected of them, emphasizing the area that needs attention. [cf. MENTAL HEALING, INNER-DIALOGUE]

MENTAL TELEPATHIC HEALING—to heal another person over a distance by use of the electricity emanating from the sender's mind; BODY CHEMISTRY is changed in the patient by the mind energy and a properly worded message from the sender; healing energy has more effect if both psychic (sender) and patient agree upon the time and meditate before the energy transfer; psychic must first get into the THOUGHT ATMOSPHERE of the patient by sending a LOVE-LINE or the suggestion will not take (suggestion must be in compliance with the patient's personality and belief system); then the psychic intensifies mind activity by concentration, changes the energy in their mind to a healing energy, and shoots it with emotion quickly to the patient; if patient does not desire to get well, consciously or unconsciously, the energy bounces off their thought atmosphere; if patient does not know it is coming, the healing energy could be overwhelming and frightening; permission should be granted before psychic sends healing energy; healings are gradual or instantaneous; to

repeat the procedure after a few days is necessary in deep-seated diseases. (Inconcl.)[cf. AFFIRMATION, MENTAL HEALING, ALTERNATIVES, MENTAL TELEPATHIC SUGGESTION]

MENTAL TELEPATHIC POLLUTION—the simultaneous spread of a psychic's thoughts among members of a gathering, excluding the leader's thoughts, if a leader is present; if psychics in a group float in and out of the ALPHA STATE OF CONSCIOUSNESS, they can easily pick up on the strongest psychic's thoughts periodically; sent deliberately or unconsciously by psychic; picked up intentionally or unconsciously by members, sometimes not realizing they are not their own ideas. [cf. SPLODGER, TELEPATHIC TWIN, MIND-LINKING]

MENTAL TELEPATHIC SUGGESTION—planned wordage sent telepathically to deliberately influence the receiver's mind; wordage can be a new ideal or belief, a change in one's present ideal or belief, an idea, instructions, or an order to perform activity when in the alert stage; sent during the sleep state so the CONSCIOUS MIND cannot make any decisions regarding the suggestion; SUBCONSCIOUS MIND accepts it as is and it manifests outwardly without question; however, if new suggestions are not in compliance with the sleeper's BELIEF SYSTEM or personality, they will reject them; sender must first get into receiver's THOUGHT ATMOSPHERE with compliments and basic emotional interests; when receiver awakens he or she feels ideas are their own; e.g., suggestions to heal a patient and the next morning he or she feels better, thinking it is their own doing; to order an individual to attend a meeting and the next morning the individual decides to attend and feels it is his or her idea to go (used by the destructive brainwashing cults). [cf. LAW OF SUGGESTION Appendix 7, LOVE-LINE, THOUGHT ATMOSPHERE, LOVE BOMBING, MENTAL HEALING]

MENTAL TELEPATHY—1. the transfer of thoughts from the mind of one person to the mind of one or more persons, regardless of distance; executed more accurately if both parties are in the ALPHA STATE OF CONSCIOUSNESS; emotional thoughts transfer more easily than asbstract thoughts; in all cases, sender must be able to reach into the THOUGHT ATMOSPHERE of the receiver; 2. types of transfer: (a) occurs spontaneously and unintentionally between both parties; this is more prevalent when there is a love-bond or hate-bond between the sender and receiver (this bond puts them in one another's thought atmosphere); receiver must be in a relaxed state of consciousness to catch the thought; (a touch of consciousness of one mind upon another mind with the ability to discern what that person is thinking at that moment); **(b)**tuning in to another person's mind deliberately, unbeknown to the thinker; recognized by some to be unethical; (c) message sent and received, deliberately, by both parties, with a compatible message to both parties; used in psychic experiments to learn about the power of the mind; used with friends and relatives who live at a distance; (d) suggestions sent deliberately to one who does not know he or she is going to receive it, and therefore, they feel the thought is their own; thought bypasses the CONSCIOUS MIND which puts the sender in the receiver's thought atmosphere, because the suggestion is usally sent during sleep; used unethically by destructive-brainwashing cults and ethically by healing practitioners; 3. accomplished by the sender first sending a LOVE-LINE to get into the thought atmosphere of the receiver; sender intensifies their brain energy by concentrating on the formulaic phrase; when ready, sender shoots their idea to the receiver with a strong emotional burst; executed silently or verbally; MEDITATION beforehand for one or both parties enhances their ability. [cf. MENTAL TELEPATHIC SUGGESTION, MENTAL TELEPATHY Appendix 2]

MENTAL TRANSFIGURATION—a change in facial features and body structure in a MEDIUM while the medium is doing psychic work; perceived clairvoyantly and psycially by others, when room is dimly lit; etheric world intelligence (medium's GUIDE) interpenetrates the medium's body to assist in either physical or mental psychic feats; medium feels no different except for an awareness that the guide is helping them; features resemble that of the guide; e.g., body appears elongated or shrinks, face grows a mustache, hair appears piled on the top of the head or in pig tails, cheekbones and eyes resemble a Chinaman; neither medium or guide will this as a part of the psychic feat; it is a necessary part of the MEDIUMSHIP process. [cf. MENTAL PSYCHISM, MENTAL PSYCHIC PROCESSES Appendix 2]

MENTAL TRANSFORMATION—see MENTAL TRANSFIGURATION.

MENTAL TRANSMUTATION—(alchemy) to change substance from one nature and form to another, by the power of the mind; ALCHEMIST intensifies his or her focus on the article to be changed; this undivided attention builds the mind energy which is transferred to the article until it dematerializes into an ethereal vibration; alchemist then rematerializes it into matter, but in a higher frequency; article appears in a different form; alchemist must accomplish this feat before they can transmute their own body into a higher vibrational frequency. (Inconcl.) [cf. ALCHEMICAL PRINCIPLES, ALCHEMY, PHYSICAL TRANSMUTATION]

MENTAL TRAVEL—see MENTAL PROJECTION.

MENTAL TV—the perceive lines, shapes, and forms being drawn by the sender, in an experiment; sender draws a simple picture on paper out of view of the receiver; no words or emotions are exchanged; sender keeps a NEUTRAL MIND; receiver tunes into the hand movement and allows their hand to move accordingly; (CLAIRVOYANCE is not involved). **Syn.** PSYCHOMETRIC TELEPATHY. [cf. TELEPATHY Appendix 2]

MENTAL UFO COMMUNCATIONS—(ufology) telepathy between the intelligence mechanism of the UFONAUT and the mind of the earthling. (Inconcl.) [cf. EARTH TELEPATHY, TARGET HUMAN, INNER-WORLD TELEPATHY]

MENTAL WALL—1. an invisible protection within one's THOUGHT ATMOSPHERE that prevents past traumatic emotions from surfacing; built unconsciously by the constant repressing of emotions that are too painful or too intense to be held in CONSCIOUSNESS; this invisible wall also makes it difficult for the individual to remember dreams, be hypnotized, and from becoming adept in psychic skills that require getting into one's past; 2. an invisible protection built into the thought atmosphere around an individual that prevents others from entering into their belief system, morals, and lifestyle; built unconsciously by a constant overprotection of her or his affairs from others; this invisible wall makes it difficult for the individual to get a good psychic reading, to become a pendulumist, and other psychic skills that tend to give advice for betterment; individual would do better to seek tarot card or hand analysis readings for news. [cf. BELIEF SYSTEM, THOUGHT ATMOSPHERE, BLOCKS, OBJECTIVE PROGRAMMING, MOOD STIMULUS, MEMORY-VISUAL DISPLAY]

MENTAL-BODY PROJECTION—the departure of an individual's mental body from their physical body to travel to very high realms in the etheric world, similar to an ASTRAL PROJECTION; accomplishable by an old soul-mind and with much practice; a necessary way to energize the physical during sleep by those whose body is a faster vibrational frequency than normal; not as easily remembered as an astral projection; (do not confuse with MENTAL PROJECTION in which the mind expands into the higher realms). (Inconcl.) [cf. CLOAK OF INSULATION, LAW OF LIKE ATTRACTS LIKE Appendix 7]

MENTAL-CONSCIOUSNESS-CORD—(Eastern) one of the five ethereal strands of the SILVER CORD; this strand extends from the SOUL-MIND located in the FIFTH PLANE to the PINEAL GLAND in the human head; from here it extends to the KANDA and is now called the SUSHUMNA; within this strand lies all of one's attributes and weaknesses as a result of one's many incarnations; a product of one's own doings; this connects a person to their invisible SUPERCONSCIOUS MIND; carries one's mental development the entire length of the spine; controls the response mechanism in the brain. [cf. MENTAL-CONSCIOUSNESS-SEED-ATOM]

MENTAL-CONSCIOUSNESS-SEED-ATOM—(ancient, Zoroastrianism) an invisible seed at the end of the MENTAL-CONSCIOUSNESS-CORD (a strand of the SILVER CORD) located in the PINEAL GLAND; contains all the qualities of mankind's past knowledge; a link between the CONSCIOUS MIND and the SUPERCONSCIOUS MIND receiving energies and knowledge from the OVERSOUL. Syn. ONE BOOK OF LIFE (Bible). [cf. THIRD-EYE AREA]

MENTAL-EMOTIONAL ACTIVITY—(future science) theory: human thoughts encased in emotions are the force behind the rate of vibration of atoms; under the LAW OF VIBRATION and the law of POLARITY (see Appendix 7), emotions contact atoms in their atomic stage influencing their colonization until mundane matter is formed; process can be compared to the crystal in the radio which sets the frequency and the energy applied to the plate circuit determines the power output (the mind is the crystal and the emotion is the energy applied to the plate circuit). (Inconcl.) [cf. EEG, ENERGY, EMOTIONS, KEY TO LIFE]

MENTAL-NEUTRAL LEVEL—(clinical) a state of consciousness wherein the CONSCIOUS MIND and physical body are asleep or resting and passive, and the SUBCONSCIOUS MIND is alert and in control; occurs during NREM, REM, a deep meditative state,

and a hypnotic state of consciousness. Syn. SLEEP-ALERT. [cf. PASSIVE VOLITION, ESSENCE OF REST, BRAIN SOOTING, CONCENTRATION]

MENTAL-REFLECTING-ETHER—(esoteric) 1. (human being) an ethereal energy that extends from the MENTAL PLANE to the physical body taking pictures of everything the individual does during his or her incarnation; these minute electronic pictures channel back and forth from the HEART-SEED-ATOM in the heart area to the AKASHIC RECORDS in the mental plane where they are filed; these miniature pictures are distributed throughout the CEREBROSPINAL NERVOUS SYSTEM and bloodstream where they are played back into action portraying the individual's KARMA; (function is indescribable in present language); when perceived clairvoyantly, the energy is a very colorful radiant field in perpetual motion. (Inconcl.) 2. (earth) an ethereal energy, similar to photographic plates, which records the incidents occurring on planet earth in minute motion-picture form; made of the more subtle substance known as ATOMIC-ETHER; these minute motion pictures are stored for karmic use. (Inconcl.) [cf. TEMPORARY AKASHIC RECORDS, THIRD-EYE AREA, NADIS, ASTRAL PICTURE GALLERY]

MENTAL-SEED-ATOM—see MENTAL-CONSCIOUSNESS-SEED-ATOM.

MENTAL-TRAVEL-IN-TIME—see PROPHECY.

MENTALIST—1. one who combines stage magic and psychism; 2. an entertainer who consciously attempts to use ordinary sensorimotor means to imitate psi phenomena; one who performs an extraordinary feat by sleight of hand and deceptive devices and infers it is a psychic feat.

MENTATION—to mentally place a positive trait of character in a specific part of the body to overcome a congested area; objective is to change a negative energy that cuases tension to a positive energy that causes relaxation; e.g., "I put patience in my shoulders"; executed through mental processing, such as VISUALIZATION, AFFIRMATIONS, HYPNOSIS, and telepathic suggestions. [cf. VISUAL-IMAGERY TECHNIQUE, SOLEMNIZING THE MIND]

MENTICIDE—(destructive-brainwashing) a systematic effort to undermine and destroy a person's values and beliefs through prolonged interrogation; a dangerous form of mental coercion by attacking the mind with feelings of fear, terror and hopelessness; coercive phraseology repeated daily results in Pavlovian conditioning and the mind can no longer exercise free will; used in some DESTRUCTIVE-BRAINWASHING CULTS. [cf. SUGGESTION, MENTAL TELEPATHY, SPELLED, MASS HYPNOSIS]

MENTIFEROUS—see MENTAL TELEPATHY.

MENTO-MENTAL ACTION —(early 1900s) a psychic impression transferred from one who is about to go through a traumatic or emotional event to a close friend or relative at the moment it is happening or about to happen; soul-mind of the victim desires to let someone know about the emotional event and unexpectedly impresses a friend or relative who is in a relaxed state, with the announcement, precise and detailed. [cf. EMOTIONAL PSI, CRISIS PHENOMENA, IMPRESSION, DOUBLE APPEARANCE, PSYCHIC YELL, SPONTANEOUS PSI]

MENTO-MENTAL ACTION CLAIRVOYANCE—see EMOTIONAL CLAIRVOYANCE.

MENTO-PHYSICAL—pertains to a type of PSYCHISM or MEDIUMSHIP that could fall in both the category of mental psychism or physical psychism; also pertains to those skills that lack sufficient research to date to know how the phenomenon is manifested; see Appendix 2 for listing of mento-physical types of skills.

MENTOR—(esoteric) see ETHERIC WORLD INTELLIGENCE.

MERCURIAL ROD—see DOWSING ROD.

MERCURIUS—see SOUL-MIND.

MERCURIUS PHILOSOPHORUM—an all-pervading, all-uniting influence that connects heaven and earth, governed by the law of sympathy; see SYMPATHETIC MAGIC. Syn. ANIMA MUNDI, MAGICIAN'S FIRE, JACOB'S LADDER. [cf. ALCHEMIST, PHILOSOPHER'S STONE, SYMBOLS, ASSOCIATED MAGIC]

MERCURY—(alchemy) one of the basic components necessary in the refining process of both metals and soul-minds; found in all matter; possesses the quality of fusibility; convertible from solid to liquid by heat; corresponds to human CONSCIOUSNESS, which when brought together or fused, becomes an instrument of expressing power and brings wakefulness into the consciousness; also called QUICKSILVER or **living silver** because it is mobile which is the basis of its importance as the

SPIRIT of alchemy. [cf. QUINTESSENCE, FIRE OF THE SAGES, ILLUMINATION]

MERCY BAND—a group of ETHERIC WORLD INTELLIGENCES that worked with Mrs. Anna Wickland for over thirty years when she helped earthlings who were haunted; Anna transferred the earthbound entity to herself and gave them understanding and knowledge so they would leave her and not attach her or himself to another earthling; the mercy band's function was to keep Anna from becoming obsessed herself. [cf. OBSESSION, HAUNTING, EARTHBOUND ENTITIES, STATIC ELECTRICITY]

MERCY GROUND—(West Africa) a magnetized, sandy area outside the church, which is set aside for EXORCISM purposes; at intervals the church holds WATCH SERVICES that diminish any inferior etheric world entities who work through those who trance; the service encourages superior ETHERIC WORLD INTELLIGENCES to replace the others. [cf. CHERUBIM AND SERAPHIM MOVEMENT, MAGNETISM]

MERIDIA—see MERIDIAN LINES.

MERIDIAN LINES—(China) twelve, invisible, electrical NERVE FLUID lines in the human body running from the tips of the feet and fingers to the head area connecting all the major organs and glands; these invisible lines have a definite relationship to one's physical health; these body nerve fluid lines behave identical with the universal movements of the sun, earth, moon, and planets; at various intervals the lines contain special areas or points of concentrated energy which compare to the nodes in the air, making the body inseparable from the whole system. Syn. BODY ZONES. [cf. ACUPUNCTURE POINTS, CYCLES, ACUPUNCTURE, REFLEXOLOGY]

MERIDIAN THERAPY—any kind of treatment that has as its basis for healing a method of releasing and breaking up the congested pressure points along the MERIDIAN LINES; this causes the flow of energy within the nerves to return, aiding the body cells to normalize, so the intelligence in the cells heal themselves; healing methods which use meridian therapy; REFLEXOLOGY, COLOR HEALING, MUSIC THERAPY, KINESIOLOGY, NEUROMUSCULAR MASSAGE, ACUPUNCTURE, ACUPRESSURE, MAGNETIC HEALING.

MERKABAH—(Kabbalah) a text containing the sacred, secret structure of the universe, the higher and the lower mansions in the invisible worlds, and how the INITIATE passes through the mansions. [**cf.** THRONE MYSTICISM, WHITE BROTHERHOOD, AKASHIC RECORDS, DEAD SEA SCROLLS]

MERKABAH MYSTICISM—(Jewish, Old Testament) a doctrine in which one main aspect consisted of mental projections into the higher realms of the etheric world; ADEPT had a clear psychic vision of the higher realms; only chosen disciples were permitted to engage in the sitting for a mystical visionary experience of divine intervention; it was called "concentration on the throne of glory" or a "chariot vision"; adept sat until he or she experienced the ascension of their soul which could take many days; e.g., from biblical passages: 1. "I saw the Lord sitting on the throne and all the host of heaven standing beside him"; 2. Ezekiel reached into the higher realms of the etheric world when he had a great vision of wheels (which was meant for the rabbis and the chosen). [**cf.** CHARIOT, SEALS, GERMAN HASIDISM, PERILS OF THE SOUL, DARKNESS OF IGNORANCE, GREY WORLD, ISLES OF THE BLEST]

MERMAIDS—one of the minor ELEMENTALS in the NATURE KINGDOM, part human and part fish; both kind and helpful or dangerous; female. [**cf.** NATURE SPIRIT, DIMENSION-SHIFTING, SOULLESS]

MERMAN—one of the minor ELEMENTALS in the NATURE KINGDOM, part human and part fish; both kind and helpful or dangerous; male.

MERUDANDA—(Hinduism) see KUNDALINI.

MESCALIN—a psychedelic drug that is used to induce an ALTERED STATE OF CONSCIOUSNESS; comes from the mescal cactus plant; under its influence time recedes and a heightened awareness of color and form is experienced. [**cf.** JIMSONWEED, PERSONAL QUEST, PSYCHEDELIC CONSCIOUSNESS]

MESCALITO—(botane) a PSYCHOTROPIC PLANT that causes hallucinations; human form ascribed to the plant; an anthropomorphic power of peyote. [**cf.** FORCED PSI Appendix 2]

MESMERIC FLUID—(hypnosis) subtle energy going from the eye of the hypnotist to the body of the subject; discovered by Franz Anton Mesmer; see MAGNETIC FLUID. **Syn.** ANIMALIZED FLUID, ANIMAL MAGNETISM, UNIVERSAL FLUID. [**cf.** Appendix 5 HYPNOTHERAPY]

MESMERISM—(1766) an early form of hypotism

discovered by a German physician Franz Anton Mesmer; he used hand passes which were thought to convey a vital essence or fluid, which dominated the patient's will; this fluid he named ANIMAL MAGNETISM; his system also consisted of the use of magnets in which the force in the magnet was transferred from the magnet to the patient aiding a cure for poor health; Mesmer made the parallel between the magnetism in humans and in the magnet, declaring human magnetism (VITAL FLUID) is transferred from the eyes and hands of the hypnotist the same as magnetism is transfered from the magnet. **Syn.** HYPNOTISM. [**cf.** ANIMAL MAGNETISM, HYPNOTHERAPY Appendix 5]

MESSAGE—personal psychic information given by a MEDIUM or PSYCHIC to a client seeking counsel or prophecy for her or himself; information can be about client's personality potentials to present solutions, problems, prophecy, deceased or living friends, relatives and pets; information is executed through CLAIRVOYANCE, CLAIRSENTIENCE, PSYCHOMETRY and other types of skills; message is usually short; i.e., two to fifteen minutes. **Syn.** READING. [**cf.** READING, PSYCHIC INFORMATION, LIFE READING, TAROT CARDS]

MESSAGE BEARER—1. a MENTAL MEDIUM who gives out psychic information which comes from the ETHERIC WORLD INTELLIGENCE; 2. a mental medium who stands on her or his feet and brings a very short (two to five minute) psychic message to persons in a public gathering; information is given to them from their etheric guide. **Syn.** STANDING READER, MESSAGE WORKER. [**cf.** ATTUNEMENT, MESSAGE, LIGHT TRANCE.]

MESSAGE HOUND—(slang) a person who goes to a different Spiritualist Church every week for the purpose of receiving the mini-message at the end of the service, with no desire to learn from the sermon. [**cf.** MESSAGE WORKERS, READINGS, STANDUP READERS, BILLET READING]

MESSAGE WORKER—a MENTAL MEDIUM who gives short readings to persons in a congregation after the religious service is over; occurs most frequently in Spiritualist churches; from one to four mediums serve each service; each worker brings forth a two to five minute reading to as many persons as possible in his or her alloted time (ten to fifteen minutes); medium works in a LIGHT TRANCE state while standing on their feet, allowing their guide to intervene and give them the information through CLAIRVOYANCE and CLAIR-SENTIENCE; psychic information pertains to one's past, future, present problems, health, spiritual growth, warnings, and living and deceased family, friends, and pets; congregation does not ask questions nor request a reading. **Syn.** STAND-UP READER, MESSAGE BEARER. [**cf.** UNDER, DEEP TRANCE, GUIDE]

MESSENGER—see GUIDE.

META—prefix meaning "above and beyond."

META-PROTO-MATTER—(Theosophy) a fast vibrational frequency of atoms in the etheric world that form the super-etheric plane. (Inconcl.) [**cf.** LAW OF VIBRATION Appendix 7, ATOMS, THOUGHT ENERGY, BUDDHIC PLANE, SEVENTH PLANE]

METABOLIC MONITOR—(invented by Maury Bonnain, innovated by June Bletzer) a tiny sophisticated BIOFEEDBACK INSTRUMENT (similar to a GSR), that measures the body's entire metabolic system; uses both pulsating and DC current; electrodes are attached to middle finger of both hands; uses a digital readout in numbers of 2,000 increments; because it is without sound, it allows the subject to use relaxation techniques that require music or a guided instructor and to hear instructions from the biofeedback therapist (without taking off the earphones, as in most styles); numbers make it possible to LOG at each session, and 2,000 numbers enables one to see even the slightest improvement in each session; immune to outside artifacts; a helpful tool for MEDITATION, HYPNOTHERAPY, psychic experiments, and for recognizing what causes stress in one's life; see BIO-STAT MONITOR. [**cf.** BIOFEEDBACK TRAINING, STRESS MONITOR]

METACOMMAND LANGUAGE—(John Lilly) concepts that one consciously and deliberately forms as she or he goes through life's experiences; these are dropped into the memory storage to surface when needed to form more decisions regarding new material related to the same subject. [**cf.** SUBCONSCIOUS MIND, METAPROGRAMMING, SUBJECTIVE PROGRAMMING, AKASHIC RECORD]

METACOSMOGRAPHY—see ASTRAL PROJECTION.

METAGNOME—(France) see MEDIUM and PSYCHIC.

METAGNOMY—(France) see PSYCHIC ART and MENTAL PSYCHISM.

METAGRAPHOLOGY—to give a short message or

an answer to one's problem by holding paper between one's hands on which the subject has written, (without reading the words on the paper); psychic tunes into the emotions of the subject that are given out from the words on the paper regardless of the words per se. **Syn.** PRACTICAL PSYCHOMETRY. [**cf.** PURE PSYCHOMETRY, BILLET READING]

METAL FROM THE SKY—(Egypt) see TAMING OF FIRE.

METALLOTHERAPY—the use of metals for healing ill persons; works especially well with hysteria. [**cf.** UNORTHODOX HEALING, HOLISTIC HEALTH, MAGNETS, CELL SALTS]

METAMORPHOSIS—transformation of one's self into a different structure, form, or substance for a time by physical means and the subsequent transformation back to one's original form; psychic makes a complete change in appearance, performs the task intended and goes back to normal; 1. an ETHERIC WORLD INTELLIGENCE can appear in human or animal form; 2. psychic can transform into animal (reptile, WEREWOLF, hawk) or a flower; 3. inanimate objects can transform into real life forms (a wax model can come alive); the EGYPTIAN BOOK OF THE DEAD carries formulas to give one metamorphic ability to return in any form one pleases after death. [**cf.** DIMENSION-SHIFTING, ALCHEMY, MENTAL TRANSMUTATION]

METANOIA—a higher state of consciousness than normal everyday awareness. [**cf.** MENTAL MANIFESTATION PROCESSES]

METAPATTERNS—(John Lilly) millions of correlated patterns lying passively in the Total Mind ready to be tapped into by living active people; made from parts of personal metapatterns that are broken up when the person dies and added to the Total Mind meta-patterns. **Syn.** COLLECTIVE UNCONSCIOUS, EARTH AKASHIC RECORDS. [**cf.** PERSONAL METAPATTERNS, BELIEF SYSTEMS, OTHER PERSONS, PROGRAMMING PROPERTIES]

METAPHOR—psychic information that comes in a word or phrase to express a feeling or concept that shows a comparison, but does not mean the words per se; occurs in a CLAIRAUDIENT message, in a dream, in AUTOMATIC WRITING; e.g., "my cup runneth over" would mean the person's life would be filled with so many wonderful experiences that they could hardly handle them. [**cf.** SYMBOLS, PAR-

ABLES, SOUL-COMPLEX, METAPHYSICAL INTERPRETATIONS]

METAPHYSICAL EMPTINESS—a state of consciousness during MEDITATION when one does not feel time, space, or movement, but feels a VOID or "pure being." [**cf.** SEED MEDITATION, SILENT INTONING, HOLY BREATH, BLISS, BLANK PERIODS]

METAPHYSICAL HEALING—to motivate a "permanent" healing that does not return, at another time or in another place in the body, in a different form; situations, events and activities are given to an individual to learn lessons and when these are not handled or settled at the time they occur, they cause a broken circuit in the emotional (electrical) nervous sytem; this is not repaired until that particular experience is resolved and is accompanied by an attitudinal change, regardless of time or incarnations; pressure point areas in which the broken circuit exists will not allow the vital magnetic fluid to flow until mentally-emotionally repaired; any healing, traditional or holistic alternatives are only temporary cures unless the cause is found and resolved. [**cf.** LAW OF HEALING Appendix 7, HOLISTIC HEALTH, ALTERNATIVES, METAPHYSICS]

METAPHYSICAL PHYSICIAN—see ALCHEMIST, and INNER BAND.

METAPHYSICALLY ARRANGED—coined by Robert Frank; to receive or gain something one has specifically asked for through VISUALIZATION or AFFIRMATIONS but one made no conventional attempts to attain it or purchase it, e.g., two irritant coworkers becoming good friends overnight with neither one making any apologies, (one worker had been repeating "harmony" affirmations), a neighbor giving a color TV to a family she hardly knew because she had too many TVs (mother of family had been visualizing a color TV for her family), a cat crying on a doorstep of a person who had been affirming, "I am free from being alone." [**cf.** VISUALIZATION, END-RESULT, VISUAL-IMAGERY TECHNIQUE]

METAPHYSICIAN—one who studies, understands and tries to practice the laws of METAPHYSICS; one working with the science of being and growing. **Syn.** METAPHYSICIST. [**cf.** HOLISTIC HEALTH, METAPHYSICS]

METAPHYSICS—(*meta,* "higher and beyond") beyond earth physics or invisible physics; 1. a philosophical doctrine that all things are a part of one main source (intelligence and energy), and that each thing, animate or inanimate, should be respected for its particular form of this one main source; therefore, each thing has an independent function and is dependent upon every other thing, and all are contributing to the main source; 2. a branch of philosophy that treats first principles; 3. (Rosicrucian) an inquiry into knowledge; 4. (Gilbert Holloway) a systematic study, refinement, and development of COSMIC CONSCIOUSNESS; 5. advanced knowledge of evolution not taught in formal education; should not be accepted unless a "compatible feeling" accompanies it (not to be intellectualized only); 6. a study of PHYSICS in which one should not attempt to solve all questions materially but accept that which happens obviously, even when no scientific explanation can account for it; 7. (metaphysical religions) imply that God is the one main source, therefore, evil, suffering, and change are aspects of GOD as well as all the good and perfectness in the world. **Syn.** PANTHEISM. [**cf.** Appendix 4 to differentiate from RELIGION]

METAPROGRAMMER—(John Lilly) the SOULMIND of a person; the life force that never dies, even when the physical body expires; carries with it into the ETHERIC WORLD all of its personal programming; this personal programming contributes to the METAPATTERNS. [**cf.** AKASHIC RECORDS, COSMIC MEMORY, REACTIVE MIND, PASSIVE SOUL]

METAPROGRAMMING—(John Lilly) an invisible operation in which a central control system holds "built-in" experiences from the past history of mankind in earth; the growth of all human beings operates in parallel simultaneously within each one's SYMPATHETIC NERVOUS SYSTEM; these built-in experiences are from genetic codes, people and their cultures and lifestyles, protomammals, reptiles, myths, etc. **Syn.** INSTINCT, COLLECTIVE UNCONSCIOUS. [**cf.** SERPENTS OF WISDOM, GOD-BRAIN, REPROGRAMMING, COSMIC STREAM]

METAPSYCHIATRY—coined by Stanley Dean; refers to the interface between psychiatry and psychic-mystic experiences; "an existence of realities that are yet beyond perceptual intellectual apprehension but are accessible to consciousness"; a developing branch of psychiatry that deals with psychic phenomena, from shamanistic practice, to chemical alteration of states of consciousness. [**cf.** PARAPSYCHOLOGY, MYSTICISM, PSYCHIC COUNSELING]

METAPSYCHIC PHENOMENOLOGY—(clinical) the study of how and why dogs and cats travel over great distances to return home. [cf. ANPSI Appendix 2]

METAPSYCHIQUE—(France) see PARAPSYCHOLOGY.

METAPSYCHISM—see PARAPSYCHOLOGY.

METAPSYCHIST—see PSYCHIC.

METAPSYCHOLOGIST—one who teaches PARAPSYCHOLOGY.

METAPSYCHOLOGY—see PARAPSYCHOLOGY.

METAPSYCHOSIS—see PSYCHIC ART.

METATHEORETICAL—a new way of looking at oneself and the world that is beyond the theory of the day; theories that are not in accordance with the majority. [cf. NEW-AGE PSYCHOLOGY Appendix 5]

METEMPSYCHOSIS—the rebirth of the SOUL-MIND in another body of either animal or human immediately after the physical death; (do not confuse with REINCARNATION). [cf. TRANSMIGRATION, KARMA]

METEMSOMATOSIS—theory: a human does not always live in this earth type of body; some incarnations in the past and in the future one will have or has had a body made of another substance. [cf. EVOLUTION, CYCLES, REINCARNATION, KARMA, MASS KARMA, STAR CHILDREN]

METETHERIAL—(F.W.H. Myers) beyond the ETHER; the transcendental spiritual world. [cf. HIGHER REALMS, MANSIONS, NIRVANIC PLANE, SIXTH PLANE]

METHOD+PATTERN—an individual ritualistic process the psychic goes through to find the level of awareness in which he or she feels comfortable where they can successfully perform; psychic found this process by practice and SITTING until they established what was best for them; patterns that have proved successful: CLOAK OF INSULATION, MEDITATION beforehand, PRAYER, repeating special phrases, sitting or standing in a particular posture, wearing a special AMULET, holding a stone, etc. **Syn.** GETTING IN TUNE, GOING-TO-LEVEL. [cf. NARROW BAND TUNING, AWAKE CONTROL, FREE-STATE OF CONSCIOUSNESS, ATTUNEMENT]

METOPOSCY—to judge one's character and destiny using the lines on the forehead. [cf. PHRENOLOGY, HAND READING, MOLESCOPY]

MEVLEVIS—see WHIRLING DERVISHES.

MI-URGE—(Gnosis) see TOTALITY.

MIB—see MEN IN BLACK.

MICAWBER—a PSYCHIC who keeps her or himself in a receptive state of consciousness for any kind of psychic information; useless and dangerous to one's physical and mental well-being; one who has their psychic doors open all the time receives from negative vibrations as well as positive ones, and could pick up atmospheric and environmental conditions, illnesses, and negative emotions of fear, anxiety, jealousy, hauntings, etc., from earthbound entities; brings mental confusion, illness and overwhelming sensations that throw one out of balance. [cf. SHIELDING, CLOAK OF INSULATION, EMPATHY CLAIRSENTIENCE, LAW OF LIKE ATTRACTS LIKE Appendix 7]

MICHAEL—an archangel who had charge over the country Israel in 500 B.C.; worked through Daniel when he was in a TRANCE state of consciousness; Michael was superlative in character with a vast knowledge to draw upon; represents the solar forces in their aspect of spiritual power; guardian of the Supernal Fire; had charge of approaches to higher consciousness from the Infernal Fire. [cf. ANGELOLOGY, GREAT ONES]

MICRO—prefix meaning "small"; a millionth part of a unit.

MICRO COFMUS—(Robert Fludd) a drawing of man within a CIRCLE; his arms are outstretched and his legs are straddled, both touching the circle edge; within the circle is a TRIANGLE and SQUARE also; depicts man as a MICROCOSM, and the universe as MACROCOSM. [cf. LAW OF MICRO/MACROCOSM Appendix 7, MACROMOLECULAR BASIS MEMORY]

MICROCOSM—(Greek, "miniature world") a human being or any other organic mass that is a miniature replica of the great MACROCOSM, the UNIVERSE; the tiniest particle in the universe that one discovers will always be the microcosm containing all that the macrocosm contains; see LAW OF MICRO/MACROCOSM Appendix 7. [cf. MACROCOSM, TOTALITY]

MICROCOSMOLOGY—the science of human beings and society as being miniature replicas of the universes.

MICROPSIA—to sense the feeling that the world is shrinking. [**cf.** ELONGATION, MENTAL PROJECTION, MACROPSIA]

MICROVOLTS—abbr. MV, millionth of a volt.

MID-DAY WOMAN—(Slavic) 1. a NATURE SPIRIT that lives in the woods and comes out during the daytime to work; hinders or helps human beings; 2. see VAMPIRES.

MID-STREAM MASTER—a SOUL-MIND who has earned the MASTER level of consciousness and chooses to serve mankind in an earthly body, but not to incarnate from the womb of a woman; master understands the law of TRANSMUTATION so he or she materializes as a full grown adult; without past personal history, they have no image to overcome and no wasted years as a child, making it easier to accomplish the task that they incarnated for; masters always serve civilization and never serve themselves. [**cf.** INCARNATIONAL EXCHANGE, MATERIALIZATION, WALK-IN]

MID-WAY SPIRITS—discarnate etheric world entities that communicate with earthlings. [**cf.** ETHERIC WORLD INTELLIGENCES Appendix 2]

MIDDLE KINGDOM—a level of consciousness in between the light regions where FAIRIES live; this vibrational frequency is deceiving to human awareness as it sometimes seems over the horizon and sometimes beneath one's feet. [**cf.** LIGHT ETHER, SUBSURFACE KINGDOMS, SYSTEM OF PROBABILITIES]

MIDDLE WORLD—the EARTH; theory: there is a world of living beings inside the earth, and living beings in the ETHERIC WORLD. [**cf.** INNER-EARTH CIVILIZATIONS, ATMOSPHERIC PHYSICS, NETWORKS OF CIVILIZATIONS]

MIDEWIWIN—(Native American) the secret society of the shamans; established by the etheric world entities. [**cf.** SUMMERLAND, SPACE BROTHERS, WHITE BROTHERHOOD, ANGELOLOGY]

MIDGARD—(Hinduism) a great cosmic serpent recognized as the lord of all serpents having no evil intentions; functions to help mankind. [**cf.** SERPENT, COSMOS, SYMBOLS, KUNDALINI POWER]

MIDSUMMER EVE FERN SEED—(William Shakespeare) has properties that can make human beings invisible; used for protection; known by its bluish flames. [**cf.** BOTANE, DIMENSION-SHIFTING, INVISIBILITY]

MIDSUMMER MEN—a purple-flowered stone-crop with the properties to answer questions regarding marriage. **Syn.** ORPINE. [**cf.** BOTANE, PLANT CONVERSATIONS, INSANE ROOT, MANDRAKE FRUITS]

MIGHTY DEAD—see ETHERIC WORLD ENTITIES.

MIGRATION—the transfer of matter in the form of solid, liquid, and gases from one form to another subject to the law of thought. [**cf.** LAW OF THOUGHT Appendix 7, MATTER, ATOMS]

MILKY WAY—(esoteric) the galaxy in which the solar system is located; visible as a luminous band in the night sky; the storehouse of soul-minds waiting to be incarnated. [**cf.** PLANETARY WORKERS, SOUL-MIND, MASTER]

MILL OF THE GODS—(esoteric) TEMPORARY AKASHIC RECORDS which are distributed from the HEART-SEED-ATOM through the blood stream and glandular system; in this way KARMA manifests one's body and one's experiences. [**cf.** AKASHIC RECORDS, LIFE-CORD-HEART-SEED-ATOM, MENTAL-REFLECTING-ETHER, EMOTIONAL-ASTRAL-SEED-ATOM]

MIMICRY—see LAW OF MIMICRY Appendix 7.

MIND—(capitalized) in the beginning was the WORD, or UNIVERSAL MIND, intelligence or thought; see TOTALITY; 2. (uncapitalized) (a) (parapsychology) an invisible source of intelligence which flows through the human brain; an ethereal vibrational frequency that contains an individual's AKASHIC RECORDS and present BELIEF SYSTEM; also called the SUBCONSCIOUS MIND, BIOCOMPUTER, and SOUL-MIND; see these for details; (b) (humanistic scientists) the term is used to acknowledge that mankind has access to another source of intelligence other than the physical brain; under research presently. [**cf.** BRAIN]

MIND EXPANSION—blanket term used if one feels he or she has reached a higher state of awareness; to allow the conscious, decision-making mind to become passive and the subconscious or superconscious mind to activate causing an awareness at another level; occurs in MENTAL PROJECTION, ASTRAL PROJECTION, MEDITATION, BIOFEEDBACK TRAINING and some MENTAL PSYCHIC PROCESSES. [**cf.** INTONING, TAMING OF THE MIND]

MIND EXPERIENCE—1. a blanket phrase encompassing any experience that pertains to psychic work, MEDITATION, or other ALTERED STATES OF

CONSCIOUSNESS; the subject has a new awareness outside the realm of the CONSCIOUS MIND; **2.** a subjective activity of the SUBCONSCIOUS MIND (pleasurable or unpleasurable) in which the person is aware of it at the time it occurs; brought about by meditation, HYPNOSIS, and with RECREATIONAL DRUGS. [**cf.** ALTERED STATES OF CONSCIOUSNESS, MENTAL ACTIVITY, NON-ORDINARY REALITY]

MIND PHOTOGRAPHY—see THOUGHTOGRAPHY.

MIND RAIDER—a psychic who practices reading the mind of those he or she comes in contact with in their everyday activity; intentionally executed. [**cf.** MENTAL TELEPATHY Appendix 2]

MIND READING—to tune into another person's mind and know what she or he is thinking or know what she or he is going to say before they say it; executed intentionally and unintentionally. [**cf.** MIND RAIDER, LOVE-LINE, MENTAL TELEPATHY, TELEPATHY]

MIND TECHNOLOGIES—see PSYCHOTECH-NOLOGIES.

MIND WANDERING—uncontrolled, INNER-MIND PICTURES of persons, figures, or scenes, induced deliberately in an exercise used to strengthen the IMAGINATION faculty; accomplished by listening to strange sounds or unfamiliar music, staring at an abstract picture or being guided by a leader; pictures are being drawn "into" the mind and therefore will not manifest in future behavior as normal thinking; (do not confuse with DAY-DREAMING, CONSCIOUS FANTASY, or HALLUCI-NATION; see Appendix 4 for clarification). **Syn.** IMAGERY. [**cf.** THOUGHT-FORMS Appendix 5]

MIND'S EYE—**1.** an imaginary area inside the forehead, between the eyes, which is used as a POINT-OF-FOCUS for many mental psychic skills, i.e., CLAIRVOYANCE, VISUALIZATION, CLAIR-AUDIENCE, CLAIRSENTIENCE; when the physical eyes are turned upward to stare at this area, the body relaxes more quickly aiding the goal achievement. Usage: "Look into your mind's eye and tell me what you perceive"; **2.** see THIRD-EYE AREA; **3.** to perceive a vision and feel that one is seeing inside the head. **Syn.** THIRD-EYE, SIXTH SENSE, PSYCHISM. [**cf.** POINT-OF-FOCUS Appendix 2, SUBJECTIVE CLAIRVOYANCE]

MIND-AWARENESS MOVEMENT—a current trend throughout the globe to seek a means of increasing one's potential, receive more satisfaction from life,

and to maintain one's self-worth; movement motivated by the AQUARIAN AGE; individuals seek new disciplines, techniques that require mind activity, a change in the style of exercise, mind therapies for physical cures, change in beliefs, food habits, etc.; reopened the study of MEDITATION, OCCULTISM, MYSTICISM, KARATE, YOGA, METAPHYSICS, etc., and opened new doors of HOLISTIC HEALTH, PARAPSYCHOLOGY, and DREAM RESEARCH LABORATORIES. (Inconcl.) [**cf.** CONSCIOUSNESS AWARENESS MOVEMENT, PLANETARY WORKERS, TRANSFORMATION]

MIND-BODY ART—(biofeedback training) (Barbara Brown) theory: one can use his or her own biofeedback patterns of lines that they created while being hooked to an EEG for therapeutic purposes. (Inconcl.) [**cf.** BIOFEEDBACK TRAINING, UNORTHODOX HEALING, LAW OF REPETITION Appendix 7]

MIND-BODY DISCIPLINE—theory: the mind can control or influence the functions of the body at will, even those classified as involuntary; a new discovery to Westerners presented through the use of BIOFEEDBACK TRAINING that shows that the mind and emotions of human beings constantly affect the physical body; ancient and Eastern philosophies have preached and demonstrated this for years; biofeedback instruments give instant evidence of what happens within the body in regards to changes of thoughts and emotions. (Inconcl.) [**cf.** MIND-LINK, BODY-LINK, HOLISM, LAW OF SUBSERVIENCE Appendix 7, BODY CONTROL Appendix 2]

MIND-BRAIN MACHINE—see EEG and ELECTRO-ENCEPHALOGRAPH.

MIND-BRAIN SCIENTISTS—individuals who study the electrical activity of the brain and its intellectual-memory function, as opposed to the study of its physical nature (such as, brain tumors). [**cf.** BIO-FEEDBACK TRAINING Appendix 5]

MIND-CAUSED ACCIDENT—coined by E. Arthur Winkler; "accidental injuries" are eighty percent of the time due to PSYCHOSOMATIC conditions of one or more persons involved in the accident; individual is unable to handle an emotional conflict any longer, becomes susceptible to having something unpleasant occur physically as well as emotionally as a necessity for him or her not to handle the present emotional conflict; accident-prone individuals can be cured by HYPNOTHERAPY. [**cf.** NEW-AGE PSYCHOLOGY, ILLNESS]

MIND-CLEANSING MEDITATION—(karate) a type of motionless quietude required for ten minutes of each hour during a KARATE session. [**cf.** MARTIAL ARTS Appendix 5]

MIND-DRIFT—a break in one's concentration when one is giving full attention to his or her meditation FOCAL POINT, BIOFEEDBACK TRAINING instructions, or to the TARGET of the psychic skill; ruins one's goal or lessens the degree of success for that time; happens less frequently as one masters control over their mind activity; thoughts and problems of the day, past experiences, guilts, and visions can surface when one is in an ALPHA STATE OF CONSCIOUSNESS; what is in the mind-drift may or may not prove helpful in PSCHOANALYSIS: if the mind consistently drifts, one can take a five minute mind-drift break and let it all float through without giving the thoughts any energy or consideration; the mind is then ready to behave and recenter its attention on the project. [**cf.** INNER-DIALOGUE, SLEEPITATE, LAW OF ATTENTION Appendix 7]

MIND-ENERGY—(esoteric) 1. ergs of electrical, intelligent, energy constantly emanating from a human being's head; rate of vibration of these ergs pertains to the individual's thoughts with their accompanying emotions; 2. a LIFE FORCE of a higher vibrational frequency than ETHERIC ENERGY or ASTRAL LIGHT energy; functions as an intricately organized network of complex fields through the neuronal network of the brain organ, controlling the synaptic connections and processes of the whole electrical system; 3. mind-energy originates from COSMIC ENERGY and enters the head constantly in minute quantities; it reaches the PINEAL GLAND where it is transmuted into electrical energy to be used by the brain area; travels to the PITUITARY GLAND where it is transmuted into physical energy suitable for use by the glands and other physical systems; travels back to the brain to be transmuted back into electrical energy for brain use; used in the thinking process and emanates out in electrical form to be utilized by the "main switchboard" (TOTALITY) to do its work; keeps in perpetual flow by the power of the UNIVERSAL SEED and is used in the body according to the emotional state of the individual and the soul-mind level. (Inconcl.) [**cf.** BRAIN Appendix 2, VIBRATIONS, LAW OF SOUL-MIND Appendix 7]

MIND-LINK/BODY-LINK—(Russia) theory: there is an intellectual, instinctual and physical link within all living things, and a change in one's instinct or intellect promotes a change in all other living things. [**cf.** PSYCHOPHYSIOLOGICAL PROCESSES, HOLISTIC THEORY, HOLISM]

MIND-LINKING—the transfer of thought, unintentionally, among members of a gathering when the group is in one accord or emotionally compatible; can be recognized from feedback of imagery exercises because many fantasize the same thing, or is recognized in psychic experiments wherein members tune into each other instead of the target. (Inconcl.) [**cf.** GROUP TELEPATHY, SELECTIVE TELEPATHY]

MIND-MACHINES—see BLACK BOX.

MIND-MIRROR—(biofeedback training) a multichannel EEG that gives feedback from each brain hemisphere simultaneously and records the unique brain wave patterns of psychic and spiritual healers; developed by C. Maxwell Cade and Nona Coxhead. (Inconcl.) [**cf.** FIFTH STATE OF CONSCIOUSNESS, SPLIT-BRAIN HEMISPHERES Appendix 5]

MIND-OVER-MATTER—1. metaphysical doctrine: human beings live in a "mental" world and everything in it is made and held together by their thoughts and emotions; humans co-create life forms, inanimate objects, atmosphereic conditions, their bodies and the earth proper; the invisible electrical impulses that emanate endlessly from their heads direct the course of the cosmic atoms; these impulses are influenced by people's daytime thinking, speaking, reading, INNER-DIALOGUE, and their dreams and sleep thinking, bringing about a three-dimensional manifestation; one can deliberately co-create what he or she desires to manifest by using VISUALIZATION, AFFIRMATIONS, HYPNOTHERAPY, and disciplined THINKING; (do not confuse with a NON-THOUGHT that does not originate from "within" the head). (Inconcl.) 2. psychic skill: to concentrate on an object with intense undivided attention until the object is moved or altered in size or condition; (Sheila Ostrander) "mind over force field"; (J.B. Rhine) "influence exerted on an external physical process, condition or object by the percipient"; see PSYCHOKINESIS. (Inconcl.) [**cf.** Appendix 4 for clarification]

MIND-TO-OBJECT COMMUNICATION—(laboratory) see PSYCHOKINESIS.

MIND-TYPE PHENOMENA—see MENTAL PSYCHISM.

MIND/BODY and MIND-BODY—(written either

way) denotes that a human being's two main functions, the thinking mind and physical body are one system; these two main functions have defined independent goals but will continue to coincide because they work constantly as agents contributing to, and dependent upon, each other, making it all one system; one cannot separate the reactions of the body from the state of mind, and one cannot separate the reactions of the mind from the state of the physical body. (Inconcl.) [cf. BLOCKS, HOLOGRAM BRAIN THEORY, GESTALT, CONSCIOUSNESS]

MINDFULNESS—to be consciously aware of one's body movements, thoughts, and emotions while in a normal waking state. [cf. SENSITIVE, INSTINCT, NARROW-BAND TUNING, INNER-DIALOGUE, NERVE ELECTRICITY]

MINDLESS SHELL—see ASTRAL SHELL.

MINERAL CONSCIOUSNESS—a vibrational frequency of minerals, stones, and gems which causes them to attract to themselves the emotions of people for miles around, and to cause them to tune into the aura of their environment; stones have been known to warn living organisms in their environment of danger and to give out special vibrations accordingly for the living organisms' use; recognized as an OVERALL CONSCIOUSNESS or an ATTRACTION CONSCIOUSNESS; stones attract emotions, and have been used as amulets, or psychic tools since the beginning of time; used for protection, for stepping up owner's psychic ability, and for healing agents. (Inconcl.) [cf. MINPSI, CRYSTAL, SCRYING, CALUNDRONIUS, GOD-AS-THE-STONE]

MINERAL KINGDOM—(esoteric) primal condition of everything that exists in earth today; atoms congregate and begin as soil or sand; they grow in consciousness and emerge into stones, minerals, and gems; these minerals evolve and grow in CONSCIOUSNESS and emerge into the PLANT KINGDOM, the ANIMAL KINGDOM, and then the HUMAN BEING KINGDOM; the human physical body still contains the minerals of the stones; because the minerals have a consciousness that gives and takes and have the same chemicals as the human, they make a good healing agent and psychic tool for the human. (Inconcl.) [cf. MINPSI, OVERALL CONSCIOUSNESS]

MINERAL SALTS—(healing) an inorganic material found in minute quantities in the body which is essential to maintain or restore the chemical balance so the body can more easily heal itself. (Inconcl.) **Syn.** CELL SALTS, TISSUE SALTS. [cf. CELLULAR THERAPY, UNORTHODOX HEALING, PSYCHIC HEALING, CURATIVE EDUCATION]

MING STICKS—(China) narrowed numbered sticks that correspond to numbered "fortunes" and "your luck for the day" which is printed in a book; a cylinder is filled with ming sticks which the querant shakes and thrusts forward so one stick falls out; this stick bears the number of this or her fortune and luck for that day. [cf. CASTING OF LOTS, I CHING, SYNCHRONICITY]

MINI-MICRO FILMS—(esoteric) minute pictures of every activity an individual performs during each incarnation in earth; taken by an invisible MENTAL-REFLECTING-ETHER that hovers close to the human physical body; these minute pictures are frequently seen by those who are clinically dead and return to life to tell others; pictures infiltrate throughout the blood stream, the heart, and possibly in the DNA of the cells; a mechanism that provides an individual with his or her KARMA that gives one experiences and a body condition that comes from one's own previous activity. (Inconcl.) [cf. DEATHBED EXPERIENCES, MENTAL PLANE, NADIS, RIPE EGO]

MINOR ARCANA—fifty-six cards as a part of the TAROT CARDS; consist of swords, pentacles, diamonds, wands and clubs; ancient tarot cards are composed of major and minor arcana. [cf. MAJOR ARCANA]

MINOR CYCLES—a complete execution of earth's magnetic field repeating its behavior in slight periodicities that can be noticeable in divisions of twenty-seven, twenty-nine, thirteen, and nine days; believed to be influenced by solar changes. (Inconcl.) [cf. CYCLES Appendix 2, LAW OF REPETITION Appendix 7]

MINOR DEITIES—(Tibet) THOUGHT-FORMS in the ETHERIC WORLD which give the appearance of a human, superhuman, or subhuman being, but have no individual real existence; thought-forms take these shapes from the karmic seeds of both the high and low impulses of man. [cf. GODDESSES, LORDS OF DEATH, DAKINIS, RAVASHIS, SOULLESS]

MINOR DEVAS—a highly intelligent, invisible, formless LIFE FORCE belonging to the ANGEL KINGDOM; minor devas have charge over lesser and smaller human responsibilities of the earthling; e.g., resident deva, parking lot deva, supermarket deva, city council deva, etc. [cf. ANGEL KINGDOM, MAGNIFICENT DEVA, GREAT ONES, GUIDE, CONTROL]

MINPSI—abbr. for MINERAL PSYCHISM; ability of stones, rocks, and gems to communicate instinctual perception with their environment, plants, animals, humans, and among themselves; minerals are attuned to auras and the instinctual activity of natural things for miles around themselves; minerals are possessed with sensibilities and power to be governed by sounds and the mind and emotions of human beings; they bear some relationship to already known forces of nature, i.e., gravity, electricity and magnetism; recognized as the transmitters of the influence from planets to earth and earthlings; minerals have a consciousness that can both give and take from its environment; minerals possess similar chemicals as the human body; all of the above make the mineral an excellent psychic tool for people; each type of mineral has its own peculiarities of usefullness to the human, to be used in bringing peace, healing, fertility, harmony, courage, protection, etc.; average everyday stones make a good psychic tool if kept close to one daily and spoken to gently; i.e., can step up the owner's psychic sensitivity in psychic skills, induce meditation, and increase one's healing abilities; hypothesis: MINERAL KINGDOM is living matter, growing and evolving in the overall plan. [cf. STONES, Appendix 2 MINPSI]

MINUS (-)—(biorhythm chart) the period of days below the 0-LINE on one's BIORHYTHM CHART; this means that the body system is at its lowest ebb, and will show reduced efficiency in that particular cycle; each phase of a person's life needs a time to rejuvenate. [cf. CRITICAL DAYS]

MIRACLE—(Latin *miraculum,* "an occurrence that excites wonder") an effect or extraordinary event which surpasses all known human or natural causes; laws ascribed to the event are not understood in their entirety; event is the outworking of human beings and their environment but seldom happens and happens only to a few; entails more than one law of physics and usually a law of final causes. [cf. LOURDES, ELECTRIC GIRLS, PHANTOM DOG, LAW OF THOUGHT Appendix 7, FAITH, MATTER]

MIRACLE HEALING—usually pertains to curing a person who was very ill or ill for a long time and instaneously healed; see INSTANTANEOUS HEAL-

ING. [cf. MASS HEALING, CHARISMATIC MEETINGS, PSYCHIC HEALING, LOURDES, FAITH]

MIRACLE IN STONE—see GIZA PYRAMID.

MIRACULOUS BIRTH—(Tibet) the transfer of the consciousness-principle (a SOUL-MIND) from one vibrational frequency to another vibrational frequency into the desired womb. (Inconcl.) **Sim:** birth by superpsychic womb. [cf. CONSCIOUSNESS-PRINCIPLE, IMMACULATE CONCEPTION]

MIRROR—serves as a good psychic tool for advanced psychics: 1. to stare intensely into the mirror after a MEDITATION period to: (a) clairvoyantly perceive one's guides who interpenetrate the body for psychic work and now desire to be identified; (b) clairvoyantly perceive a deceased loved one who superposes or stands behind one for identification; (c) clairvoyantly perceive one's own past incarnations that will be revealed by a change in facial features; (d) reveal one's own AURA; one must let the SUBCONSCIOUS MIND know which of the above one desires to perceive. (Inconcl.) 2. a highly polished mirror may be used for a SCRYING tool similar to a CRYSTAL BALL.[cf. X-RAY CLAIRVOYANCE, TRANSFIGURATION]

MIRROR CURSE—to psychically send an unpleasurable psychic attack back to the one who sent it; if one feels very emotional or slightly ill and does not believe it belongs to her or himself but comes from an outside source, one should send it back to its original source; psychic silently says "go back to where you came from." **Syn.** BOOMERANG PSI. [cf. ASSIMILATION, PSYCHIC ATTACK]

MIRROR EFFECT—(biofeedback training) to use the psychic images that surface while HOOKED-UP to a BIOFEEDBACK INSTRUMENT during a training session, as a therapeutic aid; one can externalize with the image, figure its symbology, and determine its usefulness in correcting a present situation; when the CONSCIOUS MIND is passive (the goal of the session), the SUBCONSCIOUS MIND tries to perfect itself and the psychic images will frequently pertain to the cause of the problem the subject is trying to correct by the training sessions. [cf. BIOFEEDBACK TRAINING Appendix 5, PSYCHIC CONSCIOUSNESS]

MIRROR MAGIC—see IMITATIVE MAGIC.

MIRROR OF KARMA—the MENTAL-REFLECTING-ETHER which consists of minute pictures of every

405

activity and experience one goes through during her or his incarnation in earth; pictures are of each incarnation and during the dying process one is shown these pictures in a flash of time; the individual realizes when in his or her life they performed well, and when they could have made better choices and will return to reexperience them. (Inconcl.) [cf. DEATH SCIENCE, REINCARNATION, KARMA, DEATHBED EXPERIENCES]

MIRROR WRITING—(automatism) a script brought through in AUTOMATIC WRITING that must be read by holding it up to a mirror; it is written backwards. [cf. ETHERIC SCRIPT, AUTOMATISM]

MIRROR-LIKE WISDOM—seeing within the mind during MEDITATION, a form that is isolated from materiality, such as a reflection; the first movement toward meditational depth. (Inconcl.) [cf. TRANSCENDENTAL MEDITATION, RELAXATION RESPONSE, GOING WITHIN, ESSENCE OF REST]

MIRRORED—(laboratory) to dream a picture or sound that is the TARGET of a controlled experiment; happens to students working in the laboratory. (Inconcl.) [cf. DREAM RESEARCH LABORATORIES, EOG, THETA STATE OF CONSCIOUSNESS]

MIRRORS OF DESTINY—(palmistry) the lines in the palms of the hands that tell a story of one's past and future; understood by the palm reader. [cf. PALMISTRY LINES, Appendix 2 BODY READING]

MISCARRIAGES—(psi tasks) failure of equipment, inappropriate randomization, procedural error, etc., when conducting controlled experiments. **Syn.** ERROR PHENOMENA. [cf. ESP, PSI TASKS, CHANCE]

MISINGHALIKUN—(Native American, Delaware) a psychic manifestation of an ETHERIC WORLD INTELLIGENCE who appears human, except he is wearing a mask in place of a face; manifests to help the tribe with healings and give guidance in hunts. **Syn.** LIVING SOLID FACE. [cf. APPARITION, SYMBOLISM, PROTECTOR]

MISPLACED EFFICIENCY—(psi tasks) to continually perceive the TARGET to the card preceding it or to the card following it, when working in Rhine card controlled experiments. [cf. ESP, RHINE CARDS, PSI TASKS]

MISPLACED PHENOMENA—physical psychism occurring randomly where and when not expected or when not deliberately willed; e.g., psychic knocks or raps in the home when not sitting for psychic

development, an article disappearing and reappearing later in another place; superior ETHERIC WORLD INTELLIGENCES will not perform if not asked but can perform if it is necessary to carry out a subconscious strong desire from this life or a past life; i.e., the stronger emotional desire always nullifies the weaker one; e.g., to emotionally decree that one desires to become a physical medium in six months will void a lesser statement, if necessary, that says the intelligence should work through one only in a psychic development circle. [cf. NON-HUMAN-PK, POLTERGEIST, LEVITATION TELEKINESIS, MEDIUMSHIP]

MISPLACED PSI—(laboratory) to psychically perceive information that one could not know by physical means and yet it is not the intended TARGET of the experiment; in the ALPHA STATE OF CONSCIOUSNESS when working on a psychic experiment, the PERCIPIENT tunes into another person's target, answer, emotions, thoughts, or perceives a tragedy occurring in another area, or perceives PROPHECY; percipient has tuned into the wrong wavelength or channel; with correct instructions and practice one can learn to tune into the proper channel for the target needed. [cf. PSYCHIC TRANSFER, NARROW BAND TUNING, CENTERING, MUDDY CONDITIONS, MIND-LINKING]

MISS—(psi tasks) to give an erroneous response that does not come close to the TARGET, in a controlled experiment. [cf. PSYCHIC DEVELOPMENT CIRCLE, SHEEP AND GOATS EFFECT, LISTENING MODE, GOING-TO-LEVEL]

MISSION-CONTROL—(psychotherapy) to use provoking suggestions until one finds a topic or a name that the subject tries to avoid or that appears unpleasant to the subject; this usually leads to the experience that caused the block that is making an imbalance in the body or mind. [cf. BLOCKS, WORD ASSOCIATION, PASTLIVES THERAPY, NEW AGE PSYCHOLOGY]

MISSIONARY SPIRITS—ETHERIC WORLD INTELLIGENCES whose function is to rescue, guide and uplift the soul-minds in the density when they reach out for help. [cf. MERCY BAND, DENSITY, PLANES]

MISTLETOE—1. (esoteric) a plant used in rituals because its vibrational frequency helps step up one's psychic ability; 2. has power of fertility; influenced by the lunar cycle; 3. (Druids) used it as a tool for healing because they could charge it with MAG-

NETISM. [cf. BOTANE Appendix 2, EARTH MAGNETISM]

MITOGENTIC RADIATION—coined by Alexander Gurvitch (1937); see VITAL LIFE FORCE.

MITOGENTIC RAYS—abbr. M-RAYS: (Russia, Alexander Gurvitch) radiations emanating from the cells of animals, plants, and humans creating a biological force field surrounding the organism; the vibrational frequency is similar to the ULTRA VIOLET RAYS; these rays have an influence on each other from one living organism to another; in humans, the radiations emanate from muscle tissue, cornea of the eye, blood, and nerves. (Inconcl.) [cf. SENSATION CONSCIOUSNESS, ANPSI, MASTER EYE, EVIL EYE]

MITROGENTIC WAVES—energy formed between the two frontal lobes of the brain; the quality and quantity depend on and change with the polarities of the body. (Inconcl.) [cf. POLARITY, THIRD-EYE AREA Appendix 2, PINEAL GLAND]

MOBIA—abbr. MENTAL OR BEHAVIORAL INFLUENCE OF AN AGENT; (ASPR) principle thoughts, actions, or lack of attentiveness on the part of the sender in a mental telepathic message could easily influence the message of the receiver. (Inconcl.) [cf. ACTIVE-AGENT TELEPATHY, EARTH TELEPATHY, LOVE-LINE, THOUGHT ATMOSPHERE]

MOBILE CENTER OF CONSCIOUSNESS—(laboratory) that LIFE FORCE in human beings which is capable of taking an ASTRAL PROJECTION.

MOCKING SPIRIT—(Native American) an ETHERIC WORLD INTELLIGENCE who takes on the appearance of an animal when communicating to an earthling. [cf. GUIDE, INNER BAND, REALITY, KINGDOM OF THE MIND]

MODEST MEDIUMS—those who allow the ETHERIC WORLD INTELLIGENCES to intervene to bring psychic information, new knowledge, or personal messages, but take no personal credit for the material; executed through VOICE TRANCE, or AUTOMATIC WRITING; mediums consider themselves as strangers when under the influence of the intelligence. [cf. PHYSICAL MANIFESTATIONS/MISCELLANEOUS Appendix 2, REGULATED SITUATIONS]

MOIRAE—(Greece) three goddesses of destiny who each give their rightful portion in life; make themselves present at birth or three days later; current term for naming one's rightful portion is

the BIORHYTHM cycles: PHYSICAL, EMOTIONAL, and INTELLECTUAL cycles. [cf. BIORHYTHM CHART, CYCLES, LIFE-CORD-HEART-SEED-ATOM, EMOTIONAL-ASTRAL-SEED-ATOM]

MOKSHA—(Sanskrit, Hinduism) see TOTALITY.

MOLD—see AURA.

MOLECULAR CHORUS—inaudible sound produced by the movement of each molecule in the invisible atmosphere which must harmonize with other molecules as it colonizes together in COVALENT BONDING; matter is held together by harmonious chords; can be perceived by an expert CLAIRAUDIENT or by instruments made for picking up noise that is out of physical range. [cf. COSMIC SOUND, CONDENSED CONSCIOUSNESS, CLAIRAUDIENCE]

MOLECULAR MEMORY—(esoteric) the ability of mundane material to return to its original shape after being deformed by twisting, heating, etc.; this is possible because the molecules have a memory bank, DNA.

MOLESOPHY—study of moles on the skin in relation to their indication of the individual's character and their representation of future events. [cf. BODY READING Appendix 2]

MOLY—(botane) an herb with a black root which has the vibrational frequency that gives it the power to protect its owner. [cf. BOTANE, PUSSY-WILLOW, VEGETATION MAGIC, WATCH-PLANTS]

MOMENT—(esoteric) an indefinitely short measurement of time which is psychically formless to normal senses but mathematically a form to the solar system. [cf, PRESENT MANIFESTING, SERIAL TIME, TIME FRAMEWORK]

MOMENT POINT—(Seth) instantaneous action of the entity or object performing its function simultaneously in all dimensions, visible and invisible. [cf. MULTIDIMENSIONAL TIME, PRESENT MANIFESTING, PATTERNING ACROSS TIME]

MOMENTARY ABILITY—(psi tasks) to demonstrate one's psychic ability on the spur of the moment, at will; (Spiritualist) to habitually WILL psychic skills to occur spontaneously lessens the accuracy in that skill, shows disrespect for one's psychism, and frequently proves to be harmful to the psychic's well-being; before opening one's psychic doors, it is important to choose the correct type of environment, prepare oneself by a CLOAK

OF INSULATION, and then go into an ALPHA STATE OF CONSCIOUSNESS; this leads to improvement in the skill, respect for psychism, and maintains one's psychic balance. [cf. UP-FOR-GRABS, HUMAN TRANSMITTER, MENTAL TELEPATHY, CLAIRSENTIENCE]

MONAD—(metaphysics) (Greek *monas,* "indestructible unit") a minute, ethereal, concentrated mass of energy and intelligence; contains a complete replica of TOTALITY when it was in its original perfect state; endowed with an urge to return to this perfect state which keeps it in perpetual motion; 1. (Gottfried Wilhelm Leibnitz) "units that incorporate the whole, the exquisitely orderly behavior of light indicating an underlying radical, patterned order of reality; a perpetual living mirror of the universe, closed off from one another but still sensitive to vibrations of the universe"; 2. (Giordano Bruno) "a basis and irreducible metaphysical unit that is spatial and psychically undividuated"; 3. (Karl Pribram) "lensless, indivisible entities as basic units of the universe, a MICROCOSM of it; monadic organization: (monads) contain the whole as in the HOLOGRAM"; 4. (metaphysical religions) MONAD is the Divine Spark of God in every living thing containing all the attributes of God; monads remember when God was ONE and this motivates them to unfold and evolve until they once again are *one* with God; 5. each (monad) concentrated mass contains: (a) a soul/intelligence; (b) spirit/energy (movement); (c) a consciousness; (d) memory mechanism; monads know their function and have a condensed consciousness that holds the memory of every vibrational frequency in which they have vibrated. [cf. CONDENSED MEMORY, HUMAN BEING SPECIES SEED, MICROCOSM, HOLOGRAM BRAIN THEORY]

MONAD PERCEPTIONS—(esoteric) reflections of the quality of knowledge gained in the MUNDANE WORLD vibrational frequencies are retained in the monad memory bank; used in its progress of evolution. [cf. OVERSOUL, CONDENSED CONSCIOUSNESS, DNA, COLLECTIVE UNCONSCIOUS, PRIMAL PERCEPTION]

MONADIC PLANE—the SIXTH PLANE, a very subtle, atomic, ethereal vibration; a state of consciousness in which Totality's plan begins and ends; a perfect spark of TOTALITY from this frequency, radiates from itself and projects itself into the planes below; each spark forms a SOUL-MIND

which in turn radiates to more dense vibrations under the law called INVOLUTION; the soul-mind with its memory of this peaceful, happy plane is constantly desiring to return; the soul-mind must evolve or unfold from within out; this plane requires that the monad must have endured, experienced, and learned all there is to learn in the lower planes before it is admitted home; in MEDITATION one can expand his or her mind with much practice and unselfish intent to perceive what is here. [cf. LAW OF SOUL-MIND GROWTH Appendix 7]

MONADOLOGY—a philosophy dealing with final causes; 1. (Gottfried Wilhelm von Leibnitz) "within each man is a microcosmic expression of the perfect universe, macrocosmic; 2. the UNIVERSE is filled with infinite living seeds, centers of force in the structure of reality; living seeds exist in hierarchies extending to TOTALITY; each living seed possesses potentialities of perception and movement which become self-consciousness, awareness of its function, and the will to fulfill its function; the overall goal of every MONAD is to unfold into the love of its mother, Totality. (Inconcl.) [cf. HUMAN BEING SPECIES SEED, INVOLUTION]

MONEN—(Kabbalah) to divine by observation of the heavenly bodies. [cf. POINT-OF-FOCUS Appendix 2, MANTIC ARTS]

MONITION—a warning regarding the present, perceived psychically; comes from the SUPERCONSCIOUS MIND; occurs usually through CLAIRSENTIENCE. [cf. COGNITION, FUNCTIONAL CLAIRSENTIENCE, GUT FEELING, INNER-DIRECTED]

MONITOR SWITCH—(biofeedback training) a dial on a BIOFEEDBACK INSTRUMENT that tells whether the audio sound is producing. [cf. EEG, EMG, GSR, METABOLIC MONITOR]

MONKEY CHATTER—unnecessary and irrelevant thoughts that race back and forth in the mind during MEDITATION, psychic work, or any type of concentration activity, that keeps one from accomplishing the task at hand. [cf. PENDULUM POWER, PSI TASKS, PSYCHIC READING, PK]

MONKEY—(meditation) a posture assumed in MEDITATION, wherein the arms dangle and the knees bend; this posture helps one attain a relaxed state of consciousness. **Syn.** SAMURAI POSITION. [cf. LOTUS POSTURE, PALM DOWNWARD DURING MEDITATION, PRAYER BEADS, GODFORM POSITION]

MONO-MOTIVATIONAL STATE OF TRANSCEN-DANCE—to release a repressed frustration by blurting out a single powerful thought from the SUBCONSCIOUS MIND under the influence of HYPNOSIS; when the CONSCIOUS MIND is passive, a forceful sensation or emotion can tower momentarily over all other sensations and surface to be released; one does not always choose the time or the particular sensation while she or he is in a state of hypnosis, but rather the subconscious mind frequently chooses to release the block. [**cf.** HYPNOTHERAPY, BLOCKS, TEARS, NEW-AGE PSYCHOLOGY, CLEARING, DRAINING OFF]

MONOCHROMATIC LIGHTS—the range from ULTRA-VIOLET to INFRARED.

MONOIDEASIM—(William James) "to reach one point of heaven, or to reach profound peace in one's own psyche, during meditation." [**cf.** SEED MEDITATION, BLISSING OUT, ONENESS, NIRVANA, TRANSCENDENT MOMENT]

MONOLATERALITY—to specialize and isolate one field of a whole unit but not recognize there is a function of that one field to the whole unit; opposite of the GESTALT theory. [**cf.** SYNTHESIZING, HOLISM, MONAD]

MONOLITH—(esoteric) a single stone of considerable size standing alone; found in ancient cultures; represents the first school of humanity, the aim being power, perfection, and supremacy within the laws of the universe; symbolic of human capabilities. [**cf.** NUMEROLOGY, ONE, NUMBER POWER]

MONOSPRIT—JESUS, the Christ, or the devil in an aspect of communicating with human beings; belief: only one intelligence has the power and intelligence to communicate with mankind, and this power will not send others to intercede, such as, the guides. **Syn.** UNISPRIT. [**cf.** ANGEL HIERARCHY, GUIDE, ETHERIC WORLD INTELLIGENCES, HOLY SPIRIT]

MONOSYLLABIC ANSWERS—*yes* and *no* signals coming from objects in physical phenomena, e.g., CANDLE FLAME, PENDULUM, rappings or TABLE TIPPING. [**cf.** ETHERIC SCRIPT, RAPS, OSCILLATIONS]

MONSTER ACTIVITY—study of large creatures, half man and half animal, appearing in many parts of the earth sharing similar characteristics and behaviorial patterns; 1. unable to be captured; 2. difficult to physically see; 3. give evidence of their life and presence by being destructive to animals, humans, property and environment; 4. prefer to work at night; 5. make hideous and shrieking noises; 6. appear more frequently after a UFO sighting and in the same area; 7. capable of shifting dimensions; 8. inhabit woods, water, plains, etc.; 9. theories: (**a**) belong to the giant nature spirit kingdom; (**b**) a throw back from another culture of ancient times. (Inconcl.) [**cf.** DIMENSION-SHIFTING, BIG FOOT, ABDOMINABLE SNOWMAN, INVISIBILITY]

MONSTER LILITH—(Hebrew) an etheric world female entity who travels at night to find men to "lie with." **Syn.** NIGHT HAG, LILI, SUCCUBUS, WOOD NYMPH. [**cf.** DIMENSION-SHIFTING, LAW OF LIKE ATTRACTS LIKE Appendix 7, ASTRAL PROJECTION]

MOOD ADJECTIVE CHECK LIST—(psi tasks) a record of the subject's feelings and attitude during the psi experiment which has an influence on the accuracy of hitting the TARGET; theory: ESP target may be guided by the mood state, a consequence of the subject's precognitive awareness of the nature of the task. [**cf.** ESP, SHEEP AND GOATS EFFECT, CHANCE AVERAGE, DEVIATION, PERSONAL MIND PRINTS, MONKEY CHATTER, INNER-DIALOGUE]

MOOD-PATTERN—peaks of happiness and valleys of unhappiness found to run in a universal rhythm among all human beings; these have been studied and determined by the BIOLOGICAL RHYTHM and BIORHYTHM CHARTS; also called **emotional highs** and **lows**. [**cf.** CYCLES, BIORHYTHM SPAN, CIRCADIAN RHYTHM, CIVILIZATION CYCLE]

MOOD-SHIFTS—(psi tasks) the attitude and feelings of the participant while working on a psychic experiment which influence the psychic information process and the target answer. [**cf.** PSYCHIC DOORS, NARROW-BAND TUNING, PSI CONDUCIVE STATE, THREE-FINGER TECHNIQUE]

MOOD-STIMULUS—background activity that one has intentionally learned to ignore in conscious awareness, but has an influence on one's more subtle bodies and therefore makes changes in his or her emotional state; e.g., music played for background purposes, continuous noise of a machine in one's work area, dark clouds gathering, stopping and starting of rain, a member of one's family opening and closing the refrigerator door. (Inconcl.) [**cf.** BIOFEEDBACK TRAINING, MEDITATION, MENTAL BODY, OBJECTIVE CONSCIOUSNESS, ASTRAL BODY]

MOON—(esoteric) a supreme deity having dominion over the monthly cycles, the tides and movement of the fluidic elements within and upon the earth's surface, and the humoral fluids within the human body; the moon is considered a dead planet as its energy flow has dissolved and gone back into the stratosphere; the moon has a function to the milky way parallel to the function of the SOUL-MIND to a human being; the moon has no light of its own. (Inconcl.) [**cf.** EMOTIONAL CYCLE, JET LAG, INTERNAL TIME, ACTIVE AND PASSIVE PHASES]

MOONSTONE—(esoteric) a mineral endowed with the property to transmit energy from the moon to the earth; used as an AMULET to influence the sea tides and women's menstrual cycles. (Inconcl.) [**cf.** MOON, MOOD-PATTERN, BIORHYTHM, SUBJECTIVE TIME SENSE, MINPSI Appendix 2]

MORAL PHILOSOPHIC MEDIUM—a medium whose etheric world GUIDE intervenes and the material that comes through physical mediumship centers around higher philosophies and morals. [**cf.** GUIDE, SUBJECTIVE EDUCATION, INSPIRATIONAL THOUGHT, HEAVENLY STUFF]

MORAL SUBJUGATION OBSESSION—the paralyzing of an earthling's will by an inferior etheric world DISCARNATE ENTITY; discarnate entity instigates absurd and compromising communication; discarnate constantly deceives the earthling and influences him or her to do activity that benefits and thrills the discarnate; objective of the discarnate entity is to relive earthly sensations through the earthling; see POSSESSION. [**cf.** CORPOREAL, SIMPLE OBSESSION]

MOROII—(Rome) see VAMPIRE.

MOSS PEOPLE—see NATURE SPIRITS.

MOTHER SEA—see TOTALITY.

MOTHMAN PROPHECIES—bird-like creatures who haunted the Ohio River Valley for thirteen months; capable of chasing cars at the speed of 110 miles per hour. (Inconcl.) **Syn.** DEMONID BIRD. [**cf.** MONSTER ACTIVITY, DIMENSION-SHIFTING, BIG FOOT]

MOTION—the action of a body or system shifting one position to another, completely related; (esoteric) energy patterns in the universe; common denominator between the planets and sound involving repetitive movement or cycles; caused by resonance in the universe and its transference; utilizes principle of attraction and repulsion and a result of the law of vibration. [**cf.** POLARITY, ENERGY, LAW OF VIBRATION Appendix 7]

MOTION WITHOUT CONTACT—see LAYING-ON-OF-HANDS.

MOTIONLESS MEDITATION—(karate) a technique of meditating that cleanses the mind; lasts ten minutes; executed every hour during the KARATE session. [**cf.** MARTIAL ARTS Appendix 5]

MOTIONLESSNESS—the occurrence of external motions happening too fast to be measured by mankind's present standards; the past-present-future presenting itself all at once; the mind going "blank." [**cf.** SPACIOUS PRESENT, TIMELESS PRESENT, ACTION, ALL-AT-ONCE]

MOTIVE UNCONSCIOUSNESS—(astral projection and dreams) SLEEP-WALKING performed by the PROJECTIONIST after he or she returns and is released from the astral sensations and fixity; projectionist remains unconscious and finds it necessary to release motor processes within the body. **Sim.** SOMNAMBULISTIC UNCONSCIOUS ASTRAL PROJECTION. [**cf.** HOLD-OFF POINT, HEAD-THUMPING DREAM, INCOMPLETE PROJECTION, SECOND STATE]

MOTIVITY—(astral projection) an ethereal cord or rod extended outside the physical body, full of energy and power but with no ASTRAL BODY on the other end; subject to the direction of the CONSCIOUS MIND and SUBCONSCIOUS MIND. [**cf.** IN-THE-RANGE-OF-CORD-ACTIVITY, LIFT OUT, MENTAL-BODY PROJECTION]

MOTOR APPORTATION—(alchemy) to transport one's self through space in an invisible form by the power of the mind; ALCHEMIST focuses undivided attention on his or her body until it changes VIBRATIONAL FREQUENCIES and dematerializes into an invisible state; still deep in concentration, he or she moves it to another area and rematerializes it in full form in the three-dimensional world; alchemist begins in the conscious state and through intense focalization the act proceeds in the subconscious state; never happens unwilled; the last step before TRANSMUTATION; perfected by great saints and masters, such as JESUS and Comte de St. Germain; believed to be an accomplishment of the UFOs. [**cf.** ALCHEMY, REMATERIALIZATION, TRANSMUTATION, HUMANPK, ALCHEMICAL PRINCIPLES]

MOTOR AUTOMATISM—to allow one's hand, arm, and writing tool to be moved entirely by an ETHERIC WORLD INTELLIGENCE to bring knowledge or art that far surpasses that of the MEDIUM; proceeds at a speed more rapid than an artist or author can work; medium has no artistic talent or literary education to bring forth this material; executed in any of the three levels of trance; always willed, preplanned and under DESIRED-CONTROL; types of automatism: AUTOMATIC WRITING, AUTOMATIC ART, and AUTOMATIC TYPEWRITING. [cf. MOTOR LEVITATION]

MOTOR FORCE—coined by John Worrell Keely (1880); see VITAL LIFE FORCE.

MOTOR LEVITATION—to vertically raise and suspend one's body in the air without using physical means: 1. (mediumship) to synchronize one's energies with the ETHERIC WORLD INTELLIGENCE so he or she nullifies the normal gravitational effect on the body and raises it; performed in a DEEP TRANCE state; always programmed and willed; 2. (spiritual attainment) to physically rise in the air while in a state of spiritual ECSTASY; vibrational rate in the body changes during the peak experience giving the body buoyancy and it automatically lifts off the ground a few inches; occurs spontaneously and unwilled; 3. (meditation) prolonged meditational states eventually release the drossy, materialistic atoms (that hold the body to the earth) from the body, allowing the body to rise a few feet for a short period. **Syn.** MOTOR SUSPENSION. [cf. FLY, ANTIGRAVITY, LEVITATION, TELEKINESIS, HUMAN-PK]

MOTOR PSYCHOKINESIS—abbr. MOTOR-PK; to impart motion, muscular movement, or change the position of one's physical body or the physical body of another by using mind power only; psychic focalizes his or her undivided attention on the task until the energy from the mind is densified and travels to the area needed; executed in a semi-conscious awareness or passive-alert state; e.g., MOTOR LEVITATION, WALKING-ON-WATER. [cf. GRAVITY CONTROL Appendix 2, RADIONICS]

MOTOR SUSPENSION—see MOTOR LEVITATION.

MOTOR TELEKINESIS—abbr. MOTOR-TK; to impart motion, muscular movement, or change the position of one's physical body or the physical body of another through the help of the ETHERIC WORLD INTELLIGENCES; performed in SEMITRANCE or DEEP TRANCE, pre-planned, and desired-controlled; intelligences intervene and using the energy of the medium's body perform the physical phenomena; e.g., MOTOR LEVITATION, TELEPORTATION, APPORTATION TELEKINESIS, VOICE TRANCE and TRANSFIGURATION. **Syn.** HUMAN-TK. [cf. NONHUMAN TELEKINESIS]

MOTOR TELEPATHY—the transference of a suggestion or instruction for action between two living organisms; sender intentionally, telepathically tells the receiver how to move his, her or its body; the receiver carries out the instruction believing it is their idea to perform the action; e.g., telepathically asking the squirrel to bring one a nut; telepathically asking an individual to give one a kiss. [cf. GROUP TELEPATHY, ACTION TELEPATHY, TELEPHONE TELEPATHY, SENDER]

MOTOR TELEPORTATION—see TELEPORTATION TELEKINESIS.

MOULD—(England) see AURA; also written **mold**.

MOULOU—(Missouri) see BIG FOOT.

MOUNT SINAI—(Egypt) a mountain with a special magnetic field and vibratory rate that makes it conducive to psychical feats; (Old Testament) Moses brought the ten commandments through INDEPENDENT VOICE on the top of it; (a mountain is symbolic of a higher state of consciousness). [cf. TRANCE MANIFESTATION, INDEPENDENT VOICE, PASSIVE ALERT]

MOUNTAIN ASH—(esoteric) a plant held sacred by the Druids; found growing near stones and near the stone circle of the Druids; has a vibrational frequency that evil doers cannot tolerate so it is used as protection against evil witchcraft. **Syn.** ROWAN. [cf. TREES, HAZEL, PLANT MAGIC, ROSEMARY, BOTANE]

MOUNTAIN OF PHILOSOPHERS—(alchemy) a peculiar looking mountain tower symbolic of the alchemical process of self-perfection. [cf. CIRCLE, PENTACLE, SACRED CUT, CONE OF POWER]

MOUNTING—(Voodoo, Africa) the superimposing of the LOA (etheric world intelligence) on the SHAMAN in the onset of the trance impersonation; each shaman has their own special ritual dance to invoke his or her loa; this superimposing or MOUNTING allows the loa and shaman time to synchronize their BODY CHEMISTRY and energies before the loa takes over and performs healings, or brings knowledge for the tribe. [cf. POSSESSION TRANCE, LOA, IMPERSONATION, CATALEPSY, EXCITABLE MEDIUM, FORCED PSI]

MOUNTS—(hand analysis) the puffiness or raised sections of the hand and fingers that have significant meaning to the palmist; puffiness correlates to ASTROLOGY. **Syn.** BOSSES. [cf. PALMISTRY, CHIROGNOMY]

MOVEMENT TELEPATHY—(laboratory) the transference of body movement from one group to another group located in areas closed off from one another; each one in the sending group performs the same body movement; e.g., lifting the left leg, pinching the right ear; receiver group allows their body sensations to perceive and react with no mental thought transference; can be performed with two persons. [cf. TELEPATHIC SLEEPING PILL, HERD IMPULSES, MOTOR TELEPATHY]

MOVEMENT-FOR-ALTERED-CONSCIOUSNESS-the use of preplanned or choreographed body movements until one reaches a higher state of consciousness; movements are usually rhythmic or the mode of body/mind cooperation; used in groups or singly; helpful for mental and physical psychism. [cf. Appendix 2 MOVEMENT-FOR-ALTERED-CONSCIOUSNESS for many types]

MOVEMENTS—(George Ivanovich Gurjieff) sacred dances performed during the night that were choreographed to bring courage for one to face her or himself directly; danced by those who desire to better themselves. [cf. MEDITATION-IN-MOTION, SUFI TWIRLING, HEALING DANCE]

MOVING MEDIUM—one who produces movement of an inert body without contact; see TELEPORTATION-TK.

MT. MERU—(Buddhism, Hinduism) a central core around which the layers of hell and heaven evolve; an apex in the middle of the universes compared to the sun in western astronomy. [cf. DENSITY, VEIL, SIXTH DIMENSION, SPIRITUAL PLANE, NOOSPHERE]

MU—a continent lost in the Pacific in antiquity; also known as LEMURIA; see same.

MU IGALA—(Panama, Kuna Indian) their main book of literature, consulted by the SHAMAN and priest; a manual for psychic skills.

MUDDY CONDITIONS—(laboratory) when environment or circumstances make psychism difficult. [cf. MENTAL PSYCHIC PROCESSES Appendix 2, GOING-TO-LEVEL, INCENSE, HUMAN INFORMATION PROCESSING SYSTEM, CLOAK OF INSULATION]

MUDRA—1. (Buddhism, Hinduism) a ritual of symbolic gestures, postures, dances, and body movements designed to aid one in reaching a higher state of consciousness in MEDITATION; hand gestures in sacred dances; 2. (Sanskrit, "close off") movement to close off both physically and mentally; a place in the body where the ritual is to be performed; 3. (Tibet) to lock densified psychic energy in the body by putting two palms together, pressing hard and bending the hands down; a well-known prayful position; 4. (Yoga) meditation using repetitive physical movements of the arms, legs or fingers; movements direct the awareness continually toward the process of making movement; e.g., to touch the thumb to the tip of each finger repeatedly; 5. (Sufi) the essence of the phrase as expressed in the body. [cf. MEDITATION, MANTRA, MOVEMENT-FOR-ALTERED-CONSCIOUSNESS]

MUFON—abbr. MUTUAL UFO NETWORK; civilian research organization for UFO landings. [cf. CLOSE-ENCOUNTERS-OF-THE-THIRD-KIND, CONTACTEE SYNDROME, PROJECT BLUE BOOK]

MULDHARA CHAKRA—an etheric energy source made of etheric substance at the base of the spine where the KUNDALINI is stored until it rises. **Syn.** ROOT CHAKRA, KANDA. [cf. IDA, PENGALLA, MEDULLA OBLONGATA]

MULTICONSCIOUSNESS—to project one's consciousness into an animal or plant and to become that animal or plant; a simultaneous observation of many aspects of one scene by becoming the bird, or the leaf, etc.; performed by intense concentration and desire; (do not confuse with BILOCATION). (Inconcl.) **Syn.** MULTILOCATION. [cf. MENTAL PROJECTION, FLOAT OFF, SOUL TRAVEL, ASTRAL VISION]

MULTIDIMENSIONAL—theory: many levels of consciousness and each level inhabiting life energies, remaining separate and unconscious of one another; myriads of shapes and degrees of intelligence, all finding life in the same spot but vibrating at different rates of speed; each have an awareness that does not reach into other dimensions, except the SOUL-MIND; everything coexistant. (Inconcl.) [cf. TIME Appendix 5]

MULTIFORM—(Tibet) to exist and function in two places at the same time appearing normal in both places; SOUL-MIND psychically splits and carries on for a few hours or more in a three-dimensional form wearing the same clothes; usually unknown to the multiformer until told about it later; multiformer is capable of talking, walking and thinking in both places; theory: individual has a strong emotional desire to be in the other place but mundane circumstances prevent it and the soul-mind splits and one half goes anyway; uses the energy of the emotional desire to function. **Syn.** BILOCATION, BRAHMANA VAGGA, ANGUTTARA NIKAYA. [**cf.** MULTI-CONSCIOUSNESS, SPLIT-OFF, EGO-SPLITTING]

MULTIFORM WAVES—grotesque, distorted, fleeting forms interacting, found in the etheric world DENSITY; sensitive and influenced to the temperament of human thoughts. **Syn.** ELEMENTAL ASTRAL SHAPES. [**cf.** LOW-ORDER-PSI-FORCE, LAW OF LIKE ATTRACTS LIKE Appendix 7, SUBHUMAN REALM, CLOAK OF INSULATION]

MULTILOCATION—see MULTICONSCIOUSNESS.

MULTIPLE ASPECT TARGET—(laboratory) a controlled experiment in which there is more than one TARGET to be physically received; used in COGNITION with cards; i.e., color, number and suit are the target. [**cf.** PSI-COGNITION, DOUBLE-HEADER EXPERIMENT]

MULTIPLE PERSONALITY—pertains to a person who has literally more than one personality inside their head which pours out into his or her life; person is capable of switching from one personality to another in minutes; each personality has its own body chemistry, characteristics, talents, and capabilities; personalities vary in age from a child to an elderly person; usually this personality changeover is not remembered by the real personality; current researchers feel that it occurs to children who have been badly abused mentally, physically, or sexually; have repeatedly experienced overwhelming situations; and are constantly receiving conflicting messages from adults; **possible theories**: 1. (Richard Kluft) children cannot run away from this abuse so they run within and separate themselves from that which is the overwhelming hurt; believed that these children are born with ability to dissociate, and to divide the mind; a structural pattern is formed in their minds and is repeated each time they have overwhelming experiences to keep defending themselves; this pattern develops into a personality eventually as the child gets older because of its repetition; probably the child uses self-hypnosis as a way of shifting gears; it is easily diagnosed with hypnosis which allows the patient

to switch back and forth more easily; 2. (possession) individual creates an opening in his or her etheric web because of this abuse, due to constant negative feelings, such as hate, fear, anxiety, self-condemnation, and jealousy; this opening allows earthbound drifters from the lower planes to hover close by and slide in and out of their mental atmosphere very easily; 3. personalities of past lives surface for attention to emotional situations that have never been resolved. [**cf.** HAUNTING, CONFUSED SOUL-MIND, DENSITY]

MULTIPLE SOULS—indicates the many aspects of mankind's intelligence and feeling nature; 1. (Native American, Menomini) each person is assigned one soul to the heart and one to the head; 2. (Philippines) each person has a right-hand and left-hand soul; 3. (Native American) an individual has four souls; 4. (Melanesia) everyone has seven souls of different types. [**cf.** CONSCIOUS MIND, SUBCONSCIOUS MIND, UNIVERSAL MIND, SUPERCONSCIOUS MIND, SUBLIMINAL LEVEL]

MULTIPLE-SELF-TRANSFORMATION—(Celtic, Wales) to psychically transmute one's self into one form after another, as an animal, bird, or an inanimate object. **Syn.** SHAPE-CHANGING, SELF-TRANSFORMATION. [**cf.** Appendix 2 DIMENSION-SHIFTING and SHAPE-CHANGING]

MULTIPLICITY—a rearranging of the numbers; numbers, which by their nature, simultaneously provoked and corresponded to the functions and principles for which the physical cosmos was formed. [**cf.** NUMEROLOGY, NUMBER POWER Appendix 5]

MULTISPIRIT SYSTEM—thousands of levels of consciousness in the etheric world inhabited by soul-minds according to their state of EVOLUTION; soul-minds migrate together in their own levels of understanding making a vibrational frequency suitable for their growth level. [**cf.** SOUL-MIND, HUMAN BEING, ETHERIC WORLD]

MULTITIME—(esoteric) 1. a system to express perpetual existence; the past, present, and future occurring simultaneously; past, present, and future are simply different aspects of this system; 2. a product of the universal "seed" giving it a means of growing, unfolding, and expressing its potential; 3. multitime is a succession of events which is never present as a whole, but divided into three periods that continually pass into one another so that the

413

future becomes the present and the present becomes the past; mankind's awareness of the present is where the past and future meet; 4. multitime is electromagnetic currents within the brain and subconscious mind that have pseudo-boundaries caused by the amount of awareness the physical-body-design can handle; 5. (Seth)"past exists only as a pattern of electromagnetic currents within the mind and brain; past currents constantly change, and future actions are not dependent upon a concrete finished past for the past never exists." (Inconcl.) [cf. MULTIDIMENSIONAL, TIME Appendix 5]

MULTIVARIATE APPROACH—(psi tasks) the mood and feelings of those around the experiment affect the testing. [cf. CLOAK OF INSULATION, SHEEP AND GOATS EFFECT, PSI-CONDUCIVE STATE, MEDITATION, TEXTURE OF MENTAL ACTIVITY, MONKEY CHATTER]

MULUNGU—(Central African Yaos) see VITAL LIFE FORCE.

MUMBO-JUMBO—the special formula or magic words which are used in magic rituals because they have the vibrational frequency that releases psychic energy and helps the phenomena take place. [cf. WORDS-WITH-POWER, RITUAL, AFFIRMATIONS]

MUMIA and MUNIA—(Theophrastus Paracelsus, 1530) see VITAL LIFE FORCE.

MUMMIFICATION—1. (Egypt) a process of preserving the physical body after death by special embalming and wrappings; used for the great leaders only; theory: by preserving the physical body the ETHERIC DOUBLE would stay intact and that which had been accomplished in that INCARNATION would not have to be reexperienced in the next incarnation; (a) physical body could be used if the great leader made trips to earth to help his or her country; (b) etheric double could be used by the leader in his or her next incarnation. [cf. OPENING OF THE MOUTH CEREMONY, HOUSE OF ETERNITY, BURIAL WITH THE FEET TO THE EAST] 2. to preserve perishable objects, plants, or animals by methods unknown to modern science; the psychic contacts or makes passes with the thing being preserved and a fluid emanates from the hands and head that is capable of destroying bacteria and preventing decomposition. (Inconcl.) [cf. INCORRUPTIBILITY]

MUMMY—(Persia *mumia,* "wax or preserved corpse"). [cf. DEATH SCIENCE Appendix 2, CREMATION]

MUNDANE WORLD—(esoteric) 1. a perception of three-dimensional objects, things, earth, men, etc.; anything that is visible; 2. the manifestation of the total past vibrations that can be perceived by the five senses; an energy held together by the mind; 3. (Patrick Flanagan) "a pattern of energy interferences; an illusion of solidarity and stillness in a web of emotional energy fields." [cf. THIRD DIMENSION, SECOND DIMENSION, FOURTH DIMENSION]

MUNGO—(Sudan) see VITAL LIFE FORCE.

MUNGU AND NOKUNZI—(East Congo, Pygmies) two deities representing good and evil; depicted by two men that are larger, stronger, and capable of psychic feats. [cf. POLARITY, YIN AND YANG, CONSCIOUS MIND, SUBCONSCIOUS MIND]

MUNIS—(Theophrastus Paracelsus) see VITAL LIFE FORCE.

MUREEDS—people who study SUFI philosophy and follow its tradition; see PSYCHIC.

MUSCLE FIRING—(biofeedback training) the reaction of a muscle to stress; changes in the muscle mechanism is detectable on the EMG (electromyograph) and METABOLIC MONITOR; muscle firing permits subject, who is HOOKED-UP to the instrument, to get in touch with her or himself and determine what thoughts cause muscle restraint and muscle relaxation. [cf. EEG, METABOLIC MONITOR, BIOFEEDBACK TRAINING]

MUSCLE READING—to use a PENDULUM, DOWSING ROD, OUIJA BOARD, or LOTS, in DIVINATION, whereby the psychic's muscles take part in the psychic skill; PSYCHIC is unaware of the muscle reaction as she or he concentrates on keeping their mind neutral; the SYMPATHETIC NERVOUS SYSTEM can then react with accurate psychic information. [cf. TRANCE AUTOMATISM, MECHANICAL, BREASTPLATE OF JUDGMENT]

MUSCLE TENSION PATTERNS—"unresolved" frustration or traumatic experiences which settle in the muscles of the body; gradually over the years these experiences form the shape and condition of the body. [cf. ROLFING, NEURO-MUSCULAR MASSAGE, BLOCKS, SYMPATHETIC NERVOUS SYSTEM, IRIDOLOGY, HOLISTIC HEALTH]

MUSCULAR ESP—see KINETIC TELEPATHY.

MUSCULAR TREMORS—(Native American, Chiricahua Apaches) to be given a body sign whether the situation one is to encounter is right or wrong for one's self; movement of muscles on the outside and inside of the legs or around the eyes give the psychic the diagnostic sign. **Syn.** GOOSE BUMPS. [**cf.** HUMAN OMEN, PORTENT, OMENS Appendix 2]

MUSE—an allegorical personification of angels or guides who are in charge over the arts and sciences; any goddess presiding over a particular art. [**cf.** ETHERIC WORLD INTELLIGENCE, OUTER BAND, IMPERISHABLE ONES, ANGELS]

MUSEUM OF RECORDS—manuscripts, records, and higher studies stored in an area in the ASTRAL PLANE of the ETHERIC WORLD; information contains help in the EVOLUTION of earth; kept by the GREAT WHITE BROTHERHOOD. [**cf.** SOUL JURY, LORDS OF JUSTICE, MENTAL PLANE, REALM OF IDEAS]

MUSHROOM—(Hebrew, Vedic, Hinduism, Greece, Britain) (botane) the juice of the red-spotted variety was used in ancient times for its ability to induce visions which brought insight as to how the country should be governed; information was held sacred. **Syn.** HOLY FIRE, FLY AGARIC MUSCARIA, SOMA, LAW OF SUBSERVIENCE Appendix 7, BOTANE Appendix 2, PSYCHOTROPIC PLANTS]

MUSIC ELEMENTALS—NATURE SPIRITS that show themselves and perform for humans when music is played within the sound range and rhythm for their subtle bodies; woodland fairies are joyous by nature and appreciate mankind's generosity to play music for them. (Inconcl.) [**cf.** COSMIC MUSIC, LIGHT BODIES]

MUSIC HEALING—to use sound especially choreographed to change BODY CHEMISTRY and aid the body to heal itself more quickly; rhythm, tones, and certain musical pieces loosen the block of muscle tension, bring harmony to mentally disturbed patients, and influence the patient's AURA, which in turn changes body chemistry. (Inconcl.) [**cf.** COSMIC MUSIC, BLOCKS, GREAT TONE OF NATURE, MOLECULAR CHORUS, WHITE NOISE]

MUSIC OF THE SPHERES—1. sound vibrating from objects and living organisms that cannot be heard with the physical ear but can be perceived clairaudiently or by instruments designed to amplify these sounds; when a unit, system, or organism is functioning properly its chords and melody are harmonious; every vibrational frequency of an atom makes a different sound and atoms gravitate to each other by this sound; nature is composed of a number of elements that make a musical scale unknown to the human range of hearing; **2.** a choir of angels in the ETHERIC WORLD which is consecrated to music and rhythmic chanting; music is a magnitude of various octaves and keys, produced without the vocal chords; angels speak from the mind and sing from the heart; perceived clairaudiently if in a high state of consciousness. (Inconcl.) **Syn.** COSMIC MUSIC. [**cf.** INCANTATIONS, HARP, GREGORIAN CHANTS, VIBRATIONS, COLOR]

MUSIC THERAPIST—(clinical) one who treats mentally disturbed persons with especially choreographed sound and music that brings tranquility and balance to their thinking; effective tool with depressives and schizophrenics. (Inconcl.) [**cf.** MUSIC HEALING, BLOCKS, INTONING, SHOOTING CHANT, CHANTING]

MUSICAL LIGHTS—the seven chakras which correspond to one of the seven notes of the octave; each chakra withdraws vital life force from the atmosphere for its physical plexus, according to the vibrational frequency of each note. (Inconcl.) [**cf.** KUNDALINI, CHAKRAS, SOUNDS-WITH-POWER]

MUSICAL SCIENCE—study of the fundamental principles of universal sound and rhythm; belief: every thing created from the atom to the solar system possesses a keynote of its own. (Inconcl.) [**cf.** COSMIC SOUND, CLAIRAUDIENCE, RAGAS, VIBRATIONS, COLOR]

MUSICIAN MEDIUM—1. one who plays melodious music on an instrument without touching it; ETHERIC WORLD INTELLIGENCES pick up the instrument lying close to the medium and play it; performed while medium is in a TRANCE state and his or her ECTOPLASM is used by the intelligence. [**cf.** PRECIPITATION Appendix 2] **2.** one who allows an etheric world intelligence to intervene, when in a relaxed state of consciousness, and impress upon her or his mind musical compositions far beyond their own capabilities. [**cf.** INSPIRATIONAL ART, TRANCE]

MUSING—1. absorbed in thought, contemplating; **2.** (magic) a ritual used to invoke one's personal she-god to perform psychic phenomena. [**cf.** MUSE, ETHERIC WORLD INTELLIGENCE, INSPIRATIONAL THOUGHT, INVOCATION]

MUTAGEN—an agent used by the alchemists that

415

causes biological mutation. [cf. PARTHENOGENE-SIS, FIRE OF THE SAGES, ALCHEMICAL PRINCIPLES]

MUTANTS—(ufology) colorful, living organisms inhabiting outer space that have various indefinite shapes and these shapes are constantly changing in size and form; organisms float and pulsate at different speeds; cannot be seen by the physical eye but can be photographed on special film. (Inconcl.) **Syn.** CRITTERS, AEROFORMS. [cf. UFOLOGY, EXTRA-TERRESTRIAL BEINGS, PLASMATIC FAUNA, COSMIC PULSE]

MUTATION OF ENERGY—(ufology) organisms in outer space that change from one shape and size to another shape and size so easily as if this is an important part of their function; not detectable by the physical eye but detectable with instrumentation. (Inconcl.) [cf. MUTATION, DYNAMIC TRANSITIONS, COSMIC PULSE, ETHEREAN BEINGS, LIVING CREATURES OF OUR ATMOSPHERE]

MUTI—(Sanskrit) the highest; PERFECTNESS: the ABSOLUTE: see TOTALITY.

MUTUAL LANGUAGE—(penduluming) the style, size, direction, and speed of the swing of the PENDULUM is determined by the CONSCIOUS MIND, SUBCONSCIOUS MIND and the pendulum. [cf. RADIESTHETIC SENSE, PENDULUM POWER, WITNESS, DOWSING, RESET]

MYANG-HDAS—(Tibet) to experience the true goal of peace, ENLIGHTENMENT; one's mind travels beyond all planes in the etheric world, the density, heavens, and nature; occurs during deep MEDITATION; (indescribable in today's language). **Syn.** NIRVANA. [cf. SEVENTH PLANE, SOUL PROJECTION, CAVE MEDITATION, NO-MIND STATE, BLISS]

MYCOPHAGES—nations addicted to eating mushrooms for their visionary properties. [cf. ETHNO-MYCOLOGY, MUSHROOMS, PSYCHOTROPIC DRUGS, HALLUCINATION]

MYCOPHOBES—nations afraid of mushroom eating. [cf. ETHNOMYCOLOGY]

MYOCLONIC JERK—(dreams) a spasmodic movement of the whole body or a snap of the head and neck occuring in the onset of sleep; CONSCIOUS MIND steps out of the body and a few minutes later, it steps back in the body causing an abrupt flareup of electrical activity in the brain; theories: 1. sensations of falling as one dozes off to sleep causes one

to automatically shake and retrieve itself; 2. hypnogogic images are unpleasant and sleeper attempts to drive them away; 3. ASTRAL BODY steps out of the physical body to rejuvenate itself and one feels this difference and snaps it back. (Inconcl.) [cf. ASTRAL PROJECTIONS, DREAMS Appendix 2, HYPNA-GOGIC]

MYRRH—plant used in ancient times for increasing psychic sensitivity, medicinal purposes, embalming corpses, and preserving foods. [cf. SENSATION CONSCIOUSNESS, INCENSE, BOTANE, LAW OF SUBSERVIENCE Appendix 7, DOCTRINE OF SIGNATURES, HEALING]

MYRTLE—(botane) a plant with a vibrational frequency that makes it compatible with women; (ancient) placed in a prayer book so it would reveal psychic information regarding one's lover. [cf. BOTANE, SENSATION CONSCIOUSNESS, FLOWER THERAPY, ROSEMARY]

MYSTERIES OF ANTIQUITY—schools that taught immutable laws concerning the human mind and its relationship to the body and the COSMOS; esoteric secrets that were divided into two parts: The LESSER MYSTERIES and the GREATER MYSTERIES; this wisdom was kept back from the masses until they could accept the responsibility that comes with in-depth knowledge; psychic skills and psychic healings were a normal part of this teaching. [cf. PARAPSYCHOLOGY, METAPHYSICS]

MYSTERION—(Greece) 1. one who has been nominated to the study of the secret mysteries; 2. a psychic who is well-grounded with full control over his psychic powers.

MYSTERIOUS STONE—see PHILOSOPHER'S STONE.

MYSTIC—one who: brings new knowledge of spiritual Truths (proven or not); incorporates psychic skills and psychic healings with religion; aims to experience the HIGHER SELF wherein the EGO is demolished and one transcends into a high awareness with a deep understanding of existence; believes in a superior order of things, in God, and in life eternal; constantly seeks the inner meaning to all things regardless of how traumatic the outer experience is; helps change people in a peaceful manner. **Syn.** PSYCHIC. [cf. MYSTIC CHRISTIAN, MYSTICISM]

MYSTIC CHRISTIAN—(Earlyne Chaney) one who follows the Christ teachings and is a PSYCHIC and

MEDIUM; "one whose inner life is more important than his or her outer life."

MYSTIC EXPERIENCE—1. (LeRoy Zemke) "an emotional one-time event that brings about a change in one's life that is of permanent value (a change of thought about one's self)"; 2. (Adam Smith) "episodes of intense and immediate cognition in which the total personality is absorbed in an intimate, though transient, relationship with the basic forces, cycles, and mechanisms, at work in the universe and in his own psychosomatic composite"; 3. (Christian)a direct experience of God, a spiritual marriage; 4. a direct apperception of eternal being; an experience as if one's everyday personality is dissolved or merged into all. [**cf.** MYSTICISM, MYSTERION, MYSTIC]

MYSTIC HEALING—see METAPHYSICAL HEALING.

MYSTIC MARRIAGE—the uniting of the PITUITARY GLAND and PINEAL GLAND in the purification process of the SOUL-MIND; when these two unite, the third-eye is thoroughly opened and one will accomplish great things. [**cf.** GLORIFIED BODY, THIRD-EYE AREA, CHAKRAS]

MYSTIC RING—a fleshly ring on the ring-finger of the right hand appearing spontaneously overnight; recognized to designate the betrothal of Christ to the individual; occurs to individuals who have religious hysteria, or who go through a highly emotional state pertaining to the church. (Inconcl.) [**cf.** STIGMATA, HOLY SPIRIT, ELONGATION, PSYCHIC IMPRINT]

MYSTIC ZONE—the upper half of the ETHERIC WORLD that inhabits intelligences without form; those intelligences who are merging into PURE CONSCIOUSNESS, called angels. **Syn.** EMPYREAN ZONE. [**cf.** ANGELOLOGY, ANGEL HIERARCHY, EXALTED ONES, LIGHT BODIES]

MYSTIC-TYPE STATE OF CONSCIOUSNESS—a level of awareness in which psychic information comes into the mind and one can feel comfortable that it is accurate. [**cf.** GOING-TO-LEVEL, THREE FINGER TECHNIQUE, ALTERED-STATE-OF-CONSCIOUSNESS]

MYSTICAL—pertains to psychic skills or ESOTERIC SCIENCE.

MYSTICAL ECSTASY—(Greek *es, stasis,* "to stand aside") a spontaneous experience in which one becomes entranced and an ETHERIC WORLD INTELLIGENCE steps inside the body to perform an important task; the CONSCIOUS MIND cannot handle the present emotional situation so it steps aside and allows the physical body to be momentarily taken over by the intelligence; e.g., within moments, the woman cut open the dog, removed the cancerous growth that was causing excruciating pain, and sewed up the wound, knowing absolutely nothing about surgery. [**cf.** IMPERSONATION, PSYCHIC SURGERY, ETHERIC SURGERY, VOICE TRANCE, LEVITATION-TK]

MYSTICAL THEOSOPHY—knowledge of God in its entirety; a never ending learning process of universal laws.

MYSTICISM—(Greek *mystico,* "hidden wisdom"; *mueo,* "to initiate") 1. a highly, intellectual secretive science of the relationship between visible and invisible beings and their power; (theosophy) doctrine that one can see into the INVISIBLE WORLD and train her or himself to communicate with the life there in order to learn the laws of the invisible world; an attempt of humanity to enjoy communion with the highest energies and eventually GOD; 2. to seek union with God and understand the laws that pertain to make this union; only those who were emotionally ready were considered as initiates to take the training to unite with God; (Oxford University) belief in the possibility of union with the divine nature by means of ecstatic contemplation and reliance on INTUITION for knowledge; 3. mysticism has no mundane leader, such as JESUS, ALLAH, or BRAHMA; 4.(Rosicrucian) doctrine: "man possesses an innate link with the Divine from which all things emanate and upon which they are dependent"; 5. doctrine: man goes through many steps, called initiations, in an attempt to have a personal union with his or her concept of God and to reach transcendental power; 6. (Vedic) study of the True Knowledge of God; man can attain NIRVANA, the GODHEAD, while in a human body. **Sim.** PARAPSYCHOLOGY. [**cf.** WHITE MAGIC, MENTAL PSYCHISM, PHYSICAL PSYCHISM, MANTIC ART]

MYSTICO—prefix meaning "wisdom, hidden wisdom."

MYSTICO-RELIGIOUS—a sect that has principles mysterious to scientific proof; known as the ancient philosophies of the OCCULT. [**cf.** SPIRITUALISM, MANTIC ARTS, YOGA, BUDDHISM]

MYTH—a story from true expression of historical

reality, "telling who man is, where he is going, and where he came from"; spontaneous reactions of the SOUL-MIND coming from the initial stage of its origin resulting in a belief or pattern of inner feeling long after the origin; (Joseph Campbell) "spontaneous productions of the psyche from the germ power of its source." [cf. ARCHETYPAL IMAGES, MEMORY BANK]

MYTHOLOGY—collection of stories and signs handed down throughout the ages symbolizing mankind's early beliefs and concepts of the universes, their demi-gods and deities, and their relationship to same.

N-RAYS—1. coined by Prosper Blondiot; see VITAL LIFE FORCE; 2. (France) radiation that emanates from the brain and nerve centers; see AURA; 3. PSYCHIC ENERGY.

N/UM—(Kalahari Desert) an energy in the body that can be used for healing; concentrated at the pit of the stomach and base of the spine; this energy is heated to a boiling point to make it rise up the spine by singing, rhythmic dancing, and DESIRE of the tribe to heal their sick; healer must have thoughts that are "nothing in the head," to make the energy useful; when it reaches the head it can be used to heal members of the tribe; sometimes healer loses control because of the overwhelming power, but tribe members step in to his rescue and after healer drinks cool water, he is ready to proceed. [cf. !KIA FIRE, TRANCE, PARANORMAL HEALER]

NABHI—(Old Testament) a CALLED PERSON; one who was "breathed upon" by the HOLY SPIRIT and is then able to see psychic visions, speak, or sing psychic information; roams the streets playing the flute, harp or tambourine to keep himself psyched up so he can read and prophesy for the people. [cf. GOING-TO-LEVEL, MUSIC THERAPIST, STAND-UP READER]

NADA—an internally generated sound, imaginary or natural; a sound serving as the object for MEDITATION; an inner sound current; the sound potency that never ends, the subtle elements of sound regarded as eternal, absolute and self-contained; the first sound to emerge from Nada was OM; e.g., sitting near a waterfall or windsource and concentrating on the monotonous sound of the wind or water. **Syn.** WHITE NOISE. [cf. TONING, SPHERES OF RESONANCE, OHM]

NADAM—see WHITE NOISE.

NADIS—(esoteric) the NERVOUS SYSTEM of the ASTRAL BODY connecting the ASTRAL BRAIN with the physical brain; thousands of invisible fluidic nerve canals, infiltrating the physical nervous system, which stem out from the base of the spine (KANDA) reaching various organs of the physical body; these ethereal canals are made of PHYSICAL ETHERS (LIGHT, PRANA, ELECTRICITY, MENTAL-REFLECTING-ETHER), KARMA, bone marrow, BRAIN DEWS, GOLDEN OIL, and chemicals of the glands; depends upon the SOLAR PLEXUS CHAKRA for the incoming of COSMIC ENERGY; can be manipulated by the human mind to increase in strength, and be directed where it can be useful for psychic healing and psychic skills. **Syn.** MAGNETIC FLUID. [cf. THIRD-EYE AREA, PITUITARY GLAND, PINEAL GLAND]

NAGA—(Hinduism) a male nature spirit considered semidivine; perceived psychically around water as half human and half serpent; symbolic of the negation man must overcome; can be harmful or beneficial to man; female is **nagini. Syn.** SERPENT-SPIRIT. [cf. POLARITY, NEGATIVE THOUGHT, YIN AND YANG]

NAGUAL—1. (Native Central American) an etheric world entity communicating with man by residing in an animal; 2. (don Juan) "one realm of the universe pertaining to the order of all existing matter, making up one half of the totality of man; an unseen source of all there is." [cf. ETHERIC WORLD INTELLIGENCE, SUPERCONSCIOUS MIND, MENTAL PLANE]

NAIAD—(Greece) a nymph which presides over brooks, fountains, rivers, and springs; considered to be the counterpart of the divinity of girls who purify themselves. [cf. NATURE SPIRIT, NYMPHS]

NAICIDS—see NAIAD.

NALJOR—(Buddhism) a teacher of the secret wisdoms, considered to be a saint. [cf. SAINT, ANGEL HEIRARCHY]

NAMAPATHY—(ancient) to heal through the combination of sound and music which is composed especially for the purpose of healing. **Syn.** MUSIC HEALING. [cf. SOUND HEALING, OHM, HARP, SYMPATHETIC VIBRATION]

NAMASKAR CONSCIOUSNESS—(Hinduism) "the divinity in me salutes the divinity in you"; a salutation used for opening sermons, lectures and personal conversations. [cf. AFFIRMATIONS, INCANTATIONS]

NAMASTE—(Hinduism) "I salute the divinity in you"; usually said with palms of both hands pressed together vertically in front of the bosom, and the body bows while the hands come together; used as a salutation; conventional Hindu expression on meeting or parting. [cf. SYMBOLISM, WORDS-WITH-POWER, NAMASKAR CONSCIOUSNESS]

NAME—(esoteric) a necessary tool for thought and speech in order for humanity to manipulate the atoms and shape the things of earth; patterns are formed en masse from the root sound when a word is spoken verbally or silently; root sound has been collecting in the COLLECTIVE UNCONSCIOUS since gutteral utterance began and now surfaces to mingle with humanity's conscious consciousness for a completion of an object or activity; 1. each name (or word) mankind has given something has a vibrational frequency that makes a pattern or symbol of that something in one's mind through association: (a) object: to say "table" brings a pattern of a flat surface with four legs out of the collective unconscious; "my kitchen table" brings a yellow formica table top and chrome legs out of the conscious consciousness; the table stays in tact; (b) action: to think "running" differentiates one's mode of travel from flying or walking, and the legs move in a running motion; (c) personal name: a uniqueness of the SOUL-MIND in one particular incarnation that separates one from his or her other incarnations; 2. memory "gimmicks" are used to remind one of something; an associated device both as aspects or descriptions or events; 3. theory: the vibrational frequency of the name of an object or activity puts one into the inherent power of that object. [cf. EVIL MOUTH, PRAYER POWER, MAGIC VERSE, HOLD THE THOUGHT, JACK]

NAME-SOUL—(Eskimo) a TRANSMIGRATION theory: a SOUL-MIND attaches itself to a name of another soul-mind who is in an earth vibration and eventually enters that earthly soul-mind. [cf. WALK-IN, INCARNATIONAL EXCHANGE, BIRTH SCIENCE]

NAMES-OF-POWER—1. (human) the individual name of a person, especially the first name; when spoken orally or silently, taps into the inherent characteristics and karmic qualities of that person; one's own first name is a unique pattern that resonates through the whole universe and can be used for past, present, and future psychic information pertaining to that person; by concentrating on one's own name one can receive a better message from a psychic or from themselves when doing psychic work; 2. certain words, because of their sound, have a more powerful vibratory rate and can be used to bring into effect certain things when

pronounced singularly, en masse, sung or chanted; see GRIMOIRE and MANTRA. [cf. JACK, JESUS, VERSE MAGIC, PSYCHIC SHIELD, CLOAK OF INSULATION, BLESS, DANGER CHARGED WORDS]

NAN-A-PUSH—a NATURE SPIRIT of the forest; belongs to the Leni-Lenapi nature spirit group.

NANABUSH—(Native American) the intelligences living inside the earth; willing to communicate with earthlings to bring knowledge and counsel. [cf. KICHI-MANITOU, HOLLOW EARTH]

NAPI—(Native American, Blackfoot) white old man; an ETHERIC WORLD INTELLIGENCE taking on the temporary form of an animal or bird bringing information and help to the mediumistic Indian. [cf. TRICKSTER, SPIDER, COYOTE, OUTER BAND]

NAPISTU—(Mesopotamia) throat; designates the life principle, SOUL, BREATH and LIFE. [cf. SPIRIT, HOLY SPIRIT]

NARA-LOKA—(Hinduism) planes of earth where humans dwell. [cf. MUNDANE PLANE, PHYSICAL BODY, MATERIALISTIC MAN, EVOLUTION]

NARCOLEPSY—a spontaneous attack of deep sleep lasting for a short time that unexpectedly overtakes an individual during the daytime. [cf. DREAM ANALYSIS, PSYCHOSOMATIC DREAMS]

NARROW BAND TUNING—(dowsing) to keep one's mind centered on what one wants to find under the ground; e.g., if one wants to find water, they must narrow their thoughts to that of water. [cf. DOWSING QUESTION, MONKEY CHATTER, LAW OF ATTENTION Appendix 7]

NASA—abbr. NATIONAL AERONAUTICS AND SPACE ADMINISTRATION; an organization of the United States government working with the outer space intelligences, life forms, constructs, and other space oddities. [cf. UFOLOGY Appendix 5]

NASAL GAZE—a method of quieting the emotions and mind by gazing at the tip of one's nose during MEDITATION; also beneficial for stimulating the memory mechanism. [cf. VACILLATING, QUIETUDE, TAMING OF THE MIND, ZEN SICKNESS]

NAT—(Southern Asia) an etheric world entity with evil intentions that communicates with mankind. [cf. DENSITY, HAUNTING, CLOAK OF INSULATION, LAW OF LIKE ATTRACTS LIKE Appendix 7]

NAT CULT—(Southern Asia) a group of worshipers and psychic communicators who call in the low, inferior entities of the etheric world for evil intent; (do not confuse with DESTRUCTIVE-BRAINWASH-ING CULT). [cf. GREAT BEAST, ETERNITIES, COUNTS OF HELL]

NATIONAL KARMAN—(Sanskrit) see MASS KARMA.

NATSAW—see PSYCHIC or WIZARD.

NATURAL BIRTH CONTROL—to use ASTROLOGY, lunar phases, and the traditional rhythm method for calculating fertile and infertile days of the woman. [cf. ASTROLOGICAL BIRTH CONTROL]

NATURAL CONCEPTION AVOIDANCE—study of the natural ways to control conception; 1. lunar conception; 2. ASTROLOGICAL BIRTH-CONTROL; 3. moment of ovulation; 4. mental control of conception. [cf. COSMO-BIOLOGICAL BIRTH CONTROL, BIRTH CONSCIOUSNESS]

NATURAL DISCOINCIDENCE—(astral projection) the separation of the ASTRAL BODY about an inch above the physical body; occurs in a normal sleep. [cf. MYOCLONIC JERK, SLIGHTLY-OUT-OF-BODY]

NATURAL HEALERS—pertains to healing with natural methods and natural ingredients; (do not confuse with a person who is born with healing abilities). [cf. CELL SALTS, MASSAGE, HEALEE, PRACTITIONER, LAW OF HEALING Appendix 7]

NATURAL INFRASOUND—sounds made by nature as it grows; can be perceived clairaudiently; resonates below the threshold of hearing of the physical ears. (Inconcl.) **Syn.** NOISY SILENCE, MUSIC OF THE SPHERES. [cf. THRESHOLD CONTROL, VIBRATIONS, CLAIRAUDIENCE]

NATURAL LAW—an unchangeable principle of the universes that was set in motion to govern all that had been created in the beginning; a law of nature that always existed and always will exist. [cf. Appendix 7]

NATURAL MAGIC—the use of psychic energy stored and concealed in animals, herbs, stones, numbers, and all other phenomena of the world; utilizes the principle of MACROCOSM and MICRO-COSM. [cf. WHITE MAGIC, CEREMONIAL MAGIC, ASSOCIATION MAGIC, LAW OF REPETITION Appendix 7]

NATURAL MAGNET—(psychic healing) emits a MAGNETIC FLUD similar to the magnetic fluid that hands emit; used in healing by placing the magnet

on the diseased area and then moving it away from the diseased area to draw out the congestion, or by using the POLARITY of the magnet and placing it on the body accordingly; does not have to be charged with psychic energy like an amulet. **Syn.** LODESTONE. [cf. MAGNET HEALING, MAGNE-TOLOGY Appendix 5]

NATURAL MEDIUM—one who is born with the proper NERVOUS SYSTEM and the proper chemicals in their body that can be used by the ETHERIC WORLD INTELLIGENCES for PHYSICAL PSYCHISM; aware or unaware of this ability; special characteristic of a natural-born medium is to produce physical psychic phenomena spontaneously and randomly; often occurs against their will; e.g., knocks heard within their environment, articles missing from his or her home; can be properly trained in the SEANCE room; (Allan Kardec) this ability is not proof of superiority or moral advancement, but only shows that the person has developed this ability in another life. [cf. SUBCONSCIOUSLY WILLED, KARMICALLY WILLED, GUIDE, META-PHYSICS, SPIRITUALISM]

NATURAL SOMNAMBULIST—1. one who has an ECSTATIC psychic experience without previous preparation or instruction; ETHERIC WORLD INTEL-LIGENCE makes her or himself known in some physical psychic manner, usually entering the voice box of the individual; individual is taken under into a deep hypnotic state for a few minutes for the physical phenomena to occur; sometimes the individual remembers nothing except being asleep or feeling exhilerated later, but those in their presence report to him or her the experience as they viewed it; from that time on, the physical phenomenon grows more perfect and the MEDIUM then has control over the intelligence. [cf. DEPENDENT VOICE, TRANCE] 2. one who performs physical phychism during a normal night sleep, such as PRECIPITATION PAINTING. [cf. PRECIPITATION Appendix 2]

NATURAL SPIRITISM—to allow an ETHERIC WORLD INTELLIGENCE to intervene for physical phenomena; matter is moved so that everyone can see; medium is capable of relaxing so that the intelligence can enter their body and/or mind to perform the psychism; e.g., LEVITATION-TK. **Syn.** SPONTANEOUS PHYSICAL MANIFESTATION. [cf. MEDIANIMIC, GRAVITY CONTROL, TELEKINESIS, NONHUMAN-TK]

NATURAL SYMBOLS—psychic visionary scenes of pictures that have the same interpretation among most psychics, e.g., ocean of rough waters means rough days; a flag means victory; a rainbow means a desire will be fulfilled. **Syn.** UNIVERSAL SYMBOLS. [**cf.** PSYCHIC MESSAGE, DREAM SYMBOLISM, ARCHE-TYPAL IMAGES]

NATURAL-BORN PSYCHIC—an individual who has his or her first psychic experiences without any preparation and sometimes without any knowledge of this work; occurs in childhood or in teen years; individual accomplished this ability in a past INCARNATION, which is never lost from incarnation to incarnation; results in the psychic skills of PROPHECY, INTUITION, POLTERGEIST FOCUS, daily recall of DREAMS, MENTAL TELEPATHY or DOWSING; natural-born psychic has no trouble in perfecting their skills; developing new skills are sometimes overshadowed by traits of the innate skills; psychic experiences occur randomly and spontaneously for the natural-born and are difficult to keep under control without professional training; designating a specific time daily or weekly to open psychic doors helps bring psychic experiences under obeyance; natural-born psychics' abilities began accelerating, without deliberation, in the late 1970s. [**cf.** NONINTENTIONAL ESP, CLOAK OF INSULATION]

NATURE—(esoteric) (capitalized) 1. the soul of TOTALITY in its flesh in all its forms; 2. an alive, evolving entity in itself; 3. GOD. [**cf.** MACROCOSM, LIGHT]

NATURE BEING KINGDOM—see NATURE KINGDOM.

NATURE BEINGS—see NATURE SPIRITS.

NATURE DEVA—see ANGELS.

NATURE KINGDOM—(esoteric) includes both the ANGEL KINGDOM and the nature spirit kingdom working harmoniously together as interdependent and independent intelligences; alive, invisible, formless intelligent energy fields that are responsible for forming the ETHERIC DOUBLE for all earth systems, animate and inanimate, that humanity knows as the THIRD DIMENSION; can be perceived clairvoyantly and clairaudiently in angel or nature spirit form; desire to communicate with earthlings and maintain harmony in earth; e.g., angels have charge over such things as pollution and parking lots, while NATURE SPIRITS have charge over trees, grass, etc. (Inconcl.) [**cf.** ANGEL CONSCIOUSNESS, KINGDOM]

NATURE LORDS—(esoteric) angels who have charge over large areas; when perceived clairvoyantly they appear thirty feet tall, embodied in the nature area itself; e.g., have charge over the mountains of a country, the Grand Canyon, etc.; made of ETHEREAL substance which is very close to CELESTIAL substance; working on the sixth step in the climb to GODHEAD. (Inconcl.) **Syn.** LORDSHIPS. [**cf.** GODHOOD, ANGEL HIERARCHY, ANGEL KINGDOM]

NATURE PSYCHOKINESIS—abbr. NATURE-PK; to use one's mind to alter the properties of nature; accomplished through concentration and a sincere desire to harm no person or thing of nature; possible to change nature's chemistry, form, position, age, or its normal path of life; ability includes instantaneous and long term phenomenon; e.g., to heal a plant or animal by mental energy or magnetic energy from the palms, to change the direction of the spider, to split a cloud, to direct a tree to grow a new limb in a specific spot, to project one's consciousness in the air to promote rain on one's crops, and to hold a bean sprout in one's hand bringing the sprout back to the seed stage. [**cf.** HUMAN-PSYCHOKINESIS, ARTICLE-PSYCHO-KINESIS, PK-LT]

NATURE SPIRITS—(esoteric) 1. (nature kingdom) (a) a highly intelligent force taken from the ethereal substance around the earth which emanates from humanity's minds and emotions; give form and function to fields of energy while working harmoniously with the nature blueprints of the earth; inhabit all of earth's NATURE, AIR, EARTH, WATER, and FIRE; each one has a special function in natural or in manufactured things; e.g., have charge over the trees and charge over parking lots; (b) have charge over the planet's blueprints to provide for its fulfillment and maintenance; (c) nature spirits are a lower order than the nature devas (angels), composed of denser etheric matter; generate from the FIFTH and SIXTH PLANES of earth's terrestrial atmosphere; (d) capable of shaping into a tiny person or a giant; behave in a human manner or in a half-human and half-animal manner; (e) desire to communicate with earthlings; capable of materializing for a short time in a physical level of vibration to be seen by earthlings; change dimensions frequently and easily; (f) sensitive to human emotions and act accordingly, loveable and helpful, or naughty and destructive; **(g)** have no SOUL-MIND that works out KARMA and incarnates often; some are known to live hundreds of years; seem to be limitless, unsubstantial, and free; help people work out their karma; propagate offspring and die due to disease, not for spiritual development of their own; see FAIRIES. [**cf.** Appendix 3 for individual names of each type] **2.** (Carl Jung) nature spirits are an early stage of human evolution; intelligent energy forms "involving" down into denser matter, ever seeking lower coarser and more enduring substance from which to build their forms to begin their "evolutionary" path upward. [**cf.** EVOLUTION, INVOLUTION, MONAD]

NATURE TELEPATHY—**1.** to send a mental message to any one of the three nature kingdoms and receive a response from the message; transference of thought can be between a plant, stone, fish, animal, insect, or weather elements; an inborn trait or can be learned; see ANPSI, MINPSI, and BOTANE; **2.** to have such a rapport with the atmosphere and elements of the planet that one's body responds to hurricane, volcanic eruptions, and earthquakes, etc.; body is distressed for a few days before the weather catastrophe and is relieved when it occurs; e.g., psychic is awakened in the night with an upset stomach, shivering in a warm room, and sensing death; body sensations continue for the next day until the volcano erupts; (volcano kills many persons and occurs in a cold climate). [**cf.** ATMOSPHERE CONTROL Appendix 2]

NATUROPATHY—system of treating disease employing natural agencies, such as air, sunshine; rejects the use of drugs and medicine. [**cf.** HOLISTIC HEALTH, ALTERNATIVES, UNORTHODOX HEALING, PSYCHIC HEALING]

NAUGHTY GHOST—see POLTERGEIST.

NAVAJO SHAMAN—(Native American, Navajo) three kinds: the HERBALIST, the HAND TREMBLER DIAGNOSTICIAN, and the SINGER. [**cf.** SHAMANSHIP]

NAVEL CHAKRA—See SPLEEN CHAKRA.

NDE—abbr. for NEAR-DEATH EXPERIENCE.

NEAR-DEATH EXPERIENCE—to be declared clinically dead, and return to life remembering the experience of the LIFE FORCE leaving the PHYSICAL BODY and the reason for returning; although cases vary, the following are similarities: individual sees his or her physical body and the medical staff

working on them; a microfilm of happenings of his or her present life passes swiftly by their eyes; one sees a tunnel with a bright light at the end and meets friends and relatives who speak and encourage him or her to return to earth to finish their life. [**cf.** DEATHBED EXPERIENCE, DEATH ANGEL]

NEBULAR HYPOTHESIS—the solar system came into existence as a gigantic glowing nebula which cooled and formed the present system of which earth is a part.

NECROMANCER—(Arabia, Greece, Tibet) see MEDIUM and PSYCHIC. **Syn.** NECROMANTIST.

NECROMANCY—**1.** (Latin *necromantia*, "divination by corpses") (Tibet, Greece, Arabia, Old Testament Bible) to perceive PSYCHIC INFORMATION with the help of the ETHERIC WORLD INTELLIGENCES for guidance, protection, and prophecy; used for professional, public, and private purposes. **Sim.** SPIRITUALISM. [**cf.** PARAPSYCHOLOGY, MYSTICISM, MAGIC] **2.** (French, medieval Latin *nigro mantia*, "black") calling upon inferior entities of the etheric world to perform activity for evil intent in BLACK MAGIC rituals.

NECROMANTEION—(Greece) an inner chamber within the ancient temples which was used by the mediums to contact their ETHERIC WORLD INTELLIGENCES; kept very sacred; communication from the etheric world brought forth PROPHECY and guidance for the country, knowledge and wisdom pertaining to DEATH, REBIRTH, and the principles of the invisible planes; VOICE TRANCE was the most popular skill used. [**cf.** TRUMPET, INDEPENDENT VOICE, CONTROL, SEANCE]

NECROMANTIC BELL—a tiny bell used in mediumistic sessions to summon the etheric world guides when the mediums were ready for them to intervene with psychic information or activity. (**cf.** SOUNDS-WITH-POWER; BELL, BOOK AND CANDLE; GREAT TONE OF NATURE]

NECROMANTIC INCUBATION—(dreams) to place a question with one's etheric world guides before going to sleep; answer comes in the DREAMSTUFF or in a PSYCHIC EXPERIENCE DURING SLEEP. [**cf.** INCUBATION DREAMING]

NECTAR—liquid produced by certain plants that helps to induce visions or trance; e.g., the red-top mushroom, mead, or fermented honey. [**cf.** PSYCHOTROPIC PLANTS]

NEED-DETERMINED RESPONSE—PSYCHIC IN-FORMATION or psychic activity occuring spontaneously to a PSYCHIC, regardless of conditions, because the need is great; psychism is not planned, willed, or knowingly desired but recognized to occur for a special reason; human necessities can trigger psychic phenomena; occurs in the following methods: PSYCHIC EXPERIENCE DURING SLEEP, CRISIS PHENOMENA, falling into a LIGHT STATE OF HYPNOSIS, TALKING-IN-TONGUES, AUTOMATIC WRITING impulse, OUIJA BOARD response, MENTAL DISSOCIATION during meditation, and an involuntary SECONDARY PERSONALITY coming through a medium. [**cf.** EMOTIONAL PSYCHISM, RANDOM PSYCHISM, SPONTANEOUS PSI]

NEFIA—(Sufi) see ZIKR and PSYCHIC.

NEFILM—(Genesis, Hebrew, "those who descended from heaven") human beings in some kind of form who came to planet earth in the beginning; brought life to the planet. (Inconcl.) [**cf.** SUB-SURFACE KINGDOMS, MASS KARMA, EVOLUTION]

NEGAPSI—powerful energy that reverses or inverts all psi activity in the area; psychism turns backward; a blessing could end up to be a curse. [**cf.** LAW OF LIKE ATTRACTS LIKE Appendix 7, CLOAK OF INSULATION, MOOD ADJECTIVE CHECK LIST]

NEGATIVE—1. pertains to the pole of POLARITY that compliments the positive; negative pole is anxious to team with the positive as each supplies what the other lacks; it takes both poles of polarity to make a manifestation in the etheric and MUNDANE WORLD; passive, static receptive; 2. when used in conjunction with ELECTRICITY it means the presence of an excessive amount of electrons in a unit; 3. when used in reference to a worldly experience, it means in poor taste, wrong, bad, harmful, or the opposite of what should have happened according to the morals and belief system of the person making the judgment. [**cf.** POSITIVE, PROTONS, NEGATIVE THOUGHT, NEGATIVE ELEMENTAL, LAW OF OPPOSITIVES Appendix 7]

NEGATIVE ELEMENTAL—continual thoughts of jealousy, hate, resentment, anxiety, fear, guilt or self-condemnation which build an atmosphere and hover over the thinker; as long as the feelings and thoughts are persistent, the ELEMENTAL is nourished and will seek a weak point in the thinker's AURA that it can operate through; brings harm to the thinker through disease, accidents, or a break down of appliances. [**cf.** MASS ELEMENTAL, MASS HYSTERIA]

NEGATIVE ENTROPY—coined by Erwin Schroedinger (1945); see VITAL LIFE FORCE.

NEGATIVE FLUID—ergs of energy emanating from the minds of skeptics or doubters that follow the nature of the thought; will block or try to hinder a psychic or medium from performing. [**cf.** SHEEP AND GOATS EFFECT, SHIELDING, LAW OF LIKE ATTRACTS LIKE Appendix 7, ILL-WISHING]

NEGATIVE GREEN ENERGY—(France) an energy found in the atmosphere and in the center of a pyramid; believed to be the energy that sharpens razor blades when placed in the pyramid; capable of dehydrating organic and inorganic objects. (Inconcl.) [**cf.** POSITIVE GREEN ENERGY, PYRAMID POWER]

NEGATIVE ION BEAMS—Dr. L. L. Vasiliev's theory: to set up a field of negative ions around a psychic makes him or her become artificially electrified and increases their psychic ability; (negative ions are particles with a negative electrical charge). [**cf.** GOING-TO-LEVEL, GUIDE]

NEGATIVE PSI—(psi-tasks) the element of scepticism that prevents a normal psychic experience. (Inconcl.) [**cf.** SHEEP AND GOATS EFFECT, NEGATIVE FLUID, SPONTANEOUS SYMPTOM SHIFTING, PSYCHIC BLOCK, SHIELDING]

NEGATIVE PSYCHISM—instinctual, primitive INTUITION and thoughts of persons in the environment that flow into a human's SOLAR PLEXUS unknowingly, which tend to influence the psychic's reading, making parts of it incorrect; psychic is unaware of this information until it works on the SYMPATHETIC NERVOUS SYSTEM and reaches the mental consciousness; this uncontrolled, undifferentiated information is usually difficult for the psychic to distinguish, between his or her own thoughts and psychic impressions; it is more noticeable when one opens their psychic doors; (do not confuse with EVIL information infiltrating from the inferior, invisible planes of consciousness). [**cf.** SHIELDING, CLOAK OF INSULATION, SPLODGER, BIOLOGICAL CONTACT, SYMPATHETIC INDUCTION]

NEGATIVE STRESS—a psychological response to a situation felt to be inappropriate by the one who makes the response; 1. a feeling of discomfort with one's emotional attitude toward an activity at the time of the activity, and a continual feeling of discomfort until one's point of view regarding the activity is changed; 2. the need for a decision but not having made it; 3. an outside stimuli strong enough to cause strain or distortion in the system for that individual; 4. (Hans Selye) "emotional pressures or supressed emotions stored in the NERVOUS SYSTEM causing an imbalance in the chemicals of the body"; 5. the section of the SYMPATHETIC NERVOUS SYSTEM as it increases its right to fire in the flight or fight mechanism. [cf. BLOCKS, EUSTRESS, NEGATIVE THOUGHT, KEY TO LIFE]

NEGATIVE THOUGHT—(June Bletzer) a thought instigated from within the mind of an individual which he or she feels is wrong; individual feels it is wrong because it is not in accord with his or her personal good judgment, personal or cultural value system, personal or moral standard, or personal self-worth; negativity is in the eyes of the beholder only, and will affect the body and affairs of the beholder only, until he or she corrects the thought to be compatible with their belief system; (do not confuse with an "errant" thought or a thought which does not have direction). [cf. BLOCKS, HOLISTIC HEALTH]

NEGENTROPY—term for NEGATIVE ENTROPY; (psi tasks) the target answers show no degree of sameness or similarity. Usage: psi interaction manifests as negentropy. [cf. BOOMERANG PSI, ANXIETY ATTACK, LOW VARIANCE, DECLINE EFFECT]

NELLIE—(San Blas Indians, Panama) a professional psychic who works as a TELEPATH for the whole tribe; telepath is hired by the government official to tune into the neighboring tribes telepathically to send and receive messages; there are no telephones in their culture. [cf. MENTAL TELEPATHY, LOVE-LINE, MIND-LINKING]

NEO—(Greek) preface meaning new, recent, fresh, young."

NEOPAGAN WITCHES—a new religion that descended from the ancient Mediterranean mystery schools which called themselves WICCA, "the wise one"; a small minority stayed together from 1800 to 1940 with a belief that their theology was more important than their pedigree; from the pieces of wisdom they could save they constructed this new pagan religion; belief in the universal Mother Goddess and KARMA. [cf. WITCH, WITCHDOCTOR]

NEOPHASIA—a form of TALKING-IN-TONGUES; the construction of a purely artificial language including GLOSSOLALIA and LINGUISTIC NEOFORMATION; automatic activity of fundamentalist religious groups; has no apparent grammar or prepositional vocabulary; sounds as pure gibberish but sometimes it is decipherable by another person in the group. [cf. RANDOM PSYCHISM, TENSION WAVE, SUBCONSCIOUSLY WILLED]

NEOPHYTE—a student who is in the process of changing their beliefs; a beginner; a student. [cf. DISCIPLE]

NEOPLATONISTS—(Alexandria A.D. 300) teacher of deep mysticism specializing in ANGELOLOGY and DEMONOLOGY and psychic skills.

NEOSPHERE—see ETHERIC WORLD.

NEPHELEGERETA—(Greek, "the piler of clouds") a nature spirit in charge of the clouds. [cf. NATURE SPIRITS]

NEPHESH—(Hebrew) see SOUL-MIND.

NEPHILIM—(Bible) a nature spirit that belongs to the race of giants; capable of appearing and disappearing apparently to fool people; monsters of the land. [cf. MONSTER ACTIVITY, DIMENSION-SHIFTING, NATURE SPIRITS]

NEREIDS—NATURE SPIRITS that take the title of deities, appearing fifty in number, and presiding over the seas of the earth; nymphs or daughters of the wise old man. **Syn.** NYMPHS, FAIRIES.

NERGAL—(Mesopotamia) God of the underworld in charge of wars and pestilence; identified with the red planet, Mars. [cf. DENSITY, HOLLOW EARTH, NATURE SPIRITS, DEMIGOD]

NERRIVIK—(Eskimo) nature spirit in charge of the sea animals. [cf. NATURE SPIRITS]

NERVE ELECTRICITY—psychic heat created from the heat waves that touch the retina in the back of the eye. [cf. THIRD-EYE AREA, MASTER EYE, THALAMUS]

NERVE ETHER—see NADIS.

NERVE FLUID—see NADIS and MAGNETIC FLUID.

NERVE-CENTER OF WISDOM—(Tibetan Buddhism) one of the SILVER CORD strands which extends from the SOUL-MIND to the LIFE-CORD-

HEART-SEED-ATOM. [cf. EMOTIONAL-ASTRAL-SEED-ATOM, HEART, SUBCONSCIOUS MIND, VAGUS NERVE, KARMA]

NERVOUS SYSTEM—(human) (esoteric) an invisible and visible electrical system in the body connected to the electrical system in the atmosphere, making it all one system without any breaks; the body transceiver points (the ACUPUNCTURE POINTS) correspond to and are a continuation of the NODES in the atmosphere; 1. each area of nerves has its own chemical formula, its own amps of electricity and its own power capabilities of building electrical erg forces; as the electric current runs through the nervous system it sets up MAGNETIC FIELDS which are controlled by the chemicals of the body; 2. the BRAIN is the center of this magnetic field and the brain is controlled by conscious thought impulses; EMOTIONS trigger the chemicals which activate the system and keep it regulated according to its activation; thoughts are the electricity of the system, emotions are the magnetism of the system, and the chemicals needed for the system come from the physiology of the body; all three are necessary in electrical systems; 3. a communicative method for the brain to receive data from the internal organs and transmit the appropriate messages back to those organs; 4. how one handles one's nervous system is an indication of how one is managing their incarnations; 5. the nervous system is divided into three systems which have special distinct functions; see CEREBROSPINAL NERVOUS SYSTEM, SYMPATHETIC NERVOUS SYSTEM, and VAGUS NERVE. (Inconcl.) [cf. WILL, PSYCHIC ENERGY, MATTER]

NERVOUSNESS—a vibrational frequency not compatible with the human organism or the planet; brought about by a personal decision that causes a disruption of one's basic mental conscousness; this in turn disrupts body functions; when one understands the TRUTH of his or her being and the Truth of the earth being, one will find it easier to control one's MIND, EMOTIONS and NERVOUS SYSTEM; then humanity will evolve and use another mechanism in place of the nervous system to learn soul-mind lessons. [cf. SYMPATHETIC NERVOUS SYSTEM, BRAIN, CEREBROSPINAL NERVOUS SYSTEM]

NETHERWORLD—see DENSITY.

NETTER—(ancient Egypt) the one Supreme God, creator of all there is; sacred; holy; plural **Netteru**; also spelled **nutur**; see TOTALITY.

NETWORKS OF CIVILIZATIONS—see PLANES.

NEURAL COMMUNICATION—(esoteric) the transfer of psychic information between a person's (electrical) NERVOUS SYSTEM, other parts of their body, the electrical system in the atmosphere, and the electrical system in living and inanimate things; everything has an electrical system so it is perfectly natural to receive and transmit psychic energy that is electrical in nature. [cf. CROSS-TALK, NODES, HOLOGRAM ENERGY, ACUPUNCTURE POINTS]

NEURAL DISCHARGE—everyday physical energy that one must let loose; (do not confuse with PSYCHIC ENERGY, which can be stored). [cf. SYMPATHETIC NERVOUS SYSTEM, ABDOMINAL BRAIN, SOLAR PLEXUS]

NEURIC ENERGY—coined by E. Barety (1887); see VITAL LIFE FORCE.

NEURICIDAD—coined by Barety (1887); see VITAL LIFE FORCE.

NEURO—prefix meaning "nerves."

NEUROLINGUISTIC PROGRAMMING—a system of organizing human behavior into its smallest component parts, on both the verbal and non-verbal levels.

NEUROMUSCULAR REACTION—(radiesthesia) a response of the PENDULIST to the radiations of the object the PENDULUM is blending with which results in movements of the pendulum. (Inconcl.) [cf. RADIESTHEOLOGY, MASTER EYE]

NEUROMUSCULAR THERAPY—coined and innovated by Paul St. John; a specific approach to the problem of pain by a form of deep massage combining ACUPRESSURE, SHIATSU, and numerous body techniques currently used by Western science; a natural therapy whereby a trained therapist uses pressure by the hand, thumb, elbow, or a small soft-tipped pressure bar, to specific trigger points in the body; this releases pent-up emotions that have settled in the body which prevented certain areas of the body from functioning properly; therapy allows a reversal of the stress-tension-pain cycle by interrupting afferent impulses to the spinal cord, reduces the intensity of nervous activity within the tissue and mechanically forces out toxic irritants which have accumulated at nerve receptor sites; muscles then relax and circulation increases allowing the body to return to normal. [cf. BLOCKS,

THERAPY LOCALIZATION, ROLFING, ALTERNA-TIVES, ORGAN LANGUAGE, SYSTEM OF DUCTS]

NEURON—fundamental functional unit of the NERVOUS SYSTEM. [**cf.** METABOLIC MONITOR, STRESS, EMOTION, SYNAPSE]

NEUROPHYSIOLOGIC SCIENCE—the study of subjective activities as induced by physical stimuli; how one feels and thinks about his or her behavior, environment, or another's behavior.

NEUROPSYCHIATRY—a branch of medicine concerned with organic and psychic aspects of neural disorders; the study of brain electrical impulses to help in therapy for BIOFEEDBACK TRAINING and CLINICAL PSYCHOLOGY. [**cf.** LISTENING MODE, AUTOGENTIC TRAINING, MIND-LINK/BODY-LINK, METABOLIC MONITOR, MIND-BODY DISCIPLINE]

NEUROSIS—an instinctive manipulation to shut off unpleasantries or pain; as situations repeat themselves the individual represses the original unpleasantry further into her or himself; a learning pattern of behavior to build a defense system; not a disease. [**cf.** BLOCKS, GRAPES, ROLFING, BIOFEEDBACK TRAINING, KEY TO LIFE]

NEUTER PERSONALITY—an entity that exists in a dimension where it is not possible to have sex, such as an angel. [**cf.** ETHERIC WORLD INTELLIGENCES]

NEUTRAL INNER FEELINGS—(biofeedback training) to sense a detachment and a belonging at the same time, while HOOKED-UP to an instrument and meditating. [**cf.** BIOFEEDBACK TRAINING, AWARENESS NOTEBOOK, PROBLEM-SOLVING STATE OF CONSCIOUSNESS, SKIN RESISTANCE]

NEUTRAL MIND—an unopinionated mental state; a necessary condition for the psychic to receive psychic information that is not tinted with his or her own conscious mind throughts or BELIEF SYSTEM; (do not confuse with BLANK AWARENESS). [**cf.** MONKEY CHATTER, MEDITATION, SELF-REGULATED PHRASES]

NEW AGE—a period from approximately 1920 to A.D. 2000 in which there will be a tremendous change in the thinking and lifestyle of the masses; cosmic vibrations will change as the earth passes from the PISCEAN AGE to the AQUARIAN AGE in earth's solar system; in this period the Milky Way will also change from one AGE to another age in the Great Solar System; 1. the Aquarian Age signifies the opening of COSMIC CONSCIOUSNESS to the masses; deals with etheric world laws and expansion of mind functions; the dignity of life will rise; scientists will become God oriented; interests will shift to mind recreation, mind exercise, mind industry, mind types of crime, mind philosophies, air travel, and planet exploration; the etheric world will draw attention to itself; 2. a natural process mother earth must go through as she tries to purify herself; all nature is feeling the thrust of the change; every living thing is responsible to flow with the transformation and will notice a change in its lifestyle; every living thing provokes this transformation; NEW AGE is a total globular cleansing; 3. help can come from the etheric world and other planets if humanity desires and respects this help. [**cf.** NEW-AGE PSYCHOLOGY, NEW-AGE CONSCIOUSNESS AWARENESS MOVEMENT, PLANETARY WORKER, FUTURISTS]

NEW BIRTH—1. (ancient philosophies) the graduation of the INITANT to become an INITIATE; being born into Truth; 2. (current) the rise of an individual to a new plateau in the present incarnation; noticeable by a change in interests, friends, foods, colors, education, vocation, books, and lifestyle. [**cf.** SELF-INTEGRATION, SELF-REALIZATION, SUCCESS, EVOLUTION]

NEW CONSCIOUSNESS—a current term which refers to the discovery that there is a connection between the body and mind, making it all one system; the thoughts in the mind, accompanied with emotion, (noticeable and unnoticeable) change every minute bringing a change in the BODY CHEMISTRY and a change in one's environment. [**cf.** EEG, BIOFEEDBACK TRAINING, MIND-LINK/BODY-LINK, MIND TECHNOLOGIES, LAW OF LIKE ATTRACTS LIKE Appendix 7]

NEW CONSCIOUSNESS-AWARENESS MOVEMENT—organizations springing up all over the world teaching new philosophies, new techniques of mind control, new kinds of recreation, foods, dances, and classes not found in the usual formal educational systems; this drive stems from the individual's desire to get more out of life than the usual job and family routine; to become unstereotyped and more independent and unique. [**cf.** TRANSPERSONAL GROUP THERAPY, SELF-IDENTIFICATION, HOLISM]

NEW KNOWLEDGE—pertains to UFOLOGY, mastery of GRAVITY, MUTATION OF ENERGY, and the understanding of VISUAL RAY and ORGONE

ENERGY. [cf. MUTANTS, TRANSMUTATION, MENTAL COMMUNICATIONS, CONSTRUCTS, POLARITY, SPACE CONTINUUM]

NEW PLANETARY MYTHOLOGY—the expression of human cultural change on a large scale; to work with the cosmic angelic forces to bring harmony between all levels of worlds. [cf. PLANETARY WORKERS, STAR CHILDREN, UFOLOGY, SPACE BROTHERS]

NEW THOUGHT—1. concept: the potential of the human brain is almost limitless; one has the ability to use this mind to control his or her physical body and their entire lifestyle; one has a consciousness that one makes one self, which can be changed and should be elevated to better one's affairs in each INCARNATION; this change can be accomplished by hundreds of methods which have sprung up all over the nation and universe, in the past decade which are at his or her option; 2. a collective word pertaining to the similarity of theories throughout groups, disciplines, philosophies, and religions revealing humanity's relationship to an ultimate universal energy of which everyone partakes; swings away from the usual orthodox religions and philosophies and their dominating beliefs that mankind is a victim of circumstances and the puppet of a higher source; 3. theory: planet is in a state of transformation going from one AGE to another age which requires the planet to purify herself; each individual on the planet is a part of this and should FLOW with an open mind to new concepts, new inventions, different morals, and any changes which may seem correct at the time, so as not to detain the planet in its transformation. [cf. EVOLUTION, CONSCIOUSNESS SHIFT, NEW-AGE CONSCIOUSNESS, SUFFERING, SUCCESS]

NEW-AGE CONSCIOUSNESS—awareness of the power of the MIND; realization that the mind is responsible for itself, for the body condition, and for the happenings of the day; 1. the human mind is aware of itself; 2. the mind is sensitive to LIGHT, weather, COLOR, SOUND, other people's BODY CHEMISTRY, and rules of society; this sensitivity can all be balanced with the proper knowledge, so it will influence one in a positive way; 3. humans desire to feel free and to be released from restraints of his or her mind potential and free from suppression from others; 4. there is a desire for "meaning" to life; prestige and wealth is becoming secondary; importance of being in charge of one's health is under research; people are taking another look at the value system of the culture. [cf. PLEASURE, PSYCHOSYNTHESIS, SOCIAL RENEWAL, CURATIVE EDUCATION]

NEW-AGE POLITICS—the competition among Eastern consciousness awareness disciplines for the western searcher; results in the self-designing of techniques and words for a new western philosophy, with an eastern twist. [cf. TRANSFORMATION, PLANETARY DEME, OCCULT MEDICINE, EARTH MOTHER]

NEW-AGE PSYCHOLOGY—the MIND (subconscious and conscious) has charge of the condition of one's body and the condition of one's daily activity; each person should learn about THOUGHT, INNER-DIALOGUE, THOUGHT-FORMS, emotions and attitudes; if one is concerned with what goes on inside of his or her mind, the outside daily activity will take care of itself; no one is responsible for anyone else but each one is responsible for her or himself and their contribution to the system they live in; researchers are taking another look into morals and the importance of life; see Appendix 5 NEW-AGE PSYCHOLOGY for individual suggestions.

NEWSPAPER TEST—(laboratory) the ability to PROPHESY what will be printed in the newspaper before it goes to press using any type of mental psychism. [cf. PROPHECY, PREDICTIONS, CLAIRVOYANCE, HUMAN OMEN, CLAIRSENTIENCE, DREAMS]

NEXT WORLD—see ASTRAL PLANE and ETHERIC WORLD.

NEXUS—(Buryl Payne) "a link, tie, or connection where one can receive guidance from the higher self—a place where one can move in many directions and dimensions." [cf. GOING-TO-LEVEL, MENTAL PROJECTION, CLOAK OF INSULATION]

NGAI—(Africa, Masai tribe) see VITAL LIFE FORCE.

NICHIREN SHOSHU—see CHANTING.

NIGHT FLYER—(Rome) a PSYCHIC with knowledge of ASTROLOGY.

NIGHT FLYING BLOODSUCKERS—see VAMPIRE.

NIGHT HAG—(Bible, Isaiah) see SUCCUBUS.

NIGHT LANGUAGE—the position of the body that one assumes after retiring is influenced by personality. [cf. SLEEP PARALYSIS, NINETY-MINUTE CYCLE]

NIGHT WITCHES—a force that works in the night

against one who draws this force to her or himself by negative actions and thoughts. [**cf.** WITCHCRAFT, NEGATIVE ELEMENTAL, LAW OF LIKE ATTRACTS LIKE Appendix 7]

NIGHTMARE—(dreams) PICTURE LANGUAGE during sleep that plays strongly and is clearly trying to stir the sleeper into some personal action before negativity comes into his or her life; the dream plays over and over, each night in a normal way, but if the sleeper pays no attention, this DREAMSTUFF energy builds up until one night it is forceful enough to shake the sleeper into seeing it; the emotion that accompanies the dream changes the BODY CHEMISTRY and researchers feel this has a therapeutic value to the body chemistry; not a negative dream to frighten the sleeper but meant to stir him or her into action. (Inconcl.) [**cf.** DREAM INTERPRETATION, FREE ASSOCIATION, SYMBOLIZATION]

NIGHTMARES—(Slavic) see NATURE SPIRIT.

NIGROMANTIA—(Arabic, Greek, Latin) (ancient) to communicate with a deceased person by using a corpse from a graveyard for the divination tool; to sit by the grave and talk to the soul-mind of that dead person or to dig up the corpse and talk to the decaying body. [**cf.** LETTERS TO THE DEAD, PHONE CALLS FROM THE DEAD, OPENING THE MOUTH, CORPSE LIGHT]

NIHI—(Huna) an etheric world entity who acts as a servant to an earthling; see GUIDE. [**cf.** ETHERIC WORLD INTELLIGENCE]

NIHONGI—(Japan) the cosmological bible, regarding ANGELOLOGY.

NIMBUS—emanations of light seen around the heads of great spiritual beings, and religous figures, in the form of a CIRCLE, TRIANGLE, or SQUARE; colors vary: gold, silver, red, blue, green, violet; also seen over the ships' masts, tree tops, and church spires. **Syn.** HALO. [**cf.** KIRLIAN EFFECT, AURA, CROWN CHAKRA, GLORIFIED BODY]

NIN-MA-PA—(Tantrism) see PSYCHIC.

NINE—(esoteric) important number on which all life is based; found by adding the seven chakras to the two in the center, the star and the LOTUS, equalling nine; most used number in ancient Egyptian religion and most revered; composed of three times the TRINITY; completes the cycle of numbers as ten is reduced to one; NUMEROLOGY

life cycle number: representative of one's love for his fellow man, philosophy, nobility, and mysticism; planetary link is Neptune. [**cf.** NUMBER POWER, THREE, TWELVE]

NINETY-MINUTE CYCLE—(dreams) a universal pattern of REM or dream sleep that repeats itself every ninety minutes during the night, in a normal night of sleep, regardless how long one sleeps. [**cf.** NREM, EOG, DREAMING MIND, SENSE-IMAGERY]

NIR—(Egyptian, "nothing") TOTALITY in the beginning before matter was formed.

NIRVANA—(Sanskrit, Buddhism, Vedic) awareness utterly devoid of content; a state of blissful inactivity; a state of spiritual ENLIGHTENMENT or ILLUMINATION which releases the individual from suffering, death, and birth; the diminishing of personality and identification with the HIGHER SELF; the Supreme transcendental consciousness; Paradise. **Syn.** BLISS, PURE AWARENESS. [**cf.** INTONING, TAMING THE MIND, ESTHETIC STATE, ONENESS]

NIRVANAM, KAIVALYAM—(Yoga) absolute LIBERATION where psychic energies are considered as obstacles in the path.

NIRVANIC PLANE—see SIXTH PLANE.

NIVRITTI—Sanskrit) rolling backwards, or unwrapping. **Syn.** EVOLUTION. [**cf.** CYCLES, VIBRATIONS, INVOLUTION, SOUL-MIND]

NJOM—(Africa) coined by Ekoi; see VITAL LIFE FORCE.

NO TIME OR SPACE—a property of the etheric world vibration wherein everything happens at the same time; e.g., one can see an object being born and falling apart at the same time. (Inconcl.) **Syn.** MULTIDIMENSIONAL, ALL-AT-ONCE. [**cf.** NOWNESS, PRESENT MANIFESTING, SPACIOUS PRESENT]

NO-DOWN—(Buddhism) one level in the ETHERIC WORLD where the seeds of all universal forces and things are very close together within; a STATE OF CONSCIOUSNESS where there is no fall; realm of the Buddhas. **Syn.** FOURTH PLANE, OG-MIN, DENSELY-PACKED REALM, THICKLY-FORMED. [**cf.** BUDDHIC PLANE, MENTAL PLANE, MONADIC PLANE]

NO-MIND STATE—(Zen) letting go of any need for things of the material world; becoming one with the UNIVERSE. [**cf.** LOW BREATHING, ZEN SITTING, GONG]

NO-THING-NESS—a feeling of VOID; state of pure being during MEDITATION when one does not experience any movement, time, or space. **Syn.** METAPHYSICAL EMPTINESS, NIRVANA. [cf. BEATING DOWN THOUGHT, BLANK PERIODS]

NOA—a state of normality, accomplished by ritual and by the means of cleansing agents of fire and water; ritual performed when too much mana endangered a person or situation. [cf. SPIRIT, VITAL LIFE FORCE, BREATHATERIAN, WATER, FIRE]

NOAIDE—(Lapland) see PSYCHIC.

NOCTURNAL BIRD—(Rome) one who is knowledgeable in both ASTROLOGY and PSYCHISM.

NOCTURNAL ESP—psychic experiences that happen during sleep. [cf. THETA STATE OF CONSCIOUSNESS, SLEEP EXPERIENCES, PROPHETIC DREAMS, SLEEP THINKING]

NOCTURNAL LIGHT—(ufology), a bright light in the sky giving the appearance of intelligence as opposed to being a point of source; indeterminate of linear size; varying in color or all colors of the spectrum. [cf. EXTRATERRESTRIAL BEING, CONSTRUCTS, MENTAL INTERCHANGE, ETHER-SHIP BEING]

NOCTURNAL MEDIUM—one who is capable of performing only in the dark. [cf. SEANCE, PHYSICAL PSYCHISM, MEDIUM]

NOCTURNAL PARALYSIS—a STATE OF CONSCIOUSNESS when one is getting up in the morning wherein the CONSCIOUS MIND is fully awake but the muscles and organs have not awakened, causing difficulties in moving or talking for a short time. [cf. REM, NREM, FALSE AWAKENING, DELTA STATE OF CONSCIOUSNESS]

NODE—(esoteric) a highly concentrated, invisible, minute center of ENERGY and INTELLIGENCE that acts as a transformer for the electrical wavelengths that flow throughout the universe; (Patrick Flanagan) "a point, line, or region in a standing wave where there is little or no vibration; a point of stillness in a sea of vibration"; 1. believed to have been created with CREATION; the node knows its function which is to transmit and receive the ELECTRICITY in the air connecting the entire UNIVERSE in one gigantic electrical system; 2. an ethereal ZERO POINT between wavelengths to transform the frequencies of the electrode or atom to make the elements of all substance, invisible or

visible; elements are held together by this electrical system that infiltrates all things, living and inert; in human beings, these nodes are called ACUPUNCTURE POINTS and the wavelengths are called the MERIDIAN LINES; individuals are literally "one with the universe" because of this continuation. **Syn.** LIGHT-DOT. [cf. ANTINODES]

NOETIC—(Greek *nous*, "mind") mental functions; the highest character of the mind principle consciousness; CONSCIOUSNESS. [cf. NOETIC SCIENCE, MIND ACTIVITY]

NOETIC ENERGY—(coined by Charles Muses (1972); see VITAL LIFE FORCE.

NOETIC PSI—a qualitative mental psychic experience that is followed by an overwhelming sensation of understanding; most frequently occurring in vision form. [cf. SPONTANEOUS PSI, MOMENTARY ABILITY, RANDOM PSYCHISM]

NOETIC SCIENCE—study of altered-states of consciousness and how the mind and body react in altered states. [cf. MOVEMENT-FOR-ALTERED-CONSCIOUSNESS, EMOTIONAL PSI, HYPNOTHERAPY, TRANCE]

NOISY GHOST—see POLTERGEIST.

NOISY SILENCE—sound wave frequencies too low to be heard by the physical ear, but can be heard clairaudiently; e.g., sound of nature growing. **Syn.** INFRASOUND. [cf. MUSIC OF THE SPHERES, CLAIRAUDIENT, MOLECULAR CHORUS]

NOKUNZI AND MUNGU—(Africa, Eastern Congo) two dieties of the pygmies; another man bigger and stronger than they are who is both good and bad; capable of psychic performances. [cf. ETHERIC WORLD INTELLIGENCES, POLARITY, LEARNED SPIRITS]

NON-THOUGHT—1. a psychic impression or intelligent impulse making mental mind activity, originating outside the mind and completely free from sensory stimuli; expresses the nature of its sender whether it is a living or nonliving organism or a situation; e.g., vibrations from a planet, flower, color, live person, animal, a deceased person, candle, chair, or emotions of a crowd; results in an emotion of the psychic; received knowingly and unknowingly; can be self-generated or spontaneous (subconscious or karmically self-generated): can be beneficial, pleasant, genuine, inferior, dangerous, or distorted; (do not confuse with INNER-DIA-

LOGUE that is generated from within the mind); 2. see DREAMS; 3. see OUTER MENTAL ACTIVITY. [**cf.** Appendix 4 to clarify PSYCHIC INFORMATION, IMAGERY, DAYDREAMING, THOUGHTS and NON-THOUGHTS]

NON-THOUGHT-FORMATION—(Tibet) to arrest the natural flow of the mind by suppressing mental thoughts to a condition, such as "nothing-to-do" and "nothing-to-hold." [**cf.** BLANK PERIODS, ESSENCE OF REST]

NONALERT BRAIN WAVE PATTERNS—marks on the readout of the EEG instrument showing patterns associated with nonattention of the subject who is HOOKED-UP to the instrument. [**cf.** ELECTRODES, INNER ATTENTION, PASSIVE VOLITION, ACTIVE VOLITION]

NONATTACHMENT—(Vedic) a STATE OF CONSCIOUSNESS while in the material world to be free from the desires of the material world; accomplished through study, meditation and actions; (Bible) "be in the world but not of the world." [**cf.** SELF-DISIDENTIFICATION, QUIET REFLECTION]

NONAWARENESS—something is there but one does not know it. [**cf.** SUBLIMINAL LEVEL, COLLECTIVE UNCONSCIOUS, MEMORY BANK]

NONBEING—(Seth) "a state in which probabilities and possibilities are known and anticipated, but blocked from expression; not a state of nothingness." [**cf.** BLOCKS, EMOTION, SELF-NONSELF]

NONBRAIN ALPHA WAVES—(biofeedback training) biofeedback readouts that appear to be ALPHA WAVES on the instrument but are caused by artifacts; movements of hair, muscles, twitches, gulping, and sweating in the area of the electrodes cause alpha wave patterns, which can be misleading. [**cf.** EEG, ARTIFACT, BRAIN ELECTRICAL EVENTS, BRAIN WAVE TRAINING]

NONCAUSAL PHENOMENA—what people termed FATE or *luck* is now being researched from the laws of SYNCHRONICITY. [**cf.** CHANCE, RADIESTHESIA]

NONCHANCE FACTOR—(laboratory) psychic ability is present when the answers in a controlled experiment are more than half correct, representing more than chance. [**cf.** SUBJECT VARIANCE, PRECOGNITION, PSI TASKS, ESP]

NONCHANGE—(I Ching) that which must be and cannot be altered. [**cf.** CASTING OF LOTS, SYNCHRONICITY]

NONCHEMICAL OUT-OF-BODY TRIP—(laboratory) an expansion of the mind consciousness, in which the soul-mind tunes into distant places or the etheric world. [**cf.** MENTAL PROJECTION, RIDING THE CHARIOT TO THE EXHAULTED THRONE]

NONCONSCIOUS LEVEL—(huna) laws within the human organism that take care of themselves without one consciously knowing where and what is being done; i.e., involuntary system; (Carl Jung) "that part of the SOUL-MIND that reflects both a part of a human being and a part of the universe." [**cf.** MEMORY BANK, COLLECTIVE UNCONSCIOUSNESS]

NODURATION—a place where TIME (as mankind understands time) is non-existent; motion too fast to be measured. (Inconcl.) **Syn.** ETERNAL PRESENT. [**cf.** SIMULTANEOUS SYSTEMS]

NONEMBODIES—a SOUL-MIND in the etheric world who no longer has a physical body but is very much alive. **Syn.** DISCARNATE ENTITY. [**cf.** SURVIVALISTS, PRESERVING OF SACREDNESS]

NONEXTERNAL WORLD—mental activity in the SUBJECTIVE MIND and body-feeling within the body proper, that one can perceive with the five senses; i.e., PSYCHIC ENERGY and MEDITATION sensations surfacing for attention. **Syn.** BODY-FEELING. [**cf.** MENTAL PSYCHISM, PHYSICAL PSYCHISM Appendix 2]

NONFORM-PRODUCING MATTER—(prescience) the three higher planes above the mental plane where atoms do not respond to every impulse of thought. [**cf.** LAW OF THOUGHT Appendix 7, FIFTH PLANE]

NONHOMOGENEOUS FIELD—(future science) (Russia) an energy field around the object in a PK experiment that enables it to be moved by mind energy; no longer believed to be electrostatic but having properties unknown to us. [**cf.** NONHUMAN-PK, PSYCHOKINETIC OUTBREAKS, TELENEURAL INFLUENCE, UNINTENTIONAL-PK]

NONHUMAN AGENCY—1. birds, animals, dice, coins, water, oil, etc., used in performing types of DIVINATION and RADIESTHESIA techniques; 2. natural things (excluding human beings), birds, animals, clouds, vegetation, etc., and material objects bringing omens. [**cf.** OMEN, LOTS, I CHING, MANTIC ART, PENDULUM, DOWSING ROD]

NONHUMAN FORMS—1. forms of life that do not

have a SOUL-MIND or characteristics resembling in some manner the evolutionary path of man; 2. intelligent living organisms that do not conform to man's idea of man but belong to the evolutionary cycle; 3. a life form belonging to a preterrestrial or pre-human type of development, sometimes grotesque or revolting but having features mankind can identify with. [**cf.** SOULLESS, CONSCIOUSNESS, DENSITY]

NONHUMAN INTELLIGENCES—(ufology) life forms seen in outer space and in space photographs that have a reasonable amount of intelligence but do not resemble the human species. [**cf.** OTHER WORLD INTELLIGENCES, PILOTING INTELLIGENCES, CONSTRUCTS, ETHER SHIPS]

NONHUMAN PROPHECY—to have an unordinary event happen in one's environment that predicts a future event pertaining to that individual; occurs to foretell pleasant or unfortunate information; e.g., one misses the plane because of a traffic jam and later learns the plane had an accident; one smells the fragrance of a rose very strongly while cooking supper and three days later an out of town friend, Rose, knocks on the door unannounced. **Sim.** OMEN. [**cf.** PORTENDER, OMENS, EMOTIONAL PSI]

NONHUMAN PSYCHOKINESIS—to psychically cause movement of matter by mind energy and HUMAN MAGNETISM; to have control over or interfere with external objects and living organisms (excluding the human body) without the use of regular modes of physics; movement consists of altering its position, shape, pattern of activity, or the elements within the matter; performed in a light hypnotic state, meditative relaxed state or an alpha alert state of consciousness; methods of execution: 1. to use mind discipline by constantly directing the ergs of energy that emanate from the head to the matter, with directions of what it should do; 2. to fix one's eyes on the matter with intense concentration allowing the magnetism to emanate from the eyes to the matter; 3. to call forth the magnetism within the body and direct it out of the palms of the hand and two psychic fingers while handling the matter; (manipulation of matter results in more than a human hand can normally do); 4. to solidify the magnetism and direct to it flow out of the palms of the hands with hands a few inches above the matter; magnetism alters the electromagnetic field surrounding the matter and this is transferred to the alteration of the physical

matter; two groupings: NATURE-PSYCHOKINESIS, and OBJECT-PSYCHOKINESIS. (Inconcl.)

NONHUMAN REALMS—the lower planes co-created by mankind's inferior thoughts and actions that do not resemble life, as mankind thinks of life. **Syn.** STATE OF HELL, DENSITY, HADES. [**cf.** HYPNO-GOGIC STATE, SEA OF FACES]

NONHUMAN SPIRIT—a soul-mind's shell in the etheric world that holds together after the SOUL-MIND has left with enough material thoughts to keep it together; this shell has enough intelligence to contact a psychic who is not careful in his or her contacts, and fool him or her with erroneous information for a short time; see ASTRAL SHELL. [**cf.** ANTIGOD, ASTRAL CEMETERY]

NONHUMAN TELEKINESIS—abbr. NONHUMAN TK; to move and manuever mundane matter (excluding the human body) while in a state of TRANCE; requires a well-developed MEDIUM that can synchronize with the etheric world intelligence who intervenes within his or her body and performs the physical phenomena to suit the medium; e.g., levitate an object, apport an object, and teleport an object; (do not confuse with NON-HUMAN PSYCHOKINESIS in which the subconscious mind is used). [**cf.** HUMAN TELEKINESIS, OBJECT-TK, PSYCHOKINESIS]

NONHUMAN WORLD—see ETHERIC WORLD.

NONHUMAN-PK—abbr. for NONHUMAN PSYCHO-KINESIS; see same.

NONINTENTIONAL ESP—1. (American Society for Psychical Research) psi-mediated information in one's behavior when one was not aware of being tested for ESP; 2. spontaneous psychic information motivated by an individual's momentary needs and long-term motivations; 3. a talent in art or writing in which one had no formal education and is surprised at her or his own capabilities; see INSPIRATIONAL WRITING. [**cf.** KARMIC DESIRE, INSPIRATIONAL THOUGHT]

NONMANIFEST SOUND—(India) (future science) New Testament concept of the WORD; complex tones that cannot be heard by physical ears, which are a product of mankind's thoughts (words), resulting in mundane matter and earth; theory: every ATOM vibrates a sound which gravitates to other atoms to make a harmonious chord and matter results; subconscious and conscious thoughts (words) capable of co-creating, destroying, and recreating manifold universes. (Inconcl.) **Syn.** COSMIC MUSIC. [**cf.** MOLECULAR CHORUS, GREAT TONE]

NONMATERIAL—ASTRAL PLANE material, or any level of the etheric world.

NONMATERIAL PATTERNS—PSYCHIC INFORMATION coming through in geometric forms, color rays, numbers or other symbols, instead of familiar objects that belong to the MUNDANE WORLD. [**cf.** INNER-MENTAL ACTIVITY; PSI CONTROL]

NONMEDICINAL HEALING—see UNORTHODOX HEALING and ALTERNATIVES.

NONMEDITATION—to enter into an ALPHA STATE OF CONSCIOUSNESS, in which the mind, emotions, and body are quiet without elicitation; occurs when one is deeply engrossed in one subject and unconsciously obliterates outside stimuli; e.g., deep concentration, an invention, choreographing a dance, or memorizing information; this POINT-OF-FOCUS of creativity operates from the RIGHT BRAIN HEMISPHERE and to be altered to conversation, or other LEFT BRAIN HEMISPHERE functions, makes the individual react in a peculiar manner, unable to answer, or become frustrated; e.g., the absent-minded professor forgot his name by pondering and visualizing his formula long after he left the laboratory, with such intent to solve his project, that the brain did not switch hemispheres for menial tasks and conversation. [**cf.** QUIET ATTENTIVENESS, RIGHT BRAIN HEMISPHERE]

NONORDINARY REALITY—pertains to things happening in an ALTERED STATE OF CONSCIOUSNESS, or experiencing emotions that cannot be described in the present language. [**cf.** ASTRAL CONSCIOUSNESS]

NONORDINARY REALITY EXPERIENCES—to perceive from a feeling nature as opposed to perceiving from an intellectual nature; happens when one is in another state of consciousness brought on by: in-depth psychic work, deep meditation, dreaming, and the influence of psychotropic drugs. [**cf.** NIRVANA, DETACHMENT, CAPTURING THE VISION]

NONPERSONAL SUBCONSCIOUS—thoughts and sounds one does not connect with oneself are recorded at a SUBLIMINAL LEVEL of the mind; affects one's decisions, regardless; e.g., when the radio news broadcast is on in the background, it may not interfere with one's immediate lifestyle, but the SUBCONSCIOUS MIND heard the news and will use it in future judgmental statements. [**cf.** UNCONSCIOUS]

NONPHYSICAL—the INVISIBLE.

NONPHYSICAL BODY—see ASTRAL BODY.

NONPHYSICAL PHENOMENA—see MENTAL PSYCHISM.

NONPHYSICAL PLANETS—the outer bodies of the planets made from SUPERPHYSICAL matter proving to be an important function in earth's solar system. (Inconcl.) [**cf.** ETHERIC DOUBLE, ELECTROMAGNETISM]

NONRAPID-EYE-MOVEMENT-STATE—abbr. NREM STATE; all periods of sleep except when the sleeper is having a dream (when the eyeballs are moving under closed lids); eyeballs are quiet and functionally blind; body can make large movements; sleeper reaches alpha, theta, and delta states of consciousness; includes periods of sleep when psychic experiences and thinking occur. (Inconcl.) [**cf.** REM, SLEEP THINKING, SLEEP EXPERIENCES]

NONRATIONAL PHENOMENA—see ACAUSAL RELATIONSHIPS.

NONREALITY REALITY—an ALTERED STATE OF CONSCIOUSNESS in which one feels normal while experiencing it but entirely different than that which one senses from one's five senses and conscious mind awareness; (language of the THIRD DIMENSION that hopefully describes this feeling). [**cf.** NONORDINARY REALITY EXPERIENCES, DREAMS, ETHERIC WORLD]

NONRECALLERS—(dreams) people who remember less than one dream a month. [**cf.** DREAM DIARY, DREAMED AWAKE]

NONSENSORY SIGNALS—psychic information entering the body and mind through any psychic skill, recognized to be psychic information because it is alien to stimuli entering through the physical five senses. [**cf.** CLAIRSENTIENCE, GUT FEELING, CLAIRSCENT, CLAIRAUDIENCE]

NONSPONTANEOUS MANIFESTATIONS—physical psychic phenomena occurring through proper processes; i.e., through DESIRE by the psychic, through deep CONCENTRATION, after proper PRAYER, INVOCATION, or MEDITATION, and protection of one's mind and body by cloaking. [cf. GOING-TO-LEVEL, RAISE THE VIBRATIONS]

NONSWING QUESTION—(radiethesia) a question given to the PENDULUM or DOWSING ROD that is incorrectly worded, foolish, or is answerable by physical means; e.g., "Should I eat ice cream with a spoon or fork?" "Will my mother die?" "Should I take a vacation to New York or Boston in July or August?" [cf. A COURTESY, IN THE MOOD]

NONSWING RESPONSE—(radiesthesia) stillness or slight wiggling of the PENDULUM or DOWSING ROD resulting from a poorly worded question. [cf. WARM UP THE MOTOR]

NONVERBAL COMMUNICATION—to perceive inner feelings and understanding regarding people; a form of INTUITION. [cf. INNER DIRECTED, SUPERMENTAL ACTIVITY]

NOOSPHERE—(Pierre Teilhard de Chardin) see ETHERIC DOUBLE or AURA.

NORMAL—(new-age psychology) (human) each human being serves as the "norm" for her or himself and only for themselves; no one can serve or contribute to a fixed pattern of behavior that should be standard for others; one's pattern of behavior, lifestyle, and thinking depends upon one's KARMA, BELIEF SYSTEM, and goals; one should compare one's self to one's self, and only for the purpose of evaluation. [cf. ANORM, NEW-AGE, TENSION, VALUES]

NORNS—(Nordic) NATURE SPIRITS that have been here since antiquity, similar to female FAIRIES.

NORTHERN LIGHTS—a tremendous, expressive light source that can be seen around the northern part of America at night time; a luminescence that gently moves in a curtain-like display with graceful folds and outlines; appears suspended in space; a faint crackling sound can be heard in conjunction with this display; esoteric theories: 1. caused by electrically charged particles emitted from the sun, clashing the upper atmosphere; generated and influenced by the entire universe; 2. soul-minds leading the deserving discarnate entities to parade. [cf. AURORA BOREALIS]

NOUMENAL WORLD—the physical world that appears to exist as mankind's physical faculties perceive it; opposite of PHENOMENA. [cf. NON-ORDINARY REALITY EXPERIENCES, MUNDANE WORLD, ENERGY SYSTEMS]

NOUS—(Greek, "spirit") a living energy field of intelligence; the HIGHER MIND or SPIRITUAL SOUL; (Plato) the divine soul of man or the SUPERCONSCIOUS MIND; (AMORC) "the energy, power, and force emanating from the source of all life, vibratory in character, dual in nature, triune in manifestation." (Inconcl.) **Syn.** LIFE, ZOE, MIND, PRIMAL BEING. [cf. SOUL-MIND]

NOUSE—the first emanation from the GODHEAD; LIFE. [cf. MONADOLOGY]

NOWNESS—a multidimensional time theory: all events coexist in a timeless sense. (Inconcl.) [cf. TIME DISPLACEMENT, MOTIONLESSNESS]

NOX—(Rome, Greece) see TOTALITY.

NOXIOUS AREA—(dowsing) an underground region where the veins of flowing water meet and cross underneath a building; such areas have been thought to cause illness in persons who unknowingly spend much time sitting, standing, or sleeping over it; research found that when the persons were relocated the illness disappeared; DOWSING skill can detect these veins. **Syn.** ZONES OF IRRITATION. [cf. WATER UNDULATION, GHOST VEINS]

NREM—see NONRAPID EYE MOVEMENT.

NU—(ancient Egypt) water, believed to contain everything in embryo; the ultimate primeval matter from which everything has come; possesses the properties of male and female; depicted as a deity wearing a headdress of plumes and a disk. [cf. POLARITY, TOTALITY]

NUDITY DREAMS—dreams that tell the dreamer that he or she is unprepared in some phase of their life or relates something about honesty. [cf. EXPOSURE DREAMS]

NUDITY IN MAGIC—the absence of clothing when contacting psychic information; 1. purpose is to allow the power to flow to and from the body more freely without being inhibited by clothing; 2. symbolic that shedding clothing is shedding the materialistic world; 3. makes all members feel equal. [cf. UNBOUNDED AWARENESS, PSI-CONDUCIVE STATE, SWORD]

NULIAJUK—(Eskimo) a nature spirit in charge of sea animals; mother of the beasts.

NUMBER ETHER—see CHEMICAL ETHER.

NUMBER OF THE BEAST—(Bible, Revelation) six six six.

NUMBER POWER—each single number is a receptacle for the cosmic vibrations having its own characteristics and meanings; names and letters have their own energy field with a special vibratory rate that designates a certain function and can be put to practical use; (Pythagoras) "the power of the number rests in the connection existing between the relations of things and the principles in nature." [**cf.** see each number from ONE to TWELVE]

NUMBERS—(ancient and future science) TOTALITY is the numerical disciplines of geometry, arithmetic, and music; (Pythagoras) "the qualitative distinction one makes between phenomena is fundamentally numerical"; the brain transcribes its mental activity into frequencies the person can perceive, use, and enjoy, and those the brain processes are nothing but the jiggling and rearranging of numbers; mankind's senses operate through the reception of vibrations of different frequencies or number of vibrations per second; e.g., blue is blue because of its frequency; number is ALL. [**cf.** MULTIPLICITY, COLOR, COSMIC RHYTHM]

NUMEN—(*neure*, "to nod") 1. (Rome) a movement of the head; the sign was first recognized by the administrators; when the head nodded, another force was working within the speaker and would be heard as the lecture moved along; i.e., an etheric world ·intelligence; this experience was awed and revered; 2. a sign of the head nodding for the mental psychic to now he or she is now receiving help in their PSYCHIC INFORMATION; this nod occurs spontaneously without any effort on the part of the psychic; a human omen to know one is tuned in. [**cf.** MENTAL PSYCHIC PROCESSES, INSPIRATIONAL SPEAKING]

NUMERICAL WIZARD—a PSYCHIC capable of knowing the numbers of things in his or her surroundings; willed or a subconscious knowing; this information can be used for practical purposes. [**cf.** BIBLICAL NUMEROLOGY, COVEN]

NUMEROLOGY—the study of numbers in regard to a person's character and life plan; theory: there is significance in a number which is not expressed by the figure or symbol employed to denote quantity only; the structure of the universe and the essence of a person or object can be told by turning the letters of the name into numbers; one's life can be mapped out according to the relation in which all its numbers are standing to each other. [**cf.** Appendix 5 NUMBER POWER]

NUMINOSITY—(Carl Jung) "a light in the aura drawing psychic energy to it, giving that person an intense urge to further his spirituality and knowledge of psychic skills."

NUMINOUS—pertains to the spark found in all human beings that urges them on a quest for more spirituality, more understanding of the invisible world, and more knoweldge of psychic skills; this automatically surfaces when the individual is ready; motivated by the HUMAN BEING SPECIES SEED. [**cf.** HOLY GRAIL, ALCHEMIST]

NUNC STANS—(Latin, "stable") past, present, and future is all one time. [**cf.** ETERNAL NOW, MOMENT POINT, TIME FIELD]

NYAME—(Africa, Ashanti tribe) the supreme being capable of being reached by earthlings through prayer. [**cf.** HOLY SPIRIT, REFRACTIONS OF GOD, SACRED DISK]

NYMPHS—(Rome, Greece) a NATURE SPIRIT that shows herself as a beautiful young woman having charm and psychic ability; presides over all bodies of water on the planet. **Syn.** NEREIDS.

O-LINE—see CRITICAL DAYS.

OAK PEOPLE—the Druids who lived in England.

OAK TREE—(Celtic, Germany, Slavic, Rome) (esoteric) a tree species believed to be chosen by God Himself; everyone who drew energy from it would go to heaven; worshipped in ceremonies, and used as a psychic tool for energy, protection and information; has the vibrational frequency that its leaves can speak to mankind. [**cf.** ACORN, DRUIDS, INSTINCT PERCEPTION, SENSATIONAL CONSCIOUSNESS]

OAN—(Babylonia) an intelligent NATURE SPIRIT that had the face, limbs, and speech of human beings, the skin of a fish, lived in the sea; taught his people science, art, craft, written language and how to construct temples and cities; wrote a book on such.

OBAIFO—(Africa) a phosphorescent light seen floating in the night; an ETHERIC WORLD ENTITY seeking blood from humans. [**cf.** ASTRAL VAMPIRE, DOG-GHOST]

OBE—abbr. for OUT-OF-BODY EXPERIENCES, see ASTRAL PROJECTION.

OBEAH—(Jamaica, West Indies) PSYCHISM and MEDIUMSHIP including about every kind of psychic and mediumistic skill.

OBEAH DOCTOR—(Jamaica, West Indies) see MEDICINE MAN and SHAMAN.

OBEAHMAN—(Jamaica, West Indies) psychic male who is capable of many psychic skills, mediumship skills, and possesses healing abilities; female is called **Obeahwoman**.

OBEer—(laboratory) one who has the OUT-OF-BODY EXPERIENCE.

OBI—(West Indies) psychics.

OBJECT PSYCHOKINESIS—abbr. OBJECT-PK; to manipulate inert third-dimensional matter with mind activity only; (excludes living organisms); psychic builds dense concentrated energy in her or his mind giving undivided attention to the activity desired; this puts the PSYCHIC in an ALPHA STATE OF CONSCIOUSNESS, working with the SUBCONSCIOUS MIND; methods to alter the object's shape, area of location, vibrational frequency, placement of parts, or form, varies; 1. psychic concentrates on the object with his or her eyes focused on the object until it changes; 2. psychic gathers and holds energy in his or her mind until it is dense and then stares directly at the object and shoots a mass of mind energy all at once; 3. psychic beams the concentrated energy out of the palms by placing his or her hands over the object, with palms facing the object; (controlled experiments put the object in a bottle to eliminate air movements from the hands); 4. psychic holds the object in the hand and performs feats that the hand cannot physically perform; energy is sent out of the mind, down the SYMPATHETIC NERVOUS SYSTEM and out the palm and the object is altered; e.g., matchstick is moved across a surface by staring at it (in an area without drafts); a broken watch is held in the hand and soon it is repaired by mind activity; (do not confuse with alchemical DEMATERIALIZATION or with OBJECT TELEKINESIS in which the guides perform the task). **Syn.** ARTICLE-PK, NONHUMAN-PK. [**cf.** NONHUMAN PSYCHOKINESIS, MOTOR PSYCHOKINESIS, NONHUMAN TELEKINESIS, ALCHEMY, GRAVITY CONTROL]

OBJECT READING—to perceive PSYCHIC INFORMATION by holding an article in the palms of the hands; psychic can determine data regarding the article itself or data regarding the owner of the article; see PSYCHOMETRY. [**cf.** PRACTICAL PSYCHOMETRY, PSYCHOSCOPY]

OBJECT TELEKINESIS—abbr. OBJECT-TK; to manipulate inert third-dimensional matter with the aid of the ETHERIC WORLD INTELLIGENCES, while in a TRANCE state of consciousness; accomplished in the SEANCE room with the assistance of the SITTERS, or in daylight by one's self; intelligence intervenes when directed to do so and alters matter in shape, vibrational frequency, placement of parts, or area where placed; e.g., (authenicated case) two wooden loops with no breaks in their construction were hooked together in a seance; a candy dish floated through the air, unattended, to serve the sitters; piano keys began to play without human hands touching the keys; (do not confuse with POLTERGEISTRY which is unexpected as this phenomenon is planned and willed). [**cf.** OBJECT PSYCHOKINESIS, LEVITATION TELEKINESIS, GRAVITY CONTROL, TELEPORTATION, PSYCHIC PHOTOGRAPHY]

OBJECT-KNOWING PRINCIPLE—(Tibet) the SOUL-MIND of a human being compacted with all the memories and concepts of past lives forever surfacing and used in present consciousness. **Syn.** SOUL-MIND, CONSCIOUSNESS-PRINCIPLE.

OBJECT-PK—see OBJECT PSYCHOKINESIS.

OBJECT-TK—abbr. for OBJECT TELEKINESIS; see same.

OBJECTIVE CLAIRAUDIENCE—1. to psychically perceive noise, knocks, music, or words, that appear to come from OUT-THERE in the atmosphere with no visible physical means; physical ears are not used and the PSYCHIC is the only one who perceives the sound, but it is very realistic to the psychic; transmitted through the THIRD-EYE AREA by the SUBCONSCIOUS MIND or by ETHERIC WORLD INTELLIGENCES who wish to bring information to the psychic's attention; should be kept under control as sounds coming without physical means can be startling and cause erratic action; (do not confuse with sounds in the SEANCE room which every one perceives); 2. to psychically tune into the more subtle vibrational frequencies of nature and hear the movement of growth; grass makes a noise as it grows, flowers make a noise as they open up, etc.; a rare clairaudent skill. [**cf.** SUBJECTIVE CLAIRAUDIENCE, MUSIC OF THE SPHERES, CLOAK OF INSULATION]

OBJECTIVE CLAIRVOYANCE—to psychically reach into another vibrational frequency with one's PSYCHIC EYE and perceive a VISION at a point in "outer space"; physical eyes can be opened or closed as they are not used; appears as if one were watching a play, a still picture or moving energies; picture may be full blown and realistic or may flow in fragments to make the message complete; visions out in space vary from scenes, people, colors, lights, animals, words, auras, thoughtforms, geometric figures, discarnate entities, personal guides; psychic is in a relaxed or ALPHA STATE OF CONSCIOUSNESS; should be kept under control and only happen when willed; visions have no place in everyday living as they are distractive and could cause an accident. [**cf.** SUBJECTIVE CLAIRVOYANCE, MENTAL PSYCHISM, ASTRAL VISION, CLOAK-OF-PROTECTION]

OBJECTIVE CONSCIOUSNESS—(George Ivanovich Gurdjieff) a state in MEDITATION when one is everything else as well as oneself, with full objectivity to one's ordinary awareness; has added an inner silence detaching the continuing rumbling of the mind. [**cf.** SELF-IDENTIFICATION, SELF-NON-SELF]

OBJECTIVE CONTROLLED IMAGERY—see DAY-DREAMING.

OBJECTIVE DREAM—a dream in which the dream symbol means in the dream what it means in daytime living. [**cf.** RELEASE TYPE DREAMS]

OBJECTIVE MIND—see CONSCIOUS MIND or MENTAL MIND.

OBJECTIVE PROGRAMMING—(Silva Mind Control) conscious instructions or concepts given to the subconscious mind from normal stimuli taken in by the five senses. [**cf.** FREE WILL, CRITICAL BRAIN]

OBJECTIVE PROPORTION—(AMORC) see FOURTH DIMENSION.

OBJECTIVE SENSES—the physical five senses; BETA SENSES. [**cf.** CONCRETE MIND, CONSCIOUS AWARENESS, ELECTRIC ACTUALITY]

OBJECTIVE/SUBJECTIVE PROGRAMMING—(Silva Mind Control) "when either the sender or the receiver has altered his level of consciousness in the relationship of a psychic experience but still in the physical environment of the other." [**cf.** LIGHT TRANCE, WIDE-BAND TUNING]

OBLIQUE SWING—(penduluming) pendulum swinging in a slanting or sloping movement, which is unusual. [**cf.** NONSWING QUESTION]

OBSESSED MEDIUM—one who allows a lower or inferior ETHERIC WORLD ENTITY to intervene when he or she calls upon a guide and yet is not deceived by the erroneous information. [**cf.** LAW OF LIKE ATTRACTS LIKE Appendix 7, COMPULSION, OBSESSION]

OBSESSION—parapsychological theory: the ability of an inferior ETHERIC WORLD ENTITY from the lower planes to psychically transfer his or her feelings, desires, hang-ups, or thoughts to an earthling; 1. this transferring process goes on slowly and persistently until the earthling has two standards in mutual conflict and slides back and forth between two personalities; 2. earthling harbors negative thoughts: i.e., has low self-worth, feelings of being victimized, religious conflicts, and feelings of one whom God has forsaken; as individual keeps negation uppermost in her or his mind the inferior entity becomes stronger until the individual is mentally ill; 3. occurs so gradually over the years, that it goes unnoticed by individual's close associates; individual does not admit to his or her entirely different personality because of the graduation of its process; 4. frequently diagnosed as chronic depression or other mental illnesses. [**cf.**

POSSESSION, SIMPLE OBSESSION, FASCINATION, SUBJUGATION, PHYSICAL OBSESSION]

OBSIDIAN—a natural black glass of volcanic origin used for SCRYING. [cf. QUARTZ, SOLOMON'S MIRROR]

OC—(Latin) prefix meaning "opposed to, against, inversely, oppositely, reversely."

OCCIPITAL HEMISPHERE BRAINWAVE MONITORING—to place a redbead electrode about one inch to the right or left of the skull bone, when using the EEG biofeedback instrument. [cf. ELECTROENCEPHALOGRAPH, BRAIN FREQUENCY ALTERATION]

OCCULT—(Latin *occulere*, "to conceal") 1. (ancient) that which is hidden behind outer appearances and must be studied to be understood; that which is magical or mystical; only available for the initiates; a system of methods compatible with nature to develop psychic power; knowledge of the invisible world and its relationship to mankind; 2. (current Western philosophies) to use nature to develop psychic skills and to constructively probe ancient mysteries and philosophies and to relate these to science; includes knowledge of the invisible world. **Sim.** MYSTICISM. [cf. Appendix 4 OCCULT]

OCCULT ATTACK—see PSYCHIC ATTACK.

OCCULT FIRE—see SERPENT POWER.

OCCULT FORCE—see PSYCHIC ENERGY.

OCCULT GUARDIANS OF MANKIND—see ETHERIC WORLD INTELLIGENCES.

OCCULT HYPNOTISM—(antiquity) to use the MAGNETIC FLUID in the subject's body and the operator's body to induce a deep hypnotic state which relates to the SUPERCONSCIOUS MIND whereby the subject can establish contact with her or his own OVERSOUL; subject travels through the higher planes with complete memory of the teachings received; used by Pythagoras, Rene Descartes, Theophrastus Paracelsus, Hermes, Plato, Robert Fludd, and the Druids; see ESOTERIC HYPNOSIS and HYPNOTHERAPY.

OCCULT MEDICINE—(current) alternative or unorthodox methods, therapies, and medicines that aim for HOLISTIC HEALTH. [cf. ROLFING, DANCE THERAPY, NEUROMUSCULAR MASSAGE, ALTERNATIVES]

OCCULT PHILOSOPHY—originated in the Eastern teachings of antiquity; see OCCULTISM.

OCCULT POLICE—highly intelligent ETHERIC WORLD INTELLIGENCES who concern themselves with psychism applied toward criminal ends and offense against society; answerable to anyone who needs help and calls upon them through telepathic communication. [cf. WHITE BROTHERHOOD, EMPATHY-PK, UP-FOR-GRABS, BODY BRUISES]

OCCULT SCIENCES—study of OCCULTISM; includes astrology, parapsychology, nature psi, hypnotherapy, holistic health, yoga, meditation, pyramidology, reincarnation, etc.

OCCULTISM—(Latin) the science and study of the nature of human beings; the function, operation, purpose, origin, and destiny of mankind; aim is to bring the HIGHER SELF through into manifestation in consciousness through this knowledge; study of the secrets of nature and the relationship between the invisible and visible forces pertaining to progress of the earth; suggests developing INDIVIDUALITY; this hidden material is now being released for anyone. **Sim.** MYSTICISM, PARAPSYCHOLOGY. [cf. Appendix 3 PSYCHIC ART]

OCEAN—(esoteric, Tibet) symbolizes the second layer of stratum of ethers (air) resting on the warp and woof. [cf. IMMATERIAL DIMENSION, OCEAN OF LIVING ENERGY]

OCEAN OF FIRE—(Sufi) see SOLAR PLEXUS.

OCEAN OF LIVING ENERGY—the atmosphere containing the various levels of vibrational frequency and each level having life suited to that level; meaning no emptiness; ETHERIA substance in its entirety. [cf. ETHERIC WORLD, UNSEEN REALM, HIGHER SIDE OF LIFE]

OCEAN SURF—the sound of the ocean waves breaking as it rolls up to the shore, is used for meditation: its natural sound has a soothing and hynotic effect to aid in quieting the mind, emotions and body. **Syn.** WHITE NOISE, WHITE SOUND. [cf. SELF-GENERATED, REPEATED STIMULUS, TANTRIC MEDITATION]

OCEANIDE—(Greece) a nature spirit, known as a daughter of the ocean, capable of communicating with and helping mankind; inhabiting the oceans and presiding over its function.

OCTAHEDRON—two three-dimensional triangles placed bottom to bottom giving a solid figure with eight faces; has a vibrational frequency that increases the energy of the material that is that shape, used especially with crystal. [**cf.** FORMS-WITH-POWER Appendix 2]

OCTAVE—(esoteric) waves of VIBRATIONAL FREQUENCIES in the universe; differentiates the various speeds, and motion, into ranges for further reference under the theory that every virbration emits a different sound. [**cf.** COSMIC MUSIC, PINK SOUND, HARP, MUSICAL SCIENCE]

OCULOGRAM—abbr. EOG; (*Oculo*, "eye") an instrument that is HOOKED-UP to the eyeballs of the subject in a dream research laboratory to tell the monitor when the subject's eyes are moving under the closed lids at a rapid pace; subject is then awakened to report on the dream he or she is experiencing or has just experienced; this instrument results in more accurate monitoring of the REM state. [**cf.** NREM, SLEEP BRAIN PATTERNS, SLEEP CONTROL, DREAMS]

OD—coined by Baron Karl von Reichenbach; (Norse mythology, "creator of the cosmos"; Odin, "all-pervasive") an energy power found in and around people and objects, necessary for existence; appears in greater amounts in some people, when electricity, heat, and light are present, and when the individual is relaxed; was seen by clairvoyants in the darkened room; exhibits the same laws as ordinary lighting; other findings run parallel with VITAL LIFE FORCE.

OD NEGATIVE—(Baron Karl von Reichenbach) a force attracting and repelling to the positive force of OD; perceived clairvoyantly as blue in color. **Syn.** YIN. [**cf.** VITAL LIFE FORCE]

OD POSITIVE—(Baron Karl von Reichenbach) a force attracting and repelling to the OD NEGATIVE; can be perceived clairvoyantly as yellow-red color. **Syn.** YANG. [**cf.** VITAL LIFE FORCE, POLARITY Appendix 5]

ODIC BODY—see ETHERIC DOUBLE.

ODIC COLOR—colors beyond the range of violet in the spectrum. [**cf.** ULTRAVIOLET RAYS, ULTRAVIOLET AURIC LIGHT]

ODIC LIGHT—(Baron Karl von Reichenbach) the energies that emanate from people and objects making a magnetized field around them, perceivable by visionary psychics. **Syn.** AURA.

ODIC RADIATION—(Baron Karl von Reichenbach) energy that comes from the SITTERS and MEDIUM

in the SEANCE room needed for the performance of the physical phenomena. [**cf.** ECTOPLASM, BLACKED-OUT, TESTING MEDIUMSHIP, QUALITY OF THE WORK]

ODIN—1. (Norse mythology) god of war, poetry, knowledge, wisdom, culture and the dead. [**cf.** WODAN] 2. (Germany) an ETHERIC WORLD god who communicates with his people bringing them guidance, protection and PSYCHIC INFORMATION; comes through INSPIRATIONAL THOUGHT, ECSTASY, and MEDIUMSHIP; 3. (Scandianavia, Vikings) a one-eyed etheric world GUIDE who takes astral projections to bring back knowledge to help his people; works through mediumship; 4. an ETHERIC WORLD INTELLIGENCE in charge of inspiration and developing mankind's psychic powers, and his or her understanding of physical death; 5. (Iceland) a PSYCHIC who is skilled in changing shape to a wild beast, fish, or dragon, to help others; also switches dimensions to become invisible to those around the area. [**cf.** DIMENSION-SHIFTING, APHRODITE, ASHTAR, BENEVOLENT SPIRIT]

ODOR—1. fragrances or smells used by psychics to attract or repel etheric world entities, as scents are easily detected by the etheric world; e.g., ONIONS, INCENSE, MYRRH. [**cf.** CEREMONIAL MAGIC] 2. fragrances or smells manifested by the etheric world to be perceived psychically to relay information; i.e., guide uses the same fragrances each time he or she comes into the area as notification of his or her presence; the smell of death is a prophecy for the CLAIRSCENTRIST; 3. odors affect the more subtle energies of mankind because they have a counterpart in the etheric world; (invisible bodies of human beings are affected according to the vibrational frequency of the odor). [**cf.** FOOD OF ETHEREAL ESSENCE, GHOSTLY ODORS]

ODOUR OF SANCTITY—(England) an odor of perfume or incense manifesting in the vicinity of persons of holy life, with no physical reason for the fragrance. [**cf.** CLAIRSCENT Appendix 2]

ODYLE—see OD.

ODYLLIC—coined by Baron Karl von Reichenbach (1845); see VITAL LIFE FORCE.

OFFICIAL CURSE—(medieval Greece) a punishment for criminals that puts a HEX on them or psychically attacks them with evil energy; this had a terrifying effect on the offenders and if they were unknowledgable in laws of magic or parapsychology they could not free themselves of the results of these horrendous activities; performed by the magistrates and priests. [cf. HYPNOSPELL, CHARM-STRUCK, MALADAPTIVE BEHAVIOR]

OG-MIN—(Buddhism) a plane where the seed of all universal forces and things are close together; state where there is no FALL. Syn. DENSELY PACKED REALM, THICKLY-FORMED, NO-DOWN. [cf. UNSEEN REALM, SEA OF PSI]

OHM—see AUM.

OHRMAZD AND AHRIMAN—(Zoroastrianism) represents the POLARITY in all things, positive and negative; ohrmazd is the principle of goodness and light, positive; ahriman is the principle of evil and darkness; negative. Sim. YIN AND YANG. [cf. FATHER-MOTHER GOD, LINGAM AND YONI]

OID—suffix meaning "incomplete, like, resembling."

OIL FOR ANOINTING—(ancient) used in the work of the MAGI; compounded of MYRHH, cinnamon, galingale, and very pure olive oil. [cf. CALL UP SPIRITS, SALT, SACRAMENTS]

OJAS—(Sanskrit) see VITAL LIFE FORCE.

OKI—(Native American, Iroquois) see VITAL LIFE FORCE.

OLD ORDER—formal science, narrow methods of proving a fact.

OLD PEOPLE—(esoteric) human beings living in installations underground in the earth made by STAR PEOPLE in ancient times before our records of civilization; they protect themselves with a mind-force field and are known to be here to protect the earth; at times they come out at night; have little in common with humans. Syn. EARTH GUARDIANS. [cf. POSITIVE PRIMARY ENERGY, ETHERIC STEEL, EARTH MAGNETISM]

OLD SOUL—one who has been incarnated innumerable times or who has learned a great deal during each incarnation; acts more mature than the majority of people of his or her time; an expression used as a reasonable or possible assumption why an individual has more than one of the following characteristics: an extremely high I.Q., excels in creativity that is not always understood by the masses (but this does not hinder his or her interest or activity in the research); possesses hard-to-come-by personality traits; is free from unnecessary worry both inside and outside; shows mature characteristics at a very early age; acts from a different time frame, consequently people do not easily understand this individual; people are drawn to this soul's magnetic personality rather than to what he or she stands for; is free from poor health in spite of defying many rules of good health; leads a good righteous life; feels material things are insignificant to the point that it bothers his or her close friends and relatives.

OLD VALICUS—(ufology) one of the first spacecraft to come to earth and land beneath a mountain in Copper Basin, Idaho; believed to come with good intent as there was no one lying dead afterward; it seemed to be carrying some smaller crafts. [cf. UFOLOGY Appendix 5, DYNAMIC TRANSITIONS, ETHER SHIP, BEING]

OLOGY—suffix meaning "study or science of."

OM—see AUM.

OMEGA—(Edgar Mitchell) "the symbol for consciousness and noetics." [cf. COMPOUND OF CONSCIOUSNESS, ALPHA STATE OF CONSCIOUSNESS]

OMEGA POINT—a time period designating the ending of one AGE and the beginning of another in the cycle of human evolution; occurs approximately every 2,600 years. [cf. AQUARIAN AGE, COSMOBIOLOGY, ETERNAL RHYTHM]

OMEN—a rare or extraordinary event or physical activity using a NONHUMAN AGENCY to prognosticate an emotional event; event is impossible under the normal laws of PHYSICS; occurs as a signal of an opportunity to be seized, a danger to be avoided, or news of an emotional event to happen to oneself or one's close associates; a token indication given for the one where it happens; executed by an etheric world GUIDE, a NATURE SPIRIT, a deceased close friend or relative, the UNIVERSAL MIND or the SUBCONSCIOUS MIND; e.g., a flower growing out of season; the clock chiming at an odd hour; a child's slipper found by the front door a day before an unexpected arrival of the child; a picture falling off the wall when the person in another locale dies; FATIMA PROPHECY for the world was given to three children. Syn. NONHUMAN PROPHECY, TOKEN INDICATION. [cf. Appendix 2 OMEN]

OMEN INTERPRETATOR—(Greece) a PSYCHIC hired to decipher historic omens for the country by weather condition, earth changes, or other signals of unordinary outbursts of nature; interpretations given by the etheric world guides to the psychic. **Syn.** PORTENTS. [**cf.** HUMAN OMENS, NONHUMAN AGENTS]

OMEN STICKS—(ancient, Druids) slivers of the OAK TREE were used for the casting of lots because of the oak tree's psychic properties. [**cf.** MING STICKS, BOTANE, COINCIDENTAL MATCHING]

OMENIST—one who perceives sensations in his or her body or whose body shows an unaccountable difference in its normal body behavior as a fore-warning of an unpleasant personal or earthly event; e.g., one ear turning red as a warning of a conflict in the home, one's body becoming cold and uneasy in a warm climate preceding a volcanic eruption that occurs in a cold climate and which harms many people. [**cf.** OMEN Appendix 2]

OMNI—(Latin) prefix meaning "all."

OMNIPOTENT—all powerful.

OMNISCIENT—all-knowing.

OMNIVERSE—ALL the universe.

ON YOUR FEET PSYCHIC—(England) see STAND-UP READER.

ON-THE-SPOT-HYPNOSIS—coined by Ted Patrick; a light state of DISGUISED HYPNOSIS, induced by a destructive-brainwashing cult recruiter on the first encounter of a prospective member; 1. recruiter uses preplanned ploy geared to reach the emotional level of one's basic needs and desires; individual becomes unknowingly transfixed by the eye-to-eye contact, the overuse of the pronoun *you*, the appeal to his or her Achilles heel and primal needs, and the insidious uninterrupted speech; individual becomes victimized as this ploy keeps his or her concentration narrowed and the CONSCIOUS MIND passive; 2. MAGNETISM from the eye-stare of the cult member penetrates the NERVOUS SYSTEM of the victim increasing the silencing of the decision-making mind and allowing the SUBCONSCIOUS MIND to absorb the verbiage just as it is given; victim never realizes he or she is being hypnotized; 3. future decisions regarding this encounter will be what the recruiter wants the person to decide, but the victim thinks it is his or her own decision. (Inconcl.) [**cf.** HYPNOTIC SPEECH PATTERN, SPELLED, LIGHT STATE OF HYPNOSIS, MASS HYP-NOSIS]

ON-THE-SPOT-PSYCHIC—a psychic who is fre-quented with intuition, hunches, warnings and premonitions regarding almost all of his or her activities. **Syn.** PRECOG, CLAIRSENTIENT. [**cf.** TELE-PATH, UP-FOR-GRABS, CLOAK OF INSULATION]

ONDINNONK—(Native American, Iroquois) a secret desire of the SOUL-MIND showing in PIC-TURE LANGUAGE during sleep; repressed emo-tions that surface while the conscious mind is quiet. [**cf.** ONONHAROIA, FEAST OF THE FOOLS, BLOCKS, ADVERSARIES]

ONE—(numerology) 1. unit; the most significant number for psychics, metaphyscians, and occultists; signifies the "whole"; "all is of the one"; the essence of GOD is the essence of NUMBERS; 2. represents the principle that created; "pioneering" or creating anew; a person who is dominated by the number one is always doing things before anyone else, discovering or inventing or creating ahead of the field; 3. a leadership number because if it is multiplied by itself it remains the same; if added to an odd number it makes it even, and if added to an even number it makes it odd; 4. represents the creation which is divided into three basic mean-ings: qualities of evolving life, fighting spirit, leadership and force; 5. NUMEROLOGY life cycle number one represents the basic life principle, unchangeable and immovable; it is identified with the sun, the source of all energy; 6. destiny number: persons destined to attain their goals, through dedication, perseverance, and increasing conscien-tiousness and hard work. [**cf.** NUMBER POWER Appendix 5]

ONE AGE—a period of 26,000 years. [**cf.** COSMIC WHEEL, BIOELECTROMAGNETIC INTERACTIONS]

ONE ESSENCE PRINCIPLE—everything is made from the same PRIMORDIAL SUBSTANCE, moving at different VIBRATIONAL FREQUENCIES; this primordial substance is indestructible, unchange-able, unduplicatable and everywhere; this primor-dial substance is the ATOM, or smaller particles now being discovered. [**cf.** TOTALITY]

ONE FELL STROKE—to accomplish the desired MEDIUMSHIP feats the first time one tries; thusly named because mediumship usually takes years and many sessions to perfect physical phenomena. (Inconcl.) [**cf.** DARKROOM SESSIONS, DESIRED-CONTROL, CONTROL]

ONE SPACE FRAMEWORK—(Seth) ALL-THERE-IS; the universes; total atmosphere with everything happening at the same time within that framework. [**cf.** HOLOGRAM, ONE SUPREME PRINCIPLE, LAW OF DESTINTY Appendix 7]

ONE SUPREME PRINCIPLE—see GOD or TOTALITY.

ONE-HUNDRED CYCLE—(Maxwell Wheeler) demonstrates that mankind's control of energy is predictably divided into four parts of the 100-year cycle; periods of warm-wet, warm-dry, cold-wet, and cold-dry weather. (Inconcl.) [**cf.** CYCLE PRINCIPLE, EMOTIONAL CYCLE, EXCITABILITY CYCLE]

ONE-POINTEDNESS—heavy concentration in one direction, needed for MEDITATION, HPYNOTHERAPY, TRANCE work, and most psychic skills. [**cf.** DYNATYPE, DIFFUSION, EMPIRICAL ENERGY]

ONEARTH—coined at Findhorn; one earth on earth is the aim of a new planetary culture movement at Findhorn, Scotland; a magazine of Findhorn published twice a year.

ONEIROKRITAI—(ancient) professional interpreters of DREAMS using their own ESOTERIC methods. [**cf.** DIALOGUE TECHNIQUE, ASSOCIATION FLUIDITY, DISPLACEMENT]

ONEIROLOGY—the study of DREAMS. [**cf.** ALLEGORICAL DREAMS, AWAKE-DREAMING, DEEPER DREAMLAND, DELTA WAVES]

ONEIROLYSIS—theory: DREAMS are fast, fading, elusive experiences. **Syn.** DREAM DISSOLUTION. [**cf.** EXPOSURE DREAM, ADVERSARIES, FALSE AWAKENING]

ONEIROS—(ancient) the entity or symbol appearing in the dream bringing the message. [**cf.** SYMBOLS, DREAMMAKER, DISPLACEMENT]

ONENESS—1. the realization of one great source where all ENERGY, INTELLIGENCE, and IDEAS spring from, and the realization that MAN exists as only a speck within it; 2. when one no longer feels he or she is a HUMAN BEING but just AN INTELLIGENCE; a feeling of belonging; happens in a deep meditative state. [**cf.** ANCIENT DISCIPLINES, AVATAR MEDITATION]

ONIONS—a vegetable that has the peculiar qualities to absorb negative vibrations in a room and hold these vibrations until the vegetable is burned; used where unpleasant thought or actions have transpired or used to ward off negativity in the room before unpleasant actions transpire. [**cf.** CEREMONIAL MAGIC; DAGGER; HEXAGRAM; BELL, BOOK AND CANDLE]

ONONHAROIA—(Native American, Iroquois) a community-wide celebration wherein everyone takes turns to act out a perplexing dream they have had in a sort of charade and others try to guess the meaning of the dream. [**cf.** ONDINNONK, BIRTH SYMBOL, NUDITY DREAM, COMPENSATORY DREAMS]

ONTOLOGY—(Aristotle) the study of dealing with the fundamental essence of all things, visible and invisible, as opposed to material existence; the art and science of true being. **Syn.** METAPHYSICS.

ONYX—(esoteric) a mineral under the influence of all the vibrations of Saturn; represents "out of the void came the light and all things." [**cf.** MINPSI, BLACK ONYX, CONTAINERS OF MAGICAL POWER, OVERALL CONSCIOUSNESS]

OOBE—abbr. OUT-OF-BODY EXPERIENCE; plural OOBEs; see ASTRAL PROJECTION.

OOSCOPY—see OOMANCY Appendix 6.

OPAL—a mineral that is a transmitter of Mercury's vibrations and is helpful to the PSYCHIC when taking an ASTRAL PROJECTION. [**cf.** Appendix 2 MINPSI, CHRYSOLITE, CONTAINERS OF MAGICAL POWER, BERYL]

OPAQUE POINTS—tiny bodies which are neither transparent or translucent; discs, light points, and black points in the atmosphere coming from the eye of the globe; perceived clairvoyantly and physically; (do not confuse with an ETHERIC WORLD ENTITY). **Syn.** GLOBULAR SPIRITS. [**cf.** ANTINODES, NODES, COSMO RAYS]

OPEN SYSTEM—1. a complex of components that maintain an exchange of matter with their environment through import and export, as well as through the building up and breaking down of components and are still able to attain a constant state; 2. (Seth) "a place where matter exists in three-dimensional form having its roots in man's mind which is not conformed to a set pattern." [**cf.** SYNERGY, BASIC ELEMENTS]

OPEN-EYE—(Egypt) the optic thalamus that is egg-shaped and a ganglion of the inner brain, when cut cross-sectioned it looks like a beetle; symbolizes IMMORTALITY. **Syn.** SACRED BEETLE, EGG OF IMMORTALITY, SINGLE EYE. [**cf.** HEART OF THE LOTUS, BOAT OF THE SEEKER]

443

OPEN-EYE-PSYCHIC—a slang phrase referring to a psychic that perpetrates fraud.

OPEN-FACE TRANCE—to speak out with intelligent new information with no previous preparation; psychic rambles on and when asked to repeat it, psychic cannot; new data comes from: 1. the SUPERCONSCIOUS MIND in INSPIRATIONAL SPEAKING; 2. a GUIDE that attaches to the psychic's PINEAL GLAND; occurs in normal conversation if the listener needs the information or when psychic is asked to give an impromptu speech. [cf. DIRECT KNOWLEDGE, INSPIRATIONAL THOUGHT]

OPENING OF THE MOUTH CEREMONY—(Egypt) a psychic ritual performed before the mummified body was put into the sepulcher; this ceremony would allow the body to recapture seeing, hearing, eating and speaking with the belief the corpse would then live on. [cf. DEATH SCIENCE, DEATH GLOW, COFFIN RITUALS, COMING FORTH FROM THE DAY]

OPENING OF THE SEALS—(ancient Egypt) to be transformed in a new attitude that awakens the CONSCIOUSNESS and this new attitude "starts" the vital energy fluid up the KUNDALINI. [cf. TRANSFORMATION]

OPERATING SPIRIT—an ETHERIC WORLD INTELLIGENCE working through a MEDIUM in charge of physical manifestations. [cf. PHYSICAL MANIFESTATIONS/MISCELLANEOUS]

OPERATION PRAYER POWER—an inauguration of an invention that stored human being prayer energy in a special box; prayer energy was taken from hundreds and hundreds of people on a mountain in England, ready to be released when needed in a country crisis; box invented by George King.

OPERATIVE ALCHEMY—to concentrate intensely on a substance with the desire to change its vibratory frequency to a higher level; basic principle: substance differs in degree of vibration but not in nature. [cf. ALCHEMICAL PRINCIPLE, ASANA AWAKENED, AKAM'S SLIMY EARTH]

OPERATOR—(hypnosis) a hypnotist who helps an individual reach a highly suggestible state and then gives directions or suggestions to the hypnotized person. **Syn.** GUIDE, HYPNOTHERAPIST. [cf. INDUCTION, INDUCTION RELEASE, PRESCRIPTION]

OPIUM—(esoteric) a narcotic drug prepared from the seed capsules of the opium POPPY used to induce a state of ECSTASY wherein one can travel into the psychic realm and be capable of curing illnesses or increase his or her psychic abilities; one can overdose on it's use and bring about psychic and physical horrors. [cf. FORCE-FEED, ATROPINE, DATURA INOXIA]

OPTICAL COMPUTER—see SUBCONSCIOUS MIND.

OPTICAL IMAGE DEVICE—an instrument designed to perceive the GUIDE of a MEDIUM from a point in space while the medium is reading for someone. (Inconcl.) [cf. MENTAL PSYCHIC PROCESSES]

OPTICAL THRESHOLD—a point when the colors and shapes in a MANDALA begin to shift and vibrate when one is staring at it during MEDITATION; the focused eyes seem to see the same spatial picture, but now in three dimensions. [cf. ESSENCE OF REST, HYPOTHERMIA, CENTER]

OPTIMUM HEALTH—(Robert K. Markorre Cooper) "treating health, disease, life and its purpose as one meaningful unit." **Syn.** HOLISTIC HEALTH. [cf. BREATHING RELEASE, APPLIED KINESIOLOGY, ATTITUDINAL HEALING]

OPTIONAL MEDIUM—one who has the ability to produce physical psychism at will. [cf. INVOLUNTARY MEDIUM]

ORACCU—(Wilhelm Reich) an instrument that collects and stores the life energy in the air making it usable for science and medicine. [cf. BLACK BOX, RADIESTHESIA, RADIONICS]

ORACLE—(Greece) any person, or thing that serves as an agent of divine communication; 1. a PSYCHIC capable of MENTAL PSYCHISM, especially PROPHECY; 2. the shrine where a god speaks to people through the priests or priestesses, similar to DEPENDENT VOICE trance. [cf. TRANCE MANIFESTATIONS, PORTENDER]

ORACLE AT DELPHI—a building constructed around an area on a mountain slope that emanated a peculiar vapor; Pythia, a medium and psychic, sat on a tripod over the spot; Pythia gave counsel and guidance to individuals and leaders of countries; vapor was believed to help open her psychic doors and permit Apollo, then deceased, to work through her. [cf. INVISIBLE DRUM]

ORACLE STATUE—(Greece, Egypt) a statue deity representing a necessity of life; statue encases a token appropriate to that particular necessity and named accordingly; e.g., a god that represents abundance of crops would be brown in color, contain wheat inside, and be named God of Harvest; when an answer is needed pertaining to the crops, the statue is invoked in a ritual and the question asked; oracle statues have been known to shift or move an arm, eye, or give an OMEN in some way for an answer. [cf. SYMPATHETIC MAGIC, ORACLE]

ORACS—an instrument that is a "form of energy accumulator" and emits PRANA energy at a certain intensity. [cf. RADIONICS, POLARITY]

ORACULAR POSSESSION TRANCE—(Greece, B.C.) to permit an ETHERIC WORLD INTELLIGENCE to enter one's body and use one's voice to relay important information and guidance to one's clan; breathing of MANTIS (psychic) slows down and voice becomes husky when intelligence has entered; priests were sometimes called upon to interpret the knowledge that came through. **Syn.** DEPENDENT VOICE. [cf. FRENZIED HYSTERICAL POSSESSION TRANCE, MEDIUMSHIP, POET]

ORACULAR PRIESTS—(China, Mongolia) mediums who seek information from the etheric world to help solve the country's political problems. [cf. PROPHECY, NATURE OMENS]

ORACULAR WORDS—information coming from the etheric world while MEDIUM is in a TRANCE state.

ORAL BREATHING—a technique of breathing that helps one take an ASTRAL PROJECTION; discovered by Robert Monroe. [cf. FOCUS TWO, FRINGE OF SPACE-TIME, EXTERIORIZATION]

ORANGE—(colorology) a color that has the vibrational frequency of energy, health, emotional strength and vitality; warm color relating to the sun, the life-giving source of the universe. [cf. COLOROLOGY, CHROMOPATHY, COLOR ACTIVITY]

ORANUR—(Wilhelm Reich) ORGONE ENERGY driven to a very high level of excitation; violent and full of life as opposed to the negative form of orgone energy. (Inconcl.) [cf. VIBRATIONS, CLOUD SHIFTING]

ORANUR ATMOSPHERE—(Wilhelm Reich) lightning-like flashes of yellow and white that seem to be STATIC ELECTRICITY that happen at unexpected times; perceived clairvoyantly as bluish gray, changing to reddish and purple color; e.g., electricity entering the hair and hand from skuffing a rug. [cf. COSMO RAYS, BIOCURRENTS, ENERGY GRIDS]

ORDER OF THE GOLDEN DAWN—influential OCCULT society in England founded in 1887 by the Rosicrucian Society; patterned after the Hermetic Society; brought through many great ancient truths from the ETHERIC WORLD.

ORDERING PRINCIPLE—1. the HUMAN BEING SPECIES SEED within each individual that motivates that individual to do better each day and keep him or her evolving back to the perfect state; 2. the I AM; 3. the CHRIST WITHIN; 4. AN INNATE QUALITY THAT HOLDS TOGETHER A PATTERN of archetypal non-thoughts and current thinking that reacts in the CASTING OF LOTS skill, bringing a synchronicity situation. [cf. I CHING, NON-THOUGHT, LOTS, INTERIOR COHESION, CORRESPONDENCE]

ORDINARY CONSCIOUSNESS—a mind not aware of itself; it only knows its destination. [cf. DUAL CONSCIOUSNESS, CELLULAR CONSCIOUSNESS, BETA STATE]

ORDINARY DREAMS—scenes that are uninteresting to the dreamer or psychiatrist and are not analyzed. [cf. DREAMS, ARCHETYPAL DREAMS, CAUSAL ANALYSIS, DEEPER DREAMLAND]

OREAD—(Greece) NATURE SPIRIT taking the form of a nymph to preside over the mountains and grottos in earth. [cf. NYMPHS]

ORENDA—(Native American, Iroquois and Algonquin) 1. the magic in breath necessary to all living things; see VITAL LIFE FORCE; 2. (Native American, Sioux and Monomines) a technique of HYPNOSIS so powerful that it allows the person to be completely healed, or it may be used in reverse for the person's destruction; 3. the inner power of the TOTEM of the tribes chosen animal that inspires the community to do great things, e.g., a horse could inspire one to steadfastness. [cf. HYPNOTHERAPY, ASSOCIATED MAGIC]

ORESTIAD—see OREAD.

ORGAN LANGUAGE—to unintentionally repeat a phrase, silently or orally, with a subjective and symbolic meaning which affects parts of the physical body; the SUBCONSCIOUS MIND takes CONSCIOUS MIND phrases verbatim; e.g., "I close my eyes to it" (individual has eye problems); "I can't swallow that" (affects the throat); "that is a

445

pain in the neck" (neck becomes stiff or sore). [cf. DISEASE, METAPHYSICAL HEALING, BODY ARMOR]

ORGANIZATIONAL PSYCHOLOGY—pertains to people's behavior and attitudes within an organizational setting; the effect of the organization upon the individual and the individual's effect upon the organization depends upon whether one was involved with the same individuals in a past incarnation and whether this involvement was a happy one. [cf. NEW-AGE PSYCHOLOGY, ART OF LIVING]

ORGONE ACCUMULATOR—(Wilhelm Reich) a man-sized box that produces the heat found in space; one could restore oneself to good health by sitting in it.

ORGONE ENERGY—(Wilhelm Reich) an original, mass-free universal life energy form in which everything on our planet is immersed; similar to the ETHER in ordinary physics; PRIMAL ENERGY in the atmosphere vital to all life; controls biophysical emotion, penetrating everything; has wavelike motion which electromagnetic energy modulates. [cf. PRANA, SPIRIT, ODIC, MAGNETIC FLUID]

ORGONOMY—the study of ORGONE ENERGY discovered by Wilhelm Reich.

ORGONOTIC PULSATION—(ufology) cyclic disturbances in the atmosphere.

ORPHAN PLANT—signs of a plant losing its vitality when the mother plant dies. [cf. EMPATHY CLAIRSENTIENCE, BIOTELEPATHY, BOTANE]

ORPHIC CULT—(Hinduism) began with Orpheus; proclaims salvation as a release from MATTER and from eathly bondage. [cf. PEYOTE CULT, KRIYA-MAYA, REINCARNATION]

ORPINE—(esoteric) a purple-flowered stonecrop used for its psychic properties; especially good for inducing information regarding marriage. **Syn.** MIDSUMMER MEN. [cf. BOTANE Appendix 2, BLACK BEANS, BIRTH BY HEAT AND NATURE]

ORTHODOX SLEEP—see NREM SLEEP.

OSCILLATING RECORDER—an instrument that registers the pulsation of plants, used in psychic experiments with plants. [cf. ARTIFICIAL PARADISE, MENTAL HEALING, BEAMED ENERGY]

OSCILLATION—(penduluming) the swinging of the bob of the pendulum in a straight line in one direction for the psychic to use as an answer, as opposed to swinging in a circle. [cf. COURTESY, CYCLE OF MOVEMENTS, PALLOMANCY, DOWSING]

OSCILLOSCOPE—an auxiliary piece of a BIOFEEDBACK INSTRUMENT that is connected to the person to eliminate variations in baseline drift. [cf. BIOFEEDBACK TRAINING Appendix 5, ALPHA WAVES, ACTIVE VOLITION, BALANCE CONTROL]

OSIRIAN FIELDS—a place of heaven; see MONADIC PLANE.

OSIRIS—(ancient Egypt) a symbol of the God of creation; king of the underworld; a symbol of immortality; depicted many ways; one way is the form of a mummy wearing a crown and in his hands is the emblem of sovereignity and power; the father of HORUS.

OTAHCHUK—(Native American, Algonquin) human life force (SOUL-MIND) and his outer SHADOW that can show psychically after death.

OTHER ENERGIES—an X-ENERGY that has been found recently to be consolidated in the center of particular forms and shapes; i.e., PYRAMID, SQUARE, CONICAL SHAPE; while under study, it has not been named but verified that it is prevalent, so it is known at this time as other energies. [cf. FORMS-WITH-POWER Appendix 2, PSYCHOTRONIC ENERGY]

OTHER PERSONS-PROGRAMMING PROPERTIES—data taken into one's memory storage system given by others without one's being aware it is happening; occurs because of lack of knowledge of the two functions of the mind. [cf. CONSCIOUS MIND, SUBCONSCIOUS MIND]

OTHER WORLD INTELLIGENCE—(ufology) intelligent organisms detected in UFO encounters that appear to have similarities with humans, as opposed to the construct they ride in. [cf. CREATURES OF STRATOSPHERE, CONSTRUCTS]

OTHERWHERE—(esoteric) dimension past the FOURTH PLANE where entities are dedicated to achieve betterment of the human race and choose to come to earth to work with earthlings as a WALK-IN. (Inconcl.) [cf. INCARNATIONAL EXCHANGE, COSMIC INTERVAL, CHAIN OF BEING]

OTHERWORLD—see ETHERIC WORLD; used in connection with NATURE SPIRITS.

OTOMI FIGURINES—(Mexico, Native American, Otomi) angels, saints, and demons made of the famous AMATL PAPER according to how the

Indians felt they looked; these duplicates were used in sacred rituals. [cf. CEREMONIES, ANTHROPOMORPHIC]

OUIJA BOARD—(France, Germany; *oui ja*, "yes, yes") (capitalized) trademark for a manufactured board that spells out answers to questions for the psychic; board contains the alphabet, numbers, and a *yes* and *no* written on its face; psychic asks a question verbally and places finger tips on an indicator that travels lightly over each letter needed to spell out the answer; a dangerous tool when used by one not well-grounded in psychic sciences and knowledge of beforehand preparation; when used as a game for those unfamiliar with psychic tuning it has been known to draw the inferior entities to move the indicator; this inferior entity fools the user and can lead to dangerous physical phenomena. [cf. INFERIOR SPIRITS, DENSITY, CLOAK OF INSULATION, PLANCHETTE, ASTRAL SHELL]

OUR STONE—primary substance used by ALCHEMIST; has the property to germinate and develop into the final substance. **Sim.** LAPIS NOSTER, PRIMA MATERIA. [cf. PHILOSOPHER'S STONE]

OUROBOROS—(Greece) the study of mankind and society as a miniature replica of the UNIVERSE; depicted by a serpent in a circle swallowing its own tail, expresses the LIFE FORCE in nature feeding and renewing itself eternally; also represents the UNIVERSE in its cyclic nature of completeness. [cf. ALCHEMIST'S EGG, AZOTH, CHEMICAL MARRIAGE]

OUSIA—(Greece) see VITAL LIFE FORCE.

"OUT OF THE BLUE"—information perceived clairsentiently and spontaneously; data not consciously thought out nor coming from one's background. Usage: "It came to me out of the blue to dash over here," and she found the person ill. [cf. CLAIRSENTIENCE, FUZZY FEELING, CONCEPTUAL SENSE]

OUT-BREATH—(Zen) concentration of the impulse of the air leaving the stomach during MEDITATION. [cf. SESSHIN, ZAZEN, KEISAKU]

OUT-OF-BODY-EXPERIENCE—abbr. OOBE, OBE; to leave one's physical body and sail invisibly through the air in an etheric coating that is a replica of the physical body and physical clothing; occurs randomly during sleep to replenish one's vitality or to conduct business in the higher planes; can be willed in the awake state; the etheric coating is encasing one's SOUL-MIND which remains attached to the corpse-like physical body by the SILVER CORD; see ASTRAL PROJECTION.

OUT-OF-PHASE—1. see OUT-OF-SYNC; 2. (astral projection) to take 180 degree curves, in exact opposite of POLARITY, in an astral flight. [cf. ATTRACTION-ACTION-REACTION, BACK TOGETHER, CLEAR CONSCIOUS STATE]

OUT-OF-RANGE-OF-CORD-ACTIVITY—(astral projection) refers to the stretched SILVER CORD of the PROJECTIONIST when it is longer than fifteen feet; cord has greater elasticity, is thinner in diameter, and keeps the projectionist more stable; the longer the stretch of the cord, the more smoothly the projectionists flies. [cf. IN-THE-RANGE-OF-CORD-ACTIVITY]

OUT-OF-SYNC—(astral projection) to function and operate with an abnormal biological rhythm, caused from flying through time zones; symptoms: fatigue, abnormal temperature of body, digestion upset, lack of confidence and mixed mental activity; e.g., individual feels like eating cereal and shaving but it is time for the evening meal. **Syn.** OUT OF PHASE. [cf. JET FATIGUE, TIME LAG, CIRCADIAN RHYTHM]

OUT-THERE—1. (Native American) see ETHERIC WORLD; 2. a point in space where psychic information is perceived by the psychic as opposed to perceiving it in the mind; see OBJECTIVE CLAIRAUDIENCE and OBJECTIVE CLAIRVOYANCE.

OUTER BAND—etheric world soul-minds that are drawn to earthlings to assist them as their interests, needs, and desires change; during one's lifetime one may call upon or unknowingly accept an intelligence or soul-mind who shares similarity of talent, interest, and knowledge, only on a greater scale; these soul-minds work toward their evolvement by attaching to the earthling to aid him or her; they stay only as long as their speciality is needed; soul-minds may help in sports, musical achievements, charity drives, schooling, health problems, marriage, child raising, vocations, employment, inventions, writings, psychic skills, etc.; earthling may specify a special soul-mind if he or she desires; e.g., in taking a course in engineering and the author of the text book is deceased, one may call upon them; if the soul-mind is not available, he or she will send another who agrees with their theories; earthling cannot draw to her or himself a soul-mind who far surpasses their stage of evolvement as the law of like attracts like is in force in this process; e.g., one who constantly uses profanity and abuses his associates will not receive personal collaboration from a highly evolved soul-mind; (mankind will eventually learn that brotherly love between the etheric world and the earth world is necessary to bring harmony to the universe). [cf. INNER BAND, GUIDE, DISCARNATE ENTITY, LAW OF LIKE ATTRACTS LIKE Appendix 7]

OUTER CONSCIOUS LEVEL—awareness by the MENTAL MIND only, the normal everyday level of consciousness. **Syn.** BETA STATE OF CONSCIOUSNESS. [cf. ALPHA STATE OF CONSCIOUSNESS, THETA STATE OF CONSCIOUSNESS]

OUTER MENTAL ACTIVITY—ergs of intelligent energy that enter into the BRAIN to be recognized and mingled with the normal processes of decision-making; energy is not originally put together from the MENTAL MIND; kinds: 1. PSYCHIC INFORMATION that terminates in the brain to be recognized and used respectfully; enters via the PSYCHIC SENSES, SUBCONSCIOUS MIND and SUPERCONSCIOUS MIND, and the ETHERIC WORLD INTELLIGENCES; 2. environmental stimuli that are not usually recognized unless one makes a special effort to do so; radiations from people; living organisms, EARTHBOUND ENTITIES, FLOWERS, COLOR, weather, STARS, SOUND, minerals, and inert objects. **Syn.** NON-THOUGHT. [cf. CONFIDENCE CALL, PRIMARY PERCEPTION, BLIND MENTAL PSYCHISM]

OUTER SENSES—five physical senses.

OUTLAW MEMORY—(Huna) record of an unresolved emotional event stored in the SUBCONSCIOUS MIND which was not rationalized at the time it happened; resurfaces at any time making negative behavior for the individual; see BLOCKS. [cf. MEMORY CLUSTERS, GRAPES]

OUTSIDE INVADER—thoughts that are telepathically sent during the night by adepts, hypnotists, friends, discarnates, or etheric world guides with enough power or emotion to intrude into one's dreams or daytime living; used for good or evil intent. [cf. MENTAL TELEPATHIC SUGGESTION, MENTAL TELEPATHIC HEALING]

OUTSIDE PERSONALITIES—see ETHERIC WORLD INTELLIGENCES.

OUTSIDERS—(Tibet) anyone who doesn't believe in psychic work, astrology, etheric world intelligences, etc. [cf. INSIDERS, SHEEP AND GOATS EFFECT]

OVAL—(Tattwa) fifth symbol; represents the spirit energy in the air; an elemental primordial black substance; a necessary element when tuning into the SUBCONSCIOUS MIND, CLAIRVOYANCE, and other types of psychism. **Syn.** OVOID, AKASHA. [cf. TATTWA VISIONS, CIRCLE, CONICAL SHAPE]

OVER THERE—see ETHERIC WORLD.

OVERALL CONSCIOUSNESS—(esoteric) level of awareness of the MINERAL KINGDOM; minerals, regardless of size, blend with their environment, attracting and repulsing vibrations from the environment; minerals record the atmosphere of emotions and attitudes in their immediate area and for miles around, depending upon their size; these attitudinal and emotional vibrations are radiated back into the environment influencing the conditions of the environment; the attracting and repulsing gives the mineral shape, size, and quality. [cf. MINPSI, SENSATION CONSCIOUSNESS]

OVERLOOKING—to control someone by staring at them; see SPELL.

OVERLORDS—magnanimous exalted beings who have an interest in the planet and give assistance to planetary angels, especially in this transformational period. [cf. AQUARIAN AGE, PLANETARY ANGEL, CONSCIOUSNESS AWARENESS MOVEMENT]

OVERSAW—to see something happening beyond the normal range of the physical eyes while it is happening. **Syn.** CLAIRVOYANCE-IN-SPACE. [cf. REMOTE VIEWING, EYES OF INSTINCT]

OVERSELF—(Tibet) see SUBCONSCIOUS MIND.

OVERSHADOWING—(mental mediumship) to allow interpenetration of one's etheric world GUIDE (or guides) to work within one's body and yet not be in a SEMITRANCE or DEEP TRANCE state; 1. MEDIUM calls in his or her guide after meditating, or singing of hymns, or listening to classical music and the guide stays within his or her body until dismissed; medium is in an ALPHA STATE OF CONSCIOUSNESS and finds it difficult to make decisions in speech or activity; 2. medium senses body feelings when guide has entered which assures medium that the information will come from the ETHERIC WORLD; closeness of guide can be detected by other psychics because medium looks different, sometimes taking on the facial features of the guide (more easily detected in subdued lighting); mannerisms are also changed slightly; 3. occurs in a PSYCHIC DEVELOPMENT CIRCLE, READING, INSPIRATIONAL SPEAKING and INSPIRATIONAL WRITING or whenever the medium calls in the guide for psychic purposes; etheric world guide can relay information more easily working slightly within the body; comes through CLAIRVOYANCE, CLAIRAUDIENCE, CLAIRSENTIENCE, CLAIRSCENT, CLAIRSAVORANCE, and INSPIRATIONAL THOUGHT; a normal synchronization, when the two are compatible workers for civilization. [cf. PHYSICAL MANIFESTATIONS/MISCELLANEOUS, TRANSFIGURATION]

OVERSIMPLIFIED BIOCOMPUTER LOGICS—(destructive-brainwashing cult) the continual automatic repetition of simple phrases in meetings, daytime conversation, and in sleep learning tapes during the night; this conditioning program dulls the SUBCONSCIOUS MIND (BIOCOMPUTER) and it stops working for its own purpose; takes the cult member back to the more primitive stages in which the CONSCIOUS MIND was not as active in decision-making and members then act as robots subject to the cult leader's decisions. [cf. COLLECTIVE PSYCHE, ASSOCIATION THEORY]

OVERSOUL—1. (Zoroastrianism) a part of the SOUL-MIND that separates and stores all the activities the ENTITY has experienced in earthly incarnations that were handled with the correct attitude; properly handled experiences are considered to be WISDOM and do not have to be re-experienced; incorrectly handled activities stay in the soul-mind to be worked out as KARMA; 2. (Hinduism) that part of the soul-mind that is purified and shows the perfected quality necessary for the MONAD to slip into perfect consciousness; 3. (Lama Sing, an etheric world master working through Al Miner) "a guide or mentor who is in constant contact with the external force which guides one's LIFE FORCE; 4. the GESTALT for that system, e.g., the oversoul for earth is in charge of everything on earth having a function to work with itself and the sum of the whole parts; 5. Qabalistic wisdom, the ARCHANGELS are the oversouls; 6. (Marilyn Ferguson) invisible dimension of REALITY. [cf. SUPERCONSCIOUS MIND, EVOLUTION]

OVERSOUL-CONSCIOUSNESS—functioning from the level of universal love and the wisdom that is in the OVERSOUL.

OVERWORLD—see ETHERIC WORLD; named to distinguish from the world within the earth.

OVOID—the appearance of a solid egg-shape; term used when expressing the AURA around a person; appears to clairvoyants as an oval and yet without definite boundaries.

OWL—(esoteric) associated with psychic powers due to the facial features, eyes, screams, and the nocturnal nature; (Semitic) felt to be ominous; (Persia) the angel of death; (Greece) the goddess of night; (Rome) hung stuffed owls overhead to ward off strangers, and as a talisman to combat the evil-eye; (Africa) associated with sorcery. [cf. DOVES, EAGLES]

OWL CORNER—(China) an owl ornament placed on a building to keep the building free from fire. [cf. TALISMAN, ANIMAL SPIRITS, DEER ANTLERS]

OWLS IN MADAGASCAR—the soul-mind of a SORCERER.

OWN-BEING—(Sunyavada) the immutable part of each person, arising to be existent in the earth plane; the function is to change and that which functions is relatively real.

OXYGEN INTOXICATION—to overbreathe by continually taking short breaths; this causes a giddy feeling which could eventually lead to a dissociation of the body; continuing to take short breaths ends in a hypnotic or ALTERED STATE OF CONSCIOUSNESS; dangerous if one is not familiar with breathing exercises and their purpose. Syn. HYPERVENTILATING. [cf. COMPLETE BREATH, DIVINE INTOXICATION]

OXYGEN JAG—see HYPERVENTILATING or OXYGEN INTOXICATION.

OZONIZE—the process of making ozone present in the SEANCE room by the ETHERIC WORLD INTELLIGENCES before ectoplasmic materialization. (Inconcl.) [cf. ECTOPLASM, MATERIALIZATION, ECTOPLASM WISPS]

449

P—abbr. PROBABILITY (capitalized and uncapitalized); (laboratory) the number of target hits according to the scale of probability. [**cf.** CHANCE AVERAGE, ESP SHUFFLE, BASIC TECHNIQUE]

P-VALUE—(psi task) the significance of the results of an experiment done by a table of statistics, indicating the odds against those particular results appearing by chance. [**cf.** BIDIRECTIONALITY OF PSI, CHANCE LEVEL]

PACE-MAKER—(esoteric) the heart serving as an anchor point for the vagus nerve. **Syn.** PULSE-POINT. [**cf.** THIRD-EYE AREA, VAGUS BREATHING, LIFE-CORD-SEED-aATOM]

PADMASANA—see LOTUS POSTURE.

PAGAN—(Latin *paganua*, "countryman") one who is not a Christian, a Jew, or a Moslem; current: a blanket word meaning "a heathen" or "anyone who does not believe as I do."

PAIN—(future science) a related amount of disorganization in the brain; a perception, not a sensation; each one perceives discomfort differently and in different degrees; a necessary tool in one's growth pattern; there would be no pleasure if there were no pain; see LAW OF OPPOSITES Appendix 7. [**cf.** CURATIVE EDUCATION, POLARITY, ILLNESS, CHRONIC PAIN]

PAINTING MEDIUM—one who paints under the influence of an ETHERIC WORLD ENTITY while in a trance state; work is done with considerable speed; shows characteristics of the etheric world painter; the medium need know nothing about painting. [**cf.** INSPIRATIONAL PAINTING, AUTOMATISM, AUTOMATIC ART]

PALAEOAESTHETIC CLAIRVOYANCE—name given to PSYCHOMETRY.

PALINDROME—a name for a word spelled the same backwards as forwards; gives it more powerful vibrations. e.g., *eye, noon, madam*. [**cf.** WORDS-WITH-POWER]

PALINGENESIS—1. (Greek, "coming again into being") each body of each species, e.g., frog, daisy, or human will come back into the same species at rebirth that it passed out from. [**cf.** REINCARNATION, TRANSMIGRATION OF SOULS, ANIMAL GROUP SOUL] 2. (alchemy) alchemical art that deals with the recreation of an object after it has been reduced to ashes. [**cf.** ALCHEMICAL PRINCIPLES, ALCHEMIST OF SACRED FIRE]

PALINGRAPHIA—see MIRROR WRITING.

PALLOMANCY—(Greek *pallo,* "to pendle"; *manteia,* "divination") to use a PENDULUM to measure radiations from a given object or person, or to answer questions by the use of a pendulum; the psychic is sensitive to radiations around living energy fields, nonliving energy fields, and energy fields not in one's presence; by holding a pendulum between the index finger and thumb over these radiations, one receives tangible answers that can be interpreted easily by the brain; a code is set up between the SOUL-MIND and the pendulum which then gyrates and oscillates by swinging; the swings are read for their speed, direction, length and number. **Syn.** PENDULUM POWER. [**cf.** RADIESTHETIC SENSE, CRYSTAL PENDULUM, COURTESY, NONSWING RESPONSE]

PALLOMANTIC—a PSYCHIC who is skilled with a PENDULUM.

PALM DOWNWARD DURING MEDITATION—1. (Buddhism) the right hand facing inward or down represents the total of past experiences; the first step in MEDITATION (awareness of reflections from the UNIVERSAL LIGHT); 2. (Christianity) palms downward is expressive of giving. [**cf.** HANDS, PALMING]

PALM TREE—(Ironsland) 1. one of the seven noble trees of the land; held sacred and used in ceremonies and on Palm Sunday; 2. (metaphysics, Unity) represents the realization of unlimited strength while in the flesh. [**cf.** BIODETECTORS, BIRCH, PUSSY WILLOW]

PALM UPWARD DURING MEDITATION—1. (Buddhism) left hand relaxing in the lap with the palm upward, represents the four wisdoms; expresses love for all things; 2. (Christianity) expressive of receiving.

PALMED POWER—(1860-1920) to store PSYCHIC ENERGY in an object by holding it in one's hand and concentrating on energy coming from the hands for a while; proven by over six instruments that there is a nervous (psychic) force that can be exteriorized and stored in wood, water, linen and cardboard. **Syn.** EXTERIORIZATION OF MOTORICITY. [**cf.** BIOMETER, MAGNETOMETER, SPIRITOSCOPE, HUMAN POLARITY, AMULET ENERGIZING]

PALMING—to direct PSYCHIC ENERGY out of the palms of the hands to be used in psychic skills and healing; psychic takes a few minutes to build energy in the mind and then directs it outward through the palms of the hands, the index finger, and thumb; palms are held close to the object or on the object to be affected; palming is one of the main doors of the human being for sending generated power; used in PK, AMULET ENERGIZING, LAYING-ON-OF-HANDS. [cf. PSYCHOKINESIS, AMULET, CONTACT HEALING, CONFERRING OF POWER]

PALMING THE EYES—(China) to rest and rejuvenate one's eyesight by using one's hands; the palms are rubbed together until warm, the fingers are crossed at the temple while the palms of the hands are cupped over the eyeballs with lids closed; the subject is to see "jet black"; when one sees pure black under closed lids the eyes are completely relaxed, freeing them from any strain. **Syn.** CORPSE POSE. [cf. HOLISTIC HEALTH, BATE'S METHOD, BREATHING RELEASE]

PALMIST—one who gives palm readings by psychically tuning into a person's character, future, or past by holding his or her hands face up and studying the lines, etc. **Syn.** CHIROSOPHIST, HAND-ANALYST. [cf. BODY READING Appendix 5]

PALMISTRY—encompasses all phases of analyzing one's hands to tune into one's past, future, characteristics, health and wealth situation; uses scientific facts regarding the study of the hand, fingers, wrist, for their lines, shape and texture; uses hands as a POINT-OF-FOCUS for psychic information; includes both categories: CHIROMANCY, and CHIROGNOMY. **Syn.** CHIROSOPHY, HAND-ANALYSIS, CHIROGNOSY. [cf. MOLESCOPY, IRIDOLOGY]

PALMISTRY LINES—principle lines: life line, head line, heart line, fate line, Apollo or sun line, and intuition line; secondary lines: girdle of Venus, cross line, lines of union, martian lines, travel lines, Mercury or health line, and three bracelets of health, wealth, and happiness. [cf. CHIROSOPHY, CHIROGNOMY, BUMPS]

PAMPAS—(the desert) to induce an ALTERED STATE OF CONSCIOUSNESS by two or three hours of hearty exercises, walking, carrying heavy objects and praying, in order to surface PSYCHIC INFORMATION. [cf. CIRCULAR STONE DANCE, ETHERIC ACTIVITY, SINGERS]

PAN—(uncapitalized) prefix meaning "all".

PAN—(capitalized) (Greek, "all," everywhere) a NATURE SPIRIT known as god of the ELEMENTAL world, whose purpose is to bring a reality of COSMIC CONSCIOUSNESS into the world; given many nature spirit subjects to help him; belongs to a different ray than mankind; DEITY of the countryside, and easily perceived clairvoyantly as wandering or dancing through the woods with other NYMPHS; a very beautiful spirit able to shift dimensions and to be in many places at once; depicted as half-man and half-goat; the upper half is human, with human arms, and horns on forehead, represents "intellect"; lower half is animal, with cloven hooves, fine silky hair, animal legs, represents "powerful, deep energy." [cf. FAIRIES] **2.** a continent in the Pacific Ocean that submerged 24,000 years ago in what is known as the Deluge to the Kosmon Era; also called LEMURIA. [cf. KOSMON REVELATION]

PANDORA'S BOX—(Greek myth) (Pandora is an earth goddess, meaning "all-giving") the great jar or box held all evils which had been confined; Pandora was the first woman on earth to punish men; she opened the box letting the evils loose to plague the world; everything flew out except "hope." [cf. REM REBOUND]

PANORAMIC FLASHBACK—to perceive clairvoyantly while making the TRANSITION, the ethereal, microfilm pictures of the life that is terminating; unwilled; happens to everyone; takes a few minutes to view one's whole life; a method of letting one know one's incarnational accomplishments and mistakes. (Inconcl.) [cf. DEATH SCIENCE, DEATH-BED VISIONS, MANIFESTED IN THE LIGHT]

PANPSYCHIC—(Greek, *pan* "all") all psychic; see PSYCHIC.

PANPSYCHISM—see PARAPSYCHOLOGY.

PANT NETERU—(ancient Egypt) the nine greatest gods in the ETHERIC WORLD called upon for guidance and protection; also known as **the great company of the gods. Syn.** PAUT AAT. [cf. NINE, GREAT WHITE BROTHERHOOD]

PANTHEISM—(Greek, *pan*, "all") doctrine that GOD is ALL, the sum total of everything that exists; all things, animate and inanimate, including the earth and humans are manifestations of God; suffering, evil, and change are aspects of God as much as the ultimate good in everything; denies any personality related to God. **Syn.** METAPHYSICS.

PANTOMNESIA—a sensation that one is repeating

an experience, has been in the area before, or has known a person before one was introduced for the first time; regression of the memory; theory: **1.** one knew that person, had been in the area, or had experienced the same action in a previous life; **2.** one experienced the same emotional sensations in a previous life, not necessarily the same activity, which triggers the memory. (Inconcl.) **Syn.** DEJA VU. [**cf.** DEJA ENTENDU, DISPLACEMENT]

PAPYRUS—(Egypt) the most perfect copy of the BOOK OF THE DEAD written on papyrus. [**cf.** TIBETAN BOOK OF THE DEAD, EGYPTIAN BOOK OF THE DEAD]

PAR—prefix meaning "equal to"; parallel.

PARA—(Sanskrit, Greek) prefix meaning "beyond, above, far, distant, amiss, aside"; sometimes implies alteration or modification; parallel to, but not the same.

PARABLE—(root word, *parallel*) a story of mundane experiences that can portray an inner religious truth or moral lesson in a simplified and short manner; a story that conveys meaning indirectly by comparison. [**cf.** SYMBOLISM, ALLEGORY]

PARABRAHM—(Hinduism) TOTALITY in the beginning when all was CHAOS.

PARACHEMICAL REACTIONS—the change of the alchemist's materials through concentration and prayer; to use the mind to alter matter. **Syn.** OBJECT-PK. [**cf.** PSYCHOKINESIS, TRANSMUTATION, MIND-OVER-MATTER]

PARACHERO—(Mexico) see PSYCHIC.

PARACOGNITIVE PHENOMENA—to perceive information through one's psychic senses regarding the present situation and to realize it is PSYCHIC INFORMATION. [**cf.** PSYCHIC COGNITION, COGNITIVE CLAIRSENTIENCE, ESP]

PARADIAMAGNETIQUE—(France) a PENDULUM constructed by Father Bovis to be sensitive to food radiations; used to test food's vibrational rate, etc. [**cf.** RADIESTHESIA, AURIC CHARGE]

PARADISE—(esoteric) an etheric realm beyond the FIFTH or SIXTH PLANE where one releases the flesh and is in a different energy vibration, without loss of identity; like going home; an ultimate goal of a blessed, happy vibration where one joins other paradises and where its citizens are immortal; OTHERWHERE; higher level than heaven.

PARADISE LINE—(hand analysis) a small line around the bottom edge of the palm indicating the ability to enjoy more pleasure than usual. [**cf.** DIAGNOSTIC PALMISTRY, BUMPS, BOSSES]

PARADOXAL SLEEP—see DREAM STAGE, REM.

PARAELECTRICITY—coined by Ambrose Worrall; energy that comes from the healing practitioner's hand in SPIRITUAL or MENTAL HEALING; similar to ELECTRICITY in some of its characteristics; has intelligence of a high order knowing to not destroy healthy tissues; works at a distance or on body contact; seems to alter tension and break up the congested area, controlled by the desirability and thoughts of the mental activity of the healer. (Inconcl.) [**cf.** MENTAL HEALING, THOUGHT, ATOMS, PK]

PARAFFIN MOLDS—(materialization seance) a wax pattern made from the hands that materialize without a body at the SEANCE, to be used for a cast; when the hands become dense enough, they dip themselves into hot paraffin, and cold water; after paraffin congeals, the hands carefully pull themselves out leaving a wax glove; this is filled with plaster of Paris for a cast to study and fingerprint; hands work with abnormal rapidity and obligingly to help prove their authenticity; fingerprints show that hands always belong to a deceased person. [**cf.** ECTOPLASM, EFFUVIUM, ECTOPLASM WISPS]

PARAGNOSIS—the most common types of mental psychism: MENTAL TELEPATHY, CLAIRVOYANCE, CLAIRSENTIENCE, and PSYCHIC COGNITION. **Syn.** ESP. [**cf.** CONCLUSION-LEAPING, AGENT, COVARIANCE EFFECT]

PARAGNOST—(Netherlands) a PSYCHIC and HEALER who uses esoteric and spiritual knowledge as his or her basis.

PARAKINESIS—to move an object in space by employing mind power only. **Syn.** PSYCHOKINESIS. [**cf.** ARTICLE-PK, NATURE-PK, TELEKINESIS]

PARALLEL AWARENESS—the MEDIUM STATE OF HYPNOSIS; the SUBCONSCIOUS MIND has full control, and is receiving and reacting to the suggestions given by the GUIDE but the subject is also showing enough consciousness to be aware that he or she is on the couch; a pseudo awareness subserving the subconscious mind. [**cf.** HYPNOTHERAPY, SEMI-STAGE HYPNOSIS, EYE-ROLL TEST]

PARALLEL LIVES—coined by Richard Sutphen;

453

"the simultaneous multiple incarnation of various physical entities of the same OVERSOUL, living on the earth plane at the same time, overlapping in physical manifestation"; one is in unconscious communication with one's parallels and each one could influence the other to some degree, in attitude and occurrences; one is not conscious of this influence normally. **Syn.** SEPARATE SELVES, COUNTERPARTS.

PARALYTIC CONDITION—a sensation of immobility; the whole physical body is so relaxed it cannot move; body feels too heavy to move but a comfortable heaviness; every muscle is dormant; takes place during TRANCE, in a hypnotic state, and before taking an ASTRAL PROJECTION. [**cf.** HYPNOTIC SPEECH, HYPNOTIC DISC]

PARAMNESIA—see DÉJÀ VU.

PARAMORPHIC TABLE RAPPINGS—(Canada, Laboratory) see TABLE-TIPPING.

PARANEUROPHYSIOLOGICAL—see PARAPSYCHOLOGY.

PARANOIA—(esoteric) a state of derangement and rearrangement of the SOUL-MIND as one diminishes the EGO; occurs on the last steps of one's growth path.

PARANORMAL—beyond present accepted models of science; above and beyond everyday happenings; pertains to psychic events by those who do not believe everyone is capable of developing psychism; that which is unexplainable but not "absurd." [**cf.** PSYCHIC RESEARCH, PSYCHIC SKILLS, MENTAL PSYCHIC PROCESSES]

PARANORMAL COGNITION—see PSYCHIC COGNITION.

PARANORMAL HEALER—1. see PSYCHIC SURGEON; 2. one who uses esoteric, parapsychological, or occult healing methods; (do not confuse with HOLISTIC HEALTH HEALERS). [**cf.** PSYCHIC HEALING, MEDIUMSHIP HEALING]

PARANORMAL HEALING—any healing that is performed without using conventional or orthodox methods; see PSYCHIC HEALING.

PARANORMAL ODOR PHENOMENA—see CLAIRSCENT.

PARANORMALITY—coined by Jean de Charin; term used in place of PARAPSYCHOLOGY in his lectures to the Vatican at the University in Rome,

so confusion may not arise as to the nature of miracles.

PARANORMALOLOGY—(Rome) the study of PARASONOPTIC PHENOMENA, PARAPSYCHOLOGICAL PHENOMENA, PARASPIRIT PHENOMENA, PARAPHYSICAL PHENOMENA; used in lectures to the Vatican in the University.

PARANTHROPOLOGY—study of PSYCHISM or PARAPSYCHOLOGY in regard to its effect on the reactions and feelings of people in general.

PARAOPTIC SIGHT—see EYELESS SIGHT.

PARAOPTIC VISION—to see with one's skin; to sense colors with the fingertips if blind or blindfolded; one type of EYELESS SIGHT. **Syn.** SKIN VISION. [**cf.** FINGER READING, CEREBRAL VISION]

PARAPHYSICAL—pertains to: 1. that which is above and beyond the mundane things a human being perceives with the five SENSES; 2. ETHERIC WORLD INTELLIGENCES after they have made their TRANSITION; 3. NATURE SPIRITS; 4. that which is accomplished by PSYCHISM.

PARAPHYSICAL ELECTRONIC VOICES—a human voice utterance heard on a telephone from a dead person; theory: the voice in a PSYCHIC PHONE CALL is being produced over or within the specific instrument on which the voice is received, similar to a voice coming through a seance TRUMPET; the telephone apparatus amplifies the voice; the deceased person uses energy of the WITNESS as in PHYSICAL PSYCHISM. (Inconcl.) [**cf.** ELECTROMAGNETIC THEORY, ELECTRONIC VOICES Appendix 2]

PARAPHYSICAL PHENOMENA—see PHYSICAL PSYCHISM.

PARAPHYSICISTS—those who study PARAPSYCHOLOGY or psi-fields. [**cf.** PSYCHIC ART, PSI-FIELD]

PARAPHYSICS—the study of PHYSICS in relationship to psychic phenomena; 1. study of: (**a**) physics of paranormal processes; activity that resembles physical phenomena but is without recognizable physical cause; (**b**) (B. Herbert); anomalous physical effects not explained by current physical theories; 2. (laboratory) an approach to PSYCHIC ENERGY above and beyond the usual study of physics; 3. investigations made on the borderline of both physics and psychic phenomena. **Syn.** PARAPSYCHOLOGY.

PARAPSYCHIATRY—see PARAPSYCHOLOGY.

PARAPSYCHIC—1. (J.B. Rhine) one who scores high on tests; 2. (Carl Jung) PHYSICAL PSYCHISM; that which comes from deep within the SUBCONSCIOUS MIND.

PARAPSYCHIC FACULTY—see PSYCHIC SENSES.

PARAPSYCHIC INSTRUMENT—see DOWSING ROD.

PARAPSYCHIC SYSTEM—to measure the relative values of energy in the vital energy systems from the radiations given off from the object or person, by using the DOWSING ROD and PENDULUM. (Inconcl.) [**cf.** RADIESTHESIA, RADIONICS]

PARAPSYCHOLOGICAL—psychical effects.

PARAPSYCHOLOGICAL PHENOMENA—any type of psychic skill.

PARAPSYCHOLOGY—1. the study of invisible energies around animate and inanimate things here on earth and from the ETHERIC WORLD, and their action and reaction to mankind through other means than the normal five SENSES; how to understand and direct these energies for practical good in the growth of one's SOUL-MIND, under the principles of METAPHYSICS; 2. (Charles Richet) "a science dealing with the mechanical or psychological phenomena due to forces that seem to be intelligent or to unknown powers latent in human intelligence"; 3. (J.B. Rhine) "the branch of science that deals with psi communications, e.g., behavioral or personal exchanges with the environment which are EXTRASENORIMOTOR, not dependent on the senses and muscles"; 4. (Heron) a branch of psychology that deals with phenomena not explainable through data gained by the five senses; from the word *la psychologie* meaning "unknown psychology"; 5. the study of the nature of the human PSYCHE; (do not confuse with ESP). [**cf.** PSYCHIC ART synonyms Appendix 3]

PARARELIGIOUS—see METAPHYSICS.

PARASCIENCE—the study of psychic events beyond the normal fundamental science, with an attitude that psychic events are not beyond science, only beyond the accepted models of science as they are presently understood; includes: exploring QUANTUM PHYSICS, bioscience aspects of ESP and PK, ALTERED STATE OF CONSCIOUSNESS, cosmic intelligent communication, and parabody anatomy.

PARASCIENTIFIC RESEARCH—see PARAPSY-CHOLOGY.

PARASITISM—exchange of PSYCHIC ENERGY between two persons when in close contact with each other, in relation to inborn BODY CHEMISTRY; length of time is immaterial; 1. one in need of psychic vitality draws from a vibrant, magnetically charged person, involuntarily (not realizing why he or she feels better at the end of the session); difficult to turn off if one is aware he or she is doing this; 2. a strong, dominant PSYCHIC can lap up another's psychic energy, consciously or unconsciously, to add to his or her already abundant energy; easier to take from one who is not strong in psychic or physical energy, leaving them depleted at the end of the session, if victim is not knowledgeable in psychically cloaking her or himself with protection; difficult to prevent oneself from doing this. (Inconcl.) [**cf.** SPLODGING, HUMAN BATTERIES, ATMOSPHERE SHIELDING, PSYCHIC TRANSFER, HUMAN TRANSMITTER, CLOAK OF INSULATION]

PARASOMATIC EXPERIENCE—see OUT-OF-BODY-EXPERIENCE.

PARASONOPTIC PHENOMENON—(England) see PSYCHIC HEALING.

PARASPIRIT PHENOMENON—theory: SOUL-MIND leaves the body at death and survives in the ETHERIC WORLD and can communicate with earthlings. [**cf.** SPIRITUALIST, SURVIVALISTS, DEATH-BED VISIONS]

PARASYTE—one who laps up psychic and emotional energy from other persons when in contact with them, either knowingly or unknowingly; happens frequently; parasyte's BODY CHEMISTRY is not generating a lot of PSYCHIC ENERGY and is drawn into close contact with a vibrant, magnetically endowed person so it can supply itself; willed by some; parasyte leaves contact feeling vitalized and victim feels depleted or tired. [**cf.** PSYCHIC TRANSFER, PARASITISM]

PARDES—(Kabbalah) to meditate on a few single words from a PRAYER as a point-of-focus, until the mind transcends the simple meaning of the words and ascends to higher realms. [**cf.** MANTRA, CONTEMPLATION, CORTICALLY MEDIATED STABILIZATION]

PARTIAL INCENDIUM AMORIS—to heat one region of the body to an extremely high temperature, that gives them a negative feeling about why they were born and their usefulness; handed down from generation to generation due to the incorrect birth processes mothers undergo. (Inconcl.) [cf. COLLECTIVE UNCONSCIOUS, BIRTH SCIENCE, BIRTH WITHOUT VIOLENCE]

PARENT-CHILD TELEPATHY—the inner knowing of joy, sickness or danger for one another before it happens or is actually happening; regardless of distance. [cf. MIND LINKING, MIND RAIDER, SELECTIVE TELEPATHY]

PARIETAL EYE—the invisible third eye located in the middle of the forehead; functions as a concentration point for PSYCHIC INFORMATION; named after the vertabrates that have one or two eyes on the top of their heads, in addition to the lateral eyes; this eye was found to detect eye wavelengths. [cf. THIRD-EYE AREA Appendix 5]

PARIETO-OCCIPITAL AREA—(biofeedback training) area on the head that was found to be satisfactory for placing electrodes when HOOKED-UP to the EEG instrument; an area from midway on one side of the skull to midpoint on the back of the skull. [cf. AMPLITUDE DIAL, ALPHA WAVES, AROUSAL]

PAROPTIC SENSE—to psychically see with the whole body (similar to seeing in the ASTRAL BODY), or like an animal "sees" without the use of the eyes; (do not confuse with PARAOPTIC VISION). (Inconcl.) [cf. THIRD-EYE AREA, PSYCHIC PERCEPTS, INNER SENSE]

PARTHENOGENESIS—a reproduction of organisms without conjunction of the opposite sex, i.e., virgin birth. [cf. BIRTH BY SUPERPSYCHIC WOMB, MUTAGEN]

PARTIAL AGE REGRESSION—(hypnosis) to recall scenes from one's past present life while under HYPNOSIS; subject acts as a bystander and relates what he or she is doing, wearing, etc., without going through the same emotional experience or becoming that age; subject does not need to go as deep as in complete REGRESSION; subject realizes the HYPNOTIST is speaking to her or him. (Inconcl.) [cf. REVIVIFICATION, AGE REGRESSION, INDUCTION]

PARTIAL ANESTHESIA—to allow an ETHERIC WORLD INTELLIGENCE to influence one's actions by using a part of one's body; the appendage of one's body that performs is anesthetized by the intelligence; MEDIUM is in a SEMITRANCE or LIGHT TRANCE state and appears to others to be aware and awake; always preplanned and willed; does not require a SEANCE setting; a form of IMPERSONATION that is becoming popular today; medium receives impressions in his or her head which come more swiftly than one normally thinks; the anesthetized part of the body reacts immediately and freely to the impressions; sometimes the body reacts with no control to the medium; e.g., arms and hands are anesthetized for PSYCHIC SURGERY, piano playing, and AUTOMATIC WRITING; the skin is anesthetized for SKIN WRITING. Syn. TEN PERCENT TRANCE. [cf. VOICE TRANCE.]

PARTIAL IMPERSONATION—to allow an ETHERIC WORLD INTELLIGENCE to intervene and take control of one's body and physically move parts of the body; MEDIUM is slightly aware of movements; occurs in a TRANCE state; happens during a learning process of full IMPERSONATION; takes place in many seances before full impersonation is accomplished allowing both entities to synchronize with each other in a healthy manner. [cf. TRANCE CONTROL, ONE FELL STROKE, DIVINE INTOXICATION]

PARTIAL INCENDIUM AMORIS—to heat one region of the body to an extremely high temperature, while the rest of the body remains normal, using intensified CONCENTRATION. (Inconcl.) [cf. FLAMES OF DIVINE LOVE, HYSTERIA, STIGMATA, LAW OF ACTIVITY Appendix 7]

PARTIAL MATERIALIZATION—(materialization seance) vaporous-looking forms dense enough to produce the hand, face, hair, fingers, or clothing of the ETHERIC WORLD ENTITY who will manifest whole in the future; many SEANCE sessions take place before FULL MATERIALIZATION is successful; 1. ETHERIC WORLD INTELLIGENCES use an order of MATTER that can neither reflect nor obstruct light, but set up vibrations in the atmosphere which affect the SITTERS as sound; 2. this order of matter is incapable of reflecting light that sitters can see, yet able to affect some ULTRAVIOLET RAYS and can be photographed; eventually SYNCHRONIZATION of MEDIUM and intelligence occurs and there is sufficient energy of the ECTOPLASM to produce the whole etheric intelligence. [cf. ADEPT MATERIALIZATION, BLACKED-OUT ROOM]

PARTIAL REGRESSION—(hypnotherapy) to recall scenes or parts of scenes from a past INCARNATION that relate to a problem or unwanted behavior in one's present life; subject views this event as a bystander without becoming involved emotionally; a SEMITRANCE or DEEP STATE OF HYPNOSIS is needed; HYPNOTHERAPIST asks questions to help the subject bring out the important factors; subject understands his or her feelings without becoming one with them; (whenever the CONSCIOUS MIND is passive as in HYPNOSIS, the PSYCHE is always ready to improve itself; therefore, one will regress back to a scene of a past incarnation that relates to their present life); subject and hypnotherapist talk over the event after the session and the subject is helped to work through their situation and resolve it logically; (do not confuse with COMPLETE REGRESSION). [cf. REVIVIFICATION]

PARTIAL SOMATIC DISSOCIATION—an awareness that some body parts are without feeling or feel detached from the rest of the body; happens during MEDITATION or HYPNOTHERAPY. (Inconcl.) **Syn.** DEZYGOSIS.

PARTNER CLAIRVOYANCE—psychic VISION experienced simultaneously by two persons who are together at the same time of the vision; believed to be supported by the telepathic rapport between these people. (Inconcl.) [cf. CLAIRVOYANCE]

PASSAGE OF THE SUN GOD—(esoteric) a new STATE OF CONSCIOUSNESS, like a new awakening for a person when their KUNDALINI power reaches the last two chakras (BROW and CROWN CHAKRAS); symbolic of the SOLAR CYCLE. [cf. SERPENT POWER, CROWN OF GLORY]

PASSES—(magnetic healing) movements made by the healing practitioner's hands going slowly over the patient's body, about two inches from the body per se; MAGNETIC FLUID emanates from the palm of the practitioner's hand subjected to concentrated thoughts; passes aid in repairing auric field of patient which in turn normalizes body cells so body can repair itself more quickly. (Inconcl.) **Syn.** MAGNETIC PASS. [cf. CLOUD CHAMBER, CURATIVE MESMERISM]

PASSING-THE-MANTRA—a ritual an individual goes through to receive the word or words he or she is to use for their own personal MANTRA in MEDITATION; these words are chosen for their ability to help this particular individual reach a deep ALTERED STATE OF CONSCIOUSNESS. [cf. EGO-KILLING PRACTICE, ESSENCE OF REST]

PASSION DEVAS—etheric world entities who are

still attached to the materialistic world and who latch onto earthlings to reexperience their earthly desires and passions; see HAUNTING. **Syn.** EARTH-BOUND ENTITIES. [cf. HAUNTING, ERRANT SPIRIT, APPARITION]

PASSIVE AWARENESS—(biofeedback training) a subconscious nonreaction to an outward stimuli that normally causes one to reach a deeper or meditative state of consciousness. [cf. MEDITATION, BIOFEEDBACK TRAINING]

PASSIVE CONCENTRATION—to focus one's whole attention on a single-point, allowing the body to relax, and the emotions to become quiet; this registers a decided change in the AUTONOMIC NERVOUS SYSTEM on the BIOFEEDBACK INSTRUMENT. **Sim.** PASSIVE VOLITION. [cf. INTEGRATED PSYCHOLOGICAL RESPONSE, FIXATIONS]

PASSIVE HYPNOSIS—to perform imaginary actions in the mind that feel as if one were physically doing them; a deep hypnotic state in which one functions under the suggestions of the HYPNOTIST [cf. HYPNOTHERAPY DESENSITIZATION, HYPER-ACUTE]

PASSIVE PSYCHOGRAPHIC MEDIUM—one who allows his or her hand to be used by an ETHERIC WORLD INTELLIGENCE to write information on paper, while in an unconscious state. **Syn.** MECHANICAL PSYCHOGRAPHIC MEDIUM. [cf. ETHERIC SCRIPT, AUTOMATIC WRITING]

PASSIVE SOUL—a SOUL-MIND that is dormant in the physical body due to brain damage but the physical body lives on; theory: the soul-mind chooses to be an instrument for those who care for his or her physical body to learn that type of lesson. [cf. REINCARNATION, FAMILY KARMA, COSMIC INTERVAL, BODY CHANGE]

PASSIVE VOLITION—coined by Elmer Green; (biofeedback training) "ability to reach the ALPHA STATE OF CONSCIOUSNESS by willing it, without exerting one's self physically; in an attempt to make a physiological change through the focus of attention, one must not use force or active will, but imagine the intended change while in a relaxed state, feel the body become quiet and tranquil and the thoughts stop by themselves; wanting it to happen and allowing it to happen" [cf. FIXED-BRAIN-WAVE-STATE, ENVIRONMENTAL NOISE, ELECTRONIC MEDITATION]

PASSIVE WILLING—see PASSIVE VOLITION.

457

PASSIVE-AGENT PHENOMENA—see TELEPATHY.

PAST-LIVES THEORY—if an individual dies and is still suppressing feelings of resentment, anger, fear or hate for a person or a situation, this will be carried over into other lifetimes; this suppressed feeling brings unwanted, unpleasurable, and painful behavioral patterns or physical illness in each lifetime until the charge is taken out of the original experience; many techniques have been discovered to help the patient regress to the life in which the experience occurred, and to dissipate the charge; the experience is either worked through over a period of time under the direction of a therapist, or resolved by revivification in a hypnotic state. [**cf.** PRIMAL SCREAM, PAST-LIVES THERAPY, HYPNOTHERAPY]

PAST-LIVES THERAPY— a form of REGRESSION in which the subject is in the BETA STATE OF CONSCIOUSNESS, much aware of what is happening; PRACTITIONER traces self-destructive patterns through several lives with an objective to find incidents in other lives which are influencing the present life; repeated phrases by the subject are keys for questions asked by the practitioner; traumatic events of past incarnations are worked out verbally and emotionally until subject resolves the attitude of the trauma; subject can then manage his or her present behavior and dissipate unwanted behavior. (Inconcl.) [**cf.** BACK-IN-MEMORY, ALPHA BLOCKING, BEHAVIORAL MEMORIES]

PASTORAL WITCH—(Italy) a PSYCHIC who uses her skills for only proper and beneficial endeavors and healings.

PATANJALI—(B.C.) an Indian SAGE who is capable of many psychic skills and uses them in his work.

PATANJALI'S SUTRAS—(Yoga, ancient) MEDITATION that includes strict mind-body coordination which must be practiced until the individual can perform the siddhis; this brings a change within and without the YOGI or yogin and helps in his or her growth toward ENLIGHTENMENT; includes three YOGA disciplines: KARMA YOGA, HATHA YOGA and SHAKTI. [**cf.** MUDRA, SIDDHI, QUANTUM VACUUM, SENSE WITHDRAWAL]

PATH—(Huna, Hinduism) the SILVER CORD that connects the lower self of a human being with his or her higher self (from the KANDA to the MONAD), joining all the bodies together; attainment on the path is achieved when the individual opens to a

higher state of consciousness causing the energy to flow up the SUSHUMNA. [**cf.** PATH SYMBOLISM]

PATH SYMBOLISM—a line of direction toward PERFECTNESS where humanity seems to be headed in the overall scheme of things; theory: mankind will eventually go back to Perfectness, from whence they came; with each INCARNATION the individual chooses which karmic conditions he or she wants to overcome and which new attributes he or she desires to learn; when one is working on these, one is on his or her PATH; the path is not predestined, only the goal; one can go in as many directions as he or she chooses; when one is working on the right path, he or she has an inner peace that is indescribable, a sense of self-worth, and a comfortable feeling about oneself in general; with culture changes, *path* has been changed to the term *road*. Usage: road to recovery; fell by the wayside; open road is ahead of you; there is a long, long, road awinding; on the right track. [**cf.** ACCUMULATED KARMA, EVOLUTION]

PATIENT-THERAPIST ESP—telepathic flashes and psychic dreams received by the patient of PSYCHOTHERAPY that reflect the private thoughts or activities of the therapist; these can be used to advantage for the patient. (Inconcl.) [**cf.** ASSOCIATION TELEPATHY, BIOLOGICAL COMPATIBILITY]

PATTERN—a blueprint or design surrounding all systems, biological and insentient, that is absolutely necessary for its existence; found in the energy field around the tiniest particle to the Great Central Sun; designates what rate of vibration the system should assume and its direction in the scheme of things; details see AURA, ETHERIC DOUBLE. (Inconcl.)

PATTERN WORLD—see MENTAL PLANE.

PATTERNED SYSTEM—theory: there is only one system, one unified, interrelated, whole unit having no beginning or ending; constantly prints its likeness in all sizes, shapes and forms; these shapes and forms contain monads which constantly interlock with each other throughout this system; operates by the law of order and adjustment; a small piece of the system reflects the pattern of the whole unit, only reduced.

PATTERNING—outward random results of psychic events which provide mankind with clues that the world is orderly and patterned; e.g., fall of LOTS, DOWSING ROD pull, PENDULUM swing, lines on one's hands, IRIDOLOGY, I CHING, BIORHYTHM

CHARTS, ASTROLOGY, NUMEROLOGY.

PATTERNING ACROSS TIME—many similarities of inventions, conditions and events happen around the world simultaneously, not related to or copied from one another. [**cf.** SYNCHRONICITY, CROSS-CASUALTY OF INTERACTION]

PATTERNS—(biofeedback training) the style of the lines made on the EEG printouts caused from the various levels of brain wave consciousness with enough variation and similarity to categorize a scale of these patterns for future experiments. [**cf.** EVOKED POTENTIALS, CROSS TALK]

PAWANG—(Malaya) see MEDIUM or PSYCHIC.

PEACEFUL ORDER OF DEITIES—(Tibet) personified gods in the ETHERIC WORLD, held together by THOUGHT; typify the glorified principles of sensations of the heart and most beautiful human sentiments found in the psychic HEART CHAKRA.

PEACOCK— a bird honored in the psychic field because of its alchemical traits; eats poisons and transmutes them into a beautiful array of large irridescent feathers; (Hinduism) has properties that cure disease and dispel poison; feathers are displayed in homes to ward off evil. [**cf.** ANIMAL GROUP SOUL, RAVEN, ROBIN]

PEAK EXPERIENCE—1. (psychology) a short period of time when one feels strong, self-confident, a sense of selfworth and in complete control; experiences that one likes to reflect upon and keep in the privacy of one's heart; activity that makes the whole day seem worthwhile; 2. (meditation) a very successful time when one reaches a point of indescribable ECSTASY, tenderness, love, profound BLISS, or a religious high.

PEARCE-PRATT EXPERIMENTS—(Duke University, 1933) the first time they tested ESP at a distance by placing the agent and the percipient in separate buildings.

PEARL—(esoteric) 1. a mineral so beautiful and perfect that it symbolizes both purity and the SOUL-MIND; i.e., the pearl (soul-mind) in the oyster (rough casing, the body); 2. represents that which is meaningful and worthwhile, i.e., pearls of wisdom; 3. transmits influence from the moon affecting the TWENTY-EIGHT DAY CYCLE in people; 4. used to induce psychic visions. [**cf.** BERYL, CHRYSOLITE, CONTAINERS OF MAGICAL POWER]

PEARLWORT—(esoteric) a holy plant; transfers COSMIC ENERGY from the earth to humans; (the first plant JESUS stepped on when he arose from the dead); placed over the door of homes to prevent negative energies from entering; in the fields where planted it keeps away naughty nature spirits. [**cf.** CHARGING, ELDER TREE, APPLE]

PEARLY EMPEROR—(China) the counterpart of the empress in the etheric world, capable of communicating to his people phychically. [**cf.** ETHERIC WORLD INTELLIGENCE]

PELTING GHOST—see POLTERGEIST.

PENANG-GALAN—an invisible female entity who detaches her head and entrails from her body and flies through the air at night to suck blood from a human; red lights can be seen swarming around where she is working. [**cf.** SUCCUBUS, HAG]

PENATES—(Rome) NATURE SPIRITS that are the stewards of a home; considered to be gods of the food cupboards; also direct the prosperity of the home; work with the LARES. **Syn.** PENETRALIA.

PENDULE—(Germany) 1. see PENDULUM; 2. to use a pendulum.

PENDULISANT—(France) see PENDULUMIST, PENDULIST.

PENDULIST—one who is skilled in RADIESTHETIC SENSE; one who uses the PENDULUM for diagnosing disease, finding missing persons, detecting ghost energy fields, measuring energy of fruits, vegetables, and objects, and getting yes and no answers to questions about themselves; pendulist empties his or her mind, keeps it neutral during the use of the pendulum, and concentrates on the task at hand; a code of movements for the swing of the pendulum is establsihed with the CONSCIOUS MIND and SUBCONSCIOUS MIND.[**cf.** BOB, PALLOMANCY]

PENDULOUS—hanging down loosely; refers to the manner in which the PENDULUM is used, without tension in the person holding it. [**cf.** COURTESY, FORE-AND-AFT-SWING]

PENDULUM—a radiesthetic tool made of a string, thread, or chain with a weighted object attached to one end, and the other end is held between the index finger and thumb of the PENDULUMIST; used for communicating between the SUBCONSCIOUS MIND and the force fields around any object in the universe; acts as an antenna to amplify signals coming from these force fields and in return makes movements that can be interpreted by the conscious mind of the person holding it. [**cf.** WITNESS, PENDULUM POWER, RADIESTHETIC SENSE]

PENDULUM GYRATION—the swing of the BOB of the PENDULUM in a circular motion, either clockwise or counterclockwise, as opposed to a back and forth movement; PENDULIST reads the gyration by its speed, size of circle, direction of circle, and number of circles. [**cf.** PENDULUM OSCILLATION, ATTENTIVE-EYE, AURIC CHARGE]

PENDULUM OSCILLATION—the swing of the BOB of the PENDULUM in a to and fro movement making a straight line, as opposed to a circular movement; PENDULIST reads the oscillation by its speed, length of swing, and position of the line of swing. [**cf.** PENDULUM GYRATION, CYCLE OF MOVEMENTS, DETECTOR]

PENDULUM POWER—to correctly read the meaning of the swing of the PENDULUM when held over an object, area, or when asked a question; to attune one's self to the whole universal patterned system, and with a radiesthetic sensitivity, tune into radiations around living and nonliving things in the world and one's own SOUL-MIND; a code of movements is established between the CONSCIOUS MIND and SUBCONSCIOUS MIND and the pendulum; pendulum amplifies the WAVELENGTH of the RADIATION of the object being measured, located, or the question of the soul-mind, in movements of the established code; PENDULIST must be knowledgeable in how to word the question, reset the BOB, and how to keep a neutral mind regarding the answer during the entire use of the pendulum. (Inconcl.) **Syn.** RADIESTHETIC SENSE, PALLOMANCY. [**cf.** DOWSING, MAP DOWSING, PENDULUM GYRATIONS, RADIONICS]

PENDULUM PROPHET—a PSYCHIC who uses the PENDULUM to forecast the future.

PENDULUM SEARCHING—the use of a map and a PENDULUM to locate a missing animal or person, or to locate something underground. **Syn.** REMOTE DOWSING. [**cf.** WITNESS, MAP DOWSING]

PENDULUMING—the process of using a PENDULUM to answer one's question or to measure radiations over an object or person; pendulist holds the pendulum over the object to be measured. Usage: "He is penduluming the fruit to see which ones are ripe enough to eat." [**cf.** PENDULUM POWER, UP AND DOWN MOTION, WARM UP THE MOTOR, Appendix 2 PENDULUMING]

PENDULUMIST—see PENDULIST.

PENDULUMIZE—to use a PENDULUM to receive information unknown to one's self; PSYCHIC is attuned to the electromagnetic field radiations around things of nature and things of the MUNDANE WORLD; psychic has control of his or her SYMPATHETIC NERVOUS SYSTEM; this sensitivity is accomplished by keeping one's mind neutral and one's arm and fingers relaxed while engaged in pendulumizing; MEDITATION beforehand and constructing one's own pendulum enhances one's sensitivity; the psychic is the instrumentation and the pendulum is the antenna that transmits and amplifies the signals; pendulumizing can be useful in one's lifestyle and a few examples are: to determine ripeness of fruit, the age and value of an article, sex of an unborn child, location of a ghost in the room, whether water is safe to drink, location of a lost article (by MAP DOWSING), and to determine a yes or no answer to a question. [**cf.** WITNESS, COURTESY, NO RESPONSE SWING]

PENTACLE—(French, "to hang") any TALISMAN used for psychic operations that hangs; the PENTAGRAM is the most common; the FIVE-POINTED STAR acts like a shield, passive and defensive; also used is the six-pointed star in a circle surrounded by another circle; pentacles control the forces of nature and bring the HIGHER SELF through into manifestation or mental consciousness; used to COUNTERSPELL in a PSYCHIC ATTACK. [**cf.** CEREMONIAL MAGIC, HEX]

PENTAGRAM—the FIVE-POINTED STAR, the most powerful symbol of all ceremonial rites; used for: **1.** same symbolism as the number FIVE; **2.** emblem of EARTH; **3.** representation of MAN; one point for the head pointing upward and the other points are the legs and arms reversed; **4.** a base or ground for ceremonies; acts like a shield, both passive and defensive; a solid weapon; **5.** (Levi) the sign of intellectual omnipotence and autocracy; **6.** (Dawn) representative of the DEVIL (as the devil's horns and points are parallel), used when necessary to converse with evil vibrations to keep them at bay; **7.** representing the five wounds of CHRIST; **8.** symbol of the MAGI; the star which led the Magi to the manger where the infant Christ was laid; **9.** sign of the MICROCOSM; **10.** representation of EVIL and GOOD; one point in the ascendant as the sign of

Christ, two points in the ascendant as the sign of SATAN; **11.** protection; **12.** notifying the ETHERIC WORLD INTELLIGENCES of something as its shape lights up the ASTRAL PLANE and makes the intelligences aware of mankind. **Syn.** BLAZING STAR. [**cf.** DOUBLE-TRIANGLE, CIRCLE, SYMBOLS]

PENTARBE—a mineral that has properties to absorb whatever is in its environment; glows in a fire-like red light at night; believed to have a psychic spirit within it. [**cf.** BLACK ONYX, GIFT OF HEAVEN, GOD-IN-THE-STONE]

PEOPLE OF PEACE—see NATURE SPIRITS.

PEP—abbr. for PYRAMID ENERGY PLATE; (invented by Patrick Flanagan) a plate made of anodized aluminum which has been polarized with pyramid or BIO-COSMIC ENERGY, capable of functioning as a pyramid.

PERCEIVE—**1.** (parapsychology) to become aware and detect invisible VIBRATIONAL FREQUENCIES from environmental stimuli, or from body sensations, with one's PSYCHIC SENSES; **2.** (Beth Brown) "to define the dimensions of an event or an object in time or space with enough definition to make it retrievable from memory."

PERCEIVER—a PSYCHIC who uses mental psychic skills.

PERCENT TIME METER—a dial on a BIOFEEDBACK INSTRUMENT showing the progress of the subject in the frequency in which he or she is working. [**cf.** ELECTRIC RHYTHM, ENVIRONMENTAL NOISE]

PERCEPT—(laboratory) that which is perceived by the PSYCHIC; the TARGET reached in any laboratory experiment; e.g., when clairvoyantly perceiving an apparition, the apparition is the percept; when cognizing a card with wavy lines on it, the card is the percept. [**cf.** ESP, ZENER CARDS, CYPHER CHARACTERS, ELUSIVE]

PERCEPTION OF THE SHADOW—(Plato) PSYCHIC INFORMATION received from an etheric world guide. [**cf.** INNER BAND, OUTER BAND, HELPERS]

PERCEPTIVITY—see INTUITION and CLAIR-SENTIENCE.

PERCEPTUAL DATA—(biofeedback training) the visual or auditory feedback from the instrument, such as lights and tones; as opposed to the thoughts or emotions of the subject. [**cf.** ARTIFACT, ENVIRONMENTAL NOISE, BURSTS]

PERCEPTUAL DEFENSE—**1.** to defend one's self against disturbing information coming from the SUBLIMINAL LEVEL of the mind so as to not blend it in with PSYCHIC INFORMATION; **2.** to prevent psychic information from coming into the conscious level of awareness unless it is desired and when it is desired. **Syn.** ANTIPSI. [**cf.** CLOAK OF INSULATION, FREE FLOWING, ETHERIC LINK]

PERCIPIENT—**1.** (psi tasks) one being tested for PSYCHIC ABILITY, not usually given to a person who has established the title of PSYCHIC; **2.** (Russia) the receiver of any psychic experience at any time. **Syn.** PSYCHIC. [**cf.** CENTERING, CYPHER CHARACTER]

PERCUSSION—to produce sounds without the use of physical methods by synchronizing and cooperating with one or more ETHERIC WORLD INTELLIGENCES; the striking that one material object makes against another object with such sharpness and impact that the physical ears can hear the sound; intelligence uses the ECTOPLASM of the MEDIUM and SITTERS but not the medium's body; takes place in a SEANCE or PSYCHIC DEVELOPMENT CIRCLE; a code of sounds is frequently agreed upon between the invisible etheric world intelligences and the group; researchers found an auric condensation coming from the sitter's and medium's bodies which formed into PSEUDORODS at a certain condensation point extending to the areas of the phenomenon; detected by instruments and CLAIRVOYANCE; darkness is not always necessary; one of the easiest types of physical phenomena to develop; see PERCUSSION Appendix 2 for many kinds.

PERFECTNESS—(capitalized) (esoteric) **1.** ALL-THERE-IS in its entirety; **2.** "all there was" in the beginning because mankind knows no more; the entire life of all life as humanity knows life, and life that humanity does not know yet, and that which mankind calls nonliving; **3.** ALL organized into one complete, harmonious, simplified, coherent whole, without loss of entity individuality; a deeper meaning to every fraction of the integrated whole.

PERFECTNESS PLANE—the SEVENTH PLANE: perfectness represents the highest conceivable spiritual attainment, indescribable in language, beyond human level and comprehension; on this plane, it is speculated that mankind will be free from the downward pull of materialistic desires and its karmic tie; happiness experienced beyond one's strongest imagination; a plane of light so strong that mankind cannot perceive it in their present stage of EVOLUTION. [cf. MENTAL PLANE, SIXTH PLANE]

PERFORMANCE CLINIC—(biofeedback training) a place where one goes for sessions to increase one's full potential, before one is due at an anxiety producing event; under the guidance of a therapist, the subject is HOOKED-UP to a BIOFEEDBACK INSTRUMENT and given instructions on verbiage, MEDITATION, AFFIRMATIONS, or whatever is beneficial for his or her particular situation; e.g., subjects work out at the clinic to overcome anxiety before a test or an athletic event; or to overcome fear before a dentist appointment or an airplane ride. [cf. BIOFEEDBACK TRAINING, NEW-AGE PSYCHOLOGY]

PERFUMED SAINT—to give the natural perfume of any flower to a scentless one; to make a person's skin exude delightful fragrance; to manufacture scents from the astral world that have a pleasant fragrance that stay in the air for a long time, or to put it upon an object for lasting effects; most commonly done by saints, and receives its name because of this. [cf. CLAIRSCENT, CLAIRSAVORANCE]

PERFUMES—1. (Buddhism) fragrances used to make oneself more acceptable to the DEITY in a sacrificial ceremony; 2. used to help the SOUL-MIND ascend to heaven upon a cloud of incense; 3. used to influence thoughts to a higher level of consciousness, similar to one going for mountain air to invigorate the body and mind; 4. used to call in guides, as they are very sensitive to fragrances; 5. used in reverse, the GUIDE brings the MEDIUM a fragrance to make known his or her presence. [cf. INCENSE, CLAIRSCENT]

PERI—prefix meaning "about, beyond, around."

PERILS OF THE SOUL—(Jewish; Old Testament, Bible) an initiation whereby the SOUL-MIND ascends through all the spheres of the ETHERIC WORLD overcoming the dangers of the lower spheres and then works with other celestial keepers; if all goes well he or she is found worthy of the throne. [cf. WORK OF THE CHARIOT, EXALTED THRONE]

PERINATAL EXPERIENCE—the trauma or non-trauma of being born that influences one's behavior during the rest of one's life. (Inconcl.) [cf. BIRTH TRAUMA, BIRTH WITHOUT VIOLENCE]

PERIOD—the time between the beginning and the end of one CYCLE; the microsecond, hour, day, year, decade, etc. [cf. AGE]

PERIOD LOG—a notebook used to record one's progress while taking BIOFEEDBACK TRAINING sessions; records of specific phases of emotions, feelings and experiences happening while being HOOKED-UP to the instrument; plus answers to questions given at the end of each session. [cf. BASELINE DRIFT, ANXIETY STATION, CYBERNETIC LOOP]

PERIOD PIECES—(Seth) the many incarnations that one creates for one's self. [cf. REINCARNATION, DOCTRINE OF LOCALIZATION OF SOUL, AKASHIC RECORDS]

PERIODICITY—tendency to recur at regular intervals; the lesser cycles; the study of the symphony of biorhythms playing a part in the living systems of people, animals and plants. (Inconcl.) **Sim.** BIOCLOCKS. [cf. BIOLOGICAL TIME OF DAY, DAILY CYCLE, BIORHYTHM]

PERIPHERAL VISION—to see unconsciously and not be aware one is seeing; to perceive out of the path of conscious sight; recorded on the SUBLIMINAL LEVEL of the mind and can be surfaced under HYPNOSIS; makes a slight dent in the subconscious memory bank to be utilized in future decisions. [cf. DOMINANTS OF THE UNCONSCIOUSNESS, EGO]

PERISPRIT—(Allan Kardec) a part of the whole SPIRIT in the ETHERIC WORLD made of SEMI-MATERIAL, capable of communicating with a MEDIUM; blanket name given to any form the SOUL-MIND takes after its TRANSITION. [cf. FLUIDIC LINK]

PERMANENT-SEED-ATOMS—tiny concentrated centers of energy containing all of an individual's past thinking and acting, which come with him or her in each incarnation; located in the PINEAL GLAND, the HEART, and the SOLAR PLEXUS; connected to strands of the SILVER CORD that reach to the soul-mind; (Bible) called the BOOKS OF LIFE; see LIFE-CORD-HEART-SEED-ATOM, EMOTIONAL-ASTRAL-SEED-ATOM and the MENTAL-CONSCIOUS-NESS-SEED-ATOM.

PERPETUAL PRESENCE—see TOTALITY.

PERSONA THEORY—(Hart) the ETHERIC WORLD INTELLIGENCES that communicate with a MEDIUM are temporary recreations of the personality structures of his or her unconscious dramatizing powers; sometimes they derive ingredients from actual discarnate personalities. [cf. GHOST IN THE MACHINE, HOLY GUARDIAN ANGEL]

PERSONAL DAEMON—(Greece) an ETHERIC WORLD ENTITY that stays with the same earthling throughout his or her lifetime. **Syn.** DOCTOR TEACHER, CELESTIAL GUARDIAN, GUARDIAN SPIRIT. [**cf.** INNER BAND, ELEVATED SPIRITS, EMISSARY]

PERSONAL ENCOUNTER—a natural moment of enlightenment; 1. a source of genuine personal growth 2. a pseudo-source of religious high. [**cf.** EGO-DESTRUCTION, SNAPPING, DEHUMANIZE, ARTIKA CEREMONY]

PERSONAL HAUNTING—the hovering of an earthbound entity close to an earthling, encouraging him or her to increase an unwanted habit; earthbound entity uses his or her own energy as in mental psychism; attaches periodically to an earthling who is a negative thinker, materialistic person or who shares the same frailities of the discarnate being; impresses in the earthling's mind to keep up the activity he or she desires, making it harder for the earthling to relinquish the habit; discarnate being receives pleasure by memory; (do not confuse with ENVIRONMENTAL HAUNTING in which the earthbound entity uses energy in environment and the results are physical psychism). [**cf.** HAUNTING, GHOSTOLOGY, EARTHBOUND ENTITIES]

PERSONAL HISTORY—(don Juan) the image an individual has of her or himself and the image others· have of that individual that he or she has accepted, contributing to their present personality. [**cf.** BELIEF SYSTEM, EMOTION]

PERSONAL METAPATTERNS—(John Lilly) the sum total of all the interlocking experiences, happenings and thoughts that make up an individual as he or she goes through life. **Syn.** SUBCONSCIOUS MIND.

PERSONAL MIND PRINTS—(psi tasks) any pattern or idiosyncratic mind thoughts left on the experiment material unintentionally that could be picked up by the subject. [**cf.** INNER-DIALOGUE, BEASTIES]

PERSONAL POWER—(don Juan) a force that commands one and yet obeys one; can be stored through a feeling; power in the body allows the body to do many feats; can be used on others; works well with nature; it is more of a feeling or a mood and difficult to be convinced it exists. **Syn.** PSYCHIC ENERGY. [**cf.** CLOUD SHIFTING, BRINGER OF THE ANIMALS]

PERSONAL "QUEST"—a self induced initiation because of an inward desire to have psychic skills and healing abilities; results in prolonged days of FASTING, MEDITATION, and silence, until the individual has developed these skills. [**cf.** SHAMANSHIP, RESURRECTION]

PERSONAL RADAR SET—beams of energy that are emitted from a person's eyes. **Syn.** VISUAL RAY. [**cf.** EARTH MAGNETISM, HUMAN ENERGY TRANSFER, GREAT EYE, EYE OF HORUS]

PERSONAL UNCONSCIOUSNESS—(Carl Jung) "the level of the PSYCHE just below the surface level; consists of half-forgotten relics of the individual's past experiences from infancy onwards"; TEMPORARY MEMORY BANK: surface consciousness. [**cf.** BRAIN SUBSTRATE, DOMINANTS OF THE UNCONSCIOUS]

PERSONAL WITCHES—(Africa) one creates one's own inferior and subordinate etheric world entities with thoughts of jealousy, hate, anxiety, and resentment which brings illness and poverty. [**cf.** LAW OF LIKE ATTRACTS LIKE Appendix 7, CLOAK OF INSULATION, THOUGHT-FORMS]

PERSONALITY—1. (esoteric) the CONSCIOUSNESS one is functioning from, giving certain character traits, built from all past thoughts and actions from many incarnations enmeshed with present vibrational bombardment; 2. (psychology) the organization of a set of selective skills or characteristics and skills; these skills and characteristics differ greatly among personality theorists; an innate mechanism within a person; the something that does something that makes things happen; an organization of tendencies or dispositions in a person which determine how he or she behaves in a given situation; environment plus inborn mechanisms cause personality; 3. (humanistic psychology) the total of SELF: one's body structure and muscle tone, NERVOUS SYSTEM, BRAIN, GLANDS and attitude, incapable of being totally duplicated; influenced by the past and present environment or outer stimuli; 4. (Sigmund Freud) innate drives that are channelled through structures of some past mechanism and develop as the child matures; 5. (Eastern discipline) emotional reactions to outer stimuli (perceivable by others), influencing the CEREBROSPINAL NERVOUS SYSTEM, differentiating one individual from another; the part of the self that one comes to change in each INCARNATION; 6. (metaphysics) represents those aspects of identity that one is able to actualize within a three-dimensional existence, molded by attitudinal responses to circumstances, accumulated over incarnations, making an ever-changing unified whole. [**cf.** SUPER EGO, ID, SOUL-MIND, SYMPATHETIC NERVOUS SYSTEM]

PERSONALITY CYCLES—a pattern of ups and downs in a person's emotional, intellectual and physical makeup that repeats itself in spans; has been investigated and charted to be used for practical purposes called biorhythms. [**cf.** PHYSICAL CYCLE, EMOTIONAL CYCLE, MENTAL CYCLE, BIORHYTHM]

PERSONALITY FRAGMENT—(Seth) each earth life is a fragment of the entire story of the ENTITY, operating independently but under the support of the entire story; each past INCARNATION exists within, and makes itself known to the earthling to whom it belongs, in some earthly form or manner; maintains an individual CONSCIOUSNESS of its own; controls the involuntary bodily processes. [**cf.** REINCARNATION Appendix 5]

PERSONALITY PHYSISM—the ability of the entity to duplicate itself and be in more than one place at the same time, each body functioning as if it were the whole body. **Sim.** SPLIT-OFF, BILOCATION.

PERSONALITY TRANSFORMATION—(Marilyn Ferguson) anything that disrupts the system of one's life has the potential for triggering a marked change in a movement toward greater maturity, openness, and strength, e.g., personal stress can be an agent of transformation, close relations with someone whose views differ, a book which shakes one's beliefs, a move to a foreign country, a promotion, a sudden death in the close family, etc.; the object is to fuse emotion with the intellect, and the brain will integrate and transcend the old lifestyle and bring beneficial changes in mind, brain, body, in life direction and bring a feeling of self-worth. [**cf.** LAW OF PERSONAL TRANSFORMATION Appendix 7, NEW-AGE PSYCHOLOGY]

PERSONALIZED PYRAMID—1. an open-style PYRAMID made to scale, large enough to sleep or sit under to improve one's health or mind; 2. pendant in the perfect shape of the pyramid to energize the one who wears it. [**cf.** FORCE ZONE, GOLDEN SECTION]

PERSONIFICATION—(occult) any psychic or mediumistic phenomenon is considered to be alive and to have a personality. [**cf.** INVOCATION, LAW OF PERSONIFICATION Appendix 7]

PET—(ancient Egypt) the sky or heaven; represented by the goddess Nut.

PETITION—(magnetic healing) a request written on a small piece of paper by one who desires aid in healing their body; healing PRACTITIONER holds the paper between his or her hands and mentally transfers their MAGNETISM to the healee, whose written request is the point of contact; practitioner's magnetism enters the healee's NERVOUS SYSTEM helping the healee's cells to normalize so the healee's innate healing mechanism works more quickly; distance is no barrier. [**cf.** PRAYER BASKET, CELL, MAGNETIC HEALING]

PETITIONER—(Native American, Navaho) one who uses SAND PAINTINGS to help bring PSYCHIC INFORMATION for his healings and PSYCHIC COUNSELING. [**cf.** HEALING MEMORIES, PSYCHIC HEALING, BELIEF SYSTEM]

PETRO—Voodoo; see PSYCHIC.

PEYOTE BUTTON—part of the cactus that is the "giver of visions," and helps one heal. [**cf.** EVERGREEN TREE, EVOKE RESPONSES]

PEYOTE CACTUS—(Mexico, South America) a plant hallucinogen that works on the blood chromosomes; held sacred for its illuminating qualities; used by the leaders to bring information for the tribe and to aid in healing; a narcotic and an intoxicant, non-habit forming; brings a sense of exhilaration, mental ease, a feeling of greater mental capacity, and brings visions. [**cf.** DATURA STRANONIUM, FAIRY WEED]

PEYOTE CULT—(Native American) a strict religious organization that only allows men who are morally upright to use the peyote plant as a tool to bring visions; the peyote plant is used as a teacher, healer and saviour for their race; a cult of withdrawal and submission. [**cf.** PEYOTE ROAD, SHAMANSHIP, PSYCHOTROPIC PLANTS]

PEYOTE ROAD—(Native American) represents living a long life of devotion to doing good and being "straight." **Sim.** the path. [**cf.** PATH SYMBOLISM, BHAKTI-MARGA, TREE OF LIFE]

PEYOTISM—(Mexico) 1. a religion using the peyote plant as an aid to spiritual growth; 2. denotes their seasonal ritual pilgrimage with dancing and psychic power seeking.

PHANTASM—a SOUL-MIND in the ETHERIC

WORLD showing itself to the CLAIRVOYANT as a human but hazy in texture; name used by the first psychic researchers in 1888. **Syn.** APPARITION. [**cf.** CONFUSED SOUL-MIND, ENVIRONMENTAL HAUNTING, GHOST SEERS]

PHANTASMA—see PHANTASM.

PHANTASMAGORIA—tremendous mental activity of non-thoughts; a shifting series of apparitions, illusions, or visionary deceptive appearances; seen in a dream, HYPNOGOGIC STATE, hallucinating from drugs, and optical illusions. [**cf.** HALLUCINATIONS, NON-THOUGHT]

PHANTASMATA—see ASTRAL BODY.

PHANTASMOGENTIC CENTER—see THIRD-EYE.

PHANTASMS OF THE LIVING—the APPARITION of a person going through a highly emotional state or a traumatic experience, which makes it possible for the SOUL-MIND to split and get a message through to a loved one who is not in that area, e.g., a person seen the same time he is in an accident. [**cf.** DOUBLE EGOS, SPONTANEOUS PSI, SPLIT PERSONALITIES]

PHANTASY—see FANTASY.

PHANTOM—an ASTRAL BODY showing itself clairvoyantly as a human being, only hazy or in a substance less dense than the physical body; usually full blown; term used for an etheric entity one does not recognize and is not sensed as one's GUIDE. **Syn.** APPARITION, PHANTASM. [**cf.** DOPPLEGANGER, BODIES AND PLANES Appendix 5]

PHANTOM ARMIES—soldiers in white uniforms in the ASTRAL PLANE seen by many clairvoyants at the same time. (Inconcl.) [**cf.** ERRANT SPIRIT, GIB GHOSTS, APPARITION]

PHANTOM COACH—an astral coach, similar to earth's vehicle of a coach, carrying one who is about to die; SOUL-MIND splits to make the experience known to the friend or relative, and the person is unaware of this taking place; perceived by a CLAIRVOYANT if in a relaxed state. [**cf.** CRISIS APPARITION, APPARITIONS OF THE LIVING]

PHANTOM DOG—an etheric world dog that can be called upon to guard hidden treasure that has been located by conjured up spirits; dog guards treasure until a PSYCHIC can reach it. [**cf.** GHOSTS' PRINTS, FIRES WITH BOUNDARIES]

PHANTOM FLOCK OF ANIMALS—filthy, artificial elementals that take the form of animals so they can feed upon the lowest vibrations of earth world, e.g., gallows or brothels; made from mankind's lower thoughts of lust, jealousy, resentment, hate, and fear that gather together in the etheric world and shape THOUGHT-FORMS or elementals; root subject and emotional impact give this elemental an intelligence of its own. [**cf.** DENSITY, CARRYING AN EVIL, MASS ELEMENTAL, ARTIFICIAL ELEMENTAL]

PHANTOM HITCHIKER—a SOUL-MIND in an ASTRAL BODY, clinging to an area where a traumatic accident happened, appearing in APPARITION form at certain times to hitch a ride; after a short distance in the car, he or she disappears from the seat. [**cf.** ZOMBIE, ASTRAL SHELL, GHOST]

PHANTOM LEAF EFFECT—(Kirlian effect) the auric pattern of a torn leaf when taken with a high voltage camera, will show AURA of the whole leaf as if the leaf were still intact, and yet a portion of the leaf has been removed. [**cf.** PHANTOM PAINS, ETHERIC DOUBLE, SYNERGY, GESTALT]

PHANTOM PAINS—(Kirlian effect) the feeling of pain coming from a limb that has been amputated and when photographed on the high voltage camera, the aura looks as if the limb was still there. [**cf.** PHANTOM LEAF EFFECT, LAW OF HEALING Appendix 7]

PHANTOM PHONE CALLS—see PSYCHIC PHONE CALLS.

PHANTOM VOICE—1. word or name perceived clairaudiently from an APPARITION of a dead person when showing her or himself clairvoyantly; infrequently, the discarnate person is capable of impressing the mind of the PSYCHIC with sound which is heard by the psychic only; 2. a sound or name perceived clairaudiently of a SOUL-MIND going through a traumatic accident or the death process and identifying her or himself by sound (as opposed to a vision); in both cases, it is MENTAL PSYCHISM accomplished by the emotional energy of the deceased person. [**cf.** CLAIRAUDIENCE Appendix 2]

PHAROAH—Lord of the Earthly Plane; advanced soul-minds, considered to be rulers of the world or demi-gods of this planet; those in charge of the religion, the politics and the slaves of a certain area in ancient times.

PHASE—(biological cycles) the time within the cyclic period in reference to external time; a particular action that takes place or reaches its peak or its low in a periodic process. [**cf.** CRITICAL LINE, CIRCADIAN HALF-WAVES, HIGHS AND LOWS]

PHASE SHIFT—concept: external environment and a chosen lifestyle does not influence the normal twenty-four hour pattern of flow within the body; people cannot make their own physical and mental patterns according to their wishes; e.g., pilots flying into another time zone do not change body metabolism; a man's beard will grow in the same hourly cycle regardless of clock time. (Inconcl.) **Syn.** TIME SHIFT. [**cf.** CIRCADIAN RHYTHM]

PHENOMENA—plural of PHENOMENON.

PHENOMENA BEINGS—see ETHERIC WORLD ENTITIES.

PHENOMENAL WORLD—see ETHERIC WORLD.

PHENOMENOLOGY—study of PSYCHISM by contemporary philosophy; includes: awareness in experience and a construction as it appears in the mind; extraordinary things and their relation to the mind.

PHENOMENON—an observable occurrence that impresses the observer as extraordinary; 2. (parapsychology) (a) an umbrella word meaning any kind of physical and mental psychism; (b) correct usage is for PHYSICAL PSYCHISM only, because everyone can perceive what is taking place in physical phenomenon; plural **phenomena.**

PHILEMON—an archetypal figure created by Carl Jung in his own consciousness with whom he communicated.

PHILLIP—(Canada) an invisible intelligent THOUGHTFORM that was concocted deliberately from the desires of eight dedicated persons for an experiment, and responds to the name Phillip; a make-believe person living in the ETHERIC WORLD with a story background and personal problems; comes when called each week and tilts or moves the table; eight persons sit around in table-tipping phenomena fashion. (Inconcl.) [**cf.** RAPS AND KNOCKS, ALPHABETIC TYPTOLOGY]

PHILLIP GROUP—four couples from Toronto, Canada who began in 1972 to sit around a table for TABLE-TIPPING and rappings; conjured up an imaginary ETHERIC WORLD ENTITY, they named *Phillip* who was to answer questions in table movements; an experiment to study energy fields, ghosts, etheric world entities and PERCUSSION phenomena; (do not confuse with a TULPA). [**cf.** PERCUSSION Appendix 2]

PHILOLOGY—(esoteric) study of names and their vibratory rate; theory: names and letters have their own distinct function and properties, whether written or spoken. [**cf.** WORDS-WITH-POWER, ELOHIM, BODY DNA's]

PHILOSOPHER'S EGG—a spherical glass container used by alchemists in their work; it is believed that from this, the PHILOSOPHER'S STONE would emerge; represents the whole UNIVERSE and MAN; depicted by a sphere suspended in an egg. [**cf.** ELIXIR OF LIFE, EMERALD TABLET, BODY OF GLORY]

PHILOSOPHER'S FIRE—(alchemy) a fire that does not destroy, it vivifies; the last process of refining metals and soul-minds that is kept a secret by the ALCHEMIST. **Syn.** FIRE OF THE SAGES. [**cf.** ALCHEMY Appendix 2]

PHILOSOPHER'S STONE—also **Philosophers' stone;** (China, B.C.) term used by the ALCHEMIST meaning the KEY ingredient necessary for the transmutation process; to first find the key ingredient to dematerialize baser metals and rematerialize them into a higher frequency metal (gold); then to find the key invisible ingredient to dematerialize his or her own body and to rematerialize it to a higher STATE OF CONSCIOUSNESS, a higher frequency level. [**cf.** ASCENSION, APPORTATION, PSYCHOKINESIS, GLORIFIED BODY]

PHILOSOPHICAL SCIENTISTS—those looking for ways to measure the feeling knowledge of being.

PHILOSOPHY—a conscientious pursuit of TRUTH by inquiring into origins and the nature of the human PSYCHE; a practical way of life one learns to practice through a science believed to be complete; a never ending study of the nature of nature; inquiry into the "why of things" as well as the "how of things." [**cf.** METAPHYSICS]

PHILTER—a liquid made with ingredients that give it properties to invite love; "magic love potions." [**cf.** APPLE, CHALICE, FIVE-POINTED STAR]

PHOBIA—(esoteric) a strong, abnormal, unreasonable fear of something; believed to be caused by an event in one's present or past incarnations that was not properly dealt with and is carried on, causing unwanted behavior. [**cf.** BURIED LIFE, CASE-

CRACKING, ADAPTATION RESPONSE]

PHONE CALL TO THE DEAD—a phone call to a friend, in which one has a normal conversation, then later learns that the friend had died many days before the conversation took place. (Inconcl.) [**cf.** ANSWER CASES, ELECTRONIC VOICES Appendix 2]

PHONE CALLS FROM THE DEAD—see PSYCHIC PHONE CALLS.

PHONE-VOYANCE—to give a psychic READING by tuning into the client's voice at the other end of the telephone line; given easier at night when the wires do not pick up interference; distance is no barrier. [**cf.** MENTAL MANIFESTATIONS/MISCEL-LANEOUS]

PHONY STARS—(ufology) aircraft that are capable of materializing and maneuvering in the sky and looking like stars. [**cf.** DISC OCCUPANT, ECHO, ETHER SHIPS, DOR CLOUDS]

PHOOKA—(Ireland) 1. a nature spirit of negative energy; shows itself in a rough beast-form with jet black skin and blazing eyes; 2. capable of changing shapes; shows itself as a friendly shaggy dog or a sway-back pony desiring to carry people on its back. **Syn.** GOBLIN.

PHOS—see TOTALITY.

PHOTO-CHROMOTHERAPY—the use of color and a photograph to heal a person, plant, or animal; to apply the energy of color via the spiritual bridge between a photograph and the aura of a life form; if the correct color is chosen it will result in a healing. (Inconcl.) [**cf.** CHROMA, COLOR ACTIVITY]

PHOTO-MEDIUM—one who allows the etheric world GUIDE to intervene and use one's ECTO-PLASM to "think" energy into shapes and people, or whatever the guide wants to appear on a negative or print; the guide, being of a higher vibrational frequency, can reflect light rays which impinge upon the sensitized plate; this results into words, or pictures of people or etheric world guides, imposed onto the finished picture, that were not seen by the physical eye when the picture was originally taken. (Inconcl.) [**cf.** THOUGHTOGRAPHY, EXTRAS, SPIRIT PHOTOGRAPHY]

PHOTO-TELEPATHY—to use a photograph of the person to whom one wants to send a telepathic message; photograph is stared at for a few minutes first, and then the message is beamed at the picture with emotional impact; message can be words,

motions, suggestions, or knowledge; distance is no barrier. [**cf.** MENTAL TELEPATHY, PSYCHOMETRIC TELEPATHY, PHOTO-TELEPATHY HEALING]

PHOTO-TELEPATHY HEALING—to use a photograph of the person to whom one wants to send healing energies; 1. photograph must be a picture of the person well and happy; picture is stared at for five or ten minutes after a MEDITATION period; concentration on the picture as is, with no concern as to how the patient will become well again; a form of VISUALIZATION using a real picture to enforce the mental mind picture; 2. one stares at the photograph for the meditation period; then sends words of healing with emotional impact and projects it at the photograph; (recent research: patient and healer were HOOKED-UP to biofeed-back instruments, and the exact time the thought was projected was registered on the instruments for both subjects; patient also registered BODY CHEMISTRY changes); distance is no barrier. [**cf.** MENTAL HEALING, WORDS-WITH-POWER]

PHOTOELECTRONIC MULTIPLIERS—1. (Kirlian effect) a low frequency camera using 3,000 cycles per second as compared to the high frequency of the Kirlian camera, and when photographing the aura, it shows as a glow or a luminescent fur rim around people as compared to the bright colors of the Kirlian camera. **Syn.** SUPERSENSITIVE PHOTO MULTIPLIERS, RADIATION-FIELD PHOTOGRAPHY. [**cf.** ETHERIC DOUBLE, MITOGENTIC RADIATION, EARTH'S ELECTRICAL FIELD, SEVEN BODIES OF MAN] 2. a very sensitized camera, using low fre-quencies, that is used in the psi laboratory to see what is going on in the invisible world during psi experiments. **Syn.** RADIATION-FIELD PHOTO-GRAPHY.

PHOTOFLASH CLAIRSENTIENCE—(laboratory) to flash a light on a photograph at the same time one or more persons concentrate on a section of the body of the one in the photograph; at that moment, the one in photograph feels changes in his or her body; distance being no barrier. [**cf.** DIRECTED-THOUGHT TRAINERS, BIOCOMMUNICATION]

PHOTOGRAPH LIFE READING—see PHO-TOGRAPHOLOGY.

PHOTOGRAPHIC PLATE OF NATURE—a record, in picture form, of all events that ever happened on planet earth; made of ethereal substance, hovering close to earth; constantly retakes and plays back vibrations to earth; pictures become a blueprint for future events; perceived clairvoyantly if in a high state of consciousness. **Syn.** MENTAL-REFLECTING-ETHER. [**cf.** PLANES, MENTAL PLANE]

PHOTOGRAPHOLOGY—to perceive psychic information regarding a person by staring at their portrait, without the person being present; the eyes are used as a POINT-OF-FOCUS, and when stared at for a short period, one can tune into the INNER-BEING of that person and reveal his or her past, present, future, state of health, of prosperity, traits of character, potentials, etc; information revealed is similar to that which is revealed by having the person next to oneself for a reading. **Syn.** PHOTO-GRAPH LIFE READING. [**cf.** FLOWER CLAIR-SENTIENCE]

PHOTOGRAPHY READING—see PHOTOGRAPH-OLOGY.

PHOUKA—(Ireland) see NATURE SPIRIT.

PHOWA—(Tibet) to project one's consciousness into the body of another through the thirty-eight junctions of the body; a form of POSSESSION. **Syn.** AVESHA. [**cf.** INVASION, DEMONIAC, PSYCHIC TRANSFER]

PHRASE-FOCUSING DREAM INCUBATION—to program one's self to dream an answer to a question or problem; process of writing on paper a concise question which one wants answered, using as few words as possible; to repeat them over and over until one falls asleep; answer comes during REM sleep and its symbols must be interpreted. [**cf.** LANDMARK IMAGE, INCUBATION]

PHRENO-MESMERISM—to apply the principles of HYPNOTHERAPY to the science of PHRENOLOGY; the BUMPS on the head of the subject are touched by the HYPNOTHERAPIST when the subject is in a hypnotic state, and responds to the stimulus by exhibiting the symptoms of the mental trait that corresponds to the bump being touched. [**cf.** HYPOPHENOMENALISM, HYPNOTIC TOUCH]

PHRENOLOGY—the science of the skull and head, telling one's individuality and personality; theory: various sections of the brain interact and have a specific physical location in the head which helps reveal one's mental faculties and character. [**cf.** IRIDOLOGY, HAIR ANALYSIS]

PHYIT-PYET—(Buddhism) a very powerful chant used frequently; has been known to stimulate the

mind to an awareness in which one perceives clairvoyantly the atoms coming and going, in a ceaseless changing of particles and waves. [**cf.** COLLECTING THE MIND, SOUNDS-WITH-POWER]

PHYSICAL—pertains to the mundane or third-dimensional existance; all earthly things as they are perceived by the five SENSES; used in psychic research literature so as to distinguish earthly things from the etheric world things.

PHYSICAL BIOCOMMUNICATION—(clinical) theory: nothing physical is ever transmitted, but there is a communion model of some kind that unites all human beings. [**cf.** HOLOGRAM, BRAIN THEORY, GREATH WHITE LIGHT]

PHYSICAL BODY—(esoteric, prescience)1. a divine unit within the great divine universal unit; a continuation of the electrical system of the universe, with its transceivers comparing to the nodes in the atmosphere, making it all one system; contains body fluids identical with the nature of universal energy and composition; 2. an instrument that resonates automatically to sounds that surround it, playing its harmony with the COSMIC MUSIC; 3. a temporary accessory to the SOUL-MIND, serving as a barometer telling how the soul-mind is handling or balancing with life's situations; 4. an initiation tool on the evolutionary scale of the soul-mind; works for the same overall principle as the other bodies that interpenetrate it, to complete the MONAD; 5. unique from other BODIES OF MAN or organisms, as it contains a decision mechanism, the brain; 6. contains all the substances of the seven bodies of man: solids, liquids, gases, etheric, super-etheric, sub-atomic, and atomic. (Inconcl.) [**cf.** HUMAN BODY, BRAIN, SOUL-MIND, ACUPUNCTURE POINTS, PRINCIPLES OF MAN]

PHYSICAL BODY POLARITY—right side: electric, male, action; left side: magnetic, female, heart, emotion. (Inconcl.) [**cf.** FATHER/MOTHER GOD, FIRST MATTER]

PHYSICAL CARRIER OF PSI INFORMATION—(future science) ELECTROMAGNETIC WAVES of extremely low frequency. (Inconcl.) [**cf.** ARTIFICIAL FIELDS, ALPHA SENSES, BIOACCUMULATOR]

PHYSICAL CYCLE—(biorhythm) a rhythmic pattern "within" the human body that reacts to one's health, physical strength, endurance, energy, resistance and confidence; makes the organism give out peak performance for 11½ days and relaxation performance for 11½ days, constituting 23 days and then repeats itself; begins at birth and ends at death; used in charting one's biorhythms. [cf. CYCLES, BIOLOGICAL CYCLES, CIRCADIAN RHYTHM, EMOTIONAL CYCLE]

PHYSICAL ETHERS—a few, of the several thousands of vibrational frequencies in the etheric world, which function compatibly with mankind's physical world: 1. ELECTRICITY; 2. PRANA; 3. LIGHT; 4. MENTAL-REFLECTING-ETHER. [cf. BODIES AND PLANES Appendix 5]

PHYSICAL ISOLATION—to put the physical body into conditions of visible zero-level, subsonic level, isothermal level, and with a minimum of gravity in order to open the mind to the etheric planes; in this level of awareness, one can visit the DENSITY or astral planes. [cf. GROSS COMMUNICATIONS, IMP, INITIATORY DEATH]

PHYSICAL MANIFESTATIONS—see PHYSICAL PSYCHISM.

PHYSICAL MANIFESTATIONS/MISCELLANEOUS—see Appendix 2, under this heading; lists the many types of physical psychism that have not been investigated enough, and do not happen often enough to presently require catagories of their own.

PHYSICAL MATTER—energy patterns and energy waves at a rate of frequency that can be perceived by humanity; forces of vitality finding means to express; see MUNDANE WORLD.

PHYSICAL MEDIUMSHIP—to use the ETHERIC WORLD INTELLIGENCES to perform physical psychic feats or skills; intelligences collaborate with the medium to learn and perform the wishes of the medium; everyone in the area can witness the phenomenon through the five senses; intelligences use the energy of the MEDIUM and SITTERS (as opposed to MENTAL MEDIUMSHIP in which they use their own energy); sometimes simply called phenomena. [cf. GUIDE, PHYSICAL PSYCHIC PROCESSES]

PHYSICAL OBSESSION IN A MEDIUM—activity of an inferior world entity working within a MEDIUM at its own discretion but meeting the approval of the medium; manifestations result in improper behavior and unpredictable occurrences; entity intervenes within the medium's body causing spontaneous movements of objects and noises and works through the mediumistic skills, such as AUTOMATIC WRITING, AUTOMATIC SPEECH, AUTOMATIC PAINT MEDIUM; continual allowance of the entity could result in poor physical or mental health; (do not confuse with OBSESSION within the mind). [cf. CHEMICAL PHENOMENA, OBSESSION, CRYPTOPHYSICAL]

PHYSICAL PHOTOGRAPHY—to produce a photograph on regular film or sensitized paper with no camera involved; MEDIUM works with techniques and directions from the guide, while in a LIGHT TRANCE, SEMITRANCE, or DEEP TRANCE; pictures are as detailed and clear, as if taken in a normal procedure; also produced on color film; a RITUAL or PRAYER begins the process; time of exposure and method is chosen by the GUIDE; techniques vary with medium; e.g., film lies next to the medium with no camera involved; film has been known to be worn around the neck while in a darkened room; sensitized paper has been known to contain the picture without being taken out of the package while picture is taken. [cf. EXTRAS, PSYCHIC PHOTOGRAPHY]

PHYSICAL PLANE—first plane of third-dimensional matter, created by the SOUL-MIND as a means for it to express itself and to grow in a manner that only third-dimensional matter affords; matter held together by thought energy (both CONSCIOUS MIND and SUBCONSCIOUS MIND activity); the earth and all the material things on it. Syn. PHYSICAL WORLD. [cf. Appendix 5 BODIES AND PLANES]

PHYSICAL PSYCHIC LIGHTS—a white hazy light seen around an object, an area, or a group of persons by more than one person; it could be the ASTRAL WORLD, THOUGHT FORMS of the people in that area, or the AURA of the group. (Inconcl.) [cf. CORPOREAL VISION, INVOLUNTARY INTERVENTION]

PHYSICAL PSYCHIC PROCESSES—see Appendix 2 for listings of the various methods and techniques that can be used to acquire and improve one's PHYSICAL PSYCHISM; advice as how to keep it under control, etc., researched from many sources. [cf. DESIRED-CONTROL, MEDIUMSHIP, CLOAK OF INSULATION]

PHYSICAL PSYCHISM—one of the two major categories of psychic skills; can be identified from mental psychic skills by the characteristics listed below under two sub-groupings: Personal Physical Psychism (using the SUBCONSCIOUS MIND), and

Physical Mediumship (using ETHERIC WORLD INTELLIGENCES). Both types of skills: 1. require the activity of the subconscious mind and CONSCIOUS MIND only; 2. tune into the electromagnetic field around matter; 3. show the matter moved, changed in form, shape, or size, so everyone in the area can physically see it; 4. will it to happen, consciously, subconsiously, or karmically; 5. require relaxation of mind and body. **Personal Physical Psychism:** 1. skill requires practice; 2. brain activity energy is used. **Physical Mediumship:** 1. requires desire, patience, sincerity, and sitting regularly for "unfoldment"; 2. requires a TRANCE or a sleep state; 3. MEDIUM is not always aware of what transpires until the session is over; 4. an etheric world intelligence or DISCARNATE ENTITY uses the ECTOPLASM that exudes from the medium's body (and sitters' bodies if present); 5. controlled by preplanning and trust in the etheric world intelligence. **Syn.** PHENOMENA. [**cf.** Appendix 2 for listings of types of PHYSICAL PSYCHISM]

PHYSICAL READING—to psychically scan an individual body to perceive information regarding one's mental health; scanning is performed by: AURA READING, X-RAY CLAIRVOYANCE, MAGNETIC PASSES with hands over ETHERIC DOUBLE, use of radiesthetic tools over etheric double, and POLARITY BALANCING. [**cf.** PSYCHIC HEALING, CURATIVE EDUCATION, MAGNETISM]

PHYSICAL TRANSFIGURATION—1. facial and body features of a GUIDE or guides superimposed on a MEDIUM while medium is working with etheric world guides; seen with one's physical eyes; occurs in a development circle or in lecturing; and indication of the intense interpenetration that occurs when working with guides; more easily seen in a semidark room; 2. to induce facial features and characteristics of one's past incarnations onto one's body so others can see; executed more easily after deep MEDITATION and in a semidark room; also perceived by one's self by staring into a mirror. (Inconcl.) **Syn.** PHYSICAL TRANSFORMATION. [**cf.** ELECTROSTATIC FIELD, FIERY LIVES, DARKROOM SESSIONS]

PHYSICAL TRANSFORMATION—see PHYSICAL TRANSFIGURATION.

PHYSICAL TRANSMUTATION—(mediumship) to change MATTER into ENERGY and then subsequently change this form of energy into another form of matter by the intervention of the etheric world guides; medium brings into his or her outer band an etheric world ALCHEMIST who can use the medium's ECTOPLASM for transmuting various atoms into other atoms; transacted while medium is in a SEMITRANCE or DEEP TRANCE state; (do not confuse with an earth alchemist who uses the power of mind CONCENTRATION). [**cf.** MENTAL TRANSMUTATION, ALCHEMY, MEDIUMSHIP, APPORTATION, TELEKINESIS]

PHYSICAL WORLD—see PHYSICAL PLANE.

PHYSICAL-SEED-ATOM—a tiny concentrated ethereal center of energy located in the heart; the end of one of the strands of the SILVER CORD; contains a temporary file of the akashic record pictures; subject to the physical TWENTY-THREE DAY CYCLE of biorhythms; (Bible) one of the three BOOKS OF LIFE; see LIFE-CORD-SEED-ATOM. **Syn.** HEART-SEED-ATOM. [**cf.** BIORHYTHMS, PLANES]

PHYSICALLY COERCIVE—the use of an outside agency to force electrochemical changes in the brain. [**cf.** DESTRUCTIVE-BRAINWASHING CULTS, HALLUCINOGENIC DRUGS]

PHYSICS—the science that deals with MATTER and ENERGY in terms of motion and force.

PHYSICS UNDERGROUND—list of names, considered at one time to be far-out physicists; used for relating to one another the discoveries and information that could lead to psychic functioning without their peers knowing about them.

PHYSIOCHEMICAL MECHANISM—to change the chemistry in a living organism by intensifying and focalizing one's concentration on the feat; energy can be discharged on plants, animals, humans and one's own self; research proved with medical examination that BODY CHEMISTRY changes in BIOFEEDBACK TRAINING and healing sessions. [**cf.** MENTAL HEALING, MENTAL TELEPATHY, HUMAN PSYCHOKINESIS]

PHYSIOGNOMY—ancient theory: the shape of the head, facial features, profile, lines on the face and facial expression reveal one's characteristics and personality. [**cf.** PHRENOLOGY, BODY READING Appendix 5]

PI-RAY—a life-giving ray found in a PYRAMID at an angle of 6° 15′ from the vertical axis inside the pyramid. [**cf.** KING'S CHAMBER, KING SCALE, CAPSTONE]

PI-RAY ORGON ACCUMULATOR COFFER—an ancient tool designed to be used in collaboration with individual consciousness. [**cf.** BLACK BOX, ENERGY MATRIX]

PIBS—abbr. PSI INTERACTIVE BIOMOLECULES; the connection between the intelligence in the atoms of the body, the UNIVERSAL MIND, and the SOUL-MIND. (Inconcl.) [**cf.** SUBCONSCIOUS MIND, TOTALITY, ATOMS]

PICATRIX—(Arabia) a special method of jumbled directions using esoteric COSMOLOGY, preparation of talismans, and incantations for a precise psychic treatment. [**cf.** AMULETS, TALISMAN, CONTAGION MAGIC]

PICK-TREE BRAG—see NATURE SPIRIT.

PICKED UP—to perceive PSYCHIC INFORMATION by tuning into a person, without any preparation or outward sign for this information; can be used for one's personal protection but is considered poor taste to frequently allow information about another's personal life enter one's mind without their permission. Usage: "While I was waiting for you to come, I picked up that you would have some good news for me." [**cf.** COLD READER, CLAIRSENTIENCE, FREE FLOWING, CLOAK OF INSULATION]

PICTOGRAPH—various types of pictures used as symbols by the ETHERIC WORLD INTELLIGENCES to bring psychic information through during an AUTOMATIC WRITING session; some intelligences prefer to use pictures or symbols instead of words. [**cf.** AUTOMAT, AUTOMATIC TYPEWRITING]

PICTURE LANGUAGE—see DREAMS.

PICTURE METAPHORS—(dreams) objects or living organisms used in the fabric of the dream in an activity that compares subjective feelings of the dreamer, instead of telling a story about the dreamer's daily activities. [**cf.** COMPENSATORY DREAMS, INTIMATION DREAMS]

PICTURE TELEPATHY—(laboratory) to send and receive pictures in experiments to develop telepathic sensitivity; sender and receiver in different locales tune into each other at a given time; receiver picks up on color, forms, emotion, and picture per se; picture is later disclosed to check receiver's accuracy. [**cf.** TELEPATHY, BIOLOGICAL COMPATIBILITY, LOVE-LINE, ARTISTIC TELEPATHY]

PICTURIZATION—see VISUALIZATION.

PIETISM—a religious attitude regarding personal devotion, stressing emotional behavior instead of intellect.

PILGRIM-MONADS—(esoteric) soul-minds whose function is to follow the path of the COSMOS, to go from planet to planet, planet to sphere, sun to planet, and vice versa.

PILLARS—(Kabbalah, tree of life) the three vertical parallel lines connecting the discs; known as the pillar of severity, pillar of mildness, and pillar of mercy. [**cf.** SEPHIROTH, PATHS, KABBALAH, LAW OF THREES Appendix 7]

PILLOW MESSAGE—(dreams) an answer to a question written on a piece of paper and put under the pillow with the expectation of dreaming a message. [**cf.** INCUBATION, ANNOUNCING DREAMS]

PILOTING INTELLIGENCES—(ufology) an energy field with intelligence and ability to maneuver space craft, but do not resemble earth beings. [**cf.** ETHER SHIPS, CONSTRUCTS, ETHER-SHIP BEING]

PINACYANOLE BROMIDE FILTERS—lenses used in goggles designed to help see the aura. [**cf.** AURAVISION, ACTINIC RAYS]

PINE TREES—(esoteric) have the properties of healing disorders of the NERVOUS SYSTEM; sitting under a pine tree, one feels the energy from the tree enter one's AURA; holding onto a pine needle on the tree with the two psychic fingers, one receives energy into one's body. [**cf.** BOTANE, COSMIC TREE, ELDER TREE]

PINEAL DOOR PROJECTION—to exit from the PINEAL GLAND in an ASTRAL PROJECTION; the eyes roll upward, and one feels a rushing sensation on the top of one's head. **Sim.** WHIRLWIND. [**cf.** ZIGZAGGING, SKYING]

PINEAL GLAND—(esoteric) a tiny flattened organ, shaped like a pine cone, located in the middle of the head, which acts as the controlling factor in the THIRD-EYE AREA for psychic sensitivity; connected to the THALAMUS by a hollow stalk, but is not itself a part of the brain; contains a pigment similar to that of the eyes; 1. the master gland of the etheric bodies; masculine, positive in polarity; 2. (future science) has attached antennas so it can transmute COSMIC ENERGY into electrical energy for the brain to use, mingling it with conscious and subconscious activity, and emotional energy; sends it along to the

471

PITUITARY GLAND and NERVOUS SYSTEM to be used in the body; 3. controls the action of light upon and within the body; 4. acts as an external door for etheric vibrations to penetrate, making clairvoyant sensitivity possible; 5. used by ETHERIC WORLD INTELLIGENCES who attach themselves to it, to bring higher knowledge from the SUPERCONSCIOUS MIND; 6. a part of the third-eye area; the pineal gland is becoming more awakened in mankind in the coming age, and will vivify as humanity evolves and perform its normal function as a regulator for TELEPATHY, CLAIRSENTIENCE, CLAIRVOYANCE, CLAIRAUDIENCE, etc. (Inconcl.) [cf. THIRD-EYE AREA Appendix 5]

PINGALA—(kundalini) one of two ethereal nerve canals running along the spinal column carrying a force vital to the human physical being; crosses at five physical PLEXUS in the body creating ethereal CHAKRAS; masculine, positive in polarity; located on right side of the spine. [cf. IDA, KUNDALINI, CADUCEUS WINDING]

PINK NOISE—a constant energy of sound per band width; steady energy per octave makes a pink noise response and puts one in a relaxed, meditative, neutral state of consciousness ready for psychic information, e.g., rain drops, noise on FM radio where there is no station broadcasting. [cf. SOUNDS-WITH-POWER, SELF-GENERATED STIMULUS, CORTICALLY MEDIATED STABILIZATION]

PIPE OF PEACE—a long, ornamental tobacco pipe, called a **calumet**, that is used by the Native American Indians in their ceremonies, as a token of peace; the ritual was founded by the Great Manitou in the ETHERIC WORLD and is still supervised by him. **Syn.** PEACE PIPE. [cf. GROUP TOTEM, COMMUNAL WORSHIP, SUN DANCE]

PIPER—(Cornwall, England) a small NATURE SPIRIT that can be perceived dancing in the woods and gardens; wears a green suit with a red cap, and has a long beard; mischievous and kindhearted. **Syn.** REDCAP, PISKEY.

PIRIT—(Buddhism) a collection of chants used at set intercals to protect one after one's transition. [cf. GREAT TONE OF NATURE, SOUNDS-WITH-POWER, DEATH, CHIKAHIA BARDO]

PISCEAN AGE—(Pisces, astrological sign of the fish) the age the planet is now leaving; 1. a water sign; the age of the fish and its element, water; astrological sign that included: sinking of ATLAN-TIS, flood of Noah, conquering of the "flat" sea by Columbus, disciples of JESUS becoming fishermen of men, invention of submarines; 2. identifies with Christian dispensation. [cf. GREAT YEAR, CIVILIZATION'S CYCLE]

PISKEY—(Cornwall, England) small NATURE SPIRIT; clairvoyantly seen dancing in the woods and gardens; capable of being mischievous; wears a green suit and a redcap. **Syn.** REDCAP, PIPER.

PIT—see DENSITY.

PITRI-YANA—(Yoga) the SOUL-MIND that is exceptionally virtuous but not sinless; travels through the atmosphere, winds, clouds and rain to a lesser paradise to be reborn as a person again. [cf. PATH SYMBOLISM, INITIATIONS]

PITRIS—1. (Sanskrit) beings that evolved on the moon chain preceding the earth chain; their shadows provided the archetypal molds for mankind's incarnations in this chain; they were ancestors and creators of mankind; classes: three incorporeal (ARUPA), four CORPOREAL (RUPA); (Hoult) belong to previous humanities, lunar ancestors; 2. human beings that have passed into the ETHERIC WORLD.

PITUITARY GLAND—(esoteric) a double-bean-shaped organ suspended in a bony cavity beneath the brain behind the nose, which links health and death with thinking and everyday affairs; 1. its post lobe is a part of the THIRD-EYE AREA; the frontal lobe is concerned with emotional thought and the post lobe is concerned with concrete intellectual concepts; here thoughts and emotions become translated into terms of chemistry and vice versa; 2. electrical impulses from the PINEAL GLAND and BRAIN run into the PITUITARY GLAND; here they are transmuted into physical energy; this gland regulates the release of hormones of all other glands of the ENDOCRINE SYSTEM; this adds to the common pool of blood and lymph regulating the chemical balance of the body; 3. the master gland of the physical body; all hormone-producing glands discharge their trigger substances into the blood, under orders from this gland; 4. violet in color; feminine, negative in polarity; 5. called "the seat of the mind." (Inconcl.) [cf. PINEAL GLAND, PITUITRIN, THIRD-EYE AREA]

PITUITRIN—(esoteric) the main hormone that is released from the PITUITARY GLAND that regulates and controls all other glands. [cf. PINEAL

GLAND, THALAMUS]

PIXIE—(Cornwall, England) a NATURE SPIRIT that usually wears green; has a turned up nose, red hair and squinty eyes; has an excess of speed and action, bringing the owner feelings of joy, to the extent of giggling; has happy intents; usually works with one farm family; dances in the shadows of the standing stones or tumbles on stream edges; bells can be heard when it is around; can be mischievous or hard working; likes to thresh corn at night for special rewards; also spelled **pisgie, piskie, pigsey.**

PK—abbr. for PSYCHOKINESIS; see same.

PK-BY-COMMITTEE—(Toronto, Canada) name given to a group of eight men and women who met weekly to create a ghost personality; the group was without known psychic ability and sat around a small table with their fingertips on the table top and talked to the invisible personality they made up; the desire was to know if the invisible personality was a product of the SUBCONSCIOUS MIND of the SITTERS in a PSYCHIC DEVELOPMENT CIRCLE; after a year they were able to produce RAPS and TABLE-TIPPING through their created ghost personality; some felt the personality would respond to what the majority of the committee wanted to hear. **Syn.** PHILLIP GROUP. [**cf.** CONJURING UP PHILLIP]

PK-LT—abbr. PSYCHOKINESIS-LIVING TARGET (psi tasks) to send a mental telepathic message to the consciousness of an animal or plant to make it alter its movements; e.g., to concentrate on a different direction than the pigeon seems to be going in, to get it to go your way; to influence one leaf on a stem to grow more rapidly; to send a message to heal the animal or plant. **Syn.** NATURE-PK. [**cf.** PSYCHOKINESIS, TELEKINESIS]

PK-MEDIUMSHIP—(Russia) to move an object without touching it; ETHERIC WORLD INTELLIGENCE works through the hand of the MEDIUM which is a few inches above the article; e.g., a matchstick rolls along a perfectly level table in a room in which the drafts have been made extinct. **Syn.** TELEKINESIS. [**cf.** ELECTROSTATIC FIELD, LEVITATION-TK, PSYCHOKINESIS]

PK-MT—abbr. PSYCHOKINESIS-MOVING TARGETS (psi tasks) to move an object already in motion by concentration of the mind; e.g., to will the numbers of the dice before they are thrown; to will the

pendulum on the clock to stop. **Syn.** NONHUMAN-PK. [**cf.** PSYCHOKINESIS, MIND—OVER-MATTER Appendix 4]

PK-PLACEMENT TEST—(psi tasks) to influence falling objects to land in a designated area of the throwing surface through mind concentration. [**cf.** ESP, PK]

PK-ST—abbr. PSYCHOKINESIS-STATIC INANIMATE OBJECTS (psi tasks) to move an object that cannot move itself by mundane means through the power of steady mind concentration; e.g., projecting a picture on film or moving a table. **Syn.** NONHUMAN PK. [**cf.** PSYCHOKINESIS, TELEKINESIS]

PL KYODAN—(*PL*, "perfect liberty"; *Kyodan*, "church") to heal a patient by transferring the ailment to oneself and then dispelling it; disease is diagnosed first; both patient and healer are more healthy for the transfer. [**cf.** HUMAN TRANSMITTERS, EMPATHY-PK, ASSIMILATION]

PLANCHETTE—a commercially made instrument containing a tripod table mounted on small wheel-castors, with a pencil attached; used for communicating with the ETHERIC WORLD INTELLIGENCES; one or more fingertips are placed on the tripod when in a relaxed state and the tool takes off without any effort of the medium's fingertips, spelling out words and answering questions of the medium; an offshoot of the OUIJA BOARD; theory: **1.** it is the muscular movements initiated by the SUBCONSCIOUS MIND as in the PENDULUM principle; **2.** it is moved by etheric world entities; this type of AUTOMATISM easily attracts the low inferior entities who are always anxious to interfere in physical life if the psychic is not well-grounded in psychic sciences. [**cf.** ASTRAL SHELL, GUIDE]

PLANE OF ATMA—see SPIRITUAL PLANE or FIFTH PLANE.

PLANE OF DESIRES—see ASTRAL PLANE.

PLANE OF FLAME—see FIFTH PLANE.

PLANE OF FORGETFULNESS—(esoteric) a place in the ETHERIC WORLD where one drinks of the river which has a vibrational frequency that makes one lose all remembrances of the past; one is then ready to reincarnate. [**cf.** SOUL JURY, KARMIC BOARD, SEED ATOMS]

PLANE OF ILLUSION—see ASTRAL PLANE.

PLANES—(esoteric) **1.** various levels of ENERGY

that fill the ATMOSPHERE; formed by the different number of electrons and protons attracting to themselves atoms of like nature, and colonizing until they form a special vibratory rate; this vibratory rate makes its own rules and has its own functions necessary for the various states of consciousness of the SOUL-MIND it serves; subject to the LAW OF THOUGHT, see Appendix 7; 2. a state of consciousness directed by the soul-mind, whose function is to bring the plane into existence for its own personal place of schooling; humanity named the planes they made: (0) DENSITY; the level of consciousness of a much lesser degree than the majority of individuals living in the physical plane; (1) PHYSICAL PLANE (earth); (2) ASTRAL PLANE; (3) MENTAL PLANE; (4) BUDDHIC PLANE; (5) SPIRITUAL PLANE; (6) MONADIC PLANE; (7) PERFECTNESS; within each of these planes are seven more planes and within each of these planes are seven more planes; this makes hundreds of levels of existence for the soul-mind to inhabit when one is living in the ETHERIC WORLD which is necessary for the hundreds of states of consciousness the soul-minds are in. **Syn.** LEVELS, DIMENSIONS, SPHERES, MANSIONS, STATE OF CONSCIOUSNESS, PLATEAUS, INNER KINGDOMS, STAGES OF EVOLUTION, ETHERIC WORLD. [**cf.** BODIES AND PLANES Appendix 5]

PLANES OF DARKNESS—see DENSITY.

PLANET—(esoteric) a globe or sphere containing life, some of which are felt to have human forms, similar to earth.

PLANET EARTH—1. used frequently by parapsychologists to mean anything that concerns the THIRD-DIMENSION and matter as mankind knows matter in this world; shows recognition of other planets; 2. (metaphysical) a quasi-infinite energy field of colonized embodied consciousness. **Syn.** MUNDANE WORLD.

PLANET-TO-PSYCHIC-CENTER CORRESPONDENCE—(prescience) the use of a synthesizer that changes the quality of sound over a range; to find the type of sound most suitable to provoke a psychic response in a listener. [**cf.** LOST WORD, SOUNDS-WITH-POWER, KEY NOTE]

PLANETARY ANGEL—an exalted, magnanimous ETHERIC WORLD INTELLIGENCE, high on the hierarchy of EVOLUTION, in charge of guiding harmony among the planets in the solar system; many

are now concerned with the earth and its inhabitants and earth's responsibility to other planets and the sun. [**cf.** ANGEL OF THE SUN, ANNOINTED ONES]

PLANETARY CHAIN—system of seven globes linked together in a chain equalling one solar system. [**cf.** GLOBE, ROUND]

PLANETARY CYCLES—radiations from the various planets combined together have an effect on all planets individually over a span of time and this effect then repeats itself. [**cf.** COSMIC TIMETABLE, COSMIC RHYTHM]

PLANETARY DEME—a group of common people working together psychically with the new energies coming to earth now to utilize the energies for the growth of the new culture. [**cf.** TRANSFORMATION, PLANETARY HELPERS, FUTURISTS]

PLANETARY INITIATION—(Eastern) a time when a planet is feeling an inner urge to cleanse itself, to raise its STATE OF CONSCIOUSNESS and prepare itself for its new function in the SOLAR SYSTEM; a change from one astrological sign to another; planet goes through an accelerated transformation in every aspect of its being; how the people of the planet react will determine if the initiation is passed or if the planet dies.

PLANETARY PRANA—rays from the moon that pulsate through the soles of the feet to enter the ROOT CHAKRA and into the NERVOUS SYSTEM; negative in POLARITY; necessary to mankind. [**cf.** SOLAR PRANA, COSMIC ENERGY]

PLANETARY RENAISSANCE—(future culture) a new revival of earth finding its place in the universe and then working at universal harmony; to have a planetary community composed of many planets in the solar system, working together for the overall picture of harmony in the skies. [**cf.** CONSCIOUSNESS AWARENESS MOVEMENT, FINDHORN, EVOLUTIONARY NECESSITY]

PLANETARY SCHEME—each of the seven planets which have seven globes of different densities interpenetrating them, similar to the seven invisible bodies of a human being; necessary to make a solar system. [**cf.** CHAIN OF GLOBES, BIORHYTHMIC YEAR, CYCLE]

PLANETARY SOUL—(theosophy) the MONAD or seed of each planet that is alive and evolving; contains all the potential of a perfect planet that keeps it in orbit; it is eternally unfolding its etheric blueprint, showing its changes in states of development of the people or organisms that inhabit it; this results in atmospheric and environmental forms of matter. [**cf.** SOUL-MIND, MONAD, COSMIC TIMETABLE]

PLANETARY SPIRIT—(esoteric) a lofty, mighty intelligence in the etheric world forming a ray of consciousness pure enough to be given the honor of ruling over the planets. **Syn.** PLANETARY ANGEL. [**cf.** PLANETARY SOUL, PLANETIZATION] ·

PLANETARY WORKER—(Hilliary Ellers) one who understands what the solar system and the earth are going through and are willing to reclaim earth's roots of the evolving life stream; worker will move beyond self and move into the whole in an outworking of the change in the planet; all will run smoothly as the transformation takes place. [**cf.** PLANETARY ANGEL, COSMIC CYCLE]

PLANETIZATION—(future science) coined by Jean deChardin; the building of oneness between humanity's world and the ethereal world with the help of the cosmic forces; groups of people who can find interest in building a future in which all planets come into harmony with each other or to work on a friendly basis, instead of those who find all their interests rest within humanity's world. (Inconcl.) [**cf.** COSMIC WHEEL, CONTINUITY, COSMIC RHYTHM]

PLANT BIOLOCATION—to hold a plant in the palm of the hand and with intense mind concentration will the plant to sprout branches in a matter of minutes; one must have a love for plants and understand their relationship with humans. (Inconcl.) **Syn.** PK-LT, NATURE-PK. [**cf.** BOTANE, PSYCHOKINESIS, SENSATION CONSCIOUSNESS]

PLANT CIRCULATION—the psychic ability of a plant to transfer water from itself to another plant nearby that needs it; research has shown that if one plant is out of the way of the rain, the plants who partake of the rain will automatically share their water. (Inconcl.) [**cf.** SYMPATHETIC MAGIC, EMPATHY TELEPATHY, BOTANE Appendix 2]

PLANT CONVERSATION—the reaction of a plant in sympathy with the emotions of a human, especially its owner; plants are sentient, and respond to beneficial and menacing emotions of humans; e.g., research showed that a plant died after being one hour in the presence of a very depressed person;

plant shows signs of wilting or dying before or during the illness of its owner. (Inconcl.) [**cf.** SENSATION CONSCIOUSNESS, CELLULAR CONSCIOUSNESS]

PLANT KINGDOM—(esoteric) 1. a subtle, shifting network of energies to link all life together; has a SENSATION CONSCIOUSNESS; susceptible to the thoughts and emotins of humanity; 2. energy forms and shapes to serve humans and animals with medicines, food, beauty, fragrance, and shelter; have an innate desire to go to a higher vibrational frequency by being eaten by people or animals instead of lying on the ground to rot and then dissipate back into the ethers; 3. an essential energy for a person in his or her system of balance; a transmitter of the VITAL LIFE FORCE (PRANA) found in the air which is needed by the human NERVOUS SYSTEM; 4. NATURE SPIRITS subserve the plant kingdom, designing all of nature's patterns. (Inconcl.) [**cf.** BOTANE Appendix 2, LAW OF SUBSERVIENCE Appendix 7, PLANT PERCEPTION]

PLANT MAGIC—the electrical system in plants that links the plant with the universe and all other forms of life; plants tune into the auric field of all things and sense when danger is coming from human beings, animals, insects, weather, etc., and act accordingly; have the properties to enhance psychic sensitivity and healing for a PSYCHIC. (Inconcl.) [**cf.** COSMIC RECEIVER, BIODETECTORS, CELLULAR CONSCIOUSNESS]

PLANT PERCEPTION—the ability of the nervous system in plants to react to the emotions of people, animals, and inanimate things which shows in its growth and activity patterns; can be noticed by the plant caretaker and the polygraph instrument; (Sir Jagadis Chandra Bose) "love, joy, hate, fear, pleasure, pain, and excitability, in humans, and countless other responses to outer stimuli are universal reactions in plants, also"; (Cleve Backster) "when HOOKED-UP to a POLYGRAPH the plant reacts to the attitudes, emotions, and health of people; this seems to go to the level of the atomic vibration happening in every cell in the plant"; plants are alive and feel just as important as people. [**cf.** ELECTROCULTURE, CELL MEMORY, CELL PERCEPTION]

PLASM—(Greek) suffix meaning "something molded or formed"; the fluid substance of an animal or vegetable as PROTOPLASM; see ECTOPLASM.

PLASMA—1. (theosophy) one of the four primary types of MATTER of the earth plane: solids, liquids, gases, and plasma; fire composed of plasma which are subatomic particles; (Inconcl.) 2. see PLASM.

PLASMAS—(ufology) (Trevor James Constable) pulsation of matter in outer space that looks like living organisms which emit a reddish-orange glow as they move; maybe a FOO FIGHTER discerned as SPHEROIDS. [cf. CRITTERS, ATMOSPHERE PHENOMENA, DAWN ANGELS]

PLASMATIC FAUNA—(ufology) (Trevor James Constable) pulsating life in outer space that appears to be more animal like than human; invisible and visible; uncomfortable to look at. [cf. ATMOSPHERE AMOEBA, BIOFORMS]

PLASMOLOGY—the study of ECTOPLASM; energy that exudes from the bodies of the MEDIUM and SITTERS in a SEANCE.

PLASTICS—see PSYCHIC IMPRINTS.

PLATEAU—see PLANES.

PLATFORM CLAIRVOYANCE—see STANDUP READER.

PLATONIC YEAR—(esoteric) period of approximately 26,000 years; time it takes earth's SOLAR SYSTEM to revolve around a Great Central Sun once; equal to the time required for a complete revolution of the equinoxes. **Syn.** GREAT YEAR, PRECESSION OF THE EQUINOXES, AGE, ANNUS MAGNUS. [cf. ROUND, GLOBE-ROUND, GALAXY, FOURTH ROUND OF THE PLANET EARTH]

PLEASURE—anything that releases tension; the opposite of tightness or tension in the NERVOUS SYSTEM; noticeable by and desirable to the person to whom it is happening. [cf. REWARDS AND PUNISHMENTS SYSTEM]

PLENARY TRANCE—the deepest state of HYPNOSIS that one can reach; usually takes about an hour of INDUCTION to accomplish; advantageous in research. [cf. INDUCTION RELEASE, DEEP STATE OF HYPNOTHERAPY]

PLEROMA—(Gnostic) (Greece) universal soul; that space which is divided into varying forms and shapes and is filled with a hierarchy of archons working for the good of mankind. [cf. INNER BAND, ARCHON, FORMED MEDIUM, GO-BETWEENS]

PLETHYSOMOGRAPH—an instrument that measures blood volume, changes in the heart beat, and the emotional state in the body; used in connection with psychic experiments.

PLEXUS—(esoteric) a junction in the physical body where the ASTRAL BODY connects to the physical body, and where the IDA and PENGALA cross which form the CHAKRAS. [cf. KUNDALINI]

PLOY—a maneuver in conversation to gain the advantage. [cf. ON-THE-SPOT-HYPNOSIS, MASS HYPNOSIS]

PLUMED SERPENT—(Mexico, native American) an ETHERIC WORLD INTELLIGENCE manifesting as a combination of bird and snake; identified with the morning star and the wind; a sky god bringing reconciliation between the UNDERWORLD and HEAVEN. **Syn.** QUETZALCOATL, KUKULCAN. [cf. DENSITY, HOLLOW EARTH, ETHERIC WORLD]

PLURALITY OF EXISTENCES—a concept that a human being is born into earth, dies and that same soul is born into the earth again and again. **Syn.** REINCARNATION.

PLUS—written (+); the period of days above the 0-LINE on the BIORHYTHM CHART showing when the body system is at its best for that particular cycle. [cf. CRITICAL DAYS, MINUS (-)]

PLUTO—(Greece) an etheric world DEVA in charge of the UNDERWORLD or lord of the dead, in HADES. [cf. DENSITY, LOWER ASTRAL PLANES, HELL]

PMIR—abbr. PSI-MEDITATED INSTRUMENTAL RESPONSE; (psi tasks) a spontaneous response to outer stimuli due to a scanning of the environment by the sensory and psi mechanism for a desirable answer. [cf. CLOAK OF INSULATION, FREE FLOWING, ETHERIC BRIDGE]

PNEUMA—1. (Erasistratus, 300 B.C.; Arabia, Aristotle, Greece) see VITAL LIFE FORCE; 2. (Greece) (a) the soul; (b) the spirit of God, the Holy Ghost; (c) breath, wind.

PNEUMA-TAPE-RECORDER—see TAPED VOICES.

PNEUMASPHERE—see ASTRAL WORLD.

PNEUMATIC PHENOMENA—term used loosely to denote all types of mediumship; psychism executed by etheric world intelligences. **Syn.** MEDIUMSHIP. [cf. Appendix 2 PHYSICAL PSYCHISM]

PNEUMATICIAN—see MEDIUM or SHAMAN.

PNEUMATOGRAPHIST—a MEDIUM who produces written psychic information on paper by itself; an

ETHERIC WORLD INTELLIGENCE writes the message on the paper without the aid of the medium's arm; executed close by the medium while the medium is in a trance state or asleep; some mediums do not set out the paper and pencil beforehand; always willed; see PRECIPITATION WRITING. [cf. SLATE WRITING, WINDOWGLASS CROSSES, LANDSCAPE PAINTINGS]

PNEUMATOGRAPHY—to allow an ETHERIC WORLD INTELLIGENCE to intervene and produce writing or hieroglyphics on paper without the use of one's arm or hand; intelligence uses the ECTOPLASM from the medium's body while MEDIUM is in a DEEP TRANCE state; usually performed with others around, as in a church or a SEANCE. **Syn.** DIRECT WRITING, PRECIPITATION. [cf. WATER SPRINKLING, SPIRIT ARTISTS]

PNEUMATOLOGY—1. a doctrine that emphasizes the HOLY SPIRIT; 2. pertains to the belief in intermediary intelligences in the etheric world who communicate between humanity and God; 3. (archaic psychology) doctrine of spiritual beings. **Syn.** PNEUMATICS.

PNEUMATOPHONY—spontaneous sounds coming from various parts of a medium's body made by an ETHERIC WORLD INTELLIGENCE; sometimes imitating a person, sometimes a nature creature, but always expressing intelligence and bringing a meaningful interruption; (do not confuse with CLAIRAUDIENCE). [cf. PERCUSSION, EXTERIOR PNEUMATOPHONY]

PNEUMBRA—(Haiti, Voodoo) the SPIRIT in the body or the conscience; the imperfect shadow outside the complete shadow. **Syn.** ZOMBIE, SPIRIT.

PO—1. (Polynesia) the absolute; the atoms before form was formed; see TOTALITY; 2. (Hawaii) the UNDERWORLD.

POET—1. (Greece) a SEER into the past rather than the future; poets were believed to be BREATHED INTO and then possessed by an ETHERIC WORLD INTELLIGENCE who would reveal information to the poet; points of the past were revealed and the poet would turn it into verse; 2. (A.D. 1500-1900) poets were capable of influencing the elements of nature by their rhythmic magical verse; psychic feats which were accomplished are: dispersing drifting ice, stopping volcanic eruptions and storms, killing destructive animals, forcing ghosts to disappear into the ground and putting on

a curse if needed. **Sim.** VERSE MAGIC. [cf. WORDS-WITH-POWER, ENTHUSED, RETROCOGNITION, BREATHED INTO]

POETIC MEDIUM—one who is capable of allowing the ETHERIC WORLD to intervene and receive communications of a sentimental nature (usually vague but affectionate expressions). [cf. CONSCIOUS COOPERATION, FINGERPRINTS OF PSI]

POETRY—(Greece) words composed to a special rhythmic beat for the purpose of stirring or enhancing magical powers; wordage was composed in formulaic style to be repeated silently or aloud with the mental intent of the magic occurring; poets were hired to design formulas that would psychically benefit the country or benefit an individual. [cf. RHYTHMIC PATTERNS, INCANTATIONS]

POINT-INSTANTS—(Buddhism) impersonal simple entities in the ETHERIC WORLD that are the ultimate elements of existence; have no space extension, nor time duration; they are the source of the order of all things. **Sim.** DHARMAS. [cf. OUTER BAND, ETHERIC WORLD INTELLIGENCES]

POINT-OF-FOCUS—any *one* thing that is small and will hold the attention of an individual over a period of time; with undivided attention on the *one* thing, the CONSCIOUS MIND is not needed for outside stimuli decisions, so it becomes passive; this allows the SUBCONSCIOUS MIND and SUPERCONSCIOUS MIND to flow freely; artists, scientists and inventors become so engrossed in their work that they frequently bring in help from a higher source; 1. to receive psychic information, one uses a focal point object and with intense directed attention, keeps the mind focused on it until the PSYCHIC INFORMATION flows; 2. to send PSYCHIC ENERGY, the focal point is used to consolidate the energy in the mind and when it seems densified enough to shoot it at the target; a focus point can be a candle flame, flower, cross, or the center of a MANDALA; see Appendix 2 for more ideas and types of skill that require a point-of-focus.

POINT-OF-FOCUS-READINGS—to use an object to hold one's concentration intensely to bring in psychic information; article must be compatible with psychic; article is stared at, not held, e.g., to use a photograph, flower, colored ribbon, water, the iris of the eyes of another person, or the face of cards. [cf. FOCUSED CONSCIOUSNESS, CANDLE FLAME]

477

POINTING—to use a wooden stick, a rod, or the index finger to point where the concentrated energy is desired to go; the energy automatically runs from the mind down the arm to the stick or finger and the emotion behind the message sends it to its target. [**cf.** Appendix 2 FORMS-WITH-POWER, POINT-OF-FOCUS]

POINTING BONE—(Aborigine, Australia) an animal bone used to direct one's PSYCHIC ENERGY; bone is consecrated for and by the owner; serves as his amulet also; energy is accumulated in the head, decreed for a certain task, and sent down the arm and out the bone for psychic work and healing. [**cf.** HAND, PSYCHIC SHOCK ARTICLES, ROD]

POLARITY—1. the POSITIVE or NEGATIVE state in which a system or an entity reacts to a magnetic or electrical field, and constantly seeks to balance; 2. (esoteric) everything has a positive and a negative aspect which is necessary for balance; this balancing of opposites works simultaneously with vibrations and human thought; thoughts direct its course; (Ralph Waldo Emerson) "there is a current that knows its way"; 3. (biology) (**a**) vertical polarity: a human's right side is positive, his or her left side is negative; horizontal polarity: upper half of the human body is positive and the lower half is negative; this applies to all organisms; (**b**) female gender reflects the essence of earth, receptive and respected; male gender reflects the energy of the sun; (**c**) (Native American, Chippewa) men represent FIRE and AIR, and women represent EARTH and WATER; special cermonies are performed to work with these energies. [**cf.** LAW OF POLARITY Appendix 7, POLARITY Appendix 5]

POLARITY BALANCING—a method of HEALING in which touch is a gentle, manual, manipulative technique identifying specific energy points throughout the body; POLARITY is a strong foundation system that accentuates and compliments all touch therapies; used to evaluate and correct system malfunctions; the PRACTITIONER moves his or her fingers over the top of the body, a little above the body, with an attempt to create an energy circuit between the patient and the practitioner to develop a polarity of electromagnetic charge; a physical relationship that allows the vital energy to pass between patient and practitioner. **Syn.** POLARITY THERAPY. [**cf.** MERIDIAN LINES, TRIGGER POINTS]

POLARITY THERAPISTS—one who works with the MERIDIAN LINES of a patient to bring a balance of flow through these currents of energy; uses various methods to break up the blockage of flow.

POLARITY THERAPY—see POLARITY BALANCING.

POLARITY-REVERSING PHOTOGRAPHY—(Trevor James Constable) a camera attachment is used that will photograph invisible UFOs and invisible creatures of the atmosphere which cannot be seen with the naked eye; photographed while in an airplane. (Inconcl.) [**cf.** CRITTERS, CONSTRUCTS, ENERGY TRAIL, DEVIL'S HEAD]

POLLUX—see ST. ELMO'S FIRE and NATURE SPIRIT.

POLTERGEIST—(German *polte*, "noise, racket"; *geist*, "spirit") 1. a noisy, playful, quick-moving discarnate SOUL-MIND from the ETHERIC WORLD who manipulates physical objects in unexplainable feats; entity is difficult to perceive clairvoyantly but his or her presence can be felt; desires attention and that his or her EGO be fed; 2. displays his or her presence by doing mischievous, boisterous, harmful acts, or by doing playful, kind acts; poltergeist's feats defy all laws of GRAVITY; 3. uses the energy of a FOCUS in a home and can only perform when the focus is close by or in the vicinity; entity's time is either short lived or the poltergeist lies dormant until the focus rebuilds emotional energy; 4. entity is very persistent for attention while active and should be exorcised because he or she can become more and more destructive; poltergeist is usually young in age and can be dealt with similarly as one deals with a grammar school child. [**cf.** POLTERGEIST FOCUS, GHOSTOLOGY, POLTERGEISTRY Appendix 2]

POLTERGEIST CARRIER—see POLTERGEIST FOCUS.

POLTERGEIST FOCUS—a psychic individual whose ENERGY is being used by the POLTERGEIST to manipulate matter; individual has an exuberant amount of emotional energy at that time; individual is unaware their energy is being used and does nothing consciously to stir the poltergeist into action; the following states of consciousness have been known to make a person a good generator of this emotional energy: 1. one in a weakened mental state; 2. one in a highly emotional state; 3. teenager who has an explosive quality; 4. adolescent going through puberty; 5. child hiding sibling jealousy; 6. one who is going through a traumatic experience; 7. a nun or SAINT who stays in a very high spiritual state of consciousness; 8. one who resorts to this activity as a means of release of tension, instead of drinking or gambling; **9.** an untrained member of a PSYCHIC DEVELOPMENT CIRCLE. (Inconcl.) **Syn.** POLTERGEIST GENERATOR. [**cf.** VESTIBULAR LOCALIZATION, FAMULATION, POLTERGEISTRY]

POLTERGEIST GENERATOR—see POLTERGEIST FOCUS.

POLTERGEIST MISSILES—feats that have been recorded by the unexplainable phenomena occurring from a POLTERGEIST: teleportation of articles, flinging of mud or stones when none were around; objects being smashed from a person's hand and the person remains unharmed; stones whizzing through the air and landing like a feather; turning on and off household appliances; whistling, singing and talking. [**cf.** WATER WITHOUT CAUSE]

POLTERGEIST PK-ACTIVITY—(Russia) unwanted destructive physical actions that occur around the PK laboratory area. [**cf.** ATOPICAL LOCALIZATION, BORDER PHENOMENA]

POLTERGEISTRY—psychic activity in a home performed by a young, invisible, mischievous, quick-moving SOUL-MIND from the ETHERIC WORLD; desirous of attention and of having their ego fed; displays his or her presence by raps, bangs, scratching, teleportation of articles in freak ways that defy laws of GRAVITY, and sounds projected out in a subjective place with the location difficult to determine; temperature drops when feats are occurring; can happen in the homes of all types of personalities from saints to sinners; needs emotional energy from a person to perform; daily conversations regarding the entity's actions feed him or her energy, feed their EGO, and encourage performances; more easily occurable over fault lines, large quantities of water, and stress areas in the earth; poltergeist should be exorcised, as psychic feats can become dangerous, e.g., lighting a burner on the stove during the night, throwing articles with no warning; (do not confuse with GHOSTOLOGY). [**cf.** POLTERGEISTRY Appendix 2]

POLY—prefix meaning "much, many."

POLYGLOT MEDIUM—one whose etheric world GUIDE speaks or writes in a language unknown to the MEDIUM. [**cf.** XENOGLOSSY, ETHERIC SCRIPT]

POLYGLOT WRITINGS—written phrases that are foreign to the person receiving them; can happen in AUTOMATIC WRITING, TALKING-IN-TONGUES and INSPIRATIONAL WRITING. [**cf.** ETHERIC SCRIPT, POLYGLOTTOUS NEOPHASIA]

POLYGLOTTOUS NEOPHASIA—to talk-in-tongues in a construction of many languages as opposed to just one language. [**cf.** XENOGLOSSIA]

POLYGRAPH—an instrument used by law enforcement agencies for detecting when a person is lying; hooks-up to a person by attaching electrodes to the fingers; **Sim.** SKIN-RESISTANCE RESPONSE INSTRUMENT; passes a minute amount of electricity through the body that records several parts of the nervous system giving out information regarding the SUBCONSCIOUS MIND (subconscious mind cannot lie); now also used for psychic experiments, registering dreams, testing the SENSATION CONSCIOUSNESS in plants, and in telepathic messages (capable of revealing when the receiver gets the message, whether he or she recognizes the message or not). [**cf.** BIOFEEDBACK TRAINING Appendix 5, METABOLIC MONITOR, GSR]

POLYGRAPHIC MEDIUM—an AUTOMATIST capable of AUTOMATIC WRITING that has the characteristics of the ETHERIC WORLD INTELLIGENCE and not the MEDIUM. [**cf.** ETHERIC SCRIPT, BOOK TESTS]

POLYMODE—name of a joint project between Russia and the United States, a study of the BERMUDA TRIANGLE, the area in the Atlantic Ocean noted for ship and plane disasters and disappearances. [**cf.** DIMENSION-SHIFTING]

POLYSENSORY INCANTATION—to use the same term over and over again until it takes form and stabilizes in the mind; once the phrase has concentrated into a single-pointed thought, it then has the power it is intended for. [**cf.** CEREMONIAL MAGIC, INCANTATION, CHANTING, AFFIRMATION]

POLYSPIRIT SYSTEM—(Allan Kardec) the SOUL-MIND lives on in the invisible world on the plane level according to the soul-mind's level of growth; desires to communicate with earthlings. [**cf.** SPIRITUALISM]

POLYTHEISM—(Greek, "many" and "god") the concept that many gods exist and each one has a function to preside over various aspects of nature and life. [**cf.** MONOLATERALITY, NATURE SPIRITS, ANGEL KINGDOM]

POM—(Native American, Otami) a sweet scented incense burned by the Otomi Indians to clear the air before tuning in to the etheric world. [**cf.** INCENSE, VEGETATION MAGIC]

PONIK—(St. Eleuthere, Quebec, Canada) a long black monster with several bumps on his back; lives in the lake; rises and circles swiftly at intervals, unlike any other water animal. [**cf.** MONSTER ACTIVITY, DIMENSION-SHIFTING]

POOKA—(Ireland) also called **wee people**; see NATURE SPIRIT.

POP-PARAPSYCHOLOGY—material written and printed by authors who do not realize that PARA-PSYCHOLOGY is a vast subject and who have so little knowledge about it that their material is erroneous and disrespectable to such a highly-intelligent field of study; sometimes dangerous to the reader.

POP-UP—coined by June Bletzer; a much needed idea, reminder, or thought, brought to one's attention, unintentionally, in an unusual manner that has nothing to do with the need; occurs in important matters when one has a positive frame of mind; indicates an orderly universe that is always trying to be of service; e.g., to drop an eraser which rolls on the floor and when finding it under the desk, there is a lost bill; to meet a friend while shopping and in the conversation he mentions an important meeting the next day which you had forgotten. [**cf.** SCHEME OF THINGS, SYNCHRONIC-ITY, HUMAN OMENS]

POPPY—a flower which yields OPIUM; a symbol of SLEEP; has the properties to help soothe pain. [**cf.** BOTANE, POPPY SEED DIVINATION]

POPPY SEED DIVINATION—to throw the seeds of the poppy upon burning coals to determine a good or bad OMEN by the smoke that results; if smoke hangs around closely there will be little change in the situation, if it ascends to the heavens, that means good news in the future. [**cf.** ORPINE, WATCH PLANTS, HAZEL]

PORTENDER—a PSYCHIC who triggers omens to happen in his or her vicinity as a means of psychic information; nonhuman agencies show themselves in freak or unexplainable actitivies in the psychic's home or working environment; bring warnings of traumatic events or pleasurable events about to happen; executed by learning the skill, or an innate ability. [**cf.** OMEN, NONHUMAN AGENCIES]

PORTENT—a psychic indication that something is about to happen; portrayed by an irregular movement of an inanimate of living organisms; see OMEN. [**cf.** TOKEN INDICATION, NONHUMAN PROPHECY]

PORTRAIT CLAIRVOYANCE—to tune into the ETHERIC WORLD while painting one's portrait and paint around the portrait that which is perceived clairvoyantly; it is usually a GUIDE, the OUTER BAND, a deceased close friend, scene from the astral world or energies with forms unusual to earth forms; done in oils, charcoal, or pencil. [**cf.** INSPI-RATIONAL PAINTING, PSYCHIC ART]

PORTUNES—(England) a NATURE SPIRIT that is considered to be one of the earliest and tiniest known FAIRIES; has a wrinkled face; capable of DIMENSION-SHIFTING.

POSEIDON—an ETHERIC WORLD angel in charge of the seas.

POSICONTROL—a PSYCHIC EXPERIENCE that only comes when willed. [**cf.** CONTROLLED RELAXA-TION, DEVELOPMENTAL PATTERNS]

POSITIVE—1. (metaphysics) pertains to that which is good, correct, loving, pleasurable, according to the value system and self-worth of the one or ones making the judgment; a judgment of that which should have happened, or one was glad it happened. [**cf.** POSITIVE THOUGHT, NEGATIVE THOUGHT, POSITIVE PSYCHISM] 2. (electricity) the presence of an excessive amount of protons in a body. [**cf.** LAW OF POLARITY Appendix 7]

POSITIVE DAYS—(biorhythm) the first half of each CYCLE above the 0-LINE that designates when the body-organism will be functioning at its best for each particular cycle, e.g., during the days in the upper half of the PHYSICAL CYCLE one will need less sleep, (probably) have no physical accidents, and have lots of energy. (Inconcl.) [**cf.** CYCLES, EMOTIONAL CYCLE, BIORHYTHM CHARTS]

POSITIVE EXPECTATION—(healing) (O. Carl Simonton) to have confidence and to know without a question that the treatment and the PRACTI-TIONER or doctor that one has chosen, will bring about a HEALING: a necessary factor in all types of therapies, treatments, and medicines. [**cf.** CURA-TIVE EDUCATION, NEW-AGE PSYCHOLOGY, FAITH]

POSITIVE GREEN ENERGY—the energy that comes off the apex of a PYRAMID. [**cf.** NEGATIVE GREEN ENERGY]

POSITIVE MIND-SET—a STATE OF CONSCIOUSNESS whereby one locks her or himself into a framework of unity and cannot function well in life activities; to focus one's entire attention on one particular event, object, person or achievement, during every aspect of one's life, prevents this thing from happening too; the thinker binds the atoms to him or her and congests their flow; e.g., being wildly in love; experiencing excruciating pain; determination on winning a contest. [**cf.** ELEMENTAL, THOUGHT-FORMS]

POSITIVE PRIMARY ENERGY—(ufology) (pre-science) the force that comes from a spaceman to an earthling; corresponds to a human's ORGONE ENERGY and bioplasmic energy fields. (Inconcl.) [**cf.** BIOENERGETIC PROPULSION, ELECTROGRAVITIC WAVES, BIOPLASMA FORCE FIELD]

POSITIVE PSYCHISM—to perceive PSYCHIC INFORMATION as clear as physical perception; psychism that is determined, planned, and willed; begins in the head and enters the cerebro cortex; consciously directed and controlled by the psychic and perceived as objective and clear-cut. [**cf.** NEGATIVE PSYCHISM, LAW OF POLARITY Appendix 7]

POSITIVE THOUGHT—1. a thought instigated by an individual that is in accord with his or her good judgment, cultural values, moral standards, self-worth, or personal value system, and is therefore felt to be correct for "himself"; 2. correctness, properness, or rightness is in the eye of the beholder and will only affect the body and affairs of the beholder, even if he or she changes their beliefs in the future; positivity of thought works with the BELIEF SYSTEM at hand at the time of instigation; 3. personal POSITIVE THOUGHT keeps the body working on the "ongoing life process" and a lifestyle that will bring pleasure to the thinker; one judge's his or her own thoughts; 4. a positive thought for one may be an evil thought to another, depending upon one's belief system and stage of EVOLUTION. [**cf.** NEGATIVE THOUGHT, VALUES, HUMANISTIC PSYCHOLOGY]

POSSESSING GOD—(mediumship) see GUIDE and CONTROL. [**cf.** IMPERSONATION]

POSSESSION—1. (esoteric) (to hold occupancy either with or without rights of ownership); a compulsive INVASION by a low-grade ETHERIC WORLD ENTITY into a living earthling, whose organs he or she then exercises according to their own personality and according to their own will; (a) the evil-intentioned entity acts from within the borrowed body, substituting his or her own SOUL-MIND for the length of the seizure; (b) a new personality unfolds quickly which is incoherent and incalulable; facial features change and are sometimes grotesque; voice uses language uncommon to victim; body performs mannerisms and body gestures that are impossible to do in normal consciousness; (c) entity triggers strong irresistible impulses to perform acts contrary to the victim's personality; (d) seizure is not remembered when it is over; (e) if seizure is not caused by a brain tumor, it usually is a PSYCHIC EXPERIENCE; (do not confuse it with TRANCE IMPERSONATION which is executed to benefit mankind); 2. (Allan Kardec) state of absolute subjection to which a soul-mind in the flesh may be reduced by the imperfect spirits under whose domination he or she has fallen; 3. (clinical) a pathologically-altered state of consciousness, SPLIT PERSONALITY structure, hysterical MENTAL DISSOCIATION; an invasion of personality for evil intent; types of POSSESSION Appendix 2. [**cf.** FREE-FLOATING DREAD, HYPER-VENTILATION SYNDROME, ANXIETY ATTACK, OBSESSION]

POSSESSION OF A MEDIUM—the activity of an inferior ETHERIC WORLD ENTITY on the physical organs of a MEDIUM; entity consistently provokes involuntary bodily movements; enters at his or her discretion, e.g., a writing medium could be made to spontaneously write on a wall. **Syn.** CORPOREAL SUBJUGATION OBSESSION. [**cf.** POSSESSION, OBSESSION, DESIRED-CONTROL, CLOAK OF INSULATION]

POSSESSION OF MEMORIES—(Tibet) born with more knowledge than one could have acquired by normal means; believed to be earned and learned in past incarnations. [**cf.** GENIUS, ALL-ACCOMPLISHING WISDOM, COSMIC MEMORY]

POST-DEATH CONTACT—activity of a deceased person manifesting her or himself to a loved one in some psychic manner; e.g., occurs in a SLEEP PSYCHIC EXPERIENCE, as an APPARITION, or appears clairvoyantly to the psychic in a psychic READING: purpose is for the deceased to take care of unfinished earthly business or for the deceased to let the loved one know he or she is alive; instigated by the deceased person, and the emotional impact behind the message generates the procedure; after such a contact, the deceased person is heard of no more and the earthling is relieved and ceases to mourn. [cf. DISCARNATE ENTITY SLEEP EXPERIENCE, APPARITION, OMENS]

POST-MORTEM APPARITION—a deceased person showing her or himself clairvoyantly to a loved one within a few days after death, to either say goodbye or to let the loved one know he or she is still alive; the emotion behind the desire or the psychic bond between the two is the generator that facilitates the accomplishment. [cf. POST-DEATH CONTACT]

POST-VISION—to perceive clairvoyantly into the FOURTH DIMENSION, where the AKASHIC RECORDS are kept, and be allowed to look into an individual's past records; an earned privilege. [cf. PREVISION]

POSTCOGNITION—to psychically perceive flashes of one's past incarnations. Syn. BACK-IN-MEMORY, FAR-MEMORY. [cf. FORWARD-PK]

POSTCOGNITIVE TELEPATHY—to correspond mentally with a deceased person that one had known when the person was alive; occurs in two methods: earthling can be impressed with ideas from the deceased person or it can be a two-way exchange in which an inner-mind conversation is held. Syn. INNER-WORLD TELEPATHY. [cf. MENTAL TELEPATHY, DISCARNATE ENTITY SLEEP EXPERIENCE]

POSTHYPNOTIC SUGGESTION—a specific idea, suggestion, or command that is put into the subject's mind while in a hypnotic state, but is to be carried out when the subject is in a normal state of consciousness; e.g., "you will be able to remember names when introduced the first time"; "your BODY CHEMISTRY will change and heal itself," etc. [cf. DEEP STATE OF HYPNOSIS, INDUCTION, PRESCRIPTION]

POSTURAL INTEGRATION—(Wilhelm Reich and Gestalt therapy) a specialized form of bodywork, combining principles of connective tissue manipulation, ACUPRESSURE and movement awareness: its purpose is to increase the level of internal mind-body awareness and improve one's health. [cf. ROLFING, NEUROMUSCULAR MASSAGE]

POWDER OF PROJECTION—see PHILOSOPHER'S STONE.

POWER ABOVE—(Native American) THE GREAT SPIRIT; see GOD.

POWER CENTERS IN MAN—see CHAKRA.

POWER DOCTOR—(Ozark Mountains) nonevil PSYCHIC, herb doctor, DOWSER, LAYING-ON-OF-HANDS healer. [cf. MAGNETIC HEALING, PSYCHIC HEALING]

POWER OF MIRACULOUS ACTION—(Tibet) to make one's self larger or smaller than a normal person; to go into another dimension and disappear to physical eye vision and then reappear again; these two skills seem to be compatible to the same entity; e.g. NATURE SPIRITS have this ability. [cf. DIMENSION-SHIFTING, SHAPE-SHIFTING]

POWER OF THE GAZE—a self-directed, penetrating, MAGNETIC FLUID emanating from a person's eyes that can be used to influence other persons, living organisms, and inert objects; staring intensely and steadily has an effect on that which is being stared at making it behave as starer intends; e.g., to spell a person with a transfixed glare; snake will stare at a bird until it has the bird hypnotized. [cf. ON-THE-SPOT-HYPNOSIS, SPELLED, MAGNETISM]

POWER OF THE THUNDER GOD—(Native American) a TALISMAN made into a bow with a lancehead at one end, that has the properties to bring a flow of PSYCHIC ENERGY to protect and guide the Indian. [cf. BEAR PAW, HOLED-STONE, TOTEM]

POWER-POINTS—(prescience) areas on the earth's surface that are highly energized or magnetized and seem to attract UFOs. (Inconcl.) Syn. POWER HOUSES. [cf. MONSTER ACTIVITY, SIGHTINGS]

POWER SHORTS— an abrupt stoppage of PSYCHIC ENERGY in which the psychic is knocked out, mentally distraught, or physically harmed, for minutes or for days; psychic is discharged if a noise, bodily contact or something goes wrong in the environment during her or his use of PSYCHISM; the psychic recovers, but it is an unpleasant and dangerous experience; can occur in mental psychic skills, physical phenomena and in magical rituals. [cf. ATMOSPHERE SHIELDING, CLOAK OF INSULATION]

POWER SYSTEM—(ufology) the pulsation and vibrations in the atmosphere that are manipulated as a source of power by the AEROFORMS and aerocraft using air as their habitat. [cf. ENERGY TRAIL, ETHER SHIPS, ELECTROGRAVITIC WAVES]

POWER-OF-THE-WORD—1. to make a demand, a command, or a declaration, either verbally or silently, with such meaningful EMOTION that it manifests immediately, or in the immediate future; intense emotion makes a snap in one's consciousness which abruptly changes one's lifestyle; e.g., a woman pounded her fist on the stove and declared in rage "I wish I did not have to cook any more"; her stove blew up and the family ate out for two weeks; the owner of a laundry business made a remark with anger,"I wish people would be kind enough to return our wire hangers," within a week she had so many hangers she did not know where to put them; 2. to read written words in a book or other sources and perceive the attitude of the writer while writing the material; to tune into the reason for writing the book that is not in the words per se; e.g., one could feel so much jealousy that he or she would have to put the book down; (do not confuse with PSYCHOMETRY in which one handles the book deliberately to perceive something about the author). [**cf.** WORDS-WITH-POWER, LAW OF THOUGHT Appendix 7]

POWERS OF DARKNESS—see EARTHBOUND ENTITIES and DENSITY.

POWWOW HEALING—(Native American) to use the hand in adjunct to prayer in communication with the GREAT SPIRIT in an effort to remove physical distress in man or animal. [**cf.** LAYING-ON-OF-HANDS, AFFIRMATIONS]

POWWOWER—(Native American) a healing PRACTITIONER who received POWWOW HEALING instructions from a relative; includes specific prayers and a method of channeling healing energy. [**cf.** PSYCHIC HEALING]

PRA—(Sanskrit) prefix meaning "forward or progression."

PRABHAMADALA—(Hinduism) the aureole of fire perceived clairvoyantly around people; represents the rhythm of the universe; see AURA.

PRACTICAL PSYCHOMETRY—to discern PSYCHIC INFORMATION about an individual by holding an article which the individual contacts frequently; article is pressed on the forehead, SOLAR PLEXUS, or held between the palms of the hands of the psychic; it is like tuning into an extension of the individual through the psychometrist's hands to the individual's SUBCONSCIOUS MIND; eyeglasses, wristwatch, wedding ring or items worn daily are more easily read; the collar of a dog is used to read for the dog; emotional vibrations impregnate that which one wears or handles and hold fast if the same

vibrations are repeated; vibrations reveal the owner's health, work, characteristics, inclinations, problems of the past or present; (future events cannot be detected as vibrations do not impregnate until they happen). [**cf.** PURE PSYCHOMETRY, EMANATIONS]

PRACTITIONER—one who knows and understands his or her profession and practices it proficiently; name used extensively today by alternative healers, spiritual healers, conjure men, psychic healers, professional psychics, etc. [**cf.** PSYCHIC HEALING]

PRAN-VAYU—(Yoga) movements of air in one's body produced by chanting a MANTRA, manifesting SHAKTI within. [**cf.** FAYU, SOUNDS-WITH-POWER]

PRANA—1. (Sanskrit) absolute energy; to breathe, to live; the life principle; the psycho-electrical field manifesting in humans; 2. **(Vedic) the sum total of** PRIMAL ENERGY from which all mental and physical energy has evolved; manifests in the form of MOTION, gravitation, MAGNETISM, and sustains physical life, thought force, and bodily action; 3. (Western) the principle behind life, a primordial absolute energy found everywhere; a vital force behind all vibrations under the control of the brain; 4. (Krishna) a primal COSMIC ENERGY outside the ELECTROMAGNETIC SPECTRUM and all other force systems known to official science. (Inconcl.) **Syn.** SPIRIT, VITAL LIFE FORCE.

PRANA AURA—see SOUL-MIND AURA.

PRANA LEAKAGE—damage or tear in the ETHERIC DOUBLE of an individual whereby vital pranic energy slowly leaks out; leaves the person incessantly tired, unable to close PSYCHIC DOORS, and with difficulty in coping with the world; (physical checkups will not detect this); damage or tear is brought on by malicious hypnosis or SPELL, a physical nervous breakdown, misuse of one's PSYCHIC ENERGY, or brought over from another INCARNATION. [**cf.** PSYCHIC PROTECTION, LIKE ATTRACTS LIKE, KARMICALLY SELF-GENERATED]

PRANA-IZED—to energize oneself with concentrated PRANA from the air by special breathing exercises. [**cf.** KUNDALINI, MEDITATION]

PRANAYAMA—(Hinduism) see VITAL LIFE FORCE.

PRANAYAMA BREATH—1. (Hinduism, Yoga) a special breathing exercise that stimulates the KUNDALINI and helps it rise; gives proper oxygenation, circulation, and relaxation of nerves, revitalizes one; 2. (Vedas) a method of controlling the PRANA, the breath and vital organs contributing to the awakening of the SHAKTI, by rhythmically breathing; produces DETACHMENT and LIBERATION from bondage. [cf. PRANAYAMA, SPIRIT, BREATHING]

PRANA ETHER—an invisible life force in the blood stream and other physical organs; see SPIRIT. [cf. NADIS, MAGNETIC HEALING]

PRANIC HEALING—see SPIRIT HEALING.

PRAYER—1. a continuous string of words either spoken or silent, shouted or sung, that sends power into the ethers in accordance with the emotion and faith behind the words; executed as: 1. an invitation or request to the MONAD to come from within the person in order to make changes in his or her life; 2. a method of invoking entities in the etheric world for church services and mediumistic phenomena; 3. a protection for an EXORCIST; 4. suggestions to a DEITY of one's choice with an expectation of change happening somewhere as a result; 5. four categories: **(a) low prayer;** (1) begging prayer—"please do this for me, please"; (2) petitioning prayer—"I will stop needling her if you give me a job"; (3) demanding prayer—to set forth a list of demands for God to fulfill; **(b) ethical prayer**—to ask a favor for someone else; **(c) prayer of faith**—to affirm words of Truth—"I am a perfect child of God and therefore inherit healthy lungs"; **(d) pure prayer**—(Hinduism) to pray to the Lord for the sake of the Lord. [cf. AFFIRMATIONS, TRUTH, PRAYER BEADS]

PRAYER BEADS—(Eastern) beads put together in necklace form to keep a count of the number of times the MANTRA is said silently; number of beads differ with disciplines; there is a special way of rolling the bead over the finger each time the mantra is repeated; made from a varied group of substances; e.g., SANDALWOOD, AMBER, etc. [cf. ROSARY, MANDALA]

PRAYER GROUP—an organized group of people who meet regularly to send mental telepathic help to others; mental telepathic messages tend to heal physical bodies, bring harmony in relationships, and bring abundance; mental energy sent in unison is more effective than a single message; research shows words change BODY CHEMISTRY, change attitudes and lead one to prosperity. [cf. LOVE LINE, MENTAL HEALING, MENTAL TELEPATHY]

PRAYER POWER—a strong thought-form built by a group of people saying the same words in unison, with intentions to change an outward manifestation; energy of the thought-form will hit its target and be effective to the degree of impact; impact depends upon the expectancy, emotions, and faith of the group as a whole; marching, clapping, and singing the words increases the thought-form in intensity; a spiritual tool that could enable humanity to shape their future history. [cf. OPERATION PRAYER POWER, THOUGHT-FORMS, MENTAL TELEPATHY, MENTAL HEALING]

PRAYER TEAM—many persons who pray singularly in their homes, forming a steady stream of MENTAL ENERGY for others that need help; the leader receives information of the one needing healing, prays in private, relays the information to the second link in the chain who prays privately and relays it to another link; this is continued for a designated time; usually managed by telephone. [cf. PRAYER POWER, MEDITATION, PETITIONS, VISUALIZATION]

PRAYER WHEELS—1. (Tibet) two cylinders inscribed with mantras, one on top of the other; each turns individually or they turn simultaneously; both the mechanical repetition of the mantras and the turning movement convey a BLESSING; the individual spins them and if it turns to the right, it means good news; if it turns to the left it is bad fortune; utilizes belief in REINCARNATION; used for sun worshippers; a meeting of the minds of the monks; 2. (Hinduism, Buddhism) a drum that spins: while one turns the prayer wheel, an INCANTATION is repeated silently; spinning gives power to the spoken word, putting one in tune with BRAHMA. [cf. PRAYER BEADS, MANTRA, AMULET, POWER-OF-THE-WORD, RHYTHM]

PRE—(Latin) prefix meaning "before, prior to, in advance of, early."

PREARRANGED HARMONY—(Baron Gottfried Wilhelm von Leibnitz) theory: MATTER cannot act by itself but needs spirit to move it. [cf. VITAL LIFE FORCE, CONSCIOUSNESS]

PREBIRTH—pertains to the idea that people existed in this planet or another, prior to the present life. [cf. REINCARNATION, KARMA]

PRECAUTIOUS RESISTANCE—(prescience) to persistently form a MENTAL ENERGY field around one's self to block out PSYCHIC INFORMATION until one has time and is in an area with compatible vibrations to perceive it accurately and handle it; as mankind evolves and the PINEAL GLAND opens in the majority of persons, mankind will have to know how to block the mind and protect the physical body against inferior and dangerous vibrations floating in the ethers. [cf. SPLODGER, HUMAN BATTERIES]

PRECEPTOR—an ETHERIC WORLD INTELLIGENCE who takes charge of the activity when the MEDIUM is in a state of TRANCE; blocks out anxious etheric world entities who want to be known to earthlings and are not advantageous to the phenomena; brings the phenomena to the SEANCE and gives instructions to the SITTERS so that no physical or mental harm comes to the medium. **Syn.** CONTROL, GUIDE. [cf. DOCTOR TEACHER, INNER BAND]

PRECESSION OF THE EQUINOXES—period of approximately 26,000 years; equal to the time required for a complete revolution of the equinoxes. **Syn.** GREAT YEAR, PLATONIC YEAR.

PRECIPITANT—a MEDIUM who has the BODY CHEMISTRY that emanates ECTOPLASM while asleep or in a DEEP TRANCE state, strong enough to be used by his or her etheric GUIDE to paint or write material that can be used for their mundane benefit. [cf. PRECIPITATION Appendix 2]

PRECIPITATION—to permit an ETHERIC WORLD INTELLIGENCE to use the ECTOPLASM from one's body to produce PSYCHIC INFORMATION or exquisite art on paper or canvas with no bodily movements by the MEDIUM; takes place during sleep, or deep trance; tools are left close to the medium; writing tool is levitated by the etheric intelligence and used swiftly on the material provided; medium is unaware of the phenomena taking place until in the awake state. **Syn.** DEPOSITED MATTER. [cf. Appendix 2 for kinds of PRECIPITATION]

PRECIPITATION PAINTING—to produce beautiful paintings on canvas without the use of one's hands, arms or feet; MEDIUM has the proper BODY CHEMISTRY to synchronize with the ETHERIC WORLD INTELLIGENCE while in a sleep or TRANCE state; canvas and painting tools are provided by the medium; intelligence uses the ECTOPLASM that emanates from the medium to levitate the brushes and paint an exquisite picture; medium may use the paintings to sell for a livelihood; painting is executed with superspeed and is sometimes still wet

when the medium awakens; medium is not necessarily an artist. [cf. ETHERIC SCRIPT, SPIRIT ARTISTS, SLATE WRITING, LEVITATION]

PRECIPITATION WRITING—to produce written information or symbolic pictures on paper without moving one's arms, hands, or feet; earth tools are provided beforehand; MEDIUM synchronizes with an ETHERIC WORLD INTELLIGENCE while in a DEEP TRANCE state, asleep, or giving a lecture; intelligence uses the ECTOPLASM emanating from the medium's body to levitate the pencil, descend upon the paper, and write; a message is produced more swiftly than a human can think and write; medium's physical body is not used; information is beneficial to the medium, to sell, to use as a lecture, or to inform others about the ETHERIC WORLD. **Syn.** DIRECT WRITING. [cf. PRECIPITATION Appendix 2, PRECIPITANT, LEVITATION]

PRECOG—a psychic who specializes in perceiving information pertaining to the future of people, one's self, or the nation; refers to the content of the PSYCHIC INFORMATION, not the manner in which it is perceived. [cf. COGNITION, PROPHECY, PRECOGNITION]

PRECOGNITION—(parapsychology) to perceive mentally a NON-THOUGHT or a gut feeling regarding the future of one's self, other people, or civilization; happens randomly or is willed; (J. B. Rhine) "a psychic awareness of the objective probabilities relating to the future state of the system"; one of the three aspects of ESP. **Syn.** PREDICTIONS. [cf. PSI TASKS, PREDICTIONS]

PRECOGNITIVE CLAIRSENTIENCE—to perceive psychically information regarding the future of one's self, others, the weather, the nation or the world; one feels it in one's bones, or one's stomach, just knows, or senses an uneasiness following one; (personal) data comes as a warning so that one can prepare for a highly emotional event, pleasant or unpleasant; (civilization, weather) the insecure feeling follows one before the event (sometimes a few days) and when the event occurs the psychic's uneasiness is relieved immediately; an inborn ability which is difficult to cultivate. [cf. CLAIRSENTIENCE, PRECOGNITION, PROPHECY, CLAIRVOYANCE]

PRECOGNITIVE DREAM—to perceive future events regarding one's self or one's involvements, during sleep; a PSYCHIC EXPERIENCE occurring between REM states; comes to prepare one for an

485

emotional event that is going to happen (after perceiving it during sleep one is less shocked when it comes and thus thinks more clearly to handle the emotional event); usually happens clairvoyantly or clairaudiently. [**cf.** SLEEP EXPERIENCES, COGNITION, PSYCHIC EXPERIENCE DURING SLEEP]

PRECOGNITIVE REMOTE VIEWING—(laboratory) 1. to mentally perceive the target before it is selected for the experiment; 2. to mentally perceive an event before it happens. [**cf.** COGNITION, PREDICTION, REMOTE VIEWING]

PRECOGNITIVE TELEPATHY—to perceive a thought regarding what another person in one's presence is going to do shortly before he or she does it, or the topic of a conversation beforehand. [**cf.** COGNITION PSYCHISM Appendix 2]

PRECOGNIZANT—pertains to knowledge of or an attitude toward the future that is not learned information; a spontaneous mental awareness of events before they happen. Usage: "That must have been a precognizant thought because I don't remember learning about that." [**cf.** PRECOGNITION, PROPHECY, PRECOGNITIVE]

PRECONSCIOUS—1. an awareness occurring prior to the development of CONSCIOUSNESS in mankind; 2. a consciousness mankind recognizes to be a part of the self, containing all the memory of the different VIBRATIONAL FREQUENCIES the atoms of his or her body have participated in; now formed in the SUBCONSCIOUS MIND and minutely filtering through to the CONSCIOUS MIND constantly; 3. (Pir Vilayat Inayat Khan) a DIVINE NOSTALGIA innate in all people and things. 4. (Sigmund Freud) below the level of consciousness, between the ID and the EGO; a fourth part of humanity's access to intelligence; 5. (Gestalt) the background out of which the figure emerges, meaning that only a portion of one's potential is available; 6. a storage of every memory, every item of knowledge, that can be summoned at will with difficulty; 7. duplicate AKASHIC RECORDS in the HEART-SEED-ATOM that filters through into consciousness without conscious awareness of it. [**cf.** SUBLIMINAL, INSTINCT, CELL MEMORY]

PRECONSCIOUS LEVEL—(biofeedback training) an awareness of change to the alpha level before the subject can consciously feel the experience of the change, while going though a session in BIOFEEDBACK TRAINING. [**cf.** AVERAGE EVOKED RESPONSE, ANXIETY STATION]

PREDICT—to give information about the future of one's self, other persons, personal conditions, the nation, etc.; received through various psychic skills. **Sim.** PROPHESY. [**cf.** SEERS, FORECAST PROPHECY]

PREDICTINOSIS—to diagnose before the onset of a disease as a part of a WELLNESS program; the body shows that disease is forthcoming if habits continue; can be detected by: scanning with the palm of the hand, deciphering POLARITY by a PENDULUM, using REFLEXOLOGY on one's feet, observation of one's personal plant, and reading one's aura. [**cf.** CURATIVE EDUCATION Appendix 5]

PREDICTION—information perceived psychically that pertains to the future of one's self, family, friends, country, or nation, discharged at will or spontaneously; information about pleasant, benevolent, or unfortunate, subordinate events; predictions can be changed by deliberate methods of MENTAL PSYCHISM or actual mundane attention to the situation; frequently given as a preparation for the recipient who will soon undergo an emotional experience; predictions come through DREAMS, CLAIRVOYANCE, CLAIRSENTIENCE, ASTROLOGY, SCRYING, VOICE TRANCE, OMENS, or INSPIRATIONAL THOUGHT. **Sim.** PROPHECY. [**cf.** PORTENDER, PRECOGNITIVE CLAIRSENTIENCE, CLAIRVOYANCE-IN-TIME, GUIDE]

PREDICTOR—a psychic who receives information, spontaneously or willed, regarding the future of oneself, others, current conditions, nature, or civilization; method of perceiving varies with psychic's ability. **Syn.** PROPHET. [**cf.** PREDICTIONS, CLAIRVOYANCE]

PREEMINENT PSYCHIC—(Tibet) one who remembers former existences and has the ability to trace lineage of prior human entities. [**cf.** REINCARNATION, EARTH MEMORY, FAMILY KARMA]

PREESTABLISHED HARMONY—(Baron Gottfried Wilhelm von Leibnitz) theory: the universes are a vast pattern of interrelated monads containing the inherent characteristics relating to the pattern, and an image of the universe within themselves. [**cf.** MONAD, TOTALITY]

PREEXISTENCE—theory: the SOUL-MIND has lived many lives on this planet or another planet before this INCARNATION.

PREFLIGHTING—(radiesthesia) to check the POLARITY of one's body periodically, as to one's health, with the PENDULUM or DOWSING ROD: ill health causes the pendulum to swing in the opposite direction for the polarity of that area of the body, and detects a symptom before it manifests in the physical body. [**cf.** POLARITY BALANCING, PENDULUM POWER]

PREGRESSION—to stretch one's STATE OF CONSCIOUSNESS indefinitely into the future along one's own time-track to observe what is in store for one's self; utilizes the theory that mankind lives in a multiple time system; accomplished by HYPNOSIS, after a deep MEDITATION, or in a prolonged BIOFEEDBACK TRAINING session. [**cf.** MULTIPLE DIMENSION]

PREHOUSE-CLEANING—to eliminate negative vibrations from inside a new home, before it is occupied; executed by blessings, prayers, chants, burning incense, and cultural rituals by groups or by individuals. **Syn.** HOUSE-SWEEP. [**cf.** EXORCISM Appendix 2]

PREHUMAN KINGDOMS—theory: in an evolutionary process, human beings belonged to the mineral, vegetable, and animal kingdom before they evolved into the human being species. [**cf.** EVOLUTION, INVOLUTION]

PRELUCID DREAMING—to debate with one's self whether one is awake or dreaming while the dream scenario is being shown. [**cf.** LUCIDITY, CONFRONT AND CONQUER]

PREMONITION—to be forewarned about a future event through a sensation of anxiety or anticipation within the physical body; see PRECOGNITIVE CLAIRSENTIENCE. [**cf.** PROPHECY Appendix 2]

PREMONITORY DREAMS—to perceive an accident, death or environmental tragedy in a psychic experience during sleep, which does eventually happen. [**cf.** PREDICTIONS, PSYCHIC EXPERIENCES DURING SLEEP]

PREMONITORY SIGNS—to be forewarned by an OMEN about a coming traumatic experience, a tragedy in one's life, another's life or the environment; omen can be human or nonhuman; e.g., a picture falling off the wall indicating that the person in the picture would soon be in trouble. [**cf.** PROPHESY, HUMAN OMEN, PORTENDER]

PRENATAL RECALL—to remember under hypnosis one's awareness, understanding, and feelings when in the womb and during physical birth; used in PSYCHOTHERAPY: there is an awareness at those times that is held by the SUBCONSCIOUS MIND which influences feelings during one's life. [**cf.** BIRTH TRAUMA, ASTRAL THREAD]

PRE-PHYSICAL BODY—see ETHERIC DOUBLE.

PREPHYSICAL ENERGY—see VITAL LIFE FORCE.

PRESAGED—see PREDICTION.

PRESCIENCE—1. foresight; to be aware and knowledgeable of that which will be and is in the future scheme of things; 2. events that happen but science denies they can happen; 3. (clinical) answers to scientific problems through psychic energies; 4. (ancient Mesopotamia) divination to predict the future by using entrails of dead animals, fire, smoke, stones, plants, tree whispers, serpents, dreams, etc.

PRESCRIPTION—carefully worded suggestions selected by the HYPNOTHERAPIST for the individual who is undergoing therapy; suggestions are designed to change the subject's lifestyle, personality, BODY CHEMISTRY or attitude; presented after the induction period when subject is in a deep ALTERED STATE OF CONSCIOUSNESS; e.g., "you will be able to retain what you read and use it appropriately from this time on." [**cf.** INDUCTION PERIOD, SEMI-STAGE HYPNOSIS]

PRESEANCE PHENOMENON—to experience electrical energy passing through the body hours before the SEANCE is to take place preparing the body for seance phenomenon; e.g., MEDIUM emits sparks from the hair without combing it; medium feels as if he or she were holding opposite poles of a battery. [**cf.** MATERIALIZATION, TRANCE]

PRESENT—(multitime) an ever-moving point separating one's past and future; where/when one's immediate past experience anticipates the continuance of one's experiences into the immediate future; present earth life is where/when the future and past "meet" in the multiple time continuum. [**cf.** ALL-AT-ONCE, ETERNAL PRESENT]

PRESENT MANIFESTED—(Native American, Hopi) indicates the "past," in their knowledge of the theory of MULTITIME. [**cf.** COEXISTENCE, ETERNAL NOW]

PRESENT MANIFESTING—(Native American, Hopi) the future in the Hopi's theory and understanding of space/time continuum. [**cf.** ETERNAL PRESENT, INTROJECTION]

PRESENT-CENTEREDNESS—(Gestalt) to live in the present awareness and be responsible for it; the "here and now" practicability. [cf. FULFILLMENT, HOLISTIC BIOLOGY, GESTALT PSYCHOLOGY]

PRESENTIMENT—see PREMONITION and PROPHECY.

PRESENTIMENT MEDIUM—one who is frequently impressed by his or her ETHERIC WORLD INTELLIGENCE with intuitive knowing regarding future events; specializes in professional predictions. **Syn.** PROGNOSTICATION, SOOTHSAYER, SEER. [cf. PROPHECY Appendix 2]

PRESERVING OF SACREDNESS—(Tibet) (death) to preserve a dead body by covering it with gold; performed only by a high order of priests in a sacred ritual. [cf. HALL OF INCARNATIONS, COFFIN RITUALS, DEATH CONSCIOUSNESS]

PRESLEEP—see HYPNAGOGIC.

PRESSAGE—a PSYCHIC MESSAGE about the future. [cf. PROPHECY, PREDICTIONS]

PRESSURE POINTS—see ACUPUNCTURE POINTS.

PRETA-LOKA WORLD—(Tibet) levels in consciousness close to the earth plane; here confused soul-minds float randomly and discarded astral shells coagulate in ghostly forms; both are earthbound and haunt earthlings. **Syn.** BARDO, ASTRAL PLANE. [cf. HAUNTING, ASTRAL SHELL, GHOSTS, EARTHBOUND]

PRETAS—(Tibet) unhappy and confused soul-minds and astral shells who haunt earthlings because of their desire to recapture materialistic habits, or because they are held captive by earthlings who overly mourn. [cf. HAUNTING, ASTRAL SHELL, DENSITY, ASTRAL PLANES]

PRETEMATURALISM—see OCCULTISM.

PRETERSENSUAL—see PSYCHIC.

PREVIOUS INCARNATE—(Tibet) an old soul who is raised in his earthly incarnation with prestige and is given help to accomplish his mission; old soul is proved in childhood as he recognizes articles and places of his past incarnations and proves that he has accomplished more knowledge than usual. [cf. OLD SOUL, AGENTS OF THE LORDS OF KARMA]

PREVISION—to see psychically into the MENTAL PLANE and CAUSAL PLANE of the ETHERIC WORLD to predict what will happen in the future of earth; transacted by a well trained CLAIRVOYANT. [cf. FUTURISTS, TRANSFORMATION]

PREVORST—see PSYCHIC.

PRICKING—(Europe) to prove one is PSYCHIC by psychially stopping the bloodflow and pain of another person who is pricked with a needle. [cf. MENTAL PSYCHIC HEALING Appendix 2]

PRIEST MAGICIANS—(China) psychics who were trained to have dominion over the forces of NATURE; able to divert rivers, command lightning, and imprison winds in jars. [cf. Appendix 2 ATMOSPHERE CONTROL]

PRIESTS—1. (prior to Renaissance) had the ability to receive information through the ETHERIC WORLD INTELLIGENCES from higher realms; 2. those who have reached a rank of priesthood through their stage of development; earned in the EARTH PLANE or in ETHERIC WORLD; a step in ANGELHOOD and once earned, it cannot be taken away.

PRIM—prefix meaning "primitive, first."

PRIMA MATERIA—(esoteric) 1. basic force that permeates living organisms; the source of all vital activity, thought, feeling, perception, and movement; name for PRANA: 2. a substance that is common and easily obtainable but only recognized by the initiates; presumed to be a primeval slime; 3. used in the first steps of the alchemists in their work of transmutation. (Inconcl.) **Syn.** AKAM'S SLIMY EARTH. [cf. ALCHEMIST, IMMORTAL DRAUGHT, AZOTH]

PRIMAL BEING—(Egypt) see TOTALITY.

PRIMAL ENERGY—crystallized power in the ATOM, individualized, yet connecting all of TOTALITY; third basic energy in the universe; generator of two lesser energies, physical and psychical. (Inconcl.) [cf. MATTER]

PRIMAL GERMS—1. basic seed from which all creation of the MUNDANE WORLD came; 2. the governing principle within every seed. [cf. MONAD, CELL PERCEPTION]

PRIMAL GROUND—see TOTALITY.

PRIMAL PAINS—coined by Arthur Janov; basic core pains of a baby or child that have been repressed or denied by CONSCIOUSNESS: normal feelings and physical needs that were not attended to in infancy and still hurt because the needs have not been allowed expression or fulfillment; the original emotional hurts upon which neuroses are built in later-life, irrespective of the type of neuroses; e.g., "I am not loved, I have no hope of being loved when I am really myself"; thoughts of the baby when he or she cried because of being hungry or wet and was not attended to. (Inconcl.) [cf. PRIMAL POOL, PRIMAL THERAPY, BLOCKS, GRAPES]

PRIMAL POOL—the constant build up of the original unpleasant pain in a child who represses it in his or her body, as leaders and parents unintentionally ridicule, ignore or push the child beyond their limits. [cf. PRIMAL THERAPY]

PRIMAL SCREAM—coined by Arthur Janov: "a process of overthrowing the neurotic system by a forceful upheaval": to unlock BLOCKS in body tissue stored from unpleasant childhood experiences by isolation of the individual; person eventually releases their tension by yelling and what is yelled out is an expression of the cause of that block; isolation consists of denial of all contacts; i.e., sound, light, human voice, learnable material and civilization. (Inconcl.) [cf. PRIMAL THERAPY, PAST-LIVES THEORY]

PRIMAL THERAPY—(Arthur Janov) a treatment that changes inhibitable processes which prevent the fluid access to certain brain structures; a process of unlocking stored pain of the body muscles, put there unconsciously by unpleasant, unresolved, childhood experiences; treatment prevents this emotional pain from exerting itself in unwanted behavior or mental disorders in adult life. [cf. PRIMAL SCREAM, PSYCHIC PAIN, PRIMAL POOL]

PRIMARY CLEAR LIGHT—(Tibet) the ultimate light: dazzling, colorless, and unbelievably strong; ONENESS with oneness; NIRVANA: TOTALITY; reflection of light glimpsed when one makes his or her TRANSITION. (Inconcl.) [cf. NEAR DEATH EXPERIENCE]

PRIMARY CYCLE—humanity's basic cycle for progression and growth is seven sun years; each period must be completed. (Inconcl.) [cf. CYCLES Appendix 5]

PRIMARY ENERGY—see VITAL LIFE FORCE.

PRIMARY ENERGY GESTALTS—see TOTALITY.

PRIMARY PERCEPTION—coined by Cleve Backster; an innate consciousness of each life system designed to protect itself; a deeply imbedded, invisible sensing mechanism within all organisms; faculty that senses ALL THERE IS without a choice of what it desires to sense, therefore, is constantly tuned into the basic laws of creation and can instinctively feel what is suitable or harmful for its particular structure; begins in cellular life and continues upward through animal life and into the human. (Inconcl.) [cf. MONADOLOGY, HUNCH, MINPSI, OVERALL CONSCIOUSNESS, MATTER, VIBRATION]

PRIMARY PSI PERCEPTION—an invisible sensory workshop within all of nature's organisms (including humans), which assists them to monitor their environment and to communicate with other organisms; an inner communication of the happening of any one thing in nature which affects all other things, regardless of distance or source; e.g., 1. the plant senses a spider is going to build a web among its leaves before it happens; 2. a cow can predict a storm and takes steps to protect itself; 3. parents perceive when an offspring is in trouble; 4. (Cleve Backster) a transmission of thought between plant and human as the plant reacted to the human striking a match; plant was HOOKED-UP to a polygraph instrument and displayed unusual feedback. (Inconcl.) [cf. PRIMARY PERCEPTION]

PRIMARY WAVES—(psychometry) deeply imbedded VIBRATIONS in an object or area caused by human emotions; emotional vibrations interpenetrate and surround an object or area; these are intensified by repetition of the role the object plays in the environment or by a traumatic emotional event; vibrations impregnate the DNA of the atoms in the object with these memories; the psychic tunes into these vibrations with their hands and fingers to perceive information regarding the object, the area, or the environment and any living organisms involved. [cf. SECONDARY WAVES]

PRIME-AGE—(clairvoyant vision) age that one appears to be as he or she returns in a PSYCHIC MESSAGE; deceased entity chooses the age that has meaning to them; presents the image he or she wants to remember; e.g., one who died as an elderly person would not present themselves with gray hair and a cane, but chooses the age of forty when they had accomplished a great deal and still looked young. [cf. DREAMS, CLAIRVOYANT, APPARITION, DISCARNATE ENTITY]

PRIME-INCARNATION—one of the many lives the GUIDE spent on earth that he or she chooses to use

489

when presenting themselves to an earthling. [**cf.** CONTROL, INNER BAND, OUTER BAND]

PRIMEVAL—1. (parapsychology) the atoms vibrating in space making the essence of heaven and earth; 2. (science) refers to the very first forms of life on planet earth.

PRIMEVAL ATOM—(capitalized) the concentrated, superdense, superbly intelligent seed that exploded in the beginning creating the BIG BANG THEORY. [**cf.** COSMIC CREATIVITY, COSMIC EGG, DIVINE INTELLIGENCE]

PRIMEVAL TONGUE—(Emmanuel Swedenborg) the language of the Angels used by early Spiritists to communicate with the etheric world intelligences; faded into disuse in mid-nineteenth century; a universal language that anyone can use for ANGEL communication. [**cf.** EYE-LANGUAGE, CRYSTALLINE LEVEL]

PRIMITIVE BRAIN—see SUBCONSCIOUS MIND.

PRIMORDIAL SUBSTANCE—the ELECTRON and ATOM (and similar smaller particles) used as the base or essence of all other substances. (Inconcl.) [**cf.** AETHER, BIOCURRENTS]

PRINCE OF DARKNESS—the ETHERIC WORLD INTELLIGENCE that is in charge of those in the DENSITY who are ready for help and ask for help. [**cf.** INFERNAL REGIONS]

PRINCIPALITIES—ETHERIC WORLD INTELLIGENCES who work in a graded order of helpers to carry out the divine plan. [**cf.** ANGEL HIERARCHY, DOCTOR TEACHER, MASTER]

PRINCIPLES OF MAN—seven invisible bodies of the human organism which interpenetrate and extend from the human body during earthly incarnations; each body has a personal function at its vibrational frequency level and a function as the whole; even though mankind is unaware of their interpenetration and extension, each reacts to their development unconsciously; each body plays a part in the other bodies evolvement; the earthly body is the slowest and most dense body; as one evolves he or she will shed one body at a time; this is not universal because the rate she or he sheds each body is up to their choice of choices; the overgoal of these seven bodies is to complete the MONAD (the finest, most subtle body), at which time he or she will blend into TOTALITY; each body does not necessarily take the form of a human INCARNATION;

bodies can be perceived by clairvoyants at times. **Syn.** BODIES OF MAN. [**cf.** SOUL-MIND, PLANES, MENTAL BODY, CAUSAL BODY]

PRINT-OUTS—(biofeedback training) paper charts attached to the EEG instrument which record variances in line patterns that show different states of consciousness of the subject who is HOOKED-UP; the mind energy makes the markers move back and forth on the charts to indicate tangible evidence of various states of consciousness. [**cf.** BIOFEEDBACK TRAINING Appendix 5, BRAIN RHYTHM CYCLES PER SECOND]

PRITHIVI—see SQUARE.

PRIVATE SITTING—to receive a personal psychic READING from a professional reader in privacy, where one can ask for counsel and have problems worked out. [**cf.** PSYCHIC INFORMATION, PSYCHIC COUNSELING]

PROBABILITY—(psi tasks) abbr. p or P; the statistically analyzed results of a particular test as opposed to the estimate of prior likelihood that chance alone could produce a particular result. [**cf.** CHANCE AVERAGE, COINCIDENCE, CHANCE LEVEL]

PROBABLE SELF—(Seth) a counterpart of a human being existing in the ETHERIC WORLD; an entirely new entity with similar interests as the human being, who are eager to help or communicate with the human being. **Sim.** OUTER BAND. [**cf.** INNER BAND, GUIDE]

PROBLEM SOLVING STATE OF CONSCIOUSNESS —a personal level of awareness for each PSYCHIC where the psychic knows that the psychic information which comes through at this level can be depended upon; psychic learns to recognize this level by the similarity of mind or body sensations; psychic tries to reach this level of consciousness each time he or she tunes into the etheric realm. [**cf.** HOMING IN, INNER AWARENESS]

PROCARNATION—to go forward into a life one has not experienced as yet; to see an episode from a future life one will eventually live; theory: multitime. [**cf.** CELESTIAL SEEING]

PROCEDURAL IRREGULARITIES—(laboratory) an experiment that does not inform the subject of the real purpose of the experiment or what type of psychic skill he or she should be performing; objective is that he or she can perceive this psychically. [**cf.** BLIND MENTAL PSYCHISM, DISPLACEMENT,

DOUBLE-BLIND EXPERIMENTS]

PROCESS MEDITATION—see GUIDED MEDITATION.

PROFOUND WAKEFULNESS—a level of consciousness where psychic information comes to the awareness of the psychic, is understood and remembered by the psychic, yet the body, emotions, and CONSCIOUS MIND are quiet and inactive. **Sim.** PASSIVE VOLITION. [**cf.** BIOFEEDBACK TRAINING, PSYCHIC DOORS, PROBLEM SOLVING STATE OF CONSCIOUSNESS]

PROGNOSTICATION—see PREDICTION.

PROGRAMMED BIOCOMPUTERS—(human) 1. a hidden system in the human mind that controls the feeling nature, actions, and thinking which one does not have to process from scratch; 2. belief that the human NERVOUS SYSTEM contains the history of all of one's past lives; 3. reactions to one's past thoughts and actions that seem to come instinctively. (Inconcl.) **Syn.** SOUL-MIND, SUBCONSCIOUS MIND. [**cf.** MEMORY BANK, COMPOUND OF CONSCIOUSNESS]

PROGRAMMER—(biofeedback training) one who determines the type of training for the biofeedback session; gives such rewards for subject's accomplishments during program session that subject can know of their progress without breaking his or her level of concentration by trying to absorb information from the dials. [**cf.** BIO-STAT, GSR, EEG]

PROGRAMMING—(mind activity) to impress suggestions upon the subconscious memory cells without interference by the CONSCIOUS MIND; impressed without the knowledge of the subject; accomplished by the following methods: 1. HYPNOSIS; 2. SLEEP-LEARNING; 3. disguised BRAINWASHING; 4. utilization of the shock state; 5. (SILVA METHOD) utilizing the subjective level of the mind. (Inconcl.) [**cf.** HYPNOTHERAPY, SUGGESTIONS, ON-THE-SPOT-HYPNOSIS]

PROGRAMMING DREAMS—see INCUBATION DREAMING, DREAM CONTROL.

PROGRAMMING THE SUBCONSCIOUS—(radiesthesia) to consciously tell the SUBCONSCIOUS MIND which way it should swing the PENDULUM for *yes* and *no;* 2. to tell the subconscious mind what the DOWSING ROD is looking for. (Inconcl.) [**cf.** RADIESTHETIC SENSE]

PROGRESSIVE LYCEUMS—schools in the INVISIBLE WORLD.

PROGRESSIVE RELAXATION—abbr. P.R.; method used in the training sessions with biofeedback instruments to teach the subject to achieve relaxation. [**cf.** BIOELECTRIC SIGNS, FREQUENCY ANALYSIS, FIXED-BRAIN-WAVESTATE]

PROJECT BLUE BOOK—records of twenty-two years of investigations by the United States Air Force regarding living organisms, intelligent beings, moving vehicles in the outer atmosphere, and other UFOs. [**cf.** ASTROPHYSICS, COSMIC ENTITY]

PROJECT MAGNET—a five-year study of UFOs by Wilbert B. Smith resulted in the Smith Coil which is reported to be able to pick up voices of living beings in outer space; secret of the coil was structured in a caduceus winding; sponsored by the Canadian Government. (Inconcl.) [**cf.** UFOLOGY Appendix 5]

PROJECTED ENERGY—(laboratory) to put intense concentration on a target and let the THOUGHT ENERGY go with as much force as possible, still aiming at the target. [**cf.** DIRECTED-THOUGHT TRAINER, BEAMED ENERGY]

PROJECTION—to free and send a part of the body to travel into the etheric world planes; there are three basic methods: 1. MENTAL PROJECTION or SOUL TRAVEL; 2. ASTRAL PROJECTION, OUT-OF-BODY-EXPERIENCE; 3. ETHERIC PROJECTION.

PROJECTION ART— to be able to take an astral flight at will. [**cf.** ASTRAL PROJECTION Appendix 2]

PROJECTION BY-SYMBOL—(I Ching) to mentally proejct one's mind into the astral planes to help decipher the hexagrams of an I CHING reading; a symbol of a door is used to pass through in consciousness so as to reach the astral plane that associates with each HEXAGRAM in the reading; the results are combined with the I Ching text. **Sim.** SOUL TRAVEL, MENTAL PROJECTION. [**cf.** I CHING]

PROJECTION-INCLINATION—(astral projection) to feel that one is elsewhere other than in one's bed falling sleep; dream research has found that some people astrally project at the onset of sleep, in the HYPNOGOGIC STATE. [**cf.** SLEEP EXPERIENCES, BORDERLINE STATE]

PROJECTIONIST—the person who is making the flight in an ASTRAL PROJECTION. [**cf.** ASTRAL ROUTE, ATTRACTION-ACTION-REACTION]

491

PROJECTIONS OF THE UNCONSCIOUS—(Carl Jung) to perceive visions of a previous life on earth. [cf. BACKWARD PSI, BACK-IN-MEMORY]

PROLONGED-CALLS—(electronic voices) a lengthy telephone conversation with a deceased person lasting for a half hour or more; the dead person does not admit he or she is dead and the receiver of the call does not remember the person has died until after the conversation is over. (Inconcl.) [cf. CARRY ON TALKING, BREAK-THROUGH]

PROLONGED JOGGING—twenty minutes of constant, rhythmic running or jogging can provide the preliminary step to receiving a PSYCHIC MESSAGE; serves the same purpose as a MEDITATION period prior to opening PSYCHIC DOORS; e.g., the answer to one's question in the mind before jogging often surfaces at the end of the exercise; longer periods of running or jogging make one feel detached from the body and clears the mind as in meditation; caused by the rhythmic movements of the exercise. (Inconcl.) [cf. MOVEMENT-FOR-ALTERED-CONSCIOUS-NESS]

PROP—(Tibet) the physical body.

PROPHECY—(Greek, "speaking before") 1. (ancient) a collective word meaning a PSYCHIC MESSAGE; one's principle concern in that time was the future so almost all psychic information pertained to the future of the country and its leader; recognized to be an inspiration from God; 2. (current) any information received through a means of psychic sensitivity that pertains to future conditions of a nation, the world, authoritative world figure, civilization, or other large units; (as opposed to personal events); comes spontaneously or willed; information can be warnings, or pleasant news; 3. prophecies usually come true because they are MASS KARMA and involve change in attitudes on a large scale; the KARMA is already made from years in the past and the psychic sees when it will become RIPE KARMA; 4. prophecy pertains to the contents of the psychic information, not the method of perception; prophetic skills are: CASTING OF LOTS, CLAIRVOYANCE, CLAIRSENTIENCE, PSYCHIC EXPERIENCES DURING SLEEP, ASTROLOGY, SCRYING, VOICE TRANCE, OMENS, etc. **Syn.** NABHI, MENTAL-TRAVEL-IN-TIME. [cf. PREDICTIONS, PROPHET]

PROPHESY— to indicate beforehand; to psychically tune into the future. [cf. PROPHECY]

PROPHET—(Greek *pro*, "for"; *phetes*, "to speak") a human spokesman for an etheric world DEITY; a PSYCHIC who perceives information regarding the future of nations, world leaders, weather conditions, world economics, and other phases of civilization; perceived in a variety of psychic skills; often hired by governments as a professional prophet; information received spontaneously or willed. **Sim.** PREDICTOR. [cf. OMENS, CLAIRVOYANCE, DREAMS, SEER]

PROPHETIC DREAM—to perceive an emotional event clairvoyantly during sleep and the event happens at a future time; VISION is distinguished from a DREAM as it is vivid, clear and authentic to the time period in each detail; it is easily recalled and remembered; the clairvoyant psychic experience occurs between REM dream states. [cf. PSYCHIC EXPERIENCES DURING SLEEP, DELTA WAVES]

PROPHETIC MEDIUM—a MEDIUM capable of receiving precise, distinct revelations of future events from their etheric world guides, with the impression to make this known to other people. [cf. CHANNELING, SEMITRANCE]

PROPULSION—1. (astral projection) the force that drives the ASTRAL BODY forward; 2. (ufology) the movement of creatures and vehicles in the atmosphere by manipulation of the primal element. [cf. DYNAMIC TRANSITIONS, ELECTRONIC FINGER]

PROSERPINE—see ETHERIC WORLD.

PROTEAN—living organisms that have a natural ability to change themselves into various shapes and forms with rapid speed. [cf. SHAPE-CHANGING, ALEURANTHROPY]

PROTEAN SOUL—see ASTRAL BODY.

PROTEAN SPECTRES—entities of the lower astral planes can be grotesque, distorted or floating around in confusion; seen in the HYPNOGOGIC STATE, in ASTRAL PROJECTION, or when first entering the astral world upon death; believed that one's negative thoughts attract them. [cf. DENSITY, SEA-OF-FACES]

PROTECTING GENII—an entity in the etheric world who offers a service of protection to an earthling who has earned it through his or her moral code. **Syn.** PROTECTOR. [cf. INNER BAND, DOORKEEPER[

PROTECTIVE SUPERSTITION—(foreign cultures) to make an article capable of protecting one's self;

an immense amount of MENTAL ENERGY is projected onto the article (gem, or homemade TALISMAN), which is then consecrated for the purpose of protecting its owner from negation; article is placed in an area that needs protection and will ward off negative vibrations. [**cf.** AMULET ENERGIZING, TALISMAN[

PROTECTOR—(mediumship) an ETHERIC WORLD INTELLIGENCE who shows her or himself as an American Indian and whose function is to protect the MEDIUM; serves in the INNER BAND from birth to death; reads one's AURA and helps prevent accidents for the individual if KARMA permits. [**cf.** OUTER BAND, GUIDE]

PROTO—prefix meaning "first."

PROTOANALYSIS—an exercise in the Arica discipline that helps one become more aware or more sensitive. [**cf.** MENTAL PSYCHIC PROCESSES Appendix 2]

PROTOPLASM—**1.** the living matter of all vegetable and animal cells and tissues; **2.** see ECTOPLASM.

PROTOPLASMIC CONSCIOUSNESS—**1.** (biologists) a consciousness in every living CELL that differs from another cell; the awareness of a single-celled creature lacking a NERVOUS SYSTEM; **2.** (esoteric) a STATE OF CONSCIOUSNESS where there are no boundaries between SELF and not-self; entity has no personal identity but environment and self as one; e.g., the feelings of a newborn baby. **Syn.** SYMBIOTIC CONSCIOUSNESS. [**cf.** TOTEM CULT, SYMPATHETIC MAGIC]

PROTOTYPE TELEFLASHER—(laboratory) a training device for PICTURE TELEPATHY; a simple box with a light inside that flashes behind the picture to be sent in the telepathic practice; flashing light aids the sender in focusing his or her attention on the picture; receiver in another area finds it easier to receive. (Inconcl.) **Syn.** DIRECTED-THOUGHT TRAINER, TELEPROMPTER. [**cf.** TELEPATHY, MENTAL TELEPATHY]

PROVED INCARNATIONIST—(Tibet) one who earns the right to have his third-eye opened surgically and can thus see into the ETHERIC WORLD at all times; earns this right by correct living and understanding of past incarnations; the open third-eye brings special privileges in this life. [**cf.** FLASHBACK, GERM PICTURES, HEREDITY]

PROVIDENCE—(esoteric) the ordering of events by the "laws" of the creator; an energy and principle that determines the course of events which humanity has influenced by their thinking and acting; events correlate with mankind's past and present activities whether recognized or not; laws prevail throughout all eternity regardless of mankind's interest in or knowledge of them. [**cf.** CASTING OF LOTS, SYNCHRONICITY, MONADOLOGY, RADIESTHESIA]

PROVOKING—(possession) the process in an EXORCISM rite that brings the etheric world tormentor to the surface in order for the EXORCIST to get him or her out of the possessed body. [**cf.** POSSESSION]

PROXIMAL LOCALIZATION—poltergeistry phenomena that occurs in close proximity to the POLTERGEIST GENERATOR; moving of articles and disturbances of matter happening close by and only in the presence of the human poltergeist generator. **Syn.** VESTIBULAR PHENOMENA. [**cf.** DISTALLY LOCALIZATION, FAMULATION]

PROXY SITTING—**1.** (seance) message from the medium's ETHERIC WORLD INTELLIGENCE control for a sitter who is absent from the circle; **2.** one who comes to a PSYCHIC for a reading for another person who cannot make it; psychic tunes into the absent client through the friend or relative. [**cf.** PHYSICAL MANIFESTATIONS/MISCELLANEOUS Appendix 2]

PSE—abbr. for PSYCHOLOGICAL STRESS MONITOR; see same.

PSEUDO—prefix meaning "false."

PSEUDODEATH—to experience the process of DEATH and be declared clinically dead but then recover to life and remember experiencing the death process. (Inconcl.) **Syn.** DEATHBED EXPERIENCE. [**cf.** DEATH SCIENCE Appendix 2, DEATH WISH, DEATH TRANCE, CLOSE BRUSHES]

PSEUDOELEMENTAL—a NATURE SPIRIT made of the same substance as the pure nature spirit only reduced in quality, working with destructive intent; a model of the DEVIL; a detached shadow of the PURE ELEMENTAL; when perceived clairvoyantly, appears with coarser hair, longer horns, vicious looks and a peculiar odor. [**cf.** NATURE SPIRITS Appendix 3, ANTI-PAN, GOBLINS, IMPS, SATYR]

PSEUDOMATTER—(Seth) the weaker areas of the

physical world, where the electromagnetic energy centers in the invisible world are less charged than other places. [cf. MATTER, ANTIMATTER, PSEUDOPHYSICAL IMAGES]

PSEUDOPHYSICAL IMAGES—(Seth) temporary physical beings made from heavily charged repressed energy projected from one's own fears. [cf. PSEUDOMATTER, ELEMENTAL, THOUGHT-FORMS]

PSEUDOPOD—(materialization seance) ectoplasmic hands materialized in a SEANCE room that could perform unbelievable, unexplainable things, that normal hands of a person cannot do; fingerprints of hands were checked against the deceased person claiming them and found to be same fingerprints; e.g., (documented) hands took a violin out of a locked cage without using a key and played a tune on it. [cf. PARTIAL MATERIALIZATION, FULL MATERIALIZATION, ECTOPLASMIC HAND]

PSEUDORODS—temporary psychic structures found in a SEANCE room if medium is well trained; structures are round or square beams of energy made from the condensation of the bodies of the SITTERS and MEDIUM; when energy reaches a certain point in its condensation, it forms auric rods that extend from the medium to the area of the performance. (Inconcl.) [cf. ECTOPLASMIC WISPS, ECTOPLASMIC CORD]

PSEUDOTECHNICAL INSTRUMENTS—devices that detect energy generated by the human mind; e.g., the DOWSING ROD varies in its swing speed and size of circle of each person's head it is held over when measuring human energy. (Inconcl.) [cf. BUILT-IN DIRECTIONAL SENSE, PENDULUM POWER]

PSI—1. (Heron) (the twenty-third letter of the Greek alphabet) arbitrarily chosen like the English X to represent an actual unknown quantity; psychic phenomena are brought to pass by an undefined force that is designated by the specific term *psi*; 2. (J.B. Rhine) first coined it to mean ESP, and later to mean PK and ESP; "a general term to identify a person's extrasensorimotor communication with the environment"; 3. currently popular to mean PSYCHIC.

PSI ABILITY—abbr. for PSYCHIC ABILITY; represents a quality within a person to transmit and receive PSYCHIC ENERGY, understand its meaning, know how to keep it under control, and will it to surface under proper conditions; an inborn quality or a quality capable of developing; see Appendix 2

for differentiating between PHYSICAL and MENTAL PSYCHIC SKILLS.

PSI BLOCK—vibrations of heaviness surrounding an individual that prevents another person from psychically tuning into that person's electromagnetic field; caused deliberately and unconsciously; e.g., one who hides personal information about her or himself normally is difficult to psychically tune into because of this atmosphere of heaviness that protects them which he or she built up over the years. (Inconcl.) [cf. ATMOSPHERE SHIELDING, BOOMERANG PSI, ANTI-PSI]

PSI DEXTERITY—(psi tasks) combination of manual manipulation and the exercise of PSI so the apparatus or objects are affected in a way that cannot be entirely accounted for in terms of normal sensorimotor activity. (Inconcl.) [cf. CASTING OF LOTS, NONHUMAN-PK, NATURE-PSYCHOKINESIS]

PSI ENERGY—see PSYCHIC ENERGY.

PSI EXPERIMENTER EFFECT—(psi tasks) theory: the needs, wishes, expectancies and attitude of the experimenter have effects on the target at times and interfere with the subject's ability. [cf. BIDIRECTIONALITY OF PSI, EXPERIMENTER BIAS]

PSI GIFT—inborn psychic talent of some kind; pertains to any of the many psychic skills that one is born with, as opposed to the psychic skills one practices many times to accomplish. [cf. CALLED PERSON, CONTAGIOUS ENTHUSIASM]

PSI HEALING—see PSYCHIC HEALING.

PSI JUNGLE—mind of an untrained, uncontrolled PSYCHIC who experiences psychic information and psychic energy that comes indiscriminately and contains inferior and incorrect information, which is of no benefit. [cf. UP-FOR-GRABS, CLOAK OF INSULATION, IN PROTECTION]

PSI LEAKAGE—(psi tasks) thoughts and attitudes of the experimenter that are picked up telepathically by the PERCIPIENT that influence him or her correctly or incorrectly. [cf. DISPLACEMENT, FINGERPRINTS OF PSI]

PSI MEMORY—(psi tasks) conclusion: there may be a higher mental process that is involved with both PSI and memory. [cf. SUBCONSCIOUS MIND, BIOCOMPUTER, AKASHIC RECORDS]

PSI PARTICLES—(Russia) PSYCHIC ENERGY.

PSI PLASMA—(Andrija Puharich, 1962) see VITAL

LIFE FORCE.

PSI PRACTITIONER—a psychic using her or his skills in a practical manner as a part of their vocation; one who uses PSYCHISM in mental and physical therapeutic means.

PSI RELATIVITY—the ability to interpret the symbols that come through as psychic information, to physical world activities. [**cf.** SYMBOLS, FORCED CHOICE, CONCEPTUALIZATION]

PSI RESISTANCE—the strong emotional attitude of nonbelief in PSI abilities or nonbelief in one's own ability hinders the result of the experiment in accuracy or no result at all. [**cf.** SHEEP AND GOATS EFFECT, HOMING IN]

PSI RETRIEVAL PROCESS—to try "too hard" to anticipate the TARGET results binds the PSYCHIC ENERGY to one's self and nothing happens. [**cf.** IMPRESSION, IMAGINATION, APOPSI]

PSI SCALE—a record of PSI TASKS; used to study individuals that are high in psi achievements to see if they differ in any way from other people. [**cf.** ESP]

PSI SCAN—combination of a psychic and spiritual look at a patient's physical symptoms; employs two psychics, one the leader, one the scanner; scan includes mental and emotional processes. (Inconcl.) [**cf.** LEADER, ETHERIC DIAGNOSING]

PSI TASKS—term used for "experiments" at Rhine Laboratory, in Duke University where psychic research has been conducted since the early 1930s; studies began with ESP, later added PK, and currently studies include PRECOGNITION, SURVIVAL, PHENOMENA, and others.

PSI TRAILING—(S. Feather, J.B. Rhine) a study of animals who track down lost owners regardless of distance and length of time involved. (Inconcl.) [**cf.** ANPSI Appendix 2]

PSI-CONDUCIVE STATE—1. (psi tasks) a condition of the experimental area, in which the attitude of the experimenter and subject are desiring for the PSYCHIC ABILITY to flow. (Inconcl.) 2. (parapsychology) an acute state of subconscious alertness brought about by MEDITATION for at least ten minutes beforehand; this quiets the body, emotions and CONSCIOUS MIND to bring the psychic to a higher level of AWARENESS, and helps him or her maintain a neutral and passive attitude. (Inconcl.) [**cf.** MENTAL PSYCHIC PROCESSES Appendix 2]

PSI-FAVORABLE STATES—(laboratory) frame of mind or the STATE OF CONSCIOUSNESS that produces the most hits in PSI testing. (Inconcl.) [**cf.** ESP, SHEEP AND GOATS EFFECT, EXPERIMENTER PATTERN, EXTRACHANCE]

PSI-FIELD—1. (psi tasks) an unseen mechanism within a person that brings them PSYCHIC INFORMATION. (Inconcl.) 2. (esoteric) the THIRD-EYE AREA, the SUBCONSCIOUS MIND, the SYMPATHETIC NERVOUS SYSTEM, the electromagnetic vibrations (AURA) around the PSYCHIC, and the electromagnetic vibrations around the object, animate or inanimate, that the psychic tunes into. (Inconcl.) [**cf.** SUPERCONSCIOUS MIND, SOUL-MIND]

PSI-HIT—(psi tasks) to psychically perceive the correct answers in experiments, using Rhine cards, or in other laboratory experiments. [**cf.** CHANCE AVERAGE, DECLINE EFFECT, CONCLUSION-LEAPING]

PSI-HITTER—(psi tasks) one who is able to hit the target in psychic experiments more frequently than the principle of chance. [**cf.** EXPERIMENTER EXPECTANCY, ESP SHUFFLE, GESP]

PSI-INPUTS—(laboratory) PSYCHIC INFORMATION coming into mind activity; usually refers to TELEPATHY, PRECOGNITION and PK. **Syn.** NON-THOUGHTS. [**cf.** PSYCHIC ENERGY]

PSI-INTERACTIVE BIOMOLECULES—abbr. PIBs; the connection between the intelligence in atoms of the body and intelligence of TOTAL INTELLIGENCE.

PSI-MEDIATED EXPERIMENTER EFFECTS—(psi tasks) PSYCHIC INFORMATION, other than the target, flowing into the mind of the subject that interferes with finding the experiment target; e.g., while subject is tuned into more subtle vibrations he or she perceives the experimenter thinking about the movie he or she saw, and this is not the target; subject is tuned in, but to the wrong channel. (Inconcl.) **Syn.** MISPLACED PSI. [**cf.** SHEEP AND GOATS EFFECT, SPLODGER]

PSI-MEDIATED INFORMATION—(psi tasks) PSYCHIC INFORMATION.

PSI-MEDIATED INSTRUMENTAL RESPONSE—abbr. PMIR; to unconsciously scan the environment with one's sensory and psi mechanism and respond to this outer stimuli spontaneously and unintentionally. [**cf.** CLAIRSENTIENCE, SPONTANEOUS PSI, INTUITION]

PSI-MEDIATED VEHICLE—(psi tasks) a symbol, article, or object that is used to aid the PERCIPIENT to bring information received by ESP methods, into conscious awareness; e.g., staring at a picture. [**cf.** MANDALA, CANDLE FLAME]

PSI-MEDIATOR—(laboratory) one who received the PSYCHIC INFORMATION; serves as an intermediary between the experimenter and the psychic energy field; see PSYCHIC.

PSI-MISSING—(laboratory) to avoid the target one is trying to hit more often than would be expected if only chance were operating. [**cf.** ESP, RHINE CARDS, HOMING IN, GOING-TO-LEVEL]

PSI-OPTIMIZATION—(psi tasks) to have optimistic feelings regarding ESP results in making no effort to obtain maximum efficiency. [**cf.** ARTIFICIAL SYMBOLS, APPERCEPTION, BASIC LIMITING PRINCIPLES]

PSI-ORG ENERGY—orgone energy used for psychic information or psychic skills; see VITAL LIFE FORCE.

PSI-PHENOMENOLOGY—(J.B. Rhine) the study of TELEPATHY, PRECOGNITION and PK.

PSI-Q—measurement of PSYCHIC ABILITY according to a human made scale. [**cf.** HEAVENLY STUFF, EXTINCTION PROCEDURE]

PSILAND—the fields of ESP and PK.

PSILOCYBIN MUSHROOM—(Mexico, "god's flesh") a mushroom containing psilocybin, a hallucinogen endowed with special properties that can depersonalize one and bring him or her to a state of ILLUMINATION and produce higher states of consciousness if used correctly. (Inconcl.) **Syn.** TEONANACTL. [**cf.** FLY AGARIC, DIVINE INTOXICATION]

PSIONIC MACHINE— an instrument that depends on the PSYCHIC ENERGY of a person in order to function; e.g., BLACK BOX, DOWSING ROD, DIRECTED-THOUGHT TRAINER, and other devices that make mind itself the controlling force. (Inconcl.) [**cf.** ENERGY MATRIX MACHINES, ENERGY MATRIX]

PSIONICS—1. coined by John W. Campbell (1956) see VITAL LIFE FORCE; 2. pertains to PSYCHIC INFORMATION and PSYCHIC FORCE (does not include mediumship energy or information); 3. name given to RADIONICS in the DeLaWarr Laboratory in England and in Russia; 4. applied METAPHYSICS, PARAPSYCHOLOGY, ancient art of MAGIC.

PSITRON—(laboratory) (Dobbs) particles of imaginary mass capable of interacting with particles of real mass; imaginary mass is not subject to frictional loss of energy when they travel across physical distance; emit into the psychic brain, impinging on the neurons that are a state of unstable equilibrium causing a PSYCHIC MESSAGE. **Sim.** ZOETHER.

PSYCALISTHENICS—a set of exercises that produce balance between the body, minds, and emotions combining breathing and conscious body movements. [**cf.** DANCE THERAPY, GYMNASTIC MEDICINE]

PSYCH—prefix meaning 1. "psychological, psychology"; 2. "breath, spirit, soul, mind"; also spelled **psycho.**

PSYCHE—pronounced *si ki*; (Greek, "breath, life force, soul, spirit," or "mind" (distinguished from the body); 1. (Charles Fillmore) the SOUL in its many earthly expressions encased in a physical body, in its failures and its successes; 2. (Carl Jung) soul having four levels: ego consciousness, PERSONAL UNCONSCIOUSNESS, COLLECTIVE UNCONSCIOUS, and psychological level; 3. structure of a person as a motive force; 4. one type of emanation of the One UNIVERSAL CONSCIOUSNESS; 5. a mechanism that serves the whole body. [**cf.** SPIRIT, SPIRIT, PSYCHIC ENERGY]

PSYCHE CONSCIOUSNESS—see PSYCHIC CONSCIOUSNESS.

PSYCHED-OUT—(slang) to be psychoanalyzed or analyzed by another person which is disturbing to the one being analyzed, who feels he or she is being victimized.

PSYCHED-UP—1. to be in a more receptive condition to perceive psychic impressions than usual, both mentally and physically; 2. to be favorably excited over what just transpired regarding universal Truths or soul-mind development, e.g., after a PSYCHIC DEVELOPMENT CIRCLE it is difficult to come down to a beta level; 3. to doubly insulate one's self with a coat of protection, then reach an alpha level so people around one will not be as disturbing as anticipated. [**cf.** CLOAK OF INSULATION, GROKKING IN FULLNESS, EMPIRICAL ENERGY]

PSYCHEDELIA—(J.C. Gowan) a short-lived ALTERED STATE OF CONSCIOUSNESS characterized by a sudden spasmodic, transitory ILLUMINATION in which the individual is transformed by the contents of the group's auric unconsciousness; individual appears to be in full control and in full awareness at the time. (Inconcl.) [cf. GROUP HYPNOSIS, GROUP ELEMENTAL]

PSYCHEDELIC CLAIRVOYANCE—to experience beautiful colored lights of a high vibrational frequency passing through one's CLAIRVOYANT vision during MEDITATION; colors are unlike earth colors, indescribable by present language. [cf. THETA STATE OF CONSCIOUSNESS, COLOR, DISTINGUISHING WISDOM, GOING WITHIN]

PSYCHEDELIC CONSCIOUSNESS—AWARENESS when taking a mood trip from RECREATIONAL DRUGS.

PSYCHEGENICS—(*psyche*, "mind"; *genics*, "discipline"); a discipline that studies effects which can be produced through, with, and by the mind to enhance human potential.

PSYCHIATRY-PSI—TELEPATHY, PRECOGNITIVE, RETROACTIVE-PK, and PK.

PSYCHIC—1. (Greek *psychiokos*, "psyche, soul, or that which is mental"); (a) (Tibet) vital or secret; (b) sensitivity of the mind and body to subtle vibrations; (c) (Edgar Mitchell) pertains to PARANORMAL events and abilities that cannot be explained in terms of established physical principles; (d) a collective adjective to encompass all types of mental and physical SUPERNORMAL skills; 2. one whose total MIND/BODY organization tunes into the more subtle VIBRATIONAL FREQUENCIES and who is able to decipher this sensitivity for practical purposes; accomplished through strong DESIRE, KNOWLEDGE, and practice, or through birth from a past INCARNATION; (a) total mind/body organization requires the proper BODY CHEMISTRY, NERVOUS SYSTEM, GLANDS, electromagnetic field SURROUND, and ability to recognize unusual information impressed as non-thoughts on the MIND and SOLAR PLEXUS processes; (b) one who can keep a NEUTRAL MIND, intensify concentration on a FOCAL POINT, or enter an ALTERED STATE OF CONSCIOUSNESS at will, as the supernormal skill demands; (c) one capable of having his or her SUPERCONSCIOUS MIND and SUBCONSCIOUS MIND function beyond the limits of the third-dimensional plane submitting information to the CONSCIOUS MIND for interpretation; (d) (present usage) majority of mediums are also psychic so the term *psychic* is used to include both a medium and psychic. **Syn.** ORACLE, CHANNEL, SENSITIVE, Appendix 3 PSYCHIC. [cf. non-thought]

PSYCHIC ABILITY—to sense, to understand, to interpret, and to use for practical purposes, a force that enters in and emanates out of the body and mind without the use of the five SENSES; force is sensed in the CONSCIOUS MIND and SOUL-MIND, hands, and SOLAR PLEXUS; is proejcted out of same; ability can be accomplished through the strong emotion of DESIRE, study, and practice or can be inborn and brought under control with practice. [cf. PSYCHIC Appendix 3]

PSYCHIC ACUPUNCTURE—(magnetic healing) to go over the meridians of the patient's body with the palms of the hands a little above the body; hands work with the auric pattern to make a BODY CHEMISTRY change in the AURA; helps the body normalize and heal itself. **Syn.** ACUPRESSURE. (Inconcl.) [cf. MERIDIAN LINES, ACUPUNCTURE POINTS]

PSYCHIC ANNALS—a PSYCHIC EXPERIENCE so vivid and clear that one does not forget it, as if it were meant to be a record. [cf. ECSTASY, HAND OF GLORY, INNER WISDOM]

PSYCHIC ARTS—1. pertains to all or many psychic skills grouped under one general heading whether they are performed through the SUBCONSCIOUS MIND, the SUPERCONSCIOUS MIND or through MEDIUMSHIP; not limited to one special type; see Appendix 3 for TYPES; 2. (singular) to paint or draw through mediumship or inspirational means. [cf. INSPIRATIONAL THOUGHT, AUTOMATISM]

PSYCHIC ASSEMBLY—a gathering of psychics and mental mediums in a public building to serve the public for a small fee, by giving individual psychic readings which usually last ten or fifteen minutes. **Syn.** PSYCHIC FAIR. [cf. ABSENT SITTING, COME INTO YOUR VIBRATION, DÉJÀ VU]

PSYCHIC ATMOSPHERE GAUGE—(future science) a gauge that registers the psychic intensity in the ATMOSPHERE; measures the minutest electrical impulses, their varying frequencies and duration, coming to the PSYCHIC from outer stimuli; also picks up dangerous PSI immediately. [cf. BIOLOGICAL GENERATOR, CATAPSI, CONFERRING OF POWER]

PSYCHIC ATTACK—1. the transference of NEGATIVE energy between two persons through the use of telepathic skills; the sender deliberately sends his or her feelings and thoughts of hate, jealousy, harm, resentment, etc., their confused situation, their sickness, or their unpleasant circumstances; receiver feels uncomfortable, ill, or in a negative attitude and does not always understand that it is not of his or her own doing; easily transferable if there is a strong bond of love or hate between the two psychic persons and if one leaves their PSYCHIC DOORS open all the time, or after a long encounter in which the two interacted, i.e., to spend all day together makes a transfer of emotions, attitudes, a headache, etc., easily transferable that same evening; to test unpleasant, uncomfortable body or emotional feelings that appeared for no apparent reason, silently repeat the following: "I send it back to where it came from"; the feeling will leave immediately if it does not belong to the victim; (do not confuse with a HEX in which more than telepathic skills are employed). (Inconcl.) [cf. TELEPATHY, LIKE ATTRACTS LIKE, EMPATHY CLAIRSENTIENCE, UP-FOR-GRABS, CLOAK OF INSULATION] 2. the entering of an ETHERIC WORLD ENTITY from the DENSITY into an individual's AURA because of a leakage; the entity frequently haunts the victim and encourages him or her to do and say things that he or she is not likely to do and say normally; victim does not realize it is not his or her own doings; leak in the aura can be caused from an individual low on society's scale of morality, from negative confusion, from constant degrading of one's self, from a long state of depression, or from a nervous breakdown; an EXORCIST, MAGICIAN, or well-grounded PSYCHIC can dislodge the earthbound entity, but the repair of the auric field is up to the individual. [cf. HAUNTING, EARTHBOUND ENTITIES] 3. a harmful, frightening, dark thought-form which follows an earthling around and makes his or her presence known by disrupting the earthling's lifestyle; individual's activities go down hill, friends disappear, and his or her motivation becomes lessened; thought-form is a NEGATIVE ELEMENTAL built by the victim from his or her own thoughts of hate, resentment, revenge, anger, etc.; as thoughts persist, the elemental intensifies and brings harm to the victim; victim must change his or her attitude to dissipate their elemental. [cf. ELEMENTAL, THOUGHT-FORMS]

PSYCHIC ATTUNEMENT—to reach a high level of awareness within one's body and mind and extend this awareness to the electromagnetic field of the object, person, or situation, which is the target; target is the electromagnetic field one sends PSYCHIC ENERGY or information to or from; level of AWARENESS is a particular body feeling sensation within each psychic individually that he or she recognizes to be a level where the PSYCHIC INFORMATION and energy is beneficial, accurate, and not his or her own mental awareness. [cf. ELECTROMAGNETIC RADIATION, PSYCHIC INFORMATION]

PSYCHIC AURA—one of the seven energy fields surrounding the physical body thast makes up the entire human AURA.

PSYCHIC BAND—a peculiar sensation of pressure often felt around the head when developing MEDIUMSHIP and which goes way when the developing period is finished. [cf. MENTAL PSYCHIC PROCESSES Appendix 2]

PSYCHIC BANKRUPT—to lose one's PSYCHIC ABILITY entirely or have it lessen, due to ill health or to evil thoughts and actions by the psychic himself. [cf. GOSSAMER VEIL, IN PROTECTION, IN THIS WORK]

PSYCHIC BARRIER—to deliberately set tangible, forceful, protective VIBRATIONS around an individual or around an area that he or she frequents, who is bothered or victimized by a malicious, revengeful, or negative person; certain words, objects, symbols, and incantations, have a vibrational frequency that wards off EVIL, if used in a ritual and with that intent; performed by an EXORCIST or a well-grounded PSYCHIC; these symbols, words, etc., disrupt or stir the CONSCIOUSNESS of the oncoming undesirable person; he or she feels uncomfortable and leaves, not realizing why they changed their mind; e.g., a tetragram drawn on the inside of the door, or salt sprinkled in a circle around a house makes any guests who come with evil intent feel uneasy and they do not enter; (unnecessary to see the SALT or TETRAGRAM). [cf. EXORCISM, HEX, CEREMONIAL MAGIC]

PSYCHIC BLOCK—a wall made in one's auric atmosphere that prevents a PSYCHIC from tuning into that person by: 1. a good CLOAK OF INSULATION made with AFFIRMATIONS, positive thoughts and PRAYER; 2. a cloak of skepticism; 3. a closing off, in normal life, of personal attitudes and thoughts to any outside intrusion through the years; also closed off psychic attunement. [cf. PSYCHIC ATTACK, PSYCHIC BARRIER, SPLODGER]

PSYCHIC BREEZES—(darkroom sessions) cool

currents of air combined with a drop of temperature felt in seances because apparitions can come with a chilly atmosphere; drops of 20° F have been recorded. [**cf.** SEANCES, MEDIUMSHIP, GHOSTS, DARKROOM SESSIONS]

PSYCHIC BRUISES—a mark which symbolizes trouble, appearing on a human or animal's body with no recollection to the victim as to how it got there, usually discovered in the morning; e.g., the ace of clubs on one's arm in scar form, redness, or blackened crossbones on one's neck. [**cf.** PSYCHIC TRANSFER, HEX, FIRES WITHOUT CAUSE, EXORCISM]

PSYCHIC CABLE—see SILVER CORD.

PSYCHIC CASUALTIES—frightening or disturbing psychic experiences of inferior quality; mental or physical psychic activity occurring spontaneously, unplanned, unwilled, too frequently, too overwhelming or making the psychic physically ill; happens to those: 1. who do not seek proper training of psychic principles; 2. who do not bother with PSYCHISM philosophy; 3. whose lifestyle is low in standards; 4. who do not take time to meditate before tuning in; 5. who do not insulate themselves before tuning in; 6. who try to force their PSYCHIC ABILITY too quickly; 7. who do not try to learn to control it but enjoy it spilling in normal life until it comes too frequently. [**cf.** PSYCHIC ATTACK, CLOAK OF INSULATION, LAW OF LIKE ATTRACTS LIKE Appendix 7]

PSYCHIC CENTERS—1. two places in the body where one can feel and concentrate on receiving PSYCHIC INFORMATION; the SOLAR PLEXUS area below the breast-bone and above the navel, and/or the area just above the base of the nose in the lower central forehead. [**cf.** THIRD-EYE AREA, PINEAL GLAND, SOLAR PLEXUS CHAKRA] 2. see CHAKRAS.

PSYCHIC CENTRES—see CHAKRAS.

PSYCHIC CHEMISTRY—see ALCHEMY.

PSYCHIC COGNITION—("perception") to psychically perceive data regarding the PRESENT; data is a NON-THOUGHT that is brought into mental activity by by-passing the process of thinking; data that the PSYCHIC could not have known through normal means but later found to be true; brought on by deliberate WILL; happens quickly after the preparation and leaves quickly; comes from the SUPERCONSCIOUS MIND with or without the aid of the

ETHERIC WORLD INTELLIGENCES; information is beneficial; psychic cognition skill used in PSYCHICAL RESEARCH laboratories; (do not confuse with CLAIRSENTIENCE which is not always willed and comes through a feeling sensation instead of mental activity). **Syn.** EXTENDED MIND. [**cf.** PRECOGNITION, RETROCOGNITION, Appendix 2 PSYCHIC COGNITION]

PSYCHIC COLLISION—to sense an undertow of NEGATIVE emotions among a group of people, by a supersensitive PSYCHIC, no matter how it is hidden by the intellect; the interweaving of the auras leaves the psychic feeling uncomfortable or in a sense of shock, even though no words had been said. **Sim.** PSYCHIC IMPACT. [**cf.** PSYCHIC KINSHIP, NEGATIVE PSYCHISM]

PSYCHIC CONSCIOUSNESS—an ALTERED STATE OF CONSCIOUSNESS in which the SOUL-MIND works on perfecting itself; when the CONSCIOUS MIND, the decision making mind, has relinquished its role, as in SLEEP, HYPNOSIS, MEDITATION, and the opening of PSYCHIC DOORS, the SUBCONSCIOUS MIND, the soul-mind, works on survival beyond the physical senses; soul-mind is free to work for final causes to reach itself; data for the soul-mind to reach perfection surfaces (sometimes a complete surprise as to its nature); easily willed as the soul-mind likes this state of consciousness when it is free to speak out; an awareness of self, giving a human being personal existence; also called **psyche consciousness.** [**cf.** ALPHA STATE OF CONSCIOUSNESS, SOUL-MIND, CONSCIOUS MIND]

PSYCHIC CONTAGION—transfer of NEGATIVE vibrations into a PSYCHIC DEVELOPMENT CIRCLE from a newcomer, before the group realizes it is happening; newcomer has either been dealing in BLACK MAGIC or is very jealous and these vibrations splodge out. [**cf.** WELL-GROUNDED MEDIUM, SPLODGING, CROSS-EXCITATION, CONVERSION HYSTERIA]

PSYCHIC COUNSELING—to give a private READING on a one-to-one basis that pertains to the personal information desired by the client; PSYCHIC is a professional psychic counselor; client asks pertinent questions regarding his or her job, health, relationships, family (living or deceased), vocation, investing money, and problems; psychic only tunes into aspects of the client's life that he or she inquires about, as opposed to the fortune-telling type of reading. [**cf.** PSYCHIC READER,

COME CLOSE TO YOU]

PSYCHIC CRISIS—(Native American) name given to the death initiation in the development of SHAMANSHIP, by outsiders who do not understand the culture, because it looked to outsiders to be a psychopathological sickness. [**cf.** INITIATORY DEATH, INITIATORY SICKNESS]

PSYCHIC DANCING—1. prolonged body movements in rhythm and harmony with others to reach an ALTERED STATE OF CONSCIOUSNESS. [**cf.** SUFI TWIRLING, TRIBAL DANCING] **2.** (Paris, France) Waslaw Nijinsky often watched from the ceiling, his own body float and dance; he controlled his physical form from the ASTRAL PLANE; his feet did not always touch the stage; 3. (England) dance designed after the ancient temple dancers to give off creative energy and love; audience mentally reaches into the sixth dimension before it is over. (Inconcl.) [**cf.** DANCING MANIA, MOVEMENT-FOR-ALTERED-CONSCIOUSNESS]

PSYCHIC DENTISTRY—(angel alchemy) to psychically repair teeth, gums, and other mouth problems and to change silver fillings to gold fillings en masse; authenticated psychic dentist, P.J. Esch, gives an inspirational lecture and ends with singing traditional, lively, religious songs accompanying himself on the guitar; congregation joins in the singing; during this time, the invisible TRANSMUTATION and repair takes place by his ANGELIC FORCES; congregation has their mouths examined for changes in the condition of the teeth and jaw; some cases show the repair and gold fillings at that time while others realize the healing the next day. (Inconcl.) [**cf.** ALCHEMY, TRANSMUTATION]

PSYCHIC DEVELOPMENT—to bring into activity one's PSYCHIC ABILITY by frequently taking time to prepare one's body, mind, and environment; one then sits with the mind focused on the skill one desires to surface or expand; the following routines have been tested and proven to work well for tuning into the SUBCONSCIOUS MIND and for reaching a high level of AWARENESS; 1. MENTAL PSYCHISM: sit in a straight back chair or in the LOTUS POSTURE in the same area each time; work in a group, in a laboratory, or alone; mentally cloak one's self with protective words; meditate or say affirmations and a prayer; when through meditating, stay in the ALPHA STATE OF CONSCIOUSNESS, keep the mind neutral, and put one's full attention on the type of psychic skill chosen (e.g., PENDU-LUMING, CRYSTAL BALL GAZING, THOUGHTOGRAPHY, CASTING OF LOTS, MENTAL TELEPATHY, PSYCHOMETRY, CLAIRVOYANCE, CLAIRAUDIENCE); allow non-thoughts to enter the mind; dialogue with them for clarity if necessary; when finished, thank the subconscious mind and shake the arms and legs gently to come back into beta awareness; 2. PHYSICAL PSYCHISM: preparation is the same for physical psychism, only after MEDITATION, one may have to stand to execute the skill (e.g., BODY CONTROL, NONHUMAN-PK, MAGNETIC HEALING, ALCHEMY, BOTANE); eyes are usually opened to beam the MENTAL ENERGY on the matter one is manipulating; when finished, thank the subconscious mind; entire session of either type of psychism should not last over a half hour (for many months), gradually working longer if desired; these same routines are good to perform to learn how to CONTROL one's psychism for those with natural-born psychic ability who experience random and spontaneous psychic phenomena; a person stores PSYCHIC POWER and when the subconscious mind keeps an orderly pattern of expressioning it, the compartment in the subconscious mind becomes conditioned and only surfaces the information at the planned time; (do not confuse with MEDIUMSHIP DEVELOPMENT in which the ETHERIC WORLD INTELLIGENCES intervene). [**cf.** MENTAL PSYCHISM, PHYSICAL PSYCHISM, MEDIUMSHIP, CLOAK OF INSULATION, LAW OF LIKE ATTRACTS LIKE Appendix 7]

PSYCHIC DEVELOPMENT CIRCLE—(current: mental mediumship circle) a chosen group of people who meet regularly once a week to develop themselves in MENTAL MEDIUMSHIP skills under the guidance of a trained MEDIUM; they sit in chairs in a circle in the light or semidarkness; circle holds good VIBRATIONS within the circle and closes out all negative vibrations; persons must be compatible; each one develops his own type of mental mediumship; (do not confuse with DARKROOM SESSIONS or SEANCES which are for physical mediumship phenomena). [**cf.** MENTAL MEDIUMSHIP, FORMS-WITH-POWER, GUIDE]

PSYCHIC DIAGNOSTICIAN—a PSYCHIC or MEDIUM that tunes into the patient's physical body phychically and finds the congested area and receives directions as to the patient's needs.

PSYCHIC DOORS—two parallel beams of light extending from each side of the head of the PSYCHIC, out into the various wavelengths in the

ETHERIC WORLD; seen by ETHERIC WORLD INTEL-LIGENCES and other discarnates; can be perceived clairvoyantly; psychic doors is a fitting name for perceiving PSYCHIC INFORMATION, as one can control the psychic information that comes and goes; one can close the door to low, inferior psychic information; each person is in charge of what he perceives psychically and can learn to control it; doors also signify that opening up one's psychic sensitivity is not the same as opening and closing the eyes, and it isn't. Usage: "This is not the best restaurant in town, be sure and close your psychic doors." "After I meditate for ten minutes and am sure I am at my level, then I open my psychic doors." [cf. DOORKEEPER, JOY GUIDE]

PSYCHIC DRIFTERS—people who have died and are in the lower astral planes of the etheric world; due to their lack of understanding, confusion, limited low STATE OF CONSCIOUSNESS, or their wish to recapture memories of mundane desires, they float around not wanting to leave the earth vibrations; tend to haunt earthlings and bother them. **Syn.** EARTHBOUND ENTITIES. [cf. GHOSTS, HAUNTING, DENSITY, ASTRAL PLANE]

PSYCHIC ENCOUNTER—an unusual, uninvited, occurrence happening when the receiver is in a passive mood, and the invisible sender is in a very emotional or confused state; e.g., clock striking out of turn at the moment one dies; an APPARITION appearing in one's room during sleep and awakening the sleeper. [cf. HUMAN OMENS, NONHUMAN AGENCY]

PSYCHIC ENERGY—an intelligent, powerful, invisible force formed by the friction of the blood cells running back and forth throughout the veins, and arteries filling the body with ELECTRICITY, capable of being controlled and directed by the human mind; 1. capable of being channeled into the BRAIN and SUBCONSCIOUS MIND, palms, and SOLAR PLEXUS; capable of being channeled out through the brain, palms, and eyes; 2. can be transmitted through space into other living organisms, and through MATTER; 3. dominated by the five minds and bypasses the physical five SENSES; occurs when willed or occurs spontaneously; 4. invisible energy living in all organisms and matter, connected throughout all the universes; psychic energy is an aspect of electricity and electricity runs throughout the atmosphere and throughout living organisms and inert matter connecting all to a giant switchboard; 5. an energy that can be refracted, polarized,

focused and combined with other energies; 6. controlled and employed under certain conditions that mankind does not fully understand; has a rapport with emotions; subjective part of a human being tunes into the etheric world VIBRATIONAL FREQUENCIES reaching from COSMIC CONSCIOUSNESS calling it psychic energy; 7. a mind force that can change the neurological structure of the psychic, or other living organisms by deliberate will or unconsciously by emotions; 8. a release of power through an appropriate form; 9. transmits knowledge to the mind, and manipulates matter in an unexplainable manner; 10. frequently comes from an intelligent, powerful energy field known as highly evolved soul-minds in invisible bodies; 11. by-products of the simultaneous "everywhere-matrix"; 12. a primordial form of intelligence pervading the universe and affecting its course; 13. SOUL-MIND phenomenon; 14. future science. [cf. PSYCHIC CONSCIOUSNESS, MAGNETISM]

PSYCHIC ENERGY TRANSFORMERS—see PSYCHIC ENERGY.

PSYCHIC EXPERIENCE—1. collective word pertaining to any paranormal PHENOMENON; 2. characteristics that distinguish it from other phenomenon: brevity of activity, perceiver is in a passive mood or ALTERED STATE OF CONSCIOUSNESS, noetic quality of activity, serves as an ILLUMINATION, usually undescribable in present language; 3. pertains to a spontaneous, unexpected activity which involves PSYCHIC ENERGY; 4. pertains to preplanned or desired psychic activity.

PSYCHIC EXPERIENCE DURING SLEEP—to perceive an awareness employing any of the five PSYCHIC SENSES during sleep in between the REM state (in a lower state of consciousness than the dream state); experience is like any daytime psychic experience, perceived in a vision, voice utterance, feelings, hunches, etc.; following characteristics distinguish it from a dream: 1. "easy to recall," leaving an impression on the sleeper, sometimes for years; 2. vivid, clear, even to details; 3. authenticity of each object to the time period of the scene; 4. comes during the lower alpha and theta state of sleep without paralysis of the body; 5. to be interpreted as is, or symbolically, as any psychic message, and not interpreted as a dream is interpreted. (Inconcl.) [cf. TIME BENDERS, PROPHECY, DREAMS, RECALLERS]

PSYCHIC EXTRAS—see EXTRAS.

PSYCHIC EYE—see THIRD-EYE.

PSYCHIC FAIR—a group of psychics and mediums gathered together in a public building, to serve the public with their variety of psychic talents; each one has a section, booth, or corner to work in; usually a church affair; e.g., tarot readers, clairvoyants, psychometrists, psychic counselors, numerologists, and psychic healers. **Syn.** PSYCHIC ASSEMBLY.

PSYCHIC FENCE—etheric substance that keeps the unnecessary perceptions of the astral dimension from the CONSCIOUS MIND, such as, past lives information, archetypal knowledge, earthbound entities, etc. **Syn.** VEIL. [**cf.** ASTRAL SHELLS, THOUGHT-FORMS, EARTHBOUND ENTITIES, ELEMENTALS]

PSYCHIC FEUDS—see PSYCHIC TRANSFER.

PSYCHIC FIGURINE—an image made to look as much as possible like a certain person, to be used as a psychic tool; image made of wax, clay, ceramics or cloth; used to link psychic energy sent to that person to change that person's body chemistry or life affairs; i.e., a voodoo doll or ceramic image of a deity. [**cf.** SYMPATHETIC MAGIC, LAW OF CORRESPONDENCE Appendix 7, MIMICRY]

PSYCHIC FORCE—1. (Tibet) see VITAL LIFE FORCE; 2. coined by Sergeant Cox in 1871 as a branch of psychology and used ever since; 3. ultrafrequencies that are faster than earth vibrations, giving humans information and knowledge which cannot be detected by the five senses , or normal activity of the subconscious mind. [**cf.** CLAIR SENSES, THIRD-EYE, BIOTELECOMMUNICATION, ECTENIC FORCE]

PSYCHIC GATE—see PSYCHIC DOORS.

PSYCHIC GESTALT—the human soul as a part of the "great all-there-is"; an ever-expanding energy that is capable of breaking itself down and rebuilding itself; God's manifestations; God. [**cf.** TOTALITY, ALMIGHTY CREATIVE POWER, ATMA]

PSYCHIC HEALING—a collective word encompassing all kinds of unorthodox healing methods and therapies that use PSYCHIC principles; in this dictionary MENTAL HEALING, MAGNETIC HEALING, and MEDIUMSHIP HEALING are separate categories and all others are listed in Appendix 2 under psychic healing.

PSYCHIC HEALING TECHNICIAN—one who evaluates the patient's condition so as to administer the proper type of PSYCHIC HEALING for each patient; technician must understand many types of human-healing and psychic healing alternatives to be able to choose the method compatible for each patient; patient should sign a form stating they understand the healing method is an alternative healing. [**cf.** PSI SCAN, PARANORMAL HEALING, NATURAL HEALERS, MAGIC HEALING ALTERNATIVES]

PSYCHIC HEART-CENTRE—(Tibet) keeps one's body warm in extreme cold temperatures while wrapped in wet cotton sheets; PSYCHOPHYSICAL bodily warmth made by extracting PRANA from the air and storing it in the human body battery; prana is then employed to transmute the generative fluid into a fiery energy; this in turn makes the invisible nervous system run through the NERVOUS SYSTEM in the form of heat; keeps the body completely warm in cold temperatures; this skill is also used to make the energy in the KUNDALINI rise. [**cf.** ICE SITTERS, INTERNAL EXERCISES, NADIS]

PSYCHIC HEREDITY—innate characteristics in some person's SOUL-MIND, that are similar to many but not yet universal, regarding the family, race, and the cultural beliefs; e.g., a green thumb, ability to play a musical instrument by ear, predisposition to disease. [**cf.** REINCARNATION]

PSYCHIC HEAT—to keep one's body warm in extremely cold temperatures wrapped in wet cotton sheets; psychophysical bodily warmth made by extracting PRANA from the air and storing it in the human body; prana is then employed to transmute the generative fluid into a fiery energy; this in turn makes the invisible nervous system run through the nervous system in the form of heat; keeps the body completely warm in cold temperatures; this skill is also used to make the energy in the KUNDALINI rise [**cf.** ICE SITTERS, INTERNAL EXERCISES, NADIS]

PSYCHIC HOUSE-CLEANING—the removal of ghosts (if any), and the clearing of past VIBRATIONS in a new house, or one changing tenants, by a group of psychics; team neutralizes the ATMOSPHERE by mind and hand rituals, making it ready for the new tenant's vibrations. **Syn.** HOUSESWEEP. [**cf.** EXORCISM, GHOSTS, PSYCHOMETRY]

PSYCHIC IMPACT—a transfer of incompatible energy to a person in a group who is not in agreement with the group, making him or her feel very uncomfortable; e.g., an exciting birthday party with all but Tommy having fun; Tommy does not feel comfortable around unorganized excitement, the mood being transitory leaves him shaken and bewildered. [cf. PSYCHIC COLLISION, PSYCHIC KINSHIP, NEGATIVE PSYCHISM]

PSYCHIC IMPRESSION—see CLAIRSENTIENCE, or GUT FEELING.

PSYCHIC IMPRINT—1. (materialization seance, early 1900s) a cast or mold of the objects materialized in the SEANCE for further study; soft yielding substances were brought into the seance room, such as clay, putty, flour, smoked and chemically treated surfaces, and melted paraffin; used to make a cast or mold of the arms, legs, faces or hands that were materialized; see PARAFFIN MOLDS; 2. a physical print of a foot or hoof in the ground made by an ethereal APPARITION in UFO sighting areas after the UFO appearance; e.g., hoof print of a big foot or a large manlike foot print; 3. fingerprints of the ASTRAL BODY taken when the person was not in the area where his or her fingerprints were needed; (documented cases) astral body fingerprints are found to be the exact same print as the physical body. [cf. PLASTICS, MOSTER ACTIVITY, UFO SIGHTINGS]

PSYCHIC INFORMATION—1. a NON-THOUGHT impressing the mind and/or body sensations or PSYCHIC SENSES impressing the physical body with data that were not known beforehand and could not be known by normal means; impressions come from the electromagnetic fields of outer environment (living organisms, inert objects, atmospheric conditions), the SUBCONSCIOUS MIND, the SUPERCONSCIOUS MIND, ETHERIC WORLD INTELLIGENCES, or NATURE SPIRITS; non-thoughts consist of knowledge, information, ideas symbols, impressions, feelings, smells, tastes, sounds, or visions; brings data that could not have been known before by the psychic from conscious awareness, formal education, lifetime experiences, nor logically reasoned; data must be interpreted by psychic, client, or recipient desiring the information; 2. used loosely: every psychic reaction that comes through in any of the various kinds of psychic phenomena; (do not confuse with MEDITATION); see Appendix 4 for clarification with IMAGERY, FANTASY, HALLUCINATION and DAYDREAMING).

PSYCHIC INTERMEDIARY—see MEDIUM.

PSYCHIC ISOLATION—an AURA around a person who is withdrawn, aloof, silent or a non-mingler gives the impression of being a cold person; this type of aura will shrink in size and when it doesn't stretch out far enough to easily blend with other people's auras, one considers him or her to be an introvert. [cf. EMOTIONAL PSYCHISM, EMERGENCY PSI]

PSYCHIC KINSHIP—auras in a group of persons who are on the same level of thinking leave everyone enjoying themselves; when no one in the group is acting negatively or harboring jealous thoughts, each one in the group will feel compatible as the auras will glow, expand and interweave with each other. [cf. CONTROLLED EMPATH, CROSS-EXCITATION, EMOTIONAL TELEPATHY]

PSYCHIC LASER—modern symbol for concentrated group energy focused for strength plus coherence plus distance. [cf. UPPER·FREQUENCY, UNBOUNDED AWARENESS, SHIELDING]

PSYCHIC LEAKAGE—a tear in the ETHERIC WEB, or veil, around a person; separates the physical body from the atmospheric psychic influences making that person "always tired"; person is susceptible to psychic impacts, unconsciously working as negative psychism through the SOLAR PLEXUS which flattens the NAVEL CHAKRA making it limp; this makes the person lose coordination making him or her feel exhusted for no reason as there are no physical defects; usually naturally born with the person or caused by too many drugs; (do not confuse with SPONTANEOUS PSI). [cf. PSYCHIC IMPACT, PSI LEAKAGE, SUPPRESSED DESIRE]

PSYCHIC LIGHT—to manifest light or maneuver light in a darkroom session or SEANCE; 1. light that is leaking in from the door or window is moved from place to place by the SITTERS or MEDIUM; 2. medium or sitters produce light in a BLACKED-OUT ROOM; concentration is focused on light, and by using the ethers in the room, a phosphorescent and dazzling light appears; 3. to synchronize with fire elementals who produce dancing globules of light in which they can transform themselves. [cf. DARKROOM SESSIONS, BLACKED-OUT, FIRE-ELEMENTAL, INFRARED NETWORK]

PSYCHIC LUBRICATION—to release the blocks located in the NERVOUS SYSTEM or the muscles, by special MEDITATION processes. [cf. ROLFING, NEUROMUSCULAR MASSAGE, MUSIC THERAPY, BLOCKS]

503

PSYCHIC MENTAL DIAGNOSIS—1. to psychically sense parts of the patient's body that needs attention; 2. to close the eyes and clairvoyantly tune into the CONGESTED AREA; 3. to see past the skin of the patient and locate the congestion among the organs of the body. **Syn.** X-RAY CLAIRVOYANCE. [**cf.** ETHERIC DIAGNOSING, HEALING-AT-A-DISTANCE]

PSYCHIC MESSAGE—1. see PSYCHIC INFORMATION; 2. personal information perceived psychically by one's self or by another person; 3. very short or mini reading given to individuals in a public gathering by a mental medium standing in front of the gathering. [**cf.** PSYCHIC READING, STANDING READER]

PSYCHIC MESSAGE SYMBOLS—words, sounds, body feelings, pronounced attitudinal change, numbers, tastes, odors, or visions (of scenes, colors, objects, plants, animals) perceived psychically that imply something more than their obvious and immediate meaning; symbols appear in psychic attunements because it is an immediate way of portraying an abundance of data; psychic symbols appear in readings, dreams, experiments, and psychic development sessions; e.g., to see a puppy following the client could mean that an immature person is constantly tagging along in most everything he or she does; psychic should ask silently if the perception is IMAGE or SYMBOLS; e.g., to see a bride and groom dressed in green, could mean the client would be involved in a wedding and everyone was dressed in green (image); could mean that the client was spending too much time in one area of his or her life (married to it) and another person was envious of this (green with envy) (symbol). [**cf.** DREAM SYMBOLS, UNIVERSAL SYMBOLS]

PSYCHIC MOULDS—(England) (materialization) a very thin wax glove obtained from a hand materialized in a SEANCE room, which dipped itself into molten wax, and then dissolved leaving the thin glove form; impossible for a human to do this; spelled **mold** in America. [**cf.** SEANCE, BLACKED-OUT ROOM]

PSYCHIC NAVEL CORD—an ethereal long, narrow, hazy-like string, connecting the ECTOPLASM exuding from the MEDIUM to the navel of the medium; is a part of her or his body and can cause a tremendous weight loss or even death if severed. [**cf.** MATERIALIZATION]

PSYCHIC NERVE SYSTEM—(Tibet) the invisible ethereal nervous system in the BARDO BODY. **Syn.** ASTRAL NERVOUS SYSTEM, NADIS. [**cf.** MAGNETIC HEALING, SPIRIT, MENTAL-REFLECTING ETHER]

PSYCHIC ORGAN—see PINEAL GLAND.

PSYCHIC PAIN—nicknamed **capital P;** written **P;** unpleasant emotional pain from childhood experiences that one cannot understand with childhood knowledge and which locks the emotional hurt in the brain; exerts pressure as it surfaces during life and results in mental disorders or unpleasant habits and attitudes; 2. subconscious hurt of one's pride; suppressed emotions relating to one's EGO resulting in the above. [**cf.** PRIMAL THERAPY, BLOCKS]

PSYCHIC PAINTER—medium whose body is extensively used by an ETHERIC WORLD INTELLIGENCE who was an artist in an earthly incarnation and desires to continue his or her painting on earth; works through a medium's hands or feet to paint exquisite pictures beyond the ability of the medium's talent; partial type of PERSONIFICATION. [**cf.** TEN-PERCENT TRANCE, IMPERSONATION]

PSYCHIC PARANOID—one who uses psychic abilities constantly for EVIL and is wrapped up in psychism for its evil possibilities; e.g., Hitler, Nero. [**cf.** UP-FOR-GRABS, SHIELDING, PSYCHIC THEFT, DENSITY, EARTHBOUND ENTITIES]

PSYCHIC PERCEPTORS—the human mechanism that tunes into the electromagnetic field of his or her environment and other people to perceive PSYCHIC INFORMATION; mechanism pertains to the THIRD-EYE AREA in the head, the SYMPATHETIC NERVOUS SYSTEM, the SOLAR PLEXUS region and the palms of the hands. [**cf.** SOLAR PLEXUS CHAKRA, NADIS]

PSYCHIC PERCEPTS—see PSYCHIC INFORMATION.

PSYCHIC PHONE CALL—(electronic voices) a normal telephone call except that the caller is either dying or has already made the TRANSITION; callers are all ages; calls last from one fuzzy word to a half hour of clear conversation; objectives of calls now on record: 1. caller has an urgent message for a loved one; 2. a social visit; 3. caller wishes to relate that he or she is alive; 4. one main similarity of phone calls on record, the receiver has amnesia during the call and does not remember the caller is dead until it is over. Current theories: 1. a PSYCHOKINETIC force comes from the receiver who unconsciously tuned into a mental telepathic message of the dead person; the liberated energy of the deceased person is capable of manipulating the electronic system creating electric impulses that imitate a human voice; **2.** the caller is really who he or she says; concept that people live on in the ETHERIC WORLD and the earthly bond between two persons, who have been previously involved, can easily contact one another forever; deceased person uses the energy of the earth person and manipulates the telephone system as a voice amplifier. (Inconcl.). [**cf.** SIMPLE CALLS, PRO-LONGED CALLS, CRISIS CALLS, WITNESS]

PSYCHIC PHOTOGRAPHY—encompasses all types of unconventional photography or normal photography that produces extras; performed by intense concentration of the SUBCONSCIOUS MIND or as a result of intervention of the ETHERIC WORLD INTELLIGENCES; see Appendix 2 for kinds; (do not confuse with KIRLIAN PHOTOGRAPHY). (Inconcl.) [**cf.** EXTRAS]

PSYCHIC PHYSICAL LIGHT—a WHITE LIGHT seen by many individuals with their physical eyes, around a group of people, a city, or a mountain; a form of physical phenomena that has not been explained. (Inconcl.)

PSYCHIC PLAGIARISM—great inventions and discoveries being simultaneously impressed upon the minds of many mediums scattered around the world; discoveries are necessary for advancement of mankind at that given period; new inventions are given to many with the hopes one of them will understand it and bring it to the world; if MEDIUM uses these impressions as his or her own unaided effort, it is theft; (do not confuse with SIMUL-TANEOUS INSPIRATION).

PSYCHIC PLANE—(AMORC) a level of denseness in the ETHERIC WORLD designed for those who have committed themselves to help earthlings with guidance and inspiration. [**cf.** ETHERIC WORLD INTELLIGENCES, PLANETARY HELPERS, WHITE BROTHERHOOD]

PSYCHIC PLATFORM—an invisible ETHERIC ENERGY FIELD similar to a physical platform built by the medium's etheric world guides so as to hold an object or person, making them look suspended in thin air. (Inconcl.) [**cf.** TELEKINESIS, ANTI-GRAVITY PHENOMENA, LEVITATION TELEKINESIS]

PSYCHIC PORTRAIT—to paint or draw what one perceives in the higher realms of the etheric world

that pertains to the individual sitting for the portrait; PSYCHIC is an artist in everyday life; artist puts her or himself in an ALPHA STATE OF CONSCIOUSNESS and paints what he or she feels, perceives clairvoynatly, or is impressed to paint; two kinds: **1.** an artist who paints or draws the individual's etheric world GUIDE; **2.** artist who paints or draws the portrait of the individual and while painting, he or she perceives visions and impressions of the higher realm energies around the individual and paints these on the portrait; a form of INSPI-RATIONAL ART in which the SUPERCONSCIOUS MIND is used; (do not confuse with AUTOMATISM art in which the etheric world guides use one's arm and the art talent is theirs). (Inconcl.) [**cf.** ASTRAL ART]

PSYCHIC POWER—see PSYCHIC ENERGY and PSYCHIC SKILL.

PSYCHIC PRACTITIONER—one who is a CHAN-NEL for some type of PSYCHIC HEALING or one who does psychic counseling. [**cf.** Appendix 2 PSYCHIC HEALING, PSYCHIC SKILL]

PSYCHIC PROJECTION—**1.** see CLAIRVOYANCE-IN-SPACE; **2.** see MENTAL PROJECTION.

PSYCHIC PROTECTION—to decree the ergs of energy that continuously emanate from one's head to be of a protective nature and make a protective atmosphere around one; accomplished by repeating AFFIRMATIONS of TRUTH, thinking positive thoughts, and mentally affirming a CLOAK OF INSULATION; this atmospheric condition makes the edge of the AURA remain impenetrable and insures against psychic invasion and other undesirable vibrations; to bring in the aid of the ETHERIC WORLD INTELLIGENCES also helps; (Bible) Paul called this, the "whole armor of God." [**cf.** THOUGHTS ARE THINGS, LAW OF LIKE ATTRACTS LIKE Appendix 7, ELEMENTAL, PSYCHIC ATTACK]

PSYCHIC PUSH-OVER—to unintentionally send highly emotional THOUGHT ENERGY to a friend which influences his or her attitude, because of a strong physical tie; emotional thought can be pleasurable or negative; **1.** transference of over-concern for a friend sends that thought energy to the friend and binds him or her to that concern, an image he or she may not want to have; e.g., a mother's concern about her son's ability to cope with the rules of the military service, gives the young adult unfounded anxieties about his ability to cope with military life when he really is enjoying

505

the experience. [cf. HOLD THE THOUGHT] 2. transference of negative psychic energy from a victim of a PSYCHIC ATTACK, unconsciously repeating this force, to another. [cf. PSYCHIC TRANSFER, THOUGHT-FORMS]

PSYCHIC PYROTECHNICS—(Greek *pyro* "fire, heat") to psychically cause a fire to ignite near one's self without using normal means of lighting it; happens unconsciously and unintentionally; caused by the BODY CHEMISTRY of the psychic; objects burn within an area without the fire spreading nor harming the psychic. (Inconcl.) [cf. PSYCHIC PYROTECHNIST, POLTERGEIST FOCUS]

PSYCHIC PYROTECHNIST—one who has the BODY CHEMISTRY that causes fires to ignite within their area without using matches or other normal means; psychic is the focus because of his or her natural body make-up and does not realize he or she is starting the fire until it happens. (Inconcl.) [cf. PSYCHIC HEAT, FIRES WITH BOUNDARIES]

PSYCHIC RADIO OPERATOR—(ufology) one capable of focusing their energy to transmit information with outer space intelligences. [cf. UFOLOGY, TRANCE MEDIUM]

PSYCHIC READER—one who gives PSYCHIC COUNSELING or predictions to others, sometimes for a fee; psychic information is perceived through CLAIRSENTIENCE, CLAIRVOYANCE, MENTAL MEDIUMSHIP, PSYCHOMETRY and other psychic skills. [cf. PSYCHIC MESSAGE, PSYCHIC, COME INTO YOUR VIBRATION]

PSYCHIC RECOVERY—(psychic attack) to improve one's physical condition if a psychic HEX leaves one exhausted and jittery, use the sunlight, massage, games, and physical exercise in a spa; walks in the woods or country or spending time by the water is not wise, as the psychic ELEMENTAL is more easily sent to these areas. [cf. PSYCHIC ATTACK, EXORCISM]

PSYCHIC RIPOFFS—those who profess to have super PSYCHIC ABILITY and charge extremely high prices for their services, giving a bad name to those who are sincere in this work.

PSYCHIC RODS—1. ectoplasmic tools in the SEANCE room that are used for holding objects in the air in LEVITATION, or striking objects in PERCUSSION; extendable, rigid, elastic, long rods or levers varying in thickness, length and intensity;

perceived clairvoyantly or can be photographed by INFRARED camera; extend from the medium's navel to the object being manipulated; 2. yellowish, or golden cylinders seen emanating from the head of the person one is tuned into; denotes the amount of psychic ability he or she has attained by the number of beams and the thickness of the beams; 3. yellowish orange beams seen around a candle when sitting for development, that are not the usual rays sent out by a light. [cf. PSYCHIC DEVELOPMENT CIRCLE, POINT-OF-FOCUS]

PSYCHIC SCIENCE—see PARAPSYCHOLOGY.

PSYCHIC SEED—see MONAD.

PSYCHIC SELF-PROTECTION—see PSYCHIC SHIELD.

PSYCHIC SENSE—the THIRD-EYE AREA of the head that is the controlling faculty used to perceive psychic information through the invisible counterpart of each of the physical five SENSES: CLAIRVOYANCE, CLAIRSENTIENCE, CLAIRSCENT, CLAIRSAVORANCE, CLAIRAUDIENCE: third-eye area includes the PINEAL GLAND, post lobe of the PITUITARY GLAND, THALAMUS, third ventricle, and occipital lobe; (do not confuse with MEDIUMSHIP) correctly used as singular or plural. **Syn.** THIRD-EYE, SIXTH SENSE.

PSYCHIC SENSES—see PSYCHIC SENSE.

PSYCHIC SENSITIVITY—to realize that one has an AWARENESS that cannot be attributed to the physical five SENSES and is capable of making use of this awareness; to psychically tune into the electromagnetic field of objects, living organisms, people, atmosphere, and environment; ability to interpret these feelings, tastes, visions, noises, smells, and bodily sensations; spontaneous or willed; natural-born or learned. [cf. PSYCHIC, NATURAL-BORN PSYCHIC]

PSYCHIC SENSORIUM—(Greece) to psychically perceive information in more than one type of PSYCHISM simultaneously; e.g., "I have a vision of someone cooking and I hear the name Pat." [cf. TAROT CARDS, PSYCHIC READING, CONTAGIOUS ENTHUSIASM]

PSYCHIC SHELL—(Tibet) the outer coat that is shed from the SOUL-MIND in the DENSITY and ASTRAL PLANE; capable of becoming galvanized by negative thoughts from the past earth life and keeping a life-like shape; enjoys contacting a psychic who is ignorant of the rules of psychism and thinks it is a deceased person. **Syn.** ASTRAL SHELL. [**cf.** DENSITY, EARTH-BOUND ENTITIES, OUIJA BOARD]

PSYCHIC SHIELD—an ATMOSPHERE of electrical energy built around a person by one's self or another that affords protection from low quality or negative vibrations; high quality verbiage, positive INNER-DIALOGUE, deliberate AFFIRMATIONS or prayers cling to the person according to the intensity of the emotion behind them to build this mental atmospheric wall; utilizes the law of like attracts like and offers protection accordingly; used: 1. before opening PSYCHIC DOORS; 2. before entering a crowd; 3. before going to work or driving the car; 4. as a reminder that the SOUL-MIND only accepts PSYCHIC INFORMATION that is for its highest good when in an ALPHA STATE OF CONSCIOUSNESS or hypnotized; can be built mentally telepathically by a concerned person for his or her friend who may be doing something dangerous; (believed that the CIA put a PSYCHIC SHIELD around President Ford and Henry Kissinger so mind-reading experts from communist countries could not pick their thoughts). [**cf.** CLOAK OF INSULATION, LAW OF LIKE ATTRACTS LIKE Appendix 7]

PSYCHIC SHOCK ARTICLES—(future science) 1. (Huna) a mundane object that has had mind activity transferred onto it making it give off an electric shock when people come in contact with it; mind energy is condensed and solidified with a specific purpose and projected onto the article; e.g., Hunas charged their fighting sticks so that when the stick struck the enemy, the enemy would become unconscious; 2. radionic machines have been designed to contain electrical energy whether they are connected to a power source or not; made with mind energy. [**cf.** AMULET ENERGIZING, BEAMED ENERGY, EVIL EYE, ELECTRIC GIRLS]

PSYCHIC SHUFFLE—(psi tasks) (J.B. Rhine) to select a predetermined order for the shuffle of a deck of cards; subject must match the predetermined shuffle by shuffling the deck of cards by hand; experimenter mixes the shuffle target by hand in this controlled experiment. [**cf.** PSI TASKS, CHANCE AVERAGE, BASIC TECHNIQUE]

PSYCHIC SIGHT—see CLAIRVOYANCE.

PSYCHIC SKILL—1. to have proficiency and competency in performing one or more of the various types of PSYCHISM when desired, (according to the amount of current technology or the type of psychism); ability to discern the information that is perceived; knowledgeable in the field of the type one uses so it can be controlled. [**cf.** Appendix 2 for listing of types of psychism] 2. to understand one's facility of spontaneous non-thoughts from outer stimuli and the aptitude to use them constructively (INTUITION). [**cf.** CLAIRSENTIENCE, INSPIRATIONAL THOUGHT, PROPHECY]

PSYCHIC SKIN—see AURA.

PSYCHIC SMELLS—to psychically perceive a pleasant fragrance or a disagreeable odor without any physical object present that could have given off that particular scent; 1. ETHERIC WORLD INTELLIGENCES bring the scent to signify information; e.g., the same fragrance of incense occurring each time the medium tunes into the higher realms, could be a sign the guide is present and what he or she perceives will be accurate; 2. scents come with some physical phenomena processes; e.g., sulphur or metallic odors frequently accompany physical phenomena in the SEANCE room due to the chemical change in the medium's and sitters' bodies. [**cf.** CLAIRSCENT Appendix 2]

PSYCHIC SOS SYSTEM—(Russia) (future science) a code made out of the brain impulses that show on the readouts of the EEG instrument. [**cf.** SCALE OF BRAIN RHYTHMS]

PSYCHIC SPACE—see ETHERIC WORLD.

PSYCHIC STRUCTURE—1. see PSYCHIC RODS; 2. (body) the invisible organs within the body necessary to one's physical being but not visible by the human eye or ear; e.g., NADIS, the astral nervous system; CHAKRAS imbedded in the plexus that feed humans spirit from the air. [**cf.** ETHERIC DOUBLE]

PSYCHIC SUGGESTIBILITY—to intuitively receive orders with an urgency to carry them out, and do so without logically thinking about the result of the experience. [**cf.** HUNCHABILITY, INTUITIVE KNOWING, KARMICALLY SELF-GENERATED]

PSYCHIC SUPPORT FIGURES—(laboratory) an ETHERIC WORLD INTELLIGENCE that communicates and helps the earthling with PSYCHIC INFORMATION.

PSYCHIC SURGEON—one who allows an ETHERIC WORLD INTELLIGENCE to intervene and borrow his or her arms and hands for a time to perform surgical work on needy and deserving patients; an inborn quality; MEDIUM has no knowledge in medicine or anatomy of the body; medium has a NEUTRAL MIND, and relaxes to a semi-alpha state; the discarnate doctors anesthetize and enter the lower arms and hands to perform the surgery; many are natives of the Philippines. [cf. TEN PERCENT IMPERSONATION, PSYCHIC SURGERY]

PSYCHIC SURGERY—an operation by which a MEDIUM or SHAMAN practitioner opens the patient's body without medical instruments, anesthesia or sterilization; the patient is conscious, and feels no pain; the diseased tissue is removed and the incision is closed, all in a matter of minutes; incision heals immediately or in a few days; patient notices very little recovery time; one to five discarnate doctors work through the medium performing hundreds of operations in one day; practitioner knows little about the body or medicine but allows his or her hands to be manipulated; the cells separate over the diseased area by the touch of the PRACTITIONER hands (not like a raw cut of flesh); diseased tissue rises to the surface as if it is magnetized, making it easily removed; practitioner operates in a light alpha state being aware enough to conduct an orderly turnover of patients; more prevalent in the Philippines. [cf. PSYCHIC SURGEON, SPIRITISTA, ECTOPLASM PSYCHIC SURGERY]

PSYCHIC TELEMETRY—see WORDS-WITH-POWER.

PSYCHIC TELESCOPE—see TRAVELING CLAIRVOYANCE, CLAIRVOYANCE-IN-SPACE.

PSYCHIC THEFT—the mysterious vanishing of an article from one's premises and its reappearance hours or days later in some other place with no external environmental reasons. (Inconcl.) [cf. SPONTANEOUS DEMATERIALIZATION, POLTERGEIST, GUIDE, BEAMED ENERGY]

PSYCHIC THRILL—(Tibet) to experience "release" and joy when the CONSCIOUSNESS-PRINCIPLE slides from the physical body during the death process. [cf. DEATH ANGEL, DEATHBED VISIONS, SILVER CORD, MENTAL-CONSCIOUSNESS-SEED-ATOM]

PSYCHIC TRANSFER—1. to be thrust with an abundance of PSYCHIC ENERGY, unknowingly while it is happening; changes one's attitude, heals one's attitude, heals one's body, or disturbs one's sense of emotional balance, until one realizes what has happened; can be prevented or encouraged by understanding the laws of psychism; 2. to be

drained of one's psychic energy, unknowingly, while it is happening; leaves one feeling exhausted; occurs gradually or instantaneously; can be prevented by understanding how this occurs; see Appendix 2 for types of PSYCHIC TRANSFER.

PSYCHIC TRAVEL—see ASTRAL PROJECTION.

PSYCHIC TWIN BROTHER—a child's invisible playmate, about the same age of the child but more evolved; gives the child energy, information, protection and can do things for him or her similar to a GUIDE: sometimes stays and grows with the child being a source of help throughout the years. [cf GUIDE]

PSYCHIC UNDERGROUND—psychics and mediums who work in psychic research but do not let it be known in their everyday lifestyle; psychics are careful who and where they talk about psychic matters for fear of being ridiculed and for fear that nonbelievers would lose respect for the psychics' everyday work achievements; those who have a concern for the planet as a whole; planetary helpers.

PSYCHIC VAMPIRE—one whose BODY CHEMISTRY is capable of absorbing PSYCHIC ENERGY from another person, deliberately or unknowingly; vampire feels invigorated physically and mentally; victim feels depleted, (even depressed), not realizing why; vampire gravitates to psychic givers in crowds and in relationships; people are born with this body chemistry, (not cultivated) and need energy from others to live vigorously; victims are born with body chemistry to be psychic givers; some givers do not notice a loss as they have more than enough for themselves. [cf. BROADCASTING, COSMIC GENERATOR]

PSYCHIC VOICES—human-like utterances or thought-out sentences coming from animals, birds, objects, or from parts of the psychic's body; sounds happen while one is awake, in an alpha state or during sleep. **Syn.** CLAIRAUDIENCE. [cf. HEARING MEDIUMS, DIVINE WHISPERS]

PSYCHIC WARP—the invisible path that the PSYCHIC or MEDIUM uses to perceive into the higher invisible realms or deep into the subconscious mind. **Syn.** PSYCHOLOGICAL WARP, TRANSPARENT DIMENSIONAL WARP. [cf. DIMENSION-SHIFTING and SHAPE-CHANGING]

PSYCHIC WINDS—see PSYCHIC BREEZES.

PSYCHIC WORLD—see ETHERIC WORLD

PSYCHIC YELL—a widespread, general, broadcasting of EMOTION so strong that it drowns out all other incoming psychic energy to those around the broadcaster; similar to sending out a loud volume signal overpowering all other sounds caused by a state of anxiety; the broadcaster may or may not be aware of this. **Syn.** SPLODGING. [**cf.** BROADCASTING, CONTROLLED EMPATH, CROSS-EXCITATION]

PSYCHIC-PHYSICAL CONTROL—to govern or make a particular part of the body respond to one's will by deep and prolonged concentration while practicing YOGA or while being HOOKED-UP to a BIOFEEDBACK INSTRUMENT; research found individuals who can stop bleeding, control the autonomic system, and control a single cell. [**cf.** COMBUSTIBILITY, BREATH CONTROL]

PSYCHICAL CULTURE—a time period when mankind, all over the world, is interested in psychism; scientists, psychologists, religious leaders, medical researchers, and individuals are learning to develop or accelerate their psychic potential to a higher degree and use it intelligently; earth is now in that time period and will continue to advance further as time goes on. [**cf.** TRANSFORMATION, COSMIC WHEEL]

PSYCHICAL INVASION—to allow all kinds of unnecessary psychic information and energy to flow into one's mind by leaving one's PSYCHIC DOORS open all the time; brings an imbalance in one's physical or mental state; could lead to depression or illness; caused by ignorance of the rules of psychism, or a deliberate ego trip. [**cf.** CLOAK OF INSULATION, LIKE ATTRACTS LIKE, PSYCHIC ATTACK]

PSYCHICAL POWERS—see PSYCHIC ENERGY.

PSYCHICAL RESEARCH—1. parapsychological study in the late 1800s at Cambridge University, in London, England; investigation by scientific technologies; followed two lines of study: (**a**) to find the laws that explain PARANORMAL phenomena as it appears to exist; (**b**) to disprove that the paranormal phenomena exists as it appears to exist; 2. (LeRoy Zemke) "a method or doorway of attempting to offer ways in which to look at the next dimension"; 3. (current) investigation into ancient MYSTICISM, EASTERN PHILOSOPHY, religions, the American Medicine Man, and SPIRITUALISM, by psychics, anthropologists, scientists, religious lead-

ers, and medical men; study by physicists (France, Mexico) who have split the ATOM into CONSCIOUSNESS, LOVE and MATTER; 4. two important inventions as investigation tools: biofeedback instruments and the Kirlian camera. **Syn.** PARAPSYCHOLOGY.

PSYCHICAL RESEARCHER—psychics and non-psychics who have an interest in the EVOLUTION of mankind and work to check out any PARANORMAL happening for its validity; perform experiments to increase their knowledge of PSYCHISM and its practicality.

PSYCHICIST—see PSYCHIST.

PSYCHING-UP—to prepare one's body and mind for a psychic event; i.e., a PSYCHIC ASSEMBLY, a SEANCE class, a psychic experiment or a meeting of psychics; accomplished by deep breathing exercises, programming one's self with suggestions, MEDITATION, FASTING, cloaking one's self with AFFIRMATIONS, physical exercise, and sunbathing; each psychic has a way that works best for her or himself in order to prepare for good attunement. [**cf.** PROLONGED JOGGING, BIOMUSIC]

PSYCHISM—1. study of cosmic energies as a personal exchange between the mental, physical, and nervous systems within humans, under the command, and in compatibility with, the five minds (CONSCIOUS, SUBCONSCIOUS, SUPERCONSCIOUS, UNIVERSAL, and SUBLIMINAL LEVEL); 2. study of SOUL-MIND growth through action and reaction of its decisions during its many incarnations; 3. the merging of the third-eye (psychic mechanism) with TOTALITY to bring forth informative knowledge via the three minds (CONSCIOUS, SUBCONSCIOUS, and SUPERCONSCIOUS); made possible through the law of vibration; 4. (Edgar Cayce) "psychism is not the soul—but the very force of activity of the soul in its experience of the soul itself"; 5. influences of ETHERIC WORLD INTELLIGENCES and the electromagnetic fields of living organisms and inert objects on a human body, psychic senses, behavioral and growth patterns; 6. practice and study of all types of mental and physical psychic skills including mediumship; (PSYCHISM is not interchangeable with ESP). **Sim.** PARAPSYCHOLOGY, SHAMANISM, OCCULTISM, WHITE MAGIC, MYSTICISM. See Appendix 2 for the types (listed according to how one perceives psychic energy).

PSYCHIST—a PSYCHICAL RESEARCHER or a stu-

509

dent of PARAPSYCHOLOGY.

PSYCHLES—("psychic cycles") a time lag between the cause of certain kinds of upsets and its actual happening; stimuli used with PSYCHIC ENERGY to bring about mishaps that one has created as a response for one's KARMA; based on BODY CHEMISTRY generated by COSMIC ENERGY; studies show a 36 hour range cycle based on the CIRCADIAN RHYTHM of 24 hours plus 1/2 of 24, or 36 hours in the cycle. (Inconcl.) **Sim.** HOMEOSTASIS, BALANCING THE BOOKS.

PSYCHO—(Greek *psyche*) prefix meaning "soul or mind, spirit, breath, mental process" or "soul-mind."

PSYCHO-CYBERNETICS—(Greece) (cybernetics, "the steersman"); (Maxwell Maltz) the human brain and nervous system conceived as a servo-mechanism, operating in accordance with the cybernetic principles; does not say a human is a machine but a human has a machine which he or she uses; self-image psychology; science of using the mind to control human functions.

PSYCHOACOUSTICS—(Steven Halpern) study of the psychological and physiological effects of sound. [**cf.** CLAIRAUDIENT, COSMIC MUSIC]

PSYCHOACTIVE—the action and reaction of the human mind affecting all things in the universe, utilizing the law of radioactivity; all substances in the universe have properties that permit the mind to act and react upon. [**cf.** HUMAN INFORMATION PROCESSING SYSTEM, CONSCIOUSNESS-PRINCIPLE]

PSYCHOANALYSIS—1. (Hans Selye) to analyze an abnormal mental state, having the patient review his or her past emotional experiences and relate them to their present mental life; 2. (Sigmund Freud) to uncover and release REPRESSION held back by the UNCONSCIOUS MIND from the CONSCIOUS MIND (so as not to upset it); 3. (parapsychology) to work with the past lives of the SOUL-MIND to see if the repressed emotional experience began before this life. [**cf.** HYPNO-THERAPY, DREAM ANALYSIS, BLOCKS]

PSYCHOANALYST—one who perfects psychological techniques, helping the patient to reveal his or her INNER-SELF; one trained to work with mental problems and interested in the CONSCIOUS MIND and SUBCONSCIOUS MIND functions and their relationship to the body. [**cf.** BLOCKS Appendix 5]

PSYCHOANALYZING DREAMS—to use the symbols in the dream as clues to identify memories of events which could be the cause of a complex. [**cf.** SYMBOLS, FREE ASSOCIATION]

PSYCHOBERNETICS—a practical empirical branch of psychology; employs mechanistic techniques to increase an individual's SELF-AWARENESS and well-being.

PSYCHOBIOLOGY—study of the theory that the mind has control over the body and the body serves the mind; study of a human being as a unit in relation to his or her entire present environment; application of physical and biological techniques that science uses to study the NERVOUS SYSTEM. **Syn.** HOLISTIC HEALTH. [**cf.** CURATIVE EDUCATION, BELIEF SYSTEM, MIND-BODY LINK]

PSYCHOBOLY—PSYCHOKINESIS used for malevolent purposes, as in EVIL EYE phenomena. [**cf.** ARTICLE-PK, HUMAN-PK, TELEKINESIS]

PSYCHOCRIMINOLOGIST—a PSYCHIC who uses his or her skills to help the police. [**cf.** CONTROLLED PSYCHISM, HOMING IN, BLOCKING]

PSYCHOCYCLES—(future science) a pattern of ups and downs one goes through regardless of one's decisions, that seemingly come from within. [**cf.** EMOTIONAL CYCLE, BIORHYTHM CHART]

PSYCHODRAMA—founded by J.L. Moreno; a group therapy wherein the patients form a play and dramatize roles relevant to their problems; an improvisational theater with requirements of both total attention and spontaneity; enforces an awareness of roles and role playing; contemplation of nature and other aesthetically overwhelming experiences. [**cf.** GESTALT THERAPY]

PSYCHODRAMA WHITE MAGIC—(Vienna, Austria) a role-playing therapy in which a group of people act out the psychological problem in a role-playing pretense of a friend who is absent; the absent person still picks up the idea or theme of the help portrayed; friend changes his or her attitude without knowing the sessions are going on. [**cf.** LAW OF ASSOCIATION Appendix 7, GROUP TELEPATHY]

PSYCHODYNAMICS—study of PERSONALITY in terms of past and present experiences related to motivation.

PSYCHOENERGETICS—(United States) compiling of statistics to see if PSYCHIC ENERGY exists and/or if the PSYCHIC is cheating; (Russia) the study of the laws governing psychic phenomena; a term used by their physicists who are researching the energetic aspects of PSI. [cf. PSIONICS, PARASCIENCE]

PSYCHOGALVANIC REFLEX—to measure in degrees the electrical resistance of one's conductivity with a GSR or similar instrument in order to reveal concepts of past life experiences stored in the SYMPATHETIC NERVOUS SYSTEM; each individual's conductivity differs and must be used as a baseline for him or her only. [cf. METABOLIC MONITOR]

PSYCHOGENESIS—the original development of the mind; time when EVOLUTION produced minds. **Syn.** MONAD, HUMAN BEING SEED, "I AM."

PSYCHOGENIC BLEEDING—see STIGMATA.

PSYCHOGRAM—message from the ETHERIC WORLD INTELLIGENCE appearing on a photograph which was not in view through the lens when the picture was taken. **Syn.** EXTRAS. [cf. PSYCHIC PHOTOGRAPHY]

PSYCHOGRAPH—an instrument to facilitate AUTOMATIC WRITING from an EHTERIC WORLD INTELLIGENCE; consists of a rotating disc on which the medium's finger tips are placed to carry the disc over the alphabet to spell out a message. **Sim.** OUIJA BOARD or PLANCHETTE. [cf. AUTOMATISM, DIRECT WRITING]

PSYCHOGRAPHIC MEDIUM—one who is capable of allowing an etheric world intelligence to intervene and then write under this influence. **Syn.** AUTOMAT. [cf. AUTOMATIC WRITING, ETHERIC SCRIPT]

PSYCHOGRAPHY—to perform AUTOMATISM of any style, including the use of an instrument, to bring psychic information from the ETHERIC WORLD INTELLIGENCES; includes AUTOMATIC WRITING, and use of a OUIJA BOARD. [cf. Appendix 2 AUTOMATISM]

PSYCHOHOLINESS PSYCHOKINESIS—abbr. PSYCHOHOLINESS-PK; to change the BODY CHEMISTRY of one's self or another by the use of AFFIRMATIONS of TRUTH, positive prayerful thoughts, or talking to one's cells when in an ALPHA STATE OF CONSCIOUSNESS; tested and proven. [cf. PARAELECTRIC, PRAYER BASKETS, PRAYER LISTS]

PSYCHOID—(Carl Jung) an aspect of personality, whereby the PSYCHE has not yet achieved a distinct psychological quality; an aspect of the personality in its primal chaotic state, not distinct enough for separation; corresponds to the primal CHAOS of the universe. [cf. LAW OF REPETITION Appendix 7]

PSYCHOKENIST—a PSYCHIC who can move articles with mind concentration. [cf. ARTICLE-PK, NATURE-PK]

PSYCHOKINESIS—abbr. PK; to deliberately change the position, form, or elements of a specific energy field with disciplined concentration of the CONSCIOUS and SUBCONSCIOUS MINDS; to psychically and intentionally direct one's will to act on elementary atoms of the THIRD-DIMENSION in a definite manner; performed in an AWARENESS state; sometimes it defies the laws of GRAVITY and other times gravity is in tact; theories: 1. the psychic's eyes send and return rays and the PINEAL GLAND uses these rays to pick up the energy from the environment and return it through the eyes in a changed form; 2. (Russia) an unhomogeneous PLASMA field penetrating and generating out affected by the mind and emotions of the body enabling the mind to move matter without any outside stimuli; 3. to intensify one's concentration until energy in the mind is solidified, giving a signal from within, and then directing it out through the mind and eyes on the TARGET with the intent of its accomplishment; grouped into three categories; NONHUMAN, HUMAN, and NATURE PSYCHOKINESIS; (do not confuse with TELEKINESIS wherein the etheric world intelligences perform the phenomena). (Inconcl.) See Appendix 4 for further clarification of MIND-OVER-MATTER. [cf. Appendix 2 PSYCHOKINESIS]

PSYCHOKINESIS LEVITATION—to elevate an object vertically in the air and suspend it for a period of time without using physical means; executed through deep, disciplined concentration; never spontaneous; first step in PK teleportation; (do not confuse with LEVITATION TELEKINESIS in which the ETHERIC WORLD INTELLIGENCES are employed). (Inconcl.) [cf. ECTOPLASM TELEKINESIS, PSYCHOKINESIS]

PSYCHOKINETIC—an energy that comes from the minds under intense CONCENTRATION of will that can manipulate the atomic structure of physical matter. (Inconcl.) [cf. PK, clarification of MIND-OVER-MATTER Appendix 4]

PSYCHOKINETIC OUTBREAKS—the change of a physical object in structure, form, size, or elements

511

without manipulation from external sources or deliberate CONCENTRATION with the mind; e.g., keys bending, broken clocks repairing themselves when Uri Geller is near by; broken washing machine repairing itself while the person sleeps. (Inconcl.) [**cf.** PSYCHOKINESIS, CELLULAR PSYCHO-KINESIS, BIOENERGETICS]

PSYCHOLOGICAL AURA—the second layer of the ELECTROMAGNETIC RADIATION surrounding and interpenetrating the physical body, extends two to four feet; the astral body; represents one's own true self; can be perceived clairvoyantly. [**cf.** ETHERIC DOUBLE, SOUL-MIND AURA]

PSYCHOLOGICAL BIND—see BLOCKS.

PSYCHOLOGICAL FIELD—a person plus his or her environment and activity in that environment. [**cf.** CURATIVE EDUCATION, HOLISTIC HEALTH]

PSYCHOLOGICAL HEALTH—study of a human being and his or her potential; administers therapy to help one express one's true self; helps one find one's capabilities, one's mission in life (reason of INCARNATION); client has a change in attitude, feels more confident and secure, with an inner satisfaction; makes one a happier human being. **Syn.** SELF-REALIZATION. [**cf.** NEW-AGE PSYCHO-LOGY]

PSYCHOLOGICAL IMPRISONMENT—(destructive-brainwashing cults) to function in a personality that is not one's own by right of decision; to have been cornered, and coerced into a specific set of beliefs and personality changes by MENTAL TELA-PATHIC and HYPNOTIC SUGGESTIONS without one's consent or knowledge of it happening; victim is unable to make logical decisions contrary to the dogma or rules of the destructive cult as the mental telepathic and hypnotic suggestions continue twenty-four hours a day; victim is unable to think for her or himself as he or she is always under the influence of verbal ploy or a mass mental at-mospheric field geared for the purpose and beliefs of the destructive cult; victim's mind is strapped and suppressed of previous concepts and knowl-edge by the will of another. [**cf.** DESTRUCTIVE-BRAINWASHING CULTS, CHARMED, MASS HYPNOSIS]

PSYCHOLOGICAL INTEGRATION—to unify the intellectual solving part of the problem with the EMOTION and UNDERSTANDING necessary to make a complete solution; emotion must be compatible to all solutions if that particular problem is to be dissolved; if one's emotions do not balance with the intellectualizing of the problem, it will occur at another time in one's life. [**cf.** GESTALT THERAPY, KEY TO LIFE]

PSYCHOLOGICAL STRESS EVALUATOR—a device that analyzes the spoken voice; capable of picking up the frequency indistinguishable to the physical ear that detects the truth or falseness of the voice on the device. [**cf.** THIRD FREQUENCY MODULATION, TAPED VOICE PHENOMENON, METABOLIC MONITOR]

PSYCHOLOGICAL STRUCTURES—(Sigmund Freud) dream symbols from night or waking dreams that represent the individual's hidden complexes; can be surfaced in FREE ASSOCIATION therapy. [**cf.** FLUIDIC ASSOCIATION, EXPOSURE DREAM, AWAKE DREAMING]

PSYCHOLOGICAL TIME—1. (Seth) the time in one's life that is best for that person to develop their PSYCHIC ABILITY. **Syn.** PSI-TIME. 2. a period equivalent in human time wherein the SOUL-MIND experiences peaks and valleys of intensities con-cerning emotion, making color, size, height, depth and width changes. [**cf.** EARTH ELECTRIC FIELD, COSMIC WILL]

PSYCHOLOGICAL TRAP—see PSYCHOLOGICAL IMPRISONMENT.

PSYCHOLOGICAL VARIABLES—pertains to exter-nal physical world processes as opposed to extras-ensory processes.

PSYCHOLOGICAL WARP—a "leap to" the higher realms when the PSYCHIC or MEDIUM tunes into the ETHERIC WORLD: an invisible path from the psychic to the attunement he or she is making. **Syn.** PSYCHIC WARP, TRANSPARENT DIMENSIONAL WARP. [**cf.** VEIL, AMPING, APPERCEPTION]

PSYCHOLOGICAL-DETERMINED AMNESIA—to lock emotional experiences out of one's CON-SCIOUSNESS; to suppress painful, unpleasant events after they occurred and gradually repress every similar event until one has completely forgotten the first painful experience. [**cf.** FROZEN, BURIED LIFE, ARTIFICIAL ANXIETY WAVES]

PSYCHOLOGY—science of the mind, the mental states and its capacities; study of human behavior as determined by action; three basic branches: Freu-dian, Behavior Modification, and Humanistic Psychology; the two latter psychologies are interested in the MIND and CONSCIOUSNESS and whether a man has an immaterial brain and a material brain working together. [cf. GHOST IN THE MACHINE, BLOCKS]

PSYCHOLUMINESCENCE—to psychically control photons, thus controlling light, radiant heat, ultraviolet light, and radio-waves through PK. (Inconcl.) [cf. RADIANCE, HALOS, MYSTERIOUS LIGHTS]

PSYCHOMAGNETIC RADIATION—see AURA.

PSYCHOMATIC PHENOMENON—an astral projection to a distant place on the earth in current time. [cf. ASTRAL PROJECTION Appendix 2]

PSYCHOMETER—one skilled in PSYCHOMETRY; see PSYCHIC.

PSYCHOMETRIC—pertains to VIBRATIONS that interpenetrate and surround an article or an area that are intense enough to contain information regarding the article, its environment, and any person involved with the article. [cf. SECONDARY WAVES, PRIMARY WAVES, PSYCHOMETRY]

PSYCHOMETRIC MEDIUM—one who does automatic handwriting with the ETHERIC WORLD INTELLIGENCE and the script comes in poetry form or in the form of metered lines. **Syn.** AUTOMATIST. [cf. AUTOMATIC TRANCE WRITING, COMPLIMENTARY CROSS-CORRESPONDENCE]

PSYCHOMETRIC OBJECT—an article or area that has played its role repeatedly or has been involved in an emotional trauma; article or area carries intense VIBRATIONS interpenetrating and surrounding it that can tell a story to a PSYCHIC who has sensitivity in the hands; psychic holds the article in the palms of his or her hands or holds their palms over the area and perceives this sensitivity through their SYMPATHETIC NERVOUS SYSTEM; e.g., eyeglasses or a wedding ring make a good object to hold for a personal reading because it has been worn daily by the owner and would have imbedded within it the personality of the owner; walls of a room where a shooting took place carry emotional trauma and will tell a story. **Syn.** TOKEN OBJECT. [cf. PRIMARY WAVES, SECONDARY WAVES]

PSYCHOMETRIC POWER—a manifestation of PHYSICAL PSYCHISM by an ETHERIC WORLD INTELLIGENCE that produces etheric script in poetic form.

PSYCHOMETRIC READING—see PSYCHOMETRY.

PSYCHOMETRIC SPECIMEN—an article that belongs or pertains to an individual who is under a PSYCHIC ATTACK, an article taken from the environment of a crime, or individuals under suspicion; article should carry a lot of emotional surface VIBRATIONS or carry imbedded vibrations that accumulated from a good deal of usage by the victim; article is handled with tweezers or pliers, put in a cloth, and taken to the PSYCHOMETRIST to learn information from its radiations; the following are good conductors of MAGNETISM and can be used nicely as specimens: lock of hair, piece of jewelry, crystalline substance, metals, pocketknife, silk, linen, and signet ring. [cf. PURE PSYCHOMETRY, PRACTICAL PSYCHOMETRY, SECONDARY WAVES]

PSYCHOMETRIC TELEPATHY—(laboratory) the transference of the sense of touch-feeling from one person to another, regardless of distance; 1. to perceive a target that is being stroked or touched by the palm of the hand of the experimenter; experimenter must keep a NEUTRAL MIND to allow the texture, size, shape and temperature of the target to be communicated through the palm of the hand, instead of the mind; 2. happens spontaneously also; i.e., one handles a coat at a sale and the friend standing by senses the quality of the cloth. **Syn.** TEXTURE TELEPATHY. [cf. PSYCHOMETRY, TELEPATHY]

PSYCHOMETRIST—one who has sensitivity in one's hands and can tune into the impregnated VIBRATIONS of an object and interpret the vibrations for practical purposes; a psychic who works in the field of PSYCHOMETRY. [cf. CONTACT TELEPATHY, EMANATIONS]

PSYCHOMETRIZING—to perceive PSYCHIC INFORMATION through one's hands; to hold or touch an article between one's hands, close to the forehead, or against the SOLAR PLEXUS to tune in to the vibrations of the article; signals come through the palms of the hands, up the SYMPATHETIC NERVOUS SYSTEM and the brain amplifies and interprets the signals into information the PSYCHOMETRIST can understand. [cf. BILLET READING, PRACTICAL PSYCHOMETRY, PURE PSYCHOMETRY]

PSYCHOMETRY—to handle an object or touch an area and perceive through the palms of one's hands information that was not known before about the article or the owner of the article; PSYCHIC has

513

sensitivity in his or her hands and the VIBRATIONS come through the SYMPATHETIC NERVOUS SYSTEM to the brain where they are amplified for interpretation; article can be held up to the forehead or against the SOLAR PLEXUS for clearer amplification; articles most easily read have been involved in the same role repeatedly or involved in an emotional trauma that impregnated the DNA of the atoms of th article with memories which the psychometrist's hands pick up; one does not sense future information from PSYCHOMETRIZING because the vibrations have not been impregnated as yet; e.g., a policeman brings a shoe to a psychometrist, and the psychometrist handles the shoe and brings information regarding where the shoe has been, or where it spent most of its time, and the emotional characteristics about its owner; psychic tunes out the vibrations of the policeman who brought it. Types of psychometry: 1. PURE PSYCHOMETRY; 2. PRACTICAL PSYCHOMETRY. [cf. SECONDARY WAVES, PRIMARY WAVES, BILLET READING, TOKEN OBJECT]

PSYCHOMONISM—the principle that a living entity can communicate with a DISCARNATE ENTITY.

PSYCHON—(esoteric) an invisible imprint of a traumatic earth event hanging in space; cuts into the physical world frequently after the individuals involved are deceased, causing disturbance in an area; perceived clairvoyantly by earthlings; particles of the formation are nonphysical, nonmaterial, and are emitted in radioactivity through psychic emissions which cling together and hold. [cf. GHOSTS, MENTAL-REFLECTING-ETHER]

PSYCHONUTRITION—study of how food is consumed in the body and why some foods help in one body and not in another body; (John Pageler) "nutritious food will help when the right molecule is in the right place for that particular person at the right time in that life span." [cf. FRINGE MEDICINE, CURATIVE EDUCATION]

PSYCHOPATHOLOGY—manifestations coming from a submerged or subliminal stream of consciousness; possesses powers which ordinary waking conscious does not, pushes on into the consciousness through dreams, hypnosis, hysterical tics, anaesthesia, etc. [cf. SUBLIMINAL LEVEL, KARMA]

PSYCHOPHONE—see DIRECT VOICE.

PSYCHOPHYSICAL—pertains to the mind and body functioning as one unit, with each affecting the other. **Syn.** MIND/BODY. [cf. MIND-LINK/BODY-LINK, HOLISM]

PSYCHOPHYSICAL FIELD—see ECTOPLASM.

PSYCHOPHYSICAL GERM—(esoteric) a seed within each person containing the potential and the thrust to unfold each person to be a perfect human being specimen; a man or woman is an organism like all other organisms that have a seed within and unfold to a perfect specimen of their kind. **Syn.** HOLY SEED, MONAD.

PSYCHOPHYSICAL PARALLELISM—(Baron Gottfried Wilhelm von Leibnitz) theory: the MONAD is the inherent living essence of the potentiality of the organism; body is subservient to the monad. [cf. TOTALITY, ATOMS, LIFE-CORD-HEART-SEED-ATOM]

PSYCHOPHYSICAL PHENOMENA—see PSYCHOKINESIS.

PSYCHOPHYSICS—1. study of movements and manifestations of LIFE and CONSCIOUSNESS originating from the primary cosmos. [cf. VIBRATIONS, ATOMS] 2. study of relationship of physiological parts of the BODY and MIND, the environment, PSYCHIC ENERGY, psychology and ALTERED STATES OF CONSCIOUSNESS; expresses an intelligence with a coating of some substance; research into mind energy that changes conditions in the body such as heart rate, blood flow, hormonal and gastric juices, etc.; theory: body conditions are related to psychological factors, such as stress, arousal, fear, sexual excitement, anxiety and relaxation. [cf. BIOFEEDBACK TRAINING] 3. (Charles Honorton) "denotes physical measurements of psychological phenomena; the EEG is a psychophysical tool."

PSYCHOPHYSIOLOGICAL METHOD—theory: MINDBODY relationship affords that the mind influences the body and the body influences the mind; therefore, the mind could use controlled imagination for an extended range of purposes, especially for the healing of the physical body. [cf. MENTAL HEALING, VISUALIZATION, HOLISTIC HEALTH]

PSYCHOPHYSIOLOGICAL PROCESSES—(biofeedback training) pertains to the physiological conditions that are related to psychological factors made tangible to the PRACTITIONER by instruments: 1. muscle tension can be fed back by the EMG; 2. arousal changes are fed back by the GSR; 3. peripheral bloodflow is fed back by the temperature instrument; 4. altered states of consciousness are fed back by the EEG brain wave patterns; see each instrument individually.

PSYCHOPHYSIOLOGISTS—scientists who study the relationship of electrical brain activity to human being behavior and are interested in human CONSCIOUSNESS. [**cf.** BIOFEEDBACK TRAINING Appendix 5]

PSYCHOPHYSIOLOGY—1. study of mental states and their relationship to the physiological changes in the body; 2. study of the relationships between PSI events and physiological events and its advantages and disadvantages to life experiences; 3. the use of prescribed medicine to change one's attitude as in a mental illness. **Syn.** PHYSIOLOGICAL PSYCHOLOGY. [**cf.** HOLISM]

PSYCHOPLASM—see ECTOPLASM.

PSYCHOPOMP—1. (Native American) a SHAMAN who has experienced an initiatory death-rite; this experience prepares his mind and body to become a channel for healing and helping tribesmen make their TRANSITION to the etheric world in the real death process; 2. one has charge of helping individuals enter into the ETHERIC WORLD during their death process. [**cf.** DEATH SCIENCE Appendix 2]

PSYCHOPOMPOS—(early A.D.) the ETHERIC WORLD INTELLIGENCE in charge of guiding persons through the DENSITY and lower planes upon death; helps the dying person find his or her rightful plane more easily. [**cf.** DEATH ANGEL, DEATH SCIENCE, DEATH CONSCIOUSNESS]

PSYCHOPRESIS—to psychically control heat, ignite fire, and control fire; ability to direct the speed of atoms and be in command of the atoms pertaining to the fire by intense mind focalization; (temperature is a function of the speed of atoms moving in an object. (Inconcl.) [**cf.** TEMPERATURE, ATMOSPHERE CONTROL, IGNIS FATUUS]

PSYCHORIENTOLOGY—(Silva Mind Control) the study of techniques of how to orient the subjective world and reach the various levels of the mind dimension. [**cf.** ENIGMATIC PHENOMENA, FORTEAN EVENTS]

PSYCHORRHAGY—to perceive clairvoyant visions and phantoms at will. [**cf.** CLAIRVOYANCE Appendix 2]

PSYCHOSCIENCE—the study of mind processes; see PARAPSYCHOLOGY.

PSYCHOSCOPE—(Brazil) an appliance designed to listen to the soul of a man or woman; capable of defining its vibrations and the capacity to carry out certain observations concerning matter based on ELECTRICITY, MAGNETISM, and radiant elements. [**cf.** SUBCONSCIOUS MIND]

PSYCHOSCOPY—see PSYCHOMETRY.

PSYCHOSENSITIVE—see PSYCHIC.

PSYCHOSENSOR—see PSYCHIC.

PSYCHOSOMA—(Brazil) see SOUL-MIND.

PSYCHOSOMATIC—(Greek *psycho*, "mind"; *somo*, "body") concept that disease is all in the mind even though it is manifesting in a physical way; a malfunction of the body; pain or sickness, stemming from the individual's thoughts and emotional status; an imbalance between the parasympathetic and SYMPATHETIC NERVOUS SYSTEM. [**cf.** HOLISTIC HEALTH, PERMANENT HEALING]

PSYCHOSOMATIC POWER CENTER—an invisible energy field located in the spine, necessary for life; begins as a concentrated energy field in the base of the spine and flows upward as the SOUL-MIND grows; see SUSHUMNA. [**cf.** KUNDALINI, SERPENT POWER]

PSYCHOSOMATIC SELF-REGULATION—to enter the subconscious level of the mind and function with awareness from that level; to learn to control altered states of consciousness.

PSYCHOSOPHY—see PSYCHISM.

PSYCHOSPHERE—(Edgar Mitchell) a hyperdimensional field of consciousness whereby the individual human PSYCHE transcends egoism to achieve union and a COSMIC CONSCIOUSNESS. [**cf.** EGO-KILLING PRACTICE, ESSENCE OF REST]

PSYCHOSPIRITUAL POWERS—1. a level of development in an individual wherein an individual psychically senses a correct feeling about Truths in the world and etheric world; an experience of ECSTASY in the quietness of one's sanctuary. [**cf.** DHARANIS, BLISS MEDITATION] 2. psychic skills and mediumship used in a religious nature to help the SOUL-MIND grow.

PSYCHOSURGERY—(future science) to bury sensitive electrodes deep within a person's brain, then monitor his or her BRAIN WAVES and send this information via two-way radio to a central computer; instead of being upset with conditions, the computer sends back messages of its own, inhibiting what would otherwise be violent behavior and blunting emotional response; presently against the law.

PSYCHOSYNTHESIS—integration of knowledge, techniques, and guidance pertaining to the SOUL-MIND growth; the desire for optimum relationship between one's major aspects of personality, body, mind and feelings; to disidentify with environment and to identify with SELF; to experience mastery of the WILL as the optimum motive force in choosing, planning, and directing one's life. [cf. MYSTIC CHRISTIAN, PLANETARY HELPER]

PSYCHOTECHNOLOGIES—(Marilyn Ferguson) 1. systems for a deliberate change in CONSCIOUSNESS; (a) refers to all kinds of techniques and methods using the MIND, or BRAIN/MIND that have been discovered, experienced and are now being practiced in this NEW AGE; objective: to benefit and raise the consciousness of the mental realm and MUNDANE WORLD lifestyles; (b) systems are designed to transform the individual by shifting from the LEFT BRAIN HEMISPHERE, intellectual and analytical side, to the RIGHT BRAIN HEMISPHERE which eventually brings an attitude change in one's lifestyle and goals; (c) in all varieties the main theme is "awareness on awareness," making the new focal point unbounded and indefinite; the mind is plagued by strangeness, complexity, or monotony by the use of music, WATER, CANDLE FLAME, MANTRA, BREATHING, blank wall, physical movement, a KOAN, etc.; these bring expansions of awareness that are pleasurable to the doer; 2. some systems are: SENSORY ISOLATION or overload, BIO-FEEDBACK TRAINING, AUTOGENIC TRAINING, IMAGERY, GUIDED MEDITATION, music intonation, PSYCHODRAMA, mutual help networks, HYPNOTHERAPY, SELF-HYPNOTHERAPY, jogging, dancing, innumerable types of MEDITATION and intensive weekend seminars; (do not confuse with DESTRUCTIVE-BRAINWASHING CULTS which use forced and coerced methods]

PSCHOTHERAPIST—1. one who works with the mind and emotions in dealing with disease; usually a HYPNOTHERAPIST works with PSYCHO-THERAPY; 2. (Bulgaria) one who gives MENTAL HEALING treatment through the method of SUGGESTOLOGY. [cf. SUGGESTOPEDIA, EMOTIONS]

PSYCHOTHERAPY—psychological counseling therapy that gets the individual integrated and on his or her rightful PATH; administers to the SOUL-MIND and emotions to keep the body and mind healthy; works with the SUBCONSCIOUS MIND to help release the tensions or blocks that have been pushed into the body and could be the cause of the mental or physical illness; usually carried out by the power of suggestion as in HYPNOTHERAPY or repeated AFFIRMATIONS. [cf. CURATIVE EDUCATION]

PSYCHTRON ENERGY—(Russia, Czechoslovakia) coined in Czechoslovakia; the energy in the body that does psychic work. (Inconcl.) see PSYCHIC ENERGY.

PSYCHOTRONIC GENERATORS—(Czechoslovakia) instruments that draw PSYCHIC ENERGY out of a human and use this energy for TELEPATHY, TELEKINESIS and HEALING; instrument stores this psychic energy, similar to electricity stored in a battery, and then uses it to change molecular structure; other instruments draw psychic energy out of the air to use it constructively; e.g., purifying small amounts of polluted water. [cf. OPERATION PRAYER POWER]

PSYCHOTRONICS—1. (Russia, Czechoslovakia, United States) an interdisciplinary science studying interaction (internal and external) between people, their environment, and the energy processes involved; recognizes MATTER, ENERGY, and CONSCIOUSNESS as interconnected; 2. study of paranormal processes or psychic research including RADIONICS, RADIESTHESIA, SHAPED POWER, KIRLIAN EFFECT, BOTANE, with emphasis on electrical measurements; 3. study of interactions between living and nonliving objects over a distance bound by an energy form of living matter. **Syn.** PARAPSYCHOLOGY.

PSYCHOTROPIC PLANTS—1. plants used to induce altered states of consciousness for pleasure and spiritual growth; plants that are administered under supervision or with righteous intent to bring an ALTERED STATE OF CONSCIOUSNESS which gives one a PSYCHIC EXPERIENCE that enables one to have a greater understanding of reality and the worlds; 2. (Hinduism) induce a sense of union with the universe as the identification of Brahma with

ATMAN; 3. used as drugs to change one's mood, mind, and attitude. **Syn.** HALLUCINOGENIC PLANT. [**cf.** PEYOTE PLANT, BOTANE]

PUBLIC AUGURY—(Rome) to give counsel and predict the affairs of the country by obtaining the information psychically, using omens of weather and of nature; taught by Caesar in the colleges of Rome. **Syn.** DIVINATION, SOOTHSAYING. [**cf.** AUGUR, LITUS, TEMPLUM, OMEN]

PUBLIC PORTENDER—a PSYCHIC who draws nonhuman omens to her or himself or their vicinity and is hired by the government to interpret the omens as to the future of the government and civilization; psychic understands the laws of nature and knows when nature is disturbed that nature behaves abnormally; e.g., to have a branch fall a few feet in front of one with no physical cause; to hear a rooster crow in the daytime; these are forerunners of events. [**cf.** DIVINE EYES, ARUSPEX, EXTRATEMPORAL PERCEPTION, OMEN]

PUCK—(William Shakespeare) a NATURE SPIRIT with a mischievous, teasing, tricky character but who could show compassion or kindness; not malevolent and has his own moral standards; capable of shape-shifting into a stool, horse, etc.; related to the HOBGOBLINS of the Welsh and Irish PHOUKA. **Syn.** WILL-O-THE-WISP, BROWNIE. [**cf.** NATURE SPIRITS]

PUCKWUKJINI—(Native American, Algonquin) means "little vanishing people"; see NATURE SPIRITS.

PUDAK—(Siberia) symbolic of obstacles one has to overcome; name of the density or the seven subterranean regions. [**cf.** DENSITY, ASURA-LOKA, CARRYING AN EVIL]

PUG—a wee one, sometimes meaning DEVIL; see NATURE SPIRITS.

PUGGIE—same derivation as PUCK; see NATURE SPIRITS.

PUJA—(Buddhism) offerings consisting of flowers, incense, sticks, or lights, brought to the temple or any place one worships; used as an aid to derive emotional satisfaction from BUDDHA worship. [**cf.** CAUCASIAN YOGA, COLLECTING THE MIND]

PULLING OUT THE SICKNESS—(!Kung) to force the illness out of patients, by a healer who works in a TRANCE state induced by prolonged dancing around a hot fire in the evening; 1. the fluttering hands of the entranced HEALER are placed on either side of the congested area; shaky hands draw the illness out with a sweeping motion; the negative vibrations are shaken or flicked off the healer's hands before he repeats the process; continued until the patient is free of the sickness; 2. after dancing around the hot fire, the healer wraps his sweaty body around the ill person; the sweat forces the disease to psychically transfer into the healer's body; healer must free himself of the disease; patient is well. [**cf.** KIA, PSYCHIC HEALING, ECSTASY, TRANCE]

PULOTU—(Hawaii) see ETHERIC WORLD.

PULSATION—vibrate, beat, burst; constant movement. **Syn.** VIBRATION.

PULSE-POINT—(esoteric) one of the two anchor points for the VAGUS NERVE which is located in the heart chakra. **Syn.** PACE-MAKER. [**cf.** LIFE-CORD-SEED-ATOM]

PULSED WAVE ACTIVITY—(ufology) the chopping of the radar radiation into hundreds of short bursts. [**cf.** FLYING SHIELDS, FIREFLIES, DAYLIGHT DISCS]

PUMPING—(spirit healing) to utilize the spirit in the air for healing a physical condition; hand is placed on the congested area while one breathes rhythmically; healing can be instantaneous or gradual; spirit from the air is emanated through the hands; (group healing) people form a chain, linking themselves together by body contact; the first person touches the patient, as the group breathes rhythmically in unison; this pumps the spirit in the air to the patient; the spirit from the breath goes directly to the congested area and begins a healing process (for a gradual or spontaneous healing). Usage: to be performed in accidents before the paramedics arrive, or in the home during the night when doctors are not available; requires no healing knowledge, religious belief or special faith; (do not confuse with LAYING-ON-OF-HANDS). [**cf.** MAGNET HEALING, MENTAL HEALING]

PURE ALERTNESS—a complete meditative state in which the body is sound asleep, the mind is unattached to outer things, but it is still very awake to inner realizations. [**cf.** DOING JAPA, ALERT-ASLEEP, DETACHMENT]

PURE AWARENESS—a fundamental aspect of self; the knowing of a source of knowledge and energy that one can contact. [**cf.** MEDITATION, CONSCIOUSNESS]

517

PURE COGNITIVE TECHNIQUE—(laboratory) an experiment whereby a machine generates the targets and scores the responses but records only the total scores; this rules out TELEPATHY as an explanation of extra chance results. [**cf.** CHANCE, COVARIANCE EFFECT, CHECKER]

PURE CONSCIOUSNESS—a perfect state of being, wherein living matter will have no need of direction; the very highest attainment a human or matter will have to accomplish in the evolutionary cycle; the state of awareness in this consciousness can only be speculation: perhaps one would be only totally aware, deeply relaxed, not distracted by thought, feeling, or sense impression; a grandeur or ecstasy humans cannot comprehend at this time; perfectness and etheric oneness.

PURE CREATIVITY—Totality manifesting itself in the physical world through an earth artist; see INSPIRATIONAL THOUGHT.

PURE ELEMENTAL—see NATURE SPIRITS.

PURE IMAGINATION—(Carl Jung) "perception coming from the unconscious without any conscious thought"; a NON-THOUGHT coming into the mind that was not triggered from within the mind; see INSPIRATIONAL THOUGHT.

PURE LAND—(Buddhism) a vibrational frequency in the etheric world where one will be free from pain and sorrow. [**cf.** PURE CONSCIOUSNESS, SEVENTH PLANE]

PURE LOVE—vibrates as all WHITE; see TOTALITY or PURE CONSCIOUSNESS.

PURE PSYCHOMETRY—(*psycho,* "soul"; *metron,* "measure") to psychically measure or evaluate a physical article or an area through the hands; article is held in the hands, or the area is touched by the hands, and information is perceived about the article or area "itself" that one cannot tell by looking at it; PSYCHIC has sensitivity in palms of his or her hands and first three fingers; imbedded VIBRATIONS on article pass through the palms into the SYMPATHETIC NERVOUS SYSTEM to the brain for amplification and interpretation; article reveals its origin, value, age, many uses, its inhabitants, and involvements (in happiness or resentment), etc.; every inanimate thing holds within its atoms the memory of where it has been and how involved it was; e.g., a figurine could reveal if it came from a sunny or dark, cold climate, its uses, whether presented as a gift, used in a RITUAL, etc.; a knife used to kill would be impregnated with evil vibrations; (do not confuse with PRACTICAL PSYCHOMETRY which reveals information regarding its owner); an object will not carry its future uses within its vibrations. [**cf.** PRACTICAL PSYCHOMETRY]

PURE SPIRITS—angels who have evolved high on the hierarchy into a substance that humanity could not recognize if they could contact, because of its rate of frequency. [**cf.** COSMIC ENTITY, EXALTED ONES]

PURE TELEPATHY TECHNIQUE—(psi tasks) no objective record is ever made of the targets in an ESP experiment, thus ruling out COGNITION and PRECOGNITION as an explanation for extra chance results. [**cf.** ESP, FORCED-CHOICE TEST, COGNIZE]

PURGATORY—1. (Christianity) a lower plane in the ETHERIC WORLD where a SOUL-MIND works to purify her or himself; a condition or place of spiritual cleansing for the dead; 2. a plane of darkness in the DENSITY made by and inhabited by soul-minds that have put themselves in that state of consciousness through their ignorance and low morality acts and thoughts while an earthling. [**cf.** DENSITY, HADES]

PURIFIED BODY—see GLORIFIED BODY.

PURIFYING BREATH—(Yoga) method of BREATHING that cleanses and helps to balance one's SOUL-MIND. [**cf.** BREATHING RELEASE, COMPLETE BREATH]

PURITY OF THE WORK—a psychic phrase meaning there is no fraudulent desires on part of the psychic.

PURNA—(Hinduism) the whole; see TOTALITY.

PURPORTED SPIRITS—ETHERIC WORLD INTELLIGENCES who are eager to prove their authenticity when called in by the MEDIUM; this relieves the medium's mind and he or she knows that the entities are of a high caliber.

PURUSHA—see SOUL-MIND.

PUSSY WILLOW—(Ironsland) a tree considered as one of the seven noble trees of the land, similar to Christianity's Palm for Palm Sunday; used as a psychic charm against enchantment. [**cf.** BOTANE, BIODETECTORS, CHARGING[

PUT IT ON THE SHELF—a common expression giving advice to a student of METAPHYSICS who can accept new philosophy and concepts logically and intelligently but does not "feel good" with the new

518

material. Usage: "Put it on the shelf until you can emotionally accept the new concept no matter how long it takes; do not cast it completely aside." Metaphysics is a discipline of feeling. [**cf.** METAPHYSICS, MYSTICISM]

PUTTING OUT FEELERS—the desire to tune into the experience of life and yet not open up one's PSYCHIC DOORS until the activity is examined beforehand.

PUTTY IMPRESSIONS—(materialization seance) before full materialization is accomplished, an indentation in the form of a face or hand, looking as if it was made from putty, will be seen in the ectoplasm coming from the medium's body. [**cf.** IDEOLASTICITY, ECTOPLASMIC WISPS, ECTOPLASMIC MATERIALIZATION]

PWCA—(Wales), see NATURE SPIRIT.

PYGMALION HYPOTHESIS—(Jule Eisenbud) a survival concept: while personalities may seemingly be living in certain restricted senses, they are not surviving portions of the deceased; they are recreations, by the living, of certain aspects, of the deceased; once organized, such entities may have varying degrees of autonomy, but they continue to exist only for as long as their life is sustained by the living. [**cf.** PHILLIP, ELEMENTALS]

PYGMIES—(Greek mythology) NATURE SPIRITS about thirteen inches high; a nation of them are living in the ETHERIC WORLD.

PYRAMID—a construction of four triangles attached together made to "specific dimensions" that yields a condensed energy in the middle because of its shape. (Inconcl.) See PYRAMID POWER and GIZA PYRAMID. [**cf.** FORMS-WITH-POWER]

PYRAMID ENERGY PLATE—(Patrick Flanagan) a small aluminum plate which has been electronically charged with amplified pyramid energy and can do everything a large PYRAMID does; a type of psychotronic device. [**cf.** PYRAMID POWER]

PYRAMID IN MYTHOLOGY—symbolizes the CAUSAL BODY, the body that has to conquer the three lower bodies; the causal body is the seat of the spiritual TRIAD which then unites with the higher self, or the capstone. [**cf.** BODIES AND PLANES Appendix 5]

PYRAMID MATRIX—a unit of fifteen small pyramids made to scale that generate pyramid energy from their points; food or items placed on top of them receive the same PYRAMID POWER as if placed inside a PYRAMID. [**cf.** HEADSTONE, GALACTIC CONFEDERATION]

PYRAMID MEDITATION—to sit under a suspended pyramid or inside a large pyramid for MEDITATION; individuals face the east; some may feel very relaxed and others will be rejuvenated with energy; the energy is not harmful to people but can be overwhelming and, therefore, one must know his or her own limits. [**cf.** PYRAMID POWER, PYRAMID IN MYTHOLOGY]

PYRAMID POWER—(Greek *pyr,* "fire"; *amid,* "near the center"; "fire in the center") a special condensed energy found inside every PYRAMID, made according to the exact scale of the GREAT PYRAMID at Giza; this energy follows the pattern or seed potential of the objects placed within it bringing that person or object closer to its intended perfect state; some items are enhanced and others are preserved when placed within the pyramid form; pyramid must be aligned with one side to the true north; a special condensed energy is found about one/third the way from the bottom that makes changes in animate or inanimate things when placed within the pyramid; energy also emits from the apex of the pyramid; material from which it is made is insignificant as long as it is to exact scale; a framework construction works as well as a solid form; length of time articles should be kept under the pyramid or on top is still in the experimental state. [**cf.** PYRAMIDOLOGY, FORMS-WITH-POWER]

PYRAMID TEXTS—hieroglyphic inscriptions on the chambers and passages in the pyramids make up the Heliopolitan version of the BOOK OF THE DEAD. [**cf.** GIZA PYRAMID, STEP PYRAMID]

PYRAMIDAL—pertaining to the PYRAMID.

PYRAMIDOLOGIST—one who scientifically studies how the shape makes the energy that is filled in the center of the PYRAMID, and its function, etc. [**cf.** PYRAMIDOLOGY, FORMS-WITH-POWER, CONE]

PYRAMIDOLOGY—study of the energy that is produced inside and outside the pyramids which properly constructed to the scale of the Great Giza Pyramid; (do not confuse with study of archaeology). [**cf.** PYRAMID POWER, FORMS-WITH-POWER]

PYROKINESIS—(Russia) form of PK.

PYROTECHNICS—emissions of the auric pattern picked up on the film of the Kirlian camera. [**cf.**

BIOLOGICAL PLASMA, HEAT CONVECTION CUR-
RENTS]

PYTHAGOREAN SCIENCE—an integrated study
based on the correspondence of one unique event
with another; a sympathetic consciousness resonance between two unique events wherein they
vibrate in harmony together; it then moves beyond
resonance, not to control nature, but in cooperation
with nature. [**cf.** SOUNDS-WITH-POWER.]

PYTHIA—the PSYCHIC and prophetess at Delphi
who went into trance allowing voices to speak
through her; her main voice was that of Apollo. [**cf.**
ORACLE AT DELPHI, ORACLE STATUE]

QABALAH—(Hebrew) a book that carries the esoteric tradition of Israel, the ancient Hebrew culture that gives the European spiritual culture its roots; traces back to the Chaldeans; put together in the Middle Ages; the wisdom of a sacred and hidden science; see CABALA and KABBALAH; also spelled **Cabbala, Kabala, Kabalah, Kabbala, Qabala, Quabalah, Quaballah,** and **Quabbalah.** [cf. DEUS ABSCONDITIUS, EN SOPH, TREE OF LIFE, SEFIROTH]

QI—(China) air or breath; a vital energy in the air necessary for all life; taken into the body by BREATHING and then broken down into the Yin, negative/feminine and Yang, positive/masculine; see VITAL LIFE FORCE for details. **Syn.** LIFE FORCE, PRANA, BIOSCOSMIC ENERGY.

QLIPPOTH—(Kabbalah) the demons of "positive evil"; opposite of angels; the name of powers of magic; obverse of SEPHIROTH.

QUABBALAH—see CABALA, KABBALAH, and QABALAH.

QUABBALISTIC—pertaining to the Holy Quabbalah text.

QUALITY OF THE WORK—a parapsychologist's phrase to describe whether the psychic is contacting the higher or lower ASTRAL PLANES in his or her messages. [cf. ETHERIC WORLD INTELLIGENCES, DENSITY]

QUANTUM JUMP—the energy transfer of an electron within an atom containing the knowledge that will come through psychically. (Inconcl.) [cf. SYNAPSE, VEIL, PSYCHIC WARP]

QUANTUM MECHANICS—a branch of mechanics that is applicable to systems at the atomic and nuclear level; composed of systems in which velocities are approached or equal to the speed of light and for which particles are created and destroyed. (Inconcl.)

QUANTUM PHYSICS—the smallest amount of radiant energy; (esoteric) the new basic principle is wholistic and synchronistic. (Inconcl.)

QUANTUM THEORY—(Max Planck's radiation law) changes of energy in atoms and molecules occur only in discrete quantities, each is an integral multiple of a fundamental quantity or quantum. (Inconcl.) [cf. VIBRATIONS Appendix 5]

QUANTUM VACUUM—the source of all activity where activity is unmanifest and yet infinitely correlated; where all ideas and thoughts begin; state of least excitement; quietude. (Inconcl.) **Syn.** AKSHARA. [cf. SIDHIS, SUTRAS, QUANTUM PHYSICS]

QUARTER DISTRIBUTION—abbr. QD (psi tasks) keeping track of an experiment by dividing the paper into quarters, so a decline or incline could be determined, both up and down and across, in the analysis of the number of hits and their effects. [cf. PSI TASKS, ESP]

QUARTZ—(esoteric) a mineral or rock crystal that is hexagonal in form but no two are alike; possesses the property helpful in DEMATERIALIZATION and rematerialization of a human being; can make the invisible visible and vice versa; capable of being energized from the palm of the hand; used in healing by medicine men and in their rain-making ceremonies; used for SCRYING. (Inconcl.) [cf. BOTANE, ALCHEMY Appendix 2]

QUASARS—radio stars that send out radio waves; a stellar object felt to be among the most remote bodies in the sky. [cf. UFOLOGY]

QUASI—prefix meaning "false, but similar."

QUASI-PHYSICAL SUBSTANCE—coined by Charles Richet; ECTOPLASM; see same.

QUASIELECTROSTATIC FIELD—coined by Henry Margenau (1959); see VITAL LIFE FORCE.

QUEEN OF ELPHEN—ETHERIC WORLD INTELLIGENCE that has charge over kings; appears clairvoyantly to psychics as being very pleasant. [cf. MAGNIFICENT DEVAS, MINOR DEVAS]

QUEEN OF THE BODY—(esoteric) the PITUITARY GLAND; the feminine center that radiates upon a higher vibrational level than the rest of the body; has control of the human body in its third-dimensional state, by changing electrical energy from the brain to a physical hormone used throughout the body; in charge of the SYMPATHETIC NERVOUS SYSTEM, SUBCONSCIOUS MIND, glandular system, and the blood stream; its post lobe is a part of the THIRD-EYE AREA; negative in POLARITY; holds the BROW CHAKRA; master gland of the physical body. [cf. PINEAL GLAND, THIRD-EYE AREA Appendix 5]

QUEEN SCALE—a diagram used in CEREMONIAL MAGIC, containing circles and paths; painted special colors for the devotee to use in a special ritual for becoming attuned to the universal power; reverse of the KING SCALE. [cf. CEREMONY, CONJURATION, CONE OF POWER]

QUENCHING THE SPIRIT—term used to describe individuals who have not discovered how to open up and let the HOLY SPIRIT flow through them, and talk-in-tongues. [cf. ECSTASY, GLOSSOLALIST]

QUERANT—the individual who desires to receive information psychically, through a psychic READING, from TAROT CARDS, from coins in CASTING OF LOTS, or from the I CHING; the questioner. [cf. PERCIPIENT, SUBJECT, PERCEIVER]

QUERIST—one desiring PSYCHIC INFORMATION; the questioner or recipient

QUESITED—one who answers the questioner through ASSTROLOGY or by giving PSYCHIC INFORMATION; see PSYCHIC.

QUESTIONER—individual who has a problem and is seeking an answer, used with the I CHING; and for mental PSYCHIC COUNSELING.

QUICKENED CONSCIOUSNESS—the surfacing of stagnant or uneducated energy that is stimulated by a physical experience; outer environmental events frequently occur that at first appear to be negative but result in helping a person express another part of her or himself which they would not have expressed; e.g., the spraining of one's ankle so one will have to stay home from work and read a book that needed reading; cold weather destroying one's flowers, so one has to work in the garden and receive necessary exercise. [cf. EXPANSION CONSCIOUSNESS, GROSS LEVEL]

QUICKSILVER—the name given to mercury because of its mobility; important to the ALCHEMIST because it combines opposites by being a metal and also a liquid, and a liquid, yet not wet. Syn. LIVE SILVER. [cf. ALCHEMICAL LIQUOR, ALCHEMIST OF SACRED FIRE]

QUIET ATTENTIVENESS—a state in which the body is calm and relaxed, the emotions under control, and the CONSCIOUS MIND is passive; the SUBCONSCIOUS MIND and SUPERCONSCIOUS MIND are concentrating on one special thing, to bring about a correct meditative state. [cf. COLLECTING THE MIND, CAUCASIAN YOGA]

QUIET REFLECTION—a meditative state whereby

the mind, body, and emotions are quiet and relaxed, allowing the MONAD to reflect the perfect SELF in CONSCIOUSNESS. [cf. PASSIVE VOLITION, ART OF TEA]

QUIET—a meditative state. [cf. BEATING DOWN THOUGHT, CENTER, SILENCE]

QUIETISM—(Spanish priest) to surrender ones worldly interests and passively concentrate on GOD; the body becomes lifeless with no motion or noise; a meditative level in which God can talk to the individual. [cf. PSYCHIC DOORS, INSPIRATIONAL THOUGHT, BLANK PERIODS]

QUIETUDE—see MEDITATION.

QUINTESSENCE—1. (Theophrastus Paracelsus) theory that the true value of every substance lies in the virtue of its center, the SOUL or MONAD; the life energy that fills all the universe, a magnetic light force essential for all things; 2. (alchemy) term used in ancient philosophy for the fifth element in addition to AIR, EARTH, WATER, FIRE; the most characteristic part of quality of a thing; thought to be the material of which the heavenly bodies were made and to exist later in all earthly things. [cf. MONAD, CELESTIAL DEW]

RA—(ancient Egypt) God of earth; marks the beginning of time; also represents the sun and antiquity; depicted by a hawk-headed man bearing the solar disk and the uraeus on his head.

RABBAT—see POLTERGEIST.

RACE KARMA—the past, present, and future activity, concepts, goals, economy, government, inventions, progress, etc., for each race, made by the mental and emotional equivalent of the past and present KARMA of the people (at large) who are born into it; one is born into a particular race because one needs the experiences of the karmic pattern of that race; some are sent to become leaders and to raise the CONSCIOUSNESS of that race; one race is not higher than another, but simply presents different kinds of experiences; each race must raise its own consciousness, which is added to the overall consciousness of the planet; each individual in a race is held responsible for the goals and activities of that race, unless he or she is working to change these activities. [**cf.** MASS KARMA, REINCARNATION]

RACES—a group of persons related by karmic ties and similarities in bodily capabilities, personal values, levels of CONSCIOUSNESS and needed earthly lessons; there are seven root-races that mankind must evolve through in the PLANETARY CHAIN, which forms the evolutionary cycle in the earth. [**cf.** COSMIC CYCLE, COSMIC TIME-TABLE, ROOT RACE]

RACIAL MEMORY—(Carl Jung) to recall, through regression methods, events and lives which one feels are his or her own past lives, but which are actually lives of ancestors of the race he or she was incarnated into; each race has a GROUP SOUL that telepathically links each one in the race, and one always retains this link, even though it weakens in strength. [**cf.** COLLECTIVE UNCONSCIOUS]

RACIAL UNCONSCIOUS—1. (Carl Jung) dispositions that each person inherits about human and subhuman ways of thinking; 2. a collection of thoughts and experiences of all the happenings of the human race on planet earth (both good and bad); capable of coming through the SUBCONSCIOUS MIND in DREAMS, HYPNOTHERAPY, or other alpha states of consciousness. [**cf.** SOUL-MIND MEMORY BANK, UNIVERSAL SYMBOLS]

RACING ONES—(Tibet) persons who can run at high speeds for hours; accomplished by the rhythmic, repetitive movement of the body which alters the STATE OF CONSCIOUSNESS after the first hour; in this altered state one centralizes one's thought on the upper part of the body, which frees the legs from jurisdiction of the CONSCIOUS MIND and the legs then move automatically, hardly touching the ground. [**cf.** PROLONGED JOGGING, MOVEMENT-FOR-ALTERED-CONSCIOUSNESS, DERVISHES]

RADAR ANGELS—(future science) any energy field seen in the atmosphere which cannot be identified as to what it is or as to its composition. [**cf.** ARMORED ORGANISM, ELECTRONIC FINGER, ENERGY TRAIL]

RADIANT BODY—see ETHERIC DOUBLE.

RADIATING ONE—a Buddhic meditative position, wherein both hands are on the level of the heart center, left palm turned inward, right palm turned outward; representative of uniting the outer world with the center in the human and putting the wheels of the universe in motion. [**cf.** MEDITATION, HANDS, LOTUS POSTURE]

RADIATION—(esoteric) vibrations full of life and intelligence that are emitted from a person or an object, having a uniqueness to that body; invisible to the naked eye but can be detected and measured by instruments and can be photographed; radiations are transmitted through space and become absorbed by another body or object; a collective word which encompasses the electromagnetic field, gravitational field, and other types of vibrations within and without the human spectrum range. [**cf.** VIBRATIONS Appendix 5]

RADIATION BURN—(ufology) a flesh burn on a UFO CONTACTEE that is caused by the pulsed electromagnetic energy emanating from the vehicle that overstimulates the living tissue; not noticeable until after the UFO vehicle leaves. [**cf.** COMPUTERISTS, BLIP]

RADIATION FIELD PHOTOGRAPHY—see KIRLIAN PHOTOGRAPHY.

RADIATION PATTERN—see AURA.

RADIATIONAL PARAPHYSICS—the detection of radiations beyond the range of standard physics instrumentation; see SUPERSONICS.

RADIESTHESIA—(*radii*, "rays"; *esthesia*, "sensation and feeling") feeling of the rays; a science that studies sensitivity to the RADIATION which emanates from all things (animate and inanimate), and how to detect, measure, and make use of those radiations; a measurement of micro radiating waves or vibrations emanating from a substance, plant, animal, or human, in relation to the physical universe; theories: 1. the mind tells itself what it is searching for or what it wants to know, i.e., "Where is the water located underground?"; "Is this watermelon ripe?"; the hand using an instrument (DOWSING ROD or PENDULUM) senses the radiation from the object over which the instrument is held; this sensation travels up the SYMPATHETIC NERVOUS SYSTEM to the brain; the brain tunes into the universe for the answer and sends the answer down the sympathetic nervous system through the arm and hand; the instrument amplifies the answer, and gives visible signals that the CONSCIOUS MIND can understand; 2. the mind tells itself the question, and then keeps itself neutral; the eyes react similarly to radar and bounce signals back from the radiations of the object that the instrument is held over; the signals travel down the sympathetic nervous system from the brain; they reach the instrument, and this acts as an antenna to amplify and code the answser (code is prearranged in the mind); in both theories, the process happens very quickly. (Inconcl.) [cf. RADIESTHETIC SENSE, RADIONICS, BOB, PALLOMANCY]

RADIESTHESIOLOGY—the science of radiations and their practical use.

RADIESTHESIST—one who is skilled in the use of the PENDULUM, DOWSING ROD, radionic instrumentation, and other similar tools; one who believes that the radiations from all things, animate and inanimate, have a meaning and a purpose; PSYCHIC must have ability to keep a NEUTRAL MIND until the instrument answers, to make sure the answer comes from TOTALITY; the psychic is the DIVINER, actually the instrument, and the tool (pendulum and dowsing rod) serves as the antenna to amplify the "weak" signals in the brain, so the psychic can understand them. [cf. RHABODIC FORCE, PROGRAMMING THE SUBCONSCIOUS]

RADIESTHETIC SENSE—term for RADIESTHESIA sensitivity; to receive accurate responses from the PENDULUM, and/or DOWSING ROD; to measure radiations emanating from a chosen object or person by holding a tool over the article or person under examination, and allowing the tool to react in a meaningful way, for psychic understanding; tool serves as an antenna, both receiving information from the radiations and amplifying the information back to the psychic by its movements; signals travel through the SYMPATHETIC NERVOUS SYSTEM to the brain, register faintly, and then travel down the sympathetic nervous system to the antenna; same principle is utilized when finger tips are rubbed on a rubber strip or stroker's plate on a radionic box; the plate and strip serve as the antenna. [cf. STICK, RADIATIONAL PARAPHYSICS, STROKER PLATE]

RADIOGRAPHS—photographs obtained without the use of a camera, by a MEDIUM, with the help of his or her guides; see PSYCHIC PHOTOGRAPHY.

RADIONIC CAMERA—(future science) an instrument that takes a picture of the patient's organs and tissues (similar to an x-ray picture) in the absence of the patient, by using a drop of his or her blood; invented by Ruth Drown. (Inconcl.) [cf. MIND MACHINE, RESONANT RECORDER, PSIONIC MACHINE]

RADIONIC DIAGNOSTICIAN—one who uses either the PENDULUM or DOWSING ROD to detect a change in POLARITY somewhere on the body of the patient, indicating a problem in that area; body polarity needs to be balanced for a well body. (Inconcl.) [cf. POLARITY BALANCING, CURATIVE EDUCATION]

RADIONIC HEALING—to use a black box, or similar instrumentation, for healing the body; see BLACK BOX for details. [cf. RADIONICS, RADIATION]

RADIONIC PRACTITIONER—a doctor who has used the BLACK BOX extensively for healing and diagnosing, and has become so proficient that he or she can accomplish the same kind of diagnosing with the use of their finger tips only, without relying on the dials of the box. (Inconcl.) [cf. STICK-POINT ANALYSIS]

RADIONICS—a branch of radiesthesia that deals only with human being radiations; a scientific study of body POLARITY, energy radiations and other kinds of radiations that can be used in the future for diagnosing disease. (Inconcl.) [cf. KINESIOLOGY, RADIATION, HANDS]

RAGAS—(Hinduism) consists of six basic raga, which are fixed melodic scales, each having a natural correspondence with a certain hour of the day, season of the year, and a presiding DEITY who bestows a particular potency; each raga has a minimum of five notes. [cf. MUSIC OF THE SPHERES]

RAGWEED—(esoteric) a plant used by the witches and fairies to ride through the air. **Syn.** RAGWORT. [**cf.** BOTANE, WITCH'S OIL, MANDRAKE]

RAGWORT—a plant used by fairies and witches on which to ride through the air; the stem is adaptable for the small fairy to use. **Syn.** RAGWEED.

RAIN DANCE—(Native American) a religious function of communication between GOD and MAN, having influence psychically over sky and clouds; a ceremonial dance performed by imitating the growth of crops in gestures and chants; theory; similar activity produces similar results; nature can be controlled with respect for and the mimicking of a desired event, and strong concentration on rain hitting the ground. [**cf.** LAW OF ASSOCIATION Appendix 7, ATMOSPHERE CONTROL, VISUALIZATION]

RAINBOW BODYthe highest vibrational frequency of a body in the ETHERIC WORLD that a SOUL-MIND can attain before LIBERATION; by this attainment it is possible to appear and disappear on any one of the planes at will, including the earth plane, to be helpful to other soul-minds. **Syn.** GLORIFIED BODY OF CHRIST, BODY OF GLORY. [**cf.** ALCHEMY, GLORIFICATION]

RAISE THE VIBRATIONS—to accelerate the vibrations in an area by fast, loud, jolly songs, by clapping and stamping in rhythm, or by playing loud fast music; frequently done to give energy to the etheric world intelligences to perform physical phenomena in a seance; used in charismatic meetings to put the sitters onto a spiritual high and to give energy to the healing forces working within the leader. [**cf.** SOUNDS-WITH-POWER]

RAISING THE TRUMPET—(seance) to go into a TRANCE state of consciousness and synchronize with an ETHERIC WORLD INTELLIGENCE so that the intelligence can float a TRUMPET in the air to be used as an amplifying system; trumpet magnifies the etheric world voices so they are heard by the physical ear; information brought by the etheric world is such advanced science that one could not have learned it from formal educational sources; knowledge pertains to the universal laws, growing spiritually, the etheric world planes, and PSYCHIC DEVELOPMENT; MEDIUM and SITTERS meet weekly and sit in a BLACKED-OUT ROOM; ECTOPLASM from the medium and sitters is used to form a ribbon which swoops under the trumpet and glides it through the air; trumpet stops when a voice speaks through it; questions may be asked by the sitters; takes dedication and patience, from the medium to develop. [**cf.** TRUMPET SEANCE]

RAJA YOGA—(Eastern, Tibet, "royal") the utilization of the mind to achieve balance within the body and mind, through the eight-fold path; one of the main paths of the Divine, the path of formal MEDITATION; helps to prepare one for transcendental consciousness, wisdom and understanding. [**cf.** YAMA, ASANAS, CONCENTRATION, SAMADHI]

RAM—(Hinduism) God; see TOTALITY.

RAMA—(Hinduism) abiding joy; interchangeable with RAM, or GOD.

RAMP FUNCTION—(biofeedback training) a pattern on an EEG instrument showing similarities to that of a person suffering from an overdose of a hallucinogenic drug; believed to come from the deep areas of the brain. [**cf.** EEG, GSR, PSYCHOTROPIC PLANTS, TOPSY]

RANDOM PSYCHISM—(psi tasks) psychic experiences that occur at rare and irregular intervals, independent of all known physical bases, regardless of times or space. **Syn.** SPONTANEOUS PSI. [**cf.** EMOTIONAL PSI, CRISIS PHENOMENA, SPONTANEOUS APPARITION, KARMICALLY DESIRED]

RANDOM-EXPERIMENT—(psi tasks) an experiment in which the TARGET goal is not revealed to the subject until the experiment is over. [**cf.** DOUBLE-BLIND EXPERIMENT, PSI-MEDIATED]

RANGE CONTROL—the dial on a biofeedback instrument which can be regulated to the subject's own electrical impulse cycles, establishing a baseline for that training session. **Syn.** FREQUENCY CONTROL. [**cf.** READOUT, THRESHOLD CONTROL]

RANGE SWITCH—a dial on the biofeedback instrument which sets the range for the amplification; e.g., one setting could be for a range of 5 uv to a maximum of 109 uv. [**cf.** BIOFEEDBACK TRAINING, ELECTRODE, LOWER FREQUENCY]

RANGE-OF-CORD-ACTIVITY—(astral projection) pertains to the extension of the silver cord in an astral projection; the length of the cord results in different reactions; see OUT-OF-RANGE-CORD-ACTIVITY and IN-THE-RANGE-OF-CORD-ACTIVITY. [**cf.** Appendix 2 ASTRAL PROJECTION]

RAPE OF THE SOUL—(N. Biriat, Siberia) a disease believed to be caused by the patient's SOUL-MIND being stolen or having gone astray; the shaman's duty is to find it and to return it, which results in a cured patient. [cf. ERLIK, MAGIC HEALING, SHAMAN]

RAPID MEDIUM—one who speaks or writes under the influence of an ETHERIC WORLD ENTITY, with a rapidity greater than one could voluntarily do in an ordinary state of consciousness. [cf. SEMI-TRANCE, GUIDE, INSPIRATIONAL WRITING, INSPIRATIONAL SPEAKING]

RAPID-EYE-MOVEMENT—abbr. REM; DREAM STATE of consciousness wherein the eyes of the sleeper are moving back and forth, up and down, or fluttering, under closed lids; detectable by an observer; occurs at ninety minute intervals; sleeper is in the low beta and high alpha state. **Syn.** PARADOXAL SLEEP. [cf. DREAMS, NREM, EOG, BETA STATE OF CONSCIOUSNESS, ALPHA STATE OF CONSCIOUSNESS]

RAPPER BY PROFESSION—an ETHERIC WORLD INTELLIGENCE who specializes in communicating with earthlings by means of audible sounds, i.e., RAPS, snaps, knocks, clicks; these sounds bring warnings, predictions, psychic information and knowledge to the medium; a code is set up between the medium and etheric intelligence regarding the number and intensity of the knocks. [cf. Appendix 2 PERCUSSION]

RAPPING SPIRITS—see RAPPER BY PROFESSION.

RAPS—1. (percussion) to produce psychic energy for an etheric world intelligence to use, to make audible sounds in one's presence without any physical means; sounds come from the walls, from underneath chairs or tables or from "within" the woodwork; can be willed to happen in a SEANCE or can happen at random in the home of the PERCUSSION medium; light density has no bearing; a code is established for *yes* and *no* questions; frequently results in acquiring knowledge that could not be gained by formal education; acts as a step to more difficult and dedicated phenomena; (do not confuse with POLTERGEISTRY, or CLAIRAUDIENCE). (Inconcl.) 2. noises and knocks coming from a confused earthbound, discarnate, entity, who desires sympathy and understanding. [cf. GHOST, EARTHBOUND ENTITIES] 3. rappings preceding the death of a SOUL-MIND wanting to notify a loved one of the coming event; see OMEN and NON-HUMAN AGENCY (def. 2). **Syn.** KNOCKS. [cf. PHILLIP GROUP, PERCUSSION]

RAPTURE—(Christian fundamentalists) the first activity of the final "Battle of Armageddon" when Christ will appear in the sky above the earth, unannounced; in a flash of a second every "saved" believer will disappear from earth and be lifted into the sky and kept safe for seven years.

RATE OF FLOW—(Russia, Nikolai Kozyrev) (future science) theory: the weight of any substance is changed by the rate of flow within the substance and is predictable; discovered by astrophysics researchers. [cf. GRAVITY CONTROL Appendix 2]

RATIONAL MIND—the intelligence in mankind that makes decisions and logically thinks things out; (Jose Silva) the mechanism that pertains to learning, calculation, theorizing and problem solving. **Syn.** CONSCIOUS MIND, MENTAL MIND, BRAIN. [cf. SUBCONSCIOUS MIND]

RATIONAL SOUL—(Rene Descartes) the CONSCIOUS MIND, the brain; does not include the SUBCONSCIOUS MIND.

RAUWOLFIA—a medicinal drug derived from trees and shrubs of the dogbane family which is capable of changing one's mind, mood, and attitude; calms the mind. [cf. BOTANE, SENSATION CONSCIOUSNESS, SOMA]

RAVASHIS—(Parasees) the guardian spirits who have left the heavenly sphere because they have chosen to move to the world of humans to assist them in the fight against EVIL. [cf. ANGEL HIERARCHY, GUARDIAN SPIRIT]

RAVEN—1. (Native American, Northwest Pacific) an etheric world entity temporarily taking on the form of a bird; works with and for the earthly Indian. **Syn.** TRICKSTER, WHITE MAN, SPIDER, COYOTE. [cf. SHAPE-CHANGING, GUIDE] 2. black birds used as a psychic tool; capable of knowing what is going on in a distant area and reporting this to its master. [cf. ANPSI, ANPSI PREMONITIONS, TROUT OF THE WELL]

RAVEN'S WING—(alchemy) a rock crystal formation of blue black fluid in the alchemist's receptacle, which on contact with air, will solidify and break up; this is then, an entirely new substance, unknown in nature; possesses all the properties of pure chemical elements which cannot be separated by chemical means; the "essence" of the metals, called the SOUL; will someday be released from the hermetically sealed receptacle that the ALCHEMIST so tenderly handled in the furnace. **Syn.** AL-

CHEMIST'S EGG. [cf. RESURRECTION, ALCHEMIST OF SACRED FIRE, DISTILLATION]

RAY—1. a measurement of invisible levels of AWARENESS in the etheric world; a wave-length of a certain vibratory rate usually associated with COLOR; 2. (esoteric) an invisible vitality globule that hits the spleen and breaks up into streams of different colors; each has a special function in the physical body. [cf. MAGNETIC RADIATION, WHITE COLOR, SPLEEN CHAKRA]

RAY THERAPY—see COLOR HEALING.

RDZU-UPHRUL—(Tibet *rdzu*, "power to change one's shape"; *hphrul*, "power to change one's size and number") to disappear and reappear as two or as many, at will; to appear large or small, on any plane of existence, which includes the physical plane. **Syn.** POWER OF MIRACULOUS ACTION. [cf. MATERIALIZATION, DEMATERIALIZATION, ALCHEMY, SHAPE-CHANGING, DIMENSION-SHIFTING]

RE—(ancient Egypt) the sun god; generator of all forms of life; depicted by the SCARAB BEETLE. **Syn.** KHEPRI.

REACHED—a common term used when psychic messages are being given in a public gathering, inquiring whether the person has received a message. Usage: "Have you been reached yet?" [cf. STAND-UP READER]

READER—1. one who gives psychic readings; 2. (Tibet) the LAMA or person who stays by the house of the deceased even after the corpse is removed, and reads the GUIDE SERIES to help the SOUL-MIND of the deceased into the BARDOS. [cf. GUIDE SERIES, DEATH SCIENCE]

READINESS WAVE—(esoteric) a place in the frontal cortex of the brain that sends a signal out into the surrounding environment of the thinker, pertaining to the nature of the thought, before the actual happening of the experience; these vibrations alert animals, plants, stones, and psychic persons of what is about to happen and they can then react accordingly; a PRIMARY PERCEPTION. [cf. HUNCHABILITY, SYNCHRONICITY, ANPSI, BOTANE]

READING—psychic information given by a professional PSYCHIC to an individual, regarding that person's lifestyle, personality, past, present, and future experiences, or regarding answers to ques-

tions that are on the client's mind; uses skills of CLAIRVOYANCE, CLAIRSENTIENCE, and MENTAL MEDIUMSHIP; (LeRoy Zemke) "an attunement to another individual in which one can tune into energies about that person and relate it back to him." [cf. PSYCHIC INFORMATION]

READOUT—(biofeedback training) the chart or paper that records the marks from a pen that is moved by the electrical energy emanating from the subject, who is HOOKED-UP to the EEG instrument; this chart displays the variance in electrical energy, the thoughts, and emotions of the subject; the lines made by the moving pen are vertical and patterned, relating to the states of consciousness of the subject; these patterns are similar in all persons. **Syn.** PRINT-OUTS. [cf. RANGE CONTROL, INTERNALIZATION AWARENESS]

REAL DIVINING ROD—(dowsing) the right arm and right hand of the body; to stretch out one's arm and tune into the feeling of the arm; the arm may move, twitch, quiver, or become cold or hot, to indicate to the dowser when the hidden substance has been located. [cf. RADIESTHESIA, DOWSING, PENDULUM]

REAL MAN—(theory) the "real" man is the ASTRAL BODY, and the earth man is a "reflection" of it. [cf. Appendix 3 ASTRAL BODY]

REALITY—(esoteric) 1. (capitalized) see TOTALITY; 2. (AMORC) an awareness of life that is different for each person; an "individual concept" of one's self and one's inhabitant, constructed by the mind of the individual; "that which is real to the subconscious mind or psychic mind regardless of actuality"; 3. feeling of BEING on the plane of existence where one's consciousness puts one; 4. (living organisms) the entity's individual concept of it's self and it's inhabitant, constructed by instinct, depending upon the state of EVOLUTION at the time of perception; 5. (inert objects) CONSCIOUS OF BEING within all things; the intelligence in the cells making an awareness for that object. [cf. CONSCIOUSNESS Appendix 5]

REALIZABLE CONSCIOUSNESS—a group of earthling's past lives and experiences recorded in a great knowledge pot, that all have forgotten, but of which all individuals share in its manifestations, in each incarnation. **Sim.** COLLECTIVE UNCONSCIOUS. [cf. GROUP-SOUL, UNIVERSAL CONSCIOUSNESS]

REALIZATION—(Vedic) discovery of the reality of

GOD through direct personal spiritual experience; what is realization for one is not necessarily so for another. **Syn.** ILLUMINATION.

REALIZER OF THE AIM—a statue of BUDDHA, with the right hand raised to shoulder level, representing the wisdom that accomplishes all works; if the palm is turned outward, it is a gesture of blessing to all the world. [**cf.** LAW OF MIMCRY Appendix 7, MEDITATION]

REALM OF CAUSES—(Plato) two worlds: one is the realm of cause and ideas, and the other is the realm of material. [**cf.** CAUSAL PLANE, MENTAL PLANE]

REALM OF IDEAS—(Plato) a vibrational frequency in the ETHERIC WORLD where thought plans for the material world originate. **Syn.** CAUSAL PLANE. [**cf.** MENTAL PLANE, BATTLE GROUND, CASUAL BODY]

REALM OF ILLUSION—see ASTRAL PLANE.

REALMS OF FORM—(Buddhism) a plane in the ETHERIC WORLD where one has a form similar to a human being, but where inhabitants no longer need to incarnate into the physical world; ETHERIC WORLD INTELLIGENCES come to developed voice trance mediums from this plane. [**cf.** FIFTH PLANE, MASTER, GUIDE, VOICE TRANCE]

REASSOCIATED—(astral projection) see INTERIORIZATION.

REBIRTH—theory of REEMBODIMENT: the SOUL-MIND has had many births on planet earth, in a physical body, and will have many more. **Sim.** REINCARNATION. [**cf.** KARMA, RACIAL MEMORY, RECORDERS AND ANALYSTS, DISCARNATE INTELLIGENCES]

REBIRTH DOCTRINE—(Druid) the SOUL-MIND is incarnated in a physical body on the planet many times; the soul-mind contains a memory record of all the hundreds of lives the earthling has lived and is recoverable each time the soul-mind is incarnated. **Syn.** REINCARNATION. [**cf.** KARMA OF FUNCTION, DWELLER OF THE THRESHOLD, LAW OF THE SOUL-MIND EVOLUTION Appendix 7]

REBIRTHING—a technique used to simulate the birth process to make the subject relive his or her BIRTH TRAUMA; works out negative feelings regarding ones birth process, or transforms the subconscious impression of a traumic birth to one of pleasure; subject curls in a fetal position in a pool of body-temperature water and breaths through a snorkel, under the guidance of a rebirthing therapist. [**cf.** ASSOCIATION MAGIC, CONTAGIOUS MAGIC]

RECALL—1. to remember, when back in the awake state, the feelings and visions experienced in the ALPHA STATE OF CONSCIOUSNESS and THETA STATE OF CONSCIOUSNESS while in TRANCE, under hypnosis, taking an ASTRAL PROJECTION or while DREAMING; this will not happen unless one programs oneself to remember fully everything that happens, prior to the experience; 2. spontaneous flashes of past lives during normal activity that are later verified by hypnosis or historical records and found to be accurate; flashes are usually associated with the emotional aspects of the present lifestyle correlating to those of the past life. [**cf.** REINCARNATION, KARMA, HYPNOTHERAPY]

RECALLER—(dreams) an individual who remembers many of his or her DREAMS without writing them in a DREAM DIARY and who understands much of the content without formal instruction in DREAM ANALYSIS; (dreams to the majority of persons are elusive and fuzzy). [**cf.** REM STATE]

RECEIVER OPTIMIZATION—(psi tasks) a free response task which allows the subject to respond to the ESP TARGET by verbally describing it. [**cf.** PSI-FAVORABLE STATE, PSI-MEDIATED INFORMATION]

RECEIVING MODE—an ALTERED STATE OF CONSCIOUSNESS, wherein the body is relaxed, the mind is controlled and the emotions are quiet; reached by the psychic's private technique; at this level the psychic feels comfortable that the information that comes into awareness (from the SUBCONSCIOUS MIND or the ETHERIC WORLD INTELLIGENCES) will be true and accurate; to reach "one's level," level of awareness to "receive" thoughts, not "instigate" them. [**cf.** MENTAL HEALING, BIOFEEDBACK TRAINING, MEDITATION, PSYCHIC DOORS, LISTENING MODE, GOING-TO-LEVEL]

RECEIVING THE GLOSSOLALIA—the first time one utters sounds that are foreign, and seem to simply spill out of the mouth; brought on by attaining religious ECSTASY; a religious belief that the person has received the HOLY SPIRIT and now has the GIFT OF TONGUES. [**cf.** TALKING-IN TONGUES, CHARISMATIC RENEWAL]

RECEPTIVE—(I Ching) the half of a human being that is feminine, passive; symbolically represented by the BUDDHA.

RECONCILIATION OF REINCARNATION—(Seth) "the whole self is aware of all of the experiences of all of its egos, and since one identity forms them, there are bound to be similarities between them and shared characteristics."

RECORDERS AND ANALYSTS—(Theosophy) energy fields in the etheric world who could be considered agents of KARMA; they work automatically, recording every act and thought of mankind for the ASTRAL LIGHT RECORDS. [cf. REINCARNATION, RIPE KARMA, MASS KARMA]

RECORDING ANGEL—an ETHERIC WORLD INTELLIGENCE whose function is to assist those in the process of death; appears shortly after the TRANSITION to help the deceased entity pass through the lower planes with no problem. **Syn.** DEATH ANGEL. [cf. DEATH COMA, DEATH MIST, HOUSE OF ETERNITY]

RECORDS OF THE ASTRAL LIGHT—see ASTRAL LIGHT RECORDS.

RECREATIONAL DRUGS—drugs taken for other than therapeutic purposes; usually taken so that one can hallucinate or have some kind of psychic experience. [cf. VISION, HALLUCINATION, PEYOTE PLANT]

RECREATIONAL HYPNOSIS—see STAGE HYPNOSIS.

RECREATOR—the mind of a human being; mind constantly sends out ergs of energy which use the primordial atoms in the air to arrange, formulate, construct, destruct, compose, assemble, invent, prepare, produce, reproduce, build, design, and make things, according to the nature of the thought it thinks; uses the primordial LAW OF VIBRATION, LAW OF POLARITY, and LAW OF LIKE ATTRACTS LIKE. **Syn.** CO-CREATOR. [cf. see above laws in Appendix 7, CREATION]

RECTOR—an etheric world intelligence who communicates psychically with a medium. **Sim.** GUIDE, DOCTOR TEACHER, CELESTIAL GUARDIAN.

RECURRING DREAMS—theory: dreams that occur periodically without changing in content are generated by the physiology of the BRAIN, rather than by the happenings of the day; the DREAMSTUFF leaves an emotional impact on the mind the first time it happens, but the dreamer ignores the dream and its interpretation; ignoring the dream leaves a groove in the brain cells; it occurs again to receive attention and is ignored; like a record, the more it plays, the deeper the groove; eventually the situation in the dream that needed attention is outgrown or settled, but the dream has made an emotional groove in the physical cells and can recur when stimulated from a tiny similarity of the original event, happening in a new experience. (Inconcl.) [cf. DREAM REALITY, MIRRORED, MOTIVE UNCONSCIOUSNESS]

RED—(colorology) a primary color; first color the new baby sees; represents energy, aggressiveness, vitality; (negative aspect is cowardice); symbolic of the activity principle of life, the PHYSICAL BODY, strength, FIRE, the HOLY SPIRIT, JEHOVAH, and the Law-Giver. [cf. COLOR Appendix 5]

RED CORALS—(esoteric) a mineral that has properties to prevent melancholy and evil activities, and to transmit vibrations of the sun to the owner. [cf. MINPSI, IRON, EMERALD, GOLD]

RED HOT NEEDLES—minor itchings and crawlings felt on the skin during MEDITATION or psychic activity: a good sign that one has tuned in; it goes away when the psychic or meditation period is over. [cf. MENTAL PSYCHIC PROCESS]

RED-BEADED ELECTRODES—(biofeedback training) sensors that are placed on the head for monitoring BRAIN WAVES; the necessary, active sensor is red-beaded to tell it apart from the sensor, that acts as a ground, which is black-beaded; both are placed on specific areas of the head and fastened with a band; the other end of SENSOR is plugged into the instrument. [cf. ARTIFACT, ELECTRODE RETENTION BAND]

REDCAP—(Cornwall, England) small, lively NATURE SPIRIT found dancing in gardens and woods, wearing a green suit and red cap; can be mischievous. **Syn.** PISKEY, PIPER, FAIRIE.

REDOUBLED—see BILOCATION.

REDUCTIVE ANALYSIS—(dreams) (Carl Jung) an integration of some unknown characteristics of the dreamer bringing new symbols to the dream, to help achieve useful interpretation of the dream. [cf. COMPENSATORY DREAMS, FORGOTTEN LANGUAGE]

REDUPLICATION—(alchemy) to psychically make an exact replica of an object; accomplished by intense, undivided concentration on the object, forming a mental image of it; eventually this gathers the necessary ethereal and physical substance around the mental mold, and a real object materializes; e.g., Jesus multiplied the loaves and fishes; (do not confuse with MATERIALIZATION in the seance room). [cf. ATOMIC-PSYCHOKINESIS, EXTERNAL ALCHEMY]

REEMBODIMENT—theory: after the SOUL-MIND leaves the PHYSICAL BODY in death and lives in the ETHERIC WORLD it will take on another physical body at a future date; does not exist in the etheric world forever; this also applies to other forms of living consciousness. **Syn.** REBIRTH. [cf. REINCARNATION, CONSCIOUSNESS PRINCIPLE]

REFLECTED HEALING—the process of changing the AURA (the pattern that surrounds the human body) to promote a healing; when the pattern is changed, it reflects and transforms the atoms of the physical body: 1. in ETHERIC SURGERY, the practitioner goes through an operation, imitating each step of a physical operation, but performing about four inches above the physical body in the auric pattern; 2. in MAGNETIC HEALING, the LAYING-ON-OF-HANDS and the drawing-out process is simulated about two inches above the physical body; or the practitioner works four inches out from the head, to affect the mental aura, which in turn influences the physical body. [cf. MAGNETIC HEALING, MENTAL HEALING, ETHERIC SURGERY]

REFLECTING—1. (Buddhism) to perceive clairvoyantly one's own THOUGHT-FORMS in the shape of human beings in the ASTRAL WORLD and DENSITY, during the DEATH PROCESS. [cf. BARDO, DEATH SCIENCE] 2. (Tibet) to perceive clairvoyantly one's own thought-forms in the shape of humans, subhumans, and superhumans as one goes through the second state of descipleship; helps one to overcome negative thinking and to understand intuitive thinking. [cf. LISTENING, ELEMENTALS, THOUGHT-FORMS, THINKING, INNER-DIALOGUE]

REFLECTIONS—the counterpart or parallel in the etheric world of any object in the physical world; also known as the ETHERIC DOULBE of the world. [cf. ETHERIC WORLD, AURA, ILLUSION]

REFLECTIVE ETHER—see MENTAL-REFLECTING-ETHER.

REFLECTOGRAPH—an instrument built especially for ETHERIC WORLD COMMUNICATION; has very sensitive, lettered keys for the delicate touch of the ETHERIC WORLD INTELLIGENCES; these keys are connected to a large screen which displays written words for the medium to read. [cf. PRECIPITATION Appendix 2]

REFLEXOLOGY—an ancient foot therapy used for healing physical ills, rediscovered for westerners by Eunice Ingham; compression on various parts of the foot, by the three psychic fingers of the practitioner's hand; releases a flow of electrical energy to the blocked nerve endings, which show in the feet when parts of the body are congested; there is an area in the foot that corresponds to every part of the body; this compression noramlizes the cells of the diseased area and hastens the ability of the cells to heal themselves. [cf. CURATIVE EDUCATION, ACUPUNCTURE]

REFRACTIONS OF GOD—(Nuer tribe, Upper Nile) theory: there is only one God, and all ETHERIC WORLD INTELLIGENCES are a part of that One God. [cf. TOTALITY, GOD, UNIVERSAL MIND]

REGENTS—see ETHERIC WORLD INTELLIGENCES.

REGENTS OF THE EARTH—invisible energy fields in the ETHERIC WORLD, ranking high in the ANGEL HIERARCHY; known as the four kings; rule over: 1. elements of AIR, WATER, EARTH, FIRE; 2. one's indwelling angels; 3. the functions and essences of NATURE SPIRITS, directly responsible for an individual's KARMA in each incarnation. **Syn.** CHATUR MAHARAJAS, ANGELS OF THE FOUR CARDINAL POINTS.

REGRESSION—the activation of the subconscious mind MEMORY BANK to recall parts of a past life; can happen as a spontaneous flashback occurring during an emotional period, or can be brought about by various techniques, such as HYPNOTHERAPY, MENTAL REGRESSION, and PAST-LIVES THERAPY; the past life recall consists of: 1. a very emotional experience of a past incarnation through clairvoyant visions, emotional impressions, and reliving the feelings of that trauma; see REVIVIFICATION; 2. viewing one's self as a bystander in the attire of the past life in a normal life experience or a traumatic experience. **Syn.** BACK-IN-MEMORY, BACK-IN-TIME. [cf. PARTIAL REGRESSION, PAST LIVES THEORY, REINCARNATION]

REGULATED SITUATION—(physical psychism) preparation of the MEDIUM and the area to be used before the physical phenomena is to take place; medium adheres to a regimen of special foods, exercises, sleep patterns and dwells on high qualitative thoughts, a day or two beforehand; area is freed of negative vibrations by burning candles and incense and by verbal blessings; preparation makes it possible for superior ETHERIC WORLD INTELLIGENCES to perform the psychic activity rather than spontaneous physical feats that could be done by an inferior entity. [cf. SEANCE, MEDIUMSHIP]

REIKE—(Zen) a type of healing in which the healer is a channel for universal force and COSMIC ENERGY. [cf. MAGNETIC HEALING, SPIRIT HEALING]

REINCARNATION—theory: the LIFE FORCE of the PHYSICAL BODY does not die with the physical body, but goes on living in the ETHERIC WORLD for a period of time and is then reborn in earth, repeating this hundreds of times until the life force has perfected itself: 1. there is a human being seed encased within the soul-mind of every individual that contains the essence of perfection, like all seeds; this seed declares that the soul-mind of an individual cannot and does not attain perfection in one earth life, but requires many cycles of experiences in this plane; for this purpose the soul-mind assumes a succession of personalities who are born into the different time periods of history, different cultures, different sun signs and different amounts of wealth, all carrying many kinds of emotional and intellectual experiences (to teach a variety of lessons until the soul-mind is perfected); when the lessons are learned it will burst into the next expression; 2. the soul-mind lives many years in between these incarnations in the etheric world learning lessons also; when perfected the soul-mind (life force) lives an ANGEL life, not needing to return; (do not confuse with TRANSMIGRATION OF SOULS, in which the life force returns as an animal or plant). [cf. KARMA, MASS KARMA, SOUL-MIND, PAST-LIVES THEORY, REGRESSION]

REINCARNATIONIST—one who believes that the SOUL-MIND is a MEMORY BANK of *all* past thoughts and actions contributing to the perfecting of the human; uses past life information to improve and understand his or her present life if necessary; believes in REINCARNATION and KARMA. [cf. MENTAL REGRESSION, RIPE KARMA, KARMIC BOARD]

REIYUKA—(Japan) "Association of Friends of the Spirit"; a philosophy in which the members communicate with ETHERIC WORLD INTELLIGENCES. **Syn.** MEDIUMSHIP. [cf. SPIRITUALISM]

RELATIVES—(Native American, Cherokee) (Rolling Thunder) "all spiritual people all around the world"; recognition that all humans come from the same God and have equal responsibilities and equal privileges to one another and to the EARTH MOTHER; (Russel Means, Indian) "relatives are the flowers and animals and all people who partake of the planet." **Syn.** RELATIONS. [cf. TRANSFORMATION, NEW-AGE PSYCHOLOGY]

RELAXATION RESPONSE—another term for MEDITATION, coined by Herbert Benson; by quieting the mind and emotions and relaxing the physical body one counteracts the increase in the SYMPATHETIC NERVOUS SYSTEM activity from the fight-or-flight system; the sympathetic nervous system is cyclic and needs meditation to act as the inactivity to the fight-or-flight aspect of the nervous system; the fight-or-flight system is the activity half of the cycle. [cf. BREATHING RELEASE, CONSCIOUSNESS OF INFINITE SPACE]

RELEASE TYPE DREAMS—symbolic visionary scenes during REM sleep that release physical and emotional tensions and inner anxiety while the sleeper is having the dream; dreamer awaken's feeling much better than the day before; (findings of the dream research laboratories). [cf. COMPENSATORY DREAMS, NIGHTMARES, RELEASE TYPE DREAMS]

RELIGIO-MAGICAL—contemporary term used because so many religions are involved in psychic work, and many of their philosophies combine the two disciplines. [cf. SPIRITUALISM]

RELIGION—a belief in powers higher than one's self, backed by faith rather than logic, with certain basic principles particular to that group; should not be a dogma, but rather an experience; a discipline or an order that one might achieve harmony with oneself, (Katrina Blank) "that which is loving and sufficient to the human being"; major religions of the world: CHRISTIANITY, JUDAISM, BUDDHISM, ZOROASTRIANISM, TAOISM, SUFISM, HINDUISM, ISLAM, ANIMISM.

RELIGIOUS CYCLES—theory: every 625 years, religions of the world have a peak session when hundreds of people join their sects and everyone becomes very active and interested; opposite of this peak is a relapse of interest and membership falls off. [cf. CYCLES, COSMIC WHEEL, CYCLIC PRINCIPLES]

RELIGIOUS HYSTERIA—a trait of one who makes every act of eating, sleeping, working, and recreation pertain to his or her religion and the way he or she interprets it; individual lives in a religious stupor, unable to function successfully on the avenues of life; this brings an abundance of emotional religious psychic experiences. [**cf.** STIGMATIC, ECSTATIC, GIFT OF TONGUES]

RELIGIOUS KING OF THE DEAD—(Tibet) an etheric world god depicted holding a mirror to reflect the SOUL-MIND, as seen in the WHEEL OF LIFE mandala. [**cf.** MANDALAS, DEATH SCIENCE]

RELIGIOUS MYSTIC—a PSYCHIC or MEDIUM who learned and perfected his or her talent in relation to their religious beliefs; practices this talent in connection with their religion, as a tool to help him or her grow spiritually, e.g., JESUS, Moses, Daniel, BUDDHA, Spiritists, Psychic Surgeons, Spiritualists, Shamans, Tantrists, and Witch-doctors. [**cf.** SPIRITUALISM]

REM—see RAPID-EYE-MOVEMENT.

REM REBOUND PHENOMENA—the SEA OF FACES, (hypnagogic stage), occurring in the middle of the night when an individual is withdrawing from drugs (medicinal or recreational); the repressed dream material and earthbound entities that unconsciously cling to one on drugs, clamor to the surface when one withdraws; the SOUL-MIND and CONSCIOUS MIND try to set up equilibrium while the patient sleeps, leaving an opening in the ETHERIC WEB; this opening allows the entities and dream material to explode, after their long repression; the sleeper sees grotesque, surrealistic phantoms, and pastiche visions coming rapidly and overcrowding to get in; it is frightening and unpleasant. [**cf.** HYPNAGOGIC STATE, EARTHBOUND ENTITIES, DENSITY]

REMOTE DOWSING—to hold a PENDULUM over a map until it swings in a manner to indicate the area where the underground substance is located, or where the missing person can be found. **Syn.** MAP DOWSING. [**cf.** BOB, PENDULUM POWER, NON-SWING RESPONSE]

REMOTE HEALING—to perform MENTAL HEALING over a distance; to use mental telepathic suggestions or VISUALIZATION for a patient who is not in the vicinity. **Syn.** DISTANT HEALING. [**cf.** FAITH, HEALING]

REMOTE TREATMENTS—(amuleting) to receive healing VIBRATIONS from a material object that has been charged with MAGNETISM from a healer's palms or with ergs of energy from the healer's mind; the object is placed close to the diseased area; if it is a cloth, it is placed over the diseased area. [**cf.** AMULET, MAGNETIZED OBJECTS, PALMED POWER]

REMOTE VIEWING—1. to perceive clairvoyantly that which is happening at the present time, but is out of range of the physical eyes. [**cf.** CLAIRVOYANCE-IN-SPACE, EXTENDED-CLAIRVOYANCE] 2. to visit a home or area during an ASTRAL PROJECTION and later be able to relate what was seen on the visit; in the projectionist's state details are remarkably recorded in the mind. [**cf.** MEMORY PATTERNS, SEES-IN-SLEEP, MULTICONSCIOUSNESS]

REN—(ancient Egypt) designates the individuality of the SOUL-MIND. **Syn.** MONAD.

RENUNCIATION—an Eastern discipline in which an individual gives up all worldly possessions, allows the GURU to teach and lead him or her on their own private pathway, to reach a higher STATE OF CONSCIOUSNESS; a teacher-pupil, one-to-one situation. [**cf.** PATH, SOUL-MIND]

REPERCUSSION—(astral projection) an emergency interiorization of the ASTRAL BODY into the PHYSICAL BODY causing pain to the PROJECTIONIST; fear, noise, or an emotional disturbance causes the astral body to shoot quickly into the physical body; the physical body, having been corpse-like, without a LIFE FORCE, finds it painful to normalize spontaneously when this occurs. [**cf.** IN-THE-RANGE-OF-CORD-ACTIVITY, INTERIORIZATION]

REPHAIM—(Palestine) NATURE SPIRITS that were a race of giants and communicated with earthlings.

REPRESSION—to hold back or remove from mental consciousness any experience that is unpleasant and painful, rather than to deal with it at the time it happens; because it is not resolved, it remains painful; as time goes on, other experiences that are remindful of this one, are also shut out or blocked from mental consciousness; these experiences become stored in the body and often result in physical or mental illness. [**cf.** BLOCKS, GRAPES, CLEARING, HABITS OF THOUGHT]

REPRODUCTIVE KARMA—(Buddhism) past life experiences and thoughts, determining the type of life for the next INCARNATION. [**cf.** ACCUMULATED KARMA, RIPE KARMA, SUPREME GUIDES OF HUMANITY]

REPROGRAMMING—(esoteric) (mind) a normal procedure that everyone goes through in each INCARNATION, to bring the SOUL-MIND to a more advanced STATE OF CONSCIOUSNESS; the attitude one takes toward the new experiences one encounters changes the compartments in the soul-mind that one entered earth life with, thus making new compartments, revising and updating the old; meant to be accomplished gradually and by one's own free will; gives a meaningful purpose to life. [cf. DEPROGRAMMING, SUBCONSCIOUS MIND, BIO-COMPUTER, MIND, DESTRUCTIVE-BRAINWASHING CULTS]

RESCUE CIRCLES—a dedicated group of psychics who meet regularly to help deceased entities who are earthbound through ignorance or are in need of sympathy and understanding; their purpose is to encourage the PSYCHIC DRIFTERS to go into astral schooling and into the progression realm. [cf. DENSITY, ASTRAL PLANE]

RESERVED KARMA—see DELAYED KARMA and ACCUMULATED KARMA.

RESET—(penduluming) see COURTESY.

RESIDENT DEVA—a minor ANGEL who is in charge of designing the etheric blueprints for many kinds of residents, buildings, hospitals, etc., on earth. [cf. LIGHT BODY, DEVA COMMUNICATION, EYE-LANGUAGE]

RESISTANCE—(biofeedback training) a reaction to the passage of electrical current in the body from the GSR or METABOLIC MONITOR, measured in ohms. [cf. GALVANIC SKIN RESISTANCE, BIOFEED-BACK TRAINING]

RESONANCE—amplification of the range of audibility of any speech sounds.

RESONANT BREATHING—a method of BREATH-ING to attain deep relaxation; to feel an intensive vibration of a roaring or hissing sound in the head or to psychically see patterns of light. [cf. BREATH-ING RELEASE, COMPLETE BREATH]

RESONANT CARDIOGRAPH—(India) (Jagadis Chandra Bose) an instrument that measures an infinitesimal pulsation of plants, animals, and humans. [cf. BOTANE Appendix 2]

RESONANT RECORDER—an instrument that measures the speed of conveyance of the excitatory response of PSYCHISM.

RESONATE—1. to amplify a vocal sound by the sympathetic vibration of air in certain cavities and body structure; to resound; 2. (electronics) to reinforce oscillations because the natural frequency of the device is the same as the frequency of the source. [cf. SOUNDS-WITH-POWER]

RESONATER—that which is used to amplify sound.

RESONATING GROUP CIRCUIT—(future science) (John C. Lilly) to use people as transmitters and receivers (by specific relationship to each other), creating an electric current capable of picking up and deciphering energies around the planet, that are presently undetectable. (Inconcl.) [cf. SUB-CONSCIOUS MIND, ELECTROMAGNETIC FIELD, RADIATIONS]

RESPONSE—(laboratory) psychic information regarding the target picked up by the receiver in a controlled experiment. [cf. GO WITH THE FLOW, IMPRESSION, EXPERIMENT]

RESTFUL ALERTNESS—a state of TRANSCEN-DENTAL MEDITATION in which the mind remains active and awake and the body and emotions become passive; an ALTERED STATE OF CONSCIOUS-NESS in which the PHYSICAL BODY is quiet and still, the CONSCIOUS MIND is unaware of environmental stimuli but the SUBCONSCIOUS MIND is awake to its focal point of incoming psychic energies; shows no loss of consciousness, but the metabolic rate drops lower than in sleep. [cf. MEDITATION Appendix 5]

RESTING ELECTRICAL LEVEL—(biofeedback train-ing) (Barbara Brown) "relationship of the BIO-FEEDBACK INSTRUMENT to the electrical current in man when in a normal emotional state"; this electrical level reading is necessary to reach on all types of biofeedback instruments before correct readings can be obtained; the subject is HOOKED-UP and instructed to do nothing but just "be" until the instrument comes to a stable reading point and the subject feels this is his norm. **Syn.** LEVEL-OFF. [cf. BASELINE READING, ANXIETY STATION]

RESURRECTION—(Native American) the self-cure of a close-to-death illness in a psychopatho-logical experience, during the process of earning the right to become a SHAMAN; the shaman can then give healings and psychic counsel to his tribe; a step that follows the INITIATORY DEATH-RITE, bringing on a deeper understanding of one's self. [cf. INITIATORY SICKNESS, SHAMANSHIP INSTRUCTION]

RESURRECTION BODY—see ASTRAL BODY.

RETREAT—a gathering of people of one discipline, faith, or religion for the purpose of spending time together to raise the CONSCIOUSNESS of each individual and to promote an emotional-high learning experience; consists of MEDIATION, religious rituals, health rituals or workshops, and keeps within one theme.

RETROACTIVE-PK—(psi tasks) to produce the same physical effect or outcome of a physical action that is the target of the experiment which is kept secret; this activity is recorded and compared to the target when the experiment is over. **Syn.** BACKWARD CAUSATION, BACKWARDS PSI. [**cf.** OBJECT-PK, HUMAN-PK, GRAVITY CONTROL]

RETROCOGNITION—to perceive psychic information regarding past events in this life or of another life brought through CLAIRVOYANCE, CLAIRSENTIENCE or CLAIRAUDIENCE. [**cf.** COGNITION, PRECOGNITION]

RETROGRESSION—see REGRESSION.

REVENANT—see GHOST.

REVERIE—(Elmer Green) a relaxed STATE OF CONSCIOUSNESS registering "theta level" on the EEG readout; a level associated with hypnogogic-like imagery, in which unconscious mental processes are revealed to the waking self as symbols, words, or complex patterns; a level of consciousness where creativity flows; the level most psychics reach to bring forth PSYCHIC INFORMATION. **Syn.** THETA LEVEL, HYPNOGOGIC. [**cf.** THETA STATE OF CONSCIOUSNESS]

REVERSAL SLEEP—to sleep in the daytime instead of night time; the quality of daytime sleep is not equal to night time sleep and it will take the sleeper about four weeks for the body to synchronize it's CIRCADIAN RHYTHM and for the physical organism to feel normal. [**cf.** JET LAG, CYCLES]

REVERSED EFFICIENCY—(psi tasks) obtaining scores lower than chance. [**cf.** PSI TASKS, ESP, CHANCE AVERAGE, CHANCE EXPECTATION]

REVIVIFICATION—(hypnotherapy) a form of therapeutic REGRESSION for the purpose of improving one's present life; subject is put into a deep hypnotic STATE OF CONSCIOUSNESS to relive an emotional traumatic episode from a past INCARNATION that is negatively influencing this life; when the CONSCIOUS MIND has relinquished its role of decision making, as in HYPNOSIS, the SOUL-MIND surfaces to perfect itself and will chose the correct past life and emotional episode; subject experiences the same emotional feelings as were felt at the time of the trauma and believes he or she is there; subject could cry, scream, and have physical pain; all knowledge learned from that point in time is blocked out of his or her consciousness; e.g., to be regressed to a life in Germany and only speak in German, having no knowledge of his or her present language and present personality; subject is not aware of the HYPNOTHERAPIST but answers his or her questions as to their activity and feelings; in this dramatic type of regression, the hypnotherapist has the subject face and resolve the negative aspect of the experience; this takes the CHARGE out of the episode and it is erased from his or her memory bank and their present problem is overcome; subject will remember little of this session unless it is related back to them. [**cf.** PARTIAL REGRESSION, AGE REGRESSION]

REWARDS AND PUNISHMENTS SYSTEM—(psychology) theory: pleasure emotion and pain emotion cause every outward activity in one's life; one constantly seeks pleasure rewards for oneself in every phase of one's life; emotion changes BODY CHEMISTRY, and this pleasure emotion is being studied today to see how it affects the state of health; also called **brain rewards**. [**cf.** NEW-AGE PSYCHOLOGY]

RHABDOMANCY—(Greek *rhabdos*, "rod"; *manteia*, "divination") using a rod for DIVINATION; the practice of searching for springs, well-sites, precious metals, etc., concealed within the earth, using a special kind of rod. **Syn.** DOWSING. [**cf.** DOWSING ROD, RADIESTHESIA]

RHABDOMANT—(Holland) see DOWSER.

RHABODIC FORCE—see RADIESTHETIC SENSE.

RHYTHMIC PHENOMENA—spectacular events of science, history, economy, etc., which repeat themselves over the years in a cyclic pattern, as far back as history records. [**cf.** COSMIC TIME-TABLE, CYCLES OF PROGRESSION]

RHYTHMICITY—(in mankind) a principle of recurring strong and weak elements of the basic functions innate in all humanity; appears to influence everything a person does; i.e., walk, talk, learn, play, eat, exercise. **Syn.** CYCLIC PRINCIPLE. [**cf.** CIVILIZATION CYCLE]

RIBBON CLAIRVOYANCE—(England) the use of colored ribbons as a POINT-OF-FOCUS to give psychic readings. [**cf.** FLOWER CLAIRSENTIENCE, COFFEEOGRAPHY]

RIDES—(Haiti, West Africa) to allow a god (ETHERIC WORLD INTELLIGENCE) to enter one's body and use it for a short time to heal sick tribesmen and to bring PSYCHIC INFORMATION to others; the god enters the tribesman's body during the ceremonial dance and is said to "ride" the tribesman inside the head; each tribesman needs his own particular dance pattern and drum rhythm to put himself into a TRANCE state of consciousness so the god can use his body; as the god uses the tribesman's body the body dances as if it is a horse being broken in. [**cf.** IMPERSONATION, TRANCE, GUIDES]

RIDING THE CHARIOT TO THE EXALTED THRONE—see MENTAL PROJECTION.

RIG-PA—(Tibet) CONSCIOUSNESS of the very purest aspect. **Syn.** CHRIST CONSCIOUSNESS, BLISS CONSCIOUSNESS.

RIG-VEDA—(India, Aryan) ancient hymns, of invaluable wisdom, given by word of mouth in the second millenium B.C.; written 3,000 years ago, and used today for personal guidance and understanding.

RIGHT BRAIN HEMISPHERE—research shows that each half of the brain has its role as to the various phases of one's emotions, activities, abilities, and information processing; such as: 1. predominates during all levels of sleep; 2. controls DREAMSTUFF of dreams; 3. processes patterns; 4. perceives FEELINGS, dominates emotions; 5. is preverbal and nonverbal; 6. controls perceptual ability; 7. expresses itself in pictures; 8. appreciates dancing, art, music, sculpture; 9. processes spatial awareness; 10. dominates INTUITION; 11. dominates other PSYCHIC SENSES, especially higher faculties; 12. regulates creativity; 13. controls the IMAGINATION faculty; 14. controls dominant hand; 15. controls the SUBLIMINAL LEVEL of the mind; 16. controls the parasympathetic nervous system; 17. relaxes the PHYSICAL BODY; 18. controls muscle sense; 19. shares primary processes of thought; 20. has nonlinear receptibility; 21. distinguishes between feeling and activity; 22. compartmentalizes information as given from the LEFT BRAIN HEMISPHERE; 23. understands nouns and adjectives but not verbs; 24. controls the left side of body; 25. is

susceptible to illnesses; 26. controls states of depression; 27. distorts and disorganizes (according to mundane perception); 28. views the whole as the whole. (Inconcl.)

RIGHT HAND SYMBOL—the palm of the right hand will automatically raise or point in the directions of one's CONSCIOUSNESS if one does not become too aware of these movements. [**cf.** DOWSING, REAL DIVINING ROD, CASTING OF LOTS]

RIGHT PSYCHIC NERVE—(Hinduism) a necessary, invisible, energy force, traveling up the KUNDALINI crossing at the chakras; see PINGALA. [**cf.** PINGALA, IDA, LEFT PSYCHIC NERVE]

RIGHT-HAND PATH—(Sanskrit) the path of ENLIGHTENMENT to the individual who is on it; activity accepted by the majority as being correct and good, for that time period.

RIM AURAS—glowing or hazy emanations seen clairvoyantly around inanimate objects, extending about an inch or two out from the object; the retina and visual cortex of the eyes are organizing the interpreting visual contours when this is seen; felt to be the pattern of the object. (Inconcl.)

RING—see FLOW.

RING OF WOODEN POSTS—(Native American, Algonquin) wooden posts, with the heads of ancestor spirit guides carved on top; planted in the ground in circle formation designating a holy place, where the tribe comes and pays homage to God and his helpers. [**cf.** GREAT MANITOU, TOTEM POLE]

RING-PASS-NOT—1. the outer rim of any system in this world or in the ETHERIC WORLD; (Theosophy) the border of the SOLAR SYSTEM; 2. (regarding humans) a circle with the point in the center; the circle within, where all are confined, who labor under the delusion of separateness; to not realize that one is "one with the universe" brings limitations to one's self; 3. (astral projection) determines the distance that the traveler can project her or himself. [**cf.** REALITY, CONSCIOUSNESS]

RINZIA ZEN SECT—a strict, ceremonial, ritual of long meditative periods, with an overseeing priest who strikes the meditators on the back with a stick when they are not in the correct posture or when they become drowsy. [**cf.** MEDITATION, SLEEPITATE, SITTING ZEN]

RIPE EGO—(Vedic) a SOUL-MIND full of knowledge and devotion, acting like a child and servant of God, who comes to earth to teach earthlings. [cf. RIGHT-HAND PATH]

RIPE KARMA—the pattern of circumstances that one is experiencing at present, from minute to minute, made from all one's thinking and acting during one's past incarnations; ripe karma is given to one in doses as one can handle it. [cf. ACCUMULATED KARMA, REINCARNATION, KARMA]

RISHI—(Hinduism) see PSYCHIC.

RITUAL—(Ruth Blackmer) "a prescribed event or a particular form or ceremony that is built up by tradition and carries with it a great amount of energy, light, force, and impact"; environment and dress of participants contribute to the event; repetitious activity and use of the same materials make each event more effective because they are impregnated with the emotions of the users; materials retain these emotions and emanate them to the participants of the next ceremony. [cf. SUPREME AND COMPLETE RITUAL, VIRGIN, TOTEM, TRADITION]

RITUAL MAGIC—(Europe, , West Africa) proven processes and ceremonies used repeatedly to execute PSYCHISM, known only to the MAGICIAN; processes summon large quantities of natural forces and ETHERIC WORLD INTELLIGENCES for manipulation by the magician; impressive and demonstrative ceremonies have symbolic meanings that serve psychological purposes; ritual magic is beneficial for promoting healings, EXORCISM of evil vibrations or entities, settling disputes, bringing prosperity to others, and sometimes promoting negativity; ritual necessitates: 1. especially prepared area; 2. appropriate clothing; 3. proven incantations; 4. consecrated and dedicated magician's tools; 5. patterned activity with purposeful intent (this builds energy that stays with the tools, garments, area and body motions to increase the PSYCHIC ENERGY each time). [cf. CEREMONIAL MAGIC, LAW OF RITUAL Appendix 7, AMULET]

RITUAL OBJECT—see AMULET and TALISMAN.

RIVER OF LIGHT—see KUNDALINI.

RIVER SPIRITS—(Upper Nile) Dinka priests, who seem to arise from a river; work psychically with earthlings to bring guidance and to ward off evil vibrations. [cf. ETHERIC WORLD GUIDE]

RMI-LAM BAR-DO—(Tibet) state of DREAM CONSCIOUSNESS; see DREAMS.

ROBIN—(Britain) a bird that is associated with blood, death, and fire because of its red breast; noted for its desire to cover up the dead with a pile of moss and for carrying water to put out fires. [cf. ANIMAL OVERSOUL, ANPSI RESEARCH]

ROCK CRYSTAL—(esoteric) a mineral that transmits influences from the moon; has properties that help summon one's guides, see visions, and perform healings. **Syn.** SHEWSTONE. [cf. SCRYING, BLACK DIAMOND, BISHOPS RING]

ROCK ELECTRICITY—(T. Townsend Brown) the study of TELLURIC ENERGY; research findings: energy having the characteristics of electricity can be found in stones; believed to come from the gravitational radiation from the depths of space. [cf. GRAVITATIONAL WAVES, OVERALL CONSCIOUSNESS, RADIATIONS]

ROD—a long, slender piece of wood, metal or other material that serves as a magical tool in radiesthetic phenomena, in physical feats, and in healing; used by magicians; the precise rod has a triangular prism at one end and is black resin on the other end; it is bound by rings of copper and zinc, and a long magnetized iron needle runs through it; it is more valuable if the rod is a perfectly straight branch of almond or HAZEL WOOD, cut with a golden sickle before the tree blossomed, in the early morn; the rod is consecrated to its magical uses at the new moon by another MAGICIAN who already possesses a rod; magicians kept the rod in their flowing sleeve to keep its construction a secret; (do not confuse with the DOWSING ROD). [cf. RITUAL, CEREMONIAL MAGIC]

RODS—YELLOW, ORANGE or GOLDEN BEAMS around a person's head, denoting the degree of spirituality of the person by the size and diameter of the rods; extend perpendicularly from the head and shoulders; can be perceived clairvoyantly. [cf. AURA, BLIND SPOTS, EMPIRICAL ENERGY]

ROEDELOPER—(Holland) see DOWSER.

ROGUES—(Russia) see PSYCHIC.

ROLFING—a method of manipulating the muscles to align the body's structure with the earth's gravitational field; discovered by Ida Rolf; designed to help heal the body by working with the deep muscle joints to restore structural balance; principle: the body muscles store within themselves unresolved negative thoughts and thus the body loosens the trapped negation, helping the individual to be free of the cause of the ailment. **Syn.** STRUCTURAL INTEGRATION. [**cf.** BLOCKS, SYMPATHETIC NERVOUS SYSTEM, NEGATIVE THOUGHT]

ROLL-IN—(astral projection) coined by Robert Monroe; a method of reentering the PHYSICAL BODY; the ASTRAL BODY levels on an imaginary line with the physical body and moves along into the body by turning over and over. **Syn.** INTERIORIZATION. [**cf.** BACK-TOGETHER, REPERCUSSION]

ROLLED-OUT—the turning over and over of the ASTRAL BODY as it moves out of the PHYSICAL BODY, in the beginning of an astral projection. [**cf.** ACCLIMATIZING, ASTRAL ROUTE, ASTRAL VISION]

ROOK—(anpsi) a bird used to predict oncoming weather and human affairs of the country; made possible because the repetition of its performances for the same set of conditions does not vary over the years. **Sim.** MAGPIE. [**cf.** ROBIN, FISH PSI, GOLDEN MONEY SPIDER]

ROOT ASSUMPTIONS—(Seth) built-in ideas upon which an existence is based; telepathic thoughts and emotions creating an energy field cohesive enough to hold physical environment in a manner all can perceive; contributed to subconsciously by each individual; e.g., earth-plane existence is based on time, space, and gravity.

ROOT BRAIN—a consciousness working in some people in conjunction with the generative organs, constituting their mental activity. **Syn.** THIRD BRAIN. [**cf.** ROOT CHAKRA]

ROOT CAUSE—TOTALITY must perfect itself; Totality is completing its cycle to return to the primordial state of electrons, CHAOS, PERFECTNESS, or pure BLISS. [**cf.** AQUARIAN AGE, CONSCIOUSNESS AWARENESS MOVEMENT, LAW OF TRANSFORMATION Appendix 7]

ROOT CHAKRA—a vortex of energy, made of etherael substance lying at the base of the spine, superimposing the prostrate area in the male and uterus in the female; looks like the sign of the cross when perceived clairvoyantly; brown and red in color; active when an individual's mind is focused on materialistic matters and body sensualities; represents the lowest part of human consciousness;

the seat of the KUNDALINI; first chakra. **Syn.** MULDHARA. [**cf.** CHAKRA]

ROOT RACE—pertains to the different types of civilizations in earth that humans evolve through to form the evolutionary cycle; there are seven basic root types in each globe in a PLANETARY CHAIN: humanity's first two root races were lived in the etheric planes; the third root race was during LEMURIA and the first time the SOUL-MIND was in a solid body; the fourth root race depicts the time of ATLANTIS; humanity is in the fifth root race now. [**cf.** CYCLES, GLOBE]

ROSARY—1. (Catholic) a string of 150 beads designed to assist in the ritual of a series of prayers; divided into groups of ten, joined by a chain, and forming a chalet to which a pendant is attached; 2. (Moslem) 99 beads on a string, denoting the essential names of ALLAH, with a leader on the string which acts as a terminal, representing an essential name; 3. (Sanskrit) 54 or 110 beads on a string to assist in a form of JAPA; each bead records the number of mantras said in MEDITATION by a special method of fingering the beads each time the mantra is repeated; 4. (Tibet) beads used for meditation and for help in psychic skills; the color and material of the beads have a significant bearing on the nature of their abilities. [**cf.** JAPA-MALA, MANTRA]

ROSE—the flower of the West comparable to the lotus of the East; associated with love, death, celebrations, success, etc.; (Scandinavia) the rose is always protected by the fairies and dwarfs. [**cf.** BOTANE, LOTUS, FLOWERS]

ROSE CROSS—a *T* formation consisting of two narrow pieces of various materials with one bar crossing the other about one third down; each bar ends with three scallops instead of a straight cut; a rose is in the center; emblem of the Rosicrucian Order. [**cf.** CROSS]

ROSEMARY—(esoteric) a holy and sacred plant that has properties to ward off evil spirits and negative vibrations of the physical plane; used at funerals to help the deceased through the density. [**cf.** ARTIFICIAL PARADISE, ELDER TREE, SENSATION CONSCIOUSNESS]

ROUND—1. a cosmic time period in one solar system, consisting of life waves evolving seven times around each chain; symbolizes mankind involving and evolving from their etheric Garden of Eden to their Garden of Paradise; **2.** a period of time constituting one civilization; beginning with the great flood of ATLANTIS, and moving through seven rounds for one platonic year; (mankind is in the fourth round); **3.** each round constitutes the evolvement of one of the four elements: AIR, EARTH, WATER, FIRE. [**cf.** COSMIC TIME-TABLE, LIFE WAVE, CIVILIZATION CYCLE]

ROYAL CENTER—see PINEAL GLAND.

ROYAL TOUCH—(ancient) see LAYING-ON-OF-HANDS.

RSPK—(clinical) recurrent spontaneous PSYCHO-KINESIS; see POLTERGEISTRY.

RUBY—(esoteric) a mineral that is subjected to the influence of Mars; used psychically as a transmitter of energy; represents the red earth, and the flesh of ADAM. [**cf.** CHRYSOLITE, GARNETS, BLACK ONYX]

RUH—(Moslem) see SOUL-MIND.

RUN—(psi tasks) a series of repeated ESP or PK tries under identically controlled conditions toward a target or goal. [**cf.** AVERAGE SCORE, BACKWARD CAUSATION]

RUNNER'S HIGH—state of mild euphoria, and a mental state which corresponds to that which follows a good meditational period; acquired after a thirty minute, or longer, run or jog; the body has worked out the tensions and becomes lulled by its rhythmical movement; makes it possible for answers to problems and useable inspirations to surface. [**cf.** DANCING MANIA, SUFI TWIRLING]

RUPA—(Hinduism, "the void and form"); (Buddhism, "form" or "shape"; matter, a human body) the PHYSICAL BODY existing in form of concepts and ideas. [**cf.** SKANDHAS, RUPA-LOKA]

RUPA-LOKAS—(Sanskrit) material world.

RUTENGANGER—(Germany) see DOWSER.

RUTLIMANNER—(Switzerland) see DOWSING.

538

SA-AG-GA—(Native American, Haida; British Columbia and Alaska) the village shaman; specializes in using information from his dreams to help the tribe; capable of going into trance; has earned the privilege of knowing the previous incarnation of the newborn baby. [**cf.** REINCARNATION, CHANGING WOMAN, CURANDEROS]

SACRAMENT—1. (Christian) an external sign of an inward emotion; 2. a RITUAL using the laws of nature to change vibrational frequencies, resulting in mental or physical phenomena; sacramental principle as a natural pattern of human behavior when in quest of SUPERNATURAL power or grace; 3. (Greece) a pledge to keep the teachings of the mysteries a secret; 4. an expression of desiring spiritual attainment. [**cf.** TALISMAN, CEREMONY]

SACRAMENTAL HEALER—A PRACTITIONER who works in a setting in which HEALING is invariably a part of the sacred ritual; i.e., psychedelic mushroom ceremonies. [**cf.** CEREMONIAL MAGIC, RAIN DANCE, !KUNG ENERGY, SING]

SACRED BEETLE—(esoteric) the optic THALMUS which is a part of the THIRD-EYE AREA; an egg-shaped ganglion of the inner brain; is beetle-shaped when cross-sectioned; symbolizes immortality. **Syn.** EGG OF IMMORTALITY, BOAT OF THE SEEKER, CRYSTAL LAMP, OPEN-EYE. [**cf.** SCARAB BEETLE]

SACRED CUT—phi; a mystical unending ratio that is the basic measurement of the human body; a sacred proportion that appears throughout nature; this magic ratio is the mathematical proportion of the GREAT PYRAMID; division of a line (or geometric figure) so that the proportion of the smaller section to the larger is the same as that of the larger to the whole; also called **Golden Section.**

SACRED DISC—(China) symbol of the SUN and the heavens as a whole; heavenly perfection.

SACRED FIRE—(esoteric) breath of the ETHERIC WORLD INTELLIGENCE charged with ENERGY or SPIRIT; can be released in such a manner as to help earthlings. [**cf.** EXORCISM, SPIRIT]

SACRED HALLS—(Joan O'Connell) special magnetized areas scattered around and inside the earth, safely holding the sacred, secret knowledge of the universes and holistic man. **Syn.** VAULTS. [**cf.** MAGNETISM, ARK OF THE COVENANT]

SACRED MAGIC—the study of ANGELOLOGY, PHYSICS, and METAPHYSICS with a desire to work toward raising the CONSCIOUSNESS of the planet; theory: the ETHERIC WORLD INTELLIGENCES can help the material world perfect itself and therefore, communication and harmony between the two is necessary; see PARAPSYCHOLOGY, MYSTICISM.

SACRED PATIENCE—(alchemy) the hundreds of times that the ALCHEMIST repeats his or her alchemical operations, waiting for the moment when all the conditions will be most favorable and his or her formula will be complete. [**cf.** ELIXIR OF LIFE, ALCHEMICAL THEORY]

SACRED RIVER IN MAN—(esoteric) an invisible gaseous fluid that runs through the spinal column in the hollow of the KUNDALINI; symbolized by the River Nile, Ganges River, River Jordan. **Syn.** SUSHUMA. [**cf.** BRAIN DEWS, GOLDEN OIL, IDA, PINGALA]

SACRED SCIENCE—(esoteric) the study of alchemical principles; felt by the alchemists to be so precious and important that each time a formula is written in a sacred book one ingredient is purposely left out; this is done so the formula will not be used for evil intent but used by those who have righteous intent which is shown by their persistence to find the missing ingredient. [**cf.** ALCHEMY, AZOTH, ALCHEMIST]

SACRED SEAL—(esoteric) see THALMUS.

SADDHA—(Buddhism) faith that man "can" attain a very high nature and that man has a "goal and destiny" to perfect his or herself. **Syn.** LIBERATION, NIRVANA, CHRIST CONSCIOUSNESS. [**cf.** MONADOLOGY, LAW OF DESTINY Appendix 7, CREATION]

SADHAKA—(Vedic) (male) a seeker of spiritual advancement.

SADHIKA—(Vedic) (female) a seeker of spiritual advancement.

SADHU—(India) a holy man who uses psychic skills for helping his people. **Syn.** SHAMAN, PRIEST, DRUID. [**cf.** FAKIR, SELF-DENIAL]

SAGA—(Rome) a PSYCHIC specializing in EXORCISM, PROPHECY, and ASTROLOGY. **Syn.** PROPHET, INDIAN PRIEST, CHALDEAN, MIRACLE-WORKER, MENTAL PSYCHIC.

SAGE—1. (ancient) a person of great wisdom, judgment, and experience; one who uses psychic skills to help others and to PROPHESY for the

539

townspeople. **Syn.** SPIRIT COUNSELOR, FORESEER, AGENT, VILLAGE WISE-WOMAN. **2.** (Native American) a plant that has the vibratory rate to rid the area where it is placed of negative energies. [**cf.** ATMOSPHERE CLEARING, BOTANE, SHIELDING]

SAGOMA—(Africa) WITCH-DOCTOR specializing in PSYCHISM, DREAM INTERPRETATION, HEALING, and other SHAMAN arts. **Syn.** AGENCY, MEDIUM, CLEVER MAN, MAGI, PORTENT.

SAHASRARA—(Vedic) the THOUSAND PETAL LOTUS, centered above the head, representing the center of consciousness; controls one's psychic energies; a part of the THIRD-EYE AREA; corresponds to the HALO around Christ. **Syn.** CROWN CHAKRA. [**cf.** MENTAL PLANE, SAINT]

SAHU—(ancient Egypt) a life force that leaves the physical body and lives on, intelligently, in the etheric world. **Syn.** PERISPRIT, SPIRITUAL BODY, SHEATHS, ENVELOPE, SOUL-MIND.

SAINT—a person of great holiness; considered to have earned an exalted place in the ETHERIC WORLD through the quality of his or her earthly lives, heroism, and ability to perform feats of the paranormal while living on earth; one who performs the more difficult types of mental and physical psychism, using it for the betterment of all mankind; believes that psychic skills make one more closely related to the divine because one obtains (divine) knowledge, unknown to others; will enter high on the ANGELOLOGY scale after death and be recognized in both worlds. [**cf.** COSMIC MASTERS, LORDHOOD, MELCHIZEDEK]

SAINTESS—a female who obtains knowledge through ETHERIC WORLD INTELLIGENCES, using a form of PSYCHISM, as opposed to obtaining it intellectually; see SAINT.

SAKTI—see SHAKTI.

SALAMANDER—a NATURE SPIRIT that lives easily in flames of fire and whose function is to handle the fires on earth; the lesser salamander handles the small fires in homes and factories; the larger salamander works with the huge fires of volcanoes and forests; difficult for this nature spirit to communicate with humans; see FAIRIES. [**cf.** TOTEMIC SPIRIT, FOOLISH FIRE, FOX-FIRE]

SALT—(alchemy) **1.** symbol of the element EARTH; **2.** because it's a crystalline substance it can receive and hold etheric magnetism better than other substances; has properties to ward off evil vibrations; used by the alchemists in their formula and by the magician in ceremonial magic. [**cf.** CHEMICAL MARRIAGE, CELESTIAL DEW, MAGIC CIRCLES]

SALVATION—**1.** (Hinduism) union with God; **2.** (Greek *salvos,* "health, healing and wholeness"); **3.** (Christian) deliverance from the power and penalty of sins; **4.** (esoteric) belief that humans can be saved from the cycle of REBIRTH and DEATH by learning to stay on the PATH through understanding self.

SAMADHI—**1.** (Sanskrit) state of being aware of the SOURCE of knowledge and energy, receiving peace and BLISS; **2.** (Yoga) an emptiness of CONSCIOUSNESS without loss of consciousness; **3.** (transcendental meditation) the climax; absorption, a thoughtless state, reflecting true inner-self; **4.** (Raja Yoga) step seven in the eight-fold path. **Syn.** CHRIST CONSCIOUSNESS, THETA STATE OF CONSCIOUSNESS, LIBERATION.

SAMADHI YOGA—(Tibet) leads one on the PATH to the ultimate ILLUMINATION and prepares one for the initiation at the time of death. [**cf.** INITIATORY DEATH, BARDO]

SAMASARA—(Hinduism, Tantrism) see REINCARNATION.

SAMBHOGA-KAYA—(Tibet) see ETHERIC DOUBLE.

SAMBODHI—(Buddhism) the fully awakened state; supreme consciousness; next step is ENLIGHTENMENT. **Syn.** SAMADHI, CLEAR-LIGHT, CHRIST CONSCIOUSNESS.

SAMEDI—Lord of the UNDERWORLD; works in BLACK MAGIC. **Syn.** DENSITY, EARTHBOUND ENTITIES]

SAMJNA—(Buddhism) perception of the five PSYCHIC SENSES and creativity. [**cf.** SKANDHAS, MENTAL PSYCHISM]

SAMPLE—(penduluming) see WITNESS.

SAMSKARA—(Buddhism) tendencies of CONSCIOUSNESS; i.e., predispositions, emotions, habits, impulses. [**cf.** SKANDHAS, EMOTIONS, HABITS OF THOUGHT]

SAMURAI—a yoga position of relaxation wherein the arms dangle and the knees bend. **Syn.** MONKEY. [**cf.** ESOTERIC MOVEMENT, SILENCE]

SANCHITA KARMA—(Vedic) see DELAYED

KARMA and ACCUMULATED KARMA.

SANCTUARY—an area designated to be used for CHANNELING healing energy, opening PSYCHIC DOORS, and receiving an inner peace with one's self; built from positive thoughts, prayer, soft appropriate music, or a consecrated ritual; kept free from negative thoughts; e.g., a designated area outdoors in virgin nature, a church, or a tiny corner in one's home.

SAND DIVINATION—to perceive PSYCHIC INFORMATION through sand symbols: 1. (LeRoy Zemke) a QUERANT places his or her hands on top of psychic's hands, and psychic thrusts the querant's hand into a container of smooth sand without voluntary movement by either person; SYMBOLS are traced in the sand by querant; designs are interpreted by PSYCHIC who has a background of knowledge in symbolism; designs can also lead to psychic impressions within the psychic, making the reading quite complete; 2. to make a personal psychic assessment of the imprint of the client's hand after it has been placed in a tray of sand. [**cf.** CASTING OF LOTS, POINT-OF-FOCUS, BODY READING]

SAND PAINTINGS—(Native American, Navaho) sacred SYMBOLS made in the sand to the accompaniment of sacred chants which release creativity within the painters; could employ as many as twenty Indians for many hours to express the relationship between the MEDICINE MAN and the ETHERIC WORLD; sometimes depicts a healing for a tribesman. [**cf.** CHANTING]

SAND READING—(Native American) to use the patterns made by strewn sand to give a psychic READING; the holes and hills that appear from the fallen sand have a meaning as to the tosser's future, personality, and affairs; actual meaning of patterns is handed down from father to son. [**cf.** SHAMAN, SYMBOLS, CASTING OF LOTS]

SAND WRITING—(Native American, Navaho) to allow an ETHERIC WORLD INTELLIGENCE to intervene and move one's hand in the sand, making SYMBOLS that can be deciphered to bring PSYCHIC INFORMATION and guidance; performed in the conscious or unconscious state. **Sim.** AUTOMATIC WRITING. [**cf.** AUTOMATISM Appendix 2]

SANDALWOOD—wood which has properties that make it sacred; used to make prayer beads, incense, and used in sacrificial ceremonies. [**cf.** PRAYER BEADS, INCENSE]

SANGHA—(Zen) 1. congregation of meditators; 2. a community of holy persons.

SANGSARA—(Sanskrit) "rising and rising again"; born in the earth, then born in the etheric world, and reborn in earth again. **Syn.** REINCARNATION.

SANGSARIC REGIONS—(Tibet) any level of the ethetic world that is not NIRVANA; earthling's state of consciousness other than nirvana; 1. DEVA WORLD; 2. ASURA-LOKA world; 3. HUMAN world; 4. BRUTE WORLD; 5. PRETA-LOKA WORLD; 6. HELL world.

SANKIRTANS—(Hinduism) musical gatherings used for spiritual discipline; to use intense CONCENTRATION and to become absorbed in the seed thought and the sound of the music to attain higher realms of consciousness; the music is subjective, a spiritual and an individualistic art aiming at personal harmony with the OVERSOUL. [**cf.** COSMIC MUSIC, SEED-MANTRA, TONING, SHOOTING CHANT]

SANSKRIT—an ancient Indo-European, Indic language; the most important religious and literary language of India; a mystery language of the Brahman.

SAP OF THE TREE OF KNOWLEDGE—the invisible, gaseous ETHERIC FLUID that permeates the spinal cord and carries nerve fluids throughout the entire system. **Syn.** SUSHUMNA. [**cf.** GOLDEN OIL, NADIS, BRAIN DEWS]

SAPPHIRE—(esoteric) a translucent stone, usually blue, with properties making it useful as an AMULET; helpful in inducing HYPNOSIS; influenced by the vibrations of Jupiter. [**cf.** MINPSI, QUARTZ CRYSTALS, OVERALL CONSCIOUSNESS]

SASQUATCH—(Himalayas) a giant creature, half-human, half-animal; capable of shifting dimensions; appears for a short time and disappears instantaneously; the damage it does to animals and people gives evidence of its life. (Inconcl.) **Syn.** ABOMINABLE SNOWMAN, YETI, BIG FOOT. [**cf.** MONSTER ACTIVITY, DIMENSION-SHIFTING]

SASTRAS—a science of particular training in relationship to a certain set of rules, i.e., Buddhists, yogis, Indians. **Syn.** DISCIPLINE. [**cf.** PARAPSYCHOLOGY, MAGIC]

SAT—(Sanskrit, Vedic) see TOTALITY and GOD.

SAT-CHID-ANANDA—(Yoga) eternal existence

consciousness; the "I" of life; see MONAD.

SATAN—(Hebrew, Christian) EVIL personified to emphasize lower degrees of intent; one in charge of inferior actions on planet earth for those who are in a lower state of EVOLUTION than the majority of earth's inhabitants; evil vibrations bring a balance to its opposite GOOD. [**cf.** DENSITY, POLARITY]

SATANIC FORCES—energies in the DENSITY of the ETHERIC WORLD who are earthbound and haunt earthlings; half soul-minds and half elementals. [**cf.** DENSITY Appendix 5]

SATANISM—a group of new souls who worship EVIL activities and have chosen to incarnate in a time period that is too advanced for their desires; souls who have not been incarnated enough times or who learned too little from their previous incarnations; works in opposition to the masses who have grown to a higher STATE OF CONSCIOUSNESS; eventually the earth will be rid of these low-grade entities; (do not confuse with DESTRUCTIVE-BRAIN-WASHING CULTS]

SATORI—(Zen) a sudden alteration of AWARENESS brought about by extreme CONCENTRATION on one point, during MEDITATION sessions over a period of time; when one is aware of SELF as being one with nature and the universe, and remains an impartial observer; a pure, spontaneous awareness of peacefulness and ENLIGHTENMENT; an emptiness of consciousness without the loss of consciousness (describing a nonreality experience with reality words). **Syn.** NIRVANA, BLISS. [**cf.** WHITE LIGHT, SINGLE POINTEDNESS]

SATSANG—a group which gathers together informally to listen to a spiritual leader; spiritual communion.

SATURATION PASS—(magnetic healing) a special type of hand gesture and mind discipline that transfers MAGNETISM from the healing PRACTITIONER to the patient; the practitioner releases magnetism from his or her hands to the congested area or the whole body of the patient, after he or she has decreed his or her magnetism to have healing qualities; can be accomplished by touching the body or by hand movement a few inches away from the body; to pass magnetic fluid via the palms from one NERVOUS SYSTEM to another nervous system that needs repairing or vitality. [**cf.** LAYING-ON-OF-HANDS, MAGNETISM]

SATYRS—1. (ancient Egypt) any of a group of

ETHERIC WORLD INTELLIGENCES who were the first to know the story of OSIRIS; **2.** (pre-Christian) an etheric world male entity seeking women to participate in sexual activities. **Syn.** INCUBUS, LORD OF EVIL. **3.** identified with PAN, the nature spirit that has charge of the woods and fields; depicted as part goat and part human; a sensual, lascivious musical and pleasure-loving minor elemental, eager to communicate with mankind; can be irritated into riotous actions. **Syn.** HE-GOAT, SEIRIM, FAUN. [**cf.** NATURE SPIRIT, ETHERIC WORLD ENTITIES, DENSITY]

SAUCER CULT—(ufology, 1947) a group of people who believed in flying saucers and began to investigate them on their own because they felt that government officials were withholding knowledge. [**cf.** UFOLOGY Appendix 5]

SAUCER FLAP—(ufology) outer-space vehicle that looks like a pebble skipping over the air. **Syn.** FLYING SAUCER. [**cf.** STAR TRAVELERS, UFO INVESTIGATOR, WINDOW AREA]

SAUCERNAUTS—(ufology) the intelligence assumed to be in charge of driving the spacecraft. [**cf.** ETHER SHIPS, CONSTRUCTS, EXTRATERRESTRIAL BEINGS]

SAVAGE—(esoteric) a human in the very lowest stages of development; a new SOUL-MIND who has not reached the STATE OF CONSCIOUSNESS of the masses in earth today. [**cf.** STATE OF EVOLUTION, TIME PLAN, WHEEL OF LIFE]

SAVANT—great leaders and holy men with extensive learning, who earned their knowledge and spirituality from past incarnations. [**cf.** KARMA, MASTERS, GENIUS, LORDHOOD]

SCALE OF BRAIN RHYTHM—(biofeedback training) a chart that shows the states of consciousness of a human being by measuring the emanations of electrical brain impulses in cycles per second; groupings were decided upon by hooking up hundreds of subjects to the ELECTROENCEPHALOGRAPH to determine universal measurements of these electrical emanations; four levels of consciousness have been agreed upon: 14 to 29 cycles/second = beta level, 7 to 13 cycles/second = alpha level, 4 to 6 cycles/second = theta level, 3 cycles/second = delta level. (Inconcl.) [**cf.** BIOFEEDBACK TRAINING Appendix 5]

SCALE SWITCH—a dial on the ELECTROEN-

CEPHALOGRAPH that sets the range for amplification on which the subject is working, i.e., a range runs from 5 to 100 uv's. [cf. FIXED-BRAIN-WAVE-STATE, BURSTS]

SCAPEGOAT—(Greece) a live goat used for the PSYCHIC TRANSFER of one's negative problems or sins which is then killed; the sins or negative vibrations will dissipate or be destroyed with the death of the goat. [cf. PRIMARY WAVES, TELEPATHIC TRANSMISSION OF ILLNESS, ILL-WISHING, PSYCHIC ATMOSPHERE GAUGE]

SCARAB BEETLE—(Egypt) a sacred insect of the Egyptians; *kheprer* is the Egyptian name for beetle, *khepri* is the sun god; both bring life into existence without the female, in a 28-day cycle; frequently found in their hieroglyphics; has properties to make it useful as an amulet. [cf. SCARAB BEETLE AMULET, TALISMAN, MAGNETIZED OBJECTS]

SCARAB BEETLE AMULET—(Egypt) a preserved real beetle or a replica of a beetle made from a gem, used to bring PSYCHIC INFORMATION, guidance, and insurance of eternal life to the owner; handmade scarab beetle is cut in the shape of a beetle, flat underneath with inscribed hieroglyphics; top side made convex and designed to look like a beetle; the shape, Egyptian thought form, and inscription give it psychic properties. [cf. LAW OF SIMILARITY Appendix 7, AMULET ENERGIZING, WORDS-WITH-POWER]

SCARABAEUS—(Egypt) see SCARAB BEETLE.

SCATTER EFFECT—(psi tasks) psi responses in an experiment that are displaced in time or space; theory: records show that psi responses are rarely in one-to-one agreement with the TARGET due to the fact that psi information is not in exact harmony with the target and is biologically incongruous. [cf. WIDE-BAND TUNING, ETHERIC LINK, MISCARRIAGES, HOMING-IN]

SCHEME OF THINGS—(capitalized) an intelligence and/or power that keeps things moving perpetually, with a purpose, and in an orderly fashion; this purpose is greater than one's individual purposes but needs human activities in this orderliness; see TOTALITY.

SCHIZOKINESES—(Greece) to split or to move; (clinical) the physical gap in psi response due to the NERVOUS SYSTEM; [cf. AFFERENT SCHIZO-NEUROSIS]

SCHLIEREN SYSTEM—an optical system that breaks up the convection currents in the warm airflow surrounding the body into color systems; detects the pulsating envelope of warm air created by body heat and makes it visible; looks like shimmering rainbow; Schlieren is made from a light source, viewing screen, several magnifying lenses, and screens with pinholes which are arranged to catch this range of vision; (science) theory: there is an envelope surrounding human beings that is laden with bacterial particles of inorganic matter and microscopic bits of skin and this could trap other bacteria; (not considered the same etheric level as the Kirlian effect). (Inconcl.) [cf. ETHERIC DOUBLE, KIRLIAN EFFECT]

SCHOOL OF FUNCTIONALISM—founded by William James, 1842-1910; taught PSYCHOLOGY, PHILOSOPHY, and PARAPSYCHOLOGY.]

SCHOOLS FOR PROPHETS—(early A.D.) institutions for the study of mediumship.

SCI—abbr. for SCIENCE OF CREATIVE INTELLIGENCE; (TM, Maharishi Mahesh Yogi) the study of nature, origin, range, growth, and application of the theory that in every human being is a constant source of intelligence, energy, and happiness. [cf. TRANSCENDENTAL MEDITATION]

SCIENCE—1. (conventional) the search for measurable knowledge; reductive cause and effect information; an unraveling method of knowing by the five SENSES; 2. (liberalists) a self-constructing process; an ongoing unraveling process of intuitive and factual knowledge functioning with compatibility.

SCIENCE OF CHANTING—the study of VIBRATIONAL FREQUENCIES of the various chants in relation to their sound and rhythm for altering states of consciousness; used to induce MEDITATION, HEALING, and psychic skills; when CHANTING, the mind dissolves into a liquid current of energy and becomes purified and ready for the activities the chanter wants to perform; considered a spiritual discipline of the highest order, leading to the NADAM, or the INNER-SOUND CURRENT. (Inconcl.) [cf. SOUNDS-WITH-POWER, INCANTATION, OHM]

SCIENCE OF COLOR—1. (esoteric) (ancient Egypt, China, India, Greece) the study of the functions of each COLOR and subcolor in conjunction with the sevenfold nature of mankind, etheric world planes, chakras, the rainbow, and WHITE LIGHT. (Inconcl.)

2. (general science) principle of matter and light being inseparable; the essence of matter being light. (Inconcl.) **Syn.** COLOR SCIENCE. [**cf.** COLOROLOGY Appendix 2]

SCIENCE OF CONSCIOUSNESS—(future science) modern physics, theory: the atom (and electron) contain consciousness; this consciousness knows its function and keeps track, in a memory bank within the atom, of the various levels of consciousness it experiences throughout time. (Inconcl.) [**cf.** CONSCIOUSNESS Appendix 5]

SCIENCE OF CREATIVE INTELLIGENCE—abbr. SCI; see SCI.

SCIENCE OF EXPERIENCE—the principle that science and religion cannot be separated if one wants a true, complete picture of reality; feeling and intelligence must blend into the individual's BELIEF SYSTEM before it becomes understanding for him or her.

SCIENCE OF SERVICE—(Russ Michael) to consciously sort and set forth the essential priorities, versus the nonessential, time-consuming trivia; this trivia bogs the often well-meaning but short-sighted server.

SCIENCE OF SPIRIT—the study of the ETHERIC WORLD, its inhabitants, its functions, its properties, and its relationship to the physical world.

SCIENCE RULE—(unknown) "nothing is true until it has been duplicated with a conceptual scheme explaining what has happened."

SCIENTIFIC ASTROLOGY—the study of the relationship of medicine, psychiatry, and ASTROLOGY. (Inconcl.) **Syn.** COSMOBIOLOGY.

SCIENTIFIC MEDIUM—a PSYCHIC who works with ETHERIC WORLD INTELLIGENCES who are willing to consent to various controlled experiments and test conditions for study and observation; intelligences are eager to prove their validity and abilities. [**cf.** CROSS-CORRESPONDENCE, TESTING MEDIUMSHIP, PSYCHIC IMPRINTS]

SCIENTIFIC PRAYER—to speak affirmative words that state the Truth of one's innate potential accompanied by the desire and faith to bring it into manifestation (as opposed to the begging, beseeching, or bargaining types of verbiage) has more effect if one is in an ALPHA or THETA STATE OF CONSCIOUSNESS; e.g., "I am a child of the universe growing toward perfection and, therefore, inherit all the money I need for my needs and desires." [**cf.** WORDS-WITH-POWER, AFFIRMATIONS]

SCIENTIFIC WILL—the process of the SUBCONSCIOUS MIND that allows the CONSCIOUS MIND to control a single cell's movement. [**cf.** BIOFEEDBACK TRAINING, BODY FEELING]

SCINTILLATE—to emanate sparks or to leave a trail of light behind; flowing lights have been perceived clairvoyantly following an ASTRAL PROJECTIONIST and following an APPARITION. [**cf.** REALMS OF FORM, SPIRITUAL ENERGY, SPIRITUAL LIGHT]

SCINTILLATING KALEIDOSCOPIC NEBULA—see AURA.

SCOPE—(Greek) suffix meaning "instrument for viewing"; used in words pertaining to DIVINATION and CASTING OF LOTS.

SCOPY—see SCRIPTOGRAPH.

SCOUT SHIPS—(ufology) little nocturnal lights that seem to separate from the BIG MAMA assemblage of lights for a short period to do some kind of work, then regather again into the big mama assemblage. [**cf.** PROTEAN FORMS, ANOMALOUS SHADOWS, PHONY STARS]

SCREAMING STONE—(Tara and Dublin, Ireland) a pillar that utters a noise audible to physical ears if the wrong kind of king is inaugurated. **Syn.** STONE OF FAIL, LIA FAIL. [**cf.** CONTAINERS OF MAGICAL POWER, GOD-AS-THE-STONE]

SCREENED TOUCH MATCHING—abbr. STM; an ESP card testing technique in which the pack is held by the experimenter behind a screen; the subject indicates in each try what he or she thinks the top card is by pointing to one of five key positions; the card is laid opposite that position and checked at the end of the experiment. [**cf.** EXPERIMENT EXPECTANCY, FORWARD DISPLACEMENT ESP, HIGH VARIANCE]

SCRIPT INTELLIGENCE—an ETHERIC WORLD INTELLIGENCE who writes messages on paper using the hand of the MEDIUM; as in AUTOMATIC WRITING. **Sim.** EARTH SPIRIT, ODIN, AGENT, CONTROL. [**cf.** AUTOMATIC SCRIPT, AUTOMAT, DIRECT PSYCHOGRAPHY]

SCRIPTOGRAPH—(MEDIUMSHIP) to supply energy to deceased persons so they can write messages on unexposed photographic plates; writing is done without exposure to light so it can be printed and read; handwriting can be checked, and in past cases, it was found to be the penmanship of the deceased person who claimed to have written it. [**cf.** ETHERIC SCRIPT, PSYCHIC PHOTOGRAPHY, PRECIPITATION, EXTRAS]

SCRIPTURE—writings of pure Truths in the form of PARABLE and metaphysical symbolism, contained in a sacred book (as opposed to interpreting the writings as accurate history); all words in a sacred book are not SCRIPTURE just because they are written there.

SCRYER—a PSYCHIC who is skilled at CRYSTAL GAZING. [**cf.** SCRYING]

SCRYING—(antiquity) ("seeing") to perceive psychic visions on clear, shiny surfaces that relate to the masses or to individual questions; surfaces from clear crystal, clear water, polished mirrors, shiny black ink, or polished stainless steel are effective; CRYSTAL BALL is most commonly used; material must be placed so the light strikes it at an angle; question is asked, then psychic stares at the crystal ball with a neutral mind; vision begins with a white cloud, which lifts to reveal a scene, words, or a face; PSYCHIC should be in an ALPHA STATE OF CONSCIOUSNESS; can be used for one's self or for answers for others; (do not confuse with SKRYING). **Sim.** HYDROMANCY, CYLICOMANCY, LECONOMANCY. [**cf.** MENTAL PSYCHISM, QUARTZ CRYSTAL]

SEA OF FACES—EARTHBOUND ENTITIES who show themselves clairvoyantly to an individual when there is an opening in his or her ETHERIC WEB; these faces come from various time periods; may be weird, grotesque, handsome, hazy, vivid, old, or young; they appear as if floating around in an aquarium; 1. because they hover close to earth hoping to relive earth experiences, they may slide in an opening in the etheric web unknowingly; an opening in the etheric web occurs when the CONSCIOUS MIND and SUBCONSCIOUS MIND are exchanging dominancy in their roles; when these two minds set up an equilibrium as they exchange (both on the same level at once), they leave an opening for these faces; (a) on the onset of sleep, called the HYPNAGOGIC STATE: (b) on the onset of awakening, called the HYPNAPOMPIC STATE; (c) in the middle of the night to persons on medicinal or RECREATIONAL DRUGS or alcohol; called REM REBOUND PHENOMENA; 2. a sophisticated EEG instrument was designed with twenty-two electrodes

to especially tune into these wandering souls; this instrument is called a TOPOSCOPE. (Inconcl.) [**cf.** EARTHBOUND ENTITIES]

SEA OF PSI—see ETHERIC WORLD.

SEA OF UNIVERSAL ENERGY—the ETHERIC WORLD; theory: the ATMOSPHERE has unlimited intelligence in it that is constantly vibrating at millions of VIBRATIONAL FREQUENCIES; intended to be used by the mind of every human in order to make a UNIVERSE. **Sim.** HEAVEN, PLANES, SPHERES.

SEA SPIRIT—(Melanesia) 1. deceased peson who enters a live fish and from inside the fish helps earthlings have an abundant catch; sharks make the best fish to enter psychically; 2. deceased person who enters the water and magically shoots flying fish into the air to be caught by earthlings. [**cf.** ETHERIC WORLD INTELLIGENCES, ANPSI]

SEAL OF SOLOMON—see SOLOMON'S SEAL.

SEALING OF THE AURA—to put a protection around one's self to ward off negative vibrations; to mentally or verbally say AFFIRMATIONS or a word ritual, and to have uplifting, positive, qualitative thoughts for many hours; this puts a wall of good vibrations around one to prevent accidents, psychic transfers, emotional transfers, and tuning into low-quality PSYCHIC INFORMATION; see SHIELDING. [**cf.** CLOAK OF INSULATION, THOUGHTS, LAW OF LIKE ATTRACTS LIKE Appendix 7, PSYCHIC TRANSFER]

SEANCE—a meeting of a group of dedicated persons and at least one WELL-GROUNDED MEDIUM who sit in a BLACKED-OUT ROOM to produce physical phenomena; 1. meetings are held weekly and last for two or three hours; group sits in a circular formation to keep PSYCHIC ENERGY concentrated in the center for easier manipulation by the ETHERIC WORLD INTELLIGENCES, and to keep out negative entities; 2. etheric world intelligences work during the meeting to synchronize the BODY CHEMISTRY of each member until they can produce the phenomenon; some sitters are used for batteries; harmony among the personalities of the group, both outside the meeting and within the meetings is the most important factor for success; 3. a metaphysical or a religious lesson precedes the blacked-out meeting; MEDITATION, PRAYER, and singing help to build the VIBRATIONS conducive to physical phenomena; 4. medium improves his or her ability to synchronize with the intervention of the etheric world intelligence with each meeting; ECTOPLASM emanates from the medium in an abundant quantity and in smaller amounts from the SITTERS, which is the psychic energy that is necessary for physical phenomema; however, sitters improve their MENTAL MEDIUMSHIP ability also; 5. proven facts: the number of members is not as important as the regularity of attendance and sitting in the same chair and this is the reason it is difficult for outsiders to investigate what goes on; reporters and scientists must attend regularly and be in agreement with the work in order to make it a controlled situation; skeptical thoughts hinder psychic performance. [cf. CIRCLE, MEDIUMSHIP, DESIRED-CONTROL]

SEANCE HANDS—ETHERIC WORLD INTELLIGENCES who remain invisible in the SEANCE room but the work they do with their hands is tangible evidence of their presence; i.e., stroking the sitters' faces or moving objects around the room; these intelligences are ENERGY FIELDS of matter that can neither reflect nor obstruct light; intention is always to teach about life after death. [cf. ANTIFRAUD PRECAUTION, SPIRIT HANDS, CO-PARTICIPANTS, CONTROL]

SEANCE LIGHTS—tiny globules of light which dance around in the BLACKED-OUT ROOM that are ETHERIC WORLD INTELLIGENCES who have come to join the session; some are discarnate beings and some are the guides of the sitters. **Syn.** SPIRIT LIGHTS. [cf. SEANCE, PSYCHIC STRUCTURE, HUMAN BATTERIES]

SEANCE MANIFESTATIONS—congested matter that has the appearance of earthly bodies and objects, made by the ETHERIC WORLD INTELLIGENCES at will during a materialization SEANCE; etheric world is able to act on the ECTOPLASM taken from the SITTERS and MEDIUM along with the necesary elements from the COSMOS in order to duplicate earthly things; purpose is to teach the sitters the true nature of mind and physics. [cf. MATERIALIZATION Appendix 2]

SEANCE TRUMPET—a long, narrow megaphone used by ETHERIC WORLD INTELLIGENCES during a SEANCE to amplify their voices so they can be heard by the physical ear; made in three tiers so it will collapse for easy carrying; material is lightweight, such as aluminum or heavy cardboard; the trumpet is magnetized in the sun and rain and then pro-tected in a case when not in use; handled only by the trumpet MEDIUM. [cf. TRUMPET, TRUMPET CONTROL, DESIRED-CONTROL]

SEAT OF CONSCIOUSNESS—the PINEAL GLAND in the brain area, where the mental and subconscious activity initiates a STATE OF CONSCIOUSNESS that mankind perceives as REALITY; COSMIC ENERGY enters the head, unknown to the individual and strikes the antennas of the pineal gland where it is transmuted into electrical energy so the brain can use it. (Inconcl.) [cf. THIRD-EYE AREA, THALAMUS, SUBSCONSCIOUS MIND, MENTAL MIND, PITUITARY GLAND]

SEAT OF THE RATIONAL SOUL—(Rene Descartes) the PINEAL GLAND.

SECOND BODY—see ASTRAL BODY.

SECOND DEATH—1. (Hinduism) the casting off of the three lower bodies of the individual when one is working from the middle self, called the battleground consciousness; here one prepares the self for entry into the three higher bodies. [cf. BATTLEGROUND, MATERIALISTIC MAN, BODIES OF MAN] 2. (Tibet) an initiation ritual whereby the candidate is symbolically crucified and actually placed in a stone coffin; here the candidate experiences his or her transformation in a mock episode, going through great suffering so as to bring him or her understanding regarding the reason for life. [cf. DEATH SCIENCE, INITIATORY DEATH-RITE, COFFIN RITUAL, COMING FORTH FROM THE DAY]

SECOND DIMENSION—matter that has length only and is able to move backward, forward, and sideward; when a line moves in any direction not in its own length, it generates an arc giving it two dimensions, both length and width; found when a line or direction can be taken at an angle to the first flat plane or straight line; two different lines of force, two opposing currents meet, intersect, and fuse; this gives an interaction of fusion, attraction, repulsion, and cohesion to resist; i.e., touch gives second dimension; as one contacts a surface, he or she fuses and has a sensation of what kind of surface he or she is feeling. [cf. FIRST DIMENSION, THIRD DIMENSION]

SECOND PLANE—see ASTRAL PLANE.

SECOND SELF—1. an ENERGY FIELD that is a higher intelligence than the psychic's personal intelligence; brings knowledge to the psychic through

INSPIRATIONAL THOUGHT. **Syn.** SUPERCONSCIOUS MIND. [**cf.** INSPIRATIONAL WRITING] 2. an ETHERIC WORLD INTELLIGENCE working through a MEDIUM in any type of physical phenomena. **Syn.** AGENT, GUIDE. [**cf.** AUTOMATISM, VOICE TRANCE, IMPERSONATION]

SECOND SIGHT—1. see PSYCHIC ENERGY; **2.** see CLAIRVOYANCE; **3.** (Scotland) to mentally project, at will, one's clairvoyant vision to the higher realms of the etheric world. [**cf.** MENTAL PROJECTION Appendix 2]

SECOND STAGE OF THE CHIKHAI BARDO—(Tibet) to view one's own THOUGHT-FORMS during the DEATH PROCESS after the SOUL-MIND has left the PHYSICAL BODY and is still under the direction of the reader; the realization, by the deceased person, that the physical world is not as real as the positive and negative floating thought-forms one made while still alive. [**cf.** DEATH SCIENCE, READER, PROTEAN SPECTRES]

SECOND STATE—(astral projection) (Robert Monroe) pertains to the ASTRAL BODY after it has separated from the physical body. **Syn.** PHO-WA. [**cf.** SEPARATION, ROTATION, CHANGING THE SKIN]

SECOND-RING-OF-POWER—to give attention to the nonordinary world with an indication that something significant and amazing will happen, and holding this attention firmly and trusting until it does. [**cf.** FIRST-RING-OF-POWER, CENTERING]

SECONDARY CLEAR LIGHT—(Tibet) the SECOND STAGE OF CHIKHAI BARDO, during the DEATH PROCESS, wherein one has missed the primary clear light because one is in a lower state of consciousness and the light one sees is less dazzling. [**cf.** FREEING THE SOUL, BIRTH OF THE BARDO-BODY, LORDS OF DEATH]

SECONDARY EFFECT—(psi tasks) a consistent miss or a consistent displacement in experiments; reveals significance in psi scoring even though one does not directly hit the target. [**cf.** TARGET, MISPLACED PSI]

SECONDARY GAINS—(holistic health) pertains to those who feel it is more lucrative to be sick than it is to be well; e.g., some people's lifestyles depend upon being sick because they would not know how to interact with others if they were well, relieves them from chores they dislike; prevents them from making a major lifestyle decision. [**cf.** CURATIVE EDUCATION Appendix 5]

SECONDARY PERSONALITY—an ETHERIC WORLD INTELLIGENCE who communicates through a PSYCHIC or MEDIUM; manner of communication can be VOICE TRANCE, AUTOMATIC WRITING, TRUMPET, INSPIRATIONAL MEDIUMSHIP, INDEPENDENT VOICE, etc.; theory: **1.** the intelligence the medium calls a GUIDE is a personality of one of his or her past incarnations; **2.** the intelligence portrays many characteristics and beliefs that are buried beneath the conscious awareness of the medium. (Inconcl.) **Syn.** SPLIT-OFF, SPIRIT POSSESSION, HAUNTING. [**cf.** NEED-DETERMINED RESPONSE]

SECONDARY WAVES—(psychometry) the vibrations on the "surface" of an article that have not been repeatedly exposed to it enough times to make an intense impregnation on the article; these vibrations are not as important as the impregnated ones and cannot be easily read; e.g., the mother gave the ring and lipstick of the daughter to the PSYCHOMETRIST to help locate the daughter; the vibrations of the mother are the secondary waves. [**cf.** PRIMARY WAVES, PSYCHOMETRY]

SECRET CHIEFS—1. magnanimous, intelligent soul-minds who have earned the privilege to belong to the order of the GREAT WHITE BROTHERHOOD which is in charge of planet earth's evolvement; make themselves known by entering MEDIUMSHIP DEVELOPMENT circles to teach psychic skills, laws of the universe, and to encourage advancement of the SOUL-MIND; their knowledge cannot be learned by formal education; only enter circles in which the members show an earnest, consistent desire for the Truths of the higher realms. [**cf.** GOLDEN DAWN] 2. (Hebrew Kabbalah) the supposed invisible superhumans who direct the activities of authentic dedicated fraternities. **Syn.** DEVAS, SHINING ONES, MASTERS.

SECRET DOCTRINE—a masterpiece of root knowledge written by Madam Helena Petrovna Blavatsky out of which many religions, philosophies, and sciences have grown; given to her from the AKASHIC RECORDS by the ETHERIC WORLD INTELLIGENCES.

SECRET SCIENCE—(antiquity) universal principles and philosophies which includes METAPHYSICS, PSYCHISM, MYSTICISM, and occult knowledge that is taught only to special individuals. **Syn.** WISDOM OF THE MYSTERIES.

SECT—a group of people who all believe, or who profess to believe, in the same basic principles of a religious nature.

SECULARIST VIRUS—to run from one to another of the cults, churches, and philosophies trying to find an inner meaning for oneself.

SEDNA—(Eskimo) a NATURE SPIRIT belonging to the sea animal group. **Sim.** MERMAN, NYMPH.

SEE—1. (Native American) to go into TRANCE and receive PSYCHIC INFORMATION; 2. (South Africa) psychic information brought through a WITCH-DOCTOR that gives guidance to the questioner; e.g., "The witch-doctor could *see* an answer to my problem." **Syn.** PSYCHIC COUNSELING; 3. (don Juan) to hold the world still long enough to investigate it; to *see* the world as it really is; sometimes accomplished by squinting the eyes to tiny slits.

SEED MEDITATION—a very disciplined STATE OF CONSCIOUSNESS in which the mind is controlled, the body is relaxed, the emotions are quiet, and one tries to have blank periods of the mind; going to the nucleus of TOTALITY. [**cf.** MANTRA, TM, BLANK PERIODS]

SEED-MANTRA—(meditation) the sound in which the power governing this element manifests itself. **Syn.** BIJA. [**cf.** INTONING, GREAT TONE OF NATURE]

SEED-PICTURE—an inner-mental scene showing the END-RESULT of a desire or need one wants to manifest; held in the mind subconsciously or held deliberately for a period of time which makes the manifestation appear; see VISUALIZATION. [**cf.** INNER-DIALOGUE, MEDITATION]

SEEDS—(Huna) begin with an experience that brings emotional pain when it happens and is repressed to alleviate the pain; occurs frequently when the CONSCIOUS MIND is not in condition to rationalize the experience; this reacts in the body like a seed embryo, drawing to it repressed emotional pain every time a similar situation occurs; thus a cluster of seeds forms and blocks the energy flow in the body, making one ill. [**cf.** GRAPES, BLOCKS, EMOTION]

SEEDS OF SOUND—(India) levels of noise that affect the etheric world bodies and bring irritating

or soothing reactions on the personality, without the person realizing why he or she is feeling this way; caused by: 1. subliminal levels of sound and music that are not noticeable to the physical ear; 2. background music that is blocked out by the will of the conscious mind. [**cf.** CLAIRAUDIENCE, COSMIC MUSIC, SUBLIMINAL LEVEL]

SEEING—1. (penduluming) (Howard St. L. Cookes) theory: the eyes have a relationship in making the PENDULUM respond to the question in the mind; looking toward an object, the eyes receive the reflected ELECTROMAGNETIC WAVES from that object, and these waves pass through the opening of the pupil to the optic nerve of the retina, and on to the brain; the waves spread from the brain to every part of the body making the pendulum capable of responding to the thoughts in the brain; 2. (don Juan) "responding to the perceptual solicitations of a world outside the description man has learned to call reality." [**cf.** see, REALITY, PENDULUM POWER]

SEEING A DREAM—(Greece) the feeling that one is viewing the scene of a dream instead of being in the dream. [**cf.** FALSE AWAKENING, ESSAY DREAM, DEEPER DREAMLAND]

SEEING MEDIUM—see CLAIRVOYANCE.

SEEING PROPERLY—(Kalahari Desert) to see inside the body of the patient while in a TRANCE state and to recognize the cause of the physical or mental illness; to bring on a TRANSCENDANT state of consciousness by rhythmic dancing and chanting around a campfire until thoughts stand still and fires stop floating; this makes it possible for one to see beyond appearances into other realities and to see the ghosts who are causing the problem; from this the seer or seeress can cure the patient. [**cf.** X-RAY CLAIRVOYANCE, HAUNTING]

SEEING WITH THE SKIN—see SKIN TALK.

SEEING WITH THE STOMACH—1. see HUNCHABILITY and GUT-FEELING; 2. an umbrella word for MENTAL PSYCHISM because many psychics perceive PSYCHIC INFORMATION through the SOLAR PLEXUS instead of the THIRD-EYE AREA; 3. (hypnosis) to receive answers from the SUBCONSCIOUS MIND of the hypnotized subject via the solar plexus; the HYPNOTHERAPIST puts one hand on the stomach of the hypnotized subject and directs questions to his or her other hand; the subject answers; to be used when the physical ears do not hear the questions asked by the hypnotherapist. [cf. CLAIRSEN-TIENCE, HYPNOTHERAPY]

SEEING-EYE VISION—to perceive with the psychic eye as if one were living in the FOURTH DIMENSION; to look clairvoyantly through everything, and in all directions at once; to view an object or thing from the inside and outside at the same time. Syn. ASTRAL VISION. [cf. ASTRAL PLANE, FOURTH DIMENSION]

SEELE—(Germany) ultimate reality in its feminine aspect; the womb of all things. Syn. COLLECTIVE UNCONSCIOUS, DHARMA-KAYA. [cf. BIOCOMPUTER, MEMORY BANK, HABITS OF THOUGHT]

SEER—(ancient Egypt, Bible) a male PSYCHIC specializing in CLAIRVOYANCE, CLAIRSENTIENCE, and PROPHECY; female is called seeress; Sim. AUGUA, CELT, INDIAN PRIEST, MAN OF GOD, NELLIE]

SEER PRIESTS—(ancient Egypt) priests who had acquired MEDIUMSHIP ability and used it to bring psychic knowledge for their people. Sim. MEDIUM, CHALDEAN, AGENT.

SEERSHIP—1. (Middle English, Egypt, Bible) to perceive psychic information using the skills of CLAIRVOYANCE, CLAIRSENTIENCE, and MEDIUMSHIP; information is usually prophetic; 2. (ancient Rome) to perceive psychic vision at will; psychic skill was used professionally in governmental affairs.

SEES-IN-SLEEP—(Mesopotamia) the ability to remember one's astral projections that one takes in the normal night sleep, even when not willed; recall is vivid and when earth areas are visited, found to be accurate. [cf. OUT-OF-RANGE-OF-CORD-ACTIVITY, BODY FLAPPING DREAM, DISTANT POINT ASTRAL PROJECTION]

SEFER YETSIRAH—(Kabbalah) theory of CREATION derived from the first ten numbers and twenty-two letters of the Hebrew alphabet. [cf. SEFIROTH, NUMBERS]

SEFIROTH—(Kabbalah) the revelation of God through ten spheres for mankind to use as psychic centers.

SEIDR—(Sweden) act of going into trance. [cf. SEMITRANCE, ECTOPLASM, SEANCE]

SEKHEM—(ancient Egypt) see MONAD.

SELECTIVE AMNESIA—the ability to coerce a painful or stressful life experience out of the CON-SCIOUSNESS; later the individual has amnesia whenever anything that pertains to that event occurs. (Inconcl.) [cf. BLOCKS, REPRESSION, EMOTIONS]

SELECTIVE TELEPATHY—(early 1900s) a deliberate form of INNER-WORLD TELEPATHY to prove that ETHERIC WORLD INTELLIGENCES communicate among themselves; two or more mediums were located at distant places and tuned into the etheric world at the same time; they all received the same message. [cf. CROSS-CORRESPONDENCE, MENTAL TELEPATHY]

SELECTIVITY—(dowsing) ability of the DOWSER to tell the SUBCONSCIOUS MIND what he or she is looking for underground; i.e., gas pipelines, water veins, gold, etc.; the DOWSING ROD bends in his or her hand only for that particular substance, when it is located underground. Sim. NARROW-BAND TUNING. [cf. DOWSING QUESTION, FORKED BRANCH, GHOST VEIN]

SELF—1. (capitalized) (a) (Vedic) the divine spark of the Godhead. Sim. ATMAN, MONAD. (b) the ultimate reality in the orderly, all-encompassing universe reflecting the human being; center of the soul-mind. Sim. MACROCOSM. (c) (Carl Jung) an evolutionary unit emerging from nature, functioning to develop as a human being; (d) (Hinduism) ABSOLUTE BEING, BRAHMA; 2. (uncapitalized) (a) (Theosophy) unity; unit in unity; (b) the total memory-bank of all the experiences the soul-mind has encountered in each incarnation. Sim. SOUL-MIND, SUBSCONSCIOUS MIND. (c) (Seth) a fragment of the entire entity connecting to the other fragment selves through one vital source; grows into various realities while springing from the same source. [cf. SOUL-MIND]

SELF-ACTUALIZATION—(Abraham Maslow) to unfold one's full potential of mind, body, and emotions in developing the whole organism, man; to bring into fruition one's inner capabilities, motivated from within, putting one in command of these resources; the act or process of manifesting the capabilities for which one has the potentiality; this results in higher fulfillment of life experiences; to develop a mature whole organism.

SELF-AWARENESS—1. to be acutely sensitive to bodily feelings; to distinguish between physical activity, psychic indications, and cosmic radiations flowing within the body; 2. to be keenly sensitive to mind activity; to know how to separate a thought instigated from within the mind from a NON-

THOUGHT (psychic information) entering from outside the mind. [**cf.** PSYCHIC INFORMATION, COSMIC ENERGY]

SELF-CONTROL OF INNER STATES—1. to give commands to the INVOLUNTARY FUNCTIONS of the body, at will, and to allow it to react accordingly; more easily performed when the emotions are quieted, the body is relaxed, and the mind is under control; e.g., to stop the blood flow in an area of the arm so that when it is stuck with a needle it doesn't bleed; to make one hand warm and the other cold; 2. to retain a degree of decision-making ability while in SEMI-STAGE HYPNOSIS without coming out of the hypnotic state; ability to make a small decision, i.e., "I did not go to high school, ask me another question"; two consciousnesses working at the same time. [**cf.** HYPNOTHERAPY, EEG, HYPNOSIS TRAINING]

SELF-DENIAL—to strengthen the will by relinquishing material and bodily pleasures in a desire to attain psychic skills, healing channeling, and spiritual growth; i.e., by fasting, long daily meditations, or giving up an activity that doesn't seem to be in accord with one's new standard of thinking. [**cf.** MENTAL PSYCHIC PROCESSES Appendix 2]

SELF-DIRECTING—1. pertains to a system that functions within a living entity; this system is instructed from a universal law without mankind's interference; found in humans, animals, plants, minerals, and other specimens of nature; e.g., the sun rising every morning; the digestive systems of humans and animals. [**cf.** SYMPATHETIC NERVOUS SYSTEM, NATURAL LAWS] 2. to receive information from the ETHERIC WORLD to help make decisions in life and to realize that this is guidance from TOTALITY; to follow the guidance regardless of logical reasoning in order to keep it flowing. [**cf.** ETHERIC WORLD INTELLIGENCES, CLAIRSENTIENCE]

SELF-DISCIPLESHIP—(esoteric) to become a follower and student of one's own inner feelings and directions, regardless of comments from friends, family, and the cultural system. [**cf.** TRANSFORMATION, GURU, ALTERNATIVES]

SELF-DISIDENTIFICATION—(meditation) to no longer be consciously aware of outside stimuli and physical body sensations; to be aware of the dissociated mind activity only; to feel that one belongs to the whole ethereal universe. [**cf.** GOING INTO THE SILENCE, INTERNALIZATION, NOTHING-NESS]

SELF-EDIFICATION DREAMS—picture language during REM sleep that tells the person where he or she stands mentally, spiritually, and psychologically in the world for that present day; almost all DREAMS have this one type of interpretation, purposely, to help the dreamer make decisions the next day according to how he or she feels about their present status. [**cf.** COMPENSATORY DREAMS, DREAMS FOR HEALTH, RELEASE TYPE DREAMS]

SELF-GENERATED, REPEATED STIMULUS—(meditation) to direct the mental mind to the smallest possible target by one's own volition to induce a deep state of MEDITATION; i.e., to say a MANTRA until it becomes a habit, yet the CONSCIOUS MIND must remain aware in order to keep it going (in contrast to the repeated stimulus of an air-conditioner hum). [**cf.** ROSARY BEADS, JAPA]

SELF-HYPNOSIS—to allow one's self to reach a hypnotic state of consciousness without the aid of another person; occurs unconsciously or can be programmed deliberately; types of self-hypnosis: SELF-HYPNOTHERAPY, EMOTIONAL HYPNOSIS, and SPONTANEOUS HYPNOSIS. [**cf.** MASS HYPNOSIS, STAGE HYPNOSIS, PRESCRIPTION]

SELF-HYPNOTHERAPY—to deliberately put one's self in a hypnotic state to improve or correct a health condition or a behavioral pattern; to verbally or silently give one's self the induction instructions, preplanned prescription suggestions, and the induction release. [**cf.** HYPNOTHERAPY Appendix 5]

SELF-IDENTIFICATION—to understand that one's self is a contributing factor, whether purposefully or uselessly, to the condition of the wholeness of humanity and the world; 2. to choose and be supportive of the NEW AGE and changing world by thoughts and actions as one deems logical; a characteristic of a planetary worker. [**cf.** NEW-AGE PSYCHOLOGY Appendix 5]

SELF-INDUCED TRANCE—a very deep state of hypnosis accomplished by the SYNCHRONIZATION of the MEDIUM and ETHERIC WORLD INTELLIGENCE so the intelligence can use the medium's body, in whole or in part, for the desired physical phenomena; sometimes cataleptic in nature; medium remains passive and allows the etheric world to intervene. [**cf.** MEDIUMSHIP, INDEPENDENT VOICE, ETHERIC SURGERY, DESIRED-CONTROL]

550

SELF-INDUCTION—(hypnosis) the process of putting one's self in a state of HYPNOSIS; to verbally or silently say to one's self preplanned suggestions of a relaxing nature until one feels detached from the body; the CONSCIOUS MIND is aware enough to continue the prescription or the reason for the hypnotherapeutic state. [**cf.** PRESCRIPTON, HYPNO-THERAPY, INDUCTION RELEASE]

SELF-INTEGRATION—a harmonious working of the mind, body, and emotions, and the ability to realize this harmony; to feel comfortable about one's self; e.g., to feel satisfied in one's "bones" that the decision one made is correct. [**cf.** CURATIVE EDUCATION, NEW-AGE PSYCHOLOGY]

SELF-ISOLATION—1. to be keenly aware of one's thoughts and nervous system; a necessary state before going into TRANCE, taking an ASTRAL PRO-JECTION, or applying SELF-HYPNOTHERAPY; 2. to cut out the trivia in one's life regardless of the opinions of outsiders; functioning from the sensitivity within. [**cf.** CURATIVE EDUCATION, INTUI-TION, INSTINCT]

SELF-METAPROGRAMMING—(John C. Lilly) the absorption of one's inner beliefs and emotions from one's experiences into the SUBCONSCIOUS MIND, regardless of the outward appearance one portrays; these real feelings are ready to react and will be used according to future outer environmental stimuli. [**cf.** CONSCIOUS MIND, PROGRAMMED BIOCOMPUTER]

SELF-METAPROGRAMMER—see CONSCIOUS MIND.

SELF-NONSELF—to be aware that one is a PHYSICAL BODY, a MIND, and a point in the total ALL. [**cf.** LAW OF REPETITION Appendix 7, QUIET ATTENTIVENESS]

SELF-OBSERVATION THERAPY—a technique using altered states of consciousness to help the subject understand which thoughts have occurred to make him or her cry, faint, laugh, get bored, tired, or hungry, in order to help overcome mundane problems and to balance with life.

SELF-ORGANIZING BIOGRAVITATIONAL FIELDS —masses of electrons emanating from an object that form together and generate that object. **Sim.** AURA, ORGONE FIELD, L-FIELD, BIOCOSMIC ENERGY PATTERN. [**cf.** KIRLIAN EFFECT]

SELF-REALIZATION—to be aware of oneself as a great important being necessary to the wholeness of humanity and the universe, and to use this awareness to open the avenues of one's potential that has been repressed; to use one's capabilities freely to bring self-expression, happiness, and a meaningful LIFE to oneself. [**cf.** TRANSFORMATION, CURATIVE EDUCATION, NEW-AGE PSYCHOLOGY, CONSCIOUS-NESS AWARENESS MOVEMENT]

SELF-REGULATED—(biofeedback training) coined by Elmer Green; to *voluntarily* control the INVOL-UNTARY FUNCTIONS of the body and to be sensitive to this change in the body; see SELF-CONTROL OF INNER STATES. [**cf.** BIOFEEDBACK TRAINING Appendix 5]

SELF-REGULATING PHRASES—coined by Elmer Green; preplanned statements that tell one's body what one wants it to do; such as heal its kidney; method: to meditate until one has reached a deep STATE OF CONSCIOUSNESS (mind, body, and emotions are quiet, and to then visualize the area of the body needing improvement, and silently say the proper words; this meditative mood makes the body open and receptive to the words said at that time; words make contact with that particular part of the body and start physiological changes in the body. [**cf.** BIOFEEDBACK TRAINING, DESENSITIZA-TION, LISTENING MODE, RECEIVING MODE]

SELF-RELEASE MECHANISM—coined by Richard Sutphen; a strong suggestion that one can pull him or herself out of the hypnotic REGRESSION session by themselves whenever they wish; suggestion is given during induction to the hypnotic state in group regression; if the subject does not like the life he or she has tuned into they may return to the awake state by using the suggestion; a very necessary tool to make group regression possible and pleasant. [**cf.** REINCARNATION, PAST LIVES THEORY, BLOCKS]

SELF-SUGGESTION—1. the INNER-DIALOGUE one carries on most of the time, unnoticeable to the conscious awareness; even though the dialogue is emotionless, the repetition makes it powerful; the ideas and suggestions work toward manifesting one's behavior, lifestyle, and BODY CHEMISTRY as if they were spoken aloud, or silently, but deliberately; 2. (hypnosis) to give one's self direction or positive thought, verbally or silently, after the SELF-HYP-NOSIS induction. [**cf.** SUGGESTION, HYPNOTHER-APY, INNER-DIALOGUE, AFFIRMATIONS]

SELF-TALK—see INNER-DIALOGUE.

551

SELF-TRANSFORMATION—(Hinduism, Egypt, Celtic) to change the vibrational frequency of one's body and become an animal, bird, or fish for a given time, perform a function in this new shape, and then transfer back to the human self. **Syn.** SHAPE-CHANGING. [**cf.** VIBRATIONAL FREQUENCIES, DIMENSION-SHIFTING and SHAPE-CHANGING Appendix 2]

SELFLESS UNIVERSAL LOVE—pertains to a high STATE OF CONSCIOUSNESS that is held in CONSCIOUS AWARENESS by masters who enter this earth plane; to feel at one with all humanity; to be attuned to the universe and its purpose, regardless of the opinions of the beings on earth and in spite of the hardships of earth. [**cf.** BUDDHIC PLANE, MASTERS]

SEMATOLOGY—to receive information from the ETHERIC WORLD INTELLIGENCES in a SEANCE room by the manner of the movements of the material object being used; intelligences expressing feelings in a sort of pantomime show, e.g., a gently floating handkerchief means agreement; loud, fast knocks on the wall mean anger. **Syn.** LANGUAGE OF SIGNS. [**cf.** PERCUSSION, LEVITATION, MEDIUM, DARKROOM SESSIONS]

SEMI-STAGE OF HYPNOSIS—see MEDIUM STATE OF HYPNOSIS.

SEMIHOMO PLANT—(Rome) see MANDRAKE.

SEMILIMBO—(Native American, Navaho) a level in the ETHERIC WORLD where the deceased go for rehabilitation and suggestions before they start their normal etheric world existence. [**cf.** ASTRAL PLANE, DEATH ANGEL, INITIATORY DEATH-RITE, FREEING THE SOUL]

SEMIMATERIAL—a fluidic, vaporous substance containing ETHER, SUPERETHER, subatomic and atomic properties; vibrates a little faster than physical matter and invisibly interpenetrates the physical body; (Allan Kardec) "an invisible substance having some properties of matter composing the PERISPRIT." [**cf.** ASTRAL MATTER]

SEMIMECHANICAL WRITING MEDIUM—one who allows an ETHERIC WORLD INTELLIGENCE to intervene and move his or her hand involuntarily and who has instantaneous consciousness of the words or phrases as he or she writes; (do not confuse with AUTOMATISM in which one performs in TRANCE and does not know what one is writing while writing). [**cf.** AUTOMATIC WRITING, ETHERIC SCRIPT, INSPIRATIONAL WRITING]

SEMINAR—a meeting of a group of students who are interested in further research or study of advanced material in the particular subject being offered. [**cf.** WORKSHOP, CEREMONY]

SEMIPHYSICAL BODY—see AURA.

SEMITRANCE—a neutral, dreamy, relaxed STATE OF CONSCIOUSNESS acquired by the SYNCHRONIZATION of the MEDIUM and the ETHERIC WORLD INTELLIGENCE for certain types of PHYSICAL PSYCHISM: medium preplans for this level of consciousness by preparing his or her body and mind, the area used, and mentally notifying the intelligence of his or her expectations; used in AUTOMATIC WRITING, INSPIRATIONAL SPEAKING, and PERCUSSION; recognized by certain characteristics: 1. alert enough to answer questions but does not know who asked them; 2. a feeling of being aware as to what is transpiring but unable to recall it later; 3. able to stand or sit; 4. hearing is acute; 5. speaking voice not always clear and loud. [**cf.** TABLE-TIPPING, KNOCKS]

SEMITRANSPARENT—a characteristic of an astral object or APPARITION which shows enough density to recognize its form, yet it appears hazy enough to see through; to see both the inside and outside of an object or person at the same time, as in ASTRAL VISION. [**cf.** X-RAY CLAIRVOYANCE, GHOST, FULL-BLOWN SOLUTION]

SENOI DREAM THERAPY—(Malaya) each morning household members gather to discuss their DREAMS of the previous night; the older members help to interpret the DREAMSTUFF and then bring suggestions as to what the household member must do to rectify any situation that is negative; this reconciles one's anxieties, resentments, fears, and jealousies immediately, preventing them from accumulating in the mind and body which could result in ill health, behavioral problems, or negative events at a future time. [**cf.** CONFRONT AND CONQUER, EXPOSURE DREAM, HIGH DREAM]

SENSATION—1. a memory of mental feeling which has happened many times before, that triggers mind activity and sends it throughout the body instantaneously; 2. the faculty of perception of outer stimuli; 3. (esoteric) (Seth) "a method by which consciousness knows itself." [**cf.** FEELINGS, DÉJÀ VU, NEGATIVE THOUGHT]

SENSATION CONSCIOUSNESS—(future science) (botane) an innate ability of the PLANT KINDGOM to perceive feelings from the emotions, morals, intent, and health of humans, animals, and other plants; these vibrations reach the plant's AURA and affect its growth, color, and length of life. [cf. BOTANE, ANPSI, MINSPI, MANDRAKE, VEGETATION MEMORY]

SENSATIONAL HYPNOSIS—see STAGE HYPNOSIS.

SENSE WITHDRAWAL—to turn off the physical SENSES so they no longer react to outer stimuli; this permits the body to rest and repair itself, and allows the individual to feel his or her ONENESS with TOTALITY; accomplished by a deep HYPNOTHERAPY session or by undivided attention on a small point, consistently for a length of time, during MEDITATION. [cf. BEATING DOWN THOUGHT, MANTRA]

SENSE-IMAGERY—(dreams) a PSYCHIC EXPERIENCE DURING SLEEP processed in clear, vivid, detailed picture language, using one or more of the five SENSES; e.g., to see an APPARITION full-blown, hold its hand, and feel the touch of a real hand; to perceive the smell of real flowers. [cf. SLEEP EXPERIENCES, DISCARNATE ENTITY SLEEP EXPERIENCE]

SENSES—(esoteric) any of the faculties, such as sight, hearing, smell, taste, or touch, designed to co-create objects, situations, relationships, families, jobs, nature, and a place to inhabit; this co-creation to be used as a school for learning special lessons that are unable to be learned in any other way; as opposed to the theory that the SENSES are to give an awareness of the world already created; (Seth) "function of the senses is to create a world, not to permit awareness." [cf. NEW-AGE PSYCHOLOGY]

SENSING—to distinguish between perceiving PSYCHIC INFORMATION through the five PSYCHIC SENSES and perceiving mundane information through the physical five senses; both require awareness of outer stimuli; this is accomplished through knowledge of psychism, practice of psychism, and checking the information received after a passage of time. [cf. GUT-FEELING, NON-THOUGHT, CLAIRSENTIENCE]

SENSITIVE—see PSYCHIC.

SENSITIVE ELECTROMETER—see KIRLIAN PHOTOGRAPHY.

SENSITIVE MEDIUM—1. (Allan Kardec) person who possesses a high degree of MEDIANIMIC faculties and who is able to project this animalized fluid out from his or her body to be used for PHYSICAL PSYCHISM when working with the ETHERIC WORLD INTELLIGENCES. Sim. INDIAN PRIEST, MAGI, MYSTIC. 2. one who is extremely susceptible to the presence of the etheric world intelligences and their impressions of guidance and psychic knowledge. Sim. CLAIRSENTIENT, LISTENING-MAN.

SENSITIVITY CONTROL—(biofeedback training) a dial found on many biofeedback instruments that modulates a higher accuracy adjustment of the subject; an auxiliary range designed for vernier power. [cf. SCALE OF BRAIN RHYTHM, GSR, EEG]

SENSITIVITY CYCLE—(biorhythm) a rhythmic pattern within the physical mechanism of the body which repeats itself every twenty-eight days and affects one's attitudes, emotions, sensibility, and creativity. Syn. EMOTIONAL CYCLE. [cf. CYCLES, BIORHYTHM CHART, CRITICAL DAYS, BIORHYTHM CURVES]

SENSITIVITY TRANSFER—(hypnosis) the ability of the skin of a hypnotized person to be sensitive to activity that is being carried on a short distance from the subject; in experiments it was found the hypnotized subject would have similar reactions to the one involved in the activity nearby; e.g., cutting hair off someone else and putting it in water makes the subject feel as if hair is being pulled out of him; making believe one is pin-pricking the subject's arm and although the pain is actually a few inches from the subject, he feels pricks at the corresponding places on his arm. Syn. EXTERIORIZATION OF SENSITIVITY. [cf. HYPNOTIC PHENOMENA, HYPNOTIC TOUCH, HYPNOTIZABLITY]

SENSOR—1. (biofeedback training) a tiny piece of metal on the end of a wire that is placed on the skin of the subject being HOOKED-UP to a BIOFEEDBACK INSTRUMENT; the other end of the wire plugs into the instrument; this metal sends and/or receives electrical current through the subject's body; can be attached to the fingers, toes, or over a muscle, depending upon the type of instrument. Sim. ELECTRODE. [cf. GSR, METABOLIC MONITOR, ELECTRODE RETENTION BAND, GAIN SETTING] 2. (pyramidology) a pendant that magnifies pyramid power invented by G. Patrick Flanagan to be worn around the neck; a flat design which features concentric waves of diamonds in multiple sizes;

each diamond resonates in a different frequency to an incoming electromagnetic signal; gives the wearer the same effect as sitting under a pyramid with a four-foot base. [cf. PYRAMID ENERGY]

SENSORIMOTOR LEAKAGE—(psi tasks) the feelings of others that unintentionally influence the experimenter in his or her target response. [cf. BLIND MENTAL PSYCHISM, SHEEP AND GOATS EFFECT]

SENSORY—see PSYCHIC.

SENSORY DEPRIVATION—to reduce the input from one's SENSES to nearly zero for therapeutic purposes; accomplished by isolating the subject in a room without sound, people, or light, and without anything to do but think; results in a state of mental confusion and progresses into a state of seeing psychic visions; this releases any trapped emotion that has caused blocks in the body; emotion surfaces as a VISION revealing the cause of the block. (Inconcl.) [cf. PRIMAL SCREAM, ISOLATION TANK, BLOCKS]

SENSORY HUNGER—the desire of the body organism to stay within its 24-hour circadian cycle with regard to hunger for food; a time change in one's life due to traveling through a time zone, or due to working the night shift could cause the taste buds to crave breakfast food at evening meal time. [cf. JET-LAG, REVERSAL SLEEP, CIRCADIAN RHYTHM]

SENSORY ISOLATION—see SENSORY DEPRIVATION.

SENSUOUS ELEMENT—to communicate to others the same sensation of touch that one is feeling as one handles an article. Sim. PSYCHOMETRIC TELEPATHY. [cf. COLOR TELEPATHY, FEEL-AND-SEE-COMBINATION]

SENTIENT EXISTENCE—the body of physical matter experiencing and perceiving with the physical five SENSES which is influencing the six invisible bodies, unknowingly, to the individual.

SEPARATE CONSCIOUSNESS—theory: each ATOM (or smaller particle) knows it function as an individual atom, and when colonized as a CELL, works as a cell member but never loses its individual functional consciousness; this keeps going ad infinitum to compose elements, compounds, and matter. Syn. LAW OF FUNCTION Appendix 7. [cf. HOLOGRAM BRAIN THEORY,

PRIMAL PERCEPTION]

SEPARATE REALITIES—psychic visions and/or hallucinations as perceived from an ALTERED STATE OF CONSCIOUSNESS which is brought about from the use of PSYCHOTROPIC PLANTS; while one is in the altered state of consciousness, one feels that the experience is an actuality and quite real. [cf. ARTIFICIAL PARADISE, HALLUCINATION]

SEPHIROTH—(Kabbalah) the ten holy emanations of the DEITY that made CREATION possible; symbolized on the TREE OF LIFE by circles made into a special pattern; personified as ARCHANGELS. [cf. LAW OF SYMBOLISM Appendix 7]

SEQUE PHENOMENON—psychic events happening in an uninterrupted flow. [cf. FREE-FLOWING, PSYCHIC DOORS, INNER-AWARENESS]

SER'ERA—(Ethiopia) a NATURE SPIRIT willing to help around a home; one to a household.

SERAPHIM—the highest order of angels in the ETHERIC WORLD felt to be in charge of the divine plan; soul-minds who have purified themselves from all imperfection; (Hebrew) celestial angels depicted with six wings, a human face, hands, feet, and voice; plural; singular is seraph. [cf. MASTERS, SECRET CHIEFS, GREAT WHITE BROTHERHOOD, LUMINOUS SPIRITS, HOLY SPIRIT]

SERENITY—an unruffled state of mind found when one learns how to FLOW; to be versatile and to find good where one did not expect it; (Heidi Jones) "You can't find your true heaven until you have lived your own hell."

SERGEYEV DETECTORS—(Russian secret research) an instrument used to measure the auric fields around humans and objects. [cf. HIGH-VOLTAGE PHOTOGRAPHY, AURIC RETREAT, BIO-ELECTROMAGNETIC INTERACTIONS]

SERIAL TIME—(dreams) multidimensional time indicated by images from yesterday, today, and even tomorrow, flowing at the same frequency during sleep. (Inconcl.) [cf. HYPNAGOGIC, SEA-OF-FACES]

SERIOUS MEDIUM—one who brings very knowledgeable and purposeful PSYCHIC INFORMATION from the ETHERIC WORLD because of righteous intent in his or her work and the respect given to his or her guide. Syn. WELL-GROUNDED MEDIUM. [cf. LAW OF LIKE ATTRACTS LIKE Appendix 7]

SEROTONIN—a hormone secreted from the PI-

NEAL GLAND believed to affect the CONSCIOUS-NESS mechanism. (Inconcl.) [**cf.** CONSCIOUSNESS]

SERPENT—(ancient) 1. used as a symbol of wisdom, "for is not wisdom fearful?"; 2. in the symbol, if the head of the serpent is up, ready to strike, it denotes EVIL, but if the head is down, it denotes protection. [**cf.** SYMBOLS, SERPENT POWER]

SERPENT FIRE—see SERPENT POWER.

SERPENT POWER—(esoteric) 1. a collective word pertaining to the whole function of the KUNDALINI; 2. a barely visible, intelligent, gaseous fluid lying dormant at the base of the spine when mankind makes his or her first few incarnations in the earth plane; it travels up the tiny hollow in the center of the spinal column as one progresses in his or her evolutionary cycle; this serpent energy meets the SILVER CORD at the top of the head after many incarnations; current science says this substance is a high-grade form of bioplasm, concentrated PRANA, or living ELECTRICITY; (Sigmund Freud) the LIBIDO. **Syn.** SERPENT FIRE, SERPENTS OF WISDOM, COILED SERPENT, COSMIC FIRE, SUSHUMNA. [**cf.** CHAKRAS, KANDA, ANANDA]

SERVE—the giving of psychic information to an individual in a public gathering by a psychic. Usage: "He will *serve* you tonight"; "Have you been *served* yet?" [**cf.** STANDING READER, FROM THE WORLD OF SPIRIT]

SESHA—(Hinduism) a NATURE SPIRIT in the form of a giant cosmic serpent, believed to support the world; opposite of EVIL.

SESSHIN—(Zen) in meditation, long periods of sitting still and watching. **Sim.** COLLECTING THE MIND. [**cf.** OUT-BREATH, KEISAKU, ZAZEN]

SESSION—1. (psi tasks) one complete experiment; 2. one in a series of weekly meetings of SITTING for development in a darkroom with a MEDIUM and other SITTERS. [**cf.** DEVELOPMENT CIRCLE, BLACKED-OUT]

SET—(psi tasks) a scoring unit for a consecutive group of trials, usually for the same target. [**cf.** CALL, CHANCE EXPECTATION, COVARIANCE EFFECT]

SET HIS SEAL—(Old Testament) refers to the information found on the palm of the hand; each person's history (past and future) is written on the lines of the hand and is unique to each person, i.e.,

God set his seal on men. [**cf.** LAW OF SIGNATURES Appendix 7]

SET UP DREAMING—(Native American, Yaqui Indian) (Carlos Castaneda) to have concise and pragmatic control over the general situation of a dream, comparable to the control one has when climbing up a hill. [**cf.** CONFRONT AND CONQUER, LUCID DREAMING]

SETH—a very highly evolved ETHERIC WORLD INTELLIGENCE who spoke through Jane Roberts, bringing her new scientific knowledge about the reality of man and the universe (emphasizing the MULTIDIMENSIONAL world); (Seth) "an energy personality essence no longer focused in physical reality." [**cf.** VOICE TRANCE]

SETH TWO—an exalted SOUL-MIND who is now a small mass of highly concentrated intelligent energy who worked through Jane Roberts' physical body; a seed existing in endless realities, reaching out to help earthlings with deep scientific knowledge, for those who want to learn. [**cf.** SETH, TRANCE VOICES]

SETTING THE MOOD—(psi tasks) theory: acknowledgment that enthusiasm and belief by all people involved in the experiment is necessary for "hitting the TARGET." [**cf.** MEDITATION, MEAN VARIANCE, SHEEP AND GOATS EFFECT]

SEVEN—1. (esoteric) emblematic of "completion," e.g., seven notes in the musical scale, seven bodies of man, seven colors in the spectrum, seven chakras, seven etheric world places, seven days of the week, etc.; 2. (ancient occult) the only number of ETERNITY and continuing in itself as long as the number representing eternity lasts; 3. (numerology life cycle) symbolic of pursuit, marked individuality, and philosophical thought; planetary link is Uranus. [**cf.** NUMBER POWER]

SEVEN JEWELS OF YOGA—see SEVEN MAJOR RAYS.

SEVEN MAJOR RAYS—(esoteric) colored wavelengths emanating from the GREAT WHITE LIGHT; visible to mankind in the form of a rainbow; interrelates with the seven planes in the etheric world and with the seven centers in human beings; manifestation of the seven great cosmic periods. [**cf.** COLOR, MAGNETIC RADIATION, PURE LOVE, WHITE LIGHT]

SEVEN PLANETARY CHAIN LOGOI—(Theosophy)

555

the projection of CONSCIOUSNESS of seven mighty intelligences acting as channels of TOTALITY; Totality's life forces representing the coming of evolutionary activities which flow into the world through exalted agents. **Syn.** SEVEN SEPHIROTH, SEVEN PRAJAPATIS, SEVEN MYSTERY GODS. [**cf.** COSMIC WHEEL, BIBLICAL NUMEROLOGY]

SEVEN PRINCIPLES OF MAN—(esoteric) refers to the invisible levels of awareness encompassing and interpenetrating the human SOUL-MIND; serve as ENERGY FIELDS of reality in steps of a learning process in the evolutionary path upward; man is aware of only one reality at a time; each principle or energy field will be shed when that step is accomplished; see BODIES OF MAN. [**cf.** BODIES AND PLANES Appendix 5]

SEVEN SACRED PLANETS—(ancient esoteric) the first seven planets in the earth's SOLAR SYSTEM; considered sacred because they serve the same function to earth's solar system as the chakras serve to the physical body. [**cf.** CHAKRAS, SEVEN, LAW OF REPETITION Appendix 7]

SEVEN SEALS OF SILENCE—to hold back knowledge of the "Mysteries of Wisdom" from those who are not at a level of awareness to understand it; these persons tend to use it in inferior ways which causes damage or causes wasted energies.

SEVEN SPIRITS BEFORE THE THRONE OF GOD—(Bible, Revelation) see SEVEN PLANETARY CHAIN LOGOI.

SEVEN SPIRITS OF GOD—(Bible) seven devas in the etheric world in charge of the SEVEN MAJOR RAYS. **Syn.** LORDS OF LIGHT. [**cf.** ANGEL HIERARCHY, DEVA]

SEVEN STARS AND SEVEN CHURCHES—see CHAKRA.

SEVEN-KNOTTED WAND—(esoteric) symbol used to represent the spinal column and the seven chakras. [**cf.** LAW OF SYMBOLISM Appendix 7, LADDER, CADUCEUS WINDING, CHAKRA]

SEVEN-SIDED VAULT—the tomb of Christian Rosenkreuz, designed by him, and in which his body was found, many years after his death, in a perfectly preserved state; each side of the tomb was the same size, and was lit by sunlight but contained no windows; in the center was a circular altar; concealed in each wall was a chest containing various objects that pertain to PSYCHISM and ALCHEMY, e.g.,

copies of the Rosicrucian Order's books, mirrors, burning lamps, and a statue of Christ; next to the immutable body was an inscription, "I will reappear 120 years later," written by Rosenkreuz himself. [**cf.** AMORC, IMMUTABILITY]

SEVEN-YEAR CYCLE—(cycles) theory: every seven years, a human being goes through a definite set of changes in his or her lifestyle, thinking, and his or her physical and intellectual growth patterns, which is due to the earth's rotation. [**cf.** CYCLES, BRAINWAVE PATTERNS]

SEVENTH HEAVEN—see SEVENTH PLANE.

SEVENTH PLANE—a level of consciousness of the highest conceivable spiritual attainment that each SOUL-MIND will eventually be a part of; indescribable in language and beyond human comprehension; unknown PERFECTNESS; happiness beyond one's strongest imagination, which is recognizable, understandable, and appreciated because one has experienced all the opposite of this happiness; controversial concepts regarding the time when the soul-mind slips into this CONSCIOUSNESS: 1. one keeps his or her individuality; 2. one loses his or her individuality into the TOTAL CONSCIOUSNESS; TOTALITY in its entirety; GOD consciousness. **Syn.** CLEAR LIGHT, NIRVANA, SATORI, PURE CONSCIOUSNESS, BLISS. [**cf.** MONAD, LAW OF SOUL-MIND GROWTH and LAW OF MICRO/MACROCOSM Appendix 7]

SEVENTH SENSE—to perceive PSYCHIC INFORMATION through the SUPERCONSCIOUS MIND instead of the SUBCONSCIOUS MIND; comes from the SEVENTH PLANE directly to the CONSCIOUS MIND; pure knowledge or unknown information that is not subjected to the subconscious mind's concepts or karmic memories, because it by-passes the subconscious mind. **Syn.** INSPIRATIONAL THOUGHT. [**cf.** CLAIRSENTIENCE]

SEX TRANSMUTATION—(Yoga) a process of sexual relations in which the semen is held still and the sex energy is sent up the KUNDALINI to the CROWN CHAKRA by mind power and/or special breathing techniques. **Syn.** SEXUAL MAGIC, MAITHUNA. (Inconcl.) [**cf.** BODY CONTROL Appendix 2]

SEXUAL MAGIC—(Taoism) see SEX TRANSMUTATION.

SEXUAL MYSTICISM—principle: male and female

energies are necessary to all existence; when these two are combined in balance, they are capable of activating the cosmic forces; mankind is the chief representative of this POLARITY energy. [cf. YANG AND YIN]

SHADE—1. a discarnate entity appearing flimsy, transparent, and shadowy; perceived clairvoyantly in the daytime or during sleep. **Syn.** GHOST, APPARITION. 2. (Charles W. Leadbeater) an astral corpse in the astral cemetery left to disintegrate after the SOUL-MIND has withdrawn all the lower plane desires and knowledge; (do not confuse with ASTRAL SHELL which is not devoid of lower plane desires and knowledge); 3. see ASTRAL BODY. [cf. DISCARNATE ENTITY, EARTHBOUND ENTITY]

SHADOW—1. (Dion Fortune) various kinds of formations which appear to the CLAIRVOYANT as a dark shadow in the scene; brings a degree of fear when seen; appears in dreams and psychic visions; theories: one's karmic debts that are for this INCARNATION only; the inner meaning of Self; represents the subconscious material of the present incarnation. **Syn.** SHADOW-SOUL. 2. faint copy of a DISCARNATE ENTITY perceived clairvoyantly as a transparent outline of a person. **Syn.** APPARITION, SHADE, ASTRAL SHELL, GHOST. 3. (Carl Jung) the human EGO, the imp or dark side of a person (opposite of the saint image) bringing a balance into a psychic wholeness; appears as a compensatory figure in dreams. **Syn.** TRICKSTER-TRANS-FORMER. 4. (mystic schools) the human PHYSICAL BODY; the ASTRAL BODY is the real body and the physical body is the shadow of it. [cf. ASTRAL PLANE, ILLUSIONARY BODY]

SHADOW-WATCHERS—refers to Plato's theory: "as its shadow is to a solid object, so is the object itself to its archetypal idea." [cf. MENTAL PLANE, THOUGHT-FORMS, ARCHETYPES]

SHADOWY ARC—(Theosophy) theory: every celestial body, including earth, is a member of a chain of globes surging upward in life waves toward perfectness. **Syn.** ASCENDING ARC, DESCENDING ARC, LUMINOUS ARC. [cf. CYCLES, LUNAR MONADS, UNIVERSAL LIFE CYCLE]

SHAKEY—(future science) name of the robot living in the rooms and corridors of the Stanford Research Institute in California; a complex electronic artifact with motor-driven wheels, touch-sensitive feelers, an optical range-finder and a TV camera for eyes; the brain is a large digital computer which communicates with Shakey's smaller on-board computer via radio-telemetry; it can perceive and manipulate objects in its environment. [cf. SOULLESS]

SHAKTI—1. (Hinduism, Tantric) one of the gods of the VEDAS, representing the divine creative power, time, and death; the female counterpart of the All-Good Mother, believed to be inherent in all things and necessary to all existence; sends forth radiant energy capable of activating matter in its primordial essence; negative in POLARITY; usually symbolized by a dancing white- or silver-colored man with many arms; 2. (Tibet) the female counterpart of the Divine Father-Mother God, and the female counterpart of anything. **Syn.** LORD OF DANCE, SHIVA, PARVATI, UMA. [cf. POLARITY, YIN, LINGAM]

SHAMAN—(Sanskrit "ascetic," one who is dedicated), an individual capable of many PSYCHIC and MEDIUMSHIP skills; skills are either a natural-born characteristic or can be earned through many difficult initiations; 1. (Native American, Navaho) serves the tribe as the HAND-TREMBLER, PRACTITIONER, HERBALIST, SINGER, and diagnostician for sickness; 2. (Native American, Algonquin) serves as the MEDICINE MAN and the psychic; 3. (Siberia) serves as the holy man; 4. (Orient) serves as the holy man, administering priestly rites; he is a teacher and psychic; 5. (Native American) serves mainly as the psychic, but can act as the medicine man, psychiatrist, Singer, etc., depending upon the culture and size of the tribe. **Syn.** MEDIUM, SPIRIT COUNSELOR, SIBYL, MAGICIAN, VILLAGE WISE-WOMAN. [cf. SHAMANISM]

SHAMANISM—(Native American, Siberia, Ural-Altaic, Central Asia, Orient) a very highly respected profession wherein one serves his tribe with his psychic skills and HEALING abilities which is intermingled with influential guidance, protection, and advanced knowledge from the ETHERIC WORLD INTELLIGENCES; belief is in one God and healing through natural means; shamanism is learned from a past INCARNATION or from torturous initiations and years of study. Feats of shamanism: to give psychiatric counsel; prepare Sings; interpret DREAMS and visions; preside over birth, death, and marriage rites; speak in TRANCE; take astral projections to the DENSITY to help inferior soul-minds; escort soul-minds in the DEATH PROCESS to

557

higher realms; perceive clairvoyantly-at-a-distance; control body temperature; control fire; control food intake; change into an animal and back again; foretell the future; psychically kill animals from a distance for food; control forces of nature (bring rain); become invisible; become a spirit while in the physical body; heal the sick with herbs; and substitute for the priest. [**cf.** MEDIUMSHIP, SPIRIT COUNSELOR, LAM, MAGICIAN]

SHAMANSHIP—see SHAMANISM.

SHAMANSHIP HEALING—see MEDIUMSHIP HEALING.

SHAMANSHIP INSTRUCTIONS—take many years of study to learn: 1. techniques of PSYCHISM, MEDIUMSHIP, and HEALING; 2. functions of the ETHERIC WORLD and its inhabitants; 3. mythology, genealogy, and the secret language of the clan; 4. emotional pain, suffering, and purpose of life by going through traumatic initiations. [**cf.** INITIATORY SICKNESS, RESURRECTION, SPONTANEOUS VOCATION, HEREDITY TRANSMISSION, QUEST]

SHAMBALLAH—(Buddhism) 1. believed to be the capital of the SUBTERRANEAN WORLD where the Supreme Ruler of this Empire dwells; gives orders to Tibet and Brazil for his rule of the world. (Inconcl.) 2. (legend) an underground camp in the Himalayas which has a force that can control humanity. [**cf.** SUBTERRANEAN WORLD, AGHARTA]

SHAMEER—(esoteric) a diamond that is said to be pulled from the beak of a rooster used by Moses to cut precious stones and by KING SOLOMON to open the gates of wisdom. [**cf.** ROCK ELECTRICITY, LEVITATION GEMS, MINPSI]

SHAPE-CHANGING—1. (seance) to psychically alter one's body in size with the help of the ETHERIC WORLD INTELLIGENCES; accomplished in a SEMITRANCE or DEEP TRANCE state; body can shrink, elongate, and lengthen one appendage, for a short time; 2. to psychically change into a different living organism or an inert object, perform an act, and change back again; 3. to multiply oneself in number; for many types see DIMENSION-SHIFTING and SHAPE-CHANGING Appendix 2]

SHAPE-SHIFTING—1. (Tibet, Celtic) to psychically transform one's self into an animal, bird, fish, or an inanimate object for a temporary period and be able to perform a task as that animal or object; PSYCHIC lives in the reality of the animal during

that time; performed by devas, NATURE SPIRITS, black magicians, white magicians, and ordinary people; theories: 1. psychic projects mind energy to the mental plane in the etheric world where patterns are formed and changes the pattern by intense thoughts so the earth body will change; 2. to move into an animal's body and use the animal's eyes and ears as if they are one's own, as in possession, utilizing the law of identity. **Syn.** METAMORPHOSIS. [**cf.** MENTAL PLANE, WEREWOLF, WEREBEARS, ALCHEMY, POSSESSION, DIMENSION-SHIFTING]

SHAPED POWER—coined in Czechoslovakia (future science); condensed energy that comes from within the boundaries of specific forms and positions of matter; energy is magnified due to the special form of the container or arrangement of the objects. (Inconcl.) **Syn.** PSYCHOTRON ENERGY. [**cf.** PSYCHIC DEVELOPMENT CIRCLES, LIFE FORCE SYMBOL, MAGIC SYMBOLS, FORMS-WITH-POWER]

SHAPES—(esoteric) theory: the external surface, design, and form of any natural entity, unit, or system; all formations are result of the sound they vibrate; this sound can be audible, clairaudible, or inaudible to the physical ear; the sound of each unit forms its own principles, individuality, and radiates out into various shapes for mankind to use. (Inconcl.) [**cf.** FORMS-WITH-POWER, MUSIC OF THE SPHERES]

SHARED DREAMS—1. identical DREAMSTUFF dreamt by two people the same night; happens mostly between spouses and in mother-daughter relationships; 2. visions of one another seen by two people dreaming at the same time. [**cf.** VISITATION DREAM, PREMONITORY DREAM, VERIDICAL DREAM]

SHC—abbr. for SPONTANEOUS HUMAN COMBUSTION; see same.

SHE-WOLF—a female who takes the form of a wolf in order to help children in distress; PSYCHIC transforms herself into a vibrational frequency for a passage of time long enough to travel the streets and assist children and parents that are in psychological need; known as the friendly wolf; town anticipates her visits; psychic keeps her ability a secret. [**cf.** DIMENSION-SHIFTING and SHAPE-CHANGING Appendix 2]

SHEATH—a collective word used to designate an APPARITION that has been seen in the ETHERIC

WORLD, but one is not sure who it is; could be an ASTRAL BODY, GHOST, MENTAL BODY, discarnate person, earthbound entity, etc. **Syn.** PERISPRIT, SPIRIT, ENVELOPE. [**cf.** SHADE, MENTAL PLANE, RUPA-LOKAS]

SHEE—(Ireland) a NATURE SPIRIT in charge of love, beauty, and luxury; has contempt for thrift and economy; see FAIRIES.

SHEEP AND GOATS EFFECT—(psi tasks) (early concept discovered at Rhine laboratory) those who believe in ESP were able to display their psychic ability and were named the *sheep;* the nonbelievers could not display much psychic ability and were named the *goats.* [**cf.** MISPLACED EFFICIENCY, PSI EXPERIMENTER EFFECT]

SHEEP BONES—(Germany, England) used frequently as a tool to PROPHESY; regarded as oracular significance in the Virgil book of psychism; divination from black sheep's bones, especially the shoulder blades, gives insight into the future of the country or immediate area. [**cf.** CASTING OF LOTS, SORTES SANCTORUM, SYNCHRONICITY, VIRGILIAN SORTES]

SHELLS—(esoteric) 1. have the properties that ward off negative vibrations; spread abundantly around an area for their protective properties; 2. large open shells absorb erroneous noises in an area and help to deaden background sound; 3. (Christian) an empty shell found by the grave foretells that the SOUL-MIND has left the discarded body. [**cf.** ANPSI, BOTANE, PRIMARY PSI PERCEPTION]

SHELLYCOAT—(Scotland) a NATURE SPIRIT living in water; see NYMPH.

SHEM—(Prague, Czechoslovakia) the letters spelling this name were impressed into a statue of a man; the power of these letters gave the statue a semblance of real life so it could perform menial tasks for its master (Shem is recognized as a god); (do not confuse with a TULPA). [**cf.** WORDS-WITH-POWER, FORMS-WITH-POWER]

SHEOL—(Old Testament) a level of CONSCIOUSNESS in the DENSITY of the ETHERIC WORLD inhabited by deceased earthlings whose earth lives were considered to be of low caliber; place of stagnation, darkness, crime, and other negation. **Sim.** HELL, HADES. [**cf.** EARTHBOUND ENTITIES, LAND OF THE SHADOWS]

SHEWSTONE—(esoteric) a mineral in the shape of a small crystal globe which transmits influential vibrations from the moon; used in healing, summoning one's guides, and for SCRYING. **Syn.** ROCK CRYSTAL. [**cf.** CATOPTROMANCY, MINPSI]

SHIATSU—(Japanese *shi*, "finger"; *atsu*, "pressure") a finger-pressure therapy; an oriental healing art in which the fingers are pressed on particular receptor points of the body which run along the MERIDIAN LINES; eases aches, pains, tension, fatigue, and symptoms of disease. **Sim.** ACUPRESSURE. [**cf.** ACUPUNCTURE, POINTS]

SHIELD—(dowsing) a wall made of a combination of wire mesh and rings of copper wire used to protect persons who have symptoms of disease from the earth's underground RADIATION. (Inconcl.) [**cf.** RADIESTHESIA, DOWSING]

SHIELDING—to form a protective electric ENERGY FIELD around one's body and life activity to keep out harmful mental and physical radiations; accomplished by verbally or silently saying affirmations, prayers, or uplifting, high, qualitative words; this goes into the electrical energy emanating from the brain and hovers around the body and head, because it is without direction and purpose; this electrical energy works under the LAW OF LIKE ATTRACTS LIKE, making it capable of blocking out harmful thoughts from another earthling, earthbound entity from the etheric world, and physical activity, e.g., to prevent a car accident or to prevent being cheated in a real estate deal; the more consistent the positive thoughts, the more efficiently the day will move along; e.g., (Paul, Bible) "put on the whole armor of God." [**cf.** THOUGHTS, LAW OF LIKE ATTRACTS LIKE Appendix 7, CLOAK OF INSULATION, ELEMENTAL, SEALING OF THE AURA]

SHIKHA—(Hinduism) an adornment of the Supreme Lord, worn in the center of the head over the CROWN CHAKRA; made from a crest-lock, tuft, or comb; symbolizes appreciation for the divine state a human being can achieve. [**cf.** RITUAL MAGIC, CHAKRA]

SHIN THEORY—(Hebrew) all intelligence is composed within each person's UNCONSCIOUSNESS: this unfolds for him or her to use as each evolves. **Syn.** MONADOLOGY, MICROCOSM/MACROCOSM, [**cf.** WORLD SOUL, COLLECTIVE UNCONSCIOUS]

SHINING BODY—see ETHERIC DOUBLE and AURA.

SHINING ONE—1. (capitalized) (Hinduism) the

559

total of ALL-THERE-IS; see TOTALITY. [**cf.** LAW OF MICRO/MACROCOSM Appendix 7]. **2.** (uncapitalized) (Aryan, B.C.) the intelligence (gods) in the ETHERIC WORLD who bring PSYCHIC INFORMATION and guidance to the earthlings. **Syn.** DEVAS, SKY PEOPLE, MASTERS. [**cf.** SPIRIT COMMUNICATION, MEDIUMSHIP]

SHINING-ILLUSORY BODY—(Tibet) see ASTRAL BODY.

SHIP'S NAME—theory: the name chosen for a boat will influence the destiny of that boat because of the vibrational frequency and number power of the name. [**cf.** WORDS-WITH-POWER, LAW OF NAMES Appendix 7, NUMEROLOGY]

SHIP-BURIAL—(ancient belief) the SOUL-MIND of a deceased person is carried off in a boat to reach the ETHERIC WORLD. [**cf.** RELIGIOUS KING OF THE DEAD, LADY OF DARKNESS, RECORDING ANGEL]

SHIPS-FROM-OTHER-PLANETS—(collective word) anything seen in the sky that appears to be a foreign vehicle and capable of traveling great distances; many persons *assume* that all foreign aircraft come from other planets. (Inconcl.) **Syn.** CONSTRUCTS. [**cf.** UFOLOGY, SAUCER-FLAP, SKY CRAFT, ETHER-SHIP BEING]

SHISHYA—(Hinduism) pupil of a GURU. **Syn.** CHELA, DISCIPLE. [**cf.** MASTER, PATH]

SHIVA—(Hinduism, "propitious") one of the gods of the VEDAS; the male deity; represents: **1.** divine creative power; time and death; positive POLARITY which is inherent in all things, necessary to all existence; energy capable of activating matter in its primordial essence; **2.** sometimes a slayer of demons; **3.** Lord of the Dance: dances the dance of CREATION; is depicted with four arms, stepping on a baby and with an aureola of fire around him, emanating from a LOTUS pedestal; represents the rhythm of the universe. **Syn.** LORD OF THE DANCE, DURGA, SAKTI, SHAKTI, UMA, PARVATI. [**cf.** POLARITY Appendix 2]

SHIVA AND SHAKTI—(Hinduism, Tantrism, Yoga) see VITAL LIFE FORCE and POLARITY.

SHOCK-IN-RETURN—to send negative VIBRATIONS that are not of one's own volition back to the originator, which results in a startling sensation to the originator; feelings of illness, pain, negative thoughts, or a PSYCHIC ATTACK can be transferred from one to another; one individual does not have

to be a SCAPEGOAT for another's KARMA, whether it is sent deliberately or unknowingly, one does not have to be a TARGET for jealousy or anger; to think silently to one's self, "go back to where you came from," immediately detaches these unwanted vibrations from the receiver and they hit the sender with force. [**cf.** CLOAK OF INSULATION]

SHOOT—(astral projection) term explains the expedient return of the ASTRAL BODY to the PHYSICAL BODY in cases of emergency. [**cf.** REPERCUSSION, ASTRAL PROJECTIONIST]

SHOOTING CHART—(Native American, Navaho) a special sound and rhythm that "shoots up" and will conjure up ETHERIC WORLD INTELLIGENCES for PSYCHIC INFORMATION. [**cf.** SOUNDS-WITH-POWER, CHANTING, GROUP SOUND, CONJURE UP]

SHRADDHA CEREMONY—(Hinduism) a three-day religious RITUAL after the DEATH PROCESS that helps the deceased person go through the lower astral plane in the etheric world; thought energy sent to the deceased immediately after death, while he or she is still clinging to earth memories. [**cf.** SECONDARY CLEAR LIGHT, CHONYID BARDO]

SHRI—(Hinduism, Vedanta) the overseer of spiritual activity; a divine person who earned special religious rights in his sect through deeds and acts and not through formal education.

SHRI YANTRA—(ancient India) a pattern of interlaced triangles symbolic of the GREAT MOTHER. [**cf.** TRIANGLE, LAW OF THREES Appendix 7]

SHRINE—an area or place considered sacred because of its character and past associations, built from rituals or ceremonies; place where one can meet his or her inner nature, gather the infinite energies and intelligences into his or her own being, and find peace within the self; the area can be any location from under a tree in the backyard to an elaborate cathedral in the city. [**cf.** NEW-AGE PSYCHOLOGY, SILENCE]

SHRINE IN THE ADYAR HEADQUARTERS—(India) a cupboard for storing the letters received through psychics from the great teachers of the etheric world. [**cf.** MASTERS, ANGELOLOGY]

SHUG—(Tibet) an invisible thought-form-person capable of doing menial taasks for its human creator; a large amount of condensed mind energy projected to make a tiny, invisible, human-like, soulless form; accomplished by consistent thoughts on this life-form until the thoughts colonize into making the form; the life-form lasts as long as the psychic projects consistent thoughts. [**cf.** SOULLESS, MASS ELEMENTAL, THOUGHTS ARE THINGS]

SHUNT PATHS—(Russian) low-resistance paths connected to each of the ACUPUNCTURE POINTS in the body. (Inconcl.) [**cf.** MERIDIAN LINES, NODES, TRIGGER POINTS]

SHUSTAH CARDS—a deck of cards based on the ancient knowledge of the mystery teachings; used to predict the future and to bring guidance to the recipient; contains five suits of fourteen "pages"; cards are spread and studied for the subjective meaning. [**cf.** POINT-OF-FOCUS, CASTING OF LOTS]

SHUT-EYE PSYCHIC—one who closes his or her eyes when tuning into PSYCHIC INFORMATION in order to block out impressions he or she might receive from physical eye contract; in contrast to the OPEN-EYE PSYCHIC who tries to fake the psychic information by reading facial expressions and body language.

SIBYL—(ancient) a PSYCHIC who specializes in PROPHECY and talking in trance; sibyls claim they will return one thousand years after their death and talk to earthlings by building a voice box in the air to amplify their speech. [**cf.** INDEPENDENT VOICE, TRANCE VOICE]

SICKNESS—see ILLNESS.

SICKNESS TRANSFER—the absorption of the negative condition of the patient into the body of the HEALER or PSYCHIC; happens when the healer does not cloak her or himself before beginning the healing, or is not in full understanding of the work he or she is performing. [**cf.** CLOAK OF INSULATION, PSYCHIC CONTAGION]

SIDDHI—(Buddhism, Yoga, "perfection") to accomplish extreme control over the body through intensification of thought concentration; such as: making one's self small, large, heavy, or weightless; transporting one's self anywhere, instantaneously; having control over hunger and thirst; making one's self invisible; having control over the forces of nature and people; achieving LORDSHIP over all things. [**cf.** BODY CONTROL, ATMOSPHERE CONTROL]

SIDEREAL DAY—a period in which the earth rotates once on its axis; using this data, mankind divided it into minutes, seconds, hours; this forms their calendar and from the calendar clock time began. [**cf.** PRESENT MANIFESTED, PATTERNING ACROSS TIME]

SIDEREAL KINGDOM—consists of all the stars and planets in space, divided into many universes or solar systems; all the planets and millions of stars surrounding these planets in earth's SOLAR SYSTEM come from one CENTRAL SUN; all solar systems come from the parent Central Sun; a sun is made of flaming gas and parts of this molten substance shoots away from the sun and becomes a star and a solar system is born. [**cf.** SOLAR SYSTEM]

SIDEREAL RADIATION—small amounts of substance bombarding earth in all directions at varying speeds; found everywhere; believed to be coming from the stars. (Inconcl.) [**cf.** RADIATION PATTERN, RAYS, ETHERIC CURRENTS]

SIDERISCHER PENDEL—(Germany) see DOWSING ROD.

SIDEWAY PASSES—(magnetic healing) a swaying movement of the healer's hands across the afflicted area of the patient's body made without touching the body; healer's hands are held with palms together; this movement breaks up the congested area so the patient's biological energy can flow as it is intended. [**cf.** LOOSENED UP, THERAPEUTIC TOUCH, UNRUFFLING THE FIELD]

SIDPA BARDO—(Tibet) the viewing of one's own inferior THOUGHT-FORMS in subhuman shapes; realization of the *true* REALITY; third main step in the DEATH PROCESS; the CONSCIOUSNESS begins the onset of the next birth in earth; one's material instincts take over; decision is made whether to be reborn in the earth plane or in the etheric world planes. [**cf.** BARDOS, THOUGHT-FORMS, BARDO THODOL]

SIGHT IN DARKNESS—(esoteric) pertains to the THIRD-EYE AREA of PSYCHISM; depicted by the black diamond because of its influence from Saturn. [**cf.** BRAHMA'S EYE, BOAT OF THE SEEKER, CLAIRVOYANCE]

SIGHT SENSATION—(astral projection) thrill and bewilderment of an ASTRAL PROJECTIONIST to see with the physical eyes, the astral eyes, or both at the same time; made possible by the SILVER CORD. [**cf.** ASTRAL VISION, SEES-IN-SLEEP, ROLLED-OUT]

SIGHTING—(ufology) an area or spot on earth

561

where a person saw what was felt to be UFO life or a UFO construct which could contain life; happens more than one time in the same area. Usage: "There are four sightings in Florida." [cf. SAUCER-NAUTS, FLYING SAUCERS, SPACE CRITTERS]

SIGIL—(mysticism) the exact nature of a desired object or activity states in one short sentence or phrase; used as a "sphere of influence" to bring an object or activity into manifestation; conciseness and exactness of phrase pinpoints one's attention of thought; e.g., the sigil of the MAGUS is capable of conjuring up his own special angel at will. **Syn.** SIGNATURE. [cf. WORDS-WITH-POWER, LAW OF SIGNATURES Appendix 7]

SIGN OF THE CROSS—to mark or signal with bodily gestures a simulated cross for religious, protective, or ritualistic purposes; 1. (Christian) to imitate the cross of Calvary by touching one's forehead with the first two fingers of the right hand, touch the SOLAR PLEXUS, then the left and right shoulder respectively; performed to show religious respect and intentions; 2. (mediumship) to imitate the cross of Calvary, as above, to signal to the superior ETHERIC WORLD INTELLIGENCES that the MEDIUM is going into TRANCE and desires protection from the inferior etheric world entities; (do not confuse with principle of wearing a cross necklace); 3. (occult) to simulate the EQUI-LIMBED CROSS in a ritual of EXORCISM; this gesture differs from the Christian only in the order: touch the forehead, the solar plexus, right shoulder, left shoulder; see EQUI-LIMBED CROSS. [cf. CROSS, ROSE CROSS, PSYCHIC FINGERS]

SIGNAL VALUE—(meditation) a special feeling within the body when one reaches a level of CONSCIOUSNESS during MEDITATION which means the mind is under control, the body is relaxed, and the emotions are quieted; recognizable after many meditative periods that have been effective; thereafter, this "body-feeling" will serve as a state to strive for in future meditation. [cf. KASINA MEDITATION, JUST SITTING, LOW BREATHING]

SIGNATURA RERUM—(Germany) coined by Jakob Bohme; theory: everything bears its own inherent signature or sign, and each person carries with him a sign, a unique character trait, that comes with him or her at birth. [cf. LAW OF SIGNATURES Appendix 7, KARMIC DEBT, ZODIAC]

SIGNIFICANT COINCIDENCES—(Carl Jung) see SYNCHRONICITY.

SIGNS AND WONDERS—ancient cliche; refers to omens and the markings of civilization's future on everything of nature; see MANTIC ARTS. [cf. OMENS, CASTING OF LOTS]

SIKUN—(Native American) see PSYCHIC.

SILAP INUA—(Eskimo) the supreme being; the principal that controls the whole universe; the spirit in the air, bipolar in nature; see VITAL LIFE FORCE.

SILENCE—(capitalized) 1. a deep state of CONSCIOUSNESS reached by meditating, wherein one goes back to his or her primal spark of TOTALITY and feels a ONENESS with all things; the body is relaxed, the emotions are quiet, the mind is controlled, and the concerns of the day float away; time becomes incomprehensible; a feeling of universal happiness one cannot explain; a place inside everyone where one can find one's personal God; this deep meditative state changes one's attitude to a more positive outlook; 2. a secret place of the SOUL-MIND that people carry with them at all times and which cannot be seen by human eyes. **Syn.** SEED MEDITATION. [cf. SELF-DISIDENTIFICATION, VOIDNESS, SAMADHI]

SILENT SHADOWS—(Egypt) entire expression is "land of the silent shadows"; see ASTRAL CEMETERY. [cf. EARTHBOUND ENTITIES]

SILENT WATCHER—1. angels in the etheric world who oversee whole units; i.e., in charge of all roads on planet earth. **Syn.** COSMIC BEING, DIVINE DAIMON. 2. (Theosophy) one who can claim to be ABSOLUTE; 3. an ETHERIC WORLD INTELLIGENCE who administers aid to an individual during one entire incarnation. **Syn.** PERISPRIT, CELESTIAL GUARDIAN]

SILVA METHOD—special mind-technique used to orient oneself on the various levels of the ETHERIC WORLD to receive PSYCHIC INFORMATION; taught at weekend seminars throughout the country; designed by Jose Silva.

SILVER CORD—(esoteric) an ethereal cobweb-like cable which contains an abundance of intelligence and energy and has the properties of elasticity; extends from the SUSHUMNA in the human spine to the human being seed (the MONAD); serves as a person's connecting link to the UNIVERSE making both all one unit; penetrates through one's ethereal bodies; connects the SOUL-MIND to the PHYSICAL BODY during an ASTRAL PROJECTION and, at this time, can be seen clairvoyantly, coming out of the top of the head; a vital energy source composed of five tiny strands, each with a separate function necessary to sustain the physical body which exists to perfect the human being seed. (Inconcl.) **Syn.** SPIRITUAL CORD. [**cf.** IN-THE-RANGE-OF-CORD-ACTIVITY, LIFE-CORD-HEART-SEED-ATOM, EMOTIONAL ASTRAL CORD, VAGUS NERVE]

SIMBIOTIC CLOSENESS—a spontaneous, short, psychic contact from a deceased person to an earthling for personal reasons; contact is usually to assure the earthling that deceased person is alive and still a friend; occurs by a psychic vision, or smelling a fragrance or tasting a food that can be associated with the friend but not associated with anything in the vicinity; earthling is in a relaxed state to perceive this contact. [**cf.** EMOTIONAL PSI, DISCARNATE EXPERIENCE DURING SLEEP]

SIMILE PICTURE—psychic visions that do not mean the image itself but uses a symbol to relay the message which could not be brought in any other way; e.g., seeing a cat crying outside a door does not mean the individual will have a cat to feed but, rather, it could mean one is hurt because someone has shut off loving him or her. [**cf.** LAW OF SYMBOLISM Appendix 7, METAPHOR]

SIMONTON METHOD—(future science) a VISUALIZATION technique designed by O. Carl Simonton to help cancer patients destroy cancer cells; his new psychological approach is to have the patient imagine a simulated scene over the diseased area that consists of something destroying the cancerous cells; e.g., sharks eating them, agriculturists pulling them out like weeds; is more effective if performed when in a deep meditative state; entire technique also includes goal setting, nutrition, exercise, play, and development of a good supportive system. (Inconcl.) [**cf.** MENTAL HEALING]

SIMPLE CALL—(electronic voices) a PSYCHIC PHONE CALL from a deceased person that is brief and often interrupted; some interaction between the two parties involved does take place before the line goes dead or the conversation is otherwise terminated. (Inconcl.) [**cf.** PHONE CALLS FROM THE DEAD]

SIMPLE CONSCIOUSNESS—a level of AWARENESS of some animals in which cognitive experiences beyond instinct and conditioning show the appearance of thought-processes; the animal's ability to learn and answer a person's questions by decision and not repetition; animals in this new category of EVOLUTION: monkeys, dogs, horses, and porpoises. (Inconcl.) [**cf.** INSTINCT CONSCIOUSNESS, PRIMARY PSI PERCEPTION]

SIMPLE CROSS-CORRESPONDENCE—processes of the ETHERIC WORLD INTELLIGENCES working independently through two or more automatists, or trance voice mediums, in different locations; each MEDIUM receives the same thought individually expressed or in the same wording at an approximate time; performed so the etheric world intelligences could prove their validity. [**cf.** COMPLEMENTARY CROSS-CORRESPONDENCE, ETHERIC SCRIPT]

SIMPLE MEMORY RECALL—to psychically view one's past life or lives as to vocation, sex, time period, economic situation, marriage, etc., as a bystander, instead of reliving the traumatic scenes and becoming emotional; accomplished by MEDITATION, SELF-HYPNOTHERAPY, MENTAL REGRESSION, and other techniques on the market. [**cf.** REVIVIFICATION, PARTIAL REGRESSION, AGE REGRESSION]

SIMPLE OBSESSION—(mediumship) the muddling of a medium's communications by an etheric world entity; entity constantly substitutes or mixes, information making it incorrect; brought about by the low moral standards of the medium or by a lack of knowledge as to how to protect her or himself. [**cf.** CLOAK OF INSULATION, THOUGHT-FORM]

SIMPLE REGRESSION—see SIMPLE MEMORY RECALL.

SIMULTANEOUS PARALLELS—two events happening at the same time, unrelated in nature but functioning for the same purpose. [**cf.** LAW OF CORRESPONDENCE Appendix 7, SYNCHRONICITY]

SIMULTANEOUS SYSTEMS—(Seth) theory: one has no place to go because one is the place; to simply explore the nature and experience of each living thing within one's own system until one understands the system, and then leave it. [**cf.** TIME Appendix 5]

SIMULTANEOUS THOUGHTS—to transfer one's mental atmosphere of thoughts to another individual knowingly; to unintentionally receive the exact idea another person has; e.g., not perceive the answer to another's question but to perceive the question itself. **Syn.** SUBCONSCIOUS TELEPATHY. [**cf.** MENTAL TELEPATHY, MIND-LINKING, MIND RAIDER]

563

SIMULTANEOUS TIME—(future science) theory: the past, present, and future happen at the same time only in different VIBRATIONAL FREQUENCIES; all things occurring at once make a difficult concept for mankind to conceive but make it possible for psychics to tune into the past and future. (Inconcl.) **Sim.** MULTIDIMENSIONAL. [**cf.** TIME FLOW, TIME FRAMEWORK]

SIN—(esoteric) 1. activity and behavioral patterns of an individual whose SOUL-MIND is in an earlier state of EVOLUTION than that of the masses and these activities are considered incorrect for the society he or she lives in, but considered necessary for his or her growth; lack of intelligence; 2. (Unity) "missing the mark; falling short of divine perfection; failure to express the attributes of the God qualities"; 3. the desire of the soul-mind for the sake of its own growth to have a certain experience, even though it is considered wrong by others; it will recognize this experience in the future and will not be overcome by the desire of this activity again; 4. (Huna) an act in which the SUBCONSCIOUS MIND takes over, preventing the SUPERCONSCIOUS MIND from surfacing with the correct direction; 5. there are no sins, only steps in the evolutionary cycle of the human being trying to purify itself; 6. theory: there is only one sin, and that is to be "stagnant"; lack of progression; "stagnation is death." [**cf.** EVIL, CYCLES, EVOLUTION]

SING—(Native American, Navaho) (capitalized) a HEALING ceremony of dancing, CHANTING, public speaking, and group discussions according to the kind of sickness of the patient; directed by the MEDICINE MAN; ceremony ritualized in nature as they feel illness is a manifestation within a person when he or she becomes out of harmony with nature. [**cf.** CURATIVE EDUCATION, MEDICINE MAN, SHAMANSHIP]

SING-IN-THE-SPIRIT—to emotionally express one's self in verse and song, according to how one is moved; happens in a large gathering after one's emotions have been aroused by a charismatic lecture or service; results in an even higher emotional state of ecstasy; [**cf.** PEAK EXPERIENCE, CHARISMATIC MOVEMENT, GROUP SOUND]

SINGER—(Native American, Navaho) (capitalized) the MEDICINE MAN or priest who puts together the type of SING necessary for that particular kind of illness (mental or physical); brings the patient back in harmony with nature and his fellow

tribesmen. [**cf.** SING, CHANTING, GROUP SOUND, SEEING]

SINGING STONES—(China) flat pieces of jade that give off musical tones; have therapeutic properties and are used as tools to heal sick people. [**cf.** MANDRAKE, LIGHT-BALL GEMS, MINPSI]

SINGLE EYE—(Egypt) the optic THALAMUS; an egg-shaped ganglion of the inner brain; when cross-sectioned looks like a beetle; symbol of IMMORTALITY. **Syn.** OPEN-EYE, SACRED BEETLE, EGG OF IMMORTALITY, HEART OF THE LOTUS, BOAT OF THE SEEKER. [**cf.** THIRD-EYE AREA Appendix 2]

SINGLE-POINT OF CONSCIOUSNESS—see MONAD.

SINGLE-POINTEDNESS—1. to use a very small object, sound, or MANTRA as a focus point during MEDITATION to reach a deep level of consciousness. [**cf.** SEED MEDITATION.] 2. to center one's entire attention on a subject or a situation that one has a deep-seated desire to be manifested; this situation is dwelt upon while sleeping, eating, working, and playing; this undivided attention without letting go, binds the atoms to the situation and nothing in that area flows. [**cf.** THOUGHT-FORMS, VISUALIZATION, ELEMENTAL]

SINGLES-TEST—(psi tasks) an experiment in which the aim of a subject is to try to influence dice to fall with a specified number facing up. [**cf.** NON-HUMAN-PK, MIND-TO-OBJECT COMMUNICATION, SUBJECT]

SINKS INTO THE FLOOR—(early 1900s) (materialization) describes the appearance of the ECTOPLASM when the MATERIALIZATION session is ending; the ectoplasm looks as if it melts down and sinks into the floor without any traces of melting; the ectoplasm is actually being withdrawn into the medium's body through his or her mouth and SOLAR PLEXUS. [**cf.** DEMATERIALIZATION, BLACKED-OUT ROOM]

SIRAT—(Islam) a fine, narrow pathway bridging over HELL. [**cf.** HADES, DENSITY]

SIREN—(Greece) a female etheric world entity capable of having intercourse with a human being either by remaining invisible or assuming a human form for that time. **Sim.** SUCCUBUS, NIGHT-HAG. [**cf.** DIMENSION-SHIFTING, PHYSICAL MANIFESTATIONS/MISCELLANEOUS Appendix 2]

564

SISYA—(Tantrism) a student or initiate of the mysteries of WISDOM.

SIT—to occupy a chair in the same SEANCE or PSYCHIC DEVELOPMENT CIRCLE held in the same location for many weekly sessions for the purpose of communicating with ETHERIC WORLD INTELLI-GENCES; term originated because the PSYCHIC or MEDIUM does practically nothing but take time to "sit" and allow the etheric world intelligence to figure out how to synchronize with the group and bring forth the psychic information or physical phenomena. Usage: "I sit for levitation or I sit for voice trance." [**cf.** SITTERS, BLACKED OUT ROOM]

SITTERS—1. members of a SEANCE circle who meet repeatedly to help develop one member as a physical phenomena MEDIUM; people are willing to be used as batteries for this phenomena and are able to keep a good rapport with one another so as not to detain the phenomena; 2. members of a PSYCHIC DEVELOPMENT CIRCLE who meet regularly to develop their own mental psychic abilities with a developed mental medium in attendance. [**cf.** SEANCE]

SITTING—1. a period of time when a professional PSYCHIC is answering questions, predicting the future, and giving guidance to one who has come for counseling. Usage: "I just had a sitting with June and she told me where to go for a job." **Syn.** PSYCHIC READING. 2. (Zen) the length of time one meditates in one span. [**cf.** PSYCHIC INFORMATION, JUST SITTING]

SITTING FACE TO FACE—(Tibet) to view one's THOUGHT-FORMS, whether advantageous or inferior, during the DEATH PROCESS; happens immediately upon entering the ETHERIC WORLD; brings a realization of the *real* REALITY and the realization of the strength of thought. [**cf.** DEATH SCIENCE Appendix 2]

SITTING FOR TRUMPET—repeated SEANCE sessions of a group of dedicated people and a MEDIUM with a desire to raise a TRUMPET; the trumpet is used by the ETHERIC WORLD INTELLIGENCES to amplify their messages for audibility; metaphysical or PSYCHIC SCIENCE lesson precedes session; this, plus MEDITATION and singing of songs during the session, helps to raise the VIBRATIONS for the trumpet to rise; trumpet must levitate to be used for amplification; ECTOPLASM levitates the trumpet; expression was coined due to the number of years the same group met to perfect the phenom-

enon; trumpet rises by steps: first it moves from its position on the floor, and each session it moves more until it rises and travels through the air above the SITTERS' heads; in this levitated position it amplifies the etheric voices.

SITTING ZEN—to maintain the ZEN posture, keep very still, and meditate. [**cf.** SITTING, MOTIONLESS MEDITATION]

SIX—represents cooperation; life cycle symbolizes harmony, beauty, balance, and rhythm; most stable of all vibrations; planet Venus holds sway over this number. [**cf.** SIX-SIX-SIX, ONE, NINE]

SIX-SIX-SIX—believed to be an OMEN of EVIL forces. [**cf.** SIX, NUMEROLOGY]

SIXTH BODY—see MONAD.

SIXTH PLANE—home of the monads; a level of CONSCIOUSNESS wherein the MONAD begins and ends the necessity of using a SOUL-MIND as its vehicle for the evolutionary cycle; the vibrational frequency that triggers off the INVOLUTION of the monad and gives it the potential to envelop itself in a soul-mind; implants a demand for its EVOLUTION back to this plane. **Syn.** MONADIC PLANE. [**cf.** LAW OF INVOLUTION and LAW OF SOUL-MIND Appendix 7, MONADOLOGY]

SIXTH SENSE—ability to perceive PSYCHIC INFORMATION. **Syn.** PSYCHIC SENSITIVITY. [**cf.** PSYCHIC SKILLS]

SIXTY-CYCLE HUM—see ENVIRONMENTAL NOISE.

SKANDHA—(Sanskrit, Buddhism) groups of karmic seeds that have accumulated and are being manifested in the earthly incarnations as a complex of activities, and as one's characteristics; the components of the human race; a series of momentary states successively generated from one form to another in continuous transformation, losing its principle of animation in rebirths; (do not confuse with the SOUL-MIND, who does not lose his or her principle in rebirths). [**cf.** REINCARNATION, KARMIC RECORDS]

SKIN—(human) (esoteric) 1. outer surface for the embodiment of the SOUL-MIND for the earthly incarnation; connects with membranes and organs in order to receive information from human touch and environmental radiations to help the brain make decisions; these decisions are recorded in the electrical system of the body. (Inconcl.) 2. correlates total mind capacity, making EYELESS SIGHT and GSR biofeedback training effective; 3. its psychic sensitivity relates information in psychometrizing and psychic diagnosing of sickness using radies-thesia. (Inconcl.) [**cf.** PSYCHOMETRY]

SKIN COMMUNICATION—the skin has the sensi-tivity to understand one's intentions and feelings from contact with another; theory: the skin has remnants of the primordial stone age culture when language was not used; communication was through enfolding embraces and loving touches. [**cf.** METABOLIC MONITOR, HANDS, HUMAN EVO-LUTION, GSR]

SKIN PORTRAITS—(esoteric) tiny pictures in-scribed within the skin of each human that portray the future of that individual; begins at birth. [**cf.** MENTAL-REFLECING-ETHER, SYMPATHETIC NER-VOUS SYSTEM]

SKIN POTENTIAL LEVEL—abbr. SPL, pertains to the amount of electrical voltage produced by the skin. (Inconcl.) [**cf.** EMOTIONS, GALVANIC SKIN RESISTANCE]

SKIN RESISTANCE RESPONSE INSTRUMENT—(biofeedback training) abbr. SSR; a device that detects aroused and calm states of the mind and body of the individual who is HOOKED-UP to it; used during MEDITATION or therapy sessions; passes miniscule amounts of electrical current through the body, which in turn relates back into the instrument what the SYMPATHETIC NERVOUS SYSTEM is doing by means of amplification in sound, visual lights, or numbers; measures skin resistance; see GSR. [**cf.** LOWER FREQUENCY, LUCID AWARENESS]

SKIN SIGHT—see EYELESS SIGHT.

SKIN TALK—(future science) coined by Barbara Brown: pathological and normal states of emotions, revealed through the skin when HOOKED-UP to a biofeedback amplifying instrument; the SUBCON-SCIOUS MIND sends every characteristic of emo-tional energies through the nerve endings and sweat glands; e.g., motivation stimuli, method of solving problems, level of arousal and excitation or passivity and relaxation, feedback from daily out-side stimuli, feedback from repressed or secret ex-periences, and levels of consciousness during MEDI-TATION, HYPNOTHERAPY, and psychic sensitivity. (Inconcl.) [**cf.** SWEAT GLAND ACTIVITY, BIOSTAT INSTRUMENT, GSR]

SKIN TEMPERATURE INSTRUMENT—abbr. TEMP; a biofeedback device that measures the amount of stress one is undergoing by detecting skin tempera-ture that varies with blood flow according to states of emotional stress; a tiny bead of iron oxide (a THERMISTOR) is attached to the skin surface and measures slight changes in skin temperature. (Inconcl.) [**cf.** SKIN RESISTANCE, MENTAL-EMO-TIONAL ACTIVITY]

SKIN VISION—see EYELESS SIGHT.

SKIN WRITING—to produce a PSYCHIC MESSAGE written in words or pictures on one's skin while in a TRANCE state of consciousness; performed by an ETHERIC WORLD INTELLIGENCE; stays on the skin for a few minutes or hours, just long enough for others to see and record the message; diminishes before the medium returns to the normal state of consciousness; occurs with no pain when written or disappearing; willed and desired-controlled; (do not confuse with STIGMATIZATION). **Syn.** DER-MOGRAPHY. [**cf.** TRANCE MANIFESTATIONS/ MISCELLANEOUS Appendix 2]

SKINLESS HAG—(West Indies) the egg-shaped mass of faint light or fire that follows the PSYCHIC taking an ASTRAL PROJECTION; can be seen by both physical and clairvoyant eyes. [**cf.** ASTRAL PROJECTION]

SKOTOGRAPH—(Greek, "writing in the dark") the writing on an undeveloped pack of film by the ETHERIC WORLD INTELLIGENCES using the PSYCHIC ENERGY of a MEDIUM; when film is de-veloped, the writing shows on the picture. [**cf.** PYSCHIC PHOTOGRAPHY, THOUGHTOGRAPHY, VAPOROGRAPH]

SKRYING—to travel into the ETHERIC WORLD or to project a part of the body into other planes, by will; divided into three types: 1. MENTAL PROJEC-TION with the mind; 2. ASTRAL PROJECTION with the astral body; 3. ETHERIC PROJECTION with the etheric or ectoplasmic body; (do not confuse with SCRYING). **Syn.** PROJECTION.

SKRYING IN THE SPIRIT VISION—(magic) see ASTRAL PROJECTION.

SKULLS—(esoteric) believed to retain the essence of that person's life-energy and character; skulls of holy men are kept sacred.

SKUNK APE—(Florida Everglades) see MONSTER ACTIVITY.

SKY CEREMONIES—(Native American) special rituals performed to communicate with the ETHERIC WORLD INTELLIGENCES immediately when contacted; used when the Indian needed enlightenment and guidance. [cf. TRANCE, IMPERSONATIONS, PSYCHIC HEALING]

SKY CRAFT—(ufology) intelligently designed forms seen in outer space that give the appearance of a vehicle; thought to be manipulated by an intelligent being who is similar to earth mankind. (Inconcl.) **Syn.** ETHER SHIPS, CONSTRUCTS. [cf. SPACE ANIMALS, UFO PROPULSION]

SKY PEOPLE—1. (New Guinea) soul-minds living in the ETHERIC WORLD similar to earth life; desire to communicate with earth people; 2. (Native American, Sioux) soul-minds living in the etheric world who receive messages, carried by birds, from the earth people. **Sim.** SPIRIT, VIBRATORY INTELLIGENCES, UNSEEN HELPER, PSYCHOPOMPAS. [cf. HAPPY HUNTING GROUND]

SKY-EARTH—(Native American, Nagas) the supreme god in charge of man and his communications with the etheric world entities. **Sim.** JESUS, BUDDHA, KRISHNA.

SKY-WORSHIP—(Aryan) philosophy: there are gods or intelligences in the ETHERIC WORLD who communicate with earthlings. **Sim.** MEDIUMSHIP, SPIRIT COMMUNICATION.

SKYCLAD—(Wicca) NUDE.

SKYER—1. (Aryan) one who communicates with the ETHERIC WORLD INTELLIGENCES for the purposes of receiving psychic information and performing physical psychism. **Sim.** MEDIUM, PROPHETER, CHALDEAN, MAGICIAN. [cf. SKY-WORSHIP. 2. (astral projection) one who is capable of taking an astral flight at will. **Sim.** SKYWALKER. [cf. SKYING]

SKYING—(astral projection) to will one's SOUL-MIND to leave the PHYSICAL BODY by shooting upward like a rocket to the higher etheric planes; to temporarily function in these other VIBRATIONAL FREQUENCIES in a conscious state of consciousness. **Sim.** PHOWA. [cf. OBE, FRINGE OF SPACE-TIME, INTERPLANETARY DISCOINCIDENCE]

SKYWALKER—1. a PSYCHIC capable of willing her or himself to astrally project to other planets to explore their types of life, instead of astrally projecting into the etheric world to work for earth life; 2. (*Star Wars* movie) individuals who traveled to other galaxies. **Syn.** PROJECTIONIST. [cf. WILLED ASTRAL PROJECTION, SPONTANEOUS ASTRAL PROJECTION]

SLATE WRITING—(seance) to allow an ETHERIC WORLD INTELLIGENCE to intervene and write on an old-fashioned child's slate during a SEANCE without using the medium's body; one MEDIUM must have the ability of PRECIPITATION; slate is placed: 1. in the center of the circle and seance carries on in other ways; 2. under a card table with each sitter touching the edge of the card table—chalk is placed between the underside of the table and the slate; when scratching noise stops, the writing is finished; message is for the masses, a PROPHECY, or an answer to a question from the group; takes many months to develop but once developed it is a good method of receiving answers to worldwide questions. **Sim.** AUTOGRAPHY, PNEUMATOGRAPHIC MEDIUMSHIP. [cf. ETHERIC SCRIPT, DIRECT WRITING]

SLAYING-IN-THE-SPIRIT—to lightly touch the forehead of an individual with the first two fingers of the right hand and cause the individual to fall to the floor unharmed with the intention that he or she will receive a bolt of HOLY SPIRIT energy; performed by an evangelist at a charismatic meeting that is designed to stir the emotions of the members; individual falls backward in a prone position fully relaxed, instantaneously with the touch; workers help to ease the slain individuals to the floor as they are touched one after another; they lie on the floor until normal consciousness returns; purpose is to receive a physical healing or a change in attitude; not all who fall backward are healed; theory: a GROUP ELEMENTAL is built through loud, rhythmic music and emotional ploy from the leader beforehand, composed to put the group in unison of thought; group's expectation and desire for the healings and falling backward cause it to happen. (Inconcl.) [cf. TALKING-IN-TONGUES, EMOTIONAL PSI]

SLEEP—(esoteric) to allow one's CONSCIOUS AWARENESS to become quiescent, causing the physical body systems to slow down for rest, repair, and COSMIC ENERGY replenishment (including the brain); a length of time of inactivity, absolutely necessary for the animal organism to allow time for DREAMING; to give the guiding principle an opportunity to strive for perfecting the human being without the interference of the decision-making mind (the BRAIN) through the process of dreaming; during sleep: the mind contacts other levels of awareness in the ETHERIC WORLD, the ASTRAL BODY separates and recharges the NERVOUS SYSTEM, the SUBCONSCIOUS MIND thinks, dreams, and sometimes has a PSYCHIC EXPERIENCE. (Inconcl.) [cf. REM, NREM, COMPENSATORY DREAMS, PERSONAL PSYCHIATRIST]

SLEEP ASTRAL PROJECTION—the unwilled separation of the ASTRAL BODY from the PHYSICAL BODY during SLEEP; to travel with a purpose unknown and unplanned by the sleeper; happens periodically; astral body varies its course; visits a close relative the sleeper had been thinking about the past day, visits the etheric world planes to learn or perform a duty, sails through space, etc., some projections are never recalled, some remembered in part, and some brushed off as being a dream; if one dreams during the projection, one could be sailing, flying, swimming, running, all portrayed in giant strides or distance. (Inconcl.) [cf. ASTRAL PROJECTION Appendix 2]

SLEEP BRAIN WAVE PATTERNS—four categories of different forms and lengths of lines that appear on the readouts of the EEG instrument during a normal night's sleep indicating levels of CONSCIOUSNESS; considered to be universal patterns after twenty years and thousands of sleepers being HOOKED-UP to the EEG instrument in the DREAM RESEARCH LABORATORIES; lines indicate BETA, ALPHA, THETA and DELTA WAVES.

SLEEP CONTROL—(Silva Mind Control) to enter normal, natural, physiological sleep anytime, anywhere, at will. [cf. MOTIVE UNCONSCIOUSNESS, MENTAL PSYCHIC PROCESSES]

SLEEP CYCLE—a BIOLOGICAL RHYTHM in a normal night's rest that takes the sleeper through four stages of consciousness: beta, alpha, theta, and delta; begins with the delta stage, getting less deep sleep as the night goes on; within this pattern, dreams come approximately every ninety minutes, setting a rhythmic pattern varying slightly with each individual, according to the need that night. (Inconcl.) [cf. DREAM CYCLE, FORGOTTEN LANGUAGE, BRAINWAVE RHYTHM]

SLEEP EXPERIENCE—levels of awareness that occur during a night's sleep; 1. DREAMS at ninety-minute intervals every night during a normal night's sleep, happening to everyone; 2. psychic

experiences occurring between dream periods, happening occasionally; 3. astral projections occurring during the onset of early morning sleep and between dream periods, happening infrequently. (Inconcl.) 4. hypnagogic flashes in the onset of sleep and hypnapompic flashes in the onset of awakening, recognizable to some individuals; 5. thinking consistently between all of the above levels by everyone. (Inconcl.) [cf. PSYCHIC EXPERIENCE DURING SLEEP, ASTRAL PROJECTION, HYPNAGOGIC STATE, HYPNAPOMPIC STATE, THINKING DURING SLEEP]

SLEEP LEARNING—to play cassette tapes repeatedly during the night or at the onset of sleep when the mental levels of awareness are highly suggestible; one can learn new material, reprogram their lifestyle, or change their behavioral patterns. (Inconcl.)

SLEEP PARALYSIS—(dreams) a state of limp paralysis during the REM state of sleep; the physical body is incapable of large body movements, but the fingers, toes, eyes, and genitals are free to move, and usually do. (Inconcl.) [cf. EOG, EEF, REM, NREM]

SLEEP PREACHING—to receive, upon awakening in the morning, the context of a speech designed for others to hear, without having made any preparation before one goes to bed; the MEDIUM suggests to her or himself the theme of a desired topic before retiring and during the night it is expounded upon by the ETHERIC WORLD INTELLIGENCES; in the morning, this flows clearly for the medium until he or she writes it on paper. **Syn.** INSPIRATIONAL SLEEP. [cf. INSPIRATIONAL WRITING] 2. to give a sermon or lecture on the platform while in a state of DEEP TRANCE; the etheric world inteligences work through the medium in such a way that the medium can handle her or himself as to rising, sitting, and length of lecture. [cf. LIGHT TRANCE]

SLEEP PSYCHIC EXPERIENCE—a very impressive and easily recalled experience during sleep; perceived through one or more of the five PSYCHIC SENSES; differs from a normal dream because it is detailed, vivid, clear, and authentic to one time period throughout the scene, and is sometimes remembered for years; (contrasted to a REM dream which is fuzzy, fragmented, and evasive); occurs between REM dreams in an ALPHA or THETA STATE OF CONSCIOUSNESS; not detectable by RAPID-EYE-MOVEMENT; PROPHECY and speaking with deceased loved ones are most common. (Inconcl.) [**cf.** TIME BENDERS, FALLING DREAM, PROPHETIC DREAM]

SLEEP RHYTHM OF PLANTS—daily elevation and drooping of a plant's leaves that repeats every twenty-four hours. (Inconcl.) [**cf.** CIRCADIAN CYCLE, PRIMARY PERCEPTION]

SLEEP TELEPATHY—the transference of thought during the night between the sender who is awake and the receiver who is asleep; can be used appropriately for sending mental telepathic healings and messages in laboratory experiments; used for EVIL in enforcing a HEX and enforcing mind control by the destructive cults. (Inconcl.) [**cf.** MENTAL ATMOSPHERE, MENTAL TELEPATHIC SUGESTION, MENTAL TELEPATHY]

SLEEP THINKING—constant thoughts running through the SUBCONSCIOUS MIND during the NREM state during sleep which are not preplanned or knowingly instigated; these thoughts are similar to one's daytime subconscious dialogue as to attitudes and opinions; do not use the emotional process that accompanies daily routine, such as anxiety and hostility; thoughts about recreation, recent or coming events, or mulling over worldly affairs; found to be as valid and meaningful as one's daytime thinking and adds to the ergs of energy that make one's BODY CHEMISTRY, lifestyle, and KARMA. (Inconcl.) [**cf.** THETA STATE OF CONSCIOUSNESS, ALPHA STATE OF CONSCIOUSNESS, SLEEP EXPERIENCE]

SLEEP OSMOSIS—to absorb the material in a book by putting it under one's pillow at night and sleeping on it. [**cf.** MENTAL OSMOSIS]

SLEEP-SPIRIT PROBLEMS—(destructive-brainwashing cults) to become drowsy during the long night meetings; theory: one is being attacked by the spirits of deceased persons who belong to Satan so as to prevent one from listening at the meeting; this is overcome by making the victim take a shower or squirting him or her with a water gun. [**cf.** EGO-DESTRUCTION, BLISSING OUT, DESTRUCTIVE-BRAINWASHING CULTS]

SLEEP-TALKING—to speak aloud during sleep between dream periods when the body is mobile; one can answer questions if they do not require decisions, while he or she is in this state. (Inconcl.) [**cf.** SLEEPWALKING, REDUCTIVE ANALYSIS, MEANINGLESS NOISE]

SLEEP-WAKE HYPNOSIS—to cause an individual to fall asleep or to go into a TRANCE state for a few seconds, at will; individual has no recall of what happened; distance is no barrier. [**cf.** WAKING HYPNOSIS, SENSITIVITY TRANSFER]

SLEEPING PROPHET—Nickname given to Edgar Cayce, a well-known PSYCHIC who received a tremendous amount of PSYCHIC INFORMATION while lying on a bed in a TRANCE state of consciousness; this information brought forth new knowledge and suggestions for individual people to use to regain their health.

SLEEPITATE—coined by Arthur Douet; to doze off to sleep while one is supposed to be meditating. [**cf.** JOSS-STICK, PRAYER BEADS, PURE ALERTNESS]

SLEEPWALKING—to walk while in the sleep state; occurs between dream periods when the body is able to make large movements; one should not awaken the sleeper, for physical reasons, but rather direct him or her back to bed. (Inconcl.) [**cf.** RELEASE TYPE DREAMS, RECURRING DREAMS]

SLIGHTLY-OUT-OF-BODY—(astral projection) 1. the separation of the ASTRAL BODY a few inches away from the PHYSICAL BODY during sleep every night; in this position, the astral body becomes recharged with COSMIC ENERGY and when it returns to the physical body, the energy is transmuted into physical energy. 2. the astral body steps a few inches away from the physical body during MEDITATION and the meditator finds her or himself looking at his or her own body. [**cf.** IN-THE-RANGE-OF-CORD-ACTIVITY]

SLOW VIBRATORY DROP—(astral projection) to return from an astral flight in a normal way with only a slight trembling of the two bodies as everything is under control; an interiorization when all vibrations are in harmony. [**cf.** EXTERIORIZATION, REPERCUSSION]

SMALL SPIRIT—an ETHERIC WORLD INTELLIGENCE using only a part of the medium's body for the physical phenomena and only this part is anesthetized; e.g., only the arm and hand is used in PSYCHIC SURGERY; only the feet are used in feet painting; only an arm and hand are used in AUTOMATIC WRITING. **Syn.** TEN-PERCENT TRANCE. [**cf.** see individual listings]

SMARAGDINE TABLETS—the writings of Hermes Trismegistus, the noted ancient Egyptian king.

SMITHY—the VILLAGE BLACKSMITH and the PSYCHIC of the town; see both.

SMUDGING—(Native American) to burn a special plant in an area before a ceremony, a healing, or a lecture, etc., as a customary RITUAL; resulting smoke is fanned throughout the room or area from each cardinal point, which cleanses the atmosphere of any negativity; (Native American, Chippewa) to burn sage and fan the smoke with an eagle feather. [**cf.** ATMOSPHERE CLEARING, EXORCISM]

SNAKE-HANDLING CULTS—(Native American, Southern United States) religious organizations in which the members personally hold and maneuver poisonous snakes in rituals of dancing, chanting, and praying; theory: one will not be bitten if one has enough faith in God because God has power over the devil (the snake); these rituals lead to TALKING-IN-TONGUES and suffering through overwhelming ecstatic seizures which symbolize one's spiritual attainment, increase one's healing ability, and enhance psychic skills. [**cf.** RESURRECTION, !KIA FIRE, LYSERGIC ACID]

SNAKE-STONE—(esoteric) a mineral having properties that rot substances; used by the alchemists in their formulas; used as a tool to predict the future; influenced by the vibrations of Mars; symbolizes Scorpio. [**cf.** MINPSI, WITCH BALLS, SCREAMING STONE]

SNAPPING—coined by Flo Conway and Jim Siegelman because people have voiced this word when describing what has happened to them; an abnormal mental and emotional response one reaches after an overdose of repetitious suggestions that are carefully planned for that purpose, and are forced upon one until the victim makes a complete change in personality; a critical point in the mind of the victim when the snapping happens because the attack of suggestons in the brainwashing can proceed rapidly with a willing and believing victim from then on; an overwhelming emotional release and the human mind is snapped shut with bliss; the surrender of thought, feelings, and will, instantaneously or drawn out; happens in the first encounter by ON-THE-SPOT-HYPNOSIS, while in the commune, in the weekend intensives, or (in reverse) when being deprogrammed. [**cf.** SUDDEN PERSONALITY CHANGE, MASS HYPNOSIS, DESTRUCTIVE-BRAINWASHING CULTS Appendix 2]

SOCIAL READJUSTMENT RATING SCALE—designed by T. H. Holmes and R. H. Rahe; scale assigned numerical values to painful and happy stressful experiences; totaling numerical values of the stressful events in one's immediate past indicated the amount of stress one was undergoing; research found that individuals with a high total of numerical value were more susceptible to taking on a disease; individuals who did not fall in line with the scale and became ill were individuals who had been able to cope correctly and resolve the stressful event. [**cf.** KEY TO LIFE, BLOCKS]

SOCIAL RENEWAL—to build new psychotechnological organizations into the present system to aid in a smooth transformation of the times; those who desire to help the planet purify herself will organize or promote WELLNESS centers, support networks, HOLISTIC HEALTH education, hospice groups, encounter groups, TM, and the hundreds of other conscioussness awareness organizations that bring more harmony and love into the individual and thus to the universe. [**cf.** NEW-AGE PSYCHOLOGY, FUTURISTS, CONSCIOUSNESS AWARENESS MOVEMENT]

SOCIETY FOR PSYCHICAL RESEARCH—first professional organization to study and investigate the scientific processes involved with psychics and mediums; began in 1882, Cambridge University, London, England; Prof. Henry Sidgewick, president, and Prof. Frederick Myers, vice-president.

SODO—(Zen) the monk's hall or any place designed for MEDITATION in a Zen community. [**cf.** ZAZEN, SESSHIN, KEISAKU]

SOFTWARE—(esoteric) name given the CONSCIOUS MIND because it programs the material before it goes into the SUBCONSCIOUS MIND, the BIOCOMPUTER; the conscious mind receives outer stimuli, sorts it over, determines the meaning, decides what it wants to believe, and drops this concept into the biocomputer, to be stored for future use. **Syn.** MENTAL MIND, DECISION-MAKING MIND, BRAIN, SUBJECTIVE MIND. [**cf.** SOUL-MIND]

SOL—("Sun") (capitalized); light-center; basic word for SOUL, the human soul. see SOUL-MIND.

SOLAR CYCLE—(esoteric) 1. a periodic radiation of energy from the sun into the earth; 2. the awakening of a new consciousness when one enters the last two chakras, the brow and crown chakras. **Sim.** PASSAGE OF THE SUN GOD. [**cf.** CYCLES, CHAKRA]

SOLAR DEITY—a magnanimous, lofty intelligent energy whose SOUL-MIND has been so purified that it now has charge of all the functions of the sun; works in the ANGEL KINGDOM, under the galaxy DEITY. [cf. MAGNIFICENT DEVAS]

SOLAR EDDIES—clouds of ionic gas plasma impinging upon the earth's magnetosphere; seems to have an influence upon the human body. (Inconcl.) [cf. ELECTROMAGNETIC SPECTRUM, ERGOSPHERE]

SOLAR FURNACE—see SOLAR PLEXUS.

SOLAR GOD—principle of the laws of the ZODIAC in outer space.

SOLAR IRON—an element of the VITAL LIFE FORCE within the atmosphere attracted by invisible nerve fluids; necessary to the human NERVOUS SYSTEM. [cf. PRANA, NADIS]

SOLAR LOGOS—principle ruling one SOLAR SYSTEM; creator and sustainer of our solar system. **Syn.** GOD, TOTALITY.

SOLAR PLEXUS—(esoteric) an important complex structure of nerves and ganglia located behind the stomach which acts as the coordinator of the internal economy of the body, working with the AUTONOMIC NERVOUS SYSTEM; composed of material similar to the head BRAIN; 1. (ancient) believed to be the SOUL of man; the center of the body where one feels the emotions of the universe; 2. a point of conversion where the physical body transmutes cosmic energies into usable physical energy; 3. PSYCHIC ORGAN for diffusing the sense of feeling and touch; area of the body where emotions are felt most intensely; 4. perception center for both positive and negative vibrations; (this sensitivity is greater in the NATURAL-BORN PSYCHIC). **Syn.** ABDOMINAL BRAIN, OCEAN OF FIRE. [cf. SOLAR PLEXUS CHAKRA, GUT FEELING]

SOLAR PLEXUS CHAKRA—an invisible, ethereal, concentrated center of energy, superimposing an area of the stomach and liver; looks like a whirling wheel or a flower with ten petals, alternating brown and red, with a blending of orange and yellow if seen clairvoyantly; capable of changing colors with emotional states; THIRD CHAKRA on the evolutionary scale; the PSYCHIC ORGAN for diffusing the sense of feeling and touch. **Syn.** MANIPUR, SVADHISTHANA. [cf. SOLAR PLEXUS, HUNCHABILITY]

SOLAR SYSTEM—1. (esoteric) an organized plan with one main sun around which revolve planets, stars, satellites, and asteroids; 2. (Theosophy) seven globes linked together as in a chain, respon-

sible for the EVOLUTION of all life in that system; an intelligent, evolving life-force system based on the power of a sun, and functioning according to basic laws of nature; Earth's solar system consists of the following planets and stars: sun, moon, Venus, Jupiter, Mercury, Saturn, Uranus, Neptune, Pluto, and Earth. [cf. SIDEREAL KINGDOM]

SOLAR SYSTEM CONSCIOUSNESS—an intelligence that seems to be drawing earth's solar system into a harmony of oneness at this time, as it experiences a change from one Great Cosmic Cycle to another Great Cosmic Cycle. [cf. COSMIC YEAR, AGE, ROUND]

SOLEMNIZING THE MIND—(Huna) to begin the manifestation of a desire or need by focalizing attention on the end result of this need; the process of VISUALIZATION; see same.

SOLEX MAL—(ufology) the language spoken by space beings. (Inconcl.) [cf. SAUCERNAUTS, INTELLIGENCE IN THE SKY]

SOLID ASTRAL MATTER—(esoteric) the lowest, most dense substance of lower ASTRAL CONSCIOUSNESS which is the counterpart of iron or similar substance in the earth consciousness. [cf. WAVE-VIBRATION CONCEPT, MANSIONS]

SOLID ECTOPLASM—(materialization seance) the last stage of the substance that emanates from the MEDIUM, showing the following variance from the beginning stage: 1. is tossed around and manipulated in front of the medium before it takes some kind of form; 2. looks like threads, cords, or rigid rays; 3. sometimes resembles woven fabric or net; 4. feels moist or cold to the touch; 5. can be seen easier with physical eyes; 6. sensitive to incandescent light. [cf. SITTERS, ECTOPLASM, ECTOPLASM WISPS]

SOLID-STATE LIFE FORMS—(ufology) intelligent ENERGY FIELDS in outer space that are small, cubical, or rectangular creatures; live in ethereal substance; one theory is that they come from the stratosphere. (Inconcl.) [cf. UFOLOGY Appendix 5]

SOLIDIFIED THOUGHTS—THOUGHT-FORMS that have become so dense they can be perceived clairvoyantly around the thinker or near the object or person in the thought; caused by consistent thoughts on one particular subject. [cf. THOUGHT-FORMS Appendix 2]

571

SOLIDIFYING LIGHT—to work with light and control it for a short time with no apparent damage to the eyes; 1. to bring light into a room, condense it, and project it in balls on the floors or walls; 2. to absorb light from a normal source already in the room and change it in form and area. [**cf.** PSYCHIC BREEZES, MEDIUMS FOR PHYSICAL EFFECTS]

SOLOMON'S MIRROR—polished metal used for SCRYING; see CRYSTAL BALL GAZING.

SOLOMON'S SEAL—an ancient symbol consisting of two triangles interlaced with one apex pointing up and one pointing down; constitutes the number SIX and its symbology; represents the MACROCOSM; symbol was worn by magicians during their ceremonies, wherein it was bound on their breasts or attached to their foreheads; symbol engraved on the silver reservoir of the magic lamp. [**cf.** CEREMONIES, SYMBOLS]

SOMA—a plant capable of inducing PSYCHISM; (Eastern) Vedic hymns sing of its effect in bringing visions of the worlds of splendor and deities. [**cf.** MUSHROOMS, PSYCHOTROPIC PLANTS]

SOMATIC PSYCHOLOGY—a combination of psychodiagnostics, PSYCHOTHERAPY, HYPNOTHERAPY, and MEDITATION; teaches mind-body integration. [**cf.** MIND-LINK, BODY-LINK, ROLFING, WHOLISM]

SOMATO-PSYCHIC—the flow of body-mind movement in the T'AI CHI dance that brings a balanced state in the individual whereby PSYCHIC INFORMATION can come through. [**cf.** JUMPING MAGICIANS, RUNNER'S HIGH]

SOMNAMBULES—mediums that can slide into DEEP TRANCE very easily and work phenomena while in a trance state. [**cf.** DESIRED-CONTROL, DEEP SLEEP, EXCITATIVE MEDIUM]

SOMNAMBULIC PHENOMENA—a study of humans and animals functioning in a hypnotic or sleep-like state. [**cf.** ANPSI, SELF-SUGGESTION]

SOMNAMBULISM—(esoteric) (Latin *somnum,* "sleep"; *ambulare,* "performing acts") to perform physical activity while in a DEEP TRANCE, DEEP STATE OF HYPNOSIS, or in delta sleep; the CONSCIOUS MIND has relinquished its role, and the SOUL-MIND is free to use the body for special purposes; activity can be in the prone position,

standing, or sitting; i.e., SLEEPWALKING, SLEEPTALKING, or actions of a more complicated nature; psychic ability manifests in spontaneous or artificial sleep or SEMITRANCE, whereby the soul-mind faculties operate on the body instead of the conscious mind; differs from ordinary sleep as the body is capable of its normal biological functions except the eyes stay upward and appear transfixed and one is insensitive to pain, taste, smell, and noise; unwilled and unprogrammed; two types: that which works on the SUBCONSCIOUS MIND and that which works with an ethereal GUIDE. (Inconcl.)

SOMNAMBULISM STAGE OF HYPNOSIS—see DEEP TRANCE.

SOMNAMBULIST—one who performs psychic activity in a DEEP STATE OF HYPNOSIS or sleep; works while the CONSCIOUS MIND is passive and the SUBCONSCIOUS MIND is in control; characteristics of a somnambulist: slips into a hypnotic state very quickly, speech is lowered in pitch, walk is unsteady or clumsy, eyes are staring or closed, ears are deaf to auditory impressions, and sense of taste, smell, and pain are not functioning; mannerisms reflect that of the psychic as he or she is operating from the subconscious mind; PSYCHIC has no recollection of this activity when in his or her normal state. [**cf.** FULL TRANCE, TRANCE OF INDIFFERENCE]

SOMNAMBULISTIC MEDIUM—one who goes into DEEP TRANCE and allows the ETHERIC WORLD INTELLIGENCE to intervene and use his or her body for physical phenomenon and/or his or her voice to speak; intelligence gives his or her characteristics and mannerisms to the physical body and activity; occurs for IMPERSONATION and MEDIUMSHIP HEALING; (do not confuse with POSSESSION, in which the MEDIUM does not invite the entity to enter his or her body). [**cf.** FULL TRANCE, TEN PERCENT TRANCE, SHAMANSHIP HEALING, !KIA]

SOMNAMITY—(Yoga) to stay in a closed box for a long time without fresh air coming in and without an internal pulse; to have control over one's body sytems. [**cf.** VAMPIRIC HIBERNATION, BREATH CONTROL, VAGUS BREATHING]

SONG OF LIFE—pleasant and harmonious music inaudible to the physical ear, necessary to counteract negative vibrations in the earth plane; found in places not ordinarily felt to emit sound or found vibrating from the atmosphere in areas where life is running smoothly; theory: everything in the universe emits a sound that one can tune into clairaudiently and this inaudible sound has an effect on an individual's invisible bodies; objective of life is to play chords soothing to the invisible bodies and inaudible ear by co-creating a good life style. [**cf.** BACKGROUND FILL, MOLECULAR CHORUS]

SONIFEROUS ETHER—primeval substance; atoms in space subject to the laws of creation, vibration, and polarity. **Syn.** SPIRIT, PRANA, AKASA. [**cf.** LAW OF VIBRATION Appendix 7, POLARITY]

SONS OF GOD—(Hinduism) soul-minds in the highest structure of EVOLUTION, vibrating extremely fast; more progressed than the human being kingdom but still connected to this earth; serve as an opening for mankind to evolve to this kingdom. [**cf.** LORDS OF MIND, LORDHOOD]

SONS OF THE SUN—1. (Egypt) an INITIATE after he or she graduates from an INITIANT; 2. one who is reborn or has a complete change of CONSCIOUSNESS and reaches a higher plateau in one INCARNATION. [**cf.** LAW OF THE PATH Appendix 7]

SOOTHSAYER—(A.D.) a psychic who specializes in PROPHECY and DREAM INTERPRETATION; see PSYCHIC. **Sim.** SINGER, VILLAGE WISE-WOMAN, FOREKNOWER.

SOR—(Latin) a PSYCHIC noted for general counseling and prophesying using the SORS tablets. [**cf.** SORTES SANCTORUM, CASTING OF LOTS, LOTS]

SORCERER—1. (Native American) a male PSYCHIC who has served for many years as an apprentice to an established sorcerer in order to learn BODY CONTROL, ATMOSPHERE CONTROL, physical phenomena, and to receive mental psychic information; capable of feats beyond the average psychic; serves his tribe or mankind in healing and counseling. **Syn.** SHAMAN. 2. (ancient Rome) one who used his psychic abilities for both GOOD and EVIL; female is **sorceress**.

SORCERY—1. meaning depends upon the culture and time period; 1. PSYCHISM used for EVIL only; 2. psychism used for both GOOD and EVIL; 3. psychism used for only good.

SORROWLESS LAND—(esoteric) a faster vibrational frequency in the etheric world representing the higher realms where one finds peace and tranquility. [**cf.** SIXTH PLANE, FIFTH PLANE]

SORS—(Greece, Rome) special tablets or discs containing inscriptions of human conditions and how to improve upon them; used for those who needed counseling in a system of CASTING OF LOTS. [**cf.** SORTES SANCTORUM, I CHING, LOTS, SYNCHRONICITY, RADIESTHESIA]

SORTES—(Latin *serere*, "to string") a string of discs with each disc containing an inscription pertaining to conditions which man must go through and suggestions as to how to improve these conditions; used to counsel persons in a type of CASTING OF LOTS. **Sim.** SORS. [**cf.** LOTS, I CHING, SYNCHRONICITY]

SORTES SANCTORUM—(Christianity) to fnd an answer to one's problem by blindly opening the Bible and, with eyes still closed, use a pin to prick a verse on the page; that verse pertains to the answer. [**cf.** I CHING, RADIESTHESIA]

SORTILEGE—(ancient) a method of foretelling the future by drawing lots. [**cf.** MING STICKS, READINESS WAVE]

SOTHIC CYCLE—(ancient Egypt) a period of 1,460 years, based on the relationship of Sirius (the Dog Star) and the sun.

SOTHIC YEAR—(ancient Egypt) a 365¼-day cycle determined by the rising of Sirius (the Dog Star) coincident with the sun; this fixes our calendar year of 365¼ days. [**cf.** LUNAR CYCLE, UNIVERSAL LIFE CYCLE]

SOTO SCHOOL—(Zen) a building used for MEDITATION specializing in "sitting with a single mind" or "sitting just to sit." [**cf.** MEDITATION Appendix 5]

SOUL—1. (esoteric) the condensed INTELLIGENCE in every ATOM (electron) which is conscious of its intelligence, has knowledge of its function, has knowledge of TOTALITY in its entirety, and has the capacity to remember all the frequencies it has vibrated in; this intelligence in every atom is accompanied with SPIRIT (or the law of vibration) that gives it energy to use its intelligence; see ATOM; 2. the principle *in* life and the principle *of* life; the intelligence of Totality expressing itself; 3. an essence manifesting at a very fast rate of vibration as ELECTRICITY and MAGNETISM functioning under the LAW OF POLARITY making everything in the COSMOS one structure, one grandeur, one exalted intelligence; see GREAT SOUL, DIVINE INTELLIGENCE, UNIVERSAL MIND; 4. (Siri Bletzer) synonymous with CELL from which life began; 5.

(protean term) each person or thing has its own idea and assumes this character 6. (Baba Ram Dass) everything is living (vibrating), whether animate or inanimate, and owns intelligence, and this intelligence (SOUL) gives the instructions to make and hold and sustain that formation, acting like a pattern; acts like a DNA code, a set of predisposing factors which affect how each individual pattern relates to all the rest; the pattern is a soul and it separates from the rest and has a unique set of predisposing characteristics and becomes a structure in the ETHERIC WORLD; see MONAD; 7. (AMORC) the invisible LIFE FORCE of existence found in every living thing, containing the knowledge of instinct, automation, dividing and pro-creating, and other INVOLUNTARY FUNCTIONS; the quality of every living thing is "living" and "expressing" and the soul is the energizer of this in the organism; there is only one soul and part of it is in every human being; 8. (Allan Kardec) the soul acts through the intermediary of the organism's organs, whose organs are animated by the cosmic VITAL FLUID which is distributed among them, according to the soul; 9. for human soul see SOUL-MIND. [cf. POLARITY, LAW OF POLARITY and LAW OF VIBRATION Appendix 7, MEMORY CONSCIOUSNESS, ATOM, SPIRIT]

SOUL BODY—see ASTRAL BODY.

SOUL BROTHERHOOD—(ancient Egypt) to mix the physical blood of two initiates in a formal RITUAL to form a bond of togetherness of friendship and responsibilities. [cf. INITIANT, INITIATE, CHELA]

SOUL CYCLES—a pattern of one's peak experiences and one's unpleasant experiences that comes from within, regardless of the mental mind's decisions; shows traces of influencing one's character. (Inconcl.) Syn. PERSONALITY CYCLE. [cf. LIFE GROWTH CYCLE, LIFE WAVE]

SOUL DEVELOPMENT—see LAW OF SOUL-MIND GROWTH Appendix 7]

SOUL ENERGY—see PSYCHIC ENERGY.

SOUL FLIGHT—see MENTAL PROJECTION.

SOUL JURY—(esoteric) a group of intelligent entities in the ETHERIC WORLD with a responsibility to plan the proper reincarnational entry for the SOUL-MIND when it is ready for rebirth on planet earth; they consider the necessary factors for the soul-mind to work out karmic actions and to further its

growth; i.e., the location of the planet, race, sex, sun sign, parents, physical attributes and disabilities, and economic conditions of the parents. [cf. KARMA]

SOUL OF THE UNIVERSE—(Gustav Stromberg, 1948) see VITAL LIFE FORCE.

SOUL PERSONALITY—1. see MONAD; 2. made from the total memory of the AKASHIC RECORDS; 3. (AMORC) "personality is Self, and Self is each man's own expression of God." Syn. INDIVIDUALITY, SELF, EGO. [cf. SOUL-MIND]

SOUL SCIENCE—the study of the human SOUL, the reason for its creation, and the relationship of an individual to his or her soul. [cf. SOUL-MIND, MONAD, SPIRIT]

SOUL SUBSTANCE—(esoteric) theory: if the SOUL-MIND is capable of certain functions, it must "exist" on some level of vibration even though it is invisible to the physical eye. [cf. BODIES OF MAN, MENTAL BODY]

SOUL TRAVEL—to travel from one plane to another plane in the etheric world in mind only (as opposed to ASTRAL PROJECTION); to learn from the masters at each level in a subjective experience; a mind expansion experience; (do not confuse with BLISSING OUT). Syn. MENTAL PROJECTION. [cf. THE CHARIOT, EXALTED THRONE]

SOUL'S FIELD OF KNOWLEDGE AND TRUTH—to tune into total universal knowledge through the SUPERCONSCIOUS MIND, keeping the SUBCONSCIOUS MIND and MENTAL MIND passive. [cf. INSPIRATIONAL THOUGHT Appendix 2]

SOUL-ACTION—a human being's performance that comes from his or her subconscious mind, gut feelings, and emotions, instead of current, logical opinion. [cf. CLAIRSENTIENCE Appendix 2, SPONTANEITY DISCIPLINE]

SOUL-COMPLEX—a subsconscious reaction to the memory of one's past lives in the SUBCONSCIOUS MIND, showing constantly in the daily activities, in preference to conscious mind logic. [cf. SUBJECTIVE MIND]

SOUL-MATES—two monads that have split from one monadic entity to go through evolvement capable of working as one unit of consciousness; each one is individualistic in itself, but complementary to the other; these monadic entities live in the earth plane, in the etheric world planes, on planets that are unlike ours, or in different places at the same time; unlikely these monads will make physical contact as this would defeat their purpose. **Syn.** TWIN SOUL. [**cf.** GROUP SOUL]

SOUL-MEMORY—see AKASHIC RECORDS.

SOUL-MIND—coined by June Bletzer; pertains to the HUMAN BEING KINGDOM only; (esoteric) 1. (Greek *soul* derived from *sol* meaning "sun") function of the SOUL-MIND of an individual is parallel to the sun's functions to the earth making a human being a miniature SOLAR SYSTEM; *mind* signifying the vastness and completeness of INTELLIGENCE within the soul; 2. an invisible ethereal substance in a faster vibrational frequency than the physical body; congregates around the human being seed constantly; changes and grows, furnishing various bodies for this seed to help it fulfill its potential; the soul-mind is a manifestation of the human being seed, responsible to the seed, and the seed in turn is in charge of the soul-mind; e.g., a daisy has a seed potential to be a beautiful daisy, an elephant has a seed potential to be a great elephant; a human being has a seed potential to be a perfect human being with complete knowledge and understanding. [**cf.** MONAD, EGO, PERSONALITY, EVOLUTIONARY MAN] 3. a higher dimensional frequency in relation to the physical body; this invisible frequency is concerned with the management and direction of the body; 4. a mechanism to record the sum total of a person's experiences throughout his or her incarnations, forming his or her physical bodies and lifestyles for the planet from these recordings; known as the MEMORY BANK (akashic record), 5. a permanent intellect; the consciousness that composes a person's character or individuality that never dies. **Syn.** SUBSCONSCIOUS MIND. 6. an ethereal computer for each individual; unable to make decisions; takes information from the CONSCIOUS MIND as it is given; accepts the concepts, suggestions, ideas, and emotional evaluations as the conscious mind drops this into it and neatly organizes it in compartments, **Syn.** BIOCOMPUTER. [**cf.** SOFTWARE]; 7. "energizer" of the conscious mind; acts as the motivating factor behind the brain consciousness to sustain and improve the physical body and lifestyle of the individual for the duration of the incarnation. [**cf.** BRAIN, SUBCONSCIOUS MIND] 8. (Seth) soul (mind) is a portion of the whole self; a psychological structure composed of characters belonging to the personality as a whole, organized together to form a surface iden-

tity; changes as the conscious mind feeds it, receding some traits and adapting to some; 9. (Albert Einstein) a human's soul is an electromagnetic force which holds together the protoplasmic energy that existed in the body prior to death; the human soul is an exact but invisible duplicate of the living body in the astral world; 10. (Theosophy) the domains of consciousness that compose a person's immortal selfhood, having three regions: MANAS, BUDDHI, ATMA; 11. (Allan Kardec) a moral being, distinct, independent of matter, preserving its individuality after death; a soul-mind is a cause, not an effect; 12. (Plato) consists of four faculties: reason, UNDERSTANDING, FAITH, perception; 13. (Carl Jung) consists of four faculties: THINKING, SENSATION, feeling, and INTUITION; 14. (Levi) always was and has no ending; a thought of God, just as a seed of earth holds all the attributes of the seed, the soul holds all the attributes of God; 15. some philosophies use *spirit* synonymously with *soul-mind*. [**cf.** SOL, MONADOLOGY, SPIRIT, SOUL, INDIVIDUALITY, LAW OF SOUL-MIND Appendix 7]

SOUL-MIND AURA—a BIPOLAR, electromagnetic force field surrounding the whole of a man or woman, emanating the different amps of ELECTRICITY from the body; functions as a pattern from which the human body is made, changing gradually as one's SOUL-MIND evolves; can be perceived clairvoyantly as a silvery phosphorescent mist, or as a pattern full of color; designates the individual's overall health, character, past, and future; the outer rim of the ETHERIC DOUBLE. **Syn.** BIOENERGY, AURIC AUREOLA, AURIC EGG, MATRIX, FUNCTIONAL BODY, FLUIDIC BODY, HUMAN AURA, MOULD, SAHU; (do not confuse with the MENTAL AURA that surrounds only the head area). [**cf.** KIRLIAN PHOTOGRAPHY, BODY POLARITY]

SOUL-MIND BREATH—(esoteric) a process of breathing "within," through the VAGUS NERVE, without the use of the lungs; happens involuntarily when in a very relaxed state; can be controlled voluntarily by the CONSCIOUS MIND; used by the YOGA skill of survival after being buried alive underground and left for days. [**cf.** BREATHING, BODY CONTROL]

SOUL-MIND CYCLE—(cycles) an innate influence on the personality and character of a human being in seven distinct periods in one solar year; found by beginning with the spring equinox, March 22, and charted similarly to ASTROLOGY; each period has two natures, the first half of the period produces

575

slightly different effects from the last half. (Inconcl.) [cf. LIFE WAVE, LAW OF CYCLES Appendix 7]

SOUL-MIND KEY NOTE—the sound or key of music that makes the whole chord of an EARTHLING and is as unique as his or her fingerprints; can be heard clairaudiently; each body has its own chord of music that blends in with the plane it inhabits; changes with each INCARNATION according to the change in the SOUL-MIND. [cf. RESONANCE, ENVIRONMENTAL NOISE, KEY NOTE]

SOUL-MIND MEMORY BANK—see AKASHIC RECORDS.

SOUL-RAPPORT TELEPATHY—to psychically sense the real meaning of the noises of nature; to perceive the feelings and intentions of animals; to forecast the weather and to sense grumblings of the earth, such as earthquakes and volcanic eruptions. [cf. LAW OF TRANSFER OF ENERGY PRINCIPLE Appendix 7, CLAIREMPATHY, SUPER-ESP]

SOUL-SPLITTING—(Eskimo) theory: a deceased person's soul can split and come into one or more incarnations simultaneously. **Sim.** SOUL-MATES. [cf. SUBCONSCIOUS MIND, SOUL-MIND]

SOULLESS PSYCHISM—(esoteric) ENERGY FIELDS that have a resemblance to a HUMAN BEING and enough intelligence to do human activity, giving an impression that they are activated by their own SOUL-MIND but actually have none; can exist and function in the ETHERIC WORLD, can exist and function in the MUNDANE WORLD, and exist in the etheric world but function in the mundane world; generated and directed psychically by a living person or by the leftover intelligence in the cells of the physical or astral shell (FAIRIES have no soul-mind but enough material has been written about them to warrant their own category). [cf. SOULLESS PSYCHISM Appendix 2]

SOUND—(esoteric) noise varying in tone, quality, pitch, and rhythm which fills the entire space of the universes; this noise is emitted from every object, animate or inanimate, according to its vibrational frequency; can be heard audibly or clairaudiently; sound radiates throughout all of TOTALITY making shapes, forms, and color, and organizes a uniformity of form, color, and density according to its proportions. [cf. SOUNDS-WITH-POWER, THRESHOLD OF HEARING, COSMIC MUSIC]

SOUND CURRENT—harmonious COSMIC MUSIC which connects each individual to the COSMOS;

enters the head and registers in the THIRD-EYE AREA on the same mechanism that makes one hear audible sounds; can be perceived clairaudiently. [cf. PINEAL GLAND, PITUITARY GLAND]

SOUND ETHER—the third level of VIBRATIONAL FREQUENCIES throughout all TOTALITY; level of the atmosphere wherein sound is perceived clairaudiently or audible; see CHEMICAL ETHER. [cf. VIBRATIONS, ETHERIC WORLD]

SOUND HEALING—to use a combination of LIGHT and SOUND working together in therapy of emotional problems and opening of BLOCKS in the body; creates energies which can harmonize many inner centers of the body having a different frequency; performed by a beam of light from a slide projector that focuses on the body with sounds or music being played at the same time. (Inconcl.) [cf. CHROMOTHERAPY, CURATIVE MEDICINE, HOLISTIC HEALTH]

SOUND KASINA—(Yoga) a technique that immerses one in a particular SOUND, then recalls the sound to mind and holds it in the mind in order to swamp out all other sound. [cf. WHITE NOISE, NADAM]

SOUND PLATE—a brass or plate glass disc with sand scattered over the surface which forms various patterns when plate is struck on the edge with a stick.

SOUNDS OF THE FOUR ELEMENTS—(Tibet) the psychic noise heard in the SIDPA BARDO in the afterlife (see EARTH, AIR, WATER, FIRE). **Sim.** AWE-INSPIRING SOUNDS. [cf. SEEDS OF SOUND, ULTRA-SONICS]

SOUNDS-WITH-POWER—to use specific auditory noises, music, sounds, tones, or rhythmic sounds to influence or change the vibrational frequency of a person or object; 1. accelerates one's psychic skills, increases healing abilities, brings attitudinal changes in emotions, and gives the ETHERIC WORLD INTELLIGENCES energy to work with; 2. research shows coherence and harmony in brainwave patterns from certain sounds, suggesting the two BRAIN HEMISPHERES are synchronizing; the older brain structure surfaces to mingle with the new music and this synchrony changes nerve cells, permitting physical healings, psychic experiences, and inflow of higher intelligence; 3. SOUND exercises a potent and immediate effect on many persons because the right music, pitch, and rhythm causes a temporary vibratory awakening of his or her occult spinal centers; at this moment, a dim memory of his or her divine origin comes to them and he or she is fed by the SUPERCONSCIOUS MIND or SUBCONSCIOUS MIND; e.g., the Native Americans developed effective sound rituals to control wind and rain; 4. Hindu music is a subjective, spiritual, and individualistic art aiming at personal harmony with the OVERSOUL; chants, gongs, bells, singing of the Psalms, hymns, drums, and unison PRAYER have their planned effect within a ceremony when used. [**cf.** SOUNDS-WITH-POWER Appendix 2]

SOUNDSITIVE—coined by Stephen Halpern; a person who is very sensitive to sound; usually an inborn talent.

SOURCE—(capitalized) see TOTALITY.

SOURCIER—(France) see DIVINER and DOWSER.

SPACE—(esoteric) 1. CONSCIOUS OF BEING spread out into INFINITY, full of invisible intelligence and energy, subject to the direction of THOUGHT; space stretches out and is full of places; space curves. (Inconcl.) 2. a primordial energy field from which matter is derived; a fifth-dimensional structure of hidden life being used by mankind for third-dimensional life. is not measurable when perceived in the THIRD DIMENSION; 3. a place to move about in, to think, to feel, and to find others of like nature; 4. (ufology) vibrating PRIMORDIAL SUBSTANCE with life throughout its entirety under the LAW OF INTELLIGENCES (see Appendix 7); 5. lack of EMPTINESS; 6. the VOID. **Sim.** TOTALITY, COSMOS, CREATIVE INTELLIGENCE, MONADIC WORLD. [**cf.** VIBRATIONS, ATOMS]

SPACE ANIMALS—(ufology) foreign objects in various sizes, shapes, and colors, using outer space as their home; pulsating life that appears and acts more like animals than humans; invisible to the physical eye but have been photographed by infrared camera exposures; some appear pleasant and some appear revolting. **Syn.** EXTRATERRESTRIAL ANIMALS, AEROFORMS. [**cf.** DEVIL-LIKE GOBLIN, PLASMATIC FAUNA]

SPACE BROTHERS—EXTRATERRESTRIAL soul-minds that come through mediumistic circles to bring guidance regarding the future of earth and disclose information regarding themselves; hide in the clouds to observe humanity. [**cf.** ELECTRONIC VOICES, SHIPS-FROM-OTHER-PLANETS]

SPACE BUBBLE—an area of energy around a human being, discovered by scientists in 1974; because of its different densities, it was divided into groupings: INTIMATE ZONE, personal zone, public zone, and social zone. [**cf.** SEVEN PRINCIPLES OF MAN, REALM OF ILLUSION, MENTAL BODY]

SPACE CONTINUUM—(ufology) an extended atmospheric intelligence who is individualized, but also a part of the whole. (Inconcl.) [**cf.** AEROFORMS, SPACE CRITTERS, MENTAL INTERCHANGE]

SPACE INTELLIGENCE—(Uri Geller) an energy with some degree of intelligence comparable to a human being rather than an animal; lives somewhere in the atmosphere. **Syn.** ETHEREAN BEINGS. [**cf.** DISC OCCUPANTS, ETHERIAN PHYSICS]

SPACE-BEING—(ufology) an intelligent energy field, comparable to an intelligent human being, capable of manipulating spacecraft; theories: 1. has its existence in outer space, capable of wearing a denser body when desirous of being seen by earthlings; 2. has its existence on another planet that is third-dimensional like ours; believed that they come to either help earthlings or to investigate earth's type of life. (Inconcl.) **Syn.** ETHEREANS. [**cf.** MUTATION OF ENERGY]

SPACE-BEING TRAVEL—(ufology) one theory: construct or vehicle made of congealed light which can be teleported through space from planet to planet in both invisible form and third-dimensional form; does an intelligence have the skill to make this construct shift dimensions or is the construct the intelligence? (Inconcl.) [**cf.** MUTATION OF ENERGY, CONSTRUCTS]

SPACE-TIME CONTINUA—mankind's CONSCIOUSNESS constructing an orderly vibrating universe into INFINITY. [**cf.** TIME FRAMEWORK, TIME FLOW]

SPACE-TRAVEL—(mental psychism) to perceive what is happening away from the area one is in, through CLAIRVOYANCE or CLAIRSENTIENCE. **Sim.** CLAIRVOYANCE IN SPACE. [**cf.** REMOTE VIEWING]

SPACE/TIME THEORIES—(future science, esoteric) 1. a product of CONSCIOUSNESS, held in consciousness, and divided into two categories to study and better understand this product; because the physical body flows and grows, mankind has a sense of dimension they call TIME, and another sense of existence they call SPACE, both unique to ths plane; space/time has an essence in consciousness only, made by mankind to be compatible with their body

577

design; space and time have their vibrational rate co-created in the mental activity of humanity, and have meaning in the mind only; **2.** space/time is not in the brain but read out of it; space/time is a place or region where the two blend together and have the characteristic of fluidity, and is able to be shaped to desire (varying in degrees according to the ability of the individual); **3.** physical-mundane-clock-time made by humanity for their convenience; **4.** the UNIVERSE as a four-dimensional continuum of length, breadth, depth, and time; **5.** (Albert Einstein) "space/time exists only in accordance with the weight and size of the object concerned, and the distance from which a viewpoint can be taken"; **6.** (Seth) "a plane of existence having mental and psychic events"; **7.** time is a dimension-space equal to life; *space* and *time* are synonymous. (Inconcl.) [**cf.** TIME Appendix 5]

SPACIOUS PRESENT—theory: past, present, and future happen at the same time; (Seth) "basic time in which the whole exists." **Sim.** MULTIDIMEN-SIONAL, SIMULTANEOUS TIME. [**cf.** TIME Appendix 5]

SPAGYRIC—coined by Theophrastus Paracelsus; **1.** (alchemy) the art of separating and combining atoms in the correct way in order to change their form. **Sim.** ELIXIR OF LIFE. **2.** the ALCHEMIST. [**cf.** ALCHEMY, MAGNUM OPUS, LIVE SILVER]

SPATIAL CLAIRVOYANCE—to perceive a vision in front of oneself, out in space, instead of within the head. **Syn.** OBJECTIVE CLAIRVOYANCE. [**cf.** SUBJEC-TIVE CLAIRVOYANCE, CLAIRVOYANCE-IN-SPACE]

SPATIALIZE TIME—(P. D. Ouspensky) "succession is an illusion attributed to man's dimensional infer-iority; the flux associated with phenomenal time is actually an incomplete sensation of higher space in which man is embedded. [**cf.** TIME Appendix 5]

SPEAKERS—"teaching personalities" who reach across the centuries; highly active personalities who teach throughout all aspects of existence; i.e., physical or nonphysical, waking or sleeping, in between lives, and on other levels of existence in the etheric world.

SPEAKING MEDIUM—one who talks while under the influence of the ETHERIC WORLD INTELLI-GENCES, through inspirational impressions, in a conscious state instead of in a TRANCE state. [**cf.** INSPIRATIONAL THOUGHT, DIRECT VOICE]

SPEAKING STONE—(early Christian) a stone that had psychic properties and could answer questions in an audible sound owned by Eusebius, a historian; the reply came in a high-pitched whistle-like voice or in a clear small voice; whether an ETHERIC WORLD INTELLIGENCE was using the stone as a voice amplifier or the intelligence in the stone was speaking, was not determined. [**cf.** MINPSI Appendix 2, MANDRAKE, GOD-IN-THE-STONE]

SPEAKING-IN-TONGUES—see TALKING-IN-TONGUES.

SPECIFIC NEGATIVES—(rebirthing) inherited and cultural ideas or principles that are imbedded in one's belief system and manifest as punishment to one's self; these ideas or principles have never been intelligently reasoned out and are reinforced with one's INNER-DIALOGUE and conscious thought; they are not true to mankind's real nature; e.g., "There is never enough time," "I have no right to this. . . ."; these can be surfaced in REBIRTHING, dealt with and dissolved so one will express his or her full potential. [**cf.** UNDERSIDE OF EXPERI-ENCES, LONELINESS]

SPECTER—a white, cloudy substance that appears similar to a human form; perceived clairvoyantly; a spontaneous experience; see GHOST; also spelled **spectre**.

SPECTRAL FLAMES—lights seen around churches and cemeteries; believed to be discarnate entities. [**cf.** GHOSTS, ASTRAL SHELLS, CONFUSED SOUL-MINDS]

SPECTRUM—a band of light waves that comprises a rainbow of colors when passed through a prism; seven colors (RED, ORANGE, YELLOW, GREEN, BLUE, INDIGO, VIOLET) seen with the physical eye, coming from the planetary rays. [**cf.** KILNER GOGGLES, WHITE, ULTRAVIOLET]

SPECULARII—(sixteenth century) see SCRYER.

SPECULATIVE ALCHEMY—to use the operative tools and formulas of the ALCHEMIST, with the laws of nature, to elevate the consciousness of humanity to a higher vibratory body. [**cf.** ALCHEMICAL PRIN-CIPLES, GLORIFIED BODY]

SPECULATIVE-METAPHYSICAL THEORY—states that the universe is a strong complex in an orderly and recurring theme, influenced and directed by subjective thought; (Yoga) the world is mindstuff; (Elmer Green) "Everything is crystallized thought." [**cf.** LAW OF THOUGHT Appendix 7]

SPECULUM—any light-reflecting, shining surface such as, black ink, stainless steel, a pond which can be used to focus one's attention for SCRYING. **Syn.** CRYSTAL BALL. [**cf.** CRYSTAL BALL GAZING]

SPEED OF THOUGHT—mode of travel in the ETHERIC WORLD; to think a thought bearing a locale puts one there instantaneously; this can be compared to an earthling uttering a sound and it being heard. [**cf.** ETHERIC WORLD, SPACE/TIME THEORIES]

SPELL—1. a period of time during which a person or object is held captive by a PSYCHIC for the benefit of the psychic (usually for EVIL intent); one person can stimulate another person's brain while the victim is in the ALPHA STATE OF CONSCIOUSNESS; accomplished by thought transference accompanied by such strong emotion that the resistance of the nerve gap is reduced and the ACETYLCHOLINE is undissolved; this breaks down one's resistance to another's message; emotion transferred is either extremely fearful or extremely pleasurable; in spelling, the eye-stare and emotionally planned ploy from one person puts another in the alpha state for susceptibility; period of spell can last through one encounter of twenty minutes to half a day or for many days; 2. a word, words, music, or a chant designed to have a dominating or irresistible influence over another individual; i.e., incantations, complimentary ploy. Usage: the spell of fine music. 3. to spell; to use one's eyes to stare at another individual, animal, or object for a period of time; energy is thus beamed from the eyes in an icy, destructive, fearful stare or in a pleasurable, enticing, lovable stare; either stare deprives the victim of the power of resistance; see CASTING A SPELL. [**cf.** GLAMOURED, FASCINATION, HEX, PSYCHIC HEALING, AMULET, EVIL EYE, MAGNETISM, CASTING A SPELL Appendix 2]

SPELLBOUND—to be limited as to one's freedom of mobility and thought; to be under the control of another individual to a certain degree for a designated period of time; begins with a "can't move" experience for a short time, even though the CONSCIOUS MIND is intellectually telling one's self to move; one encounters sociably with the psychic SPELLER and is "fixed on the spot" while being programmed as to length of time and extent of manipulation; victim stays under the speller's control until released, experiencing feelings and performing acts that cannot be accounted for by personal effort; speller has a super amount of PSYCHIC ENERGY beaming from his or her eyes that temporarily paralyzes the victim; with knowledge of this power one can use it for GOOD or EVIL; see CASTING A SPELL. [**cf.** LAW OF ASSOCIATION and LAW OF QUANTUM CONNECTION Appendix 7, GLAMOUR, EVIL EYE, TRANSFIXED]

SPELLED—see SPELLBOUND.

SPELLER—one who has superpowerful PSYCHIC ENERGY emanating from his or her whole body (especially the eyes), and who uses this psychic energy to cast spells. [**cf.** CASTING A SPELL, FASCINATOR]

SPHERES—(esoteric) various levels of energy in the ETHERIC WORLD formed by universal states of consciousness; each level is inhabited with soul-minds who have made their TRANSITION; see PLANES. **Sim.** DIMENSIONS, PLATEAUS, MANSIONS.

SPHERES OF RESONANCE—sound is a vibration and the function of sound is to be harmonious chords that form matter vibrating at different frequencies; all vibrations have a sound level, from the ELECTRON to the SOLAR SYSTEM, individually and collectively in their unit; one's cells, body systems, and body as a whole carry different levels of sound; can be heard clairaudiently or with special machinery. [**cf.** CELESTIAL CHORUSES, DEEPAKA RAGA, DISTORTED MUSIC, HARMONY OF THE UNIVERSE]

SPHEROIDS—(ufology) a mass seen in outer space; resembles a disc but is incomplete as to actual form. [**cf.** AEROFORMS, SPACE CRITTERS, RADAR ANGELS, FLYING SAUCERS]

SPHOTA—(Vedanta) an unexpected sound or idea impressed upon the mind spontaneously, which appears to be an answer to a prayer and the mind bursts open like a blossom; e.g., the last line of a poem which one had been struggling with, occurring at the breakfast table; a missing link in a formula occurring while taking a shower; or a healing occurring for no obvious reason. [**cf.** BLESS, CLICK]

SPIKE—(biofeedback training) a long, pointed mark on the graph of an EEG READOUT which records ten brain wave cycles per second; indicates that the subject HOOKED-UP is in a calm, relaxed state of consciousness; this amplitude frequency often produces psychic experiences, whether the subject is psychic or not. [**cf.** BETA STATE OF CONSCIOUSNESS, DELTA STATE OF CONSCIOUSNESS]

SPIN WAVES—(Akeezer) the energy given out from a MEDIUM during psychic work, as opposed to the static waves that do not move. [cf. PHYSICAL PSYCHIC PROCESSES]

SPINAL CONSCIOUSNESS—the awareness of the lower animals that comes from COSMIC CONSCIOUSNESS and gives them the intuitive direction to protect and feed themselves to be able to exist on the planet. **Sim.** INSTINCT CONSCIOUSNESS. [cf. SIMPLE CONSCIOUSNESS, PRIMAL PERCEPTION, ANPSI]

SPINAL GATE—(acupuncture) the substantia gelatinosa in the body that acts like a door through which pain signals must pass before being received in the brain; there are ACUPUNCTURE POINTS that can be stimulated to close this door and block out pain. [cf. ACUPUNCTURE Appendix 5]

SPINNING OF THE WEB—Western symbology for universal life; LAW OF THE WHEEL and WHEEL OF THE LAW. **Syn.** TAROTA, TARO-ROTA. [cf. REINCARNATION, CHAIN OF GLOBES]

SPINNING THE 'SAS'—see COSCINOMANCY Appendix 6]

SPIRAL DROP—(astral projection) the ASTRAL BODY spinning out of balance in the interiorization process as it resists gravity and withdraws into the physical body. [cf. SLOW-VIBRATING DROP, PERCUSSION, INTERIORIZING]

SPIRILLA—(esoteric) a coil (spiral) of ethereal energy which acts like an antenna, located at the tip of the PINEAL GLAND; receives COSMIC ENERGY and transforms it into electrical energy to be used by the brain; a part of the THIRD-EYE AREA; man perceives it in the brain as PSYCHIC INFORMATION, and sends it along the KUNDALINI to be felt by the body as INTUITION or BODY-FEELINGS; man has seven spirilla and, at this time, four are developed; singular **spirillae**. [cf. PITUITRIN]

SPIRIT—a collective word, but the basic theme is always "indestructible life"; **1.** the function of activity; both its cause and effect occurring simultaneously; **(a)** (capitalized) the *one* and *only* energy, absolute and neutral, broken up and distributed throughout the universe; "the energy of the universe" making movements, activities, and VIBRATIONAL FREQUENCIES; that which keeps the ATOM moving; works harmoniously with the atom's INTELLIGENCE; **(b)** (uncapitalized when speaking of its distribution) found everywhere, in inanimate things and in the NERVOUS SYSTEM of organisms; found in the human bloodstream and nervous system and considered an absolute necessity for life; i.e., (Bible) "it is the spirit that giveth life"; born *into* life, it is not life; the principle that vivifies matter. (Inconcl.) **Syn.** PRANA, ORGONE ENERGY, QI, BIOCOSMIC ENERGY. [cf. VITAL LIFE FORCE] **2.** (capitalized) (psychism) **(a)** movement of PSYCHIC ENERGY which can be perceived by earthlings in many types of psychic skills; knowledge or information that was not logically reasoned out, or gathered from past education or life experiences; perceived through intuition; an inward intuitive direction guiding an individual through life; **(b)** used as a normal PSYCHIC HEALING method, employing rhythmic breathing. [cf. MAGNETIC HEALING, GAUSS MAGNETICS] **(c)** enters through the SUPERCONSCIOUS MIND, SUBCONSCIOUS MIND, or ETHERIC WORLD INTELLIGENCES as psychic energy. **Syn.** (Bible) HOLY SPIRIT, SPIRIT OF THE LORD and SPIRIT. [cf. Appendix 4 SPIRIT for clarification] **3.** (uncapitalized) represents that essence of the individual that never dies; interchangeable for SOUL in religious philosophies; used loosely (because of lack of information) to designate any etheric world entity when it makes itself known to a PSYCHIC; i.e., GUIDE, GHOST, MASTER, EARTHBOUND ENTITIES. [cf. MEDIUMSHIP, ANGEL, SOUL-MIND] **4.** subjected to the thinking mechanism in individuals; can be controlled, stored, and moved under his or her direction. [cf. SYMPATHETIC NERVOUS SYSTEM] **5.** (Huna) a part of the mind divided into three spirits: conscious, subconscious, and superconscious; handles and manufactures the vital force. [cf. UNIHIPIPI, UHANE] **6.** (Tibet) the subconscious mind; **7.** (Native American) an intelligence in every natural object which can be contacted and communicated with; **8.** (Allan Kardec) intelligent principle outside matter, composed of soul and PERISPRIT; **9.** (E. Arthur Winkler) because Spirit is the energy of the universe, it is good and correct to say "Spirit of Christmas" and "Spirit of Thanksgiving."

SPIRIT AGENCY—see .GUIDE.

SPIRIT ARTISTS—(precipitation) ETHERIC WORLD INTELLIGENCES who work on physical canvas without physical brushes or paint, and who paint portraits or scenes of people both living and deceased; they use the energy of the MEDIUM while the medium is sleeping or in a TRANCE state; e.g., May and Lizzie Bangs left the canvas in their bedroom, and the helpers worked while they slept, leaving beautiful paintings which were discovered in the morning. [cf. PRECIPITATION PAINTING]

SPIRIT BAND—see INNER BAND.

SPIRIT BEING—1. used loosely; anyone residing in the ETHERIC WORLD, whether it is a discarnate being, an earthbound entity, or a medium's helper; 2. an ETHERIC WORLD INTELLIGENCE who communicates pyschically with a MEDIUM. **Syn.** SPIRIT. [cf. GUIDE, DISCARNATE ENTITY, EARTHBOUND ENTITIES]

SPIRIT COMMUNICATION—the transference of information back and forth between a mediumistic psychic and an etheric world intelligence; see ETHERIC WORLD COMMUNICATION. [cf. MEDIUM, GUIDE, SPIRIT (Definition 2), BEYOND PERSONAL CONSCIOUSNESS]

SPIRIT CONTROL—1. a personal ETHERIC WORLD INTELLIGENCE with high qualitative characteristics who has earned the right to work with a MEDIUM in physical phenomena. [cf. TRANCE, VOICE TRANCE] 2. one of the etheric world intelligences who exist in the .INNER BAND of an individual and who has charge of screening out inferior entities and information during mental or physical psychic work. **Syn.** JOY GUIDE, DOORKEEPER. [cf. OUTER BAND, MASTER]

SPIRIT COUNCILS—(Spiritualism) meetings held in the higher realms of the ETHERIC WORLD to determine courses of missionary action in the EARTH PLANE; God works by delegation. [cf. WHITE BROTHERHOOD]

SPIRIT DRAPERY—1. (ectoplasm materialization) a cloth effect that covers and protects the unformed parts of a materializing person; used to satisfy the modesty of this person; drawn from the actual clothing of the MEDIUM in ectoplasmic substance; disintegrates rapidly in the air when the session is over. [cf. ECTOPLASM, ECTOPLASMIC HANDS, CABINET] 2. simple, flowing garment or robe worn by an ETHERIC WORLD INTELLIGENCE when clairvoyantly showing him or herself to the medium; the intelligence feels more graceful and comfortable in this simple attire as earth plane clothing has long ago been discarded; takes less energy to show him or herself in simple, plain clothing than in garments with collars, buttons, belts, trousers, shoes, etc., and this energy can be put to a more

practical use. [cf. GUIDE, MATERIALIZED PERSONALITY, SEANCE, INNER BAND]

SPIRIT GUARDIAN—an ETHERIC WORLD INTELLIGENCE who has chosen, as his or her function, to watch over the soul-minds in the ETHERIC WORLD of those who have passed over while still children and need special attention. [cf. DOCTOR TEACHER, CELESTIAL GUARDIAN]

SPIRIT GUIDANCE—collective word encompassing all the various kinds of help the ETHERIC WORLD INTELLIGENCES can do for earthlings, whether one is a MEDIUM or not.

SPIRIT GUIDE—see ETHERIC WORLD INTELLIGENCES.

SPIRIT HANDS—1. invisible hands in the SEANCE room or DARKROOM SESSIONS that perform movements as if they were like human hands; i.e., move material objects from one place to another; stroke a sitter's face, hair, or pant leg; belong to an ETHERIC WORLD INTELLIGENCE. [cf. PYSCHIC DEVELOPMENT CIRCLE] 2. a mass of ECTOPLASM materializing as human hands in a MATERIALIZATION seance, see ECTOPLASM HANDS. **Syn.** SEANCE HANDS. [cf. ECTOPLASM MATERIALIZATION FORMS]

SPIRIT HEALING—to use SPIRIT in the air via rhythmic breathing to change BODY CHEMISTRY: 1. healing performed by group; people form a circle, or a straight chain, by making body contact with each other and the patient, and breathe rhythmically in unison; hands are linked when circle formation is used; hands are on the shoulders of one another when straight chain is used; this unison breathing powerfully directs healing energy to the weakest spot in the patient without the patient telling or even knowing where the weak spot exists at that time; acts as a tool to normalize the body cells and allows the body to heal itself more quickly; happens gradually or instantaneously. (Inconcl.) 2. one-to-one healing: the PRACTITIONER puts right palm over diseased area, left palm turned upward, and breathes rhythmically; this tends to normalize the body cells so they can heal more quickly; (do not confuse with MENTAL HEALING, MAGNETIC HEALING, or MEDIUMSHIP HEALING). (Inconcl.) 3. loosely-used term: to be a channel for an ETHERIC WORLD INTELLIGENCE to work through in any type of SPIRITUAL HEALING, usually performed in a religious setting. [cf. CON-

GREGATIONAL HEALING, LAYING-ON-OF-HANDS, PRAYER BASKET, SPIRIT, BREATHING]

SPIRIT HYPOTHESIS—there are intelligences of some breed who abide in the ETHERIC WORLD, that desire to contact earthlings to bring them information, guidance, and a clearer understanding of who man is and why humanity exists on earth; these intelligences take time to learn SYNCHRONIZATION with earthlings for the purpose of communication. [**cf.** GUIDES, HUMAN BEING KINGDOM, ANGEL BEING KINDGOM]

SPIRIT LIGHTS—dancing globules or sparks of light filling the air in a SEANCE room or PSYCHIC DEVELOPMENT CIRCLE; indicate that etheric world entities are in the room, ready to bring help to psychic manifestations. **Syn.** STARS, SEANCE LIGHTS. [**cf.** PROXY SITTING, PSYCHIC BREEZES]

SPIRIT LOVER—an ETHERIC WORLD ENTITY who is proficient in having sexual intercourse with an earthling, causing a physical orgasm. **Sim.** INCUBUS, male; SUCCUBUS, female.

SPIRIT MEDIUM—(Philippines) a person who allows the etheric world intelligence to interpenetrate his or her body and use it as a channel for healing others, especially in PSYCHIC SURGERY. **Sim.** MEDIUMSHIP HEALING. [**cf.** PSYCHIC HEALING Appendix 2]

SPIRIT NOISES—sounds with peculiar characteristics heard in darkroom sessions or seances; usually obedient to those who ask; dry-blow, hollow, feeble, light, clear, distinct, and loud noises; change from place to place; repeated with mechanical regularity or occur hit-or-miss. [**cf.** PERCUSSION Appendix 2]

SPIRIT OF EARTH—(Ashanti, people of Ghana) a feminine NATURE SPIRIT whose function is to serve the earth, acting as a mother to all humanity. **Sim.** KINDLY ONE, TUTELARY FAIRY.

SPIRIT OF GOD—1. God's spirit body (if there is such) could be countless tissues of light, unbearably overwhelming to see or experience in an earthly state of EVOLUTION; inexhaustible BLISS; see TOTALITY; 2. see PSYCHIC ENERGY; 3. see VITAL LIFE FORCE.

SPIRIT PERSONALITY—see MATERIALIZATION PERSONALITY.

SPIRIT PHOTOGRAPH—a finished picture which shows the actual images photographed, plus faces, lights, words, or objects that were not visible to the naked eye when the picture was taken; called EXTRAS. [**cf.** PHYSICAL PHOTOGRAPHY, THOUGHTOGRAPHY]

SPIRIT PHOTOGRAPHY—to take a picture in a conventional manner, and find other things on that print that were not in the visible range of the naked eye when the picture was taken; etheric world intelligences transfer the objects, words, lights, or portraits of deceased persons onto the negative when taken: these are called EXTRAS; theory: intelligences use the energy from the MEDIUM to reflect it onto the negative; sometimes extras only appear on the photograph itself; medium usually develops his or her own film. (Inconcl.) [**cf.** PSYCHIC PHOTOGRAPHY]

SPIRIT PROTECTOR—an advanced soul-mind of a deceased Native American who has chosen to serve an earthling along with other soul-minds in an earthling's INNER-BAND for his or her present INCARNATION; helps to prevent accidents in the physical body if it is karmically permissible, or helps to lessen the seriousness of the accident if it must karmically happen; also works in the darkroom session in physical phenomena. **Syn.** INDIAN GUIDE. [**cf.** MONITOR]

SPIRIT RAPPING—(seance) to allow an ETHERIC WORLD INTELLIGENCE to intervene and use one's psychic energy to make noises in the SEANCE room for communicable purposes; noises sound like a knock on wooden furniture, or a knock between the walls, or like electrical snaps in the air; a code is established between both parties to answer questions; intelligence uses the ECTOPLASM of the MEDIUM and SITTERS for energy; room lighting can be bright, subdued, or blacked-out; occurs spontaneously or is willed; (do not confuse with CLAIRAUDIENCE in which only the psychic can perceive the sound). **Syn.** RAPPINGS. [**cf.** PERCUSSION Appendix 2]

SPIRIT SCIENCE—the study of the ETHERIC WORLD, its inhabitants, its functions, its properties, and its relationship to humanity. **Sim.** PSYCHISM, SECRET SCIENCE, PARAPSYCHOLOGY, MYSTICISM.

SPIRIT SPECTATOR—an ETHERIC WORLD ENTITY in a vacant chair at an assembly in church or at a lecture; invisible, except to clairvoyants. [**cf.** GUIDE, ETHERIC WORLD INTELLIGENCES]

SPIRIT SPHERES—see PLANES and ETHERIC WORLD.

582

SPIRIT TEACHER—a special ETHERIC WORLD IN-TELLIGENCE who works psychically with an earthling upon request of the earthling; brings guidance, information, and instructions to further the earthling's evolution. **Syn.** DOCTOR TEACHER, ANGEL, TUTELARY DEITY, VIBRATORY INTELLIGENCE, SECRET CHIEF, MANITOU.

SPIRIT TORMENTOR—a discarnate entity in the etheric world who is earthbound and, because he or she desires to be back on earth, attaches him or herself to an earthling; is capable of influencing an earthling's behavior if the earthling is in a low emotional state, is a negative thinker, or has the particular habit the tormentor desires to reexperience. **Syn.** HAUNTER. [**cf.** EARTHBOUND ENTITIES, CONFUSED SOUL-MIND, HAUNTING, LAW OF LIKE ATTRACTS LIKE Appendix 7]

SPIRIT WORLD—see ETHERIC WORLD.

SPIRIT-OBJECT INFLUENCE—the use of a material object by an ETHERIC WORLD INTELLIGENCE to bring influences to earthlings in a helpful or harmful manner; whether the intelligence attaches his or her energies to the object in order to amplify them or whether the PSYCHIC ENERGY from the MEDIUM is captured and held in the object has not been disclosed; e.g., Dr. George M. Lamsa owned a glass that, when filled with water, would speak audible intelligent guidance and helpful instructions to him. [**cf.** CONFUSED SOUL-MIND, AMULETS, POSSESSION]

SPIRITISM—(France) an early form of SPIRITUALISM taught by Allan Kardec; doctrine: REINCARNATION of souls, life after death, and communication between the earth and the ETHERIC WORLD; dwells on MEDIUMSHIP.

SPIRITIST HEALER—(Aztec, Mexico, Philippines) a person who administers PSYCHIC HEALING by allowing ETHERIC WORLD INTELLIGENCES to intervene and use his or her body as a CHANNEL to work through; usually a natural-born talent, prevalent among the uneducated; intelligences are usually famous deceased doctors, Christian Saints, or leaders from their countries. [**cf.** PSYCHIC SURGERY, TEN-PERCENT IMPERSONATION]

SPIRITISTIC MEETING—a gathering for the purpose of having a MEDIUM go into TRANCE to receive information and knowledge from the etheric world helpers. **Syn.** SEANCE. [**cf.** MEDIUMSHIP]

SPIRITLIKE—pertains to a cloudy mass which is able to float through MATTER; sometimes takes the form of a human being. **Syn.** GHOSTLY, PHANTOMIC. [**cf.** APPARITIONS, WANDERING SPIRIT, SEMITRANSPARENT]

SPIRITOID—pertains to the quality of psychic messages which come from the SUBCONSCIOUS MIND and appear very emotional, dramatic, and personal. [**cf.** PSYCHIC INFORMATION, MENTAL PSYCHIC PROCESSES Appendix 2]

SPIRITOSCOPE—invention of Dr. Hare (1920); an instrument designed to test the energy force emanating from a MEDIUM in the SEANCE room, helped one understand phenomena such as PK and palming energy in objects. [**cf.** DYNAMOSCOPE, MAGNETOMETER, GALVANOMETER, EXTERIORIZATION OF MOTORICITY, EXTERIORIZATON OF SENSITIVITY]

SPIRITOUS—refers to ethereal matter that is more refined than mundane matter. [**cf.** ETHERIC WORLD]

SPIRITS OF THE ABOVE—(Nuer tribe, Upper Nile) superior intelligences, are a part of the one God, living in the air, wind, breezes, and lightning; desire to administer to individuals, families, lineages, and tribes. [**cf.** REFRACTONS OF GOD]

SPIRITS OF THE BELOW—(Nuer tribe, Upper Nile) etheric world entities of low quality; desire to communicate with earthlings; consist of TOTEMIC SPIRITS, fetishes, and some nature sprites. [**cf.** SPIRITS OF THE ABOVE, FETISH, SPRITE]

SPIRITS OF THE SEVEN RAYS—lofty, exalted angels whose function is to guide the evolutionary cycles of mankind for this planet. **Syn.** LORDS OF LIGHT, SEVEN SPIRITS OF GOD, SEVEN ANGELS WHICH STOOD BEFORE GOD. [**cf.** MAGNIFICENT DEVAS, DIVINE THRONE, ANGEL]

SPIRITUAL—1. pertains to attitudinal growth, new understanding, and progression of the SOUL-MIND; 2. that which is of a moral or religious nature; pertains to the DIVINE; 3. not material, not tangible.

SPIRITUAL ADDICT—one who has experienced a very emotional and religious STATE OF CONSCIOUSNESS, a state of BLISS during MEDITATION or CHANTING, or has had an ego-idealistic psychic experience and then lives in a world of unreality based on that experience.

583

SPIRITUAL AURA—the third layer of the SOUL-MIND AURA which extends approximately eight feet from the body; light in color when perceived clairvoyantly; a person's connecting link to COSMIC CONSCIOUSNESS and to other people; permits one to psychically perceive intentions of another person before one is very close in bodily contact with that person. [**cf.** MENTAL AURA, BIPOLAR]

SPIRITUAL BEING—an INTELLIGENCE that has evolved to a very high STATE OF CONSCIOUNESS uniting with the more subtle substances; when perceived clairvoyantly, vibrates like a light or beam and no longer has the form of a human. [**cf.** PLANES, ANGEL KINGDOM, FIFTH BODY]

SPIRITUAL BODY—1. an umbrella phrase meaning any psychic VISION that appears like a human form; sometimes perceived clearly and at other times appears hazy, cloudy, or as a white gossamer substance but still a human formation. **Syn.** APPARITION, GHOST, PHANTOM, DISCARNATE. **2.** see ATMAN BODY. [**cf.** DISCARNATE ENTITY, GHOST, ETHERIC WORLD INTELLIGENCE]

SPIRITUAL CALM—a feeling of religious security; an inner knowing that one is in the correct religion for that span of time in that particular INCARNATION.

SPIRITUAL CHEMISTRY—1. substance of the invisible bodies: ETHER, SUPERETHER, SUBATOMIC ENERGY, and ATOMIC ETHER; **2.** TRANSMUTATION of cosmic energies; cosmic radiations enter the head and are transmuted by the PINEAL GLAND into electrical energy for the brain to utilize; the electrical energy is then transmuted by the PITUITARY GLAND into physical energy for the body to utilize; (ancient Egypt) known as BRAIN DEWS when the cosmic radiations enter the body, and as GOLDEN OIL when it exists. [**cf.** BODIES AND PLANES Appendix 5, THIRD-EYE AREA]

SPIRITUAL CIRCLE—a group of people who meet regularly for a few hours and sit in a circle to concentrate on developing psychically and mediumistically; often connected with a church; see PSYCHIC DEVELOPMENT CIRCLE.

SPIRITUAL CORD—see SILVER CORD.

SPIRITUAL CREATURE—An ETHERIC WORLD INTELLIGENCE appearing to a PSYCHIC as a half-angelic/half-elfin personality, eager to serve the MEDIUM; see NATURE SPIRIT.

SPIRITUAL CYCLE—a rhythmic pattern within oneself that repeats itself influencing inspiration, creativity, SELF-REALIZATION, and PSYCHISM; the month of July is the low month and December is the high month. [**cf.** PSYCHLES, RELIGIOUS CYCLES, RHYTHMIC PHENOMENA]

SPIRITUAL DOCTOR—(Nilotes tribe, Africa) a MEDIUM who has the talent to perform EXORCISM. [**cf.** EXORCISM Appendix 2]

SPIRITUAL ENERGY—see COSMIC ENERGY.

SPIRITUAL HEALING—pertains to any type of healing carried on in a church or religious gathering or by a PRACTITIONER who learned the healing technique in a church or a religious setting; healer feels this ability is a gift from God, or that he or she is a CHANNEL for God, the HOLY SPIRIT, or an etheric world healer to work through; laxly and inappropriately used term, see Appendix 4 for clarification. [**cf.** MENTAL HEALING, MAGNETIC HEALING, and MEDIUMSHIP HEALING]

SPIRITUAL HIERARCHY—(esoteric) the theory based on a consciousness of ONE which is all-love, all-intelligent, all-powerful and an overall principle at the top command; hierarchy is according to the awareness and growth of soul-minds who have separated from this one-love; each degree of consciousness has power over the lesser, and so on down to the slowest vibrations of intelligence and awareness, which is earth; makes a scale of justice and compatibility.

SPIRITUAL HIGH—to experience an emotional state of ECSTASY stimulated by an outer condition of a religious nature; occurs instantaneously or gradually; lasts from a few minutes up to half a day; brought on by music, chants, MEDITATION, religious ploy, or a PSYCHIC EXPERIENCE. **Sim.** ECSTASY. [**cf.** PEAK EXPERIENCE, EMOTIONAL PSI]

SPIRITUAL HUSTLERS—those who gather a following based upon the pretense that they are enlightened soul-minds, or incarnations of great religious leaders who have lived before; these people actually know very little.

SPIRITUAL ILLNESS—an attitude of a person or group of people who have lost the desire to worship something or someone stronger than themselves.

SPIRITUAL INSIGHT—see PSYCHISM.

SPIRITUAL LIGHT—a web of quantum connections

near the CHRIST CONSCIOUSNESS; a light so bright, magnificent, and dazzling that when seen by earthlings they must turn away from it; fragments of this light have been seen clairvoyantly during MEDITATION, near-death experiences, or when projecting mentally into the etheric planes. **Syn.** GREAT WHITE LIGHT OF THE CHRIST, LIGHT. [**cf.** SEVENTH PLANE]

SPIRITUAL PLANE—see FIFTH PLANE.

SPIRITUAL POTENCY—a developed, well-grounded sensitivity for using psychic energies for information, physical phenomena, healing and communication with the etheric world. [**cf.** PARAPSYCHOLOGY]

SPIRITUAL SCIENCE—a study of ancient sacred teachings of psychical wisdom and Truths; Wisdom of the Mystics; study of the INVISIBLE WORLD and its relationship to this world, and the scientific properties of religious beliefs; theory: SCIENCE and RELIGION are one and the same.

SPIRITUAL SHAPE—see ETHERIC DOUBLE.

SPIRITUAL SIGHT—("a vision") (Emmanuel Swedenborg) three kinds of visions: 1. to see with eyes closed as vividly as with eyes open; 2. to see places, people, and scenes of another life in another dimension when wide awake; e.g., when walking down the street; called IN VISION; 3. to see, when in a TRANCE state, spirits and other objects that represent things of HEAVEN. [**cf.** VISIONARY]

SPIRITUAL SON—(Tibet) a young person learning spiritual advancement techniques under the direction and guidance of a LAMA. **Sim.** NOVICE, NEOPHYTE.

SPIRITUAL SOUL—(Allan Kardec) a principle of individuality after death pertaining to humans only; used to distinguish a human's soul from the soul of animals, fish, and plants. **Syn.** SOUL-MIND. [**cf.** ANIMAL GROUP-SOUL, PRIMARY PERCEPTION, INSTINCT CONSCIOUSNESS]

SPIRITUAL SUN—the Great Sun in the KOSMOS; functions for other galaxies as the sun functions for planet earth. **Syn.** CENTRAL SUN. [**cf.** COSMIC CYCLE, GLOBE-ROUND]

SPIRITUAL THERAPIST—a PRACTITIONER who uses religious beliefs or a special religious DEITY along with PSYCHOLOGY in the healing process, with emphasis on finding the cause of the illness. [**cf.** LAW OF HEALING Appendix 7, MEDIUMSHIP HEALING]

SPIRITUAL THERAPY—use of religious or philosophical knowledge in the treatment of mental and physical disorders; based on the assumption that an individual is an etheric fragment of the total etheric universe and in proportion to one's acceptance of this idea and the necessity for one's own SOUL-MIND growth, will one be successful in demonstrating it; one may control the body and material plane elements in harmony with a divine plan. [**cf.** HOLISTIC HEALTH THEORY, TOTALITY]

SPIRITUAL WORLD—see ETHERIC WORLD.

SPIRITUALISM—a SCIENCE, PHILOSOPHY, and RELIGION using the doctrine of METAPHYSICS; belief in the continuity of life after death and communication with this life for the advancement of civilization and personal growth; scientific study of the ETHERIC WORLD, its properties, functions, and relationship to mankind and God; belief in REINCARNATION; uses the Bible as a guide to show one how to perfect oneself in his or her many incarnations; uses PSYCHIC and MEDIUMSHIP skills for growth and advancement of all.

SPIRITUALIST—one who believes in the communication between this world and the INVISIBLE WORLD, and who endeavors to mold his or her character and conduct in accordance with the highest teachings derived from such communion. [**cf.** SPIRITUALISM]

SPIRITUALITY—essence distinct from matter; has no religious significance; a latent force or characteristic within each one which desires to manifest to some ideal that is bigger than the individual; to grow in mental awareness and attitude.

SPIRITUALIZING THE ETHERIC WORLD—to perform rituals and say prayers for soul-minds inhabiting the DENSITY, in order to instill in them a desire to attain higher planes of consciousness. [**cf.** HELL, PLANES]

SPIRITUALLY STUNTED—describes one who attends charismatic meetings and has the desire to talk-in-tongues, but has never been able to do so. [**cf.** GLOSSOLALIST, QUENCHING THE SPIRIT]

SPIRITUS—coined by Robert Fludd (1650); see VITAL LIFE FORCE.

SPIRITUS RECTOR—(dreams) the dreammaker that tries to regulate or balance a one-sided mind or extreme attitude of the conscious mind by sending

585

a dream containing scenes portraying the opposite of this extreme characteristic; e.g., a shy person may dream he is speaking in front of hundreds of people. [cf. COMPENSATORY DREAMS, PERSONAL PSYCHIATRIST]

SPITTLE—saliva, considered a holy fluid because it contains energy of the body, connected to the emotions; believed to have therapeutic properties.

SPL—see SKIN POTENTIAL LEVEL.

SPLEEN CHAKRA—an invisible individual power-plant of concentrated energy, shaped like a wheel with six spokes; covers the navel and extends to the spleen; absorbs the vitality from the sun and disperses it throughout the body; draws in the SPIRIT from the air to disperse it to the ETHERIC DOUBLE and the physical NERVOUS SYSTEM; when seen clairvoyantly, it is RED, ORANGE, YELLOW, GREEN, BLUE, and VIOLET. [cf. KUNDALINI, CHAKRA]

SPLIT CONSCIOUSNESS—see POSSESSION.

SPLIT PERSONALITY—see POSSESSION.

SPLIT PERSONALITY FRAGMENT—an APPARITION coming to a PSYCHIC and built from the psychic's SUBCONSCIOUS MIND. **Syn.** PERSONALITY IMAGE FRAGMENT. [cf. SPIRIT OF THE ABOVE, TAMBARAN, KWOTH]

SPLIT-BRAIN HEMISPHERE—two functions of the CEREBRAL HEMISPHERES of the brain which operate semi-independently even though connected; the two halves of the brain essentially think in different languages; memories of one hemisphere are not directly available to the other; i.e., the left brain's logical consciousness does not pay attention when the right brain does meditation, dream, inspirational thought, etc.; each half has its own private sensations, perceptions, and impulses; an individual puts emphasis on one side of the brain hemispheres at a time according to the input of the experience, which depends whether the experience is subjective or objective; dreams are elusive and irrational to the logical left brain hemisphere; e.g., when one works creatively for a long time in the right brain consciousness, it is difficult to bring out the left brain language or describe one's creative work; during the creative process, the left brain does not pay attention to where one puts items or what one eats for lunch because the left brain hemisphere is absent during the creative process; this is how the absent-minded professor received his name (his deep interest in his theory kept him functioning in the right brain hemisphere for long hours); for separate functions of the hemispheres, see RIGHT BRAIN HEMISPHERE and LEFT BRAIN HEMISPHERE [cf. MIND MIRROR, SUGGESTOPEDIA, SPLIT BRAIN HEMISPHERE Appendix 5]

SPLIT-OFF—a psychic duplication of a person in two or three places at the same time, each one functioning in an awake state; the original personality is not aware of being in another place; one theory: split-off is caused by an overwhelming desire to be somewhere else causing the SOUL-MIND to divide into pieces. (Inconcl.) **Syn.** BILOCATION, DOUBLE EGOS. [cf. NEED-DETERMINING PHENOMENA]

SPLITTING A CLOUD—to psychically divide a cloud by concentration of the mind; to stare at the cloud, beam it energy from the eyes, and silently tell it to divide and float away in two pieces; theory: ability was handed down from the witches who could sweep among the clouds. [cf. RAIN DANCE, WIND MAGIC, SPACE BROTHERS]

SPLITTING OF PERSONALITIES—see IMPERSONATION.

SPLODGER—one who is extremely psychic and whose personal emotions spread out among those around him or her, drowning out PSYCHIC INFORMATION, and preventing it from coming or going out from anyone in the immediate vicinity; emotions can be positive or negative; sent out unconsciously or deliberately. [cf. CATAPSI, SPLODGING]

SPLODGING—a widespread, general broadcasting of pleasant or uncomfortable emotions coming from one psychic which are so intense that they drown out all other competing psychism in the immediate area; other psychics tune into these emotions easily; happens unconsciously or deliberately when the psychic is in a state of anxiety or in a PSYCHIC DEVELOPMENT CIRCLE. [cf. EMOTIONAL PSI, CLOAK OF INSULATION]

SPONTANEITY DISCIPLINE—to allow one's emotions to flow freely through the NERVOUS SYSTEM and react to them immediately as they lead one to respond; objective is to learn to react openly and correctly; prevents BLOCKS from forming in the body; theory: spontaneity knows its function and will resolve all situations if allowed to do so; emotions are builders in the mental areas. [cf. AUTOMATION, LAW OF SPONTANEITY Appendix 7]

SPONTANEOUS APPARITION—an unwilled vision of a DISCARNATE ENTITY appearing in a split second and leaving the same way; theory: the discarnate made a mistake and landed on this plane instead of another, or the viewer had IN VISION for a split second and could tune into the ETHERIC WORLD in front of him or her. [**cf.** VISIONARY, APPARITION, PHANTOM, GHOST]

SPONTANEOUS ASTRAL PROJECTION—to move in one's astral body out of the physical body, unexpectedly, when in a highly emotional state of consciousness: 1. could occur when in a catastrophic situation, in anger, constant negative disturbance, state of mental exhaustion, or an unbearable negative state; experience comes for a mental problem emergency, similar to an INVOLUNTARY ASTRAL PROJECTION in a physical health emergency; leaves the PROJECTIONIST feeling better about him or herself and/or the situation; one turns inward for help, not specifying what kind, and the SOUL-MIND, always working on survival and personality improvement, takes the suggestion; the experience is vivid and whether it is a symbol or a real image, it proves to help the projectionist balance the situation; 2. occurs to a karmic need when one is seriously on the path of unfoldment; needs an ALPHA STATE OF CONSCIOUSNESS to occur, such as in MEDITATION, under HYPNOSIS, or in a psychic development sitting; one has full recall and feels elated from the experience. [**cf.** PEAK EXPERIENCE, ASTRAL PROJECTION Appendix 2]

SPONTANEOUS CASE—(psi tasks) an involuntary experience of a psychic event at home or elsewhere as opposed to an experience in a controlled laboratory. **Syn.** RANDOM PSYCHISM. [**cf.** EMPATHY CLAIRSENTIENCE, CLOAK OF INSULATION, EMOTIONAL CLAIRAUDIENCE]

SPONTANEOUS DEMATERIALIZATION—the process of an object vanishing mysteriously from one's premises; sometimes reappears hours, days, or months later, in plain sight, but not from the area where it dematerialized. **Syn.** PSYCHIC THEFT. [**cf.** POLTERGEISTRY, APPORTATION]

SPONTANEOUS HUMAN COMBUSTION—abbr. SHC; the igniting of a human body and its consumation by intense heat without physical means; each documented case has the following pecularities (seventy-five cases): body is reduced to ashes in less time than in CREMATION; body is not recognizable, with little or no anatomy left; combustible objects in the vicinity show no damage; building does not catch on fire; flesh has no burning odor (exudes a sweet, perfume-like scent); speculation on the cause: highly localized electric current occurs within the body due to certain kinds of earthpothesis, i.e., associated with earthquake phenomena in the region. (Inconcl.) [**cf.** PHYSICAL MANIFESTATIONS/ MISCELLANEOUS]

SPONTANEOUS PHYSICAL MANIFESTATIONS—the visible action of MATTER in the vicinity of a MEDIUM not consciously willed by the medium; ETHERIC WORLD INTELLIGENCE working through the medium is capable of moving the matter even when not in a SEANCE; occurs more frequently around a natural-born medium; e.g., a curtain moving without a breeze; a lost article reappearing. **Syn.** NATURAL SPIRITISM. [**cf.** NATURAL MEDIUM, PK, POLTERGEIST, GUIDE]

SPONTANEOUS PSI—(psi tasks) any PSYCHIC EXPERIENCE that happens without effort and without being willed; J. B. Rhine's theory: "experiences of spontaneous ESP outside the laboratory whether complete or incomplete are processed through psychological vehicles while asleep or awake; placed in four groupings: realistic, unrealistic, hallucinatory, and intuitive." [**cf.** ESP, CLAIRVOYANCE, UNREALISTIC EXPERIENCE, HALLUCINATION, INTUITIVE EXPERIENCES]

SPONTANEOUS PSYCHISM—any type of mental or physical phenomena that is experienced frequently, and involuntarily, without being consciously planned or willed at the time it occurs (except CLAIRSENTIENCE or INTUITION); 1. occurs from a lower entity and the quality of information or feats is inferior; hypothesis: individual needs an EGO reinforcement and feels personal achievement through these many irregular psychic events; individual is ignorant of how to close his or her PSYCHIC DOORS; 2. occurs from a higher intelligence and quality of information or feats is superior; hypothesis: individual subconsciously or karmically desires spontaneous psychic experiences, which gives the psychic mechanism the permission to perform; the SUBCONSCIOUS MIND will not operate without a command from the CONSCIOUS MIND from some INCARNATION, nor will a superior ETHERIC WORLD INTELLIGENCE perform without permission from some incarnation; (to use one's psychic abilities freely in a past incarnation is karmic permission to use it freely in the present

587

incarnation until the desire is shown to bring it under control). [cf. GUIDE, EMOTIONAL PSI, KARMICALLY WILLED]

SPONTANEOUS RECALL—to experience a flash vision of a past life or perceive a feeling of a past life (while in the awake state, meditative state, or a relaxed psychic state) without programming the experience as one does in hypnotherapy. Syn. FLASHBACK, DEJA ENTENDER. [cf. REINCARNATION, REGRESSION, REVIVIFICATION]

SPONTANEOUS REMISSION—(holistic health) a physical or mental response that comes quickly from the SUBCONSCIOUS MIND before the CONSCIOUS MIND has an opportunity to sort it over; e.g., retracting a verbal message immediately after it is said; receiving an instant health cure at a charismatic meeting.

SPONTANEOUS SELF-HYPNOSIS—a temporary, self-generated, disguised state of HYPNOSIS brought on by a preoccupied mind; to narrow one's attention to looking or listening so intently that the CONSCIOUS MIND is not functioning; this puts the SUBCONSCIOUS MIND in control, makes the body passive and relaxed, and closes the individual off to outer stimuli even in the vicinity; e.g., when one is very absorbed in a football game on TV they will not be aware of a family member passing by; the night driver of a motor car can easily lose all sense of where he is and if he made the correct turns because the constant staring at the white lines on the road and listening to the monotonous hum of the motor has a hypnotic effect. [cf. ON-THE-SPOT HYPNOSIS, EMOTIONAL HYPNOSIS, MASS HYPNOSIS]

SPONTANEOUS SYMPTOM SHIFTING—(Russia) the transference of one's illness symptoms, strong emotional feeling or attitude (whether pleasant or unpleasant), or one's karmic accident-to-be, to another person; unconsciously willed or planned; happens to a member in a gathering, a person which one is temporarily involved, or a family member; distance is no barrier. Sim. EMOTIONAL TELEPATHY, SPONTANEOUS TELEPATHY TRANSFER. [cf. CLOAK OF INSULATION, PSYCHIC TRANSFER, EMOTIONAL PSYCHISM Appendix 2]

SPONTANEOUS VOCATION—the process of SHAMANSHIP for one who is not a NATURAL-BORN PSYCHIC to receive psychic skills and healing abilities all at once; this is preceded by 1. the INITIATORY SICKNESS, which is serious and painful until the SHAMAN performs self-healing; 2. the extreme feelings of ECSTASY when one is given the instructions and techniques for becoming the shaman for one's tribe; occurs in an ALTERED STATE OF CONSCIOUSNESS. [cf. CALL, PERSONAL QUEST, HEREDITARY TRANSMISSION]

SPONTANEOUS-PK—(psi tasks) objects moving for no apparent reason. [cf. SPONTANEOUS DEMATERIALIZATION, NONHUMAN OMENS, POLTERGEIST, GELLER-TYPE PHENOMENA]

SPOOK—1. (Netherlands) see NATURE SPIRIT; 2. an ASTRAL SHELL floating in the ASTRAL CEMETERY after its SOUL-MIND has departed; held together by the strong emotions and poor habits of the departed soul-mind giving it the cohesive power to stay in a body form; noted for haunting earthlings. Syn. ASTRAL SHELL. [cf. NATURE SPIRIT, GHOST]

SPOT CARDS—(ancient Egypt) cards which bear symbols for telling the future of an individual or country; used with SORTES. [cf. CASTING OF LOTS, I CHING, SYNCHRONICITY, MONADOLOGY]

SPOTTER—(ufology) 1. one who is trained to sight a flying saucer or other strange object in the sky; one who can distinguish a natural object from the unusual. [cf. UNKNOWN FORCES, BLUE BOOK, SIGHTINGS]

SPR—abbr. SKIN POTENTIAL RESPONSE; see GALVANIC SKIN RESPONSE.

SPRIGGANS—(Cornwall, England) NATURE SPIRITS that are small, ugly, grotesque, and spiteful; capable of inflating themseles into monstrous forms at will; said to switch babies in cradles; guardians of hill treasure and skilled thieves themselves; sometimes destructive, dangerous, and bothersome to people who are working. [cf. NATURE KINGDOM Appendix 2]

SPRINGING FORTH—(Tibet) to awaken to a new STATE OF CONSCIOUSNESS with supernormal psychic powers after going through a mock DEATH PROCESS. Sim. BORN IN DISGUISE. [cf. HEREDITARY TRANSMISSION, BODY CONTROL]

SPRITE—(Tibet) a radiant, small NATURE SPIRIT whose energy blends well with good deeds for earthlings; brings guidance, confidence, honor, and security regarding money and opportunities; works better in a group of sprites; changes dimensions to be recognized by earthlings. Syn. PIXIE, LEPRE-

CHAUN, ELF, FAY.

SPUK—(Germany) see NATURE SPIRITS.

SPYANG-FU—(Tibet) a special RITUAL performed after death wherein an object is dressed in the clothes of the deceased person and a paper containing special inscriptions is appropriately placed to represent the face of the deceased. [**cf.** MIRROR OF KARMA, READER, REFLECTING]

SQUARE—(esoteric) 1. the first of the tattwa SYMBOLS, representing EARTH; a primordial element, colored YELLOW, called PRITHIVI; designed to help reach the very basic part of the SUBCONSCIOUS MIND. [**cf.** TATTWAS] 2. a symbol of the fourth level of atmospheric substance; radiation from the sun to earth; solid, purple or VIOLET, LIFE ETHER.

SQUID—abbr. SUPERCONDUCTING QUANTUM INTERFERENCE DEVICE; an instrument that can measure the brain's magnetic field in a room without elaborate shielding; shows that stimulation of the body produces a magnetic field which forms around a specific area of the brain. [**cf.** MENTAL-EMOTIONAL ACTIVITY, MIND-BRAIN SCIENTISTS, MAGNETIC FIELDS]

SRI—(Hinduism, "holy") a title of respect similar to reverend; earned by experiences performed correctly and not by a certain amount of formal education.

SRI RAGA—(Hinduism) one of the basic RAGAS; fixed melodic scales that are reserved for autumn twilights; used to attain pure love. [**cf.** MEGHA RAGA, HINDOLE RAGA]

SRID-PA BAR-DO—(Tibet) to change into a CLEAR LIGHT consciousness after going through a mock DEATH PROCESS, similar to the change of consciousness in the real death process. [**cf.** WENT OUT, PSEUDODEATH, WATCHFUL SPIRITS]

SRR—see SKIN RESISTANCE RESPONSE and .GALVANIC SKIN RESPONSE.

SRUTI—(Hinduism) ancient psychic men who acted as channels for the "Supreme" to bring poetry and hymns of revelations of eternal Truths; composed the VEDAS, which stand for "that which is heard." [**cf.** INSPIRATIONAL WRITING]

SSP—abbr. for SENSORY PERCEPTION; see INSPIRATIONAL THOUGHT.

ST. ELMO'S FIRE—electrical charges coming from the masthead, rigging, and yardarm of wooden ships, seen by sailors; named after the patron saint of sailors; theories: 1. the AURA; 2. high-voltage electricity ionizes with the gases in the surrounding air. **Syn.** CASTOR, POLLUX, DIOSCURI, CORPOS. [**cf.** CORPSE CANDLE, ELECTROMAGNETIC RADIATION]

ST. JOHN'S WORT—(esoteric) a plant that has psychic properties; used to ward off negative vibrations in the area where it is planted; gives off vibrations of therapeutic value for the sick when growing in their room; similar to a miniature sun. [**cf.** BOTANE Appendix 2]

ST. MICHAEL—(Bible) a lofty etheric world ANGEL who communicated with earthlings during the time of the Old Testament; his function was to be guardian over Israel; in the New Testament, he was the first of the seven ARCHANGELS and led the host against the DEVIL. [**cf.** ANGELOLOGY, PLANETARY ANGEL, RACIAL ANGELS]

ST. VANUS—an etheric world ANGEL whose function is to watch over the forests.

ST. VITUS'S DANCE—a religious, spiraling, rhythmic movement, done with outstretched arms, that is performed to bring the dancer knowledge that could not have been obtained in any other way; dance is repeated continuously until an ETHERIC WORLD INTELLIGENCE enters the body and works with the body or with the vocal cords in verbal language. [**cf.** MOVEMENT-FOR-ALTERED-CONSCIOUSNESS, TRANCE VOICE, IMPERSONATION]

STACKING EFFECT—(psi tasks) the possibility of a statistical error; an overestimate or underestimate of variance, when large groups are receivers for one TARGET. [**cf.** VARIABLES, PSI-HIT, PROBABILITY]

STAFF—see DOWSING ROD.

STAG—(ancient) a NATURE SPIRIT that spends time on the function of the sun and the function of the UNDERWORLD.

STAGE HYPNOSIS—hypnosis performed on stage or TV to prove how suggestion influences the subconscious mind when it is given directly to the subconscious mind, as in a hypnotic state; conducted by an operator whose concern is to entertain or show sensationalism, and who gives hypnotizability tests to pick subjects from the audience accordingly; then silly antics are suggested for the subject to perform while in the hypnotic state, to prove the power of suggestion; this is a dangerous and unhealthy mind activity if performed only for entertainment and not for mental development. [cf. HYPNOTHERAPY Appendix 5]

STAGE OF EVOLUTION—(esoteric) 1. a time frame of consciousness that puts each thing, living and nonliving, into an awareness of a reality of its own as it progresses from one existence to another, fulfilling the potential within the seed of the UNIVERSE of which it is a part. [cf. HOLOGRAM BRAIN THEORY, MONADOLOGY] 2. (referring to humans) a degree or step in the process of the SOUL-MIND unfoldment; each step makes its own rules and functions to benefit that level toward perfecting itself; each step is measured by the amount of WISDOM one has acquired through experiences of activity, emotions, and thoughts from one's various incarnations in earth; the correct reactions to these experiences make changes in the electrical vibrational frequency of the body, giving each individual a different conductivity of electricity in the body; conductivity changes according to the "quality" of correctly learned experiences, regardless of the "number" of incarnations; the soul-mind acts like a "voltage regulator" for the amount of COSMIC ELECTRICITY utilized in the body; each individual is bombarded with the same amount of cosmic electricity but the amount the body utilizes is according to the soul-mind evolution; the more cosmic energy utilized, the more refined body and lifestyle one has; the rate of vibration of each individual (stage of evolution) will be the the key as to what happens to one as the earth purifies itself. **Syn.** STATE OF EVOLUTION, STAGE OF DEVELOPMENT. [cf. OVERSOUL, COSMIC ENERGY, PERFECTNESS, HUMAN BEING SPECIES SEED, LAW OF INVOLUTION Appendix 7, EMOTIONAL STRESS, AKASHIC RECORDS]

STAINLESS INDIVIDUALITY—a never-changing PERFECTNESS potential within the seed of the human species; a minute ethereal replica of TOTALITY in its primeval state, recognized by mankind to be the human being seed; endowed with an urge to return to this perfect state. **Syn.** MONAD. [cf. VOID, CLEAR LIGHT, MICROCOSM, STATE OF EVOLUTION]

STAND-UP READER—one who gives mini-psychic messages while standing on the platform at a public gathering or church service; messages last from one to four minutes and pertain to a listener's personal problems, character, past, future, or friends; PSYCHIC does not answer verbal questions but moves along from one to another rapidly; usually more than one psychic serves in one evening, and each reads for ten to fifteen minutes; performed in a LIGHT TRANCE state of consciousness which is only noticeable to those trained in this skill. **Syn.** ON YOUR FEET PSYCHIC. [cf. STEP INTO YOUR VIBRATION, REACHED]

STANDING READING—short, concise PSYCHIC INFORMATION given to an individual in a public gathering by a professional stand-up PSYCHIC READER; usually two or more readers work at the same gathering, taking turns for approximately ten to twenty minutes each; individuals in the audience do not ask for a reading, nor ask questions when being read for, but just allow the psychic to flow; message lasts two or three minutes but is significant and important; psychic must word the information so others in the audience do not understand it; stand-up psychic must be well-grounded so skepticism in the audience does not interfere with the quality of the reading; psychic works in light trance, moving quickly, and speaking rapidly, with no pause, between readings; sometimes the ETHERIC WORLD INTELLIGENCE that works through the psychic displays his or her own mannerisms that can be noticed if one understands trance work. [cf. STAND-UP READER, LIGHT TRANCE]

STANZAS—refers to sections of the Hindu book of mysticism. [cf. VEDAS]

STAR BODY—see ETHERIC DOUBLE.

STAR PEOPLE—soul-minds who were born of earthly parents but who have had past incarnations on other planets which were more evolved than earth, and who are here as planetary helpers for the coming age; they show these similarities: have an unusual blood type, have low body temperature, feel an urgency to accomplish goals, feel displaced here, yearn for another home, were unplanned children, are very good artists and musicians, hear buzzing in ears when doing psychic work, can perform healings, had an outstanding psychic experience when a child (e.g., a visitation by one administering guidance and comfort), have frequent dreams that involve multi-moon planet environmental scenes, perform best work at night. (Inconcl.) [cf. PLANETARY WORKER]

STAR SPIRITS—(Native American, Pueblo) ETHERIC WORLD INTELLIGENCES who bring guidance, protection, and PSYCHIC INFORMATION to the Indians; related to the cloud spirits. [cf.

RAIN-MAKER, DAWN SPIRITS]

STAR TRAVELERS—used in ancient times to mean UFOs.

STAR-GAZING—(Native American, Navaho) see MEDIUMSHIP.

STAR-RUBY—(esoteric) a deep-red stone influenced by radiations of the sun; used to induce creativity, and used by the owner's guides to help in physical psychism. [**cf.** MINPSI, WATER SAPPHIRE, SCREAMING STONE]

STAR-SAPPHIRE—(esoteric) a mineral influenced by radiations of Saturn; worn to represent the "light of the soul-mind." [**cf.** GOD-AS-THE-STONE, ONYX, MINPSI Appendix 2]

STAR-SOUND—(Michael Heleus) noise, inaudible to the normal hearing, that comes from the planets and stars influencing a psychological and physical response in people; has characteristic of being predictable; felt to be the meaning of "aspects" in astrology. (Inconcl.) **Syn.** ASTROSONICS. [**cf.** ASTROLOGY, MAJESTIC MUSIC, CLAIRAUDIENCE]

STARE DOWN—to transfix one's eyes (animal or human) on a specific center, such as the eyes of another person or animal or a spot on an object; the MAGNETIC FLUID extends from the eyes of the starer to influence the person, animal, or object and puts the subject under some degree of control by the starer; used in CASTING A SPELL, AMULET ENERGIZING, HYPNOSIS, OBJECT-PK, and POINT-OF-FOCUS psychism. **Syn.** THE EVIL-EYE, BEAMING ENERGY. [**cf.** THIRD-EYE AREA, ANIMAL FLUID, ON-THE-SPOT HYPNOSIS]

STARRY ENVELOPE OF THE SOUL—(Aristotle) see ASTRAL BODY.

STARRY SOUL-CHARIOTS—(Aristotle) see ASTRAL PROJECTION.

STARS—tiny specks of light which flash through the air in DARKROOM SESSIONS or seances; intelligences from the etheric world announcing they are there, ready to help. **Sim.** SEANCE LIGHTS, PSYCHIC LIGHTS. [**cf.** GUIDE, PSYCHIC BREEZES, TESTING MEDIUMSHIP]

STASIS—a concept or feeling that TIME is nonexistent or nondurational; sometimes experienced in MEDITATION. [**cf.** MULTIDIMENSIONAL, TIME Appendix 5]

STATE—1. a set of circumstances or attributes characterizing a person or thing at a given time; a particular mental or emotional condition; 2. (W. Brugh Joy) "'a state' is bound consciousness."

STATE OF CONSCIOUSNESS—1. (pertaining to the primordial state) in the beginning was TOTAL CONSCIOUSNESS, which was CONSCIOUS OF BEING; all form is a manifestation of this consciousness, alive and eternally seeking self-expression. [**cf.** TOTALITY] 2. (pertaining to nonhuman things) a particular way of expressing for a period of time; a sense of awareness of knowing one is functioning in the UNIVERSE whether alive or inert; the reality of the vibrational frequency the entity is existing in; a way of perceiving the various dimensions of the universe through PRIMARY PERCEPTION and knowing one's function for existence; 3. (pertaining to humans) a momentary period of time reacting as LIFE affected by present stimuli of the five SENSES and organized by the NERVOUS SYTEM; what one thinks and feels about this stimuli and one's response to it; the activity of CONSCIOUSNES is one's awareness of the REALITY one is functioning in; 4. aspects of consciousness: waking (using the CONSCIOUS MIND), sleeping (using the SUBCONSCIOUS MIND), dreaming (using the subconscious mind and SUPERCONSCIOUS MIND), meditating (using the superconscious mind). [**cf.** CONSCIOUSNESS Appendix 5]

STATE OF EVOLUTION—see STAGE OF EVOLUTION.

STATE OF TRANSITION—(esoteric) the length of time of the initiation as the SOUL-MIND passes from physical life to etheric life; various levels of CONSCIOUSNESS one must go through to have a happy etheric life. **Syn.** MAKING THE TRANSITION. [**cf.** DEATH HORMONE, DEATH ANGEL, READER, BIRTH OF THE BARDO BODY]

STATE ORACLE—(Greece, Spain, Tibet) a professional PSYCHIC and MEDIUM employed by the government to foretell the future of the state or its cities, announce danger from enemies, conditions of crops, and give general counsel for the highest good of the country. [**cf.** INDIVIDUAL ORACLE, TRANCE]

STATES OF NONORDINARY REALITY—any frame of mind that is not normal waking awareness; a state in which the CONSCIOUS MIND cuts off outer stimuli, releases its duty of decision-making, and allows the SUBCONSCIOUS MIND to handle the body's existence; usually pertains to seeing into the

591

vibrational frequency of the astral or mental planes, or the DENSITY, wherein one sees with the whole body and hears more acutely.

STATIC—the condition of bodies at rest or lacking in movement but retaining equilibrium.

STATIC ELECTRICITY—1. ELECTRICITY that is by itself without a magnetic field; lacking in movement; stationary; 2. (esoteric) a type of energy that does not affect a living person but can affect a discarnate being. [**cf.** EFFECTS OF STATIC ELECTRICITY, MAGNETIC FIELDS]

STATIC INANIMATE OBJECTS-PK—abbr. PK-ST; (psi tasks) to move matter which cannot move by itself by using mind power; noninstantaneous; needs time of intensified concentration on the desired activity; e.g., to cause a match to roll off a table; to cause a picture to move over one inch while still hanging on the wall. **Syn.** ARTICLE PSYCHOKINESIS. [**cf.** NONHUMAN PSYCHOKINESIS Appendix 2]

STATIC UNIVERSE—the opposite of what the universe is now expressing; nonmovement of the atoms would mean the end of TOTALITY as it is known.

STATUE OF FOUR FACES AND FOUR ARMS—(Hinduism, Brahmanism) the highest DEITY, representing one aspect of the TRINITY; represents the CREATOR of the UNIVERSE.

STATUE OF STIGMATA—a statue of JESUS of unknown origin, from which a red substance flows out of the hands and no one can stop; occurs around Easter time. [**cf.** STIGMATISM, ORACLE AT DELPHI, FATIMA PROPHECY]

STEP INTO YOUR VIBRATION—an expression frequently verbalized by psychics as they mentally tune into the electromagnetic field around the person to whom they are giving a message. [**cf.** STANDING READER, REACHED, READING]

STEP PYRAMID—(esoteric) a PYRAMID, with steps leading to the top, which represents "ascent to the sun" or higher states of consciousness; it served as an initiation chamber into the mysteries of WISDOM by the disciples of that time; believed to be the first pyramid built, which was during the reign of Zoser at Sakkhara. (Inconcl.) [**cf.** PYRAMID ENERGY, STEPS, MYSTICISM]

STEPS—symbolizes "upward"; a means of ASCENT from one STATE OF CONSCIOUSNESS to a higher

state of consciousness; used universally in DREAM-STUFF and psychic messages. **Syn.** LADDER. [**cf.** SYMBOLS, DREAMS, PSYCHIC INFORMATION]

STEPS TO GODLINESS—seven major steps of initiation for the unfoldment of the SOUL-MIND into the ANGEL KINGDOM; prepares the soul-mind for eventually blending into Etheric Oneness; steps one through four are earthly achievements; five is Mastership and is attainted in the EARTH PLANE, e.g., Pythagoras and Lao-Tse; six is Lordhood and is attained in the ETHERIC WORLD, e.g., JESUS the Christ and Gautama BUDDHA; seven is Godhood and is attained in the etheric world. [**cf.** ANGEL HIERARCHY]

STHENOMETER—1. an instrument invented by Dr. Paul Joire (early 1900s); used in testing the POLARITY of PSYCHIC ENERGY within the MEDIUM when in a trance state. [**cf.** BIOMETER OF BARADUC, GALVANOMETER, MAGNETOSCOPE OF RUTER, HUMAN POLARITY, EXTERIORIZATION OF SENSITIVITY] 2. an instrument of radionics that responds instantly to the visual stimuli of a person's eye gaze or body radiations; used to measure these energies as they form around objects and people. [**cf.** RADIESTHESIA, RADIONICS]

STICK—1. (radionics diagnostic instrument) (a) the resistance of the tips of the fingers when rubbed over the rubber strip, denoting that the dials should be read at that point to diagnose the disease of the patient; "stick" is detected as the sound becomes crisper and the fingers adhere to the rubber plate; see ABRAM'S BOX; (b) resistance of the fingers on the STROKER PLATE as the dials are being turned with the other hand, denoting where to stop the dials to acquire the desired results; fingers get heavy and become glued to the plate. (Inconcl.). [**cf.** PSYCHIC FINGERS, RADIESTHESIA, RADIONICS] 2. (Tai Chi) the moving away from YIN or YANG in the dance exercise, allowing the center of gravity to be more fluid. [**cf.** SUFI TWIRLING, MOVEMENT-FOR-ALTERED-CONSCIOUSNESS]

STICK-POINT ANALYSIS—(Friedman) to search for expectations in the life of an individual by using a PENDULUM and a zodiacal design; design consists of all possible areas of human experience relating to the twelve houses of the ZODIAC; pendulum is held over the design and reacts differently over the houses that pertain to the inquirer. [**cf.** RADIONICS, ASTROLOGY, PALLOMANCY]

STIGMATA—marks on one's body resembling crucifixion wounds; bleeding from these points simulating the wounds of JESUS the Christ; blood pouring out of hands, feet, and side from the lance and nail wounds, bruises on the shoulder from the weight of the cross; chafing of wrists and ankles where Jesus was tied; scourge marks on the skin representing His beating; chafing of the ring finger denoting betrothal to the Christ. [cf. STIGMATIZATION, EMOTIONAL PSYCHISM Appendix 2]

STIGMATIC—1. pertaining to STIGMATA; 2. a person who has received the flowing of blood from the same spots as the wounds on Jesus' body at the time of His death. [cf. STIGMATIZATION]

STIGMATIZATION—to bleed from the body in the same spots as Jesus' injuries, resembling the wounds of the Crucifixion; bleeding may last a short time or may flow freely for a few weeks, severely incapacitating the person; does not deplete one's health; occurs showing one wound or all the wounds; can be produced and stopped spontaneously or sometimes cannot be stopped; happens at random or can be willed; Catholic Church gives causes: 1. DIVINE INTERVENTION; 2. diabolical intervention for the conversion of the faithful; 3. wakeful deliberation or unconscious suggestion. (Inconcl.) [cf. STIGMATA, STIGMATIC, EMOTIONAL PSYCHISM Appendix 2]

STILL, SMALL VOICE—a HUNCH or intuitive feeling that one should do a particular thing, change one's plans, or be careful when proceeding; one's inner guidance; see CLAIRSENTIENCE.

STONE CIRCLE—see STONEHENGE.

STONE OF FAIL—(Ireland) a stone that was known to scream during the coronation if the king was wrong for the people; located near Dublin. Syn. SCREAMING STONE, LIA-FAIL. [cf. MINPSI, LEVITATION GEMS, LIGHT BULB GEMS]

STONE OF LAZ—(Egypt) (esoteric) LAPIS LAZULI, a mineral having properties that help one make love, improve one's psychic skills, and bring radiations of Jupiter to earth. [cf. MINERAL CONSCIOUSNESS, CONTAINERS OF MAGICAL POWER]

STONE WALK—(South Pacific) to walk across burning stones without getting any burns on one's body or clothing; accomplished by praying and fasting beforehand; special stones from the native land are placed to form an oven which gives off even heat; see FIREWALKING. [cf. BODY CONTROL Appendix 2]

STONE WORSHIPPING CULTS—(Hellenic Greece, Crete, Thessaly) considered the stone to be a god because of its stability, strength, and indestructible properties which offered protection and helped in psychic skills. [cf. STONES, GOD-AS-THE-STONE, GOD-IN-THE-STONE]

STONE-AGE GRAMOPHONE RECORDS—(ufology) stone discs which look like phonograph records, found by archeologists who believe the artifacts are from outer space. (Inconcl.) [cf. STONEHENGE, ETHERIAN PHYSICS, UFOLOGY]

STONEHENGE—(Salisbury, England) a barren area surrounded by a circle of stone monuments whose structure is designed for observing and predicting the movement of heavenly bodies; an astrological calendar that marks the position of the sun and moon in inner measurements, giving the precise number of solar years (similar to the PYRAMID); the particular symmetry of the stones and the circle formation indicate its use for psychic forces; believed to be a place of worship for chiefs and kings; a place to see the operation of PSYCHISM in action; associated with the Druids and Celts, who were extremely psychic. [cf. STONES, FORMS-WITH-POWER]

STONES—(esoteric) a hard substance formed from earth and mineral material; a symbol of the eternal substance in the air (the VITAL LIFE FORCE) because of its similar property of indestructibility; has the same elements as the human body, making them both compatible; when carried close to the body, or placed in the immediate area of the body, will accelerate the owner's psychic skills, HEALING ability, and induce MEDITATION; brings stability to areas where placed; a handful of ordinary pebbles is very powerful; a stone will respond to a human voice if spoken very close to it. [cf. STONEHENGE, STONE-WORSHIPPING CULTS, MINPSI Appendix 2]

STOPPING THE WORLD—to break the flow of interpretation of what one now calls REALITY by some alien set of circumstances, and to be in another state of AWARENESS; when in the other vibrational frequency, one feels as if "it" is the reality. [cf. CONSCIOUSNESS Appendix 5]

STORAGE CLOSET—see SUBCONSCIOUS MIND.

STORING POWER—1. (in the body) (don Juan) to store up power in one's body gradually by plugging up all the points of drainage by *not* doing things; happens unnoticeably; the body learns as it goes through life and must experience drastic happenings in order for the body to profit from its learnings; power can be stored for these happenings. [cf. SYMPATHETIC NERVOUS SYSTEM] 2. (in an object) objects handled frequently become imbued with one's personal psychic and thought vibrations, unconsciously, and can then be used as a TALISMAN for one's self; objects used in rituals over the years are heavily impinged with the same vibrations; both objects frequently handled and objects used in rituals make excellent psychometric specimens. [cf. AMULETS, BEAMED ENERGY, PSYCHOMETRY]

STORM RAISING—(Native American) to tune into the vibrations of nature to manipulate rain, if it is rightfully needed; accomplished by many tribe members visualizing rain falling on the crops; giving thanks and showing respect for nature and its manner of functioning are important factors in producing rain. [cf. ATMOSPHERE CONTROL Appendix 2]

STREAM OF CONSCIOUSNESS—(William James) all the INTELLIGENCE there is to know, located in the subconscious of each person; the flow of TOTAL INTELLIGENCE from each individual's personal MONAD that could be perpetual, if one allowed it to enter his or her mind, but which one normally blocks out by one's belief systems and cultural traditions. [cf. BELIEF SYSTEM, TRADITION]

STREAM OF HALF-CONSCIOUSNESS—the involuntary thoughts that idly flow through a person's brain, filling the gaps between deliberate thoughts. Syn. INNER-DIALOGUE. [cf. INTERNAL AWARNESS, HEART]

STRAIGHT AND NARROW WAY—a cliche referring to the KUNDALINI energy which rises in the spine as a person grows in character from his or her righteous deeds and acts. [cf. KUNDALINI Appendix 5]

STRAIGHT DROP—see REPERCUSSION.

STRATA OF CREATION—various frequencies of ELECTRICITY vibrating simultaneously in the atmosphere which create levels that function independently unde their own principles yet interpenetrate and depend upon one another to make a unified whole, i.e., atomic, subatomic, cellular, and molecular VIBRATIONAL FREQUENCIES. (Inconcl.) [cf. HOLOGRAPHIC MODEL, METAPHYSICS]

STREAM OF THOUGHT—thinking in SYMBOLS, images, scenes, events, colors, and fragments of things; using the imagination faculty without enough emotion to create THOUGHT-FORMS; willed or spontaneous; similar to INNER-DIALOGUE, but in pictures instead of words; (do not confuse with psychic visions, which require a relaxed state of consciousness). Syn. INNER-MIND PICTURES. [cf. THOUGHT-FORMS, IMAGERY, FANTASY, VISION]

STREAMER REPULSION—(Kirlian effect) two auras drawing away from each other as shown by a Kirlian camera photograph of two objects taken in the same picture; thinning of the corona. (Inconcl.) [cf. AURA, HIGH-FREQUENCY FIELDS, MITOGENTIC RADIATION]

STREGA—(Italy) see PSYCHIC.

STRENGTH TRANSFERENCE—to convey PSYCHIC ENERGY between those who are harmoniously attuned, wherein the receiver benefits greatly; some individuals are born givers of psychic energy and some are born takers, a pattern which generally follows throughout one's life; to transfer psychic energy between the weak and the strong; e.g., the aged receive benefits from being with the young, and the sick from being with the healthy. [cf. PARASYTE, PSYCHIC TRANSFER, EATING COMPANIONS]

STRESS—a neutral energy which influences the body and mind with varying degrees of intensity, subservient to the attitude of the person but director of one's BODY CHEMISTRY; the measure of all the wear and tear in the physical and mental activity of the body caused by life experiences; humans form viewpoints from the ups and downs of these experiences and react accordingly, making them rewards or non-rewards; physiological and psychological consequences of stimuli coming from the environment being judged as being either POSITIVE or NEGATIVE; the body's indeterminate response to any demand placed on it, whether that demand is pleasant or not; stress has its own recognizable peculiarities, but when studied it was found to have no specific cause; the unusual results of exposure to anything for that person; see EUSTRESS for beneficial stress and NEGATIVE STRESS for undesirable stress. [cf. EMOTIONS, KEY TO LIFE]

STRESS MONITOR—a BIOFEEDBACK INSTRUMENT that helps one to quiet one's emotions, mind, and body by registering levels of CONSCIOUSNESS and feeding this information back to the subject who is HOOKED-UP to it; relates progress during MEDITATION by way of sound, lights, numbers, or print-outs; research has found that it is easier to reach lower levels of awareness when meditating if one is fed back one's progression; stress can be brought under control by regular meditating periods in biofeedback training sessions. [cf. BIOFEED-BACK TRAINING Appendix 5]

STRESSING—RADIESTHESIA theory: there is an intellgent energy already stored in a DOWSING ROD that preconditions it for a vigorous twist. [cf. DOWS-ING, PRIMAL PERCEPTION, ATOMS, SELECTIVITY]

STRESSOR—a very traumatic event in one's life that takes more than the usual time to balance with; e.g., a death in the immediate family. [cf. STRESS, BELIEF SYSTEM, HOLISTIC HEALTH]

STRIATIONS—(Kirlian effect) grains and lines shown in the human AURA on photographs taken by high-voltage cameras. [cf. PHANTOM LEAF, KIRLIAN EFFECT, AUTOEMISSIVE IMAGE]

STRIGA—(Rome) a PSYCHIC who changes into a bird to attack sleeping persons and drink their blood or visits a graveyard to eat the flesh of the dead; also spelled **strega**. Syn. STRIX, ESTRIE, VAMPIRE. [cf. SHAPE-CHANGING, WEREWOLF]

STRIGOI—(Romania) see STRIGA.

STRIP-CHART RECORDER—a device that measures the growth rate of plants per hour; used to measure the growth rate of the plant in experiments wherein the PSYCHIC sends the plant healing energy. [cf. BOTANE, SENSATION CONSCIOUS-NESS, WATCH PLANTS]

STRIPPED ROD—see DOWSING ROD.

STRIX—(Rome) PSYCHIC who specializes in EX-ORCISM, PROPHECY, and ASTROLOGY.

STROBE LIGHT—a light designed to flash in frequencies parallel to BRAIN WAVES, resulting in a hypnotic effect; used to induce HYPNOSIS, send mental telepathic messages, and to transfix the CONTACTEE in UFO encounters; (a flashing light is attached to the UFO constructs and is directed at the earthling, making him or her unable to move for a period of time). [cf. HYPNOTIC DISC, HYPNO-THERAPY, DIRECTED THOUGHT TRANSFER]

STROKE NURSING—the act of a nurse touching the shoulder or holding the hand of a patient while giving words of encouragement, as opposed to only writing on the charts and performing tasks briskly without conversation; recent research found that patients who receive touching and uplifting conversation recover faster; patients have a positive psychological reaction to warm physical contact, and feel nurses have a real concern for them; theory: primal form of love that we have not outgrown is transmitted from touching. [cf. CURATIVE EDUCATION, WELLNESS]

STROKER PLATE—(radiesthesia) a copper plate on the RADIESTHESIA instrument (BLACK BOX); the psychic rubs his or her fingers lightly over it while turning the dials with the other hand; when the psychic feels a slight drag or adhesion to the plate, it is the finest point-of-focus and he or she should leave the dial at that point. [cf. ABRAM'S BOX, RADIONICS, STICK]

STRUCTURAL INTEGRATION—a method of manipulating the muscles to align the body's structure with the earth's gravitational field; this releases stress patterns that have been unknowingly put into the body; see ROLFING. [cf. BLOCKS]

STRUCTURED MEDITATION—a group of people mentally following a leader who is speaking words designed to help them reach a state of MEDITATION; each person narrows his or her attention to the leader's voice, which brings on the meditative state more quickly; the leader can also instigate certain imagery for this process. Syn. GUIDED MEDITA-TION. [cf. IMAGERY, RED-HOT NEEDLES, ROSARY]

SUB—prefix meaning "under, below, slightly" and "in conjunction with."

SUBATOMIC ENERGY—1. (Russia) matter of which brain thoughts are made; psychic vibrations; a vibrational frequency wherein the finer forms of ELECTRICITY are transmitted as being one of the four substances to compose MATTER; known to physicists as positive nucleus. (Inconcl.) 2. (esoteric) (Theosophy) six esoteric atoms attracted together to make a hyper-meta-proto-element held together by will-force of the first aspect of the SOLAR DEITY. [cf. FIFTH PLANE, HYPER-META-PROTO-ELEMENTAL MATTER]

SUBBREATHERS—intelligent beings having a SOUL-MIND who live under the surface of the planet. [cf. HOLLOW-EARTH, REALMS OF FORM, MIDDLE WORLD]

595

SUBCONSCIOUS FORCE—see PSYCHIC ENERGY.

SUBCONSCIOUS MIND—(esoteric) 1. an invisible, ethereal energy field belonging to the PHYSICAL BODY but vibrating faster than the physical body; has no counterpart in the physical body (as does the invisible ASTRAL BODY) but its function is never separate from the brain area; 2. structure is like a computer more complex than humans will ever make; this computer mind records and holds in memory that which is given from the CONSCIOUS MIND, the data processor; from each experience the individual goes through, the conscious mind forms an attitude, a reaction, an idea, a concept, and emotional feelings (mingled with outer stimuli of smells, tastes, sounds, sights, and touch feelings); the conscious mind stores the final judgment in the SUBCONSCIOUS MIND; the new data is orderly, compartmentalized in the storage computer; new data that correlates with previously organized data adds to the total content of that data compartment, increasing it in understanding and thus perfecting it; material can be fed too fast and can be too foreign at one time; the objective is to perfect each compartment so change must come gradually; past data that corresponds to present activity and thought of the conscious mind surfaces instantaneously and automatically to help in the decision-making process; subconscious mind cannot make a decision of its own but takes data exactly as given from the conscious mind and doesn't lie in the return trip even if it has been stored from previous lives; 3. subconscious mind is director of the SYMPATHETIC NERVOUS SYSTEM but subservient to the conscious mind, having no decision-making mechanism of its own; 4. (Sigmund Freud) "governs personality"; corresponds to INSTINCT, the ID, the child; 5. (Jose Silva) "dumb mass of no sense of awareness; takes impressions from the conscious mind and creates reactons based on that information"; 6. intermingles with the conscious mind in making the pattern for one's lifestyle, BELIEF SYSTEM, daily activities, and BODY CHEMISTRY, helping the organism to unfold; 7. called the MIND in some disciplines in order to differentiate from the BRAIN; 8. a *permanent* intellect in contrast to the brain, which is a *temporary* intellect; 9. operates in an area between the conscious level of earth affairs and the mental levels of etheric world affairs; 10. helps direct the atoms in the brain along with the MENTAL MIND; supervises the sympathetic nervous system; 11. there is nothing in the UNIVERSE that is not filed away in the subconscious mind. (Inconcl.) **Syn.** SOUL-MIND, BIOCOMPUTER. [**cf.** BRAIN/MIND, UNCONSCIOUS MIND, SUBJECTIVE MIND, ID, AKASHIC RECORDS]

SUBCONSCIOUS TELEPATHY—1. to psychically tune in to a question on another person's mind, and without knowing the question per se, give the answer; 2. the transference of thoughts without speech between two persons, regardless of distance; occurs between two people who have a love or strong friendship bond. [**cf.** EARTH TELEPATHY, MIND READING, MIND-LINKING, PROTOTYPE TELEFLASHER]

SUBCONSCIOUSLY WILLED—a mental or physical psychic experience that is thought to be unplanned, undesired, and unwilled, happening spontaneously and at random (excluding the PSYCHIC EXPERIENCE that is brought on by a crisis from one's lifestyle, a deceased person, or a loved one); no guide from the "higher realms" will thrust his or her will upon the psychic to display signs of phenomena or urge to intervene with the pyschic unless called upon; the SUBCONSCIOUS MIND cannot make a decision by itself, therefore cannot be blamed for surfacing without permission; theory: unplanned PSYCHISM is a "hidden" desire in the subconscious mind; the individual wishes to excel in some phase of his or her life, wishes secretly to increase his or her psychic skills, or used psychism freely in a past life, and it now surfaces from a past-life agreement; psychic and mediumistic skills should be controlled by the psychic at all times, excluding CLAIRSENTIENCE. [**cf.** KARMICALLY SELF-GENERATED, CLOAK OF INSULATION]

SUBHUMAN BEING—(esoteric) an inferior ENTITY or a new SOUL-MIND belonging to the HUMAN BEING KINGDOM dwelling in the lower astral planes; exists in a body that appears unpleasant but shows human characteristics; is half-man and half-animal or half-bird; capable of communicating with psychics who do not know the rules of PSYCHISM; fed by the energy of low negative thoughts and acts found in the earth plane. (Inconcl.) [**cf.** DENSITY, NATURE SPIRITS]

SUBHUMAN BODIES—any living organisms that do not belong to the HUMAN BEING KINGDOM; i.e., plants, aquatic animals, reptiles, birds, quadruped animals, simian forms; all known to communicate with human beings telepathically. [**cf.** ANPSI, BOTANE]

SUBHUMAN REALM—see DENSITY.

SUBJECT—1. (hypnotherapy) the person being hypnotized; 2. (biofeedback training) the person using the instrument; 3. (dreams) the theme of the dream; 4. (ufology) the type of EXTRATERRESTRIAL LIFE or the type of craft that was spotted; 5. (psi tasks and laboratory experiments) the person who is being tested for ESP ability.

SUBJECT VARIANCE—(psi tasks) the fluctuation of a subject's total score from the theoretical mean of a series. [cf. VARIANCE-DIFFERENTIAL EFFECT, SCATTERED EFFECT]

SUBJECTIVE BEHAVIORISM—the study of inner thought experiences as compared to simple outer stimulus responses. [cf. HOLOGRAPHY, NEW-AGE PHILOSOPHY]

SUBJECTIVE CLAIRAUDIENCE—1. to hear sound, music, or voices "within the head" without the aid of physical ears; in contrast to hearing sound "in space" without the aid of physical ears; one theory: ETHERIC WORLD INTELLIGENCES transmit sound using the medium's THIRD-EYE AREA as an amplifier to be clairaudiently heard. [cf. OBJECTIVE CLAIRAUDIENCE] 2. to tune in to the sound of the processes of one's organs and bodily functions. [cf. EARTH PSYCHIC SOUND, CLAIRAUDIENCE Appendix 2]

SUBJECTIVE CLAIRVOYANCE—to reach into another vibrational frequency and see pictures "within the mind" without the use of the physical eyes, as opposed to seeing visions "in the atmosphere"; seeing on the back of the eyelids or on the back of the forehead; physical eyes closed or opened; pictures are objects, scenes, people, colors, lights, animals, words, geometric figures, etheric world friends, etheric world guides; visions are full-blown or in fragments; one can consciously will to see a psychic vision but what is seen is a product of the SUBCONSCIOUS MIND or the guides. **Syn.** INNER VISION. [cf. OBJECTIVE CLAIRVOYANCE, MENTAL PSYCHISM, ESP, COGNITION]

SUBJECTIVE COMMUNICATION—1. to perceive psychic skills "within the head" in constrast to "out in the atmosphere"; 2. to use HYPNOTHERAPY as a means of surfacing psychic or psychological information; 3. to perceive information from one's etheric world helpers; 4. to receive PSYCHIC INFORMATION when in a TRANCE state. [cf. SUBCONSCIOUS MIND]

SUBJECTIVE EDUCATION—information pertaining to levels of AWARENESS beyond the conscious level; instruction on how to extract PSYCHIC INFORMATION from these levels and use it for problem solving. **Sim.** PARAPSYCHOLOGY.

SUBJECTIVE IMAGES—see IMAGES.

SUBJECTIVE INTERPRETATION—(dreams) used when the scenes and the theme of a dream cannot be taken literally but must be allegorically compared with the dreamer's character, desires, or feelings. [cf. DREAM THERAPY, SYMBOLS, MOTIVE UNCONSCOUSNESS]

SUBJECTIVE MIND—1. the thinking and reasoning mechanism, the BRAIN; 2. (esoteric) a permanent intellect that contains knowledge of birth, dying, involuntary functions, instinctual functions, automation, etc.; includes the feeling nature with the thinking process; see SUBCONSCIOUS MIND. [cf. OBJECTIVE MIND, SOUL-MIND, CONSCIOUS MIND]

SUBJECTIVE PROGRAMMING—(Silva Mind Control) a technique used for perceiving PSYCHIC INFORMATION; to give the CONSCIOUS MIND a question and then enter an ALTERED STATE OF CONSCIOUSNESS to gain the information desired. **Syn.** AUTOSUGGESTION. [cf. PROGRAMMING, OBJECTIVE PROGRAMMING]

SUBJECTIVE PSYCHIC ATTACK—unpleasant, undesirable, negative mental activity that preoccupies one's time, depletes one's energy, and eats into the physical body; abnormal activity for that person; theories: 1. thoughts telepathically sent by a PSYCHIC with EVIL intent; 2. information surfacing from a past INCARNATION wherein the victim dealt in BLACK MAGIC; 3. negative vibrations entering the mind through a break in the ETHERIC WEB; 4. evil forces drawn to the victim through his or her own volition by dwelling on emotions of hate, fear, resentment, and jealousy. [cf. OBJECTIVE PSYCHIC ATTACK]

SUBJECTIVE SENSATION—to feel an emotion within the body and mind that has no bearing on present outer stimuli; can be attributed to tuning in to another person's feelings. **Sim.** EMPATHY CLAIRSENTIENCE. [cf. TELEPATHY, INTERCHANGE OF MAGNETISM]

SUBJECTIVE SENSES—see PSYCHIC SENSES.

SUBJECTIVE SPACE—to feel the psychic information or psychic phenomena that is happening is in space instead of inside the mind. [cf. OBJECTIVE

COMMUNICATION, OBJECTIVE CLAIRAUDIENCE]

SUBJECTS—(esoteric) all NATURE SPIRITS in the nature spirit kingdom under their rulers, PAN and ANTIPAN.

SUBJUGATION—to allow an inferior ETHERIC WORLD ENTITY to paralyze one's will, dominate one's mind, and to make one act contrary to one's own will; on the surface, the PSYCHIC seems to be out of control; see OBSESSION. [**cf.** POSSESSION Appendix 2, SUBCONSCIOUSLY WILLED]

SUBLIME UNIVERSAL SOUL—see TOTALITY.

SUBLIMINAL BIOFEEDBACK—a response that registers on the BIOFEEDBACK INSTRUMENT even though the lights and patterns shown to the subject were too fast for his or her conscious awareness. [**cf.** SUBLIMINAL LEVEL, UPPER FREQUENCY, VISUAL SCANNING]

SUBLIMINAL LEVEL—a region beneath the CONSCIOUS AWARENESS that has the capacity to receive, accept, and record outside stimuli; records material just as it is received because it bypasses the CONSCIOUS MIND without being noticed, and therefore without being sorted before filing; this is compartmentalized in the SUBCONSCIOUS MIND as if it were sorted in the conscious mind first; surfaces back into the conscious mind to help with current decisions the same as other material in the subconscious mind; e.g., an advertisement is flashed on the movie screen too fast for viewers to consciously see or hear, and in a few minutes, a large number of people from the audience go to the lobby to buy the popcorn that was shown in the subliminal flash. (Inconcl.) [**cf.** SUBCONSCIOUS MIND, UNCONSCIOUS MIND]

SUBLIMINAL PERCEPTION—(esoteric) to receive information and feelings from invisible outer stimuli which occurs in psychic readings and which passes at a speed too fast for physical perception. (Inconcl.) [**cf.** COMPOUND OF CONSCIOUSNESS]

SUBLIMINAL PLANE—counterpart in the ETHERIC WORLD that corresponds to the SUBLIMINAL LEVEL of the mind; not knowing what the subliminal level holds may account for the clairvoyant perception that one does not understand and which seems foreign to the REALITY at that time. [**cf.** UNCONSCIOUS MIND, SUBJECTIVE MIND]

SUBLIMINAL RECORDS—(future science) MEMORY BANK of all kinds of information and knowledge in each individual's mind that differs for each; surfaces secretly, and silently influencing one's belief system and conscious mind decisions; awareness level of mind undetermined at the present time; records can be surfaced under hypnotic states; theory: information perceived through RETROCOGNITION, PRECOGNITION, AUTOMATISM, CLAIRVOYANCE, and DREAMS. (Inconcl.) [**cf.** INNER-DIALOGUE, BELIEF SYSTEM]

SUBLIMINAL SELF—coined by F. W. H. Myers (1890); "the self beneath the conscious threshold"; 1. contains knowledge of internal bodily functions; 2. storage bin in the deepest level of the SUBCONSCIOUS MIND for knowledge of the world; 3. the HUMAN BEING SPECIES SEED that contains total knowledge. (Inconcl.) **Syn.** MONAD. [**cf.** ARCHETYPAL UNCONSCIOUS, EGO-ID]

SUBNUCLEAR PARTICLES—(esoteric) concentrated centers of ENERGY and INTELLIGENCE smaller than the ATOM, oscillating in the atmosphere. (Inconcl.) [**cf.** NODE]

SUBPERSONALITY—1. an ETHERIC WORLD ENTITY who communicates with a MEDIUM too frequently; thought to be a suppressed personality of the medium. (Inconcl.) 2. patterns within an individual that give one conscious and unconscious, habitual ways of thinking, feeling, and acting. **Sim.** AKASHIC RECORDS. [**cf.** SPIRIT COMMUNICATION, CELL MEMORY BANK]

SUBPLANES OF ASTRAL—lower levels of consciousness where earthbound soul-minds have their home; see DENSITY. **Syn.** HADES, HELL. [**cf.** EARTHBOUND ENTITIES, HAUNTING]

SUBSTATES OF MATTER—(esoteric) the various substances that make up MATTER: solid, liquid, gaseous, etheric, superetheric, subatomic, and atomic elements. [**cf.** BUDDHIC PLANE, FIRMAMENT, HIGHER PLANE]

SUBSTITUTION MESSAGE—information that is unknowingly repressed in a psychic READING because of its unpleasant nature, and only a clue is given; e.g., "I see an ad for carpet cleaning," but the querient has no carpets; within a few days, his or her mother's funeral notice is printed in the paper next to the carpet cleaning advertisement; thus the death message was repressed due to the unpleasantness of its nature. **Syn.** DISPLACEMENT MESSAGE. [**cf.** MISCARRIAGES, QUANTUM JUMP]

SUBSURFACE KINGDOMS—see SUBTERRANEAN

598

WORLD.

SUBTALK—see INNER-DIALOGUE.

SUBTERRANEAN WORLD—1. a place in the hollow of the earth where cities exist; believed to be a civilization of millions of inhabitants; theory: (**a**) highly intelligent beings; (**b**) a low type of life form; they frequently appear in their astral bodies to earthlings; earthlings have visited them in the flesh in caves. (Inconcl.) **Syn.** HOLLOW EARTH. **2.** (Buddhism) exists under the earth's surface, where the Supreme Ruler of the Empire or King of the World inhabits; he controls the world through secret tunnels connecting the subterranean world and Tibet (perhaps connecting the GIZEH complex); far advanced in the science of technology. **Syn.** AGHARTA. (Inconcl.) **3.** believed that some flying saucers come from here. (Inconcl.)

SUBTLE—pertains to faster vibrations than the physical SENSES can perceive; used to describe the ETHERIC WORLD or PSYCHIC ENERGY.

SUBTLE BODY—see ASTRAL BODY.

SUBVOCALIZATION—sounds made by one learning to TRANCE; slight vibrations of the throat, altered by movements of the tongue, that can be heard by the SITTERS in a SEANCE. [**cf.** TRANCE VOICES Appendix 2]

SUCCESS—to give all one has to give to whatever one is doing; this means one is "successful" at doing that thing, whether it be working for a boss, earning fame, or sweeping the floor; whether or not one meets the standards of others has nothing to do with the success of one's self. [**cf.** NEW-AGE PSYCHOLOGY]

SUCCESS MECHANISM—see GRACE.

SUCCUBUS—a female ETHERIC WORLD ENTITY who has sexual intercourse with a human male; the entity remains invisible during the act, which occurs during the dream state, or it assumes a human form for that period. [**cf.** INCUBUS, DENSITY]

SUDARIUM—see TALISMAN.

SUDDEN PERSONALITY CHANGE—coined by Flo Conway and Jim Siegelman: **1.** an abrupt, unordinary, impulsive alteration of one's character in all its many forms; a very deep and comprehensive change in individual awareness and personality; this compulsive transformation in attitude toward one's society, family, business committment,

morals, intellectual reasoning, religion, habits, and money is brought about by: (**a**) an innocent encounter with a recruiter from a DESTRUCTIVE-BRAINWASHING CULT; (**b**) a weekend intensive sponsored by the cult; (**c**) what is described as a "peak" experience by the cult's teachings brought about by repetitious rituals; the well-planned ploy and technique of the repetitious suggestions, without time in between to make any logical choices, is designed for this purpose; e.g., without warning, a college student leaves school overnight, and is discovered selling flowers on the street corner a few days later; **2.** an abnormal process of the brain function that can only be brought about by torture, an overdose of drugs, or the "coercive persuasion" of repeated suggestions; the destructive brainwashing cult uses repeated suggestions that involve the emotional aspect of the primal law of function and are difficult for any human to resist. (Inconcl.) [**cf.** WITNESS, ON-THE-SPOT-HYPNOSIS, SNAPPING, GROUP HYPNOSIS, SUGGESTION]

SUFFERING—(esoteric) **1.** a mental or physical transformation trying to happen; an energy manifestation of TOTALITY needed by everyone to "unfold"; **2.** (Herman Hesse) "one only hurts because one fears it, or flees it; if one loved it, did not resist it, and gave one's self to it, it would not hurt; it is one's aversion that hurts"; **3.** (Swami Rama) mental suffering is caused from one's attachments to people, jobs, conditions, locations, and things, and when they stop their routine of flow, one feels emotionally hurt; **4.** the only way out of suffering, mentally or physically, is through it; pain is to be transformed into joy; **5.** suffering occurs from one's outside awareness; "nothing" in the universe can hurt one, no accident, no loss of a loved one, no loss of job, no natural catastrophe, no terminal illness; it is only one's attitude toward these experiences which causes the hurt; **6.** (Pir Vilayat Inayat Khan) suffering is a blessing because it is from God bringing with it a sense of purpose; there is a blessing behind every problem; one who has had the greatest suffering can experience the greatest joy; **7.** physical pain is an aversion, healing methods are attention. [**cf.** NEW-AGE PSYCHOLOGY, BELIEF SYSTEM, EMOTIONS, HOLISTIC HEALTH, DISEASE, BLOCKS]

SUFFERING SPIRITS—discarnate soul-minds who bind themselves to the earth plane with their longing for materialistic experiences; cause trouble to earthlings by latching onto those with earthly

599

habits they wish to remember. **Syn.** EARTHBOUND ENTITIES. [**cf.** HAUNTING, CONFUSED SOUL-MINDS, DENSITY]

SUFI—("wearer of wool") one who belongs to the Sufi discipline; refers to her or himself as *fugara* or "poor in Spirit"; noted for his or her whirling movements to reach higher states of consciousness and to bring on psychic experiences. **Sim.** FAKIR. [**cf.** MEDITATION IN MOTION, ALLAH, WHIRLING DERVISHES]

SUFISM—not a sect in itself but composed of a series of philosophical systems designed to improve the human mind; no rituals, no holy city, no ecclesiastical hierarchy, but a body of knowledge bearing the same TRUTH that is at the heart of all religions and human endeavor; noted for its whirling dervish dancers. [**cf.** WHIRLING DERVISHES]

SUGGESTION—a new idea, proposition, plan, belief, or attitude mentioned or introduced to one for consideration, possible action, or to be absorbed as knowledge; (esoteric) the main factor in making thoughts manifest in the world is through suggestion by the spoken or written word or life's experiences; this is done by the CONSCIOUS MIND, which perceives from outside stimuli, forms a concept or decision, and then drops it into the computer mind, the SUBCONSCIOUS MIND; it is then compartmentalized if there is a compartment to which the new suggestion can relate; if the suggestion is completely foreign, it will be spewed out until a new compartment begins to form; before thoughts can manifest into mundane reality, the suggestion must be "accepted" by the subconscious mind; it then blends with the conscious mind's ergs of energy that emanate from the head, with meaning and purpose, which gives it the intensity it needs to manifest; (E. Arthur Winkler) inner thoughts and desires become suggestions also and manifest into reality, when they are intense enough to be lodged in the subconscious level of the mind; changing the subconscious mind is normally a gradual process as one grows; new, completely foreign compartments can be "forced" to develop and manifest REALITY by overly repeating suggestions, such as is being done in the DESTRUCTIVE-BRAINWASHING CULTS. [**cf.** HETEROSUGGESTION, AUTOSUGGESTION, HYPNOTIC SUGGESTION, TELEPATHIC SUGGESTION, SUDDEN PERSONALITY CHANGE]

SUGGESTOLOGY—see SUGGESTOPEDIA.

SUGGESTOPEDIA—(future science) (Bulgaria) founded by Dr. Georgi Lozanov; a method of speed learning by memory expansion; a technique based on stimulating background music set to a receptive learning mood and tempo; the information to be learned bypasses the CONSCIOUS MIND and is absorbed by the SUBCONSCIOUS MIND without the subconscious mind becoming knowingly involved; (subconscious mind is not alert to the incoming information as in HYPNOSIS and DREAMING); the information to be learned is presented by an instructor who modulates his or her voice according to the tempo of the music; the student focuses not on the lesson, but on the music as one would a MANTRA; the tempo of the music is timed to be compatible with the brain rhythm of the student; the music is pleasurable enough for the conscious mind to relinquish its function of sorting the incoming thought, allowing the subconscious mind to surface, focus on the music, and with another compartment accept the material read by the instructor as given, record it, and remember it. (Inconcl.) **Syn.** SUGGESTOLOGY.

SUGMAD—(Eckankar) Lord of All.

SULPHUR—(alchemy) one of the three basic components necessary for refining both metals and souls; the element in a substance which enables it to burn; a powerful disinfectant similar to purification by fire; corresponds to human emotions. [**cf.** PHILOSOPHERS' FIRE, SALT, MERCURY]

SUMMER HORMONE—a thyroid secretion appearing automatically when summer approaches, to help reduce body heat. [**cf.** CYCLES, LIFE GROWTH CYCLE]

SUMMERLAND—the first, second, and third subdivisions of the ASTRAL PLANE in the ETHERIC WORLD; (F. W. H. Myers) "PLANE OF ILLUSION appears to be a blissful land of rest and harmony, partly a creation of the inhabitant's own desires and the pleasures of earth-life, minus its drawbacks"; a temporary existence that looks like our plane, only it is superior; formed of matter by self-absorbed discarnate beings who call into temporary existence schools, cities, gardens, homes, etc. **Syn.** PARADISE CONDITIONS. [**cf.** HAPPY HUNTING GROUND, LITHISPHERE, PRINCIPLES OF MAN]

SUN—1. a star; source of all life, light, warmth, and motion on our planet earth; 2. (esoteric) contains all elements known on earth; necessary to charge and recharge the atmosphere of our earth with different types of energy used to sustain earth life; a transmitter of COSMIC ENERGY into chemical MATTER; 3. possesses a positive-masculine POLARITY working in harmony with the planets which are negative-feminine; 4. a live entity accomplishing and evolving toward the overall plan; 5. sun is to the UNIVERSE as the HEART is to a human. [cf. EVOLUTION, UNIVERSAL LIFE CYCLE]

SUN BY THE SACRED HEART—(Germany) HEART CHAKRA symbolized by the serpent around a sun over the heart area.

SUN WORSHIP—1. religions of primitive people who were aware of the sun as the main source of life; sun was their DEITY; beliefs: sun impinged upon individuals and groups, measured rhythm of days and seasons, and gave and withheld life; 2. worship of the God that keeps the sun on its path, bringing light into darkness; worshipers considered the sun to be both male and female; symbolized by a sun goddess riding in a golden chariot drawn by horses.

SUN'S JOURNEY—see SUSHUMNA.

SUN'S RAYS—invisible and visible life energy emanating from the sun, necessary to all life on the planet; contains all elements known to mankind and brings these elements to whatever it strikes. [cf. VIBRATIONS, POLARITY, SUN]

SUN-GAZE DANCE—(Native American) a personal, sacred, but agonizing dance one must go through as a part of the initiation to become a SHAMAN; this helps him earn his guardian spirits that will work with him in his new role of counselor for the tribe. [cf. INITIATORY SICKNESS, SHAMANISM, MEDIUM, VISION QUEST, WHIRLING DERVISHES, GUARDIAN SPIRIT]

SUNGNA—(Tibet) a PSYCHIC living in the church; respected as the guardian and protector for others due to his psychic ability to PROPHESY and counsel. [cf. SPIRITUALIST]

SUNSPOTS—(esoteric) dark patches which appear on the surface of the sun; caused by the breathing of the sun, which takes eleven years for each breath; the spots appear at the peak of the breath. (Inconcl.)

SUNSTONE—(Vikings) a magic gem that changes color when pointed to the sun even on the cloudiest of days. [cf. MINPSI, LIGHT-BULB GEMS, MOONSTONE]

SUNYATA—(Buddhism) (meditation) to be without a feeling of TIME, SPACE, or movement; state of pure-being; experiencing the VOID. **Syn.** BEING, IS-NESS. [cf. BLANK MIND, CAVE MEDITATION]

SUPER—prefix meaning "above and beyond."

SUPER-ESP—those types of psychic experiences that seem to reveal evidence of life in another form after this life. [cf. DEATHBED VISIONS, FREEING THE SOUL, MANIFESTED IN THE LIGHT, GO-BEYOND-DEATH EXPERIENCE]

SUPER-ETHER—(esoteric) one of the four substances that compose ETHERIC MATTER; vibrational frequency wherein light is transmitted; known in physics as neutralized nucleus. [cf. SUB-ATOMIC, ATOMIC]

SUPER-PSI—(psi tasks) see ASTRAL PROJECTION.

SUPERALERTNESS—the increase in sensitivity of the physical senses, as in HYPNOTHERAPY and MEDITATION; when the body, mind, and emotions have become relaxed and quieted, the senses become more acute; e.g., someone talking outside the window sounds to the subject as though they are talking next to him or her; a light touch on the arm can be painful. [cf. HYPERAESTHESIA]

SUPERCLAIRVOYANCE—ability of the brain to understand what the ASTRAL BODY is seeing while in the ASTRAL PLANE during an ASTRAL PROJECTION; understanding ASTRAL VISION, which is seeing with the whole body and seeing the inside and outside of each thing at the same time. [cf. INTELLIGENT BODY, DIVINE LIGHT]

SUPERCONSCIOUS MIND—(esoteric) also spelled **supraconscious**; 1. an ethereal energy field that brings knowledge and information of a higher source than the other two minds to the brain area; occurs spontaneously or intentionally; information and knowledge flow from the UNIVERSAL MIND via the SILVER CORD to the head and run along the spinal column in the KUNDALINI; an Infinite intellect; 2. this information bypasses the SUBCONSCIOUS MIND, therefore, the subconscious belief system does not filter the data; the data is "pure"; 3. data and advice flow from the superconscious mind through the PSYCHISM called INTUITION, CLAIRSENTIENCE, and HUNCHABILITY; data could not have been logically reasoned or figured out ahead of time; pure information; because it flows through the spine, psychics remark, "I have a gut feeling..."

601

or "I feel it in my bones that I should not . . ."; takes the same path as INSTINCT and therefore is the only type of psychism that does not need to be willed; 4. superconscious mind knowledge flows through the psychism called INSPIRATIONAL THOUGHT, INSPIRATIONAL WRITING, INSPIRATIONAL ART; this knowledge was not learned in past education or life experiences; knowledge is beyond the perceiver's time period; a state of consciousness that geniuses are tuned into; 5. (Jules-Bois) "is the opposite of the subconscious mind, comprises the faculties that can really make man a super-animal"; 6. (Ralph Waldo Emerson) the OVERSOUL; 7. (Sigmund Freud) SUPEREGO, parent; a fundamental aspect of self; 8. (Carl Jung) the most spiritual part of the mind, a part of universal subconscious. **Syn.** SUPEREGO, SUPRACONSCIOUS. [**cf.** CLAIRSENTIENCE, CONSCIOUS MIND]

SUPERCREATIVITY—ability of an artist or a MEDIUM to compose music, write, or paint material that exceeds his or her own talent or formal education; accomplished under ACTIVE TRANCE and occurs with great speed (compared with the person's own skill); sometimes recognizable as the style of a famous artist or writer; theory: an etheric world GUIDE or the deceased famous person is working through the artist. [**cf.** INSPIRATIONAL THOUGHT Appendix 2]

SUPEREGO—1. (Sigmund Freud) one's conscience; an aspect of the mind that passes judgment according to one's morals; founded on social standards which are represented by parents' behavior internalized into the child's PERSONALITY system; attempts to deny or restrict pleasure; the last aspect of personality to develop; the ID, EGO, and superego are in constant conflict; 2. see SUPERCONSCIOUS MIND.

SUPERGALAXY—a system of many galaxies revolving around a Great Central Sun; each one a replica of our galaxy. [**cf.** LAW OF REPETITION Appendix 7]

SUPERHUMAN BEING—(esoteric) an ETHERIC WORLD INTELLIGENCE having more knowledge and power than most etheric world entities; an angelic being working in the higher planes. **Syn.** DEVA. [**cf.** CELESTIAL HIERARCHY, LOGOI OF THE PLANETARY CHAIN]

SUPERINTELLIGENCE—the fastest vibrational frequency possible, containing all the knowledge, in-

formation, ideas, inventions, plans, colors, music, numbers, shapes, etc., humanity will ever conceive; separated in a minute, duplicate, complete form within each person. **Syn.** UNIVERSAL MIND, DIVINE MIND, GODHEAD. [**cf.** MACROCOSM, MICROCOSM]

SUPERINTELLIGENT ELECTRICITY—energy stored in the KUNDALINI ready to be used for raising one's STATE OF CONSCIOUSNESS; sometimes misinterpreted and misused as a sex drive. [**cf.** JOURNEY TO THE MOON, LIFE FLUID]

SUPERIOR MAN—see TOTALITY.

SUPERIOR MENTAL PERSPECTIVE—higher thoughts that come to an individual without one's asking and without one's conscious formation of them. **Syn.** INSPIRATIONAL THOUGHT, CLAIRSENTIENCE. [**cf.** SUPERCONSCIOUS MIND]

SUPERIOR SPIRITS—(Allan Kardec) ETHERIC WORLD INTELLIGENCES who possess purified terrestrial fluid, perfected SENSES, and have chosen to help civilization on earth; bring only advanced WISDOM and high qualitative PSYCHISM to mediums who are well-grounded and will pass the information along. **Syn.** CHIEF DEITIES. [**cf.** CONTROL, ETHERIC MENTORS, WELL-GROUNDED MEDIUM]

SUPERLIMINAL—(Michael H. Bradford) "everything an individual perceives as it is now; the beta level; the functioning of the conscious mind." [**cf.** SUBLIMINAL LEVEL]

SUPERMENTAL ACTIVITY—spontaneous PSYCHIC INFORMATION that could not have been logically reasoned or figured out from the mental mind; comes directly from the GODHEAD, and bypasses the SUBCONSCIOUS MIND, resulting in "pure" information; see CLAIRSENTIENCE. **Sim.** INTUITIVE KNOWING, HUNCH. [**cf.** SUPERCONSCIOUS MIND, CONSCIOUS MIND]

SUPERMESMERIC—(Huna) the use of a physical stimulus for the induction of HYPNOTHERAPY; e.g., a swinging PENDULUM or the HYPNOTIC DISC. [**cf.** INDUCTION, INDUCTION RELEASE]

SUPERMIND—1. a catch-all name given to the mechanism that functions in the ETHERIC WORLD to bring PSYCHIC INFORMATION; the SUBCONSCIOUS MIND or the SUPERCONSCIOUS MIND. **Sim.** PSYCHISM, THIRD-EYE. [**cf.** TRANSCENDENT SELF, MYSTICISM]

SUPERMUNDANE—that which has a higher state

of consciousness than does the material world consciousness but exists in the material world for a purposeful time. **Sim.** SPIRITUAL VALUE. [**cf.** STATE OF CONSCIOUSNESS]

SUPERNATURAL—1. pertains to events, outside the range of the five physical SENSES, that are uncommon and cannot be explained by today's scientific measurements; includes happenings beyond the understanding of the masses, within a mundane perspective, occurring infrequently; imagery faculty of a person at work; 2. (esoteric) the result of energies related to natural laws which are subject to the WILL of mankind, consciously or unconsciously. **Syn.** SUPERNORMAL, PSYCHIC SKILLS.

SUPERNATURALISTIC ART—a theory of artists: one need not expound on nature but allow the SOUL-MIND to reveal itself in the art. **Syn.** INSPIRATIONAL ART, INSPIRATIONAL COMPOSITION, INSPIRATIONAL WRITING.

SUPERNORMAL—see SUPERNATURAL.

SUPERPERSONAL ENTITY—an intelligence in the etheric world who has accomplished the art of communicating with an earthling. **Syn.** ETHERIC WORLD ENTITY, GUIDE.

SUPERPHYSICAL—1. pertains to any source of life seen or felt in the ETHERIC WORLD; 2. outer activity of physical matter without any scientific explanation. [**cf.** ETHERIC WORLD INTELLIGENCE, PSYCHISM]

SUPERPHYSICAL BODY—pertains to the ASTRAL BODY.

SUPERPHYSICAL ORDER OF MATTER—(Theosophy, Hinduism) ETHERIC, SUPERETHER, SUBATOMIC ENERGY, and ATOMIC ETHER, BUDDHIC PLANE, REALMS OF FORM.

SUPERSENSITIVE—see PSYCHIC.

SUPERSENSITIVE PHOTO MULTIPLIERS—a camera using a frequency lower than the Kirlian camera for picking up the "faint" rays of light or glow following objects. (Inconcl.) [**cf.** GLOBULES, EARTH'S ELECTRICAL FIELD, RADIATION FIELD PHOTOGRAPHY]

SUPERSENSONICS—(future science) radiations from invisible and visible matter, from zero to infinity; the study of the entire spectrum of ELECTROMAGNETIC RADIATION of the universe emanating from animate, inanimate, and ethereal substance, and their influence on the human biological system and psychic system; the spiritual physics of all radiations; detection of radiations beyond the range of standard physics' instrumentation; correlates PARAPSYCHOLOGY, PHYSICS, RADIESTHESIA, and RADIONICS. **Syn.** RADIATIONAL PARAPHYSICS.

SUPERSENSORY PERCEPTION—abbr. SSP; a collective term covering all kinds of psychic skills.

SUPERSENSUAL—1. pertains to that which is beyond the range of physical SENSES; see PSYCHIC INFORMATION; 2. pertains to spiritual emotion.

SUPERSONIC—that which is greater than the speed of sound through air; a higher frequency than is audible to the ear. [**cf.** CLAIRAUDIENCE]

SUPERSPEAKING MEDIUMSHIP—see VOICE TRANCE.

SUPERSTITION—(esoteric) (Dion Fortune) "the blind use of a form whose significance has been forgotten."

SUPERSTRUCTURES—personal laws, made consciously and unconsciously, which rule one's life; a result of education and attitudes regarding life experiences, mingled with past life experiences; cause undesirable, unwanted habits or desirable, pleasant habits; laws are not outwardly recognizable but can be detected by an awareness of INNER-DIALOGUE. [**cf.** CURATIVE EDUCATION, LAW OF THOUGHT Appendix 7]

SUPERTELEPATHY—to tune into thoughts of an etheric world entity, think they are one's own, but question why the mind wandered to another subject; (do not confuse with planned impressions that the etheric world GUIDE uses for one's guidance). [**cf.** INNER-WORLD TELEPATHY]

SUPERUNIVERSES—see CHAKRA.

SUPERWAKEFULNESS—(Russia) special hypnotic consciousness wherein one functions like the personality of a famous person performing the talent as if they were the famous person themselves; one knows they do not know the famous person; e.g., playing music like Beethoven although one has no talent in music. **Syn.** ANTITHESIS OF SLEEP. [**cf.** ARTIFICIAL REINCARNATION]

SUPRA—prefix implying "above and beyond" or sometimes "within and without."

SUPRACONSCIOUSNESS—see SUPERCONSCIOUS MIND.

SUPRAHUMAN SUPRASELF SPACES—levels of consciousness making PLANES for the ETHERIC WORLD INTELLIGENCES of the highest spiritual accomplishment, such as masters, to inhabit. [cf. CONSCIOUSNESS, FIFTH PLANE, SELFLESS UNIVERSAL LOVE]

SUPRALIMINAL—1. (F. W. H. Myers) "a highly specialized, superficial level of the human PSYCHE; developed through EVOLUTION to respond to influences from the material environment acting on the body through the sense organs; responsible for PSYCHIC INFORMATION;" 2. psychological term for mental activity above the threshold of mental consciousness; used by musicians, artists, and geniuses; see INSPIRATIONAL THOUGHT.

SUPRAMUNDANE REALITY—(esoteric) STATE OF CONSCIOUSNESS wherein earth sensations and realities have been obliterated; sensation of PURE CONSCIOUSNESS; oneness with the clear light; a feeling of life in other vibrational levels around one's self; [cf. ETHERIC WORLD, ULTRACONSCIOUSNESS]

SUPRANATURAL ACTIVITY—MENTAL and PHYSICAL PSYCHISM.

SUPRAPHYSICAL BODY—an umbrella word used to express one of the etheric world entities because each one has its own personality. [cf. ETHERIC WORLD INTELLIGENCES]

SUPRAPHYSICAL PERSONALITY—a character trait developed in a past life which frequently surfaces in this life; puzzles the earthling as to the reason or cause. [cf. BLOCKS, DELAYED KARMA, KARMA OF FUNCTION]

SUPRASELF—a higher state of consciousness of one's self communicating through one's own voice organs as if it were a separate entity, while in a state of TRANCE. [cf. VOICE TRANCE, CHANNELING]

SUPRASELF METAPROGRAMS—see ETHERIC WORLD INTELLIGENCES.

SUPRASPECIES METAPROGRAMMERS—see ETHERIC WORLD INTELLIGENCES.

SUPREME AND COMPLETE RITUAL—a special ceremony of MAGIC wherein one invokes the HOLY GUARDIAN ANGEL for mental guidance or psychic phenomena. [cf. ANGEL HIERARCHY, GUIDES]

SUPREME BLISS—(alchemy) to know how to transmute one's body back and forth from the PHYSICAL WORLD to the ETHERIC WORLD at will; the ultimate aim of the alchemists; to understand how to purify one's body so it can be easily dematerialized by a meticulous, disciplined mind, held together in its ethereal state, until needed on earth, and then rematerialized back in a physical form to be helpful to mankind. **Syn.** IMMORTAL DRAUGHT. [cf. GREAT AWAKENING, INTERNAL ALCHEMY]

SUPREME GUIDES OF HUMANITY—old soul-minds who chose to come to earth and serve from here; recognized as mighty leaders of men; avatars; e.g., JESUS, BUDDHA, KRISHNA. [cf. LORDHOOD, MASTERSHIP, AVATAR]

SUPREME STATE—see CHRIST CONSCIOUSNESS or VOID.

SUPPRESSED DESIRE—implies that even though the psychic experience is labeled "spontaneous," consent at some time was given by the SUBCONSCIOUS MIND. [cf. CLOAK OF INSULATION, SUBCONSCIOUSLY WILLED, KARMICALLY WILLED]

SUR—prefix corresponding to "super" or "before."

SURFACE DOWSING—to walk over the actual ground where one wants to locate something as opposed to MAP DOWSING; to tell the rod what it should locate and walk until there is a pull in the hands indicating that the desired substance is under the ground. [cf. DOWSING, ROD, RADIESTHESIA, ZONES OF IRRITATION]

SURFACE SUBCONSCIOUS—use of the BRAIN as a temporary MEMORY BANK with information put there in this life; ready to be used in this life enmeshed with the SUBCONSCIOUS MIND, the permanent memory bank. [cf. CEREBROSPINAL NERVOUS SYSTEM, AKASHIC RECORDS, BELIEF SYSTEM]

SURFACING—to begin speaking from one's CONSCIOUS MIND. Knowledge when one is supposed to be psychically tuned into the SUBCONSCIOUS MIND; occurs when working with an ETHERIC WORLD INTELLIGENCE, or when one is in a hypnotic state; this means the subject is coming back to a normal BETA STATE OF CONSCIOUSNESS, and must be reprogrammed if he or she is to go on with the psychic work. [cf. PSYCHED-UP, OUTER MENTAL ACTIVITY]

SURGICAL GIFT—(Philippines) ability to perform PSYCHIC SURGERY or ETHERIC SURGERY; see same.

SURNATURALISM—to put on paper or canvas that which comes from an ETHERIC WORLD INTELLIGENCE and pertains to the etheric world, especially the higher realms; (do not confuse with AUTOMATISM). [**cf.** PSYCHIC ARTIST, INSPIRATIONAL ART, AUTOMATIC]

SURREALISM—(1920) development of a type of art and literature that was not perceived by the five SENSES but came through AUTOMATISM, VISION, INSPIRATIONAL ART, and INSPIRATIONAL WRITING.

SURREALISTIC PHANTOMS—1. (biofeedback training) stream of faces and scenes passing through the mind of some people in the beginning of MEDITATION, when HOOKED-UP to the EEG; **2.** see HYPNAGOGIC. [**cf.** SEA OF FACES, REVERIE]

SURRENDER OF THE WILL—(destructive-brainwashing cults) to relinquish complete control of one's mental activity, actions, and emotions to a higher authority; letting go of the total personality; caused by a spontaneous, short-lived spiritual experience during the brainwashing program; victim is told he or she is "born again" and the brainwashing suggestions are then readily accepted and the cult organization is in control. **Syn.** SNAPPING. [**cf.** DIVINE MOMENT, PERSONAL ENCOUNTER]

SURROUND—see ETHERIC DOUBLE.

SURVIVAL—(death) pertains to continued existence after physical DEATH in some form of an energy field in the ETHERIC WORLD, for an indeterminate time; differs from IMMORTALITY as existence in varied forms is not implied but neither is it ruled out; does not infer REINCARNATION. (Inconcl.) [**cf.** DEATH SCIENCE Appendix 2, SURVIVAL RESEARCH]

SURVIVAL ELEMENTS—(death science) (ancient, Eastern) the SOUL-MIND and part of the ETHERIC DOUBLE are the ENERGY FIELDS that do not deteriorate in the ground with the PHYSICAL BODY; the soul-mind slides from the physical body upon death and takes with it into the ETHERIC WORLD the "quality" of knowledge and emotions just learned, worked-out KARMA, and ACCUMULATED KARMA not yet worked-out; the etheric double splits and part stays with the physical body and part stays with the soul-mind; within the soul-mind is the LIFE FORCE, the potential within the human being seed that lives on in the etheric world. [**cf.** REIN-CARNATION, RIPE KARMA]

SURVIVAL OF PERSONALITY—a whole unit of uniqueness and individuality of character that identifies one in the PHYSICAL WORLD and the ETHERIC WORLD; comprised of knowledge learned and attitudes taken toward every life experience in all incarnations, and forming a BELIEF SYSTEM; personality is never lost regardless of number of incarnations, but can be and should be "changed" constantly. (Inconcl.) [**cf.** AKASHIC RECORDS, NEW-AGE PSYCHOLOGY]

SURVIVAL PHENOMENA—unusual psychic experiences that indicate life after death must exist in the etheric world; e.g., an OUT-OF-BODY EXPERIENCE in the operating room, DEATHBED VISIONS, trance mediumship, etc. (Inconcl.) [**cf.** APPARITIONS, HAUNTINGS, PAST-LIVES THEORY]

SURVIVAL PROGRAM—a function in a human being that, in a clinical death phenomena, brings one back to a normal awareness without the CONSCIOUS MIND being responsible. (Inconcl.) **Syn.** EMERGENCY PROGRAM. [**cf.** MANKIND SEED, MONADOLOGY]

SURVIVAL RELATED APPARITIONS—deceased loved ones, friends, and religious figures seen by clinically dead persons who survive and tell of their visions; hundreds of documented cases all tell a similar story; formerly known deceased persons meet them and offer assistance to step over or encourage them to return to earth. **Syn.** DEATHBED VISIONS. [**cf.** DEATH SCIENCE Appendix 2]

SURVIVAL RESEARCH—scientific investigation among doctors, scientists, and parapsychologists to find tangible proof or evidence that some kind of LIFE FORCE exists after physical death; documented cases of hundreds of near-death experiences are being used. [**cf.** REBIRTHS, DEATHBED VISIONS, REGRESSION, REVIVIFICATION, THETA-AGENT, NEAR-DEATH EXPERIENCE]

SURVIVALISTS—psychic researchers who believe a LIFE FORCE of human PERSONALITY survives after physical death and can make contact with the living in many ways. [**cf.** ANTISURVIVALISTS, SOUL-MIND]

SUSCEPTIBLE MEDIUM—(Allan Kardec) those who call the etheric world entities to do their bidding and are not happy unless all information compliments them and their decisions regarding life.

SUSHUMNA—(Eastern, ancient) an ethereal and

physical, tiny, hollow nerve acting as a tube in the spinal column which is filled with VITAL LIFE FORCE; runs from the base of the spine through the MEDULLA OBLONGATA to the CROWN CHAKRA, where it connects to the SILVER CORD; because it is an extension of the silver cord, it makes a human being literally a part of the universe (the silver cord is connected to the MONAD, a nodal point); fluid in the tube is bluish in color; serves as a barometer to denote the place on the spiritual scale where the individual is functioning. [cf. CHAKRA, NADIS, SERPENT POWER]

SUSHUPTI-STATE—(Sanskrit) a state of deep sleep without dreams; see DELTA STATE. [cf. NREM, REM]

SUSPENDED ANIMATION—1. (astral projection) to astrally travel a long time in an ASTRL PROJECTION, causing the physical body to appear as lifeless as a corpse. [cf. LOOPING-THE-LOOP, OUT-OF-RANGE-OF-CORD-ACTIVITY] 2. to cause an object, such as a book, to hang in mid-air by intense concentration. Syn. LEVITATION, SUSPENSION. [cf. TELEPORTATION TELEKINESIS, ARTICLE-PSYCHO-KINESIS, PSYCHIC PLATFORM]

SUSPENSION—to raise an inert object and hold it in space without physical support; performed in an ALTERED STATE OF CONSCIOUSNESS by the SUBCONSCIOUS MIND or with the help of ETHERIC WORLD INTELLIGENCES; see LEVITATION, SUSPENDED ANIMATION. [cf. MOTOR SUSPENSION, TELEPORTATION TELEKINESIS]

SUSPENSION MEDIUM—one who allows the ETHERIC WORLD INTELLIGENCES to intervene, raise an object or the self in space, and hold it there without physical support; executed in a SEMITRANCE or DEEP TRANCE state; the first step before teleportation; e.g., a documented case: while a group of mediums were sailing on a ship together, one medium was raised in her chair to the ceiling and held there for many minutes. [cf. LEVITATION, TELEPORTATION TELEKINESES, APPORTATION]

SUTRA—a collection of aphorism relating to some aspect of life: 1. beliefs of the YOGA discipline written in simple form about 400 B.C.; 2. (Pali) a sacred terse chant; 3. (Mahayana Buddhism) a doctrine proclaiming all the ALL is emptiness. [cf. SUNYATA] 4. (TM) the use of a concise effective aphorism to reach a very high STATE OF CONSCIOUSNESS. Sim. SILENCE, SIDDHIS, BIJA. [cf. CHANT, SYMPATHETIC VIBRATION]

SUTRATMA—(Eastern) see SILVER CORD.

SVADHISTHANA CHAKRA—(India) a subservient chakra located near the generative organs. Syn. SOLAR PLEXUS CHAKRA, MANIPUR. [cf. ROOT CHAKRA, KUNDALINI]

SVARA—(India) see COSMIC SOUND.

SVAROZHICH—(Slavic, "fire") the primeval substance created in the beginning and from which all things in the universes are made. [cf. TSAR SUN, FIRE]

SVARUPA—true form in the higher planes before it takes on the type of form that we can perceive as dense MATTER. [cf. BUDDHIC PLANE, REALM OF IDEAS, NOOSPHERE]

SVECHCHHOTKRANTI—(Tantra) to psychically project one's mental consciousness into the thirty-eight junctions of another individual's body with enough power that the individual now acts as the projector wants him or her to; (do not confuse with POSSESSION). Syn. PHOWA. [cf. HEX, JUNCTIONS, POSSESSION, AVESHA, PSYCHIC TRANSFER, TRANSFIXED]

SVETOVIT—(Slavic) a NATURE SPIRIT that is in charge of harvesting crops and works beneficially with the farmers.

SWABHAVA—(Sanskrit swa, "self") to become, to grow into, to be formed; the pattern of all that is formed in the EARTH PLANE to become the potential within its seed, be it tomato or a human. [cf. MONADOLOGY, MANKIND SEED]

SWABHAVAT—(Sanskrit) energies created by UNIVERSAL LAW; primordial state of atoms before they were ETHERIC WORLD matter or PHYSICAL WORLD matter; original COSMIC CONSCIOUSNESS substance. [cf. SPIRITUALIZED CONSCIOUSNESS, SUPERMUNDANE, MEMORY CONSCIOUSNESS]

SWALLOW—(esoteric) bird with a vibrational frequency that helps heal sicknesses; stones in its belly have a medicinal value. [cf. ANPSI, ANIMAL KINGDOM]

SWAMI—(Hinduism) a holy one who has reached the highest state of spiritual progress through required initiations according to standards of his discipline; title of respect; teacher of religion, spiritual counselor, and PSYCHIC. similar to a LORD, MASTER, or PRIEST. [cf. ANGEL HIERARCHY, GODHEAD,

FIFTH PLANE]

SWAPNA—(Sanskrit) the dream state of consciousness during sleep. **Syn.** REM SLEEP. [**cf.** LANGUAGE OF DREAMS, DREAMS, DREAM FORMS]

SWARTHEIM—(Europe) a NATURE SPIRIT that is small in structure and dark skinned; communicates with humanity with an eagerness to help. **Syn.** ELF. [**cf.** WODAN, TANKWAY, FAIRIES]

SWASTIKA—a figure consisting of a cross with arms of equal length, each arm having a continuation at right angles with all four continuations turning the same way; 1. (China, India, Egypt, Greece, Scandinavia, North and South American Natives) set upright with arms in north-south, east-west positions and continuations angling ninety degrees counterclockwise to the arms; symbol for life and fertility; also used as a religious symbol; 2. (Nazism) placed tilted to the left with a center circle and continuations angling ninety degrees clockwise to the arms; became a symbol of destruction and decadence; i.e., Adolph Hitler regime and the Third Reich. [**cf.** SYMBOLISM]

SWEAT GLAND ACTIVITY—(biofeedback training) (future science) a minute change in liquid that comes from the pores of the skin in response to changes in emotional status of the human system, during which levels of arousal and relaxation initiate sweating; noticeable but more frequently unnoticeable; chemistry of flowing sweat itself; chemical changes that occur during the reabsorption of sweat all contribute to the electrical behavior of the skin; this electrical system can be amplified in tangible readouts with instrumentation for help in understanding human stress. (Inconcl.) [**cf.** BIO-STAT MONITOR, GSR, SKIN TALK]

SWEAT LODGE—(Native American, Chippewa) a closed-in area where one goes to cleanse one's self physically and mentally, to offer thanksgiving prayers to SPIRIT, and to make one's needs known to Spirit; FASTING precedes the session; one enters naked, on hands and knees; (this entering position keeps one humble; nakedness represents how one entered the earth; to be without one's jewelry is to be without vanity); rocks are heated outside previously, and then placed in the center of the area, and water poured over them to provide the steam; (the rocks represent earth mother's bones; steam represents the breath of life); BLOCKS and problems are worked out and one becomes in tune with the UNIVERSE; a personal sacred RITUAL. [**cf.** ISOLATION

TANK, PRIMAL SCREAM]

SWEET GRASS—(Native American) a plant that has the vibratory rate to draw positive energies into the area where placed; also used for SMUDGING; small pieces are energized and used as amulets. [**cf.** AMULET, ATMOSPHERE CLEARING]

SWEET ONE—(capitalized) (Vedic) name given to Sri Krishna while in the earthly vibration.

SWEET-SCENTED ROHUTU—(Leeward Islands) a level in paradise consciousness to where aristocratic ETHERIC WORLD INTELLIGENCES go because of their rank. [**cf.** FOUL-SCENTED ROHUTU, PROGRESSIVE LYCEUM]

SWIMMING DREAM—the ASTRAL BODY worming along in a horizontal position in an ASTRAL PROJECTION during sleep, making one dream of swimming or propelling one's self through space. [**cf.** UPRIGHT FORCE, ROLLED-OUT]

SWINGING TYPTOLOGY—to receive information from ETHERIC WORLD INTELLIGENCES by a table tipping on one leg to give *yes* and *no* answers. **Syn.** TYPTOLOGY. [**cf.** PERCUSSION Appendix 2]

SWISHING—(biofeedback training) sounds of "ssshhh" followed by a silence, indicating to the subject HOOKED-UP to the EEG instrument that he or she is in a low state of consciousness. [**cf.** ARTIFACTS, MICROVOLTS, ZEROING]

SWITCHBOARD—(future science) 1. (Totality) an overall consciousness of sameness and belonging to one another that flows through all things in the universes, animate and inanimate, keeping everything in the universes connected; acts like an electrical system with invisible nodes in the air to receive and transmit frequencies; sends messages through this system, motivating purification of each thing; psychics tune in to this switchboard. (Inconcl.) **Syn.** SCHEME OF THINGS, UNIVERSAL MIND, DIVINE MIND. 2. (human mind) vast network of interlocking METAPATTERNS of everyone who has ever lived, past and present, surfacing through current time periods via TELEPATHIC TRANSMISSION, influencing everyone's life. (Inconcl.) **Syn.** COLLECTIVE UNCONSCIOUS. [**cf.** METAPATTERN, METAPROGRAM]

SWITCHING HEMISPHERES—to change from one brain hemisphere to the other hemisphere through conscious will; detectable on the EEG instrument. (Inconcl.) [**cf.** BRAIN HEMISPHERES, SPLIT BRAIN

HEMISPHERES Appendix 5]

SWOON—(Tibet) a consciousness devoid of objects and experiences, after the TRANSITION of death, that retains a consciousness of pureness; individuality separated from all but grey mist and sounds; an ILLUMINATION. **Syn.** VOID.

SWORD—1. a psychic tool capable of pointing and directing PSYCHIC ENERGY from the PSYCHIC to that which is at the end of the blade; used in many cultures, anciently and currently; used in CEREMONIAL MAGIC for EVOCATION rituals, for EXORCISM as a defense against an invisible enemy, and for severing psychic bonds in hexes and psychic transfers; not used as a fighting tool; 2. (traditional sword used for PSYCHISM) wrought of steel, copper handle shaped like a crucifix, signs engraved on the guard and blade, and consecrated on a Sunday in the thrust of a SACRED FIRE; 3. the actual sword can be simulated by the extended arm and pointed finger; 4. symbolic of FIRE and of the element AIR. [**cf.** CEREMONIAL MAGIC, RITUALS, INVOCATION]

SYLPH—1. a graceful, slender female ANGEL living in the air and clouds; a highly developed INTELLIGENCE; links with a person at birth or baptism; helps this individual grow if he or she is not too materialistic; a constant and faithful energy field that can be called upon in emergenceis. **Syn.** GUARDIAN ANGEL, CELESTIAL GUARDIAN, GUIDE. 2. a NATURE SPIRIT that moves and has its being in the air; will burn in fire and drown in water; feels kindly toward humanity, desiring to help but not hinder individual freedom; considered sculptors of fairy world; dainty and feminine when seen clairvoyantly; can change to an enormous size and shift dimensions.

SYLVANUS—(Latin, "deity") a NATURE SPIRIT whose function is to oversee the physical nature of mankind; i.e., Pan. **Syn.** FAUNUS.

SYMBIOTIC CONSCIOUSNESS—feeling and living as if all were one, unable to distinguish between self and environment; e.g., the newborn baby, or the DESTRUCTIVE-BRAINWASHING CULT victim (loss of identity of his or her whole being). [**cf.** UNIVERSAL CONSCIOUSNESS, BRAHMA CONSCIOUSNESS, EGO-DESTRUCTION]

SYMBIOTIC RELATIONSHIP—two entities receiving a mutually beneficial PSYCHIC EXPERIENCE at the same time; e.g., mother and child, plant and spider. [**cf.** BOTANE, TELEPATHY, TELEPATHIC TWIN]

SYMBOLIC MAGIC—(Africa) see MIRROR MAGIC.

SYMBOLISM—(antiquity) to use something other than itself to reveal a REALITY; to make use of action, sensation, sound, or objects through resemblance, association, or convention, to portray something important; important thing can be invisible, spiritual, or objective in nature or it can be activity of persons and events, or it can be objects; e.g., a warm handshake after a business meeting could mean that the meeting was not only successful, but pleasurable, and that "I like you as a person"; a chalice on a communion table could represent the whole life story of JESUS, remind one to improve his or her life or remind one to be thankful for what he or she has; 2. (Carl Jung) "the inexpressible can only be expressed in terms of symbol or ALLEGORY"; 3. symbolism represents the language of the PSYCHIC, MEDIUM, and MAGICIAN; 4. symbolism is the language of the SOULMIND revealing itself in DREAMS; 5.a universal language that all can understand, whether one is illiterate or intelligent. [**cf.** PARABLE, MYTHOLOGY, SYMBOLS, ASSOCIATION MAGIC]

SYMBOLIST—1. one who is familiar with and capable of interpreting signs, feelings, visions, and words for oneself and others, such as a dream or PSYCHIC MESSAGE interpreter; 2. one who thinks in images rather than words; picture thinking; 3. pertains to a form of religious art that deals with the ETHERIC WORLD, not the CONSCIOUS MIND.

SYMBOLIZATION—(dreams) a method of telling a dreamer about her or himself and their world through pictures that have implications regarding their personal life, as opposed to writing, which would be uninteresting and undecipherable if the dreamer cannot read. [**cf.** DREAM OBJECTS, DREAM INTERVIEW, DREAM CONTROL]

SYMBOLS—(esoteric) 1. impressions, pictures, words, phrases, sounds, tastes, smells, touches, gestures, objects, or things that imply more than their obvious and immediate meanings; agents of power that suggest to the viewer by association or resemblance that which is in the SUBCONSCIOUS MIND, independent of conscious intention; 2. (Ruth Blackmere) "a sign or activity used to designate another thing, to indicate an event one wants understood; appears and grows naturally out of a series of events that become tradition; 3. (AMORC) "a device or object used as a sign to represent an idea; two kinds: natural and artificial"; 4. use of one thing or action to imply more than the definiteness of its manifestation; 5. (I Ching) "appearance of anything is called *symbol;* when it has received a physical form, it is called *vessel;* when regulated and used, it is the *law.*" [**cf.** CEREMONIAL MAGIC, DREAM OBJECTS, PSYCHIC INFORMATION]

SYMPATHETIC EARTHLINGS—strangers who have a close relationship caused by a tie from a previous existence; magnetic chemical balance of the two individuals brings instant harmony which is not due to material or physical relationship. Syn. TERRESTRIAL SYMPATHIES. [**cf.** SOUL-MATES, SYMBIOTIC RELATIONSHIP]

SYMPATHETIC INDUCTION—emotional vibrations in an area which are so strong that they linger and influence the incoming people who sense this emotion, consciously or unconsciously, and are inclined to act the same as those who left these emotions; e.g., nervousness sensed in the area of a microphone. [**cf.** PSYCHIC TRANSFER Appendix 2]

SYMPATHETIC MAGIC—1. to simulate a likeness of, or to imitate, a condition, object, or event in smaller form to cause a parallel in the condition, object, or event; the action of things on one another through a secret affinity which is caused by some likeness in outward structure or reciprocal condition; see following laws in Appendix 7: CONTAGION, ASSOCIATION, MIMICRY, and SIMILARITY; 2. the relationship of two similar organs in a living organism shows that one affects the other; a condition, effect, or disorder of one organ induces some effect on the other; e.g., when one elbow has a rash, the other will immediately follow with this condition. [**cf.** BOTANE, ANPSI]

SYMPATHETIC MOTIONS—(trance) movements of the body back and forth, up and down, which are needed to allow the ETHERIC WORLD ENTITY to enter the KUNDALINI and PINEAL GLAND when the MEDIUM is learning to go into a DEEP TRANCE state. [**cf.** IMPERSONATION, DANCED HIM, CO-PARTICIPANTS]

SYMPATHETIC NERVOUS SYSTEM—(esoteric) 1. a network of electrical wires running through the PHYSICAL BODY with the main transformer in the SOLAR PLEXUS; negative-feminine in POLARITY; 2. NERVOUS SYSTEM influenced by the SOUL-MIND in charge of INSTINCT, automation, INVOLUNTARY FUNCTIONS, and the MEMORY BANK of past incarnations; a permanent intellect; 3. developed before the CEREBROSPINAL NERVOUS SYSTEM, working in harmony with it; 4. this system changes a person from an animal to a human organism; 5. controller of the fight-or-flight system and the activity of the sweat glands that shows the individual's degree of excitement or calmness by activating chemicals and processes in the fight-or-flight system; this system results in invisible water in the pores detectable by a GSR and METABOLIC MONITOR. [**cf.** ABDOMINAL BRAIN]

SYMPATHETIC PAINS—unintentional telepathic transfer of a disease, sickness, or accident, unintentionally received by one closely linked emotionally or even by a total stranger; e.g., the husband feeling labor pains at the same time the wife is giving birth. [**cf.** EMOTIONAL PSI, LAW OF SYMPATHETIC MAGIC Appendix 7]

SYMPATHETIC TELEPATHY—to telepathically transfer an attitude, emotion, or idea throughout a gathering; occurs deliberately or unconsciously; each person is minutely connected by an invisible thread while in the group and will be compassionate to another's emotions, attitudes, or ideas that come from a strong PSYCHIC or a disturbed psychic; the greater the number of developed psychics in the group, the more noticeable these telepathic transfers become. [**cf.** INTUIT TELEPATHY, MENTAL TELEPATHY, EMPATHY CLAIRSENTIENCE]

SYMPATHETIC TURN-ON—(biofeedback training) an indication on the GSR, METABOLIC MONITOR, or TEMPERATURE CONTROL instrument when there is a nervous out-flow from the sympathetic nervous system of the subject, indicating the subject is upset or disturbed from thinking about or actuating a certain condition, which gives indication of the cause of the nervousness. [**cf.** SYMPATHETIC NERVOUS SYSTEM]

SYMPATHETIC VIBRATION—theory: when a particular sound is called forth and rhythmically repeated; it will intensify vibrations, which result in an event happening that apparently is out of all proportion; e.g., an army marching over a bridge in perfect step will shatter the bridge. [**cf.** MANTRA, SOUNDS-WITH-POWER]

SYMPHONY OF LIFE—(esoteric) theory: everything is vibrating a sound; the SOUL-MIND is playing one long musical song with the harmonious chords and dischords representative of one's chaos and joys. [**cf.** COSMIC SOUND, VIBRATION, SOUNDS-WITH-POWER]

SYMPTOM REVERSAL—see SYMPTOM SUBSTITUTION.

SYMPTOM SUBSTITUTION—(metaphysic) the reappearance of an unwanted behavioral pattern or stress condition after one behavioral pattern or stress condition has been overcome by HYPNOTHERAPY or PSYCHOTHERAPY sessions; unless the cause is found and the emotional situation resolved, the undesirable symptoms return in the same manifestation or a different manifestation in the future. [**cf.** LAW OF HEALING Appendix 7, HYPNOTHERAPY]

SYN, SY, SYL—prefixes meaning "with, along with," and "also."

SYNAPSE—(esoteric) (Greek, "conjunction or union") places where nerve cells hook together; a gap between the axon of one neuron and the dendrite of another neuron where electrical nerve impulses are transmitted in one direction; felt to be bridged by PSYCHIC ENERGY; known to scientists as neuro-transmitters. [**cf.** BIOFEEDBACK TRAINING, MENTAL PSYCHIC PROCESSES, DENDRITES]

SYNC—the lack of SYNCHRONIZATION in a person's body rhythms after a long airplane flight across time zones; see JET-LAG. [**cf.** CYCLES, CIRCADIAN RHYTHM]

SYNCHRONICITY—coined by Carl Jung; two separate and unsimilar events occurring simultaneously which are found to be related; these two events cannot be attributed to a cause-and-effect theory but rather a blending together simultaneously in a unexplainable but meaningful way. Syn. MEANINGFUL COINCIDENCE. [**cf.** CASTING OF LOTS, I CHING]

SYNCHRONISTIC INTERVENTION—an innate function of a human being to keep in balance with the CIRCADIAN RHYTHM of the body regardless of outside stimuli; e.g., a man working night-shifts notices a pull to sleep in the evening. (Inconcl.) [**cf.** DIURNAL CYCLE]

SYNCHRONIZATION—(Karl Pribram) brain theory: when two persons are harmoniously working together, their brains are picking up and implementing the same holographic wave forms. (Inconcl.) [**cf.** HOLOGRAM BRAIN THEORY]

SYNERGISM—the blending together of the human

WILL and the HOLY GHOST to produce something new or bring about a change; SYNCHRONIZATION of cosmic forces and the human MIND produces a change in physical matter. Syn. PSYCHISM, MONERGISM. [**cf.** PHYSICAL PHENOMENA, AUTOMATIC WRITING, DIRECT VOICE, PK]

SYNERGY—("cooperation") 1. theory: the unpredictability of behavior of a system as a whole because of the separate behaviors of any of the parts is real cooperation; 2. harmony, blending, and cooperation between two energies is necessary for physical phenomena; i.e., COSMIC ENERGY and MIND; ETHERIC WORLD INTELLIGENCES and mind; SUBCONSCIOUS MIND and CONSCIOUS MIND; works especially through skills of INSPIRATIONAL THOUGHT, AUTOMATIC WRITING, DOWSING, TRANCE. [**cf.** LAW OF SYNTHESIS Appendix 7, SYNERGISM]

SYNESTHESIA—("mixed-up senses") co-mingling of one sensory channel with another; a malfunction of the five SENSES; e.g., sound vibrations causing sight, sight vibrations causing taste; common type is visual colors produced by speech; also spelled **synaesthesia.** (Inconcl.)

SYNTHESIS—the combining of complex or unlike things, causing them to unite in harmony. [**cf.** LAW OF SYNTHESIS Appendix 7]

SYSTEM OF COLLECTIVE SOULS—theory: physical psychism depends upon the harmony of the soul-minds of the MEDIUM, the SITTERS, and the ETHERIC WORLD INTELLIGENCES; without this harmony, the phenomena cannot happen, is distorted, or is incomplete. [**cf.** PHYSICAL PSYCHISM PROCESSES Appendix 2]

SYSTEM OF DUCTS—(acupuncture) the network of the meridians in the body, acting as an electrical system. [**cf.** ACUPUNCTURE, ACUPRESSURE, BODY TRANSCEIVERS, MERIDIAN LINES]

SYSTEM OF MENTAL WAVES—(esoteric) scientific names given to the invisible vibrations from the MENTAL PLANE in the ETHERIC WORLD, where all blueprints for planet earth are formed. [**cf.** CAUSAL PLANE]

SYSTEM OF NEGATION—detrimental influences on a MEDIUM or PSYCHIC during mental or physical psychic performances brought on by negative attitudes of skeptics and nonbelievers. [**cf.** SHEEP AND GOATS EFFECT, EXPERIMENTER EFFECTS]

SYSTEM OF PROBABILITIES—(Seth) simultaneous functions in the etheric world have a relationship to the experiences one is having in the earthly world. [**cf.** HOLOGRAM BRAIN THEORY, MULTIDIMENSIONAL]

SYSTEM OF REALITIES—various levels of dimensions in the ETHERIC WORLD resulting from the different VIBRATIONAL FREQUENCIES caused by the many states of consciousness of mankind. **Syn.** PLANE, LEVELS, DIMENSIONS, KINGDOMS, SPHERES. [**cf.** ETHERIC WORLD]

SYSTEM OF WAVES—(science) patterns made by atoms, electrons, and molecules vibrating in a ceaseless, cyclic rhythm. **Syn.** PLANES, DIMENSIONS, LEVELS. [**cf.** CYCLES Appendix 5]

SYSTEMS SCIENCE—1. a complex of components in mutual interaction; 2. a grouping and outgrowth of the simultaneous rise of biological, behavioral, and social sciences; 3. (Russia) the study of scientific developments using the ACUPUNCTURE POINTS and KIRLIAN PHOTOGRAPHY.

SYZYGIES—(Gnosis) the male and female or antithetical (directly opposed) pairs of the first Principle. [**cf.** POLARITY Appendix 5]

'TI BON ANGE—(Haiti, Voodoo) the conscious mind equated with the SPIRIT, the conscience, or PNEUMBRA; referred to as the little good angel, which works simultaneously with the LARGE GOOD ANGEL, the soul-mind, within everyone; when illness occurs or problems arise, the Voodoo Priest or medicine man performs healing magic to change the attitude of the GROS BON ANGE. **Syn.** LITTLE GOOD ANGEL. [**cf.** IMORTAL SOUL, ATTITUDINAL HEALING]

T'AI CHI—(China, 1000 BC, "the whole circle") originated with Taoist monks; slow, non-strenuous exercises in specific patterns for conditioning the entire organism; a method of getting in rhythm with the universe by simple and graceful movements performed slowly in a continuous series; correct name T'AI CHI CHUAN. [**cf.** MOVEMENT-FOR-ALTERED-CONSCIOUSNESS, TEMPLE DANCERS, PSYCALISTHENICS]

T'AI CHI CHUAN—see T'AI CHI.

T'AI CHI DOH—an Oriental martial art for self-defense and bodily awareness; shadow boxing, using one's energy against one's self; includes JUDO, JUJITSU, KARATE, AIKIDO.

T-BACILLI—(Wilhelm Reich) red units of life in ORGONE ENERGY or in VITAL LIFE FORCE.

T-FIELDS—abbr. for THOUGHT FIELDS; see AURA and ETHERIC DOUBLE.

TABLE GIRARDIN—an instrument designed to be used cooperatively with the PSYCHIC and the ETHERIC WORLD ENTITY who moves its parts to spell out PSYCHIC INFORMATION; consists of an upper moveable stand with a fixed needle in the center turning freely in a circle pointing to the letters which form a dial around the edge. [**cf.** TYPOLOGY, AUTOMATISM, OUIJA BOARD]

TABLE-TALKING—see TABLE-TIPPING.

TABLE-TILTING—see TABLE-TIPPING.

TABLE-TIPPING—to receive answers from the ETHERIC WORLD INTELLIGENCES by means of a wooden table which thumps one leg in answer to questions of the SITTERS; a code is established between the etheric world intelligence, the sitters and the MEDIUM; i.e., one thump for *yes*, etc.; performed by a group of people sitting around a table with no empty spaces in between any two members; each member lightly touches all ten finger tips to the table top; the ECTOPLASM and PSYCHIC ENERGY is built by songs, prayers, etc.; this ectoplasm is used to move the table which can be quivering, tilting, thumping, and eventually walking across the floor; responds to the sitter's and medium's wishes; a practical step for those beginning physical psychism which frequently leads into more difficult phenomena. [**cf.** PERCUSSION, RAPPING SPIRITS, PHILLIP GROUP]

TABLE-TURNING—see TABLE-TIPPING.

TABOO—(Polynesian, "prohibited") danger from an overly powerful psychic influence; signifies a prohibition enforced by religious or magical power; applied to similar usages among peoples all over the world; also spelled **tabu, tapu.** [**cf.** PSYCHIC TRANSFER, UP-FOR-GRABS, UNCONTROLLED PSYCHISM]

TACHYON—(Gerald Feinberg) faster-than-light particles of a physical nature; believed to be the basis of ESP. (Inconcl.) [**cf.** SPEED OF THOUGHT, BROADCASTING]

TACTILE SENSITIVITY—see PSYCHOMETRY.

TAG—1. (biofeedback training) denotes the subject HOOKED-UP to a BIOFEEDBACK INSTRUMENT was capable of identifying his or her subjective experience, had some understanding of it, and could control it while using the machine; 2. (dreams) a short phrase or one word used to indicate the theme of the dreams in the DREAM DIARY for the purpose of comparing the dream content over a period of time. [**cf.** VISCERAL LEARNING, REDUCTIVE ANALYSIS, DREAM FRAGMENTS]

TAI CHI—see T'AI CHI.

TAI CHI CHUAN—see T'AI CHI.

TAI CHI DOH—see T'AI CHI DOH.

TAKU HE—(Little Eagle, South Dakota) a monstrous, ape-like creature, that shows evidence of its visitation by harming little animals and by his screeching in the night; appears periodically in the same area and cannot be caught. **Syn.** SASQUATCH, CHUCHUNAS. [**cf.** MONSTER ACTIVITY, DIMENSION-SHIFTING Appendix 2.]

TALENT SUBSTITUTION—(Haiti, Voodoo) to exchange one's talent (soul-mind) with that of an animal and become the animal for a period of time. **Syn.** BAKA. [**cf.** WEREWOLF, LYCANTHROPY]

TALISMAN—(Greek *teleo*, "to consecrate"; *telesma*,

"one over which a rite has been consecrated") an inanimate object consecrated with PSYCHIC ENERGY to serve its owner by bringing changes in his or her environment or lifestyle; 1. an ornament, made from a piece of paper, to a temple building; device can be manufactured, handmade, or created by the owner; device or object is constructed to attain definite results by using SYMBOLS, astrological signs, HIEROGLYPHS, special words, or that which has meaning toward its objective; 2. device is charged with PSYCHIC FORCE to be used for specific purposes by the owner by: beaming of eyes, palming between the hands, and energizing under the sun, stars, or near water, etc.; objective of the energy is always designated with each energizing process; once it is energized, it is carried or worn by the owner or kept safely wrapped until ready to use; loses little potency if in a natural setting; 3. can be consecrated to be a tool in PSYCHIC HEALING, protection for the owner and his or her surroundings, writing a book, spiritual and psychic attainment, increase in physical energy, or about anything necessary to life; 4. examples: a star carved out of a bone and worn as a necklace, a figurine placed in the bedroom or in a personal sanctuary, or a room consecrated for prayer only. [cf. AMULET, UDJAT EYE, TOTEM, MAGNETIZED OBJECTS, PALMED POWER]

TALISMANIC MAGIC—to use inert objects as storage batteries that have been consecrated and energized with PSYCHIC ENERGY by psychics who know how to recharge the object by just being close to it, by ceremony, or by creating it to link with planetary forces. [cf. RITUAL OBJECTS, REMOTE TREATMENTS, WAND]

TALISMANIC READING—(LeRoy Zemke) to attune to the level of the querant's consciousness and perceive a KEY for the querant to use later in facilitating integration of his or her potentials in life; this key is symbolically rendered in color onto a keepsake. [cf. OTOMI FIGURINES]

TALISMANING—to use a TALISMAN for psychic purposes; to place the energized object near the area or person it was energized to serve. Usage: "I am talismaning her illness." [cf. MEDICINE BUNDLE, PSYCHIC SHOCK ARTICLES, TIKI]

TALISMANTIZE—to energize an article so it will serve as a psychic instrument; preferably the article should be made by the owner but may be purchased; article can be energized by PALMED POWER, the SUN, the rain, rhythmic dancing, CHANTING, or simply by using it repeatedly in a RITUAL; article is concentrated upon at the time of energizing it, as to what it is intended to do (that is all it will be able to do); at the time it is being used, stored energy in the article should be exposed close to the psychic to release its talismantized power and between these periods it is kept wrapped in a black or special cloth; talisman will serve its owner only. [cf. AMULET ENERGIZING, CONSECRATED STATUES, GROUP TOTEM]

TALISMANIZE—see TALISMANING.

TALKING BOARD—see OUIJA BOARD.

TALKING GLASS—Dr. George M. Lamsa owned a glass that, when filled with water, became a VOICE BOX amplifier for an ETHERIC WORLD INTELLIGENCE to speak through with PSYCHIC INFORMATION and knowledge. [cf. INDEPENDENT VOICE]

TALKING MEDIUM—see DEPENDENT VOICE.

TALKING TABLE—see TYPTOLOGY.

TALKING TO THE GODS—(Kalahari Desert) an act of the healing PRACTITIONER to release the EARTHBOUND ENTITIES from haunting the patient in a healing ceremony; healing practitioner battles with, insults, and bargains with the gods (haunters) that have overcome the patient by invading his or her life, and causing disease; the healer loosens them from the patient and advises them to attend to their etheric duties. [cf. SPIRITUALISM, PROVOKING]

TALKING-IN-TONGUES—to express vocally an utterance, or a loud chatter of incoherent sounds, at a very rapid pace; speech can be: an unknown language from another planet, a foreign language from this planet, a change in pitch in chanting, or rapid nonsensical syllables which seem to have no recognizable meaning; occurs to one in a state of LIGHT TRANCE brought on by a charismatic or evangelic service which was composed with music and ploy for the purpose of bringing the mental and physical bodies into a religious state of hypnotic ECSTASY; a desire by the will of the recipient results in a release of a joyful religious excitement bringing an upliftment, a pleasureable experience or a feeling of oneness with one's DEITY: JESUS, GOD or the HOLY SPIRIT; in this state tears can roll, body can move or wiggle in light contortions and the hands are held up-raised with no effort; religious belief that the recipient has received the Holy

Spirit; one theory: it is telepathically projected from the ETHERIC WORLD INTELLIGENCE using the BRAIN as a sort of receiving apparatus of thought waves; utterance unveils eternal varieties of information in a garb of allegory, or unveils knowledge of celestial Truths that transcend the comprehension of the recipient and church members. (Inconcl.) **Syn.** GLOSSOLALIA, ALIEN TONGUES. [**cf.** EMOTIONAL HIGH, CHARISMATIC RENEWAL, QUENCHING THE SPIRIT]

TALMUD—the collection of Jewish law and tradition containing fundamental principles; a text and commetary in book form.

TAMARISK ROD—(Egypt) the DOWSING stick of the MAGI and Tartars; a symbol of the WILL and ability to apply one's energy to a task until done; see DOWSING ROD. **Syn.** WILLOW WAND, DIVINING ROD, RODS OF AARON. [**cf.** WATER UNDULATION, TELLURIC FORCE]

TAMBARAN—(New Guinea) see GUIDE.

TAMING OF FIRE—to use fire for many psychic skills; theory: if one can discipline fire, one can discipline one's self. [**cf.** VILLAGE BLACKSMITH, IRON, FIRE IMMUNITY]

TAMING THE MIND—to learn control of CONSCIOUS MIND activity and to discipline the SUBCONSCIOUS MIND and ETHERIC WORLD INTELLIGENCES by sitting daily in MEDITATION periods, before opening PSYCHIC DOORS; daily sittings, regardless of length of time, help prevent PSYCHIC INFORMATION from surfacing at random during one's daily activities (RANDOM PSYCHISM results in useless information); by meditating first, one reaches a level that is conducive to higher qualitative information; while quietly sitting, one may ask for clarification of the information and request special information: this results in usable psychism and prevents future uncontrolled events. [**cf.** IMPRESSION, RECEIVING MODE, GOING-TO-LEVEL]

TAMING WAND—(Iceland) see DOWSING ROD.

TANGALOA, TANGAROA, TA'AROA—(Tonga, Samoa) the creator who existed above the huge waters, coming from a continuous thick darkness revolving in endless space; see TOTALITY.

TANGIBILITY-MATERIALIZATION—to produce an object in a SEANCE session through the will of the ETHERIC WORLD INTELLIGENCE by transforming ethereal matter so it looks real to the SITTERS. [**cf.** PSYCHIC PHYSICAL LIGHTS, SEANCE MANIFESTATIONS]

TANGIBLE APPARITION—an ETHERIC WORLD INTELLIGENCE (a MASTER, GUIDE, or discarnate) who momentarily assumes the form of a live person; creates a complete, full-blown psychic VISION and, for a split second, has warmth and density to the touch; not researched to date but authenticated. **Syn.** AGENERES. [**cf.** MEDIANIMIC FLUID, THOUGHT-FORM CLAIRVOYANCE]

TANGRAMS—shapes of animals and humans, and silhouettes of objects made from seven TANS, used in combination with geometry to solve a variety of problems. [**cf.** MAGICAL DIAGRAMS]

TANKWAY—(Ethiopia) healing PRACTITIONER and PSYCHIC; see HEALER.

TANS—(Tantra, Sanskrit, "to weave, propagate and endure"; in the loom with emphasis on patterning and association) disciples were to make various patterns by using only five pieces, a square, two large triangles, a middle-sized triangle and a rhomboid. [**cf.** SEVEN, FORMS-WITH POWER, FIVE]

TANTAKAM—to lock one's gaze on an object, a symbol, the tip of one's nose or an object of abstract art, to induce a deep MEDITATION. **Syn.** NASAL GAZE. [**cf.** LAW OF ATTENTION Appendix 7, MIND-DRIFT]

TANTRA—(Sanskrit *tan*, "to weave, propagate and endure") rule and ritual; a version of Buddhism and Hinduism, beginning early A.D.; highly developed magical-mystical religion using CANDLES, INCENSE, bells, magical wands, spells, MAGIC CIRCLE, bodily postures and symbolical designs; INITIATE must unlearn TIME and SPACE, as they are considered illusions; brings one closer to nonspatial nature and NIRVANA; a discipline that aims to set free the spark of divine light in each human. [**cf.** BELL, MAGIC WAND, SYMBOLS, AMULETS, CEREMONIAL MAGIC, SPELL]

TANTRIC MEDITATION—(Tibet) to see forms of energy going from the VOID, penetrating each other making indescribable light and color. [**cf.** QUIET ATTENTIVENESS, INNER-SOUND CURRENT]

TANTRIK—(Tibet, Mahayana Buddhism) an offshoot of Buddhism around early A.D.; see TANTRA.

TAO—(China, Vedic, "the way") the motivation that keeps harmony between mankind and the ETHERIC WORLD; the SCHEME OF THINGS; philos-

615

ophy that doesn't prescribe a particular path but simply the uncomplicated essence of what is right; belief that all things are governed by the Tao and one should understand this nature within oneself; belief that spirits guard the stars, constellations, moon, sun, wind, clouds, kitchen, sewers, stones, intestines, tongues, etc.; everything has an opposite POLARITY, depicted by a circle divided into two equal parts by a serpentine line (half dark and half light). [cf. LAW OF POLARITY Appendix 7, PATH, PATTERNED WORLD, ANGELS, YIN AND YANG SYMBOL]

TAO TE CHING—(Vedic, China) eighty-one stanzas of classical mystical scripture of the Chinese Tao philosophy, written by the founder LAOTSE.

TAOISM—(China) a religion of China which emerged as an offshoot from CONFUCIANISM, concerned with spiritual growth; served as a major underlying influence in China from 2,500 years.

TAPAS—(Yoga) to condition the body through proper kinds and amounts of diet, rest, recreation, etc., to bring it to the greatest possible state of health and activity. [cf. CURATIVE EDUCATION, WELLNESS, ALTERNATIVES]

TAPAS SEX—(Tantrism, China, Yoga) ("heat" and "asceticism") a union between two people, wherein the sex organs are used, but not in a conventional manner; sexual energy is not obliterated, but visualized and used; theory: the generative organs are instruments of supreme magical power and should be used for more than sensual pleasure; the fluids of the sexual act are directed back into the KUNDALINI in the spine; this energy is controlled with intense concentration as it rises to a climax; the orgasm is experienced in the head, and the sexual fluid is reabsorbed into the system, giving the individuals extra PSYCHIC ENERGY; involves conquering and killing physical desire. [cf. YOGA, FEATS, BODY CONTROL, SEXUAL MAGIC]

TAPE-RECORDED, LOW-AMPLITUDE-PK—(psi tasks) to record inaudible sounds, i.e., sound, raps, whistles and voices on a low-amplitude tape recorder; this can be heard with physical ears when played back at high amplification. [cf. VOICES FROM THE UNIVERSE, ELECTRONIC VOICES]

TAPED VOICE PHENOMENON—(future science) to capture a voice or sound on the tape of a tape recorder, that is not audibly heard by the physical ear when being recorded; 1. when desiring and willing the phenomena to happen, the tape recorder is left running by the bedside during the night, in the center of a PSYCHIC DEVELOPMENT CIRCLE, or by the side of the PSYCHIC in a private development setting; when tape is played back normally or at high amplification, human voices, electrical snaps, whistles, gutteral sounds, alien languages, or background sound similar to a motor, are heard; 2. voices have identified themselves as discarnate beings, ETHERIC WORLD INTELLIGENCES, EXTRATERRESTRIAL BEINGS from other planets and inhabitants of space, or space CONSTRUCTS themselves; 3. hypothesis as to the source of recording: (a) electronic impulses of the SUBCONSCIOUS MIND registering as human utterances on the tape; (b) voices transmitted by an unknown intelligence from another planet or from outer space with recording methods superior to ours; (c) deceased persons who are still emotionally tied to someone on earth; (d) an etheric world intelligence wanting to dispel information regarding the transformation of the earth. Methods used by (c) and (d): (1) voice is impressed directly onto the tape via some kind of psychokinetic-mediated electromagnetic manipulation; (2) voice is being paraphysically created (although inaudible to the physical ear) directly in front of the tape recorder microphone or within the microphone. (Inconcl.) [cf. VOICE PRINTS, VOICE BROADCAST CONTROLLER]

TAPES—(est) stored records in one's SUBCONSCIOUS MIND of patterns made from one's past thinking and feelings which can prevent one from experiencing a full life in the present. [cf. UNCONSCIOUS NONAWARENESS, LOCKED-IN]

TAPPING INTO—psychically entering into the electromagnetic field of the thing or person one wants to perceive information about. [cf. GOING-TO-LEVEL, PSI-CONDUCIVE STATE]

TAPPING MEDIUM—one who hears taps, knocks, noises, or raps in his or her presence either in the SEANCE room or in his or her private home; performed by the ETHERIC WORLD INTELLIGENCES; if desired, a code is worked out so the intelligence can bring the MEDIUM guidance or counsel. [cf. DARKROOM SESSIONS, ECTOPLASM, TABLE TIPPING, KNOCKS]

TARGET—1. (psi tasks) in ESP experiments: the object or mental activity to which the subject is attempting to respond; in PK experiments: the objective process or object that the subject tries to influence. [cf. SUBJECT VARIANCE, SUBJECT, TARGET PACK] 2. (acupuncture) the area on the body needing the attention or healing that is acted upon when the acupuncture point is pressed, massaged, or needled. Syn. REFERRED ZONE. [cf. TRIGGERPOINTS, SHIATSU]

TARGET AREAS—(psi tasks) the goal the subject is supposed to choose psychically. [cf. ESP Appendix 2]

TARGET CARD—(psi tasks) the card that the PERCIPIENT is attempting to identify or otherwise indicate a knowledge of. [cf. ZENER CARDS, PROCEDURAL IRREGULARITIES]

TARGET FACE—(psi tasks) the face of the failing die that the subject tries to make turn up by PK. [cf. MECHANIZED-PK, NONHUMAN-PK]

TARGET HUMAN—(ufology) expression used as vehicles and creatures from outer space seem to aim for a particular person on earth; penetrating rays are sent out to immobilize the person and the encounter begins. [cf. CLOSE-ENCOUNTERS-OF-THE-SECOND-KIND, STROBE LIGHT]

TARGET PACK—(psi task) a pack of cards whose order is trying to be identified by the subject in an experiment. [cf. SECOND EFFECT, TIME BARRIER]

TARGET PREFERENCE—(psi tasks) the tendency of some subjects to call certain symbols more than others in an ESP experiment. [cf. FOCUSING EFFECT, RESPONSE BIAS]

TAROCCHI CARDS—(ancient Egypt) see TAROT CARDS.

TAROT CARDS—(antiquity; Egypt) a pack of cards for the purpose of DIVINATION using symbolism; contains seventy-eight cards forming a system of communication and a relationship between God, man, and the universe through SYMBOLS; related to ASTROLOGY, NUMEROLOGY, and Kabalistic teachings; querant shuffles the cards and makes various spreads or layouts for the purpose of prognosticating or guidance for specific questions; layout can be simple or highly complicated; sometimes symbols act as a stimuli to PSYCHIC INFORMATION along with the symbolic meaning. [cf. CARDOMANCY, SORTES, POINT-OF-FOCUS, LAYOUT, KABBALAH]

TAROT KING—one of the four court cards; representing SELF; the SPIRIT in an individual. [cf. MAJOR TRUMP CARD]

TAROT KNIGHT—one of the four court cards depicting the special focusing of energies and a personal sense of selfhood. [cf. LITTLE EGYPT]

TAROT PAGE—one of the four court cards, standing for the body or personal vehicle, corresponding to the God in Hebrew theology: YOD, HE VAU, YHVH. [cf. YHVH]

TAROT QUEEN—one of the four court cards depicting the SOUL-MIND or inner pattern part of a particular human PERSONALITY. [cf. MINOR ARCANA]

TAROTA—also written taro-rota means "WHEEL OF THE LAW and the LAW OF THE WHEEL," symbolizing universal life. Syn. SPINNING OF THE WEB. [cf. CYCLES OF PROGRESSION]

TARQUIP INUA—(Eskimo) an exalted, lofty ANGEL whose function is to help sustain the moon. [cf. SECRET CHIEFS, WINGS, MELCHIZEDEK]

TASK—1. (psi tasks) the ESP or PSI experiment or test; 2. (Britain) see APPARITION.

TASSEOGRAPHER—a psychic who uses tea leaves in a cup as a POINT-OF-FOCUS to bring PSYCHIC INFORMATION to another. Syn. TEA-LEAF READER. [cf. FOCUS ATTENTION]

TASSEOGRAPHY—to stare at tea leaves in a cup to bring PSYCHIC INFORMATION for the person who has drunk the tea previously; bulk tea should be used because it serves as a point-of-focus for the reading. Syn. TEA-CUP READING. [cf. COFFEOGRAPHY, MANTIC ART, SYNCHRONICITY, POINT-OF-FOCUS]

TAT—(psi tasks) abbr. THEME APPERCEPTION TEST; 1. the AGENT silently transmits certain words to the subject while the subject is telling a story; the TARGET is the relationship of the story to the silent words the agent was sending; 2. (Sanskrit) the beyond, "that." [cf. MENTAL TELEPATHY Appendix 2]

TAT TVAM ASI—Samkaracharya; "that am I." [cf. NEW-AGE PSYCHOLOGY]

TATHATA—(Buddhism) to reach a STATE OF CONSCIOUSNESS through prolonged MEDITATION that feels like a transcendent ocean, where material desires have diminished; one is passionless. [cf. NIRVANA]

TATTWA CHART—(Eastern) a special picture of colored circles and paths that is designed to be used in a special ritual that will stimulate an ASTRAL PROJECTION and other psychic skills. [**cf.** FOCAL POINT]

TATTWAS—(Eastern) plain, simple, unornamented geometric symbols used to stir the primordial part of the MIND, INSTINCT, and SYMPATHETIC NERVOUS SYSTEM to psychically learn information regarding CREATION and antiquity; these symbols are the SQUARE, CIRCLE, CRESCENT, TRIANGLE, and OVAL; represent the magical elements for FIRE, AIR, EARTH, WATER, and SPIRIT; meant to stimulate information before the archetypes had formed in racial consciousness.

TAU—(Hebrew) St. Anthony's cross; a T-shaped cross patterned after the last letter of the Hebrew alphabet meaning the end of the world; this cross shape has the vibrational frequency to be a tool to protect the owner against negative vibrations. [**cf.** PENTACLE, TALISMAN, CROSS]

TAULA—(South Africa) objects used to reveal the future and other PSYCHIC INFORMATION by one throwing them and then studying the pattern of their fall; taula's can be ivory engraved tablets, knuckle bones, tortoise shells, seeds, seashells, or coins. **Syn.** LOTS. [**cf.** SORTES, CASTING OF LOTS]

TC—(laboratory) see TRANSPERSONAL CONSCIOUSNESS.

TCH'I—(China) originally called **hi** or **air**; COSMIC ENERGY that flows through the MERIDIAN LINES. [**cf.** NODE, ACUPUNCTURE POINTS]

TE—(Veddas, Tao) the creative power necessary to keep TAO moving; the 10,000 creatures of the Whole. **Syn.** SHAKTI, TOTALITY.

TEA—1. (Zen, India, China) used to combat drowsiness during MEDITATION; 2. (Zen) used in a solemn ritual similar to communion. [**cf.** BOTANE, PSYCHOPATHOLOGY, SLEEPITATE]

TEA LEAF READING—see TEA-CUP READING.

TEA-CUP READING—to use the formation of tea leaves that remain in a cup, after the tea has been drunk, to receive PSYCHIC INFORMATION; tea leaf formation serves as a meaningful POINT-OF-FOCUS; the tea cup should be white china, tapered, and the tea leaves large; accomplished because: 1. the leaves can act as a stimulator for the psychic to see psychic visions after staring at the leaves; 2. the formation of the leaves are a reflection of patterns in the AURA of the recipient, giving clues to the

PSYCHIC regarding the recipient's character and health. **Syn.** TASSEOGRAPHY. [**cf.** POINT-OF-FOCUS Appendix 2]

TEACHER—(esoteric) an individual, an event, or an activity that is able to connect with the student and bring instructions or new information to the student (one who can recognize a learning situation); teacher does not have to be physically present, nor does it have to be a person.

TEACHER WITHIN—motivation within all persons bringing the desire to improve one's self; the potential within the HUMAN BEING SPECIES SEED that urges one to advance and grow (human being species' growth is measured in wisdom and righteousness, not in physical growth). **Syn.** GRACE, MONAD. [**cf.** HUMAN BEING KINGDOM, WISDOM, AWARENESS]

TEARING—(mental mediumship) eyes watering enough to run down one's cheeks, while giving a psychic READING, with no change in expression or emotional sensations of the psychic; has nothing to do with the sadness or happiness of the message coming through; to tear is a normal body process when one is working with an ETHERIC WORLD INTELLIGENCE. [**cf.** RED HOT NEEDLES, BODY SENSATION]

TEARS—1. a necessary mechanism in both male and female designed to release stress and to prevent blocks in their systems; has nothing to do with maturity or strength of character; a mechanism to clean out the fears, disappointments, and sadness of one's emotions; 2. (Pir Vilayat Inayat Khan) the waters of the plants of life; an abundance of crying (when necessary) can transform one, as it acts as an alchemical cleanser; 3. white bleeding; tears allow the hurt to heal from within, similar to red bleeding that cleans out the wound and allows it to heal from within. [**cf.** NEW-AGE PSYCHOLOGY]

TECHNICAL MUSE—a personal GUIDE or ANGEL that attaches to one, helping in one's technical adventures. [**cf.** OUTER BAND, INNER BAND]

TEJAS—see TRIANGLE.

TEKTITES—(ufology) smooth glass lumps of curious shapes, found strewn in fixed areas in the world; UFO researchers feel that some of these pieces show characteristics of a burned out missile that was traveling rapidly through the air. [**cf.** UFO RADIATION, FUSIFORM, FIREFLIES]

TELAESTHESIA—see CLAIRVOYANCE-IN-SPACE.

TELE—(Greek) prefix meaning "distance"; transmission over a distance.

TELECONFERENCE—(psi tasks) to identify the same TARGET at the same time as a group is identifying it in an experiment in which all participants are isolated independently in scattered cities; target is in the possession of the experimenter in one place only. [**cf.** CROSS-CORRESPONDENCE]

TELECULT POWER—hidden, distinct, psychic sensitivity; to bring about one's desired goal by unobserved means. [**cf.** PSYCHIC ENERGY]

TELEDIAGNOSIS—(radiesthesia) 1. to use a PENDULUM or DOWSING ROD to find information regarding things and people, without the people and things being present; e.g., to hold the pendulum over the schematics of a washing machine and observe its swing to locate the trouble in the mechanism; to use the dog's feeding dish to locate the missing dog; see WITNESS; 2. to hold a pendulum over a letter written when a person is ill, to tune into the radiations still on the letter, regarding the illness; emotional radiations cling to the written words. [**cf.** PENDULUM POWER, LAW OF CONTAGION and LAW OF SIMILARITY Appendix 7]

TELEFLASHER—(laboratory) a box designed with a flashing light behind a screen that holds cards of colors, pictures, names, symbols, etc., used in telepathic experiments; the flashing light makes the receiver more receptive. [**cf.** TELEPROMPTER, VISUALIZATION TRAINER, DIRECTED-THOUGHT TRAINER]

TELEGNOSIS—see FORECASTING, PROPHESY.

TELEKINESIS PSYCHISM—abbr. TK; (Greek *tele,* "over a distance"; *kinesis,* "movement") a psychic production of motion and movement over a distance; to act psychically on third-dimensional matter to change its position, form, or elements, (including one's own body); performed by a MEDIUM who allows the ETHERIC WORLD INTELLIGENCES to intervene and use the ECTOPLASM from his or her body and the sitters' bodies to act on the energy field around the physical matter; some events defy the LAW OF GRAVITY and some show the law of gravity intact; performed in daylight or in a BLACKED-OUT ROOM; phenomena is always willed, preplanned and desired by the medium;

medium prepares him or herself beforehand and goes into a TRANCE state for the intelligence to intercede; two main groupings: NONHUMAN TELE-KINESIS, and HUMAN TELEKINESIS; (do not confuse with PSYCHOKINESIS wherein mind concentration does the work). [**cf.** MEDIUMSHIP, GRAVITY CONTROL]

TELEKINETIC—pertains to telekinesis.

TELEKINETIC MEDIUM—one who synchronizes with an etheric world ALCHEMIST to manipulate and move MATTER, change the elements in the matter, or change the vibrational frequency of the matter; distance is no barrier; a necessary step in apportation. [**cf.** TK, APPORTATION TELEKINESIS, LEVITATION-TK]

TELEMETRY—thought transference of words that are metered, in the form of verse or poetry, coming from an ETHERIC WORLD INTELLIGENCE or from the inner thoughts of a sender; occurs when both parties are emotionally happy. [**cf.** MIND-LINKING, INNER-WORLD TELEPATHY, POETRY]

TELENEURAL INFLUENCE—transference of emotions (anxiety, sadness, depression, fear, excitement, etc.) over a distance without any words being said; usually happening between two people who are relatives or friends. **Syn.** EMOTIONAL TELEPATHY. [**cf.** EMPATHY CLAIRSENTIENCE, TELEPATHIC TWIN]

TELEOLOGICAL—(Carl Jung) within each organism is a seed containing the final purpose of that organism's life with an urge to work out that purpose. [**cf.** MONAD, TOTALITY]

TELEOLOGY—the doctrine that final causes exist; the study of evidences and purposes of nature.

TELEOTIC—transmission over a distance; see TELEPATHY.

TELEPATH—one who sends and receives thought messages, emotions and illnesses to or from others; performed deliberately and unknowingly; is an inborn trait or can be learned through practice; usually when it is an inborn trait it flows frequently, spontaneously and randomly, and it becomes a nuisance; friends may stay away to prevent mind invasion, and it is frustrating to the PSYCHIC to have emotions and diseases that are not of one's own making; strict mind discipline and daily MEDITATION periods are necessary to control this inborn trait and the same are necessary to develop it. [cf. MENTAL TELEPATHY, TELEPATHY, CLOAK OF INSULATION]

TELEPATHIC CLAIRVOYANCE—(laboratory) the transference of pictures and colors over a distance; in experiments, the sender stares at a colored picture at a designated time when the receiver in another area is in a receiving mode to tune into the picture. [cf. INTUIT TELEPATHY, TELEPATHIC MODE, FRIVOLOUS COMMUNICATIONS]

TELEPATHIC HYPNOSIS—(Russia) to hypnotize a person who is not in one's vicinity; the telepath concentrates on sending suggestions to attain the hypnotic state and then sends instructions to be performed; subject carries out the orders without realizing he or she is a victim of HYPNOSIS; easier to perform if a love or hate bond is between the two; this is a dangerous tool if used for evil. (Inconcl.) **Syn.** ETHEREAL HYPNOSIS. [cf. TELEPATHY, HYPNOSIS]

TELEPATHIC LEAKAGE—(healing) a unintentional transfer of the therapist's emotional interests to the patient; therapist's current ideas and even his or her theories about PSYCHOTHERAPY can be mirrored in the patient's lifestyle and dreams if there is a good rapport between the two. [cf. PATIENT-THERAPIST ESP, EMPATHY, CLAIRSENTIENCE]

TELEPATHIC MODE—(psi tasks) concentration on the TARGET symbol by the agent (sender) in a laboratory experiment. [cf. ESP, TARGET PREFERENCE, SESSION]

TELEPATHIC SIGNAL—to accurately sense the thought and feeling of an unseen person in a crowd; e.g., to perceive that someone is staring at you from behind and realize their inner-dialogue is about you, making you feel uneasy. [cf. MENTAL RADIO, TELEPATHIC WIRE]

TELEPATHIC SLEEP-WAKE—(Russia) to hypnotize an individual at a distance and have him or her carry out orders; a special technique is used to put the victim in a hypnotic state, but he or she appears to be in a normal state to others; the victim performs what the sender desires and when in an awake state remembers nothing (not even that there was a time lapse). **Syn.** TELEPATHIC HYPNOSIS. [cf. ETHEREAL HYPNOSIS, MENTAL TELEPATHY]

TELEPATHIC TRANSMISSION—see TELEPATHY.

TELEPATHIC TRANSMISSION OF ILLNESS—the transfer of an illness (regardless of distance) between two people who have a close relationship; an unconscious transfer results in the receiver remaining ill until the sick person is better; in a deliberate transfer the PSYCHIC absorbs the illness into his or her body to relieve the patient, and then the psychic dissipates the illness; some healing practitioners use the latter method, especially in primitive tribes; the former method can result in many admirers of a great leader taking on the symptoms of the leader and not feeling well until the leader is well. [cf. TELEPATHIC TWIN, STRENGTH TRANSFERENCE]

TELEPATHIC TRIGGERED-VISION—to clairvoyantly perceive a full blown VISION of a friend or relative at the same time the friend or relative is experiencing trauma or going through the DEATH PROCESS; the SOUL-MIND of the sender is emotional and desires to let someone know of the dilemma, which triggers a vision; distance is no barrier. [cf. CRISIS ESP, NEED-DETERMINED PHENOMENON]

TELEPATHIC TV—(laboratory) to use a TELE-FLASHER or DIRECTED-THOUGHT TRAINER to psychically project a picture to a receiver who is in another area; picture sets in front of a flashing light which helps the transference in the experiment. [cf. THOUGHT TRANSFERENCE, DIRECTED THOUGHT TRAINER]

TELEPATHIC TWIN—(laboratory) a PSYCHIC who while working on mental telepathic experiments repeatedly receives thoughts of a certain person, who is not the sender of the experiment. [cf. MIND RAIDER, POLLUTION, SOUL-RAPPORT TELEPATHY]

TELEPATHIC WIRE—an invisible ETHERIC THREAD that passes between the two people who act as terminals for the invisible wire which is held there by thought; the telepathic wire is created whenever one thinks about or talks to another person. [cf. MIND-LINKING, LOVE-LINE, SIMULTANEOUS THOUGHTS]

TELEPATHIST—a PSYCHIC who is capable of sending and receiving mental telepathic messages and emotions, and practices these skills; see TELEPATH.

TELEPATHIZE—to psychically send a message of words, colors, sounds, motions, emotions, or attitudes over a distance. [cf. MENTAL TELEPATHIC POLLUTION, MOTOR TELEPATHY]

TELEPATHY—(future science) (Greek *tele*, "distance"; *pathos*, "sensing"; "to feel afar") coined by F.W.H. Myers; 1. the coinciding of any of the five PSYCHIC SENSES of two individuals at the exact same time, one is receiving and one is sending; both individuals can be alive or one can be deceased; involuntary or voluntary, and selective and deliberate or spontaneous and undesired; 2. the fundamental process of communication; primordial communication before sound utterance and language; 3. the touch of CONSCIOUSNESS of one person upon another person with the ability to discern what that person is thinking and feeling at the present moment; the sensing can be thoughts, visions, hypnotic energy, body movements, subconscious data, feelings, illness, emotional states, psychic messages, or the train of INNER-DIALOGUE; 4. hypothesis: caused by the transmission of ELECTROMAGNETIC WAVES between all atoms connecting the UNIVERSE together (connecting particles, neutrons, bioenergetic vibrations, and radiations); these electromagnetic waves and particles, etc., can be tuned into (when one is in a passive frame of mind) by the body or the CONSCIOUS MIND; (W. Brugh Joy) "one does not have to think in images or SYMBOLS, language is automatically translated into essential thought and retranslated into the outer language of the person having the telepathic *impress*; a natural form of communication." (Inconcl.) [cf. MENTAL TELEPATHY and TELEPATHY Appendix 2]

TELEPHONE CALLS FROM THE DEAD—see PSYCHIC PHONE CALLS.

TELEPHONE TELEPATHY—to send and receive suggestions, instructions or ideas from another PSYCHIC, in the presence of others, without either one uttering a sound. [cf. THOUGHT READING, OUTSIDE INVADER]

TELEPLASM—see ECTOPLASM.

TELEPORT—a MEDIUM capable of teleportation.

TELEPORTATION PSYCHOKINESIS—abbr. TELEPORTATION-PK; to levitate an article or one's own body and transport it horizontally through the air by using mind CONCENTRATION; performed by: 1. one who has a well-disciplined mind and the understanding of the gravitational field; takes many years or incarnations to accomplish; 2. one who is in a state of spiritual ECSTASY; during the peak experience when one is free from materialistic thoughts and thus free from the law of GRAVITY, the body becomes buoyant, lifts off the ground and

floats through the air; authenticated experiences have been reported that a priest floated up the isle of his church during a service. [cf. TELEPORTATION TELEKINESIS, LEVITATION]

TELEPORTATION TELEKINESIS—abbr. TELEPORTATION-TK; to levitate an article or one's own body, and transport it away from the area, horizontally through the air, in it's original form; accomplished by a MEDIUM synchronizing with the etheric world intelligences while in DEEP TRANCE so they can use the medium's (and sitter's if necessary) ectoplasmic energy; usually performed in a SEANCE room but articles have been teleported miles away; e.g., a dish of candy moving through the air unaided and stopping at each of the sitters for them to help themselves; levitation is accomplished as the step before teleportation; see LEVITATION-TK for hypothesis of how this is performed. [cf. APPORTATION Appendix 4, DEMATERIALIZATION, SEANCE, BLACKED-OUT ROOM]

TELEPROMPTER—(laboratory) a box containing a flasher attached to a low frequency light bulb that lights up a picture placed at one end of the box; used for mental telepathic experiments; the flashing light makes it easier for the sending and receiving of the picture. **Syn.** DIRECTED-THOUGHT TRAINER, PROTOTYPE TELEFLASHER. [cf. TRACE METHOD]

TELERADIESTHESIA—to use a PENDULUM to answer questions regarding a person, animal, or situation wherein the person, animal or situation is not present; e.g., MAP DOWSING for a lost kitten, or using a WITNESS to receive answers about a sick friend.

TELERADIESTHESIOLOGIST—one who uses the skill of the PENDULUM and DOWSING ROD to locate missing articles, animals, and persons, and answer questions regarding that which is not in one's presence. [cf. RADIESTHESIA, PENDULUM POWER]

TELERGY—(late 1800s) see MENTAL TELEPATHY.

TELESMA—(Hermes Trismegistus, 350 B.C.) see VITAL LIFE FORCE.

TELESOMATIC—(Russia) to experience identical symptoms and feelings as another person at the same time the other person experiences them; e.g., a husband going through labor pains as his wife is in labor. [cf. BIOCOMMUNICATION, DOCTRINAL COMPLIANCE]

TELESTERION—(Greece) a special hall set aside for initiation into the mysteries where one proved one's ability in psychic skills.

TELETHESIA—coined by F.W.H. Myers; to psychically perceive what is happening in a distant locality as to the weather, the activity, and the attitude of the people in the area. [**cf.** TELEPATHY, HERD IMPULSES, INTUIT TELEPATHY]

TELLTALE SKIN—pertains to the function of the human skin when HOOKED-UP to a POLYGRAPH, GSR, or METABOLIC MONITOR; the instrument indicates when one lies or speaks truthfully because the electrodes attached to the skin tune into the SYMPATHETIC NERVOUS SYSTEM; this nervous system governs the subconscious mind that holds the records of one's entire past and cannot lie. [**cf.** HANDS]

TELLURIAN—an EARTHLING; an inhabitant of the planet earth or an object pertaining to the EARTH as opposed to pertaining to SPACE. [**cf.** UFOLOGY Appendix 5]

TELLURIC ENERGY—(esoteric) 1. MAGNETISM that emanates from the ground and is fed to the human body through the feet; all individuals living on the planet receive this energy which is necessary to sustain the ELECTRICITY within the body. **Syn.** EARTH MAGNETISM, GAUS MAGNETICS. 2. the force that makes the DOWSING ROD pull downward when it has located the sought after underground substance. [**cf.** FORKED STICK, L-ROD, SCHEME OF THINGS]

TEMP—(esoteric) the SIXTH SENSE associated with mental time and "tempor" (the organ of temp), providing all individuals with their own time-sense and corresponding naturally conditioned reflexes. [**cf.** CIRCADIAN RHYTHM, JET LAG, TIME]

TEMPERATURE—(body control) a function of how fast an object's atoms are vibrating and moving in SPACE; (pertains to those psychics who control body temperature so as not to freeze in subzero weather with very little clothes on). [**cf.** ATOM, BODY CONTROL, PSYCHIC PHYSICAL CONTROL]

TEMPERATURE CONTROL—(Tibet) to regulate and control one's body temperature regardless of atmospheric conditions of extreme cold and extreme heat; e.g., one initiation is for the LAMA to stay in the icy snow for hours without getting frost bitten, while wrapped in a wet sheet; theory: the VITAL LIFE FORCE that is minutely flowing in the KUNDALINI and body cells is under the control of THOUGHT and can act as a thermostat for the human who understands it; makes it possible for one to control one's body temperature through thought activity. [**cf.** PSYCHIC HEAT, SIDDHI]

TEMPERATURE CONTROL BIOFEEDBACK—an instrument that registers the temperature of the skin by attaching a THERMISTOR to the skin; body skin temperature indicates the amount of blood flow in the body, which changes with one's emotional state; skin temperature goes down when an individual becomes aroused because the heart speeds, the small arteries constrict, and blood pools in muscles near the surface of the skin and warms the skin; objective is to meditate while HOOKED-UP, and calm the NERVOUS SYSTEM to lower the skin temperature; (do not confuse with body temperature taken in the mouth); instrument is helpful in controlling blood flow in diseases regarding blood flow restriction and in testing the blood flow in subjects during psychic experiments. [**cf.** VOLUNTARY CONTROL OF INTERNAL STATES]

TEMPERATURE SENSOR—tiny THERMISTOR used to strap on the finger of one hand (in place of the usual electrodes), in the temperature control BIOFEEDBACK INSTRUMENT. [**cf.** TEMPERATURE CONTROL BIOFEEDBACK]

TEMPLE—any construction or area that serves as a meeting place for something valued; 1. (ancient Egypt) a building used as a university to learn the secret esoteric keys to universal knowledge; within the building were sacred rooms where one could test one's psychic skills as one learned (known as INITIATION RITES); temple walls were sometimes inscribed with their traditional knowledge, by NUMBERS and HIEROGLYPHS; 2. an area or building used for a religious service or RITUAL; 3. (Bible) the human body is the learning place of esoteric knowledge for the growth of the SOUL-MIND; "your body is a temple of the living God"; 4. (etheric world) an ethereal building used to educate one's soul-mind so one can advance one's STATE OF CONSCIOUSNESS, while inhabiting the etheric world.

TEMPLE DANCERS—(ancient Egypt) a group of dancers that had music, tempo, and body movements so choreographed that the audience would mentally move into the SIXTH PLANE by simply viewing the dance numbers, achieving a sense of serenity and timelessness. [**cf.** MOVEMENT-FOR-

ALTERED CONSCIOUSNESS, PSYCHIC DANCING]

TEMPLE OF LUXOR—(ancient Egypt) a building containing statuary and wall paintings with inscribed texts of the principle of EVOLUTION and the mathematical proportions employed in this growth.

TEMPLE WHEELS—(India, Tibet, Egypt, Greece, Japan) a device with wheels used to pay adoration to the angels and ETHERIC WORLD INTELLIGENCES, as an ORACLE to predict the future, and as a prayer wheel; wheels are spun with the hand or a rope imitating the rotary movement of the heavens; the wheels were spun to turn to the proper god whose function pertained to the situation one was inquiring about; e.g., an agricultural oracle to predict about the crops, etc. [**cf.** WHEEL OF LIFE, PRAYER WHEEL]

TEMPLUM—an area in the sky chosen and marked out by the AUGUR to use as a POINT-OF-FOCUS; augur uses the influence of the radiations of that particular area to tune into PSYCHIC INFORMATION. [**cf.** MANTIC ART, FOCUSING EFFECT]

TEMPORAL CONSCIOUSNESS—a materialistic awareness of life experiences. [**cf.** AWARENESS]

TEMPORAL-WORLD—that which is related to TIME and this physical world. **Syn.** MUNDANE, PHYSICAL WORLD, THIRD DIMENSION, PLANET EARTH, EARTH MOTHER.

TEMPORARY AKASHIC RECORDS—(ancient Egypt) electronic microscopic pictures that duplicate the akashic records in the ethereal world, vibrating at a speed incomprehensible to a human being; dwells within each person's HEART; pictures function as a supplier to the blood steam as records of KARMA to be worked out in *this* incarnation; (Bible) "as a man thinketh in his heart, so is he." [**cf.** MENTAL-REFLECTING-ETHER, LIFE-CORD-HEART-SEED ATOM, BOOKS OF LIFE]

TEMPORARY DEAL—(psi tasks) an agreement made with the mind and the sensorimotor nervous system. [**cf.** TARGET PREFERENCE, PSYCHOLOGICAL VARIABLES]

TEMPORARY MEMORY BANK—knowledge and experience gathered in this lifetime and stored in the CONSCIOUS MIND. **Syn.** PERSONAL UNCONSCIOUS, SURFACE SUBCONSCIOUS. [**cf.** BRAIN Appendix 5]

TEMPORARY PARALYSIS—(rebirthing) to become very stiff and unable to move all muscles, for a short time, after a session in the warm pool in the REBIRTHING process; caused by traumatic experiences that happened during the actual birth or during prenatal conditions which surfaced and, in their desire to become unblocked, restrict movement. [**cf.** BIRTH SCIENCE]

TEN SERFIROTH—(Kabbalah) the first ten numbers which include the thirty-two elements of the UNIVERSE and the first twenty-two letters of the Hebrew alphabet.

TEN-PERCENT IMPERSONATION—to allow an ETHERIC WORLD INTELLIGENCE to interpenetrate a part of one's body, anethetize that part, and use it in physical phenomena; MEDIUM is in a relaxed state or LIGHT TRANCE with the mind alert but neutral in thought; no formal education regarding the work performed is required; impersonation is always preplanned, willed, and desired-controlled; unnecessary to be accomplished in a SEANCE room; e.g., the hands and forearms of the PSYCHIC SURGEON are anesthetized before operations but his or her mind is alert; hands and forearms of the California girl who plays music of great composers, are anesthetized before playing; her music is as if the composers themselves were playing. [**cf.** IMPERSONATION, CONTROL, SMALL SPIRIT]

TEN-PERCENT TRANCE—see TEN-PERCENT IMPERSONATION.

TENSION—(new-age psychology) unlabeled suspense, reacting in the metabolic system and causing muscle constriction patterns; sometimes noticeable and sometimes suppressed quickly before the individual notices any change in the body. [**cf.** TIME PRESSURE, EMOTION, STRESS]

TENSION WAVE—(esoteric) (human) one of the forces of mechanical energy, associated with pressure wavelengths; capable of being communicated over a distance from one person to another, if it is intense enough, it also makes the receiver feel anxious. [**cf.** SHOCK WAVE, EMOTIONAL PSI]

TENSOR FIELDS—(Patrick Flanagan) an ENERGY in the air necessary for all life.

TEONANACTL—(Mexico) a hallucinogenic drug held sacred because of its properties to influence psychic visions; contains psilocybin. **Syn.** PSILOCYBIN MUSHROOM, GOD'S FLESH. [**cf.** FLY AGARIC, HALLUCINATIONS]

TERMAS—(Tibet, "treasure") 108 volumes of treasure or sacred literature regarding MYSTICISM and the growth of the SOUL-MIND. **Syn.** TERTONS.

TERRESTRIAL MAGNETISM—see AURA.

TERRESTRIAL SYMPATHIES—theory: a tie of a former INCARNATION can cause an instant intimate affection or harmony, not due to material or physical relationships; caused by the magnetical-chemical balance of the two individuals due to sharing the same area, same time period and some lifetime experience in a past incarnation. **Syn.** SYMPATHETIC EARTHLINGS. [**cf.** TRANSFERENCE, RACIAL MEMORY]

TESLA COIL—invented by Nikola Tesla; a transformer that operates on high voltages at frequencies of 120,000 to 900,000 hertz, and for this reason is used in the Kirlian camera. [**cf.** KIRLIAN EFFECT Appendix 5]

TESTAMENT OF SOLOMON—the many entities of the ETHERIC WORLD that Solomon contacted and conquered by the use of his magic ring; served as proof of life in the etheric world and proof of communicating with same. [**cf.** KEY OF SOLOMON, TALISMAN]

TESTING MEDIUMSHIP—(Allan Kardec) "persons still evolving in the field of psychic and mediumship skills, find these skills are a means to grow; one must learn PSYCHISM and MEDIUMSHIP as well as possible, just as one must learn every other field, to grow"; mediumship and psychism is a human potential and not proof of superiority or moral advancement. [**cf.** PHYSICAL PSYCHIC PROCESSES Appendix 2]

TETRAGRAM—that which has FOUR; the symbol of a four-pointed star formed by the interplacement of two pillars; 1. (magic) represents the four elements: AIR, EARTH, WATER, and FIRE; used in the CONJURATION of the elementary nature spirits: SYLPHS, GNOMES, UNDINES, and SALAMANDERS; 2. (alchemy) represents the magical elements of the formula: SALT, SULPHER, MERCURY, and AZOTH; 3. (mysticism) represents SPIRIT (motion) and MATTER (rest); 4. (hieroglyphs) represents the MAN, eagle, lion, and bull. [**cf.** ALCHEMY, ASSOCIATION MAGIC]

TETRAGRAMMATON—1. (Old Testament) the four Hebrew letters of the name of God spoken as JEHOVAH or YAHWEH, written YHVH but regarded with profound awe and rarely pronounced, usually substituted with ADONAI or **Him**; 2. name given to

the "Supreme" of the Gods; believed to be the most powerful of all names, depicted by a five pointed star and the name written inside; 3. adds one to the GODHEAD if put with the four elements of MATTER. [**cf.** LAW OF SIGNATURE Appendix 7, WORDS-WITH-POWER]

TETRAPOLAR MAGNET—a magnet with four poles; four poles of the POLARITY. [**cf.** YIN AND YANG SYMBOL]

TEXT—(I Ching) that part of the BOOK OF CHANGES that gives guidance to the question that is asked while throwing the coins or lots; coins are thrown six times and depending upon heads-up or tails-up build a HEXAGRAM; text is divided into sixty-four discussions related to each hexagram; the sixty-four discussions of the text are believed to be all the guidance necessary to life's situations. **Syn.** JUDGMENT, TUAN. [**cf.** MOVING LINES, COMMENTARY]

TEXTURE OF MENTAL ACTIVITY—the quality of the impression perceived should determine whether it is an ESP IMPRESSION or a normal thought. [**cf.** VERDICAL PSI PHENOMENA, WAITING TECHNIQUE, NON-THOUGHT]

TEXTURE TELEPATHY—to decipher the texture of an object being touched or stroked by a PSYCHIC who is in another location. **Syn.** PSYCHOMETRIC TELEPATHY. [**cf.** INTUIT TELEPATHY, PSYCHOMETRY]

THALAMUS—(esoteric) a dark section of the BRAIN that relays sensory impulses to other areas of the brain; located directly above the HYPO-THALAMUS; an important part of the THIRD-EYE AREA and physical vision; both psychic vision and physical vision must go through the thalamus before being projected upon the occipital lobe; part of the third-eye area; acts as if it were the developing room for the negative of the pictures of both physical vision and psychic vision. [**cf.** THIRD-EYE AREA Appendix 5]

THANATOLOGY—the study of the science of the DEATH PROCESS.

THANGKA—(Tibet) an exquisite or enjoyable pictured used as a POINT-OF-FOCUS for MEDITATION; one contemplates on the thangka to the point that one can close one's eyes and see every detail of the picture reproduced in the MIND'S EYE. [**cf.** TANTRA, MANTRAM, JAPAM]

THAUMATURGIST—(Greece, Egypt) a PSYCHIC who communed with the ETHERIC WORLD INTELLIGENCES, spoke with the deceased, flew to HEAVEN or HELL as the occasion demanded; performed EXORCISM, invoked celestial and nature spirits, and understood MEDIUMSHIP; recognized as an ORACLE, SORCERER, and a physician.

THAUMATURGY—(Greece) the art and science of wonderworking; a very scientific approach to psychic research. **Syn.** PARAPSYCHOLOGY.

THEBAN BOOK OF THE DEAD—(ancient Egypt) views on religion and the external existence of the SOUL-MIND; soul-mind is not altered, only by itself, even during the DEATH PROCESS. [**cf.** SURVIVAL RESEARCH, KARMIC RECALL]

THEBAN SCRIPT—letters from the magicians' alphabet used for writing incantations and spells; comes from the Atlanteans, differing slightly, from sect to sect. **Syn.** RUNES, HONORIUS. [**cf.** MUMBO JUMBO, MAGIC VERSE, SPELLBOUND]

THEMATIC APPERCEPTION TEST—see TAT.

THEMING THE DREAM—(dream interpretation) the action in the dream will briefly sum up what the dream is all about, i.e., running, observing, riding, inquiring, hesitating, etc. [**cf.** RELEASE TYPE DREAMS, PROGRAMMING DREAMS, TAG]

THEOBIOLOGY—the study of the inner aspect of life and how to disassociate SELF from being bound up in the divine.

THEOLOGY—the study of religious Truths through an analysis of GOD, his attributes and his relation to the UNIVERSE; science of divinity.

THEOSOPHICAL SOCIETY—an organization founded in New York City by Mdme. Helena Petrovna Blavatsky, a Russian noblewoman (1875); influenced by the ancient mystics: Pythagoras, Plato, the Neoplatonists, and Gnostics; Madame Blavatsky studied all the ancient sects and mastered a very high state of perfection.

THEOSOPHY—(Greek, *theos*, "god, divine"; *sophia*, "wisdom, ethics"; "divine ethics") 1. a philosophical religious system which claims absolute knowledge of the existence and nature of the DEITY; this knowledge may be obtained through the operation of some higher faculty or special individual revelation; "wisdom of the gods"; knowledge only imparted to worthy pupils of the mystery schools; 2. a complex of philosophical and religious ideas centered on an attempt to gain access to the universal spiritual REALITY beyond material existence, popularized by the THEOSOPHICAL SOCIETY, founded by Mdme. Helena Blavatsky.

THERAPEUTIC DREAMS—(dream research) majority of dreams are helpful in solving every-day problems, diagnosing an approaching illness, accentuating character weaknesses, or releasing tensions; useful in accomplishing a more healthful and satisfying life. [**cf.** COMPENSATORY DREAMS, OBJECTIVE DREAM]

THERAPEUTIC TOUCH—coined by Delores Krieger; to transfer healing energy from one's hands to the patient to promote normal healing more quickly; to use a special technique to unruffle the energy field of the congested area in the patient; to transfer energy that has been decreed healing in nature, and localized from the hand of the healer to the patient; if the healer has a deep desire to be helpful, the patient's body will show a significant change in the BODY CHEMISTRY, especially in the blood cells; the healing energy elicits a generalized relaxation response that puts the patient in a healing mode and the body can heal itself more quickly. **Syn.** LAYING-ON-OF-HANDS, MAGNETIC HEALING. [**cf.** POWWOW, HEALING, NERVE FLUID, PASSES]

THERAPEUTIST—1. (ancient Egypt) one who was versed in the healing arts, which consisted of mental and magnetic healing; utilizing the rule "energy follows thought." [**cf.** TELEPATHIC WIRE, MAGNETISM, MENTAL TELEPATHIC HEALING] 2. (current) (a collective word) encompasses anyone using a special method to promote HEALING, whether it is orthodox or unorthodox. [**cf.** HYPNOTHERAPY, MUSIC HEALING, DREAM ANALYSIS]

THERAPY LOCALIZATION—(kinesiology) a method of determining whether a nerve center of a muscle is functioning normally; the muscle is tested by the doctor, and then the patient's hand is placed over the muscle; muscle is retested for a change in muscle strength; the patient's hand has either added or subtracted energy to that area giving the doctor the ability to determine if the nerve center functions normally. [**cf.** REFLEXOLOGY, BODY READING, POSTURAL INTERGRATION]

THEREVADAN MEDITATION—to watch an object, one's breath, a color, parts of one's body, etc., until one sees it as it really is; the meditator can realize the many absorptions of the levels of consciousness there are. [cf. CONSCIOUSNESS OF INFINITE SPACE, VIPASSANS]

THERMAL IMAGES—(Seth) ethereal pictures acting as a means of communicating in the INVISIBLE WORLD; made possible by the current of heat that is directed by the degree of emotion behind the thought. [cf. VERIDICAL HALLUCINATION, MISCARRIAGES]

THERMISTOR—(biofeedback training) a tiny bead of iron oxide, a part of the skin temperature BIOFEEDBACK INSTRUMENT, attached to any skin surface; detects blood flow that varies in electrical resistance as the emotion in the body changes, making temperature changes on the skin surface. [cf. ELECTRODES, ELECTRIC RHYTHM, EVOKED POTENTIALS]

THERMOVISION—(laboratory) an instrument similar to a television camera which detects infrared RADIATION coming from MATTER and emitting heat; instrument assigns a color value to each given intensity of radiation, corresponding to the different temperatures. [cf. PHOTO-CROMOTHERAPY, ULTRA-RED, ULTRAVIOLET RAYS]

THETA—(Greek *thanatos*, "death") used today as an adjective pertaining to survival phenomena. [cf. SURVIVALISTS, DEATHBED VISIONS]

THETA ASPECT—abbr. TA (American Society for Psychical Research); see ASTRAL PROJECTION.

THETA PHENOMENA—relates to the question of survival or an inquiry into the possibility of survival after death. [cf. KARMIC REFLEXES, DEATH-MIST, DEATH ANGEL]

THETA STATE OF CONSCIOUSNESS—(biofeedback training) a state of AWARENESS in which one is functioning from the SUBCONSCIOUS MIND or SUPERCONSCIOUS MIND, with the conscious mind passive; has these characteristics: subject has no perception of reality of TIME or SPACE, mundane awareness is subdued, and subject feels tranquil or drowsy; physical body is anesthetized; acquired during SLEEP, HYPNOSIS, or deep MEDITATION, a state which the PSYCHIC or MEDIUM surfaces for PSYCHIC INFORMATION; brainwaves register on the EEG BIOFEEDBACK INSTRUMENT between four and seven cycles per second and show a slow steady rhythm. [cf. BETA, DELTA, and ALPHA STATES OF CONSCIOUSNESS]

THETA WAVES—a brain current frequency between four and seven cycles per second, in a chart of groupings of brain currents, discovered since the EEG instrument was invented; current frequency shows a slow, steady rhythm in the feedback; designates a very deep state of relaxation and quieting of the mind, emotions and body. [cf. SCALE OF BRAIN RHYTHMS, EEG INSTRUMENT]

THETA WAVES OF FANTASY—to tune into the MEMORY BANK within the SOUL-MIND and have clairvoyant perception regarding one's past. Syn. REGRESSION. [cf. REBIRTH DOCTRINE, PROVED INCARNATIONIST]

THETA-AGENT—(survivalists) the living force that slips away from the human body after death and exists in the etheric world. Syn. SOUL-MIND. [cf. SURVIVALISTS, ASTRAL BODY]

THETIS—(Greece) a NATURE SPIRIT known as a daughter of the sea that has psychic power of self-transformation. Syn. NYMPH.

THEURGISTS—psychics who practiced MEDIUMSHIP in the Theurgical philosophy; able to help their country with guidance, counselling and predictions from the ETHERIC WORLD INTELLIGENCES; about A.D. 5; noted for their ability to go into TRANCE and work with physical phenomena. Syn. MEDIUM.

THEURGY—(Greece) (Neoplatonism, A.D. 5) philosophy which practiced psychic skills and MEDIUMSHIP to attain spiritual growth; brought guidance and counseling for their country; used VOICE TRANCE, AUTOMATIC WRITING, amulets and ASTRAL PROJECTION to obtain knowledge of the ETHERIC WORLD; under Emperor Julian, the practitioners were elevated to a high office. Syn. SPIRITUALISM, PARAPSYCHOLOGY.

THICKLY-FORMED—plane where the seed of all universal forces and objects are very close together within. Syn. NO-DOWN, OG-MIN, DENSELY-PACKED-REALM. [cf. SPIRIT SPHERES, BUDDHIC PLANE]

THINGS—(esoteric, future science) all inanimate objects and animate entities in this world that are known to humanity as three-dimensional; all masses of atoms that people perceive as distinct from something else, including one's body, is a formulation of one's mental activity in the form of ideas of one's self and one's relation to the total; things and mind are one; things are the human mind in action, conscious energy; (Unity) "things are thoughts lowered in vibration to the level of sense perception"; see MATTER. [**cf.** LAW OF MATTER Appendix 7]

THINKER—"man," who controls and generates matter in the universe; the co-creator responsible for unfolding the UNIVERSE until it reaches it's perfect state. **Syn.** SOUL-MIND.

THINKING—(esoteric) 1. INNER-MIND ACTIVITY while in the PHYSICAL BODY, that one feels has been instigated through one's own power; the law of thought in action; 2. makes the ergs of energy that emanate from one's head functional by giving them intelligence and direction; 3. a necessary tool for the universe to unfold itself and grow to perfection by harmonizing the SUBCONSCIOUS MIND and CONSCIOUS MIND; the designing of relationships or functional departmentalizing between one's self and one's world; 4. a tool that makes the particles of the ATOM oscillate to the nature of mankind's intellect and emotions; the intelligence and emotions of thinking utilize the ethereal ELECTRICITY and MAGNETISM of the atom, and the movement of the thought utilizes physical chemistry of the atom; e.g., to study or think for hours, tires one physically; 5. believed to be the fastest vibrational rate that an individual can comprehend; thinking travels faster than LIGHT, generated by the EMOTION behind the thought; 6. the beginning of manifestations in the UNIVERSE; to conceive an idea in the inner mind and to build on it as if the idea were one's own; 7. recollecting and remembering what is already in the human seed and surfacing it for use; 8. (Rudolf Steiner) "an organ that can be used to perceive a spiritual world"; (do not confuse with PSYCHIC INFORMATION and DREAMS, which are non-thoughts, that come from outside to within). (Inconcl.) [**cf.** LAW OF THOUGHT Appendix 7, INNER-DIALOGUE, BRAIN, MENTAL MIND]

THINKING DURING SLEEP—(dreams) INNER-MIND ACTIVITY with as much intelligence as daytime thoughts; rambling on to one's self with the same opinions and beliefs regarding the government, economy of the country, one's job, what to wear to work, etc., as daytime thoughts; occurs ceaselessly during the NREM state (alpha, theta, and delta), except to take time to have a PSYCHIC EXPERIENCE now and then; one does not remember thought during sleep unless awakened during NREM sleep, as is done in the DREAM RESEARCH LABORATORIES. [**cf.** DREAMS, SLEEP EXPERIENCES, INNER-DIALOGUE]

THIRD ASPECT—(Theosophy) a projection from COSMIC CONSCIOUSNESS to seven great intelligences of the ETHERIC WORLD to represent the coming evolutionary activities. [**cf.** SEVEN MYSTERY GODS, SEVEN SEPHIROTH]

THIRD BRAIN—a CONSCIOUSNESS working in conjunction with the generative organs; the ROOT CHAKRA; constitutes mental activity for people in a materialistic frame of mind. **Syn.** ROOT BRAIN. [**cf.** CHAKRAS, ABDOMINAL BRAIN]

THIRD CHAKRA—see SOLAR PLEXUS CHAKRA.

THIRD DIMENSION—depth, the additional feature by which a solid object is distinguished from a second dimensional object; has depth, along with length and width; an "area' that moves out of it's plane, becomes a solid, and has three dimensions (a solid remains just a solid wherever you place it); third dimension has lines, areas, and solids; it can move backward and forward and now up and down; it takes three numbers measured in three mutually perpendicular directions to determine and mark out any particular point from the total of points; a dimension of time determined by the human nervous system; third dimension is affected by the law of gravity, and affected by motion of rotation; the earth plane and all its inhabitants are considered third dimensional. [**cf.** FIRST DIMENSION, SECOND DIMENSION, FOURTH DIMENSION, LAW OF GRAVITY Appendix 7]

THIRD FORCE—(humanistic psychology) the study of the individual in concernment of one's humanness, as opposed to viewing the individual in psychoanalytic and behavioristic terms.

THIRD FREQUENCY MODULATION—a vibrational frequency of the vocal cord indistinguishable to the physical ear, but can be detected by the PSE. [**cf.** ELECTRONIC VOICES Appendix 2, PSYCHOLOGICAL STRESS MONITOR]

THIRD PLANE—a level of consciousness consisting of THOUGHT where most negative thinking has been eliminated by astral and physical existences; a faster vibrational frequency from earth, interpenetrating it and extending out from it; composed of the seven divisions of matter: solid, liquid, gas, ETHER, SUPERETHER, SUBATOMIC ENERGY, and ATOMIC ETHER; houses the mental bodies; has two distinct levels of function: 1. upper half is the

627

region of abstract thought where plans and ideas are designed into the blueprints for earth life, called the CAUSAL PLANE; **2.** lower half is the region where these abstract thoughts begin to become concrete ideas weaving into manifestation; referred to as the MENTAL PLANE; a level where the forces of WILL find expression. **Syn.** MENTAL PLANE, MANAS PLANE. [**cf.** BATTLE GROUND, CAUSAL BODY, MENTAL BODY, SECOND PLANE]

THIRD ROUND OF THE PLANET—(Theosophy) evolovement of the element WATER mixed with AIR and FIRE.

THIRD-EYE AREA—(esoteric, future science) **1.** a region of the head that PSYCHIC INFORMATION and DREAMSTUFF uses as a mechanism to alert the CONSCIOUS MIND it is there to be perceived; consists of the PINEAL GLAND, the post-lobe of the PITUITARY GLAND, the third-ventricle and the THALAMUS; **2.** (Charles Fillmore) "the imaging faculty presides at the nerve center between the eyes (the pineal gland) and to go through this faculty the formless takes form"; **3.** on the outside we think of the area between the eyebrows called the holy spot; inside it is located between the eyes above the root of the nose and acts as the external opening for the glands within; when perceiving clairvoyantly it feels as if one is looking from that spot within; **4.** (Rene Descartes) "our mind and body interact somewhere in the body believed to the be the THIRD-EYE AREA"; the pineal gland is the focal point of the five minds and transmutes cosmic information into electrical energy so the brain can use it; travels to the pituitary gland which transmutes the electrical energy of the brain into physical energy, so the body can use it (condensely explained); **5.** in this area one perceives CLAIRVOYANCE, CLAIRAUDIENCE, and CLAIRSENTIENCE; this area is developing in all people with increasing speed, for this coming age. **Syn.** EYE OF SHIVA, EYE SINGLE, EYE OF THE LORD, ALL-SEEING EYE, SIXTH SENSE, EYE OF ODIN. [**cf.** THIRD-EYE AREA Appendix 5]

THIRD-EYE ATTAINMENT—(Tibet) the opening of the THIRD-EYE AREA to constant ethereal vision, by special surgical techniques, when the student reaches a point that new psychic power will not be used for personal gain, worldly ambition, or as proof that such powers exist. [**cf.** PATH, ANGEL BEING KINGDOM, CHAIN OF BEING, MASTERSHIP]

THIRTY-SEVEN NATS—(Southern Asia) the soul-minds of outstanding men and women who suffered violent deaths, and who are now in the ETHERIC WORLD with characteristics that are dangerous. [**cf.** NAT CULT, DAEMON IN THE DIE]

THIRTY-THREE DAY CYCLE—(biorhythm) a rhythmic pattern "within" the human body that reacts to mental productivity, creativity, ability of intelligence, memory, mental alertness, logic and decision-making; the organism gives out peak performance for 16½ days and regenerative performance for 16½ days, making 33 days total; begins at birth and ends at death, repeating itself constantly; represented by the green curve in a BIORHYTHM CHART. [**cf.** BIORHYTHM, CRITICAL LINE]

THIRTY-THREE DOORS OF THE MYSTIC HALLWAY—a symbol representing the spinal column; the KUNDALINI. [**cf.** CHAKRAS, SUSHUMNA]

THOR—(Scandinavia) the DEVA in charge of thunder, lightning, winds, and showers; depicted to be a dynamic figure of might and strength with a red beard, voracious appetite and armed with a great axe-hammer to protect gods and people from the evil forces of chaos and destruction. [**cf.** MINOR DEVAS, SOLAR DEITY, RACIAL ANGELS]

THORNAPPLE—(Mexico) a hallucinogenic drug which has the properties that bring the user psychic visions and guidance from the etheric world; taken in sacred ceremonies; containing scopolamine and atropine. **Syn.** DATURA STRAMONIUM. [**cf.** DIVINE INTOXICATION, AMBROSIA]

THOTH—(Egypt) represents DIVINE INTELLIGENCE; god of WISDOM, learning and MAGIC; the inventor of letters and numbers; broken up into many gods, one each of air, seas, and sky, each having the attributes of Thoth; creator of the world using NU, making eight elements; identified with HERMES TRISMEGISTUS; depicted holding the ink jar and the crescent moon, and depicted as an ape holding a pallette full of writing reeds. [**cf.** MAA, TOTALITY]

THOUGHT—(esoteric) (future science) **1.** an erg of ENERGY; an electrical impulse taken from pure energy, manipulated with a person's INNER-MIND ACTIVITY, that automatically sends out a negative or positive current which is chemically propelled; inner-mind activity, having a set WAVELENGTH, which makes the MENTAL PLANE; (Uri Geller) "thoughts come from one source, a field of pure energy deep within the mind, the source of millions of individual bundles of creativity, intelligence, and energy"; 2. ergs of energy, always present, alive, responsive, possessing their own kind of mobility; interact within the body and outside the body; thoughts work with other thoughts throughout all infinity; 3. ideas in expression but not manifested as yet; all force or power is derived from thought, communicated by vibrations or waves; where thought is directed a force follows; electrical impulses cause activity and the theme of the impulse attributes to the type of activity it takes on; a mental vibration that expresses its nature; 4. a tool for co-creating one's own manifestations; a method of producing activated energy in a special vibrational frequency according to the expression of intelligence brought to the fore, stimulated by outer stimuli and by the BELIEF SYSTEM within; an energy configuration that is transformed into a sequential pattern to appear as words or images in outer awareness; 5. each theme of the impulse has a set wavelength utilizing the LAW OF LIKE ATTRACTS LIKE; thoughts create an electromagnetic reality that feels "real" to the thinker; 6. thoughts have an inner "sound" value that works in harmony with other sounds in the atmosphere; 7. a product of mental activity within the BRAIN and SOUL-MIND overlapping; mental activity individually originating from within, stimulated from the monad and outer environment, deliberately stimulated or stimulated from automatic repetitive processes; 8. an expression of TOTALITY making a mental world energy field in a certain state of motion; 9. (Rene Descartes); "In essence, spatially dimensionless or extended substance but exists nowhere"; 10. (Sri Ramakrishna) "a responsive memory and limited because it can't understand the whole field...is broken up piece by piece"; 11. a modulated field of Spirit energy intensified by the emotion accompanying the thought; 12. occult theory: every human thought coalesces with one of the creatures of the ASTRAL PLANE, which temporarily embodies it; mere passing impulses of annoyance with somebody will not last long in the astral world; 13. thought's negative aspect: (Hesychius, fifth century) "enemies who are bodiless and invisible, malicious and clever at harming man; thoughts can be skillful, nimble, and used in warfare"; 14. all of the above information includes INNER-DIALOGUE as well as expressed thought; (do not confuse with a PSYCHIC IMPRESSION that originates outside the mind and is non-thought).

(Inconcl.) [cf. ELEMENTAL, ATOM, LAW OF LIKE ATTRACTS LIKE Appendix 7]

THOUGHT ATMOSPHERE—the ELECTROMAGNETIC RADIATION around each person that makes one's BELIEF SYSTEM; this belief system has jelled from attitudes and emotions which accompanied one's experiences and activities from this life and other lives; consists of learned habits, learned information, instinctive desires, repressed desires, repressed emotions, morals, opinions, and standards; it is this jelled electromagnetic field that suggestions or new information must get through in order to be accepted by the individual and compartmentalized in the belief system for future use; e.g., 1. in sending a mental telepathic message, the receiver will not receive it, if the suggestion is not in compliance with the receiver's belief system; see LOVE-LINE; 2. destructive-brainwashing cults use LOVE-BOMBING in the first encounter to break into the thought atmosphere so their ideas and suggestions will take; they also continuously repeat the beliefs of the cult to force a new compartment in the belief system; see BIOCOMPUTER. [cf. EMOTION, MENTAL TELEPATHIC HEALING, ON-THE-SPOT-HYPNOSIS, SUGGESTION]

THOUGHT CONTROL—to be aware of one's INNER-DIALOGUE and one's speech to the extent that one utters only POSITIVE words, silently and verbally; the most beneficial things one can do for one's self in this incarnation is to practice controlling one's mental activity, because the state of one's health and one's daily experiences depend upon THINKING and its accompanying degree of emotion. [cf. SEED-PICTURE, LAW OF THOUGHT Appendix 7, SUBTALK, PERSONAL MIND PRINTS]

THOUGHT ENERGY—the cohesive quality that holds MATTER of each dimension together; each dimension is mental substance, held in place by the inner-mental activity of all the soul-minds of the universe. (Inconcl.) [cf. COSMIC ENERGY, MENTAL NOISE, MASS ELEMENTAL]

THOUGHT PHOTOGRAPHER—a PSYCHIC who has the ability to project a picture mentally imaged onto sensitized paper, and when developed in a normal way, it looks as if it were taken by the camera. [cf. THOUGHTOGRAPHY, EXTRAS, VAPOR-GRAPH]

THOUGHT PHOTOGRAPHY—see THOUGHT-OGRAPHY.

629

THOUGHT PROJECTION—to deliberately image a picture of a need or a desire in one's mind with the belief that it will make a thought-form strong enough to come into manifestation; accomplished by repeatedly centralizing one's attention on the END-RESULT of the situation one wishes to happen or on the object one wishes to own; the image is held as long as possible, perferably after a meditation period; (do not confuse with IMAGERY, HALLUCINATION, DAYDREAMING or MEDITATION). **Syn.** VISUALIZATION. [**cf.** CONTROLLED IMAGINATION, INNER-MIND ACTIVITY]

THOUGHT READING—see MENTAL TELEPATHY.

THOUGHT SPHERE—(esoteric) the space used for THOUGHT-FORMS in the ETHERIC WORLD, believed to contain the fastest and most subtle of all VIBRATIONS. [**cf.** ZOETHER, PSITRONICS, LOGOIDAL]

THOUGHT TRANSFERENCE—see MENTAL TELEPATHY.

THOUGHT-BODY—(Tibet) see MENTAL BODY.

THOUGHT-FORM CLAIRVOYANCE—to psychically perceive a VISION of a thought-form in the ETHERIC WORLD when one is in the same frame of mind as the mood of the thought-form; the wave length of thought-form ENERGY FIELDS can be moved with the speed of thought and withdrawn into the subtlest level of the astral world and anchored there to an idea; if the THOUGHT-FORMS are constantly being charged with EMOTION this emotion will follow the thought-forms around and make them more vivid and easily perceived; e.g., one feeling a religious high may clairvoyantly perceive Jesus the Christ; what he perceived is the thought-form of JESUS made up of thousands of images of him, held in the minds of the masses; (Jesus is in such a fast vibration, one would not likely be able to "up" one's vibration to that speed). [**cf.** THOUGHT PROJECTION, REFLECTING]

THOUGHT-FORM CLUSTERS—(Huna) memories of light, sound, smell, or noise stamped on microscopic bits of the ASTRAL SUBSTANCE, joined together into a cluster, to convey the impressions being thought about; electrical subconscious mind impulses molding impessions in the ASTRAL BODY where these memories of complete events become records. [**cf.** AKASHIC RECORDS]

THOUGHT-FORMS—different shapes of ethereal substance, defined or cloudy, large or small, varying in color and density, that float through space or hover over persons' heads; capable of being perceived clairvoyantly; ergs of ENERGY emanating from the head area are charged with degrees of INTELLIGENCE and EMOTION and have their position in SPACE according to these degrees; formations: 1. thoughts that take on the image of the thinker and object will be impressed upon the moving fluidic plastic-like energy of the ASTRAL PLANE forming it like a mold to reproduce the theme of the thought; 2. a thought charged with emotion and no special theme will hover over the head of the thinker, taking a shape and color according to the quality and clearness of the mood; 3. thoughts that remain in space forever, but weaken in density as the thinker releases them and the mold has been used; the PSYCHIC can easily tune into these thought-forms and the more highly charged with emotion, the easier it is; (do not confuse with VISUALIZATION or IMAGERY). (Inconcl.) [**cf.** ELEMENTAL, INNER-DIALOGUE, THOUGHT-FORMS Appendix 2]

THOUGHT-OUT—(Albert Einstein) term used to mean that his ideas were drawn out of the blue, not logically reasoned with or learned from formal education. [**cf.** SUPERCONSCIOUS MIND, INSPIRATIONAL THOUGHT]

THOUGHTLIKE DREAMS—(dreams) wordy ideas without a picture. [**cf.** AWAKE-DREAMING, ABSENT DREAMS]

THOUGHTOGRAPHY—to project a picture that is imaged in the mind, onto film or sensitized paper; when developed, it looks as if it were taken normally; (sometimes vague but recognizable); accomplished by the PSYCHIC centralizing his or her attention on the image he or she wants to project, the camera is held at one's forehead and snapped; (do not confuse with EXTRAS. [**cf.** PSYCHIC PHOTOGRAPHY Appendix 2]

THOUGHTS ARE THINGS—1. in back of everything manifested on earth, and earth itself, is one or many thoughts; the theme of every thought, with its accompanying degree of EMOTION, has dominion over the atoms; the most valuable knowledge one can ever understand; 2. (Elmer Green) "the world is nothing but crystalized thought"; because explanation would be repetitious, see ATOM, ENERGY, MATTER, BIOFEEDBACK TRAINING, MENTAL MIND, SUBCONSCIOUS MIND, THOUGHTS, LAW

OF THOUGHT Appendix 7, THOUGHT-FORMS, and VISUALIZATION.

THOUGHTS OF THE HEART—(dreams) feelings, emotions, and attitudes that are not logically thought-out, are depicted in a dream to let the dreamer know about these feelings. [**cf.** DEEPER DREAMLAND, DREAMSTUFF, FLUIDIC ASSOCIATION]

THOUGHTSMANSHIP—coined by Forrest C. Shaklee; "the art of expressing thoughts; a natural law of TRANSMUTATION in which all thoughts are transmuted into the fibers of the body." [**cf.** LAW OF THOUGHT Appendix 7]

THOUSAND PETAL LOTUS—see LOTUS.

THREAD—(esoteric) a fine cord of considerable length used as a TALISMAN because it's harmonious construction of two or more filaments twisted together; worn around the neck as a medical talisman to protect against sterility and death; placed in coffins to allow the dead to ascend to heaven; placed in the formation of a circle to keep the power within the circle and negative vibrations out; symbolizes a connection between the earth and etheral planes. [**cf.** KNOTS, FORMS-WITH-POWER, MEDICINE BAG]

THREE—1. (esoteric) known as the perfect number; blends ONE and TWO making the TRINITY; used in magic quite frequently; considered a lucky number; 2. (numerology) one whose life cycle number is three is affectionate, talented, popular, creative, self-expressive, and desirous of entertainment and beauty, but not orderly or reliable; planetary link is Jupiter. [**cf.** LAW OF THREES Appendix 7]

THREE BOOKS OF LIFE—see BOOKS OF LIFE.

THREE EGG CEREMONY—(ancient Egypt) an initiation in which one was to walk over a prescribed path of hazards, danger and complications, symbolic of DEATH, BIRTH, and LIFE; if students came out alive, they would have experienced truths and would be eligible to counsel and comfort others. [**cf.** MYSTICISM, INITIATORY SICKNESS, INITIATION RITES]

THREE FINGER TECHNIQUE—a special method to help memory, designed by Silva Mind Control. [**cf.** GOING-TO-LEVEL]

THREE-DAY SMOKE—(Native American; Panama, San Blas) a tradition in which hallucinogenic drugs are smoked to induce psychic visions to bring guidance for the tribe; one-half of the tribe smokes the drug for three days reporting to the other half who remain in a normal STATE OF CONSCIOUSNESS to interpret and record the PSYCHIC INFORMATION; the next three days the system is reversed. [**cf.** FORCED PSYCHISM, BOTANE, HALLUCINATING]

THREE-KNOTTED WAND—a wand, created to represent the human spinal column, used by magicians to perform psychic skills; gives the owner KUNDALINI power because the three knots symbolized the IDA, PINGALA, and the SUSHUMNA. [**cf.** ASSOCIATED MAGIC, LAW OF MIMICRY Appendix 7]

THREE-PART COOPERATION—(Findhorn, Scotland) a working relationship to bring harmony among the HUMAN BEING KINGDOM, the nature spirit kingdom and the devic kingdom. [**cf.** KINGDOM]

THRESHOLD CONTROL—1. (biofeedback training) a dial on a BIOFEEDBACK INSTRUMENT using a meter, that establishes a baseline for each training session; dial is used to regulate the subject's electrical impulse cycle in relation to the meter. **Syn.** FREQUENCY CONTROL. [**cf.** ELECTRODES, BASELINE DRIFT, ARTIFACT] 2. an invisible line or level in the ATMOSPHERE designating that sound enters the ear, or a sound-receiving instrument, and humans perceive it as sound. [**cf.** MUSIC OF THE SPHERES, SOUND, WHITE NOISE]

THRESHOLD OF ETERNITY—the division between the physical plane and the etheric planes. **Syn.** VEIL, WALL. [**cf.** ASTRAL WORLD, BELOW LEVELS OF AWARENESS, BLACK CURTAIN]

THRESHOLD OF HEARING—the level where sound becomes audible to physical ears; varies with each person and changes in each person during a twenty-four hour period. [**cf.** CLAIRAUDIENCE]

THRESHOLD OF PROSPERPINA—(Greece) crossed when making the TRANSITION; physical death. [**cf.** DEATH CONSCIOUSNESS, DWELLERS ON THE THRESHOLD]

THRIAEAN LOTS—(Rome) handmade markers that bore generalized inscriptions that could answer many types of questions and were used to predict and guide one's future; the recipient tossed the markers and their fall determined which lot's inscription was the answer; the markers were

631

consecrated to Mercury and hence, the cliche, "the lot of Mercury is given to the olive leaf." **Syn.** SORTILEGE. [**cf.** CASTING OF LOTS, SIGNIFICANT COINCIDENCES]

THROAT CHAKRA—(Hinduism, Yoga, Sanskrit) a minute center of concentrated energy invisibly located below the larynx in the throat area, superimposing the thyroid gland; it extends to embrace the MEDULLA OBLONGATA; this chaikra is the center of creativity and mediates vocal expression; when perceived clairvoyantly it has sixteen petals with an indigo center and looks blue and silver, like shimmering ripples of water on a moonlight night; it is a sexual center, a psychic center, and its symbol is the ETHER. **Syn.** VISUDDA CHAKRA. [**cf.** KUNDALINI, ROOT CHAKRA, CHAKRA]

THRONE MYSTICISM—(Old Testament) the study of the ASCENSION of the SOUL, and instructions to achieve intervention of the DIVINE by helping students to open their visionary capabilities; when one could perceive the higher planes and clairvoyantly perceive "the Lord sitting on his throne and all the host of heaven standing beside him," one was considered an accomplished VISIONARY. **Syn.** MERKABAH MYSTICISM. [**cf.** MENTAL PROJECTION, PERILS OF THE SOUL]

THRONES—graded order of etheric world helpers to carry out the divine plan. [**cf.** ANGEL KINGDOM, WINGS, MYSTIC ZONE]

THROUGH—term used to express psychic perception in action. Usage: "Your AURA came through very visibly tonight." "The CONTROL came through with a whisper instead of his usual strong voice." [**cf.** AMPING, FALL IN WITH]

THROWING GHOST—see POLTERGEIST.

THROWING THE BONES—(Africa) to throw markers from the hand and use the pattern of their fall to have meaning for counselling and predicting the future for one's self and for others; the layman uses bones, stones, sticks or whatever is handy, and the professional psychic uses special consecrated bones or stones which are kept in a bag hung from the psychics waist gear and which no one else handles. **Syn.** CASTING OF LOTS. [**cf.** LOTS, SORTILEGE, PATTERNING ACROSS TIME, MING STICKS]

THULE—(Iceland) a type of poet who was also considered a prophet because he or she was capable of seeing into the past and writing poems regarding this. [**cf.** TIME BENDERS, RETROCOGNITION, PRESAGED, PRESCIENCE]

THUNDER PEOPLE—(Native American, Navaho) (thunder means "Truth") ETHERIC WORLD INTELLIGENCES of a very high order that communicate with the holy ones of the tribe to bring great Truths of the universe; also bring counsel, guidance, and protection. **Syn.** GUIDE, ANGEL, CELESTIAL GUARDIAN.

TI BON ANGE—see 'TI BON ANGE.

TIBETAN BOOK OF THE DEAD—a document of BUDDHISM, that gives instructions for going through an initiation when one is dying; describes how to live when in the ETHERIC WORLD; written to help one reach NIRVANA. [**cf.** BARDO THODOL]

TIBETAN ORACLES—see MEDIUMS and PSYCHICS.

TIBETAN RELIGION—a form of BUDDHISM; emphasis was on the development of the SOUL by controlling one's mind and working for the benefit of the whole planet; believed in REINCARNATION and the oneness of all mankind; used psychic skills far advanced of other cultures to attain spiritual perfection.

TIDE CYCLE—a pattern in humans that relates to the tides of the ocean, repeating itself in each twelve hour pattern; connects humans to earth. (Inconcl.) [**cf.** GROWTH CYCLE, LIFE WAVE]

TIE—(Nuer tribe, Upper Nile) see EARTHBOUND ENTITY, GHOST and ASTRAL SHELL.

TIED-IN—pertains to the PSYCHIC as he or she picks up information and emotional feelings from the subject who is receiving the reading. [**cf.** TUNED-IN, STEP INTO YOUR VIBRATION]

TIGER—(anpsi) a creature that is sensitive to psychic vibrations; capable of changing its form and its size. [**cf.** DIMENSION-SHIFTING, SHAPE-CHANGING]

TIKI—(Polynesia) a stone or natural object that is found and can be used as an AMULET; believed to have been made by the goddess of childbirth; given to a child by the father at birth to always be worn around the child's neck; has the properties to protect and bring abundance to the wearer. [**cf.** AMULET, KACHINA DOLL, TOTEM]

TIME—(esoteric) (future science) 1. a factor of CONSCIOUSNESS measured by ETERNITY; an illusionary period of measurement, when in the third dimensional plane, made by the BRAIN; rules the

PHYSICAL BODY form; a period during which something exists or continues, whether action, process or condition; 2. a mental awareness moving within consciousness affected by intensity, direction, and flow; (Validivar) "the duration of the period of consciousness"; 3. time "is," making life meaningful; (W. Brugh Joy) a useful construct of outer awareness"; 4. (Seth) "an ILLUSION brought about by the motions of apparently solidified vitality, triggered off by action and counter-action; meaningless without the necessity to counteract against other actions"; 5. an ENERGY that links all things in the UNIVERSE, maintaining the events of life in the world; experiences and thoughts imbedded in an individual's SOUL-MIND or akashic record; 6. (Charles Muses) "time may be defined as the ultimate causal pattern of all energy release"; (Nikolai A. Kozyrev) "time is an unknown kind of energy that emanates between cause and effect ends; man's ability to differentiate minute energy events is the basis of our time"; 7. current belief: time flows in two directions but one normally perceives it from past to future; time moves from left to right; time has a pattern of flow and a rate of flow; an illusionary system that is constant, and through which mankind moves; 8. (Monteith) "a geometrical aspect of BIOPLASMA expressed as static geometry, having its effect in dynamic geometry; effects the processes of construction and decay"; 9. (Albert Einstein) "a function of the gravitational field in which it exists; the stronger the gravitational field of a planet, the slower the passage of time on its surface; a second on earth would be of a slightly longer duration on the planet, Jupiter, which has a stronger gravitational field." (Inconcl.) [cf. MULTITIME, MULTIDIMENSION, SPACE/TIME THEORIES]

TIME BARRIER—(laboratory and psi tasks) the time lapse between the time when the subject (psychic) calls the TARGET and the experimenter determines the target order, which interferes with the subject's rsults. [cf. TASK, TARGET AREA, SECONDARY EFFECT]

TIME BENDER—1. (dreams) PSYCHIC EXPERIENCE DURING SLEEP that shows the dreamer a past life scene or a future life scene; can be distinguished from a dream because the scene shows authentic scenery and dress code and it is easy to recall; 2. any psychic experience that goes forward or backward in time. (Inconcl.) [cf. PROPHECY, RETROGRESSION]

TIME CYCLES—1. day is based on the earth's rotation on its axis with reference to the sun; 2. month is based on the moon's revolution around the earth; 3. year is based on the earth's revolution around the sun. [cf. ETERNAL PRESENT, INTROJECTION, AGE OF BRAHMA]

TIME DENSITY—(Russia) (Nikolai Kozyrev) a chemical reaction to thought (in the study of time as an energy). [cf. BOUNDLESS, THE COVALENT BONDING.]

TIME DISPLACEMENT—1. (psi tasks) to hit the TARGET, in a laboratory experiment, before the target was chosen or after the target was given. [cf. TIME-BAND LAG, REAL TIME, ESP] 2. to perceive clairvoyantly a dinosaur or a creature that seems to belong to millions of years ago; the clairvoyant is temporarily out of step with the stream of time. (Inconcl.) [cf. MOMENT POINT, THULR, MULTITIME]

TIME DISTORTION—to lose a mundane concept of clock time when in a theta, or delta, level of consciousness in which there is no TIME-SPACE; to have unrealistic awareness of the time that has elapsed after the following sessions: deep MEDITATION, HYPNOSIS, BIOFEEDBACK TRAINING, and lengthy jogging. [cf. DELTA and THETA STATES OF CONSCIOUSNESS, ASTRAL PLANE]

TIME FRAMEWORK—time sequence; a period of time.

TIME LAG—1. (biofeedback training) the lapse of time in the brain cells as they do their work, as opposed to working simultaneously; 2. (dowsing) a small lapse in time before the reaction of a dowser tool when picking up radiations from an earth object. [cf. DOWSING, BLOCKING, EXPECTANCY WAVE, ELECTRICAL RHYTHM]

TIME LAPSE PHOTOGRAPHY—(dream research) uses a specially designed camera that records periods of motion and immobility of the sleepers; placed in the corner of the room of the sleeper; attached to the eyeballs, chin, and brain activity, which triggers it to go off every 7½ minutes; can be used at home as well as the laboratory. (Inconcl.) [cf. EOG, DELTA STAGE OF SLEEP, ORDINARY DREAMS]

TIME LOSS—(ufology) a block in the CONSCIOUS MIND of each member of a UFO encounter that shuts out any recollection of what transpired during that time span of the encounter. (Inconcl.)

[cf. UFOLOGY, AMNESIA'S GRIP, ACTINIC RAYS]

TIME OF ACTIVITY AND TIME OF REST—(cycles) the breakdown of the biological and consciousness cyclic pattern that all things of nature go through; each unit of nature has its own cyclic time span with degrees of activity and rest; occurs within everything from the amoeba to the Great Central Sun; each cycle is divided into half, regardless of the cycle's length of time and importance of the unit in the SCHEME OF THINGS; for half of the cycle the unit does peak performance with no outer preparation; for the other half of the cycle the unit gives less of a performance, or shuts down completely, as if to regenerate for its life continuity; more noticeable in plants, animals and humans; humans can lessen the lower performance cyclic hours or days by MEDITATION, PSYCHISM, more sleep and other new-age preparations. **Syn.** HIGHS AND LOWS OF A CYCLE. [cf. SENSITIVITY CYCLE, SUMMER HORMONE]

TIME OF REPOSE—a period of restraint of the SOUL-MIND while the infant's organs grow to a mature state, when the soul-mind can then express its true self.

TIME PLAN—a measurement of incarnations on planet earth fulfulling a karmic debt. [cf. ALL-ACCOMPLISHING WISDOM, CAUSATION, DELAYED KARMA]

TIME PRESSURE—the subconscious feeling that one must be constantly doing something noticeably constructive to be accepted in today's world. [cf. NEW-AGE PSYCHOLOGY, LIVING DEAD, NORMAL]

TIME SENSE—an inner alertness to clock time, people and creatures have without looking at a clock; a subjective knowing of how long to perform an activity without a watch, even though the task is irrelevant to one's usual schedule; the mind runs in harmony with a twenty-four hour cycle as does the PHYSICAL BODY; time sense is more of a psychological feeling than a physical function; e.g., a dog knows exactly what time the master is coming home from work; to awaken one's self at the time desired without an alarm clock. (Inconcl.) [cf. JET LAG, CIRCADIAN RHYTHM, POSITIVE DAYS]

TIME SERIES ANALYSIS—(cycles) a general name for cycle-locating techniques. [cf. ASCENDING ARC, BIOLOGICAL CYCLE, PLANETARY CHAIN]

TIME STRUCTURE—a period of time; phrase used by biorhythmists and scientists studying laws of time. [cf. TIME FRAME, ACROSS TIME, ETERNAL NOW]

TIME TRAVEL—1. (astral projection) to use the ASTRAL BODY to travel back in time or forward in time for a short period, leaving the physical body on the bed; 2. (mental projection) to allow the mind to expand and travel forward or backward in time and view scenes; requires deep MEDITATION or HYPNOTHERAPY session; time travel is a rare skill but possible. (Inconcl.) [cf. MENTAL PROJECTION Appendix 2, PROJECTION ART, SUPERCLAIRVOYANCE]

TIME TRAVELERS—persons who have DREAMS and REGRESSION flashes giving evidence of past lives on earth when earth was experiencing times similar to the present TRANSFORMATION; time travelers claim lives on ATLANTIS and give evidence of knowledge of Atlantis to back their theory; believed to have incarnated to help earthlings go through this transformation period or to work out their own Atlantis KARMA in a similar setting. (Inconcl.) [cf. TIME, CONSCIOUSNESS, MULTITIME]

TIME-CONSCIOUSNESS—theory: a human is the only animal that understands, and has an outer awareness of, the frame of time; which gives a clue that time is made by the CONSCOUS MIND. (Inconcl.) [cf. TIME, CONSCIOUSNESS, MULTITIME]

TIME-FLOW—1. see VITAL LIFE FORCE; 2. (Russia) an unknown energy in the universe that is positive in nature. (Inconcl.) [cf. UNCERTAINTY PRINCIPLE, SPEED OF THOUGHT]

TIME-LOCK—an invisible energy field which guards the recycling vaults of the earth; if catastrophe comes to the planet, there are vaults or caves, scattered around the earth to house soul-minds who will be needed for the new civilization; this invisible energy field on the door to the cave will only allow soul-minds to enter who have the correct vibrational frequency. (Inconcl.) [cf. EVOLUTION, SOUL-MIND, TRANSFORMATION]

TIME-SPACE—see SPACE/TIME THEORIES.

TIME-SPATIALITY—events occuring in the vibrations that relate to a point in time. [cf. ETERNAL PRESENT, HYPERSPACE]

TIME-TRAINS—(Huna) single impressions (of seeming unimportance) that are related to traumatic past experiences join together with other like experiences, in the SUBCONSCIOUS MIND, as a cluster of grapes. **Syn.** MEMORY CLUSTER. [**cf.** AKASHIC RECORDS, LOCKED-IN]

TIMEBAND LAG—(psi tasks) the seconds it takes to change the TARGET in an experiment which seems to be just enough time for the participant to psychically sense the next target. [**cf.** PROPHECY, COGNITION, BLIND MENTAL PSYCHISM]

TIMELESS-PRESENT—a STATE OF CONSCIOUS-NESS when one blocks out all past or future moments and is enraptured into that which is happening at the present and time is no longer an awareness; one could be going through a time warp. (Inconcl.) [**cf.** ALTERED STATE OF CON-SCIOUSNESS, BLANK PERIODS, CENTERING]

TINDALO—(Melanesia) an important ETHERIC WORLD INTELLIGENCE who takes the form of an animal to communicate with the earthling. [**cf.** GUIDE, COYOTE, BAND OF COLLABORATORS]

TIP-OFFS—(psi tasks) unintentional little man-nerisms that either mislead or lead the subject to know the TARGET; therefore does not make a true experiment. [**cf.** FORCED IMPRESSIONS, EXPERI-MENT EXPECTANCY]

TIRAWA—(Native American, Sioux, "Father" or the "power above") see TOTALITY and GOD.

TISRA TIL—(Eckankar) see THIRD-EYE AREA.

TISSUE CAPSULE CONTRACTION—to feel the pulling together of the self into an ever-smaller dimension enabling the mind to travel to higher planes in the ETHERIC WORLD; occurs after a deep meditation, willed or unwilled. (Inconcl.) **Syn.** MENTAL PROJECTION. [**cf.** MENTAL PROJECTION, TRANSCENDENT]

TISSUE CAPSULE EXPANSION—to feel the exten-sion or enlargement of one's self enabling the mind to travel in planes of a very high level in the ETHERIC WORLD; can occur after a deep or long MEDITATION period; willed or unwilled. **Syn.** MENTAL PROJECTION. [**cf.** CONSCIOUSNESS PRO-JECTION, MACROPSIA]

TISSUE SALTS—twelve inorganic minerals that can be taken internally and will be assimilated into the system to restore the deficient inorganic elements; prepared homeopathically; the inorganic minerals are in minute quantities in the body but are essential in restoring balance to the BODY CHEMISTRY so the body can more easily heal itself. **Syn.** CELL SALTS, MINERAL SALTS. [**cf.** BIOCHEMIC

SYSTEM OF MEDICINE]

TITANS—(Tibet) see DENSITY.

TIWAZ—(Germany) supreme God of the sky.

TM—Abbr. TRANSCENDENTAL MEDITATION; coined by Maharishi Mahesh Yogi from India; a scientific, simple, effortless, mental technique whereby one can rid oneself of stresses of the mind and enjoy deep rest and relaxation; to be practiced twice a day; aim is to go into a STATE OF CONSCIOUSNESS beyond normal thinking and ex-perience quiet levels of the mind; to become aware of impulses, feeling and action; an aid to one's conscious awareness of oneself and a realization of one's place in the universe; makes the mind more orderly. [**cf.** MEDITATION Appendix 5]

TMU—(ancient Egypt) the sun, the first form emerging from the water; the primeval matter, in the beginning of CREATION; marks the beginning of TIME; the sun-god: (later united with RA, called TMU-RA). [**cf.** SUN, WATER, SPIRIT]

TO WORSEN—(psi tasks) to score closer to chance. [**cf.** ESP, PSI TASKS, CHANCE]

TO-MORROW—(Buddhism) the next reincar-nation.

TOADSTONE—(esoteric) a mineral used as an AMULET to protect new-born babies and their mothers because of its properties of protection; (William Shakespeare) a precious jewel found in the head of a toad. [**cf.** ATTRACTION CONSCIOUS-NESS, CONTAINER'S OF MAGICAL POWER]

TOADSTOOLS—contains a hallucinogenic drug used in rituals, or privately, to bring on clairvoyant visions of the ETHERIC WORLD; see MUSHROOM. [**cf.** ARTIFICIAL PARADISE, DATURA STRANO-NIUM]

TOBISCOPE—(Russia) invented by Victor Adamenko; a device used to detect ACUPUNCTURE POINTS; consists of two electrodes and an ampli-fier; when the therapist touches points on the skin a needle on a scale will swing according to the amount of energy at that point, helps the acu-puncturist to recognize whether there is enough energy in that circuit. [**cf.** ACUPUNCTURE, SYSTEM OF DUCTS]

TOKEN—(fifth century) (Greece, Egypt, Neo-platonists) an animal, herb stone, scent, or an

635

engraved character used as a symbol to invoke the god in charge of one's particular problem; token was hidden inside an animated statue (which resembled its function) so the identity was only known to the MAGICIAN; statue acts as an ORACLE for its owner; theory: each god has its "sympathetic" representative in the ANIMAL KINGDOM, vegetable kingdom, and MINERAL KINGDOM which is permanently in rapport with the divine; token is the "sympathetic" representative; e.g., a gem is put inside the statue of the god of wealth to bring wealth to the owner. **Syn.** SYMBOL. [**cf.** MIMICRY, AMULET, TOTEM, SYMPATHETIC MAGIC, ORACLE STATUE]

TOKEN INDICATION—see OMEN.

TOKEN OBJECT—a tangible article that makes a good PSYCHOMETRIC READING; article should be owned by one or a few owners, and used in a repetitious manner; this article has the vibrations of the owner, itself and its purpose imbedded within it. [**cf.** OBJECT READING, SECONDARY WAVES, PURE PSYCHOMETRY]

TOMB—(Egypt) a shrine built for the dead making a haven for the deceased's SOUL-MIND to inhabit if it wanted to return to earth later; bodies were carefully buried in the tomb so the soul-mind could enjoy earthly vibrations again, but in a state of serenity unknown in the physical body's incarnation. [**cf.** PRESERVING OF SACREDNESS, MUMMIFICATION]

TONAL—(Native American, Yaqui) (don Juan) one realm of the order of the UNIVERSE pertaining to the structure that people experience and produce as living organisms, and to the order of all existing MATTER; makes up one half of the total of an individual. **Syn.** MAYA, MUNDANE. [**cf.** NAGUAL, REALITY, TOTALITY]

TONAL PERSON—(don Juan) the social person; the PERSONALITY or EGO that begins at birth and ends at death; includes all humanity knows or can name, and all the categories by which humanity organizes the ordinary world. [**cf.** SUBCONSCIOUS MIND, EGO, MATERIALISTIC MAN]

TONDI—(Bataks, Pacific) see VITAL LIFE FORCE.

TONE OF THE COSMIC MUSIC—(India, "that which shines by itself") each sound of the raga is chosen because of its specific spiritual and emotional charge, making one feel that it originates from the heart or the "self." [**cf.** MUSICAL SCIENCE,

LOST WORD, TONING, RAGAS]

TONGUES—slang for TALKING-IN-TONGUES.

TONING—(future science) (esoteric) a sound used for therapeutic purposes; a special tone or music chosen because of its vibrational frequency to bring harmony in the body of one who has a particular mental or physical disease. (Inconcl.) [**cf.** ALTERNATIVES, SOUND HEALING, SCIENCE OF CHANGING]

TONTON-MACOUTE—(Haiti, Voodoo) the traveling MAGICIAN, known for owning a satchel of magical articles and medicinal plants that are used in HEALING and PSYCHIC COUNSELING; uses amulets for mothers with undisciplined children. **Sim.** JESTER. [**cf.** VOODOOISM, HERBOLOGIST, MEDICINE BUNDLE]

TONUS—(esoteric) 1. (seventeenth century) something found in the body which makes rules of its own and eludes PHYSICS and chemistry. **Sim.** HOMEOSTASIS. 2. (China) the subtle differences in the ACUPUNCTURE POINTS; abnormalities are detectable by the superior practitioner. [**cf.** MIND TECHNOLOGIES, SHUNT PATHS, ACUPUNCTURE, POLARITY BALANCING]

TOOBA TREE—(Koran) an enormous tree covered with many kinds of fruit, living in PARADISE or SEVENTH HEAVEN in the ETHERIC WORLD; sits among rivers and springs that flow with water, milk, honey and wine. [**cf.** SUMMERLAND, HAPPY HUNTING GROUND, PLANES]

TOOL—(esoteric) a method, condition, object, instrument, or technique that can be used to better one's self.

TOP FORCE—see TOTALITY.

TOPAZ—(esoteric) a mineral that has the properties to help the wearer to be wise and fearless; emblematic of the conquering of the lower man; influenced by the vibrations from the sun; linked with the lion of the ANIMAL KINGDOM. [**cf.** CARNAL MAN, MINPSI, PRIMARY PERCEPTION]

TOPOSCOPE—abbr. TOPSY; an instrument having twenty-two electrodes that attach to the head, designed for a more sophisticated job than the EEG; the instrument detects unusual states of consciousness such as seizures, HYPNAGOGIC STATES, REM REBOUND PHENOMENA, mental disturbances; grew out of the desire to research "the crowd of strangers milling around in our dear unknown" at the Burden Neurological Institute in Bristol,

England. (Inconcl.) [**cf.** ELECTRODES, ELECTRO-ENCEPHALOGRAPH, REM REBOUND PHENOMENA]

TOPSY—see TOPOSCOPE.

TORAH—(Jewish) a sacred book of teachings; an inclusive term that refers to all that God has revealed about Himself, history of the Jewish people, and the conduct that is required of them; in time the entire written revelation came to be referred to as Torah; in a narrow sense, means God's commandments; book provides the basis of common belief and conduct characterized in Jewish life binding Jews together.

TORNAIT—(Thule, Greenland; Eskimo) ETHERIC WORLD INTELLIGENCES that bring helpful information and guidance through many mediumistic skills. [**cf.** MEDIUMSHIP, TRANCE, INNER-BAND]

TORNIT—(Thule, Greenland; Eskimo) NATURE SPIRITS that show themselves as giants, willing to help earthlings by counseling and protecting. [**cf.** NATURE SPIRIT]

TORTOISE—considered in some cultures to be one of the four most important spiritual creatures. [**cf.** DRAGON, FENG-HWANG, UNICORN]

TOTAL ABSORPTION—(meditation) to become one with the aspiring thought or symbol one is focusing on, until one's self feels like the symbol or thought; a beneficial STATE OF CONSCIOUSNESS. [**cf.** NO-MIND STATE, EQUALIZING WISDOM, HOLY BREATH]

TOTAL CONSCIOUSNESS—see COSMIC CONSCIOUSNESS.

TOTAL EMPATH—a PSYCHIC who is overly sensitive (through birth or an accident) and "absorbs" the local atmosphere wherever he or she is; tunes into the feelings of an area spontaneously and remains under its influence until he or she leaves; cognitively tunes into the nation with physical and mental sensations until the trauma is over; usually defenseless against PSYCHIC ATTACK. (Inconcl.) [**cf.** PSYCHIC TRANSFER, EMPATHY CLAIRSENTIENCE, FUNCTIONAL CLAIRSENTIENCE]

TOTAL EXACTITUDE CONSCIOUSNESS—a feeling of surety about what psychically surfaced regarding past information learned, or past experiences in other lives, because of the forcefulness of the relating facts obtained. (Inconcl.) [**cf.** EXACTITUDE CRITERIA]

TOTAL INTELLIGENCE—a composite of all the sounds, colors, smells, tastes, feelings, emotions, physical structures, thoughts, words, inventions, discoveries, ethereal structures, concepts, ideas, languages, etc., that humanity will ever think of, condensed in each electron, making the overall picture of the universe; total intelligence contains ALL; orderly processes which produces things. **Syn.** UNIVERSAL MIND, DIVINE INTELLIGENCE. [**cf.** TOTALITY]

TOTAL LAW—the life force activity within the seed of the universe motivating it to express its potential; all universal laws are subservient to Total Law in order for it to evolve to perfection. [**cf.** UNIVERSAL LAW, LAW OF SUBSERVIENCE Appendix 7]

TOTAL RECALL—to remember what one experienced in an ALTERED STATE OF CONSCIOUSNESS; normally the CONSCIOUS MIND is passive and will not surface what transpires unless the psychic programs her or himself to have total recall; one should program oneself before ASTRAL PROJECTION, deep MEDITATION, TRANCE and HYPNOSIS. (Inconcl.) [**cf.** FAIR WITNESS, MENTAL REGRESSION, SIMPLE MEMORY RECALL]

TOTAL REGRESSION—to relive a past life traumatic experience, during a HYPNOTHERAPY session, that was never resolved when it occured and has been suppressed for one or many lifetimes; subject reverts back to the same emotional state experienced when the event happened; subject only has the amount of knowledge up to that point in time; e.g., if it happened in Germany, one may speak in German and not know English; subject reports the experience from the point of view perceived at the time of the trauma, because subject thinks it is happening now; if the HYPNOTHERAPIST can get the subject to put the experience in the right perspective and handle it properly this takes the charge out of the experience, and the subject will not be bothered with the negative results from that trauma anymore. (Inconcl.) **Syn.** REVIVIFICATION. [**cf.** PARALLEL AWARENESS, COMPLETE REGRESSION, SUPERALERTNESS, BLOCKS]

TOTAL SCORE—(laboratory) the polled score of all runs; the number of hits made in any given unit of trials. [**cf.** HIT, RUN, AVERAGE, SCORE]

TOTAL VISION—see ASTRAL VISION.

TOTALITY—(esoteric) (capitalized) coined by June Bletzer; "one source" of all; and "one unifying movement" of all; 1. a neutral whole; a self-contained living organism; a living entity with a SOUL, expressing what it is, evolving and growing to fulfill the potential within its seed; 2. an invisible source of *one* intelligence, *one* energy, *one* love, and *one* consciousness, broken up and distributed into atoms (and smaller particles); each ATOM contains all the attributes of the total, with one overall function, which is to vibrate at varying frequencies, in explicit order, until the total has perfected itself; (Richard Horwege) both a *cause* and *effect* occuring simultaneously; 3. (stage of evolution to date) the individual, an ENTITY within the total entity, is to direct and utilize the atoms by his or her mind, making the densities, shapes, forms and principles to carry on their overall purpose; 4. one essence behind all manifestations which is indestructable, unchangable, and eternal; 5. *X* matter having two modes, mind and substance; 6. SPACE-TIME CONTINUA consciousness; 7. underlying principles that direct, supply, maintain, organize, sustain, motivate, and love; 8. pure ENERGY and pure THOUGHT; 9. implies an order behind all; THE SCHEME OF THINGS; 10. a sea of usable and reusable atoms, perpetually in motion; 11. a magnanimous, giant, electronic switchboard forming a communication system between all things in the UNIVERSE; perceivable and unperceivable; uses its own atoms, nodes and electrons to connect all things within itself making itself one unit; a sea of trillions of VIBRATIONAL FREQUENCIES interacting, interplaying and interchanging constantly, filling this unit with myriads of shapes and densities; each shape has it's own individuality but all are connected to the electronic switchboard; switchboard drains wavelengths from its own wavelength source, gives out principles of rates of vibrations from itself, and interpenetrates these myriads of shapes and densities so each shape and density knows it's function; 12. Totality is invisible, indestructive perpetual motion of positivism and negativism, appearing and disappearing; 13. an essence so vast that only it can understand its vastness. (Inconcl.) **Syn.** see Appendix 3. [**cf.** LIGHT, TOTAL INTELLIGENCE, LOVE, MUSIC OF THE SPHERES, UNIVERSAL LAW, ATOM, LAW OF VIBRATION and LAW OF POLARITY Appendix 7]

TOTEM—(Native American; Dinka, Nilotes) an object, ploant or animal that: 1. serves as a hereditary badge or emblem for a tribe or clan; represents the spirit of the whole tribe or clan and the relationship among the members; carved on the TOTEM POLE and used as a design on tribal property; made into jewelry to be worn by tribal members to identify them and serve as a TALISMAN; usually the animal or object (totem) is that which the tribe is named after; 2. serves as a sacred personal talisman; each individual in the tribe has a private totem, which was chosen because the totem has a personal relationship to the individual, which is kept secret; individuals' personal totems can appear in their dreams or in clairvoyant visions to warn them of danger, bring strength, heal their bodies, or bring them abundance; symbol can be worn on one's body or clothing or carried; e.g., one's totem might be a white horse. [**cf.** THREE-KNOTTED WAND, UDJAT/EYE, KACHINA DOLL]

TOTEM CULTS—see TOTEMISM.

TOTEM POLE—(Native American) a post carved and painted with bright colored totemic figures erected in a site that was set aside for tribal members to come and worship the GREAT SPIRIT; marked an area of an outdoor church. [**cf.** RING OF WOODEN POSTS, ASSOCIATE MAGIC, RITUAL]

TOTEMIC SPIRITS—(Nuer tribe, Upper Nile) the intelligence, in the animal form, that is respected by their lineage and used as the badge or totem for their tribe; gives their tribe some of it's characteristics for which it is noted; e.g., the spirit of the lion is courageousness and fearlessness; spirit of the lamb is tenderness, etc. [**cf.** LAW OF ASSOCIATION, Appendix 7, SYMBOLISM]

TOTEMISM—(Native American) 1. the use of an animal emblem as a tribal leader and TALISMAN; belief: (a) their ancestors in the ETHERIC WORLD are part divine, and are capable of changing their form into an animal at will; this leads them to use the animal of the ancestor that came to them through MEDIUMSHIP skills to help the tribe, as a symbol of appreciation for guidance and protection; animal emblem was carved on poles and homes; (b) the etheric world has an animal for each shaman that can be called upon psychically for guidance, abundance and protection; 2. (Australian Aborgines) the use of an animal as one's sacred symbol that comes to one in a dream or a clairvoyant vision; this animal can be called upon psychically for counsel, guidance and protection; belief: animals can develop a human side and manifest their messages through dreams; 3. totem means close relationship, like a brother. [**cf.** AMU-

LET, TIKI, ETHERIC WORLD INTELLIGENCES, PSYCHIC FIGURINE]

TOUCH SENSE—see PSYCHOMETRY.

TOUCHED—to receive a personal READING from a STAND-UP READER. Usage: "Have you been touched yet?" Psychics working in public gatherings do not always know who has had a reading, because they stay in the ALPHA STATE OF CONSCIOUSNESS, which makes them unaware of mundane activity; they ask the above question to avoid re-reading for someone. [cf. LIGHT TRANCE]

TOUCHES—sensations of coming in contact with what seems to be a living presence when sitting for physical phenomena in darkroom sessions; e.g., a kiss on the cheek, a touch on the ear, the mussing of hair, or even a clammy, wet coldness or cobweb-like feeling over the face; believed to come from the guides. [cf. SEANCE, GUIDE, TRANSFIGURATION]

TOURMALINE—(esoteric) a mineral having the properties to be a transmitter of Mercury's vibrations; absorbs light and transfers electricity easily. [cf. MINPSI, ROCK, CRYSTAL, SIGHT IN DARKNESS, STAR-RUBY]

TOVERSTAF—(Holland) see DOWSING.

TOWERS OF SILENCE—(Parsee, Zoroastrianism) large, sacred buildings of stone structure located on the hills, surrounded by gardens; bodies of the dead are placed on the tops, exposed to the sun and flesh-eating vultures; belief: that the bodies will go back into the ethers more quickly. [cf. DEATH FEASTS, OPENING OF THE MOUTH CEREMONY, BARDOS]

TRACE METHOD—(Russia) (Ippolit Kogan) a technique of tracking telepathy in the brain waves of the receiver by means of a man-made psi field and dividing the telepathic message received into information of bits per second. (Inconcl.) [cf. SUBCONSCIOUS CODE, INNER-WORLD TELEPATHY, DIRECTED-THOUGHT TRAINER]

TRACER EFFECT—(dream laboratories) indicating the target of an experiment appearing, in specific and distinctive features, in the DREAMSTUFF of the dreamer when conducting psychic experiments with the sleeping person in the DREAM RESEARCH LABORATORIES. (Inconcl.) [cf. DREAM REALITY, SHARED DREAMS]

TRACKING—(electronic voices) to record sounds on the tape of a cassette player in a room shielded from all outside interference; in experiments, voices that were not heard by the physical ears at the time the tape was running were heard when the tapes were played back. (Inconcl.) [cf. VOICE TAPE PHENOMENA, ELECTRONIC VOICES Appendix 2]

TRADE-DOWN (hypnotherapy) to replace a serious symptom with a minor one in a HYPNOTHERAPY session; when working with behavioral patterns that the subject wishes to change, sometimes a minor symptom switch works out satisfactorily; e.g., looking from left to right in place of biting fingernails. (Inconcl.) [cf. SYMPTOM SUBSTITUTION, DISPLACEMENT PHOBIA, AUTOSUGGESTION]

TRADITION—an emotional experience that has happened and is then repeated over a number of years or centuries in a real performance or simulated form, with only a gradual change; even though the newcomers may not be knowledgeable of it's first meaning, there will be some influence and significance to those newcomers partaking of the activity, because of its repetitious performance, especially if the same articles are used over and over; e.g., hanging some style of cross around the neck for that occasion. [cf. ELECTROMAGNETIC IMAGE, RITUAL, WATER]

TRADITIONAL INSTRUCTIONS—(Native American) replica instructions of shamanic techniques, with only slight deviations over the years, received by each SHAMAN candidate; the only way to become a shaman; replica instructions include: names and functions of the spirits, mythology and geneology of the clan, and the clan's secret language. [cf. MEDIUMSHIP, INITIATORY SICKNESS, QUEST, HEREDITARY TRANSMISSION]

TRAFFIC GUIDE—see DOORKEEPER.

TRANCE—an ALTERED STATE OF CONSCIOUSNESS brought about by the willing collaboration between the MEDIUM and the ETHERIC WORLD INTELLIGENCE for the purpose of physical phenomena; in this state, the etheric world intelligence has control, in part or in whole, over the activity; accomplished by SITTING for development over a period of time, in a darkened room, with a desire for the physical phenomena; this gives the etheric world intelligence an opportunity to work with the medium's BODY CHEMISTRY making it compatible to work in or to use the body's ECTOPLASM (according to the type of phenomena); the medium sits in a passive state with a neutral frame of mind to make it easier for the intelligence to take over; trance has it's degree of the altered state of consciousness: e.g., LIGHT TRANCE, SEMITRANCE, and DEEP TRANCE; when viewed, the state of the medium appears to be similar to the hypnotic state with dissociation of consciousness; (*trance* should not be used to describe a hypnotic state that is not used for physical phenomena). [cf. TRANCE MANIFESTATIONS/MISCELLANEOUS Appendix 2]

TRANCE AUTOMATISM—to allow an ETHERIC WORLD INTELLIGENCE to use one's arms and hands or one's legs and feet, to perform physical phenomena; phenomena is performed in a mechanical manner in which the etheric world intelligence uses his or her own characteristics controlling the body from outside or controlling the body by entering it; always preplanned and desired-controlled; medium may be uneducated in the work the intelligence performs; *trance* automatism refers to the medium working in a deep ALTERED STATE OF CONSCIOUSNESS (cataleptic state) as opposed to automatism performed in a light or semistate of consciousness; the following can be accomplished in all three states of consciousness: AUTOMATIC WRITING, AUTOMATIC ART, PSYCHIC SURGERY, playing the piano, etc. (Inconcl.) [cf. IMPERSONATION, TEN-PERCENT TRANCE, OUIJA BOARD]

TRANCE-CONTROL—(voodoo) the proper synchronization of the LOA (etheric world intelligence) who has entered the medium's body, to use the body in the same pattern that is preplanned. [cf. DANCED HIM, EXCITABLE, MEDIUM, TRANCE OF INDIFFERENCE]

TRANCE EXCHANGES—the soul-mind of a medium leaves his or her body while the ETHERIC WORLD INTELLIGENCE is using it to travel to a different location and manifest through another medium. (Inconcl.) [cf. DROP-IN COMMUNICATORS, INVOLUNTARY INTERVENTION, DEEP TRANCE]

TRANCE MANIFESTATIONS—physical phenomena that require an ETHERIC WORLD INTELLIGENCE to perform; MEDIUM collaborates with the intelligence so they can synchronize the medium's BODY CHEMISTRY to make it compatible for the task to be accomplished; medium sits in weekly sessions, willingly, for the development; sometimes occurs seemingly at random (karmically willed); physical activity can be perceived by everyone in the area while the medium is in a light,

semi, or deep state of altered consciousness; etheric world intelligence enters the medium's body or uses the ECTOPLASM of the medium (and sitters); performed in a seance or lighted room with or without sitters; takes from a few sittings to many years to develop; depending upon the type of phenomena and standards of the medium; see TRANCE MANIFESTATIONS/MISCELLANEOUS, PHYSICAL MANIFESTATTIONS/MISCELLANEOUS, TRANCE VOICES, and PHYSICAL PSYCHIC PROCESSES.

TRANCE MANIFESTATIONS/MISCELLANEOUS—in this dictionary there is a grouping of various kinds of physical phenomena that require ETHERIC WORLD INTELLIGENCES to help perform the activity, but are not popular enough to be listed individually; see Appendix 2 for listings.

TRANCE MEDIUM—one who collaborates with an etheric world intelligence and performs physical phenomena; medium allows the etheric world intelligence to enter his or her body, in part or in whole, or to use the ectoplasm that emanates from his or her body in a seance; medium's body must have the proper chemistry to be manipulated by the etheric world intelligence or must sit in development sessions until the intelligence changes the medium's chemistry; always uses DESIRED-CONTROL. [cf. MEDIUMSHIP, GUIDE, CONTROL]

TRANCE OF INDEFFERENCE—(Western) the splitting of a SOUL-MIND wherein one part is in ordinary consciousness, carrying on without interruption, and the other part is being subjected to extraordinary experiences; sometimes putting the PSYCHIC in touch with planes beyond one's normal grasp. (Inconcl.) **Syn.** BILOCATION. [cf. SPLITTING OF PERSONALITIES, VACATED BODY, ASTRAL PROJECTION]

TRANCE OF WONDER—the splitting of a SOUL-MIND of an artist wherein one part of the consciousness paints a picture and the other part of the consciousness transcends to a high level in the etheric world; what one part sees and experiences influences the other part's artwork. [cf. BILOCATION, VISIONARY TRANCE, RAPTURE]

TRANCE PERSONALITY—an ETHERIC WORLD INTELLIGENCE of high order that comes as a GUIDE and informer of knowledge to the same MEDIUM for many years. **Syn.** CONTROL. [cf. INNER BAND, DOCTOR TEACHER, OUTER BAND]

TRANCE POSSESSION—see IMPERSONATION.

TRANCE VOICE—to allow an ETHERIC WORLD INTELLIGENCE to intervene and use one's vocal organs to speak through; medium's throat is anesthetized by the intelligence, to be used as a means of amplification of the etheric world's message and knowledge to be brought to the level of the physical ear threshold; MEDIUM has the proper BODY CHEMISTRY for the intervention, and remains in a neutral frame of mind; voice may be heard in the medium's own tone, or in an alien tongue, tone, or accent; medium does not remember what transpired after it is over; can occur in the SEANCE room, DARKROOM SESSION, or in a PRIVATE SITTING; medium lies or sits; always performed with DESIRED-CONTROL. [**cf.** TRANCE VOICES Appendix 2]

TRANCE VOICE MEDIUM—one who is willing and capable of allowing an ETHERIC WORLD INTELLIGENCE to intervene on a regular basis, and to use one's voice organs to bring knowledge that could not have been known in any other way; MEDIUM has proper BODY CHEMISTRY or sits until body chemistry changes; happens quickly or takes many months to perfect; medium is one who is willing to print the material and circulate it; usually developed in a SEANCE or DARKROOM SESSION; knowledge is spoken in another voice or in medium's own voice; trance voice mediums date back to thousands of years B.C. [**cf.** DEPENDENT VOICE, TEN-PERCENT IMPERSONATION]

TRANCE VOICES—the ETHERIC WORLD INTELLIGENCES have various means of amplifying their speech in the SEANCE room so it can be heard by the physical ears; see TRANCE VOICES Appendix 2 for the ways of doing this.

TRANCER—one who is a TRANCE MEDIUM.

TRANS—a prefix meaning "beyond, across, through"; (Sanskrit) "over, through."

TRANSCEND—to rise above, go beyond the limits of, to exceed; pertains to the SOUL-MIND tuning into the higher realms of the ETHERIC WORLD.

TRANSCENDENCE—1. a temporary, spontaneous, experience in which the LIFE FORCE leaves the PHYSICAL BODY to bypass the experience of physical pain; occurs when one is on the operating table or when one is going through an accident; life force (ASTRAL BODY) hovers close to the physical body but could easily go on and finish the DEATH PROCESS; individual is frequently pronounced clinically dead; authentic reports say the dying person's life force feels a sense of peace and tranquility and wishes to stay in the etheric world; life force returns because it can see the family below and has a sense of responsibility, or because it is encouraged to go back by an etheric world entity; individual lives with no damage to the brain. (Inconcl.) [**cf.** DEATH-BED EXPERIENCES, SPONTANEOUS ASTRAL PROJECTION] 2. (alchemy) see ASCENSION.

TRANSCENDENT—pertains to the realms beyond the earth plane; pertains to the FOURTH STATE OF CONSCIOUSNESS wherein one has extended one's mind to higher levels of existence and senses a reality in the higher planes; occurs when in a HYPNOTHERAPY session, in deep MEDITATION, in MENTAL PROJECTION, in ASTRAL PROJECTION, in a HIGH DREAM, in perceiving visions from hallucinogenic plants and in prolonged body movement. (Inconcl.) **Syn.** TRANSCENDENTAL. [**cf.** SOUL TRAVEL, KAIROS DIMENSION, SKRYING, TRANSCENDENTAL MEDITATION]

TRANSCENDENT INFINITE—(Sufi) see GOD; oneness of being.

TRANSCENDENT MOMENT—a short time in which one has an exalted, emotional, high feeling, a transpersonal, vagueness of reality, or an extraordinary elation of some kind that brings an extreme change in one's attitude and lifestyle; a nonordinary experience that could cause a sensation of timelessness, loss of boundaries, disconnection, and difficulty in communicating in logical description; experience cannot be intellectualized or described in today's language; after the experience is over, one feels more: freedom, kinship and unity, creative, self-assurance, capable of handling stress and plasticity of human awareness and meaning in one's life; can happen spontaneously at a religious gathering or when in an alpha or theta state of consciousness because of righteous living. (Inconcl.) [**cf.** PEAK EXPERIENCE]

TRANSCENDENT SPHERES—very high realms in the ETHERIC WORLD where one will contact angel beings or their light-forms, higher VIBRATIONAL FREQUENCIES of creatures like birds and butterflies, pure geometric forms, beams of colors, forms, sounds that surpass physical parallelism, feelings of freedom, oneness with COSMIC CONSCIOUSNESS, the vastness of the cosmic plan, and whatever is in one's BELIEF SYSTEM regarding this sphere. (Inconcl.) [**cf.** THOUGHT-BODY, LIGHT ETHER, PARADISE REALMS]

TRANSCENDENTAL—pertains to the highest planes in the ETHERIC WORLD; refers to levels of awareness one can reach by mind expansion, and which, when experienced feel like reality. **Syn.** TRANSCENDENT. [**cf.** CELESTIAL CITY, PSYCHIC PROJECTION, CHARIOT]

TRANSCENDENTAL BEING—an angel high on the hierarchical scale who may or may not show her or himself for human communication; sometimes seen as only a face, only eyes, beams of light of awesome beauty, or beautiful gems that gleam seemingly for miles. [**cf.** IMPERISHABLE ONES, DIVINE THRONE, ARCHANGELS]

TRANSCENDENTAL FUNCTIONALIST—a PSYCHIC who can see into the ETHERIC WORLD and in the physical world simultaneously much of the time; can relate to others what he or she is perceiving; lives like a human being with no more problems than the normal, as opposed to those who have this ability but find it difficult to live normally. (Inconcl.) [**cf.** SUPERPHYSICAL ORDER OF MATTER, REALM OF FORM, PLATEAU]

TRANSCENDENTAL MEDITATION—abbr. TM; a practical, simple, effortless mental technique to go beyond normal thinking where one experiences quiet levels of thought and becomes aware of impulses, feeling and action. [**cf.** MEDITATION Appendix 5]

TRANSCENDENTAL MUSIC—magnificant music perceived clairaudiently at deathbeds, funerals, and religious sanctuaries; unaccountable sounds of instruments and singing beyond physical hearing. (Inconcl.) [**cf.** MUSIC OF THE SPHERES, CLAIRAUDIENCE]

TRANSCENDENTAL PHENOMENA—UFO sightings; that which pertains to outer space activity in regard to UFOLOGY. [**cf.** ETHER SHIPS, EXTRA-TERRESTRIAL VISITATION]

TRANSCENDENTAL PHYSICS—the study of psychic phenomena that can be explained by fourth dimensional space and its functions; e.g., an APPARITION, POSSESSION, CLAIRVOYANCE-IN-TIME, and OUT-OF-BODY-EXPERIENCE etc. [**cf.** PARAPSYCHOLOGY]

TRANSCENDENTAL REASON—see INTUITION.

TRANSCENDENTAL WORLD—see TRANSCENDENT SPHERES.

TRANSCENDENTAL WORLD OF IDEAS—(Plato) a place in the ETHERIC WORLD where soul-minds spend time learning truth, beauty, and goodness; this is impressed upon the body form during sleep, arousing one to go back to one's glorious state. **Syn.** MENTAL PLANE. [**cf.** MENTAL PROJECTION, SLEEP EXPERIENCES]

TRANSCENDENTALISM—to go beyond the awareness of the physical SENSES; see PSYCHISM.

TRANSCENDENTALIST—a psychic who can reach the higher levels by mind expansion at will.

TRANSCENDERS—(Abraham Maslow) soul-minds who are living at this time, considered to be advance scouts for the race; individuals who far exceed the traditional criteria for psychological health and are drawn to each other in a room full of people; seem to be always talking about the new times. (Inconcl.) [FUTURISTS, STAR PEOPLE]

TRANSCENDING PHYSICS—(Aristotle) see PSYCHIC PHENOMENA.

TRANSFERENCE—(Tibet) (death) to dissolve the total of karmic properties into the clear light of the ETHERIC WORLD, at the end of the DEATH PROCESS. [**cf.** MANIFESTED IN THE LIGHT, DEATH MIST, COFFIN RITUAL]

TRANSFIGURATION—1. changes in the appearance of another's face and body while sitting in a PSYCHIC DEVELOPMENT CIRCLE in subdued lighting; the interpenetration of the etheric world guides can be so strong that SITTERS can see changes in the features of others, sometimes taking on the features of the GUIDE and sometimes appearances of body movement when the body is still; e.g., a pseudo appearance of a mustache, eyes blinking, or an elongated neck; 2. the building of a recognizeable likeness of a DISCARNATE ENTITY, over the face of a MEDIUM; seen more easily in dim light; happens where there was a strong bond between two people; may be seen by one's self when looking in a mirror; happening spontaneously. [**cf.** GUIDE, SENSE CURRENTS]

TRANSFIX—to pierce through one's feeling nature with an eye-stare, making that person motionless with the nature of the penetration; to penetrate to the very essence of the personality with the eyes as if they were a pointed weapon; the expression and energy coming from the eyes holds and makes the victim motionless with amazement, awe, terror, love, or delight, etc. [cf. SPELLED, ON-THE-SPOT-HYPNOSIS]

TRANSFORMATION—1. (astral projection) to take the shape of an animal and perceive one's environment like that animal for a short time; belief that the ASTRAL BODY, when separated from the PHYSICAL BODY, has the qualities of plasticity so that when it is surrounded by it's own creative power it can be moulded into various forms before it returns to the physical body; a difficult and dangerous physical feat but has been performed by many. [cf. SHAPE-CHANGING, SUCCUBUS, HAG] 2. a forming over; a restructuring; a change in condition, nature or character; a paradigm shift; pertains to the shift of civilization, countries, lifestyles, geography, morals, and values that is taking place on earth today; (I Ching) "the shutting of one door and opening of another door; effective evolvement; the results of movement because of the two primal forces, YANG and YIN, which displace each other and produce the changes and a transformation." [cf. NEW-AGE PSYCHOLOGY, LAW OF TRANSFORMATION Appendix 7]

TRANSFORMATION OF SOULS—theory; the SOUL of one who is deceased is reborn in the body of an animal; and the cycle is then reversed and the soul of the deceased animal is reborn in a body of a human [cf. REINCARNATION, TRANSMIGRATION OF SOULS]

TRANSFORMATIONISTS—those who realize the evolutionary change is here and have the insight to allow the information to come together in a new dimension by flowing with new ideas, new perspectives, and new theories; those who let go of the "old," regardless of personal inconveniences and goals, and still keep a cheerful outlook. [cf. NEW-AGE CONSCIOUSNESS, FUTURISTS, CURATIVE EDUCATION, ONEARTH]

TRANSFORMED ONES—(Sufi) those who believe they have a gift of transmitting GRACE because they receive messages from the ETHERIC WORLD INTELLIGENCES. [cf. PSYCHIC READING]

TRANSITION—the DEATH PROCESS; to move from one STATE OF CONSCIOUSNESS to another state of consciousness; to change environments. Usage: "He just made his transition and I am lonely." [cf. DEATH SCIENCE, TRANSITION HORMONE, DEATH ANGEL]

TRANSITION CENTERS—a few special places on the planet where vibrations are so high that an ordinary mortal could be seriously affected by the bombardment of sensory particles; usually located in wooded and mountainous areas with pure water streams flowing near by; screened from interlopers and maintained as meeting places for those of higher advancement; from these areas, advanced soul-minds send and receive signals from other planets; e.g., STONEHENGE and Glastonbury, England. (Inconcl.)

TRANSITION HORMONE—an ethereal substance emitted by the ENDOCRINE SYSTEM during the process of death; loosens the atoms of the astral and mental bodies from the physical body, making it possible for the LIFE FORCE to slide out of the body easily. **Syn.** DEATH HORMONE. [cf. LETTERS TO THE DEAD, DEATH CONSCIOUSNESS, DEATH TRANCE]

TRANSITION OF SUBSTANCE—(ufology) the ability of the space craft to pass material from eye visibility to material that is invisible. (Inconcl.) **Syn.** DIMENSION-SHIFTING. [cf. SUPER-ETHER, DYNAMIC TRANSITIONS]

TRANSITIONAL CONSCIOUSNESS—see TRANSMUTATION.

TRANSITIONAL STATE—(Tibet) the period one spends in the ETHERIC WORLD between death to rebirth in the earth plane. **Syn.** BARDO, INTERMEDIATE STATE. [cf. KARMA OF FULFILLMENT, RIPE KARMA]

TRANSITIONAL WORLDS—see ETHERIC WORLD.

TRANSLATED—(Eckankar) made the TRANSITION; died.

TRANSLATION—1. the transference of holy people abiding in the ETHERIC WORLD to a higher realm after their earthly work is done. [cf. ANGEL HEIRARCHY, FIFTH PLANE] 2. (death) a mental projection to the higher spheres during the DEATH PROCESS, bringing an ecstatic experience to the dying person. [cf. HOUSE OF ETERNITY, HALL OF INCARNATIONS]

TRANSMIGRATION OF SOULS—(death science) theory: the SOUL-MIND leaves the PHYSICAL BODY upon DEATH and enters another body according to past behavior and spiritual needs; new body can be human, animal, plant, reptile or anything alive; when the animate life dies, the soul-mind can come back into a human life or enter an animal again; (do not confuse with REINCARNATION).

TRANSMUTATION—(alchemy) to change the basic structure of physical matter from its vibrational frequency to a higher frequency through an alchemical process of purification by intensified mind energy focused on the object and process; 1. to dematerialize an object by rearranging the atomic structure until it is ethereal in nature, and to rematerialize these atoms into the mundane plane in a higher vibrational frequency so it does not appear as the same object; transmutation of baser metals into finer metals; 2. to dematerialize one's own body by rearranging the atomic structure until it is ethereal in nature, and to rematerialize one's body into the mundane plane in a higher vibrational frequency (keeps its patterns to some degree); ALCHEMIST can travel in the ETHERIC WORLD while in the ethereal state, distance and time span are not barriers; then changes back to a body according to the chronological time; can function intelligently under the laws of each frequency; ability to transmute does away with physical death and allows one to materialize in a place where and when needed; a glorified or purified body is accomplished after this psychic feat; see Appendix 4 for comparison with ASCENSION. **Syn.** ALCHEMICAL MATERIALIZATION. [**cf.** GLORIFIED BODY, ALCHEMICAL PRINCIPLES, ELIXIR OF LIFE]

TRANSPARENCY—(clairvoyance) psychic visions that have the property to move through third-dimensional MATTER and are perceived as hazy or sheer enough to see partially through; e.g., GHOST. [**cf.** APPARITION]

TRANSPARENT DIMENSIONAL WARP—the invisible mechanism or path in mankind that allows one to perceive into the INVISIBLE WORLD. (Inconcl.) **Syn.** PSYCHOLOGICAL WARP, PSYCHIC WARP. [**cf.** VEIL, MENTAL PSYCHIC PROCESSES Appendix 2]

TRANSPERSONAL CONSCIOUSNESS—abbr. TC; a consciousness that extends beyond the personality of the individual; to be in an ALTERED STATE OF CONSCIOUSNESS; i.e., meditating, hypnotherapy, perceiving psychically, trancing; beyond normal mental mind consciousness. (Inconcl.) [**cf.** TEMPORAL CONSCIOUSNESS, LIBERATION]

TRANSPERSONAL EXPERIENCE—to undergo any phenomena which is not included in objective reality; an encounter that transcends one's unique personality; e.g., PSYCHIC EXPERIENCE during the day or during sleep, REGRESSION in hypnotherapy, MENTAL PROJECTION, ASTRAL PROJECTION, DISASSOCIATION TRANCE during MEDITATION or BIOFEEDBACK TRAINING. [**cf.** MYSTIC EXPERIENCE]

TRANSPERSONAL GROUP THERAPY—to encounter with others, an experience designed to integrate one's spiritual and personal aspects; uses JUNGIAN dream work, FANTASY, MEDITATION, GESTALT, DHARMIC methods, or life path techniques. [**cf.** NEW-AGE PSYCHOLOGY, GESTALT THERAPY, PATH SYMBOLISM]

TRANSPERSONAL PSYCHOLOGY—the fourth major approach to the study of humanity; study concerned with the fulfillment of humanity, the development of transcendent potential as individuals and as a species; considers the spiritual aspect of humanity; SELF-ACTUALIZATION, interpersonal encounter, and COSMIC CONSCIOUSNESS.

TRANSPERSONAL UNCONSCIOUS—see COLLECTIVE UNCONSCIOUS.

TRANSPHYSICAL REALITY—the state that exists beyond the material plane into other dimensions and realms in the etheric world with life which is a replica of humans; similar to humans in some mannerisms, characters, and outward form; incorporates GHOSTS, POLTERGEISTS, DENSITY ELEMENTALS, and ETHERIC WORLD INTELLIGENCES.

TRANSPHYSICAL SCIENCE—that which is above and beyond conventional science. **Syn.** METAPHYSICS.

TRANSPORTATION—see TELEPORTATION.

TRANSPOSITION OF SENSES—mixed-up combination of mental consciousness and psychic sensitivity at the same time; i.e., seeing from the pit of the stomach, tasting from the toes, or seeing from the nose. (Inconcl.)

TRANSUBSTANTIATION—the conversion of the bread and wine of the communion table into the body and blood of JESUS the Christ; theory: when a clergy consecrates bread and wine through traditional rituals in an attitude of worship, there is an alchemical change turning the bread and wine into the Christ elements with only the external appearance of bread and wine remaining; the blood and wine are essentially the same substance coming from the same One life as His body, as opposed to being symbolic of these. [cf. TRANSMUTATION, ALCHEMIST, MERCURY, RITUAL, SALT]

TRANSVECTION—1. to visibly fly or sail through the air in one's normal form; to understand the law of gravity and have it under control using mind energy for this psychic feat; e.g., the witch on the broomstick. **Syn.** TELEPORTATION. 2. to change one's self into a bird being and fly in the air. [cf. SHAPE-CHANGING, WITCH'S OIL]

TRAPPAS—(Tibet) a medical priest specializing in metaphysical healings and psychic counseling. [cf. PSYCHIC READING, MENTAL HEALING]

TRATAKAM—an external object used in meditation to provide a focal point on which one can fix one's attention to reach an ALTERED STATE OF CONSCIOUSNESS; e.g., a stone, a candle, a vase, a light, a picture of a DEITY, a cross, etc. [cf. CENTERING, MANTRA, TANTRA]

TRATAKAM MEDITATION METHOD—a technique to reach a state of consciousness in which one feels one is gazing on supreme consciousness; using an external object for a POINT-OF-FOCUS, dwelling on its symbolic nature and attributes as one stares at it until the object disappears and ethereal energies are in its place. [cf. TM, YANTRA, SITTING ZEN]

TRAVEL DYSRHYTHMIA—scientific name given "jet lag" by the airlines; places the occurrence on the natural laws of the body and not on the airlines. [cf. CIRCADIAN RHYTHM, BIOLOGICAL RHYTHM]

TRAVELER—(astral projection) one who takes astral projections. **Syn.** OBEER, PROJECTIONIST, ETHER-GOER, ASTRAL PROJECTOR. [cf. SUPER PSI, SPIRAL DROP, SIGHT SENSATION]

TRAVELING CLAIRVOYANCE—to psychically attune to a distant place or person and see clairvoyantly what is happening in that place or to that person at the present time. **Syn.** REMOTE VIEWING, CLAIRVOYANCE-IN-SPACE, BILOCATION OF CONSCIOUSNESS. [cf. X-RAY CLAIRVOYANCE, OBJECTIVE CLAIRVOYANCE]

TREASURE MAGICIAN—(A.D. 1500) a PSYCHIC who specialized in finding hidden treasure; custom was to bury gold or money to keep it safe; psychic was hired or used this skill personally; conjured up the etheric world entities who communicated where to find the buried treasure. [cf. CONJURE UP, SORCERER]

TREASURE-SEEKING MANIA—(A.D. 1500) an epidemic of psychics using their skills to conjure up the etheric world entities and asking them to point to the hidden buried gold and money; it was a custom at the time to bury one's gold and money.

TREATMENT—(Christian Science) a special wording of PRAYER or AFFIRMATIONS used to alter one's attitude toward sickness and other things; this in turn will change what is in one's subconscious and conscious mind, which in turn changes one's BODY CHEMISTRY and allows a natural healing. (Inconcl.) [cf. MENTAL HEALING, WORDS-WITH-POWER]

TREE—(esoteric) 1. symbolizes organized life of a supreme power, unfolding from a seed; used in many disciplines and religions to symbolize man. [cf. LAW OF TOTALITY Appendix 7, MONAD] 2. has properties to be used, in whole or in part, for psychic feats; held sacred by magicians, psychics, and mediums; (a) used as an ORACLE in ancient days; (b) branches used for the DOWSING ROD, WAND and the STICK; (c) houses NATURE SPIRITS which are invaluable for human's and animals' plant food; (d) wood environment is very conducive to psychic energies. [cf. TREE ORACLE, JINNS, DOWSING ROD]

TREE OF KNOWLEDGE—known as the tree of good and evil, representative of the CEREBROSPINAL NERVOUS SYSTEM, or the system that can make choices, good or evil choices. [cf. SUBJECTIVE MIND]

TREE OF LIFE—(metaphysical) 1. (Genesis) symbolic of the human body; a human spinal cord is like the trunk of a tree with the nerves corresponding to the many branches; upturned, the roots are human hair; the branches bear many enjoyable fruits as the nerves bear enjoyable sensations of sight, sound, smell, taste, and touch; in the midst of the garden is the forbidden experience of sex, the apple at the center of the body; 2. (Yoga) the trunk of the tree represents the invisible SUSHUMNA, and the six stages of the tree's growth are the six CHAKRAS. 3. (Kabbalah) a symbolic picture of ten circles with parallel lines connecting the circles designed to reveal many aspects of the down flowing force of spirit; spirit descends step by step from its first untraveled state, until it manifests as MATTER and the force that animates it. [cf. SEPHIROTH, TETRAGRAMMATON] 4. (Scandinavia) the ash tree is emblematic of the COSMIC

TREE; the cosmic tree bears fruits which the gods eat to ensure fruits of their IMMORTALITY; 5. the tree is symbolic of the environment of the SOUL-MIND with its many branches representing the many pathways to be experienced in the quest for ILLUMINATION; when the tree has grown to its perfect state, the pathways will have been fulfilled and the individual is a whole person, free of restrictions and yet always connected or dependent upon the universal source as is a tree. [**cf.** TREE, SOUL-MIND]

TREE ORACLE—(esoteric) 1. (Armenia, Arabia, Persia, Rome, Druids, Spiritualism) trees were used to bring PSYCHIC INFORMATION to earthlings through the ETHERIC WORLD INTELLIGENCES; belief: the tree roots are connected to the UNDER-WORLD and therefore, can supply the intelligences with wisdom and foreknowledge; 2. (Old Testament) tree of the revealer; used as a source of AUGURY in Rome; kinds of trees used as oracles: mulberry, oak, WILLOW, LAUREL, cypress, ash, hawthorne, BIRCH, rowan, and YEW. [**cf.** TREE, EA, JINN, RODS, WOOD NATURE SPIRITS]

TREE SPIRIT—an earth fairy who is large, long and narrow, and who lives within the trunk; does not react quickly to people (as other NATURE SPIRITS do) because of the more dense body which is almost physical; loyal to people's desires; reacts slowly to outer stimuli learning from the cell life of its own make-up. [**cf.** EARTH FAIRES]

TRIAD—a group of three closely related parts; can be persons or things; an association of THREE. [**cf.** NUMEROLOGY]

TRIAL—(psi tasks) each psychic attempt is one trial: 1. (controlled experiments) one attempt to bring forth PSYCHIC INFORMATION in response to the question; 2. (ESP) one attempt to identify a TARGET object; 3. (PK) one unit of effect to be measured in the evaluation of results. [**cf.** ESP, PSI TASKS, CONFIDENCE CALLS, LOW VARIANCE]

TRIALECTIC LOGIC—emphasizes how the entire body systems work together, as in KARATE and ACUPUNCTURE, while the parts still have separate functions. **Syn.** GESTALT, HOLISTIC HEALTH. [**cf.** SYMPATHETIC NERVOUS SYSTEM, REFLEXOLOGY, IRIDOLOGY]

TRIANGLE—a flat, three-sided form; 1. used emblematically, based on the idea of the TRINITY or the law of threes which is found in all things; i.e., in

the DEITY, TIME and CREATION. [**cf.** LAW OF THREES Appendix 7] 2. a primary symbol representing the second level of the atmospheric substance (light ether) which is yellow, gaseous and gives mankind light; 3. (Tattwa) their fourth symbol; represents FIRE, a primordial element; colored RED; called TEJAS; designed to reach the very basis of the subconscious mind. [**cf.** TATTWAS, SYMBOLISM]

TRIBAL BLOOD KARMA—ancestral, karmic, electromagnetic, microscopic pictures which emanate from the bloodstream of each tribal member; cannot be seen physically but brings an inward, spontaneous attachment for each other; represents a past INCARNATION, when all were together. (Inconcl.) [**cf.** MENTAL-REFLECTING-ETHER, AKASHIC RECORDS]

TRIBAL DANCING—1. (Native American) repetitious, rhythmic dancing performed to the beat of a drum for the purpose of reaching an ALTERED STATE OF CONSCIOUSNESS; prolonged dancing in a circle induces a state of TRANCE, whereby ANCESTRAL SPIRITS (etheric world intelligences) intervene to bring PSYCHIC INFORMATION and counsel for the tribe, or induces a state of ecstasy, whereby one has a peak spiritual experience; 2. (Native American, Chippewa) a special ceremony performed outdoors when the tribe agrees it is time to give energy back to EARTH MOTHER; the whole family participates; the rhythm, the circle formation and the *intent* of the dance replenishes earth mother; it pleases the earth to have humans dance on it; dance ceremonies are also performed in honor of the gift of an animal to eat. [**cf.** ANTELOPE CHARMING, SUN GAZE DANCE, NEW-AGE PSYCHOLOGY]

TRIBAL MEDICINE BUNDLE—(Native American) a bag filled with a collection of sacred objects used for promoting a PSYCHIC HEALING and for prophesying for the owner or for the tribe; objects are gathered from dream images or handed down through generations; each object has its symbol, spirit and psychic ability. [**cf.** DREAM SYMBOLS, AMULET, TIKI, MEDICINE BAG]

TRIBULATION—(belief of some Christians) a period of time designed to give nonbelievers one more chance to accept JESUS the Christ in their hearts; the period will include an enormous battle in which Christ will return with the faithful to establish the millennium (a 1,000 year period of peace and prosperity) as stated in Revelation.

TRICKSTER—(Native American) a GOD or an ETHERIC WORLD INTELLIGENCE who takes the form of an animal or other guises when communicating with the Indian; brings information, guidance and protection from the ETHERIC WORLD. **Syn.** ETHERIC WORLD GUIDE, CELESTIAL GUARDIAN. [**cf.** ANIMAL KINGDOM, KACHINA DOLL, TOTEM]

TRICKSTER-TRANSFORMER—a psychic catharsis on a deep and vital level; a cultural hero who transforms aspects of the world for humanity's benefit and is a player of pranks; a comic relief; a destroyer, a giver, and a negator; depicted as a primordial being existing from the beginning of things and whose own evolution parallels with that of mankind toward a higher consciousness and social maturity; capable of SHAPE-CHANGING from a high god to a devil; sometimes represented by an old man, a rabbit, a bluejay, a mink, a raven, a spider, a coyote; uses psychic skills for good or evil; (Carl Jung) the theory of the shadow, the darker part is the "human" ego and necessary for psychic wholeness. **Syn.** SHADOW, HOLY FOOLS.

TRIFLING MEDIUM—one who uses mediumistic abilities for amusement or for frivolous things. [**cf.** CLOAK OF INSULATION, IMPERFECT SPIRITISTS, INSPIRED MEDIUM]

TRIGGER POINTS—(Western) sensitive points of the body near nerve endings, which create impulses from the decisions of the MENTAL MIND, that fire into the NERVOUS SYSTEM; when the body is not in perfect good health; the sensitive points contain toxins which disrupt the normal flow of energy and send out pain; this causes symptoms which have been named DISEASE, fatigue, TENSION, or PAIN; these areas can be temporarily relieved by ACUPUNCTURE, ACUPRESSURE, NEUROMUSCULAR MASSAGE and permanently relieved by a change in attitude or resolving the activity that causes the toxins. (Inconcl.) **Syn.** ACUPUNCTURE POINTS. [**cf.** MERIDIAN LINES, SPINAL GATE]

TRIGGERS—an object, music, pulsing light device, chant, COLOR, rhythmic beat, dance, mineral or MANDALA that aids in inducing an ALTERED STATE OF CONSCIOUSNESS; once one reaches this state using a trigger, the trigger then suggests the altered state to the SUBCONSCIOUS MIND and makes each session easier. (Inconcl.) [**cf.** GOING-TO-LEVEL, INNER-AWARENESS, BODY-FEELING]

TRIGRAMS—(I Ching) basic symbols used in the I Ching; two combinations of three lines, solid and broken, making up the hexagram symbol; eight primary TRIGRAMS. **Syn.** TUAN. [**cf.** I CHING, HEXAGRAM]

TRIKONA—inverted triangle. [**cf.** ASSOCIATION MAGIC, SYMBOLS]

TRILITHON—1. an ancient structure of two upright stones supporting a third stone, representing the law of threes; (used in STONEHENGE); 2. (Greece) two pillars and a third stone on top making an arch; symbolic of the love school combining goodwill, brotherhood, sympathy, and consideration; 3. represents the five senses and their relationship to the sun. [**cf.** LAW OF THREES Appendix 7, NUMEROLOGY, STONES]

TRINISM—the belief that everything has characteristics in triplicity representing the law of threes; theory: everything has a positive and negative aspect making the whole; each of the three aspects has a separate function to the universe. **Syn.** LAW OF THREES Appendix 7. [**cf.** NUMBER POWER, NINE]

TRINITY—the three aspects of the many things throughout the universe depicted by the symbol of the TRIANGLE or the trinity; e.g., CONSCIOUS MIND, SUBCONSCIOUS MIND, SUPERCONSCIOUS MIND; waking consciousness, dreaming consciousness, and sleep consciousness; carnal man is made from the physical, astral and mental bodies; universal chant is AUM; atoms contain chemicals, magnetism, and electricity; thought and emotion are needed to make a manifestation; Father, Son, and Holy Ghost; three primary colors RED, YELLOW, BLUE make all other colors. [**cf.** LAW OF THREES, Appendix 7, UNIVERSAL TRINITY]

TRIP OUT—to slip into a deeper ALTERED STATE OF CONSCIOUSNESS than one intended, while meditating or being hypnotized; usually the experience is so pleasant one does not want to return to the meditative state or the hypnotic suggestions or even return to the awake state, for a while; frequently occurs unintentionally with a NATURAL-BORN PSYCHIC; tripping out can be brought under control with mind discipline if one desires. [**cf.** SOMNAMBOLISTIC]

TRIP-PROJECTION—see ASTRAL PROJECTION.

TRIPLE-HEATER—composition of the three higher CHAKRAS forming a circle: THROAT CHAKRA,

647

located in the neck, meaning judgment; BROW CHAKRA, located in the PITUITARY GLAND, meaning intellect; CROWN CHAKRA, located in the PINEAL GLAND, meaning harmony. (Inconcl.) **Syn.** TRIPLE-WARMER. [**cf.** KUNDALINI]

TRIPLE-WARMER—see TRIPLE-HEATER.

TROLL—(Northern Europe) a NATURE SPIRIT that inhabits the mountains and has charge of their functions; shows itself as a dwarf or a giant; capable of SHAPE-SHIFTING; can be helpful or capricious and hostile.

TRON—suffix used in compound words denoting an "instrument."

TROOPING FAIRIES—NATURE SPIRITS that appear in groups, each one very beautiful; groups have both sexes; specific function unknown.

TROUT—a supernatural fish able to communicate with humanity psychically; held sacred by many cultures; known as "trout of the well" or guardian of the NATURE SPIRITS of the wells. [**cf.** ANPSI, FISH TELEPATHY]

TROW—(Shetland Islands) a NATURE SPIRIT which is an ally of the troll; lives in the sea or on the land; when perceived clairvoyantly, performs a curious top-sided dance; loves to invade the human mind. [**cf.** NATURE SPIRITS]

TRUE MAN—(Buddhism) see SOUL-MIND.

TRUE SEAL—(Buddhism) teachings that seem to come from the heart as opposed to the teachings that come from the intellect.

TRUE SELF—see MONAD.

TRUE-ACTION DREAMS—(research laboratory) dreams in which one is swimming, falling, flying, body-flapping, head-thumping, running in giant strides, taking two stair steps in one step, etc.; pertain to the LIFE FORCE of the sleeper in actual action taking an ASTRAL PROJECTION. [**cf.** DREAM REALITY, OBJECTIVE INTERPRETATION, HIGH LUCID DREAMS]

TRUE-SERIOUS COMMUNICATIONS—information, suggestions, and knowledge that is perceived from superior ETHERIC WORLD INTELLIGENCES inhabiting the higher realms; intelligences can be challenged by asking for proof of their validity, honesty, and authenticity; the superior intelligence welcomes the challenge and presents proof but an inferior intelligence becomes upset and rude from such inquiry. [**cf.** SENSITIVITY TRANSFER, REFRACTIONS OF GOD]

TRULKU—(Tibet) an individual who has attained the third-eye privilege through many past incarnations, and is now allowed to have the third-eye opened surgically; this individual will then see in both realms, the ETHERIC WORLD and the PHYSICAL WORLD, simultaneously. **Syn.** PROVED INCARNATION. [**cf.** KARMA, REINCARNATION, LAW OF COMPENSATION Appendix 7, THIRD-EYE AREA]

TRUMPET—1. (global) an instrument that is long, hollow and wider at one end, used to attract the voice of the supernatural; used by ETHERIC WORLD INTELLIGENCES to speak through as an amplification system to be heard by humans; this is recognized as a divine intervention; e.g., (Bible) "and when the voice of the trumpet sounded long, and waxed louder, Moses spoke"; 2. (seance) a megaphone-shape device used in a SEANCE as an amplification system for etheric world intelligences to relay knowledge that could not be known from formal education; made from light weight material, i.e., cardboard, aluminum or metal; sectioned in four pieces so as to collapse for easy carrying and storing; magnetized in the sun or rain by the MEDIUM; kept in a black case and only touched by the medium; 3. a shortened term for "raising the trumpet." Usage: "He has trumpet," meaning he has the mediumship ability to raise the trumpet and have etheric world intelligences use it to speak through. [**cf.** TRUMPET SEANCE, RAISING THE TRUMPET]

TRUMPET CONTROL—the ETHERIC WORLD INTELLIGENCE who is the main guide communicating through the trumpet in a weekly trumpet session; function is to bring knowledge about the ETHERIC WORLD, psychic communication, and to answer questions regarding PARAPSYCHOLOGY; has charge of other etheric world intelligences or deceased relatives who wish to speak through the trumpet; has control over the ECTOPLASM and alloted time for the session chosen by the MEDIUM; there is a trust in the control when the medium collaborates with the control and allows his or her body to be taken under in deep CATALEPTIC TRANCE. [**cf.** ECTOPLASM, SEANCE, SITTERS]

TRUMPET SEANCE—a group of people and a developed MEDIUM sitting in a circle in a BLACKED-OUT ROOM to communicate with ETHERIC WORLD INTELLIGENCES through a TRUMPET; intent is to gain knowledge to help in one's spiritual progress; medium sinks into a DEEP TRANCE state with the collaboration of the etheric world CONTROL; ECTO-PLASM that emanates from the SITTERS and the medium is used to swoop under the trumpet and levitate it and move it through the air above the heads of the sitters; trumpet stops when the control is using it for an amplification system to be heard by human ears; this type of physical phenomena takes many years of weekly sittings by the same basic group to achieve; object is to learn and to receive answers to questions regarding ANGEL-OLOGY and PSYCHIC SKILLS; any etheric world intelligence who specializes in various phases of these two subjects can use the amplification of the trumpet to relay knowledge; pseudotrumpet session can be detected by the quality of the information relayed; superior entities do not make frivolous or insignificant conversation but only utilize the time for advanced technologies. [**cf.** DESIRED-CONTROL, RAISING THE TRUMPET]

TRUTH—(capitalized) (esoteric) 1. an individual REALITY (not universal); all individuals have their own Truth within themselves, truth must be found within one's self; no one can teach another a Truth; 2. a function of belief. [**cf.** LAW OF PRAGMATISM Appendix 7] 3. that which is the fundamental and ultimate reality of any one thing; it is possible for Truth to transcend fact.

TSAL—(Tibet) a THOUGHT-FORM built by densified, centralized MENTAL ENERGY, to be used in the manner for which it is made; psychic delilberately begins the thought-form, concentrates on its purpose repetitiously throughout each day until it has denseness and becomes powerful enough to be utilized; may be used in psychic work, in healing, or sometimes it is large and solidified enough to perform mundane tasks for its maker; see TULPA. **Syn.** ELEMENTAL. [**cf.** THOUGHTS, SOULLESS]

TSAR SUN—(Slavic) the sun, recognized to be necessary for all life, and worshiped as a diety; all earthlings are considered to be grandchildren of the sun and to be one with the main deity. [**cf.** DAZHBOG, FIRE, SUN, SUN DANCE]

TSAS AND RTSA—(Tibet) the ethereal veins, arteries, and nerves of the etheric double that are used as aids in producing psychic feats; this ethereal substance interpenetrates one's bloodstream and NERVOUS SYSTEM and acts as minute channels to transmit the VITAL LIFE FORCE throughout one's body; subject to the law of thought and can be directed to change its function temporarily, which results in difficult psychic phenomena. (Inconcl.) [**cf.** BODY CONTROL, TUMO, SPIRIT, NADIS, VIBRIC MATTER]

TSI-PA—(Tibet) a death HOROSCOPE made by a LAMA astrologer, using the moment of death of the deceased, to foretell the soul-mind's future incarnations. [**cf.** CONTINUITY OF LIFE, SURVIVALISTS, DEATH WISH]

TU—(Polynesia) an etheric world DEITY whose function is to oversee wars.

TUAN—(I Ching) two combinations of three lines, solid and broken, making up the HEXAGRAM symbol wherein one can receive the answers to the questions posed. [**cf.** TRIGRAM, TEXT, JUDGMENT]

TUAN CHUAN—(I Ching) that part of the HEXA-GRAM passage which interprets the judgment section of the commentary more thoroughly. [**cf.** JUDGMENT, GOVERNING RULERS]

TUAT—(ancient Egypt) a level of CONSCIOUSNESS in the ETHERIC WORLD recognized as the UNDER-WORLD; has a narrow valley, mountainous housing, fearful monsters, and beasts, when perceived clairvoyantly. **Syn.** DENSITY. [**cf.** INFERNAL REGIONS, DISEMBODIED SOULS, PIT]

TUI NA—(China) a method of releasing muscle tension by manipulation or massaage with the fingers and fists; therapist works along the MERIDIAN LINES of specific places on the body to loosen congested areas; this helps the cells to normalize and hasten a natural healing. (Inconcl.) **Syn.** CHINESE MASSAGE. [**cf.** ROLFING, NEURO-MUSCULAR MASSAGE]

TULKU—(Tibet) a SOUL-MIND who was an accomplished LAMA in a past incarnation and who can prove this by identifying objects, places, and names as they were in his or her past life. [**cf.** REINCARNATION, EXPERIENTIAL HISTORIES, OLD SOUL, RACIAL MEMORY, RECALL]

TULPA—(Tibet) a colony of an enormous amount of invisible, densified, concentrated thought atoms with a unified purpose, to perform menial tasks for its owner; this thought energy takes on a human-like FORM when perceived clairvoyantly and is under the direction of the PSYCHIC; thought-form is built by continuous, repetitious thoughts on its purpose and will hover close to its thinker and stay powerful as long as the psychic can hold the thought of this form and its purpose; tulpa could last days or years; when the concentration is broken the thought-form will gradually dissipate; been known to turn on its master and do harm. [cf. ELEMENTAL, THOUGHT-FORMS, MASS ELEMENTAL]

TUMMO—(Tibet) a method of awakening the etheric nerve fluid within the NADIS (the astral nervous system), to perform many psychic feats. (Inconcl.) [cf. JOGI-FEATS, BODY CONTROL, SEXUAL MAGIC]

TUMO—(Tibet) heat; see VITAL LIFE FORCE.

TUMO CONTROL—(Tibet, Yoga) to psychically regulate one's body heat, voluntarily; theory: the TUMO (vital life force) runs invisibly in the etheric nervous system and is subject to the law of thought; psychic concentrates on the tumo to change its rate of flow, which in turn changes the temperature, and PSYCHIC adjusts the body to live comfortably in extreme weather; e.g., Yogis live in caves in icy weather without fires and a minimum of clothing. (Inconcl.) [cf. VITAL LIFE FORCE, LAW OF THOUGHT Appendix 7, PSYCHIC HEAT, TEMPERATURE CONTROL]

TUNED-IN—to pick up information regarding a person from the vibrations that surround that person; to lower one's STATE OF CONSCIOUSNESS to a level of AWARENESS that will draw one close to another's thought atmosphere with the ability to decipher some of it. Usage: "I am tuned-in now and you may ask me your question." **Syn.** STEP INTO YOUR VIBRATION. [cf. PSYCHIC READING, STATES OF NONORDINARY REALITY]

TUNING OF THE MIND—(radionics) the mind activity of the operator of a PSIONIC instrument must be neutral as to the answer and must have the question correctly formulated, in order for the instrument to be accurate; if operator's mind is conditioned properly, he or she subconsciously gathers the PSYCHIC INFORMATION and turns the dials which will register accordingly; (similar to the radio dial selecting a certain station frequency). [cf. WIDE BAND TUNING, NARROW BAND TUNING]

TUNZI—(Zulus, Africa) a person's shadow and SOUL.

TURIYA—(Sanskrit) an extremely high STATE OF CONSCIOUSNESS in a nirvanic awareness; recognized by some to be the FOURTH STATE OF CONSCIOUSNESS; brought on by MEDITATION. [cf. PURE-AWARENESS, TRANSPERSONAL CONSCIOUSNESS]

TURNED ON—to be aware of PSYCHIC INFORMATION flowing swiftly and clearly, usually happens with INSPIRATIONAL THOUGHT or with psychic readings when chemistry of both client and psychic are compatible. Usage: "I must be turned on, I need a pencil quickly before I forget what I am receiving." [cf. INSPIRATIONAL WRITING, GOING-TO-LEVEL, IMPRESSION]

TURQUOISE—(esoteric) a mineral that receives radiations from Venus; these radiations are used to transfer the VITAL LIFE FORCE from one organism to another; known as the sky stone it represents purity and power that comes from the sky. [cf. VITAL LIFE FORCE, BLACK DIAMOND, TOPAZ]

TUTELARY DEITY—an ETHERIC WORLD INTELLIGENCE who joins a baby at birth and stays with that person throughout one INCARNATION, bringing guidance, counsel, abundance, psychic skills, and healing when called upon. **Syn.** GUARDIAN ANGEL, CELESTIAL GUARDIAN, DOCTOR TEACHER. [cf. INNER BAND, OUTER BAND]

TUTELARY FAIRY—a NATURE SPIRIT who chooses a family and acts as a guardian over that one particular family. **Syn.** DOMESTIC FAIRY.

TWELVE—spiritual number that stands for that which is complete; in the coming age it will take the place of seven and mean completeness, attainment, and precision; i.e., groupings of twelve: disciples of Christ, tribes of Israel, signs of the Zodiac, months of the year. [cf. NUMBER POWER, NEW-AGE, SEVEN]

TWELVE BLESSINGS—sacred literature given to George King, an Englishman, by the astronauts from outer space; used these blessings to build PSYCHIC ENERGY to store in his instrument. [cf. OPERATION PRAYER POWER]

TWELVE PULSES—(China) (acupuncture) twelve sections that the human body can be divided into, that correspond to the twelve MERIDIAN LINES with surface sensitivity, that can be used for diagnosing illnesses. [cf. ACUPUNCTURE, SYSTEM OF DUCTS, JUNCTIONS]

TWENTY-EIGHT DAY CYCLE—(biorhythm) the blue curved line representing the physical body systems' reacing to creativity, intuition, emotions and nervousness; determined by woman's twenty-eight day fundamental cycle; found to exist in both sexes; see EMOTIONAL CYCLE. [**cf.** BIORHYTHM CHART, CRITICAL LINE, OUT-OF-SYNC]

TWENTY-THREE DAY CYCLE—(biorhythm) the red curved line representing the body systems' reaction to physical strength, energy, endurance, and resistance, determined by the twenty-three fundamental cycle found to exist in both human sexes; see PHYSICAL CYCLE. [**cf.** THIRTY-THREE DAY CYCLE, DAILY CYCLES, SEASONAL CYCLES, POSITIVE DAYS]

TWENTY-TWO PATHS—(Hebrew) the many courses or directions one may go when taking an astral projection, for the benefit of spiritual attainment. [**cf.** STARRY SOUL-CHARIOTS, PROJECTIONIST]

TWILIGHT IMAGERY—see HYPNAGOGIC STATE.

TWILIGHT LEARNER—one who uses SUGGESTOPEDIA techniques for increasing one's knowledge; method permits one to learn more quickly and retain more easily. (Inconcl.) [**cf.** TWILIGHT ZONE]

TWILIGHT ZONE—a state of mental activity when the CONSCIOUS MIND and SUBCONSCIOUS MIND are exchanging prominancy in their roles; at the time the minds meet and both are functioning at an equal level the following awarenesses occur: 1. (future science) the brain activity can retain new material learned move easily and more swiftly; in this line between the ALPHA STATE and BETA STATE OF CONSCIOUSNESS, the conscious control liberates the mind from certain constraints which are necessary to maintain the disciplined routines of thought; this state of consciousness may become an impediment to the creative leap and more primitive levels of mental organization are brought into activity; now, persons are hypersuggestible and capable of learning certain things more efficiently and painlessly than during the beta state. (Inconcl.) **Syn.** SUGGESTOPEDIA. [**cf.** REVERIE, TWILIGHT LEARNER] 2. in this in-between state, the entities from the lower astral planes and density can slip in and present themselves in the form of the SEA OF FACES; see HYPNAGOGIC STATE.

TWIN-SOULS—two soul-minds who experience a psychic affinity; when two soul-minds incarnate together over many lifetimes, there is a union of closeness of these two soul-minds whether it is on the etheric or earth plane; they are drawn together and react compatibly to each other; this does not imply they will always join together for eternity, nor does it imply that there is only one twin-soul for each individual. (Inconcl.) [**cf.** SOUL-MATES, TIME PLAN, GROSS SOUL, OLD SOUL, GROUP SOUL]

TWISTIANS—(ufology) those who, for various motives, twist and distort any type of information about outer space intelligences, vehicles or life forms. [**cf.** BLUE BOOK]

TWO—represents the DEVIL as it is the first number to break away from the creator; considered weak, a subordinate number; numerology life cycle personality traits: sociable, affectionate, diplomatic, give-and-take qualities, gentleness, perceptiveness, and helpfulness and tends to be a homemaker; planetary link is the moon; a constant number and yet ever changing. [**cf.** NUMBER POWER, THREE]

TWO-MIRROR OSCILLATION EFFECT—occurs when two people project mind pictures over one another and emphasize their own emotions so that neither one is able to pick up from the other. [**cf.** MENTAL TELEPATHY, CLOAK OF INSULATION, EMPATHY CLAIRSENTIENCE, SPLODGER]

TWO-TAILED TEST—(psi tasks) a statistical test used to evaluate the results of experiments in which the direction of deviation, either above or below chance expectation, has not been specified in advance. [**cf.** CHANCE, MEAN VARIANCE, TRIAL, ZENER CARDS]

TYCHOGRAPH—(psi tasks) an instrument that just works with CHANCE. [**cf.** REVERSED EFFICIENCY, UNINTENTIONAL PSI, BUBBLES MACHINE]

TYPTOLOGY—to receive information from the etheric world intelligences during a PHYSICAL PSYCHISM development circle by rappings on walls, tables, woodwork and within the woodwork, using monosyllabic answers to sitter's questions. **Syn.** LANGUAGE OF RAPPINGS. [**cf.** SWINGING TYPTOLOGY, RAPS]

TZAPHQIEL—(Islam) considered to be an ARCHANGEL.

UDJAT EYE—(ancient Egypt) a drawing of an open eye engraved on amulets and talismans to help the wearer have clairvoyant ability; fashioned to accompany King Tut through eternity. **Syn.** EYE OF HORUS. [**cf.** Appendix 2 AMULETING]

UFO—abbr. for UNIDENTIFIED FLYING OBJECT.

UFO AKINESIA—a temporary paralysis of one's body experienced while in the presence of a UFO or a UFO related entity, which occurs for no logical mundance reason, and without any known cessation of mental activity. (Inconcl.) [**cf.** Appendix 5 UFOLOGY]

UFO CONTROL SYSTEM—(ufology) (Jacques Vallee) belief that UFOs function under a control system, which is not within the concepts of our scientists as they are presented with continually recurring absurd messages and appearances. (Inconcl.) [**cf.** ARMORED ORGANISM, DOR CLOUDS, GODS FROM THE SKY, DEHUMANIZE]

UFO CULT—(1976) a group of people who followed the "Two," believing that if they lived an isolated life and obeyed certain laws, the UFO intelligence would take them to another planet for a life of eternity; considered themselves to be followers to the next kingdom through a window to heaven open to those who are properly prepared. [**cf.** INDIVIDUAL METAMORPHOSIS, UFOLOGY]

UFO IMPRINTS—circular patterns in the ground that appear to have been made by UFO machines, witnessed or unwitnessed by humans. (Inconcl.) [**cf.** EXTRATERRESTRIAL VISITATION, INTRUDERS, SCOUT SHIP]

UFO INTELLIGENCES—a system that is recognized as a living form with a soul-mind, as opposed to the aircraft itself that is occupied with a life-form but not as humans know a life-form; name includes a space being, other planet beings, inner-world beings, or even angel beings taking on a new guise; an energy field of some kind that seems to humans to be somewhat like humans. (Inconcl.) [**cf.** GUARDIANS, HUMANOIDS, CRITTERS, FLYING SHIELDS]

UFO INVESTIGATOR—one who has been trained in investigation techniques: radiation detection, photography, moldcasting, and UFO characteristics. [**cf.** BLUE BOOK, CONTACTEE SYNDROME, CLOSE-ENCOUNTERS-OF-THE-THIRD-KIND]

UFO LANDING—an area on earth where someone

reported spotting something that to them semed to be a space craft or a space person; each case reported is kept on record. [**cf.** BLUE BOOK, UFO RADIATION, UFO SIGHTINGS, WINDOW AREA]

UFO PHENOMENA—anything that is seen, heard or felt pertaining to foreign things in the sky. [**cf.** CLOSE ENCOUNTERS-OF-THE-FIRST-KIND, UFOCAT, TARGET HUMAN, SPACE-BEING]

UFO PROPULSION—an unknown force which drives the UFO aircraft onward. (Inconcl.) [**cf.** STAR TRAVELERS, POSITIVE PRIMARY ENERGY, PHONY STARS]

UFO RADIATION—invisible emanations that one cannot see, feel or hear, but when one is standing within the emanations, one knows of their presence. (Inconcl.) [**cf.** CLOUD BUSTER, BEAM OF HEAT, DAYLIGHT DISCS]

UFO SIGHTINGS—areas on earth where unidentified and identifed space craft or space objects have landed, or been spotted, or areas where evidence of their presence has been seen; usually occurs near deposits of metal, iron, nickel, titanium, and near caves. (Inconcl.) [**cf.** MONSTER ACTIVITY, CLOSE-ENCOUNTER-OF-THE-FIRST-KIND]

UFOCAT—(ufology) a center that maintains computer files of UFO sightings reported by private research groups over a twenty-four hour telephone hot line; researched information on sightings is relayed to over 80,000 law enforcement authorities. [**cf.** Appendix 5 UFOLOGY, PROJECT BLUE BOOK, PROPULSION, ENERGY TRAILS]

UFOLOGIST—one who scientifically studies all aspects of outer space with an open mind.

UFOLOGY—the study and scientific investigation of anything of any nature that is foreign to earth and things that come from or are seen in outer space. [**cf.** AEROFORMS, SPACE CRAFT, COSMIC ENTITY, HEAT RAYS, CONSTRUCTS]

UFONAUT—(ufology) the intelligence that manipulates an outer space craft, or is capable of coming near earth in only his or her own embodiment. [**cf.** DEVIL-LIKE GOBLIN, EXTRATERRESTRIAL LIFE, FOO FIGHTERS]

UHANE—(Huna) the CONSCIOUS MIND, recognized as a separate entity. [**cf.** BRAIN, SPLIT BRAIN, THINKER, OBJECTIVE SENSES]

ULTIMA THULE—the magic center of a vanished

653

civilization.

ULTIMATE PRIMAL—see BIRTH PRIMAL.

ULTIMATE SCIENCE—the study of the interplay between radiating and absorbing energy systems integrated in an energy universe. Syn. RADIATIONAL PHYSICS. [**cf.** NODES, POLARITY, HOLOGRAM ENERGY]

ULTIMATE WHOLENESS—see TOTALITY.

ULTRA—a prefix meaning "beyond the ordinary"; "the extreme."

ULTRA-RED—a color beyond the ordinary visible spectrum. [**cf.** GREEN RAY PERIOD, WHITE, RED]

ULTRACONSCIOUSNESS—awakened state, opposite of sleep; fantastic realism; similar to IMAGINATION; the reality of this world made through images. [**cf.** PSYCHIC SENSES, INSPIRATIONAL THOUGHT, SUPERCONSCIOUS MIND]

ULTRADIAN RHYTHM—(split brain) a change in muscular activity and brain hemisphere function occurring every ninety minutes during the twenty-four hour period; during the REM sleep state the right hemisphere has dominance and the muscles are paralyzed; during the awake state when the brain shifts to the right hemisphere there is only a slight decrease in muscular activity; the daytime ninety-minute interval is less noticeable and has only a minor influence on the behavior and body. [**cf.** ACTIVITY AND REST CYCLES, SPLIT-BRAIN HEMISPHERES Appendix 5]

ULTRAFAINT LUMINESCENCE—(Kirlian effect) a light ray or glow surrounding all things, animate or inanimate, which represents plasmic processes; picked up by low frequency cameras; believed to be different from or part of the AURA picked up by high frequency cameras. (Inconcl.) [**cf.** CORONA, ENERGY MATRIX, ELECTROPHOTOGRAPHY, ETHERIC DOUBLE, PATTERN, COLD ELECTRON EMISSION, EARTH'S ELECTRICAL FIELD]

ULTRAOUTER AURA—the third layer of atmosphere around a person; difficult to detect, but has been photographed by a high voltage camera. (Inconcl.) [**cf.** MENTAL BODY, ASTRAL BODY, HIGH VOLTAGE PHOTOGRAPHY]

ULTRASCIENCES—name given to the technology of the Atlantean culture because it far surpasses the sciences of the present. [**cf.** ATLANTIS]

ULTRASONICS—1. (science) pertaining to the sounds above the normal hearing range; 2. (parapsychology) pertaining to the clairaudient ear; MUSIC OF THE SPHERES. [**cf.** NATURAL INFRA-SOUND, RESONANCE, UNHEARD MELODIES]

ULTRASOUND—vibrations of sound that human ears can no longer detect unless perceived clairaudiently; sound that human ears heard at one time. [**cf.** INVISIBLE DRUM, STAR SOUND, OBJECTIVE CLAIRAUDIENCE, SUBJECTIVE CLAIRAUDIENCE]

ULTRATERRESTRIAL—(esoteric) an advanced race coexisting with mankind on planet earth occupying a different dimension of vibration than humans known as REALITY, either as transient visitors or as permanent residents; their dimension is known as reality to them. (Inconcl.) [**cf.** GUARDIANS, HUMANOIDS, RADAR ANGELS]

ULTRAVIOLET AURIC LIGHT—the speculative term relating the AURA to the high frequency ultraviolet light rays spectrum. (Inconcl.) [**cf.** COLD ELECTRON EMISSION, ENERGY FIELD PHOTOGRAPHY, PHOTOCHEMISTRY]

ULTRAVIOLET RAYS—color beyond the limits of the visible spectrum; believed to be the frequency rate of clairvoyant vision; moves faster than earth vibrations, giving out images to the clairvoyant eye. (Inconcl.) [**cf.** PSYCHIC FORCES, CLAIRVOYANCE]

UMA—(Tibet) the main artery, ethereal in nature, located in the ETHERIC DOUBLE of a human. [**cf.** ASTRAL BODY, NADIS]

UMBANDA—a form of Brazilian SPIRITISM combining two creeds: the African Candomble, and the Allan Kardec spiritism; combining the high and low cultures in a blending of PARAPSYCHOLOGY. [**cf.** SPIRITUALISM, MAGIC]

UN—prefix meaning "no, not, lack of"; when added to verbs it indicates a reversal of.

UNA SALUS—the ultimate, the great liberation; see TOTALITY.

UNAS TEXT—(ancient Egypt) hieroglyphics inscribed on the pyramids and other monuments, regarding life in the ETHERIC WORLD and phases of the eternal life of the SOUL-MIND.

UNBOUNDED AWARENESS—the level of the mind where PSYCHIC INFORMATION is received. [**cf.** GOING-TO-LEVEL, HOMING IN, HUNCHABILITY]

UNCARING ALERTNESS—an attitude necessary to

receive psychic messages; a relaxed and passive state, in which one is still keen to happenings that are different. **Syn.** AWARENESS ALERT. [**cf.** SENSITIVITY TRANSFER, THREE-FINGERS TECHNIQUE, PERCEIVE, NARROW BAND TUNING]

UNCOLORED MESSAGE—PSYCHIC INFORMATION that is not based on any known facts regarding the PERCIPIENT: this is easier to produce if the percipient is a stranger to the PSYCHIC. [**cf.** PSYCHIC READING, LIFE READING]

UNCONSCIOUS DEATH URGE—(rebirthers) theory: an individual could live in a physical body on earth forever, but buried deep within each individual's SUBCONSCIOUS MIND is the concept that DEATH is inevitable, put there by mass thinking over the years, and which causes one to die. [**cf.** DEATH ANGEL, ETCHING-OF-THE-SEED-ATOMS]

UNCONSCIOUS FRAUD—(psychic reading) to unintentionally submit to the interference of MENTAL MIND activity, from one's self or from those in the immediate vicinity, which flows out during the READING; happens because the reader is in the ALPHA STATE OF CONSCIOUSNESS where mind activity is acute, and he or she is not adept at precision tuning. [**cf.** CLOAK OF INSULATION, MEDITATION, MISPLACED PSI, PSYCHIC PERCEPTERS]

UNCONSCIOUS MATERIAL—see PSYCHIC INFORMATION.

UNCONSCIOUS MEDIUM—one who has the characteristics of any kind of MEDIUMSHIP whereby the MEDIUM produces phenomena spontaneously and unplanned; frequently happens because the medium is untrained and ignorant of the laws of mediumship, or subconsciously desires it to happen. [**cf.** INFERIOR ENTITIES, DESIRED CONTROL, CLOAK OF INSULATION]

UNCONSCIOUS MIND—1. the level of human intelligence that stores information and experiences that are fed to it by the CONSCIOUS MIND. **Syn.** SUBCONSCIOUS MIND, SUBJECTIVE MIND, SOUL-MIND. 2. knowledge in its entirety without conscious awareness of it; all the intelligence one is to ever know is fitted minutely in an invisible ethereal seed available to each individual. **Syn.** MONAD, HUMAN BEING SPECIES SEED. [**cf.** MONADOLOGY, SYMPATHETIC NERVOUS SYSTEM, SUBCONSICOUS MIND, CEREBROSPINAL SYSTEM] 3. the veil or wall between the conscious mind and the subconscious mind. (Inconcl.) [**cf.** VEIL]

UNCONSCIOUS MOTOR PHENOMENON— to give permission for an ETHERIC WORLD INTELLIGENCE to intervene and use one's body, in part or in whole, for physical psychism; type of activity and body movements are prearranged between MEDIUM and intelligence; occurs in a SEANCE or in front of an audience; performed in DEEP TRANCE; etheric world intelligence enters the medium's body and the medium's SOUL-MIND leaves the body; the body takes on the personality of the intelligence for that specific time, performing feats impossible for an individual to do normally. [**cf.** LEVITATION-TK, TELEPORTATION TELEKINESIS, INDEPENDENT VOICE]

UNCONSCIOUS NONAWARENESS—to build tension in the muscles by automatically holding back emotional expression during experiences that remind one of an unresolved, unpleasant past event; the event is not consciously connected with the tense muscles; this tension is built gradually over years as the memory of this emotional trauma is stimulated by similar situations; (the muscles are ready to act but repressed). [**cf.** ROLFING, NEUROMUSCULAR MASSAGE, BLOCKS]

UNCONSCIOUSNESS—1. (Sigmund Freud) coined to differentiate it from normal consciousness; used in describing mental illness; means "co-consciousness," (not subconsciousness as described in this dictionary); 2. a collective word; that which is not in the awareness of the CONSCIOUS MIND activity; 3. (Carl Jung) far below; an unruly platoon of erotic energies, archetypes, and curiosities. [**cf.** COLLECTIVE UNCONSCIOUS, SUBJECTIVE MIND, STREAM OF CONSCIOUSNESS]

UNCONTROLLED HALLUCINATION—spontaneous images or scenes from the SUBCONSCIOUS MIND which emerge and grow in intensity and interest; unlimited to unnatural environment and abnormal perception; the subject feels it is real; comes from an unsound mind, delirium, insanity, or from an obsessive illogical thought that grows. [**cf.** Appendix 4 for differences between HALLUCINATION, PSYCHIC INFORMATION, IMAGERY; PSYCHOTROPIC PLANTS]

UNCONTROLLED INNER-MIND PICTURES—see NON-THOUGHT. [**cf.** DELUSION]

UNCONTROLLED PSYCHISM—to allow one's PSYCHIC DOORS to be open all the time, in wrong settings, without proper protection, or too frequently for one's own good; 1. this can cause: (a) erroneous or harmful visions, sounds or hunches; (b) PSYCHIC TRANSFER of emotions, thoughts or health conditions from another psychic, either knowingly or unknowingly; (c) POLTERGEIST movements; (d) knocks; (e) PK in the home; 2. this can bring confusion, anxiety, fear, unnecesary sensations in the body, illness, change in appetite, change in sleep patterns, and incorrect PSYCHIC INFORMATION; 3. occurs because the rules and principles of psychic work are not followed, due to: (a) ignorance of the principles of psychism; (b) the psychic is on an "ego trip" consciously or sub-consciously desiring it to happen; (c) a karmic desire to be open to psychism; (d) a past INCAR-NATION when one was a strong psychic; (e) a time when one is in a mental turmoil which causes a leak in the ETHERIC WEB; (f) one is taking too many drugs; 4. more prevalent in a NATURAL-BORN PSYCHIC; all psychism can be brought under control by discipline and by observing the standards of the principles of psychism. [cf. CLOAK OF INSULATION, THOUGHT, LAW OF LIKE ATTRACTS LIKE Appendix 7, ELEMENTALS, DENSITY, GUIDE, PSYCHIC DEVELOPMENT]

UNCONVENTIONAL MEDICINE—medical treatment which is not prescribed nor approved by a legally licensed physician; also called UN-ORTHODOX HEALING; e.g., NEUROMUSCULAR MASSAGE, ACUPUNCTURE, jogging, PSYCHIC SURGERY. [cf. ALTERNATIVES, CURATIVE EDUCATION]

UNCRYSTALIZED MATTER—uncombined matter that is free from thought at the present; atoms in their normal state of floating through space. [cf. MATTER, VIBRATIONS, LAW OF THOUGHT Appendix 7]

UNCTION—the process of annointing with oil; a religious-magical rite performed to endow the person or object with supernatural power, grace, or sacredness; a crucial part of coronation ceremonies; administered to those near death for the health of the soul-mind. [cf. RITUALS, CEREMONIES]

UNDER—(hypnotherapy, seance) a deep ALTERED STATE OF CONSCIOUSNESS wherein the CONSCIOUS MIND and body are quieted, and free from conscious awareness; the SUBCONSCIOUS MIND is super alert and the subject is ready to: 1. accept the hypnotic prescription in HYPNOTHERAPY; 2. accept PSY-CHIC INFORMATION from the guides in a trance

state. [cf. ETHERIC COMMUNICATION, WENT OUT, WILLED, CREATIVE UPWELLINGS]

UNDERGROUND BASES—areas believed to be in the earth where civilizations of the ancient past were carried on, and which now hold mystical knowledge in vaults for humanity's use, when they are ready. [cf. GUARDIANS, HOLLOW EARTH]

UNDERSIDE OF EXPERIENCES—that which may not be intellectualized but which speaks for itself. [cf. NEW-AGE PSYCHOLOGY, METAPHYSICS]

UNDERSTANDING—(Wang Yang Ming) "that which is converted; knowledge which is converted into which is his own"; the ability to *use* knowledge received in its right perspective, and to feel comfortable with it. [cf. WISDOM]

UNDERWORLD—1. (Tumbuka, New Guinea) a realm in the ETHERIC WORLD where the departed go and where they are never old, hungry or sad; 2. one layer on the lower planes in the DENSITY, usually called HADES; an intermediate state in the density; a place or abode for soul-minds who are of inferior thoughts and who are young in development. [cf. DISCARNATES]

UNDINES—NATURE SPIRITS that live, breathe, and see easily in water; resemble people and are kind to humans; have their own language and customs; made of a different vibrational frequency than humans, but capable of mating with humans. **Syn.** WATER BABIES.

UNES—the original script of the Atlanteans. [cf. ATLANTIS]

UNFORMED THOUGHT—a HUNCH or an intuitive impression; an answer that seems to come from nowhere when one cannot reason or logically think; comes from the MONAD through the SUPERCONSCIOUS MIND and is pure information; see CLAIRSENTIENCE. [cf. MONAD, TOTALITY, NON-THOUGHTS, HUNCHABILITY]

UNGODLY SPIRITS—etheric world entities who live and die waging war with the gods above. **Syn.** EARTHBOUND ENTITIES, GHOSTS, FALLEN ANGELS. [cf. GREAT DOCTRINE OF LIBERATION, GREYLAND, DENSITY]

UNI—prefix meaning "one."

UNICORN—1. a NATURE SPIRIT that has been given so much interest and attention that when it changes dimensions to the PHYSICAL WORLD, it has the energy to live in the physical vibration for many months; a creature who combines male and female in one beast; used as symbols for travelers, biblical verse, and the alchemists; born of humanity's imagination, with a form and function that varies with each culture and religion; the one-horn beast designates supreme power; symbolized as a ram, goat, bull, fish, serpent, antelope, ass, or horse, all using the single horn: the strength associated with SINGLE-POINTEDNESS; 2. (alchemy) represents Mercury as a male-female element necessary to the accomplishment of humanity's inward victory over darkness; the unicorn's most vital function has been as a symbol for a combination of the opposites: the male horn and the female body, representing the SOUL-MIND as the spark of divine light in the darkness of matter; 3. emblematic of soul/spirit; one of the four spiritual creatures. **Syn.** KI-LIN.

UNIDENTIFIED FLYING OBJECTS—abbr. UFO; (future science) things or objects seen in the sky that cannot be recognized as belonging on earth; fall into two broad categories: 1. (Trevor James Constable) vehicles or constructs, having various shapes, sizes, colors, and sounds; seen in the sky in many places all over the world by lay persons, people in airplanes, and ufologists; travel at supersonic speed; carry intelligent life forms, or *are* intelligent life forms; visible to the physical eye or visible in a camera photograph; 2. pulsating life forms that seem to float or swim in the atmosphere, having various sizes and shapes; can be pleasant or grotesque; differ in color and brilliance; are invisible to the physical eye, but visible in a photograph. (Inconcl.) [**cf.** CRITTER, CONSTRUCTS OF INTELLIGENT DESIGN, FLYING SAUCERS, BIOLOGICAL UFO'S]

UNIFIED-FIELD THEORY—everything in the UNIVERSE is a form of ENERGY, all belonging to the whole, but each having individuality. **Syn.** GESTALT, HOLOGRAM. [**cf.** MATTER, TOTALITY, LAW OF QUANTUM CONNECTION Appendix 7]

UNIHIPILI—(Huna, "spirit") a separate ENTITY attached to the ASTRAL BODY. **Syn.** SOUL-MIND. [**cf.** SUBCONSCIOUS MIND]

UNILATERAL PATTERN—one of the five major brain wave signatures resulting from dominant left-brain activity, discovered when HOOKED-UP to the MIND-MIRROR EEG. (Inconcl.) [**cf.** ALPHA STATE, MIND-MIRROR, EEG]

UNIMANIFEST—see TOTALITY or GODHEAD.

UNINTENTIONAL-PK—(psi tasks) an unconscious movement of matter happening when the psychic is not aware that a PK effect is desired; psi results when the psychic feels detached or not responsible for the effect. [**cf.** OBJECT-PK, PSYCHOKINESIS, BLIND PK TASK]

UNIO MYSTICA—(Christian Saints) the mystical union with God; the supreme goal is reached; similar to NIRVANA or FANA, but without the loss of one's identity; the immersion of PERSONALITY with TOTALITY. [**cf.** BLISS MEDITATION, COMPANIES OF GODS, ECSTASY, PEAK EXPERIENCE]

UNIQUE PSYCHOPHYSIOLOGICAL TOOLS AND TECHNIQUES—(United States government) the study of CHAKRAS.

UNISEX—equally male and female as in the ETHERIC WORLD; earthlings lose gender identification after TRANSITION. [**cf.** POLARITY, ANGELS]

UNISPRIT—belief: only one etheric world intelligence can communicate with people; one who believes that only JESUS, the HOLY SPIRIT, or the DEVIL communicate. **Syn.** MONOSPRIT. [**cf.** SPIRIT COMMUNICATION, INNER BAND]

UNIT SEARCH—(dowsing) to work in the outdoor field where one intends to locate an underground substance; to stand in one spot and move in a circular motion until the DOWSING ROD responds, giving the direction of the substance desired, and to keep moving in that direction until the rod indicates the underground substance. **Syn.** REMOTE DOWSING METHOD. [**cf.** DOWSING QUESTION, FIELD DOWSING, INTERNAL DIRECTION]

UNITARY PRINCIPLE IN NATURE—coined by L.L. Whyte (1969) see VITAL LIFE FORCE.

UNITED MANDALAS—(Tibet) a circle containing a complete picture of the peaceful deities of the first six days of BARDO. [**cf.** SYMBOLS, DEATH ANGEL]

UNITY-MULTIPLICITY—the AWARENESS in the higher planes of the ETHERIC WORLD that one is no longer an individual, but a part of all motion. [**cf.** SIXTH PLANE, SEVENTH PLANE]

UNIVERSAL—pertains to the ALL, affecting or concerning all; that which is repeatable and unchangeable in essence.

UNIVERSAL BALM—an ELIXIR composed by the ALCHEMISTS, which formed a sovereign remedy for every malady, illness, and which brought the dead to life. [**cf.** BONDAGE OF THE FLESH, ALCHEMICAL FORMULA, PHILOSOPHER'S STONE]

UNIVERSAL BREATH—(esoteric) term used to acknowledge that the VITAL LIFE FORCE was in the air in the beginning; term used to acknowledge that an essential life force was in the air in the beginning, and is given to all in accord with one's ability to absorb and utilize it. **Syn.** VITAL LIFE FORCE.

UNIVERSAL BROTHERHOOD—theory: every living thing has as much right to love and life as all other living things; this right to love and life is equally important to each living thing, regardless of its status; e.g., the bumble bee, snake, elephant, mother, child, criminal, rose, teacher. [**cf.** META-PHYSICS, VEGETARIAN, GESTALT]

UNIVERSAL CONSCIOUSNESS—ONE total aware-ness that is CONSCIOUS OF BEING; everything in the universe is a part of, and belongs to, the "one" consciousness of being; animate and inanimate things consist of consciousness, some having lesser degrees than others; the mother universe aware-ness is distributed in all things, unevenly, in accord to the nature of the thing, but with enough awareness to know its "function"; everything is aware that it is connected to the mother conscious-ness, and to some this awareness of connection is more acute. [**cf.** DIVINE CONSCIOUSNESS, FIELD OF BEING]

UNIVERSAL DIVINE LIFE—see TOTALITY.

UNIVERSAL FLUID—see VITAL LIFE FORCE.

UNIVERSAL INTELLIGENCE—see TOTALITY.

UNIVERSAL KISS—an act of affection for the UNI-VERSE; a response to the universe by an embrace between two persons occurring at a metaphysical or religious gathering; happens when two persons feel on the same spiritual level, or when one dis-covers new knowledge and shares this discovery; a feeling of ONENESS comes over the two; can occur between man and man, woman and man, or woman and woman, without a feeling of sexual desire; one only has a feeling of accomplishment. [**cf.** TRANSFORMATION, NEW-AGE PSYCHOLOGY]

UNIVERSAL KOSMOS—ancient and esoteric philo-sophy concerned with both the inner and outer realms of the UNIVERSE. [**cf.** METAPHYSICS, MYS-TICISM, OCCULTISM]

UNIVERSAL LAW—an underlying principle found within everything necessary for the SCHEME OF THINGS, that cannot be altered, worn out, or ended; see Appendix 7 on laws.

UNIVERSAL LIFE CYCLE—begins as a rapid vibrat-ing mass of colored spirals which contain power to transmute ETHERIC ENERGY into physical sub-stance and back again. [**cf.** ETHERIC DOUBLE, AURA, TRANSMUTATION]

UNIVERSAL LIGHT—(esoteric) refers to the theory that in the beginning ALL was LIGHT (synonomous with INTELLIGENCE) and now all things are a manifestation of light or intelligence in lesser forms. [**cf.** ENERGY, TOTAL INTELLIGENCE]

UNIVERSAL MIND—(esoteric) the DNA of the whole UNIVERSE: a conglomeration of all the knowledge, principles and living forms, (animate and inert objects); all there ever was and all there ever will be; an expression, from the cockroach to Mars; all this is one stupendous whole and is imprinted within every particle regardless of its size. **Syn.** DIVINE MIND, TOTAL INTELLIGENCE, COSMIC CONSCIOUSNESS.

UNIVERSAL ONE-SELF—the placing of a SOUL-MIND with its relationship to TOTALITY, the ALL.

UNIVERSAL PRIMITIVE ELEMENT—see VITAL LIFE FORCE.

UNIVERSAL SOLVENT—an X-liquid until dis-covered by an X-method; one method of the ALCHEMIST is to grind the powder and mix it with other ingredients until it liquifies; known as the UNIVERSAL SOLVENT. **Syn.** ALCHEMICAL LIQUOR. [**cf.** ALCHEMICAL FORMULA]

UNIVERSAL SUBSTANCE—(Jean de Chardin) "the final 'stuff' of the universe is mind stuff"; (Elmer Green) "universe is crystalized thought"; (R. Gam-mon) "what we know of the world is the structure of the mind"; a system of unheard music; (esoteric) electro-chemical, magnetic vibrations balancing under the law of action and reaction (KARMA), forming various levels of energy consciousness which is subject to the law of thought. (Inconcl.) [**cf.** LAW OF THOUGHT Appendix 7, MATTER, ENERGY]

UNIVERSAL SYMBOLS—snatches of the environ-ment and objects used in human lifestyles that have come to cause similar feelings in almost all cultures throughout the ages; these symbols are used in

DREAMSTUFF and psychic messages; e.g., ocean of rough waters signifies rough days, flag means victory, baby designates birth, roof symbolizes shelter or protection, rainbow indicates your wish will come true, etc. **Sim.** ARCHETYPAL IMAGES. [**cf.** DREAMS, PSYCHIC INFORMATION]

UNIVERSAL TRINITY—represents three elements that are necessary for all existences; SPIRIT, SOUL, and a PATTERN: **1.** spirit—the movement, energy, vibration; **2.** soul—intelligence directing the rate of vibration; **3.** pattern—universal fluid, the thought, the idea. [**cf.** NUMBER POWER, SYMBOLS, LAW OF THREES Appendix 7]

UNIVERSE—all that is known to exist, the total of ALL; consists of gigantic galaxies; an ever-changing, ever-evolving energy field processing trillions of levels of INTELLIGENCE; for details see TOTALITY.

UNIVERSION—coined by George Lakhovsky; see VITAL LIFE FORCE.

UNKNOWN—see ETHERIC WORLD.

UNKNOWN FORCES—see UNIDENTIFIED FLYING OBJECTS.

UNKNOWN PLANE—see PERFECTNESS PLANE or SEVENTH PLANE.

UNKNOWN TONGUES—see TALKING-IN-TONGUES.

UNORTHODOX HEALING—any method, medicine, surgery, therapy, diet, or exercise, that is taken or used to promote the patient's well being, that is not the prescription or treatment of a medical doctor; see ALTERNATIVES. [**cf.** CURATIVE EDUCATION Appendix 5]

UNREAL INNER ACTIVITY—PSYCHIC INFORMATION that is needed for the TRANSFORMATION of the planet; information given through any one of the psychic skills which the PSYCHIC cannot comprehend, should be taken to one who can understand it; all psychic information that seems to surpass the individual, should be studied, evaluated and considered as needed information for the coming years. [**cf.** AQUARIAN AGE.]

UNREALISTIC EXPERIENCE—(J.B. Rhine) a form of presumptive psi information processed into CONSCIOUSNESS during sleep, when the imagery ranges from a slight tendency toward dramatization to symbols; sometimes this is with a feeling of conviction. [**cf.** DREAMS, FALSE AWAKENING, CONVERGENT OPERATIONS]

UNRIPE EGG—(Vedic) the part of an individual that is self-centered, arrogant, and materialistic.

UNRUFFLING THE FIELD—coined by Dolores Krieger; (magnetic healing) to change the direction of, or to sweep out, the congested body energy of the patient until the movement of the energy flow (that had been stagnant in the congestion) is felt; a special technique of the PRACTITIONER whose hands move a little above the body or touch the body. [**cf.** THERAPEUTIC TOUCH, MAGNETIC HEALING]

UNSEELIE COURT—a NATURE SPIRIT associated with particular localities; seen at twilight, and appearing as a weird and terrifying monstrosity.

UNSEEN FORCES—see ETHERIC WORLD INTELLIGENCES.

UNSEEN INTERLOCUTORS—see ETHERIC WORLD INTELLIGENCES.

UNSEEN INTERLOPERS—see ETHERIC WORLD INTELLIGENCES.

UNSEEN REALM—see ETHERIC WORLD.

UNSEEN SEER—(esoteric) the black diamond, used as symbol to represent the third-eye. [**cf.** THIRD-EYE AREA, PSYCHIC ENERGY]

UNSHIELDED PLANETARY BODIES—planets that seem to stay barren due to the lack of a shield that is necessary to keep out harmful radiations.

UNSTRESSING—the act of releasing the BLOCKS and knots which one has repressed, in order to restore the NERVOUS SYSTEM to normal function; tools used for unstressing: AUTOGENTIC TRAINING, MEDITATION, BIOFEEDBACK TRAINING, systematic DESENSITIZATION, ACTUALIZATION, RELAXATION RESPONSE, GROWTH GAMES, COLOR THERAPY, ROLFING, and NEUROMUSCULAR MASSAGE. [**cf.** BLOCKS Appendix 5]

UNSUBSTANTIALIZATION—see ECTOPLASM MATERIALIZATION.

UP THROUGH—a term used when working with ZENER CARDS; calls are made from the bottom to top, instead of top to bottom; this process tests precognition. [**cf.** DOWN THROUGH]

UP-AND-DOWN MOTION—(penduluming) a direct movement of the PENDULUM, going in a straight line away from the body and back again, as opposed to swinging sideways; this makes it possible to establish a code of *yes* or *no* with each movement of the pendulum. [cf. COURTESY, OSCILLATION, PENDULUM POWER]

UP-FOR-GRABS—to leave one's PSYCHIC DOORS open in everyday activity; when done without proper preparation and choice of time and place, exposes one to psychic attacks from other psychics (knowingly and unknowingly) and from the etheric world inferior and EARTHBOUND ENTITES; frequently results in illnesses, fatigue, and erroneous information; excluding CLAIRSENTIENCE and HUNCH-ABILITY. [cf. CLOAK OF INSULATION, TAMING THE MIND, PSYCHIC TRANSFER, CLAIRSENTIENCE]

UPADHI—(Sanskrit) the problems and chaos created by humanity, instead of the orderly manifestations within human capability.

UPADYA'S MIND—(Hinduism) see OVERSOUL.

UPANISHADS—(Sanskrit) ancient teachings of the Hindu religion; kept secret for many years until the VEDANTA was written from them; the sacred scripture which constitutes the philosophical portion of the VEDAS, teaching knowledge of God; contain records of the spiritual experiences of the sages of ancient India; the Upanishads were brought to a close as each of the four Vedas was written.

UPPER DUAD—(Theosophy) see MONAD.

UPPER FREQUENCY—(biofeedback training) denotes the highest threshold reached on the scale of brain rhythms when HOOKED-UP to the ELECTROENCEPHALOGRAPH. [cf. SCALE OF BRAIN RHYTHMS, DELTA STATE OF CONSCIOUSNESS, THETA WAVES]

UPRAISED SERPENT—name given to coiled serpent when it has reached the CROWN CHAKRA; state of KUNDALINI activity during which the third-eye is opened and remains open all the time; accomplished by properly handling growth experiences. Syn. NAGAS. [cf. CHAKRAS, SUSHUMNA, SERPENT POWER]

UPRIGHTING FORCE—an underlying principle that moves the ASTRAL BODY into a vertical position at a certain distance from the physical body during an ASTRAL PROJECTION. (Inconcl.) [cf. ASTRAL CORD, ASTRAL BODY WANDERINGS, ASTRAL ROUTE]

UR-HEKA—(Egypt) rods that were designed and then consecrated for being turned into a serpent; the rod had either a handle of a serpent, or the shape of the rod resembled a snake or the body of a ram. [cf. OBJECT-PK, TALISMAN, TOTEM]

URANOS—(Greece) name given for the atmosphere of electrons and atoms. Syn. ETHERIC WORLD, HEAVEN, WATERS OF SPACE.

URANUS—personification of the sky, heaven or the god that rules the heavens; depicted by a sky made of bronze or iron and garlanded with stars. [cf. ANGELHOOD, MAGNIFICENT DEVAS]

URIM AND THUMMIM—gems that could be used for communicating with ETHERIC WORLD INTELLIGENCES for guidance and PROPHECY; (Old Testament, Bible) worn by Aaron in the secret pocket of his breastplate, and linked to it by a gold chain. [cf. MINPSI, AMULETS, BEAMED ENERGY, PSYCHOMETRY]

URINE—(esoteric) 1. (alchemy) retains some of the vital energy of the body from which it came, therefore, provides a magical link with that body; 2. (witchcraft) in casting a SPELL, the victim's urine is put in a bottle and the spell influence can then be connected to the victim; 3. traveler's urine is bottled and sent home to predict whether the traveler will finish the trip; 4. (radionics) used as a diagnostic tool with the BLACK BOX, to diagnose the nature of the disease. [cf. LAW OF CONTAGION Appendix 7, RADIESTHESIA]

USHABTI—(Egypt) a small stone figurine with magical inscriptions placed in the tomb of a mummified body to perform tasks for the deceased in the ETHERIC WORLD. [cf. TALISMANS, WORDS-WITH-POWER, MUMMIFICATION]

USO—abbr. for UNDERWATER SUBMERGED OBJECTS.

UTCHAT—(Egypt) a sacred symbol representing the third-eye; designed with an eye, an eyebrow and a tail-like line that hinges in the corner. [cf. THIRD-EYE AREA, SACRED BEETLE, AMULET, TALISMAN, EYE OF HORUS]

UTRIUSQUE COSMI—(seventeenth century) (Robert Fludd) a picture of a man's head showing humanity's mental abilities in relation to GOD and the UNIVERSE.

UTRIUSQUE COSMI HISTORIA—(Robert Fludd) literature that expounds on the belief that man is a MICROCOSM and the universe is a MACROCOSM. [cf. LAW OF MICRO/MACROCOSM Appendix 7, MONAD, TOTALITY]

UTTERANCES—see TALKING-IN-TONGUES.

UTTERLY TRUSTWORTHY PARENTAL SELF—
(Huna) the SUPERCONSCIOUS MIND, high-self,
that does not interfere with the other two minds.
[**cf.** KUNDALINI, INSPIRATIONAL THOUGHT]

UV—(uncapitalized) abbr. MICROVOLTS; millionths
of a volt.

VACATED BODY—1. (physical phenomena) the physical body in a CATALEPTIC TRANCE state; the LIFE FORCE, the astral body, is gone and the ETHERIC WORLD INTELLIGENCE has entered the body to perform the physical phenomena at hand. [**cf.** DEEP TRANCE, IMPERSONATION] 2. (astral projection) the physical body, looking very lifeless and corpse-like, after the astral body has left it. [**cf.** DISCOINCIDENCE, ASTRAL PROJECTION]

VACH—(Sanskrit) the degree of EMOTION within a word. [**cf.** THOUGHT-FORMS, WORDS-WITH-POWER]

VACILLATING—(meditation) a normal sensation of feeling as if one is swaying or vibrating while the actual physical body is not moving. [**cf.** CORTICALLY MEDIATED STABILIZATION, DISASSOCIATION]

VACULATE—to deliberately psychically transfer the sickness from the patient to oneself to cure the patient; distance is no barrier. [**cf.** PSYCHIC TRANSFER, SCAPEGOAT]

VAGUS BREATHING—to breathe by employing the VAGUS NERVE within the body and not using the nostrils; in deep meditation, the normal breathing mechanism becomes temporarily suspended and an inner breathing mechanism assumes control; one is not always aware there is a temporary motionless mechanism operating within; the vagus nerve makes a passage for the internal soul-mind breath; used by yogis and Tibetans who can stay concealed in a cell or box for days. [**cf.** HERMIT'S CELL, BREATHING]

VAGUS NERVE—(esoteric) also known as the **pneumogastric nerve** (*pneumo*, "life-breath") a channel for the soul-mind breath; runs downward through the neck in two strands, from the MEDULLA OBLONGATA at the base of the brain to the heart and abdomen; these two strands are a part of the SILVER CORD; controls the respiratory system in humans. [**cf.** VAGUS BREATHING]

VAIROCHANA—(Tibet) the Father principle (masculine, positive); the seed of ALL-THERE-IS, the MONAD of the universe.

VAJRA-KAYA—a tremendous, luminous display of light and color seen in MEDITATION; it is form coming from the void to make itself visible to the clairvoyant eye. **Syn.** DIAMOND BODY, TRANSPARENT BODY. [**cf.** HYPOMETABOLIC STATE, INNER SILENCE, ESSENCE OF REST]

VAJRINI—(Eastern) a fine channel that runs up the KUNDALINI. **Syn.** SUSHUMNA. [**cf.** COILED SERPENT, DIVINE MARRIAGE]

VAKHARI—a state where spontaneous words of wisdom, in poetry or prose form, seem to flow. [**cf.** INNATE RESPONSE, IMPRESSION, INSPIRATIONAL WRITING]

VALHALLA—(Norse) paradise where the heroes of war were taken in the ETHERIC WORLD, overseen by the Valkyries. [**cf.** HEAVEN, AETHER, HEAVENLY FIELDS]

VALKRYIOR—a woman in the ETHERIC WORLD who comes to help men in battlefields and take the dead to heaven, (a section of the northern lights). [**cf.** CELESTIAL GUARDIANS, MAGNIFICENT DEVAS]

VALKYRIES—(Germany) believed to be the entities in the ETHERIC WORLD who have charge over war and battles. [**cf.** VALKYRIOR, MINOR DEVAS, ANCESTRAL SPIRITS]

VALUE—(colorology) a matter of how much light is reflected, and intensity of brightness; e.g., if all light is reflected then the value is white, if no light is reflected then the value is black; in between are the colors of the rainbow. [**cf.** CHROMOTHERAPY, BLUE AIR, ASPECTS OF WISDOM]

VALUES—the qualities within each person which he or she feels are important, desirable, useful, and worthwhile according to his or her present BELIEF SYSTEM; values of each person change to a higher level as the SOUL-MIND grows; values are an absolute necessity for the growth of the soul-mind. [**cf.** NEW-AGE PSYCHOLOGY]

VAMACHARINS—(Sanskrit) black magicians; those who follow the path of darkness, resulting in negative activities, according to the standard of the masses. [**cf.** BLACK MAGIC]

VAMPIRE—a person or animal who sucks and draws blood from humans during the night: 1. a deceased person living in the DENSITY; returns to earth in a semi-materialized form of a physical body during the night; preys on sleeping persons in order to draw out blood from their bodies (without killing them); seems to have powers and functions of a noncorporeal soul-mind; appears like a withered skeleton when seen clairvoyantly. [**cf.** NIGHT HAG, GOLEM] 2. a living PSYCHIC who rests by day and takes astral flights by night; changes the ASTRAL BODY to an animal form and sucks the blood from sleeping humans (without killing them); it is believed that the victim is hypnotized by the vampire; theory: these psychics refused an earlier system of life and are not in the correct time period for their state of EVOLUTION. [cf. NIGHT-FLYING BLOODSUCKERS, ASTRAL VAMPIRISM]

VAMPIRIC HIBERNATION—theory: vampires who were pronounced dead and were buried were really in a state of hibernation and could astrally project from their grave to do their work; this would account for pulses found in vampire corpses; believed to belong to another system capable of a form of subterranean hibernation. [cf. HERMIT'S CELL, VAGUS BREATHING]

VAMPIRISM—to psychically "suck out" the physical energy or blood of sleeping persons, leaving them feeling weak and drawn but still alive; performed deliberately or unconsciously; theory: these soul-minds are from an earlier system of life that needed blood to exist. [cf. ELECTRICAL VAMPIRISM, SOLEM, HAG]

VANIR—(Sweden) a CULT noted for their psychic abilities.

VAPOR ECTOPLASM—a misty, watery, vapor that is luminous or phosphorous in color and that emanates from the sitters and medium in a materialization seance; first stage of materialization and capable of forming a simple, or a lesser amount, of a body. [cf. SOLID ECTOPLASM, PARTIAL MATERIALIZATION]

VAPORGRAPH—an image appearing on cloth similar to a photographic plate; theory: body vapors can interact with special spices and produce a picture negative on cloth; e.g., the ancient burial cloth known as the Shroud of Turin with the image of a man believed by many to be that of JESUS. [cf. CLOTHOGRAPHY]

VARDOGER—(Scandinavia) forerunner; one with the ability to psychically visit a place before physically arriving there. [cf. RANDOM PSYCHISM, PSYCHIC COLLISION, SPONTANEOUS CASE]

VARIABLES—capable of being altered or changed; inconstant.

VARIANCE-DIFFERENTIAL EFFECT—(psi tasks) significant difference between variances of run scores or other units in two experimental series (designed to affect results differntially). [cf. PROCEDURAL IRREGULARITIES, DOUBLE HEADER EXPERIMENT]

VARNA—(Tantrism) the principle that SOUND is eternal and every letter of the alphabet is a GOD. [cf. WORDS-WITH-POWER, POWER-OF-THE-WORD, SUGGESTION]

VASSAGO—an ETHERIC WORLD INTELLIGENCE who is invoked by the crystal gazer and appears in the CRYSTAL BALL; its purpose is to give PSYCHIC INFORMATION in the form of visions in the crystal. [cf. SCRYING Appendix 2]

VASUS—a highranking order of etheric world helpers in the angel kingdom whose function is to carry out the overall plan of PERFECTNESS, by giving guidance in negative karmic conditions. [cf. GREAT WHITE BROTHERHOOD, INNER BAND]

VATE—(Latin) one who is a POET and a PROPHET, but who reads into the past instead of the future. **Syn.** FILI, RETROGRESSION PSYCHIC. [cf. STATE ORACLE, PROPHET, CLAIRVOYANT]

VAYU—1. (Hinduism) the five principle directions of the VITAL LIFE FORCE taken in through the chakras; 2. (Yoga) external space-sound; the movement of air in waves in the external atmosphere. **Syn.** SPACE-SOUND. [cf. CIRCLE, SPIRIT, CHAKRA]

VCIS—abbr. for VOLUNTARY CONTROL OF INTERNAL STATES; to regulate body temperature, muscle tension, nervous arousal, and levels of alpha and theta; accomplished in an ALTERED STATE OF CONSCIOUSNESS; reached through PASSIVE VOLITION in the self-conscious waking state, during MEDITATION or BIOFEEDBACK TRAINING. [cf. FIXED BRAIN WAVE STATE, EXPECTANCY WAVE, RECORD MODE]

VEDAMATA—(Yoga) the Mother of the VEDAS; a MANTRA used to carry the aspirant through the five states of the LIGHT; the consciousness of EARTH, WATER, FIRE, AIR and ETHER. [cf. ILLUMINATION, PASSING THE MANTRA, INWARD ART]

VEDANA—(Buddhism) "feeling" nature caused by the SENSES; can be pleasant, unpleasant, or neutral. [cf. SKANDHAS]

VEDANTA—(Sanskrit) the end of the VEDAS; divided into two portions: work portion and knowledge portion; a system of mystical philosophy derived from the efforts of the Sages through generations in order to interpret the UPANISHADS; theory: there is an all-pervading reality with characteristics and attributes which remain unchanged amidst the changing appearances of humanity's universe; encompasses all teachings of the East.

VEDAS—scriptures which form the basis of the Hindu religion; composed by SEERS and RISHIS of an indeterminable antiquity; received by the rishis as a revelation in sound, that is, "directly heard"; literature of chants and recitations; 100,000 couplets were orally transmitted by Brahmin priests; philosophy teaches MIND-OVER-MATTER, advanced psychology, and that there are invisible threads that will help to transform the earth into a sublime harmonious family; contributes material to the wisdom of the mysteries.

VEGANISM—see VEGETARIAN.

VEGETABLE MONAD—divine spark of TOTALITY, found in all vegetation from the least to the greatest, which endows each type of vegetation with PRIMAL PERCEPTION connecting all to the ALL. [cf. INSTINCT PERCEPTION, VEGETATION MAGIC]

VEGETAL SCIENTISTS—those who study the nature of plants and currently conduct research in the psychic ability of plants; plant psychism is known in ancient Hellenistic culture as BOTANE. [cf. BOTANE Appendix 2]

VEGETARIAN—(*vegetar* "to enliven") one who does not eat flesh food such as meat and poultry; lives on products of the plant kingdom, excluding all foods and commodities derived from animals; postulates that all animals have a right to life; plants desire to be eaten by animals and humans, so as to transmute into a higher STATE OF CONSCIOUSNESS. [cf. BREATHATARIAN, WELLNESS, LAW OF SUBSERVIENCE Appendix 7]

VEGETATION MAGIC—(ancient) the use of special rituals designed to change the VIBRATIONAL FREQUENCIES of the area, and of the clouds, to make rain as needed to grow crops. [cf. LAW OF ASSOCIATION Appendix 7, SENSATION CONSCIOUSNESS]

VEGETATIVE MEMORY—(Russia) the ability of the plant kingdom to learn and remember; experiments performed by Gruzinov proved that the plant could remember the rhythm of blinking lights. (Inconcl.) [cf. PRIMARY PERCEPTION, CELLULAR CONSCIOUSNESS]

VEHICLE—a word used interchangeably with the PHYSICAL BODY, or body of an ETHERIC WORLD

INTELLIGENCE. **Syn.** ENVELOPE. [cf. ASTRAL CURRENTS, BARDO BODY]

VEIL—1. an invisible field of etheric energy-matter that separates the physical senses from the PSYCHIC SENSES, surrounding a human being in the inside of the AURA; a dense and etheric material built into the chakras that acts as a shield to prevent one from seeing into the astral world all the time; a wall of protection from the etheric planes; 2. pertains to the dark cloud one sees sometimes before seeing a VISION; a curtain blocking out the astral world that can be raised in psychic sittings; 3. the film over some babies at birth; some feel this is nothing but a physical occurrence and to others it means the child will be PSYCHIC. **Syn.** ETHERIC WEB, BARRIER, BLACK-CLOUD, WALL. [cf. MENTAL PSYCHIC PROCESSES Appendix 2]

VENTILATED PYRAMID—a skeleton or frame of a PYRAMID made according to the proper scale of proportions, regardless of its material, will manufacture the same energy as if it was solid. [cf. FORMS-WITH-POWER, PYRAMID ENERGY]

VENTLA-TYPE VEHICLE—(ufology) a spacecraft that appears to have a white, plasmatic, quasi-spheroidal radiation with a whirling energy field around the disc. [cf. FUSIFORM, FLYING SHIELDS, POWER SOURCE]

VERIDICAL AFTER-IMAGE—(ghost) an emotional energy field of a deceased person, with enough intelligence to make it appear as a ghost; dead persons can leave a strong emotional memory in areas they frequented, which makes the places seem haunted. [cf. FAMILY GHOST, PHANTASMS, ENVIRONMENTAL HAUNTING]

VERIDICAL DREAM—a PSYCHIC EXPERIENCE DURING SLEEP that later becomes a real event. **Syn.** PROPHETIC DREAM. [cf. DREAMS, PROPHECY]

VERIDICAL HALLUCINATION—(laboratory) 1. (Edgar Mitchell) a visual or auditory psychic experience, similar to sense perception (but without sensory stimulation or without being in the range of sensory awareness) that corresponds to a real event taking place; 2. the reception of uncontrolled psychic information that corresponds to actual facts. [cf. PSYCHIC COGNITION, EXTENDED CLAIRVOYANCE]

VERIDICAL PSI PHENOMENA—PSYCHIC INFORMATION that is found to be the TRUTH, or to be truthful, instead of being distorted or erroneous.

[cf. HUMAN OMENS, UNCONSCIOUS MATERIAL]

VERIFICATION—see AUTHENTICATION.

VERIFICATION DREAM—DREAMSTUFF coming to the dreamer after a problem has been solved to indicate that the solution was correct; a complimentary dream that helps the dreamer feel satisfied about a decision. [cf. CONPENSATORY DREAMS, MOTIVE UNCONSCIOUSNESS]

VERMONT FOLK MEDICINE—(Vermont) the adoption of old physiological and biochemical laws for maintaining health and vigor in Vermont living; to condition the body in its entirety so that disease will not attack it; utilizes healing plants that are sought out by animals to cure themselves. [cf. ALTERNATIVES, HOLISTIC HEALTH]

VERONICA—(uncapitalized) a TALISMAN, such as a handkerchief, veil, or cloth, which bears a representation of the face of Christ; a symbol of the cloth given to Christ on his way to Calvary which later showed the imprint of his facial features. [cf. VAPORGRAPH, CLOTHOGRAPHY]

VERSE MAGIC—(Greece) to use metrical compositions of rhythmic beat that influence the elements of nature; given to the ancient poets through inspiration by the ETHERIC WORLD INTELLIGENCES; e.g., using compositions to stop volcanic eruptions and storms, disperse drifting ice, kill destructive animals, force ghosts to disappear into the ground or to cast a curse of evil. [cf. AFFIRMATION, MIND ACTIVITY, MUMBO-JUMBO]

VERSIFYING MEDIUM—one who is capable of AUTOMATIC WRITING or VOICE TRANCE and whose GUIDE delivers metrical lines of rhythmic verse, that can be used in rituals in calling in the etheric world entities. [cf. AUTOMATISM, VERSE MAGIC, WORDS-WITH-POWER]

VESSELS OF CONCEPTION—(China) special points on the body that act as transmitters and receivers, which store body energy reserves when one represses emotions that one does not want to face; can be released by ACUPUNCTURE or ACUPRESSURE to prevent congestion in the body. **Syn.** ACUPUNCTURE POINTS. [cf. MERIDIAN LINES]

VESTIBULAR LOCALIZATION—poltergeist phenomena that occurs in close proximity to the poltergeist foci. **Syn.** PROXIMAL LOCALIZATION. [cf. POLTERGEIST, FOCUS, NAUGHTY GHOST, PELTING GHOST]

VIBES—(slang for **vibration**); relates to how one is perceiving one's environment. Usage: "I get good vibes with that person."

VIBRANALYSIS—a combined study of NUMEROLOGY, COLOR, and ASTROLOGY; shows aspects of the vibrations of the UNIVERSE in respect to the days, months, and years for an individual's personal life.

VIBRASONIC TUNER—a tape recording of well chosen words intended to influence the pattern of an individual which in turn influences the lifestyle of that individual; best to listen at the onset of sleep and the last part of sleep. [cf. AFFIRMATION, MAGICAL VERSE]

VIBRATING RING—(sixteenth century) a ring suspended on a fine thread over a round table which is marked with the letters of the alphabet; the ring would stop at various letters, thus spelling out the answers to questions; used especially for hunting treasure. [cf. OUIJA BOARD, PLANCHETTE, AUTOMATISM]

VIBRATIONAL FREQUENCIES—see LAW OF VIBRATIONAL FREQUENCIES Appendix 7.

VIBRATIONAL LEVEL—a STATE OF CONSCIOUSNESS in which the PSYCHIC feels comfortable that the information that comes through will be correct and true; all psychics and mediums have their own place of contact, that is comparable to a wavelength of a radio station. [cf. WIDE BAND TUNING, NARROW BAND TUNING, GOING-TO-LEVEL]

VIBRATIONAL STATE—(astral projection) pulsations in the PHYSICAL BODY that occur when the ASTRAL BODY has slipped out; noticeable to the astral projectionist and to an observer. [cf. SLOW-VIBRATORY DROP, SLIGHTLY-OUT-OF-BODY, PROPULSION]

VIBRATIONS—(metaphysics, parapsychology) frequently used common word, that refers to the steady, rhythmic, cyclic movements of the atoms that never cease, whether they are visibly engaged in making an object or a PHYSICAL BODY, or invisibly making ethereal substances; governed by a power surpassing human comprehension, giving each thing a different vibrational frequency; constantly moving particles and interlacing tiny web-like connections from the dense earth to the celestial planes, makes all psychic work possible because of this vibrational connection; an innate characteristic of the ATOM usually referred to as SPIRIT, or ENERGY that keeps the atom vibrating. [cf. VITAL

LIFE FORCE, VIBRATIONS Appendix 2; LAW OF VIBRATION and LAW OF VIBRATIONAL FREQUENCIES Appendix 7]

VIBRATORY NOTE—sound emitted from each individual thing, determining its power; theory: all things, from the ATOM to the great CENTRAL SUN, emit a sound. [**cf.** LAW OF VIBRATIONAL FREQUENCIES Appendix 7]

VIBRATORY SCALE OF FOOD—a listing of foods and their rate of vibration to denote the best foods to eat to maintain health in the TRANSFORMATION age; the faster the vibratory rate, the more healthful the food. [**cf.** CURATIVE EDUCATION, FOLK MEDICINE, HERBOLOGY, CELL SALTS]

VIBRIC MATTER—substance with a different vibrational level than PHYSICAL MATTER.

VIBRO—a prefis meaning "vibrations" used in forming compound words.

VIBROSCOPE—an instrument used for detecting unusual VIBRATIONS. [**cf.** SIDEREAL RADIATION, OCTAVE]

VIBROTURGY—see PSYCHOMETRY.

VIDEHA MURTI—a belief in a bodiless liberation and then a death-surviving element. [**cf.** SURVIVALISTS, TRANSITION HORMONE, COMING FORTH]

VIDEO-MEDIC—see VISUALIZATION.

VILLAGE BLACKSMITH—a master of fire, therefore believed to be a possessor of secret knowledge; usually the village PSYCHIC; practitioner of occult skills, specializing in HEALING and CHARMING. **Syn.** FIRE DOCTOR, IRON DOCTOR. [**cf.** CLASSICAL WITCHES, FIRE IMMUNITY, FIRE WALKING]

VILLAGE HERBALIST—(Ozark Mountains) a person who had an understanding of herbs and their therapeutic uses in mental and physical healing; also a good PSYCHIC. [**cf.** FASTING, FLESH FOOD VEGETARIAN]

VILLAGE WISE-WOMAN—see PSYCHIC; given this name because of an ability to see into the future and past with accuracy. [**cf.** PROPHECY, RETROACTIVE PK, MULTIPLE TIME]

VIMANAS—see UFO.

VIOLET—color representing SPIRITUALITY or COSMIC CONSCIOUSNESS; the seventh and highest quality an individual can attain; holy love attained through the highest spiritual devotion; represents honor, spirituality and self-esteem. [**cf.** COLOROLOGY Appendix 2]

VIOLET FIRE—(alchemy) violet vibrations in the ETHERIC WORLD which are believed will eventually transmute unwanted conditions and balance all by the Light. [**cf.** TRANSMUTATION, IMMORTAL DRAUGHT]

VIPASSANA—(Burma) a form of MEDITATION; the ability to see things as they really are by focusing on one thing in meditation until the mundane appearance of it disappears leaving only the ETHERIC DOUBLE (auric vibrations). **Syn.** INSIGHT MEDITATION. [**cf.** CONSCIOUSNESS OF INFINITE SPACE]

VIRGILIAN SORTE—a PSYCHIC who specializes in the interpretation of the VIRGILIAN SORTES discs and the CASTING OF LOTS.

VIRGILIAN SORTES—(Rome) a string of discs, each inscribed with a verse taken from the poetry of Virgil; used by the PSYCHIC to predict the future, or to give counsel to the QUERIST by the skill of CASTING OF LOTS, which indicated which disc should be read. **Syn.** SORTES SANCTORIUM. [**cf.** SORTILEGE, THROWING THE BONES, YARROW STALKS]

VIRGIN—(magic, occult) the undissipated innate force in an object; anything that has never been used for any purpose; magicians make their tools and instruments from previously unused materials or buy them new; each tool is selected for its operation; theory: to use an object which is second hand, has belonged to another MAGICIAN, or has been employed for nonmagical purposes is to risk danger; previous owners may have linked the object with influences, not in harmony with the magician's good intent or with the ceremonial beliefs. [**cf.** TALISMAN, PSYCHOMETRY, WITNESS, RITUALS]

VIRGIN SPIRIT—TOTALITY, in its original form, divided itself into fractions and ensouled the egos of humans and all other forms of life, causing itself to enter the heavy, imprisoning matter of this world; slowly, patiently, fights its way back to its original virgin state. **Syn.** TOTALITY. [**cf.** INVOLUTION, EVOLUTION, EGOS]

VIRTUES AND POWERS—an order of etheric world helpers who carry out the divine plan. [**cf.** ANGEL HIERARCHY]

VIS MEDICATRIX NATURAE—(Hippocrates, 350 B.C.) see VITAL LIFE FORCE.

VIS NATURALIS—see VITAL LIFE FORCE.

VISCERAL LEARNING—to set aside the intellect temporarily and listen to the body; to learn to control involuntary muscles and movements assisted by BIOFEEDBACK TRAINING. [**cf.** SUBLIMINAL AWARENESS, SWISHING LISTENING MODE]

VISHNU—(Hinduism) an exalted GOD or ANGEL of a higher intelligence who chooses to be incarnated on earth for a particular age to help the righteous, and to bring guidance and instructions that help prevent EVIL from becoming too powerful in that age, e.g., KRISHNA, JESUS, Siddartha. [**cf.** LORD-HOOD, LORDS OF HUMANITY]

VISIBLE CONSCIOUSNESS—see MUNDANE WORLD, or PHYSICAL WORLD.

VISIBLE SPEECH—(Rudolf Steiner) a therapeutic art of movement of the human body intoning untapped sound. **Syn.** EURYTHMY. [**cf.** RHYTHMIC EMOTIONS, MUDRA, GHOST DANCE]

VISION—("elsewhere") to perceive a picture as if it were OUT-THERE in front of one, without using the physical eyes; picture can be an object, person, or a scene; full blown or in part; seen with eyes opened or closed; planned or spontaneous; usually occurs while in a relaxed state of consciousness, such as after MEDITATION, in HYPNOSIS, during sleep, in development circles, or under sedation. **Syn.** OBJECTIVE CLAIRVOYANCE. [**cf.** SUBJECTIVE CLAIR-VOYANCE]

VISION OF SELF—to perceive one's ASTRAL BODY in a psychic vision, during sleep, or clairvoyantly in a relaxed state; happens usually as a sign of approaching death, as if the astral body becomes the thinking self and sends out a notice or warning. [**cf.** EMOTIONAL PSI]

VISION QUEST—1. (Native American) to perceive a full blown clairvoyant vision of one's personal guide, brought about by tribal traditions as preparation; these visionary activities, sometimes agonizing, are necessary for receiving the highest possible etheric world intelligence, who will bring counsel, guidance, protection, and PROPHECY for the tribe; a traditional initiation is necessary for perceiving this vision to become a tribal SHAMAN; it is a very personal and spiritual experience for the Indian; opens one up to PSYCHISM, MEDIUMSHIP and HEALING abilities. [**cf.** INITIATORY SICKNESS, SUN GAZE DANCE] 2. (Native American, Chippewa) a traditional tribal preparation for clairvoyantly perceiving a vision that reveals the reason for one's INCARNATION; usually performed between the ages of twelve and fourteen; traditional activities for inducing the vision are called "crying for a vision" and can vary in the following ways: (a) to fast without food and water for four days; (b) to spend time in the sweat lodge; (c) to walk back and forth until one becomes exhausted and is in an ALTERED STATE OF CONSCIOUSNESS; (d) to lie down in a trench and cover one's self with earth; after inducement activity, one finds a place in nature that is compatible and then inquires for the vision to appear. [**cf.** VISION QUEST MOUNTAIN]

VISION QUEST MOUNTAIN—(Native American, Chippewa) a mountain, held very sacred because of its properties which helps one to see a personal vision that reveals the individual's goal or purpose in this incarnation. [**cf.** THRONE MYSTICISM]

VISIONARY—a PSYCHIC who received most of his or her PSYCHIC INFORMATION in the form of pictures or scenes perceived in front of the eyes as opposed to perceiving them within the head. **Syn.** OBJECTIVE CLAIRVOYANT. [**cf.** SUBJECTIVE CLAIR-VOYANCE, OBJECTIVE CLAIRAUDIENCE]

VISIONARY TRANCE—1. to allow an ETHERIC WORLD INTELLIGENCE to enter one's body and use one's physical senses as if they were his or her own; e.g., seeing with the eyes of the MEDIUM and performing the task at hand; intelligence helps the medium to reach the level of a CATALEPTIC TRANCE. **Syn.** IMPERSONATION. 2. to bring forth information in vivid visions at will; PSYCHIC goes into a lethargic SELF-INDUCED TRANCE, whereby his or her senses are intensified and the subconscious mind produces full blown, clear visions. [**cf.** DEPENDENT CLAIRVOYANCE, DEEP TRANCE]

VISITATION DREAM—(Native American, Iroquois) a PSYCHIC EXPERIENCE DURING SLEEP in which the ETHERIC WORLD INTELLIGENCES give information to the sleeper regarding community participation and fulfillment that will be beneficial to the tribe. [**cf.** PRECOGNITIVE DREAM]

VISUAL MANFESTATIONS—impressionable and understandable communications from the ETHERIC WORLD that can be seen and heard by anyone in the vicinity; e.g., TABLE-TIPPING, KNOCKS, TRUMPET, etc.; ETHERIC WORLD INTELLIGENCES worked in this manner in the beginning of SPIRITUALISM in the early 1900s to prove their authenticity; this is in opposition to manifesting within the mind of the medium so that only the medium perceives; see PHYSICAL MANIFESTATION. [**cf.** see Appendix 2 to differentiate between MENTAL and PHYSICAL PSYCHISM]

VISUAL RAY—a beam of ENERGY, similar to radar, that comes out of the eyes, going in the direction one is looking; makes contact with the external object, allowing the eyes to see and to make a magnetic connection. [**cf.** HYPNOTHERAPY, DOWSING, PENDULUM, THIRD-EYE AREA]

VISUAL SCANNING—(biofeedback training) to be absorbed with the CONSCIOUS MIND in the normal activities of the day, while HOOKED-UP to the BIOFEEDBACK INSTRUMENT; the instrument readings show no progress; the BETA STATE OF CONSCIOUSNESS. [**cf.** EEG, METABOLIC MONITOR, BASELINE DRIFT]

VISUAL SOUND INFORMATION—(biofeedback training) noise of degrees of tone and rhythm varying with each subject HOOKED-UP to the GSR biofeedback instrument, and varying to the states of consciousness the subject is producing; gives the therapist clues as to how the subject is progressing. [**cf.** GALVANIC SKIN RESPONSE, METABOLIC MONITOR, TELLTALE SKIN]

VISUAL-IMAGERY TECHNIQUE—see VISUALIZATION.

VISUALIZATION—to deliberately bring into manifestation a desire or need by an exercise of picturing the desire or need in the MIND'S EYE; one sits and images the END-RESULT of the request in mundane form; the picture will eventually become a thought-form strong enough to manifest in the outer world; 1. requires inner-mental discipline to not cloud one's mind with how one could or could not attain this desire or need; THOUGHT-FORMS use directions from TOTALITY to manifest, and interference from the individual confuses the direction of the atoms; 2. picture should be clear and exact as to the final product and allowed to build up in the ETHERIC WORLD by holding it as long as possible; repeated sessions are necessary; manifestations will happen more quickly if exercise is performed directly after MEDITATION or in an ALPHA STATE OF CONSCIOUSNESS where the SUBCONSCIOUS MIND accepts it; 3. can be performed for one's self or for others; usable for manifesting an increase in

prosperity, improvement in health, harmony between two persons, bringing ability to speak in public, etc.; e.g., if one desires a new car, one might visualize a new car parked in the garage and the keys in one's purse or pocket; if one desires more harmony among persons, one might visualize them in a lovely restaurant happily engaged in conversation. **Syn.** SOLEMNIZING THE MIND, HO-ANO, SEED PICTURE. [**cf.** THOUGHT-FORMS Appendix 2, DAYDREAMING]

VISUALIZED HEALING—to purposely change the BODY CHEMISTRY in a patient by techniques of VISUALIZATION: this change in body chemistry allows the body cells to normalize and heal themselves more quickly; visualization should be performed in an ALPHA STATE OF CONSCIOUSNESS, directly after MEDITATION, when the CONSCIOUS MIND is passive and the SUBCONSCIOUS MIND is in an acceptance mode; requires repetition, a disciplined mind, and an understanding of the principle of MIND-OVER-MATTER which seals it with the necessary faith; techniques: 1. to picture the patient perfectly well, happy and doing what he or she likes to do (END-RESULT); hold this picture a few minutes with strong positive, constructive emotions; executed for one's self and others; 2. to make an inner-mind scene of helpers and see these helpers destroying the diseased area and then rebuilding it; hold this picture over the diseased area; performed for one's self; e.g., to image the diseased area of the body as a garden where men are working and pulling out weeds and planting healthy vibrant flowers in their place. **Syn.** LOGURY. [**cf.** VISUALIZATION, MENTAL HEALING, CELL ACTIVITY]

VISUALIZER—one who has mind control and uses the VISUALIZATION method to make things happen or to change one's world. [**cf.** METAPHYSICALLY ARRANGED]

VISUARY—see VISIONARY.

VISUDDA CHAKRA—see THROAT CHAKRA.

VITAL BODY—see ETHERIC DOUBLE.

VITAL FLUID—see VITAL LIFE FORCE.

VITAL HEAT—(Tibet) see TUMO CONTROL.

VITAL LIFE FORCE—(esoteric) motion and the reason for motion working simultaneously; 1. primordial quality of MOTION, working in harmony with primordial intelligence; invisible neutral essence found in all motion, giving it life; 2. neutral movement, neither plus nor minus, neither positive nor negative; it is born into life but is not life; 3. scientists are not sure if it is the *principle* of vibration (motion), or if it *is* vibration (motion); 4. all cultures have known of its presence for thousands of years, but none have discovered what it is in its entirety; (global) universal principle of LIFE ENERGY or LIFE FORCE found in the air and in all things, animate and inanimate, giving them life and sustenance; principle of all CREATION; found in air and where air cannot reach; 5. it is the quality of motion of the essence of the air that brings it alive; everything is in motion, therefore, everything is alive (*alive* meaning motion or live movement); 6. an expression of specialized energy, derived from TOTALITY; 7. vital life force is in MATTER, but independent of it; 8. is the chemicalization in the ATOM that keeps it vibrating; acts as the generator of the atom, hand in hand with the intelligence of the atom; 9. primordial force capable of setting into motion the particle of the atom by mental-emotional activity of the human mind; 10. needed by person's mind to think; taken into the PHYSICAL BODY through the breath and through the chakras, distributed in the bloodstream and the CONSCIOUS MIND and filters into the NERVOUS SYSTEM and SUBCONSCIOUS MIND: utilizes the LAW OF THOUGHT; 11. emanates from the physical body through the hands, when directed by the mind, making it useful for psychic skills and psychic healing; can be stored in the BRAIN and ABDOMINAL BRAIN, like a battery; 12. cannot be duplicated, destroyed, or made visible (even clairvoyantly); 13. theory of metaphysics: each atom is made up of INTELLIGENCE and ENERGY (vital life force); said in another way: each atom has a SOUL (intelligence) and SPIRIT (vital life force); 14. (Levi) "acknowledgement that the vital life force was in the air in the beginning given to all in accord with their ability to absorb and utilize it"; 15. (Patrick Flanagan) "this energy can be conducted from humans by substances that are electrical insulators"; 16. (AMORC) "universal essence pervading all nature, even unconsciousness, matter and the electron; the basis is a lower rate than soul"; 17. (Japan) it is etymologically connected with breath; 18. (Allan Kardec) cannot be seen or touched, has no odor, nor color, but can produce results; 19. (Krishna) a primal COSMIC ENERGY outside the electromagnetic spectrum and other force systems known to official science; 20. (Sanskrit) means to breathe, to live; a psycho-electrical field manifesting in mankind; 21. (Vedanta) the sum total of PRIMAL ENERGY from which all mental and physical energy has evolved; manifests in the form of MOTION, gravitation, MAGNETISM, and the sustenance of physical life, thoughtforce, and bodily action; 22. (Bible) sometimes it is used interchangably for breath, wind, SPIRIT, and HOLY SPIRIT. (Inconcl.) **Syn.** see Appendix 3. [LAW OF CAUSE AND EFFECT Appendix 7]

VITAL MAGNETIC SERIES—the all-pervading, all-uniting influence that connects HEAVEN and EARTH, under the law of sympathy; theory: there is an underlying substance that connects all things whether they are visible or invisible; details, see ANIMA MUNDI. [**cf.** MAGICIAN'S FIRE, GOLDEN CHAIN]

VITAL MAGNETISM—coined by Charles Littlefield (1920); see VITAL LIFE FORCE.

VITAL POINTS—(Karate) places in the body where one strike can momentarily stop blood from flowing to the head; the victim loses control of his or her limbs, or certain nerves are paralyzed. [**cf.** MARTIAL ARTS, OPEN-HANDED CHOP, BREAK-FALLS]

VITAL PRINCIPLE—(Allan Kardec) see VITAL LIFE FORCE.

VITAL SOUL—(Allan Kardec) principle of all material life; see MONAD.

VITAL SPIRIT—(Hinduism) see VITAL LIFE FORCE.

VITAL-AIR—(Tibet) see VITAL LIFE FORCE.

VITALISM—(seventeenth century) theory: a living force within human beings that eludes PHYSICS and chemistry, and makes rules of its own; doctrine that phenomena are only partly controlled by mechanical forces, and are in some measure self-determining. **Sim.** HOMEOSTASIS. [**cf.** TONUS, FRINGE MEDICINE, CELLULAR MEMORY]

VITALITY—(Theosophy) an invisible force manifesting from within the ATOM which is under the will of the SOLAR DEITY; see VITAL LIFE FORCE.

VITALITY GLOBULES—(esoteric) hypermeta-proto elements; tiny drops or points of light bouncing around in the air; are best seen when the sun is behind the individual and he or she is looking into blue sky; consists of seven physical atoms charged with spirit; they are drawn into the SPLEEN

CHAKRA; replacing those that were absorbed by the ETHERIC DOUBLE, and are taken into the PHYSICAL BODY invisibly, and transmuted to a physical vibration.

VITALITY VESTURE—see ASTRAL BODY.

VITALIZED SHELL—the corpse of the ASTRAL BODY floating in the ASTRAL CEMETERY after the SOUL-MIND has left it; it is energized by the materialistic thoughts of the individual who just stepped out; this shell can haunt earthlings and be a nuisance for many months contacting uncontrolled and untrained psychics through the OUIJA BOARD and AUTOMATIC WRITING; see ASTRAL SHELL. [cf. SHADOW]

VITRIOL—one of the sayings used by alchemists meaning: "visit the interior of the earth, through purification and thou wilt find the hidden stone." [cf. PHILOSOPHER'S STONE, RESURRECTED]

VIVI—(Haiti, Voodoo) a trapped ZOMBIE who is subjected to the influence of an evil MAGICIAN, who knows how to manipulate a corpse. [cf. ANDROID, CORPSE CADAVER]

VODYANCY—(Slavic) an ETHERIC WORLD INTELLIGENCE who uses deep waters, lakes and brooks for his or her existence; has the ability to transform her or himself into a NYMPH, marry and have nymph children; seeks communication with earthlings at night at the water surface. [cf. ETHERIC WORLD INTELLIGENCES, NATURE SPIRIT]

VOICE BOX—(seance) a temporary, invisible instrument built by the ETHERIC WORLD INTELLIGENCES to be used as an amplification system for their voices; 1. voice box is fashioned after human vocal cords or a concoction of the etheric world; made from the ECTOPLASM that emanates from the SITTERS and MEDIUM in the SEANCE; when photographed by an infra-red camera the pictures show a white substance lying on the medium's shoulder or in the corner of the room near the ceiling; 2. purpose is to relay information and knowledge that could not be known by formal education at that time period; etheric voices can hear the sitters and answer their questions; knowledge is meant for the masses not for personal counseling; 3. takes many repetitious sessions and the dedication of the sitters and medium to build; this box dissipates and the ectoplasm is drawn back into the medium's body when seance is over; room is BLACKED-OUT: medium is under desired-control and always wills

the physical phenomenon to occur. **Syn.** INDEPENDENT VOICE. [cf. TRUMPET, DEPENDENT VOICE]

VOICE BROADCAST CONTROLLER—the voice of an ETHERIC WORLD INTELLIGENCE who organizes and acts as announcer for other voices on the tape recorder, in electronic voice phenomena. [cf. ELECTRONIC VOICES Appendix 2]

VOICE BROADCASTS—see TAPED VOICE PHENOMENA.

VOICE OF SILENCE—(Tibet) the UNIVERSAL MIND where intuitive and inspirational information comes from; the quietness within that can be heard when the mind, body, and emotions are quieted. [cf. SUPERCONSCIOUS MIND, INSPIRATIONAL THOUGHT, CLAIRSENTIENCE]

VOICE PHENOMENON—1. the ability of a discarnate being or an ETHERIC WORLD INTELLIGENCE to talk through an animal, bird, object or parts of the physical body of the MEDIUM; 2. see TAPED VOICE PHENOMENA.

VOICE PRINTS—patterns of a person's voice produced on the sound spectrograph, which traces the distinctive sound patterns on graph paper; it was found that each person's voice continues to make the same pattern and has its own pattern, as unique as a fingerprint. [cf. RAUDIVE VOICE, VOICE PHENOMENA]

VOICE TRANCE—to allow an ETHERIC WORLD INTELLIGENCE to intervene in one's body and use one's vocal cords to speak through; 1. medium's neck area is anesthetized by the intelligence when the MEDIUM is in a DEEP TRANCE state; the vocal cords serve as an amplification system to bring the intelligence's voice to the level of physical ear threshold; the voice, tone, and quality used may be the medium's or may be intelligence's voice which will have a foreign accent; 2. purpose is to relay knowledge regarding the ETHERIC WORLD, UNIVERSAL LAW, etc., that surpasses present day scientific knowledge; 3. medium must have the proper BODY CHEMISTRY to synchronize with the INTERVENTION, keep a NEUTRAL MIND, and have the fortitude to sit weekly for many months or years; medium is chosen because of willingness to give the knowledge to the public; medium remembers nothing or very little when session is over; a tape recorder is used or SITTERS take notes; 4. occurs in a SEANCE, DARKROOM SESSION or a PRIVATE SIT-

TING; always willed and under desired-control of the medium; sitters may ask questions (sometimes for personal counseling) and receive answers; intelligences can hear and see what transpires in the seance room; 5. voice trance phenomena has been in existence since hundreds of years B.C. and exists today; most popular way of receiving knowledge beyond the time period of the masses, regarding the etheric world, and regarding the purpose of life. **Syn.** DEPENDENT VOICE. [**cf.** TRANCE VOICES Appendix 2, CONTROL, GUIDES, BLACKED-OUT]

VOICES FROM THE UNIVERSE—see TAPED VOICE PHENOMENA.

VOICETAPE PHENOMENA—see TAPED VOICE PHENOMENA.

VOID—(esoteric) that which first existed in the process of CREATION; the beginning; essence of purification; energy that is unfruitful; the absence of all that is present now, but ultimate perfectness; (Tibet) the ultimate, shining, clear colorless light of pure reality; not an emptiness, but where the universe holds the moons, the suns, and the stars; (do not mistake it for nothingness, it is everythingness).

VOIDANCES—(Gestalt dream therapy) to relate a dream or experience repeatedly for therapy; certain facts or events that are consistently omitted are the areas that represent repressed desires or traumatic experiences that have never been resolved and keep surfacing for attention. [**cf.** DREAMS, BLOCKS, FIXATIONS, COMPLEX]

VOIDNESS—(meditation) consciousness of transcending over-all consciousness and ending in the ONENESS of all. **Syn.** DIVINE BODY OF TRUTH [**cf.** TOTAL ABSORPTION, CLOSET]

VOLANTICA—(Rome) the PSYCHIC specializing in EXORCISM, PROPHECY, and ASTROLOGY.

VOLATILE ROD—(Ootker) (Switzerland) name given to the dowsing rod by the monk of St. Gallen; see DOWSING ROD.

VOLKH—(Slavic) a NATURE SPIRIT that communicates with humans in the form of a hawk; capable of SHAPE-SHIFTING, taking the form of a grey wolf and an ant.

VOLITION—willing; choice or decision made by the WILL.

VOLUNTARIUM—(biofeedback training) coined by Marvin Karlins and Lewis M. Andres to represent an institution in the future, where patients would learn to combat medical problems by bringing their bodily functions under voluntary control. [**cf.** AUTOGENIC TRAINING, LISTENING MODE, PASSIVE VOLITION, ALPHA INDEX]

VOLUNTARY CONTROL OF INTERNAL STATES—(Elmer Green) "becoming conscious in normal unconscious parts of the body, at will"; ability to turn away from the outside world, enter the ALPHA STATE OF CONSCIOUSNESS or lower, visualize the body feeling in one particular area, and talk to the body mentally to have that area behave as you want it to; most easily attained when HOOKED-UP to a BIOFEEDBACK INSTRUMENT; has proven an aid to healing some diseases. [**cf.** BIOFEEDBACK TRAINING, ALPHA MODE, BASELINE DRIFT]

VOLVA—(Scandinavia) a MEDIUM who goes into a TRANCE state and works with the ETHERIC WORLD INTELLIGENCES; see MEDIUMSHIP.

VOODOO—(West Africa, Haiti; *vodun,* "god") ETHERIC WORLD INTELLIGENCE, spirit, or any object that is held sacred; object can be a consecrated AMULET. **Syn.** TOTEM. [**cf.** VOODOOISM, MEDIUMSHIP, SHAMANSHIP, PRESERVING OF SACREDNESS]

VOODOO DOCTOR—1. (Southern United States) an Afro-American PSYCHIC who has his or her recipes for GOOD or EVIL psychism; not related to voodoo religion in West Africa. **Syn.** CONJURE MAN, HOODOO PRACTITIONER. [**cf.** WITCHMAN, OWL, INCANTATION]

VOODOO LE CHEVAL—(Haiti) the process of going into TRANCE: the MEDIUM dances around a fire, imitating a horse; when the ETHERIC WORLD INTELLIGENCE enters, the medium appears to be riding the horse; a form of ASSIMILATION. [**cf.** VOODOOISM, MEDIUMSHIP, SUN DANCE]

VOODOOISM—1. (West Africa, Haiti; *vudu,* "the worship of a group of gods") belief that each god has its function to govern aspects of the UNIVERSE; a systematic religion of ceremonies and rituals in which the tribes dedicate and consecrate themselves; all mediums have their own ETHERIC WORLD INTELLIGENCES to call upon for guidance, counsel, PROPHECY, HEALING and protection; mediums establish a personal relationship with their own etheric world intelligences; specialize in energizing amulets and physical phenomena, emphasizing IMPERSONATION and VOICE TRANCE; very knowledgeable in the laws of nature and human psychology; **2.** (Western) means BLACK MAGIC and SUPERSTITION, having no connection to the religion of the Haitians. [**cf.** VOODOO LE CHEVAL, VOODOO, MEDIUMSHIP, AMULET, IMPERSONATION]

VRIL—**1.** (T. Levesque) believed to be the underground source of energy which could replace that of the Sun, prolonging human life; **2.** (Henry Bulwer Lytton, 1872) see VITAL LIFE FORCE.

VRITTIS—(Yoga) see HYPNAGOGIC.

WA'NKONDA—(Native American) the great power above; see TOTALITY.

WAFT—(Britain) see APPARITION.

WAI—(Huna) sometimes substituted for the word MANA, meaning "water."[**cf.** MANA-MANA, BRAIN DEWS, COSMIC ATOM]

WAITING TECHNIQUE—(psi tasks) a method of responding to ESP targets in which the subject deliberately waits for images to develop. [**cf.** WIDE BAND TUNING, CONTROLLED PSYCHISM]

WAKAN—(Native American, Sioux) see VITAL LIFE FORCE.

WAKEFUL HYPOMETABOLIC STATE OF CON-SCIOUSNESS—the greatly reduced rate at which the body consumes energy during MEDITATION; tested and found to be less than during sleep; considered by some to be the FOURTH STATE OF CON-SCIOUSNESS. (Inconcl.) [**cf.** CHRIST CONSCIOUSNESS, BEYOND PERSONAL CONSCIOUSNESS, INNER-ATTENTION]

WAKENING CONSCIOUSNESS—beta level of consciousness wherein people are aware of what is going on all around them with the sensitivity of the physical five SENSES; normal everyday awareness. **Syn.** MENTAL MIND, CONSCIOUS STATE. [**cf.** BETA STATE OF CONSCIOUSNESS, ALPHA STATE OF CON-SCIOUSNESS]

WAKING DREAMS—INNER-MIND-PICTURES that enter the mind while one is talking, as if the topic triggers off visual listening. [**cf.** FREE ASSOCIA-TION, INNER-DIALOGUE, CLOAK OF INSULATION]

WAKING HYPNOSIS—a state in which the subject functions according to prior hypnotic suggestions and yet appears to be acting normally and appears to be influenced by his or her own will, subject is acting without awareness of post-hypnotic sugges-tions. [**cf.** DESTRUCTIVE-BRAINWASHING CULT, SPELLED, SELF-HYPNOSIS]

WAKING SLEEP—BETA STATE OF CONSCIOUS-NESS; the normal everyday state of consciousness. [**cf.** SCALE OF BRAIN RHYTHMS, MENTAL MIND]

WAKING THINKING—(Sigmund Freud) a secon-dary process of thought which is verbal, abstract, logical, objective and in tune with REALITY. **Syn.** INNER DIALOGUE. [**cf.** LEFT BRAIN HEMISPHERE, LUCID AWARENESS]

WAKONDA—(Native American, Sioux) see VITAL LIFE FORCE.

WAL—(Nuer tribe, upper Nile) MAGIC or medi-cine. [**cf.** ESOTERIC HEALING, HEALING OF MEM-ORIES]

WALK-IN—coined by Ruth Montgomery; a super-ior SOUL-MIND (old soul) from the SIXTH PLANE who enters an adult PHYSICAL BODY on earth and uses it while helping the planet in trying times; in this way the superior soul-mind can bypass the process of birth and childhood, and get right at the task at hand; sometimes the entry is because the earthling longs to get out of his or her body. [**cf.** WALK-OUT, WALK-IN PROCESS]

WALK-IN PROCESS—the act of abandonment of an adult's PHYSICAL BODY to allow an advanced superior SOUL-MIND from the ETHERIC WORLD to enter his or her body and use it for another purpose; the soul-mind of the earthling slips out of the body on a prearranged date and the superior soul-mind slips in, with no illness to the physical body; it is not a surrender of, as in suicide, but an agreement between the two soul-minds; the superior soul-mind is familiarized with the AKASHIC RECORDS of the soul-mind replaced and finishes the soul-mind's immediate KARMA before getting at the purpose of this process; happens more frequently when the planet is undergoing alterations and transformations. [**cf.** DELAYED KARMA, WALK-IN, INCARNATIONAL EXCHANGE, TRANSFORMATION]

WALK-OUT—coined by Ruth Montgomery; 1. an adult earthling who mentally or subconsciously asks an ETHERIC WORLD INTELLIGENCE to take over his or her body because that earthling has lost the will to keep on living and feels that further soul advancement would be better achieved in the ETHERIC WORLD; 2. an adult earthling who pre-planned his or her life before entering this INCAR NATION and agreed to go through the birth and childhood process so that an advanced soul-mind could use the body later in life. [**cf.** WALK-IN, GROUP SOUL, HERMETIC CHANGE]

WALKING ON COALS—see FIREWALKING.

WALKING ON WATER—to move on the surface of water without physical help; one theory: requires intense CONCENTRATION on the upper part of the body or requires undivided attention on something entirely different; this method allows the lower part of the body to take care of itself, defying all laws of GRAVITY; when one breaks this concentration, the body will start sinking. [cf. PROLONGED JOGGING, LEVITATED RUNNING]

WALL OF PROTECTION—(Yoga) an ethereal energy field around mankind that was created by the adepts and saints to help shield humans from the evils of the DENSITY. **Syn.** GUARDIAN WALL. [cf. ETHERIC WEB, VEIL, BLACK CURTAIN]

WALLABY—(Australia) a form of an ETHERIC WORLD INTELLIGENCE who communicates with earthlings in dreams to relay helpful information. [cf. PITRIS, PLANETARY SPIRITS]

WALWORTH JUMPERS—an ecstatic sect whose members jump and dance up and down to induce psychic powers, such as trance and utterings; under the leadership of M.A. Girling. **Syn.** GIRLINGITES. [cf. MOVEMENT-FOR-ALTERED-CONSCIOUSNESS, WHIRLING DERVISH]

WAND—1. a symbol of AIR: 2. a slender stick or staff used by a MAGICIAN as a psychic tool; serves as an instrument to direct the energy emanating from the psychic's hand to the object, event, or phenomenon the magician wants to happen; wands are personal tools and consecrated by the owner to direct PSYCHIC ENERGY; used in ceremonies to help control the forces of nature and to bring the higher self into manifestation in the mental consciousness; (ancient) sticks were cut in a particular manner at a particular time from an almond or hazel tree. [cf. CEREMONIAL MAGIC, AMULET, DOWSING ROD, WAND OF MERCURY]

WAND OF MERCURY—a staff with wings on the top, and two snakes coiling around the staff, crossing at six intervals; 1. a symbol of HEALING; represents the spinal column and the IDA and PINGALA working up the spine crossing at the CHAKRAS; see CADUCEUS WINDING SYMBOL; 2. insignia of Mercury, the winged god of messages from the ETHERIC WORLD. [cf. KUNDALINI, NADIS, GOD]

WANDERING SOUL—(primitive) belief that disease is due to the absence of a patient's soul-mind and not due to the invasion of an EVIL force. [cf. BLOCKS, SING, HAUNTING]

WANDERING SPIRIT—an ETHERIC WORLD ENTITY that is not engrossed in learning but is going to and fro to reexperience earth sensations while waiting for his or her next INCARNATION. **Syn.** ERRANT SPIRIT, SHADE, CONFUSED SOUL-MIND. [cf. GHOST,

EARTH-BOUND ENTITY]

WANDJINA—(Australia) a NATURE SPIRIT in charge of the landscape for certain areas; has been known to paint pictures on the fences or walls showing how the land should be cared for.

WANGA—(Haiti, Voodoo) magical powder made from ground-up nail clippings, hair, food, herbs, etc., or a part of the article one is working with psychically; 1. used for casting a SPELL on the owner of the nail clippings and hair; 2. used to promote a HEALING from the herb powder; 3. used to bring about a particular event from a piece of the event, ground into the powder., e.g., ground soil and cornhusks would bring about an abundant corn crop; happens under the LAW OF QUANTUM CONNECTION and the LAW OF CORRESPONDENCE, see Appendix 7; sometimes the spell itself is called the **wanga.** [cf. MAGIC EFFECT, DIVINATION, EMANATIONS]

WANGATEUR—(Southern United States) see SHAMAN.

WANKONDA—see WA'NKONDA.

WARLOCK—(Scottish, Anglo-Saxon) a male witch; see WITCH.

WARM HOLES IN SPACE—theory: there is something in space that allows mankind to cut through the universe faster than the speed of light; inconclusive, but helps explain DIMENSION-SHIFTING. [cf. DIMENSION-SHIFTING AND SHAPE-CHANGING Appendix 2]

WARM UP THE MOTOR—(penduluming) to steady the PENDULUM while holding it between the thumb and first finger and give it time to connect with the NERVE FLUID coming from the SUBCONSCIOUS MIND; usually takes time to establish its own rhythm. [cf. OSCILLATION, COURTESY, PENDULIST]

WARMTH ETHER—heat that is in a state of expansion; considered to be the first level of vibration in the atmosphere, next to earth vibrations; can evolve into the next density of etheric substance; manifests in heat; recognized as the FOURTH STATE OF MATTER; its function is to produce spherical shaped objects and the color RED. (Inconcl.) [cf. COLOROLOGY]

WARNING DREAM—1. a dream that tells the dreamer where he or she stands according to the decisions he or she made that day; this gives the dreamer an option to change plans the next day; 2. a

PSYCHIC EXPERIENCE DURING SLEEP that foretells a mishap in the near future regarding one's self or a loved one, or in the nation. [cf. PROPHECY]

WARNING STICK—(Zen) a stick carried by the masters of the monastery, used to strike the shoulder of one who has fallen asleep during MEDITATION. **Syn.** KEISAKU. [cf. SITTING ZEN, SLEEPITATE, OUT-BREATH, DHYANA]

WARP AND WOOF—(Tibet) the constant vibrational cycle of the ethers at the base of each universe; known as BLUE AIR. [cf. ZERO + ZERO, INFRARED RHYTHMS]

WART CHARMER—the village healer who knows the art of this ritual and has faith in his or her own hands to clear a person of warts and other viruses. [cf. PSYCHIC HEALING, MENTAL HEALING, HERBALIST]

WASSERMUTER—(Germany) see DOWSER.

WASSERSCHMECKER—(Germany) see DOWSER.

WATCH PLANTS—vegetable plants believed to have a rapport of integration with their owners since the plants have the properties of being sensors and detectors for the owners. [cf. SYMBIOTIC RELATIONSHIPS, BIOTELEPATHY, BOTANE]

WATCH SERVICES—(West Africa) nightly services of singing, dancing and drumming held to build VIBRATIONS for trance messages from the etheric world. [cf. MERCY GROUND, CHERUBIM AND SERAPHIM MOVEMENT, ABSTRACT DANCING, HEALING DANCE]

WATCH YOUR BREATH—(Zen) instructions given during MEDITATION to help one narrow one's attention to the smallest possible target; to concentrate on one's breath can be an all-absorbing thing. [cf. AUTOGENIC STATE, INTERIOR SILENCE, FRINGE OF CONSCIOUSNESS]

WATCHDOGS OF THE PSYCHE—(dreams) (Ann Faraday) those scenes during sleep which put one in touch with experiences that one did not resolve during the day and that have been repressed. [cf. DREAMS, FORGOTTEN LANGUAGE, ABSENT DREAMS]

WATCHER—1. (psychic healing) an animal thought-form attached to the PRACTITIONER; built by the practitioner through concentrated mind centralization; animal thought-form is sent to the patient to take on the consciousness of the patient; this con-

sciousness is reabsorbed into the practitioner through the thought-form; practitioner now has a good understanding of the patient to be helped, and knows how to shed the disease of the patient from his or her own body. [cf. PSYCHIC HEALING, FAMILIAR, SCAPEGOAT] 2. the highest rank of angel princesses/princes having charge over many other angels. **Syn.** HOLY ONES. [cf. ANGEL HIERARCHY]

WATCHFUL SPIRITS—(Ireland) a totem of brightly painted wood sculpture of a bird holding a fish and clutching a serpent; used at burial grounds as protection against EVIL forces. [cf. DEATH SCIENCE, DWELLER IN THE ABYSS]

WATER—a vibrational frequency making a certain "quality" named *water;* 1. the third basic element; the most primary form in which liquid can exist; origin of everything; (Hebrew) refers to the primeval substance vibration in space, subject to the laws of CREATION; atoms before colonizing into MATTER; 2. an element of ENERGY depicting the SOUL-MIND; the unconscious depth of the human mind or its mystery; an aggregate of CONSCIOUSNESS; 3. negative, feminine in POLARITY; passive, receptive, joyful, soft and reposing; 4. the only liquid that stores human energy; has an affinity to the human AURA; 5. classic symbol of GOD; 6. a purifying agent; (ancient) running water has the peculiar electrical qualities that if put in front of EVIL vibrations, it will break the path of this evil and send it on another course; (Levi) "all men must be washed, symbolic of the cleansing of the soul"; water has the ability to cleanse; 7. (occultism) used in ceremonies and development circles to enhance psychic skills; (Slavic) an element of neutrality believed to be carrying positive and negative qualities that have a DIVINATION quality and HEALING effect; used for SCRYING; 8. liquids are lifegiving because they flow and move about, while lifeless things are still. [cf. CUP, WATER OF CHAOS, PSYCHIC HEALING, PSYCHIC ATTACK]

WATER BABIES—nickname for UNDINES; small happy nature spirits which play on the edge of the surf and have different qualities than land or sea fairies; (Native American) small beings in human form living in lakes, springs, and streams; have charge over small waters.

WATER FAIRIES—NATURE SPIRITS that have a fairy heart, and a body surface covered with points for suction that enables them to draw vitality from the sun; not as intelligent as land fairies; are playful, give water energy, and are in charge of the purposes of water; rhythm is important to their life, as it is designed to feel the effectiveness of the waves; not interested in humans; expressive of self-control. **Syn.** WATER SPRITE, WATER NYMPHS, NAIAD.

WATER KELPIE—nature spirit that shows itself in the form of a fish; can be harmful or beneficial.

WATER OF CHAOS—(alchemy) "perform no operation till all be made water" means that the material in the vessel of the ALCHEMIST, which parallels the spirituality of the alchemist, must be reduced to a state of watery, primeval chaos; then the "philosophical mercury" can move the waters to create either a new material in the vessel or a new condition in the alchemist. [**cf.** ALCHEMICAL LIQUOR, ELIXIR OF LIFE]

WATER POLTERGEIST—a mischievous ego-seeking entity that delights in materializing pools of water in the home. [**cf.** POLTERGEIST, FOCUS, POLTER-GEIST MISSILES]

WATER SAPPHIRE—(Vikings) a magical gem that, when held to the sky even on cloudy days, changes color if it is pointing toward the sun; when tilted on its axis—about 90 degrees—in a line between the viewer and the sun, it changes its color from light yellow to a light blue. [**cf.** STAR-RUBY, AMBER]

WATER SPRINKLING—(seance) the scattering of small drops of water or perfume on the SITTERS, walls, and furniture; an indication from the guides that they approve of the activity, or thoughts, in the SEANCE. [**cf.** WATER POLTERGEIST, ECTOPLASM MATERIALIZATION, INNER BAND, GUIDE]

WATER UNDULATION—(dowsing) abbr. WU; the reaction of the DOWSING ROD when it is over RADIATION waves from unknown underground water. [**cf.** IRRITATION ZONES, DETECTOR]

WATER WITCHER—(Ozark Mountains) a PSYCHIC capable of water DOWSING; see DOWSER.

WATER WITCHING—see DOWSING.

WATER WITHOUT CAUSE—the phenomena of water or oil dripping from the ceiling with no discernible cause; believed to be poltergeist activity. [**cf.** POLTERGEISTRY, ATOPICAL LOCALIZATION]

WATER-ELEMENT SOUND—the noise of storm-tossed ocean waves breaking on the shore; because of it natural sound, it is good to use in MEDITATION

to break up negative vibrations. [**cf.** WHITE NOISE, INNATE RESPONSE]

WATERLOPER—(Holland) see DOWSER.

WATERS OF SPACE—the whole ATMOSPHERE and its essence of all creation. **Syn.** ETHERIC WORLD, HEAVEN, COSMOS, VOID, CHAOS, TO-TALITY.

WATERWITCH—(England) see DOWSER.

WAVE FRONTS—(Czechoslovakia) see AURA.

WAVE-VIBRATION CONCEPT—theory: there is an infinite number of worlds in the atmosphere operating at different vibrational frequencies, with our world being one of them. **Syn.** EXPRESSIONS. [**cf.** FIFTH PLANE, EIGHTH SPHERE, INTERIOR LANDS]

WAVELENGTH—1. (Patrick Flanagan) "the distance between two successive points in a wave"; (esoteric) the distance between any two nodes in the ETHERIC WORLD; a measurement of DENSITY; a blend of colors; wave radiations emitting from electromagnetic energy fields, found around animate and inanimate objects; these wavelengths depend upon the objects for intensity and frequency, in accordance with the general vitality, metabolism and PSYCHOPHYSICAL tone of the object; a distance from crest to crest of a wave of RADIATION of cosmic rays; VIBRATIONS form waves as they travel and their rate of vibration is known as their FREQUENCY; electrical magnetic vibrations coming from the planets and sun; a distance between one thought ripple and another thought ripple in the sea of THOUGHT SPHERE in the etheric world, which may be as long as three miles; 2. (personal) the place of contact where the PSYCHIC or MEDIUM holds CONCENTRATED THOUGHT and is able to pick up PSYCHIC INFOR-MATION; depends upon the psychic's state of development and mood for that period. [**cf.** NODE, ZOETHER, PSITRONICS, AWARE ENERGY]

WAVES OF REINCARNATIONAL PATTERNS—similarities in cultures which repeat themselves in some sort of a CYCLE [**cf.** MASS KARMA, GROUP KARMA, DELAYED KARMA, REINCARNATION]

WAY-OF-MINDFULNESS—the goal of ZEN MEDI-TATION. [**cf.** JUST SITTING, FREE-RESPONSE SIT-TING]

WE FRIENDS—(Sufi) see WEE PEOPLE.

WE WEI—(Lao Tzu) the place of non-activity; the

supreme goal; see TOTALITY.

WEARERS OF THE RED CAP—(Tibet) see PSYCHIC.

WEATHER MAGIC—(Native American, Celtic, Druid) the ability to influence the elements of weather; to have control over rain, mist, clouds, fogs, sunsets, sunrises and to use this ability for growing crops, etc.; sometimes electrical or heat energy is applied and is effective; power behind the weather has spiritual connotations; believed to be possible because human life is closely linked with the movements of wind, rain, the earth, tides of oceans, the sun and the moon. [ATMOSPHERE CONTROL Appendix 2]

WEB—(capitalized) theory: an interlocking of the energy of every ATOM which makes energy wavelengths; the universe is a huge pattern connecting everything psychically to every other thing; all ENERGY and INTELLIGENCE is interwoven in this universal energy pattern (a pattern to supply all patterns); this intelligent interlocking energy is continually changing and continually the same; supervised by NATURE SPIRITS of the ANGEL KINGDOM. **Syn.** MICROCOSM/MACROCOSM. [**cf.** TOTALITY, VIBRATIONS]

WEB OF CAUSALITY—one huge line of network throughout all space that gathers knowledge of all civilization, both from humanity's conscious, preferred thoughts and from humanity's unconscious, unplanned thoughts; these unconscious thoughts make the information seem to be without conscious reasoning. [**cf.** SYNCHRONICITY, ACAUSAL COINCIDENCE]

WEB OF ENERGY—(Schlieren system) a variance of live, moving etheric frequencies of energy; interpenetrating and emanating from the body, forming patterns and colors which cross at the SOLAR PLEXUS. [**cf.** KIRLIAN EFFECT, CHAKRAS, SCHLIEREN SYSTEM]

WEB OF LIFE—(Rome) a myth: the fates weave the web of life; concept that the universe is a web of forces of air, as "woven and webbing"; see TOTALITY.

WEE PEOPLE—intelligent entities that constantly inhabit the earth; they live *in* the earth, in a dimension that provides means whereby they can see humans but humans cannot see them. **Syn.** NATURE SPIRITS.

WEIGHTY KARMA—(Buddhism) experiences of

past incarnations or of this INCARNATION which are of a degree that calls for immediate and influential action. [**cf.** EMOTIONAL KARMA, GROUP KARMA, HERMETIC CHAIN]

WEIRD—(Scotland) see SPELL and HAND OF GLORY.

WEIRD SISTERS—(William Shakespeare) see PSYCHIC.

WELL-GROUNDED MEDIUM—a PSYCHIC or MEDIUM who can enter into any kind of psychic feat (mental or physical), without being influenced by the lower NEGATIVE frequencies; to know how to screen out inferior ETHERIC WORLD INTELLIGENCES and invoke only superior etheric world intelligences (when PSYCHIC DOORS are opened, they are opened to both); to have complete control over one's guides so they bring psychic information or phenomenon only when invited; accomplished through training, discipline, diet, exercise, routine development sittings, aiming to lead a life of high standards, and by acquiring knowledge and understanding of the rules and philosophy relative to PSYCHISM. [**cf.** DESIREDCONTROL, LAW OF LIKE ATTRACTS LIKE Appendix 7]

WELLNESS—a degree of mental and physical HEALTH that one feels comfortable with and tries to maintain; the responbility for good health and future health rests with one's self; 1. what is good health for one is not necessarily good health for another; a STATE OF CONSCIOUSNESS wherein one can relate to one's self and feel satisfied with one's behavior and lifestyle; good health is not a measurement of one's spiritual growth; how one handles one's wealth is not a method for preventing illness; 2. to balance, resolve, and put in proper perspective the stresses of everyday experiences, without postponing these stresses for future handling, contributes to good health; 3. emphasis should be on a lifestyle that brings harmonious integration of the SOUL-MIND and the CONSCIOUS MIND to bring correct health for the body in this incarnation. [**cf.** NEW-AGE PSYCHOLOGY, CURATIVE EDUCATION, HOLISM]

WELSH TYLWYTH TEG—a very beautiful NATURE SPIRIT that wears white.

WELTSCHMERZ—(Germany) depression: basic despondency, attributed to a problem lying in the soul-mind PERSONALITY with the desire to change something that cannot be changed. [**cf.** CURATIVE

EDUCATION]

WENT OUT—designates that a person has died a physical DEATH and is now in the ETHERIC WORLD. Usage: "When this man went out, he had a leg missing." [**cf.** SURVIVALISTS, DEATH SCIENCE, MADE HIS TRANSITION]

WERE-CREATURE—(Old English, *were,* "man") "were" is half human and half creature; a human being who is capable of transforming into the shape of a creature for a period of time to perform an EVIL task which can be accomplished only in that form; while in the creature state, human being intelligence is retained; (Russia, Scandinavia) people known to change into werebears, werelions, werecrocodiles, werejackals; ability to change into a bestial form is based on the "beast within"; dual nature. [**cf.** DIMENSION-SHIFTING AND SHAPE-CHANGING Appendix 2]

WERELEOPARD(Africa) (*were,* "man") half human and half leopard who belonged to a sacred cult of leopard people; one who could transform oneself at will into a half leopard and still maintain human intelligence. [**cf.** BEOWULF, ASTRAL VAMPIRISM]

WEREWOLF—1. (Greece) a PSYCHIC who flaunts his or her ecstasies by wearing a wolf mask; 2. (Anglo-Saxon) a person temporarily or permanently transformed into a wolf, having the intelligence of a human; sometimes half human and half wolf; 3. a deceased entity in the consciousness of the DENSITY in the ETHERIC WORLD; knowledgeable in black arts, making it possible to materialize her or himself into an animal on the physical plane for a short period; an anachronism; a refuse of an earlier system. [**cf.** DYNAMIC TRANSITIONS]

WERZELYA—(Ethopia) one who uses his psychic ability for EVIL intent and brings illnesses to children, similar to the Hebrew LILITH. [**cf.** PSYCHIC TRANSFER, EMPATHY-PK, MALADAPTIVE BEHAVIOR]

WESTCAR PAPYRUS—(Egypt, 1800 B.C.) a papyrus devoted to tales of magic and enchantment; the commencement and ending are lost at present, yet enough of the subject matter has survived to enable the researchers to form a fairly accurate idea of the whole; King Cheops of the pyramid especially enjoyed having this read to him. [**cf.** MYSTICISM, I CHING, PARAPSYCHOLOGY]

WHALE—(metaphysics) a mammal personifying the great cosmic force of the universe; white whale is spirit of absolute goodness; dark whale is emblem of evil; mouth represents the gateway to the ETHERIC WORLD and belly represents the infernal regions; capable of changing size and shape. [**cf.** LYCANTHROPY, DIMENSION-SHIFTING AND SHAPE-CHANGING Appendix 2]

WHAMMY—(slang expression) casting a spell on another by staring intently, using direct eye contact, and influencing thoughts and behavior. [**cf.** SPELLED, EYES, THIRD-EYE AREA]

WHEEL BEINGS—a high order of intelligences in the etheric world, known as ANGELS, who are in charge of the chakras of the planet which parallel the chakras of a human; function is to keep the planet's chakras energized; referred to as **Galgallim** in the Bible. [**cf.** CELESTIAL HIERARCHY, LADY OF HEAVEN, CHAKRA]

WHEEL IN THE MIDDLE OF THE WHEEL—(Bible) name given by Ezekiel to a FLYING SAUCER from outer space. [**cf.** ETHERIAN COMMUNICATIONS PILOTING INTELLIGENCES]

WHEEL OF EXISTENCE—(Tibet) scriptures that tell one how to live correctly. [**cf.** BIBLE, VITAL SOUL, WHOLE SELF]

WHEEL OF FORTUNE—see WHEEL OF TIME.

WHEEL OF LIFE—(Hindusim, Buddhism, Tibet) a circle MANDALA built in three-dimensional form representing mankind's KARMA, resulting in repetitious births, deaths, and rebirths; has three hub outgrowths symbolic of ignorance, lust, and anger; has four spokes symbolic of gods, demigods, tortured souls, and human beings; circle is emblematic of immortality; theory: all people are shackled to the wheel of life and must be reborn in earth until all karma is expended. [**cf.** PERSONAL LIFE SITUATION, LIFE WAVE]

WHEEL OF THE LAW—(Buddhism) the statue of BUDDHA that has both hands on the level of the heart; the left palm is turned inward, the right palm is turned outward which represents the outer world and our world within our bodies; both are responsible for carrying out the UNIVERSAL LAW; known to the Easterners as the **Radiating One**. [**cf.** PALM UPWARD DURING MEDITATION, DIVINE BODY OF TRUTH]

WHEEL OF TIME—(India, Jainism) a wheel with twelve spokes representing the months of the year;

six are ascending and six are descending; the circle is saying that time is endless. **Syn.** WHEEL OF FORTUNE. [**cf.** CYCLES, ONE-HUNDRED YEAR CYCLE, CHAIN PERIOD]

WHIRLING DERVISHES—(Sufi, Slavic) mystics who perform a group dance that involves a moving circle and at the same time, each dervish is individually twirling and spinning; their technique keeps them from getting dizzy and the energy built up keeps the one in the center from toppling over; it is a repetitious, rhythmic, monotonous, individual movement that is done as the circle as a whole moves; sometimes sounds are used concurrently; an exercise that can cause transcending of consciousness and surfacing of answers to problems; brings both a personal and social experience; called MEDITATION-IN-MOTION; helps move one from the ego-seeking to the broader sense of the UNIVERSE; the order of MEVLEVIS. **Syn.** DERVISH. [**cf.** ZEN OF RUNNING, MOVEMENT-FOR-ALTERED CONSCIOUSNESS]

WHIRLWIND—(astral projection) a feeling of suction or being caught in a cyclone that some people experience when the ASTRAL BODY draws away from the PHYSICAL BODY. [**cf.** HORIZONTAL GLIDING, LOCOMOTION]

WHISTLING BOTTLES—(500 B.C., Peru) bottles that were used to carry water gave off an intense, high-pitched sound that could CENTER consciousness; similar to the MANTRA in MEDITATION; the sound was used to bring in SPIRIT COMMUNICATION. [**cf.** SOUND PLATE, SHOOTING CHANT, NECROMANTIC BELL]

WHITE—color that is emblematic of goodness, purity, and positiveness.

WHITE BEAM—**1.** an ENERGY FIELD that radiates seven WAVE-LENGTHS making the rainbow; enters the SOUL-MIND through the ETHERIC DOUBLE and is diffused into its seven component colors giving the chakras power; **2.** nontechnological term given to the MAGNETIC FLUID that exudes from the hands and minds of psychic healers and mediums; can be perceived clairvoyantly, differing in density and shape; flows from the NERVE FLUID of the psychic. [**cf.** GOLDEN BEAMS, GOLD, BLACK]

WHITE BLEEDING—see TEARS.

WHITE BROTHERHOOD—(capitalized) one of a number of select groups whose members are dedicated to the advancement of human evolution and fulfillment of cosmic plans; composed of incarnate and discarnate individuals who function on the INNER-PLANES: masters that once roamed the earth and are still interested in the earth; white does not mean the color of the skin, but the state of EVOLUTION (free from spot or blemish and without evil intent); borrowed from the Anglo-Saxon word *whit* meaning "to know." [**cf.** BROTHERS OF LIGHT, GROUP SOUL, GREAT WHITE BROTHERHOOD]

WHITE COLOR—the perfect blending of all the seven colors of the spectrum making white *pure* color; the combination of RED, ORANGE, YELLOW, GREEN, BLUE, INDIGO, VIOLET; the positive aspect represents good, light, purity, peace, modesty, innocence, gaiety, and happiness; negative aspect represents weakness, delicacy, infirmity, cowardice. [**cf.** LIGHT, GREAT WHITE LIGHT]

WHITE DIAMOND—a mineral that symbolizes the absolute and pure energy because of its essence of brilliance. [**cf.** DIAMOND, TOPAZ, MOONSTONE]

WHITE DWARF—a small star that lacks the gravitational impact to jam its electrons close together, which ends as a tremendously dense, hot cinder named white dwarf.

WHITE HOLES—(esoteric) sites where fountains of material and energy pour into the UNIVERSE from holes in space; opposite of BLACK HOLES. **Syn.** COSMIC GUSHERS. [**cf.** TIME]

WHITE LIGHT—(esoteric) the one ENERGY that contains the energies of all elements and chemicals found in the sun; the basis for all color, being *pure* in its essence; emanations from the SPIRITUAL SUN; represents TOTALITY, the ABSOLUTE; the TRINITY; white is *pure* love, perfect love is pure and perfect love is all, therefore the white light is ALL; all is white light and as it extends into the UNIVERSE, it is broken up or refracted and one perceives it as color; everything is an extension of the white light; light represents INTELLIGENCE; see TOTALITY. [**cf.** COLOROLOGY, WHITE, BLACK]

WHITE MAGIC—an art and discipline that relies on the technology of ceremonies and ritual to achieve psychic results; *white* meaning superior and with good intent; **1.** discipline objective: to unite the MICROCOSM to the MACROCOSM in the overall SOUL-MIND evolution; theory: if a person is a microcosm, his or her thoughts must have a parallel reality with the universe outside; **2.** art technology: (a) MAGICIAN makes an impression with his or her mind in the ASTRAL LIGHT, creating a reality in the astral world; this, in turn, projects the thought impression into the physical world; (b) accomplished through PRAYER, magical incantations, herbal medicine, breath and SUGGESTION; uses amulets for healing and protecting; (c) natural laws which make this possible: gravity, electricity, magnetism, chemistry, LAW OF SIGNATURES and LAW OF THOUGHT Appendix 7, laws of nature, and the system of correspondence (AS ABOVE, SO BELOW, AS BELOW, SO ABOVE); 3. two levels of white magic: LOW MAGIC and HIGH MAGIC; (do not confuse with BLACK MAGIC which is used for evil intent). [**cf.** CEREMONIAL MAGIC Appendix 2, ASSOCIATION MAGIC]

WHITE MAGICIAN—PSYCHIC, HEALER, psychiatrist, or PRACTITIONER in the field of MAGIC; understands nature and believes that its forces can be controlled to serve humanity; through tradition of his or her ancestors (who were in the religious priesthood) the magician has learned to invoke ANGELS, GODS, or NATURE SPIRITS to supply the power needed for his or her operations; capable of making an ELEMENTAL; can locate black witches and hinder their practice; can effect changes in the mental state of sick persons to relieve suffering or reduce illness to manageable proportions; works with ceremonies and rituals. [**cf.** MEDIUM, RITUAL]

WHITE MAN—(Native American, Cheyenne) a GOD or ETHERIC WORLD INTELLIGENCE in a temporary animal form that appears in various guises when making contact with the Indian, capable of bringing PSYCHIC INFORMATION. **Syn.** SPIDER, WIHIO, TRICKSTER.

WHITE NOISE—an unfiltered broadband noise; sound in which all frequencies have equal loudness; the frequency spectrum is a random noise source that has a constant energy per CYCLE; a sound potency that never ends; a low-level sound similar to mild static without any irregularities. [**cf.** PINK NOISE, WHITE NOISE STIMULI]

WHITE NOISE STIMULI—1. a sound that becomes so absorbing that it can deaden pain, cut one off from REALITY, and alter one's STATE OF CONSCIOUSNESS; a sound serving as the object of MEDITATION, either as an internally generated sound that is imagined, or a natural sound; sound should not have any irregularities that might distract the attention of the listener; 2. an environmental low-

key hum or noise that is not detectable to the physical ear but reacts on the etheric bodies; 3. sound that is of constant duration and can be physically suppressed; e.g., an air conditioner hum or sound of rhythmic waves of the surf become unnoticeable when one is in their presence for very long; sitting near a waterfall, wind source, or a beehive and simply listening to the monotonous repetition is beneficial for a WHITE NOISE effect. [**cf.** MEDITATION, COSMIC MUSIC, MANTRA]

WHITE RELIGIOUS RITES—(Tibet) the opposite of black rites or BLACK MAGIC.

WHITE SERPENT—symbolic of the descending path of INVOLUTION of the SOUL-MIND as it came down to earth from the MONADIC PLANE. [**cf.** LAW OF INVOLUTION Appendix 7, EVOLUTION]

WHITE SHAMAN—(Siberia, Buriat, Yakut) a PSYCHIC and HEALER who communicates with the gods in the ETHERIC WORLD, enlisting their support in helping fellow tribesmen; wears special costumes to be recognized by tribal members. [**cf.** SHAMANISM, HAND-TREMBLER]

WHITE SHELL CREATURES—(Buddhism) represent the positive of POLARITY, the LINGAM. [**cf.** YIN AND YANG]

WHITE STONE—1. the seed or soul found in all objects, inorganic and organic; the intelligence or potential of each thing which tells it to express itself as that thing. **Syn.** MONAD. 2. (alchemy) (a) an instrument that would turn all things to silver; (b) an important ingredient needed for the formula for which all alchemists strive. [**cf.** PHILOSOPHER'S STONE, MONADOLOGY]

WHITE WIZARD—(Europe, England) a semi-divine authority; believed to possess inherent power; one who practices MAGIC in order to receive guidance and knowledge. [**cf.** GENIUS, WIZARD]

WHOLE SELF—(Seth) composed of many incarnated entites, belonging to one unified entity, that function as individuals under the direction of the INNER-EGO; seem to be striving to understand their simultaneous selves. **Syn.** SOUL-MIND, SOUL. [**cf.** INCARNATION, WHEEL OF KARMA, SOUL-MIND]

WHOLISM—see HOLISM.

WHORLEY—(Scotland) a NATURE SPIRIT who lurks about ruined or deserted castles or haunts the silent cobblestone streets of towns. **Syn.** AIR WRAITH.

WICCA—(Anglo-Saxon *wicca*, "wise one") current name for WITCHCRAFT; a religion that uses simple ceremonies to achieve communion with the natural forces around mother nature; ceremonies and rituals handed down from ancestors; tools and activity are personified by a female; (do not confuse with a MAGICIAN who uses more complicated laws of nature and is associated with male vibrations; has nothing to do with satanists or DEVIL worshippers.); four groupings of Wicca: 1. Celtic; 2. Guardian; 3. Traditional; 4. Alexandrian Form; also speclled **Wica**. [**cf.** WITCHCRAFT, PSYCHIC, HEALERS]

WICCE—(Old English) the feminine form of one working in WICCA.

WICHELROEDE—(Holland) see DOWSING.

WICHTLEIN—(Southern Germany) a NATURE SPIRIT in the mines.

WIDDERSHINS—moving in a direction contrary to the sun's course, to the left, or counterclockwise; deliberate movements of the PSYCHIC or the psychic's tools in this direction when working with the EVIL or negative forces because it reverses the normal and proper order of things; believed to repudiate God's rule so this movement is used in evil ceremonies. **Syn.** WITHERSHINS. [**cf.** DEOSIL MOVEMENT, PSYCHIC ATTACK, HEX]

WIDE-BAND TUNING—to receive PSYCHIC INFORMATION from a larger range than one is aiming for; e.g., in DOWSING, the dowser locates long forgotten sewer pipes while concentrating on water for a well; the receiver in a telepathic experiment picks up colors on the person who is in the next room instead of the TARGET. [**cf.** NARROW-BAND TUNING, TUNING OF THE MIND]

WIHIO—(Native American, Cheyenne) an ETHERIC WORLD INTELLIGENCE in temporary animal form appearing in various guises when making contact with the Indian, bringing PSYCHIC INFORMATION, counsel or protection. **Syn.** WHITE MAN, SPIDER. [**cf.** TRICKSTER]

WILD HUNT—(Celtic, Britain) an event based on a belief that the soul of the dead is snatched away through the clouds. [**cf.** GWYN-AP-NUDD, FREEING THE SOUL, SHIP BURIAL]

WILD WOMAN—(Slavic) see VAMPIRE.

WILD-MAN MONSTER—(Russia) a shaggy-haired, shrill-voiced wild man who frightened people in Moscow but was never caught. **Sim.** ABOMINABLE SNOWMAN. [**cf.** MONSTER ACTIVITY, DIMENSION-SHIFTING]

WILL—1. (Taoism) the HEART, both mind and emotions; 2. (esoteric) the governing principle that activates the atoms into manifestations of all degrees in the UNIVERSE; the essential attribute of the MIND, acts as a lever on elementary MATTER, and by consecutive action reacts on its compounds, whose intimate properties can thus be transformed; (Unity) "the center in mind and body around which revolve all the activites that constitute CONSCIOUS-NESS; it is the avenue through which the I AM expresses its potentiality"; 3. (science) the substance behind a person's ability to control a single cell; 4. (psychic skills) *will* is the basis of all MENTAL and PHYSICAL PSYCHISM; *will of approval* makes the action occur; although some psychic feats appear to come at random or some seem to be instigated from another party, the SUBCONSCIOUS MIND cannot make a decision on its own, so it is *willed* consciously, subconsciously, or karmically in order for it to surface; (**a**) no superior ETHERIC WORLD INTELLIGENCE will use his or her will to work for a medium for it would cause that intelligence to be dismissed from that function; (**b**) an inferior etheric world entity will come through on its own if the psychic generalizes a *will* to be open to psychic feats at any time; (**c**) in a SPELL and ON-THE-SPOT-HYPNOSIS, the *will* comes from ignorance of the laws of PARAPSYCHOLOGY; one listens because of a desire or *will* to better oneself when one is unfamiliar with the techniques being used; the will to better oneself serves as an Achilles' heel. [**cf.** FREE WILL, THOUGHT, MATTER]

WILL OF THE CLAN—(Native American) the member of the tribe who is chosen by an ancestor from the ETHERIC WORLD to become the psychic counselor and MEDICINE MAN for the tribe; ancestor guides the chosen member through an initiation of agonizing sickness and the death process which enables the initiate to earn authority and perpetual guidance from the ETHERIC WORLD INTELLIGENCES; by enduring the physical and mental anguishes of these experiences, this individual learns much about psychic skills, healing, and the purpose of life. [**cf.** HERMIT'S CELL, INITIATORY DEATH, SHAMAN, INITIATORY SICKNESS]

WILL-O'-THE-WISP—1. (Britain) a curious light resembling a flame, sometimes seen flickering in the distance; a flitting phosphorescent light seen at night. **Syn.** IGNIS FATUUS. 2. a frivolous and mischievous NATURE SPIRIT attached to a family home, who delights in doing something with objects in the home to annoy an earthling; 3. (Russia) the soul of an unbaptized child; 4. (Germany) a wandering SOUL-MIND seeking help; 5. a white cloudy mist found hovering over grave-yards or marshy grounds, felt to be an ASTRAL SHELL; 6. (folk tales) an etheric world entity who leads night travelers astray; 7. any mysterious activity that deludes or misleads by luring. **Syn.** FOOLISH FIRE, FRIARI'S LANTERN, FAIRY-FIRE, JACK-O-LANTERN.

WILLED THOUGHT—any impulse that causes one to think; an impulse to action that one sends forth from "within" the mind mechanism; an awareness of consciously and deliberately surfacing silent or audible words in the BRAIN/MIND activity; originates from within the mind (one cannot interpret thought without using words); (do not confuse with VISUALIZATION).

WILLIAM WITH THE LITTLE FLAME—see IGNIS FATUUS.

WILLOW TREE—(China) a tree that has the qualities and properties of PSYCHISM, capable of averting harm and illnesses; to some it symbolizes death or mourning, as the "weeping willow"; began the cliche to "knock on wood" or "call upon the willow"; has been known to cure rheumatism that is caused by dampness (one psychically gives the disease to the willow which absorbs it in the bark); the acid from the willow is now used in hospitals, for rheumatism. [**cf.** BOTANE Appendix 2]

WILLOW-WAND—makes an excellent DOWSING ROD as it is a symbol of the WILL; has properties to supply one with the energy to work until the task is finished. [**cf.** DIVINING STICK, TAMARASK ROD, ELECTRIC FIELDS]

WIND MAGIC—1. (Europe, Celtic) to understand the principles of wind and be able to stop it; by tying wind energy with rope, and pulling the knots tight the energy can be used; ability to calm ships; if used for EVIL intent, it brings illness; 2. (Greece) ability to harness wind and use it when needed; the wind is tied up in a bag (called a wind bag) and used like a bellows of bagpipes; this will induce the real winds to follow the example of air being expelled. [**cf.** SYMPATHETIC MAGIC] 3. (Native American) to understand the natural process of wind and move large amounts around; the air molecules are moved around to evoke the winds; theory: an energy flows through the wind that gives humans protection and guidance, and acts as a guardian angel, so wind is under the influence of humanity's will. [**cf.** ATMOSPHERE CONTROL Appendix 2]

WIND PEOPLE—(Native American, Navaho) the ETHERIC WORLD INTELLIGENCES that intercede for the holy people, to relate PSYCHIC INFORMATION and guidance. **Syn.** GUIDES, CELESTIAL. [**cf.** CHANGING WOMAN]

WINDING ROAD—symbolic of the spinal column; see KUNDALINI.

WINDING STAIRWAY—a symbol used to represent the spinal column; see KUNDALINI.

WINDOW AREA—(ufology) a portal from one dimension to another dimension; a section of earth that can open up similar to the BERMUDA TRIANGLE; a geographical location where UFO SIGHTINGS have occurred repeatedly for many years; situated on or near known magnetic vaults; paraphysical objects become temporarily visible when travelling over such areas. [**cf.** UNKNOWN FORCES, GUARDIANS]

WINDOW ON THE UNKNOWN—name given to the photographs taken by high voltage photography. [**cf.** KIRLIAN EFFECT Appendix 5]

WINDOWGLASS CROSSES—light colored crosses, not created by physical means, seen in the panes of church windows; not attributed to reflections of light; do not disappear as time goes by; documentation exists that it happened in epidemic proportions in one area in a single year. [**cf.** PRECIPITATION, LANDSCAPE PAINTINGS]

WINDOWS OF THE SOUL—the various methods of acquiring PSYCHIC INFORMATION. [**cf.** PSYCHIC CONSCIOUSNESS]

WINGS—two appendages designed for flying, attached to the back or shoulders of an ETHERIC WORLD ENTITY when painted or drawn; 1. (folklore) both angels and devils have the power of flight; because artists have depicted angels with wings, does not necessarily mean they have wings; wings are symbolic of ability to move in the atmosphere; 2. clairvoyant theory: when one concentrates intently on beautiful thoughts, one builds an energy field of gossamer substance; if concentration is maintained, an intelligence may be seen in the center; this appears as though the gossamer substance belongs to the face and it looks like wings. [**cf.** GRAVITATIONAL WAVES, SIXTH PLANE, THOUGHT-FORM]

WINKS OUT—expression given to a star that implodes and pulls all the atoms into a dense center; the star disappears and the BLACK HOLE is born in its place.

WIRELESS WAVES—(Albert Abrams, 1914) see AURA.

WIRKENDE KRAFT—a vital energy, innate to all the archetypes, which corresponds to the great COSMOS; see MONAD.

WISDOM—1. strength; there is a strength that comes from knowing; 2. the application of KNOWLEDGE; AWARENESS happens first; practice of awareness turns it into knowledge; the correct and timely use of knowledge turns it into wisdom for that person; this wisdom is then impinged upon the SOUL-MIND permanently; e.g., if it is a proper application of a personality trait, one will have that personality trait in every INCARNATION from that time on; whatever the situation was that was handled correctly will not occur again as it is now wisdom and does not have to be reexperienced; wisdom is the correct expression of the potential within the human seed, and once learned, will not have to be handled again; (don Juan) "a man of knowledge is one who has followed truthfully the hardships of learning; who has without rushing or without faltering gone as far as he can in unraveling the secrets of personal power." [**cf.** INTELLIGENCE]

WISDOM MIND—the most humanity can comprehend of PERFECTNESS at this time; emerges into the MONAD; capable of permeating the MENTAL AURA with SUPREME BLISS. **Syn.** ADI-BUDHA.

WISDOM OF EQUALITY—(Yoga) sensed during MEDITATION when one no longer feels like the observer but becomes compassionate with all living things; considered the second movement in meditation. [**cf.** INWARD ART, INNER SOUND CURRENT]

WISDOM OF THE GREAT MIRROR—sensed in the first movement in MEDITATION, when one can see form that is isolated from materiality, similar to a reflection. [**cf.** WISDOM OF EQUALITY]

WISE LORD—see TOTALITY.

WISE MAN—(Native American) the PSYCHIC whose function is to ask the TOTEM for answers for guidance, counsel, and protection for the tribe. [**cf.** AMULET, TALISMAN]

WISE PASSIVENESS—the ability to free the CONSCIOUS MIND from preoccupation and allow the higher knowledge to enter. **Syn.** INSPIRATIONAL THOUGHT. [**cf.** CLAIRSENTIENCE, INSPIRATIONAL WRITING]

WISE SPIRITS—see ETHERIC WORLD INTELLIGENCES.

WISE WOMAN—1. (Mexico, Native American, Otomi) a PSYCHIC of the village who specializes in applied psychology, prayer meetings, and PSYCHISM; 2. (Rome. Italy) a psychic who specializes in EXORCISM and prophetic messages; 3. a psychic who uses incantations and potions to assist in births and in healing of the sick. **Syn.** CURANDERAS, SYBYL, WHITE WITCH. [**cf.** OWL, ENCHANTRESS, PRAYER PETITIONS]

WISECRAFT—see WITCHCRAFT.

WISHING ROD—a tool made of split hazel rods; see DOWSING RODS.

WISHING WELL—a place where psychic properties of water and rules of thought and emotion are used to promote the manifestation of a desire; desire is written on a note or verbalized when the coin is thrown into the water; note or coin serves as a POINT-OF-FOCUS and an outward psychological movement for the desire; another theory: in the bottom of the well live powerful spirits that will make one's wish come true. [**cf.** THOUGHT-FORMS, NYMPHS, UNDINES]

WITCH—(Old English "wise person") 1. a seeker of knowledge; uses traditions, knowledge, psychic skills, and rituals; dates back to the MAGI; one who is well versed in ASTROLOGY, astronomy, mind/-brain psychology, anatomy, PSYCHOMETRY, psychic sciences, AMULET ENERGIZING, POWER-OF-THE-WORD, and the laws of the etheric world; 2. one who uses magic phenomena in one's religion; shows repsect for the etheric world DEITY who brings SUPERNATURAL power, and is capable of projecting psychical energy on another individual's SUBCONSCIOUS MIND in order to manipulate the other; 3. (Philip Emmons Isaac Bonewitz) (*Wicca,* "bending or twisting"; *wych hazel* [witch hazel] "hazeel with the bent branches") this went from *wicca* to *wicce* to *wycche* and to modern English to *witch*; one who can bend others to his or her will; not used as a religion; 4. one who uses ceremonies

685

and rituals in psychic work; hires her or himself out professionally for his or her psychic skills (both GOOD and EVIL); one who can give a BLESSING or a HEALING with success and work the PSYCHISM for the opposite and inflict a HEX; female is **wicce** and male is **warlock**. [**cf.** SINGER, ENCHANTER, SORCERER, DRUGGER]

WITCH BALLS—glass balls hung in the home in the belief they were able to protect one from EVIL. [**cf.** MINPSI Appendix 2, CRYSTAL]

WITCH BOTTLE—a glass bottle containing blood, hair, nail parings and urine of a person being hexed for use in exorcising that person out of the HEX; the bottle is heated on a fire, at midnight, the Lord's prayer is intoned backwards until the contents of the bottle are afire; when this occurs, the person is freed from the hex. [**cf.** BANISHING, PROVOKING]

WITCH COVEN—the place where healers meet to practice PSYCHIC HEALING; so-called by those who do not approve of unorthodox methods. [**cf.** CURATIVE EDUCATION, PSYCHIC HEALING]

WITCH FINDER—see DOWSER.

WITCH MASTER—see SHAMAN.

WITCH OF ENDOR—the psychic who worked for Saul, bringing him PROPHECY and guidance.

WITCH WIGGLER—see PENDULUMIST.

WITCH'S MILL—(England, Middle Ages) the building where the witches went to practice their ancient art of making potions from herbs to heal the sick. [**cf.** WITCHCRAFT, WITCH-DOCTOR, HEALER]

WITCH'S OIL—theory: the WITCH used a special ointment to rub on the skin that would put him or her in a state of TRANCE before mounting a broomstick and flying off. [**cf.** STRIX, TRANSVECTION, BRUXA]

WITCH'S TALENT—see PSYCHIC SENSE and PSYCHIC ENERGY.

WITCH-BIRD—(*witch* comes from *wicca*, "wise one"; so "wise-bird") the SOUL-MIND of humans personified by a bird because the soul is not attached to the human brain and can fly around or leave the body in an ASTRAL PROJECTION. [**cf.** SOUL-MIND]

WITCH-DOCTOR—(Central Africa, Congo, Bushman) a PRACTITIONER skilled in magical arts and OCCULTISM; a highly respected member of the tribe; in some instances, it takes years of apprenticeship and sometimes it is a process of going through initiations of hardship and suffering; in primitive tribes, their attire is very elaborate and gay, with gaudy red and white clay on the face, and a bag of totems and healing objects dangling from the waist; some also use the basket of skins, bones, nerve fibers, herbs, etc.; their talents vary but most of them are shrewd psychologists, herbalists, philosophers, prophets, rainmakers, priests, and controllers of weather; many are women; work with the laws of nature, ceremonies and rituals; capable of going into TRANCE and working with the ETHERIC WORLD INTELLIGENCES. [**cf.** MEDICINE MAN, CEREMONIES, LAW OF ASSOCIATION Appendix 7]

WITCH-HAT—a conically structured headgear worn by the witch in belief that there is power in shapes, and that when worn, this hat will open one's brain to higher intelligences. [**cf.** CONICAL SHAPE, FORMS-WITH-POWER, PYRAMID POWER]

WITCH-HUNTER—see DOWSER.

WITCHCRAFT—(Anglo-Saxon *wicca*, "the wise one") a craft of the wise; a religion paying homage to the one GOD; belief that man has fallen from the GODHEAD and will return to the Godhead by working to perfect himself; interested in what happens within themselves rather than what happens to their environment and lifestyle; a revival of the magicians of the ancient past who had to disband during the Renaissance, while a few worked underground to save the knowledge; belief in the superiority of the mother goddess, who represents nature; emphasizes harmony with nature and tries to appeal to this harmony; uses ceremonies, rituals, and amulets; belief in life after physical death and calls upon these intelligences along with the nature spirits for guidance, counsel, and protection; three distinct divisions: CLASSICAL WITCHES, GOTHIC WITCHES and NEOPAGAN WITCHES. [**cf.** WHITE MAGIC, ASSOCIATION MAGIC, CEREMONIAL MAGIC]

WITCHCULT—see WITCHCRAFT.

WITCHHOOD—divided into three groups: GOTHIC WITCHES, NEOPAGAN WITCHES, and CLASSICAL WITCHES.

WITCHMAN—see SHAMAN.

WITCHWIFE—(Scotland, Ireland and Northern England) see PSYCHIC.

WITCRAFT—see WITCHCRAFT.

WITHDRAWAL—to center one's concentration to a small point without letting outside stimuli interfere. **Syn.** MEDITATION, GOING INTO THE SILENCE.

WINTERSHINS—see WIDDERSHINS.

WITHIN-NESS—a feeling that Totality, ALL-THERE-IS, resides within one's own being, and that this encompasses all dimensions of SPACE and TIME. [**cf.** SELFLESS UNIVERSAL LOVE, DIVINE CONSCIOUSNESS]

WITHINNESS—the center of one's being, where one talks to the etheric forces and knows that the answers are not one's own, but are truthful answers. [**cf.** GOING-TO-LEVEL, WAVELENGTH]

WITNESS—1. (penduluming) an article belonging to the person in question but who is absent; in the process of RADIESTHETIC SENSE, the left hand of the PSYCHIC is placed on the witness and the right hand holds the PENDULUM; e.g., the witness could be the dog's food dish when trying to locate the dog. [**cf.** LAW OF CONTAGION Appendix 7, TELE-DIAGNOSIS] 2. (electronic voices) the witness is the one who receives the telephone call from the deceased person and talks, not realizing that on the other end of the wire is one who has died. (Inconcl.) [**cf.** PHONE CALLS FROM THE DEAD] 3. (Bible) outer manifestations; e.g., the faithful and true witness—the beginning of the creation of God; 4. (mystical tradition) the mind behind the scenes; the part that watches the watcher, identifying with a wider dimension than a person's usual fragmented CONSCIOUSNESS; this level is consciousness of a higher dimension. **Syn.** SUPERCONSCIOUS MIND.

WITNESS EFFECT—(psi tasks) an effect resulting in a change in psi scoring level, sometimes occurring when a stranger is brought into an experiment session in the role of an observer. [**cf.** CHANCE LEVEL, PSI-CONDUCIVE STATE, CHANCE, EXPECTATION]

WITNESS MEDITATION—to merely witness the flow of thoughts without getting involved in any of the ideas; to exert no control over them but just watch the thoughts as if they belonged to somebody else. **Syn.** TELEVISION MEDITATION. [**cf.** RELAXATION RESPONSE, WATCH YOUR BREATH, QUIET ATTENTIVENESS]

WITNESSING—1. (Charismatic sects) the act of giving personal testimony of a personal experience of an encounter believed to be with the HOLY SPIRIT, in hopes of winning new converts to the movement; 2. (destructive-brainwashing cults) the endless hours spent daily by the members to recruit new members, by using special geared ploy and hypnotic techniques. [**cf.** ON-THE-SPOT-HYPNOSIS, LOVE-BOMBING]

WIZARD—(Anglo-Saxon) one who performs WIZ-ARDRY (includes both genders); a PSYCHIC who is born with natural powers, or is self-taught with the help of friends and relatives; a practitioner of magic who adheres to pagan traditions and usually acts alone; sometimes considered to be a semi-divine authority. [**cf.** PSYCHIC, PRACTITIONER, HEALER]

WIZARD'S ROD—see DOWSING ROD.

WIZARDRY—(Anglo-Saxon *wys* comes from the root word *wisdom* or *wise*; *ard* is the suffix for agent) a discipline between the ranks of witches and magicians; usually natural-born or trained by family or friends; rarely scholastically inclined as is the MAGICIAN; characteristic of medicine men and shamans; many of their psychic feats do not differentiate between natural and supernatural forces; a continuation of the old methods of MAGIC and HEALING. [**cf.** WITCHCRAFT, WIZARD]

WODAN—(Germany) an ETHERIC WORLD INTELLIGENCE who has charge of individuals making their TRANSITION; able to communicate with earthlings and finds it easier to do so on stormy nights. [**cf.** WODE, ASTRAL BODY]

WODE—(Germany) superior ETHERIC WORLD INTELLIGENCE; leader of the wodans. **Sim.** MASTER.

WOLF—(Rome) a fruitful source of AUGURY used for both GOOD and EVIL. [**cf.** WEREWOLF, ANPSI]

WONDERFUL COUNSELOR—(Isaiah) the SUPERCONSCIOUS MIND. [**cf.** INSPIRATIONAL THOUGHT]

WONG—(Gold Coast, Africa) see VITAL LIFE FORCE.

WOOD— a material which is very amenable to PSYCHIC FORCE; ETHERIC WORLD INTELLIGENCES work nicely with wood articles, e.g., wooden table for table tipping and knocks; wood is easily impregnated by vibrations, making wooden articles easy to psychometrize; wooden forked sticks work best for DOWSING; wooded area of live trees is very conducive to MEDITATION and tuning into the ETHERIC WORLD, FAIRIES most easily contacted are the tree fairies. [cf. MEN OF THE OAK TREE, DOWS-ING ROD]

WOOD GHOST—(South America) a NATURE SPIRIT that lures people to death in the wildwood.

WOOD NATURE SPIRITS—names given to these nature spirits by various cultures: JINNI, SATYR, CENTAUR, CYCLOPS, PAN, DRYADS, FAUN, FEMALE HAMADRYADS, WOOD GHOST.

WOODLAND DEITY—a highly intelligent, dynamic life force that designs the etheric blueprints for all woodlands.

WOODWOUSE—a NATURE SPIRIT living comfortably in the woods; similar to people but uncivilized, acting like a madman at times; known to play a harp and help people with literary writings; also spelled **woodwose, woodhouse.**

WOOL GATHERING—slang for DAYDREAMING. [cf. IMAGERY]

WORD—(capitalized) see GOD or TOTALITY.

WORD ASSOCIATION TEST—(Carl Jung) a method in which a series of disconnected words are given by the therapist to the subject, one by one; the subject speaks out the first word that comes to mind after each test word is given by the therapist; a system used to interpret the dream symbol or psychic information symbol and to surface repressed thoughts during PSYCHOANALYSIS sessions. [cf. COMPENSATORY DREAMS, SYMBOLS]

WORDLESS-SIGNLESS COMMUNICATION—1. the ability of both animals and humans to read auras and tell the emotional feelings of other humans or animals; 2. (Russia) the ability of an animal to telepathically pick up ideas of people. [cf. MENTAL TELEPATHY, AURIC READING, CLAIRVOYANCE]

WORDS—(esoteric) tools or vehicles that bring ideas into manifestation; a way of expressing thought; words spoken or thought put the human being in touch with psychic skills; the DNA factors of the atoms make THOUGHT-FORMS, putting one in tune with TOTALITY; words co-created the world and all that is on it; each word has an emotional vibratory rate that gives it a degree of co-creative effect. [cf. LAW OF THOUGHT Appendix 7, MATTER, CO-CREATOR]

WORDS OF INSULATION—positive and high qualitative thoughts spoken aloud, or spoken in one's INNER-DIALOGUE; a continuous stream of thoughts of this nature surround one with a wall of electrical energy that will protect one from negative events and people; e.g., to see only the good quality in others, to look at things and nature and silently declare its positive beauty and value; opposite of **grumbling and complaining.** [cf. CLOAK OF INSULATION, PSYCHIC TRANSFER, AURA OF RESPONSIBILITY, THOUGHT-FORMS]

WORDS-WITH-POWER—1. principle: certain words are able to change and influence the inner and outer reality of those saying them and those hearing them; the influence lies in the sound of the words themselves; this sound is formed with *intent* and the same intent will have the same effect on the body and outward affairs, regardless of the word meaning; words that carry an accelerated degree of emotion will step-up the mind's vibratory rate and the energy emanated from it, whether said verbally or silently; each word has its distinct vibratory rate and function; (Seth) "there is an inner-sound with suggestion, even when quietly thought about—sounds of thoughts in one's head have a greater power than exterior ones and act upon the body by affecting the atoms and molecules that compose the cells, bones, flesh, etc."; 2. law: words must be used to name things; to name something is to structure CONSCIOUSNESS; naming and wording awakens new perspectives; 3. words are used to co-create; words cannot be spoken without a thought behind them, and the thought is the CO-CREATOR of manifestation; each word carries an emotional vibratory rate with it, and when spoken, read, or placed on paper gives a degree of a co-creative effect from the emotional vibratory rate; 4. language releases the unknown from limbo, expressing it in a way that the whole brain can know it and yet language expresses in a way that the whole brain cannot express; 5. to plan words for psychic feats will enhance the activity, manipulate the skill, or will use the energy in the words themselves, to bring about the desired PSYCHISM; words or thoughts spoken, read, or silently gathered in the mind with clear realization, with intense centralized concentration, and with emotion, have a materializing value and are used in HEALING, MATERIALIZATION, PHYSICAL and MENTAL PSYCHISM; 6. loud or silent repetition of inspiring words has been found effective in HYPNOSIS, AFFIRMATIONS, systems of PSYCHOTHERAPY, religious rituals, CEREMONIAL MAGIC and in the DESTRUCTIVE-BRAINWASHING CULTS. [cf. LAW OF SIGNATURES and LAW OF THOUGHT Appendix 7,

MATTER, ATOMS, CLOAK OF INSULATION]

WORK OF THE CHARIOT—(Jewish *ma'aseh mer kabah*, "a mystical discipline") the chosen adept must learn to go through the perils and dangers of the DENSITY and the ASTRAL PLANE; the adept spirals upward until he or she reaches the CHARIOT, which represents the highest planes in the etheric world. [**cf.** THRONE MYSTICISM, PERILS OF THE SOUL]

WORK WITH US—instructions given the receiver of a psychic READING; to speak up if one can relate to the message and symbol; gives the psychic a nudge to continue in that subject. [**cf.** MENTAL PSYCHIC PROCESSES Appendix 2]

WORKING MEDITATION—to use the concept of NOWNESS; one tries to become aware of the present moment, here and now, through CONCENTRATION on each breath as a complete single expression. [**cf.** AVATAR MEDITATION, CHECKING, BREATHING]

WORKSHOP—a group of students, interested in new findings, who gather together to put this new information into practice by participating in its activity, and thereby are checking its practicality.

WORLD—see MUNDANE WORLD and MATTER.

WORLD BRAIN—see TOTALITY.

WORLD MOTHER—1. pertains to NATURE; 2. pertains to the KUNDALINI power because it is the feminine aspect of EVOLUTION. [**cf.** SERPENT POWER]

WORLD OF EIDOS—(F.W.H. Myers) the fourth sphere, a level of consciousness that is full of color. [**cf.** COLOROLOGY Appendix 2]

WORLD OF MEDITATION—a term used by some sects in reference to PSYCHIC INFORMATION and the ETHERIC WORLD; see Appendix 4 for clarification of MEDITATION and PSYCHIC DEVELOPMENT.

WORLD OF SPIRIT—(Spiritualism, Tibet) a popular expression that means (there is) life in the invisible world; pertains to PSYCHIC ENERGY that conmes from the ETHERIC WORLD INTELLIGENCES. Usage: "I bring you this message from the world of spirit." [**cf.** GUIDES, ETHERIC COMMUNICATION]

WORLD OF THOUGHT—see MENTAL PLANE.

WORLD SOUL—(Cornelius Agrippa, 1510) everything in the UNIVERSE has a SOUL, an ethereal component that is a part of the World Soul; found in metals, stones, animals, plants, weather, and humans; there is only one intelligence, World Soul, and all is a segment of the one; see TOTALITY.

WORLDS—hundreds of dimensions in the invisible atmosphere vibrating at their own frequencies and having their own properties and functions; three major groupings: 1. ETHERIC WORLD: 2. PHYSICAL WORLD; 3. UNDERWORLD (density).

WOVOKA—(Native American, Paiute, circa 1858-1932) PROPHET and founder of the messianic GHOST DANCE religion circa 1870; claimed a VISION during a solar eclipse on New Year's Day 1889 that prophesied the disappearance of whites from the earth and the return of Indian health and prosperity; to accomplish this the Indians were asked to follow his pacifist doctrine and to practice the sacred ghost dance; his stature grew from prophet to Indian messiah among most western tribes; however, his religion took on warlike aspects never intended by him (the allegedly bulletproof ghost shirts his followers wore played a tragic part in massacre of the Sioux at Wounded Knee); his prophecy failed to materialize, the ghost dance religion faded, and his Indian converts were forced onto reservations. [**cf.** MASTER, AVATAR, WALK-IN]

WRAITH—an APPARITION perceived clairvoyantly: 1. the SOUL-MIND splitting when it is in danger and showing itself to a loved one as an OMEN of this trauma; 2. a DIVINE INTERVENTION shown as a VISION, fashioned by the angels, Mary, or God. [**cf.** WRAITHFUL ORDER OF THE DEITIES]

WRAITHFUL ORDER OF THE DEITIES—(Tibet) has one etheric world intelligence typifying each aspect of mankind's mental activity: reason, memory, imagination, and logic; see ETHERIC WORLD INTELLIGENCES.

WRITING IN TONGUES—words written by an invisible source at the same time they are spoken, without the use of the medium's hand; the pen and paper moving separately from the medium; usually comes in another language; it appears as if the sound of the voice is writing the words. [**cf.** PRECIPITATION]

WRITING OF HEAVEN—(Mesopotamia) term used in the beginning of ASTROLOGY; movement of the planets in relation to the constellations of the fixed stars, in which the will of the gods signifies the future for the person or state.

WU CHI—(China) the formless; the creator of

689

movement and quietude; see TOTALITY.

WUDEWASA—(Anglo-Saxon) a giant NATURE SPIRIT which leaves evidence of its life; see MONSTER ACTIVITY. [**cf.** SASQUATCH]

WUDO—see WUDEWASA.

WUNSCHELRUTE—(Germany) see DOWSING ROD.

X—used to denote an unknown quantity while still in the experimental state.

X-BIOENERGIES—radiations which are given off from people and things and which can be photographed and studied in pictures taken by a high voltage camera; see AURA. (Inconcl.) [**cf.** KIRLIAN EFFECT, ETHERIC DOUBLE]

X-ENERGY—see VITAL LIFE FORCE.

X-FACTOR—coined by Colin Wilson (1971); see VITAL LIFE FORCE.

X-FORCE—1. coined by L.E. Eeman (1947); see VITAL LIFE FORCE; 2. the energy behind psychic skills. (Inconcl.) [**cf.** PSYCHIC ENERGY, FORCE, THIRD-EYE AREA]

X-NESS IN SPACE—1. an order of neither breadth, length, nor depth, but an order of the FOURTH DIMENSION. (Inconcl.) 2. the undetermined dimension of the minute pictures of past history of the planet in the astral picture gallery, as seen by good clairvoyants; see MENTAL-REFLECTING-ETHER. (Inconcl.) [**cf.** AKASHIC RECORDS OF THE EARTH, THIRD DIMENSION, SECOND DIMENSION]

X-RAY CLAIRVOYANCE—to see past the outer coating of MATTER into its interior; (humans) e.g., the skin disappears and every organ lies open to be seen as clear as an x-ray image; (inert objects) e.g., the letter is open to be read clairvoyantly, although it is physically in a sealed envelope; the contents of a drawer are made visible althought the drawer is closed; skill used in police work. [**cf.** X-RAY CLAIRVOYANCE DIAGNOSIS, CLAIRVOYANCE Appendix 2]

X-RAY CLAIRVOYANCE DIAGNOSIS—to see physically past the skin of a patient to detect the congested area; it looks as if the skin is peeled away and the organs exposed. [**cf.** X-RAY CLAIRVOYANCE, ASTRAL VISION]

X-RAY VIDEO CLAIRVOYANCE—(eyeless sight) 1. to psychically see and sense what is in one's immediate vicinity without the use of physical eyes; 2. to psychically see pictures as if everything were imprinted on the inside of one's forehead; this is similar to a picture negative; occurs to some blind persons studying EYELESS SIGHT; (do not confuse with CLAIRVOYANCE of the sighted). [**cf.** EYELESS SIGHT Appendix 2]

XENOGLOSSIA—1. to spontaneously utter a language that is foreign to one's self during a charismatic religious or evangelistic meeting; occurs when the individual is in an emotional state; theories: (**a**) individual is in a LIGHT TRANCE state and the foreign utterance is from the subliminal level of the SUBCONSCIOUS MIND; (**b**) (medieval) a sign that a demon is present; (**c**) (current) the HOLY SPIRIT has touched the individual and the Holy Spirit is responsible for the utterances; sometimes it comes out in CHANTING; three groupings: 1. NEOPHASIA; 2. LINGUISTIC RESTITUTION; 3. true XENOGLOSSIA. **Syn.** XENGLOSSY. [**cf.** SUPER ESP, TALKING-IN-TONGUES]

XENOGRAPHY—*xen,* "strange" *graphy,* "process or manner of writing") to write in a language that is foreign to one's self; brought on by a religious or emotional state of ECSTASY; individual is urged to write and the writing comes swiftly; three main kinds: 1. NEOPHASIS; 2. LINGUISTIC RESTITUTION (psuedo writings); 3. one's own handwriting; (do not confuse with automatism). (Inconcl.) [**cf.** ETHERIC SCRIPT, XENOGLOSSIA]

XYLONITE—(Kirlian effect) (England) a fabric used in ELECTROGRAPHY because it is impermeable to infrared, visible, and ultraviolet radiation, and does not hinder reproduction of the corona. (Inconcl.) [**cf.** ETHERIC WIRES, FLARE PATTERNS, HEAT CONVECTION CURRENTS]

Y-ROD—a forked branch in the shape of a *Y*; or two rods put together, fastened at the ends to form a *V*, used as for DOWSING. [**cf.** DOWSING QUESTION, FORKED BRANCH, DIVINING ROD, L-ROD]

YAGE—(South America) a drug used to induce a state of ECSTASY. [**cf.** HALLUCINOGEN, PSYCHOTROPIC PLANTS]

YAHOSHUA—(Jewish) pronounced YAH-HOSH-U-A; 1. name for the Messiah; 2. a name given to all, as we are all sons of the creator; sons of the Savior. [**cf.** TOTALITY, DIVINE, LAW OF MICRO/MACROCOSM Appendix 7]

YAHWEH—1. (Sanskrit) "I am what I am" and "I will become"; 2. (Old Testament) God, the sustainer of the creation; 3. (Jewish) substitution for the sound *YHVH* which was too sacred and powerful to be uttered silently or verbally; means "God," "God Almighty," and "Elohim" in its own right. [**cf.** TOTALITY, WORDS-WITH-POWER]

YAKKU—(Ceylon, Vedic) the SOUL-MIND of a deceased person living near the grave until the soul-mind realizes the necessity of going on into the ETHERIC WORLD and joining others who are dead. [**cf.** GHOST, APPARITION, DEATH PROCESS]

YAMA—(Tibet, Vedic) the monarch of the dead reigning over all the "worthy" who have departed in the outer sky; respected because he has earned the right to take care of them; seen as a realm of light. [**cf.** DEATH, FREEING THE SOUL, HOUSE OF ETERNITY]

YANG—(China) ether that has a positive electrical charge of POLARITY; is active, and has the characteristics of male, sunlight, fire, strength, and heaven; has a complimentary and opposite twin, YIN; found in every element of life with the yin; mutations of YIN AND YANG represent the universal force; in yang is contained the seed of the other. [**cf.** POLARITY Appendix 5]

YANTRA—1. (Hinduism) a diagram, symbolic in nature, used for MEDITATION; a visual image or picture used to hold one's attention in order to induce a single-pointed focus which helps one to reach a deep ALTERED STATE OF CONSCIOUSNESS; 2. (Tibet) symbolic designs. **Sim.** MANDALA. [**cf.** HYPOMETABOLIC STATE, EMPTINESS]

YARB DOCTOR—(Ozark Mountains) psychics capable of healing through the use of herbs. **Syn.** VILLAGE HERBALIST. [**cf.** CURATIVE EDUCATION, ALTERNATIVE]

YARIS—(Pacific, Tobi) see VITAL LIFE FORCE.

YARROW PLANT—a plant that has psychic properties; can induce CLAIRVOYANCE and heal ills; the plant has thin narrow stalks, uniform in size, which are used in DIVINATION of lots. [**cf.** BOTANE, RADIONICS, YARROW STALKS]

YARROW STALKS—a plant of thin narrow stalks, uniform in size, used in casting of lots; sticks of yarrow are put into a cylinder to be mixed by shaking, and are cast out at random; the cast out sticks are numbered and can be used with a book of answers to predict the future and answer problems of the PERCIPIENT; the original lots used in the I CHING. [**cf.** CASTING OF LOTS, DICE, DIVINATION]

YARTHKINS—(Lincolnshire Fens, England) a NATURE SPIRIT that was malicious, but is now believed to be extinct.

YAUHAHY—(Native American) Indian ETHERIC WORLD INTELLIGENCE who chooses to serve an earthling in the INNER BAND.

YE ARE GODS—pertains to human beings; theory: God is all; then humanity must be a division of God, or god in a lesser degree; humans have all the attributes of God in a lesser degree. [**cf.** LAW OF REPETITION Appendix 7]

YEARLY CYCLE—a pattern of mental and physical events that seems to happen without any known logical reason; repeats itself at the same time each year. [**cf.** CYCLIC PRINCIPLE]

YECHIDAH—see MONAD.

YELLOW—one of the primal colors; refers to Christ love, Sunlight, Sun God, or wisdom principle; yellow has the properties for intellectual stimulation and works with the soul-mind in culminating wisdom. [**cf.** COLOROLOGY, RED]

YELLOW CAPS—(Tibet, Bhutan) those who use their psychic skills for the good of all; holy men. **Syn.** NALJORS. [**cf.** PSYCHIC, MENTAL PSYCHIC PROCESSES Appendix 2]

YELLOW DIAMOND—(esoteric) a mineral that is influenced by the sun; used as a symbol for the lion and the sun; when worn, brings one courage, leadership and royalty; helps to neutralize the vibrations of the moon. [**cf.** CONTAINERS OF MAGICAL POWER, CAT'S EYE]

YENO—founder of ZEN philosophy, A.D. 638-813.

YESOD—(Cabalists, 350 B.C.) see VITAL LIFE FORCE.

YETI—(Himalayas; Gobi desert; Mongolia; Rocky Mountains, United States) half-creature, half-human; leaves large footprints showing evidence of its presence, but is not approachable; now associated with UFO sightings of a negative nature; one theory: yeti is a throwback of a human race, and in this STATE OF CONSCIOUSNESS it must live in seclusion; takes a different path of EVOLUTION, and is capable of shifting dimensions when people are around. [cf. DIMENSION-SHIFTING, MONSTER ACTIVITY]

YETZIRAH—(Kabbalah, Hebrew) considered the third highest in rank of the ETHERIC WORLD; where formation begins, with the angels having charge of each SEPHIROTH; choir of angels and the primal alchemical element WATER is assigned here. [cf. ATZILUTH, BRIAH, ASSIAH, TETRAGRAMMATION]

YEW—an evergreen tree or shrub that has a hollow center; symbol of IMMORTALITY and RESURRECTION; known to survive for over 3,000 years; because it symbolizes life after death, it is planted in churchyards and near graveyards in order to ward off evil spirits. [cf. INSTINCT PERCEPTION, DEATH DEMONS]

YGGDRASIL—(Scandinavia) a symbol of a tree standing at the center of the UNIVERSE, connecting HEAVEN, EARTH, and the UNDERWORLD to portray a belief it is all one world. [cf. SYMBOLS, TOTALITY]

YHVH—(Hebrew) a four letter name representing God energy; the most important of the eleven names of power; so revered and so powerful that it is not allowed to be spoken aloud or silently, except by the High Priest when in a holy room; JEHOVA is spoken in substitution. Y—(Yod) is represented by the King; stands for the first principle and is the origin of all things; H—(He) symbolizes substance; in opposition to essence; meaning the life and feminine principle, the queen; V (Vau) indicates Affinity; completes the Trinity; is pictured by the bond of love and the mystery of union; exemplified by the four knights and suit of swords; H—(He) (the second He) this page represents the second marking in transition from the metaphysical to the material world; God in man made manifest. [cf. POWER-OF-THE-WORD, SOUNDS-WITH-POWER]

YIEGH—(Nuer tribe, Upper Nile) see SOUL-MIND.

YIN—(China) 1. ETHER that has a NEGATIVE electrical charge of POLARITY; found in every element of life with YANG, its complimentary and opposite twin; the mutation of YIN AND YANG represent the universal force; yin is receptive and in yin is contained the seed of the yang; has the characteristics of female, darkness, and represents the moon, weakness, and water. [cf. YANG, LINGAM, LINGAM AND YONI, POLARITY Appendix 5]

YIN AND YANG—(China) two great opposite principles or forces whose interplay everything in the UNIVERSE depends; a vital force found in the ETHER which is divided into opposite but complementary halves; symbol of SYNTHESIS. [cf. POLARITY Appendix 5]

YIN AND YANG SYMBOL—a circle divided into two equal parts by a serpentine line; the dark half of circle is YIN, and the whilte half is YANG; circle indicates everything has opposites. [cf. LAW OF POLARITY Appendix 7]

YMIR—1. (ancient) the body of a giant that was used symbolically to represent the primeval abyss, at the time when all life had its beginning; 2. (subarctic) a giant NATURE SPIRIT living comfortably in ice and in charge of icebergs, snow, and all forms of ice.

YO-KI—(Japan) sickness, sick KI; malfunction of the VITAL FLUID energy.

YOGA—1. (Sanskrit *yoga*, "union"; to join together) philosophy that teaches the union between one's self and the one source; oldest science known today, and a disciplined way of life to those who practice it; objective is to attain at-one-ness with the divine spiritual essence within man; 2. (Vedic) union of the individual soul with the GODHEAD; methods are taught on how to harness the mind to the universe; 3. (Upanishads) lessons on how to make the CONSCIOUS MIND and five SENSES stand still by holding them back, which leads to a more satisfying life; 4. most common types of yoga are: RAJA and HATHA; other schools are: Bhakti (bucktee), JNANA (nya-na), KARMA, MANTRAM, LAYA. [cf. YOGA PHILSOPHY]

YOGA LAMA—(Astara) a special technique for advanced students that teaches one to tune into one's PSYCHIC ENERGY by the use of breath and disciplined mind activity; arouses the KUNDALINI and combines the PERSONALITY with the divine spirit. [**cf.** BREATHING, ALERT PASSIVITY]

YOGA NIDRA—(Yoga) a famous technique of relaxing based on BREATH CONTROL and CONCENTRATION. **Syn.** SLEEPLESS SLEEP. [**cf.** Appendix 5 MEDITATION]

YOGA PSYCHOLOGY—a science of CONSCIOUSNESS designed to develop and refine the HIGHER MIND; the simultaneous fostering of both the rational and intuitive faculties until they are purified and harmonious, leading to WISDOM. [**cf.** TRANSFORMATION, INTUITION]

YOGA TATWIC—the science of breath.

YOGI—a male who practices YOGA: the female is called **yogin.** **Syn.** YOGIST.

YOIK—(Lapland) songs sung to the beat of the drum to induce TRANCE. [**cf.** BODY CATALEPSY, ECSTATIC MEDIUM]

YONI—(Hinduism) the female organ which represents the NEGATIVE side of nature; the female, negative symbol of the LAW OF POLARITY, see Appendix 7. [**cf.** POLARITY]

YUGAS—(Oriental) time cycles; see CYCLES.

YUWIPI CEREMONY—(American Native, Sioux) a seance held by a gathering of Indians. [**cf.** DISSOCIATED STATE, FULL TRANCE, YOIK]

ZAR—(Ethiopia) an INTELLIGENCE in the ETHERIC WORLD who lives similarly to mankind and who has parallel activities; anxious to communicate with mediums.

ZARS—(Egypt) those in the etheric world desiring to communicate with people for EVIL intent.

ZAUBERRUTE—(Germany) see DOWSING ROD.

ZAZA—(Japan, Zen) a technique to free one's mind; a solitary form of attention to present things as they are, and then to internalize them in a manner of blankness, beginning and ending with the eyes open. [**cf.** JUST SITTING, EMPTINESS, END-STATE]

ZAZEN—(Zen) a special way of meditating called JUST SITTING. [**cf.** DHYANA, WARNING STICK, SESSHIN]

ZEN—(China, Japan) a branch of Mahayana BUD-DHISM; a highly intellectual, metaphysical philosophy; concentrates on MEDITATION to reach the SILENCE; not a religion, nor is there communication with the ETHERIC WORLD INTELLIGENCES.

ZEN MEDITATION—(Japan) a special technique used to learn how to go into the SILENCE using an exact ritual; performed under the guidance of the Zen monk for a certain length of time. [**cf.** FRINGE OF CONSCIOUSNESS, EGO-KILLING PRACTICE, BLANK PERIODS]

ZEN OF RUNNING—to reach an ALTERED STATE OF CONSCIOUSNESS by running; after sixty minutes of running there is an organic loosening of the consciousness and a mystical unity with one's surroundings; persistent hourly running brings one a feeling of well-being and euphoria, similar to the effects of a psychotropic drug. **Syn.** JOGGING MEDITATION. [**cf.** RUNNER'S HIGH, MOVEMENT-FOR-ALTERED-CONSCIOUSNESS]

ZEN SICKNESS—occurs when one comes to a spiritual pride in one's self, the ego takes over and one withdraws from meditating to support the ego trip. [**cf.** BRAIN SOOTING, COMPANIES OF GODS]

ZEN SITTING—using the MEDITATION posture and keeping still. [**cf.** WARNING STICK, OUT-BREATH, DHYANA]

ZENDO—the room used for MEDITATION in the ZEN monastery.

ZENER CARDS—a deck of cards designed at Duke University by Karl E. Zener, consisting of five cards of each of five different symbols: star, circle, cross, square, and wavy lines; used to prove or disprove ESP; (do not confuse with cards used to give a psychic READING). [**cf.** ESP Appendix 2]

ZENNIST—one who practices ZEN MEDITATION, and Soto; see SOTO SCHOOL.

ZERO DIMENSION—a point that does not move. [**cf.** FIRST DIMENSION, SECOND DIMENSION]

ZERO POINT—a superior state of AWARENESS where one feels the darkness and silence and yet one is alert to other levels of the mind; beneficial in MEDITATION, HYPNOTHERAPY, and PSYCHIC DEVELOPMENT. [**cf.** GOING-TO-LEVEL, ALPHA STATE OF CONSCIOUSNESS]

ZERO + ZERO—(biorhythm chart) indicates when two of the cycles pass on the zero-line in the same day, or when one cycle passes on the zero line and another cycle is at a very low ebb; this means that negative things could happen on this day and one should make extra preparations and take precautions; see ZERO-LINE. [**cf.** BIORHYTHM CURVES, BIORHYTHM CHARTS]

ZERO-LINE (0-LINE)—(biorhythm chart) the line that divides each of the three cycles in half, depicting the critical days of each CYCLE; at this time the body makes a "complete switch" to an opposite type of activity, and until the balance of the opposite half settles, the system is not functioning correctly; the zero-line charts many mishaps in any one of the three cycles, however, mishaps can be avoided by taking extra precautions. [**cf.** EMOTIONAL CYCLE, PHYSICAL CYCLE]

ZEROING—(biofeedback training) to reset the meter to zero in order to start a new frequency scale, when the subject has gone past the threshold range he or she was working within. [**cf.** EEG, GAIN SETTING, FREQUENCY CONTROL]

ZIGZAGGING—(astral projection) a distinct side to side movement of the ASTRAL BODY while it is rising out of the PHYSICAL BODY in preparation for going into the horizontal position. [**cf.** GETTING OUT, ACCLIMATIZING]

ZIKR—(Sufi) a sacred RITUAL, performed under the guidance of the SUFI leader, that brings the congregation into a higher STATE OF CONSCIOUSNESS; accomplished by forming double circles, with each individual in the circle twirling separately, as the whole group moves in a circular direction;

697

people also chant and shriek in tones which are chosen to help anchor one's mind on God; objectives: 1. to bring on a PSYCHIC EXPERIENCE; 2. to put one in a transfixed state of consciousness; 3. to call down a BLESSING on the group; 4. to receive masters of the past, present, and future for their guidance and instructions. **Syn.** NEFIA. [**cf.** RENUNCIATION, DERVISHES]

ZODIAC—1. (astrology) a circle in the sky, divided into twelve portions in which the sun, moon, and planets appear to move; each division is alloted thirty degrees of the circle, and influence people and events on earth differently; divisions correspond to the twelve months of a year, with one sign ruling from the twenty-first to the twenty-first of each month; **2.** (Greece) twelve signs are called "Circle of Life"; the signs are Aries, Taurus, Gemini, Cancer, Leo, Virgo, Libra, Scorpio, Sagittarius, Capricorn, Aquarius, and Pisces. [**cf.** ASTROLOGY, COSMIC CYCLE]

ZOE—see TOTALITY.

ZOETHER—(root word *zooid*) a thought cell with all the attributes of the whole word or theme from which it came; capable of separate movement and of splitting into parts; thought cells acting similar to the zooid. [**cf.** ZOETHIC WAVES, HOLD THE THOUGHT, THOUGHT-FORMS, MENTAL PLANE]

ZOETHIC WAVES—particles of thought in the air, making a universal ETHER, similar to light ether; as one finds electricity in the air, one also finds a more subtle substance comprised of humanity's thoughts; thought connects thought in one giant network throughout all ETERNITY; thought or zoethic waves travel at the rate of 250,000 miles per second to their destination; see ATOMS, and LAW OF THOUGHT Appendix 7 for process of thought. **Syn.** LOGOIDAL ETHER. [**cf.** ZOETHER, THOUGHT-FORMS Appendix 5]

ZOGO—(Australian Tribes of the Torres Strait) see VITAL LIFE FORCE.

ZOHAR—(Hebrew) the *Book of Splendor* published A.D. 1280; textbook of the Kabbalah, dealing with the exile of man from God; describes an involution of the soul down through the ten spheres that make up the universe, and then an EVOLUTION back up through them.

ZOMBIE—(Haiti, Voodoo) **1.** a person who has been deprived of his or her free will, personality, and character by being buried alive and then exhumed; a form of Haitian folk justice, used in place of capital punishment; BOCOR mixes a potion of puffer fish, highly poisonous, with other components and leaves it where the criminal will touch it; drug potion temporarily cools the brain, cuts down the flow of blood to the head; criminal remains conscious to some degree as body metabolism slows down until the criminal becomes paralyzed; this brings a semblance of death; criminal is put in a coffin and buried; oxygen needs are dramatically reduced in this state of paralyzation and there is enough oxygen in the coffin to survive until the body is exhumed; body functions at an animal level and is controlled by the bocor or owner to work as a slave or soldier; some brain cells are saved if individual is exhumed quickly enough; zombification can be identified by a shambling gait, downcast eyes, gibberish language and an appearance of insanity; theory is that either the soul-mind leaves the body or specific brain cells are damaged making the individual perform like an animal. (Inconcl.) [**cf.** SOULLESS Appendix 2] **2.** a soul-mind without a body; an initiation whereby the soul is dissociated at death, sending its spirit into the waters of death, and recapturing it in a spiritual awakening and resurrection; this is a purified zombie whose activity is controlled by an etheric world god, and not by an earthly magician. **Syn.** INITIATORY DEATH. [**cf.** INITIATORY SICKNESS]

ZONE OF IRRITATION—(radiesthesia) a danger area formed by the crossing of veins of water running underground; this can affect a person who spends much time in the building over the crossing, such as in an area where one sleeps, works, or sits frequently; these zones have been known to cause cancer and other diseases; can be detected by the DOWSING ROD. [**cf.** DOWSING, DOWSING FIELD]

ZONE OF QUIETUDE—(sleep) a period when sleep is normal and the ASTRAL BODY is about an inch above the PHYSICAL BODY, but still interpenetrating the physical body; both bodies are inactive except for the necessary act of recharging the physical body. [**cf.** CONSCIOUS DEZGOSIS, MYCLONIC JERK, HORIZONTAL GLIDING]

ZONE THERAPY—a method of healing the body by using compression on the feet with the thumb and fingers; this releases the flow of electrical energy in the nerve endings, which balances the body's POLARITY that allows the body cells to normalize and heal themselves. **Syn.** REFLEXOLOGY. [**cf.** MERIDIAN LINES, ACUPUNCTURE POINTS]

ZOROASTRIANISM—an ancient Persian religion; belief that the UNIVERSE is a creation of holy power and evil power; dualism: Ormazd is the god for good and Ahriman is the god for bad; later believed in one Creator manifesting in various aspects; the HOLY SPIRIT inspires the psychics and keeps the cosmos orderly.

PARAPSYCHOLOGY STUDY COURSES

The advanced student or the instructor of parapsychology will find this dictionary intriguing to read as a book per se or to use as a supplement to further his or her studies in some of the special courses at the end of this appendix. For the individual whose interest has just begun, or for the intermediate student who has read a dozen or so books, it may be confusing or fatiguing to read the word listings in alphabetical order. To prevent this is the main reason for the category groupings. Reading one category at a time is an easier way to digest the information. When reading page after page, one's mind shifts from subject to subject and even shifts levels of awareness.

The following study courses give information in good sequential order making the philosophy of parapsychology easier to absorb according to one's level of awareness and/or personal interest.

I. LEVELS OF AWARENESS AND PSYCHIC SKILL TRAINING

To develop psychically, to increase one's already developed psychic skills and to use these psychic skills only when willed, one should read and study parapsychological philosophy and science, and sit for psychic unfoldment. One important aspect to unfolding psychically is having a strong, sincere desire to become psychic and being able to call upon this ability at will. One proves this sincere intent to their subconscious mind and to their etheric world helpers by reading, studying, and sitting regularly in meditation and psychic development periods. "Forced" methods of inducing psychic energy without supervision are never advisable for the Westerner, at any level of parapsychological understanding. Forced methods can bring inferior or erroneous psychic information and can cause a decline in one's physical or mental health.

Using the following lessons will make the unfolding of psychic skills fun, interesting, easy, and safe.

The forty-eight graduated lessons are designed to be completed in one year at the rate of four lessons a month. If you are a natural-born psychic it will serve as an aid to help you utilize your psychic skills when willed only. If you do not consider yourself psychic, the lessons will help you develop psychically and decide which skills are best for you.

As you become acquainted with a variety of mental psychic and mental mediumistic skills throughout the course, and sit for their unfoldment, you will discover some skills will not unfold easily and others will unfold at the first sitting. This is due to your body chemistry and your ability to concentrate. The body's chemistry will not always adjust to a particular type of skill in the beginning, but will change if necessary as you go through the daily sittings.

It is advisable to keep a journal next to you during the meditation period and psychic sitting. Since you are working from your own self-discipline, you will find it rewarding to look back upon your accomplishments and chart your progress. It is almost impossible to remember the many things that happen during the meditation and psychic periods. To log your achievements also reinforces your subconscious mind and convinces your etheric world helpers that your intentions are serious.

The eight instructions that follow are the same for each lesson but will not be written repeatedly after each lesson. Reread them frequently to see if you are training yourself properly.

Instruction 1. Read the new material at the beginning of the week before sitting for your new psychic skill. Read the annotation in the main section of the dictionary under the main category listing you are to study before reading the designated word listings under that category. The word listings may be read in order and, of course, read any of the other listings you care to read under that category.

Instruction 2. Choose a small area in your home which you can use each day for your training without being disturbed. Decide upon a time of day or night that you can continue your daily meditation and psychic sittings. Use a straight back chair if you are not planning to sit in the lotus posture. A timer that has a light ring is very beneficial to clock the amount of time you allot yourself for meditation and psychic training. This allows you to put full concentration on your work without thinking about time. Burn a white candle during both the meditation and psychic periods. It is best to sit for unfoldment two or more hours after eating. Your clothing should be loose or at least not constricting around the waist. Taking off your shoes is also a good idea. *Always say a cloak of insulation to yourself or aloud before you commence.*

Instruction 3. Each day before you meditate, record in your journal the date, the length of time you are going to meditate, and the focal point you are using. Leave plenty of space for notes. Also record in the psychic achievement section the date, length of time you will spend in your psychic sitting, and the target or objective goal for that sitting. Leave plenty of room for comments.

Instruction 4. This instruction begins with lesson 3 and continues daily thereafter. When the timer rings at the end of your meditation period, set the timer again for the amount of time you have alloted yourself for psychic training, without getting out of your chair. Moving as little as possible keeps you in the psychic state of consciousness that you have achieved in meditation. Silently or aloud ask your subconscious mind or your guide to open your psychic doors, whichever the instructions call for. Follow the instructions for that lesson without surfacing to the normal beta state of consciousness.

Instruction 5. When the timer goes off the second time and your psychic session is over, shake your hands, wiggle your feet, move your head, open your eyes, and return to the normal beta state of consciousness.

Instruction 6. Record in the psychic skill training section of your journal what you psychically perceived within your mind, your body, and the room. Make comments on any impressions, visions, moods, and body feelings, before they slip away, no matter how ridiculous or beside the point to the logical mind they may seem to be. It will probably make sense at a later date; e.g., "I felt heat going down my right arm, a little light flickered in the corner of the room, one eye wanted to close." And be sure to log if you perceived the target or objective.

Instruction 7. Now record in the meditation section of the journal, what you experienced during meditation; e.g., "I felt detached from my body, mundane thoughts crowded in, it was a very peaceful state of being." And be sure to log if it was a good meditation *for you*. As you vary your focal points and background sound, these records will help you choose the best focal point for reaching a deep altered state of consciousness, as time goes on.

Instruction 8. Always construct your question(s) before meditating. Clarifying your question(s) on paper beforehand prevents you from shifting back and forth from the subconscious state of consciousness to the conscious state of consciousness and will bring a more accurate answer. Write down on paper what you think you wish to know. Analyze it and rewrite it making it more direct and concise. You will probably need to separate it as most questions have more than one aspect; e.g. would it be good for my business to make a deal with Jones & Co. when I am in New York in July on my vacation? Analyzed:

1. What would be the outcome for my business if I made a contract with Jones & Co.? (If the psychic perception is symbolic of good then proceed.)
2. Give me an indication of the month that would be practical.
3. Can I successfully handle a business deal and vacation at the same time?
4. What would happen if I invited a representative to come to my area?
5. Give me an indication as to whom I should make an appointment.
6. Will I get financial gain immediately?
7. Show me future results from a business contract made now with Jones & Co.

You can now make a wise decision because you know what the business deal would curtail and its gains. You have also clarified in your subconscious and conscious mind what you meant by 'good' in your original question. Place the paper beside you but do not think about the question or speculate the answers while meditating.

Lesson 1. MEDITATION

Look up all the starred words under the MEDITATION category found in Appendix 5. Also read: CLOAK OF INSULATION, SANCTUARY, and MEDITATION and PSYCHIC DEVELOPMENT in Appendix 4 for further clarification.

Daily sitting: Light a white candle in your sanctuary. Set your timer for a minimum of ten minutes and a maximum of twenty. Place the object you have chosen for a point of focus (not the candle) at eye level and about five or six feet from you. The objective this week is to discipline the mind and learn concentration. Stare at the visual object without letting your psychic doors open. If you begin to perceive a vision before your time is over simply tell the vision to leave until a later day. When the timer rings, follow Instruction 5. Record the necessary meditation data as stated in Instruction 7. Do not be concerned with the proper words to express yourself. The words will come to you more easily as you keep learning.

Lesson 2. EXPLANATION OF PARAPSYCHOLOGY

Look up all the starred words under PSYCHIC ARTS category in Appendix 3. Also read: CULT, MENTAL PSYCHISM, PHYSICAL PSYCHISM, PSYCHIC SKILL, PUT IT ON THE SHELF, MANTRA, OCEAN SURF, PINK NOISE, WHITE NOISE STIMULI, and BIJA MANTRA.

Daily sitting: Repeat your same meditation routine, only this week construct a mantra that you feel comfortable with. While searching for your own special mantra, you may want to try this one, "joy, joyous, joyful, joyously." The words of a mantra must be tongue twisters so you will put a small amount of attention to them. You may also use background noise. Perfect your concentration and do not allow your psychic doors to open this week either. If you begin to perceive a vision, refuse to pay any attention to it and mentally ask the vision to disappear until you ask for a vision. Be persistent and you will accomplish control of your mind.

Lesson 3. MENTAL PSYCHIC PROCESSES

Look up all the starred words under the MENTAL PSYCHIC PROCESS category in Appendix 2. Also read: MIND'S EYE, PSYCHIC ENERGY, PSYCHIC EXPERIENCE, PSYCHIC SENSITIVITY, and the LAW OF INTENT in Appendix 7.

Daily sitting: Meditate using the focal points from Lesson 1 or 2. When the timer goes off reset the timer, without stirring, for ten to twenty minutes. Close your eyes and ask your subconscious mind to open your psychic doors. Try to keep a neutral mind, sit quietly and look between your eyes with your eyes closed. Be attentive to what is happening in your mind's eye and physical body. This week you are simply establishing a rapport with your subconscious mind and opened psychic doors. You need not have any great experiences, although you may. Simply let it flow without being concerned about the meaning. The subconscious mind learns gradually. When the timer goes off the second time follow the necessary steps under Instruction numbers 5, 6 and 7 for recording in your journal.

Lesson 4. MANKIND'S RELATIONSHIP TO THE UNIVERSE

Look up all the starred words under the TOTALITY and MONAD categories in Appendix 3. Also read: COSMIC ENERGY, UNIVERSAL SUBSTANCE, PRIMAL ENERGY, PRIMORDIAL SUBSTANCE, SOUL, CANDLE FLAME, and the LAW OF VIBRATIONS in Appendix 7.

Daily sitting: Place the flame of the candle at eye level and about five or six feet from you (do not place it in front of a mirror at this time). Meditate with eyes closed. This week when you open your psychic doors, stare at the candle flame for ten to twenty minutes. You will blink and you may have to rest your eyes a few times, which is natural. Log all visions, body-feelings, and changes in the candle flame in your journal. Log your meditation results also.

Lesson 5. MENTAL TELEPATHY

Look up all the words under MENTAL TELEPATHY category in Appendix 2.

Daily sitting: Before you begin your meditation, prepare a simple message for a member of the household or a friend giving instructions to do something different; e.g., "bring home bread." Meditate. Without stirring, send the receiver of the message a love-line for a few minutes. Then repeat the message three times aloud or silently, but with emotion. Do not tell the receiver that you are sending the message. If you have more psychic development time after sending the message, simply repeat the whole process, and be sure to keep up the same amount of expectation and emotion. Send the same message three days. Send a different member of the household a message for the next three days. Log results.

Lesson 6. POWER OF THE CONSCIOUS MIND

Look up all the starred words under the BRAIN category in Appendix 5 and one-starred words under THOUGHT-FORMS category in Appendix 2. Also read: LAW OF FREE WILL and LAW OF LIKE ATTRACTS LIKE in Appendix 7.

Daily sitting: Choose a family member or a friend to send you a mental telepathic message. Both of you meditate at the same time if possible, in two separate areas. Record all your psychic perceptions before comparing with the message sent. You may perceive a body-feeling that corresponds with the words, etc. Try different persons to see if you have a better psychic rapport with one than another. Are you a better sender or receiver?

Lesson 7. FUNCTIONS OF THE SUBCONSCIOUS MIND

Look up all the starred words under the SUBCONSCIOUS MIND in Appendix 5 and SOUL-MIND in Appendix 3. Also read: HUMAN BEING; WORLD SOUL; and the LAW OF SOUL-MIND GROWTH and LAW OF THE SOUL-MIND in Appendix 7.

Daily sitting: Try a different focal point for your meditation period if you desire. Open your psychic doors, and stare at the candle flame again this week. Log results. Do you have a better rapport with the flame than you did in Lesson 4?

Lesson 8. MIND-OVER-MATTER AND VISUALIZATION

Look up all the starred words under the CONSCIOUSNESS and VIBRATIONS categories in Appendix 5 and the three-starred words under the THOUGHT-FORMS category in Appendix 2. Also read: the LAW OF MATTER and LAW OF THOUGHT in Appendix 7.

Daily sitting: Decide upon a material object you would like to own. Meditate. Without stirring, visualize yourself owning this object. Repeat the same picture daily. Record what you visualized and leave room to record when you received this object and how you got it.

Lesson 9.   PSYCHOMETRY

Look up all the words under the PSYCHOMETRY category in Appendix 2.

Daily sitting: Choose a book whether you have read it or not. Put it by your dominant-hand side. Meditate. With eyes closed, open to a page in the book. Keeping eyes closed, place your palm on the page and be attentive to what you psychically perceive. When the timer goes off, turn the page upside down before opening your eyes. Log your psychic perceptions. Look the page over thoroughly that you psychometrized and put down whether your perceptions were a plus or a minus. Do not underrate yourself, e.g., if your body felt weightless and some of the words or pictures were about the sky or airplanes, that is a plus.

Lesson 10.   REINCARNATION AND INDIVIDUAL KARMA

Look up all the one-starred words under the REINCARNATION category in Appendix 5. Also read: LAW OF KARMA, and the LAW OF KARMIC BALANCE in Appendix 7.

Daily sitting: Ask a friend to let you borrow something from their home that you have not seen before, such as a knick-knack. Meditate. Hold the article and ask your subconscious mind to perceive something about the article itself only. You are working with "pure psychometry" this week. Log results before checking with the friend. Use the same article three days and use another article the other four days. Log your pluses and minuses.

Lesson 11.   BREATHING, FASTING, AND FOODS

Look up all the three-starred words under CURATIVE EDUCATION in Appendix 5. Also read: COMPLETE BREATH; OUT-BREATH; PRANAYAMA BREATH; PRANA; UNIVERSAL BREATH; VITAL LIFE FORCE; SPIRIT; and FASTING, DIETING, STARVING under Appendix 4.

Daily sitting: Put a couple of unopened personal letters by your side before you start. From now on, take a "complete breath" before meditation and before opening your psychic doors. When there is a lull in psychic perception, take another deep breath. You are working on "practical psychometry" this week. Hold one letter unopened between the palms of your hands and tune into the mood the writer was in when writing the letter. Go to the next one. Record both the news and the emotions you perceived. Open the letter and check the pluses and minuses. Fast one day this week, if your stomach is normal. Note the difference in your psychic perceptions and meditation periods on that day and the day after.

Lesson 12.   CLAIRVOYANCE

Look up all the one-starred words under the CLAIRVOYANCE category in Appendix 2. Also read: METAPHOR; PSYCHIC MESSAGE SYMBOLS; and SYMBOLS definitions 1, 3, and 4; and Instruction 8.

706

Daily sitting: Choose your favorite meditation focal point. This week you will work on subjective clairvoyance and how to formulate a question. Do not ask a question you know the answer to nor a very traumatic question in the beginning. Meditate. Remember to look upward with your eyes closed as much as possible, after you ask the question. Log visions and any other psychic perceptions, even if you feel they do not answer the question.

Lesson 13.   ANGELS AND GUIDES

Look up all the one-starred words under the ETHERIC WORLD INTELLIGENCES in Appendix 3 and ANGELOLOGY in Appendix 5. Also read: MENTAL MEDIUMSHIP and TRUE-SERIOUS COMMUNICATION.

Daily sitting: Fix the candle for your focal point. Meditate with background music. To open your psychic doors, call in your inner band to assist your development this week. Stare at the candle flame. You and your guides are working on objective clairvoyance. When you perceive any changes in the candle flame or around it, say what you perceive silently or aloud. The guides know what they are sending but not what you perceive unless you let them know. Be patient. Your guides are learning too. If you do not perceive what they are sending, they will work in a different manner. Do not ask questions at this time, simply allow it to flow.

When your timer goes off, thank your guides and dismiss them. They are not to spill over in your everyday lifestyle. Learn to be in control of them at the very beginning. Do not tolerate any visions this week, unless you are sitting in your sanctuary and only then if you have invited your guides to come into your vibration. To be in charge of your guides means that you will always attract only superior intelligences.

Lesson 14.   CLAIRSENTIENCE, INTUITION, AND GUT FEELING

Look up all the words under the CLAIRSENTIENCE category in Appendix 2.

Daily sitting: Meditate. Ask for the guide to come into your vibration, who will be working with you in mental mediumship development. Ask for a body-feeling. Allow time for it to happen. Ask for a sign to let you know when he or she has attuned to you. Allow plenty of time and be attentive to body-feelings from your toes to the top of your head. If you feel the same sensation every day then you can be reasonably sure that your guide is with you. If it doesn't happen this week, be patient, it will happen. Thank your guide and dismiss him or her. Explain that they may give you a body-feeling any time of day. This is the only skill that can be perceived without disturbing your activity, and could be very helpful at other times.

Lesson 15.   ENVIRONMENTAL AND OTHER TYPES OF KARMA

Look up all the three-starred words under the REINCARNATION category in

Appendix 5. Also read: RECALL, EXCITABILITY CYCLE, MASS MUSIC, and MASS SUFFERING definition 2.

Daily sitting: Meditate. Ask your subconscious mind to bring you a vision or an intuitive feeling regarding a past life. Log your perception regardless of how insignificant it seems.

Lesson 16.   ESP

Read all the starred words under the ESP category in Appendix 2.

Daily sitting: If you own Zener cards, use them. Otherwise use twenty-five cards from a regular deck. Have another person shuffle the deck and turn over one card at a time where you cannot see the cards. They are not to stare at the face of the card. You are working with cognition. Check your answers with each twenty-five cards. Repeat three times. If you have over five answers correct, you are in the psychic realm.

Lesson 17.   ANIMAL AND MINERAL PSYCHISM

Look up all the starred words under ANPSI and MINPSI categories in Appendix 2. If you choose, also look up the stones of your choice by name.

Daily sitting: Go to a place where the squirrels, pigeons, or ducks are friendly. Do not take food. Meditate there. Choose an animal, send a love-line to the animal, and then mentally tell the animal to change his direction or do something. Birds that visit your home daily can be used. Do not use your own pet as you are already sending mental messages to each other.

Lesson 18.   PLANT PSYCHISM

Look up all the starred words under the BOTANE category in Appendix 2. Look up plants or trees according to their name if you choose.

Daily sitting: Bring a houseplant into your sanctuary or meditate outdoors near a tree or plant, if weather permits. Meditate. Work on a PK-LT experiment. You are to influence one leaf of the plant to grow in a different direction than it is supposed to. Silently send the plant a love-line first. Every day spend time admiring and loving the plant between psychic periods. Make the mental telepathic instructions the same every day. Keep track of the plant's progress for a couple of weeks and log.

Lesson 19.   KUNDALINI AND CHAKRAS

Look up all the starred words in the KUNDALINI category in Appendix 5.

Daily sitting: If you can find a picture of the crown chakra, copy it onto a large cardboard and color it. Use this frequently for meditation. Formulate a personal question for yourself or for another person. Place the crown chakra picture about five feet away at eye level or above eye level. Meditate on the crown chakra.

Your inner band has been close by every day awaiting to be called upon for guidance. Call in the guide who will be helping you with clairvoyance. Mentally ask the question you have formulated. With eyes closed, allow the picture or pictures to flow. If you do not understand the answer, mentally ask for clarification in another symbol. If many pictures flash by quickly, ask that they slow down. If you feel uncomfortable ask the guide to back away, he or she may have come into your vibration too closely. If you perceive nothing, take a deep breath and try again. Be sure to tell the guide exactly what you perceive so they know how they can improve. If you get an answer the first day, try another question the next day. Thank your guide and dismiss him or her.

Lesson 20.   INSPIRATIONAL THOUGHT—CREATIVITY

Look up all the starred words under the INSPIRATIONAL THOUGHT category in Appendix 2.

Daily sitting: Plan a question on how to improve your vocational work without being concerned about how it will happen; i.e., for the electrician, to make your wiring more safe; for the plumber, an easier way to fix a leak; for the administrator, how to save time on the production line; for a seamstress, how to change the sleeves in a used pattern. Put paper and pencil by your side.

Meditate on the crown chakra if you made a mandala of one. Do not think about your question while meditating. Pick up the paper and pencil and ask the question you have formulated. Write as it comes, without letting the whole message come first. It will come swiftly. Do not be concerned about spelling or how well you are writing. When you are finished, read it over for its logic. If the idea does not come, it may come while you are on your job.

Lesson 21.   LEVELS OF AWARENESS IN
THE ETHERIC WORLD

Look up all the one-starred words under the BODIES and PLANES category in Appendix 5. Because there are so many words you may save some of these words for the next lesson, but be sure to read the FIRST PLANE through the SEVENTH PLANE this week.

Daily sitting: Have paper and pencil ready. Before you start meditating, ask that you be brought a scientific fact that is advanced knowledge for you or a philosophical Truth that you do not know at this time. Meditate as usual. Pick up your paper and pencil and write whatever comes without logically reasoning with it as it flows. Study what you wrote after you are through. One day may tie in with the next day. Save your work.

Lesson 22.   SEVEN PRINCIPLES OF MAN

Look up all the three-starred words under the BODIES and PLANES category in Appendix 5.

Daily sitting: Think of someone you would like to have a more harmonious relationship with. Meditate. Use visualization and picture the "end-result," i.e., you and that person enjoying each other's company. Visualize the same picture every day. Leave room in the journal to put the results at a later date.

Lesson 23. MENTAL PROJECTION

Look up all the starred words under the MENTAL PROJECTION category in Appendix 2.

Daily sitting: Meditate a full twenty minutes with your favorite focal point. Ask your superconscious mind to clairvoyantly project to the highest plane you can reach that day. Do not allow yourself to take an astral projection. Log whatever you experienced or perceived no matter how trivial you think it is. Each day will make more sense.

Lesson 24. NATURE SPIRITS

Read: NATURE SPIRITS, FAIRIE, DIMENSION-SHIFTING, FAIRY LAND, FAIRY RINGS, FLINT ARROWHEADS, FAIRY MOUNDS, FAIRY WEED, and ELF ARROW. Also look up names of fairies that are familiar to you under the NATURE SPIRITS category in Appendix 3.

Daily sitting: If possible, use concert music or environmental nature sounds on a tape recorder for meditation. Choose a large healthy growth of bushes or trees and put the recorder in the midst of it. Virgin growth is best. Let the cassette play all during the meditation period and development period. Meditate. Concentrate with eyes open on the tree or bush to perceive the fairy or the fairie's light. Thank the fairy or light when you perceive it clairvoyantly. Using the same spot each day assures the fairy that you will not laugh at it or harm it. Log.

Lesson 25. COLOROLOGY AND AURAS

Look up all the one-starred words under the COLOROLOGY, AURA, and KIRLIAN EFFECT categories in Appendixes 5 and 3. Also read AURIC CLAIRVOYANCE.

Daily sitting: Stare at a soft yellow sheet of paper or cloth for at least ten minutes. Choose an object in your sanctuary and stare at it to perceive the rim aura. You may want to go back and stare at the yellow color at times to recondition your eyes. Squinting your eyes part of the time is helpful. Choose different articles each day.

Lesson 26. EMOTIONAL PSYCHISM

Look up both the one-starred and two-starred words under the EMOTIONAL PSYCHISM category in Appendix 5.

Daily sitting: Use a gray or tan background for another person to stand against. Meditate on the soft yellow color again this week. Have your friend stand against the gray or tan background and stare over his or her head to perceive their mental aura. A worship service is another good place to practice seeing the mental aura. Stare over the head of the clergy, and toward the end of the sermon it will be easier to perceive.

Lesson 27. OMENS, PROPHECY, AND RETROCOGNITION

Look up all the one-starred words under OMENS and PROPHECY and RETRO-COGNITION categories in Appendix 2. Also read: CHAIR TEST, PROPHECY, and RETROCOGNITION in Appendix 4.

Daily sitting: If you attend any weekly group gatherings, perform the chair test after meditation. You may also want to prophesy who will be interviewed on a TV program each day or prophesy the nature of the news broadcast each evening. Let the prophecy flow with clairvoyance, clairsentience or any of the other skills you are practicing.

Lesson 28.   STUDY OF CYCLES

Read all the one-starred words under the CYCLES category, Appendix 5.

Daily sitting: Meditate. Predict how many pieces of mail you will receive the next day. After the first three days, predict whether the mail pieces will be personal, bills, or advertising.

Lesson 29.   CLAIRAUDIENCE

Look up all the one-starred words under the CLAIRAUDIENCE category in Appendix 2.

Daily sitting: Make sure you will have complete silence in your sanctuary. Place a card table in front of you. Meditate. Rest your elbows on the table. Cup the body of your hands, and lightly rest the side of your hand on your cheek. The fingers will be above the ear and thumb on your hair but hand not touching the earlobe. Concentrate with eyes closed and listen attentively to the sounds in your head. The sounds will change. Do not move while you are perceiving.

Lesson 30.   BIORHYTHM AND CIRCADIAN RHYTHM

Look up all the three-starred words and four-starred words under the CYCLES category in Appendix 5. The three-starred words pertain to the biorhythm charts and the four-starred words pertain to the twenty-four hour cycle.

Daily sitting: If you have access to a computer that is programmed for biorhythm charting, have your chart made for at least three months. Be sure to meditate more on the critical days. For the circadian rhythm, keep track of your hunger pains each day and when you are most sleepy, for two weeks. You will find these times occur approximately at the same time each day even though your meal time is regulated by your work hours and your relaxed time is chosen by you.

Daily sitting: Work with objective clairaudience. Meditate. Call in your guide and ask him or her to make sounds in the atmosphere during your training period when you can question what it means. Do not allow your guide to make sounds in your home during other times. You are working with mental mediumship at present and you will be the only one who hears the noise.

Lesson 31.   CLAIRSAVORANCE, CLAIRSCENT, AND PSYCHIC COGNITION

Read all the words under the above categories in Appendix 2.

Daily sitting: Meditate. Ask one of your guides to send you a fragrance or odor of something that is not in the room. Remember to tell them what you perceive and thank them. Although this is little talked about, clairscent is a very good tool to receive messages symbolically.

Lesson 32. SOUNDS THAT HELP PSYCHIC ATTUNEMENT

Look up all the one-starred words under SOUNDS-WITH-POWER category in Appendix 2.

Daily sitting: If you have access to an AUM recording, use it for meditation. Chant the AUM before meditation and then again before opening your psychic doors. Call in a guide and ask if he or she can put a taste in your mouth that you can perceive psychically.

Lesson 33. PENDULUMING

Look up all the starred words under the PENDULUMING category in Appendix 2.

Daily sitting: Make yourself a pendulum out of a ten inch piece of heavy duty thread and a button. Meditate. Keeping your hand and arm absolutely steady, hold the pendulum over pieces of fruit and vegetables to perceive their degree of ripeness. The larger and faster the swing the riper the fruit. You may bring the food to your sanctuary or walk into the kitchen immediately after meditation. Use your pendulum in the grocery store to check thick shelled vegetables or fruits, such as cantaloupe and pumpkin. Do not call in guides.

Lesson 34. POLARITY

Look up all the one-starred words under the POLARITY category in Appendix 5. Also read LAW OF POLARITY and LAW OF OPPOSITES in Appendix 7.

Daily sitting: Put a card table in front of you. Formulate a few questions to ask the pendulum. Meditate. With your dominant-hand elbow resting on the table and arm upright, hold the pendulum over a clean area. Allow the wrist to be loose. Ask the pendulum what it will do for *yes*. After establishing this by questioning it many times, ask what it will do for *no*. Establish these two definite swings each day before asking the questions. They should be the same swing each day. After the week is over, you will feel confident in the meaning of the pendulum swings and need not repeat it. Do not call in guides. Ask the questions one at a time. You may even ask the pendulum a question you know the answer to, i.e., "Is it raining outside?" After ten minutes, it is best to tell it thanks and stop the training. Because your conscious mind keeps surfacing to ask the questions, you lose your psychic state of consciousness after approximately ten minutes.

Lesson 35. DOWSING

Look up all the one-starred words under the DOWSING category in Appendix 2.

Daily sitting: Construct two angle rods out of a coat hanger. Meditate. Directly after meditation, go into your backyard and mentally ask your dowsing rods to locate underground water, even if you know where the water and sewage lines are. The rods will cross, separate, or pull downward. Do this in your neighbor's yard also. It is best if only you handle your dowsing rods.

Lesson 36.   STUDY OF THE PSYCHIC INSTRUMENT

Look up all the starred words under the HUMAN BEING category in Appendix 5.

Daily sitting: Place your angle rods by your side. Meditate on a mandala. Stand up and holding the angle rods, ask them to point to a specific article in the room. Try several objects and move about the room. Ask them to point to a certain person. As long as one rod reacts, you are a dowser.

Lesson 37.   AMULETS AND TALISMANS

Look up all the starred words under the AMULETING category under Appendix 2. Be sure you understand the difference between an amulet and a talisman.

Daily sitting: Choose an object you would like to energize and a cloth to wrap it in. Each day after meditation, direct psychic or natural energy into it, using a different kind each day. Always keep it wrapped when not in use. Be sure to consecrate it for the same purpose each time you put energy in it. Use your hands, eyes, sunlight, the AUM chant, etc. Let no one touch it.

Lesson 38.   THE THIRD-EYE AREA

Look up all the starred words under the THIRD-EYE AREA category in Appendix 2.

Daily sitting: Place your amulet by your side. Meditate. Unwrap it and use it for which it was consecrated. If you consecrated it to help you play the piano better or to help you work on your invention in the garage, you may take it to another room to do this. Keep it wrapped when not in use and in your bedroom at night. You may use it for hours at a time without deenergizing it.

Lesson 39.   WORDS-WITH-POWER

Look up all the starred words under the WORDS-WITH-POWER category in Appendix 5.

Daily sitting: Construct your own affirmation to use for self-improvement. Many times you will think of a better word to be more concise and more accurate in your meaning. Change it. This is natural and the wordage is extremely important. Say the affirmation frequently during the day and expect results.

Choose one of the powerful words in the category as a focal point in meditation. You may write it in large letters on paper or repeat it over and over and see it in the mind's eye. Using the same word repeatedly increases its power for you. Have your tape recorder by your side. Meditate. Begin to speak into the microphone whatever comes into your mind. Even if the words seem garbled, let it flow. It is normal to go from subject to subject. When your timer goes off, analyze your tape for its knowledge. You are working with inspirational speaking.

713

Lesson 40.   GHOSTOLOGY AND POLTERGEISTRY

Look up all the starred words under the GHOSTOLOGY and POLTERGEISTRY category. Be sure you understand the difference between a poltergeist and a haunting ghost. The poltergeist can become dangerous.

Daily sitting: If your digestive system is normal, fast for one more day than you did in Lesson 11. During the fasting days, meditate and practice your skill twice a day. Formulate a question for yourself or a family member. It is time to contact your guide again. Meditate. Remain as neutral as possible. Ask the question by your side and work with body-feelings for your answer. If a vision comes, do not tell it to go away this time as this is your development time and your guide may be working with clairvoyance and clairsentience at the same time.

Lesson 41.   TYPES OF TELEPATHY

Look up all the starred words under the TELEPATHY category in Appendix 2. Do not confuse with mental telepathy.

Daily sitting: Choose a partner for texture telepathy. Find objects or articles with an unusual surface, such as soft soap, cotton batting, dried star fish, brillo pad, etc. If possible your partner and you should meditate at the same time. The sender should stroke and keep touching the surface of the article. The receiver is to perceive the type of texture, not the article per se. Reverse the procedure after three days. Be sure to wash the vibrations off your hands before meditating.

Lesson 42.   SCIENCE OF DEATH

Look up all the starred words under the DEATH SCIENCE category in Appendix 2.

Daily sitting: Meditate to nature sounds, birds chirping, or ocean waves breaking. Ask your gut feeling to bring you body-feelings or other signs to prophesy about the earth's weather and atmospheric conditions, i.e., storms, tornadoes, volcanoes, draught, etc. Log your gut feelings and if you perceived any dates or seasons with them, mark it on your calendar so you will be able to check your prophetic ability.

Lesson 43.   DESTRUCTIVE-BRAINWASHING CULTS

Look up all the words under DESTRUCTIVE-BRAINWASHING CULTS category in Appendix 5. Study this category well. Everyone is vulnerable to the cleverness of on-the-spot hypnosis, love-bombing, and mass hypnosis, if they do not understand parapsychological principles.

Daily sitting: Meditate. Work with subjective or objective clairaudience. Ask your doctor teacher to make a sound in the atmosphere or in your head that you can hear clairaudiently. Perhaps, by this time you have heard the telephone ringing when it really wasn't, or heard your name within your mind. This usually is your doctor teacher reminding you of something you have forgotten. Thank your guide.

714

Lesson 44.   PSYCHOKINESIS (PK)

Look up all the words under PSYCHOKINESIS category under Appendix 2. Also read the following in Appendix 4: PSYCHOKINESIS, MIND-OVER-MATTER, and TELEKINESIS.

Daily sitting: This lesson does work with physical psychism. Use the card table. Mark a chalk line on the table up close to you. Place a toothpick on it. Meditate. Stare at the toothpick and also mentally tell it to move. You are using eye and mind energy.

Lesson 45.   PHYSICAL BIRTH

Look up all the words that are NOT starred under BIRTH SCIENCE category in Appendix 2. Also read BEAMED ENERGY and HANDS.

Daily sitting: Put a chalk line on the table again with the toothpick on top of it. Meditate. Holding both hands above the toothpick, send the energy down the arms to the hands and move the toothpick. The hands must be far enough above the toothpick as to not cause a draft that could move it.

Lesson 46.   POINT-OF-FOCUS METHOD

Look up all the words under the SCRYING and POINT-OF-FOCUS categories in Appendix 2.

Daily sitting: Put water in a wide-mouth bowl, preferably a glass bowl. Stare at the water in the bowl after meditation. Be patient. It takes time to make it cloud up and show you a vision. Use a crystal ball if you have one. If this comes easy to you, you may ask a question and wait for the vision for your answer.

Lesson 47.   PSYCHIC TRANSFER

Look up all the one-starred words under the PSYCHIC TRANSFER category.

Daily sitting: Ask someone to come to you for a reading and bring a cut flower from his or her yard. The flower is to be the point-of-focus. Meditate just before they are to arrive. Keep your eyes focused on the flower. Your client may ask you questions and you are to perceive visions or body-feelings from the cut flower. Artificial flowers do not work as well. You may want to practice with a cut flower for a few days before you invite someone to read for.

Lesson 48.   PSYCHIC SHIELDING AND PROTECTING

Look up all the three-starred words under the PSYCHIC TRANSFER category in Appendix 2. Also reread: LAW OF LIKE ATTRACTS LIKE, Appendix 7; POSITIVE THOUGHT; PSYCHIC PROTECTION; and PSYCHIC SHIELD.

Daily sitting: Now read AWARENESS, KNOWLEDGE, and WISDOM, and you will understand why this course is called levels of awareness. This book and course made you aware of information you had not been exposed to before. When you studied the information and accepted it into your belief system it became knowledge for you. When

715

you sat for psychic skill training and *used* the knowledge you learned and accepted, it became wisdom for you.

Read over your log book and determine what skill you are best in. Do you work best with your hands, eyes, solar plexus, subconscious mind, superconscious mind, or your guides? Perfect the skills that work that part of the body you seem to have more psychic ability in and are compatible to you. If you have read all the assigned words and sat daily, you have no doubt experienced a shift in consciousness. This means you are choosing different foods, clothing, reading material, attitudes, and even friends. A shift in consciousness should be an enriching and joyous unfolding experience.

Please write to me: June G. Bletzer, P.O. Box 7036, St. Petersburg, FL 33734, and give me your opinion of this condensed course.

IN-DEPTH COURSE IN HOLISTIC HEALTH

Look up all the definitions under the one-starred words in the CURATIVE EDUCATION category in Appendix 5. These words give an understanding of the new-age principles underlying the holistic health theory. Look up all the two-starred words in the CURATIVE EDUCATION category. These words give many types of unconventional medicine and wellness theory alternatives. Also read: LAW OF HEALING in Appendix 7; PHYSICAL BODY, HUMAN BODY, BLOCKS, BLOCKING definition 1 & 2, and CLUSTERS, FAITH, HOLISTIC, SPIRITUAL, PSYCHIC HEALING in Appendix 4 for clarification. All the words in the NEW-AGE PSYCHOLOGY category are important. Scan through the categories for two-starred phrases. These pertain to healing alternatives.

BIOFEEDBACK TRAINING INFORMATION

Look up all the one-starred words in the BIOFEEDBACK TRAINING category in Appendix 5. These definitions give the philosophy underlying biofeedback training and give the directions pertaining to the training. Look up the three-starred words in the BIOFEEDBACK TRAINING category. These words describe the instrumentation and their parts. Familiarize yourself with the following definitions and as many one-starred words as possible under their category: MEDITATION, BRAIN, SUBCONSCIOUS MIND, BLOCKS, CLAIRVOYANCE, BODIES and PLANES.

POPULAR TYPES OF ALTERNATIVE HEALING
USING ONE'S BODY AS AN INSTRUMENT
TO CHANNEL HEALING ENERGY

Look up all the words under the following categories in Appendix 2: MENTAL HEALING, MAGNETIC HEALING, MEDIUMSHIP HEALING. Study and practice all the

716

instructions under one category at a time. Continue using the skill techniques that you are most successful and comfortable with. *Do not execute two types of healing at one time.* This scatters your energy and decreases the effectiveness of your healing channel. Also read: FAITH; LAW OF HEALING in Appendix 7; FAITH, HOLISTIC, SPIRITUAL, and PSYCHIC HEALING in Appendix 4 for clarification; and PSYCHIC HEALING category. Read as much as possible in the CURATIVE EDUCATION and NEW-AGE categories.

STUDY IN SELECTIVE CATEGORIES

Many of the lengthy categories in both the psychic skill Appendix 2 and related subjects in Appendix 5 have one-starred words. When these words are looked up, along with their cross references, you will have covered the essential data of that category. Many categories need all of the words to give well-rounded data.

There are certain skills that should be attempted only by a "well-grounded" and "well-informed" medium or psychic, e.g., ASTRAL PROJECTION, EXORCISM, HYPNO-THERAPY, and CEREMONIAL MAGIC. These need more instructions in technique than are in this book. One should also read the cross references and many more categories before feeling well-informed and follow and practice the instructions for sitting found in Lesson I in this Appendix before feeling well-grounded.

Mental psychism, mental mediumship, and physical psychism are easy and proper to develop at home. It is necessary to develop physical mediumship and forced psychism in the presence of an already developed medium or shaman; see PHYSICAL PSYCHISM.

Appendix 2

GENERAL CATEGORIES OF PSYCHIC SKILLS

The widespread interest in psychic skills divides them into two main categories: MENTAL PSYCHIC PROCESSES and PHYSICAL PSYCHIC PROCESSES. (See these listings in main section of this dictionary for complete differences.) After recording so many types of skills, and analyzing the general categories, four main groups would be more accurate for this dictionary: MENTAL PSYCHIC SKILLS, PHYSICAL PSYCHIC SKILLS, MENTO-PHYSICAL PSYCHIC SKILLS, and PSYCHIC PROCESSES USED TO PRODUCE PSYCHISM.

The main reason for further classification after categorizing them is for the sole purpose of developing the skill. The method of "attaining" each type of psychism differs considerably. Mental psychism, mental mediumship, and physical psychism are easy and proper to develop at home, but physical mediumship should be developed in the presence of an already developed medium.

Each psychic skill and each psychic process used to attain a psychic skill are categorized according to the most common name given that skill or process. Psychic skills that are not explored enough to warrant a separate grouping are listed under one heading, MENTAL MANIFESTATIONS/MISCELLANEOUS and PHYSICAL MANIFESTATIONS/MISCELLANEOUS.

Listed under each category are words and terms that are used in conjunction with that skill or process. This relays words and terms that exist, and serves as a reference to bring a well-rounded understanding of that skill. Some categories have short listings because the research or interest in that grouping is less.

Cross-references suggest further reading for an expansion of data.

MENTAL PSYCHIC SKILLS

General groups of psychic skills in which psychic information is transferred between the subconscious minds of two or more individuals, or transferred between universal mind and an individual's subconscious mind, or transferred between the subconscious mind and the brain of the individual. This psychic information is only perceived by the psychic(s).

ASTRAL PROJECTION
AURA READING (SEE
    KIRLIAN EFFECT,
    APPENDIX 5 AND AURAS,
    APPENDIX 3)
BIRTH SCIENCE
CLAIRAUDIENCE AND
    INAUDIBLE SOUNDS
CLAIRSCENT AND
    CLAIRSAVORANCE
CLAIRSENTIENCE
CLAIRVOYANCE
DEATH SCIENCE
DREAMS
ESP
EYELESS SIGHT

HYPNAGOGIC STATE
INSPIRATIONAL THOUGHT
MENTAL
    MANIFESTATIONS/
    MISCELLANEOUS
MENTAL PROJECTION
MENTAL TELEPATHY
OBSESSION
OMENS (HUMAN)
PROPHECY AND
    RETROCOGNITION
PSYCHIC COGNITION
PSYCHOMETRY
SCRYING
THOUGHT-FORMS

ASTRAL PROJECTION

Acclimatizing *
Aconcinnitous Psychism #2
Adept Materialization #1
Alphoid Pattern
Anguttara Nikaya
Astral Body Wanderings ***
Astral Bruises *
Astral Catalepsy *
Astral Cord *
Astral Diving Pool
Astral Line of Force *
Astral Plane Inhabitants *
Astral Projection *
Astral Projection Mode of Travel *
Astral Projectionist *
Astral Projector
Astral Route *
Astral Travel
Astral Vision *
Attraction-Action-Reaction
Automatic Astral Projection *
Autoscopic Hallucination
Autoscopic Vision
Autoscopy
Aviation-Type Dream
Back-Together *
Bicorporeity *
Bilocation ***
Blood-Flow Surge *
Bodies of Air
Bodies of Fire
Body of Light
Body-Flapping *
Brahmana Vagga ***
Celestial Headache *
Cerebral Click
Changing the Skin
Clear Conscious State *
Click-Clak
Clickation
Coincidence #3 *
Concavation
Conjunction *
Conscious Astral Projection *
Conscious Dezgosis
Cool Down Stage *
Cord-Activity Range *
Corpse Aspect *
Deathlike
Depersonalization

Depersonalized Experience
Dezygotic Phenomena
Disassociate *
Discoincidence
Distant-Point Astral Projection *
Diving Pool
Double Appearance ***
Double Men *
Doubling *
Dual Astral Vision *
Dynamize the Will *
Ego-Splitting
Eidolongic Kinesis #1
Ephemeral Projection
ESP Projection
Ether Goer
Etheric Projection *
Exteriorization *
Fetch #2
Flying in the Sky
Flying Spirits of Red Men
Focus Fifteen
Focus One
Focus Ten
Focus Twelve
Forerunner
Fringe of Space-Time
Giant-Stride Dream
Hagging
Head-Thumping Dream
Hold-Off Point
Horizontal Gliding *
HPHO-WA
Immotive Consciousness
In-the-Range-of-Cord-Activity *
Incomplete Projection *
Inter-Globe Trotting
Interiorizing *
Interplanetary *
Interrupted Unconscious Astral
    Projection *
Involuntary Astral Projection *
Jugamentum
Ketamines
La Reproduction Interdite
Lift-Out *
Locale
Locale II
Locomotion
Looping the Loop *

Mayavi-Rupa
Metacosmography
Mobile Center of Consciousness
Motive Unconsciousness
Motivity
Multiform ***
Near-Death Experience
Obe
Obeer *
Oobe
Oral Breathing
Out-of-Body-Experience *
Out-of-Range-of-Cord-Activity *
Parasomatic Experience
Personality Physism ***
Pineal Door Projection *
Projection
Projection Art
Projectionist
Propulsion
Psychic Imprint #3
Psychic Travel
Psychomatic Phenomenon *
Range-of-Cord-Activity *
Reassociated
Redoubled ***
Remote Viewing #2
Repercussion *
Roll-In *
Rolled-Out *
Scintillate
Second State *
Sees-in-Sleep

Shoot *
Sight Sensation
Skinless Hag
Skrying
Skrying in the Spirit Vision *
Skying
Skywalker
Sleep Astral Projection *
Slightly-Out-of-Body *
Slow-Vibratory Drop
Spiral Drop *
Split-Off ***
Spontaneous Astral Projection *
Starry Soul-Chariots
Straight Drop *
Super-PSI
Superclairvoyance
Suspended Animation
Tattwa Chart
Theta Aspect
Time Travel
Transformation #1
Traveler *
Trip-Projection
True-Action Dreams
Twenty-Two Paths
Uprighting Force *
Vacated Body *
Vibrational State
Whirlwind
Zigzagging
Zone of Quietude

BIRTH SCIENCE

Ancestral Body
Angel of Birth
Animal Birth
Astral Cable
Astral Seed Atom
Astrological Birth Control
Avatara
Birth
Birth by Heat and Moisture
Birth by Superpsychic Womb
Birth Consciousness
Birth Karma
Birth Primal **
Birth Science

Birth Symbol
Birth Trauma
Birth Without Violence **
Birthing Release **
Blue Blood
Body Change
Books of Life
Born with a Veil
Breathing Release **
Caul
Clear **
Cosmo-Biological Birth Control
Dry Rebirthing **
Embodied Anew

Gestation in Humans
Harmonious Infant
Heavenly Computers
Life Wish
Miraculous Birth
Moirae
Name-Soul
Natural Birth Control
Natural Conception Avoidance
Parent Disapproval Syndrome
Parthenogenesis

Perinatal Experience
Plane of Forgetfulness
Prenatal Recall
Rebirthing **
Soul Jury
Temporary Paralysis **
Three Books of Life
Ultimate Primal **
Walk-In
Walk-In Process
Walk-Out

CLAIRAUDIENCE AND INAUDIBLE SOUNDS

Air-Element Psychic Sound *
Anahata Shabda *
Angelic Conversation *
Astral Bell *
Astronics Pitches *
Astrosonics *
Auditive Medium *
Auditory Hallucination *
Call #2 *
Cazzamalli Waves *
Celestial Choruses
Cell Rhythm *
Clairaudience *
Clairaudient *
Collective Clairaudience *
Cosmic Chord
Cosmic Music
Divine Whispers *
Earth Cosmic Sound *
Emotional Clairaudience *
Eternal Rhythm #1
Ethereal Music *
Eurythmy
Exterior Pneumatophony *
Fire-Element Psychic Sound *
Formless Fire *
Great Tone of Nature, The
Harmony of the Universe
Hearing Mediums *
Hu *
Interior Pneumatophony *
Key-Note *

Kung
Listening *
Listening with the Third Ear *
Majestic Music
Molecular Chorus
Music of the Spheres
Musical Lights
Musical Science
Natural Infrasound *
Noisy Silence *
Objective Clairaudience *
Octave
Phantom Voice *
Psychic Voices *
Seeds of Sound
Shapes
Song of Life
Soul-Mind Key Note
Sound Current *
Sounds of the Four Elements *
Soundsitives *
Spheres of Resonance
Star-Sound
Subjective Clairaudience *
Supersonic *
Svara
Symphony of Life
Threshold of Hearing *
Transcendental Music *
Ultrasonics *
Ultrasound
Vibratory Note

CLAIRSCENT AND CLAIRSAVORANCE

Clairgustance
Clairgustant
Clairolfaction
Clairsavorance
Clairsavorant
Clairscent
Clairscent Diagnosis
Clairscentrist

Food of Ethereal Essence
Ghostly Odors
Odor
Odour of Sanctity
Paranormal Odor Phenomena
Perfumed Saint
Psychic Smells
Simbiotic Closeness

CLAIRSENTIENCE

Akuhaiamio
Arrival Case
Astral Perception #2
Celestial Phenomena
Clairempathic
Clairempathy
Clairsentience
Clairsentient
Clairsentiment People
Cognitive Clairsentience
Conceptual Sense
Dormant ESP
Educated Guess
Empath
Empathy Clairsentience
Exactitude Criteria
Exploitation of Instinct
Flashes
Functional Clairsentience
Gut Feeling
Hunch
Hunchability
Impression
Inner-Directed
Intervention
Intuiting
Intuition
Intuitionist
Intuitive Archaeology

Intuitive Awareness
Intuitive Experiences
Intuitive Knowing
Intuitive Medium
Libido #1
Mental Avenue
Monition
Nonverbal Communication
On-the-Spot-Psychic
Out of the Blue
Perceptivity
Personal Power
Precognitive Clairsentience
PSI-Mediated Instrumental
    Response
Psychic Impression
Psychic Suggestibility
Readiness Wave
Seeing with the Stomach
Soul-Action
Space-Travel
Spontaneity Discipline
Still Small Voice
Subjective Sensation
Superconscious Mind
Supermental Activity
Transcendental Reason
Unformed Thoughts

CLAIRVOYANCE

Adarsajnana *
Allegory *
Angelic Conversation
Apperception *
Archetypal Fantasy-Forms
Archetypal Symbols *

Artificial Symbols *
Astral Fantasies
Astral Perception *
Astral Vision *
Aura Reading
Aura-Vision

Auratist
Auric Clairvoyance
Auric Clairvoyant
Auric Sense
Bilocation of Consciousness
Boundless Vision
Celestial Light
Clairvoyance *
Clairvoyance-in-Space *
Clairvoyance-in-Time *
Clairvoyant *
Clairvoyant Dream
Clairvoyant Light *
Clairvoyant Projection
Clairvoyant Reconnaissance
Clairvoyant Sweep *
Collective Apparition
Collective Clairvoyance
Collective Hallucinations
Compensatory Hallucinations
Condensation
Constructive Imagination
Controlled Clairvoyant *
Corporeal Vision
Cryptoscopy
Dependent Clairvoyance *
Deuteroscopy
Direct Vision
Distant-Point Vision *
Divine Intervention
Divine Light *
Double Sight
Ecstatic Vision
Eidetic *
Eidetic Biofeedback
Eidetic Image
Eidetic Language
Eidolon
Eidolonics
Electromagnetic Image *
Emotional Clairvoyance
Entencephalic Visions
Etheric Clairvoyance *
Etheric Vision
Etheric Web
Extended Clairvoyance *
External Autoscopy
Eye Single
Eyes of Instinct *
Eyes of the Flesh
Fluidic Apparition *
Formless Visions *

Fourth Dimensional
  Clairvoyance *
Full Blown Solution *
Full Clairvoyance
Full Etheric Vision
Globular Spirits
Hallucination *
Hallucinogen *
Higher Vision
Hypnotic Clairvoyance
Image *
Imaginative Vision
In Vision *
Inner-Mind Pictures *
Interior Vision
Internal Autoscopy
Luminous Phenomena
Magnetic Sense
Materialization #3
Mechanico-Mystical Cognition
Mental Manifestation *
Mento-Mental Action
  Clairvoyance
Merkabah Mysticism
Natural Symbols *
Objective Clairvoyance *
Opaque Points
Oversaw
Partner Clairvoyance
Physical Psychic Lights *
Platform Clairvoyance
Prevision
Psychedelic Clairvoyance *
Psychic Projection
Psychic Sight
Psychic Telescope
Psychorrhagy
Remote Viewing *
See
Seeing Medium
Seeing Eye Vision
Space-Travel
Spatial Clairvoyance
Spirit Drapery
Spiritual Sight *
Spontaneous Apparition *
Subjective Clairvoyance *
Subjective Images
Telaesthesia
Thought-Form Clairvoyance
Total Vision
Traveling Clairvoyance *

723

Two-Mirror Oscillation Effect
Udjat Eye
Ultraviolet Rays
Vision *
Vision Quest
Vision Quest Mountain
Visionary *

Visuary
Wordless-Signless
    Communications
Wraith *
X-Ray Clairvoyance
X-Ray Clairvoyance Diagnosis

DEATH SCIENCE

Across the Threshold *
Advanced Spirit *
After-Death-Dream-State
Alive but Asleep and Dead
All Soul's Day
Angel of Death *
Animal-Headed Dieties
Anrakushi
Anshi-Jutsu
Antisurvivalists
Anubis
Aperture of Brahma
Ars Moriendi
Art of Dying *
Astral Hallucinations *
Astral Initiation *
Bardo Thodol
Bardos *
Birth of the Bardo Body *
Black Beans
Black-Sailed Ship of Death
Blue-Black-Egg *
Bodily Incorruption *
Body Breakers *
Book of the Dead
Books of Life
Born in Disguise
Breakers of the Dead
Burial with Feet to the East *
Ceremony of Little Death
Chikahai Bardo *
Chonyid Bardo
Close Brushes *
Coffin Rituals *
Coming Forth from the Day *
Continuity of Life *
Corpse Light *
Cremation *
Crionics
Dawn of Conscience
Death *

Death Angel *
Death Coincidences *
Death Coma *
Death Compact
Death Consciousness *
Death Demons
Death Feasts
Death Fetch
Death Glow *
Death Hormone *
Death Mist
Death Process *
Death Process Phenomena
Death Science *
Death Trance
Death Wish
Death-PK
Deathbed Experience *
Deathbed Visions
Disposers of the Dead Colony
Dweller on the Threshold
Dwellers in the Bardo
Dying *
Eater of Hearts
Egyptian Book of the Dead, The *
Electric Picture Records *
Epiphenomenalism #2
Epipneuma *
Etching of the Seed Atoms
Euthanasia
Excarnate *
Extracorporeal Intelligences
Feather Crown
First Death *
First Stage of the Chikhai Bardo
Freeing of the Soul *
Glastonbury Tor
Go-Beyond-Death Experience *
Golden Bowl
Great Camp
Great Doctrine of Liberation *

Unconscious Death Urge *
Universal Balm
Videha Mukti
Vision of Self *
Went Out
Wild Hunt
Yakku
Yama

DREAMS

Absent Dreams
Announcing Dreams
Archetypal Dreams
Association Fluidity
Awake-Dreaming
Birth Symbol
Brain Frequency Alteration
Causal Analysis
Compensatory Dreams
Condensation Dream
Confront and Conquer
Convergent Operations
Correlation
D-State
Deeper Dreamland
Delta Waves
Dialogue Technique
Discarnate Entity Sleep
    Experience
Displacement #4
Divination Dreaming
Dream Analysis
Dream Avoidances
Dream Body
Dream Clairvoyance
Dream Consciousness
Dream Control
Dream Cycle
Dream Diary
Dream Dictionary
Dream Fabric
Dream Forms
Dream Fragments
Dream Glossary
Dream Guide
Dream Interpretation
Dream Journal
Dream Log
Dream Reality
Dream Recall
Dream Research Laboratories

Dream Stage
Dream Symbolism
Dream Therapy
Dreamed Awake
Dreaming
Dreaming Mind
Dreaming True
Dreamlets
Dreammakers
Dreams
Dreams for Health
Dreamstuff
Dreamtime
Electro-Oculogram
Electrosleep
EOG
Essay Dream
Exposure Dream
Falling Dreams
Falling Spirits
False Awakening
Feast of Fools
Fifth Form of PSI
Fluidic Association
Flying Dreams
Forgotten Language
Head Snapping
Heart Thoughts
High Dream
Hypnophobia
Hypnos
Incubation Dreaming
Incubation Phrase
Individuation Process
Inspirational Sleep
Interviewer
Intimation Dreams
Jerk
K-Complex
L-Tryptophon
Landmark Imagery

726

Active-Agent-Active-Subject *
Agent #1 *
Artifactual ESP
Association Telepathy
Average Score *
Backward Causation
Backward Displacement *
Basic Technique *
Bidirectionality of PSI
Blind Mental Psychism *
BT
Bubbley Machine
Call #1
Chance *
Chance Average *
Chance Expectation *
Chance Level
Change Effect
Checker #2
Clairvoyant Mode *
Closed Pack *
Conclusion-Leaping *
Confidence Call #1
Covariance Effect
Decline Effect *
Differential Effect
Displacement #1 & #2
Double-Blind Experiments *
Down Through
Dual Task
Error Phenomenon
ESP *
ESP Cards
ESP Shuffle *
ESPatester
Expectation
Experient *
Experiment Expectancy *
Experiment-Experimenter
    Interactions
Experimenter *
Experimenter Bias
Experimenter Effect
Experimenter Pattern *
Experimenter-Subject
    Paranormal Communication *
Extinction of a Conditioned
    Response
Extrachance *
Extrasensitive Perception #1 & #2 *

Extrasensory Perception *
Extrasensory Signals
Flaw-Determined Phenomena
Forward Displacement
General Extrasensory Perception
GESP *
Goats
Hit *
Impression #3 *
Incline Effect
Low Variance
Mean Chance Expectation *
Mean Variance
Miscarriages *
Misplaced Efficiency *
Miss *
Mood Adjective Check List *
Multiple Aspect Target
Negative PSI
Negentropy *
Nonintentional ESP #1 & #2
P
P-Value
Paragnosis
Pearce-Pratt Experiments
PMIR
Probability
Procedural Irregularities
PSI Experimenter Effect
PSI Scale
PSI Tasks *
PSI-Favorable States *
PSI-Hit *
PSI-Inputs
PSI-Mediated Experimenter
    Effects *
PSI-Mediated Information
PSI-Missing *
PSI-Optimization *
Psychic Shuffle *
Psychological Variables
Quarter Distribution
Random-Experiment *
Receiver Optimization
Reversed Efficiency
Run *
Scatter Effect
Screened Touch Matching
Secondary Effect
Session #1 *

Set *
Sheep and Goats Effect *
Stacking Effect
Subject #5 *
Subject Variance
Target #1 *
Target Areas
Target Card *
Target Pack *
Target Preference
Task #1
Telepathic Mode
Temporary Deal
Time Barrier *

Time Displacement
Timeband Lag
To Worsen
Total Score *
Trial *
Two-Tailed Test
Tychograph
Up Through *
Variables
Variance-Differential Effect *
Waiting Technique *
Witness Effect *
Zener Cards *

EYELESS SIGHT

Ambient Vision
Biointroscopy #1
Blind Awareness
Cerebral Vision
Color Barrier
Cutaneous Vision
Dermal Optical Sensitivity
Dermal Vision
Dermo-Optical Perception
Dermoptics
Electrostatic Sensitivity
Extraretinal Vision
Eyeless Sight

Eyeless Vision
Finger Reading
Finger Tip Vision
Fingers
Hyperesthesia
Listening to the Skin
Paraoptic Sight
Paraoptic Vision
Skin #2
Skin Sight
Skin Vision
X-Ray Video Clairvoyance

HYPNAGOGIC STATE

Animal-Headed Deities
Bad Trip
Borderland Sleep State
Borderline State
Bridge of Consciousness
Dreamlets
Grotesques
Half-Sleep
Hypnagogic
Hypnagogic State
Hypnapompic State
Hypnogogostat
Hypnopompic
Hypnopompic State

Marginal States of Awareness
Myoclonic Jerk
Phantasmagoria
Presleep
Projection-Inclination
REM Rebound Phenomena
Sea of Faces
Serial Time
Surrealistic Phantoms
Toposcope
Topsy
Twilight Imagery
Twilight Zone
Vrittis

INSPIRATIONAL THOUGHT

Active Mental Inactivity
Afflatus *
Alpha-ESP
Astral Art *
Astral World Artist *
Aumakau
Aurascope Paintings
Breathed Into #2 *
Buddhi *
Buddhi Amitabha
Buddhi of Infinite Light
Channeling
Creative *
Creative Insight
Creative Meditation *
Creative Upwellings *
Dawning Consciousness *
Direct Knowledge *
Divine Idea *
Divine Intervention
Dual Consciousness
Enthused *
Genius #1 *
God-Brain
God-Filled
Holy Ghost
Holy Spirit #2 & #3
Inaginative Freedom
In Stream
Influenced Writing *
Innate Response
Inspirational Art *
Inspirational Compostition
Inspirational Mediumship
Inspirational Mediumship Art
Inspirational Mediumship
  Speaking
Inspirational Mediumship
  Writing
Inspirational Sleep *
Inspirational Speaking *

Inspirational Thought *
Inspirational Writing *
Inspired
Intuitive Leap
Jabberwocky Trance
Kingdom of the Mind
Knowledge Beyond that Time
  Period *
Mechanical Writing Medium
Mental Avenue
Numen *
Open-Face Trance *
Overshadowing
Portrait Clairvoyance *
Psychic Art #2
Psychic Portrait *
Pure Creativity *
Pure Imagination *
Second Self #1
Seventh Sense *
Sleep Preaching
Soul's Field of Knowledge
  and Truth
Speaking Medium
Sruti
SSP
Superconscious Mind *
Supercreativity
Superior Mental Perspective
Supernaturalistic Art
Supraconsciousness *
Supraliminal #2 *
Surnaturalism
Surrealism
Thought-Out *
Vakhari
Voice of Silence
Wise Passiveness
Wonderful Counsellor *
Yoga Psychology
Xenography

MENTAL MANIFESTATIONS / MISCELLANEOUS

Absent Sitting
Afferent Schizoneurosis
Alleged Phenomena
Alpha-ESP
Animal Familiar

Animal Spirits #1 & #3
Aspects of Self-Source
Atavistic Resurgence
Aural Memory
Aurascope Paintings

730

Client
Come Close To You
Come Into Your Vibration
Counselor
Déjà
Déjà Entendu
Déjà Vu
Displacement
Ecstasy #1 & #2
Finder
Flame Billets
Fortune Teller
Have You Been Read
Holy Fire
Human Electric Wire
Hyperaesthesia
Impressible Medium
Inner-Wisdom
Kama
Medium for Intellectual Effects
Mental Manifestations/
    Miscellaneous
Mental Osmosis
Mental Transfiguration
Micropsia
Misplaced PSI
Momentary Ability
Nonexternal World
Operation Prayer Power
Overshadowing
Pantomnesia
Paramnesia
Phone-Voyance
Physical Transfiguration

Physical Transformation
Psychic Annals
Psychic Assembly
Psychic Bankrupt
Psychic Casualties
Psychic Counseling
Psychic Fair
Psychic Isolation
Psychic Leakage
Psychic Plagiarism
Psychic Paranoid
Reached
Reading
Rescue Circles
Resonating Group Circuit
Self-Directing #2
Seque Phenomenon
Sitting
Sleep Control
Sleep-Osmosis
Sphota
Spirit Spectator
Spiritual Body
Spontaneous Psychism
Substitution Message
Touched
Transition Centers
Transposition of Senses
Uncolored Message
Uncontrolled Hallucination
Unisprit
Vardoger
Vibes

MENTAL PROJECTION

Alternate Realities
Asomatic Experience
Celestial City
Chariot, The
Consciousness Projection
Consciousness Travel
Disassociation Trance
Eckankar
Ecstatic Vision
Exalted Throne
Extreme Exaltation
Float Off
Kairos
Macropsia
Mental Projection

Mental Travel
Merkabah Mysticism
Mind Expansion
Multiconsciousness
Multilocation
Nonchemical Out-of-Body Trip
Perils of the Soul
Projection
Projection By-Symbol
Psychic Projection
Riding the Chariot to the
    Exalted Throne
Skrying
Soul Flight
Soul Travel

731

Throne Mysticism
Time Travel #2
Tissue Capsule Contraction
Tissue Capsule Expansion
Transcend

Transcendent
Transcendental
Transcendentalist
Translation
Work of the Chariot

MENTAL TELEPATHY

Active-Agent Telepathy
Agent-Percipient Pair
Artificial Brain Wave Pattern
Association Telepathy
Astral Link
Cholinergia
Direct Paragnostic Observation
Directed-Thought Trainer
Earth Telepathy
Group Mind
Inner-World Telepathy
Love-Beam
Love-Line
Mental Radio
Mental Telepathic Healing
Mental Telepathic Pollution
Mental Telepathic Suggestion
Mental Telepathy
Mental UFO Communications
Mentiferous
Mind Raider
Mind Reading
Mind-Linking
Mobia
Nellie

Outside Invader
PK-LT
Postcognitive Telepathy
Prototype Teleflasher
Simultaneous Thoughts
Sleep Telepathy
Subconscious Telepathy
Supertelepathy
TAT
Teleflasher
Telemetric
Telepath
Telepathic Twin
Telepathic TV
Telepathic Wire
Telepathist
Telepathize
Telephone Telepathy
Teleprompter
Telergy
Thought Atmosphere
Thought Reading
Thought Transference
Trace Method

OMENS

Angelic Host
Death Coincidences
Fateful Communication
Feather Crown *
Haruspex *
Human Omens *
Light Apparition
Muscular Tremors *
Nonhuman Agency *
Nonhuman Prophecy
Omen *
Omen Interpreter *
Omen Sticks *

Omenist *
Pop-Up
Portender *
Portent
Premonitory Signs *
Psychic Encounter
Public Augury
Public Portender
Raps #3 *
Signs and Wonders *
Token Indication *
Wraith *

PROPHECY AND RETROCOGNITION

Aruspex *
Back-In-Time
Backwards Time *
Celestial Eyes *
Celestial Seeing
Central Premonitions
    Registery *
Chair Test *
Clairboyance-In-Time *
Concept Recall
Divine Eyes *
Divining
ETP *
Extratemporal Perception
Eyes of Truth *
Eyes of Wisdom
Far-Memory *
Fatima
Fatima Prophecy *
Forecasting *
Foreknowledge of the Future
Foretelling
Forward-PK *
Holy Spirit #3
Hypnosentience
Indian Wheel of the Law
Kismet *
Mass Dreams *
Memory and ESP *
Mental-Travel-In-Time
Newspaper Test
Nonhuman Prophecy *
Postcognition *
Prayer Wheels

Precog *
Precognition *
Precognitive Clairsentience *
Precognitive Dream
Precognitive Remote Viewing
Predict
Prediction *
Predictor *
Premonition
Premonitory Dreams
Premonitory Signs
Presaged
Prescience #1 & #4
Presentiment
Presentiment Medium
Pressage
Prevision
Procarnation *
Prognostication
Projections of the Unconscious *
Prophecy *
Prophesy *
Prophet *
Prophetic Dream *
Prophetic Medium *
Retrocognition *
Retrogression
Spontaneous Recall *
Telegnosis
Thulr *
Time Bender *
Veridical Dream *
Warning Dreams *

PSYCHIC COGNITION

Cognit
Cognitant
Cognition
Cognitive Clairsentience
Cognitive Psychopharmacology
Cognize
ESP
ESP Cards
Field Independence
Forced-Choice Test
Free-Response Test
Hypercognition
Inanimate Cognition

Inner-Vibrational Touch
Instant Cognition
Nonchance Factor
Paracognitive Phenomena
Paranormal Cognition
Precognitive Telepathy
Precognizant
Psychic Cognition
Pure Cognitive Technique
Pure Telepathy Technique
Total Empath
Veridical Hallucination #2

PSYCHOMETRY

Billet Reading
Ceremonial Magnetising
Clairtangency
Contact Telepathy
Emanations
Fingers
Flower Psychometry
Inductor
K-Object
Metagraphology
Object Reading
Palaeoaesthetic Clairvoyance
Practical Psychometry
Primary Waves
Psychometer
Psychometric

Psychometric Object
Psychometric Reading
Psychometric Specimen
Psychometric Telepathy
Psychometrist
Psychometrizing
Psychometry
Psychoscopy
Pure Psychometry
Secondary Waves
Tactile Sensitivity
Texture Telepathy
Token Object
Touch-Sense
Vibroturgy
Wood

SCRYING

Angelical Stone
Call #3
Crystal Ball Gazing
Crystallo
Crystallography
Enochian
Gazing Crystal
Lamen
Magic Mirror
Magic Passes

Mirror #2
Obsidian
Quartz
Scryer
Scrying
Solomon's Mirror
Specularii
Speculum
Vassago
Water #7

THOUGHT-FORMS

A Priori Action
Activity
Affirmations
Animal-Headed Deities
Art of Precipitation
As If Technique
Astral Attendant *
Autogenic Training
Automatic Autosuggestion
Autosuggestion *
Babbler
Beasties *
Beasts of the Field
Beating Down Thought
Belief System *
Blank Periods
Blank Stare

Bottle Imps
Bur
Casecracking
Castles-In-Spain
Cellular Psychokinesis
Chief Deities
Cloak of Insulation
Color Visualization **
Common Auric Field
Constructive Imagination
Day Dream of Homage
Daydreaming
Daydreams
Delusion
Demonstration
Desire Elemental
Display Day-Dreaming

734

Electromagnetic Reality
Electromagnetic Unit
Elemental #1 & #4 *
Embryonic Auric Cloud
Emotional Noise
End-Result
Energy Patterns #2
Familiar Spirit
Family Ghost #1
Fantasy
Fixed Thought
Fog
Furies #3 *
Gathering Diffuseness of
   Thought
Goddesses #1
Group Elemental
Group Energy
Group Mind
Guided Fantasy
Habit Focus
Habits of Thought
Ho-ano
Hold the Thought ***
Idea Patterns
Imagery
Imagination
Imagine, To
Inner-Attention *
Inner-Dialogue
Inner-Talking
Jnana
Koan
Koan Theory
Listening
Manifest
Mass Elemental
Memory-Visual Display
Mental Chatter
Mental Elemental *
Mental Etiquette
Mental Noise
Mentation
Metaphysically Arranged ***
Mind Wandering
Mindfulness
Minor Deities
Negative Elemental *

Objective Controlled Imagery
Personal Mind Prints
Personal Witches
Phantasy
Phantom Flock of Animals
Picturization ***
Positive Mind-Set
Prayer Power
Psychic Attack
Psychic Push-Over
Psychophysiological Method
Pygmalion Hypothesis
Reflecting
Seed-Picture ***
Self-Suggestion #1
Self-Talk
Shielding
Single-Pointedness #2
Solemnizing the Mind
Solidified Thoughts
Subtalk
Thought
Thought Atmosphere
Thought Control
Thought Energy
Thought Projection ***
Thought Sphere
Thought-Form Clairvoyance
Thought-Forms ***
Thoughts Are Things *
Thoughtsmanship
Tsal
Tulpa *
Uncrystalized Matter ***
Video-Medic
Visual-Imagery Technique
Visualization ***
Visualized Healing
Visualizer ***
Waking Thinking
Web of Causality
Wings
Wishing Well
Wool Gathering
Words of Insulation *
Zoether
Zoethic Waves

PHYSICAL PSYCHIC SKILLS

These are general groups of physical skills in which psychic energy or psychic information is transferred between matter and universal mind, and/or the subconscious mind, and/or the brain of the individual. The matter is manipulated so everyone in the vicinity can perceive its change through the five physical senses.

ALCHEMY
ATMOSPHERE CONTROL
AUTOMATISM
BODY CONTROL
BOTANE
DOWSING
GRAVITY CONTROL
ECTOPLASM
   MATERIALIZATION
PENDULUMING
PERCUSSION

PHYSICAL
   MANIFESTATIONS/
   MISCELLANEOUS
POLTERGEISTRY
POSSESSION
PRECIPITATION
PSYCHIC PHOTOGRAPHY
PSYCHOKINESIS
TRANCE MANIFESTATION/
   MISCELLANEOUS
TRANCE VOICES

ALCHEMY

A-PK
Aaron's Rod #1
Ageneres
Aglow #1
Akam's Slimy Earth *
Alchemical Formula *
Alchemical Liquor *
Alchemical Materialization *
Alchemical Principles *
Alchemical Symbolism
Alchemical Theory *
Alchemist *
Alchemist of Sacred Fire
Alchemist's Egg
Alchemy *
Alkahest
Alteration of Vibration
   Phenomena
All Aglow *
Apport Objects *
Apportation Psychokinesis *
Aqua Fleur
Article Psychokinesis *
Ascend
Ascension *
Asport
Asportation *
Atomic-Psychokinesis *

Awakened
Azoth
Baaras
Beautification
Biological Transmutation *
Birth by Superpsychic Womb
Bodily Fires
Body of Glory *
Bondage of the Flesh #2
Catput Aureola
Celestial Dew
Chemical Marriage *
Circulation of the Kosmos *
Crown, The *
Crucification
Cup of Djemscheed
Dematerialization #2 *
Disintegration
Elixir
Elixir of Life *
Emerald Tablet
External Alchemy
Fire of the Sages *
Fo-Ti-Tieng
Gloria
Glorified Body *
Glory
Glow

736

Golden Lane
Great Awakening
Great Body of Radiance
Halo
Hermes Trismegistus
Holy Fire #2 *
Homunculus
Immortal Draught *
Invisible Transmutation *
Iron #4
Lapis *
Lapis Noster *
Lapis Philosophicum
Liberation
Light Body
Live Silver *
Magi *
Magic Wheel #2
Magicians' Fire
Magnum Opus #2 *
Materialization
Matter Duplication *
Mental Transmutation *
Mercurius Philosophorum
Mercury
Metamorphosis
Mid-Stream Master *
Motor Apportation *
Mutagen
Mysterious Stone
Nimbus
Operative Alchemy
Our Stone
Ouroboros
Parachemical Reactions
Philosopher's Egg

Philosopher's Fire
Philosopher's Stone *
Physical Transmutation *
Powder of Projection
Prima Materia
Psychic Chemistry
Psychic Dentistry
Psycholuminescence
Purified Body *
Quartz *
Quicksilver *
Rainbow Body
Raven's Wing
Reduplication
Sacred Patience *
Sacred Science
Salt *
Seven-Sided Vault
Spagyric
Speculative Alchemy
Sulphur *
Supreme Bliss
Tangible Apparition *
Tetragram #2
Transcendence
Transitional Consciousness *
Transmutation *
Transubstantiation
Universal Balm
Universal Solvent *
Violet Fire
Vital Magnetic Series, The
Vitriol
Water of Chaos *
White Stone

ATMOSPHERE CONTROL

Atmosphere Clearing
Atmosphere Control
Atmosphere Shielding
Bitumen
Bringer-of-the-Animals
Built-In Directional Sense
Chac
Changing Woman
Cloud Shifting
Dust Devils
Master of Fire #4

Medicine Man
Nature Telepathy
Personal Power
Priest Magicians
Psychopresis
Rain Dance
Splitting a Cloud
Storm Raising
Vitality Globules
Weather Magic
Wind Magic

AUTOMATISM

Additor
Automagraph
Automat
Automatic Art
Automatic Musical Medium
Automatic Paint Medium
Automatic Script
Automatic Trance Writing
Automatic Typewriting
Automatic Writing
Automatism
Automatist
Autoscope
Basket
Book Tests
Breastplate of Judgment
Cerebral Material
Complementary
    Cross-Correspondence
Concordant Automatism
Condensation #2
Corbeille-a-Bec
Corbeille-Toupie
Cross Reference
Cross-Correspondence
Dactylomancer
Desired-Control
Double Planchette Writing
Drawing Medium
Etheric Script

Facsimile Writing
Indirect Psychography
Involuntary Writing
Manual Psychography
Mechanical Psychographic
    Medium
Mirror Writing
Motor Automatism
Ouija Board
Painting Medium
Palingraphia
Partial Anesthesia
Pictograph
Planchette
Polyglot Medium
Polyglot Writings
Polygraphic Medium
Psychic Painter
Psychograph
Psychographic Medium
Psychography
Psychometric Medium
Psychometric Power
Sand Writing
Semimechanical Writing
    Medium
Simple Cross-Correspondence
Table Girardin
Talking Board
Trance Automatism

BODY CONTROL

Agape
Avatara
Bioclimatology **
Biological Phenomena
Biological Plasma
Bodily Incorruption
Body Control
Body Feats
Breath Control
Combustibility
Control Over Hunger and
    Thrist
Death-Like Trance
Dilation
Elongation
Ember Walk
Endurance Tests

Fire Handling
Fire Immunity
Fire Ordeal
Fire Walking
Fire Worship
Gift of Heaven
Handling of Fire
Heat Generation
Heliotherapy #2
Human Orientation
Human Psychokinesis
Human Telekinesis
Human Temperature Control
Ice-Sitter
Immunity to Fire
Immutability
Incombustibility Phenomena

Incorruptibility
Inedia
Insensibility to Fire
Internal Exercises
Internal Intonation
Internal Sex
Invisibility
Jogi-Feats
Kama-Kali
Love Feast
Magic Sleep
Magic Sleep Inducement
Maithuna
Master of Fire
Metal from the Sky
Partial Incendium Amoris
Psychic Heat

Psychic-Physical Control
Resurrection
Sex Transmutation
Sexual Magic
Siddhi
Somnamity
Soul-Mind Breath
Stigmatization
Stone Walk
Taming of Fire
Tapas Sex
Temperature
Temperature Control
Tummo
Tumo Control
Vital Heat
Walking on Coals

BOTANE

A. Muscaria *
Abyssum
Acorn
Alrune
Amanita Muscaria
Ambrosia
Angelica
Angelica Archangelica
Animate Beings *
Anthropomorphon
Apple
Apsaras #2
Artificial Paradise
Atropine *
Autophotography *
Baaras
Backster Phenomena *
Beans
Besom
Biodetectors *
Biological Phenomena #1 & #3
Birch
Birth by Heat and Moisture
Black Beans
Bo-Tree
Boswellia
Botane *
Botane Energy *
Cellular Consciousness *
Charging *
Cinquefoils
Clover

Copal
Cosmic Receiver *
Cosmic Tree *
Crescograph *
Datura Inoxia
Datura Stranonium
Devil's Head
Didjan
Divine Whispers
DMT
Dryad Fields
Ea #1
Elder Tree
Electroculture
Elf Arrow
Emotional Consciousness
Eucalyptus Tree
Evergreen Tree
Evoke Responses *
Faint
Fairy Mounds
Fairy Rings
Fairy Weed
Flint Arrowheads
Flower Psychometry
Flowers *
Fly Agaric
Fo-Ti-Tieng
Foxglove
Frankincense
Fuga Daemonum
Garlic

739

Watch Plants *
Willow Tree
Yage
Yarrow Plant
Yew

DOWSING

A Courtesy
Aaron's Rod *
Acausal Relationships *
Angle-Rod *
Assistant Dowsing *
Auric Charge
Baguette Divinatoire
Barehanded Dowsing
Biomagnetics
Biophysical Effect Method *
Blocking #4
BPE
Claw of the Dragon*
Compatability*
Conjurer's Wand
Conventional Dowsing *
Dalkarl
Detector #1
Divining Rod *
Dowser *
Dowsing *
Dowsing Question *
Dowsing Response *
Dowsing Rod *
Dowsing Zone *
Drag and Drag *
Energy Fields *
Field Dowsing *
Finkelrut
Fixity
Forked Branch *
Forked Divining Rod *
Forked Dowsing Wand
Frequency Registration
Ghost Vein *
Guettiste
Hand-Trembler*
Haze Wood
Helicopter Motions *
In the Mood *
Index *
Information Dowsing Method *
Internal Direction *
Irritation Zones *

Ivory Rod
Jacob's Rod *
L-Rod Response Position *
Lituus Rod
LL
Mental Probe *
Mercurial Rod
Narrow Band Tuning *
Noxious Area
Parapsychic Instrument
Preflighting *
Programming the
    Subconscious *
Radiesthesia
Radiesthesist *
Radiesthetic Sense
Real Divining Rod *
Rhabdomancy *
Rhabdomant
Rhabodic Force
Roedeloper
Rutenganger
Rutlimanner
Selectivity *
Shield
Siderischer Pendel
Sourcier
Staff
Stressing *
Stripped Rod
Supersensonics
Surface Dowsing *
Tamarisk Rod
Taming Wand
Telluric Energy #2 *
Time Lag #2 *
Toverstaf
Unit Search *
Volatile Rod
Wand *
Wassermuter *
Wasserschmecker
Water Undulation *
Water Witcher

Water Witching
Waterloper
Waterwitch
Wichelroede
Willow-Wand *
Wishing Rod

Witch-Hunter
Wizard's Rod
Wunschelrute
Y-Rod *
Zauberrute
Zone of Irritation

GRAVITY CONTROL

A-PK
Aerial Translation
Aerial Translation Medium
Aethrobacy
Ambient Gravitational
  Radiation
Antigravity Phenomena
Antimatter
Apportation Telekinesis
Ascend
Ascension
Ascension-Through-Meditation
Asport
Asport to Apport
Asportation
Atropa Belladonna
Bat's Blood
Besom
Biogravitational Field
Breath Levitation
Broomstick
Contra-Gravitational
Disentanglement
Disintegration
Ectoplasmic Structures
Electrogravitic Waves
Fly
Flying Ointment
Gravitational Spinning Wave
Gravitational Waves
Gravitational-Field Sense
Gravitons
Gravity
Gravity Control
Gravity Free Flight
Kinesis
Levitated Dancing
Levitated Running
Levitation
Levitation Gems
Levitation Psychokinesis
Levitation Telekinesis
Levitation-PK

Levitation-TK
Levity
Motor Levitation
Motor Psychokinesis
Motor Suspension
Motor Telekinesis
Motor Teleportation
Moving Medium
Natural Spiritism
Nonhuman Telekinesis
Object Telekinesis
Object-TK
PK-Mediumship
Psychic Platform
Psychic Rods
Psychokenist
Psychokinesis
Psychokinesis Levitation
Psychokinetic
Rate of Flow
Spontaneous Dematerialization
Structural Integration
Suspended Animation
Suspension
Suspension Medium
Telekinesis Psychism
Telekinetic
Teleport
Teleportation Psychokinesis
Teleportation Telekinesis
Transmutation
Transportation
Transvection
Walking on Water
Wings
Witch's Oil

ECTOPLASM MATERIALIZATION

Apparition Medium
Apparitional Light
Cabinet
Dematerialization
Ectoplasm
Ectoplasm Materialization
Ectoplasm Phantom
Ectoplasmic Cord
Ectoplasmic Dematerialization
Ectoplasmic Flow
Ectoplasmic Hand
Ectoplasmic Materialization
 Forms
Ectoplasmic Wisps
Ectoplasy
Effuvium
Ethereal Smoke
Etherealization
Exteriorized Protoplasm
Full Materialization
Ideoelasticity
Ideomorph
Materialization
Materialization Forms
Materialization Medium

Materialized Personality
Ozonize
Paraffin Molds
Partial Materialization
Plasmology
Plastics
Preseance Phenomenon
Pseudopod
Pseudorods
Psychic Imprint
Psychic Moulds
Psychic Naval Cord
Psychophysical Field
Psychoplasm
Putty Impressions
Quasi-Physical Substance
Seance Manifestations
Sinks into the Floor
Solid Ectoplasm
Spirit Drapery
Spirit Hands
Spirit Personality
Tangibility-Materialization
Unsubstantialization
Vapor Ectoplasm

PENDULUMING

A Courtesy *
Attentive-Eye *
Auric Charge *
Automatic-Eye Control *
Biomagnetics
Biometer
Bob *
Bobber
Body Scanning #2
Bow Pallomancy *
Compatibility
Congested Area **
Conventional Dowsing *
Courtesy
Cross-Causality of Interaction
Crystal Pendulum *
Cycle of Movements *
Detector #1
Doodlebug
Dowsing Question *
Dowsing Response *
Drops In *

Energy Fields *
Field Shifts
Fixity *
Fore-and-Aft-Swing *
Frequency Registration *
Gyrate *
Hollow Bob *
In the Mood
Inanimate Poles
Index *
King of Pendulumists
Map Dowsing *
Master Eye *
Mental Probe
Muscle Reading
Mutual Language *
Nonswing Question *
Nonswing Response *
Oblique Swing *
Oscillation *
Pallomancy *
Pallomantic

Paradiamagnetique *
Parapsychic System
Pendules *
Pendulisant
Pendulist *
Pendulous *
Pendulum *
Pendulum Gyration
Pendulum Oscillation
Pendulum Power *
Pendulum Prophets
Pendulum Searching *
Penduluming *
Pendulumist *
Pendulumize
Preflighting
Programming the
    Subconscious *

Pseudotechnical Instruments
Radiesthesia *
Radiesthesist
Radiesthetic Sense *
Remote Dowsing *
Reset *
Sample *
Seeing #1
Stick-Point Analysis
Telediagnosis *
Teleradiesthesia
Teleradiesthesiologist
Up-and-Down Motion *
Vibrating Ring
Warm up the Motor *
Witch Wiggler *
Witness *

PERCUSSION

Alphabetic Typtology
Concussion
Conjuring Up Phillip
Ectoplasmic Structures
Fox Sisters
Imaginary Ghost
Independent Bells
Interior Typtology
Knocks
Language of Rappings
Monosyllabic Answers
Paramorphic Table Rappings
Percussion
Phillip
Phillip Group
PK-by-Committee

Pneumatophony
Rappers by Profession
Rapping Spirits
Raps
Sematology
Spirit Noises
Spirit Rapping
Swinging Typtology
Table-Talking
Table-Tilting
Table-Tipping
Table-Turning
Talking Table
Tapping Medium
Typtology
Wood

PHYSICAL MANIFESTATIONS/MISCELLANEOUS

Adze
Alleged Phenomena
Ardat-Lile
Artephius
Berberlangs
Bioelectric Phenomena
Book Reading
Breath Levitation
Burning Handprints
Catalepsy Phenomena
Chemical Phenomena
Click-Out

Communal Seance
Controlled Multiple Hauntings
Corporeal Vision
Counseling Medium
Crambion
Cryptophysical
Daemon in the Die
Dairy Magic
Darshan
Diakha
Earthbound Phantom Cars
Ecstatic

744

Electric Girls
Electric Person
Electrified
Elf-Marked
Extraorgan
Faun #2
Fires with Boundaries
Flames of Divine Love
Geomantic Art
Ghosts' Prints
Gloria
Golden Plates
Greek Love Feast
Herd-Intoxication
Hot Reader
Human Generator Machines
Hyperamnesia #2
Incendium Amoris
Incubus
Infrared Network
Involuntary Intervention
Irradiance Phenomena
Isis
Jumbie
Kite-Flying
Language of Signs
Manna
Matter Through Matter
Medianimic Phenomena
Medium for Physical Effects
Miracle
Misplaced Phenomena
Monster Lilith
Moroii
Mummification
Night Flying Bloodsuckers
Obaifo
Penang-Galan
Perfumed Saint
Phantom Dog
Physical Manifestations/Miscellaneous

Physical Transfiguration
Physical Transformation
Polymode
Proxy Sitting
PSI-Q
Psychic Breezes
Psychic Casualties
Psychic Experience
Psychic Lights
Psychic Physical Lights
Psychic Plagiarism
Psychic Pyrotechnics
Psychic Winds
Psychomonism
Resonant Recorder
Sacred Fire
Shamballah #2
SHC
Solidifying Light
Spirit Hands
Spirit Lights
Spirit Lover
Spirit-Object Influence
Spontaneous Human
   Combustion
Spontaneous Physical
   Manifestations
Spontaneous Psychism
Stars
Statue of Stigmata
Talking Glass
Touches
Transfiguration
Treasure-Seeking Mania
Vagus Breathing
Vampiric Hibernation
Vampirism
Visual Manifestations
Wild Woman

POLTERGEISTRY

Agent *
Atopical Localization *
Boggle *
Border Phenomena *
Distal Localization *
Domicilium Poltergeist *
Efferent Schizoneurosis *
Eidolongic Kinesis #2

Extradomiciliation *
Famulation *
Focus *
Geist *
Kinematics
Naughty Ghost *
Noisy Ghost
Pelting Ghost

Poltergeist *
Poltergeist Carrier
Poltergeist Focus *
Poltergeist Generator
Poltergeist Missiles *
Poltergeist PK-Activity *
Poltergeistry *
Proximal Localization *

Psychic Theft *
Rabbat
RSPK
Throwing Ghost *
Vestibular Localization *
Water Poltergeist *
Water Without Cause

POSSESSION

Anxiety Attack
Avesha
Bantering Spirit
Compulsion
Convulsionary
Corporeal Subjugation
   Possession
Demon
Demoness
Demoniac
Demonic
Demonical Somnabulism
Demonomania
Demonopathy
Diabolic Possession
Dual Personality
Expressive Stereotype
Fascination Obsession
Free-Floating Dread
Giddiness

Hyperventilation Syndrome
Hysterical Absences
Incorporation
Invasion
Lucid Possession
Mercy Band
Moral Subjugation Obsession
Multiple Personality
Obsessed Medium
Obsession
Physical Obsession in a Medium
Possession
Possession of a Medium
Split Consciousness
Split Personality
Static Electricity
Subjugation
Svechchhotkranti
Voice Phenomenon #1

PRECIPITATION

Art of Precipitation
Autography
Basket Drawings
Card-Basket
Cloth Photography
Clothography
Deposited Matter
Direct Artistry
Direct Medium
Direct Writing
Dynamistograph
Etheric Writing
Hieroglyphs
Independent Etheric Writing

Landscape Paintings
Musician Medium #1
Pneumatographist
Pneumatography
Precipitant
Precipitation
Precipitation Painting
Precipitation Writing
Reflectograph
Slate Writing
Spirit Artists
Water Sprinkling
Windowglass Crosses
Writing in Tongues

746

PSYCHIC PHOTOGRAPHY

Autophotography
Burning Handprints
Chemicograph
Clothography
Delayed Photo Impression
  Phenomena
Easter Extras
Etheric Extras
Extras
Gismo
Infrared Film
Lightning Photography
Mind Photography
Photo-Medium

Physical Photography
Psychic Extras
Psychic Photography
Psychogram
Radiographs
Scotograph
Scriptograph
Skotograph
Spirit Photographs
Spirit Photography
Thought Photographer
Thought Photography
Thoughtography
Vaporgraph

PSYCHOKINESIS

Article Psychokinesis
Bioenergetics #2
Dice-PK
Electrostatic-PK
Faraday Cage
Geller-Type Phenomena
Hypergeometrical
Induced Physical Manifestations
Kinesis
Kinetic Energy Phenomena
Magnetoscope of Ruter
Mechanized-PK
Mental or Behavioral Influence
  of an Agent
Mind-over-Matter #2
Mind-to-Object
 Communication
Nature Psychokinesis
Nonhomogeneous Field
Nonhuman Psychokinesis
Nonhuman-PK
Object Psychokinesis

Object-PK
Palming
Parakinesis
PK
PK-MT
PK-Placement Test
PK-ST
PSI Dexterity
Psychoboly
Psychokenist
Psychokinesis
Psychokinetic
Psychokinetic Outbreaks
Psychophysical Phenomena
Pyrokinesis
Singles Test
Spontaneous-PK
Stare Down
Static Inanimate Objects-PK
Target Face
Unintentional-PK

TRANCE MANIFESTATIONS/MISCELLANEOUS

Accommodation
Animalized Fluid
Apportation Telekinesis
Assumed
Biometer of Baraduc
Body Catalepsy
Borrowed
Calm Medium

Candomble
Catalepsy
Cataleptic Trance
Complete Impersonation
Complete Medium
Complimentary Cross-
  Correspondence
Control

747

Coparticipants
Cryptomenesia
Decompose
Deep Sleep
Deep Trance
Dermography
Dermography Arm
Desired-Control
Dissociated State
Ecstasy #1
Ecstatic Medium
Ectoplasm
Ectoplasm Telekinesis
Ectoplasmic Structures
Effuvium
Electromedianimic
Excitable Medium
Exclusive Medium
Exteriorization of Sensation
Exteriorized Protoplasm
Fluid Motor Instrument
Frenzied Hysterical Possession
    Trance
Full Trance
Hyperventilation Syndrome
Impersonation
Intermediary Agency
Invisible Drum
La Prise Des Yeux
Light Trance
Mania
Mantic Trances
Mediamized
Medium Trance
Mediumistic Sleep
Mediumistic Trance
Mediumship Development
Message Worker
Motor Telekinesis
Mounting
Mystical Ecstasy
Partial Anesthesia
Partial Impersonation
Plasm
Realms of Form
Seance
Seance Hands
Seance Lights
See
Seidr
Self-Induced Trance
Semitrance

Skin Writing
Sleep Preaching #2
Small Spirit
Somnambules
Somnambulism
Somnambulist
Spiritistic Meeting
Splitting of Personalities
Stand-Up Reader
Standing Reading
Sthenometer
Subvocalization
Supercreativity
Sympathetic Motions
Talking Medium
Telekinesis Psychism
Telekinetic
Telekinetic Medium
Teleplasm
Ten-Percent Impersonation
Ten-Percent Trance
Trance
Trance Control
Trance Exchanges
Trance Manifestations
Trance Manifestations/
    Miscellaneous
Trance of Indifference
Trance of Wonder
Trance Possession
Trancer
Unconscious Motor
    Phenomenon
Under
Vacated Body
Visionary Trance
Voodoo Le Cheval
Yoik
Yuwipi Ceremony

TRANCE VOICES

Alien Voice
Aspects of Self-Source
Automatic Speech
Autophonic Oracle
Bull Roarer
Candomble
Cross-Correspondence
Daughter of Voice
Delphi
Dependent Voice
Direct Voice
Illiterate Medium
In-Depth Spirit Reading
Independent Voice
Inspirational Mediumship
   Speaking #2 & #3
Mount Sinai
Necromanteion
Oracle at Delphi
Oracular Possession Trance

Oracular Words
Psychophone
Pythia
Raising the Trumpet
Seance Trumpet
Simple Cross-Correspondence
Sitting for Trumpet
Superspeaking Mediumship
Supraself
Supraself Metaprograms
Trance Voice
Trance Voice Medium
Trance Voices
Trumpet
Trumpet Control
Trumpet Seance
Voice Box
Voice Phenomenon #1
Voice Trance

MENTO-PHYSICAL PSYCHIC SKILLS

These are general groups of psychism in which the result can be perceived sometimes by the psychic only and sometimes by everyone in the vicinity. Psychic information or psychic energy is transferred between mind(s) and matter (organic and inorganic, including humans).

ANPSI
CASTING A SPELL
CASTING OF LOTS
DESTRUCTIVE-
   BRAINWASHING
DIMENSION-SHIFTING AND
   SHAPE-CHANGING
ELECTRONIC VOICES
EXORCISM
GHOSTOLOGY
MAGNETIC HEALING
MANTIC ARTS (See Appendix 6)

MEDIUMSHIP HEALING
MENTAL HEALING
OMENS (Objects) (see OMENS
   under Mental Skills)
PSYCHIC HEALING
   (miscellaneous)
PSYCHIC TRANSFER
RADIONICS
SOULLESS PSYCHISM
TELEPATHY
WORDS-WITH-POWER

ANPSI

Animal Control *
Animal ESP *
Animal Group-Soul
Animal Karma *
Animal Kingdom *
Animal Liberation *

Animal Oversoul
Animal Psychism
Animal Soul
Animal Spirits #1 & #3 *
Animal Transmigration
Animate Beings

749

Anpsi *
Anpsi Premonitions *
Antelope Charming
Azoic Rock
Bat
Biodetectors
Biogenerator
Bioluminescent
Black Shell Creatures
Blackbird
Buffalo Power *
Built-In Alarm System *
Chayoth
Cockroach
Cosmic Receiver *
Coyote
Crescograph
Dairy Magic
Deer
Deer Antlers
Directional Instinct *
Dog-Ghost *
Doves
Dragon
Eagle
Earthquake Forecasters
Empathy-PK *
Fish PSI
Fish Telepathy *
Golden Money Spider
Hare
Hawk

Hen-Eggs
Homeothermic Animals *
Horse Whisperer
Instinct
Instinct Consciousness *
Instinct Perception *
Instinctual Telepathy *
Intuit #2 *
Manpsi *
Metapsychic Phenomenology
Nature Telepathy *
Owl
Owl Corner
Peacock
PK-LT *
Primary Perception
Primary PSI Perception *
PSI Trailing
Raven
Robin
Rook
Self-Directing #1
Shells
Simple Consciousness *
Spinal Consciousness *
Subhuman Bodies
Swallow
Tiger
Tortoise
Trout
Whale
Wolf

CASTING A SPELL

Becharm
Bewitcher
Bewitchery
Bewitching
Binding Deities
Black Glance
Blessing
Captivation
Casting a Spell
Casting Runes
Charm
Charm-Bound
Charm-Struck
Charmer
Charming
Counterspell
Death-Like Trance

Demonifuge
Enchant
Enchanter
Enchantress
Entrancement
Entrancer
Evil Eye
Eye-Fixation
Fascinate
Fascinator
Gaze
Glamour
Glamourie
Glamourizer
Hagridden
Hagride
Hand of Glory

750

Hypnospell
Hypnotelepathy
Iconoclast
Ill-Wishing
Incantation #1
Juju
Kalevala
Official Curse

Overlooking
Spell
Spellbound
Spelled
Speller
Weird
Whammy

CASTING OF LOTS

Acausal Coincidence *
Acausal Relationships *
Activism *
ARS Notoral
Atouts
Archetypal Experience
Beans
Bone-Throwing *
Book of Changes, The *
Book of Thoth
Casting of Lots *
Cereoscopy
Changing Lines
Coincidence *
Coincidental Matching *
Commentary
Consultant
Cooccurrence *
Correspondences-in-Time *
Court Cards
Cross-Causality of Interaction *
Dice Divination *
Divining
Domino Divination
Drawing of Lots
Eggs
Epatoscopy
Fall *
Hexagram *
Hsiang Chuan
I Ching *
Interior Cohesion
Judgment
Key to Hexagram
Lay Out *
Life Reading #2
Little Egypt
Lots *
Magic Causality *
Major Arcana
Major Trump Card

Meaningful Coincidence
  Theory *
Ming Sticks *
Minor Arcana
Noncausal Phenomena
Nonchange *
Nonrational Phenomena
Omen Sticks *
Ordering Principle *
Patterning
Patterning Across Time *
Providence
Querant
Questioner
Right Hand Symbol
Sand Divination
Sand Reading
Scope *
Sheep Bones *
Shustah-Cards
Significant Coincidences *
Simultaneous Parallels
Sor
Sors
Sortes
Sortes Sanctorum *
Sortilege
Spinning the 'Sas' *
Spot Cards
Synchronicity *
Taula
Tarocchi Cards
Tarot Cards *
Tarot King *
Tarot Knight
Tarot Page *
Tarot Queen
Text
Thriaean Lots
Throwing the Bones
Trigrams

751

Tuan
Tuan Chuan
Virgilian Sorte *
Virgilian Sortes
Yarrow Stalks *

DESTRUCTIVE-BRAINWASHING

Adaptive Reaction
Artificial Group Elemental
Artika Ceremony
Atmosphere of Affection
Automaton
Backsliding
Big Breakthrough
Binding Deities
Blank Stare
Blissing Out
Brainwashing
Centering #2
Clear #2
Cooperative Suggestion
Critical Mind
Critical Situational Response
Cult
Cult Syndrome
Dehumanize #2
Deprogramming
Destructive Manipulation
Destructive-Brainwashing Cult
Deterministic Psychology
Ego Metaprogramming
Ego-Destruction
Fair Witness
Floating
Free Choice
Group Brainwashing
Group Elemental

Group Energy
Group Hypnosis
Heavenly Deceit
Iconoclast
Information Disease
Love-Bombing
Mass Hypnosis
Mental Psychological Prison
Menticide
On-the-Spot-Hypnosis
Oversimplified Biocomputer
    Logics
Personal Encounter
Physically Coercive
Ploy
Power of the Gaze
Psychedelia
Psychic Paranoid
Psychological Imprisonment
Psychological Trap
Sleep-Spirit Problems
Sleep-Telepathy
Snapping
Stare Down
Sudden Personality Change
Suggestion
Surrender of the Will
Symbiotic Consciousness
Transfix
Witnessing

DIMENSION-SHIFTING AND SHAPE-CHANGING

Abominable Snowman
Aleuranthropy
Assumption of God Forms
Astral Vampirism
Beowulf
Bhut
Big Bird
Big Foot
Big Owl
Birds of Prey

Boanthropy
Bruxa
Buda
Chang Tang Highlands
Chuchunaa
Cockroach
Cynanthropy
Dimension-Shifting
DMT
Druid

752

Druidism
Dusil
Dynamic Transitions
Fairie
Folk Monster
Ghosts of the Gibbet
Grimms Fairy Tales
Hag
Invisibility
Kilcrop
Kuanthropy
Lansuir
Legarou
Lepanthropy
Light Body #2
Lili
Loch Ness Monster
Loogaroo
Lycanthropy
Metamorphosis
Monster Activity
Mothman Prophecies
Moulou
Multiple-Self-Transformation
Nature Spirits
Night Hag
Polymode
Ponik
Power of Miraculous Action
Protean

Psychic Imprint #2
Psychic Warp
Quartz
Rdzu-Uphrul
Sasquatch
Self-Transformation
Shape-Changing
Shape-Shifting
She-Wolf
Siddhi
Siren
Skunk Ape
Striga
Strigoi
Succubus
Taku He
Talent Substitution
Transition of Substance
Vampire
Vampirism
Warm Holes in Space
Were-Creature
Wereleopard
Werewolf
Whale
Wild-Man Monster
Wudewasa
Wudo
Yeti

ELECTRONIC VOICES

Answer Cases
Apparent Psychic Phone Calls
Biotransducer
Breakthrough
Carry-On Talking
Cassette Voice Recording
Control Personality
Crisis Calls
Electric Clairaudience
Electromagnetic Theory
Electronic Ghosts
Electronic Voices
Environmental Noise
Intention Cases
Jurgenson Voices
Laser Microphone Matrix
Paraphysical Electronic Voices
Phantom Phone Calls
Phone Call to the Dead

Phone Calls from the Dead
Pneuma-Tape-Recorder
Prolonged-Calls
Psychic Phone Call
Simple Call
Tape-Recorded,
    Low-Amplitude-PK
Taped Voice Phenomenon
Telephone Calls from the Dead
Third Frequency Modulation
Tracking
Voice Broadcast Controller
Vice Broadcasts
Voice Phenomenon
Voice Prints
Voices from the Universe
Voicetape Phenomena
Witness #2

EXORCISM

Abyssum
Banishing
Carrying an Evil
Casting Out Evil Spirits
Conjuration
Counterspell
Demonologist #1
Equi-Limbed Cross
Exorcism
Exorcist
False-Face Society
Goetric Art #1
Guiding the Ghost Service
Healing Moon-Deity Stone
    Statue
Hex Doctor
Host Woman
Houngman
House Blessing

House Sweep
Lay
Lay Ghosts
Lifter of Spells
Loosing Deities
Magic with Magic Cure
Man Shock Treatment
Mercy Ground
Monosprit
Prehouse-Cleaning
Provoking
Psychic Barrier
Psychic House-Cleaning
Smudging
Spiritual Doctor
Static Electricity
Talking to the Gods
Witch Bottle

GHOSTOLOGY

Apparition *
Border Phenomena
Chhaya *
Confused Soul-Mind *
Controlled Multiple
    Hauntings *
Counterfeit *
Crossroads *
Demonologist *
Disembodied Spirit *
Dream-Whiskey *
Drifters *
Dybbuk *
Earthbound Entities *
Earthbound Phantom Cars
Eidola
Enemy Way *
Environmental Haunting *
Errant Spirit *
Family Ghost *
Foolish Fire
Ghost *
Ghost Haunting *
Ghost Seers
Ghost Ships
Ghostery
Ghostly Odors *
Ghostology *

Gib Ghosts
Graveyard Ghosts *
Guiding the Ghost Service *
Haunted House *
Haunted Localities *
Haunting *
Ignis Fatuus
Larva
Lemur
Material Fluidic Envelope *
Passion Devas *
Personal Haunting *
Phantasm *
Phantasma
Phantom Armies
Phantom Hitchiker
Preta-Loka World
Pretas
Psychic Drifters *
Psychon *
Revenant
Semitransparent *
Specter
Spectral Flames
Spirit Tormentor
Spiritlike
Spontaneous Apparition *
Suffering Spirits

Talking to the Gods *
Tie
Transparency *
Veridical After-Image
Wandering Spirit

MAGNETIC HEALING

Apotropaic Healing Prayer
Assessing
Auric Diagnosis
Auric Healing
Bath of Rebirth
Body Scanning
Catalystic Healing
Centering
Charge
Clearing Pass
Cloud Chamber
Congested Area
Contact Healer
Contact Healing
Curative Mesmerism
Earth Magnetic Healing
Earth Magnetism
Eddy Current
Energetic Medicine
Etheric Diagnosing
Etheric Magnetic Current
Etheric Thread
Fingers
Flick
Gauss Magnetics
Handkerchief Healing
Healee
Healer
Healing Fluid
Healing Hands
Holy Oils
Holy Water
Human Energy Transfer
Human Magnetism
Interchange of Magnetism

Intuitive Healers
Joule's Heat
Laying-on-of-Hands
Leader
Localized Field
Locked-In
Long Pass
Loosened
Magic Passes
Magnetic Distance Healing
Magnetic Flux
Magnetic Healing
Magnetic Nerve Fluid
Magnetic Passes
Magnetic Practitioner
Magnetic Self-Healing
Magnetism
Magnetism Immunity
Magnetized Water
Motion Without Contact
Nadis
Nerve Fluid
Palming
Passes
Petition
Powwow Healing
Powwower
Psychic Diagnostician
Psychic Nerve System
Reflected Healing #2
Royal Touch
Saturation Pass
Sideway Passes
Therapeutic Touch
Unruffling the Field

MEDIUMSHIP HEALING

!Kia
!Kia Fire
!Kia Healing
!Kung Healer
Bone-Symmetry Healing

Brought Down
Cone of Power #2
Danced Him
Ectoplasm Psychic Surgery
Espiritista

755

Espiritista Group
Etheric Surgery
Healer
Healing by Impersonation
Healing Forces
Healing Medium
Mediumship Healing
Psychic Diagnostician
Psychic Surgeon
Psychic Surgery

Pulling Out the Sickness
Reflected Healing
Seeing Properly
Shamanship Healing
Spirit Mediums
Spiritist Healer
Surgical Gift
Ten-Percent Impersonation
Ten-Percent Trance
Third Force

MENTAL HEALING

Absent Healing
Affirmative Healing
Apotropaic Healing Prayer
Autosuggestion
Autosuggestion Healing
Baraka #2
Baruch
Biochemical
Blessing
Catalystic Healing
Cone of Power
Congregational Healing
Curanderism
Dart
Directed-Thought
Distant Healing
End-Result
Headache Control
Healee
Healing Basket
Healing by Evokation #1
Healing Current
Healing Petition
Healing-at-a-Distance

Intuitive Healers
Leader
Logurist
Logury
Medical Medium
Mental Healer
Mental Healing
Mental Mediumship Healing
Mental Self-Healing
Mental Telepathic Healing
Paraelectricity
Photo-Telepathy Healing
Physiochemical Mechanism
Prayer Group
Prayer Team
Pricking
Psychic Diagnostician
Psychic Mental Diagnosis
Psychoholiness Psychokinesis
Remote Healing
Simonton Method
Treatment
Visualized Healing

PSYCHIC HEALING

Astral Healing
Astral Projection Healing
Aura Balancing
Auric Diagnosing
Biological Phenomena #4
Black Crown Ceremony
Blessing Way
Blowing upon the Sick
Breath Healing
Charismatic Healer
Clairscent Diagnosis
Curanderos

Dental Psychism
Doctoring Session
Emotional Healing
Esoteric Healers
Esoteric Healing
Etheric Diagnosing
Group Denistry Psychism
Healee
Healer
Healing by Evocation #2
Healing by Proxy
Healing Dance

Healing Hands
Healing Reflexes
Heat Up
Lourdes
Magic Healing
Make a Prayer
Medicine
Medicine Bundle
Medicine Man
Miracle Healing
Mystic Healing
N/UM
Nonmedicinal Healing
Palming the Eyes
Paragnost
Paranormal Healer
Paranormal Healing
Parasonoptic Phenomena
Petitioner
Physical Reading
PL Kyodan
Polarity Balancing
Polarity Therapists
Power Doctor
Pranic Healing
PSI Healing

PSI Scan
Psyched-Out
Psychic Healing
Psychic Healing Technician
Psychic Practitioner
Pumping
Rape of the Soul
Reiki
Remote Treatments
Sickness Transfer
Sing
Singer
Spirit Healing
Spontaneous Remission
Sweat Lodge
Talking to the Gods
Therapeutists #1
Tonton-Macoute'
Vaculate
Wal
Wart Charmer
Watcher #1
Water
Witch Coven
Witch-Doctor

PSYCHIC TRANSFER

Accidental Psychic Attack *
Antipsi *
Apopsi ***
As If Technique *
Assimilation *
Astral Bruises *
Atmosphere Shielding ***
Aura of Respectibility
Backlash ***
Biocommunication #1 & #2 *
Biological Generator
Biorapport *
Boomerang Curse ***
Boomerang PSI ***
Broadcasting *
Catapsi *
Conferring of Power *
Controlled Empath *
Conversion Hysteria *
Cosmic Generator
Cross-Excitation
Curse
Demand Characteristics

Eating Companions *
Electric Vampirism
Emotional Telepathy *
Etheric Projection #3 *
Evil Mouth *
Fires Without Cause #2
Healing by Proxy ***
Hex *
Holy Mountain ***
Human Batteries *
Human Generator Machines *
Human Transmitter *
Ill-Wishing *
Intuit Telepathy *
Locking-Out ***
Magic With Magic Cure ***
Maladaptive Behavior *
Mental Telepathic Pollution *
Mirror Curse ***
Negapsi *
Negative Fluid *
Negative Psychism *
Occult Attacks *

757

Occult Police ***
Official Curse *
Operation Prayer Power *
Parasitism *
Parasyte
Phowa
PL Kyodan
Prana Leakage *
Precautious Resistance ***
PSI Block ***
Psychic Atmosphere Gauge ***
Psychic Attack *
Psychic Block ***
Psychic Bruises *
Psychic Collision *
Psychic Contagion *
Psychic Feuds
Psychic Impact *
Psychic Kinship
Psychic Leakage *
Psychic Protection ***
Psychic Push-Over ***
Psychic Recovery ***

Psychic Transfer *
Psychic Vampire
Psychic Yell
Psychical Invasion *
Scapegoat *
Sealing of the Aura ***
Shielding ***
Shock-in-Return
Sickness Transfer *
Splodger
Splodging *
Spontaneous Symptom Shifting
Strength Transference ***
Subjective Psychic Attack *
Svechchhotkranli
Sympathetic Induction *
Total Empath *
Twelve Blessings
Up-For-Grabs *
Vaculate *
Wall of Protection *
Water #6 ***
Werzelya

RADIONICS

Abrams Box
Anthropoflux
Biodynamics
Black Box
Black Box Concept
Book of Rates
Congested Area
De La Warr Box
E-Matrix
E.R.A.
Electronic Radiation of Abrams
Emanation #1 & #2
Energy Matrix
Energy Matrix Machines
ERA
Gallen Machine
Hand-Trembler Diagnostician
Medical Radiesthesia
Mind-Machines
Mitogenetic Rays
Oraccu
Oracs
Pi-Ray Orgon Accumulator
    Coffer

Psionic Machine
Psychic Shock Articles #2
Radiational Paraphysics
Radiesthesist
Radiesthetic Sense
Radionic Camera
Radionic Diagnostician
Radionic Healing
Radionic Practitioner
Radionics
Sthenometer #2
Stick
Stroker Plate
Tuning of the Mind
Urine #3

SOULLESS PSYCHISM

Android
Animal Familiar
Antigod
Artificial Elemental
Astral Corpses
Astral Shell
Baka
Corpse Cadaver
Counterfeit
Density Elementals
Dessounin Rite
Eidola #1
Elemental #1a
Elemental Astral Shapes
Elemental Beings #5 & #6
Elemental Essence
Fairie
Fairy Fire
Familiar Spirit #1
Golem
Homunculus
Imaginary Ghost
Inanimate Entities
Irrational Shell
Lay the Spirits

Lords of the Dark Face
Magloire
Mandrake Amulet
Mental Elementals
Minor Deities
Nature Spirits
Negative Elemental
Nonhuman
Nonhuman Forms
Nonhuman Spirit
Pseudophysical Images
Psychic Shell
Pygmalion Hypothesis
Shade
Shakey
Shem
Shug
Soulless
Spook
Tsal
Tulpa
Vitalized Shell
Vivi
Zombie

TELEPATHY

Action Telepathy *
Artistic Telepathy *
Backward PSI
Biocommunication *
Biological Compatibility *
Biotelepathy *   •
Blood-Soul *
Collective Hallucinations *
Color Telepathy
Cryptopsychism
Doctrinal Compliance
Extrasensorimotor *
Feel-and-See-Combination *
Group Telepathy *
Herd Impulses *
Intuit Telepathy *
Joint Hypnosis Telepathy *
Kinetic Telepathy *
Mental Radio
Mental TV *
Motor Telepathy
Movement Telepathy *

Muscular ESP
Parent-Child Telepathy *
Passive-Agent Phenomenon
Patient-Therapist ESP *
Photo-Telepathy *
Photoflash Clairsentience *
Picture Telepathy *
Psychometric Telepathy *
Selective Telepathy *
Senuous Element
Soul-Rapport Telepathy *
Symbiotic Relationship
Sympathetic Pains *
Sympathetic Telepathy
Synchronization *
Teleconference *
Teleneural Influence *
Teleotic
Telepath *
Telepathic Clairvoyance
Telepathic Hypnosis *
Telepathic Leakage *

759

Telepathic Signal *
Telepathic Sleep-Wake *
Telepathic Transmission
Telepathic Transmission of
   Illness *
Telepathist *
Telepathize *

Telepathy *
Telesomatic *
Telethesia *
Texture Telepathy *
Wordless-Signless
   Communications

WORDS-WITH-POWER

Ablanathtanalba
Abracadabra *
Adonai *
Affirmations *
Agala *
Agla
Aham Brahmasmi
Amen *
Ananisapta
Bible *
Bijakshara Mantra
Black Mud of Occultism *
Bless *
Bless You *
Blessed Be
Body DNA's *
Buddha Amida Butsu
Cittavisuddhiprakarana *
Cloak of Insulation *
Coat of Protection
Collective Prayer *
Court Cards
Danger-Charged Words *
Dies, Mies, Jeschet, Benedoefet,
   Dowima, Enitemaus
DNA Molecules *
Elohim *
Evil Mouth *
Gohonzon
Heterosuggestion *
Hocus Pocus
Incantation *
Jack
Japam
Jesus
Jesus Prayer
Ketab
Kyrie Eleison *
Ledi Sayadaw *
Logorhythmic *
Magic Verse *

Mantram *
Mind-Over-Matter #1 *
Mumbo-Jumbo *
Namaskar Consciousness
Namaste *
Name *
Names-of-Power *
Nonmanifest Sound
Palindrome *
Philology *
Poet #2
Poetry *
Polysensory Incantation *
Power-of-the-Word *
Prayer
Prayer Wheels
Prayer Power *
Psychic Self-Protection
Psychic Shield *
Psychic Telemetry
Scarab Beetle Amulet *
Scarabaeus
Scientific Prayer *
Shem
Ship's Name *
Sigil *
Tetragrammaton *
Theban Script
Vach *
Verse Magic *
Vibrasonic Tuner
Words *
Words-With-Power *
Yahweh *
YHVH

PSYCHIC PROCESSES USED TO PRODUCE PSYCHISM

These are general groups of psychism according to special methods of inducing either mental or physical psychism: Many cultures and early civilizations encouraged psychic experiences by everyone focusing on the same process. This resulted in a variety of psychic skills which are all acquired by the same process. These are categorized under the particular process used.

AMULETING
ASSOCIATION MAGIC AND
  SYMBOLS
CEREMONIAL MAGIC
EMOTIONAL PSYCHISM
FORCED PSYCHISM
MEDITATION (see Appendix 5)
MENTAL PSYCHIC
  PROCESSES
MINPSI

MOVEMENT-FOR-ALTERED-
  CONSCIOUSNESS
PHYSICAL PSYCHIC
  PROCESSES
POINT-OF-FOCUS
PSYCHIC EXPERIENCES
  DURING SLEEP (see
  DREAMS)
SOUNDS-WITH-POWER

AMULETING

Acorn *
Adore
Alrune
Amatl Paper
Amulet *
Amulet Energizing *
Amuleting *
Amuletizing *
Anthropomorphism
Artificial Magnet *
Bear Claw
Bear Paw
Ceremonial Magnetising *
Charm *
Charming
Churinga
Circular Stone Dance *
Consecrated Statues *
Cross of Life
Directed-Thought #2 *
Ear-Ring
Elixir
Exteriorization of Motoricity
Fairy Stone *
Fetish *
Garnets
Gris-Gris *
Group Totem *
Hammer
Hei-Tiki

Hex-Signs *
Holed Stone
Horse Shoe *
Kachina Doll *
Ketab *
Lefafa Sedq
Magloire
Main-De-Gloire
Mandrake Amulet *
Medicine Bag *
Medicine Bundle *
Otomi Figurines
Palmed Power *
Palming *
Pointing Bone *
Power of the Thunder God
Protective Superstition *
Psychic Shock Articles #1 *
Remote Treatments *
Ritual Objects *
Scarab Beetle Amulet *
Spirit-Object Influence
Storing Power *
Sudarium
Talisman *
Talismanic Magic *
Talismanic Reading
Talismaning *
Talismanitize *
Talismanize

Tau
Thread
Tiki
Totem *
Tribal Medicine Bundles *
Udjat Eye *

Ur-Keka
Ushabti
Utchat
Veronica *
Wand #2 *

ASSOCIATION MAGIC AND SYMBOLS

Abraxas
Adornation of Ashes
Allegory
Ankh
Annuit Coeptis
Apotropaic Action
Ascent
Ashes
Association Magic
Aswattha
Bat
BC/AB
Black Crown
Bowls
Butterfly
Contagious Magic
Cosmic Snake
Cup
Dagger
Dorje
Equi-Limbed Cross
Evergreen Tree
Five-Pointed Star
Golden Lotus
Guardian of the Door
Hair
Hex
Hex-Signs
Hexagram
Hexist
Holy Kiss
Holy Trinity
Image Magic
Imagination #2
Imitative Magic
Immutable One
Jacob's Ladder
Kat
Key
Knots
L-Rod
Ladder
Law of the Wheel
Lotus

Lotus of the Heart
Ma-At
Macroprospus
Magic Symbols
Magic Wheel
Magic with Magic Cure
Magical Correspondence
Magical Diagrams
Mani Padme
Micro-Cosmus
Midgard
Mimicry
Mirror Magic
Oracle Statue
Orenda
Parable
Pentacle
Picatrix
Pillars
Psychic Figurine
Psychodrama White Magic
Psychogenic Bleeding
Realizer of the Aim
Sacred Disc
Salt
Scarab Beetle
Sephiroth
Serpent
Seven Sacred Planets
Seven-Knotted Wand
Shikha
Shiva
Solomon's Seal
Statue of Four Faces and Four
    Arms
Steps
Sword
Symbolic Magic
Symbolism
Symbolist
Symbols
Sympathetic Magic
Temple Wheels
Tetragram

762

Three-Knotted Wand
Token
Totem
Totem Cults
Totem Pole
Totemic Spirits
Totemism
Tree
Tree of Knowledge
Tree of Life
Triangle
Tribal Medicine Bundles

Trikona
Trinity
Unicorn
Urine
Wanga
Wheel of the Law
White Serpent
Wicca
Witch
Witchcraft
Yggrosil

CEREMONIAL MAGIC

Ab-I-Hayat
Altar
Anointing
Arthame
Ashes
Banishing
Banishing Rituals
Bell
Bell, Book, and Candle
Black Crown
Black Crown Ceremony
Black Magic
Black Mass
Blood-Covenant
Blood-Soul
Call Up Spirits
Calls Down
Calls Up
Ceremonial Magic
Ceremonial Magnetising
Ceremony
Chalice
Charm #2 & #3
Cone of Power
Conjuration
Conjure
Conjure Up
Conjuring Lodges
Copal
Cup
Dagger
Deosil Movement
Devil's Girdle
Dorje
East
Elemental Weapons
Enemy Way
Equi-Limbed Cross

Evocation
Exsufflation
Familiar
Five-Pointed Star
Fork
Garlic
Gassho
Goat
Goetric Art
Golden Lotus
Grimoire
Group Totem
Halloween
Hex
Hexagram
Holy Oils
Indian Pipe
Individualized Conditioned
    Response
Initiatory Ceremonies
Invocation
Invocation of the Holy Guardian
    Angel
Kat
Key of Solomon
Ku-He-A
Ladder to Heaven
Lamen
Ley Lines
License to Depart
Liturgy
Low Magic
Magic Circle
Magic Wand
Magician
Maze
Mumbo-Jumbo
Musing

Nudity in Magic
Oil for Anointing
Onions
Pentacle
Perfumes
Philter
Pipe of Peace
Queen Scale
Ring of Wooden Posts
Ritual
Ritual Magic
Rod
Sacrament
Sacramental Healer
Sign of the Cross
Sky Ceremonies
Soul Brotherhood
Superstition
Supreme and Complete Ritual
Sweat Lodge
Sword

Symbolism
Symbolist
Symbols
Tantra
Tea #2
Tetragram
Tradition
Unction
Virgin
Voodoo
Voodoo Doctor
Voodooism
Warlock
White Magic
White Magician
White Wizard
Wicca
Widdershins
Witch
Witch's Mill
Withershins

EMOTIONAL PSYCHISM

Alien Tongues
Apparition of the Living *
Baptism in the Spirit
Charisma *
Charismatic Healer **
Charismatic Hymn
Charismatic Movement **
Charismatic Renewal **
Charisms
Communal Worship
Corroborator *
Crisis Apparition
Crisis Calls *
Crisis ESP
Crisis Phenomena
Crisis Telepathy *
Death Coincidences *
Death Fetch
Double Egos *
Ectasy #2 *
Emergency PSI *
Emotional Clairaudience *
Emotional Clairvoyance *
Emotional Healing **
Emotional High *
Emotional PSI *
Emotional Psychism

Emotional Psychokinesis *
Emotional Telepathy *
Empathy Clairsentience *
Etheric Materialization *
Etheric Projection #2 & #3
Fateful Communications
Fetch #1
Filled with the Spirit *
Flood of New Words, The
Giddiness
Gift of Tongues
Glossolalia
Glossolalic Utterance *
Glossolalist
Glottologue
Healing Dance **
Heat Up **
Hlambululu Emadloti *
Holy Ghost
Holy Spirit *
Hypnotic Ecstasy *
Interpretation-of-Talking-in-
  Tongues *
Inversion of Time *
Jimsonweed
Kairos
Light Apparition *

Mystic Ring *
Need-Determined Response *
Neophasia
Phantasms of the Living
Phantom Coach
Polyglottous Neophasia
Psychic Yell *
Psychogenic Bleeding
Quenching the Spirit
Random Psychism
Receiving the Glossolalia
Religious Hysteria *
Sing-in-the-Spirit *
Slaying-in-the-Spirit **
Speaking-in-Tongues
Spiritual High *
Spiritually Stunted
Splodging
Spontaneous Case

Spontaneous PSI
Spontaneous Psychism *
Spontaneous Remission **
Spontaneous Vocation *
Stigmata
Stigmatic
Stigmatization *
Talking-in-Tongues *
Telepathic Triggered-Vision
Tension Wave
Tongues
Transcendent Moment *
Unio Mystica
Unknown Tongues
Utterances
Vedana
Vision of Self *
Xenoglossia

FORCED PSYCHISM

!Kia
!Kia Fire
!Kia Healing
!Kung Healer
A. Muscaria
Amanita Muscaria
Ambrosia
Atropine
Caapi
Convulsive Medium
Datura Inoxia
Datura Stranonium
Die **
Divine Intoxication
Election **
ESP Phenomena Under LSD
Fly Agaric
Force-Feed
Forced PSI
Forced Psychism
Foxglove
Ghost Dance
God's Flesh
Group Sound **
Hand-Trembling Sickness
Healing Dance **
Healing Reflexes **
Hermit's Cell
Howling Dervishes
Hysteria

Initiation Rites
Initiatory Death
Initiatory Sickness **
Ipomea
Isolation Booth
Isolation Box
Isolation Initiation
Isolation Tank
Jimsonweed
Ketamines
Kia Fire
Kung Healer
Liber Jugorum
Lophophora Williansii
Lysergic Acid
Mantike
Mate Tea
Mescalin
Mescalito
Mushroom
Opium
Oxygen Intoxication
Oxygen Jag
Personal Quest
Peyote Cactus
Peyote Cult
Physical Isolation
Psilocybin Mushroom
Psychedelic Consciousness
Psychic Crisis

Psychotropic Plants
Recreational Drugs
Resurrection
Separate Realities
Snake-Handling Cults
Sun-Gaze Dance
Teonanactl
Think Tank

Third-Eye Attainment
Thornapple
Three-Day Smoke
Traditional Instructions
Tribal Dancing
Will of the Clan
Yage

MENTAL PSYCHIC PROCESSES

A Call
A Present
Acetylcholine
Active Ritual
Active Willing
Adrenergia
After Image *
Alladin
Alpha Senses
Amping *
Antahkarana
Apperception
Artificial Fields
Artificial Symbols *
ASC
Asceticism
Astral Telescope
Attunement
Awake Control
Baraduc's Biometer
Basic Limiting Principles
Beamed In
Bioaccumulator
Biochemical *
Bioelectric *
Bioelectric Phenomena
Biological Contact
Blank Mood
Blind Experiments
Blind Mental Psychism
Blind Spot
Blocking
Bodhi Tree
Body Chemistry #2
Body Sensation
Body-Feelings *
Buffalo Power
Called Person
Candle Flame *
Center *
Chance

Change Effect
Charismatic
Cloak of Insulation
Co-Creative Quietness
Coat of Protection
Cold
Cold Reader
Complete Breath
Compression Symbol
Concentrated Thought
Concentration *
Conceptualization
Conditioning
Confidence Call
Conformance Behavior
Conscious Cooperation
Contagious Enthusiasm *
Contradistinction to See
Controlled Psychism *
Controlled Relaxation
Coordinated Psychical Functions
Coread
Creative Quiet
Critical Facilitate *
Crutch
Cypher Characters
Deep-Dream Meditation
Demanded PSI-Try *
Demos
Detuning
Developmental Patterns
Dezygotic Phenomena
Dialogue
Double-Blind Experiments
Doubt Vibrations *
Dual Consciousness
Electromagnetic Circuit
Elements of Occultism
Elf Waves
Eliciting PSI
Elusive PSI *

Monkey Chatter
Mood-Shifts *
Monosprit
Muddy Conditions *
Multivariate Approach
Mystic-Type State of
    Consciousness
Negapsi
Negative Fluid
Negative PSI *
Neural Communication
Neutral Mind *
Nexus
Non-Thought *
Nonintentional ESP
Nonmaterial Patterns
Nonordinary Reality
Nonreality Reality
Numen
Numinosity
Objective/Subjective
    Programming
Optical Image Device
Out-There
Outer Band
Outer Mental Activity
Perceive #1 *
Percept
Perception of the Shadow
Perceptual Defense *
Percipient
Persona Theory
Personification
Physical Carrier of PSI
    Information
Picked Up
Plethysomograph
Pom
Posicontrol
Power Shorts
Prime-Age
Private Sitting
Problem Solving State of
    Consciousness
Profound Wakefulness
Projected Energy
Protoanalysis
PSI Gift
PSI Jungle
PSI Leakage
PSI Relativity
PSI Resistance

PSI Retrieval Process
PSI-Conducive State #2 *
PSI-Favorable States
PSI-Mediated Information
PSI-Mediated Vehicle
PSI-Optimization
PSI-Org Energy
PSI-Q
Psitron
Psyched-Up
Psychic Attunement *
Psychic Band
Psychic Casualties *
Psychic Centers
Psychic Development *
Psychic Development Circle
Psychic Doors *
Psychic Fence
Psychic Gate
Psychic Information *
Psychic Laser
Psychic Message
Psychic Message Symbols
Psychic Percepts
Psychic Protection
Psychic Rods
Psychic Self-Protection
Psychic Sensorium
Psychic Shield *
Psychic Skill
Psyching-Up
Psychological Warp
Psychomonism
Psychosomatic Self-Regulation
Psychotronic Generators
Purity of the Work *
Putting Out Feelers
Quantum Jump
Querant
Querist
Questioner
Receiving Mode
Red Hot Needles
Response
Resonant Recorder
Rods
Sanctuary
Scatter Effect
Schizokinesis
Second-Ring-of-Power
Self-Awareness
Sensorimotor Leakage

Serve
Session
Setting the Mood
Sign of the Cross
Silva Method
Simile Picture
Sit
Sitters
Skyclad
Spiritoid
Spiritual Circle
States of Nonordinary Reality
Step into your Vibration
Subconsciously Willed
Superphysical
Supraself
Supressed Desire
Surfacing *
Synapse
Tachyon
Taming the Mind *
Tapping Into *
Tearing
Texture of Mental Activity
Thermal Images
Three Finger Technique
Through
Tied-In

Tip-Offs
Transparent Dimensional Warp
Triggers
True-Serious Communications
Tsas and Rtsa
Tuned-In
Turned On *
Unbounded Awareness
Uncaring Alertness *
Unconscious Fraud
Unconscious Material
Uncontrolled Psychism *
Universal Symbols *
Unreal Inner Activity
Veil *
Veridical PSI Phenomena
Verification
Vibrational Level
Waiting Technique
Woft
Wide-Band Tuning
Withinness
Words of Insulation
Work with Us
World of Meditation
Zero Point*

MINPSI

Agate
Alabaster
Alexandrite *
Amber *
Amethyst
Anachitis
Anancithidus
Angelical Stone
Aquamarine **
Attraction Consciousness *
Azoic Rock *
Beryl
Bishop's Ring
Black Diamond *
Black Onyx
Brimstone
Calundronius *
Cat's Eye
Chalcedony
Chrysolite
Churinga

Containers of Magical Power *
Coral Castle
Crick Stone **
Crystals
Dinhinh Dyonrd **
Emerald *
Garnets
Gift of Heaven
Glosoperta **
Gnostic Gems *
God-as-the-Stone
God-in-the-Stone
Gold
Greenish Turquoise
Hexagonal Form *
Holed Stone
Iceland Spar
Iron
Iron Doctor *
Iron Ring
Ivory

769

Jade #1
Jewel of the Lotus
Kaustubha
Kether *
Land of Darkness #2
Lapis
Lapis Lazuli
Levitation Gems
Ley Lines *
Lia-Fail
Light-Bulb Gems *
Lorelei #2
Manimala *
Men-An-Tol **
Mineral Consciousness *
Mineral Kingdom *
Minpsi *
Monolith
Moonstone
Natural Magnet **
Onyx
Opal
Overall Consciousness *
Pearl
Pentarbe
Primary Perception *
Quartz *
Red Corals

Rock Crystal
Rock Electricity *
Ruby
Sapphire
Screaming Stone
Self-Directing #1
Shameer
Shewstone
Sight in Darkness
Singing Stones *
Snake-Stone
Speaking Stone
Star-Ruby
Star-Sapphire
Stone Circle
Stone of Fail
Stone of Laz
Stone Worshiping Cults *
Stones *
Sunstone
Toadstone
Topaz
Tourmaline
Turquoise
Unseen Seer *
Water Sapphire
White Diamond
Yellow Diamonds

MOVEMENT-FOR-ALTERED-CONSCIOUSNESS

Abstract Dancing
Belly Dancing
Carole
Cave Phenomenon
Cherubim and Seraphim
   Movement
Circular Stone Dance
Collective Trance
Dance of Life
Dance Therapy
Danced Him
Dancing Mania
Deosil Movement
Dervish
Dhikr
Diker
Double Heavy
Egyptian Temple Dancers
Etheric Activity
Etheric Running
Fana

Gymnastic Medicine
Healing Dance
Howling Dervishes
Hula
Invocation #2
Jogging Meditation
Jumping Magicians
Khikr
Kinhin
Kirtan
Loa
Lun-Gom-Pa Runners
Mass Strength
Maulavi
Meditation-in-Motion
Mental Epidemic
Movement-for-Altered
   Consciousness
Movements
Mudra
Pampas

770

Prolonged Jogging
Psycalisthenics
Psychic Dancing
Racing Ones
Rides
Runner's High
Samurai
Somato-Psychic
St. Vitus's Dance
Stick #2
T'ai Chi

T'ai Chi Chuan
Tai Chi
Tai Chi Chuan
Temple Dancers
Tribal Dancing
Visible Speech
Walworth Jumpers
Watch Services
Whirling Dervishes
Zen of Running
Zikr

PHYSICAL PSYCHIC PROCESSES

Aconcinnitous Psychism *
Antifraud Precaution
Arrhythmia *
Batteries
Battery *
Blacked-Out Room *
Breathed Into #1
Call
Catalepsy
Cataleptic Trance
Convulsive Medium
Cooperants
Dark Room *
Darkness
Darkroom Sessions *
Demanded PSI-Try *
Desired-Control *
Devil's Girdle
Diffusion
Draperies *
Drop-In Communicators *
Ectoplasm *
Ectoplasmic Flow *
Ectoplasmic Structures *
Electrostatic Field *
Electrostatic Field Meter
Elements of Occultism
Emanation #1 & #2
Emetic Ritual *
Empirical Energy
Ethereal Smoke
Etheric Energy
Etheric World Communication
False-Serious Communications
Fatal Psychic Ability
Fiery Lives *
Fluidic Link *
Furor

Galvanometer *
Hand-Trembling Sickness *
Hands
Heavy Trance *
Herd Intoxication
Hereditary Transmission *
Home Circle *
Human Hand
Imaginary Spirit
Initiant *
Intermediary Agency *
Karmically Desired *
Karmically Self-Generated *
Karmically Willed
Kiva
Kivas
Ma-at
Magnetic Somnambolism
Magnetic Scope of Ruter
Medianimic
Medianimization *
Mediate
Meditation
Mediumized
Mediumship Development *
Mento-Physical
Method + Pattern
Nonordinary Realities
Nonreality Reality
Nonspontaneous
    Manifestations *
Odic Radiation *
One Fell Stroke
One-Pointedness
Physical Psychic Processes
Physical Psychism *
Physical Transfiguration *
Plethysomograph

Power Shorts *
Protoplasm
PSI-Org Energy
Psychic Band *
Psychic Development *
Psychic Protection
Psychic Shield *
Psychic Skill
Psychomonism
Quality of the Work *
Raise the Vibrations *
Regulated Situation *
Schools for Prophets
Seance *
Self-Isolation *
Shamanship Instructions *
Sign of the Cross *

Simple Obsession
Sitters *
Spin Waves
Spiritoscope
Springing Forth
States of Nonordinary Reality
Subconsciously Willed
Sympathetic Motion
Synergy #2
System of Collective Souls
System of Negation
Taboo
Testing Mediumship *
Three Egg Ceremony *
Transfiguration
Uncontrolled Psychism *

POINT-OF-FOCUS

Altar
Candle Flame #2
Center #2
Coffeography
Concentration
Contemplation #1, #2 & #4
Crab Divination
Cup of Divination
Extispicium
Eye of Light
Flame Billets
Flower Clairsentience
Focal Point
Focusing Effect
Hearth Divination
Hen-Eggs
Hepatoscopy
Look Fixedly
Lituus Rod
Liver Gazing

Mantram
Matter Duplication
Mind's Eye #1
Mind-Drift
Mindfulness
Monen
Photograph Life Reading
Photographology
Photography Reading
Point-of-Focus
Point-of-Focus Readings
Pointing
Pointing Bone
Ribbon Clairvoyance
Single-Pointedness
Stare Down
Tasseographer
Tasseography
Tea Leaf Reading
Tea-Cup Reading

SOUNDS-WITH-POWER

Aum *
Background Fill *
Bell *
Bhairava Raga
Bioresonance *
Chanting *
Class Mantra *
Constant Sensory Input *
Daimoku

De-Tuned *
Deepaka Raga *
Distorted Music *
Drum *
Eidophone
Enchant
Eternal Rhythm #2 *
F *
Gayatri Mantra

772

Gongyo
Gregorian Chants *
Group Sound *
Habituated Stimulus *
Hagging
Harp
Hindole Raga
Hum
Incantation *
Inner-Sound Current *
Inter-Etheric Force
Intoning *
Japa *
Kaidan
Listening Fatigue *
Litany
Little Snake *
Lost Word **
Malkounsa Raga
Mantra *
Mass Music *
Megha Raga *
Mood-Stimulus *
Music Healing **
Music Therapist **
Nada *
Nadam
Namapathy **
Necromantic Bell
Nichiren Shoshu
Nonmanifest Sound
Octave
Ohm *
Om

Phyit-Pyet *
Pink Noise *
Pirit
Planet-to-Psychic-Center
    Correspondence *
Pran-Vayu *
Psychoacoustics *
Pythagorean Science
Ragas *
Raise the Vibrations *
Resonance
Resonate *
Resonater
Sand Paintings
Sankirtans *
Science of Chanting *
Seed-Mantra
Shapes
Shooting Chant *
Sound
Sound Healing **
Sound Kasina *
Sound Plate
Sounds-with-Power *
Sri Raga
Sympathetic Vibration *
Threshold Control #2 *
Tone of the Cosmic Music *
Toning **
Varna
Water-Element Sound
Whistling Bottles *
White Noise
White Noise Stimuli *

Appendix 3
SYNONYMS OF POPULAR KEY WORDS

Synonyms of popular words too numerous to list under each word or the key word.

ASTRAL BODY
AURA
ETHERIC WORLD
ETHERIC WORLD
   INTELLIGENCES
MONAD

NATURE SPIRITS
PSYCHIC
PSYCHIC ARTS & PSYCHISM
SOUL-MIND
TOTALITY
VITAL LIFE FORCE

ASTRAL BODY (Synonyms)

Astral Body
Astro-Soul
Bardo Body
Biocorporeity
Cambodian Spirit
Chhaya
Design Body
Desire Body
Disembodied Soul #1
Doppelganger
Doubleganger
Dream Body
Emotional Body

Energy Accumulator
Esprit
Essential Body
Follower
Free-Soul
Fylgja
Intermediary Body
Judel
Kama Rupa
Khaibit
Maya-Rupa
Nonphysical Body
Phantasmata

Phantom
Protean Soul
Real Man
Resurrection Body
Second Body
Shade #2 & #3
Shining-Illusory Body
Soul Body
Starry Envelope of the Soul
Subtle Body
Superphysical Body
Vitality Vesture

AURA (Synonyms)

Arc Emanations
Archetypal Pattern
Atomic and Molecular
   Attraction
Aura *
Aura-Mist *
Aureola
Auric Aureola
Auric Egg
Auric Light
Auric Rays *
Beta Body
Bienergy
Biological Field
Biological Plasma
Biological Plasma Body
Biological Radiation
Biological Radio
   Communication
Bioluminescent Electrical Field

Bioplasma Force Field *
Biotensor Field
Bipolar Aura *
Blueprint *
Body of Life and Vitality *
Chemical Aura
Collective Aura *
Corona
Counterpart Body *
Electric Aura
Electric Body
Electric Fields
Electric Magnetic Matrix
Electrobioluminescence
Electrodynamic Field
Eloptic Radiation
Energy Body
Energy Matrix
Energy Shield
Energy Surround

Energy-Electrical Field
Etheric Aura
Etheric Double *
Etheric Energy Field
Etheric Envelope
Etheric Lights *
Etheric Matrix
Etheric Mould
Etheric Physical Aura
Etherico-Physical Body
Fields of Life
First Aura *
Fluidic Energy
Formative-Force Body
Fourth State of Matter
Functional Body
Geomagnetic Field
Heat Aura
Heat Convection Currents *
Heat Envelope

774

Heloidic Rays
Holy Body
Human Air Surround
Human Atmosphere
Human Aura *
Infrared Radiation Man
Inner-Aura
Inua
Ka
L & T Fields
L-Fields
Life Field
Life Soul
Life-and-Thought Fields *
Linga Sharira
Luminescence
Luminous Body *
Luminous Eggs
Magnetic Atmosphere
Magnetic Body *
Magnetic Emanations

Magnetic Fields *
Magnetic Radiation
Magnetic Waves
Matrix
Mental Aura *
Mold
Mould
N-Rays #2
Noosphere
Odic Body
Odic Light *
Ovoid
Pattern *
Prabhamadala
Prana Aura
Prephysical Body
Psychic Aura *
Psychic Skin
Psychological Aura
Psychomagnetic Radiation
Radiant Body

Radiation Pattern
Rim Auras *
Sambhoga-Kaya
Scintillating Kaleidoscopic
    Nebula
Self-Organizing
    Biogravitational Fields
Semiphysical Body
Shining Body
Soul-Mind Aura
Spiritual Aura
Spiritual Shape
St. Elmo's Fire *
Star Body
Surround *
T-Fields
Terrestial Magnetism
Vital Body
Wave Fronts
Web of Energy
Wireless Waves

ETHERIC WORLD (Synonyms)

Acoma-Pueblo
Aether
Aethereal
Aetherial
After-Death World
Air
Atmosphere
Beyond
Celestial
Chemical Ether
Cloud of Unknowing
Concentric Spheres
Counterspace
Devanchan #1 & #3
Empty Space
Epipneuma Sphere
Eternal World
Ether #2
Ether Ocean
Ethereal
Etheric
Etheric Plane
Etheric World
Extraterrestrial
Fourth Dimension
Funerary Geography
Heaven #1, #5 & #6

Heaven of Fire
Heaven of Stars
Heavenly Fields
Hidden Dimension
Higher Plane
Higher Realities #2
Higher Side
Higher Side of Life
Homeland
Immaterial Dimensions
Inner-Planes
Invisible World
Loka
Multispirit System
Neosphere
Next World
Nonhuman World
Nonphysical
Ocean of Living Energy
Otherworld
Out-There
Over There
Overworld
Phenomenal World
Psychic Space
Pulotu
Sea of PSI

Sea of Universal Energy
Sound Ether
Space
Spirit Spheres
Spirit World
Spiritous
Spiritual World
System of Realities
Transitional Worlds
Unknown
Unseen Realm
Vibric Matter
World of Spirit

ETHERIC WORLD INTELLIGENCES (Synonyms)

Abigor #2 ***
Adversaries ***
Aerolite
Agathodemon
Agni #1 & #3 *
Ahola
Ahriman ***
Ahura Mazdah
Ahyras ***
Aio
Aiwass
Ajiva *
Akua
Akwalupo
Alchemist #2 *
An Intelligence
Ancestral Ghosts
Ancestral Spirits *
Ancestrals
Angel Doctor *
Angel of Righteousness
Angelic Sentries *
Angels of the Four Cardinal
   Points
Anthropomorphic Creations
Antigod ***
Antitheoi ***
Apothecarer
Apparition
Ardat-Lile
Ariel
Ascended Being #1
Astral Coadjutor
Asuras #1
Autonomous Secondary
   Personality
Baalzephon
Band of Collaborators *
Banshee
Being of Light *
Beneficent Daemon *
Benevolent Spirit
Bright Angel
Celestial Beings *
Celestial Guardian *
Celestial Smith
Chac
Chalchihuitlicue
Chuku
Cloud Beings *

Collaborator *
Comforting Angel
Communicant
Communicator *
Congress of Spirits
Control
Cosmic Hosts of Light
Coyote
Cult of the Dead
Daemon *
Daimon *
Daivas ****
Dark Outside-Personalities ***
Davy Jones
Dawn Spirits
Death Demons ***
Deities
Deity #1
Demiurge
Demon #1 & #2
Demoness
Demonic
Denizens in Space
Departed Spirits
Devil #3 ****
Diakka
Diamond Body
Dibbuk
Dimonion
Discarnate Entity
Discarnate Intelligence
Doctor Teacher *
Dog-Gods
Domestic Spirits
Doorkeeper *
Drop-In Communicators
Dynatype
Ea
Earth Mother
EDB
Elevated Spirits
Emissary
Enki
Entities of Seances
Entity *
Eros #3
Etheric Control
Etheric Guardian
Etheric Mentor *
Etheric World Entity *

Etheric World Intelligences *
Etimmu
Eudemon
Eumenides
Executive Order
Extrabrain-Mind Computer
Falling Spirits
Familia
Forces *
Forces of the Unseen
Fox Spirits
Fye
Genius #2 & #3
Germ God
Gila Monster
God (uncapitalized) *
Goddesses #2 *
Goinmiu #2
Great White Brotherhood
Guardian Angels
Guardian Spirit
Guide *
Hamatmas
Healer #2
Hecate
Helpers #1 & #2
Hidden Masters *
High Spirit
Higher Intelligences *
Holy Guardian Angel #3
Household Lar
Illuminators *
Imperator
Imperator Band
Impure Spirits ****
Independent Spirit
Indian Guide *
Inferior Intelligences ***
Inferior Spirits ****
Inner Band *
Intelligent Agent
Intermediaries
Invisible Intelligence #2
Invisible Master *
Invisible
Joy Guide *
Juno #1
Kachina
Kali
Koot Hoomi

776

Kuan Ti
Kukulcan
Kwoth
Lar *
Lar Familiaris
Lares *
Lares of Ancients
Learned Spirits *
Legion ***
Lilith ***
Little White God
Living Dead #2
Living Solid Face
Lleu
Loa
Lugh
Luminous Spirits
Lying Spirit ****
Maggana
Magnetizer #2
Man Force
Manasaputras
Manes #2
Manitou
Martinet
Master #2 & #5
Mazenge
Mentor
Messenger
Metaphysical Physician *
Mid-Way Spirits
Mighty Dead
Misinghalikun
Mocking Spirit
Monospirit
Mungu and Nokunzi
Muse
Nagual #1
Nanabush
Napi
Nat
Nihi
Nokunzi and Mungu

Occult Guardians of Mankind
Occult Police
Odin #2, #3 & #4
Operating Spirit
Outer Band *
Outside Personalities
Pant Neteru
Pearly Emperor
Perisprit
Personal Daemon
Personal Witches ****
Phenomena Beings
Philemon
Plumbed Serpent
Possessing God
Preceptor
Probable Self
Protecting Genii
Protector *
Psychic Support Figures *
Psychic Twin Brother
Purported Spirits
Qlippoth ***
Rappers by Profession
Rapping Spirits
Raven #1
Rector
Refractions of God *
Regents
River Spirits
Sahu
Satyrs #1
Script Intelligence
Second Self #2
Secondary Personality
Secret Chiefs
Seth
Seth Two
Shining One #2
Silent Watcher #3
Sky People *
Spirit #3 *
Spirit Agency

Spirit Band
Spirit Being #2
Spirit Control
Spirit Protector *
Spirit Teacher *
Spirits of the Above
Split Personality Fragment
Star Spirits
Subpersonality #1
Superior Spirits *
Superpersonal Entity
Supraself Metaprograms *
Supraspecies Metaprogrammers
Sylph
Tambaran
Technical Muse
Thunder People
Tindalo
Tornait
Traffic Guide
Trance Personality
Trickster
Tutelary Deity
Unseen Forces
Unseen Interlocutors
Unseen Interlopers
Vassago
Vasus
Virtues and Powers
Vodyanoy
Wallaby
White Brotherhood
White Man
Wihio
Wind People
Wise Spirits
Wodan
Wode
Wraithful Order of the Deities *
Yauhahy
Zar
Zars ***

MONAD (Synonyms)

Adoration
All-Self
Animism
Anu
Cere
Chariot of the Soul

Christ Within *
Closet #2
Cosmic Christ *
Dharma
Divine Spark
Doer, The

Dweller in the Body
Entelechy #2 & #3
Evolving Principle
God Within
Higher Self
Human Being Species Seed *

777

Human Monad
I Am *
Ib
Images Mundo
Infinitesmal Light Dots
Inner-Light
Inner-Self
Inner-Space of Man #2 *
Jiva
Jivatman
Knower of the Field
Kosmic Nous
Life-Atom
Life-Flux

Light Within
Mankind Seed
Microcosm
Monad *
Nouse
Primal Germs
Psychic Seed
Psychophysical Germ
Quintessence *
Ren
Sat-Chid-Ananda
Sekhem
Self #1, #2 & #3
Single-Point of Consciousness

Soul Personality
Stainless Individuality
Subliminal Self #3
Swabhava
Teacher Within
True Self
Unconscious Mind #2
Upper Duad
Vairochana
Vital Soul
Wirkende Kraft
Ye Are Gods
Yechidah

NATURE SPIRITS (Synonyms)

Aganent
Air Fairies
Air-Spirit
Airy Wraiths
Akualeles
Alfheim
Alpiel
Anti-Pan
Apsaras
Astral Fairies
Awd Goggie
Beasties
Black Annis
Bogey Beasts
Bogey Man
Boggart
Bogie
Border Redcap
Brown Man of the Muirs
Brownie
Bucans
Bucca Dhu
Bucca Gwidden
Buckie
Bug-A-Boos
Bugaboo
Bugs
Candle Light
Castor
Cellar Ghost
Centaur
Cereberus
Cerenunnos
Cloud Spirit
Cluricaun

Coblynau
Corn Maidens
Corpse Candle
Dakinis
Damballahwedo
Dana O'Shee
Deils
Divine Dog
Djinni
Driza
Droll
Dryads
Dunny
Dwarf
Dwarf Trolls
Earth Fairies
Earth Spirit
Elemental #2
Elemental Beings #2
Elementals
Elf
Elf Bull
Elves
Fachan
Fairie
Fairy Changeling
Fairy Midwife
Fates
Faudeur
Faun
Faunus
Fawn
Fay
Fee
Female Hamadryads

Feng
Feng-Hwang
Fermie's Fire
Fetch Light
Fey
Field Spirits
Filly Foal
Fir Darrig
Fire-Elemental
Flashing Fire
Foolish Fire
Formless Fire
Fox-Fire
Frau Holle
Freyja
Freyr
Friar's Lantern
Frivolous Spirits
Furies
Gandharvas
Genius #3
Genius Loci #1
Ghul
Giant Trolls
Giants
Gnomes
Goblin
Green Man
Griffin
Gryphon
Gwragedd Annwn
Gwyn-Ap-Nudd
Hag
Hamodryads
Harpies

Hedley Kow
Highland Banshees
Highland Glaistigs
Hippogriff
Hobgoblin
Hobs
Holda
Horned Sorcerer
Hotbrush
Humadryad
Hwang
Iblees
Iemanja
Ifreet
Imp
Ioa
Irish Banshee
Jack of the Bright Light
Jack-O-Lantern
Jann
Jinni
Juggernaut
Kelpies
Ki-Lin
Kindly Ones
Knackers
Knockers
Kobolds
Kommasso
Kurmos
Land Spirits
Laurin
Lechie
Legba
Leprechauns
Leshy
Little People
Lob
Loki
Lorelei
Madan
Magical Creatures
Marid
Mermaids
Merman
Mid-Day Woman
Moss People
Music Elementals
Naga
Naiad
Naicid
Nan-A-Push

Nature Beings
Nature Spirits
Nephelegereta
Nephilim
Nereids
Nerrivik
Nightmares
Norns
Nuliajuk
Nymphs
Oan
Oceanide
Oread
Orestiad
Pan
Penates
People of Peace
Phooka
Phouka
Pick-Tree Brag
Piper
Piskey
Pixie
Pollux
Pooka
Portunes
Pseudoelemental
Puck
Puckwudjini
Pug
Puggie
Pure Elemental
PWCA
Pygmies
Redcap
Rephaim
Salamander
Satyrs
Sedna
Ser'era
Sesha
Shee
Shellycoat
Spirit of Earth
Spirits of the Below
Spiritual Creature
Spook
Spriggans
Sprite
Spuk
Stag
Subjects

Svetovit
Swartheim
Sylph
Sylvanus
Thetis
Tornit
Tree Spirit
Troll
Trooping Fairies
Trow
Tutelary Fairy
Undines
Unicorn
Unseelie Court
Volkh
Wandjina
Water Babies
Water Fairies
Water Kelpie
We Friends
Wee People
Welsh Tylwyth Teg
Whorley
Wichtlein
Will-O'-The Wisp
William with the Little Flame
Wood Ghost
Wood Nature Spirits
Woodland Deity
Woodwouse
Yarthkins
Ymir

Abbot
Abigor #1
Aborigine
Adept
Aerial Translation Medium
Agent #1, #2 & #3a
Ame No Ma-Hitotsu No
   Kami #2
Anogoger
Angakoqs
Angokok
Anolist
Ap Thmop
Apparition Medium
Apport Medium
Arahant
Arlakeen
Auditive Medium
Augur
Auratist
Auric Clairvoyant
Automat
Auxiliaries to the Spirits
Bacoti
Bat Kol
Beggar Monk
Bewitcher
Bhikkhu
Bocor
Bonpa
Brahmana
Brothers of the Light
Brothers of the Shadow
Brujo
Bukor
Cairn Druids
Called Person
Carrying an Evil
Ceremonial Magicians
Chaldean
Changing Woman
Channel
Charmer
Chiromant
Christian Mystic
Christian Spiritists
Clairaudient
Clairempathic
Clairgustant
Clairsavorant

Clairscentrist
Clairsentient
Clairvoyant
Classic Clairvoyant
Classical Sorcerers
Classical Witches
Clever Man
Conjure Man
Conjuror
Consecrated Man
Consultant
Controller
Crafters
Cuannadero
Cunning Folk
Curandera #2
Curanderos
Dabtaras
Dactyl
Dactylomancer
Dalkarl
Dancing Sorcerer
Daughter of Voice
Dervish
Depth Psychologist
Diabolist
Direct Medium
Diver
Diviner
Drugger
Druid
Druzes
Dugpas
Dukun
Ecstat
Ecstatic
Ecstatic Medium
Eidetikers
Empath
Enchanter
Enchantress
Enoch
Entrancer
Estrie
Experimental Spiritists
Explicit Medium
Fakir
Fascinated Medium
Fascinator
Faticaria

Fierce One, The
Fili
Flexible Medium
Flyer, The
Focalizer
Fools in Christ
Formed Medium
Futurists
Gelugpa
Geomancer
Ghost Seers
Gifted Experimenters
Glamourizer
Glossolalist
Glottologue
Gnostic
Go-Betweens
Gothic Witches
Great Master
Gypsy
Hand Analyst
Hand Trembler
Hatahli
Haughty Medium
Hedge-Wizard
Hermetist
Hermit
Hexist
Hieromantis
Hierophant
Historical Medium
Holy Men of God
Hoodoo Doctor
Host Woman
Houngman
Huaca
Hugan
Hypercatholic
Hypersensitive
Iatromantis
Illiterate Medium
Illuminati #1
Imperfect Spiritists
Impressible Medium
Incorrect Mediums
Indifferent Medium
Individual Oracle
Inmost One, The
Insincere Medium
Instrument

Intermediaries
Intuit
Intuitionist
Intuitive Medium
Invocator
Involuntary Medium
Iron Doctor
Isangoma
Jack-In-Irons
Jettatore
Kahuna Nui
Kardicism
Koyemshi
Kru
Laconic Medium
Laibon
Lama
Lamia
Lanoo
Literary Medium
Logurist
Madame Zenoibia
Mage
Maggid
Magi
Magician
Magism
Magister
Magos
Magus
Mahatmas
Mambo
Mandunugu
Mantic Artist
Mantis
Master of Fire
Mediator
Medical Medium
Medicine Man
Medium
Medium for Intellectual Effects
Medium for Physical Effects
Medium for Spontaneous
   Dictations
Medium for Trivial
   Communications
Mediumistic Servitor
Men of God
Men of the Oak-Tree
Mental Healer
Mental Medium
Message Bearer

Message Worker
Metagnome
Metaphysician
Metapsychist
Mevlevis
Micawber
Modest Mediums
Moral Philosophic Medium
Mureeds
Musician Medium
Mysterion
Mystic
Mystic Christian
Nabhi
Natsaw
Natural Medium
Natural Somnambulist
Natural-Born Psychic
Navajo Shaman
Necromancer
Nefia
Neopagan Witches
Night Flyer
Night Witches
Nin-Ma-Pa
Noaide
Nocturnal Bird
Nocturnal Medium
Numerical Wizard
Oak People
Obeah Doctor
Obeahman
Obi
Odin
Omen Interpreter
Omenist
On Your Feet Psychic
Open-Eye Psychic
Optional Medium
Oracle
Oracular Priests
Pallomantic
Panpsychic
Parachero
Paragnost
Paraphysicists
Parapsychic
Passive Psychographic Medium
Pastoral Witch
Patanjali
Pawang
Pendulisant

Pendulist
Pendulum Prophets
Perceiver
Petitioner
Petro
Pneumatician
Poet
Poetic Medium
Polygraphic Medium
Portender
Power Doctor
Powwower
Practitioner
Precipitant
Precog
Pretersensual
Prevorst
Priest Magicians
Priests
Prophetic Medium
Proved Incarnationist
PSI Practitioner
PSI-Hitter
PSI-Mediator
Psychic
Psychic Diagnostician
Psychic Intermediary
Psychic Reader
Psychical Researcher
Psychicist
Psychist
Psychocriminologist
Psychokenist
Psychometer
Psychometrist
Psychopomp
Psychosensitive
Psychosensor
Public Portender
Quesited
Racing Ones
Rapid Medium
Reader
Religious Mystic
Rishi
Rogues
Sa-Ag-Ga
Sadhu
Saga
Sage
Sagoma
Scientific Medium

Scryer
Seer
Seer Priests
Semimechanical Writing
    Medium
Sensitive
Sensitive Medium
Sensory
Serious Medium
Shaman
Shut-Eye Psychic
Sibyl
Sikun
Singer
Skyer
Smithy
Somnambulist
Somnambulistic Medium
Soothsayer
Sor
Sorcerer
Sourcier
Speaking Medium
Speller
Spirit Artists
Spiritual Doctor
Spiritual Son
Spiritualist
Sruti
Stand-Up Reader
State Oracle
Strega
Strix
Sufi

Sungna
Supersensitive
Susceptible Mediums
Suspension Medium
Talking Medium
Tankway
Tapping Medium
Telekinetic Medium
Telepath
Telepathist
Teleport
Teleradiesthesiologist
Thaumaturgist
Therapeutists
Theurgists
Tibetan Oracles
Tonton-Macoute'
Total Empath
Trance Medium
Trance Voice Medium
Trancer
Transcendental Functionalist
Transcendentalist
Transcenders
Transformed Ones
Trappas
Treasure Magician
Trickster-Transformer
Trifling Medium
Trulku
Tulku
Unconscious Medium
Vamacharins
Vate

Versifying Medium
Village Blacksmith
Village Wise Woman
Village Wise-Woman
Visualizer
Visuary
Volantica
Volva
Walworth Jumpers
Wangateur
Warlock
Water Witcher
Waterloper
Waterwitch
Wearers of the Red Cap
Weird Sisters
Well-Grounded Medium
White Magician
White Shamans
Wicce
Wise Man
Wise Woman
Witch
Witch Finder
Witch Master
Witch Wiggler
Witch-Doctor
Witch-Hunter
Witchman
Witchwife
Wizard
Yarb Doctor
Yellow Caps
Yogi

PSYCHIC ARTS (Synonyms)

Adidactos
Anagogical
Ancestor Worship
Ancient Magic
Ancient Wisdom
Anthroposophy #2
Apocrypha
Arcane Records
Atavism Psychism
Atechnos
Auapicia
Augury *
Bioelectronics *
Bioenergy
Bioinformation #2 & #3

Biological Information
Bionics of Man
Bioplasma
Biopsychic
Biotelecommunication
Book of the Golden Precepts
Book of the Law
Book of the Secret
Cantrip
Chaldean Oracles
Charisms
Christamorphic
Clair-Senses
Cognitive Revolution
Cosmic Electricity

Craft of the Smith
Cryptesthesia *
Curanderism *
Daemonologie
Depth Psychology
Divination *
Divination with the Spirit
Druidism *
Ectenic Force
Endogentic Psychism
Enigmatic Phenomena
Esoteric Development
ESP *
Espiritismo
Ethereal Psychism

Exogenic Psychism
Extrasensorimotor Interaction
Extrasensory Episodes
Eyes of Wisdom*
Fetishism
Fifth Force
Fortean Events
Fortean Phenomena
Fringe Sciences
Frivolous Communications
General Extrasensory
  Perception
German Hasidism
Gestic Magic
Gifts of the Spirit
Gnosis
Gnosticism *
God Spoke
Goetia
Goetric Art
Great Eye
Great Science
Greater Mysteries
Grimoire
Haruspication
Hermetic Philosophy *
Hidden Science
Hidden Wisdom *
High Magic
Hoodooism
Human X-Factor
Hyperacuity
Hypnopsychedelic
Iddhi or Iddhis
Inductive Divination
Inner-Sight
Insight
Inspired by God *
Institutionalized Mediumship
Instructive Communications
Kahuna
Kami #2
Kardec System
Kardicism
Ken
Key of Solomon *
La Vecchia
Magianism
Magic *
Magic Art
Magical Gift
Mana Loa

Mancy
Mantic Art
Mantric Science
Master Sense
Medianimic Phenomena
Mediumistic Communication
Mediumship
Mental Culture
Merkabah
Merkabah Mysticism *
Metagnomy
Metaphysics *
Metapsychiatry
Metapsychique
Metapsychism
Metapsychology
Metapsychosis
Mind-Type Phenomena
Mu Igala
Mysteries of Antiquity
Mystical
Mysticism
Mystico-Religious
Natural Magic
Necromancy
Nonphysical Phenomena
Nonsensory Signals
Obeah
Occult *
Occult Force
Occult Philosophy
Occult Sciences *
Occultism *
Panpsychism
Paraneurophysiological
Paranormal
Paranormality
Paranormalogy *
Paranthropology
Paraphysical
Paraphysical Phenomena
Paraphysics
Parapsychiatry
Parapsychic
Parapsychological
Parapsychological Phenomena
Parapsychology *
Parascience
Parascientific Research
Phenomenology
Phenomenon
Pneumatic Phenomena

Positive Psychism
Pretematuralism
PSI *
PSI Ability *
PSI Energy
PSI Particles
PSI-Phenomenology
PSIland
PSIonic
PSIonics
Psychegenics
Psychiatry-PSI
Psychic *
Psychic Ability
Psychic Art
Psychic Energy *
Psychic Energy Transformers
Psychic Experience
Psychic Eye
Psychic Force *
Psychic Power
Psychic Science
Psychic Sense
Psychic Senses
Psychic Sensitivity
Psychical Powers
Psychical Research *
Psychism *
Psychoenergetics
Psychophysics #2
Psychorientology
Psychoscience
Psychosophy
Psychotron Energy
Psychotronics
Public Augury
Reiyuka
Religio-Magical *
Sacred Magic *
Samjna
Science of Spirit
Second Sight
Secret Science *
Seership
Sensing
Shamanism *
Shamanship
Sky-Worship *
Sorcery
Soul Energy
Soul Science
Spirit Communication

Spirit Guidance
Spirit of God #2
Spirit Science
Spiritism
Spiritual Insight
Spiritualism
Subconscious Force
Subjective Communication
Subjective Education
Subjective Programming
Subjective Senses
Subjective Space
Subliminal Perception
Supernatural *

Supernormal
Superphysical
Supersensory Perception
Supersensual
Supranatural Activity
Telecult Power
Thaumaturgy
Theurgy *
Transcendental Physics *
Transcendentalism
Transcending Physics
Transpersonal Experience
Transphysical Reality

Transphysical Science
Umbanda
Vanir
White Religious Rites
Wicca
Windows of the Soul *
Wisecraft
Witch's Talent
Witchcraft *
Witchcult
Witchhood
Witcraft
Wizardy

SOUL-MIND (Synonyms)

Akh
Alter Ego
Anima
Anima Humana
Anima Mundi
Astro-Soul
Ba
Biocomputer
Causal Body
Compound of Consciousness
Consciousness-Principle *
Dual Germs
Ego #3
Egoic
Free-Soul
Geist
Ghost in the Machine *
Glorified Soul-Mind
Greater Mind
Gros Bon Ange
Gross Soul
Heart
Higher Soul-Mind
Human Information
    Processing System
Human Soul
I
Id
Identity
Illumined Mind
Immortal Soul
Incarnal #2
Individuality
Indwelling Life

Inner-Being *
Inner-Consciousness
Inner-Space of Man
Integrative Tendency
Intellectual Soul
Intermediate Duad
Intermediate Nature
Ka-La
Khalb
King in Heaven
Liekkio
Low Self
Mercurius
Mind
Napistu
Nephesh
Nous
Old Soul
Oversoul
Own-Being
Personality Fragment *
Pilgrim-Monads
Pitri-Yana
Pneuma
Psyche *
Psycho
Psychosoma
Purusha
Ruh
Self
Sol
Soul
Soul Personality
Soul-Mate

Soul-Mind *
Spirit #6 & #8 *
Spiritual Soul *
Subjective Mind #2 *
Theta-Agent
Thetan
Thinker
True Man
Tunzi
Unihipili
Universal One-Self
Upadya' Mind
White Stone #1
Whole Self
Witch-Bird *
Yiegh

TOTALITY (Synonyms)

Absolute
Absolute Being
Acosmism
Adi-Buddhi
Ain Soph
Awka
Alaya
All
All-That-Is
All-There-Is
Allah
Almighty Creative Power
Amen #1
Amitabha
Amon-Ra
Archetypal Perfection
Atma
Aum #5
Averroes
Basic Buzz of the Universe
Be'al
Being
Brahma
Chaos
Child from the Egg
Chit
Chuntzu
Circle #3
Clear Light
Cosmic *
Cosmic Atom
Cosmic Computer *
Cosmic Consciousness *
Cosmic Creativity
Cosmic Egg
Cosmic Fire
Cosmic God
Cosmic Mass
Cosmic Mind *
Cosmo
Cosmos
Creation *
Creative Intelligence
Creative Potential
Creative Synthesis
Creator
Daiviprakriti
Dazhbog
Dazzlement
Deus Absconditius

Directive Intelligence
Divine #1 *
Divine Body
Divine Consciousness *
Divine Energy *
Divine Intelligence *
Divine Mind
Divine Order #1 *
Eck
En Soph
En Soph, Ain Soph, Ein Soph
Eternal Brahman
Fermental Aether
Fire #1 & #2
Force *
God (capitalized)
Godhead #2
Grand Man of the Universe
Great Countenance
Great Logi
Great Manitou
Great Soul
Great Spirit
Great Unmanifest
Great White Light
Great White Spirit
Guiding Principle
Heavenly Man
Holograph *
Hum
Idoiho
Immutable Light
Imperishable Light
Incal
Infinite
Infinite Creator-Creatrix
Infinite Memory Bank *
Infinity
Interior Orderedness
Io
Is-ness #1
Jehovah
Kichi-Manitou
Knower
Kosmos
Light #1, #2 & #5
Logoidal Plasm
Logos
Logos of the System
Ma

Macrocosm
Macromolecular Basis of
  Memory
Maha Maya
Mahat
Master of Fire #2
Master Soul
Mi-Urge
Micro Cofmus
Mind (capitalized) #1
Moksha
Mother Sea
Muti
Nature
Netter
Nir
Nox
Nu
Nyame
Omniverse
One #1 & #2
One Essence Principle *
One Space Framework *
One Supreme Principle
Parabrahm
Patterned System
Perfectness *
Perpetual Presence
Phos
Pleroma
Po
Power Above
Primal Being
Primal Ground
Primary Clear Light
Primary Energy Gestalts
Primeval Atom
Psychic Gestalt
Pure Love
Purna
Ram
Rama
Reality (capitalized) #1 & #5
Sat
Scheme of Things
Seventh Plane
Shining One
Solar God
Solar Logos
Source

785

Spirit of God #1
Sublime Universal Soul
Sugmad
Superintelligence
Superior Man
Switchboard *
Tangaloa, Tangaroa, Ta'aroa
Tao
Thoth
Tirawa
Tiwaz
Top Force
Total Intelligence
Total Law *

Totality *
Transcendent Infinite
Ultimate Wholeness
Una Salus
Unimanifest
Universal
Universal Divine Life
Universal Intelligence
Universal Light
Universal Mind *
Universe
Virgin Spirit *
Void

Wa' nkonda
Wankonda
Waters of Space
We Wei
Web *
Web of Life
White Light
Wise Lord
Word *
World Brain
World Soul
Wu Chi
Zoe

VITAL LIFE FORCE (Synonyms)

Ab-Soo
Absolute Energy
Akasa
Akwalu
Anamorphosis
Andriamanitra
Ani
Anima #1
Animal Magnetism
Anut
Arunquiltha
Atua
Ayik
Badi
Baraka #1
Basic Buzz of the Universe
Biocosmic Energy
Bioplasma #2
Breath of God
Breath of Life
Ch'i
Cosmic Energy
Cosmic Light
Daily Bread
Di-Electric Bio
Dielectric Biocosmic Energy
Divine Breath
Ectoplasm Energy
Elan Vital
Elf Fire
Elima
Eloptic Energy
Entelechy

Ether #1
Ether in Nature
Etheric Fluid
Etheric Force
Etheric Formative Forces
Facultas Formatrix
Fiery Intelligence
Fifth Type of Matter
Fine Media
Fohatic Power
Formative Cause
Formative Energy
Ga-Llama
Gestaltung
Guna
Ham-Sa
Han
Holy Breath #1
Hormic Energy
Immaterial Force
Inergy
It
Kalit
Kami #1
Kasinge
Ki #1
"L" Particle
Labuni
Lea
Libido
Life Energy
Life Force
Logoidal Energy

Magnale Magnum
Magnetic Fluid
Magnetic Life Force
Magnetoelectricity
Magnetoism
Mana #1
Mana, Mana-Mana, Mana Loa
Manitu
Megbe
Mitogentic Radiation
Motor Force
Mulungu
Mumia and Munia
Mungo
Munis
N-Rays #1
Negative Entropy
Neuric Energy
Neuricidad
Ngai
Njom
Noetic Energy
Od
Odyle
Odyllic
Ojas
Oki
Orenda
Orgone Energy
Ousia
Pneuma #1
Prana #2, #3 & #4
Pranayama

786

Prephysical Energy	Tensor Fields	Vital Principle
Primary Energy	Time-Flow #1	Vital Spirit
PSI Plasma	Tondi	Vital-Air
PSIonics #1	Tumo	Vitality
Psychic Force #1	Unitary Principle in Nature	Vril
Qi	Universal Breath	Wakan
Quasielectrostatic Field	Universal Fluid	Wakonda
Shiva and Shakti	Universal Primitive Element	Wong
Silap Inua	Universion	X-Energy
Soul of the Universe	Vis Medicatrix Naturae	X-Factor
Spirit (capitalized) #1 & #2	Vis Naturalis	X-Force
Spirit of God #3	Vital Fluid	Yaris
Spiritus	Vital Life Force	Yesod
Telesma	Vital Magnetism	Zogo

Appendix 4

SUMMARIZED CLARIFICATION OF COMMON PSYCHIC TERMS

This is simplified data to help one understand the language of the psychic, in which *ordinary* words are used to describe *non-ordinary* experiences and altered states of consciousness. The definition or description from the main section of this dictionary of the particular word being explained is not repeated in this summary, but it should be read for full understanding of the explanations.

FOURTH DIMENSIONAL TERMINOLOGY

Psychic states, meditation, hypnotherapy, dreams, etc., function from an ALTERED STATE OF CONSCIOUSNESS or a fourth dimensional awareness. In this state of awareness the CONSCIOUS MIND is passive, leaving the SUBCONSCIOUS MIND to talk, (if it can), in an automatic language rather than one's learned vocabulary. Some researchers feel that the RIGHT BRAIN HEMISPHERE is dominant in this state of consciousness, therefore, one finds it difficult to speak logical verbal language. Albert Einstein once remarked when referring to his psychically altered state of consciousness: "Conventional words or other signs have to be sought for laboriously when in a secondary stage, if the mentioned associative play is sufficiently established and can be reproduced at will."

Many terms appear to be grammatical errors, but are entered as spoken or written in order to preserve the essence of the intended meaning. As Mark Twain once remarked that "the difference between the right words and the almost right word is the difference between the lightning bug and lightning." For example the Spiritualists use a BLACKED-OUT ROOM to hold a SEANCE because the tiniest amount of light destroys the ECTOPLASM which is necessary for the physical phenomenon. *Blackish* is the adjective, but blackish does not indicate absolutely no trace of light. Very heavy drapes were used over the windows and door cracks, and later on, black-out material was used to block out light. So the term *blacked-out* gives the impression that there is no trace of light in that room prepared for the phenomenon.

Psychics and meditators have found that *idioms* make an excellent way to express what they need to say. For example, INNER-SPACE OF MAN has nothing to do with the physical organs within the human body. This term is describing PSYCHIC INFORMATION, the potential within each person, or the subjective feeling of the divine. Another example of an idiom is ALERT-ASLEEP in which the two words have opposite meanings. When used together, they were coined to mean the conscious mind is passive or asleep, and the subconscious mind is super awake. This is a special state of consciousness found in deep MEDITATION, BIOFEEDBACK TRAINING, the semistate of HYPNOTHERAPY, and the state induced for psychic information. Both examples are excellent ways to express a *noncustomary* state of consciousness with *customary* words.

In many instances, terms may appear rudimentary. This does not suggest that psychics are ignorant or lack formal education. For example, SINKS INTO THE FLOOR is used by the SITTERS in a materialization seance. When the materialized intelligence is ready to return, it appears as if the ectoplasm energy sinks into the floor. In more formal grammar, one could say that the ectoplasm dissipates at the floor level and gives the appearance that it is absorbed by the floor. Sitters in a materialization seance are in an ALPHA STATE OF CONSCIOUSNESS in order to contribute to the ectoplasm. In this state of consciousness, the mental activity is governed by the right brain hemisphere and the LEFT BRAIN HEMISPHERE is passive. The left brain hemisphere is responsible for the basic word-by-word language. It would be perfectly normal for the sitters to express the interiorization process in a simple-like term and to repeat it often enough until it becomes commonly used. (In my early days of research, findings of the split brain hemispheres were not in print and I am sorry now that I did not record more of these simple expressions of the right brain hemisphere.)

In many instances, the reader may feel that the definition or description is grammatically incorrect according to the part of speech of the word entry. For instance, the definition under CARD-BASKETS does not describe a basket but describes a type of PSYCHIC SKILL, because it is the name of a psychic skill. TRUMPET, another good example, means the megaphone used in a seance, but it also means a type of psychic skill. The combined phrase is "he has trumpet." This is a shortened phrase to say that a MEDIUM goes into a DEEP TRANCE state of consciousness and an ETHERIC WORLD INTELLIGENCE synchronizes with him or her to levitate an instrument (the megaphone) as an amplifying system for the etheric world intelligence to speak through. The medium does not levitate the trumpet per se. The intelligence does the work, but nonetheless, the medium is necessary, for it is his or her ectoplasm that supplies the energy for the phenomenon. So as not to explain the whole procedure each time one speaks about the SESSION, the short term was coined by the Spiritualists. It would also be appropriate to say "one is a trumpet medium."

This holds true for many types of physical phenomena; for example, one has SEANCE HANDS, or is a seance hands' medium; one has DEPOSITED MATTER, or is a deposited matter medium. In the case of a verb being used to describe the skill, it is more suitable to only use *medium* at the end of the name: ENTHUSED, an enthused medium; SPLITTING OF PERSONALITIES, splitting of personalities' medium; BREATHED INTO, breathed into medium.

If interest in psychic phenomena increases and the ability to become psychic accelerates at the present rate, and all indication is that it will, the psychic and medium will not only admit he or she is a psychic or a medium, but they will proudly name the type of psychism they possess. Because a psychic is an excellent dowser does not necessarily mean they can see auras or levitate a candy dish. The general public will need to understand terms to speak more fluently on the subject. When using the names that psychics and researchers have given to the hundreds of types of psychic skills, one finds that *they do not always adhere to standard grammar*. These names were coined because they bring forth the essence of a particular talent. There are standard words and rules, however, that will describe the psychic and their talent without violating the coined phrases that are presently being used. Anything is *not* acceptable as the following information explains.

Mediums are respectful to their etheric world helpers and are careful not to take credit for the phenomena produced in the seance room, even though they themselves are a vital part of that performance. For example, if PERCUSSION or RADIOGRAPHY takes place in the seance room, the medium does not call her or himself a percussionist or a radiographer because the etheric world helper does the activity. It is appropriate to say "he has percussion" or "he is a percussion medium," and "he has radiography" or "he is a radiography medium."

Mental psychic skills in which the psychic uses his subconscious or superconscious mind is a different story. In MENTAL PSYCHISM, it is appropriate for the psychic to describe her or himself by adding a suffix after the type of skill he or she excells in. Examples are: PREMONITION, premonitionist; DIVINE INTERVENTION, divine interventionist; PURE IMAGINATION, pure imaginationist; EXTREME EXALTATION, extreme exaltationist; BIOLOGICAL PHENOMENA, biological phenomenist or phenomenizer; ESP ATTUNEMENT, ESP Attuner; UTTERANCES, an utterer; WRITING IN TONGUES, writer of tongues; HOUSE BLESSING, house blesser; MUMMIFICATION of plants, mummificator; TOUCH-SENSE, touch sensitive; CASTING OF LOTS, caster of lots.

Some psychic skills have been given names that will not adhere to this rule; for example: CELESTIAL EYES, one cannot say "I have celestial eyes" because this ability comes from the mind and not from an etheric world intelligence, so the appropriate wordage would be: "I am a celestial eyes perceiver." The analogy of this term compared to the use of "I have" in a mediumistic skill is this: one would say "I have a child" and so one says "I have an etheric world helper who does -------"; one would not say "I have a piano player" but would say "I am a piano player"; consequently for mental psychism and the use of one's minds, it is correct only to say "I am a celestial eyes perceiver." Other examples are: FAR-MEMORY, far memory perceiver; INNER-VIBRATIONAL TOUCH, inner-vibrational touch perceiver; INSPIRATIONAL THOUGHT, inspirational thought perceiver; GUT FEELING, gut feeling sensitive; DAWNING CONSCIOUSNESS, dawning consciousness perceiver. Tibetians have been known for their extraordinary mind control which falls under another principle. They have named two of their skills COMBUSTIBILITY and INVISIBILITY. To give the psychic credence for these feats, one could say: combustion controller; invisibility controller; PALMED POWER, palmed power controller; POWER-OF-THE-WORD, power-of-the-word controller.

Other suggestions for noncustomary names: BLOWING UPON THE SICK, blowing on the sick healer; LAYING-ON-OF-HANDS, laying-on-of-hands healer; ROYAL TOUCH, royal touch healer.

One new type of psychic skill developed, executed under the influence of hypnosis, is one in which one is given instructions to perform like a famous person. Examples of these names are: SUPERWAKEFULNESS and ANTITHESIS OF SLEEP. Subject or performer is appropriate to describe this subject: super-wakefulness performer; antithesis of sleep performer.

Another newly developed psychic skill over the past decade is when invisible intelligences record their voice on a tape recorder for amplification in order to be heard by a psychic. Until further research in this field determines whether this process uses the principles of GHOSTOLOGY, POLTERGEISTRY, or MEDIUMSHIP, the appropriate word to use is TAPED-VOICE PHENOMENON RECORDER which is the coined term. In the psychic experience of PHONE CALLS FROM THE DEAD, a more suitable word would be PARTICIPANT, at least until further research is done; for example: CARRY-ON-TALKING, carry-on-talking participant; PHANTOM PHONE CALLS, phantom phone call participant.

POPULAR WORDS USED
INTERCHANGEABLY INCORRECTLY

Some words are very similar in meaning but modern studies show there are differences and therefore, they no longer should be used interchangeably. In the following groupings, misunderstandings are brought out by emphasizing the similarities and differences of the various terms. The definition or description from the main section of this dictionary is not repeated but should be read for full understanding of the explanation.

Meditation
Psychic development

Medium
Psychic

Clairvoyance
Intuition
Psychic cognition

Prophecy
Precognition

Demonology
Parapsychology
Magic

Psychokinesis (PK)
Mind-over-matter

Silent personal pryaer
Meditation
Contemplation

Bad karma
Karma

Cult
Occult
Destructive cult

Poltergeistry
Psychokinesis

Apparition
Ghost
Spirit
Guide
Etheric world intelligence
Angel
Discarnate being

Clairvoyance
Imagery
Fantasy
Hallucination
Daydreaming
Visualization

Trance
Hypnotic state

Dreams
Psychic experiences during sleep

Mental telepathy
Telepathy

Voice trance
Trance

House ghost
Poltergeist

Guided meditation
Guided hypnotherapy

Fasting
Dieting
Starving

Spirit
Holy Spirit
Spirit

Faith healing
Holistic healing
Spiritual healing
Psychic healing
Mediumship healing
Spirit healing
Magnetic healing
Mental healing

Metaphysics
Religion

Astral projection
Mental projection

Kirlian photography
Psychic photography

Knocks
Clairaudience

Elemental
Nature elemental

Psychokinesis
Telekinesis

Charm
Amulet
Talisman
Ornament

Spell
Curse
Hex
Psychic attack
Satonic forces

Possession
Obsession

Psychokinesis
Levitation
Teleportation
Apportation
Transmutation
Ascension

MEDITATION
PSYCHIC DEVELOPMENT

In both cases of sitting for *psychic development* and sitting for *meditation,* the body should be relaxed and the backbone straight trying to still the CONSCIOUS MIND and five SENSES to influences of outer environmental stimuli, desirous of tuning into a higher STATE OF CONSCIOUSNESS, but still in control. In both cases there is a need to practice for accomplishment

However, there is a pronounced difference because in *psychic development* one allows and encourages a NON-THOUGHT to enter the mind processes, and in *meditation* one encourages the mind to cut out all mind processes (thought or non-thought), focusing on the tiniest possible point or letting the mind become blank.

For example, a student may say, "While I sat in meditation I saw a vision of a friend going to Syracuse with his work brief case." Once the vision is allowed to start appearing the intent has changed and along with it the state of consciousness. Parapsychologists suggest one meditate before opening one's PSYCHIC DOORS, but when the FOCAL POINT is broken, you are no longer benefiting from a meditative state but are now benefiting from the psychic state.

MEDIUM
PSYCHIC

Within the current culture, these words are used synonymously and almost rightly so, because the majority of psychics are both a *medium* and a *psychic.* The *psychic* uses his or her SUBCONSCIOUS MIND or SUPERCONSCIOUS MIND in the psychic skill and the *medium* is a channel for the ETHERIC WORLD INTELLIGENCE to perform the psychic skill. Not all mediums profess to be psychic. There are many psychic skills that can be accomplished by either allowing the etheric world to intervene, or by using one's subconscious or superconscious mind. Physical phenomena that is elicited in the SEANCE room is through the etheric world intelligences only. There are particular skills that one should not call upon the intelligences for help, such as DOWSING, PENDULUMING, BODY CONTROL, AMULETING, CASTING OF LOTS, etc. However, it is

best if one knows when to call upon his or her intelligence for help and when to tune into one's other minds.

CLAIRVOYANCE
INTUITION
PSYCHIC COGNITION

Psychic cognition and *intition* (also known as gut feeling or HUNCHABILITY) are frequently used incorrectly interchangeably. They are similar skills, inasmuch as they both happen quickly, leave quickly, and bring information that could not have been known by normal means. The difference is that *psychic cognition* is always willed and enters through the mind. *Intuition* can be either willed or unwilled, and comes through body sensations.

Clairvoyance and *intuition* are incorrectly used interchangeably also. *Clairvoyance* is a French word meaning "clear or bright vision." Persons who have an intuitive feeling sometimes say, "I see that -----" for lack of words to designate an inner perception, and this is mistaken to mean they had a vision.

These three terms, used independently, are also misused to mean PSYCHISM in general. They are the most common types of psychism and the most easily developed and probably most people feel that *intuition,* or *clairvoyance,* or *psychic cognition* is all there is to psychism.

PROPHECY
PRECOGNITION

A very common mistake is to use these two terms in parallel with types of psychic skills. Terms designating types of psychic skills pertain to the method of perceiving the PSYCHIC INFORMATION. These two terms pertain to the kind of information perceived, meaning it will occur in the future. The "method" of perceiving *prophecy* and *precognition* varies and can come through CLAIRVOYANCE, CLAIRAUDIENCE, CLAIRSCENT, CLAIRSAVORANCE, OMENS, MANTIC ARTS, EMOTIONAL PSYCHISM, MEDIUMSHIP, etc. The better choice would be to say: dream prophecy, clairvoyant prophecy, omen prophecy, etc.

DEMONOLOGY
PARAPSYCHOLOGY
MAGIC

Each of these three disciplines study and use PSYCHIC ENERGY, believe that the SOUL-MIND of a person lives on after death and is capable of communicating with earthlings. These soul-minds can be manipulated to work according to the wishes of the PSYCHIC, along with other invisible cosmic forces.

These terms are not synonymous, and the difference lies in the intent of their usage. The student or practitioner of *parapsychology* uses psychic work to gain knowledge and to progress on the spiritual path, putting their psychic energy to use for the good of humanity, disciplining themselves to tune into only the superior intelligences. The student or practitioner of *demonology* studies the same cosmic forces, but calls upon invisible intelligences of an inferior quality to use this psychic energy for personal worldly gain, and for evil intent toward other persons or situations. *Magic* studies the same cosmic forces and uses the same principles as the other two, only it emphasizes ritualistic methods of inducing psychic energy. There are two types of magic, white and black. WHITE MAGIC is used for positive purposes, and BLACK MAGIC is used for negative purposes. If the term *magic* is used without being preceded by an adjective, the reader must consider the rest of the text to see if it refers to black or to white magic.

PSYCHOKINESIS (PK)
MIND-OVER-MATTER

Psychokinesis is a psychic skill in which one makes a deliberate attempt to move an object or change its form in the present, using heavy mind concentration. In order to explain the controversy of this term one must deal with one of the theories of metaphysics, occultism, and ancient Eastern teachings. This theory states that the world and everything in it is made and held together by man's thoughts which give it form and energy. This means that each individual's inner picture, thought, and belief constantly contributes to objects, events, and situations, whether it is conscious, unconcious, or subconscious activity. Psychics who do not adhere to this belief, label any outer manifestation to be *psychokinesis* ability when they recognize that an event or situation relates to thoughts one has dwelt upon in the past. A better choice of words for this would be *mind-over-matter*.

SILENT PERSONAL PRAYER
MEDITATION
CONTEMPLATION

These terms are frequently used interchangeably, because in essence, each term pertains to personal mind activity, requires concentration, a silent setting, a quieting of emotions and body, and is performed to better one's life or to understand one's potential.

However, they are not the same process, their objectives differ, and the processes should not be mixed when one is sitting to attain high results for him or herself.

Prayer keeps one in an aware or a BETA STATE OF CONSCIOUSNESS, releases inner feelings, and attunes one to a higher source. *Prayer* can bring tears, anger, tranquility, or a feeling of security. *Prayer* serves as an aid for continuing daily activity. Body posture is unimportant.

Meditation is a disciplined mind technique to achieve attunement to one's personal higher self, dissipate stored stress, improve health, and change one's body metabolism. *Meditation* requires practice and special body postures are important. *Meditation* brings one to an ALPHA or THETA STATE OF CONSCIOUSNESS which results in an increase of mental alertness and an attitudinal change that continues in daily activity for many hours.

Contemplation requires an open and NEUTRAL MIND on the onset of the process, with a receptive attitude as the period prolongs. One uses a prelearned technique to reach the alpha or theta state of consciousness and then allows his or her mind to wander over their chosen idea, concept, or abstract thought. The objective is to broaden one's opinions, and/or bring ENLIGHTENMENT; (do not confuse with the psychic skill, INSPIRATIONAL THOUGHT). Body posture is unimportant. *Contemplation* does not necessarily bring a feeling of peace and security like the other two techniques, but does gives one a sensation of universality.

BAD KARMA
KARMA

Esoteric science says that *karma* is the accumulation of all thoughts and attitudes one has ever thought, all the actions one has ever performed, and all the various lifestyles one has ever led, from one's past incarnations and from one's past-present life, stored in each individual's ethereal MEMORY BANK. This memory record manifests at the present time bringing reality to the individual or lies dormant ready to manifest at another time. The purpose is to aid the progression of the SOUL-MIND. Because no one is all bad or all good, there is both good and *bad karma*. The word *karma* is often misused to mean just the unpleasant things that happen in one's life. The law of cause and effect says one also earns all the good experiences one manifests.

CULT
OCCULT
DESTRUCTIVE CULT

Current usage of the term *cult* frequently means that an individual does not understand the teachings of an organization or religion, and therefore, considers it to be "bad," or a *cult*. This usage stems from the new organizations that are considered *destructive cults,* of which many persons are afraid. Webster defines a *cult* as a system of religious worship or ritual; devoted attachment to a person or principle. This means that almost all orthodox religions, many organizations, and fraternities could fall under this definition.

What makes a system of religious worship devoted to a person or principle destructive? It lies, not in what the organization teaches, but in the "method" of getting an individual to join the religious organization, and keeping him or her in it. Some of the manipulative techniques are HYPNOSIS, MENTAL TELEPATHIC SUGGESTIONS, coercive repetitive suggestions, sleep programming, a low protein diet, and forced methods of staying awake at night.

Weekly, and biweekly, meetings are mandatory in a destructive cult regardless if the member lives on the commune property or in planned outside quarters. The ploy at the meetings preys upon the individual's basic emotional needs, suppresses the normal BELIEF SYSTEM, and emphasizes suggestions that benefit the organization only. Members are kept so busy in *cult* activities and listening to this ploy that eventually they behave like an AUTOMATON, think on an animal level of consciousness, and are unable to make personal decisions. To intentionally destroy one's free will is considered immoral and inhuman. Everyone needs time to come away from a meeting or activity and evaluate the meeting or activity for her or himself.

Occultism teaches METAPHYSICS, which is foreign to many persons, so many times occultism is placed in the above categories, due to lack of understanding. The term *occult* was formed with the prefix *oc* which is a Latin term meaning, "reversely, inversely, opposite," and "against." Occultism is the opposite of a *cult* because its philosophy teaches one to do his or her own thinking and to accept no concept or theory that one cannot feel comfortable with. An *occult* organization "teaches" its members PSYCHIC SKILLS. This means that the members would be aware if the officials were using psychic skills to coerce one's thinking and would know how to protect oneself against such tactics. When one studies PSYCHIC ENERGY, one becomes sensitive to negative vibrations within a few lessons and is no longer vulnerable to DESTRUCTIVE BRAINWASHING CULTS.

POLTERGEISTRY
PSYCHOKINESIS

Because of the similarity in these two types of PSYCHISM, *psychokinesis* is frequently used to label a poltergeist event. In both types of skills, an excess of PSYCHIC ENERGY, from a particular individual, is used to move or manipulate matter. However, in *poltergeistry,* the individual's PSYCHIC ENERGY is used unknowingly and unwantedly, and the majority of researchers feel that an ETHERIC WORLD ENTITY is involved. In *psychokinesis,* the individual deliberately builds his or her psychic energy and directs it to the matter with the intent that the energy behaves as he or she so decrees it to. *Psychokinesis* is performed to develop mind concentration and for experimental purposes. No etheric world entity is involved.

APPARITION
GHOST
SPIRIT
GUIDE
ETHERIC WORLD INTELLIGENCE
ANGEL
DISCARNATE BEING

These words should not be used interchangeably but it is easy to understand why they frequently are. All seven terms have two things in common: 1. each one represents a LIFE FORCE (soul-mind) in individuals that has lived many earth lives and now abides in the ETHERIC WORLD; 2. this life force can show itself clairvoyantly as a misty, cloud-like vision appearing in a human shape, seemingly to have a purpose and a desire to communicate with people.

There are differences, however. The terms *ghost* and *apparition* also have other meanings pertaining to other energy fields in the etheric world.

The *guide, etheric world intelligence* and *angel* bring aid and knowledge to humanity, but only come when summoned (unconsciously or consciously). The *etheric world intelligences* and *angels* have other duties and all etheric world intelligences and angels do not communicate with mankind. The *guide* is called a guide because he or she is an *etheric world intelligence* that has chosen to aid an earthling to higher accomplishment.

The *ghost* and *discarnate being* come unsummoned to the earthling having an emotional desire to be heard and understood by the earthling.

A *spirit* (definition #3) is an umbrella word meaning anyone of the above terms. It is used when a life force makes its presence known to an earthling but not its identity.

The *apparition* and *ghost* are perceived clairvoyantly in outer space only. The other five terms can be perceived in outer space and also in the psychic's mind.

CLAIRVOYANCE
IMAGERY
FANTASY
HALLUCINATION
DAYDREAMING
VISUALIZATION

These terms should not be used interchangeably as each word has its own distinctions in meaning. There is one definite similarity and that is that they all pertain to INNER-MIND PICTURES. The top five terms pertain to the SUBCONSCIOUS MIND influencing and filtering into the conscious consciousness with an ongoing stream of mental activity and a fluidity of association of scenes, people, and images.

However, this mental activity is processed differently. *Hallucination* and *clairvoyance* are NON-THOUGHT mental activity coming from the outer atmosphere through the subconscious mind to the MENTAL MIND. *Clairvoyance, imagery,* and *fantasy* are induced deliberately and then allowed to go on uncontrolled. *Hallucination* begins and continues to flow uncontrolled. *Daydreaming* is induced and the stream of mental activity is consistently consciously controlled. *Clairvoyance, daydreaming,* and *fantasy* will fill a psychological need. *Imagery* is used as a practice exercise to increase the imagination faculty and used as a source of inner guidance for renewed health or self-improvement.

Visualization is deliberately induced but it is not ongoing. It is one picture held intact for a short time. This exact picture must be induced daily to accomplish a change in one's life or body. *Daydreaming* and *visualization* are the only experience that will react as a manifestation in the future behavior of one's world as other thoughts do. *Visualization, hallucination,* and *clairvoyance* require an ALTERED STATE OF CONSCIOUSNESS while *imagery, fantasy* and *daydreaming* are induced in a normal state of consciousness.

TRANCE
HYPNOTIC STATE

These words should never be used interchangeably even though they both pertain to an ALTERED STATE OF CONSCIOUSNESS. *Trance* is not a DEEP STATE OF HYPNOSIS. How one reaches the altered state of consciousness and its purpose determines which word to use.

A *hypnotic state* is used for surgery, dentistry, birthing, psychiatric therapy, regression, stage antics and hypnotherapy suggestions. One can reach a hypnotic state by self-hypnosis or by a hypnotist's guidance.

Trance is a fourth dimensional word that tells its whole story in six letters. *Trance* is an altered state of consciousness brought about by the collaboration of both the MEDIUM and the ETHERIC WORLD INTELLIGENCE for the sole purpose of performing some kind of PHYSICAL PSYCHISM.

However, both terms can mean a light, semi, or deep altered state of consciousness and should be preceded by an adjective to describe this; e.g. semi-trance or semi-hypnotic state.

DREAMS
PSYCHIC EXPERIENCES DURING SLEEP

For many years, those who studied *dreams* felt that some people have vivid, clear, detailed, and easy-to-recall dreams and other people have fuzzy, fragmented, elusive dreams. When the DREAM RESEARCH LABORATORIES began to use the electro-encephalograph instrument they found that the brain goes through four levels of altered states of consciousness during a regular night's sleep. The fuzzy, fragmented, elusive dreams occur with rapid-eye-movement and register at a particular level on the EEG. The vivid, clear, detailed, easy-to-recall dreams occur in between the normal RAPID-EYE-MOVEMENT dreams and register at another level of consciousness. Upon further research, it was found this later state of consciousness was the same level that a PSYCHIC reaches when tuning in for PSYCHIC INFORMATION. This was classified as a *psychic experience during sleep*. This later subject also had the normal fuzzy, fragmented, elusive dreams with rapid-eye-movement. For proper interpretation, it is best to determine whether the dreamer had a *psychic experience during sleep* or a *dream* because each experience is to be interpreted using different principles.

MENTAL TELEPATHY
TELEPATHY

Telepathy is not a short term for *mental telepathy* as it is frequently used. Prof. F.W.H. Myers coined the word and it meant to him "sensing over a distance." The majority of research and experiments have been in *mental telepathy* so many people are not aware of the other kinds of *telepathy,* nor are they aware that *telepathy* does not necessarily happen only between humans. Today psychics know that visions, hypnotic influence, subconscious data, physical motor movement, group suggestion, empathy, sense of touch, illnesses, etc., can be transferred; therefore, a particular adjective should always preceed the word *telepathy*.

VOICE TRANCE
TRANCE

Because the majority of persons in this field are familiar with someone who has a voice speak through them while in an ALTERED STATE OF CONSCIOUSNESS, the term *trance* is frequently used to mean *voice trance*. Upon examination, one finds that *trance* does not refer to any one kind of PSYCHIC SKILL, but rather it refers to a necessary preparation between the MEDIUM and the ETHERIC WORLD INTELLIGENCE for the purpose of performing many types of PHYSICAL PSYCHISM.

HOUSE GHOST
POLTERGIEST

It is incorrect to call every invisible living presence that makes itself known in a household, a *ghost*. Sometime it is a *poltergeist*. These two invisible etheric world entities differ in the purpose of their household interference, their antics and mannerism, and receive their energy for their existence from different sources.

The typical *house ghost* is a DISCARNATE ENTITY who clings to earth because he or she carries a traumatic emotional load and needs help. The ghost appears in the area of the home where his or her emotions are centered, which gives them the energy to appear. The ghost moves slowly, making similar noises in a periodic pattern. Sometimes he or she is perceivable clairvoyantly. This haunting can continue for many years until the ghost is dissipated or their problem is understood by the householders and they receive help.

The *poltergeist* is a young spirit who desires to feed their ego. He or she plays childish tricks with household furnishings to get attention. Their movements are swift, occuring in any area of the house, sometimes insignificant and sometimes defying the laws of gravity and physics. Their energy is generated from a household member who is in a highly emotional state. His or her antics are short-lived as they will dissipate when the household member's condition changes or they are exorcised.

GUIDED MEDITATION
GUIDED HYPNOTHERAPY

Many persons feel that *guided meditation* and *guided hypnotherapy* are the same process. Both techniques are used in a group or singularly, aid in helping the subject(s) reach an altered state of PSYCHE CONSCIOUSNESS by means of a leader speaking special phrases. The leader stimulates the state of awareness he or she intends to induce by phrasing their wordage accordingly.

Guided meditation requires the subject to sit in a lotus position or sit in a chair with the spine held straight throughout the entire period. Meditational periods last approximately fifteen minutes to one half an hour, in which time, the body becomes very relaxed, the emotions become quieted, and the MENTAL MIND becomes passive. During this period the SUPERCONSCIOUS MIND is reached and the subject accrues an attitudinal change, and more mental alertness in the aftermath, than he or she had previously.

In *guided hypnotherapy*, the subject is usually reclining or if sitting, the head is allowed to hang loosely with the chin resting on the chest. The length of the entire hypnotherapy session is approximately from half an hour to an hour. The hypnotherapy wordage is only spoken to induce a hypnotic state to the subject in the beginning of the session. The body becomes very relaxed, the emotions become quieted and the mental mind relinquishes its dominance to the SUBCONSCIOUS MIND. The hypnotherapist then proceeds with the purpose of the session.

Another pronounced difference is that the meditative subject will return to the awake state of consciousness quickly and the hypnotized subject must be brought back slowly.

FASTING
DIETING
STARVING

The similarity in these three words is the changing of one's normal eating habits to lesser amounts or to no food at all. The difference lies in the results in body functions and the attitude towards the food intake. *Starving* is a slow painful process of dying while the body consumes itself, usually done unintentionally. *Dieting* is for the physical improvement of the body, done intentionally.

Fasting is done with full acceptance of the INNER-SELF, usually seeking higher attainment of the SOUL-MIND, and improvement in psychic talents or PSYCHIC HEALING ability. As one lets loose of the visible to grasp the invisible and learns to have faith in the ETHERIC WORLD and the power of one's own mind, the experience becomes a step in the purification of both mind and body.

SPIRIT
HOLY SPIRIT

Spirit (capitalized) has two distinct meanings: 1. It pertains to the One Life Force that permeates throughout all the universes. LIFE FORCE, *movement, total energy source,* and *ceaseless vibrations* can be used synonymously with *Spirit.* 2. Because all ENERGY is accompanied with INTELLIGENCE, *Spirit* used in the psychic field means PSYCHIC INFORMATION that comes from the One Force, the DIVINE, or TOTALITY. This psychic information coming directly from Totality makes it *pure* information and is intended for the betterment of mankind. It is always information that surpasses the logical thinking of the one receiving it and surpasses his or her formal education or experiential learning.

Holy Spirit is synonymous with *Spirit (capitalized).* To call upon the *Holy Spirit* for psychic information or psychic phenomena is to decree the phenomena or information to be pure and righteous and free from one's own BELIEF SYSTEM.

Spirit (uncapitalized) has two distinct meanings: 1. It is fragments of the One Spirit, flowing through everything in the UNIVERSE, giving it life and movement. 2. It is used in some disciplines and in the Bible to mean the SOUL-MIND life-force of a deceased human, now in the ETHERIC WORLD, distinguishing it from other types of ethereal energies. It is used ambiguously to pertain to any DISCARNATE ENTITY or an etheric world GUIDE.

Spirit (capitalized) works through mankind in INSPIRATIONAL THOUGHT. The *Holy Spirit* works through mankind in inspirational thought and "some" physical phenomena. *Spirit* (uncapitalized) works through mankind by means of a guide or discarnate intelligence.

FAITH HEALING
HOLISTIC HEALING
SPIRITUAL HEALING
PSYCHIC HEALING
SPIRIT HEALING
MAGNETIC HEALING
MENTAL HEALING

Research in the field of alternative healings is fairly new, so it is understandable that these alternative methods of healing have been inappropriately named and mixed up when administering them. The above types of healing should not be put into the same parallel series because there is no one common denominator that flows through all of them. Fortunately new research helps one discriminate between them so the healing PRACTITIONER can specialize in order to bring more successful results.

All of the above types of healing are ALTERNATIVES except *faith healing* and *holistic healing*. All healings require FAITH on the part of the patient, whether it comes from a bottle, pill, surgery, cell salts, aerobic dancing, or the LAYING-ON-OF-HANDS.

Holistic healing pertains to any type of healing, if and only *if* the practitioner or doctor takes into consideration every aspect of one's lifestyle and emotional attitudes to find the cause and cure of the illness. This includes medical, dentistal, CHIROPRACTIC and MEDIUMSHIP HEALING; and PSYCHIC AND MEDICAL SURGERY; ROLFING ACUPUNCTURE.

Holistic healing is not one special method of healing, nor is it entirely a psychiatric healing.

Spiritual healing is the name given to any type

of healing that is performed in a religious setting or learned from a religious setting. *Spiritual healing* could include *magnetic, mental, mediumship,* and all *psychic healings.*

Psychic healing is a general term to mean any method of healing that includes one or more psychic skills.

Mediumship healing pertains to an individual who allows her or himself to be used as a CHANNEL for healing energies to flow from an ETHERIC WORLD INTELLIGENCE. The intelligence handles where it is to flow in the body of the patient and handles the making of the energy to be healing in nature. This healing energy can be administered through various methods, which have nothing to do with its potential, but does pertain to the mediumistic characteristic of the medium. Administering could be through personal touch, PETITION slips, PSYCHIC SURGERY, charismatic group healing, tribal SHAMANSHIP HEALING, and MENTAL MEDIUMSHIP readings (in which one is told what to do to promote correct health for the client). The talent of the medium lies in the willingness to synchronize with an etheric world intelligence, patience to develop this ability, and trust in the intelligence.

Mental, magnetic, and *spirit healing* methods have similarities that make them difficult to separate to the general public, but should be thoroughly understood by the practitioner. This allows the practitioner to attain the best results and prevents him or her from shifting from one body energy to another through lack of proper knowledge and causing her or himself fatigue.

All of these last healing methods are enhanced by breath, thought concentration and direction, and use of the natural energies of the body which flow in and out of the body constantly. These body energies are neutral in each type of healing and must be decreed to be of a healing quality before being projected to the patient.

Spirit and *magnetic healing* (laying-on-of-hands) work with body energy flow. *Spirit healing* relies on the type of breathing and concentration on the breaths. A physical contact or etheric contact is necessary. This cannot be performed at a distance. One need not know where the illness lies in the body as the spirit quickens the self-healing potential in the proper area by itself. This is performed quickly and is enhanced by group participation.

Magnetic healing is also enhanced by breaths, but concentration and direction follows the magnetic energy through the practitioner's body to the imbalance of energy flow in the patient. Practitioners have their own special hand movements over the ETHERIC DOUBLE or the body per se. This could take from three to twenty minutes to perform. (It can be used at a distance by modifying the above).

Mental healing uses the electricity that constantly emanates from one's head. This electrical energy is built up in the practitioner's head and then projected to the patient's electromagnetical field. No physical contact is ever made and distance is no barrier. This type cannot be used on one's self as can *spirit* and *magnetic healing*. Mind discipline and much concentration is important, taking approximately five to twenty minutes in length. There are many methods of *mental healing* (see main section).

All healing can be instantaneous or gradual depending upon the receptivity of the patient and has nothing to do with the ability of the healer. All healing processes, from the medical doctor to the religious practitioner, are intended to change BODY CHEMISTRY. Healings only aid the imbalance in the body chemistry, helping the cells to normalize so the intelligence in the cells can heal themselves.

METAPHYSICS
RELIGION

Because there are many religions today that profess to be metaphysically oriented, many people understand the term *metaphysical* to mean a religious sect. This is incorrect. *Metaphysics* is a doctrine which underlies many religions, but it also underlies philosophies, some sciences, and much literature.

ASTRAL PROJECTION
MENTAL PROJECTION

There are many names for these two types of invisible travel, but for simplification these are used as key words in this dictionary. In *astral projection,* the LIFE FORCE leaves the physical body

and is clothed in ASTRAL MATTER. This astral matter looks like the physical body in form and clothing to clairvoyants. The ASTRAL BODY can fly to other parts of the physical world and to parts of the astral world. The individual actually feels like he or she is flying. Psychics who are aware of taking this OUT-OF-BODY-EXPERIENCE feel as though they are in another life form similar to the physical body.

In a *mental projection,* the mind or minds expand or stretch (for lack of better terms) and visit the planes above the astral level. This is deliberately brought on by deep MEDITATION and by one who wishes to study these levels. Those who take this mind expansion trip feel that the lower bodies, the physical, astral, and mental bodies, are all intact.

Other names from different cultures and time periods are given these two types of invisible travel.

KIRLIAN PHOTOGRAPHY
PSYCHIC PHOTOGRAPHY

Both types of photography produce "something" on the photograph that was not seen with the physical eye when the picture was taken. *Kirlian photography* uses a high voltage camera that was invented by two scientists and not for the purpose of psychism. *Psychic photography* uses a normal camera and the "somethings" on the photograph are attributed to the ability of the PSYCHIC or the ability of the ETHERIC WORLD INTELLIGENCE. Psychics were quick to honor and use the Kirlian camera because it gives tangible evidence of the AURA that for many years psychics claimed existed.

KNOCKS
CLAIRAUDIENCE

These two different skills are easily confused because both are hearing sounds "out in the atmosphere." These sounds are caused, in both cases, by the ETHERIC WORLD INTELLIGENCE who has come to announce that something extraordinary is about to happen soon, or to call attention to the fact that the PSYCHIC forgot to do something. Sounds can be tappings on a window, ringing a telephone, or knocking on a door or piece of furniture. In the skill *knocks,* the sound is heard by other members of the household and in *clairaudience* the sound is heard by the psychic only (objective clairaudience).

ELEMENTAL
NATURE ELEMENTAL

When relating information about the NATURE KINGDOM, the term *elemental* is often used to distinguish the fairy form from the angel form or used to designate a mischievous or evil fairy.

Elemental is used in some cultures to mean a strong THOUGHT-FORM made by a PSYCHIC, which forms an intelligent mass of energy. If formed purposely, it can do menial human tasks, and if formed unconsciously, it haunts the thinker.

Both of these intelligent forms are felt to be composed of substance known to psychics as ELEMENTAL ESSENCE. This substance is of a slow vibration, close to earth, and amenable to being shaped into living forms. Other types of forms are made of this essence.

When speaking of a *nature elemental,* a fairy, the better choice of words would be NATURE SPIRIT.

PSYCHOKINESIS
TELEKINESIS

The frequent misuse, in this case, is to employ *psychokinesis* for both of these types of PSYCHISM. From the numerous similarities one can see why the one term is felt to fit both skills. But there is a decided difference which is understood by the PSYCHIC and clearly seen by the physical eyes of the onlookers.

Similarities: The PSYCHIC SKILL is performed deliberately, used in experiments, and everyone in the vicinity can perceive the matter being changed, manipulated, and defying the law of gravity.

Differences: In *psychokinesis,* the psychic performs in a light ALTERED STATE OF CONSCIOUSNESS, is aware of what is occurring, and has complete control of the manipulation. This feat requires a disciplined mind which can focus on the project with undivided concentration. In *telekinesis* the psychic (medium) is in a semi or deep state of altered consciousness. The medium is not aware of what is happening while it is happening and has no control over the movement of the matter

except to program its movement beforehand. The feat requires the medium to sit in a SEANCE for the ETHERIC WORLD INTELLIGENCE to synchronize with his or her body. Medium has control over the length of time he or she is in the altered state of consciousness and type of matter manipulation that is to take place.

CHARM
AMULET
TALISMAN
ORNAMENT

An *amulet* or a *talisman* is frequently called an *ornament* because amulets and talismans are worn on the body, are attractive in themselves, and enhance one's outfit. An *ornament* is just that, with no magical qualities. An *amulet* and *talisman* have been energized with PSYCHIC ENERGY to serve the wearer in some psychic manner and are not worn to adorn the clothing. *Charm* may be used synonymously with *amulet* or synonymously with *ornament* (trinket).

SPELL
HEX
CURSE
PSYCHIC ATTACK
SATANIC FORCES

Satanic forces have nothing to do with PSYCHIC SKILLS and should not be in this parellelism except that it is evilly intended. SATANISM is a religion that does not dwell on psychic skills but caters to the abuse of the body and other acts of violence that appear to be very low on the scale of today's cultural and value systems.

The other four terms also pertain to evilly intended works and are misunderstood because the average reader does not read material of this nature. Following are brief and simple descriptions of the outstanding characteristics of each feat.

There is a similarity in a *psychic attack,* a *hex,* and a *curse* that implies the victim is entertaining thoughts of hate, resentment, jealousy, anxiety, etc., or the victim is going through a very emotional trauma. In both cases this type of thinking will draw negativity to oneself. The *psychic attack, spell,* and *hex,* need personal contact between the victim and the evil doer.

A *curse* is brought about by an excellent PSYCHIC who is capable of building an ELEMENTAL and holding it in formation. This elemental hovers over the victim and through this elemental the negation is generated to the victim. This could result in severe illness, a loss in weight, a freak accident, or even death. This evilly intended PSYCHISM is usually short-lived, from one day to a few weeks, as it is difficult for the psychic to keep the elemental colonized. A *curse* is energized by an intense angry emotion inside the curser. Personal contact is not necessary at any time during the execution.

A *hex* is similar to the *curse* in its performance, as the victim can become ill, wake up with the body very mutilated, or even die. A *hex,* also can result in harm to one's property, pets, and friends. The difference lies in that the *hex* is executed through BLACK MAGIC rituals using IMITATIVE MAGIC. A *hex* can last months and years as black magic rituals take time but do not use physical energy to deplete the black magician.

A *psychic attack* is milder than the last two types, bringing a transference of the sender's illness, negative emotions, or bothersome thoughts. A *psychic attack* is sent by TELEPATHY to the victim after a personal contact. This is short-lived and can exist from one hour to a day, and is more easily exorcised than the others. The *psychic attack* that pertains to the HAUNTING by an EARTH-BOUND ENTITY could last for years, always aiming at one aspect of one's life; e.g., a jealous spouse could bother the living partner every time he or she had a date and prevent them from having any other relationship.

Another type of *psychic attack* is the making of an elemental by oneself. One can dwell on his or her problem night and day creating a negative THOUGHT-FORM and holding it colonized for days and months. This results in a nervous breakdown if one does not change their attitude and outlook on life. One attacks oneself.

A *spell* pertains to the use of hypnotic skills to keep a subject in an ALPHA STATE OF CONSCIOUSNESS for susceptibility to obey the hypnotist's wishes in regard to activity that benefits the HYPNOTIST. The victim is unaware that he or she is under the hypnotic submission and appears to act normally to strangers. This *spell* begins with personal contact between the two parties and personal contact must be kept up from time to time to keep the victim submissive. This can last from one day to many years. This is not caused from negative thinking on the part of the victim, but could happen to anyone who is uneducated in psychic skills and is highly hypnotizable.

POSSESSION
OBSESSION

These two types of psychic illnesses are similar in that they show the intrusion of an inferior ETHERIC WORLD ENTITY manifesting through an individual against his will. This entity performs to satisfy their own emotions regardless of the physical or mental harm he or she is bringing to the individual. Both illnesses must be exorcised to be corrected, but exorcised differently.

There are decided differences, however, in the manifestation. In *obsession,* which is a form of MENTAL PSYCHISM, the entity works through the mind of the individual gradually and persistently. It is as if another soul was speaking in the head with contrary ideas, presenting a conflict to the individual. The PERSONALITY changes gradually but eventually there is a complete switch of the individual's values and beliefs. The facial features do not change except to show illness. The changes are not always noticeable to immediate associates and they usually are not admitted by the individual, however, his or her behavior shows a deterioration in personality and productivity.

Possession is a form of PHYSICAL PSYCHISM in which the inferior etheric world entity manifests through the individual in their body activity. The entity enters rapidly, performs contortions that are humanly impossible in normal awareness, and exits after staying a few minutes to a few hours. During this seizure the facial features take on the grotesque look of the entity. The personality is completely different, usually using extreme vulgarity and obnoxious actions that are in reverse of the individual's personality. These seizures occur periodically and could go on for years until the individual is properly exorcised.

Parapsychologists feel that these inferior etheric world entities are either drawn to an individual by conscious evil thoughts, by subconsciously suppressed negative thoughts, or by thoughts and actions from another life expressing as KARMA. More studies have been made on *possession* than on *obsession*.

PSYCHOKINESIS
LEVITATION
TELEPORTATION
APPORTATION
TRANSMUTATION
ASCENSION

The four bottom skills are not too frequently performed today but past history shows a good deal of study in these fields. Upon close examination, one finds these are steps in the attainment of perfected mind discipline to acquire eternal life, rather than merely types of psychic skills. However, there are similarities. Each skill involves the manipulation of physical matter, is willed consciously, and proceeds in an AWARENESS state or LIGHT STATE of consciousness.

Step 1—psychic process: In *psychokinesis,* better known as PK, one works with a small inanimate object in a small area, changes the object's shape and direction, and accomplishes it in a relatively short time. It is believed that one is working with the BIOPLASMA FORCE FIELD.

Step 2—psychic process: *Levitation* needs more time, uses a larger area and raises the inanimate object without changing its shape or form. One then learns to perform this with a human body. It is believed that one is working with the gravitational field around the object.

Step 3—psychic process: *Teleportation* requires more time, utilizes a larger area because this levitated object or body is moved through space. The form is not changed. One is working with the gravitational field.

Step 4—alchemical process: *Apportation* takes a longer time to perform and requires two aspects of space, physical and etherical. Concentration becomes more difficult. An object or human body is dematerialized by changing its atomic structure to an ethereal nature, moving this through space in the etheric world, but keeping it intact. The object or body is then rematerialized in the PHYSICAL WORLD in its original form in that same operation. This skill works with the bioplasma force field and the gravitational field.

Step 5—alchemical process: *Transmutation* requires perfected mind discipline. The object is purified by rearranging its atomic structure to an ethereal state and to a higher vibrational frequency in quality and form when rematerialized in the physical world. This skill is then repeated with one's own body. The body can be held in its ethereal structure until a future time and then rematerialized in a higher vibrational frequency in the physical world as a different person, changing in appearance and ability. The time spent in space is lengthened and useful.

Step 6—spiritual process: *Ascension* means one has the freedom to live in either the ETHERIC WORLD or the physical world at will. *Ascension* requires a magnitude of time and space. Many incarnations have brought the individual to this perfect mind discipline and purified body through righteous actions and thinking. A purified body is free from the gravitational field and will rise or ascend into the air and dematerialize at will. The individual lives in the etheric world until he or she chooses to rematerialize their body in earth at a time period when his or her presence is required to help the masses. The body changes in appearance and talent to fit the occasion. This skill utilizes the bioplasma force field, gravitational field, MIND-ENERGY, SPIRITUAL CHEMISTRY, and probably many other energy laws of both the etheric and physical worlds that humans are not aware of.

SUBJECTS WHICH ARE RELATED TO PARAPSYCHOLOGY AND THEIR TERMINOLOGY

ACUPUNCTURE
ANGELOLOGY
BIOFEEDBACK TRAINING
BLOCKS
BODIES AND PLANES
BODY READING
BRAIN
COLOROLOGY
CONSCIOUSNESS
CURATIVE EDUCATION
CYCLES
DENSITY
ETHERIC VIBRATIONS/MISCELLANEOUS
FORMS-WITH-POWER
HUMAN BEING
HYPNOTHERAPY
KIRLIAN EFFECT/AURAS

KUNDALINI AND CHAKRAS
MAGNETOLOGY
MARTIAL ARTS
MEDITATION
NEW-AGE PSYCHOLOGY
NUMBER POWER
POLARITY
PYRAMIDOLOGY
REINCARNATION/KARMA
SPLIT BRAIN HEMISPHERES
SUBCONSCIOUS AND SUPERCONSCIOUS
   MINDS
SUGGESTOPEDIA
THIRD-EYE AREA
TIME
UFOLOGY

ACUPUNCTURE

Acupoints
Acupressure
Acupuncture
Acupuncture Channel Detector
Acupuncture Points
Balancing of Energy Fields
Body Transceivers
Body Zones
Book of the Yellow Emperor
Byko-Ki
CCAP
Ch'i
Chi
Chinese Massage
Compression Massage
Crystal Deposits
Echo
Electronography
Etheric Power Points
Gate Control Mechanism
Ingham Reflex Method of
   Compression Massage
Jin Shin Jyutsu

Junctions
Kyungrak System of Ducts
Light Pencil
Meridia
Meridian Lines
Meridian Therapy
Node
Pressure Points
Psychic Acupuncture
Reflexology
Shiatsu
Shunt Paths
Spinal Gate
System of Ducts
Target
Tch'i
Tobiscope
Tonus
Trigger Points
Tui Na
Twelve Pulses
Vessel of Conception
Zone of Therapy

ANGELOLOGY

Abatur
Abhamsi
Adapt
Adityas
Advanced Spirit
Aia
Airport Deva
Alaisiagae
Amaimon
Amida
Amsu
Anagamai
Angel *
Angel Axir
Angel Being Kingdom *
Angel Evolution *
Angel Hierarchy
Angel King
Angel Kingdom
Angel of the Sun
Angel of Transition
Angelhood *
Angelic Forces
Angelology *
Angels of the Four Cardinal
    Points
Anges
Annointed Ones
Anpu
Aphrodite
Archangels
Archon
Arhat
Arjuna
Arnquagssaq
Artemis
Arupa
Ascended Being #2
Ascended Master
Asexual *
Astarte
Ba
Barishad
Baron Samedi
Beriah
Bethor
Bodhisattva
Bodiless Devas

Book of Enoch
Boreas
Brotherhoods *
Buddha
Celestial Choruses
Celestial Hierarchy
Celestial Magic
Celestial Phenomena
Celestial Recorders
Celestial Spirits
Chain of being
Chatur Maharajas
Cherub
Children of the Fire Mist
Christ
Christed
Christos *
Chthonian
Circulation of the Kosmos
Color Elementals
Compita
Conclave *
Cooperative Kingdoms
Cosmic Band *
Cosmic Being
Cosmic Entity
Cosmic Master
Cosmic Messiah
Council of Masters
Couriers of Heaven
Crystalline Level
Cupid
De devel ski
Death Angel
Deification
Demigod
Demiurge
Deva *
Deva Evolution
Deva of Communication
Deva-Loka
Devachan
Devanic
Devi
Dhyan Chohans
Dhyani Buddhas
Director
Divine Progenitors

Divine Throne
Doctor of the Spirit
Dominations
Doorkeepers
Egyptian Gods and Goddesses
El
Elder Brothers
Elemental Beings
Eon Degrees
Erinnyes
Ethereal
Exalted Ones
Eye-Language *
Eye-Type Angels
Fairie Land
Fallen Angels
Fiery River
Findhorn Foundation
Form Devas
Gabriel
Galaxial Deity
Garuda
Genius Loci
Glorified Beings
Godhood
Goinmiu
Golden Chain
Good Genius
Great Logi
Great Ones
Great White Brotherhood *
Group Mind
Guardian Angels *
Guide
Guru Dev
Gurudeva
Halo
Heimdall
Hermetic Chain
Hierarchy
His Holiness
Holy Ones
Imperishable Ones
Incarnal
Inner-Brotherhood
Iris
Ishtar
Iuppiter Fulgar

Iuppiter Pluvialis
Iuppiter Tonans
Izana-Gi
Izana-Mi
Jizo
Jolly Baccus
Juno
Kanaloa, Ku, Kane
Keraunios
Keres
Kingdom
Kingdom of Elements
Kingdoms of Living Creatures
Ku
Ku, Kane, Kanaloa
Ladder of Life
Lady of Heaven
Lar Semitales
Lares Compitales
Lares Praestites
Legba
Level and Beingness
Light Bearer of the Piscean Age
Light Beings *
Light Intelligences
Lodges
Logoi of a Planetary Chain
Lordhood
Lords of Humanity
Lords of Light
Lords of Mind
Lords of the Environment
Lords of the Nature Kingdom
Lordship
Lotus Order of Deities
Luminous Train
Maat
Magnificent Deva
Manus

Master *
Mastership
Melchizedek
Michael
Minor Devas
Mystic Zone
Naljor
Nature Being Kingdom
Nature Deva
Nature Kingdom
Nature Lords
Neuter Personality
Overlords
Paradise
Peaceful Order of Deities
Pitris
Planetary Angel
Planetary Spirit
Point-Instants
Polytheism
Poseidon
Priests
Prime-Incarnation
Primeval Tongue
Principalities
Pure Spirits
Queen of Elphen
Ra
Ravashis
Regents of the Earth
Resident Deva
Saint
Saintess
Secret Chiefs
Separh
Seraphim
Seth
Seth Two
Seven planelary chain logoi

Seven spirits before the throne
    of God
Seven Spirits of God
Shrine in the Adyar
    Headquarters
Sky-Earth
Solar Diety
Sons of God
Spirit Councils
Spirit Guardian
Spirits of the Seven Rays
Spiritual Being
St. Michael
St. Vanus
Steps to Godliness
Superhuman Being
Supreme Guides of Humanity
Swami
Tarquip Inua
Te
Third Aspect
Thor
Three-Part Cooperation
Thrones
Transcendental Being
Translation
Tsar Sun
Tu
Tzaphqiel
Uranus
Valkryior
Virtues and Power
Vishnu
Watcher #2
Wheel Beings
Wings
Wovaka
Yama
Yetzirah

BIOFEEDBACK TRAINING

Active Volition *
Active Willing *
Alert Alpha Waves
Allobiofeedback
Alpha Blocking
Alpha Index ***
Alpha Mode *

Alpha Waves *
Amplitude Dial ***
Amplitude Intergration
Anthropoflux
Anxiety Station
Arousal *
Artifact ***

Audio
Autocontrol of Consciousness
Autogenic Relaxation Sequence
Autogenic Training *
Autogenics
Average Evoked Response *
Awareness Notebook *

Balance Control ***
Baseline Drift *
Baseline Reading ***
Berger Rhythm
BFT
Bio-Stat Monitor ***
Biochemical
Bioelectric Signs *
Biofeedback Desensitization *
Biofeedback Instruments ***
Biofeedback Training *
Biogram
Biologic Filter ***
Biomusic
Biosone
Black-Beaded Electrode ***
Brain Electrical Events *
Brain Frequency Alteration *
Brain Print-Outs ***
Brain Scale of Revolutions *
Brain Wave High
Brain Wave Patterns ***
Brain Wave Rhythm
Brain Wave Training *
Brain Waves *
Bumping *
Bursts *
Calm Waves *
CAT
Cerebral Cortex
Chatterbox Organ *
Clean Records
CMS
Conceptualize the Experience *
Conditioning Biofeedback *
Cortical Integration
CPS *
Cross-Examination
Cross-Talk
Cryptographers *
Cultural Noise ***
Cybernetic Loop *
Deep Psychophysiological
   Relaxation *
Delta Waves *
Desynchronized Waves
Detector #2 ***
Drowsiness Alarm Control ***
EEG ***

EEG Mind-Mirror ***
Eidetic Biofeedback
Electric Chair Effect ***
Electric Fabric
Electric Rhythm *
Electric Skin Resistance *
Electroculture
Electrode Cream ***
Electrode Retention Band ***
Electrode Windows *
Electrodermal Response
Electrodes ***
Electroencephalogram ***
Electroencephalograph ***
Electroencephalography
   Science *
Electromyography ***
Electronic Analyzer ***
Electronic Meditation *
Electronic Sensing Devices ***
Electronic Yoga
Electrophysiologist
Electrostatic Artifact ***
Electrosurogram
EMG ***
Environmental Noise ***
Evoked Potentials
Expectancy Wave *
Experiential
Externalized Thoughts *
Feedback *
Fifth State of Consciousness *
Fixed-Brain-Wave-State *
Formula **
Frequency
Frequency Analysis ***
Frequency Control ***
Frontalis Muscles ***
Gain Setting ***
Galvanic Skin Resistance *
Galvanic Skin Response
   Instrument ***
GSR ***
Habituates
Hassle-Log *
Hertz ***
Hieronymus Detector ***
Hooked-Up ***
Hypermetabolic *

Hypometabolic State *
H_2 ***
Integrated Psysiological
   Response *
Integration #1 *
Integration Control ***
Intercerebral Inhibition
Internal Awareness
Internal States *
Internalization Awareness *
Level-Off ***
Lower Frequency ***
Lucid Awareness
Magnetoencephalograph ***
Memory Record *
Memory Time *
Metabolic Monitor ***
Microvolts ***
Mind-Body Art
Mind-Body Discipline *
Mind-Brain Machine ***
Mind-Brain Scientists
Mirror Effect *
Monitor Switch ***
Muscle Firing *
Neuron
Neuropsychiatry
Neutral Inner Feelings *
Nonalert Brain Wave Patterns *
Nonbrain Alpha Waves
Occipital Hemisphere
   Brainwave Monitoring *
Oscilloscope ***
Parieto-Occipital Area
Passive Awareness *
Passive Concentration
Passive Volition *
Passive Willing *
Patterns
Percent Time Meter ***
Perceptual Data **
Performance Clinic
Period Log
Polygraph ***
Preconscious Level
Print-Outs ***
Programmer *
Progressive Relaxation *
Psychic SOS System

Psychogalvanic Reflex *
Psychophysiological Processes
Psychophysiologists
Ramp Function
Range Control ***
Range Switch ***
Readout ***
Red-Beaded Electrodes ***
Resistance ***
Resonater
Resting Electrical Level *
Reverie
Scale of Brain Rhythm *
Scale Switch ***
Seeing with the Skin *
Self-Control of Inner States
Self-Regulated
Self-Regulating Phrases *
Sensitivity Control ***

Sensor ***
Sixty Cycle Hum
Skin Potential Level *
Skin Resistance Response
    Instrument ***
Skin Talk *
Skin Temperature
    Instrument ***
Spike ***
SPL
SPR
Squid
SRR
Stress Monitor ***
Subliminal Biofeedback
Sweat Gland Activity ***
Swishing ***
Sympathetic Turn-On *
Synapse
Tag #1

Telltale Skin *
Temperature Control
    Biofeedback ***
Temperature Sensor ***
Thermistor ***
Theta Waves *
Threshold Control ***
Time Lag
Toposcope ***
Topsy ***
Upper Frequency ***
VCIS
Visceral Learning *
Visual Scanning
Visual Sound Information
Volition
Voluntarium
Voluntary Control of Internal
    States *
Zeroing

BLOCKS

Abreaction
Anniversary Symptoms *
Artificial Anxiety Waves **
Association Fluidity
Aura Balancing **
Bhavana *
Bioenergetic Bends
Bioenergetics
Bioenergetics Therapy **
Black Sack
Block *
Blocked Path
Blocking *
Blocks *
Buried Life *
Burning Karma
Capital P
Carecracking
Character Armor *
Charge *
Clear #1 **
Clearing **
Clusters *
Complex *
Conceptual Blockbusting
Conditioned Avoidance
    Response *
Conditioned Learning *

Conditioned Reflexes
Conditioned Response
CS
Cultural Trance *
Dehumanize **
Dominant Persona
    Consciousness Factors *
Draining Off **
Encounter Group **
Energy Block
Engrams #2
Experimental Histories *
Fascia *
Fixations
Fluidic Association **
Frozen
Gordian Knots *
Grapes *
Habitual Karma *
Healing of Memories **
Hold Patterns *
Hypnotherapy
    Desensitization **
Imprint
Intrapsychic Conflict
Key to Life *
Locked-In *
Lomi-Lomi

Lost Word
Mana Surcharge
Memory Clusters
Mental Wall
Mind-Caused Accident
Mission-Control
Mono-Motivational State
    of Transcendance **
Muscle Tension Patterns *
Neurosis
Neuromuscular Therapy
Outlaw Memory
Phobia
Primal Pains
Primal Pool
Primal Scream **
Primal Therapy **
Psychic Lubrication
Psychic Pain
Psychological Bind
Psychological-Determined
    Amnesia *
Repression *
Seeds
Selective Amnesia *
Sensory Deprivation **
Sensory Integration **
Tapes

Tears
Tension
Time-Trains

Ultimate Primal
Unconscious Nonawareness
Vessel of Conception

BODIES AND PLANES

Aanroo
Adam
Adi Plane *
Aether *
After-Human-Death-States
Aka ***
Aka Finger
Akashic Currents
Annu
Antaskarana #2
Arupa-Lokas *
Assiah
Astral *
Astral Body ***
Astral Brain ***
Astral Cable
Astral Cemetery
Astral Cord
Astral Counterpart *
Astral Currents
Astral Land of Light
Astral Light
Astral Light Record
Astral Matter *
Astral Medicine
Astral Picture Gallery
Astral Plane *
Astral Plane Inhabitants ***
Astral Senses ***
Astral Shell
Astral Sphere
Astral Substance
Atman Body
Atmic Matter *
Atomic Ether
Atomic Etheral Matter
Atomic Picture Images
Atomic Substance
Atomic-Molecular Matter *
Atziluth
Balcony
Barrier
Battle Ground Plane
Batysphere
Beings ***

Below Levels of Awareness
Bhutas
Bifrost
Biopsychic Energy Field ***
Biosphere *
Black Curtain
Bliss Body
Bodies of Light ***
Bodies of Man ***
Body of Light
Border *
Borderland
Briah
Bubble
Buddhic Body ***
Buddhic Plane *
Camouflage
Carnate Entity ***
Causal Body ***
Causal Plane *
Clear Light of Reality
Coput Aureola
Coordinate Points
Corporeal
Cosmic Axis
Cosmic Zones *
Counterfeit
Dead People
Dense Black-Cloud
Dense Body
Densely Packed Realm
Desire World *
Deva
Deva World
Devanchan #1 & #3
Dharma-Kaya #2
Dimensions *
Divine Plane *
Divine Throne
DNA Body Cells
Earth *
Earth Memory
Earth Plane *
Earth's Electrostatic Field
Earth's Etheric Double

Earth-Biology Plane
Earthbound Entities ***
Edge of the Unknown
Eighth Sphere *
Electromagnetic Reality
Elemental Essence
Elemental Evolution
Elementary
Elysium
Emotional Plane *
Empyrean Zone ***
Energy Trail #1
Ethereal Body ***
Etheria *
Etherial *
Etheric Double ***
Etheric Double/Earth *
Etheric Film
Etheric Matter
Expressions ***
Fairie Land
Fetch #1
Fiddler's Green
Field of Peace
Fiery Lives #2
Fifth Dimension *
Fifth Element
Fifth Plane *
Firmament
First Dimension
First Plane *
Flow of Soul ***
Fluidic Body ***
Formless Levels ***
Foul-Scented Rohutu
Four Corners
Fourth Plane *
Fulfill the Scriptures
Funis
Fye
Geomagnetic Field
Great Picture Gallery
Great White Lodge
Grey Twilight Lands
Gross Body ***

Gross Level
Guardian Wall *
Gurdjieffian Man
Hall of Learning
Hall of Sorrow *
Happy Hunting Ground *
Heaven #1 & #5
Heaven Country
Hekhaloth Texts
Hermetic Change
Hyper-Meta-Proto-Elemental
   Matter
Impure Spirits
In Transition
Individuation
Inner-Earth Civilization
Inner-Kingdoms
Intelligent Body ***
Intuitional Wisdom Plane
Intuitional World
Iron-Wall Shell
Isis' Veil
Isles of the Blest
Kama-Manas
Kama-Rupa *
Karana-Sarira
Khat
Kingdom *
Klu
Kosmic Life ***
Kriya Sakti **
Land of Golden Light
Levels
Life Ether *
Life-Cord
Linga-Sairira
Lithisphere
Macrotellurically
Mahaparanirvanic
Manes
Mansions *
Mansions of Light
Material World *
Mental Body ***
Mental Field
Mental Plane
Mental-Reflecting-Ether
Meta-Proto-Matter
Metetherial
Mid-Way Spirits
Middle Kingdom
Middle World

Mindless Shell
Monadic Plane *
Mt. Meru
Mundane World
Museum of Records
Nara-Loka
Nerve Ether
Nerve Fluid
Nerve-Center of Wisdom
Networks of Civilizations ***
Nirvanic Plane *
No-Down
Nonform-Producing Matter
Nonmaterial
Northern Lights
Objective Proportion
Ocean
Og-Min
Osirian Fields
Paradise *
Pattern World
Perfectness Plane *
Photographic Plate of Nature
Physical Ethers *
Physical Matter
Physical Plane
Physical World *
Plane of Atma
Plane of Desires
Plane of Flame
Plane of Illusion *
Planes *
Planet
Planet Earth *
Plateau
Pneuma Sphere
Pneumatology #2 & #3
Polyspirit System ***
Principles of Man
Progressive Lyceums
Psychic Cable
Psychic Nerve System
Psychic Plane *
Pure Land
Realm of Causes *
Realm of Ideas *
Realm of Illusion
Realms of Form
Reflective Ether
Rupa
Rupa-Lokas
Sahu

Sangsaric Regions
Second Plane *
Sefiroth
Semimaterial
Semitransparent ***
Seven Principles of Man ***
Seventh Heaven
Seventh Plane *
Shadow #2 & #4
Sheaths ***
Shin Theory
Sixth Plane *
Solid Astral Matter *
Sorrowless Land
Space Bubble
Spheres
Spirit Hypothesis
Spiritual Light
Spiritual Plane *
Strata of Creation
Subbreathers
Substates of Matter
Subsurface Kingdoms
Subterranean World
Summerland *
Super-Ether *
Superphysical Order of Matter
Sutratma
Svarupa
Sweet-Scented Rohutu
System of Mental Waves *
Teleological
Testament of Solomon
Thickly-Formed
Third Plane *
Thought-Body ***
Threshold of Eternity
Tonal
Tooba Tree
Transcendent Sphere
Transcendental World
Transcendental World of Ideas *
Ultraterrestrial
Uma***
Uni
Unas Text
Unity-Multiplicity ***
Unknown Plane *
Vehicle
Volhallo
Wave-Vibration Concept
World

808

World of Thought
Worlds
Yetzirah

BODY READING

Anthroposcopy
Bear Paw
Body Reading
Bosses
Bumps
Cheirognomy
Chirognomy
Chirognomy Graph
Chirognosy
Chirogonomist
Chiromant
Chirosophist
Chirosophy
Dermatoglyphic
Diagnostic Palmistry
Geloscopy

Graphology
Graphology Therapy
Hair Analysis
Hand Analysis
Hand Analyst
Hand Reflexology
Handwriting Analysis
Harmonic Intervals of Man
Health Aura
Heart Fire
Indian Medicine Wheel
Iridology
Iris Photography
Metoposcy
Mirrors of Destiny
Molesophy

Mounts
Palmist
Palmistry
Palmistry Lines
Paradise Line
Patterning
Phreno-Mesmerism
Phrenology
Physiognomy
Right Hand Symbol
Set His Seal
Signatura Rerum
Skin Communication
Skin Portraits
Skulls

BRAIN

All-Is-Within Doctrine
Analytical Mind *
Animal Brain
Archeo-Cortex
Awareness
Belief System
Beta State of Consciousness
Beta Senses *
Biocomputer
Bioinformation *
Brain *
Brain Electricity *
Brain Magnetism
Brain Sand
Brain Substrate
Brain Wave Patterns
Brain Waves
Brain/Mind *
Brainwashing
Brown Study
Cerebral Recording
Cerebrospinal Nervous System
Chitta
Co-Creator
Concrete Mind
Conscious Awareness *

Conscious Fantasy
Conscious Mind *
Creative Mental Process
Cybernetic Machines
Dendrites
Destructive-Brainwashing Cult
Dgongs-PA
DNA Molecules
Dual Unconsciousness
Educated Consciousness
Ego-Id
Electron *
Electronic Plasma
Essence of Mind
Fantasy
Feedback Control System
First Personality
Form
Form Levels
Free Will
Gateways to the Mind
Group Minds
Habit Focus
Hallucination
Heart #1 & #3
Hologram Brain Theory

Hypmocampal
Hypothalamus
I-ness
Idea Construction
Ideas
Ideation
Illumination
Information Disease
Inner-Dialogue *
Inner-Mind Activity *
Interior Monologue
Internal Awareness
Intrapsychic Machinery
Limbic System *
Linear Thinking
Little Local Self *
Little Man
Logoidal Will *
Mana-Mana
Manas #3 & #4
Mental Activity *
Mental Brain Programming *
Mental Energy *
Mental Enzymes
Mental Field
Mental Mind *

Mental Noise *
Mental Processes *
Mental Wall
Mental-Consciousness-Cord
Mental-Consciouness—Seed-
    Atom
Mental-Emotional Activity
Mental-Seed-Atom
Metacommand Language
Mind *
Mind Experience
Mind—Energy *
Mind-Link/Body-Link
Mind/Body and Mind-Body
Nervousness
Non-Thought
Objective Mind

Objective Programming *
Objective Senses
Outer Mental Activity *
Outer Senses
Personal History
Pibs
Psychoactive
Psychology
Rational Mind *
Rational Soul *
Recreator
Scale of Brain Rhythm
Self-Metaprogrammer
Self-Metaprogramming *
Software *
Stream of Half-Consciousness
Stream of Thought

Suggestion
Superliminal
Supraliminal
Surface Subconscious *
Temporary Memory Bank *
Thinking *
Thought *
Thought-Forms *
Thoughtsmanship
Uhane
Uncontrolled Inner-Mind
    Pictures
Wakening Consciousness *
Waking Dreams
Waking Sleep
Will
Willed Thought *

COLOROLOGY

Aspects of Wisdom
Astral Spectrum
Aura Energy *
Black
Black Diamond
Black Nimbus
Blue
Blue Air
Chroma
Chromatogram
Chrome Practitioner **
Chromo
Chromopath
Chromopathy
Chromotherapy **
Chromotherapy Practitioner **
Color *
Color Activity *
Color Breathing **
Color Elementals
Color Healing **
Color Organ *
Color Psychology *
Color Science *
Color Spectrum *
Color Starvation *
Color Telepathy *
Color Therapy **
Color Visualization **
Colorology *

Cosmic Octaves *
Darkness *
Divine Aura *
Electromagnetic Spectrum *
Electromagnetic Waves *
Gold
Green
Green Ray Period *
Green Rays
Heliotherapy **
Hue *
Indigo
Infrared
Infrared Film
Light *
Monochromatic Lights
Odic Color *
Orange
Photo-Chromotherapy **
Pure Love *
Ray
Ray Therapy **
Red
Science of Color *
Seven Major Rays *
Spectrum *
Tattwa Chart *
Thermovision *
Ultra-Red
Ultraviolet Rays

Value *
Vibranalysis
Violet
Warmth Ether
White
White Beam
White Color *
White Light
World of Eidos
Yellow

CONSCIOUSNESS

Age of Cosmic Consciousness
Akshara
Alpha State of Consciousness
Altered State of Awareness
Altered State of Consciousness
Angel Consciousness
ASC
Astral Consciousness
At-One-Ment
Atom-Memory Bank
Attraction Consciousness
Aware Energy
Awareness
Awareness-Raising
Bardo Consciousness
Basic Consciousness
Beta State of Consciousness
Beyond Personal Consciousness
Birth Consciousness
Blank Awareness
Bliss
Bliss Consciousness
Brahma Consciousness
Brain-Bound Consciousness
Bridge of Consciousness
Cell
Cellular Consciousness
Centers of Consciousness
Chit
Christ Consciousness
Collective Unconscious *
Collective Unconscious
   Consciousness *
Compound of Consciousness
Condensed Consciousness
Conditioned Consciousness
Conscious Cooperation
   Consciousness
Conscious of Being *
Consciousness *
Consciousness Awareness
  Movement
Consciousness Cord
Consciousness Evolution
Consciousness Junkie
Consciousness of Infinite Space
Consciousness of Self
Consciousness Shift
Consciousness-Control
   Programs

Cosmic Consciousness *
Crystalline Level
D-ASC
Deep Level of Consciousness
Delta State of Consciousness
Devachan
Divine Consciousness
Dream Consciousness
Dual Unconsciousness
Emotional Consciousness
Empyrean Zone
Enlightenment #5
Epiphenomenalism
Esthetic State
Expansion of Consciousness
FC
Field Consciousness
Field of Being
Folk Consciousness
Fringe of Consciousness
God Consciousness Supreme
Gross Level
Higher State of Consciousness
Human Being Consciousness
Individual Cellular
   Consciousness *
Individual Consciousness
Inner-Awareness
Inner-Stream of Consciousness
Instinct Consciousness
Intergalactic Consciousness *
Intuitive Level of the Psyche
Invisible Consciousness
Involuntary Functions
Jagrat
Labryinth Subconscious
Level of Being
Liberation
Life
Mass Consciousness
Mass Strength
Memory Consciousness *
Mental-Neutral Level
Mind
Mind-Awareness Movement
Molecular Memory
Mystic Experience
Mystic-Type State of
   Consciousness
New Consciousness

New Consciousness-Awareness
  Movement
Noetic
Noetic Science
Nonawareness
Nonbeing
Nonconscious Level
Nonordinary Reality
  Experiences
Nonreality Reality
Objective Consciousness
Omega
Ordinary Consciousness *
Outer Conscious Level
Overall Consciousness
Oversoul Consciousness
Preconscious
Protoplasmic Consciousness
Psyche Consciousness
Psychedelia
Psychedelic Consciousness
Psychic Consciousness
Psychological Structures
Psychosomatic Self-Regulation
Pure Awareness
Pure Consciousness
Quickened Consciousness
Reality #3 & #5
Realizable Consciousness
Rig-Pa
Sambodhi
Samskara
Science of Consciousness
Seeing #2
Self-Directing
Selfless Universal Love
Sensation Consciousness
Separate Consciousness
Simple Consciousness
Single-Point of Consciousness
Spinal Consciousness
Spiritual Hierarchy
Srid-Pa Bar-Do
State of Consciousness
Stopping the World
Stream of Consciousness *
Stream of Half-Consciousness
Supermundane
Suprahuman Supraself Spaces
Supramundane Reality

Supreme State
Swabhavat
Symbiotic Consciousness
TC
Temporal Consciousness
Theta State of Consciousness

Total Consciousness
Transpersonal Consciousness
Transpersonal Unconscious
Turiya
Ultraconsciousness
Unconsciousness

Universal Consciousness *
Visible Consciousness
Wakeful Hypometabolic State of
  Consciousness
Within-Ness
Zero Point

CURATIVE EDUCATION

Abhyantara Vritti ***
Allopathy **
Alternatives **
Antidotal Medicine *
Applied Kinesiology **
Ariosophie *
Astrological Herb Healing **
Attitudinal Healing **
Bahya Vritti ***
Bates Method **
Belief System
Biochemic System
  of Medicine **
Biochemistry Therapy *
Bioclimatology *
Biodynamic Farming *
Bioenergetic and Reichian
  Therapy *
Bioenergetics #1 *
Biomusic
Biopsychiatric *
Body Armor *
Body Is Turned On
Body Transceivers *
Breathaterian ***
Breathing ***
Breathing Release ***
Bright Spot of the Day *
Cancer Elemental
Catharsis *
Cell Salts **
Cellular Therapy **
Chiropractic Adjustment **
Chromotherapy **
Chronic Pain *
Chua K'a **
Clean Slate Psychology *
Click #2 *
Color Healing **
Color Starvation *
Complete Breath ***
Correct Health *

Cosmic Love *
Curative Education *
Curative Medicine **
Dance Therapy **
Dead Food ***
Diets for Psychics ***
Disease *
Do-In **
Doctoring Session
Dysponesis *
Earth Spirit #1 **
Electromagnet Healing **
Emotional Stress *
Esoteric Healers
Esoteric Healing
Eucalyptus Tree **
Eustress *
Experiential Histories *
Faith Healing **
Fasting ***
Feeling Therapy *
Flesh Food ***
Flower Therapy **
Fluidic Association *
Folk Medicine **
Food Scale ***
Free Association **
Free-Floating Anxiety *
Fringe Medicine **
Fruititarian ***
Fulfillment *
Functional Integration *
Geobiology *
Gestalt Psychology *
Gestalt Therapy **
Ginseng **
Glands *
Growth Games
Hair Analysis **
Hand Reflexology
Healing **
Healing by the Sun **

Healing Crisis ***
Healing Memories
Health *
Health Aura *
Heliotherapy **
Helpers #3 **
Herbalist **
Herbology *
Hindu Yoga ***
Holism *
Holistic *
Holistic Education *
Holistic Health *
Holistic Health Healer **
Holistic Health Theory
Holistic Medicine **
Hologram Energy *
Holy Breath #3 & #5 ***
Holy Fools **
Homeopathy **
Hormones *
Humanistic Therapy Groups
Hydrotherapy **
Hyperventilation ***
Illness *
Immunobiology **
Imprint *
Indian Medicine Wheel *
Inner-Attention *
Instantaneous Healing **
Insufflation **
Integration *
Intentional Suffering *
Iridology **
Iris Photography **
Kinesiology **
Kinesthetic Experience
Kinesthetic Feedback *
Kokysyu *
Kumbhakam ***
L-Tryptophon ***
Lemon ***

Licorice ***
Life Change Indent *
Lifeit ***
Lite Program *
Low Breathing ***
Massage Therapy **
Maturity *
Medical Climatology *
Meridian Therapy **
Metallotheraphy **
Metaphysical Healing *
Mineral Salts **
Mission-Control **
Muscle Tension Patterns *
Music Healing **
Music Therapist **
Namapathy **
Natural Healers **
Naturopathy *
Negative Thought *
Neuromuscular Therapy **
New Consciousness *
New-Age Psychology *
Nonmedical Healing
Occult Medicine *
Optimum Health *
Organ Language *
Orgone Accumulator **
Pain *
Positive Expectation *
Positive Thought #3 *
Postural Integration **
Predictinosis **
Psycalisthenics ***

Psychoanalysis *
Psychoanalyst *
Psychobiology *
Psychodrama **
Psychological Field *
Psychological Health *
Psychological Integration *
Psychological Stress Evaluator
Psychological Structures **
Psychonutrition ***
Psychopathology *
Psychophysiology *
Psychosomatic **
Psychotherapy *
Purifying Breath ***
Resonant Breathing ***
Reward and Punishment System
Rolfing **
Scientific Astrology *
Secondary Gains *
Self-Integration *
Self-Isolation #2 *
Self-Observation Therapy **
Self-Realization *
Senoi Dream Therapy **
Sensory Isolation
Sickness
Simonton Method **
Social Readjustment Rating
    Scale *
Somatic Psychology *
Spirit Healing ***
Spiritual Healing **
Spiritual Therapist **

Spiritual Therapy **
Spittle **
Stress *
Stressor *
Stroke Nursing *
Superstructures *
Symptom Reversal *
Symptom Substitution
Tapas ***
Tears
Therapy Localization **
Tissue Salts **
Tonus #2 *
Transpersonal Group
    Therapy **
Trialectic Logic
Unconventional Medicine **
Unorthodox Healing *
Unstressing *
Veganism ***
Vegetarian ***
Vermont Folk Medicine **
Vibratory Scale of Food ***
Village Herbalist ***
Vitalism *
Wandering Soul *
Wellness *
Weltschmerz *
White Bleeding *
Wholism *
Yarb Doctor **
Yo-Ki *
Yoga Tatwic ***

CYCLES

Active and Passive Phases ***
Activity and Rest Cycles ****
Aesthetic Perception
Age *
Age of Aquarius
Age of Brahma
Age of Love, Light and Life *
Aquarian Age *
Ascending Arc
Bioclocks ***
Biocycle ****
Bioelectromagnetic Interactions
Biological Clock #1 ****
Biological Cycle

Biological Rhythm
Biological Time of Day ****
Bionomy
Biorhythm ***
Biorhythm Chart ***
Biorhythm Curves ***
Biorhythm Cyclegraph
Biorhythm Dialgraph
Biorhythmic Span ***
Biorhythmic Year ***
Bisexuality ***
Body Rhythm Diary
Body-Time
Central Sun *

Chain of Globes
Chain Period *
Circadian Half-Waves
Circadian Rhythm ****
Civilization Cycle *
Clock
Compassion Cycle ***
Compatibility Percentage ***
Continuity *
Cosmic Biology *
Cosmic Clock
Cosmic Cycle *
Cosmic Rhythm
Cosmic Sweep *

814

DENSITY

Adversaries *
Aerial Body *
Aerial Plane
Ahriman *
Annwn
Annwyl *
Archdemons
Artificial Astral Plane *
Asura-Loka *
Avitichi
Baalzephon
Beelzebub *
Birds of Prey
Black Lodges *
Black Shaman **
Brute World *
Carrying An Evil **
Celestial Descent **
Chang Tang Highlands
Counts of Hell
Daivas
Darkness of Ignorance *
Death Mist
Demon H2
Demoness
Demoniac
Demonic
Demonologist **
Demonology *
Density *
Density Elementals *
Devil *
Devils of All Ages

Diabolic
Disembodied Soul #2
Dweller in the Abyss
Elementaries *
Erlik
Eternities *
Foul-Sceneted Rohuter
Great Beast
Gross Communications *
Hades *
Hell *
Husks *
Imp
Infernal Animals *
Infernal Beings *
Inferno
Intermediate State *
Intermediate World
Kama-Loka
Land of the Shadows *
Left-Hand Path
Lesser Key of Solomon *
Lilth
Limbo *
Lord of Evil
Low-Order-Psi-Force *
Lucifer *
Mercy Band **
Missionary Spirits **
Multiform Waves *
Nat Cult
Nergal

Netherworld
Nonhuman Realms *
Obaifo
Osiris
Phantom Flock of Animals
Pit
Planes of Darkness
Pluto
Po
Powers of Darkness
Preta-Loka World *
Prince of Darkness
Protean Spectres *
Pudak *
Purgatory *
Samedi
Satan *
Satanic Forces
Sheol
Silent Shadows *
Sirat
Spiritualizing the Etheric
  World **
Subhuman Being
Subhuman Realm
Subplanes of Astral *
Testament of Solomon **
Titans
Tuat
Underworld
Ungodly Spirits

ETHERIC VIBRATIONS/MISCELLANEOUS

Actualism
Aether
Antinodes
Archetypal Womb
Asiyyah
Assiah
Astro
Astrological Influences
Atom #1 & #2 *
Aware Energy *
Basic Elements
Biocurrents
Bions
Blue Air

Building Blocks
Cellular Memory
Charged Globule
Co-Creator *
Contour Theory
Corona of the Sun
Cosmic Electronics
Cosmic Magnetic Forces
Cosmic Mainstream
Cosmic Ray
Cosmic Stream *
Cosmic Will *
Cosmo Rays
Cosmogenesis

Cosmogony
Covalent Bonding
Dead Matter
Dense
Diamagnetic
Downward Curve of the Arc
Earth *
Earth Magnetism
Earth-Breathing
Eka-Ksana
Electric magnetic Energy
Electricity *
Electrokinetic
Electromagnetic Spectrum *

815

Electromagnetic Universe *
Electromagnetism *
Electrometric
Electromotive Force
Energeology
Energy
Energy Grid
Energy Patterns
Energy Potential
Energy Sink
Energy Systems
Ergosphere
Ether
Ether Pressure
Etheric Currents
Etheric Spaces
Etheric Warp
Ethertricity
Evolution
External World *
Field of Mind *
Fire
First Dimension
Flame and the Fire
Fourth Dimension
Fragment
Free Energy
Galactic Wave Field
Galaxy
Globules
Gravitational Waves
Gravitons
Gunas
Harpakrad
Holon
Hydronics

Hylozoism
Hypersynchronized Waves
Illusion
Inanimate Things
Innergy
Intelligence
Involution
Koilon
Life Units
Lifetrons
Light Waves
Light-Dot
Living Organism
Mana
Matter *
Maya
Mental Energy
Meta-Proto-Matter
Micro
Microcosmology
Monad Perceptions
Monadology
Motion
Natural Law
Nebular Hypothesis
Node *
Noumenal World
Od
Opaque Points
Open System
Oranur Atmosphere
Orgonomy
Physical Biocommunication
Physical Matter *
Prearranged Harmony

Preestablished Harmony
Primal Energy
Primordial Substance
Pseudomatter
Psi-Interactive Biomolecules
Psychogenesis
Pulsation
Quantum Mechanics
Quantum Physics
Quantum Theory
Radiation
Ring-Pass-Not #1
Sidereal Radiation
Solar Eddies
Soniferous Ether
Speculative-Metaphysical Theory
Spiritual Energy
Static
Static Universe
Subatomic Energy
Subnuclear Particles
Subtle
Sun's Rays
Things *
Third Round of the Planet
Ultimate Science
Unified-Field Theory
Universal Substance *
Vibrational Frequencies
Vibrations *
Vibro
Vibroscope
Wai
Wavelength
White Holes

FORMS-WITH-POWER

Abred
Adi
Akasha
Ankh
Apas
Binah
Bishop's Ring
Broomstick
Caduceus Winding Symbol
Cameron Cones
Carole
Chaterson Coils
Circle

Cone of Power
Conical Shape
Crescent
Cross
Crux Ansata
Crystals
Cube
Dagger
Dorje
Double Triangle
Dunce Hat
Equi-Limbed Cross
Fairy Rings

First Temple of the Mysteries
Five-Pointed Star
Forms
Forms-With-Power
Four-Pointed Star
Fraternity of the Rose Cross
Fu Hsi Pattern
Golden Chain
Half-Moon Shape
Hexagonal Form
Hexagram
Hieroglyphs
Horns

Horse Shoes
Hyperspace Theory
Iron Ring
King Scale
Kolam
Life Force Symbol
Magic Circle
Magic Symbols
Magical Diagrams
Magical Proportions of Man
Mandala
Men-An-Tol
Mountain of Philosophers

Octahedron
Other Energies
Oval
Pentagram
Prithivi
Psychic Development Circle
Pyramid
Ring of Wooden Posts
Rose Cross
Shaped Power
Shapes
Shri Yantra
Square

Step Pyramid
Stone Circle
Stonehenge
Swastika
Sword
Tangrams
Tans
Tattwas
Tau
Tejas
Thread
Triangle
Witch-Hat

HUMAN BEING

Adam Kadmon
Animate Beings
Annamaya-Kosha
Armored Organism *
Atomic-Molecular Matter *
Beings #2 *
Bioelectrical System *
Biogenetic Law
Blood
Body
Body Chemistry #2 *
Brains Dews *
Breath Form
Carnal Man *
Cell
Cell Activity
Central Nervous System *
Character
Chemiphysical
City of Man *
Colloidal System
Consciousness-Seed-Atom
Corporeal Envelope *
Desire #3 *
Divine Psychology *
Dynamics #2
Earthian
Earthling *
Electric Actuality *
Electric Ether
Electric Fluid
Electroauragram
Elecromagnetic Body Waves *
Electromagnetic Circuit *
Electrophysiology

Elements *
Emotional Astral Cord
Emotional Force Field *
Emotional-Astral-Seed-Atom
Emotional-Seed-Atom
Enervated *
Envelope *
Flaming Sword
Golden Urn
Hair *
Hands *
Hara
Harmonic Intervals of Man *
Human Being *
Human Being Consciousness
Human Being Kingdom
Human Being Specie Seed *
Human Body
Human Hand *
Human Transmitter *
In the Body Pent
Inner-Psychic Climate
Introjection
Instinct
Learning to Learn *
Life Units *
Life-Cord-Heart-Seed-Atom
Light Body #1 *
Light Ether
Living Tissue
Lower Self
Magnetocardiograph
Man *
Manas-Kama
Mankind *

Manna
Materialistic Man
Mind/Body and Mind-Body
Nadis *
Nervous System *
Neural Discharge *
Ocean of Fire
Pace-Maker
Permanent-Seed-Atoms
Personality
Physical Body *
Pranic Ether
Prop
Psychic Heart-Centre
Psychic Structure #2
Psychophysical *
Psychophysical Parallelism
Sentient Existence *
Signatura Rerum
Silver Cord
Skin #1 *
Skin Communication
Skulls
Solar Furnace
Solar Iron
Solar Plexus *
Stage of Evolution *
Telluric Energy *
Three Books of Life
Time of Repose *
Tonal Person *
Tonus #1
Unripe Ego
Upadhi

HYPNOTHERAPY

Abulia *
Active Trance
Age Regression *
Antithesis of Sleep *
Artificial Group Elemental *
Artificial Reincarnation
Autogenic Training #2
Autohypnosis
Autoprocedure
Autosuggestion *
Biological Marker *
Brain Wave Synchronizer *
Catalepsy
Cataleptic Stage of Hypnosis *
Clearing **
Coma State *
Community of Sensation
Complete Age Regression *
Complete Regression *
Cooperative Suggestion *
Cryptomenesia
Deep State of Hypnotherapy *
Dehypnotizing *
Detachment #4
Disassociation
Disgusied Hypnosis *
Distant Hypnosis *
Dynamometer
Ego-Strengthening *
Emotional Hypnosis *
Esoteric Hypnotism *
Ethereal Hypnosis
Etheric Magnetic Current
Everyday Trance *
Evil Eye *
Exteriorization of Sensitivity
Eye-Fixation
Eye-Roll Test *
Eyelid Fatigue *
Fair Witness
Finger Response *
Fluctuation
Free-Associating Unconscious
Fringe of Consciousness
Fringe of Space-Time
Full Recall *
Gaze
Group Hypnosis *
Guided Hypnosis *
Hand Levitation *

Healing of Memories
Heterohypnotherapy
Heterosuggestion *
Hyperacute *
Hyperamnesia *
Hypnoanalyst
Hypnography
Hypnoidal
Hypnology
Hypnomotivation
Hypnopersonation
Hypnoplasty
Hypnoreproduction
Hypnoscope
Hynosis *
Hypnotherapist *
Hypnotherapy *
Hypnotherapy Desensitization
Hypnotic Anesthesia *
Hypnotic Clairvoyance *
Hypnotic Disc *
Hypnotic Ecstasy
Hypnotic Pallomancy
Hyponotic Phenomena
Hypnotic Prescription *
Hypnotic Speech Pattern *
Hypnotic Suggestion *
Hypnotic Touch
Hypnotism *
Hypnotist
Hypnotizability *
Hypnotizable
Hypnotized Teams
Hypothermia **
Ideomotor Action *
Ideomotor Response *
Induction *
Induction Profile
Induction Release *
Joint Hypnosis Telepathy
Lethargic State of Hypnosis *
Light State Of Hypnosis *
Limb Catalepsy *
Magnet Sleep
Magnetization
Magnetizer
Magnetizing Object
Mass Hypnosis *
Medical Hypnosis *
Medium State of Hypnosis *

Mesmeric Fluid *
Mesmerism
Mono-Motivational State of
  Transcendance
Occult Hypnotism
On-The-Spot-Hypnosis *
Operator *
Orenda #2 **
Parallel Awareness
Paralytic Condition
Partial Age Regression *
Partial Regression *
Partial Somatic Dissociation
Passive Hypnosis *
Phreno-Mesmerism
Plenary Trance
Posthypnotic Suggestion
Power of the Gaze *
Prescription
Programming
Psychotherapist
Recall *
Recreational Hypnosis *
Revivification *
Seeing with the Stomach #3
Self-Control of Inner States
Self-Hypnosis
Self-Hypnotherapy *
Self-Induction
Self-Suggestion
Semi-Stage Hypnosis *
Sensational Hypnosis *
Sense Withdrawal
Sensitivity Transfer
Sleep-Wake Hypnosis *
Somnambulic Phenomena
Somnambulism Stage of
  Hypnosis
Spontaneous Self-Hypnosis *
Stage Hypnosis
Strobe Light *
Subject *
Superalertness *
Supermesmeric
Superwakefulness
Surfacing *
Symptom Substitution *
Telepathic Hypnosis *
Telepathic Sleep-Wake
Time Distortion *

Total Recall *
Total Regression *
Trade-Down

Transfix
Under *
Waking Hypnosis *

KIRLIAN EFFECT/AURA

Actinic Rays
Aura Colors *
Aura Photography
Aura Reading *
Aura-Vision *
Aura-Vision Trainer
Auric Retreat *
Auroemmissive Image
Biodynamo-Chromatic
Bioelectrode
Bioenergetics Therapy #2
Biological Plasma
Bioluminescence
Bioluminesence
Bioplasma Body
Chemiluminescent and Electro-
    Photographic Techniques
Cold Electron Emission
Cold Light
Contact Photography
Corona
Corona Patterns
Corona Photography
Dicyanain Screens
Electric State
Electrobiology

Electrodynamic Theory *
Electrography
Electron Microscope
Electron Microscopy
Electronography
Electrophotography
Electrophysiologist
Electrophysiology
Energy Field Photography
Etheric Wires
Field
Field Biology
Field Effect Monitors
Field Shifts
Finger Pad Electrographs
Flare Patterns
Haircut Effect
Halo Effect
Heat Convection Currents
High Frequency Fields
High Voltage Photography
Ikra
Integral Stimulating Intensity
    Stroboscope
Kilner Goggles *
Kilner Screen

Kirlian Effect
Kirlian Photography
Kirlian Theory
Light Hieroglyphs
Lost Leaf
Magnetic Emanations
Nimbus
Phantom Leaf Effect
Phantom Pains
Photoelectronic Multipliers
Pinacyanole Bromide Filters
Pyrotechnics
Radiation Field Photography
Schlieren System
Sensitive Electrometer
Sergeyev Detectors
Streamer Repulsion
Striations
Supersensitive Photo Multipliers
Tesla Coil
Ultrafaint Luminescence
Ultraouter Aura
Ultraviolet Auric Light
Window on the Unknown
X-Bioenergies
Xylonite

KUNDALINI AND CHAKRAS

Akasa #2
Alta Major Center *
Amrit
Anahat Chakra
Ananda
Anja Chakra
Astral Lotuses *
Baptism by Fire
Battle Ground
Brahamaranda Chakra
Brahmadanda
Brahmanical Thread
Brow Chakra *
Caduceus of Mercury
Caduceus Winding Symbol *
Cakras
Central Axis of Creation *

Chakra *
Chakra Stem *
Chakra System *
Chakram
Chamber of the Heart
Chitrini
Chrism Oil
Coiled Serpent *
Cosmic Fire *
Crown Chakra *
Dhammachakkappavattana Sutta
Divine Fire in Man
Divine Marriage *
Earth Chakras
Etheric Bowl *
Etheric Centers *
Fiery Furnace

Fiery Power
Fire of Creation
Fire of Wisdom
Fish Gate
Force Centers
Fourth Chakra *
Gates
Gateway to the Heart *
Godhead #1
Golden Oil
Heart Chakra *
Ida *
Inner-Bowl *
Journey of the Moon
Journey
Kanda
Knot of Brama

Knot of Shiva
Knot of Vishnu
Kundalini *
Kundalini Prana *
Kundalini Shakti *
Lam
Left Psychic Nerve *
Life Fluid
Long-Stemmed Unfolded Lotus
Manipur
Manna #2 *
Median-Nerve
Medulla Oblongata *
Mental Rays
Merudanda
Muldhara Chakra
Musical Lights *
N/um
Navel Chakra *
Occult Fire
Opening of the Seals *
Passage of the Sun God
Path

Pingala *
Plexus
Power Centers in Man *
Pranayama Breath
Psychic Centres *
Psychosomatic Power Center
Pulse-Point
Right Psychic Nerve *
River of Light
Root Chakra *
Sacred River in Man
Sahasrara
Sap of the Tree of Knowledge *
Serpent Fire
Serpent Power
Solar Cycle #2
Solar Plexus Chakra *
Spiritual Cord *
Spleen Chakra *
Straight and Narrow Way
Sun by the Sacred Heart
Sun's Journey

Superintelligent Electricity
Superuniverses
Sushumna *
Svadhisthana Chakra
Third Brain
Third Chakra *
Thirty-Three Doors
   of the Mystic Hallway
Thousand Petal Lotus *
Throat Chakra *
Triple-Heater *
Triple-Warmer
Unique Psychophysiological
   Tools and Techniques *
Upraised Serpent *
Vajrini
Vayu #1
Visudda Chakra
Wand of Mercury
Winding Road *
Winding Stairway
World Mother #2

MAGNETOLOGY

Electromagnet Healing
Lodestone
Magnet Dispensary
Magnet Healing
Magnet Practitioner
Magnetization
Magnetizer #3

Magnetology
Magnetometer
Magnetotherapeutic Device
Magnets
Mesmerism
Natural Magnet

MARTIAL ARTS

Acheta
Aikdo Dojo
Aikido
Aketa
Anesthetic Hold
Art of the Velvet Fist
Black Art
Black Belt
Breakfalls
Budo
Chuan
Empty Hands
Gi
Judo

Judo Touch
Karate
Karate Practitioner
Kareteka
Kendo
Knife Side
Kung-Fu
Martial Arts
Mind Cleansing Meditation
Motionless Meditation
T'Ai Chi Doh
Tai Chi Doh
Vital Points

MEDITATION

Adrogynous
Akshara
Alaya-Vijnana
Alert-Asleep
Alert-Passivity *
Alert-Wakefulness *
Alpha Mode
Angas *
Art of Tea
Asana
Ascension-Through-Meditation
At-One-Ment
Autogenic State
Avatar Meditation
Bahya Vritti
Beggar Monk
Beating Down Thought *
Bija Mantra
Blank Mind
Bodhi Tree
Brain Sooting
Bsam-Gtan Bar-Do
Buddha Amida Butsu
Burmese Meditation *
Caucasian Yoga
Cave Meditation
Cave of Energy
Cha-No-Yu
Chanoyu
Check
Checker
Checking
Chhos-Nyid Bar-Do
Christian Prayer
Closet
Collecting the Mind
Complete Breath *
Concentration
Concentration/Contemplation/
   Sam-Yama-Type
Consciousness of Infinite Space
Contemplation
Controlled Relaxation *
Cortically Mediated Stabilization
Cosmic Communion *
Creative Meditation
Deep Psychophysiological
   Relaxation
Desert Fathers *
Detachment #2 & #3

Dhammapada
Dharanis
Dhyana
Disassociation
Distinguishing Wisdom
Divine Body of Truth
Doing Japa *
Eastern Rosary
Eating Mindfully
Ecstasy #3
Ego-Killing Practice *
Egyptian Yoga ***
End-State *
Equalizing Wisdom
Essence of Rest
Experiencer
Fourth State of Consciousness *
Fringe of Consciousness
Frontal Gaze *
Ghanta Nadam
Godform Position *
Going into the Silence
Going Within *
Gong
Guffaw
Guided Fantasy
Guided Meditation
Hands at the Heart Level
Hesychasm
Hypermetabolic
Hypometabolic State *
Hypothermia
In Quietude •
Initiator
Inner-Silence
Inner-Sound Current
Interior Silence
Internalization
Inward Art
Is-Ness #2
Isolation Tank
Japa *
Japa Yoga
Japa-Mala *
Japam
Jiji-Mu-Ge
Jivanmukta
Just Sitting
Kasina Meditation
Keisaku

Kensho
Kriyas
Kyrie Eleison
Lam
Laya Yoga
Led meditation
Lotus Posture *
Lowered State
   of Consciousness *
Maitreya Asana
Mandala *
Manjursi
Mantra
Mantram Yoga
Meditation *
Meditative Palming *
Metaphysical Emptiness
Mind Expansion
Mind-Drift
Mirror-Like Wisdom *
Monkey
Monoideasim *
Mudra
Myang-Hdas
Nasal Gaze
Nirvana
No-Mind State *
No-Thing-Ness
Nonattachment
Objective Consciousness
Ocean Surf *
Oneness
Optical Threshold
Out-Breath
Padmasana
Palm Downward During
   Meditation *
Palm Upward During
   Meditation *
Pardes
Partial Somatic Dissociation *
Passing-The-Mantra
Patanjali's Sutras
Peak Experience #2
Pink Noise
Prayer Beads
Process Meditation
Psychosphere
Psychospiritual Powers
Puja

Pure Alertness
Purifying Breath
Quantum Vacuum
Quiet Attentiveness *
Quiet Reflection
Quiet
Quietism
Quietude
Radiating One
Raja Yoga
Red Hot Needles
Relaxation Response
Resonant Breathing
Restful Alertness
Rinzia Zen Sect
Rosary
Samadhi
Samuroi
Sangha #1
Satori
Sci
Science of Creative Intelligence
Seed Meditation
Self-Disidentification
Self-Generated,
    Repeated Stimulus
Self-Nonself

Sense Withdrawal *
Sesshin
Signal Value
Silence
Sitting
Sitting Zen
Sleepitate *
Sodo
Soto School
Sound Kasina
Structured Meditation
Sunyata
Sutra
Tantakam
Tantric Meditation *
Tathata
Tea *
Thangka
Therevadan Meditation
TM
Total Absorption *
Transcendental Meditation *
Tratakam
Tratakam Meditation Method
Turiya
United Mandalas
Vacillating *

Vajra-Kaya
Vedamata
Vipassana
Voidness
Wakeful Hypometabolic
    State of Consciousness *
Warning Stick
Watch Your Breath ***
Way-of-Mindfulness
White Noise Stimuli
Wisom of Equality
Wisdom of the Great Mirror
Withdrawal
Witness Meditation
Working Meditation
Yantra *
Yoga Lama
Yoga Nidra
Yoga Tatwic ***
Zaza
Zazen
Zen Meditation *
Zen Sickness
Zen Sitting
Zendo
Zennist

NEW-AGE PSYCHOLOGY

Abnormal Behavior
Actualization
Anorm
Art of Living
At
Behavioral Control
Bible
Blind Faith
Capturing the Vision
Character Armor
Click
Consciousness of Self
Consciousness Shift
Controlled Coincidences
Cosmic Education
Cosmic Love
Crisis Situation
Cultural Trance
Cultural Transformation
Deconditoning Process
Deindividualized

Denial
Desensitizing Pain
Deteriorating Self-Concept
    Syndrome
Dharmic
Distress
Divine Initiative
Divine Love
Divine Nostalgia
Divine Psychology
Education
Ego Psychology
Emotion
Emotional Stress
Emptiness
Encounter Group
Enriching Experience
Erhard Seminars Training
Esoteric Movement
Esoteric Philosophies
Esoteric Psychologies

Esoteric Science
Esotericism
Esoterist
est
Eustress
Evil
Evolutionary Necessity
Expansion of Conciousness
Faith
Flow
Fog
Fourth Way
Free Choice
Fulfillment
Futurists
Gestalt
Gestalt Psychology
Gestalt Therapy
Good
Grace
Grace of God

Grok
Group Tone
Growth Games
Gut Level Values
Habituation
Happiness
Harmony
High Plateau
Holism
Holistic
Holistic Biology
Hot Seat
Human Potential Movement
Humanist
Humanistic Psychology
Humanized Technology
Identification
Identity Theory
Illumined
Joy
Knowledge
Koan Theory
Lie
Life Change Index
Lite Program
Living Dead #1
Loneliness
Love
Luminosity
Magic Effect
Make a Prayer
Mankind
Mass Suffering
Massage Therapy
Maturity
Medicine Path
Medicine Wheel
Metatheoretical

Mind-Awareness Movement
Mystic Experience
Negative Stress
New Age
New Birth #2
New Consciousness-Awareness
New Consciousness-Awareness
    Movement
New Planetary Mythology
New Thought
New-Age Consciousness
New-Age Politics
New-Age Psychology
Normal
Onearth
Peak Experience
Performance Clinic
Personality Transformation
Planetary Deme
Planetary Worker
Planetization
Pleasure
Positive Expectation
Present-Centeredness
PSE
Psychic Underground
Psychological Health
Psychosynthesis
Psychotechnologies
Put it on the Shelf
Relatives
Ring
Rewards and Punishments
    System
Science of Service
Secondary Gains
Self-Actualization
Self-Denial

Self-Discipleship
Self-Identification
Self-Nonself
Self-Realization
Sensation
Senses
Serenity
Shrine
Sin
Social Readjustment Rating Scale
Social Renewal
Specific Negatives
Spontaneity Discipline
Storing Power #1
Stress
Subjective Behaviorism
Success
Success Mechanism
Suffering
Teacher
Tension
Time Pressure
Time Travelers
Tool
Transcenders
Transformation
Transformationists
Tribal Dancing #2
True Seal
Truth
Underside of Experiences
Understanding
Universal Brotherhood
Universal Kiss
Unreal Inner Activity
Values
Wellness
Wisdom

NUMBER POWER

Biblical Numerology
Binah
Clover
Cosmic Wheel
Coven
Eight
Eleven
Five
Forty
Forty-Nine
Four

Gematria
Great Beast
Holy Trinity
Magical Proportions of Man
Monolith
Multiplicity
Nine
Number Ether
Number of the Beast
Number Power
Numbers

Numerical Wizard
Numerology
One
Sacared Cut
Sefer Yetsirah
Seven
Seven Jewels of Yoga
Seven Major Rays
Seven Planetary Chain Logoi
Six
Six-Six-Six

Tangrams
Ten Sefiroth
Tetragram
Three
Triad
Trilithon

Trinism
Trinity
Twelve
Two
Universal Trinity
Vibrananalysis

POLARITY

An-Kheft-Ka
Archdemons *
Bipolar *
Bipolar Aura *
Body Polarity *
Body Scanning **
Byelbog and Chernobog *
Chernobog and Byelbog
Cosmic Egg #2
Cosmic Magnetic Forces *
Creative #2 *
Delilah
Devi
Devil #7 *
Dharma-Kaya #1 *
Divine Mother
Dynamoscope *
Electron
Eye of Horus *
Eye of Isis *
Eye of Siva
Father/Mother God *
First Matter
Fu Hsi Pattern
Galvanometer

Great Mother *
Holy Ghost
Holy Spirit *
Iao
Iceland Spar
Infinite
Linga *
Lingam *
Lingam Andyoni
Magnetism #1 *
Magnetocardiograph
Monosprit
Munger and Nokunzi
Negative *
Negative Ion Beams *
Negative Thought *
Od Negative *
Od Positive *
Ohrmazd and Ahriman *
Oranur
Out-of-Phase *
Physical Body Polarity *
Planetary Prana
Polarity *
Polarity Balancing **

Polarity Therapists **
Polarity Therapy **
Pole and Opposite Pole
Positive *
Positive Thought *
Qi
Receptive
Sakti
Seele
Sexual Mysticism
Shakti
Shiva
Shiva and Shakti *
Sthenometer
Sun #3 *
Syzygies
Tao
Tetrapolar Magnet
Unisex *
White Shell Creatures
Yang *
Yin *
Yin and Yang
Yin and Yang Symbol *
Yoni

PYRAMIDOLOGY

Abaka
Ark of the Covenent
BC/AB
Capstone
Coffer
East
Experimental Sensor
Force Zone
Galactic Confederation
Giza Pyramid
Gizeh Complex
Golden Mountain
Golden Section

Great Pyramid
Head Stone
House of God
King's Chamber
Magnetic Form Resonance
Miracle in Stone
Negative Green Energy
Pep
Personalized Pyramid
Pi-Ray
Positive Green Energy
Pyramid
Pyramid Energy Plate

Pyramid in Mythology
Pyramid Matrix
Pyramid Meditation
Pyramid Power
Pyramid Texts
Pyramidal
Pyramidologist
Pyramidology
Sensor
Step Pyramid
Ventilated Pyramid

Reproductive Karma
Reserved Karma
Ripe Ego
Ripe Karma *
Salvation #4
Samasara
Sanchita Karma
Sangsara
Savage ***
Savant ***
Shadow #1
Simple Memory Recall ***
Simple Regression
Skandha

Soul Jury
Soul-Memory*
Soul-Mind Memory Bank
Soul-Splitting
Stage of Evolution *
Subpersonality #2
Supraphysical Personality
Sympathetic Earthlings *
Temporary Akashic Record
Terrestial Sympathies ***
Theta Waves of Fantasy
Thought-Form Clusters ***
Time Plan ***
Time Travelers ***

Time-Lock
To-Morrow
Total Exactitude Conciousness
Transformation of Souls
Transitional State ***
Transmigration
Tribal Blood Karma ***
Tsi-Pa ***
Tulku
Twin-Souls ***
Waves of Reincarnation
   Patterns ***
Weighty Karma *

SPLIT-BRAIN HEMISPHERES

Amplitude Integration
Bilateral Alpha Rhythms
Brain Hemispheres
Brain Magnetism
Brainwave Signatures
Cerebral Hemispheres
Cerebral Lateralization
Cerebral Localization

Chemical Marriage
Convergent
Dichotomous
EEG Mind-Mirror
Intercerebral Competition
Intercerebral Dominance
Intercerebral Inhibition
Left Brain Hemisphere

Mind-Mirror
Nonmeditation
Right Brain Hemisphere
Split-Brain Hemispheres
Switching Hemispheres
Ultradian Ryhthm
Unilateral Pattern

SUBCONSCIOUS MIND AND SUPERCONSCIOUS MIND

Abdominal Brain
Active Imagination
All-Is-Within Doctrine
Ancestral Memory
Archetypal Miracle
Archetypal Region
Archetypal Unconscious
Archetypes
Association Theory
Automatic Autosuggestion
Autonomic Nervous System
Back Brain
Belief System
Below Levels of Awareness
Biocomputer *
Brain Substrate *
Brain/Mind
Collective Psyche
Collective Unconscious *
Collective Unconscious
   Consciousness
Creative Mental Process
Credology

Cryptomenesia
Dark Angel
Deep Level of Consciousness *
Depth Psychology
Deva-Yana
Dianetics
Doctrine of Subliminal
Dominant Persona
   Consciousness Factors *
Dominants of the Unconscious *
Ego *
Ego Metaprogramming *
Ego-Id
Ego-Strengthening
Facing the Shadow *
God-Brain
Greater Mind *
Habit
Habits of Thought
Heart
High Self
Higher Mind
Higher Soul-Mind

Holy Guardian Angel #1 & #2
Human Information Processing
   System
Hypnocampal
Illumination
Information Processing Theory
Inherited Complexes
Inner-Ego
Intuitive Mind
Large Good Angel
Memory Clusters
Memory Storage System *
Metaprogrammer *
Metaprogramming *
Mind *
Monad Perceptions
Multiple Souls
Nagual
Nonpersonal Subconscious
Object-Knowing Principle
Optical Computer
Other Persons-Programming
   Properties

826

Overself
Paranoia
Peripheral Vision
Personal Metapatterns
Personal Unconsciousness
Pibs
Pneumbra
Primitive Brain
Programmed Biocomputers *
Programming
Psychoscope
Racial Unconscious
Reactive Mind
Reprogramming *

Root Assumptions
Root Brain
Scientific Will
Self-Directing #1
Shadow-Watchers
Software
Soul Development
Soul Substance
Soul-Complex *
Soul-Mind
Soul-Mind Memory Bank
Stage of Evolution
State of Evolution
Storage Closet

Subconscious Mind *
Subliminal Level
Subliminal Plane
Subliminal Records
Suggestion
Superconscious Mind
Superego
Supraconsciousness
Switchboard *
Sympathetic Nervous System *
Unconscious Mind
Utterly Trustworthy
    Parental Self
Wisdom Mind

SUGGESTOPEDIA

Hypnopedia
Hyponeida
Psychotherapist #2
Sleep Learning

Suggestology
Suggestopedia
Twilight Learner
Twilight Zone

THIRD EYE AREA

Ajna Chakra *
Akshi *
All-Seeing Eye
Alpha Brain
Black Glance
Boat of the Seeker *
Brahman's Eye *
Brain Sand
Crystal Lamp
Divya Dristi
Egg of Immortality *
Eidolonics *
Evil Eye
Eye *
Eye of Balor *
Eye of Horus
Eye of Isis
Eye of the Soul *
Flaming Sword
Great Eye *
Guerwitsch Rays
Heart of the Lotus *
Hidden Door *
Holy Eggs
Holy Seed *
Hypothalamus *
Imaging Faculty *

Infinite Vision
Inner-Senses
Kingly Center *
Light of the World *
Master Eye
Mental Arena *
Mind's Eye
Mitogentic Waves
Mystic Marriage *
Nerve Electricity *
Open-Eye
Parietal Eye *
Paroptic Sense
Personal Radar Set *
Phantasmogentic Center
Pineal Gland *
Pituitary Gland *
Pituitrin *
Psi-Field *
Psychic Energy
Psychic Organ
Psychic Perceptors *
Psychic Sense
Queen of the Body
Royal Center
Sacred Beetle
Sacred Seal

Sahasrara
Seat of Consciousness *
Seat of the Rational Soul
Serotonin *
Sight in Darkness
Single Eye
Sixth Sense *
Spirilla *
Spiritual Chemistry #2
Supermind
Thalamus *
Third-Eye Area *
Third-Eye Attainment *
Tisra Til
Unseen Seer
Visual Ray *
X-Force

TIME

Across Time
Action
Age
All-At-Once
Antimatter
Astrophysics Station
Backwards Time
Black Hole
Borderland
Boundless
Chons
Coexistence
Cosmic Gushers
Day of Judgment
Dharmas
Eka-Ksana
Eternal Forms
Eternal Now
Eternal Present
Eternity
Flow Pattern
Frontierless
Geometrodynamics
Hologram Brain Theory
Holographic Model
Hyperspace
Immobility
Kala

Ksana
Levels of Reality
Life
Life Wave
Linear Dimensions
Maya
Moment
Moment Point
Motionlessness
Multidimensional
Multitime
No Time or Space
Nonduration
Nowness
Nunc Stans
One Space Framework
Pregression
Persent
Present Manifested
Present Manifesting
Second Dimension
Serial Time
Sidereal Day
Simultaneous Systems
Simultaneous Time
Sothic Year
Space

Space-Time Continua
Space/Time Theories
Spacious Present
Spatialize
Speed of Thought
Stasis
System of Probabilities
Temporal World
Third Dimension
Time
Time Cycles
Time Density
Time Displacement
Time Distortion
Time Framework
Time Sense
Time Structure
Time-Consciousness
Time-Flow
Time-Space
Time-Spatiality
Timeless-Present
Tmu
Wheel of Fortune
Wheel of Time
X-ness in Space #1
Zero Dimension

UFOLOGY

Actinic Rays
Actinism
Aeroforms
Agharta *
Alpha Creatures
Alternate Earths
Amnesia's Grip
Anomalous Shadows
Aretalogy
Ark of the Covenant *
Armored Organism
Ashtar
Astronavigation
Astrophys
Astrophysics
Astrotheology
Atmosphere Phenomena
Atmospheric Amoeba
Atmospheric Physics
Beam of Heat

Bermuda Triangle *
Big Mama
Bioenergetic Beacon
Bioenergetic Propulsion
Bioforms
Biological Signal Transducer
Biological UFO's
Blip
Blue Book
Blue Holes *
Bo and Peep
Borderline Science
Boys Downstairs
Boys from Topside
Brain Wave Synchronizer
Call Phase
Close-Encounter-of-the-First-
Kind
Close-Encounter-of-the-Fourth-
Kind

Close-Encounter-of-the-Second-
Kind
Close-Encounter-of-the-Third-
Kind
Constructs
Contactee
Contactee Syndrome
Cosmic Entity
Cosmic Pulse
Cosmic Ray
Cosmological Community
Creatures of Stratosphere
Critter Family
Critters
Dawn Angels
Daylight Discs
Dematerialization #3
Devil's Head
Devil-Like Goblin
Disc Occupant

828

Disc Sky Craft
Dor
Dor Clouds
Dynamic Transitions
Echo
Electrogravitation
Electrogravitic Waves
Electromagnetic Radiation
Electronic Finger
Energy Currents
Energy Trail
Ephidrosis
ETH
Ether Ship
Ether-Ship Being
Etherean Beings
Etherian Communications
Etherian Physics
Etheric Fauna
Etheric Life Forms
Etheric Steel
Etherically Propelled Ships
Exobiology
Extraterrestrial
Extraterrestrial Animals
Extraterrestrial Beings
Extraterrestrial Craft
Extraterrestrial Life
Extraterrestrial Visitation
Fireflies
Flashing Light
Flying Flapjack
Flying from Cloud to Cloud
Flying Saucer
Flying Saucer Disease
Flying Scroll
Flying Shields
Foo Fighters
Fusiform
Giant Amoeba
Gods From the Sky
Goosegg Instruments
Guardians #2 *
Hollow Earth *
Homo Mechanicus
Humanoids
Individual Metamorphosis
Inductopyrexia
Inner-Earth Civilization *
Intelligence in the Sky
Inter-Galactic UFO's
Interface

Interior Lands
Interplanetary
Interstellar Space
Intradimensionality
Intruders
Invisible-Physical Existence
IS
Juggernaut
Klieg Conjunctivitus
Landing
Life Forms
Living Creatures of our
    Atmosphere
Living Phemomena
Luminous Disc
Lung-Ta
Macrobacteria
Magnetic Anomaly
Manna #3 *
Men in Black
Mental Interchange
Mental UFO Communications
Mib
Mothman Prophecies *
Mufon
Mutants
Mutation of Energy
NASA
Nefilim
New Knowledge
New Planetary Mythology
Nocturnal Light
Nonhuman Intelligences
Old People *
Old Valicus
Orgonotic Pulsation
Other World Intelligences
Phony Stars
Piloting Intelligences
Plasmas
Plasmatic Fauna
Polarity-Reversing Photography
Positive Primary Energy
Power Points
Power System
Project Blue Book
Project Magnet
Propulsion
Psychic Radio Operator
Pulsed Wave Activity
Quasars *
Radar Angels

Radiation Burn
Sacred Halls *
Saucer Cult
Saucer Flap
Saucernauts
Scout Ships
Shamballah *
Ships-From-Other-Planets
Sighting
Sky Craft
Solex Mal
Solid State Life Forms
Space Animals
Space Brothers
Space Continuum
Space Intelligence
Space-Being
Space-Being Travel
Spheroids
Spotter
Star Travelers
Stone-Age Gramaphone Records
Target Human
Tektites
Tellurian
Time Loss
Transcendental Phenomena
Transition of Substance
Twistians
Twistians
Two
UFO
UFO Akinesia
UFO Control System
UFO Cult
UFO Imprints
UFO Intelligences
UFO Investigator
UFO Landing
UFO Phenomena
UFO Propulsion
UFO Radiation
UFO Sightings
UFOcat
Ufologists
Ufology
Ufonaut
Ultraterrestrial
Underground Bases *
Unidentified Flying Objects
Unknown Forces
Unshielded Planetary Bodies *

Appendix 6

MANTIC ARTS

Listing of the many mantic arts is isolated from the main section because this skill is not popular today, and because the skills are so similar in purpose. The objects and articles used to perform the divination skills are listed in alphabetical order below because the name of the ancient skill is foreign to man's present language. Each word is suffixed with "mancy." See the definition of MANTIC ART in the main section.

OBJECTS USED IN MANTIC ARTS

Animal Behavior-Theriomancy
Animal Behavior-Zoomancy
Animal Innards-Epatoscomancy
Animal Innards-Extispiciomancy
Animal Livers-Hapatomancy
Animal Shoulder Blades-
   Scapulomancy
Animals-Apantomancy
Arrows-Belomancy
Ashes-Tephramancy
Atmosphere-Alectromancy
Axe-Axinomancy
Baked Barley Bread-Alphitomancy
Barley Flour-Critomancy
Beans, Bones-Cleromancy
Bible-Bibliomancy
Birds-Ornithomancy
Books-Stichomancy
Burned Tree Branches-
   Botanomancy
Burning Objects-Pyromancy
Cake Dough, Cakes-Critomancy
Candle-Lampadomancy
Cards-Cartomancy
Cats-Felidomancy
Caul-Amniomancy
Chance Remarks-Cledonmancy
Circle Dizziness-Gyromancy
Clouds-Nephelomancy
Clouds, Wind Direction-
   Aeromancy
Cockerel-Alectryomancy
Communicating with the Dead-
   Nigromancy
Cookies, Cakes-Aleuromancy

Crystal Ball-Crystalomancy
Crystal Pieces-Crystallomancy
Diagnosing Diseases-Iatromancy
Donkey-Onomancy
Dowsing-Rhabdomancy
Dreams-Oneiromancy
Dressing Oneself-Stolisomancy
Earth-Eomancy
Eggs-Oomancy
Entrails-Anthropomancy
Etheric World Intelligences-
   Necromancy
Excrements-Scatomancy
Eyes-Oculomancy
Facial
   Features-Anthroposomancy
Fig Leaves-Sycomancy
Fingernails-Onychomancy
Fire-Causimonancy
Fire Watching-Pyromancy
Fish-Ichthyomancy
Flames, Smoke-Spodomancy
Forehead-Metopomancy
Gnomes-Geomancy
Goat, Ass-Kephalonomancy
Grains, Coins, Stones-Ars
   Geomanancy
Hands-Cheiromancy
Hands-Chiromancy
Human Shoulders-Armomancy
Incense-Empyromancy
Incense-Libanomancy
Inspirational Thought-Theomancy
Key-Clidomancy
Laughing-Geloscomancy

Laurel Branch-Daphnomancy
Lines on Hands-Cheiromancy
Lines on Hands-Chiromancy
Mantic Trances
Mediumship-Psychomancy
Melted Lead-Molybdomancy
Mirror-Enoptromancy
Moles-Moleomancy
Moon Phases-Selenomancy
Numbers-Arithmancy
Objects-Astragalomancy
Objects-Astragyromancy
Oil-Leconomancy
Olive Oil-Onimancy
Ouija Board-Dactylomancy
Palms and Hands-
   Psychotherapeutic
   Chiromancy
Patterns of Pebbles, Seeds,
   Dust-Geomancy
Pearls-Margaritomancy
Pebbles-Pessomancy
Pebbles-Psephomancy
Pendulum-Cleidomancy
Pendulum-Dactyomancy
Pendulum-Kleidomancy
Pendulum-Pallomancy
Person's Name-Onomamancy
Person's Name-Onomatomancy
Poetry-Rhapsodomancy
Poppies-Capnomancy
Precious Gems-Lithomancy
Priest Breast Plate-Urimancy
Psychometry-Hylomancy
Rats-Myomancy

830

Revolving Circle-Cyclomancy	Spot Cards-Spotomancy	Water-Cylicomancy
Rose Leaves-Phyllorhodomancy	Stamping of Horses Hooves-	Water-Hydromancy
Sacred Names-Theomancy	Hippomancy	Water Currents-Bletanomancy
Sacred Things-Heiromancy	Stars-Astromancy	Water Currents-Bletonomancy
Salt-Halomancy	Straws-Sideromancy	Water Fountain-Pegomancy
Shadow-Sciomancy	Swiss Cheese-Tiromancy	Wax-Cereomancy
Sieve-Cosinomancy	Tea Leaves-Tasseomancy	Well-Catoptromancy
Sieve-Coskiomancy	Three Candles-Lynchomancy	Whites of Eggs-Oomancy
Skulls-Cephalomancy	Three Candles-Zoanthropy	Wind-Austromancy
Smoke-Capnomancy	Trance-Aspidomancy	Wine-Oenomancy
Snakes-Ophimancy	Trance-Chresomonancy	Wine-Oinomancy
Soles of Feet-Podomancy	Urine-Uromancy	Wood-Xylomancy
Spoken Word-Transatuaumancy	Voice Trance-Gastromancy	

EGYPTIAN SUPERSTITIONS—Chiromancy—Drawn by Leopold Carl Muller.

AEROMANCY—1. forcasting events from the shapes of clouds; 2. divination involving wind direction: (a) throwing sand into the wind after asking a question, and receiving the answer in the form of the dust cloud; (b) throwing a handful of seeds into the air after asking oneself a question, and receiving the answer from the pattern created by the fallen seeds.

ALECTROMANCY—divination by observing atmospheric phenomena; weather conditions are recorded, and then use for predictions when similar events and conditions recur; e.g., the death of great men is preceded by the appearance of a comet; different types of thunder and lightening precede certain events; clouds project the future in their formations.

ALECTRYOMANCY—divinations using grains of corn that are eaten by a hen or cockerel; a circle is made of alphabetical letters on which grains of corn are placed; the hen then chooses to eat from the letters, and the order of her selections results in the answer to a given problem.

ALEUROMANCY—a general method of predicting one's future; messages are enclosed in cookies or cakes before being baked, with the idea that the message will fit the person eating that particular cookie or piece of cake; e.g., Chinese fortune cookies.

831

ALPHITOMANCY—proving guilt or innocence by using a loaf of barley bread; bread was divided among the suspects and upon eating the bread, the guilty person would become sick; each person repeated before eating; "If I am deceiving you, may this piece of bread choke me."

AMNIOMANCY—predicting the future of a new baby by the caul on its head; if it is red, happy days are ahead but if it is lead-colored, misfortune will befall the baby.

ANTHROPOMANCY—(ancient) divination using the entrails of a sacrificial human being; the viscera were used to read symbols of the future.

ANTHROPOSOMANCY—divination by observing the facial features of a person.

APANTOMANCY—using the symbolism of an animal that crosses one's path to predict one's future; utilizes the theory that nothing happens by chance; e.g., a black cat brings bad luck; a bluebird represents happiness.

ARITHMANCY—(Chaldea) using numerical values of letters and combinations of letters to foretell the overall destiny of an individual, country or universal situation; number values of the names of individuals, country and situations pertain to their characteristics. **Syn.** NUMEROLOGY

ARMOMANCY—a manner of predicting the ability of MEDIUMSHIP by inspecting the shoulders of the prospective candidate.

ARS GEOMANANCY—divination by the use of grains, coins, dice or stones. **Syn.** ARS GEOMANTICS.

ASPIDOMANCY—(East Indies) a type of RITUAL MAGIC whereby the PSYCHIC draws a circle, sits in the middle, mutters conjurations, falls into a trance state, and when back in the alert state knows the answers to the questions of the querant. **Syn.** TRANCE.

ASTRAGALOMANCY—see ASTRAGYROMANCY.

ASTRAGYROMANCY—(Anglo-Saxon) a technique of throwing dice, dominoes, coins, knucklebones, or any object bearing different sides, for determining the future or making decisions.

ASTROMANCY—divination by observing the stars.

AUSTROMANCY—divination by observing the wind.

AXINOMANCY—(Creten Greece) PROGNOS-TICATION by the use of an axe; used to find buried treasure or for obtaining PSYCHIC INFORMATION; the axe is balanced on the wrist, or heated and studied.

BELOMANCY—(Arabia, Greece, Chaldea) a number of arrows were thrown into the air and the direction in which an arrow was inclined to fall pointed out the course to be taken by the QUERANT.

BIBLIOMANCY—(Latin) (BIBLUS) using a sacred book to provide the necessary answer to one's innermost question; with eyes closed, book is opened and a section on the page is pointed to; this randomly-selected passage is the correct answer.

BLETONOMANCY—divination using patterns formed by water currents. **Syn.** BLETONISM.

BOTANOMANCY—a manner of PROGNOSTICATION using burning branches; questions are carved on a tree and some of the branches are burned; the manner of their burning denotes the answer; vervein and brier branches are best suited for divination.

CAPNOMANCY—divination using smoke: 1. sacrifices are used for the fire; if smoke rises lightly from the altar and ascends straight to the clouds, it means conditions are favorable; if the smoke hangs about, one's plans should be changed; 2. jasmine or poppy seeds thrown into a fire cause formations of smoke, which indicate certain predictions; 3. a practice of breathing the smoke from a sacrificial fire to insure good fortune.

CARTOMANCY—(ancient Egypt) divination using a pack of cards; originated with gypsies who perceived one's future, personality traits, and helpful guidance; when brought to Europe in A.D. 1300, it was not taken seriously in that culture; this resulted in many methods and types of cards used in an attempt to revive its original authenticity; the matter in which the cards are handled by the QUERANT or PSYCHIC determines their placement, and the placement is used for PSYCHIC INFORMATION. [**cf.** TAROT CARDS, SHUSTAH, I CHING]

CATOPTROMANCY—PROGNOSTICATION using a glass which is suspended over a holy well; the reflections on the glass reveal the secrets hidden in the water, giving answers to the problems of the holy organization owning the well.

CAUSIMONANCY—foretelling the future by throwing combustible objects into a fire; if they do not burn this indicates a happy future or a positive answer.

CEPHALOMANCY—divination using skulls. **Syn.** PHRENOLOGY.

CEREOMANCY—predictions made by dropping melted wax into cold water; the formations formed by the wax tell the answer to the querant's question. **Syn.** CEREOSCOPY.

CHEIROMANCY—see CHIROMANCY.

CHIROMANCY—study of lines, spaces, and creases on a person's hands and wrists; for surfacing PSYCHIC INFORMATION regarding personal general welfare, emotional maturity, and future expectations for this INCARNATION; some lines and spaces have universally predetermined meetings. **Syn.** CHEIROMANCY. [**cf.** PALMISTRY]

CHRESMONANCY—see VOICE TRANCE.

CLEDONOMANCY—to predict remarks of a conversation before it begins and by using these chance remarks for divination.

CLEIDOMANCY—see PENDULUM POWER.

CLEROMANCY—(Rome, Egypt) divination by the use of black and white beans, stones, and little bones, which are used as lots. **Syn.** SORTILEGE.

CLIDOMANCY—determining the guilt or innocence of a person suspected of a crime by using a key and a Bible' the crime is written on a key which is tied to the Bible; both are then hung from the finger of a virgin; the movement of the Bible and key according to a pre-established code determines the person's guilt; performed when the sun or moon is in Virgo; sometimes the impression of the key is found as an omen on the guilty person.

COSINOMANCY—(Theocritus, Bible) using a sieve and a pair of shears to determin who is guilty among a group of suspected people; the sieve is held between shears or tongues supported by the thumb nails of two persons; while staring at each other, so as not to influence the turn of the sieve, the question is asked "who is guilty?"; the sieve turns until the handle points to the guilty person. **Syn.** SPINNING THE SAS.'

COSKIOMANCY—see COSINOMANCY.

CRITOMANCY—1. divination by observing the paste of cakes and barley flour sprinkled over a sacrificial victim; 2. to predict the future for one's self by the unusual behavior of grains, dough, or the cakes themselves; also spelled CRITHOMANCY.

CRYSTALOMANCY—the art of divination using a crystal ball; SCRYING; see CRYSTAL BALL GAZING.

CRYSTALLOMANCY—divination using small pieces of crystals as lots; [do. not confuse with scrying].

CYCLOMANCY—divination using a wheel or revolving circle; e.g., the wheel of fortune found at carnivals is based on this practice.

CYLICOMANCY—SCRYING using a cup of water instead of a crystal.

DACTYLOMANCY—(50 B.C. Greek) (*dacty,* "fingers") a tripod (similar to the one at Delphi) is placed in a large basin, upon which the alphabet is written around the edge; fingers are placed on the tripod very lightly, and after prayers, the tripod moves by itself to spell out answers to the questions of the dactylomancers.

DACTYOMANCY—a religious method of spelling out a message by using a ring PENDULUM and a round table, inscribed on top with letters of the alphabet; the ring pendulum is suspended over the letters and swings over the letters of the psychic message.

DAPHNOMANCY—divination by the use of a laurel branch which is thrown on a fire; if it crackles while burning, it is a good sign, and if it does not, it means the prognostication is false.

EMPYROMANCY—(Pythagoras) divination using smoke from the burning of incense of laurel leaves.

ENOPTROMANCY—(antiquity) using a mirror to predict that a sick person will recover or die; a mirror is lowered into water with only the base touching, and upon gazing into the mirror, death or recovery is foretold.

EPATOSCOMANCY—divination by examining animal entrails.

EXTISPICIOMANCY—divination by examining animal entrails.

FELIDOMANCY—art of divination by observing the behavior of cats.

GASTROMANCY—divination from the belly; a trance voice coming through a PSYCHIC; because it sounded very low and hollow they felt it was issuing from the belly and thus named the ability; details see VOICE TRANCE.

GELOSCOMANCY—interpreting another person's laughter as having prophetic meaning for one's self.

GEOMANCY—(Greek *gaie,* "earth") 1. receiving answers to problems by observing the formations of pebbles scattered upon the earth, dust blown over a smooth surface, sand and seeds tossed on the ground, dead leaves thrown into a pool; 2. divination by throwing a handful of earth randomly on the ground and counseling from the lines and dots made by the throw; 3. (magic) collaborating with NATURE SPIRITS of earth, especially GNOMES, for divination purposes, guidance, and protection; 4. a method of selection of sites for cities, temples, palaces, private dwellings, and graves by the Lords and priests; a figure was made from some of the earth of the site, consecrated and thrown down on the ground, and the way it broke determined if the site was favorable.

GYROMANCY—divination by circle dizziness; the individual continously moves around in a circle that is marked with letters; when he becomes giddy and stumbles, he or she lands on the letters that spell out the message; circling excludes the interference of the will in selecting the letters; this was carried down to the children's game wherein they are blindfolded and spun in a circle before being turned loose.

HALOMANCY—divination by using salt; salt is poured on the ground and the shape it forms constitutes the answer to a given question; is the source of the expression: "Bad luck comes to those who overturn a salt cellar."

HARUSPICY—using the cracks that appear in the shoulder-blade of a roasted sheep to foretell the future.

HEPATOMANCY—inspecting animal livers for the purpose of PROGNOSTICATION.

HIEROMANCY—divination using sacred articles or observing things being used in sacrifices.

HIPPOMANCY—forecasting events from the stamping of horses hooves; 1. (Celtic) white horses kept in consecrated groves were made to walk immediately after the sacred car; the interpretations came from their movements; 2. (Germany) steeds kept in their temples which were let out at the outbreak of hostilities; if the left forefoot of the horse crossed the threshold first, it was interpreted as an evil omen, and the war was abandoned.

HYDROMANCY—(Greece) divination by water brought to Delrio by the sea angel, Nereus; 1. scrying in a bowl of water; 2. examining rain water; 3. using color and turbulence observed in the sea; each having various meanings; 4. finding treasure by spreading a thin film of oil over the surface of a bowl of water, and the oil's formations indicate where the treasure is hidden.

HYLOMANCY—see PSYCHOMETRY.

IATROMANCY—diagnosing diseases psychically.

ICHTHYOMANCY—foretelling future events from the movements of fish, and from inspecting their entrails.

KELIDOMANCY—see PENDULUMING.

KEPHALONOMANCY—a method of determining a person's guilt or innocence; ancients placed lighted carbon on the baked head of an ass or goat and pronounced the names of those suspected of a crime, if a crackling sound coincided with the utterance of the name, the person was guilty.

LAMPADOMANCY—divination from observing the flame of a torch or a candle.

LECONOMANCY—divination by pouring oil on water, or by dropping pebbles in the water and watching the ripples.

LIBANOMANCY—Divination by interpreting the shapes assumed by the smoke rising from burning incense.

LITHOMANCY—1. a method of providing an OMEN by scattering precious stones on a dark surface; stones are each assigned a particular message before scattering; the stone that reflects the most light is the answer to the querant's question' 2. to mix many small objects and allow the QUERANT to throw them randomly; the formations of the throw is used by the PSYCHIC to give the querant a psychic READING.

LYNCHOMANCY—divination using three lighted candles, which are placed in the form of a triangle.

MARGARITOMANCY—the use of pearls to establish guilt; a pearl is placed under a vase near a fire; the names of the suspected persons pronounced, and when the guilty person's name is spoken, the pearl bounds upward and pierces the bottom of the vase.

METOPOMANCY—studying the lines on an individual's forehead to presage his or her future of characteristics of PERSONALITY.

MOLEOMANCY—divination by studying moles for their shape, size, and position on the body.

MOLYBDOMANCY—receiving psychic messages by listening to the hisses made by melted lead being dropped into water.

MYOMANCY—prophesying by the use of rats; seeing evidence of their being around an area or hearing rats cry means EVIL will come.

NECROMANCY—1. (Greek *nekros,* "dead") the ability of the PSYCHIC to descend into HADES in order to consult the dead for needed information; **2.** (Italy) a form of the BLACK ARTS using EARTH-BOUND ENTITIES, by summoning them for EVIL intent.

NEPHELOMANCY—divination using cloud patterns.

NIGROMANCY—(Latin) ancient method of communicating with the dead: talking to the ghosts around the grave, or opening the grave and talking to the corpse.

OCULOMANCY—divination by examining one's eyes for the marks in the eye; (do not confuse with staring into one's eyes to perceive one's emotional state.)

OENOMANCY—see OINOMANCY.

OINOMANCY—divination by analyzing the color and taste of wines.

ONEIROMANCY—(Ancient Israel) dream interpretation; see DREAM ANALYSIS.

ONIMANCY—making decisions about one's future plans by using olive oil; oil of olives is mingled with tallow or blackening in the palm of the hand, on top of which is placed a marker or coin; if the marker turns to the east, it means one decision and to the west another; decisions for each point of the compass was pre-established; believed that the angel Uriel performed the turning.

ONOMAMANCY—(Pythagoreans) predicting the future, and the characteristics of a person by his or her personal name.

ONOMANCY—divination using a donkey; determining the future according to the stubbornness or willingness of a donkey's movements.

ONOMATOMANCY—(Pythagoras, Plato) divination by using one's name; theory: an anology existed between a person's names and their fortunes.

ONYCHOMANCY—analyzing the reflection of the sun on the nails of young boys to reveal information their future.

OOMANCY—predicting the future or answering a question by observing and analyzing egg whites dropped in hot water. **Syn.** OOSCOPY, OOMANTIA.

OPHIMANCY—divination by observing the behavior of snakes.

ORNITHOMANCY—(Greece, Rome) divination by the flight or songs of birds; ancient theory held that bird behavior has supernatural significance; became a part of the Roman religion.

PALLOMANCY—divination by the use of a PENDULUM; see PALLOMANCY in main section.

PEGOMANCY—using water fountains for divination.

PESSOMANCY—using pebbles for divination.

PHYLLORHODOMANCY—using rose leaves to judge the success of one's ambitions, by noting the sound quality from clapping the rose leaves between one's hands.

PODOMANCY—divination using the soles of the feet.

PSEPHOMANCY—prophesying by analyzing pebbles taken from a pile.

PSYCHOMANCY—communication between ETHERIC WORLD INTELLIGENCES and EARTHLINGS.

PSYCHOTHERAPEUTIC CHIROMANCY—studying an individual's palms and hands to reveal his or her weaknesses and good points; theory: this relates to the individual's mental and physical states.

PYROMANCY—1. divination by staring into the flames of a fire and perceiving psychically; 2. when burning a sacrifice, if the smoke clears, and the fire is bright red without crackling and forming a pyramidal form, this is a good sign; 3. divination by studying the burning rate of various objects thrown onto a fire.

RHABDOMANCY—(Greek *rhabdos*, "rod or wands") searching for springs, sights, and precious metals buried in the ground through a ritual practice; see DOWSING.

RHAPSODOMANCY—finding answers by opening the works of a poet at random, and reading the first verse that presents itself to the eyes.

SCAPULOMANCY—divination from the shoulder blades of animals.

SCATOMANCY—divination using one's own excrements.

SCIOMANCY—divination by one's shadow, it's size, shape and position.

SELENOMANCY—prognosticating by observing the phases of the moon.

SIDEROMANCY—predicting the future by the movements of straws placed on a red-hot iron.

SPODOMANCY—prophesying by observing the behavior of flames and smoke from the candle that is burning a paper upon which the QUERANT has written a personal question.

SPOTOMANCY—(ancient Egypt) foretelling the future of a person, country or organization using SPOT CARDS and SORTES in the skill of CASTING OF LOTS.

STICHOMANCY—obtaining information and answers to questions, by reading at random, passages in books.

STOLISOMANCY—divination by noticing the way in which one dresses one's self; certain significance is ascribed to making a mistake; e.g., buckling one's right sandal on one's left foot.

SYCOMANCY—receiving positive or negative answers to questions by writing them on a fig leaf; if they dry quickly, this is considered a negative response.

TASSEOMANCY—divination by using of tea leaves. Syn. TASSEOGRAPHY.

TEPHRAMANCY—1. (personal) counseling from the formation of the ashes of burned paper on which the querant's problems are written; 2. (government) divination by the use of ashes from a sacrificial fire; 3. divination using the ashes of burned trees; 4. reading ashes from the fire that has consumed the victim of sacrifice.

THEOMANCY—(Jewish) 1. one who studies the mysteries of the divine majesty and seeks the sacred names, will posses the future commands of nature and have power over the ANGELS and DEMONS, and will perform MIRACLES; 2. see INSPIRATIONAL THOUGHT.

THERIOMANCY—prognosticating by studying animal behavior.

TIROMANCY—forecasting events from the holes in Swiss cheese.

TRANSATUAUMANCY—divination based on remarks heard accidentally, and which are interpreted beyond their normal meaning.

URIMANCY—(Israel) determining a yes or no answer from the gods by using an object or precious metal inscribed with the symbols on that of the breast plate of the high priest; similar to the CASTING OF LOTS.

UROMANCY—divination using urine.

XYLOMANCY—using small pieces of wood found in one's path to presage the future; or forecasting by the arrangement of logs in a fire as they burn.

ZOANTHROPY—divination with lighted candles placed in the form of the TRINITY (a triangle).

ZOOMANCY—prognosticating by studying the behavior of animals.

Appendix 7

FUNCTIONAL AND PHILOSOPHICAL LAWS AND PRINCIPLES PERTAINING TO PSYCHISM, MYSTICISM, OCCULTISM, ESOTERICISM, METAPHYSICS, AND NEW-AGE PSYCHOLOGY.

ABRAMS' LAW—(Albert Abrams, inventor of the black box) "All forms of matter posses a quality that puts them in touch with each other's signals;" the basic principle behind RADIESTHESIA and RADIONICS.

ABSORPTION, LAW OF—All matter in the universes, regardless of its manifestable vibration, absorbs emanations from all other matter, and the matter is influenced by this absorption; type of manifestation regulates the degree of absorption, resulting in one gigantic unit. [**cf.** HOLOGRAM, METAPHYSICS, GESTALT, AURA, KIRLIAN EFFECT]

ACTIVITY, LAW OF—Action results from attention of thought and the nature of the action corresponds to the nature of the attention. Every thought produces an alchemical process in CONSCIOUSNESS; action is not homogeneous, but contains three elements; the THOUGHT which conceives it, the WILL which finds the means of accomplishment, and the "union" of the two, needed to bring the action to pass; e.g., cast your bread upon the waters and it shall return to you; seeds will yield up fruits after their kind (necessary for almost all types of PSYCHISM). [**cf.** PK, LAW OF THOUGHT, LEVITATION, ATMOSPHERE CONTROL, BODY CONTROL]

ALGABRAIC GROUP, LAW OF—All elements of a group are powers of one element arranged in a group so that the first elements follow the last. [**cf.** LAW OF SUBSERVIENCE, LAW OF CYCLES, CEREMONIAL MAGIC]

ALIKES, LAW OF—(Baron Gottfried Wilhelm von Liebniz) "Two things alike in every respect having the same composition and dimension, but separated in space, will experience energy transfer from one to the other in proportion to their separation; if things differ in dimension by whole numbers divided into the dimensions, we have a scale model into which energy applied to the first will flow in proportion to the scale factor simplicity and the distance." [**cf.** PSYCHIC TRANSFER APPENDIX 2]

APPERCEPTION, LAW OF—CONSCIOUS OF BEING flows within all units of the UNIVERSE, throughout

all ETERNITY; every thing (unit) has a CONSCIOUSNESS; every thing is conscious of its own consciousness; INTELLIGENCE knows it is intelligence; ENERGY knows it is energy; every single unit, from the Great Cosmos to the tiny ATOM, knows what the function of its unit is.

ASSOCIATION, LAW OF—If two or more things have something in common, the "thing in common" can be used to influence or control the other thing (or things); the degree of control depends upon the size of the "thing in common;" the more in common they both have, the more the influence; e.g., eating bread and wine and listening to the assimilated words of The Last Supper, to feel as if one were in the Upper Room. [**cf.** ASSOCIATION MAGIC APPENDIX 2]

ATTENTION, LAW OF—An unconcscious core-point-of-focus "held" in the minds of the billions of people inhabiting planet earth is necessary to hold the planet and everything on it together; changes in size, shape, color, and sounds are controlled by this basic core-point-of-focus, individualized in various sections and cultures; (don Juan) "We hold the images of the world with our attention; if I don't focus attention on the world, the world collapses." (Inconcl.). [**cf.** THOUGHTS ARE THINGS, MATTER, VIBRATIOINS, HOLD THE THOUGHT, VISUALIZATION, INNER-DIALOGUE]

ATTITUDE, LAW OF—1. "Attitude," the only weapon that can harm an individual. Nothing, absolutely nothing, in the universe can harm an earthling except his or her own attitude. No human accident, no loss of a loved one, no natural catastrophe, no personal illness, no loss of property, or job hardship can harm one. It is only the attitude one takes toward these events and experiences that hurts the individual. Traumatic experiences are meant to happen in each INCARNATION. Each experience should be put in its proper perspective, resolved in a favorable manner, analyzed for the good it brought, and balanced with emotionally. Attitude has its degree of emotion and emotion triggers off one's "ongoing-life-process" or one's

837

"ongoing-death-process" in the body. One chooses by his or her attitude which process is to prevail. 2. To whatever depths one sinks below his or her norm, materially, one can rise equally above one's norm, spiritually. One reaches a state wherein nothing material offers any hope and then the SOUL-MIND becomes ready to receive the influx of power and inspiration from the ETHERIC WORLD or the SUPERCONSCIOUS MIND.

ATTRACTION, LAW OF—The electromagnetic sensitivity field that surrounds each ATOM is either compatible with, or disturbed by, other atom's electromagnetic sensitivity field SURROUND; atoms of compatibility aggregate repeatedly with each other until MATTER that we can perceive is formed. This makes it understandable how one draws to one's self, both experiences and a physical body, resulting from the nature of the atoms that emanate from mental activity. **Syn.** LIKE ATTRACTS LIKE.

AVOIDANCE, LAW OF—To refuse to handle a highly emotional unpleasant situation, to deny living up to one's full potential, or to neglect doing something that should be done, will affect the individual's PHYSICAL BODY, MENTAL MIND, and lifestyle affairs, through each INCARNATION, until one correctly balances with the situation. (Marilyn Ferguson) "Denial is an evolutionary deadend."

BEAMED ENERGY, LAW OF—THOUGHT ENERGY focused on one central idea, with one's undivided attention, can be densified in the MIND, and then psychically transferred from the living tissue rays of the eyes, palms of the hands, sex organs, balls of the feet, and finger tips to a physical inanimate article, and organized into a definite specific external form. This energy configuration can independently direct and control unstructured atomical energy, enabling it to exhibit certain behavioral characteristics and accomplish a given result; process used to energize amulets and talismans which, in turn, serve the PSYCHIC.

BEING, LAW OF—"is *in* being."

CATASTROPHE, LAW OF—1. A severe turning point that takes place abruptly and happens, in its season to every unit on the planet, inanimate or animate, including the planet; short-lived for that particular activity; sometimes a startling and unexpected breaking point in a wavelike pattern; more noticeable in living organisms; 2. A complete change in the flux of the ACTIVITY AND REST CYCLE;

the time when the "thing" is changing in the opposite direction; everything is affected by this change in flux, some to a lesser degree than others; 3. An absolute necessity for the evolutionary process, motivated by the many laws of TOTALITY; e.g., (**a**) when a seed cracks and an outward growth begins; (**b**) when a mother goes into labor; (**c**) prison riots and stock-market crashes bring about transformational results; (**d**) earthquakes and cloudbursts make changes in people and nature; (**e**) religion conversions are a new beginning for some; (**f**) when something in a patient clicks and, from that time on, any therapy used will make the patient well; (**g**) when the SOUL-MIND is going through a traumatic death, it can split and show itself in a VISION to a loved one (incapable of this in normal times); (**h**) (destructive-brainwashing cults) when the member reaches a peak from the constant drilling of the well-structured verbiage and the mind "snaps" he or she is easy to handle from that time on. **Syn.** SHOCK WAVES. [**cf.** TRANSFORMATION, HOLISTIC HEALTH, AQUARIAN AGE]

CAUSE AND EFFECT, LAW OF—1. (science) For every action there is a reaction, equal in force but opposite in nature. 2. (esoteric) For every happening in the UNIVERSE, the earth, a personal life, or an inanimate life there has been activity or a series of activities, in the past, that are the cause of the manifestations as one perceives them in the present. Esoteric example simplified: a decision is made to go swimming; the decision is registered in the mental plane in the etheric world, which makes the blueprint for the event; this is the cause of one's action to go swimming on the material plane; the feeling about the swim, happiness or sadness is registered on the ASTRAL PLANE (emotional plane); it is this degree of emotion that is used to return to you on the physical plane, in the same degree of emotion (not necessarily in another swim but in another situation entirely; perhaps involving other people working out their causes). *Cause* and *effect* are opposite and equal. [**cf.** KARMA, LORD OF JUSTICE]

CENTER, LAW OF—A basic principle duplicated in all nature, giving everything a center from which it obtains its source of energy, intelligence, and pattern which is continually self-renewing. Each center in minutely connected to every other center and to the one Center from which all life is vitalized. (Unity) "Life is lived from center to circumference." [**cf.** MONADOLOGY]

CENTRAL COMMUNICATION SYSTEM, LAW OF— Every unit, from the single ATOM to the galaxy system appears to be plugged into one giant electronic switchboard. Each unit has its own electrical system and its own vibrational frequency, therefore, each unit, including man, is electrically connected one to another and to this giant switchboard. This electrical system provides the method of travel for PSYCHISM, making it possible for mankind to tune into all other systems. Every man and every thing has psychic possibilities. Those who are called "psychic" are the individuals who have learned to tune into the correct frequency to receive the information they desire. **Syn.** GOD, TOTALITY. [**cf.** HOLOGRAPH, HOMING IN, COME INTO YOUR VIBRATION]

CHANGE, LAW OF—The readiness of a situation to alter, modify, transform or convert is caused by a change in "inner attitude" of one or of many, and then incidental and parallel outer manifestation occurs. Change and transformation are exhibited by an attitudinal alteration. (I Ching) When this happens, "the 'I' dovetails with heaven and earth and the result that is completed interweaves with the path (Toa) of heaven and earth; fortune and misfortune are constantly overcoming one another in exact rule; there is no chance." (Rolling Thunder) "It works because the situation is at hand; there is no guarantee any prayer or medicine will work. It works because the time has come. It depends upon if your heart is in the right place and which way your blood flows."

CHOICE, LAW OF—see LAW OF FREE WILL.

COMMITMENT, LAW OF—(universal) When an individual makes a "complete" decision, pledging and obligating her or himself to a particular task, thing or belief, everything seems to fall into place, as if the individual was a magnet drawing the correct situations and people to fulfill that decision. "Naming" a change seems to awaken new perspectives. When the mind is "totally" made up to do this or that, and as long as the individual has no inkling of indecisiveness, the atoms will move around working for that individual until that manifestation is complete. Emotional desire behind the decision brings it about more quickly and gives the ETHERIC WORLD INTELLIGENCES an okay to intervene and help bring it about.

COMMONALITY CONTROLS, LAW OF—(human mind) Any datum entering the CONSCIOUS MIND correlates and then combines with previously organized data patterns in the SUBCONSCIOUS MIND, adding to the total content of the data system. This increases the knowledge of the person, whether the datum enters at the conscious or unconscious level. When this new datum associates with the old data patterns, old patterns discard, rearrange or strengthen the total data system. This system consists of millions of patterns which determine how man thinks, feels and remembers from moment to moment. Although data system changes from day to day, if the new datum is completely foreign to the system, it will not be accepted until it is broken down to correlate to an already established pattern; e.g. 1. the principle behind repeating AFFIRMATIONS: in order for one's data pattern system to accept the affirmation, it must be broken down to correlate with a previous pattern, a repetition will do this; 2. unethical methods of "quickly" making a new pattern in the system is accomplished by the DESTRUCTIVE-BRAINWASHING CULT through the constant repetitious statements, hour after hour, until the mind is "forced" to make a new pattern whether it has correlation or not, completely changing the member's PERSONALITY. The objective of each INCARNATION is to change the patterns of the data system to higher, qualitative knowledge, but to do it gradually; otherwise the mind would not be commonality controlled.

COMPENSATION, LAW OF—One is responsible for each experience in his or her life, one's physical body, and all environmental stimuli, due to one's past thinking and acting in this present life and in past incarnations. All of a person's actions, deeds, and bombardment of outer stimuli are tools for one to use to form an attitude about and to handle accordingly. This "attitude" toward life experiences is returned to him or her in the form of rewards or problems, as pleasant, joyful experiences or as confused, chaotic, and heartbreaking experiences. The rewards or punishments are returned in the next few minutes, next few weeks, next year or the next INCARNATION(s), in compatibility with the Law. "For every action there is a reaction." **Syn.** KARMA, LORDS OF JUSTICE. [**cf.** REINCARNATION]

CONSCIOUSNESS, LAW OF—TOTALITY is all CONSCIOUSNESS-ALL-THERE-IS is consciousness—and this consciousness is CONSCIOUS OF BEING. This "conscious of being" or "awareness of its existence" manifests in all forms, animate and inanimate, and each exists according to its consciousness of being in that given moment. Therefore, one lives in a world which is, in reality, only what he or she perceives in consciousness from moment to moment.

CONSEQUENCE, LAW OF—One has pure free will to think what he or she wants to think, say what one wants to say, eat what one wants to eat, work where and when one wants to work, and do what he or she wants to do, at all times. However, one is personally "responsible" for the outcome of his or her choices and must, somehow, handle the consequences. (Aleister Crowley) "Do as thou wilt, and take the consequences."

CONTACT, LAW OF—same as LAW OF CONTAGION.

CONTAGION, LAW OF—Things, animate or inanimate, once in contact with each other will continue to act upon each other even at a distance, long after the physical contact has been severed. Matter that comes into contact with other matter absorbs or influences that which it contracts; e.g., using a bracelet in a prayer ceremony to help the healing process of the owner of the bracelet; using the animal's food dish as a WITNESS in RADIESTHESIA to help locate the lost animal; (do not confuse with PSYCHOMETRY). **Syn.** LAW OF QUANTUM CONNECTION, LAW OF CONTACT. [**cf.** DISTANT HEALING, CEREMONIAL MAGIC, RADIONICS]

CONTINUITY, LAW OF—Nothing in the UNIVERSE ever dies, is lost or destroyed, it just changes form. Everything becomes a part of forever. MATTER and ENGERY are never destroyed, only transformed or changed. [**cf.** REINCARNATION, ASCENSION, MATERIALIZATION, APPORTATION]

CORRESPONDENCE, LAW OF—Each component within a system or thing retains its own characteristics and takes on the characteristics of the system or thing as a total sum of its parts. Each component then has two functions: to retain its own characteristics and to function as the whole system or thing. When separated into parts, each part remains connected to the parent system or thing and retains all the characteristics of the parent; distance is no barrier to the strength of connection; e.g., the branch of the tree has all the characteristics of the tree as a whole even when severed; the feathers of the eagle have their own characteristics and the characteristics of the whole eagle even when the eagle is dead; the MICROCOSM contains all the intelligence and energy of its parent MACROCOSM and when isolated, it is capable of doing all the macro-

cosm can do. Each person is a component of TOTALITY and endowed with all the attributes of Totality and can perform the same as Totality; therefore, it is possible to link any factor of the body with any factor of the UNIVERSE (principle behind color, sound, gem, and herbal healings). It is possible to link any unit of the body to the whole body (principle behind a BODY READING). [**cf.** RADIESTHESIA, SYMBOLS, IRIDOLOGY, PALM READING]

COSMIC RHYTHM, LAW OF—Each "thing" in the COSMOS moves in a rhythmic PERIODICITY. and this cycle governs the thing. This in turn, adds to the governing of the cosmos, harmonizing with the rhythmic periodicity vibration of the cosmos. There is a parallel evolutionary process of manifestations that everything in the universe must go through which prepares it for changing from one rate of rhythmic cycle, to a higher rate of rhythmic cycle, according to its nature and in its due season. [**cf.** AQUARIAN AGE, REBIRTH]

COSMIC WEB, LAW OF—Every point in space regardless of vibrational frequency connects with every other point in space and interconnects with every point of time; past, present, and future. [**cf.** HUNCHABILITY, REGRESSION, SHAMANSHIP, RADIESTHESIA, MEDIUMSHIP]

COUNTERPART FREE WILL, LAW OF—No highgrade intelligence in the ETHERIC WORLD will interfere or assist an earthling unless asked subconsciously or consciously by the earthling to do so. It is the prerogative of the earthling to ask for help when desired and it is the perrogative of the ETHERIC WORLD INTELLIGENCE to give help when he or she desires; etheric world entities are responsible for their actions too. [**cf.** A CALL, DESIRED—CONTROL, TRANCE]

CYCLES, LAW OF—(Greek *luklos,* "ring") A period of time divided into equal lengths and each length of time produces a certain definite effect upon the progressional path of each living organism, object, or event; this effect repeats itself in the same order, and at the same intervals, making a circle of time for each system. This circle of time, in turn, effects the evolutionary path of the COSMOS. Every manifestation is moved and responds to certain definite rhythmic circles which govern each manifestation as it expresses itself through time periods; e.g., the lunar cycle of the female, annual awakening of nature in the spring, daily sleep and wake cycle, weekly day of rest. With full knowledge of nature's cycle, man may lessen or enhance these effects if he chooses, which may prove beneficial or disastrous. (Inconcl.) [**cf.** MOTION, EMERGY PATTERNS, BIO-RHYTHM CHART, CYCLES APPENDIX 5]

DESTINY, LAW OF—(Baron Gottfried Wilhelm von Leibnitz) "preestablished harmonious universe." Everything, from the electrodes to the galaxies, is evolving back to PERFECTNESS at different speeds, different time periods, and through different experiences to complete the great evolutionary cycle. Every organism has a built-in motivation intelligence that keeps it growing and raising its consciousness until it reaches the perfect state, the ultimate TOTALITY. All happenings are a branch of destiny (perfectness) whether they result in a quick or slow return; FATE and luck are branches of this growth. All life, even inert life, is caught in the web of growing and evolving. Whether one is healthy or ill, happy or unhappy, rich or poor, is a process of raising consciousness. Mankind will someday express the fullness of what he already is by becoming perfect according to the potential in the HUMAN BEING SPECIES SEED. [**cf.** PSYCHIC CONSCIOUSNESS]

DIFFERENCES, LAW OF—A function of the group soul of each category necessary for it to complete its growth spell. Each mineral, plant, animal and human, has a uniqueness of their own, a strengthening feature they can feed into their categorical unit, their group soul, preparing both for the next step. No two things are exactly alike and should not try to be.

DOMINANT DESIRE, LAW OF—(Emil Cou'e) "An idea always tends towards realization and a stronger emotion always counteracts a weaker one." Every idea that is formulated in the mind begins on its path of manifestation but all ideas do not come into fruition. Ideas held in the mind with a stronger emotion will outrun, overpower, and nullify the weaker ones, regardless of conscious favorability. The strongest intent or desire in one's mind will manifest a general thread throughout all one's activity. This is the meaning of the "pearl of great price," because the strongest desire many be an unconscious or karmic desire, or the desire may have reservations and bring unpleasant activity into one's life in order to manifest. This law is also depicted in fairy tales in which the subject may "have but one wish." [**cf.** HOLD THE THOUGHT, THOUGHT-FORMS APPENDIX 2, EMOTION, KARMICALLY DESIRED]

DOMINION, LAW OF—(Bible) And let man have dominion over all the earth. The human mind (the interrelationship of the invisible and visible minds) is the instrument that has the privilege to change the vibrational frequency of the atoms which make this three-dimensional earth and everything that partakes within it. Man co-creates according to the speciality of the THOUGHT and the degree of intensity of the EMOTION accompanying the thought, giving each one full responsibility for the world. This is possible because the intelligence in the mind instrument is connected to the intelligence in the atoms via the electrical system that flows through all atoms. Man can form, make, change, rearrange, and manipulate MATTER in whatever way he or she chooses, "utilizing the laws of nature." Thus each one co-creates his or her own type and time of progression of EVOLUTION. Humanity individually and collectively directs the course of the universe with their minds. (Inconcl.) [**cf.** LAW OF CONSEQUENCE, THOUGHT].

DUALITY, LAW OF—(Rosicrucian) "All living situations contain both POSITIVE elements and NEGATIVE elements. A positive element by itself does not exist; together with a positive element there is always associated a negative element. Every sound follows a silence; every light casts a shadow. It is duality which gives life to a situation. It is this very duality, the combination of both positive and negative elements, which makes for perfection." All psychics are susceptible to positive and negative vibrations when they tune in psychically. Those unknowledgeable in this work will not know how to tune out the negative vibrations which could bring discomfort and erroneous information. [**cf.** POLARITY]

DUE SEASON, LAW OF—(human activity) All manifestations of man come into fruition when the project has reached completion of itself, decided by itself, similar to the cycles and seasons of nature. This completion is determined by the strongest, innermost, intent of the purpose of the project held in the minds of the individual(s) behind it (whether it be an invention, book, community drive, application form, educational course, repairing a chair, repairing the body, or taking a vacation). All projects do not reach a point of perfection but all projects reach the highest point they can go utilizing its intended purpose. The true intent of the project is psychically picked up by the project itself and it will add, subtract, draw and withdraw actions and persons that will contribute to the true purpose.

True purpose is not always consciously understood by the person (s) behind it. Manmade time of completion matters little (unless calendar time is the uppermost goal).

DUPLICATION, LAW OF—If one person can do it, it can be done by others; perhaps to a lesser or higher degree, or equally, to equalize with the activity.

DYING, LAW OF—When a unit or ENTITY has completed one stage or area of growth, it will gather all the knowledge from this area of growth, and all the knowledge from the GROUP SOUL of its element, and withdraw this into itself, ready to expand into more knowledge. The end of one expression of life gives rise to another expression of life. An overall evolutionary step in life forms and inanimate objects; to move from one vibrational frequency taking all accumulated knowledge with it, making it a faster vibrational frequency. This law was created in the beginning for all kingdoms: mineral, plant, animal, human, mature spirits, demons, angels, etc. [**cf.** REINCARNATION, CYCLES, HUMAN BEING KINGDOM]

EARTH'S SURVIVAL, LAW OF—DESIRE, desire of the SOUL-MIND of mankind. As long as the soul-mind desires, because it feels a need for a habitation to express and grow at this level of CONSCIOUSNESS, the earth will be the REALITY of mankind's thinking and emotional state. Emotion, feeling, and attitude, move atoms, and *desire* is the strongest emotion, feeling and attitude known to humanity; e.g., the soul-mind first desired this level of consciousness in its evolutionary path and so founded an EARTH PLANE consciousness and a physical body for itself. Then mankind desired food, warmth, shelter, touch, companionship, and the earth grew to satisfy these desires. Everything that lacks a purposeful need will dissolve from its uselessness. When humanity no longer needs physical earth and desires a higher state of consciousness, earth will dissolve. [**cf.** LAW OF DOMINION]

ELEMENTS, PRINCIPLE OF—Each unit has its own frequency, each element in that unit has its frequency of emanations connecting it to and compatible with the parent unit. When these elements are separated from the parent unit, they will still have the same emanations connecting them to the parent unit. Distance is no barrier for strength of emanations; i.e., the radio receiver which does what the broadcasting station is doing. **Syn.** LAW OF CORRESPONDENCE.

EMOTION, LAW OF—Emotion is the ENERGY of the UNIVERSE, the SPIRIT and the LIFE FORCE within each ATOM. The Law of Emotion refers to the internal processes of "activiation" making the NERVOUS SYSTEM act. The "push" behind motion keeps mankind out of the inertia state which is the main tool given to humanity in this earthly existence to propel one through this INCARNATION and to elevate one's state of SOUL-MIND development. Mankind uses the special earthly mechanisms: the nervous system, the five SENSES, and the BRAIN, which work compatibly with emotion. Emotions are influeneved by one's belief system, i.e., one's present beliefs, past beliefs through the many incarnations, and hidden core and cultural beliefs. As mankind perfects their understanding, their beliefs change and their emotional reactions perfect themselves. [**cf.** KEY TO LIFE, EMOTIONS]

EMOTIONAL BALANCE, LAW OF—To balance emotionally is to keep all aspects of one's personal experiences orderly and in the right perspective. This is the KEY TO LIFE. To balance with one's emotions is to make a deliberate choice (regarding an experience, event, situation, environmental stimuli outside personalities, one's own personality, etc.) and feel comfortable, satisfied, and content about the choice. This deliberate choice can be one of anger, or spiritual joy, as long as it is accepted by both the conscious and subconscious minds. The minds decide if it is a pleasureable or educational experience and then put it to rest. [**cf.** LAW OF KNOWLEDGE, EMOTIONS, KEY TO LIFE, LAW OF EMOTIONS]

ENERGY, LAW OF—All motion (vibration) was created with CREATION and carries knowledge with it, from the electron to the galaxy, making ceaseless interaction of all intelligences in the UNIVERSE possible. This includes the interaction of the ATOM and the human SOUL-MIND, resulting in various frequencies such as forms, sounds, colors, tastes, odors, etc. that mankind can perceive. Energy moves in cycles of its own pattern. (Ralph Waldo Emerson) "There is a current that knows its way."

ENVIRONMENT, LAW OF—Everything that surrounds an individual is an extension of one's self. One's home, the furnishings in the home, the automobile, pets, the yard, etc., is a physical picture of one's attitudes, feelings, emotions, and BELIEF SYSTEM. One's environment is the outpicturing of the individual's core beliefs, strong ideas and emotions about one's own existence, self-worth, cultural blanket belief, and beliefs that were taught as a child. [**cf.**COLLECTIVE UNCONSCIOUS]

EQUALITY, LAW OF—Things separately equal to the same thing are equal to each other.

ETHERIO-ATOMIC, LAW OF—All things are constantly radiating their peculiar essence and as each substance passes through another substance, each partakes of the essence of the other. Therefore, each substance's peculiar essence is constantly changing.

EVOLUTION, LAW OF—As each MONAD reaches its highest peak or perfect quality of its present habitation (or present range of status), it pushes forth to a higher range taking with it, in memory, its learned knowledge and allows its past habitation to disintegrate or dissolve. The monad now exists in a new range of status and quality, under new principles, and it is fully qualified to fit into this new range because of this past accomplishment. Everything, animate and inanimate, is going upward and onward to a higher, more perfect STATE OF CONSCIOUSNESS. Everything begins in an uncreate, unconscious, elementary form, and progressively grows through sacrifice, strife, and struggle to a "perfect" condition for that range of status. This procedure repeats itself until the monad blends into TOTALITY with no loss of individuality. (True or not true, this theory gives a hypothesis why an individual in an ALTERED STATE OF CONSCIOUSNESS, whether dreaming, tuning in psychically or mediumistically, perceives information that is in regard to how the individual (or another person) can better himself.)

EXCLUSIVENESS, LAW OF—"If it works for you, it is a law for you." PSYCHIC INFORMATION is reached and perceived in a different manner for each person. The person is the instrument and each person is unique; therefore, it is difficult to make a set of general rules that could be used by everyone. "What definitely is, is," as opposed to "what may be."

EXPERIENCE, LAW OF—To experience one must creatively respond to information; acquiring information itself is passive, experiencing it is active. When one is active, something happens inside the NERVOUS SYSTEM and midbrain recording neural patterns in the gray matter of the brain. (Ashby) "New information entering a cybernetic system destroys previous information of a similar nature; new experiences supersede the old; e.g., the world

is flat." To experience is a normal procedure, if taken slowly.

EXPERIENCES, LAW OF—(Seth) "You are what happens to you." One's everyday experiences, health, mechanical breakdowns, sex relations, family relations, job abilities, etc., can be used as a barometer telling one how one's SOUL-MIND is growing and whether the CONSCIOUS MIND and SUBCONSCIOUS MIND are functioning in harmony. Physical experience is an inexhaustible "feeling" of one's self. [**cf.** CURATIVE EDUCATION, NEW-AGE PSYCHOLOGY]

EYE FOR AN EYE, TOOTH FOR A TOOTH, LAW OF—Each individual can absorb only information or suggestions (psychic or mundane) at his or her present level of CONSCIOUSNESS, regardless of the speed, clarity, and detail of the datum. PSYCHIC ENERGY of any type must be sent at the level of awareness of the receiver or it will not penetrate his or her AURA and will be of no use; e.g., 1. to surround a hexer with love vibrations thinking he will have a change of attitude is useless; love vibrations will bounce off his or her evil THOUGHT ATMOSPHERE because they are entirely foreign to their thinking; one must fight EVIL magic skills with evil magic skills; 2. to encircle a patient in a WHITE LIGHT who doesn't understand DISTANT HEALING may frighten them and the healing be rejected. [**cf.** LOVE LINE, MAGIC WITH MAGIC CURE]

FINITE SENSES, LAW OF—Made by mankind through their desire to understand and manipulate MATTER in a three-dimensional world, as opposed to the belief that all data available to mankind must be perceived by his or her five SENSES.

FORCE, LAW OF—All energies throughout the universes, regardless of VIBRATIONAL FREQUENCY, have their origin in TOTALITY and are maintained, either directly or indirectly, by Totality. All energies are working with atoms to maintain regular and perfect movements of each unit in the universes. [**cf.** LAW OF EVOLUTION, TOTALITY]

FORM, LAW OF—(esoteric) Form is function. Certain shapes and forms act as tools to concentrate and trap energy within its boundaries. This trapped energy changes in its manner of usefulness. (Inconcl.) [**cf.** FORMS-WITH—POWER APPENDIX 2]

FOUR ELEMENTS, THE DOCTRINE OF—(Anaximander, Aristotle, astrology) Everything in the universes, including the human being, is composed of the elements EARTH, AIR, FIRE and WATER; dry, moist, cold and hot.

FREE WILL, LAW OF—Every person has absolute, pure freedon of choice every minute of the day. Mankind is never free from decision making; to not make a decision *is* a decision. Through his or her decisions mankind is *totally* in charge of his or her body and daily experiences. No outside universal or environmental stimuli dominate one's body or experiences. Therefore, one is automatically accountable for each decision, and this decision is reflected in the state of one's body and affairs. Mankind has evolved from an instinctual system and is now the only animal in earth with the free will system. Out of man's seven states of consciousness, earth consciousness is the only life in which free choice plays such an important role. One does not fail or fall, nor is one considered immature because one made a wrong choice. If people were not meant to make a wrong choice sometimes, they would not own this system. Choices which oneself judges to be incorrect or unpleasureable have a stronger impact on learning. Free will is mankind's main tool in each incarnation for learning lessons for evolvement.

FUNCTION, LAW OF—Everything, every living and nonliving construct, system, and time-period has a purposeful vibrational frequency with a directive-intelligence within iteself, guiding it ro fulfill its purpose (whether the purpose be meager or grand). This purpose is always fulfilled before the construct, system, or time-period changes to a higher vibrational frequency, as if it knows that each step must be perfected in its responsibility to TOTALITY. Simply stated "Everything knows its function!" **Syn.** LAW OF SEPARATE CONSCIOUSNESS. [**cf.** LAW OF EVOLUTION]

GIVE AND TAKE, LAW OF—All units in the UNIVERSE, animate or inanimate, are tranceivers. Each unit is capable of taking VIBRATIONS from the sea of ethers to utilize beneficially and is capable of giving out vibrations to the sea of ethers to be utilized beneficially by other units in the universe. This ability varies in degree of intensity. The auric pattern around each unit acts as a buffer to discriminate among the various vibrations coming in and going out so as to keep the unit in tune. (Inconcl.)

GOD, LAW OF—Any principle that expresses ultimate WISDOM and which benefits all mankind.

GOOD LAW OF—ALL is good, ALL-THERE-IS is good. There is no EVIL in all the universes, only a system

of opposites and POLARITY. There are no tragedies or SIN on earth, only an ultimate unfolding of each person. There are hundreds of levels of unfoldment.

GRACE, LAW OF—1. (June Bletzer) "Motivation," an innate guiding principle that promotes constant change to perfectibility in all things. The potential within each seed of living organisms that motivates it to grow to be a perfect organism of its species. Grace in mankind is the motivating force that tells one to keep going and do better, no matter what happens to one; e.g., the ability of the body to heal itself. **Syn.** LAW OF PERFECTIBILITY. 2. (Edgar Cayce) "The moment that one begins to forgive himself, he moves under the Law of Grace." When one understands the evolutionary process and the need to be a credit to the universe, one can forgive oneself and go about righting the wrong one did.

GRAVITY, LAW OF—1. A characteristic of this time dimension giving humanity perception of life as they know it in their present STATE OF CONSCIOUSNESS. The desires and needs of the SOUL-MIND for a three-dimensional world for its development was pushed and pulled to this earth by these desires and needs of the soul-mind and will stay here by the LAW OF PUSH AND PULL as long as mankind has jealousies, greed, hate, resentment, anxieties, and fears. These attitudes are the glue or action of gravity that binds mankind here. When all these drossy desires and thinking are dissipated from humanity's cells, they will not be "pushed or pulled" to work here any longer and will rise to the planes of TIME and SPACE in the etheric world. Materialistic desires are the push and pull binding human beings to earth, known as gravity. (Inconcl.) 2. Solids, liquids, and gases such as are in the PHYSICAL PLANE of existence, move according to their weight and density, determind by the emanation of MAGNETISM from the earth's core. (Inconcl.)

GROWTH, LAW OF—Growth is the change in the rate of vibration of atoms in all things, animate or inanimate, caused by the minds of man and the potential within the ATOM to return to the PERFECTNESS state from which it came. The constant movement of things, animate and inanimate, makes them better with time as they are influenced by mankind's minds, TOTAL INTELLIGENCE, environmental vibrations and the monad theory.

GUIDING PRINCIPLE, LAW OF—An innate intelligent force permeating all substance from the electron to the Great Solar System and which moves toward righteousness in various manifestations, binding all the parts to one coherent whole. The driving force behind constant change and whose laws only endure. **Syn.** DIRECTIVE INTELLIGENCE, TOTALITY.

GUILT CONSCIENCE, LAW OF—(June Bletzer) Guilt conscience is a necessary emotion that helps a person to achieve a higher qualitative life by telling him or her that the activity, speech, or thought they just enacted should not be repeated. A guilt conscience should never last longer than the time it takes to evaluate a situation or experience and make a judgment for oneself. To hold on to the guilt emotion for hours, days, months, or years is self-punishing, self-degrading, and unnecessary. Guilt conscience is an overly worked emotion encouraged by the mores of society. Each individual does the best he or she can do at the time he or she does it because their past acting and thinking has brought them to that activity, speech or thought. Each indiviual would do better if they could. (Even a planned robbery is the best that person can do at that time.) One minute after one performs an activity, speaks words, or thinks, one can pass judgment on oneself, because one then senses his or her own feeling, the feelings of others in the locale, and the property changes that occurred, which relay back to oneself whether it was right or wrong. But until the act, spoken words, or thought occured, one could not know the true reactions, and therefore, he or she was doing their best. This law does not excuse a criminal from paying for his or her crime, nor does it take away one's personal responsibility for one's actions, words, or thoughts. Manmade laws should provoke mankind to become more educated, acquire understanding, and strive for good mental health, so whatever one does (which is their best) is within the law.

HEALING, LAW OF—(holistic health, metaphysics) In order to motivate a *permanent* physical or mental healing that does not return at a future time or return in a different form of illness (as the majority of illnesses do), one must correct the cause of the illness. A true healing is to aid in a physical or mental cure and at the same time seek the reason for the disturbance. One must correctly interpret and overcome the original traumatic experience at the base of the disease, by a change in attitude regarding the traumatic experience. This attitudinal change erases the experience from one's BELIEF SYSTEM and AKASHIC RECORDS, thus stimulating repair to the body's transceiver point in that area. The repaired transceiver point stirs up the vital flow of MAGNETISM throughout the SYMPATHETIC NERVOUS SYSTEM releasing the obstruction and the body or brain cells normalize and repair themselves. Once the painful trauma is resolved properly by the patient, he or she no longer has to suppress emotions that remind them of that emotional event and the mind or body remain free of illness caused by that particular incident. Original causes can date back from one's past life or past incarnations. Every situation in one's life comes for a reason, and must be balanced with and put in its proper perspective when it is occurring, or it stays with the individual until it is emotionally translated correctly and balanced with, regardless of time. Situations cannot be put aside, suppressed, or ignored without causing havoc in the body or mind until dealt with properly; otherwise, all healings, surgery, medicine, psychic healings, holistic alternatives, traditional or unorthodox therapies, are only *temporary* cures. [**cf.** BLOCKS, REGRESSION, HOLISTIC HEALTH, CURATIVE EDUCATION APPENDIX 5]

HOLDING ON, LAW OF—Any activity one starts, whether it be a poem, a craft, a home, a love, a job, etc. should be worked at until it is finished as perfectly as one can make it. The joy is in the moments of the making, not the finished product. This Law goes further to say that one should hold onto an object or human relationship *only* as long as it makes a learning experience for one. [**cf.** LAW OF LETTING GO]

HUMAN BEING SEED, LAW OF—The guiding principle within each individual that urges one to forge ahead into activity and learning experiences that will enhance one's character and increases one's knowledge. The guiding principle is imbedded within the seed so the seed will unfold into a perfect specimen of a human being. This guiding principle stores in the AKASHIC RECORDS what the individual accomplishes in one INCARNATION to another making each incarnation an improvement. [**cf.** BIO-COMPUTER, CONSCIOUS MIND, AKASHIC RECORD]

IDENTIFICATION, LAW OF—By acquiring maximun knowledge about an entity, through association or education, and organizing it with one's SUBCONSCIOUS MIND and CONSCIOUS MIND, one can exercise power over or influence that entity, be it animal, person, or a skill. Increase in knowledge increases control. One can become another; animal, person or object. [**cf.** SHAPE-CHANGING]

845

ILLNESS, LAW OF—(holistic health) Every physical problem is caused by a psychological trauma which began from a past experience of this life or from a past INCARNATION: and every psychological problem is caused from a physical injury of some kind which happened in a past experience from this life or from a past incarnation. [cf. HOLISTIC HEALTH, PAST LIVES THEORY, REINCARNATION, KARMA, DISEASE]

IMAGINATION, LAW OF—Imagination is an agency of mental activity which can be consciously instigated to motivate the transformation of belief, past places, objects, and persons, into new images, places, beliefs, and objects. Mankind has full charge of directing this mechanism to co-create new experiences for themselves. One must dislodge unsuitable beliefs and experiences to establish new ones. This faculty interrelates with ideas and moves concepts in and out of the mind. Imagination gives mobility to ideas and beliefs. If imagination comes in conflict with "will power," will power will always lose. (Albert Einstein) "Imagination is more important than knowledge. It is man's most powerful force, not negative or positive, but it's there for man to use." To instigate new constructions in the mind is the principle source of human improvement.

IMITATION, LAW OF—The real can be influenced through the simulated and one can bring about a new situation, or alter an existing situation, regardless of distance. The symbol of a thing *is* the thing. To make a pretense through RITUAL, CONCENTRATED THOUGHT, intent, and the use of a similar sensation, color, odor, shape or function that is symbolic of the thing in the situation, is to cause it to happen; e.g., to hang a fish on a tree to bring a good crop of fish.

INATTENTION, LAW OF—In order to discriminate things, one leaves all impressions unnoticed which are valueless to him or her. Inattention is the result of mental economy. Since CONSCIOUSNESS is inherently limited in capacity, each person is given a switching-circuit that sifts and sorts out its scarce resources to the matters that are immediately important; e.g., one can't afford to notice the way one's socks feel on one's feet; a man doesn't notice a hurt wrist if he is playing tennis with a girlfriend. The mind has learned to sift out what it wants to.

INFINITE DATA, LAW OF—Mankind will never know all there is to know in any one given point in time and there is no indication of any end of data to come. There is no proof that one's finite mind can perceive everything there is to perceive in the universes. People will never run out of something to learn.

INFINITE UNIVERSES, LAW OF—No two human beings perceive the universes in the same way. This means there are innumberable universes and all existing as they appear to exist for the perceiver. (Inconcl.) [cf. LAW OF REALITY]

INFORMATION, LAW OF—Information gravitates toward a like CONSCIOUSNESS because it cannot exist by itself. It is not information until it is accompanied by those tho perceive it or originate it. Information must be held in consciousness in order for it to exist; it wants to exist and moves toward those who seek it and hold it. Information is not stored somewhere for one to dip into. (Seth) "One's consciousness attracts the consciousness that is already connected with the material; information become new and is rebron as it is interpreted through a new consciousness."

INTELLIGENCE, LAW OF—Everything living or non-living possesses intelligence and will respond to higher degrees of intelligence. However humble each form of life may be on the evolutionary ladder, it seems to revolve around an inward growth of development and awakening; e.g., a vine in a dark place will seek sunlight by extending itself until sunlight is reached; an old automobile will perform well for its owner but the broken down parts will not work properly for a borrower.

INTENT, LAW OF—Intention is the strongest element of every action of conduct. The activity one performs matters little, no matter how difficult or tedious, no matter how conscientious one's efforts, and no matter what one sacrifices to accomplish it. The purpose behind the activity, one's attitude toward the effect of one's actions or conduct, determines the whole meaning of the activity and determines the result of the action. (Is the activity performed with honest, good, evil, selfish, or helpful intentions?)

INTERRELATIONSHIP, LAW OF—There is a relationship of all things in the UNIVERSE, one to another, whether animate or inanimate, whether causal or non-causal, because all are constructed of the same atoms, and each ATOM has the ability to remember its past performance in matter before it was dissipated (functions in ASSOCIATION MAGIC).

INVOLUTION, LAW OF—(Eastern) The human being MONAD (in its seed state) projected itself to the lower planes of dense matter (mental, astral, physical) while in the ETHERIC WORLD. These lower planes serve as soil for its growth. On its path downward the monad took on a SOUL-MIND and is now encased in the soul-mind, growing and progressing in the evolutionary process (speculative, as no mind today can trace back that far, but this law utilizes the theory of repetition, which is valid). This gives a hypothesis why one tunes into the past (because he or she already experienced it) and into the future (because the monad is promoting the blossoming of itself) and the present (because this tells one his or her present status and how one can improve it). It also tells us why the purpose of DREAMS is to improve one's character.

KARMA, LAW OF—(Sanskrit) The highest form of justice; begins with a concept that everyone is created equal in the beginning. Each one is completely independent and solely responsible for his or her life and body by their thinking and acting in each life. One governs his or her incarnations, and all the experiences that come with them are from one's own doings in past incarnations. Karma is a system that returns to one, in kind, every act one has ever performed along one's evolutionary scale, showing no favoritism. The sum total of causes makes one's life wherever one is, as the result of his or her own activity and thinking in past lives and this life, bringing one good or unpleasant experiences. At the same time, one builds up from these new experiences for his or her future lives. Whatever energy is expended through thoughts, desires, and acts, a like energy is returned; e.g., "Thou shalt reap as thou didst sow." "Cast your bread upon the water and it shall return to you." **Syn.** LORDS OF JUSTICE, LAW OF COMPENSATION. [**cf.** REINCARNATION, APPENDIX 5]

KARMIC BALANCE, LAW OF—Energy expended in one INCARNATION could be so overwhelmingly bad or good that to have it all return in one incarnation would put one out of balance. Therefore, it is dispersed and returned to be worked off in more than one lifetime. [**cf.** KARMA, REINCARNATION]

KNOWLEDGE, LAW OF—The more informed one becomes through formal education and through life experiences, 1. the more understanding one has about oneself and life; 2. the more intelligent one's decisions will be; 3. the stronger one will be in all aspects of one's life (there is a strength that comes from knowing); 4. the more control one will have over the maximun data which one has learned. [**cf.** LAW OF SELF-KNOWLEDGE, CURATIVE EDUCATION]

LETTING GO, LAW OF—One should say good-bye without regrets or resentment to anything or anyone that is no longer useful and purposeful in making or adding to a learning experience for one's self (whether it be a home, record, plant, animal, former love, car, a grown child, club membership, philosophy, belief, lifestyle, book, etc.). The pleasure should be in the moment of the doing, the making, or the learning, with the object or experience. This frees one to begin another learning experience without bondage to the old image of one's self. (don Juan) "One should erase personal history by dropping past friends, relatives, cities, and events; where one has been and what one has done, so no one builds a fog around you or is angry with you." [**cf.** NEW-AGE PSYCHOLOGY]

LIFE, LAW OF—A compatible relationship between ENERGY and INTELLIGENCE working to promote the evolutionary process by guiding the atoms in sympathetic, similar patterns or units, contributing to the HOLOGRAM, and yet allowing for individualization of each ATOM; the individualizing of energy systems by radiating and absorbing with the interplay of an energy universe. (Inconcl.) [**cf.** LIFE, ENERGY, INTELLIGENCE]

LIFE AND DEATH, LAW OF—(holistic health) There are two major chemical processes in the body that are always functioning; the "ongoing life process" and the "ongoing death process." With every emotion, regardless of its degree of feeling, there is a BODY CHEMISTRY change toward one or the other of the processes. One cannot think a thought, or sit in silence, without some degree of emotion so the body is constantly working on one of these processes. There is no neutral chemical process in the body. [**cf.** CURATIVE EDUCATION]

LIKE ATTRACTS LIKE, LAW OF—Atoms will colonize because of their similarity, and thereby form various levels of matter. That which has similarity will be in sympathy or be compatible with that of like nature, working both subjectively and objectively; "birds of a feather flock together." No one escapes this principle in this plane or in the ETHERIC WORLD. Negative and inferior thoughts bring about undesirable and subordinate manifestations. Positive outlook on life brings happiness and beneficial manifestations. This law works through-out all types of PSYCHISM and MEDIUMSHIP. One should start with a neutral mind in order to perceive correct psychic information. (Robert E. Massy) "Nonsense begets nonsense, junk gives out junk and brings back junk."

LIVING ELECTRICAL STRUCTURE, LAW OF—Within every living organism is an electrical system, and conductivity factor of this system varies because if its dependence upon the condition of the living organism at any given moment. The condition of the organism changes its CONSTRUCT through normal life processes which in turn reflects upon the electrical system; e.g., in BIOFEEDBACK TRAINING, the baseline established in one session will vary with each session thereafter even though the subject is HOOKED-UP one week later in the same place, etc., psychics perform better some days than others. This law makes it impossible to have a controlled psychic experiment in the laboratory. (Inconcl.)

MANIFESTATION, LAW OF—SUGGESTION is the generator behind all operations and manifestations in the MATERIAL WORLD, and these manifestations cannot happen until suggestion hits the SUBCONSCIOUS MIND and is "taken in" by the subconscious mind. An act, object or event, begins with a mental impression of suggestion in the mind, impregnated by emotions until it is exteriorized; a normal function law is used in HYPNOTHERAPY, MENTAL TELEPATHIC HEALING, DESTRUCTIVE-BRAINWASHING CULTS, and VISUALIZATION. [**cf.** TELEPATHIC SUGGESTION]

MATTER, LAW OF—(Esoteric) All matter is composed of atoms vibrating at different frequencies made by the constant repulsion and attraction of electrons and protons trying to balance. The repulsion and attraction is activated by the human mind and emotions and keeps on until atoms of the same number of electrons aggregate together forming the various rates of vibration or mattter. (Jean Chardin) "Matter is conscious energy; mind and matter are one, poles of one continuum. Matter is the human mind in action; there is no substance except conscious energy." (Elmer Green) "Matter is crystalized thought." This law makes all types of PSYCHISM a perfectly normal function. (Inconcl.)

MEDITATION, LAW OF—When the CONSCIOUS MIND is fully occupied or locked-in on a small focul point for a period of time, the physical SENSES automatically become stilled and pure THOUGHT or ideas flow from TOTALITY which could not have flowed with the conscious senses working. Inventors, authors, artists, geniuses, scientists, all receive their new material by becoming so engrossed in their work, it stills outer senses and ideas flow. Meditation is a deliberate and pronounced holding back of the conscious mind and emotions for a set time, in a particular posture. This allows the PHYSICAL BODY to act upon itself in repair and attunes the conscious mind and emotions to a higher state of thinking, for many hours. Meditation before opening PSYCHIC DOORS will surface higher qualitative information; see MEDITATION APPENDIX 5]

MICRO/MACROCOSM, LAW OF—Law implies that something is a miniature replica of a whole, containing all the attributes of the whole. Each section of particle of a unit or system contains all the characteristics of the parent body and can function like the parent body only in lesser degrees. The macrocosm is the entire solar systems and the ATOM is a miniature SOLAR SYSTEM. The macrocosm contains Total knowledge, Total energy, and Total love and the microcosm contains these same features in minute quantities. The cup of ocean water has all the charactersitics of the ocean only in lesser degrees. (Inconcl.) [**cf.** TOTALITY, MONAD, GREAT MOTHER]

MIMICRY, LAW OF—A PSYCHIC can simulate the activity desired to be accomplished with as much detailed parallelism as possible, in color, shape, sound and activity; this parallelism will accomplish the desired activity. Distance is no barrier, size is not important, and knowledge of the desire at the distant end is not necessary. "Like produces like," the effect resembles its cause; e.g., dress a doll up as much like the patient as possible, take it out of bed and let it do something active which the patient likes to do; the patient will soon mimic this act and become well. **Syn.** LAW OF MIRROR MAGIC.

NAMES, LAW OF—Recognition of the name shows knowing the named. To know the complete and true data of a person or psychic skill gives one complete control over the person or psychic skill. Names are associated devices, memory gimmicks, used to remind one of something, both as aspects or descriptions of a phenomenon and as root (germ) sounds. To name a thing structures CONSCIOUSNESS. Naming awakens and expresses in a way the whole brain can know it. [**cf.** LAW OF SIGNATURE, WORDS-WITH-POWER]

NATURAL LAW—An immutable principle created in the beginning, or which always was, stating predictable consequences based on the way things or conditions appear to behave, having no exceptions or deviations. (If an exception seems to occur, it is because one does not understand the law in its entirety for that particular exception.)

OMNIPRESENCE, LAW OF—The UNIVERSE is represented in every one of its particles. Everything is made of one hidden stuff, TOTALITY, and Totality appears within all its parts; in every grain of sand and star in the sky. It is always present and present everywhere.

ONE SYSTEM, LAW OF—(new-age psychology) There is an intellectual, instinctual psychical and physical link between all living things and a change, small or large, in any one thing promotes a change in all other living things; given tangible evidence by psychic experiments and testing by the KIRLIAN PHOTOGRAPHY, BIOFEEDBACK INSTRUMENTS and PSYCHIC SKILLS. [cf. TRANSFORMATION, AQUARIAN AGE]

OPPOSITES, LAW OF—Everything has a reverse relationship. Anything can be split into two complete reverse characteristics and each of these reverse characteristics contains the essence of the other in its essence. Each end of POLARITY contains the potentiality of the elements of the other. One pole away from a central fixation has its reverse characteristic the same distance or density from the center; e.g., positive/negative, hot/cold, loud/quiet, yin/yang, lingam/yoni, male/female, sick/well, happy/sad, up/down, black/white, stale/fresh. The Slavs have two deities in the ETHERIC WORLD, BYEL-BOG AND CHERNOBOG; personifying DARKNESS and LIGHT, GOOD and EVIL, used together as if both were a part of the one; similar to Christianity's GOD and SATAN. [cf. LAW OF POLARITY.]

ORGANIZATION, LAW OF—A psychological, bio-electromagnetic, biogravitational, bioplasma, etc. field is only as well-organized as the contributing factor to the unit (animate or inanimate) to which these fields belong. A poorly organized field is still an organized field and functions according to its feeder.

NON-RESISTANCE, LAW OF—One can overly desire to accomplish something and keep one's mind and actions on it, constantly. This holds the atoms in rigidity and binds the accomplishment to one because of the strong emotion and activity. One should do one's part as well as one can and then let the plan or situation go, and stop letting it posses one's attention and time; let it unfold and happen; e.g., the little boy plants a tomato seed and, every day, digs it up to see how it is doing, thereby stifling its growth.

PARALLELISM, LAW OF—There is a higher, ethereal, more subtle, vibrational frequency counterpart that corresponds to everything in the UNIVERSE which one cannot perceive with the five SENSES. (Hermetics) "As above, so below; as below, so above;" (Jean Chardin) "The universe conceals and reveals constantly;" (Marilyn Ferguson) "What is above knows what is below, but what is below does not know what is above."

PATH, LAW OF—What is of worth to one is "his" path, regardless of the hardships it presents, or the length or time it takes. Each individual has a karmic journey which he or she has chosen to pursue in this INCARNATION and he will, somehow, find a way to travel on it. This road in one's journey will not go to the individual, he or she will go to it if it proves of worth to them. If it does not, one cannot hold it together successfully in one's dimension of time because it will fall apart of its uselessness. The direction one should take is within each individual, and only that individual can take that road. When one finds their "path," they will constantly have an inner drive to keep on it, and when one is not on it, he or she will feel restless and disturbed. When one finds "his" path, one will find security, happiness and fulfillment from within, regardless of outside circumstnaces, no matter how traumatic they are. [cf. PATH SYMBOLISM]

PERCEPTION, LAW OF—Mankind is aware and identifies data on all levels of his or her existence at the same time, and each of the bodies of an individual is aware and identifying data under the laws of that level only, occuring simultaneously. There is no proof that identification of data with the five SENSES is the only way to learn and understand, or that all the information one receives through the five senses is all the information there is to receive. One hasn't perceived everything in the UNIVERSE yet, and there is no indication one ever will; e.g., a candy dish floats around a room, unattended; a fairy is in view for a minute then disappears into thin air; one stares at a match and it moves.

849

PERFECTIBILITY, LAW OF—There seems to be a directive INTELLIGENCE that guides and promotes all things in the UNIVERSE—living and non-living organisms, from the Great Central Sun to the grain of sand—in an everlasting flux toward betterment. This proceeds repeatedly in an everlasting upward spiral of birth, growth, decay, and rebirth, growth and decay. This law acts through minor laws and various others as well.

PERSONAL HEALTH, LAW OF—(holistic health) The construction of the PHYSICAL BODY is constantly giving one a tangible readout of what the SOUL-MIND is doing, via illnesses or good health, vitality, or laggardness. One can use his or her physical body as an accomplishment chart to detect how one is handling life stresses, one's attitude toward experiences and people, and if the SUBCONSCIOUS MIND and CONSCIOUS MIND are synchronizing. However, a high rating of good health, vitality, and whole body ambulation does not signify that one is high on the evolutionary scale, but does testify how one is balancing with this incarnation. [**cf.** CURATIVE EDUCATION, BELIEF SYSTEM, PERMANENT HEALING, HOLISTIC HEALTH]

PERSONAL RETURN, LAW OF—Everything in nature is cyclic. When forces of thought are deliberately sent out from one's mind and are not absorbed by the object or event, to which they are directed, they will return, in due course, to the sender, as sent; otherwise, they will return rearranged or reprogrammed in their own due course. (inconcl.) [**cf.** TELEPATHY, PSYCHIC BOOMERANG]

PERSONAL SURVIVAL, LAW OF—Total life existence for each individual in each separate INCARNATION depends upon that individual's system of beliefs, values, and thinking for that particular incarnation. This changes from day to day as the thinking, values, and beliefs change. When the entity makes his or her TRANSITION, it will be because of their system of thinking. [**cf.**LAW OF LIFE AND DEATH]

PERSONAL TRANSFORMATION, LAW OF—(new age psychology) When something new appears in one's life that totally disrupts one's normal lifestyle, one must let go of old patterns, beliefs, mannerisms and activity. The new experience could be an accident, job transference, residential move, new baby, new friendships, a death, etc. The individual should take on a good frame of mind, and eagerly look forward to the new situation; otherwise, his or her growth is held back, the atoms stop flowing and the individual experiences ill health, chaotic activity, and a loss of the benefits he or she was to earn from the new lifestyle. The key is to "surrender" and go forth with joy [**cf.** HOLISTIC HEALTH, BELIEF SYSTEM, NEW-AGE PSYCHOLOGY APPENDIX 5]

PERSONAL VALUE, LAW OF—The attitude and emotional feeling one has about each daily experience is handled in accord with the individual's idea of his or her self-worth and its value to them. [**cf.** BELIEF SYSTEM, EMOTION, HOLISTIC HEALTH]

PERSONIFICATION, LAW OF—Anything can be a person. Any thing that has a real existence, such as an object, a skill, an event, a group of persons, a natural event, etc., has characteristics and a PERSONALITY of its own, and should be treated as if it were alive. This utilizes the theory that mankind makes the world and everything on it with their minds; therefore, everything else is an extension of humanity and embodies like qualities. Any phenomena is considered to be an "alive" entity; e.g., hurricanes are named after persons; cars are named, patted, and talked to; one refers to a time as "in the days of Walt Disney."

PHYSIOLOGICAL STRUCTURE, LAW OF—Because the BRAIN is connected to every system in the physiological structure, no change in the body can come about without first going through a mental phase. [**cf.** BIOFEEDBACK TRAINING]

POLARITY, LAW OF—A state of repulsion and attraction and balancing of NEGATIVE (female) and POSITIVE (male) energies of primordial essence, necessary to make the thousands of VIBRATIONAL FREQUENCIES in the entire COSMOS under the direction of mind activity. The way a CONSTRUCT reacts to a magnetic or electrical field manifesting two opposite tendencies, positive and negative. Everything can be split into two complete opposing principles and each contrasting principle will contain the potential of the opposing principle; e.g., in life is the seed of death; in death is the seed of life. (Inconcl.) [**cf.** LAW OF OPPOSITES]

POTENCY, LAW OF—That which is more powerful and influential can rule that which is less powerful and influential; e.g., PSYCHIC TRANSFER, PSYCHOKINESIS, SPLODGING.

PRAGMATISM, LAW OF—A "true" law would require infinite data, so if the character of conduct emphasizes practicality, accept it as true. (One cannot perceive everything.) Accept anything that works as true, such as MYTH, INTUITION, theory, method, system, hunches, DREAMS, RITUAL, etc.

PRIMAL DUALITY, LAW OF—Everything gives and takes. Everything is a transceiver, from the remotest particle to the great complex uniformity of the COSMOS. Everything takes in VIBRATIONS and gives out vibrations, contributing to and receiving from TOTALITY.

PROGRESSION, LAW OF—A natural law of evolutionary betterment: the higher substance operates upon the lower substance until the degree of which the lower substance is manifesting is ready to transmute to a higher degree. The lower substance, in turn, becomes the higher substance, and that which was higher before goes on to even higher VIBRATIONAL FREQUENCIES. This is repetitious throughout all ETERNITY, for all of nature. (Human being kingdom) The wise ones, the angels, serve on higher planes but rule the intelligences (humans and nature spirits) on the lower planes. They obey the laws coming from the plane above, use the laws on their own plane, and rule on the lower plane (earth) to raise the intelligences upward.

PROSPERITY, LAW OF—Anything less than today's need is not enough. Anything more than today's need is a burden and prosperity lies in between.

PSYCHE CONSCIOUSNESS, LAW OF—Whenever the conscious, decision-making mind is passive, the human PSYCHE (soul-mind) attempts to perfect itself to make a perfect specimen; anytime the CONSCIOUS MIND gives undivided attention to a FOCAL POINT, intentionally or unintentionally, this centralization of CONCENTRATION makes the conscious mind nonparticipative and submissive to the activity of the subconscious and superconscious minds. In this state the potential within the human seed pushes through the opening in the brain with knowledge and information to upgrade the individual. This could be in the form of answers to questions or ideas to stimulate new interest. It could also be a past life surfacing in visions or fragments of impressions to stimulate an interest to re-experience and handle the trauma that has been repressed for years or incarnations. Occurs when one is engrossed in an invention, writing a story or poem, during prolonged jogging, repetitious dance practice, DREAMING, ROLFING session, ACUPRESSURE session, AURA BALANCING period, or when deliberatley producing an ALTERED STATE OF CONSCIOUSNESS as in HYPNOTHERAPY or MEDITATION. [cf. GENIUS, SPLIT BRAIN, MOVEMENT-FOR-ALTERED CONSCIOUSNESS]

PSYCHIC PARALLELISM, LAW OF—Man has a counterpart to each of the five physical SENSES that operates on a higher vibrational frequency where SPACE and TIME are not limited. These PSYCHIC SENSES are capable of being released through the physical senses with no outer earth stimuli being necessary: CLAIRVOYANCE, CLAIRSCENT, CLAIRAUDIENCE, CLAIRSAVORANCE, and CLAIRSENTIENCE.

PSYCHO-ACTIVITY, LAW OF—The human mind is the highest power affecting the UNIVERSE; therefore, there is no substance on which the mind cannot act and react. The whole world is mental, held together by MENTAL ACTIVITY, and it can be altered by mental activity. (This law is used in all PSYCHISM and METAPHYSICAL practices.)

PSYCHO-PHYSIOLOGICAL PRINCIPLE—(Elmer Green) "Every change in the physiological state is accompanied by an appropriate change in the mental-emotional state; every change in the mental-emotional state, conscious or unconscious, is accompanied by appropriate change in the physiological state." [cf. BIOFEEDBACK TRAINING, EMOTION, SOLAR PLEXUS]

PSYCHOBIOLOGY CONSCIOUSNESS, LAW OF—For every state of mind, there is a corresponding physical state of the human NERVOUS SYSTEM. The human nervous system in turn affects the other systems in the body. The state of mind changes from moment to moment. The above conclusions were reached based on the results of years of biofeedback study.

PUSH AND PULL, LAW OF—A synchronization principle that causes conflict between the SOUL-MIND and CONSCIOUS MIND during earth incarnations. The individual is torn between irrelevant and harmful desires and necessary desires. Desires of the soul-mind are excited by a longing for long term knowledge and necessary experiences that will prepare itself for the perfect state. Some desires of the conscious mind are excited by the wordly satisfactions and pleasures of the five SENSES that have no bearing on or that detain from this perfect state. Negative emotions, i.e., hate, fear, anxiety, jealousy, resentment, unfriendliness, ego building, smother love, etc., excite the conscious mind into harmful activity, and push away from the soul-mind's desires. These types of emotions are temporary and will eventually be overcome. Until

851

mankind can synchronize the conscios mind with the soul-mind, they will resume earthly incarnations and be under this law, always feeling pushed and pulled, or torn in the middle. (Sigmund Freud) "We are motivated by needs of which we are not aware."

QUANTUM CONNECTION, LAW OF—All things, living and non-living, are minutely connected in the ethereal world, and when a physical contact is made and then severed, they will continue to influence and affect one another long after separation, distance being no barrier. **Syn.** LAW OF CONTAGION [**cf.** RADIESTHESIA, PSYCHIC HEALING]

QUASI-IMMORTALITY, LAW OF—Nothing in nature, including man, remains exactly the same for even one second of time. Every time an ATOM changes, everything in the UNIVERSE minutely changes and atoms are constantly vibrating and changing. Atoms travel in cycles and everything follows this cyclic path.

READINESS, LAW OF—(Eastern) "When the pupil is ready, the Master is ready also; when the student is ready, the Teacher will come." No matter how good a reputation a metaphysical or occult organization has, its only value to you is when the subjects or activities mean something to you, at that "given time." This has nothing to do with the competence or incompetence of the organization or teacher.

REALITY, LAW OF—(esoteric) There is only one real Reality, and this is broken down in perception in an infinite number of ways to be viewed in accordance with the number of entities viewing it (on the physical and etheric plane.) Each individual has atoms that have different consciousnesses, a different akashic record, which is being bombarded constantly, but differently, by environmental stimuli. Therefore, the universe, world, countries, weather, prominent people, neighborhoods, animals, plants, communication systems, etc., will be unique to each perceiver, according to his or her current BELIEF SYSTEM (because he knows no other at that time) e.g., this law is obvious when two psychics are given the same message but it is brought through in different symbols. Each person's total belief system makes their consciousness. What one has the consciousness for makes his world and body. This is "real" for him. Reality is function of belief.

REGENERATION, LAW OF—Everything in the

COSMOS, from the Great Central Sun to the glow-worm, is an everlasting work of perfection, some in less noticeable degrees than others. Each entity begins with birth, grows in CONSCIOUSNESS and CONSTRUCT, and then decays in construct. Then the entity begins again with rebirth in another more advanced construct, with growth in consciousness and construct, and decay in construct. This is constant cyclic process of betterment that the entity can detain but not stop. **Syn.** LAW OF PERFECTION.

REPETITION, LAW OF—There is an orderly purposeful arrangement of energy levels in the UNIVERSE manifested in various patterns of form, color, sound and periods of time, which is repeated in duplication up and down the scale. This law governs the tiniest particle of the greatest hologram, TOTALITY. Each energy level has its own degree of life, but all fall under the same underlying principles and are intimately connected to everything in the universe; e.g., the condition of one's body is repeated in the bottom of the foot, the condition of the tree is repeated in the leaf; the group consciousness of a neighborhood is held by each member of that neighborhood. [**cf.** BODY READING]

RITUAL, LAW OF—Any act performed repeatedly with specific conscious intent becomes a "rite" of that conscious specific intent, whether or not the person is aware of this law. All MATTER used in a customary procedure absorbs and influences the other during that procedure period until it is worn away through another repeated customary procedure; e.g., a kitchen platter absorbs odors of the meat, the attitude of the dishwasher, and the overall atmosphere in the kitchen, with each use. Glasses worn every day are influenced by the characteristics and emotions of the wearer. This is the main law behind PSYCHOMETRY.

SELF-KNOWLEDGE, LAW OF—When one is aware of oneself and has information about oneself and understands these two combinations, one will have complete control over one's behavior, making life pleasurable and joyous. The most important kind of knowledge is knowledge of oneself; "know thyself."

SELF-ORGANIZATION, LAW OF—(human) Every person is governed by an electromagnetic and biogravitational field that surrounds the physical body. This field is made from the CONSCIOUS MIND and SUBCONSCIOUS MIND activity during the present and past incarnations, forming a blueprint of the PHYS-

ICAL BODY and daily affairs to come. No change can take place in one's physical body and daily affairs without a change in one's blueprint first. Self organizes self.

SELF-PRESERVATION, LAW OF—There is an innate ability given to all living organisms to take care of themselves, some through INSTINCT and mechanical means, some through the faculty of reason, subjective, and mechanical means. This is considered the "first law of the land" for earth. All injured living organisms can heal themselves if left in a natural setting and they have the desire to live. One's desires for self-preservation extend to save one's self-image, and to preserve one's family, neighborhood, country and world, and their self-images.

SEPARATE CONSCIOUSNESS, LAW OF—Each thing in the UNIVERSE, each ENTITY, unit, system of activity, and time period, from the minutest particle to the great complex SOLAR SYSTEM, has a CONSCIOUSNESS of its being and purpose at any given time, and goes on striving to reach that purpose. Each thing works in group activities, contributing to the group consciousness, learning from the group consciousness, never losing its own individual consciousness. [**cf.** GROUP SOUL]

SEQUENT CHANGE, LAW OF—1. (esoteric) that which appears in an organic vibration will have an effect for every cause; 2. (clinical) that which appears in a mechanical vibration will have an effect for every cause.

SIGNATURES, DOCTRINE OF—see LAW OF SIGNATURES.

SIGNATURES, LAW OF—Every manmade object, natural object, event, or condition is noted for its usefulness, quality, and other outstanding characteristics. When an object, event, or condition is shown to the PSYCHIC in the form of a symbol, glyph, or metaphor, the psychic identifies with this usefulness, quality, or outstanding characteristic which belongs to the object, event, or condition shown in order to interpret the message. This Law is also utilized extensively in DREAMS, and Bible literature; e.g., "the Lamb." **Syn.** DOCTRINE OF SIGNATURES.

SIMILARITY, LAW OF—If a person, object, or condition bears any likeness or resemblance in color, shape, smell, action or sequence of events to another person, object, or condition, it can be used for many psychic purposes as if it were the person, object, or condition itself, because of this likeness. This resemblance and likeness makes the person, object, or condition partake of some of the power of the original; look alikes are alike; effects resemble causes; e.g., to use a doll, name it after the patient, hold doll in the palm of the hands with healing intentions, and the patient receives the healing energies. [**cf.** SYMPATHETIC MAGIC]

SIMULTANEITY, LAW OF—Any action going on anywhere in the UNIVERSE influences all points in the universe simultaneously, without any forces traveling through SPACE. [**cf.** HOLOGRAM, TIME]

SOUL-MIND, LAW OF—The SOUL-MIND serves the body as the "voltage regulator" governing the electrical force coming from the COSMOS. The Cosmos gives equal amounts of electrical energy to all but, each individual can only utilize amounts of this energy according to the growth of the soul-mind. This growth is measured in WISDOM and righteousness and not in physical body conditions or the number of earthly incarnations. The soul-mind keeps track of its own growth on the evolutionary scale, and with its memory of being in a heavenly condition in the beginning, strives to advance. The more it advances, the more electrical energy the body utilizes. The more electrical, COSMIC ENERGY, the more qualitative life for the individual. Tangible evidence that each body absorbs a different amount of electrical energy is shown by the GSR and METABOLIC MONITOR in which the conductivity of each individual varies when HOOKED-UP to these biofeedback instruments.

SOUL-MIND EVOLUTION, LAW OF—An innate guiding principle directs the SOUL-MIND on its evolutionary path of growth through many incarnations in earth, preparing itself for ASCENSION to its original state of PERFECTNESS. This is accomplished by overcoming SPACE (dimensional), TIME (succession), and SELF (separation from TOTALITY) while in earth incarnations. [**cf.** SUBCONSCIOUS MIND, LAW OF INVOLUTION, MONADOLOGY, AKASHIC RECORDS]

SOUL-MIND GROWTH, LAW OF—Three major aspects that contribute to the growth of the SOUL-MIND while in the PHYSICAL BODY, speeding up its vibrational rate: 1. balancing with emotional stress as it presents itself, resolving situations in their proper perspective; 2. correct breathing and utilization of the spirit in the air; 3. eating the correct food for one's physical body with the proper attitude. All activities in the physical body are variations of lessons relating to these three aspects.

SPACE, LAW OF—All space is electrical and all LIFE, and nonlife, is based upon the action and interaction between the various electrical units of the UNIVERSE, under the direction of mind.

SPONTANIETY, DOCTRINE OF—An automatic funtion of response by the SYMPATHETIC NERVOUS SYSTEM to outer stimuli blended with the subconscious mind MEMORY BANK. If this funtion is felt to be natural and right, it will give an inner satisfaction and aid the health of the PHYSICAL BODY, regardless of cultural opinion or environmental reactions.

SUBSERVIENCE, LAW OF—The greater manifestation in a system always serves the lesser manifestation in the same system in a subordinate capacity in order to promote a purposeful end. In the earth plane and etheric planes, all energy flows from the more energetic sources to the less energetic sources, never in the opposite direction. The higher aspects of consciousness always aid in the transmutation of the lower aspects of consciousness. The higher awareness subordinately serves the lower awareness because the higher forms of energy cannot perform if they do not have the lower forms with which to work. The objective is to raise the lower energy to a higher state; e.g., the INTELLIGENCE subserves the BRAIN; the hand subserves the fingers, the tree trunk subserves the branches; the GUIDES subserve the MEDIUM; the ethereal masters subserve the guides.

SUCCESSION, LAW OF—The roots of every structure in the UNIVERSE hold upon the hierarchy system.

SUFFERING, LAW OF—(new-age psychology) All misery, agony, or anguish, whether mental or physical, is caused by FEELINGS. These feelings are caused from one's attitudes or point of view, regarding what one is experiencing. One's attitude is caused by one's BELIEF SYSTEM. The whole range of one's belief system results from earthly thoughts in one's first INCARNATION to the present moment. So, one feels the way one thinks.

SUGGESTION, LAW OF—All manifestations in the physical world come from MENTAL MIND activity and within this mental mind activity are suggestions. It is when these suggestions are "accepted" by the SUBCONSCIOUS MIND that they manifest in the outer world. Any information, knowledge, encouragement or instructions given the subconscious mind must be in compliance with the compartments already there; otherwise, it will be expelled. Suggestions that are in compliance with one's PERSONALITY will take immediately and others will be mulled over and mixed with the compartments already in the subconscious mind. Suggestions are given to the subconscious mind intentionally from the decisions of the CONSCIOUS MIND through the written and spoken word, and unintentionally through INNER-DIALOGUE thinking. Suggestions are accepted directly are given when in an ALTERED STATE OF CONSCIOUSNESS such as HYPNOSIS, MEDITATION, and DREAMING, if in compliance with the personality.

SYMBOLISM, LAW OF—(Alchemy) Environmental and body happenings are a direct result of one's thinking, emotions, and attitudes, and these outward conditions appear to have much similarity and likeness to these thoughts, emotions, and attitudes. One's body, house, automobile, washing machine, lawn, trees, are an extension of one's self, and an outer symbol of attitudes and emotions; e.g., one who has no money to bank may bank fat on the body as a compensation; the brakes go wrong on the car when one needs to slow down, or one desires to stop something but cannot. [**cf.** HOLISTIC HEALTH, CURATIVE EDUCATION]

SYNCHRONICITY, LAW OF—(Carl Jung) The principle that two separate events occurring simultaneously, neither being causally connected or having an effect on each other, will show a meaningful related response, indicating some kind of link. An acausal connecting principle works through the process of linking IDEAS, THOUGHT-FORMS, ARCHETYPES, SYMBOLS, to influence external events. The regularity, order, and patterns that knowingly exist in vast areas of knowledge may be accountable for events previously thought to be random or coincidental. This principle explains some psychic events, i.e., CLAIRVOYANCE-IN-SPACE, TELEPATHY, CASTING OF LOTS, and RADIESTHESIA (asking the DOWSING ROD to react in the hands when over water only, and it does). (Inconcl.)

SYNTHESIS, LAW OF—The blending of two opposing ideas or data producing a third idea or datum which appears to be truer than either of the first two. The third idea will be something brand-new and not a compromise of the two. Synthesis builds on synthesis.

THIRD-DIMENSION, LAW OF—Believed to have its origin from the desire and need of the SOUL-MIND to learn lessons of a different nature, those of an emotional quality. So the soul-mind took on forms that could move up and down, and backward and forward. This heightens the vividness and significance of this reality. Flesh is very responsive to THOUGHT and yet capable of springing back to its original form easily. It is the level of REALITY needed for this dimension.

THOUGHT, LAW OF—The mental activity of the HUMAN BEING KINGDOM directs the course of the ATOMS to make third-dimensional manifestations, holds the manifestations in place or frees them, according to his or her needs and desires. (Briefly explained) The mental activity behind the thought sends out ergs of EMOTION and INTELLIGENCE (unstoppable radiations); this emotion and intelligence together start the rate of vibration of electrons and protons in the atoms, according to the nature and emotions behind the thought (emotion has its degrees of voltage). These atoms congregate atoms of like nature to form molecules, molecules form compounds, and compounds form physical matter that mankind can perceive and use for their needs and wants: 1. This explains the cliche "man has dominion over all things." Mental activity directs the course of the universe. 2. A person does not have a thought, he or she just unfolds what is already there within the potential of the universal seed (trying to grow to a perfect universe). 3. This law functions because of other universal laws, i.e., polarity, vibration, like attracts like. 4. Thought energy holds the world together. (Emmett Fox) "Everything manifested in earth is the mental equivalent of the thoughts of every man in earth." Thought expresses the universe in its evolutionary progress. 5. (Elmer Green) "The world is crystalized thought." 6. MIND and MATTER are one and the same. (Inconcl.) [**cf.** LAW OF POLARITY, LAW OF VIBRATION, CONSCIOUS MIND]

THREES, LAW OF—This begins with two, which is commonly recognized as positive and negative, and becomes a law only when it has a neutralizing force. These three then become a unit of themselves, neither of the two becoming more powerful or larger. Now, each behaves for itself and for the benefit of the whole; e.g., Father, Son, and HOLY SPIRIT; mother, father, child; CONSCIOUS MIND, SUBCONSCIOUS MIND, SUPERCONSCIOUS MIND; waking state, sleeping state, dreaming state; bride, groom, marriage as a unit.

TOTALITY, LAW OF—The ultimate living organism, the COSMOS, motivated by the potential within its seed to unfold and express itself to a perfect total. To do this, it is perpetually changing energy and matter giving it new direction and function in millions of degrees of VIBRATIONAL FREQUENCIES throughout all eternities.

TRANSFER OF ENERGY PRINCIPLE—(Baron Gottfried Wilhelm von Leibniz) "Two things alike in every respect, having the same composition and dimension but separated in space, will experience energy transfer from one to the other in proportion to their separation." [**cf.** NUMEROLOGY, TWIN-SOULS.

TRANSFORMATION, LAW OF—Every 26,000 years, earth moves into a restructuring of human EVOLUTION. The pendulum makes a complete swing, bringing a flowing, bursting, resurgence from within the seed of the SOLAR SYSTEM toward a new awareness of ideas, theories, lifestyles, attitudes, and characteristics. That which has outlived its potential in the old culture send up signals triggering a movement toward a higher STATE OF CONSCIOUSNESS. Each new occurrence is felt by the whole planet. That which was hidden becomes revealed. That which had been threatening will absorb, enlarge, and enrich the unknown making it exciting and compatible. The law will shift into a new dimension if there is no rebuff. Avoidances and rebukes tend to hold the restructuring back. New perspectives from the shift bring a fulfillment for all. [**cf.** FUTURISTS, NEW-AGE PSYCHOLOGY, TRANSFORMATIONISTS]

TRUE FALSEHOODS, LAW OF—1. Data that is not acceptable to the feeling nature of an individual but nonetheless works, is true. Because information does not agree with one's SOUL-MIND growth, does not mean it is false. 2. Information that contradicts the usual data regarding a method, system, subject or concept, but nonetheless works in the system or method, or fits the concept or subject, is true. Paradoxical statements that work are real, and must be understood in their entirety before being declared untrue. [**cf.** LAW OF EXCLUSIVENESS]

ULTIMATE UNITS OF MATTER, LAW OF—Unit emanations built from emotional-intensity energy move through the air just beneath the range of physical matter. They charge the air as they pass, drawing to them other units, operated by the Law of Attraction and Repulsion, making up patterns produced by all kinds of consciousness, from the molecule to large gestalts.

UNCERTAINITY PRINCIPLE—(Albert Einstein, Werner Heisenberg) Any realistic description of the universe must decribe it in all possible states at the same instant of time; e.g., a person would be alive, dead, and unborn simultaneously. (Inconcl.) [**cf.** TIME DISPLACEMENT, PATTERNING ACROSS TIME, NO TIME OR SPACE]

UNFOLDMENT, LAW OF—(angel hierarchy) There are seven major phases the SOUL-MIND must experience to purify her or himself to evolve into the divine or the "Godliness." Phases one, two, three, and four, are worked out in a PHYSICAL BODY. Phase five, initiation into MASTERSHIP may be earned in either the material plane or ETHERIC PLANE. Phase six, initiation into LORDSHIP is earned in the ETHERIC WORLD. Phase seven, initiation into the unfoldment into Godhood is earned in the higher planes. **Syn.** ANGEL EVOLUTION.

UNIVERSAL LAW, LAW OF—Principles that are absolutely necessary for this system of universes. All the laws that are necessary were created with CREATION and are existing now, whether mankind has discovered them or not. No other laws will ever be necessary to run the UNIVERSE. These principles have no exception (as do manmade laws) and if events, situations, objects, persons, phenomena and mother nature act as if an exception to a universal law, it is only because humanity does not understand the law in its entirety. Subordinate and superior laws will govern the exception. **Syn.** NATURAL LAW.

VIBRATION, LAW OF—Everything in the UNIVERSE has its foundation in the principle of constant movement and this rate of movement determines its uniqueness and expression. Because of this law, the CONSCIOUS MIND of a person can tune into the SUBCONSCIOUS MIND and UNIVERSAL MIND to receive PSYCHIC INFORMATION. **Syn.** LAW OF QUANTA STATE.

VIBRATIONAL FREQUENCIES, LAW OF—Everything in the UNIVERSE is vibrating and the rate of vibration determines its nature. There are trillions of vibrational frequencies and each thing, animate and inanimate, is formed, shaped, colored, activity oriented, intelligently endowed, and evolutionary-processed by its entire vibrational frequency and the various frequencies within its unit; e.g., the earth and its products such as steel and iron are slower frequencies than the SEVENTH PLANE and its celestial beings. [**cf.** VIBRATIONS, LAW OF VIBRATION, VIBRATORY NOTE]

SELECT BIBLIOGRAPHY

The references listed here represent only a portion of the numerous publications read and studied by the author over a period of years. Many of the publications listed contain pertinent appendices and references. Source categories are: Books; Conferences, Seminars, Lectures, and Workshops; Learning Cassettes; Magazines and Newsletters; Selected Magazine and Newspaper Articles; Booklets; Radio and Television Shows; and Miscellaneous Sources.

BOOKS

Alder, Vera Stanley. *The Finding of the Third Eye*. New York: Samuel Weiser, Inc., 1968.

_____. *The Fifth Dimension*. New York: Samuel Weiser, Inc., 1974.

Angoff, Allan. *Eileen Garrett and the World Beyond the Senses*. New York: William Morrow and Co., Inc., 1974.

Archer, Fred. *Exploring the Psychic World*. New York: Paperback Library, Inc., 1968.

Arnold, Levi, and MacDonald, Anna A. *History of the Origin of All Things*. N.p., Ca.: W.M. Publishing Trust, 1961.

Arya, Pandit Usharbudh. *Superconscious Meditation*. Glenview, Ill.: Himalayan Institute, 1974.

Assagioli, Roberto. *Synthesis I: The Realization of the Self*. Redwood City, Ca.: The Synthesis Press, 1977.

_____. *Synthesis II: The Realization of the Self*. Redwood City, Ca.: The Synthesis Press, 1978.

Bailey, Alice. *A Treatise on Cosmic Fire*. New York: Lucis Publishing Co., 1970.

Baker, Douglas. *Practical Techniques of Astral Projection*. New York: Samuel Weiser, Inc., 1976.

_____. *The Opening of the Third Eye*. New York: Samuel Weiser, Inc., 1977.

_____. *The Techniques of Astral Projection*. London: Douglas Baker, 1977.

Bander, Peter. *Voices From the Tapes*. New York: Drake Publishing, 1973.

Barbanell, Maurice. *This is Spiritualism*. London: Spiritualist Press, 1959.

Barborka, Geoffrey. *The Peopling of the Earth*. Wheaton, Ill.: Theosophical Publishing House, 1975.

Bates, W. H. *Better Eyesight Without Glasses*. New York: Pyramid Books, 1970.

Beall, James Lee. *The Adventure of Fasting*. Old Tappan, N.J.: Fleming H. Revell & Co., 1974.

Bentov, Itzhak. *Stalking the Wild Pendulum*. New York: Bantam Books, Inc., 1979.

Berlitz, Charles, and Moore, William. *The Philadelphia Experiment*. New York: Fawcett Crest, 1980.

Bernard, Raymond. *The Hollow Earth*. Secaucus, N.J.: University Books, Inc., 1969.

Besant, Annie, and Leadbeater, Charles W. *Thought Forms*. Wheaton, Ill.: Theosophical Publishing House, 1971.

Birren, Faber. *The Story of Color: From Ancient Mysticism to Modern Science*. Westport, Conn.: The Crimson Press, 1941.

Blakeslee, Thomas. *The Right Brain: A New Understanding of the Unconscious Mind and Its Creative Powers*. New York: Doubleday, Anchor Press, 1980.

Blavatsky, H. P. *Dynamics of the Psychic World*. Wheaton, Ill.: Theosophical Publishing House, 1972.

_____. *The Secret Doctrine*. 2 vols. Wheaton, Ill.: Theosophical Publishing House, 1974.

Bloomfield, Harold; Cain, Michael Peter; and Jaffe, Dennis T. *TM—Discovering Inner Energy and Overcoming Stress.* New York: Delacorte Press, 1975.

Bolen, Jean Shinoda, M.D. *The Tao of Psychology: Synchronicity.* New York: Harper and Row, 1979.

Bonewitz, P. E. *Real Magic.* New York: Berkley Medallion Books, 1971.

Borderline. *Strange Horizon.* Compiled by editors. New York: Paperback Library, Inc., 1967.

Boyd, Douglas. *Rolling Thunder.* New York: Dell Publishing Co., 1971.

Bradley, Dorothy, and Bradley, Robert. *Psychic Phenomena.* New York: Warner Paperback Library, 1969.

Bragdon, Claude. *Explorations Into the Fourth Dimension.* Lakemont, Ga.: CSA Press, 1972.

_____ *Yoga and You.* New York: Alfred A. Knopf, Inc., 1943.

Branden, Nathaniel. *The Disowned Self.* New York: Bantam Books, Inc., 1979.

Bro, Harmon H. *Edgar Cayce On Dreams.* New York: Warner Books, Inc., 1968.

Brown, Barbara. *New Mind, New Body.* New York: Harper and Row Publishers, Inc., 1974.

_____ *Stress and the Art of Biofeedback.* New York: Harper and Row Publishers, Inc., 1977.

Brown, Beth. *ESP With Plants and Animals.* New York: Simon & Schuster, 1971.

Budge, E. A. Wallis. *Egyptian Book of the Dead.* New York: Dover Publications, 1967.

Byrne, Peter. *The Search for Big Foot: Man, Myth or Monster?* New York: Pocket Books, Inc., 1976.

Cade, Maxwell, and Coxhead, Nona. *The Awakened Mind.* New York: Delacorte, 1979.

Carroll, Lewis. *Alice in Wonderland.* New York: Pocket Books, Inc., 1951.

Cartwright, Rosaline D. *Night Life: Explorations in Dreaming.* Englewood Cliffs, N.J.: Prentice-Hall, Inc., 1977.

Castaneda, Carlos. *Tales of Power.* New York: Simon & Schuster, 1974.

_____ *Journey to Ixtlan.* New York: Simon & Schuster, 1972.

_____ *A Separate Reality: Further Conversations With Don Juan.* New York: Simon & Schuster, 1974.

Cavendish, Richard, ed. *Man, Myth and Magic Encyclopedia.* 24 vols. New York: Marshall Cavendish Corp., 1978.

Cayce, Edgar Evans. *Edgar Cayce on Atlantis.* Edited by Hugh Lynn Cayce. New York: Paperback Library, 1968.

Chan, Wing-Tsit. *The Way of Lao Tzu.* New York: Bobbs-Merrill Co., 1963.

Chaney, Earlyne. *Secrets from Mount Shasta.* Upland, Ca.: Astara, Inc., 1953.

_____ *Revelations of Things to Come.* Upland, Ca.: Astara, Inc., 1982.

Chaney, Robert. *Unfolding the Third Eye.* Upland, Ca.: Astara, Inc., 1970.

_____ *Transmutation.* Upland, Ca.: Astara, Inc., 1969.

Cheiro. *Book of Numbers.* New York: Arco Publishing, Inc., 1971.

Constable, Trevor James. *Cosmic Pulse of Life: The Revolutionary Biological Power Behind UFO's.* New York: Merlin Press, 1976.

Conway, Flo, and Siegelman, Jim. *Snapping.* New York: J. B. Lippincott Co., 1978.

Cooks, Howard. *The Eyes, Brain and Nerve Systems in Relation to Earth's Magnetism.* Devon, England: Devon Rustics, 1971.

Corriere, Richard, and Hart, Joseph. *The Dream Makers.* New York: Funk & Wagnalls, Inc., 1977.

Cousins, Norman. *Anatomy of an Illness As Perceived by the Patient.* New York: Bantam Books, Inc., 1981.

Crowley, Aleister. *Magick in Theory and Practice.* New York: Dover Publications, 1976.

Davidson, Mark, and Ponnamperuma, Nirmali. *The Mystery of the Black Holes That Warp Space and Halt Time.* Van Nuys, Ca.: Van Nuys Publishing Co., 1977.

Davis, Adelle. *Let's Eat Right to Keep Fit.* New York: New American Library, 1970.

DeGivry, Grillot. *Witchcraft, Magic & Alchemy.* Translated by J. Courtenay Locke. New York: Dover Publications, Inc., 1971.

Deniston, Denise, and McWilliams, P. *The TM Book.* New York: Warner Books, 1975.

Diamond, Edwin. *The Science of Dreams.* New York: McFadden, 1967.

Diamond, John, M.D. *BK—Behavioral Kinesiology: The New Science for Positive Health Through Muscle Testing.* New York: Harper and Row, 1979.

Dubin, Reese. *Telecult Power: The American New Way to Psychic and Occult Wonders.* New York: Parker Publishing Co., 1970.

Dudley, Geoffrey. *How to Understand Your Dreams.* North Hollywood, Ca.: Wilshire Book Co., 1957.

Dumont, Theron Q. *The Solar Plexus or Abdominal Brain.* Des Plains, Ill.: Yogi Publication Society, n.d.

Dyer, Wayne W. *Your Erroneous Zones.* New York: Avon Books, 1977.

Ebon, Martin. *Psychic Discoveries by the Russians.* Bergenfield, N.J.: New American Library, n.d.

_____ *Test Your Own ESP.* North Hollywood, Ca.: Wilshire Book Co., 1969.

Ehret, Arnold. *Rational Fasting.* New York: Benedict Lust Publishers, 1971.

Eisenbud, Jule. *The World of Ted Serios.* New York: Pocket Books, 1968.

Ellison, Jerome. *Life Beyond Death: As Told to Jerome Ellison by Arthur Ford.* New York: Berkley Medallion Books, 1971.

Evans-Wentz, W. Y. *The Tibetan Book of the Dead.* New York: Oxford University Press, Inc., 1960.

_____ *Tibetan Yoga and Secret Doctrines.* New York: Oxford University Press, Inc., 1961.

Fagan, Joan, and Shepperd, Irma, eds. *Gestalt Therapy Now.* New York: Harper and Row, 1971.

Faraday, Ann. *The Dream Game.* New York: Harper and Row, 1974.

_____ *Dream Power.* New York: Berkley Medallion Books, 1973.

Farina, Mario V. *Computers—a Self-Teaching Instruction.* Englewood Cliffs, N.J.: Prentice-Hall, Inc., 1969.

Ferguson, Marilyn. *The Aquarian Conspiracy: Personal and Social Transformation in the 1980s.* Los Angeles: J. P. Tarcher, Inc., 1980.

Ferguson, Robert. *Psychic Telemetry: Key to Health, Wealth & Perfect Living.* New York: Parker Publishing Co., 1977.

Fillmore, Charles. *Atom Smashing Power of the Mind.* Unity Village, Mo.: Unity School of Christianity, 1957.

_____ *Mysteries of Genesis.* Unity Village, Mo.: Unity School of Christianity, 1957.

_____ *Twelve Powers of Man.* Unity Village, Mo.: Unity School of Christianity, 1957.

Findhorn Community. *The Findhorn Garden.* New York: Harper and Row, 1975.

_____ *Onearth 1.* Findhorn, Scotland: Findhorn Foundation, 1976.

Firth, Henry. *Practical Palmistry.* N.p., Pa.: The Penn Publishing Co., 1908.

Fitzgerald, B. J. *A New Text of Spiritual Philosophy and Religion.* Los Angeles: Universal Church of the Master, 1969.

Flanagan, G. Patrick. *Pyramid Power.* Marina Del Rey, Ca.: DeVorss & Co., 1975.

_____ *Beyond Pyramid Power.* Marina Del Rey, Ca.: DeVorss & Co., 1976.

_____ *The Pyramid and Its Relationship to Biocosmic Energy.* N.p.: G. Patrick Flanagan, 1972.

Fodor, Nandor. *Encyclopedia of Psychic Science.* Secaucus, N.J.: University Books, Inc., 1966.

Ford, Arthur, and Bro, Margueritte Harmon. *Nothing So Strange.* New York: Paperback Library, Inc., 1968.

Forem, Jack. *Transcendental Meditation.* New York: E. P. Dutton, Inc., 1974.

Fortune, Dion. *Applied Magic.* New York: Samuel Weiser, Inc., 1962.

_____ *Psychic Self-Defense.* London: Aquarian Press, 1976.

Fox, Douglas. *The Vagrant Lotus.* Philadelphia: Westminster Press, 1927.

Fox, Emmet. *The Ten Commandments.* New York: Harper and Row, 1953.

_____ *The Sermon on the Mount.* New York: Harper Brothers, 1938.

Froud, Brian, and Lee, Alan L. *Faeries.* New York: Rufus Publishers, Inc., 1978.

Fuller, John G. *The Interrupted Journey.* New York: Dell Publishing Co., Inc., 1967.

_____ *Arigo, Surgeon of the Rusty Knife.* New York: Thomas Crowell Co., 1974.

_____ *The Ghost of Flight 401.* New York: Berkley Medallion, 1976.

Furst, Charles. *Origins of the Mind: Mind-Brain Connections.* Englewood Cliffs, N.J.: Prentice-Hall, 1979.

Garfield, Patricia. *Creative Dreaming.* New York: Ballantine Books, 1979.

Gauquelin, Michel. *The Cosmic Clocks.* New York: Avon Books, 1969.

Geley, Gustave. *From the Unconscious to the Conscious.* Glasgow, Scotland: Wm. Collins & Co., 1920.

Geller, Uri. *My Story.* New York: Praeger Publishers, 1975.

Gendlin, Eugene T., Ph.D. *Focusing.* New York: Bantam Books, 1981.

Gibran, Kahlil. *The Prophet.* New York: Alfred A. Knopf, 1972.

Gibson, Walter, and Gibson, Litzka. *The Complete Illustrated Book of the Psychic Sciences.* Garden City, N.Y.: Doubleday and Co., Inc., 1966.

Gibson, Walter. *Hypnotism.* New York: Grosset & Dunlap, 1970.

Goldsmith, Joel. *God, Substance of All Form.* New York: Julian Press, 1962.

Goodman, Linda. *Sun Signs.* New York: Bantam Books, 1968.

Graham, Billy. *Angels: God's Secret Agents.* New York: Doubleday and Co., Inc., 1975.

Grant, Joan, and Kelsey, Denys. *Many Lifetimes.* New York: Doubleday and Co., Inc., 1968.

Gray, Eden. *The Tarot Revealed.* New York: Bell Publishing Co., 1960.

Greber, Johannes. *Communication With the Spirit World of God: Personal Experiences of a Catholic Priest.* Teaneck, N.J.: Greber Memorial Foundation, 1979.

Green, Elmer, and Green, Alyce. *Beyond Biofeedback.* New York: Delacorte Press, 1977.

Gregory, R. L. *Eye and Brain.* New York: McGraw-Hill Book Co., 1974.

Hall, Calvin S. *A Primer of Freudian Psychology.* New York: New American Library, 1954.

Halpern, Steven. *Tuning the Human Instrument.* Belmont, Ca.: Spectrum Research Institute, 1978.

Hanson, Virginia, ed. *Approaches to Meditation.* Wheaton, Ill.: Theosophical Publishing House, 1973.

_____. *H. P. Blavatsky and the Secret Doctrine.* Wheaton, Ill.: Theosophical Publishing House, 1973.

Helena, Theodore. *The American Indian.* La Canada, Ca.: New Age Press, 1964.

Heron, Laurence T. *ESP in the Bible.* New York: Doubleday and Co., Inc., 1974.

Hesse, Hermann. *Siddhartha.* New York: Bantam Books, 1971.

Hodson, Geoffrey. *The Miracle of Birth.* Wheaton, Ill.: Theosophical Publishing House, 1981.

Hoffa, Helynn. *Animal Spirits.* San Leandro, Ca.: Universal Church of the Master, n.d.

Holloway, Gilbert. *ESP and Your Superconscious.* N.p., Ky.: Best Books, 1966.

Holtzer, Hans. *The Psychic Side of Dreams.* New York: Doubleday and Co., Inc., 1976.

Holy Bible. St. James Version. New York: Cambridge University Press, n.d.

Houston, F. M. *The Healing Benefits of Acupressure.* New Canaan, Ct.: Keats Publishing Co., 1974.

Hubbard, L. Ron. *Dianetics, the Evolution of a Science.* Letchworth, Hertfordshire, England: Garden City Press, Ltd., 1968.

_____. *Dianetics, the Modern Science of Mental Health.* Los Angeles: Church of Scientology, The American St. Hill Organization, 1975.

Hudson, Thomas J. *The Law of Psychic Phenomena.* New York: Samuel Weiser, Inc., 1975.

Hunt, Roland. *The Seven Keys to Colour Healing.* London: C. W. Daniel Co., 1971.

Hutchins, Robert M., and Adler, Mortimer; eds. *Great Books of the Western World.* 54 vols. Chicago: Encyclopedia Brittanica, Inc., 1952.

Ingham, Eunice D. *Stories the Feet Can Tell.* Rochester, N.Y.: Eunice D. Ingham, 1938.

_____. *Stories the Feet Have Told.* Rochester, N.Y.: Eunice D. Ingham, 1963.

Irwin, Yukiko, and Wagenvoord, James. *Shiatzu.* New York: J. P. Lippincott Co., 1976.

Janov, Arthur. *The Primal Scream.* New York: Dell Publishing Co., Inc., 1970.

Joy, W. Brugh. *Joy's Way.* Los Angeles: J. P. Tarcher, Inc., 1978.

Kardec, Allan. *The Book of Mediums.* New York: Samuel Weiser, Inc., 1970.

_____. *The Spirits Book.* London: Psychic Press, 1975.

Karlins, Marvin, and Andrews, Lewis M. *Biofeedback: Turning On the Power of Your Mind.* New York: Warner Books, Inc., 1974.

Kee, Howard C.; Young, Franklin; and Froelich, Karlfried. *The Understanding of the New Testament.* Englewood Cliffs, N.J.: Prentice-Hall, 1973.

Keyes, Ken, Jr. *Handbook to Higher Consciousness.* Berkeley, Ca.: Living Love Center, 1975.

Kilner, Walter J. *The Aura.* New York: Samuel Weiser, Inc., 1973.

King, Francis, and Skinner, Stephen. *Techniques of High Magic.* New York: Warner Destiny Books, 1976.

Kloss, Jethro. *Back To Eden: Herbal Medicine and Natural Foods and Home Remedies.* Santa Barbara, Ca.: Woodbridge Press Publishing Co., 1972.

Kraeger, Hannah. *Old Time Remedies for Modern Ailments.* Boulder, Colo.: n.p., 1971.

Krieger, Dolores, Ph.D., R.N. *The Therapeutic Touch: How to Use Your Hands to Help or to Heal.* Englewood Cliffs, N.J.: Prentice-Hall, 1979.

Krippner, Stanley, and Rubin, Daniel. *The Kirlian Aura.* New York: Doubleday, Anchor Press, 1974.

Krishna, Gopi. *Kundalini: Evolutionary Energy in Man.* Berkeley, Ca.: Shambhala Publications, 1967.

Kubler-Ross, Elisabeth. *On Death and Dying.* New York: Macmillan Publishing Co., 1969.

Kueshana, Eklal. *The Ultimate Frontier.* Chicago: The Stelle Group, 1963.

La Barre, Weston. *They Shall Take Up Serpents: Psychology of the Southern Snake-Handling Cult.* New York: Schocken Books, 1976.

Lamsa, George M. *The Gospel Light.* Philadelphia: A. J. Holman Co., 1936.

_____ *New Testament Commentary: Acts to Revelation.* Philadelphia: A. J. Holman Co., 1956.

_____ *Old Testament Light.* Englewood Cliffs, N.J.: Prentice-Hall, 1957.

Langley, Noel. *Edgar Cayce on Reincarnation.* New York: Paperback Library, 1967.

Leadbeater, C. W. *Clairvoyance.* Wheaton, Ill.: Theosophical Publishing House, 1955.

_____ *Man, Visible and Invisible.* Wheaton, Ill.: Theosophical Publishing House, 1971.

_____ *The Astral Plane.* Wheaton, Ill.: Theosophical Publishing House, 1973.

_____ *The Chakras.* Wheaton, Ill.: Theosophical Publishing House, 1974.

_____ *The Monad.* Wheaton, Ill.: Theosophical Publishing House, 1974.

Le Cron, Leslie M. *Self-Hypnotism.* Englewood Cliffs, N.J.: Prentice-Hall, 1964.

Legge, James. *I Ching.* New York: Bantam Books, 1969.

Leif, Horace. *What Mediumship Is.* London: Spiritualist Press, 1963.

Lewis, H. Spencer. *Cycles of Light.* San Jose, Ca.: AMORC, 1952.

_____ *Rosicrucian Manual.* San Jose, Ca.: AMORC, 1966.

Lilly, John C. *The Center of the Cyclone.* New York: Bantam Books, 1973.

_____ *Programing and Meta-Programing in the Human Biocomputer.* New York: Bantam Books, 1974.

Locke, Courtney. *Witchcraft, Magic and Alchemy.* New York: Dover Publications, 1971.

Long, Max Freedom. *The Secret Science Behind Miracles.* Marina Del Rey, Ca.: DeVorss & Co., 1954.

_____ *The Huna Code in Religions.* Marina Del Rey, Ca.: DeVorss & Co., 1965.

Lopez, Vincent. *Numerology.* New York: New American Library, Inc., Signet, 1961.

Lucas, Richard. *Common and Uncommon Uses of Herbs for Healthful Living.* New York: Arco Publishing Co., 1969.

Luce, Gay Gaer. *Biological Rhythms in Human and Animal Physiology.* New York: Dover Publications, 1971.

_____ *Body Time.* New York: Bantam Books, 1971.

MacCollam, Joel A. *A Carnival of Souls.* New York: Seaburn Press, Crossword Books, 1979.

MacIvor, Virginia, and LaForrest, Sandra. *Vibrations: Healing Through Color, Homeopathy & Radionics.* New York: Samuel Weiser, Inc., 1979.

McKnight, Harry. *Silva Mind Control Through Psychorientology.* Laredo, Tex.: Institute of Psychorientology, 1973.

Maltz, Maxwell. *Psycho-Cybernetics.* North Hollywood, Ca.: Wilshire Book Co., 1960.

Manning, Matthew. *The Link.* New York: Holt, Rinehart & Winston, 1974.

Marks, Pat R. *The Movement of est.* Chicago: Playboy Press, 1976.

Marphet, Howard. *When Daylight Comes.* Wheaton, Ill.: Theosophical Publishing House, 1971.

Martine, Yvonne. *Health, Youth and Beauty Through Color Breathing.* Berkeley, Ca.: Celestial Arts, 1976.

Massey, Robert E. *Alive to the Universe.* Boulder Creek, Ca.: University of the Trees Press, 1976.

Masters, Robert, and Houston, Jean. *Listening to the Body.* New York: Delacorte Press, 1978.

Meek, George W., ed. *Healers and the Healing Process.* Wheaton, Ill.: Theosophical Publishing House, 1977.

Mishlove, Jeffrey. *Roots of Consciousness.* New York: Random House, 1975.

Mitchell, Edgar D. *Psychic Exploration.* New York: G. P. Putnam Sons, 1974.

Monroe, Robert. *Journeys Out-of-the-Body.* New York: Doubleday, Anchor Press, 1971.

Montagu, Ashley. *Touching.* New York: Harper and Row, 1972.

Montgomery, Ruth. *A Gift of Prophecy.* New York: William Morrow & Co., Inc., 1965.

_____ *Here and Hereafter.* Greenwich, Conn.: Fawcett Books, 1968.

_____ *Born to Heal.* New York: Coward, McCann and Geohagen, 1973.

_____ *Companions Along the Way.* New York: Coward, McCann and Geohagen, 1974.

_____ *Strangers Among Us.* New York: Coward, McCann and Geohagen, 1979.

Moody, Raymond, Jr. *Life After Life.* St. Simons Island, Ga.: Mockingbird Books, 1975.

Muldoon, Sylvan, and Carrington, Hereward. *The Projection of the Astral Body.* New York: Samuel Weiser, Inc., 1974.

Newhouse, Flower A. *Rediscovering the Angels & Natives of Eternity.* Escondido, Ca.: Christward Ministry, 1976.

Nichol, C. W. *Moving Zen, True Karate.* New York: Dell Publishing Co., Inc., 1975.

Nichols, Beverly. *Powers That Be.* New York: Popular Library, 1966.

Nielsen, Greg, and Polanski, Joseph. *Pendulum Power.* New York: Warner Destiny, 1977.

Ophiel. *The Art and Practice of Astral Projection.* New York: Samuel Weiser, Inc., 1961.

_____ *The Art and Practice of Getting Material Things Through Creative Visualization.* New York: Samuel Weiser, Inc., 1975.

Ornstein, Robert. *The Psychology of Consciousness.* New York: Penguin Books, 1978.

Ostrander, Sheila, and Schroeder, Lynn. *Psychic Discoveries Behind the Iron Curtain.* New York: Bantam Books, 1971.

_____ *The Handbook of Psychic Discoveries.* New York: Berkley Medallion, 1974.

_____ *The ESP Papers.* New York: Bantam Books, 1976.

Ostrander, Sheila, and Schroeder, Lynn; and Schroeder, Nancy. *Super Learning.* New York: Delacorte Press, 1979.

Ousley, S. G. J. *Colour Meditations, With a Guide to Colour Healing.* London: L. N. Fowler and Co., 1967.

Ouspensky, P. D. *The Psychology of Man's Possible Evolution.* New York: Random House, Inc., 1950.

Panati, Charles. *The Geller Papers.* Boston: Houghton Mifflin Co., 1976.

_____ *Supersenses: Our Potential for Parasensory Experience.* New York: Times Books, Quadrangle, 1974.

Panchadasi, Swami. *The Astral World: Its Scenes, Dwellers, and Phenomena.* Des Plains, Ill.: Yogi Publication Society, n.d.

_____ *The Human Aura.* Des Plains, Ill.: Yogi Publication Society, 1972.

Patrick, Ted. *Let Our Children Go.* New York: Ballantine Books, 1979.

Pauwels, Louis, and Bergier, Jacques. *The Morning of the Magicians.* New York: Avon Books, 1971.

Payne, Buryl, and Reitano, Carmen. *Bio-meditation.* Brookline, Mass.: BFI Inc., 1977.

Payne, Phoebe D., and Bendit, Lawrence J. *Psychic Sense.* Wheaton, Ill.: Theosophical Publishing House, 1958.

Pearson, Norman. *Space, Time and Self.* Wheaton, Ill.: Theosophical Publishing House, 1957.

Percival, Harold Waldon. *Thinking and Destiny.* New York: Word Foundation, Inc., 1971.

Perkins, James S. *Through Death to Rebirth.* Wheaton, Ill.: Theosophical Publishing House, 1973.

Perls, Frederick S. *Gestalt Therapy Verbatim.* Edited by John O. Stevens. New York: Bantam Books, 1980.

Playfair, Guy L. *The Unknown Power.* New York: Souvenir Press, 1975.

Playfair, Guy L., and Hill, Scott. *The Cycles of Heaven.* New York: St. Martin's Press, Inc., 1978.

Porter, Donald, and Taxson, Diane. *The est Experience.* New York: Award Books, 1976.

Powell, Arthur E. *The Etheric Double.* Wheaton, Ill.: Theosophical Publishing House, 1969.

Powers, Melvin. *Encyclopedia of Self-Hypnotism.* Opa-locka, Fla.: Improvement Books, 1974.

Progoff, Ira. *Jung, Synchronicity and Human Destiny.* New York: Delta Books, 1973.

Ram Dass, Baba. *The Only Dance There Is.* New York: Doubleday, Anchor Press, 1970.

Ramacharaka, Yogi. *Science of Breath.* Chicago: Yogi Publication Society, 1906.

Rampa, T. Lobsang. *The Saffron Robe.* New York: Bantam Books, Inc., 1970.

_____ *The Third Eye.* London: Corgi Books, 1975.

Rand McNally Atlas of the Body and Mind. New York, Chicago, London: Rand McNally & Co., 1976.

Rapaport, David. *Emotions and Memory.* New York: Science Editions, Inc., 1971.

Regush, June V., and Regush, Nicholas M. *Dream Worlds, the Complete Guide to Dreams & Dreaming.* New York: New American Library, Signet, 1977.

Reid, James. *God, Adam and the Universe.* Grand Rapids, Mich.: The Zondervan Publishing House, 1971.

Renard, Henry. *Philosophy of Being.* N.p., Wisc.: Bruce Publishing Co., 1946.

Restak, Richard M. *The Brain: The Last Frontier.* New York: Doubleday Publishing Co., 1979.

Reyner, J. H. *Psionic Medicine.* New York: Samuel Weiser, Inc., 1974.

Rhine, J. B. *New Frontiers of the Mind: The Story of the Duke Experiments.* New York: Farrar and Reinhardt, 1937.

Roberts, Jane. *Seth Speaks.* Englewood Cliffs, N.J.: Prentice-Hall, Inc., 1963.

_____ *The Seth Material.* Englewood Cliffs, N.J.: Prentice-Hall, Inc., 1970.

_____ *The Coming of Seth.* New York: Pocketbooks, 1976.

_____ *The Nature of Personal Reality: A Seth Book.* New York: Bantam Books, Inc., 1978.

Rogo, D. Scott, and Bayless, Raymond. *Phone Calls From the Dead.* New York: Berkley Books, 1980.

Roman, Klara G. *Handwriting: A Key to Personality.* New York: Pantheon Books, Inc., 1952.

Rossner, John. *From Ancient Magic to Future Technology.* Toward Recovery of the Primordial Tradition, vol. I, Bk.1. Washington, D.C.: University Press of America, Inc., 1979.

Russ, Michael. *Divine Psychology.* Kakemont, Ga.: Tarnhelm Press, 1972.

_____ . *The Mysteries.* Washington, D.C.: Millenium Publishing House, 1975.

_____ . *Finding Your Soulmate.* Washington, D.C.: Millenium Publishing House, 1975.

Russell, Lao. *God Will Work With You—But Not For You.* Swannonoa, Va.: University of Science and Philosophy, 1955.

Sagan, Carl. *The Dragons of Eden.* New York: Random House, Inc., 1977.

_____ . *Broca's Brain: Reflections on the Romance of Science.* New York: Random House, Inc., 1979.

Schein, Edgar. *Coercive Persuasion.* New York: W. W. Norton & Co., Inc., 1971.

Schindler, John A. *How to Live 365 Days a Year.* Greenwich, Conn.: Fawcett Crest, 1978.

Schul, Bill, and Pettit, ed. *The Secret Power of Pyramids.* Greenwich, Conn.: Fawcett Publishers, 1975.

_____ . *Psychic Power of the Pyramids.* Greenwich, Conn.: Fawcett Publishers, 1976.

Shultz, Will. *Profound Simplicity.* New York: Bantam Books, Inc., 1979.

Seiss, Joseph. *The Great Pyramid: A Miracle in Stone.* New York: Rudolf Steiner Publications, 1973.

Selye, Hans, M.D. *The Stress of Life.* New York: McGraw-Hill Book Co., 1978.

Shaklee, Forrest C., Sr. *Reflections on a Philosophy.* New York: Benjamin Publishing Co., 1975.

Sheban, Joseph, ed. *The Wisdom of Gibran: Aphorisms and Maxims.* New York: Philosophical Library, Inc., 1966.

Shepard, Leslie A. *Encyclopedia of Occultism and Parapsychology.* 2 vols. Detroit: Gale Research Co., 1978.

Shiffrin, Nancy, and Netherton, Morris. *Past Lives Therapy.* New York: Grossett & Dunlap, 1978.

Simonton, O. Carl; Simonton, Stephanie; and Creighton, James. *Getting Well Again.* New York: Bantam Books, 1978.

Singer, Jerome L. *Day Dreaming: An Introduction to the Experimental Study of Inner Experience.* New York: Random House, Inc., 1966.

Smith, Adam. *Powers of the Mind.* New York: Random House, Inc., 1975.

Smith, Cushing. *I Can Heal Myself and I Will.* New York: Frederick Fell Publishers, Inc., 1980.

Smith, Robert E. *Doc Anderson: The Healing Faith.* New York: Warner Books, Inc., 1972.

Spear, Wilfred. *Sunflower—Great Spirit Healing.* New York: Chief Sunflower Publishing Co., 1953.

Spence, Lewis. *Encyclopaedia of Occultism.* Hyde Park, N.Y.: University Books, Inc., 1960.

Stapleton, Ruth Carter. *The Gift of Inner Healing.* New York: Word Books, Inc., 1981.

Steadman, Alice. *Who's the Matter With Me?* Lakemont, Ga.: CSA Press, 1969.

Stearn, Jess. *The Search for a Soul: Taylor Caldwell's Psychic Lives.* New York: Fawcett Books, 1972.

_____ . *The Power of Alpha Thinking.* New York: New American Library, Signet, 1976.

Steiger, Brad. *The Enigma of Reincarnation.* New York: Ace Books, 1967.

Steiner, Rudolf. *Cosmic Memory: Atlantis and Lemuria.* New York: Rudolf Steiner Publishing Co., 1971.

Stoner, Carroll, and Parke, Jo Anne. *All God's Children: The Cult Experience.* New York: Penguin Books, 1977.

Sutphen, Dick. *You Were Born Again To Be Together.* New York: Pocket Books, 1976.

Swedenborg, Emanuel. *Heavenly Secrets.* Vol. 1. New York: Swedenborg Foundation, 1967.

Tabori, Paul. *Pioneers of the Unseen.* New York: Taplinger Publishing Co., Inc., 1972.

Tanous, Alex, and Ardman, Harvey. *Beyond Coincidence: One Man's Experiences With Psychic Phenomena.* New York: Doubleday and Co., Inc., 1976.

Taylor, John. *Super Minds.* New York: Warner Books, 1975.

Taylor, Ruth Mattson. *Witness From Beyond.* Chicago: Chicago Review Press, Inc.; Foreword Books, 1975.

Thomas Lewis. *The Lives of a Cell.* New York: Bantam Books, 1974.

Thommen, George S. *Is This Your Day?* New York: Avon Books, 1973.

Three Initiates. *The Kybalion: Hermetic Philosophy.* Chicago: Yogi Publication Society, 1940.

Time-Life Books editors, and *Life* editors et al. *Life Science Library.* Multiple vols. New York: Time-Life Books and Time, Inc., 1964-1971.

Toben, Bob. *Space-Time and Beyond.* New York: E. P. Dutton & Co., 1975.

Tompkins, Peter, and Bird, Christopher. *The Secret Life of Plants.* New York: Avon Books, 1974.

Trine, Ralph Waldo. *In Tune With the Infinite.* London: G. Bell & Sons, 1970.

Tromp, S. W. *Psychical Psychics.* New York: Elsevier Publishing Co., 1949.

Tulku, Tarthung. *Time, Space and Knowledge: A New Vision.* Berkeley, Ca.: Dharma Publishing, 1977.

Tuttle, Hudson. *Mediumship and Its Laws.* 98th ed., N.p., Wisc.: National Spiritualist Assn., 1890.

Twitchell, Paul. *Ekankar: Key to Secret Worlds.* San Diego: Illuminated Way Press, 1969.

Tyl, Noel. *Horoscope Construction.* Principles & Practice of Astrology Series: vol. 1. St. Paul, Minn.: Llewellyn Publications, 1977.

Tyrrell, G. N. *Science and Psychical Phenomena.* New York: Universal Books, 1961.

Underwood, Barbara, and Underwood, Betty. *Hostage to Heaven.* New York: Clarkson N. Potter, Inc., 1979.

Vander, Peter. *Voices From the Tapes: Recordings From the Other World.* New York: Drake Publishers, 1973.

Van Gelder, Dora. *The Real World of Fairies.* Wheaton, Ill.: Theosophical Publishing House, 1977.

Wade, Carlson. *Magic Minerals: Your Key to Better Health.* New York: Arco Publishing Co., Inc., 1972.

Waite, Arthur E. *The Holy Kabbalah: A Study of the Secret Tradition in Israel.* Secaucus, N.J.: University Books, 1975.

Walker, Norman W. *Colon Health.* Phoenix: O'Sullivan, Woodside & Co., 1979.

Watts, Alan. *The Way of Zen.* New York: Random House, Inc., 1974.

Wayland, Bruce, and Wayland, Shirley. *Steps to Dowsing Power.* N.p., Ill.: Life Force Press, 1976.

White, George Star. *The Story of the Human Aura.* Mokelume Hill, Ca.: Health Research, 1969.

White, John, and Krippner, Stanley, eds. *Future Science: Life Energies & the Psychics of Paranormal Phenomena.* New York: Doubleday and Co., 1977.

Wickland, Carl. *Thirty Years Among the Dead.* Amherst, Wisc.: Amherst Press, 1924.

Wilshire, Bruce. *William James and Phenomenology: A Study of "the Principles of*

Psychology." New York: Harper & Row
Publishers, Inc., 1971.

Wilson, Ernest. *The Other Half of the
Rainbow.* Los Angeles: Unity Classics,
1952.

World Almanac, ed. *World Almanac Book of
the Strange.* New York: New American
Library, Inc., Signet, 1977.

Yarbro, Chelsea Quinn. *Messages From*

Michael. New York: Playboy Paper-
backs, 1979.

Yogananda, Paramahansa. *Autobiography of
a Yogi.* Los Angeles: Self-Realization
Fellowship, 1973.

Yram. *Practical Astral Projection.* New York:
Samuel Weiser, Inc., 1974.

Zentarra, Oskar. *Simplified Astrology.* N.p.:
Astral Research Society, 1971.

CONFERENCES, SEMINARS, LECTURES, AND WORKSHOPS

Bach, Marcus. Lectures on Metaphysics and
Reincarnation. St. Petersburg, Fla.: Unity
Center of St. Petersburg, 1965, 1966,
and 1967.

Barker, Samuel P. III, D.O. "Primal
Therapy." St. Petersburg, Fla.: Psychic
Research Institute of Florida; and
Vocational, Technical, and Adult
Education; School Board of Pinellas
County, October 1978.

Beckus, Erick. "The I Ching." St. Petersburg,
Fla.: Psychic Research Institute of
Florida, n.d. 1978.

Bell, Roger, D.C. "Spinal Alignment." St.
Petersburg, Fla.: Continuing Education
of University of South Florida, 19
November 1981.

Brady, Don. Founder of Self-Center of St.
Petersburg. "Rebirthing." and "Science
of Breath." St. Petersburg, Fla.: Psychic
Research Institute of Florida; and Vocational, Technical, and Adult Education,
n.d. 1978.

Brown, Barbara. "Biofeedback." St. Petersburg, Fla.: Humanistic Institute, n.d.
1977.

Brown, Dr. William. "Etheric Surgery."
Lecture and demonstration. St. Petersburg, Fla.: Temple of the Living God,
n.d. 1978 and 1979.

Caddy, Peter, and Caddy, Eileen. "Findhorn."
Illustrated lecture. St. Petersburg, Fla.:
Ekerd College, n.d. 1978.

Campbell, John. Hypnotist. "Initiation by San
Blas Indians of Panama." St. Petersburg
and Clearwater, Fla.: Psychic Research
Institute of Florida; and Vocational,
Technical, and Adult Education; n.d.
1979.

Cayce, Hugh Lynn et al. "The Cayce Foundation." St. Petersburg, Fla.: n.d. 1975.

Chaney, Earlyne. "Initiation at Moment of
Death" and "Worship of Ancient
Wisdom." Seminar. Atlanta, Ga.: Astara
Foundation, n.d. 1977.

Cooper, Robert K.M., Ph.D., N.D. "Full-
Spectrum, Optimum Natural Health."
Clearwater, Fla.: Vocational, Technical,
and Adult Education, n.d. 1976.

Decker, Dr. Nelson C. "Oriental and Indian
Healings." St. Petersburg, Fla: First
Unity Church, n.d., 1979.

"Depression, Stress, Executive Stress." St.
Petersburg, Fla.: Horizon Mental
Health Seminars, 19 October 1976, 11
May 1977, and 27 August 1977.

"Destructive Brainwashing Cults." Tampa,
Fla.: Citizens' Freedom Foundation
National Annual Conference, 1-3
October 1981.

"est." Tampa, Fla.: "est" Lecture, June 1980.

Flax, Audrey, R.N. "Polarity Balancing." Training. Clearwater, Fla.: March 1981.

Gladden, Rose. Healer from England. Healing Demonstration. St. Petersburg, Fla.: Temple of the Living God, 4 October 1980.

Green, Elmer, and Green, Alyce. "Biofeedback" Lecture. West Palm Beach, Fla.: Unity Center, 13 March 1976.

Hollaway, Dr. Gilbert. "Psychism and Philosophy." St. Petersburg, Fla.: Self-sponsored winter seminars; 1963, 1964, and 1965.

"Humanities in Today's World." Tampa, Fla.: FWCCLACE Conference, 7 December 1979.

Khan, Pir Vilayat Inayat. Sufi Retreat and Spiritual Transformation Meditation Camp. Odessa, Fla., 24-31 January 1982.

Lamsa, Dr. George. Translator of the Holy Bible. "Metaphysics." St. Petersburg, Fla.: Unity Center, 14 April 1970.

Levitan, Jack. Founder of Yoga Society of Florida. "Your Sculptures and Your Emotions." St. Petersburg, Fla., n.p. 1980.

Martin, Timothy. Indian Sorcerer's Apprentice. "Indian Sorcery." St. Petersburg, Fla.: University of South Florida, October 1981.

Miles, Gwen. "Mind Projection." St. Petersburg, Fla.: Eckankar, n.d. 1975.

Mishra, Dr. Ramamurti. Yoga Workshop. Clearwater, Fla.: Yoga Society of Florida, 13 April 1980.

O'Connell, Pat, and O'Connell, Joan. Editors and publishers of *The New Atlantean Journal.* "Ufology." St. Petersburg, Fla.: Psychic Research Institute of Florida; and Vocational, Technical, and Adult Education; n.d. 1978.

Pacetti, R. Bruce, D.D.S. Director of Florida Holistic Medicine Centers of Clearwater. "Nutrition and Holistic Health." Clearwater, Fla.: Vocational, Technical, and Adult Education; March 1980.

_____ "Balancing Body Chemistry." St. Petersburg, Fla.: Continuing Education, University of South Florida, December 1980.

Pageler, John. Biochemist. "Nutrition." St. Petersburg, Fla.: Psychic Research Institute of Florida; and Vocational, Technical, and Adult Education, November 1977.

Psi '74 Conference. St. Petersburg, Fla., n.d. 1974.

"Psychic Sciences." St. Petersburg Beach, Fla.: Second World Congress on Science and Religion, 14-20 June 1981.

Rama, Swami et al. Conference on Wholistic Health. Tampa, Fla.: Wholistic Health Councils of St. Petersburg and Palm Harbor, September 15-17, 1979.

Reeves, John. UFO Contactee. Brooksville, Fla.: Psychic Research Institute of Florida; and Vocational, Technical, and Adult Education Field Trip; November 1977, February 1978.

Rolling Thunder. Native American Medicine Man. "Healing" and "The New Age." Tampa, Fla.: Edgar Cayce Foundation, 2 January 1982.

St. John, Paul, R.M.T. Founder of the Institute of Natural Health. "Iridology" and "Nutrition." St. Petersburg, Fla.: Psychic Research Institute of Florida; and Vocational, Technical, and Adult Education, n.d. 1977, 1979, and 1980.

Silva, Jose. Founder of Silva Mind Control. "Psycho-Orientology." St. Petersburg, Fla., 4 December 1984.

Southeastern Region Unity Centers. Metaphysical Retreat. Miami, Fla., n.d. 1965, 1968, and 1970.

Southeastern Regional Parapsychological Association Conference. Winter Park, Fla.: Rollins College, 1 February 1980.

"Stress—Business Stress." Continuing Education Seminar. St. Petersburg, Fla.: St. Petersburg Junior College, n.d. 1980.

Sun Bear, and Wabun. Chippewa Medicine Man and his wife. "Making Medicine." St. Petersburg, Fla., 4 March 1982.

——————. "Earth Awareness." St. Petersburg, Fla., 27 January 1983.

——————. "Medicine Wheel." Seminar. St. Petersburg, Fla., 12 February 1983.

Taylor, Paul W., Ph.D. "Future Lives." Clearwater, Fla.: Vocational, Technical, and Adult Education; 8 May 1980.

——————. "Chakras." St. Petersburg, Fla.: Vocational, Technical, and Adult Education; 14 May 1980.

Thorensen, Eric. "How to Practically Never Be Upset About Anything." St. Petersburg, Fla.: Psychic Research Institute of Florida, 15 April 1978.

Unity School of Christianity. Metaphysical Seminar. St. Petersburg Beach, Fla., n.d. 1975.

Van Decar, Lewis E. Prince of the Magi. "Magic and Witchcraft." Zephyrhills, Fla.: Vocational, Technical, and Adult Education Field Trips; 14 March 1981, 13 May 1981.

Wholistic Health Council. Lecture Series. St. Petersburg, Fla., 1980.

Winkler, E. Arthur, Ph.D., Th.D. "Hypnotherapy." St. Petersburg, Fla.: Psychic Research Institute of Florida; and Vocational, Technical, and Adult Education; n.d., 1978.

Wunderlich, Raymond, Jr., M.D. "Stress and Holistic Health." St. Petersburg, Fla.: Continuing Education, University of South Florida, November 1980.

LEARNING CASSETTES

Alden, Dr. Reginald J. *Why Does it Work?* Danville, Vt.: American Society of Dowsers, 1979.

Chaney, Earlyne. *Bardo.* Upland, Ca.: Astara Foundation, 1981.

Dickerson, Ric, and Paulson, J. Sig. *Secret Key to Meditation—The Miracle of Creative Meditation.* Unity Village, Mo.: Unity School of Christianity, 5 June 1975.

——————. *Secret Key to Meditation—The Lord's Prayer.* Unity Village, Mo.: Unity School of Christianity, 10 July 1976.

Farrelly, Frances, Ph.D. *How Do It Know?* Danville, Vt.: American Society of Dowsers, 1980.

Finch, Bill. *Dowsing Personalities.* Danville, Vt.: American Society of Dowsers, 1980.

Gershman, George. *Dowsing, Parapsychology, and Psychic Healing.* Danville, Vt.: American Society of Dowsers, 1978.

——————. *Advanced Pendulum Dowsing and Dowsing for Minerals and Vitamins.* Danville, Vt.: American Society of Dowsers, 1979.

Guidici, Martha. *World of Meditation.* Unity Village, Mo.: Unity School of Christianity, 1977.

Green, Elmer and Alyce. Interview: *Biofeedback.* Unity Village, Mo.: Unity School of Christianity, 1979.

Hill, Christopher. *Information & Guidance.* Boulder Creek, Ca.: University of the Trees Press, 1978.

——————. *Chants for the Heart.* Boulder Creek, Ca.: University of the Trees Press, 1978.

——————. *Perception.* Boulder Creek, Ca.: University of the Trees Press, 1978.

——————. *Nature of Light.* Boulder Creek, Ca.: University of the Trees Press, 1978.

——————. *Womb of Space.* Boulder Creek, Ca.: University of the Trees Press, 1978.

Khan, Pir Vilayat Inayat. *In Search of Meaningfulness and Fulfillment.* Unity Village, Mo.: Unity School of Christianity, 1980.

Lederer, William J. *How a Pendulum Reacts to Energy Fields.* Danville, Vt.: American Society of Dowsers, 1978.

Mermins, Rob. *Creating and Dowsing for Thought Forms.* Danville, Vt.: American Society of Dowsers, 1980.

Ostrander, Sheila; Schroeder, Lynn; and Schroeder, Nancy. *Superlearning, The Art of Learning Exercise Cycle.* New York, Superlearning, Inc. 1979, 1980.

Rabel, Ed. *Bible Interpretation.* Unity Village, Mo.: Unity School of Christianity, 1972.

_____ *Twelve Powers of Man.* Unity Village, Mo.: Unity School of Christianity, 1974.

_____ *Book of Revelation.* Unity Village, Mo.: Unity School of Christianity, 1976.

_____ *Effective Bible.* Unity Village, Mo.: Unity School of Christianity, 1978.

Rahtjen, Dr. Bruce D. *Paul and his World.* Unity Village, Mo.: Unity School of Christianity, 1978.

Rath, Charles. *Power Meditation Series.* Indianapolis: Delaware Publishing Co., 1975.

Stelle Group, The. *Tolerance, Kindness.* Chicago, Ill., 1976.

Willey, Raymond C. *The Dowsers Energy Field.* Danville, Vt.: American Society of Dowsers, 1978.

Williamson, David. *God, Self and Dreams.* Unity Village, Mo.: Unity School of Christianity, 1979.

MAGAZINES, NEWSLETTERS

Alternatives, Miami, Fla., 1978-1979.

American Dowser, The. Danville, Vt.: American Society of Dowsers, Inc., 1977-1982.

American Society for Psychical Research Newsletter. New York, 1976-1982.

The ARE Journal. Virginia Beach, Va.: ARE Publishing Co., 1979-1982.

Beyond Reality. New York: Simplex Textured Reproductions, Inc., 1974-1979.

Biofeedback Journal, The. Garden Grove, Ca.: Biofeedback Technology Inc., 1977-1979.

Brain Mind Bulletin. Los Angeles: Interface Press, 1980-1982.

Echo. Orange Park, Fla.: Rev. Al Miner, Pub., 1978-1979.

ETA Journal. Orange Park, Fla.: Enlightment Through Attunement Foundation, 1976-1977.

Expansion. Hollywood, Ca.: C C & S Publications, 1981-1982.

Fate Magazine. Highland Park, Ill.: Clark Publishing Co., 1974-1982.

Himalayan News. Honesdale, Pa.: Himalayan International Institute of Yoga Science and Philosophy, 1980-1982.

Human Behavior. Los Angeles: Manson Western Corp., 1978-1981.

Humanist, The. Amherst, N.Y.: The American Humanist Assn., 1978-1980.

International Kirlian Research Association Communications. Brooklyn, N.Y.: IKRA, 1980-1983.

Journal of the American Society for Psychical Research. New York: American Society for Psychical Research, Inc., 1976-1982.

Journal of Natural Health and Parapsychology. Ontario: Canadian Society of Geobiology and Biomagnetism, 1981-1982.

Journal of Parapsychology. Durham, N.C.: Parapsychology Press, 1976-1981.

Journal of Religion and Psychical Research.
Bloomfield, Conn.: The Academy of
Religion and Psychical Research,
1981-1982.

Leading Edge Bulletin. Los Angeles:
Frontiers of Social Information, 1982.

National Enquirer. Lantana, Fla.: National
Enquirer Inc., 1978-1980.

New Atlantean Journal. Pinellas Park, Fla.:
New Atlantean Research Society,
1977-1982.

New Horizons. Ontario: New Horizons
Research Foundation, 1975.

New Realities. San Francisco: New Realities,
Inc., 1977-1982.

Nucleous, The. Cottonwood, Ariz.: L and R
Enterprises, Inc., 1978.

Parapsychology Review. Parapsychology
Foundation, Inc., 1976-1982.

Psychic News. London, England: Psychic
Press Ltd., 1977-1982.

Psychic Observer/Chimes. Washington,
D.C.: ESPress Inc., 1963-1981.

Psychic World and The Occult. New York:
CBS Publications, 1976-1977.

Psychology Today. New York: Ziff-Davis
Publishing Co., 1977-1982.

A Public Lecture. Lama Sing channeling
through Rev. Al Miner. Jacksonville,
Fla.: Enlightment Through Attunement
Foundation, 1976-1977.

Readers Digest, The. New York: Readers
Digest Assn., Inc., 1976-1981.

Rosicrucian Digest, The. San Jose, Ca.:
Rosicrucian Order AMORC, 1976-1981.

Science Digest, The. New York: Hearst
Corp., 1977-1980.

Science News. Washington, D.C.: Science
Service, Inc., 1976-1980.

Scientific American, The. New York: W. H.
Freeman & Co., 1974-1981.

Skylight. St. Petersburg, Fla.: Center of Light,
1976 and 1977.

Smithsonian, The. Washington, D.C.: Smithsonian Associates, 1982.

Spiritualist Gazette. London: SAGA Association of Great Britain, 1978-1981.

Stelle Letters. Chicago: The Stelle Group,
1976-1979.

Two Worlds. London: Psychic Press Ltd.,
1976-1980.

UCM Magazine. San Leandro, Ca.: Universal
Church of The Master, 1980-1981.

Unity Magazine. Unity Village, Mo.: Unity
School of Christianity, 1977-1982.

Unwrapping Paper, The. Largo, Fla.: Tag
Powell, 1979-1982.

Vedanta Society of Southern California. N.p.,
Ca.: Madonna Press, 1962, 1968, 1969.

Voice of Astara. Upland, Ca.: Astara Inc.,
1966-1982.

SELECTED MAGAZINE
AND NEWSPAPER ARTICLES

Arneberg, Marianne. "The Trauma of Letting
Go." *St. Petersburg Times,* 16 July 1978.

Bird, Christopher, contributing ed. "Dowse
Me a River." *Playboy's New Age
Primer,* October 1980, p. 225.

Caffery, Bethia. "Listen to the Beat and You
Can Learn Very Quickly." *St. Petersburg
Evening Independent,* 29 July 1980, p.
B1.

Cherry, Laurence. "Can the Brain Understand the Brain?" *Family Weekly,* 9
November 1980, p. 4.

——————. "Inner Space—Sleep and
Dreams." *Science Digest,* July 1981, p.
62.

——————. "Patient, Heal Thyself." *Family
Weekly,* 12 July 1981, p. 17.

Cousins, Norman. "You are the Healer."
Modern Maturity, June-July 1981, p. 84.

Dart, John. "Hell is Not a Burning Question." *St. Petersburg Times, Crossroads,* April 1980.

Edelson, Edward. "Aura Phenomenon Puzzles Experts.*" Smithsonian,* April 1977, p. 109.

Everetz, Mary. "Plotting a Course on the Curve of Life." *St. Petersburg Times,* 25 January 1976, p. E1.

Glassman, Judith. "When Your Mind Can Cure Your Body." *McCall's,* April 1981, p. 80.

Hassan, Carl A. "Pyramid Power: The Shape of Things to Come." *St. Petersburg Times, The Floridian,* 17 October 1976.

Landers, Ann. "Coping with Crisis." *Reader's Digest,* October 1980, p. 61.

Mainwaring, Marion. "'Phys/phren'—why not to take each other at face value." *Smithsonian,* November 1980, p. 193.

McAuliffe, Kathleen. "I Sing the Body Electric." *Omni,* n.d., p. 70.

O'Roark, Mary Ann. "Life After Death: The Growing Evidence." *McCall's,* March 1981, p. 24.

Peterman, Peggy. "Belly Dancing." *St. Petersburg Times,* April 1977.

Pribram, Karl, with Goleman, Daniel. "Holographic Memory." *Psychology Today,* February 1979, p. 71.

Pugh, Jeanne. "The Anti-Cult Network." *St. Petersburg Times, Crossroads,* 7 November 1981.

_____. "Archeologists Dig Up Religion's Roots." *St. Petersburg Times, Crossroads,* 26 December 1981.

_____. "The Ark Furor." *St. Petersburg Times, Crossroads,* 22 August 1981, p. 4.

Rosenbaum, Ron. "A Mouthful of Miracles: Psychic Dentistry by Rev. Willard Fuller." *Rolling Stone,* 10 December 1981.

Ross, Robert Alan. "Explore Levels of Sensory Suspension." Isolation Tank. *St. Petersburg Times,* 21 January 1981, p. D3.

Schiller, Ronald. "Unsolved Mysteries of the Great Pyramid." *Baltimore Sun,* 10 March 1974.

Schurter, Dale, and Walter, Eugene. "All You Need To Know about the Meat You Eat." *The Plain Truth,* October-November 1970, p. 26.

Shafiroth, Benjamin, and Groff, Edward S. "Medical Applications of Kirlian Electrography." Brooklyn, N.Y.: IKRA Conference, October 1977.

Sullivan, Walter. "New Data on Neutrinos May Help Explain Cosmos." © *New York Times, St. Petersburg Times,* 11 May 1980, p. A4.

"Thermography—A Fabulous New Way of 'Seeing.'" *Baltimore Sun,* 24 November 1974.

BOOKLETS

Altered States of Awareness. Readings from *Scientific American.* New York: W. H. Freeman & Co., 1972.

Angels and Man. Miami, Fla.: Mark Age Medicenter, 1974.

Beard, Paul. *Hints on Consulting a Psychic.* London: College of Psychic Studies, n.d.

The Biochemic Handbook. London: New Era Laboratory, Ltd., 1976.

Black Box and Other Psychic Generators. St. Louis: T. & A. Publications, 1980.

Christopher, John R. *Dr. Christopher's Three Day Cleansing Program and Mucusless Diet.* Provo, Utah: John R. Christopher, 1971.

Decker, Dr. Nelson. *The Great Mystery in the Sky.* American Indian healing techniques. Hollywood, Fla.: Benu, Inc., 1979.

Heleus, Michael. *Astrosonics.* University of Sussex, England: A. A. Conference, 1975.

Martin, George. *An Introduction to Catholic Charismatic Renewal.* Ann Arbor, Mich.: Word of Life, 1975.

Orphonics—Look Within Point. N.p.: Dawn Foundation, 1968.

The Rainbow Book. Berkeley, Ca.: Shambhala Publications, 1960.

Rudeau, Charlotte, and Schnell, Dietrich. *Good Morning, Jay Brackett: Youth and Beauty Through Breathing.* N.p.: Charlotte Rudeau and Dietrich Schnell, 1969.

Saraydarian, Haroutin. *Hierarchy and the Plan.* Agoura, Ca.: Aquarian Educational Group, 1975.

Sechrist, Elsie. *Meditation—Gateway to Light.* Virginia Beach, Va.: ARE Press, 1964.

Shaklee, Forrest C., Sr. *Thoughtsmanship: Ten Rules for Happiness and Contentment.* Emeryville, Ca.: Shaklee Corporation, 1974.

Sharp, Harold. *Animals in the Spirit World.* London: Spiritualist Association of Great Britain, 1966.

Stress. New York: Metropolitan Life Insurance Co., 1958.

Studies in Alchemy. Colorado Springs: Summit Lighthouse, Inc., 1967.

Unity Tracts. Unity Village, Mo.: Unity School of Christianity, 1962-1981.

Winkler, E. A., Ph.D., Th.D. *Hypnotherapy.* Valley, Nebr.: Eastern Nebraska Christian College, 1972.

Young, Howard S. *Rational Counseling Primer.* N.p.: Institute for Rational Living, 1974.

RADIO AND TELEVISION SHOWS

"As Man Behaves." Mental Health Series. PBS Television, n.d., 1976.

Boots, Suzanne. "Cults." St. Petersburg: WDAE Radio, December 1978.

"Chariots of the Gods." PBS Television, n.d., 1976.

Flanagan, G. Patrick. "Pyramid Power." NBC Television: "The Tomorrow Show," n.d., 1977.

"Hard Choices—Behavior Control." Transcript of television show. Kent, Ohio: PTV Publications, May 1981.

"In Search of. . . ." Selected shows. PBS Television, 1978.

"The John Eastman Show." Selected shows. ABC Television, 1977-1981.

_____ Selected radio shows, 1978.

"The Long Search." Anthropology Series on Religions. PBS Television, 1978.

"Man and His Environment." Mental Health Series. PBS Television, 1977.

National Geographic Society. "The Incredible Machine." The Human Body. PBS Television, n.d., 1976.

O'Connell, Pat, and O'Connell, Joan. "Close Encounters." Tampa, Fla.: WPLP Radio, October 1978.

_____ "UFO's." Tampa, Fla.: WPLP Radio, February 1979.

"PBS Latenight." Selected shows. PBS Television, 1982.

"The Phil Donahue Show." Selected shows. ABC Television, 1977-1981.

"Relativity." Einstein's Theories. PBS Television, n.d., 1979.

Sagan, Carl. "Cosmos." Selected shows. PBS Television, 1981.

MISCELLANEOUS SOURCES

American Society for Psychical Research. Conference. St. Petersburg, Fla., 12 October 1974.

Angley, Rev. Ernest. Holy Spirit Rally and Slaying-in-the-Spirit. Tampa, Fla., April 1981.

Associate Minister's Certification. Rev. Harold C. Durbin, teacher. St. Petersburg, Fla.: Church of Aquarian Science, 3 May 1970.

Beautiful Painted Arrow (Joseph Rael). Vision Quest Sweat Lodge. Kissimmee, Fla.: 20 November 1982.

Biofeedback Training Seminar. Certification in Encephalograph, Myograph, Blood Flow, and Galvanic Skin Response Feedback Instrumentation. Rev. Hal Rosencrans and Peggy Brown, instructors. West Palm Beach, Fla.: Biofeedback Training Center, 15 November 1975.

Cassadaga Spiritualist Camp Meetings. Sessions with mental mediums, and psychic readings. Cassadaga, Fla.: Vocational, Technical, and Adult Education Field Trips; 1976, 1978, 1980, and 1981.

Chaney, Earlyne, and Chaney, Robert. *Astara's Book of Life*. Degree lessons 1-4. Los Angeles: Astara Foundation, 1959.

Dental Alchemist's Workshop. Rev. Paul Esch, Jr., alchemist. St. Petersburg, Fla.: n.d. 1977. May 1982.

Durbin, Rev. Harold. Voice trance seances with "Dr. Zellers." St. Petersburg, Fla.: St. Paul's Church of Aquarian Science, 1969-1971.

Gestalt Encounter Group. William King, facilitator. St. Petersburg, Fla., 22, 23, June 1973.

Golden Harvest Herbal Tea. Copy on tea box. Pittsburg, Pa.: Natural Sales Co., 1982.

Hines, Rev. Crystal. Voice trance seance lessons with "Master Onargo." St. Petersburg, Fla.: The Spiritual Center, 1968-1972.

Hypnosis Techniques Certification Training. Rev. Al Miner, and E. Arthur Winkler, Ph.D., Th.D., president. Valley, Neb.: Eastern Nebraska Christian College, 19 January 1975.

Hypnotherapy Instructor Certification. Dr. E. Arthur Winkler, president and mentor. Ponchatoula, La.: St. John's University, 27 October 1983.

Johnson, Rev. John. Sufi Twirling Ziker. St. Petersburg, Fla., n.d. 1977.

Magnetic Healing Training. Private instruction by Thomas Miller, osteopath and psychic healer. St. Petersburg, Fla., 1970-1974.

Masters, Roy. "How Your Mind Can Keep You Well." Phonograph record. Los Angeles: The Foundation of Human Understanding, 1971.

Ministerial Ordination. Universal Church of the Master. San Jose, Ca. Rev. Harold W. Margrave, president, Rev. Thelma Fischer and Rev. Irene Palmer, educators. St. Petersburg, Fla.: The Spiritual Center, 17 August 1972.

Palmer, Rev. Irene. Cyclic Laws. Ten lectures. St. Petersburg, Fla., n.d. 1975.

Panton, Rev. M. McBride. Trumpet seances with "White Cloud." St. Petersburg, Fla.: Church of Spiritual Philosophy and Vedanta Center, 1966-1969.

Reflexology Certification. National Institute of Reflexology. Dwight C. Byers, instructor. St. Petersburg, Fla., 28 May 1970.

Reflexology Testing for Registration with the National Institute of Reflexology. Dwight C. Byers, president and tester. St. Petersburg, Fla., n.d. 1974.

The Rosicrucian Order. "The Science of Mysticism." Phonograph record. San Jose, Ca.: AMORC, n.d.

Silva Mind Control Certification. Mind Control Institute, Inc. Laredo, Texas. Jose Silva, director. Thomas J. Masterson, trainer. N.p., 8 January 1975.

Walker, Rev. Gerry B. Slaying-in-the-Spirit and Talking-in-tongues. St. Petersburg, Fla.: Evangelistic Healing Week, 1979, 1980, 1985.

Winkler, E. Arthur. Ph.D. President of Eastern Nebraska Christian College. Voice trance lessons. St. Petersburg, Fla., 1976, 1977.